CONSTITUTIONAL INTERPRETATION

THIRD EDITION

CONSTITUTIONAL INTERPRETATION

Cases Essays Materials

THIRD EDITION

Craig R. Ducat
Professor of Political Science
Northern Illinois University

Harold W. Chase
Late Professor of Political Science
University of Minnesota

West Publishing Company
St. Paul   New York   Los Angeles   San Francisco

Library of Congress Cataloging in Publication Data

Ducat, Craig R.
    Constitutional interpretation.

    Rev. ed. of: Constitutional interpretation/Harold W. Chase. 2nd ed. 1979.
    Includes index.
    1. United States—Constitutional law—Cases.
I. Chase, Harold William, 1922–1982. Constitutional interpretation. II. Title.
KF4549.D78   1983   342.73   82–21824
ISBN 0–314–69640–7   347.302

2nd Reprint—1985

To
Mr. Justice Black, Mr. Justice Frankfurter, Mr. Justice Douglas,
mighty protagonists of diverse approaches
and
Mr. Justice Jackson,
a man for all seasons.

Though all the winds of doctrine were let loose to play upon the earth, so Truth be in the field, we do injuriously, by licensing and prohibiting, to misdoubt her strength. Let her and Falsehood grapple; who ever knew the Truth put to the worse, in a free and open encounter?

—John Milton, AREOPAGITICA

Preface

This edition of *Constitutional Interpretation* includes cases, legislation, and other materials through 1982. As we explained in the First Edition:

> We have borrowed the title "Constitutional Interpretation" from the undergraduate course, once taught at Princeton by Professor Corwin, to underscore our purpose in presenting the cases, essays, and other materials which comprise this casebook. We rejected the perennial favorite "Cases in Constitutional Law" because, as we conceive it, the purpose of an undergraduate course on the Constitution is not so much to teach what the law is as to delve into and examine the principal methods by which justices of the United States Supreme Court give meaning to constitutional provisions in the context of individual cases and concrete problems.

> Constitutional interpretation is not a static enterprise which presents the prospect of furnishing correct, certain, or ultimate legal answers to political problems but, rather, one of a continual adjustment of tensions through a process of unending dialogue among judges of fundamentally different political faiths and experiences. As much as space has permitted, we have tried in the essays and materials which follow to continually probe and test the quality of justifications which these men offer for the choices they make. In an imperfect world, where the clash of competing interests is the only certainty, where issues are therefore inherently complex, where judges are fallible, and where man-made institutions have limits, solutions to problems will inevitably be less than the optimum.

Introductory essays preface each chapter and knit together the materials which follow. As with the preceding editions, the Third Edition maintains the broad scope of the casebook without appreciably sacrificing coverage of material. This is in large part due to the inclusion of numerous charts which summarize constitutional rulings. *Constitutional Interpretation* is not intended to provide a history of constitutional developments either in the essays or through the cases and other materials selected. For those in search of a commentary on the law of the Constitution and, to a lesser extent, how it came to be, readers are referred to our latest revision of that old standard, *Corwin's The Constitution and What It Means Today*, now in its Fourteenth Edition with a 1980 Supplement, published by Princeton University Press.

Footnotes in this edition are designated by numbers and letters. Notes indicated by numerals are those of the Court; those indicated by letter or asterisk are ours.

Producing this edition was a lonely task without my partner and friend, Harold Chase. Although Hal's remarkable agility in debate, his uncommon sense, his contagious goodwill, and his indomitable vigor are now matters of memory to the hundreds of former students and colleagues who revere him, this edition could not do better than to aspire to continue Hal's consistent commitment to fair-mindedness.

In Hal's absence, the advice and help of others was doubly appreciated. I especially want to thank Judy Manelis for an endless stream of valuable editorial suggestions. Thanks, too, to Davalene Cooper, Bob Dudley, and Richard Rosswurm to whom I am indebted for enduring contributions from previous editions. Above all, this edition—like its predecessors— bears a debt to the hundreds of undergraduate students in our political science courses over the years whose favorable response and probing questions helped frame these materials. Any errors, whether old or new, are mine.

Finally, it should not go without saying that this project was eased greatly by the patience, support, and encouragement of especially dear friends. Although such intangibles can never really be appraised, I owe much to Chris Fosnaugh and Ian Fishman.

CRAIG R. DUCAT

August 1982
Chicago, Illinois

Summary of Contents

Table of Contents

**Chapter   7   The State Police Power and Business
                Regulation   *546***

Table of Cases

The principal cases are in italic type. Cases cited or discussed are in roman type. References are to pages.

CONSTITUTIONAL INTERPRETATION

THIRD EDITION

Part I

THE DISTRIBUTION OF POWER IN THE NATIONAL GOVERNMENT

Chapter 1

Judicial Power

It has become a commonplace that, as Governor (later Chief Justice) Hughes put it, "We are under a Constitution, but the Constitution is what the judges say it is * * *." Although this cliché seriously misleads when it appears to suggest that courts necessarily have the last word on questions of constitutionality and insofar as it implies that judges are free to adopt whatever reading of that document pleases them, it does contain a kernel of truth—however overblown—that the courts play a central role in interpreting the Constitution. This, as every schoolboy and girl knows, is especially true of the Supreme Court. And it is this understanding which compels us to begin the study of constitutional interpretation with an examination of judicial power.

Courts, of course, are not the only agencies of government which have shaped the meaning of the Constitution. What Presidents, Congress, federal administrators, their state counterparts, scholars, and the media say and do impact very heavily on developing the meaning of the Constitution. Important, too, is what the sovereign American people do with their votes to support or oppose assertions of power under or in spite of the Constitution. These impacts are naturally greatest where there are significant ambiguities or omissions (lacunae) in the Constitution. The Framers, after all, despite their intellectual brilliance, could not foresee that one day we would be a nation of over 200 million people, nor could they possibly envision the kinds of technological changes which would take place. With regard to some matters, they just guessed badly. For example, they omitted all reference to political parties in the Constitution because they regarded them as a bane to be avoided (see *Federalist 10* and Washington's famous Farewell Address). Surely, if they had appreciated the importance of political parties to the democratic process, they would have cast some basic ground rules for inclusion in the Constitution. Nor did the Framers, basically conservative and fearful of too much democracy,

appreciate how inexorable would be the drive for more democracy.
Recent debates over the President's war power, executive privilege, power
to act in the national security, and the power to impound funds illustrate
dramatically the host of factors which help spell out the meaning of the
Constitution. Once an exercise of power becomes accepted on the basis of
precedent, it can truly be said that such an exercise has become a part of
the constitutional *system*, although one could argue that technically it is
not a part of the Constitution. As you will see, when you read the items
under presidential power, precedent of actions uncontested or allowed to
stand is a powerful argument for legitimation. But even as to precise
constitutional provisions a myriad of extrajudicial influences can have a
crucial impact on developing the meaning of the Constitution because of
peculiarities of the American constitutional system. For example, when
President Franklin D. Roosevelt, contrary to Article IV, section 3's
express provision that "The Congress shall have power to dispose of
* * * property belonging to the United States," traded U. S. destroyers
for bases with Great Britain, no one could fashion a constitutional remedy
for challenging his action which on its face was unconstitutional. As you
will see later (p. 68), in those days no one had standing to take such a case
to court, and impeachment struck those who objected to his action as politically infeasible. Americans reflecting upon Watergate need not be
reminded of all the political considerations which must be calculated in
contemplating impeachment.

Despite all of the foregoing, the fact remains that the judiciary, particularly the Supreme Court, does play the leading role in constitutional
interpretation, primarily because of the uniquely American institution of
judicial review. Consequently, for one who wishes to learn the meaning of
the Constitution, one must know what the Supreme Court says it is—as a
beginning if not as the end-all. At the outset, then, it is imperative to
understand how the Court derived its great power as well as what ground
rules circumscribe the exercise of that power. This is precisely what this
first topic is all about.

a. The Supreme Court's Jurisdiction and Its Assumption of Judicial Review

There has been a lively debate among scholars literally throughout American history over the issue of whether or not the Framers intended that the
Supreme Court have the power of judicial review. On the one hand, it can
be demonstrated that most of the Framers knew what the concept was
and were for it. On the other hand, there is the hard fact that the Framers had considered and rejected an idea for a Council of Revision which
would have permitted the Court to join with the President in vetoing acts
of Congress. It seems a fair appraisal of what took place at Philadelphia
to suggest that proponents of judicial review like Hamilton (see *Federalist
78*) decided that it was a good tactical move not to try to resolve that issue
in the Convention but rather to leave the Constitution ambiguous. Two
factors point to such an interpretation. One, there were people at the
Convention who were bitterly opposed to judicial review. Knowing that it

would be difficult to obtain ratification, those who favored judicial review opted not to press this controversial issue which, hopefully, they could win in other ways. It was not difficult to predict at that time who would head the new government if it were achieved and who would have the initiative in interpreting the document initially—George Washington and those in whom he had great trust. And that "in group" would surely include his former chief of staff Alexander Hamilton. This is not to suggest a "conspiracy theory"; it is simply to suggest that astute negotiators calculate very shrewdly costs and benefits of taking a particular stance in a negotiation and include in such calculations whether or not the written agreement will in the long run provide desired results. There is no gainsaying the capacity of Alexander Hamilton and other champions of judicial review for shrewd calculation. And it did not take long for Chief Justice John Marshall to demonstrate how shrewd they had been.

John Marshall's opinion in *Marbury* v. *Madison* (p. 16) is a beautiful illustration of a *tour de force* in argumentation. He makes it appear that logic *requires* judicial review in a governmental system in which a written Constitution is the supreme law. The nub of his argument is that the Constitution vests the *judicial power* of the United States "in one Supreme Court, and in such inferior courts as the Congress may from time to time ordain and establish." Implicit in his argument is an assumption made explicit by the Court subsequently that "judicial power" is the power "to decide cases." Clearly, the power to decide cases carries with it certain other necessary *inherent powers.* For example, it would be impossible for courts to decide cases if they could neither force people to testify nor require that witnesses tell the truth. What Marshall does effectively in *Marbury* v. *Madison* is to make it appear that judicial review must be such an inherent power. He wrote: "It is emphatically the province and duty of the judicial department to say what the law is. Those who apply the rule to particular cases, must of necessity expound and interpret that rule. If two laws conflict with each other, the courts must decide on the operation of each. So if a law be in opposition to the Constitution; if both the law and the Constitution apply to a particular case, so that the court must either decide that case conformably to the law, disregarding the Constitution; or conformably to the Constitution, disregarding the law; the court must determine which of these conflicting rules governs the case. This is the very essence of judicial duty." Notice the use of the word "must" four times. Notice, too, that these assertions are not bolstered by empirical evidence.

As Judge Gibson of the Pennsylvania Supreme Court so eloquently pointed out in *Eakin* v. *Raub* (p. 26), a constitutional system does not necessarily require judicial review. Nor was Judge Gibson alone in his views in the early days of our history. Thomas Jefferson wrote in a letter to Spencer Roane in 1819: "My construction of the Constitution is * * * that each department is truly independent of the others, and has an equal right to decide for itself what is the meaning of the Constitution in the cases submitted to its action most especially where it is to act ultimately and without appeal. * * * Each of the three departments has equally the right to decide for itself what is its duty under the Constitution, without any regard to what the others may have decided for themselves under a similar question."

However persuasive you find the opinion of John Marshall, you should consider seriously the opinion of Judge Gibson and ask yourself whether it would be possible to operate a constitutional government without the institution of judicial review. In your consideration you should reflect upon the British experience which, by contrast, has been dominated by a different kind of Constitution but which appears to demonstrate a workable constitutional system without judicial review. Some thought should be given to how the British have been able, perhaps better than we, to safeguard civil liberties without judicial review. Here, too, you should ask yourself how our constitutional system would operate without judicial review. Courts would still, of course, decide cases. But they would assume at the outset of a case involving an act of Congress that the act was constitutional and proceed only on the basis of whether or not there was violation of law. Those who considered the law unconstitutional would be required then to battle it out in the political arena. In short, the Constitution would still be the supreme law of the land and the foundation of our system, but its primary interpretation would shift from the Court to other places and persons.

Whatever you decide about the rightness or wrongness of Marshall's position, he did win the battle. After the decision in *Marbury* v. *Madison*, judicial review did become part and parcel of our constitutional system, read into the Constitution so to speak. It is too late in our history to change that part of our system by judicial interpretation. It would require nothing short of a constitutional amendment to do away with the institution of judicial review.

As important as the decision in *Marbury* v. *Madison* was in establishing the power of judicial review over acts passed by Congress, other significant questions remained. One such issue, particularly crucial for a fledgling nation with a federal system of government, was whether the Supreme Court possessed the power to review a final judgment or decree of the highest court of a state. In its disposition of two cases, Martin v. Hunter's Lessee, 14 U.S. (1 Wheat.) 304, 4 L.Ed. 97 (1816) and Cohens v. Virginia, 19 U.S. (6 Wheat.) 264, 5 L.Ed. 257 (1821), the Court confirmed its appellate jurisdiction respectively in civil and criminal cases tried in state courts which presented federal constitutional questions. Chief Justice Marshall, whose opinions in both cases carried the day for the power of the national government in general and that of the Supreme Court in particular, rested this holding on Article III, section 2 which provides that "The judicial Power shall extend to *all* Cases, in Law and Equity, arising under this Constitution, the Laws of the United States, and Treaties made, or which shall be made, under their Authority; * * * " [emphasis supplied] and on the Supremacy Clause (Article VI, section 2) which declares, "This Constitution, and the Laws of the United States which shall be made in Pursuance thereof; and all Treaties made, or which shall be made, under the Authority of the United States, shall be the supreme Law of the Land; and the Judges in every State shall be bound thereby, any Thing in

the Constitution or Laws of any State to the Contrary notwithstanding."
Whatever doubts may be had about Marshall's wisdom in regard to judicial review of acts of Congress, his wisdom here appears less conjectural.
Although it is possible to conceive of a viable system where the decisions
of each state's highest court would not be subject to review, it is easy to
agree with Marshall that the consequences of such a procedure would be
"mischievous." In conjunction with this, it might be appropriate to consider, too, the Court's power to review acts of the state legislatures similarly predicated on the Supremacy Clause. In this regard a famous
statement by Justice Holmes seems particularly insightful. He wrote: "I
do not think the United States would come to an end if we lost our power
to declare an Act of Congress void. I do think the Union would be imperiled if we could not make that declaration as to the laws of the several
states."

It is important in the study of constitutional interpretation to understand the distinction between "judicial power" and "jurisdiction." "Jurisdiction" is the authority of a court to exercise "judicial power" in a
particular case. The Constitution vests "judicial power" in the courts;
Congress cannot enlarge or diminish it. But Congress has been granted
vast power in Article III, section 2 with respect to the jurisdiction of the
Supreme Court. In paragraph 2 of that section, after indicating the relatively few cases in which the Court shall have original jurisdiction (the
power to hear a case first), the Constitution provides that "In *all other
cases* before mentioned the Supreme Court shall have appellate jurisdiction, both as to law and fact, *with such exceptions and under such regulations as the Congress shall make.*" [Emphasis supplied.] There is no
question that Congress does have the constitutional authority to enlarge
or diminish the Court's *appellate* jurisdiction. And, as is apparent from
Ex parte McCardle (p. 32), once Congress has withdrawn the Court's
appellate jurisdiction in a particular class of cases, the Court is without
authority to render a decision in such a case even if it has already been
argued.

In periods when Congress is unhappy with the Court's decisions,
efforts are sometimes energized to curtail the appellate jurisdiction of the
Court. The decision in *McCardle* illustrates one such successful effort.
There have been others, some successful, some not (p. 219). However
much one might agree that such efforts are unwise, it cannot be contended that they are unconstitutional. If the diminution of appellate jurisdiction amounted to putting the Supreme Court out of business, perhaps a
case would be made that Congress went too far, for that portion of Article
III, section 2 quoted above does appear to grant *some* appellate jurisdiction and speaks of Congress making "exceptions" rather than granting it
full control.

The parameters of the Court's jurisdiction, both original and appellate,
are spelled out in various sections of Title 28 of the United States Code
Annotated (p. 34). Although the Supreme Court technically acts as a trial
court when it exercises its original jurisdiction, cases coming before the
Court for hearing in the first instance have not been tried to a jury since

before 1800. When the parties in a case have stipulated to the facts or where otherwise only questions of law are presented, the Court will hear argument. Where there is dispute as to the facts in the case, the Court's customary practice has been to appoint what is called a "Special Master" who functions as a kind of hearing officer. He takes testimony, hears argument, sifts evidence, and formulates conclusions both as to matters of fact and questions of law. The Master's report is advisory only and subject to exceptions and objections by the parties. The Court may then order argument on any of the findings or recommendations in dispute. In any case, the Court itself rules on all important motions and directly issues any orders granting or denying the ultimate relief sought.

Note that in the case of appellate jurisdiction there are three routes to the Court: by appeal, by certiorari, and by certification. Appeal, as the term is technically used here, denotes a route of seemingly obligatory review assigned by the statutes to cases in which a significant constitutional clash would appear to be readily indicated. When the Court takes a case on appeal, it so signifies by "not[ing] probable jurisdiction" and schedules the case for argument or disposes of it in a more summary fashion (as when it affirms or reverses the decision below without argument or issuing an opinion). The certiorari route (discussed below and so named because of the particular writ the Court grants in response to petitions in those cases) depends upon the Court's issuing of an order by which it signifies its interest in hearing a case and which is granted wholly as a matter of the Court's discretion. Certification is an infrequently used procedure by which a U. S. court of appeals or the Court of Claims asks the Supreme Court to answer a question necessary to the decision of a case pending before the lower court and as to which it is in need of guidance. (For the rules by which questions are certified to the Court and the procedures by which they are handled, see p. 37.) The provisions of Title 28 indicate which kinds of cases take which route. The Supreme Court's Rules specify differences in procedures and timing in employing the respective routes, but it is sufficient here that we be aware only that differences in these routes do exist. It is important to recognize, though, that an *appeal* where applicable is supposed to be a matter of *right*; in other words, the Court is supposed to have no discretion as to whether or not it will hear an appeal. But as a practical matter, the Court can decide that an appeal has no merit and turn it down without hearing the case. For example, the Court may dismiss an appeal "for want of jurisdiction" (see Quarles v. Texas, 404 U.S. 805, 92 S.Ct. 127 [1971] and Clark v. Craven, 404 U.S. 805, 92 S.Ct. 130 [1971]) or for "want of a substantial federal question" (see Cole v. Nigro, 404 U.S. 804, 92 S.Ct. 122 [1971]).

In some of the old cases you will come across the term "writ of error." Employed by the Court for a considerable span of its history, the writ was one means of securing review where federal law granted litigants review as a matter of right. A writ of error was issued by the Supreme Court to a state or lower federal court in a given case to signify exercise of the Court's obligatory appellate jurisdiction (1) in cases in which there was a question of "the validity of * * * an authority exercised under the United States" and the decision below was against validity, and (2) in cases where "the validity of * * * an authority exercised under any State" was challenged as "repugnant to the Constitution, treaties or laws of the United States" and the decision below was in favor of validity. But in 1928 Congress by law substituted an appeal for writ of error in all cases that were reviewable as a matter of right.

The overwhelming majority of cases which come to the Court for review come by way of writs of certiorari. The writ itself is a Court order directing that the record in a case below be sent up, and the significance of granting a petition for certiorari is, of course, that the Supreme Court will hear the case. Of the approximately 150 cases heard on the merits which the Court has averaged during recent Terms, roughly four-fifths reached the Court by the certiorari route, something less than one-fifth by appeal, and a negligible 1 or 2 percent of the matters decided by full opinion fell under the Court's original jurisdiction. In all, with an average of better than 5000 cases per Term crowding the Court's docket for consideration, the Justices have accorded review to under 6 percent. Because over nine-tenths of the Court's docket is composed of petitions for certiorari, it is important to know something of the Supreme Court's practice in making a determination as to which cases it will simply deny the writ. Those considerations are set out in Rule 19 (p. 37). At least four Justices must agree that a case presents a substantial federal question in order to grant a writ of certiorari. In a dissenting opinion in *Rogers* v. *Missouri Pacific Railroad Co.* (p. 38), in which he explained why he would not vote on the merits of a case where the Court had, through its "rule of four," granted certiorari, Justice Frankfurter illuminated the important considerations that govern the exercise of the Court's review power and ably defended the view that the Court must not become an agency for doing justice in individual cases. It is also worth noting, in terms of the kinds of cases that reach the Court, that for the last decade the Court has been mainly a Court of constitutional law. When Justice Frankfurter penned his dissent in *Rogers*, only a little more than a third of the cases on the Court's docket raised constitutional questions; two-thirds involved matters of statutory interpretation. A decade and a half later, however, constitutional cases claimed approximately 60 percent of the Court's docket, increasing threefold in fifteen years, while the Court's nonconstitutional business increased by only a third. Surely this underscores the importance of what Justice Frankfurter has to say.

What may we conclude when the Court denies a petition for a writ of certiorari in a given case? Many people think this means that the Supreme Court agreed with the lower court's treatment of the merits of the case. This is a badly mistaken impression, as Justice Frankfurter forcefully points out in the following excerpt from his statement in Maryland v. Baltimore Radio Show, Inc., 338 U.S. 912, 917–919, 70 S.Ct. 252, 254–255 (1950):

> The sole significance of such denial of a petition for writ of certiorari need not be elucidated to those versed in the Court's procedures. It simply means that fewer than four members of the Court deemed it desirable to review a decision of the lower court as a matter "of sound judicial discre-

tion." * * * A variety of considerations underlie denials of the writ, and as to the same petition different reasons may lead different Justices to the same result. This is especially true of petitions for review on writ of certiorari to a State court. Narrowly technical reasons may lead to denials. Review may be sought too late; the judgment of the lower court may not be final; it may not be the judgment of a State court of last resort; the decision may be supportable as a matter of State law, not subject to review by this Court, even though the State court also passed on issues of federal law. A decision may satisfy all these technical requirements and yet may command itself for review to fewer than four members of the Court. Pertinent considerations of judicial policy here come into play. A case may raise an important question but the record may be cloudy. It may be desirable to have different aspects of an issue further illumined by the lower courts. Wise adjudication has its own time for ripening.

Since there are these conflicting and, to the uninformed, even confusing reasons for denying petitions for certiorari, it has been suggested from time to time that the Court indicate its reasons for denial. Practical considerations preclude. In order that the Court may be enabled to discharge its indispensable duties, Congress has placed the control of the Court's business, in effect, within the Court's discretion. During the last three terms the Court disposed of 260, 217, 224 cases, respectively, on their merits. For the same three terms the Court denied, respectively, 1,260, 1,105, 1,189 petitions calling for discretionary review. If the Court is to do its work it would not be feasible to give reasons, however brief, for refusing to take these cases. The time that would be required is prohibitive, apart from the fact as already indicated that different reasons not infrequently move different members of the Court in concluding that a particular case at a particular time makes review undesirable. It becomes relevant here to note that failure to record a dissent from a denial of a petition for writ of certiorari in nowise implies that only the member of the Court who notes his dissent thought the petition should be granted.

Inasmuch, therefore, as all that a denial of a petition for a writ of certiorari means is that fewer than four members of the Court thought it should be granted, this Court has rigorously insisted that such a denial carries with it no implication whatever regarding the Court's views on the merits of a case which it has declined to review. The Court has said this again and again; again and again the admonition has to be repeated.

Justice Frankfurter's figures are now quite dated, but his observations still ring true. See Robert L. Stern and Eugene Gressman, *Supreme Court Practice* (5th ed., 1978), pp. 353–360. If anything, current figures strengthen what Justice Frankfurter said. The motivations behind denial of a petition for "cert." remain a mystery in any case, but the effect of having denied the writ, on the other hand, is clear: the decision of the highest ranking lower court in the case stands.

An understanding of "the judicial Power of the United States" would be grossly incomplete without some appreciation of the independence essential to preserving the integrity of the federal courts which is secured by the Constitution. In this regard it has long been thought useful to point out the difference between Article III and Article I courts. The third article of the Constitution vests judicial power "in one supreme

Court, and in such inferior Courts as the Congress may from time to time ordain and establish." The federal courts of appeals and district courts clearly fall within its ambit. The protections afforded tribunals deriving their authority from Article III include judicial life tenure with removability only for misconduct in office and the guarantee that judicial salaries may not be diminished during tenure in office. But all courts created by Congress do not draw their power from the judicial article of the Constitution. Courts such as the United States Tax Court and the United States Court of Military Appeals were established by Congress as "necessary and proper" under an appropriate enumerated power granted in Article I. As contrasted with "constitutional courts" created under Article III, courts created under Article I are known as "legislative courts." Not bound by the explicit or inherent requirements of the judicial article, Article I courts have judges who serve for fixed terms of office (fifteen years in the case of Tax Court and Military Appeals Court judges) and are not restricted to hearing only "cases and controversies" but may render advisory opinions or fulfill other functions permitted or directed by the Congress. Following the Supreme Court's decision in Ex parte Bakelite Corp., 279 U.S. 438, 49 S.Ct. 411 (1929), both the U. S. Court of Claims and the U. S. Court of Customs and Patent Appeals were regarded as Article I courts, but a later decision by the Court in Glidden Co. v. Zdanok, 370 U.S. 530, 82 S.Ct. 1459 (1962), recognized Congress's subsequent intent to accord these tribunals different status and confirmed them as Article III courts, although an opinion of several Justices cast doubt on the simplicity and ease with which the functions and work of Article I and Article III courts could be delineated.

b.   The Current Controversy over Judicial Review: Judicial Self-Restraint vs. the Preferred Freedoms Concept

The prospect in a democracy that appointed, life-tenured Justices hold the power to set aside policy choices made by popularly elected lawmakers has provoked a lively and ongoing debate on the Bench as well as off. All of the Justices accept judicial review as part of the American system, and all agree that the Court should exercise restraint in employing that power. But stout differences of opinion have remained as to the degree of restraint which should be exercised. Today, for example, some, like Chief Justice Burger and Justice Rehnquist, believe that judicial review should be like the shotgun behind the door—a lethal instrument to be used only in clear-cut cases where other agencies of national or state government patently violate the Constitution. Others, like Justices Brennan and Marshall, feel that with respect to the Bill of Rights and particularly the First Amendment the Court should play a more "activist" role and be prompt to vindicate important civil liberties. In bygone days such mighty protagonists as Justice Frankfurter and Justice Douglas championed the respective positions of judicial self-restraint and judicial activism. Able and eloquent expositions of these two positions are presented in turn in Justice Frankfurter's dissent in *West Virginia State Board of Education* v. *Bar-*

nette (p. 46) and in Justice Rutledge's opinion for the Court in *Thomas* v. *Collins* (p. 53).

The setting of the current debate—the greater or lesser deference to be accorded government regulation of civil liberties—may mislead the unwary observer into believing that the positions of judicial activism and self-restraint are simply covers for the judicial expression of merely personal preferences on the major policy issues of the day. It is frequently taken as a given, for example, that the position of the "activists" is the "liberal" position and that of the "restraintists" is "conservative." But history suggests that labels such as "activism" and "self-restraint" are better understood as manifestations of a judge's conception of his role rather than his personal political attitude. That positions of judicial activism and self-restraint need bear no essential relation to a particular political ideology is readily apparent from the contrast supplied by Justice Brandeis's dissent in *Burns Baking Co.* v. *Bryan*, (p. 43). In an earlier day judicial activism was employed to vindicate economic liberties and property rights, thereby preventing other institutions of government from effectively regulating economic activity. In those days liberals applauded judicial deference to national and state legislation aimed at regulating business and castigated judicial activism.

Justice Frankfurter's tenure on the Court superbly illuminates the role of judicial self-restraint. When he was appointed to the Court in 1939, he was a darling of the liberals, but his steadfast devotion to the precepts of that judicial role made him their *bête noire* by the time of his retirement in 1962. He was consistent throughout in his practice of judicial self-restraint, but the world had changed around him. The major issues with which the Court was dealing had shifted in the interim from economic regulation to civil liberties.

When coupled with a Justice's attitude toward making or merely applying law, his position on the Court's relation to other branches of government (i.e., his orientation toward judicial activism or self-restraint) forms a critical dimension to the major philosophies of constitutional adjudication that have dominated the Court in modern times. These frameworks or modes of constitutional interpretation, which justify the Court's greater or lesser invocation of judicial review and structure the response of Justices in concrete cases, are sketched out in the essay entitled, "Does the Supreme Court Have a Unique Function?" (p. 58).

c. Institutional Constraints on Judicial Problem Solving

An old cartoon from *The New Yorker* pictures the manager of a baseball team who, engaged in a heated argument with the umpire, stabs him in the chest with his finger and says, "I'll take this all the way up to the Supreme Court." It caricatures a persistent myth in American life that any issue can ultimately be brought to the Supreme Court for resolution. Yet, as a reading of the cases in this section will demonstrate, it is not so easy to get a case to the Supreme Court and, once there, to obtain a definitive decision.

Jurisdiction, we have already noted, is an indispensable requisite for Supreme Court consideration of any case. No less important a factor is justiciability, the appropriateness of the subject matter for judicial consideration. Jurisdiction is the authority of a tribunal to render a binding decision. Justiciability is a term used to characterize the structure and form of a legal dispute and denotes its suitability for adjudication. As Justice Brennan explained, speaking for the Court in *Baker* v. *Carr* (p. 102):

> The distinction between the two grounds is significant. In the instance of nonjusticiability, consideration of the cause is not wholly and immediately foreclosed; rather, the Court's inquiry necessarily proceeds to the point of deciding whether the duty asserted can be judicially identified and its breach judicially determined, and whether protection for the right asserted can be judicially molded.   *   *   *

The essence of a justiciable dispute is a real case and controversy. While other elements of justiciability are essentially for the Court itself to define (as contrasted with jurisdiction which, either as defined by the Constitution or limited by Congress, is beyond the Court's control), the necessity of a real case and controversy is mandated by Article III. Exactly what this means as a limitation on the kinds of causes the Supreme Court may hear is succinctly spelled out in the following words of Chief Justice Hughes, speaking for the Court in Aetna Life Insurance Co. v. Haworth, 300 U.S. 227, 240–242, 57 S.Ct. 461, 464 (1937):

> A "controversy" in this sense must be one that is appropriate for judicial determination.   *   *   *   A justiciable controversy is thus distinguished from a difference or dispute of a hypothetical or abstract character; from one that is academic or moot.   *   *   *   The controversy must be definite and concrete, touching the legal relations of parties having adverse legal interests.   *   *   *   It must be a real and substantial controversy admitting of specific relief through a decree of a conclusive character, as distinguished from an opinion advising what the law would be upon a hypothetical state of facts.   *   *   *   Where there is such a concrete case admitting of an immediate and definitive determination of the legal rights of the parties in an adversary proceeding upon the facts alleged, the judicial function may be appropriately exercised although the adjudication of the rights of the litigants may not require the award of process or the payment of damages.

In sum, then, the Court is barred from rendering advisory opinions, accepting hypothetical, abstract, or moot cases, and dealing with disputes which are collusive or trivial in nature, that is those without a genuine adverseness of substantial legal interests between the parties.

Yet a suit may contain a conflict between parties with substantial and adverse legal interests and still fail for other reasons of form. It may be, as the Court concluded in *International Longshoremen's & Warehousemen's Union* v. *Boyd* (p. 66), that such a controversy is not sufficiently ripe for review in its present posture. The requirement of ripeness exists to screen out disputes in which the facts have not sufficiently crystalized. In a word, a case not ripe for review is one that is premature.

A controversy of seemingly adverse and concrete legal interests may also fail to be entertained by the Court because the party bringing the suit lacks standing. Simply put, this means that the party initiating the suit must be the proper party to do so, one whose legal interests are indeed injured by the actions of another as alleged. The requirement of standing was at one time thought sufficient to exclude all taxpayer suits, as the opinion in *Frothingham* v. *Mellon* (p. 68) attests. But in 1968 the doctrine, at least with respect to that type of case, underwent a drastic change in *Flast* v. *Cohen* (p. 72). Liberalization of the standing requirement may, however, have been more apparent than real given some of the Court's more recent decisions (p. 82). And, quite apart from the matter of taxpayer suits, the dissenting Justices in Warth v. *Seldin* (p. 90) complain that in suits of all kinds the requirement of standing adopted by the present Court is set so high as to constitute a genuine impediment to legitimate causes of action.

Cases which present justiciable issues must also be contrasted with those which present "political questions." By employing this phrase to describe certain kinds of cases it will not hear, the Court is not suggesting that the disputes it does consider raise issues that are somehow apolitical. Obviously, since the Supreme Court, like all courts, is a political institution and since it accepts only cases raising substantial federal issues, the questions it decides are undeniably political questions of the most basic sort. Rather, the Court has in mind a very special meaning for the term, one which it uses to describe a certain class of cases which involve aspects of the separation of powers. The Court sets out the characteristics of cases involving "political questions" in *Baker* v. *Carr* (p. 102). The Court in *Baker* concluded that the reapportionment controversy was justiciable, at least when litigated under the Equal Protection Clause. Justice Frankfurter, on the other hand, thought in dissent that the case "presented a Guarantee Clause claim masquerading under a different label" and therefore constituted a "political question." The concept of the "political question" is also illustrated by a couple of more recent decisions, one by a federal appellate court in *Holtzman* v. *Schlesinger* (p. 118) and one by the Supreme Court in *Goldwater* v. *Carter* (p. 123).

The Court's concern with justiciability may appear dry and technical, but in fact it entails a controversy over judicial activism and self-restraint as important as that surrounding the exercise of judicial review on the merits of constitutional questions. It may appear odd at first glance that the Court should concern itself at all with the form in which suits are cast. But upon further reflection the necessity of its insistence on dealing only with justiciable matters becomes apparent. If suits were not in the proper form, the integrity of the judicial process itself would be threatened. Unless the circumstances of a dispute appear in bold relief, the Court will not be able to scrupulously observe the wise canon of adjudication that admonishes it to decide only what it has to in order to dispose of the matter. The more precise the definition of the problem at hand, the greater will be the Court's ability to see the law in relation to the dispute. The more remote or conjectural the controversy, the greater the Court's lack of confidence in speaking about the law; the more likely, too, that it will either overshoot the bounds of its proper holding (thus forcing the Court later to retract an overbroad or misleading ruling) or err entirely in disposing of a case. Indeed, insofar as the judicial process is defined "by the peculiar form of participation it accords the affected party, that of presenting proofs and arguments for a decision in his favor," [a] the lack of a sharply defined issue may seriously jeopardize the due process guarantee that the parties shall have their "day in court." The containment of the judicial process to involvement only with justiciable matters clearly serves the cause of judicial self-restraint, as is apparent in the following excerpt from Chief Justice Burger's opinion for the Court in Schlesinger v. Reservists Committee to Stop the War, 418 U.S. 208, 222, 94 S.Ct. 2925, 2932–2933 (1974): "To permit a complainant who has no concrete injury to require a court to rule on important constitutional issues in the abstract would create the potential for abuse of the judicial process, distort the role of the Judiciary in its relationship to the Executive and the Legislature and open the Judiciary to an arguable charge of providing 'government by injunction.'" But, as the decisions in *Boyd* and *Warth* attest, the other side of this coin is that tighter definitions of the elements of justiciability shrink—and perhaps close off entirely—the availability of the judicial process to disadvantaged individuals and groups in society. The wealthier plaintiff can often wait until tangible and costly injury occurs to make his complaint justiciable, but for the plaintiff of more modest means the price of admission to the judicial process may be the wager of his job or a jail term. It is the bias of this differential in what one has to put on the line to get to court that moves the judicial activist to loosen up on the requirements of case and controversy, ripeness, and standing. The dilemma in this is, of course, that there are costs involved in tightening or loosening the elements that make a case justiciable.

In appropriate justiciable cases the costliness of bringing many individual suits is obviated and the effectiveness of litigating enhanced with the filing of a "class action." These suits, where an action is brought by the plaintiff both for himself and for others similarly situated, are permitted in federal courts under conditions specified in Rule 23 of the Federal Rules of Civil Procedure:

Rule 23. Class Actions

(a) **Prerequisites to a Class Action.** One or more members of a class may sue or be sued as representative parties on behalf of all only if (1) the class is so numerous that joinder of all members is impracticable, (2) there are questions of law or fact common to the class, (3) the claims or defenses of the representative parties are typical of the claims or defenses of the class, and (4) the representative parties will fairly and adequately protect the interests of the class.

* * *

a. Fuller, *Adjudication and the Rule of Law*, 54 Proceedings of the American Society of International Law 1, 3 (1960).

(2) In any class action maintained under subdivision (b)(3), the court shall direct to the members of the class the best notice practicable under the circumstances, including individual notice to all members who can be identified through reasonable effort. * * *

The Court contracted the scope of the Rule, however, with its ruling in Eisen v. Carlisle & Jacquelin, 417 U.S. 156, 94 S.Ct. 2140 (1974), where it held that the class representative's refusal in that case to defray the cost of giving actual notice (as mandated by Rule 23(c)(2)) to 2,250,000 reasonably identifiable class members (at an estimated expense of $225,000) required dismissal of the suit. Such a ruling has an inhibiting influence particularly on consumer, environmental, civil rights, and antitrust cases that have a significant impact on large numbers of people collectively but not, perhaps, individually.

Finally, it is important to note another important constraint on the kinds of decisions available to parties coming before the Court. As the ruling in *Mississippi* v. *Johnson* (p. 124) indicates, the Court may not enjoin a coordinate branch of the government—in that case, the Executive—in the performance of entirely discretionary acts of office.

a. THE SUPREME COURT'S JURISDICTION AND ITS ASSUMPTION OF JUDICIAL REVIEW

MARBURY v. MADISON

Supreme Court of the United States, 1803
5 U.S. (1 Cranch) 137, 2 L.Ed. 60 [b]

The election of 1800 proved to be a disaster for the Federalist party. Their candidate for the Presidency, John Adams, was denied reelection and control of both houses of Congress fell to the Jeffersonians. In an effort to retain what political advantage they could—for they would never again gain a national popular mandate—the Federalists sought to entrench themselves in the federal judiciary.

---

b. Until the practice ceased with the beginning of its October 1875 Term, citations of cases decided by the Supreme Court bore the name of the Court's reporter. The reporter at the time *Marbury* v. *Madison* was decided was William Cranch who held the post until 1815. He succeeded the Court's first reporter, A. J. Dallas in 1801. Over the following years the Court's reports bore the names of Wheaton 1816–1827, Peters 1828–1842, Howard 1843–1860, Black 1861–1862, and Wallace 1863–1874. In each case the name of the reporter, appropriately abbreviated, was preceded by the volume of his reports in which the decision was to be found and followed by the page number on which the report of the case began. Though this basic format holds today, citation of cases is by series rather than reporter. The official series of the Court's decisions is known as the *United States Reports* and is abbreviated "U.S." There are also two commercially published series of the Court's decisions. The oldest is the *Lawyers' Edition*, published by the Lawyers Cooperative Publishing Company of Rochester, New York, and is abbreviated "L.Ed." or "L.Ed.2d," depending on whether it is in the first or second set of volumes. The third series of the Court's opinions is the *Supreme Court Reporter*, a unit of the National Reporter System published by West Publishing Company of St. Paul, Minnesota, and is abbreviated "S.Ct." A complete citation also includes the year in which the case was decided in parentheses at the end.

After the election but before March 4 of the following year, the date on which the Constitution prescribed that Thomas Jefferson would take the oath of office, Oliver Ellsworth, then Chief Justice, conveniently resigned for reasons of ill health, allowing President Adams to name a new Chief Justice. This he did by appointing his Secretary of State, John Marshall, an arch political enemy though a cousin of the President-elect. Marshall also retained his post in the Adams administration until it went out of office.

The Federalist-controlled "lame duck" Congress also obliged by passing legislation creating some fifty-eight additional judgeships to be filled by the party faithful. On February 3, 1801, it passed a law creating federal circuit courts designed to relieve Supreme Court Justices from the burdensome task of "riding circuit" in their dual capacity as appellate judges. These sixteen vacancies were promptly filled by Adams and commissions for them delivered before March 4. The men named to these vacancies are historically referred to as "the midnight judges" because of the late hour at which their commissions were delivered. Two weeks after it had passed the circuit court legislation, Congress passed an act which provided forty-two justices of the peace for the District of Columbia. It was this second piece of legislation which gave rise to the controversy in this case.

President Adams sent his nominations for this second wave of judicial appointments to the Senate, and they were confirmed on March 3. The commissions for these judgeships were signed by the President and the Seal of the United States affixed by Marshall as Secretary of State late the same day, but Adams's term expired before all the commissions could be delivered by John Marshall's brother, James, who returned four undelivered certificates to the Secretary of State's office. Upon entering office James Madison, the new Secretary of State, under instructions from President Jefferson refused to deliver these four remaining commissions, whereupon William Marbury, one of the four designated but uncertified judges, brought suit to recover his commission. Marbury lodged his suit directly with the Supreme Court asking that it vindicate his right to the commission under Section 13 of the Judiciary Act of 1789 by issuing a writ of mandamus (i.e., a court order commanding that the occupant of a given office fulfill a particular act within the purview of that office) directing Secretary of State Madison to deliver the certificate.

With a bare quorum of four of the six Justices participating, the Court handed down the following decision two years later. You may wonder, why the delay? The answer lies in the hostile response of the new Congress to these best-laid plans of the Federalists. Chafing under the repressive propensities of a Federalist judiciary already, as typified by the stern application of the Alien and Sedition acts, and rankled by these preinaugural maneuverings, the Jeffersonian majority voted to repeal the circuit court legislation and to cancel the Court's 1802 Term. Consequently, the Court did not meet to hear this case until its session in 1803.

[T]he following opinion of the court was delivered by the Chief Justice [MARSHALL]:

* * *

In the order in which the court has viewed this subject, the following questions have been considered and decided: 1st. Has the applicant a right to the commission he demands? 2d. If he has a right, and that right has been violated, do the laws of his country afford him a remedy? 3d. If they do afford him a remedy, is it a *mandamus* issuing from this court?

The first object of inquiry is— Has the applicant a right to the commission he demands? * * *

* * *

[Because the Constitution provides for the appointing and the commissioning of officers under separate sections of Article II, the two processes are distinctly different. The former has been completed when the President signs the commission, thus accepting the Senate's confirmation of his nominee. Chief Justice MARSHALL continued:]

Some point of time must be taken when the power of the executive over an officer, not removable at his will, must cease. That point of time must be when the constitutional power of appointment has been exercised. And this power has been exercised when the last act, required from the person possessing the power, has been performed. This last act is the signature of the commission. * * *

The signature is a warrant for affixing the great seal to the commission; and the great seal is only to be affixed to an instrument which is complete. It attests, by an act supposed to be of public notoriety, the verity of the presidential signature.

It is never to be affixed till the commission is signed, because the signature, which gives force and effect to the commission, is conclusive evidence that the appointment is made.

The commission being signed, the subsequent duty of the secretary of state is prescribed by law, and not to be guided by the will of the president. He is to affix the seal of the United States to the commission, and is to record it.

[Delivery of the commission cannot be regarded as a stage in the appointment process both because the process is concluded well before that event can take place and because, in Chief Justice MARSHALL's words, "transmission of the commission is a practice directed by convenience, but not by law." Were possession of the commission to be equated with appointment, then loss or destruction of the certificate would displace the officeholder from his post, which it surely does not. Under the law a certified copy of the commission, obtainable from the Secretary of State, is a valid substitute. Chief Justice MARSHALL concluded:]

Mr. Marbury, then, since his commission was signed by the president, and sealed by the secretary of state, was appointed; and as the law creating the office, gave the officer a right to hold for five years, independent of the executive, the appointment was not revocable, but vested in the officer legal rights, which are protected by the laws of his country. To withhold his commission, therefore, is an act deemed by the court not warranted by law, but violative of a vested legal right.

2. This brings us to the second inquiry; which is: If he has a right, and that right has been violated, do the laws of his country afford him a remedy? The very essence of civil liberty certainly consists in the right of every individual to claim the protection of the laws, whenever he receives an injury. One of the first duties of government is to afford that protection. In Great Britain, the king himself is sued in the respectful form of a petition, and he never fails to comply with the judgment of his court.

In the 3d vol. of his Commentaries (p. 23), Blackstone states two cases in which a remedy is afforded by mere operation of law. "In all other cases," he says, "it is a general and indisputable rule, that where there is a legal right, there is also a legal remedy by suit, or action at law, whenever that right is invaded."

And afterwards (p. 109, of the same vol.), he says, "I am next to consider such injuries as are cognisable by the courts of the common law. And herein I shall, for the present, only remark, that all possible injuries whatsoever, that did not fall within the exclusive cognisance of either the ecclesiastical, military or maritime tribunals, are, for that very reason, within the cognisance of the common-law courts of justice; for it is a settled and invariable principle in the laws of England, that every right, when withheld, must have a remedy, and every injury its proper redress."

The government of the United States has been emphatically termed a government of laws, and not of men. It will certainly cease to deserve this high appellation, if the laws furnish no remedy for the violation of a vested legal right. * * *

* * *

It follows, then, that the question, whether the legality of an act of the head of a department be examinable in a court of justice or not, must always depend on the nature of that act. If some acts be examinable, and others not, there must be some rule of law to guide the court in the exercise of its jurisdiction. In some instances, there may be difficulty in applying the rule to particular cases; but there cannot, it is believed, be much difficulty in laying down the rule.

By the constitution of the United States, the president is invested with certain important political powers, in the exercise of which he is to use his own discretion, and is accountable only to his country in his political character, and to his own conscience. To aid him in the performance of these duties, he is authorized to appoint certain officers, who act by his

authority, and in conformity with his orders. In such cases, their acts are his acts; and whatever opinion may be entertained of the manner in which executive discretion may be used, still there exists, and can exist, no power to control that discretion. The subjects are political: they respect the nation, not individual rights, and being entrusted to the executive, the decision of the executive is conclusive. The application of this remark will be perceived, by adverting to the act of congress for establishing the department of foreign affairs. This officer, as his duties were prescribed by that act, is to conform precisely to the will of the president: he is the mere organ by whom that will is communicated. The acts of such an officer, as an officer, can never be examinable by the courts. But when the legislature proceeds to impose on that officer other duties; when he is directed peremptorily to perform certain acts; when the rights of individuals are dependent on the performance of those acts; he is so far the officer of the law; is amenable to the laws for his conduct; and cannot, at his discretion, sport away the vested rights of others.

The conclusion from this reasoning is, that where the heads of departments are the political or confidential agents of the executive, merely to execute the will of the president, or rather to act in cases in which the executive possesses a constitutional or legal discretion, nothing can be more perfectly clear, than that their acts are only politically examinable. But where a specific duty is assigned by law, and individual rights depend upon the performance of that duty, it seems equally clear, that the individual who considers himself injured, has a right to resort to the laws of his country for a remedy.

If this be the rule, let us inquire, how it applies to the case under the consideration of the court. The power of nominating to the senate, and the power of appointing the person nominated, are political powers, to be exercised by the president, according to his own discretion. When he has made an appointment, he has exercised his whole power, and his discretion has been completely applied to the case. If, by law, the officer be removable at the will of the president, then a new appointment may be immediately made, and the rights of the officer are terminated. But as a fact which has existed, cannot be made never to have existed, the appointment cannot be annihilated; and consequently, if the officer is by law not removable at the will of the president, the rights he has acquired are protected by the law, and are not resumable by the president. They cannot be extinguished by executive authority, and he has the privilege of asserting them in like manner, as if they had been derived from any other source.

The question whether a right has vested or not, is, in its nature, judicial, and must be tried by the judicial authority. If, for example, Mr. Marbury had taken the oaths of a magistrate, and proceeded to act as one; in consequence of which, a suit has been instituted against him, in which his defence had depended on his being a magistrate, the validity of his appointment must have been determined by judicial authority. So, if he conceives that, by virtue of his appointment, he has a legal right either to the commission which has been made out for him, or to a copy of that commission, it is equally a question examinable in a court, and the

decision of the court upon it must depend on the opinion entertained of his appointment. That question has been discussed, and the opinion is, that the latest point of time which can be taken as that of which the appointment was complete, and evidence, was when, after the signature of the president, the seal of the United States was affixed to the commission.

It is, then, the opinion of the Court: 1st. That by signing the commission of Mr. Marbury, the President of the United States appointed him a justice of peace for the county of Washington, in the District of Columbia; and that the seal of the United States, affixed thereto by the secretary of state, is conclusive testimony of the verity of the signature, and of the completion of the appointment; and that the appointment conferred on him a legal right to the office for the space of five years. 2d. That, having this legal title to the office, he has a consequent right to the commission; a refusal to deliver which is a plain violation of that right, for which the laws of his country afford him a remedy.

3. It remains to be inquired whether he is entitled to the remedy for which he applies? This depends on—1st. The nature of the writ applied for; and 2d. The power of this court.

*   *   *

It is not by the office of the person to whom the writ is directed, but the nature of the thing to be done, that the propriety or impropriety of issuing a *mandamus* is to be determined. Where the head of a department acts in a case, in which executive discretion is to be exercised; in which he is the mere organ of executive will; it is again repeated, that any application to a court to control, in any respect, his conduct would be rejected without hesitation. But where he is directed by law to do a certain act, affecting the absolute rights of individuals, in the performance of which he is not placed under the particular direction of the president, and the performance of which the president cannot lawfully forbid, and therefore, is never presumed to have forbidden; as, for example, to record a commission or a patent for land, which has received all the legal solemnities; or to give a copy of such record; in such cases, it is not perceived, on what ground the courts of the country are further excused from the duty of giving judgment that right be done to an injured individual, than if the same services were to be performed by a person not the head of a department.

* * *

* * * The doctrine * * * now advanced, is by no means a novel one.

It is true, that the *mandamus*, now moved for, is not for the performance of an act expressly enjoined by statute. It is to deliver a commission; on which subject, the acts of congress are silent. This difference is not considered as affecting the case. It has already been stated, that the applicant has, to that commission, a vested legal right, of which the executive cannot deprive him. He has been appointed to an office, from which he is not removable at the will of the executive; and being so appointed, he has a right to the commission which the secretary has received from the president for his use. The act of congress does not indeed order the secretary of state to send it to him, but it is placed in his hands for the person en-

titled to it; and cannot be more lawfully withheld by him, than by any other person.

* * *

This, then, is a plain case for a *mandamus*, either to deliver the commission, or a copy of it from the record; and it only remains to be inquired, whether it can issue from this court?

The act to establish the judicial courts of the United States authorizes the supreme court, "to issue writs of *mandamus*, in cases warranted by the principles and usages of law, to any courts appointed or persons holding office, under the authority of the United States." The secretary of state, being a person holding an office, under the authority of the United States, is precisely within the letter of this description; and if this court is not authorized to issue a writ of *mandamus* to such an officer, it must be because the law is unconstitutional, and therefore, absolutely incapable of conferring the authority, and assigning the duties which its words purport to confer and assign.

The constitution vests the whole judicial power of the United States in one supreme court, and such inferior courts as congress shall, from time to time, ordain and establish. This power is expressly extended to all cases arising under the laws of the United States; and consequently, in some form, may be exercised over the present case; because the right claimed is given by a law of the United States.

In the distribution of this power, it is declared, that "the supreme court shall have original jurisdiction, in all cases affecting ambassadors, other public ministers and consuls, and those in which a state shall be a party. In all other cases, the supreme court shall have appellate jurisdiction." It has been insisted, at the bar, that as the original grant of jurisdiction to the supreme and inferior courts, is general, and the clause, assigning original jurisdiction to the supreme court, contains no negative or restrictive words, the power remains to the legislature, to assign original jurisdiction to that court, in other cases than those specified in the article which has been recited; provided those cases belong to the judicial power of the United States.

If it had been intended to leave it in the discretion of the legislature, to apportion the judicial power between the supreme and inferior courts, according to the will of that body, it would certainly have been useless to have proceeded further than to have defined the judicial power, and the tribunals in which it should be vested. The subsequent part of the section is mere surplusage—is entirely without meaning, if such is to be the construction. If congress remains at liberty to give this court appellate jurisdiction, where the constitution has declared their jurisdiction shall be original; and original jurisdiction where the constitution has declared it shall be appellate; the distribution of jurisdiction, made in the constitution, is form without substance. Affirmative words are often, in their operation, negative of other objects than those affirmed; and in this case, a negative or exclusive sense must be given to them, or they have no operation at all.

It cannot be presumed, that any clause in the constitution is intended to be without effect; and therefore, such a construction is inadmissible, unless the words require it. If the solicitude of the convention, respecting our peace with foreign powers, induced a provision that the supreme court should take original jurisdiction in cases which might be supposed to affect them; yet the clause would have proceeded no further than to provide for such cases, if no further restriction on the powers of congress had been intended. That they should have appellate jurisdiction in all other cases, with such exceptions as congress might make, is no restriction; unless the words be deemed exclusive of original jurisdiction.[c]

When an instrument organizing, fundamentally, a judicial system, di-

---

c. The relevant portion of the Judiciary Act of 1789, 1 Stat. 73, 80–81, is as follows:

Sec. 13. *And be it further enacted*, That the Supreme Court shall have exclusive jurisdiction of all controversies of a civil nature, where a state is a party, except between a state and its citizens; and except also between a state and citizens of other states, or aliens, in which latter case it shall have original but not exclusive jurisdiction. And shall have exclusively all such jurisdiction of suits or proceedings against ambassadors, or other public ministers, or their domestics, or domestic servants, as a court of law can have or exercise consistently with the law of nations; and original, but not exclusive jurisdiction of all suits brought by ambassadors, or other public ministers, or in which a consul, or vice consul, shall be a party. And the trial of issues in fact in the Supreme Court, in all actions at law against citizens of the United States, shall be by jury. *The Supreme Court shall also have appellate jurisdiction from the circuit courts and courts of the several states, in the cases herein after specially provided for; and shall have power to issue writs of prohibition to the district courts, when proceeding as courts of admiralty and maritime jurisdiction, and writs of mandamus, in cases warranted by the principles and usages of law, to any courts appointed, or persons holding office, under the authority of the United States.* [Emphasis supplied.]

vides it into one supreme, and so many inferior courts as the legislature may ordain and establish; then enumerates its powers, and proceeds so far to distribute them, as to define the jurisdiction of the supreme court, by declaring the cases in which it shall take original jurisdiction, and that in others it shall take appellate jurisdiction, the plain import of the words seems to be, that in one class of cases, its jurisdiction is original, and not appellate; in the other, it is appellate, and not original. If any other construction would render the clause inoperative, that is an additional reason for rejecting such other construction, and for adhering to their obvious meaning. To enable this court, then, to issue a *mandamus*, it must be shown to be an exercise of appellate jurisdiction, or to be necessary to enable them to exercise appellate jurisdiction.

It has been stated at the bar, that the appellate jurisdiction may be exercised in a variety of forms, and that if it be the will of the legislature that a *mandamus* should be used for that purpose, that will must be obeyed. This is true, yet the jurisdiction must be appellate, not original. It is the essential criterion of appellate jurisdiction, that it revises and corrects the proceedings in a cause already instituted, and does not create that cause. Although, therefore, a *mandamus* may be directed to courts, yet to issue such a writ to an officer, for the delivery of a paper, is, in effect, the same as to sustain an original action for that paper, and therefore, seems not to belong to appellate, but to original jurisdiction. Neither is it necessary in such a case as this, to enable the court to exercise its appellate jurisdiction. The authority, therefore, given to the supreme court by the act establishing

the judicial courts of the United States, to issue writs of *mandamus* to public officers, appears not to be warranted by the constitution; and it becomes necessary to inquire, whether a jurisdiction so conferred can be exercised.

The question, whether an act, repugnant to the constitution, can become the law of the land, is a question deeply interesting to the United States; but, happily, not of an intricacy proportioned to its interest. It seems only necessary to recognise certain principles, supposed to have been long and well established, to decide it. That the people have an original right to establish, for their future government, such principles as, in their opinion, shall most conduce to their own happiness, is the basis on which the whole American fabric has been erected. The exercise of this original right is a very great exertion; nor can it, nor ought it, to be frequently repeated. The principles, therefore, so established, are deemed fundamental: and as the authority from which they proceed is supreme, and can seldom act, they are designed to be permanent.

This original and supreme will organizes the government, and assigns to different departments their respective powers. It may either stop here, or establish certain limits not to be transcended by those departments. The government of the United States is of the latter description. The powers of the legislature are defined and limited; and that those limits may not be mistaken or forgotten, the constitution is written. To what purpose are powers limited, and to what purpose is that limitation committed to writing, if these limits may, at any time, be passed by those intended to be restrained? The distinction between a government with limited and unlimited powers is abolished, if those limits do not confine the persons on whom they are imposed, and if acts prohibited and acts allowed, are of equal obligation. It is a proposition too plain to be contested, that the constitution controls any legislative act repugnant to it; or that the legislature may alter the constitution by an ordinary act.

Between these alternatives, there is no middle ground. The constitution is either a superior paramount law, unchangeable by ordinary means, or it is on a level with ordinary legislative acts, and, like other acts, is alterable when the legislature shall please to alter it. If the former part of the alternative be true, then a legislative act, contrary to the constitution, is not law: if the latter part be true, then written constitutions are absurd attempts, on the part of the people, to limit a power, in its own nature, illimitable.

Certainly, all those who have framed written constitutions contemplate them as forming the fundamental and paramount law of the nation, and consequently, the theory of every such government must be, that an act of the legislature, repugnant to the constitution, is void. This theory is essentially attached to a written constitution, and is, consequently, to be considered, by this court, as one of the fundamental principles of our society. It is not, therefore, to be lost sight of, in the further consideration of this subject.

If an act of the legislature, repugnant to the constitution, is void, does it, notwithstanding its invalidity, bind the courts, and oblige them to give it effect? Or, in other words, though it be not law, does it constitute a rule as operative as if it was a law? This would be to overthrow, in fact, what

was established in theory; and would seem, at first view, an absurdity too gross to be insisted on. It shall, however, receive a more attentive consideration.

It is emphatically, the province and duty of the judicial department, to say what the law is. Those who apply the rule to particular cases, must of necessity expound and interpret that rule. If two laws conflict with each other, the courts must decide on the operation of each. So, if a law be in opposition to the constitution; if both the law and the constitution apply to a particular case, so that the court must either decide that case, conformable to the law, disregarding the constitution; or conformable to the constitution, disregarding the law; the court must determine which of these conflicting rules governs the case: this is of the very essence of judicial duty. If then, the courts are to regard the constitution, and the constitution is superior to any ordinary act of the legislature, the constitution, and not such ordinary act, must govern the case to which they both apply.

Those, then, who controvert the principle, that the constitution is to be considered, in court, as a paramount law, are reduced to the necessity of maintaining that courts must close their eyes on the constitution, and see only the law. This doctrine would subvert the very foundation of all written constitutions. It would declare that an act which, according to the principles and theory of our government, is entirely void, is yet, in practice, completely obligatory. It would declare, that if the legislature shall do what is expressly forbidden, such act, notwithstanding the express prohibition, is in reality effectual. It would be giving to the legislature a practical and real omnipotence, with the same breath which professes to restrict their powers within narrow limits. It is prescribing limits, and declaring that those limits may be passed at pleasure. That it thus reduces to nothing, what we have deemed the greatest improvement on political institutions, a written constitution, would, of itself, be sufficient, in America, where written constitutions have been viewed with so much reverence, for rejecting the construction. But the peculiar expressions of the constitution of the United States furnish additional arguments in favor of its rejection. The judicial power of the United States is extended to all cases arising under the constitution. Could it be the intention of those who gave this power, to say, that in using it, the constitution should not be looked into? That a case arising under the constitution should be decided, without examining the instrument under which it arises? This is too extravagant to be maintained. In some cases, then, the constitution must be looked into by the judges. And if they can open it at all, what part of it are they forbidden to read or to obey?

There are many other parts of the constitution which serve to illustrate this subject. It is declared, that "no tax or duty shall be laid on articles exported from any state." Suppose, a duty on the export of cotton, of tobacco or of flour; and a suit instituted to recover it. Ought judgment to be rendered in such a case? ought the judges to close their eyes on the constitution, and only see the law?

* * *

From these, and may other selections which might be made, it is apparent, that the framers of the constitution contemplated that instrument as a rule for the government of courts, as well as of the legislature. Why otherwise does it direct the judges to take an oath to support it? This oath certainly applies in an especial manner, to their conduct in their official character. How immoral to impose it on them, if they were to be used as the instruments, and the knowing instruments, for violating what they swear to support!

* * * If such be the real state of things, this is worse than solemn mockery. To prescribe, or to take this oath, becomes equally a crime.

It is also not entirely unworthy of observation, that in declaring what shall be the supreme law of the land, the constitution itself is first mentioned; and not the laws of the United States, generally, but those only which shall be made in pursuance of the constitution, have that rank.

Thus, the particular phraseology of the constitution of the United States confirms and strengthens the principle, supposed to be essential to all written constitutions, that a law repugnant to the constitution is void; and that courts, as well as other departments, are bound by that instrument.

The rule must be discharged.

EAKIN v. RAUB

Supreme Court of Pennsylvania, 1825
12 S. & R. 330

The facts and opinion of the court in this case have been omitted since they are of no particular importance to a study of constitutional law. Suffice it to say that the case, which was an ejectment proceeding, involved the power of the Pennsylvania Supreme Court to invalidate a state law. Justice Gibson disagreed with his colleagues on the resolution of this dispute and specifically took issue with the right of any court to exercise the power of judicial review. Gibson's opinion is considered one of the best expositions against the assertion of such judicial power. As a postscript it is interesting to note that twenty years later Justice Gibson changed his mind and retracted the position he took in the opinion excerpted below. Said Gibson, "I have changed that opinion for two reasons. The late convention [to draft a constitution for the Commonwealth of Pennsylvania], by their silence, sanctioned the pretensions of the courts to deal freely with the Acts of the Legislature; and from experience of the necessity of the case." Norris v. Clymer, 2 Pa. 277, 281 (1845).

GIBSON, J., dissenting. * * *

* * *

* * * I am aware, that a right to declare all unconstitutional acts void * * * is generally held as a professional dogma; but I apprehend, rather as a matter of faith than of reason. I admit, that I once embraced the same doctrine, but without examination, and I shall, therefore, state the arguments that impelled me to abandon it, with great respect for those by whom it is still maintained. But I may premise, that it is not a little remarkable that although the right in question has all along been claimed by the judiciary, no judge has ventured to discuss it, except Chief Justice MARSHALL * * * and if the argument of a jurist so distinguished for the strength of his ratiocinative powers be found inconclusive, it may fairly be set down to the weakness of the position which he attempts to defend. * * *

I begin, then, by observing, that in this country, the powers of the judiciary are divisible into those that are POLITICAL, and those that are purely CIVIL. Every power by which one organ of the government is enabled to control another, or to exert an influence over its acts, is a political power. The political powers of the judiciary are *extraordinary* and *adventitious*; such, for instance, as are derived from certain peculiar provisions in the constitution of the *United States*, of which hereafter: and they are derived, by direct grant from the common fountain of all political power. On the other hand, its civil, are its *ordinary* and *appropriate* powers; being part of its essence, and existing independently of any supposed grant in the constitution. But where the government exists by virtue of a *written* constitution, the judiciary does not necessarily derive from that circumstance, any other than its ordinary and appropriate powers. Our judiciary is constructed on the principles of the common law, which enters so essentially into the composition of our social institutions as to be inseparable from them, and to be, in fact, the basis of the whole scheme of our civil and political liberty. In adopting any organ or instrument of the common law, we take it with just such powers and capacities as were incident to it, at the common law, except where these are expressly, or by necessary implication, abridged or enlarged in the act of adoption; and that such act is a written instrument, cannot vary its consequences or construction. * * * Now, what are the powers of the judiciary, at the common law? They are those that necessarily arise out of its immediate business; and they are, therefore, commensurate only with the judicial execution of the municipal law, or, in other words, with the administration of distributive justice, without extending to anything of a political cast whatever. * * *

With us, although the legislature be the depository of only so much of the sovereignty as the people have thought fit to impart, it is, nevertheless, sovereign within the limit of its powers, and may relatively claim the same pre-eminence here, that it may claim elsewhere. It will be conceded, then, that the ordinary and essential powers of the judiciary do not extend to the annulling of an act of the legislature. * * *

The constitution of *Pennsylvania* contains no express grant of political powers to the judiciary. But to establish a grant by implication, the constitution is said to be a law of superior obligation; and consequently, that if it were to come into collision with an act of the legislature, the latter would have to give way; this is conceded. But it is a fallacy, to suppose, that they can come into collision *before the judiciary*. What is a constitution? It is an act of extraordinary legislation, by which the people establish the structure and mechanism of their government; and in which they prescribe fundamental rules to regulate the motion of the several parts. What is a statute? It is an act of ordinary legislation, by the appropriate organ of the government; the provisions of which are to be executed by the executive or judiciary, or by officers subordinate to them. The constitution, then, contains no practical rules for the administration of *distributive justice*, with which alone the judiciary has to do; these being furnished in acts of ordinary legislation, by that organ of the government, which, in this respect, is exclusively the representative of the people; and it is generally true, that the provisions of a constitution are to be carried into effect immediately by the legislature, and only mediately, if at all, by the judiciary. In what respect is the constitution of *Pennsylvania* inconsistent with this principle? Only, perhaps, in one particular provision, to regulate the style of process, and establish an appropriate form of conclusion in criminal prosecutions: in this alone, the constitution furnishes a rule for the judiciary, and this the legislature cannot alter, because it cannot alter the constitution. In all other cases, if the act of assembly supposed to be unconstitutional, were laid out of the question, there would remain no rule to determine the point in controversy in the cause, but the statute or common law, as it existed before the act of assembly was passed; and the constitution and act of assembly, therefore, do not furnish conflicting rules *applicable to the point before the court*; nor is it at all necessary, that the one or the other of them should give way.

The constitution and the *right* of the legislature to pass the act, may be in collision; but is that a legitimate subject for judicial determination? If it be, the judiciary must be

a peculiar organ, to revise the proceedings of the legislature, and to correct its mistakes; and in what part of the constitution are we to look for this proud preeminence? Viewing the matter in the opposite direction, what would be thought of an act of assembly in which it should be declared that the supreme court had, in a particular case, put a wrong construction on the constitution of the *United States*, and that the judgment should therefore be reversed? It would, doubtless, be thought a usurpation of judicial power. But it is by no means clear, that to declare a law void, which has been enacted according to the forms prescribed in the constitution, is not a usurpation of legislative power. It is an act of sovereignty; and sovereignty and legislative power are said by Sir William *Blackstone* to be convertible terms. It is the business of the judiciary, to interpret the laws, not scan the authority of the lawgiver; and without the latter, it cannot take cognizance of a collision between a law and the constitution. So that to affirm that the judiciary has a right to judge of the existence of such collision, is to take for granted the very thing to be proved; and that a very cogent argument may be made in this way, I am not disposed to deny.
* * *

But it has been said to be emphatically the business of the judiciary, to ascertain and pronounce what the law is; and that this necessarily involves a consideration of the constitution. It does so: but how far? If the judiciary will inquire into anything beside the form of enactment, where shall it stop? There must be some point of limitation to such an inquiry; for no one will pretend, that a judge would be justifiable in calling for the election returns, or scrutiniz-

ing the qualifications of those who composed the legislature.

* * *

[L]et it be supposed that the power to declare a law unconstitutional has been exercised. What is to be done? The legislature must acquiesce, although it may think the construction of the judiciary wrong. But why must it acquiesce? Only because it is bound to pay that respect to every other organ of the government, which it has a right to exact from each of them in turn. This is the argument. But it will not be pretended, that the legislature has not, at least, an equal right with the judiciary to put a construction on the constitution; nor that either of them is infallible; nor that either ought to be required to surrender its judgment to the other. Suppose, then, they differ in opinion as to the constitutionality of a particular law; if the organ whose business it first is to decide on the subject, is not to have its judgment treated with respect, what shall prevent it from securing the preponderance of its opinion by the strong arm of power? It is in vain to say, the legislature would be the aggressor in this; and that no argument in favor of its authority can be drawn from an abuse of its power.
* * *

* * * But, in theory, all the organs of the government are of equal capacity; or, if not equal, each must be supposed to have superior capacity only for those things which peculiarly belong to it; and as legislation peculiarly involves the consideration of those limitations which are put on the law-making power, and the interpretation of the laws when made, involves only the construction of the laws themselves, it follows, that the construction of the constitution, in

this particular, belongs to the legislature, which ought, therefore, to be taken to have superior capacity to judge of the constitutionality of its own acts. But suppose all to be of equal capacity, in every respect, why should one exercise a controlling power over the rest? That the judiciary is of superior rank, has never been pretended, although it has been said to be co-ordinate. It is not easy, however, to comprehend how the power which gives law to all the rest, can be of no more than equal rank with one which receives it, and is answerable to the former for the observance of its statutes. Legislation is essentially an act of sovereign power; but the execution of the laws by instruments that are governed by prescribed rules, and exercise no power of volition, is essentially otherwise. * * * It may be said, the power of the legislature, also, is limited by prescribed rules: it is so. But it is, nevertheless, the power of the people, and sovereign as far as it extends. It cannot be said, that the judiciary is co-ordinate, merely because it is established by the constitution; if that were sufficient sheriffs, registers of wills and recorders of deeds would be so too. Within the pale of their authority, the acts of these officers will have the power of the people for their support; but no one will pretend, they are of equal dignity with the acts of the legislature. Inequality of rank arises not from the manner in which the organ has been constituted, but from its essence and the nature of its functions; and the legislative organ is superior to every other, inasmuch as the power to will and to command, is essentially superior to the power to act and to obey. * * *

* * *

Every one knows how seldom men think exactly alike on ordinary subjects; and a government constructed on the principle of assent by all its parts, would be inadequate to the most simple operations. The notion of a complication of counter-checks has been carried to an extent in theory, of which the framers of the constitution never dreamt. When the entire sovereignty was separated into its elementary parts, and distributed to the appropriate branches, all things incident to the exercise of its powers were committed to each branch exclusively. The negative which each part of the legislature may exercise, in regard to the acts of the other, was thought sufficient to prevent material infractions of the restraints which were put on the power of the whole; for, had it been intended to interpose the judiciary as an additional barrier, the matter would surely not have been left in doubt. The judges would not have been left to stand on the insecure and ever-shifting ground of public opinion, as to constructive power; they would have been placed on the impregnable ground of an express grant; they would not have been compelled to resort to the debates in the convention, or the opinion that was generally entertained at the time. A constitution, or a statute, is supposed to contain the whole will of the body from which it emanated; and I would just as soon resort to the debates in the legislature, for the construction of an act of assembly, as to the debates in the convention, for the construction of the constitution.

The power is said to be restricted to cases that are free from doubt or difficulty. But the abstract existence of a power cannot depend on the clearness or obscurity of the case in which it is to be exercised; for that is a consideration that cannot present itself, before the question of the existence of the power shall have been determined; and if its existence be conceded, no considerations of policy, arising from the obscurity of the particular case, ought to influence the exercise of it. * * * To say, therefore, that the power is to be exercised but in perfectly clear cases, is to betray a doubt of the propriety of exercising it at all. Were the same caution used in judging of the existence of the power, that is inculcated as to the exercise of it, the profession would, perhaps, arrive at a different conclusion. The grant of a power so extraordinary, ought to appear so plain, that he who should run might read. * * *

But the judges are sworn to support the constitution, and are they not bound by it as the law of the land? In some respects they are. In the very few cases in which the judiciary, and not the legislature, is the immediate organ to execute its provisions, they are bound by it, in preference to any act of assembly to the contrary; in such cases, the constitution is a rule to the courts. But what I have in view in this inquiry is, the supposed right of the judiciary, to interfere, in cases where the constitution is to be carried into effect through the instrumentality of the legislature, and where that organ must necessarily first decide on the constitutionality of its own act. The oath to support the constitution is not peculiar to the judges, but is taken indiscriminately by every officer of the government, and is designed rather as a test of the political principles of the man, than to bind the officer in the discharge of his duty: otherwise, it were difficult to determine, what operation it is to have in the case of a recorder of deeds, for instance, who, in the execution of his office, has nothing to do with the constitution. But granting it to relate to the official conduct of the judge, as well as every other officer, and not to his political principles, still, it must be understood in reference to supporting the constitution, *only as far as that may be involved in his official duty*; and consequently, if his official duty does not comprehend an inquiry into the authority of the legislature, neither does his oath. * * *

But do not the judges do a *positive* act in violation of the constitution, when they give effect to an unconstitutional law? Not if the law has been passed according to the forms established in the constitution. The fallacy of the question is, in supposing that the judiciary adopts the acts of the legislature as its own; whereas, the enactment of a law and the interpretation of it are not concurrent acts, and as the judiciary is not required to concur in the enactment, neither is it in the breach of the constitution which may be the consequence of the enactment; the fault is imputable to the legislature, and on it the responsibility exclusively rests. * * *

* * *

But it has been said, that this construction would deprive the citizen of the advantages which are peculiar to a written constitution, by at once declaring the power of the legislature, in practice, to be illimitable. * * * But there is no magic or inherent power in parchment and ink, to command respect, and protect principles from violation. In the business of government, a recurrence to first principles answers the end of an observation at sea, with a view to correct the dead-reckoning; and for this purpose, a written constitution is an instrument of inestimable value. It is of inestimable value also, in rendering its principles familiar to the mass of the people; for, after all, there is no effectual guard against legislative usurpation, but public opinion, the force of which, in this country, is inconceivably great. * * * Once let public opinion be so corrupt, as to sanction every misconstruction of the constitution, and abuse of power, which the temptation of the moment may dictate, and the party which may happen to be predominant, will laugh at the puny efforts of a dependent power to arrest it in its course.

For these reasons, I am of opinion, that it rests with the people, in whom full and absolute sovereign power resides, to correct abuses in legislation, by instructing their representatives to repeal the obnoxious act. What is wanting to plenary power in the government, is reserved by the people, for their own immediate use; and to redress an infringement of their rights in this respect, would seem to be an accessory of the power thus reserved. It might, perhaps, have been better to vest the power in the judiciary; as it might be expected, that its habits of deliberation, and the aid derived from the arguments of counsel, would more frequently lead to accurate conclusions. On the other hand, the judiciary is not infallible; and an error by it would admit of no remedy but a more distinct expression of the public will, through the extraordinary medium of a convention; whereas, an error by the legislature admits of a remedy by an exertion of the same will, in the ordinary exercise of the right of suffrage—a mode better calculated to attain the end, without

popular excitement. It may be said, the people would probably not notice an error of their representatives. But they would as probably do so, as notice an error of the judiciary; and besides, it is a *postulate* in the theory of our government, and the very basis of the superstructure, that the people are wise, virtuous, and competent to manage their own affairs; and if they are not so, in fact, still, every question of this sort must be determined according to the principles of the constitution, as it came from the hands of its framers, and the existence of a defect which was not foreseen, would not justify those who administer the government, in applying a corrective in practice, which can be provided only by a convention.

* * *

But in regard to an act of assembly, which is found to be in collision with the constitution, laws or treaties of the *United States*, I take the duty of the judiciary to be exactly the reverse. By becoming parties to the federal constitution, the states have agreed to several limitations of their individual sovereignty, to enforce which, it was thought to be absolutely necessary, to prevent them from giving effect to laws in violation of those limitations, through the instrumentality of their own judges. Accordingly, it is declared in the sixth article and second section of the federal constitution, that "This constitution, and the laws of the *United States* which shall be made in pursuance thereof, and all treaties made, or which shall be made under the authority of the *United States*, shall be the *supreme* law of the land; and the *judges* in every *state* shall be BOUND thereby; anything in the *laws* or *constitution* of any *state* to the contrary notwithstanding.''

This is an express grant of a political power, and it is conclusive, to show that no law of inferior obligation, as every state law must necessarily be, can be executed at the expense of the constitution, laws or treaties of the *United States*. It may be said, these are to furnish a rule only when there is no state provision on the subject. But in that view, they could, with no propriety, be called supreme; for supremacy is a relative term, and cannot be predicated of a thing which exists separately and alone: and this law, which is called supreme, would change its character and become subordinate,

as soon as it should be found in conflict with a state law. But the judges are to be bound by the federal constitution and laws, notwithstanding anything in the constitution or laws of the particular state *to the contrary*. If, then, a state were to declare the laws of the *United States* not to be obligatory on her judges, such an act would unquestionably be void; for it will not be pretended, that any member of the union can dispense with the obligation of the federal constitution; and if it cannot be done directly, and by a general declaratory law, neither can it indirectly, and by by-laws dispensing with it in particular cases.
* * *

* * *

EX PARTE McCARDLE
Supreme Court of the United States, 1869
74 U.S. (7 Wall.) 506, 19 L.Ed. 264

McCardle, a newspaper editor, was under detention by the military government occupying Mississippi for trial before a military commission on charges that he had allowed to be published articles alleged to be "incendiary and libelous." As a civilian, McCardle asserted that he was being unlawfully restrained and, on appeal, sought a writ of habeas corpus (a court order based upon a determination that one in custody is being detained contrary to due process which commands that the custodian of the prisoner deliver him up for the court) from the Supreme Court. The Court heard full arguments in the case, but before it could meet in conference to arrive at a decision, Congress, under the control of the Radical Republicans, passed legislation which repealed the statute of 1867 authorizing the Court to hear appeals in such cases. The repeal, reenacted by the necessary constitutional majorities in both houses of Congress over President Andrew Johnson's veto, was typical of the efforts of the Radicals to check the efforts of both the judiciary and the executive to mitigate the harshness of post-Civil War reconstruction policy in the South. The usual adversary format is missing in the title to this case; in proceedings such as this where a petition to the court is at the demand and for the benefit of only one party, the action is said to be *ex parte*, "on the side of" or "on the application of" the party named.

The Chief Justice [CHASE] delivered the opinion of the court.

* * *

The first question necessarily is

that of jurisdiction; for, if the act of March, 1868, takes away the jurisdiction defined by the act of February, 1867, it is useless, if not improper, to enter into any discussion of other questions.

It is quite true, as was argued by the counsel for the petitioner, that the appellate jurisdiction of this court is not derived from acts of Congress. It is, strictly speaking, conferred by the Constitution. But it is conferred "with such exceptions and under such regulations as Congress shall make."

It is unnecessary to consider whether, if Congress had made no exceptions and no regulations, this court might not have exercised general appellate jurisdiction under rules prescribed by itself. For among the earliest acts of the first Congress, at its first session, was the act of September 24th, 1789, to establish the judicial courts of the United States. That act provided for the organization of this court, and prescribed regulations for the exercise of its jurisdiction.

The source of that jurisdiction, and the limitations of it by the Constitution and by statute, have been on several occasions subjects of consideration here. In the case of Durousseau v. The United States [6 Cr. 312, 3 L.Ed. 232] particularly, the whole matter was carefully examined, and the court held, that while "the appellate powers of this court are not given by the judicial act, but are given by the Constitution," they are, nevertheless, "limited and regulated by that act, and by such other acts as have been passed on the subject." The court said, further, that the judicial act was an exercise of the power given by the Constitution to Congress "of making exceptions to the appellate jurisdiction of the Supreme Court." "They have described affirmatively," said the court, "its jurisdiction, and this affirmative description has been understood to imply a negation of the exercise of such appellate power as is not comprehended within it."

The principle that the affirmation of appellate jurisdiction implies the negation of all such jurisdiction not affirmed having been thus established, it was an almost necessary consequence that acts of Congress, providing for the exercise of jurisdiction, should come to be spoken of as acts granting jurisdiction, and not as acts making exceptions to the constitutional grant of it.

The exception to appellate jurisdiction in the case before us, however, is not an inference from the affirmation of other appellate jurisdiction. It is made in terms. The provision of the act of 1867, affirming the appellate jurisdiction of this court in cases of *habeas corpus* is expressly repealed. It is hardly possible to imagine a plainer instance of positive exception.

We are not at liberty to inquire into the motives of the legislature. We can only examine into its power under the Constitution; and the power to make exceptions to the appellate jurisdiction of this court is given by express words.

What, then, is the effect of the repealing act upon the case before us? We cannot doubt as to this. Without jurisdiction the court cannot proceed at all in any cause. Jurisdiction is power to declare the law, and when it ceases to exist, the only function remaining to the court is that of announcing the fact and dismissing the cause. And this is not less clear upon authority than upon principle.

Several cases were cited by the counsel for the petitioner in support of the position that jurisdiction of this case is not affected by the repealing act. But none of them, in our judgment, afford any support to it. They are all cases of the exercise of judicial power by the legislature, or of legislative interference with courts in the exercising of continuing jurisdiction.

On the other hand, the general rule, supported by the best elementary writers, is, that "when an act of the legislature is repealed, it must be considered, except as to transactions past and closed, as if it never existed." And the effect of repealing acts upon suits under acts repealed, has been determined by the adjudications of this court. The subject was fully considered in Norris v. Crocker [13 How. 429, 14 L.Ed. 210] and more recently in Insurance Company v. Ritchie [5 Wall. 541, 18 L.Ed. 540]. In both of these cases it was held that no judgment could be rendered in a suit after the repeal of the act under which it was brought and prosecuted.

It is quite clear, therefore, that this court cannot proceed to pronounce judgment in this case, for it has no longer jurisdiction of the appeal; and judicial duty is not less fitly performed by declining ungranted jurisdiction than in exercising firmly that which the Constitution and the laws confer.

Counsel seem to have supposed, if effect be given to the repealing act in question, that the whole appellate power of the court, in cases of *habeas corpus*, is denied. But this is an error. The act of 1868 does not except from that jurisdiction any cases but appeals from Circuit Courts under the act of 1867. It does not affect the jurisdiction which was previously exercised.

The appeal of the petitioner in this case must be dismissed for want of jurisdiction.

STATUTORY PROVISIONS GOVERNING THE SUPREME COURT'S ORIGINAL AND APPELLATE JURISDICTION

The following sections of Title 28 of the United States Code Annotated govern the Supreme Court's jurisdiction:

§ 1251. Original jurisdiction

(a) The Supreme Court shall have original and exclusive jurisdiction of:

(1) All controversies between two or more States;

(2) All actions or proceedings against ambassadors or other public ministers of foreign states or their domestics or domestic servants, not inconsistent with the law of nations.

(b) The Supreme Court shall have original but not exclusive jurisdiction of:

(1) All actions or proceedings brought by ambassadors or other public ministers of foreign states or to which consuls or vice consuls of foreign states are parties;

(2) All controversies between the United States and a State;

(3) All actions or proceedings by a State against the citizens of another State or against aliens.

§ 1252. Direct appeals from decisions invalidating Acts of Congress

Any party may appeal to the Supreme Court from an interlocutory or final judgment, decree or order of any court of the United States, the

United States District Court for the District of the Canal Zone, the District Court of Guam and the District Court of the Virgin Islands and any court of record of Puerto Rico, holding an Act of Congress unconstitutional in any civil action, suit, or proceeding to which the United States or any of its agencies, or any officer or employee thereof, as such officer or employee, is a party.

A party who has received notice of appeal under this section shall take any subsequent appeal or cross appeal to the Supreme Court. All appeals or cross appeals taken to other courts prior to such notice shall be treated as taken directly to the Supreme Court.

§ 1253. Direct appeals from decisions of three-judge courts

Except as otherwise provided by law, any party may appeal to the Supreme Court from an order granting or denying, after notice and hearing, an interlocutory or permanent injunction in any civil action, suit or proceeding required by any Act of Congress to be heard and determined by a district court of three judges.

§ 1254. Courts of appeals; certiorari; appeal; certified questions

Cases in the courts of appeals may be reviewed by the Supreme Court by the following methods:

(1) By writ of certiorari granted upon the petition of any party to any civil or criminal case, before or after rendition of judgment or decree;

(2) By appeal by a party relying on a State statute held by a court of appeals to be invalid as repugnant to the Constitution, treaties or laws of the United States, but such appeal shall preclude review by writ of certiorari at the instance of such appellant, and the review on appeal shall be restricted to the Federal questions presented;

(3) By certification at any time by a court of appeals of any question of law in any civil or criminal case as to which instructions are desired, and upon such certification the Supreme Court may give binding instructions or require the entire record to be sent up for decision of the entire matter in controversy.

§ 1255. Court of Claims; certiorari; certified questions

Cases in the Court of Claims may be reviewed by the Supreme Court by the following methods:

(1) By writ of certiorari granted on petition of the United States or the claimant;

(2) By certification of any question of law by the Court of Claims in any case as to which instructions are desired, and upon such certification the Supreme Court may give binding instructions on such question.

§ 1256. Court of Customs and Patent Appeals; certiorari

Cases in the Court of Customs and Patent Appeals may be reviewed by the Supreme Court by writ of certiorari.

§ 1257. State courts; appeal; certiorari

Final judgments or decrees rendered by the highest court of a State in which a decision could be had, may be reviewed by the Supreme Court as follows:

(1) By appeal, where is drawn in question the validity of a treaty or statute of the United States and the decision is against its validity.

(2) By appeal, where is drawn in question the validity of a statute of any state on the ground of its being repugnant to the Constitution, treaties or laws of the United States, and the decision is in favor of its validity.

(3) By writ of certiorari, where the validity of a treaty or statute of the United States is drawn in question or where the validity of a State statute is drawn in question on the ground of its being repugnant to the Constitution, treaties or laws of the United States, or where any title, right, privilege or immunity is specially set up or claimed under the Constitution, treaties or statutes of, or commission held or authority exercised under, the United States.

* * *

For the purposes of this section, the term "highest court of a State" includes the District of Columbia Court of Appeals.

§ 1258.   Supreme Court of Puerto Rico; appeal; certiorari

Final judgments or decrees rendered by the Supreme Court of the Commonwealth of Puerto Rico may be reviewed by the Supreme Court as follows:

(1) By appeal, where is drawn in question the validity of a treaty or statute of the United States and the decision is against its validity.

(2) By appeal, where is drawn in question the validity of a statute of the Commonwealth of Puerto Rico on the ground of its being repugnant to the Constitution, treaties, or laws of the United States, and the decision is in favor of its validity.

(3) By writ of certiorari, where the validity of a treaty or statute of the United States is drawn in question or where the validity of a statute of the Commonwealth of Puerto Rico is drawn in question on the ground of its being repugnant to the Constitution, treaties, or laws of the United States, or where any title, right, privilege, or immunity is specially set up or claimed under the Constitution, treaties, or statutes of, or commission held or authority exercised under, the United States.

Before their repeal in 1976, 28 U.S.C.A. §§ 2281 and 2282 required the convening of three-judge federal district courts and direct appeals from them to the Supreme Court in suits to enjoin enforcement of state and federal laws on grounds of unconstitutionality. Such suits today are heard by single-judge district courts with appeals to the courts of appeals. Because use of three-judge district courts has long been thought to be outmoded and burdensome, use of such a procedure is now confined to reapportionment cases and certain suits pertaining to the 1964 Civil Rights Act, the Voting Rights Act and related statutes, the Regional Rail Reorganization Act, and the Presidential Election Campaign Fund Act. Congress, in fact, has come under increasing pressure, most recently at the unanimous and urgent request of the Justices themselves, to dispense with any obligatory character in the Court's appellate jurisdiction and to give the Supreme Court complete discretion as to the cases it will hear. A bill (S 3100) reported out of the Senate Judiciary Committee in 1978 during the 95th Congress contained provisions which would have largely abolished review as a matter of right, with certain minor exceptions. Said the committee's report recommending passage: "It [the continuation of mandatory jurisdiction] detracts from the Court's ability to control its own docket and to effectuate its constitutional mission of resolving only those matters that are of truly national significance." Although the legislation failed to pass by the end of that session or the session following, future attempts at enactment are a certainty.

RULES OF THE SUPREME COURT
CONCERNING CERTIORARI AND CERTIFICATION

Rule 19. Considerations governing review on certiorari

1. A review on writ of certiorari is not a matter of right, but of sound judicial discretion, and will be granted only where there are special and important reasons therefor. The following, while neither controlling nor fully measuring the court's discretion, indicate the character of reasons which will be considered:

(a) Where a state court has decided a federal question of substance not theretofore determined by this court, or has decided it in a way probably not in accord with applicable decisions of this court.

(b) Where a court of appeals has rendered a decision in conflict with the decision of another court of appeals on the same matter; or has decided an important state or territorial question in a way in conflict with applicable state or territorial law; or has decided an important question of federal law which has not been, but should be, settled by this court; or has decided a federal question in a way in conflict with applicable decisions of this court; or has so far departed from the accepted and usual course of judicial proceedings, or so far sanctioned such a departure by a lower court, as to call for an exercise of this court's power of supervision.

2. The same general considerations outlined above will control in respect of petitions for writs of certiorari to review judgments of the Court of Claims, of the Court of Customs and Patent Appeals, or of any other court whose determinations are by law reviewable on writ of certiorari.

Rule 28. Questions certified by a court of appeals
or by the Court of Claims

1. Where a court of appeals or the Court of Claims shall certify to this court a question or proposition of law, concerning which it desires instruction for the proper decision of a cause, the certificate shall contain a statement of the nature of the cause and of the facts on which such question or proposition of law arises. Questions of fact cannot be certified. Only questions or propositions of law may be certified, and they must be distinct and definite.

2. If in a cause certified by a court of appeals it appears that there is special reason therefor, this court may on application, or on its own motion, require that the entire record be sent up, so that it may consider and decide the entire matter in controversy.

Rule 29. Procedure in certified cases

1. When a case is certified, the certificate itself constitutes the record. The clerk will upon receipt thereof from the court below notify the appellant in the court of appeals, or the plaintiff in the Court of Claims, who shall thereupon pay the docket fee, after which the case will be placed on the docket. If the appellant or plaintiff fails to pay the fee, the appellee or defendant may do so. The appearance of counsel for the party paying the fee shall be entered at the time of payment.

2. After docketing, the certificate shall be submitted to the court for a preliminary examination to determine whether the case shall be set for argument or whether the certificate will be dismissed.

3. Any portion of the record to which the parties wish to direct the court's particular attention shall be printed in a single appendix prepared by the appellant or plaintiff in the court below under the procedures provided in Rule 36, but the fact that any part of the record has not been printed shall not prevent the parties or the court from relying on it.

* * *

ROGERS v. MISSOURI PACIFIC RAILROAD CO.

Supreme Court of the United States, 1957
352 U.S. 500, 521, 77 S.Ct. 443, 459, 1 L.Ed.2d 493, 520

The Federal Employer's Liability Act grants railroad employees a more liberal right of recovery for on-the-job injuries by replacing traditional limitations on common law remedies with a general duty imposed upon the employer to pay damages for job-related injury or death due in whole or in part to the employer's negligence. The statutory burden can be met by the employee and the employer's obligation to pay damages established by proof which is wholly circumstantial. Congress has extended the same right of recovery through the Jones Act to shipmen serving in the merchant marine. Usually the Court's attention in such cases focuses on the question of whether the employer's negligence played any part, no matter how small, in the employee's injury or death so as to warrant submission of the case to the jury. The Supreme Court granted certiorari and heard argument in three FELA cases and one Jones Act case. In one case a section gang laborer was injured in a fall while burning off grass and weeds from the company right of way; in a second, a brakeman was hurt when he slipped on an unnoticed and partially covered cinder; in a third, a conductor sustained injury when he was thrown to the floor of a caboose because the train came to a sudden stop; and in a fourth case a ship's baker accidently sliced off two of his fingers while using a butcher knife to chip hard ice cream. The Court defended its consideration of these cases by pointing out that it had a "duty to effectuate the intention of the Congress to secure the right to a jury determination, * * * to correct instances of improper administration of the Act and to prevent its erosion by narrow and niggardly construction." Justice Frankfurter voiced strong disagreement with the majority and explained his objection to according full review to these cases in the following opinion.

Mr. Justice FRANKFURTER, dissenting.

* * *

* * * For many years, I reluctantly voted on the merits of these negligence cases that had been granted review. In the last ten years, and more particularly within the past few years, as the Court has been granting more and more of these petitions, I have found it increasingly difficult to acquiesce in a practice that I regard as wholly incompatible with the certiorari policy embodied in the 1916 Act, the Judiciary Act of 1925, 43 Stat. 936, and the Rules formulated by the Court to govern certiorari jurisdiction for its own regulation and for the guidance of the bar. I have therefore felt compelled to vote to dismiss petitions for certiorari in such cases as improvidently granted without passing on the merits. In these cases I indicated briefly the reasons why I believed that this Court should not be reviewing decisions in which the sole issue is the sufficiency of the evidence for submission to the jury. In view of the increasing number of these cases that have been brought here for review—this dissent is to four decisions of the Court—and in view of the encouragement thereby given to continuing resort to this Court, I deem it necessary to enlarge upon the considerations that have guided me in the conviction that writs in this class of cases are "improvidently granted."

At the outset, however, I should deal briefly with a preliminary problem. It is sometimes said that the "integrity of the certiorari process" as expressed in the "rule of four" (that is, this Court's practice of granting certiorari on the vote of four Justices) requires all the Justices to vote on the merits of a case when four Justices have voted to grant certiorari and no new factor emerges after argument and deliberation. There are two reasons why there can be no such requirement. Last Term, for example, the Court disposed of 1,361 petitions for certiorari. With such a volume of certiorari business, not to mention the remainder of the Court's business, the initial decision to grant a petition for certiorari must necessarily be based on a limited appreciation of the issues in a case, resting as it so largely does on the partisan claims in briefs of counsel. * * * The Court does not, indeed it cannot and should not try to, give to the initial question of granting or denying a petition the kind of attention that is demanded by a decision on the merits. The assumption that we know no more after hearing and deliberating on a case than after reading the petition for certiorari and the response is

inadmissible in theory and not true in fact. * * * The course of argument and the briefs on the merits may disclose that a case appearing on the surface to warrant a writ of certiorari does not warrant it, * * * or may reveal more clearly that the only thing in controversy is an appraisal of facts on which this Court is being asked to make a second guess, to substitute its assessment of the testimony for that of the court below.

But there is a more basic reason why the "integrity of the certiorari process" does not require me to vote on the merits of these cases. The right of a Justice to dissent from an action of the Court is historic. Of course self-restraint should guide the expression of dissent. But dissent is essential to an effective judiciary in a democratic society, and especially for a tribunal exercising the powers of this Court. Not four, not eight, Justices can require another to decide a case that he regards as not properly before the Court. The failure of a Justice to persuade his colleagues does not require him to yield to their views, if he has a deep conviction that the issue is sufficiently important. Moreover, the Court operates ultimately by majority. Even though a minority may bring a case here for oral argument, that does not mean that the majority has given up its right to vote on the ultimate disposition of the case as conscience directs. This is not a novel doctrine. As a matter of practice, members of the Court have at various times exercised this right of refusing to pass on the merits of cases that in their view should not have been granted review.

This does not make the "rule of four" a hollow rule. I would not change the practice. No Justice is likely to vote to dismiss a writ of certiorari as improvidently granted after argument has been heard, even though he has not been convinced that the case is within the rules of the Court governing the granting of certiorari.

In the usual instance, a doubting Justice respects the judgment of his brethren that the case does concern issues important enough for the Court's consideration and adjudication. But a different situation is presented when a class of cases is systematically taken for review. Then a Justice who believes that such cases raise insignificant and unimportant questions—insignificant and unimportant from the point of view of the Court's duties—and that an increasing amount of the Court's time is unduly drained by adjudication of these cases cannot forego his duty to voice his dissent to the Court's action.

The "rule of four" is not a command of Congress. It is a working rule devised by the Court as a practical mode of determining that a case is deserving of review, the theory being that if four Justices find that a legal question of general importance is raised, that is ample proof that the question has such importance. This is a fair enough rule of thumb on the assumption that four Justices find such importance on an individualized screening of the cases sought to be reviewed. The reason for deference to a minority view no longer holds when a class of litigation is given a special and privileged position.

* * *

In all good conscience, what "special and important" reason for granting certiorari do the facts in any one of these cases disclose? In three of them, the trial judge had allowed a case to go to the jury, and three unanimous reviewing courts—two

Courts of Appeals and one state Supreme Court—had reversed for lack of evidence. In each of these cases, this Court has combed the record and found that there was sufficient evidence for the case to go to the jury, * * * whereas in * * * [a fourth] the Court found insufficiency of evidence to go to the jury. * * *

In any event, the Court in these four cases has merely reviewed evidence that has already been reviewed by two lower courts, and in so doing it ignores its own strictures to the bar that "We do not grant a certiorari to review evidence and discuss specific facts." United States v. Johnston, 268 U.S. 220, 227, 45 S.Ct. 496, 497. * * * If the Court does not abide by its Rules, how can it expect the bar to do so? Standards must be enforced to be respected. If they are merely left as something on paper, they might as well be written on water.

The rule that the Court does not grant certiorari to review evidence is a wise rule, indeed indispensable to the work of the Court, and is as equally applicable to negligence cases as to any other type of case. * * *

* * *

"One's deep sympathy is of course aroused by a victim of the hazards of negligence litigation in situations like the one before us. But the remedy for an obsolete and uncivilized system of compensation for loss of life or limb of crews on ships and trains is not intermittent disregard of the considerations which led Congress to entrust this Court with the discretion of certiorari jurisdiction. The remedy is an adequate and effective system of workmen's compensation," adequate in amount and especially prompt in administration. McAllister v. United States, 348 U.S. 19, 23–24, 75 S.Ct. 6, 9 (separate opinion). It deserves to be recorded that Professor John Chipman Gray, a legal scholar with social insight, taught his students fifty years ago, before the first workmen's compensation law had been enacted, that it is anachronistic to apply the common-law doctrine of negligence to injuries suffered by railroad employees rather than have society recognize such injuries as inevitable incidents of railroading and provide compensation on that basis. The persistence of this archaic and cruel system is attributable to many factors. Inertia of course. But also it is merely one illustration of the lag of reform because of the opposition of lawyers who resist change of the familiar, particularly when they have thriven under some outworn doctrine of law. Finally, one cannot acquit the encouragement given by this Court for seeking success in the lottery of obtaining heavy verdicts of contributing to the continuance of this system of compensation whose essential injustice can hardly be alleviated by the occasional "correction" in this Court of ill-success.

* * * For this Court to take a case which turns merely on such an appraisal of evidence, however much hardship in the fallible application of an archaic system of compensation for injuries to railroad employees may touch our private sympathy, is to deny due regard to the considerations which led the Court to ask and Congress to give the power to control the Court's docket. Such power carries with it the responsibility of granting review only in cases that demand adjudication on the basis of importance to the operation of our federal system; importance of the outcome merely to the parties is not enough. * * * "

* * *

This is not the supreme court of review for every case decided "unjustly" by every court in the country. The Court's practice in taking these Federal Employers' Liability Act cases discriminates against other personal injury cases, for example those in the federal courts on diversity jurisdiction. Similar questions of negligence are involved there and the opportunity for swallowing up more of the Supreme Court's energy is very great indeed. * * * Whether or not it be true that we are a litigious people, it is a matter of experience that clients, if not lawyers, have a strong urge to exhaust all possibility of further appeal, particularly when judicially encouraged to do so. Disappointed litigants and losing lawyers like to have another go at it, and why should they not try when certiorari was granted in cases like these?

* * *

* * * [E]xperience leaves no doubt, though the fact cannot be established statistically, that by granting review in these cases, the Court encourages the filing of petitions for certiorari in other types of cases raising issues that likewise have no business to be brought here. Moreover, the considerations governing discharge of the Court's function involve only in part quantitative factors. Finally, and most important, granting review in one or two cases that present a compassionate appeal on this ground and one or two that present a compassionate appeal on that ground and one or two that present a compassionate appeal on a third ground inevitably makes that

drain upon the available energy of the Court that is so inimical to the fullest investigation of, the amplest deliberation on, the most effective opinion-writing and the most critical examination of draft opinions in, the cases that have unquestioned claims upon the Court.

* * *

This unvarnished account of Federal Employers' Liability Act litigation in this Court relating to sufficiency of the evidence for submission of cases to the jury is surely not an exhilarating story. For the Supreme Court of the United States to spend two hours of solemn argument, plus countless other hours reading the briefs and record and writing opinions, to determine whether there was evidence to support an allegation that it could reasonably be foreseen that an ice-cream server on a ship would use a butcher's knife to scoop out ice cream that was too hard to be scooped with a regular scoop, is surely to misconceive the discretion that was entrusted to the wisdom of the Court for the control of its calendar. The Court may or may not be "doing justice" in the four insignificant cases it decides today; it certainly is doing injustice to the significant and important cases on the calendar and to its own role as the supreme judicial body of the country.

It is, I believe, wholly accurate to say that the Court will be enabled to discharge adequately the vital, and, I feel the increasingly vital, responsibility it bears for the general welfare only if it restricts its reviewing power to the adjudication of constitutional issues or other questions of national importance, including therein settlement of conflict among the circuits. Surely it was this conviction, born of experience, that led the

Court to ask of Congress that of the great mass of litigation in the state and federal courts only those cases should be allowed to be brought here that this Court deemed fit for review. Such was the jurisdictional policy accepted by Congress when it yielded to the Court's realization of the conditions necessary for its proper functioning.

For one thing, as the current United States Reports compared with those of even a generation ago amply prove, the types of cases now calling for decision to a considerable extent require, investigation of voluminous literature far beyond the law reports and other legal writings. If it is to yield its proper significance, this vast mass of materials, often confused and conflicting, must be passed through the seive of reflection. Judicial reflection is a process that requires time and freedom from the pressure of having more work to do than can be well done. It is not a bit of quixotism to believe that, of the 63 cases scheduled for argument during the remaining months of this Term, there are a half dozen that could alone easily absorb the entire thought of the Court for the rest of the Term.

The judgments of this Court are collective judgments. Such judgments are especially dependent on ample time for private study and reflection in preparation for discussion in Conference. Without adequate study, there cannot be adequate reflection; without adequate reflection, there cannot be adequate discussion; without adequate discussion, there cannot be that full and fruitful interchange of minds that is indispensable to wise decisions and persuasive opinions by the Court. Unless the Court vigorously enforces its own criteria for granting review of cases, it will inevitably face an accumulation of arrears or will dispose of its essential business in too hurried and therefore too shallow a way.

I would dismiss all four writs of certiorari as improvidently granted.

b. THE CURRENT CONTROVERSY OVER JUDICIAL REVIEW: JUDICIAL SELF-RESTRAINT vs. THE PREFERRED FREEDOMS CONCEPT

BURNS BAKING CO. v. BRYAN

Supreme Court of the United States, 1924
264 U.S. 504, 44 S.Ct. 412, 68 L.Ed. 813

Plaintiff in this suit was a Nebraska baking company appealing a decision of the Nebraska Supreme Court which upheld a 1921 act of the state legislature regulating the weight of loaves of bread sold in the state. A seven-man majority on the U. S. Supreme Court subsequently invalidated the legislation on grounds that such a power to legislate in the interest of the welfare of the state's inhabitants was overridden by the guarantee to the plaintiff under the Fourteenth Amendment that certain economic freedoms not be abridged without due process of law. The excerpt from Justice Brandeis's dissenting opinion below took exception to the majority's standards for assessing constitutional validity.

Mr. Justice BRANDEIS (with whom Mr. Justice HOLMES concurs) dissenting.

The purpose of the Nebraska standard weight bread law is to protect buyers from short weights and honest bakers from unfair competition. It provides for a few standard size loaves, which are designated by weight, and prohibits, as to each size, the baking or selling of a loaf which weighs either less or more than the prescribed weight. Schmidinger v. Chicago, 226 U.S. 578, 33 S.Ct. 182, * * * settled that the business of making and selling bread is a permissible subject for regulation, that the prevention of short weights is a proper end of regulation, that the fixing of standard sizes and weights of loaves is an appropriate means to that end, and that prevalent marketing frauds make the enactment of some such protective legislation permissible. The ordinance there upheld, besides defining the standard weight loaf, required that every loaf should bear a label stating the weight, and to sell a loaf weighing less than the weight stated in the label was made a misdemeanor.

The Nebraska regulation is in four respects less stringent than the ordinance upheld in the *Schmidinger* Case: (1) It provides for a tolerance; that is, it permits a deviation from the standard weight of not more than 2 ounces in a pound, provided that the prescribed standard weight shall be determined by averaging the weights of not less than 25 loaves of any one unit. (2) The prescribed weight applies for only 24 hours after the baking. (3) The weight is to be ascertained by weighing on the premises where the bread is baked. (4) No label stating the weight is required to be affixed to the loaf; that is, as a representation of the weight, the familiar size of the loaf is substituted for the label. On the other hand, the Nebraska requirement is more stringent than the Chicago ordinance, in that it prohibits making and selling loaves which exceed the prescribed weight by more than the tolerance. This prohibition of excess weights is held to deny due process of law to bakers and sellers of bread. In plain English, the prohibition is declared to be a measure so arbitrary or whimsical that no body of legislators, acting reasonably, could have imposed it. In reaching this conclusion, the court finds specifically that this prohibition "is not necessary for the protection of purchasers against imposition and fraud by short weights," that it "is not calculated to effectuate that purpose," and that the practical difficulties of compliance with the limitation are so great that the provision "subjects bakers and sellers of bread to restrictions which are essentially unreasonable and arbitrary."

To bake a loaf of any size other than the standard is made a misdemeanor. Why baking a loaf which weighs less than the standard size should be made a crime is obvious. Such a loaf is a handy instrument of fraud. Why it should be a crime to bake one which weighs more than the standard is not obvious. The reason given is that such a loaf, also, is a handy instrument of fraud. In order that the buyer may be afforded protection, the difference between the standard sizes must be so large as to be evident and conspicuous. The buyer has usually in mind the difference in appearance between a one-pound loaf and a pound and a half loaf, so that it is difficult for the dealer to palm off the former for the latter. But a loaf weighing one pound and five ounces may look so much like the buyer's memory of the pound and a half loaf that the dealer may effectuate the fraud by delivering the former. The prohibition of excess weight is imposed in order to prevent a loaf of one standard size from being increased so much that it can readily be sold for a loaf of a larger standard size.

With the wisdom of the legislation we have, of course, no concern. But, under the due process clause as construed, we must determine whether the prohibition of excess weights can reasonably be deemed necessary, whether the prohibition can reasonably be deemed an appropriate means of preventing short weights and incidental unfair practices, and whether compliance with the limitation prescribed can reasonably be deemed practicable. The determination of these questions involves an enquiry into facts. Unless we know the facts on which the legislators may have acted, we cannot properly decide whether they were (or whether their measures are) unreasonable, arbitrary or capricious. Knowledge is essential to understanding, and understanding should precede judging. Sometimes, if we would guide by the light of reason, we must let our minds be bold. But, in this case, we have merely to acquaint ourselves with the art of breadmaking and the usages of the trade, with the devices by which buyers of bread are imposed upon and honest bakers or dealers are subjected by their dishonest fellows to unfair competition, with the problems which have confronted public officials charged with the enforcement of the laws prohibiting short weights, and with their experience in administering those laws.

First. Why did legislators, bent only on preventing short weights, prohibit also excessive weights? It was not from caprice or love of symmetry. It was because experience had taught consumers, honest dealers, and public officials charged with the duty of enforcing laws concerning weights and measures that, if short weights were to be prevented, the prohibition of excessive weights was an administrative necessity. Similar experience had led to the enactment of a like prohibition of excess quantities in laws designed to prevent defrauding, by short measure, purchasers of many other articles. * * *

* * * In Nebraska the demand for the legislation under review was general and persistent. It was enacted after a prolonged public discussion carried on throughout the state as well as in the Legislature. Can it be said, in view of these facts, that the legislators had not reasonable cause to believe that prohibition of excess weights was necessary in order to protect buyers of bread from imposition and honest dealers from unfair competition?

Second. Is the prohibition of excess weights calculated to effectuate the purpose of the act? In other words, is it a provision which can reasonably be expected to aid in the enforcement of the prohibition of short weights? That it has proved elsewhere an important aid is shown by abundant evidence of the highest quality. * * *

Third. Does the prohibition of excess weight impose unreasonable burdens upon the business of making and selling bread? In other words, would compliance involve bakers in heavy costs, or necessitate the employment of persons of greater skill than are ordinarily available? Or would the probability of unintentional transgression be so great as unreasonably to expose those engaged in the business to the danger of criminal prosecution? Facts established by widespread and varied experience of the bakers under laws containing a similar provision, and the extensive investigation and experiments of competent scientists, seem to compel a negative answer to each of these questions. But we need not go so far. There is certainly reason to believe that the provision does not subject the baker to an appreciable cost; that it does not require a higher degree of skill than is commonly available to bakery concerns; and that it does not expose honest bakers to the danger of criminal proceedings. * * *

* * * The evidence contained in the record in this case is * * * ample to sustain the validity of the statute. There is in the record some evidence in conflict with it. The Legislature and the lower court have, doubtless, considered that. But with this conflicting evidence we have no concern. It is not our province to weigh evidence. Put at its highest, our function is to determine, in the light of all facts which may enrich our knowledge and enlarge our understanding, whether the measure, enacted in the exercise of an unquestioned police power and of a character inherently unobjectionable, transcends the bounds of reason; that is, whether the provision as applied is so clearly arbitrary or capricious that legislators acting reasonably could not have believed it to be necessary or appropriate for the public welfare.

To decide, as a fact, that the prohibition of excess weights "is not necessary for the protection of the purchasers against imposition and fraud by short weights," that it "is not calculated to effectuate that purpose," and that it "subjects bakers and sellers of bread" to heavy burdens, is, in my opinion, an exercise of the powers of a super-Legislature—not the performance of the constitutional function of judicial review.

WEST VIRGINIA STATE BOARD OF EDUCATION v. BARNETTE

Supreme Court of the United States, 1943
319 U.S. 624, 63 S.Ct. 1178, 87 L.Ed. 1628

Walter Barnette and others sued to restrain the West Virginia State Board of Education from enforcing its directive, issued pursuant to a statute passed by the state legislature, requiring public school children throughout the state to salute the American flag as a part of the regular program of school activities. Six Justices of the Supreme Court voted to invalidate the mandatory flag salute. Justice Frankfurter, a Jewish immigrant from Austria, cast one of the three dissenting votes. In his eloquent dissenting opinion, reproduced below, Frankfurter speaks at some length on what he perceives the role of a judge to be in the American political process. A more complete account of the background to this case and excerpts of other opinions rendered begin on p. 1313.

Mr. Justice FRANKFURTER, dissenting.

One who belongs to the most vilified and persecuted minority in history is not likely to be insensible to the freedoms guaranteed by our Constitution. Were my purely personal attitude relevant I should wholeheartedly associate myself with the general libertarian views in the Court's opinion, representing as they do the thought and action of a lifetime. But as judges we are neither Jew nor Gentile, neither Catholic nor agnostic. We owe equal attachment to the Constitution and are equally bound by our judicial obligations whether we derive our citizenship from the earliest or the latest immigrants to these shores. As a member of this Court I am not justified in writing my private notions of policy into the Constitution, no matter how deeply I may cherish them or how mischievous I may deem their disregard. The duty of a judge who must decide which of two claims before the Court shall prevail, that of a State to enact and enforce laws within its general competence or that of an individual to refuse obedience because of the demands of his conscience, is not that of the ordinary person. It can never be emphasized too much that one's own opinion about the wisdom or evil of a law should be excluded altogether when one is doing one's duty on the bench. The only opinion of our own even looking in that direction that is material is our opinion whether legislators could in reason have enacted such a law. In the light of all the circumstances, including the history of this question in this Court, it would require more daring than I possess to deny that reasonable legislators could have taken the action which is before us for review. Most unwillingly, therefore, I must differ from my brethren with regard to legislation like this. I cannot bring my mind to believe that the "liberty" secured by the Due Process Clause gives this Court authority to deny to the State of West Virginia the attainment of that which we all recognize as a legitimate legislative end, namely, the promotion of good citizenship, by employment of the means here chosen.

Not so long ago we were admonished that "the only check upon our own exercise of power is our own sense of self-restraint. For the removal of unwise laws from the statute books appeal lies, not to the courts, but to the ballot and to the processes of democratic government." United States v. Butler, 297 U.S. 1, 79, 56 S.Ct. 312, 325. We have been told that generalities do not decide concrete cases. But the intensity with which a general principle is held may determine a particular issue, and whether we put first things first may decide a specific controversy.

The admonition that judicial self-restraint alone limits arbitrary exercise of our authority is relevant every time we are asked to nullify legislation. The Constitution does not give us greater veto power when dealing with one phase of "liberty" than with another, or when dealing with grade school regulations than with college regulations that offend conscience, as was the case in Hamilton v. Regents, 293 U.S. 245, 55 S.Ct. 197. In neither situation is our function comparable to that of a legislature or are we free to act as though we were a super-legislature. Judicial self-restraint is equally necessary whenever an exercise of political or legislative power is challenged. There is no warrant in the constitutional basis of this Court's authority for attributing different roles to it depending upon the nature of the challenge to the legislation. Our power does not vary according to the particular provision of the Bill of Rights which is invoked. The right not to have property taken without just compensation has, so far as the scope of judicial power is concerned,

the same constitutional dignity as the right to be protected against unreasonable searches and seizures, and the latter has no less claim than freedom of the press or freedom of speech or religious freedom. In no instance is this Court the primary protector of the particular liberty that is invoked. This Court has recognized, what hardly could be denied, that all the provisions of the first ten Amendments are "specific" prohibitions. * * * But each specific Amendment, in so far as embraced within the Fourteenth Amendment, must be equally respected, and the function of this Court does not differ in passing on the constitutionality of legislation challenged under different Amendments.

When Mr. Justice Holmes, speaking for this Court, wrote that "it must be remembered that legislatures are ultimate guardians of the liberties and welfare of the people in quite as great a degree as the courts," * * * he went to the very essence of our constitutional system and the democratic conception of our society. He did not mean that for only some phases of civil government this Court was not to supplant legislatures and sit in judgment upon the right or wrong of a challenged measure. He was stating the comprehensive judicial duty and role of this Court in our constitutional scheme whenever legislation is sought to be nullified on any ground, namely, that responsibility for legislation lies with legislatures, answerable as they are directly to the people, and this Court's only and very narrow function is to determine whether within the broad grant of authority vested in legislatures they have exercised a judgment for which reasonable justification can be offered.

The framers of the federal Constitution might have chosen to assign an active share in the process of legislation to this Court. They had before them the well-known example of New York's Council of Revision, which had been functioning since 1777. After stating that "laws inconsistent with the spirit of this constitution, or with the public good, may be hastily and unadvisedly passed," the state constitution made the judges of New York part of the legislative process by providing that "all bills which have passed the senate and assembly shall, before they become laws," be presented to a Council of which the judges constituted a majority, "for their revisal and consideration." Art. III, New York Constitution of 1777. Judges exercised this legislative function in New York for nearly fifty years. See Art. I, § 12, New York Constitution of 1821. But the framers of the Constitution denied such legislative powers to the federal judiciary. They chose instead to insulate the judiciary from the legislative function. They did not grant to this Court supervision over legislation.

The reason why from the beginning even the narrow judicial authority to nullify legislation has been viewed with a jealous eye is that it serves to prevent the full play of the democratic process. The fact that it may be an undemocratic aspect of our scheme of government does not call for its rejection or its disuse. But it is the best of reasons, as this Court has frequently recognized, for the greatest caution in its use.

The precise scope of the question before us defines the limits of the constitutional power that is in issue. The State of West Virginia requires all pupils to share in the salute to the flag as part of school training in citizenship. The present action is one to enjoin the enforcement of this requirement by those in school attendance. We have not before us any attempt by the State to punish disobedient children or visit penal consequences on their parents. All that is in question is the right of the state to compel participation in this exercise by those who choose to attend the public schools.

We are not reviewing merely the action of a local school board. The flag salute requirement in this case comes before us with the full authority of the State of West Virginia. We are in fact passing judgment on "the power of the State as a whole." * * * Practically we are passing upon the political power of each of the forty-eight states. Moreover, since the First Amendment has been read into the Fourteenth, our problem is precisely the same as it would be if we had before us an Act of Congress for the District of Columbia. To suggest that we are here concerned with the heedless action of some village tyrants is to distort the augustness of the constitutional issue and the reach of the consequences of our decision.

Under our constitutional system the legislature is charged solely with civil concerns of society. If the avowed or intrinsic legislative purpose is either to promote or to discourage some religious community or creed, it is clearly within the constitutional restrictions imposed on legislatures and cannot stand. But it by no means follows that legislative power is wanting whenever a general non-discriminatory civil regulation in fact touches conscientious scruples or religious beliefs of an individual or a group. Regard for such scruples or beliefs undoubtedly presents one of the most reasonable claims for the exertion of legislative accommodation. It is, of course, beyond our power to rewrite the state's requirement, by providing exemptions for those who do not wish to participate in the flag salute or by making some other accommodations to meet their scruples. That wisdom might suggest the making of such accommodations and that school administration would not find it too difficult to make them and yet maintain the ceremony for those not refusing to conform, is outside our province to suggest. Tact, respect, and generosity toward variant views will always commend themselves to those charged with the duties of legislation so as to achieve a maximum of good will and to require a minimum of unwilling submission to a general law. But the real question is, who is to make such accommodations, the courts or the legislature?

This is no dry, technical matter. It cuts deep into one's conception of the democratic process—it concerns no less the practical differences between the means for making these accommodations that are open to courts and to legislatures. A court can only strike down. It can only say "This or that law is void." It cannot modify or qualify, it cannot make exceptions to a general requirement. And it strikes down not merely for a day. At least the finding of unconstitutionality ought not to have ephemeral significance unless the Constitution is to be reduced to the fugitive importance of mere legislation. When we are dealing with the Constitution of the United States, and more particularly with the great safeguards of the Bill of Rights, we are dealing with principles of liberty and justice "so rooted in the traditions and conscience of our people as to be ranked as funda-

mental"—something without which "a fair and enlightened system of justice would be impossible." Palko v. Connecticut, 302 U.S. 319, 325, 58 S.Ct. 149, 152; Hurtado v. California, 110 U.S. 516, 530, 531, 4 S.Ct. 111, 118, 119, 292. If the function of this Court is to be essentially no different from that of a legislature, if the considerations governing constitutional construction are to be substantially those that underlie legislation, then indeed judges should not have life tenure and they should be made directly responsible to the electorate. There have been many but unsuccessful proposals in the last sixty years to amend the Constitution to that end. See Sen.Doc. No. 91, 75th Cong., 1st Sess., pp. 248–51.

Conscientious scruples, all would admit, cannot stand against every legislative compulsion to do positive acts in conflict with such scruples. We have been told that such compulsions override religious scruples only as to major concerns of the state. But the determination of what is major and what is minor itself raises questions of policy. For the way in which men equally guided by reason appraise importance goes to the very heart of policy. Judges should be very diffident in setting their judgment against that of a state in determining what is and what is not a major concern, what means are appropriate to proper ends, and what is the total social cost in striking the balance of imponderables.

* * *

We are told that a flag salute is a doubtful substitute for adequate understanding of our institutions. The states that require such a school exercise do not have to justify it as the only means for promoting good citizenship in children, but merely as one of diverse means for accomplishing a worthy end. We may deem it a foolish measure, but the point is that this Court is not the organ of government to resolve doubts as to whether it will fulfill its purpose. Only if there be no doubt that any reasonable mind could entertain can we deny to the states the right to resolve doubts their way and not ours.

That which to the majority may seem essential for the welfare of the state may offend the consciences of a minority. But, so long as no inroads are made upon the actual exercise of religion by the minority, to deny the political power of the majority to enact laws concerned with civil matters, simply because they may offend the consciences of a minority, really means that the consciences of a minority are more sacred and more enshrined in the Constitution than the consciences of a majority.

We are told that symbolism is a dramatic but primitive way of communicating ideas. Symbolism is inescapable. Even the most sophisticated live by symbols. But it is not for this Court to make psychological judgments as to the effectiveness of a particular symbol in inculcating concededly indispensable feelings, particularly if the state happens to see fit to utilize the symbol that represents our heritage and our hopes. And surely only flippancy could be responsible for the suggestion that constitutional validity of a requirement to salute our flag implies equal validity of a requirement to salute a dictator. The significance of a symbol lies in what it represents. To reject the swastika does not imply rejection of the Cross. And so it bears repetition to say that it mocks reason and denies our whole history to find in the allowance of a requirement to salute our flag on fitting occasions

the seeds of sanction for obeisance to a leader. To deny the power to employ educational symbols is to say that the state's educational system may not stimulate the imagination because this may lead to unwise stimulation.

*   *   *

The flag salute exercise has no kinship whatever to the oath tests so odious in history. For the oath test was one of the instruments for suppressing heretical beliefs. Saluting the flag suppresses no belief nor curbs it. Children and their parents may believe what they please, avow their belief and practice it. It is not even remotely suggested that the requirement for saluting the flag involves the slightest restriction against the fullest opportunity on the part both of the children and of their parents to disavow as publicly as they choose to do so the meaning that others attach to the gesture of salute. All channels of affirmative free expression are open to both children and parents. Had we before us any act of the state putting the slightest curbs upon such free expression, I should not lag behind any member of this Court in striking down such an invasion of the right to freedom of thought and freedom of speech protected by the Constitution.

I am fortified in my view of this case by the history of the flag salute controversy in this Court. Five times has the precise question now before us been adjudicated. Four times the Court unanimously found that the requirement of such a school exercise was not beyond the powers of the states. Indeed in the first three cases to come before the Court the constitutional claim now sustained was deemed so clearly unmeritorious that this Court dismissed the appeals for want of a substantial federal question.   *   *   *

*   *   *

What may be even more significant than this uniform recognition of state authority is the fact that every Justice—thirteen in all—who has hitherto participated in judging this matter has at one or more times found no constitutional infirmity in what is now condemned. Only the two Justices sitting for the first time on this matter have not heretofore found this legislation inoffensive to the "liberty" guaranteed by the Constitution. And among the Justices who sustained this measure were outstanding judicial leaders in the zealous enforcement of constitutional safeguards of civil liberties—men like Chief Justice Hughes, Mr. Justice Brandeis, and Mr. Justice Cardozo, to mention only those no longer on the Court.

One's conception of the Constitution cannot be severed from one's conception of a judge's function in applying it. The Court has no reason for existence if it merely reflects the pressures of the day. Our system is built on the faith that men set apart for this special function, freed from the influences of immediacy and from the deflections of worldly ambition, will become able to take a view of longer range than the period of responsibility entrusted to Congress and legislatures. We are dealing with matters as to which legislators and voters have conflicting views. Are we as judges to impose our strong convictions on where wisdom lies? That which three years ago had seemed to five successive Courts to lie within permissible areas of legislation is now outlawed by the deciding shift of opinion of two Justices. What reason is there to be-

lieve that they or their successors may not have another view a few years hence? Is that which was deemed to be of so fundamental a nature as to be written into the Constitution to endure for all times to be the sport of shifting winds of doctrine? Of course, judicial opinions, even as to questions of constitutionality, are not immutable. As has been true in the past, the Court will from time to time reverse its position. But I believe that never before these Jehovah's Witnesses cases (except for minor deviations subsequently retraced) has this Court overruled decisions so as to restrict the powers of democratic government. Always heretofore, it has withdrawn narrow views of legislative authority so as to authorize what formerly it had denied.

In view of this history it must be plain that what thirteen Justices found to be within the constitutional authority of a state, legislators can not be deemed unreasonable in enacting. Therefore, in denying to the states what heretofore has received such impressive judicial sanction, some other tests of unconstitutionality must surely be guiding the Court than the absence of a rational justification for the legislation. But I know of no other test which this Court is authorized to apply in nullifying legislation.

In the past this Court has from time to time set its views of policy against that embodied in legislation by finding laws in conflict with what was called the "spirit of the Constitution." Such undefined destructive power was not conferred on this Court by the Constitution. Before a duly enacted law can be judicially nullified, it must be forbidden by some explicit restriction upon political authority in the Constitution.

Equally inadmissible is the claim to strike down legislation because to us as individuals it seems opposed to the "plan and purpose" of the Constitution. That is too tempting a basis for finding in one's personal views the purposes of the Founders.

The uncontrollable power wielded by this Court brings it very close to the most sensitive areas of public affairs. As appeal from legislation to adjudication becomes more frequent, and its consequences more far-reaching, judicial self-restraint becomes more and not less important, lest we unwarrantably enter social and political domains wholly outside our concern. I think I appreciate fully the objections to the law before us. But to deny that it presents a question upon which men might reasonably differ appears to me to be intolerance. And since men may so reasonably differ, I deem it beyond my constitutional power to assert my view of the wisdom of this law against the view of the State of West Virginia.

Jefferson's opposition to judicial review has not been accepted by history, but it still serves as an admonition against confusion between judicial and political functions. As a rule of judicial self-restraint, it is still as valid as Lincoln's admonition. For those who pass laws not only are under duty to pass laws. They are also under duty to observe the Constitution. And even though legislation relates to civil liberties, our duty of deference to those who have the responsibility for making the laws is no less relevant or less exacting. And this is so especially when we consider the accidental contingencies by which one man may determine constitutionality and thereby confine the political power of the Congress of the United States and the legislatures of forty-eight states. The attitude of judicial humility which these considerations enjoin is not an abdication of the judicial function. It is a due observance of its limits. Moreover, it is to be borne in mind that in a question like this we are not passing on the proper distribution of political power as between the states and the central government. We are not discharging the basic function of this Court as the mediator of powers within the federal system. To strike down a law like this is to deny a power to all government.

*   *   *

Of course patriotism cannot be enforced by the flag salute. But neither can the liberal spirit be enforced by judicial invalidation of illiberal legislation. Our constant preoccupation with the constitutionality of legislation rather than with its wisdom tends to preoccupation of the American mind with a false value. The tendency of focusing attention on constitutionality is to make constitutionality synonymous with wisdom, to regard a law as all right if it is constitutional. Such an attitude is a great enemy of liberalism. Particularly in legislation affecting freedom of thought and freedom of speech much which should offend a free-spirited society is constitutional. Reliance for the most precious interests of civilization, therefore, must be found outside of their vindication in courts of law. Only a persistent positive translation of the faith of a free society into the convictions and habits and actions of a community is the ultimate reliance against unabated temptations to fetter the human spirit.

THOMAS v. COLLINS

Supreme Court of the United States, 1945
323 U.S. 516, 65 S.Ct. 315, 89 L.Ed. 430

A Texas statute required all labor organizers to register with the Texas Secretary of State and receive a permit before undertaking such activity. Thomas, President of the United Automobile, Aircraft, and Agricultural Implements Workers Union and a vice-president of the C. I. O., came into the state to address a mass meeting sponsored by the Oil Workers Industrial Union in their effort to organize workers at the Bay Town, Texas plant of the Humble Oil & Refining Co. Anticipating noncompliance with the law, the Texas Attorney General sought and received a restraining order from the county court forbidding Thomas to address the labor rally. Upon receiving a copy of the order, Thomas determined to defy it because, he concluded, it abridged his right of free speech under the Constitution. At the conclusion of his speech to the mass meeting, Thomas openly solicited new union members. He was subsequently arrested, judged to be in contempt, and sentenced to three days in jail and a $100 fine.

Mr. Justice RUTLEDGE delivered the opinion of the Court.

* * *

The case has been twice argued here. Each time appellant has insisted, as he did in the state courts, that the statute as it has been applied to him is in contravention of the Fourteenth Amendment, as it incorporates the First, imposing a previous restraint upon the rights of freedom of speech and free assembly, and denying him the equal protection of the laws. He urges also that the application made of the statute is inconsistent with the provisions of the National Labor Relations Act, 49 Stat. 449, 29 U.S.C.A. § 151 et seq., and other objections which need not be considered. For reasons to be stated we think the statute as it was applied in this case imposed previous restraint upon appellant's rights of free speech and free assembly and the judgment must be reversed.

* * *

The case confronts us again with the duty our system places on this Court to say where the individual's freedom ends and the State's power begins. Choice on that border, now as always delicate, is perhaps more so where the usual presumption supporting legislation is balanced by the preferred place given in our scheme to the great, the indispensable democratic freedoms secured by the First Amendment. * * *

For these reasons any attempt to restrict those liberties must be justified by clear public interest, threatened not doubtfully or remotely, but by clear and present danger. The rational connection between the remedy provided and the evil to be curbed, which in other contexts might support legislation against attack on due process grounds, will not suffice. These rights rest on firmer foundation. Accordingly, whatever occasion would restrain orderly discussion and persuasion, at appropriate time and place, must have clear support in public danger, actual or impending. Only the gravest abuses, endangering paramount interests, give occasion for permissible limitation. It is therefore in our tradition to allow the widest room for discussion, the narrowest range for its restriction, particularly when this right is exercised in conjunction with peaceable assembly. It was not by accident or coincidence that the rights to freedom in speech and press were coupled in a single guaranty with the rights of the people peaceably to assemble and to petition for redress of grievances. All these, though not identical, are inseparable. They are cognate rights. * * *

This conjunction of liberties is not peculiar to religious activity and institutions alone. The First Amendment gives freedom of mind the same security as freedom of conscience. * * * Great secular causes, with small ones, are guarded. The grievances for redress of which the right of petition was insured, and with it the right of assembly, are not solely religious or political ones. And the rights of free speech and a free press are not confined to any field of human interest.

The idea is not sound therefore that the First Amendment's safeguards are wholly inapplicable to business or economic activity. And it does not resolve where the line shall be drawn in a particular case merely to urge, as Texas does, that an organization for which the rights of free speech and free assembly are claimed is one "engaged in business activities" or that the individual who leads it in exercising these rights receives compensation for doing so. Nor, on the other hand, is the answer given, whether what is done is an exercise of those rights and the restriction a forbidden impairment, by ignoring the organization's economic function, because those interests of workingmen are involved or because they have the general liberties of the citizen, as appellant would do.

These comparisons are at once too simple, too general, and too inaccurate to be determinative. Where the line shall be placed in a particular application rests, not on such generalities, but on the concrete clash of particular interests and the community's relative evaluation both of them and of how the one will be affected by the specific restriction, the other by its absence. That judgment in the first instance is for the legislative body. But in our system where the line can constitutionally be placed presents a question this Court cannot escape answering independently, whatever the legislative judgment, in the light of our constitutional tradition. * * * And the answer, under that tradition can be affirmative, to support an intrusion upon this domain, only if grave and impending public danger requires this.

That the State has power to regulate labor unions with a view to protecting the public interest is, as the Texas court said, hardly to be doubted. They cannot claim special immunity from regulation. Such regulation however, whether aimed at fraud or other abuses, must not trespass upon the domain set apart for free speech and free assembly. This Court has recognized that "in the circumstances of our times the dissemination of information concerning the facts of a labor dispute must be regarded as within that area of free discussion that is guaranteed by the Constitution. * * * Free discussion concerning the conditions in industry and the causes of labor disputes appears to us indispensable to the effective and intelligent use of the processes of popular government to shape the destiny of modern industrial society." Thornhill v. Alabama, 310 U.S. 88, 102, 103, 60 S.Ct. 736, 744. * * * The right thus to discuss, and inform people concerning, the advantages and disadvantages of unions and joining them is protected not only as part of free speech, but as part of free assembly. Hague v. Committee for Industrial Organization, 307 U.S. 496, 59 S.Ct. 954. The Texas court, in its disposition of the cause, did not give sufficient weight to this consideration, more particularly by its failure to take account of the blanketing effect of the prohibition's present application upon public discussion and also of the bearing of the clear and present danger test in these circumstances.

In applying these principles to the facts of this case we put aside the broader contentions both parties have made and confine our decision to the narrow question whether the application made of Section 5 in this case contravenes the First Amendment.

The present application does not involve the solicitation of funds or property. Neither Section 5 nor the restraining order purports to prohibit or regulate solicitation of funds, receipt of money, its management, distribution, or any other financial matter. Other sections of the Act deal with such things. And on the record Thomas neither asked nor accepted funds or property for the union at the time of his address or while he was in Texas. Neither did he "take applications" for membership, though he offered to do so "if it was necessary"; or ask anyone to join a union at any other time than the occasion of the Pelly mass meeting and in the course of his address.

Thomas went to Texas for one purpose and one only—to make the speech in question. Its whole object was publicly to proclaim the advantages of workers' organization and to persuade workmen to join Local No. 1002 as part of a campaign for members. These also were the sole objects of the meeting. The campaign, and the meeting, were incidents of an impending election for collective bargaining agent, previously ordered by national authority pursuant to the guaranties of national law. Those guaranties include the workers' right to organize freely for collective bargaining. And this comprehends whatever may be appropriate and lawful to accomplish and maintain such organization. It included, in this case, the right to designate Local No. 1002 or any other union or agency as the employees' representative. It included their right fully and freely to discuss and be informed concerning this choice, privately or in public assembly. Necessarily correlative was the right of the union, its members and officials, whether residents or nonresidents of Texas and, if the latter, whether there for a single occasion or sojourning longer, to discuss with and inform the employees concerning matters involved in their choice. These rights of assembly and discussion are protected by the First Amendment. Whatever would restrict them, without sufficient occasion, would infringe its safeguards. The occasion was clearly protected. The speech was an essential part of the occasion, unless all meaning and purpose were to be taken from it. And the invitations, both general and particular, were parts of the speech, inseparable incidents of the occasion and of all that was said or done.

That there was restriction upon Thomas' right to speak and the rights of the workers to hear what he had to say, there can be no doubt. The threat of the restraining order, backed by the power of contempt and of arrest for crime, hung over every word. A speaker in such circumstances could avoid the words "solicit," "invite," "join." It would be impossible to avoid the idea. The statute requires no specific formula. It is not contended that only the use of the word "solicit" would violate the prohibition. Without such a limitation, the statute forbids any language which conveys, or reasonably could be found to convey, the meaning of invitation. That Thomas chose to meet the issue squarely, not to hide in ambiguous phrasing, does not counteract this fact. General words create different and often particular impressions on different minds. No speaker, however careful, can convey exactly his meaning, or the same meaning, to the different members of an audience. How one might "laud unionism," as the State and the State Supreme Court concede Thomas was free to do, yet in these circumstances not imply an invitation, is hard to conceive. This is the nub of the case, which the State fails to meet because it cannot do so. Workingmen do not lack capacity for making rational connections. They would understand, or some would, that the president of U.A.W. and vice president of C.I.O., addressing an organization meeting, was not urging merely a philosophic attachment to abstract principles of unionism, disconnected from the business immediately at hand. The feat would be incredible for a national leader, addressing such a meeting, lauding unions and their principles, urging adherence to union philosophy, not also and thereby to suggest attachment to the union by becoming a member.

Furthermore, whether words intended and designed to fall short of invitation would miss that mark is a question both of intent and of effect. No speaker, in such circumstances, safely could assume that anything he might say upon the general subject would not be understood by some as an invitation. In short, the supposedly clear-cut distinction between discussion, laudation, general advocacy, and solicitation puts the speaker in these circumstances wholly at the mercy of the varied understanding of his hearers and consequently of whatever inference may be drawn as to his intent and meaning.

Such a distinction offers no security for free discussion. In these conditions it blankets with uncertainty whatever may be said. It compels the speaker to hedge and trim. He must take care in every word to create no impression that he means, in advocating unionism's most central principle, namely, that workingmen should unite for collective bargaining, to urge those present to do so. The vice is not merely that invitation, in the circumstances shown here, is speech. It is also that its prohibition forbids or restrains discussion which is not or may not be invitation. The sharp line cannot be drawn surely or securely. The effort to observe it could not be free speech, free press, or free assembly, in any sense of free advocacy of principle or cause. The restriction's effect, as applied, in a very practical sense was to prohibit Thomas not only to solicit members and memberships, but also to speak in advocacy of the cause of trade unionism in Texas, without having first procured the card. Thomas knew this and faced the alternatives it presented. When served with the order he had three choices: (1) To stand on his right and speak freely; (2) to quit, refusing entirely to speak; (3) to trim, and even thus to risk the penalty. He chose the first alternative. We think he was within his rights in doing so.

The assembly was entirely peaceable, and had no other than a wholly lawful purpose. The statements forbidden were not in themselves unlawful, had no tendency to incite to unlawful action, involved no element of clear and present, grave and immediate danger to the public welfare. Moreover, the State has shown no justification for placing restrictions on the use of the word "solicit." We have here nothing comparable to the case where use of the word "fire" in a crowded theater creates a clear and present danger which the State may undertake to avoid or against which it may protect. Schenck v. United States, 249 U.S. 47, 39 S.Ct. 247. We cannot say that "solicit" in this setting is such a dangerous word. So far as free speech alone is concerned, there can be no ban or restriction or burden placed on the use of such a word except on showing of exceptional circumstances where the public safety, morality or health is involved or some other substantial interest of the community is at stake.

If therefore use of the word or language equivalent in meaning was illegal here, it was so only because the statute and the order forbade the particular speaker to utter it. When legislation or its application can confine labor leaders on such occasions to innocuous and abstract discussion of the virtues of trade unions and so becloud even this with doubt, uncertainty and the risk of penalty, freedom of speech for them will be at an end. A restriction so destructive of the right of public discussion, without greater or more imminent danger to the public interest than existed in this case, is incompatible with the freedoms secured by the First Amendment.

We do not mean to say there is not, in many circumstances, a difference between urging a course of action and merely giving and acquiring information. On the other hand, history has not been without periods when the search for knowledge alone was banned. Of this we may assume the men who wrote the Bill of Rights were aware. But the protection they sought was not solely for persons in intellectual pursuits. It extends to more than abstract discussion, unrelated to action. The First Amendment is a charter for government, not for an institution of learning. "Free trade in ideas" means free trade in the opportunity to persuade to action, not merely to describe facts. * * * Indeed, the whole history of the problem shows it is to the end of preventing action that repression is primarily directed and to preserving the right to urge it that the protections are given.

* * *

The restraint is not small when it is considered what was restrained. The right is a national right, federally guaranteed. There is some modicum of freedom of thought, speech and assembly which all citizens of the Republic may exercise throughout its length and breadth, which no State, nor all together, nor the Nation itself, can prohibit, restrain or impede. If the restraint were smaller than it is, it is from petty tyrannies that large ones take root and grow. This fact can be no more plain than when they are imposed on the most basic rights of all. Seedlings planted in that soil grow great and, growing, break down the foundations of liberty.

In view of the disposition we make of the cause, it is unnecessary to rule upon the motion appellee has filed to require appellant to furnish security for his appearance to serve the sentence.

The judgment is reversed.

[Chief Justice STONE, Justices ROBERTS, REED, and FRANK-FURTER dissented.]

DOES THE SUPREME COURT HAVE A UNIQUE FUNCTION?

Contemporary political science has long recognized that courts are political institutions.[d] In interaction with other agencies of government the judges who comprise them resolve the problems pressed on them as to "who gets what, when, and how." Yet the observation that the judicial process is a political process and that judges are policy makers, whether wittingly or unwittingly, is not the end of the discussion but its beginning. This is all the more significant when considered in light of the Supreme Court's power of judicial review, a feature of the American system which, coupled with the independence of the judicial branch, goes a long way toward distinguishing the American judiciary from those of other political systems. Indeed, for a goodly part of our national existence—from 1803, if not before, to the present—we have continually debated the issue of whether a democracy can tolerate invalidation of policies enacted through elected representatives of the people by an appointed, independent, life-tenured Court. This is no dry academic matter. The answer to this question goes to the core of the justification for the review power held by the American judiciary. Its resolution, moreover, ultimately depends upon the assertion by the judiciary of a superior capability unpossessed by other branches of the government which can justify its basically undemocratic character. That value must be a value superior to democracy itself. There is probably only one such widely respected, superior value, and that value is justice. Therefore, to justify the exercise of the review power by an undemocratic institution like the Supreme Court, those who make the case for it must show that the Court has a unique function. In short, those who espouse the doctrine of judicial review and would actively have the Court use it must show that the Court has a unique capacity to do justice.

This essay presents three alternative resolutions to this fundamental question. Each comes to grips with this issue in formulating a judicial philosophy. These statements of judicial role reflect the intersection of two important dimensions—the relation of the judicial institution to other governmental institutions and the relation between the judge and the law. In sum, we suggest that any difference which inheres in the judicial institution exists because of the justification which judges are compelled to offer for their decisions. Roles structure political values. No political actor is valueless. All political actors are asked to resolve problems, the

---

d. Cardozo, The Nature of the Judicial Process (1921); Truman, The Governmental Process (1951); Peltason, Federal Courts in the Political Process (1955); Rosenblum, Law as a Political Instrument (1955); Krislov, The Supreme Court in the Political Process (1965); Schubert, Judicial Policy-Making (Rev. ed., 1974).

pressing of divergent claims on them by contending groups in the political system. The structure of this casebook and its problems-oriented awareness of the competing interests judges are called upon to reconcile demonstrate this. Like other government officials, judges must solve problems. In doing so there is considerable latitude for discretion, for there is no one and only true and correct solution for every problem. In the allocation of values among the competing interests of society reasonable men can and do differ. The vast majority of men who go on to become judges spend years before that intimately involved with the political process and its pressures; [e] they do not leave their values and experiences behind them merely by donning a black robe. They must respond to problems too, and if de Tocqueville's classic observation can be regarded as correct—that "There is hardly a political question in the United States which does not sooner or later turn into a judicial one" [f]—judges will be asked to respond to the same problems as legislators, executives, and administrators. In doing so, however, they will be compelled to offer written justification. They will be constrained by a need for consistency. They will be tempered by an expectation of fairness and evenhandedness. In short, the reaction of judges to problems cannot over the long run be a reflection merely of expediency, party allegiance, constituency loyalty, or personal advancement. We suggest that their solutions to problems will show a pattern of resolution—a pattern strongly colored by their response to the fundamental question we have already acknowledged. The problems the judges face may be severable, but the imperative of judicial role will pattern their solutions to those problems. We suggest that three general patterns can be discerned.

The Neutralist or Absolutist Approach

Certainly one of the most fundamental ideals in the Anglo-American legal tradition is that of the Rule of Law. Traditionally, it is contrasted with the Rule of Men. The implications in juxtaposing the two are not difficult to discern. The former implies the decision of controversies objectively according to general and impartial rules which do not acknowledge the individual identity of or personal consequences for particular litigants before a court. The second concept implies that judgments in individual cases tend to be made on the basis of "whose ox is being gored." Above all, it suggests arbitrariness.[g] The neutralist or absolutist conception of the judicial role would suggest that it is distinguished from the "political" roles of other governmental actors by virtue of a certain form which judicial decisions must partake. That form acts to bridle discretion in fashioning solutions to problems which are posed for the Court. It suggests a particular notion of justice—on the order of Kant's categorical imperative or Aristotle's concept of distributive justice—the notion of "treating like cases alike." The essence of how the judiciary's resolution of problems is

---

e. Chase, Federal Judges: The Appointing Process (1972).

f. de Tocqueville, Democracy in America (ed. Mayer, 1969), 270.

g. Shklar, Legalism (1964).

contrasted with that of other governmental institutions is perhaps best summed up by Professor Herbert Wechsler:

> The courts have both the title and the duty when a case is properly before them to review the actions of the other branches in light of constitutional provisions, even though the action involves value choices, as invariably action does. In doing so, however, they are bound to function otherwise than as a naked power organ; they participate as courts of law. This calls for facing how determinations of this kind can be asserted to have any legal quality. The answer, I suggest, inheres primarily in that they are—or are obliged to be—entirely principled. A principled decision, in the sense I have in mind, is one that rests on reasons with respect to all the issues in the case, reasons that in their generality and their neutrality transcend any immediate result that is involved.[h]

Hence the role of the judge is defined by his obligation to decide cases according to principles which "cut both ways."

A corollary of this is the belief that there are fixed standards by which cases can be adjudicated. Indeed, most of the judges who have professed this judicial role have posited that such principles are absolute and can be discovered from a reading of the Constitution itself.[i] The literal application of constitutional provisions furnishes at once the source of the standards they apply and their justification for the use of judicial power. Justices do not "make law" but merely apply the fixed principles of the original political contract to subsequent legislative and executive acts. Application of the correct principle is a matter of logic, skilled reading, and guidance given by an incisive understanding of the intentions of the Framers who wrote the Constitution.[j] Certainty is a requisite of justice. Fair warning to the citizen before he or she violates the law that such rules exist can only be afforded when constitutional rights and obligations are illumined by judicial principles stark enough to inform. Uncertain application of principles and *ad hoc* adjudication on a case-by-case basis breed arbitrariness, favoritism, and prejudice. Unprincipled adjudication results merely in the Rule of Men.

The passionate allegiance of Justices such as Hugo Black and John Harlan, Sr., to the literal provisions of the Constitution and its subsequent amendments—to single out only two of the more eloquent exponents—stems from a belief that justice is contained in the original balance of interests embodied in the document. Change of those provisions by means other than those authorized in the provisions of that contract is to change the rules of the game after play has begun. It is to alter the agreement *ex post facto*. These judges, then, see themselves not as policy makers but as mediums through which the Rule of Law, embodied in a written

---

h. Wechsler, *Toward Neutral Principles of Constitutional Law*, 73 Harv.L.Rev. 1, 19 (1959). See also Dworkin, Taking Rights Seriously (1977).

i. Black, *The Bill of Rights*, 35 N.Y.U.L. Rev. 865 (1960); A Constitutional Faith (1968).

j. For a critical evaluation, see Anderson, *The Intention of the Framers: A Note on Constitutional Interpretation*, 49 Amer.Pol. Sci.Rev. 340 (1955).

Constitution, speaks. They exercise the power of judicial review because of the supremacy of the original contract over legislative or executive power exercised pursuant to it. The power of judicial review is justified by its principled quality, and its principled quality emanates from the Constitution itself. There is, then, no contradiction between the exercise of judicial review by an appointed, life-tenured Court and the existence of a constitutional democracy, for the Justices are simply the instruments through which the Supreme Law speaks.

The Balancing of Interests or Restraintist Approach

A second school of constitutional interpretation begins by repudiating the question which this essay asks. On the issue of the exercise of judicial power, it pleads eloquently for the exercise of self-restraint. This is so because, according to its tenets, the Court has no unique function.[k] Its function in a system of checks and balances is little different than that exercised by the other two branches. The Court is unmistakably a political institution. Judges are not distinguished from legislators either by the values they hold, by the way they reach their decisions, or by the content of their policies. They comprise an equally political, but a markedly weaker, third branch of government. Indeed, the Court is caught in a perilous dilemma. After the *tour de force* scored by Chief Justice Marshall when he seized for the Court the power of judicial review, the restraintists find no way to square it with democratic theory. In short, while not wanting to give the power back, while appreciating its contribution to the system of checks and balances, they cannot justify its use in a democratic system. The Court is undeniably an undemocratic institution, and if it is, as Hamilton put it in *Federalist 78*, "the least dangerous branch," it is so because it is least powerful. Preoccupied with an acute awareness of the Court's inability to force compliance with its own decisions, the restraintists counsel prudence in the use of judicial power. They favor risking confrontation with another branch of government only on rare and auspicious occasion. Only in an instance of obviously capricious, unreasonable, or arbitrary exercise of legislative or executive power should the Court invoke its power to nullify policy.

The ethos of restraint is closely related to the method by which decision is made. Courts, like other governmental institutions, must resolve conflicts among competing social interests. Every lawsuit and criminal proceeding forces the judge to choose as to which of the rival interests personified by the plaintiff or respondent, government or defendant should prevail. This is a matter of judgment. And judgment is conditioned not by logic alone, but by experience and in accordance with the fundamental values of the society. Every decision advantages some interests in society and disadvantages others. This question of judgment must also be set in the context of democratic society. In reaching an accommodation of conflicting interests put forth in a lawsuit or criminal action, judges should endeavor to resolve the claims—to balance the interests—

---

k. Hand, The Bill of Rights (1958).

such that the solution offered maximizes as many of the claims as possible.[1]

It is no surprise, then, that the interest balancers are restraintists. For legislative policy is a product of majority rule. When legislation comes to the Court for review and interpretation, presumption is clearly in its favor because, being passed by the majority, it maximizes more claims; it satisfies more interests. The only alternative, in the view of this school of thought, would be to thwart democratic rule by extolling minority interests. Only on rare and unusual occasion, as when the majority has patently gone beyond the bounds of fair play and explicitly abridged constitutional provisions or acted arbitrarily or irrationally, should the judiciary intervene.

A final word should be added as to the scope of adjudication in response to a problem. The exercise of restraint is not only important in avoiding constitutional questions where possible, but also in avoiding as much of a constitutional question as possible. This calls for settling the issue in any given case on the narrowest possible grounds. The reason for this is fairly obvious. For a philosophy of prudence in adjudication successful resolution of problems is better achieved by incremental efforts which preserve flexibility and assume a pragmatic stance than an approach which, without adequate information or experience, seeks to lay out wide-ranging solutions that eventually lead to unworkable results or embarrassing backtracking. In the view of Justices such as Felix Frankfurter, Louis Brandeis, Oliver Wendell Holmes, Benjamin Cardozo, and John Harlan, Jr.—to cite only a few who espoused this role—law is not a fixed set of definitive principles, it is the accumulated solutions to past problems which have been fashioned with due regard to the conditions at hand and with sensitivity to the limited effectiveness of the judicial institution. Law, if anything definable, is not a series of fixed principles to be divined by dint of strict logic but a trend apparent in individual decisions which have been made on a case-by-case basis.

The Preferred Freedoms or Activist Approach

One of the tacit assumptions underlying the "balancing of interests" method is that the interests to be weighed are pretty much counted equally. It is precisely the contrary belief—that all interests are not equal—that inspired a third philosophy of constitutional interpretation. Indeed, the equal weighting of all social interests and the application of the maximizing guideline resulted in what some critics saw as exploitation of vulnerable minorities by a persistent majoritarianism. In sum, balancing came to be viewed by some as the perverse arrangement of social interests espoused, for example, by Thrasymachus in Plato's *Republic*, as justice defined as "the interest of the stronger." An early expression of concern for the problem of permanent minorities and for the potential obli-

---

1. Pound, An Introduction to the Philosophy of Law (1922); Pound, *A Survey of Social Interests*, 57 Harv.L.Rev. 1 (1943).

gation of the Court to assume a representational role on behalf of soci-
ety's disadvantaged groups is apparent in the following text of Justice
Stone's famous footnote 4 to his opinion for the Court in *United States* v.
Carolene Products Co.:

> There may be narrower scope for operation of the presumption of consti-
> tutionality when legislation appears on its face to be within a specific prohi-
> bition of the Constitution, such as those of the first ten Amendments, which
> are deemed equally specific when held to be embraced within the Four-
> teenth.   *   *   *
>
> It is unnecessary to consider now whether legislation which restricts
> those political processes which can ordinarily be expected to bring about
> repeal of undesirable legislation, is to be subjected to more exacting judicial
> scrutiny under the general prohibitions of the Fourteenth Amendment than
> are most other types of legislation.   *   *   *
>
> Nor need we enquire whether similar considerations enter into the
> review of statutes directed at particular religious,   *   *   *   or national,
> *   *   *   or racial minorities   *   *   *   whether prejudice against discrete
> and insular minorities may be a special condition, which tends seriously to
> curtail the operation of those political processes ordinarily to be relied upon
> to protect minorities, and which may call for a correspondingly more search-
> ing judicial inquiry.   *   *   * m

This third mode of constitutional interpretation sought to distinguish
the standards of adjudication applied to civil rights and liberties from
those applied to economic liberties and property rights. While preserving
the pragmatism and flexibility of the balancing approach to assess the constitutionality of legislation aimed, say, at governmental regulation of business, the advocates of this philosophy sought to justify a stiffer
constitutional standard for judging the validity of governmental regulation
of civil liberties. The justification which they offered in the use of this
double standard was an assertion that there were some liberties which
were so fundamental to the existence of the democratic order and the
maintenance of the individual personality that they merited special consideration. After all, who could imagine a democracy existing without freedoms of speech or thought or association or the press? Nor could one
envision the human personality as left unfettered without rights to religious belief and privacy, for example. Yet both democracy and individual
liberty could survive without the ownership of private property. Because,
then, these rights were essential to the preservation of all that was basic
to democratic society, these freedoms were placed in a "preferred position." That is, the mere test of reasonableness or lack of arbitrariness
used to adjudicate issues of economic regulation was thought insufficient
to protect these basic rights from abridgement. When legislation directly
infringed a fundamental freedom or unequally provided for its exercise by
all citizens or allocated rights or imposed burdens drawn along lines
thought to constitute "suspect classes," employment of the following tri-

---

m. 304 U.S. 144, 152–153, 58 S.Ct. 778,
783–784 (1938).

partite test supplanted reliance upon the traditional litmus of constitutional adjudication:

1. Where legislation abridges a preferred freedom on its face or creates legal categories that amount to "suspect classes," the usual presumption of constitutionality is reversed; that is, legislation directly infringing a fundamental right or burdening a "suspect class" is assumed to be unconstitutional until the government demonstrates otherwise.

2. The government must show that the exercise of a fundamental freedom presents a clear and imminent danger, or it must establish that the legislation advances a "compelling interest."

3. The legislation must be narrowly drawn so as to present a precise response to the problem and must not impair basic liberties by its overbreadth, which means the regulatory policy at issue must constitute the least restrictive alternative.

This mode of constitutional interpretation presented an additional consideration in the adjudication of claims. Resolution of problems involving the conflict of the exercise of governmental power and the assertion of individual rights was not to be solved somehow by merely maximizing claims. If some rights, like those contained in the First Amendment already mentioned, were in a preferred position, it stood to reason that everyone in the society was entitled to those rights before any kind of secondary rights—say, the right to dispose of your property as you saw fit—could be vindicated. Thus, in a conflict between those individuals in society who were attempting to have their basic rights vindicated as against a larger number of their fellow citizens who were seeking to have lesser rights extended, the former claims must triumph over the latter, notwithstanding the fact that the number of individuals in the first group might be considerably less than the number of persons in the second.[n]

By using this method of adjudication, liberal judges on the Court sought to guarantee equal basic rights to those who lived on the periphery of the society—the poor, religious dissenters, radicals, black and Spanish-speaking people, urbanites, juveniles, people accused of crime, and so on. In sum, like the other constitutional approaches already described, the "preferred freedoms" concept was predicated on an assertion of the Court's relation to the question about its unique capacity to do justice—here justice was embodied in the mediation of the harshness and potential exploitation of majority rule; it was embodied in a concern for guaranteeing substantive equality in the allocation of rights and responsibilities in the society. Thus, during much of the 1940s and 1960s the Court acted to integrate what had heretofore been out-groups into the political system and to extend to those individuals who had been discriminated against fuller protection and participation in society. Justices such as William O. Douglas, Earl Warren, William Brennan, Frank Murphy, Wiley Rutledge, Abe Fortas, Thurgood Marshall, Arthur Goldberg were deeply committed

n. Rawls, A Theory of Justice (1971);
Bay, The Structure of Freedom (1958).

to the belief that vindication of fundamental liberties for peripheral groups in the society took precedence over the extension of any additional rights to society's larger in-groups. In short, the Court was, because of its unique capability to do this kind of justice, actively obliged to use its power of judicial review to temper the policies of the "silent majority."

Constitutional Interpretation

This has not been nor was it intended to be a definitive discussion of the principal modes of constitutional interpretation. We did not attempt to lay out each of the variations in all its particulars or to offer critiques of each.° These tasks are what the rest of this casebook is about. While it is our intention to focus this casebook so as to point up problem areas in constitutional law and to have you examine each with an eye toward alternative solutions, that is not enough. Courts do not merely offer solutions to problems. They must come to grips with those problems through solutions that derive from the functions of the judiciary itself. The Justices do not espouse random solutions to varied problems. The positions they take form patterns, and those patterns are the modes of constitutional interpretation of which we have spoken. Thus do Justices relate their solutions to problems to the enduring question of importance as to the Court's function.

We do not mean to imply that Justices are practitioners of only one mode. We have described here pure types, and judges are individuals, not neat analytical categories. Most men personify a mix of these approaches. Yet over all, most Justices show allegiance to one role more than another.

We think it is also important to point out that this array of materials should disabuse us all of the notion that somehow there is one and only one correct constitutional interpretation or that the Court adheres to only one mode. As we have stressed before, these are issues about which reasonable people can and do disagree. Nor does it in any way follow that simply because courts are compelled to recognize precedent—to resolve present controversies with an eye toward maintaining some sense of consistency with past decisions—that the prevailing mode of interpretation does not change. The collection of materials which follows amply demonstrates the contrary. They underscore a continuing dialogue among the individuals who have sat on the Court. The key to which general philosophy prevails at any given point in time is the composition of the Court. We do not suggest that such a factor is the only variable in explaining incongruities in the Court's decisions. Surely it is not. Some inconsistencies inhere in the problems of the philosophies themselves, others in human foibles. We do suggest, however, that this political factor is a profitable starting point in the search for such explanations.

---

o. For a much more extensive treatment, see Ducat, Modes of Constitutional Interpretation (1978).

A Continuing Constitutional Convention?

Woodrow Wilson once said that the Supreme Court ought to be seen as "a kind of constitutional convention in continuous session." [p]   Certainly the men who personified the different roles we have just briefly introduced would sharply disagree in their response to such a proposal.   In light of the framework we have laid out and in the context of the materials which follow, we invite you to test out Wilson's suggestion.   Should the Court fulfill such a function?   Is it equipped for such a task?   Is it justified in such a pursuit?   And if so, what principles should guide it as it wends its way through the quagmires of constitutional adjudication?   These are questions which have provoked and sustained the attention of some of the greatest American intellects, not the least of whom are the four giants to whom we dedicated this book.   We invite you to join their debate.

c. INSTITUTIONAL CONSTRAINTS ON JUDICIAL PROBLEM SOLVING

INTERNATIONAL LONGSHOREMEN'S & WAREHOUSEMEN'S UNION v. BOYD

Supreme Court of the United States, 1954
347 U.S. 222, 74 S.Ct. 447, 98 L.Ed. 650

The facts in this case were set out in Justice Black's dissenting opinion in the following way:

Every summer members of the appellant union go from the west coast of continental United States to Alaska to work in salmon and herring canneries under collective-bargaining agreements. As the 1953 canning season approached the union and its members looked forward to this Alaska employment. A troublesome question arose, however, on account of the Immigration and Nationality Act of 1952, 66 Stat. 163. Section 212(d)(7) of this new Act has language that given one construction provides that all aliens seeking admission to continental United States from Alaska, even those previously accepted as permanent United States residents, shall be examined as if entering from a foreign country with a view to excluding them on any of the many grounds applicable to aliens generally. This new law created an acute problem for the union and its numerous members who were lawful alien residents, since aliens generally can be excluded from this country for many reasons which would not justify deporting aliens lawfully residing here. The union and its members insisted on another construction. They denied that Congress intended to require alien workers to forfeit their right to live in this country for no reason at all except that they went to Alaska, territory of the United States, to engage in lawful work under a lawfully authorized collective-bargaining contract. The defendant immigration officer announced that the union's interpretation was wrong and that workers going to Alaska would be subject to examination and exclusion. This is the controversy.

---

p. As quoted to Professor Corwin; see Chase and Ducat, Edward S. Corwin's The Constitution and What It Means Today (14th ed., 1978), p. 5.

Mr. Justice FRANKFURTER delivered the opinion of the Court.

* * *

Appellants in effect asked the District Court to rule that a statute the sanctions of which had not been set in motion against individuals on whose behalf relief was sought, because an occasion for doing so had not arisen, would not be applied to them if in the future such a contingency should arise. That is not a lawsuit to enforce a right; it is an endeavor to obtain a court's assurance that a statute does not govern hypothetical situations that may or may not make the challenged statute applicable. Determination of the scope and constitutionality of legislation in advance of its immediate adverse effect in the context of a concrete case involves too remote and abstract an inquiry for the proper exercise of the judicial function. * * * Since we do not have on the record before us a controversy appropriate for adjudication, the judgment of the District Court must be vacated, with directions to dismiss the complaint.

It is so ordered.

Mr. Justice BLACK, with whom Mr. Justice DOUGLAS concurs, dissenting.

This looks to me like the very kind of "case or controversy" courts should decide. With the abstract principles of law relied on by the majority for dismissing the case, I am not in disagreement. Of course federal courts do not pass on the meaning or constitutionality of statutes as they might be thought to govern mere "hypothetical situations." * * * Nor should courts entertain such statutory challenges on behalf of persons upon whom adverse statutory effects are "too remote and abstract an inquiry for the proper exercise of the judicial function." But as I read the record it shows that judicial action is absolutely essential to save a large group of wage earners on whose behalf this action is brought from irreparable harm due to alleged lawless enforcement of a federal statute. My view makes it necessary for me to set out the facts with a little more detail than they appear in the Court's opinion.

[The statement of facts quoted above then follows.]

* * *

It was to test the right of the immigration officer to apply § 212(d)(7) to make these workers subject to exclusion that this suit, was filed by the union and two of its officers on behalf of themselves and all union members who are aliens and permanent residents. True, the action was begun before the union members went to Alaska for the 1953 canning season. But it is not only admitted that the immigration official intended to enforce § 212(d)(7) as the union and these workers feared. It is admitted here that he has since done precisely that. All 1953 alien cannery workers have actually been subjected to the wearisome routine of immigration procedure as though they had never lived here. And some of the union members are evidently about to be denied the right ever to return to their homes on grounds that could not have been legally applied to them had they stayed in California or Washington instead of going to Alaska to work for an important American industry.

Thus the threatened injury which the Court dismisses as "remote" and "hypothetical" has come about. For going to Alaska to engage in honest employment many of these workers may lose the home this country once afforded them. This is a strange penalty to put on productive work. Maybe this is what Congress meant by passing § 212(d)(7). And maybe in these times such a law would be held constitutional. But even so, can it be that a challenge to this law on behalf of those whom it hits the hardest is so frivolous that it should be dismissed for want of a controversy that courts should decide? Workers threatened with irreparable damages, like others, should have their cases tried.

MASSACHUSETTS v. MELLON
FROTHINGHAM v. MELLON

Supreme Court of the United States, 1923
262 U.S. 447, 43 S.Ct. 597, 67 L.Ed. 1078

The opinion below rendered judgment on two challenges to the Maternity Act of 1921. Both suits were actions to enjoin the Secretary of the Treasury, Andrew Mellon, from spending federal monies pursuant to the act. While an adequate presentation of the specifics in these two cases appears in the Court's opinion, we might note by way of background that this act was a uniquely progressive piece of legislation enacted in an era not noted for the liberality of governmental programs. The act here in question was an early forerunner of those cooperative ventures, increasingly popularized since the advent of the New Deal, known as grant-in-aid programs, whereby the national government offered to match (often in generously unequal proportions) expenditures by the states to encourage them to provide certain social services. Because the Court decided that it did not have jurisdiction (for reasons explained in the decision excerpted below), it did not consider on the merits the challenge to the constitutionality of the grant-in-aid programs. In later cases in which the Court reached the constitutional issue a decade and a half later, it decisively approved such legislation (see e.g., Steward Machine Co. v. Davis [1937], p. 371).

Mr. Justice SUTHERLAND delivered the opinion of the Court.

These cases were argued and will be considered and disposed of together. The first is an original suit in this Court. The other was brought in the Supreme Court of the District of Columbia. That court dismissed the bill and its decree was affirmed by the District Court of Appeals. Thereupon the case was brought here by appeal. Both cases challenge the constitutionality of the Act of November 23, 1921, c. 135, 42 Stat. 224, commonly called the Maternity Act. Briefly, it provides for an initial appropriation and thereafter annual appropriations for a period of five years, to be apportioned among such of the several States as shall accept and comply with its provisions, for the purpose of cooperating with them to reduce maternal and infant mortality and protect the health of mothers and infants. It creates a bureau to administer the act in cooperation with state agencies, which are required to make such reports concerning their operations and expenditures as may be prescribed by the federal bureau. Whenever that bureau shall determine that funds have not been properly expended in respect of any State, payments may be withheld.

It is asserted that these appropriations are for purposes not national, but local to the States, and together with numerous similar appropriations constitute an effective means of inducing the States to yield a portion of their sovereign rights. It is further alleged that the burden of the appropriations provided by this act and similar legislation falls unequally upon the several States, and rests largely upon the industrial States, such as Massachusetts; that the act is a usurpation of power not granted to Congress by the Constitution—an attempted exercise of the power of local self-government reserved to the States by the Tenth Amendment; and that the defendants are proceeding to carry the act into operation. In the *Massachusetts* case it is alleged that the plaintiff's rights and powers as a sovereign State and the rights of its citizens have been invaded and usurped by these expenditures and acts; and that, although the State has not accepted the act, its constitutional rights are infringed by the passage thereof and the imposition upon the State of an illegal and unconstitutional option either to yield to the Federal Government a part of its reserved rights or lose the share which it would otherwise be entitled to receive of the moneys appropriated. In the *Frothingham* case plaintiff alleges that the effect of the statute will be to take her property under the guise of taxation, without due process of law.

We have reached the conclusion that the cases must be disposed of for want of jurisdiction without considering the merits of the constitutional questions.

In the first case the State of Massachusetts presents no justiciable controversy either in its own behalf or as the representative of its citizens. The appellant in the second suit has no such interest in the sub-

ject-matter, nor is any such injury inflicted or threatened, as will enable her to sue.

First. The State of Massachusetts in its own behalf, in effect, complains that the act in question invades the local concerns of the State, and is a usurpation of power viz: the power of local self government reserved to the States.

Probably, it would be sufficient to point out that the powers of the State are not invaded, since the statute imposes no obligation but simply extends an option which the State is free to accept or reject. But we do not rest here. Under Article III, § 2, of the Constitution, the judicial power of this Court extends "to controversies * * * between a State and citizens of another State" and the Court has original jurisdiction "in all cases * * * in which a State shall be party." The effect of this is not to confer jurisdiction upon the Court merely because a State is a party, but only where it is a party to a proceeding of judicial cognizance. Proceedings not of a justiciable character are outside the contemplation of the constitutional grant. * * *

* * *

What then, is the nature of the right of the State here asserted and how is it affected by this statute? Reduced to its simplest terms, it is alleged that the statute constitutes an attempt to legislate outside the powers granted to Congress by the Constitution and within the field of local powers exclusively reserved to the States. Nothing is added to the force or effect of this assertion by the further incidental allegations that the ulterior purpose of Congress thereby was to induce the States to yield a portion of their sovereign rights; that the burden of the appropriations falls unequally upon the several States; and that there is imposed upon the States an illegal and unconstitutional option either to yield to the Federal Government a part of their reserved rights or lose their share of the moneys appropriated. But what burden is imposed upon the States, unequally or otherwise? Certainly there is none, unless it be the burden of taxation, and that falls upon their inhabitants, who are within the taxing power of Congress as well as that of the States where they reside. Nor does the statute require the States to do or to yield anything. If Congress enacted it with the ulterior purpose of tempting them to yield, that purpose may be effectively frustrated by the simple expedient of not yielding.

In the last analysis, the complaint of the plaintiff State is brought to the naked contention that Congress has usurped the reserved powers of the several States by the mere enactment of the statute, though nothing has been done and nothing is to be done without their consent; and it is plain that that question as it is thus presented, is political and not judicial in character, and therefore is not a matter which admits of the exercise of the judicial power.

* * *

It follows that in so far as the case depends upon the assertion of a right on the part of the State to sue in its own behalf we are without jurisdiction. In that aspect of the case we are called upon to adjudicate, not rights of person or property, not rights of dominion over physical domain, not quasi-sovereign rights actually invaded or threatened, but abstract questions of political power, of sovereignty, of government. No rights of the State falling within the

scope of the judicial power have been brought within the actual or threatened operation of the statute and this Court is as much without authority to pass abstract opinions upon the constitutionality of acts of Congress as it was held to be, in Cherokee Nation v. Georgia [5 Pet. 1, 8 L.Ed. 25], of state statutes. If an alleged attempt by congressional action to annul and abolish an existing state government "with all its constitutional powers and privileges," presents no justiciable issue, as was ruled in Georgia v. Stanton [6 Wall. 50, 18 L.Ed. 721], no reason can be suggested why it should be otherwise where the attempt goes no farther, as it is here alleged, than to propose to share with the State the field of state power.

We come next to consider whether the suit may be maintained by the State as the representative of its citizens. To this the answer is not doubtful. We need not go so far as to say that a State may never intervene by suit to protect its citizens against any form of enforcement of unconstitutional acts of Congress; but we are clear that the right to do so does not arise here. Ordinarily, at least, the only way in which a State may afford protection to its citizens, in such cases is through the enforcement of its own criminal statutes, where that is appropriate, or by opening its courts to the injured persons for the maintenance of civil suits or actions. But the citizens of Massachusetts are also citizens of the United States. It cannot be conceded that a State, as *parens patriae*, may institute judicial proceedings to protect citizens of the United States from the operation of the statutes thereof. While the State, under some circumstances, may sue in that capacity for the protection of its citizens * * *, it is no part of its duty or power to enforce their rights in respect of their relations with the Federal Government. In that field it is the United States, and not the State, which represents them as *parens patriae*, when such representation becomes appropriate; and to the former, and not to the latter, they must look for such protective measures as flow from that status.

Second. The attack upon the statute in the *Frothingham* case is, generally, the same, but this plaintiff alleges in addition that she is a taxpayer of the United States; and her contention, though not clear, seems to be that the effect of the appropriations complained of will be to increase the burden of future taxation and thereby take her property without due process of law. The right of a taxpayer to enjoin the execution of a federal appropriation act, on the ground that it is invalid and will result in taxation for illegal purposes, has never been passed upon by this Court. In cases where it was presented, the question has either been allowed to pass *sub silentio* or the determination of it expressly withheld. * * * The case last cited came here from the Court of Appeals of the District of Columbia, and that court sustained the right of the plaintiff to sue by treating the case as one directed against the District of Columbia, and therefore subject to the rule frequently stated by this Court, that resident taxpayers may sue to enjoin an illegal use of the moneys of a municipal corporation. * * * The interest of a taxpayer of a municipality in the application of its moneys is direct and immediate and the remedy by injunction to prevent their misuse is not inappropriate. It is upheld by a large number of state cases and is the rule of this

Court. * * * Nevertheless, there are decisions to the contrary. * * * The reasons which support the extension of the equitable remedy to a single taxpayer in such cases are based upon the peculiar relation of the corporate taxpayer to the corporation, which is not without some resemblance to that subsisting between stockholder and private corporation. * * * But the relation of a taxpayer of the United States to the Federal Government is very different. His interest in the moneys of the Treasury—partly realized from taxation and partly from other sources—is shared with millions of others; is comparatively minute and indeterminable; and the effect upon future taxation, of any payment out of the funds, so remote, fluctuating and uncertain, that no basis is afforded for an appeal to the preventive powers of a court of equity.

The administration of any statute, likely to produce additional taxation to be imposed upon a vast number of taxpayers, the extent of whose several liability is indefinite and constantly changing, is essentially a matter of public and not of individual concern. If one taxpayer may champion and litigate such a cause, then every other taxpayer may do the same, not only in respect of the statute here under review but also in respect of every other appropriation act and statute whose administration requires the outlay of public money, and whose validity may be questioned. The bare suggestion of such a result, with its attendant inconveniences, goes far to sustain the conclusion which we have reached, that a suit of this character cannot be maintained. It is of much significance that no precedent sustaining the right to maintain suits like this has been called to our attention, although, since the formation of the government, as an examination of the acts of Congress will disclose, a large number of statutes appropriating or involving the expenditure of moneys for non-federal purposes have been enacted and carried into effect.

The functions of government under our system are apportioned. To the legislative department has been committed the duty of making laws; to the executive the duty of executing them; and to the judiciary the duty of interpreting and applying them in cases properly brought before the courts. The general rule is that neither department may invade the province of the other and neither may control, direct or restrain the action of the other. We are not now speaking of the merely ministerial duties of officials. * * * We have no power *per se* to review and annul acts of Congress on the ground that they are unconstitutional. That question may be considered only when the justification for some direct injury suffered or threatened, presenting a justiciable issue, is made to rest upon such an act. Then the power exercised is that of ascertaining and declaring the law applica-

ble to the controversy. It amounts to little more than the negative power to disregard an unconstitutional enactment, which otherwise would stand in the way of the enforcement of a legal right. The party who invokes the power must be able to show not only that the statute is invalid but that he has sustained or is immediately in danger of sustaining some direct injury as the result of its enforcement, and not merely that he suffers in some indefinite way in common with people generally. If a case for preventive relief be presented the court enjoins, in effect, not the execution of the statute, but the acts of the official, the statute notwithstanding. Here the parties plaintiff have no such case. Looking through forms of words to the substance of their complaint, it is merely that officials of the executive department of the government are executing and will execute an act of Congress asserted to be unconstitutional; and this we are asked to prevent. To do so would be not to decide a judicial controversy, but to assume a position of authority over the governmental acts of another and co-equal department, an authority which plainly we do not possess.

FLAST v. COHEN

Supreme Court of the United States, 1968
392 U.S. 83, 88 S.Ct. 1942, 20 L.Ed.2d 947

Florence Flast and others, whose sole common interest in this proceeding was as federal taxpayers, sued to enjoin Wilbur Cohen, Secretary of Health, Education, and Welfare, from expending funds authorized by Congress under the Elementary and Secondary Education Act of 1965. The act provided funds to finance instruction and the purchase of textbooks in reading, arithmetic, and other subjects in religious schools. A U. S. District Court in New York dismissed the suit for lack of petitioners' standing to maintain the action, and appeal was taken to the Supreme Court. Appellants contended that the act flatly abridged the prohibition on such aid contained in the Establishment and Free Exercise Clauses of the First Amendment.

Mr. Chief Justice WARREN delivered the opinion of the Court.

In Frothingham v. Mellon, 262 U.S. 447, 43 S.Ct. 597 (1923), this Court ruled that a federal taxpayer is without standing to challenge the constitutionality of a federal statute. That ruling has stood for 45 years as an impenetrable barrier to suits against Acts of Congress brought by individuals who can assert only the interest of federal taxpayers. In this case, we must decide whether the *Frothingham* barrier should be lowered when a taxpayer attacks a federal statute on the ground that it violates the Establishment and Free Exercise Clauses of the First Amendment.

* * *

This Court first faced squarely the question whether a litigant asserting only his status as a taxpayer has standing to maintain a suit in a federal court in Frothingham v. Mellon, * * * and that decision must be the starting point for analysis in this case. The taxpayer in *Frothingham* attacked as unconstitutional the Maternity Act of 1921, 42 Stat. 224, which established a federal program of grants to those States which would undertake programs to reduce maternal and infant mortality. The taxpayer alleged that Congress, in enacting the challenged statute, had exceeded the powers delegated to it under Article I of the Constitution and had invaded the legislative province reserved to the several States by the Tenth Amendment. The taxpayer complained that the result of the allegedly unconstitutional enactment would be to increase her future federal tax liability and "thereby take her property without due process of law." 262 U.S., at 486, 43 S.Ct. at 600. The Court noted that a federal

taxpayer's "interest in the moneys of the treasury * * * is comparatively minute and indeterminable" and that "the effect upon future taxation, of any payment out of the [Treasury's] funds, * * * [is] remote, fluctuating and uncertain." * * * As a result, the Court ruled that the taxpayer had failed to allege the type of "direct injury" necessary to confer standing. * * *

Although the barrier *Frothingham* erected against federal taxpayer suits has never been breached, the decision has been the source of some confusion and the object of considerable criticism. The confusion has developed as commentators have tried to determine whether *Frothingham* establishes a constitutional bar to taxpayer suits or whether the Court was simply imposing a rule of self-restraint which was not constitutionally compelled. The conflicting viewpoints are reflected in the arguments made to this Court by the parties in this case. The Government has pressed upon us the view that *Frothingham* announced a constitutional rule, compelled by the Article III limitations on federal court jurisdiction and grounded in considerations of the doctrine of separation of powers. Appellants, however, insist that *Frothingham* expressed no more than a policy of judicial self-restraint which can be disregarded when compelling reasons for assuming jurisdiction over a taxpayer's suit exist. The opinion delivered in *Frothingham* can be read to support either position. The concluding sentence of the opinion states that, to take jurisdiction of the taxpayer's suit, "would be not to decide a judicial controversy, but to assume a position of authority over the governmental acts of another and co-equal department, an authority which plainly we do not possess." * * * Yet the concrete reasons given for denying standing to a federal taxpayer suggest that the Court's holding rests on something less than a constitutional foundation. For example, the Court conceded that standing had previously been conferred on municipal taxpayers to sue in that capacity. However, the Court viewed the interest of a federal taxpayer in total federal tax revenues as "comparatively minute and indeterminable" when measured against a municipal taxpayer's interest in a smaller city treasury. * * * This suggests that the petitioner in *Frothingham* was denied standing not because she was a taxpayer but because her tax bill was not large enough. In addition, the Court spoke of the "attendant inconveniences" of entertaining that taxpayer's suit because it might open the door of federal courts to countless such suits "in respect of every other appropriation act and statute whose administration requires the outlay of public money, and whose validity may be questioned." * * * Such a statement suggests pure policy considerations.

To the extent that *Frothingham* has been viewed as resting on policy considerations, it has been criticized as depending on assumptions not consistent with modern conditions. For example, some commentators have pointed out that a number of corporate taxpayers today have a federal tax liability running into hundreds of millions of dollars, and such taxpayers have a far greater monetary stake in the Federal Treasury than they do in any municipal treasury. To some degree, the fear expressed in *Frothingham* that allowing one taxpayer to sue would inundate the federal courts with countless similar suits has been miti-

gated by the ready availability of the devices of class actions and joinder under the Federal Rules of Civil Procedure, adopted subsequent to the decision in *Frothingham*. Whatever the merits of the current debate over *Frothingham*, its very existence suggests that we should undertake a fresh examination of the limitations upon standing to sue in a federal court and the application of those limitations to taxpayer suits.

The jurisdiction of federal courts is defined and limited by Article III of the Constitution. In terms relevant to the question for decision in this case, the judicial power of federal courts is constitutionally restricted to "cases" and "controversies." As is so often the situation in constitutional adjudication, those two words have an iceberg quality, containing beneath their surface simplicity submerged complexities which go to the very heart of our constitutional form of government. Embodied in the words "cases" and "controversies" are two complementary but somewhat different limitations. In part those words limit the business of federal courts to questions presented in an adversary context and in a form historically viewed as capable of resolution through the judicial process. And in part those words define the role assigned to the judiciary in a tripartite allocation of power to assure that the federal courts will not intrude into areas committed to the other branches of government. Justiciability is the term of art employed to give expression to this dual limitation placed upon federal courts by the case-and-controversy doctrine.

Justiciability is itself a concept of uncertain meaning and scope. Its reach is illustrated by the various grounds upon which questions sought to be adjudicated in federal courts have been held not to be justiciable. Thus, no justiciable controversy is presented when the parties seek adjudication of only a political question, when the parties are asking for an advisory opinion, when the question sought to be adjudicated has been mooted by subsequent developments, and when there is no standing to maintain the action. Yet it remains true that "[j]usticiability is * * * not a legal concept with a fixed content or suceptible of scientific verification. Its utilization is the resultant of many subtle pressures." * * * Poe v. Ullman, 367 U.S. 497, 508, 81 S.Ct. 1752, 1759 (1961).

Part of the difficulty in giving precise meaning and form to the concept of justiciability stems from the uncertain historical antecedents of the case-and-controversy doctrine. For example, Mr. Justice Frankfurter twice suggested that historical meaning could be imparted to the concepts of justiciability and case and controversy by reference to the practices of the courts of Westminster when the Constitution was adopted. * * * However, the power of English judges to deliver advisory opinions was well established at the time the Constitution was drafted. 3 K. Davis, Administrative Law Treatise 127–128 (1958). And it is quite clear that "the oldest and most consistent thread in the federal law of justiciability is that the federal courts will not give advisory opinions." C. Wright, Federal Courts 34 (1963). Thus, the implicit policies embodied in Article III, and not history alone, impose the rule against advisory opinions on federal courts. When the federal judicial power is invoked to pass upon the validity of actions by the Legislative

and Executive Branches of the Government, the rule against advisory opinions implements the separation of powers prescribed by the Constitution and confines federal courts to the role assigned them by Article III. See Muskrat v. United States, 219 U.S. 346, 31 S.Ct. 250 (1911). * * * However, the rule against advisory opinions also recognizes that such suits often "are not pressed before the Court with that clear concreteness provided when a question emerges precisely framed and necessary for decision from a clash of adversary argument exploring every aspect of a multifaceted situation embracing conflicting and demanding interests." * * * Consequently, the Article III prohibition against advisory opinions reflects the complementary constitutional considerations expressed by the justiciability doctrine: Federal judicial power is limited to those disputes which confine federal courts to a rule consistent with a system of separated powers and which are traditionally thought to be capable of resolution through the judicial process.

Additional uncertainty exists in the doctrine of justiciability because that doctrine has become a blend of constitutional requirements and policy considerations. And a policy limitation is "not always clearly distinguished from the constitutional limitation." Barrows v. Jackson, 346 U.S. 249, 255, 73 S.Ct. 1031, 1034 (1953). For example, in his concurring opinion in Ashwander v. Tennessee Valley Authority, 297 U.S. 288, 345–348, 56 S.Ct. 466, 482–483 (1936), Mr. Justice Brandeis listed seven rules developed by this Court "for its own governance" to avoid passing prematurely on constitutional questions.q Because the rules operate in "cases confessedly within [the Court's] jurisdiction," id., at 346, 56 S.Ct. at 482, they find their source in policy, rather than purely constitutional, considerations. However, several of the cases cited by Mr. Justice Brandeis in illustrating the rules of self-governance articulated purely constitutional grounds for decision. * * * The "many subtle pressures" which cause policy considerations to blend into the constitutional limitations of Article III make the justiciability doctrine one of uncertain and shifting contours.

It is in this context that the standing question presented by this case

must be viewed and that the Government's argument on that question must be evaluated. As we understand it, the Government's position is that the constitutional scheme of separation of powers, and the deference owed by the federal judiciary to the other two branches of government within that scheme, present an absolute bar to taxpayer suits challenging the validity of federal spending programs. The Government views such suits as involving no more than the mere disagreement by the taxpayer "with the uses to which tax money is put." According to the Government, the resolution of such disagreements is committed to other

---

q. Justice Brandeis wrote:

* * *

The Court developed, for its own governance in the cases confessedly within its jurisdiction, a series of rules under which it has avoided passing upon a large part of all the constitutional questions pressed upon it for decision. They are:

1. The Court will not pass upon the constitutionality of legislation in a friendly, non-adversary, proceeding, declining because to decide such questions "is legitimate only in the last resort, and as a necessity in the determination of real, earnest, and vital controversy between individuals. It never was the thought that, by means of a friendly suit, a party beaten in the legislature could transfer to the courts an inquiry as to the constitutionality of the legislative act." * * *

2. The Court will not "anticipate a question of constitutional law in advance of the necessity of deciding it." * * *

"It is not the habit of the court to decide questions of a constitutional nature unless absolutely necessary to a decision of the case." * * *

3. The Court will not "formulate a rule of constitutional law broader than is required by the precise facts to which it is to be applied." * * *

4. The Court will not pass upon a constitutional question although properly presented by the record, if there is also present some

other ground upon which the case may be disposed of. This rule has found most varied application. Thus, if a case can be decided on either of two grounds, one involving a constitutional question, the other a question of statutory construction or general law, the Court will decide only the latter. * * * Appeals from the highest court of a state challenging its decision of a question under the Federal Constitution are frequently dismissed because the judgment can be sustained on an independent state ground. * * *

5. The Court will not pass upon the validity of a statute upon complaint of one who fails to show that he is injured by its operation. * * *

Among the many applications of this rule, none is more striking than the denial of the right of challenge to one who lacks a personal or property right. * * *

6. The Court will not pass upon the constitutionality of a statute at the instance of one who has availed himself of its benefits. * * *

7. "When the validity of an act of the Congress is drawn in question, and even if a serious doubt of constitutionality is raised, it is a cardinal principle that this Court will first ascertain whether a construction of the statute is fairly possible by which the question may be avoided." * * *

* * *

branches of the Federal Government and not to the judiciary. Consequently, the Government contends that, under no circumstances, should standing be conferred on federal taxpayers to challenge a federal taxing or spending program. An analysis of the function served by standing limitations compels a rejection of the Government's position.

Standing is an aspect of justiciability and, as such, the problem of standing is surrounded by the same complexities and vagaries that inhere in justiciability. Standing has been called one of "the most amorphous [concepts] in the entire domain of public law." Some of the complexities peculiar to standing problems result because standing "serves, on occasion, as a shorthand expression for all the various elements of justiciability." In addition, there are at work in the standing doctrine the many subtle pressures which tend to cause policy considerations to blend into constitutional limitations.

Despite the complexities and uncertainties, some meaningful form can be given to the jurisdictional limitations placed on federal court power by the concept of standing. The fundamental aspect of standing is that it focuses on the party seeking to get his complaint before a federal court and not on the issues he wishes to have adjudicated. The "gist of the question of standing" is whether the party seeking relief has "alleged such a personal stake in the outcome of the controversy as to assure that concrete adverseness which sharpens the presentation of issues upon which the court so largely depends for illumination of difficult constitutional questions." Baker v. Carr, 369 U.S. 186, 204, 82 S.Ct. 691, 703 (1962). In other words, when stand-

ing is placed in issue in a case, the question is whether the person whose standing is challenged is a proper party to request an adjudication of a particular issue and not whether the issue itself is justiciable. Thus, a party may have standing in a particular case, but the federal court may nevertheless decline to pass on the merits of the case because, for example, it presents a political question. A proper party is demanded so that federal courts will not be asked to decide "ill-defined controversies over constitutional issues." United Public Workers of America v. Mitchell, 330 U.S. 75, 90, 67 S.Ct. 556, 564 (1947), or a case which is of "a hypothetical or abstract character," Aetna Life Insurance Co. of Hartford, Conn. v. Haworth, 300 U.S. 227, 240, 57 S.Ct. 461, 463 (1937). So stated, the standing requirement is closely related to, although more general than, the rule that federal courts will not entertain friendly suits, * * * or those which are feigned or collusive in nature. * * *

When the emphasis in the standing problem is placed on whether the person invoking a federal court's jurisdiction is a proper party to maintain the action, the weakness of the Government's argument in this case becomes apparent. The question whether a particular person is a proper party to maintain the action does not, by its own force, raise separation of powers problems related to improper judicial interference in areas committed to other branches of the Federal Government. Such problems arise, if at all, only from the substantive issues the individual seeks to have adjudicated. Thus, in terms of Article III limitations on federal court jurisdiction, the question of standing is related only to whether the dispute sought to be adjudicated will be presented in an adversary context and in a form historically viewed as capable of judicial resolution. It is for that reason that the emphasis in standing problems is on whether the party invoking federal court jurisdiction has "a personal stake in the outcome of the controversy," Baker v. Carr * * * and whether the dispute touches upon "the legal relations of parties having adverse legal interests." *Aetna Life Insurance Co.* v. *Haworth*, supra. * * * A taxpayer may or may not have the requisite personal stake in the outcome, depending upon the circumstances of the particular case. Therefore, we find no absolute bar in Article III to suits by federal taxpayers challenging allegedly unconstitutional federal taxing and spending programs. There remains, however, the problem of determining the circumstances under which a federal taxpayer will be deemed to have the personal stake and interest that impart the necessary concrete adverseness to such litigation so that standing can be conferred on the taxpayer *qua* taxpayer consistent with the constitutional limitations of Article III.

The various rules of standing applied by federal courts have not been developed in the abstract. Rather, they have been fashioned with specific reference to the status asserted by the party whose standing is challenged and to the type of question he wishes to have adjudicated. We have noted that, in deciding the question of standing, it is not relevant that the substantive issues in the litigation might be nonjusticiable. However, our decisions establish that, in ruling on standing, it is both appropriate and necessary to look to the substantive issues for another purpose namely, to determine wheth-

er there is a logical nexus between the status asserted and the claim sought to be adjudicated. For example, standing requirements will vary in First Amendment religion cases depending upon whether the party raises an Establishment Clause claim or a claim under the Free Exercise Clause. See McGowan v. State of Maryland, 366 U.S. 420, 429–430, 81 S.Ct. 1101, 1106–1107 (1961). Such inquiries into the nexus between the status asserted by the litigant and the claim he presents are essential to assure that he is a proper and appropriate party to invoke federal judicial power. Thus, our point of reference in this case is the standing of individuals who assert only the status of federal taxpayers and who challenge the constitutionality of a federal spending program. Whether such individuals have standing to maintain that form of action turns on whether they can demonstrate the necessary stake as taxpayers in the outcome of the litigation to satisfy Article III requirements.

The nexus demanded of federal taxpayers has two aspects to it. First, the taxpayer must establish a logical link between that status and the type of legislative enactment attacked. Thus, a taxpayer will be a proper party to allege the unconstitutionality only of exercises of congressional power under the taxing and spending clause of Art. I, § 8, of the Constitution. It will not be sufficient to allege an incidental expenditure of tax funds in the administration of an essentially regulatory statute. This requirement is consistent with the limitation imposed upon state-taxpayer standing in federal courts in Doremus v. Board of Education, 342 U.S. 429, 72 S.Ct. 394 (1952). Secondly, the taxpayer must establish a nexus between that status and the precise nature of the constitutional infringement alleged. Under this requirement, the taxpayer must show that the challenged enactment exceeds specific constitutional limitations imposed upon the exercise of the congressional taxing and spending power and not simply that the enactment is generally beyond the powers delegated to Congress by Art. I, § 8. When both nexuses are established, the litigant will have shown a taxpayer's stake in the outcome of the controversy and will be a proper and appropriate party to invoke a federal court's jurisdiction.

The taxpayer-appellants in this case have satisfied both nexuses to support their claim of standing under the test we announce today. Their constitutional challenge is made to an exercise by Congress of its power under Art. I, § 8, to spend for the general welfare, and the challenged program involves a substantial expenditure of federal tax funds. In addition, appellants have alleged that the challenged expenditures violate the Establishment and Free Exercise Clauses of the First Amendment. Our history vividly illustrates that one of the specific evils feared by those who drafted the Establishment Clause and fought for its adoption was that the taxing and spending power would be used to favor one religion over another or to support religion in general. James Madison, who is generally recognized as the leading architect of the religion clauses of the First Amendment, observed in his famous Memorial and Remonstrance Against Religious Assessments that "the same authority which can force a citizen to contribute three pence only of his property for the support of any one establishment, may force him to conform to any other establishment in all cases

whatsoever." 2 Writings of James Madison 183, 186 (Hunt ed. 1901). The concern of Madison and his supporters was quite clearly that religious liberty ultimately would be the victim if government could employ its taxing and spending powers to aid one religion over another or to aid religion in general. The Establishment Clause was designed as a specific bulwark against such potential abuses of governmental power, and that clause of the First Amendment operates as a specific constitutional limitation upon the exercise by Congress of the taxing and spending power conferred by Art. I, § 8.

The allegations of the taxpayer in *Frothingham* v. *Mellon*, supra, were quite different from those made in this case, and the result in *Frothingham* is consistent with the test of taxpayer standing announced today. The taxpayer in *Frothingham* attacked a federal spending program and she, therefore, established the first nexus required. However, she lacked standing because her constitutional attack was not based on an allegation that Congress, in enacting the Maternity Act of 1921, had breached a specific limitation upon its taxing and spending power. The taxpayer in *Frothingham* alleged essentially that Congress, by enacting the challenged statute, had exceeded the general powers delegated to it by Art. I, § 8, and that Congress had thereby invaded the legislative province reserved to the States by the Tenth Amendment. To be sure, Mrs. Frothingham made the additional allegation that her tax liability would be increased as a result of the allegedly unconstitutional enactment, and she framed that allegation in terms of a deprivation of property without due process of law. However, the Due Process Clause of the Fifth

Amendment does not protect taxpayers against increases in tax liability, and the taxpayer in *Frothingham* failed to make any additional claim that the harm she alleged resulted from a breach by Congress of the specific constitutional limitations imposed upon an exercise of the taxing and spending power. In essence, Mrs. Frothingham was attempting to assert the States' interest in their legislative prerogatives and not a federal taxpayer's interest in being free of taxing and spending in contravention of specific constitutional limitations imposed upon Congress' taxing and spending power.

We have noted that the Establishment Clause of the First Amendment does specifically limit the taxing and spending power conferred by Art. I, § 8. Whether the Constitution contains other specific limitations can be determined only in the context of future cases. However, whenever such specific limitations are found, we believe a taxpayer will have a clear stake as a taxpayer in assuring that they are not breached by Congress. Consequently, we hold that a taxpayer will have standing consistent with Article III to invoke federal judicial power when he alleges that congressional action under the taxing and spending clause is in derogation of those constitutional provisions which operate to restrict the exercise of the taxing and spending power. The taxpayer's allegation in such cases would be that his tax money is being extracted and spent in violation of specific constitutional protections against such abuses of legislative power. Such an injury is appropriate for judicial redress, and the taxpayer has established the necessary nexus between his status and the nature of the allegedly unconstitutional action to support his claim of

standing to secure judicial review. Under such circumstances, we feel confident that the questions will be framed with the necessary specificity, that the issues will be contested with the necessary adverseness and that the litigation will be pursued with the necessary vigor to assure that the constitutional challenge will be made in a form traditionally thought to be capable of judicial resolution. We lack that confidence in cases such as *Frothingham* where a taxpayer seeks to employ a federal court as a forum in which to air his generalized grievances about the conduct of government or the allocation of power in the Federal System.

While we express no view at all on the merits of appellants' claims in this case, their complaint contains sufficient allegations under the criteria we have outlined to give them standing to invoke a federal court's jurisdiction for an adjudication on the merits.

Reversed.

Mr. Justice HARLAN, dissenting.

The problems presented by this case are narrow and relatively abstract, but the principles by which they must be resolved involve nothing less than the proper functioning of the federal courts, and so run to the roots of our constitutional system. The nub of my view is that the end result of *Frothingham* v. *Mellon* * * * was correct, even though, like others, I do not subscribe to all of its reasoning and premises. Although I therefore agree with certain of the conclusions reached today by the Court, I cannot accept the standing doctrine that it substitutes for *Frothingham*, for it seems to me that this new doctrine rests on premises that do not withstand analysis. Accordingly, I respectfully dissent.

It is desirable first to restate the basic issues in this case. The question here is not, as it was not in *Frothingham,* whether "a federal taxpayer is without standing to challenge the constitutionality of a federal statute." * * * It could hardly be disputed that federal taxpayers may, as taxpayers, contest the constitutionality of tax obligations imposed severally upon them by federal statute. Such a challenge may be made by way of defense to an action by the United States to recover the amount of a challenged tax debt, * * * or to a prosecution for willful failure to pay or to report the tax. * * * Moreover, such a challenge may provide the basis of an action by a taxpayer to obtain the refund of a previous tax payment. * * *

The lawsuits here and in *Frothingham* are fundamentally different. They present the question whether federal taxpayers *qua* taxpayers may, in suits in which they do not contest the validity of their previous or existing tax obligations, challenge the constitutionality of the uses for which Congress has authorized the expenditure of public funds. These differences in the purposes of the cases are reflected in differences in the litigants' interests. An action brought to contest the validity of tax liabilities assessed to the plaintiff is designed to vindicate interests that are personal and proprietary. The wrongs alleged and the relief sought by such a plaintiff are unmistakably private; only secondarily are his interests representative of those of the general population. I take it that the Court, although it does not pause to examine the question, believes that the interests of those who as taxpay-

ers challenge the constitutionality of public expenditures may, at least in certain circumstances, be similar. Yet this assumption is surely mistaken.

* * *

Presumably the Court recognizes at least certain * * * hazards, else it would not have troubled to impose limitations upon the situations in which, and purposes for which, such suits may be brought. Nonetheless, the limitations adopted by the Court are, as I have endeavored to indicate, wholly untenable. This is the more unfortunate because there is available a resolution of this problem that entirely satisfies the demands of the principle of separation of powers. This Court has previously held that individual litigants have standing to represent the public interest, despite their lack of economic or other personal interests, if Congress has appropriately authorized such suits. * * * I would adhere to that principle. Any hazards to the proper allocation of authority among the three branches of the Government would be substantially diminished if public actions had been pertinently authorized by Congress and the President. I appreciate that this Court does not ordinarily await the mandate of other branches of the Government, but it seems to me that the extraordinary character of public actions, and of the mischievous, if not dangerous, consequences they involve for the proper functioning of our constitutional system, and in particular of the federal courts, makes such judicial forbearance the part of wisdom. It must be emphasized that the implications of these questions of judicial policy are of fundamental significance for the other branches of the Federal Government.

Such a rule could readily be applied to this case. Although various efforts have been made in Congress to authorize public actions to contest the validity of federal expenditures in aid of religiously affiliated schools and other institutions, no such authorization has yet been given.

This does not mean that we would, under such a rule, be enabled to avoid our constitutional responsibilities, or that we would confine to limbo the First Amendment or any other constitutional command. The question here is not, despite the Court's unarticulated premise, whether the religious clauses of the

First Amendment are hereafter to be enforced by the federal courts; the issue is simply whether plaintiffs of an *additional* category, heretofore excluded from those courts, are to be permitted to maintain suits. The recent history of this Court is replete with illustrations, including even one announced today * * * that questions involving the religious clauses will not, if federal taxpayers are prevented from contesting federal expenditures, be left "unacknowledged, unresolved, and undecided."

Accordingly, for the reasons contained in this opinion, I would affirm the judgment of the District Court.

THE BURGER COURT AND STANDING TO SUE AS TAXPAYERS AND CITIZENS

Schlesinger v. Reservists Committee to Stop the War, 418 U.S. 208, 94 S.Ct. 2925 (1974)	Facts	Five members of a group composed of present and former members of the military reserves organized to oppose the Vietnam war launched a class action against the Secretary of Defense and the three service secretaries, attacking the constitutionality of a practice whereby several members of Congress held commissions in the reserves. The plaintiffs, also as citizens and taxpayers, contended that retention of these commissions by sitting Representatives and Senators opened the door to undue influence by the executive branch and specifically violated Art. I, § 6, cl. 2 of the Constitution which declares that "no person holding any office under the United States, shall be a Member of either House during his continuance in office."
	Decision	Plaintiffs have no standing either as citizens or as taxpayers to bring this suit.
	Vote	6–3
	Opinion of the Court	Chief Justice Burger delivered the opinion of the Court. "To have standing to sue as a class respresentative it is essential that a plaintiff must be a part of that class, that is, he must possess the same interest and suffer the same injury shared by all members of the class he represents." Although the plaintiffs' interest here was correctly characterized by the district court as "undifferentiated" from that of other citizens,

Schlesinger (*Cont.*)

Opinion of
the Court
(*Cont.*)

"[t]he only interest all citizens share in the claim advanced by respondents is one which presents injury in the abstract. Respondents seek to have the Judicial Branch compel the Executive Branch to act in conformity with the Incompatibility Clause, an interest shared by all citizens. The very language of respondents' complaint * * * reveals that it is nothing more than a matter of speculation whether the claimed nonobservance of that Clause deprives citizens of the faithful discharge of the legislative duties of Reservist Members of Congress. And that claimed nonobservance, standing alone, would adversely affect only the generalized interests of all citizens in constitutional governance, and that is an abstract injury."

"To permit a complainant who has no concrete injury to require a court to rule on important constitutional issues in the abstract would create the potential for abuse of the judicial process, distort the role of the Judiciary in its relationship to the Executive and the Legislature and open the Judiciary to an arguable charge of providing 'government by injunction.'" Only when "a court hear[s] an individual's complaint that certain specific governmental action will cause that person private competitive injury * * * or a complaint that individual enjoyment of certain natural resources has been impaired by such action, United States v. Students Challenging Regulatory Agency Procedures (SCRAP), 412 U.S. 669, 687, 93 S.Ct. 2405, 2415 (1973), * * *" is there "provide[d] the setting for a focused consideration of a concrete injury."

As for the assertion of taxpayer standing, the complaint fails the "nexus" test announced in *Flast* because "respondents d[o] not challenge an enactment under Art. I, § 8 [Congress's taxing and spending power], but rather the action of the Executive Branch in permitting Members of Congress to maintain their Reserve status."

Dissenting
Opinions

Justice Douglas dissented in an opinion which Justice Marshall joined. "While respondents have standing as taxpayers, their citizenship also gives them standing to challenge the appropriations acts financing activities of the reservists." "All the present citizens seek is to have the Constitution enforced as it is written. It is not a suit to unseat Members of Congress. Any decree that issued would run to the Secretary of Defense to take the challenged reservists off the list.

"The interest of citizens is obvious. The complaint alleges injuries to the ability of the average citizen to make his political advocacy effective whenever it touches on the vast interests of the Pentagon. It is said that all who oppose the expansion of military influence in our national affairs find

Schlesinger (*Cont.*)	Dissenting Opinions (*Cont.*)	they are met with a powerful lobby—the Reserve Officers Association—which has strong congressional allies.

"Whether this is true or not we do not know. So far as the Incompatibility Clause of the Constitution is concerned that contention is immaterial. It is as immaterial to the function of Art. I, § 6, cl. 2 of the Constitution as would be a suggestion that the establishment of a religion under the First Amendment is benign in a given case. What the Framers did in each case was to set up constitutional fences barring certain affiliations, certain kinds of appropriations. Their judgment was that the potential for evil was so great that no appropriations of that character should be made.

"The interest of citizens in guarantees written in the Constitution seems obvious. Who other than citizens have a better right to have the Incompatibility Clause enforced? It is their interests that the Incompatibility Clause was designed to protect. The Executive branch under our regime is not a fiefdom or principality competing with the Legislative as another center of power. They operate within a constitutional framework, and it is that constitutional framework that these citizens want to keep intact. * * * We have insisted that more than generalized grievances of a citizen be shown and that he must have a 'personal stake in the outcome,' Baker v. Carr, 369 U.S. 186, 204, 82 S.Ct. 691, 703. But that 'personal stake' need not be a monetary one. In *Baker* v. *Carr* it was the right to vote, an important badge of citizenship. The 'personal stake' in the present case is keeping the Incompatibility Clause an operative force in government by freeing the entanglement of the federal bureaucracy with the Legislative Branch."

Justice Brennan also dissented, concluding "that respondent Reservists Committee and its members have demonstrated sufficient 'injury in fact' to maintain this suit. * * * More stringent requirements, such as the Court's demand that these respondents satisfy *Flast's* 'nexus' requirement, are not appropriate issues for resolution under the rubric of 'standing.' Since I would find the injury-in-fact requirement met by respondents' taxpayer allegation, I have no occasion to reach the question whether respondent Reservists Committee and its members' allegations of injury to their interests as citizens would be sufficient to confer standing under the circumstances of this case."

United States v. Richardson, 418 U.S. 166, 94 S.Ct. 2940 (1974)	Facts	The Central Intelligence Agency Act provides that an accounting of agency expenditures shall be made "solely on the certificate of the Director * * * ." Richardson, a federal taxpayer at-

United States v. Richardson (*Cont.*)		
	Facts (*Cont.*)	tempting to obtain detailed information about CIA expenditures, brought suit attacking that portion of the act as a violation of Art. I, § 9, cl. 7 of the Constitution which specifies: "No Money shall be drawn from the Treasury, but in Consequence of Appropriations made by Law; and a regular Statement of Account of the Receipts and Expenditures of all public money shall be published from time to time."
	Decision	Plaintiff has not established taxpayer standing to sue.
	Vote	5–4
	Opinion of the Court	Chief Justice Burger delivered the Court's opinion. "The mere recital of the respondent's claims and an examination of the statute under attack demonstrates how far he falls short of the standing criteria of *Flast* and how neatly he falls within the *Frothingham* holding left undisturbed. Although the status he rests on is that he is a taxpayer, his challenge is not addressed to the taxing or spending power but to the statutes regulating the CIA * * *." The section of the statute in question "provides different accounting and reporting requirements and procedures for the CIA, as is also done with respect to other governmental agencies dealing in confidential areas." "Respondent makes no claim that appropriated funds are being spent in violation of a 'specific constitutional limitation upon the * * * taxing and spending power.' * * * Rather, he asks the courts to compel the Government to give him information on precisely how the CIA spends its funds. Thus there is no 'logical nexus' between the asserted status of taxpayer and the claimed failure of the Congress to require the Executive to supply a more detailed report of the expenditures of that agency." Thus, here, "[r]espondent is seeking 'to employ a federal court as a forum in which to air his generalized grievances about the conduct of the government.'" "It can be argued that if respondent is not permitted to litigate this issue, no one can do so. In a very real sense, the absence of any particular individual or class to litigate these claims gives support to the argument that the subject matter is committed to the surveillance of Congress, and ultimately to the political process."
	Concurring Opinion	Justice Powell wrote "solely to indicate that I would go further than the Court and would lay to rest the approach undertaken in *Flast*. I would not overrule *Flast* on its facts, because it is now settled that federal taxpayer standing exists in Es-

United States v. Rich-
ardson (*Cont.*)

Concurring
Opinion
(*Cont.*)

tablishment Clause cases. I would not, however, perpetuate the doctrinal confusion inherent in the *Flast* two-part 'nexus' test. The test is not a reliable indicator of when a federal taxpayer has standing, and it has no sound relationship to the question whether such a plaintiff, with no other interest at stake, should be allowed to bring suit against one of the branches of the Federal Government. In my opinion, it should be abandoned."

Dissenting
Opinions

Justice Stewart, joined by Justice Marshall, dissented. *Flast* and *Frothingham* "throw very little light on the question at issue in this case" because, unlike the plaintiffs in those cases, "Richardson's claim is of an entirely different order." He "did not bring this action asking a court to invalidate a federal statute on the ground that it was beyond the delegated power of Congress to enact or that it contravened some constitutional prohibition" but on the claim that "Art. I, § 9, cl. 7 of the Constitution, the Statement and Account Clause, gives him a right to receive, and imposes on the Government a corresponding affirmative duty to supply, a periodic report of the receipts and expenditures 'of all public Money.'" Justice Stewart continued: "In support of his standing to litigate this claim, he has asserted his status both as a taxpayer and as a citizen-voter. Whether the Statement and Account Clause imposes upon the Government an affirmative duty to supply the information requested and whether that duty runs to every taxpayer or citizen are questions that go to the substantive merits of this litigation. Those questions are not now before us, but I think that the Court is quite wrong in holding that the respondent was without standing to raise them in the trial court."

Justice Brennan also dissented, saying: "The claim was not merely that failure to publish was a violation of the Constitution. The claim went further and alleged that this violation deprived Richardson, as an individual, and not as an inseparable part of the citizenry, of a right given to him by Art. I, § 9, cl. 7. Moreover, his complaint, properly construed, alleged that the violations caused him injury not only in respect of his right as a citizen to know how Congress was spending the public fisc, but also in respect of his right as a voter to receive information to aid his decision how and for whom to vote. These claims may ultimately fail on the merits, but Richardson has 'standing' to assert them."

Justice Douglas also dissented.

Valley Forge Christian College v. Americans United for Separation of Church and State, Inc., 454 U.S. 464, 102 S.Ct. 752 (1982)	Facts	Acting under authority conferred by the Property Clause (Art. IV, § 3, cl. 2) of the Constitution, Congress passed the Federal Property and Administrative Services Act of 1949 to provide an efficient and economical means for the disposal of surplus federal property. Under the law, property which has outlived its usefulness to the government may be transferred to public or private entities. Under the act, the Secretary of Health, Education, and Welfare (now the Secretary of Education) assumes responsibility for disposing of the surplus property for educational use and is authorized to sell such property to nonprofit, tax-exempt educational institutions taking into account as consideration any benefit which has accrued or may accrue to the United States from transfer of the property. HEW conveyed to a church-related college a building formerly used as a military hospital after it was declared to be "surplus property" under the act. Although the building was appraised at over half a million dollars, HEW discounted it 100 percent, and transfer of the property was, therefore, effected at no cost at all to the religious educational institution. An organization dedicated to the separation of church and state sued to challenge the conveyance of the property as a violation of the First Amendment, alleging that each member of the organization "would be deprived of the fair and constitutional use of his (her) tax dollars."
	Decision	Plaintiff organization has neither taxpayer nor citizen standing to sue.
	Vote	5–4
	Opinion of the Court	Justice Rehnquist delivered the Court's opinion. "Unlike the plaintiffs in *Flast*, respondents fail the first prong of the test for taxpayer standing. Their claim is different in two respects. First, the source of their complaint is not a congressional action, but a decision by HEW to transfer a parcel of federal property. *Flast* limited taxpayer standing to challenges directed 'only [at] exercises of congressional power.' * * * Second, * * * the property transfer about which respondents complain was not an exercise of authority conferred by the taxing and spending clause of Art. I, § 8 * * * [but] was an evident exercise of Congress' power under the Property Clause, Art. IV, § 3, cl. 2." *Frothingham* and not *Flast*, therefore, controls this case. "[R]espondents have [also not] alleged any other basis for standing to bring this suit." "Although they claim that the Constitution has been violated, they claim nothing else. They fail to identify any personal injury suffered by the plaintiffs as a *consequence* of the alleged constitutional error, other than the psychological consequence presum-

Valley Forge Christian College (*Cont.*)	Opinion of the Court (*Cont.*)	ably produced by observation of conduct with which one disagrees. That is not an injury sufficient to confer standing under Article III, even though the disagreement is phrased in constitutional terms. It is evident that respondents are firmly committed to the constitutional principle of separation of church and State, but standing is not measured by the intensity of the litigant's interest or the fervor of his advocacy." There is "no place in our constitutional scheme" for "the philosophy that the business of the federal courts is correcting constitutional errors, and that 'cases and controversies' are at best merely convenient vehicles for doing so or at worst nuisances that may be dispensed with when they become obstacles to that transcendent endeavor. * * * It does not become more palatable when the underlying merits concern the Establishment Clause. Respondents' claim of standing implicitly rests on the presumption that violations of the Establishment Clause typically will not cause injury sufficient to confer standing under the 'traditional' view of Art. III. But '[t]he assumption that if respondents have no standing to sue, no one would have standing is not a reason to find standing.' Schlesinger v. Reservists Committee to Stop the War, 418 U.S., at 227, 94 S.Ct., at 2935. This view would convert standing into a requirement that must be observed only when satisfied. Moreover, we are unwilling to assume that injured parties are nonexistent simply because they have not joined respondents in their suit. The law of averages is not a substitute for standing."
	Dissenting Opinion	Justice Brennan dissented in an opinion in which Justices Marshall and Blackmun joined. A consequence of the fact that "[a] plaintiff's standing is a jurisdictional matter for Article III courts, and thus [constitutes] a 'threshold question' to be resolved before turning attention to more 'substantive' issues" is the "impulse to decide difficult questions of substantive law obliquely in the course of opinions purporting to do nothing more than determine what the Court labels 'standing.' * * * The serious by-product of that practice is that the Court disregards its constitutional responsibility when, by failing to acknowledge the protections afforded by the Constitution, it uses 'standing to slam the courthouse door against plaintiffs who are entitled to full consideration of their claims on the merits.' " "The opinion of the Court is a stark example of this unfortunate trend of resolving cases at the 'threshold' while obscuring the nature of the underlying rights and interests at stake." "The 'case and controversy' limitation of Article III overrides no other provision of the Constitution. To construe that Article to deny standing 'to the

Valley Forge Chris-   Dissenting   class for whose sake [a] constitutional protection
tian College (*Cont.*)   Opinion   is given' * * * simply turns the Constitution
                         (*Cont.*)   on its head." "It is clear in the light of * * *
history, that one of the primary purposes of the
Establishment Clause was to prevent the use of
tax monies for religious purposes. *The taxpayer
was the direct and intended beneficiary of the
prohibition on financial aid to religion.*" "It is
at once apparent that the test of standing formulated by the Court in *Flast* sought to reconcile the
developing doctrine of taxpayer 'standing' with
the Court's historical understanding that the Establishment Clause was intended to prohibit the
Federal Government from using tax funds for the
advancement of religion, and thus the constitutional imperative of taxpayer standing in certain
cases brought pursuant to the Establishment
Clause." Despite its general language, the two-
pronged "nexus" test, announced in *Flast* "is best
understood as 'a determinant of standing of plaintiffs alleging only injury as taxpayers who challenge alleged violations of the Establishment and
Free Exercise Clauses of the First Amendment,'
and not as a general statement of standing principles. * * * The test explains what forms of
governmental action may be attacked by someone
alleging *only* taxpayer status, and, without ruling
out the possibility that history might reveal another similarly founded provision, explains why
an Establishment Clause claim is treated differently from any other assertion that the federal
government has exceeded the bounds of law in allocating its largesse." "Each, and indeed every,
federal taxpayer suffers precisely the injury that
the Establishment Clause guards against when
the Federal Government directs that funds be
taken from the pocketbooks of the citizenry and
placed into the coffers of the ministry."

Justice Brennan then went on to explicitly reject as
both "specious" and "pernicious to our constitutional heritage" the "tortuous distinctions" put
forth by the majority in distinguishing *Flast* from
the present case. As to the first distinction—that
Flast applies to only congressional but not administrative actions—Justice Brennan responded:
"To be sure, the First Amendment is phrased as a
restriction on Congress' legislative authority; this
is only natural since the Constitution assigns the
authority to legislate and appropriate only to Congress. But it is difficult to conceive of an expenditure for which the last governmental actor, either implementing directly the legislative will, or
acting within the scope of legislatively delegated
authority is not an Executive Branch official.
The First Amendment binds the Government as a
whole, regardless of which branch is at work in a
particular instance." And, as to the distinction
drawn by the Court between actions stemming

| Valley Forge Christian College (*Cont.*) | Dissenting Opinion (*Cont.*) | from the taxing and spending power, on the one hand, and those from the Property Clause, on the other: "It can make no constitutional difference in the case before us whether the donation to the defendant here was in the form of a cash grant to build a facility * * * or in the nature of a gift of property including a facility already built. That this is a meaningless distinction is illustrated by *Tilton* [v. Richardson, 403 U.S. 672, 91 S.Ct. 2091 (1971)]. In that case, taxpayers were afforded standing to object to the fact that the Government had not received adequate assurance that if the property that it financed was later converted to religious uses, it would receive full value for the property, as the Constitution requires. The complaint here is precisely that, although the property at issue is actually being used for a sectarian purpose, the government has not received, nor demanded, full value payment. Whether undertaken pursuant to the Property Clause or the Spending Clause, the breach of the Establishment Clause, and the relationship of the taxpayer to that breach, is precisely the same." |
| | Dissenting Opinion | Justice Stevens added that "[o]ne cannot read the Court's opinion and the concurring opinions of Justice Stewart and Justice Fortas in *Flast* v. *Cohen* * * * without forming the firm conclusion that the plaintiffs' invocation of the Establishment Clause was of decisive importance in resolving the standing issue in that case." He continued, " * * * I am persuaded that the essential holding of *Flast* v. *Cohen* attaches special importance to the Establishment Clause and does not permit the drawing of a tenuous distinction between the Spending Clause and the Property Clause." |

WARTH v. SELDIN

Supreme Court of the United States, 1975
422 U.S. 490, 95 S.Ct. 2197, 45 L.Ed.2d 343

Various individuals and organizations of the Rochester, New York metropolitan area brought a class action against the suburban town of Penfield and members of its Zoning, Planning, and Town Boards. The plaintiffs asserted that the town's zoning ordinance as written and enforced effectively excluded low- and moderate-income persons from living in the town in violation of the First, Ninth, and Fourteenth Amendments as well as 42 U.S.C.A. §§ 1981, 1982, and 1983. Among the parties involved in conducting the suit were: (1) Metro-Act of Rochester, a non-profit, community action organization aimed at alerting citizens to pressing social problems and investigating the perceived critical shortage of low- and moderate-income housing in the metropolitan area; (2) several city taxpayers (plaintiffs Vinkey, Reichert, Warth, Harris, and Ortiz) who alleged that Penfield's exclusionary practices forced the City of Rochester to impose higher taxes on them than would otherwise have been necessary; (3) several low- and moderate-income city residents (plaintiffs Ortiz, Broadnax, Reyes, and Sinkler) who asserted that the town's zoning practices prevented them from purchasing or leasing property in Penfield and thus forced them to live in less attractive areas; (4) Rochester Home

Builders Association, a trade association of contractors engaged in residential construction which argued that Penfield's exclusionary zoning ordinance prevented the construction of low- and moderate-income housing and thereby deprived the builders of potential profits; and (5) Housing Council in the Monroe County Area, Inc., a non-profit corporation composed of over seventy public and private organizations interested in housing problems, seventeen of which hoped to be engaged in developing low- and moderate-income housing and one of which, Penfield Better Homes Corp., attempting to develop moderate-income housing in Penfield, asserted it was stymied by an inability to secure the necessary approvals.

The plaintiffs' complaint alleged that the exclusion of low- and moderate-income housing, which also had the effect of discriminating against minority ethnic and racial groups (since most of those persons have only low or moderate incomes), was apparent from the zoning ordinance which allocates 98 percent of the town's vacant land to single-family detached housing with such requirements as to minimum lot size, floor area, habitable space, etc., as to push the cost of housing well beyond the reach of persons of modest means. Plaintiffs also pointed out that the 0.3 percent of the available land zoned for multi-family dwellings was not feasible for development into low- and moderate-income housing because of low density and other requirements. As final evidence of the exclusionary intent and effect of the town's zoning policy and its implementation, the plaintiffs pointed to the behavior of Penfield's Zoning, Planning, and Town Boards, alleging that officials had among other things inordinately delayed action on proposals for low- and moderate-income housing, denied such proposals arbitrarily and for insubstantial reasons, refused to grant the necessary variances, and amended the zoning ordinance so as to make approval of such proposals virtually impossible.

A federal district court dismissed the complaint on grounds the plaintiffs did not have standing to sue, and this judgment was affirmed by a federal appellate court. The plaintiffs then sought review by the Supreme Court.

Mr. Justice POWELL delivered the opinion of the Court.

* * *

We address first the principles of standing relevant to the claims asserted by the several categories of petitioners in this case. In essence the question of standing is whether the litigant is entitled to have the court decide the merits of the dispute or of particular issues. This inquiry involves both constitutional limitations on federal-court jurisdiction and prudential limitations on its exercise. * * * In both dimensions it is founded in concern about the proper—and properly limited—role of the courts in a democratic society. * * *

In its constitutional dimension, standing imports justiciability: whether the plaintiff has made out a "case or controversy" between himself and the defendant within the meaning of Art. III. This is the threshold question in every federal case, determining the power of the court to entertain the suit. As an aspect of justiciability, the standing question is whether the plaintiff has "alleged such a personal stake in the outcome of the controversy" as to warrant *his* invocation of federal-court jurisdiction and to justify exercise of the court's remedial powers on his behalf. * * * The Art. III judicial power exists only to redress or otherwise to protect against injury to the complaining party, even though the court's judgment may benefit others collaterally. A federal court's jurisdiction therefore can be invoked only when the plaintiff himself has suffered "some threatened or actual injury resulting from the putatively illegal action." * * *

Apart from this minimum constitutional mandate, this Court has recognized other limits on the class of persons who may invoke the courts' decisional and remedial powers. First, the Court has held that when the asserted harm is a "generalized grievance" shared in substantially equal measure by all or a large class of citizens, that harm alone normally does not warrant exercise of jurisdiction. * * * Second, even when the plaintiff has alleged injury sufficient to meet the "case or controversy" requirement, this Court has held that the plaintiff generally must assert his own legal rights and interests, and cannot rest his claim to relief on the legal rights or interests of third parties. * * * Without such limitations—closely related to Art. III concerns but essentially matters of judicial self-governance—the courts would be called upon to decide abstract questions of wide public significance even though other governmental institutions may be more competent to address the questions and even though judicial intervention may be unnecessary to protect individual rights. * * *

Although standing in no way depends on the merits of the plaintiff's contention that particular conduct is illegal, * * * it often turns on the nature and source of the claim asserted. The actual or threatened injury required by Art. III may exist solely by virtue of "statutes creating legal rights, the invasion of which creates standing." * * * Moreover, the source of the plaintiff's claim to relief assumes critical importance with respect to the prudential rules of standing that, apart from Art. III's minimum requirements,

serve to limit the role of the courts in resolving public disputes. Essentially, the standing question in such cases is whether the constitutional or statutory provision on which the claim rests properly can be understood as granting persons in the plaintiff's position a right to judicial relief. In some circumstances, countervailing considerations may outweigh the concerns underlying the usual reluctance to exert judicial power when the plaintiff's claim to relief rests on the legal rights of third parties. * * * In such instances, the Court has found, in effect, that the constitutional or statutory provision in question implies a right of action in the plaintiff. * * * Moreover, Congress may grant an express right of action to persons who otherwise would be barred by prudential standing rules. Of course, Art. III's requirement remains: the plaintiff still must allege a distinct and palpable injury to himself, even if it is an injury shared by a large class of other possible litigants. * * * But so long as this requirement is satisfied, persons to whom Congress has granted a right of action, either expressly or by clear implication, may have standing to seek relief on the basis of the legal rights and interests of others, and, indeed, may invoke the general public interest in support of their claim. * * *

One further preliminary matter requires discussion. For purposes of ruling on a motion to dismiss for want of standing, both the trial and reviewing courts must accept as true all material allegations of the complaint, and must construe the complaint in favor of the complaining party. * * * At the same time, it is within the trial court's power to allow or to require the plaintiff to supply, by amendment to the complaint or by affidavits, further particularized allegations of fact deemed supportive of plaintiff's standing. If, after this opportunity, the plaintiff's standing does not adequately appear from all materials of record, the complaint must be dismissed.

With these general considerations in mind, we turn first to the claims of petitioners Ortiz, Reyes, Sinkler, and Broadnax, each of whom asserts standing as a person of low or moderate income and, coincidentally, as a member of a minority racial or ethnic group. We must assume, taking the allegations of the complaint as true, that Penfield's zoning ordinance and the pattern of enforcement by respondent officials have had the purpose and effect of excluding persons of low and moderate income, many of whom are members of racial or ethnic minority groups. We also assume, for purposes here, that such intentional exclusionary practices, if proved in a proper case, would be adjudged violative of the constitutional and statutory rights of the persons excluded.

But the fact that these petitioners share attributes common to persons who may have been excluded from residence in the town is an insufficient predicate for the conclusion that petitioners themselves have been excluded, or that the respondents' assertedly illegal actions have violated their rights. Petitioners must allege and show that they personally have been injured, not that injury has been suffered by other, unidentified members of the class to which they belong and which they purport to represent. Unless these petitioners can thus demonstrate the requisite case or controversy between themselves personally and respondents, "none may seek relief on behalf of himself or any other member of the class." * * *

In their complaint, petitioners Ortiz, Reyes, Sinkler, and Broadnax alleged in conclusory terms that they are among the persons excluded by respondents' actions. None of them has ever resided in Penfield; each claims at least implicitly that he desires, or has desired, to do so. Each asserts, moreover, that he made some effort, at some time, to locate housing in Penfield that was at once within his means and adequate for his family's needs. Each claims that his efforts proved fruitless. We may assume, as petitioners allege, that respondents' actions have contributed, perhaps substantially, to the cost of housing in Penfield. But there remains the question whether petitioners' inability to locate suitable housing in Penfield reasonably can be said to have resulted, in any concretely demonstrable way, from respondents' alleged constitutional and statutory infractions. Petitioners must allege facts from which it reasonably could be inferred that, absent the respondents' restrictive zoning practices, there is a substantial probability that they would have been able to purchase or lease in Penfield and that, if the court affords the relief requested, the asserted inability of petitioners will be removed. * * *

We find the record devoid of the necessary allegations. As the Court of Appeals noted, none of these petitioners has a present interest in any Penfield property; none is himself subject to the ordinance's strictures; and none has ever been denied a variance or permit by respondent officials. * * * Instead, petitioners claim that respondents' enforcement of the ordinance against third parties—developers, builders, and the like—has had the consequence of precluding the construction of housing suitable to their needs at prices they might be able to afford. The fact that the harm to petitioners may have resulted indirectly does not in itself preclude standing. When a governmental prohibition or restriction imposed on one party causes specific harm to a third party, harm that a constitutional provision or statute was intended to prevent, the indirectness of the injury does not necessarily deprive the person harmed of standing to vindicate his rights. * * * But it may make it substantially more difficult to meet the minimum requirement of Art. III: to establish that, in fact, the asserted injury was the consequence of the defendants' actions, or that prospective relief will remove the harm.

Here, by their own admission, realization of petitioners' desire to live in Penfield always has depended on the efforts and willingness of third parties to build low- and moderate-cost housing. The record specifically refers to only two such efforts: that of Penfield Better Homes Corp., in late 1969, to obtain the rezoning of certain land in Penfield to allow the construction of subsidized cooperative townhouses that could be purchased by persons of moderate income; and a similar effort by O'Brien Homes, Inc., in late 1971. But the record is devoid of any indication that these projects, or other like projects, would have satisfied petitioners' needs at prices they could afford, or that, were the court to remove the obstructions attributable to respondents, such relief would benefit petitioners. Indeed, petitioners' descriptions of their individual financial situations and housing needs suggest precisely the contrary—that their inability to reside in Penfield is

the consequence of the economics of the area housing market, rather than on respondents' assertedly illegal acts. In short, the facts alleged fail to support an actionable causal relationship between Penfield's zoning practices and petitioners' asserted injury.

In support of their position, petitioners refer to several decisions in the District Courts and Courts of Appeals, acknowledging standing in low-income, minority-group plaintiffs to challenge exclusionary zoning practices. In those cases, however, the plaintiffs challenged zoning restrictions as applied to particular projects that would supply housing within their means, and of which they were intended residents. The plaintiffs thus were able to demonstrate that unless relief from assertedly illegal actions was forthcoming, their immediate and personal interests would be harmed. Petitioners here assert no like circumstances. Instead, they rely on little more than the remote possibility, unsubstantiated by allegations of fact, that their situation might have been better had respondents acted otherwise, and might improve were the court to afford relief.

We hold only that a plaintiff who seeks to challenge exclusionary zoning practices must allege specific, concrete facts demonstrating that the challenged practices harm *him*, and that he personally would benefit in a tangible way from the court's intervention. Absent the necessary allegations of demonstrable, particularized injury, there can be no confidence of "a real need to exercise the power of judicial review" or that relief can be framed "no [broader] than required by the precise facts to which the court's ruling would be applied." * * *

The petitioners who assert standing on the basis of their status as taxpayers of the city of Rochester present a different set of problems. These "taxpayer-petitioners" claim that they are suffering economic injury consequent to Penfield's allegedly discriminatory and exclusionary zoning practices. Their argument, in brief, is that Penfield's persistent refusal to allow or to facilitate construction of low- and moderate-cost housing forces the city of Rochester to provide more such housing than it otherwise would do; that to provide such housing, Rochester must allow certain tax abatements; and that as the amount of tax-abated property increases, Rochester taxpayers are forced to assume an increased tax burden in order to finance essential public services.

"Of course, pleadings must be something more than an ingenious academic exercise in the conceivable." * * * We think the complaint of the taxpayer-petitioners is little more than such an exercise. Apart from the conjectural nature of the asserted injury, the line of causation between Penfield's actions and such injury is not apparent from the complaint. Whatever may occur in Penfield, the injury complained of— increases in taxation—results only from decisions made by the appropriate Rochester authorities, who are not parties to this case.

But even if we assume that the taxpayer-petitioners could establish that Penfield's zoning practices harm them, their complaint nonetheless was properly dismissed. Petitioners do not, even if they could, assert any personal right under the Constitution or any statute to be free of action by a neighboring municipality that may have some incidental adverse effect on Rochester. On the contrary, the only basis of the taxpayer-petitioners' claim is that Penfield's zoning ordinance and practices violate the constitutional and statutory rights of third parties, namely, persons of low and moderate income who are said to be excluded from Penfield. In short the claim of these petitioners falls squarely within the prudential standing rule that normally bars litigants from asserting the rights or legal interests of others in order to obtain relief from injury to themselves. As we have observed above, this rule of judicial self-governance is subject to exceptions, the most prominent of which is that Congress may remove it by statute. Here, however, no statute expressly or by clear implication grants a right of action, and thus standing to seek relief, to persons in petitioners' position. In several cases, this Court has allowed standing to litigate the rights of third parties when enforcement of the challenged restriction against the litigant would result indirectly in the violation of third parties' rights. * * * But the taxpayer-petitioners are not themselves subject to Penfield's zoning practices. Nor do they allege that the challenged zoning ordinance and practices preclude or otherwise adversely affect a relationship existing between them and the persons whose rights assertedly are violated. * * * No relationship, other than an incidental congruity of interest, is alleged to exist between the Rochester taxpayers and persons who have been precluded from living in Penfield. Nor do the taxpayer-petitioners show that their prosecution of the suit is necessary to insure protection of the rights asserted, as there is no indication that persons who in fact have been excluded from Penfield are disabled from asserting their own right in a proper case. In sum, we discern no justification for recognizing in the Rochester taxpayers a right of action on the asserted claim.

We turn next to the standing problems presented by the petitioner associations—Metro-Act of Rochester, Inc., one of the original plaintiffs; Housing Council in the Monroe County Area, Inc., which the original plaintiffs sought to join as a party-plaintiff; and Rochester Home Builders Association, Inc., which moved in the District Court for leave to intervene as plaintiff. There is no question that an association may have standing in its own right to seek judicial relief from injury to itself and to vindicate whatever rights and immunities the association itself may enjoy. Moreover, in attempting to secure relief from injury to itself the association may assert the rights of its members, at least so long as the challenged infractions adversely affect its members' associational ties. * * * With the limited exception of Metro-Act, however, none of the associational petitioners here has asserted injury to itself.

Even in the absence of injury to itself, an association may have standing solely as the representative of its members. * * * The possibility of such representational standing, however, does not eliminate or attenuate the constitutional requirement of a case or controversy. * * * The association must allege that its members, or any one of them, are suffering immediate or threatened injury as a result of the challenged action of the sort that would make out a justiciable case had the members themselves brought suit. * * * So long as this can be established, and so long as the nature of the claim and of the relief sought does not make the individual partici-

pation of each injured party indispensable to proper resolution of the cause, the association may be an appropriate representative of its members, entitled to invoke the court's jurisdiction.

Petitioner Metro-Act's claims to standing on its own behalf as a Rochester taxpayer, and on behalf of its members who are Rochester taxpayers or persons of low or moderate income, are precluded by our holdings * * * [above] as to the individual petitioners, and require no further discussion. Metro-Act also alleges, however, that 9% of its membership is composed of present residents of Penfield. It claims that, as a result of the persistent pattern of exclusionary zoning practiced by respondents and the consequent exclusion of persons of low and moderate income, those of its members who are Penfield residents are deprived of the benefits of living in a racially and ethnically integrated community. * * * Metro-Act argues that such deprivation is a sufficiently palpable injury to satisfy the Art. III case-or-controversy requirement, and that it has standing as the representative of its members to seek redress.

* * *

Metro-Act does not assert on behalf of its members any right of action under the 1968 Civil Rights Act, nor can the complaint fairly be read to make out any such claim. * * *

Even if we assume, *arguendo*, that apart from any statutorily created right the asserted harm to Metro-Act's Penfield members is sufficiently direct and personal to satisfy the case-or-controversy requirement of Art. III, prudential considerations strongly counsel against according them or Metro-Act standing to prosecute this action. We do not understand Metro-Act to argue that Penfield residents themselves have been denied any constitutional rights, affording them a cause of action under 42 U.S.C.A. § 1983. Instead, their complaint is that they have been harmed indirectly by the exclusion of others. This is an attempt to raise putative rights of third parties, and none of the exceptions that allow such claims is present here. In these circumstances, we conclude that it is inappropriate to allow Metro-Act to invoke the judicial process.

Petitioner Home Builders, in its intervenor-complaint, asserted standing to represent its member firms engaged in the development and construction of residential housing in the Rochester area, including Penfield. Home Builders alleged that the Penfield zoning restrictions, together with refusals by the town officials to grant variances and permits for the construction of low- and moderate-cost housing, had deprived some of its members of "substantial business opportunities and profits." * * * Home Builders claimed damages of $750,000 and also joined in the original plaintiffs' prayer for declaratory and injunctive relief.

As noted above, to justify any relief the association must show that it has suffered harm, or that one or more of its members are injured. * * * But, apart from this, whether an association has standing to invoke the court's remedial powers on behalf of its members depends in substantial measure on the nature of the relief sought. If in a proper case the association seeks a declaration, injunction, or some other form of prospective relief, it can reasonably be supposed that the remedy, if granted, will inure to the benefit of those members of the association actually injured. Indeed, in all cases in

which we have expressly recognized standing in associations to represent their members, the relief sought has been of this kind. * * *

The present case, however, differs significantly as here an association seeks relief in damages for alleged injuries to its members. Home Builders alleges no monetary injury to itself, nor any assignment of the damages claims of its members. No award therefore can be made to the association as such. Moreover, in the circumstances of this case, the damages claims are not common to the entire membership, nor shared by all in equal degree. To the contrary, whatever injury may have been suffered is peculiar to the individual member concerned, and both the fact and extent of injury would require individualized proof. Thus, to obtain relief in damages, each member of Home Builders who claims injury as a result of respondents' practices must be a party to the suit, and Home Builders has no standing to claim damages on his behalf.

Home Builders' prayer for prospective relief fails for a different reason. It can have standing as the representative of its members only if it has alleged facts sufficient to make out a case or controversy had the members themselves brought suit. No such allegations were made. The complaint refers to no specific project of any of its members that is currently precluded either by the ordinance or by respondents' action in enforcing it. There is no averment that any member has applied to respondents for a building permit or a variance with respect to any current project. Indeed, there is no indication that respondents have delayed or thwarted any project currently proposed by Home Builders'

members, or that any of its members has taken advantage of the remedial processes available under the ordinance. In short, insofar as the complaint seeks prospective relief, Home Builders has failed to show the existence of any injury to its members of sufficient immediacy and ripeness to warrant judicial intervention.
* * *

A like problem is presented with respect to petitioner Housing Council. The affidavit accompanying the motion to join it as plaintiff states that the Council includes in its membership "at least seventeen" groups that have been, are, or will be involved in the development of low- and moderate-cost housing. But, with one exception, the complaint does not suggest that any of these groups has focused its efforts on Penfield or has any specific plan to do so. Again with the same exception, neither the complaint nor any materials of record indicate that any member of Housing Council has taken any step toward building housing in Penfield, or has had dealings of any nature with respondents. The exception is the Penfield Better Homes Corp. As we have observed above, it applied to respondents in late 1969 for a zoning variance to allow construction of a housing project designed for persons of moderate income. The affidavit in support of the motion to join Housing Council refers specifically to this effort, the supporting materials detail at some length the circumstances surrounding the rejection of Better Homes' application. It is therefore possible that in 1969, or within a reasonable time thereafter, Better Homes itself and possibly Housing Council as its representative would have had standing to seek review of respondents' action. The complaint, however,

does not allege that the Penfield Better Homes project remained viable in 1972 when this complaint was filed, or that respondents' actions continued to block a then-current construction project. In short, neither the complaint nor the record supplies any basis from which to infer that the controversy between respondents and Better Homes, however vigorous it may once have been, remained a live, concrete dispute when this complaint was filed.

The rules of standing, whether as aspects of the Art. III case-or-controversy requirement or as reflections of prudential considerations defining and limiting the role of the courts, are threshold determinants of the propriety of judicial intervention. It is the responsibility of the complainant clearly to allege facts demonstrating that he is a proper party to invoke judicial resolution of the dispute and the exercise of the court's remedial powers. We agree with the District Court and the Court of Appeals that none of the petitioners here has met this threshold requirement. Accordingly, the judgment of the Court of Appeals is

Affirmed.

Mr. Justice DOUGLAS, dissenting.

With all respect, I think that the Court reads the complaint and the record with antagonistic eyes. There are in the background of this case continuing strong tides of opinion touching on very sensitive matters, some of which involve race, some class distinctions based on wealth.

* * *

Standing has become a barrier to access to the federal courts, just as "the political question" was in earlier decades. The mounting caseload of federal courts is well known. But cases such as this one reflect festering sores in our society; and the American dream teaches that if one reaches high enough and persists there is a forum where justice is dispensed. I would lower the technical barriers and let the courts serve that ancient need. They can in time be curbed by legislative or constitutional restraints if an emergency arises.

We are today far from facing an emergency. For in all frankness, no Justice of this Court need work more than four days a week to carry his burden. I have found it a comfortable burden carried even in my months of hospitalization.

As Mr. Justice BRENNAN makes clear in his dissent, the alleged purpose of the ordinance under attack was to preclude low- and moderate-income people and nonwhites from living in Penfield. The zoning power is claimed to have been used here to foist an unAmerican community model on the people of this area. I would let the case go to trial and have all the facts brought out. Indeed, it would be better practice to decide the question of standing only when the merits have been developed.

I would reverse the Court of Appeals.

Mr. Justice BRENNAN, with whom Mr. Justice WHITE and Mr. Justice MARSHALL join, dissenting.

* * * The Court today, in an opinion that purports to be a "standing" opinion but that actually, I believe, has overtones of outmoded notions of pleading and of justiciability, refuses to find that any of the variously situated plaintiffs can clear numerous hurdles, some constructed here for the first time, necessary to establish "standing." While the Court gives lip service to the principle, oft repeated in recent years, that "standing in no way depends on the merits of the plaintiff's contention that particular conduct is illegal," * * * in fact the opinion, which tosses out of court almost every conceivable kind of plaintiff who could be injured by the activity claimed to be unconstitutional, can be explained only by an indefensible hostility to the claim on the merits. I can appreciate the Court's reluctance to adjudicate the complex and difficult legal questions involved in determining the constitutionality of practices which assertedly limit residence in a particular municipality to those who are white and relatively well off, and I also understand that the merits of this case could involve grave sociological and political ramifications. But courts cannot refuse to hear a case on the merits merely because they would prefer not to, and it is quite clear, when the record is viewed with dispassion, that at least three of the groups of plaintiffs have made allegations, and supported them with affidavits and documentary evidence, sufficient to survive a motion to dismiss for lack of standing.

* * * [O]ne glaring defect of the Court's opinion is that it views each set of plaintiffs as if it were prosecuting a separate lawsuit, refusing to recognize that the interests are intertwined, and that the standing of any one group must take into account its position vis-à-vis the others. * * * The rights of low-income minority plaintiffs who desire to live in a locality, then, seem to turn on the willingness of a third party to litigate the legality of preclusion of a particular project, despite the fact that the third party may have no economic incentive to

incur the costs of litigation with regard to one project, and despite the fact that the low-income minority plaintiffs' interest is *not* to live in a particular project but to live somewhere in the town in a dwelling they can afford.

* * *

* * * [T]he portrait which emerges from the allegations and affidavits is one of total, purposeful, intransigent exclusion of certain classes of people from the town, pursuant to a conscious scheme never deviated from. Because of this scheme, those interested in building homes for the excluded groups were faced with insurmountable difficulties, and those of the excluded groups seeking homes in the locality quickly learned that their attempts were futile. Yet, the Court turns the very success of the allegedly unconstitutional scheme into a barrier to a lawsuit seeking its invalidation. In effect, the Court tells the low-income minority and building company plaintiffs they will not be permitted to prove what they have alleged—that they could and would build and live in the town if changes were made in the zoning ordinance and its application—because they have not succeeded in breaching, before the suit was filed, the very barriers which are the subject of the suit.

As recounted above, plaintiffs Ortiz, Broadnax, Reyes, and Sinkler alleged that "as a result" of respondents' exclusionary practices, they were unable, despite attempts to find the housing they desired in Penfield, and consequently have incurred high commuting expenses, received poorer municipal services, and, in some instances, have been relegated to live in substandard housing. The Court does not, as it could not, suggest

that the injuries, if proved, would be insufficient to give petitioners the requisite "personal stake in the outcome of the controversy as to assure the concrete adverseness which sharpens the presentation of issues," * * * rather, it is abundantly clear that the harm *alleged* satisfies the "injury in fact, economic or otherwise," * * * requirement which is prerequisite to standing in federal court. The harms claimed—consisting of out-of-pocket losses as well as denial of specifically enumerated services available in Penfield but not in these petitioners' present communities, * * * are obviously *more* palpable and concrete than those held sufficient to sustain standing in other cases. * * *

Instead, the Court insists that these petitioners' allegations are insufficient to show that the harms suffered were *caused* by respondents' allegedly unconstitutional practices, because "their inability to reside in Penfield [may be] the consequence of the economics of the area housing market, rather than of respondents' assertedly illegal acts." * * *

True, this Court has held that to maintain standing, a plaintiff must not only allege an injury but must also assert a " 'direct' relationship between the alleged injury and the claim sought to be adjudicated." * * * But, as the allegations recited above show, these petitioners have alleged precisely what our cases require—that *because* of the exclusionary practices of respondents, they cannot live in Penfield and have suffered harm.

Thus, the Court's real holding is not that these petitioners have not *alleged* an injury resulting from respondents' action, but that they are not to be allowed to prove one, because "realization of petitioners' desire to live in Penfield always has depended on the efforts and willingness of third parties to build low- and moderate-cost housing," * * * and "the record is devoid of any indication that * * * [any] projects, would have satisfied petitioners' needs at prices they could afford." * * *

* * *

Here, the very fact that, as the Court stresses, these petitioners' claim rests in part upon proving the intentions and capabilities of third parties to build in Penfield suitable housing which they can afford, coupled with the exclusionary character of the claim on the merits, makes it particularly inappropriate to assume that these petitioners' lack of specificity reflects a fatal weakness in their theory of causation. Obviously they cannot be expected, prior to discovery and trial, to know the future plans of building companies, the precise details of the housing market in Penfield, or everything which has transpired in 15 years of application of the Penfield zoning ordinance, including every housing plan suggested and refused. To require them to allege such facts is to require them to prove their case on paper in order to get into court at all, reverting to the form of fact pleading long abjured in the federal courts. This Court has not required such unachievable specificity in standing cases in the past, * * * and the fact that it does so now can only be explained by an indefensible determination by the Court to close the doors of the federal courts to claims of this kind. Understandably, today's decision will be read as revealing hostility to breaking down even unconstitutional zoning barriers that frustrate the deep human yearning of low-income and minority groups for decent housing they can afford in decent surroundings. * * *

Two of the petitioners are organizations among whose members are building concerns. Both of these organizations, Home Builders and Housing Council, alleged that these concerns have attempted to build in Penfield low- and moderate-income housing, but have been stymied by the zoning ordinance and refusal to grant individual relief therefrom.

* * *

The Court finds that these two organizations lacking standing to seek prospective relief for basically the same reasons: none of their members is, as far as the allegations show, *currently* involved in developing a *particular* project. * * *

Again, the Court ignores the thrust of the complaints and asks petitioners to allege the impossible. According to the allegations, the building concerns' experience in the past with Penfield officials has shown any plans for low- and moderate-income housing to be futile for, again according to the allegations, the respondents are engaged in a purposeful, conscious scheme to exclude such housing. Particularly with regard to a low- or moderate-income project, the cost of litigating, with respect to any particular project, the legality of a refusal to approve it may well be prohibitive. And the merits of the exclusion of this or that project is not at the heart of the complaint; the claim is that respondents will not approve *any* project which will provide residences for low- and moderate-income people.

When this sort of pattern-and-practice claim is at the heart of the controversy, allegations of past injury, which members of both of these organizations have clearly made, and of a future intent, if the barriers are cleared, again to develop suitable housing for Penfield, should be more than sufficient. The past experiences, if proved at trial, will give credibility and substance to the claim of interest in future building activity in Penfield. These parties, if their allegations are proved, certainly have the requisite personal stake in the outcome of *this* controversy, and the Court's conclusion otherwise is only a conclusion that *this* controversy may not be litigated in a federal court.

I would reverse the judgment of the Court of Appeals.

BAKER v. CARR

Supreme Court of the United States, 1962
369 U.S. 186, 82 S.Ct. 691, 7 L.Ed.2d 663

In 1901, the Tennessee General Assembly enacted legislation apportioning its two Houses and provided for subsequent reapportionment every ten years on the basis of the number of qualified voters resident in each of the state's counties as reported in the census. For more than sixty years, however, proposals to redistribute the legislative seats had failed to pass, while a large share of the state's population continued to drift into urban areas. Baker and others, citizens and qualified voters of the state, sued under the federal civil rights statutes, charging that as urban residents they were being denied equal protection of the laws contrary to the Fourteenth Amendment by virtue of the fact that their votes had been devalued. In the suit they named the Tennessee Secretary of State, Attorney General, and state election officials as respondents and asked the court to declare the 1901 apportionment act unconstitutional and to order state officials to either hold the election of state legislators at large without regard to counties or districts or to hold an election at which legislators would be selected from constituencies in accordance with the federal census of 1950. The U. S. District Court for the Middle District of Tennessee dismissed the suit on the ground that, while the abridgment of civil rights was clear, remedy did not lie with the courts.

Mr. Justice BRENNAN delivered the opinion of the Court.

* * *

[W]e hold today only (a) that the [District Court] possessed jurisdiction of the subject matter; (b) that a justiciable cause of action is stated upon which appellants would be entitled to appropriate relief; and (c) because appellees raise the issue before this Court, that the appellants have standing to challenge the Tennessee apportionment statutes. Beyond noting that we have no cause at this stage to doubt the District Court will be able to fashion relief if violations of constitutional rights are found, it is improper now to consider what remedy would be most appropriate if appellants prevail at the trial.

JURISDICTION
OF THE SUBJECT MATTER

The District Court was uncertain whether our cases withholding federal judicial relief rested upon a lack of federal jurisdiction or upon the inappropriateness of the subject matter for judicial consideration—what we have designated "nonjusticiability." The distinction between the two grounds is significant. In the instance of nonjusticiability, consideration of the cause is not wholly and immediately foreclosed; rather, the Court's inquiry necessarily proceeds to the point of deciding whether the duty asserted can be judicially identified and its breach judicially determined, and whether protection for the right asserted can be judicially molded. In the instance of lack of jurisdiction the cause either does not "arise under" the Federal Constitution, laws or treaties (or fall within one of the other enumerated categories of Art. III, § 2), or is not a "case or controversy" within the meaning of that section; or the cause is not one described by any jurisdictional statute. Our conclusion   *   *   * that this cause presents no nonjusticiable "political question" settles the only possible doubt that it is a case or controversy. Under the present heading of "Jurisdiction of the Subject Matter" we hold only that the matter set forth in the complaint does arise under the Constitution and is within 28 U.S.C. § 1343, 28 U.S.C.A. § 1343.

Article III, § 2, of the Federal Constitution provides that "The judicial Power shall extend to all Cases, in Law and Equity, arising under this Constitution, the Laws of the United States, and Treaties made, or which shall be made, under their Authority."   *   *   * It is clear that the cause of action is one which "arises under" the Federal Constitution. The complaint alleges that the 1901 statute effects an apportionment that deprives the appellants of the equal protection of the laws in violation of the Fourteenth Amendment. Dismissal of the complaint upon the ground of lack of jurisdiction of the subject matter would, therefore, be justified only if that claim were "so attenuated and unsubstantial as to be absolutely devoid of merit," Newburyport Water Co. v. Newburyport, 193 U.S. 561, 579, 24 S.Ct. 553, 557, or "frivolous," Bell v. Hood, 327 U.S. 678, 683, 66 S.Ct. 773, 776. That the claim is unsubstantial must be "very plain." Hart v. B. F. Keith Vaudeville Exchange, 262 U.S. 271, 274, 43 S.Ct. 540, 541. Since the District Court obviously and correctly did not deem the asserted federal constitutional claim unsubstantial and frivolous, it should not have dismissed the complaint for want of jurisdiction of the subject matter. And of course no further consideration of the merits of the claim is relevant to a determination of the court's jurisdiction of the subject matter. We said in an earlier voting case from Tennessee: "It is obvious   *   *   * that the court, in dismissing for want of jurisdiction, was controlled by what it deemed to be the want of merit in the averments which were made in the complaint as to the violation of the Federal right. But as the very nature of the controversy was Federal, and, therefore, jurisdiction existed, whilst the opinion of the court as to the want of merit in the cause of action might have furnished ground for dismissing for that reason, it afforded no sufficient ground for deciding that the action was not one arising under the Constitution and laws of the United States." Swafford v. Templeton, 185 U.S. 487, 493, 22 S.Ct. 783, 785. "For it is well settled that the failure to state a proper cause of action calls for a judgment on the merits and not for a dismissal for want of jurisdiction." Bell v. Hood, 327 U.S. 678, 682, 66 S.Ct. 773.   *   *   *

Since the complaint plainly sets forth a case arising under the Constitution, the subject matter is within the federal judicial power defined in Art. III, § 2, and so within the power of Congress to assign to the jurisdiction of the District Courts. Congress has exercised that power in 28 U.S.C. § 1343(3), 28 U.S.C.A. § 1343(3):

"The district courts shall have original jurisdiction of any civil action authorized by law to be commenced by any person * * * [t]o redress the deprivation, under color of any State law, statute, ordinance, regulation, custom or usage, of any right, privilege or immunity secured by the Constitution of the United States." * * *

An unbroken line of our precedents sustains the federal courts' jurisdiction of the subject matter of federal constitutional claims of this nature. * * *

* * *

We hold that the District Court has jurisdiction of the subject matter of the federal constitutional claim asserted in the complaint.

STANDING

A federal court cannot "pronounce any statute, either of a state or of the United States, void, because irreconcilable with the constitution, except as it is called upon to adjudge the legal rights of litigants in actual controversies." Liverpool, N. Y. & P. Steamship Co. v. Commissioners of Emigration, 113 U.S. 33, 39, 5 S.Ct. 352, 355. Have the appellants alleged such a personal stake in the outcome of the controversy as to assure that concrete adverseness which sharpens the presentation of issues upon which the court so largely depends for illumination of difficult

constitutional questions? This is the gist of the question of standing. It is, of course, a question of federal law.

The complaint was filed by residents of Davidson, Hamilton, Knox, Montgomery, and Shelby Counties. Each is a person allegedly qualified to vote for members of the General Assembly representing his county. These appellants sued "on their own behalf and on behalf of all qualified voters of their respective counties, and further, on behalf of all voters of the State of Tennessee who are similarly situated." * * * The appellees are the Tennessee Secretary of State, Attorney General, Coordinator of Elections, and members of the State Board of Elections; the members of the State Board are sued in their own right and also as representatives of the County Election Commissioners whom they appoint.

We hold that the appellants do have standing to maintain this suit. Our decisions plainly support this conclusion. Many of the cases have assumed rather than articulated the premise in deciding the merits of similar claims. * * *

These appellants seek relief in order to protect or vindicate an interest of their own, and of those similarly situated. Their constitutional claim is, in substance, that the 1901 statute constitutes arbitrary and capricious state action, offensive to the Fourteenth Amendment in its irrational disregard of the standard of apportionment prescribed by the State's Constitution or of any standard, effecting a gross disproportion of representation to voting population. The injury which appellants assert is that this classification disfavors the voters in the counties in which they reside, placing them in a position of constitutionally unjustifiable inequality *vis-à-vis* voters in irrationally favored counties. A citizen's right to a vote free of arbitrary impairment by state action has been judicially recognized as a right secured by the Constitution, when such impairment resulted from dilution by a false tally, cf. United States v. Classic, 313 U.S. 299, 61 S.Ct. 1031; or by a refusal to count votes from arbitrarily selected precincts, cf. United States v. Mosley, 238 U.S. 383, 35 S.Ct. 904, or by a stuffing of the ballot box, cf. Ex parte Siebold, 100 U.S. 371, 25 L.Ed. 717. * * *

It would not be necessary to decide whether appellants' allegations of impairment of their votes by the 1901 apportionment will, ultimately, entitle them to any relief, in order to hold that they have standing to seek it. If such impairment does produce a legally cognizable injury, they are among those who have sustained it. They are asserting "a plain, direct and adequate interest in maintaining the effectiveness of their votes," Coleman v. Miller, 307 U.S. at 438, 59 S.Ct. at p. 975 not merely a claim of "the right possessed by every citizen 'to require that the government be administered according to law'." * * * Fairchild v. Hughes, 258 U.S. 126, 129, 42 S.Ct. 274, 275. * * * They are entitled to a hearing and to the District Court's decision on their claims. "The very essence of civil liberty certainly consists in the right of every individual to claim the protection of the laws, whenever he receives an injury." Marbury v. Madison, 1 Cranch 137, 163, 2 L.Ed. 60.

Justiciability

In holding that the subject matter of this suit was not justiciable, the District Court relied on Colegrove v. Green [328 U.S. 549, 66 S.Ct. 1198] and subsequent *per curiam* cases. The court stated: "From a review of these decisions there can be no doubt that the federal rule * * * is that the federal courts * * * will not intervene in cases of this type to compel legislative reapportionment." 179 F.Supp. at 826. We understand the District Court to have read the cited cases as compelling the conclusion that since the appellants sought to have a legislative apportionment held unconstitutional, their suit presented a "political question" and was therefore nonjusticiable. We hold that this challenge to an apportionment presents no nonjusticiable "political question." The cited cases do not hold the contrary.

Of course the mere fact that the suit seeks protection of a political right does not mean it presents a political question. Such an objection "is little more than a play upon words." * * * Rather, it is argued that apportionment cases, whatever the actual wording of the complaint, can involve no federal constitutional right except one resting on the guaranty of a republican form of government, and that complaints based on that clause have been held to present political questions which are nonjusticiable.

We hold that the claim pleaded here neither rests upon nor implicates the Guaranty Clause and that its justiciability is therefore not foreclosed by our decisions of cases involving that clause. The District Court misinterpreted *Colegrove* v. *Green* and other decisions of this Court on which it relied. Appellants' claim that they are being denied equal protection is justiciable, and if "discrimination is sufficiently shown, the right to relief under the equal protection clause is not diminished by the fact that the discrimination relates to political rights." Snowden v. Hughes, 321 U.S. 1, 11, 64 S.Ct. 397, 402. To show why we reject the argument based on the Guaranty Clause, we must examine the authorities under it. But because there appears to be some uncertainty as to why those cases did present political questions, and specifically as to whether this apportionment case is like those cases, we deem it necessary first to consider the contours of the "political question" doctrine.

Our discussion, even at the price of extending this opinion, requires review of a number of political question cases, in order to expose the attributes of the doctrine—attributes which, in various settings, diverge, combine, appear, and disappear in seeming disorderliness. Since that review is undertaken solely to demonstrate that neither singly nor collectively do these cases support a conclusion that this apportionment case is nonjusticiable, we of course do not explore their implications in other contexts. That review reveals that in the Guaranty Clause cases and in the other "political question" cases, it is the relationship between the judiciary and the coordinate branches of the Federal Government, and not the federal judiciary's relationship to the States, which gives rise to the "political question."

We have said that "In determining whether a question falls within [the political question] category, the appropriateness under our system of government of attributing finality to the action of the political departments and also the lack of satisfactory criteria for a judicial determination are dominant considerations." Coleman v. Miller, 307 U.S. 433, 454–455, 59 S.Ct. 972, 982. The non-justiciability of a political question is primarily a function of the separation of powers. Much confusion results from the capacity of the "political question" label to obscure the need for case-by-case inquiry. Deciding whether a matter has in any measure been committed by the Constitution to another branch of government, or whether the action of that branch exceeds whatever authority has been committed, is itself a delicate exercise in constitutional interpretation, and is a responsibility of this Court as ultimate interpreter of the Constitution. To demonstrate this requires no less than to analyze representative cases and to infer from them the analytical threads that make up the political question doctrine. We shall then show that none of those threads catches this case.

Foreign relations: There are sweeping statements to the effect that all questions touching foreign relations are political questions. Not only does resolution of such issues frequently turn on standards that defy judicial application, or involve the exercise of a discretion demonstrably committed to the executive or legislature; but many such questions uniquely demand single-voiced statement of the Government's views. Yet it is error to suppose that every case or controversy which touches foreign relations lies beyond judicial cognizance. Our cases in this field seem invariably to show a discriminating analysis of the particular question posed, in terms of the history of its management by the political branches, of its susceptibility to judicial handling in the light of its nature and posture in the specific case, and of the possible consequences of judicial action. For example, though a court will not ordinarily inquire whether a treaty has been terminated, since on that question "governmental action * * * must be regarded as of controlling importance," if there has been no conclusive "governmental action" then a court can construe a treaty and may find it provides the answer. * * * Though a court will not undertake to construe a treaty in a manner inconsistent with a subsequent federal statute, no similar hesitancy obtains if the asserted clash is with state law. * * *

While recognition of foreign governments so strongly defies judicial treatment that without executive recognition a foreign state has been called "a republic of whose existence we know nothing," and the judiciary ordinarily follows the executive as to which nation has sovereignty over disputed territory, once sovereignty over an area is politically determined and declared, courts may examine the resulting status and decide independently whether a statute applies to that area. Similarly, recognition of belligerency abroad is an executive responsibility, but if the executive proclamations fall short of an explicit answer, a court may construe them seeking, for example, to determine whether the situation is such that statutes designed to assure American neutrality have become operative. * * * Still again, though it is the executive that determines a person's status as representative of a foreign government, * * * the executive's statements will be construed where necessary to determine the court's jurisdiction. * * * Similar judicial action in the absence of a recognizedly authoritative executive declaration occurs in cases involving the immunity from seizure of vessels owned by friendly foreign governments. * * *

Dates of duration of hostilities: Though it has been stated broadly that "the power which declared the necessity is the power to declare its cessation, and what the cessation requires," Commercial Trust Co. v. Miller, 262 U.S. 51, 57, 43 S.Ct. 486, 488, 489, here too analysis reveals insolable reasons for the presence of political questions, underlying this Court's refusal to review the political departments' determination of when or whether a war has ended. Dominant is the need for finality in the political determination, for emergency's nature demands "A prompt and unhesitating obedience," Martin v. Mott, 12 Wheat. 19, 30, 6 L.Ed. 537 (calling up of militia). Moreover, "the cessation of hostilities does not necessarily end the war power. It was stated in Hamilton v. Kentucky Distilleries & W. Co., 251 U.S. 146, 161, 40 S.Ct. 106, 110, that the war power includes the power 'to remedy the evils which have arisen from its rise and progress' and continues during that emergency." Stewart v. Kahn, 11 Wall. 493, 507. * * * But deference rests on reason, not habit. The question in a particular case may not seriously implicate considerations of finality—e.g., a public program of importance (rent control) yet not central to the emergency effort. Further, clearly definable criteria for decision may be available. In such case the political question barrier falls away: "[A] Court is not at liberty to shut its eyes to an obvious mistake, when the validity of the law depends upon the truth of what is declared. * * * [It can] inquire whether the exigency still existed upon which the continued operation of the law depended." Chastleton Corp. v. Sinclair, 264 U.S. 543, 547–548, 44 S.Ct. 405, 406. Compare Woods v. Cloyd W. Miller Co., 333

U.S. 138, 68 S.Ct. 421. On the other hand, even in private litigation which directly implicates no feature of separation of powers, lack of judicially discoverable standards and the drive for even-handed application may impel reference to the political departments' determination of dates of hostilities' beginning and ending. * * *

Validity of enactments: In *Coleman* v. *Miller*, supra, this Court held that the questions of how long a proposed amendment to the Federal Constitution remained open to ratification, and what effect a prior rejection had on a subsequent ratification, were committed to congressional resolution and involved criteria of decision that necessarily escaped the judicial grasp. Similar considerations apply to the enacting process: "The respect due to coequal and independent departments," and the need for finality and certainty about the status of a statute contribute to judicial reluctance to inquire whether, as passed, it complied with all requisite formalities. Field v. Clark, 143 U.S. 649, 672, 676–677, 12 S.Ct. 495, 497, 499. * * * But it is not true that courts will never delve into a legislature's records upon such a quest: If the enrolled statute lacks an effective date, a court will not hesitate to seek it in the legislative journals in order to preserve the enactment." * * * The political question doctrine, a tool for maintenance of governmental order, will not be so applied as to promote only disorder.

The status of Indian tribes: This Court's deference to the political departments in determining whether Indians are recognized as a tribe, while it reflects familiar attributes of political questions, * * * also has a unique element in that "the relation of the Indians to the United States is marked by peculiar and cardinal distinctions which exist no where else. * * * [The Indians are] domestic dependent nations * * * in a state of pupilage. Their relation to the United States resembles that of a ward to his guardian." Cherokee Nation v. Georgia, 5 Pet. 1, 16, 17, 8 L.Ed. 25. Yet, here too, there is no blanket rule.

While " 'It is for [Congress], * * * and not for the courts, to determine when the true interests of the Indian require his release from [the] condition of tutelage' * * *, it is not meant by this that Congress may bring a community or body of people within the range of this power by arbitrarily calling them an Indian tribe." * * * United States v. Sandoval, 231 U.S. 28, 46, 34 S.Ct. 1, 6. Able to discern what is "distinctly Indian," * * * the courts will strike down any heedless extension of that label. They will not stand impotent before an obvious instance of a manifestly unauthorized exercise of power.

It is apparent that several formulations which vary slightly according to the settings in which the questions arise may describe a political question, although each has one or more elements which identify it as essentially a function of the separation of powers. Prominent on the surface of any case held to involve a political question is found a textually demonstrable constitutional commitment of the issue to a coordinate political department; or a lack of judicially discoverable and manageable standards for resolving it; or the impossibility of deciding without an initial policy determination of a kind clearly for nonjudicial discretion; or the impossibility of a court's undertaking independent resolution without expressing lack of the respect due coordinate branches of government; or an unusual need for unquestioning adherence to a political decision already made; or the potentiality of embarrassment from multifarious pronouncements by various departments on one question.

Unless one of these formulations is inextricable from the case at bar, there should be no dismissal for nonjusticiability on the ground of a political question's presence. The doctrine of which we treat is one of "political questions," not one of "political cases." The courts cannot reject as "no law suit" a bona fide controversy as to whether some action denominated "political" exceeds constitutional authority. The cases we have reviewed show the necessity for discriminating inquiry into the precise facts and posture of the particular case, and the impossibility of resolution by any semantic cataloguing.

But it is argued that this case shares the characteristics of decisions that constitute a category not yet considered, cases concerning the Constitution's guaranty, in Art. IV, § 4, of a republican form of government. A conclusion as to whether the case at bar does present a political question cannot be confidently reached until we have considered those cases with special care. We shall discover that Guaranty Clause claims involve those elements which define a "political question," and for that reason and no other, they are nonjusticiable. In particular, we shall discover that the nonjusticiability of such claims has nothing to do with their touching upon matters of state governmental organization.

Republican form of government: Luther v. Borden, 7 How. 1, 12 L.Ed. 581, though in form simply an action

for damages for trespass was, as Daniel Webster said in opening the argument for the defense, "an unusual case." The defendants, admitting an otherwise tortious breaking and entering, sought to justify their action on the ground that they were agents of the established lawful government of Rhode Island, which State was then under martial law to defend itself from active insurrection; that the plaintiff was engaged in that insurrection; and that they entered under orders to arrest the plaintiff. The case arose "out of the unfortunate political differences which agitated the people of Rhode Island in 1841 and 1842," 7 How., at 34, and which had resulted in a situation wherein two groups laid competing claims to recognition as the lawful government. The plaintiff's right to recover depended upon which of the two groups was entitled to such recognition; but the lower court's refusal to receive evidence or hear argument on that issue, its charge to the jury that the earlier established or "charter" government was lawful, and the verdict for the defendants, were affirmed upon appeal to this Court.

Chief Justice Taney's opinion for the Court reasoned as follows: (1) If a court were to hold the defendants' acts unjustified because the charter government had no legal existence during the period in question, it would follow that all of that government's actions—laws enacted, taxes collected, salaries paid, accounts settled, sentences passed—were of no effect; and that "the officers who carried their decisions into operation [were] answerable as trespassers, if not in some cases as criminals." There was, of course, no room for application of any doctrine of *de facto* status to uphold prior acts of an officer not authorized *de jure*, for such would have defeated the plaintiff's very action. A decision for the plaintiff would inevitably have produced some significant measure of chaos, a consequence to be avoided if it could be done without abnegation of the judicial duty to uphold the Constitution.

(2) No state court had recognized as a judicial responsibility settlement of the issue of the locus of state governmental authority. Indeed, the courts of Rhode Island had in several cases held that "it rested with the political power to decide whether the charter government had been displaced or not," and that that department had acknowledged no change.

(3) Since "[t]he question relates, altogether, to the constitution and laws of [the] * * * State," the courts of the United States had to follow the state courts' decisions unless there was a federal constitutional ground for overturning them.

(4) No provision of the Constitution could be or had been invoked for this purpose except Art. IV, § 4, the Guaranty Clause. Having already noted the absence of standards whereby the choice between governments could be made by a court acting independently, Chief Justice Taney now found further textual and practical reasons for concluding that, if any department of the United States was empowered by the Guaranty Clause to resolve the issue, it was not the judiciary:

"Under this article of the Constitution it rests with Congress to decide what government is the established one in a State. For as the United States guarantee to each State a republican government, Congress must necessarily decide what government is established in the State before it can determine whether it is republican or not. And when the senators and representatives of a State are admitted into the councils of the Union, the authority of the government under which they are appointed, as well as its republican character, is recognized by the proper constitutional authority. And its decision is binding on every other department of the government, and could not be questioned in a judicial tribunal. It is true that the contest in this case did not last long enough to bring the matter to this issue; and * * * Congress was not called upon to decide the controversy. Yet the right to decide is placed there, and not in the courts.

"So, too, as relates to the clause in the above-mentioned article of the Constitution, providing for cases of domestic violence. It rested with Congress, too, to determine upon the means proper to be adopted to fulfill this guarantee. * * * [B]y the act of February 28, 1795, [Congress] provided, that, 'in case of an insurrection in any State against the government thereof, it shall be lawful for the President of the United States, on application of the legislature of such State or of the executive (when the legislature cannot be convened) to call forth such number of the militia of any other State or States, as may be applied for, as he may judge sufficient to suppress such insurrection.'

"By this act, the power of deciding whether the exigency had arisen upon which the government of the United States is bound to interfere, is given to the President. * * *

"After the President has acted and called out the militia, is a Circuit Court of the United States authorized to inquire whether his decision was right? * * * If the judicial power extends so far, the guarantee contained in the Constitution of the United States is a guarantee of anarchy, and not of order. * * *

"It is true that in this case the militia were not called out by the President. But upon the application of the governor under the charter government, the President recognized him as the executive power of the State, and took measures to call out the militia to support his authority if it should be found necessary for the general government to interfere. * * * [C]ertainly no court of the United States, with a knowledge of this decision, would have been justified in recognizing the opposing party as the lawful government. * * * In the case of foreign nations, the government acknowledged by the President is always recognized in the courts of justice." * * * 7 How., at 42–44.

Clearly, several factors were thought by the Court in *Luther* to make the question there "political": the commitment to the other branches of the decision as to which is the lawful state government; the unambiguous action by the President, in recognizing the charter government as the lawful authority; the need for finality in the executive's decision; and the lack of criteria by which a court could determine which form of government was republican.

But the only significance that *Luther* could have for our immediate purposes is in its holding that the Guaranty Clause is not a repository of judicially manageable standards which a court could utilize independently in order to identify a State's lawful government. The Court has since refused to resort to the Guaranty Clause—which alone had been invoked for the purpose—as the source of a constitutional standard for invalidating state action. See Taylor & Marshall v. Beckham (No. 1), 178 U.S. 548, 20 S.Ct. 890 (claim that Kentucky's resolution of contested gubernatorial election deprived voters of republican government held nonjusticiable); Pacific States Tel. & T. Co. v. Oregon, 223 U.S. 118, 32 S.Ct. 224 (claim that initiative and referendum negated republican government held nonjusticiable); Kiernan v. Portland, 223 U.S. 151, 32 S.Ct. 231 (claim that municipal charter amendment *per* municipal initiative and referendum negated republican government held nonjusticiable); Marshall v. Dye, 231 U.S. 250, 34 S.Ct. 92 (claim that Indiana's constitutional amendment procedure negated republican government held nonjusticiable); O'Neill v. Leamer, 239 U.S. 244, 36 S.Ct. 54 (claim that delegation to court of power to form drainage districts negated republican government held "futile"); Ohio ex rel. Davis v. Hildebrant, 241 U.S. 565, 36 S.Ct. 708 (claim that invalidation of state reapportionment statute *per* referendum negates republican government held nonjusticiable); Mountain Timber Co. v. Washington, 243 U.S. 219, 37 S.Ct. 260 (claim that workmen's compensation violates republican government held nonjusticiable); Ohio ex rel. Bryant v. Akron Metropolitan Park District, 281 U.S. 74, 50 S.Ct. 228 (claim that rule requiring invalidation of statute by all but one justice of state court negated republican government held nonjusticiable); Highland Farms Dairy v. Agnew, 300 U.S. 608, 57 S.Ct. 549 (claim that delegation to agency of power to control milk prices violated republican government, rejected).

Just as the Court has consistently held that a challenge to state action based on the Guaranty Clause presents no justiciable question so has it held, and for the same reasons, that challenges to congressional action on the ground of inconsistency with that clause present no justiciable question. In Georgia v. Stanton, 6 Wall. 50, 18 L.Ed. 721, the State sought by an original bill to enjoin execution of the Reconstruction Acts, claiming that it already possessed "A republican State, in every political, legal, constitutional, and juridical sense," and that enforcement of the new Acts "Instead of keeping the guaranty against a forcible overthrow of its government by foreign invaders or domestic insurgents, * * * is destroying that very government by force." Congress had clearly refused to recognize the republican character of the government of the suing State. It seemed to the Court that the only constitutional claim that could be presented was under the Guaranty Clause, and Congress having determined that the effects of the recent hostilities required extraordinary measures to restore governments of a republican form, this Court refused to interfere with Congress' action at the behest of a claimant relying on that very guaranty.

In only a few other cases has the Court considered Art. IV, § 4, in relation to congressional action. It has refused to pass on a claim relying on the Guaranty Clause to establish that Congress lacked power to allow the States to employ the referendum in passing on legislation redistricting for congressional seats. *Ohio ex rel. Davis* v. *Hildebrant*, supra. And it has pointed out that Congress is not required to establish republican government in the territories before

they become States, and before they have attained a sufficient population to warrant a popularly elected legislature. Downes v. Bidwell, 182 U.S. 244, 278–279, 21 S.Ct. 770, 783–784 (dictum).

We come, finally, to the ultimate inquiry whether our precedents as to what constitutes a nonjusticiable "political question" bring the case before us under the umbrella of that doctrine. A natural beginning is to note whether any of the common characteristics which we have been able to identify and label descriptively are present. We find none: The question here is the consistency of state action with the Federal Constitution. We have no question decided, or to be decided, by a political branch of government coequal with this Court. Nor do we risk embarrassment of our government abroad, or grave disturbance at home if we take issue with Tennessee as to the constitutionality of her action here challenged. Nor need the appellants, in order to succeed in this action, ask the Court to enter upon policy determinations for which judicially manageable standards are lacking. Judicial standards under the Equal Protection Clause are well developed and familiar, and it has been open to courts since the enactment of the Fourteenth Amendment to determine, if on the particular facts they must, that a discrimination reflects *no* policy, but simply arbitrary and capricious action.

This case does, in one sense, involve the allocation of political power within a State, and the appellants might conceivably have added a claim under the Guaranty Clause. Of course, as we have seen, any reliance on that clause would be futile. But because any reliance on the Guaranty Clause could not have succeeded it does not follow that appellants may not be heard on the equal protection claim which in fact they tender. True, it must be clear that the Fourteenth Amendment claim is not so enmeshed with those political question elements which render Guaranty Clause claims nonjusticiable as actually to present a political question itself. But we have found that not to be the case here.

*   *   *

We conclude then that the nonjusticiability of claims resting on the Guaranty Clause which arises from their embodiment of questions that were thought "political," can have no bearing upon the justiciability of the equal protection claim presented in this case. Finally, we emphasize that it is the involvement in Guaranty Clause claims of the elements thought to define "political questions," and no other feature, which could render them nonjusticiable. Specifically, we have said that such claims are not held nonjusticiable because they touch matters of state governmental organization. *   *   *

*   *   *

We conclude that the complaint's allegations of a denial of equal protection present a justiciable constitutional cause of action upon which appellants are entitled to a trial and a decision. The right asserted is within the reach of judicial protection under the Fourteenth Amendment.

The judgment of the District Court is reversed and the cause is remanded for further proceedings consistent with this opinion.

Reversed and remanded.

Mr. Justice WHITTAKER did not participate in the decision of this case.

Mr. Justice DOUGLAS, concurring.

*   *   * We have here a phase of the recurring problem of the relation of the federal courts to state agencies. More particularly, the question is the extent to which a State may weight one person's vote more heavily than it does another's.

*   *   *

Race, color, or previous condition of servitude is an impermissible standard by reason of the Fifteenth Amendment. *   *   *

Sex is another impermissible standard by reason of the Nineteenth Amendment.

There is a third barrier to a State's freedom in prescribing qualifications of voters and that is the Equal Protection Clause of the Fourteenth Amendment, the provision invoked here. And so the question is, may a State weight the vote of one county or one district more heavily than it weights the vote in another?

The traditional test under the Equal Protection Clause has been whether a State has made "an invidious discrimination," as it does when it selects "a particular race or nationality for oppressive treatment." See Skinner v. Oklahoma, 316 U.S. 535, 541, 62 S.Ct. 1110, 1113. Universal equality is not the test; there is room for weighting. As we stated in Williamson v. Lee Optical Co., 348 U.S. 483, 489, 75 S.Ct. 461, 465, "The prohibition of the Equal Protection Clause goes no further than the invidious discrimination."

I agree with my Brother CLARK that if the allegations in the complaint can be sustained a case for relief is established. We are told that a single vote in Moore County,

Tennessee, is worth 19 votes in Hamilton County, that one vote in Stewart or in Chester County is worth nearly eight times a single vote in Shelby or Knox County. The opportunity to prove that an "invidious discrimination" exists should therefore be given the appellants.

* * *

Mr. Justice CLARK, concurring.

* * *

Although I find the Tennessee apportionment statute offends the Equal Protection Clause, I would not consider intervention by this Court into so delicate a field if there were any other relief available to the people of Tennessee. But the majority of the people of Tennessee have no "practical opportunities for exerting their political weight at the polls" to correct the existing "invidious discrimination." Tennessee has no initiative and referendum. I have searched diligently for other "practical opportunities" present under the law. I find none other than through the federal courts. The majority of the voters have been caught up in a legislative straight jacket. Tennessee has an "informed, civically militant electorate" and "an aroused popular conscience," but it does not sear "the conscience of the people's representatives." This is because the legislative policy has riveted the present seats in the Assembly to their respective constituencies, and by the votes of their incumbents a reapportionment of any kind is prevented. The people have been rebuffed at the hands of the Assembly; they have tried the constitutional convention route, but since the call must originate in the Assembly it, too, has been fruitless. They have tried Tennessee courts with the same

result and Governors have fought the tide only to flounder. It is said that there is recourse in Congress and perhaps that may be, but from a practical standpoint this is without substance. To date Congress has never undertaken such a task in any State. We therefore must conclude that the people of Tennessee are stymied and without judicial intervention will be saddled with the present discrimination in the affairs of their state government. * * *

* * *

Mr. Justice STEWART, concurring.

The separate writings of my dissenting and concurring Brothers stray so far from the subject of today's decision as to convey, I think, a distressingly inaccurate impression of what the Court decides. For that reason, I think it appropriate, in joining the opinion of the Court, to emphasize in a few words what the opinion does and does not say.

The Court today decides three things and no more: "(a) that the court possessed jurisdiction of the subject matter; (b) that a justiciable cause of action is stated upon which appellants would be entitled to appropriate relief; and (c) * * * that the appellants have standing to challenge the Tennessee apportionment statutes." * * *

* * *

Mr. Justice FRANKFURTER, whom Mr. Justice HARLAN joins, dissenting.

The Court today reverses a uniform course of decision established by a dozen cases, including one by which the very claim now sustained was unanimously rejected only five years ago. The impressive body of rulings thus cast aside reflected the equally uniform course of our political history regarding the relationship between population and legislative representation—a wholly different matter from denial of the franchise to individuals because of race, color, religion or sex. Such a massive repudiation of the experience of our whole past in asserting destructively novel judicial power demands a detailed analysis of the role of this Court in our constitutional scheme. Disregard of inherent limits in the effective exercise of the Court's "judicial Power" not only presages the futility of judicial intervention in the essentially political conflict of forces by which the relation between population and representation has time out of mind been and now is determined. It may well impair the Court's position as the ultimate organ of "the supreme Law of the Land" in that vast range of legal problems, often strongly entangled in popular feeling, on which this Court must pronounce. The Court's authority—possessed of neither the purse nor the sword—ultimately rests on sustained public confidence in its moral sanction. Such feeling must be nourished by the Court's complete detachment, in fact and in appearance, from political entanglements and by abstention from injecting itself into the clash of political forces in political settlements.

A hypothetical claim resting on abstract assumptions is now for the first time made the basis for affording illusory relief for a particular evil even though it foreshadows deeper and more pervasive difficulties in consequence. The claim is hypothetical and the assumptions are abstract because the Court does not vouchsafe the lower courts—state and federal—guidelines for formulating specific, definite, wholly unprecedented remedies for the inevitable litigations that today's umbrageous disposition is bound to stimulate in connection with politically motivated reapportionments in so many States. In such a setting, to promulgate jurisdiction in the abstract is meaningless. It is as devoid of reality as "a brooding omnipresence in the sky," for it conveys no intimation what relief, if any, a District Court is capable of affording that would not invite legislatures to play ducks and drakes with the judiciary. For this Court to direct the District Court to enforce a claim to which the Court has over the years consistently found itself required to deny legal enforcement and at the same time to find it necessary to withhold any guidance to the lower court how to enforce this turnabout, new legal claim, manifests an odd—indeed an esoteric—conception of judicial propriety. One of the Court's supporting opinions, as elucidated by commentary, unwittingly affords a disheartening preview of the mathematical quagmire (apart from divers judicially inappropriate and elusive determinants) into which this Court today catapults the lower courts of the country without so much as adumbrating the basis for a legal calculus as a means of extrication. Even assuming the indispensable intellectual disinterestedness on the part of judges in such matters, they do not have accepted legal standards or criteria or even reliable analogies to draw upon for making judicial judgments. To charge courts with the task of accommodating the incommensurable factors of policy that underlie these mathematical puzzles is to attribute, however flatteringly, omnicompetence to judges. The Framers of the Constitution persistently rejected a proposal that embodied this assumption and Thomas Jefferson never entertained it.

Recent legislation, creating a district appropriately described as "an atrocity of ingenuity," is not unique. Considering the gross inequality among legislative electoral units within almost every State, the Court naturally shrinks from asserting that in districting at least substantial equality is a constitutional requirement enforceable by courts. Room continues to be allowed for weighting. This of course implies that geography, economics, urban-rural conflict, and all the other non-legal factors which have throughout our history entered into political districting are to some extent not to be ruled out in the undefined vista now opened up by review in the federal courts of state reapportionments. To some extent—aye, there's the rub. In effect, today's decision empowers the courts of the country to devise what should constitute the proper composition of the legislatures of the fifty States. If state courts should for one reason or another find themselves unable to discharge this task, the duty of doing so is put on the federal courts or on this Court, if State views do not satisfy this Court's notion of what is proper districting.

We were soothingly told at the bar of this Court that we need not worry about the kind of remedy a court could effectively fashion once the abstract constitutional right to have courts pass on a state-wide system of electoral districting is recognized as a matter of judicial rhetoric, because legislatures would heed the Court's admonition. This is not only a euphoric hope. It implies a sorry confession of judicial impotence in place of a frank acknowledgment that there is not under our Constitution a judicial remedy for every political mischief, for every undesirable exercise of legislative power. The Framers carefully and with deliberate forethought refused so to enthrone the judiciary. In this situation, as in others of like nature, appeal for relief does not belong here. Appeal must be to an informed, civically militant electorate. In a democratic society like ours, relief must come through an aroused popular conscience that sears the conscience of the people's representatives. In any event there is nothing judicially more unseemly nor more self-defeating than for this Court to make *in terrorem* pronouncements, to indulge in merely empty rhetoric, sounding a word of promise to the ear, sure to be disappointing to the hope.

* * *

The present case involves all of the elements that have made the Guarantee Clause cases non-justiciable. It is, in effect, a Guarantee Clause claim masquerading under a different label. But it cannot make the case more fit for judicial action that appellants invoke the Fourteenth Amendment rather than Art. IV, § 4, where, in fact, the gist of their complaint is the same—unless it can be found that the Fourteenth Amendment speaks with greater particularity to their situation. We have been admonished to avoid "the tyranny of labels." Snyder v. Massachusetts, 291 U.S. 97, 114, 54 S.Ct. 330, 335. Art. IV, § 4, is not committed by express constitutional terms to Congress. It is the nature of the controversies arising under it, nothing else, which has made it judicially unenforceable. Of course, if a controversy falls within judicial power, it depends "on how he [the plaintiff] casts his action," whether he brings himself within a jurisdictional statute. But where judicial competence is wanting, it cannot be created by invoking one clause of the Constitution rather than another. When what was essentially a Guarantee Clause claim was sought to be laid, as well, under the Equal Protection Clause in *Pacific States Telephone & Telegraph Co.* v. *Oregon*, supra, the Court had no difficulty in "dispelling any mere confusion resulting from forms of expression, and considering the substance of things." * * * 223 U.S. at 140, 32 S.Ct. at 227.

* * *

What, then, is this question of legislative apportionment? Appellants invoke the right to vote and to have their votes counted. But they are permitted to vote and their votes are counted. They go to the polls, they cast their ballots, they send their representatives to the state councils. Their complaint is simply that the representatives are not sufficiently numerous or powerful—in short, that Tennessee has adopted a basis of representation with which they are dissatisfied. Talk of "debasement" or "dilution" is circular talk. One cannot speak of "debasement" or "dilution" of the value of a vote until there is first defined a standard of reference as to what a vote should be worth. What is actually asked of the Court in this case is to choose among competing bases of representation—ultimately, really, among competing theories of political philosophy—in order to establish an appropriate frame of government for the State of Tennes-

see and thereby for all the States of the Union.

In such a matter, abstract analogies which ignore the facts of history deal in unrealities; they betray reason. This is not a case in which a State has, through a device however oblique and sophisticated, denied Negroes or Jews or redheaded persons a vote, or given them only a third or a sixth of a vote. That was Gomillion v. Lightfoot, 364 U.S. 339, 81 S.Ct. 125. What Tennessee illustrates is an old and still widespread method of representation—representation by local geographical division, only in part respective of population—in preference to others, others, forsooth, more appealing. Appellants contest this choice and seek to make this Court the arbiter of the disagreement. They would make the Equal Protection Clause the charter of adjudication, asserting that the equality which it guarantees comports, if not the assurance of equal weight to every voter's vote, at least the basic conception that representation ought to be proportionate to population, a standard by reference to which the reasonableness of apportionment plans may be judged.

To find such a political conception legally enforceable in the broad and unspecific guarantee of equal protection is to rewrite the Constitution. * * *

* * *

Dissenting opinion of Mr. Justice HARLAN, whom Mr. Justice FRANKFURTER joins.

* * *

Once one cuts through the thicket of discussion devoted to "jurisdiction," "standing," "justiciability," and "political question," there emerges a straightforward issue which, in my view, is determinative of this case. Does the complaint disclose a violation of a federal constitutional right, in other words, claim over which a United States District Court would have jurisdiction under 28 U.S.C. § 1343(3), 28 U.S.C.A. § 1343(3) and 42 U.S.C. § 1983, 42 U.S.C.A. § 1983? The majority opinion does not actually discuss this basic question, but, as one concurring Justice observes, seems to decide it *"sub silentio."* * * * However, in my opinion, appellants' allegations, accepting all of them as true, do not, parsed down or as a whole, show an infringement by Tennessee of any rights assured by the Fourteenth Amendment. Accordingly, I believe the complaint should have been dismissed for "failure to state a claim upon which relief can be granted." * * *

* * *

I can find nothing in the Equal Protection Clause or elsewhere in the Federal Constitution which expressly or impliedly supports the view that state legislatures must be so structured as to reflect with approximate equality the voice of every voter. Not only is that proposition refuted by history, as shown by my Brother FRANKFURTER, but it strikes deep into the heart of our federal system. * * *

* * *

In conclusion, it is appropriate to say that one need not agree, as a citizen, with what Tennessee has done or failed to do, in order to deprecate, as a judge, what the majority is doing today. Those observers of the Court who see it primarily as the last refuge for the correction of all inequality or injustice, no matter what its nature or source, will no doubt applaud this decision and its break with the past. Those who consider that continuing national respect for the Court's authority depends in large measure upon its wise exercise of self-restraint and discipline in constitutional adjudication, will view the decision with deep concern.

I would affirm.

In 1973, Representative Elizabeth Holtzman (D–N.Y.) sought to enjoin the Secretary of Defense and the Secretary of the Air Force from conducting intensive bombing and strafing missions in Cambodia and elsewhere in Southeast Asia. In an address to the nation and in reports to the Congress, President Nixon defended these efforts "to clean out major enemy sanctuaries on the Cambodian-Vietnam border" to combat infiltration and thereby "protect our forces in Vietnam," strengthen our bargaining position, and, ultimately, "enhance the prospects of a negotiated peace." In her complaint (in which she was joined by several Air Force officers) filed in the U. S. District Court for the Eastern District of New York, Congresswoman Holtzman asserted that the massive assault and air-combat operations were being orchestrated by the Administration in clear violation of the will of Congress. She cited as evidence many riders to appropriations bills such as the Fulbright Proviso and the Mansfield and Eagleton amendments, which provided respectively (1) that "nothing [contained in the War Forces-Military Procurement Act of 1971] shall be construed as authorizing the use of any such funds to support Vietnamese or other free world forces in actions designed to provide military support and assistance to the Government of Cambodia or Laos: *Provided further*, that nothing contained in this section shall be construed to prohibit support

of actions required to insure the safe and orderly withdrawal or disengagement of
U. S. Forces from Southeast Asia, or to aid in the release of Americans held as
prisoners of war"; (2) that the United States "terminate at the earliest practicable
date all military operations of the United States in Indochina"; and (3) that "No
funds heretofore or hereafter appropriated under any Act of Congress may be
obligated or expended to support directly or indirectly combat activities in, over, or
from the shores of Cambodia or in or over Laos by United States forces."

In Holtzman v. Richardson, 361 F.Supp. 544 (D.C.N.Y.1973), Orrin G. Judd, the
district judge, held that the Congresswoman was "a member of a specific and narrowly defined group—the House of Representatives" and, as such in view of the
facts of this case, "has been more directly affected by the conduct in question
than has the general population * * *." This was so because of her claim,
among other things, "that her right to an undiluted vote upon the declaration of
hostilities was impaired by presidential action in engaging in extensive combat in
Cambodia without Congressional authorization. She pointed out that a cease-fire
had been negotiated in Vietnam, all American servicemen had been withdrawn,
and all American prisoners of war had been released * * *." In sum, the district judge held that Representative Holtzman had standing to sue. Denying
defendants' motion to dismiss the complaint, Judge Judd found the suit presented
a real case and controversy and was not tantamount to soliciting an advisory
opinion.

Following further argument, Judge Judd enjoined the defendant secretaries
from engaging in further intensive combat operations in Cambodia. Awarding
summary judgment for the Congresswoman in Holtzman v. Schlesinger [Richard-
son's successor as Secretary of Defense], 361 F.Supp. 553 (D.C.N.Y.1973), the district judge held that "the question of the balance of constitutional authority to
declare war, as between the executive and legislative branches, is not a political
question and hence presents a justiciable issue * * *." The district court went
on to find "that there are manageable standards to resolve the controversy." Proceeding from the premise that "the principal (Congress) may limit the duration of
any authorization which it gives to the agent (the Executive)," the court
concluded:

* * *

This is not a situation where the views of a few members of Congress,
holding attitudes antithetical to the majority, are being proffered to defeat
what Congress had intended to be a grant of authority. There is no indication of a contrary majority sentiment. Majorities in both Houses had previously made plain that they were opposed to any continuation of bombing in
Cambodia. * * *

The defendants urge that Congress' will as expressed through bills
which were not enacted cannot be used as a factor in interpreting * * *
legislation. But this contention misconstrues the basic issue. The question
is not whether Congress has affirmatively acted to disavow participation,
but whether Congress has acted to authorize the continuation of hostilities
in Cambodia. While Congress can exercise its war-making power through
measures other than an express declaration of war, courts should not easily
infer the exercise of such a grave responsibility. Legislative history as evidence through bills that were vetoed is relevant to a judicial inquiry of
whether or not Congress intended to participate in the military campaign
under challenge.

It cannot be the rule that the President needs a vote of only one-third plus one of either House in order to conduct a war, but this would be the consequence of holding that Congress must override a Presidential veto in order to terminate hostilities which it has not authorized.

* * *

The court has found that there is no Congressional authorization to fight in Cambodia after the withdrawal of American troops and the release of American prisoners of war. Even though the executive and the military may consider Cambodian bombing an effective means of enforcing paragraph 20 of the Paris Agreement of January 27, 1973, it does not appear that Congress has given its authority for such acts.

* * *

* * * What is involved in this case is not the training or tactics of American forces, but whether Congress has authorized the Cambodian bombing. That question is capable of judicial resolution * * * by applying traditional processes of statutory construction.

* * *

Judge Judd delayed the effect of his ruling to give the defendants time to appeal to the U. S. Court of Appeals for the Second Circuit.

The defendant secretaries subsequently sought action by the Appeals Court to stay the judge's order pending a hearing by the Appeals Court on the merits. Without opinion the appellate court granted the stay, and Representative Holtzman and the other plaintiffs appealed to Justice Marshall to vacate the stay granted by the Court of Appeals. In his capacity as Circuit Justice but in consultation with other members of the Supreme Court, Justice Marshall refused to vacate the stay of the district court's order. See Holtzman v. Schlesinger, 414 U.S. 1304, 1321, 94 S.Ct. 1, 11 (1973). Justice Douglas entered a vigorous dissent. Holtzman v. Schlesinger, 414 U.S. 1316, 94 S.Ct. 8 (1973). The Marshall-Douglas exchange is especially interesting for the light it sheds on collegial problems which can erupt on the Court when individual Justices in their circuit capacities are asked to pass on lower court actions in highly charged constitutional cases during the Court's long summer recess.

A few days later a divided appellate panel reversed the district court's judgment in Holtzman v. Schlesinger, 484 F.2d 1307 (2d Cir. 1973). Writing for the Court of Appeals, Judge Mulligan said in part:

The most recent holding of this court now pertinent is DaCosta v. Laird, 471 F.2d 1146 (1973) where an inductee urged that the President's unilateral decision to mine the harbors of North Vietnam and to bomb targets in that country constituted an escalation of the war, which was illegal in the absence of additional Congressional authorization. Judge Kaufman found that this was a political question which was nonjusticiable, recognizing that the court was incapable of assessing the facts. He stated in part:

Judges, deficient in military knowledge, lacking vital information upon which to assess the nature of battlefield decisions, and sitting thousands of miles from the field of action, cannot reasonably or appropriately determine whether a specific military operation constitutes an "escalation" of the war or is merely a new tactical approach within a continuing strategic plan. What if, for example, the war "de-escalates" so that it is waged as it was prior to the mining of North Vietnam's harbors, and then "escalates" again? Are the courts required to oversee the conduct of the war on a daily basis, away from the scene of action? In this instance, it was the President's view that the mining of North Vietnam's harbors was necessary to preserve the lives of American soliders (*sic*) in South Vietnam and to bring the war to a close. History will tell whether or not that assessment was correct, but without the benefit of such extended hindsight we are powerless to know.

We fail to see how the present challenge involving the bombing in Cambodia is in any significant manner distinguishable from the situation discussed by Judge Kaufman in DaCosta v. Laird. Judge Judd found that the continuing bombing of Cambodia, after the removal of American forces and prisoners of war from Vietnam, represents "a basic change in the situation: which must be considered in determining the duration of prior Congressional authorization." He further found such action a tactical decision not traditionally confided to the Commander-in-Chief. These are precisely the questions of fact involving military and diplomatic expertise not vested in the judiciary, which make the issue political and thus beyond the competence of that court or this court to determine. We are not privy to the information supplied to the Executive by his professional military and diplomatic advisers and even if we were, we are hardly competent to evaluate it. If we were incompetent to judge the significance of the mining and bombing of North Vietnam's harbors and territories, we fail to see our competence to determine that the bombing of Cambodia is a "basic change" in the situation and that it is not a "tactical decision" within the competence of the President. It is true that we have repatriated American troops and have returned American ground forces in Vietnam but we have also negotiated a cease fire and have entered into the Paris Accords which mandated a cease fire in Cambodia and Laos. The President has announced that the bombing of Cambodia will terminate on August 15, 1973 and Secretary of State Rogers has submitted an affidavit to this court providing the justification for our military presence and action until that time. The situation fluctuates daily and we cannot ascertain at any fixed time either the military or diplomatic status. We are in no position to determine whether the Cambodian insurgents are patriots or whether in fact they are inspired and manned by North Vietnam Communists. While we as men may well agonize and bewail the horror of this or any war, the sharing of Presidential and Congressional responsibility particularly at this juncture is a bluntly political and not a judicial question.

We think the comments of Judge Wyzanski writing for a unanimous Court of Appeals panel in the District of Columbia are particularly apt here:

Whether President Nixon did so proceed [to end the war] is a question which at this stage in history a court is incompetent to answer. A court cannot procure the relevant evidence: some is in the hands of foreign governments, some is privileged. Even if the necessary facts were to be laid before it, a court would not substitute its judgment for that of the President, who has an unusually wide measure of discretion in this area, and who should not be judicially condemned except in a case of clear abuse amounting to bad faith. Otherwise a court would be ignoring the delicacies of diplomatic negotiation, the inevitable bargaining for the best solution of an international conflict, and the scope which in foreign affairs must be allowed to the President if this country is to play a responsible role in the council of the nations. Mitchell v. Laird, 476 F.2d 533, 538 (1973).

The court below and our dissenting Brother assume that since American ground forces and prisoners have been removed and accounted for, Congressional authorization has ceased as determined by virtue of the so-called Mansfield Amendment, P.L. 92–156, 85 Stat. 430, § 601. The fallacy of this position is that we have no way of knowing whether the Cambodian bombing furthers or hinders the goals of the Mansfield Amendment. That is precisely the holding of DaCosta v. Laird, supra, 471 F.2d at 1157. Moreover, although § 601(a)(1) of the Amendment urges the President to remove all military forces contingent upon release of American prisoners, it also in § 601(a)(2) urges him to negotiate for an immediate cease fire by all parties in the hostilities in *Indo-China*. (Emphasis added). In our view, the return and repatriation of American troops only represents the beginning and not the end of the inquiry as to whether such a basic change has occurred that the Executive at this stage is suddenly bereft of power and authority. That inquiry involves diplomatic and military intelligence which is totally absent in the record before us, and its digestion in any event is beyond judicial management. The strictures of the political question doctrine cannot be avoided by resort to the law of agency as the court did below, finding the Congress the principal and the President an agent or servant. Judicial *ipse dixits* cannot provide any proper basis particularly for the injunctive relief granted here which is unprecedented in American Jurisprudence.

The appellate court incidentally concluded that both the servicemen and Representative Holtzman lacked standing to sue. As to the officer-plaintiffs, Judge Mulligan wrote:

In Berk v. Laird, 429 F.2d 302, 306 (2d Cir. 1970), we held that a serviceman does have standing if he is under orders to fight in the combat to which he objects. Here none of the servicemen plaintiffs are presently under orders to fight in Cambodia. They have been relieved of any such military obligation and indeed one has been separated from the service. * * *

And with respect to the Congresswoman, he noted:

Neither do we see any adequate support for the standing of Representative Holtzman. She has not been denied any right to vote on Cambodia by any action of the defendants. She has fully participated in the Congressional debates which have transpired since her election to the Congress. The fact that her vote was ineffective was due to the contrary votes of her colleagues and not the defendants herein. The claim that the establishment of illegality here would be relevant in possible impeachment proceedings against the President would in effect be asking the judiciary for an advisory opinion which is precisely and historically what the "case and controversy" conditions set forth in Article III, Section 2 of the Constitution forbid. * * *

Further litigation became unnecessary since the Administration was effectively barred anyway from engaging in further bombing and air-combat activities in Southeast Asia by specific provision of the Second Supplemental Appropriations Act of 1973, 87 Stat. 99, which cut off funds effective August 15, 1973. Though the President had vetoed earlier appropriations bills containing antibombing riders, he was ultimately forced to back down and accept the mid-August cutoff date. The reason for his capitulation to congressional efforts terminating the Indochina War was a two-pronged legislative effort which, to use the words of House Appropriations Committee Chairman George H. Mahon (D–Tex.) would have brought "the U. S. Government to a screeching, grinding, unacceptable halt at midnight on June 30 [1973]." Unable to muster the votes to override presidential vetoes, war opponents hitched antibombing amendments to two crucial bills—one raising the debt limit and another funding government operations for the first three months of the fiscal year beginning on July 1. Had the President not compromised and accepted the August 15 cutoff date, the Treasury would have been forced to start liquidating its assets to begin paying off the debt, and the federal government would no longer have been able to meet its payroll. This was the first time in history Congress had used its power of the purse to force a President to terminate military operations.

A precondition to the normalization of diplomatic relations with the People's Republic of China was the cessation of all diplomatic and official relations with Taiwan and the withdrawal of American military units there. On December 23, 1978, pursuant to a presidential directive, the State Department formally notified Taiwan that its Mutual Defense Treaty with the United States would end on January 1, 1980 under a provision of the pact allowing either of the signatories to terminate the agreement upon one year's notice to the other party. President Carter acted on his own initiative in this matter and did not submit the notice of termination to either the Senate or Congress for approval. Eight Senators, a former Senator, and sixteen congressmen brought suit for declaratory and injunctive relief challenging the President's unilateral action. The U. S. District Court for the District of Columbia, at 481 F.Supp. 949 (1979), held that the President acted unconstitutionally. The district court ruled that either of two procedures, absent here, were required—consent of two-thirds of the Senate or approval by a majority of Congress. The court held that unilateral action by the President could not displace some form of legislative concurrence because the termination of a treaty impacts upon the substantial role of Congress in foreign affairs. It rejected the proposition that the conduct of foreign affairs was a plenary power of the executive branch and observed that "[t]he same separation of powers principles that dictate presidential independence and control within the executive establishment preclude the President from exerting an overriding influence in the sphere of constitutional powers that is shared with the legislative branch." Nor, reasoned the court, could the executive's action be regarded as merely ancillary to recognizing a foreign government. Alternatively, the court concluded that termination of the treaty amounted to a repeal of the "law of the land" and might then be thought to implicate congressional, as distinguished from just senatorial, action. The U. S. Court of Appeals for the District of Columbia, at 617 F.2d 697 (1979), sitting en banc reversed the judgment of the district court and upheld the President's unilateral action terminating the treaty. The court acknowledged the plaintiff legislators' standing to sue on the theory that they had been completely disenfranchised by the President's failure to submit the notice of termination for their approval. The appellate court, however, rejected the conclusions reached by the court below. As to the notion that the Senate's power to ratify treaties implies a power to consent to their termination, the court pointed out that such an inferred power is clearly absent in other circumstances, as when a President terminates the services of an American ambassador. The court also rejected the proposition that the Supremacy Clause, with its reference to treaties as part of "the supreme law of the land," had any bearing on this case since the Constitution is silent on the matter of treaty termination and the clause in Article VI is addressed to assuring supremacy over state law. In support of its ruling upholding the President's action, the appellate court noted that while the powers conferred on Congress in Article I are quite specific, those conferred on the President in Article II are general and do not speak to limitations on the conduct of foreign affairs. Observing that the President is the constitutional representative of the United States in foreign affairs, the court pointed out that *he* is given the constitutional power to enter into a treaty; and even after a treaty has obtained Senate approval, it is up to the President to decide to ratify it and to put it into effect. Article II, the court reasoned, makes it clear that the initiative in the treaty process rests with the President, not Congress. In the court's view the President's authority is at its greatest when the Senate has consented to a treaty which expressly provides that it can be terminated on one year's notice. The President's action, concluded the court, gave that notice.

In its disposition of this case, Goldwater v. Carter, 444 U.S. 996, 100 S.Ct. 533 (1979), the Supreme Court vacated the judgment of the court of appeals and remanded the case to the district court with instructions to dismiss the complaint. Justice Rehnquist, speaking for Chief Justice Burger and Justices Stewart and Stevens, explained in an opinion concurring in the judgment that he was of the view that this case presented a "political question" given that it involved foreign policy decision making, in light of the fact that the Constitution is silent on the termination of treaties and the Senate's role in the abrogation of treaties, and since "different termination procedures may be appropriate for different treaties." Justice Powell rejected the proposition that this case presented a "political question" but instead was of the view that this controversy was not ripe for review since "a dispute between Congress and the President is not ready for judicial review unless and until each branch has taken action asserting its constitutional authority." He added, "If Congress, by appropriate formal action, had challenged the President's authority to terminate the treaty with Taiwan, the resulting uncertainty could have serious consequences for our country. In that situation, it would be the duty of this Court to resolve the issue." Justice Marshall concurred in the result. Justices White and Blackmun dissented in part, voting to set the case for argument and give it plenary consideration. Justice Brennan dissented, voting to affirm the judgment of the appellate court. He rejected the idea that the question was "political" since, as he viewed it, the Court was not asked to rule on a foreign policy decision but rather on the justiciable question "whether a particular branch has been constitutionally designated as the repository of political decision-making power." Reaching the merits of the question, he concluded: "Abrogation of the defense treaty with Taiwan was a necessary incident to Executive recognition of the Peking government, because the defense treaty was predicated on the now-abandoned view that the Taiwan government was the only legitimate political authority in China. Our cases firmly establish that the Constitution commits to the President alone the power to recognize, and withdraw recognition from, foreign regimes. * * * That mandate being clear, our judicial inquiry into the treaty rupture can go no further."

MISSISSIPPI v. JOHNSON

Supreme Court of the United States, 1867
71 U.S. (4 Wall.) 475, 18 L.Ed. 437

The State of Mississippi moved to file suit with the Supreme Court directly, enjoining the President, Andrew Johnson, and General E. O. C. Ord, commander of the military district of Mississippi and Arkansas, from executing two acts of

Congress passed March 2 and 23, 1867, more commonly known as the Reconstruction Acts. Representing the President, the Attorney General objected on the ground that the Court could not properly entertain such a proceeding to restrain the Chief Executive in the performance of his constitutional duties. Speaking for the Court, Chief Justice Chase upheld the objection and denied the motion. As a further note, in subsequent litigation to secure the same objective but seeking to avoid the fatal flaw of Mississippi's suit, Georgia attempted to enjoin Secretary of War Edwin Stanton and Generals Grant and Pope from carrying the acts into effect. This suit met with the same degree of success, for the Court later the same year in Georgia v. Stanton, 6 Wall. 50, 18 L.Ed. 721, ruled that this presented a political question.

The Chief Justice [CHASE] delivered the opinion of the court.

* * *

We shall limit our inquiry to the question presented by the objection, without expressing any opinion on the broader issues discussed in argument, whether, in any case, the President of the United States may be required, by the process of this court, to perform a purely ministerial act under a positive law, or may be held amenable, in any case, otherwise than by impeachment for crime.

The single point which requires consideration is this: Can the President be restrained by injunction from carrying into effect an act of Congress alleged to be unconstitutional?

It is assumed by the counsel for the State of Mississippi, that the President, in the execution of the Reconstruction Acts, is required to perform a mere ministerial duty. In this assumption there is, we think, a confounding of the terms ministerial and executive, which are by no means equivalent in import.

A ministerial duty, the performance of which may, in proper cases, be required of the head of a department, by judicial process, is one in respect to which nothing is left to discretion. It is a simple definite duty, arising under conditions admitted or proved to exist, and imposed by law.

The case of Marbury v. Madison, * * * furnishes an illustration. A citizen had been nominated, confirmed, and appointed a justice of the peace for the District of Columbia, and his commission had been made out, signed, and sealed. Nothing remained to be done except delivery, and the duty of delivery was imposed by law on the Secretary of State. It was held that the performance of this duty might be enforced by *mandamus* issuing from a court having jurisdiction.

* * *

So, in the case of Kendall, Postmaster-General, v. Stockton & Stokes [12 Pet. 527], an act of Congress had directed the Postmaster-General to credit Stockton & Stokes with such sums as the Solicitor of the Treasury should find due to them; and that officer refused to credit them with certain sums, so found due. It was held that the crediting of this money was a mere ministerial duty, the performance of which might be judicially enforced.

In each of these cases nothing was left to discretion. There was no room for the exercise of judgment. The law required the performance of a single specific act; and that performance, it was held, might be required by *mandamus*.

Very different is the duty of the President in the exercise of the power to see that the laws are faithfully executed, and among these laws the acts named in the bill. By the first of these acts he is required to assign generals to command in the several military districts, and to detail sufficient military force to enable such officers to discharge their duties under the law. By the supplementary act, other duties are imposed on the several commanding generals, and these duties must necessarily be performed under the supervision of the President as commander-in-chief. The duty thus imposed on the President is in no just sense ministerial. It is purely executive and political.

An attempt on the part of the judicial department of the government to enforce the performance of such duties by the President might be justly characterized, in the language of Chief Justice Marshall, as "an absurd and excessive extravagance."

It is true that in the instance before us the interposition of the court is not sought to enforce action by the Executive under constitutional legislation, but to restrain such action under legislation alleged to be unconstitutional. But we are unable to perceive that this circumstance takes the case out of the general principles which forbid judicial interference with the exercise of Executive discretion.

It was admitted in the argument that the application now made to us is without a precedent; and this is of much weight against it.

Had it been supposed at the bar that this court would, in any case,

interpose, by injunction, to prevent the execution of an unconstitutional act of Congress, it can hardly be doubted that applications with that object would have been heretofore addressed to it.

* * *

The fact that no such application was ever before made in any case indicates the general judgment of the profession that no such application should be entertained.

It will hardly be contended that Congress [sic, probably should read, the Supreme Court] can interpose, in any case, to restrain the enactment of an unconstitutional law; and yet how can the right to judicial interposition to prevent such an enactment, when the purpose is evident and the execution of that purpose certain, be distinguished, in principle, from the right to such interposition against the execution of such a law by the President?

The Congress is the legislative department of the government; the President is the executive department. Neither can be restrained in its action by the judicial department; though the acts of both, when performed, are, in proper cases, subject to its cognizance.

The impropriety of such interference will be clearly seen upon consideration of its possible consequences.

Suppose the bill filed and the injunction prayed for allowed. If the President refuse obedience, it is needless to observe that the court is without power to enforce its process. If, on the other hand, the President complies with the order of the court and refuses to execute the acts of Congress, is it not clear that a collision may occur between the executive and legislative departments of the government? May not the House of Representatives impeach the President for such refusal? And in that case could this court interfere, in behalf of the President, thus endangered by compliance with its mandate, and restrain by injunction the Senate of the United States from sitting as a court of impeachment? Would the strange spectacle be offered to the public world of an attempt by this court to arrest proceedings in that court?

These questions answer themselves.

*   *   *

It has been suggested that the bill contains a prayer that, if the relief sought cannot be had against Andrew Johnson, as President, it may be granted against Andrew Johnson as a citizen of Tennessee. But it is plain that relief as against the execution of an act of Congress by Andrew Johnson, is relief against its execution by the President. A bill praying an injunction against the execution of an act of Congress by the incumbent of the presidential office cannot be received, whether it describes him as President or as a citizen of a State.

The motion for leave to file the bill is, therefore, denied.

Chapter 2

Legislative Power

That the bulk of the powers assigned to the national government appear in Article I is convincing evidence those who drafted the Constitution saw Congress as the principal architect of federal policy making. But the legislative powers enumerated in Article I, section 8 are not the only law-making powers Congress possesses. Nor do all of Congress's legislative powers bear the same scope and limitations. Furthermore, Congress has within its grasp powers other than its authority to write statutes. The cases and materials included in this chapter are designed to illuminate these broad observations.

a. The Sources and Scope of Legislative Power

In his forceful and sweeping way Chief Justice John Marshall provided in *McCulloch* v. *Maryland* (p. 137) three generalizations about the national legislative power which are essential to an understanding of the American constitutional system. First, he wrote, "This government is acknowledged by all to be one of enumerated powers." Second, he added, again in sweeping language, "If any proposition could command the universal assent of mankind, we might expect it would be this—that the government of the Union, though limited in its powers, is supreme within its sphere of action." Third, he generalized that a broad construction must be given to the Necessary and Proper Clause of Article I, section 8 and that to do so is not a violation of the concept of enumerated powers or limited government. In Marshall's words: "We admit, as all must admit, that the powers of the government are limited, and that its limits are not to be transcended. But we think the sound construction of the constitution must allow to the national legislature that discretion, with respect to the means by which the powers it confers are to be carried into execution, which will enable that body to perform the high duties assigned to it, in

128

the manner most beneficial to the people. Let the end be legitimate, let it be within the scope of the constitution, and all means which are appropriate, which are plainly adapted to that end, which are not prohibited but consist with the letter and spirit of the constitution, are constitutional."

Just as with his treatment of judicial review, Marshall makes it appear that logically there can be no other way to interpret the Necessary and Proper Clause. The advocates of states' rights saw it differently as indicated in Marshall's opinion. But, again, Marshall won the day, and over the years Congress has exercised extraordinary power in consequence of a broad interpretation of the Necessary and Proper Clause. In doing so, however, care is always taken to relate that exercise to one of the seventeen enumerated powers listed in Article I, section 8.

One might easily be misled by a reading of the *McCulloch* case into believing that all of Congress's power is derived from and limited to Article I, section 8. This is not so. The original Constitution provided for additional specific congressional power. We saw earlier that under Article III Congress was granted power with respect to establishing federal courts and defining the appellate jurisdiction of the Supreme Court. Article I, section 4, for example, gives Congress the power to make or alter regulations respecting "The times, places, and manner of holding elections for Senators and Representatives."

In addition to those powers enumerated in Article I, section 8, as enhanced by powers implied from the Necessary and Proper Clause and those deeded to the legislative branch by other provisions of the Constitution, Congress possesses what are called "inherent powers." Talk of "inherent powers" seems both contradictory and troublesome in a polity with a written constitution, but it is undeniable that the Court has recognized such a basis for legislative action (and, to an uncertain degree, for policies independently pursued by the President as well). Basically, inherent powers flow from the concept of sovereignty. These are powers, in other words, which pertain to any sovereign nation, and Congress as the incarnation of national sovereignty may exercise these powers inhering in and characteristic of a nation-state. Addressing the legitimacy of Congress's power to govern territory which the Nation acquires either by conquest or by treaty, not derivable from any specific grant of authority in the Constitution, Chief Justice Marshall, speaking for the Court in American Insurance Co. v. Canter, 26 U.S. (1 Pet.) 516, 7 L.Ed. 242 (1828), wrote: "Perhaps the power of governing a territory belonging to the United States, which has not, by becoming a state, acquired the means of self-government, may result necessarily from the facts, that it is not within the jurisdiction of any particular state, and is within the power and jurisdiction of the United States. The right to govern, may be the inevitable consequence of the right to acquire territory. *Whichever may be the source, whence the power is derived*, the possession of it is unquestioned." (Emphasis supplied.) Whether in an exact constitutional sense it results— in peaceful circumstances—from the confluence of the treaty power with Congress's power to dispose of federal territory or property (Article IV, section 3, paragraph 2), or—in more violent times—constitutes an implied consequence of the war power, the power to govern acquired territory is implicit in the concept of the modern nation-state. Later, dealing with congressional power over Indian tribes in *United States* v. *Kagama* (p. 144), the Court went further, explicitly linking Congress's power to regulate territories to sovereignty: "But this power of Congress to organize territorial governments and make laws for their inhabitants, arises not so much from the clause in the Constitution in regard to disposing of and making rules and regulations concerning the Territory and other property of the United States, as from the ownership of the country in which the Territories are, *and the right of exclusive sovereignty which must exist in the National Government* and can be found nowhere else." (Emphasis supplied.) The enormity of legislative power derived as a consequence of sovereignty is also well-illustrated in Congress's power over aliens, pointed up in *Fong Yue Ting* v. *United States* (p. 148) and *Galvan* v. *Press* (p. 151).

The awesome potential of legislative power predicated on sovereignty is not unrelated to the consequences felt by those people who are most directly affected. The nerve of this relationship was touched by Justice Brewer's dissent in *Fong Yue Ting* where he observed that "[t]his doctrine of powers inherent in sovereignty is one both indefinite and dangerous" and suggests practices more compatible with "a despotism." While it is fair to say that the national government has legitimate interests to protect with respect to both Indians and resident aliens, it is undeniably true that its treatment of them has been harsh, to say the least. Inherent powers often appear to be exercised with a patronizing, paternalistic tone accompanied by a demeaning view of those affected. Consider the Court's description of the Indians in *Kagama* as characterized by "weakness and helplessness," as "dependent," and as "wards of the nation." In these areas should the fact that the federal government has some legitimate interests to protect mean that Congress can write whatever ticket it chooses? Is the scope of interests which the Nation has in admitting people into the country the same as those it has with respect to aliens who have been residing here for years? Justice Frankfurter's admonitions in *Galvan* that precedent is voluminous, statutory construction is clear, and judgment on these matters of policy is clearly committed to Congress furnish the occasion to reflect again on the merits of judicial self-restraint and judicial activism.

The concept of inherent power similarly seems to explain in *United States* v. *Curtiss-Wright Export Corp.* (p. 157) why the power of the national government is greater in foreign than in domestic affairs. Although the controversy in *Curtiss-Wright* ostensibly revolves around the legitimacy of Congress's power to delegate authority to the President to impose an arms embargo, it might be asked in more searching terms whether the Court's opinion does not sketch out the uncharted domain of foreign relations primarily in terms of presidential rather than congressional dominance. In light of what has happened since 1936, particularly with respect to our involvement in the Korean and Vietnamese conflicts, you may want to examine the wisdom of the constitutional theory spun by Justice Sutherland.

Aside from enumerated, implied, and inherent powers, Congress derives a measure of legislative authority from constitutional grants of power by amendment. The three Civil War Amendments (XIII, XIV, and XV), for example, each contain a provision to the effect that "Congress shall have power to enforce this article by appropriate legislation." Note, too, how many other amendments grant Congress such legislative power. Congress's use of its amendment-enforcing power is at issue in both *South Carolina* v. *Katzenbach* (p. 161) and *Katzenbach* v. *Morgan* (p. 168). Notice that the test used by the Court to assess the validity of legislation passed pursuant to this power is the same as that employed to appraise the constitutionality of laws enacted under the Necessary and Proper Clause. But, though the legislative means chosen to execute the principles contained in an amendment must be reasonable, such legislation can be far-reaching. It was to one such significant alteration in the federal system worked by the Voting Rights Act which Congress passed pursuant to the Fifteenth Amendment that Justice Black objected, dissenting in the first *Katzenbach* case. The portion of the Voting Rights Act at issue in *Katzenbach* v. *Morgan*, however, was grounded on Congress's power to enforce the Fourteenth Amendment. Apart from the clarity with which the Court subjects the relevant section of the Act to judicial review, what is significant in the *Morgan* case is the potential for future use of the power by Congress that is implicit in the following statement by Justice Brennan: "More specifically, § 4(e) may be viewed as a measure to secure for the Puerto Rican community residing in New York nondiscriminatory treatment by government—both in the imposition of voting qualifications and the provision or administration of governmental services, such as public schools, public housing and law enforcement." Does this seem to suggest that in the name of enforcing equal protection of the laws Congress can require that all local public services throughout the country be shared in equally by all citizens? If so, the potential in *Morgan* is extraordinary. How do the dissenters in *Morgan* view Congress's enforcement powers? A recent decision by the Burger Court (p. 172), however, suggests a much narrower reading of Congress's enforcement power under the Fourteenth Amendment.

By virtue of the Tenth Amendment the states possess a broad undefined legislative power which Congress does not. These reserved powers we broadly refer to as "the police power." This residual power comprises a general authority to legislate for the public health, safety, welfare, and morals (although the last of these four provinces of legislation is coming under increasing constitutional attack as an infringement on the personal privacy of individuals). It is upon this general authority that the states repeatedly draw when they establish criminal and civil codes, charter corporations, provide for marriage and divorce, fund and operate institutions of public education, license doctors and nurses, enact and enforce antipollution laws, and do thousands of other things that touch our lives each day in countless ways. By contrast—as the materials in Chapter 6 illustrate—the national government possesses no general authority to legislate in the public interest; its enactments must invariably be attached to some Article I power. In its appraisal of the use of the police power the Court, as is clear from *Jacobson* v. *Massachusetts* (p. 173), looks only to the reasonableness of the legislation adopted by the state.

b. Delegation of Legislative Power

Article I, section 1 prescribes that "*All* legislative powers herein granted shall be vested in a Congress of the United States *   *   * ." (Emphasis supplied.) However jealously Congress may prize its power to make laws, the tempo and complexity of contemporary life make it necessary for Congress to delegate some law-making power to officers and agencies of the executive branch. For example, setting rates and making rules for airlines and railroads require a capacity to make changes on a day-to-day basis, something that would be difficult to accomplish by the legislative process. Establishing such rates and rules also requires special knowledge and information more easily acquired and retained by executive agencies and personnel. Furthermore, ambiguity in a statute authorizing such regulation may have been the product of legislative compromise essential to passage of the law in the first place. Nonetheless, setting rates and making rules are, strictly speaking, law-making acts.

Legal and political theory, as well as the words of the Constitution, have also created problems with respect to the delegation of power. We have long celebrated an ancient maxim of Roman law, *potestas delegata non potest delegari*. In translation this means that a delegated power must not be redelegated. Where our political theory regards the law-making power of Congress as a delegation of power to it by the people, it follows that delegation by the Congress is redelegation. John Locke, who provided much of the theory upon which our institutions were built, categorically asserted that "The Legislative neither must nor can transfer the power of making laws to anybody else, or place it anywhere but where the people have." One may well question the importance of both the legal and political theory. Why the concern about delegation? In a word, the principal reason is accountability. In human affairs it is at times important to have it clear where authority and responsibility rest. Suppose a school principal gives a certain teacher the duty to maintain order during recess, and the teacher redelegates the duty to a groundskeeper who happens to be in the area who, in turn, redelegates the duty to an older student. Who is responsible legally and otherwise if a student is injured during the recess because of inadequate supervision? In short, whatever the practical need for delegation, it would seem that there must also be some limitations. For a time the Supreme Court struggled with the issue. In 1928, in deciding *Hampton & Co.* v. *United States* (p. 177), the Court decided that "if Congress shall lay down by legislative act an intelligible principle to which the person or body authorized to fix *   *   * rates is directed to conform, such legislative action is not a forbidden delegation of legislative power." This decision was further refined in the early New Deal days in two important cases, *Panama Refining Co.* v. *Ryan* (p. 183) and *Schechter Poultry Corp.* v. *U. S.* (p. 187), where the Court held that Congress had gone too far in delegating law-making power. As the Court said in *Schechter*, "We have repeatedly recognized the necessity of adapting legislation to complex conditions involving a host of details with which the national legislature cannot deal directly. We pointed out in the *Panama Company* case that the Constitution has never been regarded as denying Congress the necessary resources of flexibility and practicality, which will enable it to perform its function in laying down policies and establishing standards, while leaving to selected instrumentalities the making of subordinate rules within prescribed limits and determination of facts to which the policy as declared by the Legislature is to apply."

Since 1935, Congress has been careful to prescribe some kind of standard for delegators to follow in delegating power. But even when these standards have been vague like "rates shall be fair and reasonable," the courts have not struck down as unconstitutional a congressional act delegating power since the mid-'thirties. This has led some eminent legal authorities to conclude that Congress now as a matter of fact can delegate as it pleases.

A measure of how the delegation of power question has substantially passed from the scene as a burning federal constitutional issue is reflected in recent legislation authorizing a variety of presidential responses to pressures threatening the economy. In the face of an energy crisis, of a concerted effort by oil-producing nations to use the sale of that commodity for purposes of exerting leverage on American foreign policy, and of inflationary pressures on our economy resulting from the escalating price of foreign oil, Congress in 1974 amended the Trade Expansion Act of 1962 so as to give the President considerable discretion in controlling foreign imports. The Court had little difficulty upholding the constitutionality of the legislation in *Federal Energy Administration* v. *Algonquin SNG, Inc.* (p. 181). Perhaps the best example of legislation in recent memory committing vast regulatory powers to the President's discretion was the Economic Stabilization Act of 1970 (p. 193). Although the Act was allowed to expire in 1974, it authorized the most comprehensive peacetime set of economic controls in American history. Given the persistent and severe inflation which has beset the economy in recent years, it is entirely possible that a congressional call for mandatory wage and price controls contemplated by the Act will come again.

Doubtless, some of the Court's concern over delegation in the 1930s was inspired by the opposition of some of the more conservative Justices to the economic programs of the New Deal. Concern about the delegation of power *per se* often is difficult to separate from disagreement with the substance of the legislation at issue, but there is another reason why delegation, such a seemingly quaint constitutional preoccupation of the 'thirties, has become a virtual dead letter in federal constitutional law today. As we noted earlier, the major reason for constraining the delegation of power is to preserve accountability. If Congress delegated its policy-making authority to unelected officers or employees of agencies in the executive branch, how could the voting public make government responsive to their wishes on matters of public policy? In other words, implicit in the concern about delegation is not only the value of accountability but the concept of legislative supremacy. The major reason for its demise was that, since delegation of power is a measure of the political balance between the legislative and executive branches, the conditions that were largely responsible for the creation of New Deal economic policies were simultaneously responsible for the rise of the modern Presidency and the transference of policy-making power and initiative to the executive branch. To the extent that Congress legislates ambiguously, it relinquishes its capacity to direct officeholders of the executive branch, and so the real policy-making power falls to them. Many of the same factors which made it increasingly difficult for Congress to write precise legislation were factors which turned Congress from an institution of policy-making leadership into a usually reactive, frequently passive body.

c. The Power to Investigate

From examinations of military mishaps during army campaigns against Indian tribes on the frontier in the 1790s and early 1800s, to exposés of political corruption during the second half of the nineteenth century, to surveys of social and economic ills in the 1930s, to probes of organized crime and labor racketeering during the 'fifties, to inquiries into presidential wrongdoing and campaign hanky-panky of the Watergate era, congressional investigations, it appears, have always been with us. Although there has been a great deal of criticism over the years of how particular investigations have been conducted and controversy over the *extent* of a legislature's power to investigate, there are few who would hold that legislatures do not (and should not) constitutionally have the power at all. First, a legislature must at times investigate in order to legislate wisely, and if that is true, the power to investigate is constitutionally inherent in the legislative power. Second, it has been agreed that legislative oversight of the executive branch is also inherent in legislative power. After all, the legislature establishes the various parts of the executive branch, defines their functions, and provides the funds to run them. Logic requires that it sees to it that these agencies perform as they were intended and financed to perform. Third, a legislature in a democratic society has an obligation to educate the public as to the need for legislation or to point up the abuses by the executive branch. Generally, this is best accomplished by debate in the legislature. But sometimes an investigation can better serve to dramatize the issues and capture the public's attention. Woodrow Wilson, long before he became President, provided the best rationale for the informing function in *Congressional Government*:

> It is the proper duty of a representative body to look diligently into every affair of government and to talk much about what it sees. It is meant to be the eyes and the voice, and to embody the wisdom and will of its constituents. Unless Congress have and use every means of acquainting itself with the acts and disposition of the administrative agents of the government, the country must remain in embarrassing crippling ignorance of the very affairs which it is most important that it should understand and direct. The informing function of Congress should be preferred even to its legislative function.

But notice that Wilson distinguishes the informing function *from* the legislative function. Since constitutionally Congress has only the legislative function, his rationale would seem to raise the question of constitutional warrant for Congress to perform the informing function. Can it be persuasively argued that the informing function is necessary to legislating or to overseeing the executive branch and hence inherent in legislative power?

As indicated earlier, there has been controversy over the *scope* of the legislative power to inquire. There are those who argue that no legislature has the power to investigate matters about which it cannot legislate. It is suggested that since no American legislature has the constitutional power to abridge First Amendment freedoms, it has no power to investigate in these areas nor the power to investigate any matter where the investigating will have the impact of abridging these freedoms. Another potent criticism leveled at legislative investigations is that they have too frequently been used to *punish* people rather than to develop the facts pertaining to a particular problem. When legislative committees have intentionally sought to mete out punishment by investigation, they have been doing what the Founding Fathers sought to prevent by inserting in the Constitution the specific prohibition against bills of attainder. According to the Supreme Court in 1866, "A bill of attainder is a legislative Act which inflicts punishment without judicial trial." Although an investigation is not a legislative "Act" in a strict legal sense, surely the Framers' abhorrence would logically extend to legislative actions of all types except in those rare instances when the legislature sits constitutionally as a court in impeachment proceedings.

The great difficulty our courts have encountered in trying to determine whether or not specific investigations have exceeded constitutional limitations is in determining what the intent of the legislative committee was in carrying out a particular investigation. Was it to limit a First Amendment freedom or truly to safeguard against subversive activities? Was it to punish or to learn facts? So much depends upon the intent, yet courts quite wisely endeavor to refrain from psychoanalyzing legislators.

To the extent that congressional committees are bound to observe extensive procedural and substantive constitutional requirements, an investigation may be deflected from its central information-gathering purpose and turned into a mini-trial. Must we choose, then, between fair or effective congressional investigations? Too often in attempting to assess the performance of a particular investigating committee or a court decision concerning a given investigation we find ourselves tempted to make the assessment on the basis of "whose ox is being gored." As you read through the cases from *McGrain* (p. 197) to *Eastland* (p. 226), you should bear in mind, therefore, that the prospect of conducting investigations which are both fair and effective hinges on the application of principles to good guys and gad guys alike. What kinds of neutral principles are apparent in the Court's decisions?

A final question, prompted by the Senate Watergate investigation of some years ago, remains: whether a committee of Congress can subpoena materials held by the President? This question presents an imposing conundrum for the American constitutional system. The doctrine of separation of powers requires a dedication to the preservation of presidential independence from congressional control. At the same time how can Congress perform its functions properly if a President can withhold from it information which it needs to perform those functions? The opinion of the federal appellate court in *Senate Select Committee on Presidential Campaign Activities* v. *Nixon* (p. 295) offers not only an answer in the case of the subpoena issued by the Ervin Committee but also some guidelines for resolving future confrontations of this type.

d. The Speech and Debate Clause (Congressional Immunity)

The Constitution specifies in Article I, section 6, paragraph 1 that congressmen "shall not be questioned in any other Place" for "any Speech or Debate in either House." The purpose of such a grant of immunity was to secure the independence of the legislative branch by preventing possible interference with or intimidation of congressmen exercising discretionary functions which are indispensable to the legislative process. Yet this absolute immunity carries with it the potential for mischief. If a member of Congress makes defamatory statements about others outside of the legislative halls, he is subject to suit for slander no less than anyone else, but if those statements are made on the floor or in committee rooms, such statements—no matter how irresponsible or damaging—cannot be held against him. The tension between maintaining the integrity of Congress, on the one hand, and creating an immunity that potentially places the legislator above the law, on the other hand, is one the Court must grapple with as it wends its way through Speech and Debate Clause cases. As you read the cases which begin with *Gravel* v. *United States* (p. 231) and end with *Hutchinson* v. *Proxmire* (p. 244), you should try to identify what sorts of conduct fall within and outside of the protection afforded by the clause and to whom the immunity conferred extends.

Much of the Court's discussion of what protection emanates from the Speech and Debate Clause in cases such as *Gravel, McMillan,* and *Proxmire* takes place against a backdrop that should be familiar to you by now—congressmen engaged in an informing function. Of two rather different delineations of the informing function—Congress informing itself or Congress informing both itself and the public—both conceivably implied in Woodrow Wilson's characterization, which has the Court accepted as describing behavior immunized by the Speech and Debate Clause?

a. THE SOURCES AND SCOPE OF LEGISLATIVE POWER

McCULLOCH v. MARYLAND

Supreme Court of the United States, 1819
17 U.S. (4 Wheat.) 316, 4 L.Ed. 579

In 1816, Congress enacted legislation creating a national bank, one branch of which was subsequently located at Baltimore. Two years later the Maryland legislature passed a statute taxing all banks operating in Maryland not chartered by the state. The act levied approximately a 2 percent tax on the value of all notes issued by the bank or, alternatively, a flat annual fee of $15,000, payable in advance. Provisions of the statute were backed by a $500 penalty for each violation. McCulloch, the cashier of the Baltimore branch of the U. S. Bank, issued notes and refused to pay the tax. The Maryland Court of Appeals upheld his conviction under the statute. The U. S. Supreme Court voted to reverse, and Chief Justice Marshall, speaking for the Court, directed the first part of his opinion to a discussion of the scope of Congress's powers under Article I.

MARSHALL, Chief Justice, delivered the opinion of the court.—In the case now to be determined, the defendant, a sovereign state denies the obligation of a law enacted by the legislature of the Union, and the plaintiff, on his part, contests the validity of an act which has been passed by the legislature of that state. The constitution of our country, in its most interesting and vital parts, is to be considered; the conflicting powers of the government of the Union and of its members, as marked in that constitution, are to be discussed; and an opinion given, which may essentially influence the great operations of the government. No tribunal can approach such a question without a deep sense of its importance, and of the awful responsibility involved in its decision. But it must be decided peacefully, or remain a source of hostile legislation, perhaps, of hostility of a still more serious nature; and if it is to be so decided, by this tribunal alone can the decision be made. On the supreme court of the United States has

the constitution of our country devolved this important duty.

The first question made in the cause is—has congress power to incorporate a bank? It has been truly said, that this can scarcely be considered as an open question, entirely unprejudiced by the former proceedings of the nation respecting it. The principle now contested was introduced at a very early period of our history, has been recognized by many successive legislatures, and has been acted upon by the judicial department, in cases of peculiar delicacy, as a law of undoubted obligation.

* * *

The power now contested was exercised by the first congress elected under the present constitution. The bill for incorporating the Bank of the United States did not steal upon an unsuspecting legislature, and pass unobserved. Its principle was completely understood, and was opposed with equal zeal and ability. After being resisted, first, in the fair and open field of debate, and afterwards, in the executive cabinet, with as much persevering talent as any measure has ever experienced, and being supported by arguments which convinced minds as pure and as intelligent as this country can boast, it became a law. The original act was permitted to expire; but a short experience of the embarrassments to which the refusal to revive it exposed the government, convinced those who were most prejudiced against the measure of its necessity, and induced the passage of the present law. * * *

In discussing this question, the counsel for the state of Maryland have deemed it of some importance, in the construction of the constitution, to consider that instrument, not as emanating from the people, but as the act of sovereign and independent states. The powers of the general government, it has been said, are delegated by the states, who alone are truly sovereign; and must be exercised in subordination to the states, who alone possess supreme dominion. It would be difficult to sustain this proposition. The convention which framed the constitution was indeed elected by the state legislatures. But the instrument, when it came from their hands, was a mere proposal, without obligation, or pretensions to it. It was reported to the then existing congress of the United States, with a request that it might "be submitted to a convention of delegates, chosen in each state by the people thereof, under the recommendation of its legislature, for their assent and ratification." This mode of proceeding was adopted; and by the convention, by congress, and by the state legislatures, the instrument was submitted to the *people*. They acted upon it in the only manner in which they can act safely, effectively

and wisely, on such a subject, by assembling in convention. It is true, they assembed in their several states—and where else should they have assembled? No political dreamer was ever wild enough to think of breaking down the lines which separate the states, and of compounding the American people into one common mass. Of consequence, when they act, they act in their states. But the measures they adopt do not, on that account, cease to be the measures of the people themselves, or become the measures of the state governments.

From these conventions, the constitution derives its whole authority. The government proceeds directly from the people; is "ordained and established," in the name of the people; and is declared to be ordained, "in order to form a more perfect union, establish justice, insure domestic tranquillity, and secure the blessings of liberty to themselves and to their posterity." The assent of the states, in their sovereign capacity, is implied, in calling a convention, and thus submitting that instrument to the people. But the people were at perfect liberty to accept or reject it; and their act was final. It required not the affirmance, and could not be negatived, by the state governments. The constitution, when thus adopted, was of complete obligation, and bound the state sovereignties.

It has been said, that the people had already surrendered all their powers to the state sovereignties, and had nothing more to give. But, surely, the question whether they may resume and modify the powers granted to government, does not remain to be settled in this country. Much more might the legitimacy of the general government be doubted, had it been created by the states.

The powers delegated to the state sovereignties were to be exercised by themselves, not by a distinct and independent sovereignty, created by themselves. * * * The government of the Union, then (whatever may be the influence of this fact on the case), is, emphatically and truly, a government of the people. In form, and in substance, it emanates from them. Its powers are granted by them, and are to be exercised directly on them, and for their benefit.

This government is acknowledged by all, to be one of enumerated powers. The principle, that it can exercise only the powers granted to it, would seem too apparent, to have required to be enforced by all those arguments, which its enlightened friends, while it was depending before the people, found it necessary to urge; that principle is now universally admitted. But the question respecting the extent of the powers actually granted, is perpetually arising, and will probably continue to arise, so long as our system shall exist. In discussing these questions, the conflicting powers of the general and state governments must be brought into view, and the supremacy of their respective laws, when they are in opposition, must be settled.

If any one proposition could command the universal assent of mankind, we might expect it would be this—that the government of the Union, though limited in its powers, is supreme within its sphere of action. This would seem to result, necessarily, from its nature. It is the government of all; its powers are delegated by all; it represents all, and acts for all. Though any one state may be willing to control its operations, no state is willing to allow others to control them. The nation, on those subjects on which it can act, must necessarily bind its component parts. But this question is not left to mere reason: the people have, in express terms, decided it, by saying, "this constitution, and the laws of the United States, which shall be made in pursuance thereof," "shall be the supreme law of the land," and by requiring that the members of the state legislatures, and the officers of the executive and judicial departments of the states, shall take the oath of fidelity to it. The government of the United States, then, though limited in its powers, is supreme; and its laws, when made in pursuance of the constitution, form the supreme law of the land, "anything in the constitution or laws of any state to the contrary notwithstanding."

Among the enumerated powers, we do not find that of establishing a bank or creating a corporation. But there is no phrase in the instrument which, like the articles of confederation, excludes incidental or implied powers; and which requires that everything granted shall be expressly and minutely described. * * *

Although, among the enumerated powers of government, we do not find the word "bank" or "incorporation," we find the great powers, to lay and collect taxes; to borrow money; to regulate commerce; to declare and conduct a war; and to raise and support armies and navies. The sword and the purse, all the external relations, and no inconsiderable portion of the industry of the nation, are intrusted to its government. It can never be pretended, that these vast powers draw after them others of inferior importance, merely because they are inferior. Such an idea can never be advanced. But it may with great reason be contended, that a government, intrusted with such ample powers, on the due execution of which the happiness and prosperity of the nation so vitally depends, must also be intrusted with ample means for their execution. The power being given, it is the interest of the nation to facilitate its execution. It can never be their interest, and cannot be presumed to have been their intention, to clog and embarrass its execution, by withholding the most appropriate means. * * *

It is not denied, that the powers given to the government imply the ordinary means of execution. That, for example, of raising revenue, and applying it to national purposes, is admitted to imply the power of conveying money from place to place, as the exigencies of the nation may require, and of employing the usual means of conveyance. But it is denied, that the government has its choice of means; or, that it may employ the most convenient means, if, to employ them, it be necessary to erect a corporation. On what foundation does this argument rest? On this alone: the power of creating a corporation, is one appertaining to sovereignty, and is not expressly conferred on congress. This is true. But all legislative powers appertain to sovereignty. The original power of giving the law on any subject whatever, is a sovereign power; and if the government of the Union is restrained from creating a corporation, as a means for performing its functions, on the single reason that the creation of a corporation is an act of sovereignty; if the sufficiency of this reason be acknowledged, there would be some difficulty in sustaining the authority of congress to pass other laws for the accomplishment of the same objects. The government which has a right to do an

act, and has imposed on it, the duty of performing that act, must, according to the dictates of reason, be allowed to select the means; and those who contend that it may not select any appropriate means, that one particular mode of effecting the object is excepted, take upon themselves the burden of establishing that exception.

The creation of a corporation, it is said, appertains to sovereignty. This is admitted. But to what portion of sovereignty does it appertain? Does it belong to one more than to another? In America, the powers of sovereignty are divided between the government of the Union, and those of the states. They are each sovereign, with respect to the objects committed to it, and neither sovereign, with respect to the objects committed to the other. We cannot comprehend that train of reasoning, which would maintain, that the extent of power granted by the people is to be ascertained, not by the nature and terms of the grant, but by its date. Some state constitutions were formed before, some since that of the United States. We cannot believe, that their relation to each other is in any degree dependent upon this circumstance. Their respective powers must, we think, be precisely the same, as if they had been formed at the same time. Had they been formed at the same time, and had the people conferred on the general government the power contained in the constitution, and on the states the whole residuum of power would it have been asserted, that the government of the Union was not sovereign, with respect to those objects which were intrusted to it, in relation to which its laws were declared to be supreme? If this could not have been asserted, we cannot well comprehend the process of reasoning which maintains, that a power appertaining to sovereignty cannot be connected with that vast portion of it which is granted to the general government, so far as it is calculated to subserve the legitimate objects of that government. The power of creating a corporation, though appertaining to sovereignty, is not, like the power of making war, or levying taxes, or of regulating commerce, a great substantive and independent power, which cannot be implied as incidental to other powers, or used as a means of executing them. It is never the end for which other powers are exercised, but a means by which other objects are accomplished. No contributions are made to charity, for the sake of an incorporation, but a corporation is created to administer the charity; no seminary of learning is instituted, in order to be incorporated, but the corporate character is conferred to subserve the purposes of education. No city was ever built, with the sole object of being incorporated, but is incorporated as affording the best means of being well governed. The power of creating a corporation is never used for its own sake, but for the purpose of effecting something else. No sufficient reason is, therefore, perceived, why it may not pass as incidental to those powers which are expressly given, if it be a direct mode of executing them.

But the constitution of the United States has not left the right of congress to employ the necessary means, for the execution of the powers conferred on the government, to general reasoning. To its enumeration of powers is added, that of making "all laws which shall be necessary and proper, for carrying into execution the foregoing powers, and all other powers vested by this constitution, in the government of the United States, or in any department thereof." The counsel for the state of Maryland have urged various arguments, to prove that this clause, though, in terms, a grant of power, is not so, in effect; but is really restrictive of the general right, which might otherwise be implied, of selecting means for executing the enumerated powers. In support of this proposition, they have found it necessary to contend, that this clause was inserted for the purpose of conferring on congress the power of making laws. That, without it, doubts might be entertained, whether congress could exercise its powers in the form of legislation.

But could this be the object for which it was inserted? A government is created by the people, having legislative, executive and judicial powers. Its legislative powers are vested in a congress, which is to consist of a senate and house of representatives. Each house may determine the rule of its proceedings; and it is declared, that every bill which shall have passed both houses, shall, before it becomes a law, be presented to the president of the United States. The 7th section describes the course of proceedings, by which a bill shall become a law; and, then, the 8th section enumerates the powers of congress. Could it be necessary to say, that a legislature should exercise legislative powers, in the shape of legislation? After allowing each house to prescribe its own course of proceeding, after describing the manner in which a bill should become a law, would it have entered into the mind of a single member of the convention, that an express power to make laws was necessary, to enable the legislature to make them? That a legislature, endowed with legislative powers, can legislate, is a proposition too self-evident to have been questioned.

But the argument on which most reliance is placed, is drawn from that peculiar language of this clause. Congress is not empowered by it to make all laws, which may have relation to the powers conferred on the government, but such only as may be *"necessary and proper"* for carrying them into execution. The word *"necessary"* is considered as controlling the whole sentence, and as limiting the right to pass laws for the execution of the granted powers, to such as are indispensable, and without which the power would be nugatory. That it excludes the choice of means, and leaves to congress, in each case, that only which is most direct and simple.

Is it true, that this is the sense in which the word "necessary" is always used? Does it always import an absolute physical necessity, so strong, that one thing to which another may be termed necessary, cannot exist without that other? We think it does not. If reference be had to its use, in the common affairs of the world, or in approved authors, we find that it frequently imports no more than that one thing is convenient, or useful, or essential to another. To employ the means necessary to an end, is generally understood as employing any means calculated to produce the end, and not as being confined to those single means, without which the end would be entirely unattainable. Such is the character of human language, that no word conveys to the mind, in all situations, one single definite idea; and nothing is more common than to use words in a figurative sense. Almost all compositions contain

words, which taken in their rigorous sense, would convey a meaning different from that which is obviously intended. It is essential to just construction, that many words which import something excessive, should be understood in a more mitigated sense—in that sense which common usage justifies. The word "necessary" is of this description. It has not a fixed character, peculiar to itself. It admits of all degrees of comparison; and is often connected with other words, which increase or diminish the impression the mind receives of the urgency it imports. A thing may be necessary, very necessary, absolutely or indispensably necessary. To no mind would the same idea be conveyed by these several phrases. The comment on the word is well illustrated by the passage cited at the bar, from the 10th section of the 1st article of the constitution. It is, we think, impossible to compare the sentence which prohibits a state from laying "imposts, or duties on imports or exports, except what may be *absolutely* necessary for executing its inspection laws," with that which authorizes congress "to make all laws which shall be necessary and proper for carrying into execution" the powers of the general government, without feeling a conviction, that the convention understood itself to change materially the meaning of the word "necessary," by prefixing the word "absolutely." This word, then, like others, is used in various senses; and, in its construction, the subject, the context, the intention of the person using them, are all to be taken into view.

Let this be done in the case under consideration. The subject is the execution of those great powers on which the welfare of a nation essentially depends. It must have been the intention of those who gave these powers, to insure, so far as human prudence could insure, their beneficial execution. This could not be done, by confiding the choice of means to such narrow limits as not to leave it in the power of congress to adopt any which might be appropriate, and which were conducive to the end. This provision is made in a constitution, intended to endure for ages to come, and consequently, to be adapted to the various *crises* of human affairs. To have prescribed the means by which government should, in all future time, execute its powers, would have been to change, entirely, the character of the instrument, and give it the properties of a legal code. It would have been an unwise attempt to provide, by immutable rules, for exigencies which, if foreseen at all, must have been seen dimly, and which can be best provided for as they occur. To have declared, that the best means shall not be used, but those alone, without which the power given would be nugatory, would have been to deprive the legislature of the capacity to avail itself of experience, to exercise its reason, and to accommodate its legislation to circumstances.

If we apply this principle of construction to any of the powers of the government, we shall find it so pernicious in its operation that we shall be compelled to discard it. * * *

* * *

In ascertaining the sense in which the word "necessary" is used in this clause of the constitution, we may derive some aid from that with which it is associated. Congress shall have power "to make all laws which shall be necessary and proper to carry into execution" the powers of the govern-

ment. If the word "necessary" was used in that strict and rigorous sense for which the counsel for the state of Maryland contend, it would be an extraordinary departure from the usual course of the human mind, as exhibited in composition, to add a word, the only possible effect of which is, to qualify that strict and rigorous meaning; to present to the mind the idea of some choice of means of legislation, not strained and compressed within the narrow limits for which gentlemen contend.

* * *

The result of the most careful and attentive consideration bestowed upon this clause is, that if it does not enlarge, it cannot be construed to restrain the powers of congress, or to impair the right of the legislature to exercise its best judgment in the selection of measures to carry into execution the constitutional powers of the government. If no other motive for its insertion can be suggested, a sufficient one is found in the desire to remove all doubts respecting the right to legislate on that vast mass of incidental powers which must be involved in the constitution, if that instrument be not a splendid bauble.

We admit, as all must admit, that the powers of the government are limited, and that its limits are not to be transcended. But we think the sound construction of the constitution must allow to the national legislature that discretion, with respect to the means by which the powers it confers are to be carried into execution, which will enable that body to perform the high duties assigned to it, in the manner most beneficial to the people. Let the end be legitimate, let it be within the scope of the constitution, and all means which are appropriate, which are plainly adapted to that end, which are not prohibited, but consistent with the letter and spirit of the constitution, are constitutional.

That a corporation must be considered as a means not less usual, not of higher dignity, not more requiring a particular specification than other means, has been sufficiently proved. * * * Had it been intended to grant this power, as one which should be distinct and independent, to be exercised in any case whatever, it would have found a place among the enumerated powers of the government. But being considered merely as a means, to be employed only for the purpose of carrying into execution the given powers, there could be no motive for particularly mentioning it.

* * *

After the most deliberate consideration, it is the unanimous and decided opinion of this court, that the act to incorporate the Bank of the United States is a law made in pursuance of the constitution, and is a part of the supreme law of the land.

The branches, proceeding from the same stock, and being conducive to the complete accomplishment of the object, are equally constitutional. It would have been unwise, to locate them in the charter, and it would be unnecessarily inconvenient, to employ the legislative power in making those subordinate arrangements. The great duties of the bank are prescribed; those duties require branches; and the bank itself may, we think, be safely trusted with the selection of places where those branches shall be fixed; reserving always to the government the right to require that a branch shall be located where it may be deemed necessary.

* * *

[Chief Justice MARSHALL went on to conclude in the second portion of his opinion, which is omitted, that the legitimate exercise of Congress's power under Article I took precedence by virtue of the Supremacy Clause over the assertion of a state's power to tax founded on the Tenth Amendment.]

UNITED STATES v. KAGAMA

Supreme Court of the United States, 1886
118 U.S. 375, 6 S.Ct. 1109, 30 L.Ed. 228

In 1885, Congress passed the Indian Appropriation Act, section 9 of which provides that it shall be a crime for one Indian to kill another on an Indian reservation and makes such an offender subject to trial by the same courts, in the same manner, and liable to the same punishment as all other persons committing the crime within the jurisdiction of the United States. Kagama, an Indian, was indicted for the murder of another Indian, Iyouse, within the confines of the Hoopa Valley Indian Reservation in California. A third Indian, Mahawaha, was indicted for aiding and abetting in the crime. This case was certified to the Supreme Court because the U. S. circuit and district judges, sitting as the Circuit Court for the District of California, divided in their opinions as to what jurisdiction the United States possessed over what seem to be exclusively Indian affairs.

Mr. Justice MILLER delivered the opinion of the court.

* * *

The Constitution of the United States is almost silent in regard to the relations of the government which was established by it to the numerous tribes of Indians within its borders.

In declaring the basis on which representation in the lower branch of the Congress and direct taxation should be apportioned, it was fixed that it should be according to numbers, *excluding Indians not taxed*, which, of course, excluded nearly all of that race, but which meant that if there were such within a State as were taxed to support the government, they should be counted for representation, and in the computation for direct taxes levied by the United States. This expression, excluding Indians not taxed, is found in the XIVth amendment, where it deals with the same subject under the new conditions produced by the emancipation of the slaves. Neither of these shed much light on the power of Congress over the Indians in their existence as tribes, distinct from the ordinary citizens of a State or Territory.

The mention of Indians in the Constitution which has received most attention is that found in the clause which gives Congress "power to regulate commerce with foreign nations and among the several States, and with the Indian tribes."

This clause is relied on in the argument in the present case, the proposition being that the statute under consideration is a regulation of commerce with the Indian tribes. But we think it would be a very strained construction of this clause, that a system of criminal laws for Indians living peaceably in their reservations, which left out the entire code of trade and intercourse laws justly enacted under that provision, and established punishments for the common-law crimes of murder, manslaughter, arson, burglary, larceny, and the like, without any reference to their relation to any kind of commerce, was authorized by the grant of power to regulate commerce with the Indian tribes. While we are not able to see, in either of these clauses of the Constitution and its amendments, any delegation of power to enact a code of criminal law for the punishment of the worst class of crimes known to civilized life when committed by Indians, there is a suggestion in the manner in which the Indian tribes are introduced into that clause, which may have a bearing on the subject before us. The commerce with foreign nations is distinctly stated as submitted to the control of Congress. Were the Indian tribes foreign nations? If so, they came within the first of the three classes of commerce mentioned, and did not need to be repeated as Indian tribes. Were they nations, in the minds of the framers of the Constitution? If so, the natural phrase would have been "foreign nations and Indian nations," or, in the terseness of language uniformly used by the framers of the instrument, it would naturally have been "foreign and Indian nations." And so in the case of The Cherokee Nation v. The State of Georgia, 5 Pet. 1, 20, brought in the Supreme Court of the United States, under the declaration that the judicial power extends to suits between a State and foreign States, and giving to the Supreme Court original jurisdiction where a State is a party, it was conceded that

Georgia as a State came within the clause, but held that the Cherokees were not a State or nation within the meaning of the Constitution, so as to be able to maintain the suit.

But these Indians are within the geographical limits of the United States. The soil and the people within these limits are under the political control of the Government of the United States, or of the States of the Union. There exist within the broad domain of sovereignty but these two. There may be cities, counties, and other organized bodies with limited legislative functions, but they are all derived from, or exist in, subordination to one or the other of these. The territorial governments owe all their powers to the statutes of the United States conferring on them the powers which they exercise, and which are liable to be withdrawn, modified, or repealed at any time by Congress. What authority the State governments may have to enact criminal laws for the Indians will be presently considered. But this power of Congress to organize territorial governments, and make laws for their inhabitants, arises not so much from the clause in the Constitution in regard to disposing of and making rules and regulations concerning the Territory and other property of the United States, as from the ownership of the country in which the Territories are, and the right of exclusive sovereignty which must exist in the National Government, and can be found nowhere else. * * *

* * *

[In earlier cases] it was held that [Indian] tribes were neither States nor nations, had only some of the attributes of sovereignty, and could not be so far recognized in that capacity as to sustain a suit in the Supreme Court of the United States. * * * It was said that they were not subject to the jurisdiction asserted over them by the State of Georgia, which, because they were within its limits, where they had been for ages, had attempted to extend her laws and the jurisdiction of her courts over them.

In the opinions in these cases they are spoken of as "wards of the nation," "pupils," as local dependent communities. In this spirit the United States has conducted its relations to them from its organization to this time. But, after an experience of a hundred years of the treaty-making system of government, Congress has determined upon a new departure—to govern them by acts of Congress. This is seen in the act of March 3, 1871, embodied in § 2079 of the Revised Statutes:

"No Indian nation or tribe, within the territory of the United States shall be acknowledged or recognized as an independent nation, tribe, or power, with whom the United States may contract by treaty; but no obligation of any treaty lawfully made and ratified with any such Indian nation or tribe prior to March third, eighteen hundred and seventy one, shall be hereby invalidated or impaired."

The case of Crow Dog, 109 U.S. 556, 3 S.Ct. 396, in which an agreement with the Sioux Indians, ratified by an act of Congress, was supposed to extend over them the laws of the United States and the jurisdiction of its courts, covering murder and other grave crimes, shows the purpose of Congress in this new departure. The decision in that case admits that if the intention of Congress had been to punish, by the United States courts, the murder of one Indian by another, the law would have been valid. But the court could not see, in the agreement with the Indians sanctioned by Congress, a purpose to repeal § 2146 of the Revised Statutes, which expressly excludes from that jurisdiction the case of a crime committed by one Indian against another in the Indian country. The passage of the act now under consideration was designed to remove that objection, and to go further by including such crimes on reservations lying within a State.

Is this latter fact a fatal objection to the law? The statute itself contains no express limitation upon the powers of a State or the jurisdiction of its courts. If there be any limitation in either of these, it grows out of the implication arising from the fact that Congress has defined a crime committed within the State, and made it punishable in the courts of the United States. But Congress *has* done this, and *can* do it, with regard to all offences relating to matters to which the Federal authority extends. Does that authority extend to this case?

It will be seen at once that the nature of the offence (murder) is one which in almost all cases of its commission is punishable by the laws of the States, and within the jurisdiction of their courts. The distinction is claimed to be that the offence under the statute is committed by an Indian, that it is committed on a reservation set apart within the State for residence of the tribe of Indians by the United States, and the fair inference is that the offending Indian shall belong to that or some other tribe. It does not interfere with the process of the State courts within the reservation, nor with the operation of State laws upon white people found there. Its effect is confined to the acts of an Indian of some tribe, of a criminal character, committed within the limits of the reservation.

It seems to us that this is within the competency of Congress. These Indian tribes *are* the wards of the nation. They are communities *dependent* on the United States. Dependent largely for their daily food. Dependent for their political rights. They owe no allegiance to the States, and receive from them no protection. Because of the local ill feeling, the people of the States where they are found are often their deadliest enemies. From their very weakness and helplessness, so largely due to the course of dealing of the Federal Government with them and the treaties in which it has been promised, there arises the duty of protection, and with it the power. This has always been recognized by the Executive and by Congress, and by this court, whenever the question has arisen.

In the case of Worcester v. The State of Georgia [6 Pet. 515, 536] * * * it was held that, though the Indians had by treaty sold their land within that State, and agreed to remove away, which they had failed to do, the State could not, while they remained on those lands, extend its laws, criminal and civil, over the tribes; that the duty and power to compel their removal was in the United States, and the tribe was under their protection, and could not be subjected to the laws of the State and the process of its courts.

* * *

The power of the General Government over these remnants of a race once powerful, now weak and diminished in numbers, is necessary to their protection, as well as to the safety of those among whom they dwell. It must exist in that government, because it never has existed anywhere else, because the theatre of its exercise is within the geographical limits of the United States, because it has never been denied, and because it alone can enforce its laws on all the tribes.

* * *

We answer the questions propounded to us: that the ninth section of the act of March 23, 1855, is a valid law in both its branches, and that the circuit court of the United States for the district of California has jurisdiction of the offense charged in the indictment in this case.

FONG YUE TING v. UNITED STATES

Supreme Court of the United States, 1893
149 U.S. 698, 13 S.Ct. 1016, 37 L.Ed. 905

In 1892, Congress enacted legislation continuing its policy of excluding persons of Chinese descent from entering the United States and providing that all Chinese laborers who were entitled to remain in the country obtain within one year a certificate of residence from the collector of internal revenue of their respective districts. The certificate was to be a kind of passport for moving about within the United States. Persons of Chinese descent convicted of illegally remaining in the country were to be punished by a year at hard labor and, along with those who were lawful residents but who had failed to obtain the certificate, then deported. The act contained a stiff penalty for forging or altering certificates. Finally, the act provided that a Chinese person seeking to land in the United States and who had been denied entry was to be refused bail and retained in custody while his petition for a writ of habeas corpus was pending.

Fong Yue Ting and two other Chinese laborers were arrested by a United States marshal for not having certificates of residence. The circuit court for the district dismissed the action for a writ of habeas corpus, and the petitioners appealed.

Mr. Justice GRAY delivered the opinion of the court:

The general principles of public law which lie at the foundation of these cases are clearly established by previous judgments of this court, and by the authorities therein referred to.

In the recent case of Ekiu v. United States, 142 U.S. 651, 659, 12 Sup. Ct.Rep. 336, the court, in sustaining the action of the executive department, putting in force an Act of Congress for the exclusion of aliens said: "It is an accepted maxim of international law, that every sovereign nation has the power, as inherent in sovereignty, and essential to self-preservation, to forbid the entrance of foreigners within its dominions, or to admit them only in such cases and upon such conditions as it may see fit to prescribe. In the United States, this power is vested in the national government, to which the Constitution has committed the entire control of international relations, in peace as well as in war. It belongs to the political department of the government, and may be exercised either through treaties made by the President and Senate, or through statutes enacted by Congress."

* * *

The right of a nation to expel or deport foreigners, who have not been naturalized or taken any steps towards becoming citizens of the country, rests upon the same grounds, and is as absolute and unqualified as the right to prohibit and prevent their entrance into the country.

* * *

The right to exclude or to expel all aliens, or any class of aliens, absolutely or upon certain conditions, in war or in peace, being an inherent and inalienable right of every sovereign and independent nation, essential to its safety, its independence and its welfare, the question now before the court is whether the manner in which Congress has exercised this right in sections 6 and 7 of the Act of 1892 is consistent with the Constitution.

The United States are a sovereign and independent nation, and are vested by the Constitution with the entire control of international relations, and with all the powers of government necessary to maintain that control and to make it effective. The only government of this country, which other nations recognize or treat with, is the government of the Union; and the only American flag known throughout the world is the flag of the United States.

The Constitution of the United States speaks with no uncertain sound upon this subject. That instrument, established by the people of the United States as the fundamental law of the land, has conferred upon the President the executive power; has made him the commander-in-chief of the army and navy; has authorized him, by and with the consent of the Senate, to make treaties, and to appoint ambassadors, public ministers and consuls; and has made it his duty to take care that the laws be faithfully executed. The Constitution has granted to Congress the power to regulate commerce with foreign nations, including the entrance of ships, the importation of goods and the bringing of persons into the ports of the United States; to establish a uniform rule of naturalization; to define and punish piracies and felonies committed on the high seas, and offenses against the law of nations; to declare war, grant letters of marque and reprisal, and make rules concerning captures on land and water; to raise and support armies, to provide and maintain a navy, and to make rules for the government and regulation of the land and naval forces; and to make all laws necessary and proper for carrying into execution these powers, and all other powers vested by the Constitution in the government of the United States, or in any department or officer thereof. And the several states are expressly forbidden to enter into any treaty, alliance or confederation; to grant letters of marque and reprisal; to enter into any agreement or compact with another state, or with a foreign power; or to engage in war, unless actually invaded, or in such imminent danger as will not admit of delay.

In exercising the great power which the people of the United States, by establishing a written Constitution as the supreme and paramount law, have vested in this court, of determining, whenever the question is properly brought before it, whether the acts of the legislature or of the executive are consistent with the Constitution, it behooves the court to be careful that it does not undertake to pass upon political questions, the final decision of which has been committed by the Constitution to the other departments of the government.

* * *

The power to exclude or to expel aliens, being a power affecting international relations, is vested in the political departments of the government, and is to be regulated by treaty or by Act of Congress, and to be executed by the executive authority according to the regulations so established, except so far as the judicial department has been authorized by treaty or by statute, or is required by the paramount law of the Constitution, to intervene.

* * *

The power to exclude aliens and the power to expel them rest upon one foundation, are derived from one source, are supported by the same reasons, and are in truth but parts of one and the same power.

The power of Congress, therefore, to expel, like the power to exclude aliens, or any specified class of aliens, from the country, may be exercised entirely through executive officers; or Congress may call in the aid of the judiciary to ascertain any contested facts on which an alien's right to be in the country has been made by Congress to depend.

Congress, having the right, as it may see fit, to expel aliens of a particular class, or to permit them to remain, has undoubtedly the right to provide a system of registration and identification of the members of that class within the country, and to take all proper means to carry out the system which it provides.

It is no new thing for the law making power, acting either through treaties made by the President and Senate, or by the more common method of acts of Congress, to submit the decision of questions, not necessarily of judicial cognizance, either to the final determination of executive officers, or to the decision of such officers in the first instance, with such opportunity for judicial review of their action as Congress may see fit to authorize or permit.

* * *

Mr. Justice BREWER dissenting:

I dissent from the opinion and judgment of the court in these cases, and the questions being of importance, I deem it not improper to briefly state my reasons therefor.

I rest my dissent on three propositions: First, that the persons against whom the penalties of section 6 of the Act of 1892 are directed are persons lawfully residing within the United States; secondly, that as such they are within the protection of the Constitution, and secured by its guarantees against oppression and wrong; and, third, that section 6 deprives them of liberty and imposes punishment without due process of law, and in disregard of constitutional guaranties, especially those found in the 4th, 5th, 6th, and 8th articles of the Amendments.

* * *

But whatever rights a resident alien might have in any other nation, here he is within the express protection of the Constitution especially in respect to those guaranties which are declared in the original amendments. It has been repeated so often as to become axiomatic, that this government is one of enumerated and delegated powers, and, as declared in Article 10 of the amendments, "the powers not delegated to the United States by the Constitution, nor prohibited by it to the states, are reserved to the states respectively, or to the people."

It is said that the power here asserted is inherent in sovereignty. This doctrine of powers inherent in sovereignty is one both indefinite and dangerous. Where are the limits to such powers to be found, and by whom are they to be pronounced? Is it within legislative capacity to declare the limits? If so, then the mere assertion of an inherent power creates it, and despotism exists. May the courts establish the boundaries? Whence do they obtain the authority for this? Shall they look to the practices of other nations to ascertain the limits? The governments of other nations have elastic powers—ours is fixed and bounded by a written constitution. The expulsion of a race may be within the inherent powers of a despotism. History, before the adoption of this Constitution, was not destitute of examples of the exercise of such a power; and its framers were familiar with history, and wisely, as it seems to me, they gave to this government no general power to banish. * * *

* * *

In * * * [Yick Wo v. Hopkins, 118 U.S. 356, 6 S.Ct. 1064 (1886)] in which was presented a municipal ordinance, fair on its face, but contrived to work oppression to a few engaged in a single occupation, this court saw no difficulty in finding a constitutional barrier to such injustice. But this greater wrong, by which a hundred thousand people are subject to arrest and forcible deportation from the country, is beyond the reach of the protecting power of the Constitution. Its grievous wrong suggests this declaration of wisdom, coming from the dawn of English history: "Verily he who dooms a worse doom to the friendless and the comer from afar than to this fellow injures himself." Laws of King Cnut, 1 Thorpe, Ancient Laws & Institutes of England, 397.

In view of this enactment of the highest legislative body of the foremost Christian nation, may not the thoughtful Chinese disciple of Confucius fairly ask, Why do they send missionaries here?

[Justice FIELD and Chief Justice FULLER also dissented.]

GALVAN v. PRESS

Supreme Court of the United States, 1954
347 U.S. 522, 74 S.Ct. 737, 98 L.Ed. 911

Galvan, an alien born in Mexico, had resided in the United States since 1918. During questioning before immigration authorities in March 1948, he admitted having been a member of the Communist Party from 1946 to 1948. One year later he was served with a deportation warrant for having been a member of an organization which advocated the overthrow of the United States government and distributed material toward that goal. In 1950, Congress passed the Internal Security Act which made membership in the Communist Party a specific ground for deportation. In a second deportation hearing in December 1950, the Hearing Officer ordered Galvan deported on the basis of that provision of the 1950 act and did not make further findings on the original charges. The Hearing Officer's conclusions were then affirmed on administrative review in the Immigration and Naturalization Service, and Galvan's petition for a writ of habeas corpus was dismissed by both the U. S. District and Circuit Courts. Galvan appealed to the Supreme Court, challenging the sufficiency of evidence to support the examiner's conclusions and arguing, in addition, that the act was unconstitutional as applied to him.

Mr. Justice FRANKFURTER, delivered the opinion of the Court.

* * *

On certiorari, petitioner challenged the sufficiency of the evidence to sustain deportation under § 22 of the Internal Security Act of 1950 and attacked the validity of the Act as applied to him. These are issues that raise the constitutionality and construction of the 1950 Act for the first time and so we granted certiorari. * * *

Petitioner's contention that there was not sufficient evidence to support the deportation order brings into question the scope of the word "member" as used by Congress in the enactment of 1950, whereby it required deportation of any alien who at the time of entering the United States, or at any time thereafter, was a "member" of the Communist Party. We are urged to construe the Act as providing for the deportation only of those aliens who joined the Communist Party fully conscious of its advocacy of violence, and who, by so joining, thereby committed themselves to this violent purpose.

But the Act itself appears to preclude an interpretation which would require proof that an alien had joined the Communist Party with full appreciation of its purposes and program. In the same section under which the petitioner's deportation is sought here as a former Communist Party member, there is another provision, subsection (2)(E), which requires the exclusion or deportation of aliens who are "members of or affiliated with" an organization required to register under the Internal Security Act of 1950, "unless such aliens establish that they did not know or have reason to believe at the time they became members of or affiliated

with such an organization * * * that such organization was a Communist organization." 64 Stat. 1007. In describing the purpose of this clause, Senator McCarran, the Act's sponsor, said: "Aliens who were innocent dupes when they joined a Communist Front organization, as distinguished from a Communist political organization [such as the Communist Party], would likewise not ipso facto be excluded or deported." 96 Cong.Rec. 14180. In view of this specific escape provision for members of other organizations, it seems clear that Congress did not exempt "innocent" members of the Communist Party.

While the legislative history of the 1950 Act is not illuminating on the scope of "member," considerable light was shed by authoritative comment in the debates on the statute which Congress enacted in 1951 to correct what it regarded as the unduly expanded interpretation by the Attorney General of "member" under the 1950 Act. 65 Stat. 28. The amendatory statute dealt with certain specific situations which had been brought to the attention of Congress and provided that where aliens had joined a proscribed organization (1) when they were children, (2) by operation of law, or (3) to obtain the necessities of life, they were not to be deemed to have been "members." In explaining the measure, its sponsor, Senator McCarran, stated repeatedly and emphatically that "member" was intended to have the same meaning in the 1950 Act as had been given it by the courts and administrative agencies since 1918, 97 Cong.Rec. 2368–2374. See S.Rep.No. 111, 82d Cong., 1st Sess. 2; H.R.Rep. No. 118, 82d Cong., 1st Sess. 2. To illustrate what "member" did not cover he inserted in the Record a memorandum containing the following language quoted from Colyer v. Skeffington, D.C., 265 F. 17, 72: "Congress could not have intended to authorize the wholesale deportation of aliens who, accidentally, artificially, or unconsciously in appearance only, are found to be members of or affiliated with an organization of whose platform and purposes they have no real knowledge." 97 Cong. Rec. 2373.

This memorandum, as a weighty gloss on what Congress wrote, indicates that Congress did not provide that the three types of situations it enumerated in the 1951 corrective statute should be the only instances where membership is so nominal as to keep an alien out of the deportable class. For example, the circumstances under which the finding of membership was rejected in *Colyer v. Skeffington*, supra, would not have been covered by the specific language in the 1951 Act. In that case, the aliens passed "from one organization into another, supposing the change to be a mere change of name, and that by assenting to membership in the new organization they had not really changed their affiliations or political or economic activities." 265 F. at 72.

On the other hand, the repeated statements that "member" was to have the same meaning under the 1950 Act as previously, preclude an interpretation limited to those who were fully cognizant of the Party's advocacy of violence. For the judicial and administrative decisions prior to 1950 do not exempt aliens who joined an organization unaware of its program and purposes.   *   *   *

It must be concluded, therefore, that support, or even demonstrated knowledge, of the Communist Party's advocacy of violence was not intended to be a prerequisite to deportation. It is enough that the alien joined the Party, aware that he was joining an organization known as the Communist Party which operates as a distinct and active political organization, and that he did so of his own free will. A fair reading of the legislation requires that this scope be given to what Congress enacted in 1950, however severe the consequences and whatever view one may have of the wisdom of the means which Congress employed to meet its desired end.

On this basis, the Hearing Officer's finding that petitioner here was a "member" of the Communist Party must be sustained. Petitioner does not claim that he joined the Party "accidentally, artificially, or unconsciously in appearance only," to use the words in Senator McCarran's memorandum. The two points on which he bases his defense against the deportation order are, first, that he did not join the Party at all, and that if he did join, he was unaware of the Party's true purposes and program. The evidence which must have been believed and relied upon for the Hearing Officer's finding that petitioner was a "member" is that petitioner was asked to join the Party by a man he assumed to be an organizer, that he attended a number of meetings and that he did not apply for citizenship because he feared his Party membership would become known to the authorities. In addition, on the basis of Mrs. Meza's testimony, the Hearing Officer was entitled to conclude that petitioner had been active in the Spanish Speaking Club, and, indeed, one of its officers. Certainly there was sufficient evidence to support a finding of membership. And even if petitioner was unaware of the Party's advocacy of violence, as he attempted to prove, the record does not show a relationship to the Party so nominal as not to make him a "member" within the terms of the Act.

This brings us to petitioner's constitutional attack on the statute. Harisiades v. Shaughnessy, 342 U.S. 580, 72 S.Ct. 512, sustained the constitutionality of the Alien Registration Act of 1940. 54 Stat. 670. That Act made membership in an organization which advocates the overthrow of the Government of the United States by force or violence a ground for deportation, notwithstanding that membership in such organization had terminated before enactment of the statute. Under the 1940 Act, it was necessary to prove in each case, where membership in the Communist Party was made the basis of deportation, that the Party did, in fact, advocate the violent overthrow of the government. The Internal Security Act of 1950 dispensed with the need for such proof. On the basis of extensive investigation Congress made many findings, including that in § 2(1) of the Act that the "Communist movement * * * is a worldwide revolutionary movement whose purpose it is, by treachery, deceit, infiltration into other groups (governmental and otherwise), espionage, sabotage, terrorism, and any other means deemed necessary, to establish a Communist totalitarian dictatorship," 50 U.S.C.A. § 781(1), and made present or former membership in the Communist Party, in and of itself, a ground for deportation. Certainly, we cannot say that this classification by Congress is so baseless as to be violative of due process and therefore beyond the power of Congress.

In this respect—the dispensation with proof of the character of the Communist Party—the present case goes beyond *Harisiades*. But insofar as petitioner's constitutional claim is based on his ignorance that the Party was committed to violence, the same issue was before the Court with respect to at least one of the aliens in *Harisiades*.

The power of Congress over the admission of aliens and their right to remain is necessarily very broad, touching as it does basic aspects of national sovereignty, more particularly our foreign relations and the national security. Nevertheless, considering what it means to deport an alien who legally became part of the American community, and the extent to which, since he is a "person," an alien has the same protection for his life, liberty and property under the Due Process Clause as is afforded to a citizen, deportation without permitting the alien to prove that he was unaware of the Communist Party's advocacy of violence strikes one with a sense of harsh incongruity. If due process bars Congress from enactments that shock the sense of fair play—which is the essence of due process—one is entitled to ask whether it is not beyond the power of Congress to deport an alien who was duped into joining the Communist Party, particularly when his conduct antedated the enactment of the legislation under which his deportation is sought. And this because deportation may, as this Court has said in Ng Fung Ho v. White, 259 U.S. 276, 284, 42 S.Ct. 492, 495, deprive a man "of all that makes life worth living"; and, as it has said in Fong Haw Tan v. Phelan, 333 U.S. 6, 10, 68 S.Ct. 374, 376, "deportation is a drastic measure and at times the equivalent of banishment or exile."

In light of the expansion of the concept of substantive due process as a limitation upon all powers of Congress, even the war power, see Hamilton v. Kentucky Distilleries & Warehouse Co., 251 U.S. 146, 155 , 40 S.Ct. 106, 107, much could be said for the view, were we writing on a clean slate, that the Due Process Clause qualifies the scope of political discretion heretofore recognized as belonging to Congress in regulating the entry and deportation of aliens. And since the intrinsic consequences of deportation are so close to punishment for crime, it might fairly be said also that the *ex post facto* Clause, even though applicable only to punitive legislation should be applied to deportation.

But the slate is not clean. As to the extent of the power of Congress under review, there is not merely "a page of history," * * * but a whole volume. Policies pertaining to the entry of aliens and their right to remain here are peculiarly concerned with the political conduct of government. In the enforcement of these policies, the Executive Branch of the Government must respect the procedural safeguards of due process. * * * But that the formulation of these policies is entrusted exclusively to Congress has become about as firmly imbedded in the legislative and judicial tissues of our body politic as any aspect of our government. And whatever might have been said at an earlier date for applying the *ex post facto* Clause, it has been the unbroken rule of this Court that it has no application to deportation.

We are not prepared to deem ourselves wiser or more sensitive to human rights than our predecessors, especially those who have been most zealous in protecting civil liberties under the Constitution, and must

therefore under our constitutional system recognize congressional power in dealing with aliens, on the basis of which we are unable to find the Act of 1950 unconstitutional. * * *

Judgment affirmed.

Mr. Justice BLACK, with whom Mr. Justice DOUGLAS concurs, dissenting.

Petitioner has lived in this country thirty-six years, having come here from Mexico in 1918 when only seven years of age. He has an American wife to whom he has been married for twenty years, four children all born here, and a stepson who served this country as a paratrooper. Since 1940 petitioner has been a laborer at the Van Camp Sea Food Company in San Diego, California. In 1944 petitioner became a member of the Communist Party. Deciding that he no longer wanted to belong to that party, he got out sometime around 1946 or 1947. As pointed out in the Court's opinion, during the period of his membership the Communist Party functioned "as a distinct and active political organization." * * * Party candidates appeared on California election ballots, and no federal law then frowned on Communist Party political activities. Now in 1954, however, petitioner is to be deported from this country solely because of his past lawful membership in that party. And this is to be done without proof or finding that petitioner knew that the party had any evil purposes or that he agreed with any such purposes that it might have had. On the contrary, there is strong evidence that he was a good, law-abiding man, a steady worker and a devoted husband and father loyal to this country and its form of government.

For joining a lawful political group years ago—an act which he had no possible reason to believe would subject him to the slightest penalty—petitioner now loses his job, his friends, his home, and maybe even his children, who must choose between their father and their native country. Perhaps a legislative act penalizing political activities legal when engaged in is not a bill of attainder. But see United States v. Lovett, 328 U.S. 303, 315–316, 66 S.Ct. 1073, 1078, 1079. Conceivably an Act prescribing exile for prior innocent conduct does not violate the constitutional prohibition of *ex post facto* laws. * * * It may be possible that this deportation order for engaging in political activities does not violate the First Amendment's clear ban against abridgment of political speech and assembly. Maybe it is not even a denial of due process and equal protection of the laws. * * * I am unwilling to say, however, that despite these constitutional safeguards this man may be driven from our land because he joined a political party that California and the Nation then recognized as perfectly legal.

Mr. Justice DOUGLAS, with whom Mr. Justice BLACK concurs, dissenting.

As Mr. Justice BLACK states in his dissent, the only charge against this alien is an act that was lawful when done. I agree that there is, therefore, no constitutional basis for deportation, if aliens, as well as citizens, are to be the beneficiaries of due process of law.

The case might, of course, be different if the past affiliation with Communism now seized upon as the basis for deportation had continued down to this date. But so far as this record shows, the alien Galvan quit the Communist Party at least six years ago. There is not a word in the present record to show that he continued his affiliations with it *sub rosa* or espoused its causes or joined in any of its activities since he ceased to be a member of it.

I cannot agree that because a man was once a Communist, he always must carry the curse. Experience teaches otherwise. It is common knowledge that though some of the leading Socialists of Asia once were Communists, they repudiated the Marxist creed when they experienced its ugly operations, and today are the most effective opponents the Communists know. So far as the present record shows, Galvan may be such a man. Or he may be merely one who transgressed and then returned to a more orthodox political faith. The record is wholly silent about Galvan's present political activities. Only one thing is clear: Galvan is not being punished for what he presently is, nor for an unlawful act, nor for espionage or conspiracy or intrigue against this country. He is being punished for what he once was, for a political faith he briefly expressed over six years ago and then rejected.

This action is hostile to our constitutional standards, as I pointed out in Harisiades v. Shaughnessy, 342 U.S. 580, 598, 72 S.Ct. 512, 523. Aliens who live here in peace, who do not abuse our hospitality, who are law-abiding members of our communities, have the right to due process of law. They too are "persons" within the meaning of the Fifth Amendment. They can be molested by the government in times of peace only when their presence here is hostile to the safety or welfare of the Nation. If they are to be deported, it must be for what they are and do, not for what they once believed.

UNITED STATES v. CURTISS-WRIGHT EXPORT CORP.

Supreme Court of the United States, 1936
299 U.S. 304, 57 S.Ct. 216, 81 L.Ed. 255

Endeavoring to contain the level of fighting between Paraguay and Bolivia over the disputed land of the Chaco, Congress passed a Joint Resolution in May 1934, empowering the President to forbid the sale of munitions by American manufacturers to these nations with such limitations and exceptions as he should determine. The President then issued a proclamation ordering an embargo on the sale of arms and charged the Secretary of State with its enforcement. The embargo was rescinded by executive action approximately a year and a half later.

In January 1936, a federal indictment was returned charging the Curtiss-Wright Corporation with conspiring to sell fifteen machine guns to Bolivia during the embargo period. The United States District Court for the Southern District of New York sustained a demurrer to the indictment (i.e., the court concluded that, had the defendant done what was alleged, no illegal act could result), and the U. S. government appealed.

Mr. Justice SUTHERLAND delivered the opinion of the Court.

* * *

First. It is contended that by the Joint Resolution the going into effect and continued operation of the resolution was conditioned (a) upon the President's judgment as to its beneficial effect upon the re-establishment of peace between the countries engaged in armed conflict in the Chaco; (b) upon the making of a proclamation, which was left to his unfettered discretion, thus constituting an attempted substitution of the President's will for that of Congress; (c) upon the making of a proclamation putting an end to the operation of the resolution, which again was left to the President's unfettered discretion; and (d) further, that the extent of its operation in particular cases was subject to limitation and exception by the President, controlled by no standard. In each of these particulars, appellees urge that Congress abdicated its essential functions and delegated them to the Executive.

Whether, if the Joint Resolution had related solely to internal affairs, it would be open to the challenge that it constituted an unlawful delegation of legislative power to the Executive, we find it unnecessary to determine. The whole aim of the resolution is to affect a situation entirely external to the United States, and falling within the category of foreign affairs. The determination which we are called to make, therefore, is whether the Joint Resolution, as applied to that situation, is vulnerable to attack under the rule that forbids a delegation of the law-making power. In other words, assuming (but not deciding) that the challenged delegation, if it were confined to internal affairs, would be invalid, may it nevertheless be sustained on the ground that its exclusive aim is to afford a remedy for a hurtful condition within foreign territory?

It will contribute to the elucidation of the question if we first consider the differences between the powers of the federal government in respect of foreign or external affairs and those in respect of domestic or internal affairs. That there are differences between them and that these differences are fundamental, may not be doubted.

The two classes of powers are different, both in respect of their origin and their nature. The broad statement that the federal government can exercise no powers except those specifically enumerated in the Constitution, and such implied powers as are necessary and proper to carry into effect the enumerated powers, is categorically true only in respect of our internal affairs. In that field, the primary purpose of the Constitution was to carve from the general mass of legislative powers *then possessed by the states* such portions as it was thought desirable to vest in the federal government, leaving those not included in the enumeration still in the states. * * * That this doctrine applies only to powers which the states had is self-evident. And since the states severally never possessed international powers, such powers could not have been carved from the mass of state powers but obviously were transmitted to the United States from some other source. During the Colonial period, those powers were possessed exclusively by and were entirely under the control of the Crown. By the Declaration of Independence, "the Representatives of the United States of America" declared the United (not the several) Colonies to be free and independent states, and as such to have "full Power to levy War, conclude Peace, contract Alliances, establish Commerce and to do all other Acts and Things which Independent States may of right do."

As a result of the separation from Great Britain by the colonies, acting as a unit, the powers of external sovereignty passed from the Crown not to the colonies severally, but to the colonies in their collective and corporate capacity as the United States of America. Even before the Declaration, the colonies were a unit in foreign affairs, acting through a common agency—namely, the Continental Congress, composed of delegates from the thirteen colonies. That agency exercised the powers of war and peace, raised an army, created a navy, and finally adopted the Declaration of Independence. Rulers come and go; governments end and forms of government change; but sovereignty survives. A political society cannot endure without a supreme will somewhere. Sovereignty is never held in suspense. When, therefore, the external sovereignty of Great Britain in respect of the colonies ceased, it immediately passed to the Union. * * * That fact was given practical application almost at once. The treaty of peace, made on September 3, 1783, was concluded between his Britannic Majesty and the "United States of America." * * *

The Union existed before the Constitution, which was ordained and established among other things to form "a more perfect Union." Prior to that event, it is clear that the Union, declared by the Articles of Confederation to be "perpetual," was the sole possessor of external sovereignty, and in the Union it remained without change save in so far as the Constitution in express terms qualified its exercise. The Framers' Convention was called and exerted its powers upon the irrefutable postulate that though the states were several their people in respect of foreign affairs were one. * * *

* * *

It results that the investment of the federal government with the powers of external sovereignty did not depend upon the affirmative grants of the Constitution. The powers to declare and wage war, to conclude peace, to make treaties, to maintain diplomatic relations with other sovereignties, if they had never been mentioned in the Constitution, would have vested in the federal government as necessary concomitants of nationality. Neither the Constitution nor the laws passed in pursuance of it have any force in foreign territory unless in respect of our own citizens. * * * and operations of the nation in such territory must be governed by treaties, international understandings and compacts, and the principles of international law. As a member of the family of nations, the right and power of the United States in that field are equal to the right and power of the other members of the international family. Otherwise, the United States is not completely sovereign. * * *

* * *

Not only, as we have shown, is the federal power over external affairs in origin and essential character different from that over internal affairs, but participation in the exercise of the power is significantly limited. In this vast external realm with its important, complicated, delicate and manifold problems, the President alone has the power to speak or listen as a representative of the nation. He *makes* treaties with the advice and consent of the Senate; but he alone negotiates. Into the field of

negotiation the Senate cannot intrude; and Congress itself is powerless to invade it. * * *

* * *

It is important to bear in mind that we are here dealing not alone with an authority vested in the President by an exertion of legislative power, but with such an authority plus the very delicate, plenary and exclusive power of the President as the sole organ of the federal government in the field of international relations—a power which does not require as a basis for its exercise an act of Congress, but which, of course, like every other governmental power, must be exercised in subordination to the applicable provisions of the Constitution. It is quite apparent that if, in the maintenance of our international relations, embarrassment—perhaps serious embarrassment—is to be avoided and success for our aims achieved, congressional legislation which is to be made effective through negotiation and inquiry within the international field must often accord to the President a degree of discretion and freedom from statutory restriction which would not be admissible were domestic affairs alone involved. Moreover, he, not Congress, has the better opportunity of knowing the conditions which prevail in foreign countries, and especially is this true in time of war. He has his confidential sources of information. He has his agents in the form of diplomatic, consular and other officials. Secrecy in respect of information gathered by them may be highly necessary, and the premature disclosure of it productive of harmful results. Indeed, so clearly is this true that the first President refused to accede to a request to lay before the House of

Representatives the instructions, correspondence and documents relating to the negotiation of the Jay Treaty—a refusal the wisdom of which was recognized by the House itself and has never since been doubted.
* * *

* * *

The marked difference between foreign affairs and domestic affairs in this respect is recognized by both houses of Congress in the very form of their requisitions for information from the executive departments. In the case of every department except the Department of State, the resolution *directs* the official to furnish the information. In the case of the State Department, dealing with foreign affairs, the President is *requested* to furnish the information "if not incompatible with the public interest." A statement that to furnish the information is not compatible with the public interest rarely, if ever, is questioned.

When the President is to be authorized by legislation to act in respect of a matter intended to affect a situation in foreign territory, the legislator properly bears in mind the important consideration that the form of the President's action—or, indeed, whether he shall act at all—may well depend, among other things, upon the nature of the confidential information which he has or may thereafter receive, or upon the effect which his action may have upon our foreign relations. This consideration, in connection with what we have already said on the subject discloses the unwisdom of requiring Congress in this field of governmental power to lay down narrowly definite standards by which the President is to be governed. As this court said in Mackenzie v. Hare, 239 U.S. 299, 311, 36

S.Ct. 106, 108, "As a government, the United States is invested with all the attributes of sovereignty. As it has the character of nationality it has the powers of nationality, especially those which concern its relations and intercourse with other countries. *We should hesitate long before limiting or embarrassing such powers.*" (Italics supplied.)

In the light of the foregoing observations, it is evident that this court should not be in haste to apply a general rule which will have the effect of condemning legislation like that under review as constituting an unlawful delegation of legislative power. The principles which justify such legislation find overwhelming support in the unbroken legislative practice which has prevailed almost from the inception of the national government to the present day.

* * *

Practically every volume of the United States Statutes contains one or more acts or joint resolutions of Congress authorizing action by the President in respect of subjects affecting foreign relations, which either leave the exercise of the power to his unrestricted judgment, or provide a standard far more general than that which has always been considered requisite with regard to domestic affairs. * * *

* * *

The result of holding that the joint resolution here under attack is void and unenforceable as constituting an unlawful delegation of legislative power would be to stamp this multitude of comparable acts and resolutions as likewise invalid. And while this court may not, and should not, hesitate to declare acts of Congress, however many times repeated, to be unconstitutional if beyond all rational doubt it finds them to be so, an impressive array of legislation such as we have just set forth, enacted by nearly every Congress from the beginning of our national existence to the present day, must be given unusual weight in the process of reaching a correct determination of the problem. A legislative practice such as we have here, evidenced not by only occasional instances, but marked by the movement of a steady stream for a century and a half of time, goes a long way in the direction of proving the presence of unassailable ground for the constitutionality of the practice, to be found in the origin and history of the power involved, or in its nature, or in both combined.

* * *

* * * It is enough to summarize by saying that, both upon principle and in accordance with precedent, we conclude there is sufficient warrant for the broad discretion vested in the President to determine whether the enforcement of the statute will have a beneficial effect upon the re-establishment of peace in the affected countries; whether he shall make proclamation to bring the resolution into operation; whether and when the resolution shall cease to operate and to make proclamation accordingly; and to prescribe limitations and exceptions to which the enforcement of the resolution shall be subject.

* * *

The judgment of the court below must be reversed and the cause remanded for further proceedings in accordance with the foregoing opinion.

It is so ordered.

[Justice McREYNOLDS dissented.]

SOUTH CAROLINA v. KATZENBACH

Supreme Court of the United States, 1966
383 U.S. 301, 86 S.Ct. 803, 15 L.Ed.2d 769

Under the Supreme Court's original jurisdiction South Carolina filed a bill of complaint seeking a declaration as to the constitutionality of several sections of the Voting Rights Act of 1965 and asking that Nicholas Katzenbach, the U. S. Attorney General, be enjoined from their enforcement. The act to which South Carolina objected was designed to identify and remedy racial discrimination in voting. The remedial provisions of the act applied to any state or political subdivision found by the U. S. Attorney Genereal to have maintained a "test or device" (e.g., literacy test, constitution interpretation test, requirement that the voter possess "good moral character," etc.) as a prerequisite to voting on November 1, 1964 and which was determined by the Director of the Census to have less than 50 percent of its voting-age residents registered or voting in the November 1964 election. The act provided, among other remedies, prompt suspension of such tests and devices, the assignment of federal registrars and poll-watchers, and that states identified by the act obtain a declaratory judgment from the U. S. District Court for the District of Columbia approving any new test or device before it could become effective.

South Carolina challenged provisions of the act principally as a violation of the Tenth Amendment though it asserted additional arguments that the act also violated due process and the principle of equal treatment of states. The Attorney General defended on the ground that such legislation was well-founded on Congress's power to legislate pursuant to provisions of the Fifteenth Amendment.

Mr. Chief Justice WARREN delivered the opinion of the Court.

* * *

The Voting Rights Act was designed by Congress to banish the blight of racial discrimination in voting, which has infected the electoral process in parts of our country for nearly a century. The Act creates stringent new remedies for voting discrimination where it persists on a pervasive scale, and in addition the statute strengthens existing remedies for pockets of voting discrimination elsewhere in the country. Congress assumed the power to prescribe these remedies from § 2 of the Fifteenth Amendment, which authorizes the National Legislature to effectuate by "appropriate" measures the constitutional prohibition against racial discrimination in voting. We hold that the sections of the Act which are properly before us are an appropriate means for carrying out Congress' constitutional responsibilities and are consonant with all other provisions of the Constitution. We therefore deny South Carolina's request that enforcement of these sections of the Act be enjoined.

The constitutional propriety of the Voting Rights Act of 1965 must be judged with reference to the historical experience which it reflects. Before enacting the measure, Congress explored with great care the problem of racial discrimination in voting. The House and Senate Committees on the Judiciary each held hearings for nine days and received testimony from a total of 67 witnesses. More than three full days were consumed discussing the bill on the floor of the House, while the debate in the Senate covered 26 days in all. At the close of these deliberations, the verdict of both chambers was overwhelming. The House approved the bill by a vote of 328–74, and the measure passed the Senate by a margin of 79–18.

Two points emerge vividly from the voluminous legislative history of the Act contained in the committee hearings and floor debates. First: Congress felt itself confronted by an insidious and pervasive evil which had been perpetuated in certain parts of our country through unremitting and ingenious defiance of the Constitution. Second: Congress concluded that the unsuccessful remedies which it had prescribed in the past would have to be replaced by sterner and more elaborate measures in order to satisfy the clear commands of the Fifteenth Amendment. We pause here to summarize the majority reports of the House and Senate Committees, which document in considerable detail the factual basis for these reactions by Congress. See H.R. Rep. No. 439, 89th Cong., 1st Sess., 8–16 (hereinafter cited as House Report); S.Rep. No. 162, pt. 3, 89th Cong., 1st Sess., 3–16, U.S.Code Congressional and Administrative News, p. 2437 (hereinafter cited as Senate Report).

The Fifteenth Amendment to the Constitution was ratified in 1870. Promptly thereafter Congress passed the Enforcement Act of 1870, which made it a crime for public officers and private persons to obstruct exercise of the right to vote. The statute was amended in the following year to provide for detailed federal supervision of the electoral process, from registration to the certification of returns. As the years passed and fervor for racial equality waned, enforcement of the laws became spotty and ineffective, and most of their provisions were repealed in 1894. The remnants have had little significance in the recently renewed battle against voting discrimination.

Meanwhile, beginning in 1890, the States of Alabama, Georgia, Louisiana, Mississippi, North Carolina, South Carolina, and Virginia enacted tests still in use which were specifically designed to prevent Negroes from voting. Typically, they made the ability to read and write a registration qualification and also required completion of a registration form. These laws were based on the fact that as of 1890 in each of the named States, more than two-thirds of the adult Negroes were illiterate while less than one-quarter of the adult whites were unable to read or write. At the same time, alternate tests were prescribed in all of the named States to assure that white illiterates would not be deprived of the franchise. These included grandfather clauses, property qualifications, "good character" tests, and the requirement that registrants "understand" or "interpret" certain matter.

The course of subsequent Fifteenth Amendment litigation in this Court demonstrates the variety and persistence of these and similar institutions designed to deprive Negroes of the right to vote. Grandfather clauses were invalidated in Guinn v. United States, 238 U.S. 347, 35 S.Ct. 926. * * * Procedural hurdles were struck down in Lane v. Wilson, 307 U.S. 268, 59 S.Ct. 872. The white primary was outlawed in Smith v. Allwright, 321 U.S. 649, 64 S.Ct. 757, and Terry v. Adams, 345 U.S. 461, 73 S.Ct. 809. Improper challenges were nullified in United States v. Thomas, 362 U.S. 58, 80 S.Ct. 612. Racial gerrymandering was forbidden by Gomillion v. Lightfoot, 364 U.S. 339, 81 S.Ct. 125. Finally, discriminatory application of voting tests was condemned in

* * * Louisiana v. United States, 380 U.S. 145, 85 S.Ct. 817.

According to the evidence in recent Justice Department voting suits, the latter strategem is now the principal method used to bar Negroes from the polls. Discriminatory administration of voting qualifications has been found in all eight Alabama cases, in all nine Louisiana cases, and in all nine Mississippi cases which have gone to final judgment. Moreover, in almost all of these cases, the courts have held that the discrimination was pursuant to a widespread "pattern or practice." White applicants for registration have often been excused altogether from the literacy and understanding tests or have been given easy versions, have received extensive help from voting officials, and have been registered despite serious errors in their answers. Negroes, on the other hand, have typically been required to pass difficult versions of all the tests, without any outside assistance and without the slightest error. The good-morals requirement is so vague and subjective that it has constituted an open invitation to abuse at the hands of voting officials. Negroes obliged to obtain vouchers from registered voters have found it virtually impossible to comply in areas where almost no Negroes are on the rolls.

In recent years, Congress has repeatedly tried to cope with the problem by facilitating case-by-case litigation against voting discrimination. The Civil Rights Act of 1957 authorized the Attorney General to seek injunctions against public and private interference with the right to vote on racial grounds. Perfecting amendments in the Civil Rights Act of 1960 permitted the joinder of States as parties defendant, gave the Attorney General access to local voting records, and authorized courts to register voters in areas of systematic discrimination. Title I of the Civil Rights Act of 1964 expedited the hearing of voting cases before three-judge courts and outlawed some of the tactics used to disqualify Negroes from voting in federal elections.

Despite the earnest efforts of the Justice Department and of many federal judges, these new laws have done little to cure the problem of voting discrimination. According to estimates by the Attorney General during hearings on the Act, registration of voting-age Negroes in Alabama rose only from 14.2% to 19.4% between 1958 and 1964; in Louisiana it barely inched ahead from 31.7% to 31.8% between 1956 and 1965; and in Mississippi it increased only from 4.4% to 6.4% between 1954 and 1964. In each instance, registration of voting-age whites ran roughly 50 percentage points or more ahead of Negro registration.

The previous legislation has proved ineffective for a number of reasons. Voting suits are unusually onerous to prepare, sometimes requiring as many as 6,000 man-hours spent combing through registration records in preparation for trial. Litigation has been exceedingly slow, in part because of the ample opportunities for delay afforded voting officials and others involved in the proceedings. Even when favorable decisions have finally been obtained, some of the States affected have merely switched to discriminatory devices not covered by the federal decrees or have enacted difficult new tests designed to prolong the existing disparity between white and Negro registration. Alternatively, certain local officials have defied and evaded court orders or have simply closed their registration offices to freeze the voting rolls. The provision of the 1960 law authorizing registration by federal officers has had little impact on local maladministration because of its procedural complexities.

* * *

The Voting Rights Act of 1965 reflects Congress' firm intention to rid the country of racial discrimination in voting. The heart of the Act is a complex scheme of stringent remedies aimed at areas where voting discrimination has been most flagrant. Section 4(a)–(d) lays down a formula defining the States and political subdivisions to which these new remedies apply. The first of the remedies, contained in § 4(a), is the suspension of literacy tests and similar voting qualifications for a period of five years from the last occurrence of substantial voting discrimination. Section 5 prescribes a second remedy, the suspension of all new voting regulations pending review by federal authorities to determine whether their use would perpetuate voting discrimination. The third remedy, covered in §§ 6(b), 7, 9, and 13(a), is the assignment of federal examiners on certification by the Attorney General to list qualified applicants who are thereafter entitled to vote in all elections.

Other provisions of the Act prescribe subsidiary cures for persistent voting discrimination. Section 8 authorizes the appointment of federal poll-watchers in places to which federal examiners have already been assigned. Section 10(d) excuses those made eligible to vote in sections of the country covered by § 4(b) of the Act from paying accumulated past poll taxes for state and local elections. Section 12(e) provides for balloting by persons denied access to the polls in areas where federal examiners have been appointed.

The remaining remedial portions of the Act are aimed at voting discrimination in any area of the country where it may occur. Section 2 broadly prohibits the use of voting rules to abridge exercise of the franchise on racial grounds. Sections 3, 6(a), and 13(b) strengthen existing procedures for attacking voting discrimination by means of litigation. Section 4(e) excuses citizens educated in American schools conducted in a foreign language from passing English-language literacy tests. Section 10(a)–(c) facilitates constitutional litigation challenging the imposition of all poll taxes for state and local elections. Sections 11 and 12(a)–(d) authorize civil and criminal sanctions against interference with the exercise of rights guaranteed by the Act.

* * *

[In the course of assessing whether those portions of the act before it for review in this case were valid enactments stemming from Congress' power to enforce the Fifteenth Amendment, the Court applied the same test of constitutionality as that governing the Congress' exercise of its Article I powers. See *Katzenbach* v. *Morgan*, and *McCulloch* v. *Maryland* generally.]

After enduring nearly a century of widespread resistance to the Fifteenth Amendment, Congress has marshalled an array of potent weapons against the evil, with authority in the Attorney General to employ them effectively. Many of the areas directly affected by this development have indicated their willingness to abide by any restraints legitimately imposed upon them. We here hold that the portions of the Voting Rights Act properly before us are a valid means for carrying out the commands of the Fifteenth Amendment. Hopefully, millions of non-white Americans will now be able to participate for the first time on an equal basis in the government under which they live. We may finally look forward to the day when truly "[t]he right of citizens of the United States to vote shall not be denied or abridged by the United States or by any State on account of race, color, or previous condition of servitude."

The bill of complaint is dismissed.

Bill dismissed.

Mr. Justice BLACK, concurring and dissenting.

I agree with substantially all of the Court's opinion sustaining the power of Congress under § 2 of the Fifteenth Amendment to suspend state literacy tests and similar voting qualifications and to authorize the Attorney General to secure the appointment of federal examiners to register qualified voters in various sections of the country. Section 1 of the Fifteenth Amendment provides that "The right of citizens of the United States to vote shall not be denied or abridged by the United States or by any State on account of race, color, or previous condition of servitude." In addition to this unequivocal command to the States and the Federal Government that no citizen shall have his right to vote denied or abridged because of race or color, § 2 of the Amendment unmistakably gives Congress specific power to go further and pass appropriate legislation to protect this right to vote against any method of abridgement no matter how subtle. Compare my dissenting opinion in Bell v. State of Maryland, 378 U.S. 226, 318, 84 S.Ct. 1814, 1864. I have no doubt whatever as to the power of Congress under § 2 to enact the provisions of the Voting Rights Act of 1965 dealing with the suspension of state voting tests that have been used as notorious means to deny and abridge voting rights on racial grounds. This same congressional power necessarily exists to authorize appointment of federal examiners. I also agree with the judgment of the Court upholding § 4(b) of the Act which sets out a formula for determining when and where the major remedial sections of the Act take effect. I reach this conclusion, however, for a somewhat different reason than that stated by the Court, which is that "the coverage formula is rational in both practice and theory." I do not base my conclusion on the fact that the formula is rational, for it is enough for me that Congress by creating this formula has merely exercised its hitherto unquestioned and undisputed power to decide when, where, and upon what conditons its laws shall go into effect. By stating in specific detail that the major remedial sections of the Act are to be applied in areas where certain conditions exist, and by granting the Attorney General and the Director of the Census unreviewable power to make the mechanical determination of which areas come within the formula of § 4(b), I believe that Congress has acted within its established power to set out preconditions upon which the Act is to go into effect.   *   *   *

Though, as I have said, I agree with most of the Court's conclusions, I dissent from its holding that every part of § 5 of the Act is constitutional. Section 4(a), to which § 5 is linked, suspends for five years all literacy tests and similar devices in those States coming within the formula of § 4(b). Section 5 goes on to provide that a State covered by § 4(b) can in no way amend its constitution or laws relating to voting without first trying to persuade the Attorney General of the United States or the Federal District Court for the District of Columbia that the new proposed laws do not have the purpose and will not have the effect of denying the right to vote to citizens on account of their race or color. I think this section is unconstitutional on at least two grounds.

(a) The Constitution gives federal courts jurisdiction over cases and controversies only. If it can be said that any case or controversy arises under this section which gives the District Court for the District of Columbia jurisdiction to approve or reject state laws or constitutional amendments, then the case or controversy must be between a State and the United States Government. But it is hard for me to believe that a justiciable controversy can arise in the constitutional sense from a desire by the United States Government or some of its officials to determine in advance what legislative provisions a State may enact or what constitutional amendments it may adopt. If this dispute between the Federal Government and the States amounts to a case or controversy it is a far cry from the traditional constitutional notion of a case or controversy as a dispute over the meaning of enforceable laws or the manner in which they are applied. And if by this section Congress has created a case or controversy, and I do not believe it has, then it seems to me that the most appropriate judicial forum for settling these important questions is this Court acting under its original Art. III, § 2, jurisdiction to try cases in which a State is a party. At least a trial in this Court would treat the

States with the dignity to which they should be entitled as constituent members of our Federal Union.

*   *   *

(b) My second and more basic objection to § 5 is that Congress has here exercised its power under § 2 of the Fifteenth Amendment through the adoption of means that conflict with the most basic principles of the Constitution. As the Court says the limitations of the power granted under § 2 are the same as the limitations imposed on the exercise of any of the powers expressly granted Congress by the Constitution. The classic formulation of these constitutional limitations was stated by Chief Justice Marshall when he said in McCulloch v. State of Maryland, 4 Wheat. 316, 421, 4 L.Ed. 579, "Let the end be legitimate, let it be within the scope of the constitution, and all means which are appropriate, which are plainly adapted to that end, *which are not prohibited, but consist with the letter and spirit of the constitution*, are constitutional." (Emphasis added.) Section 5, by providing that some of the States cannot pass state laws or adopt state constitutional amendments without first being compelled to beg federal authorities to approve their policies, so distorts our constitutional structure of government as to render any distinction drawn in the Constitution between state and federal power almost meaningless. One of the most basic premises upon which our structure of government was founded was that the Federal Government was to have certain specific and limited powers and no others, and all other power was to be reserved either "to the States respectively, or to the people."

Certainly if all the provisions of our Constitution which limit the power of the Federal Government and reserve other power to the States are to mean anything, they mean at least that the States have power to pass laws and amend their constitutions without first sending their officials hundreds of miles away to beg federal authorities to approve them. Moreover, it seems to me that § 5 which gives federal officials power to veto state laws they do not like is in direct conflict with the clear command of our Constitution that "The United States shall guarantee to every State in this Union a Republican Form of Government." I cannot help but believe that the inevitable effect of any such law which forces any one of the States to entreat federal authorities in faraway places for approval of local laws before they can become effective is to create the impression that the State or States treated in this way are little more than conquered provinces. *   *   *

*   *   *

In this and other prior Acts Congress has quite properly vested the Attorney General with extremely broad power to protect voting rights of citizens against discrimination on account of race or color. Section 5 viewed in this context is of very minor importance and in my judgment is likely to serve more as an irritant to the States than as an aid to the enforcement of the Act. I would hold § 5 invalid for the reasons stated above with full confidence that the Attorney General has ample power to give vigorous, expeditious and effective protection to the voting rights of all citizens.

KATZENBACH v. MORGAN

Supreme Court of the United States, 1966
384 U.S. 641, 86 S.Ct. 1717, 16 L.Ed.2d 828

The 1965 Voting Rights Act contained a provision that no individual who had successfully completed the sixth grade in a Puerto Rican public school or in a private school accredited by that territory in which the language used for instruction was other than English could be denied the right to vote simply because he could not read or write English. In an effort to bar the consequent enfranchisement of several hundred thousand New York City residents who had migrated from Puerto Rico, Morgan, a registered voter of New York City, sought an injunction prohibiting the U. S. Attorney General and the New York City Board of Elections from complying with the act. The district court, finding for Morgan, held that this provision of the act usurped the powers reserved to the states and therefore contravened the Tenth Amendment. On appeal, the Attorney General reasserted his argument for its validity as a proper exercise of Congress's power to legislate pursuant to the Fourteenth Amendment.

Mr. Justice BRENNAN delivered the opinion of the Court.

* * *

Under the distribution of powers effected by the Constitution, the States establish qualifications for voting for state officers, and the qualifications established by the States for voting for members of the most numerous branch of the state legislature also determine who may vote for United States Representatives and Senators, Art. I, § 2; Seventeenth Amendment; Ex parte Yarbrough, 110 U.S. 651, 663. But, of course, the States have no power to grant or withhold the franchise on conditions that are forbidden by the Fourteenth Amendment, or any other provision of the Constitution. Such exercises of state power are no more immune to the limitations of the Fourteenth Amendment than any other state action. The Equal Protection Clause itself has been held to forbid some state laws that restrict the right to vote.

The Attorney General of the State of New York argues that an exercise of congressional power under § 5 of the Fourteenth Amendment that prohibits the enforcement of a state law can only be sustained if the judicial branch determines that the state law is prohibited by the provisions of the Amendment that Congress sought to enforce. More specifically, he urges that § 4(e) cannot be sustained as appropriate legislation to enforce the Equal Protection Clause unless the judiciary decides—even with the guidance of a congressional judgment—that the application of the English literacy requirement prohibited by § 4(e) is forbidden by the Equal Protection Clause itself. We disagree. Neither the language nor history of § 5 supports such a construction. As was said with regard to § 5 in Ex parte Com. of Virginia, 100 U.S. 339, 345, 25 L.Ed. 676, "It is the power of Congress which has been enlarged. Congress is authorized to *enforce* the prohibitions by appropriate legislation. Some legislation is contemplated to make the amendments fully effective." A construction of § 5 that would require a judicial determination that the enforcement of the state law precluded by Congress violated the Amendment, as a condition of sustaining the congressional enactment, would depreciate both congressional resourcefulness and congressional responsibility for implementing the Amendment. It would confine the legislative power in this context to the insignificant role of abrogating only those state laws that the judicial branch was prepared to adjudge unconstitutional, or of merely informing the judgment of the judiciary by particularizing the "majestic generalities" of § 1 of the Amendment. * * *

Thus our task in this case is not to determine whether the New York English literacy requirement as applied to deny the right to vote to a person who successfully completed the sixth grade in a Puerto Rican school violates the Equal Protection Clause. Accordingly, our decision in Lassiter v. Northampton County Bd. of Election, 360 U.S. 45, 79 S.Ct. 985, sustaining the North Carolina English literacy requirement as not in all circumstances prohibited by the first sections of the Fourteenth and Fifteenth Amendments, is inapposite. * * * *Lassiter* did not present the question before us here: Without regard to whether the judiciary would find that the Equal Protection Clause itself nullifies New York's English literacy requirement as so applied, could Congress prohibit the enforcement of the state law by legislating under § 5 of the Fourteenth Amendment? In answering this question, our task is limited to determining whether such legislation is, as required by § 5, appropriate legislation to enforce the Equal Protection Clause.

By including § 5 the draftsmen sought to grant to Congress, by a specific provision applicable to the Fourteenth Amendment, the same broad powers expressed in the Necessary and Proper Clause, Art. I, § 8, cl. 18. * * *

* * *

We therefore proceed to the consideration whether § 4(e) is "appropriate legislation" to enforce the Equal Protection Clause, that is, under the *McCulloch* v. *Maryland* standard, whether § 4(e) may be regarded as an enactment to enforce the Equal Protection Clause, whether it is "plainly adapted to that end" and whether it is not prohibited by but is consistent with "the letter and spirit of the constitution."

There can be no doubt that § 4(e) may be regarded as an enactment to enforce the Equal Protection Clause. Congress explicitly declared that it enacted § 4(e) "to secure the rights under the fourteenth amendment of persons educated in American-flag schools in which the predominant classroom language was other than English." The persons referred to include those who have migrated from the Commonwealth of Puerto Rico to New York and who have been denied the right to vote because of their inability to read and write English, and the Fourteenth Amendment rights referred to include those emanating from the Equal Protection Clause. More specifically, § 4(e) may be viewed as a measure to secure for the Puerto Rican community residing in New York nondiscriminatory treatment by government—both in the imposition of voting qualifications and the provision or administration of governmental services, such as public schools, public housing and law enforcement.

* * * It was for Congress, as the branch that made this judgment, to assess and weigh the various conflicting considerations—the risk or

pervasiveness of the discrimination in governmental services, the effectiveness of eliminating the state restriction on the right to vote as a means of dealing with the evil, the adequacy or availability of alternative remedies, and the nature and significance of the state interests that would be affected by the nullification of the English literacy requirement as applied to residents who have successfully completed the sixth grade in a Puerto Rican school. It is not for us to review the congressional resolution of these factors. It is enough that we be able to perceive a basis upon which the Congress might resolve the conflict as it did. There plainly was such a basis to support § 4(e) in the application in question in this case. Any contrary conclusion would require us to be blind to the realities familiar to the legislators.

The result is no different if we confine our inquiry to the question whether § 4(e) was merely legislation aimed at the elimination of an invidious discrimination in establishing voter qualifications. We are told that New York's English literacy requirement originated in the desire to provide an incentive for non-English speaking immigrants to learn the English language and in order to assure the intelligent exercise of the franchise. Yet Congress might well have questioned, in light of the many exemptions provided, and some evidence suggesting that prejudice played a prominent role in the enactment of the requirement, whether these were actually the interests being served. Congress might have also questioned whether denial of a right deemed so precious and fundamental in our society was a necessary or appropriate means of encouraging persons to learn

English, or of furthering the goal of an intelligent exercise of the franchise. Finally, Congress might well have concluded that as a means of furthering the intelligent exercise of the franchise, an ability to read or understand Spanish is as effective as ability to read English for those to whom Spanish-language newspapers and Spanish-language radio and television programs are available to inform them of election issues and governmental affairs. Since Congress undertook to legislate so as to preclude the enforcement of the state law, and did so in the context of a general appraisal of literacy requirements for voting, see *State of South Carolina* v. *Katzenbach*, supra, to which it brought a specially informed legislative competence, it was Congress' prerogative to weigh these competing considerations. Here again, it is enough that we perceive a basis upon which Congress might predicate a judgment that the application of New York's English literacy requirement to deny the right to vote to a person with a sixth grade education in Puerto Rican schools in which the language of instruction was other than English constituted an invidious discrimination in violation of the Equal Protection Clause.

There remains the question whether the congressional remedies adopted in § 4(e) constitute means which are not prohibited by, but are consistent "with the letter and spirit of the constitution." The only respect in which appellees contend that § 4(e) fails in this regard is that the section itself works an invidious discrimination in violation of the Fifth Amendment by prohibiting the enforcement of the English literacy requirement only for those educated in American-flag schools (schools located within United States jurisdiction) in which the language of instruction was other than English, and not for those educated in schools beyond the territorial limits of the United States in which the language of instruction was also other than English. This is not a complaint that Congress, in enacting § 4(e), has unconstitutionally denied or diluted anyone's right to vote but rather that Congress violated the Constitution by not extending the relief effected in § 4(e) to those educated in non-American-flag schools. We need not pause to determine whether appellees have a sufficient personal interest to have § 4(e) invalidated on this ground * * * since the argument, in our view, falls on the merits.

Section 4(e) does not restrict or deny the franchise but in effect extends the franchise to persons who otherwise would be denied it by state law. Thus we need not decide whether a state literacy law conditioning the right to vote on achieving a certain level of education in an American-flag school (regardless of the language of instruction) discriminates invidiously against those educated in non-American-flag schools. We need only decide whether the challenged limitation on the relief effected in § 4(e) was permissible. In deciding that question, the principle that calls for the closest scrutiny of distinctions in laws *denying* fundamental rights is inapplicable; for the distinction challenged by appellees is presented only as a limitation on a reform measure aimed at eliminating an existing barrier to the exercise of the franchise. Rather, in deciding the constitutional propriety of the limitations in such a reform measure we are guided by the familiar principles that a "statute is not invalid under the Constitution because it might have gone farther than it did," Roschen v. Ward, 279 U.S. 337, 339, 49 S.Ct. 336, that a legislature need not "strike at all evils at the same time." Semler v. Oregon State Board of Dental Examiners, 294 U.S. 608, 610, 55 S.Ct. 570, 571 and that "reform may take one step at a time, addressing itself to the phase of the problem which seems most acute to the legislative mind," Williamson v. Lee Optical Co., 348 U.S. 483, 489, 75 S.Ct. 461, 465.

Guided by these principles, we are satisfied that appellees' challenge to this limitation in § 4(e) is without merit. In the context of the case before us, the congressional choice to limit the relief effected in § 4(e) may, for example, reflect Congress' greater familiarity with the quality of instruction in American-flag schools, a recognition of the unique historic relationship between the Congress and the Commonwealth of Puerto Rico, an awareness of the Federal Government's acceptance of the desirability of the use of Spanish as the language of instruction in Commonwealth schools, and the fact that Congress has fostered policies encouraging migration from the Commonwealth to the States. We have no occasion to determine in this case whether such factors would justify a similar distinction embodied in a voting-qualification law that denied the franchise to persons educated in non-American-flag schools. We hold only that the limitation on relief effected in § 4(e) does not constitute a forbidden discrimination since these factors might well have been the basis for the decision of Congress to go "no farther than it did."

We therefore conclude that § 4(e), in the application challenged in this case, is appropriate legislation to enforce the Equal Protection Clause and that the judgment of the District Court must be and hereby is reversed.

Reversed.

Mr. Justice HARLAN, whom Mr. Justice STEWART joins, dissenting.

* * *

[W]e have here not a matter of giving deference to a congressional estimate, based on its determination of legislative facts, bearing upon the validity *vel non* of a statute, but rather what can at most be called a legislative announcement that Congress believes a state law to entail an unconstitutional deprivation of equal protection. Although this kind of declaration is of course entitled to the most respectful consideration, coming as it does from a concurrent branch and one that is knowledgeable in matters of popular political participation. I do not believe it lessens our responsibility to decide the fundamental issue of whether in fact the state enactment violates federal constitutional rights.

* * * Federal authority, legislative no less than judicial, does not intrude unless there has been a denial by state action of Fourteenth Amendment limitations, in this instance a denial of equal protection. At least in the area of primary state concern a state statute that passes constitutional muster under the judicial standard of rationality should not be permitted to be set at naught by a mere contrary congressional pronouncement unsupported by a legislative record justifying that conclusion.

To deny the effectiveness of this congressional enactment is not of course to disparage Congress' exertion of authority in the field of civil rights; it is simply to recognize that the Legislative Branch like the other branches of federal authority is subject to the governmental boundaries set by the Constitution. To hold, on this record, that § 4(e) overrides the New York literacy requirement seems to me tantamount to allowing the Fourteenth Amendment to swallow the State's constitutionally ordained primary authority in this field. For if Congress by what, as here, amounts to mere *ipse dixit* [a bare, unproved assertion resting only on authority] can set that otherwise permissible requirement partially at naught I see no reason why it could not also substitute its judgment for that of the States in other fields of their exclusive primary competence as well.

* * *

In Pennhurst State School and Hospital v. Halderman, 451 U.S. 1, 101 S.Ct. 1531 (1981), the Court had occasion once again to address the scope of Congress's power to enforce guarantees provided by the Fourteenth Amendment. Justice Rehnquist's opinion for the Court dealt with both Congress's power under § 5 of the Fourteenth Amendment and its Article I spending power in relevant part as follows: Although the "bill of rights" provision, 42 U.S.C.A. § 6010(1) and (2), of the Developmentally Disabled Assistance and Bill of Rights Act which provides financial assistance to participating states to aid in the creation of programs to care for and treat certain mental patients, states that mentally retarded persons "have a right to appropriate treatment, services, and habilitation" in "the setting that is least restrictive of * * * personal liberty," interpretation of neither the Act nor constitutional provisions upon which the federal appeals court below held it to be based requires the closing of a state mental hospital where conditions were alleged to be unsanitary, inhumane, and dangerous or mandates that "community living arrangements" be established for its patients because these would be less restrictive of individual liberty. The federal appellate court below held that Congress had relied on both its enforcement power under the Fourteenth Amendment and its Article I Spending Power. As compared with existing legislation based on § 5 of the Fourteenth Amendment—for example, that dealing with voting rights— which prohibited certain kinds of conduct, "the case for inferring [congressional] intent is at its weakest where, as here, the rights asserted impose *affirmative* obligations on the States to fund certain services, since we may assume that Congress will not implicitly attempt to impose massive financial obligations on the States." And, with respect to Congress's Spending Power, grant-in-aid legislation constitutes a contract wherein, in return for federal funds, states agree to comply with federally-imposed conditions; "if Congress intends to impose a condition on the grant of federal moneys, it must do so unambiguously," especially where, as here, state obligations are potentially indeterminate, otherwise the states cannot be said "to exercise their choice knowingly, cognizant of the consequences of their participation." The plain language and legislative history of § 6010 disclose no congressional intent to condition funding upon state agreement to guarantee the specific rights mentioned therein.

Justice White, in a dissenting opinion in which Justices Brennan and Marshall joined, concluded that the majority had made "far too much" of the fact that Congress did not rely upon § 5 of the Fourteenth Amendment. Paraphrasing Justice White: The simple fact is that "Nothing in the statutory language refers to the Fourteenth Amendment," and since § 6010 "was but one part of a bill whose underlying purpose was to extend and modify an existing federal-state grant program, * * * all objective considerations * * * suggest that Congress enacted it pursuant to its spending clause powers." Furthermore, "[t]he language and scheme of the Act make it plain * * * that Congress intended § 6010, although couched in terms of rights, to serve as requirements that the participating States must observe in receiving federal funds under the provisions of the Act." In short, "Congress intended § 6010 to do more than *suggest* that the States act in a particular manner * * *." (Emphasis added.)

JACOBSON v. MASSACHUSETTS

Supreme Court of the United States, 1905
197 U.S. 11, 25 S.Ct. 358, 49 L.Ed. 643

Pursuant to an act passed by the Massachusetts legislature, the city of Cambridge enacted a municipal ordinance requiring all the inhabitants of the city to be vaccinated against smallpox. The state law also contained a provision punishing violators by fining them five dollars. Jacobson refused to comply with the ordinance, and he was tried and convicted. Jacobson asserted that the statute and the ordinance violated his rights under the Fourteenth Amendment. The state defended on the ground that such an act was a legitimate exercise of its police power. The Massachusetts Supreme Judicial Court sustained the legislation, and Jacobson appealed to the U. S. Supreme Court.

Mr. Justice HARLAN delivered the opinion of the court:

This case involves the validity, under the Constitution of the United States, of certain provisions in the statutes of Massachusetts relating to vaccination.

* * *

We pass without extended discussion the suggestion that the particular section of the statute of Massachusetts now in question (§ 137, chap. 75) is in derogation of rights secured by the preamble of the Constitution of the United States. Although that preamble indicates the general purposes for which the people ordained and established the Constitution, it has never been regarded as the source of any substantive power conferred on the government of the United States, or on any of its departments. Such powers embrace only those expressly granted in the body of the Constitution, and such as may be implied from those so granted. Although, therefore, one of the declared objects of the Constitution was to secure the blessings of liberty to all under the sovereign jurisdiction and authority of the United States, no power can be exerted to that end by the United States, unless, apart from the preamble, it be found in some express delegation of power, or in some power to be properly implied therefrom. 1 Story, Const. § 462.

* * *

* * * Is the statute, so construed, therefore, inconsistent with the liberty which the Constitution of the United States secures to every person against deprivation by the state?

The authority of the state to enact this statute is to be referred to what is commonly called the police power,—a power which the state did not surrender when becoming a member of the Union under the Constitution. Although this court has refrained from any attempt to define the limits of that power, yet it has distinctly recognized the authority of a state to enact quarantine laws and "health laws of every description"; indeed, all laws that relate to matters completely within its territory and which do not by their necessary operation affect the people of other states. According to settled principles, the police power of a state must be held to embrace, at least, such reasonable regulations established directly by legislative enactment as will protect the public health and the public safety.   * * *

* * *

We come, then, to inquire whether any right given or secured by the Constitution is invaded by the statute as interpreted by the state court. The defendant insists that his liberty is invaded when the state subjects him to fine or imprisonment for neglecting or refusing to submit to vaccination; that a compulsory vaccination law is unreasonable, arbitrary, and oppressive, and, therefore, hostile to the inherent right of every free man to care for his own body and health in such way as to him seems best; and that the execution of such a law against one who objects to vaccination no matter for what reason, is nothing short of an assault upon his person. But the liberty secured by the Constitution of the United States to every person within its jurisdiction does not import an absolute right in each person to be, at all times and in all circumstances, wholly freed from restraint. There are manifold restraints to which every person is necessarily subject for the common good. On any other basis organized society could not exist with safety to its members. Society based on the rule that each one is a law unto himself would soon be confronted with disorder and anarchy. Real liberty for all could not exist under the operation of a principle which recognizes the right of each individual person to use his own, whether in respect of his person or his property, regardless of the injury that may be done to others. This court has more than once recognized it as a fundamental principle that "persons and property are subjected to all kinds of restraints and burdens in order to secure the general comfort, health, and prosperity of the state; of the perfect right of the legislature to do which no question ever was, or upon acknowledged general principles ever can be made, so far as natural persons are concerned." * * *

* * *

Applying these principles to the present case, it is to be observed that the legislature of Massachusetts required the inhabitants of a city or town to be vaccinated only when in the opinion of the board of health, that was necessary for the public health or the public safety. The authority to determine for all what ought to be done in such an emergency must have been lodged somewhere or in some body; and surely it was appropriate for the legislature to refer that question, in the first instance, to a board of health composed of persons residing in the locality affected, and appointed, presumably, because of their fitness to determine such questions. To invest such a body with authority over such matters was not an unusual,

nor an unreasonable or arbitrary, requirement. Upon the principle of self-defense, of paramount necessity, a community has the right to protect itself against an epidemic of disease which threatens the safety of its members. * * * There is, of course, a sphere within which the individual may assert the supremacy of his own will, and rightfully dispute the authority of any human government,—especially of any free government existing under a written constitution,—to interfere with the exercise of that will. But it is equally true that in every well-ordered society charged with the duty of conserving the safety of its members the rights of the individual in respect of his liberty may at times, under the pressure of great dangers, be subjected to such restraint, to be enforced by reasonable regulations, as the safety of the general public may demand. * * *

* * *

Looking at the propositions embodied in the defendant's rejected offers of proof, it is clear that they are more formidable by their number than by their inherent value. Those offers in the main seem to have had no purpose except to state the general theory of those of the medical profession who attach little or no value to vaccination as a means of preventing the spread of smallpox, or who think that vaccination causes other diseases of the body. What everybody knows the court must know, and therefore the state court judicially knew, as this court knows, that an opposite theory accords with the common belief, and is maintained by high medical authority. We must assume that, when the statute in question was passed, the legislature of Massachusetts was not unaware of these opposing theories, and was compelled, of necessity, to choose between them. It was not compelled to commit a matter involving the public health and safety to the final decision of a court or jury. It is no part of the function of a court or a jury to determine which one of two modes was likely to be the most effective for the protection of the public against disease. That was for the legislative department to determine in the light of all the information it had or could obtain. It could not properly abdicate its function to guard the public health and safety. The state legislature proceeded upon the theory which recognized vaccination as at least an effective, if not the best-known, way in which to meet and suppress the evils of a smallpox epidemic that imperiled an entire population. Upon what sound principles as to the relations existing between the different departments of government can the court review this action of the legislature? If there is any such power in the judiciary to review legislative action in respect of a matter affecting the general welfare, it can only be when that which the legislature has done comes within the rule that, if a statute purporting to have been enacted to protect the public health, the public morals, or the public safety, has no real or substantial relation to those objects, or is beyond all question, a plain, palpable invasion of rights secured by the fundamental law, it is the duty of the courts to so adjudge, and thereby give effect to the Constitution. * * *

Whatever may be thought of the expediency of this statute, it cannot be affirmed to be, beyond question, in palpable conflict with the Constitution. Nor, in view of the methods employed to stamp out the disease of smallpox, can anyone confidently assert that the means prescribed by the state to that end has no real or substantial relation to the protection of the public health and the public safety. Such an assertion would not be consistent with the experience of this and other countries whose authorities have dealt with the disease of smallpox. And the principle of vaccination as a means to prevent the spread of smallpox has been enforced in many states by statutes making the vaccination of children a condition of their right to enter or remain in public schools. * * *

* * *

We are not prepared to hold that a minority, residing or remaining in any city or town where smallpox is prevalent, and enjoying the general protection afforded by an organized local government, may thus defy the will of its constituted authorities, acting in good faith for all, under the legislative sanction of the state. If such be the privilege of a minority, then a like privilege would belong to each individual of the community, and the spectacle would be presented of the welfare and safety of an entire population being subordinated to the notions of a single individual who chooses to remain a part of that population. We are unwilling to hold it to be an element in the liberty secured by the Constitution of the United States that one person, or a minority of persons, residing in any community and enjoying the benefits of its local government, should have the power thus to dominate the majority when supported in their action by the authority of the state. While this court should guard with firmness every right appertaining to life, liberty, or property as secured to the individual by the supreme law of the land, it is of the last importance that it should not invade the domain of local authority except when it is plainly necessary to do so in order to enforce that law. The safety and the health of the people of Massachusetts are, in the first instance, for that commonwealth to guard and protect. They are matters that do not ordinarily concern the national government. So far as they can be reached by any government, they depend, primarily, upon such action as the state, in its wisdom, may take; and we do not perceive that this legislation has invaded any right secured by the Federal Constitution.

* * *

* * *

The judgment of the court below must be affirmed.

It is so ordered.

[Justice BREWER and Justice PECKHAM dissented.]

b. DELEGATION OF LEGISLATIVE POWER

HAMPTON & CO. v. UNITED STATES

Supreme Court of the United States, 1928
276 U.S. 394, 48 S.Ct. 348, 72 L.Ed. 624

Section 315(a) of Title III of the Tariff Act of 1922 empowered the President to increase or decrease duties imposed by the act in order to equalize the differences in production cost of articles produced in the United States and in foreign countries. In 1924, after hearings by the United States Tariff Commission, the President issued a proclamation raising the four cents per pound duty on barium dioxide to six cents per pound. J. W. Hampton, Jr. and Company, subject to the duty, challenged the constitutionality of Section 315 as an invalid delegation of legislative power to the President. The Hampton Company appealed to the Supreme Court from adverse decisions in the lower federal courts.

Mr. Chief Justice TAFT delivered the opinion of the Court.

* * *

The issue here is as to the constitutionality of § 315, upon which depends the authority for the proclamation of the President and for two of the six cents per pound duty collected from the petitioner. The contention of the taxpayers is twofold—first, they argue that the section is invalid in that it is a delegation to the President of the legislative power, which by Article I, § 1 of the Constitution, is vested in Congress, the power being that declared in § 8 of Article I, that the Congress shall have power to lay and collect taxes, duties, imposts and excises. The second objection is that, as § 315 was enacted with the avowed intent and for the purpose of protecting the industries of the United States, it is invalid because the Constitution gives power to lay such taxes only for revenue.

First. It seems clear what Congress intended by § 315. Its plan was to secure by law the imposition of customs duties on articles of imported merchandise which should equal the difference between the cost of producing in a foreign country the articles in question and laying them down for sale in the United States, and the cost of producing and selling like or similar articles in the United States, so that the duties not only secure revenue but at the same time enable domestic producers to compete on terms of equality with foreign producers in the markets of the United States. It may be that it is difficult to fix with exactness this difference, but the difference which is sought in the statute is perfectly clear and perfectly intelligible. Because of the difficulty in practically determining what that difference is, Congress seems to have doubted that the information in its possession was such as to enable it to make the adjustment accurately, and also to have apprehended that with changing conditions the difference might vary in such a way that some readjustments would be necessary to give effect to the principle on which the statute proceeds. To avoid such difficulties, Congress adopted in § 315 the method of describing with clearness what its policy and plan was and then authorizing a member of the executive branch to carry out this policy and plan, and to find the changing difference from time to time, and to make the adjustments necessary to conform the duties to the standard underlying that policy and plan. As it was a matter of great importance, it concluded to give by statute to the President, the chief of the executive branch, the function of determining the difference as it might vary. He was provided with a body of investigators who were to assist him in obtaining needed data and ascertaining the facts justifying readjustments. There was no specific provision by which action by the President might be invoked under this Act, but it was presumed that the President would through this body of advisers keep himself advised of the necessity for investigation or change, and then

would proceed to pursue his duties under the Act and reach such conclusion as he might find justified by the investigation, and proclaim the same if necessary.

The Tariff Commission does not itself fix duties, but before the President reaches a conclusion on the subject of investigation, the Tariff Commission must make an investigation and in doing so must give notice to all parties interested and an opportunity to adduce evidence and to be heard.

The well-known maxim *"Delegata potestas non potest delegari,"* [an agent cannot redelegate his powers] applicable to the law of agency in the general and common law, is well understood and has had wider application in the construction of our Federal and State Constitutions than it has in private law. The Federal Constitution and State Constitutions of this country divide the governmental power into three branches. The first is the legislative, the second is the executive, and the third is the judicial, and the rule is that in the actual administration of the government Congress or the Legislature should exercise the legislative power, the President or the State executive, the Governor, the executive power, and the Courts or the judiciary the judicial power, and in carrying out that constitutional division into three branches it is a breach of the National fundamental law if Congress gives up its legislative power and transfers it to the President, or to the Judicial branch, or if by law it attempts to invest itself or its members with either executive power or judicial power. This is not to say that the three branches are not co-ordinate parts of one government and that each in the field of its duties may not invoke the action of the two other branches in so far as the action invoked shall not be an assumption of the constitutional field of action of another branch. In determining what it may do in seeking assistance from another branch, the extent and character of that assistance must be fixed according to common sense and the inherent necessities of the governmental co-ordination.

The field of Congress involves all and many varieties of legislative action, and Congress has found it frequently necessary to use officers of the Executive Branch, within defined limits, to secure the exact effect intended by its acts of legislation, by vesting discretion in such officers to make public regulations interpreting a statute and directing the details of its execution, even to the extent of providing for penalizing a breach of such regulations. * * *

Congress may feel itself unable conveniently to determine exactly when its exercise of the legislative power should become effective, because dependent on future conditions, and it may leave the determination of such time to the decision of an Executive, or, as often happens in matters of state legislation, it may be left to a popular vote of the residents of a district to be effected by the legislation. While in a sense one may say that such residents are exercising legislative power, it is not an exact statement, because the power has already been exercised legislatively by the body vested with that power under the Constitution, the condition of its legislation going into effect being made dependent by the legislature on the expression of the voters of a certain district. * * *

* * *

Again, one of the great functions conferred on Congress by the Feder-

al Constitution is the regulation of interstate commerce and rates to be exacted by interstate carriers for the passenger and merchandise traffic. The rates to be fixed are myriad. If Congress were to be required to fix every rate, it would be impossible to exercise the power at all. Therefore, common sense requires that in the fixing of such rates, Congress may provide a Commission, as it does, called the Interstate Commerce Commission, to fix those rates, after hearing evidence and argument concerning them from interested parties, all in accord with a general rule that Congress first lays down, that rates shall be just and reasonable considering the service given, and not discriminatory. As said by this Court in Interstate Commerce Commission v. Goodrich Transit Co., 224 U.S. 194, 214, 32 S.Ct. 436, 441, "The Congress may not delegate its purely legislative power to a commission, but, having laid down the general rules of action under which a commission shall proceed, it may require of that commission the application of such rules to particular situations and the investigation of facts, with a view to making orders in a particular matter within the rules laid down by the Congress."

* * *

It is conceded by counsel that Congress may use executive officers in the application and enforcement of a policy declared in law by Congress, and authorize such officers in the application of the Congressional declaration to enforce it by regulation equivalent to law. But it is said that this never has been permitted to be done where Congress has exercised the power to levy taxes and fix customs duties. The authorities make no such distinction. The same principle that permits Congress to exercise its rate-making power in interstate commerce, by declaring the rule which shall prevail in the legislative fixing of rates, and enables it to remit to a rate-making body created in accordance with its provisions the fixing of such rates, justifies a similar provision for the fixing of customs duties on imported merchandise. If Congress shall lay down by legislative act an intelligible principle to which the person or body authorized to fix such rates is directed to conform, such legislative action is not a forbidden delegation of legislative power. If it is thought wise to vary the customs duties according to changing conditions of production at home and abroad, it may authorize the Chief Executive to carry out this purpose, with the advisory assistance of a Tariff Commission appointed under Congressional authority. * * *

* * *

Second. The second objection to § 315 is that the declared plan of Congress, either expressly or by clear implication, formulates its rule to guide the President and his advisory Tariff Commission as one directed to a tariff system of protection that will avoid damaging competition to the country's industries by the importation of goods from other countries at too low a rate to equalize foreign and domestic competition in the markets of the United States. It is contended that the only power of Congress in the levying of customs duties is to create revenue, and that it is unconstitutional to frame the customs duties with any other view than that of revenue raising. It undoubtedly is true that during the political life of this country there has been much discussion between par-

ties as to the wisdom of the policy of protection, and we may go further and say as to its constitutionality, but no historian, whatever his view of the wisdom of the policy of protection, would contend that Congress, since the first revenue Act, in 1789, has not assumed that it was within its power in making provision for the collection of revenue, to put taxes upon importations and to vary the subjects of such taxes or rates in an effort to encourage the growth of the industries of the Nation by protecting home production against foreign competition. * * *

* * *

So long as the motive of Congress and the effect of its legislative action are to secure revenue for the benefit of the general government, the existence of other motives in the selection of the subjects of taxes can not invalidate Congressional action. As we said in the Child Labor Tax Case, 259 U.S. 20, 38, 42 S.Ct. 449, 451: "Taxes are occasionally imposed in the discretion of the legislature on proper subjects with the primary motive of obtaining revenue from them, and with the incidental motive of discouraging them by making their continuance onerous. They do not lose their character as taxes because of the incidental motive." And so here, the fact that Congress declares that one of its motives in fixing the rates of duty is so to fix them that they shall encourage the industries of this country in the competition with producers in other countries in the sale of goods in this country, can not invalidate a revenue act so framed. Section 315 and its provisions are within the power of Congress. The judgment of the Court of Customs Appeals is affirmed.

Affirmed.

As provided in § 232(b) of the Trade Expansion Act of 1962, amended by Congress in 1974, if the Secretary of the Treasury concludes that an "article is being imported into the United States in such quantities or under such circumstances as to threaten to impair the national security," the President is empowered to "take such actions, and for such time, as he deems necessary to adjust the imports of [the] article and its derivatives so that * * * imports [of the article] will not threaten to impair the national security." Following an investigation the Treasury Secretary forwarded such a finding to the President concerning the importation of crude oil and its derivatives. Accordingly, the President issued a proclamation raising the license fees on imported crude oil. Subsequently, governors of eight states, ten utility companies, and a member of Congress brought suit challenging the President's action as exceeding his authority under § 232(b). A federal district court denied relief to the plaintiffs and found § 232(b) to be a constitutional delegation of power. It also concluded that the Secretary's and President's actions were in conformity with the statute. A U. S. Court of Appeals reversed, and the federal agency charged with implementing the President's order appealed.

In Federal Energy Administration v. Algonquin SNG, Inc., 426 U.S. 548, 96 S.Ct. 2295 (1976), the Supreme Court sustained the statute as a valid delegation of power and upheld the actions of the executive branch as conforming to the law. Speaking for a unanimous Court, Justice Marshall said:

> Preliminarily, we reject respondents' suggestion that we must construe § 232(b) narrowly in order to avoid "a serious question of unconstitutional delegation of legislative power." * * * Even if § 232(b) is read to authorize the imposition of a license fee system, the standards that it provides the President in its implementation are clearly sufficient to meet any delegation doctrine attack.

> In Hampton & Co. v. United States, 276 U.S. 394, 48 S.Ct. 348 (1928), this Court upheld the constitutionality of a provision empowering the President to increase or decrease import duties in order to equalize the differences between foreign and domestic production costs for similar articles. There, the Court stated:

> > "If Congress shall lay down by legislative act an intelligible principle to which the [President] is directed to conform, such legislative action is not a forbidden delegation of legislative power." * * *

> Section 232(b) easily fulfills that test. It establishes clear preconditions to Presidential action—*inter alia*, a finding by the Secretary of the Treasury that an "article is being imported into the United States in such quantities or under such circumstances as to threaten to impair the national security." Moreover, the leeway that the statute gives the President in deciding what action to take in the event the preconditions are fulfilled is far from unbounded. The President can act only to the extent "he deems necessary to adjust the imports of such article and its derivatives so that such imports will not threaten to impair the national security." And § 232(c) * * * articulates a series of specific factors to be considered by the President in exercising his authority under § 232(b).[a] In light of these factors and our

---

a. As the Court indicated in a portion of one of its footnotes:

Section 232(c) of the Act, 19 U.S.C. § 1862(c) (Supp. IV) provides the President and the Secretary of the Treasury with guidance as to some of the factors to be considered in implementing § 232(b). It provides:

"For the purposes of this section, the Secretary and the President shall, in the light of the requirements of national security and

recognition that "[n]ecessity * * * fixes a point beyond which it is unreasonable and impracticable to compel Congress to prescribe detailed rules. * * *" American Power & Light Co. v. Securities & Exchange Commission, 329 U.S. 90, 105, 67 S.Ct. 133, 142 (1946), we see no looming problem of improper delegation that should affect our reading of § 232(b).

After an extensive examination of the legislative history behind § 232(b), Justice Marshall concluded:

Taken as a whole then, the legislative history of § 232(b) belies any suggestion that Congress, despite its use of broad language in the statute itself, intended to limit the President's authority to the imposition of quotas and to bar the President from imposing a license fee system like the one challenged here. To the contrary, the provision's original enactment, and its subsequent re-enactment in 1958, 1962, and 1974 in the face of repeated expressions from Members of Congress and the Executive Branch as to their broad understanding of its language, all lead to the conclusion that § 232(b) does in fact authorize the actions of the President challenged here. Accordingly, the judgment of the Court of Appeals to the contrary cannot stand.

A final word is in order. Our holding today is a limited one. As respondents themselves acknowledge, a license fee as much as a quota has its initial and direct impact on imports, albeit on their price as opposed to their quantity. * * * As a consequence, our conclusion here, fully supported by the relevant legislative history, that the imposition of a license fee is authorized by § 232(b) in no way compels the further conclusion that *any* action the President might take, as long as it has even a remote impact on imports, is also so authorized.

* * *

without excluding other relevant factors, give consideration to domestic production needed for projected national defense requirements, the capacity of domestic industries to meet such requirements, existing and anticipated availabilities of the human resources, products, raw materials, and other supplies and services essential to the national defense, the requirements of growth of such industries and such supplies and services including the investment, exploration, and development necessary to assure such growth, and the importation of goods in terms of their quantities, availabilities, character, and use as those affect such industries and the capacity of the United States to meet national security requirements. In the administration of this section, the Secretary and the President shall further recognize the close relation of the economic welfare of the Nation to our national security, and shall take into consideration the impact of foreign competition on the economic welfare of individual domestic industries; and any substantial unemployment, decrease in revenues of government, loss of skills or investment, or other serious effects resulting from the displacement of any domestic products by excessive imports shall be considered, without excluding other factors, in determining whether such weakening of our internal economy may impair the national security."

PANAMA REFINING CO. v. RYAN

Supreme Court of the United States, 1935
293 U.S. 388, 55 S.Ct. 241, 79 L.Ed. 446

The Panama Refining Company, an oil refining plant in Texas, sued to restrain Ryan and other federal officials from enforcing Interior Department regulations governing the transportation of petroleum and petroleum products in interstate and foreign commerce. There was a threefold basis for the imposition of these regulations. First, the President was authorized by Section 9(c) of Title I of the National Industrial Recovery Act to prohibit the transportation in interstate and foreign commerce of petroleum and petroleum products produced or withdrawn from storage in excess of the amount permitted by state authority. Second, the President issued an Executive Order on July 11, 1933 making the prohibition outlined in Section 9(c) operable. And finally, three days later, the President authorized the Secretary of the Interior to administer and enforce Section 9(c). Congress authorized the establishment of the Petroleum Code and regulations by the Executive branch to alleviate a situation in which the total supply of oil in the country had, by 1933, far exceeded the demand. To equalize supply with demand, the Department of the Interior allocated ceilings on crude oil production among several states with the approval of the President. Each state that received a quota subdivided it and thereby determined the level of crude oil that each private enterprise would be permitted to produce. Plaintiff oil company specifically attacked Section 9(c) as an unconstitutional delegation of legislative power to the President. This case came to the Supreme Court following action of a circuit court reversing a district court decision favorable to the company.

Mr. Chief Justice HUGHES delivered the opinion of the Court.

* * *

The Constitution provides that "All legislative powers herein granted shall be vested in a Congress of the United States, which shall consist of a Senate and House of Representatives." Art. I, § 1. And the Congress is empowered "To make all laws which shall be necessary and proper for carrying into execution" its general powers. Art. I, § 8, par. 18. The Congress manifestly is not permitted to abdicate, or to transfer to others, the essential legislative functions with which it is thus vested. Undoubtedly legislation must often be adapted to complex conditions involving a host of details with which the national legislature cannot deal directly. The Constitution has never been regarded as denying to the Congress the necessary resources of flexibility and practicality, which will enable it to perform its function in laying down policies and establishing standards, while leaving to selected instrumentalities the making of subordinate rules within prescribed limits and the determination of facts to which the policy as declared by the legislature is to apply. Without capacity to give authorizations of that sort we should have the anomaly of a legislative power which in many circumstances calling for its exertion would be but a futility. But the constant recognition of the necessity and validity of such provisions, and the wide range of administrative authority which has been developed by means of them, cannot be allowed to obscure the limitations of the authority to delegate, if our constitutional system is to be maintained.

The Court has had frequent occasion to refer to these limitations and to review the course of congressional action. At the very outset, amid the disturbances due to war in Europe, when the national safety was imperiled and our neutrality was disregarded, the Congress passed a series of acts, as a part of which the President was authorized, in stated circumstances, to lay and revoke embargoes, to give permits for the exportation of arms and military stores, to remit and discontinue the restraints and prohibitions imposed by acts suspending commercial intercourse with certain countries, and to permit or interdict the entrance into waters of the United States of armed vessels belonging to foreign nations. These early acts were not the subject of judicial decision and, apart from that, they afford no adequate basis for a conclusion that the Congress assumed that it possessed an unqualified power of delegation. They were inspired by the vexations of American commerce through the hostile enterprises of the belligerent powers, they were directed to the effective execution of policies repeatedly declared by the Congress, and they confided to the President, for the purposes and under the conditions stated, an authority which was cognate to the conduct by him of the foreign relations of the Government.

*   *   *

Thus, in every case in which the question has been raised, the Court has recognized that there are limits of delegation which there is no constitutional authority to transcend. We think that § 9(c) goes beyond those limits. As to the transportation of oil production in excess of state permission, the Congress has declared no policy, has established no standard, has laid down no rule. There is no requirement, no defini-

tion of circumstances and conditions in which the transportation is to be allowed or prohibited.

If § 9(c) were held valid, it would be idle to pretend that anything would be left of limitations upon the power of the Congress to delegate its law-making function. The reasoning of the many decisions we have reviewed would be made vacuous and their distinctions nugatory. Instead of performing its law-making function, the Congress could at will and as to such subjects as it chose transfer that function to the President or other officer or to an administrative body. The question is not of the intrinsic importance of the particular statute before us, but of the constitutional processes of legislation which are an essential part of our system of government.

*   *   *

We are not dealing with action which, appropriately belonging to the executive province, is not the subject of judicial review, or with the presumptions attaching to executive action. To repeat, we are concerned with the question of the delegation of legislative power. If the citizen is to be punished for the crime of violating a legislative order of an executive officer, or of a board or commission, due process of law requires that it shall appear that the order is within the authority of the officer, board or commission, and, if that authority depends on determinations of fact, those determinations must be shown. As the Court said in Wichita Railroad & Light Co. v. Public Utilities Comm'n, 260 U.S. 48, 59, 43 S.Ct. 51, 55: "In creating such an administrative agency the legislature, to prevent its being a pure delegation of legislative power, must enjoin upon it a certain course of procedure and certain rules of decision in the performance of its function. It is a wholesome and necessary principle that such an agency must pursue the procedure and rules enjoined and show a substantial compliance therewith to give validity to its action. When, therefore, such an administrative agency is required as a condition precedent to an order, to make a finding of facts, the validity of the order must rest upon the needed finding. If it is lacking, the order is ineffective. It is pressed on us that the lack of an express finding may be supplied by implication and by reference to the averments of the petition invoking the action of the Commission. We can not agree to this." Referring to the ruling in the *Wichita*, case, the Court said in Mahler v. Eby, 264 U.S. 32, 44, 44 S.Ct. 283, 288: "We held that the order in that case made after a hearing and ordering a reduction was void for lack of the express finding in the order. We put this conclusion not only on the language of the statute but also on general principles of constitutional government." We cannot regard the President as immune from the application of these constitutional principles. When the President is invested with legislative authority as the delegate of Congress in carrying out a declared policy, he necessarily acts under the constitutional restriction applicable to such a delegation.

We see no escape from the conclusion that the Executive Orders of July 11, 1933, and July 14, 1933, and the Regulations issued by the Secretary of the Interior thereunder, are without constitutional authority.

The decrees of the Circuit Court of Appeals are reversed and the causes are remanded to the District Court with direction to modify its decrees in conformity with this opinion so as to grant permanent injunctions, restraining the defendants from enforcing those orders and regulations.

Reversed.

Mr. Justice CARDOZO, dissenting.

With all that is said in the opinion of the court as to the Code of Fair Competition adopted by the President August 16, 1933, for the governance of the petroleum industry, I am fully in accord. No question is before us at this time as to the power of Congress to regulate production. No question is here as to its competence to clothe the President with a delegated power whereby a Code of Fair Competition may become invested with the force of law. The petitioners were never in jeopardy by force of such a code or of regulations made thereunder. They were not in jeopardy because there was neither statute nor regulation subjecting them to pains or penalties if they set the code at naught. One must deplore the administrative methods that brought about uncertainty for a time as to the terms of executive orders intended to be law. Even so, the petitioners do not stand in need of an injunction to restrain the enforcement of a non-existent mandate.

I am unable to assent to the conclusion that § 9(c) of the National Recovery Act, a section delegating to the President a very different power from any that is involved in the regulation of production or in the promulgation of a code, is to be nullified upon the ground that his discretion is too broad or for any other reason. My point of difference with the majority of the court is narrow. I concede that to uphold the delegation there is need to discover in the terms of the act a standard reasonably clear whereby discretion must be governed. I deny that such a standard is lacking in respect of the prohibitions permitted by this section when the act with all its reasonable implications is considered as a whole. What the standard is becomes the pivotal inquiry.

As to the nature of the *act* which the President is authorized to perform there is no need for implication. That at least is definite beyond the possibility of challenge. He may prohibit the transportation in interstate and foreign commerce of petroleum and the products thereof produced or withdrawn from storage in excess of the amount permitted by any state law or valid regulation or order prescribed thereunder. He is not left to roam at will among all the possible subjects of interstate transportation, picking and choosing as he pleases. I am far from asserting now that delegation would be valid if accompanied by all that latitude of choice. In the laying of his interdict he is to confine himself to a particular commodity, and to that commodity when produced or withdrawn from storage in contravention of the policy and statutes of the states. He has choice, though within limits, as to the occasion, but none whatever as to the means. The means have been prescribed by Congress. There has been no grant to the Executive of any roving commission to inquire into evils and then, upon discovering them, do anything he pleases. His act being thus defined, what else must he ascertain in order to regulate his discretion and bring the power into play? The answer is not given if we look to § 9(c) only, but it comes to us by implication from a view of other sections where the

standards are defined. The prevailing opinion concedes that a standard will be as effective if imported into § 9(c) by reasonable implication as if put there in so many words. If we look to the whole structure of the statute, the test is plainly this, that the President is to forbid the transportation of the oil when he believes, in the light of the conditions of the industry as disclosed from time to time, that the prohibition will tend to effectuate the declared policies of the act,—not merely his own conception of its policies, undirected by any extrinsic guide, but the policies announced by § 1 in the forefront of the statute as an index to the meaning of everything that follows.

*   *   *

In what has been written, I have stated, but without developing the argument, that by reasonable implication the power conferred upon the President by § 9(c) is to be read as if coupled with the words that he shall exercise the power whenever satisfied that by doing so he will effectuate the policy of the statute as theretofore declared. Two canons of interpretation, each familiar to our law, leave no escape from that conclusion. One is that the meaning of a statute is to be looked for, not in any single section, but in all the parts together and in their relation to the end in view. * * * The other is that when a statute is reasonably susceptible of two interpretations, by one of which it is unconstitutional and by the other valid, the court prefers the meaning that preserves to the meaning that destroys. * * * Either the statute means that the President is to adhere to the declared policy of Congress, or it means that he is to exercise a merely arbitrary will. The one construction invigorates the act; the other saps its life. A choice between them is not hard.

I am persuaded that a reference, express or implied, to the policy of Congress as declared in § 1 is a sufficient definition of a standard to make the statute valid. Discretion is not unconfined and vagrant. It is canalized within banks that keep it from overflowing. * * * [T]he separation of powers between the Executive and Congress is not a doctrinaire concept to be made use of with pedantic rigor. There must be sensible approximation, there must be elasticity of adjustment, in response to the practical necessities of government, which cannot foresee today the developments of tomorrow in their nearly infinite variety. The Interstate Commerce Commission, probing the economic situation of the railroads of the country, consolidating them into systems, shaping in numberless ways their capacities and duties, and even making or unmaking the prosperity of great communities * * * is a conspicuous illustration. * * * There could surely be no question as to the validity of an act whereby carriers would be prohibited from transporting oil produced in contravention of a statute if in the judgment of the commission the practice was demoralizing the market and bringing disorder and insecurity into the national economy. What may be delegated to a commission may be delegated to the President. "Congress may feel itself unable conveniently to determine exactly when its exercise of the legislative power should become effective, because dependent on future conditions, and it may leave the determination of such time to the discretion of the executive." *Hampton & Co.* v. *United States.* * * * In the complex life of today, the business of government could not go on without the delegation, in greater or less degree, of the power to adapt the rule to the swiftly moving facts.

* * *

There is no fear that the nation will drift from its ancient moorings as the result of the narrow delegation of power permitted by this section. What can be done under cover of that permission is closely and clearly circumscribed both as to subject matter and occasion. The statute was framed in the shadow of a national disaster. A host of unforeseen contingencies would have to be faced from day to day, and faced with a fulness of understanding unattainable by any one except the man upon the scene. The President was chosen to meet the instant need.

* * *

SCHECHTER POULTRY CORP. v. UNITED STATES

Supreme Court of the United States, 1935
295 U.S. 495, 55 S.Ct. 837, 79 L.Ed. 1570

In June 1933, the Roosevelt administration secured the passage of the National Industrial Recovery Act for the purpose of stimulating business and reducing unemployment. These social and economic objectives were to be achieved through a cooperative effort by business and government. Among other things the act authorized the establishment of codes of fair competition by business and the Executive branch operating in part through the National Recovery Administration. These codes, which were subject to the approval of the President, established standards that touched on matters such as wages, hours, employment practices, general working conditions, and methods of competition.

The Schechter brothers owned slaughterhouses in New York City that received live chickens from outside the state, killed them, and then sold them to local retail butchers. They were convicted in a district court for violating the Live Poultry Code on a number of counts which included filing false sales and price reports and selling diseased poultry. The Second Circuit Court of Appeals affirmed the conviction in part, and both the defendants and the government sought certiorari. One of the defendants' contentions was that the legislation authorizing the codes represented an unconstitutional delegation of legislative power by Congress.

In addition to the delegation of power question the Supreme Court reached an important decision on the merits, namely whether or not the business activities of the Schechter slaughterhouses could be regulated at all by the federal government. The Court concluded that the Schechters were engaged in intrastate commerce of a kind that had only an indirect effect on interstate commerce and that, therefore, their poultry business could not be regulated by Congress under the commerce power (see p. 469).

[Excerpts of opinions dealing with delegation of power]

Mr. Chief Justice HUGHES delivered the opinion of the Court.

* * *

The question of the delegation of legislative power. We recently had occasion to review the pertinent decisions and the general principles which govern the determination of this question. Panama Refining Co. v. Ryan, 293 U.S. 388, 55 S.Ct. 241. * * * We have repeatedly recognized the necessity of adapting legislation to complex conditions involving a host of details with which the national legislature cannot deal directly. We pointed out in the *Panama Company* case that the Constitution has never been regarded as denying to Congress the necessary resources of flexibility and practicality, which will enable it to perform its function in laying down policies and establishing standards, while leaving to selected instrumentalities the making of subordinate rules within prescribed limits and the determination of facts to which the policy as declared by the legislature is to apply. But we said that the constant

recognition of the necessity and validity of such provisions, and the wide range of administrative authority which has been developed by means of them, cannot be allowed to obscure the limitations of the authority to delegate, if our constitutional system is to be maintained. * * *

Accordingly, we look to the statute to see whether Congress has overstepped these limitations,— whether Congress in authorizing "codes of fair competition" has itself established the standards of legal obligation, thus performing its essential legislative function, or, by the failure to enact such standards, has attempted to transfer that function to others.

The aspect in which the question is now presented is distinct from that which was before us in the case of the *Panama Company*. There, the subject of the statutory prohibition was defined. National Industrial Recovery Act, § 9(c). That subject was the transportation in interstate and foreign commerce of petroleum and petroleum products which are produced or withdrawn from storage in excess of the amount permitted by state authority. The question was with respect to the range of discretion given to the President in prohibiting that transportation. * * * As to the "codes of fair competition," under § 3 of the Act, the question is more fundamental. It is whether there is any adequate definition of the subject to which the codes are to be addressed.

What is meant by "fair competition" as the term is used in the Act? Does it refer to a category established in the law, and is the authority to make codes limited accordingly? Or is it used as a convenient designation for whatever set of laws the formulators of a code for a particular trade or industry may propose and the President may approve (subject to certain restrictions), or the President may himself prescribe, as being wise and beneficient provisions for the government of the trade or industry in order to accomplish the broad purposes of rehabilitation, correction and expansion which are stated in the first section of Title I? [That section, under the heading "Declaration of Policy," is as follows: "Section 1. A national emergency productive of widespread unemployment and disorganization of industry, which burdens interstate and foreign commerce, affects the public welfare, and undermines the standards of living of the American people, is hereby declared to exist. It is hereby declared to be the policy of Congress to remove obstructions to the free flow of interstate and foreign commerce which tend to diminish the amount thereof; and to provide for the general welfare by promoting the organization of industry for the purpose of cooperative action among trade groups, to induce and maintain united action of labor and management under adequate

governmental sanctions and supervision, to eliminate unfair competitive practices, to promote the fullest possible utilization of the present productive capacity of industries, to avoid undue restriction of production (except as may be temporarily required), to increase the consumption of industrial and agricultural products by increasing purchasing power, to reduce and relieve unemployment, to improve standards of labor, and otherwise to rehabilitate industry and to conserve natural resources."]

The Act does not define "fair competition." "Unfair competition," as known to the common law, is a limited concept. Primarily, and strictly, it relates to the palming off of one's goods as those of a rival trader. * * * In recent years, its scope has been extended. It has been held to apply to misappropriation as well as misrepresentation, to the selling of another's goods as one's own,—to misappropriation of what equitably belongs to a competitor. * * * Unfairness in competition has been predicated of acts which lie outside the ordinary course of business and are tainted by fraud, or coercion, or conduct otherwise prohibited by law. * * * But it is evident that in its widest range, "unfair competition," as it has been understood in the law, does not reach the objectives of the codes which are authorized by the National Industrial Recovery Act. The codes may, indeed, cover conduct which existing law condemns, but they are not limited to conduct of that sort. The Government does not contend that the Act contemplates such a limitation. It would be opposed both to the declared purposes of the Act and to its administrative construction.

The Federal Trade Commission Act (§ 5) introduced the expression "unfair methods of competition," which were declared to be unlawful. That was an expression new in the law. Debate apparently convinced the sponsors of the legislation that the words "unfair competition," in the light of their meaning at common law, were too narrow. We have said that the substituted phrase has a broader meaning, that it does not admit of precise definition, its scope being left to judicial determination as controversies arise. * * * What are "unfair methods of competition" are thus to be determined in particular instances, upon evidence, in the light of particular competitive conditions and of what is found to be a specific and substantial public interest. * * * To make this possible, Congress set up a special procedure. A Commission, a quasi-judicial body, was created. Provision was made for formal complaint, for notice and hearing, for appropriate findings of fact supported by adequate evidence, and for judicial review to give assurance that the action of the Commission is taken within its statutory authority. * * *

In providing for codes, the National Industrial Recovery Act dispenses with this administrative procedure and with any administrative procedure of an analogous character. But the difference between the code plan of the Recovery Act and the scheme of the Federal Trade Commission Act lies not only in procedure but in subject matter. We cannot regard the "fair competition" of the codes as antithetical to the "unfair methods of competition" of the Federal Trade Commission Act. The "fair competition" of the codes has a much broader range and a new significance. The Recovery Act provides that it shall not be construed to impair the powers of the Federal

Trade Commission, but, when a code is approved, its provisions are to be the "standards of fair competition" for the trade or industry concerned, and any violation of such standards in any transaction in or affecting interstate or foreign commerce is to be deemed "an unfair method of competition" within the meaning of the Federal Trade Commission Act. § 3(b).

For a statement of the authorized objectives and content of the "codes of fair competition" we are referred repeatedly to the "Declaration of Policy" in section one of Title I of the Recovery Act. Thus, the approval of a code by the President is conditioned on his finding that it "will tend to effectuate the policy of this title." § 3(a). The President is authorized to impose such conditions "for the protection of consumers, competitors, employees, and others, and in furtherance of the public interest, and may provide such exceptions to and exemptions from the provisions of such code as the President in his discretion deems necessary to effectuate the policy herein declared." * * * The "policy herein declared" is manifestly that set forth in section one. That declaration embraces a broad range of objectives. Among them we find the elimination of "unfair competitive practices." But even if this clause were to be taken to relate to practices which fall under the ban of existing law, either common law or statute, it is still only one of the authorized aims decribed in section one. * * *

Under § 3, whatever "may tend to effectuate" these general purposes may be included in the "codes of fair competition." We think the conclusion is inescapable that the authority sought to be conferred by § 3 was not merely to deal with "unfair competitive practices" which offend against existing law, and could be the subject of judicial condemnation without further legislation, or to create administrative machinery for the application of established principles of law to particular instances of violation. Rather, the purpose is clearly disclosed to authorize new and controlling prohibitions through codes of laws which would embrace what the formulators would propose, and what the President would approve, or prescribe, as wise and beneficent measures for the government of trades and industries in order to bring about their rehabilitation, correction and development, according to the general declaration of policy in section one. Codes of laws of this sort are styled "codes of fair competition."

We find no real controversy upon this point and we must determine the validity of the Code in question in this aspect. As the Government candidly says in its brief: "The words 'policy of this title' clearly refer to the 'policy' which Congress declared in the section entitled 'Declaration of Policy'—§ 1. All of the policies there set forth point toward a single goal—the rehabilitation of industry and the industrial recovery which unquestionably was the major policy of Congress in adopting the National Industrial Recovery Act." And that this is the controlling purpose of the Code now before us appears both from its repeated declarations to that effect and from the scope of its requirements. It will be observed that its provisions as to the hours and wages of employees and its "general labor provisions" were placed in separate articles, and these were not included in the article on "trade practice provisions" declaring what should be deemed to constitute "un-

fair methods of competition."
* * *

* * *

The question, then, turns upon the authority which § 3 of the Recovery Act vests in the President to approve or prescribe. If the codes have standing as penal statutes, this must be due to the effect of the executive action. But Congress cannot delegate legislative power to the President to exercise an unfettered discretion to make whatever laws he thinks may be needed or advisable for the rehabilitation and expansion of trade or industry. See *Panama Refining Co.* v. *Ryan*, supra, and cases there reviewed.

Accordingly we turn to the Recovery Act to ascertain what limits have been set to the exercise of the President's discretion. *First*, the President, as a condition of approval, is required to find that the trade or industrial associations or groups which propose a code, "impose no inequitable restrictions on admission to membership" and are "truly representative." That condition, however, relates only to the status of the initiators of the new laws and not to the permissible scope of such laws. *Second*, the President is required to find that the code is not "designed to promote monopolies or to eliminate or oppress small enterprises and will not operate to discriminate against them." And, to this is added a proviso that the code "shall not permit monopolies or monopolistic practices." But these restrictions leave virtually untouched the field of policy envisaged by section one, and, in that wide field of legislative possibilities, the proponents of a code, refraining from monopolistic designs, may roam at will and the President may approve or disapprove their proposals as he may see fit. That is the precise effect of the further finding that the President is to make—that the code "will tend to effectuate the policy of this title." While this is called a finding, it is really but a statement of an opinion as to the general effect upon the promotion of trade or industry of a scheme of laws. These are the only findings which Congress has made essential in order to put into operation a legislative code having the aims decribed in the "Declaration of Policy."

Nor is the breadth of the President's discretion left to the necessary implications of this limited requirement as to his findings. As already noted, the President in approving a code may impose his own conditions, adding to or taking from what is proposed, as "in his discretion" he thinks necessary "to effectuate the policy" declared by the Act. Of course, he has no less liberty when he prescribes a code on his own motion or on complaint, and he is free to prescribe one if a code has not been approved. The Act provides for the creation by the President of administrative agencies to assist him, but the action or reports of such agencies, or of his other assistants,—their recommendations and findings in relation to the making of codes—have no sanction beyond the will of the President, who may accept, modify or reject them as he pleases. Such recommendations or findings in no way limit the authority which § 3 undertakes to vest in the President with no other conditions than those there specified. And this authority relates to a host of different trades and industries, thus extending the President's discretion to all the varieties of laws which he may deem to be beneficial in dealing with the vast array of commercial and industrial activities throughout the country.

Such a sweeping delegation of legislative power finds no support in the decisions upon which the Government especially relies. By the Interstate Commerce Act, Congress has itself provided a code of laws regulating the activities of the common carriers subject to the Act, in order to assure the performance of their services upon just and reasonable terms, with adequate facilities and without unjust discrimination. Congress from time to time has elaborated its requirements, as needs have been disclosed. To facilitate the application of the standards prescribed by the Act, Congress has provided an expert body. That administrative agency, in dealing with particular cases, is required to act upon notice and hearing, and its orders must be supported by findings of fact which in turn are sustained by evidence. * * *

* * *

To summarize and conclude upon this point: Section 3 of the Recovery Act is without precedent. It supplies no standards for any trade, industry or activity. It does not undertake to prescribe rules of conduct to be applied to particular states of fact determined by appropriate administrative procedure. Instead of prescribing rules of conduct, it authorizes the making of codes to prescribe them. For that legislative undertaking, § 3 sets up no standards, aside from the statement of the general aims of rehabilitation, correction and expansion described in section one. In view of the scope of that broad declaration, and of the nature of the few restrictions that are imposed, the discretion of the President in approving or prescribing codes, and thus enacting laws for the government of trade and industry throughout the country, is virtually unfettered. We think that the code-making authority thus conferred is an unconstitutional delegation of legislative power.

* * *

Mr. Justice CARDOZO, concurring.

The delegated power of legislation which has found expression in this code is not canalized within banks that keep it from overflowing. It is unconfined and vagrant, if I may borrow my own words in an earlier opinion. *Panama Refining Co. v. Ryan.* * * *

This court has held that delegation may be unlawful though the act to be performed is definite and single, if the necessity, time and occasion of performance have been left in the end to the discretion of the delegate. * * * I thought that ruling went too far. I pointed out in an opinion that there had been "no grant to the Executive of any roving commission to inquire into evils and then, upon discovering them, do anything he pleases." * * * Choice, though within limits, had been given him "as to the occasion, but none whatever as to the means." * * * Here, in the case before us, is an attempted delegation not confined to any single act nor to any class or groups of acts identified or described by reference to a standard. Here in effect is a roving commission to inquire into evils and upon discovery correct them.

* * *

[Justice STONE joined in this concurring opinion.]

THE ECONOMIC STABILIZATION ACT OF 1970

83 Stat. 377

§ 201. Short title

This title may be cited as the "Economic Stabilization Act of 1970."

§ 202. Findings

It is hereby determined that in order to stabilize the economy, reduce inflation, minimize unemployment, improve the Nation's competitive position in world trade, and protect the purchasing power of the dollar, it is necessary to stabilize prices, rents, wages, salaries, dividends, and interest. The adjustments necessary to carry out this program require prompt judgments and actions by the executive branch of the Government. The President is in a position to implement promptly and effectively the program authorized by this title.

§ 203. Presidential authority

(a) The President is authorized to issue such orders and regulations as he deems appropriate, accompanied by a statement of reasons for such orders and regulations, to—

(1) stabilize prices, rents, wages, and salaries at levels not less than those prevailing on May 25, 1970, except that prices may be stabilized at levels below those prevailing on such date if it is necessary to eliminate windfall profits or if it is otherwise necessary to carry out the purposes of this title; and

(2) stabilize interest rates and corporate dividends and similar transfers at levels consistent with orderly ecomonic growth.

Such orders and regulations shall provide for the making of such adjustments as may be necessary to prevent gross inequities, and shall be consistent with the standards issued pursuant to subsection (b).

(b) In carrying out the authority vested in him by subsection (a), the President shall issue standards to serve as a guide for determining levels of wages, salaries, prices, rents, interest rates, corporate dividends, and similar transfers which are consistent with the purposes of this title and orderly economic growth. Such standards shall—

(1) be generally fair and equitable;

(2) provide for the making of such general exceptions and variations as are necessary to foster orderly economic growth and to prevent gross inequities, hardships, serious market disruptions, domestic shortages of raw materials, localized shortages of labor, and windfall profits;

(3) take into account changes in productivity and the cost of living, as well as such other factors consistent with the purposes of this title as are appropriate;

(4) provide for the requiring of appropriate reductions in prices and rents whenever warranted after consideration of lower costs, labor shortages, and other pertinent factors; and

(5) call for generally comparable sacrifices by business and labor as well as other segments of the economy.

(c)(1) The authority conferred on the President by this section shall not be exercised to limit the level of any wage or salary (including any insurance or other fringe benefit offered in connection with an employment contract) scheduled to take effect after November 13, 1971, to a level below that which has been agreed to in a contract which (A) related to such wage or salary, and (B) was executed prior to August 15, 1971, unless the President determines that the increase provided in such contract is unreasonably inconsistent with the standards for wage and salary increases published under subsection (b).

(2) The president shall promptly take such action as may be necessary to permit the payment of any wage or salary increase (including any insurance or other fringe benefit offered in connection with an employment contract) which (A) was agreed to in an employment contract executed prior to August 15, 1971, (B) was scheduled to take effect prior to November 14, 1971, and (C) was not paid as a result of orders issued under this title, unless the President determines that the increase provided in such contract is unreasonably inconsistent with the standards for wage and salary increases published under subsection (b).

(3) In addition to the payment of wage and salary increases provided for under paragraphs (1) and (2), beginning on the date on which this subsection takes effect, the President shall promptly take such action as may be necessary to require the payment of any wage or salary increases (including any insurance or other fringe benefits offered in connection with employment) which have been, or in the absence of this subsection would be, withheld under the authority of this title, if the President determines that—

(A) such increases were provided for by law or contract prior to August 15, 1971; and

(B) prices have been advanced, productivity increased, taxes have been raised, appropriations have been made, or funds have otherwise been raised or provided for in order to cover such increases.

(d) Notwithstanding any other provisions of this title, this title shall be implemented in such a manner that wage increases to any individual whose earnings are substandard or who is a member of the working poor shall not be limited in any manner, until such time as his earnings are no longer substandard or he is no longer a member of the working poor.

(e) Whenever the authority of this title is implemented with respect to significant segments of the economy, the President shall require the issuance of regulations or orders providing for the stabilization of interest rates and finance charges, unless he issues a determination, accompanied by a statement of reasons, that such regulations or orders are not necessary to maintain such rates and charges at levels consonant with orderly economic growth.

(f) The authority conferred by this section shall not be exercised to preclude the payment of any increase in wages—

(1) required under the Fair Labor Standards Act of 1938, as amended [section 201 et seq. of Title 29], or effected as a result of enforcement action under such Act [section 201 et seq. of Title 29]; or

(2) required in order to comply with wage determinations made by any agency in the executive branch of the Government pursuant to law for work (A) performed under contracts with, or to be performed with financial assistance from, the United States or the District of Columbia, or any agency or instrumentality thereof, or (B) performed by aliens who are immigrants or who have been temporarily admitted to the United States pursuant to the Immigration and Nationality Act [section 1101 et seq. of Title 8]; or

(3) paid in conjunction with existing or newly established employee incentive programs which are designed to reflect directly increases in employee productivity.

(g) For the purposes of this section the term "wages" and "salaries" do not include contributions by any employer pursuant to a compensation adjustment for—

(1) any pension, profit sharing, or annuity and savings plan which meets the requirements of section 401(a), 404(a)(2), or 403(b) of the Internal Revenue Code of 1954 [Title 26];

(2) any group insurance plan; or

(3) any disability and health plan;

unless the President determines that the contributions made by any such employer are unreasonably inconsistent with the standards for wage, salary, and price increases issued under subsection (b).

(h) No State or portion thereof shall be exempted from any application of this title with respect to rents solely by virtue of the fact that it regulates rents by State or local law, regulation or policy.

(i) Rules, regulations, and orders issued under this title shall insofar as practicable be designed to encourage labor-management cooperation for the purpose of achieving increased productivity, and the Executive Director of the National Commission on Productivity shall when appropriate be consulted in the formulation of policies, rules, regulations, orders, and amendments under this title.

§ 204. Delegation

The President may delegate the performance of any function under this title to such officers, departments, and agencies of the United States as he deems appropriate, or to boards, commissions, and similar entities composed in whole or in part of members appointed to represent different sectors of the economy and the general public. Members of such boards, commissions, and similar entities shall be appointed by the President by and with the advice and consent of the Senate; except that—

(1) the foregoing requirement with respect to Senate confirmation does not apply to any member of any such board, commission, or similar entity (other than the Chairman of the Pay Board, established by section 7 of Executive Order Numbered 11627 of October 15, 1971, and the Chairman of the Price Commission, established by section 8 of such Executive order) who is serving, pursuant to appointment by the President, on such board, commission, or similar entity on the date of enactment of the Economic Stabilization Act Amendments of 1971 [Dec. 22, 1971], and who continues to serve, pursuant to such appointment, on such board, commission, or similar entity after such date [Dec. 22, 1971]; and

(2) any person serving in the office of Chairman of such Pay Board, and any person serving in the office of Chairman of such Price Commission, on the date of enactment of the Economic Stabilization Act Amendments of 1971 [Dec. 22, 1971], may continue to serve in such capacity on an interim basis without regard to the foregoing requirement with respect to Senate confirmation until the expiration of sixty days after the date of enactment of the Economic Stabilization Act Amendments of 1971 [Dec. 22, 1971], and the provisions of sections 910–913 of title 5, United States Code [sections 910–913 of Title 5], shall be applicable with respect to the procedure to be followed in the Senate in considering the nomination of any person to either of such offices submitted to the Senate by the President during such sixty-day period, except that references in such provisions to a "resolution with respect to a reorganization plan" shall be deemed for the purpose of this section to refer to such nominations.

Where such boards, commissions, and similar entities are composed in part of members who serve on less than a full-time basis, legal authority shall be placed in their chairmen who shall be employees of the United States and who shall act only in accordance with the majority vote of members. Nothing in section 203, 205, 207, 208, or 209 of title 18, United States Code [sections 203, 205, 207, 208, or 209 of Title 18], shall be deemed to apply to any member of any such board, commission, or similar entity, who serves on less than a full-time basis because of membership on such board, commission, or entity.

* * *

c. THE POWER TO INVESTIGATE

McGRAIN v. DAUGHERTY

Supreme Court of the United States, 1927
273 U.S. 135, 47 S.Ct. 319, 71 L.Ed. 580

In the course of its investigation into charges that Attorney General Harry M. Daugherty had failed, among other things, to prosecute government and oil company officials involved in the Elk Hills and Teapot Dome scandals, a Senate committee on two occasions subpoenaed Mally S. Daugherty to appear before it. When Daugherty, the brother of the Attorney General and president of a bank, failed to appear, the Senate directed that a warrant be issued to bring him into custody so that the committee might question him. John McGrain, the Deputy Sergeant at Arms, executed the warrant, whereupon Daugherty successfully petitioned the federal district court in Cincinnati for a writ of habeas corpus. In its opinion the court concluded that Daugherty had been unlawfully detained because the Senate had exceeded its constitutional powers. The case then went to the Supreme Court on direct appeal.

Mr. Justice VAN DEVANTER delivered the opinion of the Court.

*   *   *

We have given the case earnest and prolonged consideration because the principal questions involved are of unusual importance and delicacy. They are (a) whether the Senate—or the House of Representatives, both being on the same plane in this regard—has power, through its own process, to compel a private individual to appear before it or one of its committees and give testimony needed to enable it efficiently to exercise a legislative function belonging to it under the Constitution; and (b) whether it sufficiently appears that the process was being employed in this instance to obtain testimony for that purpose.

*   *   *

In approaching the principal questions * * * two observations are in order. One is that we are not now concerned with the direction in the first subpoena that the witness produce various records, books, and papers of the Midland National Bank. That direction was not repeated in the second subpoena, and is not sought to be enforced by the attachment. This was recognized by the court below * * * and is conceded by counsel for the appellant. The other is that we are not now concerned with the right of the Senate to propound or the duty of the witness to answer specific questions, for as yet no questions have been propounded to him. He is asserting—and is standing on his assertion—that the Senate is without power to interrogate him, even if the questions propounded be pertinent and otherwise legitimate, which for present purposes must be assumed.

The first of the principal questions, the one which the witness particularly presses on our attention, is as before shown, whether the Senate—or the House of Representatives, both being on the same plane in this regard—has power, through its own process, to compel a private individual to appear before it or one of its committees and give testimony needed to enable it efficiently to exercise a legislative function belonging to it under the Constitution.

The Constitution provides for a Congress, consisting of a Senate and House of Representatives, and invests it with "all legislative powers" granted to the United States, and with power "to make all laws which shall be necessary and proper" for carrying into execution these powers and "all other powers" vested by the Constitution in the United States or in any department or officer thereof. Article 1, §§ 1, 8. Other provisions show that, while bills can become laws only after being considered and passed by both houses of Congress, each house is to be distinct from the other, to have its own officers and rules, and to exercise its legislative function independently. Article 1, §§ 2, 3, 5, 7. But there is no provision expressly investing either house with power to make investigations and exact testimony, to the end that it may exercise its legislative function advisedly and effectively. So the question arises whether this power is so far incidental to the legislative function as to be implied.

In actual legislative practice, power to secure needed information by such means has long been treated as an attribute of the power to legislate. It was so regarded in the British Parliament and in the colonial Legislatures before the American Revolution, and a like view has prevailed and been carried into effect in both houses of Congress and in most of the state Legislatures.

This power was both asserted and exerted by the House of Representatives in 1792, when it appointed a select committee to inquire into the St. Clair expedition and authorized the committee to send for necessary persons, papers and records. Mr. Madison, who had taken an important part in framing the Constitution only five years before, and four of his associates in that work, were members of the House of Representatives at the time, and all voted for the inquiry. 3 Cong.Ann. 494. Other exertions of the power by the House of Representatives, as also by the Senate, are shown in the citations already made. Among those by the Senate, the inquiry ordered in 1859 respecting the raid by John Brown and his adherents on the armory and arsenal of the United States at Harper's Ferry is of special significance. The resolution directing the inquiry authorized the committee to send for persons and papers, to inquire into the facts pertaining to the raid and the means by which it was organized and supported, and to report what legislation, if any, was necessary to preserve the peace of the country and protect the public property. The resolution was briefly discussed and adopted without opposition. Cong. Globe, 36th Cong. 1st Sess. pp. 141, 152. Later on the committee reported that Thaddeus Hyatt, although subpoenaed to appear as a witness, had refused to do so; whereupon the Senate ordered that he be attached and brought before it to answer for his refusal. When he was brought in, he answered by challenging the power of the Senate to direct the inquiry and exact testimony to aid it in exercising its legislative function. The question of power thus presented was thoroughly discussed by several senators—Mr. Sumner of Massachusetts taking the lead in denying the power, and Mr. Fessenden of Maine in supporting it. Sectional and party lines were put aside, and the question was debated and determined with special regard to principle and precedent. The vote was taken on a resolution pronouncing the witness' answer insufficient and directing that he be committed until he should signify that he was ready and willing to testify. The resolution was adopted—44 senators voting for it and 10 against. Cong.Globe, 36th Cong. 1st. Sess. pp. 1100–1109, 3006, 3007. The arguments advanced in support of the power are fairly reflected by the following excerpts from the debate:

Mr. Fessenden of Maine: "Where will you stop? Stop, I say, just at that point where we have gone far enough to accomplish the purposes for which we were created; and these purposes are defined in the Constitution. What are they? The great purpose is legislation. There are some other things, but I speak of legislation as the principal purpose. Now, what do we propose to do here? We propose to legislate upon a given state of facts, perhaps, or under a given necessity. Well, sir, proposing to legislate, we want information. We have it not ourselves. It is not to be presumed that we know everything; and if any body does presume it, it is a very great mistake, as we know by experience. We want information on certain subjects. How are we to get it? The Senator says, ask for it. I am ready to ask for it; but suppose the person whom we ask will not give it to us: what then? Have we not power to compel him to come before us? Is this power, which has been exercised by Parliament, and by all legislative bodies down to the present day without dispute—the power to inquire into subjects upon which they are disposed to legislate—lost to us? Are we not in the possession of it? Are we deprived of it simply because we hold our power here under a Constitution which defines what our duties are, and what we are called upon to do?

"Congress have appointed committees after committees, time after time, to make inquiries on subjects of legislation. Had we not power to do it? Nobody questioned our authority to do it. We have given them authority to send for persons and papers during the recess. Nobody questioned our authority. We appoint committees during the session with power to send for persons and papers. Have we not that authority, if necessary to legislation? * * *

"Sir, with regard to myself, all I have to inquire into is: is this a legitimate and proper object, committed to me under the Constitution; and then, as to the mode of accomplishing it, I am ready to use judiciously, calmly, moderately, all the power which I believe is necessary and inherent, in order to do that which I am appointed to do; and I take it, I violate no rights, either of the people generally or of the individual, by that course."

"Mr. Crittenden of Kentucky: "I come now to a question where the co-operation of the two branches is not necessary. There are some things that the Senate may do. How? According to a mode of its own. Are we to ask the other branch of the Legislature to concede by law to us the power of making such an inquiry as we are now making? Has not each branch the right to make what inquiries and investigation it thinks proper who make for its own action? Undoubtedly. You say we must have a law for it. Can we have a law? Is it not, from the very nature of the case, incidental to you as a Senate, if you, as a Senate, have the power of instituting an inquiry and of proceeding with that inquiry? I have endeavored to show that we have that power. We have a right, in consequence of it, a necessary incidental power, to summon witnesses, if witnesses are necessary. Do we require the concurrence of the other house to that? It is a power of our own. If you have a right to do the thing of your own motion, you must have all powers that are necessary to do it.

"The means of carrying into effect by law all the granted powers, is given where legislation is applicable and necessary; but there are subordinate matters, not amounting to laws; there are inquiries of the one house or the other house, which each house has a right to conduct; which each has, from the beginning, exercised the power to conduct; and each has, from the beginning, summoned witnesses. This has been the practice of the government from the beginning; and if we have a right to summon the witness, all the rest follows as a matter of course."

The deliberate solution of the question on that occasion has been accepted and followed on other occasions by both houses of Congress, and never has been rejected or questioned by either.

The state courts quite generally have held that the power to legislate carries with it by necessary implication ample authority to obtain information needed in the rightful exercise of that power, and to employ compulsory process for the purpose.

* * *

Four decisions of this court are cited and more or less relied on, and we now turn to them.

The first decision was in Anderson v. Dunn, 6 Wheat. 204, 5 L.Ed. 242. The question there was wheth-

er, under the Constitution, the House of Representatives has power to attach and punish a person other than a member for contempt of its authority—in fact, an attempt to bribe one of its members. The court regarded the power as essential to the effective exertion of other powers expressly granted, and therefore as implied. * * *

The next decision was in Kilbourn v. Thompson, 103 U.S. 168, 26 L.Ed. 377. The question there was whether the House of Representatives had exceeded its power in directing one of its committees to make a particular investigation. The decision was that it had. The principles announced and applied in the case are that neither house of Congress possesses a "general power of making inquiry into the private affairs of the citizen"; that the power actually possessed is limited to inquiries relating to matters of which the particular house "has jurisdiction" and in respect of which it rightfully may take other action; that, if the inquiry relates to "a matter wherein relief or redress could be had only by a judicial proceeding," it is not within the range of this power, but must be left to the courts, conformably to the constitutional separation of governmental powers; and that for the purpose of determining the essential character of the inquiry recourse may be had to the resolution or order under which it is made. * * *

* * *

Next in order is In re Chapman, 166 U.S. 661, 17 S.Ct. 677. The inquiry there in question was conducted under a resolution of the Senate and related to charges, published in the press, that Senators were yielding to corrupt influences in considering a tariff bill then before the Senate and were speculating in stocks the value of which would be affected by pending amendments to the bill. Chapman appeared before the committee in response to a subpoena, but refused to answer questions pertinent to the inquiry, and was indicted and convicted under the act of 1857 for his refusal. The court sustained the constitutional validity of the act of 1857, and after referring to the constitutional provision empowering either house to punish its members for disorderly behavior and by a vote of two-thirds to expel a member, held that the inquiry related to the integrity and fidelity of Senators in the discharge of their duties, and therefore to a matter "within the range of the constitutional powers of the Senate" and in respect of which it could compel witnesses to appear and testify. * * *

* * *

The latest case is Marshall v. Gordon, 243 U.S. 521, 37 S.Ct. 448. The question there was whether the House of Representatives exceeded its power in punishing, as for a contempt of its authority, a person—not a member—who had written, published, and sent to the chairman of one of its committees an ill-tempered and irritating letter respecting the action and purposes of the committee. Power to make inquiries and obtain evidence by compulsory process was not involved. The court recognized distinctly that the House of Representatives has implied power to punish a person not a member for contempt, as was ruled in *Anderson v. Dunn*, supra, but held that its action in this instance was without constitutional justification. The decision was put on the ground that the letter, while offensive and vexatious, was not calculated or likely to affect

the House in any of its proceedings or in the exercise of any of its functions—in short, that the act which was punished as a contempt was not of such a character as to bring it within the rule that an express power draws after it others which are necessary and appropriate to give effect to it.

While these cases are not decisive of the question we are considering they definitely settle two propositions which we recognize as entirely sound and having a bearing on its solution: One, that the two houses of Congress, in their separate relations, possess, not only such powers as are expressly granted to them by the Constitution, but such auxiliary powers as are necessary and appropriate to make the express powers effective; and the other, that neither house is invested with "general" power to inquire into private affairs and compel disclosures, but only with such limited power of inquiry as is shown to exist when the rule of constitutional interpretation just stated is rightly applied. * * *

With this review of the legislative practice, congressional enactments, and court decisions, we proceed to a statement of our conclusions on the question.

We are of opinion that the power of inquiry—with process to enforce it—is an essential and appropriate auxiliary to the legislative function. * * *

We are further of opinion that the provisions are not of doubtful meaning, but, as was held by this court in the cases we have reviewed, are intended to be effectively exercised, and therefore to carry with them such auxiliary powers as are necessary and appropriate to that end. While the power to exact information in aid of the legislative function was not involved in those cases, the rule of interpretation applied there is applicable here. A legislative body cannot legislate wisely or effectively in the absence of information respecting the conditions which the legislation is intended to affect or change; and where the legislative body does not itself possess the requisite information—which not infrequently is true—recourse must be had to others who do possess it. Experience has taught that mere requests for such information often are unavailing, and also that information which is volunteered is not always accurate or complete; so some means of compulsion are essential to obtain what is needed. All this was true before and when the Constitution was framed and adopted. In that period the power of inquiry, with enforcing process, was regarded and employed as a necessary and appropriate attribute of the power to legislate—indeed, was treated as inhering in it. Thus there is ample warrant for thinking as we do, that the constitutional provisions which commit the legislative function to the two houses are intended to include this attribute to the end that the function may be effectively exercised.

* * * *

We come now to the question whether it sufficiently appears that the purpose for which the witness' testimony was sought was to obtain information in aid of the legislative function. The court below answered the question in the negative and put its decision largely on this ground.
* * *

We are of opinion that the court's ruling on this question was wrong, and that it sufficiently appears, when the proceedings are rightly interpreted, that the object of the investigation and of the effort to secure the witness' testimony was to obtain information for legislative purposes.

It is quite true that the resolution directing the investigation does not in terms avow that it is intended to be in aid of legislation; but it does show that the subject to be investigated was the administration of the Department of Justice—whether its functions were being properly discharged or were being neglected or misdirected, and particularly whether the Attorney General and his assistants were performing or neglecting their duties in respect of the institution and prosecution of proceedings to punish crimes and enforce appropriate remedies against the wrongdoers; specific instances of alleged neglect being recited. Plainly the subject was one on which legislation could be had and would be materially aided by the information which the investigation was calculated to elicit. This becomes manifest when it is reflected that the functions of the Department of Justice, the powers and duties of the Attorney General, and the duties of his assistants are all subject to regulation by congressional legislation, and that the department is maintained and its activities are carried on under such appropriations as in the judgment of Congress are needed from year to year.

The only legitimate object the Senate could have in ordering the investigation was to aid it in legislating, and we think the subject-matter was such that the presumption should be indulged that this was the real object. An express avowal of the object would have been better; but in view of the particular subject-matter was not indispensable.
* * *

*   *   *

While we rest our conclusion respecting the object of the investigation on the grounds just stated, it is well to observe that this view of what was intended is not new, but was shown in the debate on the resolution.

Of course, our concern is with the substance of the resolution and not with any nice questions of propriety respecting its direct reference to the then Attorney General by name. The resolution, like the charges which prompted its adoption, related to the activities of the department while he was its supervising officer; and the reference to him by name served to designate the period to which the investigation was directed.

We think the resolution and proceedings give no warrant for thinking the Senate was attempting or intending to try the Attorney General at its bar or before its committee for any crime or wrongdoing. Nor do we think it a valid objection to the investigation that it might possibly disclose crime or wrongdoing on his part.

The second resolution—the one directing that the witness be attached—declares that his testimony is sought with the purpose of obtaining "information necessary as a basis for such legislative and other action as the Senate may deem necessary and proper." This avowal of contemplated legislation is in accord with what we think is the right interpretation of the earlier resolution directing the investigation. The suggested possibility of "other action" if deemed "necessary or proper" is, of course, open to criticism in that there is no other action in the matter which would be within the power of the Senate. But we do not assent to the view that this indefinite and untenable suggestion invalidates the entire proceeding. The right view in our opinion is that it takes nothing from the lawful object avowed in the same resolution and rightly inferable from the earlier one. It is not as if an inadmissible or unlawful object were affirmatively and definitely avowed.

We conclude that the investigation was ordered for a legitimate object; that the witness wrongfully refused to appear and testify before the committee and was lawfully attached; that the Senate is entitled to have him give testimony pertinent to the inquiry, either at its bar or before the committee; and that the district court erred in discharging him from custody under the attachment.

*   *   *

What has been said requires that the final order in the district court discharging the witness from custody be reversed.

Final order reversed.

Mr. Justice STONE did not participate in the consideration or decision of the case.

WATKINS v. UNITED STATES

Supreme Court of the United States, 1957
354 U.S. 178, 77 S.Ct. 1173, 1 L.Ed.2d 1273

Watkins, an active leader in the labor movement, appeared before a subcommittee of the House Committee on Un-American Activities in 1954 to testify about the activities of himself and others in the Communist party. In his testimony, Watkins admitted that he had cooperated in Communist party functions, and, in addition, he volunteered to identify people whom he believed were still active in that organization. He refused, however, to answer questions concerning the past activity of individuals that he thought were no longer participants in the Communist movement. Petitioner believed that these questions were not relevant to the purpose of the investigation and that the subcommittee did not have the right to simply expose a person's past activities. Watkins was subsequently found guilty of contempt by two lower federal courts.

Mr. Chief Justice WARREN delivered the opinion of the Court.

* * *

We start with several basic premises on which there is general agreement. The power of the Congress to conduct investigations is inherent in the legislative process. That power is broad. It encompasses inquiries concerning the administration of existing laws as well as proposed or possibly needed statutes. It includes surveys of defects in our social, economic or political system for the purpose of enabling the Congress to remedy them. It comprehends probes into departments of the Federal Government to expose corruption, inefficiency or waste. But, broad as is this power of inquiry, it is not unlimited. There is no general authority to expose the private affairs of individuals without justification in terms of the functions of the Congress. This was freely conceded by the Solicitor General in his argument of this case. Nor is the Congress a law enforcement or trial agency. These are functions of the executive and judicial departments of government. No inquiry is an end in itself; it must be related to, and in furtherance of a legitimate task of the Congress. Investigations conducted solely for the personal aggrandizement of the investigators or to "punish" those investigated are indefensible.

It is unquestionably the duty of all citizens to cooperate with the Congress in its efforts to obtain the facts needed for intelligent legislative action. It is their unremitting obligation to respond to subpoenas, to respect the dignity of the Congress and its committees and to testify fully with respect to matters within the province of proper investigation. This, of course, assumes that the constitutional rights of witnesses will be respected by the Congress as they are in a court of justice. The Bill of Rights is applicable to investigations as to all forms of governmental action. Witnesses cannot be compelled to give evidence against themselves. They cannot be subjected to unreasonable search and seizure. Nor can the First Amendment freedoms of speech, press, religion, or political belief and association be abridged.

* * *

In the decade following World War II, there appeared a new kind of congressional inquiry unknown in prior periods of American history. Principally this was the result of the various investigations into the threat of subversion of the United States Government, but other subjects of congressional interest also contributed to the changed scene. This new phase of legislative inquiry involved a broad-scale intrusion into the lives and affairs of private citizens. It brought before the courts novel questions of the appropriate limits of congressional inquiry. Prior cases, like *Kilbourn, McGrain* and *Sinclair*, had defined the scope of investigative power in terms of the inherent limitations of the sources of that power. In the more recent cases, the emphasis shifted to problems of accommodating the interest of the Government with the rights and privileges of individuals. The central theme was the application of the Bill of Rights as a restraint upon the assertion of governmental power in this form.

It was during this period that the Fifth Amendment privilege against self-incrimination was frequently invoked and recognized as a legal limit upon the authority of a committee to require that a witness answer its questions. Some early doubts as to the applicability of that privilege before a legislative committee never matured. When the matter reached this Court, the Government did not challenge in any way that the Fifth Amendment protection was available to the witness, and such a challenge could not have prevailed. It confined its argument to the character of the answers sought and to the adequacy of the claim of privilege. * * *

A far more difficult task evolved from the claim by witnesses that the committees' interrogations were infringements upon the freedoms of the First Amendment. Clearly, an investigation is subject to the command that the Congress shall make no law abridging freedom of speech or press or assembly. While it is true that there is no statute to be reviewed, and that an investigation is not a law, nevertheless an investigation is part of lawmaking. It is justified solely as an adjunct to the legislative process. The First Amendment may be invoked against infringement of the protected freedoms by law or by lawmaking.

Abuses of the investigative process may imperceptibly lead to abridgment of protected freedoms. The mere summoning of a witness and compelling him to testify, against his will, about his beliefs, expressions or associations is a measure of governmental interference. And when those forced revelations concern matters that are unorthodox, unpopular, or even hateful to the general public, the reaction in the life of the witness may be disastrous. This effect is even more harsh when it is past beliefs, expressions or associations that are disclosed and judged by current standards rather than those contemporary with the matters exposed. Nor does the witness alone suffer the consequences. Those who are identified by witnesses and thereby placed in the same glare of publicity are equally subject to public stigma, scorn and obloquy. Beyond that, there is the more subtle and immeasurable effect upon those who tend to adhere to the most orthodox and uncontroversial views and associations in order to avoid a similar fate at some future time. That this impact is partly the result of non-governmental activity by private persons cannot relieve the investigators of their responsibility for initiating the reaction.

The Court recognized the restraints of the Bill of Rights upon congressional investigations in United States v. Rumely, 345 U.S. 41, 73 S.Ct. 543. The magnitude and complexity of the problem of applying the First Amendment to that case led the Court to construe narrowly the resolution describing the committee's authority. It was concluded that, when First Amendment rights are threatened, the delegation of power to the committee must be clearly revealed in its charter.

* * *

We have no doubt that there is no congressional power to expose for the sake of exposure. The public is, of course, entitled to be informed concerning the workings of its government. That cannot be inflated into a general power to expose where the predominant result can only be an invasion of the private rights of individuals. But a solution to our problem is not to be found in testing the motives of committee members for this purpose. Such is not our function. Their motives alone would not vitiate an investigation which had been instituted by a House of Congress if that assembly's legislative purpose is being served.

* * *

* * * It is the responsibility of the Congress, in the first instance, to insure that compulsory process is used only in furtherance of a legislative purpose. That requires that the instructions to an investigating committee spell out that group's jurisdiction and purpose with sufficient particularity. Those instructions are embodied in the authorizing resolution. That document is the committee's charter. Broadly drafted and loosely worded, however, such resolutions can leave tremendous latitude to the discretion of the investigators. The more vague the committee's charter is, the greater becomes the possibility that the committee's specific actions are not in conformity with the will of the parent House of Congress.

The authorizing resolution of the Un-American Activities Committee was adopted in 1938 when a select committee, under the chairmanship of Representative Dies, was created. Several years later, the Committee was made a standing organ of the House with the same mandate. It defines the Committee's authority as follows:

"The Committee on Un-American Activities, as a whole or by subcommittee, is authorized to make from time to time investigations of (1) the extent, character, and objects of un-American propaganda activities in the United States, (2) the diffusion within the United States of subversive and un-American propaganda that is instigated from foreign countries or of a domestic origin and attacks the principle of the form of government as guaranteed by our Constitution, and (3) all other questions in relation thereto that would aid Congress in any necessary remedial legislation."

It would be difficult to imagine a less explicit authorizing resolution. Who can define the meaning of "un-American"? What is that single, solitary "principle of the form of government as guaranteed by our Constitution"? There is no need to dwell upon the language, however. At one time, perhaps, the resolution might have been read narrowly to confine the Committee to the subject of propaganda. The events that have transpired in the fifteen years before the interrogation of petitioner make such a construction impossible at this date.

* * *

Combining the language of the resolution with the construction it has been given, it is evident that the preliminary control of the Committee exercised by the House of Representatives is slight or non-existent. No one could reasonably deduce from the charter the kind of investigation that the Committee was directed to make. As a result, we are asked to engage in a process of retroactive rationalization. Looking backward from the events that transpired, we are asked to uphold the Committee's actions unless it appears that they were clearly not authorized by the charter. As a corollary to this inverse approach, the Government urges that we must view the matter hospitably to the power of the Congress—that if there is any legislative purpose which might have been furthered by the kind of disclosure sought, the witness must be punished for withholding it. No doubt every reasonable indulgence of legality must be accorded to the actions of a coordinate branch of our Government. But such deference cannot yield to an unnecessary and unreasonable dissipation of precious constitutional freedoms.

The Government contends that the public interest at the core of the investigations of the Un-American Activities Committee is the need by the Congress to be informed of efforts to otherthrow the Government by force and violence so that adequate legislative safeguards can be erected. From this core, however, the Committee can radiate outward infinitely to any topic thought to be related in some way to armed insurrection. The outer reaches of this domain are known only by the content of "un-American activities." Remoteness of subject can be aggravated by a probe for a depth of detail even farther removed from any basis of legislative action. A third dimension is added when the investigators turn their attention to the past to collect minutiae on remote topics, on the hypothesis that the past may reflect upon the present.

The consequences that flow from this situation are manifold. In the first place, a reviewing court is unable to make the kind of judgment made by the Court in *United States* v. *Rumely*, supra. The Committee is allowed, in essence, to define its own authority, to choose the direction and focus of its activities. In deciding what to do with the power that has been conferred upon them, members of the Committee may act pursuant to motives that seem to them to be the highest. Their decisions, nevertheless, can lead to ruthless exposure of private lives in order to gather data that is neither desired by the Congress nor useful to it. Yet it is impossible in this circumstance, with constitutional freedoms in jeopardy, to declare that the Committee has ranged beyond the area committed to it by its parent assembly because the boundaries are so nebulous.

More important and more fundamental than that however, it insulates the House that has authorized the investigation from the witnesses who are subjected to the sanctions of compulsory process. There is a wide gulf between the responsibility for the use of investigative power and the actual exercise of that power. This is an especially vital consideration in assuring respect for constitutional liberties. Protected freedoms should not be placed in danger in the absence of a clear determination by the House or the Senate that a particular inquiry is justified by a specific legislative need.

It is, of course, not the function of this Court to prescribe rigid rules for the Congress to follow in drafting resolutions establishing investigating committees. That is a matter peculiarly within the realm of the legislature, and its decisions will be accepted by the courts up to the point where their own duty to enforce the constitutionally protected rights of individuals is affected. An excessively broad charter, like that of the House Un-American Activities Committee, places the courts in an untenable position if they are to strike a balance between the public need for a particular interrogation and the right of citizens to carry on their affairs free from unnecessary governmental interference. It is impossible in such a situation to ascertain whether any legislative purpose justifies the disclosures sought and, if so, the importance of that information to the Congress in furtherance of its legislative function. The reason no court can make this critical judgment is that the House of Representatives itself has never made it. Only the legislative assembly initiating an investigation can assay the relative necessity of specific disclosures.

Absence of the qualitative consideration of petitioner's questioning by the House of Representatives aggravates a serious problem, revealed in this case, in the relationship of congressional investigating committees and the witnesses who appear before them. Plainly these committees are restricted to the missions delegated to them, i.e., to acquire certain data to be used by the House or the Senate in coping with a problem that falls within its legislative sphere. No witness can be compelled to make disclosures on matters outside that area. This is a jurisdictional concept of pertinency drawn from the nature of a congressional committee's source of authority. It is not wholly different from nor unrelated to the element of pertinency embodied in the criminal statute under which petitioner was prosecuted. When the definition of jurisdictional pertinency is as uncertain and wavering as in the case of the Un-American Activities Committee, it becomes extremely

difficult for the Committee to limit its inquiries to statutory pertinency.

Since World War II, the Congress has practically abandoned its original practice of utilizing the coercive sanction of contempt proceedings at the bar of the House. The sanction there imposed is imprisonment by the House until the recalcitrant witness agrees to testify or disclose the matters sought, provided that the incarceration does not extend beyond adjournment. The Congress has instead invoked the aid of the federal judicial system in protecting itself against contumacious conduct. It has become customary to refer these matters to the United States Attorneys for prosecution under criminal law.

The appropriate statute is found in 2 U.S.C. § 192, 2 U.S.C.A. § 192. It provides:

"Every person who having been summoned as a witness by the authority of either House of Congress to give testimony or to produce papers upon any matter under inquiry before either House, or any joint committee established by a joint or concurrent resolution of the two Houses of Congress, or any committee of either House of Congress, willfully makes default, or who, having appeared, refuses to answer any question pertinent to the question under inquiry, shall be deemed guilty of a misdemeanor, punishable by a fine of not more than $1,000 nor less than $100 and imprisonment in a common jail for not less than one month nor more than twelve months."

In fulfillment of their obligation under this statute, the courts must accord to the defendants every right which is guaranteed to defendants in all other criminal cases. Among these is the right to have available, through a sufficiently precise statute, information revealing the standard of criminality before the commission of the alleged offense. Applied to persons prosecuted under § 192, this raises a special problem in that the statute defines the crime as refusal to answer "any question pertinent to the question under inquiry." Part of the standard of criminality, therefore, is the pertinency of the questions propounded to the witness.

The problem attains proportion when viewed from the standpoint of the witness who appears before a congressional committee. He must decide at the time the questions are propounded whether or not to answer. * * * An erroneous determination on his part, even if made in the utmost good faith, does not exculpate him if the court should later rule that the questions were pertinent to the question under inquiry.

It is obvious that a person compelled to make this choice is entitled to have knowledge of the subject to which the interrogation is deemed pertinent. That knowledge must be available with the same degree of explicitness and clarity that the Due Process Clause requires in the expression of any element of a criminal offense. The "vice of vagueness" must be avoided here as in all other crimes. There are several sources that can outline the "question under inquiry" in such a way that the rules against vagueness are satisfied. The authorizing resolution, the remarks of the chairman or members of the committee, or even the nature of the proceedings themselves, might sometimes make the topic clear. This case demonstrates, however, that these sources often leave the matter in grave doubt.

* * *

Having exhausted the several possible indicia of the "question under inquiry," we remain unenlightened as to the subject to which the questions asked petitioner were pertinent. Certainly, if the point is that obscure after trial and appeal, it was not adequately revealed to petitioner when he had to decide at his peril whether or not to answer. Fundamental fairness demands that no witness be compelled to make such a determination with so little guidance. Unless the subject matter has been made to appear with undisputable clarity, it is the duty of the investigative body, upon objection of the witness on grounds of pertinency, to state for the record the subject under inquiry at that time and the manner in which the propounded questions are pertinent thereto. To be meaningful, the explanation must describe what the topic under inquiry is and the connective reasoning whereby the precise questions asked relate to it.

The statement of the Committee Chairman in this case, in response to petitioner's protest, was woefully inadequate to convey sufficient information as to the pertinency of the questions to the subject under inquiry. Petitioner was thus not accorded a fair opportunity to determine whether he was within his rights in refusing to answer, and his conviction is necessarily invalid under the Due Process Clause of the Fifth Amendment.

We are mindful of the complexities of modern government and the ample scope that must be left to the Congress as the sole constitutional depository of legislative power. Equally mindful are we of the indispensable function, in the exercise of that power, of congressional investigations. The conclusions we have reached in this case will not prevent the Congress, through its committees, from obtaining any information it needs for the proper fulfillment of its role in our scheme of government. The legislature is free to determine the kinds of data that should be collected. It is only those investigations that are conducted by use of compulsory process that give rise to a need to protect the rights of individuals against illegal encroachment. That protection can be readily achieved through procedures which prevent the separation of power from responsibility and which provide the constitutional requisites of fairness for witnesses. A measure

of added care on the part of the House and the Senate in authorizing the use of compulsory process and by their committees in exercising that power would suffice. That is a small price to pay if it serves to uphold the principles of limited, constitutional government without constricting the power of the Congress to inform itself.

The judgment of the Court of Appeals is reversed, and the case is remanded to the District Court with instructions to dismiss the indictment.

It is so ordered.

[Justice CLARK dissented; Justices BURTON and WHITTAKER did not participate in the decision.]

BARENBLATT v. UNITED STATES

Supreme Court of the United States, 1959
360 U.S. 109, 79 S.Ct. 1081, 3 L.Ed.2d 1115

The facts are set out in the opinion below.

Mr. Justice HARLAN delivered the opinion of the Court.

Once more the Court is required to resolve the conflicting constitutional claims of congressional power and of an individual's right to resist its exercise. The congressional power in question concerns the internal process of Congress in moving within its legislative domain; it involves the utilization of its committees to secure "testimony needed to enable it efficiently to exercise a legislative function belonging to it under the Constitution." * * *

Broad as it is, the power is not, however, without limitation. Since Congress may only investigate into those areas in which it may potentially legislate or appropriate, it cannot

inquire into matters which are within the exclusive province of one of the other branches of the Government. * * * And the Congress, in common with all branches of the Government, must exercise its powers subject to the limitations placed by the Constitution on governmental action, more particularly in the context of this case the relevant limitations of the Bill of Rights.

The congressional power of inquiry, its range and scope, and an individual's duty in relation to it, must be viewed in proper perspective. * * * The power and the right of resistance to it are to be judged in the concrete, not on the basis of abstractions. In the present case congressional efforts to learn the extent of a nation-wide, indeed worldwide, problem have brought one of its investigating committees into the field of education. Of course, broadly viewed, inquiries cannot be made into the teaching that is pursued in any of our educational institutions. When academic teaching-freedom and its corollary learning-freedom, so essential to the well-being of the Nation, are claimed, this Court will always be on the alert against intrusion by Congress into this constitutionally protected domain. But this does not mean that the Congress is precluded from interrogating a witness merely because he is a teacher. An educational institution is not a constitutional sanctuary from inquiry into matters that may otherwise be within the constitutional legislative domain merely for the reason that inquiry is made of someone within its walls.

*   *   *

We here review petitioner's conviction under 2 U.S.C. § 192, 2 U.S.C.A. § 192 for contempt of Congress, arising from his refusal to answer certain questions put to him by a Subcommittee of the House Committee on Un-American Activities during the course of an inquiry concerning alleged Communist infiltration into the field of education.

*   *   *

Pursuant to a subpoena, and accompanied by counsel, petitioner on June 28, 1954, appeared as a witness before this congressional Subcommittee. After answering a few preliminary questions and testifying that he had been a graduate student and teaching fellow at the University of Michigan from 1947 to 1950 and an instructor in psychology at Vassar College from 1950 to shortly before

his appearance before the Subcommittee, petitioner objected generally to the right of the Subcommittee to inquire into his "political" and "religious" beliefs or any "other personal and private affairs" or "associational activities," upon grounds set forth in a previously prepared memorandum which he was allowed to file with the Subcommittee. Thereafter petitioner specifically declined to answer each of the following five questions:

"Are you now a member of the Communist Party? [Count One.]

"Have you ever been a member of the Communist Party? [Count Two.]

"Now, you have stated that you knew Francis Crowley. Did you know Francis Crowley as a member of the Communist Party? [Count Three.]

"Were you ever a member of the Haldane Club of the Communist Party while at the University of Michigan? [Count Four.]

"Were you a member while a student of the University of Michigan Council of Arts, Sciences, and Professions?" [Count Five.]

In each instance the grounds of refusal were those set forth in the prepared statement. Petitioner expressly disclaimed reliance upon "the Fifth Amendment."

*   *   *

Petitioner's various contentions resolve themselves into three propositions: First, the compelling of testimony by the Subcommittee was neither legislatively authorized nor constitutionally permissible because of the vagueness of Rule XI of the House of Representatives, Eighty-third Congress, the charter of authority of the parent Committee. Second, petitioner was not adequately apprised of the pertinency of the Subcommittee's questions to the subject matter of the inquiry. Third, the questions petitioner refused to answer infringed rights protected by the First Amendment.

Subcommittee's Authority to Compel Testimony

At the outset it should be noted that Rule XI authorized this Subcommittee to compel testimony within the framework of the investigative authority conferred on the Un-American Activities Committee. Petitioner contends that *Watkins* v. *United States* * * * nevertheless held the grant of this power in all circumstances ineffective because of the vagueness of Rule XI in delineating the Committee jurisdiction to which its exercise was to be appurtenant. * * *

The *Watkins* case cannot properly be read as standing for such a proposition. A principal contention in *Watkins* was that the refusals to answer were justified because the requirement * * * that the questions asked be "pertinent to the question under inquiry" had not been satisfied. * * * This Court reversed the conviction solely on that ground, holding that Watkins had not been adequately apprised of the subject matter of the Subcommittee's investigation or the pertinency thereto of the questions he refused to answer. * * * In so deciding the Court drew upon Rule XI only as one of the facets in the total *mise en scène* in its search for the "question under inquiry" in that particular investigation. * * * That the vagueness of Rule XI was not alone determinative is also shown by the Court's further statement that aside from the Rule "the remarks of the

chairman or members of the committee, or even the nature of the proceedings themselves, might sometimes make the topic [under inquiry] clear." * * * In short, while *Watkins* was critical of Rule XI, it did not involve the broad and inflexible holding petitioner now attributes to it.

Petitioner also contends, independently of *Watkins*, that the vagueness of Rule XI deprived the Subcommittee of the right to compel testimony in this investigation into Communist activity. We cannot agree with this contention which in its furthest reach would mean that the House Un-American Activities Committee under its existing authority has no right to compel testimony in any circumstances. Granting the vagueness of the Rule, we may not read it in isolation from its long history in the House of Representatives. Just as legislation is often given meaning by the gloss of legislative reports, administrative interpretation, and long usage, so the proper meaning of an authorization to a corgressional committee is not to be derived alone from its abstract terms unrelated to the definite content furnished them by the course of congressional actions. The Rule comes to us with a "persuasive gloss of legislative history," * * * which shows beyond doubt that in pursuance of its legislative concerns in the domain of "national security" the House has clothed the Un-American Activities Committee with pervasive authority to investigate Communist activities in this country.

* * *

In the context of these unremitting pursuits, the House has steadily continued the life of the Committee at the commencement of each new

Congress, it has never narrowed the powers of the Committee, whose authority has remained throughout identical with that contained in Rule XI; and it has continuingly supported the Committee's activities with substantial appropriations. Beyond this, the Committee was raised to the level of a standing committee of the House in 1945, it having been but a special committee prior to that time.

In light of this long and illuminating history it can hardly be seriously argued that the investigation of Communist activities generally, and the attendant use of compulsory process, was beyond the purview of the Committee's intended authority under Rule XI.

* * *

Pertinency Claim

Undeniably a conviction for contempt under 2 U.S.C. § 192, 2 U.S. C.A. § 192 cannot stand unless the questions asked are pertinent to the subject matter of the investigation. *Watkins* v. *United States.* * * * But the factors which led us to rest decision on this ground in *Watkins* were very different from those involved here.

In *Watkins* the petitioner had made specific objection to the Subcommittee's questions on the ground of pertinency; the question under inquiry had not been disclosed in any illuminating manner; and the questions asked the petitioner were not only amorphous on their face, but in some instances clearly foreign to the alleged subject matter of the investigation—"Communism in labor." * * *

In contrast, petitioner in the case before us raised no objections on the ground of pertinency at the time any of the questions were put to him. It is true that the memorandum which petitioner brought with him to the Subcommittee hearing contained the statement, "to ask me whether I am or have been a member of the Communist Party may have dire consequences. I might wish to * * * challenge the pertinency of the question to the investigation," and at another point quoted from this Court's opinion in Jones v. Securities & Exchange Comm., 298 U.S. 1, 56 S.Ct. 654, language relating to a witness' right to be informed of the pertinency of questions asked him by an administrative agency. These statements cannot, however, be accepted as the equivalent of a pertinency objection. At best they constituted but a contemplated objection to questions still unasked, and buried as they were in the context of petitioner's general challenge to the power of the Subcommittee they can hardly be considered adequate, within the meaning of what was said in *Watkins*, * * * to trigger what would have been the Subcommittee's reciprocal obligation had it been faced with a pertinency objection.

We need not, however, rest decision on petitioner's failure to object on this score, for here "pertinency" was made to appear "with undisputable clarity." * * * First of all, it goes without saying that the scope of the Committee's authority was for the House, not a witness, to determine, subject to the ultimate reviewing responsibility of this Court. What we deal with here is whether petitioner was sufficiently apprised of "the topic under inquiry" thus authorized "and the connective reasoning whereby the precise questions asked relate[d] to it." * * * In light of his prepared memorandum of constitutional objections there can be no doubt that this petitioner was well aware of the Subcommittee's authority and purpose to question him as it did. * * * In addition the other sources of this information which we recognized in *Watkins* * * * leave no room for a "pertinency" objection on this record. The subject matter of the inquiry had been identified at the commencement of the investigation as Communist infiltration into the field of education. Just prior to petitioner's appearance before the Subcommittee, the scope of the day's hearings had been announced as "in the main communism in education and the experiences and background in the party by Francis X. T. Crowley. It will deal with activities in Michigan, Boston, and in some small degree, New York." Petitioner had heard the Subcommittee interrogate the witness Crowley along the same lines as he, petitioner, was evidently to be questioned, and had listened to Crowley's testimony identifying him as a former member of an alleged Communist student organization at the University of Michigan while they both were in attendance there. Further, petitioner had stood mute in the face of the Chairman's statement as to why he had been called as a witness by the Subcommittee. And, lastly, unlike Watkins, * * * petitioner refused to answer questions as to his own Communist Party affiliations, whose pertinency of course was clear beyond doubt.

* * *

Constitutional Contentions

Our function, at this point, is purely one of constitutional adjudication in the particular case and upon the particular record before us, not to pass judgment upon the general wisdom or efficacy of the activities of this Committee in a vexing and complicated field.

* * *

* * * Undeniably, the First Amendment in some circumstances protects an individual from being compelled to disclose his associational relationships. However, the protections of the First Amendment, unlike a proper claim of the privilege against self-incrimination under the Fifth Amendment, do not afford a witness the right to resist inquiry in all circumstances. Where First Amendment rights are asserted to bar governmental interrogation resolution of the issue always involves a balancing by the courts of the competing private and public interests at stake in the particular circumstances shown. These principles were recognized in the *Watkins* case, where, in speaking of the First Amendment in relation to congressional inquiries, we said * * * "It is manifest that despite the adverse effects which follow upon compelled disclosure of private matters, not all such inquiries are barred. * * * The critical element is the existence of, and the weight to be ascribed to, the interest of the Congress in demanding disclosures from an unwilling witness." * * *

* * *

That Congress has wide power to legislate in the field of Communist activity in this Country, and to conduct appropriate investigations in aid thereof, is hardly debatable. The existence of such power has never been questioned by this Court, and it is sufficient to say, without particularization, that Congress has enacted or considered in this field a wide range of legislative measures, not a few of which have stemmed from recommendations of the very Committee whose actions have been drawn in question here. In the last analysis this power rests on the right of self-preservation, "the ultimate value of any society." * * * Justification for its exercise in turn rests on the long and widely accepted view that the tenets of the Communist Party include the ultimate overthrow of the Government of the United States by force and violence, a view which has been given formal expression by the Congress.

* * *

* * * To suggest that because the Communist Party may also sponsor peaceable political reforms the constitutional issues before us should not be judged as if that Party were just an ordinary political party from the standpoint of national security, is to ask this Court to blind itself to world affairs which have determined the whole course of our national policy since the close of World War II. * * * Indeed we do not understand petitioner here to suggest that Congress in no circumstances may inquire into Communist activity in the field of education. Rather, his position is in effect that this particular investigation was aimed not at the revolutionary aspects but at the theoretical classroom discussion of communism.

In our opinion this position rests on a too constricted view of the nature of the investigatory process, and is not supported by a fair assessment of the record before us. An investigation of advocacy of or preparation for overthrow certainly embraces the right to identify a witness as a member of the Communist Party, * * * and to inquire into

the various manifestations of the Party's tenets. The strict requirements of a prosecution under the Smith Act, * * * are not the measure of the permissible scope of a congressional investigation into "overthrow," for of necessity the investigatory process must proceed step by step. Nor can it fairly be concluded that this investigation was directed at controlling what is being taught at our universities rather than at overthrow. The statement of the Subcommittee Chairman at the opening of the investigation evinces no such intention, and so far as this record reveals nothing thereafter transpired which would justify our holding that the thrust of the investigation later changed. The record discloses considerable testimony concerning the foreign domination and revolutionary purposes and efforts of the Communist Party. That there was also testimony on the abstract philosophical level does not detract from the dominant theme of this investigation—Communist infiltration furthering the alleged ultimate purpose of overthrow. And certainly the conclusion would not be justified that the questioning of petitioner would have exceeded permissible bounds had he not shut off the Subcommittee at the threshold.

Nor can we accept the further contention that this investigation should not be deemed to have been in furtherance of a legislative purpose because the true objective of the Committee and of the Congress was purely "exposure." So long as Congress acts in pursuance of its constitutional power, the Judiciary lacks authority to intervene on the basis of the motives which spurred the exercise of that power. * * * "It is, of course, true," as was said in McCray v. United States, 195 U.S. 27,

55, 24 S.Ct. 769, 776, "that if there be no authority in the judiciary to restrain a lawful exercise of power by another department of the government, where a wrong motive or purpose has impelled to the exertion of the power, that abuses of a power conferred may be temporarily effectual. The remedy for this, however, lies, not in the abuse by the judicial authority of its functions, but in the people, upon whom, after all, under our institutions, reliance must be placed for the correction of abuses committed in the exercise of a lawful power." These principles of course apply as well to committee investigations into the need for legislation as to the enactments which such investigations may produce. * * * Thus, in stating in the *Watkins* case * * * that "there is no congressional power to expose for the sake of exposure," we at the same time declined to inquire into the "motives of committee members," and recognized that their "motives alone would not vitiate an investigation which had been instituted by a House of Congress if that assembly's legislative purpose is being served." * * *

Finally, the record is barren of other factors which in themselves might sometimes lead to the conclusion that the individual interests at stake were not subordinate to those of the state. There is no indication in this record that the Subcommittee was attempting to pillory witnesses. Nor did petitioner's appearance as a witness follow from indiscriminate dragnet procedures, lacking in probable cause for belief that he possessed information which might be helpful to the Subcommittee. And the relevancy of the questions put to him by the Subcommittee is not open to doubt.

We conclude that the balance between the individual and the governmental interests here at stake must be struck in favor of the latter, and that therefore the provisions of the First Amendment have not been offended.

We hold that petitioner's conviction for contempt of Congress discloses no infirmity, and that the judgment of the Court of Appeals must be affirmed.

Affirmed.

Mr. Justice BLACK, with whom the CHIEF JUSTICE [WARREN] and Mr. Justice DOUGLAS concur, dissenting.

* * *

* * * The Court today affirms, and thereby sanctions the use of the contempt power to enforce questioning by congressional committees in the realm of speech and association. I cannot agree with this disposition of the case for I believe that the resolution establishing the House Un-American Activities Committee and the questions that Committee asked Barenblatt violate the Constitution in several respects. (1) Rule XI creating the Committee authorizes such a sweeping, unlimited, all-inclusive and undiscriminating compulsory examination of witnesses in the field of speech, press, petition and assembly that it violates the procedural requirements of the Due Process Clause of the Fifth Amendment. (2) Compelling an answer to the questions asked Barenblatt abridges freedom of speech and association in contravention of the First Amendment. (3) The Committee proceedings were part of a legislative program to stigmatize and punish by public identification and exposure all witnesses considered by the Commit-

tee to be guilty of Communist affiliations, as well as all witnesses who refused to answer Committee questions on constitutional grounds; the Committee was thus improperly seeking to try, convict, and punish suspects, a task which the Constitution expressly denies to Congress and grants exclusively to the courts, to be exercised by them only after indictment and in full compliance with all the safeguards provided by the Bill of Rights.

It goes without saying that a law to be valid must be clear enough to make its commands understandable. * * * This is simply because it would be unthinkable to convict a man for violating a law he could not understand. * * * Vagueness becomes even more intolerable in this area if one accepts, as the Court today does, a balancing test to decide if First Amendment rights shall be protected. It is difficult at best to make a man guess—at the penalty of imprisonment—whether a court will consider the State's need for certain information superior to society's interest in unfettered freedom. It is unconscionable to make him choose between the right to keep silent and the need to speak when the statute supposedly establishing the "state's interest" is too vague to give him guidance. * * *

Measured by the foregoing standards, Rule XI cannot support any conviction for refusal to testify. * * *

* * *

I do not agree that laws directly abridging First Amendment freedoms can be justified by a congressional or judicial balancing process. There are, of course, cases suggesting that a law which primarily regulates conduct but which might also indirectly affect speech can be upheld if the effect on speech is minor in relation to the need for control of the conduct. With these cases I agree. * * * Neither these cases, nor any others, can be read as allowing legislative bodies to pass laws abridging freedom of speech, press and association merely because of hostility to views peacefully expressed in a place where the speaker had a right to be. Rule XI, on its face and as here applied, since it attempts inquiry into beliefs, not action—ideas and associations, not conduct—does just that.

To apply the Court's balancing test under such circumstances is to read the First Amendment to say "Congress shall pass no law abridging freedom of speech, press, assembly and petition, unless Congress and the Supreme Court reach the joint conclusion that on balance the interest of the Government in stifling these freedoms is greater than the interest of the people in having them exercised." This is closely akin to the notion that neither the First Amendment nor any other provision of the Bill of Rights should be enforced unless the Court believes it is *reasonable* to do so. Not only does this violate the genius of our *written* Constitution, but it runs expressly counter to the injunction to Court and Congress made by Madison when he introduced the Bill of Rights. "If they [the first ten amendments] are incorporated into the Constitution, independent tribunals of justice will consider themselves in a peculiar manner the guardians of those rights; they will be an impenetrable bulwark against *every* assumption of power in the Legislative or Executive; they will be naturally led to resist *every* encroachment upon rights expressly stipulated for in the Constitution by the declaration of rights." Unless we return to this view of our judicial function, unless we once again accept the notion that the Bill of Rights means what it says and that this Court must enforce that meaning, I am of the opinion that our great charter of liberty will be more honored in the breach than in the observance.

But even assuming what I cannot assume, that some balancing is proper in this case, I feel that the Court after stating the test ignores it completely. At most it balances the right of the Government to preserve itself against Barenblatt's right to refrain from revealing Communist affiliations. Such a balance, however, mistakes the factors to be weighed. In the first place, it completely leaves out the real interest in Barenblatt's silence, the interest of the people as a whole in being able to join organizations, advocate causes and make political "mistakes" without later being subjected to governmental penalties for having dared to think for themselves. It is this right, the right to err politically, which keeps us strong as a Nation. For no number of laws against communism can have as much effect as the personal conviction which comes from having heard its arguments and rejected them, or from having once accepted its tenets and later recognized their worthlessness. Instead, the obloquy which results from investigations such as this not only stifles "mistakes" but prevents all but the most courageous from hazarding any views which might at some later time become disfavored This result, whose importance cannot be overestimated, is doubly crucial when it affects the universities, on which we must largely rely for the

experimentation and development of new ideas essential to our country's welfare. It is these interests of society, rather than Barenblatt's own right to silence, which I think the Court should put on the balance against the demands of the Government, if any balancing process is to be tolerated. Instead they are not mentioned, while on the other side the demands of the Government are vastly overstated and called "self preservation." * * *

Moreover, I cannot agree with the Court's [n]otion that First Amendment freedoms must be abridged in order to "preserve" our country. That notion rests on the unarticulated premise that this Nation's security hangs upon its power to punish people because of what they think, speak or write about, or because of those with whom they associate for political purposes. The Government, in its brief, virtually admits this position when it speaks of the "communication of unlawful ideas." I challenge this premise, and deny that ideas can be proscribed under our Constitution. * * *

* * *

[N]o matter how often or how quickly we repeat the claim that the Communist Party is not a political party, we cannot outlaw it, as a group, without endangering the liberty of all of us. The reason is not hard to find, for mixed among those aims of communism which are illegal are perfectly normal political and social goals. And muddled with its revolutionary tenets is a drive to achieve power through the ballot, if it can be done. These things necessarily make it a political party whatever other, illegal, aims it may have. * * *

The fact is that once we allow any group which has some political aims or ideas to be driven from the ballot and from the battle for men's minds because some of its members are bad and some of its tenets are illegal, no group is safe. * * * History should teach us then, that in times of high emotional excitement minority parties and groups which advocate extremely unpopular social or governmental innovations will always be typed as criminal gangs and attempts will always be made to drive them out. * * *

* * *

Finally, I think Barenblatt's conviction violates the Constitution because the chief aim, purpose and practice of the House Un-American Activities Committee, as disclosed by its many reports, is to try witnesses and punish them because they are or have been Communists or because they refuse to admit or deny Communist affiliations. The punishment imposed is generally punishment by humiliation and public shame. * * *

I do not question the Committee's patriotism and sincerity in doing all this. I merely feel that it cannot be done by Congress under our Constitution. For, even assuming that the Federal Government can compel witnesses to testify as to Communist affiliations in order to subject them to ridicule and social and economic retaliation, I cannot agree that this is a legislative function. Such publicity is clearly punishment, and the Constitution allows only one way in which people can be convicted and punished. * * *

Ultimately all the questions in this case really boil down to one—whether we as a people will try fearfully and futilely to preserve democracy by adopting totalitarian methods, or whether in accordance with our traditions and our Constitution we will have the confidence and courage to be free.

* * *

[Justice BRENNAN dissented separately.]

COURT–CURB PROPOSALS STIMULATED BY CONTROVERSIAL DECISIONS [b]

Intermittently throughout its history, the Judicial Branch had come under attack, both from the Executive and Legislative Branches, for unpopular decisions or for general tendencies in a series of rulings. In 1937, for example, President Roosevelt proposed to "pack" the Supreme Court with his own appointees by increasing the number of justices to 15, so that the Court's "nine old men" would not be able to continue striking down New Deal legislation. The plan failed. A less overt attempt to curb the Court came in the form of a constitutional amendment (S J Res 44), which passed the Senate in 1954 but failed of enactment in the House. Designed "to fortify the independence of the Supreme Court," the amendment would have permanently set the size of the Court at nine justices and made them ineligible for the Presidency or Vice Presidency, and prohibited federal judges from serving after age 75.

---

b. Source: *Court-Curb Proposals Stimulated by Controversial Decisions,* Congress and the Nation I (Washington: Congressional Quarterly, Inc., 1965), p. 1442. Reprinted by permission.

As a result of a series of controversial decisions between 1954 and 1957, however, new and sharper criticism of the Supreme Court evolved from two factions—Southerners resentful of desegregation rulings and conservative Northern Republicans angered by decisions on federal-state relations, anti-sedition laws and contempt of Congress rulings.

In 1958, the Southerners and conservative Republicans formed an ad hoc alliance, which vigorously—but unsuccessfully—advocated imposing stringent curbs on the Court's powers. The alliance's chief complaints fell into four broad categories. They asserted that the Supreme Court had:

Upset established precedents and was basing its decisions on "sociological" rather than legal principles in order to bar racial segregation.

Ignored long-established constitutional relations between states and the Federal Government and wrongly struck down state laws under the preemption doctrine.

Intruded on Congress' right of investigation by reversing certain citations for contempt of Congress.

Endangered the national security by rulings in subversive activities cases.

Critical response to Court decisions in these areas was of two kinds. One point of view held that individual decisions might be reversed by piecemeal legislation, but that the Court's authority should remain untouched. The other held that the Judicial Branch had been exceeding its powers and should be curbed by general legislation. The former view proved most effective in the long run.

The most serious Congressional moves toward general Court curbs were embodied in two 1958 bills:

HR 3. Passed by the House July 17, 1958, by a 241–155 roll-call vote (D 100–109; R 141–46); recommitted by the Senate Aug. 21, 1958, by a 41–40 roll call (D 27–17; R 14–23). The measure would have established two new rules governing application of the preemption doctrine: (1) federal laws were to be construed as intended to invalidate laws only if Congress had stated specifically that it wished to preempt a field of legislation between a state law and a federal law, and (2) existing federal laws should not be construed as indicating Congress' intention to bar states from passing laws punishing sedition against the Federal Government.

S 2646 (the Jenner-Butler bill). Tabled by the Senate Aug. 20, 1958, by a 49–41 roll-call vote (D 30–16; R 19–25), when offered as a floor amendment to a pending bill, S 2646—the broadest of the so-called 1958 "court-curb" bills—would have hamstrung Judicial Branch powers in six ways: (1) barred the Supreme Court from assuming appellate jurisdiction in cases involving state regulations for admission to the bar; (2) provided that no past or future federal anti-sedition laws should be construed by the courts as prohibiting enforcement of otherwise valid state anti-sedition laws; (3) provided that each of the two chambers of Congress was the final judge of whether questions put to witnesses by its committees were pertinent to the authorized purpose of the committee inquiry; (4) provided that a person being tried for contempt of Congress for refusing to answer questions before a Congressional committee could not argue in defense that the questions were not pertinent unless he had raised the issue of pertinency at the time the questions were asked; (5) provided that the 1940 Smith Act made all teaching and advocacy of forcible overthrow of the U.S. Government a crime, regardless of whether such teaching and advocacy was conceived as an abstract doctrine or as an incitement to practical action; and (6) provided that the term "organize," as used in the Smith Act to make it a crime to organize a group seeking to overthrow the Government by force and violence, applied not only to the original act of bringing the groups together, but also to continuing organizational activities, such as recruiting members, conducting classes and regrouping units.

By 1959, however, the Congressional view of the Supreme Court was vastly improved. Three reasons cited for the Congressional change of attitude: the influx of "pro-Court" Northern Democrats into the Senate following the 1958 election; a series of Court decisions giving the states wider scope in taxation and other matters; and two major 1959 security rulings (*Uphaus* and *Barenblatt*) reducing fears that the Court was interfering with Government attempts to combat subversive activities.

In 1959 and for the remainder of the postwar period, the Southerner-conservative Republican coalition, from time to time, did emerge to succeed in reversing specific High Court decisions. But, despite rumblings between 1962 and 1964 on Supreme Court rulings on school prayer and reapportionment, the coalition was not successful in actually curbing the Court's powers.

GIBSON v. FLORIDA LEGISLATIVE INVESTIGATION COMMITTEE

Supreme Court of the United States, 1963
372 U.S. 539, 83 S.Ct. 889, 9 L.Ed.2d 929

During much of the late 1950s the Miami branch of the National Association for the Advancement of Colored People was under investigation by successive committees of the Florida legislature. At one point during the investigations the association was asked to reveal the list of its entire membership. The group refused to comply. In a case arising out of this controversy the Florida Supreme Court held that while a committee could not require disclosure of the membership list, it could compel the "custodian" of the records to bring them to the hearings and to refer to them while answering questions. In 1959, the Florida legislature established the Legislative Investigation Committee to resume investigations of the NAACP. The Committee, which was primarily concerned with examining Communist activities and infiltration into various organizations ordered Theodore Gibson, the president of the Miami branch, to appear before it and to bring with him the association's membership records for his own reference. Although Gibson was willing to answer questions about membership, he refused to bring the records with him. He contended that this request interfered with associational rights of members and prospective members of the NAACP protected under the First and Fourteenth Amendments. A state court found Gibson in contempt, and the Florida Supreme Court sustained that judgment whereupon Gibson appealed to the U.S. Supreme Court.

Mr. Justice GOLDBERG delivered the opinion of the Court.

* * *

We are here called upon once again to resolve a conflict between individual rights of free speech and association and governmental interest in conducting legislative investigations. Prior decisions illumine the contending principles.

This Court has repeatedly held that rights of association are within the ambit of the constitutional protections afforded by the First and Fourteenth Amendments. * * * The respondent Committee does not contend otherwise, nor could it, for, as was said in NAACP v. Alabama, * * * "It is beyond debate that freedom to engage in association for the advancement of beliefs and ideas is an inseparable aspect of the 'liberty' assured by the Due Process Clause of the Fourteenth Amendment, which embraces freedom of speech." 357 U.S., at 460, 78 S.Ct., at 1171. And it is equally clear that the guarantee encompasses protection of privacy of association in organizations such as that of which the petitioner is president; indeed, in [earlier cases] this Court held NAACP membership lists of the very type here in question to be beyond the States' power of discovery in the circumstances there presented.

The First and Fourteenth Amendment rights of free speech and free association are fundamental and highly prized and "need breathing space to survive." NAACP v. Button, 371 U.S. 415, 433, 83 S.Ct. 328, 338. "Freedoms such as these are protected not only against heavy-handed frontal attack, but also from being stifled by more subtle governmental interference." Bates v. Little Rock, * * * 361 U.S., at 523, 80 S.Ct., at 416. And, as declared in NAACP v. Alabama, * * * 357 U.S., at 462, 78 S.Ct., at 1171, "It is hardly a novel perception that compelled disclosure of affiliation with groups engaged in advocacy may constitute [an] * * * effective * * * restraint on freedom of association. * * * This Court has recognized the vital relationship between freedom to associate and privacy in one's associations. * * * Inviolability of privacy in group asso-

ciation may in many circumstances be indispensable to preservation of freedom of association, particularly where a group espouses dissident beliefs." So it is here.

At the same time, however, this Court's prior holdings demonstrate that there can be no question that the State has power adequately to inform itself—through legislative investigation, if it so desires—in order to act and protect its legitimate and vital interests. * * *

* * *

Significantly, the parties are in substantial agreement as to the proper test to be applied to reconcile the competing claims of government and individual and to determine the propriety of the Committee's demands. As declared by the respondent Committee in its brief to this Court, "Basically, this case hinges entirely on the question of whether the evidence before the Committee [was] * * * sufficient to show probable cause of nexus between the NAACP Miami Branch, and Communist activities." We understand this to mean—regardless of the label applied, be it "nexus," "foundation," or whatever—that it is an essential prerequisite to the validity of an investigation which intrudes into the area of constitutionally protected rights of speech, press, association and petition that the State convincingly show a substantial relation between the information sought and a subject of overriding and compelling state interest. Absent such a relation between the NAACP and conduct in which the State may have a compelling regulatory concern, the Committee has not "demonstrated so cogent an interest in obtaining and making public" the membership information sought to be obtained as to "justify the substantial abridgment of associational freedom which such disclosures will effect." Bates v. Little Rock, supra, 361 U.S., at 524, 80 S.Ct., at 417. "Where there is a significant encroachment upon personal liberty, the State may prevail only upon showing a subordinating interest which is compelling." * * *

Applying these principles to the facts of this case, the respondent Committee contends that the prior decisions of this Court * * * compel a result here upholding the legislative right of inquiry. In [those cases] however, it was a refusal to answer a question or questions concerning the witness' *own* past or present membership *in the Communist Party* which supported his conviction. It is apparent that the necessary preponderating governmental interest and, in fact, the very result in those cases were founded on the holding that the Communist Party is not an ordinary or legitimate political party, as known in this country, and that, because of its particular nature, membership therein is *itself* a permissible subject of regulation and legislative scrutiny. Assuming the correctness of the premises on which those cases were decided, no further demonstration of compelling governmental interest was deemed necessary, since the direct object of the challenged questions there was discovery of membership in the Communist Party, a matter held pertinent to a proper subject then under inquiry.

Here, however, it is not alleged Communists who are the witnesses before the Committee and it is not discovery of their membership in that party which is the object of the challenged inquiries. Rather, it is the NAACP itself which is the subject of the investigation, and it is its local president, the petitioner, who was called before the Committee and held in contempt because he refused to divulge the contents of its membership records. There is no suggestion that the Miami branch of the NAACP or the national organization with which it is affiliated was, or is, itself a subversive organization. Nor is there any indication that the activities or policies of the NAACP were either Communist dominated or influenced. In fact, this very record indicates that the association was and is against communism and has voluntarily taken steps to keep Communists from being members. Each year since 1950, the NAACP has adopted resolutions barring Communists from membership in the organization. Moreover, the petitioner testified that all prospective officers of the local organization are thoroughly investigated for Communist or subversive connections and, though subversive activities constitute grounds for termination of association membership, no such expulsions from the branch occurred during the five years preceding the investigation.

[T]he Committee was not here seeking from the petitioner or the records of which he was custodian any information as to whether he, himself, or even other persons were members of the Communist Party, Communist front or affiliated organizations, or other allegedly subversive groups; instead, the entire thrust of the demands on the petitioner was that he disclose whether other persons were members of the NAACP itself a concededly legitimate and nonsubversive organization. Compelling such an organization, engaged in the exercise of First and Fourteenth Amendment rights, to disclose its membership presents, under our cases, a question wholly different from compelling the Communist Party to disclose its own membership. Moreover, even to say, as in *Barenblatt* * * * that it is permissible to inquire into the subject of Communist infiltration of educational or other organizations does not mean that it is permissible to demand or require from such other groups disclosure of their membership by inquiry into their records when such disclosure will seriously inhibit or impair the exercise of constitutional rights and has not itself been demonstrated to bear a crucial relation to a proper governmental interest or to be essential to fulfillment of a proper governmental purpose. The prior holdings that governmental interest in controlling subversion and the particular character of the Communist Party and its objectives outweigh the right of individual Communists to conceal party membership or affiliations by no means require the wholly different conclusion that other groups—concededly legitimate—automatically forfeit their rights to privacy of association simply because the general subject matter of the legislative inquiry is Communist subversion or infiltration. The fact that governmental interest was deemed compelling in *Barenblatt* [and other cases] and held to support the inquiries there made into membership in the Communist Party does not resolve the issues here, where the challenged questions go to membership in an admittedly lawful organization.

* * *

In the absence of directly determinative authority, we turn, then, to consideration of the facts now before us. Obviously, if the respondent were still seeking discovery of the entire membership list, we could readily dispose of this case on the authority of *Bates* v. *Little Rock*, and *NAACP* v. *Alabama*, supra; a like result would follow if it were merely attempting to do piecemeal what could not be done in a single step. Though there are indications that the respondent Committee intended to inquire broadly into the NAACP membership records, there is no need to base our decision today upon a prediction as to the course which the Committee might have pursued if initially unopposed by the petitioner. Instead, we rest our result on the fact that the record in this case is insufficient to show a substantial connection between the Miami branch of the NAACP and Communist *activities* which the respondent Committee itself concedes is an essential prerequisite to demonstrating the immediate, substantial, and subordinating state interest necessary to sustain its right of inquiry into the membership lists of the association.

Basically, the evidence relied upon by the respondent to demonstrate the necessary foundation consists of the testimony of R. J. Strickland, an investigator for the Committee and its predecessors, and Arlington Sands, a former association official.

Strickland identified by name some 14 persons whom he said either were or had been Communists or members of Communist "front" or "affiliated" organizations. His description of their connection with the association was simply that "each of them has been a member of and/or participated in the meetings and other affairs of the NAACP in Dade County, Florida." In addition, one of the group was identified as having made, at an unspecified time, a contribution of unspecified amount to the local organization.

We do not know from this ambiguous testimony how many of the 14 were supposed to have been NAACP members. For all that appears, and there is no indicated reason to entertain a contrary belief, each or all of the named persons may have attended no more than one or two wholly public meetings of the NAACP and such attendance, like their membership, to the extent it existed, in the association, may have been wholly peripheral and begun and ended many years prior even to commencement of the present investigation in 1956. In addition, it is not clear whether the asserted Communist affiliations and the association with the NAACP, however slight, coincided in time. * * *

* * *

Of course, a legislative investigation—as any investigation—must proceed "step by step," * * * but step by step or in totality, an adequate foundation for inquiry must be laid before proceeding in such a manner as will substantially intrude upon and severely curtail or inhibit constitutionally protected activities or seriously interfere with similarly protected associational rights. No such foundation has been laid here. The respondent Committee has failed to demonstrate the compelling and subordinating governmental interest essential to support direct inquiry into the membership records of the NAACP.

Nothing we say here impairs or denies the existence of the underlying legislative right to investigate or legislate with respect to subversive activities by Communists or anyone else; our decision today deals only with the manner in which such power may be exercised and we hold simply that groups which themselves are neither engaged in subversive or other illegal or improper activities nor

demonstrated to have any substantial connections with such activities are to be protected in their rights of free and private association.
* * *

To permit legislative inquiry to proceed on less than an adequate foundation would be to sanction unjustified and unwarranted intrusions into the very heart of the constitutional privilege to be secure in associations in legitimate organizations engaged in the exercise of First and Fourteenth Amendment rights; to impose a lesser standard than we here do would be inconsistent with the maintenance of those essential conditions basic to the preservation of our democracy.

The judgment below must be and is reversed.

Reversed.

Mr. Justice BLACK, concurring.

I concur in the Court's opinion and judgment reversing the judgment of the Supreme Court of Florida although, for substantially the same reasons stated by Mr. Justice DOUGLAS in his concurring opinion, I would prefer to reach our decision by a different approach. I agree with Mr. Justice DOUGLAS that the Fourteenth Amendment makes the First Amendment applicable to the States and protects the freedoms of religion, speech, press, assembly, and petition from state abridgment with the same force and to the same degree that the First Amendment protects them from federal abridgment. That, as the cases cited by Mr. Justice DOUGLAS show, is what this Court has previously held. I agree also that these Amendments encompass freedom of the people to associate in an infinite number of organizations including the National Association for the Advancement of

Colored People, of which petitioner here was president at the time it was under investigation by the Florida committee. In my view the constitutional right of association includes the privilege of any person to associate with Communists or anti-Communists, Socialists or anti-Socialists, or, for that matter, with people of all kinds of beliefs, popular or unpopular. I have expressed these views in many other cases and I adhere to them now. Since, as I believe the National Association for the Advancement of Colored People and its members have a constitutional right to choose their own associates, I cannot understand by what constitutional authority Florida can compel answers to questions which abridge that right. Accordingly, I would reverse here on the ground that there has been a direct abridgment of the right of association of the National Association for the Advancement of Colored People and its members. But, since the Court assumes for purposes of this case that there was no direct abridgment of First Amendment freedoms, I concur in the Court's opinion, which is based on constitutional principles laid down in Schneider v. Irvington, 308 U.S. 147, 161, 60 S.Ct. 146, 150 (1939), and later cases. * * *

[Justices CLARK, HARLAN, STEWART, and WHITE dissented.]

EASTLAND v. UNITED STATES SERVICEMEN'S FUND

Supreme Court of the United States, 1975
421 U.S. 491, 95 S.Ct. 1813, 44 L.Ed.2d 324

The U.S. Servicemen's Fund was a nonprofit organization aimed at contributing to the welfare and interests of persons then serving in the military. It did this by, among other things, maintaining coffeehouses near military installations and by distributing underground newspapers. Its coffeehouses and newspapers allegedly became focal points for the expression of dissident views on the war in Southeast Asia. The Senate Subcommittee on Internal Security, chaired by James Eastland, began an investigation into the activities of the group and issued a subpoena *duces tecum* to a bank to produce records it had of the organization's financial transactions. The Fund sued to enjoin compliance with the subpoena arguing that the records constituted privileged information having First Amendment protection because they were the equivalent of confidential membership lists. A federal district court held that the organization had not made sufficient showing of irreparable injury to justify issuing an injunction and, taking the Supreme Court's decision in *Barenblatt* v. *United States* as its guide, that Congress's interest in acquiring the information should prevail over any alleged chilling of First Amendment rights. A federal appeals court reversed, citing among other cases, *Gibson* v. *Florida Legislative Investigation Committee,* and held that since the admitted goal of the subpoena was to uncover the identities of the organization's donors, the information could indeed be gained quite as readily from bank records as membership lists. It found the subpoena a substantial interference with First Amendment rights, and it ordered the district court to fashion appropriate orders. The committee sought certiorari from the Supreme Court.

Because of special circumstances, the decision of the Supreme Court turned on the Speech and Debate Clause of the Constitution unlike other cases involving congressional investigations. Because the committee issued a subpoena on a bank, a third party (which had no reason to refuse to comply), the Fund could not itself invoke judicial review by refusing to turn over subpoenaed records. Its only remedy seemed to be to get a federal court to *enjoin* the issuance by Congress of the subpoena to the bank.

Mr. Chief Justice BURGER delivered the opinion of the Court.

* * *

We conclude the actions of the Senate Subcommittee, the individual Senators, and the Chief Counsel are protected by the Speech or Debate Clause of the Constitution, Art. I, § 6, cl. 1, and are therefore immune from judicial interference. We reverse.

The question to be resolved is whether the actions of the petitioners fall within the "sphere of legislative activity." If they do, the petitioners "shall not be questioned in any other Place" about those activities since the prohibitions of the Speech and Debate Clause are absolute. * * *

Without exception, our cases have read the Speech or Debate Clause broadly to effectuate its purposes. * * * The purpose of the Clause is to insure that the legislative function the Constitution allocates to Congress may be performed independently. * * * In our system "the clause serves the additional function of reinforcing the separation of powers so deliberately established by the Founders." * * *

* * *

The applicability of the Clause to private civil actions is supported by the absoluteness of the terms "shall not be questioned," and the sweep of the terms "in any other Place." In reading the Clause broadly we have said that legislators acting within the sphere of legitimate legislative activity "should be protected not only from the consequences of litigation's

results but also from the burden of defending themselves." Dombrowski v. Eastland, 387 U.S. [82 (1967)], at 85, 87 S.Ct., at 1427. Just as a criminal prosecution infringes upon the independence which the Clause is designed to preserve, a private civil action, whether for an injunction or damages, creates a distraction and forces Members to divert their time, energy, and attention from their legislative tasks to defend the litigation. Private civil actions also may be used to delay and disrupt the legislative function. Moreover, whether a criminal action is instituted by the Executive Branch, or a civil action is brought by private parties, judicial power is still brought to bear on Members of Congress and legislative independence is imperiled. We reaffirm that once it is determined that Members are acting within the "legitimate legislative sphere" the Speech or Debate Clause is an absolute bar to interference. Doe v. McMillan, 412 U.S. [306 (1973)], at 314, 93 S.Ct., at 2025.

In determining whether particular activities other than literal speech or debate fall within the "legitimate legislative sphere" we look to see whether the activities are "done in a session of the House by one of its members in relation to the business before it." * * * More specifically, we must determine whether the activities are

"an integral part of the deliberative and communicative processes by which Members participate in committee and House proceedings with respect to the consideration and passage or rejection of proposed legislation or with respect to other matters which the Constitution places within the jurisdiction of either House."

Gravel v. United States, 408 U.S. 606, 625, 92 S.Ct., at 2627.

See Doe v. McMillan, supra, 412 U.S., at 313, 93 S.Ct., at 2025.

The power to investigate and to do so through compulsory process plainly falls within that definition. This Court has often noted that the power to investigate is inherent in the power to make laws because "[a] legislative body cannot legislate wisely or effectively in the absence of information respecting the conditions which the legislation is intended to affect or change." * * * Issuance of subpoenas such as the one in question here has long been held to be a legitimate use by Congress of its power to investigate. * * *

* * *

The particular investigation at issue here is related to and in furtherance of a legitimate task of Congress. * * * On this record the pleadings show that the actions of the Members and the Chief Counsel fall within the "sphere of legitimate legislative activity." The Subcommittee was acting under an unambiguous resolution from the Senate authorizing it to make a complete study of the "administration, operation, and enforcement of the Internal Security Act of 1950." * * * S.Res. 341, 91st Cong., 2d Sess., 116 Cong. Rec. 3419 (January 30, 1970). That grant of authority is sufficient to show that the investigation upon which the Subcommittee had embarked concerned a subject on which "legislation could be had." * * *

The propriety of making USSF a subject of the investigation and subpoena is a subject on which the scope of our inquiry is narrow. * * * Even the most cursory look at the facts presented by the pleadings reveals the legitimacy of the USSF subpoena. Inquiry into the sources of funds used to carry on activities suspected by a Subcommittee of Congress to have a potential for undermining the morale of the armed forces is within the legitimate legislative sphere. Indeed, the complaint here tells us that USSF operated on or near military and naval bases, and that its facilities became the "focus of dissent" to declared national policy. Whether USSF activities violated any statute is not relevant; the inquiry was intended to inform Congress in an area where legislation may be had. USSF asserted it does not know the sources of its funds; in light of the Senate authorization to the Subcommittee to investigate "infiltration by persons who are or may be under the control of foreign governments," * * * and in view of the pleaded facts, it is clear that the subpoena to discover USSF's bank records "may fairly be deemed within [the Subcommittee's] province." * * *

We conclude that the Speech or Debate Clause provides complete immunity for the Members for issuance of this subpoena. We draw no distinction between the Members and the Chief Counsel. In Gravel, * * * we made it clear that "the day-to-day work of such aides is so critical to the Members' performance that they must be treated as [the Members'] alter egos." * * * Here the complaint alleges that the "Subcommittee members and staff caused the * * * subpoena to be issued * * * under the authority of Senate Resolution 366. * * *" The complaint thus does not distinguish between the activities of the Members and those of the Chief Counsel. * * * Since the Members are immune because the issuance of the subpoena is "essential to legislating" their aides share that immunity.   *   *   *

*   *   *

Respondents also contend that the subpoena cannot be protected by the speech or debate immunity because the "sole purpose" of the investigation is to "force public disclosure of beliefs, opinions, expressions and associations of private citizens which may be unorthodox or unpopular."   *   *   *   Respondents view the scope of the privilege too narrowly. Our cases make clear that in determining the legitimacy of a congressional act we do not look to the motives alleged to have prompted it.   *   *   *   The wisdom of congressional approach or methodology is not open to judicial veto.   *   *   *   Nor is the legitimacy of a congressional inquiry to be defined by what it produces. The very nature of the investigative function—like any research—is that it takes the searchers up some "blind alleys" and into nonproductive enterprises. To be a valid legislative inquiry there need be no predictable end result.

Finally, respondents argue that the purpose of the subpoena was to "harass, chill, punish and deter them" in the exercise of their First Amendment rights,   *   *   *   and thus that the subpoena cannot be protected by the Clause. Their theory seems to be that once it is alleged that First Amendment rights may be infringed by congressional action the judiciary may intervene to protect those rights; the Court of Appeals seems to have subscribed to that theory. That approach, however, ignores the absolute nature of the speech or debate protection and our cases which have broadly construed that protection.

*   *   *

When the Senate case was in the Court of Appeals it was consolidated with three other cases because it was assumed that "a decision in [the Senate] case might well control the disposition of [the others]." Those cases involve subpoenas from the House Internal Security Committee to banks for the bank records of certain organizations. As in the Senate aspect of this case, the organizations whose bank records were sought sued alleging that if the subpoenas were honored their constitutional rights would be violated. The issue of speech or debate protection for Members and aides is presented in all the cases. However, the complaints in the House cases are different from the complaint in the Senate case, additional parties are involved, and consequently additional issues may be presented.

Progress in the House cases was suspended when they were in the pleading stage awaiting the outcome of the Senate aspect of this case. The issues in them, therefore, have not been joined. Additionally, it appears that the Session in which the House subpoenas were issued has expired. Since the House, unlike the Senate, is not a continuing body, *   *   *   a question of mootness may be raised. Moreover it appears that the committee that issued the subpoenas has been abolished by the House, H.Res. 5, 94th Cong., 1st Sess., January 14, 1975. In view of these problems, and because the House aspects of this case were not briefed or argued here, we conclude it would be unwise to attempt to decide any issues they might present that are not resolved in the Senate aspect of this case.   *   *   *

Judgment with respect to the Senate aspect of this case is reversed and the case is remanded to the Court of Appeals for entry of a judgment directing the District Court to dismiss the complaint. The House aspects of this case are remanded with directions to remand to the District Court for further consideration consistent with this opinion.

Reversed and remanded.

Mr. Justice MARSHALL, with whom Mr. Justice BRENNAN and Mr. Justice STEWART join, concurring in the judgment.

I agree with the Court that Speech and Debate Clause protects the actions of the Senate petitioners in this case from judicial interference, and that the House cases should be reconsidered by the District Court. As our cases have consistently held, however, the Speech and Debate Clause protects legislators and their confidential aides from suit; it does not immunize congressional action from judicial review. I write today only to emphasize that the Speech and Debate Clause does not entirely immunize a congressional subpoena from challenge by a party not in a position to assert his constitutional rights by refusing to comply with it.

* * *

The Court applies well-settled doctrine to the present case and holds that since the issuance of the subpoena fell within the sphere of legitimate legislative activity, the proceedings against the petitioners must come to an end. I do not read the Court to suggest, however, nor could I agree, that the constitutionality of a congressional subpoena is always shielded from more searching judicial inquiry. For, as the very cases on

which the Court relies demonstrate, the protection of the Speech and Debate Clause is personal. It extends to Members and their counsel acting in a legislative capacity; it does not preclude judicial review of their decisions in an appropriate case, whether they take the form of legislation or a subpoena.

* * *

The Speech and Debate Clause cannot be used to avoid meaningful review of constitutional objections to a subpoena simply because the subpoena is served on a third party. Our prior cases arising under the Speech and Debate Clause indicate only that a Member of Congress or his aide may not be called upon to defend a subpoena against constitutional objection, and not that the objection will not be heard at all.

* * *

This case does not present the questions of what would be the proper procedure, and who might be the proper parties defendant, in an effort to get before a court a constitutional challenge to a subpoena duces tecum issued to a third party. As respondent's counsel conceded at oral argument, this case is at an end if the Senate petitioners are upheld in their claim of immunity, as they must be.

Mr. Justice DOUGLAS, dissenting.

I would affirm the judgment below.

The basic issues in this case were canvassed by me in Tenney v. Brandhove, 341 U.S. 367, 381–383, 71 S.Ct. 783, 790–791 (dissenting opinion), and by the Court in Dombrowski v. Eastland, 387 U.S. 82, 87 S.Ct. 1425, in an opinion which I joined.

Under our federal regime that delegates, by the Constitution and Acts of Congress, awesome powers to individuals, that power may not be used to deprive people of their First Amendment or other constitutional rights. It is my view that no official, no matter how high or majestic his or her office, who is within the reach of judicial process, may invoke immunity for his actions for which wrong-doers normally suffer. There may be few occasions when, on the merits, it would be appropriate to invoke such a remedy. But no regime of law that can rightfully claim that name may make trustees of these vast powers immune from actions brought by people who have been wronged by official action. See Watkins v. United States, 354 U.S. 178, 198.

See *Senate Select Committee on Presidential Campaign Activities* v. *Nixon*, p. 295.

d. THE SPEECH AND DEBATE CLAUSE (CONGRESSIONAL IMMUNITY)

GRAVEL v. UNITED STATES

Supreme Court of the United States, 1972
408 U.S. 606, 92 S.Ct. 2614, 33 L.Ed.2d 583

On the evening of June 29, 1971, Senator Mike Gravel of Alaska convened the Senate Subcommittee on Public Buildings and Grounds, of which he was chairman, and proceeded to read aloud summaries of a classified Defense Department study on the decision-making process of evolving American involvement in the Vietnam conflict known as the "Pentagon Papers." When he finished reading, he introduced all forty-seven volumes of the study into the record as an exhibit. Following this, Gravel gave a copy of the materials to Beacon Press, a Boston publishing house, on the understanding it would publish the Papers (without profit to Gravel). Later, a federal grand jury was impaneled to investigate the unauthorized release of the Papers to the publisher, and it subpoenaed Leonard Rodberg, a Gravel aide, to testify. Rodberg moved to quash the subpoena, and, subsequent to the granting of a motion which allowed Gravel to intervene in the proceedings on Rodberg's behalf, a U. S. Court of Appeals issued an order resting partly on the Speech and Debate Clause which barred inquiry into the senator's actions or motives or those of his aide concerning legislative acts. While commercial publication of the Papers (or circumstances attending it) was not held to be a legislative act and thus was unprotected, the appellate court also ruled that Gravel and Rodberg could not be questioned about it because of a common law privilege analogous to an existing executive privilege. (The Court held, however, that third parties, e.g., publishers, were not exempt from a grand jury inquiry.) Both sides appealed—the government challenging the breadth of the ruling, Gravel attacking its narrowness (he asserted private publication was protected by the Speech and Debate Clause). The Supreme Court granted certiorari.

Opinion of the Court by Mr. Justice WHITE, announced by Mr. Justice BLACKMUN.

* * *

Because the claim is that a Member's aide shares the Member's constitutional privilege, we consider first whether and to what extent Senator Gravel himself is exempt from process or inquiry by a grand jury investigating the commission of a crime. Our frame of reference is Art. I, § 6, cl. 1, of the Constitution. * * *

The last sentence of the clause provides Members of Congress with two distinct privileges. Except in cases of "Treason, Felony and Breach of the Peace," the clause shields Members from arrest while attending or traveling to and from a session of their House. History reveals, and prior cases so hold, that this part of the clause exempts Members from arrest in civil cases only. * * * Indeed, implicit in the narrow scope of the privilege of freedom from arrest is, as Jefferson noted, the judgment that legislators ought not to stand above the law they create but ought generally to be bound by it as are ordinary persons. * * *

In recognition, no doubt, of the force of this part of Section 6, Senator Gravel disavows any assertion of general immunity from the criminal law. But he points out that the last portion of Section 6 affords Members of Congress another vital privilege— they may not be questioned in any other place for any speech or debate in either House. The claim is not that while one part of Section 6 generally permits prosecutions for treason, felony and breach of the peace, another part nevertheless broadly forbids them. Rather, his insistence is that the Speech or Debate Clause at the very least protects him from criminal or civil liability and from questioning elsewhere than in the Senate, with respect to the events occurring at the subcommittee hearing at which the Pentagon Papers were introduced into the public record. To

us this claim is incontrovertible. The Speech or Debate Clause was designed to assure a coequal branch of the government wide freedom of speech, debate and deliberation without intimidation or threats from the Executive Branch. It thus protects Members against prosecutions that directly impinge upon or threaten the legislative process. We have no doubt that Senator Gravel may not be made to answer—either in terms of questions or in terms of defending himself from prosecution—for the events that occurred at the subcommittee meeting. * * *

Even so, the United States strongly urges that because the Speech or Debate Clause confers a privilege only upon "Senators and Representatives," Rodberg himself has no valid claim to constitutional immunity from grand jury inquiry. In our view, both courts below correctly rejected this position. We agree with the Court of Appeals that for the purpose of construing the privilege a Member and his aide are to be "treated as one." * * * [I]t is literally impossible, in view of the complexities of the modern legislative process, with Congress almost constantly in session and matters of legislative concern constantly proliferating, for Members of Congress to perform their legislative tasks without the help of aides and assistants; that the day-to-day work of such aides is so critical to the Members' performance that they must be treated as the latters' alter ego; and that if they are not so recognized, the central role of the Speech or Debate Clause—to prevent intimidation of legislators by the executive and accountability before a possibly hostile judiciary * * * —will inevitably be diminished and frustrated.

* * *

* * * Rather than giving the clause a cramped construction, the Court has sought to implement its fundamental purpose of freeing the legislator from executive and judicial oversight that realistically threaten to control his conduct as a legislator. We have little doubt that we are neither exceeding our judicial powers nor mistakenly construing the Constitution by holding that the Speech or Debate Clause applies not only to a Member but also to his aides insofar as the conduct of the latter would be a protected legislative act if performed by the Member himself.

* * *

The United States fears the abuses that history reveals have occurred when legislators are invested with the power to relieve others from the operation of otherwise valid civil and criminal laws. But these abuses, it seems to us, are for the most part obviated if the privilege applicable to the aide is viewed, as it must be, as the privilege of the Senator, and invocable only by the Senator or by the aide on the Senator's behalf, and if in all events the privilege available to the aide is confined to those services that would be immune legislative conduct if performed by the Senator himself. This view places beyond the Speech or Debate Clause a variety of services characteristically performed by aides for Members of Congress, even though within the scope of their employment. It likewise provides no protection for criminal conduct threatening the security of the person or property of others, whether performed at the direction of the Senator in preparation for or in execution of a legislative act or done without his knowledge or direction.

Neither does it immunize Senator or aide from testifying at trials or grand jury proceedings involving third-party crimes where the questions do not require testimony about or impugn a legislative act. * * *

We are convinced also that the Court of Appeals correctly determined that Senator Gravel's alleged arrangement with Beacon Press to publish the Pentagon Papers was not protected speech or debate within the meaning of Art. I, § 6, cl. 1, of the Constitution.

* * *

But the clause has not been extended beyond the legislative sphere. That Senators generally perform certain acts in their official capacity as Senators does not necessarily make all such acts legislative in nature. Members of Congress are constantly in touch with the Executive Branch of the Government and with administrative agencies—they may cajole, and exhort with respect to the administration of a federal statute—but such conduct, though generally done, is not protected legislative activity.
* * *

Legislative acts are not all-encompassing. The heart of the clause is speech or debate in either House, and insofar as the clause is construed to reach other matters, they must be an integral part of the deliberative and communicative processes by which Members participate in committee and House proceedings with respect to the consideration and passage or rejection of proposed legislation or with respect to other matters which the Constitution places within the jurisdiction of either House. As the Court of Appeals put it, the courts have extended the privilege to matters beyond pure speech or debate in either House, but "only

when necessary to prevent indirect impairment of such deliberations."
* * *

Here private publication by Senator Gravel through the cooperation of Beacon Press was in no way essential to the deliberations of the House; nor does questioning as to private publication threaten the integrity or independence of the House by impermissibly exposing its deliberations to executive influence. The Senator had conducted his hearings, the record and any report that was forthcoming were available both to his committee and the House. Insofar as we are advised, neither Congress nor the full committee ordered or authorized the publication. We cannot but conclude that the Senator's arrangements with Beacon Press were not part and parcel of the legislative process.

There are additional considerations. Article I, § 6, cl. 1, as we have emphasized, does not purport to confer a general exemption upon Members of Congress from liability or process in criminal cases. Quite the contrary is true. While the Speech or Debate Clause recognizes speech, voting and other legislative acts as exempt from liability that might otherwise attach, it does not privilege either Senator or aide to violate an otherwise valid criminal law in preparing for or implementing legislative acts. If republication of these classified papers was a crime under an Act of Congress, it was not entitled to immunity under the Speech or Debate Clause. It also appears that the grand jury was pursuing this very subject in the normal course of a valid investigation. The Speech or Debate Clause does not in our view extend immunity to Rodberg, as a Senator's aide, from testifying before the grand jury

about the arrangement between Senator Gravel and Beacon Press or about his own participation, if any, in the alleged transaction, so long as legislative acts of the Senator are not impugned.

Similar considerations lead us to disagree with the Court of Appeals insofar as it fashioned, tentatively at least, a nonconstitutional testimonial privilege protecting Rodberg from any questioning by the grand jury concerning the matter of republication of the Pentagon Papers. This privilege, thought to be similar to that protecting executive officials from liability for libel, cf. Barr v. Matteo, 360 U.S. 564, 79 S.Ct. 1335 (1959), was considered advisable "to the extent that a congressman has responsibility to inform his constituents." * * * But we cannot carry a judicially fashioned privilege so far as to immunize criminal conduct proscribed by an Act of Congress or to frustrate the grand jury's inquiry into whether publication of these classified documents violated a federal criminal statute. The so-called executive privilege has never been applied to shield executive officers from prosecution for crime, the Court of Appeals was quite sure that third parties were neither immune from liability nor from testifying about the republication matter and we perceive no basis for conferring a testimonial privilege on Rodberg as the Court of Appeals seemed to do.

* * *

Because the Speech or Debate Clause privilege applies both to Senator and aide, it appears to us that * * * the order * * * would afford ample protection for the privilege if it forbade questioning any witness, including Rodberg: (1) concerning the Senator's conduct, or the conduct of his aides, at the June 29, 1971, meeting of the subcommittee; (2) concerning the motives and purposes behind the Senator's conduct, or that of his aides, at that meeting; (3) concerning communications between the Senator and his aides during the term of their employment and related to said meeting or any other legislative act of the Senator; (4) except as it proves relevant to investigating possible third party crime, concerning any act, in itself not criminal, performed by the Senator, or by his aides in the course of their employment, in preparation for the subcommittee hearing. * * *

Judgment of Court of Appeals vacated and case remanded.

Mr. Justice DOUGLAS, dissenting.

I would construe the Speech and Debate Clause to insulate Senator Gravel and his aides from inquiry concerning the Pentagon Papers, and Beacon Press from inquiry concerning publication of them, for that publication was but another way of informing the public as to what had gone on in the privacy of the Executive Branch concerning the conception and pursuit of the so-called "war" in Vietnam. Alternatively, I would hold that Beacon Press is protected by the First Amendment from prosecution or investigations for publishing or undertaking to publish the Pentagon Papers.

* * *

Mr. Justice BRENNAN, with whom Mr. Justice DOUGLAS and Mr. Justice MARSHALL, join dissenting.

* * *

In holding that Senator Gravel's alleged arrangement with Beacon Press to publish the Pentagon Papers is not shielded from extra-senatorial inquiry by the Speech or Debate Clause, the Court adopts what for me is a far too narrow view of the legislative function. The Court seems to assume that words spoken in debate or written in congressional reports are protected by the Clause, so that if Senator Gravel had recited part of the Pentagon Papers on the Senate floor or copied them into a Senate report, those acts could not be questioned "in any other place." Yet because he sought a wider audience, to publicize information deemed relevant to matters pending before his own committee, the Senator suddenly loses his immunity and is exposed to grand jury investigation and possible prosecution for the publication. * * *

Thus the Court excludes from the sphere of protected legislative activity a function that I had supposed lay at the heart of our democratic system. I speak, of course, of the legislator's duty to inform the public about matters affecting the administration of government. That this "informing function" falls into the class of things "generally done in a session of the House by one of its members in relation to the business before it," * * * was explicitly acknowledged by the Court in Watkins v. United States, 354 U.S. 178, 77 S.Ct. 1173 (1957).

* * *

* * * It would accomplish little toward the goal of legislative freedom to exempt an official act from intimidating scrutiny, if other conduct leading up to the act and intimately related to it could be deterred by a similar threat. * * *

Mr. Justice STEWART, dissenting in part.

* * *

Under the Court's ruling, a Congressman may be subpoenaed by a vindictive Executive to testify about informants who have not committed crimes and who have no knowledge of crime. Such compulsion can occur, because the judiciary has traditionally imposed virtually no limitations on the grand jury's broad investigatory powers; grand jury investigations are not limited in scope to specific criminal acts, and standards of materiality and relevance are greatly relaxed. But even if the Executive had reason to believe that a member of Congress had knowledge of a specific probable violation of law, it is by no means clear to me that the Executive's interest in the administration of justice must *always* override the public interest in having an informed Congress. Why should we not, given the tension between two competing interests, *each* of constitutional dimensions, balance the claims of the Speech or Debate Clause against the claims of the grand jury in the particularized contexts of specific cases? And why are not the Houses of Congress the proper institutions in most situations to impose sanctions upon a Representative or Senator who withholds information about crime acquired in the course of his legislative duties?

DOE v. McMILLAN

Supreme Court of the United States, 1973
412 U.S. 306 93 S.Ct. 2018, 36 L.Ed.2d 912

In December 1970, a congressional subcommittee filed with the Speaker of the House a report (which was subsequently ordered by the House to be printed as a public document) of its duly authorized investigation into the plight of the District of Columbia public school system. About forty-five pages of illustrative material were included in the 450-page report "to 'give a realistic view' of a troubled school and 'the lack of administrative efforts to rectify the multitudinous problems there,' to show the level of reading ability of seventh graders who were given a fifth-grade history test, and to illustrate suspension and disciplinary problems." On these pages of the report were reproduced "absence sheets, lists of absentees, copies of test papers, and documents relating to disciplinary problems of certain specifically-named students." The plaintiffs in this case were parents and children who brought suit, under pseudonyms, alleging that disclosure and dissemination of the information contained in the committee report had violated their right to privacy, hurt their reputations and future careers, and injured their physical and mental health. The proceedings for damages and injunctive relief were brought against McMillan, the chairman, and other members of the House Committee on the District of Columbia, members of the committee's staff, the Superintendent of Documents, members of the board of education, and others. A U. S. district court dismissed the suit finding that the defendants' conduct was absolutely privileged because of protections emanating from the Speech and Debate Clause and the official immunity doctrine. A U. S. court of appeals affirmed, whereupon the parents and children sought review by the Supreme Court.

Mr. Justice WHITE delivered the opinion of the Court.

* * *

[I]t is plain to us that the complaint in this case was barred by the Speech or Debate Clause insofar as it sought relief from the Congressmen-Committee members, from the committee staff, from the consultant, or from the investigator, for introducing material at committee hearings that identified particular individuals, for referring the Report that included the material to the Speaker of the House, and for voting for publication of the report. Doubtless, also, a published report may, without losing Speech or Debate Clause protection, be distributed to and used for legislative purposes by Members of Congress, congressional committees, and institutional or individual legislative functionaries. At least in these respects, the actions upon which petitioners sought to predicate liability were "legislative acts" * * * and, as such, were immune from suit.

Petitioners argue that including in the record of the hearings and in the Report itself materials describing particular conduct on the part of identified children was actionable because unnecessary and irrelevant to any legislative purpose. Cases in this Court, however, from *Kilbourn* to *Gravel* pretermit the imposition of liability on any such theory. Congressmen and their aides are immune from liability for their actions within the "legislative sphere" * * * even though their conduct, if performed in other than legislative contexts, would in itself be unconstitutional or otherwise contrary to criminal or civil statutes, although we might disagree with the Committee as to whether it was necessary, or even remotely useful, to include the names of individual children in the evidence submitted to the Committee and in the Committee Report, we have no authority to oversee the judgment of the Committee in this respect or to impose liability on them if we disagree with their legislative judgment. The acts of authorizing an investigation pursuant to which

the subject materials were gathered, holding hearings where the materials were presented, preparing a Report where they were reproduced, and authorizing the publication and distribution of that Report were all "integral part[s] of the deliberative and communicative processes by which Members participate in committee and House proceedings with respect to the consideration and passage or rejection of proposed legislation or with respect to other matters which the Constitution places within the jurisdiction of either House." * * * As such, the acts were protected by the Speech or Debate Clause.

* * *

We do not doubt the importance of informing the public about the business of Congress. However, the question remains whether the act of doing so, simply because authorized by Congress, must always be considered "an integral part of the deliberative and communicative processes by which Members participate in committee and House proceedings" with respect to legislative or other matters before the House. * * * A Member of Congress may not with impunity publish a libel from the speaker's stand in his home district, and clearly the Speech or Debate Clause would not protect such an act even though the libel was read from an official committee report. The reason is that republishing a libel under such circumstances is not an essential part of the legislative process and is not part of that deliberative process "by which members participate in committee and House proceedings." * * * By the same token, others, such as the Superintendent of Documents or the Public Printer or legislative personnel, who participate in distributions of actionable material beyond the reasonable bounds of the legislative task, enjoy no Speech or Debate Clause immunity.

Members of Congress are themselves immune for ordering or voting for a publication going beyond the reasonable requirements of the legislative function, * * * but the Speech or Debate Clause no more insulates legislative functionaries carrying out such nonlegislative directives than it protected the sergeant-at-arms in Kilbourn v. Thompson [103 U.S. 168, 26 L.Ed. 377 (1880)] when, at the direction of the House, he made an arrest that the courts subsequently found to be "without authority." * * * The Clause does not protect "criminal conduct threatening the security of the person or property of others, whether performed at the direction of the Senator in preparation for or in execution of a legislative act or done without his knowledge or direction." * * * Neither, we think, does it immunize those who publish and distribute otherwise actionable materials beyond the reasonable requirements of the legislative function.

Thus we cannot accept the proposition that in order to perform its legislative function Congress not only must at times consider and use actionable material but also must be free to disseminate it to the public at large, no matter how injurious to private reputation that material might be. We cannot believe that the purpose of the Clause * * * will suffer in the slightest if it is held that those who, at the direction of Congress or otherwise, distribute actionable material to the public at large have no automatic immunity under the Speech or Debate Clause but must respond to private suits to the extent that others must respond

in light of the Constitution and applicable laws. To hold otherwise would be to invite gratuitous injury to citizens for little if any public purpose. We are unwilling to sanction such a result, at least absent more substantial evidence that, in order to perform its legislative function, Congress must not only inform the public about the fundamentals of its business but also must distribute to the public generally materials otherwise actionable under local law.

* * *

* * * It does not expressly appear from the complaint, nor is it contended in this Court, that either the Members of Congress or the Committee personnel did anything more than conduct the hearings, prepare the Report, and authorize its publication. As we have stated, such acts by those respondents are protected by the Speech or Debate Clause and may not serve as a predicate for a suit. The complaint was therefore properly dismissed as to these respondents. Other respondents, however, are alleged to have carried out a public distribution and to be ready to continue such dissemination.

* * *

The official immunity doctrine, which "has in large part been of judicial making," Barr v. Matteo, 360 U.S. 564, 569, 79 S.Ct. 1335, 1338 (1959), confers immunity on government officials of suitable rank for the reason that "officials of government should be free to exercise their duties unembarrassed by the fear of damage suits in respect of acts done in the course of those duties—suits which would consume time and energies which would otherwise be devoted to governmental service and the threat of which might appreciably inhibit the fearless, vigorous, and effective administration of policies of government." * * * The official immunity doctrine seeks to reconcile two important considerations—

"[O]n the one hand, the protection of the individual citizens against pecuniary damage caused by oppressive or malicious action on the part of officials of the Federal Government; and on the other, the protection of the public interest by shielding responsible governmental officers against the harassment and inevitable hazards of vindictive or ill-founded damage suits brought on account of action taken in the exercise of their official responsibilities."

In the *Barr* case, the Court reaffirmed existing immunity law but made it clear that the immunity conferred might not be the same for all officials for all purposes. * * * Judges, like executive officers with discretionary functions, have been held absolutely immune regardless of their motive or good faith. Pierson v. Ray, 386 U.S. 547, 553–555, 87 S.Ct. 1213, 1217–1218 (1967). But policemen and like officials apparently enjoy a more limited privilege. * * * Also, the Court determined in *Barr* that the scope of immunity from defamation suits should be determined by the relation of the publication complained of to the duties entrusted to the officer. * * * The scope of immunity has always been tied to the "scope of authority." * * *

Because the Court has not fashioned a fixed, invariable rule of immunity but has advised a discerning inquiry into whether the contributions of immunity to effective government in particular contexts outweighs the perhaps recurring harm

to individual citizens, there is no ready-made answer as to whether the remaining federal respondents— the Public Printer and the Superintendent of Documents—should be accorded absolute immunity in this case. Of course, to the extent that they serve legislative functions, the performance of which would be immune conduct if done by congressmen, these officials enjoy the protection of the Speech or Debate Clause. Our inquiry here, however, is whether, if they participate in publication and distribution beyond the legislative sphere, and thus beyond the protection of the Speech or Debate Clause, they are nevertheless protected by the doctrine of official immunity. * * *

* * *

The duties of the Public Printer and his appointee, the Superintendent of Documents, are to print, handle, distribute, and sell government documents. The Government Printing Office acts as a service organization for the branches of the Government. What it prints is produced elsewhere and is printed and distributed at the direction of the Congress, the departments, the independent agencies and offices, or the Judicial Branch of the Government. The Public Printer and Superintendent of Documents exercise discretion only with respect to estimating the demand for particular documents and adjusting the supply accordingly. The existence of a Public Printer makes it unnecessary for every government agency and office to have a printer of its own. The Printing Office is independently created and manned and imbued with its own statutory duties; but, we do not think that its independent establishment carries with it an independent immunity. Rather, the Printing Office is immune from suit when it prints for an executive department for example, only to the extent that it would be if it were part of the department itself or, in other words, to the extent that the department head himself would be immune if he ran his own printing press and distributed his own documents. To hold otherwise would mean that an executive department could acquire immunity for non-immune materials merely by presenting the proper certificate to the Public Printer, who would then have the duty to print the material. Under such a holding, the department would have a seemingly foolproof method for manufacturing immunity for materials which the court would not otherwise hold immune if not sufficiently connected with the "official duties" of the department. * * *

Congress has conferred no express, statutory immunity on the Public Printer or the Superintendent of Documents. Congress has not provided that these officials should be immune for printing and distributing materials where those who author the materials would not be. * * * We conclude that, for the purposes of the judicially fashioned doctrine of immunity, the Printer and the Superintendent of Documents are no more free from suit in the case before us than would be a legislative aide who made copies of the materials at issue and distributed them to the public at the direction of his superiors. See Dombrowski v. Eastland, 387 U.S. 82, 87 S.Ct. 1425, (1967). The scope of inquiry becomes equivalent to the inquiry in the context of the Speech or Debate Clause, and the answer is the same. The business of Congress is to legislate; congressmen and aides are ab-

solutely immune when they are legislating. But when they act outside the "sphere of legitimate legislative activity," * * * they enjoy no special immunity from local laws protecting the good name or the reputation of the ordinary citizen.

Because we think the Court of Appeals applied the immunities of the Speech or Debate Clause and of the doctrine of official immunity too broadly, we must reverse its judgment and remand the case for appropriate further proceedings. * * *

* * *

Reversed in part and affirmed in part and case remanded.

Mr. Justice DOUGLAS, whom Mr. Justice BRENNAN and Mr. Justice MARSHALL join, concurring.

I cannot agree * * * that the question for us is "whether [public dissemination], simply because authorized by Congress, must always be considered 'an integral part of the deliberative and communicative processes by which Members participate in committee and House proceedings' with respect to legislative or other matters before the House." A legislator's function in informing the public concerning matters before Congress or concerning the administration of Government is essential to maintaining our representative democracy. Unless we are to put blinders on our Congressmen and isolate them from their constituents, the informing function must be entitled to the same protection of the Speech or Debate Clause as those activities which relate directly and necessarily to the immediate function of legislating. * * * In my view the question to which we should direct our attention is whether the House Report infringes upon the constitutional rights of petitioners and therefore is subject to scrutiny by the federal courts.

* * *

We all should be painfully aware of the potentially devastating effects of congressional accusations. There are great stakes involved when officials condemn individuals by name. The age of technology has produced data banks into which all social security numbers go; and following those numbers go data in designated categories concerning the lives of members of our communities. Arrests go in, though many arrests are unconstitutional. Acts of juvenile delinquency are permanently recorded and they and other alleged misdeeds or indiscretions may be devastating to a person in later years when he has outgrown youthful indiscretions and is trying to launch a professional career or move into a position where steadfastness is required.

Congress, in naming the students without justification exceeded the "sphere of legitimate legislative activity." * * * There can be no question that the resolution authorizing the investigation and study expressed a legitimate legislative purpose. Nevertheless, neither the investigatory nor, indeed, the informing function of Congress authorizes any "congressional power to expose for the sake of exposure." Watkins v. United States, at 200 of 354 U.S., at 1185 of 77 S.Ct. To the contrary, there is simply "no general authority to expose the private affairs of individuals without justification in terms of the functions of the Congress." * * * The names of specific students were totally irrelevant to the purposes of the study. The functions of the Committee would have

been served equally well if the students had remained anonymous.

* * * [B]oth the Public Printer and the Superintendent of Documents, official agencies entrusted by Congress with printing responsibilities, are named as defendants. And in the context of this case, such defendants may be held responsible for their actions. * * *

* * *

Mr. Chief Justice BURGER, concurring in part and dissenting in part.

I cannot accept the proposition that the judiciary has power to carry on a continuing surveillance of what Congress may and may not publish by way of reports on inquiry into subjects plainly within the legislative powers conferred on Congress by the Constitution. The inquiries conducted by Congress here were within its broad legislative authority and the specific powers conferred by cl. 17, § 8, Art. I.

It seems extraordinary to me that we grant to the staff aides of Members of the Senate and the House an immunity that the Court today denies to a very senior functionary, the Public Printer. Historically and functionally the Printer is simply the extended arm of the Congress itself, charged by law with executing congressional commands.

* * *

Mr. Justice REHNQUIST, with whom THE CHIEF JUSTICE and Mr. Justice BLACKMUN join, and with whom Mr. Justice STEWART joins * * * in part. * * *

I concur in the Court's holding that the respondent Members of Congress and their committee aides and employees are immune under the

Speech or Debate Clause for preparation of the Committee Report for distribution within the halls of Congress. I dissent from the Court's holding that Members of Congress might be held liable if they were in fact responsible for public dissemination of a committee report, and that therefore the Public Printer or the Superintendent of Documents might likewise be liable for such distribution. And quite apart from the immunity which I believe the Speech or Debate Clause confers upon congressionally authorized public distribution of committee reports, I believe that the principle of separation of powers absolutely prohibits any form of injunctive relief in the circumstances here presented.

Entirely apart from the immunity conferred by the Speech or Debate Clause on these respondents, I believe that the principle of separation of powers forbids the granting of injunctive relief by the District Court in a case such as this. We have jurisdiction to review the completed acts of the Legislative and Executive Branches. See, e.g., Marbury v. Madison, 1 Cranch 137, 2 L.Ed. 60 (1803); Youngstown Sheet and Tube Co. v. Sawyer, 343 U.S. 579, 72 S.Ct. 863 (1952); *Kilbourn* v. *Thompson*, supra. But the prospect of the District Court enjoining a committee of Congress, which, in the legislative scheme of things, is for all practical purposes Congress itself, from undertaking to publicly distribute one of its reports in the manner that Congress has by statute prescribed that it be distributed, is one that I believe would have boggled the minds of the Framers of the Constitution.

* * *

EASTLAND v. UNITED STATES SERVICEMEN'S FUND

Supreme Court of the United States, 1975
421 U.S. 491, 95 S.Ct. 1813, 44 L.Ed.2d 324

See p. 226.

OTHER RULINGS ON THE PROTECTION AFFORDED BY THE SPEECH AND DEBATE CLAUSE

Case	Facts	Ruling
United States v. Johnson, 383 U.S. 169, 86 S.Ct. 749 (1966)	At the trial of a congressman for conspiracy to defraud the government by helping to cover up irregularities at a Maryland savings and loan company, a speech which he had given on the floor of the House was used at trial—with examination into its authorship, motivation, and content—for the purpose of showing the	While a congressman may be prosecuted under a criminal statute, the government's case may not rely on legislative acts or inquire into their motivation. The Speech and Debate Clause prohibits inquiry only into those things said or done in the House in performance of official duties (and the motivation for those acts), i.e., acts generally done in the course of the process of enacting legislation. As to the seven other counts of the indictment concerning the congressman's attempts to influence members of the Justice Department and

Case	Facts	Ruling
United States v. Johnson (*Cont.*)	congressman's part in the conspiracy.	as to which the defendant congressman entered no Speech and Debate Clause objection, the Court observed that such activity by the congressman was "in no wise related to the due functioning of the legislative process."
United States v. Brewster, 408 U.S. 501, 92 S.Ct. 2531 (1972)	A former U.S. Senator, charged with soliciting and accepting bribes from a mail order company, argued that because such activity was incident to consideration of postal rate legislation then before Congress, he was immune from prosecution because of the Speech and Debate Clause.	" * * * Members of Congress engage in many activities other than the purely legislative activities protected by the Speech or Debate Clause. These include a wide range of legitimate 'errands' performed for constituents, the making of appointments with government agencies, assistance in securing government contracts, preparing so-called 'news letters' to constituents, news releases, speeches delivered outside Congress. * * * [These activities] are performed in part because they have come to be expected by constituents and because they are a means of developing continuing support for future elections. Although these are legitimate activities [as opposed to soliciting and accepting bribes], they are political in nature rather than legislative, in the sense that term has been used by the Court in prior cases. But it has never been seriously contended that these political matters, however appropriate, have the protection afforded by the Speech or Debate Clause."
United States v. Helstoski, 442 U.S. 477, 99 S.Ct. 2432 (1979)	A New Jersey congressman was indicted on charges of accepting money in return for promises to introduce or for the introduction of private bills on behalf of certain aliens to suspend the immigration laws and allow them to remain in this country. Although the federal district court refused to quash the indictment on the basis of the Speech and Debate Clause, the judge did rule that the government was barred from introducing evidence of "past legislative acts" in any form to establish motive for the congressman's sponsorship of the bills.	Although excluding evidence of past legislative acts will undoubtedly make prosecutions more difficult, the Speech and Debate Clause was intended to forbid prosecution of members of Congress for legislative acts. References to a member's legislative acts cannot be admitted without undermining the values sought to be protected by that Clause. "As to what restriction the Clause places on the admission of evidence, * * * it is clear from the language of that Clause that protection extends only to an act that has already been performed. A promise to deliver a speech, a vote, or to solicit other votes at some future date is not 'speech or debate.' Likewise a *promise* to introduce a bill is not a legislative act. * * * [T]he District Court order prohibiting the introduction of evidence 'of the performance of a *past* legislative act' was redundant."

Case	Facts	Ruling
United States v. Gillock, 445 U.S. 360, 100 S.Ct. 1185 (1980)	A Tennessee state legislator, charged with accepting bribes for using his office to block the extradition of a defendant to Illinois and for sponsoring certain special interest legislation, asserted during a *federal* prosecution that evidence pertaining to his legislative acts was inadmissible. He argued that federal recognition of a state legislative privilege comparable to that afforded by the Speech and Debate Clause was required.	Granting such a privilege to state legislators facing federal prosecution is justified by neither the separation of powers principle nor the principle of comity, and such a privilege may be denied a state legislator subjected to federal prosecution with only a minimal effect on the performance of the legislative function.

Senator William Proxmire established his "Golden Fleece of the Month Award" to draw attention to what he thinks are the most egregious examples of wasteful governmental spending. The second of these awards, in April 1975, went to the National Science Foundation for a half million dollar grant to fund the research of Hutchinson, a research behavioral scientist. The bulk of Hutchinson's research dealt with emotional behavior, and the grant was for research on aggression in particular. Both the National Aeronautics and Space Agency and the Navy were interested in the problems associated with confining humans in close quarters for extended periods of time. In the main, Hutchinson's funded research focused on aggression in animals and how they clenched their teeth and bit when confronted with aggravating and stressful stimuli. Proxmire, who relied on information supplied by Schwartz, his administrative assistant, assailed the research as transparently worthless and ridiculed it as the study of why monkeys "grind their teeth." In a speech on the Senate floor and later in a news release, in a newsletter to constituents, and in a television interview, Proxmire coupled these critical remarks with exhortations to get the federal government out of "this 'monkey business'" and to "put a stop to the bite Hutchinson and the bureaucrats who fund him have been taking of the taxpayer." Schwartz, acting at Proxmire's direction, called several federal agencies on the day the Senator delivered his speech. Hutchinson alleged these calls were to persuade the agencies to terminate his contracts and grants. Schwartz denied this was the purpose. Hutchinson subsequently sued Proxmire and Schwartz for damages, contending that the Senator's remarks humiliated him, held him up to public ridicule and scorn, damaged his professional, scholarly, and academic reputation, and impaired his income.

A federal district court granted summary judgment for Proxmire, and an appellate court affirmed. Both courts held that the Speech and Debate Clause immunized the speech on the Senate floor, and the press release was thought to be within the ambit of a legislator's "informing function." The appeals court also included the newsletter in that category of presumably protected activities. The interview was believed by both courts to be shielded by the First Amendment, and the district court placed the newsletter in that category of protected speech too. The courts ruled that Proxmire was also entitled to summary judgment on this First Amendment activity because they concluded that Hutchinson was a "public figure" and that "actual malice" could not be established within the meaning of the *New York Times* rule so as to permit the recovery of any damages against the Senator.

The Supreme Court granted certiorari "to resolve three issues: (1) Whether a Member of Congress is protected by the Speech or Debate Clause of the Constitution, Art. I, § 6, against suits for allegedly defamatory statements made by the Member in press releases and newsletters; (2) Whether petitioner Hutchinson is either a 'public figure' or a 'public official,' thereby making applicable the 'actual malice' standard of New York Times Co. v. Sullivan, 376 U.S. 254, 84 S.Ct. 710 (1964); and (3) Whether respondents [Proxmire and Schwartz] were entitled to summary judgment." The Court, in Hutchinson v. Proxmire, 443 U.S. 111, 99 S.Ct. 2675 (1979), reversed the judgment and remanded the case. Speaking for the Court and addressing the Speech and Debate Clause question, Chief Justice Burger wrote:

> Respondents * * * contend that in the modern day very little speech or debate occurs on the floor of either House; from this they argue that press releases and newsletters are necessary for Members of Congress to communicate with other Members. * * * Respondents also argue that an essential part of the duties of a Member of Congress is to inform constituents, as well as other Members, of the issues being considered.
>
> The Speech or Debate Clause has been directly passed on by this Court relatively few times in 190 years. * * * Literal reading of the Clause would, of course, confine its protection narrowly to a "Speech or Debate *in* either House." But the Court has given the Clause a practical rather than a strictly literal reading which would limit the protection to utterances made within the four walls of either Chamber. Thus, we have held that committee hearings are protected, even if held outside the Chambers; committee reports are also protected. * * *
>
> The gloss going beyond a strictly literal reading of the Clause has not, however, departed from the objective of protecting only legislative activities. * * *
>
> * * *
>
> Whatever imprecision there may be in the term "legislative activities," it is clear that nothing in history or in the explicit language of the Clause suggests any intention to create an absolute privilege from liability or suit for defamatory statements made outside the Chamber. * * * Claims under the Clause going beyond what is needed to protect legislative independence are to be closely scrutinized. * * * Indeed, the precedents abundantly support the conclusion that a Member may be held liable for republishing defamatory statements originally made in either House. We perceive no basis for departing from that long-established rule.
>
> Justice Story in his Commentaries, for example, explained that there was no immunity for republication of a speech first delivered in Congress:
>
> > "Therefore, although a speech delivered in the house of commons is privileged, and the member cannot be questioned respecting it elsewhere; *yet, if he publishes his speech, and it contains libellous matter, he is liable to an action and prosecution therefore, as in common cases of*

libel. And the same principles seem applicable to the privilege of debate and speech in congress. No man ought to have a right to defame others under colour of a performance of the duties of his office. And if he does so *in the actual discharge of his duties in congress, that furnishes no reason, why he should be enabled through the medium of the press to destroy the reputation, and invade the repose of other citizens.* It is neither within the scope of his duty, nor in furtherance of public rights, or public policy. Every citizen has as good a right to be protected by the laws from malignant scandal, and false charges, and defamatory imputations, as a member of congress has to utter them in his seat." J. Story, Commentaries on the Constitution § 863, at 329 (1833) (emphasis added).
* * *

* * *

* * * We reaffirmed that principle in Doe v. McMillan, 412 U.S. 306, 314–315, 93 S.Ct. 2018, 2025–2026 (1973). * * *

We reach a similar conclusion here. A speech by Proxmire in the Senate would be wholly immune and would be available to other Members of Congress and the public in the Congressional Record. But neither the newsletters nor the press release was "essential to the deliberations of the Senate" and neither was part of the deliberative process.

Respondents, however, argue that newsletters and press releases are essential to the functioning of the Senate; without them, they assert, a Senator cannot have a significant impact on the other Senators. We may assume that a Member's published statements exert some influence on other votes in the Congress and therefore have a relationship to the legislative and deliberative process. But in [United States v.] *Brewster* * * * [408 U.S.,] at 512, [92 S.Ct., at 2537] we rejected respondents' expansive reading of the Clause:

> "It is well known, of course, that Members of the Congress engage in many activities other than the purely legislative activities protected by the Speech or Debate Clause. These include * * * preparing so-called 'news letters' to constituents, news releases, and speeches delivered outside the Congress."

* * *

Respondents also argue that newsletters and press releases are privileged as part of the "informing function" of Congress. Advocates of a broad reading of the "informing function" sometimes tend to confuse two uses of the term "informing." In one sense, Congress informs itself collectively by way of hearings of its committees. It was in that sense that Woodrow Wilson used "informing" in a statement quoted [see p. 134] by respondents. * * *

The other sense of the term, and the one relied upon by respondents, perceives it to be the duty of Members to tell the public about their activities. Valuable and desirable as it may be in broad terms, the transmittal of such information by individual Members in order to inform the public and other Members is not a part of the legislative function or the deliberations that make up the legislative process. As a result, transmittal of such information by press releases and newsletters is not protected by the Speech or Debate Clause.

Doe v. McMillan, 412 U.S. 306, 93 S.Ct. 2018 (1973), is not to the contrary. It dealt only with reports from congressional committees, and held that Members of Congress could not be held liable for voting to publish a report. Voting and preparing committee reports are the individual and collective expressions of opinion within the legislative process. As such, they are protected by the Speech or Debate Clause. Newsletters and press releases, by contrast, are primarily means of informing those outside the legislative forum; they represent the views and will of a single Member. It does not disparage either their value or their importance to hold that they are not entitled to the protection of the Speech or Debate Clause.

The Court went on to hold that Hutchinson was not a "public figure" and that his libel claim, therefore, was not affected by the *New York Times* rule (see p. 1492). As a consequence of these answers to the first and second questions posed, the Court found the grant of summary judgment in Proxmire's favor to be erroneous and remanded the case for trial on the merits. Justice Brennan dissented, citing as reasons those given in his dissenting opinion in the *Gravel* case, and concluded that "public criticism by legislators of unnecessary governmental expenditures, whatever its form, is a legislative act shielded by the Speech or Debate Clause."

Chapter 3

Executive Power

In an oft-quoted and now famous passage in his *Autobiography*, Theodore Roosevelt wrote:

> The most important factor in getting the right spirit in my Administration, next to insistence upon courage, honesty, and a genuine democracy of desire to serve the plain people, was my insistence upon the theory that the executive power was limited only by specific restrictions and prohibitions appearing in the Constitution or imposed by Congress under its constitutional powers. My view was that every Executive officer and above all every Executive officer in high position was a steward of the people bound actively and affirmatively to do all he could for the people and not to content himself with the negative merit of keeping his talents undamaged in a napkin. I declined to adopt this view that what was imperatively necessary for the Nation could not be done by the President, unless he could find some specific authorization to do it. My belief was that it was not only his right but his duty to do anything that the needs of the Nation demanded unless such action was forbidden by the Constitution or by the laws. Under this interpretation of executive power I did and caused to be done many things not previously done by the President and the heads of the departments. I did not usurp power but I did greatly broaden the use of executive power. In other words, I acted for the common well being of all our people whenever and in whatever measure was necessary, unless prevented by direct constitutional or legislative prohibition.

Other Presidents, such as Woodrow Wilson, found this stewardship theory of executive power buttressed by the fact that "[t]he nation as a whole has chosen him, and is conscious that it has no other political spokesman." Because the President is unique among all national officeholders in his selection by all and not simply by part of the electorate, he is perceived as being specially endowed with a capacity to discern and embody the public interest. In Wilson's words, taken from his book, *Constitutional Govern-*

248

ment, "He is the representative of no constituency, but of the whole people." As a consequence, "His is the only voice in national affairs. * * * When he speaks in his true character, he speaks for no special interest."

Strong Presidents from Franklin Roosevelt on have performed in accord with the stewardship theory with the apparent approval of the American people. Despite the trauma of Vietnam and Watergate, it is probably a fair assessment that there is a consensus that the country prospers only with strong Presidents acting as stewards. Several factors, which we can only list here, contributed to this conception of the need for presidential power: the rise of an interdependent, regulated economy centralized still further by the impact of two world wars; the ascendancy since 1932 of a political coalition whose members looked to the federal government for policies of economic security and social justice; the congenital paralysis of Congress which, because of its sheer size and diversity of membership, can rarely be moved, let alone lead; the dominance of candidates' personal popularity over political issues in electoral voting; the personalities of presidential candidates which, attracted to the rigors of political battle, seek satisfaction in the use of power, not its denial; and the persistence of a global challenge to the nation's security, especially by the Soviet Union, which requires the maintenance of an enormous military establishment and accentuates the importance and impact of foreign relations. Despite the apparent need for a strong Presidency, the exercise of presidential power produces an extraordinary tension, namely, accommodation of the realities of the stewardship theory with the demands of constitutional government. That tension is plainly visible in the cases which follow.

a. The President's Appointment and Removal Power

Article II of the Constitution spells out the President's appointing powers in the following fashion: "[H]e shall nominate, and by and with the Advice and Consent of the Senate, shall appoint Ambassadors, other public Ministers and Consuls, Judges of the Supreme Court, and all other Officers of the United States, whose Appointments are not herein otherwise provided for, and which shall be established by Law; but Congress may by Law vest the Appointment of such inferior Officers, as they think proper, in the President alone, in the Courts of Law, or in the Heads of Departments." When, despite the explicitness of this provision, Congress provided by statute for officials who were not appointed in the manner prescribed by Article II, the Supreme Court in United States v. Germaine, 99 U.S. 508, 25 L.Ed. 482 (1879), held that an official who is not appointed in the manner set forth in the above provision "is not an officer, though he may be an agent or employee working for the government and paid by it, as nine-tenths of the persons rendering service to the government undoubtedly are, without thereby becoming its officers." Clearly, this decision did not alter the President's explicit power to nominate and, with the advice and consent of the Senate, appoint major *political* (outside the subsequently established civil service system) and judicial officers of the federal government and alone to appoint individuals to such inferior political and judicial offices as Congress sees fit to designate.

In view of the specificity with which the Framers dealt with the appointing process, it seems strange in retrospect that they did not make some provision for the removal of officials save by impeachment. Perhaps they felt, as Chief Justice Taft later asserted in *Myers* v. *United States* (p. 255), that removal was inherent in "executive power." Yet, as the Court recognized in *Humphrey's Executor* v. *United States* (p. 262), not all political appointments within the executive branch are subject to the unilateral exercise of the President's removal power. The determination as to which officeholders are subject to presidential ouster depends on the purpose to be served by the agency in question. As the Court pointed out, the FTC was intended to be an *independent* regulatory agency. Although Chief Justice Taft's assertion, then, came to be circumscribed somewhat, still the President does have substantial unchecked power to remove most executive officers. Justice Brandeis's dissent in *Myers*, however, offers a powerful argument for Congress's right to restrain the President and, though long-neglected, is worth serious consideration.

b. The President's Power to Pardon

The Constitution provides that the President "shall have power to grant reprieves and pardons for offenses against the United States, except in cases of impeachment." The Supreme Court's opinion in *Ex parte Grossman* (p. 266) contains a fine statement of the derivation and rationale of the pardoning power, particularly as it applies to one convicted of contempt of court. It also includes an informative discussion of the difference between civil and criminal contempt, the separation of powers, and checks and balances. However, since this decision the judges' power to summarily punish criminal contempts has been sharply curbed.

Few developments have done more to focus attention once again on the wisdom of the President's unchecked power to pardon than the parade of events which eventually culminated in the August 1974 resignation of Richard Nixon as President. Prior to his departure from office serious concern was voiced about his potential use of the pardoning power to extricate various persons implicated in the Watergate break-in and cover-up and in other extralegal activities (burglaries, campaign "dirty tricks," illegal wiretapping, illicit political fund raising, etc.) directed by individuals working out of the Committee to Re-Elect the President and the White House itself. More controversial still was President Ford's action of September 8, 1974 granting his disgraced predecessor a "full, free and absolute pardon * * * for all offenses against the United States which he * * * has committed or may have committed" during his years as President. The unconditional pardon, which had been granted in advance of any showing of criminal liability on the part of the ex-President, was upheld by a federal district court in *Murphy* v. *Ford* (p. 269). Interestingly enough (and by way of confirming Wilson's observation that the legitimacy of a President's action, taken ostensibly for the common good, follows from his election by all the people), immediately following announcement of the pardon, President Ford, who was the first Chief Executive to gain the office by appointment,[a] suffered a severe and irretrievable drop in public support and found the integrity of his administration clouded by charges that his accession resulted from a political deal. There can be little question, however, in light of *Grossman* and *Murphy* that presently the Chief Executive has virtually absolute constitutional power to grant a "reprieve" which suspends the penalties of a *federal* law or a "pardon" which remits them.

c. The Scope of Executive Power

Comparable in ambiguity to the words "judicial power" in the third article of the Constitution, the phrase "executive power" in the first sentence of Article II has also given license for varied interpretations. The fact that Article II does include a list of specific powers granted to the President and the apparent intent of the Framers only to indicate what the Chief Executive's title would be when they wrote, "The executive Power shall be vested in a President of the United States of America," are factors which strongly suggest that the opening sentence of the article was not supposed to confer additional power on the President. The history of the debate over the meaning of "executive power" has been summarized well in Edward S. Corwin's *The President: Office and Powers* (4th ed., 1957). Suffice it to say that practitioners of the stewardship theory—Lincoln, Wilson, the Roosevelts, and others—have given the phrase an independent existence.

The notion that the President possesses certain inherent but unspecified powers is clearly reflected in the following colloquy at trial in *Youngstown Sheet & Tube Co.* v. *Sawyer* between Judge David A. Pine and Assistant Attorney General Holmes Baldridge:

> The Court: And you do not assert any express constitutional power.

> Mr. Baldridge: Well, Your Honor, we base the President's power on Sections 1, 2 and 3 of Article II of the Constitution, and whatever inherent, implied or residual powers may flow therefrom.

> We do not propose to get into a discussion of semantics with counsel for plaintiffs. We say that when an emergency situation in this country arises

---

a. After Vice-President Spiro Agnew resigned on October 10, 1973, following his plea of "no contest" to criminal charges, Nixon, pursuant to the Twenty-fifth Amendment, nominated Ford who was subsequently confirmed by a majority vote of both Houses of Congress and sworn in December 6, 1973. Ford succeeded to the Presidency when Nixon resigned on August 9, 1974, and he in turn nominated Nelson Rockefeller to be Vice-President. Rockefeller was confirmed by a majority of the House and Senate and took office December 19, 1974. For the remainder of the term, then, to which Nixon and Agnew had been elected in November 1972, both top spots in the executive branch were occupied by individuals who had not been elected to office. The Twenty-fifth Amendment, of course, was largely motivated by a concern with presidential disability, and those who drafted it could not be expected to have foreseen the unusual sequence of events which unfolded throughout 1973 and 1974 or the implications of such a process for the sense of legitimacy surrounding an appointee's assumption of the office.

that is of such importance to the entire welfare of the country that something has to be done about it and has to be done now, and there is no statutory provision for handling the matter, that it is the duty of the Executive to step in and protect the national security and the national interests. * * *

The Court: So you contend the Executive has unlimited power in time of an emergency?

Mr. Baldridge: He has the power to take such action as is necessary to meet the emergency.

The Court: If the emergency is great, it is unlimited, is it?

Mr. Baldridge: I suppose if you carry it to its logical conclusion, that is true. But I do want to point out that there are two limitations on the Executive power. One is the ballot box and the other is impeachment. * * *

The Court: And that the Executive determines the emergencies and the Courts cannot even review whether it is an emergency.

Mr. Baldridge: That is correct. * * *

A comparable view of executive power is reflected in ex-President Nixon's answers to questions posed by David Frost in the third of a series of televised interviews (p. 286). Nixon's aggressive and extralegal behavior while in office, however, prompted impeachment resolutions (p. 296) which were reported out by the House Judiciary Committee in July 1974.

The clash between the vigorous exercise of executive power and the concept of constitutional government has inevitably involved the Court, for, as Chief Justice Marshall announced long ago in *Marbury* v. *Madison*, "It is emphatically, the province and duty of the judicial department, to say what the law is." So saying in its disposition of *Youngstown Sheet & Tube Co.* v. *Sawyer* (p. 272), the Court is commonly thought to have handed the presidential office a defeat. But is the conventional wisdom borne out in the Court's handling of the case? Or does the Court's performance really vindicate the stewardship theory? In addition to the Court's inability to speak with one voice and the failure of any of the opinions to provide a theory of executive power, you should also consider the following justification offered by Judge Pine in support of his ruling in federal district court against the validity of the steel seizure:

There is no express grant of power in the Constitution authorizing the President to direct this seizure. There is no grant of power from which it reasonably can be implied. There is no enactment of Congress authorizing it. On what, then, does defendant rely to sustain his acts? According to his brief, reiterated in oral argument, he relies upon the President's "broad residuum of power" sometimes referred to as "inherent" power under the Constitution, which, as I understand his counsel, is not to be confused with "implied" powers as that term is generally understood, namely, those which are reasonably appropriate to the exercise of a granted power.

This contention requires a discussion of basic fundamental principles of constitutional government, which I have always understood are immutable, absent a change in the framework of the Constitution itself in the manner provided therein. The Government of the United States was created by the ratification of the Constitution. It derives its authority wholly from the powers granted to it by the Constitution, which is the only source of power authorizing action by any branch of Government. It is a government of limited, enumerated, and delegated powers. The office of President of the United States is a branch of the Government, namely, that branch where the executive power is vested, and his powers are limited along with the powers of the two other great branches or departments of Governments, namely, the legislative and judicial.

The President therefore must derive this broad "residuum of power" or "inherent" power from the Constitution itself, more particularly Article II thereof, which contains that grant of Executive power. * * *

The non-existence of this "inherent" power in the President has been recognized by eminent writers, and I cite in this connection the unequivocal language of the late Chief Justice Taft in his treatise entitled "Our Chief Magistrate and His Powers" (1916) wherein he says: "The true view of the Executive function is, as I conceive it, that the President can exercise no power which cannot be fairly and reasonably traced to some specific grant of power or justly implied and included within such express grant as proper and necessary to its exercise. Such specific grant must be either in the Federal Constitution or in an Act of Congress passed in pursuance thereof. There is no undefined residuum of power which he can exercise because it seems to him to be in the public interest, and there is nothing in the *Neagle* case [135 U.S. 1, 10 S.Ct. 658 (1890)] and its definition of a law of the United States, or in other precedents, warranting such an inference. The grants of executive power are necessarily in general terms in order not to embarrass the Executive within the field of action plainly marked for him, but his jurisdiction must be justified and vindicated by affirmative constitutional or statutory provision, or it does not exist."

I stand on that as a correct statement of the law. * * *

Do you find it significant that the Court not only failed to adopt the literalist view of the executive office, summed up in the Taft quote, but ignored it entirely? As you reflect on *Youngstown*, consider what options the President in fact had and the merits and disadvantages of each. President Truman was faulted by some critics for not invoking the eighty-day cooling-off period under the Taft-Hartley Act. Why do you suppose he rejected that option?

The question whether the Presidency itself has been handed a defeat surfaces again in connection with the Court's decision in *United States* v. *Nixon* (p. 288). Does the Court's ruling here vindicate the thesis that the judiciary has been an effective check on executive power? To be sure, the occupant of the office in this case was dealt a severe blow strategically by the effect of this particular decision (since Nixon faced eventual impeachment given the incriminating evidence on the tapes or immediate impeachment for any refusal to obey the Court's ruling), but does the Court's opinion represent a defeat for the Presidency *per se*? Do you see in Chief Justice Burger's opinion any features which might be considered a victory in some sense for a powerful executive office? Applying much the same framework of analysis in *Senate Select Committee on Presidential Campaign Activities* v. *Nixon* (p. 295), a federal appellate court ruled against enforcement of a congressional committee's subpoena of the tapes. Why?

To what extent do subsequent decisions, such as *Nixon* v. *Administrator of General Services* (p. 299) and *Nixon* v. *Fitzgerald* (p. 303), reflect the balance struck in *United States* v. *Nixon* between maintaining the integrity and effective leadership of the Presidency and yet providing avenues of relief in time of abuse? Do those decisions demonstrate that the Court can be an effective check on executive power? Finally, given Justice Jackson's observation in his concurring opinion in *Youngstown Sheet & Tube* that "only Congress itself can prevent power from slipping through its fingers," do you think the legislative branch has been effective in that regard?

d. Executive Authority in the Conduct of Foreign Affairs

Whatever the Founding Fathers intended, over the course of American history the President has accumulated enormous power as the chief organ of our foreign relations. Perhaps this is as it should be. As John Jay's essay in the *Federalist* (p. 254) suggests, at least he was enamoured with the notion that the conduct of foreign affairs required *secrecy* and *dispatch*. Although his words now sound melodramatic, the practical considerations he suggests are repeated by Justice Sutherland speaking for the Court in *United States* v. *Curtiss-Wright Export Corp.* (p. 157), where they amplify a constitutional theory supporting presidential hegemony over foreign policy. Also, in part, presidential authority in this area is the product of past unchallenged uses of power. The Court's recent opinion in Dames & Moore v. Regan, 453 U.S. 654, 101 S.Ct. 2972 (1981), observed: "As Justice Frankfurter pointed out in *Youngstown*, 343 U.S. at 610–611, 72 S.Ct. at 897–898, 'a systematic, unbroken executive practice, long pursued to the knowledge of Congress and never before questioned * * * may be treated as a gloss on "Executive Power" vested in the President by § 1 of Art. II.' Past practice does not, by itself, create power, but 'long-continued practice, known to and acquiesced in by Congress, would raise a presumption that the [action] has been [taken] in pursuance of its consent. * * * ' United States v. Midwest Oil Co., 236 U.S. 459, 469, 35 S.Ct. 309, 311 (1915)." The legitimacy of the executive actions subjected to suit in both *Dames & Moore* (p. 313) and *Haig* v. *Agee* (p. 311) appears to confirm this observation.

With the growth of the United States both in population and military power, the conduct of foreign affairs increasingly involved the deployment of armed forces. Despite the fact that the Constitution gives to Congress alone the power to declare war, experience shows that a President's actions both as chief diplomat and commander-in-chief can involve us in shooting wars without the formalities of a congressional declaration. The erosion of Congress's power was only in part technological. In the case of the Vietnam conflict, critics argued that Congress had abdicated its control over the situation in the Gulf of Tonkin Resolution (p. 315) and periodically affirmed this *de facto* declaration of war through passage of the necessary appropriation bills. Increasing concern over unilateral presidential actions prompted not only its repeal in 1971 but enactment of the War Powers Resolution (p. 315) over President Nixon's objection two years later. Although the legislation purports to leave the constitutional powers of the two branches unaffected, you should consider whether the content of the statute belies this purpose. Assuming, then, that the intent of the act was to curb the President's war-making powers, how effective do you think the law is (or could be) in achieving that goal? As demonstrated a year and a half later when President Ford in May 1975 promptly ordered air strikes and sent in a detachment of Marines to rescue the American merchant ship *Mayaguez* and its crew after seizure by Cambodian communist troops, congressional reaction, like public opinion generally, is likely to be strongly on the President's side. And in any case, as with the *Mayaguez* incident, the entire operation, if it is to be effective, is likely to be over before any extended consultation is possible. Although it is undoubtedly true that the excesses of the Nixon Administration prompted Congress to assert itself with renewed vigor on many constitutional fronts, it is significant, finally, that when given the chance to chastise President Nixon for the secret bombing of Cambodia, the House Judiciary Committee declined to recommend an appropriate article of impeachment (p. 319).

a. THE PRESIDENT'S APPOINTMENT AND REMOVAL POWER

MYERS v. UNITED STATES

Supreme Court of the United States, 1926
272 U.S. 52, 47 S.Ct. 21, 71 L.Ed. 160

In addition to specifying a four-year term of office for postmasters, a provision of an 1876 act passed by Congress declared that first-, second-, and third-class postmasters were to be appointed and removed by the President with the consent of the Senate. Myers was appointed to a first-class postmastership at Portland, Oregon, in July 1917, in conformity with the statute. He was removed from office in February 1920, by the Postmaster General under instructions from the President but without Senate approval. After protests over his removal went unregarded, Myers sued to recover his lost salary in the U. S. Court of Claims. The Court of Claims ruled against Myers, and an appeal challenging the unfettered removal power of the President was taken to the Supreme Court by Lois Myers, the administratrix of his estate.

Mr. Chief Justice TAFT delivered the opinion of the Court.

This case presents the question whether under the Constitution the President has the exclusive power of removing executive officers of the United States whom he has appointed by and with the advice and consent of the Senate.

*   *   *

Made responsible under the Constitution for the effective enforcement of the law, the President needs as an indispensable aid to meet it the disciplinary influence upon those who act under him of a reserve power of removal. But it is contended that executive officers appointed by the President with the consent of the Senate are bound by the statutory law, and are not his servants to do his will, and that his obligation to care for the faithful execution of the law does not authorize him to treat them as such. The degree of guidance in the discharge of their duties that the President may exercise over executive officers varies with the character of their service as prescribed in the law under which they act. The highest and most important duties which his subordinates perform are those in which they act for him. In such cases they are exercising not their own but his discretion. This field is a very large one. It is sometimes described as political. Kendall v. United States, 12 Pet. 524, at page 610, 9 L.Ed. 1181. Each head of a department is and must be the President's alter ego in the matters of that department where the President is required by law to exercise authority.

* * *

The duties of the heads of departments and bureaus in which the discretion of the President is exercised and which we have described are the most important in the whole field of executive action of the government. There is nothing in the Constitution which permits a distinction between the removal of the head of a department or a bureau, when he discharges a political duty of the President or exercises his discretion, and the removal of executive officers engaged in the discharge of their other normal duties. The imperative reasons requiring an unrestricted power to remove the most important of his subordinates in their most important duties must therefore control the interpretation of the Constitution as to all appointed by him.

But this is not to say that there are not strong reasons why the President should have a like power to remove his appointees charged with

other duties than those above described. The ordinary duties of officers prescribed by statute come under the general administrative control of the President by virtue of the general grant to him of the executive power, and he may properly supervise and guide their construction of the statutes under which they act in order to secure that unitary and uniform execution of the laws which article 2 of the Constitution evidently contemplated in vesting general executive power in the President alone. Laws are often passed with specific provision for the adoption of regulations by a department or bureau head to make the law workable and effective. The ability and judgment manifested by the official thus empowered, as well as his energy and stimulation of his subordinates, are subjects which the President must consider and supervise in his administrative control. Finding such officers to be negligent and inefficient, the President should have the power to remove them. Of course there may be duties so peculiarly and specifically committed to the discretion of a particular officer as to raise a question whether the President may overrule or revise the officer's interpretation of his statutory duty in a particular instance. Then there may be duties of a quasi judicial character imposed on executive officers and members of executive tribunals whose decisions after hearing affect interests of individuals, the discharge of which the President cannot in a particular case properly influence or control. But even in such a case he may consider the decision after its rendition as a reason for removing the officer, on the ground that the discretion regularly entrusted to that officer by statute has not been on the whole intelligently or wisely exercised. Otherwise he does not discharge his own constitutional duty of seeing that the laws be faithfully executed.

We have devoted much space to this discussion and decision of the question of the presidential power of removal in the First Congress, not because a congressional conclusion on a constitutional issue is conclusive, but first because of our agreement with the reasons upon which it was avowedly based, second because this was the decision of the First Congress on a question of primary importance in the organization of the government made within two years after the Constitutional Convention and within a much shorter time after its ratification, and third because that Congress numbered among its leaders those who had been members of the convention. It must necessarily constitute a precedent upon which many future laws supplying the machinery of the new government would be based and, if erroneous, would be likely to evoke dissent and departure in future Congresses. It would come at once before the executive branch of the government for compliance and might well be brought before the judicial branch for a test of its validity. As we shall see, it was soon accepted as a final decision of the question by all branches of the government.

It was, of course, to be expected that the decision would be received by lawyers and jurists with something of the same division of opinion as that manifested in Congress, and doubts were often expressed as to its correctness. But the acquiescence which was promptly accorded it after a few years was universally recognized.

* * *

Summing up, then, the facts as to acquiescence by all branches of the government in the legislative decision of 1789 as to executive officers, whether superior or inferior, we find that from 1789 until 1863, a period of 74 years, there was no act of Congress, no executive act, and no decision of this court at variance with the declaration of the First Congress; but there was, as we have seen, clear affirmative recognition of it by each branch of the government.

Our conclusion on the merits, sustained by the arguments before stated, is that article 2 grants to the President the executive power of the government—i.e., the general administrative control of those executing the laws, including the power of appointment and removal of executive officers—a conclusion confirmed by his obligation to take care that the laws be faithfully executed; that article 2 excludes the exercise of legislative power by Congress to provide for appointments and removals, except only as granted therein to Congress in the matter of inferior offices; that Congress is only given power to provide for appointments and removals of inferior officers after it has vested, and on condition that it does vest, their appointment in other authority than the President with the Senate's consent; that the provisions of the second section of article 2, which blend action by the legislative branch, or by part of it, in the work of the executive, are limitations to be strictly construed, and not to be extended by implication; that the President's power of removal is further established as an incident to his specifically enumerated function of appointment by and with the advice of the Senate, but that such incident does not by implication extend to removals the Senate's power of checking appointments; and, finally, that to hold otherwise would make it impossible for the President, in case of political or other difference with the Senate or Congress, to take care that the laws be faithfully executed.

* * *

An argument ab inconvenienti has been made against our conclusion in favor of the executive power of removal by the President, without the consent of the Senate, that it will open the door to a reintroduction of the spoils system. The evil of the spoils system aimed at in the Civil Service Law and its amendments is in respect to inferior offices. It has never been attempted to extend that law beyond them. Indeed Congress forbids its extension to appointments confirmed by the Senate, except with the consent of the Senate. Act of January 16, 1883, 22 Stat. 403, 406, c. 27, sec. 7 (Comp.St. § 3278). Reform in the federal civil service was begun by the Civil Service Act of 1883. It has been developed from that time, so that the classified service now includes a vast majority of all the civil officers. It may still be enlarged by further legislation. The independent power of removal by the President alone under present conditions works no practical interference with the merit system. Political appointments of inferior officers are still maintained in one important class, that of the first, second and third class postmasters, collectors of internal revenue, marshals, collectors of customs, and other officers of that kind distributed through the country. They are appointed by the President with the consent of the Senate. It is the intervention of the Senate in their appointment, and not in their removal, which prevents their classification into the merit system. If

such appointments were vested in the heads of departments to which they belong, they could be entirely removed from politics, and that is what a number of Presidents have recommended. * * *

What, then, are the elements that enter into our decision of this case? We have, first, a construction of the Constitution made by a Congress which was to provide by legislation for the organization of the government in accord with the Constitution which had just then been adopted, and in which there were, as Representatives and Senators, a considerable number of those who had been members of the convention that framed the Constitution and presented it for ratification. It was the Congress that launched the government. It was the Congress that rounded out the Constitution itself by the proposing of the first 10 amendments, which had in effect been promised to the people as a consideration for the ratification. It was the Congress in which Mr. Madison, one of the first in the framing of the Constitution, led also in the organization of the government under it. It was a Congress whose constitutional decisions have always been regarded, as they should be regarded, as of the greatest weight in the interpretation of that fundamental instrument. This construction was followed by the legislative department and the executive department continuously for 73 years, and this, although the matter in the heat of political differences between the executive and the Senate in President Jackson's time, was the subject of bitter controversy, as we have seen. This court has repeatedly laid down the principle that a contemporaneous legislative exposition of the Constitution, when the founders of our government and framers of our Constitution were actively participating in public affairs, acquiesced in for a long term of years, fixes the construction to be given its provisions. * * *

We are now asked to set aside this construction thus buttressed and adopt an adverse view, because the Congress of the United States did so during a heated political difference of opinion between the then President and the majority leaders of Congress over the reconstruction measures adopted as a means of restoring to their proper status the states which attempted to withdraw from the Union at the time of the Civil War. The extremes to which the majority in both Houses carried legislative measures in that matter are now recognized by all who calmly review the history of that episode in our government leading to articles of impeachment against President Johnson and his acquittal. Without animadverting on the character of the measures taken, we are certainly justified in saying that they should not be given the weight affecting proper constitutional construction to be accorded to that reached by the First Congress of the United States during a political calm and acquiesced in by the whole government for three-quarters of a century, especially when the new construction contended for has never been acquiesced in by either the executive or the judicial departments. While this court has studiously avoided deciding the issue until it was presented in such a way that it could not be avoided, in the references it has made to the history of the question, and in the presumptions it has indulged in favor of a statutory construction not inconsistent with the legislative decision of 1789, it has indicated a trend of view that we should not and cannot ig-

nore. When on the merits we find our conclusion strongly favoring the view which prevailed in the First Congress, we have no hesitation in holding that conclusion to be correct; and it therefore follows that the Tenure of Office Act of 1867, in so far as it attempted to prevent the President from removing executive officers who had been appointed by him by and with the advice and consent of the Senate, was invalid, and that subsequent legislation of the same effect was equally so.

For the reasons given, we must therefore hold that the provision of the law of 1876 by which the unrestricted power of removal of first-class postmasters is denied to the President is in violation of the Constitution and invalid. This leads to an affirmance of the judgment of the Court of Claims.

* * *

Mr. Justice BRANDEIS, dissenting.

* * *

To imply a grant to the President of the uncontrollable power of removal from statutory inferior executive offices involves an unnecessary and indefensible limitation upon the constitutional power of Congress to fix the tenure of the inferior statutory offices. That such a limitation cannot be justified on the ground of necessity is demonstrated by the practice of our governments, state and national. In none of the original 13 states did the chief executive possess such power at the time of the adoption of the federal Constitution. In none of the 48 states has such power been conferred at any time since by a state Constitution, with a single possible exception. In a few states the Legislature has granted to the Governor, or other appointing power, the absolute power of removal. The legislative practice of most states reveals a decided tendency to limit, rather than to extend, the Governor's power of removal. The practice of the federal government will be set forth in detail.

* * *

From the foundation of the government to the enactment of the Tenure of Office Act, during the period while it remained in force, and from its repeal to this time, the administrative practice in respect to all offices has, so far as appears, been consistent with the existence in Congress of power to make removals subject to the consent of the Senate. * * *

* * *

The practice of Congress to control the exercise of the executive power of removal from inferior offices is evidenced by many statutes which restrict it in many ways besides the removal clause here in question. Each of these restrictive statutes became law with the approval of the President. Every President who has held office since 1861, except President Garfield, approved one or more of such statutes. Some of these statutes, prescribing a fixed term, provide that removal shall be made only for one of several specified causes. Some provide a fixed term, subject generally to removal for cause. Some provide for removal only after hearing. Some provide a fixed term, subject to removal for reasons to be communicated by the President to the Senate. Some impose the restriction in still other ways. * * *

* * *

The historical data submitted present a legislative practice, established by concurrent affirmative action of Congress and the President, to make consent of the Senate a condition of removal from statutory inferior, civil, executive offices to which the appointment is made for a fixed term by the President with such consent. They show that the practice has existed, without interruption, continuously for the last 58 years; that throughout this period, it has governed a great majority of all such offices; that the legislation applying the removal clause specifically to the office of postmaster was enacted more than half a century ago; and that recently the practice has, with the President's approval, been extended to several newly created offices. The data show further that the insertion of the removal clause in acts creating inferior civil offices with fixed tenures is part of the broader legislative practice, which has prevailed since the formation of our government, to restrict or regulate in many ways both removal from and nomination to such offices. A persistent legislative practice which involves a delimitation of the respective powers of Congress and the President, and which has been so established and maintained, should be deemed tantamount to judicial construction, in the absence of any decision by any court to the contrary. * * *

The persuasive effect of this legislative practice is strengthened by the fact that no instance has been found, even in the earlier period of our history, of concurrent affirmative action of Congress and the President which is inconsistent with the legislative practice of the last 58 years to impose the removal clause. Nor has any instance been found of action by Congress which involves recognition in any other way of the alleged uncontrollable executive power to remove an inferior civil officer. The action taken by Congress in 1789 after the great debate does not present such an instance. The vote then taken did not involve a decision that the President had uncontrollable power. It did not involve a decision of the question whether Congress could confer upon the Senate the right and impose upon it the duty, to participate in removals. It involved merely the decision that the Senate does not, in the absence of legislative grant thereof, have the right to share in the removal of an officer appointed with its consent, and that the President has, in the absence of restrictive legislation, the constitutional power of removal without such consent. Moreover, as Chief Justice Marshall recognized, the debate and the decision related to a high political office, not to inferior ones.

* * *

The separation of the powers of government did not make each branch completely autonomous. It left each in some measure, dependent upon the others, as it left to each power to exercise, in some respects, functions in their nature executive, legislative and judicial. Obviously the President cannot secure full execution of the laws, if Congress denies to him adequate means of doing so. Full execution may be defeated because Congress declines to create offices indispensable for that purpose; or because Congress, having created the office, declines to make the indispensable appropriation; or because Congress, having both created the office and made the appropriation, prevents by restrictions which it imposes, the appoint-

ment of officials who in quality and character are indispensable to the efficient execution of the law. If, in any such way, adequate means are denied to the President, the fault will lie with Congress. The President performs his full constitutional duty, if, with the means and instruments provided by Congress and within the limitations prescribed by it, he uses his best endeavors to secure the faithful execution of the laws enacted. * * *

Checks and balances were established in order that this should be "a government of laws and not of men." As White said in the House in 1789, an uncontrollable power of removal in the Chief Executive "is a doctrine not to be learned in American governments." Such power had been denied in colonial charters, and even under proprietary grants and royal commissions. It had been denied in the thirteen states before the framing of the federal Constitution. The doctrine of the separation of powers was adopted by the convention of 1787 not to promote efficiency but to preclude the exercise of arbitrary power. The purpose was not to avoid friction but by means of the inevitable friction incident to the distribution of the governmental powers among three departments, to save the people from autocracy. In order to prevent arbitrary executive action, the Constitution provided in terms that presidential appointments be made with the consent of the Senate, unless Congress should otherwise provide; and this Clause was construed by Alexander Hamilton in The Federalist, No. 77, as requiring like consent to removals. Limiting further executive prerogatives customary in monarchies, the Constitution empowered Congress to vest the appointment of inferior officers, "as we think proper, in the President alone, in the Courts of Law, or in the Heads of Departments." Nothing in support of the claim of uncontrollable power can be inferred from the silence of the convention of 1787 on the subject of removal. For the outstanding fact remains that every specific proposal to confer such uncontrollable power upon the President was rejected. In America, as in England, the conviction prevailed then that the people must look to representative assemblies for the protection of their liberties. And protection of the individual, even if he be an official, from the arbitrary or capricious exercise of power was then believed to be an essential of free government.

Mr. Justice HOLMES, dissenting.

My Brothers McREYNOLDS and BRANDEIS have discussed the question before us with exhaustive research and I say a few words merely to emphasize my agreement with their conclusion.

* * *

We have to deal with an office that owes its existence to Congress and that Congress may abolish tomorrow. Its duration and the pay attached to it while it lasts depend on Congress alone. Congress alone confers on the President the power to appoint to it and at any time may transfer the power to other hands. With such power over its own creation, I have no more trouble in believing that Congress has power to prescribe a term of life for it free from any interference than I have in accepting the undoubted power of Congress to decree its end. I have equally little trouble in accepting its power to prolong the tenure of an incumbent until Congress or the Senate shall have assented to his removal. The duty of the President to see that the laws be executed is a duty that does not go beyond the laws or require him to achieve more than Congress sees fit to leave within his power.

[Justice McREYNOLDS also dissented.]

HUMPHREY'S EXECUTOR v. UNITED STATES

Supreme Court of the United States, 1935
295 U.S. 602, 55 S.Ct. 869, 79 L.Ed. 1611

During the summer of 1933, William Humphrey, who had been appointed earlier to the Federal Trade Commission for the designated seven-year term by President Hoover, was asked to resign from that position by President Roosevelt. While Roosevelt stated that the reason for the request had nothing to do with Humphrey personally or his record of service as a commissioner, in correspondence with Humphrey the President wrote that the Commission would be more effective and the people's confidence in his administration heightened if the Commission consisted of individuals chosen by him. Humphrey, however, refused to resign, whereupon Roosevelt removed him from office on October 7. Although Humphrey died a few months later, the executor of his estate, Samuel Rathbun, brought suit against the United States to recover Humphrey's salary for the period between his discharge and the date of his death. During that four-month span Humphrey had refused to recognize his dismissal and had insisted on his right to continue on as a salaried member of the Commission. The decision of the Supreme Court centered on two questions certified to it by the Court of Claims. First, "Do the provisions of section 1 of the Federal Trade Commission Act, stating that 'any commissioner may be removed by the President for inefficiency, neglect of duty, or malfeasance in office,' restrict or limit the power of the President to remove a commissioner except upon one or more of the causes named?" Second, if the President is so restricted, then is that statutory limitation constitutional?

Mr. Justice SUTHERLAND delivered the opinion of the Court.

*   *   *

First. The question first to be considered is whether, by the provisions of § 1 of the Federal Trade Commission Act already quoted, the President's power is limited to removal for the specific causes enumerated therein. *   *   *

*   *   *

The commission is to be non-partisan; and it must, from the very nature of its duties, act with entire impartiality. It is charged with the enforcement of no policy except the policy of the law. Its duties are neither political nor executive, but predominantly quasi-judicial and quasi-legislative. Like the Interstate Commerce Commission, its members are called upon to exercise the trained judgment of a body of experts "appointed by law and informed by experience." *   *   *

The legislative reports in both houses of Congress clearly reflect the view that a fixed term was necessary to the effective and fair administration of the law. *   *   *

*   *   *

The debates in both houses demonstrate that the prevailing view was that the commission was not to be "subject to anybody in the government but *   *   * only to the people of the United States"; free from "political domination or control" or the "probability or possibility of such a thing"; to be "separate and apart from any existing department of the government—not subject to the orders of the President."

More to the same effect appears in the debates, which were long and thorough and contain nothing to the contrary. While the general rule precludes the use of these debates to explain the meaning of the words of the statute, they may be considered as reflecting light upon its general purposes and the evils which it sought to remedy. *   *   *

Thus, the language of the act, the legislative reports, and the general purposes of the legislation as reflected by the debates, all combine to demonstrate the Congressional intent to create a body of experts who shall gain experience by length of service—a body which shall be independent of executive authority, *except in its selection,* and free to exercise its judgment without the leave or hindrance of any other official or any department of the government. To the accomplishment of these purposes, it is clear that Congress was of opinion that length and certainty of tenure would vitally contribute. And to hold that, nevertheless, the members of the commission continue in office at the mere will of the President, might be to thwart, in large measure, the very ends which Congress sought to realize by definitely fixing the term of office.

We conclude that the intent of the act is to limit the executive power of removal to the causes enumerated, the existence of none of which is claimed here; and we pass to the second question.

Second. To support its contention that the removal provision of § 1, as we have just construed it, is an unconstitutional interference with the executive power of the President, the government's chief reliance is Myers v. United States, 272 U.S. 52, 47 S.Ct. 21. That case has been so recently decided, and the prevailing and dissenting opinion so fully review the general subject of the power of executive removal, that further discussion would add little of value to the wealth of material there collected. These opinions examine at length the historical, legislative and judicial data bearing upon the question, beginning with what is called "the decision of 1789" in the first Congress and coming down almost to the day when the opinions were delivered. They occupy 243 pages of the volume in which they are printed. Nevertheless, the narrow point actually decided was only that the President had power to remove a postmaster of the first class, without the advice and consent of the Senate as required by act of Congress. In the course of the opinion of the court, expressions occur which tend to sustain the government's contention, but these are beyond the point involved and, therefore, do not come within the rule of *stare decisis.* In so far as they are out of harmony with the views here set forth, these expressions are disapproved. * * *

* * *

The office of a postmaster is so essentially unlike the office now involved that the decision in the *Myers* case cannot be accepted as controlling our decision here. A postmaster is an executive officer restricted to the performance of executive functions. He is charged with no duty at all related to either the legislative or judicial power. The actual decision in the *Myers* case finds support in the theory that such an officer is merely one of the units in the executive department and, hence, inherently subject to the exclusive and illimitable power of removal by the Chief Executive, whose subordinate and aid he is. Putting aside *dicta,* which may be followed if sufficiently persuasive but which are not controlling, the necessary reach of the decision goes far enough to include all purely executive officers. It goes no farther;—much less does it include an officer who occupies no place in the executive department and who exercises no part of the executive power vested by the Constitution in the President.

The Federal Trade Commission is an administrative body created by Congress to carry into effect legislative policies embodied in the statute in accordance with the legislative standard therein prescribed, and to perform other specified duties as a legislative or as a judicial aid. Such a body cannot in any proper sense be characterized as an arm or an eye of the executive. Its duties are performed without executive leave and, in the contemplation of the statute, must be free from executive control. In administering the provisions of the statute in respect of "unfair methods of competition"—that is to say in filling in and administering the details embodied by that general standard—the commission acts in part quasi-legislatively and in part quasi-judicially. In making investigations and reports thereon for the information of Congress under § 6, in aid of the legislative power, it acts as a legislative agency. Under § 7, which authorizes the commission to act as a master in chancery under rules prescribed by the court, it acts as an agency of the judiciary. To the extent that it exercises any executive function—as distinguished from executive power in the constitutional sense—it does so in the discharge and effectuation of its quasi-legislative or quasi-judicial powers, or as an agency of the legislative or judicial departments of the government.

If Congress is without authority to prescribe causes for removal of members of the trade commission and limit executive power of removal accordingly, that power at once becomes practically all-inclusive in respect of civil officers with the exception of the judiciary provided for by the Constitution. The Solicitor General, at the bar, apparently recognizing this to be true, with commendable candor, agreed that his view in respect of the removability of members of the Federal Trade Commission necessitated a like view in respect of the Interstate Commerce Commission and the Court of Claims. We are thus confronted with the serious question whether not only the members of these quasi-legislative and quasi-judicial bodies, but the judges of the legislative Court of Claims, exercising judicial power * * * continue in office only at the pleasure of the President.

We think it plain under the Constitution that illimitable power of removal is not possessed by the President in respect of officers of the character of those just named. The authority of Congress, in creating quasi-legislative or quasi-judicial agencies, to require them to act in discharge of their duties independently of executive control cannot well be doubted; and that authority includes, as an appropriate incident, power to fix the period during which they shall continue in office, and to

forbid their removal except for cause in the meantime. For it is quite evident that one who holds his office only during the pleasure of another, cannot be depended upon to maintain an attitude of independence against the latter's will.

The fundamental necessity of maintaining each of the three general departments of government entirely free from the control or coercive influence, direct or indirect, of either of the others, has often been stressed and is hardly open to serious question. So much is implied in the very fact of the separation of the powers of these departments by the Constitution; and in the rule which recognizes their essential co-equality. The sound application of a principle that makes one master in his own house precludes him from imposing his control in the house of another who is master there. * * *

The power of removal here claimed for the President falls within this principle, since its coercive influence threatens the independence of a commission, which is not only wholly disconnected from the executive department, but which, as already fully appears, was created by Congress as a means of carrying into operation legislative and judicial powers, and as an agency of the legislative and judicial departments.

* * *

The result of what we now have said is this: Whether the power of the President to remove an officer shall prevail over the authority of Congress to condition the power by fixing a definite term and precluding a removal except for cause, will depend upon the character of the office; the *Myers* decision, affirming the power of the President alone to make the removal, is confined to purely executive officers; and as to officers of the kind here under consideration, we hold that no removal can be made during the prescribed term for which the officer is appointed, except for one or more of the causes named in the applicable statute.

To the extent that, between the decision in the *Myers* case, which sustains the unrestrictable power of the President to remove purely executive officers, and our present decision that such power does not extend to an office such as that here involved, there shall remain a field of doubt, we leave such cases as may fall within it for future consideration and determination as they may arise.

In accordance with the foregoing, the questions submitted are answered.

Question No. 1, Yes.

Question No. 2, Yes.

b. THE PRESIDENT'S POWER TO PARDON

EX PARTE GROSSMAN

Supreme Court of the United States, 1925
267 U.S. 87, 45 S.Ct. 332, 69 L.Ed. 527

Philip Grossman was found guilty of violating the National Prohibition Act and was issued a restraining order by a federal district court judge in 1920 to stop selling liquor. Grossman chose to ignore the injunction and, consequently, was sentenced to one-year imprisonment and a fine of $1,000 plus costs for contempt of court. In December 1923, President Coolidge commuted the penalty to the fine of $1,000. Despite the President's pardon the district court judge recommitted Grossman to serve the prison sentence. Grossman petitioned the Supreme Court for a writ of habeas corpus. In order to reach a decision on whether to grant the writ, the Court necessarily had to confront a question of constitutional significance; namely, did the President's power to pardon extend to offenses against the authority of courts as well as to offenses committed against the authority of the federal government in general?

Mr. Chief Justice TAFT delivered the opinion of the Court.

* * *

* * * The only question raised by the pleadings herein is that of the power of the President to grant the pardon.

* * *

The argument for the defendant is that the President's power extends only to offenses against the United States and a contempt of court is not such an offense, that offenses against the United States are not common-law offenses but can only be created by legislative act, that the President's pardoning power is more limited than that of the king of England at common law, which was a broad prerogative and included contempts against his courts chiefly because the judges thereof were his agents and acted in his name, that the context of the Constitution shows that the word "offenses" is used in that instrument only to include crimes and misdemeanors triable by jury and not contempts of the dignity and authority of the federal courts, and that to construe the pardon clause to include contempts of court would be to violate the fundamental principle of the Constitution in the division of powers between the legislative, executive and judicial branches, and to take from the federal courts their independence and the essential means of protecting their dignity and authority.

The language of the Constitution cannot be interpreted safely except by reference to the common law and to British institutions as they were when the instrument was framed and adopted. The statesmen and lawyers of the Convention who submitted it to the ratification of the convention of the Thirteen States, were born and brought up in the atmosphere of the common law, and thought and spoke in its vocabulary. They were familiar with other forms of government, recent and ancient, and indicated in their discussions earnest study and consideration of many of them, but when they came to put their conclusions into the form of fundamental law in a compact draft, they expressed them in terms of the common law, confident that they could be shortly and easily understood.

In a case presenting the question whether a pardon should be pleaded in bar to be effective, Chief Justice Marshall said of the power of pardon (United States v. Wilson, 7 Pet. 150, 160 [8 L.Ed. 640]):

"As this power had been exercised, from time immemorial, by the executive of that nation whose language is our language, and to whose judicial institutions ours bear a close resemblance, we adopt their principles respecting the operation and effect of a pardon, and look into their books for the rules prescribing the manner in which it is to be used by the person who would avail himself of it."

The king of England before our Revolution, in the exercise of his prerogative, had always exercised the power to pardon contempts of court, just as he did ordinary crimes and misdemeanors and as he has done to the present day. In the mind of a common-law lawyer of the eighteenth century the word "pardon" included within its scope the ending by the king's grace of the punishment of such derelictions, whether it was imposed by the court without a jury or upon indictment, for both forms of trial for contempts were had. * * *

These cases also show that long before our Constitution, a distinction had been recognized at common law between the effect of the king's pardon to wipe out the effect of a sentence for contempt in so far as it had been imposed to punish the contemnor for violating the dignity of the court and the king, in the public interest and its inefficacy to halt or interfere with the remedial part of the court's order necessary to secure the rights of the injured suitor. * * *

In our own law the same distinction clearly appears. * * * In * * * [Gompers v. Buck's Store & Range Co., 221 U.S. 418, 31 S.Ct. 492] this court points out that it is not the fact of punishment but rather its character and purpose that makes the difference between the two kinds of contempts. For civil contempts, the punishment is remedial and for the benefit of the complainant, and a pardon cannot stop it. For criminal contempts the sentence is punitive in the public interest to vindicate the authority of the Court and to deter other like derelictions.

* * *

We have given the history of the clause to show that the words "for offenses against the United States" were inserted by a Committee on Style, presumably to make clear that the pardon of the President was to operate upon offenses against the United States as distinguished from offenses against the states. It cannot be supposed that the Committee on Revision by adding these words, or the Convention by accepting them, intended sub silentio to narrow the scope of a pardon from one at common law or to confer any different power in this regard on our executive from that which the members of the Convention had seen exercised before the Revolution.

* * *

[C]riminal contempts of a federal court have been pardoned for 85 years. In that time the power has been exercised 27 times. * * *

Finally it is urged that criminal contempts should not be held within the pardoning power because it will tend to destroy the independence of the judiciary and violate the primary constitutional principle of a separation of the legislative, executive and judicial powers. This argument influenced the two District Judges below. * * *

The federal Constitution nowhere expressly declares that the three branches of the government shall be kept separate and independent. All legislative powers are vested in a Congress. The executive power is vested in a President. The judicial power is vested in one Supreme Court and in such inferior courts as Congress may from time to time establish. The judges are given life tenure and a compensation that may not be diminished during their continuance in office, with the evident pur-

pose of securing them and their courts an independence of Congress and the executive. Complete independence and separation between the three branches, however, are not attained, or intended, as other provisions of the Constitution and the normal operation of government under it easily demonstrate. By affirmative action through the veto power, the executive and one more than one-third of either House may defeat all legislation. One-half of the House and two-thirds of the Senate may impeach and remove the members of the judiciary. The executive can reprieve or pardon all offenses after their commission, either before trial, during trial or after trial, by individuals, or by classes, conditionally or absolutely, and this without modification or regulation by Congress. Ex parte Garland, 4 Wall. 333, 380, 18 L.Ed. 366. Negatively one House of Congress can withhold all appropriations and stop the operations of government. The Senate can hold up all appointments, confirmation of which either the Constitution or a statute requires, and thus deprive the President of the necessary agents with which he is to take care that the laws be faithfully executed.

These are some instances of positive and negative restraints possibly available under the Constitution to each branch of the government in defeat of the action of the other. They show that the independence of each of the other is qualified and is so subject to exception as not to constitute a broadly positive injunction or a necessarily controlling rule of construction. The fact is that the judiciary, quite as much as Congress and the executive, are dependent on the cooperation of the other two, that government may go on. Indeed while the Constitution has made the judiciary as independent of the other branches as is practicable, it is, as often remarked, the weakest of the three. It must look for a continuity of necessary cooperation, in the possible reluctance of either of the other branches, to the force of public opinion.

Executive clemency exists to afford relief from undue harshness or evident mistake in the operation or enforcement of the criminal law. The administration of justice by the courts is not necessarily always wise or certainly considerate of circumstances which may properly mitigate guilt. To afford a remedy, it has always been thought essential in popular governments, as well as in monarchies, to vest in some other authority than the courts power to ameliorate or avoid particular criminal judgments. It is a check entrusted to the executive for special cases. To exercise it to the extent of destroying the deterrent effect of judicial punishment would be to prevent it; but whoever is to make it useful must have full discretion to exercise it. Our Constitution confers this discretion on the highest officer in the nation in confidence that he will not abuse it.   *   *   *

The power of a court to protect itself and its usefulness by punishing contemnors is of course necessary, but it is one exercised without the restraining influence of a jury and without many of the guaranties which the bill of rights offers to protect the individual against unjust conviction. Is it unreasonable to provide for the possibility that the personal element may sometimes enter into a summary judgment pronounced by a judge who thinks his authority is flouted or denied? May it not be fairly said that in order to avoid possible mistake, undue prejudice or needless severity, the chance of pardon should exist at least as much in favor of a person convicted by a judge without a jury as in favor of one convicted in a jury trial? The pardoning by the President of criminal contempts has been practiced more than three-quarters of a century, and no abuses during all that time developed sufficiently to invoke a test in the federal courts of its validity.

It goes without saying that nowhere is there a more earnest will to maintain the independence of federal courts and the preservation of every legitimate safeguard of their effectiveness afforded by the Constitution than in this court. But the qualified independence which they fortunately enjoy is not likely to be permanently strengthened by ignoring precedent and practice and minimizing the importance of the co-ordinating checks and balances of the Constitution.

The rule is made absolute and the petitioner is discharged.

MURPHY v. FORD

United States District Court
Western Dist. of Michigan, 1975
390 F.Supp. 1372

On September 8, 1974, President Ford granted an unconditional pardon to former President Richard Nixon for alleged misdeeds he had committed while in office. Murphy, a Marquette, Michigan lawyer, subsequently brought suit for a declaratory judgment invalidating the pardon on grounds that a pardon could not be legally granted to an individual who had not first been indicted or convicted of a crime and that the Nixon pardon created an unequal system of law enforcement and substantially weakened the prospect of compliance with the criminal laws.

FOX, Chief Judge.

* * *

The main issue is, did President Ford have the constitutional power to pardon former President Nixon for the latter's offenses against the United States?

In The Federalist No. 74, written in 1788 in support of the proposed Constitution, Alexander Hamilton explained why the Founding Fathers gave the President a discretionary power to pardon: "The principal argument for reposing the power of pardoning * * * [in] the Chief Magistrate," Hamilton wrote, "is this: in seasons of insurrection or rebellion, there are often critical moments, when a well-timed offer of pardon to the insurgents or rebels may restore the tranquillity of the commonwealth; and which, if suffered to pass unimproved, it may never be possible afterwards to recall."

Few would today deny that the period from the break-in at the Watergate in June 1972, until the resignation of President Nixon in August 1974, was a "season of insurrection or rebellion" by many actually in the Government. Since the end of 1970, various top officials of the Nixon Administration at times during this period deliberately and flagrantly violated the civil liberties of individual citizens and engaged in criminal violations of the campaign laws in order to preserve and expand their own and Nixon's personal power beyond constitutional limitations. When many illegal activities were threatened with exposure, some Nixon Administration officials formed and executed a criminal conspiracy to obstruct justice. Evidence now available suggests a strong probability that the Nixon Administration was conducting a covert assault on American liberty and an insurrection and rebellion against constitutional government itself, an insurrection and rebellion which might have succeeded but for timely intervention by a courageous free press, an enlightened Congress, and a diligent Judiciary dedicated to preserving the rule of law.

Certainly the summer and early fall of 1974 were a period of popular discontent, as the full extent of the Nixon Administration's misdeeds became known, and public trust in government virtually collapsed. After Mr. Nixon's resignation in August, the public clamor over the whole Watergate episode did not immediately subside; attention continued to focus on Mr. Nixon and his fate. When Mr. Ford became President, the executive branch was floundering in the wreckage of Watergate, and the country was in the grips of an apparently uncontrollable inflationary spiral and an energy crisis of unprecedented proportions.

Under these circumstances, President Ford concluded that the public interest required *positive steps to end the divisions caused by Watergate and to shift the focus of attention from the immediate problem of Mr. Nixon to the hard social and economic problems which were of more lasting significance.*

By pardoning Richard Nixon, who many believed was the leader of a conspiratorial insurrection and rebellion against American liberty and constitutional government, President Ford was taking steps, in the words of Alexander Hamilton in The Federalist, to *"restore the tranquillity of the commonwealth"* by a *"well-timed offer of pardon"* to the putative rebel leader. President Ford's pardon of Richard M. Nixon was thus within the letter and the spirit of the Presidential Pardoning Power granted by the Constitution. It was a prudent public policy judgment.

The fact that Mr. Nixon had been neither indicted nor convicted of an offense against the United States does not affect the validity of the pardon. Ex parte Garland, 4 Wall. (71 U.S.) 333, 18 L.Ed. 366 (1867). In that case the Supreme Court considered the nature of the President's Pardoning Power, and the effect of a Presidential pardon. Mr. Justice Field, speaking for the court, said that the Pardoning Power is *"unlimited,"* except in cases of impeachment. "[The Power] extends to every offense known to the law, and may be exercised *at any time after its commission, either before legal proceedings are taken*, or during their pendency, or after conviction and judgment. * * * The benign prerogative of mercy reposed in [the President] cannot be fettered by any legislative restrictions.

"Such being the case, the inquiry arises as to the effect and operation of a pardon, and on this point all the authorities concur. A pardon reaches both the punishment prescribed for the offense and the guilt of the offender; and when the pardon is full, it releases the punishment and blots out of existence the guilt. * * * If granted before conviction, it prevents any of the penalties and disabilities consequent from conviction from attaching. * * *

"There is only this limitation to its operation: it does not restore offices forfeited, or property or interests vested in others in consequence of the conviction and judgment." Id. at 380–381. (Emphasis supplied.)

However, " * * * as the very essence of a pardon is forgiveness or remission of penalty, a pardon implies guilt; *it does not obliterate the fact of the commission of the crime and the conviction thereof; it does not wash out the moral stain; as has been tersely said; it involves forgiveness and not forgetfulness."* Page v. Watson, 140 Fla. 536, 192 So. 205, 208. (Emphasis supplied.)

For the above-stated reasons, plaintiff's motion to add the special prosecutor as a party defendant is denied.

The United States Attorney's amicus curiae motion to dismiss this action is hereby granted.

c. THE SCOPE OF EXECUTIVE POWER

YOUNGSTOWN SHEET & TUBE CO. v. SAWYER

Supreme Court of the United States, 1952
343 U.S. 579, 72 S.Ct. 863, 96 L.Ed. 1153

The facts are set out in the opinion below.

Mr. Justice BLACK delivered the opinion of the Court.

We are asked to decide whether the President was acting within his constitutional power when he issued an order directing the Secretary of Commerce to take possession of and operate most of the Nation's steel mills. The mill owners argue that the President's order amounts to lawmaking, a legislative function which the Constitution has expressly confided to the Congress and not to the President. The Government's position is that the order was made on findings of the President that his action was necessary to avert a national catastrophe which would inevitably result from a stoppage of steel production, and that in meeting this grave emergency the President was acting within the aggregate of his constitutional powers as the Nation's Chief Executive and the Commander in Chief of the Armed Forces of the United States. The issue emerges here from the following series of events:

In the latter part of 1951, a dispute arose between the steel companies and their employees over terms and conditions that should be included in new collective bargaining agreements. Long-continued conferences failed to resolve the dispute. On December 18, 1951, the employees' representative, United Steelworkers of America, C.I.O., gave notice of an intention to strike when the existing bargaining agreements expired on December 31. The Federal Mediation and Conciliation Service then intervened in an effort to get labor and management to agree. This failing, the President on December 22, 1951, referred the dispute to the Federal Wage Stabilization Board to investigate and make recommendations for fair and equitable terms of settlement. This Board's report resulted in no settlement. On April 4, 1952, the Union gave notice of a nation-wide strike called to begin at 12:01 a. m. April 9. The indispensability of steel as a component of substantially all weapons and other war materials led the President to believe that the proposed work stoppage would immediately jeopardize our national defense and that governmental seizure of the steel mills was necessary in order to assure the continued availability of steel. Reciting these considerations for his action, the President, a few hours before the strike was to begin, issued Executive Order 10340. * * * The order directed the Secretary of Commerce to take possession of most of the steel mills and keep them running. The Secretary immediately issued his own possessory orders, calling upon the presidents of the various seized companies to serve as operating managers for the United States. They were directed to carry on their activities in accordance with regulations and directions of the Secretary. The next morning the President sent a message to Congress reporting his action. Cong.Rec., April 9, 1952, p. 3962. Twelve days later he sent a second message. Cong. Rec., April 21, 1952, p. 4192. Congress has taken no action.

Obeying the Secretary's orders under protest, the companies brought proceedings against him in the District Court. Their complaints charged that the seizure was not authorized by an act of Congress or by any constitutional provisions. The District Court was asked to declare the orders of the President and the Secretary invalid and to issue preliminary and permanent injunctions restraining their enforcement. Opposing the motion for preliminary injunction, the United States asserted that a strike disrupting steel production for even a brief period would so endanger the well-being and safety of the Nation that the President had "inherent power" to do what he had done—power "supported by the Constitution, by historical precedent, and by court decisions." The Government also contended that in any event no preliminary injunction should be issued because the companies had made no showing that their available legal remedies were inadequate or that their injuries from seizure would be irreparable. Holding against the Government on all points, the District Court on April 30 issued a preliminary injunction restraining the Secretary from "continuing the seizure and possession of the plant * * * and from acting under the purported authority of Executive Order No. 10340." 103 F.Supp. 569. On the same day the Court of Appeals stayed the District Court's injunction. 197 F.2d 582. Deeming it best that the issues raised be promptly decided by this

Court, we granted certiorari on May 3 and set the cause for argument on May 12. * * *

* * *

The President's power, if any, to issue the order must stem either from an act of Congress or from the Constitution itself. There is no statute that expressly authorizes the President to take possession of property as he did here. Nor is there any act of Congress to which our attention has been directed from which such a power can fairly be implied. Indeed, we do not understand the Government to rely on statutory authorization for this seizure. There are two statutes which do authorize the President to take both personal and real property under certain conditions. However, the Government admits that these conditions were not met and that the President's order was not rooted in either of the statutes. The Government refers to the seizure provisions of one of these statutes (§ 201(b) of the Defense Production Act) as "much too cumbersome, involved, and time-consuming for the crisis which was at hand."

Moreover, the use of the seizure technique to solve labor disputes in order to prevent work stoppages was not only unauthorized by any congressional enactment; prior to this controversy, Congress had refused to adopt that method of settling labor disputes. When the Taft-Hartley Act was under consideration in 1947, Congress rejected an amendment which would have authorized such governmental seizures in cases of emergency. Apparently it was thought that the technique of seizure, like that of compulsory arbitration, would interfere with the process of collective bargaining. Consequently, the plan Congress adopted in that Act did not provide for seizure under any circumstances. Instead, the plan sought to bring about settlements by use of the customary devices of mediation, conciliation, investigation by boards of inquiry, and public reports. In some instances temporary injunctions were authorized to provide cooling-off periods. All this failing, unions were left free to strike after a secret vote by employees as to whether they wished to accept their employers' final settlement offer.

It is clear that if the President had authority to issue the order he did, it must be found in some provisions of the Constitution. And it is not claimed that express constitutional language grants this power to the President. The contention is that presidential power should be implied from the aggregate of his powers under the Constitution. Particular reliance is placed on provisions in Article II which say that "the executive Power shall be vested in a President" * * *; that "he shall take Care that the Laws be faithfully executed"; and that he "shall be Commander in Chief of the Army and Navy of the United States."

The order cannot properly be sustained as an exercise of the President's military power as Commander in Chief of the Armed Forces. The Government attempts to do so by citing a number of cases upholding broad powers in military commanders engaged in day-to-day fighting in a theater of war. Such cases need not concern us here. Even though "theater of war" be an expanding concept, we cannot with faithfulness to our constitutional system hold that the Commander in Chief of the Armed Forces has the ultimate power as such to take possession of private property in order to keep labor disputes from stopping production. This is a job for the Nation's lawmakers, not for its military authorities.

Nor can the seizure order be sustained because of the several constitutional provisions that grant executive power to the President. In the framework of our Constitution, the President's power to see that the laws are faithfully executed refutes the idea that he is to be a lawmaker. The Constitution limits his functions in the law-making process to the recommending of laws he thinks wise and the vetoing of laws he thinks bad. And the Constitution is neither silent nor equivocal about who shall make laws which the President is to execute. The first section of the first article says that "All legislative Powers herein granted shall be vested in a Congress of the United States." * * * After granting many powers to the Congress, Article I goes on to provide that Congress may "make all Laws which shall be necessary and proper for carrying into Execution the foregoing Powers and all other Powers vested by this Constitution in the Government of the United States, or in any Department or Officer thereof."

The President's order does not direct that a congressional policy be executed in a manner prescribed by Congress—it directs that a presidential policy be executed in a manner prescribed by the President. The preamble of the order itself, like that of many statutes, sets out reasons why the President believes certain policies should be adopted, proclaims these policies as rules of conduct to be followed, and again, like a statute, authorizes a government official to promulgate additional rules and regulations consistent with the policy proclaimed and needed to carry that policy into execution. The power of Congress to adopt such public policies as those proclaimed by the order is beyond question. It can authorize the taking of private property for public use. It can make laws regulating the relationships between employers and employees, prescribing rules designed to settle labor disputes, and fixing wages and working conditions in certain fields of our economy. The Constitution did not subject this law-making power of Congress to presidential or military supervision or control.

It is said that other Presidents without congressional authority have taken possession of private business enterprises in order to settle labor disputes. But even if this be true, Congress has not thereby lost its exclusive constitutional authority to make laws necessary and proper to carry out the powers vested by the Constitution "in the Government of the United States, or in any Department or Officer thereof."

The Founders of this Nation entrusted the law-making power to the Congress alone in both good and bad times. It would do no good to recall the historical events, the fears of power and the hopes for freedom that lay behind their choice. Such a review would but confirm our holding that this seizure order cannot stand.

The judgment of the District Court is affirmed.

Affirmed.

*   *   *

Mr. Justice FRANKFURTER, concurring.

Before the cares of the White House were his own, President Har-

ding is reported to have said that government after all is a very simple thing. He must have said that, if he said it, as a fleeting inhabitant of fairyland. The opposite is the truth. A constitutional democracy like ours is perhaps the most difficult of man's social arrangements to manage successfully. Our scheme of society is more dependent than any other form of government on knowledge and wisdom and self-discipline for the achievement of its aims. For our democracy implies the reign of reason on the most extensive scale. The Founders of this Nation were not imbued with the modern cynicism that the only thing that history teaches is that it teaches nothing. They acted on the conviction that the experience of man sheds a good deal of light on his nature. It sheds a good deal of light not merely on the need for effective power, if a society is to be at once cohesive and civilized, but also on the need for limitations on the power of governors over the governed.

To that end they rested the structure of our central government on the system of checks and balances. For them the doctrine of separation of powers was not mere theory; it was a felt necessity. Not so long ago it was fashionable to find our system of checks and balances obstructive to effective government. It was easy to ridicule that system as outmoded—too easy. The experience through which the world has passed in our own day has made vivid the realization that the Framers of our Constitution were not inexperienced doctrinaires. These long-headed statesmen had no illusion that our people enjoyed biological or psychological or sociological immunities from the hazards of concentrated power. It is absurd to see a dictator in a representative product of the sturdy democratic traditions of the Mississippi Valley. The accretion of dangerous power does not come in a day. It does come, however slowly, from the generative force of unchecked disregard of the restrictions that fence in even the most disinterested assertion of authority.

The Framers, however, did not make the judiciary the overseer of our government. They were familiar with the revisory functions entrusted to judges in a few of the States and refused to lodge such powers in this Court. Judicial power can be exercised only as to matters that were the traditional concern of the courts at Westminster, and only if they arise in ways that to the expert feel of lawyers constitute "Cases" or "Controversies." Even as to questions that were the staple of judicial business, it is not for the courts to pass upon them unless they are indispensably involved in a conventional litigation. And then, only to the extent that they are so involved. Rigorous adherence to the narrow scope of the judicial function is especially demanded in controversies that arouse appeals to the Constitution. The attitude with which this Court must approach its duty when confronted with such issues is precisely the opposite of that normally manifested by the general public. So-called constitutional questions seem to exercise a mesmeric influence over the popular mind. This eagerness to settle—preferably forever—a specific problem on the basis of the broadest possible constitutional pronouncements may not unfairly be called one of our minor national traits. * * *

* * *

The issue before us can be met, and therefore should be, without attempting to define the President's powers comprehensively. I shall not attempt to delineate what belongs to him by virtue of his office beyond the power even of Congress to contract; what authority belongs to him until Congress acts; what kind of problems may be dealt with either by the Congress or by the President or by both; * * * what power must be exercised by the Congress and cannot be delegated to the President. It is as unprofitable to lump together in an undiscriminating hotch-potch past presidential actions claimed to be derived from occupancy of the office, as it is to conjure up hypothetical future cases. The judiciary may, as this case proves, have to intervene in determining where authority lies as between the democratic forces in our scheme of government. But in doing so we should be wary and humble. Such is the teaching of this Court's rôle in the history of the country.

It is in this mood and with this perspective that the issue before the Court must be approached. We must therefore put to one side consideration of what powers the President would have had if there had been no legislation whatever bearing on the authority asserted by the seizure, or if the seizure had been only for a short, explicitly temporary period, to be terminated automatically unless Congressional approval were given. These and other questions, like or unlike, are not now here. I would exceed my authority were I to say anything about them.

The question before the Court comes in this setting. Congress has frequently—at least 16 times since 1916—specifically provided for executive seizure of production, transportation, communications, or storage facilities. In every case it has qualified this grant of power with limitations and safeguards. This body of enactments * * * demonstrates that Congress deemed seizure so drastic a power as to require that it be carefully circumscribed whenever the President was vested with this extraordinary authority. The power to seize has uniformly been given only for a limited period or for a defined emergency, or has been repealed after a short period. Its exercise has been restricted to particular circumstances such as "time of war or when war is imminent," the needs of "public safety" or of "national security or defense," or "urgent and impending need." * * *

* * *

In adopting the provisions which it did, by the Labor Management Relations Act of 1947, for dealing with a "national emergency" arising out of a breakdown in peaceful industrial relations, Congress was very familiar with Government seizure as a protective measure. On a balance of considerations Congress chose not to lodge this power in the President. It chose not to make available in advance a remedy to which both industry and labor were fiercely hostile. In deciding that authority to seize should be given to the President only after full consideration of the particular situation should show such legislation to be necessary, Congress presumably acted on experience with similar industrial conflicts in the past. It evidently assumed that industrial shutdowns in basic industries are not instances of spontaneous generation and that danger warnings are sufficiently plain before the event to give ample opportu-

nity to start the legislative process into action.

In any event, nothing can be plainer than that Congress made a conscious choice of policy in a field full of perplexity and peculiarly within legislative responsibility for choice. In formulating legislation for dealing with industrial conflicts, Congress could not more clearly and emphatically have withheld authority than it did in 1947. Perhaps as much so as is true of any piece of modern legislation, Congress acted with full consciousness of what it was doing and in the light of much recent history. Previous seizure legislation had subjected the powers granted to the President to restrictions of varying degrees of stringency. Instead of giving him even limited powers, Congress in 1947 deemed it wise to require the President, upon failure of attempts to reach a voluntary settlement, to report to Congress if he deemed the power of seizure a needed shot for his locker. The President could not ignore the specific limitations of prior seizure statutes. No more could he act in disregard of the limitation put upon seizure by the 1947 Act.

It cannot be contended that the President would have had power to issue this order had Congress explicitly negated such authority in formal legislation. Congress has expressed its will to withhold this power from the President as though it had said so in so many words. The authoritatively expressed purpose of Congress to disallow such power to the President and to require him, when in his mind the occasion arose for such a seizure, to put the matter to Congress and ask for specific authority from it, could not be more decisive if it had been written into §§ 206–210 of the Labor Management Relations Act of 1947. * * *

* * *

By the Labor Management Relations Act of 1947, Congress said to the President, "You may not seize. Please report to us and ask for seizure power if you think it is needed in a specific situation." * * *

* * *

It is not a pleasant judicial duty to find that the President has exceeded his powers and still less so when his purposes were dictated by concern for the Nation's well-being, in the assured conviction that he acted to avert danger. But it would stultify one's faith in our people to entertain even a momentary fear that the patriotism and the wisdom of the President and the Congress, as well as the long view of the immediate parties in interest, will not find ready accommodation for differences on matters which, however close to their concern and however intrinsically important, are overshadowed by the awesome issues which confront the world. * * *

* * *

Mr. Justice DOUGLAS, concurring.

* * *

The legislative nature of the action taken by the President seems to me to be clear. When the United States takes over an industrial plant to settle a labor controversy, it is condemning property. The seizure of the plant is a taking in the constitutional sense. United States v. Pewee Coal Co., 341 U.S. 114, 71 S.Ct. 670. A permanent taking would amount to the nationalization of the industry. A temporary taking falls short of that goal. But though the seizure is only for a week or a month, the condemnation is complete and the United States must pay compensation for the temporary possession. * * *

* * *

The President has no power to raise revenues. That power is in the Congress by Article I, Section 8 of the Constitution. The president might seize and the Congress by subsequent action might ratify the seizure. But until and unless Congress acted, no condemnation would be lawful. The branch of government that has the power to pay compensation for a seizure is the only one able to authorize a seizure or make lawful one that the President had effected. That seems to me to be the necessary result of the condemnation provision in the Fifth Amendment. It squares with the theory of checks and balances expounded by Mr. Justice BLACK in the opinion of the Court in which I join.

* * *

We pay a price for our system of checks and balances, for the distribution of power among the three branches of government. It is a price that today may seem exorbitant to many. Today a kindly President uses the seizure power to effect a wage increase and to keep the steel furnaces in production. Yet tomorrow another President might use the same power to prevent a wage increase, to curb trade unionists, to regiment labor as oppressively as industry thinks it has been regimented by this seizure.

Mr. Justice JACKSON, concurring in the judgment and opinion of the Court.

That comprehensive and undefined presidential powers hold both practical advantages and grave dangers for the country will impress anyone who has served as legal adviser to a President in time of transition and public anxiety. While an interval of detached reflection may temper teachings of that experience, they probably are a more realistic influence on my views than the conventional materials of judicial decision which seem unduly to accentuate doctrine and legal fiction. But as we approach the question of presidential power, we half overcome mental hazards by recognizing them. The opinions of judges, no less than executives and publicists, often suffer the infirmity of confusing the issue of a power's validity with the cause it is invoked to promote, of confounding the permanent executive office with its temporary occupant. The tendency is strong to emphasize transient results upon policies—such as wages or stabilization—and lose sight of enduring consequences upon the balanced power structure of our Republic.

A judge, like an executive adviser, may be surprised at the poverty of really useful and unambiguous authority applicable to concrete problems of executive power as they actually present themselves. Just what our forefathers did envision, or would have envisioned had they foreseen modern conditions, must be divined from materials almost as enigmatic as the dreams Joseph was called upon to interpret for Pharaoh. A century and a half of partisan debate and scholarly speculation yields no net result but only supplies more or less apt quotations from respected sources on each side of any question. They largely cancel each other. And court decisions are indecisive because of the judicial practice of dealing with the largest questions in the most narrow way.

The actual art of governing under our Constitution does not and cannot conform to judicial definitions of the power of any of its branches based on isolated clauses or even single Articles torn from context. While the Constitution diffuses power the better to secure liberty, it also contemplates that practice will integrate the dispersed powers into a workable government. It enjoins upon its branches separateness but interdependence, autonomy but reciprocity. Presidential powers are not fixed but fluctuate, depending upon their disjunction or conjunction with those of Congress. We may well begin by a somewhat over-simplified grouping of practical situations in which a President may doubt, or others may challenge, his powers, and by distinguishing roughly the legal consequences of this factor of relativity.

1. When the President acts pursuant to an express or implied authorization of Congress, his authority is at its maximum, for it includes all that he possesses in his own right plus all that Congress can delegate. In these circumstances, and in these only, may he be said (for what it may be worth), to personify the federal sovereignty. If his act is held unconstitutional under these circumstances, it usually means that the Federal Government as an undivided whole lacks power. A seizure executed by the President pursuant to an Act of Congress would be supported by the strongest of presumptions and the widest latitude of judicial interpretation, and the burden of

persuasion would rest heavily upon any who might attack it.

2. When the President acts in absence of either a congressional grant or denial of authority, he can only rely upon his own independent powers, but there is a zone of twilight in which he and Congress may have concurrent authority, or in which its distribution is uncertain. Therefore, congressional inertia, indifference or quiescence may sometimes, at least as a practical matter, enable, if not invite, measures on independent presidential responsibility. In this area, any actual test of power is likely to depend on the imperatives of events and contemporary imponderables rather than on abstract theories of law.

3. When the President takes measures incompatible with the expressed or implied will of Congress, his power is at its lowest ebb, for then he can rely only upon his own constitutional powers minus any constitutional powers of Congress over the matter. Courts can sustain exclusive Presidential control in such a case only by disabling the Congress from acting upon the subject. Presidential claim to a power at once so conclusive and preclusive must be scrutinized with caution, for what is at stake is the equilibrium established by our constitutional system.

Into which of these classifications does this executive seizure of the steel industry fit? It is eliminated from the first by admission, for it is conceded that no congressional authorization exists for this seizure. That takes away also the support of the many precedents and declarations which were made in relation and must be confined, to this category.

Can it then be defended under flexible tests available to the second category? It seems clearly eliminated from that class because Congress has not left seizure of private property an open field but has covered it by three statutory policies inconsistent with this seizure. In cases where the purpose is to supply needs of the Government itself, two courses are provided: one, seizure of a plant which fails to comply with obligatory orders placed by the Government, another, condemnation of facilities, including temporary use under the power of eminent domain. The third is applicable where it is the general economy of the country that is to be protected rather than exclusive governmental interests. None of these were invoked. In choosing a different and inconsistent way of his own, the President cannot claim that it is necessitated or invited by failure of Congress to legislate upon the occasions, grounds and methods for seizure of industrial properties.

This leaves the current seizure to be justified only by the severe tests under the third grouping, where it can be supported only by any remainder of executive power after subtraction of such powers as Congress may have over the subject. In short, we can sustain the President only by holding that seizure of such strike-bound industries is within his domain and beyond control by Congress. Thus, this Court's first review of such seizures occurs under circumstances which leave Presidential power most vulnerable to attack and in the least favorable of possible constitutional postures.

[Interestingly enough Justice Jackson felt impelled to answer the pointed references of the government's lawyers and those of his dissenting colleagues to opinions he rendered as Attorney General when President Franklin Roosevelt had seized companies during World War II. In a footnote reference to one such seizure—that of the North American Aviation Company—he pointed out that as attorney general his role was quite different from the one he presently occupied, "The North American seizure was regarded as an execution of congressional policy. I do not regard it as a precedent for this, but even if I did, I should not bind present judicial judgment by earlier partisan advocacy."]

* * *

In view of the ease, expedition and safety with which Congress can grant and has granted large emergency powers, certainly ample to embrace this crisis, I am quite unimpressed with the argument that we should affirm possession of them without statute. Such power either has no beginning or it has no end. If it exists, it need submit to no legal restraint. I am not alarmed that it would plunge us straightway into dictatorship, but it is at least a step in that wrong direction.

As to whether there is imperative necessity for such powers, it is relevant to note the gap that exists between the President's paper powers and his real powers. The Constitution does not disclose the measure of the actual controls wielded by the modern presidential office. That instrument must be understood as an Eighteenth-Century sketch of a government hoped for, not as a blueprint of the Government that is. Vast accretions of federal power, eroded from that reserved by the States, have magnified the scope of presidential activity. Subtle shifts take place in the centers of real power

that do not show on the face of the Constitution.

Executive power has the advantage of concentration in a single head in whose choice the whole Nation has a part, making him the focus of public hopes and expectations. In drama, magnitude and finality his decisions so far overshadow any others that almost alone he fills the public eye and ear. No other personality in public life can begin to compete with him in access to the public mind through modern methods of communications. By his prestige as head of state and his influence upon public opinion he exerts a leverage upon those who are supposed to check and balance his power which often cancels their effectiveness.

Moreover, rise of the party system has made a significant extraconstitutional supplement to real executive power. No appraisal of his necessities is realistic which overlooks that he heads a political system as well as a legal system. Party loyalties and interests, sometimes more binding than law, extend his effective control into branches of government other than his own and he often may win, as a political leader, what he cannot command under the Constitution. Indeed, Woodrow Wilson, commenting on the President as leader both of his party and of the Nation, observed, "If he rightly interpret the national thought and boldly insist upon it, he is irresistible. * * * His office is anything he has the sagacity and force to make it." I cannot be brought to believe that this country will suffer if the Court refuses further to aggrandize the presidential office, already so potent and so relatively immune from judicial review, at the expense of Congress.

But I have no illusion that any decision by this Court can keep power in the hands of Congress if it is not wise and timely in meeting its problems. A crisis that challenges the President equally, or perhaps primarily, challenges Congress. If not good law, there was worldly wisdom in the maxim attributed to Napoleon that "The tools belong to the man who can use them." We may say that power to legislate for emergencies belongs in the hands of Congress, but only Congress itself can prevent power from slipping through its fingers.

* * *

Such institutions may be destined to pass away. But it is the duty of the Court to be last, not first, to give them up.

Mr. Justice BURTON, concurring in both the opinion and judgment of the Court.

My position may be summarized as follows:

The validity of the President's order of seizure is at issue and ripe for decision. Its validity turns upon its relation to the constitutional division of governmental power between Congress and the President.

The Constitution has delegated to Congress power to authorize action to meet a national emergency of the kind we face. Aware of this responsibility, Congress had responded to it. It has provided at least two procedures for the use of the President.

* * *

The controlling fact here is that Congress, within its constitutionally delegated power, has prescribed for the President specific procedures, exclusive of seizure, for his use in meeting the present type of emer-gency. Congress has reserved to itself the right to determine where and when to authorize the seizure of property in meeting such an emergency. Under these circumstances, the President's order of April 8 invaded the jurisdiction of Congress. It violated the essence of the principle of the separation of governmental powers. Accordingly, the injunction against its effectiveness should be sustained.

Mr. Justice CLARK, concurring in the judgment of the Court.

* * *

The limits of presidential power are obscure. However, Article II, no less than Article I, is part of "a constitution intended to endure for ages to come, and consequently, to be adapted to the various crises of human affairs." Some of our Presidents, such as Lincoln, "felt that measures otherwise unconstitutional might become lawful by becoming indispensable to the preservation of the Constitution through the preservation of the nation." Others, such as Theodore Roosevelt, thought the President to be capable, as a "steward" of the people, of exerting all power save that which is specifically prohibited by the Constitution or the Congress. In my view—taught me not only by the decision of Chief Justice Marshall in Little v. Barreme, 2 Cranch 170, 2 L.Ed. 243, but also by a score of other pronouncements of distinguished members of this bench—the Constitution does grant to the President extensive authority in times of grave and imperative national emergency. In fact, to my thinking, such a grant may well be necessary to the very existence of the Constitution itself. As Lincoln aptly said, "[is] it possible to lose the nation and yet preserve the Constitution?" In describing this authority I care not whether one calls it "residual," "inherent," "moral," "implied," "aggregate," "emergency," or otherwise. I am of the conviction that those who have had the gratifying experience of being the President's lawyer have used one or more of these adjectives only with the utmost of sincerity and the highest of purpose.

I conclude that where Congress has laid down specific procedures to deal with the type of crisis confronting the President, he must follow those procedures in meeting the crisis; but that in the absence of such action by Congress, the President's independent power to act depends upon the gravity of the situation confronting the nation. I cannot sustain the seizure in question because here, as in Little v. Barreme, * * * Congress had prescribed methods to be followed by the President in meeting the emergency at hand.

Mr. Chief Justice VINSON, with whom Mr. Justice REED and Mr. Justice MINTON join, dissenting.

* * *

Those who suggest that this is a case involving extraordinary powers should be mindful that these are extraordinary times. A world not yet recovered from the devastation of World War II has been forced to face the threat of another and more terrifying global conflict.

Accepting in full measure its responsibility in the world community, the United States was instrumental in securing adoption of the United Nations Charter, approved by the Senate by a vote of 89 to 2. The first purpose of the United Nations is to "maintain international peace and security, and to that end: to take effective collective measures for the prevention and removal of threats to the peace, and for the suppression of acts of aggression or other breaches of the peace." * * * In 1950, when the United Nations called upon member nations "to render every assistance" to repel aggression in Korea, the United States furnished its vigorous support. For almost two full years, our armed forces have been fighting in Korea, suffering casualties of over 108,000 men. Hostilities have not abated. The "determination of the United Nations to continue its action in Korea to meet the aggression" has been reaffirmed. Congressional support of the action in Korea has been manifested by provisions for increased military manpower and equipment and for economic stabilization. * * *

* * *

One is not here called upon even to consider the possibility of executive seizure of a farm, a corner grocery store or even a single industrial plant. Such considerations arise only when one ignores the central fact of this case—that the Nation's entire basic steel production would have shut down completely if there had been no Government seizure. Even ignoring for the moment whatever confidential information the President may possess as "the Nation's organ for foreign affairs," the uncontroverted affidavits in this record amply support the finding that "a work stoppage would immediately jeopardize and imperil our national defense."

Plaintiffs do not remotely suggest any basis for rejecting the President's finding that *any* stoppage of steel production would immediately place the Nation in peril. * * *

Accordingly, if the President has any power under the Constitution to meet a critical situation in the absence of express statutory authorization, there is no basis whatever for criticizing the exercise of such power in this case.

* * *

In passing upon the grave constitutional question presented in this case, we must never forget, as Chief Justice Marshall admonished, that the Constitution is "intended to endure for ages to come, and consequently, to be adapted to the various *crises* of human affairs," and that "[i]ts means are adequate to its ends." Cases do arise presenting questions which could not have been foreseen by the Framers. In such cases, the Constitution has been treated as a living document adaptable to new situations. But we are not called upon today to expand the Constitution to meet a new situation. For, in this case, we need only look to history and time-honored principles of constitutional law—principles that have been applied consistently by all branches of the Government throughout our history. It is those who assert the invalidity of the Executive Order who seek to amend the Constitution in this case.

A review of executive action demonstrates that our Presidents have on many occasions exhibited the leadership contemplated by the Framers when they made the President Commander in Chief, and imposed upon him the trust to "take Care that the Laws be faithfully executed." With or without explicit statutory authorization, Presidents have at such times dealt with national emergencies by acting promptly and resolutely to enforce legislative programs, at least to save those programs until Con-

gress could act. Congress and the courts have responded to such executive initiative with consistent approval.

* * *

The President reported to Congress the morning after the seizure that he acted because a work stoppage in steel production would immediately imperil the safety of the Nation by preventing execution of the legislative programs for procurement of military equipment. And, while a shutdown could be averted by granting the price concessions requested by plaintiffs, granting such concessions would disrupt the price stabilization program also enacted by Congress. Rather than fail to execute either legislative program, the President acted to execute both.

* * *

The absence of a specific statute authorizing seizure of the steel mills as a mode of executing the laws—both the military procurement program and the anti-inflation program—has not until today been thought to prevent the President from executing the laws. * * *

There is no statute prohibiting seizure as a method of enforcing legislative programs. Congress has in no wise indicated that its legislation is not to be executed by the taking of private property (subject of course to the payment of just compensation) if its legislation cannot otherwise be executed. Indeed, the Universal Military Training and Service Act authorizes the seizure of *any* plant that fails to fill a Government contract or the properties of *any* steel producer that fails to allocate steel as directed for defense production. And the Defense Production Act authorizes the President to requisition equipment and condemn real property needed without delay in the defense effort. Where Congress authorizes seizure in instances not necessarily crucial to the defense program, it can hardly be said to have disclosed an intention to prohibit seizures where essential to the execution of that legislative program.

Whatever the extent of Presidential power on more tranquil occasions, and whatever the right of the President to execute legislative programs as he sees fit without reporting the mode of execution to Congress, the single Presidential purpose disclosed on this record is to faithfully execute the laws by acting in an emergency to maintain the status quo, thereby preventing collapse of the legislative programs until Congress could act. The President's action served the same purposes as a judicial stay entered to maintain the status quo in order to preserve the jurisdiction of a court. In his Message to Congress immediately following the seizure, the President explained the necessity of his action in executing the military procurement and anti-inflation legislative programs and expressed his desire to cooperate with any legislative proposals approving, regulating or rejecting the seizure of the steel mills. Consequently, there is no evidence whatever of any Presidential purpose to defy Congress or act in any way inconsistent with the legislative will.

* * *

The diversity of views expressed in the six opinions of the majority, the lack of reference to authoritative precedent, the repeated reliance upon prior dissenting opinions, the complete disregard of the uncontroverted facts showing the gravity of the emergency and the temporary nature

of the taking all serve to demonstrate how far afield one must go to affirm the order of the District Court.

The broad executive power granted by Article II to an officer on duty 365 days a year cannot, it is said, be invoked to avert disaster. Instead, the President must confine himself to sending a message to Congress recommending action. Under this messenger-boy concept of the Office, the President cannot even act to preserve legislative programs from destruction so that Congress will have something left to act upon. There is no judicial finding that the executive action was unwarranted because there was in fact no basis for the President's finding of the existence of an emergency for, under this view, the gravity of the emergency and the immediacy of the threatened disaster are considered irrelevant as a matter of law.

Seizure of plaintiffs' property is not a pleasant undertaking. Similarly unpleasant to a free country are the draft which disrupts the home and military procurement which causes economic dislocation and compels adoption of price controls, wage stabilization and allocation of materials. The President informed Congress that even a temporary Government operation of plaintiffs' properties was "thoroughly distasteful" to him, but was necessary to prevent immediate paralysis of the mobilization program. Presidents have been in the past, and any man worthy of the Office should be in the future, free to take at least interim action necessary to execute legislative programs essential to survival of the Nation. A sturdy judiciary should not be swayed by the unpleasantness or unpopularity of necessary executive action, but must independently determine for itself whether the President was acting, as required by the Constitution, to "take Care that the Laws be faithfully executed."

As the District Judge stated, this is no time for "timorous" judicial action. But neither is this a time for timorous executive action. Faced with the duty of executing the defense programs which Congress had enacted and the disastrous effects that any stoppage in steel production would have on those programs, the President acted to preserve those programs by seizing the steel mills. There is no question that the possession was other than temporary in character and subject to congression-

al direction—either approving, disapproving or regulating the manner in which the mills were to be administered and returned to the owners. The President immediately informed Congress of his action and clearly stated his intention to abide by the legislative will. No basis for claims of arbitrary action, unlimited powers or dictatorial usurpation of congressional power appears from the facts of this case. On the contrary, judicial, legislative and executive precedents throughout our history demonstrate that in this case the President acted in full conformity with his duties under the Constitution. Accordingly, we would reverse the order of the District Court.

Following is an excerpt from the third of David Frost's controversial television interviews with former President Richard Nixon aired May 20, 1977. The excerpt focuses on the issue of inherent presidential power.

* * *

FROST: The wave of dissent, occasionally violent, which followed in the wake of the Cambodian incursion prompted President Nixon to demand better intelligence about the people who were opposing him. To this end, the Deputy White House Counsel, Tom Huston, arranged a series of meetings with representatives of the C.I.A., the F.B.I. and other police and intelligence agencies.

These meetings produced a plan, the Huston Plan, which advocated the systematic use of wiretappings, burglaries, or so-called black bag jobs, mail openings and infiltration against antiwar groups and others. Some of these activities, as Huston emphasized to Nixon, were clearly illegal. Nevertheless, the President approved the plan. Five days later, after opposition from J. Edgar Hoover, the plan was withdrawn, but the President's approval was later to be listed in the Articles of Impeachment as an alleged abuse of Presidential power.

Q. So what in a sense, you're saying is that there are certain situations, and the Huston Plan or that part of it was one of them, where the President can decide that it's in the best interests of the nation or something, and do something illegal.

A. Well, when the President does it, that means that it is not illegal.

Q. By definition.

A. Exactly. Exactly. If the President, for example, approves something because of the national security, or in this case because of a threat to internal peace and order of significant magnitude, then the President's decision in that instance is one that enables those who carry it out, to carry it out without violating a law. Otherwise they're in an impossible position.

Q. So, that in other words, really you were saying in that answer, really, between the burglary and murder, again, there's no subtle way to say that there was murder of a dissenter in this country because I don't know any evidence to that effect at all. But, the point is: just the dividing line, is that in fact, the dividing line is the President's judgment?

A. Yes, and the dividing line and, just so that one does not get the impression, that a President can run amok in this country and get away with it, we have to have in mind that a President has to come up before the electorate. We also have to have in mind, that a President has to get appropriations from the Congress. We have to have in mind, for example, that as far as the C.I.A.'s covert operations are concerned, as far as the F.B.I.'s covert operations are concerned, through the years, they have been disclosed on a very, very limited basis to trusted members of Congress. I don't know whether it can be done today or not.

* * *

Q. Pulling some of our discussions together, as it were; speaking of the Presidency and in an interrogatory filed with the Church Committee, you stated, quote, "It's quite obvious that there are certain inherently government activities, which, if undertaken by the sovereign in protection of the interests of the nation's security are lawful, but which if undertaken by private persons, are not."

What, at root, did you have in mind there?

A. Well, what I, at root I had in mind I think was perhaps much better stated by Lincoln during the War between the States. Lincoln said, and I think I can remember the quote almost exactly, he said, "Actions which otherwise would be unconstitutional, could become lawful if undertaken for the purpose of preserving the Constitution and the Nation."

Now that's the kind of action I'm referring to. Of course in Lincoln's case it was the survival of the Union in war time, it's the defense of the nation and, who knows, perhaps the survival of the nation.

Q. But there was no comparison, was there, between the situation you faced and the situation Lincoln faced, for instance?

A. This nation was torn apart in an ideological way by the war in Vietnam, as much as the Civil War tore apart the nation when Lincoln was President. Now it's true that we didn't have the North and South—

Q. But when you said, as you said when we were talking about the Huston Plan, you know, "If the President orders it, that makes it legal," as it were: Is the President in that sense—is there anything in the Constitution or the Bill of Rights that suggests the President is that far of a sovereign, that far above the law?

A. No, there isn't. There's nothing specific that the Constitution contemplates in that respect. I haven't read every word, every jot and every title, but I do know this: that it has been, however, argued that as far as a President is concerned, that in war time, a President does have certain extraordinary powers which would make acts that would otherwise be unlawful, lawful if undertaken for the purpose of preserving the nation and the Constitution, which is essential for the rights we're all talking about.

* * *

UNITED STATES v. NIXON

Supreme Court of the United States, 1974
418 U.S. 683, 94 S.Ct. 3090, 41 L.Ed.2d 1039

On March 1, 1974, a federal grand jury sitting in the District of Columbia returned indictments against former Attorney General John Mitchell and six other individuals alleging conspiracy to defraud the United States and obstruction of justice, charges growing out of the cover-up of the Watergate Affair. In its findings the grand jury named President Richard M. Nixon as an unindicted co-conspirator. Following the indictments, Special Prosecutor Leon Jaworski sought and District Judge John Sirica issued on April 18, a subpoena duces tecum directed at the President as a third party to produce certain tape recordings of conversations with specifically named advisors and aides on particular dates and other memoranda then in his possession relevant to the up-coming trials of those indicted. On April 30, the President released to the public edited transcripts of forty-three conversations, twenty of which had been subpoenaed. The President declined to release additional material and through his counsel, James St. Clair, moved to quash the subpoena, asserting that the dispute did not properly lie before the district court since the controversy was nonjusticiable (involving what was postulated to be a purely internal dispute between a superior officer and his subordinate within the executive branch) and because any judicial action in the matter was precluded by the claim of executive privilege.

The district court rejected the first argument made by the President, relying upon a special regulation concerning the independence of the Special Prosecutor promulgated by the Attorney General. That court also rejected the second argument by citing the ruling of the U. S. Court of Appeals for the District of Columbia in Nixon v. Sirica, 487 F.2d 700 (D.C.Cir.1973). Further, the district court denied the President's motion to expunge the grand jury's characterization of him as a co-conspirator. The President then appealed to the U. S. Circuit Court of Appeals. At the same time the Special Prosecutor petitioned the Supreme Court for certiorari in the interest of facilitating a definitive resolution to the controversy. The Supreme Court granted the writ before any decision could be rendered by the Court of Appeals, and it heard oral argument in a special session, July 8, 1974, following the close of its October 1973 Term.

Mr. Chief Justice BURGER delivered the opinion of the Court.

* * *

THE CLAIM OF PRIVILEGE

A

[W]e turn to the claim that the subpoena should be quashed because it demands "confidential conversations between a President and his close advisors that it would be inconsistent with the public interest to produce." * * * The first contention is a broad claim that the separation of powers doctrine precludes judicial review of a President's claim of privilege. The second contention is that if he does not prevail on the claim of absolute privilege, the court should hold as a matter of constitutional law that the privilege prevails over the subpoena *duces tecum*.

In the performance of assigned constitutional duties each branch of the Government must initially interpret the Constitution, and the interpretation of its powers by any branch is due great respect from the others. The President's counsel, as we have noted, reads the Constitution as providing an absolute privilege of confidentiality for all presidential communications. Many decisions of this Court, however, have unequivocally reaffirmed the holding of Marbury v. Madison, 1 Cranch 137 (1803), that "it is emphatically the province and duty of the judicial department to say what the law is." * * *

No holding of the Court has defined the scope of judicial power specifically relating to the enforcement of a subpoena for confidential presidential communications for use in a criminal prosecution, but other exercises of powers by the Executive Branch and the Legislative Branch have been found invalid as in conflict with the Constitution. * * * In a series of cases, the Court interpreted the explicit immunity conferred by express provisions of the Constitution on Members of the House and Senate by the Speech or Debate Clause, U.S.Const. Art. I, § 6. Doe v. McMillan, 412 U.S. 306, 93 S.Ct. 2018 (1973); Gravel v. United States, 408 U.S. 606, 92 S.Ct. 2614 (1973); United States v. Brewster, 408 U.S. 501, 92 S.Ct. 2531 (1972); United States v. Johnson, 383 U.S. 169, 86 S.Ct. 749 (1966). Since this Court has consistently exercised the power to construe and delineate claims arising under express powers, it must follow that the Court has authority to interpret claims with respect to powers alleged to derive from enumerated powers.

Our system of government "requires that federal courts on occasion interpret the Constitution in a manner at variance with the construction given the document by another branch." Powell v. McCormack, 549. And in Baker v. Carr, 369 U.S., at 211, 82 S.Ct. 691, the Court stated:

"[d]eciding whether a matter has in any measure been committed by the Constitution to another branch of government, or whether the action of that branch exceeds whatever authority has been committed, is itself a delicate exercise in constitutional interpretation, and is a responsibility of this Court as ultimate interpreter of the Constitution.

Notwithstanding the deference each branch must accord the others, the "judicial power of the United States" vested in the federal courts by Art. III, § 1 of the Constitution can no more be shared with the Executive Branch than the Chief Executive, for example, can share with the Judiciary the veto power, or the Congress share with the Judiciary the power to override a presidential veto. Any other conclusion would be contrary to the basic concept of separation of powers and the checks and balances that flow from the scheme of a tripartite government. The Federalist, No. 47. * * * We therefore reaffirm that it is "emphatically the province and the duty" of this Court "to say what the law is" with respect to the claim of privilege presented in this case. *Marbury* v. *Madison*, at 177.

B

In support of his claim of absolute privilege, the President's counsel urges two grounds one of which is common to all governments and one of which is peculiar to our system of separation of powers. The first ground is the valid need for protection of communications between high government officials and those who advise and assist them in the performance of their manifold duties;

the importance of this confidentiality is too plain to require further discussion. Human experience teaches that those who expect public dissemination of their remarks may well temper candor with a concern for appearances and for their own interests to the detriment of the decisionmaking process. Whatever the nature of the privilege of confidentiality of presidential communications in the exercise of Art. II powers the privilege can be said to derive from the supremacy of each branch within its own assigned area of constitutional duties. Certain powers and privileges flow from the nature of enumerated powers; the protection of the confidentiality of presidential communications has similar constitutional underpinnings.

The second ground asserted by the President's counsel in support of the claim of absolute privilege rests on the doctrine of separation of powers. Here it is argued that the independence of the Executive Branch within its own sphere, Humphrey's Executor v. United States, 295 U.S. 602, 629–630, 55 S.Ct. 869, 874; Kilbourn v. Thompson, 103 U.S. 168, 190–191 (1880), insulates a president from a judicial subpoena in an ongoing criminal prosecution, and thereby protects confidential presidential communications.

However, neither the doctrine of separation of powers, nor the need for confidentiality of high level communications, without more, can sustain an absolute, unqualified presidential privilege of immunity from judicial process under all circumstances. The President's need for complete candor and objectivity from advisers calls for great deference from the courts. However, when the privilege depends solely on the broad, undifferentiated claim of public interest in the confidentiality of such conversations, a confrontation with other values arises. Absent a claim of need to protect military, diplomatic or sensitive national security secrets, we find it difficult to accept the argument that even the very important interest in confidentiality of presidential communications is significantly diminished by production of such material for *in camera* inspection with all the protection that a district court will be obliged to provide.

The impediment that an absolute, unqualified privilege would place in the way of the primary constitutional duty of the Judicial Branch to do justice in criminal prosecutions would plainly conflict with the function of the courts under Art. III. In designing the structure of our Government and dividing and allocating the sovereign power among three coequal branches, the Framers of the Constitution sought to provide a comprehensive system, but the separate powers were not intended to operate with absolute independence.

"While the Constitution diffuses power the better to secure liberty, it also contemplates that practice will integrate the dispersed powers into a workable government. It enjoins upon its branches separateness but interdependence, autonomy but reciprocity." Youngstown Sheet & Tube Co. v. Sawyer, 343 U.S. 579, 635, 72 S.Ct. 863, 870 (1952) (Jackson, J., concurring).

To read the Art. II powers of the President as providing an absolute privilege as against a subpoena essential to enforcement of criminal statutes on no more than a generalized claim of the public interest in confidentiality of nonmilitary and nondiplomatic discussions would upset the constitutional balance of "a workable government" and gravely impair the role of the courts under Art. III.

C

Since we conclude that the legitimate needs of the judicial process may outweigh presidential privilege, it is necessary to resolve those competing interests in a manner that preserves the essential functions of each branch. The right and indeed the duty to resolve that question does not free the judiciary from according high respect to the representations made on behalf of the President. United States v. Burr, 25 Fed.Cas. 187, 190, 191–192 (No. 14,694) (1807).

The expectation of a President to the confidentiality of his conversations and correspondence, like the claim of confidentiality of judicial deliberations, for example, has all the values to which we accord deference for the privacy of all citizens and added to those values the necessity for protection of the public interest in candid, objective, and even blunt or harsh opinions in presidential decisionmaking. A President and those who assist him must be free to explore alternatives in the process of shaping policies and making decisions and to do so in a way many would be unwilling to express except privately. These are the considerations justifying a presumptive privilege for presidential communications. The privilege is fundamental to the operation of government and inextricably rooted in the separation of powers under the Constitution. In Nixon v. Sirica, 159 U.S.App.D.C. 58, 487 F.2d 700 (1973), the Court of Appeals held that such presidential communications are "presumptively privileged," * * * and this position

is accepted by both parties in the present litigation. We agree with Mr. Chief Justice Marshall's observation, therefore, that "in no case of this kind would a court be required to proceed against the President as against an ordinary individual." United States v. Burr, 25 Fed.Cas. 187, 191 (No. 14,594) (CCD Va. 1807).

But this presumptive privilege must be considered in light of our historic commitment to the rule of law. This is nowhere more profoundly manifest than in our view that "the twofold aim [of criminal justice] is that guilt shall not escape or innocence suffer." Berger v. United States, 295 U.S. 78, 88, 55 S.Ct. 629, 633 (1935). We have elected to employ an adversary system of criminal justice in which the parties contest all issues before a court of law. The need to develop all relevant facts in the adversary system is both fundamental and comprehensive. The ends of criminal justice would be defeated if judgments were to be founded on a partial or speculative presentation of the facts. The very integrity of the judicial system and public confidence in the system depend on full disclosure of all the facts, within the framework of the rules of evidence. To insure that justice is done, it is imperative to the function of courts that compulsory process be available for the production of evidence needed either by the prosecution or by the defense.

Only recently the Court restated the ancient proposition of law, albeit in the context of a grand jury inquiry rather than a trial,

" 'that the public * * * has a right to every man's evidence' except for those persons protected by a constitutional, common law, or statutory privilege, United States v. Bryan, 339

U.S., at 331 (1949); Blackmer v. United States, 284 U.S. 421, 438, 52 S.Ct. 252, 255; Branzburg v. United States, 408 U.S. 665, 668, 92 S.Ct. 2646, 2660 (1973)."

The privileges referred to by the Court are designed to protect weighty and legitimate competing interests. Thus, the Fifth Amendment to the Constitution provides that no man "shall be compelled in any criminal case to be a witness against himself." And, generally, an attorney or a priest may not be required to disclose what has been revealed in professional confidence. These and other interests are recognized in law by privileges against forced disclosure, established in the Constitution, by statute, or at common law. Whatever their origins, these exceptions to the demand for every man's evidence are not lightly created nor expansively construed, for they are in derogation of the search for truth.

In this case the President challenges a subpoena served on him as a third party requiring the production of materials for use in a criminal prosecution on the claim that he has a privilege against disclosure of confidential communications. He does not place his claim of privilege on the ground they are military or diplomatic secrets. As to these areas of Art. II duties the courts have traditionally shown the utmost deference to presidential responsibilities. In C. & S. Air Lines v. Waterman Steamship Corp., 333 U.S. 103, 111, 68 S.Ct. 431, 436 (1948), dealing with presidential authority involving foreign policy considerations, the Court said:

"The President, both as Commander-in-Chief and as the Nation's organ for foreign affairs, has available intelligence services whose reports are not and ought not to be published to the world. It would be intolerable that courts, without the relevant information, should review and perhaps nullify actions of the Executive taken on information properly held secret." * * *

In United States v. Reynolds, 345 U.S. 1, 73 S.Ct. 528 (1952), dealing with a claimant's demand for evidence in a damage case against the Government the Court said:

"It may be possible to satisfy the court, from all the circumstances of the case, that there is a reasonable danger that compulsion of the evidence will expose military matters which, in the interest of national security, should not be divulged. When this is the case, the occasion for the privilege is appropriate, and the court should not jeopardize the security which the privilege is meant to protect by insisting upon an examination of the evidence, even by the judge alone, in chambers." No case of the Court, however, has extended this high degree of deference to a President's generalized interest in confidentiality. Nowhere in the Constitution, as we have noted earlier, is there any explicit reference to a privilege of confidentiality, yet to the extent this interest relates to the effective discharge of a President's powers, it is constitutionally based.

The right to the production of all evidence at a criminal trial similarly has constitutional dimensions. The Sixth Amendment explicitly confers upon every defendant in a criminal trial the right "to be confronted with the witnesses against him" and "to have compulsory process for obtaining witnesses in his favor." Moreover, the Fifth Amendment also guarantees that no person shall be deprived of liberty without due process of law. It is the manifest duty of the courts to vindicate those guarantees and to accomplish that it is essential that all relevant and admissible evidence be produced.

In this case we must weigh the importance of the general privilege of confidentiality of presidential communications in performance of his responsibilities against the inroads of such a privilege on the fair administration of criminal justice. The interest in preserving confidentiality is weighty indeed and entitled to great respect. However we cannot conclude that advisers will be moved to temper the candor of their remarks by the infrequent occasions of disclosure because of the possibility that such conversations will be called for in the context of a criminal prosecution.

On the other hand, the allowance of the privilege to withhold evidence that is demonstrably relevant in a criminal trial would cut deeply into the guarantee of due process of law and gravely impair the basic function of the courts. A President's acknowledged need for confidentiality in the communications of his office is general in nature, whereas the constitutional need for production of relevant evidence in a criminal proceeding is specific and central to the fair adjudication of a particular criminal case in the administration of justice. Without access to specific facts a criminal prosecution may be totally frustrated. The President's broad interest in confidentiality of communications will not be vitiated by disclosure of a limited number of conversations preliminarily shown to have some bearing on the pending criminal cases.

We conclude that when the ground for asserting privilege as to subpoenaed materials sought for use in a criminal trial is based only on the generalized interest in confidentiality, it cannot prevail over the fundamental demands of due process of law in the fair administration of criminal justice. The generalized assertion of privilege must yield to the demonstrated, specific need for evidence in a pending criminal trial.

D

We have earlier determined that the District Court did not err in authorizing the issuance of the subpoena. If a president concludes that compliance with a subpoena would be injurious to the public interest he may properly, as was done here, invoke a claim of privilege on the return of the subpoena. Upon receiving a claim of privilege from the Chief Executive, it became the further duty of the District Court to treat the subpoenaed material as presumptively privileged and to require the Special Prosecutor to demonstrate that the presidential material was "essential to the justice of the [pending criminal] case." *United States* v. *Burr*, at 192. Here the District Court treated the material as presumptively privileged, proceeded to find that the Special Prosecutor had made a sufficient showing to rebut the presumption and ordered an *in camera* examination of the subpoenaed material. On the basis of our examination of the record we are unable to conclude that the District Court erred in ordering the inspection. Accordingly we affirm the order of the District Court that subpoenaed materials be transmitted to that court. We now turn to the important question of the District Court's responsibilities in conducting the *in camera* examination of presidential materials or communications delivered under the compulsion of the subpoena *duces tecum*.

E

Enforcement of the subpoena *duces tecum* was stayed pending this Court's resolution of the issues raised by the petitions for certiorari. Those issues now having been disposed of, the matter of implementation will rest with the District Court. "[T]he guard, furnished to [President] to protect him from being harassed by vexatious and unnecessary subpoenas, is to be looked for in the conduct of the [district] court after the subpoenas have issued; not in any circumstances which is to precede their being issued." *United States* v. *Burr*, at 34. Statements that meet the test of admissibility and relevance must be isolated; all other material must be excised. At this stage the District Court is not limited to representations of the Special Prosecutor as to the evidence sought by the subpoena; the material will be available to the District Court. It is elementary that *in camera* inspection of evidence is always a procedure calling for scrupulous protection against any release or publication of material not found by the court, at that stage, probably admissible in evidence and relevant to the issues of the trial for which it is sought. That being true of an ordinary situation, it is obvious that the District Court has a very heavy responsibility to see to it that presidential conversations, which are either not relevant or not admissible, are accorded that high degree of respect due the President of the United States. Mr. Chief Justice Marshall sitting as a trial judge in the *Burr*

case, was extraordinarily careful to point out that:

"[I]n no case of this kind would a Court be required to proceed against the President as against an ordinary individual." United States v. Burr, 25 Fed.Cases 187, 191 (No. 14,694).

Marshall's statement cannot be read to mean in any sense that a President is above the law, but relates to the singularly unique role under Art. II of a President's communications and activities, related to the performance of duties under that Article. Moreover, a President's communications and activities encompass a vastly wider range of sensitive material than would be true of any "ordinary individual." It is therefore necessary in the public interest to afford presidential confidentiality the greatest protection consistent with the fair administration of justice. The need for confidentiality even as to idle conversations with associates in which casual reference might be made concerning political leaders within the country or foreign statesmen is too obvious to call for further treatment. We have no doubt that the District Judge will at all times accord to presidential records that high degree of deference suggested in *United States* v. *Burr*, and will discharge his responsibility to see to it that until released to the Special Prosecutor no *in camera* material is revealed to anyone. This burden applies with even greater force to excised material; once the decision is made to excise, the material is restored to its privileged status and should be returned under seal to its lawful custodian.

Since this matter came before the Court during the pendency of a criminal prosecution, and on representa-

tions that time is of the essence, the
mandate shall issue forthwith.
    Affirmed.

Mr. Justice REHNQUIST took no
part in the consideration or decision
of these cases.

Pursuant to a Senate resolution empowering it to investigate "illegal, improper or unethical activities" occurring in connection with the 1972 presidential campaign and election and "to determine * * * the necessity or desirability of new congressional legislation to safeguard the electoral process by which the President of the United States is chosen," the Senate Select Committee on Presidential Campaign Activities, chaired by Sen. Sam J. Ervin, Jr., held hearings at which John Dean and other former White House employees testified. When the committee learned that tape recordings of conversations between Dean and then-President Nixon were in the President's possession, it subpoenaed tapes of five such conversations in an effort to resolve serious contradictions in testimony given before the committee. When the President, asserting executive privilege, refused to comply, the committee, with statutory authorization, began a suit to force presidential compliance with its subpoena *duces tecum*. A federal district court dismissed the suit, and the committee appealed. The United States Court of Appeals for the District of Columbia Circuit heard the case en banc. In its disposition of the matter in Senate Select Committee on Presidential Campaign Activities v. Nixon, 498 F.2d 725 (1974), the appellate court relied substantially on its earlier decision in Nixon v. Sirica, 487 F.2d 700 (1973), which rejected an absolute claim of executive privilege and held that the demonstrated relevance of the tapes to pending criminal proceedings overrode even the presumptive privilege possessed by the President, an approach ultimately adopted by the Supreme Court itself in *United States* v. *Nixon* a year later.

Writing for the federal appeals court, Chief Judge David Bazelon observed at the outset that here, just as in *Nixon* v. *Sirica*, "the showing required to overcome the presumption favoring confidentiality turned, not on the nature of the presidential conduct that the subpoenaed material might reveal, but, instead, on the nature and appropriateness of the function in the performance of which the material was sought, and the degree to which the material was necessary to its fulfillment." The committee argued that it had shown this. "It contended that resolution, on the basis of the subpoenaed tapes, of the conflicts in the testimony before it 'would aid in a determination whether legislative involvement in political campaigns is necessary' and 'could help engender the public support needed for basic reforms in our electoral system.' Moreover, Congress has, according to the Committee, the power to oversee the operations of the executive branch, to investigate instances of possible corruption and malfeasance in office, and to expose the results of its investigations to public view. The Committee says that with respect to Watergate-related matters, this power has been delegated to it by the Senate, and that to exercise its power responsibly, it must have access to the subpoenaed tapes." However, the court noted: (1) the House Judiciary Committee already had begun its impeachment inquiry, an investigative authority with "an express constitutional source"; (2) "the investigative objectives of the two committees substantially overlap"; and (3) the Judiciary Committee had "in its possession copies of each of the tapes subpoenaed by the Select Committee." Consequently, since the Select Committee's immediate oversight need could only be characterized as "cumulative," the court held that "the need for the tapes premised solely on an asserted power to investigate and inform cannot justify enforcement of the Committee's subpoena." In the court's judgment, then, "[t]he sufficiency of the Committee's showing of need has come to depend   *   *   *   entirely on whether the subpoenaed materials are critical to the performance of its legislative functions." But the quality of evidence which enables Congress to legislate, the court pointed out, was not comparable to a "grand jury's need for the most precise evidence, the exact text of oral statements recorded in their original form   *   *   *." Judge Bazelon explained that "Congress frequently legislates on the basis of conflicting information provided in its hearings" while "the responsibility of the grand jury turns entirely on its ability to determine whether there is probable cause to believe that certain named individuals did or did not commit specific crimes." The committee could point "to no specific legislative decisions that cannot responsibly be made without access to materials uniquely contained in the tapes or without resolution of the ambiguities that the transcripts may contain." Because, moreover, "there is no indication that the findings of the House Committee on the Judiciary and, eventually, the House of Representatives itself, are so likely to be inconclusive or long in coming that the Select Committee needs immediate access on its own," the appeals court concluded, "the need demonstrated by the Select Committee in the peculiar circumstances of this case   *   *   *   is too attenuated and too tangential to its functions to permit a judicial judgment that the President is required to comply with the Committee's subpoena."

ARTICLES OF IMPEACHMENT AGAINST PRESIDENT RICHARD M. NIXON RECOMMENDED BY THE HOUSE JUDICIARY COMMITTEE

[In a series of extraordinary televised sessions the House Judiciary Committee debated and voted to recommend to the House of Representatives the following articles comprising a bill of impeachment against President Richard M. Nixon. Article I was approved by the committee on July 27, 1974, by a vote of 27–11; Article II was adopted on July 29 by a vote of 28–10; and Article III was accepted on July 30 by a vote of 21–17. The committee rejected 12–26 two articles dealing with income tax violations and the secret bombing of Cambodia.]

Resolved, That Richard M. Nixon, President of the United States, is impeached for high crimes and misdemeanors, and that the following arti-

cles of impeachment be exhibited to the Senate:

Articles of impeachment exhibited by the House of Representatives of the United States of America in the name of itself and of all of the people of the United States of America, against Richard M. Nixon, President of the United States of America, in maintenance and support of its impeachment against him for high crimes and misdemeanors.

ARTICLE I

In his conduct of the office of President of the United States, Richard M. Nixon, in violation of his constitutional oath faithfully to execute the office of President of the United States and, to the best of his ability, preserve, protect, and defend the Constitution of the United States, and in violation of his constitutional duty to take care that the laws be faithfully executed, has prevented, obstructed, and impeded the administration of justice, in that:

On June 17, 1972, and prior thereto, agents of the Committee for the Re-election of the President committed unlawful entry of the headquarters of the Democratic National Committee in Washington, District of Columbia, for the purpose of securing political intelligence. Subsequent thereto, Richard M. Nixon, using the powers of his high office, engaged, personally and through his subordinates and agents, in a course of conduct or plan designed to delay, impede, and obstruct the investigation of such unlawful entry; to cover up, conceal and protect those responsible; and to conceal the existence and scope of other unlawful covert activities.

The means used to implement this course of conduct or plan included one or more of the following:

1. Making or causing to be made false or misleading statements to lawfully authorized investigative officers and employees of the United States;

2. Withholding relevant and material evidence or information from lawfully authorized investigative officers and employees of the United States;

3. Approving, condoning, acquiescing in, and counseling witnesses with respect to the giving of false or misleading statements to lawfully authorized investigative officers and employees of the United States and false or misleading testimony in duly instituted judicial and congressional proceedings;

4. Interfering or endeavoring to interfere with the conduct of investigations by the Department of Justice of the United States, the Federal Bureau of Investigation, the Office of Watergate Special Prosecution Force, and Congressional committees;

5. Approving, condoning, and acquiescing in, the surreptitious payment of substantial sums of money for the purpose of obtaining the silence or influencing the testimony of witnesses, potential witnesses or individuals who participated in such illegal entry and other illegal activities;

6. Endeavoring to misuse the Central Intelligence Agency, an agency of the United States;

7. Disseminating information received from officers of the Department of Justice of the United States to subjects of investigations conducted by lawfully authorized investigative officers and employees of the United States, for the purpose of aiding and assisting such subjects in their attempts to avoid criminal liability;

8. Making false or misleading public statements for the purpose of deceiving the people of the United States into believing that a thorough and complete investigation had been conducted with respect to allegations of misconduct on the part of personnel of the executive branch of the United States and personnel of the Committee for the Re-election of the President, and that there was no involvement of such personnel in such misconduct; or

9. Endeavoring to cause prospective defendants, and individuals duly tried and convicted, to expect favored treatment and consideration in return for their silence or false testimony, or rewarding individuals for their silence or false testimony.

In all of this, Richard M. Nixon has acted in a manner contrary to his trust as President and subversive of constitutional government, to the great prejudice of the cause of law and justice and to the manifest injury of the people of the United States.

Wherefore Richard M. Nixon, by such conduct, warrants impeachment and trial, and removal from office.

ARTICLE II

Using the powers of the office of president of the United States, Richard M. Nixon, in violation of his constitutional oath faithfully to execute the office of president of the United States and, to the best of his ability, preserve, protect and defend the Constitution of the United States, and in disregard of his constitutional duty to take care that the laws be faithfully executed, has repeatedly engaged in conduct violating the constitutional rights of citizens, impairing the due and proper administration of justice and the conduct of lawful inquiries, or contravening the laws governing agencies of the executive branch and the purposes of these agencies.

This conduct has included one or more of the following:

1. He has, acting personally and through his subordinates and agents, endeavored to obtain from the Internal Revenue Service, in violation of the constitutional rights of citizens, confidential information contained in income tax returns for purposes not authorized by law and to cause, in violation of the constitutional rights of citizens, income tax audits or other income tax investigations to be initiated or conducted in a discriminatory manner.

2. He misused the Federal Bureau of Investigation, the Secret Service and other executive personnel in violation or disregard of the constitutional rights of citizens by directing or authorizing such agencies or per-

sonnel to conduct or continue electronic surveillance or other investigations for purposes unrelated to national security, the enforcement of laws or any other lawful function of his office; and he did direct the concealment of certain records made by the Federal Bureau of Investigation of electronic surveillance.

3. He has, acting personally and through his subordinates and agents, in violation or disregard of the constitutional rights of citizens, authorized and permitted to be maintained a secret investigative unit within the office of the president, financed in part with money derived from campaign contributions to him, which unlawfully utilized the resources of the Central Intelligence Agency, engaged in covert and unlawful activities and attempted to prejudice the constitutional right of an accused to a fair trial.

4. He has failed to take care that the laws were faithfully executed by failing to act when he knew or had reason to know that his close subordinates endeavored to impede and frustrate lawful inquiries by duly constituted executive, judicial and legislative entities concerning the unlawful entry into the headquarters of the Democratic National Committee and the cover-up thereof, and concerning other unlawful activities including those relating to the confirmation of Richard Kleindienst as attorney general of the United States, the electronic surveillance of private citizens, the break-in into the office of Dr. Lewis Fielding and the campaign financing practices of the Committee to Re-elect the President.

5. In disregard of the rule of law, he knowingly misused the executive power by interfering with agencies of the executive branch, in-

cluding the Federal Bureau of Investigation, the Criminal Division and the Office of Watergate Special Prosecution Force, of the Department of Justice and the Central Intelligence Agency, in violation of his duty to take care that the laws be faithfully executed.

In all of this, Richard M. Nixon has acted in a manner contrary to his trust as president and subversive of constitutional government, to the great prejudice of the cause of law and justice and to the manifest injury of the people of the United States.

Wherefore Richard M. Nixon, by such conduct, warrants impeachment and trial and removal from office.

ARTICLE III

In his conduct of the office of president of the United States, Richard M. Nixon, contrary to his oath faithfully to execute the office of president of the United States and, to the best of his ability, preserve, protect and defend the Constitution of the United States, and in violation of his constitutional duty to take care that the laws be faithfully executed, has failed without lawful cause or excuse to produce papers and things as directed by duly authorized subpoenas issued by the Committee on the Judiciary of the House of Representatives on April 11, 1974; May 15,

1974; May 30, 1974, and June 24, 1974, and willfully disobeyed such subpoenas.

The subpoenaed papers and things were deemed necessary by the committee in order to resolve by direct evidence fundamental, factual questions relating to presidential direction, knowledge or approval of actions demonstrated by other evidence to be substantial grounds for impeachment of the president.

In refusing to produce these papers and things Richard M. Nixon, substituting his judgment as to what materials were necessary for the inquiry, interposed the powers of the presidency against the lawful subpoenas of the House of Representatives, thereby assuming to himself functions and judgments necessary to the exercise of the sole power of impeachment vested by the Constitution in the House of Representatives.

In all of this, Richard M. Nixon has acted in a manner contrary to his trust as president and subversive of constitutional government, to the great prejudice of the cause of law and justice and to the manifest injury of the people of the United States.

Wherefore, Richard M. Nixon by such conduct, warrants impeachment and trial and removal from office.

* * *

Following his resignation as President, Richard Nixon entered into a depository agreement with the General Services Administration for the storage of some forty-two million documents and 880 tape recordings accumulated during his time in office. The agreement spelled out conditions of access to the materials and provided for the eventual destruction of the tape recordings. Three months after the terms of this agreement became public, Congress passed the Presidential Recordings and Materials Preservation Act. Among other things the legislation directed the Administrator of the GSA to: (1) take custody of the materials; (2) screen the materials and return to the former President those which were personal and private in nature; (3) preserve materials of historical value; and (4) maintain the availability of any materials for use in judicial proceedings conditional upon "any rights, defenses, or privileges which the Federal Government or any person may invoke." The Administrator was also directed to draw up regulations regarding public access to the materials, taking into account guidelines specified in the act, but such regulations had not yet been promulgated. On the day after President Ford signed the act, former President Nixon began a suit in federal court seeking declaratory and injunctive relief and alleging that the act violated the Constitution by infringing: (1) the separation of powers; (2) executive privilege; (3) personal privacy; (4) First Amendment guarantees of freedom of speech and association; and (5) the Bill of Attainder Clause. A three-judge federal district court rejected these arguments and denied relief, and Nixon subsequently appealed.

Focusing first on allegations that the legislation trenched upon the independence of the executive branch and infringed executive privilege, Justice Brennan, speaking for the Court in Nixon v. Administrator of General Services, 433 U.S. 425, 97 S.Ct. 2777 (1977), "reject[ed] the argument that only an incumbent President may assert such claims and h[e]ld that appellant, as a former President, may also be heard to assert them" but found all of the ex-President's constitutional contentions to be without merit. Specifically, the former President argued: (1) that by "delegat[ing] to a subordinate officer of the Executive Branch the decision whether to disclose Presidential materials and to prescribe the terms that govern any disclosure," Congress had "impermissibl[y] interfere[d] * * * [in] matters inherently the business solely of the Executive Branch"; (2) that the balancing test as employed by the lower court (as a result of which it "conclud[ed] that, notwithstanding the fact that some of the materials might legitimately be included within a claim of Presidential confidentiality, substantial public interests outweighed and justified the limited inroads on Presidential confidentiality necessitated by the Act's provision for government custody and screening of the materials"), failed to sufficiently weigh the former President's "presumptive privilege"; and (3) that the process for screening materials set up by the Act "will chill the future exercise of constitutionally protected executive functions, thereby impairing the ability of future Presidents to obtain the candid advice necessary to the conduct of their constitutionally imposed duties."

The Court disposed of the separation of powers argument by noting: (1) that screening and control of the materials pursuant to the Act still remained with an officer of the executive branch; (2) that the former President's view of the separation of powers reflected the notion of watertight compartmentalization of powers among the three coordinate branches explicitly rejected in *United States* v. *Nixon*; and (3) that the Act contained clear guidelines and conditions regulating access as protection against reckless and indiscriminate disclosure. Both Nixon's separation-of-powers contention and his argument for executive privilege, the Court concluded, were materially weakened by "the fact that neither President Ford nor President Carter supports appellant's claim * * *." Moreover, the Court found the screening process not unlike that which takes place anyway when former Presidents leave office and deposit their papers in presidential libraries, for, as the Court observed, "The expectation of the confidentiality of executive communications thus has always been limited and subject to erosion over time after an administration leaves office." Finally, the Court concluded that "adequate justifications are shown for this limited intrusion into executive confidentiality comparable to those held to justify *in camera* inspection of the District Court sustained in *United States* v. *Nixon* * * *." Among those purposes which legitimately moved Congress to pass the legislation, the Court mentioned the public's interest in, among other things: (1) insuring a complete and accurate historical record; (2) "rectify[ing] the hit-or-miss approach that has characterized past attempts to protect these substantial interests by entrusting the materials to expert handling by trusted and disinterested professionals"; (3) "restor[ing] public confidence in our political processes by preserving the materials as a source for facilitating a full airing of the events leading to appellant's resignation"; (4) enhancing "Congress' need to understand how those political processes had in fact operated in order to gauge the necessity for remedial legislation"; and (5) "shed[ding] light upon issues in civil or criminal litigation, a social interest that cannot be doubted." Summing up, Justice Brennan said, "In short, we conclude that the screening process contemplated by the Act will not constitute a more severe intrusion into Presidential confidentiality than the *in camera* inspection by the District Court approved in *United States* v. *Nixon* * * *."

The Court disposed of Nixon's other claims in short order. As for his contention that the screening process amounted to a general search and violated his right to privacy, the Court, conceding that "like [duly-authorized] electronic surveillance, [it] requires some intrusion into private communications unconnected with any legitimate governmental objectives," held that "[s]imilarly, the archival review procedure involved here is designed to serve important national interests asserted by Congress, and the unavailability of less restrictive means necessarily follows from the commingling of the documents." In response to the former President's allegation that the legislation infringed his freedoms of speech and association, Justice Brennan wrote: "Since no less restrictive way than archival screening has been suggested as a means for identification of materials to be returned to appellant, the burden of that screening is the measure of his First Amendment claim. * * * The extent of any such burden, however, is speculative in light of the Act's terms protecting appellant from improper public disclosures and guaranteeing him full judicial review before any public access is permitted." And in answer, finally, to Nixon's argument that the Act constituted a bill of attainder by singling out his papers for special treatment, the Court said: "The Presidential papers of all former Presidents from Hoover to Johnson were already housed in functioning Presidential libraries. Congress had reason for concern solely with the preservation of appellant's materials, for he alone had entered into a depository agreement, the Nixon-Sampson agreement, which by terms called for the destruction of certain of the materials. Indeed, as the Government argues, 'appellant's depository agreement * * * created an imminent danger that the tape recordings would be destroyed if appellant, who had contracted phlebitis, were to die.' * * * In short, appellant constituted a legitimate class of one, and this provides a basis for Congress' decision to proceed with dispatch with respect to his materials while accepting the status of his predecessors' papers and ordering the further consideration of generalized standards to govern his successors."

In dissent, Chief Justice Burger found "it very disturbing that fundamental principles of constitutional law are subordinated to what seem the needs of a particular situation. * * * The Court * * * has now joined a Congress, in haste to 'do something,' and has invaded historic, fundamental principles of the separate coequal Branches of government. To 'punish' one person, Congress— and now the Court—tears into the fabric of our constitutional framework." Because the Presidency is specifically provided for in the Constitution, unlike other offices, departments, and agencies of the executive branch, the Chief Justice pointed out, it "stands on a very different footing" and "is in no sense a creature of the Legislature." The "independent, constitutional origins of the Presidency" mandate, he said, that that office "as a constitutional equal of Congress, must as a general proposition be free from Congress' *coercive* powers." The effect of employing these coercive powers, in his view, was not diminished by assigning custody of the presidential papers to employees of the executive branch since "[w]hether there has been a violation of separation-of-powers principles depends not on the identity of the custodians, but upon which Branch has commanded the custodians to act. Here, Congress has given the command." By contrast, Justice Powell, concurring in part with the opinion of the Court and in its judgment, "consider[ed] it dispositive in the circumstances of this case that the [current] President has represented to this Court, through the Solicitor General, that the Act serves rather than hinders the Art. II functions of the Chief Executive." The Chief Justice also thought the Act was constitutionally offensive as "an attempt by Congress to exercise powers vested exclusively in the President—the power to control files, records and papers of the office, which are comparable to the internal workpapers of the House and Senate." In addition, he concluded that "the Act violates principles of separation of powers by intruding into the confidentiality of Presidential communications protected by the constitutionally based doctrine of Presidential privilege." Said the Chief Justice: "[N]othing remotely like the *particularized need* we found in *United States* v. *Nixon* has been shown with respect to these Presidential papers. No one has suggested that Congress will find its own 'core' functioning impaired by the lack of the impounded papers, as we expressly found the judicial function would be impaired by lack of the material subpoenaed in *United States* v. *Nixon*." He continued, "I leave to another day the question whether, under exigent circumstances, a *narrowly defined* congressional demand for Presidential materials might be justified. But * * * [the Act] fails to satisfy either the required narrowness demanded in *United States* v. *Nixon* or the requirement that the coequal powers of the Presidency not be injured by congressional legislation." Furthermore, the Chief Justice concluded that the statute's "generalized, undifferentiated goals" failed to present "paramount" or "compelling" interests such as to override or outweigh the ex-President's privacy interests. Finally, the Chief Justice saw "no escape * * * from the conclusion that, on the basis of more than 180 years' history, the appellant has been deprived of a property right enjoyed by all Presidents after leaving office, namely, the control of his Presidential papers. * * * The operative effect of * * * [the statute] is to exclude, by name, one former President and deprive him of what his predecessors—and his successor—have already been allowed."

In a separate dissent Justice Rehnquist characterized the Court's decision licensing "any future Congress to seize the official papers of an out-going President as he leaves the inaugural stand" as "a veritable sword of Damocles over every succeeding President and his advisors" which "poses a real threat to the ability of future Presidents to receive candid advice and to give candid instructions." Believing that the separation-of-powers issue was sufficient to decide the case and that it was, therefore, unnecessary to reach the other issues considered by the Court, Justice Rehnquist wrote:

My conclusion that the Act violates the principle of separation of powers is based upon three fundamental propositions. First, candid and open discourse among the President, his advisors, foreign heads of state and Ambassadors, Members of Congress, and the others who deal with the White House on a sensitive basis is an absolute prerequisite to the effective discharge of the duties of that high office. Second, the effect of the Act, and of this Court's decision upholding its constitutionality, will undoubtedly restrain the necessary free flow of information to and from present and future Presidents. Third, any substantial intrusion upon the effective discharge of the duties of the President is sufficient to violate the principle of separation of powers, and our prior cases do not permit the sustaining of an

Act such as this by "balancing" an intrusion of substantial magnitude against the interests assertedly fostered by the Act.

In the waning months of the Johnson Administration, Ernest Fitzgerald, a Pentagon management analyst, appeared before a congressional subcommittee and, to the evident embarrassment of his superiors, testified about a $2 billion cost overrun and unanticipated technical difficulties incurred in the development of a new military transport aircraft. Early on in the succeeding Nixon Administration, Fitzgerald lost his job ostensibly as part of the new administration's reduction-in-force program. Fitzgerald, however, alleged that his discharge from federal employment was not for purported reasons of governmental efficiency and economy but as retaliation for his "whistle-blowing" testimony. Although his job was itself not under civil service protection, his status as a former veteran required the government to observe certain procedures and to find him a job of comparable authority elsewhere in the federal bureaucracy. When the administration failed to observe these requirements, Fitzgerald filed a complaint with the Civil Service Commission where a hearing officer subsequently determined that, while Fitzgerald's firing was not in retaliation for his testimony, his discharge was for "reasons purely personal." Fitzgerald then sued President Nixon and presidential advisors Harlow and Butterfield, all of whom, he contended, conspired to discharge him for personal and political reasons. Lower federal courts denied summary judgment for Nixon and his advisors, rejecting their claims of absolute immunity. (Under terms of an agreement between Fitzgerald and Nixon, the defendant ex-President paid the plaintiff $142,000 and agreed to pay $28,000 more if the Supreme Court rejected his claim of absolute immunity from suit. The Supreme Court subsequently held that this agreement did not moot the controversy since "[t]he limited agreement between the parties left both * * * [of them] with a considerable financial stake in the resolution of the question presented in this Court.")

Addressing the former President's claim of absolute immunity from suit in Nixon v. Fitzgerald, —— U.S. ——, 102 S.Ct. 2690 (1982), the Court held "that petitioner, as a former President of the United States, is entitled to absolute immunity from damages liability predicated on his official acts." Speaking for a bare majority, Justice Powell continued, "We consider this immunity a functionally mandated incident of the President's unique office, rooted in the constitutional tradition of the separation of powers and supported by our history." After briefly traversing the various domains of presidential authority—domestic and foreign—and the attendant risks and sensitivities inherent in each, the Court concluded that "The President's unique status under the Constitution distinguishes him from other executive officials." The Court rejected the sort of qualified immunity afforded governors and cabinet officers respectively in Scheuer v. Rhodes, 416 U.S. 232, 94 S.Ct. 1683 (1974) and Butz v. Economou, 438 U.S. 478, 98 S.Ct. 2894 (1978), in which "the scope of the defense varied in proportion to the nature of their official functions and the range of decisions that conceivably might be taken in 'good faith.'" Justice Powell continued:

> Because of the singular importance of the President's duties, diversion of his energies by concern with private lawsuits would raise unique risks to the effective functioning of government. As is the case with prosecutors and judges—for whom absolute immunity now is established—a President must concern himself with matters likely to "arouse the most intense feelings." Pierson v. Ray, supra, 386 U.S., at 554, 87 S.Ct., at 1218. Yet, as our decisions have recognized, it is in precisely such cases that there exists

the greatest public interest in providing an official "the maximum ability to deal fearlessly and impartially with" the duties of his office. Ferri v. Ackerman, 444 U.S. 193, 203, 100 S.Ct. 402, 408 (1979) (footnote omitted). This concern is compelling where the officeholder must make the most sensitive and far-reaching decisions entrusted to any official under our constitutional system. Nor can the sheer prominence of the President's office be ignored. In view of the visibility of his office and the effect of his actions on countless people, the President would be an easily identifiable target for suits for civil damages. Cognizance of this personal vulnerability frequently could distract a President from his public duties, to the detriment not only of the President and his office but also the Nation that the Presidency was designed to serve.

Specifically rejecting the "functional" approach to immunity adopted in *Scheuer* and *Butz*, the Court observed:

In defining the scope of an official's absolute privilege, this Court has recognized that the sphere of protected action must be related closely to the immunity's justifying purposes. Frequently our decisions have held that an official's absolute immunity should extend only to acts in performance of particular functions of his office. * * * But the Court also has refused to draw functional lines finer than history and reason would support. * * * In view of the special nature of the President's constitutional office and functions, we think it appropriate to recognize absolute Presidential immunity from damages liability for acts within the "outer perimeter" of his official responsibility.

Under the Constitution and laws of the United States the President has discretionary responsibilities in a broad variety of areas, many of them highly sensitive. In many cases it would be difficult to determine which of the President's innumerable "functions" encompassed a particular action. In this case, for example, respondent argues that he was dismissed in retaliation for his testimony to Congress—a violation of 5 U.S.C.A. § 7211 and 18 U.S.C.A. § 1505. The Air Force, however, has claimed that the underlying reorganization was undertaken to promote efficiency. Assuming that the petitioner Nixon ordered the reorganization in which respondent lost his job, an inquiry into the President's motives could not be avoided under the kind of "functional" theory asserted both by respondent and the dissent. Inquiries of this kind could be highly intrusive.

Here respondent argues that petitioner Nixon would have acted outside the outer perimeter of his duties by ordering the discharge of an employee who was lawfully entitled to retain his job in the absence of "such cause as will promote the efficiency of the service." * * * Because Congress has granted this legislative protection, respondent argues, no federal official could, within the outer perimeter of his duties of office, cause Fitzgerald to be dismissed without satisfying this standard in prescribed statutory proceedings.

This construction would subject the President to trial on virtually every allegation that an action was unlawful, or was taken for a forbidden purpose. Adoption of this construction thus would deprive absolute immunity of its intended effect. It clearly is within the President's constitutional and statutory authority to prescribe the manner in which the Secretary will conduct the business of the Air Force. See 10 U.S.C.A. § 8012(b). Because this mandate of office must include the authority to prescribe reorganizations and reductions in force, we conclude that petitioner's alleged wrongful acts lay well within the outer perimeter of his authority.

Rejecting as well the proposition that absolute immunity would "place the President 'above the law,'" Justice Powell noted that "the Nation [would not be left] without sufficient protection against misconduct on the part of the chief executive" and cited impeachment, "constant scrutiny by the press," "[v]igilant oversight by Congress," and "[o]ther incentives to avoid misconduct" such as "a desire to earn re-election, the need to maintain prestige as an element of Presidential influence, and a President's traditional concern for his historical stature."

In a strong dissenting opinion, in which he also spoke for Justices Brennan, Marshall, and Blackmun, Justice White attacked the Court's creation of an absolute presidential immunity from suits for damages as "a reversion to the old notion that the King can do no wrong." Appalled at the extent to which such an immunity "places the President above the law," Justice White began by offering two "hypothetical" scenarios (strikingly similar to the allegations in *Fitzgerald* and Halperin v. Kissinger, 606 F.2d 1192 (D.C.Cir.1979), affirmed by an equally divided Court, 452 U.S. 713, 101 S.Ct. 3132 (1981)) of absolute immunity at work:

> A President acting within the outer boundaries of what Presidents normally do may, without liability, deliberately cause serious injury to any number of citizens even though he knows his conduct violates a statute or tramples on the constitutional rights of those who are injured. Even if the President in this case ordered Fitzgerald fired by means of a trumped-up reduction in force, knowing that such a discharge was contrary to the civil service laws, he would be absolutely immune from suit. By the same token, if a President, without following the statutory procedures which he knows apply to himself as well as to other federal officials, orders his subordinates to wiretap or break into a home for the purpose of installing a listening device, and the officers comply with his request, the President would be absolutely immune from suit. He would be immune regardless of the damage he inflicts, regardless of how violative of the statute and of the Constitution he knew his conduct to be, and regardless of his purpose.

Such unacceptable results would not occur, argued Justice White, had the majority adhered to the principle that characterized the Court's immunity rulings in cases such as *Butz* where "[w]e held that although public officials perform certain functions that entitle them to absolute immunity, the immunity attaches to particular functions—not to particular offices. Officials performing functions for which immunity is not absolute enjoy qualified immunity; they are liable in damages only if their conduct violated well-established law and if they should have realized that their conduct was illegal." Absent any support in constitutional history for the creation of an absolute presidential immunity (let alone anything akin to the specific textual support for congressional immunity found in the Speech and Debate Clause), he saw the Court's sweeping creation as unjustified by simply invoking the separation-of-powers principle and clearly contradictory to that sense of balance among the contending interests reflected in the approach of *United States* v. *Nixon*. Said Justice White, "This is policy, not law, and in my view, very poor policy." He continued, "The principle that should guide the Court in deciding this question was stated long ago by Chief Justice Marshall: 'The very essence of civil liberty certainly consists in the right of every individual to claim the protection of the laws, whenever he receives an injury.' Marbury v. Madison, 5 U.S. (1 Cranch) 137, 163 (1803). * * * To the extent that the Court denies an otherwise appropriate remedy, it denies the victim the right to be made whole and, therefore, denies him 'the protection of the laws.' " Justice White elaborated:

> That the President should have the same remedial obligations toward those whom he injures as any other federal officer is not a surprising proposition. The fairness of the remedial principle the Court has so far followed—that the wrongdoer, not the victim, should ordinarily bear the costs of the injury—has been found to be outweighed only in instances where potential liability is "thought to injure the governmental decisionmaking process." Imbler v. Pachtman, 424 U.S. 409, 437, 96 S.Ct. 984, 998 (1976) (White, J., concurring). The argument for immunity is that the possibility of a damages action will, or at least should, have an effect on the performance of official responsibilities. That effect should be to deter unconstitutional, or otherwise illegal, behavior. This may, however, lead officers to be more careful and "less vigorous" in the performance of their duties. Caution, of course, is not always a virtue and undue caution is to be avoided.

> The possibility of liability may, in some circumstances, distract officials from the performance of their duties and influence the performance of those duties in ways adverse to the public interest. But when this "public policy" argument in favor of absolute immunity is cast in these broad terms, it applies to all officers, both state and federal: All officers should perform their responsibilities without regard to those personal interests threatened by the possibility of a lawsuit. * * * Inevitably, this reduces the public policy argument to nothing more than an expression of judicial inclination as to which officers should be encouraged to perform their functions with "vigor," although with less care.

> The Court's response, until today, to this problem has been to apply the argument to individual functions, not offices, and to evaluate the effect of liability on governmental decisionmaking within that function, in light of the substantive ends that are to be encouraged or discouraged. In this case, therefore, the Court should examine the functions implicated by the causes of action at issue here and the effect of potential liability on the performance of those functions.

> The functional approach to the separation of powers doctrine and the Court's more recent immunity decisions converge on the following principle: The scope of immunity is determined by function, not office. The wholesale claim that the President is entitled to absolute immunity in all of his actions stands on no firmer ground than did the claim that all presidential communications are entitled to an absolute privilege, which was rejected in favor of a functional analysis, by a unanimous Court in *United States* v. *Nixon, supra.* Therefore, whatever may be true of the necessity of such a broad immunity in certain areas of executive responsibility, the only question that must be answered here is whether the dismissal of employees falls within a constitutionally assigned executive function, the performance of which would be substantially impaired by the possibility of a private action for damages. I believe it does not.

And, he added:

> It is, of course, theoretically possible that the President should be held to be absolutely immune because each of the functions for which he has constitutional responsibility would be substantially impaired by the possibility of civil liability. I do not think this argument is valid for the simple

reason that the function involved here does not have this character. On which side of the line other presidential functions would fall need not be decided in this case.

Finally, focusing on "just three contentions from which the majority draws [its] conclusion" favoring an absolute presidential immunity, Justice White wrote:

First, the majority informs us that the President occupies a "unique position in the constitutional scheme," including responsibilities for the administration of justice, foreign affairs, and management of the Executive Branch. * * * True as this may be, it says nothing about why a "unique" rule of immunity should apply to the President. The President's unique role may indeed encompass functions for which he is entitled to a claim of absolute immunity. It does not follow from that, however, that he is entitled to absolute immunity either in general or in this case in particular.

For some reason, the majority believes that this uniqueness of the President shifts the burden to respondent to prove that a rule of absolute immunity does not apply. The respondent has failed in this effort, the Court suggests, because the President's uniqueness makes "inapposite" any analogy to our cases dealing with other executive officers. * * * Even if this were true, it would not follow that the President is entitled to absolute immunity; it would only mean that a particular argument is out of place. But the fact is that it is not true. There is nothing in the President's unique role that makes the arguments used in those other cases inappropriate.

Second, the majority contends that because the President's "visibility" makes him particularly vulnerable to suits for civil damages, * * * a rule of absolute immunity is required. The force of this argument is surely undercut by the majority's admission that "there is no historical record of numerous suits against the President." * * * There is no reason to think that, in the future, the protection afforded by summary judgment procedures would not be adequate to protect the President, as they currently protect other executive officers from unfounded litigation. Indeed, given the decision today in *Harlow & Butterfield* v. *Fitzgerald,* * * * there is even more reason to believe that frivolous claims will not intrude upon the President's time. Even if judicial procedures were found not to be sufficient, Congress remains free to address this problem if and when it develops.

Finally, the Court suggests that potential liability "frequently could distract a President from his public duties." * * * Unless one assumes that the President himself makes the countless high level executive decisions required in the administration of government, this rule will not do much to insulate such decisions from the threat of liability. The logic of the proposition cannot be limited to the President; its extension, however, has been uniformly rejected by this Court. * * * Furthermore, in no instance have we previously held legal accountability in itself to be an unjustifiable cost. The availability of the courts to vindicate constitutional and statutory wrongs has been perceived and protected as one of the virtues of our system of delegated and limited powers. As I argued [earlier], our concern in fashioning absolute immunity rules has been that liability may pervert the decisionmaking process in a particular function by undercutting the values we expect to guide those decisions. Except for the empty generality that the President should have " 'the maximum ability to deal fearlessly and impartially with' the duties of his office," * * * the majority nowhere suggests a particular, disadvantageous effect on a specific presidential function. The caution that comes from requiring reasonable choices in areas that may intrude on individuals' legally protected rights has never before been counted as a cost.

The majority may be correct in its conclusion that "a rule of absolute immunity will not leave the Nation without sufficient remedies for misconduct on the part of the chief executive." * * * Such a rule will, however, leave Mr. Fitzgerald without an adequate remedy for the harms that he may have suffered. More importantly, it will leave future plaintiffs without a remedy, regardless of the substantiality of their claims. The remedies in which the Court finds comfort were never designed to afford relief for individual harms. Rather, they were designed as political safety-valves. Politics and history, however, are not the domain of the courts; the courts exist to assure each individual that he, as an individual, has enforceable rights that he may pursue to achieve a peaceful redress of his legitimate grievances.

In a concurring opinion Chief Justice Burger took aim particularly at Justice White's objections. At the outset, he observed, "[W]e do well to bear in mind that the focus must not be simply on the matter of judging individual conduct in a fact-bound setting; rather, in those familiar terms of John Marshall, it is a *Constitution* we are expounding. Constitutional adjudication often bears unpalatable fruit. But the needs of a system of government sometimes must outweigh the rights of individuals to collect damages." Faulting Justice White's reliance on *United States* v. *Nixon*, the Chief Justice pointed out that the decision in that case was set in the context of a *"criminal* prosecution." "It is one thing to say," he continued, "that a President must produce evidence relevant to a criminal case, as in *Burr* and *United States* v. *Nixon*, and quite another to say a President can be held for civil damages for dismissing a federal employee." As to Justice White's contention that creation of an absolute immunity from damages liability places the President "above the law," the Chief Justice responded:

It strains the meaning of the words used to say this places a President "above the law." Nixon v. United States, 418 U.S. 683, 94 S.Ct. 3090 (1974). The dissents are wide of the mark to the extent that they imply that the Court today recognizes sweeping immunity for a President for all acts. The Court does no such thing. The immunity is limited to civil damage claims. Moreover, a President, like Members of Congress, judges, prosecutors, or congressional aides—all having absolute immunity—are not immune for acts outside official duties. * * * Even the broad immunity of the Speech and Debate Clause has its limits.

Most of the Chief Justice's concurrence, however, was spent detailing the connection between the creation of such an absolute immunity and the separation-of-powers principle. He explained:

The essential purpose of the separation of powers is to allow for independent functioning of each co-equal branch of government within its assigned sphere of responsibility, free from risk of control, interference, or intimidation by other branches. * * * Even prior to the adoption of our Constitution, as well as after, judicial review of legislative action was recognized in some instances as necessary to maintain the proper checks and balances. * * * However, the judiciary always must be hesitant to probe into the elements of presidential decision-making, just as other branches should be hesitant to probe into judicial decision-making. Such judicial intervention is not to be tolerated absent imperative constitutional necessity. * * * The Court's opinion correctly observes that judicial intrusion through private damage actions improperly impinges on and hence interferes with the independence that is imperative to the functioning of the office of a President.

Exposing a President to civil damage actions for official acts within the scope of the Executive authority would inevitably subject presidential actions to undue judicial scrutiny as well as subject the President to harassment. The enormous range and impact of Presidential decisions—far beyond that of any one Member of Congress—inescapably means that many persons will consider themselves aggrieved by such acts. Absent absolute immunity, every person who feels aggrieved would be free to bring a suit for damages, and each suit—especially those that proceed on the merits—would involve some judicial questioning of Presidential acts, including the reasons for the decision, how it was arrived at, the information on which it was based, and who supplied the information. Such scrutiny of day-to-day decisions of the Executive Branch would be bound to occur if civil damage actions were made available to private individuals. Although the individual who claims wrongful conduct may indeed have sustained some injury, the need to prevent large scale invasion of the Executive function by the judiciary far outweighs the need to vindicate the private claims. We have decided that in a similar sense Members of both Houses of Congress—and their aides—must be totally free from judicial scrutiny for legislative acts; the public interest, in other words, outweighs the need for private redress of one claiming injury from legislative acts of a Member or aide of a Member. The Court's concern (and the even more emphatic concerns expressed by Justice White's dissent) over "unremedied wrongs" to citizens by a President seem odd when one compares the potential for "wrongs" which thousands of Congressional aides, prosecutors, and judges can theoretically inflict—with absolute immunity—on the same citizens for whom this concern is expressed. * * *

Judicial intervention would also inevitably inhibit the processes of Executive Branch decision-making and impede the functioning of the Office of the President. The need to defend damage suits would have the serious effect of diverting the attention of a President from his executive duties since defending a lawsuit today—even a lawsuit ultimately found to be frivolous—often requires significant expenditures of time and money, as many former public officials have learned to their sorrow. This very case graphically illustrates the point. When litigation processes are not tightly-controlled—and often they are not—they can be and are used as mechanisms of extortion. Ultimate vindication on the merits does not repair the damage.

In the companion case, Harlow v. Fitzgerald, —— U.S. ——, 102 S.Ct. 2727 (1982), the Court declined to afford absolute immunity to the former President's senior advisors. Relying on Gravel v. United States, 408 U.S. 606, 92 S.Ct. 2614 (1972), Harlow and Butterfield contended that "a similar 'derivative' immunity * * * [protects] the chief aides of the President of the United States. Emphasizing that the President must delegate a large measure of authority to execute the duties of his office, they argue that recognition of derivative absolute immunity is made essential by all the considerations that support absolute immunity for the President himself." Speaking for the Court once again, Justice Powell found the argument "sweeps too far" because it would logically extend to include cabinet officers and other subordinates, something implicitly rejected in the "functional" approach to immunity law taken in *Butz*. Responding to Harlow and Butterfield's reliance on *Gravel*, Justice Powell wrote: "[W]e emphasized that Senators and their aides were absolutely immune only when performing 'acts legislative in nature,' and not when taking other acts even 'in their official capacity.' * * * Our cases involving judges and prosecutors have followed a similar line. The undifferentiated extension of absolute 'derivative' immunity to the President's aides therefore could not be reconciled with the 'functional' approach that has characterized the immunity decisions of this Court, indeed including *Gravel* itself." Quoting the applicable standard from its earlier decision in Wood v. Strickland, 420 U.S. 308, 95 S.Ct. 992 (1975), the Court noted it has "held that qualified immunity would be defeated if an official 'knew or reasonably should have known that the action he took within his sphere of official responsibility would violate the constitutional rights of the [plaintiff], or if he took the action with malicious intention to cause a deprivation of constitutional rights or other injury.'" "[A]t a loss * * * to reconcile this conclusion with [the Court's] holding in *Gravel* * * * [,]" Chief Justice Burger dissented.

d. EXECUTIVE AUTHORITY IN THE CONDUCT OF FOREIGN AFFAIRS

JOHN JAY, FEDERALIST NO. 64

* * *

It seldom happens in the negotiation of treaties, of whatever nature, but that perfect *secrecy* and immediate *despatch* are sometimes requisite. There are cases where the most useful intelligence may be obtained, if the persons possessing it can be relieved from apprehensions of discovery. Those apprehensions will operate on those persons whether they are actuated by mercenary or friendly motives; and there doubtless are many of both descriptions, who would rely on the secrecy of the President, but who would not confide in that of the Senate, and still less in that of a large popular Assembly. The convention have done well,

therefore, in so disposing of the power of making treaties, that although the President must, in forming them, act by the advice and consent of the Senate, yet he will be able to manage the business of intelligence in such a manner as prudence may suggest.

They who have turned their attention to the affairs of men, must have perceived that there are tides in them; tides very irregular in their duration, strength, and direction, and seldom found to run twice exactly in the same manner or measure. To discern and to profit by these tides in national affairs is the business of those who preside over them; and they who have had much experience on this head inform us, that there frequently are occasions when days, nay, even when hours, are precious. The loss of a battle, the death of a prince, the removal of a minister, or other circumstances intervening to change the present posture and aspect of affairs, may turn the most favorable tide into a course opposite to our wishes. As in the field, so in the cabinet, there are moments to be seized as they pass, and they who preside in either should be left in capacity to improve them. So often and so essentially have we heretofore suffered from the want of secrecy and despatch, that the Constitution would have been inexcusably defective, if no attention had been paid to those objects. Those matters which in negotiations usually require the most secrecy and the most despatch, are those preparatory and auxiliary measures which are not otherwise important in a national view, than as they tend to facilitate the attainment of the objects of the negotiation. For these, the President will find no difficulty to provide; and should any circumstance occur which requires the advice and consent of the Senate, he may at any time convene them. Thus we see that the Constitution provides that our negotiations for treaties shall have every advantage which can be derived from talents, information, integrity, and deliberate investigations, on the one hand, and from secrecy and despatch on the other.

* * *

UNITED STATES v. CURTISS-WRIGHT EXPORT CORP.

Supreme Court of the United States, 1936
299 U.S. 304, 57 S.Ct. 216, 81 L.Ed. 255

See p. 157.

In Haig v. Agee, 453 U.S. 280, 101 S.Ct. 2766 (1981), the Supreme Court held that "the President, acting through the Secretary of State, has authority to revoke a passport on the ground that the holder's activities in foreign countries are causing or are likely to cause serious damage to the national security or foreign policy of the United States." Agee, an American citizen residing in West Germany and a former employee of the CIA who was, during his time with that agency, responsible for covert intelligence gathering in foreign countries, had for years been embarking on a "campaign to fight the United States CIA wherever it is operating." Said the Court in its review of the facts in this case: "To identify CIA personnel in a particular country, Agee goes to the target country and consults sources in local diplomatic circles whom he knows from his prior service in the United States Government. He recruits collaborators and trains them in clandestine techniques designed to expose the 'cover' of CIA employees and sources. Agee and his collaborators have repeatedly and publicly identified individuals and organizations located in foreign countries as undercover CIA agents, employees, or sources. The record reveals that the identifications divulge classified information, violate Agee's express contract not to make any public statements about Agency matters without prior clearance by the Agency, have prejudiced the ability of the United States to obtain intelligence, and have been followed by episodes of violence against the persons and organizations identified."

Speaking for the Court, Chief Justice Burger observed that, although the Passport Act of 1926 "does not in so many words confer upon the Secretary a power to revoke a passport," it was established by precedents, such as Kent v. Dulles, 357 U.S. 116, 78 S.Ct. 1113 (1958), and Zemel v. Rusk, 381 U.S. 1, 85 S.Ct. 1271 (1965), that "the Secretary has the power to deny a passport for reasons not specified in the statutes"—for example, for engaging in conduct violative of law or on the basis of "the weightiest considerations of national security"—and Agee conceded "that if the Secretary may deny a passport application for a certain reason, he may revoke a passport on the same ground." In addition, the Court concluded, "The history of passport controls since the earliest days of the Republic shows congressional recognition of Executive authority to withhold passports on the basis of substantial reasons of national security and foreign policy." The Court rejected Agee's contention, relying on *Kent*, "that the only way the Executive can establish implicit congressional approval is by proof of longstanding and consistent *enforcement* of the claimed power: that is, by showing that many passports were revoked on national security and foreign policy grounds." Said the Chief Justice, "The history is clear that there have been few situations involving substantial likelihood of serious damage to the national security or foreign policy of the United States as a result of a passport holder's activities abroad, and that in the cases which have arisen, the Secretary has consistently exercised his power to withhold passports." The Court also found *Kent* inapposite because "*Kent* involved denials of passports solely on the basis of political beliefs entitled to First Amendment protection" and in this case it was Agee's *conduct* that constituted the basis for revocation of his passport. As the Chief Justice pointed out, "The protection accorded beliefs standing alone is very different from the protection accorded conduct." As to Agee's constitutional contentions "first, that the revocation of his passport impermissibly burdens his freedom to travel; second, that the action was intended to penalize his exercise of free speech and deter his criticism of government policies and practices; and third, that failure to accord him a pre-revocation hearing violated his Fifth Amendment right to procedural due process," the Court responded respectively by explaining: (1) unlike the right to interstate travel which is "virtually unqualified," the constitutional right to travel internationally could be limited by a demonstration of a substantial governmental interest, such as that in "protect[ing] the secrecy of our Government's foreign intelligence operations"; (2) as distinguished from speech for the sake of political criticism, "Agee's disclosures, among other things, have the declared purpose of obstructing intelligence operations and the recruiting of intelligence personnel" and are, therefore, not pure speech but speech mixed with *action* of the sort government has the power to regulate; and (3) in keeping with the varying weights of interests and rights affected, Agee received all of the constitutional process he was due: "a statement of reasons and an opportunity for a prompt postrevocation hearing."

Observing that "this case is a prime example of the adage that 'bad facts make bad law'" because "Philip Agee is hardly a model representative of our Nation," Justice Brennan, joined by Justice Marshall, dissented. He concluded that "clearly neither *Zemel* nor *Kent* holds that a longstanding Executive *policy* or *construction* is sufficient proof that Congress has implicitly authorized the Secretary's action." He continued, "The cases hold that an administrative *practice* must be demonstrated; in fact *Kent* unequivocally states that mere *construction* by the Executive—no matter how longstanding and consistent—is *not* sufficient." In other words, "evidence of the Executive's *exercise* of discretion as opposed to its possession of discretion" must be proved. He added, "[J]ust as the Constitution protects both popular and unpopular speech, it likewise protects both popular and unpopular travelers. And it is important to remember that this decision applies not only to Philip Agee, whose activities could be perceived as harming the national security, but also to other citizens who may merely disagree with Government foreign policy and express their views."

————

Following the seizure of the American Embassy in Tehran on November 4, 1979, which resulted in the capture and holding hostage of our diplomatic personnel by the Iranians, President Carter ordered a freeze on the removal and transfer of all assets held by the Iranian government or its instrumentalities within American jurisdiction. On the day the Carter Administration left office, the hostages were released by Iran pursuant to an agreement under which the United States was obliged "to terminate all legal proceedings in United States courts involving claims of United States persons and institutions against Iran and its state enterprises, to nullify all attachments and judgments obtained therein, [and] to prohibit all future litigation based on these claims." In addition, the United States was to transfer all Iranian assets held in this country by the following July. A billion dollars of these assets were to be transferred to a security account in the Bank of England to be used to satisfy awards rendered against Iran by an Iran-United States Claims Tribunal. The day before his term of office ended, President Carter implemented the terms of the agreement through several Executive Orders which revoked all licenses permitting the exercise of power over Iranian assets, nullified all non-Iranian interests in the assets, and required banks holding Iranian funds to transfer them to the Federal Reserve Bank of New York to be held or transferred at the direction of the Secretary of the Treasury. Five weeks later, these orders were reaffirmed by the incoming Reagan Administration.

In Dames & Moore v. Regan, 453 U.S. 654, 101 S.Ct. 2972 (1981), the Supreme Court upheld the constitutionality of the President's orders. As to the President's authority to nullify attachments on the Iranian assets and order the transfer of funds, the Court concluded that such actions were within the plain language of the International Emergency Economic Powers Act (IEEPA), 50 U.S.C.A. §§ 1701–1706. Justice Rehnquist, speaking for the Court, explained:

> This Court has previously recognized that the Congressional purpose in authorizing blocking orders is "to put control of foreign assets in the hands of the President." * * * Propper v. Clark, 337 U.S. 472, 493, 69 S.Ct. 1333, 1345 (1949). Such orders permit the President to maintain the foreign assets at his disposal for use in negotiating the resolution of a declared national emergency. The frozen assets serve as a "bargaining chip" to be used by the President when dealing with a hostile country. Accordingly, it is difficult to accept petitioner's argument because the practical effect of it is to allow individual claimants throughout the country to minimize or wholly eliminate this "bargaining chip" through attachments, garnishments or similar encumbrances on property. Neither the purpose the statute was enacted to serve nor its plain language supports such a result.

> Because the President's action in nullifying the attachments and ordering the transfer of the assets was taken pursuant to specific congressional authorization, it is "supported by the strongest of presumptions and the widest latitude of judicial interpretation, and the burden of persuasion would rest heavily upon any who might attack it." Youngstown, 343 U.S., at 637, 72 S.Ct., at 871 (Jackson, J., concurring). Under the circumstances of this case, we cannot say that petitioner has sustained that heavy burden. A contrary ruling would mean that the Federal Government as a whole lacked the power exercised by the President * * * and that we are not prepared to say.

Turning to "the question of the President's authority to suspend claims pending in American courts," the Court could not find specific authorization for such action either in the IEEPA or the Hostage Act, 22 U.S.C.A. § 1732, but it declared:

> Although we have declined to conclude that the IEEPA or the Hostage Act directly authorizes the President's suspension of claims for the reasons noted, we cannot ignore the general tenor of Congress' legislation in this area in trying to determine whether the President is acting alone or at least with the acceptance of Congress. As we have noted, Congress cannot anticipate and legislate with regard to every possible action the President may find it necessary to take or every possible situation in which he might act. Such failure of Congress specifically to delegate authority does not, "especially * * * in the areas of foreign policy and national security" imply "congressional disapproval" of action taken by the Executive. Haig v. Agee, 453 U.S. 280, 291, 101 S.Ct. 2766, 2774 (1981). On the contrary, the enactment of legislation closely related to the question of the President's authority in a particular case which evinces legislative intent to accord the President broad discretion may be considered to "invite" "measures on independent presidential responsibility." Youngstown, 343 U.S., at 637, 72 S.Ct., at 871 (Jackson, J. concurring). At least this is so where there is no contrary indication of legislative intent and when as here, there is a history of congressional acquiescence in conduct of the sort engaged in by the President. * * *

> * * *

> In addition to congressional acquiescence in the President's power to settle claims, prior cases of this Court have also recognized that the President does have some measure of power to enter into executive agreements without obtaining the advice and consent of the Senate. In United States v. Pink, 315 U.S. 203, 62 S.Ct. 552 (1942), for example, the Court upheld the validity of the Litvinov Assignment, which was part of an Executive Agreement whereby the Soviet Union assigned to the United States amounts owed to it by American nationals so that outstanding claims of other American nationals could be paid. The Court explained that the resolution of such claims was integrally connected with normalizing United States' relations with a foreign state.

> * * *

> Just as importantly, Congress has not disapproved of the action taken here. Though Congress has held hearings on the Iranian Agreement itself, Congress has not enacted legislation, or even passed a resolution, indicating its displeasure with the Agreement. Quite the contrary, the relevant Senate Committee has stated that the establishment of the Tribunal is "of vital importance to the United States." * * * We are thus clearly not confronted with a situation in which Congress has in some way resisted the exercise of presidential authority.

The Court emphasized the narrowness of its decision and explicitly warned that it did "not decide that the President possesses plenary power to settle claims, even as against foreign governmental entities." Rather, "where, as here, the settlement of claims has been determined to be a necessary incident to the resolution of a major foreign policy dispute between our country and another, and where, as here, we can conclude that Congress acquiesced in the President's action, we are not prepared to say that the President lacks the power to settle such claims."

THE GULF OF TONKIN RESOLUTION

78 Stat. 384 (1964)

Whereas naval units of the Communist regime in Vietnam, in violation of the principles of the Charter of the United Nations and of international law, have deliberately and repeatedly attacked United States naval vessels lawfully present in international waters, and have thereby created a serious threat to international peace; and

Whereas these attacks are part of a deliberate and systematic campaign of aggression that the Communist regime in North Vietnam has been waging against its neighbors and the nations joined with them in the collective defense of their freedom; and

Whereas the United States is assisting the peoples of southeast Asia to protect their freedom and has no territorial, military or political ambitions in that area, but desires only that these peoples should be left in peace to work out their own destinies in their own way: Now, therefore, be it

Resolved by the Senate and House of Representatives of the United States of America in Congress assembled, That the Congress approves and supports the determination of the President, as Commander in Chief, to take all necessary measures to repel any armed attack against the forces of the United States and to prevent further aggression.

SEC. 2.   The United States regards as vital to its national interest and to world peace the maintenance of international peace and security in southeast Asia. Consonant with the Constitution of the United States and the Charter of the United Nations and in accordance with its obligations under the Southeast Asia Collective Defense Treaty, the United States is, therefore, prepared, as the President determines, to take all necessary steps, including the use of armed force, to assist any member or protocol state of the Southeast Asia Collective Defense Treaty requesting assistance in defense of its freedom.

SEC. 3.   This resolution shall expire when the President shall determine that the peace and security of the area is reasonably assured by international conditions created by action of the United Nations or otherwise, except that it may be terminated earlier by concurrent resolution of the Congress.

[Congress repealed the resolution effective January 2, 1971.]

WAR POWERS RESOLUTION

87 Stat. 555 (1973)

Resolved by the Senate and House of Representatives of the United States of America in Congress assembled, That:

Section 1. This joint resolution may be cited as the "War Powers Resolution."

Sec. 2. (a) It is the purpose of

this joint resolution to fulfill the intent of the framers of the Constitution of the United States and insure that the collective judgment of both the Congress and the President will apply to the introduction of United States Armed Forces into hostilities, or into situations where imminent involvement in hostilities is clearly indicated by the circumstances, and to the continued use of such forces in hostilities or in such situations.

(b) Under article I, section 8, of the Constitution, it is specifically provided that the Congress shall have the power to make all laws necessary and proper for carrying into execution, not only its own powers but also all other powers vested by the Constitution in the Government of the United States, or in any department or officer thereof.

(c) The constitutional powers of the President as Commander-in-Chief to introduce United States Armed Forces into hostilities, or into situations where imminent involvement in hostilities is clearly indicated by the circumstances, are exercised only pursuant to (1) a declaration of war, (2) specific statutory authorization, or (3) a national emergency created by attack upon the United States, its territories or possessions, or its armed forces.

Sec. 3.   The President in every possible instance shall consult with Congress before introducing United States Armed Forces into hostilities or into situations where imminent involvement in hostilities is clearly indicated by the circumstances, and after every such introduction shall consult regularly with the Congress until United States Armed Forces are no longer engaged in hostilities or have been removed from such situations.

Sec. 4.   (a) In the absence of a declaration of war, in any case in which United States Armed Forces are introduced—

(1) into hostilities or into situations where imminent involvement in hostilities is clearly indicated by the circumstances;

(2) into the territory, airspace or waters of a foreign nation, while equipped for combat, except for deployments which relate solely to supply, replacement, repair, or training of such forces; or

(3) in numbers which substantially enlarge United States Armed Forces equipped for combat already located in a foreign nation;

the President shall submit within 48 hours to the Speaker of the House of Representatives and to the President pro tempore of the Senate a report, in writing, setting forth—

(A) the circumstances necessitating the introduction of United States Armed Forces;

(B) the constitutional and legislative authority under which such introduction took place; and

(C) the estimated scope and duration of the hostilities or involvement.

(b) The President shall provide such other information as the Congress may request in the fulfillment of its constitutional reponsibilities with respect to committing the Nation to war and to the use of United States Armed Forces abroad.

(c) Whenever   United   States Armed Forces are introduced into hostilities or into any situation described in subsection (a) of this section, the President shall, so long as such armed forces continue to be engaged in such hostilities or situation, report to the Congress periodically on the status of such hostilities or situation as well as on the scope and duration of such hostilities or situation, but in no event shall he report to the Congress less often than once every six months.

Sec. 5. (a) Each report submitted pursuant to section 4(a)(1) shall be transmitted to the Speaker of the House of Representatives and to the President pro tempore of the Senate on the same calendar day. Each report so transmitted shall be referred to the Committee on Foreign Affairs of the House of Representatives and to the Committee on Foreign Relations of the Senate for appropriate action. If, when the report is transmitted, the Congress has adjourned sine die or has adjourned for any period in excess of three calendar days, the Speaker of the House of Representatives and the President pro tempore of the Senate, if they deem it advisable (or if petitioned by at least 30 percent of the membership of their respective Houses) shall jointly request the President to convene Congress in order that it may consider the report and take appropriate action pursuant to this section.

(b) Within sixty calendar days after a report is submitted or is required to be submitted pursuant to section 4(a)(1), whichever is earlier, the President shall terminate any use of United States Armed Forces with respect to which such report was submitted (or required to be submitted), unless the Congress (1) has declared war or has enacted a specific authorization for such use of United States Armed Forces, (2) has extended by law such sixty-day period, or (3) is physically unable to meet as a result of an armed attack upon the

United States. Such sixty-day period shall be extended for not more than an additional thirty days if the President determines and certifies to the Congress in writing that unavoidable military necessity respecting the safety of United States Armed Forces requires the continued use of such armed forces in the course of bringing about a prompt removal of such forces.

(c) Notwithstanding subsection (b), at any time that United States Armed Forces are engaged in hostilities outside the territory of the United States, its possessions and territories without a declaration of war or specific statutory authorization, such forces shall be removed by the President if the Congress so directs by concurrent resolution.

Sec. 6. (a) Any joint resolution or bill introduced pursuant to section 5(b) at least thirty calendar days before the expiration of the sixty-day period specified in such section shall be referred to the Committee on Foreign Affairs of the House of Representatives or the Committee on Foreign Relations of the Senate, as the case may be, and such committee shall report one such joint resolution or bill, together with its recommendations, not later than twenty-four calendar days before the expiration of the sixty-day period specified in such section, unless such House shall otherwise determine by the yeas and nays.

(b) Any joint resolution or bill so reported shall become the pending business of the House in question (in the case of the Senate the time for debate shall be equally divided between the proponents and the opponents), and shall be voted on within three calendar days thereafter, unless such House shall otherwise determine by yeas and nays.

(c) Such a joint resolution or bill passed by one House shall be referred to the committee of the other House named in subsection (a) and shall be reported out not later than fourteen calendar days before the expiration of the sixty-day period specified in section 5(b). The joint resolution or bill so reported shall become the pending business of the House in question and shall be voted on within three calendar days after it has been reported, unless such House shall otherwise determine by yeas and nays.

(d) In the case of any disagreement between the two Houses of Congress with respect to a joint resolution or bill passed by both Houses, conferees shall be promptly appointed and the committee of conference shall make and file a report with respect to such resolution or bill not later than four calendar days before the expiration of the sixty-day period specified in section 5(b). In the event the conferees are unable to agree within 48 hours, they shall report back to their respective Houses in disagreement. Notwithstanding any rule in either House concerning the printing of conference reports in the Record or concerning any delay in the consideration of such reports, such report shall be acted on by both Houses not later than the expiration of such sixty-day period.

Sec. 7. (a) Any concurrent resolution introduced pursuant to section 5(c) shall be referred to the Committee on Foreign Affairs of the House of Representatives or the Committee on Foreign Relations of the Senate, as the case may be, and one such concurrent resolution shall be reported out by such committee together with its recommendations within fifteen calendar days, unless such House shall otherwise determine by the yeas and nays.

(b) Any concurrent resolution so reported shall become the pending business of the House in question (in the case of the Senate the time for debate shall be equally divided between the proponents and the opponents) and shall be voted on within three calendar days thereafter, unless such House shall otherwise determine by yeas and nays.

(c) Such a concurrent resolution passed by one House shall be referred to the committee of the other House named in subsection (a) and shall be reported out by such committee together with its recommendations within fifteen calendar days and shall thereupon become the pending business of such House and shall be voted upon within three calendar days, unless such House shall otherwise determine by yeas and nays.

(d) In the case of any disagreement between the two Houses of Congress with respect to a concurrent resolution passed by both Houses, conferees shall be promptly appointed and the committee of conference shall make and file a report with respect to such concurrent resolution within six calendar days after the legislation is referred to the committee of conference. Notwithstanding any rule in either House concerning the printing of conference reports in the Record or concerning any delay in the consideration of such reports, such report shall be acted on by both Houses not later than six calendar days after the conference report is filed. In the event the conferees are unable to agree within 48 hours, they shall report back to their respective Houses in disagreement.

Sec. 8. (a) Authority to introduce United States Armed Forces into hostilities or into situations wherein involvement in hostilities is clearly indicated by the circumstances shall not be inferred—

(1) from any provision of law (whether or not in effect before the date of the enactment of this joint resolution), including any provision contained in any appropriation Act, unless such provision specifically authorizes the introduction of United States Armed Forces into hostilities or into such situations and states that it is intended to constitute specific statutory authorization within the meaning of this joint resolution; or

(2) from any treaty heretofore or hereafter ratified unless such treaty is implemented by legislation specifically authorizing the introduction of United States Armed Forces into hostilities or into such situations and stating that it is intended to constitute specific statutory authorization within the meaning of this joint resolution.

(b) Nothing in this joint resolution shall be construed to require any further specific statutory authorization to permit members of United States Armed Forces to participate jointly with members of the armed forces of one or more foreign countries in the headquarters operations of high-level military commands which were established prior to the date of enactment of this joint resolution and pursuant to the United Nations Charter or any treaty ratified by the United States prior to such date.

(c) For purposes of this joint resolution, the term "introduction of

United States Armed Forces" includes the assignment of members of such armed forces to command, coordinate, participate in the movement of, or accompany the regular or irregular military forces of any foreign country or government when such military forces are engaged, or there exists an imminent threat that such forces will become engaged, in hostilities.

(d) Nothing in this joint resolution—

(1) is intended to alter the constitutional authority of the Congress or of the President, or the provisions of existing treaties; or

(2) shall be construed as granting any authority to the President with respect to the introduction of United States Armed Forces into hostilities or into situations wherein involvement in hostilities is clearly indicated by the circumstances which authority he would not have had in the absence of this joint resolution.

Sec. 9. If any provision of this joint resolution or the application thereof to any person or circumstance is held invalid, the remainder of the joint resolution and the application of such provision to any other person or circumstance shall not be affected thereby.

Sec. 10. This joint resolution shall take effect on the date of its enactment.

[Passed over Presidential veto November 7, 1973.]

PROPOSED ARTICLE OF IMPEACHMENT REJECTED BY THE HOUSE JUDICIARY COMMITTEE

[In the course of its historic July 1974 meeting at which it considered several articles of impeachment against President Richard Nixon (see p. 296), the House Judiciary Committee rejected by a 12–26 vote the following proposed article dealing with the bombing of Cambodia.]

In his conduct of the office of President of the United States, Richard M. Nixon, in violation of his constitutional oath faithfully to execute the office of President of the United States and, to the best of his ability, preserve, protect, and defend the Constitution of the United States, and in disregard of his constitutional duty to take care that the laws be faithfully executed, on and subsequent to March 17, 1969, authorized, ordered, and ratified the concealment from the Congress of the facts and the submission to the Congress of false and misleading statements concerning the existence, scope and nature of American bombing operations in Cambodia in derogation of the power of the Congress to declare war, to make appropriations and to raise and support armies, and by such conduct warrants impeachment and trial and removal from office.

Chapter 4

The Impact of War and Emergencies on Legislative and Executive Power

The critical test for a constitutional democracy and limited government is how it behaves in wartime and emergencies. The instinct for self-preservation gives a compelling thrust to rationalizations for the uses of power to defeat the enemy be they troops or poverty. Witness Chief Justice Hughes's view that the "war power" is the power "to wage war successfully" or Abraham Lincoln's lament that "It has long been a grave question whether any government, not too strong for the liberties of its people, can be strong enough to maintain its existence in great emergencies." Consequently, it should not be surprising that there is a temptation to expand still further in crisis times the considerable powers normally exercised by the legislative and executive branches.

Article I empowers Congress "to declare war," "to raise and support armies," "to provide and maintain a navy," and "to provide for calling forth the militia * * *." Article II designates the President as commander-in-chief of the armed forces. The Constitution also authorizes Congress "to make rules for the government and regulation of the land and naval forces." The aggregate of these war powers is patently enormous. Together with the elasticity apparent in conventional legislative and executive powers, evident in periods of domestic trouble, the exercise of such broad powers poses a significant challenge at times to the notion of constitutional and limited government.

It has often been argued that in wartime and periods of domestic travail constitutional rule gives way to more expeditious governance. There is an old legal maxim, *Inter arma silent leges*—"In times of war, the laws are silent." The Court itself has never accepted it. Indeed, with respect to the need for observance of the Constitution, as Justice Davis put it speaking for the Court in *Ex parte Milligan* (p. 324), "No doctrine, involving more pernicious consequences, was ever invented by the wit of man than that any of its provisions can be suspended during any of the great

321

exigencies of government." Rather, as Chief Justice Hughes explained in *Home Building & Loan Ass'n* v. *Blaisdell* (p. 331):

> Emergency does not create power. Emergency does not increase granted power or remove or diminish the restrictions imposed upon power granted or reserved. The Constitution was adopted in a period of grave emergency. Its grants of power to the federal government and its limitations of the power of the States were determined in the light of emergency, and they are not altered by emergency. What power was thus granted and what limitations were thus imposed are questions which have always been, and always will be, the subject of close examination under our constitutional system.
>
> While emergency does not create power, emergency may furnish the occasion for the exercise of power. "Although an emergency may not call into life a power which has never lived, nevertheless emergency may afford a reason for the exertion of a living power already enjoyed." * * * The constitutional question presented in the light of an emergency is whether the power possessed embraces the particular exercise of it in response to particular conditions. * * *

It is not clear that this response is adequate to the challenge, however, since it makes little difference whether the emergency *per se* creates power if it occasions the exercise of existing powers so great as to swallow up the guarantees of liberty and due process otherwise provided in the Constitution. In any case, proof of the matter is more likely to be found by examining actual responses of the judiciary to the exercise of emergency and war powers by the executive and legislative branches than by looking to legal rhetoric.

The decisions which follow are representative of the pattern that generally characterizes the vitality of the Court as constitutional check on the exercise of war and emergency powers; that is to say, it is almost no check at all. During hostilities, the Court invariably approves whatever use is made of the war powers. Constitutional objections to wartime legislative and executive measures appear to be vindicated only after the shooting has stopped and even then constitute the exception rather than the rule. If the power to wage war evokes "a power to wage war successfully," the Justices are poorly placed, both by information and training, to question the judgment of the President and military authorities as to what measures are essential to a successful prosecution of the war. These institutional barriers to interference are doubtless reinforced by a personal reluctance to rock the boat in periods of national distress, times which call upon each citizen to do his part and pull together. In times of trouble an exhortation to achieve the common good is likely to be substituted for a climate of detached reflection. But is there something to be said for withholding judicial approval of constitutionally dubious measures in wartime even if it is likely that an adverse judgment from the Court would go unheeded or, more likely, that its judgment about the constitutionality of a challenged measure would come so long after the fact as to make the ruling of little practical consequence? Justice Jackson's dissent in *Korematsu* v. *United States* (p. 341) is addressed to precisely this concern.

And in the process he offers insight as to why, in a legalistic culture, the Court's capacity for manipulating revered symbols conveys moral approval for political acts and thus surrounds judicial rulings with a sophisticated power of legitimation that makes the Court hardly the "least dangerous branch" Hamilton once thought it to be.

In wartime, judicial deference has meant deference to executive action particularly. The vigor of Lincoln's Civil War stewardship at the expense of constitutional authority is legendary, especially but by no means exclusively during the period in 1861 between the fall of Fort Sumter and the convening of a special session of Congress. He united the President's prerogatives as commander-in-chief with his power "to take care that the laws be faithfully executed" so that

> As interpreted by President Lincoln, the war power specifically included the right to determine the existence of "rebellion" and call forth the militia to suppress it; the right to increase the regular army by calling for volunteers beyond the authorized total; the right to suspend the *habeas corpus* privilege; the right to proclaim martial law; the right to place persons under arrest without warrant and without judicially showing the cause of detention; the right to seize citizens' property if such seizure should become indispensable to the successful prosecution of the war; the right to spend money from the treasury of the United States without congressional appropriation; the right to suppress newspapers; and the right to do unusual things by proclamation, especially to proclaim freedom to the slaves of those in arms against the Government. These were some of the conspicuous powers which President Lincoln exercised, and in the exercise of which he was as a rule, though not without exception, sustained in the courts.[a]

And Congress extended its own powers as well:

> If we should seek to enumerate the war powers exercised by Congress during the sectional struggle, we would find that they included the confiscation of property; the creation of special war crimes, such as rebellion, conspiracy, and obstructing the draft; the raising of an armed force by conscription, including even aliens who had declared their intention of becoming citizens; the admission of the newly formed state of West Virginia in spite of widespread doubt as to the constitutionality of such a procedure; the approval of the President's suspension of the *habeas corpus* privilege, as well as many other executive acts savoring of legislation; the taxation of the enemy by the use of an unusual kind of "direct tax" which enabled particular pieces of real estate to be virtually confiscated by the United States; the protection of officers committing wrongs by extending immunity for acts performed under the President's orders; the extension of the jurisdiction of Federal courts so as to permit cases involving official immunity to be transferred from State to Federal tribunals; the issuance of paper money with the legal tender quality; the authorization of the President to take possession of the railroads and telegraph lines when the public

---

a. Randall, Constitutional Problems Under Lincoln (rev.ed., 1951), pp. 36–37.

safety should require it, and numerous other unusual and extraordinary measures. In addition to all this, Congress broke over into the executive field through its "Committee on the Conduct of the War" and sought to exercise control even over military operations.[b]

As we navigated our way through the century that followed, the awesome might of armed conflict centralized governmental power still further with the growth of technology and industry, intense regulation of all aspects of economic life by a seemingly endless line of alphabet agencies and boards, heightened reliance upon the universal draft, and an ever increasing sophistication and destructive capacity of weapons in the Nation's arsenal. Traditional concern as to whether the Constitution could survive further recurrence of total war, even if successfully waged, is outrun by the prospect that the next total war is likely to be very short and of such devastating consequence that concern about whether the Constitution can survive it may well border on the academic. Rather, given the legacy of the Cold War, a more pressing issue is the duration of war powers in a peacetime that appears to require a constant state of military readiness.

The event of war, of course, is the classic instance of the infusion of governmental institutions with extraordinary powers to override constitutional checks. But we habitually resort to military metaphors when we enter periods of domestic crisis. In times of escalating offenses against both life and property, we are exhorted to wage a war on crime. Confronted with the blight of economic disadvantage in a land of plenty, we were urged throughout much of the 1960s to attain the Great Society by waging a war on poverty. More recently, a President has warned us of an impending energy crisis which "is the moral equivalent of war." Concern about the limits of power in the wake of a total national effort, therefore, hardly stops with a cessation of hostilities but by analogy extends to our actions in meeting peacetime emergencies as well.

EX PARTE MILLIGAN

Supreme Court of the United States, 1866
71 U.S. (4 Wall.) 2, 18 L.Ed. 281

In October 1864, Milligan, a citizen of Indiana, was arrested by order of the commander of the military district of Indiana for "[conspiring] against the government, [affording] aid and comfort to rebels, and [inciting] the people to insurrection." Milligan was subsequently brought before a military commission, tried, found guilty, and sentenced to be hanged. In May 1865, Milligan petitioned a circuit court to issue an order that he be released from the custody of the military so that he might either have proceedings instituted against him under civil law or be discharged altogether. In addition to his contention that the Constitution guaranteed him the right to trial by jury, Milligan argued that the March 3, 1863 act of Congress prohibited the military from keeping him in confinement. Although the act authorized, after the fact, President Lincoln's suspension of the writ of habeas corpus, it also placed certain qualifications on the use of that power. One of the restrictions was that in states where "the administration of the law continued unimpaired in the Federal Courts" lists of citizens held as prisoners by the military were to be submitted to the appropriate circuit and district judges,

---

b. Ibid., pp. 43–44.

and those individuals listed who were not later indicted were to be released to a court to be discharged or dealt with through civil procedures.

In Milligan's case a grand jury met and adjourned without bringing an indictment against him. The circuit court which he thereupon petitioned was unable to reach agreement on his request (1) for a writ of habeas corpus, (2) for a discharge from military custody, and (3) that, because he was a citizen and a resident of Indiana and had never served in the military, the commission lacked jurisdiction to try and sentence him. These three unresolved questions were certified to the Supreme Court for consideration.

Mr. Justice DAVIS delivered the opinion of the court.

*   *   *

The importance of the main question presented by this record cannot be overstated; for it involves the very framework of the government and the fundamental principles of American liberty.

During the late wicked Rebellion, the temper of the times did not allow that calmness in deliberation and discussion so necessary to a correct conclusion of a purely judicial question. *Then*, considerations of safety were mingled with the exercise of power; and feelings and interests prevailed which are happily terminated. *Now* that the public safety is assured, this question, as well as all others, can be discussed and decided without passion or the admixture of any element not required to form a legal judgment. We approach the investigation of this case, fully sensible of the magnitude of the inquiry and the necessity of full and cautious deliberation.

*   *   *

The controlling question in the case is this: Upon the *facts* stated in Milligan's petition, and the exhibits filed, had the military commission mentioned in it *jurisdiction*, legally, to try and sentence him? Milligan, not a resident of one of the rebellious states, or a prisoner of war, but a citizen of Indiana for twenty years past, and never in the military or naval service, is, while at his home, arrested by the military power of the United States, imprisoned, and, on certain criminal charges preferred against him, tried, convicted, and sentenced to be hanged by a military commission, organized under the direction of the military commander of the military district of Indiana. Had this tribunal the *legal* power and authority to try and punish this man?

No graver question was ever considered by this court, nor one which more nearly concerns the rights of the whole people; for it is the birthright of every American citizen when charged with crime, to be tried and punished according to law. The power of punishment is, alone through the means which the laws have provided for that purpose, and if they are ineffectual, there is an immunity from punishment, no matter how great an offender the individual may be, or how much his crimes may have shocked the sense of justice of the country, or endangered its safety. By the protection of the law human rights are secured; withdraw that protection, and they are at the mercy of wicked rulers, or the clamor of an excited people. If there was law to justify this military trial, it is not our province to interfere; if there was not, it is our duty to declare the nullity of the whole proceedings. The decision of this question does not depend on argument or judicial precedents, numerous and highly illustrative as they are. These precedents inform us of the extent of the struggle to preserve liberty and to relieve those in civil life from military trials. The founders of our government were familiar with the history of that struggle; and secured in a written constitution every right which the people had wrested from power during a contest of ages. By that Constitution and the laws authorized by it this question must be determined. The provisions of that instrument on the administration of criminal justice are too plain and direct, to leave room for misconstruction or doubt of their true meaning. Those applicable to this case are found in that clause of the original Constitution which says, "That the trial of all crimes, except in case of impeachment, shall be by jury"; and in the fourth, fifth, and sixth articles of the amendments. * * *

Time has proven the discernment of our ancestors; for even these provisions, expressed in such plain English words, that it would seem the ingenuity of man could not evade them, are *now*, after the lapse of more than seventy years, sought to be avoided. Those great and good men foresaw that troublous times would arise, when rulers and people would become restive under restraint, and seek by sharp and decisive measures to accomplish ends deemed just and proper; and that the principles of constitutional liberty would be in peril, unless established by irrepealable law. The history of the world had taught them that what was done in the past might be attempted in the future. The Constitution of the United States is a law for rulers and people, equally in war and

in peace, and covers with the shield of its protection all classes of men, at all times, and under all circumstances. No doctrine, involving more pernicious consequences, was ever invented by the wit of man than that any of its provisions can be suspended during any of the great exigencies of government. Such a doctrine leads directly to anarchy or despotism, but the theory of necessity on which it is based is false; for the government, within the Constitution, has all the powers granted to it, which are necessary to preserve its existence; as has been happily proved by the result of the great effort to throw off its just authority.

Have any of the rights guaranteed by the Constitution been violated in the case of Milligan? and if so, what are they?

Every trial involves the exercise of judicial power; and from what source did the military commission that tried him derive their authority? Certainly no part of the judicial power of the country was conferred on them; because the Constitution expressly vests it "in one supreme court and such inferior courts as the Congress may from time to time ordain and establish," and it is not pretended that the commission was a court ordained and established by Congress. They cannot justify on the mandate of the President; because he is controlled by law, and has his appropriate sphere of duty, which is to execute, not to make, the laws; and there is "no unwritten criminal code to which resort can be had as a source of jurisdiction."

But it is said that the jurisdiction is complete under the "laws and usages of war."

It can serve no useful purpose to inquire what those laws and usages are, whence they originated, where found, and on whom they operate; they can never be applied to citizens in states which have upheld the authority of the government, and where the courts are open and their process unobstructed. This court has judicial knowledge that in Indiana the Federal authority was always unopposed, and its courts always open to hear criminal accusations and redress grievances; and no usage of war could sanction a military trial there for any offence whatever of a citizen in civil life, in nowise connected with the military service. Congress could grant no such power; and to the honor of our national legislature be it said, it has never been provoked by the state of the country even to attempt its exercise. One of the plainest constitutional provisions was, therefore, infringed when Milligan was tried by a court not ordained and established by Congress, and not composed of judges appointed during good behavior.

Why was he not delivered to the Circuit Court of Indiana to be proceeded against according to law? No reason of necessity could be urged against it; because Congress had declared penalties against the offences charged, provided for their punishment, and directed that court to hear and determine them. And soon after this military tribunal was ended, the Circuit Court met, peacefully transacted its business, and adjourned. It needed no bayonets to protect it, and required no military aid to execute its judgments. It was held in a state, eminently distinguished for patriotism, by judges commissioned during the Rebellion, who were provided with juries, upright, intelligent, and selected by a marshal appointed by the President.

The government had no right to conclude that Milligan, if guilty, would not receive in that court merited punishment; for its records disclose that it was constantly engaged in the trial of similar offences, and was never interrupted in its administration of criminal justice. If it was dangerous, in the distracted condition of affairs, to leave Milligan unrestrained of his liberty, because he "conspired against the government, afforded aid and comfort to rebels, and incited the people to insurrection," the *law* said arrest him, confine him closely, render him powerless to do further mischief; and then present his case to the grand jury of the district, with proofs of his guilt, and, if indicted, try him according to the course of the common law. If this had been done, the Constitution would have been vindicated, the law of 1863 enforced, and the securities for personal liberty preserved and defended.

Another guarantee of freedom was broken when Milligan was denied a trial by jury. The great minds of the country have differed on the correct interpretation to be given to various provisions of the Federal Constitution; and judicial decision has been often invoked to settle their true meaning; but until recently no one ever doubted that the right of trial by jury was fortified in the organic law against the power of attack. It is *now* assailed; but if ideas can be expressed in words, and language has any meaning, *this right*—one of the most valuable in a free country—is preserved to every one accused of crime who is not attached to the army, or navy, or militia in actual service. The sixth amendment affirms that "in all criminal prosecutions the accused shall enjoy the right to a speedy and public trial by an impartial jury," language broad enough to embrace all persons and cases; but the fifth, recognizing the necessity of an indictment, or presentment, before any one can be held to answer for high crimes, *"excepts cases arising in the land or naval forces, or in the militia, when in actual service, in time of war or public danger"*; and the framers of the Constitution, doubtless, meant to limit the right of trial by jury, in the sixth amendment, to those persons who were subject to indictment or presentment in the fifth.

The discipline necessary to the efficiency of the army and navy, required other and swifter modes of trial than are furnished by the common law courts; and, in pursuance of the power conferred by the Constitution, Congress has declared the kinds of trial, and the manner in which they shall be conducted, for offences committed while the party is in the military or naval service. Every one connected with these branches of the public service is amenable to the jurisdiction which Congress has created for their government, and, while thus serving, surrenders his right to be tried by the civil courts. *All other persons*, citizens of states where the courts are open, if charged with crime, are guaranteed the inestimable privilege of trial by jury. This privilege is a vital principle, underlying the whole administration of criminal justice; it is not held by sufferance, and cannot be frittered away on any plea of state or political necessity. When peace prevails, and the authority of the government is undisputed, there is no difficulty of preserving the safeguards of liberty; for the ordinary modes of trial are never neglected, and no one wishes it otherwise; but if society is disturbed by civil commotion—if the passions of men are aroused and the re-

straints of law weakened, if not disregarded—these safeguards need, and should receive, the watchful care of those intrusted with the guardianship of the Constitution and laws. In no other way can we transmit to posterity unimpaired the blessings of liberty, consecrated by the sacrifices of the Revolution.

It is claimed that martial law covers with its broad mantle the proceedings of this military commission. The proposition is this: that in a time of war the commander of an armed force (if in his opinion the exigencies of the country demand it, and of which he is to judge), has the power, within the lines of his military district, to suspend all civil rights and their remedies, and subject citizens as well as soldiers to the rule of *his will*; and in the exercise of his lawful authority cannot be restrained, except by his superior officer or the President of the United States.

If this position is sound to the extent claimed, then when war exists, foreign or domestic, and the country is subdivided into military departments for mere convenience, the commander of one of them can, if he chooses, within his limits, on the plea of necessity, with the approval of the Executive, substitute military force for and to the exclusion of the laws, and punish all persons, as he thinks right and proper, without fixed or certain rules.

The statement of this proposition shows its importance; for, if true, republican government is a failure, and there is an end of liberty regulated by law. Martial law, established on such a basis, destroys every guarantee of the Constitution, and effectually renders the "military independent of and superior to the civil power"—the attempt to do which by the King of Great Britain was deemed by our fathers such an offence, that they assigned it to the world as one of the causes which impelled them to declare their independence. Civil liberty and this kind of martial law cannot endure together; the antagonism is irreconcilable; and, in the conflict, one or the other must perish.

This nation, as experience has proved, cannot always remain at peace, and has no right to expect that it will always have wise and humane rulers, sincerely attached to the principles of the Constitution. Wicked men, ambitious of power, with hatred of liberty and contempt of law, may fill the place once occupied by Washington and Lincoln; and if this right is conceded, and the calamities of war again befall us, the dangers to human liberty are frightful to contemplate. If our fathers had failed to provide for just such a contingency, they would have been false to the trust reposed in them. They knew—the history of the world told them—the nation they were founding, be its existence short or long, would be involved in war; how often or how long continued, human foresight could not tell; and that unlimited power, wherever lodged at such a time, was especially hazardous to freemen. For this, and other equally weighty reasons, they secured the inheritance they had fought to maintain, by incorporating in a written constitution the safeguards which *time* had proved were essential to its preservation. Not one of these safeguards can the President, or Congress, or the Judiciary disturb, except the one concerning the writ of *habeas corpus*.

It is essential to the safety of every government that, in a great crisis, like the one we have just passed through, there should be a power somewhere of suspending the writ of *habeas corpus*. In every war, there are men of previously good character, wicked enough to counsel their fellow-citizens to resist the measures deemed necessary by a good government to sustain its just authority and overthrow its enemies; and their influence may lead to dangerous combinations. In the emergency of the times, an immediate public investigation according to law may not be possible; and yet, the peril to the country may be too imminent to suffer such persons to go at large. Unquestionably, there is then an exigency which demands that the government, if it should see fit in the exercise of a proper discretion to make arrests, should not be required to produce the persons arrested in answer to a writ of *habeas corpus*. The Constitution goes no further. It does not say after a writ of *habeas corpus* is denied a citizen, that he shall be tried otherwise than by the course of the common law; if it had intended this result, it was easy by the use of direct words to have accomplished it. The illustrious men who framed that instrument were guarding the foundations of civil liberty against the abuses of unlimited power; they were full of wisdom, and the lessons of history informed them that a trial by an established court, assisted by an impartial jury, was the only sure way of protecting the citizen against oppression and wrong. Knowing this, they limited the suspension to one great right, and left the rest to remain forever inviolable. But, it is insisted that the safety of the country in time of war demands that this broad claim for martial law shall be sustained. If this were true, it could be well said that a country, preserved at the sacrifice of all the cardinal principles of liberty, is not worth the cost of preservation. Happily, it is not so.

It will be borne in mind that this is not a question of the power to proclaim martial law, when war exists in a community and the courts and civil authorities are overthrown. Nor is it a question what rule a military commander, at the head of his army, can impose on states in rebellion to cripple their resources and quell the insurrection. The jurisdiction claimed is much more extensive. The necessities of the service, during the late Rebellion, required that the loyal states should be placed within the limits of certain military districts and commanders appointed in them; and, it is urged, that this, in a military sense, constituted them the theatre of military operations; and, as in this case, Indiana had been and was again threatened with invasion by the enemy, the occasion was furnished to establish martial law. The conclusion does not follow from the premises. If armies were collected in Indiana, they were to be employed in another locality, where the laws were obstructed and the national authority disputed. On *her* soil there was no hostile foot; if once invaded, that invasion was at an end, and with it all pretext for martial law. Martial law cannot arise from a *threatened* invasion. The necessity must be actual and present; the invasion real, such as effectually closes the courts and deposes the civil administration.

It is difficult to see how the *safety* of the country required martial law in Indiana. If any of her citizens were plotting treason, the power of arrest could secure them, until the government was prepared for their trial, when the courts were open and ready to try them. It was as easy to protect witnesses before a civil as a military tribunal; and as there could be no wish to convict, except on sufficient legal evidence, surely an ordained and established court was better able to judge of this than a military tribunal composed of gentlemen not trained to the profession of the law.

It follows, from what has been said on this subject, that there are occasions when martial rule can be properly applied. If, in foreign invasion or civil war, the courts are actually closed, and it is impossible to administer criminal justice according to law, *then*, on the theatre of active military operations, where war really prevails, there is a necessity to furnish a substitute for the civil authority, thus overthrown, to preserve the safety of the army and society; and as no power is left but the military, it is allowed to govern by martial rule until the laws can have their free course. As necessity creates the rule, so it limits its duration; for, if this government is continued *after* the courts are reinstated, it is a gross usurpation of power. Martial rule can never exist where the courts are open, and in the proper and unobstructed exercise of their jurisdiction. It is also confined to the locality of actual war. Because, during the late Rebellion it could have been enforced in Virginia, where the national authority was overturned and the courts driven out, it does not follow that it should obtain in Indiana, where that authority was never disputed, and justice was always administered. And so in the case of a foreign invasion, martial rule may become a necessity in one state, when, in another, it would be "mere lawless violence."

* * *

The two remaining questions in this case must be answered in the affirmative. The suspension of the privilege of the writ of *habeas corpus* does not suspend the writ itself. The writ issues as a matter of course; and on the return made to it the court decides whether the party applying is denied the right of proceeding any further with it.

If the military trial of Milligan was contrary to law, then he was entitled, on the facts stated in his petition, to be discharged from custody by the terms of the act of Congress of March 3d, 1863. The provisions of this law having been considered in a previous part of this opinion, we will not restate the views there presented. Milligan avers he was a citizen of Indiana, not in the military or naval service, and was detained in close confinement, by order of the President, from the 5th day of October, 1864, until the 2d day of January, 1865, when the Circuit Court for the District of Indiana, with a grand jury, convened in session at Indianapolis; and afterwards, on the 27th day of the same month, adjourned without finding an indictment or presentment against him. If these aver-

ments were true (and their truth is conceded for the purposes of this case), the court was required to liberate him on taking certain oaths prescribed by the law, and entering into recognizance for his good behavior.

But it is insisted that Milligan was a prisoner of war, and, therefore, excluded from the privileges of the statute. It is not easy to see how he can be treated as a prisoner of war, when he lived in Indiana for the past twenty years, was arrested there, and had not been, during the late troubles, a resident of any of the states in rebellion. If in Indiana he conspired with bad men to assist the enemy, he is punishable for it in the courts of Indiana; but, when tried for the offence, he cannot plead the rights of war; for he was not engaged in legal acts of hostility against the government, and only such persons, when captured, are prisoners of war. If he cannot enjoy the immunities attaching to the character of a prisoner of war, how can he be subject to their pains and penalties?

* * *

HOME BUILDING & LOAN ASSOCIATION v. BLAISDELL

Supreme Court of the United States, 1934
290 U.S. 398, 54 S.Ct. 231, 78 L.Ed. 413

Reacting to widespread unemployment and economic dislocation rampant in the midst of the Depression, the Minnesota legislature in 1933 passed the Minnesota Moratorium Law. The purpose of the law was to prevent widespread foreclosures on mortgages of homeowners and farmers by postponing their payments until they had a chance to get back on their feet. Part One, section four of the law authorized state courts to extend the period of redemption from foreclosure sales for such additional time. John Blaisdell and his wife, owners of a lot which was mortgaged to the Home Building & Loan Association, applied to the District Court of Hennepin County for an extension of time so that they could retain ownership of their home. The district court, however, granted a motion by the creditor Association to dismiss the Blaisdells' petition. The Minnesota Supreme Court reversed. A subsequent decision of the trial court to extend the period of redemption was sustained by the state supreme court, and the Home Building & Loan Association appealed. Throughout these proceedings the Association as creditor contended that the statute violated both the state and federal constitutions by abridging a contract and taking property without due process of law.

Mr. Chief Justice HUGHES delivered the opinion of the Court.

* * *

In determining whether the provision for this temporary and conditional relief exceeds the power of the state by reason of the clause in the Federal Constitution prohibiting impairment of the obligations of contracts, we must consider the relation of emergency to constitutional power, the historical setting of the contract clause, the development of the jurisprudence of this Court in the construction of that clause, and the principles of construction which we may consider to be established.

Emergency does not create power. Emergency does not increase granted power or remove or diminish the restrictions imposed upon power granted or reserved. The Constitution was adopted in a period of grave emergency. Its grants of power to the federal government and its limitations of the power of the States were determined in the light of emergency, and they are not altered by emergency. What power was thus granted and what limitations were thus imposed are questions which have always been, and always will be, the subject of close examination under our constitutional system.

While emergency does not create power, emergency may furnish the occasion for the exercise of power. "Although an emergency may not call into life a power which has never lived, nevertheless emergency may afford a reason for the exertion of a living power already enjoyed." Wilson v. New, 243 U.S. 332, 348, 37

S.Ct. 298, 302. The constitutional question presented in the light of an emergency is whether the power possessed embraces the particular exercise of it in response to particular conditions. Thus, the war power of the federal government is not created by the emergency of war, but it is a power given to meet that emergency. It is a power to wage war successfully, and thus it permits the harnessing of the entire energies of the people in a supreme co-operative effort to preserve the nation. But even the war power does not remove constitutional limitations safeguarding essential liberties. When the provisions of the Constitution, in grant or restriction, are specific, so particularized as not to admit of construction, no question is presented. Thus, emergency would not permit a state to have more than two Senators in the Congress, or permit the election of President by a general popular vote without regard to the number of electors to which the States are respectively entitled, or permit the States to "coin money" or to "make anything but gold and silver coin a tender in payment of debts." But, where constitutional grants and limitations of power are set forth in general clauses, which afford a broad outline, the process of construction is essential to fill in the details. That is true of the contract clause. The necessity of construction is not obviated by the fact that the contract clause is associated in the same section with other and more specific prohibitions. Even the grouping of subjects in the same clause may not require the same application to each of the subjects, regardless of differences in their nature. * * *

In the construction of the contract clause, the debates in the Constitutional Convention are of little aid. But the reasons which led to the adoption of that clause, and of the other prohibitions of section 10 of article 1, are not left in doubt, and have frequently been described with eloquent emphasis. The widespread distress following the revolutionary period and the plight of debtors had called forth in the States an ignoble array of legislative schemes for the defeat of creditors and the invasion of contractual obligations. Legislative interferences had been so numerous and extreme that the confidence essential to prosperous trade had been undermined and the utter destruction of credit was threatened. "The sober people of America" were convinced that some "thorough reform" was needed which would "inspire a general prudence and industry, and give a regular course to the business of society." The Federalist, No. 44. It was necessary to interpose the restraining power of a central authority in order to secure the foundations even of "private faith." The occasion and general purpose of the contract clause are summed up in the terse statement of Chief Justice Marshall in Ogden v. Saunders, 12 Wheat. 213, 354, 355, 6 L.Ed. 606: "The power of changing the relative situation of debtor and creditor, of interfering with contracts, a power which comes home to every man, touches the interest of all, and controls the conduct of every individual in those things which he supposes to be proper for his own exclusive management, had been used to such an excess by the state legislatures, as to break in upon the ordinary intercourse of society, and destroy all confidence between man and man. This mischief had become so great, so alarming, as not only to impair commercial intercourse, and threaten the existence of credit, but to sap the morals of the people, and destroy the sanctity of private faith. To guard against the continuance of the evil, was an object of deep interest with all the truly wise, as well as the virtuous, of this great community, and was one of the important benefits expected from a reform of the government."

But full recognition of the occasion and general purpose of the clause does not suffice to fix its precise scope. Nor does an examination of the details of prior legislation in the States yield criteria which can be considered controlling. To ascertain the scope of the constitutional prohibition, we examine the course of judicial decisions in its application. These put it beyond question that the prohibition is not an absolute one and is not to be read with literal exactness like a mathematical formula. * * *

The inescapable problems of construction have been: What is a contract? What are the obligations of contracts? What constitutes impairment of these obligations? What residuum of power is there still in the States, in relation to the operation of contracts, to protect the vital interests of the community? Questions of this character, "of no small nicety and intricacy, have vexed the legislative halls, as well as the judicial tribunals, with an uncounted variety and frequency of litigation and speculation." Story on the Constitution, § 1375.

* * *

Whatever doubt there may have been that the protective power of the

state, its police power, may be exercised—without violating the true intent of the provision of the Federal Constitution—in directly preventing the immediate and literal enforcement of contractual obligations by a temporary and conditional restraint, where vital public interests would otherwise suffer, was removed by our decisions relating to the enforcement of provisions of leases during a period of scarcity of housing.
* * *

In these cases of leases, it will be observed that the relief afforded was temporary and conditional; that it was sustained because of the emergency due to scarcity of housing; and that provision was made for reasonable compensation to the landlord during the period he was prevented from regaining possession. The Court also decided that, while the declaration by the Legislature as to the existence of the emergency was entitled to great respect, it was not conclusive; and, further, that a law "depending upon the existence of an emergency or other certain state of facts to uphold it may cease to operate if the emergency ceases or the facts change even though valid when passed." It is always open to judicial inquiry whether the exigency still exists upon which the continued operation of the law depends.
* * *

It is manifest from this review of our decisions that there has been a growing appreciation of public needs and of the necessity of finding ground for a rational compromise between individual rights and public welfare. The settlement and consequent contraction of the public domain, the pressure of a constantly increasing density of population, the interrelation of the activities of our people and the complexity of our eco-

nomic interests, have inevitably led to an increased use of the organization of society in order to protect the very bases of individual opportunity. Where, in earlier days, it was thought that only the concerns of individuals or of classes were involved, and that those of the state itself were touched only remotely, it has later been found that the fundamental interests of the state are directly affected; and that the question is no longer merely that of one party to a contract as against another, but of the use of reasonable means to safeguard the economic structure upon which the good of all depends.

* * *

Applying the criteria established by our decisions, we conclude:

1. An emergency existed in Minnesota which furnished a proper occasion for the exercise of the reserved power of the state to protect the vital interests of the community. The declarations of the existence of this emergency by the Legislature and by the Supreme Court of Minnesota cannot be regarded as a subterfuge or as lacking in adequate basis. * * * The finding of the Legislature and state court has support in the facts of which we take judicial notice. * * * It is futile to attempt to make a comparative estimate of the seriousness of the emergency shown in the leasing cases from New York and of the emergency disclosed here. The particular facts differ, but that there were in Minnesota conditions urgently demanding relief, if power existed to give it, is beyond cavil. As the Supreme Court of Minnesota said (249 N.W. 334, 337), the economic emergency which threatened "the loss of homes and lands which furnish those in possession the necessary shelter

and means of subsistence" was a "potent cause" for the enactment of the statute.

2. The legislation was addressed to a legitimate end; that is, the legislation was not for the mere advantage of particular individuals but for the protection of a basic interest of society.

3. In view of the nature of the contracts in question—mortgages of unquestionable validity—the relief afforded and justified by the emergency, in order not to contravene the constitutional provision, could only be of a character appropriate to that emergency, and could be granted only upon reasonable conditions.

4. The conditions upon which the period of redemption is extended do not appear to be unreasonable. The initial extension of the time of redemption for thirty days from the approval of the act was obviously to give a reasonable opportunity for the authorized application to the court. As already noted, the integrity of the mortgage indebtedness is not impaired; interest continues to run; the validity of the sale and the right of a mortgagee-purchaser to title or to obtain a deficiency judgment, if the mortgagor fails to redeem within the extended period, are maintained; and the conditions of redemption, if redemption there be, stand as they were under the prior law. The mortgagor during the extended period is not ousted from possession, but he must pay the rental value of the premises as ascertained in judicial proceedings and this amount is applied to the carrying of the property and to interest upon the indebtedness. The mortgagee-purchaser during the time that he cannot obtain possession thus is not left without compensation for the withholding of possession. Also important is the fact that mortgagees, as is shown by official reports of which we may take notice, are predominantly corporations, such as insurance companies, banks, and investment and mortgage companies. These, and such individual mortgagees as are small investors, are not seeking homes or the opportunity to engage in farming. Their chief concern is the reasonable protection of their investment security. It does not matter that there are, or may be, individual cases of another aspect. The Legislature was entitled to deal with the general or typical situation. The relief afforded by the statute has regard to the interest of mortgagees as well as to the interest of mortgagors. The legislation seeks to prevent the impending ruin of both by a considerate measure of relief. * * *

* * *

5. The legislation is temporary in operation. It is limited to the exigency which called it forth. While the postponement of the period of redemption from the foreclosure sale is to May 1, 1935, that period may be reduced by the order of the court under the statute, in case of a change in circumstances, and the operation of the statute itself could not validly outlast the emergency or be so extended as virtually to destroy the contracts.

We are of the opinion that the Minnesota statute as here applied does not violate the contract clause of the Federal Constitution. Whether the legislation is wise or unwise as a matter of policy is a question with which we are not concerned.

* * *

The judgment of the Supreme Court of Minnesota is affirmed.

Mr. Justice SUTHERLAND, dissenting.

Few questions of greater moment than that just decided have been submitted for judicial inquiry during this generation. He simply closes his eyes to the necessary implications of the decision who fails to see in it the potentiality of future gradual but ever-advancing encroachments upon the sanctity of private and public contracts. The effect of the Minnesota legislation, though serious enough in itself, is of trivial significance compared with the far more serious and dangerous inroads upon the limitations of the Constitution which are almost certain to ensue as a consequence naturally following any step beyond the boundaries fixed by that instrument. And those of us who are thus apprehensive of the effect of this decision would, in a matter so important, be neglectful of our duty should we fail to spread upon the permanent records of the court the reasons which move us to the opposite view.

A provision of the Constitution, it is hardly necessary to say, does not admit of two distinctly opposite interpretations. It does not mean one thing at one time and an entirely different thing at another time. If the contract impairment clause, when framed and adopted, meant that the terms of a contract for the payment of money could not be altered *in invitum* by a state statute enacted for the relief of hardly pressed debtors to the end and with the effect of postponing payment or enforcement during and because of an economic or financial emergency, it is but to state the obvious to say that it means the same now. This view, at once so rational in its application to the written word, and so necessary to the stability of constitutional principles, though from time to time challenged, has never, unless recently, been put within the realm of doubt by the decisions of this court. The true rule was forcefully declared in Ex parte Milligan, 4 Wall. 2, 120–121, 18 L.Ed. 281, in the face of circumstances of national peril and public unrest and disturbance far greater than any that exist today. In that great case this court said that the provisions of the Constitution there under consideration had been expressed by our ancestors in such plain English words that it would seem the ingenuity of man could not evade them, but that after the lapse of more than seventy years they were sought to be avoided. "Those great and good men," the court said, "foresaw that troublous times would arise, when rulers and people would become restive under restraint, and seek by sharp and decisive measures to accomplish ends deemed just and proper; and that the principles of constitutional liberty would be in peril, unless established by irrepealable law. The history of the world had taught them that what was done in the past might be attempted in the future." And then, in words the power and truth of which have become increasingly evident with the lapse of time, there was laid down the rule without which the Constitution would cease to be the "supreme law of the land," binding equally upon governments and governed at all times and under all circumstances, and become a mere collection of political maxims to be adhered to or disregarded according to the prevailing sentiment or the legislative and judicial opinion in respect of the supposed necessities of the hour:

"The Constitution of the United States is a law for rulers and people, equally in war and in peace, and covers with the shield of its protection all classes of men, at all times, and under all circumstances. No doctrine, involving more pernicious consequences, was ever invented by the wit of man than that any of its provisions can be suspended during any of the great exigencies of government. Such a doctrine leads directly to anarchy or despotism." * * *

* * *

It is quite true that an emergency may supply the occasion for the exercise of power, depending upon the nature of the power and the intent of the Constitution with respect thereto. The emergency of war furnishes an occasion for the exercise of certain of the war powers. This the Constitution contemplates, since they cannot be exercised upon any other occasion. The existence of another kind of emergency authorizes the United States to protect each of the states of the Union against domestic violence. Const. Art. IV, § 4. But we are here dealing not with a power granted by the Federal Constitution, but with the state police power, which exists in its own right. Hence the question is not whether an emergency furnishes the occasion for the exercise of that state power, but whether an emergency furnishes an occasion for the relaxation of the restrictions upon the power imposed by the contract impairment clause; and the difficulty is that the contract impairment clause forbids state action under any circumstances, if it have the effect of impairing the obligation of contracts. That clause restricts every state power in the particular specified, no matter what may be the occasion. It does not contemplate that an emergency shall furnish an occasion for softening the restriction or making it any the less a restric-

tion upon state action in that contingency than it is under strictly normal conditions.

The Minnesota statute either impairs the obligation of contracts or it does not. If it does not, the occasion to which it relates becomes immaterial, since then the passage of the statute is the exercise of a normal, unrestricted, state power and requires no special occasion to render it effective. If it does, the emergency no more furnishes a proper occasion for its exercise than if the emergency were nonexistent. And so, while, in form, the suggested distinction seems to put us forward in a straight line, in reality it simply carries us back in a circle, like bewildered travelers lost in a wood, to the point where we parted company with the view of the state court.

* * *

I quite agree with the opinion of the court that whether the legislation under review is wise or unwise is a matter with which we have nothing to do. Whether it is likely to work well or work ill presents a question entirely irrelevant to the issue. The only legitimate inquiry we can make is whether it is constitutional. If it is not, its virtues, if it have any, cannot save it; if it is, its faults cannot be invoked to accomplish its destruction. If the provisions of the Constitution be not upheld when they pinch as well as when they comfort, they may as well be abandoned. Being unable to reach any other conclusion than that the Minnesota statute infringes the constitutional restriction under review, I have no choice but to say so.

I am authorized to say that Mr. Justice VAN DEVANTER, Mr. Justice McREYNOLDS and Mr. Justice BUTLER concur in this opinion.

WOODS v. CLOYD W. MILLER CO.

Supreme Court of the United States, 1948
333 U.S. 138, 68 S.Ct. 421, 92 L.Ed. 596

Congress, utilizing the war power, passed the Housing and Rent Act of 1947 to alleviate the inflationary consequences of a widespread housing shortage resulting from curtailed construction during World War II. The legislation established a maximum rent level on housing in various "defense-rental areas." Shortly after it became effective, the Cloyd W. Miller Company violated Title II of the Act by demanding 40 percent and 60 percent rent increases from their Cleveland, Ohio tenants. Tighe Woods, the Housing Expediter, exercised his authority under section 206(a) to seek a court order enjoining these violations of Title II. The district court held the act unconstitutional principally on the ground that it transcended the notion of timeliness inherent in a legitimate exercise of the war power and appeal was taken directly to the Supreme Court.

Mr. Justice DOUGLAS delivered the opinion of the Court.

The case is here on a direct appeal * * * from a judgment of the District Court holding unconstitutional Title II of the Housing and Rent Act of 1947, 61 Stat. 193, 196.

The Act became effective on July 1, 1947, and the following day the appellee demanded of its tenants increases of 40% and 60% for rental accommodations in the Cleveland Defense-Rental Area, and admitted violation of the Act and regulations adopted pursuant thereto. Appellant thereupon instituted this proceeding under § 206(b) of the Act to enjoin the violations. A preliminary injunction issued. After a hearing it was dissolved and a permanent injunction denied.

The District Court * * * was of the view that the authority of Congress to regulate rents by virtue of the war power * * * ended with the Presidential Proclamation terminating hostilities on December 31, 1946, since that proclamation inaugurated "peace-in-fact" though it did not mark termination of the war. It also concluded that even if the war power continues, Congress did not act under it because it did not say so, and only if Congress says so, or enacts provisions so implying, can it be held that Congress intended to exercise such power. That Congress did not so intend, said the District Court, follows from the provision that the Housing Expediter can end controls in any area without regard to the official termination of the war, and from the fact that the preceding federal rent control laws (which were concededly exercises of the war power) were neither amended nor extended. The District Court expressed the further view that rent control is not within the war power because "the emergency created by housing shortage came into existence long before the war." It held that the Act "lacks in uniformity of application and distinctly constitutes a delegation of legislative power not within the grant of Congress" because of the authorization to the Housing Expediter to lift controls in any area before the Act's expiration. It also held that the Act in effect provides "low rentals for certain groups without taking the property or compensating the owner in any way." * * *

We conclude, in the first place, that the war power sustains this legislation. The Court said in Hamilton v. Kentucky Distilleries and Warehouse Co., 251 U.S. 146, 161, 40 S.Ct. 106, 110, that the war power includes the power "to remedy the evils which have arisen from its rise and progress" and continues for the duration of that emergency. Whatever may be the consequences when war is officially terminated, the war power does not necessarily end with the cessation of hostilities. We recently held that it is adequate to support the preservation of rights created by wartime legislation, Fleming v. Mohawk Wrecking and Lumber Co., 331 U.S. 111, 67 S.Ct. 1129. But it has a broader sweep. In *Hamilton* v. *Kentucky Distilleries and Warehouse Co.*, supra, and Ruppert v. Caffey, 251 U.S. 264, 40 S.Ct. 141, prohibition laws which were enacted after the Armistice in World War I were sustained as exercises of the war power because they conserved manpower and increased efficiency of production in the critical days during the period of demobilization, and helped to husband the supply of grains and cereals depleted by the war effort. * * *

The constitutional validity of the present legislation follows *a fortiori* from those cases. The legislative history of the present Act makes abundantly clear that there has not yet been eliminated the deficit in housing which in considerable measure was caused by the heavy demobilization of veterans and by the cessation or reduction in residential construction during the period of hostilities due to the allocation of building materials to military projects. Since the war effort contributed heavily to that deficit, Congress has the power even after the cessation of hostilities to act to control the forces that a short supply of the needed article created. If that were not true, the Necessary and Proper Clause, Art. I, § 8, cl. 18, would be drastically limited in its application to the several war powers. The Court has declined to follow that course in the past. * * * We decline to take it today. The result would be paralyzing. It would render Congress powerless to remedy conditions the creation of which necessarily followed from the mobilization of men and materials for successful prosecution of the war. So to read the Constitution would be to make it self-defeating.

We recognize the force of the argument that the effects of war under modern conditions may be felt in the economy for years and years, and that if the war power can be used in days of peace to treat all the wounds which war inflicts on our society, it may not only swallow up all other powers of Congress but largely obliterate the Ninth and the Tenth Amendments as well. There are no such implications in today's decision. We deal here with the consequences of a housing deficit greatly intensified during the period of hostilities by the war effort. Any power, of course, can be abused. But we cannot assume that Congress is not alert to its constitutional responsibilities. And the question whether the war power has been properly employed in cases such as this is open to judicial inquiry. * * *

The question of the constitutionality of action taken by Congress does not depend on recitals of the power which it undertakes to exercise. Here it is plain from the legislative history that Congress was invoking its war power to cope with a current condition of which the war was a direct and immediate cause. Its judgment on that score is entitled to the respect granted like legislation enacted pursuant to the police power. * * *

Under the present Act the Housing Expediter is authorized to remove the rent controls in any defense-rental area if in his judgment the need no longer exists by reason of new construction or satisfaction of demand in other ways. The powers thus delegated are far less extensive than those sustained in Bowles v. Willingham, 321 U.S. pages 512–515, 64 S.Ct. page 647. Nor is there here a grant of unbridled administrative discretion. The standards prescribed pass muster under our decisions. See Bowles v. Willingham, 321 U.S. pages 514–516, 64 S.Ct. pages 647, 648, and cases cited.

Objection is made that the Act by its exemption of certain classes of housing accommodations violates the Fifth Amendment. A similar argument was rejected under the Fourteenth Amendment when New York made like exemptions under the rent-control statute which was here for review in Marcus Brown Holding Co. v. Feldman, 256 U.S. pages 195, 198, 199, 41 S.Ct. pages 465, 466. Certainly Congress is not under greater limitations. It need not control all rents or none. It can select those areas or those classes of property where the need seems the greatest. * * * This alone is adequate answer to the objection, equally applicable to the original Act sustained in *Bowles* v. *Willingham*, supra, that the present Act lacks uniformity in application.

The fact that the property regulated suffers a decrease in value is no more fatal to the exercise of the war power * * * than it is where

the police power is invoked to the same end. * * *

Reversed.

Mr. Justice JACKSON, concurring.

I agree with the result in this case, but the arguments that have been addressed to us lead me to utter more explicit misgivings about war powers than the Court has done. The Government asserts no constitutional basis for this legislation other than this vague, undefined and undefinable "war power."

No one will question that this power is the most dangerous one to free government in the whole catalogue of powers. It usually is invoked in haste and excitement when calm legislative consideration of constitutional limitation is difficult. It is executed in a time of patriotic fervor that makes moderation unpopular. And, worst of all, it is interpreted by the Judges under the influence of the same passions and pressures. Always, as in this case, the Government urges hasty decision to forestall some emergency or serve some purpose and pleads that paralysis will result if its claims to power are denied or their confirmation delayed.

Particularly when the war power is invoked to do things to the liberties of people, or to their property or economy that only indirectly affect conduct of the war and do not relate to the management of the war itself, the constitutional basis should be scrutinized with care.

I think we can hardly deny that the war power is as valid a ground for federal rent control now as it has been at any time. We still are technically in a state of war. I would not be willing to hold that war powers may be indefinitely prolonged merely by keeping legally alive a state of war that had in fact ended. I cannot accept the argument that war powers last as long as the effects and consequences of war for if so they are permanent—as permanent as the war debts. But I find no reason to conclude that we could find fairly that the present state of war is merely technical. We have armies abroad exercising our war power and have made no peace terms with our allies not to mention our principal enemies. I think the conclusion that the war power has been applicable during the lifetime of this legislation is unavoidable.

KOREMATSU v. UNITED STATES

Supreme Court of the United States, 1944
323 U.S. 214, 65 S.Ct. 193, 89 L.Ed. 194

In March 1942, Congress passed legislation empowering the President by executive order and cabinet or military officers under his direction to restrict movement or residence in any designated military area or war zone where he felt that such restriction was necessary to national security. Amid growing fears that an invasion of the West Coast was imminent, following the attack on Peal Harbor the preceding December, and lurking suspicions about the loyalty of tens of thousands of Japanese-Americans clustered along the coast, President Roosevelt's subsequent Executive Order 9066 declaring that "the successful prosecution of the war requires every possible protection against espionage and against sabotage to national-defense material, national-defense premises, and national-defense utilities" came to be applied increasingly to people of Japanese ancestry, citizen and alien alike. These restrictions ranged from the imposition of curfews to forced removal to "relocation centers" much further inland.

The present case arose from Exclusion Order No. 34 issued by General DeWitt, the Commanding General of the Western Command in May 1942, barring all persons of Japanese descent from the "military area" of San Leandro, California. Following his failure to leave the "military area" where his home was located, Toyosaburo Korematsu, an American citizen of Japanese ancestry, was convicted of violating the act passed by Congress making it unlawful to act contrary to restrictions placed on any military area or zone. The United States Circuit Court of Appeals affirmed the conviction, and Korematsu appealed.

Mr. Justice BLACK delivered the opinion of the Court.

* * *

The 1942 Act was attacked in the *Hirabayashi* case [320 U.S. 81, 63 S.Ct. 1375] as an unconstitutional delegation of power; it was contended that the curfew order and other orders on which it rested were beyond the war powers of the Congress, the military authorities and of the President, as Commander in Chief of the Army; and finally that to apply the curfew order against none but citizens of Japanese ancestry amounted to a constitutionally prohibited discrimination solely on account of race. To these questions, we gave the serious consideration which their importance justified. We upheld the curfew order as an exercise of the power of the government to take steps necessary to prevent espionage and sabotage in an area threatened by Japanese attack.

In the light of the principles we announced in the *Hirabayashi* case, we are unable to conclude that it was beyond the war power of Congress and the Executive to exclude those of Japanese ancestry from the West Coast war area at the time they did. True, exclusion from the area in which one's home is located is a far greater deprivation than constant confinement to the home from 8 p. m. to 6 a. m. Nothing short of apprehension by the proper military authorities of the gravest imminent danger to the public safety can constitutionally justify either. But exclusion from a threatened area, no less than curfew, has a definite and close relationship to the prevention of espionage and sabotage. The military authorities, charged with the primary responsibility of defending our shores, concluded that curfew provided inadequate protection and ordered exclusion. They did so, as pointed out in our *Hirabayashi* opinion, in accordance with Congressional authority to the military to say who should, and who should not, remain in the threatened areas.

In this case the petitioner challenges the assumptions upon which we rested our conclusions in the *Hirabayashi* case. He also urges that by May 1942, when Order No. 34 was promulgated, all danger of Japanese invasion of the West Coast had disappeared. After careful consideration of these contentions we are compelled to reject them.

Here, as in the *Hirabayashi* case, 320 U.S. at page 99, 63 S.Ct. at page 1385, " * * * we cannot reject as unfounded the judgment of the military authorities and of Congress that there were disloyal members of that population, whose number and strength could not be precisely and quickly ascertained. We cannot say that the war-making branches of the Government did not have ground for

believing that in a critical hour such persons could not readily be isolated and separately dealt with, and constituted a menace to the national defense and safety, which demanded that prompt and adequate measures be taken to guard against it."

Like curfew, exclusion of those of Japanese origin was deemed necessary because of the presence of an unascertained number of disloyal members of the group, most of whom we have no doubt were loyal to this country. It was because we could not reject the finding of the military authorities that it was impossible to bring about an immediate segregation of the disloyal from the loyal that we sustained the validity of the curfew order as applying to the whole group. In the instant case, temporary exclusion of the entire group was rested by the military on the same ground. The judgment that exclusion of the whole group was for the same reason a military imperative answers the contention that the exclusion was in the nature of group punishment based on antagonism to those of Japanese origin. That there were members of the group who retained loyalties to Japan has been confirmed by investigations made subsequent to the exclusion. Approximately five thousand American citizens of Japanese ancestry refused to swear unqualified allegiance to the United States and to renounce allegiance to the Japanese Emperor, and several thousand evacuees requested repatriation to Japan.

We uphold the exclusion order as of the time it was made and when the petitioner violated it. * * * In doing so, we are not unmindful of the hardships imposed by it upon a large group of American citizens. * * * But hardships are part of war, and war is an aggregation of hardships. All citizens alike, both in and out of uniform, feel the impact of war in greater or lesser measure. Citizenship has its responsibilities as well as its privileges, and in time of war the burden is always heavier. Compulsory exclusion of large groups of citizens from their homes, except under circumstances of direst emergency and peril, is inconsistent with our basic governmental institutions. But when under conditions of modern warfare our shores are threatened by hostile forces, the power to protect must be commensurate with the threatened danger.

[The Court next turned to Korematsu's contention that at the time he was charged with remaining unlawfully within the proscribed area, there were two contradictory military orders outstanding—one making it an offense to remain within the prohibited area and another making it unlawful to leave it. The Court, agreeing that, "of course, a person cannot be convicted for doing the very thing which it is a crime to fail to do" found, however, that no real contradiction existed between the two orders but that the orders taken one at a time comprised a well-ordered, step-by-step program for evacuation of Japanese-Americans from the area to relocation centers.]

* * *

We are thus being asked to pass at this time upon the whole subsequent detention program in both assembly and relocation centers, although the only issues framed at the trial related to petitioner's remaining in the prohibited area in violation of the exclusion order. * * *

* * *

Since the petitioner has not been convicted of failing to report or to re-

main in an assembly or relocation center, we cannot in this case determine the validity of those separate provisions of the order. It is sufficient here for us to pass upon the order which petitioner violated. To do more would be to go beyond the issues raised, and to decide momentous questions not contained within the framework of the pleadings or the evidence in this case. It will be time enough to decide the serious constitutional issues which petitioner seeks to raise when an assembly or relocation order is applied or is certain to be applied to him, and we have its terms before us.

Some of the members of the Court are of the view that evacuation and detention in an Assembly Center were inseparable. After May 3, 1942, the date of Exclusion Order No. 34, Korematsu was under compulsion to leave the area not as he would choose but via an Assembly Center. The Assembly Center was conceived as a part of the machinery for group evacuation. The power to exclude includes the power to do it by force if necessary. And any forcible measure must necessarily entail some degree of detention or restraint whatever method of removal is selected. But whichever view is taken, it results in holding that the order under which petitioner was convicted was valid.

It is said that we are dealing here with the case of imprisonment of a citizen in a concentration camp solely because of his ancestry, without evidence or inquiry concerning his loyalty and good disposition towards the United States. Our task would be simple, our duty clear, were this a case involving the imprisonment of a loyal citizen in a concentration camp because of racial prejudice. Regardless of the true nature of the assembly and relocation centers—and we deem it unjustifiable to call them concentration camps with all the ugly connotations that term implies—we are dealing specifically with nothing but an exclusion order. To cast this case into outlines of racial prejudice, without reference to the real military dangers which were presented, merely confuses the issue. Korematsu was not excluded from the Military Area because of hostility to him or his race. He was excluded because we are at war with the Japanese Empire, because the properly constituted military authorities feared an invasion of our West Coast and felt constrained to take proper security measures, because they decided that the military urgency of the situation demanded that all citizens of Japanese ancestry be segregated from the West Coast temporarily, and finally, because Congress, reposing its confidence in this time of war in our military leaders—as inevitably it must—determined that they should have the power to do just this. There was evidence of disloyalty on the part of some, the military authorities considered that the need for action was great, and time was short. We cannot—by availing ourselves of the calm perspective of hindsight—now say that at that time these actions were unjustified.

Affirmed.

Mr. Justice FRANKFURTER, concurring.

According to my reading of Civilian Exclusion Order No. 34, it was an offense for Korematsu to be found in Military Area No. 1, the territory wherein he was previously living, except within the bounds of the established Assembly Center of that area. Even though the various orders issued by General DeWitt be deemed a comprehensive code of instructions, their tenor is clear and not contradictory. They put upon Korematsu the obligation to leave Military Area No. 1, but only by the method prescribed in the instructions, i.e., by reporting to the Assembly Center. * * * And so I join in the opinion of the Court, but should like to add a few words of my own.

The provisions of the Constitution which confer on the Congress and the President powers to enable this country to wage war are as much part of the Constitution as provisions looking to a nation at peace. And we have had recent occasion to quote approvingly the statement of former Chief Justice Hughes that the war power of the Government is "the power to wage war successfully." Hirabayashi v. United States, supra, 320 U.S. at page 93, 63 S.Ct. at page 1382 and see Home Bldg. & L. Ass'n v. Blaisdell, 290 U.S. 398, 426, 54 S.Ct. 231, 235. Therefore, the validity of action under the war power must be judged wholly in the context of war. That action is not to be stigmatized as lawless because like action in times of peace would be lawless. To talk about a military order that expresses an allowable judgment of war needs by those entrusted with the duty of conducting war as "an unconstitutional order" is to suffuse a part of the Constitution with an atmosphere of unconstitutionality. The respective spheres of action of military authorities and of judges are of course very different. But within their sphere, military authorities are no more outside the bounds of obedience to the Constitution than are judges within theirs. "The war power of the United States, like its other powers * * * is subject to applicable constitutional limitations," Hamilton v. Kentucky

Distilleries Co., 251 U.S. 146, 156, 40 S.Ct. 106, 108. To recognize that military orders are "reasonably expedient military precautions" in time of war and yet to deny them constitutional legitimacy makes of the Constitution an instrument for dialectic subtleties not reasonably to be attributed to the hard-headed Framers, of whom a majority had had actual participation in war. If a military order such as that under review does not transcend the means appropriate for conducting war, such action by the military is as constitutional as would be any authorized action by the Interstate Commerce Commission within the limits of the constitutional power to regulate commerce. And being an exercise of the war power explicitly granted by the Constitution for safeguarding the national life by prosecuting war effectively, I find nothing in the Constitution which denies to Congress the power to enforce such a valid military order by making its violation an offense triable in the civil courts. * * * To find that the Constitution does not forbid the military measures now complained of does not carry with it approval of that which Congress and the Executive did. That is their business, not ours.

Mr. Justice ROBERTS, dissenting.

I dissent, because I think the indisputable facts exhibit a clear violation of Constitutional rights.

This is not a case of keeping people off the streets at night as was Kiyoshi Hirabayashi v. United States, 320 U.S. 81, 63 S.Ct. 1375, nor a case of temporary exclusion of a citizen from an area for his own safety or that of the community, nor a case of offering him an opportunity to go temporarily out of an area where his presence might cause danger to himself or to his fellows. On the contrary, it is the case of convicting a citizen as a punishment for not submitting to imprisonment in a concentration camp, based on his ancestry, and solely because of his ancestry, without evidence or inquiry concerning his loyalty and good disposition towards the United States. If this be a correct statement of the facts disclosed by this record, and facts of which we take judicial notice, I need hardly labor the conclusion that Constitutional rights have been violated.

*   *   *

The Government has argued this case as if the only order outstanding at the time the petitioner was arrested and informed against was Exclusion Order No. 34 ordering him to leave the area in which he resided, which was the basis of the information against him. That argument has evidently been effective. The opinion refers to the *Hirabayashi* case, supra, to show that this court has sustained the validity of a curfew order in an emergency. The argument then is that exclusion from a given area of danger, while somewhat more sweeping than a curfew regulation, is of the same nature,—a temporary expedient made necessary by a sudden emergency. This, I think, is a substitution of an hypothetical case for the case actually before the court. * * * [T]he exclusion was but a part of an over-all plan for forceable detention. This case cannot, therefore, be decided on any such narrow ground as the possible validity of a Temporary Exclusion Order under which the residents of an area are given an opportunity to leave and go elsewhere in their native land outside the boundaries of a military area. To make the case turn on any such assumption is to shut our eyes to reality.

* * *

Mr. Justice MURPHY, dissenting.

This exclusion of "all persons of Japanese ancestry, both alien and non-alien," from the Pacific Coast area on a plea of military necessity in the absence of martial law ought not to be approved. Such exclusion goes over "the very brink of constitutional power" and falls into the ugly abyss of racism.

In dealing with matters relating to the prosecution and progress of a war, we must accord great respect and consideration to the judgments of the military authorities who are on the scene and who have full knowledge of the military facts. The scope of their discretion must, as a matter of necessity and common sense, be wide. And their judgments ought not to be overruled lightly by those whose training and duties ill-equip them to deal intelligently with matters so vital to the physical security of the nation.

At the same time, however, it is essential that there be definite limits to military discretion, especially where martial law has not been declared. Individuals must not be left impoverished of their constitutional rights on a plea of military necessity that has neither substance nor support. Thus, like other claims conflicting with the asserted constitutional rights of the individual, the military claim must subject itself to the judicial process of having its reasonableness determined and its conflicts with other interests reconciled. "What are the allowable limits of military discretion, and whether or not they have been overstepped in a

particular case, are judicial questions." Sterling v. Constantin, 287 U.S. 378, 401, 53 S.Ct. 190, 196.

The judicial test of whether the Government, on a plea of military necessity, can validly deprive an individual of any of his constitutional rights is whether the deprivation is reasonably related to a public danger that is so "immediate, imminent, and impending" as not to admit of delay and not to permit the intervention of ordinary constitutional processes to alleviate the danger. United States v. Russell, 13 Wall. 623, 627, 628, 20 L.Ed. 474. * * * Yet no reasonable relation to an "immediate, imminent, and impending" public danger is evident to support this racial restriction which is one of the most sweeping and complete deprivations of constitutional rights in the history of this nation in the absence of martial law.

It must be conceded that the military and naval situation in the spring of 1942 was such as to generate a very real fear of invasion of the Pacific Coast, accompanied by fears of sabotage and espionage in that area. The military command was therefore justified in adopting all reasonable means necessary to combat these dangers. In adjudging the military action taken in light of the then apparent dangers, we must not erect too high or too meticulous standards; it is necessary only that the action have some reasonable relation to the removal of the dangers of invasion, sabotage and espionage. But the exclusion, either temporarily or permanently, of all persons with Japanese blood in their veins has no such reasonable relation. And that relation is lacking because the exclusion order necessarily must rely for its reasonableness upon the assumption that *all* persons of Japanese ancestry may have a dangerous tendency to commit sabotage and espionage and to aid our Japanese enemy in other ways. It is difficult to believe that reason, logic or experience could be marshalled in support of such an assumption.

* * *

The military necessity which is essential to the validity of the evacuation order * * * resolves itself into a few intimations that certain individuals actively aided the enemy, from which it is inferred that the entire group of Japanese Americans could not be trusted to be or remain loyal to the United States. No one denies, of course, that there were some disloyal persons of Japanese descent on the Pacific Coast who did all in their power to aid their ancestral land. Similar disloyal activities have been engaged in by many persons of German, Italian and even more pioneer stock in our country. But to infer that examples of individual disloyalty prove group disloyalty and justify discriminatory action against the entire group is to deny that under our system of law individual guilt is the sole basis for deprivation of rights. Moreover, this inference, which is at the very heart of the evacuation orders, has been used in support of the abhorrent and despicable treatment of minority groups by the dictatorial tyrannies which this nation is now pledged to destroy. To give constitutional sanction to that inference in this case, however well-intentioned may have been the military command on the Pacific Coast, is to adopt one of the cruelest of the rationales used by our enemies to destroy the dignity of the individual and to encourage and open the door to discriminatory actions against other minority groups in the passions of tomorrow.

Moreover, there was no adequate proof that the Federal Bureau of Investigation and the military and naval intelligence services did not have the espionage and sabotage situation well in hand during this long period. Nor is there any denial of the fact that not one person of Japanese ancestry was accused or convicted of espionage or sabotage after Pearl Harbor while they were still free, a fact which is some evidence of the loyalty of the vast majority of these individuals and of the effectiveness of the established methods of combatting these evils. It seems incredible that under these circumstances it would have been impossible to hold loyalty hearings for the mere 112,000 persons involved—or at least for the 70,000 American citizens—especially when a large part of this number represented children and elderly men and women. Any inconvenience that may have accompanied an attempt to conform to procedural due process cannot be said to justify violations of constitutional rights of individuals.

* * *

Mr. Justice JACKSON, dissenting.

Korematsu was born on our soil, of parents born in Japan. The Constitution makes him a citizen of the United States by nativity and a citizen of California by residence. No claim is made that he is not loyal to this country. There is no suggestion that apart from the matter involved here he is not law-abiding and well disposed. Korematsu, however, has been convicted of an act not commonly a crime. It consists merely of being present in the state whereof he is a citizen, near the place where he was born, and where all his life he has lived.

Even more unusual is the series of military orders which made this conduct a crime. They forbid such a one to remain, and they also forbid him to leave. They were so drawn that the only way Korematsu could avoid violation was to give himself up to the military authority. This meant submission to custody, examination, and transportation out of the territory, to be followed by indeterminate confinement in detention camps.

A citizen's presence in the locality, however, was made a crime only if his parents were of Japanese birth. Had Korematsu been one of four—the others being, say, a German alien enemy, an Italian alien enemy, and a citizen of American-born ancestors, convicted of treason but out on parole—only Korematsu's presence would have violated the order. The difference between their innocence and his crime would result, not from anything he did, said, or thought, different than they, but only in that he was born of different racial stock.

Now, if any fundamental assumption underlies our system, it is that guilt is personal and not inheritable. Even if all of one's antecedents had been convicted of treason, the Constitution forbids its penalties to be visited upon him, for it provides that "no Attainder of Treason shall work Corruption of Blood, or Forfeiture except during the Life of the Person attained." Article 3, § 3, cl. 2. But here is an attempt to make an otherwise innocent act a crime merely because this prisoner is the son of parents as to whom he had no choice, and belongs to a race from which there is no way to resign. If Congress in peace-time legislation should

enact such a criminal law, I should suppose this Court would refuse to enforce it.

But the "law" which this prisoner is convicted of disregarding is not found in an act of Congress, but in a military order. Neither the Act of Congress nor the Executive Order of the President, nor both together, would afford a basis for this conviction. It rests on the orders of General DeWitt. And it is said that if the military commander had reasonable military grounds for promulgating the orders, they are constitutional and become law, and the Court is required to enforce them. There are several reasons why I cannot subscribe to this doctrine.

It would be impracticable and dangerous idealism to expect or insist that each specific military command in an area of probable operations will conform to conventional tests of constitutionality. When an area is so beset that it must be put under military control at all, the paramount consideration is that its measures be successful, rather than legal. The armed services must protect a society, not merely its Constitution. The very essence of the military job is to marshal physical force, to remove every obstacle to its effectiveness, to give it every strategic advantage. Defense measures will not, and often should not, be held within the limits that bind civil authority in peace. No court can require such a commander in such circumstances to act as a reasonable man; he may be unreasonably cautious and exacting. Perhaps he should be. But a commander in temporarily focusing the life of a community on defense is carrying out a military program; he is not making law in the sense the courts know the term. He issues orders, and they may have a certain authority as military commands, although they may be very bad as constitutional law.

But if we cannot confine military expedients by the Constitution, neither would I distort the Constitution to approve all that the military may deem expedient. That is what the Court appears to be doing, whether consciously or not. I cannot say, from any evidence before me, that the orders of General DeWitt were not reasonably expedient military precautions, nor could I say that they were. But even if they were permissible military procedures, I deny that it follows that they are constitutional. If, as the Court holds, it does follow, then we may as well say that any military order will be constitutional and have done with it.

The limitation under which courts always will labor in examining the necessity for a military order are illustrated by this case. How does the Court know that these orders have a reasonable basis in necessity? No evidence whatever on that subject has been taken by this or any other court. There is sharp controversy as to the credibility of the DeWitt report. So the Court, having no real evidence before it, has no choice but to accept General DeWitt's own unsworn, self-serving statement, untested by any cross-examination, that what he did was reasonable. And thus it will always be when courts try to look into the reasonableness of a military order.

In the very nature of things military decisions are not susceptible of intelligent judicial appraisal. They do not pretend to rest on evidence, but are made on information that often would not be admissible and on assumptions that could not be proved. Information in support of

an order could not be disclosed to courts without danger that it would reach the enemy. Neither can courts act on communications made in confidence. Hence courts can never have any real alternative to accepting the mere declaration of the authority that issued the order that it was reasonably necessary from a military viewpoint.

Much is said of the danger to liberty from the Army program for deporting and detaining these citizens of Japanese extraction. But a judicial construction of the due process clause that will sustain this order is a far more subtle blow to liberty than the promulgation of the order itself. A military order, however unconstitutional, is not apt to last longer than the military emergency. Even during that period a succeeding commander may revoke it all. But once a judicial opinion rationalizes such an order to show that it conforms to the Constitution, or rather rationalizes the Constitution to show that the Constitution sanctions such an order, the Court for all time has validated the principle of racial discrimination in criminal procedure and of transplanting American citizens. The principle then lies about like a loaded weapon ready for the hand of any authority that can bring forward a plausible claim of an urgent need. Every repetition imbeds that principle more deeply in our law and thinking and expands it to new purposes. All who observe the work of courts are familiar with what Judge Cardozo described as "the tendency of a principle to expand itself to the limit of its logic." A military commander may overstep the bounds of constitutionality, and it is an incident. But if we review and approve, that passing incident becomes the doctrine of the Constitution. There it has a generative power of its own, and all that it creates will be in its own image. Nothing better illustrates this danger than does the Court's opinion in this case.

It argues that we are bound to uphold the conviction of Korematsu because we upheld one in Kiyshi Hirabayashi v. United States, 320 U.S. 81, 63 S.Ct. 1375, when we sustained these orders in so far as they applied a curfew requirement to a citizen of Japanese ancestry. I think we should learn something from that experience.

In that case we were urged to consider only the curfew feature, that being all that technically was involved, because it was the only count necessary to sustain Hirabayashi's conviction and sentence. We yielded, and the Chief Justice guarded the opinion as carefully as language will do. He said: "Our investigation here does not go beyond the inquiry whether, in the light of all the relevant circumstances preceding and attending their promulgation, the challenged orders and statute *afforded a reasonable basis for the action taken in imposing the curfew.*" 320 U.S. at page 101, 63 S.Ct. at page 1386. "We decide only the issue as we have defined it—we decide only that the *curfew order* as applied, and at the time it was applied, was within the boundaries of the war power." 320 U.S. at page 102, 63 S.Ct. at page 1386. And again: "It is unnecessary to consider whether or to what extent *such findings would support orders differing from the curfew order.*" 320 U.S. at page 105, 63 S.Ct. at page 1387. [Italics supplied.] However, in spite of our limiting words we did validate a discrimination on the basis of ancestry for mild and temporary deprivation of liberty. Now the principle of racial discrimi-

nation is pushed from support of mild measures to very harsh ones, and from temporary deprivations to indeterminate ones. And the precedent which it is said requires us to do so is *Hirabayashi*. The Court is now saying that in *Hirabayashi* we did decide the very things we there said we were not deciding. Because we said that these citizens could be made to stay in their homes during the hours of dark, it is said we must require them to leave home entirely; and if that, we are told they may also be taken into custody for deportation; and if that, it is argued they may also be held for some undetermined time in detention camps. How far the principle of this case would be extended before plausible reasons would play out, I do not know.

I should hold that a civil court cannot be made to enforce an order which violates constitutional limitations even if it is a reasonable exercise of military authority. The courts can exercise only the judicial power, can apply only law, and must abide by the Constitution, or they cease to be civil courts and become instruments of military policy.

Of course the existence of a military power resting on force, so vagrant, so centralized, so necessarily heedless of the individual, is an inherent threat to liberty. But I would not lead people to rely on this Court for a review that seems to me wholly delusive. The military reasonableness of these orders can only be determined by military superiors. If the people ever let command of the war power fall into irresponsible and unscrupulous hands, the courts wield no power equal to its restraint. The chief restraint upon those who command the physical forces of the country, in the future as in the past, must be their responsibility to the political judgments of their contemporaries and to the moral judgments of history.

My duties as a justice as I see them do not require me to make a military judgment as to whether General DeWitt's evacuation and detention program was a reasonable military necessity. I do not suggest that the courts should have attempted to interfere with the Army in carrying out its task. But I do not think they may be asked to execute a military expedient that has no place in law under the Constitution. I would reverse the judgment and discharge the prisoner.

Justice Jackson's dissent proved prophetic indeed. Six years after the Court's ruling in *Korematsu*, Congress passed as Title II of the Internal Security Act of 1950, the Emergency Detention Act, 64 Stat. 1019. The legislation empowered the President, in a self-proclaimed "internal security emergency," "to apprehend and by order detain, pursuant to the provisions of this title, each person as to whom there is reasonable ground to believe that such person probably will engage in, or probably will conspire with others to engage in, acts of espionage or of sabotage." Eighteen years later a report of the House Un-American Activities Committee recommended the use of such camps for certain categories of persons arrested in urban riots, a proposal which understandably enraged blacks especially. The Emergency Detention Act was eventually repealed by Congress in 1971. The repealer also declared that "[n]o citizen shall be imprisoned or otherwise detained by the United States except pursuant to an Act of Congress." 85 Stat. 347.

Part II

THE DISTRIBUTION OF POWER BETWEEN THE NATIONAL GOVERNMENT AND THE STATES

Chapter 5

General Issues of the Federal Relationship

Federalism is one of the hallmarks of the American political system. Briefly put, it can be defined as a principle of government which provides for the division of powers between a national government and a collection of state governments operating over the same geographical area. As a design for the operation of government, this concept is as fraught with conflict as would be the game plan of a football team with two quarterbacks. If we are not to be subjected to the kind of turmoil and paralysis that surfaced during the era of the Articles of Confederation, some sorting and allocation of functions must occur, and that is the principal focus of this and the three succeeding chapters.

At the outset it would be appropriate to consider whether or not any extended discussion is necessary. Many observers have long questioned the utility of such an eighteenth-century system in a twentieth-century world and concluded that the confusion it spawns isn't worth the price we pay. You will have to make your own judgment, but we think it is important in giving the concept fair consideration to state its justification boldly at the beginning. Moreover, that justification cannot be merely legal or historical. It is undeniable that the contractual theory of government had considerable bearing on the genesis of the federal system—that the Union was the creation of an agreement providing that the states give up certain powers to a national government and retain certain other powers and that, as to the former, the national government was to be supreme—but stale arguments over who signed the contract and which powers were which are unlikely to present any substantial refutation to the charge that the system is outmoded today. Nor is historical discussion of the origins of the federal system likely to do much better. Whatever Hamilton may have thought of a more unitary system and Jeffersonian partisans distinctly to the contrary, a unique bargain struck nearly 200 years ago doesn't carry much weight by itself as to why such a system should continue. Legal and historical arguments are not likely to survive unless they come to grips with more pressing and powerful political considerations.

Though there are other points to be made in its behalf, such as administrative convenience and the diversity of the population, the crux of the argument for a federal system comes down to the asserted relationship between the dispersion of governmental power and the preservation of personal freedom. As such, federalism, shares the same justification as does the concept of checks and balances which was the primary focus of attention in the preceding four chapters.

The argument goes something like this: the centralization of governmental power breeds tyranny, where tyranny is essentially defined as the systematic exploitation of most of the populace by a narrow self-serving few. To avoid this possibility, governmental power is diffused—on several levels of government (as well as among various branches on each of the levels) operating over large areas of land. This dispersion of power multiplies the points of government by which people can influence and control the coercive power that is government's. By diffusing power broadly you minimize the possibility that any faction or narrow interest group can go around and sew up enough of these access points so as to push through the kind of policy that would exploit everybody else. This diffusion of power forces groups to engage in coalition building since only a substantial coalition would be large enough to control enough access points to enact and sustain policy. As the size of the coalition grows, the narrow interest of factions comprising it must broaden to accommodate other groups. As the coalition grows in size, compromise will increase the breadth of its interests until, at the point it is large enough to capture government, it represents something broad enough to approximate the public interest. In the words of James Madison in *Federalist No. 51*:

> * * * But what is government itself but the greatest of all reflections on human nature? If men were angels, no government would be necessary. If angels were to govern men, neither external nor internal controls on government would be necessary. In framing a government which is to be administered by men over men, the great difficulty lies in this: You must first enable the government to control the governed; and in the next place, oblige it to control itself. A dependence on the people is no doubt the primary control on the government; but experience has taught mankind the necessity of auxiliary precautions.

> This policy of supplying by opposite and rival interests, the defect of better motives, might be traced through the whole system of human affairs, private as well as public. We see it particularly displayed in all the subordinate distributions of power; where the constant aim is to divide and arrange the several offices in such a manner as that each may be a check on the other; that the private interest of every individual, may be a centinel over the public rights. These inventions of prudence cannot be less requisite in the distribution of the supreme powers of the state.

It is this justification together with all the suppositions which support or detract from it (such as the primacy of self-interest, the vigilance of the electorate, the equal chance of all groups for political participation, etc.)

which must be weighed against the confusion and conflict inherent in a federal system and in the context of specific problems. Needless to say, the answer to this vexing question cannot be achieved by dismissing the federal system out of hand.

From the birth of the Constitution to the present, two broad schools of thought have dominated the discussion of the nature and scope of the federal relationship. For our purposes, we designate these views as the schools of dual and cooperative federalism. It goes without saying, of course, that an endless variety of both positions has been articulated since and before 1787, but we mean to focus only on the general contours of the dispute not a cataloging of all the different views espoused.

The philosophy of dual federalism is essentially the exposition of the states' rights position. It is that conception of the federal system which views the powers of the national government and the states as mutually exclusive, conflicting, and antagonistic. It finds Madison's observation on the purpose of the federal system in helping to diffuse power best served by adopting a mode of constitutional interpretation which sets the powers of national and state governments in conflict. This tension, which is desirable for its assumed capacity to check tyranny, is made possible by the supposition that the functions of national and state governments are distinct and separable. There is thought to be no confusion if the national government confines itself to those powers enumerated in Article I, section 8 of the Constitution; those not so enumerated are reserved to the states. In the words of the late Professor Morton Grodzins, such a philosophy pictures the federal system as "a layer cake"—each level of government clearly distinct from the other. James Bryce, writing in the late nineteenth century in his book, *The American Commonwealth*, relied upon a different analogy. Said Bryce, "The system is like a great factory wherein two sets of machinery are at work, their revolving wheels apparently intermixed, their bands crossing one another, yet each set doing its own work without touching or hampering the other." Regardless of which analogy you prefer, the point is the same: in terms of the divisibility of governmental functions, everything had a place and the Constitution put everything in its place.

From time to time this view of the federal system was buttressed by its own interpretation of the contractual origins of the Constitution. This could be summed up by the view that the national government and the states were dual sovereigns. This was so because the Constitution was a compact among the states which, on certain enumerated issues, ceded a portion of their sovereignty to the national government. That portion of their sovereignty not ceded was retained.

The legal application of this philosophy found several outlets. First and foremost was a literal interpretation given to the enumerated powers of the national government and an extraordinarily limited reliance on any amplification which these powers received from the Necessary and Proper Clause contained in Article I, section 8. In sum, the dual federalists came to read Article I, section 8 much as one would read a statute—closely. Unless the national government were granted a power specifically, the assumption was against the exercise of power. Secondly, the dual federalists saw the Tenth Amendment as a viable base of support which could be used to rule actions of the national government unconstitutional. Congress, in their view, may not invade the reserved powers of the states. In their heyday advocates of dual federalism took the position that if, in the exercise of its enumerated powers, the national government happened to touch upon the functions reserved to the states, then the action of the national government was unconstitutional.

An extreme manifestation of this philosophy was unilateral action by the states, severally or individually, invalidating either single acts of the national government (as, for example, South Carolina's response to the national tariff in 1833) or the constitutional contract itself. The Civil War, of course, settled once and for all the legal quality of such acts as nullification and secession.

While the more virulent expressions of states' rights philosophy have never been countenanced by the Court, a majority of the Justices have entertained a somewhat dualist position during two periods, the first coinciding roughly with the tenure of Chief Justice Roger Taney (1835–1864) and the second covering the four decades between 1895 and 1937. In the next and succeeding chapters you will be examining Court opinions of these periods which utilize dualist approaches to constitutional interpretation, particularly in striking down congressional attempts to regulate business. More emphatic statements of the dualist position have come from outside the judicial arena. Madison and Jefferson's authorship of The Virginia and Kentucky Resolutions, Haynes's side of the debate with Webster, Calhoun's arguments on the nature of the Union, and more recently, the efforts of Governors Faubus and Wallace to interpose state authority against federal court desegregation rulings, all share a common heritage in the dualist position.

An alternative view of the national-state relationship is offered by the philosophy of cooperative federalism. Although the phrase is of fairly recent origin and has been used by some scholars to denote merely a meshing of national and state interests and policies, we use the term here in a more expansive and inclusive sense. Cooperative federalism, in our view, is a concept of partnership between the national and state governments which acknowledges the fact of national supremacy and the reality that the terms of the partnership are almost entirely fixed by the strength and power of the central government. The crush of modern-day conditions, generated by industrialism and war, has created conditions of nationwide and world interdependence which have moved groups to demand more and more of government. The role of positive government in the life of a developed nation has made the negative assumption of the dualist view (namely, that government governs best which governs least) increasingly inappropriate. The long and short of it is that the industrialism and commercial development which we have achieved, and which was anticipated by Hamilton, simply overtook and rendered obsolete the agrarian democracy envisioned by Jefferson which substantially motivated the earliest expression of the dual federalist view.

Despite the acceptance of the primacy of the central government in the federal relationship, the cooperative federalist approach searches for ways to maintain and exploit the utility of the states in serving the general populace. This has led, most notably, to efforts at dovetailing the superior experimental and administrative capacities of the states with the greater financial resources of the national government. These efforts, which date from the Northwest Ordinance to the contemporary grant-in-aid programs for highway and mass transit construction, housing, health, education, worker's compensation—to name only a few—epitomize the cooperative joining of national money and guidelines with the administrative organization of the states. Thus the central government seeks to coordinate attacks on problems lying traditionally within the purview of the states but which, because states cannot or will not eradicate them, have cumulatively assumed national proportions. More recently, the ineffectiveness or unresponsiveness of the states in treating these ills, which have centered increasingly in urban areas, has led to the emergence of a newer and competing federal relationship—that between the national government and the cities.

In the nationalistic outlook of cooperative federalism the Constitution is not seen as a contract among the states but as a contract among "We the People" to take from the states certain of their powers and vest them in a national government. In somewhat more legalistic language, then, the Union is not comprised of dual sovereigns, but of only one—the ultimate sovereign—the people. Experience verifies what logic would convey: the extreme manifestations of dualism, nullification and secession, have been accorded no standing or tolerance whatsoever in this view of the federal relationship.

The mode of constitutional interpretation to be favored likewise follows. Where dualists rely consistently on a literal or strict reading of the powers enumerated in Article I, section 8, advocates of cooperative federalism have long championed a broad and expansive view. As Chief Justice Marshall made clear in his opinion for the Court in *McCulloch* v. *Maryland* (p. 137), the enumerated powers of the national government are not to be read solely as the only means by which the national government is capable of acting, but as means which carry with them the power to achieve certain ends. Unlike the dualists, then, who read the Constitution rather like a statute, Marshall warned, "we must never forget that it is *a constitution* we are expounding." These enumerated powers must be considered, as *McCulloch* makes clear, in the light of an amplifying Necessary and Proper Clause.

A second tool of constitutional interpretation relied upon by cooperative federalism, in conjunction with broad construction, is the Supremacy Clause (Article VI, paragraph 2). In its sphere, regardless of what state powers and functions it may touch or what spillover effects it may create by its actions, the national government is supreme, and its policies are of exclusive effect when it uses its combination of enumerated and implied powers. In answering the second question to be considered in *McCulloch*, namely, "Whether the State of Maryland may, without violating the constitution, tax that branch [bank of the United States]," Marshall observed:

> In making this construction, no principle not declared, can be admissible, which would defeat the legitimate operations of a supreme government. It is of the very essence of supremacy to remove all obstacles to its action within its own sphere, and so to modify every power vested in subordinate governments, as to exempt its own operations from their own influence. This effect need not be stated in terms. It is so involved in the declaration of supremacy, so necessarily implied in it that the expression of it could not make it more certain.

Hence, it follows that the answer to the question must be "No":

> That the power to tax involves the power to destroy; that the power to destroy may defeat and render useless the power to create; that there is a plain repugnance, in conferring on one government a power to control the constitutional measures of another, which other, with respect to those very measures, is declared to be supreme over that which exerts the control, are propositions not to be denied.

A final and correlative tool in the application of the cooperative federalist view is an emasculative interpretation of the Tenth Amendment. The manner of doing so is to deny that the amendment constitutes any affirmative base of power from which the states may challenge the wide-ranging effects of national legislation. Part of this interpretation was achieved by Marshall in *McCulloch* when, with regard to the Tenth Amendment (which reads: "The powers not delegated to the United States by the Constitution, nor prohibited by it to the States, are reserved to the States respectively, or to the people."), he observed, "Even the 10th amendment, which was framed for the purpose of quieting the excessive jealousies which had been excited [by the adoption of the Constitution], omits the word 'expressly' * * *." The point was driven home again over a hundred years later by Justice Stone, speaking for the Court in the *Darby* case which you will encounter in the next chapter:

> The amendment states but a truism that all is retained which has not been surrendered. There is nothing in the history of its adoption to suggest that it was more than declaratory of the relationship between the national and state governments as it had been established by the Constitution before the amendment or that its purpose was other than to allay fears that the new national government might seek to exercise powers not granted, and that the states might not be able to exercise fully their reserved powers.

The nationalistic tenor of the cooperative view is superbly illustrated not only by the opinions of the Marshall Court (1801–1835), but also by Hamilton's financial plan, Webster's reply to Hayne in the nullification debate, Lincoln's view of the Union, the "New Nationalism" of Theodore Roosevelt, and the "New Deal" of Franklin Roosevelt.

Whether out of personal choice or compelling circumstances, most of the Justices over the last half century have come resolutely to adopt the philosophy of cooperative federalism. Most of the cases which follow in this chapter illustrate some variation on this theme.

As we have noted, the interests of national supremacy were given an extraordinary boost by the Court under Chief Justice Marshall. We have already examined the pivotal importance of his opinion for the Court in *McCulloch* v. *Maryland* (p. 137). Consider again the cases of Cohens v. Virginia, 19 U.S. (6 Wheat.) 264, 5 L.Ed. 257 (1821) and Martin v. Hunter's Lessee, 14 U.S. (1 Wheat.) 304, 4 L.Ed. 97 (1816), discussed in Chapter 1. Those decisions on the binding quality of Supreme Court decisions resolving controversies appealed from state tribunals are part and parcel of this theme of national supremacy, and, as you will find in Chapter 6, Marshall's opinion for the Court in *Gibbons* v. *Ogden* in 1824, interpreting the scope of the Commerce Clause, runs in the same direction. These decisions were crucial to overcoming the strong centrifugal forces in the federal system that threatened the survival of the Nation in its infant years.

While later courts never overruled any of these critical decisions of the Marshall Court, some of them, under dual federalist influence, did succeed in overturning Marshall's dictum in *McCulloch*. There Marshall heatedly denied that "every argument which would sustain the right of the general government to tax banks chartered by the states will equally sustain the right of the state to tax banks chartered by the general government." The difference in the arguments is the element of supremacy in favor of the national government. This position was modified by the Supreme Court later in Collector v. Day, 78 U.S. (11 Wall.) 113, 20 L.Ed. 122 (1871), a decision holding that the salaries of state judges were immune from the effects of a national income tax. The basis for such a decision was the Court's acceptance of a doctrine of intergovernmental tax immunity, predicated on the necessary assumption that both governments were due equal deference. As more decisions followed *Collector* v. *Day*, the scope of the reciprocal immunity grew to include, for example, tax exemption of the earnings of companies doing business with those governments. As the Court expanded the concept of what were considered to be instrumentalities of federal and state government, both governments came progressively to be denied more and more sources of revenue. Eventually, in Graves v. People of State of New York ex rel. O'Keefe, 306 U.S. 466, 59 S.Ct. 595 (1939), the Court overruled *Collector* v. *Day* and reestablished the tax liability of the personnel of both governments. The loophole was closed still further in *New York* v. *United States* (p. 365) seven years later when the Court had occasion to rule on the tax liability of New York for mineral water it bottled and sold. In that case the Court was divided as to whether to apply its prior ruling in South Carolina v. United States, 199 U.S. 437, 26 S.Ct. 110 (1905), taxing that state's monopoly on the sale of liquor on the basis that such a function was not governmental but "proprietary" and hence no different from any activity that, if carried on by private business, would be taxable. Consider the *New York* case carefully, not only in reaching your own conclusion as to whether you think the Court reached a sound judgment in applying the *South Carolina* precedent, but also in examining the distinction between the assignment of tax liability on the basis of "governmental" or "nongovernmental" functions.

From either a legal or political science standpoint, is this dichotomy defensible?

The financial aspects of the cooperative approach to the federal relationship are forcefully illustrated in *Steward Machine Co.* v. *Davis* (p. 371). We noted earlier that we have had a long tradition of joint cooperation between the two levels of government—whether or not the Court has chosen at times to recognize it—in financing programs traditionally regarded as falling within the province of the states. The social security program, the constitutionality of which was at stake in the *Steward Machine Co.* case, is a classic illustration of how these programs operate—the exchange of federal money, usually on a liberal matching basis, for the acceptance by the states of federally imposed guidelines. Note carefully how this program follows the contours of the federal relationship even as Justice Cardozo acknowledges the national magnitude of the unemployment and welfare problems brought on by the Great Depression. Since the national government has no general power to legislate for the general welfare, its program, in accordance with the first provision of Article I, section 8, must be hitched to a taxing and spending scheme. You should also give close attention to the debate between Justice Cardozo, speaking for the majority, and the four dissenters as to the contention that states are coerced to participate in such a program. Have the states been raped, as conservative opponents of the program contend, or were they merely seduced? It is interesting, years later, to watch how some contemporary liberals sought to put a new slant on the use of the Tenth Amendment in order to further increase the involvement of the national government in welfare responsibilities. Consider the novel argument made by the mayor and other New York City officials trying to meet critical urban problems in the face of a declining revenue base (p. 377).

When we speak of a cooperative federal enterprise, but one in which the central government is conceded to have the decisive word, we frequently encounter the vexing problem of whether the national government has meant to entirely or only partially occupy a given policy field. We must persistently deal with the issue of whether Congress has chosen, explicitly or implicitly, to exercise exclusive or concurrent supervision. When Congress has chosen to occupy the entire field, we say that it has "preempted" state action. Since very often Congress is less than clear about its intent or has deliberately left the question unsettled, the Court as "umpire of the federal system" is left to make the determination subject, of course, to any corrective legislation which Congress may choose to enact after looking at the Court's conclusion. In doing so, the Court is necessarily moved to balance contending national and state interests. Speaking for the Court in *Pennsylvania* v. *Nelson* (p. 378), Chief Justice Warren spelled out the primary considerations in resolving such a question. As applied in that case, the criteria resulted in invalidating a state sedition statute because of Congress's perceived intent to occupy the field with the Smith Act of 1940. The case is particularly instructive because its aftermath indicates what a risky business this process of trying to second-guess the Congress can be. A significant number of congressmen were so incensed by what they saw as the Court's heavy-handed use of the preemption doctrine that proposals to overturn the ruling were only narrowly foiled. (See the discussion of the Court-curbing legislation considered by Congress in the late 'fifties at p. 219.) Finally, as the note to the *Nelson* case makes clear, the interest-balancing method necessitated by the preemption doctrine takes place on an *ad hoc* basis and is heavily, if not decisively, influenced by the specifics of the case at hand. More recently, the Court employed the preemption doctrine along the lines sketched out in *Nelson* in reaching its decision holding unconstitutional a municipal noise abatement ordinance in *City of Burbank* v. *Lockheed Air Terminal* (p. 579).

Affection for the principles and values of dual federalism, out of favor with the Court for so much of its modern history (that period dating from the Great Depression), appears to have been rekindled in several rulings of the Burger Court, two of which are included here. In *Younger* v. *Harris* (p. 395), one of its early decisions, the Court heralded a renewed interest in "Our Federalism," which it described as embodying "a proper respect for state functions, a recognition of the fact that the entire country is made up of a Union of separate state governments, and a continuance of the belief that the National Government will fare best if the States and their institutions are left free to perform their separate functions in their separate ways." Allegiance to this concept infused new life into the Tenth Amendment in *National League of Cities* v. *Usery* (p. 384) over the stiff protest of Justice Brennan. Subsequent decisions (p. 393), however, suggest that the decision in *National League of Cities* may prove to be of very limited applicability. Indeed, succeeding decisions crystalizing and applying the test sketched out in *National League of Cities* suggest an analysis strikingly similar to that reviewed by the Court in *New York* v. *United States*. Also illustrative of increased deference to the exercise of state prerogatives in the federal system is, as we have noted, the decision in *Younger* v. *Harris*. In that case the Court ruled that, apart from exceptional circumstances, federal courts ought not to interfere in state criminal prosecutions until such proceedings have run their course. In the Court's view the prospect that employment of a state's criminal sanctions may have a "chilling effect" on the exercise of an individual's constitutional rights did not furnish an adequate reason for what it saw as premature federal judicial intervention. In both of these cases the Burger Court advanced a conception of the federal system quite different from that held by the Warren Court whose rulings in Maryland v. Wirtz, 392 U.S. 183, 88 S.Ct. 2017 (1968) and Dombrowski v. Pfister, 380 U.S. 479, 85 S.Ct. 1116 (1965), were overturned by *National League of Cities* and *Younger* respectively.

Whatever may be said of the Court's newfound deference to the states' prerogative of pursuing prosecutions pending before their tribunals, the Court has never held that any deference was constitutionally due the states in their compliance with judgments announced by the federal courts. Just as the Supremacy Clause insures the right to appeal a state court judgment on a federal constitutional question to the United States Supreme Court, the clause binds the states to comply with the Court's ruling when it is rendered. In *Cooper* v. *Aaron* (p. 710), for example, the

Court, adamant in its determination to stand by its 1954 school desegregation decision, underscored this canon of constitutional law.

Thus far, our focus in examining the Court's application of cooperative federalism and the concomitant doctrine of national supremacy has been on domestic sources of controversy. A final problem area is raised when we turn your attention to the impact of international agreements on the structure of the federal relationship. Recall that Article VI, paragraph 2 of the Constitution provides: "This Constitution and the Laws of the United States which shall be made in Pursuance thereof; and all Treaties made, or which shall be made, under the Authority of the United States, shall be the supreme Law of the Land * * *." In 1880, in Hauenstein v. Lynham, 100 U.S. 483, 25 L.Ed. 628, a unanimous Court had no difficulty concluding that Virginia was barred from enforcing a statute, which provided that real estate of aliens dying without a will defaulted to the state, against Swiss heirs to the property by virtue of a treaty signed between Switzerland and the United States in 1850 giving the heirs title to the property.

Missouri v. *Holland* (p. 400) would certainly appear to suggest that treaties which contradict an express provision of the Constitution would be null and void. Dualists, however, worry about a more subtle problem: could the national government alter the federal relationship by taking powers away from the states under the treaty power, thus avoiding the customary constitutional procedure of amendment? Justice Holmes's treatment of the issue in *Missouri* v. *Holland* underscores the possibility. Certainly his fleeting treatment of the Tenth Amendment is not encouraging to dualists, but the opinion is equivocal. Much emphasis, for example, is put on a feature of the controversy peculiar to this case—the migratory quality of the birds and the consequent lack of a substantial state claim. Fears of the dualists were heightened by the *Belmont* decision (p. 402) which presented the spector of a state's public policy being thwarted by a simple executive agreement. The proliferation of executive agreements and the decline in the use of the formalities of the treaty power magnify what seem to some observers to be the dangers of this loophole in the federal relationship. One of the sharpest manifestations of this concern surfaced in the proposed Bricker Amendment (p. 405) which was aimed at terminating both the self-executing quality of treaties, like that in the *Hauenstein* case, as well as the possibility that the treaty power could be used to make an end run around the formal amendment process. The effort failed, though probably less from any burning persuasiveness of the cooperative federalist view on the part of the administration than from the personal concern of President Eisenhower over what he saw as the isolationist motivation behind the measure.

McCULLOCH v. MARYLAND

Supreme Court of the United States, 1819
17 U.S. (4 Wheat.) 316, 4 L.Ed. 579

See p. 137.

NEW YORK v. UNITED STATES

Supreme Court of the United States, 1946
326 U.S. 572, 66 S.Ct. 310, 90 L.Ed. 326

Under a federal revenue act passed in 1932, producers, bottlers, and importers of mineral water were subject to a two-cent tax on every gallon sold at over $12\frac{1}{2}$ cents each. Like other states which had taken over the operation of certain commercial enterprises, New York State, through a public corporation, bottled and sold mineral water. It, however, refused to pay the tax claiming that, since this was a governmental function, it was, as such, immune from taxation. The United States brought suit in federal district court to recover the taxes, and the decision of that court in favor of the national government was affirmed subsequently by a U. S. Circuit Court of Appeals.

Mr. Justice FRANKFURTER announced the judgment of the Court and delivered an opinion in which Mr. Justice RUTLEDGE joined.

*   *   *

On the basis of authority the case is quickly disposed of. When States sought to control the liquor traffic by going into the liquor business, they were denied immunity from federal taxes upon the liquor business. State of South Carolina v. United States, 199 U.S. 437, 26 S.Ct. 110. * * * And in rejecting a claim of immunity from federal taxation when Massachusetts took over the street railways of Boston, this Court a decade ago said: "We see no reason for putting the operation of a street railway [by a State] in a different category from the sale of liquors." Helvering v. Powers, 293 U.S. 214, 227, 55 S.Ct. 171. We certainly see no reason for putting soft drinks in a different constitutional category from hard drinks. * * *

One of the greatest sources of strength of our law is that it adjudi-

cates concrete cases and does not pronounce principles in the abstract. But there comes a time when even the process of empiric adjudication calls for a more rational disposition than that the immediate case is not different from preceding cases. The argument pressed by New York and the forty-five other States who, as amici curiae, have joined her deserves an answer.

*   *   *

But the fear that one government may cripple or obstruct the operations of the other early led to the assumption that there was a reciprocal immunity of the instrumentalities of each from taxation by the other. It was assumed that there was an equivalence in the implications of taxation by a State of the governmental activities of the National Government and the taxation by the National Government of State instrumentalities. This assumed equivalence was nourished by the phrase of Chief Justice Marshall that "the power to tax involves the power to destroy." McCulloch v. Maryland, 4 Wheat. 316, 431, 4 L.Ed. 579. To be sure, it was uttered in connection with a tax of Maryland which plainly discriminated against the use by the United States of the Bank of the United States as one of its instruments. What he said may not have been irrelevant in its setting. But Chief Justice Marshall spoke at a time when social complexities did not so clearly reveal as now the practical limitations of a rhetorical absolute. * * * The phrase was seized upon as the basis of a broad doctrine of intergovernmental immunity, while at the same time an expansive scope was given to what were deemed to be "instrumentalities of the government" for purposes of tax immunity. As a result, immunity was until recently accorded to all officers of one government from taxation by the other, and it was further assumed that the economic burden of a tax on any interest derived from a government imposes a burden on that government so as to involve an interference by the taxing government with the functioning of the other government. * * *

" * * * When a state enters the market place seeking customers it divests itself of its quasi sovereignty pro tanto, and takes on the character of a trader, so far, at least, as the taxing power of the federal government is concerned." State of Ohio v. Helvering, 292 U.S. at page 369, 54 S.Ct. at page 726. * * *

When this Court came to sustain the federal taxing power upon a transportation system operated by a State, it did so in ways familiar in developing the law from precedent to precedent. It edged away from reliance on a sharp distinction between the "governmental" and the "trading" activities of a State, by denying immunity from federal taxation to a State when it "is undertaking a business enterprise of a sort that is normally within the reach of the federal taxing power and is distinct from the usual governmental functions that are immune from federal taxation in order to safeguard the necessary independence of the state." Helvering v. Powers, * * * 293 U.S. at page 227, 55 S.Ct. at page 174. * * * But this likewise does not furnish a satisfactory guide for dealing with such a practical problem as the constitutional power of the United States over State activities. To rest the federal taxing power on what is "normally" conducted by private enterprise in contradiction to the "usual" governmental functions is too shifting a basis for determining constitutional power and too entangled in expediency to serve as a dependable legal criterion. The essential nature of the problem cannot be hidden by an attempt to separate manifestations of indivisible governmental powers. * * *

The present case illustrates the sterility of such an attempt. New York urges that in the use it is making of Saratoga Springs it is engaged in the disposition of its natural resources. And so it is. But in doing so it is engaged in an enterprise in which the State sells mineral waters in competition with private waters, the sale of which Congress has found necessary to tap as a source of revenue for carrying on the National Government. To say that the States cannot be taxed for enterprises generally pursued, like the sale of mineral water, because it is somewhat connected with a State's conservation policy, is to invoke an irrelevance to the federal taxing power. Liquor control by a State certainly concerns the most important of a State's natural resources—the health and well-being of its people. * * * If in its wisdom a State engages in the liquor business and may be taxed by Congress as others engaged in the liquor business are taxed, so also Congress may tax the States when they go into the business of bottling water as others in the mineral water business are taxed even though a State's sale of its mineral waters has relation to its conservation policy.

* * *

* * * There are, of course, State activities and State-owned property that partake of uniqueness from the point of view of intergovernmental relations. These inherently constitute a class by themselves. Only a State can own a Statehouse; only a State can get income by taxing. These could not be included for purposes of federal taxation in any abstract category of taxpayers without taxing the State as a State. But so long as Congress generally taps a source of revenue by whomsoever earned and not uniquely capable of being earned only by a State, the Constitution of the United States does not forbid it merely because its incidence falls also on a State. If Congress desires, it may of course leave untaxed enterprises pursued by States for the public good while it taxes like enterprises organized for private ends. * * * If Congress makes no such differentiation and, as in this case, taxes all vendors of mineral water alike, whether State vendors or private vendors, it simply says, in effect, to a State: "You may carry out your own notions of social policy in engaging in what is called business, but you must pay your share in having a nation which enables you to pursue your policy." After all, the representatives of all the States, having, as the appearance of the Attorneys General of forty-six States at the bar of this Court shows, common interests, alone can pass such a taxing measure and they alone in their wisdom can grant or withhold immunity from federal taxation of such State activities.

The process of Constitutional adjudication does not thrive on conjuring up horrible possibilities that never happen in the real world and devising doctrines sufficiently comprehensive in detail to cover the remotest contingency. Nor need we go beyond what is required for a reasoned disposition of the kind of controversy now before the Court. The restriction upon States not to make laws that discriminate against interstate commerce is a vital constitutional principle, even though "discrimination" is not a code of specifics but a continuous process of application. So we decide enough when we reject limitations upon the taxing power of Congress derived from such untenable criteria as "proprietary" against "governmental" activities of the States, or historically sanctioned activities of Government or activities conducted merely for profit, and find no restriction upon Congress to include the States in levying a tax exacted equally from private persons upon the same subject matter.

Judgment affirmed.

Mr. Justice JACKSON took no part in the consideration or decision of this case.

Mr. Justice RUTLEDGE, concurring.

I join in the opinion of Mr. Justice FRANKFURTER and in the result. I have no doubt upon the question of power. The shift from immunity to taxability has gone too far, and with too much reason to sustain it, as respects both state functionaries and state functions, for backtracking to doctrines founded in philosophies of sovereignty more current and perhaps more realistic in an earlier day. Too much is, or may be, at stake for the nation to permit relieving the states of their duty to support it, financially as otherwise, when they take over increasingly the things men have been accustomed to carry on as private, and therefore taxable, enterprise. Competitive considerations unite with the necessity for securing the federal revenue, in a time when the federal burden grows heavier proportionately than that of the states, to forbid that they be free to undermine rather than obligated to sustain the nation's financial requirements.

* * *

With the passing of the former broad immunity, I should think two considerations well might be taken to require that, before a federal tax can be applied to activities carried on directly by the states, the intention of Congress to tax them should be stated expressly and not drawn merely from general wording of the statute applicable ordinarily to private sources of revenue. One of these is simply a reflection of the old immunity, in the presence of which, of course, it would be inconceivable that general wording, such as the statute now in question contains, could be taken as intended to apply to the states. The other is that, quite apart from reflections of that immunity, I should expect that Congress would say so explicitly, were its purpose actually to include state functions, where the legal incidence of the tax falls upon the state. And the concurring opinion of Mr. Justice Brad-

ley in United States v. Baltimore & Ohio R. Co., 17 Wall. 322, 333, 21 L.Ed. 597, indicates that he may have been of this general view.

Nevertheless, since *State of South Carolina* v. *United States*, supra, such a rule of construction seems not to have been thought required. Accordingly, although I gravely doubt that when Congress taxed every "person" it intended also to tax every state, the ruling has been made and I therefore acquiesce in this case.

Mr. Chief Justice STONE, concurring.

Mr. Justice REED, Mr. Justice MURPHY, Mr. Justice BURTON and I concur in the result. We are of the opinion that the tax here involved should be sustained and the judgment below affirmed.

In view of our [earlier] decisions * * * we would find it difficult not to sustain the tax in this case, even though we regard as untenable the distinction between "governmental" and "proprietary" interests on which those cases rest to some extent. But we are not prepared to say that the national government may constitutionally lay a nondiscriminatory tax on every class of property and activities of States and individuals alike.

Concededly a federal tax discriminating against a State would be an unconstitutional exertion of power over a coexisting sovereignty within the same framework of government. But our difficulty with the formula, now first suggested as offering a new solution for an old problem is that a federal tax which is not discriminatory as to the subject matter may nevertheless so affect the State, merely because it is a State that is being taxed, as to interfere unduly with the State's performance of its sovereign functions of government. The counterpart of such undue interference has been recognized since Marshall's day as the implied immunity of each of the dual sovereignties of our constitutional system from taxation by the other. McCulloch v. Maryland, 4 Wheat. 316, 4 L.Ed. 519. We add nothing to this formula by saying, in a new form of words, that a tax which Congress applies generally to the property and activities of private citizens may not be in some instances constitutionally extended to the States, merely because the States are included among those who pay taxes on a like subject of taxation.

Mr. Justice DOUGLAS, with whom Mr. Justice BLACK concurs, dissenting.

If *State of South Carolina* v. *United States* * * * is to stand, the present judgment would have to be affirmed. For I agree that there is no essential difference between a federal tax on South Carolina's liquor business and a federal tax on New York's mineral water business. Whether *State of South Carolina* v. *United States* reaches the right result is another matter.

Mr. Justice Brandeis stated that "Stare decisis is usually the wise policy, because in most matters it is more important that the applicable rule of law be settled than that it be settled right." * * * But throughout the history of the Court stare decisis has had only a limited application in the field of constitutional law. And it is a wise policy which largely restricts it to those areas of the law where correction can be had by legislation. Otherwise the Constitution loses the flexibility nec-

essary if it is to serve the needs of successive generations.

I do not believe *State of South Carolina* v. *United States* states the correct rule. A State's project is as much a legitimate governmental activity whether it is traditional, or akin to private enterprise, or conducted for profit. * * * A State may deem it as essential to its economy that it own and operate a railroad, a mill, or an irrigation system as it does to own and operate bridges, street lights, or a sewage disposal plant. * * *

One view, just announced, purports to reject the distinction which *State of South Carolina* v. *United States* drew between those activities of a State which are and those which are not strictly governmental, usual, or traditional. But it is said that a federal tax on a State will be sustained so long as Congress "does not attempt to tax a State because it is a State." Yet if that means that a federal real estate tax of general application (apportioned) would be valid if applied to a power dam owned by a state but invalid if applied to a state-house, the old doctrine has merely been poured into a new container. If, on the other hand, any federal tax on any state activity were sustained unless it discriminated against the State, then a constitutional rule would be fashioned which would undermine the sovereignty of the States as it has been understood throughout our history. Any such change should be accomplished only by constitutional amendment. The doctrine of state immunity is too intricately involved in projects which have been launched to be whittled down by judicial fiat.

* * *

A tax is a powerful, regulatory instrument. Local government in this free land does not exist for itself. The fact that local government may enter the domain of private enterprise and operate a project for profit does not put it in the class of private business enterprise for tax purposes. Local government exists to provide for the welfare of its people, not for a limited group of stockholders. If the federal government can place the local governments on its tax collector's list, their capacity to serve the needs of their citizens is at once hampered or curtailed. The field of federal excise taxation alone is practically without limits. Many state activities are in marginal enterprises where private capital refuses to venture. Add to the cost of these projects a federal tax and the social program may be destroyed before it can be launched. In any case, the repercussions of such a fundamental change on the credit of the States and on their programs to take care of the needy and to build for the future would be considerable. To say the present tax will be sustained because it does not impair the State's functions of government is to conclude either that the sale by the State of its mineral water is not a function of government or that the present tax is so slight as to be no burden. The former obviously is not true. The latter overlooks the fact that the power to tax lightly is the power to tax severely. The power to tax is indeed one of the most effective forms of regulation. And no more powerful instrument for centralization of government could be devised. For with the federal government immune and the States sub-

ject to tax, the economic ability of the federal government to expand its activities at the expense of the States is at once apparent. That is the result whether the rule of *State of South Carolina* v. *United States* be perpetuated or a new rule of discrimination be adopted.

* * *

Those who agreed with *State of South Carolina* v. *United States* had the fear that an expanding program of state activity would dry up sources of federal revenues and thus cripple the national government. * * * That was in 1905. That fear is expressed again today when we have the federal income tax, from which employees of the States may not claim exemption on constitutional grounds. * * * The fear of depriving the national government of revenue if the tax immunity of the States is sustained has no more place in the present decision than the spectre of socialism, the fear of which, said Holmes "was translated into doctrines that had no proper place in the Constitution or the common law."

There is no showing whatsoever that an expanding field of state activity even faintly promises to cripple the federal government in its search for needed revenues. If the truth were known, I suspect it would show that the activity of the States in the fields of housing, public power and the like have increased the level of income of the people and have raised the standards of marginal or submarginal groups. Such conditions affect favorably, not adversely, the tax potential of the federal government.

STEWARD MACHINE CO. v. DAVIS

Supreme Court of the United States, 1937
301 U.S. 548, 57 S.Ct. 883, 81 L.Ed. 1279

The Social Security Act of 1935 required employers of eight or more workers to pay a federal excise tax on a certain percentage of their employees' wages. The funds were not earmarked but were collected as general revenue and deposited in the United States Treasury. In addition, the act permitted employers who made contributions to a state unemployment fund to credit such payments against up to 90 percent of the federal tax. The state unemployment compensation program, however, had to be approved by the federal government as meeting certain minimum requirements to insure that it was a program of substance before the credit would be allowed. Also, to guard against loss of the monies, the state had to deposit its unemployment fund in the U.S. Treasury.

Under the 1935 act the Steward Machine Company paid the federal government taxes of $46.14. The company then sued Harwell Davis, an Internal Revenue official, to recover payment, contending that the Social Security Act was unconstitutional. A federal district court dismissed the complaint, and its judgment was affirmed by a U.S. Circuit Court whereupon the Steward Machine Company appealed to the Supreme Court.

Mr. Justice CARDOZO delivered the opinion of the Court.

* * *

The assault on the statute proceeds on an extended front. Its assailants take the ground that the tax is not an excise; that it is not uniform throughout the United States as excises are required to be; that its exceptions are so many and arbitrary as to violate the Fifth Amendment; that its purpose was not revenue, but an unlawful invasion of the reserved powers of the states; and that the states in submitting to it have yielded to coercion and have abandoned governmental functions which they are not permitted to surrender.

The objections will be considered seriatim with such further explanation as may be necessary to make their meaning clear.

First: The tax, which is described in the statute as an excise, is laid with uniformity throughout the United States as a duty, an impost, or an excise upon the relation of employment.

1. We are told that the relation of employment is one so essential to the pursuit of happiness that it may not be burdened with a tax. Appeal is made to history. From the precedents of colonial days, we are supplied with illustrations of excises common in the colonies. They are said to have been bound up with the enjoyment of particular commodities. Appeal is also made to principle or the analysis of concepts. An excise, we are told, imports a tax upon a privilege; employment, it is said, is a right, not a privilege, from which it follows that employment is not subject to an excise. Neither the one appeal nor the other leads to the desired goal.

As to the argument from history: Doubtless there were many excises in colonial days and later that were associated, more or less intimately, with the enjoyment or the use of property. This would not prove, even if no others were then known, that the forms then accepted were not subject to enlargement. * * *

The historical prop failing, the prop or fancied prop of principle remains. We learn that employment for lawful gain is a "natural" or "inherent" or "inalienable" right, and not a "privilege" at all. But natural rights, so called, are as much subject to taxation as rights of less importance. An excise is not limited to vocations or activities that may be prohibited altogether. It is not limited to those that are the outcome of a franchise. It extends to vocations or activities pursued as of common right. What the individual does in the operation of a business is amenable to taxation just as much as what he owns, at all events if the classification is not tyrannical or arbitrary. "Business is as legitimate an object of the taxing power as property." * * * Indeed, ownership itself, as we had occasion to point out the other day, is only a bundle of rights and privileges invested with a single name. * * * "A state is at liberty, if it pleases, to tax them all collectively, or to separate the faggots and lay the charge distributively." Id. Employment is a business relation, if not itself a business. It is a relation without which business could seldom be carried on effectively. The power to tax the activities and relations that constitute a calling considered as a unit is the power to tax any of them. The whole includes the parts. * * *

The subject-matter of taxation open to the power of the Congress is as comprehensive as that open to the power of the states, though the method of apportionment may at times be different. "The Congress shall have Power to lay and collect Taxes, Duties, Imposts and Excises." Article I, § 8. If the tax is a direct one, it shall be apportioned according to the census or enumeration. If it is a duty, impost, or excise, it shall be uniform throughout the United States. Together, these classes include every form of tax appropriate to sovereignty. * * * Whether the tax is to be classified as an "excise" is in truth not of critical importance. If not that, it is an "impost." * * * A capitation or other "direct" tax it certainly is not. "Although there have been, from time to time, intimations that there might be some tax which was not a direct tax, nor included under the words 'duties, imposts, and excises,' such a tax, for more than 100 years of national existence, has as yet remained undiscovered, notwithstanding the stress of particular circumstances has invited thorough investigation into sources of revenue." Pollock v. Farmers' Loan & Trust Co., 157 U.S. 429, 557, 15 S.Ct. 673, 680. There is no departure from that thought in later cases, but rather a new emphasis of it. * * *

The tax being an excise, its imposition must conform to the canon of uniformity. There has been no departure from this requirement. According to the settled doctrine, the uniformity exacted is geographical, not intrinsic. * * *

Second: The excise is not invalid under the provisions of the Fifth Amendment by force of its exemptions.

The statute does not apply, as we have seen, to employers of less than eight. It does not apply to agricultural labor, or domestic service in a private home or to some other classes of less importance. Petitioner contends that the effect of these restrictions is an arbitrary discrimination vitiating the tax.

The Fifth Amendment unlike the Fourteenth has no equal protection clause. * * * But even the states, though subject to such a clause, are not confined to a formula of rigid uniformity in framing measures of taxation. * * * They may tax some kinds of property at one rate, and others at another, and exempt others altogether. * * * They may lay an excise on the operations of a particular kind of business, and exempt some other kind of business closely akin thereto. * * * If this latitude of judgment is lawful for the states, it is lawful, a fortiori, in legislation by the Congress, which is subject to restraints less narrow and confining. * * *

The classifications and exemptions directed by the statute now in controversy have support in considerations of policy and practical convenience that cannot be condemned as arbitrary. The classifications and exemptions would therefore be upheld if they had been adopted by a state and the provisions of the Fourteenth Amendment were invoked to annul them. * * *

Third: The excise is not void as involving the coercion of the states in contravention of the Tenth Amendment or of restrictions implicit in our federal form of government.

The proceeds of the excise when collected are paid into the Treasury at Washington, and thereafter are subject to appropriation like public moneys generally. * * * No presumption can be indulged that they will be misapplied or wasted. Even if they were collected in the hope or expectation that some other and collateral good would be furthered as an incident, that without more would not make the act invalid. * * * This indeed is hardly questioned.

The case for the petitioner is built on the contention that here an ulterior aim is wrought into the very structure of the act, and what is even more important that the aim is not only ulterior, but essentially unlawful. In particular, the 90 per cent. credit is relied upon as supporting that conclusion. But before the statute succumbs to an assault upon these lines, two propositions must be made out by the assailant. Cincinnati Soap Co. v. United States [301 U.S. 308, 57 S.Ct. 764]. There must be a showing in the first place that separated from the credit the revenue provisions are incapable of standing by themselves. There must be a showing in the second place that the tax and the credit in combination are weapons of coercion, destroying or impairing the autonomy of the states. The truth of each proposition being essential to the success of the assault, we pass for convenience to a consideration of the second, without pausing to inquire whether there has been a demonstration of the first.

To draw the line intelligently between duress and inducement, there is need to remind ourselves of facts as to the problem of unemployment that are now matters of common knowledge. * * * During the years 1929 to 1936, when the country was passing through a cyclical depression, the number of the unemployed mounted to unprecedented heights. Often the average was more than 10 million; at times a peak was attained of 16 million or more. Disaster to the breadwinner meant disaster to dependents. Accordingly the roll of the unemployed, itself formidable enough, was only a partial roll of the destitute or needy. The fact developed quickly that the states were unable to give the requisite relief. The problem had become national in area and dimensions. There was need of help from the nation if the people were not to starve. It is too late today for the argument to be heard with tolerance that in a crisis so extreme the use of the moneys of the nation to relieve the unemployed and their dependents is a use for any purpose narrower than the promotion of the general welfare. * * *

* * *

The Social Security Act is an attempt to find a method by which all these public agencies may work together to a common end. Every dollar of the new taxes will continue in all likelihood to be used and needed by the nation as long as states are unwilling, whether through timidity or for other motives, to do what can be done at home. At least the inference is permissible that Congress so believed, though retaining undiminished freedom to spend the money as it pleased. On the other hand, fulfillment of the home duty will be lightened and encouraged by crediting the taxpayer upon his account with the Treasury of the nation to the extent that his contributions under the laws of the locality have simplified or diminished the problem of relief and the probable demand upon the resources of the fisc. Duplicated taxes, or burdens that approach them are recognized hardships that government, state or national, may properly avoid. * * * If Congress believed that the general welfare would better be promoted by relief through local units than by the system then in vogue, the co-operating localities ought not in all fairness to pay a second time.

Who then is coerced through the operation of this statute? Not the taxpayer. He pays in fulfillment of the mandate of the local legislature.

Not the state. Even now she does not offer a suggestion that in passing the unemployment law she was affected by duress. * * * For all that appears, she is satisfied with her choice, and would be sorely disappointed if it were now to be annulled. The difficulty with the petitioner's contention is that it confuses motive with coercion. "Every tax is in some measure regulatory. To some extent it interposes an economic impediment to the activity taxed as compared with others not taxed." Sonzinsky v. United States, 300 U.S. 506, 57 S.Ct. 554. In like manner every rebate from a tax when conditioned upon conduct is in some measure a temptation. But to hold that motive or temptation is equivalent to coercion is to plunge the law into endless difficulties. The outcome of such a doctrine is the acceptance of a philosophical determinism by which choice becomes impossible. Till now the law has been guided by a robust common sense which assumes the freedom of the will as a working hypothesis in the solution of its problems. The wisdom of the hypothesis has illustration in this case. Nothing in the case suggests the exertion of a power akin to undue influence, if we assume that such a concept can ever be applied with fitness to the relations between state and nation. Even on that assumption the location of the point at which pressure turns into compulsion, and ceases to be inducement, would be a question of degree, at times, perhaps, of fact. The point had not been reached when Alabama made her choice. We cannot say that she was acting, not of her unfettered will, but under the strain of a persuasion equivalent to undue influence, when she chose to have relief administered under laws of her own making, by agents of her own selection, instead of under federal laws, administered by federal officers, with all the ensuing evils, at least to many minds, of federal patronage and power. There would be a strange irony, indeed, if her choice were now to be annulled on the basis of an assumed duress in the enactment of a statute which her courts have accepted as a true expression of her will. * * * We think the choice must stand.

In ruling as we do, we leave many questions open. We do not say that a tax is valid, when imposed by act of Congress, if it is laid upon the condition that a state may escape its operation through the adoption of a statute unrelated in subject-matter to activities fairly within the scope of national policy and power. No such question is before us. * * *

The judgment is affirmed.

* * *

Separate opinion of Mr. Justice McREYNOLDS.

That portion of the Social Security legislation here under consideration, I think, exceeds the power granted to Congress. It unduly interferes with the orderly government of the state by her own people and otherwise offends the Federal Constitution.

* * *

Ordinarily, I must think, a denial that the challenged action of Congress and what has been done under it amount to coercion and impair freedom of government by the people of the state would be regarded as contrary to practical experience. Unquestionably our federate plan of government confronts an enlarged peril.

Separate opinion of Mr. Justice SUTHERLAND.

With most of what is said in the opinion just handed down, I concur. I agree that the pay roll tax levied is an excise within the power of Congress; that the devotion of not more than 90 per cent. of it to the credit of employers in states which require the payment of a similar tax under so-called unemployment-tax laws is not an unconstitutional use of the proceeds of the federal tax; that the provision making the adoption by the state of an unemployment law of a specified character a condition precedent to the credit of the tax does not render the law invalid. I agree that the states are not coerced by the federal legislation into adopting unemployment legislation. The provisions of the federal law may operate to induce the state to pass an employment law if it regards such action to be in its interest. But that is not coercion. If the act stopped here, I should accept the conclusion of the court that the legislation is not unconstitutional.

But the question with which I have difficulty is whether the administrative provisions of the act invade the governmental administrative powers of the several states reserved by the Tenth Amendment. A state may enter into contracts; but a state cannot, by contract or statute, surrender the execution, or a share in the execution, of any of its governmental powers either to a sister state or to the federal government, any more than the federal government can surrender the control of any of its governmental powers to a foreign nation. The power to tax is vital and fundamental, and, in the highest degree, governmental in character. Without it, the state could not exist.

Fundamental also, and no less important, is the governmental power to expend the moneys realized from taxation, and exclusively to administer the laws in respect of the character of the tax and the methods of laying and collecting it and expending the proceeds.

The people of the United States, by their Constitution, have affirmed a division of internal governmental powers between the federal government and the governments of the several states—committing to the first its powers by express grant and necessary implication; to the latter, or to the people, by reservation, "the powers not delegated to the United States by the Constitution, nor prohibited by it to the States." The Constitution thus affirms the complete supremacy and independence of the state within the field of its powers. Carter v. Carter Coal Co., 298 U.S. 238, 295, 56 S.Ct. 855, 865. The federal government has no more authority to invade that field than the state has to invade the exclusive field of national governmental powers; for, in the oft-repeated words of this court in Texas v. White, 7 Wall. 700, 725, 19 L.Ed. 227, "the preservation of the States, and the maintenance of their governments, are as much within the design and care of the Constitution as the preservation of the Union and the maintenance of the National government." The necessity of preserving each from every form of illegitimate intrusion or interference on the part of the other is so imperative as to require this court, when its judicial power is properly invoked, to view with a careful and discriminating eye any legislation challenged as constituting such an intrusion or interference.
* * *

The precise question, therefore, which we are required to answer by an application of these principles is whether the congressional act contemplates a surrender by the state to the federal government, in whole or in part, of any state governmental power to administer its own unemployment law or the state pay roll-tax funds which it has collected for the purposes of that law. An affirmative answer to this question, I think, must be made.

I do not, of course, doubt the power of the state to select and utilize a depository for the safe-keeping of its funds; but it is quite another thing to agree with the selected depository that the funds shall be withdrawn for certain stipulated purposes, and for no other. Nor do I doubt the authority of the federal government and a state government to co-operate to a common end, provided each of them is authorized to reach it. But such co-operation must be effectuated by an exercise of the powers which they severally possess, and not by an exercise, through invasion or surrender, by one of them of the governmental power of the other.

* * *

If we are to survive as the United States, the balance between the powers of the nation and those of the states must be maintained. There is grave danger in permitting it to dip in either direction, danger—if there were no other—in the precedent thereby set for further departures from the equipoise. The threat implicit in the present encroachment upon the administrative functions of the states is that greater encroachments, and encroachments upon other functions, will follow.

For the foregoing reasons, I think the judgment below should be reversed.

Mr. Justice VAN DEVANTER joins in this opinion.

[Justice BUTLER also dissented.]

The coercion argument so prominently advanced by conservatives in the *Steward* case surfaced again, this time in City of New York v. Richardson, 473 F.2d 923 (2d Cir. 1973), where it was being pushed by liberals. This suit against the Secretary of Health, Education, and Welfare presented an attack on the constitutionality of the Social Security Act using the Tenth Amendment in an attempt to force complete funding of welfare expenditures by the national government. The argument ran as follows: welfare is a truly national problem. Given the growing difficulty of raising revenue to support city expenditures—particularly in funding welfare—federal appropriations are essential. Under the cooperative federal design of the Social Security Act, however, funds are available only on a matching basis. Because the city is forced to make the requisite outlay in order to receive the crucial federal funds, it is deprived of resources necessary to defray the costs of local functions reserved to the states under the Tenth Amendment. The U.S. Court of Appeals, Second Circuit, rejected the ploy and, per Judge Kaufman, said in part:

> We are fully aware that metropolitan communities, faced with rising costs of local services and declining tax bases, are experiencing severe fiscal overburdening. But it seems clear that the imagination to devise a proper remedy for most of these urban ills must come from the legislative and not the judicial branch of government. The argument so forcefully advanced in this forum against the federal defendants is more properly addressed to the Congress for, even assuming *arguendo* that the welfare problem is national in character, we can detect no constitutional infirmity in the Congressional scheme embodied in the Social Security Act. We have already noted that the Act provides a mechanism of "cooperative federalism" * * * in which the states join on a voluntary basis. To be sure, the carrot provided by the federal government in the form of financial aid has proven, in many instances, too tempting to resist. But, to label this type of assistance as a form of coercion or compulsion is to read into the act language and a purpose that are simply not there.

> Similarly, there is little weight to the argument that the federal government, having once entered the field of public assistance, must assume the entire burden of the nation's welfare expenses. Although Article I, Section 8 does indeed permit Congress to expend funds for the general welfare * * * the judgment whether to do so, and to what degree, rests with that branch of government. Appellants' argument, if pressed to its logical end, would compel us to require the Congress to pay the full share of local law enforcement or educational expenses, for example, simply because the Congress has seen fit to make some funds available to the states for those purposes. The appellants concede that Congress has not assumed the burden of full financing of these "local" concerns and we see no reason to reach a contrary rule where public assistance is involved.

PENNSYLVANIA v. NELSON

Supreme Court of the United States, 1956
350 U.S. 497, 76 S.Ct. 477, 100 L.Ed. 640

Steve Nelson, a member of the Communist party, was fined and sentenced to twenty years in prison for violating the Pennsylvania Sedition Act which, in addition to protecting analogous interests of the state, made it a crime intentionally to defame or arouse hatred of the federal government. After an unsuccessful appeal to a state superior court, Nelson was able to obtain a reversal of his conviction by the Pennsylvania Supreme Court. That tribunal held that Nelson could not be convicted under the state law since the Smith Act, passed by Congress in 1940, superseded it. The state appealed this decision to the United States Supreme Court.

Mr. Chief Justice WARREN delivered the opinion of the Court.

* * *

It should be said at the outset that the decision in this case does not affect the right of States to enforce their sedition laws at times when the Federal Government has not occupied the field and is not protecting the entire country from seditious conduct. The distinction between the two situations was clearly recognized by the court below. Nor does it limit the jurisdiction of the States where the Constitution and Congress have specifically given them concurrent jurisdiction, as was done under the Eighteenth Amendment and the Volstead Act, 27 U.S.C.A., United States v. Lanza, 260 U.S. 377, 43 S.Ct. 141. Neither does it limit the right of the State to protect itself at any time against sabotage or attempted violence of all kinds. Nor does it prevent the State from prosecuting where the same act constitutes both a federal offense and a state offense under the police power.
* * *

Where, as in the instant case, Congress has not stated specifically whether a federal statute has occupied a field in which the States are otherwise free to legislate, different criteria have furnished touchstones for decision. Thus, "[t]his Court, in considering the validity of state laws in the light of * * * federal laws touching the same subject, has made use of the following expressions: conflicting; contrary to; occupying the field; repugnance; difference; irreconcilability; inconsistency; violation; curtailment; and interference. But none of these expressions provides an infallible constitutional test or an exclusive constitutional yardstick. In the final analysis, there can be no one crystal clear distinctly marked formula." Hines v. Davidowitz, 312 U.S. 52, 67, 61 S.Ct. 399. * * * In this case, we think that each of several tests of supersession is met.

First, "[t]he scheme of federal regulation [is] so pervasive as to make reasonable the inference that Congress left no room for the States to supplement it." Rice v. Santa Fe Elevator Corp., 331 U.S. at page 230, 67 S.Ct. at page 1152. The Congress determined in 1940 that it was necessary for it to re-enter the field of antisubversive legislation, which had been abandoned by it in 1921. In that year, it enacted the Smith Act which proscribes advocacy of the overthrow of any government—federal, state or local—by force and violence and organization of and knowing membership in a group which so advocates. Conspiracy to commit any of these acts is punishable under the general criminal conspiracy provisions in 18 U.S.C. § 371, 18 U.S.C.A. § 371. The Internal Security Act of 1950 is aimed more directly at Communist organizations. It distinguishes between "Communist-action organizations" and "Communist-front organizations," requiring such organizations to register and to file annual reports with the Attorney General giving complete details as to their officers and funds. Members of Communist-action organizations who have not been registered by their organization must register as individuals. Failure to register in accordance with the requirements of Sections 786–787 is punishable by a fine of not more than $10,000 for an offending organization and by a fine of not more than $10,000 or imprisonment for not more than five years or both for an individual offender—each day of failure to register constituting a separate offense. And the Act imposes certain sanctions upon both "action" and "front" organizations and their members. The Communist Control Act of 1954 declares "that the Communist Party of the United States, although purportedly a political party, is in fact an instrumentality of a conspiracy to overthrow the Government of the United States" and that "its role as the agency of a hostile foreign power renders its existence a clear present and continuing danger to the security of the United States." It also contains a legislative finding that the Communist Party is a " 'Communist-action' organization" within the meaning of the Internal Security Act of 1950 and provides that "knowing" members of the Communist Party are "subject to all the provisions and penalties" of that Act. It furthermore sets up a new classification of "Communist-infiltrated organizations" and provides for the imposition of sanctions against them.

We examine these Acts only to determine the congressional plan. Looking to all of them in the aggregate, the conclusion is inescapable that Congress has intended to occupy the field of sedition. Taken as a whole, they evince a congressional plan which makes it reasonable to determine that no room has been left for the States to supplement it. Therefore, a state sedition statute is superseded regardless of whether it purports to supplement the federal law. As was said by Mr. Justice Holmes in Charleston & Western Carolina R. Co. v. Varnville Furniture Co., 237 U.S. 597, 604, 35 S.Ct. 715, 717:

"When Congress has taken the particular subject-matter in hand, coincidence is as ineffective as opposition, and a state law is not to be declared a help because it attempts to go farther than Congress has seen fit to go."

Second, the federal statutes "touch a field in which the federal interest is so dominant that the federal system [must] be assumed to preclude enforcement of state laws on the same subject." Rice v. Santa Fe Elevator Corp., 331 U.S. at page 230, 67 S.Ct. at page 1152, citing *Hines* v. *Davidowitz*, supra. Congress has devised an all-embracing program for resistance to the various forms of totalitarian aggression. Our external defenses have been strengthened, and a plan to protect against internal subversion has been made by it. It has appropriated vast sums, not only for our own protection, but also to strengthen freedom throughout the world. It has charged the Federal Bureau of Investigation and the Central Intelligence Agency with responsibility for intelligence concerning Communist seditious activities against our Government, and has denominated such activities as part of a world conspiracy. It accordingly proscribed sedition against all government in the nation—national, state and local. Congress declared that these steps were taken "to provide for the common defense, to preserve the sovereignty of the United States as an independent nation, and to guarantee to each State a republican form of government." * * * Congress having thus treated seditious conduct as a matter of vital national concern, it is in no sense a local enforcement problem. As was said in the court below:

"Sedition against the United States is not a *local* offense. It is a crime against the *Nation*. As such, it should be prosecuted and punished in the Federal courts where this defendant has in fact been prosecuted and convicted and is now under sentence. It is not only important but vital that such prosecutions should be exclusively within the control of the Federal Government." * * *

Third, enforcement of state sedition acts presents a serious danger of conflict with the administration of the federal program. Since 1939, in order to avoid a hampering of uniform enforcement of its program by sporadic local prosecutions, the Federal Government has urged local authorities not to intervene in such matters, but to turn over to the federal authorities immediately and unevaluated all information concerning subversive activities. The President made such a request on Septem-

ber 6, 1939, when he placed the Federal Bureau of Investigation in charge of investigation in this field:

"The Attorney General has been requested by me to instruct the Federal Bureau of Investigation of the Department of Justice to take charge of investigative work in matters relating to espionage, sabotage, and violations of the neutrality regulations.

"This task must be conducted in a comprehensive and effective manner on a national basis, and all information must be carefully sifted out and correlated in order to avoid confusion and irresponsibility.

"To this end I request all police officers, sheriffs, and all other law enforcement officers in the United States promptly to turn over to the nearest representative of the Federal Bureau of Investigation any information obtained by them relating to espionage, counterespionage, sabotage, subversive activities and violations of the neutrality laws."

And in addressing the Federal-State Conference on Law Enforcement Problems of National Defense, held on August 5 and 6, 1940, only a few weeks after the passage of the Smith Act, the Director of the Federal Bureau of Investigation said:

"The fact must not be overlooked that meeting the spy, the saboteur and the subverter is a problem that must be handled on a nation-wide basis. An isolated incident in the middle west may be of little significance, but when fitted into a national pattern of similar incidents, it may lead to an important revelation of subversive activity. It is for this reason that the President requested all of our citizens and law enforcing agencies to report directly to the Federal Bureau of Investigation any complaints or information dealing with espionage, sabotage or subversive activities. In such matters, time is of the essence. It is unfortunate that in a few States efforts have been made by individuals not fully acquainted with the far-flung ramifications of this problem to interject superstructures of agencies between local law enforcement and the FBI to sift what might be vital information, thus delaying its immediate reference to the FBI. This cannot be, if our internal security is to be best served. This is no time for red tape or amateur handling of such vital matters. There must be a direct and free flow of contact between the local law enforcement agencies and the FBI. The job of meeting the spy or saboteur is one for experienced men of law enforcement."

Moreover, the Pennsylvania Statute presents a peculiar danger of interference with the federal program. For, as the court below observed:

"Unlike the Smith Act, which can be administered only by federal officers acting in their offical capacities, indictment for sedition under the Pennsylvania statute can be initiated upon an information made by a private individual. The opportunity thus present for the indulgence of personal spite and hatred or for furthering some selfish advantage or ambition need only be mentioned to be appreciated. Defense of the Nation by law, no less than by arms, should be a public and not a private undertaking. It is important that punitive sanctions for sedition *against the United States* be such as have been promulgated by the central governmental authority and administered under the supervision and review of that authority's judiciary. If that be done, sedition will be detected and punished, no less, wherever it may be found, and the right of the individual to speak freely and without fear, even in criticism of the government, will at the same time be protected."

In his brief, the Solicitor General states that forty-two States plus Alaska and Hawaii have statutes which in some form prohibit advocacy of the violent overthrow of established government. These statutes are entitled anti-sedition statutes, criminal anarchy laws, criminal syndicalist laws, etc. Although all of them are primarily directed against the overthrow of the United States Government, they are in no sense uniform. And our attention has not been called to any case where the prosecution has been successfully directed against an attempt to destroy state or local government. Some of these Acts are studiously drawn and purport to protect fundamental rights by appropriate definitions, standards of proof and orderly procedures in keeping with the avowed congressional purpose "to protect freedom from those who would destroy it, without infringing upon the freedom of all our people." Others are vague and are almost wholly without such safeguards. Some even purport to punish mere membership in subversive organizations which the federal statutes do not punish where federal registration requirements have been fulfilled.

When we were confronted with a like situation in the field of labor-management relations, Mr. Justice Jackson wrote:

"A multiplicity of tribunals and a diversity of procedures are quite as apt to produce incompatible or conflicting adjudications as are different rules of substantive law."

Should the States be permitted to exercise a concurrent jurisdiction in this area, federal enforcement would encounter not only the difficulties mentioned by Mr. Justice Jackson, but the added conflict engendered by different criteria of substantive offenses.

Since we find that Congress has occupied the field to the exclusion of parallel state legislation, that the dominant interest of the Federal Government precludes state intervention, and that administration of state Acts would conflict with the operation of the federal plan, we are convinced that the decision of the Supreme Court of Pennsylvania is unassailable.

We are not unmindful of the risk of compounding punishments which would be created by finding concurrent state power. In our view of the case, we do not reach the question whether double or multiple punishment for the same overt acts directed against the United States has constitutional sanction. Without compelling indication to the contrary, we will not assume that Congress intended to permit the possibility of double punishment. * * *

The judgment of the Supreme Court of Pennsylvania is affirmed.

Affirmed.

Mr. Justice REED, with whom Mr. Justice BURTON and Mr. Justice MINTON join, dissenting.

The problems of governmental power may be approached in this case free from the varied viewpoints that focus on the problems of national security. This is a jurisdictional problem of general importance because it involves an asserted limitation on the police power of the States when it is applied to a crime that is punishable also by the Federal Government. As this is a recurring problem, it is appropriate to explain our dissent.

Congress has not, in any of its statutes relating to sedition, specifically barred the exercise of state power to punish the same Acts under state law. And, we read the majority opinion to assume for this case that, absent federal legislation, there is no constitutional bar to punishment of sedition against the United States by both a State and the Nation. The majority limits to the federal courts the power to try charges of sedition against the Federal Government.

First, the Court relies upon the pervasiveness of the antisubversive legislation embodied in the Smith Act of 1940. * * *

* * *

We cannot agree that the federal criminal sanctions against sedition directed at the United States are of such a pervasive character as to indicate an intention to void state action.

Secondly, the Court states that the federal sedition statutes touch a field "in which the federal interest is so dominant" they must preclude state laws on the same subject. * * *

We look upon the Smith Act as a provision for controlling incitements to overthrow by force and violence the Nation, or any State, or any political subdivision of either. Such an exercise of federal police power carries, we think, no such dominancy over similar state powers as might be attributed to continuing federal regulations concerning foreign affairs or coinage, for example. In the responsibility of national and local governments to protect themselves against sedition, there is no "dominant interest."

* * *

Thirdly, the Court finds ground for abrogating Pennsylvania's antisedition statute because, in the Court's view, the State's administration of the Act may hamper the enforcement of the federal law. Quotations are inserted from statements of President Roosevelt and Mr. Hoover, the Director of the Federal Bureau of Investigation, to support the Court's position. But a reading of the quotations leads us to conclude that their purpose was to gain prompt knowledge of evidence of subversive activities so that the federal agency could be fully advised. We find no suggestion from any official source that state officials should be less alert to ferret out or punish subversion.

* * *

Mere fear by courts of possible difficulties does not seem to us in these circumstances a valid reason for ousting a State from exercise of its police power. Those are matters for legislative determination.

Finally, and this one point seems in and of itself decisive, there is an independent reason for reversing the Pennsylvania Supreme Court. The Smith Act appears in Title 18 of the United States Code, 18 U.S.C.A., which Title codifies the federal criminal laws. Section 3231 of that Title provides:

"Nothing in this title shall be held to take away or impair the jurisdiction of the courts of the several States under the laws thereof."

That declaration springs from the federal character of our Nation. It recognizes the fact that maintenance of order and fairness rests primarily with the States. The section was first enacted in 1825 and has appeared successively in the federal criminal laws since that time. This Court has interpreted the section to mean that States may provide concurrent legislation in the absence of explicit congressional intent to the contrary. Sexton v. People of State of California, 189 U.S. 319, 324–325, 23 S.Ct. 543, 545. The majority's position in this case cannot be reconciled with that clear authorization of Congress.

The law stands against any advocacy of violence to change established governments. Freedom of speech allows full play to the processes of reason. The state and national legislative bodies have legislated within constitutional limits so as to allow the widest participation by the law enforcement officers of the respective governments. The individual States were not told that they are powerless to punish local acts of sedition, nominally directed against the United States. Courts should not interfere. We would reverse the judgment of the Supreme Court of Pennsylvania.

CITY OF BURBANK v. LOCKHEED AIR TERMINAL

Supreme Court of the United States, 1973
411 U.S. 624, 93 S.Ct. 1854, 36 L.Ed.2d 547

See p. 579.

NATIONAL LEAGUE OF CITIES v. USERY

Supreme Court of the United States, 1976
426 U.S. 833, 96 S.Ct. 2465, 49 L.Ed.2d 245

The Fair Labor Standards Act was amended in 1974 to extend its provisions concerning minimum wages and maximum hours to employees of the states and their political subdivisions. Several states and cities brought suit against the Secretary of Labor seeking declaratory and injunctive relief. A three-judge federal district court dismissed the suit for failure to state a complaint upon which relief could be given, and the plaintiffs appealed.

Mr. Justice REHNQUIST delivered the opinion for the Court.

* * *

It is established beyond peradventure that the Commerce Clause of Art. I of the Constitution is a grant of plenary authority to Congress. That authority is, in the words of Chief Justice Marshall in Gibbons v. Ogden, 9 Wheat. (21 U.S.) 1 (1824), " * * * the power to regulate; that is to prescribe the rule by which commerce is to be governed." Id., at 196.

When considering the validity of asserted applications of this power to wholly private activity, the Court has made it clear that

"[e]ven activity that is purely intrastate in character may be regulated by Congress, where the activity, combined with like conduct by others similarly situated, affects commerce among the States or with foreign nations." Fry v. United States, 421 U.S. 542, 547, 95 S.Ct. 1792, 1795.

Congressional power over areas of private endeavor, even when its exercise may pre-empt express state law determinations contrary to the result which has commended itself to collective wisdom of Congress, has been held to be limited only by the requirement that "the means chosen by [Congress] must be reasonably adapted to the end permitted by the Constitution." Heart of Atlanta Motel, Inc. v. United States, 379 U.S. 241, 262, 85 S.Ct. 348, 360.

Appellants in no way challenge these decisions establishing the breadth of authority granted Congress under the commerce power. Their contention, on the contrary, is that when Congress seeks to regulate directly the activities of States as public employers, it transgresses an affirmative limitation on the exercise of its power akin to other commerce power affirmative limitations contained in the Constitution. Congressional enactments which may be fully within the grant of legislative authority contained in the Commerce Clause may nonetheless be invalid because found to offend against the right to trial by jury contained in the Sixth Amendment, United States v. Jackson, 390 U.S. 570, 88 S.Ct. 1209, or the Due Process Clause of the Fifth Amendment, Leary v. United States, 395 U.S. 6, 89 S.Ct. 1532.

Appellants' essential contention is that the 1974 amendments to the Act, while undoubtedly within the scope of the Commerce Clause, encounter a similar constitutional barrier because they are to be applied directly to the States and subdivisions of States as employers.

This court has never doubted that there are limits upon the power of Congress to override state sovereignty, even when exercising its otherwise plenary powers to tax or to regulate commerce which are conferred by Art. I of the Constitution. In [Maryland v.] *Wirtz* [392 U.S. 183, 88 S.Ct. 2017 (1968)], for example, the Court took care to assure the appellants that it had "ample power to prevent * * * 'the utter destruction of the State as a sovereign political entity,'" which they feared. * * * Appellee Secretary in this case, both in his brief and upon oral argument, has agreed that our federal system of government imposes definite limits upon the authority of Congress to regulate the activities of the States as States by means of the commerce power. * * * In *Fry*, supra, the Court recognized that an express declaration of this limitation is found in the Tenth Amendment:

"While the Tenth Amendment has been characterized as a 'truism,' stating merely that 'all is retained which has not been surrendered,' United States v. Darby, 312 U.S. 100, 124, 61 S.Ct. 451, 462, it is not without significance. The Amendment expressly declares the constitutional policy that Congress may not exercise power in a fashion that impairs the States' integrity or their ability to function effectively in a federal system. * * *" 421 U.S., at 547, 95 S.Ct., at 1795, n. 7.

* * *

Appellee Secretary argues that the cases in which this Court has upheld sweeping exercises of authority by Congress, even though those exercises pre-empted state regulation of the private sector, have already curtailed the sovereignty of the States quite as much as the 1974 amendments to the Fair Labor Standards Act. We do not agree. It is one thing to recognize the authority of Congress to enact laws regulating individual businesses necessarily subject to the dual sovereignty of the government of the Nation and of the State in which they reside. It is quite another to uphold a similar exercise of congressional authority directed not to private citizens, but to the States as States. We have repeatedly recognized that there are attributes of sovereignty attaching to every state government which may not be impaired by Congress not because Congress may lack an affirmative grant of legislative authority to reach the matter, but because the Constitution prohibits it from exercising the authority in that manner. * * *

One undoubted attribute of state sovereignty is the States' power to determine the wages which shall be paid to those whom they employ in order to carry out their governmental functions, what hours those persons will work, and what compensation will be provided where these employees may be called upon to work overtime. The question we must resolve in this case, then, is whether these determinations are "functions essential to separate and independent existence," * * * so that Congress may not abrogate the States' otherwise plenary authority to make them.

In their complaint appellants advanced estimates of substantial costs which will be imposed upon them by the 1974 amendments. Since the District Court dismissed their complaint, we take its well-pleaded allegations as true, although it appears from appellee's submissions in the District Court and in this Court that resolution of the factual disputes as to the effect of the amendments is not critical to our disposition of the case.

Judged solely in terms of increased costs in dollars, these allegations show a significant impact on the functioning of the governmental bodies involved.   *   *   *   The State of Arizona alleged that the annual additional expenditures which will be required if it is to continue to provide essential state services may total $2½ million dollars. The State of California, which must devote significant portions of its budget to fire suppression endeavors, estimated that application of the Act to its employment practices will necessitate an increase in its budget of between $8 million and $16 million.

Increased costs are not, of course, the only adverse effects which compliance with the Act will visit upon state and local governments, and in turn upon the citizens who depend upon those governments. In its complaint in intervention, for example, California asserted that it could not comply with the overtime costs (approximately $750,000 per year) which the Act required to be paid to California Highway Patrol cadets during their academy training program. California reported that it had thus been forced to reduce its academy training program from 2,080 hours to only 960 hours, a compromise undoubtedly of substantial importance to those whose safety and welfare may depend upon the preparedness of the California Highway Patrol.

This type of forced relinquishment of important governmental activities is further reflected in the complaint's allegation that the City of Inglewood, California, has been forced to curtail its affirmative action program for providing employment opportunities for men and women interested in a career in law enforcement. The Inglewood police department has abolished a program for police trainees who split their week between on the job training and the classroom. The city could not abrogate its contractual obligations to these trainees, and it concluded that compliance with the Act in these circumstances was too financially burdensome to permit continuance of the classroom program. The city of Clovis, Cal., has been put to a similar choice regarding an internship program it was running in cooperation with a California State University. According to the complaint, because the interns' compensation brings them within the purview of the Act the city must decide whether to eliminate the program entirely or to substantially reduce its beneficial aspects by doing away with any pay for the interns.

Quite apart from the substantial costs imposed upon the States and their political subdivisions, the Act displaces state policies regarding the manner in which they will structure delivery of those governmental services which their citizens require. The Act, speaking directly to the States *qua* States, requires that they shall pay all but an extremely limited minority of their employees the minimum wage rates currently chosen by Congress. It may well be that as a matter of economic policy it would be desirable that States, just as private employers, comply with these minimum wage requirements. But it cannot be gainsaid that the federal requirement directly supplants the considered policy choices of the States' elected officials and administrators as to how they wish to structure pay scales in state employment. The State might wish to employ persons with little or no training, or those who wish to work on a casual basis, or those who for some other reason do not possess minimum employment requirements, and pay them less than the federally prescribed minimum wage. It may wish to offer part time or summer employment to teenagers at a figure less than the minimum wage, and if unable to do so may decline to offer such employment at all. But the Act would forbid such choices by the States. The only "discretion" left to them under the Act is either to attempt to increase their revenue to meet the additional financial burden imposed upon them by paying congressionally prescribed wages to their existing complement of employees, or to reduce that complement to a number which can be paid the federal minimum wage without increasing revenue.

This dilemma presented by the minimum wage restrictions may seem not immediately different from that faced by private employers, who have long been covered by the Act and who must find ways to increase their gross income if they are to pay higher wages while maintaining current earnings. The difference, however, is that a State is not merely a factor in the "shifting economic arrangements" of the private sector of the economy, Kovacs v. Cooper, 336 U.S. 77, 95, 69 S.Ct. 448, 458 (Frankfurter, J., concurring), but is itself a coordinate element in the system established by the framers for governing our federal union.

The degree to which the FLSA amendments would interfere with traditional aspects of state sovereignty can be seen even more clearly upon examining the overtime requirements of the Act. The general effect of these provisions is to require the States to pay their employees at premium rates whenever their work exceeds a specified number of hours in a given period. The asserted reason for these provisions is to provide a financial disincentive upon using employees beyond the work period deemed appropriate by Congress. According to appellee,

"[t]his premium rate can be avoided if the [State] uses other employees to do the overtime work. This, in effect, tends to discourage overtime work and to spread employment, which is the result Congress intended." * * *

We do not doubt that this may be a salutary result, and that it has a sufficiently rational relationship to commerce to validate the application of the overtime provisions to private employers. But, like the minimum wage provisions, the vice of the Act as sought to be applied here is that it directly penalizes the States for choosing to hire governmental employees on terms different from those which Congress has sought to impose.

This congressionally imposed displacement of state decisions may substantially restructure traditional ways in which the local governments have arranged their affairs. Although at this point many of the actual effects under the proposed Amendments remain a matter of some dispute among the parties, enough can be satisfactorily anticipated for an outline discussion of their general import. The requirement imposing premium rates upon any employment in excess of what Congress has decided is appropriate for a governmental employee's work-week, for example, appears likely to have the effect of coercing the States to structure work periods in some employment areas, such as police and fire protection, in a manner substantially different from practices which have long been commonly accepted among local governments of this Nation. In addition, appellee represents that the Act will require that the premium compensation for over-time worked must be paid in cash, rather than with compensatory time off, unless such compensatory time is taken in the same pay period. * * * This too appears likely to be highly disruptive of accepted employment practices in many governmental areas where the demand for a number of employees to perform important jobs for extended periods on short notice can be both unpredictable and critical. Another example of congressional choices displacing those of the States in the area of what are without doubt essential governmental decisions may be found in the practice of using volunteer firemen, a source of manpower crucial to many of our smaller towns' existence. Under the regulations proposed by appellee, whether individuals are indeed "volunteers" rather than "employees" subject to the minimum wage provisions of the Act are questions to be decided in the courts. * * * It goes without saying that provisions such as these contemplate a significant reduction of traditional volunteer assistance which has been in the past drawn on to complement the operation of many local governmental functions.

Our examination of the effect of the 1974 amendments, as sought to be extended to the States and their political subdivisions, satisfies us that both the minimum wage and the maximum hour provisions will impermissibly interfere with the integral governmental functions of these bodies. We earlier noted some disagreement between the parties regarding the precise effect the amendments will have in application. We do not believe particularized assessments of actual impact are crucial to resolution of the issue presented, however. For even if we accept appellee's assessments concerning the impact of the amendments, their application will nonetheless significantly alter or displace the States' abilities to structure employer-employee relationships in such areas as fire prevention, police protection, sanitation, public health, and parks and recreation. These activities are typical of those performed by state and local governments in discharging their dual functions of administering the public law and furnishing public services. Indeed, it is functions such as these which governments are created to provide, services such as these which the States have traditionally afforded their citizens. If Congress may withdraw from the States the authority to make those fundamental employment decisions upon which their systems for performance of these functions must rest, we think there would be little left of the States' "separate and independent existence." * * * Thus, even if appellants may have overestimated the effect which the Act will have upon their current levels and patterns of governmental activity, the dispositive factor is that Congress has attempted to exercise its Commerce Clause authority to prescribe minimum wages and maximum hours to be paid by the States in their capacities as sovereign governments. In so doing, Congress has sought to wield its power in a fashion that would impair the States' "ability to function effectively within a federal system," *Fry*, supra, at 547, 95 S.Ct., at 1796, n. 7. This exercise of congressional authority does not comport with the federal system of government embodied in the Constitution. We hold that insofar as the challenged amendments operate to directly displace the States' freedom to structure integral operations in areas of traditional governmental functions, they are not within the authority granted Congress by Art. I, § 8, cl. 3.

* * *

[W]e have reaffirmed today that the States as States stand on a quite different footing than an individual or a corporation when challenging the exercise of Congress' power to regulate commerce. * * * Congress may not exercise that power so as to force directly upon the States its choices as to how essential decisions regarding the conduct of integral governmental functions are to be made. * * *

The judgment of the District Court is accordingly reversed and the case is remanded for further proceedings consistent with this opinion.

So ordered.

Mr. Justice BRENNAN, with whom Mr. Justice WHITE and Mr. Justice MARSHALL join, dissenting.

The Court concedes, as of course it must, that Congress enacted the 1974 amendments pursuant to its exclusive power under Art. I, § 8, cl. 3, of the Constitution "To regulate Commerce * * * among the several States." It must therefore be surprising that my Brethren should

choose this Bicentennial year of our independence to repudiate principles governing judicial interpretation of our Constitution settled since the time of Chief Justice John Marshall, discarding his postulate that the Constitution contemplates that restraints upon exercise by Congress of its plenary commerce power lie in the political process and not in the judicial process. For 152 years ago Chief Justice Marshall enunciated that principle to which, until today, his successors on this Court have been faithful.

"[T]he power over commerce * * * is vested in Congress as absolutely as it would be in a single government, having in its constitution the same restrictions on the exercise of the power as are found in the constitution of the United States. *The wisdom and the discretion of Congress, their identity with the people, and the influence which their constituents possess at elections, are * * * the sole restraints on which they have relied, to secure them from its abuse. They are the restraints on which the poeple must often rely solely, in all representative governments.*" Gibbons v. Ogden, 9 Wheat. 1, 197 (1824) (emphasis added).

Only 34 years ago, Wickard v. Filburn, 317 U.S. 111, 120, 63 S.Ct. 82, 87, reaffirmed that "[a]t the beginning Chief Justice Marshall * * * made emphatic the embracing and penetrating nature of [Congress' commerce] power by warning that effective restraints on its exercise must proceed from political rather than from judicial processes."

* * *

My Brethren thus have today manufactured an abstraction without substance, founded neither in the words of the Constitution nor on precedent. An abstraction having such profoundly pernicious consequences is not made less so by characterizing the 1974 amendments as legislation directed against the "States *qua* States." * * * Of course, regulations that this Court can say are not regulations of "commerce" cannot stand. Santa Cruz Fruit Packing Co. v. NLRB, 303 U.S. 453, 466, 58 S.Ct. 656, 660, and in this sense "[t]he Court has ample power to prevent * * * 'the utter destruction of the State as a sovereign political entity.'" Maryland v. Wirtz, 392 U.S. 183, 196, 88 S.Ct. 2017, 2024. But my Brethren make no claim that the 1974 amendments are not regulations of "commerce"; rather they overrule *Wirtz* in disagreement with historic principles that *United States* v. *California*, supra, reaffirmed: "[W]hile the commerce power has limits, valid general regulations of commerce do not cease to be regulations of commerce because a State is involved. If a state is engaging in economic activities that are validly regulated by the federal government when engaged in by private persons, the State too may be forced to conform its activities to federal regulation." 392 U.S., at 196–197, 88 S.Ct., at 2024. Clearly, therefore, my Brethren are also repudiating the long line of our precedents holding that a judicial finding that Congress has not unreasonably regulated a subject matter of "commerce" brings to an end the judicial role. "Let the end be legitimate, let it be within the scope of the constitution, and all means which are appropriate, which are plainly adapted to that end, which are not prohibited, but consist with the letter and spirit of the constitution, are constitutional." *McCulloch* v. *Maryland*, supra,

4 Wheat. at 421.

The reliance of my Brethren upon the Tenth Amendment as "an express declaration of [a state sovereignty] limitation," * * * not only suggests that they overrule governing decisions of this Court that address this question but must astound scholars of the Constitution. For not only early decisions, *Gibbons* v. *Ogden*, supra, 9 Wheat., at 196; *McCulloch* v. *Maryland*, supra, 4 Wheat., 404–407; and Martin v. Hunter's Lessee, 1 Wheat. 304, 324–325 (1816), hold that nothing in the Tenth Amendment constitutes a limitation on congressional exercise of powers delegated by the Constitution to Congress. See F. Frankfurter, The Commerce Power Under Marshall, Taney, and Waite 39–40 (1937). Rather, as the Tenth Amendment's significance was more recently summarized:

"The amendment states but a truism that all is retained which has not been surrendered. *There is nothing in the history of its adoption to suggest that it was more than declaratory of the relationship between the national and state governments as it had been established by the Constitution before the amendment* or that its purpose was other than to allay fears that the new national government might seek to exercise powers not granted, and that the states might not be able to exercise fully their reserved powers. * * *

"From the beginning and for many years the amendment has been construed as not depriving the national government of authority to resort to all means for the exercise of a granted power which are appropriate and plainly adapted to the permitted end." *United States* v. *Darby*, supra, 312 U.S., at 124, 61 S.Ct., at 462 (emphasis added).

*   *   *

Today's repudiation of this unbroken line of precedents that firmly reject my Brethren's ill-conceived abstraction can only be regarded as a transparent cover for invalidating a congressional judgment with which they disagree. The only analysis even remotely resembling that adopted today is found in a line of opinions dealing with the Commerce Clause and the Tenth Amendment that ultimately provoked a constitutional crisis for the Court in the 1930's. E.g., Carter v. Carter Coal Co., 298 U.S. 238, 56 S.Ct. 855; United States v. Butler, 297 U.S. 1, 56 S.Ct. 312; Hammer v. Dagenhart, 247 U.S. 251, 38 S.Ct. 529. See Stern, The Commerce Clause and the National Economy, 1933–1946, 59 Harv.L.Rev. 645 (1946). We tend to forget that the Court invalidated legislation during the Great Depression, not solely under the Due Process Clause, but also and primarily under the Commerce Clause and the Tenth Amendment. It may have been the eventual abandonment of that overly restrictive construction of the commerce power that spelled defeat for the Court-packing plan, and preserved the integrity of this institution, id., at 682, see, e.g., *United States* v. *Darby*, supra; Mulford v. Smith, 307 U.S. 38, 59 S.Ct. 648; NLRB v. Jones & Laughlin Steel Corp., 301 U.S. 1, 57 S.Ct. 615, but my Brethren today are transparently trying to cut back on that recognition of the scope of the commerce power. My Brethren's approach to this case is not far different from the dissenting opinions in the cases that averted the crisis. See, e.g., Mulford v. Smith, 307 U.S.

at 51, 59 S.Ct., at 653 (Butler, J., dissenting); NLRB v. Jones & Laughlin Steel Corp., 301 U.S., at 76, 57 S.Ct., at 630 (McReynolds, J., dissenting).

*   *   *

My Brethren do more than turn aside longstanding constitutional jurisprudence that emphatically rejects today's conclusion. More alarming is the startling restructuring of our federal system, and the role they create therein for the federal judiciary. This Court is simply not at liberty to erect a mirror of its own conception of a desirable governmental structure. If the 1974 amendments have any "vice," * * * my Brother Stevens is surely right that it represents "merely * * * a policy issue which has been firmly resolved by the branches of government having power to decide such questions." * * * It bears repeating "that effective restraints on * * * exercise [of the Commerce power] must proceed from political rather than from judicial processes." * * *

It is unacceptable that the judicial process should be thought superior to the political process in this area. Under the Constitution the judiciary has no role to play beyond finding that Congress has not made an unreasonable legislative judgment respecting what is "commerce." * * *

Judicial restraint in this area merely recognizes that the political branches of our Government are structured to protect the interests of the States, as well as the Nation as a whole, and that the States are fully able to protect their own interests in the premises. * * *

*   *   *

We are left then with a catastrophic judicial body blow at Congress' power under the Commerce Clause. Even if Congress may nevertheless accomplish its objectives—for example by conditioning grants of federal funds upon compliance with federal minimum wage and overtime standards, cf. Oklahoma v. United States Civil Service Comm'n, 330 U.S. 127, 144, 67 S.Ct. 544, 554—there is an ominous portent of disruption of our constitutional structure implicit in today's mischievous decision. I dissent.

[In a concluding footnote, Justice Brennan made the following wry and significant observation: "In contrast, my Brethren frequently remand powerless individuals to the political process by invoking doctrine of standing, justiciability, and remedies. For example, in Warth v. Seldin, 422 U.S. 490, 95 S.Ct. 2197, the Court suggested that some residents of Rochester, New York, "not overlook the normal democratic process," * * * even though they were challenging a suburban zoning ordinance and had no voice in the suburb's political affairs. In this case, however, those entities with perhaps the greatest representation in the political process have lost a legislative battle, but when they enter the courts and repeat the arguments made in the political branches, the Court welcomes them with open arms, embraces their political cause, and overrides Congress' political decision."]

Mr. Justice STEVENS, dissenting.

The Court holds that the Federal Government may not interfere with a sovereign state's inherent right to pay a substandard wage to the janitor at the state capitol. The principle on which the holding rests is difficult to perceive.

The Federal Government may, I believe, require the State to act impartially when it hires or fires the janitor, to withhold taxes from his pay check, to observe safety regulations when he is performing his job, to forbid him from burning too much soft coal in the capitol furnace, from dumping untreated refuse in an adjacent waterway, from overloading a state-owned garbage truck or from driving either the truck or the governor's limousine over 55 miles an hour. Even though these and many other activities of the capitol janitor are activities of the state *qua* state, I have no doubt that they are subject to federal regulation.

I agree that it is unwise for the Federal Government to exercise its power in the ways described in the Court's opinion. For the proposition that regulation of the minimum price of a commodity—even labor—will increase the quantity consumed is not one that I can readily understand. That concern, however, applies with even greater force to the private sector of the economy where the exclusion of the marginally employable does the greatest harm and, in all events, merely reflects my views on a policy issue which has been firmly resolved by the branches of government having power to decide such questions. As far as the complexities of adjusting police and fire departments to this sort of federal control are concerned, I presume that appropriate tailor-made regulations would soon solve their most pressing problems. After all, the interests adversely affected by this legislation are not without political power.

My disagreement with the wisdom of this legislation may not, of course, affect my judgment with respect to its validity. On this issue there is no dissent from the proposition that the Federal Government's power over the labor market is adequate to embrace these employees. Since I am unable to identify a limitation on that federal power that would not also invalidate federal regulation of state activities that I consider unquestionably permissible, I am persuaded that this statute is valid. Accordingly, with respect and a great deal of sympathy for the views expressed by the Court, I dissent from its constitutional holding.

RECENT CASES APPLYING THE DOCTRINE OF *NATIONAL LEAGUE OF CITIES* v. *USERY*

Case	Facts	Holding/Reasoning	Vote
Hodel v. Virginia Surface Mining & Reclamation Ass'n, Inc., 452 U.S. 264, 101 S.Ct. 2352 (1981)	An association of coal producers, several coal companies, some individual landowners, and the Commonwealth of Virginia brought suit challenging the constitutionality of the Surface Mining Control & Reclamation Act, a statute enacted by Congress to establish a nationwide program to protect society and the environment from the adverse effects of surface mining and authorizing the Secretary of the Interior to promulgate regulations implementing provisions of the statute. Plaintiffs argued in part that the legislation exceeded Congress's authority under the Commerce Clause and transgressed limitations on that power contained in the Tenth Amendment which, it was contended, left the matter of land use regulations to the states and their subdivisions.	Congress could rationally have concluded that, although seemingly conducted intrastate, many surface mining operations might burden or adversely affect interstate commerce and that, therefore, national regulation was necessary. Furthermore, "in order to succeed, a claim that congressional commerce power legislation is invalid under the reasoning of *National League of Cities* must satisfy *each* of three requirements. First, there must be a showing that the challenged statute regulates the 'States as States.' * * * Second, the federal regulation must address matters that are indisputably 'attributes of state sovereignty' * * *. And third, it must be apparent that the States' compliance with the federal law would directly impair their ability 'to structure integral operations in areas of traditional functions.' * * * When the Surface Mining Act is examined in light of these principles, it is clear that [the] Tenth Amendment challenge must fail because the first of these requirements is not satisfied." "[I]n contrast to the situation in *National League of Cities*, the statute at issue regulates only 'individuals and businesses necessarily subject to the dual sovereignty of the government of the Nation and the State in which they reside.' "	9–0

Case	Facts	Holding/Reasoning	Vote
United Transportation Union v. Long Island Railroad Co., 455 U.S. 678, 102 S.Ct. 1349 (1982)	At the conclusion of a thirty-day cooling-off period triggered by the failure of collective bargaining and mediation to resolve a labor-management dispute, the Railway Labor Act permits a union to resort to a strike. The union brought suit for a declaratory judgment that the Railway Labor Act, a federal statute, governed the impasse in labor-management negotiations which had developed at a state-owned railroad operating in interstate commerce. The state-controlled railroad contended that the union members had no right to strike because, as seemingly public employees, they had no right to strike against the state under explicit provision of New York's Taylor Law. The state-controlled railroad argued that the Tenth Amendment barred application of the Railway Labor Act and that the Taylor Law governed the dispute.	"The key prong of the *National League of Cities* test applicable to this case is the third one, which examines whether 'the States' compliance with the federal law would directly impair their ability "to structure integral operations in areas of traditional functions."' * * * Operation of passenger railroads, no less than operation of freight railroads, has traditionally been a function of private industry, not state or local governments. * * * Federal regulation of state-owned railroads simply does not impair a State's ability to function as a State." Furthermore, "[t]o allow individual States, by acquiring railroads, to circumvent the federal system of railroad bargaining, or any of the other elements of federal regulation of railroads, would destroy the uniformity thought essential by Congress and would endanger the efficient operation of the interstate rail system." The state knew of and accepted federal regulation when it entered the field.	9–0
Federal Energy Regulatory Commission v. Mississippi, — U.S. —, 102 S.Ct. 2126 (1982)	Congress enacted the Public Utility Regulatory Policies Act of 1978 as a legislative package designed to deal with the national energy crisis. The legislation mandates state	The statutory provisions do not infringe the Tenth Amendment. There is ample evidence to support Congress's conclusion that limited regulation of retail sales of electricity and natural gas and of the relationship between cogenerators and electric utilities was	5–4; Chief Justice Burger and Justices Powell, Rehnquist, and O'Connor dissented.

Case	Facts	Holding/Reasoning	Vote
Federal Energy Regulatory Commission (*Cont.*)	utility regulatory agencies and non-regulated utilities to "consider" the adoption and execution of certain "rate design" and regulatory standards and requires state agencies to follow particular notice and comment procedures when acting on standards proposed by the federal government. The law also encourages the development of cogeneration (a facility that produces both electric energy and steam or heat) and small power facilities and directs the Federal Energy Regulatory Commission to issue rules to accomplish this goal. Another section of the statute requires state officials, following notice and hearing, to implement these rules and permits the federal agency to exempt cogenerators and small power facilities from certain state and federal regulations.	necessary to protect interstate commerce and the national economy. In authorizing the federal commission to exempt qualified power facilities from state regulations, the statute pre-empts conflicting state laws in the traditional and legitimate way. Congress could, if it wished, completely pre-empt the states in the regulation of retail sales of electricity and natural gas and in the regulation of transactions between cogenerators and utilities because of the substantial effect of these activities on interstate commerce. The "mandatory considerations" set out in the law do not infringe Mississippi's sovereign power or dictate in a discretionary area reserved to state legislators and administrators but only establish requirements for the continuance of state activity in a field Congress has authority to pre-empt. And, if Congress may require a state agency to consider proposed federal regulations as a condition of its continued involvement in a field Congress is entitled to pre-empt, Congress may certainly set down guidelines for minimum procedures to be followed.	

YOUNGER v. HARRIS

Supreme Court of the United States, 1971
401 U.S. 37, 91 S.Ct. 746, 27 L.Ed.2d 669

John Harris was indicted for violation of California's Criminal Syndicalism Act. The act punishes the advocacy or teaching of doctrine, the organizing or assisting in the organization of groups, and the publication and dissemination of printed material to further the spread of "criminal syndicalism" which is defined as an ideology which encourages "the commission of crime, sabotage * * * or unlawful acts of force and violence or unlawful methods of terrorism as a means of accomplishing a change in industrial ownership or control, or effecting any political change." He filed a complaint in federal district court seeking to enjoin Los Angeles District Attorney Evelle Younger from prosecuting him under the statute on grounds the act had a chilling effect on his First Amendment rights. After concluding that it had jurisdiction, a three-judge panel held the act unconstitutional because it was vague and overbroad and granted the injunction. The state appealed the ruling to the U.S. Supreme Court.

Mr. Justice BLACK delivered the opinion of the Court.

* * *

Since the beginning of this country's history Congress has, subject to few exceptions, manifested a desire to permit state courts to try state cases free from interference by federal courts. In 1793 an Act unconditionally provided: "[N]or shall a writ of injunction be granted to stay proceedings in any court of a state." * * * 1 Stat. 335, c. 22, § 5. A comparison of the 1793 Act with 28 U.S.C.A. § 2283, its present-day successor, graphically illustrates how few and minor have been the exceptions granted from the flat, prohibitory language of the old Act. During all this lapse of years from 1793 to 1970 the statutory exceptions to the 1793 congressional enactment have been only three: (1) "except as expressly authorized by Act of Congress"; (2) "where necessary in aid of its jurisdiction"; and (3) "to protect or effectuate its judgments." In addition, a judicial exception to the longstanding policy evidenced by the statute has been made where a person about to be prosecuted in a state court can show that he will, if the proceeding in the state court is not enjoined, suffer irreparable damages. See Ex parte Young, 209 U.S. 123, 28 S.Ct. 441 (1908).

The precise reasons for this longstanding public policy against federal court interference with state court proceedings have never been specifically identified but the primary sources of the policy are plain. One is the basic doctrine of equity jurisprudence that courts of equity should not act, and particularly should not act to restrain a criminal prosecution, when the moving party has an adequate remedy at law and will not suffer irreparable injury if denied equitable relief. The doctrine may originally have grown out of circumstances peculiar to the English judicial system and not applicable in this country, but its fundamental purpose of restraining equity jurisdiction within narrow limits is equally important under our Constitution, in order to prevent erosion of the role of the jury and avoid a duplication of legal proceedings and legal sanctions where a single suit would be adequate to protect the rights asserted. This underlying reason for restraining courts of equity from interfering with criminal prosecutions is reinforced by an even more vital consideration, the notion of "comity," that is, a proper respect for state functions, a recognition of the fact that the entire country is made up of a Union of separate state governments, and a continuance of the belief that the National Government will fare best if the States and their institutions are left free to perform their separate functions in their separate ways. This, perhaps for lack of a better and clearer way to describe it, is referred to by many as "Our Federalism," and one familiar with the profound debates that ushered our Federal Constitution into existence is bound to respect those who remain loyal to the ideals and dreams of "Our Federalism." The concept does not mean blind deference to "States' Rights" any more than it means centralization of control over every important issue in our National Government and its courts. The Framers rejected both these courses. What the concept does represent is a system in which there is sensitivity to the legitimate interests of both State and National Governments, and in which the National Government, anxious though it may be to vindicate and protect federal rights and federal interests, always endeavors to do so in ways that will not unduly interfere with the legitimate activities of the States. It should never be forgotten that this slogan, "Our Federalism," born in the early struggling days of our Union of States, occupies a highly important place in our Nation's history and its future.

This brief discussion should be enough to suggest some of the reasons why it has been perfectly natural for our cases to repeat time and time again that the normal thing to do when federal courts are asked to enjoin pending proceedings in state courts is not to issue such injunctions. * * *

[In previous] cases the Court stressed the importance of showing irreparable injury, the traditional prerequisite to obtaining an injunction. In addition, however, the Court also made clear that in view of the fundamental policy against federal interference with state criminal prosecutions, even irreparable injury is insufficient unless it is "both great and immediate." * * * Certain types of injury, in particular, the cost, anxiety, and inconvenience of having to defend against a single criminal prosecution, could not by themselves be considered "irreparable" in the special legal sense of that

term. Instead, the threat to the plaintiff's federally protected rights must be one that cannot be eliminated by his defense against a single criminal prosecution. * * *

And similarly, in *Douglas* v. *City of Jeanette* we made clear, after reaffirming this rule, that:

"It does not appear from the record that petitioners have been threatened with any injury other than that incidental to every criminal proceeding brought lawfully and in good faith." * * * 319 U.S., at 164, 63 S.Ct., at 881.

This is where the law stood when the Court decided Dombrowski v. Pfister, 380 U.S. 479, 85 S.Ct. 1116 (1965), and held that an injunction against the enforcement of certain state criminal statutes could properly issue under the circumstances presented in that case. In *Dombrowski*, unlike many of the earlier cases denying injunctions, the complaint made substantial allegations that:

"the threats to enforce the statutes against appellants are not made with any expectation of securing valid convictions, but rather are part of a plan to employ arrests, seizures, and threats of prosecution under color of the statutes to harass appellants and discourage them and their supporters from asserting and attempting to vindicate the constitutional rights of Negro citizens of Louisiana," 380 U.S., at 482, 85 S.Ct., at 1118–1119.

* * *

For these reasons, fundamental not only to our federal system but also to the basic functions of the Judicial Branch of the National Government under our Constitution, we hold that the *Dombrowski* decision should not be regarded as having upset the settled doctrines that have always confined very narrowly the availability of injunctive relief against state criminal prosecutions. We do not think that opinion stands for the proposition that a federal court can properly enjoin enforcement of a statute solely on the basis of a showing that the statute "on its face" abridges First Amendment rights. There may, of course, be extraordinary circumstances in which the necessary irreparable injury can be shown even in the absence of the usual prerequisites of bad faith and harassment. For example, as long ago as * * * [*Watson* v. *Buck*] we indicated:

"It is of course conceivable that a statute might be flagrantly and patently violative of express constitutional prohibitions in every clause, sentence and paragraph, and in whatever manner and against whomever an effort might be made to apply it." 313 U.S., at 402, 61 S.Ct., at 967. Other unusual situations calling for federal intervention might also arise, but there is no point in our attempting now to specify what they might be. It is sufficient for purposes of the present case to hold, as we do, that the possible unconstitutionality of a statute "on its face" does not in itself justify an injunction against good-faith attempts to enforce it, and that appellee Harris has failed to make any showing of bad faith, harassment, or any other unusual circumstance that would call for equitable relief. Because our holding rests on the absence of the factors necessary under equitable principles to justify federal intervention, we have no occasion to consider whether 28 U.S.C.A. § 2283, which prohibits an injunction against state court proceedings "except as expressly authorized by Act of Congress" would in and of itself be con-

trolling under the circumstances of this case.

The judgment of the District Court is reversed, and the case is remanded for further proceedings not inconsistent with this opinion.

Reversed.

Mr. Justice BRENNAN, with whom Mr. Justice WHITE and Mr. Justice MARSHALL join, concurring in the result.

I agree that the judgment of the District Court should be reversed. Appellee Harris had been indicted for violations of the California Criminal Syndicalism Act before he sued in federal court. He has not alleged that the prosecution was brought in bad faith to harass him. His constitutional contentions may be adequately adjudicated in the state criminal proceeding, and federal intervention at his instance was therefore improper.

* * *

Mr. Justice STEWART, with whom Mr. Justice HARLAN joins, concurring.

The questions the Court decides today are important ones. Perhaps as important, however, is a recognition of the areas into which today's holdings do not necessarily extend. In all of these cases, the Court deals only with the proper policy to be followed by a federal court when asked to intervene by injunction or declaratory judgment in a criminal prosecution which is contemporaneously pending in a state court.

In basing its decisions on policy grounds, the Court does not reach any questions concerning the independent force of the federal anti-injunction statute, 28 U.S.C.A. § 2283. Thus we do not decide whether the word "injunction" in § 2283 should be interpreted to include a declaratory judgment, or whether an injunction to stay proceedings in a state court is "expressly authorized" by § 1 of the Civil Rights Act of 1871, now 42 U.S.C.A. § 1983. And since all these cases involve state criminal prosecutions, we do not deal with the considerations that should govern a federal court when it is asked to intervene in state civil proceedings, where, for various reasons, the balance might be struck differently. Finally, the Court today does not resolve the problems involved when a federal court is asked to give injunctive or declaratory relief from *future* state criminal prosecutions.

*   *   *

Mr. Justice DOUGLAS, dissenting.

The fact that we are in a period of history when enormous extrajudicial sanctions are imposed on those who assert their First Amendment rights in unpopular causes emphasizes the wisdom of Dombrowski v. Pfister, 380 U.S. 479, 85 S.Ct. 1116. There we recognized that in times of repression, when interests with powerful spokesmen generate symbolic pogroms against nonconformists, the federal judiciary, charged by Congress with special vigilance for protection of civil rights, has special responsibilities to prevent an erosion of the individual's constitutional rights.

Dombrowski represents an exception to the general rule that federal courts should not interfere with state criminal prosecutions. The exception does not arise merely because prosecutions are threatened to which the First Amendment will be the proffered defense. *Dombrowski* governs statutes which are a blunderbuss by themselves or when used *en masse*—those that have an "over-

broad" sweep. "If the rule were otherwise, the contours of regulation would have to be hammered out case by case—and tested only by those hardy enough to risk criminal prosecution to determine the proper scope of regulation." Id., at 487, 85 S.Ct., at 1121. It was in the context of overbroad state statutes that we spoke of the "chilling effect upon the exercise of First Amendment rights" caused by state prosecutions. Ibid.

As respects overbroad statutes we said at least as early as 1940 that when dealing with First Amendment rights we would insist on statutes "narrowly drawn to prevent the supposed evil." Cantwell v. Connecticut, 310 U.S. 296, 307, 60 S.Ct. 900, 905.

The special circumstances when federal intervention in a state criminal proceeding is permissible are not restricted to bad faith on the part of state officials or the threat of multiple prosecutions. They also exist where for any reason the state statute being enforced is unconstitutional on its face. *   *   *

*   *   *

Dombrowski and 42 U.S.C.A. § 1983 indicate why *   *   * federal intervention against enforcement of the state laws is appropriate. *   *   * [Here] the state statute challenged is the prototype of the one we held unconstitutional in Brandenburg v. Ohio [395 U.S. 444, 89 S.Ct. 1827].

The eternal temptation, of course, has been to arrest the speaker rather than to correct the conditions about which he complains. I see no reason why these appellees should be made to walk the treacherous ground of these statutes. They, like other citizens, need the umbrella of the First Amendment as they study, analyze, discuss, and debate the troubles of these days. When criminal prosecu-tions can be leveled against them because they express unpopular views, the society of the dialogue is in danger.

COOPER v. AARON

Supreme Court of the United States, 1958
358 U.S. 1, 78 S.Ct. 1401, 3 L.Ed.2d 5

See p. 710.

MISSOURI v. HOLLAND

Supreme Court of the United States, 1920
252 U.S. 416, 40 S.Ct. 382, 64 L.Ed. 641

Great Britain and the United States signed a treaty in 1916 to save from extinction various species of birds that migrated through both the United States and Canada. In addition to provisions for protecting the birds, the treaty stipulated that both countries would attempt to institute measures necessary to fulfill the purposes of the agreement. In 1918, Congress passed the Migratory Bird Treaty Act which authorized the Secretary of Agriculture to issue regulations concerning the killing, capturing, and selling of those birds named in the treaty. The State of Missouri brought a complaint in federal district court to prevent Ray Holland, a game warden, from enforcing the act and the Secretary's regulations. Among other objections, Missouri claimed that the statute was unconstitutional by virtue of the Tenth Amendment and that its sovereign right as a state had been violated. The district court held the Migratory Bird Treaty Act constitutional, and Missouri appealed.

Mr. Justice HOLMES delivered the opinion of the court.

* * *

[T]he question raised is the general one whether the treaty and statute are void as an interference with the rights reserved to the States.

To answer this question it is not enough to refer to the Tenth Amendment, reserving the powers not delegated to the United States, because by Article II, § 2, the power to make treaties is delegated expressly, and by Article VI treaties made under the authority of the United States, along with the Constitution and laws of the United States made in pursuance thereof, are declared the supreme law of the land. If the treaty is valid there can be no dispute about the validity of the statute under Article I, § 8, as a necessary and proper means to execute the powers of the Government. The language of the Constitution as to the supremacy of treaties being general, the question before us is narrowed to an inquiry into the ground upon which the present supposed exception is placed.

It is said that a treaty cannot be valid if it infringes the Constitution, that there are limits, therefore, to the treaty-making power, and that one such limit is that what an act of Congress could not do unaided, in derogation of the powers reserved to the States, a treaty cannot do. An earlier act of Congress that attempted by itself and not in pursuance of a treaty to regulate the killing of migratory birds within the

States had been held bad in the District Court. United States v. Shauver, 214 Fed.Rep. 154. United States v. McCullagh, 221 Fed.Rep. 288. Those decisions were supported by arguments that migratory birds were owned by the States in their sovereign capacity for the benefit of their people, and that under cases like Geer v. Connecticut, 161 U.S. 519, 16 S.Ct. 600, this control was one that Congress had no power to displace. The same argument is supposed to apply now with equal force.

Whether the two cases cited were decided rightly or not they cannot be accepted as a test of the treaty power. Acts of Congress are the supreme law of the land only when made in pursuance of the Constitution, while treaties are declared to be so when made under the authority of the United States. It is open to question whether the authority of the United States means more than the formal acts prescribed to make the convention. We do not mean to imply that there are no qualifications to the treaty-making power; but they must be ascertained in a different way. It is obvious that there may be matters of the sharpest exigency for the national well being that an act of Congress could not deal with but that a treaty followed by such an act could, and it is not lightly to be assumed that, in matters requiring national action, "a power which must belong to and somewhere reside in every civilized government" is not to be found. Andrews v. Andrews, 188 U.S. 14, 33, 23 S.Ct. 237. What was said in that case with regard to the powers of the States applies with equal force to the powers of the nation in cases where the States individually are incompetent to act. We are not yet discussing the particular case before

us but only are considering the validity of the test proposed. With regard to that we may add that when we are dealing with words that also are a constituent act, like the Constitution of the United States, we must realize that they have called into life a being the development of which could not have been foreseen completely by the most gifted of its begetters. It was enough for them to realize or to hope that they had created an organism; it has taken a century and has cost their successors much sweat and blood to prove that they created a nation. The case before us must be considered in the light of our whole experience and not merely in that of what was said a hundred years ago. The treaty in question does not contravene any prohibitory words to be found in the Constitution. The only question is whether it is forbidden by some invisible radiation from the general terms of the Tenth Amendment. We must consider what this country has become in deciding what that Amendment has reserved.

The State as we have intimated founds its claim of exclusive authority upon an assertion of title to migratory birds, an assertion that is embodied in statute. No doubt it is true that as between a State and its inhabitants the State may regulate the killing and sale of such birds, but it does not follow that its authority is exclusive of paramount powers. To put the claim of the State upon title is to lean upon a slender reed. Wild birds are not in the possession of anyone; and possession is the beginning of ownership. The whole foundation of the State's rights is the presence within their jurisdiction of birds that yesterday had not arrived, tomorrow may be in another State and in a week a thousand miles away. If we are to be accurate we cannot put the case of the State upon higher ground than that the treaty deals with creatures that for the moment are within the state borders, that it must be carried out by officers of the United States within the same territory, and that but for the treaty the State would be free to regulate this subject itself.

* * *

Here a national interest of very nearly the first magnitude is involved. It can be protected only by national action in concert with that of another power. The subject-matter is only transitorily within the State and has no permanent habitat therein. But for the treaty and the statute there soon might be no birds for any powers to deal with. We see nothing in the Constitution that compels the Government to sit by while a food supply is cut off and the protectors of our forests and our crops are destroyed. It is not sufficient to rely upon the States. The reliance is vain, and were it otherwise, the question is whether the United States is forbidden to act. We are of opinion that the treaty and statute must be upheld.

Decree affirmed.

Mr. Justice VAN DEVANTER and Mr. Justice PITNEY dissent.

UNITED STATES v. BELMONT

Supreme Court of the United States, 1937
301 U.S. 324, 57 S.Ct. 758, 81 L.Ed. 1134

Prior to 1918, the Petrograd Metal Works had deposited a sum of money with a private banker in New York City, August Belmont & Company. In 1918, the Soviet government nationalized the company and appropriated its assets, thus acquiring title to the deposit in Belmont's bank. When President Roosevelt and representatives of the Soviet Union concluded an exchange of diplomatic correspondence in November 1933, establishing diplomatic relations, they also agreed to a settlement of claims between the two countries. In the agreement it was stipulated that, rather than have each government prosecute claims against citizens of the other, the Soviet Union would assign title to claims in the United States to the United States government and vice versa. Belmont died in the interim, and the executors of his estate refused to honor a request from the United States government for the funds, whereupon the United States sued to recover them. The U.S. District Court, in a judgment affirmed by the U.S. Circuit Court on appeal, ruled against the United States on the ground that the property could not rightly be regarded as falling within Soviet jurisdiction. Since the bank was located in New York, the policy of that state was controlling, and acquisition of property by confiscation was contrary to that state's expressed public policy; therefore, the United States could not have title.

———

Mr. Justice SUTHERLAND delivered the opinion of the Court.

* * *

[T]he case * * * presents a question of public concern, the determination of which well might involve the good faith of the United States in the eyes of a foreign government.

The court below held that the assignment thus effected embraced the claim here in question; and with that we agree.

That court, however, took the view that the situs of the bank deposit was within the state of New York; that in no sense could it be regarded as an intangible property right within Soviet territory; and that the nationalization decree, if enforced, would put into effect an act of confiscation. And it held that a judgment for the United States could not be had, because, in view of that result, it would be contrary to the controlling public policy of the state of New York. The further contention is made by respondents that the public policy of the United States would likewise be infringed by such a judgment. The two questions thus presented are the only ones necessary to be considered.

First. We do not pause to inquire whether in fact there was any policy of the state of New York to be infringed, since we are of opinion that no state policy can prevail against the international compact here involved.

This court has held, Underhill v. Hernandez, 168 U.S. 250, 18 S.Ct. 83, that every sovereign state must recognize the independence of every other sovereign state; and that the courts of one will not sit in judgment upon the acts of the government of another, done within its own territory.

* * *

* * * This court held that the conduct of foreign relations was committed by the Constitution to the political departments of the government and the propriety of what may be done in the exercise of this political power was not subject to judicial inquiry or decision; that who is the sovereign of a territory is not a judicial question, but one the determination of which by the political departments conclusively binds the courts; and that recognition by these departments is retroactive and validates all actions and conduct of the government so recognized from the commencement of its existence. "The principle," we said [in Oetjen v. Central Leather Co.], 246 U.S. 297, at page 303, 38 S.Ct. 309, 311 "that the conduct of one independent government cannot be successfully questioned in the courts of another is as applicable to a case involving the title to property brought within the custody of a court, such as we have here, as it was held to be to the cases cited, in which claims for damages were based upon acts done in a foreign country, for it rests at last upon the highest considerations of international comity and expediency. To permit the validity of the acts of one sovereign state to be reexamined and perhaps condemned by the courts of another would very certainly 'imperil the amicable relations between governments and vex the peace of nations.'" * * *

* * *

We take judicial notice of the fact that coincident with the assignment set forth in the complaint, the President recognized the Soviet government, and normal diplomatic relations were established between that government and the government of the United States, followed by an exchange of ambassadors. The effect of this was to validate, so far as this country is concerned, all acts of the Soviet government here involved from the commencement of its existence. The recognition, establishment of diplomatic relations, the assignment, and agreements with respect thereto, were all parts of one transaction, resulting in an international compact between the two governments. That the negotiations, acceptance of the assignment and agreements and understandings in respect thereof were within the competence of the President may not be doubted. Governmental power over internal affairs is distributed between the national government and the several states. Governmental power over external affairs is not distributed, but is vested exclusively in the national government. And in respect of what was done here, the Executive had authority to speak as the sole organ of that government. The assignment and the agreements in connection therewith did not, as in the case of treaties, as that term is used in the treaty making clause of the Constitution (article 2, § 2), require the advice and consent of the Senate.

A treaty signifies "a compact made between two or more independent nations, with a view to the public welfare." * * * But an international compact, as this was, is not always a treaty which requires the participation of the Senate. There are many such compacts, of which a protocol, a modus vivendi, a postal convention, and agreements like that now under consideration are illustrations. * * * The distinction was pointed out by this court in the *Altman* Case * * * which arose under section 3 of the Tariff Act of 1897 (30 Stat. 151, 203), authorizing the President to conclude commercial agreements with foreign countries in certain specified matters. We held that although this might not be a treaty requiring ratification by the Senate, it was a compact negotiated and proclaimed under the authority of the President, and as such was a "treaty" within the meaning of the Circuit Court of Appeals Act (26 Stat. 826), the construction of which might be reviewed upon direct appeal to this court.

Plainly, the external powers of the United States are to be exercised without regard to state laws or policies. The supremacy of a treaty in this respect has been recognized from the beginning. Mr. Madison, in the Virginia Convention, said that if a treaty does not supersede existing state laws, as far as they contravene its operation, the treaty would be ineffective. "To counteract it by the supremacy of the state laws, would bring on the Union the just charge of national perfidy and involve us in war." * * * And while this rule in respect of treaties is established by the express language of clause 2, article 6, of the Constitution, the same rule would result in the case of all international compacts and agreements from the very fact that complete power over international affairs is in the national government and is not and cannot be subject to any curtailment or interference on the part of the several states. * * * In respect of all international negotiations and compacts, and in respect of our foreign relations generally, state lines disappear. As to such purposes the state of New York does not exist. Within the field of its powers, whatever the United States rightfully undertakes, it necessarily has warrant to consummate. And when judicial authority is invoked in aid of such consummation, State Constitutions, state laws, and state policies are irrelevant to the inquiry and decision. It is inconceivable that any of them can be interposed as an obstacle to the effective operation of a federal constitutional power. * * *

Second. The public policy of the United States relied upon as a bar to the action is that declared by the Constitution, namely, that private property shall not be taken without just compensation. But the answer is that our Constitution, laws, and policies have no extraterritorial operation, unless in respect of our own citizens. * * * What another country has done in the way of taking over property of its nationals, and especially of its corporations, is not a matter for judicial consideration here. Such nationals must look to their own government for any redress to which they may be entitled. So far as the record shows, only the rights of the Russian corporation have been affected by what has been done; and it will be time enough to consider the rights of our nationals when, if ever, by proper judicial proceeding, it shall be made to appear that they are so affected as to entitle them to judicial relief. The substantive right to the moneys, as now disclosed, became vested in the Soviet government as the successor to the corporation; and this right that government has passed to the United States. It does not appear that respondents have any interest in the matter beyond that of a custodian. Thus far no question under the Fifth Amendment is involved.

* * *

Judgment reversed.

Late in January 1954, the U.S. Senate began debate on a proposed constitutional amendment introduced by Senator John W. Bricker (R–Ohio) and cosponsored by over sixty other senators. S.J.Res. 1, known as the Bricker Amendment, was a response to the perceived threat of international agreements to the American constitutional structure. Given the Supreme Court's holding in *Missouri* v. *Holland*, supra, its sponsors feared that provisions of treaties which the United States had signed, particularly recently signed U.N. treaties on human rights, might be applied to significantly alter protections guaranteed by the Constitution, (e.g., property rights, rights reserved to the states, etc.). Their fears were not entirely unfounded. See Fujii v. State, 217 P.2d 481 (Cal.App.1950), but see also decision on appeal to California Supreme Court, 38 Cal.2d 718, 242 P.2d 617 (1952). The proposed amendment also reflected irritation with the possible impact of executive agreements. Many of the senators, still critical of President Roosevelt's Yalta Accords, sought to contain the internal application of this type of agreement.

The Bricker Amendment was reported out of the Senate Judiciary Committee by a 9–5 vote in the following form:

Section 1. A provision of a treaty which conflicts with this Constitution shall not be of any force or effect.

Section 2. A treaty shall become effective as internal law in the United States only through legislation *which would be valid in the absence of treaty.*

Section 3. Congress shall have power to regulate all executive and other agreements with any foreign power or international organization. All such agreements shall be subject to the limitations imposed on treaties by this article.

Section 4. The Congress shall have power to enforce this article by appropriate legislation.

Section 5. This article shall be inoperative unless it shall have been ratified as an amendment to the Constitution by the legislatures of three-fourths of the several States within seven years from the date of its submission. [Emphasis supplied.]

While there were numerous modifications offered over the course of the month-long debate—some by the Senate Republican leadership hoping to allay the opposition of President Eisenhower—the most significant proposal came from Senator Walter F. George (D–Ga.). Subsequently accepted as the final version of the Amendment when it was considered for passage, the George substitute proposal read as follows:

> Sec. 1. A provision of a treaty or other international agreement which conflicts with this Constitution shall not be of any force or effect.
>
> Sec. 2. An international agreement other than a treaty shall become effective as internal law in the United States only by an act of the Congress.
>
> Sec. 3. On the question of advising and consenting to the ratification of a treaty the vote shall be determined by yeas and nays, and the names of the persons voting for and against shall be entered on the Journal of the Senate.
>
> Sec. 4. This article shall be inoperative unless it shall have been ratified as an amendment to the Constitution by the legislatures of three-fourths of the several States within 7 years from the date of its submission.

The alterations were aimed chiefly at eradicating the "which clause" [see italicized portion of Sec. 2, supra] in the Committee's version—a feature of the Amendment that raised considerable opposition from the more internationally minded senators. The George proposal also contained a new section, authored initially by Senator William F. Knowland (R–Calif.), which required a roll call vote in the Senate on the ratification of treaties.

On February 26, the Senate voted on passage of the Bricker Amendment in the form of the George substitute proposal, and it was defeated. The vote was 60–31, one vote short of the constitutionally required two-thirds majority necessary for passage. That vote was the high-water mark of the Amendment's support. Similar amendments were introduced in the next two Congresses, but these died in committee.

Chapter 6

The Exercise of National Power

Inasmuch as the concept of cooperative federalism has come to have controlling effect, it makes sense to begin a more detailed consideration of the federal relationship by looking at the exercise of power by the national government. As you will find, perhaps the most significant power possessed by the central government is its power to regulate interstate and foreign commerce. From the clause granting this power flows the authority of the national government to supervise interstate traffic, regulate production, and control navigation. Another national power which has come to have considerable importance within the federal system is the taxing and spending power. Taken together, the commerce power, its correlates, and the taxing and spending power give the national government commanding influence in orchestrating public policy in the American political system, but, as you will also see, it has not always been so. From time to time the application of a dual federalist philosophy by some members of the Court has resulted in intermittent contraction of those powers or delayed their expansion.

a. The General Scope of Congress's Power to Regulate Interstate Commerce

It soon became readily apparent to anyone even remotely connected with the buying and selling of goods—which meant just about everyone—that one of the most serious difficulties plaguing the economic life of the Nation in the days following the Revolutionary War was the absence of any stabilizing system of interstate commercial regulation. Because supervisory power over commerce inhered in the sovereignty of each state, regulation was spotty at best and most often was laden with attempts by states to secure every conceivable competitive advantage. Obstacles to the free flow of trade, particularly in the form of high interstate tariffs, abounded. The Articles of Confederation furnished a notoriously weak answer to the problem, and the mounting chaos, unchecked by the debilitated power of the central government, loomed as one of the principal motivations for convening the convention which gathered in Philadelphia in the summer of 1787 to draft the Constitution. It was with vivid remembrances of the commercial anarchy in those postcolonial days that Chief Justice Marshall confronted the Court's first opportunity to articulate the scope of the new national government's power to regulate interstate commerce.

Gibbons v. *Ogden* (p. 420) presented the Court with an ideal occasion to hand down a precedent-setting decision that would come to grips with the question of just how far the interstate commerce power could be taken into geographical areas that would customarily be regarded as lying within the bailiwick of the state police power. When the New York legislature granted Robert Fulton a monopoly on all of the state's steamboat traffic, including that on interstate waterways, the stage was set.

In the manner that it deals with the concept of interstate commerce, Marshall's opinion is significant in two respects. First, he endeavored to define "commerce" in expansive terms. He interpreted the term to connote commercial intercourse generally and certainly the express power to regulate navigation. Secondly, the control of interstate carriers was not limited to their operation in those geographical areas between states, but national regulatory power could cross state lines and follow into the interior of the states in order to protect the free flow of interstate commerce.

As if it were not already apparent, the cooperative federalist quality of Marshall's opinion becomes obvious in his treatment of the status of such a national power *vis-à-vis* any state authority. As with the currency power interpreted in *McCulloch*, where the national government legislates pursuant to the Commerce Clause of the Constitution (as it did in granting a federal license to Gibbons), the central government's authority is supreme and absolute. Because it has these characteristics, we say that the national government exercises a "plenary" or exclusive power. Note, however, that Marshall's decision in this case is conditioned by the fact that here the national government has already acted. Marshall does not say that when the national government has not acted, then too, all state legislation must fall. This was left an open question, and later in Willson v. Black Bird Creek Marsh Co., 27 U.S. (2 Pet.) 245, 7 L.Ed. 412 (1829), Marshall intimated that there might well be a limited role for the states in filling such gaps, provided they do not infringe interstate interests. This topic, however, will be taken up in the next chapter.

The controlling effect of Marshall's position in *Gibbons*, particularly as it applied to interstate carriers, is amply illustrated by succeeding opinions of the Court—some of them written at times when the Court on other matters was demonstrating considerable enthusiasm for a dualist perspective. The note to *Gibbons*, for example, discussing *Pensacola Telegraph Co.* v. *Western Union Telegraph Co.* (p. 427), shows a direct application of the *Gibbons* holding to a communications case involving federal-state conflict in the licensing of telegraph companies.

Consistent with Marshall's expansive view of interstate commerce, especially as it reaches into the interior of the states, are the Court's opinions in *Stafford* v. *Wallace* (p. 427) and *Houston, East & West Texas Railway Co.* v. *United States* (p. 429), more commonly known as *The Shreveport Rate Case*. Notice how the Court articulates the "stream of commerce" test in *Stafford* to sustain the constitutionality of national legislation passed to regulate stockyards. A more penetrating illustration of the interstate commerce power is its use by the Court in the *Shreveport* case to compel a readjustment of purely intrastate rates allowed by the Texas Railroad Commission. The reason for intervention by the national government lay in the clearly discriminatory effect of those state-approved railway rates inhibiting the flow of competitively priced goods from Shreveport, Louisiana to east Texas markets.

A broad interpretation of the commerce power has also led to the involvement of the national government in the regulation of criminal activity. It may seem strange at first to talk of a federal police power since the states, with their reserved powers, are customarily regarded as the protectors of public safety, health, and welfare and as the custodians of the criminal law. No such inherent authority resides with the national government. However, since the Court's celebrated decision in *Champion* v. *Ames* (p. 431) affirmed Congress's efforts to prohibit the interstate sale of lottery tickets, the national government has sought to punish and prohibit activity in other varieties of illicit commerce. Examples abound. Congress enacted the Mann Act to deal with the problem of what was called "white slavery"—the interstate transportation of prostitutes. It has since enacted legislation aimed at the interstate transportation of kidnapped persons (the so-called Lindbergh Act) and the interstate flight of fugitives. A provision in Title I of the Civil Rights Act of 1968 makes it a federal crime to travel interstate for the purpose of inciting, organizing, or participating in a riot or civil disorder (and the Court has not found it unconstitutional, see Dellinger, et al. v. United States, 472 F.2d 340 [7th Cir. 1972], cert. denied, 410 U.S. 970, 93 S.Ct. 1443 [1973]). The invention and subsequent widespread ownership of motor vehicles gave rise to the crime which, in turn, inspired the congressional response the constitutionality of which was at issue in *Brooks* v. *United States* (p. 438). We might also add that that technological development was the principal catalyst in many, if not most, of the other exercises of the federal police power.

Given the breadth of the holding in *Gibbons* and the support given that scope of the commerce power by subsequent cases, it is both surprising and puzzling to discover that there were and, in at least one instance, continue to be some exceptions to the expectation that commercial enterprises doing business interstate would be liable to regulation by the national government. For years, one of the exceptions was the insurance business. In Paul v. Virginia, 75 U.S. (8 Wall.) 168, 9 L.Ed. 357 (1869), the Court held that insurance companies were local enterprises not liable to national regulation even though contracts were negotiated across state lines. The Court's decision in United States v. South-Eastern Underwriters Ass'n, 322 U.S. 533, 64 S.Ct. 1162 (1944), overturned that ruling. Insurance companies were at last recognized as interstate businesses that could not logically be excluded from the application of federal antitrust legislation. Insurance, once perhaps the trade of small companies on pretty much a local basis, had increasingly grown to become a big business dominated by sprawling interstate corporations. Recently, in *Goldfarb* v. *Virginia State Bar* (p. 439), the Court also extended the application of the Sherman Act to prohibit price setting by the bar associations. The monopolistic practices of professional baseball, however, continue to represent an enclave of special favor as the decision in *Flood* v. *Kuhn* (p. 442) shows. Whatever the team owners may say about the necessity of the reserve clause to maintain competition among clubs in the sport, exactly why the enforcement of such clauses should be accorded a different legal status in pro baseball than in other professional sports is difficult to understand. Apart from the Court's mechanical recitation of precedents and blind deference to Congress's perception at one time that pro baseball was "the national pastime"—a view which, given the popularity of professional football today, is something less than convincing—one may be hard pressed to justify the continuation of such an exception. The dissenters in the *Flood* case, Justices Douglas, Brennan, and Marshall, make the point that pro baseball, like the sale of insurance, is big business and, therefore, indistinguishable from other interstate commercial activity such as to justify its special privilege. Would you agree?

When we spoke earlier about the concept of a federal police power, we were making the point that the Commerce Clause can be used for broader purposes than customary commercial regulation. The ancillary use of the commerce power—to protect the health, safety, and welfare of people—is also well illustrated by three decisions of the Supreme Court upholding and applying the public accommodations provisions of the 1964 Civil Rights Act.

It may seem puzzling and perhaps dehumanizing to you that, in its efforts to eradicate racial discrimination throughout the United States, Congress turned to the commerce power rather than the seemingly more appropriate provisions of the Fourteenth Amendment. As you will find later, however, when you read the Court's decision in the *Civil Rights Cases of 1883*, included in Chapter 9, private discrimination was held to be outside the coverage of that Amendment. Rather than risk invalidation of the legislation because of this precedent and lacking broad police powers like those of the states, Congress used the Commerce Clause in its sweeping attack on racial discrimination in public accommodations. Look at the sweep of the Commerce Clause when you read the Court's decisions in *Heart of Atlanta Motel* v. *United States* (p. 446) and the two decisions which follow it, *Katzenbach* v. *McClung* (p. 451) and *Daniel* v. *Paul* (p. 455). In view of the pervasive coverage of the act and its sweeping application by the Court, particularly in *Daniel* v. *Paul*, would any commercial establishment fail to come within its scope?

b. Congress's Power to Regulate Production under the Commerce Clause

When Chief Justice Marshall elaborated on the definition of commerce in *Gibbons* v. *Ogden,* he did not indicate if the production as well as the distribution of goods was an economic function the regulation of which was consigned to the national government. Until 1895, this remained an open question. Unfortunately—from Marshall's perspective, at least—when the Court initially furnished an answer, it rejected such an extension of national power. Beginning with the decision in *United States* v. *E. C. Knight Co.* (p. 456) and continuing on into the mid-1930s, a prevailing majority of the Justices adopted a profoundly dual federalist stance on the use of the commerce power for the national supervision of business. Relying on both a niggardly definition of commerce and a vigorous use of the Tenth Amendment, the Court consistently whacked away at national legislation aimed at economic reform. It frustrated the application of federal antitrust statutes, invalidated congressional child labor laws, and killed off New Deal economic recovery measures.

The first line of attack on national legislation targeted to regulate production consisted of neatly distinguishing economic functions and then parceling them out to different levels of government. Thus the Court came to distinguish manufacturing (in *E. C. Knight* and in *Hammer* v. *Dagenhart,* p. 463), mining (in *Carter* v. *Carter Coal Co.,* p. 472), and farming (in *United States* v. *Butler,* p. 528) as elements of production which were subjects of state regulation though they were only in a limited sense local in scope. These varieties of production were analytically separated from means of distribution like those considered in the preceding section of cases. Having segmented the economic process and assigned the two principal functions—production and distribution—to competing levels of government, that ended the matter. From here on, it simply became a matter of cataloging business activity in one or the other category and mechanically applying the constitutional rules appropriate to each category.

The corollary of this tactic was, as we mentioned, a stultifying use of the Tenth Amendment. Spill-over effects from national regulatory efforts would not be tolerated when they touched the protected haven of state powers. Thus any vigorous use of the commerce power to regulate the distribution of goods which might directly affect or influence production was unconstitutional. Classic illustrations of this mode of interpretation appear in *Hammer* v. *Dagenhart* (p. 463) and the *Carter Coal* case (p. 472).

So vigilant was the Court in the protection of state prerogatives that, in the language of the *Schechter Poultry* case (p. 469), the national government might only regulate business activity which had "direct" effects on interstate commerce. The conclusion that a business, such as the Schechters', might have only "indirect" effects precluded federal interference. Though it pursued such sterile analysis with rare gusto, the Court had difficulty articulating with any precision exactly what the difference was between "direct" and "indirect" effects that would warrant treating them as different in kind.

The reason for the Court's newfound love affair with the dualist philosophy is not difficult to uncover. It stemmed less from an infatuation with any dogma of the federal relationship than from the utility such a legal ideology came to have in the late nineteenth and early twentieth centuries as it helped to actualize the economic philosophy of *laissez-faire* capitalism—that view that the economic life of a nation is best served by the noninterference of government with business, putting exclusive reliance on the operation of the free market. This self-serving outlook was not entirely foreign to the Court since many of the Justices had prior experience as corporation lawyers. As you will see later, the Court's emasculation of the Interstate Commerce Clause—especially at a time when the rise of enormous business and financial conglomerates spanning many states made their description as "local" enterprises laughable—was coordinated with other constitutional tools to achieve the goal of no governmental regulation of business at all.

It is important to understanding discussions of the national-state relationship that we see the connection between the competing federal conceptions and the advancement or hindrance of certain economic interests or political values at a given period in time. It is significant, for example, that neither liberals nor conservatives have sustained enthusiasm for a consistent view of the federal system. The liberals' concern for the exploitation of the "have nots" which led Jefferson and others to adopt a dual federalist view in the early years of the nation led twentieth-century liberals to champion heady versions of cooperative federalism, notably illustrated in the domestic programs of Franklin Roosevelt, Harry Truman, and Lyndon Johnson. The propertied and business interests, on the other hand, enthusiastic about the stabilizing and protective effects of Marshall's vigorous efforts on behalf of the national government in the early nineteenth century, found by the end of that century that the limited government bias inherent in dual federalism better fit their purposes. Discussion of federal doctrines, then, should not come to be an abstract, academic exercise. Such doctrines have edges which can cut and cut deeply.

It was the Court's insensitivity to the deleterious effects of applying its dual federalist philosophy that led the Supreme Bench into supreme difficulty in the 1930s. The Great Depression brought home with cruel candor what the prevailing majority of Justices had chosen to ignore: that the days of agrarian supremacy and cottage industry—the stuff of which economic localism is made—had long since been replaced by an interdependent *national* economy which could not tolerate the luxury of being left on automatic pilot. As the Court repeatedly sallied forth to hatchet New Deal legislation, such as the National Recovery Act and the Guffey Coal Act, designed to help the nation back on its feet, the gulf between legal image and economic reality grew. Tenacious adherence to an artificial view of the economy, fueled by a mechanical, unthinking application of legal concepts, ultimately set the Executive and the Court on a collision course.

Returned to office for a second term by the largest popular mandate in American history up to that time and with a Congress that showed Republican opposition reduced to a shadow of what it once had been, President Roosevelt launched a proposal to overhaul the Supreme Court. It provided a comfortable retirement for Justices leaving the Court and, more significantly, authorized the President to appoint one additional Justice for each sitting Justice on the Court who was seventy years of age or older. Though the formal debate was focused on whether an institution dominated by such elderly men (six were over seventy) could effectively manage a burgeoning caseload, the real debate was political. Said Roosevelt, defending his plan in a "fireside chat" to the American public on March 9, 1937:

> We have * * * reached the point as a Nation where we must take action to save the Constitution from the Court and the Court from itself. We must find a way to take an appeal from the Supreme Court to the Constitution itself. We want a Supreme Court which will do justice under the Constitution—not over it. In our courts we want a government of laws and not of men.
>
> I want—as all Americans want—an independent judiciary as proposed by the framers of the Constitution. That means a Supreme Court that will enforce the Constitution as written—that will refuse to amend the Constitution by the arbitrary exercise of judicial power—amendment by judicial say-so. It does not mean a judiciary so independent that it can deny the existence of facts universally recognized. * * *

Franklin Roosevelt was unsuccessful in persuading Congress to adopt the proposal to "pack the Court"—many Democratic legislators deserted him sensing public outrage at any attack on the independence of so sacred an institution as the Supreme Court—but the goal of attaining a more receptive Judiciary was nonetheless realized when, in a marked shift from previous voting patterns, the Court's moderate bloc, composed of Chief Justice Hughes and Justice Roberts—taking the hint—aligned with the Court's three liberals, Justices Brandeis, Cardozo, and Stone, to create a majority sustaining the constitutionality of future New Deal legislation over the dissenting votes of the four hard-core conservatives, Justices Sutherland, Van Devanter, McReynolds, and Butler. Concluding the cause was now lost, the conservatives one by one retired shortly thereafter, and, by 1941, President Roosevelt had named eight Justices to the Court. Needless to say, the appointments were given to those who had been Roosevelt's staunchest supporters in the Court-packing controversy and who had been openly critical of the old Court's activism.

To be sure, Congress's unwillingness to acquiesce in the Executive's proposal spared the Court outright humiliation, but the ultimate decision to back down is in keeping with the overall pattern of other such confrontations. Under threats of impeachment and removal by a hostile Jeffersonian Congress, the Marshall Court chose to bite its tongue and tone down some of its Federalist excesses rather than to battle it out. The same behavior is equally descriptive of a more dualist-oriented Court in the post-Civil War years when a Radical Republican Congress began taking away seats on the Court and shaving down its appellate jurisdiction. These episodes underscore the combative weakness of the judicial institution as compared to the other two branches. Faced with the prospect of decisive open confrontation, the Court will—because it has to—tuck its tail. It is the style of abandonment and the ultimate wholehearted acceptance of the initially unacceptable cooperative federalist philosophy that ties together the remaining three cases in this section.

In its retreat from such a confrontation the Court has three possibilities. It can ignore the irritating precedents that gave rise to the conflict. It can distinguish a case presently before it, thus pulling the teeth of the irritating precedents with a maximum of judicial grace and telegraphing to the antagonist that it has gotten the message and decided to retire from the battle. Finally, the Court can overrule itself, openly confessing it was wrong. This last option, however, is costly to the judicial image.

The forgetting of irritating precedents was not possible in 1937. As we have seen, the Court affirmed the use of its dual federalist doctrines too often to make that strategy possible. So, in *National Labor Relations Board* v. *Jones & Laughlin Steel Corp.* (p. 479), the Court engaged in the second mode of retreat, elaborately explaining why what before might have seemed like "indirect effects" on national commerce suddenly were now somehow different. The activities of Jones & Laughlin now miraculously yielded the kinds of "direct effects" on interstate commerce that would warrant sustaining the constitutionality of the National Labor Relations Act. To the chagrin of the four conservatives, the majority here was engaged in the use of "word magic"—the abstract distinguishing of seemingly like cases to achieve significant political results. As the Court became more progressively transformed with the appearance of new Justices, the option of simply overruling those disagreeable precedents became more feasible. Consequently, Justice Stone, speaking for the Court in *United States* v. *Darby* (p. 488) four years later, explicitly overruled *Hammer* v. *Dagenhart*. Note the majority's cavalier treatment of the Tenth Amendment. By now the Court appears to have developed such disdain for the dualist approach it no longer is even willing to consider the direct-indirect effects mode of analysis. Finally, a new majority solidly in place, the Court, in *Wickard* v. *Filburn* (p. 494), not only reaffirmed the enthusiastic embrace it gave cooperative federalism in *Darby*, it settled new frontiers of national power to control the economy, now justifying the reach of the Commerce Clause to touch even "potential" effects of what is truly local activity. The metamorphosis was complete. And it will take more than one ruling to the contrary to derail this train of events. It remains to be seen whether the Burger Court's decision in *National League of Cities* v. *Usery* (p. 384)—the single exception to the fact that the Tenth Amendment has been effectively moribund since 1941—constitutes a funny little exception in the law or whether it signals the prospect of a constitutional crisis, reminiscent of the 1930s, alluded to in dissent by Justice Brennan.

c. The Navigation Power

Unlike the power to regulate production, Congress's power to superintend navigation has never been subject to the ping-pong effect of Justices subscribing to different controlling views of the federal relationship. You will recall from Chief Justice Marshall's discussion in *Gibbons* v. *Ogden* that the navigation power is included in the power of the national government to regulate interstate commerce and, as such, is supreme and absolute. The power not only covers all those who operate ships on navigable waters, but, as the ensuing cases show, the power has become a super power which can be exercised with serious adverse consequences on those who own property connected with navigable waterways.

Those who own property fronting on watercourses are said to possess riparian rights, that is, rights relating to the use of the water including such legal rights, for example, as the right to utilize some of the water for domestic purposes, the right to wharf out to navigability, and the right to gain access to more navigable waterways. Such rights are property rights and are legally considered to be valid against infringement by other parties. Some of the cases which follow involve suits to obtain fair value from the national government not simply for the worth of the land taken in condemnation proceedings, but also to gain additional compensation for the loss such property owners suffer in giving up their riparian rights. Against other parties, claims based on the loss of riparian rights are viable, but not so against actions of the national government. To be sure, where government takes land or other property from its owner, government must, given the concept of eminent domain protected by the provisions of the Fifth Amendment, pay "just compensation." However, if the waterway is navigable, the national government is under no obligation to compensate property owners for the loss of their riparian rights since the navigation power, granted by the Constitution, affords the national government supreme and absolute regulatory power—the constitutional right to direct the waters of navigable rivers however it chooses in the public interest. Property owners may *never* use their riparian rights to challenge actions of the national government as they pertain to a navigable waterway. When the national government, using its navigation power over a navigable river, touches what would have been considered riparian rights had the infringer been a private party, there is never a "taking" of property (and, therefore, the consequent obligation to pay fair value) but only constitutional, though perhaps devastating, regulation.

Consider the decisions in *United States* v. *Chandler-Dunbar Water Power Co.* (p. 499) and *United States* v. *Rands* (p. 506). As you can see from the *Chandler-Dunbar* case, the financial losses to the property holder caused by the exercise of the navigation power can be enormous. The *Rands* case makes the point that the small landowner can experience equal, if not proportionately greater, financial injury from the effect of such a national power. Would you agree with Justice White that the exercise of riparian rights against the national government has to be emasculated in order to prevent the private property owner from "receiv[ing] a windfall to which he is not entitled"? Do these cases show a windfall to the national government? If so, is this justifiable? If *Chandler-Dunbar* and *Rands* appear to suggest that the effect of the navigation power on private property rights is virtually without limit, the Burger Court's decision in *Kaiser Aetna* v. *United States* (p. 506) would seem to indicate to the contrary. What limits on Congress's power does the Court recognize in *Kaiser Aetna*? How does it harmonize the decision in *Kaiser Aetna* with its preexisting rulings in *Chandler-Dunbar* and *Rands*? In other words, what aspects of the facts in *Kaiser Aetna* distinguish it from the earlier cases?

An additional point in *Chandler-Dunbar* is worth mentioning. Note the Court's express statement that, given a navigable river, if Congress or its authorized agent concludes that structures in the river are an impediment to navigation, such a finding is conclusive and not reviewable by the courts. Far from any issue of compensating Chandler-Dunbar for their power-generating structures, could the national government not only compel their removal and, failing the power company's efforts to remove them, remove them itself and then charge the power company for their removal?

United States v. *Appalachian Electric Power Co.* (p. 509) points to an almost limitless extension of the navigation power. Navigability, we find, is not a quality merely confined to the natural condition of a river but extends to an ability to make a waterway suitable for navigation through "reasonable improvements." Given the Court's great reluctance to question congressional findings on other aspects of navigability, is there any stream or creek in the entire nation that wouldn't qualify as a navigable waterway and thus fall within the purview of national power?

The navigation power has also been used along with other sources of authority, such as the war power and the power of Congress to dispose of the national government's property, to sustain the generation and sale of electric power in direct competition with private generating companies. See *Ashwander* v. *Tennessee Valley Authority* (p. 514). Even without relying on such massive national powers, the Court in *Alabama Power Co.* v. *Ickes* (p. 518) sustained, without much effort, the generation and sale of power by four Alabama municipalities. The lack of a valid legal argument by the plaintiff power company is underscored by the fact that the Court's decision was written by one of its archconservative Justices, George Sutherland, a devout defender of the free enterprise system.

Finally, the awesome potential of the navigation power is handsomely illustrated by the Court's ruling in *City of Tacoma* v. *Taxpayers of Tacoma* (p. 519). The Court underscored the legally subordinate position of cities to states decades earlier in City of Trenton v. State of New Jersey, 262 U.S. 182, 43 S.Ct. 534 (1923), where it said: "In the absence of state constitutional provisions safeguarding it to them, municipalities have no inherent right of self-government which is beyond the legislative control of the State. A municipality is merely a department of the State, and the State may withhold, grant or withdraw powers and privileges as it sees fit. However great or small its sphere of action, it remains the creature of the State exercising and holding powers and privileges subject to the sovereign will." In the *Tacoma* case, Congress's navigation power, embodied in the federal license, furnishes the basis for reversing that traditional position of legal subordination in this case.

d. The Taxing and Spending Power

Government which must subsist on voluntary contributions is, as we found during the days of the Confederation, weak and ineffective government. The inability of the central government in those days to legitimately compel the collection of revenue by which it could sustain its operations was the straw that broke the Confederation's back and triggered the call for a constitutional convention. As a consequence, the new Constitution sought to give the national government revenue-raising power free from the exercise of any discretion by the states.

The taxing power, the very first of the enumerated powers, carried one exception and two qualifications. As Article I, section 9 makes clear, the national government is forbidden to lay any tax on exports. The same section of the Constitution also qualifies the manner in which other taxes may be levied and distinguishes for this purpose between direct and indirect taxes. The former were to be apportioned among the states according to population for which purpose a census was to be taken; the latter were to be laid uniformly—geographically uniformly, that is—such that these taxes would be collected throughout the country on the same basis and at the same rate. The Constitution is vague as to exactly what are to be considered direct taxes other than to offer the clue that a head tax would certainly fall in that category. Very soon the Court was asked to determine into which category a federal carriage tax fell. In Hylton v. United States, 3 U.S. (3 Dall.) 171, 1 L.Ed. 556 (1796), the Court reasoned that only capitation and land taxes could be regarded as direct taxes; the carriage tax was an indirect tax. This was so because of the nature of the carriage tax and the impossibility of fairly apportioning it.

The view that the category of direct taxes was so limited remained the controlling constitutional rule until the Court's decision in Pollock v. Farmers' Loan & Trust Co., 158 U.S. 601, 15 S.Ct. 912 (1895), a century later. Dominated by Justices partial to the defense of private property, as we noted earlier, the Court struck down a federal income tax by a narrow 5–4 margin. In doing so the majority reasoned that the category of direct taxes was not limited to the *Hylton* description but also included taxes on the income derived from land and other property. Given the conclusion that an income tax was a direct tax and the unrealistic option of apportioning such a tax, Congress was denied this source of revenue until the *Pollock* decision was overturned in 1913 by the adoption of the Sixteenth Amendment. As further illustration of the Court's flourishing attachment to the defense of that core of interests surrounding private property and dual federalism symptomatic of the period, you should also reconsider the discussion from the preceding chapter (at p. 361) as to the effects of the inter-governmental taxing immunity doctrine. Passage of the Sixteenth Amendment and the fact that the personal income tax has become the largest single source of revenue for the national government combined to render largely academic further discussion of the federal taxing power in terms of direct and indirect taxes.

Prior to the twentieth century, consideration of the national taxing power focused principally on the means of raising revenue. Taxes, however, do not merely finance; they may also regulate. It is the use of the national taxing and spending power for the latter purpose which has sparked a modern-day controversy, and, as you might anticipate, how you resolve the dispute is largely contingent upon your view of the federal relationship.

The Court's initial verdict on any examination of the revenue-raising as opposed to the regulatory use of the taxing power is suggested by its decision in *McCray* v. *United States* (p. 522), a case involving the constitutionality of what was clearly an inhibiting federal tax on the sale of oleomargarine colored to look like butter. Speaking for the Court, Justice White made it plain that the chronic examination of congressional motives, a prerequisite to establishing any conclusion that the margarine tax was passed for regulatory purposes, was an improper judicial activity, displaying a lack of due regard for the discretion of a coordinate branch of government. The dualist zeal of the Court during the twenties and thirties, however, dampened any long-term effect of the holding in *McCray*. *McCray* became a precedent to be distinguished, not one to be followed.

After experiencing ignominious defeat at the hands of the Court in *Hammer* v. *Dagenhart*, Congress turned to the taxing power to deal with the problem of child labor. The fruit of its efforts, the Child Labor Tax Act, reached the Court in 1922, four years after the ruling in *Hammer*. Speaking for the Court in *Bailey* v. *Drexel Furniture Co.*, (p. 525), which held the act unconstitutional, Chief Justice Taft wasted no time asking the telltale question: Did the Child Labor Tax Act impose a tax or a penalty? How successful do you think he was in differentiating between the two? How well do these criteria operate to distinguish the "tax" in *McCray* from the "penalty" in *Bailey*? The very construction of such a dichotomy, of course, lays bare the precepts of dual federalism. Note the majority's devastating use of the Tenth Amendment to cut off any intrusion by the national government into the cloisters of state power. Though reform elements in the Congress subsequently pushed for the adoption of a constitutional amendment to abolish child labor, the Court later overruled the decision in *Hammer* itself (see *United States* v. *Darby*, p. 488), sustaining the constitutionality of such legislation.

What is regarded as the classic dual federalist response by the Court to the regulatory uses of the taxing and spending power by the national government lies in Justice Roberts's opinion in *United States* v. *Butler* (p. 528). At stake was the constitutionality of the first New Deal program to do something about the depressed state of farm prices. Justice Roberts's now famous mechanistic characterization of the judging process furnishes a clue at the outset as to the likely dualist tenor of the opinion. Consider that characterization carefully. Why is this description of the judicial function inaccurate? Is the inaccurate quality of such a description peculiar to modern-day adjudication or is it essentially mistaken with respect to all adjudication—including Roberts's?

The majority's encouraging acceptance—from a cooperative federalist view—of Hamilton's view on the scope of the taxing and spending power, as opposed to Madison's, is soured by the narrow and stunted application given his view. Though the Court accepts the proposition that the taxing and spending power is an independent power—the national government may tax and spend for the general welfare, rather than simply be permitted to tax and spend to carry into successful execution the enumerated powers of Article I, section 8—the majority exhibits a particularly limited and superficial view as to what constitutes the general welfare. How aware is Justice Roberts of the interdependence of a national economy? Quite apart from economics, how good is his political science? He says that "A tax, in the general understanding of the term, and as used in the Constitution, signifies an exaction for the support of the Government. The word has never been thought to connote the expropriation of money from one group to another." Given a contemporary pluralistic view of the political process, would you agree?

Consistent with the spirit of cooperative federalism which returned to the Court in the Constitutional Revolution of 1937 is the Court's decision in *Steward Machine Co.* v. *Davis* (p. 371), examined earlier. The tenor of Justice Stone's dissent in *Butler* eventually became the dominant tone of the Court. The *Butler* decision, however, was not overruled, and its impact, forcing a separation of the taxing and spending powers to avoid the charge that legislation is not for the *general* welfare, is apparent. The philosophy of cooperative federalism is also evident in *Mulford* v. *Smith* (p. 537), a case in which the Court validated the Second Agricultural Adjustment Act. Reflecting a change of heart, the Court accepted as constitutional the imposition of a penalty on appellants for overproduction of tobacco in violation of a marketing quota set under regulatory legislation grounded on the national government's power over interstate commerce.

A more extraordinary illustration of cooperative federalism in the context of the taxing and spending power is furnished by the Court's decision some years later in Cleveland v. United States, 323 U.S. 329, 65 S.Ct. 280 (1945). In that case, the Court sustained federal power to condemn land and construct low-cost public housing under housing legislation which was passed pursuant to the authority of the national government to expend monies and so promote the general welfare.

As demonstrated by its opinion upholding a federal gambling tax in *United States* v. *Kahriger* (p. 539), the Court has once again returned to that appreciation of the regulatory capacity of the taxing power evident initially in the *McCray* decision. Cooperation between national and state governments in a federal system, however, is not an unqualified good. It is pregnant with the possibilities of mangling individual rights, as Justices Black and Douglas so forcefully contend in dissent. As it turned out, their argument was not wide of the mark but only a little early. Their view as to the compulsion of self-incrimination, inherent in such a taxation scheme, was fully adopted by the Court fifteen years later in *Marchetti* v. *United States* (p. 543) and a companion case, *Grosso* v. *United States* (p. 545).

a. THE GENERAL SCOPE OF CONGRESS'S POWER TO REGULATE INTERSTATE COMMERCE

GIBBONS v. OGDEN

Supreme Court of the United States, 1824
22 U.S. (9 Wheat.) 1, 6 L.Ed. 23

Aaron Ogden filed a bill in the Court of Chancery of New York seeking an injunction to restrain Thomas Gibbons, a citizen of New Jersey, from operating his two steamboats between Elizabethtown, New Jersey, and New York City. Previously, the New York legislature passed a statute granting exclusive rights to use steam vessels on its waters to Robert Fulton and Robert Livingston. Ogden, who obtained permission from the two franchise holders through John Livingston, claimed exclusive rights to navigate between New York City and New Jersey. Gibbons, on the other hand, was operating his boats with a federal license granted under an act of Congress. He maintained that the New York laws conflicted with the Constitution and the laws of the United States. Nevertheless, a permanent injunction was granted and later affirmed by the state Court of Errors. Gibbons appealed to the Supreme Court.

Mr. Chief Justice MARSHALL delivered the opinion of the Court.

* * *

The appellant contends that this decree is erroneous, because the laws which purport to give the exclusive privilege it sustains, are repugnant to the constitution and laws of the United States.

They are said to be repugnant:

* * * To that clause in the constitution which authorizes Congress to regulate commerce.

* * *

As preliminary to the very able discussions of the constitution, which we have heard from the bar, and as having some influence on its construction, reference has been made to the political situation of these states, anterior to its formation. It has been said that they were sovereign, were completely independent, and were connected with each other only by a league. This is true. But when these allied sovereigns converted their league into a government, when they converted their Congress of Ambassadors, deputed to deliberate on their common concerns, and to recommend measures of general utility, into a legislature, empowered to enact laws on the most interesting subjects, the whole character in which the states appear, underwent a change, the extent of which must be determined by a fair consideration of the instrument by which that change was effected.

This instrument contains an enumeration of powers expressly granted by the people to their government. It has been said that these powers ought to be construed strictly. But why ought they to be so construed? Is there one sentence in the constitution which gives countenance to this rule? In the last of the enumerated powers, that which grants, expressly, the means of carrying all others into execution, Congress is authorized "to make all laws which shall be necessary and proper" for the purpose. But this limitation on the means which may be used, is not extended to the powers which are conferred; nor is there one sentence in the constitution which has been pointed out by the gentlemen of the bar, or which we have been able to discern, that prescribes this rule. We do not, therefore, think ourselves justified in adopting it. What do gentlemen mean by a strict construction? If they contend only against that enlarged construction which would extend words beyond their natural and obvious import, we might question the application of the term, but should not controvert the principle. If they contend for that narrow construction which, in support of some theory not to be found in the constitution, would deny to the government those powers which the words of the grant, as usually understood, import, and which are consistent with the general views and objects of the instrument; for that narrow construction, which would cripple the government and render it unequal to the objects for which it is declared to be instituted, and to which the powers given, as fairly understood, render it competent; then we cannot perceive the propriety of this strict construction, nor adopt it as the rule by which the constitution is to be expounded. As men, whose intentions require no concealment, generally employ the words which most directly and aptly express the ideas they intend to convey, the enlightened patriots who framed our constitution, and the people who adopted it, must be understood to have employed words in their natural sense, and to

have intended what they have said. If, from the imperfection of human language, there should be serious doubts respecting the extent of any given power, it is a well-settled rule that the objects for which it was given, especially when those objects are expressed in the instrument itself, should have great influence in the construction. We know of no reason for excluding this rule from the present case. The grant does not convey power which might be beneficial to the grantor, if retained by himself, or which can enure solely to the benefit of the grantee, but is an investment of power for the general advantage, in the hands of agents selected for that purpose; which power can never be exercised by the people themselves, but must be placed in the hands of agents or lie dormant. We know of no rule for construing the extent of such powers, other than is given by the language of the instrument which confers them, taken in connection with the purposes for which they were conferred.

The words are: "Congress shall have power to regulate commerce with foreign nations, and among the several states, and with the Indian tribes."

The subject to be regulated is commerce; and our constitution being, as was aptly said at the bar, one of enumeration, and not of definition, to ascertain the extent of the power it becomes necessary to settle the meaning of the word. The counsel for the appellee would limit it to traffic, to buying and selling, or the interchange of commodities, and do not admit that it comprehends navigation. This would restrict a general term, applicable to many objects, to one of its significations. Commerce, undoubtedly, is traffic, but it is something more; it is intercourse.

It describes the commercial intercourse between nations, and parts of nations, in all its branches, and is regulated by prescribing rules for carrying on that intercourse. The mind can scarcely conceive a system for regulating commerce between nations, which shall exclude all laws concerning navigation, which shall be silent on the admission of the vessels of the one nation into the ports of the other, and be confined to prescribing rules for the conduct of individuals, in the actual employment of buying and selling, or of barter.

If commerce does not include navigation, the government of the Union has no direct power over that subject, and can make no law prescribing what shall constitute American vessels, or requiring that they shall be navigated by American seamen. Yet this power has been exercised from the commencement of the government, has been exercised with the consent of all, and has been understood by all to be a commercial regulation. All America understands, and has uniformly understood, the word "commerce" to comprehend navigation. It was so understood, and must have been so understood, when the constitution was framed. The power over commerce, including navigation, was one of the primary objects for which the people of America adopted their government, and must have been contemplated in forming it. The convention must have used the word in that sense; because all have understood it in that sense, and the attempt to restrict it comes too late.

* * *

The word used in the constitution, then, comprehends, and has been always understood to comprehend, navigation within its meaning; and a power to regulate navigation is as expressly granted as if that term had been added to the word "commerce."

To what commerce does this power extend? The constitution informs us, to commerce "with foreign nations, and among the several states, and with the Indian tribes."

It has, we believe, been universally admitted that these words comprehend every species of commercial intercourse between the United States and foreign nations. No sort of trade can be carried on between this country and any other, to which this power does not extend. It has been truly said, that commerce, as the word is used in the constitution, is a unit, every part of which is indicated by the term.

If this be the admitted meaning of the word, in its application to foreign nations, it must carry the same meaning throughout the sentence, and remain a unit, unless there be some plain intelligible cause which alters it.

The subject to which the power is next applied, is to commerce "among the several states." The word "among" means intermingled with. A thing which is among others, is intermingled with them. Commerce among the states cannot stop at the external boundary line of each state, but may be introduced into the interior.

It is not intended to say that these words comprehend that commerce which is completely internal, which is carried on between man and man in a state, or between different parts of the same state, and which does not extend to or affect other states. Such a power would be inconvenient, and is certainly unnecessary.

Comprehensive as the word "among" is, it may very properly be restricted to that commerce which concerns more states than one. The phrase is not one which would probably have been selected to indicate the completely interior traffic of a state, because it is not an apt phrase for that purpose; and the enumeration of the particular classes of commerce to which the power was to be extended, would not have been made had the intention been to extend the power to every description. The enumeration presupposes something not enumerated; and that something, if we regard the language or the subject of the sentence, must be the exclusively internal commerce of a state. The genius and character of the whole government seem to be, that its action is to be applied to all the external concerns of the nation, and to those internal concerns which affect the states generally; but not to those which are completely within a particular state, which do not affect other states, and with which it is not necessary to interfere, for the purpose of executing some of the general powers of the government. The completely internal commerce of a state, then, may be considered as reserved for the state itself.

But, in regulating commerce with foreign nations, the power of Congress does not stop at the jurisdictional lines of the several states. It would be a very useless power if it could not pass those lines. The commerce of the United States with foreign nations, is that of the whole United States. Every district has a right to participate in it. The deep streams which penetrate our country in every direction, pass through the interior of almost every state in the Union, and furnish the means of exercising this right. If Congress has the power to regulate it, that power must be exercised whenever the subject exists. If it exists within the states, if a foreign voyage may commence or terminate at a port within a state, then the power of Congress may be exercised within a state.

* * *

We are now arrived at the inquiry, What is this power?

It is the power to regulate; that is, to prescribe the rule by which commerce is to be governed. This power, like all others vested in Congress, is complete in itself, may be exercised to its utmost extent, and acknowledges no limitations, other than are prescribed in the constitution. These are expressed in plain terms, and do not affect the questions which arise in this case, or which have been discussed at the bar. If, as has always been understood, the sovereignty of Congress, though limited to specified objects, is plenary as to those objects, the power over commerce with foreign nations, and among the several States, is vested in Congress as absolutely as it would be in a single government, having in its constitution the same restrictions on the exercise of the power as are found in the constitution of the United States. The wisdom and the discretion of Congress, their identity with the people, and the influence which their constituents possess at election, are, in this, as in many other instances, as that, for example, of declaring war, the sole restraints on which they have relied, to secure them from its abuse. They are the restraints on which the people must often rely solely, in all representative governments.

The power of Congress, then, comprehends navigation within the limits of every state in the Union; so far as that navigation may be, in any manner, connected with "commerce with foreign nations, or among the several states, or with the Indian tribes." It may, of consequence, pass the jurisdictional line of New York, and act upon the very waters to which the prohibition now under consideration applies.

But it has been urged with great earnestness, that although the power of Congress to regulate commerce with foreign nations, and among the several states, be co-extensive with the subject itself, and have no other limits than are prescribed in the constitution, yet the states may severally exercise the same power within their respective jurisdictions. In support of this argument, it is said that they possessed it as an inseparable attribute of sovereignty, before the formation of the constitution, and still retain it, except so far as they have surrendered it by that instrument; that this principle results from the nature of the government, and is secured by the tenth amendment; that an affirmative grant of power is not exclusive, unless in its own nature it be such that the continued exercise of it by the former possessor is inconsistent with the grant, and that this is not of that description.

The appellant, conceding these postulates, except the last, contends that full power to regulate a particular subject, implies the whole power, and leaves no residuum; that a grant of the whole is incompatible with the existence of a right in another to any part of it.

Both parties have appealed to the constitution, to legislative acts, and judicial decisions; and have drawn arguments from all these sources to support and illustrate the propositions they respectively maintain.

The grant of the power to lay and collect taxes is, like the power to regulate commerce, made in general terms, and has never been understood to interfere with the exercise of the same power by the states; and hence has been drawn an argument which has been applied to the question under consideration. But the two grants are not, it is conceived, similar in their terms or their nature. Although many of the powers formerly exercised by the states, are transferred to the government of the Union, yet the state governments remain, and constitute a most important part of our system. The power of taxation is indispensable to their existence, and is a power which, in its own nature, is capable of residing in, and being exercised by, different authorities at the same time. We are accustomed to see it placed, for different purposes, in different hands. * * * In imposing taxes for state purposes, they are not doing what Congress is empowered to do. Congress is not empowered to tax for these purposes which are within the exclusive province of the states. When, then, each government exercises the power of taxation, neither is exercising the power of the other. But, when a state proceeds to regulate commerce with foreign nations, or among the several states, it is exercising the very power that is granted to Congress, and is doing the very thing which Congress is authorized to do. There is no analogy, then, between the power of taxation and the power of regulating commerce.

* * *

[T]he inspection laws are said to be regulations of commerce, and are certainly recognized in the constitution, as being passed in the exercise of a power remaining with the states.

That inspection laws may have a remote and considerable influence on commerce, will not be denied; but that a power to regulate commerce is the source from which the right to pass them is derived, cannot be admitted. The objects of inspection laws is to improve the quality of articles produced by the labor of the country; to fit them for exportation; or, it may be, for domestic use. They act upon the subject before it becomes an article of foreign commerce, or of commerce among the states and prepared it for that purpose. They form a portion of that immense mass of legislation which embraces everything within the territory of a state not surrendered to the general government; all which can be most advantageously exercised by the states themselves. Inspection laws, quarantine laws, health laws of every description, as well as laws for regulating the internal commerce of a state, and those which respect turnpike-roads, ferries, etc., are component parts of this mass.

No direct general power over these objects is granted to Congress; and, consequently, they remain subject to state legislation. If the legislative power of the Union can reach them, it must be for national purposes; it must be where the power is expressly given for a special purpose, or is clearly incidental to some power which is expressly given. It is obvious, that the government of the Union, in the exercise of its express powers, that, for example, of regulating commerce with foreign nations and among the states, may use means that may also be employed by a state, in the exercise of its acknowledged power; that, for example, of regulating commerce within the state. * * *

In our complex system, presenting the rare and difficult scheme of one general government, whose action extends over the whole, but which possesses only certain enumerated powers, and of numerous state governments, which retain and exercise all powers not delegated to the Union, contests respecting power must arise. Were it even otherwise, the measures taken by the respective governments to execute their acknowledged powers, would often be of the same description, and might, sometimes, interfere. This, however, does not prove that the one is exercising, or has a right to exercise, the powers of the other.

* * *

[I]n exercising the power of regulating their own purely internal affairs, whether of trading or police, the states may sometimes enact laws, the validity of which depends on their interfering with, and being contrary to, an act of Congress passed in pursuance of the constitution, the court will enter upon the inquiry, whether the laws of New York, as expounded by the highest tribunal of that state, have, in their application to this case, come into collision with an act of Congress, and deprived a citizen of a right to which that act entitles him. Should this collision exist, it will be immaterial whether those laws were passed in virtue of a concurrent power "to regulate commerce with foreign nations and among the several states," or in virtue of a power to regulate their domestic trade and police. In one case and the other, the acts of New York must yield to the law of Congress; and the decision sustaining the privilege they confer, against a right given by a law of the Union, must be erroncous.

This opinion has been frequently expressed in this court, and is founded as well on the nature of the government as on the words of the constitution. In argument, however, it has been contended that if a law, passed by a state in the exercise of its acknowledged sovereignty, comes into conflict with a law passed by Congress in pursuance of the constitution, they affect the subject, and each other, like equal opposing powers.

But the framers of our constitution foresaw this state of things, and provided for it, by declaring the supremacy not only of itself, but of the laws made in pursuance of it. The nullity of any act, inconsistent with the constitution, is produced by the declaration that the constitution is the supreme law. The appropriate application of that part of the clause which confers the same supremacy on laws and treaties, is to such acts of the state legislatures as do not transcend their powers, but, though enacted in the execution of acknowledged state powers, interfere with, or are contrary to the laws of Congress, made in pursuance of the constitution, or some treaty made under the authority of the United States. In every such case, the act of Congress, or the treaty, is supreme; and the law of the state, though enacted in the exercise of powers not controverted, must yield to it.

* * *

[The Act of Congress] demonstrates the opinion of Congress, that steamboats may be enrolled and li-

censed, in common with vessels using sails. They are, of course, entitled to the same privileges, and can no more be restrained from navigating waters, and entering ports which are free to such vessels, than if they were wafted on their voyage by the winds, instead of being propelled by the agency of fire. The one element may be as legitimately used as the other, for every commercial purpose authorized by the laws of the Union; and the act of a state inhibiting the use of either to any vessel having a license under the act of Congress, comes, we think, in direct collision with that act.

Powerful and ingenious minds, taking, as postulates, that the powers expressly granted to the government of the Union are to be contracted, by construction, into the narrowest possible compass, and that the original powers of the States are retained, if any possible construction will retain them, may, by a course of well digested, but refined and metaphysical reasoning, founded on these premises, explain away the constitution of our country, and leave it a magnificent structure indeed, to look at, but totally unfit for use. They may so entangle and perplex the understanding, as to obscure principles which were before thought quite plain, and induce doubts where, if the mind were to pursue its own course, none would be perceived. In such a case, it is peculiarly necessary to recur to safe and fundamental principles to sustain those principles, and, when sustained, to make them the tests of the arguments to be examined.

[The concurring opinion of Justice JOHNSON is omitted.]

In Pensacola Telegraph Co. v. Western Union Telegraph Co., 96 U.S. 1, 24 L.Ed. 708 (1878), the Supreme Court held a monopoly conferred on the Pensacola Telegraph Company in 1866 by the State of Florida invalid when it conflicted with a federal statute passed in the same year under the powers of the national government to regulate interstate commerce and to establish post offices and post roads. The federal statute provided that any telegraph company had the right to string and operate lines over any portion of the public domain provided that company gave first priority to government transmissions and agreed to accept compensation for the conveyance of official business at rates fixed annually by the Postmaster General. On the basis of this legislation Western Union, which had undertaken an agreement with the federal government pursuant to the statute, sued to restrain the Pensacola company from exercising its exclusive state-granted franchise to service the counties of western Florida.

Speaking for the majority, (Justices Field and Hunt dissented), Chief Justice Waite said:

> Since the case of Gibbons v. Ogden, 9 Wheat., 1, it has never been doubted that commercial intercourse is an element of commerce which comes within the regulating power of Congress. Postoffices and postroads are established to facilitate the transmission of intelligence. Both commerce and the postal service are placed within the power of Congress, because, being national in their operation, they should be under the protecting care of the National Government.
>
> The powers thus granted are not confined to the instrumentalities of commerce, or the postal service known or in use when the Constitution was adopted, but they keep pace with the progress of the country, and adapt themselves to the new developments of time and circumstances. They extend from the horse with its rider to the stage-coach, from the sailing vessel to the steamboat, from the coach and the steamboat to the railroad, and from the railroad to the telegraph, as these new agencies are successively brought into use to meet the demands of increasing population and wealth. They were intended for the government of the business to which they relate, at all times and under all circumstances. As they were intrusted to the General Government for the good of the nation, it is not only the right but the duty of Congress to see to it that intercourse among the States and the transmission of intelligence are not obstructed or unnecessarily incumbered by state legislation.

STAFFORD v. WALLACE

Supreme Court of the United States, 1922
258 U.S. 495, 42 S.Ct. 397, 66 L.Ed. 735

After investigations disclosed fraud, price fixing, and manipulation rampant in the livestock and meat processing industry by the "Big Five" meatpackers (Swift, Armour, Cudahy, Wilson, and Morris), Congress enacted the Packers and Stockyards Act of 1921. Among other things it sought to regulate the exploitive practices which characterized the wholesale meat market by empowering the Secretary of Agriculture to regulate prices and oversee business methods in the stockyards. Stafford, who was engaged in buying and selling livestock, sued to enjoin Wallace, the Secretary of Agriculture, from such regulation, contending that the statute was an unconstitutional use of the commerce power by Congress. The federal district court denied the injunction, and Stafford appealed to the Supreme Court.

Mr. Chief Justice TAFT * * *
delivered the opinion of the Court.

* * *

The object to be secured by the act is the free and unburdened flow of live stock from the ranges and farms of the West and the Southwest through the great stockyards and slaughtering centers on the borders of that region, and thence in the form of meat products to the consuming cities of the country in the Middle West and East, or, still, as live stock, to the feeding places and fattening farms in the Middle West or East for further preparation for the market.

The chief evil feared is the monopoly of the packers, enabling them unduly and arbitrarily to lower prices to the shipper, who sells, and unduly and arbitrarily to increase the price to the consumer, who buys. Congress thought that the power to maintain this monopoly was aided by control of the stockyards. Another evil, which it sought to provide against by the act, was exorbitant charges, duplication of commissions, deceptive practices in respect of prices, in the passage of the live stock through the stockyards, all made possible by collusion between the stockyards management and the commission men, on the one hand, and the packers and dealers, on the other. Expenses incurred in the passage through the stockyards necessarily reduce the price received by the shipper, and increase the price to be paid by the consumer. If they be exorbitant or unreasonable, they are an undue burden on the commerce which the stockyards are intended to facilitate. Any unjust or deceptive practice or combination that unduly and directly enhances them is an unjust obstruction to that commerce. The shipper, whose live stock are be-

ing cared for and sold in the stockyards market, is ordinarily not present at the sale, but is far away in the West. He is wholly dependent on the commission men. The packers and their agents and the dealers, who are the buyers, are at the elbow of the commission men, and their relations are constant and close. The control that the packers have had in the stockyards by reason of ownership and constant use, the relation of landlord and tenant between the stockyards owner, on the one hand, and the commission men and the dealers, on the other, the power of assignment of pens and other facilities by that owner to commission men and dealers, all create a situation full of opportunity and temptation, to the prejudice of the absent shipper and owner in the neglect of the live stock, in the mala fides of the sale, in the exorbitant prices obtained, and in the unreasonableness of the charges for services rendered.

The stockyards are not a place of rest or final destination. Thousands of head of live stock arrive daily by carload and trainload lots, and must be promptly sold and disposed of and moved out, to give place to the constantly flowing traffic that presses behind. The stockyards are but a throat through which the current flows, and the transactions which occur therein are only incident to this current from the West to the East, and from one state to another. Such transactions cannot be separated from the movement to which they contribute and necessarily take on its character. The commission men are essential in making the sales, without which the flow of the current would be obstructed, and this, whether they are made to packers or dealers. The dealers are essential to the sales to the stock farmers and feeders. The sales are not in this aspect merely local transactions. They create a local change of title, it is true, but they do not stop the flow; they merely change the private interests in the subject of the current, not interfering with, but, on the contrary, being indispensable to, its continuity. The origin of the live stock is in the West; its ultimate destination, known to, and intended by, all engaged in the business, is in the Middle West and East, either as meat products or stock for feeding and fattening. This is the definite and well-understood course of business. The stockyards and the sales are necessary factors in the middle of this current of commerce.

The act, therefore, treats the various stockyards of the country as great national public utilities to promote the flow of commerce from the ranges and farms of the West to the consumers in the East. It assumes that they conduct a business affected by a public use of a national character and subject to national regulation. That it is a business within the power of regulation by legislative action needs no discussion. That has been settled since the case of Munn v. Illinois, 94 U.S. 113, 24 L.Ed. 77. Nor is there any doubt that in the receipt of live stock by rail and in their delivery by rail the stockyards are an interstate commerce * * * agency. The only question here is whether the business done in the stockyards, between the receipt of the live stock in the yards and the shipment of them therefrom, is a part of interstate commerce, or is so associated with it as to bring it within the power of national regulation. * * *

* * *

As already noted, the word "commerce," when used in the act, is defined to be interstate and foreign commerce. Its provisions are carefully drawn to apply only to those practices and obstructions which in the judgment of Congress are likely to affect interstate commerce prejudicially. Thus construed and applied, we think the act clearly within Congressional power and valid.

* * *

The orders of the District Court refusing the interlocutory injunctions are

Affirmed.

Mr. Justice McREYNOLDS dissents.

Mr. Justice DAY did not sit in these cases and took no part in their decision.

HOUSTON, EAST & WEST TEXAS RAILWAY CO. v. UNITED STATES [THE SHREVEPORT RATE CASE]

Supreme Court of the United States, 1914
234 U.S. 342, 34 S.Ct. 833, 58 L.Ed. 1341

The Louisiana Railroad Commission initiated proceedings before the Interstate Commerce Commission against three railroads, including the Houston Railway Company, for discriminating against interstate commerce between Louisiana and Texas. The gist of the complaint was that these railroads charged lower rates for intrastate shipments among east Texas locations than for interstate shipments over similar distances and territory. The impact of this preferred rate structure— a scheme sanctioned by the Texas Railroad Commission in the maximum rates it allowed on intrastate transport—was to encourage trade among east Texas cities at the expense of trade with Shreveport, Louisiana, a natural focal point of commerce for such Texas cities as Dallas. After hearings, the ICC set reasonable maximum rates for both interstate and intrastate hauls and ordered the railroads to cease their discriminatory practices. The railroads were thus obliged to raise their rates for intrastate transport to a leval equal with the interstate rates, despite the fact that this increase conflicted with the maximum rates set for intrastate hauls by the Texas Railroad Commission. The Houston Railway unsuccessfully appealed the ICC order to the Commerce Court. On subsequent appeal to the U.S. Supreme Court, the company asserted that (1) Congress or an agency created by it could not regulate intrastate traffic, and (2) if Congress could, it had chosen not to do so, and the ICC had therefore exceeded its authority.

Mr. Justice HUGHES delivered the opinion of the court:

* * *

The point of the objection to the order is that, as the discrimination found by the Commission to be unjust arises out of the relation of intrastate rates, maintained under state authority, to interstate rates that have been upheld as reasonable, its correction was beyond the Commission's power. Manifestly the order might be complied with, and the discrimination avoided, either by reducing the interstate rates from Shreveport to the level of the competing intrastate rates, or by raising these intrastate rates to the level of the interstate rates, or by such reduction in the one case and increase in the other as would result in equality. But it is urged that, so far as the interstate rates were sustained by the Commission as reasonable, the Commission was without authority to compel their reduction in order to equalize them with the lower intrastate rates. The holding of the commerce court was that the order relieved the appellants from further obligation to observe the instrastate rates, and that they were at liberty to comply with the Commission's requirements by increasing these rates sufficiently to remove the forbidden discrimination. * * *

* * *

* * * It is unnecessary to repeat what has frequently been said by this court with respect to the complete and paramount character of the power confided to Congress to regulate commerce among the several states. It is of the essence of this power that, where it exists, it dominates. Interstate trade was not left to be destroyed or impeded by the rivalries of local government. The purpose was to make impossible the recurrence of the evils which had overwhelmed the Confederation, and to provide the necessary basis of national unity by insuring "uniformity of regulation against conflicting and discriminating state legislation." By virtue of the comprehensive terms of the grant, the authority of Congress is at all times adequate to meet the varying exigencies that arise, and to protect the national interest by securing the freedom of interstate commercial intercourse from local control. * * *

* * *

* * * It is for Congress to supply the needed correction where the relation between intrastate and interstate rates presents the evil to be corrected, and this it may do completely, by reason of its control over the interstate carrier in all matters having such a close and substantial relation to interstate commerce that it is necessary or appropriate to exer-

cise the control for the effective government of that commerce.

It is also clear that, in removing the injurious discriminations against interstate traffic arising from the relation of intrastate to interstate rates, Congress is not bound to reduce the latter below what it may deem to be a proper standard, fair to the carrier and to the public. Otherwise, it could prevent the injury to interstate commerce only by the sacrifice of its judgment as to interstate rates. Congress is entitled to maintain its own standard as to these rates, and to forbid any discriminatory action by interstate carriers which will obstruct the freedom of movement of interstate traffic over their

lines in accordance with the terms it establishes.

Having this power, Congress could provide for its execution through the aid of a subordinate body; and we conclude that the order of the Commission now in question cannot be held invalid upon the ground that it exceeded the authority which Congress could lawfully confer.

* * *

The decree of the Commerce Court is affirmed in each case.

Affirmed.

Mr. Justice LURTON and Mr. Justice PITNEY dissent.

CHAMPION v. AMES
[THE LOTTERY CASE]

Supreme Court of the United States, 1903
188 U.S. 321, 23 S.Ct. 321, 47 L.Ed. 492

Charles Champion deposited lottery tickets with the Wells-Fargo Express Company in Texas to have them sent to California where they would be sold. The tickets were for an alleged lottery run by the Pan American Lottery Company which held monthly drawings for prizes in Asuncion, Paraguay. John Ames, a United States marshal, arrested Champion in Chicago to bring him to Texas to stand trial for violating an 1895 act of Congress which made it unlawful to transport lottery tickets across state lines. Champion petitioned a federal court sitting in Chicago for a writ of habeas corpus, contending that the statute was unconstitutional since it attempted to regulate what he argued was not an interstate commercial activity. The federal court dismissed Champion's application, and he appealed to the Supreme Court.

Mr. Justice HARLAN delivered the opinion of the court:

* * *

The appellant insists that the carrying of lottery tickets from one state to another state by an express company engaged in carrying freight and packages from state to state, although such tickets may be contained in a box or package, does not constitute, and cannot by any act of Congress be legally made to constitute, commerce among the states within the meaning of the clause of the Constitution of the United States providing that Congress shall have power "to regulate commerce with foreign nations, and among the several states, and with the Indian tribes"; consequently, that Congress cannot make it an offense to cause such tickets to be carried from one state to another.

The government insists that express companies, when engaged, for hire, in the business of transportation from one state to another, are instrumentalities of commerce among the states; that the carrying of lottery tickets from one state to another is commerce which Congress may regulate; and that as a means of executing the power to regulate interstate commerce Congress may make it an offense against the United States to cause lottery tickets to be carried from one state to another.

The questions presented by these opposing contentions are of great moment, and are entitled to receive, as they have received, the most careful consideration.

What is the import of the word "commerce" as used in the Constitution? It is not defined by that instrument. Undoubtedly, the carrying from one state to another by independent carriers of things or commodities that are ordinary subjects of traffic, and which have in themselves a recognized value in money, constitutes interstate commerce. But does not commerce among the several states include something more? Does not the carrying from one state to another, by independent carriers, of lottery tickets that entitle the holder to the payment of a certain amount of money therein specified, also constitute commerce among the states?

* * *

[R]eference to prior adjudications could be extended if it were necessary to do so. The cases * * * however, sufficiently indicate the grounds upon which this court has proceeded when determining the meaning and scope of the commerce clause. They show that commerce among the states embraces navigation, intercourse, communication, traffic, the transit of persons, and the transmission of messages by telegraph. They also show that the power to regulate commerce among the several states is vested in Congress as absolutely as it would be in a single government, having in its constitution the same restrictions on the exercise of the power as are found in the Constitution of the United States; that such power is plenary, complete in itself, and may be exerted by Congress to its utmost extent, subject *only* to such limitations as the Constitution imposes upon the exercise of the powers granted by it; and that in determining the character of the regulations to be adopted Congress has a large discretion which is not to be controlled by the courts, simply because, in their opinion, such regulations may not be the best or most effective that could be employed.

We come then, to inquire whether there is any solid foundation upon which to rest the contention that Congress may not regulate the carrying of lottery tickets from one state to another, at least by corporations or companies whose business it is, for hire, to carry tangible property from one state to another.

It was said in argument that lottery tickets are not of any real or substantial value in themselves, and therefore are not subjects of commerce. If that were conceded to be the only legal test as to what are to be deemed subjects of the commerce that may be regulated by Congress, we cannot accept as accurate the broad statement that such tickets are of no value. Upon their face they showed that the lottery company offered a large capital prize, to be paid to the holder of the ticket winning the prize at the drawing advertised to be held at Asuncion, Paraguay. Money was placed on deposit in different banks in the United States to be applied by the agents representing the lottery company to the prompt payment of prizes. These tickets were the subject of traffic; they could have been sold; and the holder was assured that the company would pay to him the amount of the prize drawn. That the holder might not have been able to enforce his claim in the courts of any country making the drawing of lotteries illegal, and forbidding the circulation of lottery tickets, did not change the fact that the tickets issued by the foreign company represented so much money payable to the person holding them and who might draw the prizes affixed to them. Even if a holder did not draw a prize, the tickets, before the drawing, had a money value in the market among those who chose to sell or buy lottery tickets. In short, a lottery ticket is a subject of traffic, and is so designated in the act of 1895. * * *

We are of opinion that lottery tickets are subjects of traffic, and therefore are subjects of commerce, and the regulation of the carriage of such tickets from state to state, at least by independent carriers, is a regulation of commerce among the several states.

But it is said that the statute in question does not regulate the carrying of lottery tickets from state to state, but by punishing those who cause them to be so carried Congress in effect prohibits such carrying; that in respect of the carrying from one state to another of articles or things that are, in fact, or according to usage in business, the subjects of commerce, the authority given Congress was not to *prohibit*, but only to *regulate*. * * *

* * *

* * * Are we prepared to say that a provision which is, in effect, a *prohibition* of the carriage of such articles from state to state is not a fit or appropriate mode for the *regulation* of that particular kind of commerce? If lottery traffic, *carried on through interstate commerce*, is a matter of which Congress may take cognizance and over which its power may be exerted, can it be possible that it must tolerate the traffic, and simply regulate the manner in which it may be carried on? Or may not Congress, for the protection of the people of all the states, and under the power to regulate interstate commerce devise such means, within the scope of the Constitution, and not prohibited by it, as will drive that traffic out of commerce among the states?

In determining whether regulation may not under some circumstances properly take the form or have the effect of prohibition, the nature of the interstate traffic which it was sought by the act of May 2d, 1895, to suppress cannot be overlooked. When enacting that statute Congress no doubt shared the views upon the subject of lotteries heretofore expressed by this court. In Phalen v. Virginia, 8 How. 163, 168, 12 L.Ed. 1030, after observing that the suppression of nuisances injurious to public health or morality is among the most important duties of government, this court said: "Experience has shown that the common forms of gambling are comparatively innocuous when placed in contrast with the widespread pestilence of lotteries. The former are confined to a few persons and places, but the latter infests the whole community; it enters every dwelling; it reaches every class; it preys upon the hard earnings of the poor; it plunders the ignorant and simple." In other cases we have adjudged that authority given by legislative enactment to carry on a lottery, although based upon a consideration in money, was not protected by the contract clause of the Constitution; this, for the reason that no state may bargain away its power to protect the public morals, nor excuse its failure to perform a public duty by saying that it had agreed, by legislative enactment, not to do so. Stone v. Mississippi, 101 U.S. 814, 25 L.Ed. 1079; Douglas v. Kentucky, 168 U.S. 488, 18 Sup.Ct. Rep. 199.

If a state, when considering legislation for the suppression of lotteries within its own limits, may properly take into view the evils that inhere in the raising of money, in that mode, why may not Congress, invested with the power to regulate commerce among the several states, provide that such commerce shall not be polluted by the carrying of lottery tickets from one state to another? In this connection it must not be forgotten that the power of Congress to regulate commerce among the states is plenary, is complete in itself, and is subject to no limitations except such as may be found in the Constitution. What provision in that instrument can be regarded as limiting the exercise of the power granted? What clause can be cited which, in any degree, countenances the suggestion that one may, of right, carry or cause to be carried from one state to another that which will harm the public morals? We cannot think of any clause of that instrument that could possibly be invoked by those who assert their right to send lottery tickets from state to state except the one providing that no person shall be deprived of his liberty without due process of law. We have said that

the liberty protected by the Constitution embraces the right to be free in the enjoyment of one's faculties; "to be free to use them in all lawful ways; to live and work where he will; to earn his livelihood by any lawful calling; to pursue any livelihood or avocation, and for that purpose to enter into all contracts which may be proper." Allgeyer v. Louisiana, 165 U.S. 578, 589, 17 Sup.Ct. Rep. 427, 431. But surely it will not be said to be a part of anyone's liberty, as recognized by the supreme law of the land, that he shall be allowed to introduce into commerce among the states an element that will be confessedly injurious to the public morals.

If it be said that the act of 1895 is inconsistent with the 10th Amendment, reserving to the states respectively, or to the people, the powers not delegated to the United States, the answer is that the power to regulate commerce among the states has been expressly delegated to Congress.

Besides Congress, by that act, does not assume to interfere with traffic or commerce in lottery tickets carried on exclusively within the limits of any state, but has in view only commerce of that kind among the several states. It has not assumed to interfere with the completely internal affairs of any state, and has only legislated in respect of a matter which concerns the people of the United States. As a state may, for the purpose of guarding the morals of its own people, forbid all sales of lottery tickets within its limits, so Congress, for the purpose of guarding the people of the United States against the "widespread pestilence of lotteries" and to protect the commerce which concerns all the states, may prohibit the carrying of lottery tickets from one state to another. In legislating upon the subject of the traffic in lottery tickets, as carried on through interstate commerce, Congress only supplemented the action of those states—perhaps all of them—which, for the protection of the public morals, prohibit the drawing of lotteries, as well as the sale or circulation of lottery tickets, within their respective limits. It said, in effect, that it would not permit the declared policy of the states, which sought to protect their people against the mischiefs of the lottery business, to be overthrown or disregarded by the agency of interstate commerce. We should hesitate long before adjudging that an evil of such appalling character, carried on through interstate commerce, cannot be met and crushed by the only power competent to that end. We say competent to that end, because Congress alone has the power to occupy, by legislation, the whole field of interstate commerce.   *   *   *

*   *   *

It is said, however, that if, in order to suppress lotteries carried on through interstate commerce, Congress may exclude lottery tickets from such commerce, that principle leads necessarily to the conclusion that Congress may arbitrarily exclude from commerce among the states any article, commodity, or thing, of whatever kind or nature, or however useful or valuable, which it may choose, no matter with what motive, to declare shall not be carried from one state to another. It will be time enough to consider the constitutionality of such legislation when we must do so. The present case does not require the court to declare the full extent of the power that Congress may exercise in the regulation of commerce among the states. We may, however, repeat, in this connection, what the court has heretofore said, that the power of Congress to regulate commerce among the states, although plenary, cannot be deemed arbitrary, since it is subject to such limitations or restrictions as are prescribed by the Constitution. This power, therefore, may not be exercised so as to infringe rights secured or protected by that instrument. It would not be difficult to imagine legislation that would be justly liable to such an objection as that stated, and be hostile to the objects for the accomplishment of which Congress was invested with the general power to regulate commerce among the several states. But, as often said, the possible abuse of a power is not an argument against its existence. There is probably no governmental power that may not be exerted to the injury of the public. If what is done by Congress is manifestly in excess of the powers granted to it, then upon the courts will rest the duty of adjudging that its action is neither legal nor binding upon the people. But if what Congress does is within the limits of its power, and is simply unwise or injurious, the remedy is that suggested by Chief Justice Marshall in *Gibbons* v. *Ogden*, when he said: "The wisdom and the discretion of Congress, their identity with the people, and the influence which their constituents possess at elections, are, in this, as in many other instances, as that, for example, of declaring war, the sole restraints on which they have relied, to secure them from its abuse. They are the restraints on which the people must often rely solely, in all representative governments."

* * *

The judgment is affirmed.

Mr. Chief Justice FULLER, with whom concur Mr. Justice BREWER, Mr. Justice SHIRAS, and Mr. Justice PECKHAM, dissenting:

* * *

The naked question is whether the prohibition by Congress of the carriage of lottery tickets from one state to another by means other than the mails is within the powers vested in that body by the Constitution of the United States. That the purpose of Congress in this enactment was the suppression of lotteries cannot reasonably be denied. That purpose is avowed in the title of the act, and is its natural and reasonable effect, and by that its validity must be tested. * * *

The power of the state to impose restraints and burdens on persons and property in conservation and promotion of the public health, good order, and prosperity is a power originally and always belonging to the states, not surrendered by them to the general government, nor directly restrained by the Constitution of the United States, and essentially exclusive, and the suppression of lotteries as a harmful business falls within this power, commonly called, of police. * * *

It is urged, however, that because Congress is empowered to regulate commerce between the several states, it, therefore, may suppress lotteries by prohibiting the carriage of lottery matter. Congress may, indeed, make all laws necessary and proper for carrying the powers granted to it into execution, and doubtless an act prohibiting the carriage of lottery matter would be necessary and proper to the execution of a power to suppress lotteries; but that power belongs to the states and not to Congress. To hold that Congress has general police power would be to hold that it may accomplish objects not intrusted to the general government, and to defeat the operation of the 10th Amendment.

* * *

The ground on which prior acts forbidding the transmission of lottery matter by the mails was sustained, was that the power vested in Congress to establish postoffices and post roads embraced the regulation of the entire postal system of the country, and that under that power Congress might designate what might be carried in the mails and what excluded. * * *

* * * Mr. Justice Field, delivering the unanimous opinion of the court [in Ex parte Jackson, 96 U.S. 727, 24 L.Ed. 877] said: "But we do not think that Congress possesses the power to prevent the transportation in other ways, as merchandise, of matter which it excludes from the mails. To give efficiency to its regulations and prevent rival postal systems, it may, perhaps, prohibit the carriage by others for hire, over postal routes, of articles which legitimately constitute mail matter, in the sense in which those terms were used when the Constitution was adopted, consisting of letters, and of newspapers and pamphlets, when not sent as merchandise; but further than this its power of prohibition cannot extend." And this was repeated in the *Case of Rapier* [143 U.S. 110, 12 S.Ct. 374].

* * *

But apart from the question of bona fides, this act cannot be brought within the power to regulate commerce among the several states, unless lottery tickets are articles of commerce, and, therefore, when carried across state lines, of interstate commerce; or unless the power to regulate interstate commerce includes the absolute and exclusive power to prohibit the transportation of anything or anybody from one state to another.

* * *

Is the carriage of lottery tickets from one state to another commercial intercourse?

The lottery ticket purports to create contractual relations, and to furnish the means of enforcing a contract right.

This is true of insurance policies, and both are contingent in their nature. Yet this court has held that the issuing of fire, marine, and life insurance policies, in one state, and sending them to another, to be there delivered to the insured on payment of premium, is not interstate commerce. Paul v. Virginia, 8 Wall. 168, 19 L.Ed. 357. * * *

* * *

If a lottery ticket is not an article of commerce, how can it become so when placed in an envelope or box or other covering, and transported by an express company? To say that the mere carrying of an article which is not an article of commerce in and of itself nevertheless becomes such the moment it is to be transported from one state to another, is to transform a non-commercial article into a commercial one simply because it is transported. I cannot conceive

that any such result can properly follow.

It would be to say that everything is an article of commerce the moment it is taken to be transported from place to place, and of interstate commerce if from state to state.

An invitation to dine, or to take a drive, or a note of introduction, all become articles of commerce under the ruling in this case, by being deposited with an express company for transportation. This in effect breaks down all the differences between that which is, and that which is not, an article of commerce, and the necessary consequence is to take from the states all jurisdiction over the subject so far as interstate communication is concerned. It is a long step in the direction of wiping out all traces of state lines, and the creation of a centralized government.

* * *

It will not do to say—a suggestion which has heretofore been made in this case—that state laws have been found to be ineffective for the suppression of lotteries, and therefore Congress should interfere. The scope of the commerce clause of the Constitution cannot be enlarged because of present views of public interest.

* * *

The power to prohibit the transportation of diseased animals and infected goods over railroads or on steamboats is an entirely different thing, for they would be in themselves injurious to the transaction of interstate commerce, and, moreover, are essentially commercial in their nature. And the exclusion of diseased persons rests on different ground, for nobody would pretend that persons could be kept off the trains because they were going from one state to another to engage in the lottery business. However enticing that business may be, we do not understand these pieces of paper themselves can communicate bad principles by contact.

* * *

I regard this decision as inconsistent with the views of the framers of the Constitution, and of Marshall, its great expounder. Our form of government may remain notwithstanding legislation or decision, but, as long ago observed, it is with governments, as with religions: the form may survive the substance of the faith.

Chief Justice Taft, speaking for a unanimous Court in Brooks v. United States, 267 U.S. 432, 45 S.Ct. 345 (1925), upheld the validity of the National Motor Vehicle Theft Act. The act levied a $5,000 fine or a maximum of five years imprisonment for "whoever shall receive, conceal, store, barter, sell or dispose of any motor vehicle, moving as, or which is a part of, or which constitutes interstate or foreign commerce, knowing the same to have been stolen." Said the Court in sustaining the constitutionality of the legislation:

It is known of all men that the radical change in transportation of persons and goods effected by the introduction of the automobile, the speed with which it moves, and the ease with which evil-minded persons can avoid capture have greatly encouraged and increased crimes. One of the crimes which have been encouraged is the theft of the automobiles themselves and their immediate transportation to places remote from homes of the owners. Elaborately organized conspiracies for the theft of automobiles and the spiriting them away into some other state and their sale or other disposition far away from the owner and his neighborhood have roused Congress to devise some method for defeating the success of these widely spread schemes of larceny. The quick passage of the machines into another state helps to conceal the trail of the thieves, gets the stolen property into another police jurisdiction and facilitates the finding of a safer place in which to dispose of the body at a good price. This is a gross misuse of interstate commerce. Congress may properly punish such interstate transportation by any one with knowledge of the theft because of its harmful result and its defeat of the property rights of those whose machines against their will are taken into other jurisdictions.

The Court also noted other cases that, like *Brooks*, sustained the use of the commerce power for purposes of criminal regulation in a manner like that originally approved by the Court in *Champion* v. *Ames*, supra:

* * * Congress can certainly regulate interstate commerce to the extent of forbidding and punishing the use of such commerce as an agency to promote immorality, dishonesty or the spread of any evil or harm to the people of other states from the state of origin. In doing this it is merely exercising the police power, for the benefit of the public, within the field of interstate commerce. * * * In Reid v. Colorado, 187 U.S. 137, 23 S.Ct. 92, it was held that Congress could pass a law excluding diseased stock from interstate commerce in order to prevent its use in such a way as

thereby to injure the stock of other states. * * * In Hipolite Egg Co. v. United States, 220 U.S. 45, 31 S.Ct. 364, it was held that it was within the regulatory power of Congress to punish the transportation in interstate commerce of adulterated articles which if sold in other states from the one from which they were transported would deceive or injure persons who purchased such articles. In Hoke v. United States, 227 U.S. 308, 33 S.Ct. 281, and Caminetti v. United States, 242 U.S. 470, 37 S.Ct. 192, the so-called White Slave Traffic Act, which was construed to punish any person engaged in enticing a woman from one state to another for immoral ends, whether for commercial purposes or otherwise, was valid because it was intended to prevent the use of interstate commerce to facilitate prostitution or concubinage and other forms of immorality. In Clark Distilling Co. v. Western Maryland Railway Co., 242 U.S. 311, 37 S.Ct. 180, it was held that Congress had power to forbid the introduction of intoxicating liquors into any state in which their use was prohibited in order to prevent the use of interstate commerce to promote that which was illegal in the state. In Weber v. Freed, 239 U.S. 325, 36 S.Ct. 131, it was held that Congress had power to prohibit the importation of pictorial representations of prize fights designed for public exhibition because of the demoralizing effect of such exhibitions in the state of destination.

* * *

GOLDFARB v. VIRGINIA STATE BAR

Supreme Court of the United States, 1975
421 U.S. 773, 95 S.Ct. 2004, 44 L.Ed.2d 572

‣In 1971, Lewis Goldfarb and his wife contracted to buy a house. The financing agency required them to take out title insurance which, in turn, necessitated a title examination, a function which could only be legally performed by a member of the state bar association. An attorney sought out by the Goldfarbs for this purpose quoted them a fee of 1 percent of the property involved—the precise minimum fee suggested in the fee schedule published by the county bar association. After a survey of other lawyers turned up none who would charge less than that specified in the fee schedule, the Goldfarbs sued for injunctive relief and damages, alleging that the minimum fee schedule disseminated by the county bar and the support given its enforcement by the state bar constituted price fixing in violation of the Sherman Act. A federal district court found for the Goldfarbs and enjoined the county bar association from publication of its fee schedule. This decision was reversed on appeal, and the Goldfarbs sought certiorari from the U.S. Supreme Court.

Mr. Chief Justice BURGER delivered the opinion of the Court.

* * *

Our inquiry can be divided into four steps: did respondents engage in price fixing? If so, are their activities in interstate commerce or do they affect interstate commerce? If so, are the activities exempt from the Sherman Act because they involve a "learned profession?" If not, are the activities "state action" within the meaning of Parker v. Brown, 317 U.S. 341, 63 S.Ct. 307, and therefore exempt from the Sherman Act?

* * *

[I]n terms of restraining competition and harming consumers like petitioners the price-fixing activities found here are unusually damaging. A title examination is indispensable in the process of financing a real estate purchase, and since only an attorney licensed to practice in Virginia may legally examine a title, * * * consumers could not turn to alternative sources for the necessary service. All attorneys, of course, were practicing under the constraint of the fee schedule. * * * The County Bar makes much of the fact that it is a voluntary organization; however, the ethical opinions issued by the State Bar provide that any lawyer, whether or not a member of his county bar, may be disciplined for "*habitually* charg[ing] less than the suggested minimum fee schedule adopted by his local bar Association." * * * These factors coalesced to create a pricing system that consumers could not realistically escape. On this record respondent's activities constitute a classic illustration of price fixing.

* * *

* * * Given the substantial volume of commerce involved, and the inseparability of this particular legal service from the interstate aspects of real estate transactions we conclude that interstate commerce has been sufficiently affected. * * *

The fact that there was no showing that home buyers were discouraged by the challenged activities does not mean that interstate commerce was not affected. Otherwise, the magnitude of the effect would control, and our cases have shown that, once an effect is shown, no specific magnitude need be proved. * * * Nor was it necessary for petitioners to prove that the fee schedule raised fees. Petitioners

clearly proved that the fee schedule fixed fees and thus "deprive[d] purchasers or consumers of the advantages which they derive from free competition." * * *

Where, as a matter of law or practical necessity, legal services are an integral part of an interstate transaction, a restraint on those services may substantially affect commerce for Sherman Act purposes. Of course, there may be legal services that involve interstate commerce in other fashions, just as there may be legal services that have no nexus with interstate commerce and thus are beyond the reach of the Sherman Act.

* * *

In arguing that learned professions are not "trade or commerce" the County Bar seeks a total exclusion from antitrust regulation. Whether state regulation is active or dormant, real or theoretical, lawyers would be able to adopt anticompetitive practices with impunity. We cannot find support for the proposition that Congress intended any such sweeping exclusion. The nature of an occupation, standing alone, does not provide sanctuary from the Sherman Act, * * * nor is the public service aspect of professional practice controlling in determining whether § 1 includes professions. * * * Congress intended to strike as broadly as it could in § 1 of the Sherman Act, and to read into it so wide an exemption as that urged on us would be at odds with that purpose. * * * In the modern world it cannot be denied that the activities of lawyers plays an important part in commercial intercourse, and that anticompetitive activities by lawyers may exert a restraint on commerce.

In Parker v. Brown, 317 U.S. 341, 63 S.Ct. 307, the Court held that an anticompetitive marketing program "which derived its authority and efficacy from the legislative command of the state" was not a violation of the Sherman Act because the Act was intended to regulate private practices and not to prohibit a State from imposing a restraint as an act of government.   * * *   Respondent State Bar and respondent County Bar both seek to avail themselves of this so-called state action exemption.

* * *

The fact that the State Bar is a state agency for some limited purposes does not create an antitrust shield that allows it to foster anticompetitive practices for the benefit of its members. * * * The State Bar, by providing that deviation from County Bar minimum fees may lead to disciplinary action, has voluntarily joined in what is essentially a private anticompetitive activity, and in that posture cannot claim it is beyond the reach of the Sherman Act. * * * Its activities resulted in a rigid price floor from which petitioners, as consumers, could not escape if they wished to borrow money to buy a home.

We recognize that the States have a compelling interest in the practice of professions within their boundaries, and that as part of their power to protect the public health, safety, and other valid interests they have broad power to establish standards for licensing practitioners and regulating the practice of professions. We also recognize that in some instances the State may decide that "forms of competition usual in the business world may be demoralizing to the ethical standards of a profession." United States v. Oregon State Medical Society, 343 U.S. 326, 336, 72 S.Ct. 690, 697, see also Semler v. Oregon State Board of Dental Examiners, 294 U.S. 608, 611–613, 55 S.Ct. 570, 571–572. The interest of the States in regulating lawyers is especially great since lawyers are essential to the primary governmental function of administering justice, and have historically been "officers of the courts." See Sperry v. Florida, 373 U.S. 379, 383, 83 S.Ct. 1322, 1325; Cohen v. Hurley, 366 U.S. 117, 123–124, 81 S.Ct. 954, 958; Law Students Research Council v. Wadmond, 401 U.S. 154, 157, 91 S.Ct. 720, 723. In holding that certain anticompetitive conduct by lawyers is within the reach of the Sherman Act we intend no diminution of the authority of the State to regulate its professions.

The judgment of the Court of Appeals is reversed and the case is remanded to the Court of Appeals with orders to remand to the District Court for further proceedings consistent with this opinion.

Reversed and remanded.

Mr. Justice POWELL took no part in the consideration or decision of this case.

CASES SINCE *GOLDFARB* ON THE SHERMAN ACT AND ECONOMIC REGULATION BY PROFESSIONAL ORGANIZATIONS

Case	Ruling
Bates v. State Bar of Arizona, 433 U.S. 350, 97 S.Ct. 2691 (1977)	See p. 1384
Arizona v. Maricopa County Medical Society, — U.S. —, 102 S.Ct. 2466 (1982)	The Sherman Act's absolute prohibition on price fixing applies to an agreement among member doctors forming a foundation which established *maximum* fees the doctors could claim in full payment for health services provided to policyholders of specified insurance plans. Whatever might be said for the procompetitive justifications advanced for the foundation plan as an alternative to existing health insurance plans, "[t]he *per se* rule [of the Sherman Act] 'is grounded on faith in price competition as a market force [and not] on a policy of low selling prices as the price of eliminating competition.' * * * In this case the rule is violated by a price restraint that tends to provide the same economic rewards to all practitioners regardless of their skill, their experience, their training, or their willingness to employ innovative and different procedures in individual cases. Such a restraint also may discourage entry into the market and may deter experimentation and new developments by individual entrepreneurs. It may be a masquerade for an agreement to fix uniform prices, or it may in the future take on that character."

FLOOD v. KUHN

Supreme Court of the United States, 1972
407 U.S. 258, 92 S.Ct. 2099, 32 L.Ed.2d 728

Curt Flood, formerly a center fielder for the St. Louis Cardinals, was traded in October 1969, without his consent, to the Philadelphia Phillies in a multiplayer transaction. When told of the trade only after it had been consummated, Flood complained to Baseball Commissioner Bowie Kuhn and requested that he be made a free agent to strike his own bargain with a major league team. His request denied, Flood sued Kuhn under the Clayton Act for triple the damages and costs as allowed, asserting that baseball's "reserve clause" [a] was evidence of a monopolistic practice within the meaning of the antitrust statutes. In view of the precedents which accorded baseball a special status because it was "the national pastime," thereby exempting it from antitrust regulation (unlike other profes-

---

a. In a footnote the Court described the reserve system in this way: "The reserve system, publicly introduced into baseball contracts in 1887, see Metropolitan Exhibition Co. v. Ewing, 42 F. 198, 202–204 (C.Ct.SDNY 1890), centers in the uniformity of player contracts; the confinement of the player to the club which has him under the contract; the assignability of the player's contract; and the ability of the club annually to renew the contract unilaterally, subject to a stated salary minimum."

sional sports), a federal district court dismissed Flood's suit, and that decision was affirmed later by a U.S. Court of Appeals. The Supreme Court granted certiorari.

Mr. Justice BLACKMUN delivered the opinion of the Court.

[The following summary and conclusions followed after a systematic review of earlier cases dealing with professional athletes *vis-à-vis* the antitrust statutes:]

*   *   *

1. Professional baseball is a business and it is engaged in interstate commerce.

2. With its reserve system enjoying exemption from the federal antitrust laws, baseball is, in a very distinct sense, an exception and an anomaly. *Federal Baseball* [v. National League, 259 U.S. 200, 42 S.Ct. 465 (1922)] and *Toolson* [v. New York Yankees, Inc., 346 U.S. 356, 74 S.Ct. 78 (1953)] have become an aberration confined to baseball.

3. Even though others might regard this as "unrealistic, inconsistent, or illogical," see *Radovich* [v. National Football League, 352 U.S. 445, 77 S.Ct. 390 (1957)], the aberration is an established one, and one that has been recognized not only in *Federal Baseball* and *Toolson*, but in [United States v. Schubert, 348 U.S. 222, 75 S.Ct. 277 (1955); United States v. International Boxing Club, 358 U.S. 242, 79 S.Ct. 245 (1959)], and *Radovich*, as well, a total of five consecutive cases in this Court. It is an aberration that has been with us now for half a century, one heretofore deemed fully entitled to the benefit of *stare decisis*, and one that has survived the Court's expanding concept of interstate commerce. It rests on a recognition and an accept-

ance of baseball's unique characteristics and needs.

4. Other professional sports operating interstate—football, boxing, basketball, and, presumably, hockey and golf—are not so exempt.

5. The advent of radio and television, with their consequent increased coverage and additional revenues, has not occasioned an overruling of *Federal Baseball* and *Toolson*.

6. The Court has emphasized that since 1922 baseball, with full and continuing congressional awareness, has been allowed to develop and to expand unhindered by federal legislative action. Remedial legislation has been introduced repeatedly in Congress but none has ever been enacted. The Court, accordingly, has concluded that Congress as yet has had no intention to subject baseball's reserve system to the reach of the antitrust statutes. This, obviously, has been deemed to be something other than mere congressional silence and passivity. *   *   *

7. The Court has expressed concern about the confusion and the retroactivity problems that inevitably would result with a judicial overturning of *Federal Baseball*. It has voiced a preference that if any change is to be made, it come by legislative action that, by its nature, is only prospective in operation.

8. The Court noted in *Radovich* *   *   * that the slate with respect to baseball, is not clean. Indeed, it has not been clean for half a century.

This emphasis and this concern are still with us. We continue to be loathe, 50 years after *Federal Baseball* and almost two decades after *Toolson*, to overturn those cases judicially when Congress, by its positive inaction, has allowed those decisions to stand for so long and, far beyond mere inference and implication, has clearly evinced a desire not to disapprove them legislatively.

Accordingly, we adhere once again to *Federal Baseball* and *Toolson* and to their application to professional baseball. We adhere also to *International Boxing* and *Radovich* and to their respective applications to professional boxing and professional football. If there is any inconsistency or illogic in all this, it is an inconsistency and illogic of long standing that is to be remedied by the Congress and not by this Court. If we were to act otherwise, we would be withdrawing from the conclusion as to congressional intent made in *Toolson* and from the concerns as to retrospectivity therein expressed. Under these circumstances, there is merit in consistency even though some might claim that beneath that consistency is a layer of inconsistency.

The petitioner's argument as to the application of state antitrust laws deserves a word. Judge Cooper [the District Court judge in the case below] rejected the state law claims because state antitrust regulation would conflict with federal policy and because national "uniformity [is required] in any regulation of baseball and its reserve system." 316 F.Supp., at 280. The Court of Appeals, in affirming, stated, "[A]s the burden on interstate commerce outweighs the states' interest in regulating baseball's reserve system, the Commerce Clause precludes the application here of state antitrust law." 443 F.2d, at 268. As applied to or-

ganized baseball, and in the light of this Court's observations and holdings in *Federal Baseball*, in *Toolson*, in *Schubert*, in *International Boxing*, and in *Radovich*, and despite baseball's allegedly inconsistent position taken in the past with respect to the application of state law, these statements adequately dispose of the state law claims.

The conclusion we have reached makes it unnecessary for us to consider the respondents' additional argument that the reserve system is a mandatory subject of collective bargaining and that federal labor policy therefore exempts the reserve system from the operation of federal antitrust laws.

We repeat for this case what was said in *Toolson*:

"Without re-examination of the underlying issues, the [judgment] below [is] affirmed on the authority of *Federal Baseball Club of Baltimore* v. *National League of Baseball Professional Clubs*, supra, so far as that decision determines that Congress had no intention of including the business of baseball within the scope of the federal antitrust laws." 346 U.S., at 357, 74 S.Ct., at 79.

And what the Court said in *Federal Baseball* in 1922 and what it said in *Toolson* in 1953, we say again here in 1972: the remedy, if any is indicated, is for congressional, and not judicial, action.

The judgment of the Court of Appeals is affirmed.

Judgment affirmed.

Mr. Justice POWELL took no part in the consideration or decision of this case.

Mr. Chief Justice BURGER, concurring.

I concur in [part] of the Court's opinion but, like Mr. Justice Douglas I have grave reservations as to the correctness of *Toolson* v. *New York Yankees, Inc.*, supra; as he notes in his dissent, he joined that holding but has "lived to regret it." The error, if such it be, is one on which the affairs of a great many people have rested for a long time. Courts are not the forum in which this tangled web ought to be unsnarled. I agree with Mr. Justice Douglas that congressional inaction is not a solid base, but the least undesirable course now is to let the matter rest with Congress; it is time the Congress acted to solve this problem.

Mr. Justice DOUGLAS, with whom Mr. Justice BRENNAN concurs, dissenting.

This Court's decision in Federal Baseball Club v. National League, 259 U.S. 200, 42 S.Ct. 465, made in 1922, is a derelict in the stream of the law that we, its creator, should remove. Only a romantic view of a rather dismal business account over the last 50 years would keep that derelict in midstream.

In 1922 the Court had a narrow, parochial view of commerce. With the demise of the old landmarks of that era, particularly United States v. E. C. Knight Co., 156 U.S. 1, 15 S.Ct. 249, Hammer v. Dagenhart, 247 U.S. 251, 38 S.Ct. 529, and Paul v. Virginia, 8 Wall. 168, 19 L.Ed. 357, the whole concept of commerce has changed.

*   *   *

Baseball is today big business that is packaged with beer, with broadcasting, and with other industries. The beneficiaries of the *Federal Baseball Club* decision are not the Babe Ruths, Ty Cobbs, and Lou Gehrigs.

The owners, whose records many say reveal a proclivity for predatory practices, do not come to us with equities. The equities are with the victims of the reserve clause. I use the word "victims" in the Sherman Act sense, since a contract which forbids anyone to practice his calling is commonly called an unreasonable restraint of trade. *   *   *

If congressional inaction is our guide, we should rely upon the fact that Congress has refused to enact bills broadly exempting professional sports from antitrust regulation. *   *   * The only statutory exemption granted by Congress to professional sports concerns broadcasting rights. 15 U.S.C.A. §§ 1291–1295. I would not ascribe a broader exemption through inaction than Congress has seen fit to grant explicitly.

There can be no doubt "that were we considering the question of baseball for the first time upon a clean slate" we would hold it to be subject to federal antitrust regulation. Radovich v. National Football League, 352 U.S. 445, 452, 77 S.Ct. 390. The unbroken silence of Congress should not prevent us from correcting our own mistakes.

Mr. Justice MARSHALL, with whom Mr. Justice BRENNAN joins, dissenting.

*   *   *

*   *   * I would overrule *Federal Baseball Club* and *Toolson* and reverse the decision of the Court of Appeals.

This does not mean that petitioner necessarily prevails, however. Lurking in the background is a hurdle of recent vintage that petitioner still must overcome. In 1966, the

Major League Players Association was formed. It is the collective-bargaining representative for all major league baseball players. Respondents argue that the reserve system is now part and parcel of the collective-bargaining agreement and that because it is a mandatory subject of bargaining, the federal labor statutes are applicable, not the federal antitrust laws. The lower courts did not rule on this argument, having decided the case solely on the basis of the antitrust exemption.

* * *

In light of these considerations, I would remand this case to the District Court for consideration of whether petitioner can state a claim under the antitrust laws despite the collective-bargaining agreement, and if so, for a determination of whether there has been an antitrust violation in this case.

HEART OF ATLANTA MOTEL v. UNITED STATES

Supreme Court of the United States, 1964
379 U.S. 241, 85 S.Ct. 348, 13 L.Ed.2d 258

The facts are set out in the opinion.

Mr. Justice CLARK delivered the opinion of the Court.

This is a declaratory judgment action, 28 U.S.C.A. § 2201 and § 2202 (1958 ed.) attacking the constitutionality of Title II of the Civil Rights Act of 1964, 78 Stat. 241, 243. * * * A three-judge court * * * sustained the validity of the Act and issued a permanent injunction * * * restraining appellant from continuing to violate the Act which remains in effect. * * * We affirm the judgment.

* * * Appellant owns and operates the Heart of Atlanta Motel which has 216 rooms available to transient guests. The motel is located on Courtland Street, two blocks from downtown Peachtree Street. It is readily accessible to interstate highways 75 and 85 and state highways 23 and 41. Appellant solicits patronage from outside the State of Georgia through various national advertising media, including magazines of national circulation; it maintains over 50 billboards and highway signs within the State, soliciting patronage for the motel; it accepts convention trade from outside Georgia and approximately 75% of its registered guests are from out of State. Prior to passage of the Act the motel had followed a practice of refusing to rent rooms to Negroes, and it alleged that it intended to continue to do so. In an effort to perpetuate that policy this suit was filed.

* * *

It is admitted that the operation of the motel brings it within the provisions of § 201(a) of the Act and that appellant refused to provide lodging for transient Negroes because of their race or color and that it intends to continue that policy unless restrained.

The sole question posed is, therefore, the constitutionality of the Civil Rights Act of 1964 as applied to these facts. The legislative history of the Act indicates that Congress based the Act on § 5 and the Equal Protection Clause of the Fourteenth Amendment as well as its power to regulate interstate commerce under Art. I, § 8, cl. 3, of the Constitution.

The Senate Commerce Committee made it quite clear that the fundamental object of Title II was to vindicate "the deprivation of personal dignity that surely accompanies denials of equal access to public establishments." At the same time, however, it noted that such an objective has been and could be readily achieved "by congressional action based on the commerce power of the Constitution." S.Rep. No. 872, supra, at 16–17. Our study of the legislative record, made in the light of prior cases, has brought us to the conclusion that Congress possessed ample power in this regard, and we have therefore not considered the other grounds relied upon. This is not to say that the remaining authority upon which it acted was not adequate, a question upon which we do not pass, but merely that since the commerce power is sufficient for our decision here we have considered it alone. * * *

* * *

While the Act as adopted carried no congressional findings the record of its passage through each house is replete with evidence of the burdens that discrimination by race or color places upon interstate commerce. * * * This testimony included the fact that our people have become increasingly mobile with millions of people of all races traveling from State to State; that Negroes in particular have been the subject of discrimination in transient accommodations, having to travel great distances to secure the same; that often they have been unable to obtain accommodations and have had to call upon friends to put them up overnight, * * * and that these conditions had become so acute as to require the listing of available lodging for Negroes in a special guidebook which was itself "dramatic testimony to the difficulties" Negroes encounter in travel. * * * These exclusionary practices were found to be nationwide, the Under Secretary of Commerce testifying that there is "no question that this discrimination in the North still exists to a large degree" and in the West and Midwest as well. * * * This testimony indicated a qualitative as well as quantitative effect on interstate travel by Negroes. The former was the obvious impairment of the Negro traveler's pleasure and convenience that resulted when he continually was uncertain of finding lodging. As for the latter, there was evidence that this uncertainty stemming from racial discrimination had the effect of discouraging travel on the part of a substantial portion of the Negro community. * * * This was the conclusion not only of the Under Secretary of Commerce but also of the Administrator of the Federal Aviation Agency who wrote the Chairman of the Senate Commerce Committee that it was his "belief that air commerce is adversely affected by the denial to a substantial segment of the traveling public of adequate and desegregated public accommodations." * * * We shall not burden this opinion with further details since the voluminous testimony presents overwhelming evidence that discrimination by hotels and motels impedes interstate travel.

* * *

That Congress was legislating against moral wrongs in many * * * areas rendered its enactments no less valid. In framing Title II of this Act Congress was also dealing with what it considered a moral problem. But that fact does not detract from the overwhelming evidence of the disruptive effect that racial discrimination has had on commercial intercourse. It was this burden which empowered Congress to enact appropriate legislation, and, given this basis for the exercise of its power, Congress was not restricted by the fact that the particular obstruction to interstate commerce with which it was dealing was also deemed a moral and social wrong.

It is said that the operation of the motel here is of a purely local character. But, assuming this to be true, "[i]f it is interstate commerce that feels the pinch, it does not matter how local the operation which applies the squeeze." United States v. Women's Sportswear Mfg. Ass'n, 336 U.S. 460, 464, 69 S.Ct. 714, 716 (1949). * * *

Thus the power of Congress to promote interstate commerce also includes the power to regulate the local incidents thereof, including local activities in both the States of origin and destination, which might have a substantial and harmful effect upon that commerce. One need only examine the evidence which we have discussed above to see that Congress may—as it has—prohibit racial discrimination by motels serving travelers, however "local" their operations may appear.

Nor does the Act deprive appellant of liberty or property under the Fifth Amendment. The commerce power invoked here by the Congress is a specific and plenary one author-

ized by the Constitution itself. The only questions are: (1) whether Congress had a rational basis for finding that racial discrimination by motels affected commerce, and (2) if it had such a basis, whether the means it selected to eliminate that evil are reasonable and appropriate. If they are, appellant has no "right" to select its guests as it sees fit, free from governmental regulation.

* * *

It is doubtful if in the long run appellant will suffer economic loss as a result of the Act. Experience is to the contrary where discrimination is completely obliterated as to all public accommodations. But whether this be true or not is of no consequence since this Court has specifically held that the fact that a "member of the class which is regulated may suffer economic losses not shared by others * * * has never been a barrier" to such legislation. Bowles v. Willingham, [321 U.S.] at 518, 64 S.Ct. at 649. Likewise in a long line of cases this Court has rejected the claim that the prohibition of racial discrimination in public accommodations interferes with personal liberty. See District of Columbia v. John R. Thompson Co., 346 U.S. 100, 73 S.Ct. 1007 (1953). * * *

* * *

We, therefore, conclude that the action of the Congress in the adoption of the Act as applied here to a motel which concededly serves interstate travelers is within the power granted it by the Commerce Clause of the Constitution, as interpreted by this Court for 140 years. It may be argued that Congress could have pursued other methods to eliminate the obstructions it found in interstate commerce caused by racial discrimination. But this is a matter of policy that rests entirely with the Congress not with the courts. How obstructions in commerce may be removed— what means are to be employed—is within the sound and exclusive discretion of the Congress. It is subject only to one caveat—that the means chosen by it must be reasonably adapted to the end permitted by the Constitution. We cannot say that its choice here was not so adapted. The Constitution requires no more.

Affirmed.

Mr. Justice BLACK, concurring.

*   *   *

Congress in § 201 declared that the racially discriminatory "operations" of a motel of more than five rooms for rent or hire do adversely affect interstate commerce if it "provides lodging to transient guests" *   *   * and that a restaurant's "operations" affect such commerce if (1) "it serves or offers to serve interstate travelers" or (2) "a substantial portion of the food which it serves *   *   * has moved in [interstate] commerce." Congress thus described the nature and extent of operations which it wished to regulate, excluding some establishments from the Act either for reasons of policy or because it believed its powers to regulate and protect interstate commerce did not extend so far. There can be no doubt that the operations of both the motel and the restaurant here fall squarely within the measure Congress chose to adopt in the Act and deemed adequate to show a constitutionally prohibitable adverse effect on commerce. The choice of policy is of course within the exclusive power of Congress; but whether particular operations affect interstate commerce sufficiently to come

under the constitutional power of Congress to regulate them is ultimately a judicial rather than a legislative question, and can be settled finally only by this Court. I agree that as applied to this motel and this restaurant the Act is a valid exercise of congressional power, in the case of the motel because the record amply demonstrates that its practice of discrimination tended directly to interfere with interstate travel, and in the case of the restaurant because Congress had ample basis for concluding that a widespread practice of racial discrimination by restaurants buying as substantial a quantity of goods shipped from other States as this restaurant buys could distort or impede interstate trade.

*   *   *

*   *   * I recognize that every remote, possible, speculative effect on commerce should not be accepted as an adequate constitutional ground to uproot and throw into the discard all our traditional distinctions between what is purely local, and therefore controlled by state laws, and what affects the national interest and is therefore subject to control by federal laws. I recognize too that some isolated and remote lunchroom which sells only to local people and buys almost all its supplies in the locality may possibly be beyond the reach of the power of Congress to regulate commerce, just as such an establishment is not covered by the present Act. But in deciding the constitutional power of Congress in cases like the two before us we do not consider the effect on interstate commerce of only one isolated, individual, local event, without regard to the fact that this single local event when added to many others of a similar nature may impose a burden on interstate commerce by reducing its volume or distorting its flow. * * * There are approximately 20,000,000 Negroes in our country. Many of them are able to, and do, travel among the States in automobiles. Certainly it would seriously discourage such travel by them if, as evidence before the Congress indicated has been true in the past, they should in the future continue to be unable to find a decent place along their way in which to lodge or eat. * * * And the flow of interstate commerce may be impeded or distorted substantially if local sellers of interstate food are permitted to exclude all Negro consumers. Measuring, as this Court has so often held is required, by the aggregate effect of a great number of such acts of discrimination, I am of the opinion that Congress has constitutional power under the Commerce and Necessary and Proper Clauses to protect interstate commerce from the injuries bound to befall it from these discriminatory practices.

Long ago this Court, again speaking through Mr. Chief Justice Marshall, said: "Let the end be legitimate, let it be within the scope of the constitution, and all means which are appropriate, which are plainly adapted to that end, which are not prohibited, but consist with the letter and spirit of the constitution, are constitutional." M'Culloch v. State of Maryland, 4 Wheat. 316, 421, 4 L.Ed. 579.

By this standard Congress acted within its power here. In view of the Commerce Clause it is not possible to deny that the aim of protecting interstate commerce from undue burdens is a legitimate end. In view of the Thirteenth, Fourteenth and Fifteenth Amendments, it is not possible to deny that the aim of protecting Negroes from discrimination is also a legitimate end. The means adopted to achieve these ends are also appropriate, plainly adopted to achieve them and not prohibited by the Constitution but consistent with both its letter and spirit.

* * *

Mr. Justice DOUGLAS, concurring.

Though I join the Court's opinions, I am somewhat reluctant here, * * * to rest solely on the Commerce Clause. My reluctance is not due to any conviction that Congress lacks power to regulate commerce in the interests of human rights. It is rather my belief that the right of people to be free of state action that discriminates against them because of race, like the "right of persons to move freely from State to State" (Edwards v. People of State of California, 314 U.S. at 177, 62 S.Ct. at 169), "occupies a more protected position in our constitutional system than does the movement of cattle, fruit, steel and coal across state lines." * * *

Hence I would prefer to rest on the assertion of legislative power contained in § 5 of the Fourteenth Amendment which states: "The Congress shall have power to enforce, by appropriate legislation, the provisions of this article"—a power which the Court concedes was exercised at least in part in this Act.

A decision based on the Fourteenth Amendment would have a more settling effect, making unnecessary litigation over whether a particular restaurant or inn is within the commerce definitions of the Act or whether a particular customer is an interstate traveler. Under my construction, the Act would apply to all customers in all the enumerated places of public accommodation. And that construction would put an

end to all obstructionist strategies and finally close one door on a bitter chapter in American history.

* * *

KATZENBACH v. McCLUNG

Supreme Court of the United States, 1964
379 U.S. 294, 85 S.Ct. 377, 13 L.Ed.2d 290

The facts are set out in the opinion.

Mr. Justice CLARK delivered the opinion of the Court.

This case was argued with * * * Heart of Atlanta Motel v. United States, decided this date, * * * in which we upheld the constitutional validity of Title II of the Civil Rights Act of 1964 against an attack by hotels, motels, and like establishments. This complaint for injunctive relief against appellants attacks the constitutionality of the Act as applied to a restaurant. The case was heard by a three-judge United States District Court and an injunction was issued restraining appellants from enforcing the Act against the restaurant. * * * We now reverse the judgment.

* * *

Ollie's Barbecue is a family-owned restaurant in Birmingham, Alabama, specializing in barbecued meats and homemade pies, with a seating capacity of 220 customers. It is located on a state highway 11 blocks from an interstate one and a somewhat greater distance from railroad and bus stations. The restaurant caters to a family and white-collar trade with a take-out service for Negroes. It employs 36 persons, two-thirds of whom are Negroes.

In the 12 months preceding the passage of the Act, the restaurant

purchased locally approximately $150,000 worth of food, $69,683 or 46% of which was meat that it bought from a local supplier who had procured it from outside the State. The District Court expressly found that a substantial portion of the food served in the restaurant had moved in interstate commerce. The restaurant has refused to serve Negroes in its dining accommodations since its original opening in 1927, and since July 2, 1964, it has been operating in violation of the Act. The court below concluded that if it were required to serve Negroes it would lose a substantial amount of business.

On the merits, the District Court held that the Act could not be applied under the Fourteenth Amendment because it was conceded that the State of Alabama was not involved in the refusal of the restaurant to serve Negroes. It was also admitted that the Thirteenth Amendment was authority neither for validating nor for invalidating the Act. As to the Commerce Clause, * * * [t]here must be, it said, a close and substantial relation between local activities and interstate commerce which requires control of the former in the protection of the latter. The court concluded, however, that the Congress, rather than finding facts sufficient to meet this rule, had legislated a conclusive presumption that a restaurant affects interstate commerce if it serves or offers to serve interstate travelers or if a substantial portion of the food which it serves has moved in commerce. This, the court held, it could not do because there was no demonstrable connection between food purchased in interstate commerce and sold in a restaurant and the conclusion of Congress that discrimination in the restaurant would affect that commerce.

The basic holding in *Heart of Atlanta Motel*, answers many of the contentions made by the appellees. * * * In this case we consider its application to restaurants which serve food a substantial portion of which has moved in commerce.

* * * Sections 201(b)(2) and (c) place any "restaurant * * * principally engaged in selling food for consumption on the premises" under the Act "if * * * it serves or offers to serve interstate travelers or a substantial portion of the food which it serves * * * has moved in commerce."

Ollie's Barbecue admits that it is covered by these provisions of the Act. The Government makes no contention that the discrimination at the restaurant was supported by the State of Alabama. There is no claim that interstate travelers frequented the restaurant. The sole question, therefore, narrows down to whether Title II, as applied to a restaurant annually receiving about $70,000 worth of food which has moved in commerce, is a valid exercise of the power of Congress. * * *

As we noted in *Heart of Atlanta Motel* both Houses of Congress conducted prolonged hearings on the Act. And, as we said there, while no formal findings were made, which of course are not necessary, it is well that we make mention of the testimony at these hearings the better to understand the problem before Congress and determine whether the Act is a reasonable and appropriate means toward its solution. The record is replete with testimony of the burdens placed on interstate commerce by racial discrimination in restaurants. A comparison of per capita spending by Negroes in restaurants, theaters, and like establishments indicated less spending, after discounting income differences, in areas where discrimination is widely practiced. This condition, which was especially aggravated in the South, was attributed in the testimony of the Under Secretary of Commerce to racial segregation. * * * This diminutive spending springing from a refusal to serve Negroes and their total loss as customers has, regardless of the absence of direct evidence, a close connection to interstate commerce. The fewer customers a restaurant enjoys the less food it sells and consequently the less it buys. * * * In addition, the Attorney General testified that this type of discrimination imposed "an artificial restriction on the market" and interfered with the flow of merchandise. * * * In addition, there were many references to discriminatory situations causing wide unrest and having a depressant effect on general business conditions in the respective communities. * * *

Moreover there was an impressive array of testimony that discrimination in restaurants had a direct and highly restrictive effect upon interstate travel by Negroes. This resulted, it was said, because discriminatory practices prevent Negroes from buying prepared food served on the premises while on a trip, except in isolated and unkempt restaurants and under most unsatisfactory and often unpleasant conditions. This obviously discourages travel and obstructs interstate commerce for one can hardly travel without eating. Likewise, it was said, that discrimination deterred professional, as well as skilled, people from moving into areas where such practices occurred and thereby caused industry to be reluctant to establish there. * * *

We believe that this testimony afforded ample basis for the conclusion that established restaurants in such areas sold less interstate goods because of the discrimination, that interstate travel was obstructed directly by it, that business in general suffered and that many new businesses refrained from establishing there as a result of it. Hence the District Court was in error in concluding that there was no connection between discrimination and the movement of interstate commerce. The court's conclusion that such a connection is outside "common experience" flies in the face of stubborn fact.

It goes without saying that, viewed in isolation, the volume of food purchased by Ollie's Barbecue from sources supplied from out of state was insignificant when compared with the total foodstuffs moving in commerce. But, as our late Brother Jackson said for the Court in Wickard v. Filburn, 317 U.S. 111, 63 S.Ct. 82 (1942):

"That appellee's own contribution to the demand for wheat may be trivial by itself is not enough to remove him from the scope of federal regulation where, as here, his contribution, taken together with that of many others similarly situated, is far from trivial." At 127–128, 63 S.Ct. at 90.

We noted in *Heart of Atlanta Motel* that a number of witnesses attested to the fact that racial discrimination was not merely a state or regional problem but was one of nationwide scope. Against this background, we must conclude that while the focus of the legislation was on the individual restaurant's relation to interstate commerce, Congress appropriately considered the importance of that connection with the knowledge that the discrimination was but "representative of many others throughout the country, the total incidence of which if left unchecked may well become far-reaching in its harm to commerce." Polish National Alliance of U. S. v. National Labor Relations Board, 322 U.S. 643, 648, 64 S.Ct. 1196, 1199 (1944).

With this situation spreading as the record shows, Congress was not required to await the total dislocation of commerce. * * *

Article I, § 8, cl. 3, confers upon Congress the power "[t]o regulate Commerce * * * among the several States" and Clause 18 of the same Article grants it the power "[t]o make all Laws which shall be necessary and proper for carrying into Execution the foregoing Powers." * * * This grant, as we have pointed out in *Heart of Atlanta Motel* "extends to those activities intrastate which so affect interstate commerce, or the exertion of the power of Congress over it, as to make regulation of them appropriate means to the attainment of a legitimate end, the effective execution of the granted power to regulate interstate commerce." United States v. Wrightwood Dairy Co., 315 U.S. 110, 119, 62 S.Ct. 523, 526 (1942). Much is said about a restaurant business being local but "even if appellee's ac-

tivity be local and though it may not
be regarded as commerce, it may
still, whatever its nature, be reached
by Congress if it exerts a substantial
economic effect on interstate commerce." * * * Wickard v. Filburn, supra, at 125, 63 S.Ct. at 89.
The activities that are beyond the
reach of Congress are "those which
are completely within a particular
State, which do not affect other
States, and with which it is not necessary to interfere, for the purpose
of executing some of the general
powers of the government." Gibbons v. Ogden, 9 Wheat. 1, 195, 6
L.Ed. 23 (1824). This rule is as good
today as it was when Chief Justice
Marshall laid it down almost a century and a half ago.

* * *

The appellees contend that Congress has arbitrarily created a conclusive presumption that all restaurants meeting the criteria set out in
the Act "affect commerce." Stated
another way, they object to the omission of a provision for a case-by-case
determination—judicial or administrative—that racial discrimination in
a particular restaurant affects commerce.

But Congress' action in framing
this Act was not unprecedented. In
United States v. Darby, 312 U.S. 100,
657, 61 S.Ct. 451 (1941), this Court
held constitutional the Fair Labor
Standards Act of 1938. There Congress determined that the payment
of substandard wages to employees
engaged in the production of goods
for commerce, while not itself commerce, so inhibited it as to be subject
to federal regulation. The appellees
in that case argued, as do the appellees here, that the Act was invalid
because it included no provision for
an independent inquiry regarding the

effect on commerce of substandard
wages in a particular business.
* * *

Here, as there, Congress has determined for itself that refusals of
service to Negroes have imposed
burdens both upon the interstate
flow of food and upon the movement
of products generally. Of course,
the mere fact that Congress has said
when particular activity shall be
deemed to affect commerce does not
preclude further examination by this
Court. But where we find that the
legislators, in light of the facts and
testimony before them, have a rational basis for finding a chosen regulatory scheme necessary to the protection of commerce, our
investigation is at an end. * * *

* * *

Confronted as we are with the
facts laid before Congress, we must
conclude that it had a rational basis
for finding that racial discrimination
in restaurants had a direct and adverse effect on the free flow of interstate commerce. * * * We think
in so doing that Congress acted well
within its power to protect and foster
commerce in extending the coverage
of Title II only to those restaurants
offering to serve interstate travelers
or serving food, a substantial portion
of which has moved in interstate
commerce.

The absence of direct evidence
connecting discriminatory restaurant
service with the flow of interstate
food, a factor on which the appellees
place much reliance, is not, given the
evidence as to the effect of such
practices on other aspects of commerce, a crucial matter.

The power of Congress in this
field is broad and sweeping; where it
keeps within its sphere and violates

no express constitutional limitation it has been the rule of this Court, going back almost to the founding days of the Republic, not to interfere. The Civil Rights Act of 1964, as here applied, we find to be plainly appropriate in the resolution of what the Congress found to be a national commercial problem of the first magnitude. We find it in no violation of any express limitations of the Constitution and we therefore declare it valid.

The judgment is therefore reversed.

Reversed.

In Daniel v. Paul, 395 U.S. 298, 89 S.Ct. 1697 (1969), the Supreme Court was confronted with a more remote application of Title II of the 1964 Civil Rights Act. Daniel, a Negro resident of Little Rock, Arkansas, brought suit in federal district court to enjoin Euell Paul, the owner of the Lake Nixon Club, a recreational facility, from operating that establishment on a discriminatory basis. The district court dismissed the complaint on the ground that the Lake Nixon Club was not a "public accommodation" within the terms of the act. The U.S. Circuit Court of Appeals for the Eighth Circuit affirmed the decision. The Supreme Court reversed.

According to the Court's description, the Lake Nixon Club was "a 232-acre amusement area with swimming, boating, sun bathing, picnicking, miniature golf, dancing facilities, and a snack bar." Though the resort was located at a remote spot some twelve miles west of Little Rock and well away from any major interstate arteries of travel, Justice Brennan, speaking for the Court, nevertheless found the facility involved in interstate commerce. He noted first that a substantial portion of the food served at the snack bar had come by way of interstate commerce and that three of the four items served at the snack bar (hot dogs and hamburgers on buns, soft drinks, and milk) had ingredients produced outside the state. Second, Brennan observed that "it would be unrealistic to assume that none of the 100,000 patrons actually served by the club each season was an interstate traveler." In addition, Paul advertised the facility in newspapers and media in a manner reflecting an intent to appeal to interstate travelers. The Court also noted that the club leased some fifteen paddle boats from an Oklahoma company and another boat was purchased from the same company. Finally, the Court found the club's juke box and the records played on it to be manufactured outside the state.

In the lone dissent, Justice Black objected to the extent to which the commerce power had been applied in this case. Said Justice Black:

* * *

Did Lake Nixon serve or offer to serve interstate travelers? There is not a word of evidence showing that such an interstate traveler was ever there or ever invited there or ever dreamed of going there. Nixon Lake can be reached only by country roads. The record fails to show whether these country roads are passable in all kinds of weather. They seem to be at least six to eight miles off the state or interstate roads over which interstate travelers are accustomed to travel. Petitioners did not offer evidence to show whether Lake Nixon is a natural lake, or whether it is simply a small body of water obtained by building a dam across a little creek in a narrow hollow between the hills. * * *

* * *

* * * If the facts here are to be left to such "iffy" conjectures, one familiar with country life and traveling would, it seems to me, far more likely conclude that travelers on interstate journeys would stick to their interstate highways, and not go miles off them by way of what, for all this record shows, may well be dusty, unpaved, "country" roads to go to a purely local swimming hole where the only food they could buy was hamburgers, hot dogs, milk, and soft drinks (but not beer). This is certainly not the pattern of interstate movements I would expect interstate travelers in search of tourist attractions to follow.

* * *

It seems clear to me that neither the paddle boats nor the locally leased juke box is sufficient to justify a holding that the operation of Lake Nixon affects interstate commerce within the meaning of the Act. While it is the duty of courts to enforce this important Act, we are not called on to hold nor should we hold subject to that Act this country people's recreation center, lying in what may be, so far as we know, a little "sleepy hollow" between Arkansas hills miles away from any interstate highway. This would be stretching the Commerce Clause so as to give the Federal Government complete control over every little remote country place of recreation in every nook and cranny of every precinct and county in every one of the 50 States. This goes too far for me. I would affirm the judgments of the two courts below.

b. CONGRESS'S POWER TO REGULATE PRODUCTION UNDER THE COMMERCE CLAUSE

UNITED STATES v. E. C. KNIGHT CO.

Supreme Court of the United States, 1895
156 U.S. 1, 15 S.Ct. 249, 39 L.Ed. 325

The Sherman Antitrust Act, passed by Congress in 1890, made it illegal to monopolize or restrain or attempt to monopolize or restrain interstate or foreign commerce through any contract, combination, or conspiracy. Under this act the United States filed a bill in a federal court against five sugar manufacturing companies to prevent their consolidation after one of them, a New Jersey firm, purchased the stock of the other four, E. C. Knight and three other Philadelphia companies. By this and earlier transactions the American Sugar Refining Company had obtained control over 98 percent of the country's sugar refining business. The lower federal courts held there was no violation of the Sherman Act by this combination, and the United States appealed.

Mr. Chief Justice FULLER * * * delivered the opinion of the court.

By the purchase of the stock of the four Philadelphia refineries with shares of its own stock the American Sugar Refining Company acquired nearly complete control of the manufacture of refined sugar within the United States. The bill charged that the contracts under which these purchases were made constituted combinations in restraint of trade, and that in entering into them the defendants combined and conspired to restrain the trade and commerce in refined sugar among the several states and with foreign nations, contrary to the act of congress of July 2, 1890.

The relief sought was the cancellation of the agreements under which the stock was transferred, the redelivery of the stock to the parties respectively, and an injunction against the further performance of the agreements and further violations of the act. *   *   *

*   *   *

The fundamental question is whether, conceding that the existence of a monopoly in manufacture is established by the evidence, that monopoly can be directly suppressed under the act of congress in the mode attempted by this bill.

It cannot be denied that the power of a state to protect the lives, health, and property of its citizens, and to preserve good order and the public morals, "the power to govern men and things within the limits of its dominion," is a power originally and always belonging to the states, not surrendered by them to the general government, nor directly restrained by the constitution of the United States, and essentially exclusive. The relief of the citizens of each state from the burden of monopoly and the evils resulting from the restraint of trade among such citizens was left with the states to deal with, and this court has recognized their possession of that power even

to the extent of holding that an employment or business carried on by private individuals, when it becomes a matter of such public interest and importance as to create a common charge or burden upon the citizen,—in other words, when it becomes a practical monopoly, to which the citizen is compelled to resort, and by means of which a tribute can be exacted from the community,—is subject to regulation by state legislative power. On the other hand, the power of congress to regulate commerce among the several states is also exclusive. The constitution does not provide that interstate commerce shall be free, but, by the grant of this exclusive power to regulate it, it was left free, except as congress might impose restraints. Therefore it has been determined that the failure of congress to exercise this exclusive power in any case is an expression of its will that the subject shall be free from restrictions or impositions upon it by the several states, and if a law passed by a state in the exercise of its acknowledged powers comes into conflict with that will, the congress and the state cannot occupy the position of equal opposing sovereignties, because the constitution declares its supremacy, and that of the laws passed in pursuance thereof; and that which is not supreme must yield to that which is supreme. "Commerce undoubtedly is traffic," said Chief Justice Marshall, "but it is something more; it is intercourse. It describes the commercial intercourse between nations and parts of nations in all its branches, and is regulated by prescribing rules for carrying on that intercourse." That which belongs to commerce is within the jurisdiction of the United States, but that which does not belong to commerce is within the jurisdiction of the police power of the state. * * *

The argument is that the power to control the manufacture of refined sugar is a monopoly over a necessary of life, to the enjoyment of which by a large part of the population of the United States interstate commerce is indispensable, and that, therefore, the general government, in the exercise of the power to regulate commerce, may repress such monopoly directly, and set aside the instruments which have created it. But this argument cannot be confined to necessaries of life merely, and must include all articles of general consumption. Doubtless the power to control the manufacture of a given thing involves, in a certain sense, the control of its disposition, but this is a secondary, and not the primary, sense; and, although the exercise of that power may result in bringing the operation of commerce into play, it does not control it, and affects it only incidentally and indirectly. Commerce succeeds to manufacture, and is not a part of it. The power to regulate commerce is the power to prescribe the rule by which commerce shall be governed, and is a power independent of the power to suppress monopoly. But it may operate in repression of monopoly whenever that comes within the rules by which commerce is governed, or whenever the transaction is itself a monopoly of commerce.

It is vital that the independence of the commercial power and of the police power, and the delimitation between them, however sometimes perplexing, should always be recognized and observed, for, while the one furnishes the strongest bond of union, the other is essential to the preservation of the autonomy of the states as required by our dual form of govern-

ment; and acknowledged evils, however grave and urgent they may appear to be, had better be borne, than the risk be run, in the effort to suppress them, of more serious consequences by resort to expedients of even doubtful constitutionality.

It will be perceived how far-reaching the proposition is that the power of dealing with a monopoly directly may be exercised by the general government whenever interstate or international commerce may be ultimately affected. The regulation of commerce applies to the subjects of commerce, and not to matters of internal police. Contracts to buy, sell, or exchange goods to be transported among the several states, the transportation and its instrumentalities, and articles bought, sold, or exchanged for the purposes of such transit among the states, or put in the way of transit, may be regulated; but this is because they form part of interstate trade or commerce. The fact that an article is manufactured for export to another state does not of itself make it an article of interstate commerce, and the intent of the manufacturer does not determine the time when the article or product passes from the control of the state and belongs to commerce. This was so ruled in Coe v. Errol, 116 U.S. 517, 6 Sup.Ct. 475, in which the question before the court was whether certain logs cut at a place in New Hampshire, and hauled to a river town for the purpose of transportation to the state of Maine, were liable to be taxed like other property in the state of New Hampshire. Mr. Justice Bradley, delivering the opinion of the court, said: "Does the owner's state of mind in relation to the goods— that is, his intent to export them, and his partial preparation to do so—exempt them from taxation? This is the precise question for solution. * * * There must be a point of time when they cease to be governed exclusively by the domestic law, and begin to be governed and protected by the national law of commercial regulation; and that moment seems to us to be a legitimate one for this purpose in which they commence their final movement from the state of their origin to that of their destination."

* * *

Contracts, combinations, or conspiracies to control domestic enterprise in manufacture, agriculture, mining, production in all its forms, or to raise or lower prices or wages, might unquestionably tend to restrain external as well as domestic trade, but the restraint would be an indirect result, however inevitable, and whatever its extent, and such result would not necessarily determine the object of the contract, combination, or conspiracy.

Again, all the authorities agree that, in order to vitiate a contract or combination, it is not essential that its result should be a complete monopoly; it is sufficient if it really tends to that end, and to deprive the public of the advantages which flow from free competition. Slight reflection will show that, if the national power extends to all contracts and combinations in manufacture, agriculture, mining, and other productive industries, whose ultimate result may affect external commerce, comparatively little of business operations and affairs would be left for state control.

It was in the light of well-settled principles that the act of July 2, 1890, was framed. Congress did not attempt thereby to assert the power to deal with monopoly directly as

such; or to limit and restrict the rights of corporations created by the states or the citizens of the states in the acquisition, control, or disposition of property; or to regulate or prescribe the price or prices at which such property or the products thereof should be sold; or to make criminal the acts of persons in the acquisition and control of property which the states of their residence or creation sanctioned or permitted. Aside from the provisions applicable where congress might exercise municipal power, what the law struck at was combinations, contracts, and conspiracies to monopolize trade and commerce among the several states or with foreign nations; but the contracts and acts of the defendants related exclusively to the acquisition of the Philadelphia refineries and the business of sugar refining in Pennsylvania, and bore no direct relation to commerce between the states or with foreign nations. The object was manifestly private gain in the manufacture of the commodity, but not through the control of interstate or foreign commerce. It is true that the bill alleged that the products of these refineries were sold and distributed among the several states, and that all the companies were engaged in trade or commerce with the several states and with foreign nations; but this was no more than to say that trade and commerce served manufacture to fulfill its function. Sugar was refined for sale, and sales were probably made at Philadelphia for consumption, and undoubtedly for resale by the first purchasers throughout Pennsylvania and other states, and refined sugar was also forwarded by the companies to other states for sale. Nevertheless it does not follow that an attempt to monopolize, or the actual monopoly of, the manufacture was an attempt, whether executory or consummated, to monopolize commerce, even though, in order to dispose of the product, the instrumentality of commerce was necessarily invoked. There was nothing in the proofs to indicate any intention to put a restraint upon trade or commerce, and the fact, as we have seen, that trade or commerce might be indirectly affected, was not enough to entitle complainants to a decree. * * *

Decree affirmed.

Mr. Justice HARLAN, dissenting.

* * *

"The object," the court below said, "in purchasing the Philadelphia refineries was to obtain a greater influence or more perfect control over the business of refining and selling sugar in this country." This characterization of the object for which this stupendous combination was formed is properly accepted in the opinion of the court as justified by the proof. I need not, therefore, analyze the evidence upon this point. In its consideration of the important constitutional question presented this court assumes on the record before us that the result of the transactions disclosed by the pleadings and proof was the creation of a monopoly in the manufacture of a necessary of life. If this combination, so far as its operations necessarily or directly affect interstate commerce, cannot be restrained or suppressed under some power granted to congress, it will be cause for regret that the patriotic statesmen who framed the constitution did not foresee the necessity of investing the national government with power to deal with gigantic monopolies holding in their grasp, and injuriously controlling in their own interest, the entire trade

among the states in food products that are essential to the comfort of every household in the land.

* * *

It would seem to be indisputable that no combination of corporations or individuals can, of right, impose unlawful restraints upon interstate trade, whether upon transportation or upon such interstate intercourse and traffic as precede transportation, any more than it can, of right, impose unreasonable restraints upon the completely internal traffic of a state. The supposition cannot be indulged that this general proposition will be disputed. If it be true that a combination of corporations or individuals may, so far as the power of congress is concerned, subject interstate trade, in any of its stages, to unlawful restraints, the conclusion is inevitable that the constitution has failed to accomplish one primary object of the Union, which was to place commerce among the states under the control of the common government of all the people, and thereby relieve or protect it against burdens or restrictions imposed, by whatever authority, for the benefit of particular localities or special interests.

* * *

But there is a trade among the several states which is distinct from that carried on within the territorial limits of a state. The regulation and control of the former are committed by the national constitution to congress. Commerce among the states, as this court has declared, is a unit, and in respect of that commerce this is one country, and we are one people. It may be regulated by rules applicable to every part of the United States, and state lines and state jurisdiction cannot interfere with the enforcement of such rules. The jurisdiction of the general government extends over every foot of territory within the United States. Under the power with which it is invested, congress may remove unlawful obstructions, of whatever kind, to the free course of trade among the states. In so doing it would not interfere with the "autonomy of the states," because the power thus to protect interstate commerce is expressly given by the people of all the states. Interstate intercourse, trade, and traffic are absolutely free, except as such intercourse, trade, or traffic may be incidentally or indirectly affected by the exercise by the states of their reserved police powers. Sherlock v. Alling, 99 U.S. 99, 103. It is the constitution, the supreme law of the land, which invests congress with power to protect commerce among the states against burdens and exactions arising from unlawful restraints by whatever authority imposed. Surely, a right secured or granted by that instrument is under the protection of the government which that instrument creates. Any combination, therefore, that disturbs or unreasonably obstructs freedom in buying and selling articles manufactured to be sold to persons in other states, or to be carried to other states,—a freedom that cannot exist if the right to buy and sell is fettered by unlawful restraints that crush out competition,—affects, not incidentally, but directly, the people of all the states; and the remedy for such an evil is found only in the exercise of powers confided to a government which, this court has said, was the government of all, exercising powers delegated by all, representing all, acting for all. M'Culloch v. Maryland, 4 Wheat. 405.

It has been argued that a combi-

nation between corporations of different states, or between the stockholders of such corporations, with the object and effect of controlling not simply the manufacture, but the price, of refined sugar throughout the whole of the United States,— which is the case now before us,— cannot be held to be in restraint of "commerce among the states," and amenable to national authority, without conceding that the general government has authority to say what shall and what shall not be manufactured in the several states. * * *

* * *

It may be admitted that an act which did nothing more than forbid, and which had no other object than to forbid, the mere refining of sugar in any state, would be in excess of any power granted to congress. But the act of 1890 is not of that character. It does not strike at the manufacture simply of articles that are legitimate or recognized subjects of commerce, but at combinations that unduly restrain, because they monopolize, the buying and selling of articles which are to go into interstate commerce. * * *

* * *

The power of congress covers and protects the absolute freedom of such intercourse and trade among the states as may or must succeed manufacture and precede transportation from the place of purchase. This would seem to be conceded, for the court in the present case expressly declare that "contracts to buy, sell, or exchange goods to be transported among the several states, the transportation and its instrumentalities, and articles bought, sold, or exchanged for the purpose of such transit among the states, or put in the way of transit, may be regulated, but this is because they form part of interstate trade or commerce." Here is a direct admission—one which the settled doctrines of this court justify—that contracts to buy, and the purchasing of goods to be transported from one state to another, and transportation, with its instrumentalities, are all parts of interstate trade or commerce. Each part of such trade is then under the protection of congress. And yet, by the opinion and judgment in this case, if I do not misapprehend them, congress is without power to protect the commercial intercourse that such purchasing necessarily involves against the restraints and burdens arising from the existence of combinations that meet purchasers, from whatever state they come, with the threat—for it is nothing more nor less than a threat—that they shall not purchase what they desire to purchase, except at the prices fixed by such combinations. A citizen of Missouri has the right to go in person, or send orders, to Pennsylvania and New Jersey for the purpose of purchasing refined sugar. But of what value is that right if he is confronted in those states by a vast combination, which absolutely controls the price of that article by reason of its having acquired all the sugar refineries in the United States in order that they may fix prices in their own interest exclusively?

In my judgment, the citizens of the several states composing the Union are entitled of right to buy goods in the state where they are manufactured, or in any other state, without being confronted by an illegal combination whose business extends throughout the whole country, which, by the law everywhere, is an enemy to the public interests, and which prevents such buying, except at prices arbitrarily fixed by it. I insist that the free course of trade among the states cannot coexist with such combinations. When I speak of trade I mean the buying and selling of articles of every kind that are recognized articles of interstate commerce. Whatever improperly obstructs the free course of interstate intercourse and trade, as involved in the buying and selling of articles to be carried from one state to another, may be reached by congress under its authority to regulate commerce among the states. The exercise of that authority so as to make trade among the states in all recognized articles of commerce absolutely free from unreasonable or illegal restrictions imposed by combinations is justified by an express grant of power to congress, and would redound to the welfare of the whole country. I am unable to perceive that any such result would imperil the autonomy of the states, especially as that result cannot be attained through the action of any one state.

* * *

While the opinion of the court in this case does not declare the act of 1890 to be unconstitutional, it defeats the main object for which it was passed, for it is, in effect, held that the statute would be unconstitutional if interpreted as embracing such unlawful restraints upon the purchasing of goods in one state to be carried to another state as necessarily arise from the existence of combinations formed for the purpose and with the effect, not only of monopolizing the ownership of all such goods in every part of the country, but of controlling the prices for them in all the states. This view of the scope of the act leaves the public, so far as national power is concerned, entirely at the mercy of combinations which arbitrarily control the prices of articles purchased to be transported from one state to another state. I cannot assent to that view. In my judgment, the general government is not placed by the constitution in such a condition of helplessness that it must fold its arms and remain inactive while capital combines, under the name of a corporation, to destroy competition, not in one state only, but throughout the entire country, in the buying and selling of articles—especially the necessaries of life—that go into commerce among the states. The doctrine of the autonomy of the states cannot properly be invoked to justify a denial of power in the national government to meet such an emergency, involving, as it does, that freedom of commercial intercourse among the states which the constitution sought to attain.

* * *

To the general government has been committed the control of commercial intercourse among the states, to the end that it may be free at all times from any restraints except such as congress may impose or permit for the benefit of the whole country. The common government of all the people is the only one that can adequately deal with a matter which directly and injuriously affects the entire commerce of the country, which concerns equally all the people of the Union, and which, it must be confessed, cannot be adequately controlled by any one state. Its authority should not be so weakened by construction that it cannot reach and eradicate evils that, beyond all question, tend to defeat an object which that government is entitled, by the constitution, to accomplish. "Powerful and ingenious minds," this court has said, "taking, as postulates, that the powers expressly granted to the government of the Union are to be contracted by construction into the narrowest possible compass, and that the original powers of the states are retained, if any possible construction will retain them, may, by a course of well-digested but refined and metaphysical reasoning, founded on these premises, explain away the constitution of our country, and leave it, a magnificent structure, indeed, to look at, but totally unfit for use. They may so entangle and perplex the understanding as to obscure principles which were before thought quite plain, and induce doubts where, if the mind were to pursue its own course, none would be perceived." Gibbons v. Ogden, 9 Wheat. 1, 222.

* * *

For the reasons stated, I dissent from the opinion and judgment of the court.

HAMMER v. DAGENHART
[THE CHILD LABOR CASE]

Supreme Court of the United States, 1918
247 U.S. 251, 38 S.Ct. 529, 62 L.Ed. 1101

The Federal Child Labor Act of 1916 barred from shipment in interstate commerce products of factories which either employed children under the age of fourteen or allowed children between the ages of fourteen and sixteen to work more than eight hours a day or more than six days a week or at night. Roland Dagenhart filed a bill in federal district court on behalf of himself and his two minor sons,

employees in a cotton mill in North Carolina, against W. C. Hammer, a United States attorney, to enjoin the enforcement of the act. The district court held the act unconstitutional, and appeal was made to the Supreme Court.

Mr. Justice DAY delivered the opinion of the Court.

* * *

The attack upon the act rests upon three propositions: First: It is not a regulation of interstate and foreign commerce; second: It contravenes the Tenth Amendment to the Constitution; third: It conflicts with the Fifth Amendment to the Constitution.

* * *

The power essential to the passage of this act, the government contends, is found in the commerce clause of the Constitution which authorizes Congress to regulate commerce with foreign nations and among the states.

In Gibbons v. Ogden, 9 Wheat. 1, 6 L.Ed. 23, Chief Justice Marshall, speaking for this court, and defining the extent and nature of the commerce power, said, "It is the power to regulate; that is, to prescribe the rule by which commerce is to be governed." In other words, the power is one to control the means by which commerce is carried on, which is directly the contrary of the assumed right to forbid commerce from moving and thus destroying it as to particular commodities. But it is insisted that adjudged cases in this court establish the doctrine that the power to regulate given to Congress incidentally includes the authority to prohibit the movement of ordinary commodities and therefore that the subject is not open for discussion. The cases demonstrate the contrary. They rest upon the character of the particular subjects dealt with and the fact that the scope of governmental authority, state or national, possessed over them is such that the authority to prohibit is as to them but the exertion of the power to regulate.

The first of these cases is Champion v. Ames, 188 U.S. 321, 23 Sup. Ct. 321, the so-called Lottery Case, in which it was held that Congress might pass a law having the effect to keep the channels of commerce free from use in the transportation of tickets used in the promotion of lottery schemes. In Hipolite Egg Co. v. United States, 220 U.S. 45, 31 Sup.Ct. 364, this court sustained the power of Congress to pass the Pure Food and Drug Act * * * which prohibited the introduction into the states by means of interstate commerce of impure foods and drugs. In Hoke v. United States, 227 U.S. 308, 33 Sup.Ct. 281, this court sustained the constitutionality of the so-called "White Slave Traffic Act" * * * whereby the transportation of a woman in interstate commerce for the purpose of prostitution was forbidden. * * *

In Caminetti v. United States, 242 U.S. 470, 37 Sup.Ct. 192, we held that Congress might prohibit the transportation of women in interstate commerce for the purposes of debauchery and kindred purposes. In Clark Distilling Co. v. Western Maryland Railway Co., 242 U.S. 311, 37 Sup.Ct. 180, the power of Congress over the transportation of intoxicating liquors was sustained. * * *

In each of these instances the use of interstate transportation was necessary to the accomplishment of harmful results. In other words, although the power over interstate transportation was to regulate, that could only be accomplished by prohibiting the use of the facilities of interstate commerce to effect the evil intended.

This element is wanting in the present case. The thing intended to be accomplished by this statute is the denial of the facilities of interstate commerce to those manufacturers in the states who employ children within the prohibited ages. The act in its effect does not regulate transportation among the states, but aims to standardize the ages at which children may be employed in mining and manufacturing within the states. The goods shipped are of themselves harmless. The act permits them to be freely shipped after thirty days from the time of their removal from the factory. When offered for shipment, and before transportation begins, the labor of their production is over, and the mere fact that they were intended for interstate commerce transportation does not make their production subject to federal control under the commerce power.

Commerce "consists of intercourse and traffic * * * and includes the transportation of persons and property, as well as the purchase, sale and exchange of commodities." The making of goods and the mining of coal are not commerce, nor does the fact that these things are to be afterwards shipped, or used in interstate commerce, make their production a part thereof. Delaware, Lackawanna & Western R. R. Co. v. Yurkonis, 238 U.S. 439, 35 Sup.Ct. 902.

Over interstate transportation, or its incidents, the regulatory power of Congress is ample, but the production of articles, intended for interstate commerce, is a matter of local regulation. * * * If it were otherwise, all manufacture intended for interstate shipment would be brought under federal control to the practical exclusion of the authority of the states, a result certainly not contemplated by the framers of the Constitution when they vested in Congress the authority to regulate commerce among the States. Kidd v. Pearson, 128 U.S. 1, 21, 9 Sup.Ct. 6.

It is further contended that the authority of Congress may be exerted to control interstate commerce in the shipment of child-made goods because of the effect of the circulation of such goods in other states where the evil of this class of labor has been recognized by local legislation, and the right to thus employ child labor has been more rigorously restrained than in the state of production. In other words, that the unfair competition, thus engendered, may be controlled by closing the channels of interstate commerce to manufacturers in those states where the local laws do not meet what Congress deems to be the more just standard of other states.

There is no power vested in Congress to require the states to exercise their police power so as to prevent possible unfair competition. Many causes may cooperate to give one state, by reason of local laws or conditions, an economic advantage over others. The commerce clause was not intended to give to Congress a general authority to equalize such conditions. In some of the states laws have been passed fixing minimum wages for women, in others the local law regulates the hours of labor of women in various employments. Business done in such states may be at an economic disadvantage when compared with states which have no such regulations; surely, this fact does not give Congress the power to deny transportation in interstate commerce to those who carry on business where the hours of labor and the rate of compensation for women have not been fixed by a standard in use in other states and approved by Congress.

* * *

That there should be limitations upon the right to employ children in mines and factories in the interest of their own and the public welfare, all will admit. That such employment is generally deemed to require regulation is shown by the fact that the brief of counsel states that every state in the Union has a law upon the subject, limiting the right to thus employ children. In North Carolina, the state wherein is located the factory in which the employment was had in the present case, no child under twelve years of age is permitted to work.

It may be desirable that such laws be uniform, but our federal government is one of enumerated powers; "this principle," declared Chief Justice Marshall in McCulloch v. Maryland, 4 Wheat. 316, 4 L.Ed. 579, "is universally admitted."

A statute must be judged by its natural and reasonable effect. * * * The control by Congress over interstate commerce cannot authorize the exercise of authority not entrusted to it by the Constitution. * * * The maintenance of the authority of the states over matters purely local is as essential to the preservation of our institutions as is the conservation of the supremacy of the federal power in all matters entrusted to the nation by the federal Constitution.

* * *

We have neither authority nor disposition to question the motives of Congress in enacting this legislation. The purposes intended must be attained consistently with constitutional limitations and not by an invasion of the powers of the states. This court has no more important function than that which devolves upon it the obligation to preserve inviolate the constitutional limitations upon the exercise of authority federal and state to the end that each may continue to discharge, harmoniously with the other, the duties entrusted to it by the Constitution.

In our view the necessary effect of this act is, by means of a prohibition against the movement in interstate commerce of ordinary commercial commodities to regulate the hours of labor of children in factories and mines within the states, a purely state authority. Thus the act in a two-fold sense is repugnant to the Constitution. It not only transcends the authority delegated to Congress over commerce but also exerts a power as to a purely local matter to which the federal authority does not extend. The far reaching result of upholding the act cannot be more plainly indicated than by pointing out that if Congress can thus regulate matters entrusted to local authority by prohibition of the movement of commodities in interstate commerce, all freedom of commerce will be at an end, and the power of the states over local matters may be eliminated, and thus our system of government be practically destroyed.

For these reasons we hold that this law exceeds the constitutional authority of Congress. It follows that the decree of the District Court must be

Affirmed.

Mr. Justice HOLMES, dissenting.

* * * The objection urged against the power is that the States have exclusive control over their methods of production and that Congress cannot meddle with them, and taking the proposition in the sense of direct intermeddling I agree to it and suppose that no one denies it. But if an act is within the powers specifically conferred upon Congress, it seems to me that it is not made any less constitutional because of the indirect effects that it may have, however obvious it may be that it will have those effects, and that we are not at liberty upon such grounds to hold it void.

The first step in my argument is to make plain what no one is likely to dispute—that the statute in question is within the power expressly given to Congress if considered only as to its immediate effects and that if invalid it is so only upon some collateral ground. The statute confines itself to prohibiting the carriage of certain goods in interstate or foreign commerce. Congress is given power to regulate such commerce in unqualified terms. It would not be argued today that the power to regulate does not include the power to prohibit. Regulation means the prohibition of something, and when interstate commerce is the matter to be regulated I cannot doubt that the regulation may prohibit any part of such commerce that Congress sees fit to forbid. At all events it is established by the *Lottery* Case and others that have followed it that a

law is not beyond the regulative power of Congress merely because it prohibits certain transportation out and out. Champion v. Ames, 188 U.S. 321, 355, 359, 23 Sup.Ct. 321. So I repeat that this statute in its immediate operation is clearly within the Congress's constitutional power.

The question then is narrowed to whether the exercise of its otherwise constitutional power by Congress can be pronounced unconstitutional because of its possible reaction upon the conduct of the States in a matter upon which I have admitted that they are free from direct control. I should have thought that that matter had been disposed of so fully as to leave no room for doubt. I should have thought that the most conspicuous decisions of this Court had made it clear that the power to regulate commerce and other constitutional powers could not be cut down or qualified by the fact that it might interfere with the carrying out of the domestic policy of any State.

The manufacture of oleomargarine is as much a matter of State regulation as the manufacture of cotton cloth. Congress levied a tax upon the compound when colored so as to resemble butter that was so great as obviously to prohibit the manufacture and sale. * * * Fifty years ago a tax on state banks, the obvious purpose and actual effect of which was to drive them, or at least their circulation, out of existence, was sustained, although the result was one that Congress had no constitutional power to require. The Court made short work of the argument as to the purpose of the Act. "The Judicial cannot prescribe to the Legislative Departments of the Government limitations upon the exercise of its acknowledged powers." Veazie Bank v. Fenno, 8 Wall. 533, 19 L.Ed. 482.

* * * And to come to cases upon interstate commerce notwithstanding United States v. E. C. Knight Co., * * * the Sherman Act has been made an instrument for the breaking up of combinations in restraint of trade and monopolies, using the power to regulate commerce as a foothold, but not proceeding because that commerce was the end actually in mind. The objection that the control of the States over production was interfered with was urged again and again but always in vain. Standard Oil Co. v. United States, 221 U.S. 1, 68, 69, 31 Sup.Ct. 502; United States v. American Tobacco Co., 221 U.S. 106, 184, 31 Sup.Ct. 632. * * *

The Pure Food and Drug Act which was sustained in Hipolite Egg Co. v. United States, 220 U.S. 45, 57, 31 Sup.Ct. 364, 367, with the intimation that "no trade can be carried on between the States to which it [the power of Congress to regulate commerce] does not extend," applies not merely to articles that the changing opinions of the time condemn as intrinsically harmful but to others innocent in themselves, simply on the ground that the order for them was induced by a preliminary fraud. * * * It does not matter whether the supposed evil precedes or follows the transportation. It is enough that in the opinion of Congress the transportation encourages the evil. I may add that in the cases on the so-called White Slave Act it was established that the means adopted by Congress as convenient to the exercise of its power might have the character of police regulations. Hoke v. United States, 227 U.S. 308, 323, 33 Sup.Ct. 281; Caminetti v. United States, 242 U.S. 470, 492, 37 Sup.Ct. 192. * * * I see no reason for that proposition not applying here.

The notion that prohibition is any less prohibition when applied to things now thought evil I do not understand. But if there is any matter upon which civilized countries have agreed—far more unanimously than they have with regard to intoxicants and some other matters over which this country is now emotionally aroused—it is the evil of premature and excessive child labor. I should have thought that if we were to introduce our own moral conceptions where in my opinion they do not belong, this was preeminently a case for upholding the exercise of all its powers by the United States.

But I had thought that the propriety of the exercise of a power admitted to exist in some cases was for the consideration of Congress alone and that this Court always had disavowed the right to intrude its judgment upon questions of policy or morals. It is not for this Court to pronounce when prohibition is necessary to regulation if it ever may be necessary—to say that it is permissible as against strong drink but not as against the product of ruined lives.

The Act does not meddle with anything belonging to the States. They may regulate their internal affairs and their domestic commerce as they like. But when they seek to send their products across the State line they are no longer within their rights. If there were no Constitution and no Congress their power to cross the line would depend upon their neighbors. Under the Constitution such commerce belongs not to the States but to Congress to regulate. It may carry out its views of public policy whatever indirect effect they may have upon the activities of the States. Instead of being encountered by a prohibitive tariff at her boundaries the State encounters the public policy of the United States which it is for Congress to express. The public policy of the United States is shaped with a view to the benefit of the nation as a whole. If, as has been the case within the memory of men still living, a State should take a different view of the propriety of sustaining a lottery from that which generally prevails, I cannot believe that the fact would require a different decision from that reached in *Champion* v. *Ames.* Yet in that

case it would be said with quite as much force as in this that Congress was attempting to intermeddle with the State's domestic affairs. The national welfare as understood by Congress may require a different attitude within its sphere from that of some self-seeking State. It seems to me entirely constitutional for Congress to enforce its understanding by all the means at its command.

Mr. Justice McKENNA, Mr. Justice BRANDEIS, and Mr. Justice CLARKE concur in this opinion.

SCHECHTER POULTRY CORP. v. UNITED STATES

Supreme Court of the United States, 1935
295 U.S. 495, 55 S.Ct. 837, 79 L.Ed. 1570

For a statement of the facts and a discussion of the delegation of power issue, see p. 187.

[Excerpts of opinions dealing with the Commerce Clause]

Mr. Chief Justice HUGHES delivered the opinion of the Court.

* * *

The Question of the Application of the Provisions of the Live Poultry Code to Intrastate Transactions.— * * * This aspect of the case presents the question whether the particular provisions of the Live Poultry Code, which the defendants were convicted for violating and for having conspired to violate, were within the regulating power of Congress.

These provisions relate to the hours and wages of those employed by defendants in their slaughterhouses in Brooklyn and to the sales there made to retail dealers and butchers.

Were these transactions "*in*" interstate commerce? Much is made of the fact that almost all the poultry coming to New York is sent there from other states. But the code provisions, as here applied, do not concern the transportation of the poultry from other states to New York, or the transactions of the commission men or others to whom it is consigned, or the sales made by such consignees to defendants. When defendants had made their purchases, whether at the West Washington Market in New York City or at the railroad terminals serving the city, or elsewhere, the poultry was trucked to their slaughterhouses in Brooklyn for local disposition. The interstate transactions in relation to that poultry then ended. Defendants held the poultry at their slaughterhouse markets for slaughter and local sale to retail dealers and butchers who in turn sold directly to consumers.

Neither the slaughtering nor the sales by defendants were transactions in interstate commerce. * * *

The undisputed facts thus afford no warrant for the argument that the poultry handled by defendants at their slaughterhouse markets was in a *"current"* or *"flow"* of interstate commerce, and was thus subject to congressional regulation. The mere fact that there may be a constant flow of commodities into a state does not mean that the flow continues after the property has arrived and has become commingled with the mass of property within the state and is there held solely for local disposition and use. So far as the poultry here in question is concerned, the flow in interstate commerce had ceased. The poultry had come to a permanent rest within the state. It was not held, used, or sold by defendants in relation to any further transactions in interstate commerce and was not destined for transportation to other states. Hence decisions which deal with a stream of interstate commerce—where goods come to rest within a state temporarily and are later to go forward in interstate commerce—and with the regulations of transactions involved in that practical continuity of movement, are not applicable here. See Swift & Company v. United States, 196 U.S. 375, 387, 388, 25 S.Ct. 276, * * * Stafford v. Wallace, 258 U.S. 495, 519, 42 S.Ct. 397. * * *

Did the defendants' transactions directly *"affect"* interstate commerce so as to be subject to federal regulation? The power of Congress extends, not only to the regulation of transactions which are part of interstate commerce, but to the protection of that commerce from injury. It matters not that the injury may be due to the conduct of those engaged in intrastate operations. * * *

* * *

In determining how far the federal government may go in controlling intrastate transactions upon the ground that they "affect" interstate commerce, there is a necessary and well-established distinction between direct and indirect effects. The precise line can be drawn only as individual cases arise, but the distinction is clear in principle. Direct effects are illustrated by the railroad cases we have cited, as, e.g., the effect of failure to use prescribed safety appliances on railroads which are the highways of both interstate and intrastate commerce, injury to an employee engaged in interstate transportation by the negligence of an employee engaged in an intrastate movement, the fixing of rates for intrastate transportation which unjustly discriminate against interstate commerce. But where the effect of intrastate transactions upon interstate commerce is merely indirect, such transactions remain within the domain of state power. If the commerce clause were construed to reach all enterprises and transactions which could be said to have an indirect effect upon interstate commerce, the federal authority would embrace practically all the activities of the people, and the authority of the state over its domestic concerns would exist only by sufferance of the federal government. * * *

* * *

[T]he distinction between direct and indirect effects of intrastate transactions upon interstate commerce must be recognized as a fundamental one, essential to the maintenance of our constitutional system.

Otherwise, as we have said, there would be virtually no limit to the federal power, and for all practical purposes we should have a completely centralized government. We must consider the provisions here in question in the light of this distinction.

The question of chief importance relates to the provisions of the code as to the hours and wages of those employed in defendants' slaughterhouse markets. It is plain that these requirements are imposed in order to govern the details of defendants' management of their local business. The persons employed in slaughtering and selling in local trade are not employed in interstate commerce. Their hours and wages have no direct relation to interstate commerce. The question of how many hours these employees should work and what they should be paid differs in no essential respect from similar questions in other local businesses which handle commodities brought into a state and there dealt in as a part of its internal commerce. This appears from an examination of the considerations urged by the government with respect to conditions in the poultry trade. Thus, the government argues that hours and wages affect prices; that slaughterhouse men sell at a small margin above operating costs; that labor represents 50 to 60 per cent. of these costs; that a slaughterhouse operator paying lower wages or reducing his cost by exacting long hours of work translates his saving into lower prices; that this results in demands for a cheaper grade of goods; and that the cutting of prices brings about a demoralization of the price structure. Similar conditions may be adduced in relation to other businesses. The argument of the government proves too much. If the federal govern-

ment may determine the wages and hours of employees in the internal commerce of a state, because of their relation to cost and prices and their indirect effect upon interstate commerce, it would seem that a similar control might be exerted over other elements of costs, also affecting prices, such as the number of employees, rents, advertising, methods of doing business, etc. All the processes of production and distribution that enter into costs could likewise be controlled. If the cost of doing an intrastate business is in itself the permitted object of federal control, the extent of the regulation of cost would be a question of discretion and not of power.

The government also makes the point that efforts to enact state legislation establishing high labor standards have been impeded by the belief that, unless similar action is taken generally, commerce will be diverted from the states adopting such standards, and that this fear of diversion has led to demands for federal legislation on the subject of wages and hours. The apparent implication is that the federal authority under the commerce clause should be deemed to extend to the establishment of rules to govern wages and hours in intrastate trade and industry generally throughout the country, thus overriding the authority of the states to deal with domestic problems arising from labor conditions in their internal commerce.

It is not the province of the Court to consider the economic advantages or disadvantages of such a centralized system. It is sufficient to say that the Federal Constitution does not provide for it. Our growth and development have called for wide use of the commerce power of the federal government in its control over the expanded activities of interstate commerce and in protecting that commerce from burdens, interferences, and conspiracies to restrain and monopolize it. But the authority of the federal government may not be pushed to such an extreme as to destroy the distinction, which the commerce clause itself establishes, between commerce "among the several States" and the internal concerns of a state. The same answer must be made to the contention that is based upon the serious economic situation which led to the passage of the Recovery Act—the fall in prices, the decline in wages and employment, and the curtailment of the market for commodities. Stress is laid upon the great importance of maintaining wage distributions which would provide the necessary stimulus in starting "the cumulative forces making for expanding commercial activity." Without in any way disparaging this motive, it is enough to say that the recuperative efforts of the federal government must be made in a manner consistent with the authority granted by the Constitution.

We are of the opinion that the attempt through the provisions of the code to fix the hours and wages of employees of defendants in their intrastate business was not a valid exercise of federal power.

* * *

Mr. Justice CARDOZO (concurring).

I find no authority in that grant for the regulation of wages and hours of labor in the intrastate transactions that make up the defendants' business. As to this feature of the case, little can be added to the opinion of the court. There is a view of causation that would obliterate the distinction between what is national and what is local in the activities of commerce. Motion at the outer rim is communicated perceptibly, though minutely, to recording instruments at the center. A society such as ours "is an elastic medium which transmits all tremors throughout its territory; the only question is of their size." Per Learned Hand, J., in the court below. The law is not indifferent to considerations of degree. Activities local in their immediacy do not become interstate and national because of distant repercussions. What is near and what is distant may at times be uncertain. * * * There is no penumbra of uncertainty obscuring judgment here. To find immediacy or directness here is to find it almost everywhere. If centripetal forces are to be isolated to the exclusion of the forces that oppose and counteract them, there will be an end to our federal system.

I am authorized to state that Mr. Justice STONE joins in this opinion.

CARTER v. CARTER COAL CO.

Supreme Court of the United States, 1936
298 U.S. 238, 56 S.Ct. 855, 80 L.Ed. 1160

Congress passed the Bituminous Coal Conservation Act, more popularly known as the Guffey Act, in 1935 for the purpose of stabilizing the coal industry through regulations on prices, methods of competition, and labor relations. The act established the National Bituminous Coal Commission, authorized to formulate a code within certain guidelines, and district boards with the authority to determine maximum and minimum prices on coal. Coal producers were subject to an excise tax of 15 percent on the sale price of coal at the mine but were exempt from 90 percent of the tax if they accepted the Bituminous Coal Code. In addition the act contained labor provisions (which were not in effect as of the time of this case) relating to collective bargaining, hours, wages, and the creation of a labor board to adjudicate disputes. James Carter, a principal stockholder, brought suit against the Carter Coal Company to enjoin the company from complying with the code and paying the tax. A federal court in the District of Columbia held that while the labor provisions were unconstitutional, the regulations on fair trade practices and the tax provisions were valid and dismissed Carter's bill of complaint. Carter and Guy Helvering, the Commissioner of Internal Revenue, cross-petitioned the Supreme Court for certiorari. Several other cases challenging the act were consolidated for hearing before the Court.

Mr. Justice SUTHERLAND delivered the opinion of the Court.

* * *

* * * Certain recitals contained in the act plainly suggest that its makers were of opinion that its constitutionality could be sustained under some general federal power, thought to exist, apart from the specific grants of the Constitution. The fallacy of that view will be apparent when we recall fundamental principles which, although hitherto often expressed in varying forms of words, will bear repetition whenever their accuracy seems to be challenged. The recitals to which we refer are contained in section 1 (which is simply a preamble to the act), and, among others, are to the effect that the distribution of bituminous coal is of national interest, affecting the health and comfort of the people and the general welfare of the Nation; that this circumstance, together with the necessity of maintaining just and rational relations between the public, owners, producers, and employees, and the right of the public to constant and adequate supplies at reasonable prices, require regulation of the industry as the act provides. These affirmations—and the further ones that the production and distribution of such coal "directly affect

interstate commerce," because of which and of the waste of the national coal resources and other circumstances, the regulation is necessary for the protection of such commerce—do not constitute an exertion of the will of Congress which is legislation, but a recital of considerations which in the opinion of that body existed and justified the expression of its will in the present act. Nevertheless, this preamble may not be disregarded. On the contrary it is important, because it makes clear, except for the pure assumption that the conditions described "directly" affect interstate commerce, that the powers which Congress undertook to exercise are not specific but of the most general character—namely, to protect the general public interest and the health and comfort of the people, to conserve privately-owned coal, maintain just relations between producers and employees and others, and promote the general welfare, by controlling nation-wide production and distribution of coal. These, it may be conceded, are objects of great worth; but are they ends, the attainment of which has been committed by the Constitution to the federal government? This is a vital question; for nothing is more certain than that beneficent aims, however great or well directed, can never serve in lieu of constitutional power.

The ruling and firmly established principle is that the powers which the general government may exercise are only those specifically enumerated in the Constitution, and such implied powers as are necessary and proper to carry into effect the enumerated powers. Whether the end sought to be attained by an act of Congress is legitimate is wholly a matter of constitutional power and not at all of legislative discretion. Legislative congressional discretion begins with the choice of means and ends with the adoption of methods and details to carry the delegated powers into effect. The distinction between these two things—power and discretion—is not only very plain but very important. For while the powers are rigidly limited to the enumerations of the Constitution, the means which may be employed to carry the powers into effect are not restricted, save that they must be appropriate, plainly adapted to the end, and not prohibited by, but consistent with, the letter and spirit of the Constitution. McCulloch v. Maryland, 4 Wheat. 316, 421, 4 L.Ed. 579. Thus, it may be said that to a constitutional end many ways are open; but to an end not within the terms of the Constitution, all ways are closed.

The proposition, often advanced as often discredited, that the power of the federal government inherently extends to purposes affecting the Nation as a whole with which the states severally cannot deal or cannot adequately deal, and the related notion that Congress, entirely apart from those powers delegated by the Constitution, may enact laws to promote the general welfare, have never been accepted but always definitely rejected by this court. * * * In the Framers Convention, the proposal to confer a general power akin to

that just discussed was included in Mr. Randolph's resolutions, the sixth of which, among other things, declared that the National Legislature ought to enjoy the legislative rights vested in Congress by the Confederation, and "moreover to legislate in all cases to which the separate States are incompetent, or in which the harmony of the United States may be interrupted by the exercise of individual Legislation." The convention, however, declined to confer upon Congress power in such general terms; instead of which it carefully limited the powers which it thought wise to intrust to Congress by specifying them, thereby denying all others not granted expressly or by necessary implication. It made no grant of authority to Congress to legislate substantively for the general welfare * * * and no such authority exists, save as the general welfare may be promoted by the exercise of the powers which are granted. * * *

There are many subjects in respect of which the several states have not legislated in harmony with one another, and in which their varying laws and the failure of some of them to act at all have resulted in injurious confusion and embarrassment. * * * The state laws with respect to marriage and divorce present a case in point; and the great necessity of national legislation on that subject has been from time to time vigorously urged. Other pertinent examples are laws with respect to negotiable instruments, desertion and nonsupport, certain phases of state taxation, and others which we do not pause to mention. In many of these fields of legislation, the necessity of bringing the applicable rules of law into general harmonious relation has been so great that a Commission on Uniform State Laws, composed of commissioners from every state in the Union, has for many years been industriously and successfully working to that end by preparing and securing the passage by the several states of uniform laws. If there be an easier and constitutional way to these desirable results through congressional action, it thus far has escaped discovery.

* * *

The general rule with regard to the respective powers of the national and the state governments under the Constitution is not in doubt. The states were before the Constitution; and, consequently, their legislative powers antedated the Constitution. Those who framed and those who adopted that instrument meant to carve from the general mass of legislative powers, then possessed by the states, only such portions as it was thought wise to confer upon the federal government; and in order that there should be no uncertainty in respect of what was taken and what was left, the national powers of legislation were not aggregated but enumerated—with the result that what was not embraced by the enumeration remained vested in the states without change or impairment.

* * *

* * *

We have set forth, perhaps at unnecessary length, the foregoing principles, because it seemed necessary to do so in order to demonstrate that the general purposes which the act recites, and which, therefore, unless the recitals be disregarded, Congress undertook to achieve, are beyond the power of Congress except so far, and only so far, as they may be realized by an exercise of some specific power granted by the Constitution. Proceeding by a process of elimination, which it is not necessary to follow in detail, we shall find no grant of power which authorizes Congress to legislate in respect of these general purposes unless it be found in the commerce clause—and this we now consider.

* * * Since the validity of the act depends upon whether it is a regulation of interstate commerce, the nature and extent of the power conferred upon Congress by the commerce clause becomes the determinative question in this branch of the case. * * * In exercising the authority conferred by this clause of the Constitution, Congress is powerless to regulate anything which is not commerce, as it is powerless to do anything about commerce which is not regulation. * * *

* * *

[T]he word "commerce" is the equivalent of the phrase "intercourse for the purposes of trade." Plainly, the incidents leading up to and culminating in the mining of coal do not constitute such intercourse. The employment of men, the fixing of their wages, hours of labor, and working conditions, the bargaining in respect of these things—whether carried on separately or collectively—each and all constitute intercourse for the purposes of production, not of trade. The latter is a thing apart from the relation of employer and employee, which in all producing occupations is purely local in character. Extraction of coal from the mine is the aim and the completed result of local activities. Commerce in the coal mined is not brought into being by force of these activities, but by negotiations, agreements and circumstances entirely apart from production. Mining brings the subject-matter of commerce into existence. Commerce disposes of it.

A consideration of the foregoing * * * renders inescapable the conclusion that the effect of the labor provisions of the act, including those in respect of minimum wages, wage agreements, collective bargaining, and the Labor Board and its powers, primarily falls upon production and not upon commerce; and confirms the further resulting conclusion that production is a purely local activity. It follows that none of these essential antecedents of production constitutes a transaction in or forms any part of interstate commerce. Schechter Poultry Corp. v. United States, 295 U.S. 495, at page 542 et seq., 55 S.Ct. 837. Everything which moves in interstate commerce has had a local origin. Without local production somewhere, interstate commerce, as now carried on, would practically disappear. Nevertheless, the local character of mining, of manufacturing, and of crop growing is a fact, and remains a fact, whatever may be done with the products.

* * *

But section 1 (the Preamble) of the act now under review declares that all production and distribution of bituminous coal "bear upon and directly affect its interstate commerce"; and that regulation thereof is imperative for the protection of such commerce. The contention of the government is that the labor provisions of the act may be sustained in that view.

That the production of every commodity intended for interstate sale and transportation has some effect upon interstate commerce may be, if it has not already been, freely granted; and we are brought to the final and decisive inquiry, whether here that effect is direct, as the "Preamble" recites, or indirect. The distinction is not formal, but substantial in the highest degree, as we pointed out in the Schechter Case, supra. * * *

Whether the effect of a given activity or condition is direct or indirect is not always easy to determine. The word "direct" implies that the activity or condition invoked or blamed shall operate proximately—not mediately, remotely, or collaterally—to produce the effect. It connotes the absence of an efficient intervening agency or condition. And the extent of the effect bears no logical relation to its character. The distinction between a direct and an indirect effect turns, not upon the magnitude of either the cause or the effect, but entirely upon the manner in which the effect has been brought about. If the production by one man of a single ton of coal intended for interstate sale and shipment, and actually so sold and shipped, affects interstate commerce indirectly, the effect does not become direct by multiplying the tonnage, or increasing the number of men employed, or adding to the expense or complexities of the business, or by all combined. It is quite true that rules of law are sometimes qualified by considerations of degree, as the government argues. But the matter of degree has no bearing upon the question here, since that question is not—What is the extent of the local activity or condition, or the extent of the effect produced upon interstate commerce? but—What is the relation between the activity or condition and the effect?

Much stress is put upon the evils which come from the struggle between employers and employees over the matter of wages, working conditions, the right of collective bargaining, etc., and the resulting strikes, curtailment, and irregularity of production and effect on prices; and it is insisted that interstate commerce is greatly affected thereby. But, in addition to what has just been said, the conclusive answer is that the evils are all local evils over which the federal government has no legislative control. The relation of employer and employee is a local relation. At common law, it is one of the domestic relations. The wages are paid for the doing of local work. Working conditions are obviously local conditions. The employees are not engaged in or about commerce, but exclusively in producing a commodity. And the controversies and evils, which it is the object of the act to regulate and minimize, are local controversies and evils affecting local work undertaken to accomplish that local result. Such effect as they may have upon commerce, however extensive it may be, is secondary and indirect. An increase in the greatness of the effect adds to its importance. It does not alter its character.

The government's contentions in defense of the labor provisions are really disposed of adversely by our decision in the *Schechter* Case, supra. The only perceptible difference between that case and this is that in the *Schechter* Case the federal power was asserted with respect to commodities which had come to rest after their interstate transportation; while here, the case deals with commodities at rest before interstate commerce has begun. That difference is without significance. The federal regulatory power ceases when interstate commercial intercourse ends; and, correlatively, the

power does not attach until interstate commercial intercourse begins. There is no basis in law or reason for applying different rules to the two situations. * * * A reading of the entire opinion makes clear, what we now declare, that the want of power on the part of the federal government is the same whether the wages, hours of service, and working conditions, and the bargaining about them, are related to production before interstate commerce has begun, or to sale and distribution after it has ended.

*   *   *

[Reversed.]

Separate opinion of Mr. Chief Justice HUGHES.

I agree that the stockholders were entitled to bring their suits; that, in view of the question whether any part of the act could be sustained, the suits were not premature; that the so-called tax is not a real tax, but a penalty; that the constitutional power of the federal government to impose this penalty must rest upon the commerce clause, as the government concedes; that production—in this case mining—which precedes commerce is not itself commerce; and that the power to regulate commerce among the several states is not a power to regulate industry within the state.

*   *   *

Mr. Justice CARDOZO, dissenting. * * *

*   *   *

* * * I am satisfied that the act is within the power of the central government in so far as it provides for minimum and maximum prices upon sales of bituminous coal in the transactions of interstate commerce and in those of intrastate commerce where interstate commerce is directly or intimately affected. Whether it is valid also in other provisions that have been considered and condemned in the opinion of the Court, I do not find it necessary to determine at this time. Silence must not be taken as importing acquiescence. Much would have to be written if the subject, even as thus restricted were to be explored through all its implications, historical and economic as well as strictly legal. The fact that the prevailing opinion leaves the price provisions open for consideration in the future makes it appropriate to forego a fullness of elaboration that might otherwise be necessary. * * *

[T]he obvious and sufficient answer is, so far as the act is directed to interstate transactions, that sales made in such conditions constitute interstate commerce, and do not merely "affect" it. * * * To regulate the price for such transactions is to regulate commerce itself, and not alone its antecedent conditions or its ultimate consequences. The very act of sale is limited and governed. Prices in interstate transactions may not be regulated by the states. * * * They must therefore be subject to the power of the Nation unless they are to be withdrawn altogether from governmental supervision. * * * If such a vacuum were permitted, many a public evil incidental to interstate transactions would be left without a remedy. This does not mean, of course, that prices may be fixed for arbitrary reasons or in an arbitrary way. The commerce power of the Nation is subject to the requirement of due process like the police power of the states. * * * Heed must be giv-

en to similar considerations of social benefit or detriment in marking the division between reason and oppression. The evidence is overwhelming that Congress did not ignore those considerations in the adoption of this act. * * *

Regulation of prices being an exercise of the commerce power in respect of interstate transactions, the question remains whether it comes within that power as applied to intrastate sales where interstate prices are directly or intimately affected. Mining and agriculture and manufacture are not interstate commerce considered by themselves, yet their relation to that commerce may be such that for the protection of the one there is need to regulate the other. Sometimes it is said that the relation must be "direct" to bring that power into play. In many circumstances such a description will be sufficiently precise to meet the needs of the occasion. But a great principle of constitutional law is not susceptible of comprehensive statement in an adjective. The underlying thought is merely this, that "the law is not indifferent to considerations of degree." Schechter Poultry Corporation v. United States, supra, concurring opinion, 295 U.S. at page 554, 55 S.Ct. 853. It cannot be indifferent to them without an expansion of the commerce clause that would absorb or imperil the reserved powers of the states. At times, as in the case cited, the waves of causation will have radiated so far that their undulatory motion, if discernible at all, will be too faint or obscure, too broken by cross-currents, to be heeded by the law. In such circumstances the holding is not directed at prices or wages considered in the abstract, but at prices or wages in particular conditions. The relation may be tenuous or the opposite according to the facts. Always the setting of the facts is to be viewed if one would know the closeness of the tie. Perhaps, if one group of adjectives is to be chosen in preference to another, "intimate" and "remote" will be found to be as good as any. At all events, "direct" and "indirect," even if accepted as sufficient, must not be read too narrowly. * * * A survey of the cases shows that the words have been interpreted with suppleness of adaptation and flexibility of meaning. The power is as broad as the need that evokes it.

One of the most common and typical instances of a relation characterized as direct has been that between interstate and intrastate rates for carriers by rail where the local rates are so low as to divert business unreasonably from interstate competitors. In such circumstances Congress has the power to protect the business of its carriers against disintegrating encroachments. Houston, E. & W. T. R. Co. v. U. S. (Shreveport Case), 234 U.S. 342, 351, 352, 34 S.Ct. 833. * * * To be sure, the relation even then may be character-ized as indirect if one is nice or over-literal in the choice of words. Strictly speaking, the intrastate rates have a primary effect upon the intrastate traffic and not upon any other, though the repercussions of the competitive system may lead to secondary consequences affecting interstate traffic also. * * * What the cases really mean is that the causal relation in such circumstances is so close and intimate and obvious as to permit it to be called direct without subjecting the word to an unfair or excessive strain. There is a like immediacy here. Within rulings the most orthodox, the prices for intrastate sales of coal have so inescapable a relation to those for interstate sales that a system of regulation for transactions of the one class is necessary to give adequate protection to the system of regulation adopted for the other. * * *

* * *

I am authorized to state that Mr. Justice BRANDEIS and Mr. Justice STONE join in this opinion.

NATIONAL LABOR RELATIONS BOARD v. JONES & LAUGHLIN STEEL CORP.

Supreme Court of the United States, 1937
301 U.S. 1, 57 S.Ct. 615, 81 L.Ed. 893

In 1935, Congress passed the National Labor Relations Act, commonly known as the Wagner Act, to replace the collective bargaining guarantee provision of the NIRA which had been declared unconstitutional in the *Schechter* case (p. 469). The Wagner Act guaranteed the right of collective bargaining and authorized the National Labor Relations Board to prevent specified unfair labor practices that affected commerce. The rationale for the act was, in part, that the unfair practices led to strikes and disputes which, in turn, obstructed the free flow of commerce. An affiliate of the Amalgamated Association of Iron & Tin Workers of America initiated proceedings before the NLRB against the Jones & Laughlin Corporation, the fourth largest steel producer in the country. The affiliate charged that the corporation was discouraging employees from joining the union and that it had, in fact, fired ten men because of their union activities. After hearings the board sustained the charge and, among other things, ordered the corporation to offer to reinstate the ten men. The corporation refused to comply, maintaining that the Wagner Act regulated labor relations, not commerce and was consequently unconstitutional. The NLRB petitioned a U.S. circuit court to enforce the order, but that court denied the petition. The board appealed. On hearing by the Court, this case was consolidated with several others involving challenges to the act.

Mr. Chief Justice HUGHES delivered the opinion of the Court.

The facts as to the nature and scope of the business of the Jones & Laughlin Steel Corporation have been found by the Labor Board, and, so far as they are essential to the determination of this controversy, they are not in dispute. The Labor Board has found: The corporation is organized under the laws of Pennsylvania and has its principal office at Pittsburgh. It is engaged in the business of manufacturing iron and steel in plants situated in Pittsburgh and nearby Aliquippa, Pa. It manufactures and distributes a widely diversified line of steel and pig iron, being the fourth largest producer of steel in the United States. With its subsidiaries—nineteen in number—it is a completely integrated enterprise, owning and operating ore, coal and limestone properties, lake and river transportation facilities and terminal railroads located at its manufacturing plants. It owns or controls mines in Michigan and Minnesota. It operates four ore steamships on the Great Lakes, used in the transportation of ore to its factories. It owns coal mines in Pennsylvania. It operates towboats and steam barges used in carrying coal to its factories. It owns limestone properties in various places in Pennsylvania and West Virginia. It owns the Monongahela connecting railroad which connects the plants of the Pittsburgh works and forms an interconnection with the Pennsylvania, New York Central and Baltimore & Ohio Railroad systems.

It owns the Aliquippa & Southern Railroad Company, which connects the Aliquippa works with the Pittsburgh & Lake Erie, part of the New York Central system. Much of its product is shipped to its warehouses in Chicago, Detroit, Cincinnati and Memphis,—to the last two places by means of its own barges and transportation equipment. In Long Island City, New York, and in New Orleans it operates structural steel fabricating shops in connection with the warehousing of semifinished materials sent from its works. Through one of its wholly-owned subsidiaries it owns, leases, and operates stores, warehouses, and yards for the distribution of equipment and supplies for drilling and operating oil and gas mills and for pipe lines, refineries and pumping stations. It has sales offices in twenty cities in the United States and a wholly-owned subsidiary which is devoted exclusively to distributing its product in Canada. Approximately 75 per cent. of its product is shipped out of Pennsylvania.

Summarizing these operations, the Labor Board concluded that the works in Pittsburgh and Aliquippa "might be likened to the heart of a self-contained, highly integrated body. They draw in the raw materials from Michigan, Minnesota, West Virginia, Pennsylvania in part through arteries and by means controlled by the respondent; they transform the materials and then pump them out to all parts of the nation through the vast mechanism which the respondent has elaborated."

To carry on the activities of the entire steel industry, 33,000 men mine ore, 44,000 men mine coal, 4,000 men quarry limestone, 16,000 men manufacture coke, 343,000 men manufacture steel, and 83,000 men transport its product. Respondent has about 10,000 employees in its Aliquippa plant, which is located in a community of about 30,000 persons.

* * *

While respondent criticizes the evidence and the attitude of the Board, which is described as being hostile toward employers and particularly toward those who insisted upon their constitutional rights, respondent did not take advantage of its opportunity to present evidence to refute that which was offered to show discrimination and coercion. In this situation, the record presents no ground for setting aside the order of the Board so far as the facts pertaining to the circumstances and purpose of the discharge of the employees are concerned. Upon that point it is sufficient to say that the evidence supports the findings of the Board that respondent discharged these men "because of their union activity and for the purpose of discouraging membership in the union." We turn to the questions of law which respondent urges in contesting the validity and application of the act.

First. The Scope of the Act.— The act is challenged in its entirety as an attempt to regulate all industry, thus invading the reserved powers of the States over their local concerns. It is asserted that the references in the act to interstate and foreign commerce are colorable at best; that the act is not a true regulation of such commerce or of

matters which directly affect it, but on the contrary has the fundamental object of placing under the compulsory supervision of the federal government all industrial labor relations within the nation. * * *

* * *

We think it clear that the National Labor Relations Act may be construed so as to operate within the sphere of constitutional authority. The jurisdiction conferred upon the Board, and invoked in this instance, is found in section 10(a), 29 U.S.C.A. § 160(a), which provides:

"Sec. 10(a). The Board is empowered, as hereinafter provided, to prevent any person from engaging in any unfair labor practice (listed in section 8 [section 158]) affecting commerce."

The critical words of this provision, prescribing the limits of the Board's authority in dealing with the labor practices, are "affecting commerce." The act specifically defines the "commerce" to which it refers (section 2(6), 29 U.S.C.A. § 152(6):

"The term 'commerce' means trade, traffic, commerce, transportation, or communication among the several States, or between the District of Columbia or any Territory of the United States and any State or other Territory, or between any foreign country and any State, Territory, or the District of Columbia, or within the District of Columbia or any Territory, or between points in the same State but through any other State or any Territory or the District of Columbia or any foreign country."

There can be no question that the commerce thus contemplated by the act * * * is interstate and foreign commerce in the constitutional sense. The act also defines the term "affecting commerce" section 2(7), 29 U.S.C.A. § 152(7):

"The term 'affecting commerce' means in commerce, or burdening or obstructing commerce or the free flow of commerce, or having led or tending to lead to a labor dispute burdening or obstructing commerce or the free flow of commerce."

This definition is one of exclusion as well as inclusion. The grant of authority to the Board does not purport to extend to the relationship between all industrial employees and employers. Its terms do not impose collective bargaining upon all industry regardless of effects upon interstate or foreign commerce. It purports to reach only what may be deemed to burden or obstruct that commerce and, thus qualified, it must be construed as contemplating the exercise of control within constitutional bounds. It is a familiar principle that acts which directly burden or obstruct interstate or foreign commerce, or its free flow, are within the reach of the congressional power. Acts having that effect are not rendered immune because they grow out of labor disputes.   *   *   *   It is the effect upon commerce, not the source of the injury, which is the criterion.   *   *   *   Whether or not particular action does affect commerce in such a close and intimate fashion as to be subject to federal control, and hence to lie within the authority conferred upon the Board, is left by the statute to be determined as individual cases arise. We are thus to inquire whether in the instant case the constitutional boundary has been passed.

Second. The Unfair Labor Practices in Question.—   *   *   *

[I]n its present application, the statute goes no further than to safeguard the right of employees to self-organization and to select representatives of their own choosing for collective bargaining or other mutual protection without restraint or coercion by their employer.

That is a fundamental right. Employees have as clear a right to organize and select their representatives for lawful purposes as the respondent has to organize its business and select its own officers and agents. Discrimination and coercion to prevent the free exercise of the right of employees to self-organization and representation is a proper subject for condemnation by competent legislative authority. Long ago we stated the reason for labor organizations. We said that they were organized out of the necessities of the situation; that a single employee was helpless in dealing with an employer; that he was dependent ordinarily on his daily wage for the maintenance of himself and family; that, if the employer refused to pay him the wages that he thought fair, he was nevertheless unable to leave the employ and resist arbitrary and unfair treatment; that union was essential to give laborers opportunity to deal on an equality with their employer. American Steel Foundries v. Tri-City Central Trades Council, 257 U.S. 184, 209, 42 S.Ct. 72, 78. We reiterated these views when we had under consideration the Railway Labor Act of 1926, 44 Stat. 577. Fully recognizing the legality of collective action on the part of employees in order to safeguard their proper interests, we said that Congress was not required to ignore this right but could safeguard it. Congress could seek to make appropriate collective action of employees an instrument of peace rather than of strife. We said that such collective action would be a mockery if representation were made futile by interference with freedom of choice. Hence the prohibition by Congress of interference with the selection of representatives for the purpose of negotiation and conference between employers and employees, "instead of being an invasion of the constitutional right of either, was based on the recognition of the rights of both." * * *

Third. The Application of the Act to Employees Engaged in Production.—The Principle Involved.— Respondent says that, whatever may be said of employees engaged in interstate commerce, the industrial relations and activities in the manufacturing department of respondent's enterprise are not subject to federal regulation. The argument rests upon the proposition that manufacturing in itself is not commerce. Kidd v. Pearson, 128 U.S. 1, 20, 21, 9 S.Ct. 6; Coronado Coal Co. v. United Mine Workers, 268 U.S. 295, 310, 45 S.Ct. 551, 556; Schechter Corporation v. United States, supra, 295 U.S. 495, at page 547, 55 S.Ct. 837, 850; Carter v. Carter Coal Co., 298 U.S. 238, 304, 317, 327, 56 S.Ct. 855, 869, 875, 880.

The government distinguishes these cases. The various parts of respondent's enterprise are described as interdependent and as thus involving "a great movement of iron ore, coal and limestone along well-defined paths to the steel mills, thence through them, and thence in the form of steel products into the consuming centers of the country—a definite and well-understood course of business." It is urged that these activities constitute a "stream" or "flow" of commerce, of which the Aliquippa manufacturing plant is the focal point, and that industrial strife

at that point would cripple the entire movement. Reference is made to our decision sustaining the Packers and Stockyards Act. Stafford v. Wallace, 258 U.S. 495, 42 S.Ct. 397. * * *

Respondent contends that the instant case presents material distinctions. Respondent says that the Aliquippa plant is extensive in size and represents a large investment in buildings, machinery and equipment. The raw materials which are brought to the plant are delayed for long periods and, after being subjected to manufacturing processes "are changed substantially as to character, utility and value." The finished products which emerge "are to a large extent manufactured without reference to pre-existing orders and contracts and are entirely different from the raw materials which enter at the other end." Hence respondent argues that, "If importation and exportation in interstate commerce do not singly transfer purely local activities into the field of congressional regulation, it should follow that their combination would not alter the local situation." * * *

We do not find it necessary to determine whether these features of defendant's business dispose of the asserted analogy to the "stream of commerce" cases. The instances in which that metaphor has been used are but particular, and not exclusive, illustrations of the protective power which the government invokes in support of the present act. The congressional authority to protect interstate commerce from burdens and obstructions is not limited to transactions which can be deemed to be an essential part of a "flow" of interstate or foreign commerce. Burdens and obstructions may be due to injurious action springing from other sources. The fundamental principle is that the power to regulate commerce is the power to enact "all appropriate legislation" for its "protection or advancement" (The Daniel Ball, 10 Wall. 557, 564, 19 L.Ed. 999); to adopt measures "to promote its growth and insure its safety" (County of Mobile v. Kimball, 102 U.S. 691, 696, 697, 26 L.Ed. 238); "to foster, protect, control, and restrain" (Second Employers' Liability Cases, supra, 223 U.S. 1, at page 47, 32 S.Ct. 169, 174). That power is plenary and may be exerted to protect interstate commerce "no matter what the source of the dangers which threaten it." Second Employers' Liability Cases, 223 U.S. 1, at page 51, 32 S.Ct. 169, 176. Although activities may be intrastate in character when separately considered, if they have such a close and substantial relation to interstate commerce that their control is essential or appropriate to protect that commerce from burdens and obstructions, Congress cannot be denied the power to exercise that control. * * * Undoubtedly the scope of this power must be considered in the light of our dual system of government and may not be extended so as to embrace effects upon interstate commerce so indirect and remote that to embrace them, in view of our complex society, would effectually obliterate the distinction between what is national and what is local and create a completely centralized government. The question is necessarily one of degree. * * *

That intrastate activities, by reason of close and intimate relation to interstate commerce, may fall within federal control is demonstrated in the case of carriers who are engaged in both interstate and intrastate transportation. There federal control has been found essential to secure the freedom of interstate traffic from interference or unjust discrimination and to promote the efficiency of the interstate service. The *Shreveport* Case (Houston, E. & W. T. R. Co. v. United States), 234 U.S. 342, 351, 352, 34 S.Ct. 833. * * *

The close and intimate effect which brings the subject within the reach of federal power may be due to activities in relation to productive industry although the industry when separately viewed is local. This has been abundantly illustrated in the application of the Federal Anti-Trust Act. * * *

* * *

It is thus apparent that the fact that the employees here concerned were engaged in production is not determinative. The question remains as to the effect upon interstate commerce of the labor practice involved. In the *Schechter* Case, supra, we found that the effect there was so remote as to be beyond the federal power. To find "immediacy or directness" there was to find it "almost everywhere," a result inconsistent with the maintenance of our federal system. In the *Carter* Case, supra, the Court was of the opinion that the provisions of the statute relating to production were invalid upon several grounds,—that there was improper delegation of legislative power, and that the requirements not only went beyond any sustainable measure of protection of interstate commerce but were also inconsistent with due process. These cases are not controlling here.

Fourth. Effects of the Unfair Labor Practice in Respondent's Enterprise.—Giving full weight to respondent's contention with respect to a break in the complete continuity of the "stream of commerce" by reason of respondent's manufacturing operations, the fact remains that the stoppage of those operations by industrial strife would have a most serious effect upon interstate commerce. In view of respondent's far-flung activities, it is idle to say that the effect would be indirect or remote. It is obvious that it would be immediate and might be catastrophic. We are asked to shut our eyes to the plainest facts of our national life and to deal with the question of direct and indirect effects in an intellectual vacuum. Because there may be but indirect and remote effects upon interstate commerce in connection with a host of local enterprises throughout the country, it does not follow that other industrial activities do not have such a close and intimate relation to interstate commerce as to make the presence of industrial strife a matter of the most urgent national concern. When industries organize themselves on a national scale, making their relation to interstate commerce the dominant factor in their activities, how can it be maintained that their industrial labor relations constitute a forbidden field into which Congress may not enter when it is necessary to protect interstate commerce from the paralyzing consequences of industrial war? We have often said that interstate commerce itself is a practical conception. It is equally true that interferences with that commerce must be appraised by a judgment that does not ignore actual experience.

Experience has abundantly demonstrated that the recognition of the right of employees to self-organization and to have representatives of their own choosing for the purpose of collective bargaining is often an essential condition of industrial peace. Refusal to confer and negoti-

ate has been one of the most prolific causes of strife. This is such an outstanding fact in the history of labor disturbances that it is a proper subject of judicial notice and requires no citation of instances. * * *

These questions have frequently engaged the attention of Congress and have been the subject of many inquiries. The steel industry is one of the great basic industries of the United States, with ramifying activities affecting interstate commerce at every point. The Government aptly refers to the steel strike of 1919–1920 with its far-reaching consequences. The fact that there appears to have been no major disturbance in that industry in the more recent period did not dispose of the possibilities of future and like dangers to interstate commerce which Congress was entitled to foresee and to exercise its protective power to forestall. It is not necessary again to detail the facts as to respondent's enterprise. Instead of being beyond the pale, we think that it presents in a most striking way the close and intimate relation which a manufacturing industry may have to interstate commerce and we have no doubt that Congress had constitutional authority to safeguard the right of respondent's employees to self-organization and freedom in the choice of representatives for collective bargaining.

* * *

Our conclusion is that the order of the Board was within its competency and that the act is valid as here applied. The judgment of the Circuit Court of Appeals is reversed and the cause is remanded for further proceedings in conformity with this opinion. It is so ordered.

Reversed and remanded.

Mr. Justice McREYNOLDS delivered the following dissenting opinion.

Mr. Justice VAN DEVANTER, Mr. Justice SUTHERLAND, Mr. Justice BUTLER and I are unable to agree with the decisions just announced.

We conclude that these causes were rightly decided by the three Circuit Courts of Appeals and that their judgments should be affirmed. * * *

Considering the far-reaching import of these decisions, the departure from what we understand has been consistently ruled here, and the extraordinary power confirmed to a Board of three, the obligation to present our views becomes plain.

The Court as we think departs from well-established principles followed in Schechter Poultry Corporation v. United States, and Carter v. Carter Coal Co. * * *.

By its terms the Labor Act extends to employers—large and small—unless excluded by definition, and declares that, if one of these interferes with, restrains, or coerces any employee regarding his labor affiliations, etc., this shall be regarded as unfair labor practice. And a "labor organization" means any organization of any kind or any agency or employee representation committee or plan which exists for the purpose in whole or in part of dealing with employers concerning grievances, labor disputes, wages, rates of pay, hours of employment or conditions of work.

The three respondents happen to be manufacturing concerns—one large, two relatively small. The act is now applied to each upon grounds common to all. Obviously what is determined as to these concerns may gravely affect a multitude of employers who engage in a great variety of private enterprises—mercantile, manufacturing, publishing, stock-raising, mining, etc. It puts into the hands of a Board power of control over purely local industry beyond anything heretofore deemed permissible.

* * *

Any effect on interstate commerce by the discharge of employees shown here would be indirect and remote in the highest degree, as consideration of the facts will show. In [Jones & Laughlin] ten men out of ten thousand were discharged; in the other cases only a few. The immediate effect in the factor may be to create discontent among all those employed and a strike may follow, which, in turn, may result in reducing production, which ultimately may reduce the volume of goods moving in interstate commerce. By this chain of indirect and progressively remote events we finally reach the evil with which it is said the legislation under consideration undertakes to deal. A more remote and indirect interference with interstate commerce or a more definite invasion of the powers reserved to the states is difficult, if not impossible, to imagine.

The Constitution still recognizes the existence of states with indestructible powers; the Tenth Amendment was supposed to put them beyond controversy.

We are told that Congress may protect the "stream of commerce" and that one who buys raw material without the state, manufactures it therein, and ships the output to another state is in that stream. Therefore it is said he may be prevented from doing anything which may interfere with its flow.

This, too, goes beyond the constitutional limitations heretofore enforced. If a man raises cattle and regularly delivers them to a carrier for interstate shipment, may Congress prescribe the conditions under which he may employ or discharge helpers on the ranch? The products of a mine pass daily into interstate commerce; many things are brought to it from other states. Are the owners and the miners within the power of Congress in respect of the latter's tenure and discharge? May a mill owner be prohibited from closing his factory or discontinuing his business because so to do would stop the flow of products to and from his plant in interstate commerce? May employees in a factory be restrained from quitting work in a body because this will close the factory and thereby stop the flow of commerce? May arson of a factory be made a federal offense whenever this would interfere with such flow? If the business cannot continue with the existing wage scale, may Congress command a reduction? If the ruling of the Court just announced is adhered to, these questions suggest some of the problems certain to arise.

And if this theory of a continuous "stream of commerce" as now defined is correct, will it become the duty of the federal government hereafter to suppress every strike which by possibility it may cause a blockade in that stream? * * * Moreover, since Congress has intervened, are labor relations between most manufacturers and their employees removed from all control by the state? * * *

* * *

There is no ground on which reasonably to hold that refusal by a manufacturer, whose raw materials come from states other than that of his factory and whose products are regularly carried to other states, to bargain collectively with employees in his manufacturing plant, directly affects interstate commerce. In such business, there is not one but two distinct movements or streams in interstate transportation. The first brings in raw material and there ends. Then follows manufacture, a separate and local activity. Upon completion of this and not before, the second distinct movement or stream in interstate commerce begins and the products go to other states. Such is the common course for small as well as large industries. It is unreasonable and unprecedented to say the commerce clause confers upon Congress power to govern relations between employers and employees in these local activities. * * *

It is gravely stated that experience teaches that if an employer discourages membership in "any organization of any kind" "in which employees participate, and which exists for the purpose in whole or in part of dealing with employers concerning grievances, labor disputes, wages, rates of pay, hours of employment or conditions of work," discontent may follow and this in turn may lead to a strike, and as the outcome of the strike there may be a block in the stream of interstate commerce. Therefore Congress may inhibit the discharge! Whatever effect any cause of discontent may ultimately have upon commerce is far too indirect to justify congressional regulation. Almost anything—marriage, birth, death—may in some fashion affect commerce.

* * *

UNITED STATES v. DARBY

Supreme Court of the United States, 1941
312 U.S. 100, 61 S.Ct. 451, 85 L.Ed. 609

The Fair Labor Standards Act of 1938 prohibited the shipment in interstate commerce of goods produced by employees who were paid less than a minimum wage (set at twenty-five cents per hour for the first year following the passage of the act) or who had worked over forty-four hours a week without overtime pay. In addition, the act required employers covered by it to keep records of workers' wages and hours of employment. Fred Darby, who operated a lumber business in Georgia, was indicted for violating these provisions. A federal district court quashed the indictment. It held the act unconstitutional on the grounds that Congress could not regulate manufacturing because this activity was not part of interstate commerce. The United States appealed directly to the Supreme Court.

Mr. Justice STONE delivered the opinion of the Court.

The two principal questions raised by the record in this case are, first, whether Congress has constitutional power to prohibit the shipment in interstate commerce of lumber manufactured by employees whose wages are less than a prescribed minimum or whose weekly hours of labor at that wage are greater than a prescribed maximum, and, second, whether it has power to prohibit the employment of workmen in the production of goods "for interstate commerce" at other than prescribed wages and hours. * * *

* * *

The prohibition of shipment of the proscribed goods in interstate commerce. Section 15(a)(1) prohibits, and the indictment charges, the shipment in interstate commerce, of goods produced for interstate commerce by employees whose wages and hours of employment do not conform to the requirements of the Act. * * * [T]he only question arising under the commerce clause with respect to such shipments is whether Congress has the constitutional power to prohibit them.

While manufacture is not of itself interstate commerce the shipment of manufactured goods interstate is such commerce and the prohibition of such shipment by Congress is indubitably a regulation of the commerce. The power to regulate commerce is the power "to prescribe the rule by which commerce is to be governed." Gibbons v. Ogden, 9 Wheat. 1, 196, 6 L.Ed. 23. It extends not only to those regulations which aid, foster and protect the commerce, but embraces those which prohibit it. * * * It is conceded that the power of Congress to prohibit transportation in interstate commerce includes noxious articles, * * * stolen articles, * * * kidnapped persons, * * * and articles such as intoxicating liquor or convict made goods, traffic in which is forbidden or restricted by the laws of the state of destination. * * *

But it is said that the present prohibition falls within the scope of none of these categories; that while the prohibition is nominally a regulation of the commerce its motive or purpose is regulation of wages and hours of persons engaged in manufacture, the control of which has been reserved to the states and upon which Georgia and some of the states of destination have placed no restriction; that the effect of the present statute is not to exclude the prescribed articles from interstate commerce in aid of state regulation as in Kentucky Whip & Collar Co. v. Illinois Central R. Co., [299 U.S. 334, 57 S.Ct. 277] but instead, under the guise of a regulation of interstate commerce, it undertakes to regulate wages and hours within the state contrary to the policy of the state which has elected to leave them unregulated.

The power of Congress over interstate commerce "is complete in itself, may be exercised to its utmost extent, and acknowledges no limitations, other than are prescribed by the constitution." Gibbons v. Ogden, supra, 9 Wheat. 196, 6 L.Ed. 23. That power can neither be enlarged nor diminished by the exercise or non-exercise of state power. * * * Congress, following its own conception of public policy concerning the restrictions which may appropriately be imposed on interstate commerce, is free to exclude from the commerce articles whose use in the states for which they are destined it may conceive to be injurious to the public health, morals or welfare, even though the state has not sought to regulate their use. * * *

Such regulation is not a forbidden invasion of state power merely because either its motive or its consequence is to restrict the use of articles of commerce within the states of destination and is not prohibited unless by other Constitutional provisions. It is no objection to the assertion of the power to regulate interstate commerce that its exercise is attended by the same incidents which attend the exercise of the police power of the states. * * *

The motive and purpose of the present regulation is plainly to make effective the Congressional conception of public policy that interstate commerce should not be made the instrument of competition in the distribution of goods produced under substandard labor conditions, which competition is injurious to the commerce and to the states from and to which the commerce flows. The motive and purpose of a regulation of interstate commerce are matters for the legislative judgment upon the exercise of which the Constitution places no restriction and over which the courts are given no control. McCray v. United States, 195 U.S. 27, 24 S.Ct. 769. * * * "The judicial cannot prescribe to the legislative departments of the government limitations upon the exercise of its acknowledged power." Veazie Bank v. Fenno, 8 Wall. 533, 548, 19 L.Ed. 482. Whatever their motive and purpose, regulations of commerce which do not infringe some constitutional prohibition are within the plenary power conferred on Congress by the Commerce Clause. Subject only to that limitation, presently to be considered, we conclude that the prohibition of the shipment interstate of goods produced under the forbidden substandard labor conditions is within the constitutional authority of Congress.

In the more than a century which has elapsed since the decision of *Gibbons* v. *Ogden*, these principles of constitutional interpretation have been so long and repeatedly recognized by this Court as applicable to the Commerce Clause, that there would be little occasion for repeating them now were it not for the decision of this Court twenty-two years ago in Hammer v. Dagenhart, 247 U.S. 251, 38 S.Ct. 529. In that case it was held by a bare majority of the Court over the powerful and now classic dissent of Mr. Justice Holmes setting forth the fundamental issues involved, that Congress was without power to exclude the products of child labor from interstate commerce. The reasoning and conclusion of the Court's opinion there cannot be reconciled with the conclusion which we have reached, that the power of Congress under the Commerce Clause is plenary to exclude any article from interstate commerce subject only to the specific prohibitions of the Constitution.

Hammer v. *Dagenhart* has not been followed. The distinction on which the decision was rested that Congressional power to prohibit interstate commerce is limited to articles which in themselves have some harmful or deleterious property—a distinction which was novel when made and unsupported by any provision of the Constitution—has long since been abandoned. * * * The thesis of the opinion that the motive of the prohibition or its effect to control in some measure the use or production within the states of the article thus excluded from the commerce can operate to deprive the regulation of its constitutional authority has long since ceased to have force. * * *

The conclusion is inescapable that *Hammer* v. *Dagenhart*, was a departure from the principles which have prevailed in the interpretation of the commerce clause both before and since the decision and that such vitality, as a precedent, as it then had has long since been exhausted. It should be and now is overruled.

Validity of the wage and hour requirements. Section 15(a)(2) and §§ 6 and 7 require employers to conform to the wage and hour provi-sions with respect to all employees engaged in the production of goods for interstate commerce. As appellee's employees are not alleged to be "engaged in interstate commerce" the validity of the prohibition turns on the question whether the employment, under other than the prescribed labor standards, of employees engaged in the production of goods for interstate commerce is so related to the commerce and so affects it as to be within the reach of the power of Congress to regulate it.

To answer this question we must at the outset determine whether the particular acts charged in the counts which are laid under § 15(a)(2) as they were construed below, constitute "production for commerce" within the meaning of the statute. As the Government seeks to apply the statute in the indictment, and as the court below construed the phrase "produced for interstate commerce," it embraces at least the case where an employer engaged, as are appellees, in the manufacture and shipment of goods in filling orders of extrastate customers, manufactures his product with the intent or expectation that according to the normal course of his business all or some part of it will be selected for shipment to those customers.

Without attempting to define the precise limits of the phrase, we think the acts alleged in the indictment are within the sweep of the statute. The obvious purpose of the Act was not only to prevent the interstate transportation of the proscribed product, but to stop the initial step toward transportation, production with the purpose of so transporting it. Congress was not unaware that most manufacturing businesses shipping their product in interstate commerce make it in their shops without reference to its ultimate destination and then after manufacture select some of it for shipment interstate and some intrastate according to the daily demands of their business, and that it would be practically impossible, without disrupting manufacturing businesses, to restrict the prohibited kind of production to the particular pieces of lumber, cloth, furniture or the like which later move in interstate rather than intrastate commerce. * * *

The recognized need of drafting a workable statute and the well known circumstances in which it was to be applied are persuasive of the conclusion, which the legislative history supports, * * * that the "production for commerce" intended includes at least production of goods, which, at the time of production, the employer, according to the normal course of his business, intends or expects to move in interstate commerce although, through the exigencies of the business, all of the goods may not thereafter actually enter interstate commerce.

There remains the question whether such restriction on the production of goods for commerce is a permissible exercise of the commerce power. The power of Congress over interstate commerce is not confined to the regulation of commerce among the states. It extends to those activities intrastate which so affect interstate commerce or the exercise of the power of Congress over it as to make regulation of them appropriate means to the attainment of a legitimate end, the exercise of the granted power of Congress to regulate interstate commerce. * * *

While this Court has many times found state regulation of interstate commerce, when uniformity of its

regulation is of national concern, to be incompatible with the Commerce Clause even though Congress has not legislated on the subject, the Court has never implied such restraint on state control over matters intrastate not deemed to be regulations of interstate commerce or its instrumentalities even though they affect the commerce. * * * In the absence of Congressional legislation on the subject state laws which are not regulations of the commerce itself or its instrumentalities are not forbidden even though they affect interstate commerce. * * *

But it does not follow that Congress may not by appropriate legislation regulate intrastate activities where they have a substantial effect on interstate commerce. * * * A recent example is the National Labor Relations Act, 29 U.S.C.A. § 151 et seq., for the regulation of employer and employee relations in industries in which strikes, induced by unfair labor practices named in the Act, tend to disturb or obstruct interstate commerce. See National Labor Relations Board v. Jones & Laughlin Steel Corp., 301 U.S. 1, 38, 40, 57 S.Ct. 615, 625. * * * But long before the adoption of the National Labor Relations Act, this Court had many times held that the power of Congress to regulate interstate commerce extends to the regulation through legislative action of activities intrastate which have a substantial effect on the commerce or the exercise of the Congressional power over it.

In such legislation Congress has sometimes left it to the courts to determine whether the intrastate activities have the prohibited effect on the commerce, as in the Sherman Act, 15 U.S.C.A. §§ 1–7, 15 note. It has sometimes left it to an administrative board or agency to determine whether the activities sought to be regulated or prohibited have such effect, as in the case of the Interstate Commerce Act, 49 U.S.C.A. § 1 et seq., and the National Labor Relations Act or whether they come within the statutory definition of the prohibited Act as in the Federal Trade Commission Act, 15 U.S.C.A. § 41 et seq. And sometimes Congress itself has said that a particular activity affects the commerce as it did in the present act, the Safety Appliance Act, 15 U.S.C.A. § 1 et seq., and the Railway Labor Act, 45 U.S.C.A. § 181 et seq. In passing on the validity of legislation of the class last mentioned the only function of courts is to determine whether the particular activity regulated or prohibited is within the reach of the federal power. * * *

Congress, having by the present Act adopted the policy of excluding from interstate commerce all goods produced for the commerce which do not conform to the specified labor standards, it may choose the means reasonably adapted to the attainment of the permitted end, even though they involve control of intrastate activities. Such legislation has often been sustained with respect to powers, other than the commerce power granted to the national government, when the means chosen, although not themselves within the granted power, were nevertheless deemed appropriate aids to the accomplishment of some purpose within an admitted power of the national government. * * * A familiar like exercise of power is the regulation of intrastate transactions which are so commingled with or related to interstate commerce that all must be regulated if the interstate commerce is to be effectively controlled. Shreveport Case, 234 U.S. 342, 34 S.Ct. 833.

* * * Similarly Congress may require inspection and preventive treatment of all cattle in a disease infected area in order to prevent shipment in interstate commerce of some of the cattle without the treatment. Thornton v. United States, 271 U.S. 414, 46 S.Ct. 585. It may prohibit the removal, at destination, of labels required by the Pure Food & Drugs Act, 21 U.S.C.A. § 1 et seq., to be affixed to articles transported in interstate commerce. McDermott v. Wisconsin, 228 U.S. 115, 33 S.Ct. 431. * * *

We think also that § 15(a)(2), now under consideration, is sustainable independently of § 15(a)(1), which prohibits shipment or transportation of the proscribed goods. As we have said the evils aimed at by the Act are the spread of substandard labor conditions through the use of the facilities of interstate commerce for competition by the goods so produced with those produced under the prescribed or better labor conditions; and the consequent dislocation of the commerce itself caused by the impairment or destruction of local businesses by competition made effective through interstate commerce. The Act is thus directed at the suppression of a method or kind of competition in interstate commerce which it has in effect condemned as "unfair", as the Clayton Act, 38 Stat. 730, has condemned other "unfair methods of competition" made effective through interstate commerce. * * *

The Sherman Act and the National Labor Relations Act are familiar examples of the exertion of the commerce power to prohibit or control activities wholly intrastate because of their effect on interstate commerce. * * *

The means adopted by § 15(a)(2) for the protection of interstate commerce by the suppression of the production of the condemned goods for interstate commerce is so related to the commerce and so affects it as to be within the reach of the commerce power. * * * Congress, to attain its objective in the suppression of nationwide competition in interstate commerce by goods produced under substandard labor conditions, has made no distinction as to the volume or amount of shipments in the commerce or of production for commerce by any particular shipper or producer. It recognized that in present day industry, competition by a small part may affect the whole and that the total effect of the competition of many small producers may be great. * * * The legislation aimed at a whole embraces all its parts. * * *

So far as Carter v. Carter Coal Co., 298 U.S. 238, 56 S.Ct. 855, is inconsistent with this conclusion, its doctrine is limited in principle by the decisions under the Sherman Act and the National Labor Relations Act, which we have cited and which we follow. * * *

Our conclusion is unaffected by the Tenth Amendment which provides: "The powers not delegated to the United States by the Constitution, nor prohibited by it to the States, are reserved to the States respectively, or to the people." The amendment states but a truism that all is retained which has not been surrendered. There is nothing in the history of its adoption to suggest that it was more than declaratory of the relationship between the national and state governments as it had been established by the Constitution before the amendment or that its purpose was other than to allay fears that the new national government might seek to exercise powers not granted, and that the states might not be able to exercise fully their reserved powers. * * *

From the beginning and for many years the amendment has been construed as not depriving the national government of authority to resort to all means for the exercise of a granted power which are appropriate and plainly adapted to the permitted end. * * * Whatever doubts may have arisen of the soundness of that conclusion they have been put at rest by the decisions under the Sherman Act and the National Labor Relations Act which we have cited. * * *

Validity of the requirement of records of wages and hours. § 15(a)(5) and § 11(c). These requirements are incidental to those for the prescribed wages and hours, and hence validity of the former turns on validity of the latter. Since, as we have held, Congress may require production for interstate commerce to conform to those conditions, it may require the employer, as a means of enforcing the valid law, to keep a record showing whether he has in fact complied with it. The requirement for records even of the intrastate transaction is an appropriate means to the legitimate end. * * *

* * *

Reversed.

WICKARD v. FILBURN

Supreme Court of the United States, 1942
317 U.S. 111, 63 S.Ct. 82, 87 L.Ed. 122

The Agricultural Adjustment Act of 1938, as amended in 1941, directed the Secretary of Agriculture, Claude Wickard, to establish within certain limits a national acreage allotment for wheat. This figure was subdivided several times into quotas for individual farmers. Penalties were fixed for farmers who exceeded their quota. Filburn owned a small farm in Ohio that was allotted 11.1 acres for the 1941 wheat crop. Instead, he grew twenty-three acres of wheat, intending to keep the excess crop for his own consumption. From this additional acreage Filburn harvested 239 bushels to which the government affixed a penalty of forty-nine cents each, for a total penalty of $117.11. Filburn refused to pay the penalty or to deliver the excess wheat to the Department of Agriculture. Instead, he filed a complaint in federal district court to have the enforcement of the penalty enjoined and for a declaratory judgment that the act as applied to him was unconstitutional under both the Commerce Clause and the Fifth Amendment. The district court granted the injunction but on the basis of other issues surrounding the 1941 amendment, whereupon the government appealed.

Mr. Justice JACKSON delivered the opinion of the Court.

* * *

It is urged that under the Commerce Clause of the Constitution, Article I, § 8, clause 3, Congress does not possess the power it has in this instance sought to exercise. The question would merit little consideration since our decision in *United States* v. *Darby*, sustaining the federal power to regulate production of goods for commerce except for the fact that this Act extends federal regulation to production not intended in any part for commerce but wholly for consumption on the farm. The Act includes a definition of "market" and its derivatives so that as related to wheat in addition to its conventional meaning it also means to dispose of "by feeding (in any form) to poultry or livestock which, or the products of which, are sold, bartered, or exchanged, or to be so disposed of." Hence, marketing quotas not only embrace all that may be sold without penalty but also what may be consumed on the premises. Wheat pro-

duced on excess acreage is designated as "available for marketing" as so defined and the penalty is imposed thereon. Penalties do not depend upon whether any part of the wheat either within or without the quota is sold or intended to be sold. The sum of this is that the Federal Government fixes a quota including all that the farmer may harvest for sale or for his own farm needs, and declares that wheat produced on excess acreage may neither be disposed of nor used except upon payment of the penalty or except it is stored as required by the Act or delivered to the Secretary of Agriculture.

Appellee says that this is a regulation of production and consumption of wheat. Such activities are, he urges, beyond the reach of Congressional power under the Commerce Clause, since they are local in character, and their effects upon interstate commerce are at most "indirect." In answer the Government argues that the statute regulates neither production nor consumption, but only marketing; and, in the alternative, that if the Act does go beyond the regulation of marketing it is sustainable as a "necessary and proper" implementation of the power of Congress over interstate commerce.

The Government's concern lest the Act be held to be a regulation of production or consumption rather than of marketing is attributable to a few dicta and decisions of this Court which might be understood to lay it down that activities such as "production," "manufacturing," and "mining" are strictly "local" and, except in special circumstances which are not present here, cannot be regulated under the commerce power because their effects upon interstate commerce are, as matter of law, only "indirect." Even today, when this power has been held to have great latitude, there is no decision of this Court that such activities may be regulated where no part of the product is intended for interstate commerce or intermingled with the subjects thereof. We believe that a review of the course of decision under the Commerce Clause will make plain, however, that questions of the power of Congress are not to be decided by reference to any formula which would give controlling force to nomenclature such as "production" and "indirect" and foreclose consideration of the actual effects of the activity in question upon interstate commerce.

At the beginning Chief Justice Marshall described the federal commerce power with a breadth never yet exceeded. Gibbons v. Ogden, 9 Wheat. 1, 194, 195, 6 L.Ed. 23. He made emphatic the embracing and penetrating nature of this power by warning that effective restraints on its exercise must proceed from political rather than from judicial processes. 9 Wheat. at page 197, 6 L.Ed. 23.

For nearly a century, however, decisions of this Court under the Commerce Clause dealt rarely with questions of what Congress might do in the exercise of its granted power under the Clause and almost entirely with the permissibility of state activity which it was claimed discriminated against or burdened interstate commerce. During this period there was perhaps little occasion for the affirmative exercise of the commerce power, and the influence of the Clause on American life and law was a negative one, resulting almost wholly from its operation as a restraint upon the powers of the states. In discussion and decision the point of reference instead of being what was "necessary and proper" to the exercise by Congress of its granted power, was often some concept of sovereignty thought to be implicit in the status of statehood. Certain activities such as "production," "manufacturing," and "mining" were occasionally said to be within the province of state governments and beyond the power of Congress under the Commerce Clause.

It was not until 1887 with the enactment of the Interstate Commerce Act that the interstate commerce power began to exert positive influence in American law and life. This first important federal resort to the commerce power was followed in 1890 by the Sherman Anti-Trust Act and, thereafter, mainly after 1903, by many others. These statutes ushered in new phases of adjudication, which required the Court to approach the interpretation of the Commerce Clause in the light of an actual exercise by Congress of its power thereunder.

When it first dealt with this new legislation, the Court adhered to its earlier pronouncements, and allowed but little scope to the power of Congress. *United States* v. *E. C. Knight Co.* * * * These earlier pronouncements also played an important part in several of the five cases in which this Court later held that Acts of Congress under the Commerce Clause were in excess of its power [E.g., *Hammer* v. *Dagenhart, Schechter Corp.* v. *United States, Carter* v. *Carter Coal Co.*]

Even while important opinions in this line of restrictive authority were being written, however, other cases called forth broader interpretations of the Commerce Clause destined to supersede the earlier ones, and to bring about a return to the principles first enunciated by Chief Justice Marshall in *Gibbons* v. *Ogden,* supra.

Not long after the decision of *United States* v. *E. C. Knight Co.,* supra, Mr. Justice Holmes, in sustaining the exercise of national power over intrastate activity, stated for the Court that "commerce among the states is not a technical legal conception, but a practical one, drawn from the course of business." Swift & Co. v. United States, 196 U.S. 375, 398, 25 S.Ct. 276, 280. It was soon demonstrated that the effects of many kinds of intrastate activity upon interstate commerce were such as to make them a proper subject of federal regulation. In some cases sustaining the exercise of federal power over intrastate matters the term "direct" was used for the purpose of stating, rather than of reaching, a result; in others it was treated as synonymous with "substantial" or "material"; and in others it was not used at all. Of late its use has been abandoned in cases dealing with questions of federal power under the Commerce Clause.

*   *   *

The Court's recognition of the relevance of the economic effects in the application of the Commerce Clause exemplified by this statement has made the mechanical application of legal formulas no longer feasible. Once an economic measure of the reach of the power granted to Congress in the Commerce Clause is accepted, questions of federal power cannot be decided simply by finding the activity in question to be "production" nor can consideration of its economic effects be foreclosed by calling them "indirect." * * *

Whether the subject of the regulation in question was "production," "consumption," or "marketing" is, therefore, not material for purposes of deciding the question of federal power before us. That an activity is of local character may help in a doubtful case to determine whether Congress intended to reach it. The same consideration might help in determining whether in the absence of Congressional action it would be permissible for the state to exert its power on the subject matter, even though in so doing it to some degree affected interstate commerce. But even if appellee's activity be local and though it may not be regarded as commerce, it may still, whatever its nature, be reached by Congress if it exerts a substantial economic effect on interstate commerce and this irrespective of whether such effect is what might at some earlier time have been defined as "direct" or "indirect."

The parties have stipulated a summary of the economics of the wheat industry. Commerce among the states in wheat is large and important. Although wheat is raised in every state but one, production in most states is not equal to consumption. * * *

The wheat industry has been a problem industry for some years. Largely as a result of increased foreign production and import restrictions, annual exports of wheat and flour from the United States during the ten-year period ending in 1940 averaged less than 10 per cent of total production, while during the 1920's they averaged more than 25 per cent. The decline in the export trade has left a large surplus in production which in connection with an abnormally large supply of wheat and other grains in recent years caused congestion in a number of markets; tied up railroad cars; and caused elevators in some instances to turn away grains, and railroads to institute embargoes to prevent further congestion.

* * *

In the absence of regulation the price of wheat in the United States would be much affected by world conditions. During 1941 producers who cooperated with the Agricultural Adjustment program received an average price on the farm of about $1.16 a bushel as compared with the world market price of 40 cents a bushel.

Differences in farming conditions, however, make these benefits mean different things to different wheat growers. There are several large areas of specialization in wheat, and the concentration on this crop reaches 27 per cent of the crop land, and the average harvest runs as high as 155 acres. Except for some use of wheat as stock feed and for seed, the practice is to sell the crop for cash. Wheat from such areas constitutes the bulk of the interstate commerce therein.

On the other hand, in some New England states less than one per cent of the crop land is devoted to wheat, and the average harvest is less than five acres per farm. In 1940 the average percentage of the total wheat production that was sold in each state as measured by value ranged from 29 per cent thereof in Wisconsin to 90 per cent in Washington. Except in regions of large-scale production, wheat is usually grown in rotation with other crops; for a nurse crop for grass seeding; and as a cover crop to prevent soil erosion and leaching. Some is sold, some kept for seed, and a percentage of the total production much larger than in areas of specialization is consumed on the farm and grown for such purpose. Such farmers, while growing some wheat, may even find the balance of their interest on the consumer's side.

The effect of consumption of homegrown wheat on interstate commerce is due to the fact that it constitutes the most variable factor in the disappearance of the wheat crop. Consumption on the farm where grown appears to vary in an amount greater than 20 per cent of average production. The total amount of wheat consumed as food varies but relatively little, and use as seed is relatively constant.

The maintenance by government regulation of a price for wheat undoubtedly can be accomplished as effectively by sustaining or increasing the demand as by limiting the supply. The effect of the statute before us is to restrict the amount which may be produced for market and the extent as well to which one may forestall resort to the market by producing to meet his own needs. That appellee's own contribution to the demand for wheat may be trivial by itself is not enough to remove him from the scope of federal regulation where, as here, his contribution, taken together with that of many others similarly situated, is far from trivial. * * *

It is well established by decisions of this Court that the power to regulate commerce includes the power to regulate the prices at which commodities in that commerce are dealt in and practices affecting such prices. One of the primary purposes of the Act in question was to increase the market price of wheat and to that end to limit the volume thereof that could affect the market. It can hardly be denied that a factor of such volume and variability as home-consumed wheat would have a substantial influence on price and market conditions. This may arise because being in marketable condition such wheat overhangs the market and if induced by rising prices tends to flow into the market and check price increases. But if we assume that it is never marketed, it supplies a need of the man who grew it which would otherwise be reflected by purchases in the open market. Home-grown wheat in this sense competes with wheat in commerce. The stimulation of commerce is a use of the regulatory function quite as definitely as prohibitions or restrictions thereon. This record leaves us in no doubt that Congress may properly have considered that wheat consumed on the farm where grown if wholly outside the scheme of regulation would have a substantial effect in defeating and obstructing its purpose to stimulate trade therein at increased prices.

* * *

The statute is also challenged as a deprivation of property without due process of law contrary to the Fifth Amendment, both because of its regulatory effect on the appellee and because of its alleged retroactive effect. * * *

Appellee's claim that the Act works a deprivation of due process even apart from its allegedly retroactive effect is not persuasive. Control of total supply, upon which the whole statutory plan is based, depends upon control of individual supply. Appellee's claim is not that his quota represented less than a fair share of the national quota, but that the Fifth Amendment requires that he be free from penalty for planting wheat and disposing of his crop as he sees fit.

We do not agree. In its effort to control total supply, the Government gave the farmer a choice which was, of course, designed to encourage cooperation and discourage non-cooperation. The farmer who planted within his allotment was in effect guaranteed a minimum return much above what his wheat would have brought if sold on a world market basis. Exemption from the applicability of quotas was made in favor of small producers. The farmer who produced in excess of his quota might escape penalty by delivering his wheat to the Secretary or by storing it with the privilege of sale without penalty in a later year to fill out his quota, or irrespective of quotas if they are no longer in effect, and he could obtain a loan of 60 per cent of the rate for cooperators, or about 59 cents a bushel, on so much of his wheat as would be subject to penalty if marketed. Finally, he might make other disposition of his wheat, subject to the penalty. It is agreed that as the result of the wheat programs he is able to market his wheat at a price "far above any world price based on the natural reaction of supply and demand." We can hardly find a denial of due process in these circumstances, particularly since it is even doubtful that appellee's burdens under the program outweigh his benefits. It is hardly lack of due process for the Government to regulate that which it subsidizes.

* * *

Reversed.

NATIONAL LEAGUE OF CITIES v. USERY

Supreme Court of the United States, 1976
426 U.S. 833, 96 S.Ct. 2465, 49 L.Ed.2d 245

See p. 384.

c. THE NAVIGATION POWER

UNITED STATES v. CHANDLER–DUNBAR WATER POWER CO.

Supreme Court of the United States, 1913
229 U.S. 53, 33 S.Ct. 667, 57 L.Ed. 1063

The St. Marys River is the only outlet for the waters of Lake Superior. In the river are falls and rapids which total some 3,000 feet in length and span a distance of 4,000 feet bank to bank. These rapids and falls are both a serious obstacle to navigation and a great boon as the source of waterpower. Pursuant to an act of Congress passed in March 1909, the Secretary of War began acquisition and condemnation proceedings against private waterpower companies which had been generating power under a license granted previously by the Secretary. The 1909 legislation revoked these permits and called upon the companies to remove constructions they had put in the river to harness the waterpower. This legislation was part of a plan by Congress to increase navigability around the rapids and falls and to better enable the federal government to control the water level of the Great Lakes, both serious concerns in view of the rapidly increasing level of commerce in the area.

In its judgment at the conclusion of the condemnation proceedings, a U.S. district court awarded $652,332 to the Chandler-Dunbar Company as compensation for property taken. Of this award, $550,000 was given against the loss of riparian rights to the waterpower generated in the falls and rapids. This figure was arrived at by assessing the value of the waterpower in excess of that necessary for navigational purposes. From this award both the government and the power company appealed. The government argued that its navigation powers preempted the exercise of any such riparian rights, that the power company consequently could not claim compensation for the loss of such rights, and that, therefore, Chandler-Dunbar's award should be reduced accordingly. The power company, on the contrary, asserted that the compensation it had been given for such a justifiable loss was grossly inequitable and that compensation for the loss of the value of such waterpower should be fixed at $3,450,000.

———

Mr. Justice LURTON * * * delivered the opinion of the court:

From the foregoing it will be seen that the controlling questions are, first, whether the Chandler-Dunbar Company has any private property in the water power capacity of the rapids and falls of the St. Marys river which has been "taken," and for which compensation must be made under the 5th Amendment to the Constitution; and, second, if so, what is the extent of its water power right and how shall the compensation be measured?

That compensation must be made for the upland taken is not disputable. The measure of compensation may in a degree turn upon the relation of that species of property to the alleged water power rights claimed by the Chandler-Dunbar Company. We therefore pass for the present the errors assigned which concern the awards made for such upland.

The technical title to the beds of the navigable rivers of the United States is either in the states in which the rivers are situated, or in the owners of the land bordering upon such rivers. Whether in one or the other is a question of local law. * * * Upon the admission of the state of Michigan into the Union the bed of the St. Marys river passed to the state, and under the law of that state the conveyance of a tract of land upon a navigable river carries the title to the middle thread. * * *

The technical title of the Chandler-Dunbar Company, therefore, includes the bed of the river opposite its upland on the bank to the middle thread of the stream, being the boundary line at that point between the United States and the Dominion of Canada. Over this bed flows about two thirds of the volume of water constituting the falls and rapids of the St. Marys river. By reason of that fact, and the ownership of the shore, the company's claim is, that it is the owner of the river and of the inherent power in the falls and rapids, subject only to the public right of navigation. While not denying that this right of navigation is the dominating right, yet the

claim is that the United States, in the exercise of the power to regulate commerce, may not exclude the rights of riparian owners to construct in the river and upon their own submerged lands such appliances as are necessary to control and use the current for commercial purposes, provided only that such structures do not impede or hinder navigation, and that the flow of the stream is not so diminished as to leave less than every possible requirement of navigation, present and future. This claim of a proprietary right in the bed of the river and in the flow of the stream over that bed, to the extent that such flow is in excess of the wants of navigation, constitutes the ground upon which the company asserts that a necessary effect of the act of March 3, 1909, and of the judgment of condemnation in the court below, is a taking from it of a property right or interest of great value, for which, under the 5th Amendment, compensation must be made.

This is the view which was entertained by Circuit Judge Dennison in the court below, and is supported by most careful findings of fact and law and an elaborate and able opinion. The question is therefore one which, from every standpoint, deserves careful consideration.

This title of the owner of fast land upon the shore of a navigable river to the bed of the river is, at best, a qualified one. It is a title which inheres in the ownership of the shore; and, unless reserved or excluded by implication, passed with it as a shadow follows a substance, although capable of distinct ownership. It is subordinate to the public right of navigation, and however helpful in protecting the owner against the acts of third parties, is of no avail against the exercise of the great and absolute power of Congress over the improvement of navigable rivers. That power of use and control comes from the power to regulate commerce between the states and with foreign nations. It includes navigation and subjects every navigable river to the control of Congress. All means having some positive relation to the end in view which are not forbidden by some other provision of the Constitution are admissible. If, in the judgment of Congress, the use of the bottom of the river is proper for the purpose of placing therein structures in aid of navigation, it is not thereby taking private property for a public use, for the owner's title was in its very nature subject to that use in the interest of public navigation. If its judgment be that structures placed in the river and upon such submerged land are an obstruction or hindrance to the proper use of the river for purposes of navigation, it may require their removal and forbid the use of the bed of the river by the owner in any way which, in its judgment, is injurious to the dominant right of navigation. So, also, it may permit the construction and maintenance of tunnels under or bridges over the river, and may require the removal of every such structure placed there with or without its license, the element of contract out of the way, which it shall require to be removed or altered as an obstruction to navigation. In Gilman v. Philadelphia, 3 Wall. 713, 724, 18 L.Ed. 96, 99, this court said:

"Commerce includes navigation. The power to regulate commerce comprehends the control for that purpose, and to the extent necessary, of all the navigable waters of the United States which are accessible from a state other than those in which they lie. For this purpose they are the public property of the nation, and subject to all the requisite legislation by Congress. This necessarily includes the power to keep them open and free from any obstructions to their navigation, interposed by the states or otherwise; to remove such obstructions when they exist; and to provide, by such sanctions as they may deem proper, against the occurrence of the evil and for the punishment of offenders. For these purposes, Congress possesses all the powers which existed in the states before the adoption of the national Constitution, and which have always existed in the Parliament in England.

"It is for Congress to determine when its full power shall be brought into activity, and as to the regulations and sanctions which shall be provided."

* * *

So unfettered is this control of Congress over navigable streams of the country that its judgment as to whether a construction in or over such a river is or is not an obstacle and a hindrance to navigation is conclusive. Such judgment and determination is the exercise of legislative power in respect of a subject wholly within its control.

* * *

The conclusion to be drawn is, that the question of whether the proper regulation of navigation of this river at the place in question required that no construction of any kind should be placed or continued in the river by riparian owners, and whether the whole flow of the stream should be conserved for the use and safety of navigation, are questions legislative in character; and when Congress determined, as it did by the act of March 3, 1909, that the whole river between the American bank and the international line, as well as all of the upland north of the present ship canal, throughout its entire length, was "necessary for the purposes of navigation of said waters and the waters connected therewith," that determination was conclusive.

So much of the zone covered by this declaration as consisted of fast land upon the banks of the river, or in islands which were private property, is, of course, to be paid for. But the flow of the stream was in no sense private property, and there is no room for a judicial review of the judgment of Congress that the flow of the river is not in excess of any possible need of navigation, or for a determination that, if in excess, the riparian owners had any private property right in such excess which must be paid for if they have been excluded from the use of the same.

That Congress did not act arbitrarily in determining that "for the purposes of navigation of said waters and the waters connected therewith," the whole flow of the stream should be devoted exclusively to that end, is most evident when we consider the character of this stream and its relation to the whole problem of lake navigation. The river St. Marys is the only outlet for the waters of Lake Superior. The stretch of water called the falls and rapids of the river is about 3,000 feet long, and from bank to bank has a width of about 4,000 feet. About two-thirds of the volume of the stream flows over the submerged lands of the Chandler-Dunbar Company, the rest over like lands on the Canadian side of the boundary. The fall in the rapids is about 18 feet. This turbulent water, substantially unnavigable without the artificial aid of canals around the stream, constitutes both a tremendous obstacle to navigation and an equally great source of water power, if devoted to commercial purposes. That the wider needs of navigation might not be hindered by the presence in the river of the construction works necessary to use it for the development of water power for commercial uses under private ownership was the judgment and determination of Congress. There was also present in the mind of Congress the necessity of controlling the outflow from Lake Superior, which averages some 64,000 cubic feet per second. That outflow has great influence both upon the water level of Lake Superior and also upon the level of the great system of lakes below, which receive that outflow. A difference of a foot in the level of Lake Superior may influence adversely access to the harbors on that lake. The same fall in the water level of the lower lakes will perceptibly affect access to their ports. This was a matter of international consideration, for Canada, as well as the United States, was interested in the control and regulation of the lake water levels. And so we find in the act of 1909 a request that the President of the United States will open negotiations with the government of Great Britain, "for the purpose of effectually providing, by suitable treaty * * * for maintaining ample water levels for the uses of navigation in the Great Lakes and the waters connected therewith, by the construction of such controlling and remedial works in the connecting rivers and channels of such lakes as may be agreed upon by the said governments under the provisions of said treaty."

The falls and rapids are at the exit of the river from the lake. Mil-

lions of public money have already been expended in the construction of canals and locks, by this government upon the American side, and by the Canadian government upon its own side of the rapids, as a means by which water craft may pass around the falls and rapids in the river. The commerce using these facilities has increased by leaps and bounds.
* * *

The upland belonging to the Chandler-Dunbar Company consists of a strip of land some 2,500 feet long and from 50 to 150 feet wide. It borders upon the river on one side, and on the government canal strip on the other. Under permits from the Secretary of War, revocable at will, it placed in the rapids, in connection with its upland facilities, the necessary dams, dykes, and forebays for the purpose of controlling the current and using its power for commercial purposes, and has been for some years engaged in using and selling water power. What it did was by the revocable permission of the Secretary of War, and every such permit or license was revoked by the act of 1909. (See act of September 19, 1890, 26 Stat. at L. pp. 426, 454, chap. 907, forbidding the construction of any dam, pier, or breakwater in any navigable river without permission of the Secretary of War, or the creation of any obstruction, not affirmatively authorized by law, "to the navigable capacity of such rivers." See also the later act of March 3, 1899, 30 Stat. at L. pp. 1151, 1155, chap. 425, U.S.Comp.Stat.1901, p. 3540, and United States v. Rio Grande Dam & Irrig. Co., 174 U.S. 690, 19 Sup.Ct.Rep. 770, construing and applying the act of 1890.) That it did not thereby acquire any right to maintain these constructions in the river longer than the government

should continue the license needs no argument. They were placed in the river under a permit which the company knew was likely to be revoked at any time. There is nothing in the facts which savors of estoppel in law or equity. The suggestion by counsel that the act of 1909 contemplates that the owner should be compensated not only for its tangible property, movable or real, but for its loss and damage by the discontinuance of the company's license and its exclusion from the right to use the water power inherent in the falls and rapids, for commercial purposes, is without merit. The provisions of the act in respect of compensation apply only to compensation for such "property described" as shall be held private property taken for public uses. Unless, therefore, the water power rights asserted by the Chandler-Dunbar Company are determined to be private property, the court below was not authorized to award compensation for such rights.

It is a little difficult to understand the basis for the claim that in appropriating the upland bordering upon this stretch of water, the government not only takes the land, but also the great water power which potentially exists in the river. The broad claim that the water power of the stream is appurtenant to the bank owned by it, and not dependent upon ownership of the soil over which the river flows, has been advanced. But whether this private right to the use of the flow of the water and flow of the stream be based upon the qualified title which the company had to the bed of the river over which it flows, or the ownership of land bordering upon the river, is of no prime importance. In neither event can there be said to arise any ownership of the river.

Ownership of a private stream wholly upon the lands of an individual is conceivable; but that the running water in a great navigable stream is [capable] of private ownership is inconceivable.

Whatever substantial private property rights exist in the flow of the stream must come from some right which that company has to construct and maintain such works in the river, such as dams, walls, dykes, etc., essential to the utilization of the power of the stream for commercial purposes. We may put out of view altogether the class of cases which deal with the right of riparian owners upon non-navigable stream to the use and enjoyment of the stream and its waters. The use of the fall of such a stream for the production of power may be a reasonable use consistent with the rights of those above and below. The necessary dam to use the power might completely obstruct the stream, but if the effect was not injurious to the property of those above, or to the equal rights of those below, none could complain, since no public interest would be affected. We may also lay out of consideration the cases cited which deal with the rights of riparian owners upon navigable or non-navigable streams as between each other. Nor need we consider cases cited which deal with the rights of riparian owners under state laws and private or public charters conferring rights. That riparian owners upon public navigable rivers have in addition to the rights common to the public, certain rights to the use and enjoyment of the stream, which are incident to such ownership of the bank, must be conceded. These additional rights are not dependent upon title to the soil over which the river flows, but are incident to ownership upon the bank. Among these rights of use and enjoyment is the right, as against other riparian owners, to have the stream come to them substantially in its natural state, both in quantity and quality. They have also the right of access to deep water, and when not forbidden by public law may construct for this purpose, wharves, docks, and piers in the shallow water of the shore. But every such structure in the water of a navigable river is subordinate to the right of navigation, and subject to the obligation to suffer the consequences of the improvement of navigation, and must be removed if Congress, in the assertion of its power over navigation, shall determine that their continuance is detrimental to the public interest in the navigation of the river.   *   *   *

To utilize the rapids and fall of the river which flows by the upland of the Chandler-Dunbar Company, it has been and will be necessary to construct and maintain in the river the structures necessary to control and direct the flow so that it may be used for commercial purposes. *   *   *

Upon what principle can it be said that, in requiring the removal of the development works which were in the river upon sufferance, Congress has taken private property for public use without compensation? In deciding that a necessity existed for absolute control of the river at the rapids, Congress has, of course, excluded, until it changes the law, every such construction as a hindrance to its plans and purposes for the betterment of navigation. The qualified title to the bed of the river affords no ground for any claim of a right to construct and maintain therein any structure which Congress has, by the act of 1909, decided in effect to be an obstruction to navigation, and a hindrance to its plans for improvement. That title is absolutely subordinate to the right of navigation, and no right of private property would have been invaded if such submerged lands were occupied by structures in aid of navigation, or kept free from such obstructions in the interest of navigation.   *   *   *   We need not consider whether the entire flow of the river is necessary for the purposes of navigation, or whether there is a surplus which is to be paid for, if the Chandler-Dunbar Company is to be excluded from the commercial use of that surplus.   The answer is found in the fact that Congress has determined that the stream from the upland, taken to the international boundary, is necessary for the purposes of navigation.   That determination operates to exclude from the river forever the structures necessary for the commercial use of the water power.   That it does not deprive the Chandler-Dunbar Company of private property rights follows from the considerations before stated.

*   *   *

The conclusion, therefore, is that the court below erred in awarding $550,000, or any other sum, for the value of what is called "raw water," that is, the present money value of the rapids and falls to the Chandler-Dunbar Company as riparian owners of the shore and appurtenant submerged land.

Coming now to the award for the upland taken:

[The Court then reviewed compensation, in excess of the fair market value of the company's land holdings, which the district court had awarded because of the strategic position of the land and the profitable use to which various pieces of the upland area could be put by the government, given the waterpower.   The fair market value of the land was put at $42,332.   The additional value of the land due to its location and its utility with respect to the waterpower, some $60,000, was struck from the judgment.]

*   *   *

Having decided that the Chandler-Dunbar Company, as riparian owners, had no such vested property right in the water power inherent in the falls and rapids of the river, and no right to place in the river the works essential to any practical use of the flow of the river, the government cannot be justly required to pay for an element of value which did not inhere in these parcels as upland.   The government had dominion over the water power of the rapids and falls, and cannot be required to pay any hypothetical additional value to a riparian owner who had no right to appropriate the current to his own commercial use.   These additional values represent, therefore, no actual loss, and there would be no justice in paying for a loss suffered by no one in fact.   "The requirement of the 5th Amendment is satisfied when the owner is paid for what is taken from him.   The question is what has the owner lost, and not what has the taker gained."   Boston Chamber of Commerce v. Boston, 217 U.S. 189, 194, 195, 30 Sup.Ct.Rep. 459.

Neither can consideration be given to probable advancement in the value of such riparian property by reason of the works to be constructed in the river by the government, or the use to which the flow of the stream might be directed by the government.   The value should be fixed as of the date of the proceedings, and with reference to the loss the owner sustains, considering the property in its condition and situation at the time it is taken, and not as enhanced by the purpose for which it was taken. * * *

* * *

The judgment of the court below must be reversed and the cases remanded with direction to enter a judgment in accordance with this opinion.

In United States v. Rands, 389 U.S. 121, 88 S.Ct. 265 (1967), the Supreme Court speaking through Justice White held that the United States was not constitutionally required to compensate owners of condemned land for its value as a port site. Rands and his wife owned land along the Columbia River and had leased the land to the State of Oregon with the option to purchase it, contemplating that the land would be used "as an industrial park, part of which would function as a port." Before Oregon had exercised the option, however, the land was taken by the federal government as part of a master plan by it for the development of the Columbia River. The land was then conveyed under federal law to Oregon "at a price considerably less than the option price at which respondents had hoped to sell." The district court judge assessed the land at "its value for sand, gravel, and agricultural purposes"—a figure which "was about one-fifth the claimed value of the land as a port." Its value as a port site, he ruled, could not be considered. The Ninth Circuit U.S. Court of Appeals reversed and was in turn overruled by the Supreme Court which reinstated the district court's judgment. Said the Court, "[S]tate law may give the riparian owner valuable rights of access to navigable waters good against other riparian owners or against the State itself. But * * * these rights and values are not assertable against the superior rights of the United States, are not property within the meaning of the Fifth Amendment, and need not be paid for when appropriated by the United States * * *." The Court continued, "[S]pecial values arising from access to a navigable stream are allocable to the public, and not to private interest. Otherwise the private owner would receive a windfall to which he is not entitled."

Kaiser Aetna developed the Hawaii Kai Marina on the island of Oahu by dredging and filling Kuapa Pond, a shallow lagoon separated from a navigable bay and the Pacific Ocean by a barrier beach. Besides creating a marina-style subdivision with its modifications to the pond, the developer ultimately connected the marina to the nearby bay by cutting a channel through the barrier beach, thus allowing boat traffic in the marina ready access to the bay. The developer controlled access to and use of the pond which under Hawaii law was private property and charged fees for maintaining the pond. Although at the onset of improvements to the pond the Army Corps of Engineers advised the developer that no permits were necessary for operations in the pond, the federal government sometime later filed suit to resolve a dispute about whether the developer/owner, Kaiser Aetna, was required to obtain authorization for future improvements in the marina and whether the developer could deny public access to the pond since, the government argued, these improvements had made the marina a "navigable water of the United States." A federal district court agreed that the pond was a navigable waterway subject to the Corps' regulation but otherwise held that the federal government lacked authority to open the pond to the public without payment of compensation to the owner. A federal appellate court subsequently affirmed the district court's finding as to the Corps' regulatory power but reversed the finding denying public access and held that when the owner/developer converted the pond into a marina and then connected it to what was admittedly a navigable bay, the marina fell under the "navigational servitude" of the federal government which gave the public a right of access to what was once the owner/developer's private pond.

Focusing on the question of a right of public access to the pond, the Supreme Court reversed the decision of the appeals court in Kaiser Aetna v. United States, 444 U.S. 164, 100 S.Ct. 383 (1979). The Court acknowledged at the outset that, "[w]ith respect to the Hawaii Kai Marina, * * * there is no doubt Congress may prescribe the rules of the road, define the conditions under which running lights shall be displayed, require the removal of obstructions to navigation, and exercise its authority for such other reason as may seem to it in the interest of furthering navigation or commerce." Indeed, "[i]n light of its expansive authority under the Commerce Clause, there is no question but that Congress could assure the public a free right of access to the Hawaii Kai Marina if it so chose." But, observed the Court, "Whether a statute or regulation that went so far amounts to a 'taking' [of property], * * * is an entirely separate question." Speaking to the separability of that issue, Justice Rehnquist, for the Court, contrasted various riparian access cases (e.g., United States v. Chandler-Dunbar Water Power Co., 229 U.S. 53, 33 S.Ct. 667 (1913); United States v. Rands, 389 U.S. 121, 88 S.Ct. 265 (1967)):

> For over a century, a long line of cases decided by this Court involving government condemnation of "fast lands" delineated the elements of compensable damages that the government was required to pay because the lands were riparian to navigable streams. The Court was often deeply divided, and the results frequently turned on what could fairly be described as quite narrow distinctions. But this is not a case in which the government recognizes any obligation whatever to condemn "fast lands" and pay just compensation under the Eminent Domain Clause of the Fifth Amendment to the Bill of Rights of the United States Constitution. It is instead a case in which the owner of what was once a private pond, separated from concededly navigable water by a barrier beach and used for aquatic agriculture, has invested substantial amounts of money in making improvements. The government contends that as a result of one of these improvements, the pond's connection to the navigable water in a manner approved by the Corps of Engineers, the owner has somehow lost one of the most essential sticks in the bundle of rights that are commonly characterized as property—the right to exclude others.

>   *   *   *

> There is no denying that the strict logic of the more recent cases limiting the Government's liability to pay damages for riparian access, if carried to its ultimate conclusion, might completely swallow up any private claim for "just compensation" under the Fifth Amendment even in a situation as different from the riparian condemnation cases as this one. But, as Mr. Justice Holmes observed in a very different context, the life of the law has not been logic, it has been experience. The navigational servitude, which exists by virtue of the Commerce Clause in navigable streams, gives rise to an authority in the Government to assure that such streams retain their capacity to serve as continuous highways for the purpose of navigation in inter-

state commerce. Thus, when the Government acquires fast lands to improve navigation, it is not required under the Eminent Domain Clause to compensate landowners for certain elements of damage attributable to riparian location, such as the land's value as a hydro-electric site, * * * or a port site. * * * But none of these cases ever doubted that when the Government wished to acquire fast lands, it was required by the Eminent Domain Clause of the Fifth Amendment to condemn and pay fair value for that interest. * * *

And he took care to point up the distinctive features of the present case that led to the Court's conclusion:

Here the Government's attempt to create a public right of access to the improved pond goes so far beyond ordinary regulation or improvement for navigation as to amount to a taking under the logic of Pennsylvania Coal Co. v. Mahon [260 U.S. 393, 43 S.Ct. 158 (1922)]. More than one factor contributes to this result. It is clear that prior to its improvement, Kuapa Pond was incapable of being used as a continuous highway for the purpose of navigation in interstate commerce. Its maximum depth at high tide was a mere two feet, it was separated from the adjacent bay and ocean by a natural barrier beach, and its principal commercial value was limited to fishing. It consequently is not the sort of "great navigable stream" that this Court has previously recognized as being "[in]capable of private ownership." See, e.g., United States v. Chandler-Dunbar, supra, 389 U.S., at 66, 33 S.Ct., at 673; United States v. Twin City Power Co., supra, 350 U.S., at 228, 76 S.Ct., at 262. And, as previously noted, Kuapa Pond has always been considered to be private property under Hawaiian law. Thus, the interest of petitioners in the now dredged marina is strikingly similar to that of owners of fast land adjacent to navigable water.

We have not the slightest doubt that the Government could have refused to allow such dredging on the ground that it would have impaired navigation in the bay, or could have conditioned its approval of the dredging on petitioners' agreement to comply with various measures that it deemed appropriate for the promotion of navigation. But what petitioners now have is a body of water that was private property under Hawaiian law, linked to navigable water by a channel dredged by them with the consent of the respondent. While the consent of individual officials representing the United States cannot "estop" the United States, * * * it can lead to the fruition of a number of expectancies embodied in the concept of "property,"—expectancies that, if sufficiently important, the Government must condemn and pay for before it takes over the management of the landowner's property. In this case, we hold that the "right to exclude," so universally held to be a fundamental element of the property rights, falls within this category of interests that the Government cannot take without compensation. This is not a case in which the Government is exercising its regulatory power in a manner that will cause an insubstantial devaluation of petitioners' private property; rather, the imposition of the navigational servitude in this context will result in an actual physical invasion of the privately owned marina. * * * Thus, if the Government wishes to make what was formerly Kuapa Pond into a public aquatic park after petitioners have proceeded as far as they have here, it may not, without invoking its eminent domain power and paying just compensation, require them to allow free access to the dredged pond while petitioners' agreement with their customers calls for an annual $72 regular fee.

In a dissenting opinion in which he also spoke for Justices Brennan and Marshall, Justice Blackmun rejected the Court's conclusion as injurious to "the freedom of commerce that the navigational servitude is intended to safeguard." In his view consideration of whether the navigability of waters had been "privately created or enhanced" was irrelevant to time-honored tests of navigability gleaned from the Court's own precedents. And he emphasized that the values for which the owner/developer were to be compensated in this case stemmed from the navigability of the water. Said Justice Blackmun:

* * * The chief value of the Pond in its present state obviously is a value of access to navigable water. Development was undertaken to improve and enhance this value, not to improve the value of the Pond as some aquatic species of "fast land." Petitioners do not question the Federal Government's plenary control over the waters of the Bay, and they have no vested right in access to its open water. Since the value of the Pond and the motive for improving it lie in access to a highway of commerce, I am drawn to the conclusion that the petitioners' interest in the improved waters of the Pond is not subject to compensation. Whatever expectancy petitioners may have had in control over the Pond for use as a fishery was surrendered in exchange for the advantages of access when they cut a channel into the Bay.

UNITED STATES v. APPALACHIAN ELECTRIC POWER CO.

Supreme Court of the United States, 1940
311 U.S. 377, 61 S.Ct. 291, 85 L.Ed. 243

According to the Rivers and Harbors Act of 1899, it is unlawful to construct a dam in navigable waters without the consent of Congress. The power to approve such projects, provided they met certain conditions and did not adversely affect interstate and foreign commerce, was delegated to the Federal Power Commission when it was created in 1920. In May 1934, the commission filed for an injunction in federal district court to prevent the Appalachian Electric Power Company from completing construction of a hydroelectric dam in the New River located just above Radford, Virginia. After years of vacillation the commission finally concluded that the river was navigable and that the proposed dam would adversely affect commerce. The district court, however, concluded that the river was not navigable and refused to enjoin the power company from construction and operation of the dam. This judgment was affirmed on appeal.

———

Mr. Justice REED delivered the opinion of the Court.

* * *

Concurrent Findings. The district court's finding that the New River was not navigable was concurred in by the circuit court of appeals after a careful appraisal of the evidence in the record. Both courts stated in detail the circumstantial facts relating to the use of the river and its physical characteristics, such as volume of water, swiftness and obstructions. There is no real disagreement between the parties here concerning these physical and historical evidentiary facts. But there are sharp divergencies of view as to their reliability as indicia of navigability and the weight which should be attributed to them. The disagreement is over the ultimate conclusion upon navigability to be drawn from this uncontroverted evidence.

The respondent relies upon this Court's statement that "each determination as to navigability must stand on its own facts," and upon the conventional rule that factual findings concurred in by two courts will be accepted by this Court unless clear error is shown.

In cases involving the navigability of water courses, this Court, without expressly passing on the finality of the findings, on some occasions has entered into consideration of the facts found by two courts to determine for itself whether the courts have correctly applied to the facts found the proper legal tests. When we deal with issues such as these before us, facts and their constitutional significance are too closely connected to make the two-court rule a serviceable guide. The legal concept of navigability embraces both public and private interests. It is not to be determined by a formula which fits every type of stream under all circumstances and at all times. Our past decisions have taken due account of the changes and complexities in the circumstances of a river. We do not purport now to lay down any single definitive test. We draw from the prior decisions in this field and apply them, with due regard to the dynamic nature of the problem, to the particular circumstances presented by the New River. To these circumstances certain judicial standards are to be applied for determining whether the complex of the conditions in respect to its capacity for use in interstate commerce render it a navigable stream within the Constitutional requirements. Both the

standards and the ultimate conclusion involve questions of law inseparable from the particular facts to which they are applied.

Navigability. The power of the United States over its waters which are capable of use as interstate highways arises from the commerce clause of the Constitution, art. 1, § 8, cl. 3. "The Congress shall have Power * * * To regulate Commerce * * * among the several States." It was held early in our history that the power to regulate commerce necessarily included power over navigation. To make its control effective the Congress may keep the "navigable waters of the United States" open and free and provide by sanctions against any interference with the country's water assets. It may legislate to forbid or license dams in the waters; its power over improvements for navigation in rivers is "absolute."

The states possess control of the waters within their borders, "subject to the acknowledged jurisdiction of the United States under the constitution in regard to commerce and the navigation of the waters of rivers." It is this subordinate local control that, even as to navigable rivers, creates between the respective governments a contrariety of interests relating to the regulation and protection of waters through licenses, the operation of structures and the acquisition of projects at the end of the license term. But there is no doubt that the United States possesses the power to control the erection of structures in navigable waters.

The navigability of the New River is, of course, a factual question but to call it a fact cannot obscure the diverse elements that enter into the application of the legal tests as to navigability. We are dealing here with the sovereign powers of the Union, the Nation's right that its waterways be utilized for the interests of the commerce of the whole country. It is obvious that the uses to which the streams may be put vary from the carriage of ocean liners to the floating out of logs; that the density of traffic varies equally widely from the busy harbors of the seacoast to the sparsely settled regions of the Western mountains. The tests as to navigability must take these variations into consideration.

Both lower courts based their investigation primarily upon the generally accepted definition of The Daniel Ball. [10 Wall. 557, 563, 19 L.Ed. 999:

" * * * Those rivers must be regarded as public navigable rivers in law which are navigable in fact. And they are navigable in fact when they are used, or are susceptible of being used, in their ordinary condition, as highways for commerce, over which trade and travel are or may be conducted in the customary modes of trade and travel on water. And they constitute navigable waters of the United States within the meaning of the acts of Congress, in contradistinction from the navigable waters of the States, when they form in their ordinary condition by themselves, or by uniting with other waters, a continued highway over which commerce is or may be carried on with other States or foreign countries in the customary modes in which such commerce is conducted by water."] In so doing they were in accord with the rulings of this Court on the basic concept of navigability. Each application of this test, however, is apt to uncover variations and refinements which require further elaboration.

* * *

To appraise the evidence of navigability on the natural condition only of the waterway is erroneous. Its availability for navigation must also be considered. "Natural or ordinary conditions" refers to volume of water, the gradients and the regularity of the flow. A waterway, otherwise suitable for navigation, is not barred from that classification merely because artificial aids must make the highway suitable for use before commercial navigation may be undertaken. Congress has recognized this in section 3 of the Water Power Act by defining "navigable waters" as those "which either in their natural or improved condition" are used or suitable for use. The district court is quite right in saying there are obvious limits to such improvements as affecting navigability. These limits are necessarily a matter of degree. There must be a balance between cost and need at a time when the improvement would be useful. When once found to be navigable, a waterway remains so. This is no more indefinite than a rule of navigability in fact as adopted below based upon "useful interstate commerce" or "general and common usefulness for purposes of trade and commerce" if these are interpreted as barring improvements. Nor is it necessary that the improvements should be actually completed or even authorized. The power of Congress over commerce is not to be hampered because of the necessity for reasonable improvements to make an interstate waterway available for traffic. * * * The plenary federal power over commerce must be able to develop with the needs of that commerce which is the reason for its existence. It cannot properly be said that the federal power over navigation is enlarged by the improvements to the waterways. It is merely that improvements make applicable to certain waterways the existing power over commerce. In determining the navigable character of the New River it is proper to consider the feasibility of interstate use after reasonable improvements which might be made.

Nor is it necessary for navigability that the use should be continuous. The character of the region, its products and the difficulties or dangers of the navigation influence the regularity and extent of the use. Small traffic compared to the available commerce of the region is sufficient. Even absence of use over long periods of years, because of changed conditions, the coming of the railroad or improved highways does not affect the navigability of rivers in the constitutional sense. It is well recognized too that the navigability may be of a substantial part only of the waterway in question. Of course, these evidences of nonnavigability in whole or in part are to be appraised in totality to determine the effect of all. With these legal tests in mind we proceed to examine the facts to see whether the 111-mile reach of this river from Allisonia to Hinton, across the Virginia-West Virginia state line, has "capability of use by the public for purposes of transportation and commerce."

[The Court found the New River navigable.]

* * *

License Provisions. The determination that the New River is navigable eliminates from this case issues which may arise only where the river involved is nonnavigable. But even accepting the navigability of the New River, the respondent urges that certain provisions of the license,

which seek to control affairs of the licensee, are unconnected with navigation and are beyond the power of the Commission, indeed beyond the constitutional power of Congress to authorize.

* * *

The respondent is a riparian owner with a valid state license to use the natural resources of the state for its enterprise. Consequently it has as complete a right to the use of the riparian lands, the water, and the river bed as can be obtained under state law. The state and respondent, alike, however, hold the waters and the lands under them subject to the power of Congress to control the waters for the purpose of commerce. The power flows from the grant to regulate, i.e., to "prescribe the rule by which commerce is to be governed." This includes the protection of navigable waters in capacity as well as use. This power of Congress to regulate commerce is so unfettered that its judgment as to whether a structure is or is not a hindrance is conclusive. Its determination is legislative in character. The Federal Government has domination over the water power inherent in the flowing stream. It is liable to no one for its use or non-use. The flow of a navigable stream is in no sense private property; "that the running water in a great navigable stream is capable of private ownership is inconceivable." Exclusion of riparian owners from its benefits without compensation is entirely within the Government's discretion.

Possessing this plenary power to exclude structures from navigable waters and dominion over flowage and its product, energy, the United States may make the erection or maintenance of a structure in a navigable water dependent upon a license. This power is exercised through section 9 of the Rivers and Harbors Act of 1899 prohibiting construction without Congressional consent and through section 4(e) of the present Power Act.

* * *

In our view, it cannot properly be said that the constitutional power of the United States over its waters is limited to control for navigation. By navigation respondent means no more than operation of boats and improvement of the waterway itself. In truth the authority of the United States is the regulation of commerce on its waters. Navigability, in the sense just stated, is but a part of this whole. Flood protection, watershed development, recovery of the cost of improvements through utilization of power are likewise parts of commerce control. As respondent soundly argues, the United States cannot by calling a project of its own "a multiple purpose dam" give to itself additional powers, but equally truly the respondent cannot, by seeking to use a navigable waterway for power generation alone, avoid the authority of the Government over the stream. That authority is as broad as the needs of commerce. Water power development from dams in navigable streams is from the public's standpoint a by-product of the general use of the rivers for commerce. To this general power, the respondent must submit its single purpose of electrical production. The fact that the Commission is willing to give a license for a power dam only is of no significance in appraising the type of conditions allowable. It may well be that this portion of the river is not needed for navigation at this time. Or that the dam pro-

posed may function satisfactorily with others, contemplated or intended. It may fit in as a part of the river development. The point is that navigable waters are subject to national planning and control in the broad regulation of commerce granted the Federal Government. The license conditions to which objection is made have an obvious relationship to the exercise of the commerce power. Even if there were no such relationship the plenary power of Congress over navigable waters would empower it to deny the privilege of constructing an obstruction in those waters. It may likewise grant the privilege on terms. It is no objection to the terms and to the exertion of the power that "its exercise is attended by the same incidents which attend the exercise of the police power of the states." The Congressional authority under the commerce clause is complete unless limited by the Fifth Amendment.

Reversed and remanded.

The Chief Justice [HUGHES] took no part in the consideration or decision of this case.

Mr. Justice ROBERTS (dissenting).

The judgment of reversal rests on the conclusion that New River is navigable,—a conclusion resting on findings of fact, made here de novo, and in contradiction of the concurrent findings of the two courts below. I am of opinion that the judgment of the Circuit Court of Appeals should be affirmed, first, because this court ought to respect and give effect to such concurrent findings which have substantial support in the evidence; secondly, because the evidence will not support contrary findings if the navigability of New River be tested by criteria long established.

* * *

* * * If anything has been settled by our decisions it is that, in order for a water to be found navigable, navigability in fact must exist under "natural and ordinary conditions." This means all conditions, including a multiplicity of obstacles, falls and rapids which make navigation a practical impossibility. The court now, however, announces that "natural and ordinary conditions" refers only to volume of water, gradients, and regularity of flow. No authority is cited and I believe none can be found for thus limiting the connotation of the phrase. But further the court holds, contrary to all that has heretofore been said on the subject, that the natural and ordinary condition of the stream, however impassable it may be without improvement, means that if, by "reasonable" improvement, the stream may be rendered navigable then it is navigable without such improvement; that "there must be a balance between cost and need at a time when the improvement would be useful." No authority is cited and I think none can be cited which countenances any such test. * * *

* * *

In the light of the grounds upon which the decision of the court is based it hardly seems necessary to comment on the evidence, for it is in the main addressed to issues no longer in the case. The two courts below have analyzed it and examined it in detail and reference to their carefully considered opinions suffices. I think the conclusion reached by the courts below must stand unless the two novel doctrines now announced be thrown into the scale to overcome it.

Mr. Justice McREYNOLDS concurs in this opinion.

ASHWANDER v. TENNESSEE VALLEY AUTHORITY

Supreme Court of the United States, 1936
297 U.S. 288, 56 S.Ct. 466, 80 L.Ed. 688

In January 1934, the Tennessee Valley Authority, a public agency created under congressional authority, contracted with the Alabama Power Company to sell to the company "surplus power" generated from a federal project, Wilson Dam. As part of the agreement, the company contracted to sell T.V.A. certain transmission lines, substations, and other real property. Ashwander was one of several stockholders in the power company who objected to these arrangements as being hurtful to the company by allowing T.V.A. to cut in on its market. He and others failed to convince the company's board of directors to seek annulment of the contracts, and they even refused to call a general stockholders' meeting to discuss the matter. As a consequence, Ashwander sued to have the contracts annulled and thereby to open up a general challenge to the constitutionality of the entire T.V.A. program.

The U.S. District Court returned a judgment in Ashwander's favor and annulled the contracts. It also enjoined any of the municipalities, also defendants in the litigation, from making or executing any contracts with T.V.A. for the purchase of power or from accepting any funds from federal agencies toward the goal of creating a public power system. This decision was subsequently overturned by the U.S. Circuit Court of Appeals. That court, confining itself to the circumstances of these contracts and the constitutional authority for the construction of Wilson Dam alone, held for the United States, and Ashwander appealed.

Mr. Chief Justice HUGHES delivered the opinion of the Court.

*   *   *

The Scope of the Issue. We agree with the Circuit Court of Appeals that the question to be determined is limited to the validity of the contract of January 4, 1934. The pronouncements, policies, and program of the Tennessee Valley Authority and its directors, their motives and desires, did not give rise to a justiciable controversy save as they had fruition in action of a definite and concrete character constituting an actual or threatened interference with the rights of the persons complaining. The judicial power does not extend to the determination of abstract questions. *   *   *

*   *   *

There is a further limitation upon our inquiry. As it appears that the transmission lines in question run from the Wilson Dam and that the electric energy generated at that dam is more than sufficient to supply all the requirements of the contract, the questions that are properly before us relate to the constitutional authority for the construction of the Wilson Dam and for the disposition, as provided in the contract, of the electric energy there generated.

The Constitutional Authority for the Construction of the Wilson Dam. The Congress may not, "under the pretext of executing its powers, pass laws for the accomplishment of objects not intrusted to the government." Chief Justice Marshall, in McCulloch v. Maryland, 4 Wheat. 316, 423, 4 L.Ed. 579. *   *   * The government's argument recognizes this essential limitation. The government's contention is that the Wilson Dam was construct-

ed, and the power plant connected with it was installed, in the exercise by the Congress of its war and commerce powers (Const. art. 1, § 8, cls. 3, 11); that is, for the purposes of national defense and the improvement of navigation.

Wilson Dam is described as a concrete monolith one hundred feet high and almost a mile long, containing two locks for navigation and eight installed generators. Construction was begun in 1917 and completed in 1926. Authority for its construction is found in section 124 of the National Defense Act of June 3, 1916. It authorized the President to cause an investigation to be made in order to determine "the best, cheapest, and most available means for the production of nitrates and other products for munitions of war"; to designate for the exclusive use of the United States "such site or sites, upon any navigable or nonnavigable river or rivers or upon the public lands, as in his opinion will be necessary for carrying out the purposes of this Act [section]"; and "to construct, maintain, and operate" on any such site "dams, locks, improvements to navigation, power houses, and other plants and equipment or other means than water power as in his judgment is the best and cheapest, necessary or convenient for the generation of electrical or other power and for the production of nitrates or other products needed for munitions of war and useful in the manufacture of fertilizers and other useful products." The President was authorized to lease or acquire by condemnation or otherwise such lands as might be necessary, and there was further provision that "the products of such plants shall be used by the President for military and naval purposes to the extent that he may deem necessary, and any surplus which he shall determine is not required shall be sold and disposed of by him under such regulations as he may prescribe."

We may take judicial notice of the international situation at the time the act of 1916 was passed, and it cannot be successfully disputed that the Wilson Dam and its auxiliary plants, including the hydroelectric power plant, are, and were intended to be, adapted to the purposes of national defense. While the District Court found that there is no intention to use the nitrate plants or the hydroelectric units installed at Wilson Dam for the production of war materials in time of peace, "the maintenance of said properties in operating condition and the assurance of an abundant supply of electric energy in the event of war, constitute national defense assets." This finding has ample support.

The act of 1916 also had in view "improvements to navigation." Commerce includes navigation. "All America understands, and has uniformly understood," said Chief Justice Marshall in Gibbons v. Ogden, 9 Wheat. 1, 190, 6 L.Ed. 23, "the word 'commerce,' to comprehend navigation." The power to regulate interstate commerce embraces the power to keep the navigable rivers of the United States free from obstructions to navigation and to remove such obstructions when they exist. "For these purposes," said the Court in Gilman v. Philadelphia, 3 Wall. 713, 725, 18 L.Ed. 96, "Congress possesses all the powers which existed in the States before the adoption of the national Constitution, and which have always existed in the Parliament in England." * * *

The Tennessee river is a navigable stream, although there are obstructions at various points because of shoals, reefs, and rapids. The improvement of navigation on this river has been a matter of national concern for over a century. * * *

While, in its present condition, the Tennessee river is not adequately improved for commercial navigation, and traffic is small, we are not at liberty to conclude either that the river is not susceptible of development as an important waterway, or that Congress has not undertaken that development, or that the construction of the Wilson Dam was not an appropriate means to accomplish a legitimate end.

The Wilson Dam and its power plant must be taken to have been constructed in the exercise of the constitutional functions of the federal government.

The Constitutional Authority to Dispose of Electric Energy Generated at the Wilson Dam. The government acquired full title to the dam site, with all riparian rights. The power of falling water was an inevitable incident of the construction of the dam. That water power came into the exclusive control of the federal government. The mechanical energy was convertible into electric energy, and the water power, the right to convert it into electric energy, and the electric energy thus produced constitute property belonging to the United States. * * *

Authority to dispose of property constitutionally acquired by the United States is expressly granted to the Congress by section 3 of article 4 of the Constitution. This section provides:

"The Congress shall have Power to dispose of and make all needful Rules and Regulations respecting the Territory or other Property belonging to the United States; and nothing in this Constitution shall be so construed as to Prejudice any Claims of the United States, or of any particular State."

To the extent that the power of disposition is thus expressly conferred, it is manifest that the Tenth Amendment is not applicable. And the Ninth Amendment (which petitioners also invoke), in insuring the maintenance of the rights retained by the people, does not withdraw the rights which are expressly granted to the federal government. The question is as to the scope of the grant and whether there are inherent limitations which render invalid the disposition of property with which we are now concerned.

[Following a discussion of the right of the federal government to mine coal and mineral deposits and to develop water power found on its own property, the Court concluded that there are no inherent limitations on the power of Congress to dispose of the fruits of such property.]

*   *   *

The argument is stressed that, assuming that electric energy generated at the dam belongs to the United States, the Congress has authority to dispose of this energy only to the extent that it is a surplus necessarily created in the course of making munitions of war or operating the works for navigation purposes; that is, that the remainder of the available energy must be lost or go to waste. We find nothing in the Constitution which imposes such a limitation. It is not to be deduced from the mere fact that the electric energy is only potentially available until the generators are operated. The government has no less right to the energy thus available by letting the

water course over its turbines than it has to use the appropriate processes to reduce to possession other property within its control, as, for example, oil which it may recover from a pool beneath its lands, and which is reduced to possession by boring oil wells and otherwise might escape its grasp.   *   *   *   And it would hardly be contended that, when the government reserves coal on its lands, it can mine the coal and dispose of it only for the purpose of heating public buildings or for other governmental operations. Or, if the government owns a silver mine, that it can obtain the silver only for the purpose of storage or coinage. Or that, when the government extracts the oil it has reserved, it has no constitutional power to sell it. Our decisions recognize no such restriction.   *   *   *
The United States owns the coal, or the silver, or the lead, or the oil, it obtains from its lands, and it lies in the discretion of the Congress, acting in the public interest, to determine of how much of the property it shall dispose.

*   *   *

We limit our decision to the case before us, as we have defined it. The argument is earnestly presented that the government by virtue of its ownership of the dam and power plant could not establish a steel mill and make and sell steel products, or a factory to manufacture clothing or shoes for the public, and thus attempt to make its ownership of energy, generated at its dam, a means of carrying on competitive commercial enterprises, and thus drawing to the federal government the conduct and management of business having no relation to the purposes for which the federal government was established. The picture is eloquently drawn, but we deem it to be irrelevant to the issue here. The government is not using the water power at the Wilson Dam to establish any industry or business. It is not using the energy generated at the dam to manufacture commodities of any sort for the public. The government is disposing of the energy itself which simply is the mechanical energy, incidental to falling water at the dam, converted into the electric energy which is susceptible of transmission. The question here is simply as to the acquisition of the transmission lines as a facility for the disposal of that energy. And the government rightly conceded at the bar, in substance, that it was without constitutional authority to acquire or dispose of such energy except as it comes into being in the operation of works constructed in the exercise of some power delegated to the United States. As we have said, these transmission lines lead directly from the dam, which has been lawfully constructed, and the question of the constitutional right of the government to acquire or operate local or urban distribution systems is not involved. We express no opinion as to the validity of such an effort, as to the status of any other dam or power development in the Tennessee Valley, whether connected with or apart from the Wilson Dam, or as to the validity of the Tennessee Valley Authority Act or of the claims made in the pronouncements and program of the Authority apart from the questions we have discussed in relation to the particular provisions of the contract of January 4, 1934, affecting the Alabama Power Company.

The decree of the Circuit Court of Appeals is affirmed.

Affirmed.

[Justice McREYNOLDS dissented.]

Under Title II of the National Industrial Recovery Act, Harold Ickes, the Federal Emergency Administrator of Public Works, made "loan and grant agreements" with four Alabama municipalities to finance municipally owned power systems. According to state law each municipality was empowered to construct and operate public power facilities, to allocate revenue derived from the sale of electricity, and to make agreements with the federal government regarding the financing of such projects. These agreements were made without any coercion from the federal government and contained no provisions for any federal control beyond the completion of construction. In addition, each municipality held an election before any of these agreements were made, and a majority of the qualified voters in each municipality approved the projects. As a private corporation chartered to do business, the Alabama Power Company had a nonexclusive franchise to generate, supply, and sell electricity throughout the state. The power company was a taxpayer in each of the municipalities and of the state and the federal government. It sued to enjoin execution of these agreements on grounds the administrator had no lawful statutory or constitutional power to make them and because the tax monies would be used by the municipalities to engage in destructive competition, thereby ruining the private power company.

In Alabama Power Co. v. Ickes, 302 U.S. 464, 58 S.Ct. 300 (1938), the Supreme Court held for the government and affirmed decisions of the lower federal courts. Speaking for the Court, Justice Sutherland said:

First. Unless a different conclusion is required from the mere fact that petitioner will sustain financial loss by reason of the lawful competition which will result from the use by the municipalities of the proposed loans and grants, it is clear that petitioner has no such interest and will sustain no such legal injury as enables it to maintain the present suits. Petitioner alleges that it is a taxpayer; but the interest of a taxpayer in the moneys of the federal treasury furnishes no basis for an appeal to the preventive powers of a court of equity. Massachusetts v. Mellon, 262 U.S. 447, 486 et seq., 43 S.Ct. 597, 601. The principle established by the case just cited is that the courts have no power to consider in isolation and annul an act of Congress on the ground that it is unconstitutional; but may consider that question "only when the justification for some direct injury suffered or threatened, presenting a justiciable issue, is made to rest upon such an act." The term "direct injury" is there used in its legal sense, as meaning a wrong which directly results in the violation of a legal right. "An injury, legally speaking, consists of a wrong done to a person, or, in other words, a violation of his right. It is an ancient maxim, that a damage to one, without an injury in this sense (damnum absque injuria), does not lay the foundation of an action; because, if the act complained of does not violate any of his legal rights, it is obvious, that he has no cause to complain. * * *" Parker v. Griswold, 17 Conn. 288, 302, 303, 42 Am.Dec. 739. * * *

Second. The only pertinent inquiry, then, is, What enforceable legal right of petitioner do the alleged wrongful agreements invade or threaten? If conspiracy or fraud or malice or coercion were involved, a different case would be presented, but in their absence, plainly enough, the mere consummation of the loans and grants will not constitute an actionable wrong. Nor will the subsequent application by the municipalities of the moneys derived therefrom give rise to an actionable wrong, since such application, being lawful, will invade no legal right of petitioner. The claim that petitioner will be injured, perhaps ruined, by the competition of the municipalities brought about by the use of the moneys, therefore, presents a clear case of damnum absque injuria. Stated in other words, these municipalities have the right under state law to engage in the business in competition with petitioner, since it has been given no exclusive franchise. If its business be curtailed or destroyed by the operations of the municipalities, it will be by lawful competition from which no legal wrong results.

What petitioner anticipates, we emphasize, is damage to something it does not possess—namely, a right to be immune from lawful municipal competition. No other claim of right is involved. * * *

* * *

CITY OF TACOMA v. TAXPAYERS OF TACOMA

Supreme Court of the United States, 1958
357 U.S. 320, 78 S.Ct. 1209, 2 L.Ed.2d 1345

In August 1948, the City of Tacoma filed an application with the Federal Power Commission for permission to construct a power project including two rather high dams across the Cowlitz River. The project also provided for fish-handling facilities which would permit fish to pass to spawning grounds upstream and let their young swim out to sea. Some time later the commission held public hearings at which the state attorney general appeared and argued against granting the license. Aside from violating a state law which expressly limited the size of dams that could be constructed on the tributaries of the Columbia River (of which the Cowlitz River was one), the attorney general argued that "the reservoirs which would be created by the proposed dams would inundate a valuable and irreplaceable fish hatchery owned by the State of Washington, as well as * * * productive spawning grounds." In sum, he concluded, the dams and fish-handling facilities would destroy the fishery resources of the state. Nevertheless, in November 1951, the commission handed down a decision to grant the license. Following a motion for rehearing and its subsequent denial by the commission, the state petitioned the Ninth U. S. Circuit Court of Appeals for review of the decision. In support of its petition the state argued that "Tacoma, as a creature of the State of Washington, cannot act in opposition to the policy of the State or in derogation of its laws." In its ruling the U. S. Court of Appeals held that "state laws cannot prevent the Federal Power Commission from issuing a license or bar the licensee from acting under the license to build a dam on a navigable stream since the stream is under the dominion of the United States." The state petitioned the U. S. Supreme Court for certiorari, and it was denied.

While the case was pending in the court of appeals, the City of Tacoma commenced proceedings against the taxpayers and the state's fish and game directors to obtain a judgment validating a large issue of bonds authorized by the city to finance construction. (The taxpayers were impleaded as defendants since Washington law requires it when a municipality comes to court seeking a judgment vindicating its right to float bond issues.) What followed was a series of suits and countersuits culminating in the petition to the United States Supreme Court by the city for a determination as to whether or not it could market its bonds.

Mr. Justice WHITTAKER delivered the opinion of the Court.

This is the latest episode in litigation beginning in 1948 which has been waged in five tribunals and has produced more than 125 printed pages of administrative and judicial opinions. It concerns the plan of the City of Tacoma, a municipal corporation in the State of Washington, to construct a power project on the Cowlitz River, a navigable water of the United States, in accordance with a license issued by the Federal Power Commission under the Federal Power Act. The question presented for decision here is whether under the facts of this case the City of Tacoma has acquired federal eminent domain power and capacity to take, upon the payment of just compensation, a fish hatchery owned and operated by the State of Washington, by virtue of the license issued to the City under the Federal Power Act and more particularly § 21 thereof. The project cannot be built without

taking the hatchery because it necessarily must be inundated by a reservoir that will be created by one of the project's dams.

* * *

We come now to the core of the controversy between the parties, namely, whether the license issued by the Commission under the Federal Power Act to the City of Tacoma gave it capacity to act under that federal license in constructing the project and delegated to it federal eminent domain power to take, upon the payment of just compensation, the State's fish hatchery—essential to the construction of the project—in the absence of state legislation specifically conferring such authority.

* * *

It is no longer open to question that the Federal Government under the Commerce Clause of the Constitution (Art. I, § 8, cl. 3) has dominion, to the exclusion of the States, over navigable waters of the United States. Gibbons v. Ogden, 9 Wheat. 1, 196, 6 L.Ed. 23; * * * United States v. Appalachian Electric Power Co., 311 U.S. 377, 424, 61 S.Ct. 291, 307. * * * Congress has elected to exercise this power under the detailed and comprehensive plan for development of the Nation's water resources, which it prescribed in the Federal Power Act, to be administered by the Federal Power Commission. * * *

* * *

But respondents say that the Court of Appeals did not decide the question of legal capacity of the City to act under the license and, therefore, its decision is not final on that question, but left it open to further litigation. They rely upon the following language of the opinion:

"However, we do not touch the question as to the legal capacity of the City of Tacoma to initiate and act under the license once it is granted. There may be limitations in the City Charter, for instance, as to indebtedness limitations. Questions of this nature may be inquired into by the Commission as relevant to the practicability of the plan, but the Commission has no power to adjudicate them." * * *

We believe that respondents' construction of this language is in error. The questioned language expressly refers to possible "indebtedness limitations" in the City's Charter and "questions of this nature," not to the

right of the City to receive and perform, as licensee of the Federal Government under the Federal Power Act, the federal rights determined by the Commission and delegated to the City as specified in the license. That this was the meaning of the court, if its meaning might otherwise be doubtful, is made certain by the facts that the court did not disturb a single one of the Commission's findings; affirmed its order without modification; and said, in the sentence immediately preceding the questioned language: "Consistent with the First Iowa case, supra, we conclude that the state laws cannot prevent the Federal Power Commission from issuing a license *or bar the licensee from acting under the license* to build a dam on a navigable stream since the stream is under the dominion of the United States." * * * (Emphasis added.)

* * *

We conclude that the judgment of the Court of Appeals, upon this Court's denial of the State's petition for certiorari, became final under § 313(b) of the Act, and is binding upon the State of Washington, its Directors of Fisheries and of Game, and its citizens, including the taxpayers of Tacoma. * * * Therefore, the judgment of the Supreme Court of Washington is reversed and the cause is remanded for further proceedings not inconsistent with this opinion.

Reversed and remanded.

d. THE TAXING AND SPENDING POWER

McCRAY v. UNITED STATES

Supreme Court of the United States, 1904
195 U.S. 27, 24 S.Ct. 769, 49 L.Ed. 78

Congress enacted legislation to tax oleomargarine which had been colored to look like butter at the rate of ten cents a pound. Uncolored margarine, however, was taxed at only one-fourth cent per pound. McCray, a retail dealer in oleomargarine, had purchased a fifty-pound package of the colored product for resale to which were affixed revenue stamps at the one-fourth cent per pound rate. When he refused to pay tax at the specified rate, the government sued to collect the fifty dollar penalty for noncompliance prescribed by the statute. Among the defenses he offered, McCray asserted that the legislation was unconstitutional because (1) it was intended to and would effect the ruin of the oleomargarine industry to the advantage of the butter producers, and thus this scheme of taxation took property without due process of law; and (2) that in regulating a product it interfered with the police powers reserved to the states under the Tenth Amendment. The U. S. District Court held for the government, and McCray appealed.

Mr. Justice WHITE * * * delivered the opinion of the court:

* * *

Whilst, as a result of our written constitution, it is axiomatic that the judicial department of the government is charged with the solemn duty of enforcing the Constitution, and therefore, in cases properly presented, of determining whether a given manifestation of authority has exceeded the power conferred by that instrument, no instance is afforded from the foundation of the government where an act which was within a power conferred, was declared to be repugnant to the Constitution, because it appeared to the judicial mind that the particular exertion of constitutional power was either unwise or unjust. To announce such a principle would amount to declaring that, in our constitutional system, the judiciary was not only charged with the duty of upholding the Constitution, but also with the responsibility of correcting every possible abuse arising from the exercise by the other departments of their conceded authority. So to hold would be to overthrow the entire distinction between the legislative, judicial, and executive departments of the government, upon which our system is founded, and would be a mere act of judicial usurpation.

It is, however, argued, if a lawful power may be exerted for an unlawful purpose, and thus, by abusing the power, it may be made to accomplish a result not intended by the Constitution, all limitations of power must disappear, and the grave function lodged in the judiciary, to confine all the departments within the authority conferred by the Constitution, will be of no avail. This, when reduced to its last analysis, comes to this: that, because a particular department of the government may exert its lawful powers with the object or motive of reaching an end not justified, therefore it becomes the duty of the judiciary to restrain the exercise of a lawful power wherever it seems to the judicial mind that such lawful power has been abused. But this reduces itself to the contention that, under our constitutional system, the abuse by one department of the government of its lawful powers is to be corrected by the abuse of its powers by another department.

The proposition, if sustained, would destroy all distinction between the powers of the respective departments of the government, would put an end to that confidence and respect for each other which it was the purpose of the Constitution to uphold, and would thus be full of danger to the permanence of our institutions. * * *

It is, of course, true, as suggested, that if there be no authority in the judiciary to restrain a lawful exercise of power by another department of the government, where a wrong motive or purpose has impelled to the exertion of the power, that abuses of a power conferred may be temporarily effectual. The remedy for this, however, lies, not in the abuse by the judicial authority of its functions, but in the people, upon whom, after all, under our institutions, reliance must be placed for the correction of abuses committed in the exercise of a lawful power. * * *

The decisions of this court from the beginning lend no support whatever to the assumption that the judiciary may restrain the exercise of lawful power on the assumption that a wrongful purpose or motive has caused the power to be exerted. As we have previously said: from the beginning no case can be found announcing such a doctrine, and, on the contrary, the doctrine of a number of cases is inconsistent with its existence. * * *

* * *

1. Undoubtedly, in determining whether a particular act is within a granted power, its scope and effect is to be considered. Applying this rule to the acts assailed, it is self-evident that on their face they levy an excise tax. That being their necessary scope and operation, it follows that the acts are within the grant of power. The argument to the contrary rests on the proposition that, although the tax be within the power, as enforcing it will destroy or restrict the manufacture of artificially colored oleomargarine, therefore the power to levy the tax did not obtain. This, however, is but to say that the question of power depends, not upon the authority conferred by the Constitution, but upon what may be the consequence arising from the exercise of the lawful authority.

Since, as pointed out in all the decisions referred to, the taxing power conferred by the Constitution knows no limits except those expressly stated in that instrument, it must follow, if a tax be within the lawful power, the exertion of that power may not be judicially restrained because of the results to arise from its exercise. * * *

* * *

2. The proposition that where a tax is imposed which is within the grant of powers, and which does not conflict with any express constitutional limitation, the courts may hold the tax to be void because it is deemed that the tax is too high, is absolutely disposed of by the opinions in the cases hitherto cited, and which expressly hold, to repeat again the language of one of the cases (*Spencer* v. *Merchant* [125 U.S. 345, 8 S.Ct. 921]) that "The judicial department cannot prescribe to the legislative department limitations upon

the exercise of its acknowledged powers. The power to tax may be exercised oppressively upon persons; but the responsibility of the legislature is not to the courts, but to the people by whom its members are elected."

3. Whilst undoubtedly both the 5th and 10th Amendments qualify, in so far as they are applicable, all the provisions of the Constitution, nothing in those amendments operates to take away the grant of power to tax conferred by the Constitution upon Congress. The contention on this subject rests upon the theory that the purpose and motive of Congress in exercising its undoubted powers may be inquired into by the courts, and the proposition is therefore disposed of by what has been said on that subject.

The right of Congress to tax within its delegated power being unrestrained, except as limited by the Constitution, it was within the authority conferred on Congress to select the objects upon which an excise should be laid. It therefore follows that, in exerting its power, no want of due process of law could possibly result, because that body chose to impose an excise on artificially colored oleomargarine, and not upon natural butter artificially colored. * * *

* * * Conceding, merely for the sake of argument, that the due process clause of the 5th Amendment would avoid an exertion of the taxing power which, without any basis for classification, arbitrarily taxed one article and excluded an article of the same class, such concession would be wholly inapposite to the case in hand. The distinction between natural butter artificially colored, and oleomargarine artificial-

ly colored so as to cause it to look like butter, has been pointed out in previous adjudications of this court. Capital City Dairy Co. v. Ohio, 183 U.S. 238, 46 L.Ed. 171, 22 Sup.Ct. Rep. 120, and authorities there cited. Indeed, in the cases referred to, the distinction between the two products was held to be so marked, and the aptitude of oleomargarine when artificially colored, to deceive the public into believing it to be butter, was decided to be so great, that it was held no violation of the due process clause of the 14th Amendment was occasioned by state legislation absolutely forbidding the manufacture, within the state, of oleomargarine artificially colored. As it has been thus decided that the distinction between the two products is so great as to justify the absolute prohibition of the manufacture of oleomargarine artificially colored, there is no foundation for the proposition that the difference between the two was not sufficient, under the extremest view, to justify a classification distinguishing between them.

4. Lastly we come to consider the argument that, even though as a general rule a tax of the nature of the one in question would be within the power of Congress, in this case the tax should be held not to be within such power, because of its effect. This is based on the contention that, as the tax is so large as to destroy the business of manufacturing oleomargarine artificially colored to look like butter, it thus deprives the manufacturers of that article of their freedom to engage in a lawful pursuit, and hence, irrespective of the distribution of powers made by the Constitution, the taxing laws are void, because they violate those fundamental rights which it is the duty of every free government to safe-

guard, and which, therefore, should be held to be embraced by implied, though none the less potential, guaranties, or, in any event, to be within the protection of the due process clause of the 5th Amendment.

Let us concede, for the sake of argument only, the premise of fact upon which the proposition is based. * * *

Such concession, however, is not controlling in this case. This follows when the nature of oleomargarine, artificially colored to look like butter, is recalled. As we have said, it has been conclusively settled by this court that the tendency of that article to deceive the public into buying it for butter is such that the states may, in the exertion of their police powers, without violating the due process clause of the 14th Amendment, absolutely prohibit the manufacture of the article. * * *

Let us concede that if a case was presented where the abuse of the taxing power was so extreme as to

be beyond the principles which we have previously stated, and where it was plain to the judicial mind that the power had been called into play, not for revenue, but solely for the purpose of destroying rights which could not be rightfully destroyed consistently with the principles of freedom and justice upon which the Constitution rests, that it would be the duty of the courts to say that such an arbitrary act was not merely an abuse of a delegated power, but was the exercise of an authority not conferred. This concession, however, like the one previously made, must be without influence upon the decision of this cause for the reasons previously stated; that is, that the manufacture of artificially colored oleomargarine may be prohibited by a free government without a violation of fundamental rights.

Affirmed.

The CHIEF JUSTICE [FULLER], Mr. Justice BROWN, and Mr. Justice PECKHAM dissent.

BAILEY v. DREXEL FURNITURE CO.
[THE CHILD LABOR TAX CASE]

Supreme Court of the United States, 1922
259 U.S. 20, 42 S.Ct. 449, 66 L.Ed. 817

The facts are set out in the Court's opinion.

Mr. Chief Justice TAFT delivered the opinion of the Court.

This case presents the question of the constitutional validity of the Child Labor Tax Law. The plaintiff below, the Drexel Furniture Company, is engaged in the manufacture of furniture in the Western district of North Carolina. On September 20, 1921, it received a notice from Bailey, United States collector of inter-

nal revenue for the district, that it had been assessed $6,312.79 for having during the taxable year 1919 employed and permitted to work in its factory a boy under 14 years of age, thus incurring the tax of 10 per cent. on its net profits for that year. The company paid the tax under protest, and, after rejection of its claim for a refund, brought this suit. On demurrer to an amended complaint, judgment was entered for the company against the collector for the full amount, with interest. * * *

The Child Labor Tax Law is title No. XII of an act entitled "An act to provide revenue and for other purposes," approved February 24, 1919, 40 Stat. 1057, 1138. * * * The heading of the title is "Tax on Employment of Child Labor." * * *

* * *

The law is attacked on the ground that it is a regulation of the employment of child labor in the states—an exclusively state function under the federal Constitution and within the reservations of the Tenth Amendment. It is defended on the ground that it is a mere excise tax levied by the Congress of the United States under its broad power of taxation conferred by section 8, article 1, of the federal Constitution. We must construe the law and interpret the intent and meaning of Congress from the language of the act. The words are to be given their ordinary meaning unless the context shows that they are differently used. Does this law impose a tax with only that incidental restraint and regulation which a tax must inevitably involve? Or does it regulate by the use of the so-called tax as a penalty? If a tax, it is clearly an excise. If it were an excise on a commodity or other thing of value, we might not be permitted under previous decisions of this court to infer solely from its heavy burden that the act intends a prohibition instead of a tax. But this act is more. It provides a heavy exaction for a departure from a detailed and specified course of conduct in business. That course of business is that employers shall employ in mines and quarries, children of an age greater than 16 years; in mills and factories, children of an age greater than 14 years, and

shall prevent children of less than 16 years in mills and factories from working more than 8 hours a day or 6 days in the week. If an employer departs from this prescribed course of business, he is to pay to the government one-tenth of his entire net income in the business for a full year. The amount is not to be proportioned in any degree to the extent or frequency of the departures, but is to be paid by the employer in full measure whether he employs 500 children for a year, or employs only one for a day. Moreover, if he does not know the child is within the named age limit, he is not to pay; that is to say, it is only where he knowingly departs from the prescribed course that payment is to be exacted. Scienters are associated with penalties, not with taxes. The employer's factory is to be subject to inspection at any time not only by the taxing officers of the Treasury, the Department normally charged with the collection of taxes, but also by the Secretary of Labor and his subordinates, whose normal function is the advancement and protection of the welfare of the workers. In the light of these features of the act, a court must be blind not to see that the so-called tax is imposed to stop the employment of children within the age limits prescribed. Its prohibitory and regulatory effect and purpose are palpable. All others can see and understand this. How can we properly shut our minds to it?

It is the high duty and function of this court in cases regularly brought to its bar to decline to recognize or enforce seeming laws of Congress, dealing with subjects not intrusted to Congress, but left or committed by the supreme law of the land to the control of the states. We cannot avoid the duty, even though it require us to refuse to give effect to legislation designed to promote the highest good. The good sought in unconstitutional legislation is an insidious feature, because it leads citizens and legislators of good purpose to promote it, without thought of the serious breach it will make in the ark of our covenant, or the harm which will come from breaking down recognized standards. In the maintenance of local self-government, on the one hand, and the national power, on the other, our country has been able to endure and prosper for nearly a century and a half.

Out of a proper respect for the acts of a co-ordinate branch of the government, this court has gone far to sustain taxing acts as such, even though there has been ground for suspecting, from the weight of the tax, it was intended to destroy its subject. But in the act before us the presumption of validity cannot prevail, because the proof of the contrary is found on the very face of its provisions. Grant the validity of this law, and all that Congress would need to do, hereafter, in seeking to take over to its control any one of the great number of subjects of public interest, jurisdiction of which the states have never parted with, and which are reserved to them by the Tenth Amendment, would be to enact a detailed measure of complete regulation of the subject and enforce it by a so-called tax upon departures from it. To give such magic to the word "tax" would be to break down all constitutional limitation of the powers of Congress and completely wipe out the sovereignty of the states.

The difference between a tax and a penalty is sometimes difficult to define, and yet the consequences of the distinction in the required method of their collection often are important.

Where the sovereign enacting the law has power to impose both tax and penalty, the difference between revenue production and mere regulation may be immaterial, but not so when one sovereign can impose a tax only, and the power of regulation rests in another. Taxes are occasionally imposed in the discretion of the Legislature on proper subjects with the primary motive of obtaining revenue from them and with the incidental motive of discouraging them by making their continuance onerous. They do not lose their character as taxes because of the incidental motive. But there comes a time in the extension of the penalizing features of the so-called tax when it loses its character as such and becomes a mere penalty, with the characteristics of regulation and punishment. Such is the case in the law before us. Although Congress does not invalidate the contract of employment or expressly declare that the employment within the mentioned ages is illegal, it does exhibit its intent practically to achieve the latter result by adopting the criteria of wrongdoing and imposing its principal consequence on those who transgress its standard.

The case before us cannot be distinguished from that of Hammer v. Dagenhart, 247 U.S. 251, 38 Sup.Ct. 529. Congress there enacted a law to prohibit transportation in interstate commerce of goods made at a factory in which there was employment of children within the same ages and for the same number of hours a day and days in a week as are penalized by the act in this case.

*   *   *

In the case at the bar, Congress in the name of a tax which on the face of the act is a penalty seeks to do the same thing, and the effort must be equally futile.

The analogy of the *Dagenhart* Case is clear. The congressional power over interstate commerce is, within its proper scope, just as complete and unlimited as the congressional power to tax, and the legislative motive in its exercise is just as free from judicial suspicion and inquiry. Yet when Congress threatened to stop interstate commerce in ordinary and necessary commodities, unobjectionable as subjects of transportation, and to deny the same to the people of a state in order to coerce them into compliance with Congress' regulation of state concerns, the court said this was not in fact regulation of interstate commerce, but rather that of state concerns and was invalid. So here the so-called tax is a penalty to coerce people of a state to act as Congress wishes them to act in respect of a matter completely the business of the state government under the federal Constitution. This case requires as did the *Dagenhart* Case the application of the principle announced by Chief Justice Marshall in McCulloch v. Maryland, 4 Wheat. 316, 423 (4 L.Ed. 579), in a much-quoted passage:

"Should Congress, in the execution of its powers, adopt measures which are prohibited by the Constitution; or should Congress, under the pretext of executing its powers, pass laws for the accomplishment of objects not intrusted to the government; it would become the painful duty of this tribunal, should a case requiring such a decision come before it, to say that such an act was not the law of the land."

*   *   *

For the reasons given, we must hold the Child Labor Tax Law invalid and the judgment of the District Court is

Affirmed.

Mr. Justice CLARKE, dissents.

UNITED STATES v. BUTLER

Supreme Court of the United States, 1936
297 U.S. 1, 56 S.Ct. 312, 80 L.Ed. 477

In order to deal with the chronic overproduction of farm products and consequent depression of farm income, Congress enacted the Agricultural Adjustment Act of 1933. Under terms of the act, farmers were to receive payments from the government in return for agreeing to reduce crop production. Money for this subsidy was to come from a tax levied on the processor of the commodity. The tax was to be levied at a fluctuating annual rate equal to the difference between the current average farm price and the value of the commodity during the "fair exchange" base period 1909–1914. Butler, the receiver for Hoosac Mills, a processor of cotton, refused to pay the tax. The U. S. District Court found for the United States and ordered Butler to pay the tax. The U. S. Circuit Court of Appeals reversed, and the government appealed.

Mr. Justice ROBERTS delivered the opinion of the Court.

*   *   *

The tax can only be sustained by ignoring the avowed purpose and operation of the act, and holding it a measure merely laying an excise upon processors to raise revenue for the support of government. Beyond cavil the sole object of the legislation is to restore the purchasing power of agricultural products to a parity with that prevailing in an earlier day; to take money from the processor and bestow it upon farmers who will reduce their acreage for the accomplishment of the proposed end, and, meanwhile, to aid these farmers during the period required to bring the prices of their crops to the desired level.

The tax plays an indispensable part in the plan of regulation. As stated by the Agricultural Adjustment Administrator, it is "the heart of the law"; a means of "accomplishing one or both of two things intended to help farmers attain parity prices and purchasing power." A tax automatically goes into effect for a commodity when the Secretary of Agriculture determines that rental or benefit payments are to be made for reduction of production of that commodity. The tax is to cease when rental or benefit payments cease. The rate is fixed with the purpose of bringing about crop reduction and price raising. It is to equal the difference between the "current average farm price" and "fair exchange value." It may be altered to such amount as will prevent accumulation of surplus stocks. If the Secretary finds the policy of the act will not be promoted by the levy of the tax for a given commodity, he may exempt it. * * * The whole revenue from the levy is appropriated in aid of crop control; none of it is made available for general governmental use. The entire agricultural adjustment program embodied in title 1 of the act is to become inoperative when, in the judgment of the President, the national economic emergency ends; and as to any commodity he may ter-

minate the provisions of the law, if he finds them no longer requisite to carrying out the declared policy with respect to such commodity. * * *

The statute not only avows an aim foreign to the procurement of revenue for the support of government, but by its operation shows the exaction laid upon processors to be the necessary means for the intended control of agricultural production.

* * *

It is inaccurate and misleading to speak of the exaction from processors prescribed by the challenged act as a tax, or to say that as a tax it is subject to no infirmity. A tax, in the general understanding of the term, and as used in the Constitution, signifies an exaction for the support of the government. The word has never been thought to connote the expropriation of money from one group for the benefit of another. We may concede that the latter sort of imposition is constitutional when imposed to effectuate regulation of a matter in which both groups are interested and in respect of which there is a power of legislative regulation. But manifestly no justification for it can be found unless as an integral part of such regulation. The exaction cannot be wrested out of its setting, denominated an excise for raising revenue, and legalized by ignoring its purpose as a mere instrumentality for bringing about a desired end. To do this would be to shut our eyes to what all others than we can see and understand. Child Labor Tax Case, 259 U.S. 20, 37, 42 S.Ct. 449.

We conclude that the act is one regulating agricultural production; that the tax is a mere incident of such regulation; and that the respondents have standing to challenge the legality of the exaction.

It does not follow that, as the act is not an exertion of the taxing power and the exaction not a true tax, the statute is void or the exaction uncollectible. For, to paraphrase what was said in the Head Money Cases, * * * 112 U.S. 580, page 596, 5 S.Ct. 247, 252, if this is an expedient regulation by Congress, of a subject within one of its granted powers, "and the end to be attained is one falling within that power, the act is not void because, within a loose and more extended sense than was used in the constitution," the exaction is called a tax.

* * * The government asserts that even if the respondents may question the propriety of the appropriation embodied in the statute, their attack must fail because article 1, § 8 of the Constitution, authorizes the contemplated expenditure of the funds raised by the tax. This contention presents the great and the controlling question in the case. We approach its decision with a sense of our grave responsibility to render judgment in accordance with the principles established for the governance of all three branches of the government.

There should be no misunderstanding as to the function of this court in such a case. It is sometimes said that the court assumes a power to overrule or control the action of the people's representatives. This is a misconception. The Constitution is the supreme law of the land ordained and established by the people. All legislation must conform to the principles it lays down. When an act of Congress is appropriately challenged in the courts as not conforming to the constitutional mandate, the judi-

cial branch of the government has only one duty; to lay the article of the Constitution which is invoked beside the statute which is challenged and to decide whether the latter squares with the former. All the court does, or can do, is to announce its considered judgment upon the question. The only power it has, if such it may be called, is the power of judgment. This court neither approves nor condemns any legislative policy. Its delicate and difficult office is to ascertain and declare whether the legislation is in accordance with, or in contravention of, the provisions of the Constitution; and, having done that, its duty ends.

The question is not what power the federal government ought to have, but what powers in fact have been given by the people. It hardly seems necessary to reiterate that ours is a dual form of government; that in every state there are two governments; the state and the United States. Each state has all governmental powers save such as the people, by their Constitution, have conferred upon the United States, denied to the states, or reserved to themselves. The federal union is a government of delegated powers. It has only such as are expressly conferred upon it and such as are reasonably to be implied from those granted. In this respect we differ radically from nations where all legislative power, without restriction or limitation, is vested in a parliament or other legislative body subject to no restrictions except the discretion of its members.

Article 1, § 8, of the Constitution, vests sundry powers in the Congress. But two of its clauses have any bearing upon the validity of the statute under review.

The third clause endows the Congress with power "to regulate Commerce * * * among the several States." Despite a reference in its first section to a burden upon, and an obstruction of the normal currents of, commerce, the act under review does not purport to regulate transactions in interstate or foreign commerce. Its stated purpose is the control of agricultural production, a purely local activity, in an effort to raise the prices paid the farmer. Indeed, the government does not attempt to uphold the validity of the act on the basis of the commerce clause, which, for the purpose of the present case, may be put aside as irrelevant.

The clause thought to authorize the legislation, the first, confers upon the Congress power "to lay and collect Taxes, Duties, Imposts and Excises, to pay the Debts and provide for the common Defence and general Welfare of the United States." * * * It is not contended that this provision grants power to regulate agricultural production upon the theory that such legislation would promote the general welfare. The government concedes that the phrase "to provide for the general welfare" qualifies the power "to lay and collect taxes." The view that the clause grants power to provide for the general welfare, independently of the taxing power, has never been authoritatively accepted. Mr. Justice Story points out that, if it were adopted, "it is obvious that under color of the generality of the words, to 'provide for the common defence and general welfare', the government of the United States, is, in reality, a government of general and unlimited powers, notwithstanding the subsequent enumeration of specific powers." The true construc-

tion undoubtedly is that the only thing granted is the power to tax for the purpose of providing funds for payment of the nation's debts and making provision for the general welfare.

Nevertheless, the government asserts that warrant is found in this clause for the adoption of the Agricultural Adjustment Act. The argument is that Congress may appropriate and authorize the spending of moneys for the "general welfare"; that the phrase should be liberally construed to cover anything conducive to national welfare; that decision as to what will promote such welfare rests with Congress alone, and the courts may not review its determination; and, finally, that the appropriation under attack was in fact for the general welfare of the United States.

The Congress is expressly empowered to lay taxes to provide for the general welfare. Funds in the Treasury as a result of taxation may be expended only through appropriation. Article 1, § 9, cl. 7. They can never accomplish the objects for which they were collected, unless the power to appropriate is as broad as the power to tax. The necessary implication from the terms of the grant is that the public funds may be appropriated "to provide for the general welfare of the United States." These words cannot be meaningless, else they would not have been used. The conclusion must be that they were intended to limit and define the granted power to raise and to expend money. How shall they be construed to effectuate the intent of the instrument?

Since the foundation of the nation, sharp differences of opinion have persisted as to the true interpretation of the phrase. Madison asserted it amounted to no more than a reference to the other powers enumerated in the subsequent clauses of the same section; that, as the United States is a government of limited and enumerated powers, the grant of power to tax and spend for the general national welfare must be confined to the enumerated legislative fields committed to the Congress. In this view the phrase is mere tautology, for taxation and appropriation are or may be necessary incidents of the exercise of any of the enumerated legislative powers. Hamilton, on the other hand, maintained the clause confers a power separate and distinct from those later enumerated, is not restricted in meaning by the grant of them, and Congress consequently has a substantive power to tax and to appropriate, limited only by the requirement that it shall be exercised to provide for the general welfare of the United States. Each contention has had the support of those whose views are entitled to weight. This court has noticed the question, but has never found it necessary to decide which is the true construction. Mr. Justice Story, in his Commentaries, espouses the Hamiltonian position. We shall not review the writings of public men and commentators or discuss the legislative practice. Study of all these leads us to conclude that the reading advocated by Mr. Justice Story is the correct one. While, therefore, the power to tax is not unlimited, its confines are set in the clause which confers it, and not in those of section 8 which bestow and define the legislative powers of the Congress. It results that the power of Congress to authorize expenditure of public moneys for public purposes is not limited by the direct grants of legislative power found in the Constitution.

But the adoption of the broader construction leaves the power to spend subject to limitations.

As Story says: "The Constitution was, from its very origin, contemplated to be the frame of a national government, of special and enumerated powers, and not of general and unlimited powers."

Again he says: "A power to lay taxes for the common defence and general welfare of the United States is not in common sense a general power. It is limited to those objects. It cannot constitutionally transcend them."

That the qualifying phrase must be given effect all advocates of broad construction admit. Hamilton, in his well known Report on Manufactures, states that the purpose must be "general, and not local." Monroe, an advocate of Hamilton's doctrine, wrote: "Have Congress a right to raise and appropriate the money to any and to every purpose according to their will and pleasure? They certainly have not." Story says that if the tax be not proposed for the common defense or general welfare, but for other objects wholly extraneous, it would be wholly indefensible upon constitutional principles. And he makes it clear that the powers of taxation and appropriation extend only to matters of national, as distinguished from local, welfare.

* * *

We are not now required to ascertain the scope of the phrase "general welfare of the United States" or to determine whether an appropriation in aid of agriculture falls within it. Wholly apart from that question, another principle embedded in our Constitution prohibits the enforcement of the Agricultural Adjustment Act.

The act invades the reserved rights of the states. It is a statutory plan to regulate and control agricultural production, a matter beyond the powers delegated to the federal government. The tax, the appropriation of the funds raised, and the direction for their disbursement, are but parts of the plan. They are but means to an unconstitutional end.

From the accepted doctrine that the United States is a government of delegated powers, it follows that those not expressly granted, or reasonably to be implied from, such as are conferred, are reserved to the states or to the people. To forestall any suggestion to the contrary, the Tenth Amendment was adopted. The same proposition, otherwise stated, is that powers not granted are prohibited. None to regulate agricultural production is given, and therefore legislation by Congress for that purpose is forbidden.

It is an established principle that the attainment of a prohibited end may not be accomplished under the pretext of the exertion of powers which are granted.

*   *   *

The power of taxation, which is expressly granted, may, of course, be adopted as a means to carry into operation another power also expressly granted. But resort to the taxing power to effectuate an end which is not legitimate, not within the scope of the Constitution, is obviously inadmissible.

*   *   * If the taxing power may not be used as the instrument to enforce a regulation of matters of state concern with respect to which the Congress has no authority to interfere, may it, as in the present case, be employed to raise the money necessary to purchase a compliance which the Congress is powerless to command? The government asserts that whatever might be said against the validity of the plan, if compulsory, it is constitutionally sound because the end is accomplished by voluntary co-operation. There are two sufficient answers to the contention. The regulation is not in fact voluntary. The farmer, of course, may refuse to comply, but the price of such refusal is the loss of benefits. The amount offered is intended to be sufficient to exert pressure on him to agree to the proposed regulation. The power to confer or withhold unlimited benefits is the power to coerce or destroy. *   *   *

*   *   *

But if the plan were one for purely voluntary co-operation it would stand no better so far as federal power is concerned. At best, it is a scheme for purchasing with federal funds submission to federal regulation of a subject reserved to the states.

*   *   *

Congress has no power to enforce its commands on the farmer to the ends sought by the Agricultural Adjustment Act. It must follow that it may not indirectly accomplish those ends by taxing and spending to purchase compliance. The Constitution and the entire plan of our government negative any such use of the power to tax and to spend as the act undertakes to authorize. It does not help to declare that local conditions throughout the nation have created a situation of national concern; for this is but to say that whenever there is a widespread similarity of local conditions, Congress may ignore constitutional limitations upon its

own powers and usurp those reserved to the states. If, in lieu of
compulsory regulation of subjects
within the states' reserved jurisdiction, which is prohibited, the Congress could invoke the taxing and
spending power as a means to accomplish the same end, clause 1 of section 8 of article 1 would become the
instrument for total subversion of
the governmental powers reserved to
the individual states.

If the act before us is a proper
exercise of the federal taxing power,
evidently the regulation of all industry throughout the United States
may be accomplished by similar exercises of the same power. It would
be possible to exact money from one
branch of an industry and pay it to
another branch in every field of activity which lies within the province
of the states. The mere threat of
such a procedure might well induce
the surrender of rights and the compliance with federal regulation as the
price of continuance in business.
* * *

* * *

Until recently no suggestion of
the existence of any such power in
the federal government has been advanced. The expressions of the
framers of the Constitution, the decisions of this court interpreting that
instrument and the writings of great
commentators will be searched in
vain for any suggestion that there
exists in the clause under discussion
or elsewhere in the Constitution, the
authority whereby every provision
and every fair, implication from that
instrument may be subverted, the independence of the individual states
obliterated, and the United States
converted into a central government
exercising uncontrolled police power
in every state of the Union, super-

seding all local control or regulation
of the affairs or concerns of the
states.

* * *

The judgment is affirmed.

Mr. Justice STONE (dissenting).

I think the judgment should be reversed.

The present stress of widely held
and strongly expressed differences
of opinion of the wisdom of the Agricultural Adjustment Act makes it important, in the interest of clear thinking and sound result, to emphasize at
the outset certain propositions which
should have controlling influence in
determining the validity of the act.
They are:

1. The power of courts to declare a statute unconstitutional is
subject to two guiding principles of
decision which ought never to be absent from judicial consciousness.
One is that courts are concerned only
with the power to enact statutes, not
with their wisdom. The other is that
while unconstitutional exercise of
power by the executive and legislative branches of the government is
subject to judicial restraint, the only
check upon our own exercise of power is our own sense of self-restraint.
For the removal of unwise laws from
the statute books appeal lies, not to
the courts, but to the ballot and to
the processes of democratic government.

2. The constitutional power of
Congress to levy an excise tax upon
the processing of agricultural products is not questioned. The present
levy is held invalid, not for any want
of power in Congress to lay such a
tax to defray public expenditures, including those for the general welfare, but because the use to which its
proceeds are put is disapproved.

3. As the present depressed state of agriculture is nation wide in its extent and effects, there is no basis for saying that the expenditure of public money in aid of farmers is not within the specifically granted power of Congress to levy taxes to "provide for the * * * general welfare." The opinion of the Court does not declare otherwise.

4. No question of a variable tax fixed from time to time by fiat of the Secretary of Agriculture, or of unauthorized delegation of legislative power, is now presented. The schedule of rates imposed by the secretary in accordance with the original command of Congress has since been specifically adopted and confirmed by act of Congress, which has declared that it shall be the lawful tax. Act of August 24, 1935, 49 Stat. 750, 7 U.S.C.A. § 602 et seq. That is the tax which the government now seeks to collect. Any defects there may have been in the manner of laying the tax by the secretary have now been removed by the exercise of the power of Congress to pass a curative statute validating an intended, though defective, tax. * * * The Agricultural Adjustment Act as thus amended declares that none of its provisions shall fail because others are pronounced invalid.

It is with these preliminary and hardly controverted matters in mind that we should direct our attention to the pivot on which the decision of the Court is made to turn. It is that a levy unquestionably within the taxing power of Congress may be treated as invalid because it is a step in a plan to regulate agricultural production and is thus a forbidden infringement of state power. The levy is not any the less an exercise of taxing power because it is intended to defray an expenditure for the general welfare rather than for some other support of government. Nor is the levy and collection of the tax pointed to as effecting the regulation. While all federal taxes inevitably have some influence on the internal economy of the states, it is not contended that the levy of a processing tax upon manufacturers using agricultural products as raw material has any perceptible regulatory effect upon either their production or manufacture. The tax is unlike the penalties which were held invalid in the Child Labor Tax Case, 259 U.S. 20, 42 S.Ct. 449, * * * because they were themselves the instruments of regulation by virtue of their coercive effect on matters left to the control of the states. Here regulation, if any there be, is accomplished not by the tax, but by the method by which its proceeds are expended, and would equally be accomplished by any like use of public funds, regardless of their source.

* * *

Of the assertion that the payments to farmers are coercive, it is enough to say that no such contention is pressed by the taxpayer, and no such consequences were to be anticipated or appear to have resulted from the administration of the act. The suggestion of coercion finds no support in the record or in any data showing the actual operation of the act. Threat of loss, not hope of gain, is the essence of economic coercion. * * *

* * *

It is upon the contention that state power is infringed by purchased regulation of agricultural production that chief reliance is placed. It is insisted that, while the Constitution gives to Congress, in specific and unambiguous terms, the power to tax and spend, the power is subject to limitations which do not find their origin in any express provision of the Constitution and to which other expressly delegated powers are not subject.

*　*　*

*　*　* The spending power of Congress is in addition to the legislative power and not subordinate to it. This independent grant of the power of the purse, and its very nature, involving in its exercise the duty to insure expenditure within the granted power, presuppose freedom of selection among divers ends and aims, and the capacity to impose such conditions as will render the choice effective. It is a contradiction in terms to say that there is power to spend for the national welfare, while rejecting any power to impose conditions reasonably adapted to the attainment of the end which alone would justify the expenditure.

The limitation now sanctioned must lead to absurd consequences. The government may give seeds to farmers, but may not condition the gift upon their being planted in places where they are most needed or even planted at all. The government may give money to the unemployed, but may not ask that those who get it shall give labor in return, or even use it to support their families. It may give money to sufferers from earthquake, fire, tornado, pestilence, or flood, but may not impose conditions, health precautions, designed to prevent the spread of disease, or induce the movement of population to safer or more sanitary areas. All that, because it is purchased regulation infringing state powers, must be left for the states, who are unable or unwilling to sup-

ply the necessary relief. *　*　* Do all its activities collapse because, in order to effect the permissible purpose in myriad ways the money is paid out upon terms and conditions which influence action of the recipients within the states, which Congress cannot command? The answer would seem plain. If the expenditure is for a national public purpose, that purpose will not be thwarted because payment is on condition which will advance that purpose. The action which Congress induces by payments of money to promote the general welfare, but which it does not command or coerce, is but an incident to a specifically granted power, but a permissible means to a legitimate end. If appropriation in aid of a program of curtailment of agricultural production is constitutional, and it is not denied that it is, payment to farmers on condition that they reduce their crop acreage is constitutional. It is not any the less so because the farmer at his own option promises to fulfill the condition.

That the governmental power of the purse is a great one is not now for the first time announced. Every student of the history of government and economics is aware of its magnitude and of its existence in every civilized government. Both were well understood by the framers of the Constitution when they sanctioned the grant of the spending power to the federal government, and both were recognized by Hamilton and Story, whose views of the spending power as standing on a parity with the other powers specifically granted, have hitherto been generally accepted.

The suggestion that it must now be curtailed by judicial fiat because it may be abused by unwise use hardly rises to the dignity of argument. So may judicial power be abused. "The power to tax is the power to destroy," but we do not, for that reason, doubt its existence, or hold that its efficacy is to be restricted by its incidental or collateral effects upon the states. * * * The power to tax and spend is not without constitutional restraints. One restriction is that the purpose must be truly national. Another is that it may not be used to coerce action left to state control. Another is the conscience and patriotism of Congress and the Executive. "It must be remembered that legislatures are ultimate guardians of the liberties and welfare of the people in quite as great a degree as the courts." Justice Holmes, in Missouri, Kansas & Texas R. Co. v. May, 194 U.S. 267, 270, 24 S.Ct. 638, 639.

A tortured construction of the Constitution is not to be justified by recourse to extreme examples of reckless congressional spending which might occur if courts could not prevent—expenditures which, even if they could be thought to effect any national purpose, would be possible only by action of a legislature lost to all sense of public responsibility. Such suppositions are addressed to the mind accustomed to believe that it is the business of courts to sit in judgment on the wisdom of legislative action. Courts are not the only agency of government that must be assumed to have capacity to govern. Congress and the courts both unhappily may falter or be mistaken in the performance of their constitutional duty. But interpretation of our great charter of government which proceeds on any assumption that the responsibility for the preservation of our institutions is the exclusive concern of any one of the three branches of government, or that it alone can save them from destruction is far more likely, in the long run, "to obliterate the constituent members" of "an indestructible union of indestructible states" than the frank recognition that language, even of a constitution, may mean what it says: that the power to tax and spend includes the power to relieve a nationwide economic maladjustment by conditional gifts of money.

Mr. Justice BRANDEIS and Mr. Justice CARDOZO join in this opinion.

MULFORD v. SMITH

Supreme Court of the United States, 1939
307 U.S. 38, 59 S.Ct. 648, 83 L.Ed. 1092

The facts are set out in the opinion below.

Mr. Justice ROBERTS delivered the opinion of the Court.

The appellants, producers of flue-cured tobacco, assert that the Agricultural Adjustment Act of 1938, is unconstitutional as it affects their 1938 crop.

The portions of the statute involved are those included in Title III, providing marketing quotas for flue-cured tobacco. The Act directs that when the supply is found to exceed the level defined in the Act as the "reserve supply level" a national marketing quota shall become effective which will permit enough flue-cured tobacco to be marketed during the ensuing marketing year to maintain the supply at the reserve supply level. The quota is to be apportioned to the farms on which tobacco is grown. Penalties are to be paid by tobacco auction warehousemen for marketing tobacco from a farm in excess of its quota.

Section 311 is a finding by the Congress that the marketing of tobacco is a basic industry which directly affects interstate and foreign commerce; that stable conditions in such marketing are necessary to the general welfare; that tobacco is sold on a national market and it and its products move almost wholly in interstate and foreign commerce; that without federal assistance the farmers are unable to bring about orderly marketing, with the consequence that abnormally excessive supplies are produced and dumped indiscriminately on the national market; that this disorderly marketing of excess supply burdens and obstructs interstate and foreign commerce, causes reduction in prices and consequent injury to commerce, creates disparity between the prices of tobacco in interstate and foreign commerce and the prices of industrial products in such commerce, and diminishes the volume of interstate commerce in industrial products; and that the establishment of quotas as provided by the Act is necessary and appropriate to promote, foster and obtain an orderly flow of tobacco in interstate and foreign commerce. [The opinion goes on to describe the mechanism for establishing the quotas: (1) the setting of a national quota per commodity by the secretary of agriculture; (2) ratification of the quota by two-thirds of the farmers producing the crop and voting in a referendum; (3) apportionment of the quota

among the states; (4) subsequent division of the state quotas by local committees to individual farmers; and (5) provisions for appeal of quota assignments in individual cases.]

* * *

Section 314 provides that if tobacco in excess of the quota for the farm on which the tobacco is produced is marketed through a warehouseman, the latter must pay to the Secretary a penalty equal to fifty per cent. of the market price of the excess, and may deduct an amount equivalent to the penalty from the price paid the producer.

Section 376 gives the United States a civil action for the recovery of unpaid penalties.

A few days before the 1938 auction sales were to take place, the appellants, who produce flue-cured tobacco in southern Georgia and northern Florida, filed a bill in equity in a Georgia state court against local warehousemen to restrain them from deducting penalties under the Act from the sales price of tobacco to be sold at their auction warehouses on behalf of appellants. The bill alleged that the Act is unconstitutional
* * *

* * *

The appellants plant themselves upon three propositions: (1) that the Act is a statutory plan to control agricultural production and, therefore, beyond the powers delegated to Congress; (2) that the standard for calculating farm quotas is uncertain, vague, and indefinite, resulting in an unconstitutional delegation of legislative power to the Secretary; (3) that, as applied to appellants' 1938 crop, the Act takes their property without due process of law.

* * * The statute does not purport to control production. It sets no limit upon the acreage which may be planted or produced and imposes no penalty for the planting and producing of tobacco in excess of the marketing quota. It purports to be solely a regulation of interstate commerce, which it reaches and affects at the throat where tobacco enters the stream of commerce,—the marketing warehouse. The record discloses that at least two-thirds of all flue-cured tobacco sold at auction warehouses is sold for immediate shipment to an interstate or foreign destination. In Georgia nearly one hundred per cent. of the tobacco so sold is purchased by extrastate purchasers. In markets where tobacco is sold to both interstate and intrastate purchasers it is not known, when the grower places his tobacco on the warehouse floor for sale, whether it is destined for interstate or intrastate commerce. Regulation to be effective, must, and therefore may constitutionally, apply to all sales. This court has recently declared that sales of tobacco by growers through warehousemen to purchasers for removal outside the state constitute interstate commerce. Any rule, such as that embodied in the Act, which is intended to foster, protect and conserve that commerce, or to prevent the flow of commerce from working harm to the people of the nation, is within the competence of Congress. Within these limits the exercise of the power, the grant being unlimited in its terms, may lawfully extend to the absolute prohibition of such commerce, and a fortiori to limitation of the amount of a given commodity which may be transported in such commerce. The motive of Congress in exerting the power is irrelevant to the validity of the legislation.

The provisions of the Act under review constitute a regulation of interstate and foreign commerce within the competency of Congress under the power delegated to it by the Constitution.

* * *

[The Court found no validity to the two remaining contentions.]

The decree is affirmed.

[Justices BUTLER and McREYNOLDS dissented.]

STEWARD MACHINE CO. v. DAVIS

Supreme Court of the United States, 1937
301 U.S. 548, 57 S.Ct. 883, 81 L.Ed. 1279

See p. 371.

UNITED STATES v. KAHRIGER

Supreme Court of the United States, 1953
345 U.S. 22, 73 S.Ct. 510, 97 L.Ed. 754

In addition to imposing a 10 percent excise tax on all wagers, the Revenue Act of 1951 required the payment of a fifty-dollar tax from those persons engaged in taking bets. Persons paying this occupational tax were required to register with a district collector of internal revenue to receive the tax stamp which was issued as proof of payment. Kahriger was accused of running a gambling operation without paying the tax. At a hearing in U.S. District Court, Kahriger moved to dismiss

the charge on the ground that the legislation was unconstitutional. The district
court granted the motion, whereupon the government appealed.

Mr. Justice REED delivered the opinion of the Court.

* * *

* * * The District Court sustained the motion on the authority of our opinion in United States v. Constantine, 296 U.S. 287, 56 S.Ct. 223. The court reasoned that while "the subject matter of this legislation so far as revenue purposes is concerned is within the scope of Federal authorities," the tax was unconstitutional in that the information called for by the registration provisions was "peculiarly applicable to the applicant from the standpoint of law enforcement and vice control," and therefore the whole of the legislation was an infringement by the Federal Government on the police power reserved to the states by the Tenth Amendment. United States v. Kahriger, D.C., 105 F.Supp. 322, 323.

The result below is at odds with the position of the seven other district courts which have considered the matter, and, in our opinion, is erroneous.

In the term following the *Constantine* opinion, this Court pointed out in Sonzinsky v. United States, 300 U.S. 506, at page 513, 57 S.Ct. 554, at page 555 (a case involving a tax on a "limited class" of objectionable firearms alleged to be prohibitory in effect and "to disclose unmistakably the legislative purpose to regulate rather than to tax"), that the subject of the tax in *Constantine* was "described or treated as criminal by the taxing statute." The tax in the *Constantine* case was a special additional excise tax of $1,000,

placed only on persons who carried on a liquor business in violation of state law. The wagering tax with which we are here concerned applies to all persons engaged in the business of receiving wagers regardless of whether such activity violates state law.

The substance of respondent's position with respect to the Tenth Amendment is that Congress has chosen to tax a specified business which is not within its power to regulate. The precedents are many upholding taxes similar to this wagering tax as a proper exercise of the federal taxing power. * * *

Appellee would have us say that because there is legislative history indicating a congressional motive to suppress wagering, this tax is not a proper exercise of such taxing power. In the *License Cases*, supra, it was admitted that the federal license "discouraged" the activities. The intent to curtail and hinder, as well as tax, was also manifest in the following cases, and in each of them the tax was upheld: Veazie Bank v. Fenno, 8 Wall. 533, 19 L.Ed. 482 (tax on paper money issued by state banks); McCray v. United States, 195 U.S. 27, 59, 24 S.Ct. 769, 777 (tax on colored oleomargarine); United States v. Doremus, 249 U.S. 86, 39 S.Ct. 214, and Nigro v. United States, 276 U.S. 332, 48 S.Ct. 388 (tax on narcotics); Sonzinsky v. United States, 300 U.S. 506, 57 S.Ct. 554 (tax on firearms); United States v. Sanchez, 340 U.S. 42, 71 S.Ct. 108 (tax on marihuana).

It is conceded that a federal excise tax does not cease to be valid merely because it discourages or deters the activities taxed. Nor is the tax invalid because the revenue obtained is negligible. Appellee, however, argues that the sole purpose of the statute is to penalize only illegal gambling in the states through the guise of a tax measure. As with the above excise taxes which we have held to be valid, the instant tax has a regulatory effect. But regardless of its regulatory effect, the wagering tax produces revenue. As such it surpasses both the narcotics and firearms taxes which we have found valid.

It is axiomatic that the power of Congress to tax is extensive and sometimes falls with crushing effect on businesses deemed unessential or inimical to the public welfare, or where, as in dealings with narcotics, the collection of the tax also is difficult. As is well known, the constitutional restraints on taxing are few. * * *

The difficulty of saying when the power to lay uniform taxes is curtailed, because its use brings a result beyond the direct legislative power of Congress, has given rise to diverse decisions. In that area of abstract ideas, a final definition of the line between state and federal power has baffled judges and legislators.

* * * Where federal legislation has rested on other congressional powers, such as the Necessary and Proper Clause or the Commerce Clause, this Court has generally sustained the statutes, despite their effect on matters ordinarily considered state concern. When federal power to regulate is found, its exercise is a matter for Congress. Where Congress has employed the taxing clause a greater variation in the decisions has resulted. The division in this

Court has been more acute. Without any specific differentiation between the power to tax and other federal powers, the indirect results from the exercise of the power to tax have raised more doubts. * * * It is hard to understand why the power to tax should raise more doubts because of indirect effects than other federal powers.

Penalty provisions in tax statutes added for breach of a regulation concerning activities in themselves subject only to state regulation have caused this Court to declare the enactments invalid. Unless there are provisions, extraneous to any tax need, courts are without authority to limit the exercise of the taxing power. All the provisions of this excise are adapted to the collection of a valid tax.

Nor do we find the registration requirements of the wagering tax offensive. All that is required is the filing of names, addresses, and places of business. This is quite general in tax returns. Such data are directly and intimately related to the collection of the tax and are "obviously supportable as in aid of a revenue purpose." Sonzinsky v. United States, 300 U.S. 506, at page 513, 57 S.Ct. 554, at page 555. The registration provisions make the tax simpler to collect.

Appellee's second assertion is that the wagering tax is unconstitutional because it is a denial of the privilege against self-incrimination as guaranteed by the Fifth Amendment.

Since appellee failed to register for the wagering tax, it is difficult to see how he can now claim the privilege even assuming that the disclosure of violations of law is called for. * * *

Assuming that respondent can raise the self-incrimination issue, that privilege has relation only to past acts, not to future acts that may or may not be committed. 8 Wigmore (3d ed., 1940) § 2259(c). If respondent wishes to take wagers subject to excise taxes under § 3285, supra, he must pay an occupational tax and register. Under the registration provisions of the wagering tax, appellee is not compelled to confess to acts already committed, he is merely informed by the statute that in order to engage in the business of wagering in the future he must fulfill certain conditions.

* * *

Reversed.

Mr. Justice JACKSON, concurring.

I concur in the judgment and opinion of the Court, but with such doubt that if the minority agreed upon an opinion which did not impair legitimate use of the taxing power I probably would join it. But we deal here with important and contrasting values in our scheme of government, and it is important that neither be allowed to destroy the other.

[Justice JACKSON went on to express grave concern over the self-incrimination aspects of the tax.]

* * *

Of course, all taxation has a tendency proportioned to its burdensomeness to discourage the activity taxed. One cannot formulate a revenue-raising plan that would not have economic and social consequences. Congress may and should place the burden of taxes where it will least handicap desirable activities and bear most heavily on useless or harmful ones. If Congress may tax one citizen to the point of discouragement for making an honest living, it is hard to say that it may not do the same to another just because he makes a sinister living. If the law-abiding must tell all to the tax collector, it is difficult to excuse one because his business is law-breaking.

* * *

But here is a purported tax law which requires no reports and lays no tax except on specified gamblers whose calling in most states is illegal. It requires this group to step forward and identify themselves, not because they like others have income, but because of its source. This is difficult to regard as a rational or good-faith revenue measure, despite the deference that is due Congress. On the contrary, it seems to be a plan to tax out of existence the professional gambler whom it has been found impossible to prosecute out of existence. Few pursuits are entitled to less consideration at our hands than professional gambling, but the plain unwelcome fact is that it continues to survive because a large and influential part of our population patronizes and protects it.

The United States has a system of taxation by confession. That a people so numerous, scattered and individualistic, annually assesses itself with a tax liability, often in highly burdensome amounts, is a reassuring sign of the stability and vitality of our system of self-government. What surprised me in once trying to help administer these laws was not to discover examples of recalcitrance, fraud or self-serving mistakes in reporting, but to discover that such derelictions were so few. It will be a sad day for the revenues if the good will of the people toward their taxing system is frittered away in efforts to accomplish by taxation moral reforms that cannot be accomplished by direct legislation. But the evil that can come from this statute will probably soon make itself manifest to Congress. The evil of a judicial decision impairing the legitimate taxing power by extreme constitutional interpretations might not be transient. Even though this statute approaches the fair limits of constitutionality, I join the decision of the Court.

Mr. Justice FRANKFURTER, dissenting.

The Court's opinion manifests a natural difficulty in reaching its conclusion. Constitutional issues are likely to arise whenever Congress draws on the taxing power not to raise revenue but to regulate conduct. This is so, of course, because of the distribution of legislative power as between the Congress and the State Legislatures in the regulation of conduct.

* * *

It is a wholly different thing to hold that Congress, which cannot constitutionally grapple directly with gambling in the States, may compel self-incriminating disclosures for the enforcement of State gambling laws, merely because it does so under the guise of a revenue measure obviously passed not for revenue purposes. The motive of congressional legislation is not for our scrutiny, provided only that the ulterior purpose is not expressed in ways which negative what the revenue words on their face express and, which do not seek enforcement of the formal revenue purpose through means that of-

fend those standards of decency in our civilization against which due process is a barrier.

I would affirm this judgment.

Mr. Justice DOUGLAS while not joining in the entire opinion, agrees with the views expressed herein that this tax is an attempt by the Congress to control conduct which the Constitution has left to the responsibility of the States.

Mr. Justice BLACK, with whom Mr. Justice DOUGLAS concurs, dissenting.

The Fifth Amendment declares that no person "shall be compelled in any criminal case to be a witness against himself." The Court nevertheless here sustains an Act which requires a man to register and confess that he is engaged in the business of gambling. I think this confession can provide a basis to convict him of a federal crime for having gambled before registration without paying a federal tax. * * * Whether or not the Act has this effect, I am sure that it creates a squeezing device contrived to put a man in federal prison if he refuses to confess himself into a state prison as a violator of state gambling laws. The coercion of confessions is a common but justly criticized practice of many countries that do not have or live up to a Bill of Rights. But we have a Bill of Rights that condemns coerced confessions, however refined or legalistic may be the technique of extortion. I would hold that this Act violates the Fifth Amendment. * * *

In Marchetti v. United States, 390 U.S. 39, 88 S.Ct. 697 (1968), the Supreme Court, Chief Justice Warren dissenting and Justice Marshall not participating, overruled *Kahriger*. Justice Harlan, speaking for the majority, focused the issue squarely on the ground of Justice Black's dissent in that case:

> The issue before us is *not* whether the United States may tax activities which a State or Congress has declared unlawful. The Court has repeatedly indicated that the unlawfulness of an activity does not prevent its taxation, and nothing that follows is intended to limit or diminish the vitality of those cases. * * * The issue is instead whether the methods employed by Congress in the federal wagering tax statutes are, in this situation, consistent with the limitations created by the privilege against self-incrimination guaranteed by the Fifth Amendment. * * *

Justice Harlan described several specific features of the statute, flowing from the act of registration, which bore on the self-incrimination issue:

> In addition, registrants are obliged to post the revenue stamps which denote payment of the occupational tax "conspicuously" in their principal places of business, or, if they lack such places, to keep the stamps on their persons, and to exhibit them upon demand to any Treasury officer. * * * They are required to preserve daily records indicating the gross amount of the wagers as to which they are liable for taxation, and to permit inspection of their books of account. 26 U.S.C.A. §§ 4403, 4423. Moreover, each principal internal revenue office is instructed to maintain for public inspection a listing of all who have paid the occupational tax, and to provide certified copies of the listing upon request to any state or local prosecuting officer. * * * Finally, payment of the wagering taxes is declared not to "exempt any person from any penalty provided by a law of the United States or of any State for engaging" in any taxable activity. * * *

In light of the fact that every state except Nevada outlawed gambling, the Court took notice of the role played by the information gained by way of compliance with this statute:

> Information obtained as a consequence of the federal wagering tax laws is readily available to assist the efforts of state and federal authorities to enforce these penalties. Section 6107 of Title 26 requires the principal internal revenue offices to provide to prosecuting officers a listing of those who have paid the occupational tax. Section 6806(c) obliges taxpayers either to post the revenue stamp "conspicuously" in their principal places of business, or to keep it on their persons, and to produce it on the demand of Treasury officers. Evidence of the possession of a federal wagering tax stamp, or of payment of the wagering taxes, has often been admitted at trial in state and federal prosecutions for gambling offenses; such evidence has doubtless proved useful even more frequently to lead prosecuting authorities to other evidence upon which convictions have subsequently been obtained. Finally, we are obliged to notice that a former Commissioner of Internal Revenue has acknowledged that the Service "makes available" to law enforcement agencies the names and addresses of those who have paid the wagering taxes, and that it is in "full cooperation" with the efforts of the Attorney General of the United States to suppress organized gambling. * * *

All of this led to the Court's conclusion that:

> * * * Petitioner was confronted by a comprehensive system of fed-
> eral and state prohibitions against wagering activities; he was required, on
> pain of criminal prosecution, to provide information which he might reason-
> ably suppose would be available to prosecuting authorities, and which
> would surely prove a significant "link in a chain" of evidence tending to
> establish his guilt. Unlike the income tax return * * * every portion of
> these requirements had the direct and unmistakable consequence of incrimi-
> nating petitioner; the application of the constitutional privilege to the entire
> registration procedure was in this instance neither "extreme" nor "extrava-
> gant." * * * It would appear to follow that petitioner's assertion of the
> privilege as a defense to this prosecution was entirely proper, and accord-
> ingly should have sufficed to prevent his conviction.

The Court, therefore, struck down Marchetti's conviction for refusing to comply
with the occupational tax portion of the 1951 act. In doing so, however, it emphasized the narrow nature of its holding:

> We emphasize that we do not hold that these wagering tax provisions are
> as such constitutionally impermissible; we hold only that those who prop-
> erly assert the constitutional privilege as to these provisions may not be
> criminally punished for failure to comply with their requirements. If, in
> different circumstances, a taxpayer is not confronted by substantial
> hazards of self-incrimination, or if he is otherwise outside the privilege's
> protection, nothing we decide today would shield him from the various pen-
> alties prescribed by the wagering tax statutes.

In a companion case, Grosso v. United States, 390 U.S. 62, 88 S.Ct. 709 (1968),
the Court similarly struck down the excise tax provisions of the same statute.
There the Court found submission of the required monthly reports necessary to
compute the 10 percent excise tax " * * * evidence in the most direct fashion
[of] the fact of the taxpayer's wagering activities."

Chapter 7

The State Police Power and Business Regulation

The Supreme Court's important role as umpire of the federal system comes to light most clearly in those circumstances when it is asked to settle conflicts between the national interest served by maintaining an unobstructed flow of interstate commerce and a state's exercise of its reserved powers to protect the health, safety, and welfare of its residents. While the Court, as we have seen, gives a very generous, not to say pre-emptive, weight to national power when exercised by Congress to regulate interstate commerce, it has never accepted the proposition that, even when dormant, the commerce power necessarily precludes the exercise of state power. This decision to leave some play in the joints of the federal system inescapably involves the Court in the methodology of interest balancing.

As we noted earlier, even Chief Justice Marshall acknowledged the possibility several years after the decision in *Gibbons* v. *Ogden* that, absent congressional action, state legislation regulating business which happened to touch interstate commerce was not necessarily unconstitutional. It remained, however, for the Court under the influence of Marshall's successor, Roger Taney, fully to develop the possibility. In Mayor of City of New York v. Miln, 36 U.S. (11 Pet.) 102, 9 L.Ed. 648 (1837), the Court upheld a state statute designed to control the size of the welfare rolls by discouraging the immigration of indigents through the port of New York. Among other things the act required the master of a ship entering the port from any state or foreign country to submit a report containing specified information about the passengers on board and, upon demand of the mayor, to pay bonds for the support of foreign passengers who later became public charges. Speaking for the Court, Justice Barbour found the act was "not a regulation of commerce, but of police," likening it to an "inspection law." Said the Court, "We think it as competent and as necessary for a State to provide precautionary measures against the moral pestilence of paupers, vagabonds, and possibly convicts, as it is to guard against the physical pestilence which may arise from unsound and infectious articles imported, or from a ship, the crew of which may be laboring under an infectious disease." In dissent, Justice Story characterized the law as an unconstitutional restraint on interstate and foreign commerce and allowed as how, from a personal conversation with John Marshall, New York's barrier to discourage the arrival of welfare recipients "fell directly within the principles established in the case of *Gibbons* v. *Ogden*" and went further than anything the late chief justice would have sanctioned. The position the Taney Court took in *Miln* is also further than any the Court would be willing to take today. In Edwards v. California, 314 U.S. 160, 62 S.Ct. 164 (1941), the Court unanimously held unconstitutional a California law which made it a misdemeanor to bring "into the state any indigent person who is not a resident of the state, knowing him to be an indigent person." Five Justices agreed it was clearly "an unconstitutional barrier to interstate commerce"; the remaining four were of the view that the right to travel interstate was "an incident of *national* citizenship protected by the privileges and immunities clause of the Fourteenth Amendment against state interference." More recently, the Court has reaffirmed its repudiation of the outlook in *Miln* by holding in *Shapiro* v. *Thompson* (p. 828) that a state may not even impose a one-year residency requirement as a prerequisite to eligibility for public assistance.

The Taney Court's best-remembered and most influential effort at coming to grips with the clash of national and state interests in the regulation of commerce appeared in *Cooley* v. *Board of Wardens of the Port of Philadelphia* (p. 551). Writing some fifteen years after *Miln*, Justice Curtis sustained the constitutionality of a Pennsylvania law requiring every ship under penalty of a fee to employ a local pilot when entering or leaving the port of Philadelphia. What is significant in the opinion is not only the Court's acceptance of the proposition that under some conditions the regulation of commerce can be a concurrent power of the national and state governments, but also the beginning of the search for a standard which would separate commerce constitutionally susceptible to state regulation from that within the exclusive purview of Congress, even though Congress may not have already occupied the field. In the words of the opinion the national government would exercise exclusive power only over "subjects of this power [which] are in their nature national, or admit only of one uniform system, or plan of regulation * * *." Given the increasing centralization of power in transportation and communications and the prevalence of economic interdependence as a fact of everyday life in the twentieth century, does the *Cooley* rule have any contemporary value?

The Court, of course, has concluded that there is wisdom in the *Cooley* approach as is apparent from the cases that follow. Such a manner of approaching problems, however, carries with it an obligation to be acutely sensitive to the centrifugal forces in the federal system, particularly insofar as the Court may become the handmaiden of economic Balkanization— that phenomenon of commercial anarchy that helped to make life under the Articles of Confederation so intolerable. For this reason the Court has necessarily been concerned about state regulatory activities that impose burdens on interstate commerce. It has generally invalidated legislation designed primarily to secure for a state a competitive advantage over her sister states. On the other hand, the Court has been reasonably tolerant in upholding state legislation reflecting a real and significant interest in protecting the health and safety of residents, even though such legislation may heavily burden interstate commerce. As always, it is a question of degree and countervailing justification. Such an approach has necessarily led the Court to solve the problems that come to it in a case-by-case balancing of the interests. Balancing yields flexibility, but it can also produce arbitrariness. As you read the cases which follow, you will want to keep an eye on the method of the Court's opinions as well as their substance. You should also ask yourself if the Court is the kind of institution that is best suited to play such a role. Is the Supreme Court the institution most qualified to harmonize the conflicting interests?

A superb example of the Court's application of the balancing-of-interests approach appears in *South Carolina State Highway Dept.* v. *Barnwell Bros.* (p. 554). Consider the difference between the trial court and the Supreme Court's assessment of the factors relevant to establishing the burden South Carolina's trailer truck statute put on interstate commerce. How are they different? What does the Supreme Court suggest as the proper way for courts to examine the reasonableness of such legislation? How is it different from a legislative balancing of interests? Above all, note the impact of *Cooley* in framing the issues of the case. Do you regard the Court's statement about the primacy of local responsibility for the building and upkeep of roads as persuasive in view of the massive federal interstate highway program that has been in operation for the last two-and-a-half decades? Does the Burger Court's decision in *Kassel* v. *Consolidated Freightways Corp.* (p. 560) shed any light on whether the Court would decide the *Barnwell* case the same way today?

We mentioned that one of the problems with the balancing approach is possible arbitrariness. Arbitrariness is the product of inconsistency—the failure to treat "like cases alike." Examine the Court's decisions in two railroad regulation cases, *Southern Pacific Co.* v. *Arizona* (p. 564) and *Smith* v. *Alabama* (p. 569). Some observers have criticized the Court for what they see as the inconsistent treatment of state interests here in the light of almost equally heavy burdens the legislation put on the flow of interstate commerce. Would you agree? Or do you think the two cases can be distinguished so as to justify the burden imposed in *Smith*, but not in *Southern Pacific*?

Bibb v. *Navajo Freight Lines* (p. 572) presents a fine example of such a discrepancy between the end of protecting public safety and the means used to secure that end, the curved mudguards, that the Court had no trouble at all striking down the practice as an unjustified burden on interstate commerce. The greater the burden imposed on interstate commerce, the better the justification by the state and the effectiveness of its means must be. That balance is easily frustrated here by what appears to be the lack of any redeeming qualities whatsoever in the mudguards.

More recently, the Court has been confronted with state action endeavoring to protect the environment. As you can see from three cases involving pollution control efforts, *Huron Portland Cement Co.* v. *Detroit* (p. 576), *City of Burbank* v. *Lockheed Air Terminal* (p. 579), and *Northern States Power Co.* v. *Minnesota* (p. 582), the mere articulation of a worthy purpose or even the effective relationship between means and ends may not necessarily be enough to constitutionally salvage state legislation which imposes extensive burdens on interstate commerce. Unlike many other areas of public policy, such as civil rights legislation for example, where for years federal regulation substantially outdistanced the policies of most states, the Court's reliance on federal preemption in recent environmental cases has often meant that stringent regulation enacted by particularly progressive states has had to give way to more relaxed standards imposed by the national government. Indeed, as contrasted with the Court's preoccupation fifty to ninety years ago with problems caused by diverse attempts to regulate industrial production, today it is the issue of waste disposal that is on the cutting edge of constitutional interpretation with respect to the state police power. As the Court's decision in *City of Philadelphia* v. *State of New Jersey* (p. 584) shows, waste products are clearly within the meaning of "commerce," and their disposition poses knotty problems both for the quality of life and the principle of "free trade" implicit in the federal union. The Commerce Clause principles reaffirmed in the *Philadelphia* case established a base against which the facts in succeeding state regulation cases (p. 590) have been measured.

In view of what Justice Stone told us in the *Barnwell* case about the unconstitutionality of states discriminating against interstate commerce to secure a competitive advantage, consider *Dean Milk Co.* v. *City of Madison* (p. 591). Is Madison's milk marketing ordinance an effort to favor vicinity milk producers, or is it a piece of legitimate public welfare legislation? How do you know? Also, in view of *Barnwell's* statement of the proper role courts should play in assessing the reasonableness of legislation, did Justice Clark and the rest of the majority in *Dean Milk* give due regard to the city council's prerogatives in enacting the ordinance, or did they merely substitute their own judgment in favor of what they thought was a preferable regulatory scheme? The continuing vitality of *Dean Milk* as a precedent is attested to by the Court's treatment of the Mississippi regulation at issue in the *A & P* milk case (p. 596).

Even more problematic—and unfortunately beyond the focus taken in this chapter—is the constitutionality of state regulatory legislation aimed at stabilizing local produce markets. Just as the Great Depression taught the Nation much about the perils of leaving the national economy unregulated and, therefore, subject to recurrent booms and busts, so it taught much the same lesson about economic health to the states. As federal legislation since the New Deal has sought to keep the national economy on an even keel, so New York, for example, acted to protect the milk industry in that state from the ravages of destructive competition; California acted to maintain the stability of its raisin industry; and so on and so forth. Yet such regulatory actions, even from the best of motives, create a good deal of tension for the Commerce Clause. As Justice Jackson put it, speaking for the Court in one New York milk regulation case, H. P. Hood & Sons v. Du Mond, 336 U.S. 525, 69 S.Ct. 657 (1949):

> Our system, fostered by the Commerce Clause, is that every farmer and every craftsman shall be encouraged to produce by the certainty that he will have free access to every market in the Nation, that no home embargoes will withhold his export, and no foreign state will by customs duties or regulations exclude them. Likewise, every consumer may look to the free competition from every producing area in the Nation to protect him from exploitation by any. Such was the vision of the Founders; such has been the doctrine of this Court which has given it reality.

If the command of the Commerce Clause, then, is seen as "free trade," but the states have enacted regulatory legislation to maintain the economic health of their local markets precisely because unrestrained competition has such periodically devastating consequences, the Court faces a genuine dilemma as it threads its way through state economic regulation cases, trying to determine when economic regulation has gone so far that it amounts to the sort of "protectionist" legislation our constitutional system cannot tolerate. In such cases the methodology of interest balancing will be even more essential as the Court tries to harmonize not only competing federal and state interests but rival economic theories of *laissez-faire* and economic regulation as well.

The exercise of the police power is not, however, the only means by which states can run afoul of the Commerce Clause. Although limitations of space prohibit extensive discussion of the matter here, it is important to note that the states' taxing powers can violate the Constitution by unduly burdening interstate businesses. In assessing the constitutionality of state legislation levying a tax on interstate businesses, the Court again relies on an interest balancing approach that weighs the burden imposed on interstate commerce against the justification proferred by the state. The Court has long recognized that interstate business can and should be made to pay its fair share for benefits furnished by the states. In such state taxation cases the Court focuses on such issues as whether the conduct of business by a given interstate company has some nexus to the state interest; in other words, whether the business in fact receives at least some minimal benefit for which the state can expect to be compensated. The Court has also been sensitive to burdens which can fall on interstate corporations from simultaneous taxation by several jurisdictions resulting in a burdensome multiple taxation of the same income. As a result the Court has had to look at the specific effects of different kinds of state taxes imposed simultaneously on business corporations doing business across several boundary lines.

COOLEY v. THE BOARD OF WARDENS OF THE PORT OF PHILADELPHIA

Supreme Court of the United States, 1852
53 U.S. (12 How.) 299, 13 L.Ed. 996

A Pennsylvania law passed in 1803 required ships entering or leaving Philadelphia to employ a pilot from the city for navigation purposes. It further stated that vessels failing to conform to this requirement would have to pay one-half of the pilotage fees into a fund for retired pilots and their dependents. Exceptions were made for ships of less than seventy-five tons, ships sailing to or from a port on the Delaware River, and ships engaged in the Pennsylvania coal trade. The Board of Wardens brought action against Aaron Cooley to recover fees due when two of his ships did not use pilots. The Pennsylvania Supreme Court affirmed a judgment in favor of the board by a court of common pleas, and the case was then brought to the United States Supreme Court. Although Congress had passed an act in 1789 that permitted states to regulate pilots, Cooley argued that the Pennsylvania law was an unconstitutional tax on commerce, not a pilot regulation.

Mr. Justice CURTIS delivered the opinion of the court:

* * *

That the power to regulate commerce includes the regulation of navigation, we consider settled. And when we look to the nature of the service performed by pilots, to the relations which that service and its compensations bear to navigation between the several States, and between the ports of the United States, and foreign countries, we are brought to the conclusion, that the regulation of the qualifications of pilots, of the modes and times of offering and rendering their services, of the responsibilities which shall rest upon them, of the powers they shall possess, of the compensation they may demand, and of the penalties by which their rights and duties may be enforced, do constitute regulations of navigation, and consequently of commerce, within the just meaning of this clause of the Constitution.

* * *

It becomes necessary, therefore, to consider whether this law of Penn-sylvania, being a regulation of commerce, is valid.

The Act of Congress of the 7th of August, 1789, sec. 4, is as follows:

"That all pilots in the bays, inlets, rivers, harbors, and ports of the United States, shall continue to be regulated in conformity with the existing laws of the States, respectively, wherein such pilots may be, or with such laws as the States may respectively hereafter enact for the purpose, until further legislative provision shall be made by Congress."

If the law of Pennsylvania, now in question, had been in existence at the date of this Act of Congress, we might hold it to have been adopted by Congress, and thus made a law of the United States, and so valid. Because this Act does, in effect, give the force of an Act of Congress, to the then existing state laws on this subject, so long as they should continue unrepealed by the State which enacted them.

But the law on which these actions are founded was not enacted till 1803. What effect, then, can be attributed to so much of the Act of

1789 as declares that pilots shall continue to be regulated in conformity "with such laws as the States may respectively hereafter enact for the purpose, until further legislative provision shall be made by Congress?"

If the States were devested of the power to legislate on this subject by the grant of the commercial power to Congress, it is plain this Act could not confer upon them power thus to legislate. If the Constitution excluded the States from making any law regulating commerce, certainly Congress cannot regrant, or in any manner reconvey to the States that power. And yet this Act of 1789 gives its sanction only to laws enacted by the States. This necessarily implies a constitutional power to legislate; for only a rule created by the sovereign power of a state acting in its legislative capacity, can be deemed a law, enacted by a State; and if the State has so limited its sovereign power that it no longer extends to a particular subject, manifestly it cannot, in any proper sense, be said to enact laws thereon. Entertaining these views we are brought directly and unavoidably to the consideration of the question, whether the grant of the commercial power to Congress, did per se deprive the States of all power to regulate pilots. This question has never been decided by this court, nor, in our judgment, has any case depending upon all the considerations which must govern this one, come before this court. The grant of commercial power to Congress does not contain any terms which expressly exclude the States from exercising an authority over its subject matter. If they are excluded it must be because the nature of the power, thus granted to Congress, requires that a similar authority should not exist in the States. If it were conceded on the one side, that the nature of this power, like that to legislate for the District of Columbia, is absolutely and totally repugnant to the existence of similar power in the States, probably no one would deny that the grant of the power to Congress, as effectually and perfectly excludes the States from all future legislation on the subject, as if express words have been used to exclude them. And on the other hand, if it were admitted that the existence of this power in Congress, like the power of taxation, is compatible with the existence of a similar power in the States, then it would be in conformity with the contemporary exposition of the Constitution (Federalist, No. 32), and with the judicial construction, given from time to time by this court, after the most deliberate consideration, to hold that the mere grant of such a power to Congress, did not imply a prohibition on the States to exercise the same power; that it is not the mere existence of such a power, but its exercise by Congress, which may be incompatible with the exercise of the same power by the States, and that the States may legislate in the absence of congressional regulations. Sturges v. Crowinshield, 4 Wheat. 193; Moore v. Houston, 5 Wheat. 1; Wilson v. Black Bird Creek Marsh Co., 2 Peters, 251.

The diversities of opinion, therefore, which have existed on this subject, have arisen from the different views taken of the nature of this power. But when the nature of a power like this is spoken of, when it is said that the nature of the power requires that it should be exercised exclusively by Congress, it must be intended to refer to the subjects of that power, and to say they are of such a nature as to require exclusive legislation by Congress. Now, the power to regulate commerce, embraces a vast field, containing not only many, but exceedingly various subjects, quite unlike in their nature; some imperatively demanding a single uniform rule, operating equally on the commerce of the United States in every port; and some like the subject now in question, as imperatively demanding that diversity, which alone can meet the local necessities of navigation.

Either absolutely to affirm, or deny, that the nature of this power requires exclusive legislation by Congress, is to lose sight of the nature of the subjects of this power, and to assert concerning all of them, what is really applicable but to a part. Whatever subjects of this power are in their nature national, or admit only of one uniform system, or plan of regulation, may justly be said to be of such a nature as to require exclusive legislation by Congress. That this cannot be affirmed of laws for the regulation of pilots and pilotage is plain. The Act of 1789 contains a clear and authoritative declaration by the first Congress, that the nature of this subject is such, that until Congress should find it necessary to exert its power, it should be left to the legislation of the States; that it is local and not national; that it is likely to be the best provided for, not by one system, or plan of regulations, but by as many as the legislative discretion of the several States should deem applicable to the local peculiarities of the ports within their limits.

Viewed in this light, so much of this Act of 1789 as declares that pilots shall continue to be regulated "by such laws as the States may respectively hereafter enact for that purpose," instead of being held to be inoperative, as an attempt to confer

on the States a power to legislate, of which the Constitution had deprived them, is allowed an appropriate and important signification. It manifests the understanding of Congress, at the outset of the government, that the nature of this subject is not such as to require its exclusive legislation. The practice of the States, and of the national government, has been in conformity with this declaration, from the origin of the national government to this time; and the nature of the subject, when examined, is such as to leave no doubt of the superior fitness and propriety, not to say the absolute necessity, of different systems of regulation, drawn from local knowledge and experience, and conformed to local wants. How, then, can we say, that by the mere grant of power to regulate commerce, the States are deprived of all the power to legislate on this subject, because from the nature of the power the legislation of Congress must be exclusive. This would be to affirm that the nature of the power is, in any case, something different from the nature of the subject to which, in such case, the power extends, and that the nature of the power necessarily demands, in all cases, exclusive legislation by Congress, while the nature of one of the subjects of that power, not only does not require such exclusive legislation, but may be best provided for by many different systems enacted by the States, in conformity with the circumstances of the ports within their limits. In construing an instrument designed for the formation of a government, and in determining the extent of one of its important grants of power to legislate, we can make no such distinction between the nature of the power and the nature of the subject on which that power was intended practically to operate, nor consider the grant more extensive by affirming of the power, what is not true of its subject now in question.

It is the opinion of a majority of the court that the mere grant to Congress of the power to regulate commerce, did not deprive the States of power to regulate pilots, and that although Congress has legislated on this subject, its legislation manifests an intention, with a single exception, not to regulate this subject, but to leave its regulation to the several States. To these precise questions, which are all we are called on to decide, this opinion must be understood to be confined. It does not extend to the question what other subjects, under the commercial power, are within the exclusive control of Congress, or may be regulated by the States in the absence of all congressional legislation; nor to the general question how far any regulation of a subject by Congress may be deemed to oper-

ate as an exclusion of all legislation by the States upon the same subject. We decide the precise questions before us, upon what we deem sound principles, applicable to this particular subject in the state in which the legislation of Congress has left it. We go no farther.

We are of opinion that this state law was enacted by virtue of a power, residing in the State to legislate; that it is not in conflict with any law of Congress; that it does not interfere with any system which Congress has established by making regulations, or by intentionally leaving individuals to their own unrestricted action; that this law is therefore valid, and the judgment of the Supreme Court of Pennsylvania in each case must be affirmed.

* * * Justices McLEAN and WAYNE dissented. Mr. Justice DANIEL, although he concurred in the judgment of the court, yet dissented from its reasoning.

SOUTH CAROLINA STATE HIGHWAY DEPT. v. BARNWELL BROS.

Supreme Court of the United States, 1938
303 U.S. 177, 58 S.Ct. 510, 82 L.Ed. 734

Barnwell Brothers, truckers engaged in interstate commerce, brought suit against the South Carolina Highway Department to enjoin it from enforcing a state statute which prohibited trucks over 20,000 pounds and wider than ninety inches from using state highways. The statute was passed to promote safety and to conserve the roads. After considering evidence relating to such matters as the typical weight and width of trucks hauling interstate loads, the amount of stress concrete roads could bear, and the relative quality of South Carolina's highways, a federal district court concluded that the state's regulations were an unreasonable burden on interstate commerce and, in effect, substituted its own restrictions. The width limitation was increased to ninety-six inches, and the weight limitation was eliminated altogether with exemptions from the court's decree allowed for bridges that were either too narrow or of insufficient strength. The Highway Department appealed to the Supreme Court.

Mr. Justice STONE delivered the opinion of the Court.

* * *

The trial court rested its decision that the statute unreasonably burdens interstate commerce, upon findings, not assailed here, that there is a large amount of motortruck traffic passing interstate in the southeastern part of the United States, which would normally pass over the highways of South Carolina, but which will be barred from the state by the challenged restrictions if enforced, and upon its conclusion that, when viewed in the light of their effect upon interstate commerce, these restrictions are unreasonable.

To reach this conclusion the court weighed conflicting evidence and made its own determinations as to the weight and width of motortrucks commonly used in interstate traffic and the capacity of the specified highways of the state to accommodate such traffic without injury to them or danger to their users. It found that interstate carriage by motortrucks has become a national industry; that from 85 to 90 per cent of the motor trucks used in interstate transportation are 96 inches wide and of a gross weight, when loaded, of more than 10 tons; that only four other states prescribe a gross load weight as low as 20,000 pounds; and that the American Association of State Highway Officials and the National Conference on Street and Highway Safety in the Department of Commerce have recommended for adoption weight and width limitations in which weight is limited to axle loads of 16,000 to 18,000 pounds and width is limited to 96 inches.

It found in detail that compliance with the weight and width limitations demanded by the South Carolina act would seriously impede motortruck traffic passing to and through the state and increase its cost; that 2,417 miles of state highways, including most of those affected by the injunction, are of the standard construction of concrete or concrete base with asphalt surface, $7\frac{1}{2}$ or 8 inches thick at the edges and 6 or $6\frac{1}{2}$ inches thick at the center; that they are capable of sustaining without injury a wheel load of 8,000 to 9,000 pounds or an axle load of double those amounts, depending on whether the wheels are equipped with high-pressure or low-pressure pneumatic tires; that all but 100 miles of the specified highways are from 18 to 20 feet in width; that they constitute a connected system of highways which have been improved with the aid of federal money grants, as a part of a national system of highways; and that they constitute one of the best highway systems in the southeastern part of the United States.

It also found that the gross weight of vehicles is not a factor to be considered in the preservation of concrete highways, but that the appropriate factor to be considered is wheel or axle weight; that vehicles engaged in interstate commerce are so designed and the pressure of their weight is so distributed by their wheels and axles that gross loads of more than 20,000 pounds can be carried over concrete roads without damage to the surface; that a gross weight limitation of that amount, especially as applied to semitrailer motortrucks, is unreasonable as a means of preserving the highways; that it has no reasonable relation to safety of the public using the highways; and that the width limitation of 90 inches is unreasonable when applied to standard concrete highways of the state, in view of the fact that all other states permit a width of 96 inches, which is the standard width of trucks engaged in interstate commerce.

In reaching these conclusions, and at the same time holding that the weight and width limitations do not infringe the Fourteenth Amendment, the court proceeded upon the assumption that the commerce clause, Const. art. 1, § 8, cl. 3, imposes upon state regulations to secure the safe and economical use of highways a standard of reasonableness which is more exacting when applied to the interstate traffic than that required by the Fourteenth Amendment as to all traffic; that a standard of weight and width of motor vehicles which is an appropriate state regulation when applied to intrastate traffic may be prohibited because of its effect on interstate commerce, although the conditions attending the two classes of traffic with respect to safety and protection of the highways are the same.

South Carolina has built its highways and owns and maintains them. It has received from the federal government, in aid of its highway improvements, money grants which have been expended upon the highways to which the injunction applies. But appellees do not challenge here the ruling of the District Court that Congress has not undertaken to regulate the weight and size of motor vehicles in interstate motor traffic, and has left undisturbed whatever authority in that regard the states have retained under the Constitution.

While the constitutional grant to Congress of power to regulate interstate commerce has been held to operate of its own force to curtail state power in some measure, it did not forestall all state action affecting interstate commerce. Ever since Willson v. Black Bird Creek Marsh Co., 2 Pet. 245, 7 L.Ed. 412, and Cooley v. Board of Port Wardens, 12 How. 299, 13 L.Ed. 996, it has been recognized that there are matters of local concern, the regulation of which unavoidably involves some regulation of interstate commerce but which, because of their local character and their number and diversity, may never be fully dealt with by Congress. Notwithstanding the commerce clause, such regulation in the absence of congressional action has for the most part been left to the states by the decisions of this Court, subject to the other applicable constitutional restraints.

The commerce clause by its own force, prohibits discrimination against interstate commerce, whatever its form or method, and the decisions of this Court have recognized that there is scope for its like operation when state legislation nominally of local concern is in point of fact aimed at interstate commerce, or by its necessary operation is a means of gaining a local benefit by throwing the attendant burdens on those without the state. * * * The commerce clause has also been thought to set its own limitation upon state control of interstate rail carriers so as to preclude the subordination of the efficiency and convenience of interstate traffic to local service requirements.

But the present case affords no occasion for saying that the bare possession of power by Congress to regulate the interstate traffic forces the states to conform to standards which Congress might, but has not adopted, or curtails their power to take measures to insure the safety and conservation of their highways which may be applied to like traffic moving intrastate. Few subjects of state regulation are so peculiarly of local concern as is the use of state highways. There are few, local regulation of which is so inseparable from a substantial effect on interstate commerce. Unlike the railroads, local highways are built, owned, and maintained by the state or its municipal subdivisions. The state has a primary and immediate concern in their safe and economical administration. The present regulations, or any others of like purpose, if they are to accomplish their end, must be applied alike to interstate and intrastate traffic both moving in large volume over the highways. The fact that they affect alike shippers in interstate and intrastate commerce in large number within as well as without the state is a safeguard against their abuse.

From the beginning it has been recognized that a state can, if it sees fit, build and maintain its own highways, canals, and railroads, and that in the absence of congressional action their regulation is peculiarly within its competence, even though interstate commerce is materially affected. * * * Congress not acting, state regulation of intrastate carriers has been upheld regardless of its effect upon interstate commerce. * * * With respect to the extent and nature of the local interests to be protected and the unavoidable effect upon interstate and intrastate commerce alike, regulations of the use of the highways are akin to local regulation of rivers, harbors, piers, and docks, quarantine regulations, and game laws, which, Congress not acting, have been sustained even though they materially interfere with interstate commerce.

The nature of the authority of the state over its own highways has often been pointed out by this Court. It may not, under the guise of regulation, discriminate against interstate commerce. But, "In the absence of national legislation especially covering the subject of interstate commerce, the state may rightly prescribe uniform regulations adapted to promote safety upon its highways

and the conservation of their use, applicable alike to vehicles moving in interstate commerce and those of its own citizens." Morris v. Duby, 274 U.S. 135, 143, 47 S.Ct. 548, 550. * * * This Court has often sustained the exercise of that power, although it has burdened or impeded interstate commerce. It has upheld weight limitations lower than those presently imposed, applied alike to motor traffic moving interstate and intrastate. *Morris* v. *Duby,* supra. * * * Restrictions favoring passenger traffic over the carriage of interstate merchandise by truck have been similarly sustained, * * * as has the exaction of a reasonable fee for the use of the highways. * * *

In each of these cases regulation involves a burden on interstate commerce. But so long as the state action does not discriminate, the burden is one which the Constitution permits because it is an inseparable incident of the exercise of a legislative authority, which, under the Constitution, has been left to the states.

Congress, in the exercise of its plenary power to regulate interstate commerce, may determine whether the burdens imposed on it by state regulation, otherwise permissible, are too great, and may, by legislation designed to secure uniformity or in other respects to protect the national interest in the commerce, curtail to some extent the state's regulatory power. But that is a legislative, not a judicial, function, to be performed in the light of the congressional judgment of what is appropriate regulation of interstate commerce, and the extent to which, in that field, state power and local interests should be required to yield to the national authority and interest. In the absence of such legislation the judicial function, under the commerce clause, Const. art. 1, § 8, cl. 3, as well as the Fourteenth Amendment, stops with the inquiry whether the state Legislature in adopting regulations such as the present has acted within its province, and whether the means of regulation chosen are reasonably adapted to the end sought. * * *

Here the first inquiry has already been resolved by our decisions that a state may impose nondiscriminatory restrictions with respect to the character of motor vehicles moving in interstate commerce as a safety measure and as a means of securing the economical use of its highways. In resolving the second, courts do not sit as Legislatures, either state or national. They cannot act as Congress does when, after weighing all the conflicting interests, state and national, determines when and how much the state regulatory power shall yield to the larger interests of a national commerce. And in reviewing a state highway regulation where Congress has not acted, a court is not called upon, as are state Legislatures, to determine what, in its judgment, is the most suitable restriction to be applied of those that are possible, or to choose that one which in its opinion is best adapted to all the diverse interests affected. * * * When the action of a Legislature is within the scope of its power, fairly debatable questions as to its reasonableness, wisdom, and propriety are not for the determination of courts, but for the legislative body, on which rests the duty and responsibility of decision. * * * This is equally the case when the legislative power is one which may legitimately place an incidental burden on interstate commerce. It is not any the less a legislative power committed to the states because it affects interstate

commerce, and courts are not any the more entitled, because interstate commerce is affected, to substitute their own for the legislative judgment. * * *

Since the adoption of one weight or width regulation, rather than another, is a legislative, not a judicial, choice, its constitutionality is not to be determined by weighing in the judicial scales the merits of the legislative choice and rejecting it if the weight of evidence presented in court appears to favor a different standard. * * * Being a legislative judgment it is presumed to be supported by facts known to the Legislature unless facts judicially known or proved preclude that possibility. Hence, in reviewing the present determination, we examine the record, not to see whether the findings of the court below are supported by evidence, but to ascertain upon the whole record whether it is possible to say that the legislative choice is without rational basis. * * * Not only does the record fail to exclude that possibility but it shows affirmatively that there is adequate support for the legislative judgment.

At the outset it should be noted that underlying much of the controversy is the relative merit of a gross weight limitation as against an axle or wheel weight limitation. While there is evidence that weight stresses on concrete roads are determined by wheel rather than gross load weights, other elements enter into choice of the type of weight limitation. * * * The choice of a weight limitation based on convenience of application and consequent lack of need for rigid supervisory enforcement is for the Legislature, and we cannot say that its preference for the one over the other is in any sense arbitrary or unreasonable. The choice is not to be condemned because the Legislature prefers a workable standard, less likely to be violated than another under which the violations will probably be increased but more easily detected. It is for the Legislature to say whether the one test or the other will in practical operation better protect the highways from the risk of excessive loads.

If gross load weight is adopted as the test, it is obvious that the permissible load must be somewhat lighter than if the axle or wheel weight test were applied. With the latter the gross weight of a loaded motortruck can never exceed twice the axle and four times the wheel limit. But the fact that the rear axle may and often does support as much as 70 or 80 per cent. of the gross load, with wheel weight in like be fixed at considerably less than four times the permissible wheel limit.

There was testimony before the court to support its conclusion that the highways in question are capable of sustaining without injury a wheel load of 8,000 or 9,000 pounds, the difference depending upon the character of the tire in use. * * * Much of this testimony appears to have been based on theoretical strength of concrete highways laid under ideal conditions, and none of it was based on an actual study of the highways of South Carolina or of the subgrade and other road building conditions which prevail there and which have a material bearing on the strength and durability of such highways. There is uncontradicted testimony that approximately 60 per cent. of the South Carolina standard paved highways in question were built without a longitudinal center joint which has since become standard practice, the portion of the concrete surface adjacent

to the joint being strengthened by reinforcement or by increasing its thickness; and that owing to the distribution of the stresses on concrete roads when in use, those without a center joint have a tendency to develop irregular longitudinal cracks. As the concrete in the center of such roads is thinner than that at the edges, the result is that the highway is split into two irregular segments, each with a weak inner edge which, according to the expert testimony, is not capable of supporting indefinitely wheel loads in excess of 4,200 pounds.

* * *

These considerations, with the presumption of constitutionality, afford adequate support for the weight limitation without reference to other items of the testimony tending to support it. Furthermore, South Carolina's own experience is not to be ignored. Before adoption of the limitation South Carolina had had experience with higher weight limits. * * * The present weight limitation was recommended by the commission after a full consideration of relevant data, including a report by the state engineer who had constructed the concrete highways of the state and who advised a somewhat lower limitation as necessary for their preservation. The fact that many states have adopted a different standard is not persuasive. The conditions under which highways must be built in the several states, their construction, and the demands made upon them, are not uniform. The road building art, as the record shows, is far from having attained a scientific certainty and precision, and scientific precision is not the criterion for the exercise of the constitutional regulatory power of the states.

* * * The Legislature, being free to exercise its own judgment, is not bound by that of other Legislatures. It would hardly be contended that if all the states had adopted a single standard none, in the light of its own experience and in the exercise of its judgment upon all the complex elements which enter into the problem, could change it.

Only a word need be said as to the width limitation. While a large part of the highways in question are from 18 to 20 feet in width, approximately 100 miles are only 16 feet wide. On all the use of a 96-inch truck leaves but a narrow margin for passing. On the road 16 feet wide it leaves none. The 90-inch limitation has been in force in South Carolina since 1920, and the concrete highways which it has built appear to be adapted to vehicles of that width. The record shows without contradiction that the use of heavy loaded trucks on the highways tends to force other traffic off the concrete surface onto the shoulders of the road adjoining its edges, and to increase repair costs materially. It appears also that as the width of trucks is increased it obstructs the view of the highway, causing much inconvenience and increased hazard in its use. It plainly cannot be said that the width of trucks used on the highways in South Carolina is unrelated to their safety and cost of maintenance, or that a 90-inch width limitation, adopted to safeguard the highways of the state, is not within the range of the permissible legislative choice.

The regulatory measures taken by South Carolina are within its legislative power. They do not infringe the Fourteenth Amendment, and the resulting burden on interstate commerce is not forbidden.

Reversed.

Mr. Justice CARDOZO and Mr. Justice REED took no part in the consideration or decision of this case.

Iowa law generally banned the use within the state of a tractor-trailer combination known as a double or twin, which consists of a "two-axle tractor pulling a single-axle trailer which, in turn, pulls a single-axle dolly and a second single-axle trailer." As such, a double measures some sixty-five feet overall. Iowa permitted the use of a single or "semi" which is fifty-five feet in length and "consists of a three-axle tractor pulling a forty-foot trailer." Trucking companies, however, increasingly prefer to use doubles in the transportation of certain commodities because they have larger capacities and because the trailers can be unhitched and routed separately. Doubles with an odd-size second trailer, mobile homes, trucks carrying farm equipment, and singles hauling livestock were allowed to be sixty feet in length. Iowa's statute also permitted cities near the state line to adopt the length limitations of the neighboring state, and permits were allowed for Iowa truck manufacturers to ship trucks that could be as long as seventy feet and for the movement of oversize mobile homes provided the unit was being moved from a point in the state or was being delivered for an Iowa resident. Iowa's general ban on sixty-five-foot doubles forced Consolidated Freightways, one of the nation's largest common carriers, desiring to move commodities across the country to choose from among four alternatives: (1) use fifty-five-foot singles, (2) use relatively rare sixty-foot doubles, (3) unhitch the trailers of sixty-five-foot doubles and move them through the state separately, or (4) divert its sixty-five-foot doubles around Iowa. Consolidated sued to invalidate the Iowa statute alleging it constituted an unconstitutional burden on interstate commerce. Iowa defended the restriction as a reasonable measure to protect public safety, asserted that sixty-five-foot doubles were more dangerous than fifty-five-foot singles, and argued that in any event the statute promoted both safety and reduced the wear and tear on its roads by diverting much of the truck traffic to other states. A federal district court held the statute to be unconstitutional, and a federal appellate court affirmed.

In its consideration of this case, Kassel v. Consolidated Freightways Corp., 450 U.S. 662, 101 S.Ct. 1309 (1981), the Supreme Court affirmed that judgment. Announcing the judgment of the Court in an opinion in which he was joined by Justices White, Blackmun, and Stevens, Justice Powell began by pointing out that while state regulations bearing upon public safety—especially highway safety— deserve judicial deference; nevertheless, ultimately the judgment as to their constitutionality hinges on " 'a sensitive consideration of the weight and nature of the state regulatory concern in light of the extent of the burden imposed on the course of interstate commerce.' " The " 'strong presumption of validity' " normally accorded such legislation was overcome in this case, Justice Powell said, because

> the State failed to present any persuasive evidence that 65-foot doubles are less safe than 55-foot singles. Moreover, Iowa's law is now out of step with the laws of all other midwestern and western States. Iowa thus substantially burdens the interstate flow of goods by truck. In the absence of congressional action to set uniform standards, some burdens associated with state safety regulations must be tolerated. But where, as here, the State's safety interest has been found to be illusory, and its regulations impair significantly the federal interest in efficient and safe interstate transportation, the state law cannot be harmonized with the Commerce Clause.

The four-man plurality observed that evidence presented to the district court clearly showed "that the 65-foot double was at least the equal of the 55-foot single in the ability to brake, turn, and maneuver." Furthermore, "[t]he double, because of its axle placement, produces less splash and spray in wet weather. And, because of its articulation in the middle, the double is less susceptible to dangerous 'off-tracking' ['the extent to which the rear wheels of a truck deviate from the path of the front wheels while turning'] and to wind." In response, the state asserted that the fifty-five-foot single was superior to the sixty-five-foot double in three ways: "singles take less time to be passed and to clear intersections; they may back up for longer distances; and they are somewhat less likely to jackknife." Characterizing these claims as "arguable," the plurality noted that "[t]he first two of these * * * are of limited relevance on modern interstate highways" while the "65-foot doubles actually are less likely to jackknife than [the] 60-foot doubles" Iowa permitted. Moreover, the annual cost to trucking companies in dealing with Iowa's ban on sixty-five-foot doubles through the four alternatives outlined above amounted to $12.6 million. "Consolidated alone incurred about $2 million per year in increased costs." Finally, the plurality concluded that

> Less deference to the legislative judgment is due, however, where the local regulation bears disproportionately on out-of-state residents and businesses. Such a disproportionate burden is apparent here. Iowa's scheme, although generally banning large doubles from the State, nevertheless has several exemptions that secure to Iowans many of the benefits of large trucks

while shunting to neighboring States many of the costs associated with their use.

Concurring in the Court's judgment in an opinion in which Justice Marshall joined, Justice Brennan observed that resolution of this case "does not require * * * that I engage in the debate between my Brothers Powell and Rehnquist over what the District Court record shows on the question whether 65-foot doubles are more dangerous than shorter trucks." He continued:

My Brothers Powell and Rehnquist make the mistake of disregarding the intention of Iowa's lawmakers and assuming that resolution of the case must hinge upon the argument offered by Iowa's attorneys: that 65-foot doubles are more dangerous than shorter trucks. They then canvass the factual record and findings of the courts below and reach opposite conclusions as to whether the evidence adequately supports that empirical judgment. I repeat: my Brothers Powell and Rehnquist have asked and answered the wrong question. For although Iowa's lawyers in this litigation have defended the truck length regulation on the basis of the safety advantages of 55-foot singles and 60-foot doubles over 65-foot doubles, Iowa's actual rationale for maintaining the regulation had nothing to do with these purported differences. Rather, Iowa sought to discourage interstate truck traffic on Iowa's highways. Thus, the safety advantages and disadvantages of the types and lengths of trucks involved in this case are irrelevant to the decision.

Justice Brennan argued that the record and legislative history of the Iowa statute clearly disclosed that the purpose of the law was not that of promoting highway safety. As originally enacted in 1947, the legislation was entitled "An Act *to promote uniformity with other states* in the matter of limitations on the size, weight and speed of motor vehicles * * *." [Emphasis is Justice Brennan's.] In 1974, however, when the legislature voted to increase the permissible length of trucks so that Iowa's regulation would be more in line with that of other states, the governor adopted a position quite different from that evidenced in prior state policy and vetoed the change. In his veto message, Justice Brennan pointed out

* * * Governor Ray did not rest his decision on the conclusion that 55-foot singles and 60-foot doubles are any safer than 65-foot doubles, or on any other safety consideration inherent in the type or size of the trucks. Rather, his principal concern was that to allow 65-foot doubles would "basically open our state to literally thousands and thousands more trucks per year." * * * This increase in interstate truck traffic would, in the Governor's estimation, greatly increase highway maintenance costs, which are borne by the citizens of the State, * * * and increase the number of accidents and fatalities within the State. * * * The legislative response was not to override the veto, but to accede to the Governor's action, and in accord with his basic premise, to enact a "border cities exemption."
* * *

Justice Brennan faulted the plurality for "fail[ing] to recognize that this purpose, being *protectionist* in nature, is *impermissible* under the Commerce Clause." And he concluded:

Iowa may not shunt off its fair share of the burden of maintaining interstate truck routes, nor may it create increased hazards on the highways of
neighboring States in order to decrease the hazards on Iowa highways.
Such an attempt has all the hallmarks of the "simple * * * protectionism" this Court has condemned in the economic area. Philadelphia v. New
Jersey, 437 U.S. 617, 624, 98 S.Ct. 2531, 2535 (1978). Just as a State's
attempt to avoid interstate competition in economic goods may damage the
prosperity of the Nation as a whole, so Iowa's attempt to deflect interstate
truck traffic has been found to make the Nation's highways as a whole
more hazardous. That attempt should therefore be subject to "a virtually
per se rule of invalidity." * * *

Opening his dissenting opinion by paraphrasing Justice Jackson to the effect
that "the only state truck length limit 'that is valid is one which this court has not
been able to get its hands on,' " Justice Rehnquist (joined by Chief Justice Burger
and Justice Stewart) lamented "the analysis in both [Justice Powell's and Justice
Brennan's] opinions [for] overstep[ping] our 'limited authority to review state legislation under the commerce clause,' * * * and seriously intrud[ing] upon the
fundamental right of the States to pass laws to secure the safety of their citizens." As to the plurality's portrayal of Iowa's ban on sixty-five-foot doubles as
burdensome because it was out of step with the position occupied by its sister
states, Justice Rehnquist responded:

Iowa's action in limiting the length of trucks which may travel on its highways is in no sense unusual. Every State in the Union regulates the length
of vehicles permitted to use the public roads. Nor is Iowa a renegade in
having length limits which operate to exclude the 65-foot doubles favored
by Consolidated. These trucks are prohibited in other areas of the country
as well, some 17 States and the District of Columbia, including all of New
England and most of the Southeast. While pointing out that Consolidated
carries commodities through Iowa on Interstate 80, "the principal east-west
route linking New York, Chicago, and the West Coast," * * * the plurality neglects to note that both Pennsylvania and New Jersey, through
which Interstate 80 runs before reaching New York, also ban 65-foot
doubles. In short, the persistent effort in the plurality opinion to paint
Iowa as an oddity standing alone to block commerce carried in 65-foot
doubles is simply not supported by the facts.

Moreover, he observed, "[t]here can be no question that the particular limit chosen
by Iowa—60 feet—is rationally related to Iowa's safety objective. Most truck limits are between 55 and 65 feet * * * and Iowa's choice is thus well within the
widely accepted range." He noted that Iowa presented a substantial body of evidence before the district court which "undermin[ed] the probative value of Consolidated's evidence." The gist of Justice Rehnquist's objection to the Court's
judgment was not that Iowa's evidence positively established the fact that sixty-
five-foot doubles were unsafe, but simply that the conclusion as to their relative
safety was an open question upon which the Iowa legislature was entitled to have
its judgment respected. The proper judicial posture, he reminded the Court, was
not close scrutiny but mere rationality. And he added:

Any direct balancing of marginal safety benefits against burdens on
commerce would make the burdens on commerce the sole significant factor,
and make likely the odd result that similar state laws enacted for identical

safety reasons might violate the Commerce Clause in one part of the country but not another. For example, Mississippi and Georgia prohibit trucks over 55 feet. Since doubles are not operated in the Southeast, the demonstrable burden on commerce may not be sufficient to strike down these laws, while Consolidated maintains that it is in this case, even though the doubles here are given an additional five feet. On the other hand, if Consolidated were to win this case it could shift its 65-foot doubles to routes leading into Mississippi or Georgia (both States border States in which 65-foot trucks are permitted) and claim the same constitutional violation it claims in this case. Consolidated Freightways, and not this Court, would become the final arbiter of the Commerce Clause.

* * * Striking down Iowa's law because Consolidated has made a voluntary business decision to employ 65-foot doubles, a decision based on the actions of other state legislatures, would essentially be compelling Iowa to yield to the policy choices of neighboring States. Under our Constitutional scheme, however, there is only one legislative body which can pre-empt the rational policy determination of the Iowa Legislature and that is Congress. Forcing Iowa to yield to the policy choices of neighboring States perverts the primary purpose of the Commerce Clause, that of vesting power to regulate interstate commerce in Congress, where all the States are represented. * * *

* * *

Furthermore, the effort in both the plurality and concurring opinions to portray the legislation involved here as protectionist is in error. Whenever a State enacts more stringent safety measures than its neighbors, in an area which affects commerce, the safety law will have the incidental effect of deflecting interstate commerce to the neighboring States. Indeed, the safety and protectionist motives cannot be separated: The whole purpose of safety regulation of vehicles is to *protect* the State from unsafe vehicles. If a neighboring State chooses *not* to protect its citizens from the danger discerned by the enacting State, that is its business, but the enacting State should not be penalized when the vehicles it considers unsafe travel through the neighboring State.

The other States with truck length limits that exclude Consolidated's 65-foot doubles would not at all be paranoid in assuming that they might be next on Consolidated's "hit list." The true problem with today's decision is that it gives no guidance whatsoever to these States as to whether their laws are valid or how to defend them. For that matter, the decision gives no guidance to Consolidated or other trucking firms either. Perhaps, after all is said and done, the Court today neither says nor does very much at all. We know only that Iowa's law is invalid and that the jurisprudence of the "negative side" of the Commerce Clause remains hopelessly confused.

SOUTHERN PACIFIC CO. v. ARIZONA

Supreme Court of the United States, 1945
325 U.S. 761, 65 S.Ct. 1515, 89 L.Ed. 1915

For safety reasons the Arizona Train Limit Law prohibited passenger trains of more than fourteen cars and freight trains of more than seventy cars from operating in the state. Both of these restrictions were violated when longer trains operated by the Southern Pacific Company traveled across Arizona on an interstate route. At the time Arizona brought suit in a state court against the Southern Pacific, the Interstate Commerce Commission had not yet exercised its statutory

authority to suspend state train limit laws during emergencies (which it later did following the country's entrance into World War II). The trial court held in favor of the company, but the Arizona Supreme Court reversed. Southern Pacific appealed to the United States Supreme Court contending, in part, that the state law conflicted with the federal power to regulate interstate commerce.

Mr. Chief Justice STONE delivered the opinion of the Court.

* * *

Although the commerce clause conferred on the national government power to regulate commerce, its possession of the power does not exclude all state power of regulation. Ever since Willson v. Black Bird Creek Marsh Co., 2 Pet. 245, 7 L.Ed. 412, and Cooley v. Board of Wardens, 12 How. 299, 13 L.Ed. 996, it has been recognized that, in the absence of conflicting legislation by Congress, there is a residuum of power in the state to make laws governing matters of local concern which nevertheless in some measure affect interstate commerce or even, to some extent, regulate it. * * * Thus the states may regulate matters which, because of their number and diversity, may never be adequately dealt with by Congress. * * * When the regulation of matters of local concern is local in character and effect, and its impact on the national commerce does not seriously interfere with its operation, and the consequent incentive to deal with them nationally is slight, such regulation has been generally held to be within state authority. * * *

But ever since Gibbons v. Ogden, 9 Wheat. 1, 6 L.Ed. 23, the states have not been deemed to have authority to impede substantially the free flow of commerce from state to state, or to regulate those phases of the national commerce which, because of the need of national uniformity, demand that their regulation, if any, be prescribed by a single authority. * * * Whether or not this long recognized distribution of power between the national and the state governments is predicated upon the implications of the commerce clause itself, * * * or upon the presumed intention of Congress, where Congress has not spoken, * * * the result is the same.

In the application of these principles some enactments may be found to be plainly within and others plainly without state power. But between these extremes lies the infinite variety of cases in which regulation of local matters may also operate as a regulation of commerce, in which reconciliation of the conflicting claims of state and national power is to be attained only by some appraisal and accommodation of the competing demands of the state and national interests involved. * * *

For a hundred years it has been accepted constitutional doctrine that the commerce clause, without the aid of Congressional legislation, thus affords some protection from state legislation inimical to the national commerce, and that in such cases, where Congress has not acted, this Court, and not the state legislature, is under the commerce clause the final arbiter of the competing demands of state and national interests. * * *

Congress has undoubted power to redefine the distribution of power over interstate commerce. It may either permit the states to regulate the commerce in a manner which would otherwise not be permissible, * * * or exclude state regulation even of matters of peculiarly local concern which nevertheless affect interstate commerce. * * *

But in general Congress has left it to the courts to formulate the rules thus interpreting the commerce clause in its application, doubtless because it has appreciated the destructive consequences to the commerce of the nation if their protection were withdrawn, * * * and has been aware that in their application state laws will not be invalidated without the support of relevant factual material which will "afford a sure basis" for an informed judgment. * * * Meanwhile, Congress has accommodated its legislation, as have the states, to these rules as an established feature of our constitutional system. There has thus been left to the states wide scope for the regulation of matters of local state concern, even though it in some measure affects the commerce, provided it does not materially restrict the free flow of commerce across state lines, or interfere with it in matters with respect to which uniformity of regulation is of predominant national concern.

Hence the matters for ultimate determination here are the nature and extent of the burden which the state regulation of interstate trains, adopted as a safety measure, imposes on interstate commerce, and whether the relative weights of the state and national interests involved are such as to make inapplicable the rule, generally observed, that the free flow of interstate commerce and its freedom from local restraints in matters requiring uniformity of regulation are interests safeguarded by the commerce clause from state interference.

While this Court is not bound by the findings of the state court, and may determine for itself the facts of a case upon which an asserted federal right depends, * * * the facts found by the state trial court showing the nature of the interstate commerce involved, and the effect upon it of the train limit law, are not seriously questioned. Its findings with respect to the need for and effect of the statute as a safety measure, although challenged in some particulars which we do not regard as material to our decision, are likewise supported by evidence. Taken together the findings supply an adequate basis for decision of the constitutional issue.

The findings show that the operation of long trains, that is trains of more than fourteen passenger and more than seventy freight cars, is standard practice over the main lines of the railroads of the United States, and that, if the length of trains is to be regulated at all, national uniformity in the regulation adopted, such as only Congress can prescribe, is practically indispensable to the operation of an efficient and economical national railway system. On many railroads passenger trains of more than fourteen cars and freight trains of more than seventy cars are operated, and on some systems freight trains are run ranging from one hundred and twenty-five to one hundred and sixty cars in length. Outside of Arizona, where the length of trains is not restricted, appellant runs a substantial proportion of long trains. In 1939 on its comparable route for through traffic through Utah and Nevada from 66 to 85% of its freight trains were over 70 cars in length and over 43% of its passenger trains included more than fourteen passenger cars.

In Arizona, approximately 93% of the freight traffic and 95% of the passenger traffic is interstate. Because of the Train Limit Law appellant is required to haul over 30% more trains in Arizona than would otherwise have been necessary. The record shows a definite relationship between operating costs and the length of trains, the increase in length resulting in a reduction of operating costs per car. The additional cost of operation of trains complying with the Train Limit Law in Arizona amounts for the two railroads traversing that state to about $1,000,000 a year. The reduction in train lengths also impedes efficient operation. More locomotives and more manpower are required; the necessary conversion and reconversion of train lengths at terminals and the delay caused by breaking up and remaking long trains upon entering and leaving the state in order to comply with the law, delays the traffic and diminishes its volume moved in a given time, especially when traffic is heavy.

* * *

The unchallenged findings leave no doubt that the Arizona Train Limit Law imposes a serious burden on the interstate commerce conducted by appellant. It materially impedes the movement of appellant's interstate trains through that state and interposes a substantial obstruction to the national policy proclaimed by Congress, to promote adequate, economical and efficient railway transportation service. * * * Enforcement of the law in Arizona, while train lengths remain unregulated or are regulated by varying standards in other states, must inevitably result in an impairment of uniformity of efficient railroad operation be-

cause the railroads are subjected to regulation which is not uniform in its application. Compliance with a state statute limiting train lengths requires interstate trains of a length lawful in other states to be broken up and reconstituted as they enter each state according as it may impose varying limitations upon train lengths. The alternative is for the carrier to conform to the lowest train limit restriction of any of the states through which its trains pass, whose laws thus control the carriers' operations both within and without the regulating state.

* * *

We think, as the trial court found, that the Arizona Train Limit Law, viewed as a safety measure, affords at most slight and dubious advantage, if any, over unregulated train lengths, because it results in an increase in the number of trains and train operations and the consequent increase in train accidents of a character generally more severe than those due to slack action. [Slack action is the amount of free movement of one car before it transmits its motion to an adjoining coupled car.] Its undoubted effect on the commerce is the regulation, without securing uniformity, of the length of trains operated in interstate commerce, which lack is itself a primary cause of preventing the free flow of commerce by delaying it and by substantially increasing its cost and impairing its efficiency. In these respects the case differs from those where a state, by regulatory measures affecting the commerce, has removed or reduced safety hazards without substantial interference with the interstate movement of trains. Such are measures abolishing the car stove, * * * requiring locomotives to be supplied with electric headlights, * * * providing for full train crews, * * * and for the equipment of freight trains with cabooses. * * *

The principle that, without controlling Congressional action, a state may not regulate interstate commerce so as substantially to affect its flow or deprive it of needed uniformity in its regulation is not to be avoided by "simply invoking the convenient apologetics of the police power." * * *

* * *

Appellees especially rely on the full train crew cases * * * and also on *South Carolina Highway Dept.* v. *Barnwell Bros.* * * * as supporting the state's authority to regulate the length of interstate trains. While the full train crew laws undoubtedly placed an added financial burden on the railroads in order to serve a local interest, they did not obstruct interstate transportation or seriously impede it. They had no effects outside the state beyond those of picking up and setting down the extra employees at the state boundaries; they involved no wasted use of facilities or serious impairment of transportation efficiency, which are among the factors of controlling weight here. In sustaining those laws the Court considered the restriction a minimal burden on the commerce comparable to the law requiring the licensing of engineers as a safeguard against those of reckless and intemperate habits, sustained in Smith v. Alabama, 124 U.S. 465, 8 S.Ct. 564, or those afflicted with color blindness, * * * and other similar regulations. * * *

South Carolina State Highway Dept. v. *Barnwell Bros.* * * * was concerned with the power of the state to regulate the weight and width of motor cars passing interstate over its highways, a legislative field over which the state has a far more extensive control than over interstate railroads. In that case, * * * we were at pains to point out that there are few subjects of state regulation affecting interstate commerce which are so peculiarly of local concern as is the use of the state's highways. Unlike the railroads local highways are built, owned and maintained by the state or its municipal subdivisions. The state is responsible for their safe and economical administration. Regulations affecting the safety of their use must be applied alike to intrastate and interstate traffic. The fact that they affect alike shippers in interstate and intrastate commerce in great numbers, within as well as without the state, is a safeguard against regulatory abuses. Their regulation is akin to quarantine measures, game laws, and like local regulations of rivers, harbors, piers, and docks, with respect to which the state has exceptional scope for the exercise of its regulatory power, and which, Congress not acting, have been sustained even though they materially interfere with interstate commerce. * * *

The contrast between the present regulation and the full train crew laws in point of their effects on the commerce, and the like contrast with the highway safety regulations, in point of the nature of the subject of regulation and the state's interest in it, illustrate and emphasize the considerations which enter into a determination of the relative weights of state and national interests where state regulation affecting interstate commerce is attempted. Here examination of all the relevant factors makes it plain that the state interest is outweighed by the interest of the nation in an adequate, economical and efficient railway transportation service, which must prevail.

Reversed.

Mr. Justice BLACK, dissenting.

* * *

[T]he determination of whether it is in the interest of society for the length of trains to be governmentally regulated is a matter of public policy. Someone must fix that policy—either the Congress, or the state, or the courts. A century and a half of constitutional history and government admonishes this Court to leave that choice to the elected legislative representatives of the people themselves, where it properly belongs both on democratic principles and the requirements of efficient government.

* * *

* * * The attention of the members of Congress and of the Senate have been focused on the particular problem of the length of railroad trains. We cannot assume that they were ignorant of the commonly known fact that a long train might be more dangerous in some territories and on some particular types of railroad. The history of congressional consideration of this problem leaves little if any room to doubt that the choice of Congress to leave the state free in this field was a deliberate choice, which was taken with a full knowledge of the complexities of the problems and the probable need for diverse regulations in different localities. I am therefore compelled to reach the conclusion that today's decision is the result of the belief of a majority of this Court that both the legislature of Arizona and the Congress made wrong policy decisions in permitting a law to stand which limits the length of railroad trains.

* * *

* * *

This record in its entirety leaves me with no doubt whatever that many employees have been seriously injured and killed in the past, and that many more are likely to be so in the future, because of "slack movement" in trains. Everyday knowledge as well as direct evidence presented at the various hearings, substantiates the report of the Senate Committee that the danger from slack movement is greater in long trains than in short trains. It may be that offsetting dangers are possible in the operation of short trains. The balancing of these probabilities, however, is not in my judgment a matter for judicial determination, but one which calls for legislative consideration. Representatives elected by the people to make their laws, rather than judges appointed to interpret those laws, can best determine the policies which govern the people. That at least is the basic principle on which our democratic society rests. I would affirm the judgment of the Supreme Court of Arizona.

Mr. Justice DOUGLAS, dissent[ed].

Compare the Court's holding in *Southern Pacific*, supra, with that in Smith v. Alabama, 124 U.S. 465, 8 S.Ct. 564 (1888), involving an Alabama law requiring locomotive engineers who operated trains in the state to be examined and licensed by a state board of examiners. Smith, the engineer on a train that traveled between points in Alabama, Missouri, and Mississippi, was indicted and taken into custody for violating the law. He petitioned a municipal court in Mobile for a writ of habeas corpus contending that the state law conflicted with the power of the national government to regulate interstate commerce. The court denied the application for discharge, and its decision was affirmed on appeal by the Alabama Supreme Court. The case was brought to the United States Supreme Court on a writ of error.

The Supreme Court, Justice Bradley dissenting, upheld the validity of the state law. Speaking for the Court, Justice Matthews said, in part:

[T]he provisions on the subject contained in the statute of Alabama under consideration are not regulations of interstate commerce. It is a misnomer to call them such. Considered in themselves, they are parts of that body of the local law which, as we have already seen, properly governs the relation between carriers of passengers and merchandise, and the public who employ them, which are not displaced until they come in conflict with express enactments of congress in the exercise of its power over commerce, and which, until so displaced, according to the evident intention of congress, remain as the law governing carriers, in the discharge of their obligations, whether engaged in the purely internal commerce of the state or in commerce among the states. No objection to the statute, as an impediment to the free transaction of commerce among the states, can be found in any of its special provisions. It requires that every locomotive engineer shall have a license, but it does not limit the number of persons who may be licensed, nor prescribe any arbitrary conditions to the grant. The fee of five dollars to be paid by an applicant for his examination is not a provision for raising revenue, but it is no more than an equivalent for the service rendered, and cannot be considered in the light of a tax or burden upon transportation. The applicant is required, before obtaining his license, to satisfy a board of examiners in reference to his knowledge of practical mechanics, his skill in operating a locomotive engine, and his general competency as an engineer, and the board, before issuing the license, is required to inquire into his character and habits, and to withhold the license if he be found to be reckless or intemperate. Certainly it is the duty of every carrier, whether engaged in the domestic commerce of the state or in interstate commerce, to provide and furnish itself with locomotive engineers of this precise description; competent and well qualified, skilled and sober; and if, by reason of carelessness in the selection of an engineer not so qualified, injury or loss are caused, the carrier, no matter in what business engaged, is responsible according to the local law admitted to govern in such cases, in the absence of congressional legislation.

The statute in question further provides that any engineer licensed under the act shall forfeit his license if at any time found guilty by the board of examiners of an act of recklessness, carelessness, or negligence while running an engine, by which damage to person or property is done, or who shall immediately preceding or during the time he is engaged in running an engine be in a state of intoxication; and the board are authorized to revoke and cancel the license whenever they shall be satisfied of the unfitness or incompetency of the engineer by reason of any act or habit unknown at the time of his examination, or acquired or formed subsequent to it. The eighth section of the act declares that any engineer violating its provisions shall be guilty of a misdemeanor, and upon conviction inflicts upon him the punishment of a fine not less than $50 nor more than $500, and also that he may be sentenced to hard labor for the county for not more than six months. If a locomotive engineer, running an engine, as was the petitioner in this case, in the business of transporting passengers and goods between Alabama and other states should, while in that state, by mere negligence and recklessness in operating his engine, cause the death of one or more passengers carried, he might certainly be held to answer to the criminal laws of the state if they declare the offense in such a case to be manslaughter. The power to punish for the offense after it is committed certainly includes the power to provide penalties directed, as are those in the statute in question, against those acts of omission which, if performed, would prevent the commission of the larger offense. It is to be remembered that railroads are not natural highways of trade and commerce. They are artificial creations; they are constructed within the territorial limits of a state, and by the authority of its laws, and ordinarily by means of corporations exercising their franchises by limited grants from the state. The places where they may be located, and the plans according to which they must be constructed, are prescribed by the legislation of the state. Their operation requires the use of instruments and agencies attended with special risks and dangers, the proper management of which involves peculiar knowledge, training, skill, and care. The safety of the public in person and property demands the use of specific guards and precautions. The width of the gauge, the character of the grades, the mode of crossing streams by culverts and bridges, the kind of cuts and tunnels, the mode of crossing other highways, the placing of watchmen and signals at points of special danger, the rate of speed at stations and through villages, towns, and cities, are all matters naturally and peculiarly within the provisions of that law from the authority of which these modern highways of commerce derive their existence. The rules prescribed for their construction and for their management and operation, designed to protect persons and property, otherwise endangered by their use, are strictly within the limits of the local law. They are not *per se* regulations of commerce; it is only when they operate as such in the circumstances of their application, and conflict with the expressed or presumed will of congress exerted on the same subject, that they can be required to give way to the supreme authority of the constitution.

In conclusion, we find, therefore—*First*, that the statute of Alabama, the validity of which is under consideration, is not, considered in its own nature, a regulation of interstate commerce, even when applied as in the case under consideration; *secondly*, that it is properly an act of legislation within the scope of the admitted power reserved to the states to regulate the relative rights and duties of persons being and acting within its territorial jurisdiction, intended to operate so as to secure for the public safety of person and property; and, *thirdly*, that, so far as it affects transactions of commerce among the states, it does so only indirectly, incidentally, and remotely, and not so as to burden or impede them, and, in the particulars in which it touches those transactions at all, it is not in conflict with any express enactment of congress on the subject, nor contrary to any intention of congress to be presumed from its silence. For these reasons, we hold this statute, so far as it is alleged to contravene the constitution of the United States, to be a valid law. The judgment of the supreme court of Alabama is therefore affirmed.

BIBB v. NAVAJO FREIGHT LINES, INC.

Supreme Court of the United States, 1959
359 U.S. 520, 79 S.Ct. 962, 3 L.Ed.2d 1003

Navajo Freight Lines, truckers engaged in interstate commerce, brought action against Joseph Bibb, the director of the Illinois Department of Public Safety, seeking to enjoin the enforcement of a state statute that required the use of special contoured mudguards on trucks traveling on the state's highways. A federal district court held that the statute was an unconstitutional burden on interstate commerce, whereupon Bibb appealed to the Supreme Court.

Mr. Justice DOUGLAS delivered the opinion of the Court.

* * *

Appellees, interstate motor carriers holding certificates from the Interstate Commerce Commission, challenged the constitutionality of the Illinois Act. A specially constituted three-judge District Court concluded that it unduly and unreasonably burdened and obstructed interstate commerce, because it made the conventional or straight mudflap, which is legal in at least 45 States, illegal in Illinois, and because the statute, taken together with a Rule of the Arkansas Commerce Commission requiring straight mudflaps, rendered the use of the same motor vehicle equipment in both States impossible. The statute was declared to be violative of the Commerce Clause and appellants were enjoined from enforcing it. 159 F.Supp. 358. * * *

The power of the State to regulate the use of its highways is broad and pervasive. We have recognized the peculiarly local nature of this subject of safety, and have upheld state statutes applicable alike to interstate and intrastate commerce, despite the fact that they may have an impact on interstate commerce. South Carolina State Highway Dept. v. Barnwell Bros., 303 U.S. 177, 58 S.Ct. 510; Maurer v. Hamilton, 309 U.S. 598, 60 S.Ct. 726; Sproles v. Binford, 286 U.S. 374, 52 S.Ct. 581.

* * *

These safety measures carry a strong presumption of validity when challenged in court. If there are alternative ways of solving a problem, we do not sit to determine which of them is best suited to achieve a valid state objective. Policy decisions are for the state legislature, absent federal entry into the field. Unless we can conclude on the whole record that "the total effect of the law as a safety measure in reducing accidents and casualties is so slight or problematical as not to outweigh the national interest in keeping interstate commerce free from interferences which seriously impede it" (Southern Pacific Co. v. State of Arizona, supra, 325 U.S. at pages 775–776, 65 S.Ct. at page 1523) we must uphold the statute.

The District Court found that "since it is impossible for a carrier operating in interstate commerce to determine which of its equipment will be used in a particular area, or on a particular day, or days, carriers operating into or through Illinois * * * will be required to equip all their trailers in accordance with the requirements of the Illinois Splash Guard statute." With two possible exceptions the mudflaps required in those States which have mudguard regulations would not meet the standards required by the Illinois statute. The cost of installing the contour mudguards is $30 or more per vehicle. The District Court found that the initial cost of installing those mudguards on all the trucks owned by the appellees ranged from $4,500 to $45,840. There was also evidence in the record to indicate that the cost of maintenance and replacement of these guards is substantial.

Illinois introduced evidence seeking to establish that contour mudguards had a decided safety factor in that they prevented the throwing of debris into the faces of drivers of passing cars and into the windshields of a following vehicle. But the District Court in its opinion stated that it was "conclusively shown that the contour mudflap possesses no advantages over the conventional or straight mudflap previously required in Illinois and presently required in most of the states," (159 F.Supp. at page 388) and that "there is rather convincing testimony that use of the contour flap creates hazards previously unknown to those using the highways." Id., at page 390. These hazards were found to be occasioned by the fact that this new type of mudguard tended to cause an accumulation of heat in the brake drum, thus decreasing the effectiveness of brakes, and by the fact that they were susceptible of being hit and bumped when the trucks were backed up and of falling off on the highway.

These findings on cost and on safety are not the end of our problem. Local regulation of the weight of trucks using the highways upheld in *Sproles* v. *Binford*, supra, also involved increased financial burdens for interstate carriers. State control of the width and weight of motor

trucks and trailers sustained in *South Carolina State Highway Dept.* v. *Barnwell Bros.*, supra, involved nice questions of judgment concerning the need of those regulations so far as the issue of safety was concerned. That case also presented the problem whether interstate motor carriers, who were required to replace all equipment or keep out of the State, suffered an unconstitutional restraint on interstate commerce. The matter of safety was said to be one essentially for the legislative judgment; and the burden of redesigning or replacing equipment was said to be a proper price to exact from interstate and intrastate motor carriers alike. And the same conclusion was reached * * * where a state law prohibited any motor carrier from carrying any other vehicle above the cab of the carrier vehicle or over the head of the operator of that vehicle. Cost taken into consideration with other factors might be relevant in some cases to the issue of burden on commerce. But it has assumed no such proportions here. If we had here only a question whether the cost of adjusting an interstate operation to these new local safety regulations prescribed by Illinois unduly burdened interstate commerce, we would have to sustain the law under the authority of the [previous] cases. The same result would obtain if we had to resolve the much discussed issues of safety presented in this case.

This case presents a different issue. The equipment in the [previous] cases could pass muster in any State, so far as the records in those cases reveal. We were not faced there with the question whether one State could prescribe standards for interstate carriers that would conflict with the standards of another State, making it necessary, say, for an interstate carrier to shift its cargo to differently designed vehicles once another state line was reached. We had a related problem in *Southern Pacific Co. v. State of Arizona.* * * * More closely in point is Morgan v. Commonwealth of Virginia, 328 U.S. 373, 375, 66 S.Ct. 1050, 1052, * * * where a local law required a reseating of passengers on interstate busses entering Virginia in order to comply with a local segregation law. Diverse seating arrangements for people of different races imposed by several States interfered, we concluded, with "the need for national uniformity in the regulations for interstate travel." Id., 328 U.S. at page 386, 66 S.Ct. at page 1058. Those cases indicate the dimensions of our present problem.

An order of the Arkansas Commerce Commission, * * * requires that trailers operating in that State be equipped with straight or conventional mudflaps. Vehicles equipped to meet the standards of the Illinois statute would not comply with Arkansas standards, and vice versa. Thus if a trailer is to be operated in both States, mudguards would have to be interchanged, causing a significant delay in an operation where prompt movement may be of the essence. It was found that from two to four hours of labor are required to install or remove a contour mudguard. Moreover, the contour guard is attached to the trailer by welding and if the trailer is conveying a cargo of explosives (e.g., for the United States Government) it would be exceedingly dangerous to attempt to weld on a contour mudguard without unloading the trailer.

It was also found that the Illinois statute seriously interferes with the "interline" operations of motor carriers—that is to say, with the interchanging of trailers between an originating carrier and another carrier when the latter serves an area not served by the former. These "interline" operations provide a speedy through-service for the shipper. Interlining contemplates the physical transfer of the entire trailer; there is no unloading and reloading of the cargo. The interlining process is particularly vital in connection with shipment of perishables, which would spoil if unloaded before reaching their destination, or with the movement of explosives carried under seal. Of course, if the originating carrier never operated in Illinois, it would not be expected to equip its trailers with contour mudguards. Yet if an interchanged trailer of that carrier were hauled to or through Illinois, the statute would require that it contain contour guards. Since carriers which operate in and through Illinois cannot compel the originating carriers to equip their trailers with contour guards, they may be forced to cease interlining with those who do not meet the Illinois requirements. Over 60 percent of the business of 5 of the 6 plaintiffs is interline traffic. For the other it constitutes 30 percent. All of the plaintiffs operate extensively in interstate commerce, and the annual mileage in Illinois of none of them exceeds 7 percent of total mileage.

This in summary is the rather massive showing of burden on interstate commerce which appellees made at the hearing.

Appellants did not attempt to rebut the appellees' showing that the statute in question severely burdens interstate commerce. Appellants' showing was aimed at establishing that contour mudguards prevented the throwing of debris into the faces of drivers of passing cars and into the windshields of a following vehicle. They concluded that, because the Illinois statute is a reasonable exercise of the police power, a federal court is precluded from weighing the relative merits of the contour mudguard against any other kind of mudguard and must sustain the validity of the statute notwithstanding the extent of the burden it imposes on interstate commerce. They rely in the main on *South Carolina State Highway Dept.* v. *Barnwell Bros.*, supra. There is language in that opinion which, read in isolation from such later decisions as *Southern Pacific Co.* v. *State of Arizona*, supra, and *Morgan* v. *Commonwealth of Virginia*, supra, would suggest that no showing of burden on interstate commerce is sufficient to invalidate local safety regulations in absence of some element of discrimination against interstate commerce.

The various exercises by the States of their police power stand, however, on an equal footing. All are entitled to the same presumption of validity when challenged under the Due Process Clause of the Fourteenth Amendment. * * * Similarly the various state regulatory statutes are of equal dignity when measured against the Commerce Clause. * * * Local regulations which would pass muster under the Due Process Clause might nonetheless fail to survive other challenges to constitutionality that bring the Supremacy Clause into play. Like any local law that conflicts with federal regulatory measures * * * state regulations that run afoul of the policy of free trade reflected in the Commerce Clause must also bow.

This is one of those cases—few in number—where local safety measures that are nondiscriminatory place an unconstitutional burden on interstate commerce. This conclusion is especially underlined by the deleterious effect which the Illinois law will have on the "interline" operation of interstate motor carriers. The conflict between the Arkansas regulation and the Illinois regulation also suggests that this regulation of mudguards is not one of those matters "admitting of diversity of treatment, according to the special requirements of local conditions," to use the words of Chief Justice Hughes in Sproles v. Binford, supra, 286 U.S. at page 390, 52 S.Ct. at page 585. A State which insists on a design out of line with the requirements of almost all the other States may sometimes place a great burden of delay and inconvenience on those interstate motor carriers entering or crossing its territory. Such a new safety device—out of line with the requirements of the other States—may be so compelling that the innovating State need not be the one to give way. But the present showing—balanced against the clear burden on commerce—is far too inconclusive to make this mudguard meet that test.

We deal not with absolutes but with questions of degree. The state legislatures plainly have great leeway in providing safety regulations for all vehicles—interstate as well as local. Our decisions so hold. Yet the heavy burden which the Illinois mudguard law places on the interstate movement of trucks and trailers seems to us to pass the permissible limits even for safety regulations.

Affirmed.

HURON PORTLAND CEMENT CO. v. DETROIT

Supreme Court of the United States, 1960
362 U.S. 440, 80 S.Ct. 813, 4 L.Ed.2d 852

Detroit brought criminal proceedings against appellant, a Michigan manufacturer and seller of cement which transported its product to distributing plants in other states, for operating ships in the city's port which emitted levels of smoke that exceeded the amounts allowed under a city smoke abatement ordinance. The cement company, in turn, sought to have the city enjoined from enforcing the smoke ordinance and from continuing prosecution. Appellant argued that because its vessels were inspected and licensed in accordance with congressional regulations, Detroit could not impose additional standards. The company also maintained that questions of pollution involving interstate commerce required uniform national standards. A county circuit court held in favor of the city, and the Michigan Supreme Court affirmed. Portland Cement appealed to the United States Supreme Court.

Mr. Justice STEWART delivered the opinion of the Court.

* * *

The ordinance was enacted for the manifest purpose of promoting the health and welfare of the city's inhabitants. Legislation designed to free from pollution the very air that people breathe clearly falls within the exercise of even the most traditional concept of what is compendiously known as the police power. In the exercise of that power, the states and their instrumentalities may act, in many areas of interstate commerce and maritime activities, concurrently with the federal government. * * *

The basic limitations upon local legislative power in this area are clear enough. The controlling principles have been reiterated over the years in a host of this Court's decisions. Evenhanded local regulation to effectuate a legitimate local public interest is valid unless pre-empted by federal action, * * * or unduly burdensome on maritime activities or interstate commerce. * * *

In determining whether state regulation has been pre-empted by fed-

eral action, "the intent to supersede the exercise by the state of its police power as to matters not covered by the Federal legislation is not to be inferred from the mere fact that Congress has seen fit to circumscribe its regulation and to occupy a limited field. In other words, such intent is not to be implied unless the act of Congress, fairly interpreted, is in actual conflict with the law of the state." Savage v. Jones, 225 U.S. 501, 533, 32 S.Ct. 715, 726. * * *

In determining whether the state has imposed an undue burden on interstate commerce, it must be borne in mind that the Constitution when "conferring upon Congress the regulation of commerce, * * * never intended to cut the States off from legislating on all subjects relating to the health, life, and safety of their citizens, though the legislation might indirectly affect the commerce of the country. Legislation, in a great variety of ways, may affect commerce and persons engaged in it without constituting a regulation of it, within the meaning of the Constitution." Sherlock v. Alling, 93 U.S. 99, 103, 23 L.Ed. 819. * * * But a state may not impose a burden which materially affects interstate commerce in an area where uniformity of regulation is necessary. * * *

Although verbal generalizations do not of their own motion decide concrete cases, it is nevertheless within the framework of these basic principles that the issues in the present case must be determined.

For many years Congress has maintained an extensive and comprehensive set of controls over ships and shipping. Federal inspection of steam vessels was first required in 1838 * * * and the requirement has been continued ever since. * * * Steam vessels which carry passengers must pass inspection annually, * * * and those which do not, every two years. * * * Failure to meet the standards invoked by law results in revocation of the inspection certificate, or refusal to issue a new one. * * * It is unlawful for a vessel to operate without such a certificate. * * * These inspections are broad in nature. * * *

As is apparent on the face of the legislation, however, the purpose of the federal inspection statutes is to insure the seagoing safety of vessels subject to inspection. * * * The thrust of the federal inspection laws is clearly limited to affording protection from the perils of maritime navigation. * * *

By contrast, the sole aim of the Detroit ordinance is the elimination of air pollution to protect the health and enhance the cleanliness of the local community. Congress recently recognized the importance and legitimacy of such a purpose, when in 1955 it provided:

"[I]n recognition of the dangers to the public health and welfare, injury to agricultural crops and live-

stock, damage to and deterioration of property, and hazards to air and ground transportation, from air pollution, it is hereby declared to be the policy of Congress to preserve and protect the primary responsibilities and rights of the States and local governments in controlling air pollution, to support and aid technical research to devise and develop methods of abating such pollution, and to provide Federal technical services and financial aid to State and local government air pollution control agencies and other public or private agencies and institutions in the formulation and execution of their air pollution abatement research programs." 69 Stat. 322, 42 U.S.C.A. § 1857.

Congressional recognition that the problem of air pollution is peculiarly a matter of state and local concern is manifest in this legislation. * * *

We conclude that there is no overlap between the scope of the federal ship inspection laws and that of the municipal ordinance here involved. For this reason we cannot find that the federal inspection legislation has pre-empted local action. To hold otherwise would be to ignore the teaching of this Court's decisions which enjoin seeking out conflicts between state and federal regulation where none clearly exists. * * *

An additional argument is advanced, however, based not upon the mere existence of the federal inspection standards, but upon the fact that the appellant's vessels were actually licensed. * * * It is asserted that the vessels have thus been given a dominant federal right to the use of the navigable waters of the United States, free from the local impediment that would be imposed by the Detroit ordinance.

* * *

The mere possession of a federal license, however, does not immunize a ship from the operation of the normal incidents of local police power, not constituting a direct regulation of commerce. * * * [T]he Detroit ordinance requires no more than compliance with an orderly and reasonable scheme of community regulation. The ordinance does not exclude a licensed vessel from the Port of Detroit, nor does it destroy the right of free passage. We cannot hold that the local regulation so burdens the federal license as to be constitutionally invalid.

The claim that the Detroit ordinance, quite apart from the effect of federal legislation, imposes as to the appellant's ships an undue burden on interstate commerce needs no extended discussion. State regulation, based on the police power, which does not discriminate against interstate commerce or operate to disrupt its required uniformity, may constitutionally stand. * * *

It has not been suggested that the local ordinance, applicable alike to "any person, firm or corporation" within the city, discriminates against interstate commerce as such. It is a regulation of general application, designed to better the health and welfare of the community. And while the appellant argues that other local governments might impose differing requirements as to air pollution, it has pointed to none. The record contains nothing to suggest the existence of any such competing or conflicting local regulations. Cf. Bibb v. Navajo Freight Lines, Inc., 359 U.S. 520, 79 S.Ct. 962. We conclude that no impermissible burden on commerce has been shown.

The judgment is affirmed.

Mr. Justice DOUGLAS, with whom Mr. Justice FRANKFURTER concurs, dissenting.

The Court treats this controversy as if it were merely an inspection case with the City of Detroit supplementing a federal inspection system as the State of Washington did in Kelly v. State of Washington, 302 U.S. 1, 58 S.Ct. 87. There a state inspection system touched matters "which the federal laws and regulations" left "untouched." * * * This is not that type of case. Nor is this the rare case where state law adopts the standards and requirements of federal law and is allowed to exact a permit in addition to the one demanded by federal law. * * * Here we have a criminal prosecution against a shipowner and officers of two of its vessels for using the very equipment on these vessels which the Federal Government says may be used. At stake are a possible fine of $100 on the owner and both a fine and a 30-day jail sentence on the officers.

* * *

The federal statutes give the Coast Guard the power to inspect "the boilers" of freight vessels every two years, and provide that when the Coast Guard approves the vessel and her equipment throughout, a certificate to that effect shall be made.

The requirements of the Detroit smoke ordinance are squarely in conflict with the federal statute. * * *

Thus it is plain that the ordinance requires not only the inspection and approval of equipment which has been inspected and approved by the Coast Guard but also the sealing of equipment, even though it has been approved by the Coast Guard. Under the Detroit ordinance a certificate of operation would not issue for a hand-fired Scotch marine boiler, even though it had been approved by the Coast Guard. In other words, this equipment approved and licensed by the Federal Government for use on navigable waters cannot pass muster under local law.

If local law required federally licensed vessels to observe local speed laws, obey local traffic regulations, or dock at certain times or under prescribed conditions, we would have local laws not at war with the federal license, but complementary to it. * * *

* * * The boats of appellant * * * have credentials good for any port; and I would not allow this local smoke ordinance to work in derogation of them. The fact that the Federal Government in certifying equipment applies standards of safety for seagoing vessels, while Detroit applies standards of air pollution seems immaterial. Federal pre-emption occurs when the boilers and fuel to be used in the vessels are specified in the certificate. No state authority can, in my view, change those specifications. Yet that is in effect what is allowed here.

* * *

CITY OF BURBANK v. LOCKHEED AIR TERMINAL

Supreme Court of the United States, 1973
411 U.S. 624, 93 S.Ct. 1854, 36 L.Ed.2d 547

The facts are set out in the opinion.

Mr. Justice DOUGLAS delivered the opinion of the Court.

The Court in Cooley v. Board of Wardens, 12 How. 299, first stated the rule of pre-emption which is the critical issue in the present case. Speaking through Justice Curtis, it said:

"Now the power to regulate commerce, embraces a vast field, containing not only many, but exceedingly various subjects, quite unlike in their nature; some imperatively demanding a single uniform rule, operating equally on the commerce of the United States in every port; and some, like the subject now in question, as imperatively demanding that diversity, which alone can meet the local necessities of navigation. * * * Whatever subjects of this power are in their nature national, or admit only of one uniform system, or plan of regulation, may justly be said to be of such a nature as to require exclusive legislation by Congress."

This suit brought by appellees asked for an injunction against the enforcement of an ordinance adopted by the City Council of Burbank, California, which made it unlawful for a so-called pure jet aircraft to take off from the Hollywood-Burbank Airport between 11 p. m. of one day and 7 a. m. the next day, and making it unlawful for the operator of that airport to allow any such aircraft to take off from that airport during such periods. The only regularly scheduled flight affected by the ordinance was an intrastate flight of Pacific Southwest Airlines originating in Oakland, California, and departing from Hollywood-Burbank Airport for

San Diego every Sunday night at 11:30 p. m.

The District Court found the ordinance to be unconstitutional on both Supremacy Clause and Commerce Clause grounds, 318 F.Supp. 914. The Court of Appeals affirmed on the grounds of the Supremacy Clause both as respects pre-emption and as respects conflict. 457 F.2d 667. * * * We affirm the Court of Appeals.

The Federal Aviation Act of 1958, 72 Stat. 737, 49 U.S.C.A. § 1301 et seq., as amended by the Noise Control Act of 1972, 86 Stat. 1234, and the regulations under it * * * are central to the question of pre-emption.

Section 1508 provides in part, "The United States of America is declared to possess and exercise complete and exclusive national sovereignty in the airspace of the United States." * * * By § 1348 the Administrator of the Federal Aeronautics Act (FAA) has been given broad authority to regulate the use of the navigable airspace, "in order to insure the safety of aircraft and the efficient utilization of such airspace * * *" and "for the protection of persons and property on the ground." * * *

Curfews, such as Burbank has imposed, would according to the testimony at the trial and the District Court's findings increase congestion, cause a loss of efficiency, and aggravate the noise problem. FAA has occasionally operated curfews. * * * But the record shows that FAA has consistently opposed curfews, unless managed by it, in the interests of its management of the "navigable airspace."

As stated by Judge Dooling in American Airlines v. Hempstead, 272 F.Supp. 226, 230, aff'd 398 F.2d 369:

"The aircraft and its noise are indivisible; the noise of the aircraft extends outward from it with the same inseparability as its wings and tail assembly; to exclude the aircraft noise from the Town is to exclude the aircraft; to set a ground level decible limit for the aircraft is directly to exclude it from the lower air that it cannot use without exceeding the decible limit."

The Noise Control Act of 1972, 86 Stat. 1234, which was approved October 27, 1972, provides that the Administrator "after consultation with appropriate Federal, State, and local agencies and interested persons" shall conduct a study of various facets of the aircraft "noise" problems and report to the Congress within nine months, i.e., by July 1973. The 1972 Act by amending § 611 of the Federal Aviation Act, also involves the Environmental Protection Agency (EPA) in the comprehensive scheme of federal control of the aircraft noise problem. * * *

* * *

There is to be sure no express provision of pre-emption in the 1972 Act. That, however, is not decisive. * * * It is the pervasive nature of the scheme of federal regulation of aircraft noise that leads us to conclude that there is pre-emption. * * *

* * *

If we were to uphold the Burbank ordinance and a significant number of municipalities followed suit, it is obvious that fractionalized control of the timing of take-offs and landings would severely limit the flexibility of the FAA in controlling air traffic flow. The difficulties of scheduling flights to avoid congestion and the concomitant decrease in safety would be compounded. In 1960 the FAA rejected a proposed restriction on jet operations at the Los Angeles airport between 10 p. m. and 7 a. m. because such restrictions could "create critically serious problems to all air transportation patterns." 25 Fed. Reg. 1764–1765. The complete FAA statement said:

"The proposed restriction on the use of the airport by jet aircraft between the hours of 10 p. m. and 7 a. m. under certain surface wind conditions has also been reevaluated and this provision has been omitted from the rule. The practice of prohibiting the use of various airports during certain specific hours could create critically serious problems to all air transportation patterns. The network of airports throughout the United States and the constant availability of these airports are essential to the maintenance of a sound air transportation system. The continuing growth of public acceptance of aviation as a major force in passenger transportation and the increasingly significant role of commercial aviation in the nation's economy are accomplishments which cannot be inhibited if the best interest of the public is to be served. It was concluded therefore that the extent of relief from the noise problem which this provision must have achieved would not have compensated the degree of restriction it would have imposed on domestic and foreign Air Commerce."

This decision, announced in 1960, remains peculiarly within the competence of the FAA, supplemented now by the input of the EPA. We are not at liberty to diffuse the powers given by Congress to FAA and EPA by letting the States or municipalities in on the planning. If that change is to be made, Congress alone must do it.

Affirmed.

Mr. Justice REHNQUIST, with whom Mr. Justice STEWART, Mr. Justice WHITE, and Mr. Justice MARSHALL join, dissenting.

The Court concludes that congressional legislation dealing with aircraft noise has so "pervaded" that field that Congress has *impliedly* pre-empted it, and therefore the ordinance of the city of Burbank here challenged is invalid under the Supremacy Clause of the Constitution. The Court says that "we need not, however, dwell long on the earlier versions of the Federal Aviation Act, for a 1972 Act put the question completely at rest." * * * Yet the House and Senate committee reports explicitly state that the 1972 Act to which the Court refers was *not* intended to alter the balance between state and federal regulation which had been struck by earlier congressional legislation in this area. The House Report, H.R.Rep.No.92–842, in discussing the general pre-emptive effect of the entire bill, stated:

"The authority of State and local government to regulate use, operation or movement of products is not effected at all by the bill. (The pre-emption provision discussed in this paragraph does not apply to aircraft. See discussion of aircraft noise below.)"

The report went on to state specifically:

"No provision of the bill is intended to alter in any way the relationship between the authority of the Federal Government and that of State and local governments that existed with respect to matters covered by section 611 of the Federal Aviation Act of

1958 prior to the enactment of the bill."

* * *

Appellees do not contend that the noise produced by jet engines could not reasonably be deemed to affect adversely the health and welfare of persons constantly exposed to it; control of noise, sufficiently loud to be classified as a public nuisance at common law, would be a type of regulation well within the traditional scope of the police power possessed by States and local governing bodies. Because noise regulation has traditionally been an area of local, not national, concern, in determining whether congressional legislation has, by implication, foreclosed remedial local enactments "we start with the assumption that the historic police powers of the States were not to be superseded by the Federal Act unless that was the clear and manifest purpose of Congress." Rice v. Santa Fe Elevator Corp., 331 U.S. 218, 230, 67 S.Ct. 1146, 1152. This assumption derives from our basic constitutional division of legislative competence between the States and Congress; from "due regard for the presuppositions of our embracing federal system, *including the principle of diffusion of power not as a matter of doctrinaire localism but as a promoter of democracy.*" * * * San Diego Building Trades Council v. Garmon, 359 U.S. 236, 243, 79 S.Ct. 773, 779 (emphasis added). Unless the requisite pre-emptive intent is abundantly clear, we should hesitate to invalidate state and local legislation for the added reason that "the

State is powerless to remove the ill effects of our decision, while the national government, which has the ultimate power, remains free to remove the burden." Penn Dairies, Inc. v. Milk Control Commission, 318 U.S. 261, 275, 63 S.Ct. 617, 624.

* * *

The District Court found that the Burbank ordinance would impose an undue burden on interstate commerce, and held it invalid under the Commerce Clause for that reason. Neither the Court of Appeals nor this Court's opinion, in view of their determination as to pre-emption, reached that question. The District Court's conclusion appears to be based at least in part on a consideration of the effect on interstate commerce that would result if all municipal airports in the country enacted ordinances such as that of Burbank. Since the proper determination of the question turns on an evaluation of the facts of each case, see, e.g., Bibb v. Navajo Freight Lines, Inc., 359 U.S. 520, 79 S.Ct. 962, and not on a predicted proliferation of possibilities, the District Court's conclusion is of doubtful validity. The Burbank ordinance did not affect emergency flights, and had the total effect of prohibiting one scheduled commercial flight each week and several additional private flights by corporate executives; such a result can hardly be held to be an unreasonable burden on commerce. Since the Court expresses no opinion on the question, however I refrain from any further analysis of it.

Another case, noteworthy for its timely illustration of the clash between federal and state jurisdiction in the area of environmental regulation, is Northern States Power Co. v. Minnesota, 447 F.2d 1143 (8th Cir. 1971). The issue in that case, as framed by a federal appellate court, was "whether the United States Government has the sole authority under the doctrine of pre-emption to regulate radioactive waste releases from nuclear power plants to the exclusion of the states." Northern States Power Company, a Minnesota corporation which generated electric power and then sold it in an interstate market (Northern distributed power in the neighboring states of North and South Dakota and Wisconsin, aside from Minnesota), obtained a permit from the Atomic Energy Commission in June 1967, for construction of a nuclear power plant on the Mississippi River at Monticello, Minnesota. The permit was issued by the federal agency pursuant to the Atomic Energy Act of 1954, as amended. Two years later, Northern received a waste disposal permit from Minnesota to operate the Monticello plant under conditions governing the level of gaseous emissions and radioactive liquids which were markedly more stringent than existing federal standards. In January 1971, the AEC issued a provisional operating license under which the plant was generating power when the litigation in this case began. Northern brought suit seeking a declaration that Minnesota had no constitutional right to regulate the discharges from the Monticello plant. Minnesota defended, relying generally on the police power reserved to it under the Tenth Amendment. A federal district court ruled against the state, and Minnesota appealed.

The U.S. Court of Appeals for the Eighth Circuit affirmed the lower court's decision. Speaking for the court, Chief Judge Matthes wrote:

> *   *   *   Minnesota vigorously maintains that the subject matter regulated in the instant case is confined to the narrow area of pollution control over the radioactive effluents discharged from the Monticello plant and that this is peculiarly related to the public health and safety of its state's citizens and therefore within their police powers to control. See Huron Portland Cement Co. v. Detroit, 362 U.S. 440, 80 S.Ct. 813 (1960). They contend that this is not an area which by its very nature admits only of national supervision nor one demanding exclusive federal regulation in order to achieve uniformity vital to national interests.   *   *   *

> We cannot acquiesce in this microcosmic approach to the subject matter to be regulated.   *   *   *   As Northern points out and as the record reveals, major generating plants not only produce electric power for customers in their own and neighboring states, but are part of an interstate transmission system which makes possible the purchase and sale of electric power between major systems across the nation. Congressional objectives expressed in the 1954 Act evince a legislative design to foster and encourage the development, use and control of atomic energy so as to make the maximum contribution to the general welfare and to increase the standard of living. 42 U.S.C.A. §§ 2011, 2012. However, these objectives were to be effectuated "to the maximum extent consistent with the common defense and security and with the health and safety of the public." 42 U.S. C.A. § 2013. Thus, through direction of the licensing scheme for nuclear reactors, Congress vested the AEC with the authority to resolve the proper balance between desired industrial progress and adequate health and safety standards. Only through the application and enforcement of uniform standards promulgated by a national agency will these dual objectives be assured. Were the states allowed to impose stricter standards on the level of radioactive waste releases discharged from nuclear power plants, they might conceivably be so overprotective in the area of health and safety as to unnecessarily stultify the industrial development and use of atomic energy for the production of electric power.

*   *   *

Accordingly, for the reasons stated, we hold that the federal government has exclusive authority under the doctrine of pre-emption to regulate the construction and operation of nuclear power plants, which necessarily includes regulation of the levels of radioactive effluents discharged from the plant.

The Supreme Court summarily affirmed this judgment, 405 U.S. 1035, 92 S.Ct. 1307 (1972), with Justices Douglas and Stewart dissenting.

CITY OF PHILADELPHIA v. STATE OF NEW JERSEY

Supreme Court of the United States, 1978
437 U.S. 617, 98 S.Ct. 2531, 57 L.Ed.2d 475

Chapter 363 of the 1973 New Jersey Laws prohibits the importation of most "solid or liquid waste which originated or was collected outside the territorial limits of the State." The legislature prefaced its enactment with findings "that * * * the volume of solid and liquid waste continues to rapidly increase, that the treatment and disposal of these wastes continues to pose an even greater threat to the quality of the environment of New Jersey, that the available and appropriate land fill sites within the State are being diminished, that the environment continues to be threatened by the treatment and disposal of waste which originated or was collected outside the State and that the public health, safety and welfare require that the treatment and disposal within this State of all wastes generated outside of the State be prohibited." Operators of private New Jersey landfills and several cities in other states with whom these collectors had contracts for waste disposal brought suit attacking the law as an unconstitutional burden on interstate commerce.

Mr. Justice STEWART delivered the opinion of the Court.

* * *

Before it addressed the merits of the appellants' claim, the New Jersey Supreme Court questioned whether the interstate movement of those wastes banned by ch. 363 is "commerce" at all within the meaning of the Commerce Clause. Any doubts on that score should be laid to rest at the outset.

The state court expressed the view that there may be two definitions of "commerce" for constitutional purposes. When relied on "to support some exertion of federal control or regulation," the Commerce Clause permits "a very sweeping concept" of commerce. * * * But when relied on "to strike down or restrict state legislation," that Clause and the term "commerce" have a "much more confined * * * reach." * * *

The state court reached this conclusion in an attempt to reconcile modern Commerce Clause concepts with several old cases of this Court holding that States can prohibit the importation of some objects because they "are not legitimate subjects of trade and commerce." Bowman v. Chicago & Northwestern R. Co., 125 U.S. 465, 489, 8 S.Ct. 689. These articles include items "which, on account of their existing condition, would bring in and spread disease, pestilence, and death, such as rags or other substances infected with the germs of yellow fever or the virus of small-pox, or cattle or meat or other provisions that are diseased or decayed, or otherwise, from their condition and quality, unfit for human use or consumption." * * * See also Baldwin v. G. A. F. Seelig, 294 U.S. 511, 525, 55 S.Ct. 497, 501, and cases cited therein. The state court found that ch. 363 as narrowed by the state regulations, * * * banned only "those wastes which can[not] be put to effective use," and therefore those wastes were not commerce at all, unless "the mere transportation and disposal of valueless waste between states constitutes interstate commerce within the meaning of the constitutional provision." * * *

We think the state court misread our cases, and thus erred in assuming that they require a two-tiered definition of commerce. In saying that innately harmful articles "are not legitimate subjects of trade and commerce," the *Bowman* Court was stating its conclusion, not the starting point of its reasoning. All objects of interstate trade merit Commerce Clause protection; none is excluded by definition at the outset. In *Bowman* and similar cases, the Court held simply that because the articles' worth in interstate commerce was far outweighed by the dangers inhering in their very movement, States could prohibit their transportation across state lines. Hence, we reject the state court's suggestion that the banning of "valueless" out-of-state wastes by ch. 363 implicates no constitutional protection. Just as Congress has power to regulate the interstate movement of these wastes, States are not free from constitutional scrutiny when they restrict that movement. * * *

Although the Constitution gives Congress the power to regulate commerce among the States, many subjects of potential federal regulation under that power inevitably escape congressional attention "because of their local character and their number and diversity." South Carolina State Highway Dept. v. Barnwell Bros., Inc., 303 U.S. 177, 185, 58 S.Ct. 510, 513. In the absence of federal legislation, these subjects are open to control by the States so long as they act within the restraints imposed by the Commerce Clause itself. * * * The bounds of these restraints appear nowhere in the words of the Commerce Clause, but have emerged gradually in the decisions of this Court giving effect to its basic purpose. That broad purpose as well expressed by Mr. Justice Jackson in his opinion for the Court in H. P. Hood & Sons, Inc. v. Du Mond, 336 U.S. 525, 537–538, 69 S.Ct. 657, 665:

"This principle that our economic unit is the Nation, which alone has the gamut of powers necessary to control of the economy, including the vital power of erecting customs barriers against foreign competition, has as its corollary that the states are not separable economic units. As the Court said in Baldwin v. Seelig, 294 U.S. 511, 527, 55 S.Ct. 497, 'what is ultimate is the principle that one state in its dealings with another may not place itself in a position of economic isolation.' "

The opinions of the Court through the years have reflected an alertness to the evils of "economic isolation" and protectionism, while at the same time recognizing that incidental burdens on interstate commerce may be unavoidable when a State legislates to safeguard the health and safety of its people. Thus, where simple economic protectionism is effected by state legislation, a virtually per se

rule of invalidity has been erected.
* * * The clearest example of
such legislation is a law that overtly
blocks the flow of interstate commerce at a State's borders. * * *
But where other legislative objectives are credibly advanced and there
is no patent discrimination against interstate trade, the Court has adopted
a much more flexible approach, the
general contours of which were outlined in Pike v. Bruce Church, Inc.,
397 U.S. 137, 142, 90 S.Ct. 844, 847:

"Where the statute regulates even-
handedly to effectuate a legitimate
local public interest, and its effects
on interstate commerce are only incidental, it will be upheld unless the
burden imposed on such commerce is
clearly excessive in relation to the
putative local benefits. * * * If a
legitimate local purpose is found
then the question becomes one of degree. And the extent of the burden
that will be tolerated will of course
depend on the nature of the local interest involved, and on whether it
could be promoted as well with lesser
impact on interstate activities."
* * *

The crucial inquiry, therefore, must
be directed to determining whether
ch. 363 is basically a protectionist
measure, or whether it can fairly be
viewed as a law directed to legitimate local concerns, with effects upon interstate commerce that are only
incidental.

* * *

The New Jersey Supreme Court
accepted * * * [the] statement
of the state legislature's purpose.
The state court additionally found
that New Jersey's existing landfill
sites will be exhausted within a few
years; that to go on using these sites
or to develop new ones will take a
heavy environmental toll, both from

pollution and from loss of scarce
open lands; that new techniques to
divert waste from landfills to other
methods of disposal and resource recovery processes are under development, but that these changes will require time; and finally, that "the
extension of the lifespan of existing
landfills, resulting from the exclusion of out-of-state waste, may be of
crucial importance in preventing further virgin wetlands or other unde-
veloped lands from being devoted to
landfill purposes." * * * Based
on these findings, the court concluded that ch. 363 was designed to protect not the State's economy, but its
environment, and that its substantial
benefits outweigh its "slight" burden
on interstate commerce. * * *

The appellants strenuously contend that ch. 363, "while outwardly
cloaked 'in the currently fashionable
garb of environmental protection,'
* * * is actually no more than a
legislative effort to suppress competition and stabilize the cost of solid
waste disposal for New Jersey residents." * * * They cite passages
of legislative history suggesting that
the problem addressed by ch. 363 is
primarily financial: Stemming the
flow of out-of-state waste into certain landfill sites will extend their
lives, thus delaying the day when
New Jersey cities must transport
their waste to more distant and expensive sites.

The appellees, on the other hand,
deny that ch. 363 was motivated by
financial concerns or economic protectionism. In the words of their
brief, "No New Jersey commercial
interests stand to gain advantage
over competitors from outside the
state as a result of the ban on dumping out-of-state waste." Noting that
New Jersey landfill operators are
among the plaintiffs, the appellees

argue that "[t]he complaint is not that New Jersey has forged an economic preference for its own commercial interests, but rather that it has denied a small group of its entrepreneurs an economic opportunity to traffic in waste in order to protect the health, safety and welfare of the citizenry at large."

This dispute about ultimate legislative purpose need not be resolved, because its resolution would not be relevant to the constitutional issue to be decided in this case. Contrary to the evident assumption of the state court and the parties, the evil of protectionism can reside in legislative means as well as legislative ends. Thus, it does not matter whether the ultimate aim of ch. 363 is to reduce the waste disposal costs of New Jersey residents or to save remaining open lands from pollution, for we assume New Jersey has every right to protect its residents' pocketbooks as well as their environment. And it may be assumed as well that New Jersey may pursue those ends by slowing the flow of *all* waste into the State's remaining landfills, even though interstate commerce may incidentally be affected. But whatever New Jersey's ultimate purpose, it may not be accomplished by discriminating against articles of commerce coming from outside the State unless there is some reason, apart from their origin, to treat them differently. Both on its face and in its plain effect, ch. 363 violates this principle of nondiscrimination.

* * *

The New Jersey law at issue in this case falls squarely within the area that the Commerce Clause puts off-limits to state regulation. On its face, it imposes on out-of-state commercial interests the full burden of

conserving the State's remaining landfill space. It is true that in our previous cases the scarce natural resource was itself the article of commerce, whereas here the scarce resource and the article of commerce are distinct. But that difference is without consequence. In both instances, the State has overtly moved to slow or freeze the flow of commerce for protectionist reasons. It does not matter that the State has shut the article of commerce inside the State in one case and outside the State in the other. What is crucial is the attempt by one State to isolate itself from a problem common to many by erecting a barrier against the movement of interstate trade.

The appellees argue that not all laws which facially discriminate against out-of-state commerce are forbidden protectionist regulations. In particular, they point to quarantine laws, which this Court has repeatedly upheld even though they appear to single out interstate commerce for special treatment. See Baldwin v. G. A. F. Seelig, supra, 294 U.S., at 525, 55 S.Ct., at 501; Bowman v. Chicago & Northwestern R. Co., supra, 125 U.S., at 489, 8 S.Ct., at 700. In the appellees' view, ch. 363 is analogous to such health-protective measures, since it reduces the exposure of New Jersey residents to the allegedly harmful effects of landfill sites.

It is true that certain quarantine laws have not been considered forbidden protectionist measures, even though they were directed against out-of-state commerce. See Asbell v. Kansas, 209 U.S. 251, 28 S.Ct. 485; Reid v. Colorado, 187 U.S. 137, 23 S.Ct. 92; Bowman v. Chicago & Northwestern R. Co., supra, at 489. But those quarantine laws banned the importation of articles such as diseased livestock that required destruction as soon as possible because their very movement risked contagion and other evils. Those laws thus did not discriminate against interstate commerce as such, but simply prevented traffic in noxious articles, whatever their origin.

The New Jersey statute is not such a quarantine law. There has been no claim here that the very movement of waste into or through New Jersey endangers health, or that waste must be disposed of as soon and as close to its point of generation as possible. The harms caused by waste are said to arise after its disposal in landfill sites, and at that point, as New Jersey concedes, there is no basis to distinguish out-of-state waste from domestic waste. If one is inherently harmful, so is the other. Yet New Jersey has banned the former while leaving its landfill sites open to the later. The New Jersey law blocks the importation of waste in an obvious effort to saddle those outside the State with the entire burden of slowing the flow of refuse into New Jersey's remaining landfill sites. That legislative effort is clearly impermissible under the Commerce Clause of the Constitution.

Today, cities in Pennsylvania and New York find it expedient or necessary to send their waste into New Jersey for disposal, and New Jersey claims the right to close its borders to such traffic. Tomorrow, cities in New Jersey may find it expedient or necessary to send their waste into Pennsylvania or New York for disposal, and those States might then claim the right to close their borders. The Commerce Clause will protect New Jersey in the future, just as it protects her neighbors now, from efforts by one State to isolate itself in the stream of interstate commerce from a problem shared by all.

The judgment is reversed.

Mr Justice REHNQUIST, with whom THE CHIEF JUSTICE [BURGER] joins, dissenting.

* * *

The question presented in this case is whether New Jersey must also continue to receive and dispose of solid waste from neighboring States, even though these will inexorably increase the health problems discussed above. The Court answers this question in the affirmative. New Jersey must either prohibit *all* landfill operations, leaving itself to cast about for a presently nonexistent solution to the serious problem of disposing of the waste generated within its own borders, or it must accept waste from every portion of the United States, thereby multiplying the health and safety problems which would result if it dealt only with such wastes generated within the State. Because past precedents establish that the Commerce Clause does not present appellees with such a Hobson's choice, I dissent.

* * *

In my opinion, these cases are dispositive of the present one. Under them, New Jersey may require germ-infected rags or diseased meat to be disposed of as best as possible within the State, but at the same time prohibit the *importation* of such items for disposal at the facilities that are set up within New Jersey for disposal of such material generated *within* the State. The physical fact of life that New Jersey must somehow dispose of its own noxious items does not mean that it must serve as a depository for those of every other

State. Similarly, New Jersey should be free under our past precedents to prohibit the importation of solid waste because of the health and safety problems that such waste poses to its citizens. The fact that New Jersey continues to, and indeed must continue to, dispose of its own solid waste does not mean that New Jersey may not prohibit the importation of even more solid waste into the State. I simply see no way to distinguish solid waste, on the record of this case, from germ-infected rags, diseased meat, and other noxious items.

The Court's effort to distinguish these prior cases is unconvincing. It first asserts that the quarantine laws which have previously been upheld "ban the importation of articles such as diseased livestock that required destruction as soon as possible because their very movement risked contagion and other evils." * * * According to the Court, the New Jersey law is distinguishable from these other laws, and invalid, because the concern of New Jersey is not with the *movement* of solid waste but of the present inability to safely *dispose* of it once it reaches its destination. But I think it far from clear that the State's law has as limited a focus as the Court imputes to it: Solid waste which is a health hazard when it reaches its destination may in all likelihood be an equally great health hazard in transit.

Even if the Court is correct in its characterization of New Jersey's concerns, I do not see why a State may ban the importation of items whose movement risks contagion, but cannot ban the importation of items which, although they may be transported into the State without undue hazard, will then simply pile up in an ever increasing danger to the public's health and safety. The Commerce Clause was not drawn with a view to having the validity of state laws turn on such pointless distinctions.

Second, the Court implies that the challenged laws must be invalidated because New Jersey has left its landfills open to domestic waste. But, as the Court notes, * * * this Court has repeatedly upheld quarantine laws "even though they appear to single out interstate commerce for special treatment." The fact that New Jersey has left its landfill sites open for domestic waste does not, of course, mean that solid waste is not innately harmful. Nor does it mean that New Jersey prohibits importation of solid waste for reasons other than the health and safety of its population. New Jersey must out of sheer necessity treat and dispose of its solid waste in some fashion, just as it must treat New Jersey cattle suffering from hoof-and-mouth disease. It does not follow that New Jersey must, under the Commerce Clause, accept solid waste or diseased cattle from outside its borders and thereby exacerbate its problems.

The Supreme Court of New Jersey expressly found that ch. 363 was passed "to preserve the health of New Jersey residents by keeping their exposure to solid waste and landfill areas to a minimum." * * * The Court points to absolutely no evidence that would contradict this finding by the New Jersey Supreme Court. Because I find no basis for distinguishing the laws under challenge here from our past cases upholding state laws that prohibit the importation of items that could endanger the population of the State, I dissent.

STATE REGULATION CASES SINCE *CITY OF PHILADELPHIA* v. *STATE OF NEW JERSEY*

Case	Facts	Holding/Reasoning
Minnesota v. Clover Leaf Creamery Co., 449 U.S. 457, 101 S.Ct. 715 (1981)	A Minnesota statute "bann[ed] the retail sale of milk in plastic nonreturnable, nonrefillable containers, but permitt[ed] such sale in other nonreturnable, nonrefillable containers, such as paperboard milk cartons" as a measure to promote conservation of resources, ease solid waste disposal problems, and save energy.	Since the statute "regulates 'even-handedly' by prohibiting all milk retailers from selling their products in plastic, nonreturnable milk containers, without regard to whether the milk, the containers, or the sellers are from outside the State" it "does not discriminate between interstate and intrastate commerce * * *." The "incidental burden imposed on commerce" is "relatively minor" and is not excessive considering the interests Minnesota seeks to further, even if "the out-of-state plastics industry is burdened relatively more heavily than the Minnesota pulpwood industry * * *."
New England Power Co. v. New Hampshire, 455 U.S. 331, 102 S.Ct. 1096 (1982)	A New Hampshire statute prohibits a corporation engaged in generating electric power from water from transmitting such energy outside the state unless prior approval has been received from the state public utilities commission. The state law authorizes the commission to ban the exportation of electrical energy when it finds that such energy "is reasonably required for use within this state and the public good requires that it be delivered for such use." Acting pursuant to the statute, the commission withdrew its approval for a power company, which sold most of its electricity in Massachusetts and Rhode Island, to transmit its power out of the state and ordered the firm to arrange to sell its previously exported power within the state.	"The order of the New Hampshire Commission * * * is precisely the sort of protectionist regulation that the Commerce Clause declares off-limits to the States. The Commission has made clear that its order is designed to gain an economic advantage for New Hampshire citizens at the expense of New England Power's customers in neighboring States. Moreover, it cannot be disputed that the Commission's 'exportation ban' places direct and substantial burdens on transactions in interstate commerce. * * * Such state-imposed burdens cannot be squared with the Commerce Clause when they serve only to advance 'simple economic protectionism.'" Nor did Congress, in any part of the Federal Power Act, authorize the states to impose such restrictions.

STATE REGULATION CASES (*Cont.*)

Case	Facts	Holding/Reasoning
Sporhase v. Nebraska, ___ U.S. ___, 102 S.Ct. 3456 (1982)	A Nebraska law requires anyone intending to withdraw ground water from a well located in the state and transport it for use in a neighboring state to first obtain a permit from a state agency. The agency grants permission if the withdrawal is (1) reasonable, (2) not contrary to the conservation and use of ground water, (3) not otherwise detrimental to the public welfare; and (4) if a reciprocal agreement exists between Nebraska and the state to which the ground water is to be transported permitting ground water from that state to be removed to Nebraska.	Ground water is an article of commerce, and conservation and preservation of it in the dry western states has an interstate dimension. The agricultural markets supplied by irrigated farms are included in the sort of federal interest that gave rise to the Commerce Clause. There is a significant federal interest in the conservation of scarce ground water and in its equitable allocation. While permit conditions (1) through (3) do not facially infringe the federal interest protected by the Commerce Clause, the reciprocity requirement constitutes an explicit barrier to interstate trade and impermissibly burdens the Commerce Clause.

DEAN MILK CO. v. CITY OF MADISON

Supreme Court of the United States, 1951
340 U.S. 349, 71 S.Ct. 295, 95 L.Ed. 329

A Madison, Wisconsin ordinance prohibited the sale of milk in the city that either came from a farm located further than twenty-five miles from Madison's central square or was bottled outside a five-mile radius from the square. Dean Milk Company, an Illinois corporation distributing milk in Illinois and Wisconsin, was denied a license to sell milk in Madison because its pasteurization plants were not within the five-mile limit. The company brought action against the city to test the validity of the restrictions. A county circuit court upheld the ordinance, and the Wisconsin Supreme Court affirmed. Dean Milk appealed to the U. S. Supreme Court.

Mr. Justice CLARK delivered the opinion of the Court.

* * *

The City of Madison is the county seat of Dane County. Within the county are some 5,600 dairy farms with total raw milk production in excess of 600,000,000 pounds annually and more than ten times the requirements of Madison. Aside from the milk supplied to Madison, fluid milk produced in the county moves in large quantities to Chicago and more distant consuming areas, and the remainder is used in making cheese, butter and other products. At the time of trial the Madison milkshed was not of "Grade A" quality by the standards recommended by the United States Public Health Service, and no milk labeled "Grade A" was distributed in Madison.

The area defined by the ordinance with respect to milk sources encompasses practically all of Dane County and includes some 500 farms which supply milk for Madison. Within the five-mile area for pasteurization are plants of five processors, only three of which are engaged in the general wholesale and retail trade in Madison. Inspection of these farms and plants is scheduled once every thirty days and is performed by two municipal inspectors, one of whom is full-time. The courts below found that the ordinance in question promotes convenient, economical and efficient plant inspection.

Appellant purchases and gathers milk from approximately 950 farms in northern Illinois and southern Wisconsin, none being within twenty-five miles of Madison. Its pasteurization plants are located at Chemung and Huntley, Illinois, about 65 and 85 miles respectively from Madison. Appellant was denied a license to sell its products within Madison solely because its pasteurization plants were more than five miles away.

It is conceded that the milk which appellant seeks to sell in Madison is supplied from farms and processed in plants licensed and inspected by public health authorities of Chicago, and is labeled "Grade A" under the Chicago ordinance which adopts the rating standards recommended by the United States Public Health Service. * * *

Madison contends and we assume that in some particulars its ordinance is more rigorous than that of Chicago.

* * *

This is not an instance in which an enactment falls because of federal legislation which, as a proper exercise of paramount national power over commerce, excludes measures which might otherwise be within the police power of the states. * * * There is no pertinent national regulation by the Congress, and statutes enacted for the District of Columbia indicate that Congress has recognized the appropriateness of local regulation of the sale of fluid milk. * * * It is not contended, however, that Congress has authorized the regulation before us.

Nor can there be objection to the avowed purpose of this enactment. We assume that difficulties in sanitary regulation of milk and milk products originating in remote areas may present a situation in which "upon a consideration of all the relevant facts and circumstances it appears that the matter is one which may appropriately be regulated in the interest of the safety, health and well-being of local communities." * * * Parker v. Brown, 1943, 317 U.S. 341, 362–363, 63 S.Ct. 307, 319. * * * We also assume that since Congress has not spoken to the contrary, the subject matter of the ordinance lies within the sphere of state regulation even though interstate commerce may be affected. * * *

But this regulation, like the provision invalidated in *Baldwin* v. *G. A. F. Seelig, Inc.,* * * * in practical effect excludes from distribution in Madison wholesome milk produced and pasteurized in Illinois. "The importer * * * may keep his milk or drink it, but sell it he may not." Id., 294 U.S. at page 521, 55 S.Ct. at page 500. In thus erecting an economic barrier protecting a major local industry against competition from without the State, Madison plainly discriminates against interstate commerce. This it cannot do, even in the exercise of its unquestioned power to protect the health and safety of its people, if reasonable nondiscriminatory alternatives, adequate to conserve legitimate local interests, are available. * * * A different view, that the ordinance is valid simply because it professes to be a health measure, would mean that the Commerce Clause of itself imposes no limitations on state action other than those laid down by the Due Process Clause, save for the rare instance where a state artlessly discloses an avowed purpose to discriminate against interstate goods. * * * Our issue then is whether the discrimination inherent in the Madison ordinance can be justified in view of the character of the local interests and the available methods of protecting them. * * *

It appears that reasonable and adequate alternatives are available. If the City of Madison prefers to rely upon its own officials for inspection of distant milk sources, such inspection is readily open to it without hardship for it could charge the actual and reasonable cost of such inspection to the importing producers and processors. * * * Moreover, appellee Health Commissioner of Madison testified that as proponent of the local milk ordinance he had submitted the provisions here in controversy and an alternative proposal based on § 11 of the Model Milk Ordinance recommended by the United States Public Health Service. The model provision imposes no geographical limitation on location of milk sources and processing plants but excludes from the municipality milk not produced and pasteurized conformably to standards as high as those enforced by the receiving city. In implementing such an ordinance, the importing city obtains milk ratings based on uniform standards established by health authorities in the jurisdiction where production and

processing occur. The receiving city may determine the extent of enforcement of sanitary standards in the exporting area by verifying the accuracy of safety ratings of specific plants or of the milkshed in the distant jurisdiction through the United States Public Health Service, which routinely and on request spot checks the local ratings. The Commissioner testified that Madison consumers "would be safeguarded adequately" under either proposal and that he had expressed no preference. The milk sanitarian of the Wisconsin State Board of Health testified that the State Health Department recommends the adoption of a provision based on the Model Ordinance. Both officials agreed that a local health officer would be justified in relying upon the evaluation by the Public Health Service of enforcement conditions in remote producing areas.

To permit Madison to adopt a regulation not essential for the protection of local health interests and placing a discriminatory burden on interstate commerce would invite a multiplication of preferential trade areas destructive of the very purpose of the Commerce Clause. Under the circumstances here presented, the regulation must yield to the principle that "one state in its dealings with another may not place itself in a position of economic isolation." Baldwin v. G. A. F. Seelig, Inc., * * * 294 U.S. at page 527, 55 S.Ct. at page 502.

For these reasons we conclude that the judgment below sustaining the five-mile provision as to pasteurization must be reversed.

The Supreme Court of Wisconsin thought it unnecessary to pass upon the validity of the twenty-five-mile limitation, apparently in part for the reason that this issue was made academic by its decision upholding the five-mile section. In view of our conclusion as to the latter provision, a determination of appellant's contention as to the other section is now necessary. As to this issue, therefore, we vacate the judgment below and remand for further proceedings not inconsistent with the principles announced in this opinion. It is so ordered.

Judgment vacated and cause remanded.

Mr. Justice BLACK, with whom Mr. Justice DOUGLAS and Mr. Justice MINTON concur, dissenting.

* * * I disagree with the Court's premises, reasoning, and judgment.

(1) This ordinance does not exclude wholesome milk coming from Illinois or anywhere else. It does require that all milk sold in Madison must be pasteurized within five miles of the center of the city. But there was no finding in the state courts, nor evidence to justify a finding there or here, that appellant, Dean Milk Company, is unable to have its milk pasteurized within the defined geographical area. As a practical matter, so far as the record shows, Dean can easily comply with the ordinance whenever it wants to. Therefore, Dean's personal preference to pasteurize in Illinois, not the ordinance, keeps Dean's milk out of Madison.

(2) Characterization of § 7.21 as a "discriminatory burden" on interstate commerce is merely a statement of the Court's result, which I think incorrect. The section does prohibit the sale of milk in Madison by interstate and intrastate producers who prefer to pasteurize over five miles distant from the city. But

both state courts below found that § 7.21 represents a good-faith attempt to safeguard public health by making adequate sanitation inspection possible. While we are not bound by these findings, I do not understand the Court to overturn them. Therefore, the fact that § 7.21, like all health regulations, imposes some burden on trade, does not mean that it "discriminates" against interstate commerce.

(3) This health regulation should not be invalidated merely because the Court believes that alternative milk-inspection methods might insure the cleanliness and healthfulness of Dean's Illinois milk. I find it difficult to explain why the Court uses the "reasonable alternative" concept to protect trade when today it refuses to apply the same principle to protect freedom of speech. Feiner v. People of State of New York, 340 U.S. 315, 71 S.Ct. 303. For while the "reasonable alternative" concept has been invoked to protect First Amendment rights, e.g., Schneider v. State of New Jersey, 308 U.S. 147, 162, 60 S.Ct. 146, 151, it has not heretofore been considered an appropriate weapon for striking down local health laws. * * * In my view, to use this ground now elevates the right to traffic in commerce for profit above the power of the people to guard the purity of their daily diet of milk.

If, however, the principle announced today is to be followed, the Court should not strike down local health regulations unless satisfied beyond a reasonable doubt that the substitutes it proposes would not lower health standards. I do not think that the Court can so satisfy itself on the basis of its judicial knowledge. And the evidence in the record leads me to the conclusion that the substitute health measures suggested by the Court do not insure milk as safe as the Madison ordinance requires.

One of the Court's proposals is that Madison require milk processors to pay reasonable inspection fees at the milk supply "sources." Experience shows, however, that the fee method gives rise to prolonged litigation over the calculation and collection of the charges.   *   *   *   To throw local milk regulation into such a quagmire of uncertainty jeopardizes the admirable milk-inspection systems in force in many municipalities.   Moreover, nothing in the record before us indicates that the fee system might not be as costly to Dean as having its milk pasteurized in Madison. Surely the Court is not resolving this question by drawing on its "judicial knowledge" to supply information as to comparative costs, convenience, or effectiveness.

The Court's second proposal is that Madison adopt § 11 of the "Model Milk Ordinance." The state courts made no findings as to the relative merits of this inspection ordinance and the one chosen by Madison. The evidence indicates to me that enforcement of the Madison law would assure a more healthful quality of milk than that which is entitled to use the label of "Grade A" under the Model Ordinance.   *   *   *   The Model Ordinance does not provide for continuous investigation of all pasteurization plants as does § 7.21 of the Madison ordinance. Under § 11, moreover, Madison would be required to depend on the Chicago inspection system since Dean's plants, and the farms supplying them with raw milk, are located in the Chicago milkshed. But there is direct and positive evidence in the record that milk produced under Chicago standards did not meet the Madison requirements.

Furthermore, the Model Ordinance would force the Madison health authorities to rely on "spot checks" by the United States Public Health Service to determine whether Chicago enforced its milk regulations. The evidence shows that these "spot checks" are based on random inspection of farms and pasteurization plants: the United States Public Health Service rates the ten thousand or more dairy farms in the Chicago milkshed by a sampling of no more than two hundred farms. The same sampling technique is employed to inspect pasteurization plants. There was evidence that neither the farms supplying Dean with milk nor Dean's pasteurization plants were necessarily inspected in the last "spot check" of the Chicago milkshed made two years before the present case was tried.

From what this record shows, and from what it fails to show, I do not think that either of the alternatives suggested by the Court would assure the people of Madison as pure a supply of milk as they receive under their own ordinance. On this record I would uphold the Madison law. At the very least, however, I would not invalidate it without giving the parties a chance to present evidence and get findings on the ultimate issues the Court thinks crucial—namely, the relative merits of the Madison ordinance and the alternatives suggested by the Court today.

A regulation promulgated by the Mississippi State Board of Health provided that milk and milk products from another state may be sold in Mississippi only if the other state permitted Mississippi to market her milk products there. The Atlantic and Pacific Tea Company, with milk processing plants in Louisiana, was denied a permit to distribute its milk products in Mississippi solely because Louisiana had not signed a reciprocity agreement as required by the regulation. A three-judge federal district court upheld the Mississippi regulation as a valid exercise of the police power although it incidentally burdened interstate commerce, but the Supreme Court reversed this judgment in Great Atlantic & Pacific Tea Co. v. Cottrell, 424 U.S. 366, 96 S.Ct. 923 (1976). The Court reasoned that the district court erred in balancing the contending interests, attaching too much weight to the justifications advanced by Mississippi and too little to the burden on interstate commerce. Characterizing the public health justification proffered by Mississippi as "border[ing] on the frivolous," the Court pointed out that the regulatory scheme actually disserved the goal of maintaining or promoting higher milk quality standards by allowing the sale of milk products by a reciprocating state in Mississippi even if the standards of that state were below those of Mississippi. Citing *Dean Milk*, the Court also observed that "substantially less burdensome" methods than imposing reciprocity were available to Mississippi to insure that high standards for milk products were maintained; for example, "Mississippi has the obvious alternative of applying her own standards of inspection to shipments of milk from a nonreciprocating State." Mississippi also argued that the reciprocity requirement promoted free trade among the states by "eliminat[ing] 'hypertechnical' inspection standards that vary between different States" and constituted an appropriate response to Louisiana's alleged bad faith in refusing reciprocity with Mississippi and erecting "economic barriers to the sale of Mississippi milk in Louisiana under the guise of health and inspection regulations." Addressing these arguments, the Court rejected the notion that Mississippi's self-help was necessary to guarantee free trade since "the Commerce Clause itself creates the necessary reciprocity: Mississippi and her producers may pursue their constitutional remedy by suit in state or federal court challenging Louisiana's actions as violative of the Commerce Clause." And, said Justice Brennan, speaking for a unanimous Court, "Mississippi may offer reciprocity to States with substantially equivalent health standards, and insist on enforcement of its own, somewhat different standards as the alternative. But Mississippi may not use the threat of economic isolation as a weapon to force sister States to enter into even a desirable reciprocity agreement." To allow this to happen, the Court explained, would be to sanction the very sort of interstate protectionism the Commerce Clause was intended to prevent. Justice Stevens did not participate in the decision.

Part III

THE DISTRIBUTION OF POWER
BETWEEN GOVERNMENT
AND THE INDIVIDUAL

Chapter 8

Property Rights and Economic Liberties

In a recent dissenting opinion, Justice Thurgood Marshall wrote of the Supreme Court and its constitutional role in reviewing alleged infringements of personal rights:

> [I]t seems to me inescapably clear that this Court has consistently adjusted the care with which it will review state discrimination in light of the constitutional significance of the interests affected and the invidiousness of the particular classification. In the context of economic interests, we find that discriminatory state action is almost always sustained, for such interests are generally far removed from constitutional guarantees.[a] * * * But the situation differs markedly when discrimination against important individual interests with constitutional implications and against particularly disadvantaged or powerless classes is involved. The majority [opinion] suggests, however, that a variable standard of review would give this Court the appearance of a "superlegislature." I cannot agree. Such an approach seems to me a part of the guarantees of our Constitution and of the historic experiences with oppression of and discrimination against discrete, powerless minorities which underlie that Document.

Justice Marshall's view may have failed to carry the day in the decision of a particular case by the Burger Court (San Antonio Independent School District v. Rodriguez, 411 U. S. 1, 93 S.Ct. 1278 (1973)), but it stands as an apt characterization of the Supreme Court's role as the defender of outgroups in American society, particularly during the Court's activist days

---

a. Dissenting three years earlier in Dandridge v. Williams, 397 U.S. 471, 90 S.Ct. 1153 (1970), he said of these economic interests, "The extremes to which the Court has gone in dreaming up rational bases for state regulation in that area may in many instances be ascribed to a healthy revulsion from the Court's earlier excesses in using the Constitution to protect interests that have more than enough power to protect themselves in the legislative halls."

of the 1940s and 1960s. However, even at those times when a majority of modern-day Justices have rejected the assumption underlying Marshall's view—that civil liberties stand on a higher plane than property rights—virtually all of the Justices, at least since the Court's celebrated constitutional about-face in the mid-'thirties, have agreed that the constitutionality of legislation bearing upon property interests is to be assessed by balancing the competing public and private interests. The remaining chapters of this book explore the disagreement between the balancers and the preferred freedoms advocates, like Thurgood Marshall, in the context of civil liberties issues, but this chapter focuses on their common treatment of economic claims, especially insofar as the majoritarian effects of their balancing of interests distinguished that mode of constitutional interpretation from the orientation of the pre-1937 Court.

Implicit in the excerpt of Justice Marshall's dissent is a recognition that the preferred freedoms approach can be distinguished from that of ordinary balancing by virtue of the fact that, for whatever reason, it selects a particular segment of society as the Court's favored clientele. So far as it does with respect to civil liberties claims at least, the modern activist Court shares some similarity with the Supreme Court during much of the nineteenth and early twentieth centuries. Any resemblance ends here, however, for the Court in those days was usually allied with the "haves" of society—those with substantial property holdings and economic clout. Though reference to a strict "in-group–out-group" dichotomy may seem somewhat simplistic in describing the orientation of the Court given the heterogeniety of American society, it would be entirely accurate to say that, out of sympathy for institutions of industrial and finance capitalism, the Court consciously articulated constitutional doctrines based upon the Contract Clause and the Fourteenth Amendment to protect the sanctity of private property. In the case of recurring reform efforts by popularly elected legislative bodies, both national and state, the Court frequently thwarted attempts to curb corporate power, improve the lot of the laborer, farmer, and small businessman, and more equitably distribute the costs and responsibilities of government.

a. The Contract Clause and the State Police Power

In the view of Madison and other Framers, one of the principal reasons for the creation of the social compact that gave rise to civil society was the protection of what we call "vested rights." In the aggregate this concept refers to a bundle of claims which can be subsumed under the general right to own and acquire private property and which, in turn, rests upon a fundamental moral assumption that a person should be able to reap and profit from the fruits of his labor. To many of the political thinkers responsible for the Constitution, this concept of the primacy of property rights not only antedated government but constituted a significant, authoritative principle which circumscribed the regulatory power of government. As such, the doctrine of vested rights not only precluded infringements on the present accumulation of capital, such as the expropriation of land or other tangible property without just compensation, but it extended as well to damaging interference with future property interests such as obligations embodied in contractual arrangements. In sum, then, the document that created government was thought necessarily to include guarantees that property holders would be secure in their possessions and contractual assets.

Countervailing these private considerations are important public interests embodied in the states' inherent power to legislate for the public health, safety, and welfare. The problem of arriving at a balance between the doctrine of vested rights and that of the states' police power is intensified when the form of government is a democracy. What a popularly elected legislative majority sees as the legitimate regulation of private property interests in the broader view of the welfare of all citizens, property holders may well see as an effort by the people to "soak the rich." This tension puts the judicial institution in the difficult position of assessing constitutionally whether the exercise of the police power in a given instance is related to legitimate regulatory interests or whether the state has crossed the line and taken property for which just compensation must be paid. As we have seen from examining the Supreme Court's interpretation of the navigation power, such a question about the difference between the "regulation" and "taking" of property is no dry, academic matter; it can cut deeply with severe financial consequences. Moreover, the conflict between the competing public and private interests becomes all the more acute as a nation develops an industrialized, integrated, interdependent economy. The luxury of leaving private economic arrangements alone becomes increasingly less tolerable since the vast power accumulated and exercised by private property holders has such a significant effect on the welfare of all.

Despite the Framers' significant concern over the prospect of attacks on the institutions of private property by radical state legislatures, the original Constitution contained only two provisions, aside from the prohibition on bills of attainder, that might be read as protective of vested rights. Both of these constitute prohibitions on certain exercises of state power and appear together in the context of general limitations placed on the states in Article I, section 10. The relevant passage reads as follows: "No State shall * * * pass any * * * ex post facto Law, or Law impairing the Obligation of Contracts * * *." The provision precluding states from the passage of *ex post facto* laws, however, received a very narrow interpretation from the Court in 1798 when, in Calder v. Bull, 3 U.S. (3 Dall.) 386, 1 L.Ed. 648, it was held to bar only retroactive penal legislation (i.e., legislation affecting an individual either by making something a crime after the act was committed or heightening the penalty for an existing offense after commission of the crime) and not retroactive state enactments which affected property interests or contractual obligations. The net effect, of course, was to leave the Contract Clause as the only barrier to state legislative intrusion on vested rights. It subsequently fell to the Marshall Court to take up the cudgels by putting some meaning into the Contract Clause.

The articulation of constitutional doctrines hospitable to commercial development and advantageous to the propertied classes did not come hard to the Marshall Court for the Chief Justice saw the nation's future as inseparably linked to the fortunes of industry and commerce. Strong and effective national government of the kind typified by the decisions in *McCulloch* and *Gibbons* was essential to providing the economic stability in which business enterprise could flourish, but it was not sufficient. A climate of economic stability and investment security was equally dependent on the inviolability of contractual agreements.

The contribution of the Marshall Court in fostering business enterprise through generous interpretation of the Contract Clause manifested itself in two ways. One of these was the vigor with which it resisted state encroachment on presently existing creditor-debtor relations. In Sturges v. Crowninshield, 17 U.S. (4 Wheat.) 122, 4 L.Ed. 529 (1819), for example, the Court, speaking through Marshall, invalidated New York's newly enacted bankruptcy law which operated to easily relieve debtors of preexisting financial obligations.

The second dimension to the Marshall Court's reading of the Contract Clause lay in the expanded scope of the term "contract." Promissory notes executed between two individuals, like those abrogated by the legislation at issue in *Sturges*, were a widely recognized form of contract, but what about the status of other arrangements, say those made in the name of the state, for example? The answer to that question was furnished in two decisions which substantially expanded the constitutional definition of contract and, therefore, the effect of the Contract Clause. In *Fletcher* v. *Peck* (p. 611), Chief Justice Marshall, speaking for the Court, held that a public grant qualified as a contractual obligation and could not be abrogated without fair compensation even if the legislature which struck the land deal did so under corrupt influence. The State of Georgia no more than a common debtor would be free to wriggle out of a bad bargain. Nine years later in *Dartmouth College* v. *Woodward* (p. 613), Marshall, again speaking for the Court, held that corporate charters were also contracts protected against impairment. The doctrine of vested rights was now firmly cemented in place, for the decision in *Dartmouth College* meant that the charters of all profit-making corporations as well were inviolable. With these decisions the effect of the Contract Clause in protecting vested rights reached its apex.

By contrast with the decisions in *Fletcher* and *Dartmouth College*, the Court under Marshall's successor, Roger Taney, exhibited much less attachment to the belief that the Constitution required the subordination of state interests to the interests of business enterprise. We noted before in our consideration of the federal relationship that the Taney Court demonstrated a markedly greater fondness for allowing state power wide latitude. The change in emphasis is reflected in Chief Justice Taney's opinion in *Charles River Bridge Co.* v. *Warren Bridge Co.* (p. 617). Compare his affirmation of the police power with Marshall's proposition in the *Dartmouth College* case that ambiguity in a corporate charter must be resolved in favor of the entrepreneur and against the state.

The decline of any rigid constitutional adherence to the vested rights position begun in *Charles River Bridge* became increasingly apparent the more the Marshall Court faded into history. By the end of the century, the exigencies of economic and social development had substantially eroded the Court's enthusiasm for using the Contract Clause as a vehicle to restrain state regulatory power. As the decisions in *Stone* v. *Mississippi* (p. 621) and *Atlantic Coast Line Railroad Co.* v. *City of Goldsboro* (p. 623) show, the Court had swung decisively to upholding the supremacy of the state's police power in the protection of public morals and safety as opposed to claims embodied in previously existing business franchises and public grants.

The decline of the Contract Clause as an effective vehicle with which to challenge the states' regulatory power is even more apparent in two more modern cases. As Chief Justice Hughes's opinion in the Minnesota Moratorium case, *Home Building & Loan Ass'n* v. *Blaisdell* (p. 331) observes, the economic effects of private contractual arrangements are sufficiently connected with the public welfare in a mature, national economy to warrant regulation. Moreover, the Court takes it for granted that considerations of the public interest are an unwritten constituent of all contracts. Such considerations of public policy lie dormant until occasions arise to give them effect. A legislature which effects these latent understandings by postponing mortgage payments, for example, is not usurping power but legitimately exercising its inherent power to act in the public interest. In light of this regard for an interest broader than that of the bondholder, consider the Court's treatment of the dispute in *City of El Paso* v. *Simmons* (p. 624). Does Justice White's opinion in this case evidence any regard for the concept of vested rights? Or does the Court here so broadly extend the public interest supporting the exercise of the police power that, as Justice Black contends, it effectively defines a bad bargain struck by the state as *ipso facto* contrary to the public interest and, in effect, overrules *Fletcher* v. *Peck*? Twelve years later, however, the Court announced in *United States Trust Co. of New York* v. *State of New Jersey* (p. 627) that, "[c]ontrary to Mr. Justice Black's fear * * *," it "had not 'balanced away' the limitation on state action imposed by the Contract Clause."

b. The Rise and Decline of Economic Substantive Due Process

The Contract Clause faded principally, however, because it possessed limited utility in protecting property and business interests, particularly given the growing scope and volume of social legislation which began to appear in the late nineteenth and early twentieth centuries. In the face of state efforts to regulate rates and business practices, to enable the formation of labor unions, to outlaw child labor, and to set limits as to minimum wages and maximum hours for one's job, defenders of existing economic institutions and privileges turned from the body of the Constitution itself to take refuge in the amendments, notably the Fourteenth. Their chief success in that regard lay in enlarging the concept of due process from that of a constitutional standard assuring procedural regularity and fairness in government's treatment of the individual to that of a constitutional standard capable of circumscribing the content of governmental policy, especially when it was aimed at economic regulation.

The Fourteenth Amendment commands, "nor shall any State deprive any person of life, liberty or property, without due process of law * * *." To create a doctrine that would fasten limits on what the police power might constitutionally regulate (as distinguished from the traditional concept of due process which would void the operation of a statute in a given case because it was irregularly or arbitrarily applied), an important assumption was necessary. This assumption lay in the meaning assigned to the term "liberty" which appeared in the Due Process Clause quoted above. Whether as a result of the values gained as a product of their prior attachment to business enterprise (many of the Justices on the Supreme Court at this time were, as we previously noted, corporation lawyers) or out of a more abstract belief that an utterly free market, unfettered by governmental regulation, was both more just and more socially useful than any other economic system in promoting long-range growth and evolving a higher standard of living, a majority of the Justices came to define "liberty" as "economic liberty." More specifically, this meant "the liberty of contract"—the economic freedom to strike a bargain in the free market. Legislation which limited this absolute freedom was almost invariably adjudged a denial of due process and, hence, unconstitutional.

That the interpretation of several constitutional provisions during the late nineteenth and early twentieth centuries was predicated on what many of the Justices thought was the good and proper separation of the state from the economic order is borne out not simply by the development of substantive due process, but also by how this doctrine fit into the context of applying other constitutional provisions. Earlier, we saw how the doctrine of dual federalism was applied by the Supreme Court in commerce (p. 411) and taxing and spending (p. 418) cases to invalidate regulatory legislation enacted by the Congress. When such legislation was invalidated on the national level as infringing the exercise of the states' reserved powers and the states responded by exercising those powers, the Court countered by nullifying the legislation as a violation of the Fourteenth Amendment. Taken together, then, the doctrines of dual federalism and substantive due process constituted a lethal sequence of knock-out punches which killed off almost all social legislation. The end product of applying these two doctrines was not, however, the maintenance of a *laissez-faire* capitalist economy as is commonly thought. Such a system of political economy envisions a total separation of government from economic institutions and would have necessarily entailed an end to any government aid which fostered business enterprise. Government's economic support of business continued unabated; it was only governmental *regulation* of business enterprise which the Supreme Court forbade.

The usual legislative clout which business and propertied interests possessed was backstopped, in times when it failed, by an unusually hospitable judiciary. Urged on by such men as Stephen J. Field and William Howard Taft, who repeatedly exhorted their brethren to take up the cudgels of private property against the attack of "radical" legislatures bent on "socialistic experimentation," the Supreme Court truly became a "super-legislature." Under the guise of an ostensibly neutral and almost mechanical process of constitutional interpretation which talked of everyone's right to bargain in the marketplace and receive his due, the gap between legal equality and real economic power suggested something else—that some were more equal than others. To many observers this seems to underscore but not to justify the inherently undemocratic character of judicial review.

The birth of substantive due process came in a state case, *Wynehamer* v. *New York* (p. 629), in 1856. That case involved the criminal prosecution of a Buffalo tavern owner for violation of the state's prohibition law. By a split vote the New York Court of Appeals threw out the conviction and with it the statute. Such an exercise of the police power was held to infringe the economic liberty of the tavern proprietor to practice his livelihood and, therefore, denied him due process of law. Seemingly, property rights and economic liberties were above the law and constituted some "higher law" which could be used to test the validity of state legislation. The notion that due process encompassed these "higher law" elements and could be used to assess the substance of legislation, not simply how the legislation was applied, reached the U. S. Supreme Court forty years later.

In the meantime a Court less enthusiastic about its prospective role as the defender of capitalist enterprise temporarily repelled assaults on the exercise of the states' police power. In 1873, in *Butchers' Benevolent Ass'n* v. *Crescent City Livestock Landing & Slaughterhouse Co.* (p. 632), more commonly known as *The Slaughterhouse Cases*, it narrowly turned aside a challenge by independent New Orleans butchers to a Louisiana statute rigidly controlling the landing and slaughtering of livestock in the city and assigning sole franchise in that regard to one slaughterhouse. The Court rejected any notion that the butchers' right to practice their profession constituted one of those privileges and immunities of citizens of the United States alleged to be protected from state infringement by the Fourteenth Amendment. Four years later in *Munn* v. *Illinois* (p. 637), the Court sustained an act of the Illinois legislature setting maximum rates which could be charged farmers by grain elevator operators. What is significant in Chief Justice Waite's opinion is the standard by which constitutional exercise of the state police power is to be measured—whether the business is "clothed with a public interest." However, inasmuch as it was impossible to calibrate and measure a quality that could not be defined with any degree of certainty from the beginning, the standard, though eloquently defended, was not too successfully applied.

Over the next two decades the Court experienced a significant change in its membership. By the end of that period only two Justices who had sat in the *Munn* case were left, Harlan and Field, and only the latter remained from the days of the *Slaughterhouse* decision, and he dissented. The alteration in the composition of the Court, however, was not merely quantitative, but qualitative. Gone was the alliance of old-line Democrats like Nathan Clifford and Lincolnian Republicans like Samuel Miller and

David Davis capable of sustaining the state police power against assault. Now the Court was staffed predominantly with corporate and railroad lawyers anxious to examine the potential of the substantive due process doctrine for dismantling economic regulation. Their growing numbers produced two significant decisions which paved the way. In Santa Clara County v. Southern Pacific Railroad Co., 118 U.S. 394, 6 S.Ct. 1132 (1886), the Court, without any elaborating discussion, held that corporations were "persons" within the meaning of the Fourteenth Amendment. And the following year in Mugler v. Kansas, 123 U.S. 623, 8 S.Ct. 273 (1887), the Court, in the course of upholding a state prohibition law, warned that it would begin examining the substantive reasonableness of legislation. Speaking for the Court, Justice Harlan, who had also delivered the opinion in the *Santa Clara* case, announced that not all legislation supported by an exercise of the police power would pass. The Court would look to the substance of the legislation and would not be "misled by mere pretenses." If the exercise of the police power, said Justice Harlan, "has no real or substantial relation to those objects [for which the legislation was enacted], or is a palpable invasion of rights secured by the fundamental law, it is the duty of the courts to so adjudge."

Twenty years after the *Munn* decision and ten years after the ominous announcement in *Mugler*, the Court, relying on the substantive due process doctrine, invalidated its first piece of state legislation. The significance of the Court's decision in *Allgeyer* v. *Louisiana* (p. 640) lay not in the particulars of the case which involved that state's attempt to regulate out-of-state insurance companies doing business in the state, but in Justice Peckham's nullification of such legislation by finding it to be an infringement of "the liberty of contract." The articulation of this freedom by the Court as a constituent of those "higher laws" which Justice Harlan had previously characterized as "fundamental" in *Mugler* was important because the concept would soon find ready application in the area of labor-management relations. An economic liberty used to preserve the right of consumers to be preyed upon by unscrupulous insurance companies soon became the vehicle by which to enforce "equal" bargaining rights between employees and employers.

Sympathetic legislatures by the turn of the century sought to modify the enormous disparity in bargaining power between the individual employee and the giant corporation which, thanks to a legal fiction, was now a "person" within the meaning of the Fourteenth Amendment. The use of the state police power either to encourage workers to band together and through unionization achieve real parity in bargaining strength with a corporate employer or to set outside limits on the provisions of labor contracts—wages, hours, working conditions—which management might offer received a generally hostile response from the Court. Relying upon the Due Process Clause of the Fourteenth Amendment to invalidate state legislation and an identical clause in the Fifth Amendment to strike down reform legislation passed by Congress for the District of Columbia, the Supreme Court in *Adair* v. *United States* and *Coppage* v. *Kansas* (p. 642) declared unconstitutional acts which outlawed "yellow dog" clauses (promises by laborers not to join or, if a member, to withdraw from a union) in employment contracts. Utilizing the same concept of substantive due process with regard to those two amendments, the Court also struck down minimum wage legislation. See Adkins v. Children's Hospital, 261 U.S. 525, 43 S.Ct. 394 (1923), and Morehead v. New York ex rel. Tipaldo, 298 U.S. 587, 56 S.Ct. 918 (1936).

The Court was somewhat less rigid though still exacting when it scrutinized legislative efforts to regulate the maximum number of hours one might be compelled to work. It found redeeming merit and the requisite relation to protecting health when, in Holden v. Hardy, 169 U.S. 366, 18 S.Ct. 383 (1898), it sustained the constitutionality of a Utah statute limiting the workday to eight hours for those employees in the mining and smelting industry. In *Lochner* v. *New York* (p. 644) seven years later, however, the Supreme Court failed to discover any convincing justification for New York's maximum hours legislation covering bakers. Dissenting, Justice Holmes pleaded eloquently for the exercise of self-restraint and protested this process by which Justices in the majority were riveting into the Constitution their own personal economic values.

Though *Lochner's* reputation lived on as a classic period piece in the history of the Court's jurisprudence, its constitutional effect was fleeting. In two cases which followed, Muller v. Oregon, 208 U.S. 412, 28 S.Ct. 324 (1908), and Bunting v. Oregon, 243 U.S. 426, 37 S.Ct. 435 (1917), the Court upheld the constitutionality respectively of state acts to limit the workday for women to ten hours and to extend this maximum hours limitation to all mill and factory workers. The *Bunting* decision was significant principally because it accomplished *de facto* the overturning of *Lochner*. The effect of the *Muller* case was more subtle. It rested on the Court's acceptance of a novel form of argument presented by the man who was then counsel for the state, Louis Brandeis. To substantiate the legislature's claim that a ten-hour workday limitation for women was reasonable and bore a direct and substantial relation to their health and welfare, Brandeis presented in his brief sociological data supporting that connection. The significance of the "Brandeis brief," which in this case drew extensively on physiological and medical studies to show that long hours of standing or lifting had devastating effects on women's health, was that it took legal argument out of the exclusive province of precedents and deductive logic and gave it the added dimension of empirical and behavioral research. As contrasted with the rigid adherence of the usually prevailing majority on the Court to what the Justices saw as manifest and immutable economic values, the "Brandeis brief" was genuinely reflective of Holmes's observation made a decade earlier in a piece which he wrote for the *Harvard Law Review* entitled "The Path of the Law":

> The fallacy to which I refer is the notion that the only force at work in the development of the law is logic. In the broadest sense, indeed, that notion would be true. The postulate on which we think about the universe is that there is a fixed quantitative relation between every phenomenon and its antecedents and consequents. If there is such a thing as a phenomenon without these fixed quantitative relations, it is a miracle. It is outside the law of cause and effect, and as such transcends our power of thought, or at

least is something to or from which we cannot reason. The condition of our thinking about the universe is that it is capable of being thought about rationally, or, in other words, that every part of it is effect and cause in the same sense in which those parts are with which we are most familiar. So in the broadest sense it is true that the law is a logical development, like everything else. The danger of which I speak is not the admission that the principles governing other phenomena also govern the law, but the notion that a given system, ours, for instance, can be worked out like mathematics from some general axioms of conduct. This is the natural error of the schools, but it is not confined to them. I once heard a very eminent judge say that he never let a decision go until he was absolutely sure that it was right. So judicial dissent often is blamed as if it meant simply that one side or the other were not doing their sums right, and, if they would take more trouble, agreement inevitably would come.

This mode of thinking is entirely natural. The training of lawyers is a training in logic. The processes of analogy, discrimination, and deduction are those in which they are most at home. The language of judicial decision is mainly the language of logic. And the logical method and form flatter that longing for certainty and for repose which is in every human mind. But certainty generally is illusion, and repose is not the destiny of man. Behind the logical form lies a judgment as to the relative worth and importance of competing legislative grounds, often an inarticulate and unconscious judgment, it is true, and yet the very root and nerve of the whole proceeding. You can give any conclusion a logical form. You always can imply a condition in a contract. But why do you imply it? It is because of some belief as to the practice of the community or of a class, or because of some opinion as to policy, or, in short, because of some attitude of yours upon a matter not capable of exact quantitative measurement, and therefore not capable of founding exact logical conclusions. Such matters really are battle grounds where the means do not exist for determinations that shall be good for all time, and where the decision can do no more than embody the preference of a given body in a given time and place. We do not realize how large a part of our law is open to reconsideration upon a slight change in the habit of the public mind. No concrete proposition is self-evident, no matter how ready we may be to accept it.   *   *   * b

It must also be remembered that the Court's reliance upon substantive due process as a doctrine with which to support the established economic order was not an isolated phenomenon. The antilabor bias inherent in vindicating the liberty of contract was equally if not more evident in the application of the provisions of the Sherman Anti-Trust Act to work stoppages, particularly the secondary boycott (coercion applied to customers or suppliers to get them to withhold their business from an employer experiencing labor difficulties). In a host of cases, notably Loewe v. Lawlor, 208 U.S. 274, 28 S.Ct. 301 (1908), Duplex Printing Co. v. Deering, 254 U.S. 443, 41 S.Ct. 172 (1921), Coronado Coal Co. v. United Mine Workers of America, 268 U.S. 295, 45 S.Ct. 551 (1925), and Bedford Cut Stone Co. v. Journeymen Stone Cutters' Ass'n, 274 U.S. 37, 47 S.Ct. 522 (1927), the

---

b. Reprinted by permission of the publisher from 10 Harv.L.Rev. 457, 465–466.

Copyright 1897 by the Harvard Law Review Association.

Court repeatedly found strike practices to be "unlawful restraints on trade." By narrowly circumscribing the Clayton Act's exemption of strikes from the application of the antitrust statutes, the judiciary became a haven of business interests—issuing a flurry of injunctions to halt labor protests, using the contempt power to punish strikers for continued disobedience to court orders, and awarding triple damages to the corporations for any injury they sustained because of these union activities.

As the Court made abundantly clear in *Wolff Packing Co.* v. *Court of Industrial Relations* (p. 648), freedom—economic freedom, that is—was to be the rule and restraint the exception. In every sense the Court of this era had exalted economic liberties to the status of "preferred freedoms."

The rigid logic and high abstraction of substantive due process, like its constitutional blood brother, dual federalism, was overtaken in the end by experience—and that experience was the Great Depression. The neat, stale categories of judicial construction were simply done in by the reality of violent industrial disputes, massive unemployment, and long bread lines. The convulsion of a national, industrialized, interdependent economy had suffused the dissenting opinions of Holmes in *Lochner* and Brandeis in *Burns Baking Co.* v. *Bryan* (p. 43) with a pressing relevance.

A harbinger of the limited future ahead for substantive due process was the Supreme Court's decision in *Nebbia* v. *New York* (p. 652), a 1934 case involving the constitutionality of New York's legislation aimed at shoring up plummeting milk prices. Concluding that the perils of destructive competition were sufficient to justify the imposition of a schedule of minimum and maximum prices for the sale of milk by the state Milk Control Board, the Court rejected the claim that such regulation contravened the Fourteenth Amendment. What is significant about the ruling is not simply that it turned aside a substantive due process challenge, but that in doing so the Court overturned as insubstantial the most liberal existing regulatory standard. Reviewing the business-affected-with-the-public-interest doctrine enunciated in *Munn* v. *Illinois*, Justice Roberts, speaking for the majority, remarked that "there is no closed class or category of business affected with a public interest * * *." All business was subject to regulation, and legislation accomplishing that purpose was not to be invalidated unless "arbitrary, discriminatory, or demonstrably irrelevant to the policy the legislature is free to adopt * * *." Above all, legislation was not to be nullified because the Justices thought it to be "unwise."

The demise of substantive due process in economic matters was not only a dimension to the Constitutional Revolution of 1937 but, in fact, provided the opening shot. The decisions in *National Labor Relations Board* v. *Jones & Laughlin Steel Corp.* and *Steward Machine Co.* v. *Davis*, overturning the doctrine of dual federalism, were announced respectively on April 12 and May 24, 1937. The decision in *West Coast Hotel Co.* v. *Parrish* (p. 655) preceded the ruling in *Jones & Laughlin* by two weeks. Speaking for the new majority, Chief Justice Hughes, feigning astonishment that a "liberty of contract" could have been gleaned from anywhere in the Constitution, laid substantive due process to rest and articulated the new norm of self-restraint to be followed in the future review of economic legislation. The Court's four hard-core conservatives entered bitter dissents.

The Court's subsequent adherence to a restraintist position in evaluating economic claims usually advantaged liberal interests, that is to say those groups who had little influence in the determination of governmental policy prior to the advent of the New Deal. It had been, after all, the Court's activism in using judicial review to assert the primacy of economic liberties which generally impeded the interests of workers and consumers. As the decision in *Lincoln Federal Labor Union* v. *Northwestern Iron & Metal Co.* (p. 658) illustrates, however, the practice of judicial self-restraint did not *always* yield liberal results. The role of self-restraint on the judicial review of economic policy, said Justice Black, meant restraint across the board—when it hurt labor as well as when it helped. To do otherwise, reminded Black, would be to turn the new Court into what the old Court had been. As if to confirm the demise of judicial activism in the realm of economic policy, the Court in *City of New Orleans* v. *Dukes* (p. 660) also ended the vitality of its only post-1937 precedent for vindicating a challenge to the constitutionality of business regulation via the Equal Protection Clause and underscored its commitment to judicial self-restraint in the area of economic and business regulation with its even more recent decision in *Minnesota* v. *Clover Leaf Creamery Co.* (p. 661).

As the dust settled from the fracas over what role the Court ought to play in economic affairs and the New Deal appointees took control of the Bench, the new majority began to turn its attention to the next major question: must a Court committed to the practice of self-restraint in adjudicating economic claims be equally bound to practice that role in evaluating infringements of civil liberties?

c. Regulation and "Taking" of Property

A third major area of constitutional interpretation bearing upon property rights and economic liberties is that encompassed by the procedural and substantive protections contained in the Fifth Amendment. As to the first of these, the amendment guarantees—paralleling its protection of "life" and "liberty"—that "No person shall * * * be deprived of * * * property, without due process of law"; and secondly, in a more substantive vein, it assures "nor shall private property be taken for public use, without just compensation." To some extent—albeit a very limited one—the procedural protection of property rights is touched upon by some of the cases in Chapter 11, section d. This section focuses principally on the protection afforded by what is popularly called the "Takings Clause" of the Fifth Amendment.

The text of the Fifth Amendment specifies that government is legally obligated to pay "just compensation" only when private property is "taken" for public use. Government has no constitutional responsibility to compensate owners for any diminution in the value of private property which results from the employment of its legitimate regulatory power.

The question of whether government's action is regulatory or whether it is instead tantamount to a "taking" of private property is, therefore, crucial—especially for the property owner—in any case. The principles animating the Court's application of the Takings Clause are traversed at length and in depth by Justice Brennan's opinion for the Court in *Penn Central Transportation Co.* v. *City of New York* (p. 662). As he notes, the Takings and Just Compensation Clauses of the Fifth Amendment have been held to bind both the national government *and the states* (see also p. 906). More recent decisions of the Court (p. 673) provide additional illustrations of the basic principles canvassed by the Court in the *Penn Central* case. Illumination of the impact of the difference between regulation and the "taking" of property is also provided by the discussion of Congress's navigation power which comprises Chapter 6, section c.

a. THE CONTRACT CLAUSE AND THE STATE POLICE POWER

FLETCHER v. PECK

Supreme Court of the United States, 1810
10 U.S. (6 Cranch) 87, 3 L.Ed. 162

Fletcher brought suit against John Peck for breach of covenant on land that Peck sold to him in 1803. The property was originally part of a larger purchase from the State of Georgia by four land companies after they had bribed several members of the state legislature in 1795 to support the passage of an act authorizing the sale. The next year the legislature declared the act of 1795 and all the rights or claims derived from it to be null and void. Peck obtained possession of the land in 1800. In his deed, which he signed over to Fletcher three years later, Peck stated that all of the past sale transactions involving the land had been lawful. Fletcher contended that the original sale of land by the legislature was void and, therefore, Peck was guilty of breach of covenant since the property was not legally his to sell. The circuit court rendered a judgment for Peck, and the case came before the U. S. Supreme Court on a writ of error.

MARSHALL, Chief Justice, delivered the opinion of the court as follows:

* * *

If a suit be brought to set aside a conveyance obtained by fraud, and the fraud be clearly proved, the conveyance will be set aside, as between the parties; but the rights of third persons, who are purchasers without notice, for a valuable consideration, cannot be disregarded. Titles which, according to every legal test, are perfect, are acquired with that confidence which is inspired by the opinion that the purchaser is safe. If there be any concealed defect, arising from the conduct of those who had held the property long before he acquired it, of which he had no notice, that concealed defect cannot be set up against him. He has paid his money for a title good at law, he is innocent, whatever may be the guilt of others, and equity will not subject him to the penalties attached to that guilt. All titles would be insecure, and the intercourse between man and man would be very seriously obstructed, if this principle be overturned.

* * *

If the legislature felt itself absolved from those rules of property which are common to all the citizens of the United States, and from those principles of equity which are acknowledged in all our courts, its act is to be supported by its power alone, and the same power may devest any other individual of his lands, if it shall be the will of the legislature so to exert it.

It is not intended to speak with disrespect of the legislature of Georgia, or of its acts. Far from it. The question is a general question and is treated as one. For although such powerful objections to a legislative grant, as are alleged against this, may not again exist, yet the principle, on which alone this rescinding act is to be supported, may be applied to every case to which it shall be the will of any legislature to apply it. The principle is this: that a legislature may, by its own act, devest the vested estate of any man whatever, for reasons which shall, by itself, be deemed sufficient.

* * *

Is the power of the legislature competent to the annihilation of such title, and to a resumption of the property thus held?

The principle asserted is, that one legislature is competent to repeal any act which a former legislature was competent to pass; and that one legislature cannot abridge the powers of a succeeding legislature.

The correctness of this principle, so far as respects general legislation, can never be controverted. But, if an act be done under a law, a suc-

ceeding legislature cannot undo it. The past cannot be recalled by the most absolute power. Conveyances have been made; those conveyances have vested legal estates, and, if those estates may be seized by the sovereign authority, still, that they originally vested is a fact, and cannot cease to be a fact.

When, then, a law is in its nature a contract, when absolute rights have vested under that contract; a repeal of the law cannot devest those rights; and the act of annulling them, if legitimate, is rendered so by a power applicable to the case of every individual in the community.

* * * The constitution of the United States declares that no state shall pass any bill of attainder, ex post facto law or law impairing the obligation of contracts.

Does the case now under consideration come within this prohibitory section of the constitution?

In considering this very interesting question, we immediately ask ourselves what is a contract? Is a grant a contract?

A contract is a compact between two or more parties, and is either executory or executed. An executory contract is one in which a party binds himself to do, or not to do, a particular thing; such was the law under which the conveyance was made by the governor. A contract executed is one in which the object of contract is performed; and this, says Blackstone, differs in nothing from a grant. The contract between Georgia and the purchasers was executed by the grant. A contract executed, as well as one which is executory, contains obligations binding on the parties. A grant, in its own nature, amounts to an extinguishment of the right of the grantor, and implies a contract not to re-assert that right. A party is, therefore, always estopped by his own grant.

Since, then, in fact, a grant is a contract executed, the obligation of which still continues, and since the constitution uses the general term contract, without distinguishing between those which are executory and those which are executed, it must be construed to comprehend the latter as well as the former. A law annulling conveyances between individuals, and declaring that the grantors should stand seized of their former estates, notwithstanding those grants, would be as repugnant to the constitution as a law discharging the vendors of property from the obligation of executing their contracts by conveyances. It would be strange if a contract to convey was secured by the constitution, while an absolute conveyance remained unprotected.

If, under a fair construction of the constitution, grants are comprehended under the term contracts, is a grant from the state excluded from the operation of the provision? Is the clause to be considered as inhibiting the state from impairing the obligation of contracts between two individuals, but as excluding from that inhibition contracts made with itself?

The words themselves contain no such distinction. They are general, and are applicable to contracts of every description. If contracts made with the state are to be exempted from their operation, the exception must arise from the character of the contracting party, not from the words which are employed.

* * *

It is, then, the unanimous opinion of the court, that, in this case, the estate having passed into the hands of a purchaser for a valuable consideration, without notice, the state of Georgia was restrained, either by general principles, which are common to our free institutions, or by the particular provisions of the constitution of the United States, from passing a law whereby the estate of the plaintiff in the premises so purchased could be constitutionally and legally impaired and rendered null and void.

* * *

TRUSTEES OF DARTMOUTH COLLEGE v. WOODWARD
[THE DARTMOUTH COLLEGE CASE]

Supreme Court of the United States, 1819
17 U.S. (4 Wheat.) 518, 4 L.Ed. 629

In 1769, Dartmouth College received from the British Crown a corporate charter which authorized a twelve-member board of trustees to govern the college and to appoint their own successors. The charter, however, was amended in 1816 by the New Hampshire legislature when it passed several acts increasing the number of trustees to twenty-one and creating a board of overseers with the power to review important decisions of the trustees. In addition, the state governor was empowered to appoint the nine new trustees and to fill positions on the board of overseers. The effect of these acts was to take power from the incumbent trustees of the college. They responded by refusing to recognize the legislation as binding upon them and by bringing action against William Woodward, the secretary and treasurer of the college, to recover corporate property that was temporarily entrusted to him by one of the 1816 acts. The trial court's special verdict left unresolved the issue as to whether or not the three acts violated the United States

Constitution. A state superior court upheld the legislation, whereupon the incumbent trustees brought the case to the U.S. Supreme Court.

The opinion of the court was delivered by MARSHALL, Chief Justice:

* * *

It can require no argument to prove that the circumstances of this case constitute a contract. An application is made to the crown for a charter to incorporate a religious and literary institution. In the application, it is stated that large contributions have been made for the object, which will be conferred on the corporation as soon as it shall be created. The charter is granted, and on its faith the property is conveyed. Surely in this transaction every ingredient of a complete and legitimate contract is to be found.

The points for consideration are:

1. Is this contract protected by the constitution of the United States?

2. Is it impaired by the acts under which the defendant holds?

1. * * *

[I]t appears that Dartmouth College is an eleemosynary institution, incorporated for the purpose of perpetuating the application of the bounty of the donors, to the specified objects of that bounty; that its trustees or governors were originally named by the founder, and invested with the power of perpetuating themselves; that they are not public officers, nor is it a civil institution, participating in the administration of government; but a charity school, or a seminary of education, incorporated for the preservation of its property, and the perpetual application of that property to the objects of its creation.

Yet a question remains to be considered, of more real difficulty, on which more doubt has been entertained than on all that have been discussed. The founders of the college, at least those whose contributions were in money, have parted with the property bestowed upon it, and their representatives have no interest in that property. The donors of land are equally without interest, so long as the corporation shall exist. Could they be found, they are unaffected by any alteration in its constitution, and probably regardless of its form, or even of its existence. The students are fluctuating, and no individual among our youth has a vested interest in the institution, which can be asserted in a court of justice. Neither the founders of the college nor the youth for whose benefit it was founded, complain of the alteration made in its charter, or think themselves injured by it. The trustees alone complain, and the trustees have no beneficial interest to be protected. Can this be such a contract as the constitution intended to withdraw from the power of state legislation? Contracts, the parties to which have a vested beneficial interest, and those only, it has been said, are the objects about which the constitution is solicitous, and to which its protection is extended.

The court has bestowed on this argument the most deliberate consideration, and the result will be stated. Dr. Wheelock, acting for himself, and for those who, at his solicitation, had made contributions to his school, applied for this charter, as the instrument which should enable him, and them, to perpetuate their beneficent intention. It was granted. An artificial, immortal being, was created by the crown, capable of receiving and distributing forever, according to the will of the donors, the donations which should be made to it. On this being, the contributions which had been collected were immediately bestowed. These gifts were made, not, indeed, to make a profit for the donors, or their posterity, but for something in their opinion of inestimable value; for something which they deemed a full equivalent for the money with which it was purchased. The consideration for which they stipulated, is the perpetual application of the fund to its object, in the mode prescribed by themselves. Their descendants may take no interest in the preservation of this consideration. But in this respect their descendants are not their representatives. They are represented by the corporation. The corporation is the assignee of their rights, stands in their place, and distributes their bounty, as they would themselves have distributed it, had they been immortal. So with respect to the students who are to derive learning from this source. The corporation is a trustee for them also. Their potential rights, which, taken distributively, are imperceptible, amount collectively to a most important interest. These are, in the aggregate, to be exercised, asserted and protected, by the corporation. They were as completely out of the donors, at the instant of their being vested in the corporation, and as incapable of being asserted by the students, as at present.

*   *   *

This is plainly a contract to which the donors, the trustees, and the crown (to whose rights and obligations New Hampshire succeeds), were the original parties. It is a contract made on a valuable consideration. It is a contract for the security and disposition of property. It is a contract, on the faith of which real and personal estate has been conveyed to the corporation. It is then a contract within the letter of the constitution, and within its spirit also, unless the fact that the property is invested by the donors in trustees for the promotion of religion and education, for the benefit of persons who are perpetually changing, though the objects remain the same, shall create a particular exception, taking this case out of the prohibition contained in the constitution.

It is more than possible that the preservation of rights of this description was not particularly in the view of the framers of the constitution when the clause under consideration was introduced into that instrument. It is probable that interferences of more frequent recurrence, to which the temptation was stronger, and of which the mischief was more extensive, constituted the great motive for imposing this restriction on the state legislatures. But although a particular and a rare case may not, in itself, be of sufficient magnitude to induce a rule, yet it must be governed by the rule, when established unless some plain and strong reason for excluding it can be given. It is not enough to say that this particular case was not in the mind of the convention when the article was framed, nor of the American people when it was adopted. It is necessary to go farther, and to say that, had this particular case been suggested, the language would have been so varied, as to exclude it, or it would have been made a special exception. The case being within the words of the rule, must be within its operation likewise, unless there be something in the literal construction so obviously absurd, or mischievous, or repugnant to the general spirit of the instrument, as to justify those who expound the constitution in making it an exception.

On what safe and intelligible ground can this exception stand. There is no exception in the constitution, no sentiment delivered by its contemporaneous expounders, which would justify us in making it. In the absence of all authority of this kind, is there, in the nature and reason of the case itself, that which would sustain a construction of the constitution, not warranted by its words? Are contracts of this description of a character to excite so little interest that we must exclude them from the provisions of the constitution, as being unworthy of the attention of those who framed the instrument? Or does public policy so imperiously demand their remaining exposed to legislative alteration, as to compel us, or rather permit us to say that these words, which were introduced to give stability to contracts, and which in their plain import comprehend this contract, must yet be so construed as to exclude it?

Almost all eleemosynary corporations, those which are created for the promotion of religion, of charity, or of education, are of the same character. The law of this case is the law of all. *   *   *

*   *   *

The opinion of the court, after mature deliberation, is, that this is a contract, the obligation of which cannot be impaired without violating the constitution of the United States. This opinion appears to us to be equally supported by reason, and by the former decisions of this court.

2. We next proceed to the inquiry whether its obligation has been impaired by those acts of the legislature of New Hampshire to which the special verdict refers.

*   *   *

*   *   *   The founders of the college contracted, not merely for the perpetual application of the funds which they gave, to the objects for which those funds were given; they contracted also to secure that application by the constitution of the corporation. They contracted for a system which should, as far as human foresight can provide, retain forever the government of the literary institution they had formed, in the hands of persons approved by themselves. This system is totally changed. The charter of 1769 exists no longer. It is re-organized; and re-organized in such a manner as to convert a literary institution, moulded according to the will of its founders, and placed under the control of private literary men, into a machine entirely subservient to the will of government. This may be for the advantage of this college in particular, and may be for the advantage of literature in general, but it is not according to the will of the donors, and is subversive of that contract, on the faith of which their property was given.

*   *   *

It results from this opinion, that the acts of the legislature of New Hampshire, which are stated in the special verdict found in this cause, are repugnant to the constitution of the United States; and that the judgment on this special verdict ought to have been for the plaintiffs. The judgment of the State Court must therefore be reversed.

[Justices WASHINGTON and STORY delivered separate opinions concurring in the decision of the Court. Justice DUVALL dissented.]

CHARLES RIVER BRIDGE CO. v. WARREN BRIDGE CO.

Supreme Court of the United States, 1837
36 U.S. (11 Pet.) 420, 9 L.Ed. 773

The Massachusetts legislature passed an act in 1785 incorporating the Charlestown Bridge Company and authorizing it to build a bridge over the Charles River and to collect tolls for its use. The charter specified certain requirements pertaining to the construction and maintenance of the bridge and obligated the company to pay Harvard College £200 a year as compensation in lieu of the right to operate a ferry which Massachusetts had granted to the college in 1650. The company fulfilled these requirements, and in 1792, the state extended its charter for seventy years. However, in 1828, the legislature incorporated the Warren Bridge Company and authorized it to build a bridge located within 275 yards of the Charles River Bridge. The plaintiff bridge company brought action to enjoin the construction of the Warren Bridge. The Massachusetts Supreme Judicial Court dismissed this complaint. By the time this case came before the United States Supreme Court, the operators of the Warren Bridge, under terms of their 1828 charter, had surrendered that bridge to the state for free public use after being reimbursed for expenses of constructing and operating the bridge. The Charles River Bridge Company argued that the legislation of 1828 impaired Massachusetts's obligation under the existing contract by violating what the bridge company regarded as the implied exclusiveness of its franchise.

Mr. Chief Justice TANEY delivered the opinion of the court:

*   *   *

[U]pon what ground can the plaintiffs in error contend that the ferry rights of the college have been transferred to the proprietors of the bridge? If they have been thus transferred, it must be by some mode of transfer known to the law, and the evidence relied on to prove it can be pointed out in the record. How was it transferred? It is not suggested that there ever was in point of fact, a deed of conveyance executed by the college to the bridge company. Is there any evidence in the record from which such a conveyance may, upon legal principle, be presumed? The testimony before the court, so far from laying the foundation for such a presumption, repels it in the most positive terms. The petition to the Legislature in 1785, on which the charter was granted, does not suggest an assignment, nor any agreement or consent on the part of the college; and the petitioners do not appear to have regarded the wishes of that institution, as by any means necessary to insure their success. They place their application entirely on considerations of public interest and public convenience, and the superior advantages of a communication across Charles River by a bridge instead of a ferry. The Legislature, in granting the charter, show, by the language of the law, that they acted on the principles assumed by the petitioners. The preamble recites that the bridge "will be of great public utility"; and that is the only reason they assign for passing the law which incorporates this company. The validity of the charter is not made to depend on the consent of the college, nor of any assignment or surrender on their part; and the Legislature deal with the subject, as if it were one exclusively within their own power, and as if the ferry right were not to be transferred to the bridge company, but to be extinguished; and they appear to have acted on the principle that the State, by virtue of its sovereign powers and eminent domain, had a right to take away the franchise of the ferry; because in their judgment, the public interest and convenience would be better promoted by a bridge in the same place; and upon that principle they proceed to make a pecuniary compensation to the college for the franchise thus taken away. * * *

* * *

This brings us to the Act of the Legislature of Massachusetts of 1785, by which the plaintiffs were incorporated by the name of "The Proprietors of the Charles River Bridge"; and it is here, and in the law of 1792, prolonging their charter, that we must look for the extent and nature of the franchise conferred upon the plaintiffs.

Much has been said in the argument of the principles of construction by which this law is to be expounded, and what undertakings, on the part of the State, may be implied. The court think there can be no serious difficulty on that head. It is the grant of certain franchises by the public to a private corporation, and in a matter where the public interest is concerned. The rule of construction in such cases is well settled, both in England, and by the decisions of our own tribunals. In 2 Barn. & Adol. 793, in the case of The Proprietors of the Stourbridge Canal v. Wheely et al., the court say, "the canal having been made under an act of Parliament, the rights of the plaintiffs are derived entirely from that act. This, like many other cases, is a bargain between a company of adventurers and the public, the terms of which are expressed in the statute; and the rule of construction in all such cases, is now fully established to be this— that any ambiguity in the terms of the contract, must operate against the adventurers, and in favor of the public, and the plaintiffs can claim nothing that is not clearly given them by the act." And the doctrine thus laid down is abundantly sustained by the authorities referred to in this decision. * * *

* * *

[T]he object and end of all government is to promote the happiness and prosperity of the community by which it is established, and it can never be assumed that the government intended to diminish its power of accomplishing the end for which it was created. And in a country like ours, free, active and enterprising, continually advancing in numbers and wealth; new channels of communication are daily found necessary, both for travel and trade, and are essential to the comfort, convenience, and prosperity of the people. A State ought never to be presumed to surrender this power, because, * * * the whole community have an interest in preserving it undiminished. And when a corporation alleges that a State has surrendered for seventy years its power of improvement and public accommodation, in a great and important line of travel, along which a vast number of its citizens must daily pass; the community have a right to insist, in the language of this court above quoted, "that its abandonment ought not to be presumed, in a case in which the deliberate purpose of the State to abandon it does not appear." The continued existence of a government would be of no great value, if by implications and presumptions, it was disarmed of the powers necessary to accomplish the ends of its creation, and the functions it was designed to perform, transferred to the hands of privileged corporations. The rule of construction announced by the court was not confined to the taxing power, nor is it so limited in the opinion delivered. On the contrary, it was distinctly placed on the ground that the interests of the community were concerned in preserving, undiminished, the power then in question; and whenever any power of the State is said to be surrendered or diminished, whether it be the taxing power or any other affecting the public interest, the same principle applies, and the rule of construction must be the same. No one will question that the interests of the great body of the people of the State, would, in this instance, be affected by the surrender of this great line of travel to a single corporation, with the right to exact toll, and exclude competition for seventy years. While the rights of private property are sacredly guarded, we must not forget that the community also have rights, and that the happiness and well being of every citizen depends on their faithful preservation.

Adopting the rule of construction above stated as the settled one, we proceed to apply it to the charter of 1785, to the proprietors of the Charles River Bridge. This act of incorporation is in the usual form, and the privileges such as are commonly given to corporations of that kind. It confers on them the ordinary faculties of a corporation, for the purpose of building the bridge; and establishes certain rates of toll, which the company are authorized to take. This is the whole grant. There is no exclusive privilege given to them over the waters of Charles River, above or below their bridge. No right to erect another bridge themselves, nor to prevent other persons from erecting one. No engagement from the State that another shall not be erected, and no undertaking not to sanction competition, nor to make improvements that may diminish the amount of its income. Upon all these subjects the charter is silent, and nothing is said in it about a line of travel, so much insisted on in the argument, in which they are to have exclusive privileges. No words are used from which an intention to grant any of these rights can be inferred. If the plaintiff is entitled to them, it must be implied simply from the nature of the grant, and cannot be inferred from the words by which the grant is made.

The relative position of the Warren Bridge has already been described. It does not interrupt the passage over the Charles River Bridge nor make the way to it or from it less convenient. None of the faculties or franchises granted to that corporation have been revoked by the Legislature; and its right to take the tolls granted by the charter remains unaltered. In short, all the franchises and rights of property enumerated in the charter, and there mentioned to have been granted to it, remain unimpaired. But its income is destroyed by the Warren Bridge; which, being free, draws off the passengers and property which would have gone over it, and renders their franchise of no value. This is the gist of the complaint. For it is not pretended that the erection of the Warren Bridge would have done them any injury, or in any degree affected their right of property, if it had not diminished the amount of their tolls. In order, then, to entitle themselves to relief, it is necessary to show that the Legislature contracted not to do the act of which they complain; and that they impaired, or in other words violated, that contract, by the erection of the Warren Bridge.

The inquiry then is, does the charter contain such a contract on the part of the State? Is there any such stipulation to be found in that instrument? It must be admitted on all hands, that there is none—no words that even relate to another bridge, or to the diminution of their tolls, or to the line of travel. If a contract on that subject can be gathered from the charter, it must be by implication, and cannot be found in the words used. Can such an agreement be implied? The rule of construction before stated is an answer to the question. In charters of this description, no rights are taken from the public or given to the corporation, beyond those which the words of the charter, by their natural and proper construction, purport to convey. There are no words which import such a contract as the plaintiffs in error contend for, and none can be implied. * * *

* * *

Indeed, the practice and usage of almost every State in the Union, old enough to have commenced the work of internal improvement, is opposed to the doctrine contended for on the part of the plaintiffs in error. Turn-

pike roads have been made in succession, on the same line of travel; the latter ones interfering materially with the profits of the first. These corporations have, in some instances, been utterly ruined by the introduction of newer and better modes of transportation and traveling. In some cases railroads have rendered the turnpike roads on the same line of travel so entirely useless, that the franchise of the turnpike corporation is not worth preserving. Yet in none of these cases have the corporations supposed that their privileges were invaded, or any contract violated on the part of the State. * * *

And what would be the fruits of this doctrine of implied contracts on the part of the States, and of property in a line of travel by a corporation, if it should now be sanctioned by this court? To what results would it lead us? If it is to be found in the charter to this bridge, the same process of reasoning must discover it in the various acts which have been passed within the last forty years, for turnpike companies. And what is to be the extent of the privileges of exclusion on the different sides of the road? The counsel who have so ably argued this case, have not attempted to define it by any certain boundaries. How far must the new improvement be distant from the old one? How near may you approach without invading its rights in the privileged line? If this court should establish the principles now contended for, what is to become of the numerous railroads established on the same line of travel with turnpike companies; and which have rendered the franchises of the turnpike corporations of no value? * * * The millions of property which have been invested in railroads and canals, upon lines of travel which had been before occupied by turnpike corporations, will be put in jeopardy. We shall be thrown back to the improvements of the last century, and obliged to stand still until the claims of the old turnpike corporations shall be satisfied, and they shall consent to permit these States to avail themselves of the lights of modern science, and to partake of the benefit of those improvements which are now adding to the wealth and prosperity,

and the convenience and comfort, of every other part of the civilized world. * * *

The judgment of the Supreme Judicial Court of the Commonwealth of Massachusetts, dismissing the plaintiffs' bill, must, therefore, be affirmed with costs.

[Justice STORY dissented in an opinion in which Justice THOMPSON concurred.]

STONE v. MISSISSIPPI

Supreme Court of the United States, 1880
101 U.S. 814, 25 L.Ed. 1079

In 1867, the Mississippi legislature granted John Stone and others a twenty-five-year franchise to sell tickets for their lottery. Two years later, however, Mississippi adopted a new constitution which prohibited the authorization of the sale of lottery tickets. In addition, the legislature enacted a statute in 1870 that made it unlawful to conduct a lottery in the state. The attorney general of the state filed an information against Stone and others in a state court. The case came to the U. S. Supreme Court after two state courts ruled against the defendants.

Mr. Chief Justice WAITE delivered the opinion of the court:

* * *

* * * If the Legislature that granted this charter had the power to bind the people of the State and all succeeding Legislatures to allow the corporation to continue its corporate business during the whole term of its authorized existence, there is no doubt about the sufficiency of the language employed to effect that object, although there was an evident purpose to conceal the vice of the transaction by the phrases that were used. Whether the alleged contract exists therefore, or not, depends on the authority of the Legislature to bind the State and the people of the State in that way.

All agree that the Legislature cannot bargain away the police pow-

er of a State. * * * Many attempts have been made in this court and elsewhere to define the police power, but never with entire success. It is always easier to determine whether a particular case comes within the general scope of the power, than to give an abstract definition of the power itself which will be in all respects accurate. No one denies, however, that it extends to all matters affecting the public health or the public morals. * * *

If lotteries are to be tolerated at all, it is, no doubt, better that they should be regulated by law, so that the people may be protected as far as possible against the inherent vices of the system; but that they are demoralizing in their effects, no matter how carefully regulated, cannot admit of a doubt. When the government is untrammeled by any claim of vested rights or chartered privileges, no one has ever supposed that lotteries could not lawfully be suppressed, and those who manage them punished severely as violators of the rules of social morality. * * * There is now scarcely a State in the Union where lotteries are tolerated, and Congress has enacted a special statute, the object of which is to close the mails against them. * * *

The question is, therefore, directly presented, whether, in view of these facts, the Legislature of a State can, by the charter of a lottery company, defeat the will of the People, authoritatively expressed, in relation to the further continuance of such business in their midst. We think it cannot. No Legislature can bargain away the public health or the public morals. The People themselves cannot do it, much less their servants. The supervision of both these subjects of governmental power is continuing in its nature, and they are to be dealt with as the special exigencies of the moment may require. Government is organized with a view to their preservation, and cannot devest itself of the power to provide for them. For this purpose, the largest legislative discretion is allowed, and the discretion cannot be parted with any more than the power itself. * * *

* * *

But the power of governing is a trust committed by the People to the government, no part of which can be granted away. The People, in their sovereign capacity, have established their agencies for the preservation of the public health and the public morals, and the protection of public and private rights. These several agencies can govern according to

their discretion, if within the scope of their general authority, while in power; but they cannot give away nor sell the discretion of those that are to come after them, in respect to matters the government of which, from the very nature of things, must "vary with varying circumstances." They may create corporations, and give them, so to speak, a limited citizenship; but as citizens, limited in their privileges, or otherwise, these creatures of the government creation are subject to such rules and regulations as may from time to time be ordained and established for the preservation of health and morality.

The contracts which the Constitution protects are those that relate to property rights, not governmental. It is not always easy to tell on which side of the line which separates governmental from property rights a particular case is to be put; but in respect to lotteries there can be no difficulty. They are not, in the legal acceptation of the term, mala in se, but as we have just seen, may properly be made mala prohibita. They are a species of gambling, and wrong in their influences. They disturb the checks and balances of a well ordered community. Society built on such a foundation would almost of necessity bring forth a population of speculators and gamblers, living on the expectation of what, "by the casting of lots, or by lot, chance or otherwise," might be "awarded" to them from the accumulations of others. Certainly the right to stop them is governmental, to be exercised at all times by those in power, at their discretion. Anyone, therefore, who accepts a lottery charter, does so with the implied understanding that the People, in their sovereign capacity and through their properly constituted agencies, may resume it at any time when the public good shall require, and this whether it be paid for or not. All that one can get by such a charter is a suspension of certain governmental rights in his favor, subject to withdrawal at will. He has, in legal effect, nothing more than a license to continue on the terms named for the specified time, unless sooner abrogated by the sovereign power of the State. It is a permit, good as against existing laws, but subject to future legislative and constitutional control or withdrawal.

On the whole, we find no error in the record and the judgment is, consequently, affirmed.

The Atlantic Coast Line Railroad Company obtained ownership of railroad lines and a surrounding 130-foot-wide strip of land running along the tracks that were originally chartered to another railroad company by the North Carolina legislature in 1833. Goldsboro, a growing town along the train route, was incorporated nearly fourteen years after the charter was granted. The company did not object when the town established its two main streets on the railroad's land adjacent to the tracks. In 1909, Goldsboro, now a city, passed ordinances designed to promote safety and lessen the inconvenience which the tracks posed to Goldsboro's citizens. The plaintiff railroad company challenged certain of the ordinances in court on grounds that the state legislature did not authorize the city to pass the regulations and that the railroad's rights protected by the Due Process Clause of the Fourteenth Amendment and the Contract Clause were violated. The contested ordinances prohibited trains from shifting cars along a specified four-block stretch of track except during two hours each morning and two hours each afternoon and prohibited railroad cars from standing at a stop along the same stretch of track for more than five minutes. Another ordinance to which the railroad company objected required the company to lower its tracks at certain points to street level and to fill them in between the rails. The railroad company appealed to the U. S. Supreme Court after two state courts refused to restrain enforcement of the ordinances.

A unanimous Court in Atlantic Coast Line Railroad Co. v. City of Goldsboro, 232 U.S. 548, 34 S.Ct. 364 (1914), affirmed the judgment of the state courts. Speaking for the Court, Justice Pitney reasoned that the existing broad delegation of police power from the state to the city to legislate for the public's health, safety, and welfare was adequate to rebut the company's claim that the state had not specifically authorized the regulations. The Court also dismissed the notion that the obligation of contract could be used to check the state's police power. Said Justice Pitney:

> [I]t is settled that neither the "contract" clause nor the "due process" clause has the effect of overriding the power of the state to establish all regulations that are reasonably necessary to secure the health, safety, good order, comfort, or general welfare of the community; that this power can neither be abdicated nor bargained away, and is inalienable even by express grant; and that all contract and property rights are held subject to its fair exercise.

Moreover, the Court rejected the railroad's contention that the ordinances necessarily took property without the kind of due process and fair compensation required of an eminent domain proceeding under the Constitution. Justice Pitney posited this as the conclusion only if it could be shown that the municipality had legislated beyond the bounds of the police power or, in other words, where "the regulation under criticism is not in any way designed to promote the health, comfort, safety, or welfare of the community, or that the means employed have no real and substantial relation to the avowed purpose, or that there is wanton or arbitrary interference with private rights * * * ." In the final segment of his opinion Justice Pitney found the requisite close and substantial relation between the ordinances at issue and the purposes of public health and safety.

HOME BUILDING & LOAN ASS'N v. BLAISDELL

Supreme Court of the United States, 1934
290 U.S. 398, 54 S.Ct. 231, 78 L.Ed. 413

See p. 331.

CITY OF EL PASO v. SIMMONS

Supreme Court of the United States, 1965
379 U.S. 497, 85 S.Ct. 577, 13 L.Ed.2d 446

Beginning in 1876, Texas offered land for sale in order to raise revenue to support a public school system and in order to encourage settlement of the state. Texas law provided that the land could be purchased with a down payment of one-fortieth of the price and payment of interest annually at a rate of 3 percent. The law also stipulated that if the purchaser missed an interest payment, the land was forfeited to the state, but the buyer retained the right to reinstate his claim at any time if he paid the interest owed before a third party obtained title to the property. Greenberry Simmons, a resident of Kentucky, purchased forfeited land which he, in turn, was forced to relinquish to the state in 1947. Five years and two days later Simmons, offering to pay the interest that had accumulated, applied to have his claim to the land reinstated. His application was denied, however, because under a 1941 amendment to the land law the right to reinstate a claim could no longer be exercised beyond five years from the forfeiture date. In 1955, Texas sold the land to the City of El Paso. Simmons filed suit in federal district court maintaining that title to the land rightfully belonged to him. He challenged the 1941 amendment on the grounds that it abrogated the state's contractual obligations in violation of the United States Constitution. The district court's decision for the city was reversed by the U. S. Circuit Court of Appeals, whereupon El Paso appealed to the Supreme Court.

Mr. Justice WHITE delivered the opinion of the Court.

* * *

* * * The City seeks to bring this case within the long line of cases recognizing a distinction between contract obligation and remedy and permitting a modification of the remedy as long as there is no substantial impairment of the value of the obligation. * * *

* * *

We do not pause * * * to chart again the dividing line under federal law between "remedy" and "obligation." * * * For it is not every modification of a contractual promise that impairs the obligation of contract under federal law, any more than it is every alteration of existing remedies that violates the Contract Clause. * * *

The decisions "put it beyond question that the prohibition is not an absolute one and is not to be read with literal exactness like a mathematical formula," as Chief Justice Hughes said in Home Building & Loan Assn. v. Blaisdell, 290 U.S. 398, 428, 54 S.Ct. 231, 236. The *Blaisdell* opinion, which amounted to a comprehensive restatement of the principles underlying the application of the Contract Clause, makes it quite clear that "[n]ot only is the constitutional provision qualified by the measure of control which the state retains over remedial processes, but the state also continues to possess authority to safeguard the vital interests of its people." * * *

Of course, the power of a State to modify or affect the obligation of contract is not without limit. * * * But we think the objects of the Texas statute make abundantly clear that it impairs no protected right under the Contract Clause.

* * *

The circumstances behind the 1941 amendment are well described in the Reports of the Commissioner of the General Land Office. The general purpose of the legislation enacted in 1941 was to restore confidence in the stability and integrity of land titles and to enable the State to protect and administer its property in a businesslike manner. * * *

The State's policy of quick resale of forfeited lands did not prove entirely successful; forfeiting purchasers who repurchased the lands again defaulted and other purchasers bought without any intention of complying with their contracts unless mineral wealth was discovered. The market for land contracted during the depression. * * * These developments hardly to be expected or

foreseen, operated to confer considerable advantages on the purchaser and his successors and a costly and difficult burden on the State. * * * Laws which restrict a party to those gains reasonably to be expected from the contract are not subject to attack under the Contract Clause, notwithstanding that they technically alter an obligation of a contract. The five-year limitation allows defaulting purchasers with a bona fide interest in their lands a reasonable time to reinstate. It does not and need not allow defaulting purchasers with a speculative interest in the discovery of minerals to remain in endless default while retaining a cloud on title.

* * * The measure taken to induce defaulting purchasers to comply with their contracts, requiring payment of interest in arrears within five years, was a mild one indeed, hardly burdensome to the purchaser who wanted to adhere to his contract of purchase, but nonetheless an important one to the State's interest. The Contract Clause does not forbid such a measure.

The judgment is reversed.

Mr. Justice BLACK, dissenting.

I have previously had a number of occasions to dissent from judgments of this Court balancing away the First Amendment's unequivocally guaranteed rights of free speech, press, assembly and petition. In this case I am compelled to dissent from the Court's balancing away the plain guarantee of Art. 1, § 10, that

"No State shall * * * pass any * * * Law impairing the Obligation of Contracts * * *,"

a balancing which results in the State of Texas taking a man's private property for public use without compensation in violation of the equally plain guarantee of the Fifth Amendment, made applicable to the States by the Fourteenth, that

" * * * private property [shall not] be taken for public use, without just compensation."

* * *

This Court now reverses the Court of Appeals and holds that Texas was justified in dishonoring its contractual obligation because of a state law passed in 1941 which attempted to change the obligation of this contract and the many others like it from one unconditionally allowing reinstatement, provided no rights of third parties had intervened, to one which cast off that right unless "exercised within five (5) years from the date of the forfeiture." The Court says that the State, after making a contractual obligation voluntarily and eagerly when the property was a drug on the market, was nevertheless free to enact the 1941 statute which not only impaired but flatly repudiated its former obligation after the land had greatly increased in value. And strange as it sounds, one of the reasons the Court gives as justification for Texas' repudiation of its obligation to Simmons and many others is that these contracts had turned out to be a bad bargain and Texas had lost millions of dollars by honoring them in the past. If the hope and realization of profit to a contract breaker are hereafter to be given either partial or sufficient weight to cancel out the unequivocal constitutional command against impairing the obligations of contracts, that command will be nullified by what is the most common cause for breaking contracts. I cannot subscribe to such a devitalizing constitutional doctrine.

* * *

In its opinion the Court's discussion of the Contract Clause and this Court's past decisions applying it is brief. For the most part the Court instead discusses the difficulties and regret which the Government of Texas has experienced on account of the contracts it entered. I therefore think that the first thing it is important to point out is that there is no support whatever in history or in this Court's prior holdings for the decision reached in this case. Indeed, I believe that the relevant precedents all point the opposite way.

* * *

I do not believe that any or all of the things * * * on which the Court relies are reasons for relieving Texas of the unconditional duty of keeping its contractual obligations as required by the Contract Clause. At most the Court's reasons boil down to the fact that Texas' contracts, perhaps very wisely made a long time ago, turned out when land soared in value, and particularly after oil was discovered, to be costly to the State. As the Court euphemistically puts it, the contracts were "not wholly effectual to serve the objectives of the State's land program many decades later. Settlement was no longer the objective, but revenues" * * * among other things were. In plainer language, the State decided it had made a bad deal and wanted out. There is nothing unusual in this. It is a commonplace that land values steadily rise when population increases and rise sharply when valuable minerals are discovered, and that many sellers would be much richer and happier if when lands go up in value they were able to welch on their sales. No plethora of words about state school funds can conceal the fact that to get money easily, without having to tax the whole public, Texas took the easy way out and violated the Contract Clause of the Constitution as written and as applied up to now. If the values of these lands and of valid contracts to buy them have increased, that increase belongs in equity as well as in sound constitutional interpretation not to Texas, but to the many people who agreed to these contracts under what now turns out to have been a mistaken belief that Texas would keep the obligations it gave to those who dealt with it.

All this for me is just another example of the delusiveness of calling "balancing" a "test." With its deprecatory view of the equities on the side of Simmons and other claimants and its remarkable sympathy for the State, the Court through its balancing process states the case in a way inevitably destined to bypass the Contract Clause and let Texas break its solemn obligation. As the Court's opinion demonstrates, constitutional adjudication under the balancing method becomes simply a matter of this Court's deciding for itself which result in a particular case

seems in the circumstances the more acceptable governmental policy and then stating the facts in such a way that the considerations in the balance lead to the result. Even if I believed that we as Justices of this Court had the authority to rely on our judgment of what is best for the country instead of trying to interpret the language and purpose of our written Constitution, I would not agree that Texas should be permitted to do what it has done here. But more importantly, I most certainly cannot agree that constitutional law is simply a matter of what the Justices of this Court decide is not harmful for the country, and therefore is "reasonable." * * * James Madison said that the Contract Clause was intended to protect people from the "fluctuating policy" of the legislature. The Federalist, No. 44, at 301 (Cooke ed. 1961). Today's majority holds that people are not protected from the fluctuating policy of the legislature, so long as the legislature acts in accordance with the fluctuating policy of this Court.

* * *

An interstate compact between New York and New Jersey, executed in 1962, limited the ability of the Port Authority to subsidize mass transit from revenues and reserves pledged to secure bonds floated by the Authority. In the wake of a national energy crisis twelve years later, the New York and New Jersey legislatures, acting concurrently, retroactively repealed the 1962 covenant. United States Trust Company of New York, a trustee and bondholder of the Port Authority, brought suit in a New Jersey superior court attacking the 1974 repealer as a violation of the Contract Clause and seeking declaratory relief. The trial court dismissed the complaint on grounds the statute repealing the covenant was a legitimate exercise of New Jersey's police power. The New Jersey Supreme Court affirmed the decision.

This judgment was reversed by the United States Supreme Court in United States Trust Co. of New York v. State of New Jersey, 431 U.S. 1, 97 S.Ct. 1505 (1977). Speaking for the Court, Justice Blackmun observed at the outset that "a finding that there has been a technical impairment" of the Contract Clause does not dispose of the matter but "is merely a preliminary step" in resolving the constitutional conflict between the dictates of the Contract Clause and "the 'essential attributes of sovereign power,' * * * necessarily reserved by the States to safeguard the welfare of their citizens." He continued:

> The instant case involves a financial obligation and thus as a threshold matter may not be said automatically to fall within the reserved powers that cannot be contracted away. Not every security provision, however, is necessarily financial. For example, a revenue bond might be secured by the State's promise to continue operating the facility in question; yet such a promise surely could not validly be construed to bind the State never to close the facility for health or safety reasons. The security provision at issue here, however, is different: the States promised that revenues and reserves securing the bonds would not be depleted by the Port Authority's operation of deficit-producing passenger railroads beyond the level of "permitted deficits." Such a promise is purely financial and thus not necessarily a compromise of the State's reserved powers.

Although, "[a]s with laws impairing the obligation of private contracts, an impairment may be constitutional if it is reasonable and necessary to serve an important public purpose," the Court pointed out that, "[i]n applying this standard, * * * complete deference to a legislative assessment of reasonableness and necessity is not appropriate because the State's self-interest is at stake." In short, while "the Contract Clause does not require a State to adhere to a contract that surrenders an essential attribute of its sovereignty," still, "[w]hen a State impairs the obligation of its own contract, the reserved power doctrine has a different basis." Rejecting the contention that the goals of mass transportation, energy conservation, and environmental protection "are so important that any harm to bondholders from repeal of the 1962 covenant is greatly outweighed by the public benefit," the Court refused to accept "this invitation to engage in a utilitarian comparison of public benefit and private loss." In this light, the Court found that the repealer failed to pass constitutional muster for the following reasons:

> First, it cannot be said that total repeal of the covenant was essential; a less drastic modification would have permitted the contemplated plan without entirely removing the covenant's limitations on the use of Port Authority revenues and reserves to subsidize commuter railroads. Second, without modifying the covenant at all, the States could have adopted alternative means of achieving their twin goals of discouraging automobile use and improving mass transit. Appellees contend, however, that choosing among these alternatives is a matter for legislative discretion. But a State is not completely free to consider impairing the obligations of its own contracts on a par with other policy alternatives. Similarly, a State is not free to impose a drastic impairment when an evident and more moderate course would serve its purposes equally well. * * *

Noting that "[a]s early as 1922, * * * there were pressures to involve the Port Authority in mass transit," the Court concluded that the concerns which were the purpose of the 1974 repealer were not unknown in 1962, and, more to the point, "the covenant was specifically intended to protect the pledged revenues and reserves against the possibility that such concerns would lead the Port Authority into greater involvement in deficit mass transit."

Justice Brennan, in a dissent which Justices White and Marshall joined, protested that this decision flew in the face of a century of rulings which "established the principle that lawful exercises of a State's police powers stand paramount to private rights held under contract" and "construed the Contract Clause largely to be powerless in binding a State to contracts limiting the authority of successor legislatures to enact laws in furtherance of the health, safety, and similar collective interests of the polity." Arguing that the elevation of the Contract Clause at the expense of "sound legislative policymaking" was "as demonstrably unwise as it is unnecessary," Justice Brennan predicted that, since the states' "credibility in the credit market obviously is highly dependent on exercising their vast lawmaking powers with self-restraint and discipline, * * * few, if any, jurisdictions would choose to use their authority 'so foolish[ly] as to kill a goose that lays golden eggs for them,' * * *." Justices Stewart and Powell did not participate in the decision.

b. THE RISE AND DECLINE OF ECONOMIC SUBSTANTIVE DUE PROCESS

WYNEHAMER v. NEW YORK

Court of Appeals of New York, 1856
13 N.Y. 378

Wynehamer, a tavern keeper, was indicted under a prohibition statute passed by the New York legislature in 1855. He was convicted of violating the "act for the prevention of intemperance, pauperism and crime" in an Erie county court, and he appealed to a department of the state supreme court and finally to the New York Court of Appeals. Wynehamer challenged the statute as a violation of that provision of the New York Constitution which declared that "no person shall be deprived of life, liberty, or property, without due process of law." He contended that by prohibiting the sale of intoxicating beverages the statute effectively took away his tavern business in violation of the constitutional guarantee.

COMSTOCK, J. * * *

* * *

In determining the question, whether the "act for the prevention of intemperance, pauperism and crime" was an exercise of power prohibited to the legislature, an accurate perception of the subject to which it relates is the first requisite. It is, then, I believe, universally admitted that when this law was passed, intoxicating liquors, to be used as a beverage, were *property* in the most absolute and unqualified sense of the term; and, as such, as much entitled to the protection of the constitution as lands, houses or chattels of any description. * * * In this country the right of property in them was never, so far as I know, for an instant questioned. In this state, they were bought and sold like other property; they were seized and sold upon legal process, for the payment of debts; they were, like other goods, the subject of actions at law; and when the owner died, their value constituted a fund for the benefit of his creditors, or went to his children and kindred, according to law or the will of the deceased. They entered largely into the foreign and internal commerce of the state, and when subjected to the operation of this statute, many millions in value were invested in them. In short, I do not understand it to be denied that they were property in just as high a sense as any other possession which a citizen can acquire. * * *

* * *

* * * If intoxicating liquors are property, the constitution does not permit a legislative estimate to be made of its usefulness, with a view to its destruction. In a word, that which belongs to the citizen in the sense of property, and as such has to him a commercial value, cannot be pronounced worthless or pernicious, and so destroyed or deprived of its essential attributes. * * *

* * * In a government like ours, theories of public good or public necessity may be so plausible, or even so truthful, as to command popular majorities. But whether truthful or plausible merely, and by whatever numbers they are assented to, there are some absolute private rights beyond their reach, and among these the constitution places the right of property.

The views thus far expressed, the substance of which I think must command a general assent, would seem to narrow the field of inquiry. Do the prohibitions and penalties of the "act for the prevention of intemperance, pauperism and crime" pass the utmost boundaries of mere regulation and police, and by their own force, assuming them to be valid and faithfully obeyed and executed, work the essential loss or destruction of the property at which they are aimed? * * * In my judgment, they do plainly work this result.

* * *

It has been urged upon us, that the power of the legislature is restricted, not only by the express provisions of the written constitution, but by limitations implied from the nature and form of our government; that, aside from all special restrictions, the right to enact such laws is not among the delegated powers of the legislature, and that the act in question is void, as against the fundamental principles of liberty, and against common reason and natural rights. * * *

* * *

It is scarcely necessary, perhaps, to observe, that in the views which have been expressed, it is not intended to narrow the field of legislative discretion in regulating and controlling the traffic in intoxicating liquors. We only say that, in all such legislation, the essential right of the citizen to his property must be preserved; a right which includes the power of disposition and sale, to be exercised under such restraints as a just regard both to the public good and private rights may suggest.

I am not insensible to the delicacy and importance of the duty we assume in overruling an act of the legislature, believed by so many intelligent and good men to afford the best remedy for great and admitted evils in society; but we cannot forget that the highest function intrusted to us is that of maintaining inflexibly the fundamental law. And believing, as I do, that the prohibitory act transcends the constitutional limits of the legislative power, it must be adjudged to be void.

The judgments of the supreme court and of the court of sessions must, therefore, be reversed.

A. S. JOHNSON, J. * * *

* * *

The legislature * * * has power to create offences, and to declare in what cases the consequences of loss of life, of liberty or of property, shall be attached to the commission of offences, they being ascertained "by due process of law" to have been committed. But the form of this declaration of right, "no person shall be deprived of life, liberty or property, without due process of law," necessarily imports that the legislature cannot make the mere existence of the rights secured the occasion of depriving a person of any of them, even by the forms which belong to "due process of law." For if it does not necessarily import this, then the legislative power is absolute.

* * *

T. A. JOHNSON, J. (Dissenting.)
* * *

* * *

It is claimed that courts, independent of constitutional limitations upon legislative power, have the right to annul statutes and pronounce them void, whenever, in their judgment, they are in conflict with the fundamental principles of the government and tend to individual oppression, although not in conflict with any provision of the constitution of the United States or of the state. I know of no such power vested in the courts, and they should never attempt to usurp it. The limitations upon legislative power are written in the fundamental law, and that is the standard by which all questions of power exercised by the legislature must be tried. * * *

Should the time ever come when the courts, instead of promptly sustaining and enforcing the legislative will become forward to thwart and defeat it, and assume to prescribe limits to its exercise other than those prescribed in the constitution; to substitute their discretion and notions of expediency for constitutional restraints; and to declare enactments void for want of conformity to such standards; or when, to defeat unpalatable acts, they shall habitually resort to subtleties and refinements and strained constructions to bring them into conflict with the constitution, the end of all just and salutary authority, judicial as well as legislative, will not be remote. * * *
The people have a far more certain and reliable security and protection against mere impolitic, over-stringent or uncalled-for legislation than courts can ever afford, in their reserved power of changing, annually and biennially, the representatives of their legislative sovereignty; and to that final and ultimate tribunal should all such errors and mistakes in legislation be referred for correction.

As there is nothing, therefore, in the constitution, either of this state or of the United States, which takes away or limits the rights of the legislature to make such regulations in regard to the traffic in property amongst the citizens of the state, and to impose such restrictions and prohibitions upon it as it shall deem necessary for the public good, this act, so far as it restricts and prohibits the sale of intoxicating drinks, must be pronounced a valid, constitutional act and entitled to obedience from every citizen of the state.

* * *

I am accordingly of the opinion that the conviction should be affirmed.

* * *

On deciding the case, the court passed upon and affirmed the following propositions:

1. That the prohibitory act, in its operation upon property in intoxicating liquors existing in the hands of any person within this state when the act took effect, is a violation of the provision in the constitution of this state which declares that no person shall be "deprived of life, liberty or property, without due process of law." That the various provisions, prohibitions and penalties contained in the act do substantially destroy the property in such liquors, in violation of the terms and spirit of the constitutional provision.

2. That inasmuch as the act does not discriminate between such liquors existing when it took effect as a law, and such as might thereafter be acquired by importation or manufacture, and does not countenance or warrant any defence based upon the distinction referred to, it cannot be sustained in respect to any such liquor, whether existing at the time the act took effect or acquired subsequently; although all the judges were of opinion that it would be competent for the legislature to pass such an act as the one under consideration * * * provided such act should be plainly and distinctly prospective as to the property on which it should operate.

* * *

DENIO, C. J., A. S. JOHNSON, COMSTOCK, SELDEN and HUBBARD, JJ., concurred. * * *

T. A. JOHNSON, MITCHELL, J., and WRIGHT, JJ., dissented. * * *

BUTCHERS' BENEVOLENT ASS'N v. CRESCENT CITY LIVESTOCK LANDING & SLAUGHTERHOUSE CO. [THE SLAUGHTERHOUSE CASES]

Supreme Court of the United States, 1873
83 U.S. (16 Wall.) 36, 21 L.Ed. 394

In the face of a faltering response to the problem by the New Orleans city government, the Louisiana legislature passed an act in 1869 to clean up the Mississippi River. The cause of the pollution and resulting contamination of the city's water supply (which was producing a mounting incidence of cholera) was the dumping of refuse into the river from the many small independent slaughterhouses. What feeble ordinances the city council had managed to enact were ignored or were evaded by the movement of butchering facilities north of the city on the river beyond its jurisdiction. In the act the legislature prohibited all landing and slaughtering of livestock in the city or surrounding parishes except at one large slaughterhouse which was granted an exclusive franchise for twenty-five years. Aside from laying out the usual corporate specifications, the act also established maximum rates to be charged for the landing and slaughtering of livestock. The Butchers' Benevolent Association, a group of the small independent slaughterers who had been displaced by the legislation, challenged the act on the grounds that it violated the Thirteenth Amendment and the Privileges and Immunities, Due Process, and Equal Protection Clauses of the Fourteenth Amendment in taking away their livelihood. Both a state district court and the Louisiana Supreme Court rendered decisions in favor of the state-created monopoly held by the Crescent City Livestock Landing & Slaughterhouse Company. This case came to the U. S. Supreme Court on a writ of error along with two other cases involving the same controversy.

Mr. Justice MILLER delivered the opinion of the Court:

*   *   *

The plaintiffs in error accepting this issue, allege that the statute is a violation of the Constitution of the United States in these several particulars:

That it creates an involuntary servitude forbidden by the 13th article of amendment;

That it abridges the privileges and immunities of citizens of the United States;

That it denies to the plaintiffs the equal protection of the laws; and,

That it deprives them of their property without due process of law; contrary to the provisions of the 1st section of the 14th article of amendment.

This court is thus called upon for the first time to give construction to these articles.

*   *   *

The next observation is more important in view of the arguments of counsel in the present case. It is that the distinction between citizenship of the United States and citizenship of a state is clearly recognized and established. Not only may a man be a citizen of the United States without being a citizen of a state, but an important element is necessary to convert the former into the latter. He must reside within the state to make him a citizen of it, but it is only necessary that he should be born or naturalized in the United States to be a citizen of the Union.

It is quite clear, then, that there is a citizenship of the United States and a citizenship of a state, which are distinct from each other and which depend upon different characteristics or circumstances in the individual.

We think this distinction and its explicit recognition in this Amendment of great weight in this argument, because the next paragraph of this same section, which is the one mainly relied on by the plaintiffs in error, speaks only of privileges and immunities of citizens of the United States, and does not speak of those of citizens of the several states. The argument, however, in favor of the plaintiffs, rests wholly on the assumption that the citizenship is the same and the privileges and immunities guaranteed by the clause are the same.

The language is: "No state shall make or enforce any law which shall abridge the privileges or immunities of citizens of the United States." It is a little remarkable, if this clause was intended as a protection to the citizen of a state against the legislative power of his own state, that the words "citizen of the state" should be left out when it is so carefully used, and used in contradistinction to "citizens of the United States" in the very sentence which precedes it. It is too clear for argument that the change in phraseology was adopted understandingly and with a purpose.

Of the privileges and immunities of the citizens of the United States, and of the privileges and immunities of the citizen of the state, and what they respectively are, we will presently consider; but we wish to state here that it is only the former which are placed by this clause under the protection of the Federal Constitution, and that the latter, whatever they may be, are not intended to have any additional protection by this paragraph of the Amendment.

If, then, there is a difference between the privileges and immunities belonging to a citizen of the United States as such, and those belonging to the citizen of the state as such, the latter must rest for their security and protection where they have heretofore rested; for they are not embraced by this paragraph of the Amendment.

* * *

We repeat, then, in the light of this recapitulation of events, almost too recent to be called history, but which are familiar to us all; and on the most casual examination of the language of these amendments, no one can fail to be impressed with the one pervading purpose found in them all, lying at the foundation of each, and without which none of them would have been even suggested; we mean the freedom of the slave race, the security and firm establishment of that freedom, and the protection of the newly made freeman and citizen from the oppressions of those who had formerly exercised unlimited dominion over him. It is true that only the 15th Amendment, in terms, mentions the negro by speaking of his color and his slavery. But it is just as true that each of the other articles was addressed to the grievances of that race, and designed to remedy them as the fifteenth.

We do not say that no one else but the negro can share in this protection. Both the language and spir-

it of these articles are to have their fair and just weight in any question of construction. Undoubtedly, while negro slavery alone was in the mind of the Congress which proposed the 13th article, it forbids any other kind of slavery, now or hereafter. If Mexican peonage or the Chinese coolie labor system shall develop slavery of the Mexican or Chinese race within our territory, this Amendment may safely be trusted to make it void. And so, if other rights are assailed by the states which properly and necessarily fall within the protection of these articles, that protection will apply though the party interested may not be of African descent. But what we do say, and what we wish to be understood, is, that in any fair and just construction of any section or phrase of these amendments, it is necessary to look to the purpose which we have said was the pervading spirit of them all, the evil which they were designed to remedy, and the process of continued addition to the Constitution until that purpose was supposed to be accomplished, as far as constitutional law can accomplish it.

* * *

The constitutional provision there alluded to did not create those rights, which it called privileges and immunities of citizens of the states. It threw around them in that clause no security for the citizen of the state in which they were claimed or exercised. Nor did it profess to control the power of the state governments over the rights of its own citizens.

Its sole purpose was to declare to the several states, that whatever those rights, as you grant or establish them to your own citizens, or as you limit or qualify, or impose restrictions on their exercise, the same, neither more nor less, shall be the measure of the rights of citizens of other states within your jurisdiction.

* * *

[T]he reversal of the judgments of the supreme court of Louisiana in these cases would constitute this court a perpetual censor upon all legislation of the states, on the civil rights of their own citizens, with authority to nullify such as it did not approve as consistent with those rights, as they existed at the time of the adoption of this Amendment. The argument, we admit, is not always the most conclusive which is drawn from the consequences urged against the adoption of a particular construction of an instrument. But when, as in the case before us, these consequences are so serious, so far reaching and pervading, so great a departure from the structure and spirit of our institutions; when the effect is to fetter and degrade the state governments by subjecting them to the control of Congress, in the exercise of powers heretofore universally conceded to them of the most ordinary and fundamental character; when in fact it radically changes the whole theory of the relations of the state and Federal governments to each other and of both these governments to the people; the argument has a force that is irresistible, in the absence of language which expresses such a purpose too clearly to admit of doubt.

We are convinced that no such results were intended by the Congress which proposed these amendments, nor by the legislatures of the states, which ratified them.

* * *

But lest it should be said that no such privileges and immunities are to be found if those we have been considering are excluded, we venture to suggest some which owe their existence to the Federal government, its national character, its Constitution, or its laws.

One of these is well described in the case of Crandall v. Nevada, 6 Wall. 36, 18 L.Ed. 745. It is said to be the right of the citizen of this great country, protected by implied guaranties of its Constitution, "to come to the seat of government to assert any claim he may have upon that government, to transact any business he may have with it, to seek its protection, to share its offices, to engage in administering its functions. He has the right of free access to its seaports, through which all operations of foreign commerce are conducted, to the subtreasuries, land-offices, and courts of justice in the several states." * * *

Another privilege of a citizen of the United States is to demand the care and protection of the Federal government over his life, liberty, and property when on the high seas or within the jurisdiction of a foreign government. Of this there can be no doubt, nor that the right depends upon his character as a citizen of the United States. The right to peaceably assemble and petition for redress of grievances, the privilege of the writ of habeas corpus, are rights of the citizen guarantied by the Federal Constitution. The right to use the navigable waters of the United States, however they may penetrate the territory of the several states, and all rights secured to our citizens by treaties with foreign nations, are dependent upon citizenship of the United States, and not citizenship of a state. One of these privileges is conferred by the very article under consideration. It is that a citizen of

the United States can, of his own volition, become a citizen of any state
of the Union by a bona fide residence
therein, with the same rights as other citizens of that state. To these
may be added the rights secured by
the 13th and 15th articles of Amendment, and by the other clause of the
Fourteenth, next to be considered.

But it is useless to pursue this
branch of the inquiry, since we are of
opinion that the rights claimed by
these plaintiffs in error, if they have
any existence, are not privileges and
immunities of citizens of the United
States within the meaning of the
clause of the 14th Amendment under
consideration.

* * *

The argument has not been much
pressed in these cases that the defendant's charter deprives the plaintiffs of their property without due
process of law, or that it denies to
them the equal protection of the law.
* * *

We are not without judicial interpretation, therefore, both state and
national, of the meaning of this
clause. And it is sufficient to say
that under no construction of that
provision that we have ever seen, or
any that we deem admissible, can the
restraint imposed by the state of
Louisiana upon the exercise of their
trade by the butchers of New Orleans be held to be a deprivation of
property within the meaning of that
provision.

* * *

[W]e do not see in those Amendments any purpose to destroy the
main features of the general system.
Under the pressure of all the excited
feeling growing out of the war, our
statesmen have still believed that the

existence of the states with powers
for domestic and local government,
including the regulation of civil
rights, the rights of person and of
property, was essential to the perfect
working of our complex form of government, though they have thought
proper to impose additional limitations on the states, and to confer additional power on that of the nation.

But whatever fluctuations may be
seen in the history of public opinion
on this subject during the period of
our national existence, we think it
will be found that this court, so far
as its functions required, has always
held, with a steady and an even
hand, the balance between state and
Federal power, and we trust that
such may continue to be the history
of its relation to that subject so long
as it shall have duties to perform
which demand of it a construction of
the Constitution, or of any of its
parts.

*The judgments of the Supreme
Court of Louisiana in these cases
are affirmed.*

Mr. Justice FIELD, dissenting:

* * *

* * * The provisions of the
Fourteenth Amendment, which is
properly a supplement to the thirteenth, cover, in my judgment, the
case before us, and inhibit any legislation which confers special and exclusive privileges like these under
consideration. * * *

* * *

What, then, are the privileges and
immunities which are secured
against abridgement by state legislation?

* * *

* * * The privileges and immunities designated are those which of right belong to the citizens of all free governments. Clearly among these must be placed the right to pursue a lawful employment in a lawful manner, without other restraint than such as equally affects all persons. * * *

* * *

* * * [E]quality of right, with exemption from all disparaging and partial enactments, in the lawful pursuits of life, throughout the whole country, is the distinguishing privilege of citizens of the United States. To them, everywhere, all pursuits, all professions, all avocations are open without other restrictions than such as are imposed equally upon all others of the same age, sex and condition. The state may prescribe such regulations for every pursuit and calling of life as will promote the public health, secure the good order and advance the general prosperity of society, but when once prescribed, the pursuit or calling must be free to be followed by every citizen who is within the conditions designated, and will conform to the regulations. This is the fundamental idea upon which our institutions rest, and unless adhered to in the legislation of the country our government will be a Republic only in name. The 14th Amendment, in my judgment, makes it essential to the validity of the legislation of every state that this equality of right should be respected. * * *

I am authorized by Mr. Chief Justice CHASE, Mr. Justice SWAYNE and Mr. Justice BRADLEY, to state that they concur with me in this dissenting opinion.

Mr. Justice BRADLEY, dissenting:

* * *

[A]ny law which establishes a sheer monopoly, depriving a large class of citizens of the privilege of pursuing a lawful employment, does abridge the privileges of those citizens.

* * *

In my view, a law which prohibits a large class of citizens from adopting a lawful employment, or from following a lawful employment previously adopted, does deprive them of liberty as well as property, without due process of law. Their right of choice is a portion of their liberty; their occupation is their property. Such a law also deprives those citizens of the equal protection of the laws, contrary to the last clause of the section.

* * *

MUNN v. ILLINOIS

Supreme Court of the United States, 1877
94 U.S. 113, 24 L.Ed. 77

Amid growing pressure from the Granger movement to prevent the continued exploitation of farmers by grain elevator operators, the Illinois legislature passed an act in 1871 which established maximum rates that warehouses and elevators could charge for the storage of grain and, in addition, required these businesses to obtain operating licenses. The state filed a complaint in Cook County Court against Ira Munn and another grain elevator operator for conducting their business in violation of the statute. Munn challenged the legislation on several constitutional grounds: (1) the act conflicted with the interstate commerce power of the Congress under Article I of the Constitution; (2) it gave preferential treatment to commerce in a state port; and (3) it conflicted with the Due Process Clause of the Fourteenth Amendment. The county court decided against Munn, and its judgment was affirmed on appeal by the Illinois Supreme Court, whereupon Munn appealed to the U. S. Supreme Court.

Mr. Chief Justice WAITE delivered the opinion of the court:

*   *   *

Every statute is presumed to be constitutional. The courts ought not to declare one to be unconstitutional, unless it is clearly so. If there is doubt, the expressed will of the Legislature should be sustained.

The Constitution contains no definition of the word "deprive," as used in the 14th Amendment. To determine its signification, therefore, it is necessary to ascertain the effect which usage has given it, when employed in the same or a like connection.

*   *   *

[I]t is apparent that, down to the time of the adoption of the 14th Amendment, it was not supposed that statutes regulating the use, or even the price of the use, of private property necessarily deprived an owner of his property without due process of law. Under some circumstances they may, but not under all. The Amendment does not change the law in this particular; it simply prevents the States from doing that which will operate as such a deprivation.

This brings us to inquire as to the principles upon which this power of regulation rests, in order that we may determine what is within and what without its operative effect. Looking, then, to the common law, from whence came the right which

the Constitution protects, we find that when private property is "affected with a public interest, it ceases to be juris privati only." This was said by Lord Chief Justice Hale more than two hundred years ago, in his treatise De Portibus Maris, 1 Harg L.Tr., 78, and has been accepted without objection as an essential element in the law of property ever since. Property does become clothed with a public interest when used in a manner to make it of public consequence, and affect the community at large. When, therefore, one devotes his property to a use in which the public has an interest, he, in effect, grants to the public an interest in that use, and must submit to be controlled by the public for the common good, to the extent of the interest he has thus created. He may withdraw his grant by discontinuing the use; but, so long as he maintains the use, he must submit to the control.

*   *   *

*   *   * It remains only to ascertain whether the warehouses of these plaintiffs in error, and the business which is carried on there, come within the operation of this principle.

*   *   *

[I]t is difficult to see why, if the common carrier, or the miller, or the ferryman, or the innkeeper, or the wharfinger or the baker, or the cartman, or the hackney-coachman, pursues a public employment and exercises "a sort of public office," these plaintiffs in error do not. They stand, to use again the language of their counsel, in the very "gateway of commerce," and take toll from all who pass. Their business most certainly "tends to a common charge, and is become a thing of public interest and use." Every bushel of grain for its passage "pays a toll, which is a common charge," and, therefore, according to Lord Hale, every such wharehouseman "ought to be under public regulation, viz.: that he   *   *   *   take but reasonable toll." Certainly, if any business can be clothed "with a public interest, and cease to be juris privati only," this has been. It may not be made so by the operation of the Constitution of Illinois or this statute, but it is by the facts.

*   *   *

It is insisted, however, that the owner of property is entitled to a reasonable compensation for its use, even though it be clothed with a public interest, and that what is reasonable is a judicial and not a legislative question.

As has already been shown, the practice has been otherwise. *   *   *

*   *   *

We know that this is a power which may be abused; but that is no argument against its existence. For protection against abuses by Legislatures the people must resort to the polls, not to the courts.

*   *   *

We come now to consider the effect upon this statute of the power of Congress to regulate commerce. *   *   *   The warehouses of these plaintiffs in error are situated

and their business carried on exclusively within the limits of the State of Illinois. They are used as instruments by those engaged in State as well as those engaged in interstate commerce, but they are no more necessarily a part of commerce itself than the dray or the cart by which, but for them, grain would be transferred from one railroad station to another. Incidentally they may become connected with interstate commerce, but not necessarily so. Their regulation is a thing of domestic concern and, certainly, until Congress acts in reference to their interstate relations, the State may exercise all the powers of government over them, even though in so doing it may indirectly operate upon commerce outside its immediate jurisdiction. We do not say that a case may not arise in which it will be found that a State, under the form of regulating its own affairs, has encroached upon the exclusive domain of Congress in respect to interstate commerce, but we do say that, upon the facts as they are represented to us in this record, that has not been done.

*   *   *

The judgment is affirmed.

Mr. Justice FIELD, dissenting:

I am compelled to dissent from the decision of the court in this case, and from the reasons upon which that decision is founded. The principle upon which the opinion of the majority proceeds is, in my judgment, subversive of the rights of private property, heretofore believed to be protected by constitutional guaranties against legislative interference, and is in conflict with the authorities cited in its support.

*   *   *

* * * No prerogative or privilege of the Crown to establish warehouses was ever asserted at the common law. The business of a warehouseman was, at common law, a private business, and is so in its nature. It has no special privileges connected with it, nor did the law ever extend to it any greater protection than it extended to all other private business. No reason can be assigned to justify legislation interfering with the legitimate profits of that business, that would not equally justify an intermeddling with the business of every man in the community, so soon, at least, as his business became generally useful.

I am of opinion that the judgment of the Supreme Court of Illinois should be reversed.

[Justice STRONG concurred in the dissent.]

ALLGEYER v. LOUISIANA

Supreme Court of the United States, 1897
165 U.S. 578, 17 S.Ct. 427, 41 L.Ed. 832

In 1894, the Louisiana legislature enacted a statute which prohibited the issuance of marine insurance on any property within the state by any company which had not complied fully with the laws of the state. The legislation specified a $1,000 fine to be paid by anyone effecting such an illegal insurance policy. Allgeyer & Company maintained such a policy with a New York insurance firm not doing business in Louisiana by mailing premiums from its offices in New Orleans. Allgeyer was charged with violating the law when in accordance with the terms of the policy he notified the New York firm of the shipment of 100 pounds of cotton destined for foreign ports to effect coverage under the marine policy. When the state attorney general sued to recover the penalty provided by the statute, Allgeyer challenged the constitutionality of the statute on grounds it denied due process guaranteed by the Fourteenth Amendment. The Louisiana Supreme Court upheld the statute, and Allgeyer appealed to the U. S. Supreme Court.

Mr. Justice PECKHAM * * * delivered the opinion of the court.

There is no doubt of the power of the state to prohibit foreign insurance companies from doing business within its limits. The state can impose such conditions as it pleases upon the doing of any business by those companies within its borders, and unless the conditions be complied with the prohibition may be absolute. * * *

A conditional prohibition in regard to foreign insurance companies doing business within the state of Louisiana is to be found in article 236 of the constitution of that state, which reads as follows: "No foreign corporation shall do any business in this state without having one or more known places of business and an authorized agent or agents in the state upon whom process may be served."

It is not claimed in this suit that the Atlantic Mutual Insurance Company has violated this provision of the constitution by doing business within the state.

* * *

In the course of the opinion delivered in this case by the supreme court of Louisiana that court said:

"The open policy in this case is conceded to be a New York contract;

hence the special insurance effected on the cotton complained of here was a New York contract.

"The question presented is the simple proposition whether under the act a party while in the state can insure property in Louisiana in a foreign insurance company, which has not complied with the laws of the state, under an open policy,—the special contract of insurance and the open policy being contracts made and entered into beyond the limits of the state."

*   *   *

The general contract contained in the open policy, as well as the special insurance upon each shipment of goods of which notice is given to the insurance company, being contracts made in New York and valid there, the state of Louisiana claims notwithstanding such facts that the defendants have violated the act of 1894, by doing an act in that state to effect for themselves insurance on their property then in that state in a marine insurance company which had not complied in all respects with the laws of that state, and that such violation consisted in the act of mailing a letter or sending a telegram to the insurance company in New York describing the cotton upon which the defendants desired the insurance under the open marine policy to attach. It is claimed on the part of the state that its legislature had the power to provide that such an act should be illegal, and to subject the offender to the penalties provided in the statute.
*   *   *

*   *   *

It is natural that the state court should have remarked that there is in this "statute an apparent interference with the liberty of defendants in restricting their rights to place insurance on property of their own whenever and in what company they desired." Such interference is not only apparent, but it is real, and we do not think that it is justified for the purpose of upholding what the state says is its policy with regard to foreign insurance companies which had not complied with the laws of the state for doing business within its limits. In this case the company did no business within the state, and the contracts were not therein made.

The supreme court of Louisiana says that the act of writing within that state the letter of notification was an act therein done to effect an insurance on property then in the state, in a marine insurance company which had not complied with its laws, and such act was therefore prohibited by the statute. As so construed, we think the statute is a violation of the fourteenth amendment of the federal constitution, in that it deprives the defendants of their liberty without due process of law. The statute which forbids such act does not become due process of law, because it is inconsistent with the provisions of the constitution of the Union. The "liberty" mentioned in that amendment means, not only the right of the citizen to be free from the mere physical restraint of his person, as by incarceration, but the term is deemed to embrace the right of the citizen to be free in the enjoyment of all his faculties; to be free to use them in all lawful ways; to live and work where he will; to earn his livelihood by any lawful calling; to pursue any livelihood or avocation; and for that purpose to enter into all contracts which may be proper, necessary, and essential to his carrying out to a successful conclusion the purposes above mentioned.

* * *

* * * To deprive the citizen of such a right as herein described without due process of law is illegal. Such a statute as this in question is not due process of law, because it prohibits an act which under the federal constitution the defendants had a right to perform. This does not interfere in any way with the acknowledged right of the state to enact such legislation in the legitimate exercise of its police or other powers as to it may seem proper. In the exercise of such right, however, care must be taken not to infringe upon those other rights of the citizen which are protected by the federal constitution.

In the privilege of pursuing an ordinary calling or trade, and of acquiring, holding, and selling property, must be embraced the right to make all proper contracts in relation thereto; and although it may be conceded that this right to contract in relation to persons or property or to do business within the jurisdiction of the state may be regulated, and sometimes prohibited, when the contracts or business conflict with the policy of the state as contained in its statutes, yet the power does not and cannot extend to prohibiting a citizen from making contracts of the nature involved in this case outside of the limits and jurisdiction of the state, and which are also to be performed outside of such jurisdiction; nor can the state legally prohibit its citizens from doing such an act as writing this letter of notification, even though the property which is the subject of the insurance may at the time when such insurance attaches be within the limits of the state. The mere fact that a citizen may be within the limits of a particular state does not prevent his making a contract outside its limits while he himself remains within it. * * * The contract in this case was thus made. It was a valid contract, made outside of the state, to be performed outside of the state, although the subject was property temporarily within the state. As the contract was valid in the place where made and where it was to be performed, the party to the contract, upon whom is devolved the right or duty to send the notification in order that the insurance provided for by the contract may attach to the property specified in the shipment mentioned in the notice, must have the liberty to do that act and to give that notification within the limits of the state, any prohibition of the state statute to the contrary notwithstanding. The giving of the notice is a mere collateral matter. It is not the contract itself, but is an act performed pursuant to a valid contract, which the state had no right or jurisdiction to prevent its citizen from making outside the limits of the state.

* * *

For these reasons we think the statute in question was a violation of the federal constitution, and afforded no justification for the judgment awarded by that court against the plaintiffs in error. That judgment must therefore be reversed. * * *

In 1898, Congress enacted an omnibus labor-management law providing for the settlement of industrial disputes involving interstate carriers. Most of the provisions dealt with the structuring of arbitration proceedings. Section 10 of the act, however, focused on the discrimination against union members by employers. In sum, this provision of the act outlawed the signing of "yellow dog" contracts—employment agreements signed by workers which contained clauses in which they agreed not to join unions. This section of the act also barred employers from dismissing employees from their jobs simply because of their union membership. Adair, an agent of the Louisville & Nashville Railroad Company, dismissed one O. B. Coppage, a railroad employee, from his job because of the latter's union affiliation. Adair was subsequently indicted and convicted under the statute, whereupon he appealed to the Supreme Court. In Adair v. United States, 208 U.S. 161, 28 S.Ct. 277 (1908), the Court, speaking through Justice Harlan, reversed the conviction and declared Section 10 of the act unconstitutional. The Court found no close or substantial connection between the provisions of Section 10 and the public health, safety, or welfare to justify interference with the liberty of the parties to contract. The Court concluded that Section 10 arbitrarily intruded into the free and open negotiations between labor and management. Said Justice Harlan:

> While * * * the right of liberty and property guaranteed by the Constitution against deprivation without due process of law is subject to such reasonable restraints as the common good or the general welfare may require, it is not within the functions of government—at least, in the absence of contract between the parties—to compel any person, in the course of his business and against his will, to accept or retain the personal services of another, or to compel any person, against his will, to perform personal services for another. The right of a person to sell his labor upon such terms as he deems proper is, in its essence, the same as the right of the purchaser of labor to prescribe the conditions upon which he will accept such labor from the person offering to sell it. So the right of the employee to quit the service of the employer, for whatever reason, is the same as the right of the employer, for whatever reason, to dispense with the services of such employee. It was the legal right of the defendant, Adair,—however unwise such a course might have been,—to discharge Coppage because of his being a member of a labor organization, as it was the legal right of Coppage, if he saw fit to do so,—however unwise such a course on his part might have been,—to quit the service in which he was engaged, because the defendant employed some persons who were not members of a labor organization. In all such particulars the employer and the employee have equality of right, and any legislation that disturbs that equality is an arbitrary interference with the liberty of contract which no government can legally justify in a free land. * * *

Justices McKenna and Holmes dissented. Justice Moody did not participate in consideration of the case.

Seven years after its ruling in *Adair*, the Court had an occasion to evaluate similar legislation at the state level outlawing the "yellow dog" contract. In 1909, Kansas passed an act which made it a criminal offense to coerce an employee into signing an agreement to give up or refrain from union membership as a condition of employment. Under the statute T. B. Coppage, a superintendent at the St. Louis & San Francisco Railway Company, was indicted and convicted in state court for dismissing from his job one Hedges, a switchman, who refused to sign the agreement and terminate his union membership. Coppage's conviction was affirmed by the Kansas Supreme Court, and he appealed to the U. S. Supreme Court. The Court in Coppage v. Kansas, 236 U.S. 1, 35 S.Ct. 240 (1915), finding no material difference between the statute at issue in this case and that invalidated in

Adair, reversed Coppage's conviction and declared the Kansas statute unconstitutional. Speaking for the Court, Justice Pitney said:

As to the interest of the employed, it is said by the Kansas supreme court to be a matter of common knowledge that "employees, as a rule, are not financially able to be as independent in making contracts for the sale of their labor as are employers in making a contract of purchase thereof." No doubt; wherever the right of private property exists, there must and will be inequalities of fortune; and thus it naturally happens that parties negotiating about a contract are not equally unhampered by circumstances. This applies to all contracts, and not merely to that between employer and employee. Indeed, a little reflection will show that wherever the right of private property and the right of free contract coexist, each party when contracting is inevitably more or less influenced by the question whether he has much property, or little, or none; for the contract is made to the very end that each may gain something that he needs or desires more urgently than that which he proposes to give in exchange. And, since it is self-evident that, unless all things are held in common, some persons must have more property than others, it is from the nature of things impossible to uphold freedom of contract and the right of private property without at the same time recognizing as legitimate those inequalities of fortune that are the necessary result of the exercise of those rights. But the 14th Amendment, in declaring that a state shall not "deprive any person of life, liberty, or property without due process of law," gives to each of these an equal sanction; it recognizes "liberty" and "property" as coexistent human rights, and debars the states from any unwarranted interference with either.

And since a state may not strike them down directly, it is clear that it may not do so indirectly, as by declaring in effect that the public good requires the removal of those inequalities that are but the normal and inevitable result of their exercise, and then invoking the police power in order to remove the inequalities, without other object in view. The police power is broad, and not easily defined, but it cannot be given the wide scope that is here asserted for it, without in effect nullifying the constitutional guaranty.

Justices Holmes, Day, and Hughes dissented.

LOCHNER v. NEW YORK

Supreme Court of the United States, 1905
198 U.S. 45, 25 S.Ct. 539, 49 L.Ed. 937

Joseph Lochner was found guilty and fined fifty dollars for violating an 1897 New York law that prohibited employers from allowing employees to work more than sixty hours per week in a bakery. The case was brought on a writ of error to the U. S. Supreme Court after two state courts affirmed Lochner's conviction.

Mr. Justice PECKHAM delivered the opinion of the court:
* * * The mandate of the statute, that "no employee shall be required or permitted to work," is the substantial equivalent of an enactment that "no employee shall contract or agree to work," more than ten hours per day; and, as there is no provision for special emergencies,

the statute is mandatory in all cases. It is not an act merely fixing the number of hours which shall constitute a legal day's work, but an absolute prohibition upon the employer permitting, under any circumstances, more than ten hours' work to be done in his establishment. The employee may desire to earn the extra money which would arise from his working more than the prescribed time, but this statute forbids the employer from permitting the employee to earn it.

The statute necessarily interferes with the right of contract between the employer and employees, concerning the number of hours in which the latter may labor in the bakery of the employer. The general right to make a contract in relation to his business is part of the liberty of the individual protected by the 14th Amendment of the Federal Constitution. Allgeyer v. Louisiana, 165 U.S. 578, 17 Sup.Ct.Rep. 427. Under that provision no state can deprive any person of life, liberty, or property without due process of law. The right to purchase or to sell labor is part of the liberty protected by this amendment, unless there are circumstances which exclude the right. There are, however, certain powers, existing in the sovereignty of each state in the Union, somewhat vaguely termed police powers, the exact description and limitation of which have not been attempted by the courts. Those powers, broadly stated, and without, at present, any attempt at a more specific limitation, relate to the safety, health, morals, and general welfare of the public. Both property and liberty are held on such reasonable conditions as may be imposed by the governing power of the state in the exercise of those powers, and with such conditions the

14th Amendment was not designed to interfere. * * *

The state, therefore, has power to prevent the individual from making certain kinds of contracts, and in regard to them the Federal Constitution offers no protection. If the contract be one which the state, in the legitimate exercise of its police power, has the right to prohibit, it is not prevented from prohibiting it by the 14th Amendment. Contracts in violation of a statute, either of the Federal or state government, or a contract to let one's property for immoral purposes, or to do any other unlawful act, could obtain no protection from the Federal Constitution, as coming under the liberty of person or of free contract. Therefore, when the state, by its legislature, in the assumed exercise of its police powers, has passed an act which seriously limits the right to labor or the right of contract in regard to their means of livelihood between persons who are *sui juris* (both employer and employee), it becomes of great importance to determine which shall prevail,—the right of the individual to labor for such time as he may choose, or the right of the state to prevent the individual from laboring, or from entering into any contract to labor, beyond a certain time prescribed by the state.

This court has recognized the existence and upheld the exercise of the police powers of the states in many cases which might fairly be considered as border ones, and it has, in the course of its determination of questions regarding the asserted invalidity of such statutes, on the ground of their violation of the rights secured by the Federal Constitution, been guided by rules of a very liberal nature, the application of which has resulted, in numerous instances, in upholding the validity of state statutes thus assailed. * * *

* * *

It must, of course, be conceded that there is a limit to the valid exercise of the police power by the state. * * * Otherwise the 14th Amendment would have no efficacy and the legislatures of the states would have unbounded power, and it would be enough to say that any piece of legislation was enacted to conserve the morals, the health, or the safety of the people; such legislation would be valid, no matter how absolutely without foundation the claim might be. The claim of the police power would be a mere pretext,—become another and delusive name for the supreme sovereignty of the state to be exercised free from constitutional restraint. * * * In every case that comes before this court, therefore, where legislation of this character is concerned, and where the protection of the Federal Constitution is sought, the question necessarily arises: Is this a fair, reasonable, and appropriate exercise of the police power of the state, or is it an unreasonable, unnecessary, and arbitrary interference with the right of the individual to his personal liberty, or to enter into those contracts in relation to labor which may seem to him appropriate or necessary for the support of himself and his family? Of course the liberty of contract relating to labor includes both parties to it. The one has as much right to purchase as the other to sell labor.

This is not a question of substituting the judgment of the court for that of the legislature. If the act be within the power of the state it is valid, although the judgment of the court might be totally opposed to the enactment of such a law. * * *

The question whether this act is valid as a labor law, pure and simple, may be dismissed in a few words. There is no reasonable ground for interfering with the liberty of person or the right of free contract, by determining the hours of labor, in the occupation of a baker. There is no contention that bakers as a class are not equal in intelligence and capacity to men in other trades or manual occupations, or that they are not able to assert their rights and care for themselves without the protecting arm of the state, interfering with their independence of judgment and of action. They are in no sense wards of the state. Viewed in the light of a purely labor law, with no reference whatever to the question of health, we think that a law like the one before us involves neither the safety, the morals, nor the welfare, of the public, and that the interest of the public is not in the slightest degree affected by such an act. The law must be upheld, if at all, as a law pertaining to the health of the individual engaged in the occupation of a baker. It does not affect any other portion of the public than those who are engaged in that occupation. Clean and wholesome bread does not depend upon whether the baker works but ten hours per day or only sixty hours a week. The limitation of the hours of labor does not come within the police power on that ground.

It is a question of which of two powers or rights shall prevail,—the power of the state to legislate or the right of the individual to liberty of person and freedom of contract. The mere assertion that the subject relates, though but in a remote degree, to the public health, does not necessarily render the enactment valid. The act must have a more direct relation, as a means to an end, and the end itself must be appropriate and legitimate, before an act can be held to be valid which interferes with the general right of an individual to be free in his person and in his power to contract in relation to his own labor.

* * *

We think the limit of the police power has been reached and passed in this case. There is, in our judgment, no reasonable foundation for holding this to be necessary or appropriate as a health law to safeguard the public health, or the health of the individuals who are following the trade of a baker. If this statute be valid, and if, therefore, a proper case is made out in which to deny the right of an individual, *sui juris*, as employer or employee, to make contracts for the labor of the latter under the protection of the provisions of the Federal Constitution, there would seem to be no length to which legislation of this nature might not go. * * *

We think that there can be no fair doubt that the trade of a baker, in and of itself, is not an unhealthy one to that degree which would authorize the legislature to interfere with the right to labor, and with the right of free contract on the part of the individual, either as employer or employee. In looking through statistics regarding all trades and occupations, it may be true that the trade of a baker does not appear to be as healthy as some other trades, and is also vastly more healthy than still others. To the common understanding the trade of a baker has never been regarded as an unhealthy one. * * *

* * *

* * * It seems to us that the real object and purpose were simply to regulate the hours of labor between the master and his employees * * * in a private business, not dangerous in any degree to morals, or in any real and substantial degree to the health of the employees. Under such circumstances the freedom of master and employee to contract with each other in relation to their employment, and in defining the same, cannot be prohibited or interfered with, without violating the Federal Constitution.

* * *

Reversed.

Mr. Justice HOLMES, dissenting:

* * *

This case is decided upon an economic theory which a large part of the country does not entertain. If it were a question whether I agreed with that theory, I should desire to study it further and long before making up my mind. But I do not conceive that to be my duty, because I strongly believe that my agreement or disagreement has nothing to do with the right of a majority to embody their opinions in law. It is settled by various decisions of this court that state constitutions and state laws may regulate life in many ways which we as legislators might think as injudicious, or if you like as tyrannical, as this, and which, equally with this, interfere with the liberty to contract. Sunday laws and usury laws are ancient examples. A more modern one is the prohibition of lotteries. The liberty of the citizen to do as he likes so long as he does not interfere with the liberty of others to do the same, which has been a shibboleth for some well-known writers, is interfered with by school laws, by the Postoffice, by every state or municipal institution which takes his money for purposes thought desirable, whether he likes it or not. The 14th Amendment does not enact Mr. Herbert Spencer's Social Statics. * * * Some of these laws embody convictions or prejudices which judges are likely to share. Some may not. But a Constitution is not intended to embody a particular economic theory, whether of paternalism and the organic relation of the citizen to the state or of *laissez faire*. It is made for people of fundamentally differing views, and the accident of our finding certain opinions natural and familiar, or novel, and even shocking, ought not to conclude our judgment upon the question whether statutes embodying them conflict with the Constitution of the United States.

General propositions do not decide concrete cases. The decision will depend on a judgment or intuition more subtle than any articulate major premise. But I think that the proposition just stated, if it is accepted, will carry us far toward the end. Every opinion tends to become a law. I think that the word "liberty," in the 14th Amendment, is perverted when it is held to prevent the natural outcome of a dominant opinion, unless it can be said that a rational and fair man necessarily would admit that the statute proposed would infringe fundamental principles as they have been understood by the traditions of our people and our law. It does not need research to show that no such sweeping condemnation can be passed upon the statute before us.

A reasonable man might think it a proper measure on the score of health. Men whom I certainly could not pronounce unreasonable would uphold it as a first instalment of a general regulation of the hours of work. Whether in the latter aspect it would be open to the charge of inequality I think it unnecessary to discuss.

Mr. Justice HARLAN (with whom Mr. Justice WHITE and Mr. Justice DAY concurred) dissenting:

* * *

[T]he state is not amenable to the judiciary, in respect of its legislative enactments, unless such enactments are plainly, palpably, beyond all question, inconsistent with the Constitution of the United States. We are not to presume that the state of New York has acted in bad faith. Nor can we assume that its legislature acted without due deliberation, or that it did not determine this question upon the fullest attainable information and for the common good. We cannot say that the state has acted without reason, nor ought we to proceed upon the theory that its action is a mere sham. Our duty, I submit, is to sustain the statute as not being in conflict with the Federal Constitution, for the reason—and such is an all-sufficient reason—it is not shown to be plainly and palpably inconsistent with that instrument. * * *

* * *

WOLFF PACKING CO. v. COURT OF INDUSTRIAL RELATIONS

Supreme Court of the United States, 1923
262 U.S. 522, 43 S.Ct. 630, 67 L.Ed. 1103

A Kansas statute enacted in 1920 established an industrial relations court with authority to settle labor-management disputes growing out of certain essential industries when it concluded that the peace and health of the public were threatened. A complaint was filed with the industrial court by the meat cutter's union when the Wolff Packing Company reduced the wages of its employees. The court decided to set wages higher than the amount Wolff Packing had been willing to pay, and the company refused to comply with the court order. The industrial court initiated action against the packing company before the Kansas Supreme Court where its order was subsequently sustained. Wolff Packing Company, contending that the statute conflicted with its right to contract as guaranteed by the Due Process Clause of the Fourteenth Amendment, brought the case to the U. S. Supreme Court on a writ of error.

Mr. Chief Justice TAFT delivered the opinion of the Court.

The necessary postulate of the Industrial Court Act is that the state, representing the people, is so much interested in their peace, health, and comfort that it may compel those engaged in the manufacture of food and clothing, and the production of fuel, whether owners or workers, to continue in their business and employment on terms fixed by an agency of the state, if they cannot agree. Under the construction adopted by the state Supreme Court the act gives the industrial court authority to permit the owner or employer to go out of the business, if he shows that he can only continue on the terms fixed at such heavy loss that collapse will follow. * * * A laborer dissatisfied with his wages is permitted to quit, but he may not agree with his fellows to quit or combine with others to induce them to quit.

These qualifications do not change the essence of the act. It curtails the right of the employer on the one hand, and of the employee on the other, to contract about his affairs. This is part of the liberty of the individual protected by the guaranty of the due process clause of the Fourteenth Amendment. * * * While there is no such thing as absolute freedom of contract, and it is subject to a variety of restraints,

they must not be arbitrary or unreasonable. Freedom is the general rule, and restraint the exception. The legislative authority to abridge can be justified only by exceptional circumstances. * * *

* * *

Businesses said to be clothed with a public interest justifying some public regulation may be divided into three classes:

(1) Those which are carried on under the authority of a public grant of privileges which either expressly or impliedly imposes the affirmative duty of rendering a public service demanded by any member of the public. Such are the railroads, other common carriers and public utilities.

(2) Certain occupations, regarded as exceptional, the public interest attaching to which, recognized from earliest times, has survived the period of arbitrary laws by Parliament or colonial Legislatures for regulating all trades and callings. Such are those of the keepers of inns, cabs, and gristmills. * * *

(3) Businesses which, though not public at their inception, may be fairly said to have risen to be such and have become subject in consequence to some government regulation. They have come to hold such a peculiar relation to the public that this is superimposed upon them. In the

language of the cases, the owner by devoting his business to the public use, in effect grants the public an interest in that use and subjects himself to public regulation to the extent of that interest although the property continues to belong to its private owner and to be entitled to protection accordingly. * * *

It is manifest from an examination of the cases cited under the third head that the mere declaration by a Legislature that a business is affected with a public interest is not conclusive of the question whether its attempted regulation on that ground is justified. The circumstances of its alleged change from the status of a private business and its freedom from regulation into one in which the public have come to have an interest are always a subject of judicial inquiry.

In a sense, the public is concerned about all lawful business because it contributes to the prosperity and well being of the people. The public may suffer from high prices or strikes in many trades, but the expression "clothed with a public interest," as applied to a business, means more than that the public welfare is affected by continuity or by the price at which a commodity is sold or a service rendered. The circumstances which clothe a particular kind of business with a public interest, in the sense of *Munn* v. *Illinois* and the other cases, must be such as to create a peculiarly close relation between the public and those engaged in it, and raise implications of an affirmative obligation on their part to be reasonable in dealing with the public.

It is urged upon us that the declaration of the Legislature that the business of food preparation is affected with a public interest and devoted to a public use should be most persuasive with the court, and that nothing but the clearest reason to the contrary will prevail with the court to hold otherwise. * * *

It has never been supposed, since the adoption of the Constitution, that the business of the butcher, or the baker, the tailor, the wood chopper, the mining operator, or the miner was clothed with such a public interest that the price of his product or his wages could be fixed by state regulation. It is true that in the days of the early common law an omnipotent parliament did regulate prices and wages as it chose, and occasionally a colonial legislature sought to exercise the same power; but nowadays one does not devote one's property or business to the public use or clothe it with a public interest merely because one makes commodities for and sells to, the public in the common callings of which those above mentioned are instances.

* * *

In nearly all the businesses included under the third head above, the thing which gave the public interest was the indispensable nature of the service and the exorbitant charges and arbitrary control to which the public might be subjected without regulation.

* * *

It is very difficult under the cases to lay down a working rule by which readily to determine when a business has become "clothed with a public interest." All business is subject to some kinds of public regulation, but when the public becomes so peculiarly dependent upon a particular business that one engaging therein subjects himself to a more intimate public regulation is only to be determined by the process of exclusion and inclusion and to gradual establishment of a line of distinction. We are relieved from considering and deciding definitely whether preparation of food should be put in the third class of quasi public businesses, noted above, because, even so, the valid regulation to which it might be subjected as such, could not include what this act attempts.

To say that a business is clothed with a public interest is not to determine what regulation may be permissible in view of the private rights of the owner. The extent to which an inn or a cab system may be regulated may differ widely from that allowable as to a railroad or other common carrier. It is not a matter of legislative discretion solely. It depends on the nature of the business, on the feature which touches the public, and on the abuses reasonably to be feared. To say that a business is clothed with a public interest is not to import that the public may take over its entire management and run it at the expense of the owner. The extent to which regulation may reasonably go varies with different kinds of business. * * *

If, as, in effect, contended by counsel for the state, the common callings are clothed with a public interest by a mere legislative declaration, which necessarily authorizes full and comprehensive regulation within legislative discretion, there must be a revolution in the relation of government to general business. This will be running the public interest argument into the ground. * * * It will be impossible to reconcile such result with the freedom of contract and of labor secured by the Fourteenth Amendment.

* * *

It is urged that under this act the exercise of the power of compulsory arbitration rests upon the existence of a temporary emergency as in Wilson v. New [243 U.S. 332, 37 S.Ct. 298]. * * * [I]t is enough to say that the great temporary public exigencies, recognized by all and declared by Congress, were very different from that upon which the control under this act is asserted. Here it is said to be the danger that a strike in one establishment may spread to all the other similar establishments of the state and country, and thence to all the national sources of food supply so as to produce a shortage. Whether such danger exists has not been determined by the Legislature, but is determined under the law by a subordinate agency, and on its findings and prophecy owners and employers are to be deprived of freedom of contract and workers of a most important element of their freedom of labor. * * *

* * *

The minutely detailed government supervision, including that of their relations to their employees, to which the railroads of the country have been gradually subjected by Congress through its power over interstate commerce, furnishes no precedent for regulation of the business of the plaintiff in error, whose classification as public is at the best doubtful. It is not too much to say that the ruling in *Wilson* v. *New* went to the border line, although it concerned an interstate common carrier in the presence of a nation-wide emergency and the possibility of great disaster. Certainly there is nothing to justify extending the drastic regulation sustained in that exceptional case to the one before us.

*   *   *

The judgment of the court below must be reversed.

NEBBIA v. NEW YORK

Supreme Court of the United States, 1934
291 U.S. 502, 54 S.Ct. 505, 78 L.Ed. 940

In response to falling milk prices, a condition that was causing considerable hardship to the families of milk producers, the New York legislature passed an act in 1933 establishing a milk control board with authority to fix minimum and maximum retail prices on milk. Nebbia, the proprietor of a grocery store in Rochester, was convicted of selling milk for less than the nine cents a quart minimum price set by the board. Two state courts affirmed his conviction, whereupon Nebbia appealed to the Supreme Court contending that the 1933 statute and the board's minimum price order conflicted with his rights under the Fourteenth Amendment.

Mr. Justice ROBERTS delivered the opinion of the Court.

*   *   *

The question for decision is whether the Federal Constitution prohibits a state from so fixing the selling price of milk. We first inquire as to the occasion for the legislation and its history.

During 1932 the prices received by farmers for milk were much below the cost of production. The decline in prices during 1931 and 1932 was much greater than that of prices generally. The situation of the families of dairy producers had become desperate and called for state aid similar to that afforded the unemployed, if conditions should not improve.

*   *   *

The Legislature adopted chapter 158 as a method of correcting the evils which [a report of a legislative committee] showed could not be expected to right themselves through the ordinary play of the forces of supply and demand, owing to the pe-

culiar and uncontrollable factors affecting the industry.   *   *   *

*   *   *

Under our form of government the use of property and the making of contracts are normally matters of private and not of public concern. The general rule is that both shall be free of governmental interference. But neither property rights nor contract rights are absolute; for government cannot exist if the citizen may at will use his property to the detriment of his fellows, or exercise his freedom of contract to work them harm. Equally fundamental with the private right is that of the public to regulate it in the common interest.
*   *   *

*   *   *

Thus has this court from the early days affirmed that the power to promote the general welfare is inherent in government. Touching the matters committed to it by the Constitution the United States possesses the power, as do the states in their sovereign capacity touching all subjects jurisdiction of which is not surrendered to the federal government, as shown by the quotations above given. These correlative rights, that of the citizen to exercise exclusive dominion over property and freely to contract about his affairs, and that of the state to regulate the use of property and the conduct of business, are always in collision. No exercise of the private right can be imagined which will not in some respect, however slight, affect the public; no exercise of the legislative prerogative to regulate the conduct of the citizen which will not to some extent abridge his liberty or affect his property. But subject only to constitutional restraint the private right must yield to the public need.

The Fifth Amendment, in the field of federal activity, and the Fourteenth, as respects state action, do not prohibit governmental regulation for the public welfare. They merely condition the exertion of the admitted power, by securing that the end shall be accomplished by methods consistent with due process. And the guaranty of due process, as has often been held, demands only that the law shall not be unreasonable, arbitrary, or capricious, and that the means selected shall have a real and substantial relation to the object sought to be attained. It results that a regulation valid for one sort of business, or in given circumstances, may be invalid for another sort, or for the same business under other circumstances, because the reasonableness of each regulation depends upon the relevant facts.

* * *

The court has repeatedly sustained curtailment of enjoyment of private property, in the public interest. The owner's rights may be subordinated to the needs of other private owners whose pursuits are vital to the paramount interests of the community. * * *

* * *

The Constitution does not guarantee the unrestricted privilege to engage in a business or to conduct it as one pleases. Certain kinds of business may be prohibited; and the right to conduct a business, or to pursue a calling may be conditioned. Regulation of a business to prevent waste of the state's resources may be justified. And statutes prescribing the terms upon which those conducting certain businesses may contract, or imposing terms if they do enter into agreements, are within the state's competency.

Legislation concerning sales of goods, and incidentally affecting prices, has repeatedly been held valid. In this class fall laws forbidding unfair competition by the charging of lower prices in one locality than those exacted in another, by giving trade inducements to purchasers, and by other forms of price discrimination. The public policy with respect to free competition has engendered state and federal statutes prohibiting monopolies, which have been upheld. On the other hand, where the policy of the state dictated that a monopoly should be granted, statutes having that effect have been held inoffensive to the constitutional guarantees. Moreover, the state or a municipality may itself enter into business in competition with private proprietors, and thus effectively although indirectly control the prices charged by them.

* * *

It is clear that there is no closed class or category of businesses affected with a public interest, and the function of courts in the application of the Fifth and Fourteenth Amendments is to determine in each case whether circumstances vindicate the challenged regulation as a reasonable exertion of governmental authority or condemn it as arbitrary or discriminatory. * * *

* * *

* * * The Constitution does not secure to any one liberty to conduct his business in such fashion as to inflict injury upon the public at large, or upon any substantial group of the people. Price control, like any other form of regulation, is unconstitutional only if arbitrary, discriminatory, or demonstrably irrelevant to the policy the Legislature is free to adopt, and hence an unnecessary and unwarranted interference with individual liberty.

Tested by these considerations we find no basis in the due process clause of the Fourteenth Amendment for condemning the provisions of the Agriculture and Markets Law here drawn into question.

The judgment is affirmed.

Separate opinion of Mr. Justice McREYNOLDS.

* * *

The Fourteenth Amendment wholly disempowered the several states to "deprive any person of life, liberty, or property, without due process of law." The assurance of each of these things is the same. If now liberty or property may be struck down because of difficult circumstances, we must expect that hereafter every right must yield to the voice of an impatient majority when stirred by distressful exigency. * * * Constitutional guaranties are not to be "thrust to and fro and

carried about with every wind of doctrine." They were intended to be immutable so long as within our charter. Rights shielded yesterday should remain indefeasible today and tomorrow. Certain fundamentals have been set beyond experimentation; the Constitution has released them from control by the state. Again and again this Court has so declared.

* * *

Regulation to prevent recognized evils in business has long been upheld as permissible legislative action. But fixation of the price at which A, engaged in an ordinary business, may sell, in order to enable B, a producer, to improve his condition, has not been regarded as within legislative power. This is not regulation, but management, control, dictation— it amounts to the deprivation of the fundamental right which one has to conduct his own affairs honestly and along customary lines. The argument advanced here would support general prescription of prices for farm products, groceries, shoes, clothing, all the necessities of modern civilization, as well as labor, when some Legislature finds and declares such action advisable and for the public good. This Court has declared that a state may not by legislative fiat convert a private business into a public utility. * * * And if it be now ruled that one dedicates his property to public use whenever he embarks on an enterprise which the Legislature may think it desirable to bring under control, this is but to declare that rights guaranteed by the Constitution exist only so long as supposed public interest does not require their extinction. To adopt such a view, of course, would put an end to liberty under the Constitution.

* * *

But plainly, I think, this Court must have regard to the wisdom of the enactment. At least, we must inquire concerning its purpose and decide whether the means proposed have reasonable relation to something within legislative power— whether the end is legitimate, and the means appropriate. If a statute to prevent conflagrations, should require householders to pour oil on their roofs as a means of curbing the spread of fire when discovered in the neighborhood, we could hardly uphold it. Here, we find direct interference with guaranteed rights defended upon the ground that the purpose was to promote the public welfare by increasing milk prices at the farm. Unless we can affirm that the end proposed is proper and the means adopted have reasonable relation to it, this action is unjustifiable.

* * *

Not only does the statute interfere arbitrarily with the rights of the little grocer to conduct his business according to standards long accepted—complete destruction may follow; but it takes away the liberty of 12,000,000 consumers to buy a necessity of life in an open market. It imposes direct and arbitrary burdens upon those already seriously impoverished with the alleged immediate design of affording special benefits to others. * * *

* * *

Mr. Justice VAN DEVANTER, Mr. Justice SUTHERLAND, and Mr. Justice BUTLER authorize me to say that they concur in this opinion.

WEST COAST HOTEL CO. v. PARRISH

Supreme Court of the United States, 1937
300 U.S. 379, 57 S.Ct. 578, 81 L.Ed. 703

Elsie Parrish, an employee of the West Coast Hotel Company, and her husband brought suit to recover the difference between her wage and the minimum wage of $14.50 per week of forty-eight hours set by the Industrial Welfare Committee of the State of Washington under a state law enacted in 1913. The law was passed by the state legislature to protect the health and welfare of women and minors by assuring them a minimum wage from their employers. The trial court's decision against Parrish was reversed by the state supreme court. West Coast Hotel appealed to the U. S. Supreme Court challenging the state law on grounds it conflicted with the Due Process Clause of the Fourteenth Amendment.

Mr. Chief Justice HUGHES delivered the opinion of the Court.

This case presents the question of the constitutional validity of the minimum wage law of the state of Washington.

* * *

The appellant relies upon the decision of this Court in Adkins v. Children's Hospital, 261 U.S. 525, 43 S.Ct. 394, * * * which held invalid the District of Columbia Minimum Wage Act (40 Stat. 960) * * * under the due process clause of the Fifth Amendment. * * *

The recent case of Morehead v. New York ex rel. Tipaldo, 298 U.S. 587, 56 S.Ct. 918, * * * came here on certiorari to the New York court which had held the New York minimum wage act for women to be invalid. * * * [The Court affirmed the judgment because it] considered that the only question before it was whether the *Adkins* Case was distinguishable and that reconsideration of that decision had not been sought. * * *

We think that the question which was not deemed to be open in the *Morehead* Case is open and is necessarily presented here. The Supreme Court of Washington has upheld the minimum wage statute of that state. * * * The state court has refused to regard the decision in the *Adkins* Case as determinative and has pointed to our decisions both before and since that case as justifying its position. We are of the opinion that this ruling of the state court demands on our part a re-examination of the *Adkins* Case. The importance of the question, in which many states having similar laws are concerned, the close division by which the decision in the *Adkins* Case was reached, and the economic conditions which have supervened, and in the light of which the reasonableness of the exercise of the protective power of the state must be considered, make it not only appropriate, but we think imperative, that in deciding the present case the subject should receive fresh consideration.

* * *

The principle which must control our decision is not in doubt. The constitutional provision invoked is the due process clause of the Fourteenth Amendment governing the states, as the due process clause invoked in the *Adkins* Case governed Congress. In each case the violation alleged by those attacking minimum wage regulation for women is deprivation of freedom of contract. What is this freedom? The Constitution does not speak of freedom of contract. It speaks of liberty and prohibits the deprivation of liberty without due process of law. In prohibiting that deprivation, the Constitution does not recognize an absolute and uncontrollable liberty. Liberty in each of its phases has its history and connotation. But the liberty safeguarded is liberty in a social organization which requires the protection of law against the evils which menace the health, safety, morals, and welfare of the people. Liberty under the Constitution is thus necessarily subject to the restraints of due process, and regulation which is reasonable in relation to its subject and is adopted in the interests of the community is due process.

* * *

This power under the Constitution to restrict freedom of contract has had many illustrations. That it may be exercised in the public interest with respect to contracts between employer and employee is undeniable. Thus statutes have been sustained limiting employment in underground mines and smelters to eight hours a day; * * * in requiring redemption in cash of store orders or other evidences of indebtedness issued in the payment of wages; * * * in forbidding the payment of seamen's wages in advance; * * * in making it unlawful to contract to pay miners employed at quantity rates upon the basis of screened coal instead of the weight of the coal as originally produced in the mine; * * * in prohibiting contracts limiting liability for injuries to employees; * * * in limiting hours of work of employees in manufacturing establishments; * * * and in maintaining workmen's compensation laws. * * * In dealing with the relation of employer and employed, the Legislature has necessarily a wide field of discretion in order that there may be suitable protection of health and safety, and that peace and good order may be promoted through regulations designed to insure wholesome conditions of work and freedom from oppression. * * *

* * *

We think that the views thus expressed are sound and that the decision in the *Adkins* Case was a departure from the true application of the principles governing the regulation by the state of the relation of employer and employed. * * *

* * *

There is an additional and compelling consideration which recent economic experience has brought into a strong light. The exploitation of a class of workers who are in an unequal position with respect to bargaining power and are thus relatively defenseless against the denial of a living wage is not only detrimental to their health and well being, but casts a direct burden for their support upon the community. What these workers lose in wages the taxpayers are called upon to pay. The bare cost of living must be met. We may take judicial notice of the unparalleled demands for relief which arose during the recent period of depression and still continue to an alarming extent despite the degree of economic recovery which has been achieved. It is unnecessary to cite official statistics to establish what is of common knowledge through the length and breadth of the land. While in the instant case no factual brief has been presented, there is no reason to doubt that the state of Washington has encountered the same social problem that is present elsewhere. The community is not bound to provide what is in effect a subsidy for unconscionable employers. The community may direct its law-making power to correct the abuse which springs from their selfish disregard of the public interest. * * *

* * *

Our conclusion is that the case of *Adkins* v. *Children's Hospital*, supra, should be, and it is, overruled. The judgment of the Supreme Court of the state of Washington is affirmed.

Affirmed.

Mr. Justice SUTHERLAND.

Mr. Justice VAN DEVANTER, Mr. Justice McREYNOLDS, Mr. Justice BUTLER, and I think the judgment of the court below should be reversed.

* * *

It is urged that the question involved should now receive fresh consideration, among other reasons, because of "the economic conditions which have supervened"; but the meaning of the Constitution does not change with the ebb and flow of economic events. We frequently are told in more general words that the Constitution must be construed in the light of the present. If by that it is meant that the Constitution is made up of living words that apply to every new condition which they include, the statement is quite true. But to say, if that be intended, that the words of the Constitution mean today what they did not mean when written—that is, that they do not apply to a situation now to which they would have applied then—is to rob that instrument of the essential element which continues it in force as the people have made it until they, and not their official agents, have made it otherwise.

*   *   *

The judicial function is that of interpretation; it does not include the power of amendment under the guise of interpretation. To miss the point of difference between the two is to miss all that the phrase "supreme law of the land" stands for and to convert what was intended as inescapable and enduring mandates into mere moral reflections.

If the Constitution, intelligently and reasonably construed in the light of these principles, stands in the way of desirable legislation, the blame must rest upon that instrument, and not upon the court for enforcing it according to its terms. The remedy in that situation—and the only true remedy—is to amend the Constitution.   *   *   *

*   *   *

LINCOLN FEDERAL LABOR UNION v. NORTHWESTERN IRON & METAL CO.

Supreme Court of the United States, 1949
335 U.S. 525, 69 S.Ct. 251, 93 L.Ed. 212

An amendment to the Nebraska Constitution adopted in 1946 provided that "No person shall be denied employment because of membership in or affiliation with, or resignation or expulsion from a labor organization or because of refusal to join or affiliate with a labor organization; nor shall any individual or corporation or association of any kind enter into any contract, written or oral, to exclude persons from employment because of membership in or nonmembership in a labor organization." This amendment and similar "right to work" laws passed in North Carolina and Arizona were challenged by several labor unions asserting that such enactments violated rights of speech and assembly, impaired the obligations of existing labor-management contracts, and denied unions and employers due process of law. In this case the Lincoln Federal Labor Union was seeking equitable relief and a declaratory judgment invalidating the amendment. It was appealing an adverse judgment of the Nebraska Supreme Court. In its disposition of the issues the U. S. Supreme Court found no merit in the First Amendment and Contract Clause claims of the union. The excerpt of the Court's opinion below focuses on the due process contention.

———————

Mr. Justice BLACK delivered the opinion of the Court.

*   *   *

*   *   * It is contended that these state laws deprive appellants of their liberty without due process of law in violation of the Fourteenth Amendment. Appellants argue that the laws are specifically designed to deprive all persons within the two states of "liberty" (1) to refuse to hire or retain any person in employment because he is or is not a union member, and (2) to make a contract or agreement to engage in such employment discrimination against union or non-union members.

*   *   *

Many cases are cited by appellants in which this Court has said that in some instances the due process clause protects the liberty of persons to make contracts. But none of these cases, even those according the broadest constitutional protection to the making of contracts, ever went so far as to indicate that the due process clause bars a state from prohibiting contracts to engage in conduct banned by a valid state law. So here, if the provisions in the state laws against employer discrimination are valid, it follows that the contract prohibition also is valid. * * * We therefore turn to the decisive question under the due process contention, which is: Does the due process clause forbid a state to pass laws clearly designed to safeguard the opportunity of non-union members to get and hold jobs, free from discrimination against them because they are non-union workers?

There was a period in which labor union members who wanted to get and hold jobs were the victims of widespread employer discrimination practices. Contracts between employers and their employees were used by employers to accomplish this anti-union employment discrimination. Before hiring workers, employers required them to sign agreements stating that the workers were not and would not become labor union members. Such anti-union practices were so obnoxious to workers that they gave these required agreements the name of "yellow dog contracts." This hostility of workers also prompted passage of state and federal laws to ban employer discrimination against union members and to outlaw yellow dog contracts.

* * *

The *Allgeyer-Lochner-Adair-Coppage* constitutional doctrine was for some years followed by this Court. It was used to strike down laws fixing minimum wages and maximum hours in employment, laws fixing prices and laws regulating business activities. * * *

* * *

This Court beginning at least as early as 1934, when the *Nebbia* case was decided, has steadily rejected the due process philosophy enunciated in the *Adair-Coppage* line of cases. In doing so it has consciously returned closer and closer to the earlier constitutional principle that states have power to legislate against what are found to be injurious practices in their internal commercial and business affairs, so long as their laws do not run afoul of some specific federal constitutional prohibition, or of some valid federal law. * * * Under this constitutional doctrine the due process clause is no longer to be so broadly construed that the Congress and state legislatures are put in a strait jacket when they attempt to suppress business and industrial conditions which they regard as offensive to the public welfare.

Appellants now ask us to return, at least in part, to the due process philosphy that has been deliberately discarded. Claiming that the Federal Constitution itself affords protection for union members against discrimination, they nevertheless assert that the same Constitution forbids a state from providing the same protection for non-union members. Just as we have held that the due process clause erects no obstacle to block legislative protection of union mem-

bers, we now hold that legislative protection can be afforded non-

union workers.
Affirmed.

As originally enacted, a New Orleans ordinance barred vendors from selling foodstuffs from pushcarts in the city's Vieux Carre, or French Quarter, but an amendment adopted in 1972 excepted from that ban "vendors who have continually operated the same business within the Vieux Carre * * * for eight years prior to January 1, 1972 * * *." Dukes, the owner of a pushcart business operating throughout the city but selling in the Vieux Carre for only two years before the ordinance was amended, was barred from doing business there. She sued the city for declaratory and injunctive relief. Originally, her complaint challenged the old version of the ordinance, but she modified it to attack the 1972 amendment as a violation of equal protection. A federal district court granted the city's motion for summary judgment, but that decision was reversed on appeal. Relying on Morey v. Doud, 354 U.S. 457, 77 S.Ct. 1344 (1957), the appeals court focused on the "exclusionary character" of the ordinance and highlighted its "creation of a protected monopoly for the favored class member." The court concluded that there was an "insubstan[tial] * * * relation between the nature of the discrimination and the legitimate governmental interest in conserving the traditional assets of the Vieux Carre" since the criteria chosen to distinguish permissible vending from impermissible vending bore no relation to either (1) assuring that the favored class members would "continue to operate in a manner more consistent with the traditions of the [French] Quarter than would any other operator," or (2) "instil[ling] in the [favored] licensed vendors (or their likely transient operators) the kind of appreciation for the conservation of the [French] Quarter's tradition." The appeals court declared the ordinance a violation of the Equal Protection Clause and remanded the case for consideration as to the severability of the "grandfather clause" portion from the remainder of the ordinance.

In City of New Orleans v. Dukes, 427 U.S. 297, 96 S.Ct. 2513 (1976), the Supreme Court reversed the appellate court judgment. Speaking to the legitimacy of the ordinance's purpose, the Court observed:

The city's classification rationally furthers the purpose which the Court of Appeals recognized the city had identified as its objective in enacting the provision, that is, as a means "to preserve the appearance and custom valued by the Quarter's residents and attractive to tourists." * * * The legitimacy of that objective is obvious. The city council plainly could further that objective by making the reasoned judgment that street peddlers and hawkers tend to interfere with the charm and beauty of an historic area and disturb tourists and disrupt their enjoyment of that charm and beauty, and that such vendors in the Vieux Carre, the heart of the city's tourist industry, might thus have a deleterious effect on the economy of the city. They therefore determined that to ensure the economic vitality of that area, such businesses should be substantially curtailed in the Vieux Carre, if not totally banned.

And it concluded that the means chosen were neither arbitrary nor irrational:

The city could reasonably decide that newer businesses were less likely to have built up substantial reliance interests in continued operation in the Vieux Carre and that the two vendors which qualified under the "grandfather clause"—both of which had operated in the area for over 20 years rather than only eight—had themselves become part of the distinctive character and charm that distinguishes the Vieux Carre. We cannot say that these judgments so lack rationality that they constitute a constitutionally impermissible denial of equal protection.

Reasoning from the contemporary premise that "the judiciary may not sit as a superlegislature to judge the wisdom or desirability of legislative policy determinations made in areas that neither affect fundamental rights nor proceed along suspect lines, * * * [but] in the local economic sphere, it is only the invidious discrimination, the wholly arbitrary act, which cannot stand consistently with the Fourteenth Amendment," the Court found that *Morey* v. *Doud* "was a needlessly intrusive judicial infringement on the State's legislative powers, and * * * concluded that the equal protection analysis employed in that opinion should no longer be followed. * * * [Accordingly,] it should be, and it is, overruled." c

Relying on the kind of analysis invoked to treat constitutional challenges to legislation affecting economic interests which the Court reaffirmed its commitment to in *Dukes*, the Supreme Court five years later in Minnesota v. Clover Leaf Creamery Co., 449 U.S. 457, 101 S.Ct. 715 (1981), turned its attention to the constitutionality of a state statute which "bann[ed] the retail sale of milk in plastic, nonreturnable, nonrefillable containers, but permitt[ed] such sale in other nonreturnable, nonrefillable containers, such as paperboard milk cartons." Opponents of the legislation argued and presented empirical evidence to support their claims that the legislation would not further environmental interests, that it would increase the retail price of milk, and that it would only prolong the use of paperboard milk containers. Speaking for the Court, Justice Brennan observed at the outset that "[t]he parties agree that the standard of review applicable to this case under the Equal Protection Clause is the familiar 'rational basis' test" and that "they agree that the purposes of the Act cited by the legislature * * * are legitimate state purposes" so that "the controversy in this case centers on the narrow issue whether the legislative classification between plastic and nonplastic nonreturnable milk containers is rationally related to achievement of the statutory purposes." Noting that the states "are not required to convince courts of the correctness of their legislative judgments" and are entitled to have the benefit of the doubt where "the question is at least debatable," Justice Brennan went on to canvass four reasons identified by the state why the discrimination between plastic and nonplastic, nonreturnable containers was rationally related to the purposes articulated in the statute: (1) the "elimination of the popular plastic milk jug will encourage the use of environmentally superior containers"; (2) the "ban on plastic nonreturnable milk containers will reduce the economic dislocation foreseen from the movement toward greater use of environmentally superior containers"; (3) "the Act will help to conserve energy"; and (4) "the Act will ease the State's

c. In that case the Court struck down an Illinois statute "excepting money orders of the American Express Company from the requirement that any firm selling or issuing money orders in the State must secure a license and submit to state regulation." The Court rejected the state's contention that "[b]ecause the American Express Company is a world-wide enterprise of unquestioned solvency and high financial standing, * * * the legislative classification is reasonable," on the grounds that corporate size was not a sufficient index of financial strength such as to justify treating that company differently under the law from smaller money order vendors.

solid waste disposal problem." Because of "the theoretical connection between a ban on plastic nonreturnables and the[se] purposes articulated by the legislature," he found there to be "a rational relation to the State's objectives   *   *   *   ."

c. REGULATION AND "TAKING" OF PROPERTY

PENN CENTRAL TRANSPORTATION CO. v. CITY OF NEW YORK

Supreme Court of the United States, 1978
438 U.S. 104, 98 S.Ct. 2646, 57 L.Ed.2d 631

New York City adopted a Landmark Preservation Law in 1965. What motivated the city to act was "the conviction that 'the standing of [New York City] as a worldwide tourist center and world capital of business, culture, and government' would be threatened if legislation were not enacted to protect historic landmarks and neighborhoods from precipitate decisions to destroy or fundamentally alter their character." The law is typical of many such municipal enactments in that it mainly seeks to achieve its purpose of heritage preservation not by acquisition of historic properties but instead by involving public bodies in land use decisions involving those properties. The law does not place special restrictions on landmark properties per se and does seek to insure owners of such properties a "reasonable return" on their investments and maximum latitude to use the properties for purposes which are not inconsistent with preservation goals. Where permission is not given for further development of a landmark site, the law allows a transfer of development rights to another parcel of land nearby if it is held by the owner.

The Penn Central Transportation Company owns Grand Central Station and other land on the city block on which it stands. Built in 1913, the terminal is one of the city's most famous buildings. The edifice "is regarded not only as providing an ingenious engineering solution to the problems presented by urban railroad stations, but also as a magnificent example of the French Beaux Arts style." Shortly after the legislation went into effect, the city's Landmark Preservation Commission, created by the law, designated the terminal a "landmark" and the city block a "landmark site." In 1968, Penn Central signed a fifty-year, renewable agreement with a British corporation for construction of a fifty-story-plus office building on land adjacent to the terminal which is only an eight-story structure housing the railroad, its offices, and numerous commercial establishments renting space from Penn Central. In its agreement to lease the property the British corporation agreed to pay Penn Central $1 million a year during construction and at least $3 million a year thereafter. This money, however, would have been offset in part by the loss of up to $1 million a year then paid to Penn Central by concessionaires who used the property. The commission denied permission for construction, calling the plan "an aesthetic joke" since the "sheer mass" of the tower would "overwhelm" the terminal and would reduce it "to the status of a curiosity." Penn Central subsequently filed suit for a declaratory judgment, injunctive relief, and damages, alleging that the city, through application of the landmark preservation legislation, had "taken" the company's property without just compensation in violation of the Fifth and Fourteenth Amendments. The trial court granted declaratory and injunctive relief, but an intermediate state appellate court reversed this ruling. Judgment in the city's favor was affirmed by the New York Court of Appeals whereupon Penn Central sought review by the U.S. Supreme Court.

Mr. Justice BRENNAN delivered the opinion of the Court.

The question presented is wheth-er a city may, as part of a comprehensive program to preserve historic landmarks and historic districts, place restrictions on the development of individual historic landmarks—in addition to those imposed by applicable zoning ordinances—without effecting a "taking" requiring the payment of "just compensation." Specifically, we must decide whether the application of New York City's Landmark's Preservation Law to the parcel of land occupied by Grand Central Terminal has "taken" its owners' property in violation of the Fifth and Fourteenth Amendments.

* * *

[The guarantee against] * * * a "taking" of * * * property [without payment of just compensation] for a public use within the meaning of the Fifth Amendment, * * * of course is made applicable to the States through the Fourteenth Amendment, see Chicago, B. & Q. R. Co. v. Chicago, 166 U.S. 226, 239, 17 S.Ct. 581, 585 (1897). * * *

A

Before considering appellants' specific contentions, it will be useful to review the factors that have shaped the jurisprudence of the Fifth Amendment injunction "nor shall private property be taken for public use, without just compensation." The question of what constitutes a "taking" for purposes of the Fifth Amendment has proved to be a problem of considerable difficulty. While this Court has recognized that the "Fifth Amendment's guarantee [is] designed to bar Government from forcing some people alone to bear public burdens which, in all fairness and justice, should be borne by the public as a whole," Armstrong v. United States, 364 U.S. 40, 49, 80 S.Ct. 1563, 1569 (1960), this Court,

quite simply, has been unable to develop any "set formula" for determining when "justice and fairness" require that economic injuries caused by public action be compensated by the Government, rather than remain disproportionately concentrated on a few persons. See Goldblatt v. Hempstead, 369 U.S. 590, 594, 82 S.Ct. 987, 990 (1962). Indeed, we have frequently observed that whether a particular restriction will be rendered invalid by the Government's failure to pay for any losses proximately caused by it depends largely "upon the particular circumstances [in that] case." United States v. Central Eureka Mining Co., 357 U.S. 155, 168, 78 S.Ct. 1097, 1104 (1958); see United States v. Caltex, Inc., 344 U.S. 149, 156, 73 S.Ct. 200, 203 (1952).

In engaging in these essentially ad hoc, factual inquiries, the Court's decisions have identified several factors that have particular significance. The economic impact of the regulation on the claimant and, particularly, the extent to which the regulation has interfered with distinct investment backed expectations are of course relevant considerations. See Goldblatt v. Hempstead, supra, 369 U.S., at 594, 82 S.Ct., at 990. So too is the character of the governmental action. A "taking" may more readily be found when the interference with property can be characterized as a physical invasion by Government, see, e.g., Causby v. United States, 328 U.S. 256, 66 S.Ct. 1062 (1946), than when interference arises from some public program adjusting the benefits and burdens of economic life to promote the common good.

"Government could hardly go on if to some extent values incident to property could not be diminished without paying for every such change in the general law," Pennsylvania Coal Co. v. Mahon, 260 U.S. 393, 413, 43 S.Ct. 158, 159 (1922), and this Court has accordingly recognized, in a wide variety of contexts, that Government may execute laws or programs that adversely affect recognized economic values. Exercises of the taxing power are one obvious example. A second are the decisions in which this Court has dismissed "taking" challenges on the ground that, while the challenged Government action caused economic harm, it did not interfere with interests that were sufficiently bound up with the reasonable expectations of the claimant to constitute "property" for Fifth Amendment purposes. See, e.g., United States v. Willow River Power Co., 324 U.S. 499, 65 S.Ct. 761 (1945) (interest in high water level of river for run off for tail waters to maintain power head is not property); United States v. Chandler-Dunbar Water Power Co., 229 U.S. 53, 33 S.Ct. 667 (1913) (no property interest can exist in navigable waters); see also Demorest v. City Bank Co., 321 U.S. 36, 64 S.Ct. 384 (1944); Muhlker v. Harlem R. Co., 197 U.S. 544, 25 S.Ct. 522 (1905); Sax, Takings and the Police Power, 74 Yale L.J. 36, 61–62 (1963).

More importantly for the present case, in instances in which a state tribunal reasonably concluded that "the health, safety, morals or general welfare" would be promoted by prohibiting particular contemplated uses of land, this Court has upheld land use regulations that destroyed or adversely affected recognized real property interests. See Nectow v. City of Cambridge, 277 U.S. 183, 188, 48 S.Ct. 447, 448 (1928). Zoning laws are of course the classic example, see Euclid v. Ambler Realty Co., 272 U.S.

365, 47 S.Ct. 114 (1926) (prohibition of industrial use); Gorieb v. Fox, 274 U.S. 603, 608, 47 S.Ct. 675, 677 (1927) (requirement that portions of parcels be left unbuilt); Welch v. Swasey, 214 U.S. 91, 29 S.Ct. 567 (1909) (height restriction), which have been viewed as permissible governmental action even when prohibiting the most beneficial use of the property. See Goldblatt v. Town of Hempstead, supra, 369 U.S., at 592–593, 82 S.Ct., at 988–989, and cases cited; see also Eastlake v. Forest City Enterprises, Inc., 426 U.S. 668, 674, n. 8, 96 S.Ct. 2358, 2362 n. 8 (1976).

Zoning laws generally do not affect existing uses of real property, but taking challenges have also been held to be without merit in a wide variety of situations when the challenged governmental actions prohibited a beneficial use to which individual parcels had previously been devoted and thus caused substantial individualized harm. Miller v. Schoene, 276 U.S. 272, 48 S.Ct. 246 (1928), is illustrative. In that case, a state entomologist, acting pursuant to a state statute, ordered the claimants to cut down a large number of ornamental red cedar trees because they produced cedar rust fatal to apple trees cultivated nearby. Although the statute provided for recovery of any expense incurred in removing the cedars, and permitted claimants to use the felled trees, it did not provide compensation for the value of the standing trees or for the resulting decrease in market value of the properties as a whole. A unanimous Court held that this latter omission did not render the statute invalid. The Court held that the State might properly make "a choice between the preservation of one class of property and that of the other" and since the apple industry was

important in the State involved, concluded that the State had not exceeded "its constitutional powers by deciding upon the destruction of one class of property [without compensation] in order to save another, which, in the judgment of the legislature, is of greater value to the public."
* * *

Again, Hadacheck v. Sebastian, 239 U.S. 394, 36 S.Ct. 143 (1915), upheld a law prohibiting the claimant from continuing his otherwise lawful business of operating a brickyard in a particular physical community on the ground that the legislature had reasonably concluded that the presence of the brickyard was inconsistent with neighboring uses.
* * *

Goldblatt v. *Hempstead*, supra, is a recent example. There, a 1958 city safety ordinance banned any excavations below the water table and effectively prohibited the claimant from continuing a sand and gravel mining business that had been operated on the particular parcel since 1927. The Court upheld the ordinance against a "taking" challenge, although the ordinance prohibited the present and presumably most beneficial use of the property and had, like the regulations in *Miller* and *Hadacheck* impacted severely on a particular owner. The Court assumed that the ordinance did not prevent the owner's reasonable use of the property since the owner made no showing for an adverse effect on the value of the land. Because the restriction served a substantial public purpose, the Court thus held no taking had occurred. It is of course implicit in *Goldblatt* that a use restriction on real property may constitute a "taking" if not reasonably necessary to the effectuation of a substantial public purpose, see

Nectow v. *Cambridge*, supra * * * or perhaps if it has an unduly harsh impact upon the owner's use of the property.

Pennsylvania Coal Co. v. Mahon, 260 U.S. 393, 43 S.Ct. 158 (1922), is the leading case for the proposition that a state statute that substantially furthers important public policies may so frustrate distinct investment-backed expectations as to amount to a "taking." There the claimant had sold the surface rights to particular parcels of property, but expressly reserved the right to remove the coal thereunder. A Pennsylvania statute, enacted after the transactions, forbade any mining of coal that caused the subsidence of any house, unless the house was the property of the owner of the underlying coal and was more than 150 feet from the improved property of another. Because the statute made it commercially impracticable to mine the coal, * * * and thus had nearly the same effect as the complete destruction of rights claimant had purchased from the owners of the surface land, * * * the Court held that the statute was invalid as effecting a "taking" without just compensation. * * * See generally Michelman, Property, Utility, and Fairness: Comments on the Ethical Foundations of "Just Compensation" Law, 80 Harv.L.Rev. 1165, 1229–1234 (1967).

Finally, Government actions that may be characterized as acquisitions of resources to permit or facilitate uniquely public functions have often been held to constitute "takings." *Causby* v. *United States*, supra, is illustrative. In holding that direct overflights above the claimant's land, that destroyed the present use of the land as a chicken farm, constituted a "taking," *Causby* emphasized that

Government had not "merely destroyed property [but was] using a part of it for the flight of its planes." * * * See also Griggs v. Allegheny County, 369 U.S. 84, 82 S.Ct. 531 (1962) (overflights held a taking); Portsmouth Co. v. United States, 260 U.S. 327, 43 S.Ct. 135 (1922) (United States' military installations repeated firing of guns over claimant's land is a taking); United States v. Cress, 243 U.S. 316, 37 S.Ct. 380 (1917) (repeated floodings of land caused by water project is taking); but see YMCA v. United States, 395 U.S. 85, 89 S.Ct. 1511 (1969) (damage caused to building when federal officers who were seeking to protect building were attacked by rioters held not a taking). * * *

B

In contending that the New York City law has "taken" their property in violation of the Fifth and Fourteenth Amendments, appellants make a series of arguments, which, while tailored to the facts of this case, essentially urge that any substantial restriction imposed pursuant to a landmark law must be accompanied by just compensation if it is to be constitutional. Before considering these, we emphasize what is not in dispute. Because this Court has recognized, in a number of settings, that States and cities may enact land use restrictions or controls to enhance the quality of life by preserving the character and desirable aesthetic features of a city, see City of New Orleans v. Dukes, 427 U.S. 297, 96 S.Ct. 2513 (1976); Young v. American Mini Theatres, Inc., 427 U.S. 50, 96 S.Ct. 2440 (1976); Village of Belle Terre v. Boraas, 416 U.S. 1, 9–10, 94 S.Ct. 1536 (1974) * * *, appellants do not contest that New York City's

objective of preserving structures and areas with special historic, architectural, or cultural significance is an entirely permissible governmental goal. They also do not dispute that the restrictions imposed on its parcel are appropriate means of securing the purposes of the New York City law. Finally, appellants do not challenge any of the specific factual premises of the decision below. They accept for present purposes both that the parcel of land occupied by Grand Central Terminal must, in its present state, be regarded as capable of earning a reasonable return, and that the transferable development rights afforded appellants by virtue of the Terminal's designation as a landmark are valuable, even if not as valuable as the rights to construct above the Terminal. In appellants' view none of these factors derogate from their claim that New York City's law has effected a "taking."

They first observe that the air space above the Terminal is a valuable property interest, citing *United States* v. *Causby*, supra. They urge that the Landmarks Law has deprived them of any gainful use of their "air rights" above the Terminal and that, irrespective of the value of the remainder of their parcel, the city has "taken" their right to this superadjacent air space, thus entitling them to "just compensation" measured by the fair market value of these air rights.

Apart from our own disagreement with appellants' characterization of the effect of the New York law, * * * the submission that appellants may establish a "taking" simply by showing that they have been denied the ability to exploit a property interest that they heretofore had believed was available for development is quite simply untenable. Were this the rule, this Court would have erred not only in upholding laws restricting the development of air rights, see *Welch* v. *Swasey*, supra, but also in approving those prohibiting both the subjacent, see *Goldblatt* v. *Hempstead*, supra, and the lateral development, see *Gorieb* v. *Fox*, supra, of particular parcels. "Taking" jurisprudence does not divide a single parcel into discrete segments and attempt to determine whether rights in a particular segment have been entirely abrogated. In deciding whether a particular governmental action has effected a taking, this Court focuses rather both on the character of the action and on the nature and extent of the interference with rights in the parcel as a whole, here, the city tax block designated as the "landmark site."

Secondly, appellants, focusing on the character and impact of the New York City law, argue that it effects a "taking" because its operation has significantly diminished the value of the Terminal site. Appellants concede that the decisions sustaining other land use regulations, which, like the New York law, are reasonably related to the promotion of the general welfare, uniformly reject the proposition that diminution in property value, standing alone, can establish a taking, see *Euclid* v. *Ambler Realty Co.*, supra (75% diminution in value caused by zoning law); *Hadacheck* v. *Sebastian*, supra, (87½% diminution in value) * * *, and that the taking issue in these contexts is resolved by focusing on the uses the regulations permit. * * * Appellants, moreover, also do not dispute that a showing of diminution in property value would not establish a taking if the restriction had been imposed as a result of historic district legislation, * * * but appellants argue that New York City's regulation of individual landmarks is fundamentally different from zoning or from historic district legislation because the controls imposed by New York City's law apply only to individuals who own selected properties.

Stated baldly, appellants' position appears to be that the only means of ensuring that selected owners are not singled out to endure financial hardship for no reason is to hold that any restriction imposed on individual landmarks pursuant to the New York scheme is a "taking" requiring the payment of "just compensation." Agreement with this argument would of course invalidate not just New York City's law, but all comparable landmark legislation in the Nation. We find no merit in it.

It is true, as appellants emphasize, that both historic district legislation and zoning laws regulate all properties within given physical communities whereas landmark laws apply only to selected parcels. But, contrary to appellants' suggestions, landmark laws are not like discriminatory, or "reverse spot," zoning: that is, a land use decision which arbitrarily singles out a particular parcel for different, less favorable treatment than the neighboring ones. * * * In contrast to discriminatory zoning, which is the antithesis of land use control as part of some comprehensive plan, the New York City law embodies a comprehensive plan to preserve structures of historic or aesthetic interest wherever they might be found in the city, and * * * over 400 landmarks and 31 historic districts have been designated pursuant to this plan.

Equally without merit is the related argument that the decision to designate a structure as a landmark "is inevitably arbitrary or at least subjective because it basically is a matter of taste," * * * thus unavoidably singling out individual landowners for disparate and unfair treatment. The argument has a particularly hollow ring in this case. For appellants not only did not seek judicial review of either the designation or of the denials of the certificates of appropriateness and of no exterior effect, but do not even now suggest that the Commission's decisions concerning the Terminal were in any sense arbitrary or unprincipled. But, in any event, a landmark owner has a right to judicial review of any Commission decision, and, quite simply, there is no basis whatsoever for a conclusion that courts will have any greater difficulty identifying arbitrary or discriminatory action in the context of landmark regulation than in the context of classic zoning or indeed in any other context.

Next, appellants observe that New York City's law differs from zoning laws and historic district ordinances in that the Landmarks Law does not impose identical or similar restrictions on all structures located in particular physical communities. It follows, they argue, that New York City's law is inherently incapable of producing the fair and equitable distribution of benefits and burdens of governmental action which is characteristic of zoning laws and historic district legislation and which they maintain is a constitutional requirement if "just compensation" is not to be afforded. It is of course true that the Landmarks Law has a more severe impact on some landowners than on others, but that in it-

self does not mean that the law effects a "taking." Legislation designed to promote the general welfare commonly burdens some more than others. The owners of the brickyard in *Hadacheck*, of the cedar trees in *Miller* v. *Schoene*, and of the gravel and sand mine in *Goldblatt* v. *Hempstead*, were uniquely burdened by the legislation sustained in those cases. Similarly, zoning laws often impact more severely on some property owners than others but have not been held to be invalid on that account. For example, the property owner in *Euclid* who wished to use his property for industrial purposes was affected far more severely by the ordinance than his neighbors who wished to use their land for residences.

In any event, appellants' repeated suggestions that they are solely burdened and unbenefited is factually inaccurate. This contention overlooks the fact that the New York City law applies to vast numbers of structures in the city in addition to the Terminal—all the structures contained in the 31 historic districts and over 400 individual landmarks, many of which are close to the Terminal. Unless we are to reject the judgment of the New York City Council that the preservation of landmarks benefit all New York citizens and all structures, both economically and by improving the quality of life in the city as a whole—which we are unwilling to do—we cannot conclude that the owners of the Terminal have in no sense been benefited by the Landmarks Law. Doubtless appellants believe they are more burdened than benefited by the law, but that must have been true too of the property owners in *Miller, Hadacheck, Euclid,* and *Goldblatt.*

Appellants' final broad-based attack would have us treat the law as an instance, like that in *United States* v. *Causby*, supra, in which Government, acting in an enterprise capacity, has appropriated part of their property for some strictly governmental purpose. Apart from the fact that *Causby* was a case of invasion of airspace that destroyed the use of the farm beneath and this New York City law has in no wise impaired the present use of the Terminal, the Landmarks Law neither exploits appellants' parcel for city purposes nor facilitates nor arises from any entrepreneurial operations of the city. The situation is not remotely like that in *Causby* when the airspace above the Terminal was in the flight pattern for military aircraft. The Landmarks Law's effect is simply to prohibit appellants or anyone else from occupying portions of the airspace above the Terminal, while permitting appellants to use the remainder of the parcel in a gainful fashion. This is no more an appropriation of property by Government for its own uses than is a zoning law prohibiting, for "aesthetic" reasons, two or more adult theatres within a specified area, see *Young* v. *American Mini Theatres, Inc.*, supra, or a safety regulation prohibiting excavations below a certain level. See *Goldblatt* v. *City of Hempstead*, supra.

C

Rejection of appellants' broad arguments is not however the end of our inquiry, for all we thus far have established is that the New York law is not rendered invalid by its failure to provide "just compensation" whenever a landmark owner is restricted in the exploitation of property interests, such as air rights, to a greater extent than provided for under applicable zoning laws. We now must consider whether the interference with appellants' property is of such a magnitude that "there must be an exercise of eminent domain and compensation to sustain [it]." Pennsylvania Coal Co. v. Mahon, 260 U.S., at 413, 43 S.Ct., at 159. That inquiry may be narrowed to the question of the severity of the impact of the law on appellants' parcel, and its resolution in turn requires a careful assessment of the impact of the regulation on the Terminal site.

Unlike the governmental acts in *Goldblatt, Miller, Causby, Griggs,* and *Hadacheck*, the New York City law does not interfere in any way with the present uses of the Terminal. Its designation as a landmark not only permits but contemplates that appellants may continue to use the property precisely as it has for the past 65 years: as a railroad terminal containing office space and concessions. So the law does not interfere with what must be regarded as Penn Central's primary expectation concerning the use of the parcel. More importantly, on this record, we must regard the New York City law as permitting Penn Central not only to profit from the Terminal but to obtain a "reasonable return" on its investment.

Appellants, moreover, exaggerate the effect of the Act on its ability to make use of the air rights above the Terminal in two respects. First, it simply cannot be maintained, on this record, that appellants have been prohibited from occupying *any* portion of the airspace above the Terminal. While the Commission's actions in denying applications to construct an office building in excess of 50 stories above the Terminal may indicate that it will refuse to issue a certificate of appropriateness for any comparably sized structure, nothing the Commission has said or done suggests an intention to prohibit *any* construction above the Terminal. The Commission's report emphasized that whether any construction would be allowed depended upon whether the proposed addition "would harmonize in scale, material, and character with [the Terminal]." * * * Since appellants have not sought approval for the construction of a smaller structure, we do not know that appellants will be denied any use of any portion of the airspace above the Terminal.

Second, to the extent appellants have been denied the right to build above the Terminal, it is not literally accurate to say that they have been denied *all* use of even those pre-existing air rights. Their ability to use these rights has not been abrogated; they are made transferable to at least eight parcels in the vicinity of the Terminal, one or two of which have been found suitable for the construction of new office buildings. Although appellants and others have argued that New York City's transferable development rights program is far from ideal, the New York courts here supportably found that, at least in the case of the Terminal, the rights afforded are valuable. While these rights may well not have constituted "just compensation" if a "taking" had occurred, the rights nevertheless undoubtedly mitigate whatever financial burdens the law has imposed on appellants and, for that reason, are to be taken into account in considering the impact of regulation. * * *

On this record we conclude that the application of New York City's Landmarks Preservation Law has not effected a "taking" of appellants'

property. The restrictions imposed are substantially related to the promotion of the general welfare and not only permit reasonable beneficial use of the landmark site but afford appellants opportunities further to enhance not only the Terminal site proper but also other properties.

Affirmed.

Mr. Justice REHNQUIST, with whom THE CHIEF JUSTICE [BURGER] and Mr. Justice STEVENS join, dissenting.

* * *

Only in the most superficial sense of the word can this case be said to involve "zoning." Typical zoning restrictions may, it is true, so limit the prospective uses of a piece of property as to diminish the value of that property in the abstract because it may not be used for the forbidden purposes. But any such abstract decrease in value will more than likely be at least partially offset by an increase in value which flows from similar restrictions as to use on neighboring properties. All property owners in a designated area are placed under the same restrictions, not only for the benefit of the municipality as a whole but for the common benefit of one another. In the words of Mr. Justice Holmes, speaking for the Court in Pennsylvania Coal Co. v. Mahon, 260 U.S. 393, 415, 43 S.Ct. 158, 160 (1922), there is "an average reciprocity of advantage."

Where a relatively few individual buildings, all separated from one another, are singled out and treated differently from surrounding buildings, no such reciprocity exists. The cost to the property owner which results from the imposition of restrictions applicable only to his property and not that of his neighbors may be substantial—in this case, several million dollars—with no comparable reciprocal benefits. And the cost associated with landmark legislation is likely to be of a completely different order of magnitude than that which results from the imposition of normal zoning restrictions. Unlike the regime affected by the latter, the landowner is not simply prohibited from using his property for certain purposes, while allowed to use it for all other purposes. Under the historic landmark preservation scheme adopted by New York, the property owner is under an affirmative duty to *preserve* his property *as a landmark* at his own expense. To suggest that because traditional zoning results in some limitation of use of the property zoned, the New York landmark preservation scheme should likewise be upheld, represents the ultimate in treating as alike things which are different. The rubric of "zoning" has not yet sufficed to avoid the well-established proposition that the Fifth Amendment bars the "Government from forcing some people alone to bear public burdens which, in all fairness and justice, should be borne by the public as a whole." Armstrong v. United States, 364 U.S. 40, 80 S.Ct. 1563 (1960). * * *

* * *

Appellees do not dispute that valuable property rights have been destroyed. And the Court has frequently emphasized that the term "property" as used in the Taking Clause includes the entire "group of rights inhering in the citizen's [ownership]." United States v. General Motors Corp., 323 U.S. 373, 65 S.Ct. 357 (1945). * * *

While neighboring landowners are free to use their land and "air rights" in any way consistent with

the broad boundaries of New York zoning, Penn Central, absent the permission of appellees, must forever maintain its property in its present state. The property has been thus subjected to a nonconsensual servitude not borne by any neighboring or similar properties.

Appellees have thus destroyed—in a literal sense, "taken"—substantial property rights of Penn Central. * * *

* * *

Appellees are not prohibiting a nuisance. The record is clear that the proposed addition to the Grand Central Terminal would be in full compliance with zoning, height limitations, and other health and safety requirements. Instead, appellees are seeking to preserve what they believe to be an outstanding example of Beaux Arts architecture. Penn Central is prevented from further developing its property basically because it did *too good* of a job in designing and building it. The city of New York, because of its unadorned admiration for the design, has decided that the owners of the building must preserve it unchanged for the benefit of sightseeing New Yorkers and tourists.

Unlike in the case of land use regulations, appellees are not *prohibiting* Penn Central from using its property in a narrow set of noxious ways. Instead, appellees have placed an *affirmative* duty on Penn Central to maintain the Terminal in its present state and in "good repair." Appellants are not free to use their property as they see fit within broad outer boundaries but must strictly adhere to their past use except where appellees conclude that alternative uses would not detract from the Landmark. While Penn

Central may continue to use the Terminal as it is presently designed, appellees otherwise "exercise complete dominion and control over the surface of the land," United States v. Causby, 328 U.S. 256, 262, 66 S.Ct. 1062, 1066 (1946), and must compensate the owner for his loss. * * * "Property is taken in the constitutional sense when inroads are made upon an owner's use of it to an extent that, as between private parties, a servitude has been acquired." United States v. Dickinson, 331 U.S. 745, 748, 67 S.Ct. 1382, 1385 (1947). * * *

Even where the government prohibits a noninjurious use, the Court has ruled that a taking does not take place if the prohibition applies over a broad cross section of land and thereby "secure[s] an average reciprocity of advantage." Pennsylvania Coal Co. v. Mahon, 260 U.S. 393, 415, 43 S.Ct. 158, 160 (1922). It is for this reason that zoning does not constitute a "taking." While zoning at times reduces *individual* property values, the burden is shared relatively evenly and it is reasonable to conclude that on a whole an individual who is harmed by one aspect of the zoning will be benefited by another.

Here, however, a multimillion dollar loss has been imposed on appellants; it is uniquely felt and is not offset by any benefits flowing from the preservation of some 500 other "Landmarks" in New York. Appellees have imposed a substantial cost on less than one one-tenth of one percent of the buildings in New York for the general benefit of all its people. It is exactly this imposition of general costs on a few individuals at which the "taking" protection is directed. * * *

* * *

Appellees in response would argue that a taking only occurs where a property owner is denied *all* reasonable value of his property. The Court has frequently held that, even where a destruction of property rights would not *otherwise* constitute a taking, the inability of the owner to make a reasonable return on his property requires compensation under the Fifth Amendment. * * * But the converse is not true. A taking does not become a noncompensable exercise of police power simply because the government in its grace allows the owner to make some "reasonable" use of his property. "[I]t is the character of the invasion, not the amount of damage resulting from it, so long as the damage is substantial, that determines the question whether it is a taking." United States v. Cress, 243 U.S. 316, 328, 37 S.Ct. 380, 385 (1917); United States v. Causby, 328 U.S. 256, 266, 66 S.Ct. 1062, 1068 (1946). * * *

Appellees, apparently recognizing that the constraints imposed on a Landmark site constitute a taking for Fifth Amendment purposes, do not leave the property owner empty handed. As the Court notes, * * * the property owner may theoretically "transfer" his previous right to develop the Landmark property to adjacent properties if they are under his control. Appellees have coined this system "Transfer Development Rights," or TDRs.

Of all the terms used in the Taking Clause, "just compensation" has the strictest meaning. The Fifth Amendment does not allow simply an approximate compensation but requires "a full and perfect equivalent for the property taken." Monongahela Navigation Co. v. United States,

148 U.S. 312, 326, 13 S.Ct. 622, 626 (1893). * * * And the determination of whether a "full and perfect equivalent" has been awarded is a "judicial function." * * * The fact that *appellees* may believe that TDRs provide full compensation is irrelevant. * * *

Appellees contend that, even if they have "taken" appellants' property, TDRs constitute "just compensation." Appellants, of course, argue that TDRs are highly imperfect compensation. Because the lower courts held that there was no "taking," they did not have to reach the question of whether or not just compensation has already been awarded. * * * [I]n other cases the Court of Appeals has noted that TDRs have an "uncertain and contingent market value" and do "not adequately preserve" the value lost when a building is declared to be a Landmark. * * * On the other hand, there is evidence in the record that Penn Central has been offered substantial amounts for its TDRs. Because the record on appeal is relatively slim, I would remand to the Court of Appeals for a determination of whether TDRs constitute a "full and perfect equivalent for the property taken."

Over 50 years ago, Justice Holmes, speaking for the Court, warned that the courts were "in danger of forgetting that a strong public desire to improve the public condition is not enough to warrant achieving the desire by a shorter cut than the constitutional way of paying for the change." Pennsylvania Coal Co. v. Mahon, 260 U.S., at 416, 43 S.Ct., at 160. The Court's opinion in this case demonstrates that the danger thus foreseen has not abated. The city of New York is in a precarious financial state, and some may believe that the costs of landmark preservation will be more easily borne by corporations such as Penn Central than the overburdened individual taxpayers of New York. But these concerns do not allow us to ignore past precedents construing the Eminent Domain Clause to the end that the desire to improve the public condition is, indeed, achieved by a shorter cut than the constitutional way of paying for the damage.

MORE RECENT CASES PERTAINING TO THE TAKINGS CLAUSE

Andrus v. Allard, 444 U.S. 51, 100 S.Ct. 318 (1979)	Facts	Pursuant to the Eagle Protection Act and the Migratory Bird Treaty Act passed by Congress to prevent the destruction of certain species of birds, the Secretary of the Interior promulgated regulations which prohibited commercial transactions (i.e., importing, exporting, purchasing, selling, trading, bartering, or offering for purchase, sale, trade, or barter) in parts of such birds legally killed even before the birds came under statutory protection. Plaintiffs, engaged in the trade of Indian artifacts, many of which were composed of the feathers from birds currently protected but which existed before the birds came under statutory protection, challenged the regulations as violative of the Takings Clause.

Andrus (*Cont.*)	Decision	"The regulations here do not compel the surrender of the artifacts, and there is no physical invasion or restraint upon them. Rather, a significant restriction has been imposed on one means of disposing of the artifacts. But the denial of one traditional property right does not always amount to a taking. At least where an owner possesses a full 'bundle' of property rights, the destruction of one 'strand' of the bundle is not a taking, because the aggregate must be viewed in its entirety. * * * In this case, it is crucial that appellees retain the rights to possess and transport their property, and to donate or devise the protected birds." While "the regulations here prevent the most profitable use of appellees' property," this is not controlling because "it is not clear that appellees will be unable to derive economic benefit from the artifacts; for example, they might exhibit the artifacts for an admission charge." Observing that "[p]rediction of profitability is essentially a matter of reasoned speculation that courts are not especially competent to perform," the Court pointed out that "perhaps because of its very uncertainty, the interest in anticipated gains has traditionally been viewed as less compelling than other property-related interests."
Kaiser Aetna v. United States, 444 U.S. 164, 100 S.Ct. 383 (1979)		See p. 506.
PruneYard Shopping Center v. Robins, 447 U.S. 74, 100 S.Ct. 2035 (1980)		See p. 1299.
Agins v. City of Tiburon, 447 U.S. 255, 100 S.Ct. 2138 (1980)	Facts	Plaintiffs, owners of five acres of unimproved land of great value because of the scenic view it afforded of San Francisco Bay, argued that a city zoning ordinance which permitted only the construction of single-family dwellings each on a minimum lot size of one acre effected a taking of their property by preventing significant residential development of the land and thus destroyed much of its value.
	Decision	Relying on Village of Euclid v. Ambler Realty Co., 272 U.S. 365, 47 S.Ct. 114 (1926), which upheld the facial constitutionality of zoning ordinances on the grounds they bore a substantial relationship to the public welfare despite an alleged diminution in the value of the owner's land, the Court observed that California's mandate that municipalities develop local open-space plans "will discourage the 'premature and unnecessary conversion of open-space land to urban uses.'" "The zoning ordinances benefit the appellants as well as the public by serving the city's interest in assuring careful and orderly

Agins (*Cont.*)	Decision (*Cont.*)	development of residential property with provision for open-space areas. There is no indication that the appellants' five-acre tract is the only property affected by the ordinances. Appellants therefore will share with other owners the benefits and burdens of the city's exercise of its police power." "Although the ordinances limit development, they neither prevent the best use of appellants' land * * * nor extinguish a fundamental attribute of ownership." Since the property owners may build as many as five houses on their five-acre site and "are free to pursue their reasonable investment expectations by submitting a development plan to local officials * * * it cannot be said that the impact of general land use regulations has denied appellants the 'justice and fairness' guaranteed by the Fifth and Fourteenth Amendments."
Loretto v. Teleprompter Manhattan CATV Corp. — U.S. —, 102 S.Ct. 3164 (1982)	Facts	A New York statute prohibited a landlord from interfering with a cable TV company's installation of cables and boxes on his building and specified that a property owner may not demand compensation in excess of the limit determined by a state commission to be reasonable. The commission subsequently ruled that a one-time payment of one dollar to the landlord was reasonable. A property owner brought a class action for damages and injunctive relief, alleging that the statute constituted a "taking" of property without just compensation.
	Decision	"[W]hen the 'character of the governmental action' * * * is a permanent physical invasion of property, [as distinguished from regulation of the use of property to promote the public interest] our cases uniformly have found a taking to the extent of the occupation, without regard to whether the action achieves an important public benefit or has only minimal economic impact on the owner." "Such an appropriation is perhaps the most serious form of invasion of an owner's property interests," implicating "the rights 'to possess, use and dispose of it.' * * * To the extent that the government permanently occupies physical property, it effectively destroys *each* of these rights. First, the owner has no right to possess the occupied space himself, and also has no power to exclude the occupier from possession and use of the space. The power to exclude has traditionally been considered one of the most treasured strands in an owner's bundle of property rights. * * * Second, the permanent physical occupation of property forever denies the owner any power to control the use of the property; he not only cannot exclude others, but can make no non-possessory use of the property. * * * Finally, even though the owner may retain the bare legal right to dispose of the occupied space by transfer or sale, the permanent occupation of that space by a stranger will ordinarily

Loretto (*Cont.*)	Decision (*Cont.*)	empty the right of any value, since the purchaser will also be unable to make any use of the property."
		"To borrow a metaphor, * * * [here] the government does not simply take a single 'strand' from the 'bundle' of property rights; it chops through the bundle, taking a slice of every strand." "Teleprompter's cable installation on appellant's building constitutes a taking under the traditional test. The installation involved a direct physical attachment of plates, boxes, wires, bolts and screws to the building, completely occupying space immediately above and upon the roof and along the building's exterior wall."

In City of Oakland v. Oakland Raiders, 32 Cal.3d 60, 183 Cal.Rptr. 673, 646 P.2d 835 (1982), the California Supreme Court reversed a decision by a state superior court that, as a matter of law, the city could not use its power of eminent domain to acquire a professional football team. The state supreme court overturned the lower court's award of summary judgment for the Raiders and remanded the case for trial on the merits. When the owners of the team announced their intention to move the NFL franchise to Los Angeles, the city began eminent domain proceedings to prevent the move. The city argued that what it sought to condemn was property, thus a fit subject for eminent domain, and further contended that whether such a "taking" was for a valid "public use" had to await a full trial at which all the facts could be aired. In response, the owners of the Raiders urged that the law of eminent domain did not extend to "intangible property not connected with realty" (the Oakland Colosseum, after all, is municipally owned; the team itself consists of contractual agreements) and that, in any event, such a "taking" was not for any "public use." The court acknowledged that two issues therefore were presented, "the first dealing with the intangible nature of the property to be taken, and the second focusing on the scope of the condemning power as limited by the doctrine of public use."

Speaking for the court, Justice Richardson pointed out that as long ago as 1848, the United States Supreme Court rejected the notion that intangible property could not be condemned. Said the Court in West River Bridge Co. v. Dix, 47 U.S. (6 How.) 507, 12 L.Ed. 535, with respect to the power of government " 'to resume or extinguish a franchise' ": " 'We are aware of nothing peculiar to a franchise which can class it higher, or render it more sacred, than other property. A franchise is property and nothing more; it is incorporeal property * * *.' " Justice Richardson wrote, "For eminent domain purposes, neither the federal nor the state Constitution distinguishes between property which is real or personal, tangible or intangible." He continued, "[W]e conclude that our eminent domain law authorizes the taking of intangible property. To the extent that the trial court based its summary judgment on a contrary conclusion it erred." Turning to the issue of "public use," the California court acknowledged that the question whether a municipality could acquire and operate a professional football team was truly one of first impression. However, the court noted that the U.S. Supreme Court "established years ago that 'what is public use frequently and largely depends upon the facts and circumstances surrounding the particular subject-matter in regard to which the character of the use is questioned.' (Fallbrook Irrigation District v. Bradley, 164 U.S., at 159–160, 17 S.Ct., at 63 * * *.) Further,

'Public uses are not limited, in the modern view, to matters of mere business necessity and ordinary convenience, but may extend to matters of public health, recreation and enjoyment.' (Rindge Co. v. Los Angeles County, 262 U.S. 700, 707, 43 S.Ct. 689, 693 [1923].)" Taking extensive note of the fact that municipalities across the country have long been involved with baseball fields, opera houses, amphitheaters, and the like, Justice Richardson wrote: "The obvious difference between managing and owning the facility in which the game is played, and managing and owning the team which plays in the facility, seems legally insubstantial. If acquiring, erecting, owning and/or operating a sports stadium is a permissible municipal function, we discern no valid legal reason why owning and operating a sports franchise which fields a team to play in the stadium is not equally permissible." He concluded that "the acquisition and, indeed, the operation of a sports franchise may well be an appropriate municipal function." The court left for a full trial discussion of more particular questions of "public use" pressed by the Raiders' owners. Said the court, "Our conclusion requiring a trial on the merits is reinforced by the long recognized and fundamental importance of the 'facts and circumstances' of each case in determining whether a proposed use is an appropriate public use."

Although "forced by the current state of the law to agree with the result reached by the majority," Chief Justice Bird did not sign their opinion "because it endorses * * * unprecedented application of eminent domain law without even pausing to consider the ultimate consequences of their expansive decision." She went on to say:

> There are two particularly disturbing questions in this case. First, does a city have the power to condemn a viable, ongoing business and sell it to another private party merely because the original owner has announced his intention to move his business to another city? For example, if a rock concert impresario, after some years of producing concerts in a municipal stadium, decides to move his productions to another city, may the city condemn his business, including his contracts with the rock stars, in order to keep the concerts at the stadium? If a small business that rents a storefront on land originally taken by the city for a redevelopment project decides to move to another city in order to expand, may the city take the business and force it to stay at its original location? May a city condemn *any* business that decides to seek greener pastures elsewhere under the unlimited interpretation of eminent domain law that the majority appear to approve?

> Second, even if a city were legally able to do so, is it proper for a municipality to drastically invade personal property rights to further the policy interests asserted here?

> The rights both of the owners of the Raiders and of its employees are threatened by the City's action. Thus, one unexplored aspect of the majority's decision is the ruling that contract rights can be taken by eminent domain. The cases relied on by the majority in support of this holding chiefly concerned inverse condemnation suits. Those cases essentially held that when a state condemns a business, the government is obligated to compensate the business owner for the value of the contract rights destroyed by the taking. In this case, the City seeks to condemn employment contracts between the Raiders and dozens of its employees. Can the City acquire personal employment contracts as simply as it can acquire a tract of land? Are an employee's rights violated by this non-consensual taking of an employment contract or personal services agreement?

At what point in the varied and complex business relationships involved herein would this power to condemn end? In my view, this court should proceed most cautiously before placing a constitutional imprimatur upon this aspect of creeping statism. These difficult questions are deserving of more thorough attention than they have yet received in this litigation.

It strikes me as dangerous and heavy-handed for the government to take over a business, including all of its intangible assets, for the sole purpose of preventing its relocation. The decisional law appears to be silent as to this particular question. It appears that the courts have not yet been confronted with a situation such as that presented by this case. However, a review of the pertinent case law demonstrates that decisions as to the proper scope of the power of eminent domain generally have been considered legislative, rather than judicial, in nature. Therefore, in the absence of a legislative bar to the use of eminent domain in this manner, there appears to be no ground for judicial intervention.

* * *

[T]he wisdom of the City's decision here may not be successfully challenged in the courts unless it can be shown that the municipality acted in an arbitrary or capricious fashion, or its act represents a "gross abuse of discretion." Given this present state of the law, on this limited record, respondents have not demonstrated that there has been a violation of these standards. Unless it can be shown that the City's decision to use its power of eminent domain in this fashion was completely irrational, there is no relief available for respondents in the courts. Any relief must come from legislatively imposed restrictions.

Chapter 9

Equal Protection of the Laws

When a legislative body enacts public policy, it inescapably creates legal categories. Its judgment about who is entitled to receive what service or who is to be accorded what treatment or who is to be taxed at what rate singles out this or that group for some kind of attention. As such, legal categories necessarily discriminate. The interesting question that we turn to when we consider the Fourteenth Amendment's guarantee to all citizens of equal protection of the laws is not some constitutional requirement that legislators make indiscriminate use of their power, but rather as to what are and are not permissible bases for the creation of legal categories.

We say that categories which are constructed along impermissible lines "invidiously discriminate." The Fourteenth Amendment was passed to eradicate such invidious discrimination, yet the term is far from self-defining. Certainly—at least since the Civil War—race is presumed to be such a factor. Nationality, religion, wealth, and sex among other grounds also have received attention. The problem, however, is not solved merely by isolating the telltale dimension. Even such a clearly proscribed discriminant as race, for example, comes to be at least partially tolerated when values such as federalism, private action, and the war power enter the picture. This would certainly suggest that in at least some instances we are willing to balance the interests. At other times we are more absolute. And on other occasions we seem to hold equality in such a preferred position as to command the legislature to revise its policies allocating rights and services, especially to the poor. Many of these deviations and apparent inconsistencies are, of course, a product of the Court's changing composition. They are explained more clearly, however, when also seen in terms of the rival modes of constitutional interpretation we discussed at the beginning of this book. As you read the materials concerning equal protection which follow, be especially aware of the dialogue among the major modes of constitutional interpretation as to what scope should be

679

given the Equal Protection Clause. Should it be defined so as to encompass only formal or procedural equality? And to what extent? Or should the clause be read so as to guarantee substantive equality among citizens too?

a. Racial Discrimination

In at least two instances following the adoption of the Fourteenth Amendment in 1868, the Supreme Court clearly acknowledged the purpose of the amendment as abolishing racial discrimination. One of these was the decision in the *Slaughterhouse Cases* (p. 632). The other was the Court's opinion in Strauder v. West Virginia, 100 U.S. 303, 25 L.Ed. 664 (1880). In that case, Strauder, a black man, sought to have his murder trial removed to a federal court since West Virginia law did not permit Negroes to be eligible for service on petit juries. The Supreme Court sustained Strauder's request and, through Justice Strong, said:

> The words of the amendment * * * contain a necessary implication of a positive immunity, or right, most valuable to the colored race,—the right to exemption from unfriendly legislation against them distinctively as colored,—exemption from legal distinctions, implying inferiority in civil society, lessening the security of their enjoyment of the rights which others enjoy, and discriminations which are steps towards reducing them to the condition of a subject race. * * * The very fact that colored people are singled out and expressly denied by statute all right to participate in the administration of the law, as jurors, because of their color, though they are citizens, and may be in other respects fully qualified, is practically a brand upon them, affixed by the law, an assertion of their inferiority, and a stimulant to that race prejudice which is an impediment to securing to individuals of that race that equal justice which the law aims to secure to all others.

Thus, when the Court came to decide *Plessy* v. *Ferguson* (p. 693) in 1896, the Court could hardly be said to be writing on a clean slate. As you read *Plessy*, then, you will want to determine on what basis the Court could possibly uphold Plessy's conviction under a Louisiana statute denying nonwhites access to certain train cars reserved for whites without overruling *Strauder*.

Plessy and its doctrine of "separate but equal" facilities for blacks is significant, however, for reasons other than mere inconsistency with clear precedents. It is most important because it provided the legalistic smoke screen behind which an exploitive society operated for the next six decades; for while things were separate, they were rarely, if ever, equal. The Court, if not responsible in fact for the oppression and further economic and social decline of the Negro after 1896, was at least a willing rationalizer.

What is interesting from the standpoint of constitutional interpretation is the way in which the Court rationalized the acceptability of this new policy and, indeed, how the method of the Court's justification repeated itself in succeeding decades until at last it did in the "separate but equal" standard itself. In short, the materials on racial discrimination not only ask us to consider the constitutionality of color as a categorizing device, they invite us to examine the role of sociology in judicial decisions.

When the Court handed down its decision in *Brown v. Board of Education (Brown I)* (p. 699) in 1954, critics of the decision assailed the Court for letting its ruling be guided by social science hypotheses instead of legal reasoning. Indeed, some writers have suggested that *Brown I* in overruling *Plessy* failed to state any principle at all but rested merely on sociological citations. You will want to reach your own conclusion on this issue. Nevertheless, we think it is interesting to note—especially in light of all the flack which the Court took for citing those social science studies—that the Court in *Plessy* can be seen as equally influenced by the sociological beliefs of its age. Indeed, you may want to consider the prospect that the only difference in justification offered for the social policies which the Court announced at those different times was that the *Plessy* Court was imbued with the sociological theories of its time—that racial antagonisms were rooted in immutable human instincts and couldn't be legislated away—while the *Brown* Court tended to accept the prevalent twentieth-century sociological view that racial prejudice is caused by environmental factors. Given these premises, weren't both Courts, then, practitioners of "social engineering"?

The relevance of sociology to judicial justification is also underscored in a series of post-*Plessy* cases which ultimately ended in undermining the "separate but equal" standard. As time went by, it was no accident that attention came to be focused on the constitutionality of segregation in education since the socializing function of the schools was the linchpin of racial oppression in society. It groomed the white kids for leadership and the black kids to "stay in their place." Though the Court never questioned the *Plessy* standard, it came repeatedly to ask how equal separate facilities were. Increasingly, the Court was driven to scrutinize the material equality of disparate facilities until it finally acknowledged in *Sweatt v. Painter* (p. 697), a case involving professional education, that preparation for an occupation depended not merely on equal facilities but on those priceless intangibles such as experiences which were open only to white students—experiences which could only be gained through interaction not isolation from others. Education which denied the opportunity for such interaction could not be equal no matter how good the material indices.

The alternative justification of policy resting exclusively upon principle is epitomized in Justice Harlan's dissenting opinion in *Plessy*. Writing foursquare in the tradition of *Strauder*, Harlan suggested the Court take judicial notice of what was common knowledge—that the purpose of this discrimination was the oppression of the Negro and was thus counter to the intent of the Fourteenth Amendment. Said Justice Harlan, the Louisiana statute must fall because "Our Constitution is color blind, and neither knows nor tolerates classes among citizens." Moreover, Harlan was an acute social observer. Note how he characterizes the majority's justification for separate facilities as something which today we call a "self-fulfilling prophecy," and consider, too, the accuracy of his observation that the "equal" in "separate but equal" was going to turn out to be little more than eyewash.

That the decision in *Brown I* seemed to hinge so closely on the social science evidence cited also caused problems. Enterprising segregationists countered by massing similar evidence to prove their point that desegregation would be harmful to both races as the district court decision in *Stell* v. *Savannah-Chatham County Board of Education* (p. 704) shows. How persuasive do you think they were? How well did the appellate court rebuff this challenge to the holding in *Brown?* Do you think the *Stell* case betrays a fatal mistake in letting *Brown* rest so substantially on sociological materials? Would it have been better for the Court in achieving the aim of ending segregation to have handed down a decision on the order of Harlan's dissent in *Plessy?* Why didn't it?

Since the Equal Protection Clause of the Fourteenth Amendment applies only to the states, the Court had to deal with segregation in the District of Columbia separately. In *Bolling* v. *Sharpe* (p. 702), decided at the same time as *Brown I*, the Court found such practice violative of the Due Process Clause of the Fifth Amendment. How convincingly do you think the Court established the principle that a denial of equal protection might also result in a denial of due process? The answer to this question is significant since the Court in later years would use this same line of argument to fasten standards of equal protection on national legislation even though, as we have said, the Fourteenth Amendment does not apply to the national government.

Aside from the justification it offered for its ruling in *Brown*, the Court ran into serious problems of compliance. Following its 1954 decision on the merits of the controversy, the Court set the case for reargument the following Term as to the remedy. As a consequence, the Court ordered in *Brown II* (p. 709) that desegregation proceed with "all deliberate speed." Since one of the prerequisites of compliance is a clear understanding of what is commanded, how well do you think the Court informed local school boards, lower federal judges, and state officials what would constitute compliance with the decision? In other words, when would people know they were fully obeying the Court's order? Would the standard have been clearer had the Court commanded integration rather than desegregation?

Some critics—including Justice Black in a now-historic television interview which he gave in December 1968—have suggested that including the reservation of "with all deliberate speed" in the *Brown II* opinion retarded rather than advanced the prospects of compliance. Said Justice Black:

> Looking back at it now, it seems to me that it's delayed the process of outlawing segregation. It seems to me, probably, with all due deference to the opinion and my brethren, all of them, that it would have been better— maybe—I don't say positively—not to have that sentence. To treat that case as an ordinary lawsuit and force that judgment on the counties it affected that minute. That's true, that it would have only been one school

and each case would have been only one case. But that fitted into my ideas of the Court not making policies for the nation.[a]

Would you agree? Did the Court encourage disobedience to its order by this and other things it said in *Brown II*?

We need not document here the disappointment, delay, and frustration that set in following the 1955 implementation decision and which continued until the Court fourteen years later in Alexander v. Holmes County Board of Education, 396 U.S. 19, 90 S.Ct. 29 (1969), announced, "[A]llowing 'all deliberate speed' for desegration is no longer constitutionally permissible. * * * [E]very school district is to terminate dual school systems at once and to operate now and hereafter only unitary schools." Through it all the Court remained unanimously committed to the goal of dismantling segregated schools, emphasizing its commitment on one occasion, in *Cooper* v. *Aaron* (p. 710) in 1958, with an opinion authored by all nine Justices. Compliance, however, was dependent upon the continued and aggressive support of others: Presidents like Kennedy and Johnson ready and willing to send in federal marshals or troops to force compliance, an active Attorney General like Robert Kennedy persistently filing suits against segregated districts, a federal agency like HEW willing to cut off federal school aid to noncomplying areas, ever-present interest groups such as the NAACP which provided financial help, lawyers, and research support to black plaintiffs bringing suit to challenge segregated facilities, and a lower federal judiciary whose members had to withstand enormous community pressures.

Several serious problems remain however. One of these is the question of how far the 1954–55 rulings should be carried. As the decisions in *Swann* v. *Charlotte-Mecklenburg Board of Education* (p. 714) and *Milliken* v. *Bradley* (p. 723) demonstrate, the Court presently reads the Equal Protection Clause to proscribe only *de jure* and not *de facto* segregation, that is state-imposed separation of the races, not distance between the races resulting from happenstance, as, for example, with housing patterns. The key to understanding the difference between the two terms is "intent," for only intentional discrimination by the state on the basis of race violates the Fourteenth Amendment. An appreciation of this difference is critical in turn to understanding the limits the Court has placed on the remedies that can legally be fashioned by federal district courts. As the Court allows in *Swann*, it may be necessary for a district court to require busing in the achievement of racial balance among schools afflicted with *de jure* segregation so as to effectively dismantle a dual educational system. But it is never permissible, as the Court decrees in *Milliken*, for a district court to impose such a remedy on governmental units which themselves have not intentionally discriminated. However, as the dissenters in *Milliken* rightly point out, such a limitation of the remedy—in that case, one limited to redrawing attendance zones and busing solely within the Detroit city limits—will become less and less meaningful,

---

a. 1969 Cong.Quart.Weekly Report, 7.

given that urban areas are becoming increasingly black, encircled by largely all-white suburbs. In short, failure to address the reality of segregated housing patterns will likely mean a return in stark geographical terms to "separate but equal" in education.

To say that federal court-ordered desegregation of public schools has generally not been well received would, of course, be the grossest understatement. Indeed, the stiffness of public reaction to such court orders gave Justice Powell pause for concern in the *Columbus* busing case (p. 730). In his dissenting opinion, Justice Powell makes a forceful case for holding lower federal judges to strict observance of the distinction between *de jure* and *de facto* segregation, not merely as a matter of legality, but more importantly because of its impact on the courts' political environment. The relevance of those remarks appears to be underscored by the successful efforts initiated by voters in several states to place measures on the general election ballot putting the lid on busing aimed at achieving integration (p. 735).

If *de jure* discrimination is distinguished from *de facto* discrimination by the element of intent to discriminate, another serious problem lies in the proof of intent. Although it has held in a few instances that discriminatory effect is in itself sufficient to outlaw a practice—notably in dealing with job qualification exams which test knowledge rather far afield from know-how which the job at hand requires—the Court has been reluctant to accept the broad proposition that simply showing a practice has a racially disparate effect is enough to invoke relief. Were it to be otherwise, the *de facto* segregation apparent in the housing patterns of most metropolitan areas would be sufficient to warrant federal court intervention, which *Swann* has already made clear it does not. True, some actions produce such obviously discriminatory results that the actions themselves belie a clear intent, but cases such as *Gomillion* v. *Lightfoot* (p. 792) are the exception, not the rule. As the Court indicates in *Village of Arlington Heights* v. *Metropolitan Housing Development Corp.* (p. 741), the requisite proof of discriminatory intent must usually come from an appraisal of many factors. The rub, of course, lies in the fact that ostensibly legitimate justifications can mask ugly motives. Consider *Palmer* v. *Thompson* (p. 737) and the dilemma rapidly becomes apparent. How far can a court scrutinize a city's decision to discontinue public services on grounds of financial retrenchment or public safety and still avoid adopting the position Chief Justice Burger fears, that once a service is provided by government its recipients necessarily have an unlimited claim to its future delivery? The hazards of making prohibited discrimination turn on proof of an intent to discriminate are even more extensively illustrated in *City of Memphis* v. *Greene* (p. 773).

Last, but by no means least, is the controversial matter of whether *Brown* forbids all use of racial criteria, even when the motive of a governmental agency is to better the opportunities of the traditionally disadvantaged. Apart from questions of legality, such an enterprise is socially risky. Many of these concerns are highlighted in the following excerpt from Justice Brennan's concurring opinion in United Jewish Organizations of Williamsburgh, Inc. v. Carey, 430 U.S. 144, 97 S.Ct. 966 (1977), a decision approving the use of racial quotas in the reapportionment of state legislative districts:

> *First,* a purportedly preferential race assignment may in fact disguise a policy that perpetuates disadvantageous treatment of the plan's supposed beneficiaries. Accordingly courts might face considerable difficulty in ascertaining whether a given race classification truly furthers benign rather than illicit objectives. An effort to achieve proportional representation, for example, might be aimed at aiding a group's participation in the political processes by guaranteeing safe political offices, or, on the other hand, might be a "contrivance to segregate" the group, * * * thereby frustrating its potentially successful efforts at coalition building across racial lines. * * *

> *Second,* even in the pursuit of remedial objectives, an explicit policy of assignment by race may serve to stimulate our society's latent race consciousness, suggesting the utility and propriety of basing decisions on a factor that ideally bears no relationship to an individual's worth or needs. * * * Furthermore, even preferential treatment may act to stigmatize its recipient groups, for although intended to correct systemic or institutional inequities, such a policy may imply to some the recipients' inferiority and especial need for protection. * * *

> *Third,* especially when interpreting the broad principles embraced by the Equal Protection Clause, we cannot well ignore the social reality that even a benign policy of assignment by race is viewed as unjust by many in our society, especially by those individuals who are adversely affected by a given classification. This impression of injustice may be heightened by the natural consequence of our governing processes that the most "discrete and insular" of whites often will be called upon to bear the immediate, direct costs of benign discrimination. * * *

> In my view, if and when a decisionmaker embarks on a policy of benign racial sorting, he must weigh the concerns that I have discussed against the need for effective social policies promoting racial justice in a society beset by deep-rooted racial inequities. * * *

The decision in *Regents of the University of California* v. *Bakke* (p. 743) represents the Court's first attempt at addressing the constitutionality of "benign" discrimination. Although it rejected the notion of a quota, *Bakke* approved of considering race along with other factors in the admissions decision. It is clear from *Bakke* and subsequent cases (p. 747), however, that the Court has yet to find a coherent framework for the evaluation of affirmative action programs which can command support from a majority of the Justices.

b. "Private" Discrimination and the Concept of "State Action"

The materials in the preceding section focused on the constitutionality of state-imposed discrimination. But what about the discrimination that results from the actions of private individuals? It is generally conceded that the amendments to the Constitution do not protect persons from infringements of those rights by other individuals; they are binding only as against governmental invasion. Nevertheless, Congress may legislate protections against private discrimination pursuant to them, and the states have often taken similar action pursuant to their own constitutions. The principal problem which we had with national legislation which endeavored to eradicate private discrimination was an initial hostile reception given by the Court. It took decades to recover ground lost by the early grudging interpretations given the Thirteenth and Fourteenth Amendments in the *Civil Rights Cases of 1883* (p. 749). Only Justice Harlan gave sympathetic consideration to the kind of broad interpretation, particularly of the Thirteenth Amendment, which would have quickly and resolutely affirmed the constitutionality of this early legislation.

Because of the Court's narrow initial interpretation of the Thirteenth Amendment—a position that was not reversed until eighty-five years later in *Jones* v. *Alfred H. Mayer Co.* (p. 766) and *Griffin* v. *Breckenridge* (p. 770)—attention was focused on the Fourteenth Amendment. Yet to qualify for review under that Amendment, those who were discriminated against had to show that the unequal treatment they received was the product of "state action," that is that it was somehow sanctioned or supported by the power and authority of the state. Needless to say, this proved to be a very frustrating and roundabout way to confront racial discrimination. Yet, following a milestone decision by the Vinson Court in 1948 in *Shelley* v. *Kraemer* (p. 755), the Court began bit by bit to expand the concept of state action. In the hands of the more activist Warren Court, the concept was expanded to what you may think are extraordinary lengths. How good a substitute do you think it was for the kind of position stated by Harlan in the *1883* cases? Given the logic of a decision like *Reitman* v. *Mulkey* (p. 761), do there appear to be any limits to what might be considered "state action"?

Moreover, when the Court takes this incrementalist route of using one constitutional provision to do the work that another provision should be doing, there are substantial risks of inconsistency and unevenness in the application of the distorted doctrine. This is especially true when the composition of the Court is materially changed. Consider the *Moose Lodge* case (p. 760). Can you square this decision with previous decisions of the Court dating from *Shelley*? The problem of concluding that there has not been the requisite state involvement is intensified in *Jackson* v. *Metropolitan Edison Co.* (p. 762). Although this is a case involving due process, consideration of the "state action" question remains crucial. The connection to our present discussion is readily apparent when Justice Marshall, in dissent, asks whether the Court would reach the same conclusion about the absence of "state action" had the utility made it a practice of refusing to serve certain customers on the basis of race.

It is clear from the concurring opinions in *Runyon* v. *McCrary* (p. 770) that, while at least two members of the present Court believed the *Mayer Co.* case was wrongly decided, they concluded it was more important to stand by that decision than vindicate what they saw as the real legislative intent. It is worth pondering whether, were *Mayer* before the Court today, that decision would still win support from a majority of the Court.

Clearly, though, the impact of *Mayer* and *Runyon* is such as to effectively bury the ruling of the *Civil Rights Cases*. Given this impact, is further concern about the scope of "state action" warranted? Although it is true that the Thirteenth Amendment has experienced a new vitality, it is equally fair to say, however, that the perplexing problems of discerning an intent to discriminate, encountered earlier, persist here too, as *City of Memphis* v. *Greene* (p. 773) attests.

c. Voting Rights and Electoral Discrimination

The influence of race also spilled over into the electoral system where it joined with other factors, notably wealth, to exercise an inhibiting effect on the scope of the democratic process. This became possible because under our system of government responsibility for the allocation of voting rights and governing the conduct of the electoral process lies principally with the states. It is yet another manifestation of our commitment to the decentralization of power which a federal system provides. Unfortunately, state government has shown an unusual vulnerability to be overtaken by powerful in-groups in society which then use their muscle to block participation in the political process by racial minorities and other out-groups. Ultimately, a fundamental tension surfaces in the area of voting rights and electoral discrimination. Briefly stated, it is the question of how we can accommodate our interest in the maintenance of a decentralized system for the administration of the electoral process with the value we put on the assurance of equal opportunity for all citizens to participate in that process. Needless to say, the resolution of this problem has the most direct implications for the legitimacy we attribute to democratic government. Our interest, in turn, is further heightened since the recent reforms which have opened up participation are almost entirely the doing of some branch of the national government. In sum, there has been a gradual nationalizing of the electoral process both by Congress and the Court.

The extraordinary control of voting rights which the national government is constitutionally capable of assuming is amply illustrated by cases such as *South Carolina* v. *Katzenbach* (p. 161) and *Katzenbach* v. *Morgan* (p. 168) which we looked at earlier. The Voting Rights Act of 1965 was intended to get at the invidiously discriminatory use of such devices as the literacy test, the constitutional interpretation requirement, and the requisite of "good moral character" which had been used to seal off the electoral process from participation especially by racial minorities.

The Court not only upheld these efforts by Congress to strike at the racial barrier to voting, it had earlier attacked the semiprivate election system by which the white segregationist minority dominated the Southern states. This attack centered principally on the pre-election stages of the process. You will want to examine carefully, from the discussion in *Smith* v. *Allwright* (p. 787) and the decision in *Terry* v. *Adams* (p. 791), how the Court pushed the constitutional guarantees of the Fourteenth and Fifteenth Amendments back through the "private" stages of the electoral process—to the party primary and beyond—opening up popular participa-

tion. Nor did the Court allow political units such as municipalities to dis-
enfranchise minorities by the manipulation of political boundary lines, see
Gomillion v. *Lightfoot* (p. 792). A sophisticated variation on this old
theme—at least in the opinion of the dissenters—is presented to the Court
in *City of Richmond* v. *United States* (p. 793).

The remaining cases in this section concern other kinds of invidious
discrimination in the electoral process. Note how the Warren Court deals
with the problem. It typically adopts the preferred freedoms method recognizing the priority of the right to vote in the scale of fundamental liberties and then applies the tripartite test developed by the Court earlier in
Thomas v. *Collins* (p. 53) to assess the constitutionality of the state regulation. The most thorough application of this approach is evidenced in
Kramer v. *Union Free School District No. 15* (p. 801), but it is apparent
to one degree or another in other decisions involving restrictions placed by
the states on the right to vote or to have one's name appear as a candidate
for public office (p. 805).

d. Malapportionment

The equal opportunity to cast a vote can mean very little, however, if the
strength of that vote is not equal. Thus, the Court came to examine the
constitutionality of that variety of political discrimination which results in
unequal representation due to the malapportionment of legislative districts. This problem became particularly acute since the apportionment of
legislative seats in virtually all of the states had not kept pace with the
flow of the population to urban areas. The end product of such inertia or
lag was, in a large number of states, a legislature which badly underrepresented the urban majority and, as a consequence, was felt to be unresponsive to the mounting problems of the cities. Earlier, you will recall,
we examined the ruling in *Baker* v. *Carr* (p. 102) in which the Court sustained a challenge to the constitutionality of such diluted votes as a justiciable issue under the Equal Protection Clause where it previously had not
been a problem for which the judiciary could offer a remedy under that
clause in Article IV guaranteeing to each state a republican form of government. Our focus here is on the development and application of the
standard by which the Court would judge the constitutionality of legislative apportionments.

The Court handed down its now-familiar "one man-one vote" standard
in *Reynolds* v. *Sims* (p. 808) two years after its decision in *Baker*. This
standard was amplified in succeeding cases until its application at the
hands of the Warren Court could be summed up roughly by the following
propositions:

1. Structural requirements of state constitutions which violate this
standard may not be heeded even if they are approved by majority vote.

2. When a reapportionment scheme is challenged in the courts, the burden of proof is on the defending political unit to justify deviations from
perfect equality.

3. *Small absolute* deviations will be tolerated only if the justification offered by the government is compelling (e.g., compactness, contiguity, respect for the boundary lines of important political subdivisions).

4. Equality in apportionment applies not only to the states but to the political subdivisions they create as well.

Note the influence of the preferred freedoms concept in this approach.

Do you think any other rules except those embodied in the above approach could provide a resolution to the controversy through the use of standards which are, in the words of Justice Frankfurter dissenting in *Baker*, "judicially manageable"? And what about the quality of the Court's political science? Consider Chief Justice Warren's opinion in *Reynolds*, and compare it with Justice Stewart's dissent in *Lucas* v. *Forty-Fourth Colorado General Assembly* (p. 814). Does the majority's view of the political system comport well with the prevailing pluralist view of contemporary political science? Some critics have suggested that Chief Justice Warren envisioned the political process more on the order of New England town meeting democracy than modern pluralist society. Does Stewart's view offer a better understanding of the modern American political process? If so, then do we have a dilemma: must the Court choose between intervention according to the "one man-one vote" standard because it is the only manageable standard, even though it reflects a view of the political system political science long ago disowned, and total abstention suggested both by the lack of any other manageable standard and the awareness of a more sophisticated understanding of pluralist democracy?

Finally, in view of what we have already seen of the Burger Court's affection for the value of "Our Federalism" in Chapter 5, it would not be surprising to find that the Court's present regard for implementing "one man-one vote" (p. 825) has not rivaled the vigor which characterized the approach of the Warren Court. Indeed, Justice Brennan, dissenting from several Burger Court reapportionment decisions in 1973, assailed the newer rulings as a "retreat" from the *Reynolds* standard. Would you agree? In what ways has the present Court amended the content and application of the "one man-one vote" principle? What mitigating factors have the Court's most recent decisions taken into account? Can the Court continue to take into account such interests—or, more accurately, defer to legislative decisions to take such factors into account—without running a serious risk of backing into the very quagmire which Justice Frankfurter warned of (i.e., the lack of "judicially manageable standards" for deciding what is adequate representation for various political interests)?

e. Economic and Social Discrimination

This section concludes our consideration of equal protection by highlighting Court decisions on the constitutionality of legislation drawn on the basis of certain factors—such as indigency, sex, illegitimacy, alienage, and age—that might generally be combined under the rubric "economic and social discrimination." Much of the controversy in these cases deals with the question whether these are "suspect classifications" within the meaning of federal constitutional law. Other cases in this section, arising principally out of contexts in which various kinds of public welfare benefits were denied, implicate what the plaintiffs, at least, assert are "fundamental" rights. When these classifications and rights are considered against a background that also includes those classifications and rights discussed in earlier sections of this chapter, the central theme of this section quickly becomes the current judicial debate over the applicability of the principal frameworks of constitutional interpretation. Although for some time now there has been a consensus on the Court that recognizes a two-tier framework for equal protection analysis—an upper tier of interests composed of "suspect classes" and "fundamental" rights which, when directly implicated in legislation, triggers "strict scrutiny" and a lower tier of interests containing nonsuspect classes and nonfundamental rights, regulation of which must meet only the test of reasonableness—a spirited debate persists over which interests inhabit each tier.

Support for an enlarged view of "suspect classes" and an expanded list of "fundamental" rights is apparent in the decisions of the Warren Court and in the opinions of such liberal stalwarts as Justices Brennan and Marshall who, as did Douglas before his departure, continue the Warren Court tradition in dissent from many rulings of the present Court. Moved by the belief that the Court has a unique obligation to protect peripheral and powerless groups in society from unfriendly, class-based legislation, these activist, liberal holdovers from the Warren Court would push the notion of "suspect class" beyond the traditional "insular and discrete" minorities identified by race, alienage, and religion (see footnote 4 of the *Carolene Products* case, p. 63) to include the poor, illegitimate children, and women. They would also subject to "strict scrutiny" an enlarged body of "fundamental" rights, reaching beyond the Bill of Rights to create other guarantees such as the right to equal educational opportunity.

By contrast, the majority which dominates the Burger Court has shown little enthusiasm for expanding the number of upper-tier interests, as the Court's opinion in *San Antonio Indepedent School District* v. *Rodriguez* (p. 841) shows. Indeed, the current Court's refusal to regard classifications based on wealth as suspect is clear from the following statement by Justice Powell for the Court in the context of disposing of a constitutional challenge to state legislation limiting the expenditure of public funds for abortions to only those women whose lives would be endangered by carrying a fetus to term: "In a sense, every denial of welfare to an indigent creates a wealth classification as compared to nonindigents who are able to pay for the desired goods or services. But this Court has never held that financial need alone identifies a suspect class for purposes of equal protection analysis." Maher v. Roe, 432 U.S. 464, 97 S.Ct. 2376 (1977). A graphic example of the difference between the Warren and Burger Courts on the disposition of equal protection claims in welfare cases is provided by the contrast between *Shapiro* v. *Thompson* (p. 828), on the one hand, and *Rodriguez*, on the other.

The treatment of illegitimate children as a potentially "suspect class" furnishes another example of the difference between the two approaches.

Justice Black's opinion for the Court in *Labine* v. *Vincent* (p. 857) takes care to distinguish the facts of that case from a previous Warren Court ruling, Levy v. Louisiana, 391 U.S. 68, 88 S.Ct. 1509 (1968), and thereby declines the invitation to bring legislation directly affecting illegitimates within the purview of "strict scrutiny." Through its rulings in *Labine* and subsequent cases, the present Court has indicated what criteria would have to be satisfied for the creation of any additional "suspect classes" beyond that of race (the status of which as a "suspect class" is obvious in view of the background of the Fourteenth Amendment). A recognition of three such conditions has emerged: (1) whether membership in the class "carr[ies] an obvious badge, as race and sex do"; (2) whether treatment of the class members has "approached the severity or pervasiveness of the historic legal and political discrimination against women and Negroes"; and (3) whether the disadvantaged class has been subjected to an "absolute deprivation" of the benefit available to others. The Burger Court has also established a comparable upper-tier limitation on the recognition of "fundamental" rights. As Justice Powell points out in *Rodriguez*, identification of such basic liberties depends upon whether they are "explicitly or implicitly guaranteed by the Constitution" not on "the importance of a service performed by the State * * *."

In view of the first two precepts above, we might expect legislation discriminating on the basis of sex to undergo "strict scrutiny." But in fact, the early treatment of gender-based classifications by the Burger Court reflected considerable ambivalence. In its first encounter with a gender-based classification in Reed v. Reed, 404 U.S. 71, 92 S.Ct. 251 (1971), the Court held unconstitutional an Idaho statute which automatically gave preference to the father over the mother in the appointment of an administrator for the estate of a minor who died without leaving a will. Characterizing the question as "whether a difference in the sex of the competitive applicants for letters of administration bears a *rational* relationship to a state objective that is sought to be advanced" [emphasis supplied], the Court found it to be "the very kind of *arbitrary* legislative choice forbidden by the Equal Protection Clause of the Fourteenth Amendment." [Emphasis supplied.] Two years later, speaking for a plurality that also included Justices Douglas, White, and Marshall, in Frontiero v. Richardson, 411 U.S. 677, 93 S.Ct. 1764 (1973), Justice Brennan concluded that "classifications based upon sex, like classifications based upon race, alienage, and national origin, are inherently suspect and must therefore be subjected to close judicial scrutiny." In that case the Court declared unconstitutional federal statutes which provided that married servicemen automatically qualified to receive increased quarters allowances and medical and dental benefits for their wives, but female personnel in the armed services could not receive these fringe benefits unless their husbands were, in fact, dependent on them for over half their support. Justice Powell, who concurred in the judgment and was joined by Chief Justice Burger and Justice Blackmun, resisted "invoking the strictest test of judicial scrutiny" in view of the fact that the Equal Rights Amendment was then pending and "if adopted will resolve the substance of this precise question * * *." In the years that followed, the Court hopscotched between

Reed and *Frontiero,* alternately citing each as precedent but without any declaration by a majority that gender-based distinctions were in fact "suspect." In *Craig* v. *Boren* (p. 861), a majority of the Court finally agreed but to a different standard, one that has since been characterized variously as "middle-tier" analysis or "intermediate scrutiny." This standard, that the classification in question "must serve important governmental objectives and must be substantially related to the achievement of those objectives," was also employed, you may recall, by Justice Brennan speaking for a four-Justice plurality in *Bakke.*

That the standard of "intermediate scrutiny," articulated in *Craig,* has gained wider acceptance on the Court is apparent from its use most recently in *Plyler* v. *Doe* (p. 887) where a majority relied upon it to strike down state legislation barring the children of illegal aliens from public school. Consider *Plyler* in combination with the Court's decision in *Ambach* v. *Norwick* (p. 881). For the most part, an interest—whether it be a class or a right—is assigned as a unit to a particular tier (see the chart below). Race, for example, is a suspect classification and is, therefore, an upper-tier interest along with the right to vote, which is "fundamental." Indigency and age are nonsuspect classes and, like the nonfundamental right to equal educational opportunity, are consigned to the lower tier. But, given the decisions in *Ambach* and *Plyler,* alienage is a classification whose pieces are spread among all three tiers.

THE COURT'S MULTI–TIER APPROACH TO EQUAL PROTECTION ANALYSIS

Category of Interests	Constitutional Standard	Examples	
		Classifications	Rights
UPPER TIER (Suspect Classifications and Fundamental Rights)	Strict scrutiny	Race (*Bolling,* p. 702) Alienage, generally (*Ambach*)	Vote (*Lucas,* p. 814); *Kramer,* p. 801) Interstate travel (*Shapiro*)
MIDDLE TIER	Intermediate scrutiny	Sex (*Craig*) Race, in affirmative action cases (Brennan in *Bakke,* p. 745) Illegitimacy (p. 861) Alienage, where children of illegal aliens are barred from public education (*Plyler*)	
LOWER TIER (Nonsuspect classifications and nonfundamental rights)	Reasonableness	Indigency (*Rodriquez; Maher,* p. 1215); *McRae,* p. 1217) Age (*Murgia*) Alienage, where a "governmental function" is implicated (*Ambach*)	International travel (*Aznavorian,* p. 839) Education Welfare Housing } (*Rodriguez*)

Finally, consider Justice Marshall's dissenting opinions in *Rodriguez* and *Massachusetts Board of Retirement* v. *Murgia* (p. 874). He has been a persistent critic of the Court's reliance upon two-tier analysis in equal protection cases. Why? Given the Court's recognition now of "intermediate scrutiny" and particularly the approach reflected in the *Ambach* and *Plyler* decisions taken together, has the Court already begun to take significant steps away from the two-tier approach and in the direction of the sliding scale of interests that Marshall advocates? If so, is this a wise and useful development? If the Court has come, in a roundabout way, to accept something akin to the approach Justice Marshall proposes, can it do so and not become a "super-legislature"?

a. RACIAL DISCRIMINATION

PLESSY v. FERGUSON

Supreme Court of the United States, 1896
163 U.S. 537, 16 S.Ct. 1138, 41 L.Ed. 256

In 1890, the Louisiana legislature enacted a statute requiring railroad companies to provide equal but separate accommodations for the white and black races. The law made it a criminal offense for anyone to insist on occupying a seat reserved for passengers of the other race. Plessy, who was seven-eighths white and one-eighth black, refused to relinquish a seat assigned to a white passenger. During the course of his trial, Plessy petitioned the state supreme court to enjoin the trial judge, John Ferguson, from continuing the proceedings against him. The court rejected the petition, whereupon Plessy brought the case to the United States Supreme Court on a writ of error. The 1890 law, Plessy argued, violated the guarantees of the Thirteenth and Fourteenth Amendments.

Mr. Justice BROWN * * * delivered the opinion of the court.

* * *

The constitutionality of this act is attacked upon the ground that it conflicts both with the thirteenth amendment of the constitution, abolishing slavery, and the fourteenth amendment, which prohibits certain restrictive legislation on the part of the states.

1. That it does not conflict with the thirteenth amendment, which abolished slavery and involuntary servitude, except as a punishment for crime, is too clear for argument. Slavery implies involuntary servitude,—a state of bondage; the own-ership of mankind as a chattel, or, at least, the control of the labor and services of one man for the benefit of another, and the absence of a legal right to the disposal of his own person, property, and services. * * *

* * *

A statute which implies merely a legal distinction between the white and colored races—a distinction which is founded in the color of the two races, and which must always exist so long as white men are distinguished from the other race by color—has no tendency to destroy the legal equality of the two races, or reestablish a state of involuntary servitude. Indeed, we do not understand that the thirteenth amendment is strenuously relied upon by the plaintiff in error in this connection.

2. By the fourteenth amendment, all persons born or naturalized in the United States, and subject to the jurisdiction thereof, are made citizens of the United States and of the state wherein they reside; and the states are forbidden from making or enforcing any law which shall abridge the privileges or immunities of citizens of the United States, or shall deprive any person of life, liberty, or property without due process of law, or deny to any person within their jurisdiction the equal protection of the laws.

* * *

The object of the amendment was undoubtedly to enforce the absolute equality of the two races before the law, but, in the nature of things, it could not have been intended to abolish distinctions based upon color, or to enforce social, as distinguished from political, equality, or a commingling of the two races upon terms unsatisfactory to either. Laws permitting, and even requiring, their separation, in places where they are liable to be brought into contact, do not necessarily imply the inferiority of either race to the other, and have been generally, if not universally, recognized as within the competency of the state legislatures in the exercise of their police power. The most common instance of this is connected with the establishment of separate schools for white and colored children, which have been held to be a valid exercise of the legislative power even by courts of states where the political rights of the colored race have been longest and most earnestly enforced.

One of the earliest of these cases is that of Roberts v. City of Boston, 5 Cush. 198, in which the supreme judicial court of Massachusetts held that the general school committee of Boston had power to make provision for the instruction of colored children in separate schools established exclusively for them, and to prohibit their attendance upon the other schools. * * *

Laws forbidding the intermarriage of the two races may be said in a technical sense to interfere with the freedom of contract, and yet have been universally recognized as within the police power of the state. State v. Gibson, 36 Ind. 389.

The distinction between laws interfering with the political equality of the negro and those requiring the separation of the two races in schools, theaters, and railway carriages has been frequently drawn by this court. * * *

* * *

So far, then, as a conflict with the fourteenth amendment is concerned, the case reduces itself to the question whether the statute of Louisiana is a reasonable regulation, and with respect to this there must necessarily be a large discretion on the part of the legislature. In determining the question of reasonableness, it is at liberty to act with reference to the established usages, customs, and traditions of the people, and with a view to the promotion of their comfort, and the preservation of the public peace and good order. Gauged by this standard, we cannot say that a law which authorizes or even requires the separation of the two races in public conveyances is unreasonable, or more obnoxious to the fourteenth amendment than the acts of congress requiring separate schools for colored children in the District of Columbia, the constitutionality of which does not seem to have been questioned, or the corresponding acts of state legislatures.

We consider the underlying fallacy of the plaintiff's argument to consist in the assumption that the enforced separation of the two races stamps the colored race with a badge of inferiority. If this be so, it is not by reason of anything found in the act, but solely because the colored race chooses to put that construction upon it. The argument necessarily assumes that if, as has been more than once the case, and is not unlikely to be so again, the colored race should become the dominant power in the state legislature, and should enact a law in precisely similar terms, it would thereby relegate the white race to an inferior position. We imagine that the white race, at least, would not acquiesce in this assumption. The argument also assumes that social prejudices may be overcome by legislation, and that equal rights cannot be secured to the negro except by an enforced commingling of the two races. We cannot accept this proposition. If the two races are to meet upon terms of social equality, it must be the result of natural affinities, a mutual appreciation of each other's merits, and a voluntary consent of individuals. * * * Legislation is powerless to eradicate racial instincts, or to abolish distinctions based upon physical differences, and the attempt to do so can only result in accentuating the difficulties of the present situation. If the civil and political rights of both races be equal, one cannot be inferior to the other civilly or politically. If one race be inferior to the other socially, the constitution of the United

States cannot put them upon the same plane.

It is true that the question of the proportion of colored blood necessary to constitute a colored person, as distinguished from a white person, is one upon which there is a difference of opinion in the different states; some holding that any visible admixture of black blood stamps the person as belonging to the colored race * * *; others, that it depends upon the preponderance of blood * * *; and still others, that the predominance of white blood must only be in the proportion of three-fourths. * * * But these are questions to be determined under the laws of each state, and are not properly put in issue in this case. Under the allegations of his petition, it may undoubtedly become a question of importance whether, under the laws of Louisiana, the petitioner belongs to the white or colored race.

The judgment of the court below is therefore affirmed.

Mr. Justice BREWER did not hear the argument or participate in the decision of this case.

Mr. Justice HARLAN dissenting.

* * *

In respect of civil rights, common to all citizens, the constitution of the United States does not, I think, permit any public authority to know the race of those entitled to be protected in the enjoyment of such rights. Every true man has pride of race, and under appropriate circumstances, when the rights of others, his equals before the law, are not to be affected, it is his privilege to express such pride and to take such action based upon it as to him seems proper. But I deny that any legislative body or judicial tribunal may have regard to the race of citizens when the civil rights of those citizens are involved. Indeed, such legislation as there here in question is inconsistent not only with that equality of rights which pertains to citizenship, national and state, but with the personal liberty enjoyed by every one within the United States.

The thirteenth amendment does not permit the withholding or the deprivation of any right necessarily inhering in freedom. It not only struck down the institution of slavery as previously existing in the United States, but it prevents the imposition of any burdens or disabilities that constitute badges of slavery or servitude. It decreed universal civil freedom in this country. This court has so adjudged. But, that amendment having been found inadequate to the protection of the rights of those who had been in slavery, it was followed by the fourteenth amendment, which added greatly to the dignity and glory of American citizenship, and to the security of personal liberty. * * * Finally, and to the end that no citizen should be denied, on account of his race, the privilege of participating in the political control of his country * * * was declared by the fifteenth amendment. * * *

These notable additions to the fundamental law were welcomed by the friends of liberty throughout the world. They removed the race line from our governmental systems. * * *

* * *

[I]n view of the constitution, in the eye of the law, there is in this country no superior, dominant, ruling class of citizens. There is no caste here. Our constitution is color-blind,

and neither knows nor tolerates classes among citizens. In respect of civil rights, all citizens are equal before the law. The humblest is the peer of the most powerful. The law regards man as man, and takes no account of his surroundings or of his color when his civil rights as guarantied by the supreme law of the land are involved. It is therefore to be regretted that this high tribunal, the final expositor of the fundamental law of the land, has reached the conclusion that it is competent for a state to regulate the enjoyment by citizens of their civil rights solely upon the basis of race.

* * *

* * * The present decision, it may well be apprehended, will not only stimulate aggressions, more or less brutal and irritating, upon the admitted rights of colored citizens, but will encourage the belief that it is possible, by means of state enactments, to defeat the beneficent purposes which the people of the United States had in view when they adopted the recent amendments of the constitution, by one of which the blacks of this country were made citizens of the United States and of the states in which they respectively reside, and whose privileges and immunities, as citizens, the states are forbidden to abridge. Sixty millions of whites are in no danger from the presence here of eight millions of blacks. The destinies of the two races, in this country, are indissolubly linked together, and the interests of both require that the common government of all shall not permit the seeds of race hate to be planted under the sanction of law. What can more certainly arouse race hate, what more certainly create and perpetuate a

feeling of distrust between these races, than state enactments which, in fact, proceed on the ground that colored citizens are so inferior and degraded that they cannot be allowed to sit in public coaches occupied by white citizens? That, as all will admit, is the real meaning of such legislation as was enacted in Louisiana.

The sure guaranty of the peace and security of each race is the clear, distinct, unconditional recognition by our governments, national and state, of every right that inheres in civil freedom, and of the equality before the law of all citizens of the United States, without regard to race. * * *

* * *

* * * We boast of the freedom enjoyed by our people above all other peoples. But it is difficult to reconcile that boast with a state of the law which, practically, puts the brand of servitude and degradation upon a large class of our fellow citizens,— our equals before the law. The thin disguise of "equal" accommodations for passengers in railroad coaches will not mislead any one, nor atone for the wrong this day done.

* * *

SWEATT v. PAINTER

Supreme Court of the United States, 1950
339 U.S. 629, 70 S.Ct. 848, 94 L.Ed. 1114

Homan Sweatt was denied admission to the University of Texas Law School because he was a Negro. He brought suit against Theophilis Painter and other school officials to compel the university to admit him. The trial court denied the relief sought after extending the case six months to allow Texas time to provide a law school for Negro students. Sweatt refused to attend the new law school and continued his action against the university officials. The trial court's decision against Sweatt was affirmed by the Texas Court of Civil Appeals, and petitioner's subsequent application to the Texas Supreme Court for a writ of error was denied. Sweatt petitioned the United States Supreme Court for certiorari.

Mr. Chief Justice VINSON delivered the opinion of the Court.

* * *

The University of Texas Law School, from which petitioner was excluded, was staffed by a faculty of sixteen full-time and three part-time professors, some of whom are nationally recognized authorities in their field. Its student body numbered 850. The library contained over 65,000 volumes. Among the other facilities available to the students were a law review, moot court facilities, scholarship funds, and Order of the Coif affiliation. The school's alumni occupy the most distinguished positions in the private practice of the law and in the public life of the State. It may properly be considered one of the nation's ranking law schools.

The law school for Negroes which was to have opened in February, 1947, would have had no independent faculty or library. The teaching was to be carried on by four members of the University of Texas Law School faculty, who were to maintain their offices at the University of Texas while teaching at both institutions. Few of the 10,000 volumes ordered for the library had arrived; nor was there any full-time librarian. The school lacked accreditation.

Since the trial of this case, respondents report the opening of a law school at the Texas State University for Negroes. It is apparently on the road to full accreditation. It has a faculty of five full-time professors; a student body of 23; a library of some 16,500 volumes serviced by a full-time staff; a practice court and legal aid association; and one alumnus who has become a member of the Texas Bar.

Whether the University of Texas Law School is compared with the original or the new law school for Negroes, we cannot find substantial equality in the educational opportunities offered white and Negro law students by the State. In terms of number of the faculty, variety of courses and opportunity for specialization, size of the student body, scope of the library, availability of law review and similar activities, the University of Texas Law School is superior. What is more important, the University of Texas Law School possesses to a far greater degree those qualities which are incapable of objective measurement but which make for greatness in a law school. Such qualities, to name but a few, include reputation of the faculty, experience of the administration, position and influence of the alumni, standing in the community, traditions and prestige. It is difficult to believe

that one who had a free choice between these law schools would consider the question close.

Moreover, although the law is a highly learned profession, we are well aware that it is an intensely practical one. The law school, the proving ground for legal learning and practice, cannot be effective in isolation from the individuals and institutions with which the law interacts. Few students and no one who has practiced law would choose to study in an academic vacuum, removed from the interplay of ideas and the exchange of views with which the law is concerned. The law school to which Texas is willing to admit petitioner excludes from its student body members of the racial groups which number 85% of the population of the State and include most of the lawyers, witnesses, jurors, judges and other officials with whom petitioner will inevitably be dealing when he becomes a member of the Texas Bar. With such a substantial and significant segment of society excluded, we cannot conclude that the education offered petitioner is substantially equal to that which he would receive if admitted to the University of Texas Law School.

* * *

We hold that the Equal Protection Clause of the Fourteenth Amendment requires that petitioner be admitted to the University of Texas Law School. The judgment is reversed and the cause is remanded for proceedings not inconsistent with this opinion.

Reversed.

BROWN v. BOARD OF EDUCATION OF TOPEKA I

Supreme Court of the United States, 1954
347 U.S. 483, 74 S.Ct. 686, 98 L.Ed. 873

The facts are set out in the opinion.

Mr. Chief Justice WARREN delivered the opinion of the Court.

These cases come to us from the States of Kansas, South Carolina, Virginia, and Delaware. They are premised on different facts and different local conditions, but a common legal question justifies their consideration together in this consolidated opinion.

In each of the cases, minors of the Negro race, through their legal representatives, seek the aid of the courts in obtaining admission to the public schools of their community on a nonsegregated basis. In each instance, they have been denied admission to schools attended by white children under laws requiring or permitting segregation according to race. This segregation was alleged to deprive the plaintiffs of the equal protection of the laws under the Fourteenth Amendment. In each of the cases other than the Delaware case, a three-judge federal district court denied relief to the plaintiffs on the so-called "separate but equal" doctrine announced by this Court in Plessy v. Ferguson, 163 U.S. 537, 16 S.Ct. 1138. Under that doctrine, equality of treatment is accorded when the races are provided substantially equal facilities, even though these facilities be separate. In the Delaware case, the Supreme Court of Delaware adhered to that doctrine, but ordered that the plaintiffs be admitted to the white schools because of their superiority to the Negro schools.

The plaintiffs contend that segregated public schools are not "equal" and cannot be made "equal," and that hence they are deprived of the equal protection of the laws. Because of the obvious importance of the question presented, the Court took jurisdiction. Argument was heard in the 1952 Term, and reargument was heard this Term on certain questions propounded by the Court.

Reargument was largely devoted to the circumstances surrounding the adoption of the Fourteenth Amendment in 1868. It covered exhaustively consideration of the Amendment in Congress, ratification by the states, then existing practices in racial segregation, and the views of proponents and opponents of the Amendment. This discussion and our own investigation convince us that, although these sources cast some light, it is not enough to resolve the problem with which we are faced. At best, they are inconclusive. The most avid proponents of the post-War Amendments undoubtedly intended them to remove all legal distinctions among "all persons born or naturalized in the United States." Their opponents, just as certainly, were antagonistic to both the letter and the spirit of the Amendments and wished them to have the most limited effect. What others in Congress and the state legislatures had in mind cannot be determined with any degree of certainty.

An additional reason for the inconclusive nature of the Amendment's history, with respect to segregated schools, is the status of public education at that time. In the South, the movement toward free common schools, supported by general taxation, had not yet taken hold. Education of white children was largely in the hands of private groups. Education of Negroes was almost nonexistent, and practically all of the race were illiterate. In fact, any education of Negroes was forbidden by law in some states. Today, in contrast, many Negroes have achieved outstanding success in the arts and sciences as well as in the business and professional world. It is true that public school education at the time of the Amendment had advanced further in the North, but the effect of the Amendment on Northern States was generally ignored in the congressional debates. Even in the North, the conditions of public education did not approximate those existing today. The curriculum was usually rudimentary; ungraded schools were common in rural areas; the school term was but three months a year in many states; and compulsory school attendance was virtually unknown. As a consequence, it is not surprising that there should be so little in the history of the Fourteenth Amendment relating to its intended effect on public education.

In the first cases in this Court construing the Fourteenth Amendment, decided shortly after its adoption, the Court interpreted it as proscribing all state-imposed discriminations against the Negro race. The doctrine of "separate but equal" did not make its appearance in this Court until 1896 in the case of *Plessy* v. *Ferguson,* supra, involving not education but transportation. American courts have since labored with the doctrine for over half a century.

* * *

In the instant cases, that question is directly presented. Here, unlike *Sweatt* v. *Painter,* there are findings below that the Negro and white schools involved have been equalized, or are being equalized, with respect to buildings, curricula, qualifications and salaries of teachers, and other "tangible" factors. Our decision, therefore, cannot turn on merely a comparison of these tangible factors in the Negro and white schools involved in each of the cases. We must look instead to the effect of segregation itself on public education.

In approaching this problem, we cannot turn the clock back to 1868 when the Amendment was adopted, or even to 1896 when *Plessy* v. *Ferguson* was written. We must consider public education in the light of its full development and its present place in American life throughout the Nation. Only in this way can it be determined if segregation in public schools deprives these plaintiffs of the equal protection of the laws.

Today, education is perhaps the most important function of state and local governments. Compulsory school attendance laws and the great expenditures for education both demonstrate our recognition of the importance of education to our democratic society. It is required in the performance of our most basic public responsibilities, even service in the armed forces. It is the very foundation of good citizenship. Today it is a principal instrument in awakening the child to cultural values, in preparing him for later professional training, and in helping him to adjust normally to his environment. In these days, it is doubtful that any child may reasonably be expected to succeed in life if he is denied the opportunity of an education. Such an opportunity, where the state has undertaken to provide it, is a right which must be made available to all on equal terms.

We come then to the question presented: Does segregation of children in public schools solely on the basis of race, even though the physical facilities and other "tangible" factors may be equal, deprive the children of the minority group of equal educational opportunities? We believe that it does.

In Sweatt v. Painter, supra [339 U.S. 629, 70 S.Ct. 850], in finding that a segregated law school for Negroes could not provide them equal educational opportunities, this Court relied in large part on "those qualities which are incapable of objective measurement but which make for greatness in a law school." In McLaurin v. Oklahoma State Regents, supra [339 U.S. 637, 70 S.Ct. 853], the Court, in requiring that a Negro admitted to a white graduate school be treated like all other students, again resorted to intangible considerations: " * * * his ability to study, to engage in discussions and exchange views with other students, and, in general, to learn his profession." Such considerations apply with added force to children in grade and high schools. To separate

them from others of similar age and qualifications solely because of their race generates a feeling of inferiority as to their status in the community that may affect their hearts and minds in a way unlikely ever to be undone. The effect of this separation on their educational opportunities was well stated by a finding in the Kansas case by a court which nevertheless felt compelled to rule against the Negro plaintiffs:

"Segregation of white and colored children in public schools has a detrimental effect upon the colored children. The impact is greater when it has the sanction of the law; for the policy of separating the races is usually interpreted as denoting the inferiority of the Negro group. A sense of inferiority affects the motivation of a child to learn. Segregation with the sanction of law, therefore, has a tendency to [retard] the educational and mental development of Negro children and to deprive them of some of the benefits they would receive in a racial[ly] integrated school system."

Whatever may have been the extent of psychological knowledge at the time of *Plessy* v. *Ferguson*, this finding is amply supported by modern authority.[11] Any language in *Plessy* v. *Ferguson* contrary to this finding is rejected.

We conclude that in the field of public education the doctrine of "separate but equal" has no place. Separate educational facilities are inher-

---

11. K. B. Clark, Effect of Prejudice and Discrimination on Personality Development (Midcentury White House Conference on Children and Youth, 1950); Witmer and Kotinsky, Personality in the Making (1952), c. VI; Deutscher and Chein, The Psychological Effects of Enforced Segregation: A Survey of Social Science Opinion, 26 J.Psychol. 259 (1948);

Chein, What are the Psychological Effects of Segregation Under Conditions of Equal Facilities?, 3 Int.J.Opinion and Attitude Res. 229 (1949); Brameld, Educational Costs in Discrimination and National Welfare (MacIver, ed., 1949), 44–48; Frazier, The Negro in the United States (1949), 674–681. And see generally Myrdal, An American Dilemma (1944).

ently unequal. Therefore, we hold that the plaintiffs and others similarly situated for whom the actions have been brought are, by reason of the segregation complained of, deprived of the equal protection of the laws guaranteed by the Fourteenth Amendment. This disposition makes unnecessary any discussion whether such segregation also violates the Due Process Clause of the Fourteenth Amendment.[12]

Because these are class actions, because of the wide applicability of this decision, and because of the great variety of local conditions, the formulation of decrees in these cases presents problems of considerable complexity. On reargument, the consideration of appropriate relief was necessarily subordinated to the primary question—the constitutionality of segregation in public education. We have now announced that such segregation is a denial of the equal protection of the laws. In order that we may have the full assistance of the parties in formulating decrees, the cases will be restored to the docket, and the parties are requested to present further argument on Questions 4 and 5 previously propounded by the Court for the reargument this Term.[13] The Attorney General of the United States is again invited to participate. The Attorneys General of the states requiring or permitting segregation in public education will also be permitted to appear as *amici curiae* upon request to do so by September 15, 1954, and submission of briefs by October 1, 1954.

It is so ordered.

Cases ordered restored to docket for further argument on question of appropriate decrees.

BOLLING v. SHARPE

Supreme Court of the United States, 1954
347 U.S. 497, 74 S.Ct. 693, 98 L.Ed. 884

The facts are set out in the opinion below.

---

12. See Bolling v. Sharpe, 347 U.S. 497, 74 S.Ct. 693, concerning the Due Process Clause of the Fifth Amendment.

13. "4. Assuming it is decided that segregation in public schools violates the Fourteenth Amendment

"(a) would a decree necessarily follow providing that, within the limits set by normal geographic school districting, Negro children should forthwith be admitted to schools of their choice, or

"(b) may this Court, in the exercise of its equity powers, permit an effective gradual adjustment to be brought about from existing segregated systems to a system not based on color distinctions?

"5. On the assumption on which question 4(a) and (b) are based, and assuming further that this Court will exercise its equity powers to the end described in question 4(b),

"(a) should this Court formulate detailed decrees in these cases;

"(b) if so, what specific issues should the decrees reach;

"(c) should this Court appoint a special master to hear evidence with a view to recommending specific terms for such decrees;

"(d) should this Court remand to the courts of first instance with directions to frame decrees in these cases, and if so what general directions should the decrees of this Court include and what procedures should the courts of first instance follow in arriving at the specific terms of more detailed decrees?"

Mr. Chief Justice WARREN delivered the opinion of the Court.

This case challenges the validity of segregation in the public schools of the District of Columbia. The petitioners, minors of the Negro race, allege that such segregation deprives them of due process of law under the Fifth Amendment. They were refused admission to a public school attended by white children solely because of their race. They sought the aid of the District Court for the District of Columbia in obtaining admission. That court dismissed their complaint. The Court granted a writ of certiorari before judgment in the Court of Appeals because of the importance of the constitutional question presented. * * *

We have this day held that the Equal Protection Clause of the Fourteenth Amendment prohibits the states from maintaining racially segregated public schools. The legal problem in the District of Columbia is somewhat different, however. The Fifth Amendment, which is applicable in the District of Columbia, does not contain an equal protection clause as does the Fourteenth Amendment which applies only to the states. But the concepts of equal protection and due process, both stemming from our American ideal of fairness, are not mutually exclusive. The "equal protection of the laws" is a more explicit safeguard of prohibited unfairness than "due process of law," and, therefore, we do not imply that the two are always interchangeable phrases. But, as this Court has recognized, discrimination may be so unjustifiable as to be violative of due process.

Classifications based solely upon race must be scrutinized with particular care, since they are contrary to our traditions and hence constitutionally suspect. As long ago as 1896, this Court declared the principle "that the constitution of the United States, in its present form, forbids, so far as civil and political rights are concerned, discrimination by the general government, or by the states, against any citizen because of his race." And in Buchanan v. Warley, 245 U.S. 60, 38 S.Ct. 16, the Court held that a statute which limited the right of a property owner to convey his property to a person of another race was, as an unreasonable discrimination, a denial of due process of law.

Although the Court has not assumed to define "liberty" with any great precision, that term is not confined to mere freedom from bodily restraint. Liberty under law extends to the full range of conduct which the individual is free to pursue, and it cannot be restricted except for a proper governmental objective. Segregation in public education is not reasonably related to any proper governmental objective, and thus it imposes on Negro children of the District of Columbia a burden that constitutes an arbitrary deprivation of their liberty in violation of the Due Process Clause.

In view of our decision that the Constitution prohibits the states from maintaining racially segregated public schools, it would be unthinkable that the same Constitution would impose a lesser duty on the Federal Government. We hold that racial segregation in the public schools of the District of Columbia is a denial of the due process of law guaranteed by the Fifth Amendment to the Constitution.

* * *

STELL v. SAVANNAH–CHATHAM COUNTY
BOARD OF EDUCATION

United States District Court,
Southern Dist. of Georgia, 1963
220 F.Supp. 667

The facts are stated in the findings of the U. S. District Court set out below.

SCARLETT, District Judge.

* * *

FINDINGS

The Parties

1. The minor plaintiffs are Negro students in the primary or secondary public schools of Savannah-Chatham County. The minor intervenors are white students in the primary or secondary white schools of Savannah-Chatham County. The defendant Board of Education and the individual defendants are in control of and administer the primary and secondary public schools of Savannah-Chatham County, and have the necessary authority to place in effect any orders of this court with respect thereto.

The Schools

2. The primary and secondary public schools of Savannah-Chatham County are divided into schools for white pupils and schools for Negro pupils. Admission thereto is limited to applicants of the respective races. The evidence does not show any application of any Negroes to schools operated for whites.

3. The teaching and administrative staffs of the white and Negro schools are white and Negro, respectively, up to and including the direct assistant to the superintendent of schools. Principals of both Negro and white schools are part of the superintendent's staff and participate in the adaptation of their particular schools to pupil requirements and the educational effectiveness of the several parts of the school system. The schools are equal in all respects except as to a slight advantage in favor of the Negro teaching staff in terms of graduate training and salaries. The same total curriculum is made available to all schools. Responsiveness to the attitudes and needs of the pupils in each is secured by arranging a choice of elective subjects to be selected by the school on the basis of student request and guidance counseling.

Student-test Grouping

4. All pupils in three significant grades of the Savannah-Chatham County school system have been tested annually since 1954 for psychometric intelligence and correlative academic achievement through a battery of nationally accepted tests administered by local personnel, supervised and processed by the University of Georgia. This program was initiated prior to May, 1954, at the request of the superintendent of schools for Savannah-Chatham County as part of a comprehensive study of mental growth and school achievement for pupil placement and course selection and content recommendations. The result of this testing program has been considered by the Sa-

vannah-Chatham County Board of Education in arranging school curricula responsive to the abilities and learning characteristics of the two student groups.

5. The psychometric-test results have conclusively demonstrated that the differences between white and Negro students in learning capabilities and school performance vary in increasing degree from the preschool period to the completion of high school. The differences between white and Negro students were consistent on all types of tests and increased with chronological age at a predictable and constant rate. The Negro overlap of the median white scores dropped from approximately 15 per cent in the lowest grades to 2 per cent in the highest, and indicated that the Negro group reached an educational plateau approximately four years before the white group. When a special control group was selected for identity of age and intelligence quotient in the lower grades, the Negro students lagged by two to four years when the entire group reached the twelfth grade.

6. The tests covered general intelligence, reading and arithmetic achievement and mental maturity. On the last, the white average was 20 points above the Negro average. The achievement tests showed major ability-pattern differences. On reading comprehension and arithmetic fundamentals there was virtually no overlap between the two groups.

Basis of Test Variations

7. These differences in test results in Savannah-Chatham County are not the result of the educational system or of the social or economic differences in status or in environment of the students. These test results agree on a point-for-point basis with substantially identical results obtained from similar tests made in other areas of this country and abroad, and in both segregated and integrated situations. Additionally, quantitative and qualitative distinctions in the Savannah-Chatham County and other test results have shown the same variation in learning rates between the two ethnic groups, even after the socio-economic factors of the test students have been equated.

8. All the evidence before the Court was to the effect that the differences in test results between the white and Negro students is attributable in large part to hereditary factors, predictably resulting from a difference in the physiological and psychological characteristics of the two races. The evidence establishes, and the court so finds, that of the 20-point difference in maturity-test results between Negro and white students in Savannah-Chatham County a negligible portion can be attributed to environmental factors. Furthermore, no evidence whatsoever was offered to this court to show that racial integration of the schools could reduce these differences. Substantially, all the differences between these two groups of children is inherent in the individuals, and must be dealt with by the defendants as an unchangeable fact or in programing the schools for the best educational results.

Group Integration

9. The students in Savannah-Chatham County schools are 60 per cent white, 40 per cent Negro. A school class mixed on this basis would have a median progress rate 12 points below that of the former white class, and 8 points above the progress rate of the comparable former Negro class. Two thirds of the Negro stu-

dents would fail in this situation, particularly in the upper grades. This would place in the same schoolroom Negro students two to four years older in chronological age than the white students. White students in such a class lose any challenge to further academic accomplishment.

10. Failure to attain the existing white standards would create serious psychological problems of frustration on the part of the Negro child, which would require compensation via tension-creating anti-social behavior. In other cities, this effect has created serious discipline problems for the teachers and school administrators with consequent loss of school time. In New York, 37 per cent of Negro truants questioned in a study stated that they had run away from home because of failure to keep up in school.

11. The congregation of two substantial and identifiable student groups in a single classroom under circumstances of distinct group identification and varying abilities would lead to conflict impairing the educational process. It is essential for an individual to identify himself with a reference group for healthy personality development. Physical and psychological differences are the common basis of group identification; indeed, they compel such self-identification. To increase this divisive tendency, it has been established without contradiction that selective association is a universal human trait; that physically observable racial differences form the basis for preferential association, and that patterns of racial preference are formed and firmly established at a preschool age.

12. The effects of intergroup association are reasonably predictable on the basis of that branch of psychology known as social dynamics. In the case of two identifiable groups in the same classroom, intergroup tensions and conflicts result. These become substantial when the groups have a high identification index in a situation where the difference between them is as great as that existing between white and Negro children in the Savannah-Chatham County schools.

13. In each city referred to in the evidence where large-scale integration had taken place or had existed continuously, the predicted level or even a greater degree of conflict existed and substantially impaired the efficacy of the entire educational system.

14. Total group integration as requested by plaintiffs would seriously injure both white and Negro students in the Savannah-Chatham County schools and adversely affect the educational standards and accomplishments of the public-school system.

Selective Integration

15. Throughout the trial, counsel for plaintiffs emphasized the conceded ability of certain superior Negro children to meet the progress norms of the white classes and implied that at least selective transfers of such students to white schools would not cause injury similar to the effects of group integration. The court finds that such selective integration would cause even greater psychological harm to individual Negro children involved and to the balance of their group.

16. Negro children so transferred would not only lose their right of achievement in their own group but would move to a class where

they would be inescapably conscious of social rejection by the dominant group. Such children must try to identify themselves with the white children while unable to free themselves from continuing identification with other Negro children. Additionally, the children involved, while able to maintain the rate of the white class at first, would according to all of the test results, thereafter tend to fall further back in each succeeding term.

17. The effects on the remaining Negro children would be even more injurious. The loss of the better group members would greatly increase any existing sense of inferiority. The competitive drive to educational accomplishment for those not transferred would be taken away. The court finds that selective integration would cause substantial and irremovable psychological injury both to the individual transferee and to other Negro children.

Segregation Injury

18. Plaintiffs' assumption of injury to Negro students by the continuance of segregated schools is not supported by any evidence in this case. Whatever psychological injury may be sustained by a Negro child out of his sense of rejection by white children is increased rather than abated by forced intermixture, and this increase is in direct proportion to the number and extent of his contacts with white children.

19. Each study presented to the court, confirmed by the opinions of the witnesses, showed that the damaging assumption of inferiority increased whenever the child is brought into forced association with white children. The principal author of the studies relied on by the Supreme Court in the Brown case [Brown v. Board of Education, 1954] used students from integrated schools in Northern States in getting the race-rejection results which were then cited as showing such effects occurring from segregation. Moreover, the same author in an earlier study came to the conclusion that compulsory intermixture rather than racial separation in school was the principle source of damaging loss of race identification.

20. The adverse effects of compulsory congregation are particularly harmful in the early, formative school years. Intervenors' witnesses noted that integration at the collegiate levels is not only possible, but on a voluntary basis might be of advantage to both white and Negro students. The findings herein are accordingly limited to children of primary and secondary-school ages.

Conclusions

1. The white and Negro school children have equivalent rights before this court and are equally entitled to be considered in determining the scope and content of constitutional rights.

2. A reasonable classification within the meaning of the equal-protection clause of the Constitution would be one which secures the maximum result in the educational process for all students, and the minimum injury to any.

3. The classification of children in the Savannah-Chatham County schools by division on the basis of coherent groups having distinguishable educability capabilities is such a reasonable classification.

On appeal, the U. S. Court of Appeals for the Fifth Circuit reversed. See Stell v. Savannah-Chatham County Board of Education, 333 F.2d 55 (5th Cir. 1964). Speaking for a unanimous court, Circuit Judge Griffin Bell said:

> [T]he question presented by the pleadings of the intervenors in the *Savannah* case, the evidence adduced on the hearing therein, and by the ruling of the court thereon * * * is whether a state is forbidden by the equal protection clause of the Fourteenth Amendment from reasonably classifying its children in schools on the basis of their educational aptitudes because the difference in aptitude is also a racial characteristic. We must add for clarity: "with the result that the schools continue separate as to race."

> The District Court answered this question in the negative, on the uncontested facts presented in support of the classification predicate. The conclusion reached was that a reasonable classification within the meaning of the equal protection clause of the Fourteenth Amendment might be secured by division of the schools "on the basis of coherent groups having distinguishable educability capabilities * * * ."

> On the application to this court for interim relief * * * we noted that the District Court permitted the intervention so that proof might be adduced as a factual basis for an effort to ask the Supreme Court to reverse its decision in Brown v. Board of Education, 1954. * * * We also noted that the District Court was bound by the decision of the Supreme Court in *Brown*. We reiterate that no inferior federal court may refrain from acting as required by that decision even if such a court should conclude that the Supreme Court erred either as to its facts or as to the law.
> * * *

> [T]he *Savannah* case ended then [with *Brown I* and *II*] and there it must end now. We do not read the major premise of the decision of the Supreme Court in the first *Brown* case as being limited to the facts of the cases there presented. We read it as proscribing segregation in the public education process on the stated ground that separate but equal schools for the races were inherently unequal. This being our interpretation of the teaching of that decision, it follows that it would be entirely inappropriate for it to be rejected or obviated by this court. * * *

> In this connection, it goes without saying that there is no constitutional prohibition against an assignment of individual students to particular schools on a basis of intelligence, achievement or other aptitudes upon a uniformly administered program, but race must not be a factor in making the assignments. However, this is a question for educators and not courts.

> The real fallacy, Constitutionwise, of the classification theory is that many of the Negro pupils overlap many of the white pupils in achievement and aptitude but are nevertheless to be segregated on the basis of race. They are to be separated, regardless of how great their ability as individuals, into schools with members of their own race because of the differences in test averages as between the races. Therein is the discrimination. The individual Negro student is not to be treated as an individual and allowed to proceed along with other individuals on the basis of ability alone without regard to race.

* * *

BROWN v. BOARD OF EDUCATION OF TOPEKA II

Supreme Court of the United States, 1955
349 U.S. 294, 75 S.Ct. 753, 99 L.Ed. 1083

The facts are set out in the opinion.

Mr. Chief Justice WARREN delivered the opinion of the Court.

These cases were decided on May 17, 1954. The opinions of that date, declaring the fundamental principle that racial discrimination in public education is unconstitutional, are incorporated herein by reference. All provisions of federal, state, or local law requiring or permitting such discrimination must yield to this principle. There remains for consideration the manner in which relief is to be accorded.

Because these cases arose under different local conditions and their disposition will involve a variety of local problems, we requested further argument on the question of relief. In view of the nationwide importance of the decision, we invited the Attorney General of the United States and the Attorneys General of all states requiring or permitting racial discrimination in public education to present their views on that question. The parties, the United States, and the States of Florida, North Carolina, Arkansas, Oklahoma, Maryland, and Texas filed briefs and participated in the oral argument.

These presentations were informative and helpful to the Court in its consideration of the complexities arising from the transition to a system of public education freed of racial discrimination. The presentations also demonstrated that substantial steps to eliminate racial discrimination in public schools have already been taken, not only in some of the communities in which these cases arose, but in some of the states appearing as *amici curiae*, and in other states as well. Substantial progress has been made in the District of Columbia and in the communities in Kansas and Delaware involved in this litigation. The defendants in the cases coming to us from South Carolina and Virginia are awaiting the decision of this Court concerning relief.

Full implementation of these constitutional principles may require solution of varied local school problems. School authorities have the primary responsibility for elucidating, assessing, and solving these problems; courts will have to consider whether the action of school authorities constitutes good faith implementation of the governing constitutional principles. Because of their proximity to local conditions and the possible need for further hearings, the courts which originally heard these cases can best perform this judicial appraisal. Accordingly, we believe it appropriate to remand the cases to those courts.

In fashioning and effectuating the decrees, the courts will be guided by equitable principles. Traditionally, equity has been characterized by a practical flexibility in shaping its remedies and by a facility for adjusting and reconciling public and private needs. These cases call for the exercise of these traditional attributes of equity power. At stake is the personal interest of the plaintiffs in admission to public schools as soon as practicable on a nondiscriminatory basis. To effectuate this interest may call for elimination of a variety of obstacles in making the transition to school systems operated in accordance with the constitutional principles set forth in our May 17, 1954, decision. Courts of equity may properly take into account the public interest in the elimination of such obstacles in a systematic and effective manner. But it should go without saying that the vitality of these constitutional principles cannot be allowed to yield simply because of disagreement with them.

While giving weight to these public and private considerations, the courts will require that the defendants make a prompt and reasonable start toward full compliance with our May 17, 1954, ruling. Once such a start has been made, the courts may find that additional time is necessary to carry out the ruling in an effective manner. The burden rests upon the defendants to establish that such time is necessary in the public interest and is consistent with good faith compliance at the earliest practicable date. To that end, the courts may consider problems related to administration, arising from the physical condition of the school plant, the school transportation system, personnel, revision of school districts and attendance areas into compact units

to achieve a system of determining admission to the public schools on a nonracial basis, and revision of local laws and regulations which may be necessary in solving the foregoing problems. They will also consider the adequacy of any plans the defendants may propose to meet these problems and to effectuate a transition to a racially nondiscriminatory school system. During this period of transition, the courts will retain jurisdiction of these cases.

The judgments below, except that in the Delaware case, are accordingly reversed and the cases are remanded to the District Courts to take such proceedings and enter such orders and decrees consistent with this opinion as are necessary and proper to admit to public schools on a racially nondiscriminatory basis with all deliberate speed the parties to these cases. The judgment in the Delaware case—ordering the immediate admission of the plaintiffs to schools previously attended only by white children—is affirmed on the basis of the principles stated in our May 17, 1954, opinion, but the case is remanded to the Supreme Court of Delaware for such further proceedings as that Court may deem necessary in light of this opinion.

It is so ordered.

*   *   *

COOPER v. AARON

Supreme Court of the United States, 1958
358 U.S. 1, 78 S.Ct. 1401, 3 L.Ed.2d 5

In February 1958, William Cooper, along with other members of the Little Rock School Board and the Superintendent of Schools, filed a petition in federal district court for a two-and-one-half-year postponement of their program for school desegregation. They argued that public hostility to desegregation was so intense that Central High School could no longer offer a sound educational program. To end the disruption they proposed that John Aaron and other Negro students, who had enrolled in the school in September 1957 under the plan, be transferred to segregated schools. The controversy in this case arose out of attempts by the Governor of Arkansas and the state legislature to frustrate the implementation of the Board's court-approved desegregation program.

In an effort to comply with the Supreme Court's decisions in *Brown* v. *Board of Education*, school officials had devised a plan in 1955 that called for complete desegregation of the school system by 1963. The first stage of the plan scheduled the admission of nine Negro students to Central High School on September 3, 1957. There were several indications that the plan would succeed. From discussions with citizen groups, the school board was able to conclude that the large majority of citizens thought that desegregation was in the best interests of the students. The mayor believed that the police force was adequate to deal with any incidents, and up until two days prior to the opening of school, there had been no crowds gathering or threats of violence. State government officials, however, had already adopted measures designed to maintain segregated schools in the state. In 1956, an amendment was added to the Arkansas Constitution which required the General Assembly to oppose "in every constitutional manner" the Supreme Court decisions in the two *Brown* cases. In February 1957, the legislature passed laws making attendance at racially mixed schools voluntary and establishing a State Sovereignty Commission. And finally, on September 2, 1957, Governor Orval Faubus sent Arkansas national guard units to Little Rock to prevent Negro students from attending the high school. This unsolicited action, which considerably escalated the opposition of the city's residents to the plan, prompted the Board to request that Negro students not attend Central High School and to petition the federal district court for instructions. Although the district court ordered school officials to proceed with the desegregation program, the national guard continued to prevent Negro students from attending the school. An investigation was ordered, hearings were held, and on September 20, the district court enjoined the Governor and the national guard from interfering with the plan. On September 23, Negro students attended the high school under police protection but were later withdrawn that day when it became too difficult for the police to control crowds that gathered around the school. Two days later the students were once again admitted, this time under the protection of federal troops sent to Little Rock by President Eisenhower to enforce the order of the federal district court.

It was because of these events and the general disruption of education in the school, which the Board attributed to the actions of the Governor and the General Assembly, that Cooper and the others petitioned the district court for the postponement. The district court ruled favorably on the petition and was reversed on appeal by the U. S. Court of Appeals for the Eighth Circuit.

Opinion of the Court by The CHIEF JUSTICE [WARREN], Mr. Justice BLACK, Mr. Justice FRANKFURTER, Mr. Justice DOUGLAS, Mr. Justice BURTON, Mr. Justice CLARK, Mr. Justice HARLAN, Mr. Justice BRENNAN, and Mr. Justice WHITTAKER.

As this case reaches us it raises questions of the highest importance to the maintenance of our federal system of government. It necessarily involves a claim by the Governor and Legislature of a State that there is no duty on state officials to obey federal court orders resting on this Court's considered interpretation of the United States Constitution. Specifically it involves actions by the Governor and Legislature of Arkansas upon the premise that they are not bound by our holding in Brown v. Board of Education, 347 U.S. 483, 74 S.Ct. 686. That holding was that the Fourteenth Amendment forbids States to use their governmental powers to bar children on racial grounds from attending schools where there is state participation through any arrangement, management, funds or property. We are urged to uphold a suspension of the Little Rock School Board's plan to do away with segregated public schools in Little Rock until state laws and efforts to upset and nullify our holding in *Brown* v. *Board of Education* have been further challenged and tested in the courts. We reject these contentions.

*   *   *

In affirming the judgment of the Court of Appeals which reversed the District Court we have accepted without reservation the position of the School Board, the Superintendent of Schools, and their counsel that they displayed entire good faith in the conduct of these proceedings and in dealing with the unfortunate and distressing sequence of events which has been outlined. We likewise have accepted the findings of the District Court as to the conditions at Central High School during the 1957–1958 school year, and also the findings that the educational progress of all the students, white and colored, of that school has suffered and will continue to suffer if the conditions which prevailed last year are permitted to continue.

The significance of these findings, however, is to be considered in light of the fact, indisputably revealed by the record before us, that the conditions they depict are directly traceable to the actions of legislators and executive officials of the State of Arkansas, taken in their official capacities, which reflect their own determination to resist this Court's decision in the *Brown* case and which have brought about violent resistance to that decision in Arkansas. In its petition for certiorari

filed in this Court, the School Board itself describes the situation in this language: "The legislative, executive, and judicial departments of the state government opposed the desegregation of Little Rock schools by enacting laws, calling out troops, making statements villifying federal law and federal courts, and failing to utilize state law enforcement agencies and judicial processes to maintain public peace."

One may well sympathize with the position of the Board in the face of the frustrating conditions which have confronted it, but, regardless of the Board's good faith, the actions of the other state agencies responsible for those conditions compel us to reject the Board's legal position. Had Central High School been under the direct management of the State itself, it could hardly be suggested that those immediately in charge of the school should be heard to assert their own good faith as a legal excuse for delay in implementing the constitutional rights of these respondents, when vindication of those rights was rendered difficult or impossible by the actions of other state officials. The situation here is in no different posture because the members of the School Board and the Superintendent of Schools are local officials; from the point of view of the Fourteenth Amendment, they stand in this litigation as the agents of the State.

The constitutional rights of respondents are not to be sacrificed or yielded to the violence and disorder which have followed upon the actions of the Governor and Legislature. As this Court said some 41 years ago in a unanimous opinion in a case involving another aspect of racial segregation: "It is urged that this proposed segregation will promote the public peace by preventing race conflicts. Desirable as this is, and important as is the preservation of the public peace, this aim cannot be accomplished by laws or ordinances which deny rights created or protected by the federal Constitution." * * * Thus law and order are not here to be preserved by depriving the Negro children of their constitutional rights. The record before us clearly establishes that the growth of the Board's difficulties to a magnitude beyond its unaided power to control is the product of state action. Those difficulties, as counsel for the Board forthrightly conceded on the oral argument in this Court, can also be brought under control by state action.

The controlling legal principles are plain. The command of the Fourteenth Amendment is that no "State" shall deny to any person within its jurisdiction the equal protection of the laws. "A State acts by its legislative, its executive, or its judicial, authorities. It can act in no other way. The constitutional provision, therefore, must mean that no agency of the State, or of the officers or agents by whom its powers are exerted, shall deny to any person within its jurisdiction the equal protection of the laws. Whoever, by virtue of public position under a State government * * * denies or takes away the equal protection of the laws, violates the constitutional inhibition; and as he acts in the name and for the State, and is clothed with the State's power, his act is that of the State. This must be so, or the constitutional prohibition has no meaning." * * *

Thus the prohibitions of the Fourteenth Amendment extend to all action of the State denying equal protection of the laws; whatever the agency of the State taking the action; * * * or whatever the guise in which it is taken. * * * In short, the constitutional rights of children not to be discriminated against in school admission on grounds of race or color declared by this Court in the *Brown* case can neither be nullified openly and directly by state legislators or state executive or judicial officers, nor nullified indirectly by them through evasive schemes for segregation whether attempted "ingeniously or ingenuously." * * *

What has been said, in the light of the facts developed, is enough to dispose of the case. However, we should answer the premise of the actions of the Governor and Legislature that they are not bound by our holding in the *Brown* case. It is necessary only to recall some basic constitutional propositions which are settled doctrine.

Article VI of the Constitution makes the Constitution the "supreme Law of the Land." In 1803, Chief Justice Marshall, speaking for a unanimous Court, referring to the Constitution as "the fundamental and paramount law of the nation," declared in the notable case of Marbury v. Madison * * * that "It is emphatically the province and duty of the judicial department to say what the law is." This decision declared the basic principle that the federal judiciary is supreme in the exposition of the law of the Constitution, and that principle has ever since been respected by this Court and the Country as a permanent and indispensable feature of our constitutional system. It follows that the interpretation of the Fourteenth Amendment enunciated by this Court in the *Brown* case is the supreme law of the land, and Art. VI of the

Constitution makes it of binding effect on the States "any Thing in the Constitution or Laws of any State to the Contrary notwithstanding." Every state legislator and executive and judicial officer is solemnly committed by oath taken pursuant to Art. VI, ¶ 3 "to support this Constitution." Chief Justice Taney, speaking for a unanimous Court in 1859, said that this requirement reflected the framers' "anxiety to preserve it [the Constitution] in full force, in all its powers, and to guard against resistance to or evasion of its authority, on the part of a State." * * *

No state legislator or executive or judicial officer can war against the Constitution without violating his undertaking to support it. Chief Justice Marshall spoke for a unanimous Court in saying that: "If the legislatures of the several states may, at will, annul the judgments of the courts of the United States, and destroy the rights acquired under those judgments, the constitution itself becomes a solemn mockery." * * *

It is, of course, quite true that the responsibility for public education is primarily the concern of the States, but it is equally true that such responsibilities, like all other state activity, must be exercised consistently with federal constitutional requirements as they apply to state action.

The Constitution created a government dedicated to equal justice under law. The Fourteenth Amendment embodied and emphasized that ideal. State support of segregated schools through any arrangement, management, funds, or property cannot be squared with the Amendment's command that no State shall deny to any person within its jurisdiction the equal protection of the laws. The right of a student not to be segregated on racial grounds in schools so maintained is indeed so fundamental and pervasive that it is embraced in the concept of due process of law. * * * The basic decision in *Brown* was unanimously reached by this Court only after the case had been briefed and twice argued and the issues had been given the most serious consideration. Since the first *Brown* opinion three new Justices have come to the Court. They are at one with the Justices still on the Court who participated in that basic decision as to its correctness, and that decision is now unanimously reaffirmed. The principles announced in that decision and the obedience of the States to them, according to the command of the Constitution, are indispensable for the protection of the freedoms guaranteed by our fundamental charter for all of us. Our constitutional ideal of equal justice under law is thus made a living truth.

SWANN v. CHARLOTTE-MECKLENBURG BOARD OF EDUCATION

Supreme Court of the United States, 1971
402 U.S. 1, 91 S.Ct. 1267, 28 L.Ed.2d 554

Under a desegregation plan approved by a federal district court in 1965 for the Charlotte-Mecklenburg school system in North Carolina, nearly 60 percent of the Negro students attended schools that were at least 99 percent black (approximately 71 percent of the students in the entire school system were white). James Swann and others initiated proceedings in federal district court seeking further desegregation of the school system. The school board and a court-appointed expert, Dr. John Finger, each submitted a desegregation plan for approval. The district court accepted a modified version of the board's plan for the faculty and for the secondary schools and Finger's plan for the elementary schools. The court-approved plan, which was essentially the Finger plan, called for a greater degree of desegregation than the board was willing to accept. An appeal was taken to the U.S. Circuit Court of Appeals where that part of the district court's order relating to the faculty and secondary schools was affirmed and that part of the order relating to the elementary schools was vacated because the latter, according to the circuit court, would place an unreasonable burden on the board and the students. After further court proceedings and consideration of additional desegregation plans, the district court ordered that the Finger plan be put into effect. Both parties petitioned the Supreme Court for a writ of certiorari.

Mr. Chief Justice BURGER delivered the opinion of the Court.

*   *   *

This case and those argued with it arose in States having a long history of maintaining two sets of schools in a single school system deliberately operated to carry out a governmental policy to separate pupils in schools solely on the basis of race. That was what *Brown* v. *Board of Education* was all about. These cases present us with the problem of defining in more precise terms than heretofore the scope of the duty of school authorities and district courts in implementing *Brown I* and the mandate to eliminate dual systems and establish unitary systems at once. *   *   *

*   *   *

Nearly 17 years ago this Court held, in explicit terms, that state-imposed segregation by race in public schools denies equal protection of the laws. At no time has the Court deviated in the slightest degree from that holding or its constitutional underpinnings. *   *   *

*   *   *

Over the 16 years since *Brown II*, many difficulties were encountered in implementation of the basic constitutional requirement that the State

not discriminate between public school children on the basis of their race. Nothing in our national experience prior to 1955 prepared anyone for dealing with changes and adjustments of the magnitude and complexity encountered since then. Deliberate resistance of some to the Court's mandates has impeded the good-faith efforts of others to bring school systems into compliance. The detail and nature of these dilatory tactics have been noted frequently by this Court and other courts.

By *   *   * 1968, very little progress had been made in many areas where dual school systems had historically been maintained by operation of state laws. *   *   *

*   *   *

The objective today remains to eliminate from the public schools all vestiges of state-imposed segregation. Segregation was the evil struck down by *Brown I* as contrary to the equal protection guarantees of the Constitution. That was the violation sought to be corrected by the remedial measures of *Brown II*. *   *   *

If school authorities fail in their affirmative obligations under these holdings, judicial authority may be invoked. Once a right and a violation have been shown, the scope of a district court's equitable powers to remedy past wrongs is broad, for breadth and flexibility are inherent in equitable remedies.

* * *

School authorities are traditionally charged with broad power to formulate and implement educational policy and might well conclude, for example, that in order to prepare students to live in a pluralistic society each school should have a prescribed ratio of Negro to white students reflecting the proportion for the district as a whole. To do this as an educational policy is within the broad discretionary powers of school authorities; absent a finding of a constitutional violation, however, that would not be within the authority of a federal court. * * *

The school authorities argue that the equity powers of federal district courts have been limited by Title IV of the Civil Rights Act of 1964, 42 U.S.C.A. § 2000c et seq. The language and the history of Title IV show that it was enacted not to limit but to define the role of the Federal Government in the implementation of the *Brown I* decision. It authorizes the Commissioner of Education to provide technical assistance to local boards in the preparation of desegregation plans, to arrange "training institutes" for school personnel involved in desegregation efforts, and to make grants directly to schools to ease the transition to unitary systems. It also authorizes the Attorney General, in specified circumstances, to initiate federal desegregation suits. Section 2000c(b) defines "desegregation" as it is used in Title IV:

" 'Desegregation' means the assignment of students to public schools and within such schools without re-

gard to their race, color, religion, or national origin, but 'desegregation' shall not mean the assignment of students to public schools in order to overcome racial imbalance."

Section 2000c–6, authorizing the Attorney General to institute federal suits, contains the following proviso:

"nothing herein shall empower any official or court of the United States to issue any order seeking to achieve a racial balance in any school by requiring the transportation of pupils or students from one school to another or one school district to another in order to achieve such racial balance, or otherwise enlarge the existing power of the court to insure compliance with constitutional standards."

On their face, the sections quoted support only to insure that the provisions of Title IV of the Civil Rights Act of 1964 will not be read as granting new powers. The proviso in § 2000c–6 is in terms designed to foreclose any interpretation of the Act as expanding the *existing* powers of federal courts to enforce the Equal Protection Clause. There is no suggestion of an intention to restrict those powers or withdraw from courts their historic equitable remedial powers. The legislative history of Title IV indicates that Congress was concerned that the Act might be read as creating a right of action under the Fourteenth Amendment in the situation of so-called "de facto segregation," where racial imbalance exists in the schools but with no showing that this was brought about by discriminatory action of state authorities. In short, there is nothing in the Act that provides us material assistance in answering the question of remedy for state-imposed segregation in violation of *Brown I*. The basis of our decision must be the prohibition of the Fourteenth Amendment that no State shall "deny to any person within its jurisdiction the equal protection of the laws."

We turn now to the problem of defining with more particularity the responsibilities of school authorities in desegregating a state-enforced dual school system in light of the Equal Protection Clause. Although the several related cases before us are primarily concerned with problems of student assignment, it may be helpful to begin with a brief discussion of other aspects of the process. * * * Independent of student assignment where it is possible to identify a "white school" or a "Negro school" simply by reference to the racial composition of teachers and staff, the quality of school buildings and equipment, or the organization of sports activities, a *prima facie* case of violation of substantive constitutional rights under the Equal Protection Clause is shown.

When a system has been dual in these respects, the first remedial responsibility of school authorities is to eliminate invidious racial distinctions. With respect to such matters as transportation, supporting personnel, and extracurricular activities, no more than this may be necessary. Similar corrective action must be taken with regard to the maintenance of buildings and the distribution of equipment. In these areas, normal administrative practice should produce schools of like quality, facilities, and staffs. Something more must be said, however, as to faculty assignment and new school construction.

In the companion *Davis* case, 402 U.S. 33, 91 S.Ct. 1289, the Mobile school board has argued that the Constitution requires that teachers be assigned on a "color blind" basis.

It also argues that the Constitution prohibits district courts from using their equity power to order assignment of teachers to achieve a particular degree of faculty desegregation. We reject that contention.

* * *

The central issue in this case is that of student assignment, and there are essentially four problem areas:

(1) to what extent racial balance or racial quotas may be used as an implement in a remedial order to correct a previously segregated system;

(2) whether every all-Negro and all-white school must be eliminated as an indispensable part of a remedial process of desegregation;

(3) what the limits are, if any, on the rearrangement of school districts and attendance zones, as a remedial measure; and

(4) what the limits are, if any, on the use of transportation facilities to correct state-enforced racial school segregation.

(1) *Racial Balances or Racial Quotas.*

* * *

We see therefore that the use made of mathematical ratios was no more than a starting point in the process of shaping a remedy, rather than an inflexible requirement. From that starting point the District Court proceeded to frame a decree that was within its discretionary powers, as an equitable remedy for the particular circumstances. As we said in *Green*, a school authority's remedial plan or a district court's remedial decree is to be judged by its effectiveness. Awareness of the racial composition of the whole school system is likely to be a useful starting point in shaping a remedy to correct past constitutional violations. In sum, the very limited use made of mathematical ratios was within the equitable remedial discretion of the District Court.

(2) *One-race Schools.*

* * *

[I]t should be clear that the existence of some small number of one-race, or virtually one-race, schools within a district is not in and of itself the mark of a system that still practices segregation by law. The district judge or school authorities should make every effort to achieve the greatest possible degree of actual desegregation and will thus necessarily be concerned with the elimination of one-race schools. No *per se* rule can adequately embrace all the difficulties of reconciling the competing interests involved; but in a system with a history of segregation the need for remedial criteria of sufficient specificity to assure a school authority's compliance with its constitutional duty warrants a presumption against schools that are substantially disproportionate in their racial composition. * * *

An optional majority-to-minority transfer provision has long been recognized as a useful part of every desegregation plan. Provision for optional transfer of those in the majority racial group of a particular school to other schools where they will be in the minority is an indispensable remedy for those students willing to transfer to other schools in order to lessen the impact on them of the state-imposed stigma of segregation. In order to be effective, such a transfer arrangement must grant the transferring student free transportation and space must be made available in the school to which he desires

to move. * * * The court orders in this and the companion *Davis* case now provide such an option.

(3) *Remedial Altering of Attendance Zones.*

* * *

We hold that the pairing and grouping of noncontiguous school zones is a permissible tool and such action is to be considered in light of the objectives sought. Judicial steps in shaping such zones going beyond combinations of contiguous areas should be examined in light of what is said in subdivisions (1), (2) and (3) of this opinion concerning the objectives to be sought. Maps do not tell the whole story since noncontiguous school zones may be more accessible to each other in terms of the critical travel time, because of traffic patterns and good highways, than schools geographically closer together. Conditions in different localities will vary so widely that no rigid rules can be laid down to govern all situations.

(4) *Transportation of Students.*

* * *

The importance of bus transportation as a normal and accepted tool of educational policy is readily discernible in this and the companion case *Davis*, supra. The Charlotte school authorities did not purport to assign students on the basis of geographically drawn zones until 1965 and then they allowed almost unlimited transfer privileges. The District Court's conclusion that assignment of children to the school nearest their home serving their grade would not produce an effective dismantling of the dual system is supported by the record.

Thus the remedial techniques used in the District Court's order were within that court's power to provide equitable relief; implementation of the decree is well within the capacity of the school authority.

The decree provided that the buses used to implement the plan would operate on direct routes. Students would be picked up at schools near their homes and transported to the schools they were to attend. The trips for elementary school pupils average about seven miles and the District Court found that they would take "not over 35 minutes at the most." This system compares favorably with the transportation plan previously operated in Charlotte under which each day 23,600 students on all grade levels were transported an average of 15 miles one way for an average trip requiring over an hour. In these circumstances, we find no basis for holding that the local school authorities may not be required to employ bus transportation as one tool of school desegregation. Desegregation plans cannot be limited to the walk-in school.

An objection to transportation of students may have validity when the time or distance of travel is so great as to either risk the health of the children or significantly impinge on the educational process. District courts must weigh the soundness of any transportation plan in light of what is said in subdivisions (1), (2), and (3) above. It hardly needs stating that the limits on time of travel will vary with many factors, but probably with none more than the age of the students. The reconciliation of competing values in a desegregation case is, of course, a difficult task with many sensitive facets but fundamentally no more so than remedial measures courts of equity have traditionally employed.

*　*　* On the facts of this case, we are unable to conclude that the order of the District Court is not reasonable, feasible and workable. However, in seeking to define the scope of remedial power or the limits on remedial power of courts in an area as sensitive as we deal with here, words are poor instruments to convey the sense of basic fairness inherent in equity. Substance, not semantics, must govern, and we have sought to suggest the nature of limitations without frustrating the appropriate scope of equity.

At some point, these school authorities and others like them should have achieved full compliance with this Court's decision in *Brown I.* The systems would then be "unitary" in the sense required by our decisions in *Green* and *Alexander.*

It does not follow that the communities served by such systems will remain demographically stable, for in a growing, mobile society, few will do so. Neither school authorities nor district courts are constitutionally required to make year-by-year adjustments of the racial composition of student bodies once the affirmative duty to desegregate has been accomplished and racial discrimination through official action is eliminated from the system. This does not mean that federal courts are without power to deal with future problems; but in the absence of a showing that either the school authorities or some other agency of the State has deliberately attempted to fix or alter demographic patterns to affect the racial composition of the schools, further intervention by a district court should not be necessary.

For the reasons herein set forth, the judgment of the Court of Appeals is affirmed as to those parts in which it affirmed the judgment of the District Court. The order of the District Court, dated August 7, 1970, is also affirmed. It is so ordered.

* * *

During the desegregation controversy involving the Charlotte-Mecklenburg school system, the North Carolina legislature enacted a law which prohibited busing and the assignment of students to schools for the purpose of achieving racial balance. Swann sought relief against the statute before a federal district court. The court declared the statute unconstitutional and enjoined its enforcement, whereupon the state board of education appealed to the Supreme Court. In North Carolina State Board of Education v. Swann, 402 U.S. 43, 91 S.Ct. 1284 (1971), the Supreme Court affirmed the decision of the district court. Speaking for a unanimous Court, Chief Justice Burger said:

We observed in *Swann* * * * that school authorities have wide discretion in formulating school policy, and that as a matter of educational policy school authorities may well conclude that some kind of racial balance in the schools is desirable quite apart from any constitutional requirements. However, if a state-imposed limitation on a school authority's discretion operates to inhibit or obstruct the operation of a unitary school system or impede the disestablishing of a dual school system, it must fall; state policy must give way when it operates to hinder vindication of federal constitutional guarantees.

The legislation before us flatly forbids assignment of any student on account of race or for the purpose of creating a racial balance or ratio in the schools. The prohibition is absolute, and it would inescapably operate to obstruct the remedies granted by the District Court in the *Swann* case. But more important the statute exploits an apparently neutral form to control school assignment plans by directing that they be "color blind"; that requirement, against the background of segregation, would render illusory the promise of Brown v. Board of Education. * * * Just as the race of students must be considered in determining whether a constitutional violation has occurred, so also must race be considered in formulating a remedy. To forbid, at this stage, all assignments made on the basis of race would deprive school authorities of the one tool absolutely essential to fulfillment of their constitutional obligation to eliminate existing dual school systems.

Similarly, the flat prohibition against assignment of students for the purpose of creating a racial balance must inevitably conflict with the duty of school authorities to disestablish dual school systems. As we have held in *Swann*, the Constitution does not compel any particular degree of racial balance or mixing, but when past and continuing constitutional violations are found, some ratios are likely to be useful starting points in shaping a remedy. An absolute prohibition against use of such a device—even as a starting point—contravenes the implicit command * * * that all reasonable methods be available to formulate an effective remedy.

We likewise conclude that an absolute prohibition against transportation of students assigned on the basis of race, "or for the purpose of creating a balance or ratio," will similarly hamper the ability of local authorities to effectively remedy constitutional violations. As noted in *Swann*, * * * bus transportation has long been an integral part of all public educational systems, and it is unlikely that a truly effective remedy could be devised without continued reliance upon it.

SCHOOL DESEGREGATION CASES, 1968–1973

Green v. County School Bd. of New Kent Cty., Va., 391 U.S. 430, 88 S.Ct. 1689 (1968)	Facts	In response to *Brown*, school board adopted a "freedom of choice" plan which allowed a pupil to choose his own school for the purpose of creating a system of determining admission on a nonracial basis.
	Vote	9–0
	Ruling	Where not a single white student had chosen to attend a "former" Negro public school during the three-year existence of the program and 85 percent of the Negro children in the system still attended that school, the plan failed to comply with the directive in *Brown*, and the school board must immediately formulate a new response which promises to produce realistic and prompt desegregation.
Wright v. Council of City of Emporia, 407 U.S. 451, 92 S.Ct. 2196 (1972)	Facts	Two weeks after a federal district court ordered public schools throughout the county to implement a court-approved desegregation plan, the city decided to exercise its option under Virginia law to operate its own separate school system.
	Vote	5–4
	Ruling	District court injunction against creation of separate school system upheld. "[A] new school district may not be created where its effect would be to impede the process of dismantling a dual system."
	Dissenting Opinion	Chief Justice Burger, joined by Justices Blackmun, Powell, and Rehnquist, believed that the record did not support such findings and concluded that "the District Court abused its discretion in preventing Emporia from exercising its lawful right to provide for the education of its own children." "Local control is not only vital to continued public control of the schools, but it is of overriding importance from an educational standpoint as well." The district court's discretion is particularly limited "where, as here, it deals with separate political entities. * * * To bar the city of Emporia from operating its own school system, is to strip it of its most important govern-

Wright (*Cont.*)	Dissenting Opinion (*Cont.*)	mental responsibility, and thus largely to deny its existence as an independent governmental entity."
United States v. Scotland Neck City Bd. of Educ., 407 U.S. 484, 92 S.Ct. 2214 (1972)	Facts	A North Carolina statute authorized creation of a new school district for Scotland Neck, a city which at the time was part of a larger school district then in the process of dismantling a dual school system.
	Vote	9–0
	Ruling	The statute would have the effect of carving out of the existing district a new district which would be 57 percent white and 43 percent Negro, while leaving the remainder of the original district 89 percent Negro, and thus clearly impede the dismantling of a dual system.
	Concurring Opinion	Chief Justice Burger, joined by Justices Blackmun, Powell, and Rehnquist, specifically distinguished the decision in this case from that in *Emporia* on grounds that "Scotland Neck's action cannot be seen as the fulfillment of its destiny as an independent governmental entity. * * * The movement toward the creation of a separate school system in Scotland Neck was prompted solely by the likelihood of desegregation in the county, not by any change in the political status of the municipality." "[I]t is undisputed, that the Scotland Neck severance was substantially motivated by the desire to create a predominantly white system more acceptable to the parents of Scotland Neck."
Keyes v. School Dist. No. 1, Denver, Colo., 413 U.S. 189, 93 S.Ct. 2686 (1973)	Facts	(First school desegregation case to reach the Court involving a major city outside the South.) Marked difference in racial composition of public schools depending on the area of the city, it was argued, resulted from discriminatory practices of city school authorities (rather than from any state laws or local zoning or housing ordinances).
	Vote	7–1
	Ruling	1. Hispanos "constitute an identifiable class for purposes of the Fourteenth Amendment" and, as a minority, "have a great many things in common" with blacks. "[S]chools with a combined predominance of Negroes and Hispanos" can be "included in the category of 'segregated' schools." 2. "[A] finding of intentionally segregative school board actions in a meaningful portion of a school system, as in this case, creates a presumption that other segregated schooling within the system is not adventitious. It establishes, in other words, a prima facie case

| Keyes *(Cont.)* | Ruling *(Cont.)* | of unlawful segregative design on the part of school authorities, and shifts to those authorities the burden of proving that other segregated schools within the system are not also the result of intentionally segregative actions." |
| | Dissenting Opinion | Justice Rehnquist was of the view that the holdings concerning the equation of attendance zone gerrymandering with statutes or ordinances requiring segregation and the newly created rule with respect to burden of proof on the school board were not justified by the Court's prior rulings. |

MILLIKEN v. BRADLEY

Supreme Court of the United States, 1974
418 U.S. 717, 94 S.Ct. 3112, 41 L.Ed.2d 1069

Ronald Bradley, other black students, and the Detroit branch of the NAACP brought a class action against Governor William Milliken, the state board of education, other state officials, and the city school board and superintendent, alleging racial segregation in the past and present operation of the Detroit public school system, particularly in the drawing of school district and attendance zone boundaries. This challenge was upheld by a federal district court which, finding violations of constitutional rights by both city and state officials, ordered the Detroit school board to formulate desegregation plans for the city school system and ordered state officials to devise arrangements for a nondiscriminatory, unitary system of education for the three-county metropolitan area. The district court then permitted some eighty-five surrounding school districts, not original parties to the litigation and not themselves found to have engaged in constitutional violations, to appear and present arguments relevant to the formulation of a regional plan for racial balance in the schools but foreclosed any further argument on the merits. Acting on the premise that "[s]chool district lines are simply matters of political convenience and may not be used to deny constitutional rights," the district court ultimately appointed a panel to devise a regional plan including the Detroit system and fifty-three of the eighty-five suburban districts. The court also ordered the city school board to acquire an additional 295 school buses for the purpose of transporting students to and from outlying districts. The U. S. Court of Appeals affirmed the substance of the district court's ruling but remanded the case for more extensive participation by the affected suburban districts and tentatively rescinded the order to the Detroit board concerning immediate acquisition of the additional buses. The Governor and other state officials sought certiorari from the United States Supreme Court.

Mr. Chief Justice BURGER delivered the opinion of the Court.

We granted certiorari in these consolidated cases to determine whether a federal court may impose a multidistrict, areawide remedy to a single district *de jure* segregation problem absent any finding that the other included school districts have failed to operate unitary school systems within their districts, absent any claim or finding that the boundary lines of any affected school district were established with the purpose of fostering racial segregation in public schools, absent any finding that the included districts committed acts which effected segregation within the other districts, and absent a meaningful opportunity for the included neighboring school districts to present evidence or be heard on the propriety of a multidistrict remedy or on the question of constitutional violations by those neighboring districts.

* * *

Viewing the record as a whole, it seems clear that the District Court and the Court of Appeals shifted the primary focus from a Detroit remedy to the metropolitan area only because of their conclusion that total desegregation of Detroit would not produce the racial balance which they perceived as desirable. Both courts proceeded on an assumption that the Detroit schools could not be truly desegregated—in their view of what constituted desegregation—unless the racial composition of the student body of each school substantially reflected the racial composition of the population of the metropolitan area as a whole. The metropolitan area was then defined as Detroit plus 53 of the outlying school districts. * * *

* * *

The record before us, voluminous as it is, contains evidence of *de jure* segregated conditions only in the Detroit schools; indeed, that was the theory on which the litigation was initially based and on which the District Court took evidence. * * * With no showing of significant violation by the 53 outlying school districts and no evidence of any interdistrict violation or effect, the court went beyond the original theory of the case as framed by the pleadings and mandated a metropolitan area remedy. To approve the remedy ordered by the court would impose on the outlying districts, not shown to have committed any constitutional vi-

olation, a wholly impermissible remedy based on a standard not hinted at in *Brown I* and *II* or any holding of this Court.

In dissent Mr. Justice WHITE and Mr. Justice MARSHALL undertake to demonstrate that agencies having statewide authority participated in maintaining the dual school system found to exist in Detroit. They are apparently of the view that once such participation is shown, the District Court should have a relatively free hand to reconstruct school districts outside of Detroit in fashioning relief. Our assumption, *arguendo*, * * * that state agencies did participate in the maintenance of the Detroit system, should make it clear that it is not on this point that we part company. The difference between us arises instead from established doctrine laid down by our cases. *Brown, Green, Swann, Scotland Neck* and *Emporia* each addressed the issue of constitutional wrong in terms of an established geographic and administrative school system populated by both Negro and White children. In such a context, terms such as "unitary" and "dual" systems, and "racially identifiable schools," have meaning, and the necessary federal authority to remedy the constitutional wrong is firmly established. But the remedy is necessarily designed, as all remedies are, to restore the victims of discriminatory conduct to the position they would have occupied in the absence of such conduct. Disparate treatment of White and Negro students occurred within the Detroit school system, and not elsewhere, and on this record the remedy must be limited to that system. * * *

The constitutional right of the Negro respondents residing in Detroit is to attend a unitary school system in that district. Unless petitioners drew the district lines in a discriminatory fashion, or arranged for White students residing in the Detroit district to attend schools in Oakland and Macomb Counties, they were under no constitutional duty to make provisions for Negro students to do so. The view of the dissenters, that the existence of a dual system *in Detroit* can be made the basis for a decree requiring cross-district transportation of pupils cannot be supported on the grounds that it represents merely the devising of a suitably flexible remedy for the violation of rights already established by our prior decisions. It can be supported only by drastic expansion of the constitutional right itself, an expansion without any support in either constitutional principle or precedent.

* * *

* * * Accepting, *arguendo*, the correctness of * * * [the lower courts'] finding of State responsibility for the segregated conditions within the city of Detroit, it does not follow that an interdistrict remedy is constitutionally justified or required. With a single exception, * * * there has been no showing that either the State or any of the 85 outlying districts engaged in activity that had a cross-district effect. The boundaries of the Detroit School District, which are coterminous with the boundaries of the city of Detroit, were established over a century ago by neutral legislation when the city was incorporated; there is no evidence in the record, nor is there any suggestion by the respondents, that either the original boundaries of the Detroit School District, or any other school district in Michigan, were established for the purpose of creating, maintaining or perpetuating segrega-

tion of races. There is no claim and there is no evidence hinting that petitioners and their predecessors, or the 40-odd other school districts in the tri-county area—but outside the District Court's "desegregation area"— have ever maintained or operated anything but unitary school systems. Unitary school systems have been required for more than a century by the Michigan Constitution as implemented by state law. Where the schools of only one district have been affected, there is no constitutional power in the courts to decree relief balancing the racial composition of that district's schools with those of the surrounding districts.

* * *

We conclude that the relief ordered by the District Court and affirmed by the Court of Appeals was based upon an erroneous standard and was unsupported by record evidence that acts of the outlying districts affected the discrimination found to exist in the schools of Detroit. Accordingly, the judgment of the Court of Appeals is vacated and the case is remanded for further proceedings consistent with this opinion leading to prompt formulation of a decree directed to eliminating the segregation found to exist in Detroit city schools, a remedy which has been delayed since 1970.

Reversed and remanded.

Mr. Justice DOUGLAS, dissenting.

* * *

[A]s the Court of Appeals held there can be no doubt that as a matter of Michigan law the State herself has the final say as to where and how school district lines should be drawn.

When we rule against the metropolitan area remedy we take a step that will likely put the problems of the Blacks and our society back to the period that antedated the "separate but equal" regime of Plessy v. Ferguson, 163 U.S. 537, 16 S.Ct. 1138 (1896). The reason is simple.

The inner core of Detroit is now rather solidly black; and the blacks, we know, in many instances are likely to be poorer, just as were the Chicanos in San Antonio Independent School District v. Rodriguez, 411 U.S. 1, 93 S.Ct. 1278 (1973). By that decision the poorer school districts must pay their own way. It is therefore a foregone conclusion that we have now given the States a formula whereby the poor must pay their own way.

Today's decision given *Rodriguez* means that there is no violation of the Equal Protection Clause though the schools are segregated by race and though the Black schools are not only "separate" but "inferior."

So far as equal protection is concerned we are now in a dramatic retreat from the 8-to-1 decision in 1896 that Blacks could be segregated in public facilities provided they received equal treatment.

* * *

* * * It is conceivable that ghettos develop on their own without any hint of state action. But since Michigan by one device or another has over the years created black school districts and white school districts, the task of equity is to provide a unitary system for the affected area where, as here, the State washes its hands of its own creations.

Mr. Justice WHITE, with whom Mr. Justice DOUGLAS, Mr. Justice BRENNAN, and Mr. Justice MARSHALL join, dissenting.

* * *

Regretfully, and for several reasons, I can join neither the Court's judgment nor its opinion. The core of my disagreement is that deliberate acts of segregation and their consequences will go unremedied, not because a remedy would be infeasible or unreasonable in terms of the usual criteria governing school desegregation cases, but because an effective remedy would cause what the Court considers to be undue administrative inconvenience to the State. The result is that the State of Michigan, the entity at which the Fourteenth Amendment is directed, has successfully insulated itself from its duty to provide effective desegregation remedies by vesting sufficient power over its public schools in its local school districts. If this is the case in Michigan, it will be the case in most States.

* * *

I am surprised that the Court, sitting at this distance from the State of Michigan, claims better insight than the Court of Appeals and the District Court as to whether an interdistrict remedy for equal protection violations practiced by the State of Michigan would involve undue difficulties for the State in the management of its public schools. In the area of what constitutes an acceptable desegregation plan, "we must of necessity rely to a large extent, as this Court has for more than 16 years, on the informed judgment of the district courts in the first instance and on courts of appeals." Swann v. Charlotte-Mecklenburg Board of Education, 402 U.S. 1, 28, 91 S.Ct. 1267, 1282 (1971). Obviously, whatever difficulties there might be, they are surmountable; for the Court itself concedes that had there been sufficient evidence of an interdistrict violation, the District Court could have fashioned a single remedy for the districts implicated rather than a different remedy for each district in which the violation had occurred or had an impact.

I am even more mystified how the Court can ignore the legal reality that the constitutional violations, even if occurring locally, were committed by governmental entities for which the State is responsible and that it is the State that must respond to the command of the Fourteenth Amendment. An interdistrict remedy for the infringements that occurred in this case is well within the confines and powers of the State, which is the governmental entity ultimately responsible for desegregating its schools.   *   *   *

*   *   *

Finally, I remain wholly unpersuaded by the Court's assertion that "the remedy is necessarily designed, as all remedies are, to restore the victims of discriminatory conduct to the position they would have occupied in the absence of such conduct." * * * In the first place, under this premise the Court's judgment is itself infirm; for had the Detroit school system not followed an official policy of segregation throughout the 1950's and 1960's, Negroes and whites would have been going to school together. There would have been no, or at least not as many, recognizable Negro schools and no, or at least not as many, white schools, but "just schools," and neither Negroes nor whites would have suffered from the effects of segregated education, with all its shortcomings.

Surely the Court's remedy will not restore to the Negro community, stigmatized as it was by the dual school system, what it would have enjoyed over all or most of this period if the remedy is confined to present-day Detroit; for the maximum remedy available within that area will leave many of the schools almost totally black, and the system itself will be predominantly black and will become increasingly so. Moreover, when a State has engaged in acts of official segregation over a lengthy period of time, as in the case before us, it is unrealistic to suppose that the children who were victims of the State's unconstitutional conduct could now be provided the benefits of which they were wrongfully deprived. Nor can the benefits which accrue to school systems in which school children have not been officially segregated, and to the communities supporting such school systems, be fully and immediately restored after a substantial period of unlawful segregation. The education of children of different races in a desegregated environment has unhappily been lost along with the social, economic, and political advantages which accompany a desegregated school system as compared with an unconstitutionally segregated system. It is for these reasons that the Court has consistently followed the course of requiring the effects of past official segregation to be eliminated "root and branch" by imposing, in the present, the duty to provide a remedy which will achieve "the greatest possible degree of actual desegregation, taking into account the practicalities of the situation." It is also for these reasons that once a constitutional violation has been found, the District Judge obligated to provide such a remedy "will thus necessarily be concerned with the elimination of one-race schools." These concerns were properly taken into account by the District Judge in this case. Confining the remedy to the boundaries of the Detroit district is quite unrelated either to the goal of achieving maximum desegregation or to those intensely practical considerations, such as the extent and expense of transportation, that have imposed limits on remedies in cases such as this. The Court's remedy, in the end, is essentially arbitrary and will leave serious violations of the Constitution substantially unremedied.

*   *   *

Mr. Justice MARSHALL, with whom Mr. Justice DOUGLAS, Mr. Justice BRENNAN, and Mr. Justice WHITE join, dissenting.

*   *   *

Nowhere in the court's opinion does the majority confront, let alone respond to, the District Court's conclusion that a remedy limited to the city of Detroit would not effectively desegregate the Detroit city schools.
*   *   *

*   *   *

*   *   * The rippling effects on residential patterns caused by purposeful acts of segregation do not automatically subside at the school district border. With rare exceptions, these effects naturally spread through all the residential neighborhoods within a metropolitan area.
*   *   *

The State must also bear part of the blame for the white flight to the suburbs which would be forthcoming from a Detroit-only decree and would render such a remedy ineffective. Having created a system where whites and Negroes were intentionally kept apart so that they could not become accustomed to learning together, the State is responsible for the fact that many whites will react to the dismantling of that segregated system by attempting to flee to the suburbs. Indeed, by limiting the District Court to a Detroit-only remedy and allowing that flight to the suburbs to succeed, the Court today allows the State to profit from its own wrong and to perpetuate for years to come the separation of the races it achieved in the past by purposeful state action.

*   *   *

One final set of problems remains to be considered. We recognized in *Brown II*, and have re-emphasized ever since, that in fashioning relief in desegregation cases, "the courts will be guided by equitable principles. Traditionally equity has been characterized by a practical flexibility in shaping its remedies and by a facility for adjusting and reconciling public and private needs." *Brown II*, 349 U.S., at 300. See also *Swann*.

Though not resting its holding on this point, the majority suggests that various equitable considerations militate against inter-district relief. The Court refers to, for example, financing and administrative problems, the logistical problems attending large-scale transportation of students, and the prospect of the District Court's becoming a "de facto 'legislative authority' " and " 'school superintendent' for the entire area." *   *   * The entangling web of problems woven by the Court, however, appears on further consideration to be constructed of the flimsiest of threads.

*   *   *

Some disruption, of course, is the inevitable product of any desegregation decree, whether it operates within one district or on an inter-district basis. * * *

Desegregation is not and was never expected to be an easy task. Racial attitudes ingrained in our Nation's childhood and adolescence are not quickly thrown aside in its middle years. But just as the inconvenience of some cannot be allowed to stand in the way of the rights of others, so public opposition, no matter how strident, cannot be permitted to divert this Court from the enforcement of the constitutional principles at issue in this case. Today's holding, I fear, is more a reflection of a perceived public mood that we have gone far enough in enforcing the Constitution's guarantee of equal justice than it is the product of neutral principles of law. In the short run, it may seem to be the easier course to allow our great metropolitan areas to be divided up each into two cities—one white, the other black—but it is a course, I predict, our people will ultimately regret. I dissent.

DESEGREGATION CASES OF 1976

Hills v. Gautreaux, 425 U.S. 284, 96 S.Ct. 1538 (1976)	Facts	Black plaintiffs charged that the Chicago Housing Authority had deliberately confined public housing sites to within the city limits so as to avoid placing black families in white suburban neighborhoods. It was also alleged that the U. S. Dept. of Housing & Urban Development had supported and financially assisted CHA's discriminatory actions. Observing that "there was evidence of suburban discrimination and of the likelihood that there had been an 'extra-city impact' of the [defendants'] * * * 'intra-city discrimination,'" and that "the metropolitan area is a single relevant locality for low rent housing purposes and that a city-only remedy will not work," a federal appellate court overturned a district court order which restricted the focus of relief to discriminatory actions within the city and remanded the case to the lower court for "the adoption of a comprehensive metropolitan area plan that will not only disestablish the segregated public housing system in the City of Chicago * * * but will increase the supply of dwelling units as rapidly as possible."
	Vote	8–0
	Ruling	"Nothing in the *Milliken* decision suggests a *per se* rule that federal courts lack authority to order parties found to have violated the Constitution to undertake remedial efforts beyond the municipal boundaries of the city where the violation occurred. * * * Here, unlike the desegregation remedy found erroneous in *Milliken,* a judicial order directing relief beyond the boundary lines of Chicago will not necessarily entail coercion of uninvolved governmental units, because both CHA and HUD

Hills (*Cont.*)	Ruling (*Cont.*)	have the authority to operate outside the Chicago city limits." "[I]t is entirely appropriate and consistent with *Milliken* to order CHA and HUD to attempt to create housing alternatives for the respondents in the Chicago suburbs. Here the wrong committed * * * confined the respondents to segregated public housing."
Pasadena City Bd. of Educ. v. Spangler, 427 U.S. 424, 96 S.Ct. 2697 (1976)	Facts	After four years of judicial supervision following an initial determination that its operation of the schools violated the Fourteenth Amendment, the school board sought relief from further federal court supervision of the school system and particularly from the retention of jurisdiction by the district court until full compliance was achieved with its order that no school in the system ever have "a majority of minority students."
	Vote	6–2
	Ruling	Jurisdiction of the district court ceased when the segregative practices of the school system chargeable to the school authorities had been eradicated. "[T]he District Court was not entitled to require the School District to rearrange its attendance zones each year so as to ensure that the racial mix desired by the court was maintained in perpetuity." Once a racially neutral attendance pattern had been implemented to afford relief from unconstitutional discrimination, the board need not be compelled to continually redraw zone lines to take account of the "quite normal pattern of human migration [which] resulted in some changes in the demographics of Pasadena's residential patterns, with resultant shifts in the racial makeup of some of the schools."
	Dissenting Opinion	Justice Marshall, joined by Justice Brennan, dissented on the ground that there was still reason to believe the dual system had not been dismantled and, therefore, that ending the lower court's "no majority of minority students" order could be premature.

In relatively brief opinions by Justice White which concluded that lower federal courts had correctly applied the principles enunciated by *Swann* and *Keyes*, the Supreme Court affirmed rulings ordering massive school desegregation in the public school systems of Columbus and Dayton, Ohio. In Columbus Board of Education v. Penick, 443 U.S. 449, 99 S.Ct. 2941 (1979), and Dayton Board of Education v. Brinkman, 443 U.S. 526, 99 S.Ct. 2971 (1979), the Court accepted lower court determinations that, at the time *Brown* was decided in 1954, the public school systems of both cities were officially segregated on the basis of race, not perhaps by state law but by the policies pursued by the city boards of education, and that school authorities continued policies which reflected intentional segregation in the years that followed. The lower courts found that, for example, by 1976, 70 percent of all students in the Columbus public schools attended schools that were at least 80 percent black or 80 percent white, and half of all students there attended schools that were 90 percent one-race. This distribution, the courts concluded, was not the product of housing patterns and could only be explained by the pursuit of racially discriminatory policies. The Court upheld the remedies mandated by the lower courts. In the words of Justice Rehnquist, who described the remedies imposed on the Columbus public school system: "Pursuant to the District Court's order, 42,000 of the system's 96,000 students are reassigned to new schools. There are like reassignment of teachers, staff, and administrators, reorganization of the grade structure of virtually every elementary school in the system, the closing of 33 schools, and the additional transportation of 37,000 students."

Justice Stewart, joined by Chief Justice Burger, dissented in the Dayton case and concurred only in the judgment in the Columbus case. Although it seemed to him that "the Court of Appeals in both of these cases ignored the crucial role of the federal district courts in school desegregation litigation" (as primary fact-finders), what distressed him most was the weight attached to findings that the Columbus and Dayton boards maintained segregative policies in 1954. Said Justice Stewart:

> As I understand the Court's opinions in these cases, if such an officially authorized segregated school system can be found to have existed in 1954, then any current racial separation in the schools will be presumed to have been caused by acts in violation of the Constitution. Even if, as the Court says, this presumption is rebuttable, the burden is on the school board to rebut it. And, when the factual issues are as elusive as these, who bears the burden of proof can easily determine who prevails in the litigation.
> *   *   *
> I agree that a school district in violation of the Constitution in 1954 was under a duty to remedy that violation. So was a school district violating the Constitution in 1964, and so is one violating the Constitution today. But this duty does not justify a complete shift of the normal burden of proof.
>
> Presumptions are sometimes justified because in common experience some facts are likely to follow from others. *   *   * A constitutional violation in 1954 might be presumed to make the existence of a constitutional violation 20 years later more likely than not in one of two ways. First, because the school board then had an invidious intent, the continuing existence of that collective state of mind might be presumed in the absence of proof to the contrary. Second, quite apart from the current intent of the school board, an unconstitutionally discriminatory school system in 1954 might be presumed still to have major effects on the contemporary system. Neither of these possibilities seems to me likely enough to support a valid presumption.
>
> Much has changed in 25 years, in the Nation at large and in Dayton and Columbus in particular. Minds have changed with respect to racial relationships. Perhaps more importantly, generations have changed. The prejudices of the school boards of 1954 (and earlier) cannot realistically be assumed to haunt the school boards of today. Similarly, while two full generations of students have progressed from kindergarten through high school, school systems have changed. Dayton and Columbus are both examples of the dramatic growth and change in urban school districts. It is unrealistic to assume that the hand of 1954 plays any major part in shaping

the current school systems in either city. For these reasons, I simply cannot accept the shift in the litigative burden of proof adopted by the Court.

* * *

Justice Rehnquist, joined by Justice Powell, dissented in both cases in an extensive and detailed opinion which scrutinized the findings and remedies of the lower courts. He concluded that the findings of *de jure* segregation were erroneous and clearly ran counter to the expectation that "the existence of violations of constitutional rights be carefully and clearly defined before a federal court invades the ambit of local control, and that the subsequent displacement of local authority be limited to that necessary to correct the identified violations." Far from heeding this admonition, he found "[i]t * * * difficult to conceive of a more serious supplantation" of local authority. In his view, given the breadth of what the majority was prepared to recognize as *de jure* segregation and the sweep of the remedies imposed, "a school system's only hope of avoiding a judicial receivership would be a voluntary dismantling of its neighborhood school program."

The majority's sternest critic appeared to be Justice Powell. He was "profoundly disturb[ed]" by these decisions and entered a solo dissent born of a "conviction that the Court's opinions condone the creation of bad constitutional law and will be even worse for public education—an element of American life that is essential, especially for minority children." In an opinion that pulled few punches, he wrote:

> [T]he Court's decisions mark a break with both precedent and principle. The Court indulges the courts below in their stringing together of a chain of "presumptions," not one of which is close enough to reality to be reasonable. * * * This claim leads inexorably to the remarkable conclusion that the absence of integration found to exist in a high percentage of the 241 schools in Columbus and Dayton was caused entirely by intentional violations of the Fourteenth Amendment by the school boards of these two cities. Although this conclusion is tainted on its face, is not supported by evidence in either case, and as a general matter seems incredible, the courts below accepted it as the necessary premise for requiring as a matter of *constitutional law* a systemwide remedy prescribing racial balance in each and every school.
>
> There are unintegrated schools in every major urban area in the country that contains a substantial minority population. This condition results primarily from familiar segregated housing patterns, which—in turn—are caused by social, economic, and demographic forces for which no school board is responsible. These causes of the greater part of the school segregation problem are not newly discovered. * * * Federal courts, including this Court today, continue to ignore these indisputable facts. Relying upon fictions and presumptions in school cases that are irreconcilable with principles of equal protection law applied in all other cases, * * * federal courts prescribe systemwide remedies without relation to the causes of the segregation found to exist, and implement their decrees by requiring extensive transportation of children of all school ages.
>
> The type of state-enforced segregation that *Brown* properly condemned no longer exists in this country. This is not to say that school boards—particularly in the great cities of the North, Midwest, and West—are taking all reasonable measures to provide integrated educational opportunities. As I indicated in my separate opinion in Keyes v. School District No. 1, 413

U.S. 189, 223–236 (1973), *de facto* segregation has existed on a large scale in many of these cities, and often it is indistinguishable in effect from the type of *de jure* segregation outlawed by *Brown*. Where there is proof of intentional segregative action or inaction, the federal courts must act, but their remedies should not exceed the scope of the constitutional violation. * * * Systemwide remedies such as were ordered by the courts below, and today are approved by this Court, lack any principled basis when the absence of integration in all schools cannot reasonably be attributed to discriminatory conduct.

* * *

Holding the school boards of these two cities responsible for *all* of the segregation in the Dayton and Columbus systems and prescribing fixed racial ratios in every school as the constitutionally required remedy necessarily implies a belief that the same school boards—under court supervision—will be capable of bringing about and maintaining the desired racial balance in each of these schools. The experience in city after city demonstrates that this is an illusion. The process of resegregation, stimulated by resentment against judicial coercion and concern as to the effect of court supervision of education, will follow today's decisions as surely as it has in other cities subjected to similar sweeping decrees.

The orders affirmed today typify intrusions on local and professional authorities that affect adversely the quality of education. They require an extensive reorganization of both school systems, including the reassignment of almost half of the 96,000 students in the Columbus system and the busing of some 15,000 students in Dayton. They also require reassignments of teachers and other staff personnel, reorganization of grade structures, and the closing of certain schools. The orders substantially dismantle and displace neighborhood schools in the face of compelling economic and educational reasons for preserving them. This wholesale substitution of judicial legislation for the judgments of elected officials and professional educators derogates the entire process of public education. Moreover, it constitutes a serious interference with the private decisions of parents as to how their children will be educated. These harmful consequences are the inevitable byproducts of a judicial approach that ignores other relevant factors in favor of an exclusive focus on racial balance in every school.

These harmful consequences, moreover, in all likelihood will provoke responses that will defeat the integrative purpose of the courts' order. Parents, unlike school officials, are not bound by these decrees and may frustrate them through the simple expedient of withdrawing their children from a public school system in which they have lost confidence. In spite of the substantial costs often involved in relocation of the family or in resort to private education, experience demonstrates that many parents view these alternatives as preferable to submitting their children to court-run school systems. * * *

At least where inner-city populations comprise a large proportion of racial minorities and surrounding suburbs remain white, conditions that exist in most large American cities, the demonstrated effect of compulsory integration is a substantial exodus of whites from the system. * * * It would be unfair and misleading to attribute this phenomenon to a racist response to integration *per se*. It is at least as likely that the exodus is in substantial part a natural reaction to the displacement of professional and local control that occurs when courts go into the business of restructuring and operating school systems.

Nor will this resegregation be the only negative effect of court-coerced integration on minority children. Public schools depend on community support for their effectiveness. When substantial elements of the community are driven to abandon these schools, their quality tends to decline, sometimes markedly. Members of minority groups, who have relied especially on education as a means of advancing themselves, also are likely to react to this decline in quality by removing their children from public schools. As a result, public school enrollment increasingly will become limited to children from families that either lack the resources to choose alternatives or are indifferent to the quality of education. The net effect is an overall deterioration in public education, the one national resource that traditionally has made this country a land of opportunity for diverse ethnic and racial groups. * * *

If public education is not to suffer further, we must "return to a more balanced evaluation of the recognized interests of our society in achieving desegregation with other educational and societal interests a community may legitimately assert." * * * The ultimate goal is to have quality school systems in which racial discrimination is neither practiced nor tolerated. It has been thought that ethnic and racial diversity in the classroom is a desirable component of sound education in our country of diverse populations, a view to which I subscribe. The question that courts in their single-minded pursuit of racial balance seem to ignore is how best to move toward this goal.

For a decade or more after *Brown*, the courts properly focused on dismantling segregated school systems as a means of eliminating state-imposed discrimination and furthering wholesome diversity in the schools. Experience in recent years, however, has cast serious doubt upon the efficacy of far-reaching judicial remedies directed not against specific constitutional violations, but rather imposed on an entire school system on the fictional assumption that the existence of identifiable black or white schools is caused entirely by intentional segregative conduct, and is evidence of systemwide discrimination. In my view, some federal courts—now led by this Court—are pursuing a path away from rather than toward the desired goal. While these courts conscientiously view their judgments as mandated by the Constitution (a view that would have astonished constitutional scholars throughout most of our history), the fact is that restructuring and overseeing the operation of major public school systems—as ordered in these cases—fairly can be viewed as social engineering that hardly is appropriate for the federal judiciary.

The time has come for a thoughtful re-examination of the proper limits of the role of courts in confronting the intractable problems of public education in our complex society. Proved discrimination by state or local authorities should never be tolerated, and it is a first responsibility of the judiciary to put an end to it where it has been proved. But many courts have continued also to impose wide-ranging decrees, and to retain ongoing supervision over school systems. Local and state legislative and administrative authorities have been supplanted or relegated to initiative-stifling roles as minions of the courts. Indeed, there is reason to believe that some legislative bodies have welcomed judicial activism with respect to a subject so inherently difficult and so politically sensitive, that the prospect of others confronting it seems inviting. Federal courts no longer should encourage this deference by the appropriate authorities—no matter how willing they may be to defer. Courts are the branch least competent to provide long-range solutions acceptable to the public and most conducive to achieving both diversity in the classroom and quality education.

*   *   *

After all, and in spite of what many view as excessive government regulation, we are a free society—perhaps the most free of any in the world. Our people instinctively resent coercion, and perhaps most of all when it affects their children and the opportunities that only education affords them. It is now reasonably clear that the goal of diversity that we call integration, if it is to be lasting and conducive to quality education, must have the support of parents who so frequently have the option to choose where their children will attend school. Courts, of course, should confront discrimination wherever it is found to exist. But they should recognize limitations on judicial action inherent in our system and also the limits of effective judicial power. The primary and continuing responsibility for public education, including the bringing about and maintaining of desired diversity, must be left with school officials and public authorities.

THE CONSTITUTIONALITY OF ANTI-BUSING VOTER INITIATIVES

In the waning days of its October 1981 Term, the Supreme Court addressed the constitutionality of statewide ballot propositions adopted in Washington and California aimed at putting limits on the busing of public school children. It was the first time the Court considered the legality of any antibusing initiatives. The Court struck down the Washington initiative but upheld that adopted by California's voters.

Washington v. Seattle School Dist. No. 1, — U.S. —, 102 S.Ct. 3187 (1982)	Facts	Receiving nearly 66 percent of the vote statewide, Initiative 350 was designed to end the use of mandatory busing for purposes of racial integration in the state's public schools. It barred school boards from requiring any student to attend a school other than that nearest or next nearest his home. Among the exceptions recognized in the ballot proposition were nonintegrative purposes for transportation such as the student's need for special education programs or if neighborhood schools were overcrowded or unsafe or lacked the necessary physical facilities.
	Vote	5–4; Chief Justice Burger and Justices Powell, Rehnquist, and O'Connor dissented.
	Ruling	Relying on Hunter v. Erickson, 393 U.S. 385, 89 S.Ct. 557 (1969), the Court held that "when the State allocates governmental power non-neutrally, by explicitly using the *racial* nature of a decision to determine the decisionmaking process," it " 'places *special* burdens on racial minorities within the gov-

Washington (*Cont.*)	Ruling (*Cont.*)	ernmental process,' * * * thereby 'making it *more* difficult for certain racial and religious minorities [than for other members of the community] to achieve legislation that is in their interest' " and "[s]uch a structuring of the political process * * * [is] 'no more permissible than is denying [members of a racial minority] the vote, on an equal basis with others.' " In this case, Initiative 350 "work[s] a reallocation of power of the kind condemned in *Hunter*" since "the authority to address a racial problem—and only a racial problem— [is removed] from the existing decisionmaking body, in such a way as to burden minority interests. Those favoring the elimination of *de facto* school segregation must now seek relief from the state legislature, or from the electorate" while "authority over all other student assignment decisions, as well as over most other areas of educational policy, remains vested in the local school board."
Crawford v. Los Angeles Board of Education, —— U.S. ——, 102 S.Ct. 3211 (1982)	Facts	Following a California Supreme Court decision holding that the *state* constitution prohibited both *de facto* and *de jure* segregation, California voters adopted Proposition I, amending the state constitution to provide that state courts could not order mandatory pupil assignment or busing unless a federal court "would be permitted under federal decisional law" to do so in order to remedy a violation of the Equal Protection Clause of the Fourteenth Amendment.
	Vote	8–1; Justice Marshall dissented.
	Ruling	"[H]aving gone beyond the requirements of the Federal Constitution, the State was free to return in part to the standard prevailing generally throughout the United States. It could have conformed its law to the Federal Constitution in every respect. That it chose to pull back only in part, and by preserving a greater right to desegregation than exists under the Federal Constitution, most assuredly does not render the Proposition unconstitutional on its face." "Proposition I in no way purports to limit the power of state courts to remedy the effects of intentional segregation with its accompanying stigma. The benefits of neighborhood schools are racially neutral. This manifestly is true in Los Angeles where over 75% of the public school body is composed of groups viewed as racial minorities. * * * [T]he Proposition simply removes one means of achieving the state created right to desegregated education. School districts retain the obligation to alleviate segregation regardless of cause. And the state courts still may order desegregation measures other than pupil school assignment or pupil transportation."

PALMER v. THOMPSON

Supreme Court of the United States, 1971
403 U.S. 217, 91 S.Ct. 1940, 29 L.Ed.2d 438

In 1962, a federal district court ruled that continued operation of a number of public facilities on a segregated basis by the city government of Jackson, Mississippi denied Negro residents equal protection of the laws. This decision was affirmed on appeal by the Fifth U. S. Circuit Court of Appeals. The city agreed to desegregate the public parks, auditoriums, golf courses, and the city zoo, but the city council voted to close the city's swimming pools. Hazel Palmer and other black residents of Jackson brought suit against the mayor, Allen Thompson, and others to force the reopening of the swimming pools on a desegregated basis. A federal district court denied relief, and its decision was affirmed by the U. S. Court of Appeals. The Supreme Court granted certiorari.

Mr. Justice BLACK delivered the opinion of the Court.

*   *   *

Petitioners rely chiefly on the first section of the Fourteenth Amendment which forbids any State to "deny to any person within its jurisdiction the equal protection of the laws." There can be no doubt that a major purpose of this amendment was to safeguard Negroes against discriminatory state laws—state laws that fail to give Negroes protection equal to that afforded white people. *   *   * Here there has unquestionably been "state action" because the official local government legislature, the city council, has closed the public swimming pools of Jackson. The question, however, is whether this closing of the pools is state action that denies "the equal protection of the laws" to Negroes. It should be noted first that neither the Fourteenth Amendment nor any Act of Congress purports to impose an affirmative duty on a State to begin to operate or to continue to operate swimming pools. Furthermore, this is not a case where whites are permitted to use public facilities while blacks are denied access. It is not a case where a city is maintain-

ing different sets of facilities for blacks and whites and forcing the races to remain separate in recreational or educational activities. *   *   *

Unless, therefore, as petitioners urge, certain past cases require us to hold that closing the pools to all denied equal protection to Negroes, we must agree with the courts below and affirm.

*   *   *

It is true there is language in some of our cases interpreting the Fourteenth and Fifteenth Amendments which may suggest that the motive or purpose behind a law is relevant to its constitutionality. *   *   * But the focus in those cases was on the actual effect of the enactments, not upon the motivation which led the States to behave as they did. In *Griffin* [v. County School Board of Prince Edward County, 377 U.S. 218, 84 S.Ct. 1226 (1964)] *   *   * the State was in fact perpetuating a segregated public school system by financing segregated "private" academies. And in *Gomillion* [v. Lightfoot, 364 U.S. 339, 81 S.Ct. 125 (1960)] the Alabama Legislature's gerrymander of the boundaries of Tuskegee excluded virtually all Negroes from voting in town elections. Here the record indicates only that Jackson once ran segregated public swimming pools and that no public pools are now maintained by the city. Moreover, there is no evidence in this record to show that the city is now covertly aiding the maintenance and operation of pools which are private in name only. It shows no state action affecting blacks differently from whites.

Petitioners have argued strenuously that a city's possible motivations to ensure safety and save money cannot validate an otherwise impermissible state action. This proposition is, of course, true. Citizens may not be compelled to forgo their constitutional rights because officials fear public hostility or desire to save money. * * * But the issue here is whether black citizens in Jackson *are* being denied their constitutional rights when the city has closed the public pools to black and white alike. Nothing in the history or the language of the Fourteenth Amendment nor in any of our prior cases persuades us that the closing of the Jackson swimming pools to all its citizens constitutes a denial of "the equal protection of the laws."

* * *

The judgment is affirmed.

Mr. Chief Justice BURGER, concurring.

* * *

The elimination of any needed or useful public accommodation or service is surely undesirable and this is particularly so of public recreational facilities. Unfortunately the growing burdens and shrinking revenues of municipal and state governments may lead to more and more curtail-

ment of desirable services. Inevitably every such constriction will affect some groups or segments of the community more than others. To find an equal protection issue in every closing of public swimming pools, tennis courts, or golf courses would distort beyond reason the meaning of that important constitutional guarantee. To hold, as petitioners would have us do, that every public facility or service, once opened, constitutionally "locks in" the public sponsor so that it may not be dropped * * * would plainly discourage the expansion and enlargement of needed services in the long run.

We are, of course, not dealing with the wisdom or desirability of public swimming pools; we are asked to hold on a very meager record that the Constitution *requires* that public swimming pools, once opened, may not be closed. But all that is good is not commanded by the Constitution and all that is bad is not forbidden by it. We would do a grave disservice, both to elected officials and to the public, were we to require that every decision of local governments to terminate a desirable service be subjected to a microscopic scrutiny for forbidden motives rendering the decision unconstitutional.

Mr. Justice DOUGLAS, dissenting.

My conclusion is that the Ninth Amendment has a bearing on the present problem. * * *

Rights, not explicitly mentioned in the Constitution, have at times been deemed so elementary to our way of life that they have been labeled as basic rights. Such is the right to travel from State to State. United States v. Guest, 383 U.S. 745, 758, 86 S.Ct. 1170, 1178. Such is also the right to marry. Loving v. Virginia, 388 U. S. 1, 12, 87 S.Ct. 1817, 1823. The "rights" retained by the people within the meaning of the Ninth Amendment may be related to those "rights" which are enumerated in the Constitution. Thus the Fourth Amendment speaks of the "right of the people to be secure in their persons, houses, papers, and effects" and protects it by well-known procedural devices. But we have held that that enumerated "right" also has other facets commonly summarized in the concept of privacy. Griswold v. Connecticut, 381 U. S. 479, 85 S.Ct. 1678.

There is of course, not a word in the Constitution, unlike many modern constitutions, concerning the right of the people to education or to work or to recreation by swimming or otherwise. Those rights, like the right to pure air and pure water, may well be rights "retained by the people" under the Ninth Amendment. May the people vote them down as well as up?

* * * We stated in West Virginia State Board of Education v. Barnette, 319 U. S. 624, 638, 63 S.Ct. 1178, 1185, that: "One's right to life, liberty, and property * * * and other fundamental rights may not be submitted to vote; they depend on the outcome of no elections." And we added in Lucas v. Forty-Fourth Colorado General Assembly, 377 U. S. 713, 736–737, 84 S.Ct. 1459, 1474, "A citizen's constitutional rights can hardly be infringed simply because a majority of the people choose that [they] be." * * *

In determining what municipal services may not be abolished the Court of Appeals drew the line between "an essential public function" and other public functions. Whether state constitutions draw that line is not our concern. Certainly there are no federal constitutional provisions which make that distinction.

Closing of the pools probably works a greater hardship on the poor than on the rich; and it may work greater hardship on poor Negroes than on poor whites, a matter on which we have no light. Closing of the pools was at least in part racially motivated. And, as stated by the dissenters in the Court of Appeals:

"The closing of the City's pools has done more than deprive a few thousand Negroes of the pleasures of swimming. It has taught Jackson's Negroes a lesson: In Jackson the price of protest is high. Negroes there now know that they risk losing even segregated public facilities if they dare to protest segregation. Negroes will now think twice before protesting segregated public parks, segregated public libraries, or other segregated facilities. They must first decide whether they wish to risk living without the facility altogether, and at the same time engendering further animosity from a white community which has lost its public facilities also through the Negroes' attempts to desegregate these facilities."

* * *

I believe that freedom from discrimination based on race, creed, or color has become by reason of the Thirteenth, Fourteenth, and Fifteenth Amendments one of the "enumerated rights" under the Ninth Amendment that may not be voted up or voted down.

* * *

I conclude that though a State may discontinue any of its municipal services—such as schools, parks, pools, athletic fields, and the like—it may not do so for the purpose of perpetuating or installing *apartheid* or because it finds life in a multi-racial community difficult or unpleasant. If that is its reason, then abolition of a designated public service becomes a device for perpetuating a segregated way of life. That a State may not do.

* * *

Mr. Justice WHITE, with whom Mr. Justice BRENNAN and Mr. Justice MARSHALL join, dissenting.

I agree with the majority that the central purpose of the Fourteenth Amendment is to protect Negroes from invidious discrimination. Consistent with this view, I had thought official policies forbidding or discouraging joint use of public facilities by Negroes and whites were at war with the Equal Protection Clause. Our cases make it unquestionably clear, as all of us agree, that a city or State may not enforce such a policy by maintaining officially separate facilities for the two races. It is also my view, but apparently not that of the majority, that a State may not have an official stance against desegregating public facilities and implement it by closing those facilities in response to a desegregation order.

* * *

It must be noted here that none of Jackson's public recreational facilities was desegregated until after the appellate proceedings in *Clark* v. *Thompson* [the 1962 case] were fully concluded. This was true despite that fact that under this Court's prior decisions the only possible result of such review would have been a broadening of the relief granted by the District Judge. Moreover, from the time of the trial court's decision in *Clark* v. *Thompson*, the mayor of Jackson made public statements, of record in this case, indicating his dedication to maintaining segregated facilities. * * *

* * *

There is no dispute that the closing of the pools constituted state action. Similarly, there can be no disagreement that the desegregation ruling in *Clark* v. *Thompson* was the event that precipitated the city's decision to cease furnishing public swimming facilities to its citizens. Although the secondary evidence of what the city officials thought and believed about the wisdom of desegregation is relevant, it is not necessary to rely on it to establish the causal link between *Clark* v. *Thompson* and the closings. The officials' sworn affidavits, accepted by the courts below, stated that loss of revenue and danger to the citizens would obviously result from operating the pools on an integrated basis. Desegregation, and desegregation alone, was the catalyst that would produce these undesirable consequences. Implicit in this official judgment were assumptions that the citizens of Jackson were of such a mind that they would no longer pay the 10- or 20-cent fee imposed by the city if their swimming and wading had to be done with their neighbors of another race, that some citizens would direct violence against their neighbors for using pools previously closed to them, and that the anticipated violence would not be controllable by the authorities. Stated more simply, although the city officials knew what the Constitution required after *Clark* v. *Thompson* became final, their judgment was that compliance with that mandate, at least with respect to swimming pools, would be intolerable to Jackson's citizens.

*   *   *

Metropolitan Housing Development Corporation contracted to purchase a tract within the boundaries of Arlington Heights contingent upon securing a zoning variance to construct racially integrated, low and moderate income housing. The Village Plan Commission declined to rezone the land in question from single-family (R–3) to multiple-family dwelling (R–5) apparently for two reasons: (1) the area had always been zoned single-family dwelling; and (2) it had been village policy to restrict multiple-family dwellings to act as a sort of buffer zone between areas zoned commercial and those designated single-family dwelling. No commercial or manufacturing areas lay adjacent to the tract in question. When the village declined to rezone the area, the corporation and various minority individuals sued for declaratory and injunctive relief, arguing that the village was engaging in racial discrimination in violation of both the Equal Protection Clause and the Fair Housing Act of 1968. A federal district court concluded that the decision not to rezone was motivated by desires to protect property values and maintain the village's current zoning plan. A federal appeals court reversed that judgment, finding that the ultimate effect of the decision not to rezone was racially discriminatory.

In Village of Arlington Heights v. Metropolitan Housing Development Corp., 429 U.S. 252, 97 S.Ct. 555 (1977), the Supreme Court reversed the appeals court decision and remanded the case. Speaking for the Court, Justice Powell wrote:

Our decision last Term in Washington v. Davis, 426 U.S. 229, 96 S.Ct. 2040, (1976), made it clear that official action will not be held unconstitutional solely because it results in a racially disproportionate impact. "Disproportionate impact is not irrelevant, but it is not the sole touchstone of an invidious racial discrimination." * * * Proof of racially discriminatory intent or purpose is required to show a violation of the Equal Protection Clause. * * *

Davis does not require a plaintiff to prove that the challenged action rested solely on racially discriminatory purposes. Rarely can it be said that a legislature or administrative body operating under a broad mandate made a decision motivated solely by a single concern, or even that a particular purpose was the "dominant" or "primary" one. In fact, it is because legislators and administrators are properly concerned with balancing numerous competing considerations that courts refrain from reviewing the merits of their decisions, absent a showing of arbitrariness or irrationality. But racial discrimination is not just another competing consideration. When there is a proof that a discriminatory purpose has been a motivating factor in the decision, this judicial deference is no longer justified.

Determining whether invidious discriminatory purpose was a motivating factor demands a sensitive inquiry into such circumstantial and direct evidence of intent as may be available. The impact of the official action—whether it "bears more heavily on one race than another," * * * —may provide an important starting point. Sometimes a clear pattern, unexplainable on grounds other than race, emerges from the effect of the state action even when the governing legislation appears neutral on its face. * * *

The evidentiary inquiry is then relatively easy. But such cases are rare. Absent a pattern as stark as that in *Gomillion* [v. Lightfoot, 364 U.S. 399, 81 S.Ct. 125 (1960)] * * * impact alone is not determinative, and the Court must look to other evidence.

The historical background of the decision is one evidentiary source, particularly if it reveals a series of official actions taken for invidious purposes. * * * The specific sequence of events leading up the challenged decision also may shed some light on the decisionmaker's purpose. * * * For example, if the property involved here always had been zoned R-5 but suddenly was changed to R-3 when the town learned of MHDC's plans to erect integrated housing, we would have a far different case. Departures from the normal procedural sequence also might afford evidence that improper purposes are playing a role. Substantive departures too may be relevant, particularly if the factors usually considered important by the decisionmaker strongly favor a decision contrary to the one reached.

The legislative or administrative history may be highly relevant, especially where there are contemporary statements by members of the decisionmaking body, minutes of its meetings, or reports. In some extraordinary instances the members might be called to the stand at trial to testify concerning the purpose of the official action, although even then such testimony frequently will be barred by privilege. * * *

* * *

We also have reviewed the evidence. The impact of the Village's decision does arguably bear more heavily on racial minorities. Minorities comprise 18% of the Chicago area population, and 40% of the income groups said to be eligible for Lincoln Green. But there is little about the sequence of events leading up to the decision that would spark suspicion. The area around the Viatorian property has been zoned R-3 since 1959, the year when Arlington Heights first adopted a zoning map. Single-family homes surround the 80-acre site, and the Village is undeniably committed to single-family homes as its dominant residential land use. The rezoning request progressed according to the usual procedures. The Plan Commission even scheduled two additional hearings, at least in part to accommodate MHDC and permit it to supplement its presentation with answers to questions generated at the first hearing.

The statements by the Plan Commission and Village Board members, as reflected in the official minutes, focused almost exclusively on the zoning aspects of the MHDC petition, and the zoning factors on which they relied are not novel criteria in the Village's rezoning decisions. There is no reason to doubt that there has been reliance by some neighboring property owners on the maintenance of single-family zoning in the vicinity. The Village originally adopted its buffer policy long before MHDC entered the picture and has applied the policy too consistently for us to infer discriminatory purpose from its application in this case. Finally, MHDC called one member of the Village Board to the stand at trial. Nothing in her testimony supports an inference of invidious purpose.

The opinion of the Court did not deal with any of the statutory claims, and the majority remanded the case to the appeals court to consider those claims. Justices Brennan, White, and Marshall voted to remand the case also for consideration of the constitutional issue in light of *Washington* v. *Davis*. Justice Stevens did not participate in the decision.

CITY OF MEMPHIS v. GREENE

Supreme Court of the United States, 1981
451 U.S. 100, 101 S.Ct. 1584, 67 L.Ed.2d 769

See p. 773.

In order to guarantee that each entering class contained students from certain minority groups, the medical school of the University of California at Davis maintained two separate admissions programs. The school filled eighty-four of the 100 class positions through the regular admissions program but set aside sixteen positions to be filled through its special admissions program. Applicants were asked if they wanted to be considered as "economically and/or educationally disadvantaged" and as members of certain minorities (blacks, Chicanos, Asians, or American Indians). Applications of those deemed "disadvantaged" were forwarded to a special admissions committee, a majority of whose members were from minority groups. These special candidates for admission did not have to meet the regular 2.5 grade point average cutoff point that otherwise would have triggered summary rejection, and these applicants were not rated in competition with those candidates in the regular admissions program. Though numerous disadvantaged whites applied, none were admitted. A result of applying separate and preferential standards in filling the sixteen positions was that a number of minority students were admitted with academic credentials of substantially poorer quality than a number of white applicants who were rejected through the regular admission process. Allan Bakke, a white applicant, was twice denied admission to the medical school. Since his credentials were of higher caliber by the University's own standards than a number of the minority applicants admitted under the quota system, Bakke sued alleging that he had been denied admission on grounds of race. The University filed a cross-complaint seeking a declaratory judgment vindicating its affirmative action program. A state superior court held that the special admissions procedures constituted unlawful discrimination and violated Title VI, § 601 of the 1964 Civil Rights Act,[b] the Equal Protection Clause of the Fourteenth Amendment, and a provision of the California constitution but refused to order Bakke's admission since, it concluded, he would not have been admitted even if there had been no special admissions program. The state supreme court, resting its decision solely on equal protection grounds, declared that the use of race in admissions procedures failed to survive "strict scrutiny" (because it was not the least restrictive means of furthering the admittedly compelling state interests of integrating the medical profession and increasing the number of doctors who wanted to serve minority patients) and enjoined future use of racial criteria, but directed the trial court to order Bakke's admission because, it concluded, the University had failed to meet the burden of showing that he would not otherwise have been admitted.

With results that appeared to split the difference on affirmative action—and itself as well—the United States Supreme Court in Regents of the University of California v. Bakke, 438 U.S. 265, 98 S.Ct. 2733 (1978), struck down the special admissions program because "[i]t tells applicants who are not Negro, Asian, or 'Chicano' that they are totally excluded from a specific percentage of the seats in an entering class," but otherwise held that in college admissions programs "race

---

b. Discussion of Title VI has been omitted from all but Justice Stevens's opinion in the summary of the *Bakke* decision that follows since those Justices not subscribing to his opinion concluded that Title VI prohibits those classifications that would violate the Equal Protection Clause.

or ethnic background may be deemed a 'plus' in a particular applicant's file * * * .'' Announcing the judgment of the Court in an opinion in which he spoke only for himself, Justice Powell joined Chief Justice Burger and Justices Stewart, Rehnquist, and Stevens to reach the first result (and direct that Bakke be admitted) and with Justices Brennan, White, Marshall, and Blackmun to reach the second.

Since the rights created in the first section of the Fourteenth Amendment are " 'by its terms, guaranteed to the individual' " and are thus " 'personal rights,' " Justice Powell began from the premise that "[r]acial and ethnic distinctions of any sort are inherently suspect and thus call for the most exacting judicial scrutiny." Reviewing the justifications proffered by the medical school for its special admissions program,[c] he found only one which rose to the level of a compelling interest—"the attainment of a diverse student body." This interest, Justice Powell pointed out, implicated academic freedom, which "though not a specifically enu-

---

c. The other purposes purportedly served by the special admissions program were: (1) "reducing the historic deficit of traditionally disfavored minorities in medical schools and the medical profession"; (2) "countering the effects of societal discrimination"; and (3) "increasing the number of physicians who will practice in communities currently underserved." In rejoinder and addressing each of these proffered justifications in turn, Justice Powell wrote:

If petitioner's purpose is to assure within its student body some specified percentage of a particular group merely because of its race or ethnic origin, such a preferential purpose must be rejected not as insubstantial but as facially invalid. Preferring members of any one group for no reason other than race or ethnic origin is discrimination for its own sake. This the Constitution forbids. * * *

The State certainly has a legitimate and substantial interest in ameliorating, or eliminating where feasible, the disabling effects of identified discrimination. The line of school desegregation cases, commencing with *Brown*, attests to the importance of this state goal and the commitment of the judiciary to affirm all lawful means towards its attainment. In the school cases, the States were required by court order to redress the wrongs worked by specific instances of racial discrimination. That goal was far more focused than the remedying of the effects of "societal discrimination," an amorphous concept of injury that may be ageless in its reach into the past.

We have never approved a classification that aids persons perceived as members of relatively victimized groups at the expense of other innocent individuals in the absence of judicial, legislative, or administrative findings of constitutional or statutory violations. * * *

Petitioner does not purport to have made, and is in no position to make, such findings. Its broad mission is education, not the formulation of any legislative policy or the adjudication of particular claims of illegality. * * * [I]solated segments of our vast governmental structures are not competent to make those decisions, at least in the absence of legislative mandates and legislatively determined criteria. * * * Before relying upon these sorts of findings in establishing a racial classification, a governmental body must have the authority and capability to establish, in the record, that the classification is responsive to identified discrimination. * * * Lacking this capability, petitioner has not carried its burden of justification on this issue.

* * *

Petitioner identifies, as another purpose of its program, improving the delivery of health care services to communities currently underserved. It may be assumed that in some situations a State's interest in facilitating the health care of its citizens is sufficiently compelling to support the use of a suspect classification. But there is virtually no evidence in the record indicating that petitioner's special admissions program is either needed or geared to promote that goal. * * *

Petitioner simply has not carried its burden of demonstrating that it must prefer members of particular ethnic groups over all other individuals in order to promote better health care delivery to deprived citizens. Indeed, petitioner has not shown that its preferential classification is likely to have any significant effect on the problem.

merated constitutional right, has long been viewed as a special concern of the
First Amendment." He continued, "[I]n arguing that its universities must be
accorded the right to select those students who will contribute the most to the
'robust exchange of ideas,' petitioner invokes a countervailing constitutional interest, that of the First Amendment. In this light, petitioner must be viewed as seeking to achieve a goal that is of paramount importance in the fulfillment of its
mission." But, he observed, "the diversity that furthers a compelling state interest encompasses a far broader array of qualifications and characteristics of which
racial or ethnic origin is but a single though important element." Such qualities,
he explained, "could include exceptional personal talents, unique work or service
experience, leadership potential, maturity, demonstrated compassion, a history of
overcoming disadvantage, ability to communicate with the poor, or other qualifications deemed important." However, the special admissions program, which
"focused *solely* on ethnic diversity, would hinder rather than further attainment
of genuine diversity." By contrast, "an admissions program * * * [which
was] operated * * * [so as] to consider all pertinent elements of diversity in
light of the particular qualifications of each applicant, and to place them on the
same footing for consideration, although not necessarily according them the same
weight" would contribute to diversity "without the factor of race being decisive
 * * * ." Justice Powell concluded: "This kind of program treats each applicant
as an individual in the admissions process. The applicant who loses out on the last
available seat to another candidate receiving a 'plus' on the basis of ethnic background will not have been foreclosed from all consideration for that seat simply
because he was not the right color or had the wrong surname. It would mean
only that his combined qualifications, which may have included similar non-objec-
tive factors, did not outweigh those of the other applicant. His qualifications
would have been weighed fairly and competitively, and he would have no basis to
complain of unequal treatment under the Fourteenth Amendment."

Asserting at the outset that "racial classifications are not *per se* invalid under
the Fourteenth Amendment," the plurality, speaking through Justice Brennan,
rejected the constitutional evaluation of racial and ethnic categories both in terms
of the strict scrutiny approach, because "this case does not fit neatly into our prior
analytic framework for race," and the mere reasonableness standard, "because of
the significant risk that racial classifications established for ostensibly benign purposes can be misused, causing effects not unlike those created by invidious classifications * * * ." The plurality chose instead to assess the constitutionality of
the special admissions program in light of a framework "developed in gender discrimination cases but which carr[ies] even more force when applied to racial classifications," namely, that "racial classifications designed to further remedial
purposes 'must serve important governmental objectives and must be substantially related to the achievement of those objectives' "; in other words: (1) "to
justify such a classification an important and articulated purpose for its use must
be shown," and (2) "any statute must be stricken that stigmatizes any group or
that singles out those least well represented in the political process to bear the
brunt of a benign program."

With respect to the first of these elements, the plurality concluded that "Davis'
articulated purpose of remedying the effects of past social discrimination is
 * * * sufficiently important to justify the use of race-conscious admissions programs where there is a sound basis for concluding that minority underrepresentation is substantial and chronic, and that the handicap of past discrimination is
impeding access of minorities to the medical school." The plurality found such a
basis existed. And, as to the second prong of the test, Justice Brennan explained
that the special admissions program did "not * * * in any way operat[e] to

746 CIVIL RIGHTS AND LIBERTIES PART III

stigmatize or single out any discrete and insular, or even any identifiable, nonminority group. Nor will harm comparable to that imposed on racial minorities by exclusion or separation on grounds of race to be the likely result of the program. It does not, for example, establish an exclusive preserve for minority students apart from and exclusive of whites. Rather, its purpose is to overcome the effects of segregation by bringing the races together." He continued, "Unlike discrimination against racial minorities, the use of racial preferences for remedial purposes does not inflict a pervasive injury upon whites, in the sense that wherever they go or whatever they do there is a significant likelihood that they will be treated as second-class citizens because of their color. This distinction does not mean that the exclusion of a white resulting from the preferential use of race is not sufficiently serious to require justification; but it does mean that the injury inflicted by such a policy is not distinguishable from disadvantages caused by a wide range of government actions, none of which has ever been thought impermissible for that reason alone."

After ranging over a spectrum of inequalities that separate blacks from whites in American society—from infant mortality, to income, to unemployment, to representation in the professions—Justice Marshall, in a separate opinion, wondered aloud over the irony that "after several hundred years of class-based discrimination against Negroes, the Court is unwilling to hold that a class-based remedy for that discrimination is permissible." "It is unnecessary in 20th century America," he urged, "to have individual Negroes demonstrate that they have been victims of racial discrimination; the racism of our society has been so pervasive that none, regardless of wealth or position, has managed to escape its impact." "[F]ear[ing] that we have come full circle," he likened the position of the Court, "again stepping in, this time to stop affirmative action programs of the type used by the University of California," to the post-Civil War decisions in the *Civil Rights Cases* and *Plessy* v. *Ferguson*, which "destroyed movement toward complete equality."

In another separate statement, Justice Blackmun found it "gratifying to know that the Court at least finds it constitutional for an academic institution to take race and ethnic background into consideration as one factor, among many, in the administration of its admissions program," especially in view of the fact that "educational institutions have always used geography, athletic ability, anticipated financial largess, alumni pressure, and other factors of that kind." Although he "hope[d] that the time will come when an 'affirmative action' program is unnecessary and is, in truth, only a relic of the past," he concluded: "I suspect that it would be impossible to arrange an affirmative action program in a racially neutral way and have it successful. To ask that this be so is to demand the impossible. In order to get beyond racism, we must first take account of race. There is no other way. And in order to treat some persons equally, we must treat them differently. We cannot—we dare not—let the Equal Protection Clause perpetrate racial supremacy."

The second plurality, speaking through Justice Stevens, concluded that "[t]he University's special admissions program violated Title VI of the Civil Rights Act of 1964 by excluding Bakke from the medical school because of his race." Justice Stevens explained: "The plain language of the statute ᵈ * * * requires affirmance of the judgment below. A different result cannot be justified unless that

---

d. Section 601 of the Civil Rights Act of 1964 provides:

"No person in the United States shall, on the ground of race, color, or national origin, be excluded from participation in, be denied the benefits of, or be subjected to discrimination under any program or activity receiving Federal financial assistance."

language misstates the actual intent of the Congress that enacted the statute or the statute is not enforceable in a private action. Neither conclusion is warranted." And, he added: "In unmistakable terms the Act prohibits the exclusion of individuals from federally funded programs because of their race. As succinctly phrased during the Senate debate, under Title VI it is not 'permissible to say 'yes' to one person, but to say 'no' to another person, only because of the color of his skin.' " Consistent with "[o]ur settled practice * * * to avoid the decision of a constitutional issue if a case can be fairly decided on a statutory ground" and in view of the fact that "there is no outstanding injunction forbidding any consideration of racial criteria in processing applications," Justice Stevens observed it was therefore "perfectly clear that the question whether race can ever be used as a factor in an admissions decision is not an issue in this case, and that discussion of that issue is inappropriate."

AFFIRMATIVE ACTION DECISIONS FOLLOWING *BAKKE*

United Steelworkers of America v. Weber, 443 U.S. 193, 99 S.Ct. 2721 (1979)	Facts	A collective bargaining agreement voluntarily negotiated between a private employer and a union contained an affirmative action plan to overcome conspicuous racial imbalances in the company's virtually all-white craft work force by requiring that at least half of the trainees in an in-plant craft training program be black. The affirmative action program was to remain in effect until the proportion of black skilled craft workers in the plant matched the proportion of blacks in the local work force. The program was challenged as a violation of Title VII of the 1964 Civil Rights Act which prohibits "discriminat[ion] * * * because of * * * race."
	Decision and Vote	The affirmative action program was sustained 5–2; Justices Powell and Stevens did not participate.
	Opinion of the Court	Speaking for the Court, Justice Brennan concluded that, despite the wording of the act and many aspects of its legislative history, the affirmative action program was consistent with the spirit of the law.
	Dissents	Chief Justice Burger and Justice Rehnquist dissented, chiding the majority for a ruling that squarely contradicted both the words of the statute and its legislative history and for subordinating such evidence to the majority's own values and the achievement of a "good result."
Fullilove v. Klutznick, 448 U.S. 448, 100 S.Ct. 2758 (1980)	Facts	A provision of the Public Works Employment Act of 1977 required that 10 percent of the federal funds expended for local public works projects must be used to procure services or supplies from minority-controlled businesses. This set-aside provision was challenged under the equal protection component of the Due Process Clause of the Fifth Amendment.

Fullilove (*Cont.*)

Decision and Vote	The 10 percent set-aside provision was upheld 6–3.
Plurality Opinion	Adopting none of the frameworks of analysis used in *Bakke*, Chief Justice Burger, who announced the judgment of the Court in an opinion in which Justices White and Stevens joined, focused instead on "whether the *objectives* of this legislation are within the powers of Congress" and secondly, on "whether the limited use of racial and ethnic criteria, in the context of the case presented, is a constitutionally permissible *means* for achieving the congressional objectives" and did not violate the Fifth Amendment. He concluded that Congress would have been entitled under either the Commerce Clause or § 5 of the Fourteenth Amendment to accomplish the purpose of the 10 percent set-aside provision. In view of the Court's decision in Swann v. Charlotte-Mecklenburg Board of Education, 402 U.S. 1, 91 S.Ct. 1267 (1971), Chief Justice Burger "reject[ed] the contention that in the remedial context the Congress must act in a wholly 'color-blind' fashion" and went on to conclude that the 10 percent set-aside provision was both reasonably related to the end sought to be achieved and also reasonably free of the misapplication of racial and ethnic criteria. The burden falling on nonminority businesses as a result of the provision he described as relatively light and far from "invidious" in its discriminatory impact.
Concurring Opinion	Justice Powell, applying strict scrutiny, concluded that the 10 percent set-aside provision was "justified as a remedy that serves the compelling interest in eradicating the continuing effects of past discrimination identified by Congress."
Opinion Concurring in the Judgment	Justice Marshall, joined by Justices Brennan and Blackmun, concluded that "the racial classifications employed in the set-aside provision are substantially related to the achievement of the important and congressionally articulated goal of remedying the present effects of past racial discrimination."
Dissents	Justice Stewart, joined by Justice Rehnquist, concluded that the 10 percent set-aside provision flatly contradicted the constitutional principle, articulated in dissent by Justice Harlan in *Plessy*, that "Our Constitution is color-blind, and neither knows nor tolerates classes among citizens."
	Justice Stevens dissented on the grounds that the relief afforded by the 10 percent set-aside provision failed to address the different degrees of injury sustained by the various minorities (Blacks, Indians, Eskimos, Hispanos, etc.) and treated

Fullilove (*Cont.*)	Dissents (*Cont.*)	them as equally eligible regardless of past or present circumstances. Said Justice Stevens, "Because racial characteristics so seldom provide a relevant basis for disparate treatment, and because classifications based on race are potentially so harmful to the entire body politic, it is especially important that the reasons for any such classification be clearly identified and unquestionably legitimate. * * * Racial classifications are simply too pernicious to permit any but the most exact connection between justification and classification."

b. "PRIVATE" DISCRIMINATION AND THE CONCEPT OF "STATE ACTION"

THE CIVIL RIGHTS CASES

Supreme Court of the United States, 1883
109 U.S. 3, 3 S.Ct. 18, 27 L.Ed. 835

The Civil Rights Act of 1875 prohibited any person from denying a citizen "the full and equal enjoyment of the accommodations, advantages, facilities, and privileges of inns, public conveyances on land or water, theaters, and other places of amusement * * *." In each of the five cases heard together under the above title, Negroes were denied access to business establishments or facilities covered by the act because of their race. The United States brought action against the persons guilty of violating the act in four of the cases, and in the fifth case two individuals initiated proceedings against a railroad company. The cases came to the Supreme Court from U. S. Circuit Courts on writs of error (in the two instances in which decisions were rendered for the defendants) and on certificates of division of opinion (in the other three cases).

BRADLEY, J.

* * *

Has congress constitutional power to make such a law? Of course, no one will contend that the power to pass it was contained in the constitution before the adoption of the last three amendments. The power is sought, first, in the fourteenth amendment, and the views and arguments of distinguished senators, advanced while the law was under consideration, claiming authority to pass it by virtue of that amendment, are the principal arguments adduced in favor of the power. * * *

The first section of the fourteenth amendment,—which is the one relied on,—after declaring who shall be citizens of the United States, and of the several states, is prohibitory in its character, and prohibitory upon the states. It declares that "no state shall make or enforce any law which shall abridge the privileges or immunities of citizens of the United States; nor shall any state deprive any person of life, liberty, or property without due process of law; nor deny to any person within its jurisdiction the equal protection of the laws." It is state action of a particular character that is prohibited. Individual invasion of individual rights is not the subject-matter of the amendment. It has a deeper and broader scope. It nullifies and makes void all state legislation, and state action of every kind, which impairs the privileges and immunities of citizens of the United States, or which injures them in life, liberty, or property without due process of law, or which denies to any of them the equal protection of the laws. It not only does this, but, in order that the national will, thus declared, may not be a mere *brutum fulmen*, the last section of the amendment invests congress with power to enforce it by appropriate legislation. To enforce what? To enforce the prohibition. To adopt appropriate legislation for correcting the effects of such prohibited state law and state acts, and thus to render them effectually null, void, and innocuous. This is the legislative power conferred upon congress, and this is the whole of it. It does not invest congress with power to legislate upon subjects which are within the domain of state legislation; but to provide modes of relief against state legislation, or state action, of the kind referred to. It does not authorize congress to create a code of municipal law for the regulation of private rights; but to provide modes of redress against the operation of state laws, and the action of state officers, executive or judicial, when these are subversive of the fundamental rights specified in the amendment. Positive rights and privileges are undoubtedly secured by the fourteenth amendment; but they are secured by way of prohibition against state laws and state proceedings affecting those rights and privileges, and by power given to congress to legislate for the purpose of carrying such prohibition into effect; and such legislation must necessarily be predicated upon such supposed state laws or state proceedings, and be directed to the correction of their operation and effect. * * *

* * *

And so in the present case, until some state law has been passed, or some state action through its officers or agents has been taken, adverse to the rights of citizens sought to be protected by the fourteenth amendment, no legislation of the United States under said amendment, nor any proceeding under such legislation, can be called into activity, for the prohibitions of the amendment are against state laws and acts done under state authority. * * * In fine, the legislation which congress is authorized to adopt in this behalf is not general legislation upon the rights of the citizen, but corrective legislation; that is, such as may be necessary and proper for counteracting such laws as the states may adopt or enforce, and which by the amendment they are prohibited from making or enforcing, or such acts and proceedings as the states may commit or take, and which by the amendment they are prohibited from committing or taking. It is not necessary for us to state, if we could, what legislation would be proper for congress to adopt. It is sufficient for us to examine whether the law in question is of that character.

An inspection of the law shows that it makes no reference whatever to any supposed or apprehended violation of the fourteenth amendment on the part of the states. It is not predicated on any such view. It proceeds *ex directo* to declare that certain acts committed by individuals shall be deemed offenses, and shall be prosecuted and punished by proceedings in the courts of the United States. It does not profess to be corrective of any constitutional wrong committed by the states; it does not make its operation to depend upon any such wrong committed. It applies equally to cases arising in states which have the justest laws respecting the personal rights of citizens, and whose authorities are ever ready to enforce such laws as to those which arise in states that may have violated the prohibition of the amendment. In other words, it steps into the domain of local jurisprudence, and lays down rules for the conduct of individuals in society towards each other, and imposes sanctions for the enforcement of those rules, without referring in any manner to any supposed action of the state or its authorities.

If this legislation is appropriate for enforcing the prohibitions of the amendment, it is difficult to see where it is to stop. Why may not congress, with equal show of authority, enact a code of laws for the enforcement and vindication of all rights of life, liberty, and property? If it is supposable that the states may deprive persons of life, liberty, and property without due process of law, (and the amendment itself does suppose this,) why should not congress proceed at once to prescribe due process of law for the protection of every one of these fundamental rights, in every possible case, as well as to prescribe equal privileges in inns, public conveyances, and theaters. The truth is that the implication of a power to legislate in this manner is based upon the assumption that if the states are forbidden to legislate or act in a particular way on a particular subject, and power is conferred upon congress to enforce the prohibition, this gives congress power to legislate generally upon that subject, and not merely power to provide modes of redress against such state legislation or action. The assumption is certainly unsound. It is repugnant to the tenth amendment of the constitution, which declares that powers not delegated to the United States by the constitution, nor prohibited by it to the states, are reserved to the states respectively or to the people.

[I]t is proper to state that civil rights, such as are guarantied by the constitution against state aggression, cannot be impaired by the wrongful acts of individuals, unsupported by state authority in the shape of laws, customs, or judicial or executive proceedings. The wrongful act of an individual, unsupported by any such authority, is simply a private wrong, or a crime of that individual; an invasion of the rights of the injured party, it is true, whether they affect his person, his property, or his reputation; but if not sanctioned in some way by the state, or not done under state authority, his rights remain in full force, and may presumably be vindicated by resort to the laws of the state for redress. * * *

[T]he power of congress to adopt direct and primary, as distinguished from corrective, legislation on the subject in hand, is sought, in the second place, from the thirteenth amendment, which abolishes slavery. * * * [A]nd it gives congress power to enforce the amendment by appropriate legislation.

This amendment, * * * [b]y its own unaided force and effect * * * abolished slavery, and established universal freedom. Still, legislation may be necessary and proper to meet all the various cases and circumstances to be affected by it, and to prescribe proper modes of redress for its violation in letter or spirit. And such legislation may be primary and direct in its character; for the amendment is not a mere prohibition of state laws establishing or upholding slavery, but an absolute declaration that slavery or involuntary servitude shall not exist in any part of the United States.

* * *

After giving to these questions all the consideration which their importance demands, we are forced to the conclusion that such an act of refusal [of accommodations] has nothing to do with slavery or involuntary servitude, and that if it is violative of any right of the party, his redress is to be sought under the laws of the state; or, if those laws are adverse to his rights and do not protect him, his remedy will be found in the corrective legislation which congress has adopted, or may adopt, for counteracting the effect of state laws, or state action, prohibited by the fourteenth amendment. It would be running the slavery argument into the ground to make it apply to every act of discrimination which a person may see fit to make as to the guests he will entertain, or as to the people he will take into his coach or cab or car, or admit to his concert or theater, or deal with in other matters of intercourse or business. * * *

* * *

On the whole, we are of opinion that no countenance of authority for the passage of the law in question can be found in either the thirteenth or fourteenth amendment of the constitution; and no other ground of authority for its passage being suggested, it must necessarily be

declared void, at least so far as its operation in the several states is concerned.

* * *

HARLAN, J., dissenting. The opinion in these cases proceeds, as it seems to me, upon grounds entirely too narrow and artificial. the substance and spirit of the recent amendments of the constitution have been sacrificed by a subtle and ingenious verbal criticism. * * * Constitutional provisions, adopted in the interest of liberty, and for the purpose of securing, through national legislation, if need be, rights inhering in a state of freedom, and belonging to American citizenship, have been so construed as to defeat the ends the people desired to accomplish, which they attempted to accomplish, and which they supposed they had accomplished by changes in their fundamental law. * * *

* * *

The thirteenth amendment, my brethren concede, did something more than to prohibit slavery as an *institution*, resting upon distinctions of race, and upheld by positive law. They admit that it established and decreed universal *civil freedom* throughout the United States. But did the freedom thus established involve nothing more than exemption from actual slavery? Was nothing more intended than to forbid one man from owning another as property? Was it the purpose of the nation simply to destroy the institution, and then remit the race, theretofore held in bondage, to the several states for such protection, in their civil rights, necessarily growing out of freedom, as those states, in their discretion, choose to provide? Were the states, against whose solemn protest the institution was destroyed, to be left perfectly free, so far as national interference was concerned, to make or allow discriminations against that race, as such, in the enjoyment of those fundamental rights that inhere in a state of freedom? * * *

That there are burdens and disabilities which constitute badges of slavery and servitude, and that the express power delegated to congress to enforce, by appropriate legislation, the thirteenth amendment, may be exerted by legislation of a direct and primary character, for the eradication, not simply of the institution, but of its badges and incidents, are propositions which ought to be deemed indisputable. They lie at the very foundation of the civil rights act of 1866. Whether that act was fully authorized by the thirteenth amendment alone, without the support which it afterwards received from the fourteenth amendment, after the adoption of which it was re-enacted with some additions, the court, in its opinion, says it is unnecessary to inquire. But I submit, with all respect to my brethen, that its constitutionality is conclusively shown by other portions of their opinion. It is expressly conceded by them that the thirteenth amendment established freedom; that there are burdens and disabilities, the necessary incidents of slavery, which constitute its substance and visible form; that congress, by the act of 1866, passed in view of the thirteenth amendment, before the fourteenth was adopted, undertook to remove certain burdens and disabilities, the necessary incidents of slavery, and to secure to all citizens of every race and color, and without regard to previous servitude, those fundamental rights which are the essence of civil freedom, namely, the same right to make and enforce

contracts, to sue, be parties, give evidence, and to inherit, purchase, lease, sell, and convey property as is enjoyed by white citizens; that under the thirteenth amendment congress has to do with slavery and its incidents; and that legislation, so far as necessary or proper to eradicate all forms and incidents of slavery and involuntary servitude, may be direct and primary, operating upon the acts of individuals, whether sanctioned by state legislation or not. These propositions being conceded, it is impossible, as it seems to me, to question the constitutional validity of the civil rights act of 1866. * * *

* * *

[Turning, then, to the Fourteenth Amendment, Justice HARLAN began, as the first stage of his argument, by focusing on the relationship between private property—such as the inns, public conveyances, and places of amusement described in the statute—and state regulation, noting that an agency of the state, namely local government, was implicated because it licenses and regulates such facilities. Said Justice HARLAN:]

The doctrines of Munn v. Illinois [94 U.S. 113, 24 L.Ed. 77 (1877)] have never been modified by this court, and I am justified, upon the authority of that case, in saying that places of public amusement, conducted under the authority of the law, are clothed with a public interest, because used in a manner to make them of public consequence and to affect the community at large. The law may therefore regulate, to some extent, the mode in which they shall be conducted, and consequently the public have rights in respect of such places which may be vindicated by the law. It is consequently not a matter purely of private concern.

Congress has not, in these matters, entered the domain of state control and supervision. It does not assume to prescribe the general conditions and limitations under which inns, public conveyances, and places of public amusement shall be conducted or managed. It simply declares in effect that since the nation has established universal freedom in this country for all time, there shall be no discrimination, based merely upon race or color, in respect of the legal rights in the accommodations and advantages of public conveyances, inns, and places of public amusement.

[Justice HARLAN, secondly, was of the view that Congress had broad legislative power under the Fourteenth Amendment. Tying his conclusion that "[t]he colored race is part of that public" and therefore has rights where private property is "clothed with a public interest" to Congress's power under § 5 of the Fourteenth Amendment to enforce the Privileges and Immunities Clause, he said:]

It is, therefore, an essential inquiry what, if any, right, privilege, or immunity was given by the nation to colored persons when they were made citizens of the state in which they reside? Did the national grant of state citizenship to that race, of its own force, invest them with any rights, privileges, and immunities whatever? That they became entitled, upon the adoption of the fourteenth amendment, "to all privileges and immunities of citizens in the several states," within the meaning of section 2 of article 4 of the constitution, no one, I suppose, will for a moment question. What are the privileges and immunities to which, by that clause of the constitution, they became entitled? To this it may be

answered, generally, upon the authority of the adjudged cases, that they are those which are fundamental in citizenship in a free government, "common to the citizens in the latter states under their constitutions and laws by virtue of their being citizens." Of that provision it has been said, with the approval of this court, that no other one in the constitution has tended so strongly to constitute the citizens of the United States one people. * * *

* * *

But what was secured to colored citizens of the United States—as between them and their respective states—by the grant to them of state citizenship? With what rights, privileges, or immunities did this grant from the nation invest them? There is one, if there be no others—exemption from race discrimination in respect of any civil right belonging to citizens of the white race in the same state. That, surely, is their constitutional privilege when within the jurisdiction of other states. And such must be their constitutional right, in their own state, unless the recent amendments be "splendid baubles," thrown out to delude those who deserved fair and generous treatment at the hands of the nation. Citizenship in this country necessarily imports equality of civil rights among citizens of every race in the same state. It is fundamental in American citizenship that, in respect of such rights, there shall be no discrimination by the state, or its officers, or by individuals, or corporations exercising public functions or authority, against any citizen because of his race or previous condition of servitude. * * *

Much light is thrown upon this part of the discussion by the language of this court in reference to the fifteenth amendment. In U. S. v. Cruikshank [92 U.S. at 555, 23 L.Ed. at 588 (1876)] it was said:

"In U. S. v. Reese, 92 U.S. 214, 23 L.Ed. 563 (1876), we held that the fifteenth amendment has invested the citizens of the United States with a new constitutional right, which is exemption from discrimination in the exercise of the elective franchise on account of race, color, or previous condition of servitude. From this it appears that the right of suffrage is not a necessary attribute of national citizenship, but that exemption from discrimination in the exercise of that right on account of race, etc., is. The right to vote in the states comes from the states; but the right of exemption from the prohibited discrimination comes from the United States. The first has not been granted or secured by the constitution of the United States, but the last has been."

Here, in language at once clear and forcible, is stated the principle for which I contend. It can hardly be claimed that exemption from race discrimination, in respect of civil rights, against those to whom state citizenship was granted by the nation, is any less for the colored race a new constitutional right, derived from and secured by the national constitution, than is exemption from such discrimination in the exercise of the elective franchise. It cannot be that the latter is an attribute of national citizenship, while the other is not essential in national citizenship, or fundamental in state citizenship.

If, then, exemption from discrimination in respect of civil rights is a new constitutional right, secured by the grant of state citizenship to colored citizens of the United States, why may not the nation, by means of its own legislation of a primary direct character, guard, protect, and enforce that right? It is a right and privilege which the nation conferred. It did not come from the states in which those colored citizens reside. It has been the established doctrine of this court during all its history, accepted as vital to the national supremacy, that congress, in the absence of a positive delegation of power to the state legislatures, may by legislation enforce and protect any right derived from or created by the national constitution. * * *

* * *

SHELLEY v. KRAEMER

Supreme Court of the United States, 1948
334 U.S. 1, 68 S.Ct. 836, 92 L.Ed. 1161

This dispute involved purchase of a parcel of land by Shelley, a Negro, from one Fitzgerald in a St. Louis neighborhood where deeds held by three-quarters of the property owners contained a prohibition against sale of their land to buyers "of the Negro or Mongolian race." The neighborhood restriction had been operative since 1911 when the holders of the properties agreed in a fifty-year contract pledging not to sell to persons of the two races specified. Shelley purchased the property from Fitzgerald without knowing it was covered by the restrictive covenant. When he refused to reconsider the purchase after learning of the racial exclusion, Kraemer, a resident of the neighborhood whose deed bore a similar restriction, sued to restrain Shelley from taking possession of the property. The trial court held the covenant technically faulty but was reversed on appeal by Kraemer to the Missouri Supreme Court. That court held the agreement valid, concluded that it violated no rights guaranteed by the U. S. Constitution, and directed the trial court to issue the injunction. Shelley appealed to the United States Supreme Court. This case was heard together with another controversy from Michigan involving a similar restrictive covenant.

Mr. Chief Justice VINSON delivered the opinion of the Court.

* * *

Whether the equal protection clause of the Fourteenth Amendment inhibits judicial enforcement by state courts of restrictive covenants based on race or color is a question which this Court has not heretofore been called upon to consider. * * *

* * *

It is well, at the outset, to scrutinize the terms of the restrictive agreements involved in these cases. In the Missouri case, the covenant declares that no part of the affected property shall be * * * "occupied by any person not of the Caucasian race, it being intended hereby to restrict the use of said property * * * against the occupancy as owners or tenants of any portion of said property for resident or other purpose by people of the Negro or Mongolian Race." Not only does the restriction seek to proscribe use and occupancy of the affected properties by members of the excluded class, but as construed by the Missouri courts, the agreement requires that title of any person who uses his property in violation of the restriction shall be divested. * * *

It should be observed that these covenants do not seek to proscribe any particular use of the affected properties. Use of the properties for residential occupancy, as such, is not forbidden. The restrictions of these agreements, rather, are directed toward a designated class of persons and seek to determine who may and who may not own or make use of the properties for residential purposes. The excluded class is defined wholly in terms of race or color; "simply that and nothing more."

It cannot be doubted that among the civil rights intended to be protected from discriminatory state action by the Fourteenth Amendment are the rights to acquire, enjoy, own and dispose of property. Equality in the enjoyment of property rights was regarded by the framers of that Amendment as an essential pre-condition to the realization of other basic civil rights and liberties which the Amendment was intended to guarantee. Thus § 1978 of the Revised Statutes, derived from § 1 of the Civil Rights Act of 1866 which was enacted by Congress while the Fourteenth Amendment was also under consideration, provides:

"All citizens of the United States shall have the same right, in every State and Territory, as is enjoyed by white citizens thereof to inherit, purchase, lease, sell, hold, and convey real and personal property."

It is likewise clear that restrictions on the right of occupancy of the sort sought to be created by the private agreements in these cases could not be squared with the requirements of the Fourteenth Amendment if imposed by state statute or local ordinance. * * *

* * *

But the present cases * * * do not involve action by state legislatures or city councils. Here the particular patterns of discrimination and the areas in which the restrictions are to operate, are determined, in the first instance, by the terms of agreements among private individuals. Participation of the State consists in the enforcement of the restrictions so defined. The crucial issue with which we are here confronted is whether this distinction removes these cases from the operation of the prohibitory provisions of the Fourteenth Amendment.

Since the decision of this Court in the Civil Rights Cases, 1883, 109 U.S. 3, 3 S.Ct. 18, the principle has become firmly embedded in our constitutional law that the action inhibited by the first section of the Fourteenth Amendment is only such action as may fairly be said to be that of the States. That Amendment erects no shield against merely private conduct, however discriminatory or wrongful.

We conclude, therefore, that the restrictive agreements standing alone cannot be regarded as a violation of any rights guaranteed to petitioners by the Fourteenth Amendment. So long as the purposes of those agreements are effectuated by voluntary adherence to their terms, it would appear clear that there has been no action by the State and the provisions of the Amendment have not been violated. * * *

But here there was more. These are cases in which the purposes of the agreements were secured only by judicial enforcement by state courts of the restrictive terms of the agreements. The respondents urge that judicial enforcement of private agreements does not amount to state action; or, in any event, the participation of the State is so attenuated

in character as not to amount to state action within the meaning of the Fourteenth Amendment.
* * *

That the action of state courts and of judicial officers in their official capacities is to be regarded as action of the State within the meaning of the Fourteenth Amendment, is a proposition which has long been established by decisions of this Court.
* * *

* * *

The short of the matter is that from the time of the adoption of the Fourteenth Amendment until the present, it has been the consistent ruling of this Court that the action of the States to which the Amendment has reference, includes action of state courts and state judicial officials. Although, in construing the terms of the Fourteenth Amendment, differences have from time to time been expressed as to whether particular types of state action may be said to offend the Amendment's prohibitory provisions, it has never been suggested that state court action is immunized from the operation of those provisions simply because the act is that of the judicial branch of the state government.

* * *

We hold that in granting judicial enforcement of the restrictive agreements in these cases, the States have denied petitioners the equal protection of the laws and that, therefore, the action of the state courts cannot stand. We have noted that freedom from discrimination by the States in the enjoyment of property rights was among the basic objectives sought to be effectuated by the framers of the

Fourteenth Amendment. That such discrimination has occurred in these cases is clear. * * *

Reversed.

Mr. Justice REED, Mr. Justice JACKSON, and Mr. Justice RUTLEDGE took no part in the consideration or decision of these cases.

BURTON v. WILMINGTON PARKING AUTHORITY

Supreme Court of the United States, 1961
365 U.S. 715, 81 S.Ct. 856, 6 L.Ed.2d 45

The facts are set out in the opinion below.

Mr. Justice CLARK delivered the opinion of the Court.

In this action for declaratory and injunctive relief it is admitted that the Eagle Coffee Shoppe, Inc., a restaurant located within an off-street automobile parking building in Wilmington, Delaware, has refused to serve appellant food or drink solely because he is a Negro. The parking building is owned and operated by the Wilmington Parking Authority, an agency of the State of Delaware, and the restaurant is the Authority's lessee. Appellant claims that such refusal abridges his rights under the Equal Protection Clause of the Fourteenth Amendment to the United States Constitution. The Supreme Court of Delaware has held that Eagle was acting in "a purely private capacity" under its lease; that its action was not that of the Authority and was not, therefore, state action within the contemplation of the prohibitions contained in that Amendment. It also held that under 24 Del.Code § 1501, Eagle was a restaurant, not an inn, and that as such it "is not required [under Delaware law] to serve any and all persons entering its place of business." * * * On the merits we have concluded that the exclusion of appellant under the circumstances shown to be present here was discriminatory state action in violation of the Equal Protection Clause of the Fourteenth Amendment.

The Authority * * * is "a public body corporate and politic, exercising public powers of the State as an agency thereof." Its statutory purpose is to provide adequate parking facilities for the convenience of the public and thereby relieve the "parking crisis, which threatens the welfare of the community." * * *

* * *

The land and building were publicly owned. As an entity, the building was dedicated to "public uses" in performance of the Authority's "essential governmental functions." * * * The costs of land acquisition, construction, and maintenance are defrayed entirely from donations by the City of Wilmington, from loans and revenue bonds and from the proceeds of rentals and parking services out of which the loans and bonds were payable. * * * [T]he commercially leased areas were not surplus state property, but constituted a physically and financially integral and, indeed, indispensable part of the State's plan to operate its project as a self-sustaining unit. Upkeep and maintenance of the building, including necessary repairs, were responsibilities of the Authority and were payable out of public funds. It cannot be doubted that the peculiar relationship of the restaurant to the parking facility in which it is located confers on each an incidental variety of mutual benefits. Guests of the restaurant are afforded a convenient place to park their automobiles, even if they cannot enter the restaurant directly from the parking area. Similarly, its convenience for diners may well provide additional demand for the Authority's parking facilities. Should any improvements effected in the leasehold by Eagle become part of the realty, there is no possibility of increased taxes being passed on to it since the fee is held by a tax-exempt government agency. Neither can it be ignored, especially in view of Eagle's affirmative allegation that for it to serve Negroes would injure its business, that profits earned by discrimination not only contribute to, but also are indispensable elements in, the financial success of a governmental agency.

Addition of all these activities, obligations and responsibilities of the Authority, the benefits mutually conferred, together with the obvious fact that the restaurant is operated as an integral part of a public building devoted to a public parking service, indicates that degree of state participation and involvement in discriminatory action which it was the design of the Fourteenth Amendment to condemn. * * * By its inaction, the Authority, and through it the State, has not only made itself a party to the refusal of service, but has elected to place its power, property and prestige behind the admitted discrimination. The State has so far insinuated itself into a position of interdependence with Eagle that it must be recognized as a joint participant in the challenged activity, which, on that account, cannot be considered to have been so "purely private" as to fall without the scope of the Fourteenth Amendment.

* * * Specifically defining the limits of our inquiry, what we hold today is that when a State leases public property in the manner and for the purpose shown to have been the case here, the proscriptions of the Fourteenth Amendment must be complied with by the lessee as certainly as though they were binding covenants written into the agreement itself.

* * *

Reversed and remanded.

[Justices FRANKFURTER, HARLAN, and WHITTAKER dissented.]

THE WARREN COURT AND OTHER "PRIVATE" DISCRIMINATION CASES

Case	Link to "state action"	Vote
Peterson v. City of Greenville, 373 U.S. 244, 83 S.Ct. 1119 (1963)	Even though store manager may have acted on basis of his own views when he ordered black customers to leave after they insisted on being served at all-white lunch counter, conviction of the defendants for trespass could not stand where city had on its books an ordinance requiring segregated restaurants; existence of ordinance negated presumption store manager acted on his own	8–1

"PRIVATE" DISCRIMINATION CASES (*Cont.*)

Case	Link to "state action"	Vote
Lombard v. Louisiana, 373 U.S. 267, 83 S.Ct. 1122 (1963)	Conviction of black customers under state criminal mischief statute for demanding service at all-white lunch counter overturned because mayor and police chief had announced policy of not tolerating any "sit-ins" to desegregate eating places	8–1
Robinson v. Florida, 378 U.S. 153, 84 S.Ct. 1693 (1964)	Conviction of black and white defendants, who together had demanded service at all-white restaurant and refused to leave when asked, overturned. Store restaurant had refused service because it would not have been in compliance with state statutes which specified that "where colored persons are employed or accommodated" separate toilet and washroom facilities must be provided. While these "regulations do not directly and expressly forbid restaurants to serve both white and colored people together, they certainly embody a state policy putting burdens upon any restaurant which serves both races, burdens bound to discourage the serving of the two races together"	9–0
Evans v. Newton, 382 U.S. 296, 86 S.Ct. 486 (1966)	Where, under conditions of a will controlling use of the property, city was to utilize land as a park for the enjoyment of whites only, and where the park was maintained for years by the city, became an integral part of municipal activities, and was granted tax exemption, mere removal of city as trustee and transfer of land title to private trustees, without altering the fact that city continued to care for and maintain the park, would not permit segregation in the park	6–3
Reitman v. Mulkey, 387 U.S. 369, 87 S.Ct. 1627 (1967)	Proposition 14 passed by public referendum, which amended the California constitution by prohibiting the state or any of its subdivisions from interfering with "the right of any person who is willing or desires to sell, lease or rent any part or all of his real property, to decline to sell, lease or rent such property to such person or persons as he, in his absolute discretion chooses," did not merely effect repeal of existing open housing laws but "involve[d] the State in private racial discriminations to an unconstitutional degree" because "[t]he right to discriminate, including the right to discriminate on racial grounds, was now embodied in the State's basic charter, immune from legislative, executive, or judicial regulation at any level of the state government. * * * All individuals, partnerships, corporations and other legal entities, as well as their agents and representatives, * * * [would have been able to] discriminate with respect to their real property, which is defined as any interest in real property of any kind or quality, 'irrespective of how obtained or financed,' and seemingly irrespective of the relationship of the State to such interests in real property. Only the State * * * [would have been] excluded with respect to property owned by it."	5–4

Leroy Irvis, a Negro, was refused service solely on account of his race by a branch of the Moose Lodge located in Harrisburg, Pennsylvania to which he had been invited as a guest. Irvis subsequently sued for injunctive relief in a federal district court charging that the discrimination was "state action" because the club possessed a liquor license issued by the Pennsylvania liquor board. The district court held the club's membership and guest policies to be racially discriminatory and ordered the club's liquor license revoked until these practices ceased. On Moose Lodge's petition, the Supreme Court granted certiorari. In Moose Lodge No. 107 v. Irvis, 407 U.S. 163, 92 S.Ct. 1965 (1972), the Supreme Court dismissed any challenge to the club's exclusionary membership policy on grounds Irvis as a guest had no standing to challenge it and reversed the finding of "state action" in the discrimination to which he was subjected. Speaking for the six-man majority, Justice Rehnquist said:

> The Court has never held, of course, that discrimination by an otherwise private entity would be violative of the Equal Protection Clause if the private entity receives any sort of benefit or service at all from the State, or if it is subject to state regulation in any degree whatever. Since state-furnished services include such necessities of life as electricity, water, and police and fire protection, such a holding would utterly emasculate the distinction between private as distinguished from State conduct set forth in *The Civil Rights Cases* and adhered to in subsequent decisions. Our holdings indicate that where the impetus for the discrimination is private, the State must have "significantly involved itself with invidious discriminations," * * * in order for the discriminatory action to fall within the ambit of the constitutional prohibition.

The Court then went on to distinguish the circumstances of this case from those in *Peterson* and *Burton*. In answer to the charge that by its "pervasive regulation" of licensees and the limited availability of the licenses which produced a quasi-monopoly the state had become a partner in the discrimination, Justice Rehnquist concluded:

> However detailed this type of regulation may be in some particulars, it cannot be said to in any way foster or encourage racial discrimination. Nor can it be said to make the State in any realistic sense a partner or even a joint venturer in the club's enterprise. The limited effect of the prohibition against obtaining additional club licenses when the maximum number of retail licenses allotted to a municipality has been issued, when considered together with the availability of liquor from hotel, restaurant, and retail licensees falls far short of conferring upon club licensees a monopoly in the dispensing of liquor in any given municipality or in the State as a whole. We therefore hold that, with the exception hereafter noted, the operation of the regulatory scheme enforced by the Pennsylvania Liquor Control Board does not sufficiently implicate the State in the discriminatory guest policies of Moose Lodge so as to make the latter "State action" within the ambit of the Equal Protection Clause of the Fourteenth Amendment.

Justice Brennan dissented in an opinion in which Justice Marshall joined. Quoting generously from the lower court opinion, Justice Brennan found liquor regulation substantially different from other types of state licensing and thus justifying a finding of "state action." In sum, he said:

> When Moose Lodge obtained its liquor license, the State of Pennsylvania became an active participant in the operation of the Lodge bar. Liquor licensing laws are only incidently revenue measures; they are primarily pervasive regulatory schemes under which the State dictates and continually supervises virtually every detail of the operation of the licensee's business. Very few, if any, other licensed businesses experience such complete state involvement. Yet the Court holds that that involvement does not constitute "state action" making the Lodge's refusal to serve a guest liquor solely because of his race a violation of the Fourteenth Amendment. The vital flaw in the Court's reasoning is its complete disregard of the fundamental value underlying the "state action" concept. * * *

Justice Douglas dissented in a separate opinion.

JACKSON v. METROPOLITAN EDISON CO.

Supreme Court of the United States, 1974
419 U.S. 345, 95 S.Ct. 449, 42 L.Ed.2d 477

Metropolitan Edison Company, a privately owned corporation delivering electric power and operating under a certificate from the Pennsylvania Public Utilities Commission, terminated service to Catherine Jackson. Several years before, her electric service had been discontinued for failure to pay the bills, and she subsequently had arranged to have an account with the company opened in the name of another occupant of the residence. No payments were made however, and when agents of the electric company came to inquire, they discovered that the meter had been tampered with so that it did not accurately measure the electricity which was being used. Ms. Jackson denied any knowledge of this, and several days later, without additional notice, the electric company shut off her power. Ms. Jackson brought suit under the Civil Rights Act, 42 U.S.C.A. § 1983, for failure to provide electricity until she had been afforded notice, hearing, and an opportunity to pay any amounts due. The federal district court dismissed her complaint finding no element of "state action" in the company's actions, and that conclusion was affirmed on appeal. The Supreme Court granted her petition for certiorari.

Mr. Justice REHNQUIST delivered the opinion of the Court.

* * *

The Due Process Clause of the Fourteenth Amendment provides "nor shall any State deprive any person of life, liberty, or property, without due process of law." In 1883, this Court in The Civil Rights Cases, 109 U.S. 3, 3 S.Ct. 18, affirmed the essential dichotomy set forth in that Amendment between deprivation by the State, subject to scrutiny under its provisions, and private conduct, "however discriminatory and wrongful," against which the Fourteenth Amendment offers no shield. * * *

We have reiterated that distinction on more than one occasion since then. * * * While the principle that private action is immune from the restrictions of the Fourteenth Amendment is well established and easily stated, the question whether particular conduct is "private," on the one hand, or "state action," on the other, frequently admits of no easy answer. * * *

Here the action complained of was taken by a utility company which is privately owned and operated, but which in many particulars of its business is subject to extensive state regulation. The mere fact that a business is subject to state regulation does not by itself convert its action into that of the State for purposes of the Fourteenth Amendment. * * * Nor does the fact that the regulation is extensive and detailed, as in the case of most public utilities, do so. * * * It may well be that acts of a heavily regulated utility with at least something of a governmentally protected monopoly will more readily be found to be "state" acts than will the acts of an entity lacking these characteristics. But the inquiry must be whether there is a sufficiently close nexus between the State and the challenged action of the regulated entity so that the action of the latter may be fairly treated as that of the State itself. * * * The true nature of the State's involvement may not be immediately obvious, and detailed inquiry may be required in order to determine whether the test is met. * * *

* * *

Metropolitan is a privately owned corporation, and it does not lease its facilities from the State of Pennsylvania. It alone is responsible for the provision of power to its customers. In common with all corporations of the State it pays taxes to the State, and it is subject to a form of extensive regulation by the State in a way that most other business enterprises are not. But this was likewise true of the appellant club in *Moose Lodge No. 107* v. *Irvis,* [407 U.S. 163, 173, 92 S.Ct. 1965, 1971 (1972)] where we said:

"However detailed this type of regulation may be in some particulars, it cannot be said to in any way foster or encourage racial discrimination. Nor can it be said to make the State in any realistic sense a partner or even a joint venturer in the club's enterprise." Id., 407 U.S. at 177, 92 S.Ct. at 1973.

All of petitioner's arguments taken together show no more than that Metropolitan was a heavily regulated private utility, enjoying at least a partial monopoly in the providing of electrical service within its territory, and that it elected to terminate service to petitioner in a manner which the Pennsylvania Public Utilities Commission found permissible under state law. Under our decision this is not sufficient to connect the State of Pennsylvania with respondent's action so as to make the latter's conduct attributable to the State for purposes of the Fourteenth Amendment.

We conclude that the State of Pennsylvania is not sufficiently connected with respondent's action in terminating petitioner's service so as to make respondent's conduct in so doing attributable to the State for purposes of the Fourteenth Amendment. We therefore have no occasion to decide whether petitioner's claim to continued service was "property" for purposes of that Amendment, or whether "due process of law" would require a State taking similar action to accord petitioner the procedural rights for which she contends. The judgment of the Court of Appeals for the Third Circuit is therefore

Affirmed.

Mr. Justice DOUGLAS, dissenting.

I reach the opposite conclusion from that reached by the majority on the state action issue.

The injury alleged took place when respondent discontinued its service to this householder without notice or opportunity to remedy or contest her alleged default, even though its tariff provided that respondent might "discontinue its service on reasonable notice." May a State allow a utility—which in this case has no competitor—to exploit its monopoly in violation of its own tariff? May a utility have complete immunity under federal law when the State allows its regulatory agency to become the prisoner of the utility or, by a listless attitude of no concern, to permit the utility to use its monopoly power in a lawless way?

* * *

It is said that the mere fact of respondent's monopoly status assuming *arguendo* that that status is state-conferred or state-protected, "is not determinative in considering whether Metropolitan's termination of service to petitioner was 'state action' for purposes of the Fourteenth Amendment." * * * Even so, a state-protected monopoly status is highly relevant in assessing the aggregate weight of a private entity's ties to the State.

It is said that the fact that respondent's services are "affected with a public interest" is not determinative. I agree that doctors, lawyers, and grocers are not transformed into state actors simply because they provide arguably essential goods and services and are regulated by the State. In the present case, however, respondent is not just one person among many; it is the only public utility furnishing electric power to the town. When power is

denied a householder, the home, under modern conditions, is likely to become unlivable.

* * *

In the aggregate, [a review of the facts] depict a monopolist providing essential public services as a licensee of the State and within a framework of extensive state supervison and control. The particular regulations at issue, promulgated by the monopolist, were authorized by state law and were made enforceable by the weight and authority of the State. Moreover, the State retains the power of oversight to review and amend the regulations if the public interest so requires. Respondent's actions are sufficiently intertwined with those of the State, and its termination-of-service provisions are sufficiently buttressed by state law, to warrant a holding that respondent's actions in terminating this householder's service were "state action" for the purpose of giving federal jurisdiction over respondent under 42 U.S.C.A. § 1983. Though the Court pays lip service to the need for assessing the totality of the State's involvement in this enterprise, * * * its underlying analysis is fundamentally sequential rather than cumulative. In that perspective, what the Court does today is to make a significant departure from our previous treatment of state action issues.

* * *

Mr. Justice BRENNAN, dissenting.

I do not think that a controversy existed between petitioner and respondent entitling petitioner to be heard in this action. * * * I would therefore intimate no view upon the correctness of the holdings below whether the termination of service on October 6, 1971, constituted state action but would vacate the judgment of the Court of Appeals with direction that the case be remanded to the District Court with instruction to enter a new judgment dismissing the complaint. * * *

Mr. Justice MARSHALL, dissenting.

I agree with my Brother Brennan that this case is a very poor vehicle for resolving the difficult and important questions presented today. The confusing sequence of events leading to the challenged termination make it unclear whether petitioner has a property right under state law to the service she was receiving from the respondent company. Because these complexities would seriously hamper resolution of the merits of the case, I would dismiss the writ as improvidently granted. Since the Court has disposed of the case by finding no state action, however, I think it appropriate to register my dissent on that point.

* * *

When the State confers a monopoly on a group or organization, this Court has held that the organization assumes many of the obligations of the State. * * * Even when the Court has not found state action based solely on the State's conferral of a monopoly, it has suggested that the monopoly factor weighs heavily in determining whether constitutional obligations can be imposed on formally private entities. * * * Indeed, in Moose Lodge No. 107 v. Irvis, 407 U.S. 163, 177, 92 S.Ct. 1965, 1973 (1972), the court was careful to point out that the Pennsylvania liquor licensing scheme "falls far short of conferring upon club licensees a monopoly in the dis-

pensing of liquor in any given municipality or in the State as a whole."

The majority distinguishes this line of cases with a cryptic assertion that public utility companies are "natural monopolies." * * * The theory behind the distinction appears to be that since the State's purpose in regulating a natural monopoly is not to aid the company but to prevent its charging monopoly prices, the State's involvement is somehow less significant for state action purposes. I cannot agree that so much should turn on so narrow a distinction. Initially, it is far from obvious that an electric company would not be subject to competition if the market were unimpeded by governmental restrictions. Certainly the "start-up" costs of initiating electric service are substantial, but the rewards available in a relatively inelastic market might well be sufficient under the right circumstances to attract competitive investment. Instead, the State has chosen to forbid the high profit margins that might invite private competition or increase pressure for state ownership and operation of electric power facilities.

The difficulty inherent in this kind of economic analysis counsels against excusing natural monopolies from the reach of state action principles. To invite inquiry into whether a particular state-sanctioned monopoly might have survived without the State's express approval grounds the analysis in hopeless speculation. Worse, this approach ignores important implications of the State's policy of utilizing private monopolies to provide electric service. Encompassed within this policy is the State's determination not to permit governmental competition with the selected private company, but to cooperate with and regulate the company in a multitude of ways to ensure that the company's service will be the functional equivalent of service provided by the State.

* * *

The majority's conclusion that there is no state action in this case is likely guided in part by its reluctance to impose on a utility company burdens that might ultimately hurt consumers more than they would help them. Elaborate hearings prior to termination might be quite expensive, and for a responsible company there might be relatively few cases in which such hearings would do any good. The solution to this problem, however, is to require only abbreviated pretermination procedures for all utility companies, not to free the "private" companies to behave however they see fit. At least on occasion, utility companies have failed to demonstrate much sensitivity to the extreme importance of the service they render, and in some cities, the percentage of error in service termination is disturbingly high. * * * Accordingly, I think that at the minimum, due process would require ad-

vance notice of a proposed termination with a clear indication that a responsible company official can readily be contacted to consider any claim of error.

What is perhaps most troubling about the Court's opinion is that it would appear to apply to a broad range of claimed constitutional violations by the company. The Court has not adopted the notion, accepted elsewhere, that different standards should apply to state action analysis when different constitutional claims are presented. * * * Thus, the majority's analysis would seemingly apply as well to a company that refused to extend service to Negroes, welfare recipients, or any other group that the company preferred, for its own reasons, not to serve. I cannot believe that this Court would hold that the State's involvement with the utility company was not sufficient to impose upon the company an obligation to meet the constitutional mandate of nondiscrimination. Yet nothing in the analysis of the majority opinion suggests otherwise.

I dissent.

JONES v. ALFRED H. MAYER CO.

Supreme Court of the United States, 1968
392 U.S. 409, 88 S.Ct. 2186, 20 L.Ed.2d 1189

The facts are contained in the opinion.

Mr. Justice STEWART delivered the opinion of the Court.

In this case we are called upon to determine the scope and constitutionality of an Act of Congress, 42 U.S. C.A. § 1982, which provides that:

"All citizens of the United States shall have the same right, in every State and Territory, as is enjoyed by

white citizens thereof to inherit, purchase, lease, sell, hold, and convey real and personal property."

On September 2, 1965, the petitioners filed a complaint in the District Court for the Eastern District of Missouri, alleging that the respondents had refused to sell them a home in the Paddock Woods community of St. Louis County for the sole reason that petitioner Joseph Lee Jones is a Negro. Relying in part upon § 1982, the petitioners sought injunctive and other relief. The District Court sustained the respondents' motion to dismiss the complaint, and the Court of Appeals for the Eighth Circuit affirmed, concluding that § 1982 applies only to state action and does not reach private refusals to sell. * * * [W]e reverse the judgment of the Court of Appeals. We hold that § 1982 bars *all* racial discrimination, private as well as public, in the sale or rental of property, and that the statute, thus construed, is a valid exercise of the power of Congress to enforce the Thirteenth Amendment.

At the outset, it is important to make clear precisely what this case does *not* involve. Whatever else it may be, 42 U.S.C.A. § 1982 is not a comprehensive open housing law. In sharp contrast to the Fair Housing Title (Title VIII) of the Civil Rights Act of 1968, 82 Stat. 81, the statute in this case deals only with racial discrimination and does not address itself to discrimination on grounds of religion or national origin. It does not deal specifically with discrimination in the provision of services or facilities in connection with the sale or rental of a dwelling. It does not prohibit advertising or other representations that indicate discriminatory preferences. It does not refer explicitly to discrimination in financing arrangements or in the provision of brokerage services. It does not empower a federal administrative agency to assist aggrieved parties. It makes no provision for intervention by the Attorney General. And, although it can be enforced by injunction, it contains no provision expressly authorizing a federal court to order the payment of damages.

Thus, although § 1982 contains none of the exemptions that Congress included in the Civil Rights Act of 1968, it would be a serious mistake to suppose that § 1982 in any way diminishes the significance of the law recently enacted by Congress. Indeed, the Senate Subcommittee on Housing and Urban Affairs was informed in hearings held after the Court of Appeals had rendered its decision in this case that § 1982 might well be "a presently valid federal statutory ban against discrimination by private persons in the sale or lease of real property." The Subcommittee was told, however, that even if this Court should so construe § 1982, the existence of that statute would not "eliminate the need for congressional action" to spell out "responsibility on the part of the federal government to enforce the rights it protects." The point was made that, in light of the many difficulties confronted by private litigants seeking to enforce such rights on their own, "legislation is needed to establish federal machinery for enforcement of the rights guaranteed under Section 1982 of Title 42 even if the plaintiffs in *Jones* v. *Alfred H. Mayer Company* should prevail in the United States Supreme Court."

* * *

We begin with the language of the statute itself. In plain and unambiguous terms, § 1982 grants to all citizens, without regard to race or color, "the same right" to purchase and lease property "as is enjoyed by white citizens." As the Court of Appeals in this case evidently recognized, that right can be impaired as effectively by "those who place property on the market" as by the State itself. * * *

On its face, therefore, § 1982 appears to prohibit *all* discrimination against Negroes in the sale or rental of property—discrimination by private owners as well as discrimination by public authorities. Indeed, even the respondents seem to concede that, if § 1982 "means what it says"—to use the words of the respondents' brief—then it must encompass every racially motivated refusal to sell or rent and cannot be confined to officially sanctioned segregation in housing. Stressing what they consider to be the revolutionary implications of so literal a reading of § 1982, the respondents argue that Congress cannot possibly have intended any such result. Our examination of the relevant history, however, persuades us that Congress meant exactly what it said.

* * *

The remaining question is whether Congress has power under the Constitution to do what § 1982 purports to do: to prohibit all racial discrimination, private and public, in the sale and rental of property. Our starting point is the Thirteenth Amendment. * * *

As its text reveals, the Thirteenth Amendment "is not a mere prohibition of state laws establishing or upholding slavery, but an absolute declaration that slavery or involuntary servitude shall not exist in any part of the United States." Civil Rights Cases, 109 U.S. 3, 20, 3 S.Ct. 18, 28. It has never been doubted, therefore, "that the power vested in Congress to enforce the article by appropriate legislation," * * * includes the power to enact laws "direct and primary, operating upon the acts of in-

dividuals, whether sanctioned by state legislation or not." * * *

Thus, the fact that § 1982 operates upon the unofficial acts of private individuals, whether or not sanctioned by state law, presents no constitutional problem. If Congress has power under the Thirteenth Amendment to eradicate conditions that prevent Negroes from buying and renting property because of their race or color, then no federal statute calculated to achieve that objective can be thought to exceed the constitutional power of Congress simply because it reaches beyond state action to regulate the conduct of private individuals. The constitutional question in this case, therefore, comes to this: Does the authority of Congress to enforce the Thirteenth Amendment "by appropriate legislation" include the power to eliminate all racial barriers to the acquisition of real and personal property? We think the answer to that question is plainly yes.

* * *

* * * Surely Congress has the power under the Thirteenth Amendment rationally to determine what are the badges and the incidents of slavery, and the authority to translate that determination into effective legislation. Nor can we say that the determination Congress has made is an irrational one. For this Court recognized long ago that, whatever else they may have encompassed, the badges and incidents of slavery—its "burdens and disabilities"—included restraints upon "those fundamental rights which are the essence of civil freedom, namely, the same right * * * to inherit, purchase, lease, sell and convey property, as is enjoyed by white citizens." Civil

Rights Cases, 109 U.S. 3, 22, 3 S.Ct. 18, 29. * * *

Negro citizens, North and South, who saw in the Thirteenth Amendment a promise of freedom—freedom to "go and come at pleasure" and to "buy and sell when they please"— would be left with "a mere paper guarantee" if Congress were powerless to assure that a dollar in the hands of a Negro will purchase the same thing as a dollar in the hands of a white man. At the very least, the freedom that Congress is empowered to secure under the Thirteenth Amendment includes the freedom to buy whatever a white man can buy, the right to live wherever a white man can live. If Congress cannot say that being a free man means at least this much, then the Thirteenth Amendment made a promise the Nation cannot keep.

*   *   *

Reversed.

Mr. Justice HARLAN, whom Mr. Justice WHITE joins, dissenting.

The decision in this case appears to me to be most ill-considered and ill-advised.

*   *   *

For reasons which follow, I believe that the Court's construction of § 1982 as applying to purely private action is almost surely wrong, and at the least is open to serious doubt. The issues of the constitutionality of § 1982, as construed by the Court, and of liability under the Fourteenth Amendment alone, also present formidable difficulties. Moreover, the political processes of our own era

have, since the date of oral argument in this case, given birth to a civil rights statute embodying "fair housing" provisions which would at the end of this year make available to others, though apparently not to the petitioners themselves, the type of relief which the petitioners now seek. It seems to me that this latter factor so diminishes the public importance of this case that by far the wisest course would be for this Court to refrain from decision and to dismiss the writ as improvidently granted.

*   *   *

The court rests its opinion chiefly upon the legislative history of the Civil Rights Act of 1866. I shall endeavor to show that those debates do not, as the Court would have it, overwhelmingly support the result reached by the Court, and in fact that a contrary conclusion may equally well be drawn. * * * [Discussion omitted.]

The foregoing, I think, amply demonstrates that the Court has chosen to resolve this case by according to a loosely worded statute a meaning which is open to the strongest challenge in light of the statute's legislative history. In holding that the Thirteenth Amendment is sufficient constitutional authority for § 1982 as interpreted, the Court also decides a question of great importance. Even contemporary supporters of the aims of the 1866 Civil Rights Act doubted that those goals could constitutionally be achieved under the Thirteenth Amendment, and this Court has twice expressed similar doubts. * * *

*   *   *

CASES ON PRIVATE DISCRIMINATION SINCE *JONES*

Griffin v. Brecken- ridge, 403 U.S. 88, 91 S.Ct. 1790 (1971)	Facts	Black plaintiffs, mistaken for civil rights workers, were forced from their car, physically assaulted, and threatened with murder. They brought suit against two white citizens of Mississippi under 42 U.S.C.A. § 1985(3), the Ku Klux Klan Act, a statute derived from the Civil Rights Acts of 1866 and 1871 which allowed persons to recover damages against conspiracies formed by private citizens to abridge their enjoyment of "equal protection of the laws or of equal privileges and immunities under the laws." Lower federal courts denied relief on the grounds that existing interpretation of the statute made it applicable only to those conspiracies "under color of state law."
	Opinion of the Court	Speaking for a unanimous Court, Justice Stewart reasoned that a broad interpretation of the statute to reach entirely private action was justified by both the wording and legislative history of the act, although he took care to note that it was not intended "to apply to all tortious, conspiratorial interferences with the rights of others." Said Justice Stewart: "The language requiring intent to deprive of *equal* protection, or *equal* privileges and immunities, means that there must be some racial, or perhaps otherwise class-based, invidiously discriminatory animus behind the conspirators' action. The conspiracy, in other words, must aim at a deprivation of an equal enjoyment of rights secured by the law to all." Since the right of interstate travel was a privilege of the sort the act was intended to protect, plaintiffs should have the opportunity on remand to establish if they had engaged in or intended to engage in interstate travel.
Runyon v. McCrary, 427 U.S. 160, 96 S.Ct. 2586 (1976)	Facts	Runyon and his wife, proprietors of a private school, denied admission to McCrary on racial grounds, McCrary, a black, brought suit through his parents for declaratory and injunctive relief under 42 U.S.C.A. § 1981 which provides in part that "All persons within the jurisdiction of the United States shall have the same right in every State * * * to make and enforce contracts * * * as is enjoyed by white citizens * * * *"
	Questions Presented	[1] "Whether § 1981 prohibits private, commercially operated, nonsectarian schools from denying admission to prospective students because they are Negroes, and, if so, [2] whether that federal law is constitutional as so applied." This case does not present any question of the right of a private

Runyon (*Cont.*)

Questions Presented (*Cont.*)	social organization to discriminate or of exclusion on religious grounds or restricting admission on the basis of sex.

Opinion of the Court	1. "It is now well established that § 1 of the Civil Rights Act of 1866, 14 Stat. 27, 42 U.S.C.A. § 1981 (1970), prohibits racial discrimination in the making and enforcement of private contracts." Since the school was engaged in commercial, contractual relations, it falls within the ambit of the statute. To argue "that § 1981 does not reach private acts of racial discrimination * * * is wholly inconsistent with *Jones'* interpretation of the legislative history of § 1 of the Civil Rights Act of 1866" as reaffirmed in subsequent cases. Enacting the Equal Employment Opportunity Act of 1972, Congress "specifically considered and rejected an amendment that would have repealed the Civil Rights Act of 1866, as interpreted by this Court in *Jones*, insofar as it affords private sector employees a right of action based on racial discrimination in employment. * * * There could hardly be a clearer indication of congressional agreement with the view that § 1981 *does* reach private acts of racial discrimination."

2. "The question remains whether § 1981, as applied, violates constitutionally protected rights of free association and privacy, or a parent's right to direct the education of his children." As to freedom of association, "parents have a First Amendment right to send their children to educational institutions that promote the belief that racial segregation is desirable, and * * * children have an equal right to attend such institutions. But it does not follow that the practice of excluding racial minorities from such institutions is also protected by the same principle." Discrimination "has never been accorded affirmative constitutional protections" and is, in fact, "subject to special remedial legislation in certain circumstances under § 2 of the Thirteenth Amendment * * *." As to parental rights, the cases hold only that, while a state may establish educational standards, it may not preempt the field and deny parents the right to send their children to private school. "No challenge in made to the petitioners' right to operate their private schools or to the rights of parents to send their children to a particular private school rather than a public school." And, as to the claim of a right of privacy, while certain of the Court's rulings protect "a person's decision whether to bear a child * * * it does not follow that because government is largely or even entirely precluded from regulating the childbearing decision, it is similarly restricted by the Constitution from regulating the implementation of parental decisions concerning a child's educa-

Runyon (*Cont.*)	Opinion of the Court (*Cont.*)	tion." As the Court has repeatedly pointed out, "while parents have a constitutional right to send their children to private schools and a constitutional right to select private schools that offer specialized instruction, they have no constitutional right to provide their children with private school education unfettered by reasonable government regulation."
	Concurring Opinions	Justice Powell wrote: "If the slate were clean I might well be inclined to agree with Mr. Justice White that § 1981 was not intended to restrict private contractual choices. Much of the review of the history and purpose of this statute set forth in his dissenting opinion is quite persuasive. It seems to me, however, that it comes too late." Observing also that "[a] small kindergarten or music class, operated on the basis of personal invitations extended to a limited number of preidentified students * * * would present a far different case" because it would seem the essence of a "private" contract, Justice Powell pointed out that this case was much nearer the reach of the statute because of the "public offer" apparent in the Runyons' advertisement in the yellow pages and their extensive mail-order solicitation.
		"[P]ersuaded * * * that we must either apply the rationale of *Jones* or overrule that decision," Justice Stevens decided to follow *Jones* and cases decided subsequent to it, despite his conviction that they constituted "a line of authority which I firmly believe to have been incorrectly decided," because of "the interest in stability and orderly development of the law" and the fact that "even if *Jones* did not accurately reflect the sentiments of the Reconstruction Congress, it surely accords with the prevailing sense of justice today." Given the movement of recent years "in the direction of eliminating racial segregation in all sections of society," he added, "for the Court now to overrule *Jones* would be a significant step backwards, with effects that would not have arisen from a correct decision in the first instance."
	Dissent	Justice White, joined by Justice Rehnquist, concluded "The legislative history of 42 U.S.C.A. § 1981 confirms that the statute means what it says and no more, i.e., that it outlaws any legal rule disabling any person from making or enforcing a contract, but does not prohibit private racially motivated refusals to contract."
McDonald v. Santa Fe Trail Transportation Co., 427 U.S. 273, 96 S.Ct. 2574 (1976)	Facts	Title VII of the Civil Rights Act of 1964 prohibits the discharge of an employee on the basis of race. Two discharged white employees brought suit under that statute and under 42 U.S.C.A. § 1981 when they were fired for misappropriating cargo

McDonald (*Cont.*)	Facts (*Cont.*)	while a black employee charged with the same offense was not.
	Opinion of the Court	Justice Marshall, speaking for the Court, held that the legislative history of both statutes made it clear that the ban on racial discrimination in private employment and the guarantee of contractual equality protected whites as well as nonwhites.
	Dissent	Justices White and Rehnquist dissented, consistent with their position in *Runyon*, on the grounds that § 1981 was not applicable in this case.

CITY OF MEMPHIS v. GREENE

Supreme Court of the United States, 1981
451 U.S. 100, 101 S.Ct. 1584, 67 L.Ed.2d 769

Hein Park, a small residential community in Memphis, Tennessee, is bounded on three sides by thoroughfares and on the fourth by the campus of Southwestern University. West Drive, one of three streets entering Hein Park from the north, is a two-lane, half-mile-long thoroughfare passing through the center of Hein Park. To the south, West Drive ends with the entrance to Overton Park; to the north, it terminates at the intersection of Jackson Avenue and Springdale Street, two heavily traveled, four-lane arteries. The area to the north of Hein Park is predominantly black. At the time the decision was made to close West Drive, Hein Park was all white.

In 1970, the Hein Park Civic Association filed an application, signed by a number of property owners with lots along West Drive, to close that street for twenty-five feet south of Jackson Avenue. After extensive hearings the city granted the request and gave the following reasons: to reduce the flow of through traffic using the subdivision's streets; to reduce "traffic pollution" (i.e., noise, litter, and the interruption of community living) in a residential area; and to increase the safety of school children. Several individuals and civic organizations representing residents living north of Jackson Avenue and west of Springdale Street then sought an injunction to keep West Drive open to through traffic.

After trial in federal district court, Judge McRae granted judgment for the city, concluding that the city, by closing West Drive, did not confer on white residents along that street a benefit that it had refused to confer on similarly situated black neighborhoods over the years; that a racially discriminatory purpose or intent had not been proved; and that the city had not significantly departed from the usual procedures when it authorized the street closing. A federal appellate court subsequently reversed this decision. Although not rejecting any of the district court's findings of fact, the appeals court concluded that the trial judge "erred in limiting his focus to the issue of whether the city had granted a street closing application made by whites while denying comparable benefits to blacks." Instead, the appellate court held that the black plaintiffs "could demonstrate that this particular street closing was a 'badge of slavery' under [42 U.S.C.A.] § 1982 and the Thirteenth Amendment without reference to the equal treatment issue."

Justice STEVENS delivered the opinion of the Court.

The question presented is whether a decision by the city of Memphis to close the north end of West Drive, a street that traverses a white residential community, violated § 1 of the Civil Rights Act of 1866, 14 Stat. 27, codified at 42 U.S.C.A. § 1982, or the Thirteenth Amendment to the United States Constitution. The city's action was challenged by respondents, who resided in a predominantly black area to the north. The Court of Appeals ultimately held the street closing invalid because it adversely affected respondents' ability to hold and enjoy their property. * * * We reverse because the record does not support that holding.

Most of the relevant facts concerning the geography, the decision to close the street, and the course of the litigation are not in dispute. The inferences to be drawn from the evidence, however, are subject to some disagreement.

* * *

The Court of Appeals recognized that a street closing may be a legitimate and effective means of preserving the residential character of a neighborhood and protecting it from the problems caused by excessive traffic. * * * The Court of Appeals concluded, however, that relief under § 1982 was required here by the facts: (1) that the closing would benefit a white neighborhood and adversely affect blacks; (2) that a "barrier was to be erected precisely at the point of separation of these neighborhoods and would undoubtedly have the effect of limiting contact between them"; (3) that the closing was not part of a city-wide plan but rather was a "unique step to protect one neighborhood from outside influence which the residents considered to be 'undesirable'"; and (4) that there was evidence of "an economic depreciation in the property values in the predominantly black residential

area." Before addressing the legal issues, we consider the extent to which each of these conclusions is supported by the record and the District Court's findings.

The first of the four factual predicates for the Court of Appeals' holding relates to the effect of the closing on black residents and is squarely rooted in the District Court's findings. Judge McRae expressly found that the City Council action "will have disproportionate impact on certain black citizens." * * * He described the traffic that will be diverted by the closing as "overwhelming black," * * * and noted that the white residents of West Drive will have less inconvenience. We must note, however, that although neither Judge McRae nor the Court of Appeals focused on the extent of the inconvenience to residents living north of Jackson Ave., the record makes it clear that such inconvenience will be minimal. A motorist southbound on Springdale St. could continue south on West Drive for only a half mile before the end of West Drive at Overton Park would necessitate a turn. Thus unless the motorist is going to Overton Park, the only effect of the street closing for traffic proceeding south will be to require a turn sooner without lengthening the entire trip or requiring any more turns. Moreover, even the motorist going to Overton Park had to make a turn from West Drive and a short drive down North Parkway to reach the entrance to the park. The entire trip from Springdale St. to the park will be slightly longer with West Drive closed, but it will not be significantly less convenient. Thus although it is correct that the motorists who will be inconvenienced by the closing are primarily black, the extent of the inconvenience is not great.

As for the Court of Appeals' second point, the court attached greater significance to the closing as a "barrier" between two neighborhoods than appears warranted by the record. The physical barrier is a curb that will not impede the passage of municipal vehicles. Moreover, because only one of the several streets entering Hein Park is closed to vehicular traffic, the other streets will provide ample access to the residences in Hein Park. The diversion of through traffic around the Hein Park residential area affects the diverted motorists, but does not support the suggestion that such diversion will limit the social or commercial contact between residents of neighboring communities.

The Court of Appeals' reference to protecting the neighborhood from "undesirable" outside influences may be read as suggesting that the court viewed the closure as motivated by the racial attitude of the residents of Hein Park. The District Court's findings do not support that view of the record. Judge McRae expressly discounted the racial composition of the traffic on West Drive in evaluating its undesirable character; he noted that "excessive traffic in any residential neighborhood has public welfare factors such as safety, noise, and litter, regardless of the race of the traffic and the neighborhood." * * * The transcript of the City Council hearings indicates that the residents of West Drive perceived the traffic to be a problem because of the number and speed of the cars traveling down West Drive. Even if the statements of the residents of West Drive are discounted as self-serving, there is no evidence that the closing was motivated by any racial-

ly exclusionary desire. The City Council members who favored the closing expressed concerns similar to those of the West Drive residents. Those who opposed the resolution did so because they believed that a less drastic response to the traffic problems would be adequate and that the closing would create a dangerous precedent. The one witness at trial who testified that "someone" soliciting signatures for a petition favoring the closure had described the traffic on West Drive as "undesirable traffic," stated that the solicitor mentioned excess traffic and danger to children as reasons for signing. Unlike the Court of Appeals, we therefore believe that the "undesirable" character of the traffic flow must be viewed as a factor supporting, rather than undermining the validity of the closure decision. To the extent that the Court of Appeals' opinion can be read as making a finding of discriminatory intent, the record requires us to reject that finding in favor of the District Court's contrary conclusion. Judge McRae expressly found that the respondents had not proved that the City Council had acted with discriminatory intent. * * *

Finally, the Court of Appeals was not justified in inferring that the closure would cause "an economic depreciation in the property values in the predominantly black residential area * * *." * * * The only expert testimony credited by the District Court on that issue was provided by a real estate broker called by the plaintiffs. His expert opinion, as summarized by the District Court, was that "there will not be a decrease in value experienced by property owners located to the north of West Drive because of the closure." * * * After the witness had expressed that opinion, he admittedly

speculated that some property owners to the north might be envious of
the better housing that they could
not afford and therefore might be
less attentive to the upkeep of their
own property, which in turn "could
have a detrimental effect on the
property values in the future." In
our opinion the District Court correctly refused to find an adverse impact on black property values based
on that speculation.

In summary, then, the critical
facts established by the record are
these: The city's decision to close
West Drive was motivated by its interest in protecting the safety and
tranquility of a residential neighborhood. The procedures followed in
making the decision were fair and
were not affected by any racial or
other impermissible factors. The
city has conferred a benefit on certain white property owners but there
is no reason to believe that it would
refuse to confer a comparable benefit on black property owners. The
closing has not affected the value of
property owned by black citizens, but
it has caused some slight inconvenience to black motorists.

Under the Court's recent decisions in Washington v. Davis, 426
U.S. 229, 96 S.Ct. 2040 and Arlington
Heights v. Metropolitan Housing
Corp., 429 U.S. 252, 97 S.Ct. 555, the
absence of proof of discriminatory intent forecloses any claim that the official action challenged in this case
violates the Equal Protection Clause
of the Fourteenth Amendment. Petitioners ask us to hold that respondents' claims under § 1982 and the
Thirteenth Amendment are likewise
barred by the absence of proof of
discriminatory purpose. We note initially that the coverage of both
§ 1982 and the Thirteenth Amendment is significantly different from

the coverage of the Fourteenth
Amendment. The prohibitions of the
latter apply only to official action, or,
as implemented by 42 U.S.C.A.
§ 1983, to action taken under color
of state law. We have squarely decided, however, that § 1982 is directly applicable to private parties, Jones
v. Alfred H. Mayer Co., 392 U.S. 409,
88 S.Ct. 2186; cf. Runyon v. McCrary, 427 U.S. 160, 170–174, 96 S.Ct.
2586, 2594–96; and it has long been
settled that the Thirteenth Amendment "is not a mere prohibition of
State laws establishing or upholding
slavery, but an absolute declaration
that slavery or involuntary servitude
shall not exist in any part of the
United States." Civil Rights Cases,
109 U.S. 3, 20, 3 S.Ct. 18, 27. Thus,
although respondents challenge official action in this case, the provisions
of the law on which the challenge is
based cover certain private action as
well. Rather than to confront prematurely the rather general question
whether either § 1982 or the Thirteenth Amendment requires proof of
a specific unlawful purpose, we first
consider the extent to which either
provision applies at all to this street
closing case. We of course deal first
with the statutory question.

In relevant part, § 1982 provides:

"All citizens of the United States
shall have the same right, in every
State and Territory, as is enjoyed by
white citizens thereof to inherit, purchase, lease, sell, hold, and convey
real and personal property."

To effectuate the remedial purposes
of the statute, the Court has broadly
construed this language to protect
not merely the enforceability of property interest acquired by black citizens but also their right to acquire
and use property on an equal basis
with white citizens. * * *

[A]s applied to this case, the threshold inquiry under § 1982 must focus on the relationship between the street closing and the property interests of the respondents. As the Court of Appeals correctly noted in its first opinion, the statute would support a challenge to municipal action benefiting white property owners that would be refused to similarly situated black property owners. For official action of that kind would prevent blacks from exercising the same property rights as whites. But respondents' evidence failed to support this legal theory. Alternatively, as the Court of Appeals held in its second opinion, the statute might be violated by official action that depreciated the value of property owned by black citizens. But this record discloses no effect on the value of property owned by any member of the respondent class. Finally, the statute might be violated if the street closing severely restricted access to black homes, because blacks would then he hampered in the use of their property. Again, the record discloses no such restriction.

The injury to respondents established by the record is the requirement that one public street rather than another must be used for certain trips within the city. We need not assess the magnitude of that injury to conclude that it does not involve any impairment to the kind of property interests that we have identified as being within the reach of § 1982. We therefore must consider whether the street closing violated respondents' constitutional rights.

In relevant part, the Thirteenth Amendment provides:

"Neither slavery nor involuntary servitude, except as a punishment for crime whereof the party shall have been duly convicted, shall exist within the United States, or any place subject to their jurisdiction."

In this case respondents challenge the conferring of a benefit upon white citizens by a measure that places a burden on black citizens as a unconstitutional "badge of slavery." Relying on Justice Black's opinion for the Court in Palmer v. Thompson, 403 U.S. 217, 91 S.Ct. 1940, the city argues that in the absence of a violation of specific enabling legislation enacted pursuant to § 2 of the Thirteenth Amendment, any judicial characterization of an isolated street closing as a badge of slavery would constitute the usurpation of "a lawmaking power far beyond the imagination of the Amendment's authors."

* * *

Pursuant to the authority created by § 2 of the Thirteenth Amendment, Congress has enacted legislation to abolish both the conditions of involuntary servitude and the "badges and incidents of slavery." The exercise of that authority is not inconsistent with the view that the Amendment has self-executing force. As the Court noted in Jones v. Alfred H. Mayer Co., 392 U.S. 409, 439, 88 S.Ct. 2186, 2203:

" 'By its own unaided force and effect,' the Thirteenth Amendment 'abolished slavery' and 'established universal freedom.' Civil Rights Cases, 109 U.S. 3, 20, 3 S.Ct. 18, 27. Whether or not the Amendment *itself* did any more than that—a question not involved in this case—it is at least clear that the Enabling Clause of that Amendment empowered Congress to do much more."

In *Jones*, the Court left open the question whether § 1 of the Amendment by its own terms did anything more than abolish slavery. It is also appropriate today to leave that question open because a review of the justification for the official action challenged in this case demonstrates that its disparate impact on black citizens could not, in any event, be fairly characterized as a badge or incident of slavery.

We begin our examination of respondents' Thirteenth Amendment argument by reiterating the conclusion that the record discloses no racially discriminatory motive on the part of the City Council. Instead, the record demonstrates that the interests that did motivate the Council are legitimate. Proper management of the flow of vehicular traffic within a city requires the accommodation of a variety of conflicting interests: the motorist's interest in unhindered access to his destination, the city's interest in the efficient provision of municipal services, the commercial interest in adequate parking, the residents' interest in relative quiet, and the pedestrians' interest in safety. Local governments necessarily exercise wide discretion in making the policy decisions that accommodate these interests.

In this case the city favored the interests of safety and tranquility. As a matter of constitutional law a city's power to adopt rules that will avoid anticipated traffic safety problems is the same as its power to correct those hazards that have been revealed by actual events. The decision to reduce the flow of traffic on West Drive was motivated, in part, by an interest in the safety of children walking to school. That interest is equally legitimate whether it provides support for an arguably unnecessary preventive measure or for a community's reaction to a tragic accident that adequate planning might have prevented. * * *

The residential interest in comparative tranquility is also unquestionably legitimate. That interest provides support for zoning regulations, designed to protect a "quiet place where yards are wide, people few, and motor vehicles restricted." * * * Village of Belle Terre v. Boraas, 416 U.S. 1, 9, 94 S.Ct. 1536, 1541, * * * and for the accepted view that a man's home is his castle. The interest in privacy has the same dignity in a densely populated apartment complex, * * * or in an affluent neighborhood of single family homes. In either context, the protection of the individual interest may involve the imposition of some burdens on the general public.

Whether the individual privacy interests of the residents of Hein Park, coupled with the interest in safety, should be considered strong enough to overcome the more general interest in the use of West Drive as a thoroughfare is the type of question that a multitude of local governments must resolve every day. Because there is no basis for concluding that the interests favored by the city in its decision were contrived or pretextual, the District Court correctly concluded that it had no authority to review the wisdom of the city's policy decision. * * *

The interests motivating the city's action are thus sufficient to justify an adverse impact on motorists who are somewhat inconvenienced by the street closing. That inconvenience cannot be equated to an actual restraint on the liberty of black citizens that is in any sense comparable to the odious practice the Thirteenth Amendment was designed to eradicate. The argument that the closing violates the Amendment must therefore rest, not on the actual consequences of the closing, but rather on the symbolic significance of the fact that most of the drivers who will be inconvenienced by the action are black.

But the inconvenience of the drivers is a function of where they live and where they regularly drive—not a function of their race; the hazards and the inconvenience that the closing is intended to minimize are a function of the number of vehicles involved, not the race of their drivers or of the local residents. Almost any traffic regulation—whether it be a temporary detour during construction, a speed limit, a one-way street, or a no parking sign—may have a differential impact on residents of adjacent or nearby neighborhoods. Because urban neighborhoods are so frequently characterized by a common ethnic or racial heritage, a regulation's adverse impact on a particular neighborhood will often have a disparate effect on an identifiable ethnic or racial group. To regard an inevitable consequence of that kind as a form of stigma so severe as to violate the Thirteenth Amendment would trivialize the great purpose of that charter of freedom. Proper respect for the dignity of the residents of any neighborhood requires that they accept the same burdens as well as the same benefits of citizenship regardless of their racial or ethnic origin.

This case does not disclose a violation of any of the enabling legislation enacted by Congress pursuant to § 2 of the Thirteenth Amendment. To decide the narrow constitutional question presented by this record we need not speculate about the sort of impact on a racial group that might be prohibited by the Amendment itself. We merely hold that the impact of the closing of West Drive on nonresidents of Hein Park is a rou-

tine burden of citizenship; it does not reflect a violation of the Thirteenth Amendment.

The judgment of the Court of Appeals is

Reversed.

Justice WHITE concurring.

In this civil rights action, respondents sought relief under the Thirteenth and Fourteenth Amendments as well as under 42 U.S.C.A. §§ 1982–1983. The District Court held that while the closure of West Drive in Memphis, Tenn., would have a disproportionate impact upon certain black residents of Memphis, the evidence did not support a finding of a purpose or intent to discriminate. Neither was the disparate impact "so stark that a purpose or intent of racial discrimination" could be inferred. As a consequence, and following instructions from the initial remand, the District Court concluded that respondents had failed to prove a violation of either § 1982 or § 1983. The District Court did not specifically address the alleged constitutional violations, but implicitly those allegations fell on the same basis. The Court of Appeals for the Sixth Circuit reversed the District Court's ultimate conclusion that there was no violation of § 1982, but the appellate court did not disturb the trial court's finding that there was no purposeful discrimination. Without explicitly saying so, the Court of Appeals necessarily held that a violation of § 1982 could be established without proof of discriminatory intent. The petition for a writ of certiorari sought review of that precise point.

We granted review to answer the question presented in the petition for a writ of certiorari. The parties in their briefs proceeded on the same assumption. However, instead of addressing the question which was explicitly presented by the findings and holdings below, raised by the petitioner, granted by this Court and briefed by the parties, the Court inexplicably assumes the role of factfinder, peruses the cold record, rehashes the evidence and *sua sponte* purports to resolve questions that the parties have neither briefed nor argued. It is not surprising that the dissent has taken this same record and interpreted it in quite another way. In any event, rather than becoming involved in the imbroglio between the majority and the dissent, I much prefer as a matter of policy and common sense to answer the question for which we took the case. There is no good reason here to disregard our own Rule 21.1(a) which states that "Only the questions set forth in the petition as fairly included therein will be considered by the Court."

We are called upon to determine whether a nonintentional adverse impact upon black citizens is a sufficient basis for relief under 42 U.S. C.A. § 1982. * * *

* * *

The Civil Rights Act of 1866 thus was a response to the perception held by Congress that former slaves were being denied basic civil rights. The Act would give practical effect to the Thirteenth Amendment. * * * But nothing in the legislative history of this Act suggests that Congress was concerned with facially neutral measures which happened to have an incidental impact on former slaves. On the contrary, the theme of the debates surrounding this statute is that the former slaves continued to be subject to direct, intentional abuses at the hands of their former masters. That was the problem Congress in-

tended to address and that focus should determine the reach and scope of this statute. We have no basis for concluding anything other than that a violation of § 1982 requires some showing of racial animus or an intent to discriminate on the basis of race. The Court of Appeals proceeded on a contrary basis and reversed the District Court's judgment without disturbing the District Court's conclusion that no discriminatory purpose had been found. This was error, and for that reason I concur in the judgment of reversal, but would remand for further proceedings not inconsistent with this opinion.

Justice MARSHALL, with whom Justice BRENNAN and Justice BLACKMUN join, dissenting.

This case is easier than the majority makes it appear. Petitioner city of Memphis, acting at the behest of white property owners, has closed the main thoroughfare between an all-white enclave and a predominantly-Negro area of the city. The stated explanation for the closing is of a sort all too familiar: "protecting the safety and tranquility of a residential neighborhood" by preventing "undesirable traffic" from entering it. Too often in our Nation's history, statements such as these have been little more than code phrases for racial discrimination. These words may still signify racial discrimination, but apparently not, after today's decision, forbidden discrimination. The majority, purporting to rely on the evidence developed at trial, concludes that the city's stated interests are sufficient to justify erection of the barrier. Because I do not believe that either the Constitution or federal law permits a city to carve out racial enclaves I dissent.

* * *

The majority treats this case as involving nothing more then a dispute over a city's race-neutral decision to place a barrier across a road. My own examination of the record suggests, however, that far more is at stake here than a simple street closing. The picture that emerges from a more careful review of the record is one of a white community, disgruntled over sharing its street with Negroes, taking legal measures to keep out the "undesirable traffic," and of a city, heedless of the harm to its Negro citizens, acquiescing in the plan.

I readily accept much of the majority's summary of the circumstances that led to this litigation. I would, however, begin by emphasizing three critical facts. First, as the District Court found, Hein Park "was developed well before World War II as an exclusive neighborhood for white citizens and these characteristics have been maintained." * * * Second, the area to the north of Hein Park, like the "undesirable traffic" that Hein Park wants to keep out, is predominantly Negro. And third, the closing of West Drive stems entirely from the efforts of residents of Hein Park. Up to this point, the majority and I are in agreement. But we part company over our characterizations of the evidence developed in the course of the trial of this case. At the close of the evidence, the trial court described this as "a situation where an all white neighborhood is seeking to stop the traffic from an overwhelmingly black neighborhood from coming through their street." * * * In the legal and factual context before us, I find that a revealing summary of the case. The majority apparently does not.

* * *

The majority does not seriously dispute the first of the four facts relied on by the Court of Appeals. In fact it concedes that the trial court "clearly concluded * * * that the adverse impact on blacks was greater than on whites." * * * The majority suggests, however, that this "impact" is limited to the "inconvenience" that will be suffered by drivers who live in the predominantly-Negro area north of Hein Park and who will no longer be able to drive through the subdivision. This, says the majority, is because residents of the area north of Hein Park will still be able to get where they are going; they will just have to go a little out of their way and thus will take a little longer to complete the trip.

This analysis ignores the plain and powerful symbolic message of the "inconvenience." Many places to which residents of the area north of Hein Park would logically drive lie to the south of the subdivision. Until the closing of West Drive, the most direct route for those who lived on or near Springdale St. was straight down West Drive. Now the Negro drivers are being told in essence, "You must take the long way around because you don't live in this 'protected' white neighborhood." Negro residents of the area north of Hein Park testified at trial that this is what they thought the city was telling them by closing West Drive. * * * Even the District Court, which granted judgment for petitioners, conceded that "[o]bviously, the black people north of [Hein Park] * * * are being told to stay out of the subdivision." * * * In my judgment, this message constitutes a far greater adverse impact on respondents than the majority would prefer to believe.

The majority also does not challenge the Sixth Circuit's second finding, that the barrier is being erected at the point of contact of the two communities. Nor could it do so, because the fact is not really in dispute. The Court attempts instead to downplay the significance of this barrier by calling it "a curb that will not impede the passage of municipal vehicles." * * * But that is beside the point. Respondents did not bring this suit to challenge the exclusion of municipal vehicles from Hein Park. Their goal is to preserve access for their own vehicles. But in fact, they may not even be able to preserve access for their own persons. The city is creating the barrier across West Drive by deeding public property to private landowners. Nothing will prevent the residents of Hein Park from excluding "undesirable" pedestrians as well as vehicular traffic if they so choose. * * * What is clear is that there will be a barrier to traffic that is to be erected precisely at the point where West Drive (and thus, all-white Hein Park) ends and Springdale St. (and the mostly-Negro section) begins.

The psychological effect of this barrier is likely to be significant. In this unchallenged expert testimony in the trial court, Dr. Marvin Feit, a professor of psychiatry at the University of Tennessee, predicted that the barrier between West Drive and Springdale St. will reinforce feelings about the city's "favoritism" toward whites and will "serve as a monument to racial hostility." * * * The testimony of Negro residents and of a real estate agent familiar with the area provide powerful sup-

port for this prediction. As the District Court put it: "[Y]ou are not going to be able to convince those black people out there that they didn't do it because they were black. They are helping a white neighborhood. Now, that is a problem that somebody is going to have to live with * * *." * * * I cannot subscribe to the majority's apparent view that the city's erection of this "monument to racial hostility" amounts to nothing more than a "slight inconvenience." Thus, unlike the majority, I do not minimize the significance of the barrier itself in determining the harm respondents will suffer from its erection.

The majority does not attempt to question the third conclusion by the Court of Appeals, that the closing of West Drive is intended as a protection of Hein Park against "undesirable" outside influences. Rather, its disagreement with the Court of Appeals is over the inference to be drawn. The majority insists that to the extent that the Court of Appeals found racially discriminatory intent, that finding is not supported by the record. The majority also asserts, * * * that there is "no evidence" that either the residents of Hein Park or the city officials were motivated by any racial considerations. A proper reading of the record demonstrates to the contrary that respondents produced at trial precisely the kind of evidence of intent that we deemed probative in Arlington Heights v. Metropolitan Housing Development Corp., 429 U.S. 252, 267–268, 97 S.Ct. 555, 564, 565 (1977).

The term "undesirable traffic" first entered this litigation through the trial testimony of Sarah Terry. Terry, a West Drive resident who opposed the closing, testified that she was urged to support the barrier by an individual who explained to her that "the traffic on the street was undesirable traffic." * * * The majority apparently reads the term "undesirable" as referring to the prospect of having any traffic at all on West Drive. But the common sense understanding of Terry's testimony must be that the word "undesirable" was meant to describe the traffic that was actually using the street, as opposed to any traffic that might use it. Of course, the traffic that was both actually using the street and would be affected by the barrier was predominantly Negro.

But Terry's testimony is not, as the majority implies, the only *Arlington Heights*-type evidence produced at trial. The testimony of city planning officials, for example, strongly suggests that the city deviated from its usual procedures in deciding to close West Drive. In particular, despite an unambiguous requirement that applications for street closings be signed by "all" owners of property abutting on the thoroughfare to be closed, the city here permitted this application to go through without the signature or the consent of Sarah Terry. Perhaps more important, the city gave no notice to the Negro property owners living north of Hein Park that the Planning Commission was considering an application to close West Drive. The Planning Commission held its hearing without participation by any of the affected Negro residents and it declined to let them examine the file on the West Drive closing. It gave no notice that the City Council would be considering the issue. When respondents found out about it, they sought to state their case. But the Council gave opponents of the proposal only 15 minutes, even though some members objected that that was not

enough time. Furthermore, although the majority treats West Drive as just another closing, it is, according to the city official in charge of closings, the *only* time the city has *ever* closed a street for traffic control purposes. * * * And it cannot be disputed that all parties were aware of the disparate racial impact of the erection of the barrier. The city of Memphis, moreover, has an unfortunate but very real history of racial segregation—a history that has in the past led to intercession by this Court. All these factors represent precisely the kind of evidence that we said in *Arlington Heights* was relevant to an inquiry into motivation. Regardless of whether this evidence is viewed as conclusive, it can hardly be stated with accuracy that "no evidence" exists.

Most important, I believe that the findings of the District Court and the record in this case fully support the Court of Appeals' conclusion that Negro property owners are likely to suffer economic harm as a result of the construction of the barrier. In attempting to demonstrate to the trial court that the closing of West Drive would adversely affect their property, respondents first introduced the testimony of Harrell C. Moore, a real estate agent with 17 years experience in the field. Moore began by predicting that after West Drive was closed, Hein Park would become "more or less a Utopia within the city of Memphis," families who had left the inner city for the suburbs would probably return in order to live there, and the property values in Hein Park "would be enhanced greatly." * * * Moore was then asked what effect the closing would have on the property values in the Springdale area. He responded: "From an economic standpoint there would not be a lessening of value in those properties in the Springdale area, but from a psychological standpoint, it would have a tendency to have a demoralizing—" * * *. At this point, counsel for petitioners interposed an objection, but Moore was eventually permitted to answer the question, and he testified as follows:

"In my opinion, with the 17 years experience in the real estate industry, psychologically it would have a deterring, depressing effect on those individuals who might live north of the Hein Park area. With the closure of the street, the creation of another little haven, the fact that these people are in a lower economic social group and wouldn't be able to actually afford housing with the illustrious price tags of those houses in the Hein Park area, it would be, in my opinion, like the individual looking in the pastry store who doesn't have a dime and who can't afford it. And consequently, as a result of such, their moralistic values on their properties could tend to be such that the upkeep would not be nearly so great and it could have a detrimental effect on the property values in the future." * * *

Surely Moore's uncontroverted expert testimony is evidence of an impairment of property values, an impairment directly traceable to the closing of West Drive. The majority dismisses this aspect of Moore's testimony as "speculation." * * * Yet the majority has no trouble crediting Moore's brief and conclusory testimony that the immediate impact of the closing would be negligible. Unlike the majority, I am unable to dismiss so blithely the balance of his comments.

The majority also gives insufficient weight to the testimony of Dr. Feit on this point. Dr. Feit testified, based on his experience as Director of Planning for Allegheny County, Pa., that the shift in traffic patterns as a result of the closing of West Drive would lower the property values for owners living north of Hein Park. He further testified that the closing of West Drive would lead to increased hostility toward Hein Park residents and, ultimately, to increased police harassment of residents of the Springdale area. * * * I would have thought it indisputable that increased police harassment of property owners must be construed as a significant impairment of their property interests. In my view, the combined testimony of Dr. Feit and real-estate expert Moore is sufficient to demonstrate that the closing of West Drive will cause genuine harm to the property rights of the Negro residents of the area north of Hein Park.

In sum, I cannot agree with the majority's suggestion that "[t]he injury to respondents established by the record is the requirement that one public street rather than another must be used for certain trips within the city," * * * and that this requirement amounts to no more than "some slight inconvenience." * * * Indeed, as should be clear from the foregoing, the problem is less the closing of West Drive in particular than the establishment of racially determined districts which the closing effects. I can only agree with the Court of Appeals, which viewed the city's action as nothing more than "one more of the many humiliations which society has historically visited" on Negro citizens. * * * In my judgment, respondents provided ample evidence that erection of the challenged barrier will harm them in several significant ways. Respondents are being sent a clear, though sophisticated, message that because of their race, they are to stay out of the all-white enclave of Hein Park and should instead take the long way around in reaching their destinations to the south. Combined with this message are the prospects of increased police harassment and of a decline in their property values. It is on the basis of these facts, all firmly established by the record, that I evaluate the legal questions presented by this case.

When Congress enacted § 1 of the Civil Rights Act of 1866, 14 Stat. 27, now 42 U.S.C.A. § 1982, it intended "to prohibit all racial discrimination, whether or not under color of law with respect to the rights enumerated therein." * * * Jones v. Alfred H. Mayer Co., 392 U.S. 409, 436, 88 S.Ct. 2186, 2201 (1968). * * * These enumerated rights include the rights "to inherit, purchase, lease, sell, hold, and convey real and personal property." 42 U.S. C.A. § 1982. At bottom, as the majority recognizes, § 1982 creates a right in Negroes "not to have property interests impaired because of their race." * * * Our decisions have recognized that the language of the statute is to be broadly construed. We have said that " '[w]e are not at liberty to seek ingenious analytical instruments,' " to carve exceptions from § 1982. Jones v. Alfred H. Mayer Co., supra, at 437, 88 S.Ct. at 2202, quoting United States v. Price, 383 U.S. 787, 801, 86 S.Ct. 1152, 1160 (1966). On the contrary, "[a] narrow construction of the language of § 1982 would be quite inconsistent with the broad and sweeping nature of the protection meant to be afforded by § 1 of the Civil Rights Act

of 1866." * * * Sullivan v. Little Hunting Park, 396 U.S. 229, 237, 90 S.Ct. 400, 404 (1969). If the language of the statute is given the broad reading that our cases require, then it is difficult to see how respondents can avoid its effect.

The majority concludes that the kind of harm that § 1982 was meant to prohibit does not exist in this case, but as I have stated, a proper reading of the record demonstrates substantial harm to respondents' property rights as a result of the establishment of a barrier at the northern edge of Hein Park. The closing will both burden respondents' ability to enjoy their property and also depress its value, thus falling within the literal language of § 1982. Even the majority concedes that "the statute might be violated by official action that depreciated the value of property owned by [Negro] citizens." * * * I believe that that is precisely what is challenged in this case.

The legislative history of § 1982 also supports my conclusion that the carving out of racial enclaves within a city is precisely the kind of injury that the statute was enacted to prevent. In Jones v. Alfred H. Mayer Co., supra, at 422–437, 88 S.Ct. 2186, 2194–2202, this Court discussed the legislative history of the Civil Rights Act of 1866 in some detail, and there is no need to duplicate all of that discussion here. * * *

* * *

I do not, of course, mean to suggest that the Reconstruction Congress that enacted § 1982 anticipated the precise situation presented by this case. Nor do I wish to imply that the Act prevents government from ever closing a street when the effect is to inflict harm on Negro property owners. But because of our Nation's sad legacy of discrimination and the broad remedial purpose of § 1982, I believe that official actions whose effects fall within its terms ought to be closely scrutinized. When, as here, the decisionmaker takes action with full knowledge of its enormously disproportionate racial impact, I believe that § 1982 requires that the government carry a heavy burden in order to justify its action. Absent such a justification, the injured property owners are entitled to relief. There is no need to suggest here just how great the government's burden should be, because the reasons set forth by the city for the closing of West Drive could not, on the facts of this case, survive any but the most minimal scrutiny.

In sustaining the closing of West Drive, the majority points to petitioners' "[p]roper management of the flow of vehicular traffic within a city," and their exercise of the "unquestionably legitimate" "residential interest in comparative tranquility." * * * Those interests might well, as the majority contends, prove "sufficient to justify an adverse impact on motorists who are somewhat inconvenienced by the street closing," * * * but that is not the impact that the city must explain in this case. It must instead justify the substantial injury that it has inflicted on Negro citizens solely for the benefit of the white residents of Hein Park. For that purpose, the proffered explanations are insufficient. "[A] city's possible motivations to ensure safety and save money cannot validate an otherwise impermissible state action." Palmer v. Thompson, 403 U.S. 217, 226, 91 S.Ct. 1940, 1945 (1971). * * * It is simply unrealistic to suggest, as does the Court, that the harm suffered by respondents has no more than "symbolic

significance," * * * and it defies the lessons of history and law to assert that if the harm is only symbolic, then the federal courts cannot recognize it. Compare Plessy v. Ferguson, 163 U.S. 537, 551, 16 S.Ct. 1138, 1143 (1896) ("We consider the underlying fallacy of the plaintiff's argument to consist in the assumption that the enforced separation of the two races stamps the colored race with a badge of inferiority. If this be so, it is not by reason of anything found in the act, but solely because the colored race chooses to put that construction upon it.") with Brown v. Board of Education, 347 U.S. 483, 494, 74 S.Ct. 686, 691 (1954) ("To separate them from others * * * solely because of their race generates a feeling of inferiority as to their status in the community that may affect their hearts and minds in a way unlikely to be undone. * * * Whatever may have been the extent of psychological knowledge at the time of *Plessy* v. *Ferguson*, this finding is amply supported by modern authority"). The message the city is sending to Negro residents north of Hein Park is clear, and I am at a loss to understand why the majority feels so free to ignore it.

Indeed, until today I would have thought that a city's erection of a barrier, at the behest of a historically all-white community, to keep out predominantly-Negro traffic, would have been among the least of the statute's prohibitions. Certainly I suspect that the Congress that enacted § 1982 would be surprised to learn that it has no application to such a case. Even the few portions of debate that I have cited make clear that a major concern of the statute's supporters was the elimination of the effects of local prejudice on Negro residents. In my view, the evidence before us supports a strong inference that the operation of such prejudice is precisely what has led to the closing of West Drive. And against this record, the government should be required to do far more than it has here to justify an action that so obviously damages and stigmatizes a racially identifiable group of its citizens.

In short, I conclude that the plain language of § 1982 and its legislative history show that the harm established by a fair reading of this record falls within the prohibition of the statute. Because the Court of Appeals reached the same conclusion, I would affirm its judgment.

I end, then, where I began. Given the majority's decision to characterize this case as a mere policy decision on the part of the City of Memphis to close a street for valid municipal reasons, the conclusion that it reaches follows inevitably. But the evidence in this case, combined with a dab of common sense, paints a far different picture from the one emerging from the majority's opinion. In this picture a group of white citizens has decided to act to keep Negro citizens from traveling through their urban "utopia," and the city has placed its seal of approval on the scheme. It is this action that I believe is forbidden, and it is for that reason that I dissent.

c. VOTING RIGHTS AND ELECTORAL DISCRIMINATION

SMITH v. ALLWRIGHT

Supreme Court of the United States, 1944
321 U.S. 649, 64 S.Ct. 757, 88 L.Ed. 987

Pursuant to a law enacted by the Texas legislature in 1927 authorizing political parties to establish qualifications for party membership, the state Democratic party adopted the following resolution at its convention in May 1932: "Be it resolved that all white citizens of the State of Texas who are qualified to vote under the Constitution and laws of the State shall be eligible to membership in the Democratic party and, as such, entitled to participate in its deliberations." Lonnie Smith, a Negro, brought suit against Allwright, an election judge, who refused to allow him to vote in a Democratic primary at which candidates for state and national office were to be selected.

Mr. Justice REED delivered the opinion of the Court.

*   *   *

Texas is free to conduct her elections and limit her electorate as she may deem wise, save only as her action may be affected by the prohibitions of the United States Constitution or in conflict with powers delegated to and exercised by the

National Government. The Fourteenth Amendment forbids a state from making or enforcing any law which abridges the privileges or immunities of citizens of the United States and the Fifteenth Amendment specifically interdicts any denial or abridgement by a state of the right of citizens to vote on account of color. Respondents appeared in the District Court and the Circuit Court of Appeals and defended on the ground that the Democratic party of Texas is a voluntary organization with members banded together for the purpose of selecting individuals of the group representing the common political beliefs as candidates in the general election. As such a voluntary organization, it was claimed, the Democratic party is free to select its own membership and limit to whites participation in the party primary. Such action, the answer asserted, does not violate the Fourteenth, Fifteenth or Seventeenth Amendment as officers of government cannot be chosen at primaries and the Amendments are applicable only to general elections where governmental officers are actually elected. Primaries, it is said, are political party affairs, handled by party not governmental officers.   *   *   *

The right of a Negro to vote in the Texas primary has been considered heretofore by this Court. The first case was Nixon v. Herndon, 273 U.S. 536, 47 S.Ct. 446. At that time, 1924, the Texas statute   *   *   *   declared "in no event shall a Negro be eligible to participate in a Democratic party primary election   *   *   *   in the State of Texas." Nixon was refused the right to vote in a Democratic primary and brought a suit for damages against the election officers.   *   *   *   It was urged to this Court that the denial of the franchise to Nixon violated his Constitutional rights under the Fourteenth and Fifteenth Amendments. Without consideration of the Fifteenth, this Court held that the action of Texas in denying the ballot to Negroes by statute was in violation of the equal protection clause of the Fourteenth Amendment and reversed the dismissal of the suit.

The legislature of Texas reenacted the article but gave the State Executive Committee of a party the power to prescribe the qualifications of its members for voting or other participation. This article remains in the statutes. The State Executive Committee of the Democratic party adopted a resolution that white Democrats and none other might participate in the primaries of that party. Nixon was refused again the privilege of voting in a primary and again brought suit for damages.   *   *   * This Court again reversed the dismissal of the suit for the reason that the Committee action was deemed to be State action and invalid as discriminatory under the Fourteenth Amendment. The test was said to be whether the Committee operated as representative of the State in the discharge of the State's authority. Nixon v. Condon, 286 U.S. 73, 52 S.Ct. 484. The question of the inherent power of a political party in Texas "without restraint by any law to determine its own membership" was left open.   *   *   *

In Grovey v. Townsend, 295 U.S. 45, 55 S.Ct. 622, this Court had before it another suit for damages for the refusal in a primary of a county clerk, a Texas officer with only public functions to perform, to furnish petitioner, a Negro, an absentee ballot. The refusal was solely on the ground of race. This case differed from *Nixon* v. *Condon*   *   *   *   in that a state convention of the Democratic party had passed the resolution.   *   *   *   It was decided that the determination by the state convention of the membership of the Democratic party made a significant change from a determination by the Executive Committee. The former was party action, voluntary in character. The latter, as had been held in the *Condon* case, was action by authority of the State. The managers of the primary election were therefore declared not to be state officials in such sense that their action was state action. A state convention of a party was said not to be an organ of the state. This Court went on to announce that to deny a vote in a primary was a mere refusal of party membership with which "the state need have no concern," * * * while for a state to deny a vote in a general election on the ground of race or color violated the Constitution. Consequently, there was found no ground for holding that the county clerk's refusal of a ballot because of racial ineligibility for party membership denied the petitioner any right under the Fourteenth or Fifteenth Amendments.

Since *Grovey* v. *Townsend* and prior to the present suit, no case from Texas involving primary elections has been before this Court. We did decide, however, United States v. Classic, 313 U.S. 299, 61 S.Ct. 1031. We there held that Section 4 of Article I of the Constitution authorized Congress to regulate primary as well as general elections * * * "where the primary is by

law made an integral part of the election machinery." * * * Consequently, in the *Classic* case, we upheld the applicability to frauds in a Louisiana primary of [provisions] of the [federal] Criminal Code. * * * Thereby corrupt acts of election officers were subjected to Congressional sanctions because that body had power to protect rights of Federal suffrage secured by the Constitution in primary as in general elections. * * * This decision depended, too, on the determination that under the Louisiana statutes the primary was a part of the procedure for choice of Federal officials. * * * The *Nixon* cases were decided under the equal protection clause of the Fourteenth Amendment without a determination of the status of the primary as a part of the electoral process. The exclusion of Negroes from the primaries by action of the State was held invalid under that Amendment. The fusing by the *Classic* case of the primary and general elections into a single instrumentality for choice of officers has a definite bearing on the permissibility under the Constitution of excluding Negroes from primaries.[e] This is not to say that the *Classic* case cuts directly into the ra-

---

e. The Court's conclusion in *Classic* that the Democratic party primary was an integral party of the election process in the choice of a representative from Louisiana's Second Congressional District was based upon observations that state law: (1) required all parties polling over 5 percent of the total vote in specified preceding elections to hold a primary; (2) governed the time, place, and manner of holding such primaries; (3) provided for recording and certification of the results by the Louisiana Secretary of State; (4) prohibited any losers in the primary from appearing on the general election ballot; (5) barred the counting of any write-in votes on the general election ballot for losers of primary contests; and (6) required any independent candidate

seeking a position on the general election ballot to present nominating petitions signed only by qualified voters who had not voted in a party primary for that office. Chief Justice Stone, speaking for the Court, concluded that "the practical operation of the primary law * * * is such as to impose serious restrictions upon the choice of candidates by the voters save by voting at the primary election." Noting that, since 1900, the only congressmen the Second District had elected were the winners of the Democratic primary, he continued:

Interference with the right to vote in the Congressional primary in the Second Congressional District for the choice of Democratic candidate for Congress is thus as a matter of

tionale of *Grovey* v. *Townsend*. This latter case was not mentioned in the opinion. *Classic* bears upon *Grovey* v. *Townsend* not because exclusion of Negroes from primaries is any more or less state action by reason of the unitary character of the electoral process but because the recognition of the place of the primary in the electoral scheme makes clear that state delegation to a party of the power to fix the qualifications of primary elections is delegation of a state function that may make the party's action the action of the state. When *Grovey* v. *Townsend* was written, the Court looked upon the denial of a vote in a primary as a mere refusal by a party of party membership. * * * As the Louisiana statutes for holding primaries are similar to those of Texas, our ruling in *Classic* as to the unitary character of the electoral process calls for a reexamination as to whether or not the exclusion of Negroes from a Texas party primary was state action.

* * *

It may now be taken as a postulate that the right to vote in such a primary for the nomination of candidates without discrimination by the State, like the right to vote in a general election, is a right secured by the Constitution. * * * By the terms of the Fifteenth Amendment that right may not be abridged by any state on account of race. Under our Constitution the great privilege of the ballot may not be denied a

man by the State because of his color.

We are thus brought to an examination of the qualifications for Democratic primary electors in Texas, to determine whether state action or private action has excluded Negroes from participation. * * *

* * *

[The Court took note of the following aspects of Texas's primary system in which state involvement was manifested through statutory requirements: (1) payment of a poll tax as a prerequisite to participation; (2) selection of county and state party officers; (3) holding of and specification of various rules to be observed at county, district, and state party conventions; (4) conduct of primaries according to prescribed procedures; (5) certification of the primary winner for each office by party officials; (6) exclusion of all but party-certified candidates from the general election ballot except the names of independent candidates nominated by petitions signed by voters who were required to stipulate under oath that they had not participated in any primary for the selection of a candidate for that office; and (7) jurisdiction of state courts to resolve primary election disputes and to compel party officials to perform their statutory functions.]

We think that this statutory system for the selection of party nominees for inclusion on the general election ballot makes the party which

---

law and in fact an interference with the effective choice of the voters at the only stage of the election procedure when their choice is of significance, since it is at the only stage when such interference could have any practical effect on the ultimate result, the choice of the Congressman to represent the district. The

primary in Louisiana is an integral part of the procedure for the popular choice of Congressman. The right of qualified voters to vote at the Congressional primary in Louisiana and to have their ballots counted is thus the right to participate in that choice.

is required to follow these legislative directions an agency of the state in so far as it determines the participants in a primary election. The party takes its character as a state agency from the duties imposed upon it by state statutes; the duties do not become matters of private law because they are performed by a political party. The plan of the Texas primary follows substantially that of Louisiana. * * * When primaries become a part of the machinery for choosing officials, state and national, as they have here, the same tests to determine the character of discrimination or abridgement should be applied to the primary as are applied to the general election. If the state requires a certain electoral procedure, prescribes a general election ballot made up of party nominees so chosen and limits the choice of the electorate in general elections for state offices, practically speaking, to those whose names appear on such a ballot, it endorses, adopts and enforces the discrimination against Negroes, practiced by a party entrusted by Texas law with the determination of the qualifications of participants in the primary. This is state action within the meaning of the Fifteenth Amendment. * * *

The United States is a constitutional democracy. Its organic law grants to all citizens a right to participate in the choice of elected officials without restriction by any state because of race. This grant to the people of the opportunity for choice is not to be nullified by a state through casting its electoral process in a form which permits a private organization to practice racial discrimination in the election. Constitutional rights would be of little value if they could be thus indirectly denied. * * *

The privilege of membership in a party may be, as this Court said in *Grovey* v. *Townsend* * * * no concern of a state. But when, as here, that privilege is also the essential qualification for voting in a primary to select nominees for a general election, the state makes the action of the party the action of the state. * * * Here we are applying, contrary to the recent decision in *Grovey* v. *Townsend*, the well established principle of the Fifteenth Amendment, forbidding the abridgement by a state of a citizen's right to vote. *Grovey* v. *Townsend* is overruled.

Judgment reversed.

[Justice FRANKFURTER concurred in the result. Justice ROBERTS dissented.]

Nine years later, in Terry v. Adams, 345 U.S. 461, 73 S.Ct. 809 (1953), the Court dealt a death blow to another attempt to elude the "state action" label and further privatize the electoral process. In that case, black voters were barred from membership in the Jaybird Association, ostensibly a private club, by the club's bylaws. However, white residents were automatically members if their names appeared on the county's voting lists. The club maintained a stranglehold on offices in Fort Bend County, Texas by use of a club primary. Club-endorsed candidates, being victors in that primary, always went on to win the Democratic party primary, invariably unopposed, and, subsequently, the general election. A federal district court found the association's practices "state action" and a denial of the Negro plaintiffs' rights under the Fifteenth Amendment. This decision was reversed on appeal by the U. S. Court of Appeals for the Fifth Circuit which ruled that the association was a private club. The Supreme Court reversed and reinstated the judgment of the district court. In a plurality opinion announcing the judgment of the Court, Justice Black found the Jaybird Association to be an "auxiliary" of the Democratic party and thus the result in this case controlled by the principle enunciated in *Smith* v. *Allwright*. Justice Minton dissented.

GOMILLION v. LIGHTFOOT

Supreme Court of the United States, 1960
364 U.S. 339, 81 S.Ct. 125, 5 L.Ed.2d 110

An act passed by the Alabama legislature in 1957 redefined the boundaries of Tuskegee from a square shape to that of a figure with twenty-eight sides which excluded from the city nearly all of its black voters but no voters who were white. Charles Gomillion and other Negro residents brought suit against the mayor, Phil Lightfoot, and other city officials challenging the constitutionality of the act. A federal district court dismissed the complaint and its decision was affirmed on appeal, whereupon Gomillion petitioned the Supreme Court and it granted certiorari.

Mr. Justice FRANKFURTER delivered the opinion of the Court.

* * *

It is difficult to appreciate what stands in the way of adjudging a statute having this inevitable effect invalid in light of the principles by which this Court must judge, and uniformly has judged, statutes that, howsoever speciously defined, obviously discriminate against colored citizens. "The [Fifteenth] Amendment nullifies sophisticated as well as simpleminded modes of discrimination." Lane v. Wilson, 307 U.S. 268, 275, 59 S.Ct. 872, 876.

The complaint amply alleges a claim of racial discrimination. Against this claim the respondents have never suggested, either in their brief or in oral argument, any countervailing municipal function which Act 140 is designed to serve. The respondents invoke generalities expressing the State's unrestricted power—unlimited, that is, by the United States Constitution—to establish, destroy, or reorganize by contraction or expansion its political subdivisions, to

wit, cities, counties, and other local units. We freely recognize the breadth and importance of this aspect of the State's political power. To exalt this power into an absolute is to misconceive the reach and rule of this Court's decisions. * * *

* * *

[T]he Court has never acknowledged that the States have power to do as they will with municipal corporations regardless of consequences. Legislative control of municipalities, no less than other state power, lies within the scope of relevant limitations imposed by the United States Constitution. * * *

[S]uch power, extensive though it is, is met and overcome by the Fifteenth Amendment to the Constitution of the United States, which forbids a State from passing any law which deprives a citizen of his vote because of his race. The opposite conclusion, urged upon us by respondents, would sanction the achievement by a State of any impairment of voting rights whatever so long as it was cloaked in the garb of the realignment of political subdivisions. "It is inconceivable that guaranties embedded in the Constitution of the United States may thus be manipulated out of existence." Frost & Frost Trucking Co. v. Railroad Commission of California, 271 U.S. 583, 594, 46 S.Ct. 605, 607.

* * *

When a State exercises power wholly within the domain of state interest, it is insulated from federal judicial review. But such insulation is not carried over when state power is used as an instrument for circumventing a federally protected right. This principle has had many applications. It has long been recognized in cases which have prohibited a State from exploiting a power acknowledged to be absolute in an isolated context to justify the imposition of an "unconstitutional condition." What the Court has said in those cases is equally applicable here, viz., that "Acts generally lawful may become unlawful when done to accomplish an unlawful end, * * * and a constitutional power cannot be used by way of condition to attain an unconstitutional result." * * * The petitioners are entitled to prove their allegations at trial.

* * *

Reversed.

SOUTH CAROLINA v. KATZENBACH

Supreme Court of the United States, 1966
383 U.S. 301, 86 S.Ct. 803, 15 L.Ed.2d 769

See p. 161.

KATZENBACH v. MORGAN

Supreme Court of the United States, 1966
384 U.S. 641, 86 S.Ct. 1717, 16 L.Ed.2d 828

See p. 168.

CITY OF RICHMOND v. UNITED STATES

Supreme Court of the United States, 1975
422 U.S. 358, 95 S.Ct. 2296, 45 L.Ed.2d 245

In 1969, a state court approved Richmond's annexation of adjacent territory in Chesterfield County, Virginia. The effect of the annexation was to reduce the black proportion of the population residing within the city limits from 52 to 42 percent. Prior to annexation, three members of the nine-member city council, which was elected at large, were endorsed by a black civic group as were the same number following a 1970 post-annexation election. Following the Supreme Court's ruling in Perkins v. Matthews, 400 U.S. 379, 91 S.Ct. 431 (1971), that § 5 of the Voting Rights Act extended to cover annexations, which along with other potentially discriminatory electoral devices and qualifications demanded prior approval either by the U. S. Attorney General or the U. S. District Court for the District of Columbia, the city sought authorization from the Attorney General (for a discussion of these provisions of the Voting Rights Act, see p. 161). In the meantime, Curtis Holt, a black resident, brought suit in a federal district court within Virginia alleging that the annexation was unconstitutional since it had been undertaken for the racial purpose of diluting the electoral strength of blacks. The district court so ruled and ordered a new election for the city council (seven members to run at large in the old city and two to run in the annexed area), but a federal appeals court reversed, finding no violation of the Fifteenth Amendment. Holt then started a second suit in district court under § 5 of the Voting Rights Act alleging that the annexation was invalid since the city had not received approval *beforehand* as § 5 dictated. Decision in this suit was held up pending the Supreme Court's decision in the present case.

Having been given no response by the Attorney General, the city started the present suit seeking approval of the annexation by the U. S. District Court for the District of Columbia. Shortly after filing this suit, however, that district court handed down a ruling in City of Petersburg v. United States, 354 F.Supp. 1021 (1973), aff'd, 410 U.S. 962, 93 S.Ct. 1441 (1973), striking down an annexation by another Virginia community where council elections were held at large but indicating approval should the system of elections there be modified by the adoption of a ward system, for example, to stem any adverse effect at-large elections would have on the electoral strength of blacks. After the *Petersburg* ruling, the City of Richmond and the Attorney General agreed to an amendment of Richmond's electoral scheme that would partition the city into nine wards, four with substantial black majorities, four with substantial white majorities, and one ward roughly three-fifths white and two-fifths black, one councilman to be elected from each ward. A special master appointed by the district court, however, concluded that annexation still diluted the political power of blacks and that any arguments advanced by the city failed to outweigh this finding. The district court held that the proportion of city residents who were black was substantially less following annexation and that, consequently, the annexation diluted the voting power of blacks. It left the fashioning of any remedy to await an appeal to the Supreme Court. In the face of the district court's adverse decision, the City of Richmond appealed to the Supreme Court.

Mr. Justice WHITE delivered the opinion of the Court.

[T]he issue is whether the city in its declaratory judgment action brought in the District Court for the District of Columbia has carried its burden of proof of demonstrating that the annexation had neither the purpose nor the effect of denying or abridging the right to vote of the Richmond Negro community on account of its race or color.

*   *   *

We deal first with whether the annexation involved here had the effect of denying or abridging the right to vote within the contemplation of § 5 of the Voting Rights Act.

*   *   *

*   *   * If a city having a ward system for the election of a nine-man council annexes a largely white area,

the wards are fairly redrawn, and as a result Negroes have only two rather than the four seats they had before, these facts alone do not demonstrate that the annexation has the effect of denying or abridging the right to vote. As long as the ward system fairly reflects the strength of the Negro community as it exists after the annexation, we cannot hold, without more specific legislative directions, that such an annexation is nevertheless barred by § 5. It is true that the black community, if there is block racial voting, will command fewer seats on the city council; and the annexation will have effected a decline in the Negroes' relative influence in the city. But a different city council and an enlarged city are involved after the annexation. Furthermore, Negro power in the new city is not undervalued, and Negroes will not be underrepresented on the council.

As long as this is true, we cannot hold that the effect of the annexation is to deny or abridge the right to vote. To hold otherwise would be either to forbid all such annexations or to require, as the price for approval of the annexation, that the black community be assigned the same proportion of council seats as before, hence perhaps permanently overrepresenting them and underrepresenting other elements in the community, including the nonblack citizens in the annexed area. We are unwilling to hold that Congress intended either consequence in enacting § 5.

We are also convinced that the annexation now before us, in the context of the ward system of election finally proposed by the city and then agreed to by the United States, does not have the effect prohibited by § 5. The findings on which this case was decided and is presented to us were that the postannexation population of the city was 42% Negro as compared with 52% prior to annexation. The nine-ward system finally submitted by the city included four wards each of which had greater than a 64% black majority. Four wards were heavily white. The ninth had a black population of 40.9%. In our view, such a plan does not undervalue the black strength in the community after annexation; and we hold that the annexation in this context does not have the effect of denying or abridging the right to vote within the meaning of § 5. To the extent that the District Court rested on a different view, its judgment cannot stand.

The foregoing principles should govern the application of § 5 insofar as it forbids changes in voting procedures having the effect of denying or abridging the right to vote on the grounds of race or color. But the section also proscribes changes that are made with the purpose of denying the right to vote on such grounds. The District Court concluded that when the annexation eventually approved in 1969 took place, it was adopted by the city with a discriminatory racial purpose, the precise purpose prohibited by § 5, and that to purge itself of that purpose the city was required to prove two factors, neither of which had been successfully or satisfactorily shown: (1) that the city had some objectively verifiable, legitimate purpose for the annexation at the time of adopting the ward system of electing councilmen in 1973; and (2) "that the ward plan not only reduced, but also effectively eliminated, the dilution of black voting power caused by the annexation." * * * 376 F.Supp., at 1353 (footnote omitted). The Master's findings were accepted to the effect that there were no current, legitimate economic or administrative reasons warranting the annexation. As for the second requirement, the ward plan failed to afford Negroes the political potential comparable to that which they would have enjoyed without the annexation, because they would soon have had a majority of the voting population in the old city and would have controlled the council, and because, in any event, it was doubtful that their political power under the proposed ward system in the enlarged community was equivalent to their influence in the old city under an at-large election system.

The requirement that the city allocate to the Negro community in the larger city the voting power or the seats on the city council in excess of its proportion in the new community and thus permanently to underrepresent other elements in the community is fundamentally at odds with the position we have expressed earlier in this opinion, and we cannot approve treating the failure to satisfy it as evidence of any purpose proscribed by § 5.

Accepting the findings of the Master in the District Court that the annexation, as it went forward in 1969, was infected by the impermissible purpose of denying the right to vote based on race through perpetuating white majority power to exclude Negroes from office through at-large elections, we are nevertheless persuaded that if verifiable reasons are now demonstrable in support of the annexation, and the ward plan proposed is fairly designed, the city need do no more to satisfy the requirements of § 5. We are also convinced that if the annexation cannot be sustained on sound, nondiscriminatory grounds, it would be only in the most extraordinary circumstances that the annexation should be permitted on condition that the Negro community be permanently overrepresented in the governing councils of the enlarged city. We are very doubtful that those circumstances exist in this case; for as far as this record is concerned, the County of Chesterfield was and still is quite ready to receive back the annexed area, to compensate the city for its capital improvements, and to resume governance of the area. It would also seem obvious that if there are no verifiable economic or administrative benefits from the annexation that would accrue to the city, its financial or other prospects would not be worsened by deannexation.

We need not determine this matter now, however; for if, as we have made clear, the controlling factor in this case is whether there are now objectively verifiable, legitimate reasons for the annexation, we agree with the United States that further proceedings are necessary to bring up to date and reassess the evidence bearing on the issue. We are not satisfied that the Special Master and the District Court gave adequate consideration to the evidence in this case in deciding whether there are now justifiable reasons for the annexation which took place on January 1, 1970. The special, three-judge court of the State of Virginia made the annexation award, giving great weight to the compromise agreement, but nevertheless finding that "Richmond is entitled to some annexation in this case. * * * Obviously cities must in some manner be permitted to grow in territory and population or they will face disastrous economic and social problems." * * * The court went on to find that the annexation met all of the "requirements of necessity and, most important of all, expediency," * * * expediency in the sense that it is " 'advantageous' and in furtherance of the policy of the State that 'urban areas should be under urban government and rural areas under county government'." * * *

* * *

In making his findings, however, it appears to us that the Special Master may have relied solely on the testimony of the county administrator of Chesterfield County who had opposed any annexation and was an obviously interested witness. At least there is no indication from the Special Master's findings or conclusions that he gave any attention to the contrary evidence in the record. The city now claims that the issues before the Special Master did not encompass the possible economic and administrative advantages of the annexation agreed upon in 1969. Given our responsibilities under § 5, we should be confident of the evidentiary record and the adequacy of the lower court's consideration of it. In this case * * * we have sufficient doubt that the record is complete and up to date with respect to whether there are now justifiable reasons for the city to retain the annexed area that we believe further proceedings with respect to this question are desirable.

We have held that an annexation reducing the relative political strength of the minority race in the enlarged city as compared with what it was before the annexation is not a statutory violation as long as the post-annexation electoral system fairly recognizes the minority's political potential. If this is so, it may be asked how it could be forbidden by § 5 to have the purpose and intent of achieving only what is a perfectly legal result under that section and why we need remand for further proceedings with respect to purpose alone. The answer is plain, and we need not labor it. An official action, whether an annexation or otherwise, taken for the purpose of discriminating against Negroes on account of their race has no legitimacy at all under our Constitution or under the statute. Section 5 forbids voting changes taken with the purpose of denying the vote on the grounds of race or color. Congress surely has the power to prevent such gross racial slurs, the only point of which is "to despoil colored citizens, and only colored citizens, of their theretofore enjoyed voting rights." Gomillion v. Lightfoot, 364 U.S. 339, 347, 81 S.Ct. 125, 130 (1960). Annexations animated by such a purpose have no credentials whatsoever; for "[a]cts generally lawful may become unlawful when done to accomplish an un-

lawful end." * * * Western Union Telegraph Company v. Foster, 247 U.S. 105, 114, 38 S.Ct. 438, 439 (1918); Gomillion v. Lightfoot, supra, 364 U.S., at 347, 81 S.Ct., at 130. An annexation proved to be of this kind and not proved to have a justifiable basis is forbidden by § 5, whatever its actual effect may have been or may be.

The judgment of the District Court is vacated and the case is remanded to that court for further proceedings consistent with this opinion.

So ordered.

Mr. Justice POWELL took no part in the consideration or decision of this case.

Mr. Justice BRENNAN, with whom Mr. Justice DOUGLAS and Mr. Justice MARSHALL join, dissenting.

The District Court, applying proper legal standards, found that the city of Richmond had failed to prove that its annexation of portions of Chesterfield County, Virginia, on January 1, 1970, had neither the purpose nor the effect of abridging or diluting the voting rights of Richmond's black citizens. I believe that that finding, far from being clearly erroneous, was amply supported by the record below, and that the District Court properly denied the declaratory judgment sought by Richmond. I therefore dissent.

* * *

[T]he settlement represented a clear victory for Richmond's entrenched white political establishment: the city realized a net gain of 44,000 white citizens, its black population was reduced from 52% to 42% of the total population, and the predominantly white Richmond Forward organization retained its 6–3 majority on the City Council.

Having succeeded in this patently discriminatory enterprise, Richmond now argues that it can purge the taint of its impermissible purpose by dredging up supposed objective justifications for the annexation and by replacing its practice of at-large councilmanic elections with a ward-voting system. * * * I have grave difficulty with the idea that the taint of an illegal purpose can, under § 5, be dispelled by the sort of post hoc rationalization which the city now offers.

* * *

To hold that an annexation agreement reached under such circumstances can be validated by objective economic justifications offered many years after the fact, in my view, wholly negates the prophylactic purpose of § 5. The Court nevertheless, at the suggestion of the United States, remands for the taking of further evidence on the presence of any "objectively verifiable, legitimate reasons for the annexation." Even assuming, as the District Court did, that such reasons could now validate an originally illegal annexation, I cannot agree that a remand is necessary.

The District Court, adopting the findings of the Master * * * squarely held that Richmond "has failed to establish any counterbalancing economic or administrative benefits of the annexation." 376 F.Supp., at 1353. The record before the Master, including the entire record in Holt v. City of Richmond, 334 F.Supp. 228 (ED Va.1971), rev'd, 459 F.2d 1093 (CA4), cert. denied, 408 U.S. 931, 92 S.Ct. 2510 (1972), to which the parties stipulated, contained ample evidence on the econom-

ic and administrative consequences of the annexation. The Master and the District Court weighed this often conflicting evidence and found that Richmond had failed to carry its burden of proof by showing any legitimate purpose for the annexation as consummated in 1969.

Fed.Rule Civ.Proc. 52(a) compels us to accept that finding unless it can be called clearly erroneous. I find it impossible, on this record, to attach that label to the findings below, and indeed, the Court never goes so far as to do so. Nevertheless, in apparent disagreement with the manner in which conflicting evidence was weighed and resolved by the lower court, the Court remands for further evidentiary proceedings, perhaps in hopes that a re-evaluation of the evidence will produce a more acceptable result. This course of action is to me wholly inconsistent with the proper role of an appellate court operating under the strictures of Rule 52(a).

The second prong of any § 5 inquiry is whether the voting change under consideration will have the effect of denying or abridging the right to vote on account of race or color. * * *

[T]he dilutive effect of Richmond's annexation is clear, both as a matter of semantics and as a matter of political realities. Blacks constituted 52% of the preannexation population and 44.8% of the preannexation voting-age population in Richmond, but now constitute only 42% of the postannexation population and only 37.3% of the postannexation voting-age population. I cannot agree that such a significant dilution of black voting strength can be remedied, for § 5 purposes, simply by allocating to blacks a reasonably proportionate share of voting power within the postannexation community.

The history of the Voting Rights Act * * * discloses the intent of Congress to impose a stringent system of controls upon changes in state voting practices in order to thwart even the most subtle attempts to dilute black voting rights. We have elsewhere described the Act as "an unusual, and in some aspects a severe, procedure for insuring that States would not discriminate on the basis of race in the enforcement of their voting laws." Congress was certainly aware of the hardships and inconvenience which § 5 and other portions of the Act could impose upon covered States and localities; but in passing the Act in its final form, Congress unmistakeably declared that those hardships are outweighed by the need to ensure effective protection for black voting rights.

Today's decision seriously weakens the protection so emphatically accorded by the Act. Municipal politicians who are fearful of losing their political control to emerging black voting majorities are today placed on notice that their control can be made secure as long as they can find concentrations of white citizens into which to expand their municipal boundaries. Richmond's black population, having finally begun to approach an opportunity to elect responsive officials and to have a significant voice in the conduct of its municipal affairs, now finds its voting strength reduced by a plan which "guarantees" four seats on the City Council but which makes the elusive fifth seat more remote than it was before. The Court would offer, as consolation, the fact that blacks will enjoy a fair share of the voting power available under a ward system operating within the boundaries of the postannexation community; but that same rationale would support a plan which added far greater concentrations of whites to the city and reduced black voting strength to the equivalent of three seats, two seats, or even fractions of a seat. The reliance upon postannexation fairness of representation is inconsistent with what I take to be the fundamental objective of § 5, namely, the protection of *present* levels of voting effectiveness for the black population.

It may be true, as the Court suggests, that this interpretation would effectively preclude some cities from undertaking desperately needed programs of expansion and annexation. Certainly there is nothing in § 5 which suggests that black voters could or should be given a disproportionately high share of the voting power in a postannexation community; where the racial composition of an annexed area is substantially different from that of the annexing area, it may well be impossible to protect preannexation black voting strength without invidiously diluting the voting strength of other racial groups in the community. I see no reason to assume that the demographics of the situation are such that this would be an unsuperable problem for all or even most cities covered by the Act; but in any event, if there is to be a "municipal hardship" exception for annexations vis-à-vis § 5, that exception should originate with Congress and not with the courts.

At the very least, therefore, I would adopt the *Petersburg* standard relied upon by the District Court, namely, that the dilutive effect of an annexation of this sort can be cured only by a ward plan "calculated to neutralize to the extent possible any adverse effect upon the political participation of black voters." 376 F.Supp., at 1352. * * *

More than five years has elapsed since the last municipal elections were held in Richmond. Hopes which were lifted by the District Court decision over a year ago are today again dashed, as the case is remanded for what may prove to be several additional years of litigation; Richmond will continue to be governed, as it has been for the last five years, by a slate of councilmen elected in clear violation of § 5. The black population of Richmond may be justifiably suspicious of the "protection" its voting rights are receiving when these rights can be suspended in limbo, and the people deprived of the right to select their local officials in an election meeting constitutional and statutory standards, for so many years. I would affirm the judgment below, and let the United States District Court for the Eastern District of Virginia set about the business of fashioning an appropriate remedy as expeditiously as possible.

The Voting Rights Act, widely regarded as the most effective piece of civil rights legislation ever passed, was extended for twenty-five years. The extension was passed by Congress and signed into law by President Reagan in June 1982. It was originally enacted in 1965 and was renewed in 1970 and 1975. Provisions and operation of the Act are set out in the headnotes to the two *Katzenbach* cases (see p. 161 and p. 168) and *City of Richmond* (p. 793).

On the occasion of its third extension, Congress addressed several features of the Act whose interpretation recently divided the Court. As the *Richmond* case illustrates, the Court has confronted, as of late, cases involving changes in the structure of city government, often with respect to the districting of commissioners or councilmen. Black plaintiffs have repeatedly alleged that such plans aim at diluting their voting strength. Provisions added by Congress in its newest extension of the Voting Rights Act reveal a mixed reaction to the Court's treatment of the contending interests of local jurisdictions in their quest for greater autonomy on such matters and of black voters seeking to exercise newfound political power.

Consistent with much of what the Court said in *Richmond*, the Voting Rights Extension declares there is no right to proportional representation for a minority group and that the absence of proportional representation is only one factor among several a court can consider. In what would appear rather sharp contrast to the Burger Court's recent decision in City of Mobile v. Bolden, 446 U.S. 55, 100 S.Ct. 1490 (1980),[f] in which a four-justice plurality (speaking through Stewart and including Burger, Powell, and Rehnquist) had declared that plaintiffs must be able to show evidence of *purposeful* discrimination, Congress provided that a voting rights violation could be demonstrated by showing that an election law or procedure operated in a manner that *resulted* in voting discrimination. Apparently aligning itself with Justice White's dissenting opinion in *Bolden*, Congress specified that a court should look at the "totality of the circumstances" to determine whether an abridgment of voting rights had been proved. In that case, for exam-

---

f. And the Court's newer decision in Rogers v. Lodge, — U.S.—, 102 S.Ct. 3272 (1982), which relied on *Bolden*. For extensive criticism of what he saw as the subjectivity inherent in the intention-to-discriminate standard applied in the vote dilution cases, see Justice Steven's dissenting opinion in *Lodge*.

ple, Justice White had stressed the confluence of several factors: the unresponsiveness of city officials to the demands of black citizens, the racial polarization apparent in voting patterns, and the adverse impact of a system of at-large elections on minority representation. Next, by adding a new "bail out" section, Congress made a bow in the direction of greater local autonomy and away from the Court's recent decision in City of Rome v. United States, 446 U.S. 156, 100 S.Ct. 1548 (1980), in which Justice Marshall held that the preclearance provisions of the Voting Rights Act still applied to a city that had been free of any signs of voting discrimination for at least seventeen years since only states, and not their subdivisions, could seek to "bail out" of the Act's coverage. Effective in 1984, the Voting Rights Extension would allow a jurisdiction freedom from the Act if it could show a federal three-judge panel in the District of Columbia that it had a clean record on voting rights for the preceding decade. The Voting Rights Extension provided that a clean record meant a ten-year period free of the use of discriminatory tests or devices, without any consent decrees or agreements resulting from voting rights violations, and unmarked by the presence of federal examiners to help register voters. Congress also expected that a jurisdiction qualified to "bail out" of the Act's coverage would reflect a past record of full compliance and make "constructive efforts" to bring minorities into the political process. Moreover, Congress extended until 1992 those provisions of the Act requiring certain areas of the country to furnish bilingual election materials. It also authorized assistance to blind and disabled voters.

In the House, the vote on passage was 389–24 and in the Senate, 85–8. Reflecting both a change in political and social values and a dramatic increase in black electoral participation since 1965, Southern Representatives and Senators—especially Democrats—gave the extension of the Voting Rights Act significant support.

KRAMER v. UNION FREE SCHOOL DISTRICT NO. 15

Supreme Court of the United States, 1969
395 U.S. 621, 89 S.Ct. 1886, 23 L.Ed.2d 583

The facts are set out in the opinion.

Mr. Chief Justice WARREN delivered the opinion of the Court.

In this case we are called on to determine whether § 2012 of the New York Education Law * * * is constitutional. The legislation provides that in certain New York school districts residents who are otherwise eligible to vote in state and federal elections may vote in the school district election only if they (1) own (or lease) taxable real property within the district, or (2) are parents (or have custody of) children enrolled in the local public schools. Appellant, a bachelor who neither owns

nor leases taxable real property, filed suit in federal court claiming that § 2012 denied him equal protection of the laws in violation of the Fourteenth Amendment. With one judge dissenting, a three-judge District Court dismissed appellant's complaint. Finding that § 2012 does violate the Equal Protection Clause of the Fourteenth Amendment, we reverse.

* * *

* * * The sole issue in this case is whether the *additional* requirements of § 2012—requirements

which prohibit some district residents who are otherwise qualified by age and citizenship from participating in district meetings and school board elections—violate the Fourteenth Amendment's command that no State shall deny persons equal protection of the laws.

[I]n this case, we must give the statute a close and exacting examination. "[S]ince the right to exercise the franchise in a free and unimpaired manner is preservative of other basic civil and political rights, any alleged infringement of the right of citizens to vote must be carefully and meticulously scrutinized." Reynolds v. Sims, 377 U.S. 533, 562, 84 S.Ct. 1362, 1381 (1964). * * * This careful examination is necessary because statutes distributing the franchise constitute the foundation of our representative society. Any unjustified discrimination in determining who may participate in political affairs or in the selection of public officials undermines the legitimacy of representative government.

Thus, state apportionment statutes, which may *dilute* the effectiveness of some citizens' votes, receive close scrutiny from this Court. * * * No less rigid an examination is applicable to statutes *denying* the franchise to citizens who are otherwise qualified by residence and age. Statutes granting the franchise to residents on a selective basis always post the danger of denying some citizens any effective voice in the governmental affairs which substantially affect their lives. Therefore, if a challenged state statute grants the right to vote to some bona fide residents of requisite age and citizenship and denies the franchise to others, the Court must determine whether the exclusions are necessary to promote a compelling state interest. * * *

And, for these reasons, the deference usually given to the judgment of legislators does not extend to decisions concerning which resident citizens may participate in the election of legislators and other public officials. Those decisions must be carefully scrutinized by the Court to determine whether each resident citizen has, as far as is possible, an equal voice in the selections. Accordingly, when we are reviewing statutes which deny some residents the right to vote, the general presumption of constitutionality afforded state statutes and the traditional approval given state classifications if the Court can conceive of a "rational basis" for the distinctions made are not applicable. * * * The presumption of constitutionality and the approval given "rational" classifications in other types of enactments are based on an assumption that the institutions of state government are structured so as to represent fairly all the people. However, when the challenge to the statute is in effect a challenge of this basic assumption, the assumption can no longer serve as the basis for presuming constitutionality. And, the assumption is no less under attack because the legislature which decides who may participate at the various levels of political choice is fairly elected. Legislation which delegates decision making to bodies elected by only a portion of those eligible to vote for the legislature can cause unfair representation. Such legislation can exclude a minority of voters from any voice in the decisions just as effectively as if the decisions were made by legislators the minority had no voice in selecting.

The need for exacting judicial scrutiny of statutes distributing the franchise is undiminished simply because, under a different statutory scheme, the offices subject to election might have been filled through appointment. States do have latitude in determining whether certain public officials shall be selected by election or chosen by appointment and whether various questions shall be submitted to the voters.   *   *   * However, "once the franchise is granted to the electorate, lines may not be drawn which are inconsistent with the Equal Protection Clause of the Fourteenth Amendment."

*   *   *

Besides appellant and others who similarly live in their parents' homes, the statute also disenfranchises the following persons (unless they are parents or guardians of children enrolled in the district public school): senior citizens and others living with children or relatives; clergy, military personnel, and others who live on tax-exempt property; boarders and lodgers; parents who neither own nor lease qualifying property and whose children are too young to attend school; parents who neither own nor lease qualifying property and whose children attend private schools.

Appellant asserts that excluding him from participation in the district elections denies him equal protection of the laws. He contends that he and others of his class are substantially interested in and significantly affected by the school meeting decisions. All members of the community have an interest in the quality and structure of public education, appellant says, and he urges that "the decisions taken by local boards *   *   * may have grave conse

quences to the entire population." Appellant also argues that the level of property taxation affects him, even though he does not own property, as property tax levels affect the price of goods and services in the community.

We turn therefore to question whether the exclusion is necessary to promote a compelling state interest. First appellees argue that the State has a legitimate interest in limiting the franchise in school district elections to "members of the community of interest"—those "primarily interested in such elections." Second, appellees urge that the State may reasonably and permissibly conclude that "property taxpayers" (including lessees of taxable property who share the tax burden through rent payments) and parents of the children enrolled in the district's schools are those "primarily interested" in school affairs.

We do not understand appellees to argue that the State is attempting to limit the franchise to those "subjectively concerned" about school matters. Rather, they appear to argue that the State's legitimate interest is in restricting a voice in school matters to those "directly affected" by such decisions. The State apparently reasons that since the schools are financed in part by local property taxes, persons whose out-of-pocket expenses are "directly" affected by property tax changes should be allowed to vote. Similarly, parents of children in school are thought to have a "direct" stake in school affairs and are given a vote.

Appellees argue that it is necessary to limit the franchise to those "primarily interested" in school affairs because "the ever increasing complexity of the many interacting phases of the school system and structure make it extremely difficult for the electorate fully to understand the whys and wherefores of the detailed operations of the school system." Appellees say that many communications of school boards and school administrations are sent home to the parents through the district pupils and are "not broadcast to the general public"; thus, nonparents will be less informed than parents. Further, appellees argue, those who are assessed for local property taxes (either directly or indirectly through rent) will have enough of an interest "through the burden on their pocketbooks, to acquire such information as they may need."

We need express no opinion as to whether the State in some circumstances might limit the exercise of the franchise to those "primarily interested" or "primarily affected." Of course, we therefore do not reach the issue of whether these particular elections are of the type in which the franchise may be so limited. For, assuming, *arguendo*, that New York legitimately might limit the franchise in these school district elections to those "primarily interested in school affairs," close scrutiny of the § 2012 classifications demonstrates that they do not accomplish this purpose with sufficient precision to justify denying appellant the franchise.

Whether classifications allegedly limiting the franchise to those resident citizens "primarily interested" deny those excluded equal protection of the laws depends, *inter alia*, on whether all those excluded are in fact substantially less interested or affected than those the statute includes. In other words, the classifications must be tailored so that the exclusion of appellant and members of his class is necessary to achieve the articulated state goal. Section 2012 does not meet the exacting standard of precision we require of statutes which selectively distribute the franchise. The classifications in § 2012 permit inclusion of many persons who have, at best, a remote and indirect interest, in school affairs and, on the other hand, exclude others who have a distinct and direct interest in the school meeting decisions.

Nor do appellees offer any justification for the exclusion of seemingly interested and informed residents—other than to argue that the § 2012 classifications include those "whom the State could understandably deem to be the most intimately interested in actions taken by the school board," and urge that "the task of * * * balancing the interest of the community in the maintenance of orderly school district elections against the interest of any individual in voting in such elections should clearly remain with the Legislature." But the issue is not whether the legislative judgments are rational. A more exacting standard obtains. The issue is whether the § 2012 requirements do in fact sufficiently further a compelling state interest to justify denying the franchise to appellant and members of his class. The requirements of § 2012 are not sufficiently tailored to limiting the franchise to those "primarily interested" in school affairs to justify the denial of the franchise to appellant and members of his class.

The judgment of the United States District Court for the Eastern District of New York is therefore reversed. The case is remanded for further proceedings consistent with this opinion.

It is so ordered.

Mr. Justice STEWART, with whom Mr. Justice BLACK, and Mr. Justice HARLAN join, dissenting.

In Lassiter v. Northampton County Election Bd., 360 U.S. 45, 79 S.Ct. 985 this Court upheld against constitutional attack a literacy requirement, applicable to voters in all state and federal elections, imposed by the State of North Carolina.   *   *   * Believing that the appellant in this case is not the victim of any "discrimination which the Constitution condemns," I would affirm the judgment of the District Court.

*   *   *

[I]t seems to me that under *any* equal protection standard, short of a doctrinaire insistence that universal suffrage is somehow mandated by the Constitution, the appellant's claim must be rejected. First of all, it must be emphasized—despite the Court's undifferentiated references to what it terms "the franchise"—that we are dealing here, not with a general election, but with a limited, special-purpose election. The appellant is eligible to vote in all state, local, and federal elections in which general governmental policy is determined. He is fully able, therefore, to participate not only in the processes by which the requirements for school district voting may be changed, but also in those by which the levels of state and federal financial assistance to the District are determined. He clearly is not locked into any self-perpetuating status of exclusion from the electoral process.

Secondly, the appellant is of course limited to asserting his own rights, not the purported rights of hypothetical childless clergymen or parents of preschool children, who neither own nor rent taxable property. The appellant's status is merely that of a citizen who says he is interested in the affairs of his local public schools. If the Constitution requires that he must be given a decision-making role in the governance of those affairs, then it seems to me that any individual who seeks such a role must be given it. For as I have suggested, there is no persuasive reason for distinguishing constitutionally between the voter qualifications New York has required for its Union Free School District elections and qualifications based on factors such as age, residence, or literacy.

Today's decision can only be viewed as irreconcilable with the established principle that "[t]he States have *   *   * broad powers to determine the conditions under which the right of suffrage may be exercised." *   *   * Since I think that principle is entirely sound, I respectfully dissent from the Court's judgment and opinion.

"STRICT SCRUTINY" IN VOTING RIGHTS AND BALLOT ACCESS CASES

Case	Result and Vote	Restriction at issue	Dissents
Carrington v. Rash, 380 U.S. 89, 85 S.Ct. 775 (1965)	Struck down, 7–1	Provision of the Texas constitution precluded any member of the armed forces who moved to Texas during	Harlan

"STRICT SCRUTINY" (*Cont.*)

Case	Result and Vote	Restriction at issue	Dissents
Carrington (*Cont.*)		his term of duty from establishing residency and thus the right to vote in the state so long as he remained in the military	
Harper v. Virginia State Bd. of Elections, 383 U.S. 663, 86 S.Ct. 1079 (1966)	Struck down, 6–3	Virginia law required payment of a poll tax as prerequisite to voting in state elections	Black, Harlan, and Stewart
Williams v. Rhodes, 393 U.S. 23, 89 S.Ct. 5 (1968)	Struck down, 6–3	Provisions of Ohio election law made it nearly impossible for a new political party to get on the ballot by requiring the collection of signatures equal to 15 percent of total vote polled in last gubernatorial election (while allowing the two major parties to remain on the ballot merely by polling 10 percent of the vote) and by requiring elaborate party organization	Warren, Stewart, and White
Cipriano v. City of Houma, 395 U.S. 701, 89 S.Ct. 1897 (1969)	Struck down, 9–0	Louisiana law gave only property taxpayers the right to vote on municipal bond issues	
Evans v. Cornman, 398 U.S. 419, 90 S.Ct. 1752 (1970)	Struck down, 8–0	Maryland law denied right to vote to individuals who lived on grounds of federal enclaves	
City of Phoenix v. Kolodziejski, 399 U.S. 204, 90 S.Ct. 1990 (1970)	Struck down, 5–3	State constitution and statute excluded nonproperty owners from voting in municipal bond elections	Burger, Harlan, and Stewart
Gordon v. Lance, 403 U.S. 1, 91 S.Ct. 1889 (1971)	Upheld, 9–0	West Virginia law required 60 percent approval by voters in referendum election for passage of bond issues and tax increases	
Jenness v. Fortson, 403 U.S. 431, 91 S.Ct. 1970 (1971)	Upheld, 9–0	Provision of Georgia election code required independent candidates and nominees of political organizations receiving less than 20 percent of vote in last gubernatorial election to collect signatures equal to 5 percent of the number of eligible voters in a 180-day period to qualify for place on the ballot	
Bullock v. Carter, 405 U.S. 134, 92 S.Ct. 849 (1972)	Struck down, 7–0	Texas law required payment of a filing fee, ranging as high as $8900 for some offices, as absolute prerequi-	

"STRICT SCRUTINY" (*Cont.*)

Case	Result and Vote	Restriction at issue	Dissents
Bullock (*Cont.*)		site to having candidate's name appear on primary ballot; no write-in votes counted	
Dunn v. Blumstein, 405 U.S. 330, 92 S.Ct. 995 (1972)	Struck down, 6–1	Tennessee had a durational residency requirement of one year in state and three months in county in order to vote	Burger
Kusper v. Pontikes, 414 U.S. 51, 94 S.Ct. 303 (1973)	Struck down, 7–2	Provision of the Illinois election code prohibits a person from voting in a primary election if he has voted in the primary of another party within preceding twenty-three months	Blackmun and Rehnquist
Rosario v. Rockefeller, 410 U.S. 752, 93 S.Ct. 1245 (1973)	Upheld, 5–4	To prevent "cross-over voting," New York law provided for "closed primaries" in that eligibility to vote in a party primary depended on whether voter was a registered member of that political party as of the last general election; party registration was permitted for one month prior to last general election	Douglas, Brennan, Marshall, and Powell
Storer v. Brown, 415 U.S. 724, 94 S.Ct. 1274 (1974)	Upheld (1) remanded (2), 6–3	California's election law required that (1) independent candidates for office be politically disaffiliated for one year before immediately preceding primary election; and (2) that such candidate collect signatures equal to between 5 percent and 6 percent of entire vote cast in constituency from which he seeks election	Douglas, Brennan, and Marshall
American Party of Texas v. White, 415 U.S. 767, 94 S.Ct. 1296 (1974)	Upheld (1) struck down (2), 8–1	Complex Texas law provided (1) four methods of nominating candidates for public office depending on electoral strength, with independent candidates required to get signatures; and that (2) absentee ballots bear only the names of candidates from the two major parties, not third party or independent candidates	Douglas
Lubin v. Panish, 415 U.S. 709, 94 S.Ct. 1315 (1974)	Struck down, 9–0	California statute required candidates to pay fixed filing fee to be placed on primary election ballot without providing any alternative means of access to indigents seeking a ballot position	
Hill v. Stone, 421 U.S. 289, 95 S.Ct. 1637 (1975)	Struck down, 5–3	Dual box election procedure used in Texas municipal bond elections specified that property taxpayers deposit their votes in one box and all other	Burger, Stewart, and Rehnquist

"STRICT SCRUTINY" (*Cont.*)

Case	Result and Vote	Restriction at issue	Dissents
Hill (*Cont.*)		voters deposit theirs in a separate box; passage of the bond issue required majority vote in favor from both boxes	
Town of Lockport v. Citizens for Community Action, 430 U.S. 259, 97 S.Ct. 1047 (1977)	Upheld, 9–0	New York law provided that a new county charter could go into effect only if approved by concurrent majorities of voters living within cities in the county and voters living outside the cities	

d.   MALAPPORTIONMENT

BAKER v. CARR

Supreme Court of the United States, 1962
369 U.S. 186, 82 S.Ct. 691, 7 L.Ed.2d 663

See p. 102

REYNOLDS v. SIMS

Supreme Court of the United States, 1964
377 U.S. 533, 84 S.Ct. 1362, 12 L.Ed.2d 506

Sims and other Alabama residents brought suit against state and political party officials challenging the apportionment of the state legislature. The state constitution provided that the legislature be reapportioned every ten years on the basis of population, but with the qualification that each county be allocated at least one representative and no county be entitled to more than one senator. No apportionment, however, had taken place since 1901. Under the existing scheme approximately a quarter of the population could elect a majority of the state senators and about the same proportion could elect a majority of the state representatives. Voting power of constituents (ratios of people to legislators) varied by as much as 41–1 among senate districts and up to 16–1 among districts in the lower house. A federal district court held this apportionment to be a violation of plaintiffs' rights to equal protection of the laws under the Fourteenth Amendment. In response to pressure from the district court, the Alabama legislature adopted two reapportionment plans, neither of which, however, apportioned the legislative districts solely on the basis of population, whereupon the district court held the plans unconstitutional. Reynolds and the other defendants in the suit appealed to the Supreme Court.

Mr. Chief Justice WARREN delivered the opinion of the Court.

* * *

* * * Our problem * * * is to ascertain, in the instant cases, whether there are any constitutionally cognizable principles which would justify departures from the basic standard of equality among voters in the apportionment of seats in state legislatures.

A predominant consideration in determining whether a State's legislative apportionment scheme constitutes an invidious discrimination violative of rights asserted under the Equal Protection Clause is that the rights allegedly impaired are individual and personal in nature. * * * While the result of a court decision in a state legislative apportionment controversy may be to require the restructuring of the geographical distribution of seats in a state legislature, the judicial focus must be concentrated upon ascertaining whether there has been any discrimination against certain of the State's citizens which constitutes an impermissible impairment of their constitutionally protected right to vote. * * * Undoubtedly, the right of suffrage is a fundamental matter in a free and democratic society. Especially since the right to exercise the franchise in a free and unimpaired manner is preservative of other basic civil and political rights, any alleged infringement of the right of citizens to vote must be carefully and meticulously scrutinized. * * *

Legislators represent people, not trees or acres. Legislators are elected by voters, not farms or cities or economic interests. As long as ours is a representative form of government, and our legislatures are those instruments of government elected directly by and directly representative of the people, the right to elect legislators in a free and unimpaired fashion is a bedrock of our political system. It could hardly be gainsaid that a constitutional claim had been asserted by an allegation that certain otherwise qualified voters had been entirely prohibited from voting for members of their state legislature. * * * It would appear extraordinary to suggest that a State could be constitutionally permitted to enact a law providing that certain of the State's voters could vote two, five, or 10 times for their legislative representatives, while voters living elsewhere could vote only once. And it is inconceivable that a state law to the affect that, in counting votes for legislators, the votes of citizens in one part of the State would be multiplied by two, five, or 10, while the votes of persons in another area would be counted only at face value, could be constitutionally sustainable. Of course, the effect of state legislative districting schemes which give the same number of representatives to unequal numbers of constituents is identical. Overweighting and overvaluation of the votes of those living here has the certain effect of dilution and undervaluation of the votes of those living there. The resulting discrimination against those individual voters living in disfavored areas is easily demonstrable mathematically. Their right to vote is simply not the same right to vote as that of those living in a favored part of the State. Two, five, or 10 of them must vote before the effect of their voting is equivalent to that of their favored neighbor. Weighting the votes of citizens differently, by any method or means, merely because of where they happen to reside, hardly seems justifiable. * * *

* * *

Logically, in a society ostensibly grounded on representative government, it would seem reasonable that a majority of the people of a State could elect a majority of that State's legislators. To conclude differently, and to sanction minority control of state legislative bodies, would appear to deny majority rights in a way that far surpasses any possible denial of minority rights that might otherwise be thought to result. Since legislatures are responsible for enacting laws by which all citizens are to be governed, they should be bodies which are collectively responsive to the popular will. And the concept of equal protection has been traditionally viewed as requiring the uniform treatment of persons standing in the same relation to the governmental action questioned or challenged. With respect to the allocation of legislative representation, all voters, as citizens of a State, stand in the same relation regardless of where they live. Any suggested criteria for the differentiation of citizens are insufficient to justify any discrimination, as to the weight of their votes, unless relevant to the permissible purposes of legislative apportionment. Since the achieving of fair and effective representation for all citizens is concededly the basic aim of legislative apportionment, we conclude that the Equal Protection Clause guarantees the opportunity for equal participation by all voters in the election of state legislators. Diluting the weight of votes because of place of residence impairs basic constitutional rights under the Fourteenth Amendment just as much as invidious discriminations based upon factors such as race * * * or economic status. * * *

We are told that the matter of apportioning representation in a state legislature is a complex and many-faceted one. We are advised that States can rationally consider factors other than population in apportioning legislative representation. We are admonished not to restrict the power of the States to impose differing views as to political philosophy on their citizens. We are cautioned about the dangers of entering into political thickets and mathematical quagmires. Our answer is this: a denial of constitutionally protected rights demands judicial protection; our oath and our office require no less of us. * * * To the extent that a citizen's right to vote is debased, he is that much less a citizen. The fact that an individual lives here or there is not a legitimate reason for overweighting or diluting the efficacy of his vote. * * * Population is, of necessity, the starting point for consideration and the controlling criterion for judgment in legislative apportionment controversies. * * *

We hold that, as a basic constitutional standard, the Equal Protection Clause requires that the seats in both houses of a bicameral state legislature must be apportioned on a population basis. Simply stated, an individual's right to vote for state legislators is unconstitutionally impaired when its weight is in a substantial fashion diluted when compared with votes of citizens living in other parts of the State. * * *

* * *

Since neither of the houses of the Alabama Legislature, under any of the three plans considered by the District Court, was apportioned on a population basis, we would be justified in proceeding no further. However, one of the proposed plans, that contained in the so-called 67-Senator Amendment, at least superficially resembles the scheme of legislative representation followed in the Federal Congress. * * *

* * * We agree with the District Court, and find the federal anal-

ogy inapposite and irrelevant to state legislative districting schemes. Attempted reliance on the federal analogy appears often to be little more than an after-the-fact rationalization offered in defense of maladjusted state apportionment arrangements. The original constitutions of 36 of our States provided that representation in both houses of the state legislatures would be based completely, or predominantly, on population. And the Founding Fathers clearly had no intention of establishing a pattern or model for the apportionment of seats in state legislatures when the system of representation in the Federal Congress was adopted. * * *

* * *

Political subdivisions of States—counties, cities, or whatever—never were and never have been considered as sovereign entities. Rather, they have been traditionally regarded as subordinate governmental instrumentalities created by the State to assist in the carrying out of state governmental functions. * * * The relationship of the States to the Federal Government could hardly be less analogous.

* * *

We do not believe that the concept of bicameralism is rendered anachronistic and meaningless when the predominant basis of representation in the two state legislative bodies is required to be the same—population. A prime reason for bicameralism, modernly considered, is to insure mature and deliberate consideration of, and to prevent precipitate action on, proposed legislative measures. Simply because the controlling criterion for apportioning representation is required to be the

same in both houses does not mean that there will be no differences in the composition and complexion of the two bodies. Different constituencies can be represented in the two houses. One body could be composed of single-member districts while the other could have at least some multimember districts. The length of terms of the legislators in the separate bodies could differ. The numerical size of the two bodies could be made to differ, even significantly, and the geographical size of districts from which legislators are elected could also be made to differ. And apportionment in one house could be arranged so as to balance off minor inequities in the representation of certain areas in the other house. In summary, these and other factors could be, and are presently in many States, utilized to engender differing complexions and collective attitudes in the two bodies of a state legislature, although both are apportioned substantially on a population basis.

By holding that as a federal constitutional requisite both houses of a state legislature must be apportioned on a population basis, we mean that the Equal Protection Clause requires that a State make an honest and good faith effort to construct districts, in both houses of its legislature, as nearly of equal population as is practicable. We realize that it is a practical impossibility to arrange legislative districts so that each one has an identical number of residents, or citizens, or voters. Mathematical exactness or precision is hardly a workable constitutional requirement.

* * * For the present, we deem it expedient not to attempt to spell out any precise constitutional tests. What is marginally permissible in one State may be unsatisfac-

tory in another, depending on the particular circumstances of the case. Developing a body of doctrine on a case-by-case basis appears to us to provide the most satisfactory means of arriving at detailed constitutional requirements in the area of state legislative apportionment. * * *

A State may legitimately desire to maintain the integrity of various political subdivisions, insofar as possible, and provide for compact districts of contiguous territory in designing a legislative apportionment scheme. Valid considerations may underlie such aims. Indiscriminate districting, without any regard for political subdivision or natural or historical boundary lines, may be little more than an open invitation to partisan gerrymandering. Single-member districts may be the rule in one State, while another State might desire to achieve some flexibility by creating multimember or floterial districts. Whatever the means of accomplishment, the overriding objective must be substantial equality of population among the various districts, so that the vote of any citizen is approximately equal in weight to that of any other citizen in the State. * * * So long as the divergences from a strict population standard are based on legitimate considerations incident to the effectuation of a rational state policy, some deviations from the equal-population principle are constitutionally permissible with respect to the apportionment of seats in either or both of the two houses of a bicameral state legislature. But neither history alone, nor economic or other sorts of group interests, are permissible factors in attempting to justify disparities from population-based representation. Citizens, not history or economic interests, cast votes. Considerations

of area alone provide an insufficient justification for deviations from the equal-population principle. * * *

A consideration that appears to be of more substance in justifying some deviations from population-based representation in state legislatures is that of insuring some voice to political subdivisions, as political subdivisions. * * *

* * *

We do not consider here the difficult question of the proper remedial devices which federal courts should utilize in state legislative apportionment cases. Remedial techniques in this new and developing area of the law will probably often differ with the circumstances of the challenged apportionment and a variety of local conditions. It is enough to say now that, once a State's legislative apportionment scheme has been found to be unconstitutional, it would be the unusual case in which a court would be justified in not taking appropriate action to insure that no further elections are conducted under the invalid plan. * * *

Affirmed and remanded.

Mr. Justice CLARK, concurring in the affirmance.

The Court goes much beyond the necessities of this case in laying down a new "equal population" principle for state legislative apportionment. * * *

It seems to me that all that the Court need say in this case is that each plan considered by the trial court is "a crazy quilt," clearly revealing invidious discrimination in each house of the Legislature and therefore violative of the Equal Protection Clause. * * *

I * * * do not reach the question of the so-called "federal analogy." But in my view, if one house of the State Legislature meets the population standard, representation in the other house might include some departure from it so as to take into account, on a rational basis, other factors in order to afford some representation to the various elements of the State. * * *

Mr. Justice STEWART. * * *

All of the parties have agreed with the District Court's finding that legislative inaction for some 60 years in the face of growth and shifts in population has converted Alabama's legislative apportionment plan enacted in 1901 into one completely lacking in rationality. Accordingly, * * * I would affirm the judgment of the District Court holding that this apportionment violated the Equal Protection Clause.

* * *

Mr. Justice HARLAN, dissenting.

In these cases the Court holds that seats in the legislatures of six States are apportioned in ways that violate the Federal Constitution. Under the Court's ruling it is bound to follow that the legislatures in all but a few of the other 44 States will meet the same fate. * * * Once again, I must register my protest.

* * *

Generalities cannot obscure the cold truth that cases of this type are not amenable to the development of judicial standards. No set of standards can guide a court which has to decide how many legislative districts a State shall have, or what the shape of the districts shall be, or where to draw a particular district line. No judicially manageable standard can determine whether a State should have single-member districts or mul-

timember districts or some combination of both. No such standard can control the balance between keeping up with population shifts and having stable districts. In all these respects, the courts will be called upon to make particular decisions with respect to which a principle of equally populated districts will be of no assistance whatsoever. Quite obviously, there are limitless possibilities for districting consistent with such a principle. Nor can these problems be avoided by judicial reliance on legislative judgments so far as possible. Reshaping or combining one or two districts, or modifying just a few district lines, is no less a matter of choosing among many possible solutions, with varying political consequences, than reapportionment broadside.

* * *

Although the Court—necessarily as I believe—provides only generalities in elaboration of its main thesis, its opinion nevertheless fully demonstrates how far removed these problems are from fields of judicial competence. Recognizing that "indiscriminate districting" is an invitation to "partisan gerrymandering," * * * the Court nevertheless excludes virtually every basis for the formation of electoral districts other than "indiscriminate districting." * * *

* * * What is done today deepens my conviction that judicial entry into this realm is profoundly ill-advised and constitutionally impermissible. * * *

[N]o thinking person can fail to recognize that the aftermath of these cases, however desirable it may be thought in itself, will have been achieved at the cost of a radical alteration in the relationship between the States and the Federal Government, more particularly the Federal Judiciary. Only one who has an overbearing impatience with the federal system and its political processes will believe that that cost was not too high or was inevitable.

Finally, these decisions give support to a current mistaken view of the Constitution and the constitutional function of this Court. This view, in a nutshell, is that every major social ill in this country can find its cure in some constitutional "principle," and that this Court should "take the lead" in promoting reform when other branches of government fail to act. The Constitution is not a panacea for every blot upon the public welfare, nor should this Court, ordained as a judicial body, be thought of as a general haven for reform movements. The Constitution is an instrument of government, fundamental to which is the premise that in a diffusion of governmental authority lies the greatest promise that this Nation will realize liberty for all its citizens. This Court, limited in function in accordance with that premise, does not serve its high purpose when it exceeds its authority, even to satisfy justified impatience with the slow workings of the political process. For when, in the name of constitutional interpretation, the Court *adds* something to the Constitution that was deliberately excluded from it, the Court in reality substitutes its view of what should be so for the amending process.

* * *

LUCAS v. FORTY–FOURTH GENERAL ASSEMBLY OF COLORADO

Supreme Court of the United States, 1964
377 U.S. 713, 84 S.Ct. 1459, 12 L.Ed.2d 632

Andres Lucas and other residents of Denver initiated action against the Colorado legislature challenging the validity of a legislative apportionment scheme authorized in an amendment to the state constitution. Amendment No. 7, which provided for the apportionment of the lower house on the basis of population but took into account additional factors together with population in drawing state senate districts, was approved by the Colorado electorate in November 1962, by a margin of 305,700 to 172,725. In the same election the voters defeated 311,749 to 149,822, Amendment No. 8 which provided for the apportionment of both houses of the state legislature solely on a population basis. A federal district court upheld the validity of the apportionment based on Amendment No. 7, and the case was brought to the Supreme Court on appeal. The case was docketed for hearing together with the other reapportionment cases during the October 1963 Term including Reynolds v. Sims and WMCA v. Lomenzo, 377 U.S. 633, 84 S.Ct. 1418, an action challenging the county-based apportionment of the New York legislature in which, like Colorado, factors other than population had been taken into account in drawing district lines.

Mr. Chief Justice WARREN delivered the opinion of the Court.

* * *

Several aspects of this case serve to distinguish it from the other cases involving state legislative apportionment also decided this date. Initially, one house of the Colorado Legislature is at least arguably apportioned substantially on a population basis under Amendment No. 7 and the implementing statutory provisions. Under the apportionment schemes challenged in the other cases, on the other hand, clearly neither of the houses in any of the state legislatures is apportioned sufficiently on a population basis so as to be constitutionally sustainable. Additionally, the Colorado scheme of legislative apportionment here attacked is one adopted by a majority vote of the Colorado electorate almost contemporaneously with the District Court's decision on the merits in this litigation. Thus, the plan at issue did not result from prolonged legislative inaction. * * *

As appellees have correctly pointed out, a majority of the voters in every county of the State voted in favor of the apportionment scheme embodied in Amendment No. 7's provisions, in preference to that contained in proposed Amendment No. 8, which, subject to minor deviations, would have based the apportionment of seats in both houses on a population basis. * * *

Finally, this case differs from the others decided this date in that the initiative device provides a practicable political remedy to obtain relief against alleged legislative malapportionment in Colorado. * * *

In Reynolds v. Sims * * * we held that the Equal Protection Clause requires that both houses of a bicameral state legislature must be apportioned substantially on a population basis. * * * Under neither Amendment No. 7's plan, nor, of course, the previous statutory scheme, is the overall legislative representation in the two houses of the Colorado Legislature sufficiently

grounded on population to be constitutionally sustainable under the Equal Protection Clause.

Except as an interim remedial procedure, justifying a court in staying its hand temporarily, we find no significance in the fact that a nonjudicial, political remedy may be available for the effectuation of asserted rights to equal representation in a state legislature. Courts sit to adjudicate controversies involving alleged denials of constitutional rights. While a court sitting as a court of equity might be justified in temporarily refraining from the issuance of injunctive relief in an apportionment case in order to allow for resort to an available political remedy, such as initiative and referendum, individual constitutional rights cannot be deprived, or denied judicial effectuation, because of the existence of a nonjudicial remedy through which relief against the alleged malapportionment, which the individual voters seek, might be achieved. An individual's constitutionally protected right to cast an equally weighted vote cannot be denied even by a vote of a majority of a State's electorate, if the apportionment scheme adopted by the voters fails to measure up to the requirements of the Equal Protection Clause. Manifestly, the fact that an apportionment plan is adopted in a popular referendum is insufficient to sustain its constitutionality or to induce a court of equity to refuse to act. As stated by this Court in West Virginia State Bd. of Educ. v. Barnette, 319 U.S. 624, 638, 63 S.Ct. 1178, 1185, "One's right to life, liberty, and property * * * and other fundamental rights may not be submitted to vote; they depend on the outcome of no elections." A citizen's constitutional rights can hardly be infringed simply because a majority of the people choose that it be. We hold that the fact that a challenged legislative apportionment plan was approved by the electorate is without federal constitutional significance, if the scheme adopted fails to satisfy the basic requirements of the Equal Protection Clause, as delineated in our opinion in *Reynolds* v. *Sims*. And we conclude that the fact that a practicably available political remedy, such as initiative and referendum, exists under state law provides justification only for a court of equity to stay its hand temporarily while recourse to such a remedial device is attempted or while proposed initiated measures relating to legislative apportionment are pending and will be submitted to the State's voters at the next election.

* * *

Reversed and remanded.

Dissenting opinion by Mr. Justice HARLAN printed in * * * Reynolds v. Sims. * * *

Mr. Justice CLARK, dissenting.

* * *

I would refuse to interfere with this apportionment for several reasons. First Colorado enjoys the initiative and referendum system which it often utilizes and which, indeed, produced the present apportionment. * * * Next, as my Brother Stewart has pointed out, there are rational and most persuasive reasons for some deviations in the representation in the Colorado Assembly. The State has mountainous areas which divide it into four regions, some parts of which are almost impenetrable. There are also some depressed areas, diversified industry and varied climate, as well as enormous recreational regions and difficulties in transportation. These factors give rise to problems indigenous to Colorado, which only its people can intelligently solve. This they have done in the present apportionment.

Finally, I cannot agree to the arbitrary application of the "one man, one vote" principle for both houses of a State Legislature. In my view, if one house is fairly apportioned by population (as is admitted here) then the people should have some latitude in providing, on a rational basis, for representation in the other house. The Court seems to approve the federal arrangement of two Senators from each State on the ground that it was a compromise reached by the framers of our Constitution and is a part of the fabric of our national charter. But what the Court overlooks is that Colorado, by an overwhelming vote, has likewise written the organization of its legislative body into its Constitution, and our dual federalism requires that we give it recognition. * * *

* * *

Mr. Justice STEWART, whom Mr. Justice CLARK joins, dissenting.

* * *

What the Court has done is to convert a particular political philosophy into a constitutional rule, binding upon each of the 50 States, from Maine to Hawaii, from Alaska to Texas, without regard and without respect for the many individualized and differentiated characteristics of each State, characteristics stemming from each State's distinct history, distinct geography, distinct distribution of population, and distinct political heritage. * * * I could not join in the fabrication of a constitutional mandate which imports and forever freezes one theory of political thought into our Constitution, and forever denies to every State any opportunity for enlightened and progressive innovation in the design of its democratic institutions, so as to accommodate within a system of representative government the interests and aspirations of diverse groups of people, without subjecting any group or class to absolute domination by a geographically concentrated or highly organized majority.

Representative government is a process of accommodating group interests through democratic institutional arrangements. Its function is to channel the numerous opinions, interests, and abilities of the people of a State into the making of the State's public policy. Appropriate legislative apportionment, therefore, should ideally be designed to insure effective representation in the State's legislature, in cooperation with other organs of political power, of the various groups and interests making up the electorate. In practice, of course, this ideal is approximated in the particular apportionment system of any State by a realistic accommodation of the diverse and often conflicting political forces operating within the State.

* * *

* * * The very fact of geographic districting, the constitutional validity of which the Court does not question, carries with it an acceptance of the idea of legislative representation of regional needs and interests. Yet if geographical residence is irrelevant, as the Court suggests, and the goal is solely that of equally "weighted" votes, I do not understand why the Court's constitutional rule does not require the abolition of districts and the holding of all elections at large.

[T]hroughout our history the apportionments of State Legislatures have reflected the strongly felt American tradition that the public interest is composed of many diverse interests, and that in the long run it can better be expressed by a medley of component voices than by the majority's monolithic command. What constitutes a rational plan reasonably designed to achieve this objective will vary from State to State, * * * [b]ut so long as a State's apportionment plan reasonably achieves, in the light of the State's own characteristics, effective and balanced representation of all substantial interests, without sacrificing the principle of effective majority rule, that plan cannot be considered irrational.

This brings me to what I consider to be the proper constitutional standards to be applied in these cases. Quite simply, I think the cases should be decided by application of accepted principles of constitutional adjudication under the Equal Protection Clause. * * *

* * *

* * * I think that the Equal Protection Clause demands but two basic attributes of any plan of state legislative apportionment. First, it demands that, in the light of the State's own characteristics and needs, the plan must be a rational one. Secondly, it demands that the plan must be such as not to permit the systematic frustration of the will of a majority of the electorate of the State. I think it is apparent that any plan of legislative apportionment which could be shown to reflect no policy, but simply arbitrary and capricious action or inaction, and that any plan which could be shown sys-

tematically to prevent ultimate effective majority rule, would be invalid under accepted Equal Protection Clause standards. But, beyond this, I think there is nothing in the Federal Constitution to prevent a State from choosing any electoral legislative structure it thinks best suited to the interests, temper, and customs of its people. * * *

* * *

In the allocation of representation in their State Legislatures, Colorado and New York have adopted completely rational plans which reflect an informed response to their particularized characteristics and needs.

The plans are quite different, just as Colorado and New York are quite different. But each State, while clearly ensuring that in its legislative councils the will of the majority of the electorate shall rule, has sought to provide that no identifiable minority shall be completely silenced or engulfed. The Court today holds unconstitutional the considered governmental choices of these two sovereign States. By contrast, I believe that what each State has achieved fully comports with the letter and the spirit of our constitutional traditions. * * *

THE WARREN COURT AND REAPPORTIONMENT—OTHER SELECTED CASES, 1964–1969

Case	Vote	Ruling	Dissents
Wesberry v. Sanders, 376 U.S. 1, 84 S.Ct. 526 (1964)	6–3	"[T]he command of Art. I, § 2, that Representatives be chosen 'by the People of the several States' means that as nearly as practicable one man's vote in a congressional election is to be worth as much as another's."	Clark, Harlan, Stewart
WMCA, Inc. v. Lomenzo, 377 U.S. 633, 84 S.Ct. 1418 (1964)	6–3	Reapportionment provisions of New York constitution and statutes which would give the ten most urban counties in the state with 75.3 percent of the population only 64.9 percent of the state Senate seats and 61.3 percent of the Assembly seats is unconstitutional	Clark, Harlan, Stewart
Davis v. Mann, 377 U.S. 678, 84 S.Ct. 1441 (1964)	8–1	Reapportionment of the Virginia legislature violates the Constitution where districts with 41.1 percent of the state's population elected a majority of the state senate and where residents of one city were underrepresented by 30 percent and residents of a rural county received 38 percent more than their fair share of representation in state house	Harlan
Roman v. Sincock, 377 U.S. 695, 84 S.Ct. 1449 (1964)	8–1	Apportionment of the Delaware legislature declared unconstitutional where ratio of representation (i.e., value of a vote cast by a constituent for his representative) between most and least populous state house districts was 1:12 and a majority of state senate could be elected by dis-	Harlan

WARREN COURT AND REAPPORTIONMENT (*Cont.*)

Case	Vote	Ruling	Dissents
Roman (*Cont.*)		tricts representing 21 percent of state's population	
Fortson v. Dorsey, 379 U.S. 433, 85 S.Ct. 498 (1965)	8–1	Reliance upon at-large election of several legislators from Georgia's two most urban counties, while other legislators were elected from single-member districts, did not violate one man-one vote	Douglas
Swann v. Adams, 385 U.S. 440, 87 S.Ct. 569 (1967)	7–2	No justifications offered for deviations from mean district population ranging of +15.07 percent to −10.56 percent among Florida state senate districts and of +18.28 percent to −15.27 percent among state house districts. "*De minimis* deviations are unavoidable, but variations of 30% among senate districts and 40% among house districts can hardly be deemed *de minimis* and none of our cases suggests that differences of this magnitude will be approved without a satisfactory explanation grounded on acceptable state policy."	Harlan, Stewart
Kilgarlin v. Hill, 386 U.S. 120, 87 S.Ct. 820 (1967)	6–3	Population variances of from +14.84 percent to −11.64 percent among Texas state house districts cannot survive scrutiny in absence of any justification, given that state law permits creation of multimember and floterial districts and in view of fact that other plans under consideration provided for lower variances	Clark, Harlan, Stewart
Sailors v. Bd. of Educ. of County of Kent, 387 U.S. 105, 87 S.Ct. 1549 (1967)	9–0	Selection of members to serve on county school board by delegates from local school boards did not call for application of one man-one vote principle since selection process amounts to appointment rather than popular election and because county board performs essentially administrative as opposed to legislative functions	
Dusch v. Davis, 387 U.S. 112, 87 S.Ct. 1554 (1967)	9–0	Election of 11-member council in city which adopted a borough structure, where 4 members were elected at large without regard to residence and 7 others were also elected at large but where each of the latter were required to reside in a different one of the 7 boroughs, is constitutional	
Kirkpatrick v. Preisler, 394 U.S. 526, 89 S.Ct. 1225 (1969)	6–3	Rejected the argument that "there is a fixed numerical or percentage population variance small enough to be considered *de minimis* and to satisfy without question the 'as nearly as practicable' standard." "[T]he command of Art. I, § 2, that States create congressional districts which provide equal representation for equal numbers of people permits only the limited population variances which are unavoidable despite a good	Harlan, Stewart, White

WARREN COURT AND REAPPORTIONMENT (*Cont.*)

Case	Vote	Ruling	Dissents
Kirkpatrick (*Cont.*)		faith effort to achieve absolute equality, or for which justification is shown." Unless population variances among districts are shown to have resulted despite such good faith efforts, "the State must justify each variance, no matter how small." Variance of 3.3 percent between Missouri's largest and smallest congressional districts was unjustified either by "considerations of practical politics," the "creat[ion] of districts with specific interest orientations," or nonuniform regard for large concentrations of military personnel or college students	
Wells v. Rockefeller, 94 U.S. 542, 89 S.Ct. 1234 (1969)	6–3	New York's reapportionment of congressional districts held unconstitutional where 31 of the state's 41 districts were designed with reference to 7 homogeneous regions within the state even though the numerical population variance among districts within each of the regions never exceeded 500 because construction of congressional districts on the basis of a "specific interest orientation" did not constitute a legitimate justification for deviations from absolute equality among all congressional districts in the state	Harlan, Stewart, White

AVERY v. MIDLAND COUNTY, TEXAS

Supreme Court of the United States, 1968
390 U.S. 474, 88 S.Ct. 1114, 20 L.Ed.2d 45

The facts are contained in the opinion.

Mr. Justice WHITE delivered the opinion of the Court.

Petitioner, a taxpayer and voter in Midland County, Texas, sought a determination by this Court that the Texas Supreme Court erred in concluding that selection of the Midland County Commissioners Court from single-member districts of substantially unequal population did not necessarily violate the Fourteenth Amendment. We granted review, * * * because application of the one man, one vote principle of Reynolds v. Sims * * * to units of local government is of broad public importance. * * *

Midland County has a population of about 70,000. The Commissioners Court is composed of five members. One, the County Judge, is elected at large from the entire county, and in practice casts a vote only to break a tie. The other four are Commissioners chosen from districts. The population of those districts, according to the 1963 estimates that were relied upon when this case was tried, was respectively 67,906; 852; 414; and 828. This vast imbalance resulted from placing in a single district virtually the entire city of Midland, Midland County's only urban center, in which 95% of the county's population resides.

The Commissioners Court is assigned by the Texas Constitution and by various statutory enactments with a variety of functions. According to the commentary to Vernon's Texas Statutes, the court:

"is the general governing body of the county. It establishes a courthouse and jail, appoints numerous minor officials such as the county health officer, fills vacancies in the county offices, lets contracts in the name of the county, builds roads and bridges, administers the county's public welfare services, performs numerous duties in regard to elections, sets the county tax rate, issues bonds, adopts the county budget, and serves as a board of equalization for tax assessments."

The court is also authorized, among other responsibilities, to build and run a hospital, * * * an airport, * * * and libraries. * * * It fixes boundaries of school districts within the county, * * * may establish a regional public housing authority, * * * and determines the districts for election of its own members. * * *

* * *

The Equal Protection Clause reaches the exercise of state power however manifested, whether exercised directly or through subdivisions of the State. * * * Although the forms and functions of local government and the relationships among the various units are matters of state concern, it is now beyond question that a State's political subdivisions must comply with the Fourteenth Amendment. The actions of local government *are* the actions of the State. A city, town, or county may no more deny the equal protection of the laws than it may abridge freedom of speech, establish an official religion, arrest without probable cause, or deny due process of law.

[W]hen the State delegates lawmaking power to local government and provides for the election of local officials from districts specified by statute, ordinance, or local charter, it must insure that those qualified to vote have the right to an equally effective voice in the election process. If voters residing in oversize districts are denied their constitutional right to participate in the election of state legislators, precisely the same kind of deprivation occurs when the members of a city council, school board, or county governing board are elected from districts of substantially unequal population. * * *

That the state legislature may itself be properly apportioned does not exempt subdivisions from the Fourteenth Amendment. While state legislatures exercise extensive power over their constituents and over the various units of local government, the States universally leave much policy and decisionmaking to their governmental subdivisions. * * * What is more, in providing for the governments of their cities, counties, towns, and districts, the States characteristically provide for representative government—for decisionmaking at the local level by representatives elected by the people. And, not infrequently, the delegation of power to local units is contained in constitutional provisions for local home rule which are immune from legislative interference. In a word, institutions of local government have always been a major aspect of our system, and their responsible and re-

sponsive operation is today of increasing importance to the quality of life of more and more of our citizens.
* * *

We are urged to permit unequal districts for the Midland County Commissioners Court on the ground that the court's functions are not sufficiently "legislative." The parties have devoted much effort to urging that alternative labels—"administrative" versus "legislative"—be applied to the Commissioners Court. As the brief description of the court's functions above amply demonstrates, this unit of local government cannot easily be classified in the neat categories favored by civics texts. The Texas commissioners courts are assigned some tasks which would normally be thought of as "legislative," others typically assigned to "executive" or "administrative" departments, and still others which are "judicial." In this regard Midland County's Commissioners Court is representative of most of the general governing bodies of American cities, counties, towns, and villages. One knowledgeable commentator has written of "the states' varied, pragmatic approach in establishing   governments."   * * *
That approach has produced a staggering number of governmental units—the preliminary calculation by the Bureau of the Census for 1967 is that there are 81,304 "units of government" in the United States—and an even more staggering diversity. Nonetheless, while special-purpose organizations abound and in many States the allocation of functions among units results in instances of overlap and vacuum, virtually every American lives within what he and his neighbors regard as a unit of local government with general responsibility and power for local affairs.

In many cases citizens reside within and are subject to two such governments, a city and a county.

The Midland County Commissioners Court is such a unit. While the Texas Supreme Court found that the Commissioners court's legislative functions are "negligible," 406 S.W.2d, at 426, the court does have power to make a large number of decisions having a broad range of impacts on all the citizens of the county. * * *

* * *

This Court is aware of the immense pressures facing units of local government, and of the greatly varying problems with which they must deal. The Constitution does not require that a uniform straitjacket bind citizens in devising mechanisms of local government suitable for local needs and efficient in solving local problems. Last Term, for example, the Court upheld a procedure for choosing a school board that placed the selection with school boards of component districts even though the component boards had equal votes and served unequal populations. Sailors v. Board of Education of Kent County, 387 U.S. 105, 87 S.Ct. 1549 (1967). The Court rested on the administrative nature of the area school board's functions and the essentially appointive form of the scheme employed. In Dusch v. Davis, 387 U.S. 112, 87 S.Ct. 1554 (1967), the Court permitted Virginia Beach to choose its legislative body by a scheme that included at-large voting for candidates, some of whom had to be residents of particular districts, even though the residence districts varied widely in population.

The *Sailors* and *Dusch* cases demonstrate the the Constitution and this Court are not roadblocks in the path of innovation, experiment, and development among units of local government. * * * Our decision today is only that the Constitution imposes one ground rule for the development of arrangements of local government: a requirement that units with general governmental powers over an entire geographic area not be apportioned among single-member districts of substantially unequal population.

* * *

Judgment vacated and case remanded.

Mr. Justice MARSHALL took no part in the consideration or decision of this case.

Mr. Justice HARLAN, dissenting.

I continue to think that these adventures of the Court in the realm of political science are beyond its constitutional powers. * * * However, now that the Court has decided otherwise, judicial self-discipline requires me to follow the political dogma now constitutionally embedded in consequence of that decision. I am not foreclosed, however, from remonstrating against the extension of that decision to new areas of government. * * *

* * *

There is another reason why the Court should at least wait for a suitable period before applying the *Reynolds* dogma to local governments. The administrative feasibility of judicial application of the "one man, one vote" rule to the apportionment even of state legislatures has not yet been demonstrated. A number of significant administrative questions remain unanswered,[5] and the burden on the federal courts has been substantial. When this has thus far been the outcome of applying the rule to 50 state legislatures, it seems most unwise at this time to extend it to some 80,000 units of local government, whose bewildering variety is sure to multiply the problems which have already arisen and to cast further burdens, of imponderable dimension, on the federal courts. I am frankly astonished at the ease with which the Court has proceeded to fasten upon the entire country at its lowest political levels the strong arm of the federal judiciary, let alone a particular political ideology which has been the subject of wide debate and differences from the beginnings of our Nation.

There are also convincing functional reasons why the *Reynolds* rule should not apply to local governmental units at all. * * * [N]o "practical necessity" has been asserted to justify application of the rule to local governments. More important, the greater and more varied range of functions performed by local governmental units implies that flexibility in the form of their structure is even more important than at the state level, and that by depriving local governments of this needed adaptability the Court's holding may indeed defeat the very goals of *Reynolds*.

* * *

With deference, I think that the only sure-footed way of avoiding, on the one hand, the inequities inherent in today's decision, and on the other, the morass of pitfalls that would fol-

---

5. One such question is the extent to which an apportionment may take into account population changes which occur between decennial censuses. * * * Another is the degree of population variation which is constitutionally permissible. * * *

low from my Brother Fortas' approach, is for this Court to decline to extend the constitutional experiment of *Reynolds*, and to leave the structuring of local governmental units to the political process where it belongs.

Mr. Justice FORTAS, dissenting.

* * *

* * * I believe * * * that in the circumstances of this case equal protection of the laws may be achieved—and perhaps can only be achieved—by a system which takes into account a complex of values and factors, and not merely the arithmetic simplicity of one equals one. *Dusch* and *Sailors* were wisely and prudently decided. They reflect a reasoned, conservative, empirical approach to the intricate problem of applying constitutional principle to the complexities of local government. I know of no reason why we now abandon this reasonable and moderate approach to the problem of local suffrage and adopt an absolute and inflexible formula which is potentially destructive of important political and social values. There is no reason why we should insist that there is and can be only one rule for voters in local governmental units—that districts for units of local government must be drawn solely on the basis of population. * * *

Constitutional commandments are not surgical instruments. They have a tendency to hack deeply—to amputate. And while I have no doubt that, with the growth of suburbia and exurbia, the problem of allocating local government functions and benefits urgently requires attention, I am persuaded that it does not call for the hatchet of one man, one vote. It is our duty to insist upon due regard for the value of the individual

vote but not to ignore realities or to bypass the alternatives that legislative alteration might provide.

* * *

I have said that in my judgment we should not decide this case but should give Texas a chance to come up with an acceptable result. Texas' own courts hold that the present system is constitutionally intolerable. The 1963 population estimates relied upon in this case show that the district which includes most of the City of Midland with 67,906 people has one representative, and the three rural districts, each of which has its own representative, have 852; 414; and 828 people respectively. While it may be that this cannot be regarded as satisfying the Equal Protection Clause under any view, I suggest that applying the Court's formula merely errs in the opposite direction: Only the city population will be represented, and the rural areas will be eliminated from a voice in the county government to which they must look for essential services. With all respect, I submit that this is a destructive result. It kills the very value which it purports to serve. Texas should have a chance to devise a scheme which, within wide tolerance, eliminates the gross underrepresentation of the city, but at the same time provides an adequate, effective voice for the nonurban, as well as the urban, areas and peoples.

Mr. Justice STEWART, dissenting.

I would dismiss the writ as improvidently granted for the reasons stated by Mr. Justice Harlan and Mr. Justice Fortas.

Since the Court does reach the merits, however, I add that I agree with most of what is said in the thorough dissenting opinion of Mr. Justice Fortas. Indeed, I would join that opinion were it not for the author's unquestioning endorsement of the doctrine of Reynolds v. Sims. * * * I continue to believe that the Court's opinion in that case misapplied the Equal Protection Clause of the Fourteenth Amendment—that the apportionment of the legislative body of a sovereign State, no less than the apportionment of a county government, is far too subtle and complicated a business to be resolved as a matter of constitutional law in terms of sixth-grade arithmetic. * * *

THE BURGER COURT AND REAPPORTIONMENT— SELECTED CASES, 1970–1977

Case	Vote	Ruling	Dissents
Hadley v. Junior College Dist., 397 U.S. 50, 90 S.Ct. 791 (1970)	6–3	Election of junior college district trustees on other than one man-one vote basis unconstitutional since "education has traditionally been a vital governmental function and these trustees, whose election the State has opened to all qualified voters, are governmental officials in every relevant sense of that term." "[W]henever a state or local government decides to select persons by popular election to perform governmental functions, the Equal Protection Clause of the Fourteenth Amendment requires that each qualified voter must be given an equal opportunity to participate in that election, and when members of an elected body are chosen from separate districts, each district must be established on a basis that will insure, as far as is practicable, that equal numbers of voters can vote for proportionally equal numbers of officials."	Burger, Harlan, Stewart
Abate v. Mundt, 403 U.S. 182, 91 S.Ct. 1904 (1971)	7–2	Apportionment of 18-member county board chosen from 5 districts (towns) did not violate equal protection where each district was assigned legislators in proportion of its population to that of smallest town despite a maximum deviation in population of 11.9 percent between largest and smallest districts. Plan did not contain any built-in geographical or political favoritism. "[S]lightly greater percentage deviations may be tolerable for local government apportionment schemes" because of greater need to preserve integrity of political subdivisions, fewer legislators, and smaller populations per district.	Douglas, Brennan
67th Minnesota State Senate v. Beens, 406 U.S. 187, 92 S.Ct. 1477 (1972)	8–1	While federal district court was constitutionally entitled to devise reapportionment plan for state legislative districts in absence of action by state legislature, the court exceeded its authority by adopting plans which, contrary to	Stewart

BURGER COURT AND REAPPORTIONMENT (*Cont.*)

Case	Vote	Ruling	Dissents
67th Minnesota State Senate (*Cont.*)		state law, reduced the size of the state senate from 67 to 35 members and reduced the size of the state house from 135 to 105	Stewart
Salyer Land Co. v. Tulare Lake Basin Water Storage Dist., 410 U.S. 719, 93 S.Ct. 1224 (1973)	6–3	Election of board of directors of water storage district, limiting the franchise to landholders and weighting their votes according to the assessed valuation of their property, was justified since the activities of the district were so specialized as to distinguish them from the functions of general governmental units. The greater interest of a landholder as opposed to tenant and that of a large landholder as against one smaller established sufficient nexus to warrant deviation from equal electoral participation, and it was not irrational for votes to be allocated in proportion to benefits received and expenses sustained	Douglas, Brennan, Marshall
Associated Enterprises, Inc. v. Toltec Watershed Improvement Dist., 410 U.S. 743, 93 S.Ct. 1237 (1973)	6–3	Ruling similar to that in *Salyer* sustained a Wyoming statute governing creation of a watershed improvement district and specifying that voting in referendum to create the district was restricted to landholders with votes weighted according to acreage held	Douglas, Brennan, Marshall
Mahan v. Howell, 410 U.S. 315, 93 S.Ct. 979 (1973)	5–3	The 16 percent + maximum deviation in population among Virginia state house districts contained in reapportionment plan passed by the legislature did not exceed constitutional limits. Court put aside a federal court redistricting plan which, though it ignored lines of political subdivisions, cut the maximum variance to 10 percent. "[I]n the implementation of the basic constitutional principle—equality of population among districts—more flexibility was constitutionally permissible with respect to state legislative reapportionment than in congressional districting." Given that there are invariably more state legislative seats to be apportioned that U.S. House seats in any state, "it may be feasible for a State to use political subdivision lines to a greater extent in establishing state legislative districts while affording adequate statewide representation."	Douglas, Brennan, Marshall
Gaffney v. Cummings, 412 U.S. 735, 93 S.Ct. 2321 (1973)	6–3	In view of only 1.9 percent average deviation from perfect equality among all legislative districts, plan to reapportion Connecticut state house and senate districts was constitutionally justified in achieving proportional representation for the two major political parties. There was no "warrant to invalidate a state plan, otherwise within tolerable population limits,	Douglas, Brennan, Marshall

BURGER COURT AND REAPPORTIONMENT (*Cont.*)

Case	Vote	Ruling	Dissents
Gaffney (*Cont.*)		because it undertakes, not to minimize or eliminate the political strength of any group or party, but to recognize it and, through districting, provide a rough sort of proportional representation in the legislative halls of the State."	
White v. Regester, 412 U.S. 755, 93 S.Ct. 2332 (1973)	6–3	Reiterating the principle that "state reapportionment statutes are not subject to the same strict standards applicable to the reapportionment of congressional seats," the Court upheld the Texas legislature's plan to redistrict the state house despite a maximum population variance of 10 percent between largest and smallest districts, but affirmed and remanded for further action by district court a finding that Mexican-Americans were entitled to relief from the discriminatory impact of multimember districts on their voting power	Douglas, Brennan, Marshall
White v. Weiser, 412 U.S. 783, 93 S.Ct. 2348 (1973)	9–0	Texas legislature's plan to redraw U.S. House districts with 2½ percent maximum population variance among districts violated equal protection because another plan was available which would have reduced the maximum variance to .149 percent. The Court went on to point out that it did "not disparage th[e] interest" underlying the legislature's plan which was "a policy frankly aimed at maintaining existing relationships between incumbent congressmen and their constituents and preserving the seniority the members of the State's delegation have achieved in the United States House of Representatives."	
Chapman v. Meier, 420 U.S. 1, 95 S.Ct. 751 (1975)	9–0	A court-ordered reapportionment plan of a state legislature should avoid the use of multimember districts and rely upon single-member districts unless there is persuasive justification. In view of state constitutional provision requiring use of single-member districts, federal court, in absence of persuasive justification, erred in requiring use of multimember districts in reapportioning the North Dakota legislature. Court-mandated plan is subject to stricter standards than state's own plan. Court-mandated plan must achieve goal of population equality among single-member districts with no more than *de minimis* variation unless justified by important and significant factors. Here court-imposed plan with maximum population variance of 20 percent between most and least populous districts, some of which were multimember constituencies, could not pass muster	

BURGER COURT AND REAPPORTIONMENT (*Cont.*)

Case	Vote	Ruling	Dissents
Connor v. Finch, 407 U.S. 431, 97 S.Ct. 1828 (1977)	7–1	Deference to Mississippi's historic respect for county lines failed to justify the gross variances among districts in federal court-imposed reapportionment plan of state legislature, which is expected to meet stricter standards than a districting plan devised by legislative body. "The maximum population deviations of 16.5% in the Senate districts and 19.3% in the House districts can hardly be characterized as *de minimis*; they substantially exceed the 'under 10%' deviations the Court has previously considered to be of prima facie constitutional validity only in the context of legislatively enacted apportionments." Case remanded to redraw the district lines. "In view of the serious questions raised concerning the purpose and effect of the present decree's unusually shaped legislative districts in areas with concentrations of Negro population, the District Court on remand should either draw legislative districts that are reasonably contiguous and compact, so as to put to rest suspicions that Negro voting strength is being impermissibly diluted, or explain precisely why in a particular instance that goal cannot be accomplished."	Powell
Ball v. James, 451 U.S. 355, 101 S.Ct. 1811 (1981)	5–4	By analogy to the decision in *Salyer*, a system for electing the directors of a large Arizona water reclamation district, which limits voting power according to the amount of land a voter owns, is released from the demands of the one man-one vote principle because the district's purpose is sufficiently specialized and narrow and its activities bear on landowners so disproportionately even though to subsidize its water operations it sells electricity to nearly a quarter of a million customers	Brennan, White, Marshall, and Blackmun

e.   ECONOMIC AND SOCIAL DISCRIMINATION

SHAPIRO v. THOMPSON

Supreme Court of the United States, 1969
394 U.S. 618, 89 S.Ct. 1322, 22 L.Ed.2d 600

Vivian Thompson, a nineteen-year-old unwed mother of one child and pregnant with another, moved to Connecticut from Massachusetts in June 1966. When she filed an application in August of that year for public assistance money under the Aid to Families with Dependent Children program, it was denied on the sole ground that she had not met the state's one-year residency requirement which was a prerequisite for eligibility to receive aid. She brought suit against Bernard Shapiro, the Connecticut welfare commissioner, in the U. S. District Court for the

District of Connecticut. That court found the state residency requirement unconstitutional because of its "chilling effect on the right to travel" and as a violation
of the Equal Protection Clause of the Fourteenth Amendment. Shapiro appealed
to the Supreme Court. The Court consolidated similar cases from Pennsylvania
and the District of Columbia for hearing with the *Shapiro* case. Each involved the
validity of a one-year residency requirement.

Mr. Justice BRENNAN delivered the opinion of the Court.

*   *   *

Primarily, appellants justify the waiting-period requirement as a protective device to preserve the fiscal integrity of state public assistance programs. It is asserted that people who require welfare assistance during their first year of residence in a State are likely to become continuing burdens on state welfare programs. Therefore, the argument runs, if such people can be deterred from entering the jurisdiction by denying them welfare benefits during the first year, state programs to assist long-time residents will not be impaired by a substantial influx of indigent newcomers.

There is weighty evidence that exclusion from the jurisdiction of the poor who need or may need relief was the specific objective of these provisions. In the Congress, sponsors of federal legislation to eliminate all residence requirements have been consistently opposed by representatives of state and local welfare agencies who have stressed the fears of the States that elimination of the requirements would result in a heavy influx of individuals into States providing the most generous benefits. *   *   *

We do not doubt that the one-year waiting period device is well suited to discourage the influx of poor families in need of assistance. An indigent who desires to migrate, resettle, find a new job, and start a new life will doubtless hesitate if he knows that he must risk making the move without the possibility of falling back on state welfare assistance during his first year of residence, when his need may be most acute. But the purpose of inhibiting migration by needy persons into the State is constitutionally impermissible.

This Court long ago recognized that the nature of our Federal Union and our constitutional concepts of personal liberty unite to require that all citizens be free to travel throughout the length and breadth of our land uninhibited by statutes, rules, or regulations which unreasonably burden or restrict this movement. That proposition was early stated by Chief Justice Taney in the Passenger Cases, 7 How. 283, 492, 12 L.Ed. 702 (1849). *   *   *

We have no occasion to ascribe the source of this right to travel interstate to a particular constitutional provision. It suffices that, as Mr. Justice Stewart said for the Court in United States v. Guest, 383 U.S. 745, 757–758, 86 S.Ct. 1170, 1178 (1966):

"The constitutional right to travel from one State to another *   *   * occupies a position fundamental to the concept of our Federal Union. It is a right that has been firmly established and repeatedly recognized.

" *   *   * [The] right finds no explicit mention in the Constitution. The reason, it has been suggested, is that a right so elementary was conceived from the beginning to be a necessary concomitant of the stronger Union the Constitution created. In any event, freedom to travel throughout the United States has long been recognized as a basic right under the Constitution."

Thus, the purpose of deterring the in-migration of indigents cannot serve as justification for the classification created by the one-year waiting period, since that purpose is constitutionally impermissible. If a law has "no other purpose * * * than to chill the assertion of constitutional rights by penalizing those who choose to exercise them, then it [is] patently unconstitutional." United States v. Jackson, 390 U.S. 570, 581, 88 S.Ct. 1209, 1216 (1968).

Alternatively, appellants argue that even if it is impermissible for a State to attempt to deter the entry of all indigents, the challenged classification may be justified as a permissible state attempt to discourage those indigents who would enter the State solely to obtain larger benefits. We observe first that none of the statutes before us is tailored to serve that objective. Rather, the class of barred newcomers is all-inclusive, lumping the great majority who come to the State for other purposes with those who come for the sole purpose of collecting higher benefits. In actual operation, therefore, the three statutes enact what in effect are non-rebuttable presumptions that every applicant for assistance in his first year of residence came to the jurisdiction solely to obtain higher benefits. Nothing whatever in any of these records supplies any basis in fact for such a presumption.

More fundamentally, a State may no more try to fence out those indigents who seek higher welfare benefits than it may try to fence out indigents generally. Implicit in any such distinction is the notion that indigents who enter a State with the hope of securing higher welfare benefits are somehow less deserving than indigents who do not take this consideration into account. But we do not perceive why a mother who is seeking to make a new life for herself and her children should be regarded as less deserving because she considers, among other factors, the level of a State's public assistance. Surely such a mother is no less deserving than a mother who moves into a particular State in order to take advantage of its better educational facilities.

Appellants argue further that the challenged classification may be sustained as an attempt to distinguish between new and old residents on the basis of the contribution they have made to the community through the payment of taxes. We have difficulty seeing how long-term residents who qualify for welfare are making a greater present contribution to the State in taxes than indigent residents who have recently arrived. If the argument is based on contributions made in the past by the long-term residents, there is some question, as a factual matter, whether this argument is applicable in Pennsylvania where the record suggests that some 40% of those denied public assistance because of the waiting period had lengthy prior residence in the State. But we need not rest on the particular facts of these cases. Appellants' reasoning would logically permit the State to bar new residents from schools, parks, and libraries or deprive them of police and fire protection. Indeed it would permit the State to apportion all benefits and services according to the past tax contributions of its citizens. The

Equal Protection Clause prohibits such an apportionment of state services.

We recognize that a State has a valid interest in preserving the fiscal integrity of its programs. It may legitimately attempt to limit its expenditures, whether for public assistance, public education, or any other program. But a State may not accomplish such a purpose by invidious distinctions between classes of its citizens. It could not, for example, reduce expenditures for education by barring indigent children from its schools. Similarly, in the cases before us, appellants must do more than show that denying welfare benefits to new residents saves money. The saving of welfare costs cannot justify an otherwise invidious classification.

In sum, neither deterrence of indigents from migrating to the State nor limitation of welfare benefits to those regarded as contributing to the State is a constitutionally permissible state objective.

Appellants next advance as justification certain administrative and related governmental objectives allegedly served by the waiting-period requirement. They argue that the requirement (1) facilitates the planning of the welfare budget; (2) provides an objective test of residency; (3) minimizes the opportunity for recipients fraudulently to receive payments from more than one jurisdiction; and (4) encourages early entry of new residents into the labor force.

At the outset, we reject appellants' argument that a mere showing of a rational relationship between the waiting period and these four admittedly permissible state objectives will suffice to justify the classification. * * * The waiting-period provi-

sion denies welfare benefits to otherwise eligible applicants solely because they have recently moved into the jurisdiction. But in moving from State to State or to the District of Columbia appellees were exercising a constitutional right, and any classification which serves to penalize the exercise of that right, unless shown to be necessary to promote a *compelling* governmental interest, is unconstitutional. * * *

The argument that the waiting-period requirement facilitates budget predictability is wholly unfounded. The records in all three cases are utterly devoid of evidence that either State or the District of Columbia in fact uses the one-year requirement as a means to predict the number of people who will require assistance in the budget year. None of the appellants takes a census of new residents or collects any other data that would reveal the number of newcomers in the State less than a year. Nor are new residents required to give advance notice of their need for welfare assistance. Thus, the welfare authorities cannot know how many new residents come into the jurisdiction in any year, much less how many of them will require public assistance. In these circumstances, there is simply no basis for the claim that the one-year waiting requirement serves the purpose of making the welfare budget more predictable. * * *

The argument that the waiting period serves as an administratively efficient rule of thumb for determining residency similarly will not withstand scrutiny. * * *

Similarly, there is no need for a State to use the one-year waiting period as a safeguard against fraudulent receipt of benefits; for less drastic means are available, and are employed, to minimize that hazard. * * *

Pennsylvania suggests that the one-year waiting period is justified as a means of encouraging new residents to join the labor force promptly. But this logic would also require a similar waiting period for long-term residents of the State. A State purpose to encourage employment provides no rational basis for imposing a one-year waiting-period restriction on new residents only.

We conclude therefore that appellants in these cases do not use and have no need to use the one-year requirement for the governmental purposes suggested. Thus, even under traditional equal protection tests a classification of welfare applicants according to whether they have lived in the State for one year would seem irrational and unconstitutional. But, of course, the traditional criteria do not apply in these cases. Since the classification here touches on the fundamental right of interstate movement, its constitutionality must be judged by the stricter standard of whether it promotes a *compelling* state interest. Under this standard, the waiting-period requirement clearly violates the Equal Protection Clause.[21]

Connecticut and Pennsylvania argue, however, that the constitutional challenge to the waiting-period requirements must fail because Congress expressly approved the imposition of the requirement by the States as part of the jointly funded AFDC program.

Section 402(b) of the Social Security Act of 1935, as amended, 42 U.S. C.A. § 602(b), provides that:

"The Secretary shall approve any [state assistance] plan which fulfills the conditions specified in subsection (a) of this section, except that he shall not approve any plan which imposes as a condition of eligibility for aid to families with dependent children, a residence requirement which denies aid with respect to any child residing in the State (1) who has resided in the State for one year immediately preceding the application for such aid, or (2) who was born within one year immediately preceding the application, if the parent or other relative with whom the child is living has resided in the State for one year immediately preceding the birth."

On its face, the statute does not approve, much less prescribe, a one-year requirement. It merely directs the Secretary of Health, Education, and Welfare not to disapprove plans submitted by the States because they include such a requirement. The suggestion that Congress enacted that directive to encourage state participation in the AFDC program is completely refuted by the legislative history of the section. That history discloses that Congress enacted the directive to curb hardships resulting from lengthy residence requirements. Rather than constituting an approval or a prescription of the requirement in state plans, the directive was the means chosen by Congress to deny federal funding to any State which persisted in stipulating excessive residence requirements as

---

21. We imply no view of the validity of waiting-period *or* residence requirements determining eligibility to vote, eligibility for tuition-free education, to obtain a license to practice a profession, to hunt or fish, and so forth.

Such requirements may promote compelling state interests one the one hand or, on the other, may not be penalties upon the exercise of the constitutional right of interstate travel.

a condition of the payment of benefits.

One year before the Social Security Act was passed, 20 of the 45 States which had aid to dependent children programs required residence in the State for two or more years. Nine other States required two or more years of residence in a particular town or county. And 33 jurisdictions required at least one year of residence in a particular town or county. Congress determined to combat this restrictionist policy. Both the House and Senate Committee Reports expressly stated that the objective of § 402(b) was to compel "[l]iberality of residence requirement." Not a single instance can be found in the debates or committee reports supporting the contention that § 402(b) was enacted to encourage participation by the States in the AFDC program. To the contrary, those few who addressed themselves to waiting-period requirements emphasized that participation would depend on a State's repeal or drastic revision of existing requirements. A congressional demand on 41 States to repeal or drastically revise offending statutes is hardly a way to enlist their cooperation.

But even if we were to assume, *arguendo*, that Congress did approve the imposition of a one-year waiting period, it is the responsive *state* legislation which infringes constitutional rights. By itself § 402(b) has absolutely no restrictive effect. It is therefore not that statute but only the state requirements which pose the constitutional question.

Finally, even if it could be argued that the constitutionality of § 402(b) is somehow at issue here, it follows from what we have said that the provision, insofar as it permits the one-year waiting-period requirement, would be unconstitutional. Congress may not authorize the States to violate the Equal Protection Clause. Perhaps Congress could induce wider state participation in school construction if it authorized the use of joint funds for the building of segregated schools. But could it seriously be contended that Congress would be constitutionally justified in such authorization by the need to secure state cooperation? Congress is without power to enlist state cooperation in a joint federal-state program by legislation which authorizes the States to violate the Equal Protection Clause. * * *

The waiting-period requirement in the District of Columbia Code involved in No. 33 is also unconstitutional even though it was adopted by Congress as an exercise of federal power. In terms of federal power, the discrimination created by the one-year requirement violates the Due Process Clause of the Fifth Amendment. "[W]hile the Fifth Amendment contains no equal protection clause, it does forbid discrimination that is 'so unjustifiable as to be violative of due process.'" Schneider v. Rusk, 377 U.S. 163, 168, 84 S.Ct. 1187, 1190 (1964); Bolling v. Sharpe, 347 U.S. 497, 74 S.Ct. 693 (1954). For the reasons we have stated in invalidating the Pennsylvania and Connecticut provisions, the District of Columbia provision is also invalid—the Due Process Clause of the Fifth Amendment prohibits Congress from denying public assistance to poor persons otherwise eligible solely on the ground that they have not been residents of the District of Columbia for one year at the time their applications are filed. * * *

* * *

Affirmed.

Mr. Chief Justice WARREN, with whom Mr. Justice BLACK joins, dissenting.

In my opinion the issue before us can be simply stated: May Congress, acting under one of its enumerated powers, impose minimal nationwide residence requirements or authorize the States to do so? Since I believe that Congress does have this power and has constitutionally exercised it in these cases, I must dissent.

* * *

* * * I am convinced that Congress does have power to enact residence requirements of reasonable duration or to authorize the States to do so and that it has exercised this power.

The Court's decision reveals only the top of the iceberg. Lurking beneath are the multitude of situations in which States have imposed residence requirements including eligibility to vote, to engage in certain professions or occupations or to attend a state-supported university. Although the Court takes pains to avoid acknowledging the ramifications of its decision, its implications cannot be ignored. I dissent.

Mr. Justice HARLAN, dissenting.

The Court today holds unconstitutional Connecticut, Pennsylvania, and District of Columbia statutes which restrict certain kinds of welfare benefits to persons who have lived within the jurisdiction for at least one year immediately preceding their applications. The Court has accomplished this result by an expansion of the comparatively new constitutional doctrine that some state statutes will be deemed to deny equal protection

of the laws unless justified by a "compelling" governmental interest, and by holding that the Fifth Amendment's Due Process Clause imposes a similar limitation on federal enactments. Having decided that the "compelling interest" principle is applicable, the Court then finds that the governmental interests here asserted are either wholly impermissible or are not "compelling." For reasons which follow, I disagree both with the Court's result and with its reasoning.

* * *

Against this indirect impact on the right to travel must be set the interests of the States, and of Congress with respect to the District of Columbia, in imposing residence conditions. There appear to be four such interests. First, it is evident that a primary concern of Congress and the Pennsylvania and Connecticut Legislatures was to deny welfare benefits to persons who moved into the jurisdiction primarily in order to collect those benefits. This seems to me an entirely legitimate objective. A legislature is certainly not obliged to furnish welfare assistance to every inhabitant of the jurisdiction, and it is entirely rational to deny benefits to those who enter primarily in order to receive them, since this will make more funds available for those whom the legislature deems more worthy of subsidy.

A second possible purpose of residence requirements is the prevention of fraud. A residence requirement provides an objective and workable means of determining that an applicant intends to remain indefinitely within the jurisdiction. It therefore may aid in eliminating fraudulent collection of benefits by nonresidents and persons already receiving assistance in other States. There can be no doubt that prevention of fraud is a valid legislative goal. Third, the requirement of a fixed period of residence may help in predicting the budgetary amount which will be needed for public assistance in the future. While none of the appellant jurisdictions appears to keep data sufficient to permit the making of detailed budgetary predictions in consequence of the requirement, it is probable that in the event of a very large increase or decrease in the number of indigent newcomers the waiting period would give the legislature time to make needed adjustments in the welfare laws. Obviously, this is a proper objective. Fourth, the residence requirements conceivably may have been predicated upon a legislative desire to restrict welfare payments financed in part by state tax funds to persons who have recently made some contribution to the State's economy, through having been employed, having paid taxes, or having spent money in the State. This too would appear to be a legitimate purpose.

The next question is the decisive one: whether the governmental interests served by residence requirements outweigh the burden imposed upon the right to travel. In my view, a number of considerations militate in favor of constitutionality. First, as just shown, four separate, legitimate governmental interests are furthered by residence requirements. Second, the impact of the requirements upon the freedom of individuals to travel interstate is indirect and, according to evidence put forward by the appellees themselves, insubstantial. Third, these are not cases in which a State or States, acting alone, have attempted to interfere with the right of citizens to trav-

el, but one in which the States have acted within the terms of a limited authorization by the National Government, and in which Congress itself has laid down a like rule for the District of Columbia. Fourth, the legislatures which enacted these statutes have been fully exposed to the arguments of the appellees as to why these residence requirements are unwise, and have rejected them. This is not, therefore, an instance in which legislatures have acted without mature deliberation.

Fifth, and of longer-range importance, the field of welfare assistance is one in which there is a widely recognized need for fresh solutions and consequently for experimentation. Invalidation of welfare residence requirements might have the unfortunate consequence of discouraging the Federal and State Governments from establishing unusually generous welfare programs in particular areas on an experimental basis, because of fears that the program would cause an influx of persons seeking higher welfare payments. Sixth and finally, a strong presumption of constitutionality attaches to statutes of the types now before us. Congressional enactments come to this Court with an extremely heavy presumption of validity. * * * A similar presumption of constitutionality attaches to state statutes, particularly when, as here, a State has acted upon a specific authorization from Congress. * * *

I do not consider that the factors which have been urged to outweigh these considerations are sufficient to render unconstitutional these state and federal enactments. It is said, first, that this Court * * * has acknowledged that the right to travel interstate is a "fundamental" freedom. Second it is contended that the governmental objectives mentioned above either are ephemeral or could be accomplished by means which do not impinge as heavily on the right to travel, and hence that the requirements are unconstitutional because they "sweep unnecessarily broadly and thereby invade the area of protected freedoms." NAACP v. Alabama, 377 U.S. 288, 307, 84 S.Ct. 1302, 1314 (1964). The appellees claim that welfare payments could be denied those who come primarily to collect welfare by means of less restrictive provisions, such as New York's Welfare Abuses Law; that fraud could be prevented by investigation of individual applicants or by a much shorter residence period; that budgetary predictability is a remote and speculative goal; and that assurance of investment in the community could be obtained by a shorter residence period or by taking into account prior intervals of residence in the jurisdiction.

Taking all of these competing considerations into account, I believe that the balance definitely favors constitutionality. In reaching that conclusion, I do not minimize the importance of the right to travel interstate. However, the impact of residence conditions upon that right is indirect and apparently quite insubstantial. On the other hand, the governmental purposes served by the requirements are legitimate and real, and the residence requirements are clearly suited to their accomplishment. To abolish residence requirements might well discourage highly worthwhile experimentation in the welfare field. The statutes come to us clothed with the authority of Congress and attended by a correspondingly heavy presumption of constitutionality. Moreover, although the appellees assert that the same objec-

tives could have been achieved by less restrictive means, this is an area in which the judiciary should be especially slow to fetter the judgment of Congress and of some 46 state legislatures in the choice of methods. Residence requirements have advantages, such as administrative simplicity and relative certainty, which are not shared by the alternative solutions proposed by the appellees. In these circumstances, I cannot find that the burden imposed by residence requirements upon ability to travel outweighs the governmental interests in their continued employment. Nor do I believe that the period of residence required in these cases— one year—is so excessively long as to justify a finding of unconstitutionality on that score.

I conclude with the following observations. Today's decision, it seems to me, reflects to an unusual degree the current notion that this Court possesses a peculiar wisdom all its own whose capacity to lead this Nation out of its present troubles is contained only by the limits of judicial ingenuity in contriving new constitutional principles to meet each problem as it arises. For anyone who, like myself, believes that it is an essential function of this Court to maintain the constitutional divisions between state and federal authority and among the three branches of the Federal Government, today's decision is a step in the wrong direction. This resurgence of the expansive view of "equal protection" carries the seeds of more judicial interference with the state and federal legislative process, much more indeed than does the judicial application of "due process" according to traditional concepts (see my dissenting opinion in Duncan v. Louisiana, 391 U.S. 145, 171, 88 S.Ct. 1444, 1458 (1968)), about which some members of this Court have expressed fears as to its potentialities for setting us judges "at large." I consider it particularly unfortunate that this judicial road-block to the powers of Congress in this field should occur at the very threshold of the current discussions regarding the "federalizing" of these aspects of welfare relief.

The following chart canvasses more recent decisions concerning the constitutional validity of durational residency requirements:

Case	Issue	Outcome	Vote	Holding	Dissents
Dunn v. Blumstein, 405 U.S. 330, 92 S.Ct. 995 (1972)	One year state and three month county residency as prerequisites to vote	Struck down	6–1	Given that right to vote is fundamental and calls into play strict scrutiny, these requirements do not further a compelling state interest and are overbroad	Burger
Vlandis v. Kline, 412 U.S. 441, 93 S.Ct. 2230 (1973)	Irrebuttable presumption, for tuition purposes, that out-of-state students who come to Connecticut to attend a state college continue to hold nonresident status for the entire period of their attendance	Struck down	6–3	Such a rigid presumption is a denial of due process where it is not necessarily or universally true in fact and where a reasonable and much less restrictive alternative exists for determining residency	Burger, Douglas, Rehnquist
Memorial Hospital v. Maricopa County, 415 U.S. 250, 94 S.Ct. 1076 (1974)	Arizona statute requires one year county residency as condition of receiving non-emergency hospitalization or medical care at county's expense	Struck down	8–1	Since right to travel is fundamental, state has failed to show any compelling interest and has chosen means that unnecessarily burden a protected right	Rehnquist
Sosna v. Iowa, 419 U.S. 393, 95 S.Ct. 553 (1975)	One year residency requirement as prerequisite to initiating divorce proceedings	Upheld	6–3	Not an unconstitutional denial of equal protection in view of weighty property division and child custody is-	Brennan, White, Marshall

Case	Issue	Outcome	Vote	Holding	Dissents
Sosna (*Cont.*)				sues possibly at stake and given the interests of avoiding intermeddling in matters where another state has paramount rights and in minimizing the risk of having Iowa divorces subjected to collateral attack	
Zobel v. Williams, — U.S. —, 102 S.Ct. 2309 (1982)	After Alaska amended its Constitution to establish a permanent fund into which at least 25 percent of its mineral income would be deposited each year, the state legislature enacted a plan to redistribute some of the fund's earnings directly to the state's adult residents, with each resident receiving one dividend unit for each year of residency since 1959	Struck down	8–1	Neither the state's asserted interests in creating a financial incentive for individuals to remain in Alaska nor prudent management of the fund is rationally related to the distinction between individuals who were residents before 1959 and those who became residents since. And Alaska's interest in rewarding citizens for past contributions is not a legitimate state purpose. Accepting the reasoning behind the last of these asserted state interests could open the door to the impermissible result of distributing rights, benefits, and services according to length of residency and thereby divide the citizenry in-	Rehnquist

Case	Issue	Outcome	Vote	Holding	Dissents
Zobel (*Cont.*)				to expanding numbers of permanent classes	

In enacting the Supplemental Security Income program, which provides aid to the needy aged, blind, and disabled, Congress specified that no benefits are to be paid to a recipient for any month which he or she spends entirely outside the United States. In Califano v. Aznavorian, 439 U.S. 170, 99 S.Ct. 471 (1978), the Court sustained the statute against constitutional attack. Said Justice Stewart, speaking for the Court:

Social welfare legislation, by its very nature, involves drawing lines among categories of people, lines that necessarily are sometimes arbitrary. This Court has consistently upheld the constitutionality of such classifications in federal welfare legislation where a rational basis existed for Congress's choice.

"The basic principle that must govern an assessment of any constitutional challenge to a law providing for governmental payments of monetary benefits is well established. * * * In enacting legislation of this kind a government does not deny equal protection 'merely because the classifications made by its law are imperfect. If the classification has some "reasonable basis," it does not offend the Constitution simply because the classification "is not made with mathematical nicety or because in practice it results in some inequality."' Dandridge v. Williams, 397 U.S. 471, 485, 90 S.Ct. 1153, 1161.

"To be sure, the standard by which legislation such as this must be judged 'is not a toothless one,' Mathews v. Lucas, 427 U.S. 495, 510, 96 S.Ct. 2755, 2764. But the challenged statute is entitled to a strong presumption of constitutionality." Mathews v. de Castro, 429 U.S. 181, 185, 97 S.Ct. 431, 434. * * *

Aznavorian argues that, even though * * * [the statutory provision] may under this standard be valid as against an equal protection or due process attack, a more stringent standard must be applied in a constitutional appraisal * * * because this statutory provision limits the freedom of international travel. We have concluded, however, that * * * [the statutory provision], fortified by its presumption of constitutionality, readily withstands attack from that quarter as well.

The freedom to travel abroad has found recognition in at least three decisions of this Court. In Kent v. Dulles, 357 U.S. 116, 78 S.Ct. 1113, the Secretary of State had refused to issue a passport to a person because of his links with leftwing political groups. The Court held that Congress had not given the Secretary discretion to deny passports on such grounds. Although the holding was one of statutory construction, the Court recognized that freedom of international travel is "basic in our scheme of values" and an "important aspect of the citizen's 'liberty.'" * * * Aptheker v. Secretary of State, 378 U.S. 500, 84 S.Ct. 1659, dealt with § 6 of the Subversive Activities Control Act, 50 U.S.C.A. § 785, which made it a criminal offense for a member of the Communist Party to apply for a passport. The Court again recognized that the freedom of international travel is protected by the Fifth Amendment. Congress had legislated too broadly by restricting this liberty for all members of the Party. In Zemel v. Rusk, 381 U.S. 1, 85 S.Ct. 1271, the Court upheld the Secretary's decision not to validate passports for travel to Cuba. The Court pointed out that "the fact that a liberty cannot be inhibited without due process of law does not mean that it can under no circumstances be inhibited." * * *

Aznavorian urges that the freedom of international travel is basically equivalent to the constitutional right to interstate travel, recognized by this Court for over a hundred years. * * * But this Court has often pointed out the crucial difference between the freedom to travel internationally and the right of interstate travel.

> "The constitutional right of interstate travel is virtually unqualified, United States v. Guest, 383 U.S. 745, 757–758, 86 S.Ct. 1170, 1177–1178; Griffin v. Breckenridge, 403 U.S. 88, 105–106, 91 S.Ct. 1790, 1799–1800. By contrast the 'right' of international travel has been considered to be no more than an aspect of the 'liberty' protected by the Due Process Clause of the Fifth Amendment. * * * As such, this 'right,' the Court has held, can be regulated within the bounds of due process." (Citations omitted). Califano v. Torres, 435 U.S. 1, 4 n. 6, 98 S.Ct. 906, 908.

See Shapiro v. Thompson, 394 U.S. 618, 643 n. 1, 89 S.Ct. 1322, 1336 (concurring opinion). Thus, legislation which is said to infringe the freedom to travel abroad is not to be judged by the same standard applied to laws that penalize the right of interstate travel, such as durational residency requirements imposed by the States. See Memorial Hospital v. Maricopa County, 415 U.S. 250, 254–262, 94 S.Ct. 1076, 1080–1084; Dunn v. Blumstein, 405 U.S. 330, 338–342, 92 S.Ct. 995, 1001–1003; Shapiro v. Thompson, supra, 394 U.S., at 634, 89 S.Ct., at 1331.

Unlike cases involving the right of interstate travel, this case involves legislation providing governmental payments of monetary benefits that has an incidental effect on a protected liberty, similar to the legislation considered in Califano v. Jobst, 434 U.S. 47, 98 S.Ct. 95. There, another section of the Social Security Act was challenged because it "penalized" some beneficiaries upon their marriage. The Court recognized that the statutory provisions "may have an impact on a secondary beneficiary's desire to marry, and may make some suitors less welcome than others," * * * but nonetheless upheld the constitutional validity of the challenged legislation.

The statutory provision in issue here does not have nearly so direct an impact on the freedom to travel internationally as occurred in the *Kent, Aptheker,* or *Zemel* cases. It does not limit the availability or validity of passports. It does not limit the right to travel on grounds that may be in tension with the First Amendment. It merely withdraws a governmental benefit during and shortly after an extended absence from this country. Unless the limitation imposed by Congress is wholly irrational, it is constitutional in spite of its incidental effect on international travel.

The Court noted that several considerations supported the payment limitation:

Congress may simply have decided to limit payments to those who need them in the United States. The needs to which this program responds might vary dramatically in foreign countries. The Social Security Administration would be hard pressed to monitor the continuing eligibility of persons outside the country. And, indeed, Congress may only have wanted to increase the likelihood that these funds would be spent inside the United States.

Justice Stewart observed, "These justifications for the legislation in question are not, perhaps, compelling. But its constitutionality does not depend on compelling justifications. It is enough if the provision is rationally based." Justices Brennan and Marshall concurred in the judgment.

SAN ANTONIO INDEPENDENT SCHOOL DISTRICT v. RODRIGUEZ

Supreme Court of the United States, 1973
411 U.S. 1, 93 S.Ct. 1278, 36 L.Ed.2d 16

The Texas public school system is financed by local, state, and federal funds. The state program is designed to provide a minimum level of education in all school districts by funding a large share of teachers' salaries, operating expenses, and transportation costs. Each school district provides additional funds for its own schools by taxing local property. However, because the value of local property varies among districts, there exist wide disparities in per-pupil expenditures. Demetrio Rodriguez, a Mexican-American, and others brought a class action suit against their school district on behalf of all children attending schools in districts with low property tax bases. A federal district court held that this system of school finance violated the Equal Protection Clause because it discriminated against the less wealthy districts. The case came to the Supreme Court on appeal. [It should be noted that although the title of the case when it reached the Supreme Court still indicated the school district to be the principal appellant-respondent, the school district had in fact withdrawn from that role at a pretrial conference and from that point on sided with Rodriguez; it submitted an amicus curiae brief challenging the maldistribution of educational resources. The State Board of Education, the Commissioner of Education, the Attorney General of Texas, and the Bexar County Board of Trustees remained as respondents.]

Mr. Justice POWELL delivered the opinion of the Court.

* * *

Until recent times Texas was a predominantly rural State and its population and property wealth were spread relatively evenly across the State. Sizable differences in the value of assessable property between local school districts became increasingly evident as the State became more industrialized and as rural-to-urban population shifts became more pronounced. The location of commercial and industrial property began to play a significant role in determining the amount of tax resources available to each school

district. These growing disparities in population and taxable property between districts were responsible in part for increasingly notable differences in levels of local expenditure for education.

* * *

The school district in which appellees reside, the Edgewood Independent School District, has been compared throughout this litigation with the Alamo Heights Independent School District. This comparison between the least and most affluent districts in the San Antonio area serves to illustrate the manner in which the dual system of finance operates and to indicate the extent to which substantial disparities exist despite the State's impressive progress in recent years. Edgewood is one of seven public school districts in the metropolitan area. Approximately 22,000 students are enrolled in its 25 elementary and secondary schools. The district is situated in the core-city sector of San Antonio in a residential neighborhood that has little commercial or industrial property. The residents are predominantly of Mexican-American descent: approximately 90% of the student population is Mexican-American and over 6% is Negro. The average assessed property value per pupil is $5,960—the lowest in the metropolitan area—and the median family income ($4,686) is also the lowest. At an equalized tax rate of $1.05 per $100 of assessed property—the highest in the metropolitan area—the district contributed $26 to the education of each child for the 1967–1968 school year above its Local Fund Assignment for the Minimum Foundation Program. The Foundation Program contributed $222 per pupil for a state-local total of $248. Federal funds added another $108 for a total of $356 per pupil.

Alamo Heights is the most affluent school district in San Antonio. Its six schools housing approximately 5,000 students, are situated in a residential community quite unlike the Edgewood District. The school population is predominantly Anglo, having only 18% Mexican-Americans and less than 1% Negroes. The assessed property value per pupil exceeds $49,000 and the median family income is $8,001. In 1967–1968 the local tax rate of $.85 per $100 of valuation yielded $333 per pupil over and above its contribution to the Foundation Program. Coupled with the $225 provided from that Program, the district was able to supply $558 per student. Supplemented by a $36 per pupil grant from federal sources, Alamo Heights spent $594 per pupil.

* * *

Texas virtually concedes that its historically rooted dual system of financing education could not withstand the strict judicial scrutiny that this Court has found appropriate in reviewing legislative judgments that interfere with fundamental constitutional rights or that involve suspect classifications. If, as previous decisions have indicated, strict scrutiny means that the State's system is not entitled to the usual presumption of validity, that the State rather than the complainants must carry a "heavy burden of justification," that the State must demonstrate that its educational system has been structured with "precision" and is "tailored" narrowly to serve legitimate objectives and that it has selected the "least drastic means" for effectuating its objectives, the Texas financing system and its counterpart in virtually every other State will not pass muster. The State candidly admits that "[n]o one familiar with the Texas system would contend that it has yet achieved perfection." Apart from its concession that educational finance in Texas has "defects" and "imperfections," the State defends the system's rationality with vigor and disputes the District Court's finding that it lacks a "reasonable basis."

* * * We must decide, first, whether the Texas system of financing public education operates to the disadvantage of some suspect class or impinges upon a fundamental right explicitly or implicitly protected by the Constitution, thereby requiring strict judicial scrutiny. If so, the judgment of the District Court should be affirmed. If not, the Texas scheme must still be examined to determine whether it rationally furthers some legitimate, articulated state purpose and therefore does not constitute an invidious discrimination in violation of the Equal Protection Clause of the Fourteenth Amendment.

* * *

The wealth discrimination discovered by the District Court in this case, and by several other courts that have recently struck down school-financing laws in other States, is quite unlike any of the forms of wealth discrimination heretofore reviewed by this Court. Rather than focusing on the unique features of the alleged discrimination, the courts in these cases have virtually assumed their findings of a suspect classification through a simplistic process of analysis: since, under the traditional systems of financing public schools, some poorer people receive less expensive educations than other more affluent people, these systems discriminate on the basis of wealth. This approach largely ignores the hard threshold questions, including whether it makes a difference for purposes of consideration under the Constitution that the class of disadvantaged "poor" cannot be identified or defined in customary equal protection terms, and whether the relative—rather than absolute—nature of the asserted deprivation is of significant consequence. Before a State's laws and the justifications for the classifications they create are subjected to strict judicial scrutiny, we think these threshold considerations must be analyzed more closely than they were in the court below.

The case comes to us with no definitive description of the classifying facts or delineation of the disfavored class. Examination of the District Court's opinion and of appellees' complaint, briefs, and contentions at oral argument suggests, however, at least three ways in which the discrimination claimed here might be described. The Texas system of school financing might be regarded as discriminating (1) against "poor" persons whose incomes fall below some identifiable level of poverty or who might be characterized as functionally "indigent," or (2) against those who are relatively poorer than others, or (3) against all those who, irrespective of their personal incomes, happen to reside in relatively poorer school districts. Our task must be to ascertain whether, in fact, the Texas system has been shown to discriminate on any of these possible bases and, if so, whether the resulting classification may be regarded as suspect.

The precedents of this Court provide the proper starting point. The individuals, or groups of individuals, who constituted the class discriminated against in our prior cases shared two distinguishing characteristics: because of their impecunity they were completely unable to pay for some desired benefit, and as a consequence, they sustained an absolute deprivation of a meaningful opportunity to enjoy that benefit. In Griffin v. Illinois, 351 U.S. 12, 76 S.Ct. 585 (1956), and its progeny, the Court invalidated state laws that prevented an indigent criminal defendant from acquiring a transcript, or an adequate substitute for a transcript, for use at several stages of the trial and appeal process. The payment requirements in each case were found to occasion *de facto* discrimination against those who, because of their indigency, were totally unable to pay for transcripts. And the Court in each case emphasized that no constitutional violation would have been shown if the State had provided some "adequate substitute" for a full stenographic transcript. * * *

Likewise, in Douglas v. California, 372 U.S. 353, 83 S.Ct. 814 (1963), a decision establishing an indigent defendant's right to court-appointed counsel on direct appeal, the Court dealt only with defendants who could not pay for counsel from their own resources and who had no other way of gaining representation. *Douglas* provides no relief for those on whom the burdens of paying for a criminal defense are relatively speaking, great but not insurmountable. Nor does it deal with relative differences in the quality of counsel acquired by the less wealthy.

Williams v. Illinois, 399 U.S. 235, 90 S.Ct. 2018 (1970), and Tate v. Short, 401 U.S. 395, 91 S.Ct. 668 (1971), struck down criminal penalties that subjected indigents to incarceration simply because of their inability to pay a fine. Again, the disadvantaged class was composed only of persons who were totally unable to pay the demanded sum. Those cases do not touch on the question whether equal protection is denied to persons with relatively less money on whom designated fines impose heavier burdens. The Court has not held that fines must be structured to reflect each person's ability to pay in order to avoid disproportionate burdens. Sentencing judges may, and often do, consider the defendant's ability to pay, but in such circumstances they are guided by sound judicial discretion rather than by constitutional mandate.

Finally, in Bullock v. Carter, 405 U.S. 134, 92 S.Ct. 849 (1972), the Court invalidated the Texas filing-fee requirement for primary elections. Both of the relevant classifying facts found in the previous cases were present there. The size of the fee, often running into the thousands of dollars and, in at least one case, as high as $8,900, effectively barred all potential candidates who were unable to pay the required fee. As the system provided "no reasonable alternative means of access to the ballot" * * * inability to pay occasioned an absolute denial of a position on the primary ballot.

Only appellees' first possible basis for describing the class disadvantaged by the Texas school-financing system—discrimination against a class of definably "poor" persons—might arguably meet the criteria established in these prior cases. Even a cursory examination, however, demonstrates that neither of the two distinguishing characteristics of wealth classifications can be found here. First, in support of their charge that the system discriminates against the "poor," appellees have made no effort to demonstrate that it operates to the peculiar disadvantage of any class fairly definable as indigent, or as composed of persons whose incomes are beneath any designated poverty level. Indeed, there is reason to believe that the poorest families are not necessarily clustered in the poorest property districts. A recent and exhaustive study of school districts in Connecticut concluded that "[i]t is clearly incorrect * * * to contend that the 'poor' live in 'poor' districts. * * * Thus, the major factual assumption * * *—that the educational financing system discriminates against the 'poor'—is simply false in Connecticut." Defining "poor" families as those below the Bureau of the Census "poverty level," the Connecticut study found, not surprisingly, that the poor were clustered around commercial and industrial areas—those same areas that provide the most attractive sources of property tax income for school districts. Whether a similar pattern would be discovered in Texas is not known, but there is no basis on the record in this case for assuming that the poorest people—defined by reference to any level of absolute impecunity—are concentrated in the poorest districts.

Second, neither appellees nor the District Court addressed the fact that, unlike each of the foregoing cases, lack of personal resources has not occasioned an absolute deprivation of the desired benefit. The argument here is not that the children in districts having relatively low assessable property values are receiving no public education; rather, it is that they are receiving a poorer quality education than that available to children in districts having more assessable wealth. Apart from the unsettled and disputed question whether the quality of education may be determined by the amount of money expended for it, a sufficient answer to appellees' argument is that, at least where wealth is involved, the Equal Protection Clause does not require absolute equality or precisely equal advantages. Nor indeed, in view of the infinite variables affecting the educational process, can any system assure equal quality of education except in the most relative sense. * * * The State repeatedly asserted in its briefs in this Court that it * * * assures "every child in every school district an adequate education." No proof was offered at trial persuasively discrediting or refuting the State's assertion.

For these two reasons—the absence of any evidence that the financing system discriminates against any definable category of "poor" people or that it results in the absolute deprivation of education—the disadvantaged class is not susceptible of identification in traditional terms.

As suggested above, appellees and the District Court may have embraced a second or third approach, the second of which might be characterized as a theory of relative or comparative discrimination based on family income. Appellees sought to prove that a direct correlation exists between the wealth of families within each district and the expenditures therein for education. That is, along a continuum, the poorer the family the lower the dollar amount of education received by the family's children.

* * *

If, in fact, these correlations could be sustained, then it might be argued that expenditures on education—equated by appellees to the quality of education—are dependent on personal wealth. Appellees' comparative-discrimination theory would still face serious unanswered questions, including whether a bare positive correlation or some higher degree of correlation is necessary to provide a basis for concluding that the financing system is designed to operate to the peculiar disadvantage of the comparatively poor, and whether a class of this size and diversity could ever claim the special protection accorded "suspect" classes. These questions need not be addressed in this case, however, since appellees' proof fails to support their allegations or the District Court's conclusions.

* * *

This brings us, then, to the third way in which the classification scheme might be defined—*district* wealth discrimination. Since the only correlation indicated by the evidence is between district property wealth and expenditures, it may be argued that discrimination might be found without regard to the individual income characteristics of district residents. Assuming a perfect correlation between district property wealth and expenditures from top to bottom, the disadvantaged class might be viewed as encompassing every child in every district except the district that has the most assessable wealth and spends the most on education. Alternatively, as suggested in Mr. Justice Marshall's dissenting opinion, * * * the class might be defined more restrictively to include children in districts with assessable property which falls below the statewide average, or median, or below some other artificially defined level.

However described, it is clear that appellees' suit asks this Court to extend its most exacting scrutiny to review a system that allegedly discriminates against a large, diverse, and amorphous class, unified only by the common factor of residence in districts that happen to have less taxable wealth than other districts. The system of alleged discrimination and the class it defines have none of the traditional indicia of suspectness: the class is not saddled with such disabilities, or subjected to such a history of purposeful unequal treatment, or relegated to such a position of political powerlessness as to command extraordinary protection from the majoritarian political process.

We thus conclude that the Texas system does not operate to the peculiar disadvantage of any suspect class. But in recognition of the fact that this Court has never heretofore held that wealth discrimination alone provides an adequate basis for invoking strict scrutiny, appellees have not relied solely on this contention. They also assert that the State's system impermissibly interferes with the exercise of a "fundamental" right and that accordingly the prior decisions of this Court require the application of the strict standard of judicial review. * * * It is this question—whether education is a fundamental right, in the sense that it is among the rights and liberties protected by the Constitution—which has so consumed the attention of courts and commentators in recent years.

In Brown v. Board of Education, 347 U.S. 483, 74 S.Ct. 686 (1954), a unanimous Court recognized that "education is perhaps the most important function of state and local governments." * * *

* * * But the importance of a service performed by the State does not determine whether it must be regarded as fundamental for purposes of examination under the Equal Protection Clause. Mr. Justice Harlan, dissenting from the Court's application of strict scrutiny to a law impinging upon the right of interstate travel, admonished that "[v]irtually every state statute affects important rights." Shapiro v. Thompson, 394 U.S., at 655, 661, 89 S.Ct., at 1342, 1345. In his view, if the degree of judicial scrutiny of state legislation fluctuated, depending on a majority's view of the importance of the interest affected, we would have gone "far toward making this Court a 'super-legislature.'" * * * We would, indeed, then be assuming a legislative role and one for which the Court lacks both authority and competence. But Mr. Justice Stewart's response in *Shapiro* to Mr. Justice Harlan's concern correctly articulates the limits of the fundamental-rights rationale employed in the Court's equal protection decisions:

"The Court today does *not* 'pick out particular human activities, characterize them as "fundamental," and give them added protection.' * * * To the contrary, the Court simply recognizes, as it must, an established constitutional right, and gives to that right no less protection than the Constitution itself demands." * * * (Emphasis in original.)

Mr. Justice Stewart's statement serves to underline what the opinion of the Court in *Shapiro* makes clear. In subjecting to strict judicial scrutiny state welfare eligibility statutes that imposed a one-year durational residency requirement as a precondition to receiving AFDC benefits, the Court explained:

"[I]n moving from State to State * * * appellees were exercising a constitutional right, and any classification which serves to penalize the exercise of that right, unless shown to be necessary to promote a *compelling* governmental interest, is unconstitutional." * * * (Emphasis in original.)

The right to interstate travel had long been recognized as a right of constitutional significance, and the Court's decision, therefore, did not require an ad hoc determination as to the social or economic importance of that right.

Lindsey v. Normet, 405 U.S. 56, 92 S.Ct. 862 (1972), decided only last Term, firmly reiterates that social importance is not the critical determinant for subjecting state legislation to strict scrutiny. The complainants in that case, involving a challenge to the procedural limitations imposed on tenants in suits brought by landlords under Oregon's Forcible Entry and Wrongful Detainer Law, urged the Court to examine the operation of the statute under "a more stringent standard than mere rationality." * * * The tenants argued that the statutory limitations implicated "fundamental interests which are particularly important to the poor," such as the " 'need for decent shelter' " and the " 'right to retain peaceful possession of one's home.' " * * * Mr. Justice White's analysis, in his opinion for the Court is instructive:

"We do not denigrate the importance of decent, safe and sanitary housing. But the Constitution does not provide judicial remedies for every social and economic ill. We are unable to perceive in that document any constitutional guarantee of access to dwellings of a particular quality or any recognition of the right of a tenant to occupy the real property of his landlord beyond the term of his lease, without the payment of rent. * * * *Absent constitutional mandate*, the assurance of adequate housing and the definition of landlord-tenant relationships are legislative, not judicial, functions." * * * (Emphasis supplied.)

Similarly, in Dandridge v. Williams, 397 U.S. 471, 90 S.Ct. 1153 (1970), the Court's explicit recognition of the fact that the "administration of public welfare assistance * * * involves the most basic economic needs of impoverished human beings," * * * provided no basis for departing from the settled mode of constitutional analysis of legislative classifications involving questions of economic and social policy. As in the case of housing, the central importance of welfare benefits to the poor was not an adequate foundation for requiring the State to justify its law by showing some compelling state interest.

The lesson of these cases in addressing the question now before the Court is plain. It is not the province of this Court to create substantive constitutional rights in the name of guaranteeing equal protection of the laws. Thus, the key to discovering whether education is "fundamental" is not to be found in comparisons of the relative societal significance of education as opposed to subsistence or housing. Nor is it to be found by weighing whether education is as important as the right to travel. Rather, the answer lies in assessing whether there is a right to education explicitly or implicitly guaranteed by the Constitution. * * *

Education, of course, is not among the rights afforded explicit protection under our Federal Constitution. Nor do we find any basis for saying it is implicitly so protected. As we have said, the undisputed importance of education will not alone cause this Court to depart from the usual standard for reviewing a State's social and economic legislation. It is appellees' contention, however, that education is distinguishable from other services and benefits provided by the State because it bears a peculiarly close relationship to other rights and liberties accorded protection under the Constitution. Specifically, they insist that education is itself a fundamental personal right because it is essential to

the effective exercise of First Amendment freedoms and to intelligent utilization of the right to vote. In asserting a nexus between speech and education, appellees urge that the right to speak is meaningless unless the speaker is capable of articulating his thoughts intelligently and persuasively. The "marketplace of ideas" is an empty forum for those lacking basic communicative tools. Likewise, they argue that the corollary right to receive information becomes little more than a hollow privilege when the recipient has not been taught to read, assimilate, and utilize available knowledge.

A similar line of reasoning is pursued with respect to the right to vote. Exercise of the franchise, it is contended, cannot be divorced from the educational foundation of the voter. The electoral process, if reality is to conform to the democratic ideal, depends on an informed electorate: a voter cannot cast his ballot intelligently unless his reading skills and thought processes have been adequately developed.

We need not dispute any of these propositions. The Court has long afforded zealous protection against unjustifiable governmental interference with the individual's rights to speak and to vote. Yet we have never presumed to possess either the ability or the authority to guarantee to the citizenry the most *effective* speech or the most *informed* electoral choice. That these may be desirable goals of a system of freedom of expression and of a representative form of government is not to be doubted. These are indeed goals to be pursued by a people whose thoughts and beliefs are freed from governmental interference. But they are not values to be implemented by judicial intrusion into otherwise legitimate state activities.

Even if it were conceded that some identifiable quantum of education is a constitutionally protected prerequisite to the meaningful exercise of either right, we have no indication that the present levels of educational expenditures in Texas provide an education that falls short. Whatever merit appellees' argument might have if a State's financing system occasioned an absolute denial of educational opportunities to any of its children, that argument provides no basis for finding an interference with fundamental rights where only relative differences in spending levels are involved and where—as is true in the present case—no charge fairly could be made that the system fails to provide each child with an opportunity to acquire the basic minimal skills necessary for the enjoyment of the rights of speech and of full participation in the political process.

Furthermore, the logical limitations on appellees' nexus theory are difficult to perceive. How, for instance, is education to be distinguished from the significant personal interests in the basics of decent food and shelter? Empirical examination might well buttress an assumption that the ill-fed, ill-clothed, and ill-housed are among the most ineffective participants in the political process, and that they derive the least enjoyment from the benefits of the First Amendment. * * *

We have carefully considered each of the arguments supportive of the District Court's finding that education is a fundamental right or liberty and have found those arguments unpersuasive. In one further respect we find this a particularly inappropriate case in which to subject state action to strict judicial scrutiny. The present case, in another basic sense, is significantly different from any of the cases in which the Court has applied strict scrutiny to state or federal legislation touching upon constitutionally protected rights. Each of our prior cases involved legislation which "deprived," "infringed," or "interfered" with the free exercise of some such fundamental personal right or liberty.
* * *

* * *

[After reviewing intensively the Texas system of school financing, the Court went on to state the following:]

The foregoing considerations buttress our conclusion that Texas' system of public school finance is an inappropriate candidate for strict judicial scrutiny. These same considerations are relevant to the determination whether that system, with its conceded imperfections, nevertheless bears some rational relationship to a legitimate state purpose. * * *

* * *

In its reliance on state as well as local resources, the Texas system is comparable to the systems employed in virtually every other State. The power to tax local property for educational purposes has been recognized in Texas at least since 1883. When the growth of commercial and industrial centers and accompanying shifts in population began to create disparities in local resources, Texas undertook a program calling for a considerable investment of state funds.

* * *

* * * While assuring a basic education for every child in the State, it permits and encourages a large measure of participation in and control of each district's schools at the local level. In an era that has witnessed a consistent trend toward centralization of the functions of government, local sharing of responsibility for public education has survived. The merit of local control was recognized last Term in both the majority and dissenting opinions in Wright v. Council of the City of Emporia, 407 U.S. 451, 92 S.Ct. 2196 (1972). * * *

The persistence of attachment to government at the lowest level where education is concerned reflects the depth of commitment of its supporters. In part, local control means * * * the freedom to devote more money to the education of one's children. Equally important, however, is the opportunity it offers for participation in the decisionmaking process that determines how those local tax dollars will be spent. Each locality is free to tailor local programs to local needs. Pluralism also affords some opportunity for experimentation, innovation, and a healthy competition for educational excellence. An analogy to the Nation-State relationship in our federal system seems uniquely appropriate. Mr. Justice Brandeis identified as one of the peculiar strengths of our form of government each State's freedom to "serve as a laboratory; and try novel social and economic experiments." No area of social concern stands to profit more from a multiplicity of viewpoints and from a diversity of approaches than does public education.

* * *

Appellees further urge that the Texas system is unconstitutionally arbitrary because it allows the availability of local taxable resources to turn on "happenstance." They see no justification for a system that allows, as they contend, the quality of education to fluctuate on the basis of the fortuitous positioning of the boundary lines of political subdivisions and the location of valuable commercial and industrial property. But any scheme of local taxation—indeed the very existence of identifiable local governmental units—requires the establishment of jurisdictional boundaries that are inevitably arbitrary. It is equally inevitable that some localities are going to be blessed with more taxable assets than others. Nor is local wealth a static quantity. Changes in the level of taxable wealth within any district may result from any number of events, some of which local residents can and do influence. For instance, commercial and industrial enterprises may be encouraged to locate within a district by various actions—public and private.

Moreover, if local taxation for local expenditures were an unconstitutional method of providing for education then it might be an equally impermissible means of providing other necessary services customarily financed largely from local property taxes, including local police and fire protection, public health and hospitals, and public utility facilities of various kinds. We perceive no justification for such a severe denigration of local property taxation and control as would follow from appellees' contentions. It has simply never been within the constitutional prerogative of this Court to nullify statewide measures for financing public services merely beause the burdens or benefits thereof fall unevenly depending upon the relative wealth of the political subdivisions in which citizens live.

In sum, to the extent that the Texas system of school financing results in unequal expenditures between children who happen to reside in different districts, we cannot say that such disparities are the product of a system that is so irrational as to be invidiously discriminatory. Texas has acknowledged its shortcomings and has persistently endeavored—not without some success—to ameliorate the differences in levels of expenditures without sacrificing the benefits of local participation. The Texas plan is not the result of hurried, ill-conceived legislation. It certainly is not the product of purposeful discrimination against any group or class. * * *

* * *

* * * We hardly need add that this Court's action today is not to be viewed as placing its judicial imprimatur on the status quo. The need is apparent for reform in tax systems which may well have relied too long and too heavily on the local property tax. And certainly innovative thinking as to public education, its methods, and its funding is necessary to assure both a higher level of quality and greater uniformity of opportunity. These matters merit the continued attention of the scholars who already have contributed much by their challenges. But the ultimate solutions must come from the lawmakers and from the democratic pressures of those who elect them.

Reversed.

Mr. Justice WHITE, with whom Mr. Justice DOUGLAS and Mr. Justice BRENNAN join, dissenting.

* * *

I cannot disagree with the proposition that local control and local decisionmaking play an important part in our democratic system of government. * * * Much may be left to local option, and this case would be quite different if it were true that the Texas system, while insuring minimum educational expenditures in every district through state funding, extended a meaningful option to all local districts to increase their per-pupil expenditures and so to improve their children's education to the extent that increased funding would achieve that goal. The system would then arguably provide a rational and sensible method of achieving the stated aim of preserving an area for local initiative and decision.

The difficulty with the Texas system, however, is that it provides a meaningful option to Alamo Heights and like school districts but almost none to Edgewood and those other districts with a low per-pupil real estate tax base. In these latter districts, no matter how desirous parents are of supporting their schools with greater revenues, it is impossible to do so through the use of the real estate property tax. In these districts, the Texas system utterly fails to extend a realistic choice to parents because the property tax, which is the only revenue-raising mechanism extended to school districts, is practically and legally unavailable. That this is the situation may be readily demonstrated.

* * *

Both the Edgewood and Alamo Heights districts are located in Bexar County, Texas. Student enrollment in Alamo Heights is 5,432, in Edgewood 22,862. The per-pupil market value of the taxable property in Alamo Heights is $49,078, in Edgewood $5,960. In a typical relevant year, Alamo Heights had a maintenance tax rate of $1.20 and a debt service (bond) tax rate of 20¢ per $100 assessed evaluation, while Edgewood had a maintenance rate of 52¢ and a bond rate of 67¢. These rates, when applied to the respective tax bases, yielded Alamo Heights $1,433,473 in maintenance dollars and $236,074 in bond dollars, and Edgewood $223,034 in maintenance dollars and $279,023 in bond dollars. As is readily apparent, because of the variance in tax bases between the districts, results, in terms of revenues, do not correlate with effort, in terms of tax rate. Thus, Alamo Heights, with a tax base approximately twice the size of Edgewood's base, realized approximately six times as many maintenance dollars as Edgewood by using a tax rate only approximately two and one-half times larger. Similarly, Alamo Heights realized slightly fewer bond dollars by using a bond tax rate less than one-third of that used by Edgewood.

* * *

Plainly, were Alamo Heights or North East to apply the Edgewood tax rate to its tax base, it would yield far greater revenues than Edgewood is able to yield applying those same rates to its base. Conversely, were Edgewood to apply the Alamo Heights or North East rates to its base, the yield would be far smaller than the Alamo Heights or North East yields. The disparity is, therefore, currently operative and its impact on Edgewood is undeniably serious. * * *

In order to equal the highest yield in any other Bexar County district, Alamo Heights would be required to tax at the rate of 68¢ per $100 of assessed valuation. Edgewood would be required to tax at the prohibitive rate of $5.76 per $100. But state law places a $1.50 per $100 ceiling on the maintenance tax rate, a limit that would surely be reached long before Edgewood attained an equal yield. Edgewood is thus precluded in law, as well as in fact, from achieving a yield even close to that of some other districts.

The Equal Protection Clause permits discriminations between classes but requires that the classification bear some rational relationship to a permissible object sought to be attained by the statute. It is not enough that the Texas system before us seeks to achieve the valid, rational purpose of maximizing local initiative; the means chosen by the State must also be rationally related to the end sought to be achieved. * * * If the State aims at maximizing local initiative and local choice, by permitting school districts to resort to the real property tax if they choose to do so, it utterly fails in achieving its purpose in districts with property tax bases so low that there is little if any opportunity for interested parents, rich or poor, to augment school district revenues. Requiring the State to establish only that unequal treatment is in furtherance of a permissible goal, without also requiring the State to show that the means chosen to effectuate that goal are rationally related to its achievement, makes equal protection analysis no more than an empty gesture. In my view, the parents and children in Edgewood, and in like districts, suffer from an invidious discrimination violative of the Equal Protection Clause.

* * *

Mr. Justice MARSHALL, with whom Mr. Justice DOUGLAS concurs, dissenting.

The Court today decides, in effect, that a State may constitutionally vary the quality of education which it offers its children in accordance with the amount of taxable wealth located in the school districts within which they reside. The majority's decision represents an abrupt departure from the mainstream of recent state and federal court decisions concerning the unconstitutionality of state educational financing schemes dependent upon taxable local wealth. More unfortunately, though, the majority's holding can only be seen as a retreat from our historic commitment to equality of educational opportunity and as unsupportable acquiescence in a system which deprives children in their earliest years of the chance to reach their full potential as citizens. The Court does this despite the absence of any substantial justification for a scheme which arbitrarily channels educational resources in accordance with the fortuity of the amount of taxable wealth within each district.

In my judgment, the right of every American to an equal start in life, so far as the provision of a state service as important as education is concerned, is far too vital to permit state discrimination on grounds as tenuous as those presented by this record. Nor can I accept the notion that it is sufficient to remit these appellees to the vagaries of the political process which, contrary to the majority's suggestion, has proved singularly unsuited to the task of providing a remedy for this discrimination. I, for one, am unsatisfied with the hope of an ultimate "political" solution sometime in the indefinite future while, in the meantime, countless children unjustifiably receive inferior educations that "may affect their hearts and minds in a way unlikely ever to be undone." Brown v. Board of Education, 347 U.S. 483, 494, 74 S.Ct. 686, 691 (1954). I must therefore respectfully dissent.

* * *

* * * I must * * * voice my disagreement with the Court's rigidified approach to equal protection analysis. * * * The Court apparently seeks to establish today that equal protection cases fall into one of two neat categories which dictate the appropriate standard of review—strict scrutiny or mere rationality. But this Court's decisions in the field of equal protection defy such easy categorization. A principled reading of what this Court has done reveals that it has applied a spectrum of standards in reviewing discrimination allegedly violative of the Equal Protection Clause. This spectrum clearly comprehends variations in the degree of care with which the Court will scrutinize particular classifications, depending, I believe, on the constitutional and societal importance of the interest adversely affected and the recognized invidiousness of the basis upon which the particular classification is drawn. I find in fact that many of the Court's recent decisions embody the very sort of reasoned approach to equal protection analysis for which I previously argued—that is, an approach in which "concentration [is] placed upon the character of the classification in question, the relative importance to individuals in the class discriminated against of the governmental benefits that they do not receive, and the asserted state interests in support of the classification." Dandridge v. Williams, * * * 397 U.S., at

520–521, 90 S.Ct., at 1180 (dissenting opinion).

I therefore cannot accept the majority's labored efforts to demonstrate that fundamental interests, which call for strict scrutiny of the challenged classification, encompass only established rights which we are somehow bound to recognize from the text of the Constitution itself. To be sure, some interests which the Court has deemed to be fundamental for purposes of equal protection analysis are themselves constitutionally protected rights. Thus, discrimination against the guaranteed right of freedom of speech has called for strict judicial scrutiny. See Police Dept. of City of Chicago v. Mosley, 408 U.S. 92, 92 S.Ct. 2286 (1972). Further, every citizen's right to travel interstate, although nowhere expressly mentioned in the Constitution, has long been recognized as implicit in the premises underlying that document: the right "was conceived from the beginning to be a necessary concomitant of the stronger Union the Constitution created." United States v. Guest, 383 U.S. 745, 758, 86 S.Ct. 1170, 1178 (1966). * * * Consequently, the Court has required that a state classification affecting the constitutionally protected right to travel must be "shown to be necessary to promote a *compelling* governmental interest." Shapiro v. Thompson, 394 U.S., at 634, 89 S.Ct., at 1331. But it will not do to suggest that the "answer" to whether an interest is fundamental for purposes of equal protection analysis is *always* determined by whether that interest "is a right * * * explicitly or implicitly guaranteed by the Constitution." * * *

I would like to know where the Constitution guarantees the right to procreate, Skinner v. Oklahoma ex rel. Williamson, 316 U.S. 535, 541, 62 S.Ct. 1110, 1113 (1942), or the right to vote in state elections, e.g., Reynolds v. Sims, 377 U.S. 533, 84 S.Ct. 1362 (1964), or the right to an appeal from a criminal conviction, e.g., Griffin v. Illinois, 351 U.S. 12, 76 S.Ct. 585 (1956). These are instances in which, due to the importance of the interests at stake, the Court has displayed a strong concern with the existence of discriminatory state treatment. But the Court has never said or indicated that these are interests which independently enjoy fullblown constitutional protection.

* * *

The majority is, of course, correct when it suggests that the process of determining which interests are fundamental is a difficult one. But I do not think the problem is insurmountable. And I certainly do not accept the view that the process need necessarily degenerate into an unprincipled, subjective "picking-and-choosing" between various interests or that it must involve this Court in creating "substantive constitutional rights in the name of guaranteeing equal protection of the laws." * * * Although not all fundamental interests are constitutionally guaranteed, the determination of which interests are fundamental should be firmly rooted in the text of the Constitution. The task in every case should be to determine the extent to which constitutionally guaranteed rights are dependent on interests not mentioned in the Constitution. As the nexus between the specific constitutional guarantee and the nonconstitutional interest draws closer, the nonconstitutional interest becomes more fundamental and the degree of judicial scrutiny applied when the interest is infringed on a discriminatory basis must be adjusted accordingly. Thus, it cannot be denied that interests such as procreation, the exercise of the state franchise, and access to criminal appellate processes are not fully guaranteed to the citizen by our Constitution. But these interests have nonetheless been afforded special judicial consideration in the face of discrimination because they are, to some extent, interrelated with constitutional guarantees. Procreation is now understood to be important because of its interaction with the established constitutional right of privacy. The exercise of the state franchise is closely tied to basic civil and political rights inherent in the First Amendment. And access to criminal appellate processes enhances the integrity of the range of rights implicit in the Fourteenth Amendment guarantee of due process of law. Only if we closely protect the related interests from state discrimination do we ultimately ensure the integrity of the constitutional guarantee itself. This is the real lesson that must be taken from our previous decisions involving interests deemed to be fundamental.

*   *   *

A similar process of analysis with respect to the invidiousness of the basis on which a particular classification is drawn has also influenced the Court as to the appropriate degree of scrutiny to be accorded any particular case. The highly suspect character of classifications based on race, nationality, or alienage is well established. The reasons why such classifications call for close judicial scrutiny are manifold. Certain racial and ethnic groups have frequently been recognized as "discrete and insular

minorities" who are relatively powerless to protect their interests in the political process. See * * * United States v. Carolene Products Co., 304 U.S. 144, 152–153, n. 4, 58 S.Ct. 778, 783–784 (1938). Moreover, race, nationality, or alienage is " 'in most circumstances irrelevant' to any constitutionally acceptable legislative purpose, Kiyoshi Hirabayashi v. United States, 320 U.S. 81, 100, 63 S.Ct. 1375." McLaughlin v. Florida, 379 U.S., at 192, 85 S.Ct., at 288. Instead, lines drawn on such bases are frequently the reflection of historic prejudices rather than legislative rationality. It may be that all of these considerations, which make for particular judicial solicitude in the face of discrimination on the basis of race, nationality, or alienage, do not coalesce—or at least not to the same degree—in other forms of discrimination. Nevertheless, these considerations have undoubtedly influenced the care with which the Court has scrutinized other forms of discrimination.

*   *   *

James [v. Strange, 407 U.S. 128, 92 S.Ct. 2027 (1972)] and *Reed* [v. Reed, 404 U.S. 71, 92 S.Ct. 251 (1971)] can only be understood as instances in which the particularly invidious character of the classification caused the Court to pause and scrutinize with more than traditional care the rationality of state discrimination. Discrimination on the basis of past criminality and on the basis of sex posed for the Court the specter of forms of discrimination which it implicitly recognized to have deep social and legal roots without necessarily having any basis in actual differences. Still, the Court's sensitivity to the invidiousness of the basis for discrimination is perhaps most apparent in its decisions protecting the interests of children born out of wedlock from discriminatory state action. See Weber v. Aetna Casualty & Surety Co., 406 U.S. 164, 92 S.Ct. 1400 (1972); Levy v. Louisiana, 391 U.S. 68, 88 S.Ct. 1509 (1968).

* * * Status of birth, like the color of one's skin, is something which the individual cannot control, and should generally be irrelevant in legislative considerations. Yet illegitimacy has long been stigmatized by our society. Hence, discrimination on the basis of birth—particularly when it affects innocent children—warrants special judicial consideration.

In summary, it seems to me inescapably clear that this Court has consistently adjusted the care with which it will review state discrimination in light of the constitutional significance of the interests affected and the invidiousness of the particular classification. In the context of economic interests, we find that discriminatory state action is almost always sustained, for such interests are generally far removed from constitutional guarantees. Moreover, "[t]he extremes to which the Court has gone in dreaming up rational bases for state regulation in that area may in many instances be ascribed to a healthy revulsion from the Court's earlier excesses in using the Constitution to protect interests that have more than enough power to protect themselves in the legislative halls." Dandridge v. Williams, 397 U.S. at 520, 90 S.Ct., at 1179 (dissenting opinion). But the situation differs markedly when discrimination against important individual interests with constitutional implications and against particularly disadvantaged or powerless classes is involved. The majority suggests, how-

ever, that a variable standard of review would give this Court the appearance of a "super-legislature." * * * I cannot agree. Such an approach seems to me a part of the guarantees of our Constitution and of the historic experiences with oppression of and discrimination against discrete, powerless minorities which underlie that document. In truth, the Court itself will be open to the criticism raised by the majority so long as it continues on its present course of effectively selecting in private which cases will be afforded special consideration without acknowledging the true basis of its action.

* * *

[T]he majority today attempts to force this case into the same category for purposes of equal protection analysis as decisions involving discrimination affecting commercial interests. By so doing, the majority singles this case out for analytic treatment at odds with what seems to me to be the clear trend of recent decisions in this Court, and thereby ignores the constitutional importance of the interest at stake and the invidiousness of the particular classification, factors that call for far more than the lenient scrutiny of the Texas financing scheme which the majority pursues. Yet if the discrimination inherent in the Texas scheme is scrutinized with the care demanded by the interest and classification present in this case, the unconstitutionality of that scheme is unmistakable.

* * *

[T]he majority seeks refuge in the fact that the Court has "never presumed to possess either the ability or the authority to guarantee to the citizenry the most *effective* speech or the most *informed* electoral choice." * * * This serves only to blur what is in fact at stake. With due respect, the issue is neither provision of the most *effective* speech nor of the most *informed* vote. Appellees do not now seek the best education Texas might provide. They do seek, however, an end to state discrimination resulting from the unequal distribution of taxable district property wealth that directly impairs the ability of some districts to provide the same educational opportunity that other districts can provide with the same or even substantially less tax effort. The issue is, in other words, one of discrimination that affects the quality of the education which Texas has chosen to provide its children; and, the precise question here is what importance should attach to education for purposes of equal protection analysis of that discrimination. As this Court held in Brown v. Board of Education, 347 U.S., at 493, 74 S.Ct., at 691, the opportunity of education, "where the state has undertaken to provide it, is a right which must be made available to all on equal terms." * * * [F]actors * * * including the relationship between education and the social and political interests enshrined within the Constitution, compel us to recognize the fundamentality of education and to scrutinize with appropriate care the bases for state discrimination affecting equality of educational opportunity in Texas' school districts—a conclusion which is only strengthened when we consider the character of the classification in this case.

* * *

In my judgment, any substantial degree of scrutiny of the operation of the Texas financing scheme reveals that the State has selected means wholly inappropriate to secure its purported interest in assuring its school districts local fiscal control. At the same time, appellees have pointed out a variety of alternative financing schemes which may serve the State's purported interest in local control as well as, if not better than, the present scheme without the current impairment of the educational opportunity of vast numbers of Texas school-children. I see no need, however, to explore the practical or constitutional merits of those suggested alternatives at this time for, whatever their positive or negative features, experience with the present financing scheme impugns any suggestion that it constitutes a serious effort to provide local fiscal control. If for the sake of local education control, this Court is to sustain interdistrict discrimination in the educational opportunity afforded Texas school children, it should require that the State present something more than the mere sham now before us.

* * *

See also *Maher* v. *Roe* (p. 1215) and *Harris* v. *McRae* (p. 1217).

LABINE v. VINCENT

Supreme Court of the United States, 1971
401 U.S. 532, 91 S.Ct. 1017, 28 L.Ed.2d 288

The facts are contained in the following opinion.

Mr. Justice BLACK delivered the opinion of the Court.

* * * On March 15, 1962, a baby girl, Rita Vincent, was born to Lou Bertha Patterson (now Lou Bertha Labine) in Calcasieu Parish, Louisiana. On May 10, 1962, Lou Bertha Patterson and Ezra Vincent, as authorized by Louisiana law, jointly executed before a notary a Louisiana State Board of Health form acknowledging that Ezra Vincent was the "natural father" of Rita Vincent. This public acknowledgment of parentage did not, under Louisiana law, give the child a legal right to share equally with legitimate children in the parent's estate but it did give her a right to claim support from her parents or their heirs. The acknowledgment also gave the child the capacity under Louisiana law to be a limited beneficiary under her father's will in the event he left a will naming her, which he did not do here.

Ezra Vincent died intestate (that is, without a will) on September 16, 1968, in Rapides Parish, Louisiana, leaving substantial property within the State, but no will to direct its distribution. Appellant, as the guardian of Rita Vincent, petitioned in state court for the appointment of an administrator for the father's estate; for a declaration that Rita Vincent is the sole heir of Ezra Vincent, and for an order directing the administrator to pay support and maintenance for the child. In the alternative, appellant sought a declaration that the child was entitled to support and maintenance of $150 per month under a Louisiana child support law.

Relatives of Ezra Vincent answered the petition claiming that they were entitled to the whole estate. * * * The court ruled that the relatives of the father were his

collateral relations and that under Louisiana's laws of intestate succession took his property to the exclusion of acknowledged, but not legitimated, illegimate children. The court, therefore, dismissed with costs the guardian mother's petition to recognize the child as an heir. The court also ruled that in view of Social Security payments of $60 per month and Veterans Administration payments of $40 per month available for the support of the child, the guardian for the child was not entitled to support or maintenance from the succession of Ezra Vincent. The Louisiana Court of Appeal, Third Circuit, affirmed * * * and the Supreme Court of Louisiana denied a petition for writ of certiorari. * * *

In this Court appellant argues that Louisiana's statutory scheme for intestate succession that bars this illegitimate child from sharing in her father's estate constitutes an invidious discrimination against illegitimate children that cannot stand under the Due Process and Equal Protection Clauses of the Constitution. Much reliance is placed upon the Court's decisions in Levy v. Louisiana, 391 U.S. 68, 88 S.Ct. 1509 (1968), and Glona v. American Guarantee & Liability Ins. Co., 391 U.S. 73, 88 S.Ct. 1515 (1968). For the reasons set out below, we find appellant's reliance on those cases misplaced, and we decline to extend the rationale of those cases where it does not apply. Accordingly, we affirm the decision below.

In *Levy* the Court held that Louisiana could not consistently with the Equal Protection Clause bar an illegitimate child from recovering for the wrongful death of its mother when such recoveries by legitimate children were authorized. The cause of action alleged in *Levy* was in tort.

It was undisputed that Louisiana had created a statutory tort and had provided for the survival of the deceased's cause of action, so that a large class of persons injured by the tort could recover damages in compensation for their injury. Under those circumstances the Court held that the State could not totally exclude from the class of potential plaintiffs illegitimate children who were unquestionably injured by the tort that took their mother's life. *Levy* did not say and cannot fairly be read to say that a State can never treat an illegitimate child differently from legitimate offspring.

The people of Louisiana, through their legislature have carefully regulated many of the property rights incident to family life. * * * Once marriage is contracted there, husbands have obligations to their wives. Fathers have obligations to their children. Should the children prosper while the parents fall upon hard times, children have a statutory obligation to support their parents. To further strengthen and preserve family ties, Louisiana regulates the disposition of property upon the death of a family man. The surviving spouse is entitled to an interest in the deceased spouse's estate. Legitimate children have a right of forced heirship in their father's estate and can even retrieve property transferred by their father during his lifetime in reduction of their rightful interests.

Louisiana also has a complex set of rules regarding the rights of illegitimate children. Children born out of wedlock and who are never acknowledged by their parents apparently have no right to take property by intestate succession from their father's estate. In some instances, their father may not even bequeath

property to them by will. Illegitimate children acknowledged by their fathers are "natural children." Natural children can take from their father by intestate succession "to the exclusion only of the State." They may be bequeathed property by their father only to the extent of either one-third or one-fourth of his estate and then only if their father is not survived by legitimate children or their heirs. Finally, children born out of wedlock can be legitimated or adopted, in which case they may take by intestate succession or by will as any other child.

* * *

We emphasize that this is not a case, like *Levy* where the State has created an insurmountable barrier to this illegitimate child. There is not the slightest suggestion in this case that Louisiana has barred this illegitimate from inheriting from her father. Ezra Vincent could have left one-third of his property to his illegitimate daughter had he bothered to follow the simple formalities of executing a will. He could, of course, have legitimated the child by marrying her mother in which case the child could have inherited his property either by intestate succession or by will as any other legitimate child. Finally, he could have awarded his child the benefit of Louisiana's intestate succession statute on the same terms as legitimate children simply by stating in his acknowledgement of paternity his desire to legitimate the little girl. * * *

In short, we conclude that in the circumstances presented in this case, there is nothing in the vague generalities of the Equal Protection and Due Process Clauses which empower this Court to nullify the deliberate choices of the elected representatives of the people of Louisiana.

Affirmed.

Mr. Justice BRENNAN, with whom Mr. Justice DOUGLAS, Mr. Justice WHITE, and Mr. Justice MARSHALL join, dissenting.

In my view, Louisiana's intestate succession laws, insofar as they treat illegitimate children whose fathers have publicly acknowledged them differently from legitimate children, plainly violate the Equal Protection Clause of the Fourteenth Amendment. The Court today effectively concedes this, and to reach its result, resorts to the startling measure of simply excluding such illegitimate children from the protection of the Clause, in order to uphold the untenable and discredited moral prejudice of by-gone centuries which vindictively punished not only the illegitimates' parents, but also the hapless, and innocent, children. Based upon such a premise, today's decision cannot even pretend to be a principled decision. This is surprising from Justices who have heretofore so vigorously decried decision-making rested upon personal predilections, to borrow the Court's words, of "life-tenured judges of this Court." * * *

* * *

* * * *Levy* holds squarely to the contrary specifically in the context of discrimination against illegitimate children. And numerous other cases in this Court establish the general proposition that discriminations which "merely" disadvantage a class of persons or businesses are as subject to the command of the Fourteenth Amendment as discriminations which are in some sense more absolute.

In short, the Court has not analyzed, or perhaps simply refuses to analyze, Louisiana's discrimination against acknowledged illegitimates in terms of the requirements of the Fourteenth Amendment. * * *

* * *

The Court nowhere mentions the central reality of this case: Louisiana punishes illegitimate children for the misdeeds of their parents. * * * It is certainly unusual in this country for a person to be legally disadvantaged on the basis of factors over which he never had any control. * * * The state court below explicitly upheld the statute on the ground that the punishment of the child might encourage the parents to marry. If that is the State's objective, it can obviously be attained far more directly by focusing on the parents whose actions the State seeks to influence. Given the importance and nature of the decision to marry, * * * I think that disinheriting the illegitimate child must be held to "bear no intelligible proper relation to the consequences that are made to flow" from the State's classification. * * *

In my judgment, only a moral prejudice, prevalent in 1825 when the Louisiana statutes under consideration were adopted, can support Louisiana's discrimination against illegitimate children. Since I can find no rational basis to justify the distinction Louisiana creates between an acknowledged illegitimate child and a legitimate one, that discrimination is clearly invidious. * * * I think the Supreme Court of North Dakota stated the correct principle in invalidating an analogous discrimination in that State's inheritance laws: "This statute, which punishes innocent children for their parents' transgressions has no place in our system of government which has as one of its

basic tenets equal protection for all."

*   *   *

Recently, the Court appears to have repudiated the clear implication in *Labine* that illegitimacy is a lower-tier interest and that legislation drawn along such lines would have to clear only the hurdle of "reasonableness." Speaking for a plurality in Lalli v. Lalli, 439 U.S. 259, 99 S.Ct. 518 (1978), Chief Justice Burger wrote: "Although, as decided in Mathews v. Lucas, 427 U.S. 495, 96 S.Ct. 2755 (1976), and reaffirmed in *Trimble* [v. Gordon, 430 U.S. 762, 97 S.Ct. 1459 (1977)], classifications based on illegitimacy are not subject to 'strict scrutiny,' they nevertheless are invalid under the Fourteenth Amendment if they are not substantially related to permissible state interests." Of the nearly dozen and a half cases involving plaintiffs challenging legislation discriminating against illegitimate children heard by the Court beginning with *Levy* in 1968, the Court has sided with those attacking the statutes roughly three-quarters of the time, so it seems fair to say that legislation drawn along such lines has been disfavored by the Court. The extent of that disfavor is reflected in the Court's most recent rulings, referred to above, which would seem clearly to indicate that illegitimates are a quasi-suspect class and that legislation discriminating against them warrants intermediate scrutiny.

CRAIG v. BOREN

Supreme Court of the United States, 1976
429 U.S. 191, 97 S.Ct. 451, 50 L.Ed.2d 397

Oklahoma law prohibits the sale of 3.2 percent beer to males under twenty-one and to females under eighteen. Craig, a male between the ages of eighteen and twenty-one, and Whitener, a licensed vendor of 3.2 percent beer, brought suit for declaratory and injunctive relief against the governor and other state officials, asserting that the gender-based age difference in the statute constituted invidious discrimination in violation of the Equal Protection Clause. A three-judge federal district court denied relief, and the plaintiffs appealed.

Mr. Justice BRENNAN delivered the opinion of the Court.

The interaction of two sections of an Oklahoma statute, Okla.Stat., Tit. 37, §§ 241 and 245 (1958 and Supp. 1976), prohibits the sale of "nonintoxicating" 3.2% beer to males under the age of 21 and to females under the age of 18. The question to be decided is whether such a gender-based differential constitutes a denial to males 18–20 years of age of the equal protection of the laws in violation of the Fourteenth Amendment.

*   *   *

Analysis may appropriately begin with the reminder that *Reed* [v. *Reed*] emphasized that statutory classifications that distinguish between males and females are "subject to scrutiny under the Equal Protection Clause." 404 U.S., at 75, 92 S.Ct., at 253. To withstand constitutional challenge, previous cases establish that classifications by gender must serve important governmental objectives and must be substantially related to achievement of those objectives. Thus, in *Reed*, the objectives of "reducing the workload on probate courts," *   *   * and "avoiding intrafamily controversy,"

* * * were deemed of insufficient importance to sustain use of an overt gender criterion in the appointment of administrators of intestate decedents' estates. Decisions following *Reed* similarly have rejected administrative ease and convenience as sufficiently important objectives to justify gender-based classifications. * * * And only two Terms ago, Stanton v. Stanton, 421 U.S. 7, 95 S.Ct. 1373 (1975), expressly stating that *Reed* v. *Reed* was "controlling," * * * held that *Reed* required invalidation of a Utah differential age-of-majority statute, notwithstanding the statute's coincidence with and furtherance of the State's purpose of fostering "old notions" of role typing and preparing boys for their expected performance in the economic and political worlds. * * *

Reed v. *Reed* has also provided the underpinning for decisions that have invalidated statutes employing gender as an inaccurate proxy for other, more germane bases of classification. Hence, "archaic and over-broad" generalizations, Schlesinger v. Ballard, 419 U.S., at 508, 95 S.Ct., at 577, concerning the financial position of servicewomen, Frontiero v. Richardson, 411 U.S., at 689 n. 23, 93 S.Ct., at 1772, and working women, Weinberger v. Wiesenfeld, 420 U.S. 636, 643, 95 S.Ct. 1225, 1230 (1975), could not justify use of a gender line in determining eligibility for certain governmental entitlements. Similarly, increasingly outdated misconceptions concerning the role of females in the home rather than in the "marketplace and world of ideas" were rejected as loose-fitting characterizations incapable of supporting state statutory schemes that were premised upon their accuracy. * * * In light of the weak congruence between gender and the characteristic

or trait that gender purported to represent, it was necessary that the legislatures choose either to realign their substantive laws in a gender-neutral fashion, or to adopt procedures for identifying those instances where the sex-centered generalization actually comported with fact. * * *

* * * We turn then to the question whether, under *Reed*, the difference between males and females with respect to the purchase of 3.2% beer warrants the differential in age drawn by the Oklahoma statute. We conclude that it does not.

The District Court recognized that *Reed* v. *Reed* was controlling. In applying the teachings of that case, the court found the requisite important governmental objective in the traffic-safety goal proffered by the Oklahoma Attorney General. It then concluded that the statistics introduced by the appellees established that the gender-based distinction was substantially related to achievement of that goal.

We accept for purposes of discussion the District Court's identification of the objective underlying §§ 241 and 245 as the enhancement of traffic safety. Clearly, the protection of public health and safety represents an important function of state and local governments. However, appellees' statistics in our view cannot support the conclusion that the gender-based distinction closely serves to achieve that objective and therefore the distinction cannot under *Reed* withstand equal protection challenge.

The appellees introduced a variety of statistical surveys. First, an analysis of arrest statistics for 1973 demonstrated that 18–20-year-old male arrests for "driving under the influence" and "drunkenness" substantially exceeded female arrests for that same age period. Similarly, youths aged 17–21 were found to be overrepresented among those killed or injured in traffic accidents, with males again numerically exceeding females in this regard. Third, a random roadside survey in Oklahoma City revealed that young males were more inclined to drive and drink beer than were their female counterparts. Fourth, Federal Bureau of Investigation nationwide statistics exhibited a notable increase in arrests for "driving under the influence." Finally, statistical evidence gathered in other jurisdictions, particularly Minnesota and Michigan, was offered to corroborate Oklahoma's experience by indicating the pervasiveness of youthful participation in motor vehicle accidents following the imbibing of alcohol. Conceding that "the case is not free from doubt," * * * the District Court nonetheless concluded that this statistical showing substantiated "a rational basis for the legislative judgment underlying the challenged classification." * * *

Even were this statistical evidence accepted as accurate, it nevertheless offers only a weak answer to the equal protection question presented here. The most focused and relevant of the statistical surveys, arrests of 18–20-year-olds for alcohol-related driving offenses, exemplifies the ultimate unpersuasiveness of this evidentiary record. Viewed in terms of the correlation between sex and the actual activity that Oklahoma seeks to regulate—driving while under the influence of alcohol—the statistics broadly establish that .18% of females and 2% of males in that age group were arrested for that offense. While such a disparity is not trivial in a statistical sense, it hardly can form the basis for employment of a gender line as a classifying device. Certainly if maleness is to serve as a proxy for drinking and driving, a correlation of 2% must be considered an unduly tenuous "fit." Indeed, prior cases have consistently rejected the use of sex as a decision-making factor even though the statutes in question certainly rested on far more predictive empirical relationships than this.

Moreover, the statistics exhibit a variety of other shortcomings that seriously impugn their value to equal protection analysis. Setting aside the obvious methodological problems, the surveys do not adequately justify the salient features of Oklahoma's gender-based traffic-safety law. None purports to measure the use and dangerousness of 3.2% beer as opposed to alcohol generally, a detail that is of particular importance since, in light of its low alcohol level, Oklahoma apparently considers the 3.2% beverage to be "nonintoxicating." * * * Moreover, many of the studies, while graphically documenting the unfortunate increase in driving while under the influence of alcohol, make no effort to relate their findings to age-sex differentials as involved here. Indeed, the only survey that explicitly centered its attention upon young drivers and their use of beer—albeit apparently not of the diluted 3.2% variety—reached results that hardly can be viewed as impressive in justifying either a gender or age classification.

There is no reason to belabor this line of analysis. It is unrealistic to expect either members of the judiciary or state officials to be well versed in the rigors of experimental or statistical technique. But this merely illustrates that proving broad sociological propositions by statistics is a dubious business, and one that inevitably is in tension with the normative philosophy that underlies the Equal Protection Clause. Suffice to say that the showing offered by the appellees does not satisfy us that sex represents a legitimate, accurate proxy for the regulation of drinking and driving. In fact, when it is further recognized that Oklahoma's statute prohibits only the selling of 3.2% beer to young males and not their drinking the beverage once acquired (even after purchase by their 18–20-year-old female companions), the relationship between gender and traffic safety becomes far too tenuous to satisfy *Reed's* requirement that the gender-based difference be substantially related to achievement of the statutory objective.

We hold, therefore, that under *Reed*, Oklahoma's 3.2% beer statute invidiously discriminates against males 18–20 years of age.

* * *

[In the remainder of its opinion, addressing the argument that the Twenty-first Amendment "strengthened" the states' police power with regard to the regulation of alcoholic beverages, the Court concluded that neither the Amendment's text, history, nor any of the Court's decisions interpreting it modified the protections guaranteed by the Fourteenth Amendment.]

* * * In sum, the principles embodied in the Equal Protection Clause are not to be rendered inapplicable by statistically measured but loose-fitting generalities concerning the drinking tendencies of aggregate groups. We thus hold that the operation of the Twenty-first Amendment does not alter the application of equal protection standards that otherwise govern this case.

We conclude that the gender-based differential contained in Okla. Stat., Tit. 37, § 245 (1976 Supp.) constitutes a denial of the equal protection of the laws to males aged 18–20 and reverse the judgment of the District Court.

It is so ordered.

Mr. Justice POWELL, concurring.

* * *

With respect to the equal protection standard, I agree that Reed v. Reed, 404 U.S. 71, 92 S.Ct. 251 (1971), is the most relevant precedent. But I find it unnecessary, in deciding this case, to read that decision as broadly as some of the Court's language may imply. *Reed* and subsequent cases involving gender-based classifications make clear that the Court subjects such classifications to a more critical examination than is normally applied when "fundamental" constitutional rights and "suspect classes" are not present.*

---

* As is evident from our opinions, the Court has had difficulty in agreeing upon a standard of equal protection analysis that can be applied consistently to the wide variety of legislative classifications. There are valid reasons for dissatisfaction with the "two-tier" approach that has been prominent in the Court's decisions in the past decade. Although viewed by many as a result-oriented substitute for more critical analysis, that approach—with its narrowly limited "upper-tier"—now has substantial precedential support. As has been true of *Reed* and its progeny, our decision today will be viewed by some as a "middle-tier" approach. While I would not endorse that characterization and would not welcome a further subdividing of equal protection analysis, candor compels the recog-

I view this as a relatively easy case. No one questions the legitimacy or importance of the asserted governmental objective: the promotion of highway safety. The decision of the case turns on whether the state legislature, by the classification it has chosen, had adopted a means that bears a " 'fair and substantial relation' " to this objective. Id., at 76, 92 S.Ct., at 254, quoting Royster Guano Co. v. Virginia, 253 U.S. 412, 415, 40 S.Ct. 560, 561, 64 L.Ed. 989 (1920).

It seems to me that the statistics offered by appellees and relied upon by the District Court do tend generally to support the view that young men drive more, possibly are inclined to drink more, and—for various reasons—are involved in more accidents than young women. Even so, I am not persuaded that these facts and the inferences fairly drawn from them justify this classification based on a three-year age differential between the sexes, and especially one that it so easily circumvented as to be virtually meaningless. Putting it differently, this gender-based classification does not bear a fair and substantial relation to the object of the legislation.

Mr. Justice STEWART, concurring in the judgment.

* * *

The disparity created by these Oklahoma statutes amounts to total irrationality. For the statistics upon which the State now relies, whatever their other shortcomings, wholly fail to prove or even suggest that 3.2% beer is somehow more deleterious

when it comes into the hands of a male aged 18–20 than of a female of like age. The disparate statutory treatment of the sexes here, without even a colorably valid justification or explanation, thus amounts to invidious discrimination. See Reed v. Reed, 404 U.S. 71, 92 S.Ct. 251.

Mr. Justice REHNQUIST, dissenting.

The Court's disposition of this case is objectionable on two grounds. First is its conclusion that *men* challenging a gender-based statute which treats them less favorably than women may invoke a more stringent standard of judicial review than pertains to most other types of classifications. Second is the Court's enunciation of this standard, without citation to any source, as being that "classifications by gender must serve *important* governmental objectives and must be *substantially* related to achievement of those objectives." * * * The only redeeming feature of the Court's opinion, to my mind, is that it apparently signals a retreat by those who joined the plurality opinion in Frontiero v. Richardson, 411 U.S. 677, 93 S.Ct. 1764 (1973), from their view that sex is a "suspect" classification for purposes of equal protection analysis. I think the Oklahoma statute challenged here need pass only the "rational basis" equal protection analysis expounded in cases such as McGowan v. Maryland, 366 U.S. 420, 81 S.Ct. 1101 (1961), and Williamson v. Lee Optical Co., 348 U.S. 483, 75 S.Ct. 461 (1955), and I believe that it is constitutional under that analysis.

* * *

---

nition that the relatively deferential "rational basis" standard of review normally applied takes on a sharper focus when we address a

gender-based classification. So much is clear from our recent cases. * * *

The Court's conclusion that a law which treats males less favorably than females "must serve important governmental objectives and must be substantially related to achievement of those objectives" apparently comes out of thin air. The Equal Protection Clause contains no such language, and none of our previous cases adopt that standard. I would think we have had enough difficulty with the two standards of review which our cases have recognized—the norm of "rational basis," and the "compelling state interest" required where a "suspect classification" is involved—so as to counsel weightily against the insertion of still another "standard" between those two. How is this Court to divine what objectives are important? How is it to determine whether a particular law is "substantially" related to the achievement of such objective, rather than related in some other way to its achievement? Both of the phrases used are so diaphanous and elastic as to invite subjective judicial preferences or prejudices relating to particular types of legislation, masquerading as judgments whether such legislation is directed at "important" objectives or, whether the relationship to those objectives is "substantial" enough.

I would have thought that if this Court were to leave anything to decision by the popularly elected branches of the Government, where no constitutional claim other than that of equal protection is invoked, it would be the decision as to what governmental objectives to be achieved by law are "important," and which are not. As for the second part of the Court's new test, the Judicial Branch is probably in no worse position than the Legislative or Executive Branches to determine if there is *any* ra-

tional relationship between a classification and the purpose which it might be thought to serve. But the introduction of the adverb "substantially" requires courts to make subjective judgments as to operational effects, for which neither their expertise nor their access to data fits them. And even if we manage to avoid both confusion and the mirroring of our own preferences in the development of this new doctrine, the thousands of judges in other courts who must interpret the Equal Protection Clause may not be so fortunate.

* * *

The Court's criticism of the statistics relied on by the District Court conveys the impression that a legislature in enacting a new law is to be subjected to the judicial equivalent of a doctoral examination in statistics. Legislatures are not held to any rules of evidence such as those which may govern courts or other administrative bodies, and are entitled to draw factual conclusions on the basis of the determination of probable cause which an arrest by a police officer normally represents. In this situation, they could reasonably infer that the incidence of drunk driving is a good deal higher than the incidence of arrest.

And while, as the Court observes, relying on a report to a Presidential Commission which it cites in a footnote, such statistics may be distorted as a result of stereotyping, the legislature is not required to prove before a court that its statistics are perfect. In any event, if stereotypes are as pervasive as the Court suggests, they may in turn influence the conduct of the men and women in question, and cause the young men to conform to the wild and reckless image which is their stereotype.

* * *

The Oklahoma Legislature could have believed that 18–20-year-old males drive substantially more, and tend more often to be intoxicated than their female counterparts; that they prefer beer and admit to drinking and driving at a higher rate than females; and that they suffer traffic injuries out of proportion to the part they make up of the population. Under the appropriate rational-basis test for equal protection, it is neither irrational nor arbitrary to bar them from making purchases of 3.2% beer, which purchases might in many cases be made by a young man who immediately returns to his vehicle with the beverage in his possession. The record does not give any good indication of the true proportion of males in the age group who drink and drive (except that it is no doubt greater than the 2% who are arrested), but whatever it may be I cannot see that the mere purchase right involved could conceivably raise a due process question. There being no violation of either equal protection or due process, the statute should accordingly be upheld.

SELECTED CASES ON THE CONSTITUTIONALITY OF GENDER-BASED DISTINCTIONS BEFORE AND AFTER *CRAIG* v. *BOREN*

The following chart presents Supreme Court decisions on the constitutionality of sex-based distinctions contained in various state and federal statutes. These selected cases span the entire period since *Reed* v. *Reed* and are rulings based upon constitutional (as distinguished from statutory) interpretation. With the exception of the decisions in *Taylor* and *Duren*, which were based on the jury trial guarantee of the Sixth Amendment (applicable to the states through the Due Process Clause of the Fourteenth), all of the cases below involving challenges to state legislation turn on the Equal Protection Clause of the Fourteenth Amendment. The disposition of those cases which involve attacks on the constitutionality of federal statutes—usually provisions of the Social Security Act—hinges on a parallel construction of the Due Process Clause in the Fifth Amendment. (Recall that in *Bolling* v. *Sharpe* (p. 702) the Court held that a denial of equal protection may be so great as to deny due process.)

Case	Issue	Outcome	Vote	Precedent Cited	Reasons for Decision	Other Opinions
Kahn v. Shevin, 416 U.S. 351, 94 S.Ct. 1734 (1974)	Florida law gives to widows but not widowers a $500 property tax exemption	Upheld	6–3	*Reed*	Rational because financial disabilities of women greater than men—they have more difficult time getting jobs, especially when older and anyway generally earn less	Brennan, Marshall, and White dissented relying on *Frontiero*
Geduldig v. Aiello, 417 U.S. 484, 94 S.Ct. 2485 (1974)	California disability insurance pays benefits to private employees disabled by injury and not covered by Workmen's Compensation, excludes coverage for normal pregnancy as well as certain other disabilities	Upheld	6–3		Rational because program need not constitutionally have a wider scope of benefits if they would jeopardize program's solvency. Pregnancy was merely one of many expensive disabilities not included	Brennan, Douglas, and Marshall dissented citing *Frontiero*

Case	Issue	Outcome	Vote	Precedent Cited	Reasons for Decision	Other Opinions
Schlesinger v. Ballard, 419 U.S. 498, 95 S.Ct. 572 (1975)	Federal statutes providing for mandatory discharge of Naval officers who have twice been passed over for promotion deal with men and women differently; women are guaranteed 13 years of service, men have no such guarantee	Upheld	5–4	*Reed*	Rational because women have less chance for sea duty and combat service, therefore less chance for promotion. This justification supported because other Navy service where men and women are similarly situated makes no distinction	Brennan, Douglas, Marshall, and White dissented
Taylor v. Louisiana, 419 U.S. 522, 95 S.Ct. 692 (1975)	Louisiana constitutional and statutory provisions exclude women from jury duty unless they file written declaration indicating a desire to serve. Louisiana juries are thus virtually always all-male	Struck down	8–1		No rational, let alone compelling reason for such categorical exclusion which violates constitutional expectation that juries will present a fair cross-section of the community. That some women could not serve because of family responsibilities did not justify excluding women as an entire class	Rehnquist dissented
Weinberger v. Wiesenfeld, 420 U.S. 636, 95 S.Ct. 1225 (1975)	Social Security Act grants survivors benefits to widows and minor children but only to minor children in the case where a husband survives his working spouse	Struck down	8–0	*Frontiero*	Fact that men are more likely to have jobs and therefore income is true, but not a compelling reason. Treats earning ability as congruent with sex and therefore denies possible individual need on basis that a class of people as a whole does not need benefits	Burger, Powell, and Rehnquist concurred in the result on grounds denial frustrates purpose of the act to provide *family* support
Stanton v. Stanton, 421 U.S. 7, 95 S.Ct. 1373 (1975)	Utah law specifies lower age of majority for girls than boys in the context of a parent's obligation to pay child support and has the effect of cutting off payments to girls at 18 but continuing those to boys until they reach 21	Struck down	8–1	*Reed*	Nothing rational in the distinction here	Rehnquist dissented
Califano v. Goldfarb, 430 U.S. 199, 97 S.Ct. 1021 (1977)	Social Security Act pays survivor's benefits to a widow based on earnings of deceased husband, but such benefits on the earnings of a deceased wife are not paid to a widower unless he was receiving half his support from his deceased spouse	Struck down	5–4	*Frontiero* and *Wiesenfeld*	Combination of old notions, archaic and overbroad generalizations about dependency, and sheer administrative convenience do not suffice to justify the gender-based discrimination in the distribution of employment-related benefits	Stevens concurred in the judgment; Burger, Stewart, Blackmun, and Rehnquist dissented
Califano v. Webster, 430 U.S. 313, 97 S.Ct. 1192 (1977)	With respect to formula for computing old-age benefits, Social Security Act allows women to exclude from computation of her "average monthly wage" three more lower earning years than similarly situated male worker	Upheld	9–0	*Kahn* and *Ballard*	Allowing women who as such have been unfairly hindered from earning as much as men, to eliminate additional low-earning years from calculation of retirement benefits works directly to remedy some part of the effect of past discrimination	Burger, Stewart, Blackmun, and Rehnquist concurred in judgment

Case	Issue	Outcome	Vote	Precedent Cited	Reasons for Decision	Other Opinions
Duren v. Missouri, 439 U.S. 357, 99 S.Ct. 664 (1979)	State law grants women automatic exemption from jury duty upon request, so that women make up only about 15 percent of the prospective jurors on the average as compared with fact that women comprise 54 percent of adult population of county where this criminal case was tried	Struck down	8–1	*Taylor*	The exemption is overbroad (i.e., insufficiently tailored to excuse only particular women whose jury service would create hardship for a family) and violates Sixth Amendment guarantee that juries present a "fair cross-section of the community" applicable to the states through the Fourteenth Amendment	Rehnquist dissented
Orr v. Orr, 440 U.S. 268, 99 S.Ct. 1102 (1979)	Alabama law provides that husbands but not wives may be required to pay alimony following divorce	Struck down	6–3	*Craig*	Gender-based distinction is overbroad and premised on sexual stereotypes insufficiently related to financial need as basis for awarding alimony. Alimony statute based upon spouse's ability to pay would protect interest of dependent housewife without providing unequal treatment in atypical case where husband is dependent on working wife	Burger, Powell, and Rehnquist dissented
Caban v. Mohammed, 441 U.S. 380, 99 S.Ct. 1760 (1979)	New York law allows an unwed mother, but not an unwed father, to block the adoption of their child by withholding consent	Struck down	5–4	*Craig*	"[U]ndifferentiated distinction between unwed mothers and unwed fathers, applicable in all circumstances where adoption of a child of theirs is at issue," is overbroad since father may share a relationship with the child fully as close as that of the mother	Burger, Stewart, Rehnquist, and Stevens dissented
Califano v. Westcott, 443 U.S. 76, 99 S.Ct. 2655 (1979)	Section of Social Security Act provides benefits to families with needy dependent children who have been deprived of parental support because of the father's unemployment, but does not provide such benefits when the mother becomes unemployed	Struck down	9–0	*Orr, Stanton, Taylor,* and *Craig*	Gender classification is not substantially related to the achievement of any important and valid statutory goals, but is part of the "baggage of sexual stereotypes" that automatically presumes that a woman's place is in the home	
Wengler v. Druggists Mutual Insurance Co., 446 U.S. 142, 100 S.Ct. 1540 (1980)	A provision of Missouri's workers' compensation law denies a widower benefits on his wife's work-related death unless "he is either mentally or physically incapacitated from wage earning or proves actual dependence on his wife's earnings. In contrast, a widow qualifies for death benefits without having to prove actual dependence on her husband's earnings"	Struck down	8–1	*Craig*	While there may be "empirical support for the proposition that men are more likely to be the principal supporters of their spouses and families, * * * the bare assertion of this argument falls far short of justifying gender-based discrimination on the grounds of administrative convenience"	Rehnquist dissented
Kirchberg v. Feenstra, 450 U.S. 455, 101 S.Ct. 1195 (1981)	Louisiana law gives a husband, as "head and master" of property owned jointly with his wife, the unilateral right to dispose of the property without her consent	Struck down	9–0	*Craig*	State failed to offer any justification for this gender-based discrimination since its original contention that someone had to be appointed manager of the property was rejected as	

Case	Issue	Outcome	Vote	Precedent Cited	Reasons for Decision	Other Opinions
Kirchberg (*Cont.*)					clearly insufficient by the federal district court and the state abandoned this argument on appeal. The fact that the wife could have executed a declaration prohibiting her husband from executing a mortgage on her home without her consent cannot redeem an otherwise unconstitutionally discriminatory statute	
Michael M. v. Superior Court of Sonoma County, 450 U.S. 464, 101 S.Ct. 1200 (1981)	California law punishes men but not women for the commission of "statutory rape" by defining the crime as "an act of sexual intercourse accomplished with a female not the wife of the perpetrator, where the female is under the age of 18 years"	Upheld	5–4	*Craig*	Legislature may take account of the special problems of women without violating the Equal Protection Clause. "Only women may become pregnant and they suffer disproportionately the profound physical, emotional and psychological consequences of sexual activity. The statute at issue here protects women from sexual intercourse at an age when those consequences are particularly severe." In addition, "the State has a strong interest in preventing such pregnancy" since "teenage pregnancies, which have increased dramatically over the last two decades, have significant social, medical and economic consequences for both the mother and her child, and the State"	Brennan, White, Marshall, and Stevens dissented
Rostker v. Goldberg, 453 U.S. 57, 101 S.Ct. 2646 (1981)	The Military Selective Service Act empowers the President to require the registration of men but not women for possible later duty in the armed forces	Upheld	6–3	*Craig* and *Ballard*	Congress has broad authority conferred by the Constitution to raise and support armies and " 'is permitted to legislate both with greater breadth and with greater flexibility' when the statute governs military society * * *." "No one could deny that * * * the Government's interest in raising and supporting armies is an 'important governmental interest.' " Registering men but not women is substantially related to this important interest because "[r]egistration is not an end in itself but rather the first step" in principally "prepar[ing] for a draft *of combat troops*" and, under the explicit provisions of federal statutes, "women as a group, * * * unlike men as a group, are not eligible for combat."	Brennan, White, and Marshall dissented

Case	Issue	Outcome	Vote	Precedent Cited	Reasons for Decision	Other Opinions
Mississippi University for Women v. Hogan, ___ U.S. ___, 102 S.Ct. 3331 (1982)	A state-supported university for women denied qualified men the right to enroll for credit in its nursing school	Struck down	5–4	*Wengler*	"Rather than compensate for discriminatory barriers faced by women, MUW's policy of excluding males from admission to the School of Nursing tends to perpetuate the stereotyped view of nursing as an exclusively woman's job. By assuring that Mississippi allots more openings in its state-supported nursing schools to women than it does to men, MUW's admissions policy lends credibility to the old view that women, not men, should become nurses, and makes the assumption that nursing is a field for women a self-fulfilling prophecy." Furthermore, "the State has made no showing that the gender-based classification is substantially and directly related to its proposed compensatory objective."	Burger, Blackmun, Powell, and Rehnquist dissented

A canvass of the cases involving gender-based distinctions suggests the Court is divided more or less into three camps. At the left end of the continuum are Justices Brennan, Marshall, White, and, until his retirement in 1975, Douglas (the four Justices forming the plurality in *Frontiero* v. *Richardson* in 1973) who regard sex as a suspect classification and would require that gender-based legislation be subjected to strict scrutiny. Occupying a "traditional" equal protection position at the opposite end of the spectrum are Chief Justice Burger and Justice Rehnquist, with the latter the least inclined of any member of the Court to invalidate a gender-based distinction. Arrayed in order from left to right between White and Burger, and forming a middle group, are Justices Stevens, Powell, Blackmun, and Stewart (who retired in 1981), with Stevens perhaps twice as likely as any other Justice in the center group to join with those Justices at the left end of the spectrum to hold a piece of gender-based legislation unconstitutional. The apparent lack of consistency in the sex discrimination cases is largely attributable to the lack of consensus in approach to the evaluation of gender-based distinctions among Justices in the middle. From a political standpoint, the rise of "intermediate" or "middle-tier" scrutiny in sex discrimination cases, at least, might be seen as an attempt by the Justices on the left of the spectrum to build support with the middle group by adopting, as a bridge, a framework of constitutional analysis more compatible with the generally less liberal political outlook of the Justices in the center.

Massachusetts law provides that all veterans who qualify for state civil service positions must be given preference over any qualifying nonveterans. Helen Feeney, who was not a veteran, took and passed several competitive civil service examinations. In 1971, for example, she received the second best score on an examination for a position with the Board of Dental Examiners, and two years later she registered the third highest score on a test for a post as administrative assistant at a mental health center. Her scores, however, did not secure a place for her on the certified eligible list. Because of the veterans' preference she was placed sixth in the competition for the dental board position, behind five male veterans one of whom got the job even though his score was lower than hers. Following the second of these exams, she was placed on a list behind a dozen male veterans, eleven of whom had lower scores. She subsequently brought suit and argued that the absolute, lifetime veterans' preference violated the Equal Protection Clause because it invariably operated so as to exclude women from the best of the state's civil service positions. A three-judge federal district court agreed.

In Personnel Administrator of Massachusetts v. Feeney, 442 U.S. 256, 99 S.Ct. 2282 (1979), the Supreme Court, addressing the question "whether Massachusetts, in granting an absolute lifetime preference to veterans, has discriminated against women in violation of the Equal Protection Clause," reversed the judgment of the federal district court. At the outset, Justice Stewart, speaking for the Court, observed that, of some 47,000 state civil service appointees, roughly 57 percent were men and 43 percent were women and that of the women under 2 percent were veterans while 54 percent of the male appointees had such status. Moreover, he noted, "A large unspecified percentage of the female appointees were serving in lower paying positions for which males traditionally have not applied." Justice Stewart then prefaced the Court's consideration of the constitutionality of the veterans' preference by sketching out some accepted principles of equal protection analysis:

> The Equal Protection Guarantee of the Fourteenth Amendment does not take from the States all power of classification. * * * Most laws classify, and many affect certain groups unevenly, even though the law itself treats them no differently from all other members of the class described by the law. When the basic classification is rationally based, uneven effects upon particular groups within a class are ordinarily of no constitutional concern. * * * The calculus of effects, the manner in which a particular law reverberates in a society, is a legislative and not a judicial responsibility. * * * In assessing an equal protection challenge, a court is called upon only to measure the basic validity of the legislative classification. * * * When some other independent right is not at stake, * * * and when there is no "reason to infer antipathy," * * * it is presumed that "even improvident decisions will eventually be rectified by the democratic process." * * *

Certain classifications, however, in themselves supply a reason to infer antipathy. Race is the paradigm. A racial classification, regardless of purported motivation, is presumptively invalid and can be upheld only upon an extraordinary justification. * * * This rule applies as well to a classification that is ostensibly neutral but is an obvious pretext for racial discrimination. Yick Wo v. Hopkins, 118 U.S. 356, 6 S.Ct. 1064 (1886); Guinn v. United States, 238 U.S. 347, 35 S.Ct. 926 (1914); * * * Gomillion v. Lightfoot, 364 U.S. 339, 81 S.Ct. 125 (1960). But, as was made clear in Washington v. Davis, 426 U.S. 229, 96 S.Ct. 2040 (1976), and Village of Arlington Heights v. Metropolitan Housing Development Corp., 429 U.S. 252, 97 S.Ct. 555 (1977), even if a neutral law has a disproportionately adverse effect upon a racial minority, it is unconstitutional under the Equal Protection Clause only if that impact can be traced to a discriminatory purpose.

Classifications based upon gender, not unlike those based upon race, have traditionally been the touchstone for pervasive and often subtle discrimination. * * * This Court's recent cases teach that such classifications must bear a "close and substantial relationship to important governmental objectives," Craig v. Boren, 429 U.S. 190, 197, 97 S.Ct. 451 (1977), and are in many settings unconstitutional. * * * Although public employment is not a constitutional right, * * * and the States have wide discretion in framing employee qualifications, * * * these precedents dictate that any state law overtly or covertly designed to prefer males over females in public employment would require an exceedingly persuasive justification to withstand a constitutional challenge under the Equal Protection Clause of the Fourteen Amendment.

The cases of *Washington* v. *Davis,* supra, and *Village of Arlington Heights* v. *Metropolitan Housing Development Corp.,* supra, recognize that when a neutral law has a disparate impact upon a group that has historically been the victim of discrimination, an unconstitutional purpose may still be at work. But those cases signalled no departure from the settled rule that the Fourteenth Amendment guarantees equal laws, not equal results. *Davis* upheld a job-related employment test that white people passed in proportionately greater numbers than Negroes, for there had been no showing that racial discrimination entered into the establishment or formulation of the test. *Arlington Heights* upheld a zoning board decision that tended to perpetuate racially segregated housing patterns, since, apart from its effect, the board's decision was shown to be nothing more than an application of constitutionally neutral zoning policy. Those principles apply with equal force to a case involving alleged gender discrimination.

He concluded, "If the impact of this statute could not be plausibly explained on a neutral ground, impact itself would signal that the real classification made by the law was in fact not neutral." The question, then, in this case was "whether this veteran preference excludes significant numbers of women from preferred state jobs because they are women or because they are nonveterans." "Apart from the fact that the definition of 'veterans' in the statute had always been neutral as to gender and that Massachusetts has consistently defined veteran status in a way that has been inclusive of women who have served in the military, this is not a law that can plausibly be explained only as a gender-based classification," said Justice Stewart. And, he explained: "Veteran status is not uniquely male. Although few women benefit from the preference, the nonveteran class is not substantially all-female. To the contrary, significant numbers of nonveterans are men, and all nonveterans—male as well as female—are placed at a disadvantage. Too many men are affected * * * to permit the inference that the statute is but a pretext for preferring men over women." Moreover, while it was surely clear to members of the legislature enacting the veterans' preference that it would proportionately aid men much more than women simply because more men than women have served in the military, Justice Stewart pointed out it did not follow that knowledge of such an effect was tantamount to a "discriminatory purpose":

"Discriminatory purpose," * * * implies more than intent as volition or intent as awareness of consequences. * * * It implies that the decision-maker, in this case a state legislature, selected or reaffirmed a particular course of action at least in part "because of," not merely "in spite of," its adverse effects upon an identifiable group. Yet nothing in the record demonstrates that this preference for veterans was originally devised or subsequently re-enacted because it would accomplish the collateral goal of keeping women in a stereotypic and predefined place in the Massachusetts Civil Service.

In dissent, Justice Marshall, joined by Justice Brennan, concluded that "Massachusetts' choice of an absolute veterans' preference system evinces purposeful gender-based discrimination   *   *   *   [which] bears no substantial relationship to a legitimate governmental objective,   *   *   *   [and therefore] cannot withstand scrutiny under the Equal Protection Clause." Apart from the fact that "Massachusetts' choice of a formula   *   *   *   so severely restricts public employment for women [that it] cannot reasonably be thought gender-neutral," he reasoned that none of the interests invoked by the state to justify the veterans' preference ("assisting veterans in their readjustment to civilian life"; "encouraging military enlistment"; and "rewarding those who have served their country") was sufficient to counterbalance its highly discriminatory effect, especially in light of many less restrictive alternative means for advancing the same purposes.

MASSACHUSETTS BOARD OF RETIREMENT v. MURGIA

Supreme Court of the United States, 1976
427 U.S. 307, 96 S.Ct. 2562, 49 L.Ed.2d 520

Robert Murgia, a uniformed officer in the Massachusetts State Police, was forced to retire by law upon reaching his fiftieth birthday. Murgia, who was in excellent physical and mental health, argued that such compulsory retirement, occasioned only by age, discriminated in violation of the Equal Protection Clause. A three-judge federal district court ultimately held the statute unconstitutional as lacking "a rational basis in furthering any substantial state interest" and enjoined its enforcement. The Retirement Board appealed.

———————

PER CURIAM.

*   *   *

The primary function of the Uniformed Branch of the Massachusetts State Police is to protect persons and property and maintain law and order. Specifically, uniformed officers participate in controlling prison and civil disorders, respond to emergencies and natural disasters, patrol highways in marked cruisers, investigate crime, apprehend criminal suspects, and provide back-up support for local law enforcement personnel. As the District Court observed, "service in this branch is, or can be, arduous." 376 F.Supp., at 754. "[H]igh versatility is required, with few, if any, backwaters available for the partially superannuated."   *   *   *.   Thus,

"even [appellee's] experts concede that there is a general relationship between advancing age and decreasing physical ability to respond to the demands of the job."   *   *   *.

These considerations prompt the requirement that uniformed state officers pass a comprehensive physical examination biennially until age 40. After that, until mandatory retirement at age 50, uniformed officers must pass annually a more rigorous examination, including an electrocardiogram and tests for gastro-intestinal bleeding. Appellee Murgia had passed such an examination four months before he was retired, and there is no dispute that, when he retired, his excellent physical and mental health still rendered him capable of performing the duties of a uniformed officer.

The record includes the testimony of three physicians: that of the State Police Surgeon, who testified to the physiological and psychological demands involved in the performance of uniformed police functions; that of an associate professor of medicine, who testified generally to the relationship between aging and the ability to perform under stress; and that of a surgeon, who also testified to aging and the ability safely to perform police functions. The testimony clearly established that the risk of physical failure, particularly in the cardiovascular system, increases with age, and that the number of individuals in a given age group incapable of performing stress functions increases with the age of the group. * * *. The testimony also recognized that particular individuals over 50 could be capable of safely performing the functions of uniformed officers. The associate professor of medicine, who was a witness for the appellee, further testified that evaluating the risk of cardiovascular failure in a given individual would require a detailed number of studies. * * *.

In assessing appellee's equal protection claim, the District Court found it unnecessary to apply a strict scrutiny test, see Shapiro v. Thompson, 394 U.S. 618, 89 S.Ct. 1322, for it determined that the age classification established by the Massachusetts statutory scheme could not in any event withstand a test of rationality, see Dandridge v. Williams, 397 U.S. 471, 90 S.Ct. 1153. Since there had been no showing that reaching age 50 forecast even "imminent change" in an officer's physical condition, the District Court held that compulsory retirement at age 50 was

irrational under a scheme that assessed the capabilities of officers individually by means of comprehensive annual physical examinations. We agree that rationality is the proper standard by which to test whether compulsory retirement at age 50 violates equal protection. We disagree, however, with the District Court's determination that the age 50 classification is not rationally related to furthering a legitimate state interest.

We need state only briefly our reasons for agreeing that strict scrutiny is not the proper test for determining whether the mandatory retirement provision denies appellee equal protection. San Antonio Independent School District v. Rodriguez, 411 U.S. 1, 16, 93 S.Ct. 1278, 1287 (1973), reaffirmed that equal protection analysis requires strict scrutiny of a legislative classification only when the classification impermissibly interferes with the exercise of a fundamental right or operates to the peculiar disadvantage of a suspect class. Mandatory retirement at age 50 under the Massachusetts statute involves neither situation.

This Court's decisions give no support to the proposition that a right of governmental employment per se is fundamental. See San Antonio Independent School District v. Rodriguez, supra; Lindsey v. Normet, 405 U.S. 56, 73, 92 S.Ct. 862, 874; Dandridge v. Williams, supra, 397 U.S., at 485, 90 S.Ct., at 1162. Accordingly, we have expressly stated that a standard less than strict scrutiny "has consistently been applied to state legislation restricting the availability of employment opportunities." * * *

Nor does the class of uniformed state police officers over 50 constitute a suspect class for purposes of

876 CIVIL RIGHTS AND LIBERTIES PART III

equal protection analysis. *Rodriguez*, supra, 411 U.S., at 28, 93 S.Ct., at 1294, observed that a suspect class is one "saddled with such disabilities, or subjected to such a history of purposeful unequal treatment, or relegated to such a position of political powerlessness as to command extraordinary protection from the majoritarian political process." While the treatment of the aged in this Nation has not been wholly free of discrimination, such persons, unlike, say, those who have been discriminated against on the basis of race or national origin, have not experienced a "history of purposeful unequal treatment" or been subjected to unique disabilities on the basis of stereotyped characteristics not truly indicative of their abilities. The class subject to the compulsory retirement feature of the Massachusetts statute consists of uniformed state police officers over the age of 50. It cannot be said to discriminate only against the elderly. Rather, it draws the line at a certain age in middle life. But even old age does not define a "discrete and insular" group, United States v. Carolene Products Co., 304 U.S. 144, 152–153, n. 4, 58 S.Ct. 778, 783, in need of "extraordinary protection from the majoritarian political process." Instead, it marks a stage that each of us will reach if we live out our normal span. Even if the statute could be said to impose a penalty upon a class defined as the aged, it would not impose a distinction sufficiently akin to those classifications that we have found suspect to call for strict judicial scrutiny.

Under the circumstancs, it is unnecessary to subject the State's resolution of competing interests in this case to the degree of critical examination that our cases under the Equal Protection Clause recently have characterized as "strict judicial scrutiny."

We turn then to examine this state classification under the rational basis standard. This inquiry employs a relatively relaxed standard reflecting the Court's awareness that the drawing of lines that create distinctions is peculiarly a legislative task and an unavoidable one. Perfection in making the necessary classifications is neither possible nor necessary. * * * Such action by a legislature is presumed to be valid.

In this case, the Massachusetts statute clearly meets the requirements of the Equal Protection Clause, for the State's classification rationally furthers the purpose identified by the State: Through mandatory retirement at age 50, the legislature seeks to protect the public by assuring physical preparedness of its uniformed police. Since physical ability generally declines with age, mandatory retirement at 50 serves to remove from police service those whose fitness for uniformed work presumptively has diminished with age. This clearly is rationally related to the State's objective. There is no indication that § 26(3)(a) has the effect of excluding from service so few officers who are in fact unqualified as to render age 50 a criterion wholly unrelated to the objective of the statute.

That the State chooses not to determine fitness more precisely through individualized testing after age 50 is not to say that the objective of assuring physical fitness is not rationally furthered by a maximum age limitation. It is only to say that with regard to the interest of all concerned, the State perhaps has not chosen the best means to accomplish this purpose. But where rationality is the test, a State "does not violate the Equal Protection Clause merely because the classifications made by its laws are imperfect." Dandridge v. Williams, 397 U.S., at 485, 90 S.Ct., at 1161.

We do not make light of the substantial economic and psychological effects premature and compulsory retirement can have on an individual; nor do we denigrate the ability of elderly citizens to continue to contribute to society. The problems of retirement have been well documented and are beyond serious dispute. But "[w]e do not decide today that the [Massachusetts statute] is wise, that it best fulfills the relevant social and economic objectives that [Massachusetts] might ideally espouse, or that a more just and humane system could not be devised." Id., at 487, 90 S.Ct., at 1162. We decide only that the system enacted by the Massachusetts Legislature does not deny appellee equal protection of the law.

The judgment is reversed.

Mr. Justice STEVENS took no part in the consideration or decision of this case.

Mr. Justice MARSHALL, dissenting.

Today the Court holds that it is permissible for the Commonwealth of Massachusetts to declare that members of its state police force who have been proven medically fit for service are nonetheless legislatively unfit to be policemen and must be terminated—involuntarily "retired"—because they have reached the age of 50. Although we have called the right to work "of the very essence of the personal freedom and opportunity that it was the purpose of the [Fourteenth] Amendment to secure," Truax v. Raich, 239 U.S. 33,

41, 36 S.Ct. 7, 10, the Court finds that the right to work is not a fundamental right. And, while agreeing that "the treatment of the aged in this Nation has not been wholly free of discrimination," * * * the Court holds that the elderly are not a suspect class. Accordingly, the Court undertakes the scrutiny mandated by the bottom tier of its two-tier equal protection framework, finds the challenged legislation not to be "wholly unrelated" to its objective, and holds, therefore, that it survives equal protection attack. I respectfully dissent.

Although there are signs that its grasp on the law is weakening, the rigid two-tier model still holds sway as the Court's articulated description of the equal protection test. Again, I must object to its perpetuation. The model's two fixed modes of analysis, strict scrutiny and mere rationality, simply do not describe the inquiry the Court has undertaken—or should undertake—in equal protection cases. Rather, the inquiry has been much more sophisticated and the Court should admit as much. It has focused upon the character of the classification in question, the relative importance to individuals in the class discriminated against of the governmental benefits that they do not receive, and the state interests asserted in support of the classification. * * *

Although the Court outwardly adheres to the two-tier model, it has apparently lost interest in recognizing further "fundamental" rights and "suspect" classes. See San Antonio School District v. Rodriguez, supra (rejecting education as a fundamental right); Frontiero v. Richardson, 411 U.S. 677, 93 S.Ct. 1764 (declining to treat women as a suspect class). In my view, this result is the natural consequence of the limitations of the Court's traditional equal protection analysis. If a statute invades a "fundamental" right or discriminates against a "suspect" class, it is subject to strict scrutiny. If a statute is subject to strict scrutiny, the statute always, or nearly always * * * is struck down. Quite obviously, the only critical decision is whether strict scrutiny should be invoked at all. It should be no surprise, then, that the Court is hesitant to expand the number of categories of rights and classes subject to strict scrutiny, when each expansion involves the invalidation of virtually every classification bearing upon a newly covered category.[1]

But however understandable the Court's hesitancy to invoke strict scrutiny, all remaining legislation should not drop into the bottom tier, and be measured by the mere rationality test. For that test, too, when applied as articulated, leaves little doubt about the outcome; the challenged legislation is always upheld. See New Orleans v. Dukes, 427 U.S. 297, 96 S.Ct. 2513 (overruling Morey v. Doud, 354 U.S. 457, 77 S.Ct. 1344, the only modern case in which this Court has struck down an economic classification as irrational). It cannot be gainsaid that there remain rights, not now classified as "fundamental," that remain vital to the flourishing of a free society, and classes, not now classified as "sus-

pect," that are unfairly burdened by invidious discrimination unrelated to the individual worth of their members. Whatever we call these rights and classes, we simply cannot forgo all judicial protection against discriminatory legislation bearing upon them, but for the rare instances when the legislative choice can be termed "wholly irrelevant" to the legislative goal. McGowan v. Maryland, 366 U.S. 420, 425, 81 S.Ct. 1101, 1104.

While the Court's traditional articulation of the rational basis test does suggest just such an abdication, happily the Court's deeds have not matched its words. Time and again, met with cases touching upon the prized rights and burdened classes of our society, the Court has acted only after a reasonably probing look at the legislative goals and means, and at the significance of the personal rights and interests invaded. Stanton v. Stanton, 421 U.S. 7, 95 S.Ct. 1373; Weinberger v. Weisenfeld, 420 U.S. 636, 95 S.Ct. 1225; United States Dept. of Agriculture v. Moreno, 413 U.S. 528, 93 S.Ct. 2821; Frontiero v. Richardson, 411 U.S., at 691, 93 S.Ct., at 1772 (Powell, J., concurring in the judgment); James v. Strange, 407 U.S. 128, 92 S.Ct. 2027; Weber v. Aetna Casualty & Surety Co., 406 U.S. 164, 92 S.Ct. 1400; Eisenstadt v. Baird, 405 U.S. 438, 92 S.Ct. 1029; Reed v. Reed, 404 U.S. 71, 92 S.Ct. 251. See San Antonio

---

1. Some classifications are so invidious that they should be struck down automatically absent the most compelling state interest, and by suggesting the limitations of strict scrutiny analysis I do not mean to imply otherwise. The analysis should be accomplished, however, not by stratified notions of "suspect" classes and "fundamental" rights, but by individualized assessments of the particular classes and rights involved in each case.

Of course, the traditional suspect classes and fundamental rights would still rank at the top of the list of protected categories, so that in cases involving those categories analysis would be functionally equivalent to strict scrutiny. Thus, the advantages of the approach I favor do not appear in such cases, but rather emerge in those dealing with traditionally less protected classes and rights. * * *

School District v. Rodriguez, 411 U.S., at 98–110, 93 S.Ct., at 1330 (Marshall, J., dissenting). These cases make clear that the Court has rejected, albeit *sub silentio*, its most deferential statements of the rationality standard in assessing the validity under the Equal Protection Clause of much noneconomic legislation.

But there are problems with deciding cases based on factors not encompassed by the applicable standards. First, the approach is rudderless, affording no notice to interested parties of the standards governing particular cases and giving no firm guidance to judges who, as a consequence, must assess the constitutionality of legislation before them on an *ad hoc* basis. Second, and not unrelatedly, the approach is unpredictable and requires holding this Court to standards it has never publicly adopted. Thus, the approach presents the danger that, as I suggest has happened here, relevant factors will be misapplied or ignored. All interests not "fundamental" and all classes not "suspect" are not the same; and it is time for the Court to drop the pretense that, for purposes of the Equal Protection Clause, they are.

The danger of the Court's verbal adherence to the rigid two-tier test, despite its effective repudiation of that test in the cases, is demonstrated by its efforts here. There is simply no reason why a statute that tells able-bodied police officers, ready and willing to work, that they no longer have the right to earn a living in their chosen profession merely because they are 50 years old should be judged by the same minimal standards of rationality that we use to test economic legislation that discriminates against business interests. See *New Orleans* v. *Dukes*,

supra; Williamson v. Lee Optical Co., 348 U.S. 483, 75 S.Ct. 461. Yet, the Court today not only invokes the minimal level of scrutiny, it wrongly adheres to it. Analysis of the three factors I have identified above—the importance of the governmental benefits denied, the character of the class, and the asserted state interests—demonstrates the Court's error.

Whether "fundamental" or not, "the right of the individual * * * to engage in any of the common occupations of life" has been repeatedly recognized by this Court as falling within the concept of liberty guaranteed by the Fourteenth Amendment. Board of Regents v. Roth, 408 U.S. 564, 572, 92 S.Ct. 2701, quoting Meyer v. Nebraska, 262 U.S. 390, 399, 43 S.Ct. 625, 626. As long ago as the *Slaughterhouse Cases*, Justice Bradley wrote that this right "is an inalienable right; it was formulated as such under the phrase 'pursuit of happiness' in the Declaration of Independence. * * * This right is a large ingredient in the civil liberty of the citizen." 111 U.S. 746, 762, 4 S.Ct. 652, 657 (1884) (concurring opinion). And in Smith v. Texas, 233 U.S. 630, 34 S.Ct. 681, in invalidating a law that criminally penalized anyone who served as a freight train conductor without having previously served as a brakeman, and that thereby excluded numerous equally qualified employees from that position, the Court recognized that "all men are entitled to the equal protection of the law in their right to work for the support of themselves and families." * * * Even if the right to earn a living does not include the right to work for the government, it is settled that because of the importance of the interest involved, we have always carefully looked at the reasons asserted for depriving a government employee of his job.

While depriving any government employee of his job is a significant deprivation, it is particularly burdensome when the person deprived is an older citizen. Once terminated, the elderly cannot readily find alternative employment. The lack of work is not only economically damaging, but emotionally and physically draining. Deprived of his status in the community and of the opportunity for meaningful activity, fearful of becoming dependent on others for his support, and lonely in his newfound isolation, the involuntarily retired person is susceptible to physical and emotional ailments as a direct consequence of his enforced idleness. Ample clinical evidence supports the conclusion that mandatory retirement poses a direct threat to the health and life expectancy of the retired person, and these consequences of termination for age are not disputed by appellant. Thus, an older person deprived of his job by the government loses not only his right to earn a living, but, too often, his health as well, in sad contradiction of Browning's promise, "The best is yet to be/The last of life, for which the first was made."

Not only are the elderly denied important benefits when they are terminated on the basis of age, but the classification of older workers is itself one that merits judicial attention. Whether older workers constitute a "suspect" class or not, it cannot be disputed that they constitute a class subject to repeated and arbitrary discrimination in employment. See U. S. Dept. of Labor, the Older American Worker: Age Discrimination in Employment (1965); M. Barron, The Aging American 55–68 (1961). As Congress found in passing the Age Discrimination in Employment Act in 1967,

"[I]n the face of rising productivity and affluence, older workers find themselves disadvantaged in their efforts to retain employment, and especially to regain employment when displaced from jobs[.]

"[T]he setting of arbitrary age limits regardless of potential for job performance has become a common practice, and certain otherwise desirable practices may work to the disadvantage of older persons[.]

"[T]he incidence of unemployment, especially long-term unemployment with resultant deterioration of skill, morale, and employer acceptability is, relative to the younger ages, high among older workers; their numbers are great and growing; and their employment problems grave[.]" 29 U.S.C.A. § 621 (subsection numbers omitted). * * *

Of course, the Court is quite right in suggesting that distinctions exist between the elderly and traditional suspect classes such as Negroes, and between the elderly and "quasi-suspect" classes such as women or illegitimates. The elderly are protected not only by certain anti-discrimination legislation, but by legislation that provides them with positive benefits not enjoyed by the public at large. Moreover, the elderly are not isolated in society, and discrimination against them is not pervasive but is centered primarily in employment. The advantage of a flexible equal protection standard, however, is that it can readily accommodate such variables. The elderly are undoubtedly discriminated against, and when legislation denies them an important benefit—employment—I conclude that to sustain the legislation the Commonwealth must show a reasonably substantial interest and a scheme reasonably closely tailored to achieving that interest. Cf. San Antonio School District v. Rodriguez, 411 U.S., at 124–126, 93 S.Ct. at 1343 (Marshall, J., dissenting). * * *

Turning, then, to the Commonwealth's arguments, I agree that the purpose of the mandatory retirement law is legitimate, and indeed compelling. The Commonwealth has every reason to assure that its state police officers are of sufficient physical strength and health to perform their jobs. In my view, however, the means chosen, the forced retirement of officers at age 50, is so overinclusive that it must fall.

All potential officers must pass a rigorous physical examination. Until age 40, this same examination must be passed every two years—when the officer re-enlists—and, after age 40, every year. The Commonwealth has conceded that "[w]hen a member passes his re-enlistment or annual physical, he is found to be qualified to perform all of the duties of the Uniformed Branch of the Massachusetts State Police." * * * If a member fails the examination, he is immediately terminated or refused re-enlistment. Thus, the only members of the state police still on the force at age 50 are those who have been determined—repeatedly—by the Commonwealth to be physically fit for the job. Yet, all of these physically fit officers are automatically terminated at age 50. The Commonwealth does not seriously assert that its testing is no longer effective at age 50, nor does it claim that continued testing would serve no purpose because officers over 50 are no longer physically able to perform their jobs. Thus the Commonwealth is in the position of already individually testing its police officers for physical fitness, conceding that such testing is adequate to determine the physical ability of an officer to continue on the job, and conceding that that ability may continue after age 50. In these circumstances, I see no reason at all for automatically terminating those officers who reach the age of 50; indeed, that action seems the height of irrationality.

Accordingly, I conclude that the Commonwealth's mandatory retirement law cannot stand when measured against the significant deprivation the Commonwealth's action works upon the terminated employees. I would affirm the judgment of the District Court.

AMBACH v. NORWICK

Supreme Court of the United States, 1979
441 U.S. 68, 99 S.Ct. 1589, 60 L.Ed.2d 49

Certification by the New York State Department of Education is required in order to teach in the state's public elementary and secondary schools. Section 3001(3) of the state's Education Law denies teacher certification to any person who is not an American citizen unless the individual has declared his or her intent to become a citizen. Norwick and another, resident aliens married to American citizens, refused to seek citizenship despite their eligibility to do so and were consequently denied teacher certification. They brought suit against the New York State Commissioner of Education alleging a denial of equal protection. Applying "strict scrutiny," a three-judge federal district court declared the blanket ban on resident aliens from teaching unconstitutional for overbreadth because it excluded all resident aliens from all teaching positions without regard to subject taught, national-

ity, relationship of alien's country to the United States, or willingness of the alien to substitute some other sign of loyalty, such as taking an oath of allegiance. The state appealed.

Mr. Justice POWELL delivered the opinion of the Court.

This case presents the question whether a State, consistently with the Equal Protection Clause of the Fourteenth Amendment, may refuse to employ as elementary and secondary school teachers aliens who are eligible for United States citizenship but who refuse to seek naturalization.

* * *

The decisions of this Court regarding the permissibility of statutory classifications involving aliens have not formed an unwavering line over the years. State regulation of the employment of aliens long has been subject to constitutional constraints. In Yick Wo v. Hopkins, 118 U.S. 356, 6 S.Ct. 1064 (1886), the Court struck down an ordinance which was applied to prevent aliens from running laundries, and in Truax v. Raich, 239 U.S. 33, 36 S.Ct. 7 (1915), a law requiring at least 80% of the employees of certain businesses to be citizens was held to be an unconstitutional infringement of an alien's "right to work for a living in the common occupations of the community * * *." * * * At the same time, however, the Court also has recognized a greater degree of latitude for the States when aliens were sought to be excluded from public employment. At the time *Truax* was decided, the governing doctrine permitted States to exclude aliens from various activities when the restriction pertained to "the regulation or distribution of the public domain, or of the common property

or resources of the people of the State, * * *." * * * Hence, as part of a larger authority to forbid aliens from owning land, Frick v. Webb, 263 U.S. 326, 44 S.Ct. 115 (1923); Webb v. O'Brien, 263 U.S. 313, 44 S.Ct. 112 (1923); Porterfield v. Webb, 263 U.S. 225, 44 S.Ct. 21 (1923); Terrace v. Thompson, 263 U.S. 197, 44 S.Ct. 15 (1923); Blythe v. Hinkley, 180 U.S. 333, 21 S.Ct. 390 (1901); Hauenstein v. Lynham, 100 U.S. 483, 25 L.Ed. 628 (1880), harvesting wildlife, Patsone v. Pennsylvania, 232 U.S. 138, 34 S.Ct. 281 (1914); McCready v. Virginia, 94 U.S. 391, 24 L.Ed. 248 (1877), or maintaining an inherently dangerous enterprise, Clarke v. Deckebach, 274 U.S. 392, 47 S.Ct. 630 (1927), States permissibly could exclude aliens from working on public construction projects, Crane v. New York, 239 U.S. 195, 36 S.Ct. 85 (1915), and, it appears, from engaging in any form of public employment at all, see *Truax*, 239 U.S. at 40, 36 S.Ct. at 10.

Over time, the Court's decisions gradually have restricted the activities from which States are free to exclude aliens. The first sign that the Court would question the constitutionality of discrimination against aliens even in areas affected with a "public interest" appeared in Oyama v. California, 332 U.S. 633, 68 S.Ct. 269 (1948). The Court there held that statutory presumptions designed to discourage evasion of California's ban on alien landholding discriminated against the citizen children of aliens. The same Term, the Court held that the "ownership" a State exercises over fish found in its territorial waters "is inadequate to justify California in excluding any or all aliens who are lawful residents of the State from making a living by fishing in the ocean off its shores while permitting all others to do so." Takahashi v. Fish & Game Comm'n, 334 U.S. 410, 421, 68 S.Ct. 1138, 1144 (1948). This process of withdrawal from the former doctrine culminated in Graham v. Richardson, 403 U.S. 365, 91 S.Ct. 1848 (1971), which for the first time treated classifications based on alienage as "inherently suspect and subject to close judicial scrutiny." * * * Applying *Graham*, this Court has held invalid statutes that prevented aliens from entering a State's classified civil service, Sugarman v. Dougall, 413 U.S. 634, 93 S.Ct. 2842 (1973), practicing law, In re Griffiths, 413 U.S. 717, 93 S.Ct. 2851 (1973), working as an engineer, Examining Bd. v. Flores de Otero, 426 U.S. 572, 96 S.Ct. 2264 (1976), and receiving state educational benefits, Nyquist v. Mauclet, 432 U.S. 1, 97 S.Ct. 2120 (1977).

Although our more recent decisions have departed substantially from the public interest doctrine of *Truax's* day, they have not abandoned the general principle that some state functions are so bound up with the operation of the State as a governmental entity as to permit the exclusion from those functions of all persons who have not become part of the process of self-government. In *Sugarman*, we recognized that a State could, "in an appropriately defined class of positions, require citizenship as a qualification for office." We went on to observe:

"Such power inheres in the State by virtue of its obligation, already noted above, 'to preserve the basic conception of a political community.' * * * And this power and respon-

sibility of the State applies, not only to the qualifications of voters, but also to persons holding state elective or important nonelective executive, legislative, and judicial positions, for officers who participate directly in the formulation, execution, or review of broad public policy perform functions that go to the heart of representative government." Id., 413 U.S. at 647, 93 S.Ct. at 2850 (citation omitted).

The exclusion of aliens from such governmental positions would not invite as demanding scrutiny from this Court. * * *

Applying the rational basis standard, we held last Term that New York could exclude aliens from the ranks of its police force. Foley v. Connelie, 435 U.S. 291, 98 S.Ct. 1067 (1978). Because the police function fulfilled "a most fundamental obligation of government to its constituency" and by necessity cloaked policemen with substantial discretionary powers, we view the police force as being one of those appropriately defined classes of positions for which a citizenship requirement could be imposed. * * * Accordingly, the State was required to justify its classification only "by a showing of some rational relationship between the interest sought to be protected and the limiting classification." * * *

The rule for governmental functions, which is an exception to the general standard applicable to classifications based on alienage, rests on important principles inherent in the Constitution. The distinction between citizens and aliens, though ordinarily irrelevant to private activity, is fundamental to the definition and government of a State. The Constitution itself refers to the distinction no less than 11 times, * * * indicating that the status of citizenship was meant to have significance in the structure of our government. The assumption of that status, whether by birth or naturalization, denotes an association with the polity which, in a democratic republic, exercises the powers of governance. * * * The form of this association is important: an oath of allegiance or similar ceremony cannot substitute for the unequivocal legal bond citizenship represents. It is because of this special significance of citizenship that governmental entities, when exercising the functions of government, have wider latitude in limiting the participation of noncitizens.

In determining whether, for purposes of equal protection analysis, teaching in public schools constitutes a governmental function, we look to the role of public education and to the degree of responsibility and discretion teachers possess in fulfilling that role. * * * Each of these considerations supports the conclusion that public school teachers may be regarded as performing a task "that go[es] to the heart of representative government." Sugarman v. Dougall, supra, 413 U.S., at 647, 93 S.Ct., at 2850.

Public education, like the police function, "fulfills a most fundamental obligation of government to its constituency." *Foley*, 435 U.S., at 297, 98 S.Ct., at 1071. The importance of public schools in the preparation of individuals for participation as citizens, and in the preservation of the values on which our society rests, long has been recognized by our decisions. * * * Other authorities have perceived public schools as an "assimilative force" by which diverse and conflicting elements in our society are brought to-

gether on a broad but common ground. See, e.g., J. Dewey, Democracy and Education 26 (1929); N. Edwards & H. Richey, The School in the American Social Order 623–624 (1963). These perceptions of the public schools as inculcating fundamental values necessary to the maintenance of a democratic political system have been confirmed by the observations of social scientists. See R. Dawson & K. Prewitt, Political Socialization 146–167 (1969); R. Hess & J. Torney, The Development of Political Attitudes in Children, 114, 158–171, 217–220 (1967); V. O. Key, Public Opinion and American Democracy 323–343 (1961).

Within the public school system, teachers play a critical part in developing students' attitude toward government and understanding of the role of citizens in our society. Alone among employees of the system, teachers are in direct, day-to-day contact with students both in the classrooms and in the other varied activities of a modern school. In shaping the students' experience to achieve educational goals, teachers by necessity have wide discretion over the way the course material is communicated to students. They are responsible for presenting and explaining the subject matter in a way that is both comprehensible and inspiring. No amount of standardization of teaching materials or lesson plans can eliminate the personal qualities a teacher brings to bear in achieving these goals. Further, a teacher serves as a role model for his students, exerting a subtle but important influence over their perceptions and values. Thus, through both the presentation of course materials and the example he sets, a teacher has an opportunity to influence the attitudes of students toward government, the political process, and a citizen's social responsibilities. This influence is crucial to the continued good health of a democracy.

Furthermore, it is clear that all public school teachers, and not just those responsible for teaching the courses most directly related to government, history, and civic duties, should help fulfill the broader function of the public school system. Teachers, regardless of their specialty, may be called upon to teach other subjects, including those expressly dedicated to political and social subjects. More importantly, a State properly may regard all teachers as having an obligation to promote civic virtues and understanding in their classes, regardless of the subject taught. Certainly a State also may take account of a teacher's function as an example for students, which exists independently of particular classroom subjects. In light of the foregoing considerations, we think it clear that public school teachers come well within the "governmental function" principle recognized in *Sugarman* and *Foley*. Accordingly, the Constitution requires only that a citizenship requirement applicable to teaching in the public schools bears a rational relationship to the legitimate state interest. * * *

As the legitimacy of the State's interest in furthering the educational goals outlined above is undoubted, it remains only to consider whether § 3001(3) bears a rational relationship to this interest. The restriction is carefully framed to serve its purpose, as it bars from teaching only those aliens who have demonstrated their unwillingness to obtain United States citizenship. Appellees, and aliens similarly situated, in effect have chosen to classify themselves. They prefer to retain citizenship in a

foreign country with the obligations it entails of primary duty and loyalty. They have rejected the open invitation extended to qualify for eligibility to teach by applying for citizenship in this country. The people of New York, acting through their elected representatives, have made a judgment that citizenship should be a qualification for teaching the young of the State in the public schools, and § 3001(3) furthers that judgment.

Reversed.

Mr. Justice BLACKMUN, with whom Mr. Justice BRENNAN, Mr. Justice MARSHALL, and Mr. Justice STEVENS join, dissenting.

* * *

* * * [T]he Court has held more than once that state classifications based on alienage are "inherently suspect and subject to close judicial scrutiny." Graham v. Richardson, 403 U.S. 365, 372, 91 S.Ct. 1848, 1852 (1971). * * * And "[a]lienage classifications by a State that do not withstand this stringent examination cannot stand." Ibid.

There is thus a line, most recently recognized in Foley v. Connelie, between those employments that a State in its wisdom constitutionally may restrict to United States citizens, on the one hand, and those employments, on the other that the State may not deny to resident aliens. For me, the present case falls on the *Sugarman-Griffiths-Flores de Otero-Mauclet* side of that line, rather than on the narrowly isolated *Foley* side.

* * *

* * * [T]he Court, to the disadvantage of appellees, crosses the

line from *Griffiths* to *Foley* by saying * * * that the "distinction between citizens and aliens, though ordinarily irrelevant to private activity, is fundamental to the definition and government of a State." It then concludes that public school teaching "constitutes a governmental function," * * * and that public school teachers may be regarded as performing a task that goes "to the heart of representative government." * * * The Court speaks of the importance of public schools in the preparation of individuals for participation as citizens, and in the preservation of the values on which our society rests. After then observing that teachers play a critical part in all this, the Court holds that New York's citizenship requirement is constitutional because it bears a rational relationship to the State's interest in furthering these educational goals.

I perceive a number of difficulties along the easy road the Court takes to this conclusion:

First, the New York statutory structure itself refutes the argument. Section 3001.3, the very statute at issue here, provides for exceptions with respect to alien teachers "employed pursuant to regulations adopted by the commissioner of education permitting such employment." Section 3001–a provides another exception for persons ineligible for United States citizenship because of oversubscribed quotas. Also, New York is unconcerned with any citizenship qualification for teachers in the private schools of the State, even though the record indicates that about 18% of the pupils at the elementary and secondary levels attend private schools. The education of those pupils seems not to be inculcat-

ed with something less than what is desirable for citizenship and what the Court calls an influence "crucial to the continued good health of a democracy." * * * The State apparently, under § 3001.3, would not hesitate to employ an alien teacher while he waits to attain citizenship, even though he may fail ever to attain it. And the stark fact that the State permits some aliens to sit on certain local school boards * * * reveals how shallow and indistinct is New York's line of demarcation between citizenship and noncitizenship. The Court's attempted rationalization of this fact * * * hardly extinguishes the influence school board members, including these otherwise "disqualified" resident aliens, possess in school administration, in the selection of faculty, and in the approval of textbooks and instructional materials.

Second, the New York statute is all-inclusive in its disqualifying provisions: "No person shall be employed or authorized to teach in the public schools of the state who is * * * [n]ot a citizen." It sweeps indiscriminately. * * *

Third, the New York classification is irrational. Is it better to employ a poor citizen-teacher than an excellent resident alien teacher? Is is preferable to have a citizen who has never seen Spain or a Latin American country teach Spanish to eighth graders and to deny that opportunity to a resident alien who may have lived for 20 years in the culture of Spain or Latin America? The State will know how to select its teachers responsibly, wholly apart from citizenship, and can do so selectively and intelligently. That is the way to accomplish the desired result.

An artificial citizenship bar is not a rational way. * * *

Fourth, it is logically impossible to differentiate between this case concerning teachers and *In re Griffiths* concerning attorneys. If a resident alien *may not* constitutionally be barred from taking a state bar examination and thereby becoming qualified to practice law in the courts of a State, how is one to comprehend why a resident alien *may* constitutionally be barred from teaching in the elementary and secondary levels of a State's public schools? One may speak proudly of the role model of the teacher, of his ability to mold young minds, of his inculcating force as to national ideals, and of his profound influence in the impartation of our society's values. Are the attributes of an attorney any less? He represents us in our critical courtroom controversies even when citizenship and loyalty may be questioned. He stands as an officer of every court in which he practices. He is responsible for strict adherence to the announced and implied standards of professional conduct, to the requirements of evolving ethical codes, and for honesty and integrity in his professional and personal life. Despite the almost continuous criticism leveled at the legal profession, he, too, is an influence in legislation, in the community, and in the role model figure that the professional person enjoys. * * *

If an attorney has a constitutional right to take a bar examination and practice law, despite his being a resident alien, it is impossible for me to see why a resident alien, otherwise completely competent and qualified, as these appellees concededly are, is constitutionally disqualified from teaching in the public schools of the great State of New York. The District Court expressed it well and forcefully when it observed that New York's exclusion "seems repugnant to the very heritage the State is seeking to inculcate." 417 F.Supp. 913, 922 (SDNY 1976).

I respectfully dissent.

PLYLER v. DOE

Supreme Court of the United States, 1982
— U.S. —, 102 S.Ct. 2382, 72 L.Ed.2d 786

In 1975, the Texas legislature revised its education laws to withhold from local school districts any funds for the education of children who had not been "legally admitted" into the United States. The legislation, § 21.031 of the Texas Education Code, also empowered local school districts to deny enrollment in public schools to these children. A class action challenging the legislation as a violation of equal protection of the laws was brought against a local school superintendent on behalf of certain school-age children of Mexican origin who could not establish that they had been "legally admitted" into this country. On appeal to the Supreme Court from decisions below favorable to the plaintiff children, this case was consolidated for hearing and decision with another suit attacking the constitutionality of Texas's statutes curtailing access to public education by illegal alien children.

Justice BRENNAN delivered the opinion of the Court.

The question presented by these cases is whether, consistent with the Equal Protection Clause of the Fourteenth Amendment, Texas may deny to undocumented school-age children the free public education that it provides to children who are citizens of the United States or legally admitted aliens.

* * *

[At the outset the Court rejected Texas's arguments that aliens were neither "persons" nor within the state's jurisdiction and, therefore, without standing to raise a Fourteenth Amendment claim. The Court pointed out that "the protection of the Fourteenth Amendment extends to anyone, citizen or stranger, who *is* subject to the laws of a State, and reaches into every corner of a State's territory."]

The Equal Protection Clause directs that "all persons similarly circumstanced shall be treated alike." F. S. Royster Guano Co. v. Virginia, 253 U.S. 412, 415, 40 S.Ct. 560, 561 (1920). But so too, "The Constitution does not require things which are different in fact or opinion to be treated in law as though they were the same." Tigner v. Texas, 310 U.S. 141, 147, 60 S.Ct. 879, 882 (1940). The initial discretion to determine what is "different" and what is "the same" resides in the legislatures of the States. A legislature must have substantial latitude to establish classifications that roughly approximate the nature of the problem perceived, that accommodate competing concerns both public and private, and that account for limita-

tions on the practical ability of the State to remedy every ill. In applying the Equal Protection Clause to most forms of state action, we thus seek only the assurance that the classification at issue bears some fair relationship to a legitimate public purpose.

But we would not be faithful to our obligations under the Fourteenth Amendment if we applied so deferential a standard to every classification. The Equal Protection Clause was intended as a restriction on state legislative action inconsistent with elemental constitutional premises. Thus we have treated as presumptively invidious those classifications that disadvantage a "suspect class," or that impinge upon the exercise of a "fundamental right." With respect to such classifications, it is appropriate to enforce the mandate of equal protection by requiring the State to demonstrate that its classification has been precisely tailored to serve a compelling governmental interest. In addition, we have recognized that certain forms of legislative classification, while not facially invidious, nonetheless give rise to recurring constitutional difficulties; in these limited circumstances we have sought the assurance that the classification reflects a reasoned judgment consistent with the ideal of equal protection by inquiring whether it may fairly be viewed as furthering a substantial interest of the State.[16] We turn to a consideration of the

---

16. See Craig v. Boren, 429 U.S. 190, 97 S.Ct. 451 (1976); Lalli v. Lalli, 439 U.S. 259, 99 S.Ct. 518 (1978). This technique of "intermediate" scrutiny permits us to evaluate the rationality of the legislative judgment with reference to well-settled constitutional principles. "In expounding the Constitution, the Court's role is to discern 'principles sufficiently absolute to give them roots throughout the com-

munity and continuity over significant periods of time, and to lift them above the level of the pragmatic political judgments of a particular time and place.'" University of California Regents v. Bakke, 438 U.S. 265, 299, 98 S.Ct. 2733, 2752 (1978) (Opinion of Powell, J.), quoting A. Cox, The Role of the Supreme Court in American Government 114 (1976). Only when concerns sufficiently absolute and enduring

standard appropriate for the evaluation of § 21.031.

Sheer incapability or lax enforcement of the laws barring entry into this country, coupled with the failure to establish an effective bar to the employment of undocumented aliens, has resulted in the creation of a substantial "shadow population" of illegal migrants—numbering in the millions—within our borders. This situation raises the specter of a permanent caste of undocumented resident aliens, encouraged by some to remain here as a source of cheap labor, but nevertheless denied the benefits that our society makes available to citizens and lawful residents. The existence of such an underclass presents most difficult problems for a Nation that prides itself on adherence to principles of equality under law.

The children who are plaintiffs in these cases are special members of this underclass. Persuasive arguments support the view that a State may withhold its beneficence from those whose very presence within the United States is the product of their own unlawful conduct. These arguments do not apply with the same force to classifications imposing disabilities on the minor *children* of such illegal entrants. At the least, those who elect to enter our territory by stealth and in violation of our law should be prepared to bear the consequences, including, but not limited to, deportation. But the children of those illegal entrants are not comparably situated. Their "parents have the ability to conform their conduct to societal norms," and presumably the ability to remove themselves

from the State's jurisdiction; but the children who are plaintiffs in these cases "can affect neither their parents' conduct nor their own status." Trimble v. Gordon, 430 U.S. 762, 770, 97 S.Ct. 1459, 1465 (1977). Even if the State found it expedient to control the conduct of adults by acting against their children, legislation directing the onus of a parent's misconduct against his children does not comport with fundamental conceptions of justice. * * *

Of course, undocumented status is not irrelevant to any proper legislative goal. Nor is undocumented status an absolutely immutable characteristic since it is the product of conscious, indeed unlawful, action. But § 21.031 is directed against children, and imposes its discriminatory burden on the basis of a legal characteristic over which children can have little control. It is thus difficult to conceive of a rational justification for penalizing these children for their presence within the United States. Yet that appears to be precisely the effect of § 21.031.

Public education is not a "right" granted to individuals by the Constitution. *San Antonio School District*, supra, 411 U.S., at 35, 93 S.Ct., at 1298. But neither is it merely some governmental "benefit" indistinguishable from other forms of social welfare legislation. Both the importance of education in maintaining our basic institutions, and the lasting impact of its deprivation on the life of the child, mark the distinction. * * * We have recognized "the public school as a most vital civic institution for the preservation of a democratic system of government,"

---

can be clearly ascertained from the Constitution and our cases do we employ this standard

to aid us in determining the rationality of the legislative choice.

Abington School District v. Schempp, 374 U.S. 203, 230, 83 S.Ct. 1560, 1575 (1963) (Brennan, J., concurring), and as the primary vehicle for transmitting "the values on which our society rests." Ambach v. Norwick, 441 U.S. 68, 76, 99 S.Ct. 1589, 1594 (1979). As noted early in our history, "some degree of education is necessary to prepare citizens to participate effectively and intelligently in our open political system if we are to preserve freedom and independence." Wisconsin v. Yoder, 406 U.S. 205, 221, 92 S.Ct. 1526, 1536 (1972). And these historic "perceptions of the public schools as inculcating fundamental values necessary to the maintenance of a democratic political system have been confirmed by the observations of social scientists." Ambach v. Norwick, supra, 411 U.S., at 77, 99 S.Ct., at 1594. In addition, education provides the basic tools by which individuals might lead economically productive lives to the benefit of us all. In sum, education has a fundamental role in maintaining the fabric of our society. We cannot ignore the significant social costs borne by our Nation when select groups are denied the means to absorb the values and skills upon which our social order rests.

In addition to the pivotal role of education in sustaining our political and cultural heritage, denial of education to some isolated group of children poses an affront to one of the goals of the Equal Protection Clause: the abolition of governmental barriers presenting unreasonable obstacles to advancement on the basis of individual merit. Paradoxically, by depriving the children of any disfavored group of an education, we foreclose the means by which that group might raise the level of esteem in which it is held by the majority.

But more directly, "education prepares individuals to be self-reliant and self-sufficient participants in society." Wisconsin v. Yoder, supra, 406 U.S, at 221, 92 S.Ct., at 1536. Illiteracy is an enduring disability. The inability to read and write will handicap the individual deprived of a basic education each and every day of his life. The inestimable toll of that deprivation on the social, economic, intellectual and psychological well-being of the individual, and the obstacle it poses to individual achievement, makes it most difficult to reconcile the cost or the principle of a status-based denial of basic education with the framework of equality embodied in the Equal Protection Clause. * * *

These well-settled principles allow us to determine the proper level of deference to be afforded § 21.031. Undocumented aliens cannot be treated as a suspect class because their presence in this country in violation of federal law is not a "constitutional irrelevancy." Nor is education a fundamental right; a State need not justify by compelling necessity every variation in the manner in which education is provided to its population. See San Antonio School Dist. v. Rodriguez, 411 U.S. 1, 28–39, 93 S.Ct. 1278, 1293–1300 (1973). But more is involved in this case than the abstract question whether § 21.031 discriminates against a suspect class, or whether education is a fundamental right. Section 21.031 imposes a lifetime hardship on a discrete class of children not accountable for their disabling status. The stigma of illiteracy will mark them for the rest of their lives. By denying these children a basic education, we deny them the ability to live within the structure of our civic institutions, and foreclose any realistic possibility that they will contribute in even the smallest way to the progress of our Nation. In determining the rationality of § 21.031, we may appropriately take into account its costs to the Nation and to the innocent children who are its victims. In light of these countervailing costs, the discrimination contained in § 21.031 can hardly be considered rational unless it furthers some substantial goal of the State.

It is the State's principal argument, and apparently the view of the dissenting Justices, that the undocumented status of these children *vel non* establishes a sufficient rational basis for denying them benefits that a State might choose to afford other residents. The State notes that while other aliens are admitted "on an equality of legal privileges with all citizens under nondiscriminatory laws," Takahashi v. Fish & Game Comm'n, 334 U.S. 410, 420, 68 S.Ct. 1138, 1143 (1948), the asserted right of these children to an education can claim no implicit congressional imprimatur. Indeed, on the State's view, Congress' apparent disapproval of the presence of these children within the United States, and the evasion of the federal regulatory program that is the mark of undocumented status, provides authority for its decision to impose upon them special disabilities. Faced with an equal protection challenge respecting the treatment of aliens, we agree that the courts must be attentive to congressional policy; the exercise of congressional power might well affect the State's prerogatives to afford differential treatment to a particular class of aliens. But we are unable to find in the congressional immigration scheme any statement of policy that might weigh significantly in arriving at an equal protection balance concerning the State's authority to deprive these children of an education.

The Constitution grants Congress the power to "establish a uniform Rule of Naturalization." Art. I., § 8. Drawing upon this power, upon its plenary authority with respect to foreign relations and international commerce, and upon the inherent power of a sovereign to close its borders, Congress has developed a complex scheme governing admission to and status within our borders. See Mathews v. Diaz, 426 U.S. 67, 96 S.Ct. 1883 (1976); Harrisades v. Shaughnessy, 342 U.S. 580, 588–589, 72 S.Ct. 512, 518–519 (1952). The obvious need for delicate policy judgments has counselled the Judicial Branch to avoid intrusion into this field. *Mathews*, supra, 426 U.S., at 81, 96 S.Ct., at 1892. But this traditional caution does not persuade us that unusual deference must be shown the classification embodied in § 21.031. The States enjoy no power with respect to the classification of aliens. See Hines v. Davidowitz, 312 U.S. 52, 61 S.Ct. 399 (1941). This power is "committed to the political branches of the Federal Government." *Mathews*, supra, 426 U.S., at 81, 96 S.Ct., at 1892. Although it is "a routine and normally legitimate part" of the business of the Federal Government to classify on the basis of alien status, * * * and to "take into account the character of the relationship between the alien and this country," * * * only rarely are such matters relevant to legislation by a State. * * *

As we recognized in DeCanas v. Bica, 424 U.S. 351, 96 S.Ct. 933 (1976), the States do have some authority to act with respect to illegal aliens, at least where such action mirrors federal objectives and furthers a legitimate state goal. In *De-*

Canas, the State's program reflected Congress' intention to bar from employment all aliens except those possessing a grant of permission to work in this country. * * * In contrast, there is no indication that the disability imposed by § 21.031 corresponds to any identifiable congressional policy. The State does not claim that the conservation of state educational resources was ever a congressional concern in restricting immigration. More importantly, the classification reflected in § 21.031 does not operate harmoniously within the federal program.

* * *

We are reluctant to impute to Congress the intention to withhold from these children, for so long as they are present in this country through no fault of their own, access to a basic education. In other contexts, undocumented status, coupled with some articulable federal policy, might enhance State authority with respect to the treatment of undocumented aliens. But in the area of special constitutional sensitivity presented by this case, and in the absence of any contrary indication fairly discernible in the present legislative record, we perceive no national policy that supports the State in denying these children an elementary education. The State may borrow the federal classification. But to justify its use as a criterion for its own discriminatory policy, the State must demonstrate that the classification is reasonably adapted to *"the purposes for which the state desires to use it."* Oyama v. California, 332 U.S. 633, 664–665, 68 S.Ct. 269, 284 (1948) (Murphy, J., concurring) (emphasis added). We therefore turn to the state objectives that are said to support § 21.031.

Appellants argue that the classification at issue furthers an interest in the "preservation of the state's limited resources for the education of its lawful residents." * * * Of course, a concern for the preservation of resources standing alone can hardly justify the classification used in allocating those resources. * * * The State must do more than justify its classification with a concise expression of an intention to discriminate. * * * Apart from the asserted state prerogative to act against undocumented children solely on the basis of their undocumented status—an asserted prerogative that carries only minimal force in the circumstances of this case—we discern three colorable state interests that might support § 21.031.

First, appellants appear to suggest that the State may seek to protect the State from an influx of illegal immigrants. While a State might have an interest in mitigating the potentially harsh economic effects of sudden shifts in population, § 21.031 hardly offers an effective method of dealing with an urgent demographic or economic problem. There is no evidence in the record suggesting that illegal entrants impose any significant burden on the State's economy. To the contrary, the available evidence suggests that illegal aliens underutilize public services, while contributing their labor to the local economy and tax money to the State fisc. * * * The dominant incentive for illegal entry into the State of Texas is the availability of employment; few if any illegal immigrants come to this country, or presumably to the State of Texas, in order to avail themselves of a free education. Thus, even making the doubtful assumption that the net impact of illegal aliens on the economy of the State is negative, we think it clear that "[c]harging tuition to undocumented children constitutes a ludicrously ineffectual attempt to stem the tide of illegal immigration," at least when compared with the alternative of prohibiting the employment of illegal aliens. * * *

Second, while it is apparent that a state may "not * * * reduce expenditures for education by barring [some arbitrarily chosen class of] children from its schools," Shapiro v. Thompson, 394 U.S. 618, 633, 89 S.Ct. 1322, 1330 (1969), appellants suggest that undocumented children are appropriately singled out for exclusion because of the special burdens they impose on the State's ability to provide high quality public education. But the record in no way supports the claim that exclusion of undocumented children is likely to improve the overall quality of education in the State. As the District Court * * * noted, the State failed to offer any "credible supporting evidence that a proportionately small diminution of the funds spent on each child [which might result from devoting some State funds to the education of the excluded group] will have a grave impact on the quality of education." * * * And, after reviewing the State's school financing mechanism, the District Court * * * concluded that barring undocumented children from local schools would not necessarily improve the quality of education provided in those schools. * * * Of course, even if improvement in the quality of education were a likely result of barring some *number* of children from the schools of the State, the State must support its selection of *this* group as the appropriate target for exclusion. In terms of educa-

tional cost and need, however, undocumented children are "basically indistinguishable" from legally resident alien children. * * *

Finally, appellants suggest that undocumented children are appropriately singled out because their unlawful presence within the United States renders them less likely than other children to remain within the boundaries of the State, and to put their education to productive social or political use within the State. Even assuming that such an interest is legitimate, it is an interest that is most difficult to quantify. The State has no assurance that any child, citizen or not, will employ the education provided by the State within the confines of the State's borders. In any event, the record is clear that many of the undocumented children disabled by this classification will remain in this country indefinitely, and that some will become lawful residents or citizens of the United States. It is difficult to understand precisely what the State hopes to achieve by promoting the creation and perpetuation of a subclass of illiterates within our boundaries, surely adding to the problems and costs of unemployment, welfare, and crime. It is thus clear that whatever savings might be achieved by denying these children an education, they are wholly insubstantial in light of the costs involved to these children, the State, and the Nation.

If the State is to deny a discrete group of innocent children the free public education that it offers to other children residing within its borders, that denial must be justified by a showing that it furthers some substantial state interest. No such showing was made here. Accordingly, the judgment of the Court of Appeals in each of these cases is

Affirmed.

Justice MARSHALL, concurring.

While I join the Court opinion, I do so without in any way retreating from my opinion in San Antonio School District v. Rodriguez, 411 U.S. 1, 70–133, 93 S.Ct. 1278, 1315–1348 (Marshall, J., dissenting). I continue to believe that an individual's interest in education is fundamental, and that this view is amply supported "by the unique status accorded public education by our society, and by the close relationship between education and some of our most basic constitutional values." * * * Furthermore, I believe that the facts of these cases demonstrate the wisdom of rejecting a rigidified approach to equal protection analysis, and of employing an approach that allows for varying levels of scrutiny depending upon "the constitutional and societal importance of the interest adversely affected and the recognized invidiousness of the basis upon which the particular classification is drawn." * * * It continues to be my view that a class-based denial of public education is utterly incompatible with the Equal Protection Clause of the Fourteenth Amendment.

Justice BLACKMUN, concurring.

I join the opinion and judgment of the Court.

Like Justice Powell, I believe that the children involved in this litigation "should not be left on the streets uneducated." * * * I write separately, however, because in my view the nature of the interest at stake is crucial to the proper resolution of this case.

The "fundamental rights" aspect of the Court's equal protection analysis—the now-familiar concept that governmental classifications bearing on certain interests must be closely scrutinized—has been the subject of some controversy. Justice Harlan, for example, warned that "[v]irtually every state statute affects important rights. * * * [T]o extend the 'compelling interest' rule to all cases in which such rights are affected would go far toward making this Court a 'super-legislature.'" Shapiro v. Thompson, 394 U.S. 618, 661, 89 S.Ct. 1322, 1345 (1969) (dissenting opinion). Others have noted that strict scrutiny under the Equal Protection Clause is unnecessary when classifications infringing enumerated constitutional rights are involved, for "a state law that impinges upon a substantive right or liberty created or conferred by the Constitution is, of course, presumptively invalid, whether or not the law's purpose or effect is to create any classifications." San Antonio Independent School Dist. v. Rodriguez, 411 U.S. 1, 61, 93 S.Ct. 1278, 1311 (1973) (Stewart, J., concurring). See Shapiro v. Thompson, 394 U.S., at 659, 89 S.Ct., at 1344 (Harlan, J., dissenting). Still others have suggested that fundamental rights are not properly a part of equal protection analysis at all, because they are unrelated to any defined principle of equality.

These considerations, combined with doubts about the judiciary's ability to make fine distinctions in assessing the effects of complex social policies, led the Court in *Rodriguez* to articulate a firm rule: fundamental rights are those that "explicitly or implicitly [are] guaranteed by the Constitution." * * * It therefore squarely rejected the notion that "an ad hoc determination as to the social or economic importance" of a given interest is relevant to the level of scrutiny accorded classifications involving that interest, * * * and made clear that "[i]t is not the province of this Court to create substantive constitutional rights in the name of guaranteeing equal protection of the laws." * * *

I joined Justice Powell's opinion for the Court in *Rodriguez*, and I continue to believe that it provides the appropriate model for resolving most equal protection disputes. Classifications infringing substantive constitutional rights necessarily will be invalid, if not by force of the Equal Protection Clause, then through operation of other provisions of the Constitution. Conversely, classifications bearing on nonconstitutional interests—even those involving "the most basic economic needs of impoverished human beings," Dandridge v. Williams, 397 U.S. 471, 485, 90 S.Ct. 1153, 1161 (1970)—generally are not subject to special treatment under the Equal Protection Clause, because they are not distinguishable in any relevant way from other regulations in "the area of economics and social welfare." * * *

With all this said, however, I believe the Court's experience has demonstrated that the *Rodriguez* formulation does not settle every issue of "fundamental rights" arising under the Equal Protection Clause. Only a pedant would insist that there are *no* meaningful distinctions among the multitude of social and political interests regulated by the States, and *Rodriguez* does not stand for quite so absolute a proposition. To the contrary, *Rodriguez* implicitly acknowledged that certain interests, though not constitutionally guaranteed, must be accorded a special place in equal protection analysis.

Thus, the Court's decisions long have accorded strict scrutiny to classifications bearing on the right to vote in state elections, and *Rodriguez* confirmed the "constitutional underpinnings of the right to equal treatment in the voting process." * * * Yet "the right to vote, *per se*, is not a constitutionally protected right." * * * See Harper v. Virginia Board of Elections, 383 U.S. 663, 665, 86 S.Ct. 1079, 1080 (1966); *Rodriguez*, 411 U.S., at 59, n. 2, 93 S.Ct., at 1310, n. 2 (Stewart, J., concurring). Instead, regulation of the electoral process receives unusual scrutiny because "the right to exercise the franchise in a free and unimpaired manner is preservative of other basic civil and political rights." Reynolds v. Sims, 377 U.S. 533, 562, 84 S.Ct. 1362, 1381 (1964). See Dunn v. Blumstein, 405 U.S. 330, 336, 92 S.Ct. 995, 999 (1972). In other words, the right to vote is accorded extraordinary treatment because it is, in equal protection terms, an extraordinary right: a citizen cannot hope to achieve any meaningful degree of individual political equality if granted an inferior right of participation in the political process. Those denied the vote are relegated, by state fiat, in a most basic way to second-class status.

It is arguable, of course, that the Court never should have applied fundamental rights doctrine in the fashion outlined above. Justice Harlan, for one, maintained that strict equal protection scrutiny was appropriate only when racial or analogous classifications were at issue. Shapiro v. Thompson, 394 U.S., at 658–663, 89 S.Ct., at 1344–1346 (dissenting opinion). See Reynolds v. Sims, 377 U.S., at 590–591, 84 S.Ct., at 1396 (Harlan, J., dissenting). But it is too late to debate that point, and I believe that accepting the principle of the voting cases—the idea that state classifications bearing on certain interests pose the risk of allocating rights in a fashion inherently contrary to any notion of "equality"—dictates the outcome here. * * *

In my view, when the State provides an education to some and denies it to others, it immediately and inevitably creates class distinctions of a type fundamentally inconsistent with those purposes, mentioned above, of the Equal Protection Clause. Children denied an education are placed at a permanent and insurmountable competitive disadvantage, for an uneducated child is denied even the opportunity to achieve. And when those children are members of an identifiable group, that group—through the State's action—will have been converted into a discrete underclass. Other benefits provided by the State, such as housing and public assistance, are of course important; to an individual in immediate need, they may be more desirable than the right to be educated. But classifications involving the complete denial of education are in a sense unique, for they strike at the heart of equal protection values by involving the State in the creation of permanent class distinctions. * * * In a sense, then, denial of an education is the analogue of denial of the right to vote: the former relegates the individual to second-class social status; the latter places him at a permanent political disadvantage.

* * *

Justice POWELL, concurring.

I join the opinion of the Court, and write separately to emphasize the unique character of the case before us.

The classification in question severely disadvantages children who are the victims of a combination of circumstances. Access from Mexico into this country, across our 2,000 mile border, is readily available and virtually uncontrollable. Illegal aliens are attracted by our employment opportunities, and perhaps by other benefits as well. This is a problem of serious national proportions, as the Attorney General recently has recognized. * * * Perhaps because of the intractability of the problem, Congress—vested by the Constitution with the responsibility of protecting our borders and legislating with respect to aliens—has not provided effective leadership in dealing with this problem. It therefore is certain that illegal aliens will continue to enter the United States and, as the record makes clear, an unknown percentage of them will remain here. I agree with the Court that their children should not be left on the streets uneducated.

* * *

Our review in a case such as this is properly heightened. * * * Cf. Craig v. Boren, 429 U.S. 190, 97 S.Ct. 451 (1976). The classification at issue deprives a group of children of the opportunity for education afforded all other children simply because they have been assigned a legal status due to a violation of law by their parents. These children thus have been singled out for a lifelong penalty and stigma. A legislative classification that threatens the creation of an underclass of future citizens and residents cannot be reconciled with one of the fundamental purposes of the Fourteenth Amendment. In these unique circumstances, the Court properly may require that the State's interests be substantial and that the means bear a "fair and substantial relation" to these interests. See Lalli v. Lalli, 439 U.S. 259, 265, 99 S.Ct. 518, 523 ("classifications based on illegitimacy * * * are invalid under the Fourteenth Amendment if they are not substantially related to permissible state interests"); Id. at 271, 99 S.Ct. at 526 ("[a]s the State's interests are substantial, we now consider the means adopted").

* * *

In reaching this conclusion, I am not unmindful of what must be the exasperation of responsible citizens and government authorities in Texas and other states similarly situated. Their responsibility, if any, for the influx of aliens is slight compared to that imposed by the Constitution on the federal government. So long as the ease of entry remains inviting, and the power to deport is exercised infrequently by the federal government, the additional expense of admitting these children to public schools might fairly be shared by the federal and state governments. But it hardly can be argued rationally that anyone benefits from the creation within our borders of a subclass of illiterate persons many of whom will remain in the State, adding to the problems and costs of both State and National Governments attendant upon unemployment, welfare and crime.

Chief Justice BURGER, with whom Justice WHITE, Justice REHNQUIST, and Justice O'CONNOR join, dissenting.

Were it our business to set the Nation's social policy, I would agree without hesitation that it is senseless for an enlightened society to deprive any children—including illegal aliens—of an elementary education.

I fully agree that it would be folly—and wrong—to tolerate creation of a segment of society made up of illiterate persons, many having a limited or no command of our language. However, the Constitution does not constitute us as "Platonic Guardians" nor does it vest in this Court the authority to strike down laws because they do not meet our standards of desirable social policy "wisdom," or "common sense." * * * We trespass on the assigned function of the political branches under our structure of limited and separated powers when we assume a policymaking role as the Court does today.

The Court makes no attempt to disguise that it is acting to make up for Congress' lack of "effective leadership" in dealing with the serious national problems caused by the influx of uncountable millions of illegal aliens across our borders. * * * The failure of enforcement of the immigration laws over more than a decade and the inherent difficulty and expense of sealing our vast borders have combined to create a grave socio-economic dilemma. It is a dilemma that has not yet even been fully assessed, let alone addressed. However, it is not the function of the judiciary to provide "effective leadership" simply because the political branches of government fail to do so.

The Court's holding today manifests the justly criticized judicial tendency to attempt speedy and wholesale formulation of "remedies" for the failures—or simply the laggard pace—of the political processes of our system of government. The Court employs, and in my view abuses, the Fourteenth Amendment in an effort to become an omnipotent and omniscient problem solver. That the motives for doing so are noble and compassionate does not alter the fact that the Court distorts our constitutional function to make amends for the defaults of others.

* * *

The Court acknowledges that, except in those cases when state classifications disadvantage a "suspect class" or impinge upon a "fundamental right," the Equal Protection Clause permits a State "substantial latitude" in distinguishing between different groups of persons. * * * Moreover, the Court expressly—and correctly—rejects any suggestion that illegal aliens are a suspect class, * * * or that education is a fundamental right. * * * Yet by patching together bits and pieces of what might be termed quasi-suspect-class and quasi-fundamental-rights analysis, the Court spins out a theory custom-tailored to the facts of these cases.

In the end, we are told little more than that the level of scrutiny employed to strike down the Texas law applies only when illegal alien children are deprived of a public education. * * * If ever a court was guilty of an unabashedly result-oriented approach, this case is a prime example.

The Court first suggests that these illegal alien children, although not a suspect class, are entitled to special solicitude under the Equal Protection Clause because they lack "control" over or "responsibility" for their unlawful entry into this country. * * * Similarly, the Court appears to take the position that § 21.031 is presumptively "irrational" because it has the effect of imposing "penalties" on "innocent" children. * * * However, the Equal Protection Clause does not preclude legislators from classifying among persons on the basis of fac-

tors and characteristics over which individuals may be said to lack "control." Indeed, in some circumstances persons generally, and children in particular, may have little control over or responsibility for such things as their ill-health, need for public assistance, or place of residence. Yet a state legislature is not barred from considering, for example, relevant differences between the mentally-healthy and the mentally-ill, or between the residents of different counties, simply because these may be factors unrelated to individual choice or to any "wrongdoing." The Equal Protection Clause protects against arbitrary and irrational classifications, and against invidious discrimination stemming from prejudice and hostility; it is not an all-encompassing "equalizer" designed to eradicate every distinction for which persons are not "responsible."

The Court does not presume to suggest that appellees' purported lack of culpability for their illegal status prevents them from being deported or otherwise "penalized" under federal law. Yet would deportation be any less a "penalty" than denial of privileges provided to legal residents? Illegality of presence in the United States does not—and need not—depend on some amorphous concept of "guilt" or "innocence" concerning an alien's entry. Similarly, a State's use of federal immigration status as a basis for legislative classification is not necessarily rendered suspect for its failure to take such factors into account.

* * *

The second strand of the Court's analysis rests on the premise that, although public education is not a constitutionally-guaranteed right, "neither is it merely some governmental 'benefit' indistinguishable from other forms of social welfare legislation." * * * Whatever meaning or relevance this opaque observation might have in some other context, it simply has no bearing on the issues at hand. Indeed, it is never made clear what the Court's opinion means on this score.

The importance of education is beyond dispute. Yet we have held repeatedly that the importance of a governmental service does not elevate it to the status of a "fundamental right" for purposes of equal protection analysis. San Antonio School District v. Rodriguez, 411 U.S. 1, 30–31, 93 S.Ct. 1278, 1295 (1973); Lindsey v. Normet, 405 U.S. 56, 73–74, 92 S.Ct. 862, 874 (1972). In San Antonio School District, supra, Justice Powell, speaking for the Court, expressly rejected the proposition that state laws dealing with public education are subject to special scrutiny under the Equal Protection Clause. Moreover, the Court points to no meaningful way to distinguish between education and other governmental benefits in this context. Is the Court suggesting that education is more "fundamental" than food, shelter, or medical care?

The Equal Protection Clause guarantees similar treatment of similarly situated persons, but it does not mandate a constitutional hierarchy of governmental services. Justice Powell, speaking for the Court in San Antonio School District, supra, 411 U.S., at 31, 93 S.Ct., at 1295, put it well in stating that to the extent this Court raises or lowers the degree of "judicial scrutiny" in equal protection cases according to a transient Court majority's view of the societal importance of the interest affected, we "assum[e] a legislative role and one for which the Court lacks both authority and competence." Yet

that is precisely what the Court does today. * * *

The central question in these cases, as in every equal protection case not involving truly fundamental rights "explicitly or implicitly guaranteed by the Constitution," San Antonio School District, supra, 411 U.S. at 33–34, 93 S.Ct., at 1296–1297, is whether there is some legitimate basis for a legislative distinction between different classes of persons. The fact that the distinction is drawn in legislation affecting access to public education—as opposed to legislation allocating other important governmental benefits, such as public assistance, health care, or housing—cannot make a difference in the level of scrutiny applied.

Once it is conceded—as the Court does—that illegal aliens are not a suspect class, and that education is not a fundamental right, our inquiry should focus on and be limited to whether the legislative classification at issue bears a rational relationship to a legitimate state purpose. Vance v. Bradley, 440 U.S. 93, 97, 99 S.Ct. 939, 942 (1979); Dandridge v. Williams, 397 U.S. 471, 485–487, 90 S.Ct. 1153, 1161–1162 (1970). * * *

The State contends primarily that § 21.031 serves to prevent undue depletion of its limited revenues available for education, and to preserve the fiscal integrity of the State's school financing system against an ever-increasing flood of illegal aliens—aliens over whose entry or continued presence it has no control. Of course such fiscal concerns alone could not justify discrimination against a suspect class or an arbitrary and irrational denial of benefits to a particular group of persons. Yet I assume no member of this Court would argue that prudent conservation of finite state revenues is per se an illegitimate goal. Indeed, the numerous classifications this Court has sustained in social welfare legislation were invariably related to the limited amount of revenues available to spend on any given program or set of programs. See, e.g., Jefferson v. Hackney, 406 U.S. 535, 549–551, 92 S.Ct. 1724, 1733–1734 (1972); Dandridge v. Williams, 397 U.S. 471, 487, 90 S.Ct. 1153, 1162 (1970). The significant question here is whether the requirement of tuition from illegal aliens who attend the public schools—as well as from residents of other States, for example—is a rational and reasonable means of furthering the State's legitimate fiscal ends.

Without laboring what will undoubtedly seem obvious to many, it simply is not "irrational" for a State to conclude that it does not have the same responsibility to provide benefits for persons whose very presence in the State and this country is illegal as it does to provide for persons lawfully present. By definition, illegal aliens have no right whatever to be here, and the State may reasonably, and constitutionally, elect not to provide them with governmental services at the expense of those who are lawfully in the State. In DeCanas v. Bica, 424 U.S. 351, 357, 96 S.Ct. 933, 937 (1976), we held that a State may protect its "fiscal interests and lawfully resident labor force from the deleterious effects on its economy resulting from the employment of illegal aliens." And only recently this Court made clear that a State has a legitimate interest in protecting and preserving the quality of its schools and "the right of its own *bona fide residents* to attend such institutions on a preferential tuition basis." Vlandis v. Kline, 412 U.S. 441, 452–453, 93 S.Ct. 2230, 2236–2237 (1973) (emphasis added).   *   *   *

The Court has failed to offer even a plausible explanation why illegality of residence in this country is not a factor that may legitimately bear upon the bona fides of state residence and entitlement to the benefits of lawful residence.

It is significant that the federal government has seen fit to exclude illegal aliens from numerous social welfare programs, such as the food stamp program,   *   *   *   the old age assistance, aid to families with dependent children, aid to the blind, aid to the permanently and totally disabled, and supplemental security income programs,   *   *   *   the medicare hospital insurance benefits program,   *   *   *   and the medicaid hospital insurance benefits for the aged and disabled program.   *   *   * Although these exclusions do not conclusively demonstrate the constitutionality of the State's use of the same classification for comparable purposes, at the very least they tend to support the rationality of excluding illegal alien residents of a State from such programs so as to preserve the State's finite revenues for the benefit of lawful residents. *   *   *

The Court maintains—as if this were the issue—that "barring undocumented children from local schools would not necessarily improve the quality of education provided in those schools."   *   *   * However, the legitimacy of barring illegal aliens from programs such as medicare or medicaid does not depend on a showing that the barrier would "improve the quality" of medical care given to persons lawfully entitled to participate in such programs. Modern education, like medical care, is enormously expensive, and there can be no doubt that very large added costs will fall on the State or its local school districts as a result of the inclusion of illegal aliens in the tuition-free public schools. The State may, in its discretion, use any savings resulting from its tuition requirement to "improve the quality of education" in the public school system, or to enhance the funds available for other social programs, or to reduce the tax burden placed on its residents; each of these ends is "legitimate." The State need not show, as the Court implies, that the incremental cost of educating illegal aliens will send it into bankruptcy, or have a "grave impact on the quality of education" * * *; that is not dispositive under a "rational basis" scrutiny. In the absence of a constitutional imperative to provide for the education of illegal aliens, the State may "rationally" choose to take advantage of whatever savings will accrue from limiting access to the tuition-free public schools to its own lawful residents, excluding even citizens of neighboring States.

Denying a free education to illegal alien children is not a choice I would make were I a legislator. Apart from compassionate considerations, the long-range costs of excluding any children from the public schools may well outweigh the costs of educating them. But that is not the issue; the fact that there are sound *policy* arguments against the Texas legislature's choice does not render that choice an unconstitutional one.

The Constitution does not provide a cure for every social ill, nor does it vest judges with a mandate to try to remedy every social problem. * * * Moreover, when this Court rushes in to remedy what it perceives to be the failings of the political processes, it deprives those processes of an opportunity to function. When the political institutions are not forced to exercise constitutionally allocated powers and responsibilities, those powers, like muscles not used, tend to atrophy. Today's cases, I regret to say, present yet another example of unwarranted judicial action which in the long run tends to contribute to the weakening of our political processes.

Congress, "vested by the Constitution with the responsibility of protecting our borders and legislating with respect to aliens," * * * bears primary responsibility for addressing the problems occasioned by the millions of illegal aliens flooding across our southern border. Similarly, it is for Congress, and not this Court, to assess the "social costs borne by our Nation when select groups are denied the means to absorb the values and skills upon which our social order rests." * * * While the "specter of a permanent caste" of illegal Mexican residents of the United States is indeed a disturbing one, * * * it is but one segment of a larger problem, which is for the political branches to solve. I find it difficult to believe that Congress would long tolerate such a self-destructive result—that it would fail to deport these illegal alien families or to provide for the education of their children. Yet instead of allowing the political processes to run their course—albeit with some delay—the Court seeks to do Congress' job for it, compensating for congressional inaction. It is not unreasonable to think that this encourages the political branches to pass their problems to the judiciary.

The solution to this seemingly intractable problem is to defer to the political processes, unpalatable as that may be to some.

Chapter 10

Due Process of Law

Despite the fairly widespread acclaim which federalism received for the diversity and experimentation it fostered in the innovation of political institutions and in the design of public policy, particularly social legislation, decentralization was seen by many observers as much less desirable when it came to the administration of the law or the preservation of important personal rights. Deference to the discretion of state legislatures in these realms at least was thought to be incompatible with any notion of justice—a concept which, after all, is commonly thought of as a universal and not a relative proposition. [In search of minimal constitutional standards capable of transcending state boundaries, attention naturally came to be focused on the provisions of the first eight amendments.]

a. Due Process and the Federal System: The Selective Incorporation of the Bill of Rights into the Fourteenth Amendment

In 1833, when it first encountered the argument that the Bill of Rights applied to limit acts of the states as well as those of the national government, the Supreme Court emphatically rejected the overture. Speaking for a unanimous Court in *Barron* v. *The Mayor and City Council of Baltimore* (p. 919), Chief Justice Marshall held that it was clear from the wording and intent in passage of the amendments that their provisions were directed against infringement by the national government only. For reliance on the protection of basic liberties at the state level, one had to look to the provisions of the individual state constitutions. Moreover, this position remained unchallenged until the ratification of the Fourteenth Amendment in 1868 reopened the possibility of circumscribing the reserved powers of the states with minimal constitutional guarantees.

902

The Fourteenth Amendment presented two significant possibilities for altering the existing balance of the federal system by enlarging substantive limitations on the exercise of state power. Both of these prospective vehicles were contained in consecutive clauses of section 1 of the amendment which provided: "No State shall make or enforce any law which shall abridge the privileges or immunities of citizens of the United States; nor shall any State deprive any person of life, liberty or property, without due process of law * * *." The post-Civil War Court, however, unenthusiastic about the potential for radically changing the federal system, took a narrow view of these provisions. To begin with, its 1873 decision in *Butchers' Benevolent Ass'n* v. *Crescent City Livestock Landing & Slaughterhouse Co.* (The Slaughterhouse Cases) (p. 632) virtually emasculated the Privileges and Immunities Clause. Invited to recognize the existence of certain substantive national rights, among them the right to practice one's lawful occupation, the majority emerged from its reading of the amendment with a remarkably conservative interpretation. Speaking for five of the Justices, Justice Miller ascribed a narrow purpose to the postwar amendments—the guarantee of freedom for blacks (and presumably for other minorities as well) within the existing federal context. He emphatically rejected the proposition that the Privileges and Immunities Clause was intended to impose specific substantive rights as a concomitance of state as well as national citizenship. Instead, the Clause was perceived as maintaining the phenomenon of dual citizenship with the proviso that a given state not discriminate among any of the people coming within its borders whatever their place of residence. As we noted in Chapter 9, the dissenters in *Slaughterhouse* were perhaps less concerned with the use of the Privileges and Immunities Clause to extend the scope of civil liberties generally than they were in the immediate vindication of certain economic interests.

A second possibility for underwriting a national guarantee of personal rights appeared in the Due Process Clause. You will recall in this connection that the Court's initial involvement with this clause gave rise to the creation of certain substantive economic rights, notably the liberty of contract, which were used to circumscribe the content of state regulatory policy. Beyond this concern with the quality of state economic policy, the Court saw the Due Process Clause as only a very general guarantee of procedural fairness in the legal process at the state level—a point forcefully articulated by a nearly unanimous Court in *Hurtado* v. *California* (p. 921) in 1884. Speaking for the majority, Justice Matthews sustained the constitutionality of California's substitution of indictment by information in place of indictment by grand jury as consistent with assuring the fundamental value of fairly treating those individuals accused of crime embodied in the evolution of Anglo-American legal institutions. The significance of the *Hurtado* decision and those in two cases which followed, Maxwell v. Dow, 176 U.S. 581, 20 S.Ct. 448 (1900) (in which the Court sustained the constitutionality of a Utah law providing for trial before an eight instead of a twelve-man jury) and Twining v. State of New Jersey, 211 U.S. 78, 29 S.Ct. 14 (1908) (in which the Court sustained as constitutional the act of a state trial judge drawing attention to the fact that two defendants in an embezzlement case had refused to testify on their own behalf), was that they defined due process of law as equivalent to fundamental fairness and applied this standard on a case-by-case basis to evaluate the totality of procedures by which government treated the individual in the criminal justice process.

More modern expressions of this same case-by-case fairness or balancing approach appear in Justice Frankfurter's opinions in *Adamson* v. *California* (p. 929) and *Rochin* v. *California* (p. 934) and in the opinions of Justice John Harlan, Jr. The fairness standard implicit in "the law of the land" reference in *Hurtado* becomes explicit in *Rochin's* proscription of "conduct that shocks the conscience" and which "offend[s] the community's sense of fair play and decency." Such a standard typifies the balancers' wide regard for the necessity of judicial discretion and flexibility and for all possible deference to the federal relationship.

Dissenting alone in *Hurtado, Maxwell,* and *Twining* was Justice John Harlan, Sr. What distinguished Harlan's reading of the Due Process Clause from that of his contemporaries was his insistence that the word "liberty" was intended to be a shorthand reference to the protections contained in the Bill of Rights. To Harlan, the whole import of the Fourteenth Amendment was to undo *Barron* v. *Baltimore* and the ante-bellum federal system and to nationalize the substantive guarantees of personal liberty contained in the first eight amendments. Such a total incorporation of the provisions of the Bill of Rights into the Fourteenth Amendment by way of the Due Process Clause would not only make them applicable against state infringement, it would also simultaneously incorporate any interpretation of those amendments.

The total incorporation approach was taken up several decades later by Justice Hugo Black, notably in his dissenting opinion to the Supreme Court's decision in *Adamson* v. *California* (p. 929). In this now classic opinion, Black reacted sharply to what he saw as the unbridled discretion and resulting arbitrariness inherent in the case-by-case fairness approach. To bolster the argument for total and literal incorporation of the Bill of Rights through the Due Process Clause, Black, in an appendix to his opinion, examined extensively numerous historical materials with the aim of showing that it was the intention of the Framers of the Fourteenth Amendment so to incorporate the first eight amendments and apply them to the states. Assuming that discovery of the Framers' intention is both possible and relevant—matters far from settled—Black's reading of the proceedings of the Thirty-ninth Congress which proposed the amendment and statements of several backers of the amendment are bolstered by the conclusions of Professor Horace Flack in his book, *The Adoption of the Fourteenth Amendment* (1908). Black's analysis, however, has been severely challenged as deliberately distorted by Harvard law professor Charles Fairman in his article, "Does the Fourteenth Amendment Incorporate the Bill of Rights? The Original Understanding" (2 Stanford Law Review 5 [1949]) and by other scholars.

Black reiterated the total incorporation position he espoused in *Adamson* continually during his remaining tenure on the Court, as his opinions in *Rochin* v. *California* (p. 934) and *Duncan* v. *Louisiana* (p. 937) illustrate. Moreover, faithful adherence to this absolute position led Black to dissent in *Griswold* v. *Connecticut* (p. 1192) in 1965 when the majority began to reach out and incorporate fundamental personal rights not contained in the Bill of Rights. In his view the incorporation of more than the first eight amendments was fully as fraught with unbounded discretion, and therefore was fully as obnoxious, as the incorporation of less.

Ultimately, a majority on the Court came to accept a compromise between no incorporation and total incorporation. Known as "selective incorporation," this eclectic approach to resolving the conflict between nationalized protection of specific individual rights and the federal system was first enunciated by Justice Cardozo speaking for the Court in *Palko* v. *Connecticut* (p. 926) in 1937. What this approach entailed, essentially, was a selective nationalization of portions of the Bill of Rights, the incorporation of a given right dependent upon whether it was "found to be implicit in the concept of ordered liberty * * *." Absorption of those rights implicit in national citizenship through the Due Process Clause of the Fourteenth Amendment on the basis "that neither liberty nor justice would exist if they were sacrificed" had the advantage over total incorporation of guaranteeing fundamental personal rights, such as free speech, without imposing on the states frivolous requirements, such as providing the option of a jury trial in all civil suits involving twenty dollars or more, and it confined the sweeping discretion inherent in the case-by-case fairness approach by permanently incorporating whole fundamental rights and imposing them alike at both the national and state levels. Such a pragmatic approach, however, lacked any historical justification and was alternately assailed for its imprecision and rigidity. Nevertheless, by a slow and evolutionary process of picking and choosing, largely dependent on the composition of the Court, individual liberties one by one were read into the Fourteenth Amendment. As is evident from the steps in the absorption process, set out in the following chart, the Court first included those Fifth Amendment protections restricting government's exercise of the power of eminent domain, a focus consistent with its initial enthusiasm for protecting economic liberties and property rights shown in so many of its constitutional rulings before 1937. Next, the spotlight on incorporation shifts to First Amendment rights, the absorption of which appears to be roughly coincident with the emergence of the preferred freedoms approach. And, rounding out the list of rights included, is the substantial body of procedural guarantees secured by the Warren Court as essential to insuring fair treatment of individuals accused of crime. By the end of the 1960s, not only had the body of incorporated rights swollen but several early decisions against the absorption of certain rights were reversed. For example, the initial position taken in both the *Twining* and *Adamson* cases that the right against self-incrimination was not applicable against state infringement was reversed by the Warren Court in *Malloy* v. *Hogan* (p. 993) and *Murphy* v. *Waterfront Com'n of New York Harbor* (p. 995) in 1964. The Warren Court also overturned the ruling in the *Palko* case with its 1969 decision in *Benton* v. *Maryland* which absorbed into the Fourteenth Amendment the guarantee against double jeopardy.

THE PROCESS OF SELECTIVE INCORPORATION

Provision	Amendment	Year	Case
"Public use" and "just compensation" conditions in the taking of private property by government	V	1896 and 1897	Missouri Pacific Railway Co. v. Nebraska, 164 U.S. 403, 17 S.Ct. 130; Chicago, Burlington & Quincy Railway Co. v. Chicago, 166 U.S. 226, 17 S.Ct. 581
Freedom of speech	I	1927	Fiske v. Kansas, 274 U.S. 380, 47 S.Ct. 655; Gitlow v. New York, 268 U.S. 652, 45 S.Ct. 625 (1925) (dictum only); Gilbert v. Minnesota, 254 U.S. 325, 41 S.Ct. 125 (1920) (dictum only)
Freedom of the press	I	1931	Near v. Minnesota, 283 U.S. 697, 51 S.Ct. 625
Fair trial and right to counsel in capital cases	VI	1932	Powell v. Alabama, 287 U.S. 45, 53 S.Ct. 55
Freedom of religion	I	1934	Hamilton v. Regents of Univ. of California, 293 U.S. 245, 55 S.Ct. 197 (dictum only)
Freedom of assembly and, by implication, freedom to petition for redress of grievances	I	1937	DeJonge v. Oregon, 299 U.S. 353, 57 S.Ct. 255
Free exercise of religious belief	I	1940	Cantwell v. Connecticut, 310 U.S. 296, 60 S.Ct. 900
Separation of church and state; right against the establishment of religion	I	1947	Everson v. Board of Educ., 330 U.S. 1, 67 S.Ct. 504
Right to public trial	VI	1948	In re Oliver, 333 U.S. 257, 68 S.Ct. 499
Right against unreasonable searches and seizures	IV	1949	Wolf v. Colorado, 338 U.S. 25, 69 S.Ct. 1359
Freedom of association	I	1958	NAACP v. Alabama, 357 U.S. 449, 78 S.Ct. 1163
Exclusionary rule as concomitant of unreasonable searches and seizures	IV	1961	Mapp v. Ohio, 367 U.S. 643, 81 S.Ct. 1684
Right against cruel and unusual punishments	VIII	1962	Robinson v. California, 370 U.S. 660, 82 S.Ct. 1417
Right to counsel in all felony cases	VI	1963	Gideon v. Wainwright, 372 U.S. 335, 83 S.Ct. 792

SELECTIVE INCORPORATION (*Cont.*)

Provision	Amendment	Year	Case
Right against self-incrimination	V	1964	Malloy v. Hogan, 378 U.S. 1, 84 S.Ct. 1489; Murphy v. Waterfront Com'n, 378 U.S. 52, 84 S.Ct. 1594
Right to confront witnesses	VI	1965	Pointer v. Texas, 380 U.S. 400, 85 S.Ct. 1065
Right to privacy	Various	1965	Griswold v. Connecticut, 381 U.S. 479, 85 S.Ct. 1678
Right to impartial jury	VI	1966	Parker v. Gladden, 385 U.S. 363, 87 S.Ct. 468
Right to speedy trial	VI	1967	Klopfer v. North Carolina, 386 U.S. 213, 87 S.Ct. 988
Right to compulsory process for obtaining witnesses	VI	1967	Washington v. Texas, 388 U.S. 14, 87 S.Ct. 1920
Right to jury trial in cases of serious crime	VI	1968	Duncan v. Louisiana, 391 U.S. 145, 88 S.Ct. 1444
Right against double jeopardy	V	1969	Benton v. Maryland, 395 U.S. 784, 89 S.Ct. 2056
Right to counsel in all criminal cases entailing a jail term	VI	1972	Argersinger v. Hamlin, 407 U.S. 25, 92 S.Ct. 2006

Other Incorporated Provisions

Right of petition	I	Included by implication of other First Amendment incorporations
Right to be informed of the nature and cause of the accusation	VI	Included by implication of other Sixth Amendment incorporations

	Amendment	Provision(s) Not Incorporated
Provisions of the First Eight Amendments Not Incorporated	II	All
	III	All
	V	Right to indictment by grand jury
	VII	All
	VIII	Right against excessive bail; right against excessive fines

A fourth approach to the incorporation issue is illustrated by Justice Murphy's dissenting opinion in the *Adamson* case. Speaking for Justice Rutledge and himself, Murphy argued for a "total incorporation plus" position. Succinctly put, this school of thought would agree with Black that all of the provisions of the Bill of Rights should be read into the Fourteenth Amendment supplemented by the absorption of any other fundamental liberties which, though not contained in the first eight amendments, are necessary to "a scheme of ordered liberty." Judging by his concurrence in Justice Black's *Adamson* dissent and his authorship of the majority opinion in the *Griswold* case eighteen years later, Justice Douglas could also be presumed to reflect the "total incorporation plus" philosophy. As an examination of the cases reproduced in this chapter tends to show, the Court's selective approach to absorbing the provisions of the first eight amendments plus the *Griswold* holding has not meant so much the acceptance of the "total incorporation plus" position so much as it has reflected a trend toward "selective incorporation plus."

The most recent round of the incorporation debate was occasioned by litigation in the aftermath of the Court's 1968 holding in *Duncan* v. *Louisiana* (p. 937) that defendants charged at the state level with serious crimes were constitutionally entitled to trial by jury. In *Williams* v. *Florida* (p. 943) and *Apodaca* v. *Oregon* (p. 949) four years later, the Burger Court held respectively that the Sixth Amendment, though absorbing the jury option in certain criminal proceedings, did not guarantee either the traditional twelve-man jury or the requirement that decisions of such bodies had to be unanimous to be decisive. Presumably, these modifications in the jury trial guarantee resulted in part from the obvious burdens in cost and delay that would have fallen on the states had unanimous decision by a twelve-man common-law jury been required. This ostensible retreat from the existing assumption that the Sixth Amendment's reference to a jury trial embodied the common-law understanding led Justice John Harlan, Jr. in particular, as an advocate of the case-by-case fairness approach, to wonder if the Court, now stuck with the incorporation of the jury trial guarantee in *Duncan*, was not engaging in the very destructive practice of watering down federal rights to escape from the "incorporationist straightjacket." In your view, does the merit of such criticism justify reversion to the case-by-case fairness approach as an acceptable alternative to the various modes of incorporation, all of which possess the common feature of absorbing rights whole and applying them alike at the national and state levels? Be sure to consider Justice Black's rejoinder at p. 945 where he states that the Court's decision in *Williams* "is in no way attributable to any desire to dilute the Sixth Amendment in order more easily to apply it to the States" and warns that rather "the danger of diluting the Bill of Rights protections lies * * * in the 'shock the conscience' test on which my Brother Harlan would rely instead—a test which depends, not on the language of the Constitution, but solely on the views of a majority of the Court as to what is 'fair' and 'decent.' "

b. The Right to Counsel

Few of us would deny that all but the most gifted and exceptional defendants are ill-equipped to defend themselves in a criminal prosecution. The maze of procedures and technicalities which govern the criminal justice process has long been recognized as demanding the skills of a trained lawyer to preserve some parity between the state and the individual so that the defendant can be given a meaningful chance to tell his side of the story. Giving the defendant "his day in court" is of the essence of due process of law. Interestingly enough, however, it was not until 1932, in one of the celebrated Scottsboro cases, *Powell* v. *Alabama* (p. 954), that the Supreme Court began to speak of any constitutional right to a fair trial which defendants possessed. While there were many breaches from a full and fair observance of the criminal justice process—violations of such magnitude as to reduce the proceedings against the Scottsboro defendants to a travesty—the Court zeroed in on the effective denial of counsel as particularly offensive. By recognizing "the fundamental nature" of the right to counsel "at least in cases like the present," *Powell* is commonly thought to have partially incorporated the Sixth Amendment right, insofar, that is, as it was deemed essential to insuring the fairness of trials in capital cases.

In cases subsequent to *Powell*, the Court went on to hold in Johnson v. Zerbst, 304 U.S. 458, 58 S.Ct. 1019 (1938), that the Sixth Amendment's specific guarantee of counsel applied to *all federal* cases, but in Betts v. Brady, 316 U.S. 455, 62 S.Ct. 1252 (1942), it refused to recognize any constitutionally guaranteed right to counsel in state prosecutions of noncapital felonies, saying "[t]he due process clause of the Fourteenth Amendment does not incorporate, as such, the specific guarantees found in the Sixth Amendment," though on a case-by-case basis, denial of any guarantee contained in the first eight amendments might be so fundamentally unfair as "to deprive a litigant of due process of law in violation of the Fourteenth." This dichotomy of constitutionally assuring the right to counsel for defendants accused of crimes the sentence for which could take away their lives and denying it in trials for lesser crimes, no matter how serious, persisted until the mid-1960s despite the fact that this criterion had been eroded in several succeeding cases as a basis for distinguishing the scope of constitutional rights (e.g., see Uveges v. Pennsylvania, 335 U.S. 437, 69 S.Ct. 184 [1948] and Reid v. Covert, 354 U.S. 1, 77 S.Ct. 1222 [1957]).

The expansion of the right to counsel that came with the overruling of *Betts* v. *Brady* in 1963 took two paths. The path of least resistance was the growth of the right to counsel within the courtroom itself. Speaking for a unanimous Court in *Gideon* v. *Wainwright* (p. 957), Justice Black announced the demise of the *Betts* doctrine and held instead that the right to counsel extended to the state level to include indigent defendants in all felony prosecutions. Nine years later in *Argersinger* v. *Hamlin* (p. 960), the Court further extended the Sixth Amendment's guarantee of counsel to any defendant without funds being tried for an offense the sentence for which carried a jail term. By the early 'seventies, then, the indigent defendant's right to have counsel provided for him at trial extended to all but petty offenses at the state level.

The right to counsel at trial, no matter how liberal its sweep in terms of the offenses at issue, is unlikely to be very meaningful, however, if the most crucial phase of the proceedings has already taken place. Since defendants often emerged from secret, pretrial interrogation by the police having made statements implicating themselves in a crime or having signed confessions admitting guilt, the Warren Court developed an understandable suspicion that these covert proceedings preyed upon the fear and ignorance of suspects and were used to amass a case against the defendant with the result that the guarantee of counsel at trial became a sham. Striving to maintain the integrity of the adversary system outside the courtroom as well as within, a majority on the Court expanded the right to counsel in a second direction—to include the critical investigative phases of the criminal justice process. Speaking for the Court in disposing of *Escobedo* v. *Illinois* (p. 965) the Term following *Gideon*, Justice Goldberg announced that the right to have counsel present would adhere whenever "the investigation is no longer a general inquiry into an unsolved crime but has begun to focus on a particular suspect * * *." Two years later the Court bolstered the *Escobedo* ruling in *Miranda* v. *Arizona* (p. 969) with a set of specific requirements governing pretrial questioning. These included standards imposing necessary warnings which the defendant must receive, ground rules for the conduct of interrogation, provision for the appointment of counsel in case of indigence, and understandings pertaining to the defendant's waiver of rights. By formulating these constitutional requirements, the majority of Justices on the Warren Court sought to transform the prevailing inquisitorial operation of the criminal justice process to fit the adversary model commanded by the Sixth Amendment.

Expansion of the right to counsel to pretrial investigative operations evoked considerable controversy and resistance. Critics on and off the Bench assailed the *Escobedo* and *Miranda* decisions for impairing effective law enforcement. To those concerned about the preservation of "law and order," the Warren Court's decisions inequitably balanced the contending interests of personal rights and public safety too heavily in favor of the former. The spiraling crime rate and large-scale civil disorders of the late 'sixties intensified these misgivings. Fresh from what it read as a conservative mandate in the 1968 election, the Nixon Administration sought to halt and trim the expansive policies of the Warren Court, particularly in the area of criminal procedure, by naming to the Court Justices who would echo the values of the dissenters in *Escobedo* and *Miranda*. By 1972, the administration had availed itself of four such opportunities, and the result was a tribunal which differed substantially from the outlook of the Warren Court.

A typical example of the difference in emphasis between the Warren and Burger Courts on the matter of expanding the right to counsel in pretrial proceedings appears in a comparison of cases bearing on the right to have counsel present at pretrial line-ups. Concerned about the possibility of prejudice resulting from irregularities in the use of "line-ups" or "show-ups" during which witnesses are asked to identify suspects in criminal investigations, the Warren Court in 1967, in *Wade* v. *United States* (p. 977) (and a companion state case, *Gilbert* v. *California*) held that an accused may not be exhibited to prosecution witnesses in advance of trial in the absence of the defendant's lawyer and that, if testimony offered at trial is tainted by participation in such an illicit identification, the evidence must be held inadmissible. The effect of the *Wade-Gilbert* rule was significantly curtailed by the Burger Court five years later in *Kirby* v. *Illinois* (p. 982) when, in a 5–4 decision, the new majority refused to extend it to pretrial line-ups which took place *before* the accused had been indicted.

c. Confessions and Self-Incrimination

The principal reason for guaranteeing the right to counsel when criminal investigations reach the accusatory stage is to insure that the defendant will not be forced to incriminate himself. The requirement that government establish the guilt of the accused beyond a reasonable doubt and without compelling him to produce the incriminating evidence himself—the foundation of the adversary system—is premised on the fundamental value in our society of protecting the integrity of the individual. That fundamental value is violated when law enforcement officers coerce the defendant into making incriminating statements or signing a confession.

It is important to understand that this basic value of respect for the individual, regardless of the crime for which he is accused and until he is convicted, is *the basic value* which governs our criminal procedures. Of course we strive to reconstruct the truth concerning the commission of a crime as accurately as we can and properly to assign responsibility for it, but learning the truth is not the ultimate value. If it were, we surely would not try to reconstruct it by letting two, often highly charged partisans, the prosecutor and the defense counsel—frequently by deliberate distortion, cunning, and emotion—endeavor to persuade a jury composed of individuals of only average knowledge and intelligence. If all we wanted were the truth, we would shoot the defendant full of truth serum and let him tell us. That we choose the adversary system *despite* its telltale deficiencies in reconstructing the truth tells us that we regard reliable fact finding as an important, but secondary value. The fundamental purpose apparent in the design of the adversary system is to assure the defense countervailing powers to equalize the awesome resources which the state can bring to bear in a criminal prosecution.

The fundamental quality of the Fifth Amendment right against self-incrimination was recognized by the Supreme Court in two cases, *Malloy* v. *Hogan* (p. 993) and *Murphy* v. *Waterfront Com'n of New York Harbor* (p. 995) in 1964 when it incorporated the guarantee into the Fourteenth Amendment. To incorporate a right, however, is not necessarily to define it, and we have to have some idea of what it is that the amendment forbids the state from compelling as distinguished from other types of evidence which the state might legitimately demand. The Court's 1966 decision in *Schmerber* v. *California* (p. 1003) appears instructive on this point. Speaking for a bare majority, Justice Brennan distinguished between situations in which a defendant was forced verbally to incriminate himself in the sense of admitting guilt and situations in which marks or material were taken from him for identification purposes (e.g., fingerprinting, photographing, participation in line-ups) or to prevent the dissipation of evidence (e.g., taking a blood test). Consider the problem in *California* v. *Byers* (p. 1007). Is the distinction between testimonial and nontestimonial compulsion more satisfying in the abstract than in the context of concrete problems such as the constitutionality of a state "hit and run" statute? Why?

Regardless of how one settles the problem of drawing a line between what constitute identifying marks and what constitute verbal admissions of guilt, one conclusion is unmistakable, and it is that coerced confessions violate the Fifth and Fourteenth Amendments. But what is it that marks a confession as coerced? As the Court tells us in *Rogers* v. *Richmond* (p. 992), the legitimacy of a confession is not based upon its reliability or trustworthiness, but its *voluntariness*. Yet, how will we know whether admissions of guilt or incriminating statements were not made voluntarily?

The answer to this question inheres in several factors which often appear in cases where a lawyer has not been present during pretrial interrogation and which render a confession obtained under those circumstances highly suspect. One of these elements is an unreasonable delay in arraignment, that is an excessive lapse of time between the point at which an accused is taken into custody and the point at which he is brought before a magistrate, formally apprised of the charges against him, and asked to state his plea. As the Court in *Mallory* v. *United States* (p. 986) indicates, a confession obtained during an unreasonably long delay in getting the accused before a magistrate is presumed to be coerced and, thus, is inadmissible. The holding in *Mallory*, however, applies only to the federal courts since it was based on the statutory power of the Supreme Court to supervise federal law enforcement procedures; it is not a constitutional requirement.

A second circumstance which taints a confession is lengthy interrogation. In Ashcraft v. Tennessee, 322 U.S. 143, 64 S.Ct. 921 (1944), the Court held that thirty-six hours of relay questioning was inherently coercive, and in Watts v. Indiana, 338 U.S. 49, 69 S.Ct. 1347, five years later, the Court held that five days of noncontinuous interrogation was likewise unconstitutional.

As indicated by the Court in *Spano* v. *New York* (p. 988), a confession must be the result of "free and rational choice." Very little pressure applied by the police is too much pressure. This does not mean that interrogators may not resort to trickery in dealing with the accused, but it does mean that when the police engage in deceit, they are on unsteady ground. Mere trickery will not taint a confession, but trickery which causes coercion will, and, in the absence of counsel, substantial use of tricks by the police is constitutionally risky. Trickery aside, incriminating statements made, for example, by the defendant in *Mincey* v. *Arizona* (p. 1100) also violate the principle of voluntariness necessary to effect a waiver of one's right to silence when those statements are obtained through relentless interrogation of a painfully wounded and intermittently conscious suspect.

Inducements to confess are likewise unconstitutional because they violate the "free and rational choice" test. Thus, in Haynes v. Washington, 373 U.S. 503, 83 S.Ct. 1336 (1963), the Court vacated the conviction of the defendant for robbery because he was held incommunicado and told that he could not call his wife until after he had made a confession. In Lynumn v. Illinois, 372 U.S. 528, 83 S.Ct. 917, the same year, the Court also set aside the conviction of a woman defendant prosecuted for unlawful possession of marijuana when she was induced to confess by threats that she would lose custody of her children and that welfare checks would be cut off. Finally, as a third example of inducement to confess, the Minnesota Supreme Court in State v. Biron, 266 Minn. 272, 123 N.W.2d 392 (1963), held that where police officers coaxed the eighteen-year-old defendant to confess to a purse snatching which culminated in the death of the victim by holding out to him the prospect of keeping the case in juvenile court (as opposed to the regular trial court), the admission of guilt was not voluntary. However, a guilty plea to a reduced charge, entered subsequent to bargaining between the prosecution and the defense, was held in Brady v. United States, 397 U.S. 742, 90 S.Ct. 1463 (1970), not to be induced. Though the courts will not interfere to upset such pleas, provided they are "intelligible" and "voluntary" and after the defendant has consulted with his lawyer, the courts will intervene on the defendant's side if the state does not keep its part of the bargain. See Santobello v. New York, 404 U.S. 257, 92 S.Ct. 495 (1971).

Consistent with the preferred position accorded the right against self-incrimination in *Malloy* v. *Hogan*, if a defendant repudiates his confession at trial, alleging coercion, the burden, as *Miranda* v. *Arizona* (p. 969) states, is on the state to show otherwise. Moreover, not only is a tainted confession to be excluded, but any evidence obtained from leads acquired as a result of that confession is likewise tainted and, hence, inadmissible.

But does the exclusionary rule mandate the suppression of incriminating statements made by the defendant in all circumstances where there has been some deficiency in giving the *Miranda* warnings or where, after indicating his wish first to speak with an attorney, the defendant has been prevailed upon to make some damaging admissions? Recent decisions by the Burger Court, such as *Oregon* v. *Hass* (p. 997), say that while such statements may not be admitted as evidence directly bearing on the defendant's guilt, inculpatory statements made to the police by the accused in such circumstances legitimately may be offered for the purpose of impeaching the credibility of trial testimony given by him on his own behalf and thought to be perjured. (As the decision in *Doyle* v. *Ohio* (p. 1001) establishes, though, cross-examining the defendant about his silence at the time of arrest is out of bounds.) The Court's opinion in *Hass* is also noteworthy for at least three other reasons: first, it stands as another example of the efforts of the Burger Court to circumscribe important Warren Court rulings on criminal procedure. Second, the justification presented in the Court's opinion reflects the greater emphasis given by the present Court to the attainment of truth as the overarching goal of the criminal trial and thus reveals a tendency to evaluate the admissibility of evidence in terms of its trustworthiness or reliability. Finally, *Hass* is a superb example of a new appreciation by the Court's liberal wing of deference to decisions possibly made on state constitutional grounds where, as here, such readings of state constitutional provisions afford a basis for maintaining generous interpretations of constitutional rights in the face of tightening federal constitutional standards at the hands of the majority dominating the Burger Court.

d. Procedural Guarantees and the Administrative Process

In a sense the creation of a separate heading under which to present an overview of due process problems in the administrative process is redundant because we have been looking at judicial efforts to control the police under the last two headings, and the police are nothing if not a law enforcement bureaucracy. Yet, our focus is somewhat different for here we are looking principally at the noncriminal fact-finding or regulatory operations of the executive branch.

The specialized orientation of administrative agencies which presumably have a wealth of expertise to bring to the solution of problems in a given policy area distinguishes them from the generalized approach and, hopefully, the principled quality of judicial institutions. Courts, as we saw in Chapter 1, are notoriously constrained in the solution of problems by the adversary form of their proceedings. Administrative agencies, while concededly knowledgeable and often efficient and effective in fashioning and executing technical policies, can treat individuals and groups appearing before them harshly and unfairly. The difficulty is how to preserve the strength of the specialist, which agencies can bring to the solution of problems, without unduly compromising the just and fair treatment of those people with whom they deal.

The subject of administrative law is something about which whole treatises are written, and we cannot pretend here to give anything but the most fleeting acquaintance with some of the problems in the clash of the judicial and administrative processes. Nevertheless, two important generalizations about judicial review of agency decisions are so important in establishing the parameters of the conflict that we should lay them out clearly at the outset. First, courts will generally not inject themselves into the review process, if at all, until the individual or group alleging a denial of due process has exhausted all administrative remedies, that is until the complaining party has availed himself of all avenues of appeal within the bureaucracy. Second, courts will not, as a rule, substitute their judgment on the merits of an administrative decision for that of the agency. Otherwise, there would be no need for administrative agencies. Consequently, the scope of judicial review of administrative action is limited to roughly four kinds of questions: (1) whether the agency in rendering its decision exceeded the bounds of its authority and acted on a matter beyond its jurisdiction; (2) whether the conclusion reached by the agency was patently unreasonable, arbitrary, or capricious and thus constituted an abuse of discretion; (3) whether the agency failed to accord the complaining party adequate procedural guarantees (e.g., right to notice of the charges or the fact that administrative sanctions are pending, right to a hearing, right to counsel, right to call witnesses, right to confront and cross-examine opposing witnesses, right to a written record, right to appeal, etc.) commensurate with the importance of the interest at stake; and (4) whether the agency infringed substantive constitutional rights (e.g., freedom of speech, freedom of religion, right to privacy, right to travel, etc.) possessed by the affected party. These cardinal principles, sweeping distillations of complex issues as they may be, are critical to providing some boundary between the administrative and judicial processes. Difficult as that line may be to draw, some demarcation is essential, for otherwise parties to an administrative proceeding may suffer unwarranted losses at the hands of an agency trying to operate efficiently and effectively, or alternatively, courts, in their overzealous efforts to insure fairness, may be forced to confront problems for which the judicial process provides wholly unsatisfactory solutions.

The cases presented in this section focus on the question of how much procedural due process is the right of an affected party in various situations involving the operations of administrative agencies. The maintenance of procedural guarantees has long been thought the most reliable insurance against arbitrary or unfair treatment of individuals by investigatory, policy-making, or service-delivery agencies. Particularly in proceedings which could result in substantial jeopardy, deprivation, or injury to an individual, the Supreme Court has been careful to require trial-type hearings. The same concern motivated Congress to adopt the Administrative Procedure Act. Passed in 1946 and subsequently amended in 1966 and 1967, the Act seeks to regularize the rule-making and adjudicative processes of federal agencies.

Neither statutes nor the Constitution require a trial-type hearing in every instance where an aggrieved party demands it. Rather, the Court addresses the question of how much process is due by effecting a balance between competing interests. This method of interest balancing is well illustrated in *Mathews* v. *Eldridge* (p. 1014), a case in which the Court concluded that due process did not require a trial-type hearing before Social Security disability payments could be terminated. Justice Powell's discussion in *Eldridge* is particularly helpful since the justification adopted by the Court took care to distinguish the circumstances at hand from those in a previous ruling, Goldberg v. Kelly, 397 U.S. 254, 90 S.Ct. 1011 (1970), in which it ruled that due process did require a trial-type hearing prior to the termination of welfare benefits. Applying the same framework as in *Eldridge*, the Court concluded in *Memphis Light, Gas & Water Div.* v. *Craft* (p. 1022), that due process required government to afford a customer the opportunity to present his side of the story prior to the termination of utility service but held in *Mackey* v. *Montrym* (p. 1027), that a driver who had his operator's license temporarily but summarily lifted for refusing to take a breathalyzer test received all the process he was due with the availability of a prompt postsuspension hearing.

The imposition of extensive procedural requirements on the administrative process may not only be costly and time-consuming, as *Eldridge* suggests, but requiring the disposition of disputed matters in an adversary format, which is the inescapable product of mandating more and more procedural guarantees, may seriously disrupt or destroy the purpose and functioning of the organization. It is concern over this dysfunctional effect which moved the Court to take the position it did in *Board of Curators of University of Missouri* v. *Horowitz* (p. 1024), where it sharply distinguished dismissals for academic reasons from those prompted by disciplinary problems, limiting the more extensive procedural safeguards to cases of the latter. This same concern, that imposition of an adversary format could seriously deflect an agency's attention from pursuing its primary function of information gathering, is evident in *Hannah* v. *Larche* (p. 1013). As the majority in *Hannah* tells us, the disparity in the Court's treatment of the confrontation and cross-examination claims in cases of administrative fact finding as opposed to administrative adjudication is explained by the fact that the purposes of these two kinds of investigations are different. In your view, does the fact that jeopardy may attach to the Southern voting registrars only remotely and in an attenuated way justify balancing the competing interests in *Hannah* such as to subordinate the value of confrontation and cross-examination of witnesses to that of efficient agency fact finding? Despite the almost certain retribution which would follow if the identity of black complainants to the commission were divulged, Justices Douglas and Black felt compelled as a matter of constitutional principle to defend the Sixth Amendment rights of the registrars, even though they personally despised such racist practices.

The argument for effective judicial oversight of the administrative process, for all the complex matters of judgment it entails, is probably never better illustrated than when the Court appears to have abdicated its responsibility. Such an instance was its decision in the *Shaughnessy* case (p. 1010). Exalting the doctrines of judicial self-restraint and administrative finality to new heights, the Vinson Court's disposition of that case is likely to be best explained only by the fears and insecurities that beset the Nation at the height of the Cold War. It fell to Justice Jackson in dissent to illuminate with rare insight the importance of maintaining procedural due process.

e. Due Process in Punishment and Rehabilitation

Of all the areas of due process development, few are of more recent vintage than that pertaining to the institutions and processes of punishment and rehabilitation. The newness of the Supreme Court's venture is underscored by the fact that none of the decisions reproduced here bears a date earlier than 1962. Judicial concern with unconstitutional deprivations in the processes of punishment and rehabilitation have taken on two principal thrusts. One of these is substantive and has centered on the interpretation of the Eighth Amendment's guarantee against the imposition of cruel and unusual punishments. The second tack is procedural and has focused generally on assuring due process through trial-type hearings in institutions, some of which are ostensibly judicial but which had been overtaken in the past by an administrative orientation common to treatment-type institutions and processes.

When the Supreme Court handed down its decision in *Robinson* v. *California* (p. 1029) at the close of its October 1961 Term, it unveiled a constitutional mechanism of enormous potential for revising the content and sanctions of criminal laws throughout the country. The Court's holding in *Robinson* is significant both for what it said and what it implied. First, it incorporated the constitutional guarantee against the imposition of cruel and unusual punishments into the Fourteenth Amendment, thus making it applicable at the state as well as the national level. Second, it set as an absolute minimum condition of validity that *all* criminal statutes assign liability on the basis of behavior and not the status or condition of an alleged offender. Finally, it appeared to recognize in the Eighth Amendment a general constitutional command that the punishment fit the crime. The sweep of these propositions taken individually, let alone collectively, is awesome. And subsequent decisions have only begun to scratch the surface. In *Powell* v. *Texas* (p. 1032) six years later, for example, the Court came within one vote of extending, so as to exculpate behavior, the lack-of-free-will element that characterized the majority's description of status and illness in *Robinson*. The effect of reaching such a conclusion, as Justice Marshall points out, would have been to necessitate laying out a complete theory of criminal responsibility in constitutional law terms replete with a test for insanity (and, presumably, criteria which would establish other defenses as well).

More recently, the Court's attention in a number of cases has been absorbed by the question of whether and under what conditions capital punishment offends the ban on cruel and unusual punishment. The Court's consideration of the matter in these cases reflects a significant shift from the insensitive days of 1947 when, in Louisiana ex rel. Francis v. Resweber, 329 U.S. 459, 67 S.Ct. 374 (1947), it held that a young black man, convicted of murder and sentenced to be executed, was not made to suffer cruel and unusual punishment when he was ordered to face death again due to a malfunction in the electric chair the first time. A measure of the controversy surrounding this undertaking, however, has been the fact that the Court has never been able to speak about the constitutionality of the death penalty at any length with even majority support among the Justices, let alone with one voice. Piecing together the *per curiam* and plurality opinions, the Court's position appears to be that, while the death penalty *per se* is not unconstitutional (*Gregg* v. *Georgia*, p. 1041), the imposition of capital punishment does constitute cruel and unusual punishment where, among other things, it is imposed without any standards to guide the discretion of judges and juries (*Furman* v. *Georgia*, p. 1034), where it is mandatory (*Woodson* v. *North Carolina*, p. 1046), where it is imposed as the sentence for rape (*Coker* v. *Georgia*, p. 1048), and where the law does not provide sufficient consideration of mitigating circumstances or otherwise limits the right of the defendant to be heard (*Roberts* v. *Louisiana*, p. 1048; *Lockett* v. *Ohio*, p. 1049). You should consider whether these and other recent decisions (p. 1050) have moved the Court significantly along the path toward a clear statement of what the Eighth Amendment requires or whether, as Justice White has argued, the Court's recent decisions have brought it full circle from its initial ruling in *Furman*. In any case, whatever may be said in the collected death penalty decisions of the Court's tendency to see the Eighth Amendment as authorization for the principle that the punishment should fit the crime, or—more precisely—the criminal, it is clear from the ruling in *Rummel* v. *Estelle* (p. 1053) that the Burger Court means to confine evaluations of disproportionality to the imposition of capital punishment.

In one of his most celebrated dissenting opinions, Justice Brandeis warned: "Experience should teach us to be most on our guard to protect liberty when the government's purposes are beneficent. Men born to freedom are naturally alert to repel invasion of their liberty by evil-minded rulers. The greatest dangers to liberty lurk in insidious encroachment by men of zeal, well-meaning but without understanding." (Olmstead v. United States, 277 U.S. 438, 479, 48 S.Ct. 564, 572–573 [1928].) Though the do-gooders to whom he was referring were the "Drys" of the Prohibition Era, Brandeis's warning is equally applicable to more modern reformers who have endeavored to turn what heretofore had generally been regarded as punitive institutions into institutions of treatment. Due process in the context of rehabilitative institutions was regarded by the enlightened as inappropriate in theory and dysfunctional in practice. No one was being "punished." Legal procedures simply impeded the effective "treatment" of an "illness" and only provided a set of means by which the unwilling but "troubled" individual could resist. The cases which follow touch upon two such rehabilitative institutions—juvenile courts and mental hospitals.

Few opinions have so astutely described the incongruous goals which we often assign to a single social institution as Justice Fortas's portrayal of juvenile court in *In re Gault* (p. 1055). Ostensibly a judicial institution, juvenile courts succumbed in the reformism of the 1930s to becoming rehabilitative structures preoccupied very little, if at all, by a concern for the guarantees of the adversary system than by a paternalistic outlook that turned the institutions into administrative structures. Juvenile court became much less a fact-finding body (since adjudication implied blame laying) than an organization concerned about the best disposition which could be made of the deviant children who appeared before it. The significant feature of the *Gault* decision is not that it makes a fork-in-the-road choice between the competing but incompatible goals of adjudication and rehabilitation, for it does not, but that it heightens the ambiguity (and probably increases the dysfunction) still further by picking and choosing among procedural guarantees in the hope of preserving the juvenile court's dual role (p. 1061). In yet another case involving juveniles, *Ingraham* v. *Wright* (p. 1062), the Court rejected arguments that prompt corporal punishment of public school students violated either the prohibition on cruel and unusual punishment or the guarantee of due process.

The federal judiciary has also been drawn into disputes involving the mental hospitalization process which implicate constitutional guarantees. Although decisions by the lower federal courts, tightening up on commitment procedures, insuring periodic review of patients concerning their fitness to be discharged, and developing a "Bill of Rights" for patients during hospitalization, would fill volumes, several decisions of the Burger Court are instructive. In *O'Connor* v. *Donaldson* (p. 1064), the Court ruled that an individual cannot constitutionally be committed to a mental institution without evidence that he is dangerous either to himself or to others. More recent decisions (p. 1069) have focused on other procedural issues. One of the most controversial questions spawned by judicial involvement in reviewing institutionalization of the mentally ill, however, is whether there exists a constitutional right to treatment. In *Donaldson*, the Court averted consideration of the claim, one which Chief Justice Burger wanted to confront and repudiate. In one of its more recent decisions, *Youngberg* v. *Romeo* (p. 1070), the Court, though, appears to have recognized a narrowly drawn right to training or treatment as well as other valuable substantive rights possessed by individuals committed to mental hospitals.

a. DUE PROCESS AND THE FEDERAL SYSTEM: THE SELECTIVE INCORPORATION OF THE BILL OF RIGHTS INTO THE FOURTEENTH AMENDMENT

BARRON v. THE MAYOR AND CITY COUNCIL OF BALTIMORE

Supreme Court of the United States, 1833
32 U.S. (7 Pet.) 243, 8 L.Ed. 672

John Barron, the surviving co-owner of a wharf located in Baltimore, brought action against city officials seeking compensation for the loss of value to his property. Barron alleged that by redirecting the course of several streams which fed water into that part of the harbor where the wharf was situated, the city administration had caused to accumulate around the wharf large deposits of sand and dirt which lessened the depth of the water to a level that rendered the wharf inaccessible to ships. A county court awarded Barron $4,500 in damages, but an appellate court reversed this decision. Barron appealed, maintaining that the Fifth Amendment prohibited the states as well as the national government from taking private property without just compensation. The case subsequently came to the U.S. Supreme Court on a writ of error.

Mr. Chief Justice MARSHALL delivered the opinion of the court:

* * *

The question * * * presented is, we think, of great importance, but not of much difficulty.

The Constitution was ordained and established by the people of the United States for themselves, for their own government, and not for the government of the individual States. Each State established a constitution for itself, and in that constitution provided such limitations and restrictions on the powers of its particular government as its judgment dictated. The people of the United States framed such a government for the United States as they supposed best adapted to their situation, and best calculated to promote their interests. The powers they conferred on this government were to be exercised by itself; and the limitations on power, if expressed in general terms, are naturally, and, we think, necessarily applicable to the government created by the instrument. They are limitations of power granted in the instrument itself; not of distinct governments, framed by different persons and for different purposes.

If these propositions be correct, the fifth amendment must be understood as restraining the power of the general government, not as applicable to the States. In their several constitutions they have imposed such restrictions on their respective governments as their own wisdom suggested; such as they deemed most proper for themselves. It is a subject on which they judge exclusively, and with which others interfere no farther than they are supposed to have a common interest.

The counsel for the plaintiff in error insists that the Constitution was intended to secure the people of the several States against the undue exercise of power by their respective State governments; as well as against that which might be attempted by their general government. In support of this argument he relies on the inhibitions contained in the tenth section of the first article.

We think that section affords a strong if not a conclusive argument in support of the opinion already indicated by the court.

The preceding section contains restrictions which are obviously intended for the exclusive purpose of restraining the exercise of power by the departments of the general government. Some of them use language applicable only to Congress, others are expressed in general terms. The third clause, for example, declares that "no bill of attainder or ex post facto law shall be passed." No language can be more general; yet the demonstration is complete that it applies solely to the government of the United States. * * *

The ninth section having enumerated, in the nature of a bill of rights, the limitations intended to be imposed on the powers of the general government, the tenth proceeds to enumerate those which were to operate on the State legislatures. These restrictions are brought together in the same section, and are by express words applied to the States. "No State shall enter into any treaty," etc. Perceiving that in a Constitution framed by the people of the United States for the government of all, no limitation of the action of government on the people would apply to the State government unless expressed in terms; the restrictions contained in the tenth section are in direct words so applied to the States.

* * *

If the original Constitution, in the ninth and tenth sections of the first article, draws the plain and marked line of discrimination between the limitations it imposes on the powers of the general government and on those of the States; if in every inhibition intended to act on State power, words are employed which directly express that intent, some strong reason must be assigned for departing from this safe and judicious course in framing the amendments, before that departure can be assumed.

We search in vain for that reason.

Had the people of the several States, or any of them, required changes in their constitutions; had they required additional safeguards to liberty from the apprehended encroachments of their particular governments, the remedy was in their own hands, and would have been applied by themselves. A convention would have been assembled by the discontented State, and the required improvements would have been made by itself. The unwieldy and cumbrous machinery of procuring a recommendation from two-thirds of Congress and the assent of three-fourths of their sister States, could never have occurred to any human being as a mode of doing that which might be effected by the State itself. Had the framers of these amendments intended them to be limitations on the powers of the State governments they would have imitated the framers of the original Constitution, and have expressed that intention. Had Congress engaged in the extraordinary occupation of improving the constitutions of the several States by affording the people additional protection from the exercise of power by their own governments in matters which concerned themselves alone, they would have declared this purpose in plain and intelligible language.

But it is universally understood, it is a part of the history of the day, that the great revolution which established the Constitution of the United States was not effected without immense opposition. Serious fears were extensively entertained that those powers which the patriot statesmen who then watched over the interests of our country, deemed essential to union, and to the attain-

ment of those invaluable objects for which union was sought, might be exercised in a manner dangerous to liberty. In almost every convention by which the Constitution was adopted, amendments to guard against the abuse of power were recommended. These amendments demanded security against the apprehended encroachments of the general government—not against those of the local governments.

In compliance with a sentiment thus generally expressed, to quiet fears thus extensively entertained, amendments were proposed by the required majority in Congress, and adopted by the States. These amendments contain no expression indicating an intention to apply them to the State governments. This court cannot so apply them. *   *   *

This court, therefore, has no jurisdiction of the cause, and is dismissed.

BUTCHERS' BENEVOLENT ASS'N v. CRESCENT CITY LIVESTOCK LANDING & SLAUGHTERHOUSE CO. [THE SLAUGHTERHOUSE CASES]

Supreme Court of the United States, 1873
83 U.S. (16 Wall.) 36, 21 L.Ed. 394

See p. 632.

HURTADO v. CALIFORNIA

Supreme Court of the United States, 1884
110 U.S. 516, 4 S.Ct. 111, 28 L.Ed. 232

The California Constitution of 1879 provided that prosecution of crimes, formerly requiring indictment by a grand jury, could be initiated on the basis of an information [a formal accusation drawn up by a prosecutor] after review by a magistrate. A district attorney filed an information against Hurtado charging him with murder. Found guilty of the crime and sentenced to death, Hurtado appealed, but two state courts upheld the conviction over his objection that proceedings initiated by an information were forbidden by the Due Process Clause of the Fourteenth Amendment. Hurtado subsequently petitioned the U. S. Supreme Court for a writ of error.

MATTHEWS, J.

* * *

It is claimed on behalf of the prisoner that the conviction and sentence are void, on the ground that they are repugnant to that clause of the fourteenth article of amendment to the constitution of the United States, which is in these words: "Nor shall any state deprive any person of life, liberty, or property without due process of law." The proposition of law we are asked to affirm is that an indictment or presentment by a grand jury, as known to the common law of England, is essential to that "due process of law," when applied to prosecutions for felonies, which is secured and guarantied by this provision of the constitution of the United States, and which accordingly it is forbidden to the states, respectively, to dispense with in the administration of criminal law. * * *

[I]t is maintained on behalf of the plaintiff in error that the phrase "due process of law" is equivalent to "law of the land," as found in the twenty-ninth chapter of *Magna Charta*; that by immemorial usage it has acquired a fixed, definite, and technical meaning; that it refers to and includes, not only the general principles of public liberty and private right, which lie at the foundation of all free government, but the very institutions which, venerable by time and custom, have been tried by experience and found fit and necessary for the preservation of those principles, and which, having been the birthright and inheritance of every English subject, crossed the Atlantic with the colonists and were transplanted and established in the fundamental laws of the state; that, having been originally introduced into the constitution of the United States

as a limitation upon the powers of the government, brought into being by that instrument, it has now been added as an additional security to the individual against oppression by the states themselves; that one of these institutions is that of the grand jury, an indictment or presentment by which against the accused in cases of alleged felonies is an essential part of due process of law, in order that he may not be harassed and destroyed by prosecutions founded only upon private malice or popular fury.

* * *

* * *

It is urged upon us, however, in argument, that the claim made in behalf of the plaintiff in error is supported by the decision of this court in Murray's Lessee v. Hoboken Land & Imp. Co., 18 How. 272. There, Mr. Justice CURTIS, delivering the opinion of the court, after showing that due process of law must mean something more than the actual existing law of the land, for otherwise it would be no restraint upon legislative power, proceeds as follows: "To what principle, then, are we to resort to ascertain whether this process, enacted by congress, is due process? To this the answer must be twofold. We must examine the constitution itself to see whether this process be in conflict with any of its provisions. If not found to be so, we must look to those settled usages and modes of proceeding existing in the common and statute law of England before the emigration of our ancestors, and which are shown not to have been unsuited to their civil and political condition by having been acted on by them after the settlement of this country." This, it is argued, furnishes an indispensable test of what constitutes "due process of law"; that any proceeding otherwise authorized by law, which is not thus sanctioned by usage, or which supersedes and displaces one that is, cannot be regarded as due process of law. But this inference is unwarranted. The real syllabus of the passage quoted is that a process of law, which is not otherwise forbidden, must be taken to be due process of law, if it can show the sanction of settled usage both in England and in this country; but it by no means follows, that nothing else can be due process of law. The point in the case cited arose in reference to a summary proceeding, questioned on that account as not due process of law. The answer was, however exceptional it may be, as tested by definitions and principles of ordinary procedure, nevertheless, this, in substance, has been immemorially the actual law of the land, and, therefore, is due process of law. But to hold that such a characteristic is essential to due process of law, would be to deny every quality of the law but its age, and to render it incapable of progress or improvement. It would be to stamp upon our jurisprudence the unchangeableness attributed to the laws of the Medes and Persians.

This would be all the more singular and surprising, in this quick and active age, when we consider that, owing to the progressive development of legal ideas and institutions in England, the words of *Magna Charta* stood for very different things at the time of the separation of the American colonies from what they represented originally. * * *

* * *

The constitution of the United States was ordained, it is true, by descendants of Englishmen, who inherited the traditions of the English law

and history; but it was made for an undefined and expanding future, and for a people gathered, and to be gathered, from many nations and of many tongues; and while we take just pride in the principles and institutions of the common law, we are not to forget that in lands where other systems of jurisprudence prevail, the ideas and processes of civil justice are also not unknown. Due process of law, in spite of the absolutism of continental governments, is not alien to that Code which survived the Roman empire as the foundation of modern civilization in Europe, and which has given us that fundamental maxim of distributive justice, *suum cuique tribuere*. There is nothing in *Magna Charta*, rightly construed as a broad charter of public right and law, which ought to exclude the best ideas of all systems and of every age; and as it was the characteristic principle of the common law to draw its inspiration from every fountain of justice, we are not to assume that the sources of its supply have been exhausted. On the contrary, we should expect that the new and various experiences of our own situation and system will mould and shape it into new and not less useful forms.

* * *

We are to construe this phrase in the fourteenth amendment by the *usus loquendi* of the constitution itself. The same words are contained in the fifth amendment. That article makes specific and express provision for perpetuating the institution of the grand jury, so far as relates to prosecutions for the more aggravated crimes under the laws of the United States. It declares that "no person shall be held to answer for a capital or otherwise infamous crime, unless on a presentment or indictment of a grand jury, except in cases arising in the land or naval forces, or in the militia when in actual service in time of war or public danger; nor shall any person be subject for the same offense to be twice put in jeopardy of life or limb; nor shall he be compelled in any criminal case to be a witness against himself." It then immediately adds: "nor be deprived of life, liberty, or property without due process of law." According to a recognized canon of interpretation, especially applicable to formal and solemn instruments of constitutional law, we are forbidden to assume, without clear reason to the contrary, that any part of this most important amendment is superfluous. The natural and obvious inference is that, in the sense of the constitution, "due process of law" was not meant or intended to include [by force of the term] the institution and procedure of a grand jury in any case. The conclusion is equally irresistible, that when the same phrase was employed in the fourteenth amendment to restrain the action of the states, it was used in the same sense and with no greater extent; and that if in the adoption of that amendment it had been part of its purpose to perpetuate the institution of the grand jury in all the states, it would have embodied, as did the fifth amendment, express declarations to that effect. Due process of law in the latter refers to that law of the land which derives its authority from the legislative powers conferred upon congress by the constitution of the United States, exercised within the limits therein prescribed, and interpreted according to the principles of the common law. In the fourteenth amendment, by parity of reason, it refers to that law of the land in each state which derives its authority

from the inherent and reserved powers of the state, exerted within the limits of those fundamental principles of liberty and justice which lie at the base of all our civil and political institutions, and the greatest security for which resides in the right of the people to make their own laws, and alter them at their pleasure. "The fourteenth amendment," as was said by Mr. Justice BRADLEY in Missouri v. Lewis, 101 U.S. 22-31, "does not profess to secure to all persons in the United States the benefit of the same laws and the same remedies. Great diversities in these respects may exist in two states separated only by an imaginary line. On one side of this line there may be a right of trial by jury, and on the other side no such right. Each state prescribes its own modes of judicial proceeding."

But it is not to be supposed that these legislative powers are absolute and despotic, and that the amendment prescribing due process of law is too vague and indefinite to operate as a practical restraint. It is not every act, legislative in form, that is law. Law is something more than mere will exerted as an act of power. It must be not a special rule for a particular person or a particular case, but, in the language of Mr. Webster, in his familiar definition, "the general law, a law which hears before it condemns, which proceeds upon inquiry, and renders judgment only after trial," so "that every citizen shall hold his life, liberty, property, and immunities under the protection of the general rules which govern society," and thus excluding, as not due process of law, acts of attainder, bills of pains and penalties, acts of confiscation, acts reversing judgments, and acts directly transferring one man's estate to another, legislative judgments and decrees, and other similar special, partial, and arbitrary exertions of power under the forms of legislation. Arbitrary power, enforcing its edicts to the injury of the persons and property of its subjects, is not law, whether manifested as the decree of a personal monarch or of an impersonal multitude. And the limitations imposed by our constitutional law upon the action of the governments, both state and national, are essential to the preservation of public and private rights, notwithstanding the representative character of our political institutions. The enforcement of these limitations by judicial process is the device of self-governing communities to protect the rights of individuals and minorities, as well against the power of numbers, as against the violence of public agents transcending the limits of lawful authority, even when acting in the name and wielding the force of the government.

* * *

It follows that any legal proceeding enforced by public authority, whether sanctioned by age and custom, or newly devised in the discretion of the legislative power in furtherance of the general public good, which regards and preserves these principles of liberty and justice, must be held to be due process of law.

* * *

Tried by these principles, we are unable to say that the substitution for a presentment or indictment by a grand jury of the proceeding by information after examination and commitment by a magistrate, certifying to the probable guilt of the defendant, with the right on his part to the aid of counsel, and to the cross-examination of the witnesses pro-

duced for the prosecution, is not due process of law. It is, as we have seen, an ancient proceeding at common law, which might include every case of an offense of less grade than a felony, except misprision of treason; and in every circumstance of its administration, as authorized by the statute of California, it carefully considers and guards the substantial interest of the prisoner. It is merely a preliminary proceeding, and can result in no final judgment, except as the consequence of a regular judicial trial, conducted precisely as in cases of indictments. * * *

For these reasons, finding no error therein, the judgment of the supreme court of California is affirmed.

HARLAN, J., dissenting.

* * *

* * * The people were not content with the provision in section 2 of article 3 that "the trial of all crimes, except in cases of impeachment, shall be by jury." They desired a fuller and broader enunciation of the fundamental principles of freedom, and therefore demanded that the guaranties of the rights of life, liberty, and property, which experience had proved to be essential to the safety and security of the people, should be placed beyond all danger of impairment or destruction by the general government through legislation by congress. They perceived no reason why, in respect of those rights, the same limitations should not be imposed upon the general government that had been imposed upon the states by their own constitutions. Hence the prompt adoption of the original amendments, by the fifth of which it is, among other things, provided that "no person shall be deprived of life, liberty, or property

without due process of law." This language is similar to that of the clause of the fourteenth amendment now under examination. That similarity was not accidental, but evinces a purpose to impose upon the states the same restrictions, in respect of proceedings involving life, liberty, and property, which had been imposed upon the general government.

"Due process of law," within the meaning of the national constitution, does not import one thing with reference to the powers of the states and another with reference to the powers of the general government. If particular proceedings, conducted under the authority of the general government, and involving life, are prohibited because not constituting that due process of law required by the fifth amendment of the constitution of the United States, similar proceedings, conducted under the authority of a state, must be deemed illegal, as not being due process of law within the meaning of the fourteenth amendment. The words "due process of law," in the latter amendment, must receive the same interpretation they had at the common law from which they were derived, and which was given to them at the formation of the general government. * * *

* * *

[A]ccording to the settled usages and modes of proceeding existing under the common and statute law of England at the settlement of this country, information in capital cases was not consistent with the "law of the land" or with "due process of law." Such was the understanding of the patriotic men who established free institutions upon this continent. Almost the identical words of *Magna Charta* were incorporated into most of the state constitutions before the adoption of our national constitution. When they declared, in substance, that no person shall be deprived of life, liberty, or property except by the judgment of his peers or the law of the land, they intended to assert his right to the same guaranties that were given in the mother country by the great charter and the laws passed in furtherance of its fundamental principles.

* * *

PALKO v. CONNECTICUT

Supreme Court of the United States, 1937
302 U.S. 319, 58 S.Ct. 149, 82 L.Ed. 288

Frank Palko was found guilty of second-degree murder and sentenced to life imprisonment. However, the state was permitted to appeal the decision under a Connecticut statute, and it chose to do so. The state's Supreme Court of Errors set aside the trial court's judgment and ordered a new trial. This time Palko was found guilty of first-degree murder and sentenced to death. The conviction was affirmed by the Supreme Court of Errors, and the case was appealed to the U. S. Supreme Court. Palko contended that the Connecticut statute was unconstitutional because the Due Process Clause of the Fourteenth Amendment protected individuals from being tried twice for the same offense.

Mr. Justice CARDOZO delivered the opinion of the Court.

*   *   *

The argument for appellant is that whatever is forbidden by the Fifth Amendment is forbidden by the Fourteenth also. The Fifth Amendment, which is not directed to the States, but solely to the federal government, creates immunity from double jeopardy. No person shall be "subject for the same offense to be twice put in jeopardy of life or limb." The Fourteenth Amendment ordains, "nor shall any State deprive any person of life, liberty, or property, without due process of law." To retry a defendant, though under one indictment and only one, subjects him, it is said, to double jeopardy in violation of the Fifth Amendment, if the prosecution is one on behalf of the United States. From this the consequence is said to follow that there is a denial of life or liberty without due process of law, if the prosecution is one on behalf of the people of a state. *   *   *

*   *   *

We have said that in appellant's view the Fourteenth Amendment is to be taken as embodying the prohibitions of the Fifth. His thesis is even broader. Whatever would be a violation of the original bill of rights (Amendments 1 to 8) if done by the federal government is now equally unlawful by force of the Fourteenth Amendment if done by a state. There is no such general rule.

The Fifth Amendment provides, among other things, that no person shall be held to answer for a capital or otherwise infamous crime unless on presentment or indictment of a grand jury. This court has held that, in prosecutions by a state, present-

ment or indictment by a grand jury may give way to informations at the instance of a public officer. Hurtado v. California, 110 U.S. 516, 4 S.Ct. 111, 292. The Fifth Amendment provides also that no person shall be compelled in any criminal case to be a witness against himself. *   *   * Twining v. New Jersey, 211 U.S. 78, 106, 111, 112, 29 S.Ct. 14. *   *   * The Sixth Amendment calls for a jury trial in criminal cases and the Seventh for a jury trial in civil cases at common law where the value in controversy shall exceed $20. This court has ruled that consistently with those amendments trial by jury may be modified by a state or abolished altogether. Walker v. Sauvinet, 92 U.S. 90, 23 L.Ed. 678; Maxwell v. Dow, 176 U.S. 581, 20 S.Ct. 448, 494 *   *   *.

On the other hand, the due process clause of the Fourteenth Amendment may make it unlawful for a state to abridge by its statutes the freedom of speech which the First Amendment safeguards against encroachment by the Congress (De Jonge v. Oregon, 299 U.S. 353, 364, 57 S.Ct. 255, 260; Herndon v. Lowry, 301 U.S. 242, 259, 57 S.Ct. 732, 740) or the like freedom of the press (Grosjean v. American Press Co., 297 U.S. 233, 56 S.Ct. 444; Near v. Minnesota, 283 U.S. 697, 707, 51 S.Ct. 625, 627), or the free exercise of religion (Hamilton v. Regents of University, 293 U.S. 245, 262, 55 S.Ct. 197, 204, *   *   *), or the right of peaceable assembly, without which speech would be unduly trammeled (*De Jonge* v. *Oregon*, supra; *Herndon* v. *Lowry*, supra), or the right of one accused of crime to the benefit of counsel (Powell v. Alabama, 287 U.S. 45, 53 S.Ct. 55). In these and other situations immunities that are valid as against the federal government by force of the specific pledges of particular amendments have been found to be implicit in the concept of ordered liberty, and thus, through the Fourteenth Amendment, become valid as against the states.

The line of division may seem to be wavering and broken if there is a hasty catalogue of the cases on the one side and the other. Reflection and analysis will induce a different view. There emerges the perception of a rationalizing principle which gives to discrete instances a proper order and coherence. The right to trial by jury and the immunity from prosecution except as the result of an indictment may have value and importance. Even so, they are not of the very essence of a scheme of ordered liberty. To abolish them is not to violate a "principle of justice so rooted in the traditions and conscience of our people as to be ranked as fundamental." Snyder v. Massachusetts, 291 U.S. 97, at page 105, 54 S.Ct. 330, 332. * * * Few would be so narrow or provincial as to maintain that a fair and enlightened system of justice would be impossible without them. What is true of jury trials and indictments is true also, as the cases show, of the immunity from compulsory self-incrimination. * * * This too might be lost, and justice still be done. * * *

We reach a different plane of social and moral values when we pass to the privileges and immunities that have been taken over from the earlier articles of the Federal Bill of Rights and brought within the Fourteenth Amendment by a process of absorption. These in their origin were effective against the federal government alone. If the Fourteenth Amendment has absorbed

them, the process of absorption has had its source in the belief that neither liberty nor justice would exist if they were sacrificed. * * * This is true, for illustration, of freedom of thought and speech. Of that freedom one may say that it is the matrix, the indispensable condition, of nearly every other form of freedom. With rare aberrations a pervasive recognition of that truth can be traced in our history, political and legal. So it has come about that the domain of liberty, withdrawn by the Fourteenth Amendment from encroachment by the states, has been enlarged by latter-day judgments to include liberty of the mind as well as liberty of action. The extension became, indeed, a logical imperative when once it was recognized, as long ago it was, that liberty is something more than exemption from physical restraint, and that even in the field of substantive rights and duties the legislative judgment, if oppressive and arbitrary, may be overridden by the courts. * * *

Our survey of the cases serves, we think, to justify the statement that the dividing line between them, if not unfaltering throughout its course, has been true for the most part to a unifying principle. On which side of the line the case made out by the appellant has appropriate location must be the next inquiry and the final one. Is that kind of double jeopardy to which the statute has subjected him a hardship so acute and shocking that our polity will not endure it? Does it violate those "fundamental principles of liberty and justice which lie at the base of all our civil and political institutions"? Hebert v. Louisiana, supra. The answer surely must be "no." What the answer would have to be if the state were permitted after a trial free from error to try the accused over again or to bring another case against him, we have no occasion to consider. We deal with the statute before us and no other. The state is not attempting to wear the accused out by a multitude of cases with accumulated trials. It asks no more than this, that the case against him shall go on until there shall be a trial free from the corrosion of substantial legal error. * * * This is not cruelty at all, nor even vexation in any immoderate degree. If the trial had been infected with error adverse to the accused, there might have been review at his instance, and as often as necessary to purge the vicious taint. A reciprocal privilege, subject at all times to the discretion of the presiding judge * * * has now been granted to the state. There is here no seismic innovation. The edifice of justice stands, its symmetry, to many, greater than before.

* * *

The judgment is affirmed.

Mr. Justice BUTLER dissents.

ADAMSON v. CALIFORNIA

Supreme Court of the United States, 1947
332 U.S. 46, 67 S.Ct. 1672, 91 L.Ed. 1903

The California constitution and penal code permitted the trial judge and attorneys to comment on and juries to consider as evidence of guilt failure of a defendant to testify on his own behalf. Adamson, who was convicted of first-degree murder and sentenced to death, had declined to testify during his trial. In the presentation of the case to the jury, the prosecuting attorney argued that Adamson's refusal to testify was an indication of his guilt. Adamson's conviction was affirmed by the state supreme court. On appeal to the U. S. Supreme Court, Adamson challenged the constitutionality of California's provision for this kind of comment as a violation of the Privileges and Immunities and Due Process Clauses of the Fourteenth Amendment. At the outset of its opinion, the Court dismissed the privileges and immunities claim as being without any merit.

Mr. Justice REED delivered the opinion of the Court.

* * *

[A]ppellant relies upon the due process of law clause of the Fourteenth Amendment to invalidate the provisions of the California law * * * and as applied (a) because comment on failure to testify is permitted, (b) because appellant was forced to forego testimony in person because of danger of disclosure of his past convictions through cross-examination and (c) because the presumption of innocence was infringed by the shifting of the burden of proof to appellant in permitting comment on his failure to testify.

* * *

Appellant * * * contends that if the privilege against self-incrimination is not a right protected by the privileges and immunities clause of the Fourteenth Amendment against state action, this privilege, to its full scope under the Fifth Amendment, inheres in the right to a fair trial. A right to a fair trial is a right admittedly protected by the due process clause of the Fourteenth Amendment. Therefore, appellant argues, the due process clause of the

Fourteenth Amendment protects his privilege against self-incrimination. The due process clause of the Fourteenth Amendment, however, does not draw all the rights of the federal Bill of Rights under its protection. That contention was made and rejected in Palko v. Connecticut, 302 U.S. 319, 323, 58 S.Ct. 149, 150. Nothing has been called to our attention that either the framers of the Fourteenth Amendment or the states that adopted intended its due process clause to draw within its scope the earlier amendments to the Constitution. *Palko* held that such provisions of the Bill of Rights as were "implicit in the concept of ordered liberty," * * * became secure from state interference by the clause. But it held nothing more.

* * * For a state to require testimony from an accused is not necessarily a breach of a state's obligation to give a fair trial. Therefore, we must examine the effect of the California law applied in this trial to see whether the comment on failure to testify violates the protection against state action that the due process clause does grant to an accused. The due process clause forbids compulsion to testify by fear of hurt, torture or exhaustion. It forbids any other type of coercion that falls within the scope of due process. * * * So our inquiry is directed, not at the broad question of the constitutionality of compulsory testimony from the accused under the due process clause, but to the constitutionality of the provision of the California law that permits comment upon his failure to testify. * * *

Generally, comment on the failure of an accused to testify is forbidden in American jurisdictions. * * * California, however, is one of a few states that permit limited comment

upon a defendant's failure to testify. That permission is narrow. * * * This does not involve any presumption, rebuttable or irrebuttable, either of guilt or of the truth of any fact, that is offered in evidence. * * * It allows inferences to be drawn from proven facts. Because of this clause, the court can direct the jury's attention to whatever evidence there may be that a defendant could deny and the prosecution can argue as to inferences that may be drawn from the accused's failure to testify. * * * California has prescribed a method for advising the jury in the search for truth. However sound may be the legislative conclusion that an accused should not be compelled in any criminal case to be a witness against himself, we see no reason why comment should not be made upon his silence. It seems quite natural that when a defendant has opportunity to deny or explain facts and determines not to do so, the prosecution should bring out the strength of the evidence by commenting upon defendant's failure to explain or deny it. The prosecution evidence may be of facts that may be beyond the knowledge of the accused. If so, his failure to testify would have little if any weight. But the facts may be such as are necessarily in the knowledge of the accused. In that case a failure to explain would point to an inability to explain.

* * *

Affirmed.

Mr. Justice FRANKFURTER (concurring).

* * *

For historical reasons a limited immunity from the common duty to testify was written into the Federal Bill of Rights, and I am prepared to agree that, as part of that immunity, comment on the failure of an accused to take the witness stand is forbidden in federal prosecutions. It is so, of course, by explicit act of Congress. * * * But to suggest that such a limitation can be drawn out of "due process" in its protection of ultimate decency in a civilized society is to suggest that the Due Process Clause fastened fetters of unreason upon the States. * * *

Between the incorporation of the Fourteenth Amendment into the Constitution and the beginning of the present membership of the Court—a period of 70 years—the scope of that Amendment was passed upon by 43 judges. Of all these judges, only one, who may respectfully be called an eccentric exception, ever indicated the belief that the Fourteenth Amendment was a shorthand summary of the first eight Amendments theretofore limiting only the Federal Government, and that due process incorporated those eight Amendments as restrictions upon the powers of the States. * * *

* * * The notion that the Fourteenth Amendment was a covert way of imposing upon the States all the rules which it seemed important to Eighteenth Century statesmen to write into the Federal Amendments, was rejected by judges who were themselves witnesses of the process by which the Fourteenth Amendment became part of the Constitution. Arguments that may now be adduced to prove that the first eight Amendments were concealed within the historic phrasing of the Fourteenth Amendment were not unknown at the time of its adoption. A surer estimate of their bearing was possible for judges at the time than distorting distance is likely to vouchsafe. Any evidence of design or purpose not

contemporaneously known could hardly have influenced those who ratified the Amendment. Remarks of a particular proponent of the Amendment, no matter how influential, are not to be deemed part of the Amendment. What was submitted for ratification was his proposal, not his speech. Thus, at the time of the ratification of the Fourteenth Amendment the constitutions of nearly half of the ratifying States did not have the rigorous requirements of the Fifth Amendment for instituting criminal proceedings through a grand jury. It could hardly have occurred to these States that by ratifying the Amendment they uprooted their established methods for prosecuting crime and fastened upon themselves a new prosecutorial system.

Indeed, the suggestion that the Fourteenth Amendment incorporates the first eight Amendments as such is not unambiguously urged. Even the boldest innovator would shrink from suggesting to more than half the States that they may no longer initiate prosecutions without indictment by grand jury, or that thereafter all the States of the Union must furnish a jury of 12 for every case involving a claim above $20. There is suggested merely a selective incorporation of the first eight Amendments into the Fourteenth Amendment. Some are in and some are out, but we are left in the dark as to which are in and which are out. Nor are we given the calculus for determining which go in and which stay out. If the basis of selection is merely that those provisions of the first eight Amendments are incorporated which commend themselves to individual justices as indispensable to the dignity and happiness of a free man, we are thrown back to a merely subjective test. * * * If all that is meant is that due process contains within itself certain minimal standards which are "of the very essence of a scheme of ordered liberty," * * * putting upon this Court the duty of applying these standards from time to time, then we have merely arrived at the insight which our predecessors long ago expressed. We are called upon to apply to the difficult issues of our own day the wisdom afforded by the great opinions in this field. * * *

It may not be amiss to restate the pervasive function of the Fourteenth Amendment in exacting from the States observance of basic liberties. * * * The Amendment neither comprehends the specific provisions by which the founders deemed it appropriate to restrict the federal government nor is it confined to them. The Due Process Clause of the Fourteenth Amendment has an independent potency, precisely as does the Due Process Clause of the Fifth Amendment in relation to the Federal Government. It ought not to require argument to reject the notion that due process of law meant one thing in the Fifth Amendment and another in the Fourteenth. * * * Are Madison and his contemporaries in the framing of the Bill of Rights to be charged with writing into it a meaningless clause? To consider "due process of law" as merely a shorthand statement of other specific clauses in the same amendment is to attribute to the authors and proponents of this Amendment ignorance of, or indifference to, a historic conception which was one of the great instruments in the arsenal of constitutional freedom which the Bill of Rights was to protect and strengthen.

* * *

Mr. Justice MURPHY, with whom Mr. Justice RUTLEDGE concurs, dissenting.

While in substantial agreement with the views of Mr. Justice BLACK, I have one reservation and one addition to make.

I agree that the specific guarantees of the Bill of Rights should be carried over intact into the first section of the Fourteenth Amendment. But I am not prepared to say that the latter is entirely and necessarily limited by the Bill of Rights. Occasions may arise where a proceeding falls so far short of conforming to fundamental standards of procedure as to warrant constitutional condemnation in terms of a lack of due process despite the absence of a specific provision in the Bill of Rights.

* * *

Mr. Justice BLACK, dissenting.

* * *

This decision reasserts a constitutional theory spelled out in Twining v. New Jersey, 211 U.S. 78, 29 S.Ct. 14, that this Court is endowed by the Constitution with boundless power under "natural law" periodically to expand and contract constitutional standards to conform to the Court's conception of what at a particular time constitutes "civilized decency" and "fundamental principles of liberty and justice." Invoking this *Twining* rule, the Court concludes that although comment upon testimony in a federal court would violate the Fifth Amendment, identical comment in a state court does not violate today's fashion in civilized decency and fundamentals and is therefore not prohibited by the Federal Constitution as amended.

* * * I would not reaffirm the *Twining* decision. I think that decision and the "natural law" theory of the Constitution upon which it relies, degrade the constitutional safeguards of the Bill of Rights and simultaneously appropriate for this Court a broad power which we are not authorized by the Constitution to exercise. * * *

* * *

My study of the historical events that culminated in the Fourteenth Amendment, and the expressions of those who sponsored and favored, as well as those who opposed its submission and passage, persuades me that one of the chief objects that the provisions of the Amendment's first section, separately, and as a whole, were intended to accomplish was to make the Bill of Rights, applicable to the states. With full knowledge of the import of the *Barron* decision, the framers and backers of the Fourteenth Amendment proclaimed its purpose to be to overturn the constitutional rule that case had announced. This historical purpose has never received full consideration or exposition in any opinion of this Court interpreting the Amendment.

* * *

[O]ur prior decisions, including *Twining*, do not prevent our carrying out * * * [the] purpose * * * of making applicable to the states, not a mere part, as the Court has, but the full protection of the Fifth Amendment's provision against compelling evidence from an accused to convict him of crime. And I further contend that the "natural law" formula which the Court uses to reach its conclusion in this case should be abandoned as an incongruous excrescence on our Constitution.

I believe that formula to be itself a violation of our Constitution, in that it subtly conveys to courts, at the expense of legislatures, ultimate power over public policies in fields where no specific provision of the Constitution limits legislative power. * * *

* * *

I cannot consider the Bill of Rights to be an outworn 18th Century "strait jacket" as the *Twining* opinion did. Its provisions may be thought outdated abstractions by some. And it is true that they were designed to meet ancient evils. But they are the same kind of human evils that have emerged from century to century wherever excessive power is sought by the few at the expense of the many. In my judgment the people of no nation can lose their liberty so long as a Bill of Rights like ours survives and its basic purposes are conscientiously interpreted, enforced and respected so as to afford continuous protection against old, as well as new, devices and practices which might thwart those purposes. I fear to see the consequences of the Court's practice of substituting its own concepts of decency and fundamental justice for the language of the Bill of Rights as its point of departure in interpreting and enforcing that Bill of Rights. If the choice must be between the selective process of the *Palko* decision applying some of the Bill of Rights to the States, or the *Twining* rule applying none of them, I would choose the *Palko* selective process. But rather than accept either of these choices. I would follow what I believe was the original purpose of the Fourteenth Amendment—to extend to all the people of the nation the complete protection of the Bill of Rights. To hold that this Court can determine what, if any, provisions of the Bill of Rights will be enforced, and if so to what degree, is to frustrate the great design of a written Constitution.

Conceding the possibility that this Court is now wise enough to improve on the Bill of Rights by substituting natural law concepts for the Bill of Rights. I think the possibility is entirely too speculative to agree to take that course. I would therefore hold in this case that the full protection of the Fifth Amendment's proscription against compelled testimony must be afforded by California. This I would do because of reliance upon the original purpose of the Fourteenth Amendment.

* * *

Mr. Justice DOUGLAS, joins in this opinion.

ROCHIN v. CALIFORNIA

Supreme Court of the United States, 1952
342 U.S. 165, 72 S.Ct. 205, 96 L.Ed. 183

Police officers, having information that Rochin was selling narcotics, went to his residence and entered the premises illegally. They found him partially clothed, sitting on the side of the bed. When asked, "Whose stuff is this?" referring to two capsules lying on the nightstand, Rochin reached for the pills and swallowed them. After efforts by the officers to force Rochin to regurgitate the capsules failed, they took him to a hospital where they ordered his stomach to be pumped. A report confirming that the capsules contained morphine was used to convict the defendant in a California court. The conviction was subsequently affirmed by two higher state courts, whereupon Rochin successfully petitioned the U. S. Supreme Court for certiorari.

Mr. Justice FRANKFURTER delivered the opinion of the Court.

* * *

In our federal system the administration of criminal justice is predominantly committed to the care of the States. The power to define crimes belongs to Congress only as an appropriate means of carrying into execution its limited grant of legislative powers. * * * Broadly speaking, crimes in the United States are what the laws of the individual States make them, subject to the limitations of Art. I, § 10, cl. 1, in the original Constitution, prohibiting bills of attainder and *ex post facto* laws, and of the Thirteenth and Fourteenth Amendments.

These limitations, in the main, concern not restrictions upon the powers of the States to define crime, except in the restricted area where federal authority has pre-empted the field, but restrictions upon the manner in which the States may enforce their penal codes. Accordingly, in reviewing a State criminal conviction under a claim of right guaranteed by the Due Process Clause of the Fourteenth Amendment, from which is derived the most far-reaching and most frequent federal basis of challenging State criminal justice, "we must be deeply mindful of the responsibilities of the States for the enforcement of criminal laws, and exercise with due humility our merely negative function in subjecting convictions from state courts to the very narrow scrutiny which the Due Process Clause of the Fourteenth Amendment authorizes." * * * Due process of law, "itself a historical product" * * * is not to be turned into a destructive dogma against the States in the administration of their systems of criminal justice.

However, this Court too has its responsibility. Regard for the requirements of the Due Process Clause "inescapably imposes upon this Court an exercise of judgment upon the whole course of the proceedings [resulting in a conviction] in order to ascertain whether they offend those canons of decency and fairness which express the notions of justice of English-speaking peoples even toward those charged with the most heinous offenses." * * * These standards of justice are not authoritatively formulated anywhere as though they were specifics. Due process of law is a summarized constitutional guarantee of respect for those personal immunities which, as Mr. Justice Cardozo twice wrote for the Court, are "so rooted in the traditions and conscience of our people as to be ranked as fundamental," Snyder v. Commonwealth of Massachusetts, 291 U.S. 97, 105, 54 S.Ct. 330, 332, or are "implicit in the concept of ordered liberty." Palko v. State of Connecticut, 302 U.S. 319, 325, 58 S.Ct. 149, 152.

* * *

The vague contours of the Due Process Clause do not leave judges at large. We may not draw on our merely personal and private notions and disregard the limits that bind judges in their judicial function. Even though the concept of due process of law is not final and fixed, these limits are derived from considerations that are fused in the whole nature of our judicial process. * * * The Due Process Clause places upon this Court the duty of exercising a judgment, within the narrow confines of judicial power in reviewing State convictions, upon interests of society pushing in opposite directions.

Due process of law thus conceived is not to be derided as resort to a revival of "natural law." To believe that this judicial exercise of judgment could be avoided by freezing "due process of law" at some fixed stage of time or thought is to suggest that the most important aspect of constitutional adjudication is a function for inanimate machines and not for judges, for whom the independence safeguarded by Article III of the Constitution was designed and who are presumably guided by established standards of judicial behavior. Even cybernetics has not yet made that haughty claim. To practice the requisite detachment and to achieve sufficient objectivity no doubt demands of judges the habit of self-discipline and self-criticism, incertitude that one's own views are incontestable and alert tolerance toward views not shared. But these are precisely the presuppositions of our judicial process. They are precisely the qualities society has a right to expect from those entrusted with ultimate judicial power.

Restraints on our jurisdiction are self-imposed only in the sense that there is from our decisions no immediate appeal short of impeachment or constitutional amendment. But that does not make due process of law a matter of judicial caprice. The faculties of the Due Process Clause may be indefinite and vague, but the mode of their ascertainment is not self-willed. In each case "due process of law" requires an evaluation based on a disinterested inquiry pursued in the spirit of science, on a balanced order of facts exactly and fairly stated, on the detached consideration of conflicting claims, * * * on a judgment not *ad hoc* and episodic but duly mindful of reconciling the needs both of continuity and of change in a progressive society.

Applying these general considerations to the circumstances of the present case, we are compelled to conclude that the proceedings by which this conviction was obtained do more than offend some fastidious squeamishness or private sentimentalism about combatting crime too energetically. This is conduct that shocks the conscience. Illegally breaking into the privacy of the petitioner, the struggle to open his mouth and remove what was there, the forcible extraction of his stomach's contents—this course of proceeding by agents of government to obtain evidence is bound to offend even hardened sensibilities. They are methods too close to the rack and the screw to permit of constitutional differentiation.

* * *

* * * The judgment below must be reversed.

* * *

Mr. Justice MINTON took no part in the consideration or decision of this case.

Mr. Justice BLACK, concurring.

Adamson v. People of State of California, 332 U.S. 46, 68–123, 67 S.Ct. 1672, 1683, 1684–1711, sets out reasons for my belief that state as well as federal courts and law enforcement officers must obey the

Fifth Amendment's command that "No person * * * shall be compelled in any criminal case to be a witness against himself." I think a person is compelled to be a witness against himself not only when he is compelled to testify, but also when as here, incriminating evidence is forcibly taken from him by a contrivance of modern science. * * *

In the view of a majority of the Court, however, the Fifth Amendment imposes no restraint of any kind on the states. They nevertheless hold that California's use of this evidence violated the Due Process Clause of the Fourteenth Amendment. Since they hold as I do in this case, I regret my inability to accept their interpretation without protest. But I believe that faithful adherence to the specific guarantees in the Bill of Rights insures a more permanent protection of individual liberty than that which can be afforded by the nebulous standards stated by the majority.

* * *

Some constitutional provisions are stated in absolute and unqualified language such, for illustration, as the First Amendment stating that no law shall be passed prohibiting the free exercise of religion or abridging the freedom of speech or press. Other constitutional provisions do require courts to choose between competing policies, such as the Fourth Amendment which, by its terms, necessitates a judicial decision as to what is an "unreasonable" search or seizure. There is, however, no express constitutional language granting judicial power to invalidate *every* state law of *every* kind deemed "unreasonable" or contrary to the Court's notion of civilized decencies; yet the constitutional philosophy used by the majority has, in the past, been used to deny a state the right to fix the price of gasoline, Williams v. Standard Oil Co. of Louisiana, 278 U.S. 235, 49 S.Ct. 115; and even the right to prevent bakers from palming off smaller for larger loaves of bread, Jay Burns Baking Co. v. Bryan, 264 U.S. 504, 44 S.Ct. 412. These cases, and others, show the extent to which the evanescent standards of the majority's philosophy have been used to nullify state legislative programs passed to suppress evil economic practices. What

paralyzing role this same philosophy will play in the future economic affairs of this country is impossible to predict. Of even graver concern, however, is the use of the philosophy to nullify the Bill of Rights. I long ago concluded that the accordion-like qualities of this philosophy must inevitably imperil all the individual liberty safeguards specifically enumerated in the Bill of Rights. Reflection and recent decisions[3] of this Court sanctioning abridgment of the freedom of speech and press have strengthened this conclusion.

GRISWOLD v. CONNECTICUT

Supreme Court of the United States, 1965
381 U.S. 479, 85 S.Ct. 1678, 14 L.Ed.2d 510

See p. 1192.

DUNCAN v. LOUISIANA

Supreme Court of the United States, 1968
391 U.S. 145, 88 S.Ct. 1444, 20 L.Ed.2d 491

A Louisiana court convicted Gary Duncan, a Negro, of simple battery for slapping a white boy on the elbow (under state law the maximum sentence for an offense of this kind—a misdemeanor—was two years' imprisonment and a $300 fine). During the court proceedings Duncan requested a jury trial, but the judge denied the request because the state constitution permitted jury trials only in instances where hard labor or capital punishment might be imposed. Sentenced to sixty days in prison and a fine of $150, he petitioned the Louisiana Supreme Court for a writ of certiorari. The court denied the application, whereupon Duncan appealed to the U. S. Supreme Court contending that the Sixth and Fourteenth Amendments guaranteed the right to a jury trial in state prosecutions for crimes punishable by two years' imprisonment or more.

Mr. Justice WHITE delivered the opinion of the Court.

*   *   *

The Fourteenth Amendment denies the States the power to "deprive any person of life, liberty, or property, without due process of law." In

resolving conflicting claims concerning the meaning of this spacious language, the Court has looked increasingly to the Bill of Rights for guidance; many of the rights guaranteed by the first eight Amendments to the Constitution have been held to be protected against state ac-

---

3. American Communications Ass'n v. Douds, 339 U.S. 382, 70 S.Ct. 674; Feiner v. People of State of New York, 340 U.S. 315, 71

S.Ct. 303, 328; Dennis v. United States, 341 U.S. 494, 71 S.Ct. 857.

tion by the Due Process Clause of the Fourteenth Amendment. That clause now protects the right to compensation for property taken by the State; the rights of speech, press, and religion covered by the First Amendment; the Fourth Amendment rights to be free from unreasonable searches and seizures and to have excluded from criminal trials any evidence illegally seized; the right guaranteed by the Fifth Amendment to be free of compelled self-incrimination; and the Sixth Amendment rights to counsel, to a speedy and public trial, to confrontation of opposing witnesses, and to compulsory process for obtaining witnesses.

The test for determining whether a right extended by the Fifth and Sixth Amendments with respect to federal criminal proceedings is also protected against state action by the Fourteenth Amendment has been phrased in a variety of ways in the opinions of this Court. The question has been asked whether a right is among those " 'fundamental principles of liberty and justice which lie at the base of all our civil and political institutions,' " Powell v. State of Alabama, 287 U.S. 45, 67, 53 S.Ct. 55, 63 (1932); whether it is "basic in our system of jurisprudence," In re Oliver, 333 U.S. 257, 273, 68 S.Ct. 499, 507 (1948). * * * The claim before us is that the right to trial by jury guaranteed by the Sixth Amendment meets these tests. The position of Louisiana, on the other hand, is that the Constitution imposes upon the States no duty to give a jury trial in any criminal case, regardless of the seriousness of the crime or the size of the punishment which may be imposed. Because we believe that trial by jury in criminal cases is fundamental to the American scheme of justice, we hold that the Fourteenth

Amendment guarantees a right of jury trial in all criminal cases which—were they to be tried in a federal court—would come within the Sixth Amendment's guarantee. Since we consider the appeal before us to be such a case, we hold that the Constitution was violated when appellant's demand for jury trial was refused.

The history of trial by jury in criminal cases has been frequently told. It is sufficient for present purposes to say that by the time our Constitution was written, jury trial in criminal cases had been in existence in England for several centuries and carried impressive credentials traced by many to Magna Carta. * * *

Jury trial continues to receive strong support. The laws of every State guarantee a right to jury trial in serious criminal cases; no State has dispensed with it; nor are there significant movements underway to do so. * * *

We are aware of prior cases in this Court in which the prevailing opinion contains statements contrary to our holding today that the right to jury trial in serious criminal cases is a fundamental right and hence must be recognized by the States as part of their obligation to extend due process of law to all persons within their jurisdiction. Louisiana relies especially on Maxwell v. Dow, 176 U.S. 581, 20 S.Ct. 448 (1900); Palko v. State of Connecticut, 302 U.S. 319, 58 S.Ct. 149 (1937); and Snyder v. Commonwealth of Massachusetts, 291 U.S. 97, 54 S.Ct. 330 (1934). None of these cases, however, dealt with a State which had purported to dispense entirely with a jury trial in serious criminal cases. *Maxwell* held that no provision of the Bill of Rights applied to the States—a position long since repudiated—and that the Due Process Clause of the Fourteenth Amendment did not prevent a State from trying a defendant for a noncapital offense with fewer than 12 men on the jury. It did not deal with a case in which no jury at all had been provided. In ьeither *Palko* nor *Snyder* was jury trial actually at issue, although both cases contain important dicta asserting that the right to jury trial is not essential to ordered liberty and may be dispensed with by the States regardless of the Sixth and Fourteenth Amendments. These observations, though weighty and respectable, are nevertheless dicta, unsupported by holdings in this Court that a State may refuse a defendant's demand for a jury trial when he is charged with a serious crime. * * * Respectfully, we reject the prior dicta regarding jury trial in criminal cases.

The guarantees of jury trial in the Federal and State Constitutions reflect a profound judgment about the way in which law should be enforced and justice administered. A right to jury trial is granted to criminal defendants in order to prevent oppression by the Government. * * *

* * *

The State of Louisiana urges that holding that the Fourteenth Amendment assures a right to jury trial will cast doubt on the integrity of every trial conducted without a jury. Plainly, this is not the import of our holding. Our conclusion is that in the American States, as in the federal judicial system, a general grant of jury trial for serious offenses is a fundamental right, essential for preventing miscarriages of justice and for assuring that fair trials are provided for all defendants. We would not assert, however, that every criminal trial—or any particular trial—held before a judge alone is unfair or that a defendant may never be as fairly treated by a judge as he would be by a jury. Thus we hold no constitutional doubts about the practices, common in both federal and state courts, of accepting waivers of jury trial and prosecuting petty crimes without extending a right to jury trial. However, the fact is that in most places more trials for serious crimes are to juries than to a court alone; a great many defendants prefer the judgment of a jury to that of a court. Even where defendants are satisfied with bench trials, the right to a jury trial very likely serves its intended purpose of making judicial or prosecutorial unfairness less likely.

Louisiana's final contention is that even if it must grant jury trials in serious criminal cases, the conviction before us is valid and constitutional because here the petitioner was tried for simple battery and was sentenced to only 60 days in the parish prison. We are not persuaded. It is doubtless true that there is a category of petty crimes or offenses which is not subject to the Sixth Amendment jury trial provision and should not be subject to the Fourteenth Amendment jury trial requirement here applied to the States. Crimes carrying possible penalties up to six months do not require a jury trial if they otherwise qualify as petty offenses. * * *

* * *

* * * We need not, however, settle in this case the exact location of the line between petty offenses and serious crimes. It is sufficient for our purposes to hold that a crime punishable by two years in prison is, based on past and contemporary

standards in this country, a serious crime and not a petty offense. Consequently, appellant was entitled to a jury trial and it was error to deny it.

* * *

Reversed and remanded.

Mr. Justice BLACK, with whom Mr. Justice DOUGLAS joins, concurring.

* * * With this holding I agree for reasons given by the Court. I also agree because of reasons given in my dissent in Adamson v. People of State of California. * * * I am very happy to support this selective process through which our Court has since the *Adamson* case held most of the specific Bill of Rights' protections applicable to the States to the same extent they are applicable to the Federal Government. Among these are the right to trial by jury decided today, the right against compelled self-incrimination, the right to counsel, the right to compulsory process for witnesses, the right to confront witnesses, the right to a speedy and public trial, and the right to be free from unreasonable searches and seizures.

* * *

Mr. Justice FORTAS, concurring.

* * *

[A]lthough I agree with the decision of the Court, I cannot agree with the implication * * * that when we hold, influenced by the Sixth Amendment, that "due process" requires that the States accord the right of jury trial for all but petty offenses, we automatically import all of the ancillary rules which have been or may hereafter be developed incidental to the right to jury trial in the federal courts. I see no reason whatever, for example, to assume that our decision today should require us to impose federal requirements such as unanimous verdicts or a jury of 12 upon the States. We may well conclude that these and other features of federal jury practice are by no means fundamental—that they are not essential to due process of law—and that they are not obligatory on the States.

I would make these points clear today. Neither logic nor history nor the intent of the draftsmen of the Fourteenth Amendment can possibly be said to require that the Sixth Amendment or its jury trial provision be applied to the States together with the total gloss that this Court's decisions have supplied. The draftsmen of the Fourteenth Amendment intended what they said, not more or less: that no State shall deprive any person of life, liberty, or property without due process of law. It is ultimately the duty of this Court to interpret, to ascribe specific meaning to this phrase. There is no reason whatever for us to conclude that, in so doing, we are bound slavishly to follow not only the Sixth Amendment but all of its bag and baggage, however securely or insecurely affixed they may be by law and precedent to federal proceedings. To take this course, in my judgment, would be not only unnecessary but mischievous because it would inflict a serious blow upon the principle of federalism. * * * [T]he Constitution's command, in my view, is that in our insistence upon state observance of due process, we should, so far as possible, allow the greatest latitude for state differences. * * * Our Constitution sets up a federal union, not a monolith.

* * *

Mr. Justice HARLAN, whom Mr. Justice STEWART joins, dissenting.

Every American jurisdiction provides for trial by jury in criminal cases. The question before us is not whether jury trial is an ancient institution, which it is; nor whether it plays a significant role in the administration of criminal justice, which it does; nor whether it will endure, which it shall. The question in this case is whether the State of Louisiana, which provides trial by jury for all felonies, is prohibited by the Constitution from trying charges of simple battery to the court alone. In my view, the answer to that question, mandated alike by our constitutional history and by the longer history of trial by jury, is clearly "no."

* * *

* * * I have raised my voice many times before against the Court's continuing undiscriminating insistence upon fastening on the States federal notions of criminal justice, and I must do so again in this instance. With all respect, the Court's approach and its reading of history are altogether topsy-turvy.

* * *

Apart from the approach taken by the absolute incorporationists, I can see only one method of analysis that has any internal logic. That is to start with the words "liberty" and "due process of law" and attempt to define them in a way that accords with American traditions and our system of government. This approach, involving a much more discriminating process of adjudication than does "incorporation," is, albeit difficult, the one that was followed throughout the 19th and most of the present century. It entails a "gradual process of judicial inclusion and exclusion," seeking, with due recognition of constitutional tolerance for state experimentation and disparity, to ascertain those "immutable principles * * * of justice which inhere in the very idea of free government which no member of the Union may disregard." Due process was not restricted to rules fixed in the past, for that "would be to deny every quality of the law but its age, and to render it incapable of progress or improvement." Nor did it impose nationwide uniformity in details. * * *

* * *

The relationship of the Bill of Rights to this "gradual process" seems to me to be twofold. In the first place it has long been clear that the Due Process Clause imposes some restrictions on state action that parallel Bill of Rights restrictions on federal action. Second, and more important than this accidental overlap, is the fact that the Bill of Rights is evidence, at various points, of the content Americans find in the term "liberty" and of American standards of fundamental fairness.

* * *

Today's Court still remains unwilling to accept the total incorporationists' view of the history of the Fourteenth Amendment. This, if accepted, would afford a cogent reason for applying the Sixth Amendment to the States. The Court is also, apparently, unwilling to face the task of determining whether denial of trial by jury in the situation before us, or in other situations, is fundamentally unfair. Consequently the Court has compromised on the ease of the incorporationist position, without its internal logic. It has simply assumed that the question before us is whether the Jury Trial Clause of the Sixth Amendment should be incorporated into the Fourteenth, jot-for-jot and case-for-case, or ignored. Then the Court merely declares that the clause in question is "in" rather than "out."

The Court has justified neither its starting place nor its conclusion. If the problem is to discover and articulate the rules of fundamental fairness in criminal proceedings, there is no reason to assume that the whole body of rules developed in this Court constituting Sixth Amendment jury trial must be regarded as a unit. The requirement of trial by jury in federal criminal cases has given rise to numerous subsidiary questions respecting the exact scope and content of the right. It surely cannot be that every answer the Court has given, or will give, to such a question is attributable to the Founders; or even that every rule announced carries equal conviction of this Court; still less can it be that every such subprinciple is equally fundamental to ordered liberty.

Examples abound. I should suppose it obviously fundamental to fairness that a "jury" means an "impartial jury." I should think it equally obvious that the rule, imposed long ago in the federal courts, that "jury" means "jury of exactly twelve," is not fundamental to anything: there is no significance except to mystics in the number 12. Again, trial by jury has been held to require a unanimous verdict of jurors in the federal courts, although unanimity has not been found essential to liberty in Britain, where the requirement has been abandoned.

* * *

The argument that jury trial is not a requisite of due process is quite simple. The central proposition of

Palko, a proposition to which I would adhere, is that "due process of law" requires only that criminal trials be fundamentally fair. * * * [A]part from the theory that it was historically intended as a mere shorthand for the Bill of Rights, I do not see what else "due process of law" can intelligibly be thought to mean. If due process of law requires only fundamental fairness, then the inquiry in each case must be whether a state trial process was a fair one. The Court has held, properly I think, that in an adversary process it is a requisite of fairness, for which there is no adequate substitute, that a criminal defendant be afforded a right to counsel and to cross-examine opposing witnesses. But it simply has not been demonstrated, nor, I think, can it be demonstrated, that trial by jury is the only fair means of resolving issues of fact.

* * *

That trial by jury is not the only fair way of adjudicating criminal guilt is well attested by the fact that it is not the prevailing way, either in England or in this country. * * * * * * I * * * see no reason why this Court should reverse the conviction of appellant, absent any suggestion that his particular trial was in fact unfair, or compel the State of Louisiana to afford jury trial in an as yet unbounded category of cases that can, without unfairness, be tried to a court.

* * *

In sum, there is a wide range of views on the desirability of trial by jury, and on the ways to make it most effective when it is used; there is also considerable variation from State to State in local conditions such as the size of the criminal caseload, the ease or difficulty of summoning jurors, and other trial conditions bearing on fairness. We have before us, therefore, an almost perfect example of a situation in which the celebrated dictum of Mr. Justice Brandeis should be invoked. It is, he said,

"one of the happy incidents of the federal system that a single courageous state may, if its citizens choose, serve as a laboratory." * * * New State Ice Co. v. Liebmann, 285 U.S. 262, 280, 311, 52 S.Ct. 371, 386 (dissenting opinion).

This Court, other courts, and the political process are available to correct any experiments in criminal procedure that prove fundamentally unfair to defendants. That is not what is being done today: instead, and quite without reason, the Court has chosen to impose upon every State one means of trying criminal cases; it is a good means, but it is not the only fair means, and it is not demonstrably better than the alternatives States might devise.

I would affirm the judgment of the Supreme Court of Louisiana.

WILLIAMS v. FLORIDA

Supreme Court of the United States, 1970
399 U.S. 78, 90 S.Ct. 1893, 26 L.Ed.2d 446

Williams was tried and convicted of robbery in Dade County criminal court. During the proceedings he objected to being tried before a six-man jury, allowed under Florida law in all cases not involving capital offenses. Williams asserted that denial of a hearing before a twelve-man jury violated his rights under the Sixth Amendment as made applicable to the states through the Fourteenth. Despite this and other challenges, a state district court of appeal affirmed the conviction, and the defendant obtained certiorari from the United States Supreme Court.

Mr. Justice WHITE delivered the opinion of the Court.

* * *

In Duncan v. Louisiana, 391 U.S. 145, 88 S.Ct. 1444 (1968), we held that the Fourteenth Amendment guarantees a right to trial by jury in all criminal cases that—were they to be tried in a federal court—would come within the Sixth Amendment's guarantee. Petitioner's trial for robbery * * * clearly falls within the scope of that holding. * * * The question in this case then is whether the constitutional guarantee of a trial by "jury" necessarily requires trial by exactly 12 persons, rather than some lesser number—in

this case six. We hold that the 12-man panel is not a necessary ingredient of "trial by jury," and that respondent's refusal to impanel more than the six members provided for by Florida law did not violate petitioner's Sixth Amendment rights as applied to the States through the Fourteenth.

We had occasion in *Duncan* v. *Louisiana*, supra, to review briefly the oft-told history of the development of trial by jury in criminal cases. * * * In short, while sometime in the 14th century the size of the jury at common law came to be fixed generally at 12, that particular feature of the jury system appears to have been a historical accident, unrelated to the great purposes which gave rise to the jury in the first place. The question before us is whether this accidental feature of the jury has been immutably codified into our Constitution.

* * *

We do not pretend to be able to divine precisely what the word "jury" imported to the Framers, the First Congress, or the States in 1789. It may well be that the usual expectation was that the jury would consist of 12, and that hence, the most likely conclusion to be drawn is simply that little thought was actually given to the specific question we face today. But there is absolutely no indication in "the intent of the Framers" of an explicit decision to equate the constitutional and common-law characteristics of the jury. Nothing in this history suggests, then, that we do violence to the letter of the Constitution by turning to other than purely historical considerations to determine which features of the jury system, as it existed at common law, were preserved in the Constitution. The relevant inquiry, as we see it, must be the function that the particular feature performs and its relation to the purposes of the jury trial. Measured by this standard, the 12-man requirement cannot be regarded as an indispensable component of the Sixth Amendment.

The purpose of the jury trial, as we noted in *Duncan*, is to prevent oppression by the Government. * * * Given this purpose, the essential feature of a jury obviously lies in the interposition between the accused and his accuser of the commonsense judgment of a group of laymen, and in the community participation and shared responsibility that results from that group's determina-

tion of guilt or innocence. The performance of this role is not a function of the particular number of the body that makes up the jury. To be sure, the number should probably be large enough to promote group deliberation, free from outside attempts at intimidation, and to provide a fair possibility for obtaining a representative cross-section of the community. But we find little reason to think that these goals are in any meaningful sense less likely to be achieved when the jury numbers six, than when it numbers 12—particularly if the requirement of unanimity is retained. And, certainly the reliability of the jury as a factfinder hardly seems likely to be a function of its size.

* * *

We conclude, in short, as we began: the fact that the jury at common law was composed of precisely 12 is a historical accident, unnecessary to effect the purposes of the jury system and wholly without significance "except to mystics." * * * To read the Sixth Amendment as forever codifying a feature so incidental to the real purpose of the Amendment is to ascribe a blind formalism to the Framers which would require considerably more evidence than we have been able to discover in the history and language of the Constitution or in the reasoning of our past decisions. * * * Legislatures may well have their own views about the relative value of the larger and smaller juries, and may conclude that, wholly apart from the jury's primary function, it is desirable to spread the collective responsibility for the determination of guilt among the larger group. In capital cases, for example, it appears that no State provides for less than 12 jurors—a

fact that suggests implicit recognition of the value of the larger body as a means of legitimating society's decision to impose the death penalty. Our holding does no more than leave these considerations to Congress and the States, unrestrained by an interpretation of the Sixth Amendment that would forever dictate the precise number that can constitute a jury. Consistent with this holding, we conclude that petitioner's Sixth Amendment rights, as applied to the States through the Fourteenth Amendment, were not violated by Florida's decision to provide a six-man rather than a 12-man jury.
* * *

Affirmed.

Mr. Justice BLACKMUN took no part in the consideration or decision of this case.

Mr. Justice BLACK, with whom Mr. Justice DOUGLAS joins, concurring. * * *

The Court today holds that a State can, consistently with the Sixth Amendment to the United States Constitution, try a defendant in a criminal case with a jury of six members. I agree with that decision for substantially the same reasons given by the Court. My Brother Harlan, however, charges that the Court's decision on this point is evidence that the "incorporation doctrine," through which the specific provisions of the Bill of Rights are made fully applicable to the States under the same standards applied in federal courts will somehow result in a "dilution" of the protections required by those provisions. * * * Today's decision is in no way attributable to any desire to dilute the Sixth Amendment in order more easily to apply it to the States, but follows solely as a necessary consequence of our duty to re-

examine prior decisions to reach the correct constitutional meaning in each case. The broad implications in early cases indicating that only a body of 12 members could satisfy the Sixth Amendment requirement arose in situations where the issue was not squarely presented and were based, in my opinion, on an improper interpretation of that amendment. Had the question presented here arisen in a federal court before our decision in *Duncan* v. *Louisiana* * * * this Court would still, in my view, have reached the result announced today. In my opinion the danger of diluting the Bill of Rights protections lies not in the "incorporation doctrine," but in the "shock the conscience" test on which my Brother Harlan would rely instead—a test which depends, not on the language of the Constitution, but solely on the views of a majority of the Court as to what is "fair" and "decent."

* * *

Mr. Justice MARSHALL, dissenting. * * *

* * *

I adhere to the holding of *Duncan* v. *Louisiana.* * * * And I agree with the Court that the *same* "trial by jury" is guaranteed to state defendants by the Fourteenth Amendment as to federal defendants by the Sixth. * * *

At the same time, I adhere to the decision of the Court in Thompson v. Utah, 170 U.S. 343, 349, 18 S.Ct. 620 (1898), that the jury guaranteed by the Sixth Amendment consists "of twelve persons, neither more nor less." As I see it, the Court has not made out a convincing case that the Sixth Amendment should be read differently. * * * The arguments made by Mr. Justice Harlan in

* * * his opinion persuade me that *Thompson* was right when decided and still states sound doctrine. I am equally convinced that the requirement of 12 should be applied to the States.

Mr. Justice HARLAN * * * concurring in the result. * * *

* * *

The historical argument by which the Court undertakes to justify its view that the Sixth Amendment does not require 12-member juries is, in my opinion, much too thin to mask the true thrust of this decision. The decision evinces, I think, a recognition that the "incorporationist" view of the Due Process Clause of the Fourteenth Amendment, which underlay *Duncan* and is now carried forward * * * must be tempered to allow the States more elbow room in ordering their own criminal systems. With that much I agree. But to accomplish this by diluting constitutional protections within the federal system itself is something to which I cannot possibly subscribe. Tempering the rigor of *Duncan* should be done forthrightly, by facing up to the fact that at least in this area the "incorporation" doctrine does not fit well with our federal structure, and by the same token that *Duncan* was wrongly decided.

* * *

* * * With all respect, I consider that before today it would have been unthinkable to suggest that the Sixth Amendment's right to a trial by jury is satisfied by a jury of six, or less, as is left open by the Court's opinion * * * or by less than a unanimous verdict, a question also reserved in today's decision.

The Court, in stripping off the livery of history from the jury trial, relies on a two-step analysis. With arduous effort the Court first liberates itself from the "intent of the Framers" and "the easy assumption in our past decisions that if a given feature existed in a jury at common law in 1789, then it was necessarily preserved in the Constitution." * * * Unburdened by the yoke of history the Court then concludes that the policy protected by the jury guarantee does not require its perpetuation in common-law form.

* * *

The principle of *stare decisis* is multifaceted. It is a solid foundation for our legal system; yet care must be taken not to use it to create an unmovable structure. It provides the stability and predictability required for the ordering of human affairs over the course of time and a basis of "public faith in the judiciary as a source of impersonal and reasoned judgments." * * * Surely if the principle of *stare decisis* means anything in the law, it means that precedent should not be jettisoned when the rule of yesterday remains viable, creates no injustice, and can reasonably be said to be no less sound than the rule sponsored by those who seek change, let alone incapable of being demonstrated wrong. The decision * * * however, casts aside workability and relevance and substitutes uncertainty. The only reason I can discern for today's decision that discards numerous judicial pronouncements and historical precedent that sound constitutional interpretation would look to as controlling, is the Court's disquietude with the tension between the jurisprudential consequences wrought by "incorporation" in *Duncan* * * * and the counter-pulls of the situation in *Williams* which present the prospect of invalidating the common practice in the States of providing less than a 12-member jury for the trial of misdemeanor cases.

These decisions demonstrate that the difference between a "due process" approach, that considers each particular case on its own bottom to see whether the right alleged is one "implicit in the concept of ordered liberty," * * * and "selective incorporation" is not an abstract one whereby different verbal formulae achieve the same results. The internal logic of the selective incorporation doctrine cannot be respected if the Court is both committed to interpreting faithfully the meaning of the federal Bill of Rights and recognizing the governmental diversity that exists in this country. The "backlash" in *Williams* exposes the malaise, for there the Court dilutes a federal guarantee in order to reconcile the logic of "incorporation," the "jot-for-jot and case-for-case" application of the federal right to the States, with the reality of federalism. Can one doubt that had Congress tried to undermine the common-law right to trial by jury before *Duncan* came on the books the history today recited would have barred such action? Can we expect repeat performances when this Court is called upon to give definition and meaning to other federal guarantees that have been "incorporated"?

* * *

But the best evidence of the vitality of federalism is today's decision in *Williams.* The merits or demerits of the jury system can, of course, be debated and those States that have diluted the common-law requirements evince a conclusion that the protection as known at common law is not necessary for a fair trial, or is only such marginal assurance of a fair trial that the inconvenience of assembling 12 individuals outweighs other gains in the administration of justice achieved by using only six individuals. * * *

* * *

It is time, I submit, for this Court to face up to the reality implicit in today's holdings and reconsider the "incorporation" doctrine before its leveling tendencies further retard development in the field of criminal procedure by stifling flexibility in the States and by discarding the possibility of federal leadership by example.

Mr. Justice STEWART * * * concurring in the result. * * *

I substantially agree with the separate opinion Mr. Justice HARLAN has filed in these cases—an opinion that fully demonstrates some of the basic errors in a mechanistic "incorporation" approach to the Fourteenth Amendment. I cannot subscribe to his opinion in its entirety, however, if only for the reason that it relies in part upon certain dissenting and concurring opinions in previous cases in which I did not join.

* * *

Surely Mr. Justice HARLAN is right when he says it is time for the Court to face up to reality.

In Ballew v. Georgia, 435 U.S. 223, 98 S.Ct. 1029 (1978), the Court held that a state criminal trial where the case had been tried to a jury of less than six members violated the Sixth and Fourteenth Amendments. The defendant in this instance had been indicted and convicted by a five-man jury of violating Georgia's obscenity statute. Announcing the judgment of the Court in an opinion in which only Justice Stevens joined, Justice Blackmun observed at the outset that the Court's earlier decision in Williams v. Florida, 399 U.S. 78, 90 S.Ct. 1893 (1970), held only that a jury of twelve members was not mandated by the Constitution and that some lesser number was permissible so long as it was "of sufficient size to promote group deliberation, to insulate members from outside intimidation, and to provide a representative cross-section of the community." He continued:

> When the Court in *Williams* permitted the reduction in jury size—or, to put it another way, when it held that a jury of six was not unconstitutional—it expressly reserved ruling on the issue whether a number smaller than six passed constitutional scrutiny.   *   *   *
>
> *Williams* v. *Florida* and Colgrove v. Battin, 413 U.S. 149, 93 S.Ct. 2448 (1973) (where the Court held that a jury of six members did not violate the Seventh Amendment right to a jury trial in a civil case), generated a quantity of scholarly work on jury size. These writings do not draw or identify a bright line below which the number of jurors would not be able to function as required by the standards enunciated in *Williams*. On the other hand, they raise significant questions about the wisdom and constitutionality of a reduction below six.   *   *   *

Among the concerns which he elaborated and which the empirical studies tended to show would be heightened by too small a jury were: (1) the reduced motivation and critical facility of the group to reason toward a sound and objective decision based on evidence not prejudice; (2) the higher risk of inaccuracy and inconsistency in group decision making; (3) the decreasing prospect for hung juries, to the detriment of the defense; and (4) the markedly reduced chances that the jury would represent a fair cross section of the community by grossly underrepresenting minorities. In light of these concerns, Justice Blackmun wrote:

> While we adhere to, and reaffirm our holding in *Williams* v. *Florida*, these studies, most of which have been made since *Williams* was decided in 1970, lead us to conclude that the purpose and functioning of the jury in a criminal trial is seriously impaired, and to a constitutional degree, by a reduction in size to below six members. We readily admit that we do not pretend to discern a clear line between six members and five. But the assembled data raise substantial doubt about the reliability and appropriate representation of panels smaller than six. Because of the fundamental importance of the jury trial to the American system of criminal justice, any further reduction that promotes inaccurate and possibly biased decisionmaking, that causes untoward differences in verdicts, and that prevents juries from truly representing their communities, attains constitutional significance.

Moreover, the Court found the justifications put forth by Georgia on behalf of the five-man jury (it was used only in misdemeanor cases; the unanimity rule was still maintained; there was no arbitrary exclusion of any particular class; it was both less costly and more efficient) unpersuasive.

Justice White concurred in the judgment, preferring to rest his decision against the five-man jury on its inability to "satisfy the fair cross-section requirement of the Sixth and Fourteenth Amendments." Speaking for himself, Chief Justice Burger, and Justice Rehnquist, Justice Powell, while agreeing that "a line has to be drawn somewhere if the substance of jury trial is to be preserved," nonetheless expressed strong reservations "as to the wisdom—as well as the necessity—of Mr. Justice Blackmun's heavy reliance on numerology derived from statistical studies" since "neither the validity nor the methodology employed by the studies cited was subjected to the traditional testing mechanisms of the adversary process." And in another opinion Justice Brennan, joined by Justices Stewart and Marshall, agreed with the Court's holding but dissented from the decision to remand the case for a new trial due to the view that Georgia's obscenity statute was "overbroad and therefore facially unconstitutional."

APODACA v. OREGON

Supreme Court of the United States, 1972
406 U.S. 404, 92 S.Ct. 1628, 32 L.Ed.2d 184

Apodaca and two others, defendants in three separate prosecutions for assault with a deadly weapon, burglary in a dwelling, and grand larceny, were convicted when the jury in each instance returned a guilty verdict by a split vote. The votes for convicting Apodaca and another of the defendants were 11–1 and for the third defendant, 10–2, the minimum margin necessary to convict under Oregon law. Apodaca and the others appealed the decisions charging that conviction by less than a unanimous jury vote denied them rights guaranteed by the Sixth and Fourteenth Amendments. The convictions were affirmed by the Oregon Court of Appeals, and review was denied by the state supreme court, whereupon defendants successfully sought certiorari from the U. S. Supreme Court.

Mr. Justice WHITE announced the judgment of the Court in an opinion in which The CHIEF JUSTICE [BURGER], Mr. Justice BLACKMUN, and Mr. Justice REHNQUIST joined.

* * *

Like the requirement that juries consist of 12 men, the requirement of unanimity arose during the Middle Ages and had become an accepted feature of the common-law jury by the 18th century. But, as we observed in *Williams*, "the relevant constitutional history casts considerable doubt on the easy assumption * * * that if a given feature existed in a jury at common law in 1789, then it was necessarily preserved in the Constitution." * * *

Our inquiry must focus upon the function served by the jury in contemporary society. * * * As we said in *Duncan*, the purpose of trial by jury is to prevent oppression by the Government by providing a "safeguard against the corrupt or overzealous prosecutor and against the complaint, biased, or eccentric judge." * * * "Given this purpose, the essential feature of a jury obviously lies in the interposition between the accused and his accuser of the commonsense judgment of a group of laymen. * * * " *Williams* v. *Florida*. * * * A requirement of unanimity, however, does not materially contribute to the exercise of this commonsense judgment. [A] jury will come to such a judgment as long as it consists of a group of laymen representative of a cross section of the community who have the duty and the opportunity to deliberate, free from outside attempts at intimidation, on the question of a defendant's guilt. In terms of this function we perceive no difference between juries required to act unanimously and those permitted to convict or acquit by votes of 10 to two or 11 to one. Requiring unanimity would obviously produce hung juries in some situations where nonunanimous juries will convict or acquit. But in either case, the interest of the defendant in having the judgment of his peers interposed between himself and the officers of the State who prosecute and judge him is equally well served.

Petitioners nevertheless argue that unanimity serves other purposes constitutionally essential to the continued operation of the jury system. Their principal contention is that a Sixth Amendment "jury trial" made mandatory on the States by virtue of the Due Process Clause of the Fourteenth Amendment, *Duncan* v. *Louisiana*, supra, should be held to require a unanimous jury verdict in order to give substance to the reasonable doubt standard otherwise mandated by the Due Process Clause. * * *

We are quite sure, however, that the Sixth Amendment itself has never been held to require proof beyond a reasonable doubt in criminal cases. The reasonable doubt standard developed separately from both the jury trial and the unanimous verdict. * * *

Petitioners' argument that the Sixth Amendment requires jury unanimity in order to give effect to the reasonable doubt standard thus founders on the fact that the Sixth Amendment does not require proof beyond a reasonable doubt at all. The reasonable doubt argument is rooted, in effect, in due process and has been rejected in Johnson v. Louisiana [406 U.S. 356, 92 S.Ct. 1620 (1972)].

Petitioners also cite quite accurately a long line of decisions of this Court upholding the principle that the Fourteenth Amendment requires jury panels to reflect a cross section of the community. * * * They then contend that unanimity is a necessary precondition for effective application of the cross section requirement, because a rule permitting less than unanimous verdicts will make it possible for convictions to occur without the acquiescence of minority elements within the community.

There are two flaws in this argument. One is petitioners' assumption that every distinct voice in the community has a right to be represented on every jury and a right to prevent conviction of a defendant in any case. All that the Constitution forbids, however, is systematic exclusion of identifiable segments of the community from jury panels and from the juries ultimately drawn from those panels. * * * No group, in short, has the right to block convictions; it has only the right to participate in the overall legal processes by which criminal guilt and innocence are determined.

We also cannot accept petitioners' second assumption—that minority groups, even when they are represented on a jury, will not adequately represent the viewpoint of those groups simply because they may be outvoted in the final result. They will be present during all deliberations, and their views will be heard. * * * We simply find no proof for the notion that a majority will disregard its instructions and cast its votes for guilt or innocence based on prejudice rather than the evidence.

* * *

Judgment affirmed.

Mr. Justice STEWART, with whom Mr. Justice BRENNAN and Mr. Justice MARSHALL join, dissenting.

In *Duncan* v. *Louisiana* * * * the Court squarely held that the Sixth Amendment right to trial by jury in a federal criminal case is made wholly applicable to state criminal trials by the Fourteenth Amendment. Unless *Duncan* is to be overruled, therefore, the only relevant question here is whether the Sixth Amendment's guarantee of trial by jury embraces a guarantee that the verdict of the jury must be unanimous. The answer to that question is clearly "yes." * * *

Until today, it has been universally understood that a unanimous verdict is an essential element of a Sixth Amendment jury trial. * * *

* * *

Mr. Justice BLACKMUN, concurring.

* * * My vote means only that I cannot conclude that the system is constitutionally offensive. Were I a legislator, I would disfavor it as a matter of policy. Our task here, however, is not to pursue and strike down what happens to impress us as undesirable legislative policy.

I do not hesitate to say, either, that a system employing a 7–5 standard, rather than a 9–3 or 75% minimum, would afford me great difficulty. * * *

Mr. Justice POWELL, concurring
* * *

* * *

* * * I concur in the plurality opinion in this case insofar as it concludes that a defendant in a state court may constitutionally be convicted by less than a unanimous verdict, but I am not in accord with a major premise upon which that judgment is based. Its premise is that the concept of jury trial, as applicable to the States under the Fourteenth Amendment, must be identical in every detail to the concept required in federal courts by the Sixth Amendment. I do not think that all of the elements of jury trial within the meaning of the Sixth Amendment are necessarily embodied in or incorporated into the Due Process Clause of the Fourteenth Amendment. * * *

Mr. Justice DOUGLAS, with whom Mr. Justice BRENNAN and Mr. Justice MARSHALL concur, dissenting.

* * *

I had * * * assumed that there was no dispute that the Federal Constitution required a unanimous jury in all criminal cases. After all, it has long been explicit constitutional doctrine that the Seventh Amendment civil jury must be unanimous. * * *

The result of today's decision is anomalous: though unanimous jury decisions are not required in state trials, they are constitutionally required in federal prosecutions. How can that be possible when both decisions stem from the Sixth Amendment?

* * *

But if we construe the Bill of Rights and the Fourteenth Amendment to permit States to "experiment" with the basic rights of people, we open a veritable Pandora's box. For hate and prejudice are versatile forces that can degrade the constitutional scheme.

That, however, is only one of my concerns when we make the Bill of

Rights, as applied to the States, a "watered down" version of what that charter guarantees. My chief concern is one often expressed by the late Justice Black who was alarmed at the prospect of nine men appointed for life sitting as a super-legislative body to determine whether government has gone too far. The balancing was done when the Constitution and Bill of Rights were written and adopted. For this Court to determine, say, whether one person but not another is entitled to free speech is a power never granted it. But that is the ultimate reach of a decision that lets the States, subject to our veto, to experiment with rights guaranteed by the Bill of Rights.

I would construe the Sixth Amendment, when applicable to the States, precisely as I would when applied to the Federal Government.

* * *

Mr. Justice BRENNAN, with whom Mr. Justice MARSHALL joins, dissenting.

Readers of today's opinions may be understandably puzzled why convictions by 11–1 and 10–2 jury votes are affirmed * * * when a majority of the Court agrees that the Sixth Amendment requires a unanimous verdict in federal criminal jury trials, and a majority also agrees that the right to jury trial guaranteed by the Sixth Amendment is to be enforced against the States according to the same standards that protect that right against federal encroachment. The reason is that while my Brother POWELL agrees that a unanimous verdict is required in federal criminal trials, he does not agree that the Sixth Amendment right to a jury trial is to be applied in the same way to State and Federal

Governments. In that circumstance, it is arguable that the affirmance of the convictions of Apodaca, Madden, and Cooper is not inconsistent with a view that today's decision * * * is a holding that only a unanimous verdict will afford the accused in a state criminal prosecution the jury trial guaranteed him by the Sixth Amendment. In any event, the affirmance must not obscure that the majority of the Court remains of the view that, as in the case of every specific of the Bill of Rights that extends to the States, the Sixth Amendment's jury trial guarantee, however it is to be construed, has identical application against both State and Federal Governments.

* * *

Mr. Justice MARSHALL, with whom Mr. Justice BRENNAN joins, dissenting.

* * *

[T]he question is too frighteningly simple to bear much discussion. We are asked to decide what is the nature of the "jury" that is guaranteed by the Sixth Amendment. I would have thought that history provided the appropriate guide, and as Mr. Justice Powell has demonstrated so convincingly, history compels the decision that unanimity is an essential feature of that jury. But the majority has embarked on a "functional" analysis of the jury that allows it to strip away, one by one, virtually all the characteristic features of the jury as we know it. Two years ago, over my dissent, the Court discarded as an essential feature the traditional size of the jury. *Williams* v. *Florida.* * * * Today the Court discards, at least in state trials, the traditional requirement of unanimity. It seems utterly and ominously clear that so long as the tribunal bears the label "jury," it will meet Sixth Amendment requirements as they are presently viewed by this Court. The Court seems to require only that jurors be laymen, drawn from the community without systematic exclusion of any group, who exercise common sense judgment.

* * *

Louisiana law permitted conviction for a nonpetty offense by a nonunanimous six-person jury. Burch, the defendant in a criminal prosecution for exhibiting obscene motion pictures, was found guilty by a 5–1 vote. The Louisiana Supreme Court affirmed. In Burch v. Louisiana, 441 U.S. 130, 99 S.Ct. 1623 (1979), the U. S. Supreme Court reversed the judgment, holding that "conviction by a nonunanimous six-person jury in a state criminal trial for a nonpetty offense deprives an accused of his constitutional right to trial by jury." Speaking for the Court, Justice Rehnquist said:

[T]his case lies at the intersection of our decisions concerning jury size and unanimity. As in *Ballew* [v. Georgia, 435 U.S. 223, 98 S.Ct. 1029 (1978)], we do not pretend the ability to discern *a priori* a bright line below which the number of jurors participating in the trial or in the verdict would not permit the jury to function in the manner required by our prior cases. * * * But having already departed from the strictly historical requirements of jury trial, it is inevitable that lines must be drawn somewhere if the substance of the jury trial right is to be preserved. * * *

This line drawing process, "although essential, cannot be wholly satisfactory, for it requires attaching different consequences to events which, when they lie near the line, actually differ very little." * * * However, much the same reasons that led us in *Ballew* to decide that use of a five-member jury threatened the fairness of the proceeding and the proper role of the jury, lead us to conclude now that conviction for a nonpetty offense by only five members of a six-person jury presents a similar threat to preservation of the substance of the jury trial guarantee and justifies our requiring verdicts rendered by six-person juries to be unanimous. We are buttressed in this view by the current jury practices of the several States. It appears that of those States that utilize six-member juries in trials of nonpetty offenses, only two, including Louisiana, also allow nonunanimous verdicts. We think that this near-uniform judgment of the Nation provides a useful guide in delimiting the line between those jury practices that are constitutionally permissible and those that are not. * * *

The State seeks to justify its use of nonunanimous six-person juries on the basis of the "considerable time" savings that it claims results from trying cases in this manner. It asserts that under its system, juror deliberation time is shortened and the number of hung juries is reduced. * * * Undoubtedly, the State has a substantial interest in reducing the time and expense associated with the administration of its system of criminal justice. But that interest cannot prevail here. First, on this record, any benefits that might accrue by allowing five members of a six-person jury to render a verdict, as compared with requiring unanimity of a six-member jury, are speculative, at best. More importantly, we think that when a State has reduced the size of its juries to the minimum number of jurors permitted by the Constitution, the additional authorization of nonunanimous verdicts by such juries sufficiently threatens the constitutional principles that led to the establishment of the size threshold that any countervailing interest of the State should yield.

b. THE RIGHT TO COUNSEL

POWELL v. ALABAMA

Supreme Court of the United States, 1932
287 U.S. 45, 53 S.Ct. 55, 77 L.Ed. 158

Ozie Powell and two other defendants were charged with rape and pleaded "not guilty." At the conclusion of each trial—all of which were completed in a single day—the juries convicted the defendants and imposed the death penalty. The trial judge overruled motions for new trials and sentenced the defendants as the juries directed. The judgments were affirmed by the Alabama Supreme Court. Defendants subsequently appealed to the United States Supreme Court alleging a denial of due process and equal protection of the laws because: (1) they had not been given a fair and impartial trial; (2) they were denied the right to counsel and the corresponding opportunity for effective consultation and preparation for trial; and (3) they had been deprived of trials before juries of their peers since Negroes were systematically excluded from jury service. [The last of these challenges was sustained by the Supreme Court in Norris v. Alabama, 294 U.S. 587, 55 S.Ct. 579 (1935). Together, the *Powell* and *Norris* controversies were popularly known as "The Scottsboro Cases."] Additional facts in this case appear in the opinion.

Mr. Justice SUTHERLAND delivered the opinion of the Court.

* * *

The record shows that on the day when the offense is said to have been committed, these defendants, together with a number of other negroes, were upon a freight train on its way through Alabama. On the same train were seven white boys and the two white girls. A fight took place between the negroes and the white boys, in the course of which the white boys, with the exception of one named Gilley, were thrown off the train. A message was sent ahead, reporting the fight and asking that every negro be gotten off the train. The participants in the fight, and the two girls, were in an open gondola car. The two girls testified that each of them was assaulted by six different negroes in turn, and they identi-

fied the seven defendants as having been among the number. None of the white boys was called to testify, with the exception of Gilley, who was called in rebuttal.

Before the train reached Scottsboro, Ala., a sheriff's posse seized the defendants and two other negroes. Both girls and the negroes then were taken to Scottsboro, the county seat. Word of their coming and of the alleged assault had preceded them, and they were met at Scottsboro by a large crowd. It does not sufficiently appear that the defendants were seriously threatened with, or that they were actually in danger of, mob violence; but it does appear that the attitude of the community was one of great hostility. The sheriff thought it necessary to call for the militia to assist in safeguarding the prisoners. Chief Justice Anderson pointed out in his opinion that every step taken from the arrest and arraignment to the sentence was accompanied by the military. Soldiers took the defendants to Gadsden for safe-keeping, brought them back to Scottsboro for arraignment, returned them to Gadsden for safe-keeping while awaiting trial, escorted them to Scottsboro for trial a few days later, and guarded the courthouse and grounds at every stage of the proceedings. It is perfectly apparent that the proceedings, from beginning to end, took place in an atmosphere of tense, hostile, and excited public sentiment. During the entire time, the defendants were closely confined or were under military guard. The record does not disclose their ages, except that one of them was nineteen; but the record clearly indicates that most, if not all, of them were youthful, and they are constantly referred to as "the boys." They were ignorant and illiterate. All of them were residents of other states, where alone members of their families or friends resided.

[W]e confine ourselves * * * to the inquiry whether the defendants were in substance denied the right of counsel, and if so, whether such denial infringes the due process clause of the Fourteenth Amendment.

First. The record shows that immediately upon the return of the indictment defendants were arraigned and pleaded not guilty. Apparently they were not asked whether they had, or were able to employ, counsel, or wished to have counsel appointed; or whether they had friends or relatives who might assist in that regard if communicated with. That it would not have been an idle ceremony to have given the defendants reasonable opportunity to communicate with

their families and endeavor to obtain counsel is demonstrated by the fact that very soon after conviction, able counsel appeared in their behalf.
* * *

It is hardly necessary to say that the right to counsel being conceded, a defendant should be afforded a fair opportunity to secure counsel of his own choice. Not only was that not done here, but such designation of counsel as was attempted was either so indefinite or so close upon the trial as to amount to a denial of effective and substantial aid in that regard. * * *

* * *

It * * * will be seen that until the very morning of the trial no lawyer had been named or definitely designated to represent the defendants. Prior to that time, the trial judge had "appointed all the members of the bar" for the limited "purpose of arraigning the defendants." Whether they would represent the defendants thereafter, if no counsel appeared in their behalf, was a matter of speculation only, or, as the judge indicated, of mere anticipation on the part of the court. Such a designation, even if made for all purposes, would, in our opinion, have fallen far short of meeting, in any proper sense, a requirement for the appointment of counsel. How many lawyers were members of the bar does not appear; but, in the very nature of things, whether many or few, they would not, thus collectively named, have been given that clear appreciation of responsibility or impressed with that individual sense of duty which should and naturally would accompany the appointment of a selected member of the bar, specifically named and assigned.

[T]his action of the trial judge in respect of appointment of counsel was little more than an expansive gesture, imposing no substantial or definite obligation upon any one * * *. In any event, the circumstance lends emphasis to the conclusion that during perhaps the most critical period of the proceedings against these defendants, that is to say, from the time of their arraignment until the beginning of their trial, when consultation, thorough-going investigation and preparation were vitally important, the defendants did not have the aid of counsel in any real sense, although they were as much entitled to such aid during that period as at the trial itself. * * *

* * * The defendants, young, ignorant, illiterate, surrounded by hostile sentiment, haled back and forth under guard of soldiers, charged with an atrocious crime regarded with especial horror in the community where they were to be tried, were thus put in peril of their lives within a few moments after counsel for the first time charged with any degree of responsibility began to represent them.

* * * Under the circumstances disclosed, we hold that defendants were not accorded the right of counsel in any substantial sense. To decide otherwise, would simply be to ignore actualities. * * * The prompt disposition of criminal cases is to be commended and encouraged. But in reaching that result a defendant, charged with a serious crime, must not be stripped of his right to have sufficient time to advise with counsel and prepare his defense. To do that is not to proceed promptly in the calm spirit of regulated justice but to go forward with the haste of the mob.

* * *

Second. The Constitution of Alabama * * * provides that in all criminal prosecutions the accused shall enjoy the right to have the assistance of counsel; and a state statute * * * requires the court in a capital case, where the defendant is unable to employ counsel, to appoint counsel for him. The state Supreme Court held that these provisions had not been infringed. * * * The question, however, which it is our duty, and within our power, to decide, is whether the denial of the assistance of counsel contravenes the due process clause of the Fourteenth Amendment to the Federal Constitution.

* * *

In the light of the facts outlined in the forepart of this opinion—the ignorance and illiteracy of the defendants, their youth, the circumstances of public hostility, the imprisonment and the close surveillance of the defendants by the military forces, the fact that their friends and families were all in other states and communication with them necessarily difficult, and above all that they stood in deadly peril of their lives—we think the failure of the trial court to give them reasonable time and opportunity to secure counsel was a clear denial of due process.

But passing that, and assuming their inability, even if opportunity had been given, to employ counsel, as the trial court evidently did assume, we are of opinion that, under the circumstances just stated, the necessity of counsel was so vital and imperative that the failure of the trial court to make an effective appointment of counsel was likewise a denial of due process within the meaning of the Fourteenth Amendment. Whether this would be so in other criminal prosecutions, or under other circumstances, we need not determine. All that it is necessary now to decide, as we do decide, is that in a capital case, where the defendant is unable to employ counsel, and is incapable adequately of making his own defense because of ignorance, feeblemindedness, illiteracy, or the like, it is the duty of the court, whether requested or not, to assign counsel for him as a necessary requisite of due process of law; and that duty is not discharged by an assignment at such a time or under such circumstances as to preclude the giving of effective aid in the preparation and trial of the case. To hold otherwise would be to ignore the fundamental postulate, already adverted to, "that there are certain immutable principles of justice which inhere in the very idea of free government which no member of the Union may disregard." * * * In a case such as this, whatever may be the rule in other cases, the right to have counsel appointed, when necessary, is a logical corollary from the constitutional right to be heard by counsel. * * *

* * *

The judgments must be reversed and the causes remanded for further proceedings not inconsistent with this opinion.

* * *

[Justice BUTLER dissented in an opinion in which Justice McREYNOLDS concurred.]

GIDEON v. WAINWRIGHT

Supreme Court of the United States, 1963
372 U.S. 335, 83 S.Ct. 792, 9 L.Ed.2d 799

Clarence Gideon was charged with breaking and entering a pool hall with the intent to commit a crime—a felony under Florida law. When he appeared for trial, Gideon, who did not have a lawyer or the money with which to retain one, requested the trial judge to appoint one for him. The trial judge declined, citing a Florida statute which permitted the appointment of counsel only in capital cases. Gideon then proceeded to conduct his own defense. The jury found him guilty, and the judge sentenced him to five years in prison. Gideon subsequently sued out a writ of habeas corpus against Wainwright, the state director of corrections. The Florida Supreme Court denied relief, and Gideon appealed to the United States Supreme Court, asserting that the trial judge's refusal to appoint counsel for him was a denial of rights guaranteed by the Sixth and Fourteenth Amendments.

Mr. Justice BLACK delivered the opinion of the Court.

* * * Since 1942, when Betts v. Brady, 316 U.S. 455, 62 S.Ct. 1252, was decided by a divided Court, the problem of a defendant's federal constitutional right to counsel in a state court has been a continuing source of controversy and litigation in both state and federal courts. To give this problem another review here, we granted certiorari. * * * Since Gideon was proceeding *in forma pauperis*, we appointed counsel to represent him and requested both sides to discuss in their briefs and oral arguments the following: "Should this Court's holding in *Betts*

v. *Brady* * * * be reconsidered?"

The facts upon which Betts claimed that he had been unconstitutionally denied the right to have counsel appointed to assist him are strikingly like the facts upon which Gideon here bases his federal constitutional claim. * * *

Treating due process as "a concept less rigid and more fluid than those envisaged in other specific and particular provisions of the Bill of Rights," the Court held that refusal to appoint counsel under the particular facts and circumstances in the *Betts* case was not so "offensive to the common and fundamental ideas of fairness" as to amount to a denial of due process. Since the facts and circumstances of the two cases are so nearly indistinguishable, we think the *Betts* v. *Brady* holding if left standing would require us to reject Gideon's claim that the Constitution guarantees him the assistance of counsel. Upon full reconsideration we conclude that *Betts* v. *Brady* should be overruled.

* * *

We think the Court in *Betts* had ample precedent for acknowledging that those guarantees of the Bill of Rights which are fundamental safeguards of liberty immune from federal abridgment are equally protected against state invasion by the Due Process Clause of the Fourteenth Amendment. This same principle was recognized, explained, and applied in *Powell* v. *Alabama*. * * *

We accept *Betts* v. *Brady's* assumption, based as it was on our prior cases, that a provision of the Bill of Rights which is "fundamental and essential to a fair trial" is made obligatory upon the States by the Four-teenth Amendment. We think the Court in *Betts* was wrong, however, in concluding that the Sixth Amendment's guarantee of counsel is not one of these fundamental rights. Ten years before *Betts* v. *Brady*, this Court, after full consideration of all the historical data examined in *Betts*, had unequivocally declared that "the right to the aid of counsel is of this fundamental character." *Powell* v. *Alabama*, 287 U.S. 45, 68, 53 S.Ct. 55, 63 (1932). While the Court at the close of its *Powell* opinion did by its language, as this Court frequently does, limit its holding to the particular facts and circumstances of that case, its conclusions about the fundamental nature of the right to counsel are unmistakable. * * *

In light of these and many other prior decisions of this Court, it is not surprising that the *Betts* Court, when faced with the contention that "one charged with crime, who is unable to obtain counsel, must be furnished counsel by the state," conceded that "[e]xpressions in the opinions of this court lend color to the argument." * * * The fact is that in deciding as it did—that "appointment of counsel is not a fundamental right, essential to a fair trial"—the Court in *Betts* v. *Brady* made an abrupt break with its own well-considered precedents. In returning to these old precedents, sounder we believe than the new, we but restore constitutional principles established to achieve a fair system of justice. Not only these precedents but also reason and reflection require us to recognize that in our adversary system of criminal justice, any person haled into court, who is too poor to hire a lawyer, cannot be assured a fair trial unless counsel is provided for him. This seems to us to be an obvious truth. Governments, both state and federal, quite properly spend vast sums of money to establish machinery to try defendants accused of crime. Lawyers to prosecute are everywhere deemed essential to protect the public's interest in an orderly society. Similarly, there are few defendants charged with crime, few indeed, who fail to hire the best lawyers they can get to prepare and present their defenses. That government hires lawyers to prosecute and defendants who have the money hire lawyers to defend are the strongest indications of the widespread belief that lawyers in criminal courts are necessities, not luxuries. The right of one charged with crime to counsel may not be deemed fundamental and essential to fair trials in some countries, but it is in ours. From the very beginning, our state and national constitutions and laws have laid great emphasis on procedural and substantive safeguards designed to assure fair trials before impartial tribunals in which every defendant stands equal before the law. This noble ideal cannot be realized if the poor man charged with crime has to face his accusers without a lawyer to assist him. * * *

The Court in *Betts* v. *Brady* departed from the sound wisdom upon which the Court's holding in *Powell* v. *Alabama* rested. Florida, supported by two other States, has asked that *Betts* v. *Brady* be left intact. Twenty-two States, as friends of the Court, argue that Betts was "an anachronism when handed down" and that it should now be overruled. We agree.

The judgment is reversed and the cause is remanded to the Supreme Court of Florida for further action not inconsistent with this opinion.

* * *

Mr. Justice CLARK, concurring in the result.

* * *

* * * The Court's decision today * * * does no more than erase a distinction which has no basis in logic and an increasingly eroded basis in authority. * * *

I must conclude * * * that the Constitution makes no distinction between capital and noncapital cases. The Fourteenth Amendment requires due process of law for the deprival of "liberty" just as for deprival of "life," and there cannot constitutionally be a difference in the quality of the process based merely upon a supposed difference in the sanction involved. How can the Fourteenth Amendment tolerate a procedure which it condemns in capital cases on the ground that deprival of liberty may be less onerous than deprival of life—a value judgment not universally accepted—or that only the latter deprival is irrevocable? I can find no acceptable rationalization for such a result, and I therefore concur in the judgment of the Court.

Mr. Justice HARLAN, concurring.

I agree that *Betts* v. *Brady* should be overruled, but consider it entitled to a more respectful burial than has been accorded, at least on the part of those of us who were not on the Court when that case was decided.

I cannot subscribe to the view that *Betts* v. *Brady* represented "an abrupt break with its own well-considered precedents." * * * In 1932, in *Powell* v. *Alabama*, * * * a capital case, this Court declared that under the particular facts there presented—"the ignorance and illiteracy of the defendants, their youth, the circumstances of public hostility * * * and above all that they stood in deadly peril of their lives" * * * the state court had a duty to assign counsel for the trial as a necessary requisite of due process of law. It is evident that these limiting facts were not added to the opinion as an afterthought; they were repeatedly emphasized * * * and were clearly regarded as important to the result.

Thus when this Court, a decade later, decided *Betts* v. *Brady*, it did no more than to admit of the possible existence of special circumstances in noncapital as well as capital trials, while at the same time insisting that such circumstances be shown in order to establish a denial of due process. The right to appointed counsel had been recognized as being considerably broader in federal prosecutions, see Johnson v. Zerbst, 304 U.S. 458, 58 S.Ct. 1019, but to have imposed these requirements on the States would indeed have been "an abrupt break" with the almost immediate past. The declaration that the right to appointed counsel in state prosecutions, as established in *Powell* v. *Alabama*, was not limited to capital cases was in truth not a departure from, but an extension of, existing precedent.

* * *

In agreeing with the Court that the right to counsel in a case such as this should now be expressly recognized as a fundamental right embraced in the Fourteenth Amendment, I wish to make a further observation. When we hold a right or immunity, valid against the Federal Government, to be "implicit in the concept of ordered liberty" and thus valid against the States, I do not read our past decisions to suggest that by so holding, we automatically carry over an entire body of federal law and apply it in full sweep to the States. Any such concept would disregard the frequently wide disparity between the legitimate interests of the States and the Federal Government, the divergent problems that they face, and the significantly different consequences of their actions. * * * In what is done today I do not understand the Court to depart from the principles laid down in *Palko* v. *Connecticut* * * * or to embrace the concept that the Fourteenth Amendment "incorporates" the Sixth Amendment as such.

On these premises I join in the judgment of the Court.

The scope of the right to counsel protection was broadened further—this time by a unanimous Court—in Argersinger v. Hamlin, 407 U.S. 25, 92 S.Ct. 2006 (1972). Argersinger, an indigent, was charged with carrying a concealed weapon, an offense under Florida law which carried a penalty of up to six months imprisonment and a fine of $1,000. After the case had been tried to a judge and in which petitioner was not represented by counsel, Argersinger was sentenced to serve ninety days in jail. He subsequently brought action for habeas corpus against Hamlin, the local sheriff, challenging the constitutionality of his conviction on grounds he had been denied the capability of developing an adequate defense without the services of counsel guaranteed by the Sixth and Fourteenth Amendments. The Florida Supreme Court dismissed the petition for relief relying on *Duncan* v. *Louisiana* so as conclude "that the right to court-appointed counsel extends only to trials for non-petty offenses punishable by more than six months imprisonment."

On certiorari from the almost equally divided Florida Supreme Court, the United States Supreme Court, per Justice Douglas, reversed, holding "that absent a knowing and intelligent waiver, no person may be imprisoned for any offense, whether classified as petty, misdemeanor, or felony, unless he was represented by counsel at his trial." Reasoned Justice Douglas:

> Both *Powell* and *Gideon* involved felonies. But their rationale has relevance to any criminal trial, where an accused is deprived of his liberty. *Powell* and *Gideon* suggest that there are certain fundamental rights applicable to all such criminal prosecutions.　*　*　*
>
> The requirement of counsel may well be necessary for a fair trial even in a petty offense prosecution. We are by no means convinced that legal and constitutional questions involved in a case that actually leads to imprisonment even for a brief period are any less complex than when a person can be sent off for six months or more.　*　*　*
>
> In addition, the volume of misdemeanor cases, far greater in number than felony prosecutions, may create an obsession for speedy dispositions, regardless of the fairness of the result.　*　*　*
>
> That picture is seen in almost every report. "The misdemeanor trial is characterized by insufficient and frequently irresponsible preparation on the part of the defense, the prosecution, and the court. Everything is rush, rush."　*　*　*
>
> There is evidence of the prejudice which results to misdemeanor defendants from this "assembly-line justice." One study concluded that "Misdemeanants represented by attorneys are five times as likely to emerge from police court with all charges dismissed as are defendants who face similar charges without counsel." ACLU, Legal Counsel for Misdemeanants, Preliminary Report, 1 (1970).

Justice Powell, speaking for himself and Justice Rehnquist, concurred. Preferring a decision based on the concept of due process embodied in the Fourteenth Amendment to the majority's reliance on the Sixth Amendment, he said:

> There is a middle course, between the extremes of Florida's six-month rule and the Court's rule, which comports with the requirements of the Fourteenth Amendment. I would adhere to the principle of due process that requires fundamental fairness in criminal trials, a principle which I believe encompasses the right to counsel in petty cases whenever the assistance of counsel is necessary to assure a fair trial.
>
> I am in accord with the Court that an indigent accused's need for the assistance of counsel does not mysteriously evaporate when he is charged with an offense punishable by six months or less. In *Powell* v. *Alabama* and *Gideon*, both of which involved felony prosecutions, this Court noted that few laymen can present adequately their own cases, much less identify and argue relevant legal questions. Many petty offenses will also present complex legal and factual issues that may not be fairly tried if the defendant is not assisted by counsel. Even in relatively simple cases, some defendants, because of ignorance or some other handicap, will be incapable of defending themselves. The consequences of a misdemeanor conviction, whether they be a brief period served under the sometimes deplorable con-

ditions found in local jails or the effect of a criminal record on employability, are frequently of sufficient magnitude not to be casually dismissed by the label "petty."

Serious consequences also may result from convictions not punishable by imprisonment. Stigma may attach to a drunken driving conviction or a hit-and-run escapade. Losing one's driver's license is more serious for some individuals than a brief stay in jail. * * * When the deprivation of property rights and interest is of sufficient consequence, denying the assistance of counsel to indigents who are incapable of defending themselves is a denial of due process.

This is not to say that due process requires the appointment of counsel in all petty cases, or that assessment of the possible consequences of conviction is the sole test for the need for assistance of counsel. The flat six-month rule of the Florida court and the equally inflexible rule of the majority opinion apply to *all* cases within their defined areas regardless of circumstances. It is precisely because of this mechanistic application that I find these alternatives unsatisfactory. Due process, perhaps the most fundamental concept in our law, embodies principles of fairness rather than immutable line drawing as to every aspect of a criminal trial. While counsel is often essential to a fair trial, this is by no means a universal fact. Some petty offense cases are complex; others are exceedingly simple. * * * Nor does every defendant who can afford to do so hire lawyers to defend petty charges. Where the possibility of a jail sentence is remote and the probable fine seems small, or where the evidence of guilt is overwhelming, the costs of assistance of counsel may exceed the benefits. It is anomalous that the Court's opinion today will extend the right of appointed counsel to indigent defendants in cases where the right to counsel would rarely be exercised by nonindigent defendants.

Indeed, one of the effects of this ruling will be to favor defendants classified as indigents over those not so classified yet who are in low income groups where engaging counsel in a minor petty offense case would be a luxury the family could not afford. The line between indigency and assumed capacity to pay for counsel is necessarily somewhat arbitrary, drawn differently from State to State and often resulting in serious inequities to accused persons. The Court's new rule will accent the disadvantage of being barely self-sufficient economically.

* * *

The rule adopted today does not go all the way. It is limited to petty offense cases in which the sentence is some imprisonment. The thrust of the Court's position indicates, however, that when the decision must be made, the rule will be extended to all petty offense cases except perhaps the most minor traffic violations. * * *

* * *

Thus, although the new rule is extended today only to the imprisonment category of cases, the Court's opinion foreshadows the adoption of a broad prophylactic rule applicable to all petty offenses. No one can foresee the consequences of such a drastic enlargement of the constitutional right to free counsel. But even today's decision could have a seriously adverse impact upon the day to day functioning of the criminal justice system. We should be slow to fashion a new constitutional rule with consequences of such unknown dimensions, especially since it is supported neither by history nor precedent.

* * *

There are thousands of statutes and ordinances which authorize imprisonment for six months or less, usually as an alternative to a fine. These offenses include some of the most trivial of misdemeanors, ranging from spitting on the sidewalk to certain traffic offenses. They also include a variety of more serious misdemeanors. This broad spectrum of petty offense cases daily floods the lower criminal courts. The rule laid down today will confront the judges of each of these courts with an awkward dilemma. If counsel is not appointed or knowingly waived, no sentence of imprisonment for any duration may be imposed. The judge will therefore be forced to decide in advance of trial—and without hearing the evidence— whether he will forgo entirely his judicial discretion to impose some sentence of imprisonment and abandon his responsibility to consider the full range of punishments established by the legislature. His alternatives, assuming the availability of counsel, will be to appoint counsel and retain the discretion vested in him by law, or to abandon this discretion in advance and proceed without counsel.

* * *

To avoid * * * problems and to preserve a range of sentencing options as prescribed by law, most judges are likely to appoint counsel for indigents in all but the most minor offenses where jail sentences are extremely rare. It is doubtful that the States possess the necessary resources to meet this sudden expansion of the right to counsel. * * *

* * *

Perhaps the most serious potential impact of today's holding will be on our already overburdened local courts. The primary cause of "assembly line" justice is a volume of cases far in excess of the capacity of the system to handle efficiently and fairly. The Court's rule may well exacerbate delay and congestion in these courts. We are familiar with the common tactic of counsel of exhausting every possible legal avenue, often without due regard to its probable payoff. In some cases this may be the lawyer's duty; in other cases it will be done for purposes of delay. The absence of direct economic impact on the client, plus the omnipresent ineffective assistance of counsel claim, frequently produces a decision to litigate every issue. * * *

There is an additional problem. The ability of various States and localities to furnish counsel varies widely. Even if there were adequate resources on a national basis, the uneven distribution of these resources— of lawyers, of facilities and available funding—presents the most acute problem. * * *

* * *

I would hold that the right to counsel in petty offense cases is not absolute but is one to be determined by the trial courts exercising a judicial discretion on a case-by-case basis. The determination should be made before the accused formally pleads; many petty cases are resolved by guilty pleas in which the assistance of counsel may be required. If the trial court should conclude that the assistance of counsel is not required in any case, it should state its reasons so that the issue could be preserved for review. The trial court would then become obligated to scrutinize carefully the subsequent proceedings for the protection of the defendant. * * * Formal trial rules should not be applied strictly against unrepresented defendants. Finally, appellate courts should carefully scrutinize all decisions not to appoint counsel and the proceedings which follow.

It is impossible, as well as unwise, to create a precise and detailed set of guidelines for judges to follow in determining whether the appointment of counsel is necessary to assure a fair trial. Certainly three general factors should be weighed. First, the court should consider the complexity of the offense charged. * * *

Second, the court should consider the probable sentence that will follow if a conviction is obtained. The more serious the likely consequences, the greater is the probability that a lawyer should be appointed. * * *

Third, the court should consider the individual factors peculiar to each case. These, of course, would be the most difficult to anticipate. One relevant factor would be the competency of the individual defendant to present his own case. The attitude of the community toward a particular defendant or particular incident would be another consideration. But there might be other reasons why a defendant would have a peculiar need for a lawyer which would compel the appointment of counsel in a case where the court would normally think this unnecessary. Obviously, the sensitivity and diligence of individual judges would be crucial to the operation of a rule of fundamental fairness requiring the consideration of the varying factors in each case.

* * *

——————

Ambiguity remained after the Court announced its holding in *Argersinger*, namely whether constitutionally mandated provision of counsel to an indigent accused obtained only in instances where the defendant was in fact sentenced to a term of imprisonment or whether the guarantee extended to the trial of all offenses which carried a possible penalty of imprisonment even if the defendant was not ultimately sentenced to a period of confinement but was ordered to pay a fine instead. In Scott v. Illinois, 440 U.S. 367, 99 S.Ct. 1158 (1979), the Court resolved the conflict by selecting the first alternative as the proper interpretation of the holding in *Argersinger*. Said Justice Rehnquist, speaking for the Court:

Although the intentions of the *Argersinger* Court are not unmistakably clear from its opinion, we conclude today that *Argersinger* did indeed delimit the constitutional right to appointed counsel in state criminal proceedings. * * * [W]e believe that the central premise of *Argersinger*—that actual imprisonment is a penalty different in kind from fines or the mere threat of imprisonment—is eminently sound and warrants adoption of actual imprisonment as the line defining the constitutional right to appointment of counsel. *Argersinger* has proved reasonably workable, whereas any extension would create confusion and impose unpredictable, but necessarily substantial, costs on 50 quite diverse States. We therefore hold that the Sixth and Fourteenth Amendments to the United States Constitution require only that no indigent criminal defendant be sentenced to a term of imprisonment unless the State has afforded him the right to assistance of appointed counsel in his defense. * * *

Recognizing the moral stigma that attaches to conviction for a criminal offense, Justice Brennan, in a dissent which was joined in by Justices Marshall and Stevens, argued for a "standard that would require the appointment of counsel for indigents accused of any offense for which imprisonment for any time is authorized." Justice Blackmun, dissenting separately voted to extend the right to counsel "at least as far as the right to jury trial secured by * * * [the Sixth and Fourteenth] amendments. Accordingly, I would hold that an indigent defendant in a state criminal case must be afforded appointed counsel whenever the defendant is prosecuted for a nonpetty criminal offense, that is, one punishable by more than six months' imprisonment, * * * or whenever the defendant is convicted of an offense and is actually subjected to a term of imprisonment * * * "

ESCOBEDO v. ILLINOIS

Supreme Court of the United States, 1964
378 U.S. 478, 84 S.Ct. 1758, 12 L.Ed.2d 977

The facts are set out in the opinion.

Mr. Justice GOLDBERG delivered the opinion of the Court.

The critical question in this case is whether, under the circumstances, the refusal by the police to honor petitioner's request to consult with his lawyer during the course of an interrogation constitutes a denial of "the Assistance of Counsel" in violation of the Sixth Amendment to the Constitution as "made obligatory upon the States by the Fourteenth Amendment," * * * and thereby renders inadmissible in a state criminal trial any incriminating statement elicited by the police during the interrogation.

On the night of January 19, 1960, petitioner's brother-in-law was fatally shot. In the early hours of the next morning, at 2:30 a. m., petitioner was arrested without a warrant and interrogated. Petitioner made no statement to the police and was released at 5 that afternoon. * * *

On January 30, Benedict DiGerlando, who was then in police custody and who was later indicted for the murder along with petitioner, told

the police that petitioner had fired the fatal shots. Between 8 and 9 that evening, petitioner and his sister, the widow of the deceased, were arrested and taken to police headquarters. En route to the police station, the police "had handcuffed the defendant behind his back," and "one of the arresting officers told defendant that DiGerlando had named him as the one who shot" the deceased. Petitioner testified, without contradiction, that the "detectives said they had us pretty well, up pretty tight, and we might as well admit to this crime," and that he replied, "I am sorry but I would like to have advice from my lawyer." A police officer testified that although petitioner was not formally charged "he was in custody" and "couldn't walk out the door."

Shortly after petitioner reached police headquarters, his retained lawyer arrived. * * *

Petitioner testified that during the course of the interrogation he repeatedly asked to speak to his lawyer and that the police said that his lawyer "didn't want to see" him. The testimony of the police officers confirmed these accounts in substantial detail.

Notwithstanding repeated requests by each, petitioner and his retained lawyer were afforded no opportunity to consult during the course of the entire interrogation. At one point, as previously noted, petitioner and his attorney came into each other's view for a few moments but the attorney was quickly ushered away. Petitioner testified "that he heard a detective telling the attorney the latter would not be allowed to talk to [him] 'until they were done' " and that he heard the attorney being refused permission to remain in the adjoining room. A police officer testified that he had told the lawyer that he could not see petitioner until "we were through interrogating" him.

There is testimony by the police that during the interrogation, petitioner, a 22-year-old of Mexican extraction with no record of previous experience with the police, "was handcuffed" in a standing position and that he "was nervous, he had circles under his eyes and he was upset" and was "agitated" because "he had not slept well in over a week."

It is undisputed that during the course of the interrogation Officer Montejano, who "grew up" in petitioner's neighborhood, who knew his family, and whose uses "Spanish language in [his] police work," conferred alone with petitioner "for about a quarter of an hour." * * * Petitioner testified that the officer said to him "in Spanish that my sister and I could go home if I pinned it on Benedict DiGerlando," that "he would see to it that we would go home and be held only as witnesses, if anything, if we had made a statement against DiGer-

lando * * * , that we would be able to go home that night." Petitioner testified that he made the statement in issue because of this assurance. Officer Montejano denied offering any such assurance.

A police officer testified that during the interrogation the following occurred:

"I informed him of what DiGerlando told me and when I did, he told me that DiGerlando was [lying] and I said, 'Would you care to tell DiGerlando that?' and he said, 'Yes, I will.' So, I brought * * * Escobedo in and he confronted DiGerlando and he told him that he was lying and said, 'I didn't shoot Manuel, you did it.' "

In this way, petitioner, for the first time admitted to some knowledge of the crime. After that he made additional statements further implicating himself in the murder plot. At this point an Assistant State's Attorney * * * was summoned "to take" a statement. Mr. Cooper, an experienced lawyer who was assigned to the Homicide Division to take "statements from some defendants and some prisoners that they had in custody," "took" petitioner's statement by asking carefully framed questions apparently designed to assure the admissibility into evidence of the resulting answers. Mr. Cooper testified that he did not advise petitioner of his constitutional rights, and it is undisputed that no one during the course of the interrogation so advised him.

Petitioner moved both before and during trial to suppress the incriminating statement, but the motions were denied. Petitioner was convicted of murder and he appealed the conviction.

         * * *

The interrogation here was conducted before petitioner was formally indicted. But in the context of this case, that fact should make no difference. When petitioner requested, and was denied, an opportunity to consult with his lawyer, the investigation had ceased to be a general investigation of "an unsolved crime." * * * Petitioner had become the accused, and the purpose of the interrogation was to "get him" to confess his guilt despite his constitutional right not to do so. At the time of his arrest and throughout the course of the interrogation, the police told petitioner that they had convincing evidence that he had fired the fatal shots. Without informing him of his absolute right to remain silent in the face of this accusation, the police urged him to make a statement. * * * Petitioner, a layman, was undoubtedly unaware that under Illinois law an admission of "mere" complicity in the murder plot was legally as damaging as an admission of firing of the fatal shots. * * * The "guiding hand of counsel" was essential to advise petitioner of his rights in this delicate situation. * * * This was the "stage when legal aid and advice" were most critical to petitioner. * * * What happened at this interrogation could certainly "affect the whole trial." * * * It would exalt form over substance to make the right to counsel, under these circumstances, depend on whether at the time of the interrogation, the authorities had secured a formal indictment. Petitioner had, for all practical purposes, already been charged with murder.

*   *   *

In *Gideon* v. *Wainwright* * * * we held that every person accused of a crime, whether state or federal, is entitled to a lawyer at trial. The rule sought by the State here, however, would make the trial no more than an appeal from the interrogation; and the "right to use counsel at the formal trial [would be] a very hollow thing [if], for all practical purposes, the conviction is already assured by pretrial examination." * * * "One can imagine a cynical prosecutor saying: 'Let them have the most illustrious counsel, now. They can't escape the noose. There is nothing that counsel can do for them at the trial.' " * * *

It is argued that if the right to counsel is afforded prior to indictment, the number of confessions obtained by the police will diminish significantly, because most confessions are obtained during the period between arrest and indictment, and "any lawyer worth his salt will tell the suspect in no uncertain terms to make no statement to police under any circumstances." * * * This argument, of course, cuts two ways. The fact that many confessions are obtained during this period points up its critical nature as a "stage when legal aid and advice" are surely needed. * * * The right to counsel would indeed be hollow if it began at a period when few confessions were obtained. There is necessarily a direct relationship between the importance of a stage to the police in their quest for a confession and the criticalness of that stage to the accused in his need for legal advice. Our Constitution, unlike some others, strikes the balance in favor of the right of the accused to be advised by his lawyer of his privilege against self-incrimination. * * *

We have learned the lesson of history, ancient and modern, that a system of criminal law enforcement which comes to depend on the "confession" will, in the long run, be less reliable and more subject to abuses than a system which depends on extrinsic evidence independently secured through skillful investigation. * * *

* * *

We hold, therefore, that where, as here, the investigation is no longer a general inquiry into an unsolved crime but has begun to focus on a particular suspect, the suspect has been taken into police custody, the police carry out a process of interrogations that lends itself to eliciting incriminating statements, the suspect has requested and been denied an opportunity to consult with his lawyer, and the police have not effectively warned him of his absolute constitutional right to remain silent, the accused has been denied "the Assistance of Counsel" in violation of the Sixth Amendment to the Constitution as "made obligatory upon the States by the Fourteenth Amendment," * * * and that no statement elicited by the police during the interrogation may be used against him at a criminal trial.

* * *

Reversed and remanded.

Mr. Justice HARLAN, dissenting.

* * * I think the rule announced today is most ill-conceived and that it seriously and unjustifiably fetters perfectly legitimate methods of criminal law enforcement.

Mr. Justice STEWART, dissenting.

* * *

* * * Under our system of criminal justice the institution of for-mal, meaningful judicial proceedings, by way of indictment, information, or arraignment, marks the point at which a criminal investigation has ended and adversary proceedings have commenced. It is at this point that the constitutional guarantees attach which pertain to a criminal trial. Among those guarantees are the right to a speedy trial, the right of confrontation, and the right to trial by jury. Another is the guarantee of the assistance of counsel. * * *

The confession which the Court today holds inadmissible was a voluntary one. It was given during the course of a perfectly legitimate police investigation of an unsolved murder. The Court says that what happened during this investigation "affected" the trial. I had always supposed that the whole purpose of a police investigation of a murder was to "affect" the trial of the murderer, and that it would be only an incompetent, unsuccessful, or corrupt investigation which would not do so. The Court further says that the Illinois police officers did not advise the petitioner of his "constitutional rights" before he confessed to the murder. This Court has never held that the Constitution requires the police to give any "advice" under circumstances such as these.

Supported by no stronger authority that its own rhetoric, the Court today converts a routine police investigation of an unsolved murder into a distorted analogue of a judicial trial. It imports into this investigation constitutional concepts historically applicable only after the onset of formal prosecutorial proceedings. By doing so, I think the Court perverts those precious constitutional guarantees, and frustrates the vital interests of society in preserving the legitimate and proper function of honest and purposeful police investigation.

* * *

Mr. Justice WHITE, with whom Mr. Justice CLARK and Mr. Justice STEWART join, dissenting.

* * *

The Court chooses * * * to rely on the virtues and morality of a system of criminal law enforcement which does not depend on the "confession." No such judgment is to be found in the Constitution. It might be appropriate for a legislature to provide that a suspect should not be consulted during a criminal investigation; that an accused should never be called before a grand jury to answer, even if he wants to, what may well be incriminating questions; and that no person, whether he be a suspect, guilty criminal or innocent bystander, should be put to the ordeal of responding to orderly noncompulsory inquiry by the State. But this is not the system our Constitution re-

quires. The only "inquisitions" the Constitution forbids are those which compel incrimination. Escobedo's statements were not compelled and the Court does not hold that they were.

This new American judges' rule, which is to be applied in both federal and state courts, is perhaps thought to be a necessary safeguard against the possibility of extorted confessions. To this extent it reflects a deep-seated distrust of law enforcement officers everywhere, unsupported by relevant data or current material based upon our own experience. Obviously law enforcement officers can make mistakes and exceed their authority, as today's decision shows that even judges can do, but I have somewhat more faith than the Court evidently has in the ability and desire of prosecutors and of the power of the appellate courts to discern and correct such violations of the law.

* * *

MIRANDA v. ARIZONA

Supreme Court of the United States, 1966
384 U.S. 436, 86 S.Ct. 1602, 16 L.Ed.2d 694

This case was heard by the Supreme Court together with three others [*Vignera* v. *New York, Westover* v. *United States,* and *California* v. *Stewart*], all raising the issue of the admissibility into evidence of statements obtained from defendants during custodial interrogations in possible violation of Fifth, Sixth, and—in three of the cases—Fourteenth Amendment guarantees. The specific facts of the *Miranda* case appear in the excerpt of Justice Harlan's dissenting opinion which follows:

[I]t may make the analysis more graphic to consider the actual facts of one of the four cases reversed by the Court. *Miranda* v. *Arizona* serves best, being neither the hardest nor easiest of the four under the Court's standards.

On March 3, 1963, an 18-year-old girl was kidnapped and forcibly raped near Phoenix, Arizona. Ten days later, on the morning of March 13, petitioner Miranda was arrested and taken to the police station. At this time Miranda was 23 years old, indigent, and educated to the extent of completing half the ninth grade. He had 'an emotional illness' of the schizophrenic type, according to the doctor who eventually examined him; the doctor's report also stated that Miranda was 'alert and oriented as to time, place, and person,' intelligent within normal limits, competent to stand trial, and sane within the legal definition. At the police station, the victim picked Miranda out of a line-up, and two officers then took him into a separate room to interrogate him, starting about 11:30 a. m. Though at first denying his guilt, within a short time Miranda gave a detailed oral confession and then wrote out in his own hand and signed a brief statement admitting and describing the crime. All this was accomplished in two hours or less without any force, threats or promises and—I will assume this though the record is uncertain * * * without any effective warnings at all.

Mr. Chief Justice WARREN delivered the opinion of the Court.

* * *

We start here, as we did in *Escobedo*, with the premise that our holding is not an innovation in our jurisprudence, but is an application of principles long recognized and applied in other settings. We have undertaken a thorough re-examination of the *Escobedo* decision and the principles it announced, and we reaffirm it. That case was but an explication of basic rights that are enshrined in our Constitution—that "No person * * * shall be compelled in any criminal case to be a witness against himself," and that "the accused shall * * * have the Assistance of Counsel"—rights which were put in jeopardy in that case through official overbearing. These precious rights were fixed in our Constitution only after centuries of persecution and struggle. And in the words of Chief Justice Marshall, they were secured "for ages to come, and * * * designed to approach immortality as nearly as human institutions can approach it," Cohens v. Commonwealth of Virginia, 6 Wheat. 264, 387, 5 L.Ed. 257 (1821).

* * *

Our holding will be spelled out with some specificity in the pages which follow but briefly stated it is this: the prosecution may not use statements, whether exculpatory or inculpatory, stemming from custodial interrogation of the defendant unless it demonstrates the use of procedural safeguards effective to secure the privilege against self-incrimination. By custodial interrogation, we mean questioning initiated by law enforcement officers after a person has been taken into custody or otherwise deprived of his freedom of action in any significant way. As for the procedural safeguards to be employed, unless other fully effective means are devised to inform accused persons of their right of silence and to assure a continuous opportunity to exercise it, the following measures are required. Prior to any questioning, the person must be warned that he has a right to remain silent, that any statement he does make may be used as evidence against him, and that he has a right to the presence of an attorney, either retained or appointed. The defendant may waive effectuation of these rights, provided the waiver is made voluntarily, knowingly and intelligently. If, however, he indicates in any manner and at any stage of the process that he wishes to consult with an attorney before speaking there can be no questioning. Likewise, if the individual is alone and indicates in any manner that he does not wish to be interrogated, the police may not question him. The mere fact that he may have answered some questions or volunteered some statements on his own does not deprive him of the right to refrain from answering any further inquiries until he has consulted with an attorney and thereafter consents to be questioned.

The constitutional issue we decide in each of these cases is the admissibility of statements obtained from a defendant questioned while in custody or otherwise deprived of his freedom of action in any significant way. In each, the defendant was questioned by police officers, detectives, or a prosecuting attorney in a room in which he was cut off from the outside world. In none of these cases was the defendant given a full and effective warning of his rights at the outset of the interrogation process. In all the cases, the questioning elicited oral admissions, and in three of them, signed statements as well which were admitted at their trials. They all thus share salient features—incommunicado interrogation of individuals in a police-dominated atmosphere, resulting in self-incriminating statements without full warnings of constitutional rights.

An understanding of the nature and setting of this in-custody interrogation is essential to our decisions today. The difficulty in depicting what transpires at such interrogations stems from the fact that in this country they have largely taken place incommunicado. From extensive factual studies undertaken in the early 1930's, including the famous Wickersham Report to Congress by a Presidential Commission, it is clear that police violence and the "third degree" flourished at that time.

In a series of cases decided by this Court long after these studies, the police resorted to physical brutality—beatings, hanging, whipping— and to sustained and protracted questioning incommunicado in order to extort confessions. The Commission on Civil Rights in 1961 found much evidence to indicate that "some policemen still resort to physical force to obtain confessions."
* * *

The examples given above are undoubtedly the exception now, but they are sufficiently widespread to be the object of concern. Unless a proper limitation upon custodial interrogation is achieved—such as these decisions will advance—there can be no assurance that practices of this nature will be eradicated in the foreseeable future. * * *

[W]e stress that the modern practice of in-custody interrogation is psychologically rather than physically oriented. As we have stated before, "Since Chambers v. State of Florida, 309 U.S. 227, 60 S.Ct. 472, this Court has recognized that coercion can be mental as well as physical, and that the blood of the accused is not the only hallmark of an unconstitutional inquisition." Blackburn v. State of Alabama, 361 U.S. 199, 206, 80 S.Ct. 274, 279 (1960). Interrogation still takes place in privacy. Privacy results in secrecy and this in turn results in a gap in our knowledge as to what in fact goes on in the interrogation rooms. A valuable source of information about present police practices, however, may be found in various police manuals and texts which document procedures employed with success in the past, and which recommend various other effective tactics. These texts are used by law enforcement agencies themselves as guides. It should be noted that these texts professedly present the most enlightened and effective means presently used to obtain statements through custodial interrogation. By considering these texts and other data, it is possible to describe procedures observed and noted around the country.

* * *

From * * * representative samples of interrogation techniques, the setting prescribed by the manuals and observed in practice becomes clear. In essence, it is this: To be alone with the subject is essential to prevent distraction and to deprive him of any outside support. The aura of confidence in his guilt undermines his will to resist. He merely confirms the preconceived story the police seek to have him describe. Patience and persistence, at times relentless questioning, are employed. To obtain a confession, the interrogator must "patiently maneuver himself or his quarry into a position from which the desired objective may be attained." When normal procedures fail to produce the needed result, the police may resort to deceptive stratagems such as giving false legal advice. It is important to keep the subject off balance, for example, by trading on his insecurity about himself or his surroundings. The police then persuade, trick, or cajole him out of exercising his constitutional rights.

Even without employing brutality, the "third degree" or the specific stratagems described above, the very fact of custodial interrogation exacts a heavy toll on individual liberty and trades on the weakness of individuals. * * *

* * *

[T]he constitutional foundation underlying the privilege [against self-incrimination] is the respect a government—state or federal—must accord to the dignity and integrity of its citizens. To maintain a "fair state-individual balance," to require the government "to shoulder the entire load," * * * to respect the inviolability of the human personality, our accusatory system of criminal justice demands that the government seeking to punish an individual produce the evidence against him by its own independent labors, rather than by the cruel, simple expedient of compelling it from his own mouth. * * * In sum, the privilege is fulfilled only when the person is guaranteed the right "to remain silent unless he chooses to speak in the unfettered exercise of his own will." * * *

The question in these cases is whether the privilege is fully applicable during a period of custodial interrogation. In this Court, the privilege has consistently been accorded a liberal construction. * * * We are satisfied that all the principles embodied in the privilege apply to informal compulsion exerted by law-enforcement officers during in-custody questioning. An individual swept from familiar surroundings into police custody, surrounded by antagonistic forces, and subjected to the techniques of persuasion described above cannot be otherwise than under compulsion to speak. As a practical matter, the compulsion to speak in the isolated setting of the police station may well be greater than in courts or other official investigations, where there are often impartial observers to guard against intimidation or trickery.

* * *

Today, then, there can be no doubt that the Fifth Amendment privilege is available outside of criminal court proceedings and serves to protect persons in all settings in which their freedom of action is curtailed in any significant way from being compelled to incriminate themselves. We have concluded that without proper safeguards the process of in-custody interrogation of persons suspected or accused of crime contains inherently compelling pressures which work to undermine the individual's will to resist and to compel him to speak where he would not otherwise do so freely. In order to combat these pressures and to permit a full opportunity to exercise the privilege against self-incrimination, the accused must be adequately and effectively apprised of his rights and the exercise of those rights must be fully honored.

It is impossible for us to foresee the potential alternatives for protecting the privilege which might be devised by Congress or the States in the exercise of their creative rule-making capacities. Therefore we cannot say that the Constitution necessarily requires adherence to any particular solution for the inherent compulsions of the interrogation process as it is presently conducted. Our decision in no way creates a constitutional straitjacket which will handicap sound efforts at reform, nor is it intended to have this effect. We encourage Congress and the States to continue their laudable search for increasingly effective ways of protecting the rights of the individual while promoting efficient enforcement of our criminal laws. However, unless we are shown other procedures which are at least as effective in apprising accused persons of their right of silence and in assuring a continuous opportunity to exercise it, the following safeguards must be observed.

*   *   *

A recurrent argument made in these cases is that society's need for interrogation outweighs the privilege. This argument is not unfamil-iar to this Court. *   *   * The whole thrust of our foregoing discussion demonstrates that the Constitution has prescribed the rights of the individual when confronted with the power of government when it provided in the Fifth Amendment that an individual cannot be compelled to be a witness against himself. *   *   *

*   *   *

[Before summing up, the Court had made the following points:]

The principles announced today deal with the protection which must be given to the privilege against self-incrimination when the individual is first subjected to police interrogation while in custody at the station or otherwise deprived of his freedom of action in any significant way. It is at this point that our adversary system of criminal proceedings commences, distinguishing itself at the outset from the inquisitorial system recognized in some countries. Under the system of warnings we delineate today or under any other system which may be devised and found effective, the safeguards to be erected about the privilege must come into play at this point.

Our decision is not intended to hamper the traditional function of police officers in investigating crime. *   *   * When an individual is in custody on probable cause, the police may, of course, seek out evidence in the field to be used at trial against him. Such investigation may include inquiry of persons not under restraint. General on-the-scene questioning as to facts surrounding a crime or other general questioning of citizens in the fact-finding process is not affected by our holding. It is an act of responsible citizenship for individuals to give whatever information they may have to aid in law enforcement. In such situations the compelling atmosphere inherent in the process of in-custody interrogation is not necessarily present.

* * * There is no requirement that police stop a person who enters a police station and states that he wishes to confess to a crime, or a person who calls the police to offer a confession or any other statement he desires to make. Volunteered statements of any kind are not barred by the Fifth Amendment and their admissibility is not affected by our holding today.

To summarize, we hold that when an individual is taken into custody or otherwise deprived of his freedom by the authorities in any significant way and is subjected to questioning, the privilege against self-incrimination is jeopardized. Procedural safeguards must be employed to protect the privilege and unless other fully effective means are adopted to notify the person of his right of silence and to assure that the exercise of the right will be scrupulously honored, the following measures are required. He must be warned prior to any questioning that he has the right to remain silent, that anything he says can be used against him in a court of law, that he has the right to the presence of an attorney, and that if he cannot afford an attorney one will be appointed for him prior to any questioning if he so desires. Opportunity to exercise these rights must be afforded to him throughout the interrogation. After such warnings have been given, and such opportunity afforded him, the individual may knowingly and intelligently waive these rights and agree to answer questions or make a statement. But unless and until such warnings and waiver are demonstrated by the prosecution at trial, no evidence obtained as a result of interrogation can be used against him.

* * *

In announcing these principles, we are not unmindful of the burdens which law enforcement officials must bear, often under trying circumstances. We also fully recognize the obligation of all citizens to aid in enforcing the criminal laws. This Court, while protecting individual rights, has always given ample latitude to law enforcement agencies in the legitimate exercise of their duties. The limits we have placed on the interrogation process should not constitute an undue interference with a proper system of law enforcement. As we have noted, our decision does not in any way preclude police from carrying out their traditional investigatory functions. Although confessions may play an important role in some convictions, the cases before us present graphic examples of the overstatement of the "need" for confessions. In each case authorities conducted interrogations ranging up to five days in duration despite the presence, through standard investigating practices, of considerable evidence against each defendant. * * *

* * *

Because of the nature of the problem and because of its recurrent significance in numerous cases, we have to this point discussed the relationship of the Fifth Amendment privilege to police interrogation without specific concentration on the facts of the cases before us. We turn now to these facts to consider the application to these cases of the constitutional principles discussed above. In each instance, we have concluded that statements were obtained from the defendant under circumstances that did not meet constitutional standards for protection of the privilege.

* * *

[Reversed.]

[Justice CLARK dissented.]

Mr. Justice HARLAN, whom Mr. Justice STEWART and Mr. Justice WHITE join, dissenting.

I believe the decision of the Court represents poor constitutional law and entails harmful consequences for the country at large. How serious these consequences may prove to be only time can tell. But the basic flaws in the Court's justification seem to me readily apparent now once all sides of the problem are considered.

* * *

While the fine points of this scheme are far less clear than the Court admits, the tenor is quite apparent. The new rules are not designed to guard against police brutality or other unmistakably banned forms of coercion. Those who use third-degree tactics and deny them in court are equally able and destined to lie as skillfully about warnings and waivers. Rather, the thrust of the new rules is to negate all pressures, to reinforce the nervous or ignorant suspect, and ultimately to discourage any confession at all. The aim in short is toward "voluntariness" in a utopian sense, or to view it from a different angle, voluntariness with a vengeance.

* * * Viewed as a choice based on pure policy, these new rules prove to be a highly debatable, if not one-sided, appraisal of the competing interests, imposed over widespread objection, at the very time when judi-

cial restraint is most called for by the circumstances.

* * *

Without at all subscribing to the generally black picture of police conduct painted by the Court, I think it must be frankly recognized at the outset that police questioning allowable under due process precedents may inherently entail some pressure on the suspect and may seek advantage in his ignorance or weaknesses. The atmosphere and questioning techniques, proper and fair though they be, can in themselves exert a tug on the suspect to confess, and in this light "[t]o speak of any confessions of crime made after arrest as being 'voluntary' or 'uncoerced' is somewhat inaccurate, although traditional. A confession is wholly and incontestably voluntary only if a guilty person gives himself up to the law and becomes his own accuser." Ashcraft v. State of Tennessee, 322 U.S. 143, 161, 64 S.Ct. 921, 929 (Jackson, J., dissenting). Until today, the role of the Constitution has been only to sift out *undue* pressure, not to assure spontaneous confessions.

* * *

What the Court largely ignores is that its rules impair, if they will not eventually serve wholly to frustrate, an instrument of law enforcement that has long and quite reasonably been thought worth the price paid for it. There can be little doubt that the Court's new code would markedly decrease the number of confessions. To warn the suspect that he may remain silent and remind him that his confession may be used in court are minor obstructions. To require also an express waiver by the suspect and an end to questioning whenever he demurs must heavily handicap questioning. And to suggest or provide counsel for the suspect simply invites the end of the interrogation. * * *

How much harm this decision will inflict on law enforcement cannot fairly be predicted with accuracy. Evidence on the role of confessions is notoriously incomplete. * * * We do know that some crimes cannot be solved without confessions, that ample expert testimony attests to their importance in crime control, and that the Court is taking a real risk with society's welfare in imposing its new regime on the country. The social costs of crime are too great to call the new rules anything but a hazardous experimentation.

While passing over the costs and risks of its experiment, the Court portrays the evils of normal police questioning in terms which I think are exaggerated. Albeit stringently confined by the due process standards interrogation is no doubt often inconvenient and unpleasant for the suspect. However, it is no less so for a man to be arrested and jailed, to have his house searched, or to stand trial in court, yet all this may properly happen to the most innocent given probable cause, a warrant, or an indictment. Society has always paid a stiff price for law and order, and peaceful interrogation is not one of the dark moments of the law.

This brief statement of the competing considerations seems to me ample proof that the Court's preference is highly debatable at best and therefore not to be read into the Constitution. * * *

* * *

* * * Nothing in the letter or the spirit of the Constitution or in the precedents squares with the heavy-handed and one-sided action that is so precipitously taken by the Court in the name of fulfilling its constitutional responsibilities. * * *

* * *

Defendant, who was eventually convicted of kidnapping, armed robbery, and felonious assault by a North Carolina trial court, was arrested on a fugitive warrant by FBI agents in New York. After he was given the *Miranda* warnings, he was taken to a Bureau office where agents determined that he had an eleventh-grade education and was literate. He was given the FBI's "Advice of Rights" form which he read and said he understood. He refused to sign the waiver at the bottom of the form, however. Agents told him that he did not have to speak or sign the form but that they wanted to talk with him. He replied by saying, "I will talk to you but I am not signing any form." An agent testified that the defendant gave no response when advised of his right to an attorney. The defendant then went on to make several incriminating statements. At no time during the interview did the defendant request the presence of a lawyer or seek to terminate the questioning. The defendant sought unsuccessfully to suppress the statements at trial, but the state supreme court reversed the conviction on grounds that, pursuant to Miranda v. Arizona, no statement made during custodial interrogation by a defendant could be admitted absent an explicit waiver of the right to counsel.

The U. S. Supreme Court vacated the judgment of the state supreme court in North Carolina v. Butler, 441 U.S. 369, 99 S.Ct. 1755 (1979). Said Justice Stewart speaking for the Court:

> An express written or oral statement of waiver of the right to remain silent or of the right to counsel is usually strong proof of the validity of that waiver, but is not inevitably either necessary or sufficient to establish waiver. The question is not one of form, but rather whether the defendant in fact knowingly and voluntarily waived the rights delineated in the *Miranda* case. As was unequivocally said in *Miranda*, mere silence is not enough. That does not mean that the defendant's silence, coupled with an understanding of his rights and a course of conduct indicating waiver, may never support a conclusion that a defendant has waived his rights. The courts must presume that a defendant did not waive his rights; the prosecution's burden is great; but in at least some cases waiver can be clearly inferred from the actions and words of the person interrogated.

Justice Brennan dissented in an opinion, in which Justices Marshall and Stevens concurred, saying in part: "The Court * * * shrouds in half-light the question of waiver, allowing courts to construct inferences from ambiguous words and gestures. But the very premise of *Miranda* requires that ambiguity be interpreted against the interrogator. That premise is the recognition of the 'compulsion inherent in custodial' interrogation, * * * and of its purpose 'to subjugate the individual to the will of [the] examiner' * * *. Under such conditions, only the most explicit waivers of rights can be considered knowingly and freely given." He concluded, "Had Agent Martinez simply elicited a clear answer from Willie Butler to the question, 'Do you waive your right to a lawyer?,' this journey through three courts would not have been necessary."

UNITED STATES v. WADE

Supreme Court of the United States, 1967
388 U.S. 218, 87 S.Ct. 1926, 18 L.Ed.2d 1149

The facts are contained in the Court's opinion. [This case was decided concurrently with Gilbert v. California, 388 U.S. 263, 87 S.Ct. 1951, which raised a parallel challenge on the state level and extended the holding in *Wade* through the Fourteenth Amendment against state action.]

Mr. Justice BRENNAN delivered the opinion of the Court.

The question here is whether courtroom identifications of an accused at trial are to be excluded from evidence because the accused was exhibited to the witnesses before trial at a post-indictment lineup conducted for identification purposes without notice to and in the absence of the accused's appointed counsel.

The federally insured bank in Eustace, Texas, was robbed on September 21, 1964. A man with a small strip of tape on each side of his face entered the bank, pointed a pistol at the female cashier and the vice president, the only persons in the bank at the time, and forced them to fill a pillowcase with the bank's money. The man then drove away with an accomplice who had been waiting in a stolen car outside the bank. On March 23, 1965, an indictment was returned against respondent, Wade, and two others for conspiring to rob the bank, and against Wade and the accomplice for the robbery itself. Wade was arrested on April 2, and counsel was appointed to represent him on April 26. Fifteen days later an FBI agent, without notice to Wade's lawyer, arranged to have the two bank employees observe a lineup made up of Wade and five or six other prisoners and conducted in a courtroom of the local county courthouse. Each person in the line wore strips of tape such as allegedly worn by the robber and upon direction each said something like "put the money in the bag," the words allegedly uttered by the robber. Both bank employees identified Wade in the lineup as the bank robber.

At trial the two employees, when asked on direct examination if the robber was in the courtroom, pointed to Wade. The prior lineup identification was then elicited from both employees on cross-examination. At the close of testimony, Wade's counsel moved for a judgment of acquittal or, alternatively, to strike the bank officials' courtroom identifications on the ground that conduct of the lineup, without notice to and in the absence of his appointed counsel, violated his Fifth Amendment privilege against self-incrimination and his Sixth Amendment right to the assistance of counsel. The motion was denied, and Wade was convicted. The Court of Appeals for the Fifth Circuit reversed the conviction and ordered a new trial. * * * We granted certiorari. * * * We reverse the judgment of the Court of Appeals and remand to that court with direction to enter a new judgment vacating the conviction and remanding the case to the District

Court for further proceedings consistent with this opinion.

Neither the lineup itself nor anything shown by this record that Wade was required to do in the lineup violated his privilege against self-incrimination. We have only recently reaffirmed that the privilege "protects an accused only from being compelled to testify against himself, or otherwise provide the State with evidence of a testimonial or communicative nature." * * * Schmerber v. State of California, 384 U.S. 757, 761, 86 S.Ct. 1826, 1830. * * *

We have no doubt that compelling the accused merely to exhibit his person for observation by a prosecution witness prior to trial involves no compulsion of the accused to give evidence having testimonial significance. It is compulsion of the accused to exhibit his physical characteristics, not compulsion to disclose any knowledge he might have. * * * [C]ompelling Wade to speak within hearing distance of the witnesses, even to utter words purportedly uttered by the robber, was not compulsion to utter statements of a "testimonial" nature; he was required to use his voice as an identifying physical characteristic, not to speak his guilt. * * *

The fact that the lineup involved no violation of Wade's privilege against self-incrimination does not, however, dispose of his contention that the courtroom identifications should have been excluded because the lineup was conducted without notice to and in the absence of his counsel. * * *

* * *

[T]he principle of *Powell* v. *Alabama* and succeeding cases requires that we scrutinize *any* pretrial confrontation of the accused to determine whether the presence of his counsel is necessary to preserve the defendant's basic right to a fair trial as affected by his right meaningfully to cross-examine the witnesses against him and to have effective assistance of counsel at the trial itself. It calls upon us to analyze whether potential substantial prejudice to defendant's rights inheres in the particular confrontation and the ability of counsel to help avoid that prejudice.

The Government characterizes the lineup as a mere preparatory step in the gathering of the prosecution's evidence, not different—for Sixth Amendment purposes—from various other preparatory steps, such as systematized or scientific analyzing of the accused's fingerprints, blood sample, clothing, hair, and the like. We think there are differences which preclude such stages being characterized as critical stages at which the accused has the right to the presence of his counsel. Knowledge of the techniques of science and technology is sufficiently available, and the variables in techniques few enough, that the accused has the opportunity for a meaningful confrontation of the Government's case at trial through the ordinary processes of cross-examination of the Government's expert witnesses and the presentation of the evidence of his own experts. The denial of a right to have his counsel present at such analyses does not therefore violate the Sixth Amendment; they are not critical stages since there is minimal risk that his counsel's absence at such stages might derogate from his right to a fair trial.

But the confrontation compelled by the State between the accused and the victim or witnesses to a crime to elicit identification evidence is peculiarly riddled with innumerable dangers and variable factors which might seriously, even crucially, derogate from a fair trial. The vagaries of eyewitness identification are well-known; the annals of criminal law are rife with instances of mistaken identification. Mr. Justice Frankfurter once said: "What is the worth of identification testimony even when uncontradicted? The identification of strangers is proverbially untrustworthy. The hazards of such testimony are established by a formidable number of instances in the records of English and American trials. These instances are recent— not due to the brutalities of ancient criminal procedure." The Case of Sacco and Vanzetti 30 (1927). * * * And the dangers for the suspect are particularly grave when the witness' opportunity for observation was insubstantial, and thus his susceptibility to suggestion the greatest.

Moreover, "[i]t is a matter of common experience that, once a witness has picked out the accused at the line-up, he is not likely to go back on his word later on, so that in practice the issue of identity may (in the absence of other relevant evidence) for all practical purposes be determined there and then, before the trial."

[T]he defense can seldom reconstruct the manner and mode of lineup identification for judge or jury at trial. Those participating in a lineup with the accused may often be police officers; in any event, the participants' names are rarely recorded or divulged at trial. The impediments to an objective observation are increased when the victim is the witness. Lineups are prevalent in rape and robbery prosecutions and present a particular hazard that a victim's understandable outrage may excite vengeful or spiteful motives. In any event, neither witnesses nor lineup participants are apt to be alert for conditions prejudicial to the suspect. And if they were, it would likely be of scant benefit to the suspect since neither witnesses nor lineup participants are likely to be schooled in the detection of suggestive influences. Improper influences may go undetected by a suspect, guilty or not, who experiences the emotional tension which we might expect in one being confronted with potential accusers. Even when he does observe abuse, if he has a criminal record he may be reluctant to take the stand and open up the admission of prior convictions. Moreover any protestations by the suspect of the fairness of the lineup made at trial are likely to be in vain; the jury's choice is between the accused's unsupported version and that of the police officers present. In short, the accused's inability effectively to reconstruct at trial any unfairness that occurred at the lineup may deprive him of his only opportunity meaningfully to attack the credibility of the witness' courtroom identification.

Insofar as the accused's conviction may rest on a courtroom identification in fact the fruit of a suspect pretrial identification which the accused is helpless to subject to effective scrutiny at trial, the accused is deprived of that right of cross-examination which is an essential safeguard to his right to confront the witnesses against him. Pointer v. State of Texas, 380 U.S. 400, 85 S.Ct. 1065. And even though cross-examination is a precious safeguard to a fair trial, it cannot be viewed as an absolute assurance of accuracy and reliability. Thus in the present con-

text, where so many variables and pitfalls exist, the first line of defense must be the prevention of unfairness and the lessening of the hazards of eyewitness identification at the lineup itself. The trial which might determine the accused's fate may well not be that in the courtroom but that at the pretrial confrontation, with the State aligned against the accused, the witness the sole jury, and the accused unprotected against the overreaching, intentional or unintentional, and with little or no effective appeal from the judgment there rendered by the witness—"that's the man."

Since it appears that there is grave potential for prejudice, intentional or not, in the pretrial lineup, which may not be capable of reconstruction at trial, and since presence of counsel itself can often avert prejudice and assure a meaningful confrontation at trial, there can be little doubt that for Wade the postindictment lineup was a critical stage of the prosecution at which he was "as much entitled to such aid [of counsel] * * * as at the trial itself." Powell v. State of Alabama, 287 U.S. 45, at 57, 53 S.Ct. 55, at 60. Thus both Wade and his counsel should have been notified of the impending lineup, and counsel's presence should have been a requisite to conduct of the lineup, absent an "intelligent waiver." * * *

* * *

Mr. Justice BLACK, dissenting in part and concurring in part.

* * *

* * * Being forced by the Government to help convict himself and to supply evidence against himself by talking outside the courtroom is equally violative of his constitu-

tional right not to be compelled to be a witness against himself. Consequently, because of this violation of the Fifth Amendment, and not because of my own personal view that the Government's conduct was "unfair," "prejudicial," or "improper," I would prohibit the prosecution's use of lineup identification at trial.

I agree with the Court, in large part because of the reasons it gives, that failure to notify Wade's counsel that Wade was to be put in a lineup by government officers and to be forced to talk and wear tape on his face denied Wade the right to counsel in violation of the Sixth Amendment. Once again, my reason for this conclusion is solely the Sixth Amendment's guarantee that "the accused shall enjoy the right * * * to have the Assistance of Counsel for his defence." * * *

* * *

I would reverse Wade's conviction without further ado had the prosecution at trial made use of his lineup identification either in place of courtroom identification or to bolster in a harmful manner crucial courtroom identification. But the prosecution here did neither of these things. After prosecution witnesses under oath identified Wade in the courtroom, it was the defense, and not the prosecution, which brought out the prior lineup identification. While stating that "a *per se* rule of exclusion of courtroom identification would be unjustified," the Court, nevertheless remands this case for "a hearing to determine whether the in-court identifications had an independent source," or were the tainted fruits of the invalidly conducted lineup. From this holding I dissent.

* * *

I would affirm Wade's conviction.

Mr. Justice WHITE, with whom Mr. Justice HARLAN and Mr. Justice STEWART join, dissenting in part and concurring in part.

The Court has again propounded a broad constitutional rule barring the use of a wide spectrum of relevant and probative evidence, solely because a step in its ascertainment or discovery occurs outside the presence of defense counsel. This was the approach of the Court in Miranda v. State of Arizona, 384 U.S. 436, 86 S.Ct. 1602, 16 L.Ed.2d 694. I objected then to what I thought was an uncritical and doctrinaire approach without satisfactory factual foundation. I have much the same view of the present ruling and therefore dissent from the judgment. * * *

* * *

I would not extend [the adversary system], at least as it presently operates, to police investigations and would not require counsel's presence at pretrial identification procedures. Counsel's interest is in not having his client placed at the scene of the crime, regardless of his whereabouts. Some counsel may advise their clients to refuse to make any movements or to speak any words in a lineup or even to appear in one. To that extent the impact on truthful factfinding is quite obvious. Others will not only observe what occurs and develop possibilities for later cross-examination but will hover over witnesses and begin their cross-examination then, menacing truthful factfinding as thoroughly as the Court fears the police now do. * * * I therefore doubt that the Court's new rule, at least absent some clearly defined limits on counsel's role, will measurably contribute to more reliable pretrial identifications. My fears are that it will have precisely the opposite result. * * *

* * *

Mr. Justice FORTAS, with whom The CHIEF JUSTICE [WARREN] and Mr. Justice DOUGLAS join, concurring in part and dissenting in part.

I agree with the Court that the exhibition of the person of the accused at a lineup is not itself a violation of the privilege against self-in-

crimination. * * *

In my view, however, the accused may not be compelled in a lineup to speak the words uttered by the person who committed the crime. I am confident that it could not be compelled in court. It cannot be compelled in a lineup. It is more than passive, mute assistance to the eyes of the victim or of witnesses. It is the kind of volitional act—the kind of forced cooperation by the accused—which is within the historical perimeter of the privilege against compelled self-incrimination.

* * *

Five years later in Kirby v. Illinois, 406 U.S. 682, 92 S.Ct. 1877 (1972), the Burger Court had occasion to scale down the potential of *Wade-Gilbert*. Kirby and an associate, Bean, were convicted of robbing one Willie Shard. When they were initially stopped and questioned because Kirby looked like an individual for whom the police were then looking in connection with another matter, petitioners were asked to identify themselves. In the course of producing identification, both men revealed items bearing Shard's name and were then arrested. After being taken to the police station where the officers learned that Shard had been robbed a few days before, the defendants were soon identified by the victim as the two men who had robbed him. Kirby and Bean were not advised of their right to a lawyer and did not ask for legal assistance. They were indicted several weeks later. At trial a defense motion to exclude Shard's testimony was overruled, and he recalled his earlier identification of the two men and repeated it in court. The defendants appealed charging a violation of Sixth and Fourteenth Amendment rights and cited *Wade-Gilbert* as authority. An Illinois appellate court held Shard's testimony admissible, whereupon Kirby and his associate petitioned the U. S. Supreme Court for certiorari. The Supreme Court affirmed their conviction.

Justice Stewart announced the judgment of the Court and delivered a plurality opinion in which Chief Justice Burger and Justices Blackmun and Rehnquist concurred. Reasoning that "it has been firmly established that a person's Sixth and Fourteenth Amendment right to counsel attaches only at or after the time that adversary judicial proceedings have been initiated against him," Stewart found *Wade-Gilbert* inapplicable in the present context since the post-arrest, preindictment period could not be defined as the starting point of the adversary system of criminal justice. Said Stewart:

In this case we are asked to import into a routine police investigation an absolute constitutional guarantee historically and rationally applicable only after the onset of formal prosecutorial proceedings. We decline to do so. Less than a year after *Wade* and *Gilbert* were decided, the Court explained the rule of those decisions as follows: "The rationale of those cases was that an accused is entitled to counsel at any 'critical stage of the *prosecution*,' and that a post-indictment lineup is such a 'critical stage.'" (Emphasis supplied.) Simmons v. United States, 390 U.S. 377, 382–383, 88 S.Ct. 967, 970. We decline to depart from that rationale today by imposing a *per se* exclusionary rule upon testimony concerning an identification that took place long before the commencement of any prosecution whatever.

Justice Powell concurred separately.

Justice Brennan wrote the principal dissenting opinion. Speaking for himself and Justices Douglas and Marshall, he took issue with the majority and found *Wade-Gilbert* to be controlling:

> A primary, and frequently sole, purpose of the confrontation for identification at that stage is to accumulate proof to buttress the conclusion of the police that they have the offender in hand. The plurality offers no reason, and I can think of none, for concluding that a post-arrest confrontation for identification, unlike a post-charge confrontation, is not among those "critical confrontations of the accused by the prosecution at pretrial proceedings where the results might well settle the accused's fate and reduce the trial itself to a mere formality." * * *
>
> The highly suggestive form of confrontation employed in this case underscores the point. This showup was particularly fraught with the peril of mistaken identification. In the setting of a police station squad room where all present except petitioner and Bean were police officers, the danger was quite real that Shard's understandable resentment might lead him too readily to agree with the police that the pair under arrest, and the only persons exhibited to him, were indeed the robbers. "It is hard to imagine a situation more clearly conveying the suggestion to the witness that the one presented is believed guilty by the police." * * * The State had no case without Shard's identification testimony, and safeguards against that consequence were therefore of critical importance. Shard's testimony itself demonstrates the necessity for such safeguards. On direct examination, Shard identified petitioner and Bean not as the alleged robbers on trial in the courtroom, but as the pair he saw at the police station. * * *

Dissenting separately, Justice White simply cited *Wade-Gilbert* as precedent.

RECENT RULINGS OF THE RIGHT TO COUNSEL

Case	Ruling	Vote
Faretta v. California, 422 U.S. 806, 95 S.Ct. 2525 (1975)	Defendant in a criminal trial has a constitutional right to proceed *without counsel* if he voluntarily and intelligently chooses to do so; government may not force a lawyer upon him if he is determined to conduct his own defense	6–3; Chief Justice Burger and Justices Blackmun and Rehnquist dissented
Geders v. United States, 425 U.S. 80, 96 S.Ct. 1330 (1976)	Trial judge's blanket order to defendant not to talk with his lawyer about anything during an overnight trial recess falling between direct testimony on his own behalf and his cross-examination	8–0

THE RIGHT TO COUNSEL (*Cont.*)

Case	Ruling	Vote
Geders (*Cont.*)	deprived the defendant of his right to the assistance of counsel	
Brewer v. Williams, 430 U.S. 387, 97 S.Ct. 1232 (1977)	Where defendant was being transported from Davenport, Iowa to Des Moines to stand trial for murder, where his attorney in Davenport advised him not to make any statements until he consulted with his lawyer in Des Moines, and where police officers agreed not to question him during the trip, incriminating statements made by the defendant (which also led to recovery of the body of the young female victim) were inadmissible when, despite defendant's initial refusal to make any statements, he acceded to an appeal to his deeply religious character by a detective who, during the ride, expressed view that given the poor weather conditions it might be impossible to find the body and that "the parents of this little girl should be entitled to a Christian burial for the little girl who was snatched away from them on Christmas Eve and murdered."	5–4; Chief Justice Burger and Justices White, Blackmun, and Rehnquist dissented (on grounds the defendant had freely chosen to talk, the police misconduct had not been "egregious," and the evidence garnered was trustworthy and reliable)
Rhode Island v. Innis, 446 U.S. 291, 100 S.Ct. 1682 (1980)	Where defendant, identified as the armed robber of a taxicab driver, was arrested, informed of his rights three different times, indicated he wanted to speak to a lawyer, then placed in a police car to be driven to the police station in the company of several police officers who had been instructed not to interrogate or intimidate him in any way, sawed-off shotgun was admissible at trial as the fruit of a legitimate waiver of his rights, as were incriminating statements he made to the officers at the time, even though defendant's action of leading police to the exact location of the weapon followed a couple of "off-hand remarks" by two of the officers to the effect that there were "a lot of handicapped children running around this area" and "God forbid one of them might find a weapon with shells and they might hurt themselves" (prior to leading police to the location of the weapon, the defendant had been given the *Miranda* warnings a fourth time). Defendant was not "interrogated" within the meaning of *Miranda* or subjected to the "functional equivalent" of questioning, i.e., "subjected * * * to words or actions	6–3; Justices Brennan, Marshall, and Stevens dissented. Justice Stevens concluded that the remarks by the police officers here had "the same purpose or effect as a direct question." Justice Brennan observed: "This is not a case where police officers speaking among themselves are accidentally overheard by a suspect. These officers were 'talking back and forth' in close quarters with the hand-

THE RIGHT TO COUNSEL *(Cont.)*

Case	Ruling	Vote
Innis *(Cont.)*	that the police should have known were reasonably likely to elicit an incriminating response from him"	cuffed suspect, traveling past the very place where they believed the weapon was located. They knew petitioner would hear and attend to their conversation, and they are chargeable with knowledge of and responsibility for the pressures to speak which they created"
United States v. Henry, 447 U.S. 264, 100 S.Ct. 2183 (1980)	Where, following defendant's indictment for armed robbery of a bank and while he was in jail awaiting trial, federal agents contacted an informant in the same cellblock and instructed him to be alert to statements defendant might make but not to initiate conversations with or question defendant about the crime, where informant reported to the agents incriminating statements defendant had made in conversations, where informant was paid for furnishing this information, and where informant appeared at defendant's trial and testified about those statements, such activity amounted to an unconstitutional interference with defendant's right to counsel under the Sixth Amendment. In light of the fact that defendant was in custody under indictment, that informant was acting under government's instruction, and that informant was paid on a contingent basis for the information, the agents intentionally created a situation likely to induce defendant to make incriminating statements in the absence of counsel. Since defendant did not know fellow inmate was an informant, defendant could not be said to have voluntarily waived his right to counsel. It can be said, then, that the agents "deliberately elicited" statements from the defendant in the absence of counsel and without a knowing waiver of his constitutional rights	6–3; Justices White, Blackmun, and Rehnquist dissented, the former two on grounds the Court had unwarrantedly and unwisely expanded the scope of the "deliberately elicited" standard and the latter additionally for the reason that talk of a violation of the right to counsel in circumstances such as this "is difficult to reconcile with traditional notions of the role of an attorney"

THE RIGHT TO COUNSEL (*Cont.*)

Case	Ruling	Vote
Edwards v. Arizona, 451 U.S. 477, 101 S.Ct. 1880 (1981)	Where, after being arrested and informed of his rights as required by *Miranda*, defendant was questioned until he said he wanted an attorney, it was a violation of his Fifth Amendment right to have counsel present at the interrogation for the state to introduce at trial incriminating statements made by the defendant when police officers came to the jail the next morning and, after saying that they wanted to talk with him and giving him the *Miranda* warnings again, obtained a confession after he said he was willing to talk. It was error for the state supreme court to focus on the voluntariness of the confession rather than on whether the defendant understood his right to counsel and knowingly and intelligently waived it. Where, as here, the accused indicated he wanted counsel present at the interrogation, a valid waiver of that right cannot be shown by the fact that he responded to police-initiated questioning but only if the defendant himself initiated further conversation or communication with the police	9–0; Chief Justice Burger and Justices Powell and Rehnquist concurred only in the judgment because they took exception to the new requirement that the defendant himself must initiate further conversation with the police. In their view it would be entirely proper for police to ask him if he has changed his mind about declining to answer further questions
Estelle v. Smith, 451 U.S. 454, 101 S.Ct. 1866 (1981)	See chart, p. 1002	

c. CONFESSIONS AND SELF-INCRIMINATION

MALLORY v. UNITED STATES

Supreme Court of the United States, 1957
354 U.S. 449, 77 S.Ct. 1356, 1 L.Ed.2d 1479

Andrew Mallory was arrested early one afternoon on suspicion of raping a woman in the laundry room of an apartment house located in Washington, D. C. He was taken to a police station where he was intermittently questioned for the rest of the day. During his detention Mallory confessed, but it was not until the next morning that he was brought before a U. S. commissioner for arraignment. At trial, the confession was introduced in evidence, and Mallory was subsequently convicted and sentenced to death. Mallory appealed, challenging the admissibility of the confession, but the judgment was affirmed by a U. S. Court of Appeals. The question before the Supreme Court was whether or not the conviction could stand in light of the requirement of Rule 5(a) of the Federal Rules of Criminal Procedure and a previous decision of the Court, McNabb v. United States, 318 U.S. 332, 63 S.Ct. 608 (1943), both of which are detailed in the Court's opinion below.

Mr. Justice FRANKFURTER delivered the opinion of the Court.

The case calls for the proper application of Rule 5(a) of the Federal Rules of Criminal Procedure, promulgated in 1946, 327 U.S. 821. That Rule provides:

"(a) Appearance before the Commissioner. An officer making an arrest under a warrant issued upon a complaint or any person making an arrest without a warrant shall take the arrested person without unnecessary delay before the nearest available commissioner or before any other nearby officer empowered to commit persons charged with offenses against the laws of the United States. When a person arrested without a warrant is brought before a commissioner or other officer, a complaint shall be filed forthwith."

This provision has both statutory and judicial antecedents for guidance in applying it. The requirement that arraignment be "without unnecessary delay" is a compendious restatement, without substantive change, of several prior specific federal statutory provisions. * * * Nearly all the States have similar enactments.

In McNabb v. United States, 318 U.S. 332, 343–344, 63 S.Ct. 608, 614, we spelled out the important reasons of policy behind this body of legislation:

"The purpose of this impressively pervasive requirement of criminal procedure is plain. * * * The awful instruments of the criminal law cannot be entrusted to a single functionary. The complicated process of criminal justice is therefore divided into different parts, responsibility for which is separately vested in the various participants upon whom the criminal law relies for its vindication. Legislation such as this, requiring that the police must with reasonable promptness show legal cause for detaining arrested persons, constitutes an important safeguard—not only in assuring protection for the innocent but also in securing conviction of the guilty by methods that commend themselves to a progressive and self-confident society. For this procedural requirement checks resort to those reprehensible practices known as the 'third degree' which, though universally rejected as indefensible, still find their way into use. It aims to avoid all the evil implications of secret interrogation of persons accused of crime."

Since such unwarranted detention led to tempting utilization of intensive interrogation, easily gliding into the evils of "the third degree," the Court held that police detention of defendants beyond the time when a committing magistrate was readily accessible constituted "wilful disobedience of law." In order adequately to enforce the congressional requirement of prompt arraignment, it was deemed necessary to render inadmissible incriminating statements elicited from defendants during a period of unlawful detention.

* * *

The requirement of Rule 5(a) is part of the procedure devised by Congress for safeguarding individual rights without hampering effective and intelligent law enforcement. Provisions related to Rule 5(a) contemplate a procedure that allows arresting officers little more leeway than the interval between arrest and the ordinary administrative steps required to bring a suspect before the nearest available magistrate.

* * *

The scheme for initiating a federal prosecution is plainly defined.

The police may not arrest upon mere suspicion but only on "probable cause." The next step in the proceeding is to arraign the arrested person before a judicial officer as quickly as possible so that he may be advised of his rights and so that the issue of probable cause may be promptly determined. The arrested person may, of course, be "booked" by the police. But he is not to be taken to police headquarters in order to carry out a process of inquiry that lends itself, even if not so designed, to eliciting damaging statements to support the arrest and ultimately his guilt.

The duty enjoined upon arresting officers to arraign "without unnecessary delay" indicates that the command does not call for mechanical or automatic obedience. Circumstances may justify a brief delay between arrest and arraignment, as for instance, where the story volunteered by the accused is susceptible of quick verification through third parties. But the delay must not be of a nature to give opportunity for the extraction of a confession.

The circumstances of this case preclude a holding that arraignment was "without unnecessary delay." Petitioner was arrested in the early afternoon and was detained at headquarters within the vicinity of numerous committing magistrates. Even though the police had ample evidence from other sources than the petitioner for regarding the petitioner as the chief suspect, they first questioned him for approximately a half hour. When this inquiry of a nineteen-year-old lad of limited intelligence produced no confession, the police asked him to submit to a "lie-detector" test. He was not told of his rights to counsel or to a preliminary examination before a magistrate, nor was he warned that he might keep silent and "that any statement made by him may be used against him." After four hours of further detention at headquarters, during which arraignment could easily have been made in the same building in which the police headquarters were housed, petitioner was examined by the lie-detector operator for another hour and a half before his story began to waver. Not until he had confessed, when any judicial caution had lost its purpose, did the police arraign him.

We cannot sanction this extended delay, resulting in confession, without subordinating the general rule of prompt arraignment to the discretion of arresting officers in finding exceptional circumstances for its disregard. In every case where the police resort to interrogation of an arrested person and secure a confession, they may well claim, and quite sincerely, that they were merely trying to check on the information given by him. Against such a claim and the evil potentialities of the practice for which it is urged stands Rule 5(a) as a barrier. * * *

Reversed and remanded.

SPANO v. NEW YORK

Supreme Court of the United States, 1959
360 U.S. 315, 79 S.Ct. 1202, 3 L.Ed.2d 1265

The facts appear in the Court's opinion.

Mr. Chief Justice WARREN delivered the opinion of the Court.

This is another in the long line of cases presenting the question whether a confession was properly admitted into evidence under the Fourteenth Amendment. As in all such cases, we are forced to resolve a conflict between two fundamental interests of society; its interest in prompt and efficient law enforcement, and its interest in preventing the rights of its individual members from being abridged by unconstitutional methods of law enforcement. * * *

The State's evidence reveals the following: Petitioner Vincent Joseph Spano is a derivative citizen of this country, having been born in Messina, Italy. He was 25 years old at the time of the shooting in question and had graduated from junior high school. He had a record of regular employment. The shooting took place on January 22, 1957.

On that day, petitioner was drinking in a bar. The decedent, a former professional boxer weighing almost 200 pounds who had fought in Madison Square Garden, took some of petitioner's money from the bar. Petitioner followed him out of the bar to recover it. A fight ensued, with the decedent knocking petitioner down and then kicking him in the head three or four times. Shock from the force of these blows caused petitioner to vomit. After the bartender applied some ice to his head, petitioner left the bar, walked to his apartment, secured a gun, and walked eight or nine blocks to a candy store where the decedent was frequently to be found. He entered the store in which decedent, three friends of decedent, at least two of whom were ex-convicts, and a boy who was supervising the store were present.

He fired five shots, two of which entered the decedent's body, causing his death. The boy was the only eyewitness; the three friends of decedent did not see the person who fired the shot. Petitioner then disappeared for the next week or so.

On February 1, 1957, the Bronx County Grand Jury returned an indictment for first-degree murder against petitioner. Accordingly, a bench warrant was issued for his arrest, commanding that he be forthwith brought before the court to answer the indictment, or, if the court had adjourned for the term, that he be delivered into the custody of the Sheriff of Bronx County. * * *

On February 3, 1957, petitioner called one Gaspar Bruno, a close friend of 8 or 10 years' standing who had attended school with him. Bruno was a fledgling police officer, having at that time not yet finished attending police academy. According to Bruno's testimony, petitioner told him "that he took a terrific beating, that the deceased hurt him real bad and he dropped him a couple of times and he was dazed; he didn't know what he was doing and that he went and shot at him." Petitioner told Bruno that he intended to get a lawyer and give himself up. Bruno relayed this information to his superiors.

The following day, February 4, at 7:10 p. m., petitioner, accompanied by counsel, surrendered himself to the authorities in front of the Bronx County Building, where both the office of the Assistant District Attorney who ultimately prosecuted his case and the courtroom in which he was ultimately tried were located. His attorney had cautioned him to answer no questions, and left him in the custody of the officers. He was promptly taken to the office of the Assistant District Attorney and at 7:15 p. m. the questioning began, being conducted by Assistant District Attorney Goldsmith, Lt. Gannon, Detectives Farrell, Lehrer and Motta, and Sgt. Clarke. The record reveals that the questioning was both persistent and continuous. Petitioner, in accordance with his attorney's instructions, steadfastly refused to answer. * * *

* * *

[P]etitioner persisted in his refusal to answer, and again requested permission to see his attorney, this time from Detective Lehrer. His request was again denied.

It was then that those in charge of the investigation decided that petitioner's close friend, Bruno, could be of use. He had been called out on the case around 10 or 11 p. m., although he was not connected with the 46th Squad or Precinct in any way. Although, in fact, his job was in no way threatened, Bruno was told to tell petitioner that petitioner's telephone call had gotten him "in a lot of trouble," and that he should seek to extract sympathy from petitioner for Bruno's pregnant wife and three children. Bruno developed this theme with petitioner without success, and petitioner, also without success, again sought to see his attorney, a request which Bruno relayed unavailingly to his superiors. After this first session with petitioner, Bruno was again directed by Lt. Gannon to play on petitioner's sympathies, but again no confession was forthcoming. But the Lieutenant a third time ordered Bruno falsely to importune his friend to confess but again petitioner clung to his attorney's advice. Inevitably, in the fourth such session directed by the Lieutenant,

lasting a full hour, petitioner succumbed to his friend's prevarications and agreed to make a statement. Accordingly, at 3:25 a. m. the Assistant District Attorney, a stenographer, and several other law enforcement officials entered the room where petitioner was being questioned, and took his statement in question and answer form with the Assistant District Attorney asking the questions. The statement was completed at 4:05 a. m.

But this was not the end. At 4:30 a. m. three detectives took petitioner to Police Headquarters in Manhattan. On the way they attempted to find the bridge from which petitioner said he had thrown the murder weapon. They crossed the Triborough Bridge into Manhattan, arriving at Police Headquarters at 5 a. m., and left Manhattan for the Bronx at 5:40 a. m. via the Willis Avenue Bridge. When petitioner recognized neither bridge as the one from which he had thrown the weapon, they re-entered Manhattan via the Third Avenue Bridge, which petitioner stated was the right one, and then returned to the Bronx well after 6 a. m. During that trip the officers also elicited a statement from petitioner that the deceased was always "on [his] back," "always pushing" him and that he was "not sorry" he had shot the deceased. All three detectives testified to that statement at the trial.

Court opened at 10 a. m. that morning, and petitioner was arraigned at 10:15.

At the trial, the confession was introduced in evidence over appropriate objections. The jury was instructed that it could rely on it only if it was found to be voluntary. The jury returned a guilty verdict and petitioner was sentenced to death. The

New York Court of Appeals affirmed the conviction over three dissents * * * and we granted certiorari. * * *

Petitioner's first contention is that his absolute right to counsel in a capital case * * * became operative on the return of an indictment against him, for at that time he was in every sense a defendant in a criminal case, the grand jury having found sufficient cause to believe that he had committed the crime. He argues accordingly that following indictment no confession obtained in the absence of counsel can be used without violating the Fourteenth Amendment. * * * We find it unnecessary to reach that contention, for we find use of the confession obtained here inconsistent with the Fourteenth Amendment under traditional principles.

The abhorrence of society to the use of involuntary confessions does not turn alone on their inherent untrustworthiness. It also turns on the deep-rooted feeling that the police must obey the law while enforcing the law; that in the end life and liberty can be as much endangered from illegal methods used to convict those thought to be criminals as from the actual criminals themselves. Accordingly, the actions of police in obtaining confessions have come under scrutiny in a long series of cases. * * * [A]s law enforcement officers become more responsible, and the methods used to extract confessions more sophisticated, our duty to enforce federal constitutional protections does not cease. It only becomes more difficult because of the more delicate judgments to be made. Our judgment here is that, on all the facts, this conviction cannot stand.

Petitioner was a foreign-born young man of 25 with no past history of law violation or of subjection to official interrogation, at least insofar as the record shows. He had progressed only one-half year into high school and the record indicates that he had a history of emotional instability. He did not make a narrative statement, but was subject to the leading questions of a skillful prosecutor in a question and answer confession. He was subjected to questioning not by a few men, but by many. * * * [T]he effect of such massive official interrogation must have been felt. Petitioner was questioned for virtually eight straight hours before he confessed, with his only respite being a transfer to an arena presumably considered more appropriate by the police for the task at hand. Nor was the questioning conducted during normal business hours, but began in early evening, continued into the night, and did not bear fruition until the not-too-early morning. The drama was not played out, with the final admissions obtained, until almost sunrise. In such circumstances slowly mounting fatigue does, and is calculated to, play its part. The questioners persisted in the face of his repeated refusals to answer on the advice of his attorney, and they ignored his reasonable requests to contact the local attorney whom he had already retained and who had personally delivered him into the custody of these officers in obedience to the bench warrant.

The use of Bruno, characterized in this Court by counsel for the State as a "childhood friend" of petitioner's, is another factor which deserves mention in the totality of the situation. Bruno's was the one face visible to petitioner in which he could put some trust. There was a bond of friendship between them going back a decade into adolescence. It was with this material that the officers felt that they could overcome petitioner's will. They instructed Bruno falsely to state that petitioner's telephone call had gotten him into trouble, that his job was in jeopardy, and that loss of his job would be disastrous to his three children, his wife and his unborn child. And Bruno played this part of a worried father, harried by his superiors, in not one, but four different acts, the final one lasting an hour. * * * Petitioner was apparently unaware of John Gay's famous couplet:

"An open foe may prove a curse,
But a pretended friend is worse,"

and he yielded to his false friend's entreaties.

We conclude that petitioner's will was overborne by official pressure, fatigue and sympathy falsely aroused after considering all the facts in their post-indictment setting. * * * Accordingly, we hold that petitioner's conviction cannot stand under the Fourteenth Amendment.

* * *

Reversed.

See *Mincey* v. *Arizona*, p. 1100.

ROGERS v. RICHMOND

Supreme Court of the United States, 1961
365 U.S. 534, 81 S.Ct. 735, 5 L.Ed.2d 760

Harold Rogers was arrested for attempted robbery of a hotel in New Haven, Connecticut. The police soon discovered from a ballistics test that the gun which Rogers had in his possession at the time of his arrest was probably the weapon used in a killing during a previous armed robbery of a liquor store. While he was waiting to be tried for the hotel robbery, the police decided to question him about the possibility of his involvement in the fatal shooting. After approximately six hours of interrogation, the assistant chief of police successfully threatened to have Rogers's wife taken into custody if he did not confess. At the trial the confession was entered in evidence, and Rogers was convicted of murder. Fairly involved state and federal court proceedings followed the conviction. Eventually, however, a U. S. Court of Appeals affirmed a decision by a federal district court dismissing a petition for a writ of habeas corpus brought by Rogers against his warden, Mark Richmond. The Supreme Court granted certiorari.

Mr. Justice FRANKFURTER delivered the opinion of the Court.
* * *

A critical analysis of the Connecticut proceedings leads to * * * the conclusion that the trial judge in admitting the confessions as "voluntary," and the Supreme Court of Errors in affirming the conviction into which the confessions entered, failed to apply the standard demanded by the Due Process Clause of the Fourteenth Amendment for determining the admissibility of a confession.

Our decisions under that Amendment have made clear that convictions following the admission into evidence of confessions which are involuntary, i.e., the product of coercion, either physical or psychological, cannot stand. This is so not because such confessions are unlikely to be true but because the methods used to extract them offend an underlying principle in the enforcement of our criminal law: that ours is an accusatorial and not an inquisitorial system—a system in which the State must establish guilt by evidence independently and freely secured and may not by coercion prove its charge against an accused out of his own mouth. * * *

[W]e cannot but conclude that the question whether Rogers' confessions were admissible into evidence was answered by reference to a legal standard which took into account the circumstance of probable truth or falsity. And this is not a permissible standard under the Due Process Clause of the Fourteenth Amendment. The attention of the trial judge should have been focused, for purposes of the Federal Constitution, on the question whether the behavior of the State's law enforcement officials was such as to overbear petitioner's will to resist and bring about confessions not freely self-determined—a question to be answered with complete disregard of whether or not petitioner in fact spoke the truth. The employment instead, by the trial judge and the Supreme Court of Errors, of a standard infected by the inclusion of references to probable reliability resulted in a con-

stitutionally invalid conviction, pursuant to which Rogers is now detained "in violation of the Constitution." A defendant has the right to be tried according to the substantive and procedural due process requirements of the Fourteenth Amendment. This means that a vital confession, such as is involved in this case, may go to the jury only if it is subjected to screening in accordance with correct constitutional standards. To the extent that in the trial of Rogers evidence was allowed to go to the jury on the basis of standards that departed from constitutional requirements, to that extent he was unconstitutionally tried and the conviction was vitiated by error of constitutional dimension.

* * *

* * * It was error for the court below to affirm the District Court's denial of petitioner's application for habeas corpus. The case is remanded to the Court of Appeals to be held in order to give the State opportunity to retry petitioner, in light of this opinion, within a reasonable time. In default thereof the petitioner is to be discharged.

Reversed.

[Justices STEWART and CLARK dissented but did so principally on grounds of the remedy which the Court ought to have invoked.]

MALLOY v. HOGAN

Supreme Court of the United States, 1964
378 U.S. 1, 84 S.Ct. 1489, 12 L.Ed.2d 653

William Malloy, a convicted gambler, was ordered to testify in a state investigation of gambling activities. However, when he refused to answer questions relating to his past criminal involvement, a Connecticut court held him in contempt and directed that he be imprisoned until he was willing to cooperate. Malloy then brought habeas corpus proceedings against Patrick Hogan, a county sheriff, but two state courts denied relief, overruling petitioner's objection that his privilege against self-incrimination had been violated. The U. S. Supreme Court granted certiorari.

Mr. Justice BRENNAN delivered the opinion of the Court.

In this case we are asked to reconsider prior decisions holding that the privilege against self-incrimination is not safeguarded against state action by the Fourteenth Amendment. Twining v. New Jersey, 211 U.S. 78, 29 S.Ct. 14; Adamson v. California, 332 U.S. 46, 67 S.Ct. 1672.

* * *

We hold today that the Fifth Amendment's exception from compulsory self-incrimination is also protected by the Fourteenth Amendment against abridgment by the States. Decisions of the Court since *Twining* and *Adamson* have departed from the contrary view expressed in those cases. * * *

* * *

We turn to the petitioner's claim that the State of Connecticut denied him the protection of his federal privilege. It must be considered irrelevant that the petitioner was a witness in a statutory inquiry and not a defendant in a criminal prosecution, for it has long been settled that the privilege protects witnesses in similar federal inquiries. * * *

* * *

* * * The interrogation was part of a wide-ranging inquiry into crime, including gambling, in Hartford. It was admitted on behalf of the State at oral argument—and indeed it is obvious from the questions themselves—that the State desired to elicit from the petitioner the identity of the person who ran the pool-selling operation in connection with which he had been arrested in 1959. It was apparent that petitioner might apprehend that if this person were still engaged in unlawful activity, disclosure of his name might furnish a link in a chain of evidence sufficient to connect the petitioner with a more recent crime for which he might still be prosecuted.

* * * An affirmative answer to the question[s] might well have either connected petitioner with a more recent crime, or at least have operated as a waiver of his privilege with reference to his relationship with a possible criminal. * * * We conclude, therefore, that as to each of the questions, it was "evident from the implications of the question, in the setting in which it [was] asked, that a responsive answer to the question or an explanation of why it [could not] be answered might be dangerous because injurious disclosure could result," Hoffman v. United States, 341 U.S., at 486–487, 71 S.Ct. 818. * * *

Reversed.

Mr. Justice HARLAN, whom Mr. Justice CLARK joins, dissenting.

I can only read the Court's opinion as accepting in fact what it rejects in theory: the application to the States, via the Fourteenth Amendment, of the forms of federal criminal procedure embodied within the first eight Amendments to the Constitution. While it is true that the Court deals today with only one aspect of state criminal procedure, and rejects the wholesale "incorporation" of such federal constitutional requirements, the logical gap between the Court's premises and its novel constitutional conclusion can, I submit, be bridged only by the additional premise that the Due Process Clause of the Fourteenth Amendment is a shorthand directive to this Court to pick and choose among the provisions of the first eight Amendments and apply those chosen, freighted with their entire accompanying body of federal doctrine, to law enforcement in the States.

I accept and agree with the proposition that continuing re-examination of the constitutional conception of Fourteenth Amendment "due process" of law is required, and that development of the community's sense of justice may in time lead to expansion of the protection which due process affords. * * * I do not understand, however, how this process of re-examination, which must refer always to the guiding standard of due process of law, including, of course, reference to the particular guarantees of the Bill of Rights, can be short-circuited by the simple device of incorporating into due process, without critical examination, the whole body of law which surrounds a specific prohibition directed against the Federal Government. The consequence of such an approach to due process as it pertains to the States is inevitably disregard of all relevant differences which may exist between state and federal criminal law and its enforcement. The ultimate result is compelled uniformity, which is inconsistent with the purpose of our federal system and which is achieved either by encroachment on the States' sovereign powers or by dilution in federal law enforcement of the specific protections found in the Bill of Rights.

* * *

The Court's approach in the present case is in fact nothing more or less than "incorporation" in snatches. If, however, the Due Process Clause *is* something more than a reference to the Bill of Rights and protects only those rights which derive from fundamental principles, as the majority purports to believe, it is just as contrary to precedent and just as illogical to incorporate the provisions of the Bill of Rights one at a time as it is to incorporate them all at once.

* * *

Mr. Justice WHITE, with whom Mr. Justice STEWART joins, dissenting.

The Fifth Amendment safeguards an important complex of values, but it is difficult for me to perceive how these values are served by the Court's holding that the privilege was properly invoked in this case. While purporting to apply the prevailing federal standard of incrimination—the same standard of incrimination that the Connecticut courts applied—the Court has all but stated that a witness' invocation of the privilege to any question is to be automatically, and without more, accepted. With deference, I prefer the rule permitting the judge rather than the witness to determine when an answer sought is incriminating.

* * *

In a related case, one William Murphy and others were subpoenaed to appear and answer questions before the New York Harbor Waterfront Commission in regard to a stoppage of work on certain New Jersey docks. They refused to testify on grounds their answers would tend to incriminate them and were given immunity from prosecution in both New Jersey and New York. When pressed again for testimony, petitioners continued to decline, asserting that any answers they might give would leave them open to prosecution under federal law. The New Jersey Supreme Court affirmed civil contempt judgments against them by a lower state court, vindicating the state's position that it had the power to force testimony even though admissions made before the commission constituted evidence liable to be used by federal authorities in a prosecution by the United States government. Murphy and the others subsequently petitioned the U. S. Supreme Court for certiorari challenging violation of Fifth Amendment rights.

In this case, Murphy v. Waterfront Commission of New York Harbor, 378 U.S. 52, 84 S.Ct. 1594 (1964), a companion case to *Malloy*, a unanimous Court held that petitioners could not be prosecuted by federal authorities using their testimony and, consequently, that they could be compelled to answer the questions put to them by the waterfront commission. Speaking for the Court, Justice Goldberg said:

> The privilege against self-incrimination * * * reflects many of our fundamental values and most noble aspirations: our unwillingness to subject those suspected of crime to the cruel trilemma of self-accusation, perjury or contempt; our preference for an accusatorial rather than an inquisitorial system of criminal justice; our fear that self-incriminating statements will be elicited by inhumane treatment and abuses; our sense of fair play which dictates "a fair state-individual balance by requiring the government to leave the individual alone until good cause is shown for disturbing him and by requiring the government in its contest with the individual to shoulder the entire load," * * * ; our respect for the inviolability of the human personality and of the right of each individual "to a private enclave where he may lead a private life," * * * ; our distrust of self-deprecatory statements; and our realization that the privilege, while sometimes "a shelter to the guilty," is often "a protection to the innocent." * * *

> Most, if not all, of these policies and purposes are defeated when a witness "can be whipsawed into incriminating himself under both state and federal law even though" the constitutional privilege against self-incrimination is applicable to each. * * * This has become especially true in our age of "cooperative federalism," where the Federal and State Governments are waging a united front against many types of criminal activity.

In a concurring opinion, Justice White, joined by Justice Stewart, emphasized a limitation on the Court's holding:

> In reaching its result the Court does not accept the far-reaching and in my view wholly unnecessary constitutional principle that the privilege requires not only complete protection against any use of compelled testimony in any manner in other jurisdictions but also absolute immunity in these jurisdictions from any prosecution pertaining to any of the testimony given. * * *

Finally, in a second concurring opinion, Justice Harlan, joined by Justice Clark, protested against the Court's decision predicated on a "mixing together" of the Fifth and Fourteenth Amendments. In his view, the Court's holding should have been supported by relying on the supervisory power given the Court by statute to oversee federal law enforcement.

MIRANDA v. ARIZONA

Supreme Court of the United States, 1966
384 U.S. 436, 86 S.Ct. 1602, 16 L.Ed.2d 694

See p. 969.

DUNAWAY v. NEW YORK

Supreme Court of the United States, 1979
442 U.S. 200, 99 S.Ct. 2248, 60 L.Ed.2d 824

See p. 1147.

OREGON v. HASS

Supreme Court of the United States, 1975
420 U.S. 714, 95 S.Ct. 1215, 43 L.Ed.2d 570

Hass was arrested and charged with burglary in the theft of a bicycle. At the time of arrest he was given and acknowledged that he understood the full *Miranda* warnings. On the ride back to the police station, Hass said that he would like to telephone a lawyer and was told that he could do so once they reached the station. During the course of the ride Hass made several incriminating statements. At trial, he took the stand in his own defense. He testified to facts which were directly contrary to the remarks he had made in the police car. In rebuttal, the prosecutor called one of the police officers who testified to the statements Hass had made in the squad car. Hass retook the stand and swore that the officer's statements were "wrong." The trial judge instructed the jury that while the officer's testimony could not be relied upon as proof of Hass's guilt, it could be used to assess the credibility of Hass's testimony and thereby impeach his credibility as a witness. The jury returned a guilty verdict, and Hass was sentenced to two years on probation and a $250 fine. The state appeals court reversed, holding that the officer's testimony as to Hass's statements in the squad car was inadmissible, and the Oregon Supreme Court affirmed that ruling by a narrow majority. The state sought certiorari from the U. S. Supreme Court, arguing that a previous U. S. Supreme Court ruling in Harris v. New York, 401 U.S. 222, 91 S.Ct. 643 (1971), which narrowed somewhat the scope of statements excluded by *Miranda*, controlled the present case.

Mr. Justice BLACKMUN delivered the opinion of the Court.

This case presents a variation of the fact situation encountered by the Court in Harris v. New York, 401 U.S. 222, 91 S.Ct. 643 (1971): When a suspect, who is in the custody of a state police officer, has been given full *Miranda* warnings and accepts them, and then later states that he would like to telephone a lawyer but is told that this cannot be done until the officer and the suspect reach the station, and the suspect then provides inculpatory information, is that information admissible in evidence solely for impeachment purposes after the suspect has taken the stand and testified contrarily to the inculpatory information, or is it inadmissible under the Fifth and Fourteenth Amendments?

* * *

* * * Hass suggests that "when state law is more restrictive against the prosecution than federal law," this Court has no power "to compel a state to conform to federal law." * * * This, apparently, is proffered as a reference to our expressions that a State is free *as a matter of its own law* to impose greater restrictions on police activity than those this Court holds to be necessary upon federal constitutional standards. * * * But, of course, a State may not impose such greater restrictions as a matter of *federal constitutional law* when this Court specifically refrains from imposing them. * * *

Although Oregon has a constitutional provision against compulsory self-incrimination in any criminal prosecution, Ore.Const., Art. 1, § 12, the present case was decided by the Oregon courts on Fifth and Fourteenth Amendment grounds. The decision did not rest on the Oregon Constitution or state law; neither was cited. The fact that the Oregon courts found it necessary to attempt to distinguish *Harris* v. *New York*, supra, reveals the federal basis.

* * *

This takes us to the real issue, namely, that of the bearing of *Harris* v. *New York* upon this case.

In *Harris*, the defendant was charged by the State in a two-count indictment with twice selling heroin to an undercover police officer. The prosecution introduced evidence of the two sales. Harris took the stand in his own defense. He denied the first sale and described the second as one of baking powder utilized as part of a scheme to defraud the purchaser. On cross-examination, Harris was asked whether he had made specified statements to the police immediately following his arrest; the statements partially contradicted

Harris' testimony. In response, Harris testified that he could not remember the questions or answers recited by the prosecutor. The trial court instructed the jury that the statements attributed to Harris could be used only in passing on his credibility and not as evidence of guilt. The jury returned a verdict of guilty on the second count of the indictment.

The prosecution had not sought to use the statements in its case in chief, for it conceded that they were inadmissible under *Miranda* because Harris had not been advised of his right to appointed counsel. The Chief Justice, speaking for the Court, observed, id., 401 U.S., at 224, 91 S.Ct., at 645, "It does not follow from *Miranda* that evidence inadmissible against an accused in the prosecution's case in chief is barred for all purposes, provided of course that the trustworthiness of the evidence satisfies legal standards." Relying on Walder v. United States, 347 U.S. 62, 74 S.Ct. 354 (1954), a Fourth Amendment case, we ruled that there was "no difference in principle" between *Walder* and *Harris*; that the "impeachment process here undoubtedly provided valuable aid to the jury in assessing petitioner's credibility"; that the "benefits of this process should not be' lost"; that, "[a]ssuming that the exclusionary rule has a deterrent effect on proscribed police conduct, sufficient deterrence flows when the evidence in question is made unavailable to the prosecution in its case in chief," 401 U.S., at 225, 91 S.Ct., at 645, and that the "shield provided by *Miranda* cannot be perverted into a license to use perjury by way of a defense, free from the risk of confrontation with prior inconsistent utterances." Id., at 226, 91 S.Ct., at 646. It was held, accordingly, that Harris' credibility was appropriately impeached by the use of his earlier conflicting statements.

We see no valid distinction to be made in the application of the principles of *Harris* to his case and to Hass' case. Hass' statements were made after the defendant knew Osterholme's opposing testimony had been ruled inadmissible for the prosecution's case in chief.

As in *Harris*, it does not follow from *Miranda* that evidence inadmissible against Hass in the prosecution's case in chief is barred for all purposes, always provided that "the trustworthiness of the evidence satisfies legal standards." Again, the impeaching material would provide valuable aid to the jury in assessing the defendant's credibility; again, "the benefits of this process should not be lost"; and again, making the deterrent effect assumption, there is sufficient deterrence when the evidence in question is made unavailable to the prosecution in its case in chief. If all this sufficed for the result in *Harris*, it supports and demands a like result in Hass' case. Here, too, the shield provided by *Miranda* is not to be perverted to a license to testify inconsistently, or even perjuriously, free from the risk of confrontation with prior inconsistent utterances.

We are, after all, always engaged in a search for truth in a criminal case so long as the search is surrounded with the safeguards provided by our Constitution. There is no evidence or suggestion that Hass' statements to Officer Osterholme on the way to Moyina Heights were involuntary or coerced. He properly sensed, to be sure, that he was in "trouble"; but the pressure on him was no greater than that on any person in like custody or under inquiry by any investigating officer.

The only possible factual distinction between *Harris* and this case lies in the fact that the *Miranda* warnings given Hass were proper whereas those given *Harris* were defective. The deterrence of the exclusionary rule, of course, lies in the necessity to give the warnings. That these warnings, in a given case, may prove to be incomplete, and therefore defective, as in *Harris*, does not mean that they have not served as a deterrent to the officer who is not then aware of their defect; and to the officer who is aware of the defect the full deterrence remains. The effect of inadmissibility in the *Harris* case and in this case is the same: inadmissibility would pervert the constitutional right into a right to falsify free from the embarrassment of impeachment evidence from the defendant's own mouth.

One might concede that when proper *Miranda* warnings have been given, and the officer then continues his interrogation after the suspect asks for an attorney, the officer may be said to have little to lose and perhaps something to gain by way of possibly uncovering impeachment material. This speculative possibility, however, is even greater where the warnings are defective and the defect is not known to the officer. In any event, the balance was struck in *Harris*, and we are not disposed to change it now. If, in a given case, the officer's conduct amounts to an abuse, that case, like those involving coercion or duress, may be taken care of when it arises measured by the traditional standards for evaluating voluntariness and trustworthiness.

We therefore hold that the Oregon appellate courts were in error when they ruled that Officer Osterholme's testimony on rebuttal was inadmissible on Fifth and Fourteenth Amendment grounds for purposes of Hass' impeachment. The judgment of the Supreme Court of Oregon is reversed.

It is so ordered.

Reversed.

Mr. Justice DOUGLAS took no part in the consideration or decision of this case.

Mr. Justice BRENNAN, with whom Mr. Justice MARSHALL joins, dissenting.

* * *

The Court's decision today goes beyond *Harris* in undermining *Miranda*. Even after *Harris*, police had some incentive for following *Miranda* by warning an accused of his right to remain silent and his right to counsel. If the warnings were given, the accused might still make a statement which could be used in the prosecution's case-in-chief. Under today's holding, however, once the warnings are given, police have almost no incentive for following *Miranda's* requirement that "[i]f the individual states that he wants an attorney, the interrogation must cease until an attorney is present." *Miranda*, supra, 384 U.S., at 474, 86 S.Ct., at 1628. If the requirement is followed there will almost surely be no statement since the attorney will advise the accused to remain silent. If, however, the requirement is disobeyed, the police may obtain a statement which can be used for impeachment if the accused has the temerity to testify in his own defense. Thus, after today's decision, if an individual states that he wants an attorney, police interrogation will doubtless

now be vigorously pressed to obtain statements before the attorney arrives. I am unwilling to join this fundamental erosion of Fifth and Sixth Amendment rights and therefore dissent. I would affirm or, at least, remand for further proceedings for the reasons given in Mr. Justice MARSHALL's opinion.

Mr. Justice MARSHALL, with whom Mr. Justice BRENNAN joins, dissenting.

While I agree with my Brother BRENNAN that on the merits the judgment of the Oregon Supreme Court was correct, I think it appropriate to add a word about this Court's increasingly common practice of reviewing state court decisions upholding constitutional claims in criminal cases. * * *

In my view, we have too often rushed to correct state courts in their view of federal constitutional questions without sufficiently considering the risk that we will be drawn into rendering a purely advisory opinion. Plainly, if the Oregon Supreme Court had expressly decided that Hass' statement was inadmissible as a matter of state as well as federal law, this Court could not upset that judgment. * * *

Where we have been unable to say with certainty that the judgment rested solely on federal law grounds, we have refused to rule on the federal issue in the case; the proper course is then either to dismiss the writ as improvidently granted or to remand the case to the state court to clarify the basis of its decision. * * * Of course, it may often be unclear whether a state court has relied in part on state law in reaching its decision. * * *

* * * The Constitution of Oregon contains an independent prohibi-

tion against compulsory self-incrimination, and there is a distinct possibility that the state court intended to express its view of state as well as federal constitutional law. The majority flatly states that the case was decided below solely on federal constitutional grounds, but I am not so certain. Although the state court did not expressly cite state law in support of its judgment, its opinion suggests that it may well have considered the matter one of state as well as federal law. * * *

In addition to the importance of avoiding jurisdictional difficulties, it seems much the better policy to permit the state court the freedom to strike its own balance between individual rights and police practices, at least where the state court's ruling violates no constitutional prohibitions. It is peculiarly within the competence of the highest court of a state to determine that in its jurisdiction the police should be subject to more stringent rules than are required as a federal constitutional minimum.

The Oregon court's decision in this case was not premised on a reluctant adherence to what it deemed federal law to require, but was based on its independent conclusion that admitting evidence such as that held admissible today will encourage police misconduct in violation of the right against compulsory self-incrimination. This is precisely the setting in which it seems most likely that the state court would apply the State's self-incrimination clause to lessen what it perceives as an intolerable risk of abuse. Accordingly, in my view the Court should not review a state decision reversing a conviction unless it is quite clear that the state court has resolved all applicable state law questions adversely to the defendant and that it feels compelled by its view of the federal constitutional issue to reverse the conviction at hand.

Even if the majority is correct that the Oregon Supreme Court did not intend to express a view of state as well as federal law, this Court should, at the very least, remand the case for such further proceedings as the state court deems appropriate. I can see absolutely no reason for departing from the usual course of remanding the case to permit the state court to consider any other claims, including the possible applicability of state law to the issue treated here. * * * Surely the majority does not mean to suggest that the Oregon Supreme Court is foreclosed from considering the respondent's state law claims or even ruling *sua sponte* that the statement in question is not admissible as a matter of state law. If so, then I should think this unprecedented assumption of authority will be as much a surprise to the Supreme Court of Oregon as it is to me.

I dissent.

OTHER RECENT RULINGS ON COMPELLED SELF-INCRIMINATION

Case	Holding	Vote
Doyle v. Ohio, 426 U.S. 610, 96 S.Ct. 2240 (1976)	Because of the ambiguity that necessarily surrounds the reasons for a defendant's silence after being given the *Miranda* warning and because the warning itself implies that no	6–3; Blackmun, Rehnquist, and Stevens dissented

COMPELLED SELF-INCRIMINATION (*Cont.*)

Case	Holding	Vote
Doyle (*Cont.*)	penalty will attach to a suspect's silence, a state prosecutor may not seek to impeach the credibility of defendant's alibi, told for the first time at trial, by cross-examining him about his failure to tell the story at the time of his arrest	
Lakeside v. Oregon, 435 U.S. 333, 98 S.Ct. 1091 (1978)	As distinguished from Court's previous ruling in Griffin v. California, 380 U.S. 609, 85 S.Ct. 1229 (1965), that a trial judge must refrain from telling the jury that defendant's failure to take the stand in his own defense constitutes an unfavorable reflection upon him, the Fifth Amendment does not require that, upon defendant's request, a trial judge must also refrain from giving a cautionary instruction that the jury draw no adverse conclusion from defendant's failure to take the stand	6–2; Marshall and Stevens dissented
New Jersey v. Portash, 440 U.S. 450, 99 S.Ct. 1292 (1979)	Defendant's testimony before grand jury given under a grant of immunity was the essence of compelled testimony and could not be used later to impeach his credibility at trial	7–2; Burger and Blackmun dissented
Jenkins v. Anderson, 447 U.S. 231, 100 S.Ct. 2124 (1980)	Where defendant, on trial for murder, took the stand and testified that the killing occurred in self-defense, it was not a violation of the Fifth (and Fourteenth) Amendment for prosecutor to impeach the credibility of the defendant's testimony by pointing up the fact that, after the killing occurred, the defendant did not stick around to talk to police but some two weeks passed before the defendant was arrested and before he talked to police about the matter. Questioning of defendant about his prearrest silence here distinguished from the defendant's silence in Doyle v. Ohio, supra, which followed reading of Miranda warnings and thus may have been induced by them	7–2; Brennan and Marshall dissented
Carter v. Kentucky, 450 U.S. 288, 101 S.Ct. 1112 (1981)	Upon proper request, a state trial judge has a constitutional obligation under the Fifth and Fourteenth Amendments to instruct the jury that the defendant is not required to testify and the fact that he declines to do so cannot be used to infer guilt and should not prejudice him in any way	8–1; Rehnquist dissented
Estelle v. Smith, 451 U.S. 454, 101 S.Ct. 1866 (1981)	Admission of doctor's testimony at penalty phase of defendant's trial violated Fifth Amendment guarantee against compelled self-incrimination because defendant was not advised at time of his pretrial psychiatric examination that he had the right to remain silent and that any statement he made could be used against him at a capital sentencing proceeding. Defendant's Sixth Amendment	9–0; Stewart and Powell failed to reach the Fifth Amendment issue; Rehnquist dissented from the Fifth Amendment holding

COMPELLED SELF-INCRIMINATION (*Cont.*)

Case	Holding	Vote
Estelle (*Cont.*)	guarantee of right to counsel was also abridged because examination of defendant in jail clearly took place at a "critical stage" of the proceedings against him and defense counsel was not notified in advance that the doctor's interview with the defendant would touch on the matter of the defendant's future dangerousness, which would be directly relevant at the penalty phase, and that the doctor's testimony could be used by the state at that stage of the proceedings	
Edwards v. Arizona, 451 U.S. 477, 101 S.Ct. 1880 (1981)	See chart, p. 986	
Taylor v. Alabama, — U.S. —, 102 S.Ct. 2664 (1982)	Defendant was arrested for the robbery of a grocery store without either a warrant or probable cause, based on an uncorroborated tip from an informant, and taken to the police station where he was given the *Miranda* warnings, booked, fingerprinted, and put in a line-up. Six hours later he signed a confession after he was told his fingerprints matched those on grocery store items handled by one of the participants in the robbery and after a short visit with his girlfriend. Here there was no meaningful event occurring to purge the confession of the taint accruing from the illegal search and seizure. Neither the lapse of time between arrest and confession, nor the apparent willingness with which the confession was given, nor the visit with his girlfriend, nor the lack of physical abuse by the police sufficed to cure the taint. Where police, after the defendant was in custody, procured an arrest warrant based on the match in fingerprints, such a warrant did not alleviate the taint because the fingerprints themselves were tainted under the "fruit of the poisonous tree" doctrine.	5–4; Burger and Powell, Rehnquist, and O'Connor dissented

SCHMERBER v. CALIFORNIA

Supreme Court of the United States, 1966
384 U.S. 757, 86 S.Ct. 1826, 16 L.Ed.2d 908

The facts are contained in the opinion.

Mr. Justice BRENNAN delivered the opinion of the Court.

Petitioner was convicted in Los Angeles Municipal Court of the criminal offense of driving an automobile while under the influence of intoxicating liquor. He had been arrested at a hospital while receiving treatment for injuries suffered in an accident involving the automobile that he had apparently been driving. At the direction of a police officer, a blood sample was then withdrawn from petitioner's body by a physician at the hospital. The chemical analysis of this sample revealed a percent by weight of alcohol in his blood at the time of the offense which indicated intoxication, and the report of this analysis was admitted in evidence at the trial. Petitioner objected to receipt of this evidence of the analysis on the ground that the blood had been withdrawn despite his refusal, on the advice of his counsel, to consent to the test. He contended that in that circumstance the withdrawal of the blood and the admission of the analysis in evidence denied him due process of law under the Fourteenth Amendment, as well as specific guarantees of the Bill of Rights secured against the States by that Amendment: [among those were] his privilege against self-incrimination under the Fifth Amendment * * * and his right not to be subjected to unreasonable searches and seizures in violation of the Fourth Amendment. The Appellate Department of the California Superior Court rejected these contentions and affirmed the conviction. * * * We affirm.

THE DUE PROCESS
CLAUSE CLAIM

Breithaupt [v. Abram, 352 U.S. 432, 77 S.Ct. 408] was also a case in which police officers caused blood to be withdrawn from the driver of an automobile involved in an accident, and in which there was ample justification for the officer's conclusion that the driver was under the influence of alcohol. There, as here, the extraction was made by a physician in a simple, medically acceptable manner in a hospital environment. There, however, the driver was unconscious at the time the blood was withdrawn and hence had no opportunity to object to the procedure. We affirmed the conviction there resulting from the use of the test in evidence, holding that under such circumstances the withdrawal did not offend "that 'sense of justice' of which we spoke in Rochin v. [People of] California, 1952, 342 U.S. 165, 72 S.Ct. 205." Breithaupt thus requires the rejection of petitioner's due process argument, and nothing in the circumstances of this case or in supervening events persuades us that this aspect of Breithaupt should be overruled.

THE PRIVILEGE AGAINST
SELF-INCRIMINATION
CLAIM

Breithaupt summarily rejected an argument that the withdrawal of blood and the admission of the analysis report involved in that state case violated the Fifth Amendment privilege of any person not to "be compelled in any criminal case to be a witness against himself," citing Twining v. State of New Jersey, 211 U.S. 78, 29 S.Ct. 14. But that case, holding that the protections of the Fourteenth Amendment do not embrace this Fifth Amendment privilege, has been succeeded by Malloy v. Hogan. * * * We therefore must now decide whether the withdrawal of the blood and admission in evidence of the analysis involved in this case violated petitioner's privilege. We hold that the privilege protects an accused only from being compelled to testify against himself, or otherwise provide the State with evidence of a testimonial or communicative nature, and that the withdrawal of blood and use of the analysis in question in this case did not involve compulsion to these ends.

It could not be denied that in requiring petitioner to submit to the withdrawal and chemical analysis of his blood the State compelled him to submit to an attempt to discover evidence that might be used to prosecute him for a criminal offense. He submitted only after the police officer rejected his objection and directed the physician to proceed. The officer's direction to the physician to administer the test over petitioner's objection constituted compulsion for the purposes of the privilege. The critical question, then, is whether petitioner was thus compelled "to be a witness against himself."

If the scope of the privilege coincided with the complex of values it helps to protect, we might be obliged to conclude that the privilege was violated. * * * The withdrawal of blood necessarily involves puncturing the skin for extraction, and the percent by weight of alcohol in that blood, as established by chemical analysis, is evidence of criminal guilt. Compelled submission fails on one view to respect the "inviolability of the human personality." Moreover, since it enables the State to rely on evidence forced from the accused, the compulsion violates at least one meaning of the requirement that the State procure the evidence against an accused "by its own independent labors."

* * * History and a long line of authorities in lower courts have consistently limited its protection to situations in which the State seeks to submerge those values by obtaining the evidence against an accused through "the cruel, simple expedient

of compelling it from his own mouth. * * * In sum, the privilege is fulfilled only when the person is guaranteed the right 'to remain silent unless he chooses to speak in the unfettered exercise of his own will.' " * * *

It is clear that the protection of the privilege reaches an accused's communications, whatever form they might take, and the compulsion of responses which are also communications, for example, compliance with a subpoena to produce one's papers. Boyd v. United States, 116 U.S. 616, 6 S.Ct. 524. On the other hand, both federal and state courts have usually held that it offers no protection against compulsion to submit to fingerprinting, photographing, or measurements, to write or speak for identification, to appear in court, to stand, to assume a stance, to walk, or to make a particular gesture. The distinction which has emerged, often expressed in different ways, is that the privilege is a bar against compelling "communications" or "testimony," but that compulsion which makes a suspect or accused the source of "real or physical evidence" does not violate it.

* * *

* * * Since the blood test evidence, although an incriminating product of compulsion, was neither petitioner's testimony nor evidence relating to some communicative act or writing by the petitioner, it was not inadmissible on privilege grounds.

* * *

THE SEARCH AND SEIZURE CLAIM

In *Breithaupt*, as here, it was also contended that the chemical analysis should be excluded from evidence as the product of an unlawful search and seizure in violation of the Fourth and Fourteenth Amendments. * * *

The overriding function of the Fourth Amendment is to protect personal privacy and dignity against unwarranted intrusion by the State.

* * *

Because we are dealing with intrusions into the human body rather than with state interferences with property relationships or private papers—"houses, papers, and effects"—we write on a clean slate. * * * We begin with the assumption that once the privilege against self-incrimination has been found not to bar compelled intrusions into the body for blood to be analyzed for alcohol content, the Fourth Amendment's proper function is to constrain, not against all intrusions as such, but against intrusions which are not justified in the circumstances, or which are made in an improper manner. In other words, the questions we must decide in this case are whether the police were justified in requiring petitioner to submit to the blood test, and whether the means and procedures employed in taking his blood respected relevant Fourth Amendment standards of reasonableness.

In this case, as will often be true when charges of driving under the influence of alcohol are pressed, these questions arise in the context of an arrest made by an officer without a warrant. Here, there was plainly probable cause for the officer to arrest petitioner and charge him with driving an automobile while under the influence of intoxicating liquor. The police officer who arrived at the scene shortly after the acci-

dent smelled liquor on petitioner's breath, and testified that petitioner's eyes were "bloodshot, watery, sort of a glassy appearance." The officer saw petitioner again at the hospital, within two hours of the accident. There he noticed similar symptoms of drunkenness. He thereupon informed petitioner "that he was under arrest and that he was entitled to the services of an attorney, and that he could remain silent, and that anything that he told me would be used against him in evidence."

* * *

Although the facts which established probable cause to arrest in this case also suggested the required relevance and likely success of a test of petitioner's blood for alcohol, the question remains whether the arresting officer was permitted to draw these inferences himself, or was required instead to procure a warrant before proceeding with the test. Search warrants are ordinarily required for searches of dwellings, and absent an emergency, no less could be required where intrusions into the human body are concerned. The requirement that a warrant be obtained is a requirement that inferences to support the search "be drawn by a neutral and detached magistrate instead of being judged by the officer engaged in the often competitive enterprise of ferreting out crime." * * * The importance of informed, detached and deliberate determinations of the issue whether or not to invade another's body in search of evidence of guilt is indisputable and great.

The officer in the present case, however, might reasonably have believed that he was confronted with an emergency, in which the delay necessary to obtain a warrant, under the circumstances, threatened "the destruction of evidence," Preston v. United States, 376 U.S. 364, 367, 84 S.Ct. 881, 883. We are told that the percentage of alcohol in the blood begins to diminish shortly after drinking stops, as the body functions to eliminate it from the system. * * *

* * *

Finally, the record shows that the test was performed in a reasonable manner. Petitioner's blood was taken by a physician in a hospital environment according to accepted medical practices. We are thus not presented with the serious questions which would arise if a search involving use of a medical technique, even of the most rudimentary sort, were made by other than medical personnel or in other than a medical environment—for example, if it were administered by police in the privacy of the stationhouse. To tolerate searches under these conditions might be to invite an unjustified element of personal risk of infection and pain.

We thus conclude that the present record shows no violation of petitioner's right under the Fourth and Fourteenth Amendments to be free of unreasonable searches and seizures. It bears repeating, however, that we reach this judgment only on the facts of the present record. The integrity of an individual's person is a cherished value of our society. That we today hold that the Constitution does not forbid the States minor intrusions into an individual's body under stringently limited conditions in no way indicates that it permits more substantial intrusions, or intrusions under other conditions.

Affirmed.

Mr. Justice HARLAN, whom Mr. Justice STEWART joins, concurring.

* * * While agreeing with the Court that the taking of this blood test involved no testimonial compulsion, I would go further and hold that apart from this consideration the case in no way implicates the Fifth Amendment. * * *

Mr. Justice BLACK with whom Mr. Justice DOUGLAS joins, dissenting.

I would reverse petitioner's conviction. * * *

* * *

* * * How can it reasonably be doubted that the blood test evidence was not in all respects the actual equivalent of "testimony" taken from petitioner when the result of the test was offered as testimony, was considered by the jury as testimony, and the jury's verdict of guilt rests in part on that testimony? The refined, subtle reasoning and balancing process used here to narrow the scope of the Bill of Rights' safeguard against self-incrimination provides a handy instrument for further narrowing of that constitutional protection, as well as others, in the future. * * *

* * *

[Chief Justice WARREN and Justice FORTAS also dissented.]

California's "hit and run" statute requires the driver of a motor vehicle involved in an accident that causes damage to another's property to stop at the scene and give his name and address to the owner. Jonathan Byers was involved in such an accident but did not comply with the requirements of the statute. Demurring to an indictment, he contended that compliance with this "stop and report" provision of the state vehicle code constituted an infringement of the Fifth and Fourteenth Amendments. The California Supreme Court agreed, holding that Byers faced "substantial hazards of self-incrimination" as this statute was applied to him and affirmed the ruling of a state superior court granting a writ of prohibition to quash prosecution before the trial court.

The United States Supreme Court in California v. Byers, 402 U.S. 424, 91 S.Ct. 1535 (1971), vacated the judgment and remanded the case. Chief Justice Burger announced the judgment of the Court and delivered an opinion in which Justices Stewart, White, and Blackmun concurred. The Chief Justice said:

> Tension between the State's demand for disclosures and the protection of the right against self-incrimination is likely to give rise to serious questions. Inevitably these must be resolved in terms of balancing the public need on the one hand, and the individual claim to constitutional protections on the other; neither interest can be treated lightly.
>
> An organized society imposes many burdens on its constituents. It commands the filing of tax returns for income; it requires producers and distributors of consumer goods to file informational reports on the manufacturing process and the content of products, on the wages, hours, and working conditions of employees. Those who borrow money on the public market or issue securities for sale to the public must file various information reports; industries must report periodically the volume and content of pollutants discharged into our waters and atmosphere. Comparable examples are legion.
>
> In each of these situations there is some possibility of prosecution—often a very real one—for criminal offenses disclosed by or deriving from the information that the law compels a person to supply. Information revealed by these reports could well be "a link in the chain" of evidence leading to prosecution and conviction. But under our holdings the mere possibility of incrimination is insufficient to defeat the strong policies in favor of a disclosure called for by statutes like the one challenged here.

After comparing previous decisions of the Court in which analogous disclosure had been upheld, particularly in regard to the filing of income tax returns (see United States v. Sullivan, 274 U.S. 259, 47 S.Ct. 607 [1927]), with those in which compulsion to register such information had been struck down (e.g., gambling activities, Marchetti v. United States [p. 543] and Grosso v. United States [p. 545]; Communist party affiliation, Albertson v. Subversive Activities Control Board, 382 U.S. 70, 86 S.Ct. 194 [1965]), Chief Justice Burger concluded:

> In all of these cases the disclosures condemned were only those extracted from a "highly selective group inherently suspect of criminal activities" and the privilege was applied only in "an area permeated with criminal statutes"—not in "an essentially noncriminal and regulatory area of inquiry." * * *
>
> * * *
>
> In contrast [the "stop and report" statute] like income tax laws, is directed at all persons—here all persons who drive automobiles in California. This group, numbering as it does in the millions, is so large as to render [it] a statute "directed at the public at large." * * * It is difficult to

consider this group as either "highly selective" or "inherently suspect of criminal activities." Driving an automobile, unlike gambling, is a lawful activity. Moreover, it is not a criminal offense under California law to be a driver "involved in an accident." An accident may be the fault of others; it may occur without any driver having been at fault. No empirical data are suggested in support of the conclusion that there is a relevant correlation between being a driver and criminal prosecution of drivers. So far as any available information instructs us, most accidents occur without creating criminal liability even if one or both of the drivers are guilty of negligence as a matter of tort law.

The disclosure of inherently illegal activity is inherently risky. * * * But disclosures with respect to automobile accidents simply do not entail the kind of substantial risk of self-incrimination involved in *Marchetti* [and] *Grosso*. * * * Furthermore, the statutory purpose is noncriminal and self-reporting is indispensable to its fulfillment.

The Chief Justice added that, even conceding the requirement to divulge one's name and address (he termed it "an essentially neutral act") was incriminating, it would be an "extravagant" extension of the privilege to rule that it was testimonial and thus of a variety precluded by the Fifth Amendment.

Justice Harlan concurred in the judgment of the Court. In agreeing with the conclusion of the majority, he said:

I am * * * constrained to hold that the presence of a "real" and not "imaginary" risk of self-incrimination is not a sufficient predicate for extending the privilege against self-incrimination to regulatory schemes of the character involved in this case.

* * *

Considering the noncriminal governmental purpose in securing the information, the necessity for self-reporting as a means of securing the information, and the nature of the disclosures involved, I cannot say that the purposes of the Fifth Amendment warrant imposition of a use restriction as a condition on the enforcement of this statute. To hold otherwise would, it seems to me, embark us on uncharted and treacherous seas. * * *

Justice Black dissented in an opinion joined by Justices Douglas and Brennan. Justice Black said:

* * *

The plurality opinion also seeks to distinguish this case from our previous decisions on the ground that [the "stop and report" law] requires disclosure in an area not "permeated with criminal statutes" and because it is not aimed at a "highly selective group inherently suspect of criminal activities." * * * Of course, these suggestions ignore the fact that *this particular respondent* would have run a serious risk of self-incrimination by complying with the disclosure statute. Furthermore, it is hardly accurate to suggest that the activity of driving an automobile in California is not "an area permeated with criminal statutes." * * * And it is unhelpful to say the statute is not aimed at an "inherently suspect" group because it applies to "all persons who drive automobiles in California." * * * The compelled disclosure is required of all persons who drive automobiles in California *who are involved in accidents causing property damage.* If this group is not "suspect" of illegal activities, it is difficult to find such a group.

* * *

My Brother HARLAN's opinion makes it clear that today the Court "balances" the importance of a defendant's Fifth Amendment right not to be forced to help convict himself against the government's interest in forcing him to do so. As in previous decisions, this balancing inevitably results in the dilution of constitutional guarantees. * * * By my Brother HARLAN's reasoning it appears that the scope of the Fifth Amendment's protection will now depend on what value a majority of nine Justices chooses to place on this explicit constitutional guarantee as opposed to the government's interest in convicting a man by compelling self-incriminating testimony. In my view, vesting such power in judges to water down constitutional rights does indeed "embark us" on Brother HARLAN's "uncharted and treacherous seas." * * *

I can only assume that the unarticulated premise of the decision is that there is so much crime abroad in this country at present that Bill of Rights' safeguards against arbitrary government must not be completely enforced. I can agree that there is too much crime in the land for us to treat criminals with favor. But I can never agree that we should depart in the slightest way from the Bill of Rights' guarantees that give this country its high place among the free nations of the world. * * *

* * *

Justice Marshall also dissented.

d. PROCEDURAL GUARANTEES AND THE ADMINISTRATIVE PROCESS

SHAUGHNESSY v. UNITED STATES EX REL. MEZEI

Supreme Court of the United States, 1953
345 U.S. 206, 73 S.Ct. 625, 97 L.Ed. 956

Ignatz Mezei, an alien immigrant, was born in Gibralter of Hungarian or Rumanian parents and for twenty-five years, beginning in 1923, resided in Buffalo, New York. In May 1948, he left the country apparently with the intention of visiting his dying mother in Rumania. He was denied entry there and subsequently spent some nineteen months in Hungary due "to difficulty in securing an exit permit." After being given a quota immigrant visa by the American Consul in Budapest, he headed back to the United States. On arrival in New York in February 1950, he was temporarily excluded by an immigration inspector acting under the provisions of the Passport Act. Awaiting disposition of his case he stayed on Ellis Island. After review of the case, the Attorney General ordered that the exclusion be made permanent and refused in so ruling to accord Mezei a hearing or to disclose the reasons for his decision on grounds that it "would be prejudicial to the public interest for security reasons." Mezei then tried to seek entry into other countries. France and Britain refused him entry, and Hungary denied him readmission. Approximately a dozen Latin American countries also gave a negative response. Advising the Immigration and Naturalization Service that he would make no further efforts to seek foreign refuge, Mezei, after having been detained on Ellis Island for twenty-one months, sued out a writ of habeas corpus against Shaughnessy, the District Director of Immigration and Naturalization.

A U. S. district court granted the writ finding that further detention would be excessive and unjustified if the government could not produce affirmative evidence of the risk in admitting Mezei. The government refused to disclose any evidence, and the judge conditionally paroled petitioner on bond. The Circuit Court of Appeals affirmed, and the immigration director appealed.

Mr. Justice CLARK delivered the opinion of the Court.

* * *

Courts have long recognized the power to expel or exclude aliens as a fundamental sovereign attribute exercised by the Government's political departments largely immune from judicial control. * * * In the exercise of these powers, Congress expressly authorized the President to impose additional restrictions on aliens entering or leaving the United States during periods of international tension and strife. That authorization, originally enacted in the Passport Act of 1918, continues in effect during the present emergency. Under it, the Attorney General, acting for the President, may shut out aliens whose "entry would be prejudicial to the interests of the United States." And he may exclude without a hearing when the exclusion is based on confidential information the disclosure of which may be prejudicial to the public interest. The Attorney General in this case proceeded in accord with these provisions; he made the necessary determinations and barred the alien from entering the United States.

* * *

[W]e do not think that respondent's continued exclusion deprives him of any statutory or constitutional right. It is true that resident aliens temporarily detained pending expeditious consummation of deportation proceedings may be released on bond by the Attorney General whose discretion is subject to judicial review. * * * By that procedure aliens uprooted from our midst may rejoin the community until the Government effects their leave. An exclusion proceeding grounded on danger to the national security, however, presents different considerations; neither the rationale nor the statutory authority for such release exists. * * * Whatever our individual estimate of that policy and the fears on which it rests, respondent's right to enter the United States depends on the congressional will, and courts cannot substitute their judgment for the legislative mandate. * * *

Reversed.

[Justices BLACK and DOUGLAS dissented.]

Mr. Justice JACKSON, whom Mr. Justice FRANKFURTER joins, dissenting.

Fortunately it still is startling, in this country, to find a person held indefinitely in executive custody without accusation of crime or judicial trial. Executive imprisonment has been considered oppressive and lawless since John, at Runnymede, pledged that no free man should be imprisoned, dispossessed, outlawed, or exiled save by the judgment of his peers or by the law of the land. The judges of England developed the writ of habeas corpus largely to preserve these immunities from executive restraint. Under the best tradition of Anglo-American law, courts will not deny hearing to an unconvicted prisoner just because he is an alien whose keep, in legal theory, is just outside our gates. * * *

* * *

I conclude that detention of an alien would not be inconsistent with substantive due process, provided— and this is where my dissent begins—he is accorded procedural due process of law.

Procedural fairness, if not all that originally was meant by due process of law, is at least what it most uncompromisingly requires. Procedural due process is more elemental and less flexible than substantive due process. It yields less to the times, varies less with conditions, and defers much less to legislative judgment. Insofar as it is technical law, it must be a specialized responsibility within the competence of the judiciary on which they do not bend before political branches of the Government, as they should on matters of policy which compromise substantive law.

If it be conceded that in some way this alien could be confined, does it matter what the procedure is? Only the untaught layman or the charlatan lawyer can answer that procedures matter not. Procedural fairness and regularity are of the indispensable essence of liberty. Severe substantive laws can be endured if they are fairly and impartially applied. Indeed, if put to the choice, one might well prefer to live under Soviet substantive law applied in good faith by our common-law procedures than under our substantive law enforced by Soviet procedural practices. Let it not be overlooked that due process of law is not for the sole benefit of an accused. It is the best insurance for the Government itself against those blunders which leave lasting stains on a system of justice but which are bound to occur on *ex parte* consideration. * * *

Our law may, and rightly does, place more restrictions on the alien than on the citizen. But basic fairness in hearing procedures does not vary with the status of the accused. If the procedures used to judge this alien are fair and just, no good reason can be given why they should not be extended to simplify the condemnation of citizens. If they would be unfair to citizens, we cannot defend the fairness of them when applied to the more helpless and handicapped alien. This is at the root of our holdings that the resident alien must be given a fair hearing to test an official claim that he is one of a deportable class. * * *

* * *

Congress has ample power to determine whom we will admit to our shores and by what means it will effectuate its exclusion policy. The only limitation is that it may not do so by authorizing United States officers to take without due process of law the life, the liberty or the property of an alien who has come within our jurisdiction; and that means he must meet a fair hearing with fair notice of the charges.

It is inconceivable to me that this measure of simple justice and fair dealing would menace the security of this country. No one can make me believe that we are that far gone.

[It should be noted by way of a postscript that considerable national publicity eventually forced the Attorney General to relent and, by administrative action, admit Mezei, though it was not, of course, before the principle of his unreviewable authority under the statute was vindicated by the Vinson Court.]

Suits were brought against John Hannah and other members of the U. S. Civil Rights Commission challenging the constitutionality of certain rules of procedure which were to govern the commission's investigation of alleged Negro voting deprivation in Louisiana. Specifically, Margaret Larche, other registrars of voters, and several private citizens of the state objected to the commission's rules which permitted the identity of persons submitting complaints for investigation to be kept secret and which precluded witnesses before the commission from cross-examining others who gave testimony. A federal district court held that the challenged rules were unauthorized and enjoined the commission from conducting hearings so long as the rules remained in effect. The Supreme Court granted certiorari.

In Hannah v. Larche, 363 U.S. 420, 80 S.Ct. 1502 (1960), the Supreme Court concluded that the procedures employed by the commission were authorized by Congress and comported with the Due Process Clause of the Fifth Amendment. After he inventoried the procedural safeguards Congress intended the commission to follow (e.g., the chairman was obliged to make an opening statement indicating the subject of the hearing; a copy of the commission's rules was to be made available to all witnesses; witnesses were entitled to be accompanied by counsel for the purpose of advising them on their constitutional rights; potentially defamatory or incriminating information was to be received in executive session; a witness implicated by defamatory or incriminating testimony had the opportunity to appear voluntarily as a witness and to request that the commission call additional witnesses; testimony taken in executive session was to be released only with the commission's consent; witnesses were entitled to submit brief and pertinent sworn statements for the record), Chief Justice Warren, speaking for the Court, observed, "The absence of any reference to appraisal, confrontation, and cross-examination, in addition to the fact that counsel's role is specifically limited to advising witnesses of their constitutional rights, creates a presumption that Congress did not intend witnesses appearing before the Commission to have the rights claimed by respondents. This initial assumption is strengthened beyond any reasonable doubt by an investigation of the legislative history of the [Civil Rights] Act [of 1957]" (the authorizing legislation). After reviewing the functions to be performed by the commission (investigating written sworn allegations of the denial of voting rights; collecting and studying information bearing upon denials of equal protection; and reporting its findings to both the President and Congress), the Court concluded that, in light of the fact that the commission had only fact-finding functions and no adjudicative functions (i.e., it could not issue orders, determine civil liability, indict, or punish), those procedures associated with trial-type hearings and claimed by the registrars were not constitutionally required. As to the respondent registrars' contention that such procedures were required lest they be subjected "to public opprobrium and scorn, the distinct likelihood of losing their jobs, and the possibility of criminal prosecutions," the Court termed these consequences "purely conjectural." These speculative effects were clearly offset, the Court explained, by the disruptive effect imposing the rights in question would have on the commission's fact-finding mission:

[T]he investigative process could be completely disrupted if investigative hearings were transformed into trial-like proceedings, and if persons who might be indirectly affected by an investigation were given an absolute right to cross-examine every witness called to testify. Fact-finding agencies without any power to adjudicate would be diverted from their legitimate duties and would be plagued by the injection of collateral issues that would make the investigation interminable. Even a person not called as a witness could demand the right to appear at the hearing, cross-examine any witness whose testimony or sworn affidavit allegedly defamed or incriminated him, and call an unlimited number of witnesses of his own selection. This type of proceeding would make a shambles of the investigation and stifle the agency in its gathering of facts.

Finally, Chief Justice Warren observed that the limited procedural rights afforded before the commission were analogous to comparably limited guarantees found in other investigative settings, such as hearings conducted by congressional committees or inquiries undertaken by grand juries.

Although they had no sympathy whatever for the behavior of the registrars that gave rise to their appearance before the commission, Justices Black and Douglas dissented. Said Justice Douglas, speaking for the duo:

> [I]mportant as these civil rights are, it will not do to sacrifice other civil rights in order to protect them. We live and work under a Constitution. The temptation of many men of goodwill is to cut corners, take short cuts, and reach the desired end regardless of the means. Worthy as I think the ends are which the Civil Rights Commission advances in these cases, I think the particular means used are unconstitutional.

*   *   *

> The   *   *   *   path which we take today leads to trial of separate essential parts of criminal prosecutions by commissions, by executive agencies, by legislative committees. Farming out pieces of trials to investigative agencies is fragmentizing the kind of trial the Constitution authorizes. It prejudices the ultimate trial itself; and it puts in the hands of officials the awesome power which the Framers entrusted only to judges, grand jurors and petit jurors drawn from the community where the accused lives. It leads to government by inquisition.

*   *   *

MATHEWS v. ELDRIDGE

Supreme Court of the United States, 1976
424 U.S. 319, 96 S.Ct. 893, 47 L.Ed.2d 18

Eldridge, a recipient of worker disability benefits under the Social Security Act brought suit against Secretary of Health, Education and Welfare F. David Mathews, seeking reinstatement of the payments. Eldridge argued that initial agency procedures which resulted in the termination of benefits denied him due process.

During its program of continually monitoring the medical conditions of aid recipients, a state agency reached a determination that Eldridge's disability had ended and recommended that benefits to him no longer continue. The agency informed Eldridge of its conclusion and, in a letter to him, indicated its reasons. The letter also advised Eldridge that he might request additional time to submit any other relevant information. In his letter of response to the agency, Eldridge took issue with one characterization of his medical condition but indicated that he thought the agency had sufficient information already on hand to warrant a conclusion that he was still disabled. The state agency then made its final determination that Eldridge's eligibility had terminated and forwarded its recommendation to the Social Security Administration which, in a letter to Eldridge, notified him that he would be receiving no future payments and advised him of his right to have the agency reconsider its initial determination within six months. Instead of

going this route, Eldridge launched his suit alleging that due process required he be given a pretermination hearing at which to respond to the evidence and present his side of the story. The HEW Secretary, in response, argued that present agency procedures were constitutionally adequate and that in any case Eldridge, by electing not to seek reconsideration by the state agency, failed to exhaust all available administrative remedies. A federal district court found in Eldridge's favor, and its ruling as to the unconstitutionality of the administrative procedures was affirmed on appeal, whereupon Mathews sought certiorari from the Supreme Court.

Mr. Justice POWELL delivered the opinion of the Court.

The issue in this case is whether the Due Process Clause of the Fifth Amendment requires that prior to the termination of Social Security disability benefit payments the recipient be afforded an opportunity for an evidentiary hearing.

*   *   *

*   *   * In support of his contention that due process requires a pretermination hearing, Eldridge relied exclusively upon this Court's decision in Goldberg v. Kelly, 397 U.S. 254, 90 S.Ct. 1011 (1970), which established a right to an "evidentiary hearing" prior to termination of welfare benefits.[4] The Secretary contended that Goldberg was not controlling since eligibility for disability benefits, unlike eligibility for welfare benefits, is not based on financial need and since issues of credibility and veracity do not play a significant role in the disability entitlement decision, which turns primarily on medical evidence.

The District Court concluded that the administrative procedures pursuant to which the Secretary had terminated Eldridge's benefits abridged his right to procedural due process. The court viewed the interest of the disability recipient in uninterrupted benefits as indistinguishable from that of the welfare recipient in Goldberg. It further noted that decisions subsequent to Goldberg demonstrated that the due process requirement of pretermination hearings is not limited to situations involving the deprivation of vital necessities. See Fuentes v. Shevin, 407 U.S. 67, 88–89, 92 S.Ct. 1983, 1998–1999 (1972); Bell v. Burson, 402 U.S. 535, 91 S.Ct. 1586 (1971). Reasoning that disability determinations may involve subjective judgments based on conflicting medical and nonmedical evidence the District Court held that prior to termination of benefits Eldridge must be afforded an evidentiary hearing of the type required for welfare beneficiaries under Title IV of the Social Security Act. * · * * Relying entirely upon the District Court's opinion, the Court of Appeals

4. In Goldberg, the Court held that the pretermination hearing must include the following elements: (1) "timely and adequate notice detailing the reasons for a proposed termination"; (2) "an effective opportunity [for the recipient] to defend by confronting any adverse witnesses and by presenting his own arguments and evidence orally"; (3) retained counsel, if desired; (4) an "impartial" decision maker; (5) a decision resting "solely on the legal rules and evidence adduced at the hearing"; (6) a statement of reasons for the decision and the evidence relied on. 397 U.S., at 266–271, 90 S.Ct., at 1019–1022. In this opinion the term "evidentiary hearing" refers to a hearing generally of the type required in Goldberg.

for the Fourth Circuit affirmed the injunction barring termination of Eldridge's benefits prior to an evidentiary hearing. * * * We reverse.

* * *

Procedural due process imposes constraints on governmental decisions which deprive individuals of "liberty" or "property" interests within the meaning of the Due Process Clause of the Fifth or Fourteenth Amendments. The Secretary does not contend that procedural due process is inapplicable to terminations of social security disability benefits. He recognizes, as has been implicit in our prior decisions, e.g., Richardson v. Belcher, 404 U.S. 78, 80–81, 92 S.Ct. 254, 256–257 (1971); Richardson v. Perales, 402 U.S. 389, 401–402, 91 S.Ct. 1420, 1427–1428 (1971); Flemming v. Nestor, 363 U.S. 603, 611, 80 S.Ct. 1367, 1372–1373 (1960), that the interest of an individual in continued receipt of these benefits is a statutorily created "property" interest protected by the Fifth Amendment. * * * Rather, the Secretary contends that the existing administrative procedures * * * provide all the process that is constitutionally due before a recipient can be deprived of that interest.

This Court consistently has held that some form of hearing is required before an individual is finally deprived of a property interest. Wolff v. McDonnell, 418 U.S. 539, 557–558, 94 S.Ct. 2963, 2975–2976 (1974). * * * The "right to be heard before being condemned to suffer grievous loss of any kind, even though it may not involve the stigma and hardships of criminal conviction, is a principle basic to our society." Joint Anti-Fascist Committee v. McGrath, 341 U.S. 123, 168, 71 S.Ct. 624, 646 (1951) (Frankfurter, J.,

concurring). The fundamental requirement of due process is the opportunity to be heard "at a meaningful time and in a meaningful manner." Armstrong v. Manzo, 380 U.S. 545, 552, 85 S.Ct. 1187, 1191 (1965). * * * Eldridge agrees that the review procedures available to a claimant before the initial determination of ineligibility becomes final would be adequate if disability benefits were not terminated until after the evidentiary hearing stage of the administrative process. The dispute centers upon what process is due prior to the initial termination of benefits, pending review.

In recent years this Court increasingly has had occasion to consider the extent to which due process requires an evidentiary hearing prior to the deprivation of some type of property interest even if such a hearing is provided thereafter. In only one case, Goldberg v. Kelly, 397 U.S. 254, 266–271, 90 S.Ct. 1011, 1019–1022 (1970), has the Court held that a hearing closely approximating a judicial trial is necessary. In other cases requiring some type of pretermination hearing as a matter of constitutional right the Court has spoken sparingly about the requisite procedures. Sniadach v. Family Finance Corp., 395 U.S. 337, 89 S.Ct. 1820 (1969), involving garnishment of wages, was entirely silent on the matter. In Fuentes v. Shevin, 407 U.S. 67, 96–97, 92 S.Ct. 1983, 2002–2003 (1972), the Court said only that in a replevin suit between two private parties the initial determination required something more than an *ex parte* proceeding before a court clerk. Similarly, Bell v. Burson, 402 U.S. 535, 540, 91 S.Ct. 1586, 1590 (1971), held, in the context of the revocation of a state-granted driver's license, that due process required only that the prerevocation hearing involve a probable-cause determination as to the fault of the licensee, noting that the hearing "need not take the form of a full adjudication of the question of liability." See also North Georgia Finishing, Inc. v. DiChem, Inc., 419 U.S. 601, 607, 95 S.Ct. 719 (1975). More recently in Arnett v. Kennedy, 416 U.S. 134, 94 S.Ct. 1633 (1974), we sustained the validity of procedures by which a federal employee could be dismissed for cause. They included notice of the action sought, a copy of the charge, reasonable time for filing a written response, and an opportunity for an oral appearance. Following dismissal, an evidentiary hearing was provided. * * *

These decisions underscore the truism that " '[d]ue process,' unlike some legal rules, is not a technical conception with a fixed content unrelated to time, place and circumstances." Cafeteria & Restaurant Workers Local 473 v. McElroy, 367 U.S. 886, 895, 81 S.Ct. 1743, 1748 (1961). "[D]ue process is flexible and calls for such procedural protections as the particular situation demands." Morrissey v. Brewer, 408 U.S. 471, 481, 92 S.Ct. 2593, 2600 (1972). Accordingly, resolution of the issue whether the administrative procedures provided here are constitutionally sufficient requires analysis of the governmental and private interests that are affected. * * * More precisely, our prior decisions indicate that identification of the specific dictates of due process generally requires consideration of three distinct factors: first, the private interest that will be affected by the official action; second, the risk of an erroneous deprivation of such interest through the procedures used, and the probable value, if any, of addi-

tional or substitute procedural safeguards; and finally, the government's interest, including the function involved and the fiscal and administrative burdens that the additional or substitute procedural requirement would entail. See, e.g., Goldberg v. Kelly, supra, 397 U.S., at 263–271, 90 S.Ct., at 1018–1022.

* * *

Despite the elaborate character of the administrative procedures provided by the Secretary, the courts below held them to be constitutionally inadequate, concluding that due process requires an evidentiary hearing prior to termination. In light of the private and governmental interests at stake here and the nature of the existing procedures, we think this was error.

Since a recipient whose benefits are terminated is awarded full retroactive relief if he ultimately prevails, his sole interest is in the uninterrupted receipt of this source of income pending final administrative decision on his claim. His potential injury is thus similar in nature to that of the welfare recipient in Goldberg, see 397 U.S., at 263–264, 90 S.Ct., at 1018–1019, the nonprobationary federal employee in Arnett, see 416 U.S., at 146, 94 S.Ct., at 1640, 1641, and the wage earner in Sniadach. See 395 U.S., at 341–342, 89 S.Ct., at 1822–1823.

Only in Goldberg has the Court held that due process requires an evidentiary hearing prior to a temporary deprivation. It was emphasized there that welfare assistance is given to persons on the very margin of subsistence:

"The crucial factor in this context—a factor not present in the case of * * * virtually anyone else whose governmental entitlements are ended—is that termination of aid pending resolution of a controversy over eligibility may deprive an *eligible* recipient of the very means by which to live while he waits." 397 U.S., at 264, 90 S.Ct., at 1018 (emphasis in original).

Eligibility for disability benefits, in contrast, is not based upon financial need. Indeed, it is wholly unrelated to the worker's income or support from many other sources, such as earnings of other family members, workmen's compensation awards, tort claims awards, savings, private insurance, public or private pensions, veterans' benefits, food stamps, public assistance, or the "many other important programs both public and private, which contain provisions for disability payments affecting a substantial portion of the work force." * * * Richardson v. Belcher, 404 U.S., at 85–87, 92 S.Ct., at 259 (Douglas, J., dissenting). See Staff of the House Comm. on Ways & Means, Report on the Disability Insurance Program, 93d Cong., 2d Sess., 9–10, 419–429 (1974) (hereinafter Staff Report).

As *Goldberg* illustrates, the degree of potential deprivation that may be created by a particular decision is a factor to be considered in assessing the validity of any administrative decision-making process. Cf. Morrissey v. Brewer, 408 U.S. 471, 92 S.Ct. 2593 (1972). The potential deprivation here is generally likely to be less than in *Goldberg*, although the degree of difference can be overstated. As the District Court emphasized, to remain eligible for benefits a recipient must be "unable to engage in substantial gainful activity." 42 U.S.C.A. § 423; 361 F.Supp., at 523. Thus, in contrast to the discharged federal employee in *Arnett*,

there is little possibility that the terminated recipient will be able to find even temporary employment to ameliorate the interim loss.

As we recognized last Term in Fusari v. Steinberg, 419 U.S. 379, 389, 95 S.Ct. 533, 540 (1975), "the possible length of wrongful deprivation of * * * benefits [also] is an important factor in assessing the impact of official action on private interests." The Secretary concedes that the delay between a request for a hearing before an Administrative Law Judge and a decision on the claim is currently between 10 and 11 months. Since a terminated recipient must first obtain a reconsideration decision as a prerequisite to invoking his right to an evidentiary hearing, the delay between the actual cut-off of benefits and final decision after a hearing exceeds one year.

In view of the torpidity of this administrative review process, cf. id., at 383–384, 386, 95 S.Ct., at 536–537, 538, and the typically modest resources of the family unit of the physically disabled worker, the hardship imposed upon the erroneously terminated disability recipient may be significant. Still, the disabled worker's need is likely to be less than that of a welfare recipient. In addition to the possibility of access to private resources, other forms of government assistance will become available where the termination of disability benefits places a worker or his family below the subsistence level. See Arnett v. Kennedy, supra, 416 U.S., at 169, 94 S.Ct., at 1651–1652 (Powell, J., concurring), id., at 201–202, 94 S.Ct., at 1667–1668 (White, J., concurring in part and dissenting in part). In view of these potential sources of temporary income, there is less reason here than in

Goldberg to depart from the ordinary principle, established by our decisions, that something less than an evidentiary hearing is sufficient prior to adverse administrative action.

An additional factor to be considered here is the fairness and reliability of the existing pretermination procedures, and the probable value, if any, of additional procedural safeguards. Central to the evaluation of any administrative process is the nature of the relevant inquiry. * * *
In order to remain eligible for benefits the disabled worker must demonstrate by means of "medically acceptable clinical and laboratory diagnostic techniques," 42 U.S.C.A. § 423(d)(3), that he is unable "to engage in any substantial gainful activity by reason of any *medically determinable* physical or mental impairment." * * * § 423(d)(1) (A) (emphasis supplied). In short, a medical assessment of the worker's physical or mental condition is required. This is a more sharply focused and easily documented decision than the typical determination of welfare entitlement. In the latter case, a wide variety of information may be deemed relevant, and issues of witness credibility and veracity often are critical to the decision-making process. *Goldberg* noted that in such circumstances "written submissions are a wholly unsatisfactory basis for decision." 397 U.S., at 269, 90 S.Ct., at 1021.

By contrast, the decision whether to discontinue disability benefits will turn, in most cases, upon "routine, standard, and unbiased medical reports by physician specialists," Richardson v. Perales, 402 U.S., at 404, 91 S.Ct., at 1428, concerning a subject whom they have personally examined. In *Richardson* the Court recognized the "reliability and proba-

tive worth of written medical reports," emphasizing that while there may be "professional disagreement with the medical conclusions" the "specter of questionable credibility and veracity is not present." Id., at 405, 407, 91 S.Ct., at 1428, 1430. To be sure, credibility and veracity may be a factor in the ultimate disability assessment in some cases. But procedural due process rules are shaped by the risk of error inherent in the truth-finding process as applied to the generality of cases, not the rare exceptions. The potential value of an evidentiary hearing, or even oral presentation to the decision-maker is substantially less in this context than in *Goldberg*.

The decision in *Goldberg* also was based on the Court's conclusion that written submissions were an inadequate substitute for oral presentation because they did not provide an effective means for the recipient to communicate his case to the decisionmaker. Written submissions were viewed as an unrealistic option, for most recipients lacked the "educational attainment necessary to write effectively" and could not afford professional assistance. In addition, such submissions would not provide the "flexibility of oral presentations" or "permit the recipient to mold his argument to the issues the decision maker appears to regard as important." 397 U.S., at 269, 90 S.Ct., at 1021. In the context of the disability-benefits-entitlement assessment the administrative procedures under review here fully answer these objections.

The detailed questionnaire which the state agency periodically sends the recipient identifies with particularity the information relevant to the entitlement decision, and the recipient is invited to obtain assistance from the local SSA office in completing the questionnaire. More important, the information critical to the entitlement decision usually is derived from medical sources, such as the treating physician. Such sources are likely to be able to communicate more effectively through written documents than are welfare recipients or the lay witnesses supporting their cause. The conclusions of physicians often are supported by X-rays and the results of clinical or laboratory tests, information typically more amenable to written than to oral presentation. Cf. W. Gellhorn & C. Byse, Administrative Law—Cases and Comments 860–863 (6th ed. 1974).

A further safeguard against mistake is the policy of allowing the disability recipient or his representative full access to all information relied upon by the state agency. In addition, prior to the cut-off of benefits the agency informs the recipient of its tentative assessment, the reasons therefor, and provides a summary of the evidence that it considers most relevant. Opportunity is then afforded the recipient to submit additional evidence or arguments, enabling him to challenge directly the accuracy of information in his file as well as the correctness of the agency's tentative conclusions. These procedures, again as contrasted with those before the Court in *Goldberg*, enable the recipient to "mold" his argument to respond to the precise issues which the decisionmaker regards as crucial.

Despite these carefully structured procedures, *amici* point to the significant reversal rate for appealed cases as clear evidence that the current process is inadequate. Depending upon the base selected and the line of analysis followed, the relevant

reversal rates urged by the contending parties vary from a high of 58.6% for appealed reconsideration decisions to an overall reversal rate of only 3.3%. Bare statistics rarely provide a satisfactory measure of the fairness of a decisionmaking process. Their adequacy is especially suspect here since the administrative review system is operated on an open-file basis. A recipient may always submit new evidence, and such submissions may result in additional medical examinations. Such fresh examinations are held in approximately 30% to 40% of the appealed cases, either at the reconsideration or evidentiary hearing stage of the administrative process. Staff Report 238. In this context, the value of reversal rate statistics as one means of evaluating the adequacy of the pretermination process is diminished. Thus, although we view such information as relevant, it is certainly not controlling in this case.

In striking the appropriate due process balance the final factor to be assessed is the public interest. This includes the administrative burden and other societal costs that would be associated with requiring as, a matter of constitutional right, an evidentiary hearing upon demand in all cases prior to the termination of disability benefits. The most visible burden would be the incremental cost resulting from the increased number of hearings and the expense of providing benefits to ineligible recipients pending decision. No one can predict the extent of the increase, but the fact that full benefits would continue until after such hearings would assure the exhaustion in most cases of this attractive option. Nor would the theoretical right of the Secretary to recover undeserved benefits result, as a practical matter, in any substantial offset to the added outlay of public funds. The parties submit widely varying estimates of the probable additional financial cost. We only need say that experience with the constitutionalizing of government procedures suggests that the ultimate additional cost in terms of money and administrative burden would not be insubstantial.

Financial cost alone is not a controlling weight in determining whether due process requires a particular procedural safeguard prior to some administrative decision. But the Government's interest, and hence that of the public, in conserving scarce fiscal and administrative resources, is a factor that must be weighed. At some point the benefit of an additional safeguard to the individual affected by the administrative action and to society in terms of increased assurance that the action is just, may be outweighed by the cost. Significantly, the cost of protecting those whom the preliminary administrative process has identified as likely to be found undeserving may in the end come out of the pockets of the deserving since resources available for any particular program of social welfare are not unlimited.

* * *

But more is implicated in cases of this type than ad hoc weighing of fiscal and administrative burdens against the interests of a particular category of claimants. The ultimate balance involves a determination as to when, under our constitutional system, judicial-type procedures must be imposed upon administrative action to assure fairness. We reiterate the wise admonishment of Mr. Justice Frankfurter that differences in the origin and function of administrative agencies "preclude wholesale transplantation of the rules of procedure, trial and review which have evolved from the history and experience of the courts." FCC v. Pottsville Broadcasting Co., 309 U.S. 134, 143, 60 S.Ct. 437, 441 (1940). The judicial model of an evidentiary hearing is neither a required, nor even the most effective, method of decisionmaking in all circumstances. The essence of due process is the requirement that "a person in jeopardy of serious loss [be given] notice of the case against him and opportunity to meet it." Joint Anti-Facist Refugee Committee v. McGrath, 341 U.S., at 171–172, 71 S.Ct., at 649. (Frankfurter, J., concurring.) All that is necessary is that the procedures be tailored, in light of the decision to be made, to "the capacities and circumstances of those who are to be heard," Goldberg v. Kelly, supra, 397 U.S., at 268–269, 90 S.Ct., at 1021 (footnote omitted), to insure that they are given a meaningful opportunity to present their case. In assessing what process is due in this case, substantial weight must be given to the good-faith judgments of the individuals charged by Congress with the administration of the social welfare system that the procedures they have provided assure fair consideration of the entitlement claims of individuals. See Arnett v. Kennedy, 416 U.S., at 202, 94 S.Ct., at 1667–1668 (White, J., concurring and dissenting in part). This is especially so where, as here, the prescribed procedures not only provide the claimant with an effective process for asserting his claim prior to any administrative action, but also assure a right to an evidentiary hearing, as well as to subsequent judicial review, before the denial of his claim becomes final. Cf. Boddie v. Connecticut, 401 U.S. 371, 378, 91 S.Ct. 780, 786 (1971).

We conclude that an evidentiary hearing is not required prior to the termination of disability benefits and that the present administrative procedures fully comport with due process.

The judgment of the Court of Appeals is

Reversed.

Mr. Justice STEVENS took no part in the consideration or decision of this case.

[Justice BRENNAN dissented in an opinion in which Justice MARSHALL joined. Citing his earlier dissenting opinion in Richardson v. Wright, 405 U.S. 208, 212, 92 S.Ct. 788, 791 (1972), he found Goldberg v. Kelly to be controlling and deviations from it to be unjustified. In Richardson, he argued that pretermination hearings constituted a valuable opportunity to afford an individual a chance to confront information the factual accuracy of which may be open to serious dispute and which may occasion the exercise of considerable discretion on the part of the agency. Offering other criticisms of the decision in Mathews, Justice BRENNAN wrote:

" * * * I would add that the Court's consideration that a discontinuance of disability benefits may cause the recipient to suffer only a limited deprivation is no argument. It is speculative. Moreover, the very legislative determination to provide disability benefits, without any prerequisite determination of need in fact, presumes a need by the recipient which is not this Court's to denigrate. Indeed, in the present case, it is indicated that because disability benefits were terminated there was a foreclosure upon the Eldridge home and the family's furniture was repossessed, forcing Eldridge, his wife and children to sleep in one bed. * * * Finally, it is also no argument that a worker, who has been placed in the untenable position of having been denied disability benefits, may still seek other forms of public assistance."]

When the Crafts moved into their newly purchased home, they discovered that two separate sets of gas and electric meters had been installed. During the following months, they received duplicate utility bills from Memphis Light, Gas and Water, a division of the city government. The Crafts' persistent efforts to obtain an explanation from MLG&W for the double billings and to clear things up were to no avail. After recurrently receiving "final notices" on their duplicate bills, utility service was discontinued five times for nonpayment. They continued to receive no adequate guidance from MLG&W as to how the matter could be resolved. Eventually, the Crafts brought suit against the municipal utility for injunctive relief and damages, alleging that MLG&W failed to accord them due process by not providing them an opportunity to explain the matter. A federal district court held that the Crafts had no property interest in receiving continued utility service while a disputed bill remained unpaid and that, at any rate, the utility's termination procedures (e.g., giving customers notice before shutting off service) were sufficient. Although the court acknowledged that the Crafts had not been given adequate notice of any procedure by which they could discuss the disputed bills with management, the court, nonetheless, held that the Crafts were not denied the opportunity to be heard. The court of appeals reversed, and this judgment was in turn affirmed by the Supreme Court in Memphis Light, Gas and

Water Division v. Craft, 436 U.S. 1, 98 S.Ct. 1554 (1978). Speaking for the Court, Justice Powell concluded that MLG&W's "notification procedure, while adequate to apprise the Crafts of the threat of termination of service, was not 'reasonably calculated' to inform them of the availability of 'an opportunity to present their objections' to their bills." Justice Powell continued, "The purpose of notice under the Due Process Clause is to apprise the affected individual of, and permit adequate preparation for, an impending 'hearing.' Notice in a case of this kind does not comport with constitutional requirements when it does not advise the customer of the availability of a procedure for protesting a proposed termination of utility service as unjustified." In support of this conclusion, the Court reasoned:

> Our decision in Mathews v. Eldridge, 424 U.S. 319, 96 S.Ct. 893 (1976), provides a framework of analysis for determining the "specific dictates of due process" in this case.
>
> > "[O]ur prior decisions indicate that identification of the specific dictates of due process generally requires consideration of three distinct factors: First, the private interest that will be affected by the official action; second, the risk of an erroneous determination of such interest through the procedures used, and the probable value, if any, of additional or substitute procedural safeguards; and finally, the Government's interest, including the function involved and the fiscal and administrative burdens that the additional or substitute procedural safeguards would entail." id., at 334–335.
>
> Under the balancing approach outlined in *Mathews*, some administrative procedure for entertaining customer complaints prior to determination is required to afford reasonable assurance against erroneous or arbitrary withholding of essential services. The customer's interest is self-evident. Utility service is a necessity of modern life; indeed, the discontinuance of water or heating for even short periods of time may threaten health and safety. And the risk of an erroneous deprivation, given the necessary reliance on computers, is not insubstantial.
>
> The utility's interests are not incompatible with affording the notice and procedure described above. Quite apart from its duty as a public service company, a utility—in its own business interests—may be expected to make all reasonable efforts to minimize billing errors and the resulting customer dissatisfaction and possible injury. * * * Nor should "some kind of hearing" prove burdensome. The opportunity for a meeting with a responsible employee empowered to resolve the dispute could be afforded well in advance of the scheduled date of termination. And petitioners would retain the option to terminate service after affording this opportunity and concluding that the amount billed was justly due.

The Court rejected MLG&W's argument that common-law remedies such as a pretermination injunction or a post-termination suit were adequate to deal with any problems. Justice Powell wrote:

> Judicial remedies are particularly unsuited to the resolution of factual disputes typically involving sums of money too small to justify engaging counsel or bringing a lawsuit. An action in equity to halt an improper termination, because it is less likely to be pursued and less likely to be effective, even if pursued, will not provide the same assurance of accurate decisionmaking as would an adequate administrative procedure. In these

circumstances, an informal administrative remedy, along the lines suggested above, constitutes the process that is "due."

Justice Stevens dissented in an opinion in which Chief Justice Burger and Justice Rehnquist joined. The dissent concluded that the record failed to show any facts which warranted the necessity of imposing the pretermination hearing requirement. Said Justice Stevens:

> In deciding that more process is due, the Court relies on two quite different hypothetical considerations. First, the Court stresses the fact that disconnection of water or heating "may threaten health and safety." * * * Second, the Court discounts the value of the protection afforded by the available judicial remedies because the "factual disputes typically [involve] sums of money too small to justify engaging counsel or bringing a lawsuit." * * * Neither of these examples is disclosed by this record. The Crafts' dispute involved only about $35, but they did obtain counsel and thereafter they encountered no billing problems.
>
> Although the Division's terminations number about 2,000 each month, the record does not reveal any actual case of harm to health or safety. The District Court found that the Division does not discontinue service when there is illness in a home. Since a customer can always avoid termination by the simple expedient of paying the disputed bill and claiming a refund, it is not surprising that the real emergency case is rare, if indeed it exists at all. When a true emergency does present a serious threat to health or safety, the customer will have ample motivation to take the important step of consulting counsel or filing suit even if the amount of his disputed bill is small. A potential loss of utility service sufficiently grievous to qualify as a constitutional deprivation can hardly be too petty to justify invoking the aid of counsel or the judiciary. Conversely, routine billing disputes too petty for the bench or the bar can hardly merit extraordinary constitutional protection.

Charlotte Horowitz was enrolled at the University of Missouri-Kansas City Medical School. The academic performance of students there is periodically assessed by the Council of Evaluation, a joint faculty-student body with the power to recommend probation or dismissal. The council's recommendations are subject to the approval of a faculty committee and the Dean. Dissatisfaction voiced by several faculty members over Horowitz's clinical performance during a pediatrics rotation prompted the council to recommend that she enter her last year of study on probation. Negative feedback continued during the next year. At midyear, the council again reviewed her performance and reached the conclusion that, unless she showed "radical improvement," she be dismissed and that, at any rate, she not be permitted to graduate that year. She was allowed to take a set of oral and practical exams as an appeal of the decision not to graduate her in June. The judgment of an outside panel evaluating her performance was split: two physicians recommended that she be immediately dismissed, two favored allowing her to graduate on schedule, and three voted that she be continued on probation pending future evaluations of her performance, whereupon the council reaffirmed its previous decision. In May, the council met yet again to review Horowitz's progress. When reports of her performance on two other rotations also turned out to be negative, the council recommended that she not be permitted to re-enroll. This decision was approved in turn by the faculty committee and the Dean. Upon appeal, the Provost sustained the decision to drop her from the school. Horowitz subsequently brought suit against the University's governing board alleging that she had been denied due process. A federal district court found the procedures employed by the school adequate to afford due process and denied relief, but this judgment was overturned by the court of appeal. The Supreme Court granted certiorari "to consider what procedures must be accorded to a student at a state educational institution whose dismissal may constitute a deprivation of 'liberty' or 'property' within the meaning of the Fourteenth Amendment." In Board of Curators of Univ. of Missouri v. Horowitz, 435 U.S. 78, 98 S.Ct. 948 (1978), the Court, per Justice Rehnquist, found that "[a]ssuming the existence of a liberty or property interest, respondent has been awarded at least as much due process as the Fourteenth Amendment requires." Indeed, the majority agreed with the district court that, by affording Horowitz with the opportunity to be examined by seven independent physicians so as to insure the accuracy of its assessment of her performance, the medical school had gone above and beyond what was legally required.

Justice Rehnquist took care to distinguish the kind of constitutionally required procedures necessary in cases involving dismissal on academic grounds from those instances where a student's suspension or departure is prompted by disciplinary reasons:

> In Goss v. Lopez, 419 U.S. 565, 95 S.Ct. 729 (1975), we held that due process requires, in connection with the suspension of a student from public school for disciplinary reasons, "that the student be given oral or written notice of the charges against him and, if he denies them, an explanation of the evidence the authorities have and an opportunity to present his side of the story." * * * The Court of Appeals apparently read Goss as requiring some type of formal hearing at which respondent could defend her academic ability and performance. All that Goss required was an "informal give-and-take" between the student and the administrative body dismissing him that would, at least, give the student "the opportunity to characterize his conduct and put it in what he deems the proper context." * * * But we have frequently emphasized that "[t]he very nature of due process negates any concept of inflexible procedures universally applicable to every imaginable situation." Cafeteria Workers v. McElroy, 367 U.S. 886, 895, 81 S.Ct. 1743, 1748 (1961). The need for flexibility is well illustrated by the significant difference between the failure of a student to meet academic standards and the violation by a student of valid rules of conduct. This difference calls for far less stringent procedural requirements in the case of an academic dismissal.

> * * * [P]rior decisions of state and federal courts, over a period of 60 years, unanimously holding that formal hearings before decision-making bodies need not be held in the case of academic dismissals, cannot be rejected lightly. * * *

> Reason, furthermore, clearly supports the perception of these decisions. A school is an academic institution, not a courtroom or administrative hearing room. In Goss, this Court felt that suspensions of students for disciplinary reasons have a sufficient resemblance to traditional judicial and administrative fact-finding to call for a "hearing" before the relevant school authority. While recognizing that school authorities must be afforded the necessary tools to maintain discipline, the Court concluded that

"it would be a strange disciplinary system in an educational institution if no communication was sought by the disciplinarian with the student in an effort to inform him of his dereliction and to let him tell his side of the story in order to make sure that an injustice is not done. * * * [R]equiring effective notice and informal hearing permitting the student to give his version of the events will provide a meaningful hedge against erroneous action. At least the disciplinarian will be alerted to the existence of disputes about facts and arguments about cause and effect." * * *

Even in the context of a school disciplinary proceeding, however, the Court stopped short of requiring a *formal* hearing since "further formalizing the suspension process and escalating its formality and adversary nature may not only make it too costly as a regular disciplinary tool but also destroy its effectiveness as a part of the teaching process." * * *

Academic evaluations of a student, in contrast to disciplinary determinations, bear little resemblance to the judicial and administrative fact-finding proceedings to which we have traditionally attached a full hearing requirement. In *Goss*, the school's decision to suspend the students rested on factual conclusions that the individual students had participated in demonstrations that had disrupted classes, attacked a police officer, or caused physical damage to school property. The requirement of a hearing, where the student could present his side of the factual issue, could under such circumstances "provide a meaningful hedge against erroneous action." * * * The decision to dismiss respondent, by comparison, rested on the academic judgment of school officials that she did not have the necessary clinical ability to perform adequately as a medical doctor and was making insufficient progress toward that goal. Such a judgment is by its nature more subjective and evaluative than the typical factual questions presented in the average disciplinary decision. Like the decision of an individual professor as to the proper grade for a student in his course, the determination whether to dismiss a student for academic reasons requires an expert evaluation of cumulative information and is not readily adapted to the procedural tools of judicial or administrative decisionmaking.

Under such circumstances, we decline to ignore the historic judgment of educators and thereby formalize the academic dismissal process by requiring a hearing. The educational process is not by nature adversarial; instead it centers around a continuing relationship between faculty and students, "one in which the teacher must occupy many roles—educator, adviser, friend, and, at times, parent-substitute." Goss v. Lopez, 419 U.S. 565, 594, 95 S.Ct. 729, 746 (1975) (Powell, J., dissenting). This is especially true as one advances through the varying regimes of the educational system, and the instruction becomes both more individualized and more specialized. In *Goss*, this Court concluded that the value of some form of hearing in a disciplinary context outweighs any resulting harm to the academic environment. Influencing this conclusion was clearly the belief that disciplinary proceedings, in which the teacher must decide whether to punish a student for disruptive or insubordinate behavior, may automatically bring an adversarial flavor to the normal student-teacher relationship. The same conclusion does not follow in the academic context. We decline to further enlarge the judicial presence in the academic community and thereby risk deterioration of many beneficial aspects of the faculty-student relationship. * * *

Three members of the Court (Justices Brennan, Blackmun, and Marshall) concluded that it was unnecessary to discuss "whether respondent's dismissal was for academic or disciplinary reasons" and thought it was sufficient to say that she "received all the procedural process that was due her under the Fourteenth Amendment." Justice Marshall, however, took specific exception to the majority's "dictum suggesting that respondent was entitled to even less procedural protection than she received."

———

Massachusetts's implied consent law requires the suspension of a driver's license for refusal to take a breathalyzer test upon arrest for drunken driving. The Registrar of Motor Vehicles, according to the statute, must order a ninety-day suspension of the license upon receiving a police report that the driver refused to take the breath test. After the driver has surrendered his license, the law entitles him to an immediate hearing before the Registrar. Donald Montrym was involved in a collision. After arriving at the scene, a police officer noticed that Montrym was "glassy eyed," unsteady on his feet, slurring his speech, and smelled of alcohol. Montrym was arrested and taken to the police station where he was asked to take a breathalyzer test. He refused and later unsuccessfully sought to retract his refusal by volunteering to take the test. His license was suspended, and he then brought suit against Alan Mackey, the Registrar of Motor Vehicles, to recover his license. Approximately a month after the license had been surrendered, a federal district judge issued a temporary restraining order against suspension of the license, pending further order of the court. A three-judge federal district court subsequently declared the statute unconstitutional as a violation of the Due Process Clause of the Fourteenth Amendment, whereupon Massachusetts appealed.

The Supreme Court, per Chief Justice Burger, upheld the Massachusetts statute in Mackey v. Montrym, 443 U.S. 1, 99 S.Ct. 2612 (1979). In an analysis that closely followed "the balancing process mandated by Eldridge," the Court first noted that the private interest affected was a "substantial one"—the driver's interest in operating a motor vehicle pending the outcome of the hearing due him—although its substantiality was diminished by the fact that the suspension was for a maximum of ninety days and because "a post-suspension hearing is available *immediately* upon a driver's suspension and may be initiated by him simply by walking into one of the Registrar's local offices and requesting a hearing." Focusing, secondly, on the likelihood of an erroneous deprivation of the private interest involved, the Court observed that "[t]he Due Process Clause simply does not mandate that all governmental decisionmaking comply with standards that assure perfect, error-free determinations." Indeed, the Chief Justice pointed out, "when prompt post-deprivation review is available for correction of administrative error, we have generally required no more than that the pre-deprivation procedures used be designed to provide a reasonably reliable basis for concluding that the facts justifying the official action are as a responsible governmental official warrants them to be." Here, the Chief Justice explained, the facts of the arrest and the driver's refusal are within the knowledge of a trained and experienced officer who has every incentive to ascertain and truthfully report the facts because of civil liability for an unlawful arrest and criminal penalties for willful misrepresentation of facts. Moreover, the driver's refusal must be witnessed by two officers. Furthermore, observed Chief Justice Burger, "there will rarely be any genuine dispute as to the historical facts providing cause for a suspension." The Court continued, "The third leg of the Eldridge balancing test requires us to identify the governmental function involved; also, to weigh in the balance the state interests served by the summary procedures used, as well as the administrative and fiscal burdens, if any, that would result from the substitute procedures sought." Characterizing as "paramount" the Commonwealth's interest "in preserving the safety of its public highways," the Chief Justice observed that this interest "is substantially served" by the summary suspension of the licenses of those drivers refusing to take a breathalyzer test in the following ways: (1) by serving as a deterrent to drunk driving; (2) by providing a strong incentive to take the breathalyzer test, thus effectuating the government's interest in obtaining reliable evidence on the question of intoxication; and (3) by promptly removing such drivers from the road. The Court emphasized the importance of the summary and automatic character of the suspension. "A pre-suspension hearing would substantially undermine the state interest in public safety by giving drivers significant incentive to refuse the breathalyzer test and demand a pre-suspension hearing as a dilatory tactic [and] * * * the incentive to delay arising from the availability of a pre-suspension hearing would generate a sharp increase in the number of hearings sought and therefore impose a substantial fiscal and administrative burden on the Commonwealth."

Justice Stewart dissented in an opinion in which Justices Brennan, Marshall, and Stevens joined. He began by pointing out that precedents, such as Bell v. Burson, 402 U.S. 535, 91 S.Ct. 1586 (1971) and Dixon v. Love, 431 U.S. 105, 97 S.Ct. 1723 (1977), "made clear that a person's interest in his driver's license is 'property' that a State may not take away without satisfying the requirements of the due process guarantee of the Fourteenth Amendment. And the constitutional guarantee of procedural due process has always been understood to embody a presumptive requirement of notice and a meaningful opportunity to be heard before the State acts finally to deprive a person of his property." Considering the extent to which automobiles are depended upon in modern society, the suspension of a license could well be a substantial deprivation. And, the dissent pointed out, the government's action amounts to an irreversible deprivation; its effect can be shortened but not undone. Moreover, Justice Stewart hastened to add, a presuspension hearing "protects not simply against the risk of an erroneous decision. It also protects a 'vulnerable citizenry from the overbearing concern for efficiency * * * that may characterize praiseworthy government officials no less * * * than mediocre ones.'" More disturbingly, the dissent continued, the driver is given no notice that he is entitled to a "same day" hearing before the registrar, and Montrym argued that he was not even informed of the sanction which would be imposed for his refusal to take the breathalyzer test. Justice Stewart emphasized that the real reason behind the summary suspension was "plainly not * * * to remove an irresponsible driver from the road as swiftly as possible. For if a motorist submits to the test and fails it, he keeps his driver's license—a result wholly at odds with any notion that summary suspension upon refusal to take the test serves an emergency protective purpose." "A suspension for refusal to take the test is obviously premised not on intoxication," concluded Justice Stewart, "but on non-cooperation with the police." And, as to the arguments put forward by the government for shoving the driver in this direction, Justice Stewart responded, "A State is simply not free to manipulate Fourteenth Amendment procedural rights to coerce a person into compliance with its substantive rules, however important it may consider those rules to be." As for the fiscal and administrative burdens, he added, "[I]f costs were the criterion, the basic procedural protections of the Fourteenth Amendment could be read out of the Constitution. Happily, the Constitution recognizes higher values than 'speed' and 'efficiency.'" Finally, the dissent cast doubt on the effectiveness of the purported prompt hearing. Apart from the failure to notify drivers of the right to such a hearing, Justice Stewart argued that "the 'walk-in' procedure provides little more than a right to request the scheduling of a later hearing." Indeed, as he read the statute, it was far from clear whether the registrar had much capacity to alleviate the sanction at all, let alone to do so promptly.

e.   DUE PROCESS IN PUNISHMENT AND REHABILITATION

ROBINSON v. CALIFORNIA

Supreme Court of the United States, 1962
370 U.S. 660, 82 S.Ct. 1417, 8 L.Ed.2d 758

Lawrence Robinson was convicted in Los Angeles Municipal Court for violation of a California statute that made it a misdemeanor for a person to be addicted to narcotics. At the time of his arrest, Robinson was not under the influence of drugs. However, a police officer took him into custody after observing scars, scales, and needle marks on Robinson's arms. A state appellate court affirmed the conviction after which Robinson appealed to the U. S. Supreme Court.

Mr. Justice STEWART delivered the opinion of the Court.

*   *   *

This statute *   *   * is not one which punishes a person for the use of narcotics, for their purchase, sale or possession, or for antisocial or disorderly behavior resulting from their administration. It is not a law which even purports to provide or require medical treatment. Rather, we deal with a statute which makes the "status" of narcotic addiction a criminal offense, for which the offender may be prosecuted "at any time before he reforms." California has said that a person can be continuously guilty of this offense, whether or not he has ever used or possessed any narcotics within the State, and whether or not he has been guilty of any antisocial behavior there.

It is unlikely that any State at this moment in history would attempt to make it a criminal offense for a person to be mentally ill, or a leper, or to be afflicted with a venereal disease. A State might deter-mine that the general health and welfare require that the victims of these and other human afflictions be dealt with by compulsory treatment, involving quarantine, confinement, or sequestration. But, in the light of contemporary human knowledge, a law which made a criminal offense of such a disease would doubtless be universally thought to be an infliction of cruel and unusual punishment in violation of the Eighth and Fourteenth Amendments. *   *   *

We cannot but consider the statute before us as of the same category. In this Court counsel for the State recognized that narcotic addiction is an illness. Indeed, it is apparently an illness which may be contracted innocently or involuntarily. We hold that a state law which imprisons a person thus afflicted as a criminal, even though he has never touched any narcotic drug within the State or been guilty of any irregular behavior there, inflicts a cruel and unusual punishment in violation of the Fourteenth Amendment. To be sure, imprisonment for ninety days is not, in the abstract, a punishment which is either cruel or unusual. But the question cannot be considered in the abstract. Even one day in prison would be a cruel and unusual punishment for the "crime" of having a common cold.

We are not unmindful that the vicious evils of the narcotics traffic have occasioned the grave concern of government. There are * * * countless fronts on which those evils may be legitimately attacked. We deal in this case only with an individual provision of a particularized local law as it has so far been interpreted by the California courts.

Reversed.

Mr. Justice FRANKFURTER took no part in the consideration or decision of this case.

Mr. Justice CLARK, dissenting.

* * *

Apart from prohibiting specific acts such as the purchase, possession and sale of narcotics, California has taken certain legislative steps in regard to the status of being a narcotic addict—a condition commonly recognized as a threat to the State and to the individual. * * *

* * * There was no suggestion that the term "narcotic addict" as * * * used [in the statute] included a person who acted without volition or who had lost the power of self-control. Although the section is penal in appearance—perhaps a carry-over from a less sophisticated approach—its present provisions are quite similar to those for civil commitment and treatment of addicts who have lost the power of self-control. * * *

Where narcotic addiction has progressed beyond the incipient, volitional stage, California provides for commitment of three months to two years in a state hospital. * * *

Thus, the "criminal" provision applies to the incipient narcotic addict who retains self-control, requiring confinement of three months to one year and parole with frequent tests to detect renewed use of drugs. Its overriding purpose is to cure the less seriously addicted person by preventing further use. On the other hand, the "civil" commitment provision deals with addicts who have lost the power of self-control, requiring hospitalization up to two years. Each deals with a different type of addict but with a common purpose. This is most apparent when the sections overlap: if after civil commitment of an addict it is found that hospital treatment will not be helpful, the addict is confined for a minimum period of three months in the same manner as is the volitional addict under the "criminal" provision.

* * *

The majority strikes down the conviction primarily on the grounds that petitioner was denied due process by the imposition of criminal penalties for nothing more than being in a status. This viewpoint is premised upon the theme that [the statute] is a "criminal" provision authorizing a punishment, for the majority admits that "a State might establish a program of compulsory treatment for those addicted to narcotics" which "might require periods of involuntary confinement." I submit that California has done exactly that. The majority's error is in instructing the California Legislature that hospitalization is the *only treatment* for narcotics addiction—that anything less is a punishment denying due process. * * *

However, the case in support of the judgment below need not rest solely on this reading of California law. For even if the overall statutory scheme is ignored and a purpose and effect of punishment is attached to [the statute] that provision still does not violate the Fourteenth Amendment. The majority acknowledges, as it must, that a State can punish persons who purchase, possess or use narcotics. Although none of these acts are harmful to society *in themselves*, the State constitutionally may attempt to deter and prevent them through punishment because of the grave threat of future harmful conduct which they pose. Narcotics addiction—including the incipient, volitional addiction to which this provision speaks—is no different. * * *

It is no answer to suggest that we are dealing with an involuntary status and thus penal sanctions will be ineffective and unfair. The section at issue applies only to persons who use narcotics often or even daily but not to the point of losing self-control. When dealing with involuntary addicts California moves only through [the civil commitment provision] of its Welfare Institutions Code which clearly is not penal. * * *

* * *

Mr. Justice WHITE, dissenting.

* * *

I am not at all ready to place the use of narcotics beyond the reach of the States' criminal laws. I do not consider appellant's conviction to be a punishment for having an illness or for simply being in some status or condition, but rather a conviction for the regular, repeated or habitual use of narcotics immediately prior to his arrest and in violation of the Califor-

nia law. As defined by the trial court, addiction *is* the regular use of narcotics and can be proved only by evidence of such use. To find addiction in this case the jury had to believe that appellant had frequently used narcotics in the recent past. California is entitled to have its statute. * * *

* * *

The Court clearly does not rest its decision upon the narrow ground that the jury was not expressly instructed not to convict if it believed appellant's use of narcotics was beyond his control. The Court recognizes no degrees of addiction. The Fourteenth Amendment is today held to bar any prosecution for addiction regardless of the degree or frequency of use, and the Court's opinion bristles with indications of further consequences. * * *

* * *

Finally, I deem this application of "cruel and unusual punishment" so novel that I suspect the Court was hard put to find a way to ascribe to the Framers of the Constitution the result reached today rather than to its own notions of ordered liberty. If this case involved economic regulation, the present Court's allergy to substantive due process would surely save the statute and prevent the Court from imposing its own philosophical predilections upon state legislatures for Congress. I fail to see why the Court deems it more appropriate to write into the Constitution its own abstract notions of how best to handle the narcotics problem, for it obviously cannot match either the States or Congress in expert understanding.

I respectfully dissent.

Leroy Powell was found guilty of being drunk in a public place in violation of Texas penal law. He eventually appealed his conviction to the United States Supreme Court contending that his drunken behavior was "not of his own volition" because he suffered from "the disease of chronic alcoholism" and that, therefore, the fifty-dollar fine imposed constituted cruel and unusual punishment. (This was approximately the 100th time appellant had been convicted for the offense.)

In this case, Powell v. Texas, 392 U.S. 514, 88 S.Ct. 2145 (1968), the Court narrowly rejected the invitation to extend *Robinson*. Justice Marshall announced the judgment of the Court in a plurality opinion in which he spoke for Chief Justice Warren and Justices Black and Harlan. He found *Robinson* inapposite:

> On its face the present case does not fall within that holding, since appellant was convicted, not for being a chronic alcoholic, but for being in public while drunk on a particular occasion. The State of Texas thus has not sought to punish a mere status, as California did in *Robinson*; nor has it attempted to regulate appellant's behavior in the privacy of his own home. Rather, it has imposed upon appellant a criminal sanction for public behavior which may create substantial health and safety hazards, both for appellant and for members of the general public, and which offends the moral and esthetic sensibilities of a large segment of the community. This seems a far cry from convicting one for being an addict, being a chronic alcoholic, being "mentally ill, or a leper * * *." * * *

> *Robinson* so viewed brings this Court but a very small way into the substantive criminal law. And unless *Robinson* is so viewed it is difficult to see any limiting principle that would serve to prevent this Court from becoming, under the aegis of the Cruel and Unusual Punishment Clause, the ultimate arbiter of the standards of criminal responsibility, in diverse areas of the criminal law, throughout the country.

> * * * The entire thrust of *Robinson's* interpretation of the Cruel and Unusual Punishment Clause is that criminal penalties may be inflicted only if the accused has committed some act, has engaged in some behavior, which society has an interest in preventing. * * * It thus does not deal with the question of whether certain conduct cannot constitutionally be punished because it is, in some sense, "involuntary" or "occasioned by a compulsion."

> * * *

> Ultimately, * * * the most troubling aspects of this case, were *Robinson* to be extended to meet it, would be the scope and content of what could only be a constitutional doctrine of criminal responsibility. * * *

Concluded Justice Marshall in affirming the trial court's judgment, "Nothing could be less fruitful than for this Court to be compelled into defining some sort of insanity test in constitutional terms. Yet, that task would seem to follow inexorably from an extension of *Robinson* to this case." Justice White concurred in the result only, saying:

> * * * The sober chronic alcoholic has no compulsion to be on the public streets; many chronic alcoholics drink at home and are never seen drunk in public. Before and after taking the first drink, and until he becomes so drunk that he loses the power to know where he is or to direct his move-

ments, the chronic alcoholic with a home or financial resources is as capable as the nonchronic drinker of doing his drinking in private, of removing himself from public places and, since he knows or ought to know that he will become intoxicated, of making plans to avoid his being found drunk in public. For these reasons, I cannot say that the chronic alcoholic who proves his disease and a compulsion to drink is shielded from conviction when he has knowingly failed to take feasible precautions against committing a criminal act, here the act of going to or remaining in a public place. On such facts the alcoholic is like a person with smallpox, who could be convicted for being on the street but not for being ill, or, like the epileptic, who would be punished for driving a car but not for his disease.

The fact remains that some chronic alcoholics must drink and hence must drink *somewhere*. Although many chronics have homes, many others do not. For all practical purposes the public streets may be home for these unfortunates, not because their disease compels them to be there, but because, drunk or sober, they have no place else to go and no place else to be when they are drinking. This is more a function of economic station than of disease, although the disease may lead to destitution and perpetuate that condition. For some of these alcoholics I would think a showing could be made that resisting drunkenness is impossible and that avoiding public places when intoxicated is also impossible. As applied to them this statute is in effect a law which bans a single act for which they may not be convicted under the Eighth Amendment—the act of getting drunk.

It is also possible that the chronic alcoholic who begins drinking in private at some point becomes so drunk that he loses the power to control his movements and for that reason appears in public. The Eighth Amendment might also forbid conviction in such circumstances, but only on a record satisfactorily showing that it was not feasible for him to have made arrangements to prevent his being in public when drunk and that his extreme drunkenness sufficiently deprived him of his faculties on the occasion in issue.

These prerequisites to the possible invocation of the Eighth Amendment are not satisfied on the record before us.

Justice Fortas dissented in an opinion joined by Justices Douglas, Brennan, and Stewart. Beginning with the premise that chronic alcoholism is a disease—an issue which the plurality skirted—the dissenters found *Robinson* directly applicable:

Robinson stands upon a principle which, despite its subtlety, must be simply stated and respectfully applied because it is the foundation of individual liberty and the cornerstone of the relations between a civilized state and its citizens: Criminal penalties may not be inflicted upon a person for being in a condition he is powerless to change. In all probability, Robinson at some time before his conviction elected to take narcotics. But the crime as defined did not punish this conduct. The statute imposed a penalty for the offense of "addiction"—a condition which Robinson could not control. Once Robinson had become an addict, he was utterly powerless to avoid criminal guilt. He was powerless to choose not to violate the law.

In the present case, appellant is charged with a crime composed of two elements—being intoxicated and being found in a public place while in that condition. The crime, so defined, differs from that in *Robinson*. The statute covers more than a mere status. But the essential constitutional defect here is the same as in *Robinson*, for in both cases the particular defendant was accused of being in a condition which he had no capacity to change or avoid. The trial judge sitting as trier of fact found upon the medical and other relevant testimony, that Powell is a "chronic alcoholic." He defined appellant's "chronic alcoholism" as "a disease which destroys the afflicted person's will power to resist the constant, excessive consumption of alcohol." He also found that "a chronic alcoholic does not appear in public by his own volition but under a compulsion symptomatic of the disease of chronic alcoholism." I read these findings to mean that appellant was powerless to avoid drinking; that having taken his first drink, he had "an uncontrollable compulsion to drink" to the point of intoxication; and that, once intoxicated, he could not prevent himself from appearing in public places.

And, after accepting the trial judge's findings, the dissenters concluded that they "call into play the principle that a person may not be punished if the condition essential to constitute the defined crime is part of the pattern of his disease and is occasioned by a compulsion symptomatic of the disease."

FURMAN v. GEORGIA

Supreme Court of the United States, 1972
408 U.S. 238, 92 S.Ct. 2726, 33 L.Ed.2d 346

The Supreme Court granted certiorari to review three state court decisions affirming the imposition of the death penalty in William Furman's case for murder and for rape in the other two.

PER CURIAM.

* * * Certiorari was granted limited to the following question: "Does the imposition and carrying out of the death penalty in [these cases] constitute cruel and unusual punishment in violation of the Eighth and Fourteenth Amendments?" * * * The Court holds that the imposition and carrying out of the death penalty in these cases constitutes cruel and unusual punishment in violation of the Eighth and Fourteenth Amendments. The judgment in each case is therefore reversed insofar as it leaves undisturbed the death sentence imposed, and the cases are remanded for further proceedings. So ordered.

* * *

Mr. Justice DOUGLAS, Mr. Justice BRENNAN, Mr. Justice STEWART, Mr. Justice WHITE, and Mr. Justice MARSHALL have filed separate opinions in support of the judgments.

The CHIEF JUSTICE [BURGER], Mr. Justice BLACKMUN, Mr. Justice POWELL, and Mr. Justice REHNQUIST have filed separate dissenting opinions.

Mr. Justice DOUGLAS, concurring.

* * *

The generalities of a law inflicting capital punishment is one thing. What may be said of the validity of a law on the books and what may be done with the law in its application do or may lead to quite different conclusions.

It would seem to be incontestable that the death penalty inflicted on one defendant is "unusual" if it discriminates against him by reason of his race, religion, wealth, social position, or class, or if it is imposed under a procedure that gives room for the play of such prejudices.

*   *   *

The words "cruel and unusual" certainly include penalties that are barbaric. But the words, at least when read in light of the English proscription against selective and irregular use of penalties, suggest that it is "cruel and unusual" to apply the death penalty—or any other penalty—selectively to minorities whose numbers are few, who are outcasts of society, and who are unpopular, but whom society is willing to see suffer though it would not countenance general application of the same penalty across the boards. *   *   *

*   *   *

In a Nation committed to Equal Protection of the laws there is no permissible "caste" aspect of law enforcement. Yet we know that the discretion of judges and juries in imposing the death penalty enables the penalty to be selectively applied, feeding prejudices against the accused if he is poor and despised, poor and lacking political clout, or if he is a member of a suspect or unpopular minority, and saving those who by social position may be in a more protected position. *   *   *

The high service rendered by the "cruel and unusual" punishment clause of the Eighth Amendment is to require legislatures to write penal laws that are evenhanded, nonselective, and nonarbitrary, and to require judges to see to it that general laws are not applied sparsely, selectively, and spottily to unpopular groups.

*   *   *

Any law which is nondiscriminatory on its face may be applied in such a way as to violate the Equal Protection Clause of the Fourteenth Amendment. *   *   * Such conceivably might be the fate of a mandatory death penalty, where equal or lesser sentences were imposed on the elite, a harsher one on the minorities or members of the lower castes. Whether a mandatory death penalty would otherwise be constitutional is a question I do not reach.

*   *   *

Mr. Justice BRENNAN, concurring.

*   *   *

*   *   * At bottom *   *   * the Cruel and Unusual Punishments Clause prohibits the infliction of uncivilized and inhuman punishments. The State, even as it punishes, must treat its members with respect for their intrinsic worth as human beings. A punishment is "cruel and unusual," therefore, if it does not comport with human dignity.

*   *   *

In sum, the punishment of death is inconsistent with *   *   * four principles: Death is an unusually severe and degrading punishment; there is a strong probability that it is inflicted arbitrarily; its rejection by contemporary society is virtually total; and there is no reason to believe that it serves any penal purpose more effectively than the less severe punishment of imprisonment. The function of these principles is to enable a court to determine whether a punishment comports with human dignity. Death, quite simply, does not.

* * *

Mr. Justice STEWART, concurring.

The penalty of death differs from all other forms of criminal punishment, not in degree but in kind. It is unique in its total irrevocability. It is unique in its rejection of rehabilitation of the convict as a basic purpose of criminal justice. And it is unique, finally, in its absolute renunciation of all that is embodied in our concept of humanity.

For these and other reasons, at least two of my Brothers have concluded that the infliction of the death penalty is constitutionally impermissible in all circumstances under the Eighth and Fourteenth Amendments. Their case is a strong one. But I find it unnecessary to reach the ultimate question they would decide.
* * *

* * *

Legislatures—state and federal—have sometimes specified that the penalty of death shall be the mandatory punishment for every person convicted of engaging in certain designated criminal conduct.
* * *

* * *

* * * I simply conclude that the Eighth and Fourteenth Amendments cannot tolerate the infliction of a sentence of death under legal systems that permit this unique penalty to be so wantonly and so freakishly imposed.

* * *

Mr. Justice WHITE, concurring.

* * * In joining the Court's judgment, therefore, I do not at all intimate that the death penalty is unconstitutional *per se* or that there is no system of capital punishment that would comport with the Eighth Amendment. That question, ably argued by several of my Brethren, is not presented by these cases and need not be decided.

* * *

* * * I add only that past and present legislative judgment with respect to the death penalty loses much of its force when viewed in light of the recurring practice of delegating sentencing authority to the jury and the fact that a jury, in its own discretion and without violating its trust or any statutory policy, may refuse to impose the death penalty no matter what the circumstances of the crime. Legislative "policy" is thus necessarily defined not by what is legislatively authorized but by what juries and judges do in exercising the discretion so regularly conferred upon them. In my judgment what was done in these cases violated the Eighth Amendment.

* * *

Mr. Justice MARSHALL, concurring.

* * *

There are six purposes conceivably served by capital punishment: retribution, deterrence, prevention of repetitive criminal acts, encouragement of guilty pleas and confessions, eugenics, and economy. * * *

[Justice MARSHALL then exhaustively considered each purpose in turn and rejected it.]

* * *

[E]ven if capital punishment is not excessive, it nonetheless violates the Eighth Amendment because it is morally unacceptable to the people of the United States at this time in their history.

In judging whether or not a given penalty is morally acceptable, most courts have said that the punishment is valid unless "it shocks the conscience and sense of justice of the people."

Judge Frank once noted the problems inherent in the use of such a measuring stick:

"[The court,] before it reduces a sentence as 'cruel and unusual,' must have reasonably good assurances that the sentence offends the 'common conscience.' And, in any context, such a standard—the community's attitude—is usually an unknowable. It resembles a slithery shadow, since one can seldom learn, at all accurately, what the community, or a majority, actually feels. Even a carefully-taken 'public opinion poll' would be inconclusive in a case like this."

While a public opinion poll obviously is of some assistance in indicating public acceptance or rejection of a specific penalty, its utility cannot be very great. This is because whether or not a punishment is cruel and unusual depends, not on whether its mere mention "shocks the conscience and sense of justice of the people," but on whether people who were fully informed as to the purposes of the penalty and its liabilities would find the penalty shocking, unjust, and unacceptable.

In other words, the question with which we must deal is not whether a substantial proportion of American citizens would today, if polled, opine that capital punishment is barbarous-

ly cruel, but whether they would find it to be so in the light of all information presently available.

This is not to suggest that with respect to this test of unconstitutionality people are required to act rationally; they are not. With respect to this judgment, a violation of the Eighth Amendment is totally dependent on the predictable subjective, emotional reactions of informed citizens.

It has often been noted that American citizens know almost nothing about capital punishment. Some of the conclusions arrived at in the preceding section and the supporting evidence would be critical to an informed judgment on the morality of the death penalty: e.g., that the death penalty is no more effective a deterrent than life imprisonment, that convicted murderers are rarely executed, but are usually sentenced to a term in prison; that convicted murderers usually are model prisoners, and that they almost always become lawabiding citizens upon their release from prison; that the costs of executing a capital offender exceed the costs of imprisoning him for life; that while in prison, a convict under sentence of death performs none of the useful functions that life prisoners perform; that no attempt is made in the sentencing process to ferret out likely recidivists for execution; and that the death penalty may actually stimulate criminal activity.

This information would almost surely convince the average citizen that the death penalty was unwise, but a problem arises as to whether it would convince him that the penalty was morally reprehensible. This problem arises from the fact that the public's desire for retribution, even though this is a goal that the legislature cannot constitutionally pursue as its sole justification for capital punishment, might influence the citizenry's view of the morality of capital punishment. The solution to the problem lies in the fact that no one has ever seriously advanced retribution as a legitimate goal of our society. Defenses of capital punishment are always mounted on deterrent or other similar theories. This should not be surprising. It is the people of this country who have urged in the past that prisons rehabilitate as well as isolate offenders, and it is the people who have injected a sense of purpose into our penology. I cannot believe that at this stage in our history, the American people would ever knowingly support purposeless vengeance. Thus, I believe that the great mass of citizens would conclude on the basis of the material already considered that the death penalty is immoral and therefore unconstitutional.

But, if this information needs supplementing, I believe that the following facts would serve to convince even the most hesitant of citizens to condemn death as a sanction: capital punishment is imposed discriminatorily against certain identifiable classes of people; there is evidence that innocent people have been executed before their innocence can be proved; and the death penalty wreaks havoc with our entire criminal justice system.   *   *   *

*   *   *

Mr. Chief Justice BURGER, with whom Mr. Justice BLACKMUN, Mr. Justice POWELL, and Mr. Justice REHNQUIST join, dissenting.

*   *   *

If we were possessed of legislative power, I would either join with Mr. Justice BRENNAN and Mr. Justice MARSHALL or, at the very least, restrict the use of capital punishment to a small category of the most heinous crimes. Our constitutional inquiry, however, must be divorced from personal feelings as to the morality and efficacy of the death penalty and be confined to the meaning and applicability of the uncertain language of the Eighth Amendment. There is no novelty in being called upon to interpret a constitutional provision that is less than self-defining, but of all our fundamental guarantees, the ban on "cruel and unusual punishments" is one of the most difficult to translate into judicially manageable terms. The widely divergent views of the Amendment expressed in today's opinions reveal the haze that surrounds this constitutional command. Yet it is essential to our role as a court that we not sieze upon the enigmatic character of the guarantee as an invitation to enact our personal predilections into law.

Although the Eighth Amendment literally reads as prohibiting only those punishments that are both "cruel" and "unusual," history compels the conclusion that the Constitution prohibits all punishments of extreme and barbarous cruelty, regardless of how frequently or infrequently imposed.

*   *   *

[W]here, as here, we consider a punishment well known to history, and clearly authorized by legislative enactment, it disregards the history of the Eighth Amendment and all the judicial comment that has followed to rely on the term "unusual" as affecting the outcome of these cases. Instead, I view these cases as turning on the single question whether capital punishment is "cruel" in the constitutional sense. The term "unusual" cannot be read as limiting the ban on "cruel" punishments or as somehow expanding the meaning of the term "cruel." For this reason I am unpersuaded by the facile argument that since capital punishment has always been cruel in the everyday sense of the word, and has become unusual due to decreased use, it is, therefore, now "cruel and unusual."

* * *

Today the Court has not ruled that capital punishment is *per se* violative of the Eighth Amendment; nor has it ruled that the punishment is barred for any particular class or classes of crimes. The substantially similar concurring opinions of Mr. Justice STEWART and Mr. Justice WHITE, which are necessary to support the judgment setting aside petitioners' sentences, stop short of reaching the ultimate question. * * *

* * *

The critical factor in the concurring opinions of both Mr. Justice STEWART and Mr. Justice WHITE is the infrequency with which the penalty is imposed. This factor is taken not as evidence of society's abhorrence of capital punishment—the inference that petitioners would have the Court draw—but as the earmark of a deteriorated system of sentencing. * * *

* * *

* * * The decisive grievance of the opinions not translated into Eighth Amendment terms—is that the present system of discretionary sentencing in capital cases has failed to produce evenhanded justice; the problem is not that too few have been sentenced to die, but that the selection process has followed no rational pattern. This claim of arbitrariness is not only lacking in empirical support, but it manifestly fails to establish that the death penalty is a "cruel and unusual" punishment. The Eighth Amendment was included in the Bill of Rights to assure that certain types of punishments would never be imposed, not to channelize the sentencing process. The approach of these concurring opinions has no antecedent in the Eighth Amendment cases. It is essentially and exclusively a procedural due process argument.

* * *

Since there is no majority of the Court on the ultimate issue presented in these cases, the future of capital punishment in this country has been left in an uncertain limbo. Rather than providing a final and unambiguous answer on the basic constitutional question, the collective impact of the majority's ruling is to demand an undetermined measure of change from the various state legislatures and the Congress. While I cannot endorse the process of decisionmaking that has yielded today's result and the restraints which that result imposes on legislative action, I am not altogether displeased that legislative bodies have been given the opportunity, and indeed unavoidable responsibility, to make a thorough re-evaluation of the entire subject of capital punishment. If today's opinions demonstrate nothing else, they starkly show that this is an area where legislatures can act far more effectively than courts.

* * *

The highest judicial duty is to recognize the limits on judicial power and to permit the democratic processes to deal with matters falling outside of those limits. The "hydraulic pressures" that Holmes spoke of as being generated by cases of great import have propelled the Court to go beyond the limits of judicial power, while fortunately leaving some room for legislative judgment.

Mr. Justice BLACKMUN, dissenting.

I join the respective opinions of THE CHIEF JUSTICE, Mr. Justice POWELL, and Mr. Justice REHNQUIST, and add only the following, somewhat personal, comments.

Cases such as these provide for me an excruciating agony of the spirit. I yield to no one in the depth of my distaste, antipathy, and, indeed, abhorrence, for the death penalty, with all its aspects of physical distress and fear and of moral judgment exercised by finite minds. That distaste is buttressed by a belief that capital punishment serves no useful purpose that can be demonstrated. For me, it violates childhood's training and life's experiences, and is not compatible with the philosophical convictions I have been able to develop. It is antagonistic to any sense of "reverence for life." Were I a legislator, I would vote against the death penalty for the policy reasons argued by counsel for the respective petitioners and expressed and adopted in the several opinions filed by the Justices who vote to reverse these convictions.

* * *

Although personally I may rejoice at the Court's result, I find it difficult to accept or to justify as a matter of history, of law, or of constitu-

tional pronouncement. I fear the Court has overstepped. It has sought and has achieved an end.

Mr. Justice POWELL, with whom THE CHIEF JUSTICE, Mr. Justice BLACKMUN, and Mr. Justice REHNQUIST join, dissenting.

* * * It is the judgment of five Justices that the death penalty, as customarily prescribed and implemented in this country today, offends the constitutional prohibition against cruel and unusual punishment. The reasons for that judgment are stated in five separate opinions, expressing as many separate rationales. In my view, none of these opinions provides a constitutionally adequate foundation for the Court's decision.

* * *

* * * On virtually every occasion that any opinion has touched on the question of the constitutionality of the death penalty, it has been asserted affirmatively, or tacitly assumed, that the Constitution does not prohibit the penalty. No Justice of the Court, until today, has dissented from this consistent reading of the Constitution. * * *

* * *

* * * It seems to be that the sweeping judicial action undertaken today reflects a basic lack of faith and confidence in the democratic process. Many may regret, as I do, the failure of some legislative bodies to address the capital punishment issue with greater frankness or effectiveness. Many might decry their failure either to abolish the penalty entirely or selectively, or to establish standards for its enforcement. But impatience with the slowness, and even the unresponsiveness, of legis-

latures is no justification for judicial intrusion upon their historic powers.

* * *

Mr. Justice REHNQUIST, with whom THE CHIEF JUSTICE, Mr. Justice BLACKMUN, and Mr. Justice POWELL join, dissenting.

* * * Whatever its precise rationale, today's holding necessarily brings into sharp relief the fundamental question of the role of judicial review in a democratic society. How can government by the elected representatives of the people co-exist with the power of the federal judiciary, whose members are constitutionally insulated from responsiveness to the popular will, to declare invalid laws duly enacted by the popular branches of government?

* * *

* * * While overreaching by the Legislative and Executive Branches may result in the sacrifice of individual protections that the Constitution was designed to secure against action of the State, judicial overreaching may result in sacrifice of the equally important right of the people to govern themselves.

* * *

The very nature of judicial review * * * makes the courts the least subject to Madisonian check in the event that they shall, for the best of motives, expand judicial authority beyond the limits contemplated by the Framers. It is for this reason that judicial self-restraint is surely an implied, if not an expressed, condition of the grant of authority of judicial review. The Court's hold in these cases has been reached, I believe, in complete disregard of that implied condition.

The legislative response which Chief Justice Burger predicted in his *Furman* dissent quickly materialized, and the Court was promptly confronted with the problem again. In July 1976, the Court handed down a covey of controversial, complex, and anxiously awaited decisions focusing once more on the death penalty. Although the Court dealt at length with specific issues raised by the state laws involved in the cases, with respect to constitutional interpretation what is most important in these decisions was the Court's response to two basic questions: (1) Is the punishment of death for the crime of murder "under all circumstances, 'cruel and unusual' in violation of the Eighth and Fourteenth Amendments of the Constitution"? (2) Does a death sentence "returned pursuant to a law imposing a mandatory death penalty for a broad category of homicidal offenses" constitute cruel and unusual punishment?

Announcing the judgment of the Court in an opinion in Gregg v. Georgia, 428 U.S. 153, 96 S.Ct. 2909 (1976), in which he spoke for Justices Powell and Stevens as well as himself, Justice Stewart answered the first question with a "No":

The Court on a number of occasions has both assumed and asserted the constitutionality of capital punishment. In several cases that assumption provided a necessary foundation for the decision, as the Court was asked to decide whether a particular method of carrying out a capital sentence would be allowed to stand under the Eighth Amendment. But until Furman v. Georgia, 408 U.S. 238, 92 S.Ct. 2726 (1972), the Court never confronted squarely the fundamental claim that the punishment of death always, regardless of the enormity of the offense or the procedure followed in imposing the sentence, is cruel and unusual punishment in violation of the Constitution. Although this issue was presented and addressed in *Furman*, it was not resolved by the Court. Four Justices would have held that capital punishment is not unconstitutional *per se*; two Justices would have reached the opposite conclusion; and three Justices, while agreeing that the statutes then before the Court were invalid as applied, left open the question whether such punishment may ever be imposed. We now hold that the punishment of death does not invariably violate the Constitution.

* * *

[W]hile we have an obligation to insure that constitutional bounds are not overreached, we may not act as judges as we might as legislators.

* * *

Therefore, in assessing a punishment selected by a democratically elected legislature against the constitutional measure, we presume its validity. We may not require the legislature to select the least severe penalty possible so long as the penalty selected is not cruelly inhumane or disproportionate to the crime involved. And a heavy burden rests on those who would attack the judgment of the representatives of the people.

* * *

The most marked indication of society's endorsement of the death penalty for murder is the legislative response to *Furman*. The legislatures of at least 35 States have enacted new statutes that provide for the death penalty for at least some crimes that result in the death of another person. And the Congress of the United States, in 1974, enacted a statute providing the death penalty for aircraft piracy that results in death. These recently adopted statutes have attempted to address the concerns expressed by the Court in *Furman* primarily (i) by specifying the factors to be weighed and the procedures to be followed in deciding when to impose a capital sentence, or (ii) by making the death penalty mandatory for specified crimes. But all of the post-*Furman* statutes make clear that capital punishment itself has not been rejected by the elected representatives of the people.

In the only statewide referendum occurring since *Furman* and brought to our attention, the people of California adopted a constitutional amendment that authorized capital punishment, in effect negating a prior ruling by the Supreme Court of California in People v. Anderson, 6 Cal.3d 628, 493 P.2d 880, cert. denied, 406 U.S. 958, 92 S.Ct. 2060 (1972), that the death penalty violated the California Constitution.

The jury also is a significant and reliable objective index of contemporary values because it is so directly involved. * * * The Court has said that "one of the most important functions any jury can perform in making * * * a selection [between life imprisonment and death for a defendant convicted in a capital case] is to maintain a link between contemporary community values and the penal system." Witherspoon v. Illinois, 391 U.S. 510, 519 n. 15, 88 S.Ct. 1770, 1775 (1968). It may be true that evolving standards have influenced juries in recent decades to be more discriminating in imposing the sentence of death. But the relative infrequency of jury verdicts imposing the death sentence does not indicate rejection of capital punishment *per se*. Rather, the reluctance of juries in many cases to impose the sentence may well reflect the humane feeling that this most irrevocable

of sanctions should be reserved for a small number of extreme cases.
* * * Indeed, the actions of juries in many States since *Furman* is fully
compatible with the legislative judgments, reflected in the new statutes, as
to the continued utility and necessity of capital punishment in appropriate
cases. At the close of 1974 at least 254 persons had been sentenced to
death since *Furman*, and by the end of March 1976, more than 460 persons
were subject to death sentences.

As we have seen, however, the Eighth Amendment demands more than
that a challenged punishment be acceptable to contemporary society. The
Court also must ask whether it comports with the basic concept of human
dignity at the core of the Amendment. Trop v. Dulles, 356 U.S., at 100, 78
S.Ct., at 597 (plurality opinion). Although we cannot "invalidate a category
of penalties because we deem less severe penalties adequate to serve the
ends of penology," *Furman* v. *Georgia*, supra, at 451 (Powell, J., dissenting), the sanction imposed cannot be so totally without penological justification that it results in the gratuitous infliction of suffering. * * *

The death penalty is said to serve two principal social purposes: retribution and deterrence of capital crimes by prospective offenders.

* * *

The value of capital punishment as a deterrent of crime is a complex
factual issue the resolution of which properly rests with the legislatures,
which can evaluate the results of statistical studies in terms of their own
local conditions and with a flexibility of approach that is not available to the
courts. * * * Indeed, many of the post-*Furman* statutes reflect just
such a responsible effort to define those crimes and those criminals for
which capital punishment is most probably an effective deterrent.

In sum, we cannot say that the judgment of the Georgia legislature that
capital punishment may be necessary in some cases is clearly wrong. Considerations of federalism, as well as respect for the ability of a legislature
to evaluate, in terms of its particular state the moral consensus concerning
the death penalty and its social utility as a sanction, require us to conclude,
in the absence of more convincing evidence, that the infliction of death as a
punishment for murder is not without justification and thus is not unconstitutionally severe.

* * *

Justice Marshall dissented, saying:

In Furman v. Georgia, 408 U.S. 238, 314, 92 S.Ct., at 2834 (1972), I set
forth at some length my views on the basic issue presented to the Court in
these cases. The death penalty, I concluded, is a cruel and unusual punishment prohibited by the Eighth and Fourteenth Amendments. That continues to be my view.

* * *

Since the decision in *Furman*, the legislatures of 35 States have enacted
new statutes authorizing the imposition of the death sentence for certain
crimes, and Congress has enacted a law providing the death penalty for air
piracy resulting in death. 49 U.S.C.A. §§ 1472, 1473. I would be less than
candid if I did not acknowledge that these developments have a significant
bearing on a realistic assessment of the moral acceptability of the death

penalty to the American people. But if the constitutionality of the death penalty turns, as I have urged, on the opinion of an *informed* citizenry, then even the enactment of new death statutes cannot be viewed as conclusive. In *Furman*, I observed that the American people are largely unaware of the information critical to a judgment on the morality of the death penalty, and concluded that if they were better informed they would consider it shocking, unjust, and unacceptable. 408 U.S., at 360–369. A recent study, conducted after the enactment of the post-*Furman* statutes, has confirmed that the American people know little about the death penalty, and that the opinions of an informed public would differ significantly from those of a public unaware of the consequences and effects of the death penalty.

* * *

The * * * contentions—that society's expression of moral outrage through the imposition of the death penalty pre-empts the citizenry from taking the law into its own hands and reinforces moral values—are not retributive in the purest sense. They are essentially utilitarian in that they portray the death penalty as valuable because of its beneficial results. These justifications for the death penalty are inadequate because the penalty is, quite clearly I think, not necessary to the accomplishment of those results.

There remains for consideration, however, what might be termed the purely retributive justification for the death penalty—that the death penalty is appropriate, not because of its beneficial effect on society, but because the taking of the murderer's life is itself morally good. Some of the language of the plurality's opinion appears positively to embrace this notion of retribution for its own sake as a justification for capital punishment. * * *

It is this latter notion, in particular, that I consider to be fundamentally at odds with the Eighth Amendment. * * * The mere fact that the community demands the murderer's life in return for the evil he has done cannot sustain the death penalty, for as the plurality reminds us, "the Eighth Amendment demands more than that a challenged punishment be acceptable to contemporary society." * * * To be sustained under the Eighth Amendment, the death penalty must "[comport] with the basic concept of human dignity at the core of the Amendment," * * * (opinion of Stewart, Powell, and Stevens, JJ.); the objective in imposing it must be "[consistent] with our respect for the dignity of other men." * * * Under these standards, the taking of life "because the wrong-doer deserves it" surely must fall, for such a punishment has as its very basis the total denial of the wrong-doer's dignity and worth.

* * *

Turning to the question of what kinds of statutory systems permitting the death penalty do not violate the Constitution, again in *Gregg*, the plurality per Justice Stewart continued:

* * * Georgia's new sentencing procedures require as a prerequisite to the imposition of the death penalty, specific jury findings as to the circumstances of the crime or the character of the defendant. Moreover to guard further against a situation comparable to that presented in *Furman*, the Supreme Court of Georgia compares each death sentence with the sentences imposed on similarly situated defendants to ensure that the sentence of death in a particular case is not disproportionate. On their face these procedures seem to satisfy the concerns of *Furman*. No longer should there be "no meaningful basis for distinguishing the few cases in which [the death penalty] is imposed from the many cases in which it is not." * * *

                              * * *

The provision for appellate review in the Georgia capital-sentencing system serves as a check against the random or arbitrary imposition of the death penalty. In particular, the proportionality review substantially eliminates the possibility that a person will be sentenced to die by the action of an aberrant jury. If a time comes when juries generally do not impose the death sentence in a certain kind of murder case, the appellate review procedures assures that no defendant convicted under such circumstances will suffer a sentence of death.

The basic concern of *Furman* centered on those defendants who were being condemned to death capriciously and arbitrarily. Under the procedures before the Court in that case, sentencing authorities were not directed to give attention to the nature or circumstances of the crime committed or to the character or record of the defendant. Left unguided, juries imposed the death sentence in a way that could only be called freakish. The new Georgia sentencing procedures, by contrast, focus the jury's attention on the particularized nature of the crime and the particularized characteristics of the individual defendant. While the jury is permitted to consider any aggravating or mitigating circumstances, it must find and identify at least one statutory aggravating factor before it may impose a penalty of death. In this way the jury's discretion is channeled. No longer can a jury wantonly and freakishly impose the death sentence; it is always circumscribed by the legislative guidelines. In addition, the review function of the Supreme Court of Georgia affords additional assurance that the concerns that prompted our decision in *Furman* are not present to any significant degree in the Georgia procedure applied here.

For the reasons expressed in this opinion, we hold that the statutory system under which Gregg was sentenced to death does not violate the Constitution. Accordingly, the judgment of the Georgia Supreme Court is affirmed.

The Court went on in two more cases, Proffitt v. Florida, 428 U.S. 242, 96 S.Ct. 2960 (1976), and Jurek v. Texas, 428 U.S. 262, 96 S.Ct. 2950 (1976), to uphold the capital-sentencing laws of two other states.[a]

---

a. The Florida statute survived review because it provided "specific and detailed guidance" to trial judges in deciding whether to impose the death penalty and mandated state supreme court review "to ensure that similar results are reached in similar cases." The Texas law was upheld because it "require[d] that one of five aggravating circumstances be found before a defendant can be found guilty of capital-murder, and that in considering whether to impose a death sentence the jury may be asked to consider whatever evidence of mitigating circumstances the defense can bring before it" and because it "provid[ed] prompt judicial review of the jury's decision in a court with statewide jurisdiction * * * [as] a means to promote the evenhanded, rational, and consistent imposition of death sentences under law."

The Court then turned its attention to the second question posed in the 1976 death penalty cases, "whether a death sentence returned pursuant to a law imposing a mandatory death penalty for a broad category of homicidal offenses constitutes cruel and unusual punishment," and answered it in the affirmative. Unlike Georgia, Florida, and Texas, North Carolina "responded to the *Furman* decision by making death the mandatory sentence for all persons convicted of first-degree murder." The statute distinguished this kind of offense from second-degree murder (which carried a prison term of from two years to life) by defining murder in the first degree as "murder which shall be perpetrated by means of poison, lying in wait, imprisonment, starving, torture, or by any other kind of willful, deliberate and premeditated killing, or which shall be committed in the perpetration or attempt to perpetrate any arson, rape, robbery, kidnapping, burglary or other felony * * *." Speaking once again for the plurality, in Woodson v. North Carolina, 428 U.S. 280, 96 S.Ct. 2978 (1976), Justice Stewart observed at the outset that "[t]he issue, like that explored in *Furman*, involves the procedure employed by the State to select persons for the unique and irreversible penalty of death," and then wrote:

[T]here is general agreement that American juries have persistently refused to convict a significant portion of persons charged with first-degree murder of that offense under mandatory death penalty statutes. * * * Moreover, as a matter of historic fact, juries operating under discretionary sentencing statutes have consistently returned death sentences in only a minority of first-degree murder cases. In view of the historic record, it is only reasonable to assume that many juries under mandatory statutes will continue to consider the grave consequences of a conviction in reaching a verdict. North Carolina's mandatory death penalty statute provides no standards to guide the jury in its inevitable exercise of the power to determine which first-degree murderers shall live and which shall die. And there is no way under the North Carolina law for the judiciary to check arbitrary and capricious exercise of that power through a review of death sentences. Instead of rationalizing the sentencing process, a mandatory scheme may well exacerbate the problem identified in *Furman* by resting the penalty determination on the particular jury's willingness to act lawlessly. While a mandatory death penalty statute may reasonably be expected to increase the number of persons sentenced to death, it does not fulfill *Furman's* basic requirement by replacing arbitrary and wanton jury discretion with objective standards to guide, regularize, and make rationally reviewable the process for imposing a sentence of death.

[Another] shortcoming of the North Carolina statute is its failure to allow the particularized consideration of relevant aspects of the character and record of each convicted defendant before the imposition upon him of a sentence of death. In *Furman*, members of the Court acknowledged what cannot fairly be denied—that death is a punishment different from all other sanctions in kind rather than degree. * * * A process that accords no significance to relevant facets of the character and record of the individual offender or the circumstances of the particular offense excludes from consideration in fixing the ultimate punishment of death the possibility of compassionate or mitigating factors stemming from the diverse frailties of humankind. It treats all persons convicted of a designated offense not as uniquely individual human beings, but as members of a faceless, undifferentiated mass to be subjected to the blind infliction of the penalty of death.

* * * While the prevailing practice of individualizing sentencing determinations generally reflects simply enlightened policy rather than a constitutional imperative, we believe that in capital cases the fundamental respect for humanity underlying the Eighth Amendment, see Trop v. Dulles, 356 U.S., at 100 (plurality opinion), requires consideration of the character and record of the individual offender and the circumstances of the particular offense as a constitutionally indispensable part of the process of inflicting the penalty of death.

This conclusion rests squarely on the predicate that the penalty of death is qualitatively different from a sentence of imprisonment, however long. Death, in its finality, differs more from life imprisonment than a 100-year prison term differs from one of only a year or two. Because of that qualitative difference, there is a corresponding difference in the need for reliability in the determination that death is the appropriate punishment in a specific case.

For the reasons stated, we conclude that the death sentences imposed upon the petitioners under North Carolina's mandatory death sentence statute violated the Eighth and Fourteenth Amendments and therefore must be set aside. * * *

In another case, Roberts v. Louisiana, 428 U.S. 325, 96 S.Ct. 3001 (1976), the plurality, although acknowledging that Louisiana's death penalty law differed from North Carolina's, nonetheless concluded that the difference was "not of controlling constitutional significance." [b]

It bears emphasis that all of the 1976 death penalty decisions were "announced" by a plurality of only three Justices: Stewart, Powell, and Stevens. They were able to fashion a majority in these cases by virtue of the concurrences of Chief Justice Burger and Justices White, Blackmun, and Rehnquist in *Gregg*, *Proffitt*, and *Jurek* and the concurrences of Justices Brennan and Marshall (who, throughout, held to the view previously expressed in *Furman* that the death penalty *per se* constitutes cruel and unusual punishment in violation of the Eighth and Fourteenth Amendments) in *Woodson* and *Roberts*.

---

b. The plurality explained:

There are two major differences between the Louisiana and North Carolina statutes governing first-degree murder cases. First, the crime of first-degree murder in North Carolina includes any willful, deliberate, and premeditated homicide and any felony murder, whereas Louisiana limits first-degree murder to five categories of homicide—killing in connection with the commission of certain felonies; killing of a fireman or a peace officer in the performance of his duties; killing for remuneration; killing with the intent to inflict harm on more than one person; and killing by a person with a prior murder conviction or under a current life sentence. Second, Louisiana employs a unique system of responsive verdicts under which the jury in every first-degree murder case must be instructed on the crimes of first-degree murder, second-degree murder, and manslaughter and must be provided with the verdicts of guilty, guilty of second-degree murder, guilty of manslaughter, and not guilty. * * * By contrast, in North Carolina instructions on lesser included offenses must have a basis in the evidence adduced at trial. * * *

Although it conceded the range of capital offenses had been narrowed, the plurality concluded that this was insufficient to mitigate "the harshness and inflexibility of a mandatory death sentence statute." Said Justice Stewart, "As in North Carolina, there are no standards to guide the jury in the exercise of its power to select those first-degree murderers who will receive death sentences, and there is no meaningful appellate review of the jury's decision."

In June 1977, the Court handed down two rulings which tied up some loose ends left by its decisions in the Death Penalty Cases of the preceding year. At issue in Roberts v. Louisiana, 431 U.S. 633, 97 S.Ct. 1993 (1977), was the constitutionality of a state statute which imposed a mandatory death penalty for the murder of a policeman or fireman. In a *per curiam* opinion, a bare majority of the Court held that the decisions reached in the 1976 Death Penalty Cases resolved this question by mandating that before any capital sentence is imposed there must be an opportunity "for consideration of whatever mitigating circumstances may be relevant to either the particular offender or the particular offense." In the case of a police officer who is murdered, the Court suggested such mitigating factors might be: the youth of the offender; the absence of any prior conviction; the influence of drugs, alcohol, or emotional disturbance; and even possibly the moral justification which conceivably might be offered by the offender. Chief Justice Burger and Justices White, Blackmun, and Rehnquist dissented. Speaking for himself and Justice White, Justice Rehnquist observed that while "the factors weighing on the defendant's side of the scale are constant" in this case and the 1976 decisions "significantly different factors * * * weigh on the State's side of the scale." Specifically, he said, "Policemen on the beat are exposed, in the service of society, to all the risks which the constant effort to prevent crime and apprehend criminals entails. Because these people are literally the foot soldiers of society's defense of ordered liberty, the State has an especial interest in their protection." And as to the last of the possible mitigating factors set out by the Court, Justice Rehnquist wrote:

> * * * I cannot believe that States are constitutionally required to allow a defense, even at the sentencing stage, which depends on nothing more than the convict's moral belief that he was entitled to kill a peace officer in cold blood. John Wilkes Booth may well have thought he was morally justified in murdering Abraham Lincoln, whom, while fleeing from the stage of Ford's Theater, he characterized as a "tyrant"; I am appalled to believe that the Constitution would have *required* the government to allow him to argue that as a "mitigating factor" before it could sentence him to death if he were found guilty. I am equally appalled that a State should be required to instruct a jury that such individual beliefs must or should be considered as a possible balancing factor against the admittedly proper aggravating factor.

In a second case, Coker v. Georgia, 433 U.S. 584, 97 S.Ct. 2861 (1977), Justice White, speaking for a plurality composed of himself and Justices Stewart, Blackmun, and Stevens, held that the death sentence for the crime of rape is grossly disproportionate and, therefore, violates the Eighth Amendment's ban on cruel and unusual punishments. The plurality offered two bases of support for this conclusion: (1) the response of state legislatures in redesigning death penalty statutes to comply with the Court's decision in *Furman* v. *Georgia* was such that a far greater number of states chose to reimpose capital punishment for the crime of murder than chose to reimpose the death penalty also for the crime of rape; and (2) the evidence showed that there was a demonstrable reluctance on the part of jurors to impose the death penalty in rape cases. Justices Brennan and Marshall concurred in the judgment only, adhering to their views previously elaborated in *Furman* and reaffirmed in the 1976 Death Penalty Cases that capital punishment always violates the Eighth Amendment's proscription on cruel and unusual punishments. Chief Justice Burger dissented in an opinion in which Justice Rehnquist joined. Observing at the outset that the issue of proportionality ought to be addressed in terms of the specifics of Coker's crime and background—matters the Chief Justice argued were sufficient to sustain imposition of the death penalty in the case at hand—Burger turned "reluctantly * * * to what * * * [he saw] as the broader issues raised by this holding." He went on to charge that: (1) the plurality, by focusing only on legislative policy-making since *Furman*, had willfully shut its eyes to the longer historical view which showed that a significant number of legislatures concluded capital punishment was an appropriate penalty for rape; (2) the plurality substituted its views on the wisdom and desirability of the death penalty in rape cases in place of interpreting the Eighth Amendment; and (3) the plurality showed insufficient respect for the diversity, flexibility, and experimentation that are the well-springs of the federal system. Justice Powell concurred in the judgment but dissented from the plurality's "expansive pronouncement" which "draws a bright line between murder and all rapes—regardless of the degree of brutality of the rape or the effect upon the victim." Continued Justice Powell, "I dissent because I am not persuaded that such a bright line is appropriate. * * * Some victims are so grievously injured physically or psychologically that life *is* beyond repair." He concluded, "Thus it may be that the death penalty is not disproportionate punishment for the crime of aggravated rape."

Ohio law provided that once a defendant was convicted of murder aggravated by at least one of seven enumerated factors, the death penalty had to be imposed unless, after "considering the nature and circumstance of the offense" and the defendant's "history, character, and condition," the trial judge found by a preponderance of the evidence that the victim had induced or facilitated the offense or that it was unlikely the crime would have been committed had the defendant not acted under "duress, coercion, or strong provocation," or that "[t]he offense was primarily the product of the offender's psychosis or mental deficiency" (and such condition was insufficient to establish an insanity defense). Sandra Lockett was convicted of aggravated murder in the death of a pawnbroker which occurred in the course of an armed robbery. She was not the triggerman but drove the getaway car and was one of four who devised and executed the robbery. The Supreme Court reversed the imposition of the death penalty and remanded the case in Lockett v. Ohio, 438 U.S. 586, 98 S.Ct. 2954 (1978).

Chief Justice Burger announced the judgment of the Court on the death penalty issue in an opinion in which Justices Stewart, Powell, and Stevens joined. The plurality concluded that "the Eighth and Fourteenth Amendments require that the sentencer, in all but the rarest kind of capital case, not be precluded from considering *as a mitigating factor*, any aspect of a defendant's character or record and any of the circumstances of the offense that the defendant proffers as a basis for a sentence less than death." The merit of this conclusion, reasoned the plurality, was established by the fact that "the imposition of death by public authority is so profoundly different from all other penalties" that "an individualized decision is essential" and because of "[t]he nonavailability of corrective or modifying mechanisms with respect to an executed capital sentence * * * ." By contrast, "a statute that prevents the sentencer in all capital cases from giving independent mitigating weight to aspects of the defendant's character and record and to circumstances of the offense proffered in mitigation creates the risk that the death penalty will be imposed in spite of factors which may call for a less severe penalty." Such relevant factors, the plurality pointed out, might include, for example, the defendant's age, or the absence of intent to cause the death of the victim, or the defendant's comparatively minor role in the offense. "The limited range of mitigating circumstances which may be considered by the sentencer under the Ohio statute" was, therefore, "incompatible with the Eighth and Fourteenth Amendments."

Justice Marshall, "adher[ing] to * * * [the] view that the death penalty is, under all circumstances, a cruel and unusual punishment prohibited by the Eighth Amendment," concurred in the judgment. Justice White, dissented in part and concurring in the judgment, concluded that "it violates the Eighth Amendment to impose the penalty of death without a finding that the defendant possessed a purpose to cause the death of the victim." He continued, "[T]he infliction of death upon those who had no intent to bring about the death of the victim is not only grossly out of proportion to the severity of the crime but also fails to significantly contribute to acceptable or, indeed, any perceptible goals of punishment." Justice Blackmun also cited the "gross disproportionality" in Lockett's sentence and coupled this objection with another—that, under Ohio law, "the sentencing court has full discretion to prevent imposition of a capital sentence 'in the interests of justice' if a defendant pleads guilty or no contest, but wholly lacks such discretion if the defendant goes to trial."

Justice White, however, argued that with its announcement of this decision the Court had "completed its about-face since _Furman_ v. _Georgia_." Specifically, White "fear[ed] that the effect of the Court's decision * * * will be to constitutionally compel a restoration of the state of affairs at the time _Furman_ was decided, where the death penalty is imposed so erratically and the threat of execution is so attenuated for even the most atrocious murders that 'its imposition would then be the pointless and needless extinction of life with only marginal contributions to any discernible social or public purposes.' " Justice White also wondered to what extent the Court's previous holdings in _Proffitt_ v. _Florida_ and _Jurek_ v. _Texas_ had been undone by "call[ing] into question any other death penalty statute that permits only a limited number of mitigating circumstances to be placed before the sentencing authority or to be used in its deliberations." Justice Rehnquist, who dissented from the judgment, agreed, observing that the Court's ruling "encouraging * * * consideration [of] anything under the sun as a 'mitigating circumstance' * * * will not guide sentencing discretion but will totally unleash it." In his view, rather than contributing a seminal ruling on the Eighth Amendment, the Court's decision "represents a third false start * * within the past six years." Justice Brennan did not participate in the Court's disposition of the case.

——————

RECENT SUPREME COURT DECISIONS ON THE IMPOSITION OF CAPITAL PUNISHMENT

Case	Facts	Result	Vote	Reasons	Dissenters
Godfrey v. Georgia, 446 U.S. 420, 100 S.Ct. 1759 (1980)	Defendant was convicted of two murders and one aggravated assault on a third victim and was sentenced to death under a state law which permitted the	Imposition of the death penalty struck down	6–3	The Georgia courts here failed to adhere to meaningfully specific definitions of the otherwise vague terms of the statute so as to avoid standardless sentencing	Burger, White, and Rehnquist

CAPITAL PUNISHMENT (*Cont.*)

Case	Facts	Result	Vote	Reasons	Dissenters
Godfrey (*Cont.*)	jury to impose capital punishment if a murder was found to be "outrageously or wantonly vile, horrible or inhuman in that it involved torture, depravity of mind, or an aggravated battery to the victim"			discretion. The defendant did not torture or commit an aggravated battery upon his two murder victims or inflict upon them any physical injury prior to their deaths. Nor can the depravity of the defendant's mind be said, on the basis of the facts here, to be greater than that of any other person convicted of murder	
Beck v. Alabama, 447 U.S. 625, 100 S.Ct. 2382 (1980)	Defendant was tried and convicted of robbery-intentional killing, a capital offense, and the death penalty was imposed. State law gave the jury two options: to find the defendant guilty of that offense or to find the defendant guilty of no offense, and prohibited the jury from returning a verdict of a lesser included offense (in this case, felony murder) even though evidence in the case would have supported such a finding	Imposition of the death penalty struck down	7–2	Where evidence establishes that the defendant has committed a serious violent offense, but leaves some doubt whether one of the essential elements of a capital offense has been established, failure to give the jury the third option (of finding the defendant guilty of a lesser included offense) inescapably enhances the risk of unwarranted conviction and the prospect of this risk is unacceptable where the defendant's life is at stake. Forcing the jury to	White and Rehnquist

CAPITAL PUNISHMENT (*Cont.*)

Case	Facts	Result	Vote	Reasons	Dissenters
Beck (*Cont.*)				choose between only these two alternatives may well introduce extraneous considerations in making such an extreme choice. These concerns are not outweighed by the possibility of a hung jury (and thus a mistrial) or by the judge's discretion in sentencing	
Eddings v. Oklahoma, 455 U.S. 104, 102 S.Ct. 869 (1982)	Defendant, a sixteen-year-old runaway unable to be controlled by his parents, was signalled to pull over by a state highway patrolman after he briefly lost control of the car, whereupon he killed the officer with a shotgun. After defendant pleaded nolo contendere to the murder charge, the judge refused to consider in mitigation of the death penalty defendant's history of both emotional disturbance and violent and excessive punishment by his father	Imposition of the death penalty vacated and case remanded for rehearing on sentencing	5–4	The decision in *Lockett* requires that "the sentencer not be precluded from considering, *as a mitigating factor,* any aspect of a defendant's character or record and any of the circumstances of the offense that the defendant proffers as a basis for a sentence less than death." Just as a state may not preclude the sentencer from considering any mitigating factor by statute, neither may the sentencer refuse to consider, *as a matter of law,* any relevant mitigating evidence put forward by the defendant	Burger, White, Blackmun, and Rehnquist

CAPITAL PUNISHMENT (*Cont.*)

Case	Facts	Result	Vote	Reasons	Dissenters
Enmunds v. Florida, —— U.S. ——, 102 S.Ct. 3368 (1982)	Defendant was sitting in the getaway car some 200 yards from the spot where one of two armed robbers shot an elderly couple to death in the course of a robbery. Because he was in the car presumably to help the robbers make off with the money, defendant was found guilty of first-degree murder and sentenced to death as an aider and abettor of the felony which culminated in the two deaths	Reversed and remanded	5–4	Where the defendant did not kill the victims himself, was not physically present at the killings, and did not intend death or anticipate that deadly force would be used in the perpetration of the robbery, imposition of the death sentence for felony-murder, as was committed here, violates the Eighth and Fourteenth Amendments. Imposition of the death penalty in such a case as this is allowed only in a small number of states, has overwhelmingly been rejected by juries, is excessive as punishment, and serves neither the end of retribution nor deterrence	Burger, Powell, Rehnquist, and O'Connor

In 1964, Rummel was convicted of felony theft in the fraudulent use of a credit card to obtain $80 in goods and services and was sentenced to three years' imprisonment. Five years later he pleaded guilty to passing a forged check in the amount of $28.36 and was given a four year prison term. In 1973, Rummel was charged with obtaining $120.75 by false pretenses. Because the amount was greater than $50, he was charged with felony theft, by itself punishable by from two to ten years in prison. The prosecution, however, elected to proceed under the Texas recidivist statute which requires the imposition of a life sentence upon conviction for a third felony. The jury convicted Rummel of the felony theft charged and also returned a finding that he had been convicted of the two prior felonies. As a consequence, Rummel received a life sentence. After direct appeal and collateral attacks on his imprisonment proved unsuccessful, he filed a petition for a writ of habeas corpus in a federal district court against Estelle, the Director of the state Department of Corrections, alleging that his life sentence was so disproportionate to the crimes he had committed as to constitute cruel and unusual punishment in violation of the Eighth and Fourteenth Amendments. The federal district court rejected this contention and denied relief. A panel of the Court of Appeals for the Fifth Circuit reversed, but this judgment was overturned by an en banc decision of the appeals court affirming the district judge's ruling. Rummel then sought certiorari from the Supreme Court.

Speaking for a bare majority of the Court, Justice Rehnquist upheld the constitutionality of the Texas recidivist statute in Rummel v. Estelle, 445 U.S. 263, 100 S.Ct. 1133 (1980). Observing at the start that Rummel did not contest either "the constitutionality of Texas' recidivist statute as a general proposition" or "Texas' authority to punish each of his offenses as felonies," the Court pointed out that the question was therefore that "of the State's authority to impose a sentence of life imprisonment, as opposed to a substantial term of years, for his third felony." Rejecting the contention that the recidivist statute as applied in this case violated the Eighth Amendment, the Court offered substantially a five-part justification. First, it differentiated the proportionality principle applied in its capital punishment decisions by noting that "the unique nature of the death penalty for purposes of Eighth Amendment analysis, has been repeated time and time again in our opinions." Second, Justice Rehnquist distinguished the present case from Weems v. United States, 217 U.S. 349, 30 S.Ct. 544 (1910), the Court's only nondeath penalty case to adopt the disproportionality argument, on the grounds: (1) that it was such an extreme case—one in which an "impressive * * * minimum term of imprisonment" lasting twelve years at hard labor and close confinement, accompanied by "extraordinary * * * 'accessories,'" was imposed for the "trivial" offense "of falsifying a public document, a crime apparently complete upon the knowing entry of a simple item of false information in a public record" without any proof required of some resulting injury or even the intent to defraud; and (2) that the Court in subsequent cases expressly repudiated the general proposition that the Eighth Amendment afforded a basis for some judicially applied principle that the punishment fit the crime. Third, although extreme cases such as Weems might be susceptible to resolution by objective standards, "a more extensive intrusion into the basic line-drawing process that is pre-eminently the province of the legislature when it makes an act criminal would be difficult to square with the view expressed in Coker that the Court's Eighth Amendment judgments should neither be nor appear to be merely the subjective views of individual Justices." Fourth, "the interest of the State of Texas here is not simply that of making criminal the unlawful acquisition of another person's property; it is in addition the interest, expressed in all recidivist statutes, in dealing in a harsher manner with those who by repeated criminal acts have shown that they are simply incapable of conforming to the norms of society as established by its criminal law. By conceding the validity of recidivist statutes generally, Rummel himself concedes that the State of Texas, or any other State, has a valid interest in so dealing with that class of persons." Conviction and imprisonment for two preceding felonies, as required by the statute, show that "[o]ne in Rummel's position has been both graphically informed of the consequences of lawlessness and given an opportunity to reform, all to no avail," so that the operation of the recidivist statute is "nothing more than a societal decision that when such a person commits yet another felony, he should be subjected to the admittedly serious penalty of incarceration for life, subject only to the State's judgment as to whether to grant him parole." And fifth, Rummel's attempt to show by interjurisdictional comparison that Texas is way out of line with other states in imposing life imprisonment in this case fails to take account of the facts that Texas is very liberal with good-time credits and that complex and sophisticated variations that mark the approaches of other states make simple, straightforward comparisons misleading.

Justice Powell dissented and was joined by Justices Brennan, Marshall, and Stevens. He began by noting that "[d]isproportionality analysis measures the relationship between the nature and number of offenses committed and the severity of the punishment inflicted on the offender. The inquiry focuses on whether a person deserves such a punishment, not simply on whether punishment would serve a utilitarian goal. A statute that levied a mandatory life sentence for overtime parking might well deter vehicular lawlessness, but it would offend our felt sense of justice." Justice Powell "[r]ecognize[d] that the difference between this petitioner's grossly disproportionate sentence and other prisoners' constitutionally valid sentences is not separated by the clear distinction that separates capital from noncapital punishment," but, he argued, "[s]uch a limitation finds no support in the history of Eighth Amendment jurisprudence." Said Justice Powell, "The Court has, in my view, chosen the easiest line rather than the best." Moreover, he pointed out, while Rummel might well be eligible for parole in ten to twelve years, there was certainly no right to such an early release and, given the Texas governor's recent action refusing parole to 79 percent of those persons recommended for it, such an eventuality was purely speculative. Finally, relying on a three-part series of "certain objective factors"—including "the nature of the offense, * * * the sentence imposed for commission of the same crime in other jurisdictions, * * * and * * * the sentence imposed upon other criminals in the same jurisdiction"—Justice Powell concluded that the sentence imposed on Rummel was inconsistent with Texas's treatment of much more serious offenders and well out of line in light of habitual offender statutes on the books in other jurisdictions. He added: "The jurisdictions that currently employ habitual offender statutes either (i) require the commission of more than three offenses, (ii) require the commission of at least one violent crime, (iii) limit a mandatory penalty to less than life, or (iv) grant discretion to the sentencing authority. In none of the jurisdictions could the petitioner have received a mandatory life sentence merely upon the showing that he committed three nonviolent property-related offenses."

IN RE GAULT

Supreme Court of the United States, 1967
387 U.S. 1, 87 S.Ct. 1428, 18 L.Ed.2d 527

Gerald Gault, fifteen years old, and a friend were arrested by police on the complaint of a neighbor, Mrs. Cook, that they made lewd remarks to her over the phone. Gault's parents were not notified by the police of the arrest; they later learned of their son's predicament secondhand. Nor did the Gaults receive a copy of a petition filed by the police for a court hearing. Their son was not advised of his right to remain silent and to be represented by counsel. In addition, Mrs. Cook did not appear at any time in court as a witness, nor was there any record made of the proceedings. The judge subsequently declared Gault to be a juvenile delinquent and committed him to a state industrial school for a maximum of six years (i.e., until he reached twenty-one years of age). Since Arizona law precluded appeal in juvenile cases, the Gaults filed a petition in a state court for a writ of habeas corpus. They challenged the constitutionality of Arizona's Juvenile Code on the grounds it permitted juvenile court proceedings which lacked numerous procedural guarantees provided under the Fourteenth Amendment in adult criminal trials. A state superior court dismissed the writ, and the Arizona Supreme Court affirmed, whereupon the Gaults appealed to the U. S. Supreme Court.

Mr. Justice FORTAS delivered the opinion of the court.

* * *

[A]ppellants * * * urge that we hold the Juvenile Code of Arizona invalid on its face or as applied in this case because, contrary to the Due Process Clause of the Fourteenth Amendment, the juvenile is taken from the custody of his parents and committed to a state institution pursuant to proceedings in which the Juvenile Court has virtually unlimited discretion, and in which the following basic rights are denied:

1. Notice of the charges;

2. Right to counsel;

3. Right to confrontation and cross examination;

4. Privilege against self-incrimination;

5. Right to a transcript of the proceedings; and

6. Right to appellate review.

* * *

* * * As to these proceedings, there appears to be little current dissent from the proposition that the Due Process Clause has a role to play. The problem is to ascertain the precise impact of the due process requirement upon such proceedings.

From the inception of the juvenile court system, wide differences have been tolerated—indeed insisted upon—between the procedural rights accorded to adults and those of juveniles. In practically all jurisdictions, there are rights granted to adults which are withheld from juveniles. In addition to the specific problems involved in the present case, for example, it has been held that the juvenile is not entitled to bail, to indictment by grand jury, to a public trial or to trial by jury. It is frequent practice that rules governing the arrest and interrogation of adults by the police are not observed in the case of juveniles.

The history and theory underlying this development are well-known, but a recapitulation is necessary for purposes of this opinion. The Juvenile Court movement began in this country at the end of the last century. From the juvenile court statute adopted in Illinois in 1899, the system has spread to every State in the Union, the District of Columbia, and Puerto Rico. The constitutionality of juvenile court laws has been sustained in over 40 jurisdictions against a variety of attacks.

The early reformers were appalled by adult procedures and penalties, and by the fact that children could be given long prison sentences and mixed in jails with hardened criminals. They were profoundly convinced that society's duty to the child could not be confined by the concept of justice alone. They believed that society's role was not to ascertain whether the child was "guilty" or "innocent," but "What is he, how has he become what he is, and what had best be done in his interest and in the interest of the state to save him from a downward career." The child—essentially good, as they saw it—was to be made "to feel that he is the object of [the state's] care and solicitude," not that he was under arrest or on trial. The rules of criminal procedure were therefore altogether inapplicable. The apparent rigidities, technicalities, and harshness which they observed in both substantive and procedural criminal law were therefore to be discarded. The idea of crime and punishment was to be abandoned. The child was to be "treated" and "rehabilitated" and the procedures, from apprehension through institutionalization, were to be "clinical" rather than punitive.

These results were to be achieved, without coming to conceptual and constitutional grief, by insisting that the proceedings were not adversary, but that the state was proceeding as *parens patriae*. The Latin phrase proved to be a great help to those who sought to rationalize the exclusion of juveniles from the constitutional scheme; but its meaning is murky and its historic credentials are of dubious relevance. The phrase was taken from chancery practice, where, however, it was used to describe the power of the state to act *in loco parentis* for the purpose of protecting the property interests and the person of the child. But there is no trace of the doctrine in the history of criminal jurisprudence. At common law, children under seven were considered incapable of possessing criminal intent. Beyond that age, they were subjected to arrest, trial, and in theory to punishment like adult offenders. In these old days, the state was not deemed to have authority to accord them fewer procedural rights than adults.

The right of the state, as *parens patriae*, to deny to the child procedural rights available to his elders was elaborated by the assertion that a child, unlike an adult, has a right "not to liberty but to custody." He can be made to attorn to his parents, to go to school, etc. If his parents default in effectively performing their custodial functions—that is, if the child is "delinquent"—the state

may intervene. In doing so, it does not deprive the child of any rights, because he has none. It merely provides the "custody" to which the child is entitled. On this basis, proceedings involving juveniles were described as "civil" not "criminal" and therefore not subject to the requirements which restrict the state when it seeks to deprive a person of his liberty.

Accordingly, the highest motives and most enlightened impulses led to a peculiar system for juveniles, unknown to our law in any comparable context. The constitutional and theoretical basis for this peculiar system is—to say the least—debatable. And in practice * * * the results have not been entirely satisfactory. Juvenile Court history has again demonstrated that unbridled discretion, however benevolently motivated, is frequently a poor substitute for principle and procedure. In 1937, Dean Pound wrote: "The powers of the Star Chamber were a trifle in comparison with those of our juvenile courts." * * * The absence of substantive standards has not necessarily meant that children receive careful, compassionate, individualized treatment. The absence of procedural rules based upon constitutional principle has not always produced fair, efficient, and effective procedures. Departures from established principles of due process have frequently resulted not in enlightened procedure, but in arbitrariness. The Chairman of the Pennsylvania Council of Juvenile Court Judges has recently observed: "Unfortunately, loose procedures, high-handed methods and crowded court calendars, either singly or in combination, all too often, have resulted in depriving some juveniles of fundamental rights that have resulted in a denial of due process."

* * *

It is claimed that juveniles obtain benefits from the special procedures applicable to them which more than offset the disadvantages of denial of the substance of normal due process. As we shall discuss, the observance of due process standards, intelligently and not ruthlessly administered, will not compel the States to abandon or displace any of the substantive benefits of the juvenile process. But it is important, we think, that the claimed benefits of the juvenile process should be candidly appraised. Neither sentiment nor folklore should cause us to shut our eyes, for example, to such startling findings as that reported in an exceptionally reliable study of repeaters or recidivism conducted by the Stanford Research Institute for the President's Commission on Crime in the District of Columbia. This Commission's Report states:

"In fiscal 1966 approximately 66 percent of the 16- and 17-year-old juveniles referred to the court by the Youth Aid Division had been before the court previously. In 1965, 56 percent of those in the Receiving Home were repeaters. The SRI study revealed that 61 percent of the sample Juvenile Court referrals in 1965 had been previously referred at least once and that 42 percent had been referred at least twice before."

* * *

Certainly, these figures and the high crime rates among juveniles to which we have referred * * * could not lead us to conclude that the absence of constitutional protections reduces crime, or that the juvenile system, functioning free of constitutional inhibitions as it has largely done, is ef-

fective to reduce crime or rehabilitate offenders. We do not mean by this to denigrate the juvenile court process or to suggest that there are not aspects of the juvenile system relating to offenders which are valuable. But the features of the juvenile system which its proponents have asserted are of unique benefit will not be impaired by constitutional domestication. For example, the commendable principles relating to the processing and treatment of juveniles separately from adults are in no way involved or affected by the procedural issues under discussion. Further, we are told that one of the important benefits of the special juvenile court procedures is that they avoid classifying the juvenile as a "criminal." The juvenile offender is now classed as a "delinquent." There is, of course, no reason why this should not continue. It is disconcerting, however, that this term has come to involve only slightly less stigma than the term "criminal" applied to adults. It is also emphasized that in practically all jurisdictions, statutes provide that an adjudication of the child as a delinquent shall not operate as a civil disability or disqualify him for civil service appointment. There is no reason why the application of due process requirements should interfere with such provisions.

* * *

Further, it is urged that the juvenile benefits from informal proceedings in the court. The early conception of the Juvenile Court proceeding was one in which a fatherly judge touched the heart and conscience of the erring youth by talking over his problems, by paternal advice and admonition, and in which, in extreme situations, benevolent and wise institutions of the State provided guidance and help "to save him from a downward career." Then, as now, goodwill and compassion were admirably prevalent. But recent studies have, with surprising unanimity, entered sharp dissent as to the validity of this gentle conception. They suggest that the appearance as well as the actuality of fairness, impartiality and orderliness—in short, the essentials of due process—may be a more impressive and more therapeutic attitude so far as the juvenile is concerned. * * *

Ultimately, however, we confront the reality of that portion of the Juvenile Court process with which we deal in this case. A boy is charged with misconduct. The boy is committed to an institution where he may be restrained of liberty for years. It is of no constitutional consequence—and of limited practical meaning—that the institution to which he is committed is called an Industrial School. The fact of the matter is that, however euphemistic the title, a "receiving home" or an "industrial school" for juveniles is an institution of confinement in which the child is incarcerated for a greater or lesser time. His world becomes "a building with whitewashed walls, regimented routine and institutional hours." * * * Instead of mother and father and sisters and brothers and friends and classmates, his world is peopled by guards, custodians, state employees, and "delinquents" confined with him for anything from waywardness to rape and homicide.

In view of this, it would be extraordinary if our Constitution did not require the procedural regularity and the exercise of care implied in the phrase "due process." Under our Constitution, the condition of being a boy does not justify a kangaroo court. The traditional ideas of Juvenile Court procedure, indeed, contemplated that time would be available and care would be used to establish precisely what the juvenile did and why he did it—was it a prank of adolescence or a brutal act threatening serious consequences to himself or society unless corrected? Under traditional notions, one would assume that in a case like that of Gerald Gault, * * * the Juvenile Judge would have made a careful inquiry and judgment as to the possibility that the boy could be disciplined and dealt with at home, despite his previous transgressions. Indeed, so far as appears in the record before us, * * * the points to which the judge directed his attention were little different from those that would be involved in determining any charge of violation of a penal statute. The essential difference between Gerald's case and a normal criminal case is that safeguards available to adults were discarded in Gerald's case. The summary procedure as well as the long commitment was possible because Gerald was 15 years of age instead of over 18.

* * *

[The Court went on to hold that with respect to juvenile proceedings: (1) due process requires adequate and timely notice; (2) there is right to counsel; (3) the privilege against self-incrimination is applicable; and (4) "absent a valid confession, a determination of delinquency and an order to a state institution cannot be sustained in the absence of sworn testimony subjected to the opportunity for cross-examination." It explicitly did not rule on the failure to provide a transcript or on the right to appellate review.]

Judgment reversed and cause remanded with directions.

Mr. Justice HARLAN, concurring in part and dissenting in part.

* * *

I must first acknowledge that I am unable to determine with any certainty by what standards the Court decides that Arizona's juvenile courts do not satisfy the obligations of due process. The Court's premise, itself the product of reasoning which is not described, is that the "constitutional and theoretical basis" of state systems of juvenile and family courts is "debatable"; it buttresses these doubts by marshaling a body of opinion which suggests that the accomplishments of these courts have often fallen short of expectations. * * * Its failure to provide any discernible standard for the measurement of due process in relation to juvenile proceedings unfortunately might be understood to mean that the Court is concerned principally with the wisdom of having such courts at all.

If this is the source of the Court's dissatisfaction, I cannot share it. I should have supposed that the constitutionality of juvenile courts was beyond proper question under the standards now employed to assess the substantive validity of state legislation under the Due Process Clause of the Fourteenth Amendment. It can scarcely be doubted that it is within the State's competence to adopt measures reasonably calculated to meet more effectively the persistent problems of juvenile delinquency. * * *

The proper issue here is, however, not whether the State may constitutionally treat juvenile offenders through a system of specialized courts, but whether the proceedings in Arizona's juvenile courts include procedural guarantees which satisfy the requirements of the Fourteenth Amendment. Among the first premises of our constitutional system is the obligation to conduct any proceeding in which an individual may be deprived of liberty or property in a fashion consistent with the "traditions and conscience of our people."
* * *

* * *

Measured by these criteria, only three procedural requirements should, in my opinion, now be deemed required of state juvenile courts by the Due Process Clause of the Fourteenth Amendment: first, timely notice must be provided to parents and children of the nature and terms of any juvenile court proceeding in which a determination affecting their rights or interests may be made; second, unequivocal and timely notice must be given that counsel may appear in any such proceeding in behalf of the child and its parents, and that in cases in which the child may be confined in an institution, counsel may, in circumstances of indigency, be appointed for them; and third, the court must maintain a written record, or its equivalent, adequate to permit effective review on appeal or in collateral proceedings. These requirements would guarantee to juveniles the tools with which their rights could be fully vindicated, and yet permit the States to pursue without unnecessary hindrance the purposes which they believe imperative in this field. Further, their imposition now would later permit more intelligent assessment of the necessity under the Fourteenth Amendment of additional requirements, by creating suitable records from which the character and deficiencies of juvenile proceedings could be accurately judged. * * *

* * *

Finally, I turn to assess the validity of this juvenile court proceeding under the criteria discussed in this opinion. Measured by them, the judgment below must, in my opinion, fall. Gerald Gault and his parents were not provided adequate notice of the terms and purposes of the proceedings in which he was adjudged delinquent; they were not advised of their rights to be represented by counsel; and no record in any form was maintained of the proceedings. It follows, for the reasons given in this opinion, that Gerald Gault was deprived of his liberty without due process of law, and I therefore concur in the judgment of the Court.

Mr. Justice STEWART, dissenting.

The Court today uses an obscure Arizona case as a vehicle to impose upon thousands of juvenile courts throughout the Nation restrictions that the Constitution made applicable to adversary criminal trials. I believe the Court's decision is wholly unsound as a matter of constitutional law, and sadly unwise as a matter of judicial policy.

Juvenile proceedings are not criminal trials. They are not civil trials. They are simply not adversary proceedings. Whether treating with a delinquent child, a neglected child, a defective child, or a dependent child, a juvenile proceeding's whole purpose and mission is the very opposite of the mission and purpose of a prosecution in a criminal court. The object of the one is correction of a condition. The object of the other is conviction and punishment for a criminal act.

* * *

I possess neither the specialized experience nor the expert knowledge to predict with any certainty where may lie the brightest hope for progress in dealing with the serious problems of juvenile delinquency. But I am certain that the answer does not lie in the Court's opinion in this case, which serves to convert a juvenile proceeding into a criminal prosecution.

The inflexible restrictions that the Constitution so wisely made applicable to adversary criminal trials have no inevitable place in the proceedings of those public social agencies known as juvenile or family courts. And to impose the Court's long catalog of requirements upon juvenile proceedings in every area of the country is to invite a long step backwards into the nineteenth century. * * *

* * *

I would dismiss the appeal.

OTHER RULINGS ON THE CONSTITUTIONAL RIGHTS OF DEFENDANTS IN JUVENILE COURT

Case	Holding	Vote
In re Winship, 397 U.S. 358, 90 S.Ct. 1068 (1970)	"[P]roof beyond reasonable doubt [as opposed to proof by a preponderance of the evidence] is among the 'essentials of due process and fair treatment' required during the adjudica-	6–3; Burger and Black and Stewart dissented

RIGHTS IN JUVENILE COURT (*Cont.*)

Case	Holding	Vote
In re Winship (*Cont.*)	tory stage when a juvenile is charged with an act which would constitute a crime if committed by an adult."	
McKeiver v. Pennsylvania, 403 U.S. 528, 91 S.Ct. 1976 (1971)	"[T]rial by jury in the juvenile court's adjudicative stage is not a constitutional requirement."	6–3; Black, Douglas, and Marshall dissented
Breed v. Jones, 421 U.S. 519, 95 S.Ct. 1779 (1975)	Jeopardy attaches at an adjudicatory hearing in juvenile court when the judge as trier of the facts begins to hear evidence, and retrial of defendant in adult trial court for same offense as he had been tried in juvenile court violates guarantee against double jeopardy notwithstanding fact that the defendant faced only punishment imposed by the adult trial court	9–0
Fare v. Michael C., 442 U.S. 707, 99 S.Ct. 2560 (1979)	The court below erred in ruling that a juvenile's request to have his probation officer present at custodial interrogation, like "an accused's request for an attorney is *per se* an invocation of his Fifth Amendment rights, requiring that all interrogation cease." "[W]hether the statements obtained during the subsequent interrogation of a juvenile who has asked to see his probation officer, but who has not asked to consult an attorney or expressly asserted his right to remain silent, are admissible on the basis of waiver remains a question to be resolved on the totality of the circumstances surrounding the interrogation"	5–4; Brennan, Marshall, Powell, and Stevens dissented

In Ingraham v. Wright, 430 U.S. 651, 97 S.Ct. 1401 (1977), the Supreme Court addressed two "questions concerning the use of corporal punishment in public schools: first, whether the paddling of students as a means of maintaining school discipline constitutes cruel and unusual punishment in violation of the Eighth Amendment; and second, to the extent that paddling is constitutionally permissible, whether the Due Process Clause of the Fourteenth Amendment requires prior notice and an opportunity to be heard." Speaking for the Court, Justice Powell observed that twenty-three states have addressed the problem through legislation, twenty-one of which "authorized the moderate use of corporal punishment in public schools," generally consistent with the traditional common-law principles that "teachers may impose reasonable but not excessive force to discipline a child," and two of which (Massachusetts and New Jersey) prohibit the use of corporal punishment. He concluded, with respect to the first question, that "[a]n examination of the history of the [Eighth] Amendment and the decisions of this Court construing the proscription against cruel and unusual punishment confirms that it was designed to protect those convicted of crimes [and] * * * does not apply to the paddling of children as a means of maintaining discipline in public schools." He elaborated:

> The schoolchild has little need for the protection of the Eighth Amendment. Though attendance may not always be voluntary, the public school remains an open institution. Except perhaps when very young, the child is not physically restrained from leaving school during school hours; and at the end of the school day, the child is invariably free to return home. Even while at school, the child brings with him the support of family and friends and is rarely apart from teachers and other pupils who may witness and protest any instances of mistreatment.

> The openness of the public school and its supervision by the community afford significant safeguards against the kinds of abuses from which the Eighth Amendment protects the prisoner. In virtually every community where corporal punishment is permitted in the schools, these safeguards are reinforced by the legal constraints of the common law. Public school teachers and administrators are privileged at common law to inflict only such corporal punishment as is reasonably necessary for the proper education and discipline of the child; any punishment going beyond the privilege may result in both civil and criminal liability.   *   *   *   As long as the schools are open to public scrutiny, there is no reason to believe that the common law constraints will not effectively remedy and deter excesses such as those alleged in this case.

In answer to the second question, the Court held that, while "corporal punishment in public schools implicates a constitutionally protected liberty interest,   *   *   * the traditional common law remedies are fully adequate to afford due process." Balancing the benefit of an additional safeguard to the individual against the social cost, Justice Powell explained:

> In view of the low incidence of abuse, the openness of our schools, and the common law safeguards that already exist, the risk of error that may result in violation of a schoolchild's substantive rights can only be regarded as minimal. Imposing additional administrative safeguards as a constitutional requirement might reduce that risk marginally, but would also entail a significant intrusion into an area of primary educational responsibility. We conclude that the Due Process Clause does not require notice and a hearing prior to the imposition of corporal punishment in the public schools, as that practice is authorized and limited by the common law.

In a pointed dissent, Justice White, joined by Justices Brennan, Marshall, and Stevens, took exception to the Court's holding "that corporal punishment in public schools, no matter how severe, can never be the subject of the protections afforded by the Eighth Amendment." He wrote:

> The Eighth Amendment places a flat prohibition against the infliction of "cruel and unusual punishments." This reflects a societal judgment that there are some punishments that are so barbaric and inhumane that we will not permit them to be imposed on anyone, no matter how opprobrious the offense.   *   *   *   If there are some punishments that are so barbaric that they may not be imposed for the commission of crimes, designated by our social system as the most thoroughly reprehensible acts an individual can commit, then *a fortiori*, similar punishments may not be imposed on per-

sons for less culpable acts, such as breaches of school discipline. Thus, if it is constitutionally impermissible to cut off someone's ear for the commission of murder, it must be unconstitutional to cut off a child's ear for being late to class. Although there were no ears cut off in this case, the record reveals beatings so severe that if they were inflicted on a hardened criminal for the commission of a serious crime, they might not pass constitutional muster.

Absent an express limitation in the text of the Eighth Amendment, the dissent emphatically rejected the proposition that the ban on cruel and unusual punishments applied only to protect individuals convicted of crimes. Added Justice White, "No one can deny that spanking of school children is 'punishment' under any reasonable reading of the word, for the similarities between spanking in public schools and other forms of punishment are too obvious to ignore."

O'CONNOR v. DONALDSON

Supreme Court of the United States, 1975
422 U.S. 563, 95 S.Ct. 2486, 45 L.Ed.2d 396

For nearly fifteen years, following the initiation of commitment proceedings against him by his father who said he suffered from delusions, Kenneth Donaldson was confined as a mental patient in the Florida State Hospital. Despite Donaldson's repeated requests to be released and interventions on his behalf by responsible people outside the hospital who were prepared to look after him, hospital officials refused to release him. Donaldson finally brought suit against O'Connor, the hospital superintendent, and others on the staff alleging an intentional deprivation of his liberty and seeking damages. Donaldson contended that he was dangerous neither to himself nor others and that, if he were sick, the hospital was not providing any treatment. O'Connor, as a defense, asserted that he had acted in good faith, that Florida law authorized custodial confinement of individuals who were "sick" even if they were not receiving treatment and lacking evidence that such individuals were harmful, and that, therefore, he was immune from liability. A jury in federal court found in Donaldson's favor and awarded him both compensatory and punitive damages. A federal appeals court affirmed, resting its decision on broad Fourteenth Amendment grounds, and the Supreme Court granted certiorari.

Mr. Justice STEWART delivered the opinion of the Court.

* * *

The Court of Appeals affirmed the judgment of the District Court in a broad opinion dealing with "the far-reaching question whether the Fourteenth Amendment guarantees a right to treatment to persons involuntarily civilly committed to state mental hospitals." 493 F.2d, at 509. The appellate court held that when, as in Donaldson's case, the rationale for confinement is that the patient is in need of treatment, the Constitution requires that minimally adequate treatment in fact be provided. * * * The court further expressed the view that, regardless of the grounds for involuntary civil commitment, a person confined against his will at a state mental institution has "a constitutional right to receive such individual treatment as will give him a reasonable opportunity to be cured or to improve his mental condition." * * * Conversely, the court's opinion implied that it is constitutionally permissible for a State to confine a mentally ill person against his will in order to treat his illness, regardless of whether his illness renders him dangerous to himself or others. * * *

We have concluded that the difficult issues of constitutional law dealt with by the Court of Appeals are not presented by this case in its present posture. Specifically, there is no reason now to decide whether mentally ill persons dangerous to themselves or to others have a right to treatment upon compulsory confinement by the State, or whether the State may compulsorily confine a nondangerous, mentally ill individual for the purpose of treatment. As we view it, this case raises a single, relatively simple, but nonetheless important question concerning every man's constitutional right to liberty.

The jury found that Donaldson was neither dangerous to himself nor dangerous to others, and also found that, if mentally ill, Donaldson had not received treatment. That verdict, based on abundant evidence, makes the issue before the Court a narrow one. We need not decide whether, when, or by what procedures, a mentally ill person may be confined by the State on any of the grounds which, under contemporary statutes, are generally advanced to justify involuntary confinement of such a person—to prevent injury to the public, to ensure his own survival or safety, or to alleviate or cure his illness. See Jackson v. Indiana, 406 U.S. 715, 736–737, 92 S.Ct. 1845, 1857–1858; Humphrey v. Cady, 405 U.S. 504, 509, 92 S.Ct. 1048, 1052. For the jury found that none of the above grounds for continued confinement was present in Donaldson's case.

Given the jury's findings, what was left as justification for keeping Donaldson in continued confinement? The fact that state law may have authorized confinement of the harmless mentally ill does not itself establish a constitutionally adequate purpose for the confinement. * * * Nor is it enough that Donaldson's original confinement was founded upon a constitutionally adequate basis, if in fact it was, because even if his involuntary confinement was initially permissible, it could not constitutionally continue after that basis no longer existed. * * *

A finding of "mental illness" alone cannot justify a State's locking a person up against his will and keeping him indefinitely in simple custodial confinement. Assuming that that term can be given a reasonably precise content and that the "mentally ill" can be identified with reasonable accuracy, there is still no constitutional basis for confining such persons involuntarily if they are dangerous to no one and can live safely in freedom.

May the State confine the mentally ill merely to ensure them a living standard superior to that they enjoy in the private community? That the State has a proper interest in providing care and assistance to the unfortunate goes without saying. But the mere presence of mental illness does not disqualify a person from preferring his home to the comforts of an institution. Moreover, while the State may arguably confine a person to save him from harm, incarceration is rarely if ever a necessary condition for raising the living standards of those capable of surviving safely in freedom, on their own or with the help of family or friends. * * *

May the State fence in the harmless mentally ill solely to save its citizens from exposure to those whose ways are different? One might as well ask if the State, to avoid public unease, could incarcerate all who are physically unattractive or socially eccentric. Mere public intolerance or animosity cannot constitutionally justify the deprivation of a person's physical liberty. * * *

In short, a State cannot constitutionally confine without more a nondangerous individual who is capable of surviving safely in freedom by himself or with the help of willing and responsible family members or friends. Since the jury found, upon ample evidence, that O'Connor, as an agent of the State, knowingly did so confine Donaldson, it properly concluded that O'Connor violated Donaldson's constitutional right to freedom.

O'Connor contends that in any event he should not be held personally liable for monetary damages because his decisions were made in "good faith." Specifically, O'Connor argues that he was acting pursuant to state law which, he believed authorized confinement of the mentally ill even when their release would not compromise their safety or constitute a danger to others, and that he could not reasonably have been expected to know that the state law as he understood it was constitutionally invalid. A proposed instruction to this effect was rejected by the District Court.

The District Court did instruct the jury, without objection, that monetary damages could not be assessed against O'Connor if he had believed reasonably and in good faith that Donaldson's continued confinement was "proper," and that punitive damages could be awarded only if O'Connor had acted "maliciously or wantonly or oppressively." The Court of Appeals approved those instructions. But that court did not consider whether it was error for the trial judge to refuse the additional instruction concerning O'Connor's claimed reliance on state law as authorization for Donaldson's continued confinement. Further, neither the District Court nor the Court of Appeals acted with the benefit of this Court's most recent decision on the scope of the qualified immunity possessed by state officials under 42 U.S.C.A. § 1983. Wood v. Strickland, 420 U.S. 308, 95 S.Ct. 992.

Under that decision, the relevant question for the jury is whether O'Connor "knew or reasonably should have known that the action he took within his sphere of official responsibility would violate the constitutional rights of [Donaldson], or if he took the action with the malicious intention to cause a deprivation of constitutional rights or other injury to [Donaldson]." Id., 420 U.S. 322, 95 S.Ct. 1001. See also Scheuer v. Rhodes, 416 U.S. 232, 247–248, 94 S.Ct. 1683, 1692; Wood v. Strickland, supra, 420 U.S. at 330, 95 S.Ct. at 1005 (opinion of POWELL, J.). For purposes of this question, an official has, of course, no duty to anticipate unforeseeable constitutional developments. * * *

Accordingly, we vacate the judgment of the Court of Appeals and remand the case to enable that court to consider, in light of *Wood* v. *Strickland*, whether the District Judge's failure to instruct with regard to the effect of O'Connor's claimed reliance on state law rendered inadequate the instructions as to O'Connor's liability for compensatory and punitive damages.

It is so ordered.

Mr. Chief Justice BURGER, concurring.

Although I join the Court's opinion and judgment in this case, it seems to me that several factors merit more emphasis than it gives them. I therefore add the following remarks.

With respect to the remand to the Court of Appeals on the issue of official immunity, it seems to me not entirely irrelevant that there was substantial evidence that Donaldson consistently refused treatment that was offered to him, claiming that he was not mentally ill and needed no treatment. The Court appropriately takes notice of the uncertainties of psychiatric diagnosis and therapy, and the reported cases are replete with evidence of the divergence of medical opinion in this vexing area. * * * Nonetheless, one of the few areas of agreement among behavioral specialists is that an uncooperative patient cannot benefit from therapy and that the first step in effective treatment is acknowledgement by the patient that he is suffering from an abnormal condition. * * * Donaldson's adamant refusal to do so should be taken into account in considering petitioner's good-faith defense.

Perhaps more important to the issue of immunity is a factor referred to only obliquely in the Court's opinion. On numerous occasions during the period of his confinement Donaldson unsuccessfully sought release in the Florida courts; indeed, the last of these proceedings was terminated only a few months prior to the bringing of this action. * * * Whatever the reasons for the state courts'

repeated denials of relief, and regardless of whether they correctly resolved the issue tendered to them, petitioner and the other members of the medical staff at Florida State Hospital would surely have been justified in considering each such judicial decision as an approval of continued confinement and an independent intervening reason for continuing Donaldson's confinement. Thus, this fact is inescapably related to the issue of immunity and must be considered by the Court of Appeals on remand and, if a new trial is ordered, by the District Court.

* * *

[T]he idea that States may not confine the mentally ill except for the purpose of providing them with treatment is of very recent origin, and there is no historical basis for imposing such a limitation on state power. Analysis of the sources of the civil commitment power likewise lends no support to that notion. There can be little doubt that in the exercise of its police power a State may confine individuals solely to protect society from the dangers of significant antisocial acts or communicable disease. * * * Additionally, the States are vested with the historic *parens patriae* power, including the duty to protect "persons under legal disabilities to act for themselves." * * * The classic example of this role is when a State undertakes to act as " 'the general guardian of all infants, idiots, and lunatics.' " * * *

Of course, an inevitable consequence of exercising the *parens patriae* power is that the ward's personal freedom will be substantially restrained, whether a guardian is appointed to control his property, he is placed in the custody of a private third party, or committed to an institution. Thus, however the power is implemented, due process requires that it not be invoked indiscriminately. At a minimum, a particular scheme for protection of the mentally ill must rest upon a legislative determination that it is compatible with the best interests of the affected class and that its members are unable to act for themselves. * * *

However, the existence of some due process limitations on the *parens patriae* power does not justify the further conclusion that it may be exercised to confine a mentally ill person only if the purpose of the confinement is treatment. Despite many recent advances in medical knowledge, it remains a stubborn fact that there are many forms of mental illness which are not understood, some which are untreatable in the sense that no effective therapy has yet been discovered for them, and that rates of "cure" are generally low. * * *

Alternatively, it has been argued that a Fourteenth Amendment right to treatment for involuntarily confined mental patients derives from the fact that many of the safeguards of the criminal process are not present in civil commitment. The Court of Appeals described this theory as follows:

"[A] due process right to treatment is based on the principle that when the three central limitations on the government's power to detain— that detention be in retribution for a specific offense; that it be limited to a fixed term; and that it be permitted after a proceeding where the fundamental procedural safeguards are observed—are absent, there must be a *quid pro quo* extended by the gov-

ernment to justify confinement. And the *quid pro quo* most commonly recognized is the provision of rehabilitative treatment." 493 F.2d, at 522.

To the extent that this theory may be read to permit a State to confine an individual simply because it is willing to provide treatment, regardless of the subject's ability to function in society, it raises the gravest of constitutional problems, and I have no doubt the Court of Appeals would agree on this score. As a justification for a constitutional right to such treatment, the *quid pro quo* theory suffers from equally serious defects.

* * *

The *quid pro quo* theory is a sharp departure from, and cannot coexist with, * * * due process principles. As an initial matter, the theory presupposes that essentially the same interests are involved in every situation where a State seeks to confine an individual; that assumption, however, is incorrect. It is elementary that the justification for the criminal process and the unique deprivation of liberty which it can impose requires that it be invoked only for commission of a specific offense prohibited by legislative enactment. * * * But it would be incongruous to apply the same limitation when quarantine is imposed by the State to protect the public from a highly communicable disease. * * *

A more troublesome feature of the *quid pro quo* theory is that it elevates a concern for essentially procedural safeguards into a new substantive constitutional right. Rather than inquiring whether strict standards of proof or periodic redetermination of a patient's condition are required in civil confinement, the theory accepts the absence of such safeguards but insists that the State provide benefits which, in the view of a court, are adequate "compensation" for confinement. In light of the wide divergence of medical opinion regarding the diagnosis of and proper therapy for mental abnormalities, that prospect is especially troubling in this area and cannot be squared with the principle that "courts may not substitute for the judgments of legislators their own understanding of the public welfare, but must instead concern themselves with the validity of the methods which the legislature has selected." In re Gault, 387 U.S., at 71, 87 S.Ct., at 1466 (opinion of Harlan, J.). Of course, questions regarding the adequacy of procedure and the power of a State to continue particular confinements are ultimately for the courts, aided by expert opinion to the extent that is found helpful. But I am not persuaded that we should abandon the traditional limitations on the scope of judicial review.

In sum, I cannot accept the reasoning of the Court of Appeals and can discern no other basis for equating an involuntarily committed mental patient's unquestioned constitutional right not to be confined without due process of law with a constitutional right to *treatment*. Given the present state of medical knowledge regarding abnormal human behavior and its treatment, few things would be more fraught with peril than to irrevocably condition a State's power to protect the mentally ill upon the providing of "such treatment as will give [them] a realistic opportunity to be cured." Nor can I accept the theory that a State may lawfully confine an individual thought to need treatment and justify that deprivation of liberty solely by providing some treatment. Our concepts of due process would not tolerate such a "trade-off." Because the Court of Appeals' analysis could be read as authorizing those results, it should not be followed.

RIGHTS IN THE
REHABILITATION PROCESS—OTHER
RECENT CASES

Case	Ruling
Addington v. Texas, 441 U.S. 418, 99 S.Ct. 1804 (1979)	Due process requires that the standard employed in civil commitment proceedings be greater than the "preponderance of the evidence" standard used to decide other kinds of civil cases, but the fact-finder need not be required to meet the much more rigorous standard of finding proof "beyond a reasonable doubt." Rather, "a middle level burden of proof that strikes a fair balance between the rights of the individual and the legitimate concerns of the state" is reflected in a standard that would have the fact-finder in civil commitment proceedings see "clear and convincing evidence" to warrant hospitalization.

RIGHTS IN REHABILITATION PROCESS (*Cont.*)

Case	Ruling
Parham v. J. R., 442 U.S. 584, 99 S.Ct. 2493 (1979)	"[T]he risk of error inherent in the parental decision to have a child institutionalized for mental health is sufficiently great that some kind of inquiry should be made by a 'neutral factfinder' [not necessarily law-trained; could be medically trained or a lay fact-finder] to determine whether the statutory requirements for admission are satisfied. * * * That inquiry must carefully probe the child's background using all available sources, including, but not limited to, parents, schools and other social agencies. Of course, the review must include an interview with the child. It is necessary that the decision-maker have the authority to refuse to admit any child who does not satisfy the medical standards for admission. Finally, it is necessary that the child's continuing need for commitment be reviewed periodically by a similarly independent procedure."
Vitek v. Jones, 445 U.S. 480, 100 S.Ct. 1254 (1980)	An inmate at a state prison may not be transferred to a mental institution for treatment merely because a physician or psychologist has determined that he is suffering from mental disease or defect. Involuntary transfer of a prisoner to a mental hospital may constitutionally be undertaken only after the following minimum procedures have been observed: written notice to the inmate that transfer to a mental hospital is being considered; a hearing, with time for the prisoner to prepare, at which evidence relied upon for the transfer is disclosed to the inmate and on which occasion he is given an opportunity to be heard in person and to present evidence; opportunity at the hearing to call witnesses on his behalf and to cross-examine witnesses for the other side; an independent decision-maker; a written statement by the factfinder indicating the evidence he relied upon and giving reasons for his decision; availability of independent and qualified assistance to help the inmate present his side of the story, but this advisor need not be a licensed attorney; and effective and timely notice of these rights.
Pennhurst State School & Hospital v. Halderman, 451 U.S. 1, 101 S.Ct. 1531 (1981)	See p. 172.

Nicholas Romeo, a thirty-three-year-old, severely retarded person with an I.Q. of between 8 and 10 and the mental capacity of a one-and-a-half-year-old child, was involuntarily committed to a state mental institution. As the Supreme Court noted, "He cannot talk and lacks the most basic self-care skills." When she became concerned about injuries he received, his mother brought suit on his behalf under 42 U.S.C.A. § 1983 against officials of the institution, arguing that he had rights to safe confinement, freedom from physical restraint, and training or "habilitation." Moreover, she contended, Youngberg and the other officials knew, or should have known, about his injuries and failed to take proper preventive measures, thus violating his Eighth and Fourteenth Amendment rights. At trial, the federal district judge instructed the jury using an Eighth Amendment cruel-and-unusual-punishment standard, and the jury found for the defendant institution officials. A federal appeals court subsequently reversed and remanded the case on grounds that the Fourteenth Amendment, rather than the Eighth, was the proper locus of the plaintiff's rights, and the institution officials then sought review by the Supreme Court.

In its disposition of this case, Youngberg v. Romeo, —— U.S. ——, 102 S.Ct. 2452 (1982), the Supreme Court "consider[ed] * * * for the first time the substantive rights of involuntarily-committed mentally retarded persons under the Fourteenth Amendment * * *." Speaking for the Court, Justice Powell noted that "the state concedes that respondent has a right to adequate food, shelter, clothing, and medical care." The question before the Court, then, was "whether liberty interests also exist in safety, freedom of movement, and training." Observing that if prior Court decisions have held "that the right to personal security * * * is not extinguished by lawful confinement, even for penal purposes," Justice Powell concluded, "it must be unconstitutional to confine the involuntarily committed—who may not be punished at all—in unsafe conditions." Similarly, just as " '[l]iberty from bodily restraint always has been recognized as the core of the liberty protected by the Due Process Clause from arbitrary governmental action,' " and is an "interest [which] survives criminal conviction and incarceration, * * * it must also survive involuntary commitment."

Romeo's remaining claim as to "habilitation," that is for treatment or "training and development of needed skills," the Court found "more troubling." Emphasizing at the outset: (1) that Romeo conceded no amount of habilitation would make possible his eventual release; (2) that, as a general rule, the states are under no constitutional obligations to offer services to those individuals within their jurisdiction and, when they do, they enjoy considerable discretion; and (3) that this case did not present the question whether the involuntarily committed have a right to habilitation even when such training would not lead to greater freedom, the Court narrowed its focus to the question whether Romeo was entitled to some minimal training related to bodily safety and a minimum of physical restraint. But it took care to point out that "[t]he question * * * is not simply whether a liberty interest has been infringed but whether the extent or nature of the restraint or lack of absolute safety is such as to violate due process." In other words, a court must weigh "the liberty interest of the individual against the legitimate interests of the State, including the fiscal and administrative burdens additional procedures would entail." The Court held that the Fourteenth Amendment requires that courts make certain that professional judgment was, in fact, exercised. Said Justice Powell:

> [W]e agree that respondent is entitled to minimally adequate training. In this case, the minimally adequate training required by the Constitution is such training as may be reasonable in light of respondent's liberty interests in safety and freedom from unreasonable restraints. In determining what is "reasonable"—in this and in any case presenting a claim for training by a state—we emphasize that courts must show deference to the judgment exercised by a qualified professional. By so limiting judicial review of challenges to conditions in state institutions, interference by the federal judiciary with the internal operations of these institutions should be minimized. Moreover, there certainly is no reason to think judges or juries are better qualified than appropriate professionals in making such decisions. * * * For these reasons, the decision, if made by a professional, is presumptively

valid; liability may be imposed only when the decision by the professional is such a substantial departure from accepted professional judgment, practice or standards as to demonstrate that the person responsible actually did not base the decision on such a judgment. In an action for damages against a professional in his individual capacity, however, the professional will not be liable if he was unable to satisfy his normal professional standards because of budgetary constraints; in such a situation, good-faith immunity would bar liability. * * *

Thus, in addition to the duties already conceded by the state and those recognized in addition by the Court, the state is also "under a duty to provide respondent with such training as an appropriate professional would consider reasonable to ensure his safety and to facilitate his ability to function free from bodily restraints," keeping in mind such things as the state's simultaneous "duty to provide reasonable safety for all residents and personnel within the institution" and the context of heightened demands and stresses resulting from overcrowding and understaffing.

In a concurring opinion in which he was joined by Justices Brennan and O'Connor, Justice Blackmun pointed up two questions which the Court did not address given the state of the record in the case at hand. The first of these was whether the state could order a mentally retarded person committed for "care *and* treatment" and then refuse him treatment. The second was whether the state could be compelled to furnish "training necessary to *preserve* those basic self-care skills he possessed when he first entered" the institution; that is, "such training as is reasonably necessary to prevent a person's pre-existing self-care skills from *deteriorating* because of his commitment." The concurring opinion implied an affirmative response to both these questions, at least as a matter of general constitutional doctrine.

Chief Justice Burger, writing alone and concurring in the judgment, "would [have held] flatly that respondent has no constitutional right to training, or 'habilitation,' *per se*." The Chief Justice's opinion implied that, at least in the context of the procedures employed in the present case and in light of Romeo's very limited capacity and the circumstances of his confinement, it was a frivolous issue.

Chapter 11

Obtaining Evidence

The Fourth Amendment provides, "The right of the people to be secure in their persons, houses, papers, and effects, against unreasonable searches and seizures, shall not be violated * * *." In other words, the amendment establishes at the outset that people cannot claim immunity from all searches and seizures, but only those falling short of a standard of reasonableness. Even so staunch an absolutist as Justice Black readily conceded that the constitutional sanction given judicial discretion under this amendment permitted latitude which the First Amendment, for example, did not. Such wording invites the Court to strike a balance between the principal competing values of the criminal justice process: on the one hand, the need we have for the kind of thorough and efficient law enforcement which affords all of us safety and, on the other hand, the future need each of us has in wanting to assure that individual rights will be respected when we are suspected or accused of committing a crime. Friction results because frequently methods which the police find most efficient or convenient are of a kind which transgress standards predicated on respect for the worth of the individual's privacy. As the crime rate mounts and as legal standards, by which police conduct is assessed, become more stringent, concern for a balance between these values heightens.

Many of the more stringent controls which were applied to bridle police conduct were the product of the Warren Court's interpretation of Fourth, Fifth, and Sixth Amendment guarantees. It was not surprising that by the late 1960s some critics came to assail the Court for decisions which "handcuffed the police" by "making crime easy and convictions hard." One of these was Richard Nixon who, ironically assuming the role of a "law and order" candidate said, "As a judicial conservative, I believe some Court decisions have gone too far in weakening the peace forces as against the criminal forces in our society." Having won the 1968 election, he succeeded, although with some difficulty, in redeeming his pledge "to

1073

nominate to the Supreme Court individuals who share my judicial philosophy which is basically a conservative philosophy." His subsequent legacy, the Burger Court, reflected a balance of interests in this policy area, among others, different from that of the Warren Court. As a result of this significant change in the Court's composition, you will not only want to examine the materials which follow for the ways in which they amplify the meaning of the Fourth Amendment's ambiguous provisions, you will also want to keep an eye out for the subtle and sometimes not-so-subtle changes in interpretation of such ambiguous provisions which are the product of the Court's changing orientation.

a. The Exclusionary Rule

Our first task is to understand the parameters of the Fourth Amendment's general command that evidence be obtained in reasonable fashion and its more specific requirement that warrants not issue unless probable cause has been established. Clearly, the very ratification of the amendment made such limitations operative against the national government. It is a comparatively recent development, though, that constitutional standards contained in the amendment were deemed equally applicable to the states. Indeed, the Fourth Amendment was not incorporated into the Due Process Clause of the Fourteenth until the Court's decision in Wolf v. Colorado, 338 U.S. 25, 69 S.Ct. 1359 (1949). However, this was little more than the incorporation of rhetoric since the amendment itself contains no mechanism for securing compliance by law enforcement officers.

We should point out that at common law seizure of evidence by illegal means was not viewed as affecting the quality of the materials obtained. As a consequence of this thinking that evidence was evidence however it was obtained, courts did not refuse to admit materials into evidence merely because they were not obtained according to the rules. And this view prevailed until 1914 when the Supreme Court ruled in Weeks v. United States, 232 U.S. 383, 34 S.Ct. 341, that evidence seized in disregard of Fourth Amendment standards was to be inadmissible in federal court. This prohibition came to be known as "the exclusionary rule" and was thought to provide a deterrent to illegal conduct by law enforcement personnel. Twelve years after the incorporation of the Fourth Amendment in *Wolf*, the Court incorporated the exclusionary rule as a necessary adjunct of those protections, see *Mapp* v. *Ohio* (p. 1082). As the majority in *Mapp* indicated, the exclusionary rule was incorporated because other means by which illegal police behavior might be controlled had failed. What kinds of options would these be? Why might such alternatives as suits for damages, review boards, etc., fail to deter police illegalities? The exclusionary rule came to be a real bone of contention between the Warren Court's liberal majority and dissenters such as Justices Harlan and White. Do their arguments about the virtues of federalism and the latitude which should be given police methods seem persuasive as against the majority position? A decade later, Chief Justice Burger, dissenting in *Bivens* v. *Six Unknown Named Agents of the Bureau of Narcotics* (p. 1088), suggested the Court and Congress seek other alternatives. How good a case do you think the Chief Justice makes for abandoning the exclusionary rule? Is his proposal an alternative that would provide an acceptable remedy to the problem of police abuse of power?

Chief Justice Burger's dissenting opinion in *Bivens* proved to be only the opening shot of an approaching attack on the wide-ranging application of the exclusionary rule. Following the interest-balancing form, if not the increasingly strident tenor, of his criticism of the rule, subsequent Court decisions have somewhat pinched back application of the rule, as in *Stone* v. *Powell* (p. 1092), or simply refused to extend it further, as indicated in the note on the *Calandra* and *Janis* cases (p. 1099). Still, for all of the Burger Court's pruning, *Mapp* itself remains good law, though for how long is a matter that is likely to be decisively influenced by the occasion of any new appointments to the Court.

It is also important to establish that *Mapp* did not bind the states to follow *all* interpretations of the federal judiciary in the area of criminal procedure, but only those rulings which stemmed from constitutional guarantees. As the Court itself subsequently pointed out in Ker v. California, 374 U.S. 23, 83 S.Ct. 1623 (1963), the Supreme Court is also authorized by statute to promulgate rules for the supervision of federal law enforcement. Rulings which it hands down based on this statutory authority apply only in federal courts. Consequently, you will want to examine the Court's holdings on questions of criminal procedure very carefully so as to ascertain whether the Court's decision is based on constitutional or statutory authority in order to be sure of the scope of its application.

The application of the exclusionary rule, moreover, is not limited solely to evidence which is directly seized in unconstitutional fashion by the police. Under the "fruit of the poisonous tree" doctrine, which the Court first espoused in cases such as Silverthorne Lumber Co. v. United States, 251 U.S. 385, 40 S.Ct. 182 (1920), and Nardone v. United States, 308 U.S. 338, 60 S.Ct. 266 (1939), evidence which is obtained through tips resulting from illegally seized evidence is also inadmissible. The doctrine also came to be applied to evidence gained as a result of leads which were produced by coerced confessions. In other words, if the government still wanted to proceed against a defendant on a criminal charge and the evidence which it had dug up so far was the product of an illegal search or a coerced confession, it would have to find other evidence to prove its charges—evidence sufficiently far removed from the context of its own illegal activities so as to dissipate any taint of illegality.

b. Warrantless Searches and Seizures

It is clear that the general rule with regard to the conduct of searches and seizures is that they are to be executed pursuant to a warrant. Only a few well-specified exceptions which we will discuss below can justify a departure from this procedure. But what is required to obtain a warrant? Briefly put, the procedure requires the police officer to fill out an application which *particularly* describes what the authorities expect to find and where they expect to find it. Not only must this affidavit deal in specifics, but it must set them out to the extent that a neutral and detached magistrate can independently determine if such information demonstrates that there is "probable cause" to justify the issuing of the warrant. The affidavit may not merely recite conclusions which the police believe to be true; it must set out sufficient facts to enable the judge to reach his independent conclusion that probable cause exists. As the Court makes clear in *Coolidge* v. *New Hampshire* (p. 1109), the independent role of the magistrate must be preserved to insure judicial oversight of police operations so that constitutional guarantees may be scrupulously observed. Warrant procedures also provide that, after a search has been conducted and materials seized, a copy of the warrant is to be returned to the magistrate with an account of the evidence obtained so that judicial supervision can be continually maintained. In executing a search pursuant to a warrant, officers are limited to the specific areas indicated and are not entitled to enlarge the scope of the search into a general hunt for evidence. Materials not specified in the warrant may be seized only when they are in plain sight; officers are not compelled to close their eyes when, in the course of an authorized search, they accidently stumble upon other evidence of criminal activity.

While the Warren Court made it abundantly clear in *Chimel* v. *California* (p. 1105) that getting a warrant was the rule, it did recognize some exceptions to this requirement, though it also pointed out that these exceptions were to be interpreted narrowly. First, the Court has always recognized the legality of a search to which the suspect has consented. The Justices all agree that such consent must be voluntary and given completely free from any intimidation. Yet the Burger Court in *Schneckloth* v. *Bustamonte* (p. 1104) has clearly taken the view that voluntariness does not necessitate an explicit notice to the suspect that he has the right to refuse his consent to such a search. Although in everyday life the casualness of consent might raise a problem, particularly in assessing whether there has been a voluntary and knowing waiver, the Court had little difficulty in *United States* v. *Mendenhall* (p. 1154) concluding that the defendant consented to the search.

A second exception is a search conducted incident to an arrest. This kind of search has been justified on two grounds: (1) to protect the officer's life by allowing a search for possible weapons the suspect may use to resist arrest, and (2) to prevent the destruction of evidence by the suspect. After these exceptions had been recognized by the Court in United States v. Rabinowitz, 339 U.S. 56, 70 S.Ct. 430 (1950), the scope of such searches increased until the situation reached a paradoxical point: an individual was generally safer in the privacy of his possessions when he was not at home (since probable cause would have to be established for a warrant to issue) than when he was (since searches incident to arrest sometimes ballooned to become general exploratory searches). As a result, in *Chimel* the Court clearly indicated that this exception extended only to those areas within the possible reach of the defendant.

A third exception extends to instances of "hot pursuit" such as those depicted in *Warden* v. *Hayden* (p. 1119) and *United States* v. *Santana* (p. 1124). When police are chasing a suspect and he runs into a building, they are not compelled to risk losing him by having to go back to the court-house to get a warrant. But the test in such instances is immediacy. The more remote in time the sequence of events becomes, the faster this exception fades. In sum, the exception covers emergencies only.

A fourth exception is that created for motor vehicles. First recognized in Carroll v. United States, 267 U.S. 132, 45 S.Ct. 280 (1925), and affirmed in Chambers v. Maroney, 399 U.S. 42, 90 S.Ct. 1975 (1970), the automobile exception is aimed at preventing evidence from being whisked out of the police officer's grasp and either destroyed or moved beyond the reach of the jurisdiction in which a warrant for search and seizure must be issued. Because of both the mobility of an automobile and the reduced expectation of privacy one has in it (compared to that which a person has within his home), the police officer may search a motor vehicle on the spot if he has probable cause. The parameters of this exception to the warrant require-ment are sketched out in *Coolidge* (p. 1109), the note on the *Chadwick, Sanders,* and *Ross* cases (p. 1114), and the chart on other auto search cases (p. 1119). Recently, the scope of the automobile exception has been hotly contested when police have conducted warrantless searches of con-tainers within motor vehicles. As Justice Marshall's dissent in *Ross* points up, although all of the Justices agree that an automobile exception exists, there is sharp dispute as to both the conditions which call it into play and the extent of such a search.

Finally, as with searches executed pursuant to a warrant where the officer stumbles upon evidence accidently, he may seize what he finds in plain sight. As we noted before, he need not avert his eyes from evidence of crime which is starkly before him. Note how all of these exceptions are reviewed by the Court in its consideration of the seizure at issue in the *Coolidge* case. As that instance clearly shows, these rules are more clearly stated and agreed to in the abstract than in the realities of concrete application.

Moreover, it has become apparent from several Burger Court decisions, one of which is *Cupp* v. *Murphy* (p. 1102), that searches may still be law-fully carried out in the absence of a warrant, even if they do not fit the above exceptions, so long as probable cause exists. In such cases, the present Court has emphasized, the test to be employed is not whether the police had adequate opportunity to procure a warrant, but whether the search itself was reasonable in light of all the circumstances. This shift of attention from the reasonableness of the opportunity to get a warrant to the reasonableness of the search *per se* constitutes one of the major threads running through the Burger Court's interpretation of the Fourth Amendment. A second theme, which characterizes its search and seizure rulings, is the drift away from treating exceptions to the warrant require-ment narrowly.

Cupp v. *Murphy* involved a kind of body search. Other varieties of body searches raise more provocative questions about how far we are prepared to let such searches go. By what standards should this kind of search be guided? Is the standard we found in *Rochin* v. *California* (p. 934) adequate? More particularly, does it seem adequate when used to legitimate the body search that took place in the *Blackford* case (p. 1129)?

Apart from guidelines which we have just reviewed that relate to how evidence is to be seized, other specifications have attempted to limit what can be seized as evidence. In *Schmerber* v. *California* (p. 1003) the Court established that evidence of a testimonial variety could not be used to convict the defendant. Notice in that case how the Fourth Amendment's prohibition on unreasonable searches and seizures interlocks with the guarantee against self-incrimination contained in the Fifth Amendment to bar the admission of such evidence. This conjoining relationship between the amendments was of special importance to Justice Black, for his literal interpretation of constitutional provisions afforded no way to sanction an exclusionary rule emanating alone from the Fourth Amendment. Justice Black repeatedly held to the position that evidence gathered in violation of the Fourth Amendment could only be excluded from consideration when it was of a kind which was also forbidden by the Fifth so that the exclusionary rule of that amendment could be brought to bear on the evidence.

A second and equally interesting limitation on the seizure of evidence— but one the Court no longer adheres to—is discussed in *Warden* v. *Hayden* (p. 1119). Some forty-six years earlier the Court held in Gouled v. United States, 255 U.S. 298, 41 S.Ct. 261 (1921), that seizure was conditioned on certain consideration of property rights. In other words, government had a right to seize certain materials because either the defendant had no property right to them at all or else had forfeited what property right he had by virtue of their illegal use; other materials labeled "mere evidence" were his, and even though—like articles of clothing worn in a robbery—they were connected with the crime, they remained his and could not be seized. The *Hayden* case abolished this distinction as to the seizability of evidence based on such a consideration of property rights. In your opinion, did this action by the Court overturning the *Gouled* rule materially weaken civil liberties protections? If so, does this experience lend credibility to the traditional argument of conservatives that the maintenance of property rights is essential if civil liberties are to be protected from governmental intrusion? Considering his background as the arch exponent of the preferred freedoms approach, a mode of interpretation which makes much of the opposite view—that democracy and personal liberties can exist without economic freedoms—don't you think it is somewhat ironic that the lone dissenter in *Hayden* should be—of all people— Justice Douglas? And where are the Court's conservatives, such as Justice Harlan, who worry about the protection of property rights on other occasions?

A related matter, identified by Justice Stevens as an outgrowth of the ruling in *Hayden*, is the question of whether the Fourth Amendment now requires that police normally proceed by subpoena *duces tecum* rather than by search warrant to obtain materials deemed to be relevant to a criminal investigation—what would have been called "mere evidence" under the *Gouled* rule—and thought to be in the possession of a third party. What reasons do the majority in *Zurcher* v. *Stanford Daily* (p. 1125) give for refusing to "rewrite" the amendment? Do these reasons seem to you to be convincing in light of the fact that the third party here is a newspaper? Judging by its enactment of corrective legislation (p. 1128) two years later, Congress apparently thought not.

You will also want to take a look at two other problems concerning search and seizure—questions which fall, perhaps, on the periphery of the practice. The first is a query over the status we accord those investigations by government outside the strictly criminal context. Are visits by the building inspector or fire marshal "searches" within the meaning of the Fourth Amendment? Until the Court's ruling in the *Camara* case (p. 1129) in 1967, they were not. In view of the mounting problems of the cities, making such regulatory inspections more necessary for all of us, are the decisions in *Camara* and *See* (p. 1131) mixed blessings particularly for liberals? Do the dissenters in *Camara* have a point that requiring the wholesale issuing of warrants in such instances would significantly diminish the quality of the warrant and reduce the process to a mindless routine which would endanger its capacity to protect important interests of even the criminal justice process? Controversy over the warrant requirement for administrative inspections has not abated, as *Michigan* v. *Tyler* (p. 1132) and other recent decisions (p. 1131) show.

A second issue at the periphery of search and seizure is the "stop and frisk" incident. How clearly do you think the Court develops standards for the conduct of such street searches? Does the standard of probable cause, espoused by Justice Douglas, have any realistic application when the police officer is compelled in view of his own experience to make a speedy judgment to intervene? Compare *Terry* v. *Ohio* (p. 1138), *Sibron* v. *New York* (p. 1142), and *Peters* v. *New York* (p. 1142). The Court seems to indicate clearly enough how and why such "searches" may be conducted. Note, however, that it has much greater difficulty specifying *when* such intrusions are justified, and for this reason you should give careful attention to Justice Harlan's concurring opinion in *Terry*. The issue is first whether the police officer has "reasonable suspicion" to compel a suspect to stop. Does this standard strike you as adequate to accommodate the competing interests of the criminal justice process we sketched out at the beginning? *Dunaway* v. *New York* (p. 1147), *United States* v. *Mendenhall* (p. 1154), and other recent rulings (p. 1154) from the Court have built upon the principles of *Terry*, but not without generating continued controversy.

Terry-type stops and ensuing frisks have not been limited to street encounters involving pedestrians. The controversy over applicable Fourth Amendment standards extends as well to auto stops and driver frisks. As the Court held in *Delaware* v. *Prouse* (p. 1159), police may not stop a vehicle on a public highway for the purpose of checking the driver's license or car registration, absent probable cause or reasonable suspicion to believe that some motor vehicle law has been violated or that any of its occupants is subject to seizure or detention in connection with the violation of some other law. But where police may legitimately stop a vehicle, recent cases

(p. 1165) have held that *Terry*-type precautions are in order. A further perspective on auto stops is provided by the Court's rulings concerning certain techniques employed by the U.S. Border Patrol on inland highways in search of illegal aliens (p. 1165). Border searches normally pose no particular Fourth Amendment problem since they are a sort of *quid pro quo* for the privilege of entering the country. But searches some distance from the border pose knottier problems, not the least of which is the prospect that such stops may be based solely on the ethnicity of a vehicle's occupants, a development which raises the ugly specter of racial discrimination.

c. Wiretapping and Eavesdropping

Few eras in our national experience have more forcefully raised the question about how far government should be allowed to go in combatting "crime" than Prohibition. A combination of frustration with other methods of law enforcement and the development of technology provided the genesis of a new method of obtaining evidence—the wiretap. In *Olmstead* v. *United States* (p. 1166) the Court confronted the constitutionality of this approach for the first time. Compare the encrusted literalism of the majority's narrow holding—that the Fourth Amendment guarantees apply only to physical trespass on private property and only to tangible things—with the breadth, insight, and eloquence of Justice Brandeis's dissent. It is stunning, years later, especially in light of the Watergate Affair and other governmental intrusions which have now become routine, to contemplate how true the Brandeis prophecy has become. You should also read Justice Butler's dissent with care. Unlike Justice Brandeis's view, Butler's position is predicated on the sanctity of property rights. In line with our query about the relation between property rights and civil liberties which we raised earlier in the context of *Warden* v. *Hayden*, would a holding along the lines Justice Butler suggested have accorded better protection for individual liberties than any the Court came to adopt?

Several measures were introduced in Congress to modify the policy embodied in the *Olmstead* decision, but these efforts were unavailing until the enactment of § 605 of the Federal Communications Act of 1934. That provision declared that "no person not being authorized by the sender shall intercept any communication and divulge or publish the existence, contents, substance * * * of such intercepted communication to any person." In Nardone v. United States, 302 U.S. 379, 58 S.Ct. 275 (1937), the Court held § 605 to apply against the national government as well as private individuals. Wiretap evidence thus became inadmissible in federal court as did the fruits of any such surveillance in the second *Nardone* case, 308 U.S. 338, 60 S.Ct. 266, two years later. Wiretapping by federal agents, however, did not stop since U.S. Attorneys General subsequently interpreted these rulings to apply only to surveillance that intercepted communications, contents of which were afterward divulged, and not to wiretapping which remained secret. In Goldman v. United States, 316 U.S. 129, 62 S.Ct. 993 (1942), this same policy was extended to cover eavesdropping carried out, like wiretapping, without physical intrusion into constitutionally protected premises such as one's home or rented hotel room. Electronic surveillance came to be used by federal agents chiefly against organized crime and suspected subversives until 1965 when President Johnson ordered a sharp curtailment in surveillance activities, limiting their use to selected instances approved by the President or the Attorney General involving possible threats to the national security.

The post-*Olmstead* limitations on electronic surveillance, however, had no binding effect at the state level. In the absence of legislation by a particular state that would proscribe such activities, the Court held in Schwartz v. Texas, 344 U.S. 199, 73 S.Ct. 232 (1952), that § 605's prohibition on the interception and divulgence of communications did not preclude admissibility of such evidence in state court proceedings. State authorities, therefore, continued to wiretap and eavesdrop and were entitled to make direct use of what they heard.

The limited scope of judicial rulings in this area had the effect of encouraging an ominous kind of "cooperative federalism" between national and state law enforcement agents. Federal authorities escaped application of the exclusionary rule in federal courts by merely accepting evidence willingly procured for them by state authorities unconstrained by § 605. This cross-roughing between federal and state agents continued until the Supreme Court's ruling in Benanti v. United States, 355 U.S. 96, 78 S.Ct. 155 (1957), that evidence obtained via wiretapping by state law enforcement authorities was inadmissible in federal court. The Court then plugged the remaining loophole in Lee v. Florida, 392 U.S. 378, 88 S.Ct. 2096 (1968), by holding § 605 applicable also against state-undertaken surveillance netting evidence which was then used in state proceedings.

In 1967, the Court finally vindicated the views expressed by Justice Brandeis by overruling *Olmstead* and *Goldman*. As *Katz* v. *United States* (p. 1175) and *Berger* v. *New York* (p. 1171) make abundantly clear, both wiretapping and eavesdropping are to be considered searches, and intercepted communications are to be regarded as seized materials under the terms of the Fourth and Fourteenth Amendments. In line with this holding, legislation authorizing such searches must be able to withstand the exacting scrutiny demanded of the Fourth Amendment and, above all, comply with constitutional commands for close continual judicial supervision of all such activities. In sum, the Court demanded that electronic searches and seizures be brought back into line with the constitutional standards governing more usual kinds of searches and seizures typified in the *Chimel* case. We should hasten to add, however, as the Court pointed out in *Smith* v. *Maryland* (p. 1178), that the procedures spelled out in *Berger* and *Katz* govern, for example, only the interception of telephone messages and not, by contrast, the use of a pen register which discloses merely the phone number dialed.

A nagging problem which remains in the area of electronic surveillance is evidenced by the case of *United States* v. *United States District Court* (p. 1179), namely, to what extent interpretation of the Fourth Amendment compels the judiciary to oversee surveillance related to the national security. In pointed terms it suggests the potential for a clash between a Court intent on stringently enforcing the constitutional guarantee of judicial supervision and the constitutional commitment of protecting the national security to the Executive. Does the Court's interpretation of Title III of the Omnibus Crime Control and Safe Streets Act of 1968 furnish a clue as to how far the standards of *Katz* will be applied to wiretapping and eaves-dropping in cases involving possible subversion? More importantly, do the provisions of Title III or the Court's interpretation, as evidenced in the *U. S. District Court* case suggest any loopholes through which agents of the Executive branch might escape judicial oversight of surveillance activi-ties? In 1978, Congress responded to the perceived abuse of government wiretapping and eavesdropping in the name of national security by enact-ing a foreign intelligence surveillance law (p. 1183). To what extent, do you think, did this statute close up any remaining loopholes left by the Court's decision in *United States District Court*?

One final issue is worth mentioning. It is the notion of implied con-sent. All of the cases reviewed above involved the use of conversations which were divulged by a third party—agents of federal or state govern-ment. *Hoffa* v. *United States* (p. 1184) graphically illustrates, however, a far greater latitude accorded government in the use of communications when one of the parties to the conversation is an informer. The imputa-tion of the defendant's consent is the critical element in such cases which operates to put divulgence of these conversations on a different plane. Is it fair to talk of the defendant as "consenting" to the seizure of such a conversation in such instances? Given the *Lopez* decision cited in *Hoffa*, which upheld the defendant's implied consent even where an agent fraudu-lently secured admission to the defendant's presence and then engaged the defendant in an incriminating conversation, do you think such trickery by government vitiates any real notion of consent and makes any such seizure of the conversation unreasonable? Note how, at this point, such activities by government agents begin to verge on entrapment.

a. THE EXCLUSIONARY RULE

MAPP v. OHIO

Supreme Court of the United States, 1961
367 U.S. 643, 81 S.Ct. 1684, 6 L.Ed.2d 1081

Dollree Mapp was convicted under Ohio law for possession of obscene books, pic-tures, and photographs. She challenged the conviction on the grounds that the evidence used against her was unlawfully seized.

One day in May 1957, several Cleveland police officers came to Miss Mapp's residence looking for a fugitive who was believed to be hiding out in her home. They requested entrance, but Miss Mapp refused to admit them without a search warrant. After she refused a second time, the police broke into the apartment and then physically assaulted and handcuffed her when she grabbed a piece of paper that they told her was a valid search warrant. The officers searched the entire house and discovered the obscene materials which were later used to convict her. The Ohio Supreme Court affirmed the conviction, and the U.S. Supreme Court granted certiorari.

Mr. Justice CLARK delivered the opinion of the Court.

* * *

The State says that even if the search were made without authority, or otherwise unreasonably, it is not prevented from using the unconstitutionally seized evidence at trial, citing Wolf v. People of State of Colorado, 1949, 338 U.S. 25, 69 S.Ct. 1359, in which this Court did indeed hold "that in a prosecution in a State court for a State crime the Fourteenth Amendment does not forbid the admission of evidence obtained by an unreasonable search and seizure." * * * [I]t is urged once again that we review that holding.

Seventy-five years ago, in Boyd v. United States, 1886, 116 U.S. 616, 630, 6 S.Ct. 524, 532, considering the Fourth and Fifth Amendments as running "almost into each other" on the facts before it, this Court held that the doctrines of those Amendments

"apply to all invasions on the part of the government and its employes of the sanctity of a man's home and the privacies of life. It is not the breaking of his doors, and the rummaging of his drawers, that constitutes the essence of the offence; but it is the invasion of his indefeasible right of personal security, personal liberty and private property. * * * Breaking into a house and opening boxes and drawers are circumstances of aggravation; but any forcible and compulsory extortion of a man's own testimony or of his private papers to be used as evidence to convict him of crime or to forfeit his goods, is within the condemnation * * * [of those Amendments]."

The Court noted that

"constitutional provisions for the security of person and property should be liberally construed." * * *

Less than 30 years after *Boyd*, this Court, in Weeks v. United States, 1914, 232 U.S. 383, 34 S.Ct. 341, stated that "the 4th Amendment * * * put the courts of the United States and Federal officials, in the exercise of their power and authority, under limitations and restraints [and] * * * forever secure[d] the people, their persons, houses, papers, and effects, against all unreasonable searches and seizures under the guise of law * * * and the duty of giving to it force and effect is obligatory upon all entrusted under our Federal system with the enforcement of the laws." * * *

[T]he Court in that case clearly stated that use of the seized evidence involved "a denial of the constitutional rights of the accused." * * * Thus, in the year 1914, in the *Weeks* case, this Court "for the first time" held that "in a federal prosecution the Fourth Amendment barred the use of evidence secured through an illegal search and seizure." * * * This Court has ever since required of federal law officers a strict adherence to that command which this Court has held to be a clear, specific, and constitutionally required—even if judicially implied—deterrent safeguard without insistence upon which the Fourth Amendment would have been reduced to "a form of words." * * *

* * *

In 1949, 35 years after *Weeks* was announced, this Court, in Wolf v. People of State of Colorado, * * * again for the first time, discussed the effect of the Fourth

Amendment upon the States through the operation of the Due Process Clause of the Fourteenth Amendment. It said:

"[W]e have no hesitation in saying that were a State affirmatively to sanction such police incursion into privacy it would run counter to the guaranty of the Fourteenth Amendment." * * *

Nevertheless, after declaring that the "security of one's privacy against arbitrary intrusion by the police" is "implicit in 'the concept of ordered liberty' and as such enforceable against the States through the Due Process Clause," * * * and announcing that it "stoutly adhere[d]" to the *Weeks* decision, the Court decided that the *Weeks* exclusionary rule would not then be imposed upon the States as "an essential ingredient of the right." * * * The Court's reasons for not considering essential to the right to privacy, as a curb imposed upon the States by the Due Process Clause, that which decades before had been posited as part and parcel of the Fourth Amendment's limitation upon federal encroachment of individual privacy, were bottomed on factual considerations.

While they are not basically relevant to a decision that the exclusionary rule is an essential ingredient of the Fourth Amendment as the right it embodies is vouchsafed against the States by the Due Process Clause, we will consider the current validity of the factual grounds upon which *Wolf* was based.

The Court in *Wolf* first stated that "[t]he contrariety of views of the States" on the adoption of the exclusionary rule of *Weeks* was "particularly impressive" * * * and, in this connection, that it could not "brush aside the experience of States

which deem the incidence of such conduct by the police too slight to call for a deterrent remedy * * * by overriding the [States'] relevant rules of evidence." * * * While in 1949, prior to the *Wolf* case, almost two-thirds of the States were opposed to the use of the exclusionary rule, now, despite the *Wolf* case, more than half of those since passing upon it, by their own legislative or judicial decision, have wholly or partly adopted or adhered to the *Weeks* rule. * * * Significantly, among those now following the rule is California, which, according to its highest court, was "compelled to reach that conclusion because other remedies have completely failed to secure compliance with the constitutional provisions." * * * In connection with this California case, we note that the second basis elaborated in *Wolf* in support of its failure to enforce the exclusionary doctrine against the States was that "other means of protection" have been afforded "the right to privacy." * * * The experience of California that such other remedies have been worthless and futile is buttressed by the experience of other States. The obvious futility of relegating the Fourth Amendment to the protection of other remedies has, moreover, been recognized by this Court since *Wolf.* * * *

[Moreover] the force of [the] reasoning [behind *Wolf*] has been largely vitiated by later decisions of this Court. These include the recent discarding of the "silver platter" doctrine which allowed federal judicial use of evidence seized in violation of the Constitution by state agents, * * * the relaxation of the formerly strict requirements as to standing to challenge the use of evidence thus seized, so that now the procedure of exclusion, "ultimately referable to constitutional safeguards," is available to anyone even "legitimately on [the] premises" unlawfully searched, * * * and finally, the formulation of a method to prevent state use of evidence unconstitutionally seized by federal agents. * * *

It, therefore, plainly appears that the factual considerations supporting the failure of the *Wolf* Court to include the *Weeks* exclusionary rule when it recognized the enforceability of the right to privacy against the States in 1949, while not basically relevant to the constitutional consideration, could not, in any analysis, now be deemed controlling.

* * * Today we once again examine *Wolf's* constitutional documentation of the right to privacy free from unreasonable state intrusion, and, after its dozen years on our books, are led by it to close the only courtroom door remaining open to evidence secured by official lawlessness in flagrant abuse of that basic right, reserved to all persons as a specific guarantee against that very same unlawful conduct. We hold that all evidence obtained by searches and seizures in violation of the Constitution is, by that same authority, inadmissible in a state court.

Since the Fourth Amendment's right of privacy has been declared enforceable against the States through the Due Process Clause of the Fourteenth, it is enforceable against them by the same sanction of exclusion as is used against the Federal Government. Were it otherwise, then just as without the *Weeks* rule the assurance against unreasonable federal searches and seizures would be "a form of words", valueless and undeserving of mention in a perpetual charter of inestimable human liberties, so too, without that rule the freedom from state invasions of privacy would be so ephemeral and so neatly severed from its conceptual nexus with the freedom from all brutish means of coercing evidence as not to merit this Court's high regard as a freedom "implicit in 'the concept of ordered liberty.'" At the time that the Court held in *Wolf* that the amendment was applicable to the States through the Due Process Clause, the cases of this Court, as we have seen, had steadfastly held that as to federal officers the Fourth Amendment included the exclusion of the evidence seized in violation of its provisions. Even *Wolf* "stoutly adhered" to that proposition. * * * [T]he admission of the new constitutional right by *Wolf* could not consistently tolerate denial of its most important constitutional privilege, namely, the exclusion of the evidence which an accused had been forced to give by reason of the unlawful seizure. To hold otherwise is to grant the right but in reality to withhold its privilege and enjoyment. Only last year the Court itself recognized that the purpose of the exclusionary rule "is to deter—to compel respect for the constitutional guaranty in the only effectively available way—by removing the incentive to disregard it." * * *

Indeed, we are aware of no restraint, similar to that rejected today, conditioning the enforcement of any other basic constitutional right. The right to privacy, no less important than any other right carefully and particularly reserved to the people, would stand in marked contrast to all other rights declared as "basic to a free society." * * * This Court has not hesitated to enforce as strictly against the States as it does against the Federal Government the rights of free speech and of a free press, the rights to notice and to a fair, public trial, including, as it does, the right not to be convicted by use of a coerced confession, however logically relevant it be, and without regard to its reliability. * * * And nothing could be more certain than that when a coerced confession is involved, "the relevant rules of evidence" are overridden without regard to "the incidence of such conduct by the police," slight or frequent. Why should not the same rule apply to what is tantamount to coerced testimony by way of unconstitutional seizure of goods, papers, effects, documents, etc.? * * *

Moreover, our holding that the exclusionary rule is an essential part of both the Fourth and Fourteenth Amendments is not only the logical dictate of prior cases, but it also makes very good sense. There is no war between the Constitution and common sense. Presently, a federal prosecutor may make no use of evidence illegally seized, but a State's attorney across the street may, although he supposedly is operating under the enforceable prohibitions of the same Amendment. Thus the State, by admitting evidence unlawfully seized, serves to encourage disobedience to the Federal Constitution which it is bound to uphold. * * * In non-exclusory States, federal officers, being human, were by it invited to and did, as our cases indicate, step across the street to the State's attorney with their unconstitutionally seized evidence. Prosecution on the basis of that evidence was then had in a state court in utter disregard of the enforceable Fourth Amendment. If the fruits of an unconstitutional search had been inadmissible in both state and federal courts, this inducement to evasion would have been sooner eliminated. * * *

Federal-state cooperation in the solution of crime under constitutional standards will be promoted, if only by recognition of their now mutual obligation to respect the same fundamental criteria in their approaches. "However much in a particular case insistence upon such rules may appear as a technicality that inures to the benefit of a guilty person, the history of the criminal law proves that tolerance of shortcut methods in law enforcement impairs its enduring effectiveness." * * *

There are those who say, as did Justice (then Judge) Cardozo, that under our constitutional exclusionary doctrine "[t]he criminal is to go free because the constable has blundered." * * * In some cases this will undoubtedly be the result. But, as was said in Elkins [v. United States], "there is another consideration—the imperative of judicial integrity." 364 U.S. at page 222, 80 S.Ct. at page 1447. The criminal goes free, if he must, but it is the law that sets him free. Nothing can destroy a government more quickly than its failure to observe its own laws, or worse, its disregard of the charter of its own existence. * * *

The ignoble shortcut to conviction left open to the State tends to destroy the entire system of constitutional restraints on which the liberties of the people rest. Having once recognized that the right to privacy embodied in the Fourth Amendment is enforceable against the States, and that the right to be secure against rude invasions of privacy by state officers is, therefore, constitutional in origin, we can no longer permit that right to remain an empty promise.

Because it is enforceable in the same manner and to like effect as other basic rights secured by the Due Process Clause, we can no longer permit it to be revocable at the whim of any police officer who, in the name of law enforcement itself, chooses to suspend its enjoyment. Our decision, founded on reason and truth, gives to the individual no more than that which the Constitution guarantees him, to the police officer no less than that to which honest law enforcement is entitled, and, to the courts, that judicial integrity so necessary in the true administration of justice.

The judgment of the Supreme Court of Ohio is reversed and the cause remanded for further proceedings not inconsistent with this opinion.

* * *

Mr. Justice BLACK, concurring.

* * *

I am still not persuaded that the Fourth Amendment, standing alone, would be enough to bar the introduction into evidence against an accused of papers and effects seized from him in violation of its commands. For the Fourth Amendment does not itself contain any provision expressly precluding the use of such evidence, and I am extremely doubtful that such a provision could properly be inferred from nothing more than the basic command against unreasonable searches and seizures. Reflection on the problem, however, in the light of cases coming before the Court since *Wolf*, has led me to conclude that when the Fourth Amendment's ban against unreasonable searches and seizures is considered together with the Fifth Amendment's ban against compelled self-incrimination, a consti-

tutional basis emerges which not only justifies but actually requires the exclusionary rule.

* * *

Memorandum of Mr. Justice STEWART.

* * * I would * * * reverse the judgment in this case, because I am persuaded that the provision of * * * the Ohio [obscenity law] upon which the petitioner's conviction was based, is, in the words of Mr. Justice Harlan, not "consistent with the rights of free thought and expression assured against state action by the Fourteenth Amendment."

Mr. Justice HARLAN, whom Mr. Justice FRANKFURTER and Mr. Justice WHITTAKER join, dissenting.

* * *

From the Court's statement of the case one would gather that the central, if not controlling, issue on this appeal is whether illegally state-seized evidence is Constitutionally admissible in a state prosecution, an issue which would of course face us with the need for re-examining *Wolf*. However, such is not the situation. For, although that question was indeed raised here and below among appellant's subordinate points, the new and pivotal issue brought to the Court by this appeal is whether § 2905.34 of the Ohio Revised Code making criminal the *mere* knowing possession or control of obscene material, and under which appellant has been convicted, is consistent with the rights of free thought and expression assured against state action by the Fourteenth Amendment. That was the principal issue which was decided by the Ohio Supreme Court, which was tendered by appellant's

Jurisdictional Statement, and which was briefed and argued in this Court.

In this posture of things, I think it fair to say that five members of this Court have simply "reached out" to overrule *Wolf.* With all respect for the views of the majority, and recognizing that *stare decisis* carries different weight in Constitutional adjudication than it does in nonconstitutional decision, I can perceive no justification for regarding this case as an appropriate occasion for re-examining *Wolf.*

* * *

I would not impose upon the States this federal exclusionary remedy. The reasons given by the majority for now suddenly turning its back on *Wolf* seem to me notably unconvincing.

First, it is said that "the factual grounds upon which *Wolf* was based" have since changed, in that more States now follow the *Weeks* exclusionary rule than was so at the time *Wolf* was decided. While that is true, a recent survey indicates that a present one-half of the States still

adhere to the common-law non-exclusionary rule. * * * But in any case surely all this is beside the point, as the majority itself indeed seems to recognize. Our concern here, as it was in *Wolf,* is not with the desirability of that rule but only with the question whether the States are Constitutionally free to follow it or not as they may themselves determine, and the relevance of the disparity of views among the States on this point lies simply in the fact that the judgment involved is a debatable one. Moreover, the very fact on which the majority relies, instead of lending support to what is now being done, points away from the need of replacing voluntary state action with federal compulsion.

The preservation of a proper balance between state and federal responsibility in the administration of criminal justice demands patience on the part of those who might like to see things move faster among the States in this respect. Problems of criminal law enforcement vary widely from State to State. * * *

* * *

Webster Bivens brought suit in U.S. District Court against six federal narcotics agents seeking $15,000 in damages from each of them. The agents had entered his apartment without probable cause or a warrant, arrested and shackled him in the presence of his wife and children, conducted an exhaustive search of the apartment, and then hauled him off to a federal courthouse for interrogation. Bivens contended that he should be compensated for the "humiliation, embarrassment, and mental suffering" which the agents caused by their unlawful and unreasonable conduct. The district court dismissed the complaint on two principal grounds: (1) that the suit failed to state a federal cause of action, and (2) that the agents, because of their official position, were immune from suit. The U.S. Circuit Court of Appeals affirmed. The Supreme Court reversed the decision by a 6–3 vote.

Speaking for the Court in Bivens v. Six Unknown Named Agents of the Federal Bureau of Narcotics, 403 U.S. 388, 91 S.Ct. 1999 (1971), Justice Brennan rejected the proposition that the only mode of relief open to the plaintiff was a suit in state court and concluded that inasmuch as "petitioner's complaint states a cause of action under the Fourth Amendment * * * we hold that [he] is entitled to recover money damages for any injuries he has suffered as a result of the agents' violation of the Amendment." (The Court did not reach the immunity grounds.) Chief Justice Burger and Justices Black and Blackmun dissented separately but generally objected to the creation of a damage remedy by the Court rather than Congress.

The Chief Justice wrote the principal dissenting opinion. It was particularly notable because he ventured considerably beyond the issue at hand to a searching examination and critique of the exclusionary rule. Noting that the exclusionary rule has at times been justified by "the 'sporting contest' thesis that the government must 'play the game fairly' and cannot be allowed to profit from its own illegal acts" and, alternatively, "the theory that the relationship between the Self-Incrimination Clause of the Fifth Amendment and the Fourth Amendment requires the suppression of evidence seized in violation of the latter," Chief Justice Burger observed that it was the "deterrent rationale" that really undergirded the rule. He said:

> I do not question the need for some remedy to give meaning and teeth to the constitutional guarantees against unlawful conduct by government officials. Without some effective sanction, these protections would constitute little more than rhetoric. Beyond doubt the conduct of some officials requires sanctions. * * * But the hope that this objective could be accomplished by the exclusion of reliable evidence from criminal trials was hardly more than a wistful dream. Although I would hesitate to abandon it until some meaningful substitute is developed, the history of the suppression doctrine demonstrates that it is both conceptually sterile and practically ineffective in accomplishing its stated objective. This is illustrated by the paradox that an unlawful act against a totally innocent person—such as petitioner claims to be—has been left without an effective remedy, and hence the Court finds it necessary now—55 years later—to construct a remedy of its own.

The Chief Justice ascribed what he saw as the failure of the exclusionary rule to several factors:

> The rule does not apply any direct sanction to the individual official whose illegal conduct results in the exclusion of evidence in a criminal trial. * * * The immediate sanction triggered by the application of the rule is visited upon the prosecutor whose case against a criminal is either weakened or destroyed. The doctrine deprives the police in no real sense; except that apprehending wrongdoers is their business, police have no more stake in successful prosecutions than prosecutors or the public.
>
> The suppression doctrine vaguely assumes that law enforcement is a monolithic governmental enterprise. * * * But the prosecutor who loses his case because of police misconduct is not an official in the police department; he can rarely set in motion any corrective action or administrative penalties. Moreover, he does not have control or direction over police procedures or police actions that lead to the exclusion of evidence. It is the rare exception when a prosecutor takes part in arrests, searches, or seizures so that he can guide police action.
>
> Whatever educational effect the rule conceivably might have in theory is greatly diminished in fact by the realities of law enforcement work. Police-

men do not have the time, inclination, or training to read and grasp the nuances of the appellate opinions that ultimately define the standards of conduct they are to follow. *   *   * Nor can judges, in all candor, forget that opinions sometimes lack helpful clarity.

The presumed educational effect of judicial opinions is also reduced by the long time lapse—often several years—between the original police action and its final judicial evaluation. Given a policeman's pressing responsibilities, it would be surprising if he ever becomes aware of the final result after such a delay. Finally, the exclusionary rule's deterrent impact is diluted by the fact that there are large areas of police activity that do not result in criminal prosecutions—hence the rule has virtually no applicability and no effect in such situations. *   *   *

Today's holding seeks to fill one of the gaps of the suppression doctrine—at the price of impinging on the legislative and policy functions that the Constitution vests in Congress. Nevertheless, the holding serves the useful purpose of exposing the fundamental weaknesses of the suppression doctrine. Suppressing unchallenged truth has set guilty criminals free but demonstrably has neither deterred deliberate violations of the Fourth Amendment nor decreased those errors in judgment that will inevitably occur given the pressures inherent in police work having to do with serious crimes.

Although unfortunately ineffective, the exclusionary rule has increasingly been characterized by a single, monolithic, and drastic judicial response to all official violations of legal norms. Inadvertent errors of judgment that do not work any grave injustice will inevitably occur under the pressure of police work. These honest mistakes have been treated in the same way as deliberate and flagrant *   *   * violations of the Fourth Amendment. *   *   *

And he noted that "[t]his Court's decision announced today in *Coolidge* v. *New Hampshire*" (see p. 1109) "dramatically illustrates the extent to which the doctrine represents a mechanically inflexible response to widely varying degrees of police error and the resulting high price that society pays."

Following his portrayal of exclusionary rule deficiencies, Chief Justice Burger sounded the call to consider new alternatives:

In characterizing the suppression doctrine as an anomalous and ineffective mechanism with which to regulate law enforcement, I intend no reflection on the motivation of those members of this Court who hoped it would be a means of enforcing the Fourth Amendment. Judges cannot be faulted for being offended by arrests, searches, and seizures that violate the Bill of Rights or statutes intended to regulate public officials. But we can and should be faulted for clinging to an unworkable and irrational concept of law. My criticism is that we have taken so long to find better ways to accomplish these desired objectives. And there are better ways.

Instead of continuing to enforce the suppression doctrine inflexibly, rigidly, and mechanically, we should view it as one of the experimental steps in the great tradition of the common law and acknowledge its shortcomings. But in the same spirit we should be prepared to discontinue what the experience of over half a century has shown neither deters errant officers nor affords a remedy to the totally innocent victims of official misconduct.

I do not propose, however, that we abandon the suppression doctrine until some meaningful alternative can be developed. In a sense our legal system has become the captive of its own creation. To overrule *Weeks* and *Mapp*, even assuming the Court was now prepared to take that step, could raise yet new problems. Obviously the public interest would be poorly served if law enforcement officials were suddenly to gain the impression, however erroneous, that all constitutional restraints on police had somehow been removed—that an open season on "criminals" had been declared. I am concerned lest some such mistaken impression might be fostered by a flat overruling of the suppression doctrine cases.   *   *   *

Reasonable and effective substitutes can be formulated if Congress would take the lead, as it did for example in 1946 in the Federal Tort Claims Act. I see no insuperable obstacle to the elimination of the suppression doctrine if Congress would provide some meaningful and effective remedy against unlawful conduct by government officials.

The problems of both error and deliberate misconduct by law enforcement officials call for a workable remedy. Private damage actions against individual police officers concededly have not adequately met this requirement, and it would be fallacious to assume today's work of the Court in creating a remedy will really accomplish its stated objective. There is some validity to the claims that juries will not return verdicts against individual officers except in those unusual cases where the violation has been flagrant or where the error has been complete, as in the arrest of the wrong person or the search of the wrong house.   *   *   *

I conclude, therefore, that an entirely different remedy is necessary but it is one that in my view is as much beyond judicial power as the step the Court takes today. Congress should develop an administrative or quasi-judicial remedy against the government itself to afford compensation and restitution for persons whose Fourth Amendment rights have been violated. The venerable doctrine of *respondeat superior* [literally, "let the master answer"] in our tort law provides an entirely appropriate conceptual basis for this remedy. If, for example, a security guard privately employed by a department store commits an assault or other tort on a customer such as an improper search, the victim has a simple and obvious remedy—an action for money damages against the guard's employer, the department store. *   *   * Such a statutory scheme would have the added advantage of providing some remedy to the completely innocent persons who are sometimes the victims of illegal police conduct—something that the suppression doctrine, of course, can never accomplish.

A simple structure would suffice. For example, Congress could enact a statute along the following lines:

(a) a waiver of sovereign immunity as to the illegal acts of law enforcement officials committed in the performance of assigned duties;

(b) the creation of a cause of action for damages sustained by any person aggrieved by conduct of governmental agents in violation of the Fourth Amendment or statutes regulating official conduct;

(c) the creation of a tribunal quasi-judicial in nature or perhaps patterned after the United States Court of Claims to adjudicate all claims under the statute;

(d) a provision that this statutory remedy is in lieu of the exclusion of evidence secured for use in criminal cases in violation of the Fourth Amendment; and

(e) a provision directing that no evidence, otherwise admissible, shall be excluded from any criminal proceeding because of violation of the Fourth Amendment.

I doubt that lawyers serving on such a tribunal would be swayed either by undue sympathy for officers or by the prejudice against "criminals" that has sometimes moved lay jurors to deny claims. In addition to awarding damages, the record of the police conduct that is condemned would undoubtedly become a relevant part of an officer's personnel file so that the need for additional training or disciplinary action could be identified or his future usefulness as a public official evaluated. Finally, appellate judicial review could be made available on much the same basis that it is now provided as to district courts and regulatory agencies. This would leave to the courts the ultimate responsibility for determining and articulating standards.

Once the constitutiional validity of such a statute is established, it can reasonably be assumed that the States would develop their own remedial systems on the federal model. Indeed there is nothing to prevent a State from enacting a comparable statutory scheme without waiting for the Congress. * * *

In a country that prides itself on innovation, inventive genius, and willingness to experiment, it is a paradox that we should cling for more than a half century to a legal mechanism that was poorly designed and never really worked. I can only hope now that the Congress will manifest a willingness to view realistically the hard evidence of the half-century history of the suppression doctrine revealing thousands of cases in which the criminal was set free because the constable blundered and virtually no evidence that innocent victims of police error—such as petitioner claims to be—have been afforded meaningful redress.

STONE v. POWELL

Supreme Court of the United States, 1976
428 U.S. 465, 96 S.Ct. 3037, 49 L.Ed.2d 1067

Powell and three friends entered a liquor store, and soon thereafter he became involved in a fight with the manager over the theft of a bottle of wine. In the ruckus that ensued, Powell shot and killed the store manager's wife. Ten hours later and miles away, Powell was arrested for violation of a town vagrancy ordinance. In a search incident to arrest it was discovered that he was carrying a .38 caliber revolver with six expended cartridges in the cylinder. At trial a criminologist subsequently identified the gun as that which killed the store manager's wife, and Powell was convicted of second-degree murder. The conviction was affirmed on appeal, and later the California Supreme Court denied habeas corpus relief. While in prison, Powell next instituted an action for federal habeas corpus under 28 U.S.C.A. § 2254 against his warden alleging that he was illegally confined because the vagrancy ordinance was unconstitutionally vague and, therefore, admission of the revolver into evidence was error since it was the fruit of an unlawful search, the search being incident to an unlawful arrest. A federal district court rejected Powell's argument concluding that the officer had probable cause, and even if the vagrancy ordinance was void for vagueness, the deterrent purpose of the exclusionary rule would not be served by ruling the revolver inadmissible. Moreover, even if this argument failed, the court continued, admission of the revolver was harmless error in the face of other uncontrovertible evidence given at trial. A federal appeals court reversed the district court's judgment, and the government appealed.

Mr. Justice POWELL delivered the opinion of the Court.

* * *

* * * The question is whether state prisoners—who have been afforded the opportunity for full and fair consideration of their reliance upon the exclusionary rule with respect to seized evidence by the state courts at trial and on direct review—may invoke their claim again on federal habeas corpus review. The answer is to be found by weighing the utility of the exclusionary rule against the costs of extending it to collateral review of Fourth Amendment claims.

The costs of applying the exclusionary rule even at trial and on direct review are well known: the focus of the trial, and the attention of the participants therein, is diverted from the ultimate question of guilt or innocence that should be the central concern in a criminal proceeding. Moreover, the physical evidence sought to be excluded is typically reliable and often the most probative information bearing on the guilt or innocence of the defendant. As Mr. Justice Black emphasized in his dissent in *Kaufman* [v. *United States*]:

"A claim of illegal search and seizure under the Fourth Amendment is crucially different from many other constitutional rights; ordinarily the evidence seized can in no way have been rendered untrustworthy by the means of its seizure and indeed often this evidence alone establishes beyond virtually any shadow of a doubt that the defendant is

guilty." 394 U.S., at 237, 89 S.Ct., at 1079.

Application of the rule thus deflects the truthfinding process and often frees the guilty. The disparity in particular cases between the error committed by the police officer and the windfall afforded a guilty defendant by application of the rule is contrary to the idea of proportionality that is essential to the concept of justice. Thus, although the rule is thought to deter unlawful police activity in part through the nurturing of respect for Fourth Amendment values, if applied indiscriminately it may well have the opposite effect of generating disrespect for the law and administration of justice. These long-recognized costs of the rule persist when a criminal conviction is sought to be overturned on collateral review on the ground that a search-and-seizure claim was erroneously rejected by two or more tiers of state courts.

Evidence obtained by police officers in violation of the Fourth Amendment is excluded at trial in the hope that the frequency of future violations will decrease. Despite the absence of supportive empirical evidence, we have assumed that the immediate effect of exclusion will be to discourage law enforcement officials from violating the Fourth Amendment by removing the incentive to disregard it. More importantly, over the long term, this demonstration that our society attaches serious consequences to violation of constitutional rights is thought to encourage those who formulate law enforcement policies, and the officers who implement them, to incorporate Fourth Amendment ideals into their value system.

We adhere to the view that these considerations support the implementation of the exclusionary rule at trial and its enforcement on direct appeal of state court convictions. But the additional contribution, if any, of the consideration of search-and-seizure claims of state prisoners on collateral review is small in relation to the costs. To be sure, each case in which such claim is considered may add marginally to an awareness of the values protected by the Fourth Amendment. There is no reason to believe, however, that the overall educative effect of the exclusionary rule would be appreciably diminished if search-and-seizure claims could not be raised in federal habeas corpus review of state convictions. Nor is there reason to assume that any specific disincentive already created by the risk of exclusion of evidence at trial or the reversal of convictions on direct review would be enhanced if there were the further risk that a conviction obtained in state court and affirmed on direct review might be overturned in collateral proceedings often occurring years after the incarceration of the defendant. The view that the deterrence of Fourth Amendment violations would be furthered rests on the dubious assumption that law enforcement authorities would fear that federal habeas review might reveal flaws in a search or seizure that went undetected at trial and on appeal. Even if one rationally could assume that some additional incremental deterrent effect would be present in isolated cases, the resulting advance of the legitimate goal of furthering Fourth Amendment rights would be outweighed by the acknowledged costs

to other values vital to a rational system of criminal justice.

In sum, we conclude that where the State has provided an opportunity for full and fair litigation of a Fourth Amendment claim, a state prisoner may not be granted federal habeas corpus relief on the ground that evidence obtained in an unconstitutional search or seizure was introduced at his trial. In this context the contribution of the exclusionary rule, if any, to the effectuation of the Fourth Amendment is minimal and the substantial societal costs of application of the rule persist with special force.

Accordingly, the judgments of the Courts of Appeals are

Reversed.

Mr. Chief Justice BURGER, concurring.

I concur in the Court's opinion. By way of dictum, and somewhat hesitantly, the Court notes that the holding in this case leaves undisturbed the exclusionary rule as applied to criminal trials. For reasons stated in my dissent in Bivens v. Six Unknown Named Federal Agents, 403 U.S. 388, 411, 91 S.Ct. 1999, 2012 (1971), it seems clear to me that the exclusionary rule has been operative long enough to demonstrate its flaws. The time has come to modify its reach, even if it is retained for a small and limited category of cases.

Over the years, the strains imposed by reality, in terms of the costs to society and the bizarre miscarriages of justice that have been experienced because of the exclusion of reliable evidence when the "constable blunders," have led the Court to vacillate as to the rationale for deliberate exclusion of truth from the factfinding process. The rhetoric has varied with the rationale to the point where the rule has become a doctrinaire result in search of validating reasons.

In evaluating the exclusionary rule, it is important to bear in mind exactly what the rule accomplishes. Its function is simple—the exclusion of truth from the factfinding process. * * * The operation of the rule is therefore unlike that of the Fifth Amendment's protection against compelled self-incrimination. A confession produced after intimidating or coercive interrogation is inherently dubious. If a suspect's will has been overborne, a cloud hangs over his custodial admissions; the exclusion of such statements is based essentially on their lack of reliability. This is not the case as to *reliable* evidence—a pistol, a packet of heroin, counterfeit money, or the body of a murder victim—which may be judicially declared to be the result of an "unreasonable" search. The reliability of such evidence is beyond question; its probative value is certain.

* * *

* * * Despite its avowed deterrent objective, proof is lacking that the exclusionary rule, a purely judge-created device based on "hard cases," serves the purpose of deterrence. Notwithstanding Herculean efforts, no empirical study has been able to demonstrate that the rule does in fact have any deterrent effect. In the face of dwindling support for the rule some would go so far as to extend it to *civil* cases. *United States* v. *Janis,* [428 U.S. 433, 96 S.Ct. 3021 (1976)].

To vindicate the continued existence of this judge-made rule, it is incumbent upon those who seek its retention—and surely its *extension*—to demonstrate that it serves its declared deterrent purpose and to show

that the results outweigh the rule's heavy costs to rational enforcement of the criminal law. See, e.g., Killough v. United States, 315 F.2d 241 (1962). The burden rightly rests upon those who ask society to ignore trustworthy evidence of guilt, at the expense of setting obviously guilty criminals free to ply their trade.

In my view, it is an abdication of judicial responsibility to exact such exorbitant costs from society purely on the basis of speculative and unsubstantiated assumptions. * * *

In *Bivens*, I suggested that, despite its grave shortcomings, the rule need not be totally abandoned until some meaningful alternative could be developed to protect innocent persons aggrieved by police misconduct. With the passage of time, it now appears that the continued existence of the rule, as presently implemented, inhibits the development of rational alternatives. The reason is quite simple: incentives for developing new procedures or remedies will remain minimal or non-existent so long as the exclusionary rule is retained in its present form.

It can no longer be assumed that other branches of government will act while judges cling to this Draconian, discredited device in its present absolutist form. Legislatures are unlikely to create statutory alternatives, or impose direct sanctions on errant police officers or on the public treasury by way of tort actions, so long as persons who commit serious crimes continue to reap the enormous and undeserved benefits of the exclusionary rule. And of course, by definition the direct beneficiaries of this rule can be none but persons guilty of crimes. With this extraordinary "remedy" for Fourth Amendment violations, however slight, inadvertent or technical, legislatures might assume that nothing more should be done, even though a grave defect of the exclusionary rule is that it offers no relief whatever to victims of overzealous police work who never appear in court. * * * And even if legislatures were inclined to experiment with alternative remedies, they have no assurance that the judicially created rule will be abolished or even modified in response to such legislative innovations. The unhappy result, as I see it, is that alternatives will inevitably be stymied by rigid adherence on our part to the exclusionary rule. I venture to predict that overruling this judicially contrived doctrine—or limiting its scope to egregious, bad-faith conduct—would inspire a surge of activity toward providing some kind of statutory remedy for persons injured by police mistakes or misconduct.

* * *

Mr. Justice BRENNAN, with whom Mr. Justice MARSHALL concurs, dissenting.

* * *

[T]he real ground of today's decision—a ground that is particularly troubling in light of its portent for habeas jurisdiction generally—is the Court's novel reinterpretation of the habeas statutes; this would read the statutes as requiring the District Courts routinely to deny habeas relief to prisoners "in custody in violation of the Constitution or laws of the United States" as a matter of judicial "discretion"—a "discretion" judicially manufactured today contrary to the express statutory language—because such claims are "different in kind" from other constitutional violations in that they "do not 'impugn

the integrity of the fact-finding process,' " * * * and because application of such constitutional strictures "often frees the guilty." * * *

* * * [W]e are told that "[r]esort to habeas corpus, especially for purposes other than to assure that no innocent person suffers an unconstitutional loss of liberty, results in serious intrusions on values important to our system of government," including waste of judicial resources, lack of finality of criminal convictions, friction between the federal and state judiciaries, and incursions on "federalism." * * * We are told that federal determination of Fourth Amendment claims merely involves "an issue that has no bearing on the basic justice of [the defendant's] incarceration," * * * and that "the ultimate question [in the criminal process should invariably be] guilt or innocence." * * * We are told that the "policy arguments" of respondents to the effect that federal courts must be the ultimate arbiters of federal constitutional rights, and that our certiorari jurisdiction is inadequate to perform this task, "stem from a basic mistrust of the state courts as fair and competent forums for the adjudication of federal constitutional rights"; the Court, however, finds itself "unwilling to assume that there now exists a general lack of appropriate sensitivity to constitutional rights in the trial and appellate courts of the several States," and asserts that it is "unpersuaded" by "the argument that federal judges are more expert in applying federal constitutional law" because "there is 'no intrinsic reason why the fact that a man is a federal judge should make him more competent, or conscientious, or learned with respect to the [consider-

ation of Fourth Amendment claims] than his neighbor in the state courthouse.'" * * * Finally, we are provided a revisionist history of the genesis and growth of federal habeas corpus jurisdiction. * * * If today's decision were only that erroneous state court resolution of Fourth Amendment claims did not render the defendant's resultant confinement "in violation of the Constitution," these pronouncements would have been wholly irrelevant and unnecessary. I am therefore justified in apprehending that the groundwork is being laid today for a drastic withdrawal of federal habeas jurisdiction, if not for all grounds of alleged unconstitutional detention, then at least for claims—for example, of double jeopardy, entrapment, self-incrimination, *Miranda* violations, and use of invalid identification procedures—that this Court later decides are not "guilt-related."

* * *

I would address the Court's concerns for effective utilization of scarce judicial resources, finality principles, federal-state friction, and notions of "federalism" only long enough to note that such concerns carry no more force with respect to non-"guilt-related" constitutional claims than they do with respect to claims that affect the accuracy of the fact-finding process. Congressional conferral of federal habeas jurisdiction for the purpose of entertaining petitions from state prisoners necessarily manifested a conclusion that such concerns could not be controlling, and any argument for discriminating among constitutional rights must therefore depend on the nature of the constitutional right involved.

* * * The procedural safeguards mandated in the Framers'

Constitution are not admonitions to be tolerated only to the extent they serve functional purposes that ensure that the "guilty" are punished and the "innocent" freed; rather, every guarantee enshrined in the Constitution, our basic charter and the guarantor of our most precious liberties, is by it endowed with an independent vitality and value, and this Court is not free to curtail those constitutional guarantees even to punish the most obviously guilty. Particular constitutional rights that do not affect the fairness of fact-finding procedures cannot for that reason be denied at the trial itself. What possible justification then can there be for denying vindication of such rights on federal habeas when state courts do deny those rights at trial? To sanction disrespect and disregard for the Constitution in the name of protecting society from lawbreakers is to make the government itself lawless and to subvert those values upon which our ultimate freedom and liberty depend. * * * Enforcement of *federal* constitutional rights that redress constitutional violations directed against the "guilty" is a particular function of *federal* habeas review, lest judges trying the "morally unworthy" be tempted not to execute the supreme law of the land. State judges popularly elected may have difficulty resisting popular pressures not experienced by federal judges given lifetime tenure designed to immunize them from such influences, and the federal habeas statutes reflect the Congressional judgment that such detached federal review is a salutary safeguard against *any* detention of an individual "in violation of the Constitution or laws of the United States."

* * *

In summary, while unlike the Court I consider that the exclusionary rule is a constitutional ingredient of the Fourth Amendment, any modification of that rule should at least be accomplished with some modicum of logic and justification not provided today. * * * The Court does not disturb the holding of *Mapp* v. *Ohio* that, as a matter of federal constitutional law, illegally obtained evidence must be excluded from the trial of a criminal defendant whose rights were transgressed during the search that resulted in acquisition of the evidence. In light of that constitutional rule it is a matter for Congress, not this Court, to prescribe what federal courts are to review state prisoners' claims of constitutional error committed by state courts. Until this decision, our cases have never departed from the construction of the habeas statutes as embodying a congressional intent that, however substantive constitutional rights are delineated or expanded, those rights may be asserted as a procedural matter under federal habeas jurisdiction. Employing the transparent tactic that today's is a decision construing the Constitution, the Court usurps the authority—vested by the Constitution in the Congress—to reassign federal judicial responsibility for reviewing state prisoners' claims of failure of state courts to redress violations of their Fourth Amendment rights. Our jurisdiction is eminently unsuited for that task, and as a practical matter the only result of today's holding will be that denials by the state courts of claims by state prisoners of violations of their Fourth Amendment rights will go unreviewed by a federal tribunal. I fear that the same treatment ultimately will be accorded state prisoners' claims of violations of other constitu-

tional rights; thus the potential ramifications of this case for federal habeas jurisdiction generally are ominous. The Court, no longer content just to restrict forthrightly the constitutional rights of the citizenry, has embarked on a campaign to water down even such constitutional rights as it purports to acknowledge by the device of foreclosing resort to the federal habeas remedy for their redress.

I would affirm the judgments of the Courts of Appeals.

Mr. Justice WHITE, dissenting.

For many of the reasons stated by Mr. Justice BRENNAN, I cannot agree that the writ of habeas corpus should be any less available to those convicted of state crimes where they allege Fourth Amendment violations than where other constitutional issues are presented to the federal court. Under the amendments to the habeas corpus statute, which were adopted after Fay v. Noia, 372 U.S. 391, 83 S.Ct. 822 (1963), and represented an effort by Congress to lend a modicum of finality to state criminal judgments, I cannot distinguish between Fourth Amendment and other constitutional issues.

* * *

I feel constrained to say, however, that I would join four or more other Justices in substantially limiting the reach of the exclusionary rule as presently administered under the Fourth Amendment in federal and state criminal trials.

Whether I would have joined the Court's opinion in Mapp v. Ohio, * * [367 U.S. 643, 81 S.Ct. 1684 (1961)], had I then been a Member of the Court, I do not know. But as time went on after coming to this bench, I became convinced that both

Weeks v. United States, 232 U.S. 383, 34 S.Ct. 341 (1914), and *Mapp* v. *Ohio* had overshot their mark insofar as they aimed to deter lawless action by law enforcement personnel and that in many of its applications the exclusionary rule was not advancing that aim in the slightest and that in this respect it was a senseless obstacle to arriving at the truth in many criminal trials.

The rule has been much criticized and suggestions have been made that it should be wholly abolished, but I would overrule neither *Weeks v. United States* nor *Mapp v. Ohio*. I am nevertheless of the view that the rule should be substantially modified so as to prevent its application in those many circumstances where the evidence at issue was seized by an officer acting in the good-faith belief that his conduct comported with existing law and having reasonable grounds for this belief. These are recurring situations; and recurringly

evidence is excluded without any realistic expectation that its exclusion will contribute in the slightest to the purposes of the rule, even though the trial will be seriously affected or the indictment dismissed.

* * *

When law enforcement personnel have acted mistakenly, but in good faith and on reasonable grounds, and yet the evidence they have seized is later excluded, the exclusion can have no deterrent effect. The officers, if they do their duty, will act in similar fashion in similar circumstances in the future; and the only consequence of the rule as presently administered is that unimpeachable and probative evidence is kept from the trier of fact and the truth-finding function of proceedings is substantially impaired or a trial totally aborted.

* * *

The Court also restricted the reach of the exclusionary rule in two other cases. In United States v. Janis, 428 U.S. 433, 96 S.Ct. 3021 (1976), decided the same day as *Stone*, the Court, employing a similar interest-balancing analysis, held that illegally seized evidence need not be barred from trial in civil cases brought by the United States. In that case the government introduced gambling records, obtained as a result of an illegal search and seizure, in a suit to recover unpaid federal taxes. Two years earlier in United States v. Calandra, 414 U.S. 338, 94 S.Ct. 613 (1974), the Court held that the Fourth Amendment did not preclude the use of illegally seized evidence by a grand jury. In a stiff dissent, Justice Brennan objected to the Court's "downgrading of the exclusionary rule to a determination whether its application in a particular type of proceeding furthers deterrence of future police misconduct * * *." Emphasis on the rule's capability for deterrence, he pointed out, "reflects a startling misconception * * * of the historical objective and purpose of the rule." Justice Brennan continued:

[C]urtailment of the evil, if a consideration at all, was at best only a hoped-for effect of the exclusionary rule, not its ultimate objective. Indeed, there is no evidence that the possible deterrent effect of the rule was given any attention by the judges chiefly responsible for its formulation. Their concern as guardians of the Bill of Rights was to fashion an enforcement tool to give content and meaning to the Fourth Amendment's guarantees. * * * The exclusionary rule, if not perfect, accomplished the twin goals

of enabling the judiciary to avoid the taint of partnership in official lawlessness and of assuring the people—all potential victims of unlawful government conduct—that the government would not profit from its lawless
behavior, thus minimizing the risk of seriously undermining popular trust in
government.

———

In the course of a narcotics raid on the defendant's apartment, an undercover
police officer was killed, and the defendant and two others were wounded. In
accord with departmental policy that officers personally involved not conduct the
investigation at hand, the remaining officers left after arranging medical assistance for those injured in the shooting. Homicide detectives arrived shortly to
take charge of the investigation. A four-day warrantless search ensued in which,
among other things, police officers ripped up the carpeting, opened drawers, and
seized more than 200 items. Later the same day of the raid, one of the detectives
went to the hospital's intensive care unit where the defendant was confined.
After giving him the *Miranda* warnings, the detective began and persisted in
interrogating the defendant who was barely conscious and hooked up to a breathing apparatus. The defendant protested several times, asked that the questioning
stop, and demanded to see a lawyer. At his trial on charges of murder, assault,
and various narcotics offenses, evidence obtained as a result of the search and
several statements made during the course of the interrogation, which were used
to impeach the credibility of his testimony, were admitted. The state supreme
court reversed the murder and assault convictions on points of state law but sustained the narcotics convictions, holding that a warrantless search at the scene of
a homicide constituted a procedure justified by an emergency situation and that
the statements made by the defendant at the hospital were given voluntarily. The
Supreme Court reversed this judgment and remanded the case for a new trial in
Mincey v. Arizona, 437 U.S. 385, 98 S.Ct. 2408 (1978).

In his opinion for a nearly unanimous Court in this case, Justice Stewart
addressed both the Fourth and Fifth Amendment issues. Turning first to the
search and seizure question, the Court found no exigent circumstances to justify
the warrantless search. In its consideration of the arguments advanced by the
state to justify the admissibility of the evidence obtained from the apartment, the
Court rejected the following propositions: (1) that the defendant forfeited any
expectation of privacy by shooting the undercover police officer and that the
search was not significantly more intrusive than the original narcotics raid; (2)
that a possible homicide *per se* constitutes an emergency demanding immediate
investigative action sufficient to cancel the warrant requirement; (3) that the vital
public interest in the prompt investigation of a very serious crime such as murder
overrides the usual requirement of a search warrant; and (4) that the murder
scene exception approved by the state supreme court constitutes a narrowly delineated exception to the warrant requirement. Justice Stewart concluded: "There
was no indication that evidence would be lost, destroyed or removed during the
time required to obtain a search warrant. Indeed, the police guard at the apartment minimized that possibility. And there is no suggestion that a search warrant
could not easily and conveniently have been obtained." Summing up, the Court
noted that the murder scene circumstance "would usually be constitutionally sufficient to warrant a search of substantial scope. But the Fourth Amendment
requires that this judgment in each case be made in the first instance by a neutral
magistrate." Because "there will presumably be a new trial in this case," the
Court went on to rule on the admissibility of the defendant's statements made in
the hospital. Reiterating the principle that voluntariness and not trustworthiness

is the touchstone of analysis governing the admissibility of statements by a criminal defendant, Justice Stewart explained:

> It is hard to imagine a situation less conducive to the exercise of "a rational intellect and a free will" than Mincey's. He had been seriously wounded just a few hours earlier, and had arrived at the hospital "depressed almost to the point of coma," according to his attending physician. Although he had received some treatment, his condition at the time of Hust's interrogation was still sufficiently serious that he was in the intensive care unit. He complained to Hust that the pain in his leg was "unbearable." He was evidently confused and unable to think clearly about either the events of that afternoon or the circumstances of his interrogation, since some of his written answers were on their face not entirely coherent. Finally, while Mincey was being questioned he was lying on his back on a hospital bed, encumbered by tubes, needles, and breathing apparatus. He was, in short, "at the complete mercy" of Detective Hust, unable to escape or resist the thrust of Hust's interrogation. * * *

> In this debilitated and helpless condition, Mincey clearly expressed his wish not to be interrogated. As soon as Hust's questions turned to the details of the afternoon's events, Mincey wrote: "This is all I can say without a lawyer." Hust nonetheless continued to question him, and a nurse who was present suggested it would be best if Mincey answered. Mincey gave unresponsive or uninformative answers to several more questions, and then said again that he did not want to talk without a lawyer. Hust ignored that request and another made immediately thereafter. Indeed, throughout the interrogation Mincey vainly asked Hust to desist. Moreover, he complained several times that he was confused or unable to think clearly, or that he could answer more accurately the next day. But despite Mincey's entreaties to be let alone, Hust ceased the interrogation only during intervals when Mincey lost consciousness or received medical treatment, and after each such interruption returned relentlessly to his task. The statements at issue were thus the result of virtually continuous questioning of a seriously and painfully wounded man on the edge of consciousness.

Justice Marshall wrote a concurring opinion, in which Justice Brennan joined, "to emphasize a point that is illustrated by the instant case, but that applies more generally to all cases in which we are asked to review Fourth Amendment issues arising out of state criminal convictions." Observing that it was doubtful whether "we would have granted certiorari to resolve the Fifth Amendment issue in this case, for that could have been resolved on federal habeas corpus," Justice Marshall pointed out, "With regard to the Fourth Amendment issue, however, we had little choice but to grant review, because our decision in Stone v. Powell, 428 U.S. 465, 96 S.Ct. 3037 (1976), precludes federal habeas corpus consideration of such issues." Justice Marshall explained:

> Prior to *Stone* v. *Powell*, there would have been no need to grant certiorari in a case such as this, since the federal habeas remedy would have been available to the defendant. Indeed, prior to *Stone* petitioner here probably would not even have had to utilize federal habeas, since the Arizona courts were at that earlier time more inclined to follow the federal constitutional pronouncements of the Ninth Circuit. * * * But *Stone* eliminated the habeas remedy with regard to Fourth Amendment violations, thus allowing state court rulings to diverge from lower federal court rulings on these

issues and placing a correspondingly greater burden on this Court to ensure uniform federal law in the Fourth Amendment area.

At the time of *Stone* my Brother Brennan wrote that "institutional constraints totally preclude any possibility that his Court can adequately oversee whether state courts have properly applied federal law." * * * Because of these constraints, we will often be faced with a Hobson's choice in cases of less than national significance that could formerly have been left to the lower federal courts: either to deny certiorari and thereby let stand divergent state and federal decisions with regard to Fourth Amendment rights; or to grant certiorari and thereby add to our calendar, which many believe is already overcrowded, cases that might better have been resolved elsewhere. In view of this problem and others, I hope that the Court will at some point reconsider the wisdom of *Stone* v. *Powell*.

Justice Rehnquist, concurring in part and dissenting in part, took exception to the Court's ruling on the admissibility of the defendant's statements. Said Rehnquist, " * * * I think the Court today goes too far in substituting its own judgment for the judgment of a trial court and the highest court of a State, both of whom decided these disputed issues differently than does this Court, and both of whom were a good deal closer to the factual occurrences than is this Court. * * * I believe that the trial court was entitled to conclude that, notwithstanding Mincey's medical condition, his statements in the intensive care unit were admissible. The fact that the same court might have been equally entitled to reach the opposite conclusion does not justify this Court's adopting the opposite conclusion."

b. WARRANTLESS SEARCHES AND SEIZURES

CUPP v. MURPHY

Supreme Court of the United States, 1973
412 U.S. 291, 93 S.Ct. 2000, 36 L.Ed.2d 900

Upon being informed of the murder of his wife, Daniel Murphy promptly telephoned the Portland police and voluntarily appeared at the Portland police station for questioning. Murphy's wife had died of strangulation in her home in Portland, and abrasions and lacerations were found on her throat. There was no sign of a break-in or a robbery. Soon after Murphy's arrival at the police station, the police noticed a dark spot on his finger. The police, believing that the dark spot might be blood and knowing that evidence of strangulation is often found under the assailant's fingernails, requested of Murphy that they be allowed to take a sample of scrapings from his fingernails. At this time Murphy was not under arrest, although he was detained and there was probable cause to believe that he had committed the murder. Murphy refused the request, but the police, over Murphy's protest and without a warrant, proceeded to take the samples. The samples turned out to contain traces of skin and blood cells and fabric from the victim's nightgown, all of which were admitted into evidence at the trial. Murphy appealed his conviction, claiming that the samples taken by the police were the product of an unconstitutional search in violation of the Fourth and Fourteenth Amendments. The Oregon Court of Appeals affirmed the conviction, and the United States Supreme Court denied certiorari. Murphy then appealed to a U. S. District Court for habeas corpus relief against Cupp, the Superintendent of the Oregon State Penitentiary. The district court denied the petition for habeas corpus, but the U. S. Court of Appeals for the Ninth Circuit reversed, holding that in the absence of an arrest the search was unconstitutional even though the probable cause to make an arrest existed. The Supreme Court granted the state's petition for certiorari.

Mr. Justice STEWART delivered the opinion of the Court.

* * *

On the facts of this case, considering the existence of probable cause, the very limited intrusion undertaken incident to the station house detention, and the ready destructibility of the evidence, we cannot say that this search violated the Fourth and Fourteenth Amendments. Accordingly, the judgment of the Court of Appeals is reversed.

Reversed.

Mr. Justice WHITE joins the opinion of the Court but does not consider the issue of probable cause to have been decided here or to be foreclosed on remand to the Court of Appeals where it has never been considered.

Mr. Justice BLACKMUN, with whom The CHIEF JUSTICE [BURGER] joins, concurring.

The Court today permits a search for evidence without an arrest but under circumstances where probable cause for an arrest existed, where the officers had reasonable cause to believe that the evidence was on respondent's person, and where that evidence was highly destructible. The Court, however, restricts the permissible quest to "the very limited search necessary to preserve the highly evanescent evidence they found under [respondent's] fingernails."

While I join the Court's opinion, I do so with the understanding that what the Court says here applies only where no arrest has been made. Far different factors, in my view, govern the permissible scope of a search incident to a lawful arrest.

Mr. Justice BRENNAN, dissenting in part.

Without effecting an arrest, and without first seeking to obtain a search warrant from a magistrate, the police decided to scrape respondent's fingernails for potentially destructible evidence. In upholding this search, the Court engrafts another, albeit limited, exception on the warrant requirement. Before we take the serious step of legitimating even limited searches merely upon probable cause—without a warrant or as incident to an arrest—we ought first be certain that such probable cause in fact existed. Here, as my Brother Douglas convincingly demonstates "[w]hether there was or was not probable cause is difficult to determine on this record." * * * And, since the Court of Appeals did not consider that question, the proper course would be to remand to that court so that it might decide in the first instance whether there was probable cause to arrest or search. There is simply no need for this Court to decide, upon a disputed record and at this stage of the litigation, whether the instant search would be permissible if probable cause existed.

[Justice DOUGLAS also dissented in part.]

SCHNECKLOTH v. BUSTAMONTE

Supreme Court of the United States, 1973
412 U.S. 218, 93 S.Ct. 2041, 36 L.Ed.2d 854

During a routine patrol of Sunnyvale, California, Police Officer James Rand stopped an automobile driven by one Joe Gonzales when he noticed that one headlight and the license plate light were burned out. Aside from the driver, five other men were seated in the car. Joe Alcala and the defendant, Robert Bustamonte, were seated in the front seat, while three older men were in the back seat. Officer Rand asked Gonzales for his driver's license. Following Gonzales's failure to produce identification, the officer asked if any of the men had evidence of identification. Only Joe Alcala produced a license, and he explained that the car was his brother's. At Officer Rand's request, the six men stepped out of the automobile. Officer Rand then asked Alcala if he could search the automobile. Alcala's reply was, "Sure, go ahead." At this point no one had been arrested or threatened with arrest, and the atmosphere was later characterized by Officer Rand as "very congenial." In fact, when Officer Rand asked Alcala if the trunk opened, Alcala responded by giving Officer Rand the key to the trunk. Inspection of the automobile turned up three checks, found wadded up under the left rear seat. These checks were identified as having been previously stolen from a carwash. At his trial, Bustamonte moved to suppress the introduction of the checks on the ground that they had been acquired through an unconstitutional search and seizure. The trial judge conducted an evidentiary hearing at the conclusion of which he ruled that the evidence had been gathered in a manner not inconsistent with the Constitution. Using the checks and additional evidence, Bustamonte was convicted of possessing a check with the intent to defraud. On appeal to the California Court of Appeal for the First Appellate District, the conviction was affirmed. The appellate court held that the state had proven the constitutionality of the search and seizure by demonstrating that Alcala had consented voluntarily to the search without any threat on the part of the police officer. Thereafter, Bustamonte .sought a writ of habeas corpus in federal district court against Schneckloth, the superintendent of the penal institution where he was confined. The petition for the writ was denied. On appeal to the U. S. Court of Appeals, Ninth Circuit, the lower court's decision was set aside. The court of appeals reasoned that a consent to search was a waiver of a person's Fourth and Fourteenth Amendment rights. Therefore, the court concluded, it was the state's obligation to prove not only that the consent had been uncoerced, but that it had been given with the understanding that it could be freely and effectively withheld. Since the state had failed to demonstrate that Alcala had known that his consent could be withheld, the court of appeals vacated the order denying the writ and remanded the case for further proceedings. The Supreme Court then granted the state's petition for certiorari.

Mr. Justice STEWART delivered the opinion of the Court.

It is well settled under the Fourth and Fourteenth Amendments that a search conducted without a warrant issued upon probable cause is "per se unreasonable * * * subject only to a few specifically established and well-delineated exceptions." * * * It is equally well settled that one of the specifically established exceptions to the requirements of both a warrant and probable cause is a search that is conducted pursuant to consent. * * * The constitutional question in the present case concerns the definition of "consent" in this Fourth and Fourteenth Amendment context.

* * *

Our decision today is a narrow one. We hold only that when the subject of a search is not in custody and the State attempts to justify a search on the basis of his consent, the Fourth and Fourteenth Amendments require that it demonstrate that the consent was in fact voluntarily given, and not the result of duress or coercion, express or implied. Voluntariness is a question of fact to be determined from all the circumstances, and while the subject's knowledge of a right to refuse is a factor to be taken into account, the prosecution is not required to demonstrate such knowledge as a prerequisite to establishing a voluntary consent. Because the California courts followed these principles in affirming the respondent's conviction, and because the Court of Appeals for the Ninth Circuit in remanding for an evidentiary hearing required more, its judgment must be reversed.

It is so ordered.

Judgment of Court of Appeals reversed.

Mr. Justice DOUGLAS, dissenting.

I agree with the Court of Appeals that "verbal assent" to a search is not enough; that the fact that consent was given to the search does not imply that the suspect knew that the alternative of a refusal existed. 448 F.2d, at 700. As that court stated "under many circumstances a rea-

sonable person might read an officer's 'May I' as the courteous expression of a demand backed by force of law." Id., at 701.

A considerable constitutional guarantee rides on this narrow issue. At the time of the search there was no probable cause to believe that the car contained contraband or other unlawful articles. The car was stopped only because a headlight and the license plate light were burned out. The car belonged to Alcala's brother from whom it was borrowed and Alcala had a driver's license. Traffic citations were appropriately issued. The car was searched, the present record showing that Alcala consented. But whether Alcala knew he had the right to refuse, we do not know. All the Court of Appeals did was to remand the case to the District Court for a finding—and if necessary, a hearing on that issue.

I would let the case go forward on that basis. The long, time-consuming contest in this Court might well wash out. At least we could be assured that, if it came back, we would not be rendering an advisory opinion. Had I voted to grant this petition, I would suggest we dismiss it as improvidently granted. But being in the minority, I am bound by the rule of four.

[Justices BRENNAN and MARSHALL also dissented.]

CHIMEL v. CALIFORNIA

Supreme Court of the United States, 1969
395 U.S. 752, 89 S.Ct. 2034, 23 L.Ed.2d 685

Carrying a warrant for arrest in connection with the burglary of a coin shop, three police officers arrived one afternoon to serve it on Chimel at his home. They were admitted to the house by his wife and waited there for a few minutes until he returned from work. After serving the arrest warrant, the policemen conducted a search of the house lasting about an hour which turned up several items—mostly coins. These items were later admitted into evidence at Chimel's trial over his objection, and he was subsequently convicted. The California Supreme Court affirmed the conviction, and the defendant appealed.

Mr. Justice STEWART delivered the opinion of the Court.

This case raises basic questions concerning the permissible scope under the Fourth Amendment of a search incident to a lawful arrest.

*   *   *

In 1950, [the Court announced its ruling in] United States v. Rabinowitz, 339 U.S. 56, 70 S.Ct. 430, the decision upon which California primarily relies in the case now before us. In *Rabinowitz*, federal authorities had been informed that the defendant was dealing in stamps bearing forged overprints. On the basis of that information they secured a warrant for his arrest, which they executed at his one-room business office. At the time of the arrest, the officers "searched the desk, safe, and file cabinets in the office for about an hour and a half," * * * and seized 573 stamps with forged overprints. The stamps were admitted into evidence at the defendant's trial, and this Court affirmed his conviction, rejecting the contention that the warrantless search had been unlawful. The Court held that the search in its entirety fell within the principle giving law enforcement authorities "[t]he right 'to search the place where the arrest is made in order to find and seize things connected with the crime.'" * * * The test, said the Court, "is not whether it is reasonable to procure a search warrant, but whether the search was reasonable." * * *

Rabinowitz has come to stand for the proposition, *inter alia*, that a warrantless search "incident to a lawful arrest" may generally extend to the area that is considered to be in the "possession" or under the "control" of the person arrested. And it was on the basis of that proposition that the California courts upheld the search of the petitioner's entire house in this case. That doctrine, however, at least in the broad sense in which it was applied by the California courts in this case, can withstand neither historical nor rational analysis.

Even limited to its own facts, the *Rabinowitz* decision was, as we have seen, hardly founded on an unimpeachable line of authority. * * * [After going on to recount the vague and dubious heritage of the *Rabinowitz* holding, Justice Stewart observed:] The [Fourth] Amendment was in large part a reaction to the general warrants and warrantless searches that had so alienated the colonists and had helped speed the movement for independence. In the scheme of the Amendment, therefore, the requirement that "no Warrants shall issue, but upon probable cause," plays a crucial part. * * *

*   *   *

A similar analysis underlies the "search incident to arrest" principle, and marks its proper extent. When an arrest is made, it is reasonable for the arresting officer to search the person arrested in order to remove any weapons that the latter might seek to use in order to resist arrest or effect his escape. Otherwise, the officer's safety might well be endangered, and the arrest itself frustrated. In addition, it is entirely reasonable for the arresting officer to search for and seize any evidence on the arrestee's person in order to prevent its concealment or destruction. And the area into which an arrestee might reach in order to grab a weapon or evidentiary items must, of course, be governed by a like rule. A gun on a table or in a drawer in front of one who is arrested can be as dangerous to the arresting officer as one concealed in the clothing of the person arrested. There is ample justification, therefore, for a search of the arrestee's person and the area "within his immediate control"—construing that phrase to mean the area from within which he might gain possession of a weapon or destructible evidence.

There is no comparable justification, however, for routinely searching any room other than that in which an arrest occurs—or, for that matter, for searching through all the desk drawers or other closed or concealed areas in that room itself. Such searches, in the absence of well-recognized exceptions, may be made only under the authority of a search warrant.   *   *   *

*   *   *

It is argued in the present case that it is "reasonable" to search a man's house when he is arrested in it. But that argument is founded on little more than a subjective view regarding the acceptability of certain sorts of police conduct, and not on considerations relevant to Fourth Amendment interests. Under such an unconfined analysis, Fourth Amendment protection in this area would approach the evaporation point. It is not easy to explain why, for instance, it is less subjectively

"reasonable" to search a man's house when he is arrested on his front lawn—or just down the street—than it is when he happens to be in the house at the time of arrest.
*   *   *

*   *   *

The petitioner correctly points out that one result of decisions such as *Rabinowitz* and *Harris* [v. United States, 331 U.S. 145, 67 S.Ct. 1098] is to give law enforcement officials the opportunity to engage in searches not justified by probable cause, by the simple expedient of arranging to arrest suspects at home rather than elsewhere. We do not suggest that the petitioner is necessarily correct in his assertion that such a strategy was utilized here, but the fact remains that had he been arrested earlier in the day, at his place of employment rather than at home, no search of his house could have been made without a search warrant. In any event, even apart from the possibility of such police tactics, the general point so forcefully made by Judge Learned Hand in United States v. Kirschenblatt, 2 Cir., 16 F.2d 202, remains:

"After arresting a man in his house, to rummage at will among his papers in search of whatever will convict him, appears to us to be indistinguishable from what might be done under a general warrant; indeed, the warrant would give more protection, for presumably it must be issued by a magistrate. True, by hypothesis the power would not exist, if the supposed offender were not found on the premises; but it is small consolation to know that one's papers are safe only so long as one is not at home."   *   *   *

Rabinowitz and *Harris* have been the subject of critical commentary for many years, and have been relied upon less and less in our own decisions. It is time, for the reasons we have stated, to hold that on their own facts, and insofar as the principles they stand for are inconsistent with those that we have endorsed today, they are no longer to be followed.

Application of sound Fourth Amendment principles to the facts of this case produces a clear result. The search here went far beyond the petitioner's person and the area from within which he might have obtained either a weapon or something that could have been used as evidence against him. There was no constitutional justification, in the absence of a search warrant, for extending the search beyond that area. The scope of the search was, therefore, "unreasonable" under the Fourth and Fourteenth Amendments and the petitioner's conviction cannot stand.

Reversed.

Mr. Justice HARLAN, concurring.

*　*　*

The only thing that has given me pause in voting to overrule *Harris* and *Rabinowitz* is that as a result of Mapp v. Ohio, 367 U.S. 643, 81 S.Ct. 1684 (1961), and Ker v. California, 374 U.S. 23, 83 S.Ct. 1623 (1963), every change in Fourth Amendment law must now be obeyed by state officials facing widely different problems of local law enforcement. We simply do not know the extent to which cities and towns across the Nation are prepared to administer the greatly expanded warrant system which will be required by today's decision; nor can we say with assurance that in each and every local situation, the warrant requirement plays an essential role in the protection of those fundamental liberties protected against state infringement by the Fourteenth Amendment.

*　*　*

This federal-state factor has not been an easy one for me to resolve, but in the last analysis I cannot in good conscience vote to perpetuate bad Fourth Amendment law.

*　*　*

Mr. Justice WHITE, with whom Mr. Justice BLACK joins, dissenting.

Few areas of the law have been as subject to shifting constitutional standards over the last 50 years as that of the search "incident to an arrest." There has been a remarkable instability in this whole area, which has seen at least four major shifts in emphasis. Today's opinion makes an untimely fifth. In my view, the Court should not now abandon the old rule.

[Justice WHITE then proceeded to find the search in this case "reasonable" under the terms of *Rabinowitz* and related cases.]

*　*　*

ARRESTS, SEARCHES, AND DETENTIONS
IN AND ABOUT THE HOME

Case	Ruling	Dissenting Votes
Payton v. New York, 445 U.S. 573, 100 S.Ct. 1371 (1980)	By contrast with the holding in the *Watson* case, supra, in the absence of exigent circumstances, police may not make a nonconsensual entry of a private residence without a warrant to effect a routine felony arrest	Burger, White, and Rehnquist
Steagald v. United States, 451 U.S. 204, 101 S.Ct. 1642 (1981)	In the absence of consent or emergency circumstances, a law enforcement officer may not constitutionally search for an individual named in an arrest warrant in the home of a third party without first obtaining a search warrant	White and Rehnquist
Michigan v. Summers, 452 U.S. 692, 101 S.Ct. 2587 (1981)	Where police officers executing a warrant to search a house for narcotics ran into the defendant coming down the front steps and requested his aid in gaining entry, their detention of him inside while they searched the premises until they turned up evidence establishing probable cause to arrest him did not violate the Fourth Amendment since a warrant to search for contraband implicitly carries with it limited authority to detain occupants of the premises while the search is being conducted. The arrest of the defendant and subsequent search of his person (which turned up some heroin in his coat pocket) was constitutional	Brennan, Stewart, and Marshall
Washington v. Chrisman, 455 U.S. 1, 102 S.Ct. 812 (1982)	Where a police officer arrested a college student for underage drinking and where the student then asked to go to his room so that he could get some identification, it was not a violation of the Fourth Amendment for the officer to accompany the student and, once in the room, to seize contraband in plain sight	Brennan, White, and Marshall

COOLIDGE v. NEW HAMPSHIRE

Supreme Court of the United States, 1971
403 U.S. 443, 91 S.Ct. 2022, 29 L.Ed.2d 564

During their investigation of the brutal murder of a fourteen-year-old girl near Manchester, New Hampshire, the police obtained evidence that appeared to implicate Edward Coolidge in the crime. Two witnesses had told police that on the night the girl disappeared and at the site where her body was eventually found, they assisted a man in a parked 1951 Pontiac similar to the one owned by Coolidge. In addition, petitioner's wife had voluntarily handed over to the police four weapons and some clothing which he owned. (A laboratory test of the guns revealed that one of them was used to kill the girl, although conflicting test results were later presented at the trial.) This and other evidence was brought before the attorney general of the state who was in charge of the investigation and who subsequently helped prosecute the case. Acting in his capacity also as a justice of the peace, he issued an arrest warrant and four search warrants including one authorizing seizure of Coolidge's 1951 Pontiac. (Under a New Hampshire law, all justices of the peace were empowered to issue search warrants.) The police then arrested Coolidge at his home and had the Pontiac, which was parked in the driveway at the time, towed to the police station. An inspection of the car yielded further evidence which was used at the trial to convict Coolidge. The New Hampshire Supreme Court affirmed, and the United States Supreme Court granted certiorari. Among several objections raised by petitioner was his contention that the warrant authorizing the seizure and search of his automobile was invalid because it had been issued by someone with a direct and substantial interest in the outcome of the proceedings instead of by a "neutral and detached magistrate" as required by the Fourth and Fourteenth Amendments.

Mr. Justice STEWART delivered the opinion of the Court.

* * *

The petitioner's first claim is that the warrant authorizing the seizure and subsequent search of his 1951 Pontiac automobile was invalid because not issued by a "neutral and detached magistrate." Since we agree with the petitioner that the warrant was invalid for this reason, we need not consider his further argument that the allegations under oath supporting the issuance of the warrant were so conclusory as to violate relevant constitutional standards. * * *

The classic statement of the policy underlying the warrant requirement of the Fourth Amendment is that of Mr. Justice Jackson, writing for the Court in Johnson v. United States, 333 U.S. 10, 13–14, 68 S.Ct. 367, 369:

"The point of the Fourth Amendment, which often is not grasped by zealous officers, is not that it denies law enforcement the support of the usual inferences which reasonable men draw from evidence. Its protection consists in requiring that those inferences be drawn by a neutral and detached magistrate instead of being judged by the officer engaged in the often competitive enterprise of ferreting out crime. Any assumption that evidence sufficient to support a magistrate's disinterested determination to issue a search warrant will justify the officers in making a search without a warrant would reduce the Amendment to a nullity and leave the people's homes secure only in the discretion of police officers. * * * When the right of privacy must reasonably yield to the right of search is, as a rule, to be decided by a judicial officer, not by a policeman or Government enforcement agent." * * *

In this case, the determination of probable cause was made by the chief "government enforcement agent" of the State—the Attorney General—who was actively in charge of the investigation and later was to be chief prosecutor at the trial. * * * [T]he State argues that the Attorney General, who was unquestionably authorized as a justice of the peace to issue warrants under then-existing state law, did in fact act as a "neutral and detached magistrate." * * * [I]t is enough to answer that there could hardly be a more appropriate setting than this for a *per se* rule of disqualification rather than a case-by-case evaluation of all the circumstances. Without disrespect to the state law enforcement agent here involved, the whole point of the basic rule so well expressed by Mr. Justice Jackson is that prosecutors and policemen simply cannot be asked to maintain the requisite neutrality with regard to their own investigations—the "competitive enterprise" that must rightly engage their single-minded attention. * * *

* * *

We find no escape from the conclusion that the seizure and search of the Pontiac automobile cannot constitutionally rest upon the warrant issued by the state official who was the chief investigator and prosecutor in this case. Since he was not the neutral and detached magistrate required by the Constitution, the search stands on no firmer ground than if there had been no warrant at all. If the seizure and search are to be justified, they must, therefore, be justified on some other theory.

The State proposes three distinct theories to bring the facts of this case within one or another of the exceptions to the warrant requirement. * * *

[T]he most basic constitutional rule in this area is that "searches conducted outside the judicial process, without prior approval by judge or magistrate, are *per se* unreasonable under the Fourth Amendment—subject only to a few specifically established and well-delineated exceptions." The exceptions are "jealously and carefully drawn," and there must be "a showing by those who seek exemption * * * that the exigencies of the situation made that course imperative." "[T]he burden is on those seeking the exemption to show the need for it." In times of unrest, whether caused by crime or racial conflict or fear of internal sub-

version, this basic law and the values that it represents may appear unrealistic or "extravagant" to some. But the values were those of the authors of our fundamental constitutional concepts. * * *

The State's first theory is that the seizure * * * and subsequent search of Coolidge's Pontiac were "incident" to a valid arrest. * * *

* * *

Even assuming, *arguendo*, that the police might have searched the Pontiac in the driveway when they arrested Coolidge in the house, Preston v. United States, 376 U.S. 364, 84 S.Ct. 881, makes plain that they could not legally seize the car, remove it, and search it at their leisure without a warrant. In circumstances virtually identical to those here, Mr. Justice Black's opinion for a unanimous Court held that "[o]nce an accused is under arrest and in custody, then a search [of his car] made at another place, without a warrant, is simply not incident to the arrest." * * * Search incident doctrine, in short, has no applicability to this case.

The second theory put forward by the State to justify a warrantless seizure and search of the Pontiac car is that under Carroll v. United States, 267 U.S. 132, 45 S.Ct. 280, the police may make a warrantless search of an automobile whenever they have probable cause to do so, and, under our decision last Term in Chambers v. Maroney, 399 U.S. 42, 90 S.Ct. 1975, whenever the police may make a legal contemporaneous search under *Carroll*, they may also seize the car, take it to the police station, and search it there. But even granting that the police had probable cause to search the car, the application of the *Carroll* case to these facts would extend it far beyond its original rationale.

[The rationale, set forth in *Carroll* and affirmed in *Chambers*, was that, as distinguished from the search of a house or other building, in stopping an automobile on the highway "it is not practicable to secure a warrant because the vehicle can be quickly moved out of the locality or jurisdiction in which the warrant must be sought." The Court held that it was the prospect of flight of the evidence that produced the exception.]

* * *

Since *Carroll* would not have justified a warrantless search of the Pontiac at the time Coolidge was arrested, the later search at the station house was plainly illegal, at least so far as the automobile exception is concerned. * * *

The State's third theory in support of the warrantless seizure and search of the Pontiac car is that the car itself was an "instrumentality of the crime," and as such might be seized by the police on Coolidge's property because it was in plain view. * * *

* * *

[A]n object that comes into view during a search incident to arrest that is appropriately limited in scope under existing law may be seized without a warrant. Chimel v. California, 395 U.S., at 762–763, 89 S.Ct., at 2039–2040. Finally, the "plain view" doctrine has been applied where a police officer is not searching for evidence against the accused, but nonetheless inadvertently comes across an incriminating object. * * *

* * *

[I]t is apparent that the "plain view" exception cannot justify the police seizure of the Pontiac car in this case. The police had ample opportunity to obtain a valid warrant; they knew the automobile's exact description and location well in advance; they intended to seize it when they came upon Coolidge's property. And this is not a case involving contraband or stolen goods or objects dangerous in themselves.

The seizure was therefore unconstitutional, and so was the subsequent search at the station house. Since evidence obtained in the course of the search was admitted at Coolidge's trial, the judgment must be reversed and the case remanded to the New Hampshire Supreme Court. Mapp v. Ohio, 367 U.S. 643, 81 S.Ct. 1684.

* * *

Mr. Justice HARLAN, concurring.

From the several opinions that have been filed in this case it is apparent that the law of search and seizure is due for an overhauling. State and federal law enforcement officers and prosecutorial authorities must find quite intolerable the present state of uncertainty, which extends even to such an everyday question as the circumstances under which police may enter a man's property to arrest him and seize a vehicle believed to have been used during the commission of a crime.

I would begin this process of re-evaluation by overruling Mapp v. Ohio * * * and Ker v. California, 374 U.S. 23, 83 S.Ct. 1623 (1963). The former of these cases made the federal "exclusionary rule" applicable to the States. The latter forced the States to follow all the ins and outs of this Court's Fourth Amendment decisions, handed down in federal cases.

In combination *Mapp* and *Ker* have been primarily responsible for bringing about serious distortions and incongruities in this field of constitutional law. Basically these have had two aspects, as I believe an examination of our more recent opinions and certiorari docket will show. First, the States have been put in a federal mold with respect to this aspect of criminal law enforcement, thus depriving the country of the opportunity to observe the effects of different procedures in similar settings. * * * Second, in order to leave some room for the States to cope with their own diverse problems, there has been generated a tendency to relax federal requirements under the Fourth Amendment, which now govern state procedures as well. * * *

* * *

Mr. Chief Justice BURGER, dissenting in part and concurring in part.

This case illustrates graphically the monstrous price we pay for the exclusionary rule in which we seem to have imprisoned ourselves. See my dissent in Bivens v. Six Unknown Named Agents of Federal Bureau of Narcotics, 403 U.S. 388, 91 S.Ct. 1999.

On the merits of the case I find not the slightest basis in the record to reverse this conviction. Here again the Court reaches out, strains, and distorts rules that were showing some signs of stabilizing, and directs a new trial which will be held more than seven years after the criminal acts charged.

* * *

Mr. Justice BLACK, concurring and dissenting.

* * *

* * * With respect to the rifle voluntarily given to the police by petitioner's wife, the majority holds that it was properly received in evidence. I agree. But the Court reverses petitioner's conviction on the ground that the sweepings taken from his car were seized during an illegal search and for this reason the admission of the sweepings into evidence violated the Fourth Amendment. I dissent.

* * * The truth is that the source of the exclusionary rule simply cannot be found in the Fourth Amendment. That Amendment [unlike the Fifth] did not when adopted, and does not now, contain any constitutional rule barring the admission of illegally seized evidence.

[Justice BLACK went on to find the seizure in this case incident to a valid arrest. He also chided the majority for "reject[ing] the test of reasonableness provided in the Fourth Amendment and substitut[ing] a *per se* rule—if the police could have obtained a warrant and did not, the seizure, no matter how reasonable, is void. Continued Justice BLACK, "But the Fourth Amendment does not require that every search be made pursuant to a warrant. It prohibits only 'unreasonable searches and seizures.' The relevant test is not the reasonableness of the opportunity to procure a warrant, but the reasonableness of the seizure under all the circumstances. The test of reasonableness cannot be fixed by *per se* rules; each case must be decided on its own facts."]

* * *

Mr. Justice BLACKMUN joins Mr. Justice BLACK in [p]arts * * * of this opinion. * * *

Mr. Justice WHITE, with whom THE CHIEF JUSTICE joins, concurring and dissenting.

I would affirm the judgment. In my view, Coolidge's Pontiac was lawfully seized as evidence of the crime in plain sight and thereafter was lawfully searched. * * *

[Justice WHITE examined at considerable length the consequences of the inadvertence rule imposed by the Court in searches conducted without a warrant concluding that it "seems a punitive and extravagant application of the exclusionary rule."]

OF CARS AND LUGGAGE: THE *CHADWICK*, *SANDERS*, AND *ROSS* DECISIONS

In a trilogy of major cases decided over a five-year period beginning in 1977, the Court shaped its reading of the automobile exception as it bears upon the search of containers found within a vehicle. In United States v. Chadwick, 433 U.S. 1, 97 S.Ct. 2476 (1977), the Court held that a locked footlocker could not be searched in the absence of a warrant even though it had been loaded into the trunk of an automobile because of the owner's significant expectation of privacy in the secured container. Subsequent cases posed for the Court the question whether they fell in the *Chadwick* category, thus requiring police to first obtain a warrant before searching such containers, or whether they fell within the automobile exception, recognized in Chambers v. Maroney, 399 U.S. 42, 90 S.Ct. 1975 (1970) and Carroll v. United States, 267 U.S. 132, 45 S.Ct. 280 (1925), which permitted warrantless searches of automobiles and their contents. Warrantless searches within the automobile exception were, of course, initially justified by the factor of the mobility of contraband in a motor vehicle and were fortified in later cases by the recognition that a car affords a reduced expectation of privacy.

Arkansas v. Sanders, 442 U.S. 753, 99 S.Ct. 2586 (1979), presented an occasion for considering the interface between these two categories. In that case, Little Rock police officers staked out the airport following a tip from an informant that Sanders would be arriving carrying a green suitcase containing marijuana. After he arrived, they watched as he retrieved the suitcase from the baggage claim area, placed it in the trunk of a taxi, and got into the vehicle with a companion. Two police officers followed the taxi after it drove off, stopped the vehicle a few blocks from the airport, and asked the driver to open the trunk. Without obtaining Sanders's permission, the officers opened the suitcase and found the marijuana. Addressing the issue of "whether the warrantless search of respondent's suitcase falls on the *Chadwick* or the *Chambers/Carroll* side of the Fourth Amendment line," Justice Powell, speaking for the Court, wrote:

> The only question * * * is whether the police, rather than immediately searching the suitcase without a warrant, should have taken it, along with respondent, to the police station and there obtained a warrant for the search. A lawful search of luggage generally may be performed only pursuant to a warrant. In *Chadwick* we declined an invitation to extend the *Carroll* exception to all searches of luggage, noting that neither of the two policies supporting warrantless searches of automobiles applies to luggage. Here, as in *Chadwick*, the officers had seized the luggage and had it exclu-

sively within their control at the time of the search. Consequently, "there was not the slightest danger that [the luggage] or its contents could have been removed before a valid search warrant could be obtained." 433 U.S., at 13, 97 S.Ct., at 2484. And, as we observed in that case, luggage is a common repository for one's personal effects, and therefore is inevitably associated with the expectation of privacy. * * *

* * *

In sum, we hold that the warrant requirement of the Fourth Amendment applies to personal luggage taken from an automobile to the same degree it applies to such luggage in other locations. Thus, insofar as the police are entitled to search such luggage without a warrant, their actions must be justified under some exception to the warrant requirement other than that applicable to automobiles stopped on the highway. Where—as in the present case—the police, without endangering themselves or risking loss of the evidence, lawfully have detained one suspected of criminal activity and secured his suitcase, they should delay the search thereof until after judicial approval has been obtained. In this way, the unconstitutional right of suspects to prior judicial review of searches will be fully protected.

As in *Chadwick*, Justices Blackmun and Rehnquist dissented. Justice Blackmun, writing for the two in *Sanders*, objected to the Court's decision on the grounds that it undermined the automobile exception and invited interminable litigation as to the constitutional status of "the briefcase, the wallet, the package, the paper bag, and every other kind of container."

In United States v. Ross, — U.S. —, 102 S.Ct. 2157 (1982), the Court considered a case in which, after being tipped off by an informant that the defendant was selling narcotics he kept in the trunk of a car parked at a particular location, District of Columbia police drove there, stopped the car sometime later as it was being moved, and arrested the driver who matched the description of Ross given to them by the informant. One of the police officers then opened the trunk where he found a brown paper bag containing glassine bags which held powder later identified as heroin. Another warrantless search of the trunk, which occurred after the vehicle had been moved to the station house, turned up a zippered leather pouch containing cash. The defendant was subsequently convicted of possessing heroin with the intent to distribute after the drugs and money were admitted into evidence over his objection. A federal appeals court reversed, however, holding that, while the officers had probable cause to stop and search the car, including the trunk, a warrant was required before opening either the paper bag or the leather pouch. The Supreme Court reversed the judgment of the appeals court and upheld the admissibility of the evidence. Speaking for the Court, Justice Stevens held that "police officers—who have legitimately stopped an automobile and who have probable cause to believe that contraband is concealed somewhere within it—may conduct a probing search of compartments and containers within the vehicle whose contents are not in plain view." Furthermore, "they may conduct a search of the vehicle that is as thorough as a magistrate could authorize in a warrant 'particularly describing the place to be searched' "; in other words, such authority extends to "every part of the vehicle and its contents that may conceal the object of the search." This rule, the Court concluded, was a logical adjunct to the automobile exception to the warrant requirement. Said Justice Stevens:

As we have stated, the decision in *Carroll* was based on the Court's appraisal of practical considerations viewed in the perspective of history. It is therefore significant that the practical consequences of the *Carroll* decision would be largely nullified if the permissible scope of a warrantless search of an automobile did not include containers and packages found inside the vehicle. Contraband goods rarely are strewn across the trunk or floor of a car; since by their very nature such goods must be withheld from public view, they rarely can be placed in an automobile unless they are enclosed within some form of container. The Court in *Carroll* held that "contraband goods *concealed* and illegally transported in an automobile or other vehicle may be searched for without a warrant." 267 U.S., at 153, 45 S.Ct., at 285 (emphasis added). As we noted in Henry v. United States, 361 U.S. 98, 104, 80 S.Ct. 168, 172, the decision in *Carroll* "merely relaxed the requirements for a warrant on grounds of impracticability." It neither broadened nor limited the scope of a lawful search based on probable cause.

Such a rule, of course, "applies only to searches of vehicles that are supported by probable cause." And the Court continued, "In this class of cases, a search is not unreasonable if based on facts that would justify the issuance of a warrant, even though a warrant has not actually been obtained."

The Court's holding in *Ross* squarely contradicted its disposition the previous Term of Robbins v. California, 453 U.S. 420, 101 S.Ct. 2841 (1981). In that case police officers stopped a station wagon in the early morning hours because it was being driven erratically and smelled marijuana smoke when the driver opened the door of the vehicle. A pat-down of the defendant turned up a vial of liquid, and a search of the passenger compartment produced some marijuana as well as some paraphernalia for using it. After the defendant was placed in the patrol car, the officers opened the tailgate of the station wagon, located a handle set flush in the deck, lifted it up to uncover a recessed luggage compartment, and seized two packages of marijuana wrapped in green garbage bags. Citing both *Sanders* and *Chadwick*, the Court ruled that, because of the separate interest in privacy with respect to such a package, a wrapped container in the trunk of a car may not be searched without a warrant despite the fact there was probable cause to search the vehicle and even though probable cause existed to search the container as well.

In *Ross* the Court overruled *Robbins* but maintained the validity of *Chadwick* and most of *Sanders*. As Justice Stevens pointed out, "the Court in *Chadwick* declined to extend the rationale of the 'automobile exception' to permit the warrantless search of any movable container found in a public place." And looking back at *Sanders*, he observed, "As in *Chadwick*, the mere fact that the suitcase had been placed in the trunk of the vehicle did not render the automobile exception of *Carroll* applicable; the police had probable cause to seize the suitcase before it was placed in the trunk of the cab and did not have probable cause to search the taxi itself. Since the suitcase had been placed in the trunk, no danger existed that its contents could have been secreted elsewhere in the vehicle." Thus "in neither *Chadwick* nor *Sanders* did the police have probable cause to search the vehicle or anything within it except the footlocker in the former case and the green suitcase in the latter." *Robbins*, however, "was a case in which suspicion was not directed at a specific container." In overruling *Robbins*, the Court affirmed the vitality of *Chadwick* and of *Sanders*, except insofar as the Court had "broadly suggested [in the latter case] that a warrantless search of a container found in an automobile could never be sustained as part of a warrantless search of the automobile itself." Justice Stevens added:

As Justice Stewart stated in *Robbins*, the Fourth Amendment provides protection to the owner of every container that conceals its contents from plain view. * * * But the protection afforded by the Amendment varies in different settings. The luggage carried by a traveler entering the country may be searched at random by a customs officer; the luggage may be searched no matter how great the traveler's desire to conceal the contents may be. A container carried at the time of arrest often may be searched without a warrant and even without any specific suspicion concerning its contents. A container that may conceal the object of a search authorized by a warrant may be opened immediately; the individual's interest in privacy must give way to the magistrate's official determination of probable cause.

In the same manner, an individual's expectation of privacy in a vehicle and its contents may not survive if probable cause is given to believe that the vehicle is transporting contraband. Certainly the privacy interests in a car's trunk or glove compartment may be no less than those in a movable container. An individual undoubtedly has a significant interest that the upholstery of his automobile will not be ripped or a hidden compartment within it opened. These interests must yield to the authority of a search, however, which—in light of *Carroll*—does not itself require the prior approval of a magistrate. The scope of a warrantless search based on probable cause is no narrower—and no broader—than the scope of a search authorized by a warrant supported by probable cause. Only the prior approval of the magistrate is waived; the search otherwise is as the magistrate could authorize.

The scope of a warrantless search of an automobile thus is not defined by the nature of the container in which the contraband is secreted. Rather, it is defined by the object of the search and the places in which there is probable cause to believe that it may be found. Just as probable cause to believe that a stolen lawnmower may be found in a garage will not support a warrant to search an upstairs bedroom, probable cause to believe that undocumented aliens are being transported in a van will not justify a warrantless search of a suitcase. Probable cause to believe that a container placed in the trunk of a taxi contains contraband or evidence does not justify a search of the entire cab.

Justice Marshall, joined in dissent by Justice Brennan, "conclude[d] that any movable container found within an automobile deserves precisely the same degree of Fourth Amendment warrant protection that it would deserve if found at a location outside the automobile." Laying down a barrage of criticism on the rule adopted by the majority in *Ross*, Justice Marshall wrote in part:

The majority's rule is flatly inconsistent with * * * established Fourth Amendment principles concerning the scope of the automobile exception and the importance of the warrant requirement. Historically, the automobile exception has been limited to those situations where its application is compelled by the justifications [of mobility and a reduced expectation of privacy]. Today, the majority makes no attempt to base its decision on these justifications. This failure is not surprising, since the traditional rationales for the automobile exception plainly do not support extending it to the search of a container found inside a vehicle.

The practical mobility problem—deciding what to do with both the car and the occupants if an immediate search is not conducted—is simply not present in the case of movable containers, which can easily be seized and brought to the magistrate. * * * The lesser expectation of privacy rationale also has little force. A container, as opposed to the car itself, does not reflect diminished privacy interests. * * * Moreover, the practical corollary that this Court has recognized—that depriving occupants of the use of a car may be a greater intrusion than an immediate search—is of doubtful relevance here, since the owner of a container will rarely suffer significant inconvenience by being deprived of its use while a warrant is being obtained.

Ultimately, the majority, unable to rely on the justifications underlying the automobile exception, simply creates a new "probable cause" exception to the warrant requirement for automobiles. We have soundly rejected attempts to create such an exception in the past, see Coolidge v. New Hampshire, 403 U.S. 443, 91 S.Ct. 2022 (1971), and we should do so again today.

In purported reliance on *Carroll* v. *United States*, supra, the Court defines the permissible scope of a search by reference to the scope of a probable cause search that a magistrate could authorize. Under *Carroll*, however, the mobility of an automobile is what is critical to the legality of a warrantless search. Of course, *Carroll* properly confined the search to the probable cause limits that would also limit a magistrate, but it did not suggest that the search could be as *broad* as a magistrate could authorize upon a warrant. A magistrate could authorize a search encompassing containers, even though the mobility rationale does not justify such a broad search. Indeed, the Court's reasoning might have justified the search of the entire car in *Coolidge* despite the fact that the car was not "mobile" at all. Thus, in blithely suggesting that *Carroll* "neither broadened nor limited the scope of a lawful search based on probable cause," * * * the majority assumes what has never been the law: that the scope of the automobile-mobility exception to the warrant requirement is as broad as the scope of a "lawful" probable cause search of an automobile, i.e., one authorized by a magistrate.

The majority's sleight-of-hand ignores the obvious differences between the function served by a magistrate in making a determination of probable cause and the function of the automobile exception. It is irrelevant to a magistrate's function whether the items subject to search are mobile, may be in danger of destruction, or are impractical to store, or whether an immediate search would be less intrusive than a seizure without a warrant. A magistrate's only concern is whether there is probable cause to search them. Where suspicion has focused not on a particular item but only on a vehicle, home, or office, the magistrate might reasonably authorize a search of closed containers at the location as well. But an officer on the beat who searches an automobile without a warrant is not entitled to conduct a broader search than the exigency obviating the warrant justifies. After all, what justifies the warrantless search is not probable cause alone, but *probable cause coupled with the mobility of the automobile*. Because the scope of a *warrantless* search should depend on the scope of the justification for dispensing with a warrant, the entire premise of the majority's opinion fails to support its conclusion.

The majority's rule masks the startling assumption that a policeman's determination of probable cause is the functional equivalent of the determination of a neutral and detached magistrate. This assumption ignores a major premise of the warrant requirement—the importance of having a neutral and detached magistrate determine whether probable cause exists. * * * The majority's explanation that the scope of the warrantless automobile search will be "limited" to what a magistrate could authorize is thus inconsistent with our cases, which firmly establish that an on-the-spot determination of probable cause is *never* the same as a decision by a neutral and detached magistrate.

Justice White also dissented, substantially agreeing with Justice Marshall.

OTHER AUTOMOBILE SEARCH CASES

Case	Ruling	Dissenting Votes
Texas v. White, 423 U.S. 67, 96 S.Ct. 304 (1976)	Where police had probable cause to search defendant's car immediately after he had been arrested at the scene for attempting to pass fraudulent checks, probable cause was still held to exist and thus support warrantless search of defendant's auto at the station house.	Brennan and Marshall
United States v. Watson, 423 U.S. 411, 96 S.Ct. 820 (1976)	Regardless of the opportunity to secure a warrant, arrest in a public place for a previously committed felony does not require a warrant; since arrest was legal, defendant's consent to search car comported with the Fourth Amendment.	Brennan and Marshall
South Dakota v. Opperman, 428 U.S. 364, 96 S.Ct. 3092 (1976)	Since cars afford much less expectation of privacy than homes, police can routinely search and inventory contents of impounded cars so as to adequately secure and guard same even if the car was already locked but where some valuables sitting on the dashboard and rear seat were visible.	Brennan, Stewart, White, and Marshall
Rakas v. Illinois, 439 U.S. 128, 99 S.Ct. 421 (1978)	A legitimate occupant of an automobile does not have standing to challenge a search of the vehicle unless he happens to own or have a property interest in it.	Brennan, White, Marshall, and Stevens
New York v. Belton, 453 U.S. 454, 101 S.Ct. 2860 (1981)	"When the occupant of an automobile is subjected to a lawful custodial arrest, * * * the constitutionally permissible scope of a search incident to his arrest include[s] the passenger compartment of the vehicle in which he was riding * * * *."	Brennan, White, and Marshall

WARDEN v. HAYDEN

Supreme Court of the United States, 1967
387 U.S. 294, 87 S.Ct. 1642, 18 L.Ed.2d 782

The facts are set out in the Court's opinion.

Mr. Justice BRENNAN delivered the opinion of the Court.

We review in this case the validity of the proposition that there is under the Fourth Amendment a "distinction between merely evidentiary materials, on the one hand, which may not be seized either under the authority of a search warrant or during the course of a search incident to arrest, and on the other hand, those objects which may validly be seized including the instrumentalities and means by which a crime is committed, the fruits of crime such as stolen property, weapons by which escape of the person arrested might be effected, and property the possession of which is a crime."

*   *   *

About 8 a.m. on March 17, 1962, an armed robber entered the business premises of the Diamond Cab Company in Baltimore, Maryland. He took some $363 and ran. Two cab drivers in the vicinity, attracted by shouts of "Hold-up," followed the man to 2111 Cocoa Lane. One driver notified the company dispatcher by radio that the man was a Negro about 5'8" tall, wearing a light cap and dark jacket, and that he had entered the house on Cocoa Lane. The dispatcher relayed the information to police who were proceeding to the scene of the robbery. Within minutes, police arrived at the house in a number of patrol cars. An officer knocked and announced their presence. Mrs. Hayden answered, and the officers told her they believed that a robber had entered the house, and asked to search the house. She offered no objection.

The officers spread out through the first and second floors and the cellar in search of the robber. Hayden was found in an upstairs bedroom feigning sleep. He was arrested when the officers on the first floor and in the cellar reported that no other man was in the house.

Meanwhile an officer was attracted to an adjoining bathroom by the noise of running water, and discovered a shotgun and a pistol in a flush tank; another officer who, according to the District Court, "was searching the cellar for a man or the money" found in a washing machine a jacket and trousers of the type the fleeing man was said to have worn. A clip of ammunition for the pistol and a cap were found under the mattress of Hayden's bed, and ammunition for the shotgun was found in a bureau drawer in Hayden's room. All these items of evidence were introduced against respondent at his trial.

We agree with the [Maryland] Court of Appeals that neither the entry without warrant to search for the robber, nor the search for him without warrant was invalid. *   *   * The police were informed that an armed robbery had taken place, and that the suspect had entered 2111 Cocoa Lane less than five minutes before they reached it. They acted reasonably when they entered the house and began to search for a man of the description they had been given and for weapons which he had used in the robbery or might use against them. The Fourth Amendment does not require police officers to delay in the course of an investigation if to do so would gravely endanger their lives or the lives of others. Speed here was essential, and only a thorough search of the house for persons and weapons could have insured that Hayden was the only man present and that the police had control of all weapons which could be used against them or to effect an escape.

*   *   *

We come, then, to the question whether, even though the search was lawful, the Court of Appeals was correct in holding that the seizure and introduction of the items of clothing violated the Fourth Amendment because they are "mere evidence." The distinction made by some of our cases between seizure of items of evidential value only and seizure of instrumentalities, fruits, or contraband has been criticized by courts and commentators. The Court of Appeals, however, felt "obligated to adhere to it." * * * We today reject the distinction as based on premises no longer accepted as rules governing the application of the Fourth Amendment.

Nothing in the language of the Fourth Amendment supports the distinction between "mere evidence" and instrumentalities, fruits of crime, or contraband. On its face, the provision assures the "right of the people to be secure in their persons, houses, papers, and effects," * * * without regard to the use to which any of these things are applied. This "right of the people" is certainly unrelated to the "mere evidence" limitation. Privacy is disturbed no more by a search directed to a purely evidentiary object than it is by a search directed to an instrumentality, fruit, or contraband. A magistrate can intervene in both situations, and the requirements of probable cause and specificity can be preserved intact. Moreover, nothing in the nature of property seized as evidence renders it more private than property seized, for example, as an instrumentality; quite the opposite may be true. Indeed, the distinction is wholly irrational, since, depending on the circumstances, the same "papers and effects" may be "mere evidence" in one case and "instrumentality" in another. * * *

In Gouled v. United States, 255 U.S. 298, 309, 41 S.Ct. 261, 265, the Court said that search warrants "may not be used as a means of gaining access to a man's house or office and papers solely for the purpose of making search to secure evidence to be used against him in a criminal or penal proceeding." * * * The Court derived from Boyd v. United States [116 U.S. 616, 6 S.Ct. 524], the proposition that warrants "may be resorted to only when a primary right to such search and seizure may be found." * * *

The items of clothing involved in this case are not "testimonial" or "communicative" in nature and their introduction therefore did not compel respondent to become a witness against himself in violation of the Fifth Amendment. Schmerber v. State of California, 384 U.S. 757, 86 S.Ct. 1826. This case thus does not require that we consider whether there are items of evidential value whose very nature precludes them from being the object of a reasonable search and seizure.

The Fourth Amendment ruling in *Gouled* was based upon the dual, related premises that historically the right to search for and seize property depended upon the assertion by the Government of a valid claim of superior interest, and that it was not enough that the purpose of the search and seizure was to obtain evidence to use in apprehending and convicting criminals. The common law of search and seizure after Entick v. Carrington, 19 How.St.Tr. 1029 [1765], reflected Lord Camden's view, derived no doubt from the political thought of his time, that the "great end, for which men entered into society, was to secure their property." * * * Warrants were "allowed only where the primary right to such a search and seizure is in the interest which the public or complainant may have in the property seized." * * * Thus stolen property—the fruits of crime—was always subject to seizure. And the power to search for stolen property was gradually extended to cover "any property which the private citizen was not permitted to possess," which included instrumentalities of crime (because of the early notion that items used in crime were forfeited to the State) and contraband. * * * No separate governmental interest in seizing evidence to apprehend and convict criminals was recognized; it was required that some property interest be asserted. The remedial structure also reflected these dual premises. Trespass, replevin, and the other means of redress for persons aggrieved by searches and seizures, depended upon proof of a superior property interest. And since a lawful seizure presupposed a superior claim, it was inconceivable that a person could recover property lawfully seized. As Lord Camden pointed out in *Entick* v. *Carrington*, supra, at 1066, a general warrant enabled "the party's own property [to be] seized before and without conviction, and he has no power to reclaim his goods, even after his innocence is cleared by acquittal."

The premise that property interests control the right of the Government to search and seize has been discredited. Searches and seizures may be "unreasonable" within the Fourth Amendment even though the Government asserts a superior property interest at common law. We have recognized that the principal object of the Fourth Amendment is the protection of privacy rather than property, and have increasingly dis-

carded fictional and procedural barriers rested on property concepts.
* * *

* * *

The premise in *Gouled* that government may not seize evidence simply for the purpose of proving crime has * * * been discredited. The requirement that the Government assert in addition some property interest in material it seizes has long been a fiction, obscuring the reality that government has an interest in solving crime. *Schmerber* settled the proposition that it is reasonable, within the terms of the Fourth Amendment, to conduct otherwise permissible searches for the purpose of obtaining evidence which would aid in apprehending and convicting criminals. The requirements of the Fourth Amendment can secure the same protection of privacy whether the search is for "mere evidence" or for fruits, instrumentalities or contraband. There must, of course, be a nexus—automatically provided in the case of fruits, instrumentalities or contraband—between the item to be seized and criminal behavior. Thus in the case of "mere evidence," probable cause must be examined in terms of cause to believe that the evidence sought will aid in a particular apprehension or conviction. In so doing, consideration of police purposes will be required. * * * But no such problem is presented in this case. The clothes found in the washing machine matched the description of those worn by the robber and the police therefore could reasonably believe that the items would aid in the identification of the culprit.

* * *

The survival of the *Gouled* distinction is attributable more to chance than considered judgment. Legislation has helped perpetuate it. * * * *Mapp* v. *Ohio* * * * only recently made the "mere evidence" rule a problem in the state courts. Pressure against the rule in the federal courts has taken the form rather of broadening the categories of evidence subject to seizure, thereby creating considerable confusion in the law. * * *

The rationale most frequently suggested for the rule preventing the seizure of evidence is that "limitations upon the fruit to be gathered tend to limit the quest itself." * * * But privacy "would be just as well served by a restriction on search to the even-numbered days of the month. * * * And it would have the extra advantage of avoiding hair-splitting questions." * * * The "mere evidence" limitation has spawned exceptions so numerous and confusion so great, in fact, that it is questionable whether it affords meaningful protection. But if its rejection does enlarge the area of permissible searches, the intrusions are nevertheless made after fulfilling the probable cause and particularity requirements of the Fourth Amendment and after the intervention of "a neutral and detached magistrate." * * * The Fourth Amendment allows intrusions upon privacy under these circumstances, and there is no viable reason to distinguish intrusions to secure "mere evidence" from intrusions to secure fruits, instrumentalities, or contraband.

The judgment of the Court of Appeals is reversed.

*   *   *

Mr. Justice FORTAS with whom THE CHIEF JUSTICE [WARREN] joins, concurring.

While I agree that the Fourth Amendment should not be held to require exclusion from evidence of the clothing as well as the weapons and ammunition found by the officers during the search, I cannot join in the majority's broad—and in my judgment, totally unnecessary—repudiation of the so-called "mere evidence" rule.

*   *   *

Mr. Justice DOUGLAS, dissenting.

*   *   *

The constitutional philosophy is, I think, clear. The personal effects and possessions of the individual (all contraband and the like excepted) are sacrosanct from prying eyes, from the long arm of the law, from any rummaging by police. Privacy involves the choice of the individual to disclose or to reveal what he believes, what he thinks, what he possesses. The article may be a nondescript work of art, a manuscript of a book, a personal account book, a diary, invoices, personal clothing, jewelry, or whatnot. Those who wrote the Bill of Rights believed that every individual needs both to communicate with others and to keep his affairs to himself. That dual aspect of privacy means that the individual should have the freedom to select for himself the time and circumstances when he will share his secrets with others and decide the extent of that sharing. This is his prerogative not the States'. The Framers, who were as knowledgeable as we, knew what police surveillance meant and how the practice of rummaging through one's personal effects could destroy freedom.

* * *

[The] right of privacy, sustained in *Griswold* [v. Connecticut, 381 U.S. 479, 85 S.Ct. 1678 (1965)], is kin to the right of privacy created by the Fourth Amendment. That there is a zone that no police can enter—whether in "hot pursuit" or armed with a meticulously proper warrant—has been emphasized by *Boyd* and by *Gouled*. They have been consistently and continuously approved. I

would adhere to them and leave with the individual the choice of opening his private effects (apart from contraband and the like) to the police or keeping their contents a secret and their integrity inviolate. The existence of that choice is the very essence of the right to privacy. Without it the Fourth Amendment and the Fifth are ready instruments for the police state that the Framers sought to avoid.

After undercover police officers passed marked bills in a narcotics "buy," subsequently arrested one suspect for dealing in heroin, and then learned that the rest of the money together with more narcotics was in the hands of one "Moms" Santana, they drove to her address where they saw her standing in the doorway of the building holding a paper bag. They pulled up to within fifteen feet of her, jumped out of the van in which they were riding, flashed their badges, and yelled "Police," whereupon Santana retreated to the vestibule of the building. The officers followed through the open door, caught up with her in the vestibule, and, as she tried to pull away from them, two bundles of heroin packets fell out of the bag. When she was told to empty her pockets, the officers found seventy dollars in marked money. In United States v. Santana, 427 U.S. 38, 96 S.Ct. 2406 (1976), the Supreme Court upheld the admissibility of the heroin and money used to secure Santana's conviction. The Court, per Justice Rehnquist, held first that the threshold of the house was a place in which she had no expectation of privacy so that the police, who concededly already had probable cause to arrest her, could do so without a warrant in view of the Court's earlier decision in United States v. Watson, 423 U.S. 411, 96 S.Ct. 820 (1976), where it ruled that "the warrantless arrest of an individual in a public place upon probable cause did not violate the Fourth Amendment." Turning, then, to "[t]he only remaining question * * * whether her act of retreating into her house could thwart an otherwise proper arrest," the Court held it could not. It concluded that this was a case of "hot pursuit" controlled by *Warden* v. *Hayden*. Said Justice Rehnquist: "The fact that the pursuit here ended almost as soon as it began did not render it any the less a 'hot pursuit' sufficient to justify the warrantless entry into Santana's home. Once Santana saw the police, there was likewise a realistic expectation that any delay would result in destruction of evidence. * * * Once she had been arrested the search, incident to that arrest, which produced the drugs and money was clearly justified." Justices Brennan and Marshall dissented and would have required the police to get an arrest warrant first, absent any emergency which, they concluded, simply was not present in this case. (See chart p. 1125.)

In Zurcher v. Stanford Daily, 436 U.S. 547, 98 S.Ct. 1970 (1978), the Court addressed the question of "how the Fourth Amendment is to be construed and applied to * * * [a] 'third party' search, the recurring situation where state authorities have probable cause to believe that fruits, instrumentalities, or other evidence of crime is located on identified property but do not then have probable cause to believe that the owner or possessor of the property is himself implicated in the crime that has occurred or is occurring." The *Stanford Daily*, a student newspaper, published several articles and photographs about a violent clash between demonstrators and police seeking to remove them from university hospital premises. In the police effort forcibly to evict the protestors from their barricaded position, nine officers were injured after being set upon by stick- and club-wielding demonstrators. The pictures and certain eyewitness accounts indicated that a newspaper photographer was at the end of the corridor where the assault on police officers occurred and that he could have taken pictures which would lead to identification of the assailants. The following day a warrant was obtained on a finding that probable cause for the possession of such photos and negatives existed, and a police search of the *Daily's* photographic laboratories, filing cabinets, desks, and waste paper baskets ensued. The *Daily* and several of its staff subsequently sought declaratory and injunctive relief against officials connected with obtaining, issuing, and executing the warrant. A federal district court denied injunctive relief but entered a declaratory judgment in favor of the complainants. While conceding the existence of probable cause both as to the commission of a crime and as to the fact that the materials identified would be found on the *Daily's* premises, a federal district court ruled, as later described in the Supreme Court's opinion, that "the Fourth and Fourteenth Amendments forbade the issuance of a warrant to search for materials in possession of one not suspected of crime unless there is probable cause to believe, based on facts presented in a sworn affidavit, that a subpoena *duces tecum* would be impractical. Moreover, the failure to honor a subpoena would not alone justify a warrant; it must also appear that the possessor of the objects sought would disregard a court order not to remove or destroy them. The District Court further held that where the innocent object of the search is a newspaper, First Amendment interests are also involved and that such a search is constitutionally permissible 'only in the rare circumstance where there is a *clear showing* that (1) important materials will be destroyed or removed from the jurisdiction; *and* (2) a restraining order would be futile.' " In the absence of meeting these preconditions, the district court held the search was illegal. This judgment was affirmed by the court of appeals.

SELECTED RECENT DECISIONS ON SEARCHES AND SEIZURES WITH A WARRANT

Case	Ruling	Dissenting Votes
United States v. Miller, 425 U.S. 435, 96 S.Ct. 1619 (1976)	Expectation of privacy does not extend to checks, deposit slips, and other records of defendant's bank account; these are not confidential communications but commercial transactions voluntarily disclosed to third party (bank) and hence legitimately subpoenaed by federal authorities	Brennan, Marshall
Andresen v. Maryland, 427 U.S. 463, 96 S.Ct. 2737 (1976)	Seizure and admission into evidence of defendant's business records did not violate Fifth Amendment; seizure was not unreasonable since warrant generally specified items pertaining to particular real estate transaction "together with other fruits, instrumentalities, and evidence at this [time] unknown" and, though some items seized related to another transaction, they could reasonably be thought to bear on specified transaction	Brennan, Marshall

---

The Supreme Court reversed this judgment. Characterizing the district court's ruling as a "sweeping revision" of the Fourth Amendment, the Court found "[n]othing on the face of the Amendment" to suggest "that a third-party search warrant should not normally issue," and asserted that it was "untenable to conclude that property may not be searched unless its occupant is reasonably suspected of crime and is subject to arrest." Observed the Court, "Search warrants are not directed at persons; they authorize the search of 'places' and the seizure of 'things,' and as a constitutional matter they need not even name the person from whom the things will be seized." Reiterating that "the overriding test of compliance with the Fourth Amendment" is reasonableness, the Court concluded there was "no occasion or justification for a court to revise the Amendment and strike a new balance ["between privacy and public need"] by denying the search warrant in the circumstances present here and by insisting that the investigation proceed by subpoena *duces tecum*, whether on the theory that the latter is a less intrusive alternative, or otherwise." Indeed, the Court observed, "whether the third-party occupant is suspect or not, the State's interest in enforcing the criminal law and recovering the evidence remains the same * * * ." Furthermore, said Justice White, speaking for the Court, it was not at all clear that "the District Court's new rule denying search warrants against third parties and insisting on subpoenas would substantially further privacy interests without seriously undermining law enforcement efforts." He continued:

> As the District Court understands it, denying third-party search warrants would not have substantial adverse effects on criminal investigations because the nonsuspect third party, once served with a subpoena, will preserve the evidence and ultimately lawfully respond. The difficulty with this assumption is that search warrants are often employed early in an investigation, perhaps before the identity of any likely criminal and certainly before all the perpetrators are or could be known. The seemingly blameless third party in possession of the fruits or evidence may not be innocent at all; and if he is, he may nevertheless be so related to or so sympathetic with the culpable that he cannot be relied upon to retain and preserve the articles that may implicate his friends, or at least not to notify those who would be damaged by the evidence that the authorities are aware of its location. In any event, it is likely that the real culprits will have access to the property, and the delay involved in employing the subpoena *duces tecum*, offering as it does the opportunity to litigate its validity, could easily result in the disappearance of the evidence, whatever the good faith of the third party.

In response to the argument that the district court's order in this case reflected a justified concern for the protected First Amendment interests of a particular kind of third party, namely the press, Justice White pointed out that the Framers, well aware "of the long struggle between the Crown and the press * * * nevertheless did not forbid warrants where the press was involved, did not require special showings that subpoenas would be impractical, and did not insist that the owner of the place to be searched, if connected with the press, must be shown to be implicated in the offense being investigated." Observing further that the number of instances involving the issuance of warrants for searching newspaper offices has been precious few, the Court concluded, "Properly administered, the preconditions for a warrant—probable cause, specificity with respect to the place to be searched and the things to be seized, and overall reasonableness—should afford sufficient protection against the harms that are assertedly threatened by warrants for searching newspaper offices."

In a dissenting opinion, in which he was joined by Justice Marshall, Justice Stewart wrote:

> It seems to me self-evident that police searches of newspaper offices burden the freedom of the press. The most immediate and obvious First Amendment injury caused by such a visitation by the police is physical disruption of the operation of the newspaper. Policemen occupying a newsroom and searching it thoroughly for what may be an extended period of time will inevitably interrupt its normal operations, and thus impair or even temporarily prevent the processes of newsgathering, writing, editing, and publishing. By contrast, a subpoena would afford the newspaper itself an opportunity to locate whatever material might be requested and produce it.

> But there is another and more serious burden on a free press imposed by an unannounced police search of a newspaper office: the possibility of disclosure of information received from confidential sources, or of the identity of the sources themselves. Protection of those sources is necessary to ensure that the press can fulfill its constitutionally designated function of informing the public, because important information can often be obtained only by an assurance that the source will not be revealed. * * *

>   *   *   *

> A search warrant allows police officers to ransack the files of a newspaper, reading each and every document until they have found the one named in the warrant, while a subpoena would permit the newspaper itself to produce only the specific documents requested. A search, unlike a subpoena, will therefore lead to the needless exposure of confidential information completely unrelated to the purpose of the investigation. The knowledge that police officers can make an unannounced raid on a newsroom is thus bound to have a deterrent effect on the availability of confidential news sources. The end result, wholly inimical to the First Amendment, will be a diminishing flow of potentially important information to the public.

>   *   *   *

> On the other hand, a subpoena would allow a newspaper, through a motion to quash, an opportunity for an adversary hearing with respect to the production of any material which a prosecutor might think is in its possession. * * * If, in the present case, The Stanford Daily had been served with a subpoena, it would have had an opportunity to demonstrate to the court what the police ultimately found to be true—that the evidence sought did not exist. The legitimate needs of government thus would have been served without infringing the freedom of the press.

In another dissenting opinion, Justice Stevens also concluded that the search was unconstitutional. He restricted his discussion to Fourth Amendment issues, focusing on the impact of the Court's decision in Warden v. Hayden, 387 U.S. 294, 87 S.Ct. 1642 (1967), and saying:

> A showing of probable cause that was adequate to justify the issuance of a warrant to search for stolen goods in the 18th century does not automatically satisfy the new dimensions of the Fourth Amendment in the post-*Hayden* era. In *Hayden* itself, the Court recognized that the meaning of

probable cause should be reconsidered in the light of the new authority it conferred on the police. The only conceivable justification for an unannounced search of an innocent citizen is the fear that, if notice were given, he would conceal or destroy the object of the search. Probable cause to believe that the custodian is a criminal, or that he holds a criminal's weapons, spoils, or the like, justifies that fear, and therefore such a showing complies with the Clause. But if nothing said under oath in the warrant application demonstrates the need for an unannounced search by force, the probable cause requirement is not satisfied. In the absence of some other showing of reasonableness, the ensuing search violates the Fourth Amendment.

Justice Brennan did not participate in the decision.

———

When it passed the Privacy Protection Act of 1980, 94 Stat. 1879, Congress substantially modified the Supreme Court's ruling in the *Stanford Daily* case. The act specifically makes it "unlawful for a government officer or employee, in connection with the investigation or prosecution of a criminal offense, to search for or seize any work product materials possessed by a person reasonably believed to have a purpose to disseminate to the public a newspaper, book, broadcast, or other similar form of public communication, in or affecting interstate or foreign commerce" unless "there is probable cause to believe that the person possessing such materials has committed or is committing the criminal offense to which the materials relate"; or "the offense to which the materials relate consists of the receipt, possession, or communication of information relating to the national defense, classified information, or restricted data" under specifically enumerated sections of the U.S. Code; or "there is reason to believe that the immediate seizure of such materials is necessary to prevent the death of, or serious bodily injury to, a human being." Subsequent provisions of the statute also bar searches for and seizures of "documentary materials, other than work product materials" unless these same circumstances are present; or unless "there is reason to believe that the giving of notice pursuant to a subpoena duces tecum would result in the destruction, alteration, or concealment of such materials"; or where "such materials have not been produced in response to a court order directing compliance with a subpoena duces tecum" and all appellate remedies have been exhausted or where delay would "threaten the interests of justice."

Other sections of the law define the terms "work product materials" (materials recording one's opinions, conclusions, mental impressions, or theories in anticipation of communicating matters to the public and excluding contraband, fruits and instrumentalities of crime) and "documentary materials, other than work product materials" (materials on which raw information or data are contained, such as printed matter, photographs, audio tapes, video tapes, cards, or discs and excluding contraband, fruits and instrumentalities of crime); authorize civil suits against the government or against law enforcement officers who violate the act's provisions; direct the Attorney General to formulate guidelines for the implementation of the statute; and require annual reports to Congress.

The legislation applies not only to the conduct of national law enforcement officers, but to that of state law enforcement officers as well. The reach of this legislation across the entire federal system has been questioned; see Comment, "The Constitutionality of Congressional Legislation to Overrule *Zurcher* v. *Stanford Daily*," 71 Journal of Criminal Law & Criminology 147 (1980).

ROCHIN v. CALIFORNIA

Supreme Court of the United States, 1952
342 U.S. 165, 72 S.Ct. 205, 96 L.Ed. 183

See p. 934.

In Blackford v. United States, 247 F.2d 745 (9th Cir. 1957), the U.S. Court of Appeals, Ninth Circuit, held by a 2–1 vote that the forced extraction of a container of heroin from defendant's rectum was not an unreasonable search in violation of the Fourth and Fifth Amendments. Charles Blackford was stopped at the Mexican border and ordered to disrobe when customs officials observed needle marks on his arm and learned from the defendant that he had previously been convicted for possession of marijuana. After a subsequent examination of Blackford and his admission that he was carrying narcotics (Blackford denied making the statement), physicians were called upon to remove the heroin. Blackford resisted while unsuccessful manual attempts were made, but eventually the heroin was extracted with the use of forceps and the administration of several enemas. In affirming the district court's decision, Judge Barnes held that the search was reasonable because it was incident to a lawful arrest. "Blackford was treated civilly throughout," and the examinations were conducted under sanitary conditions by qualified doctors. In addition, Judge Barnes concluded that there was no constitutional requirement "to sacrifice the abiding interest of all citizens of the United States to be free and safe from these insidious drugs to avoid offending the sensibilities of admitted narcotics importers * * *." The Supreme Court denied certiorari, 356 U.S. 914, 78 S.Ct. 672 (1958).

SCHMERBER v. CALIFORNIA

Supreme Court of the United States, 1966
384 U.S. 757, 86 S.Ct. 1826, 16 L.Ed.2d 908

See p. 1003.

CAMARA v. MUNICIPAL COURT

Supreme Court of the United States, 1967
387 U.S. 523, 87 S.Ct. 1727, 18 L.Ed.2d 930

Section 503 of San Francisco's Housing Code provided that "Authorized employees of the City departments or City agencies, so far as may be necessary for the performance of their duties, shall, upon presentation of proper credentials, have the right to enter, at reasonable times, any building, structure, or premises in the City to perform any duty imposed upon them by the Municipal Code." Roland Camara was charged with violating this ordinance when he refused several times to admit a city building inspector in the course of his annual inspection and without a warrant to the portion of an apartment building that petitioner was leasing. When Camara's demurrer to the charge was overruled by the municipal court, he sought a writ of prohibition to prevent any judicial action on the complaint filed against him. Two state courts denied him relief, and Camara appealed to the U.S. Supreme Court.

Mr. Justice WHITE delivered the opinion of the Court.

In Frank v. State of Maryland, 359 U.S. 360, 79 S.Ct. 804, this Court upheld, by a five-to-four vote, a state court conviction of a homeowner who refused to permit a municipal health inspector to enter and inspect his premises without a search warrant. * * * Since [then] more intensive efforts at all levels of government to contain and eliminate urban blight have led to increasing use of such inspection techniques, while numerous decisions of this Court have more fully defined the Fourth Amendment's effect on state and municipal action. * * * In view of the growing nationwide importance of the problem, we noted probable jurisdiction * * * to re-examine whether administrative inspection programs, as presently authorized and conducted, violate Fourth Amendment rights as those rights are enforced against the States through the Fourteenth Amendment. * * *

* * *

[W]e hold that administrative searches of the kind at issue here are significant intrusions upon the interests protected by the Fourth Amendment, that such searches when authorized and conducted without a warrant procedure lack the traditional safeguards which the Fourth Amendment guarantees to the individual, and that the reasons put forth in *Frank* v. *State of Maryland* and in other cases for upholding these warrantless searches are insufficient to justify so substantial a weakening of the Fourth Amendment's protections. Because of the nature of the municipal programs under consideration, however, these conclusions must be the beginning, not the end, of our inquiry. * * *

* * *

In this case, appellant has been

charged with a crime for his refusal to permit housing inspectors to enter his leasehold without a warrant. There was no emergency demanding immediate access; in fact, the inspectors made three trips to the building in an attempt to obtain appellant's consent to search. Yet no warrant was obtained and thus appellant was unable to verify either the need for or the appropriate limits of the inspection. * * * [W]e therefore conclude that appellant had a constitutional right to insist that the inspectors obtain a warrant to search and that appellant may not constitutionally be convicted for refusing to consent to the inspection. * * *

* * *

Judgment vacated and case remanded.

Mr. Justice CLARK with whom Mr. Justice HARLAN and Mr. Justice STEWART join, dissenting.

* * *

* * * For me [the constitutional issue] was settled in *Frank* v. *State of Maryland*, supra. I would adhere to that decision and the reasoning therein. * * * Time has not shown any need for change. Indeed the opposite is true. * * * The majority [here has] set up a new test for the long-recognized and enforced Fourth Amendment's "probable-cause" requirement for the issuance of warrants. They would permit the issuance of paper warrants, in area inspection programs, with probable cause based on area inspection standards as set out in municipal codes, and with warrants issued by the rubber stamp of a willing magistrate. In my view, this degrades the Fourth Amendment.

* * *

* * * Frankly, I cannot understand how the Court can authorize warrants in wholesale fashion in the case of an area inspection, but hold the hand of the inspector when a specific dwelling is hazardous to the health and safety of its neighbors.

SELECTED CASES ON ADMINISTRATIVE SEARCHES SINCE *CAMARA*

Case	Ruling	Dissenting Votes
See v. City of Seattle, 387 U.S. 541, 87 S.Ct. 1737 (1967)	Extended the holding in *Camara* to include business properties; in this case it held unconstitutional a warrantless examination of a locked, commercial warehouse by a city fire inspector	Clark, Harlan, and Stewart
Wyman v. James, 400 U.S. 309, 91 S.Ct. 381 (1971)	Home visitation with advance notice by caseworkers to insure compliance with state regulations by individuals receiving public welfare payments is not a search within the meaning of the Fourth Amendment and thus does not require a search warrant	Douglas, Brennan, and Marshall
Air Pollution Variance Bd. of Colorado v. Western Alfalfa Corp., 416 U.S. 861, 94 S.Ct. 2114 (1974)	Opacity test of smoke being emitted from company's smokestacks was lawfully conducted where inspector undertook the test merely by stepping on to outdoor premises of the company open to the general public and looking at the plumes of smoke (the inspector did not enter the building to examine boilers, furnaces, stacks, etc.)	None
Marshall v. Barlow's, Inc., 436 U.S. 307, 98 S.Ct. 1816 (1978)	Routine warrantless inspections conducted so as to assess compliance with federal health and safety standards under the Occupational Safety and Health Act of 1970 violate the Fourth Amendment. Although appellee's electrical and plumbing business is clearly within the Warrant Clause protection announced by the Court in *See* v. *Seattle*, supra, "[c]ertain industries have such a history of government oversight that no reasonable expectation of privacy * * * could exist for a proprietor over the stock of such an enterprise. Liquor * * * and firearms * * * are industries of this type; when an entrepreneur embarks upon such a business, he has voluntarily chosen to submit himself to a full arsenal of government regulation."	Blackmun, Rehnquist, and Stevens
Donovan v. Dewey, 452 U.S. 594, 101 S.Ct. 2534 (1981)	Warrantless inspections of stone quarries by federal mine inspectors under the Federal Mine Safety and Health Act of 1977 are compatible with the Fourth Amendment given the pervasiveness of federal regulation of surface mining with the consequent implicit	Stewart

ADMINISTRATIVE SEARCHES (*Cont.*)

Case	Ruling	Dissenting Votes
Donovan (*Cont.*)	notice close and continuous federal oversight affords mine operators, because the mining industry is among the most hazardous businesses in the country and since "a constitutionally adequate substitute for a warrant" is provided by "the certainty and regularity" of the inspection program.	

MICHIGAN v. TYLER

Supreme Court of the United States, 1978
436 U.S. 499, 98 S.Ct. 1942, 56 L.Ed.2d 486

Shortly before midnight on January 21, 1970, a fire broke out in Tyler and Tompkins's furniture store. Two hours later when the fire chief arrived at the scene as the smoldering embers were being hosed down, he learned that two plastic containers of flammable liquid had been found. He entered the building, examined the containers, and called a police detective to investigate the possibility of arson. The detective subsequently took pictures of the containers and the gutted building but ceased his efforts due to the smoke and the steam. When the fire had been completely extinguished at approximately 4 A.M., the fire chief and the detective left and took the containers with them. Four hours later the fire chief and one of his assistants returned for a brief examination of the building, and an hour after that the assistant and the detective showed up again for another inspection of the premises in the course of which additional pieces of evidence were removed. Nearly a month later a state police arson investigator took still more photographs of the building; this visit was followed by several other inspections which turned up further evidence and information. None of these inspections or searches was conducted with a warrant or with the defendants' consent. Evidence and testimony based upon these searches were admitted at trial to convict the defendants. The state supreme court reversed the convictions, however, ruling that "[once] the blaze [has been] extinguished and the firefighters have left the premises, a warrant is required to reenter and search the premises, unless there is consent or the premises have been abandoned."

Mr. Justice STEWART delivered the opinion of the Court.

* * *

The decisions of this Court firmly establish that the Fourth Amendment extends beyond the paradigmatic entry into a private dwelling by a law enforcement officer in search of the fruits or instrumentalities of crime. As this Court stated in Camara v. Municipal Court, 387 U.S., at 528, 87 S.Ct., at 1730, the "basic purpose of this Amendment * * * is to safeguard the privacy and se- curity of individuals against arbitrary invasions by government officials." The officials may be health, fire, or building inspectors. Their purpose may be to locate and abate a suspected public nuisance, or simply to perform a routine periodic inspection. The privacy that is invaded may be sheltered by the walls of a warehouse or other commercial establishment not open to the public. See v. City of Seattle, 387 U.S. 541, 87 S.Ct. 1737; Marshall v. Barlow's, Inc., 436 U.S. 307, 98 S.Ct. 1816 (1978). * * * These deviations from the typical police search are thus clearly within the protection of the Fourth Amendment.

The petitioner argues, however, that an entry to investigate the cause of a recent fire is outside that protection because no individual privacy interests are threatened. If the occupant of the premises set the blaze, then, in the words of the petitioner's brief, his "actions show that he has no expectation of privacy" because "he has abandoned those premises within the meaning of the Fourth Amendment." And if the fire had other causes, "the occupants of the premises are treated as victims by police and fire officials." In the petitioner's view, "[t]he likelihood that they will be aggrieved by a possible intrusion into what remains of their privacy in badly burned premises is negligible."

This argument is not persuasive. For even if the petitioner's contention that arson establishes abandonment be accepted, its second proposition—that innocent fire victims inevitably have no protectible expectations of privacy in whatever remains of their property—is contrary to common experience. People may go on living in their homes or working in their offices after a fire. Even when that is impossible, private effects often remain on the fire-damaged premises. The petitioner may be correct in the view that most innocent fire victims are treated courteously and welcome inspections of their property to ascertain the origin of the blaze, but "even if true, [this contention] is irrelevant to the question whether the * * * inspection is reasonable within the meaning of the Fourth Amendment." *Camara*, supra, at 536. Once it is recognized that innocent fire victims retain the protection of the Fourth

Amendment, the rest of the petitioner's argument unravels. For it is of course impossible to justify a warrantless search on the ground of abandonment by arson when that arson has not yet been proved, and a conviction cannot be used *ex post facto* to validate the introduction of evidence used to secure that same conviction.

Thus, there is no diminution in a person's reasonable expectation of privacy nor in the protection of the Fourth Amendment simply because the official conducting the search wears the uniform of a firefighter rather than a policeman, or because his purpose is to ascertain the cause of a fire rather than to look for evidence of a crime, or because the fire might have been started deliberately. Searches for administrative purposes, like searches for evidence of crime, are encompassed by the Fourth Amendment. And under that Amendment, "one governing principle, justified by history and by current experience, has consistently been followed: except in certain carefully defined classes of cases, a search of private property without proper consent is 'unreasonable' unless it has been authorized by a valid search warrant." *Camara*, supra, at 528–529. The showing of probable cause necessary to secure a warrant may vary with the object and intrusiveness of the search, but the necessity for the warrant persists.

The petitioner argues that no purpose would be served by requiring warrants to investigate the cause of a fire. This argument is grounded on the premise that the only fact that need be shown to justify an investigatory search is that a fire of undetermined origin has occurred on those premises. The petitioner contends that this consideration distinguishes this case from *Camara*, which concerned the necessity for warrants to conduct routine building inspections. Whereas the occupant of premises subjected to an unexpected building inspection may have no way of knowing the purpose or lawfulness of the entry, it is argued that the occupant of burned premises can hardly question the factual basis for fire officials wanting access to his property. And whereas a magistrate performs the significant function of assuring that an agency's decision to conduct a routine inspection of a particular dwelling conforms with reasonable legislative or administrative standards, he can do little more than rubber stamp an application to search fire-damaged premises for the cause of the blaze. In short, where the justification for the search is as simple and as obvious to everyone as the fact of a recent fire, a magistrate's review would be a time-consuming formality of negligible protection to the occupant.

The petitioner's argument fails primarily because it is built on a faulty premise. To secure a warrant to investigate the cause of a fire, an official must show more than the bare fact that a fire has occurred. The magistrate's duty is to assure that the proposed search will be reasonable, a determination that requires inquiry into the need for the intrusion on the one hand, and the threat of disruption to the occupant on the other. For routine building inspections, a reasonable balance between these competing concerns is usually achieved by broad legislative or administrative guidelines specifying the purpose, frequency, scope, and manner of conducting the inspections. In the context of investigatory fire searches, which are not programmatic but are responsive to

individual events, a more particularized inquiry may be necessary. The number of prior entries, the scope of the search, the time of day when it is proposed to be made, the lapse of time since the fire, the continued use of the building, and the owner's efforts to secure it against intruders might all be relevant factors. Even though a fire victim's privacy must normally yield to the vital social objective of ascertaining the cause of the fire, the magistrate can perform the important function of preventing harassment by keeping that invasion to a minimum. * * *

In addition, even if fire victims can be deemed aware of the factual justification for investigatory searches, it does not follow that they will also recognize the legal authority for such searches. As the Court stated in *Camara*, "when the inspector demands entry [without a warrant], the occupant has no way of knowing whether enforcement of the municipal code involved requires inspection of his premises, no way of knowing the lawful limits of the inspector's power to search, and no way of knowing whether the inspector himself is acting under proper authorization." 387 U.S., at 532. Thus, a major function of the warrant is to provide the property owner with sufficient information to reassure him of the entry's legality. * * *

In short, the warrant requirement provides significant protection for fire victims in this context, just as it does for property owners faced with routine building inspections. As a general matter, then, official entries to investigate the cause of a fire must adhere to the warrant procedures of the Fourth Amendment. In the words of the Michigan Supreme Court: "Where the cause [of the fire] is undetermined, and the purpose of the investigation is to determine the cause and to prevent such fires from occurring or recurring, a * * * search may be conducted pursuant to a warrant issued in accordance with reasonable legislative or administrative standards or, absent their promulgation, judicially prescribed standards; if evidence of wrongdoing is discovered, it may, of course, be used to establish probable cause for the issuance of a criminal investigative search warrant or in prosecution." But "[i]f the authorities are seeking evidence to be used in a criminal prosecution, the usual standard [of probable cause] will apply." 399 Mich., at 584, 250 N.W.2d, at 477. Since all the entries in this case were "without proper consent" and were not "authorized by a valid search warrant," each one is illegal unless it falls within one of the "certain carefully defined classes of cases" for which warrants are not mandatory. *Camara*, supra, at 528–529, 87 S.Ct., at 1731.

Our decisions have recognized that a warrantless entry by criminal law enforcement officials may be legal when there is compelling need for official action and no time to secure a warrant. Warden v. Hayden, 387 U.S. 294, 87 S.Ct. 1642 (warrantless entry of house by police in hot pursuit of armed robber); Ker v. California, 374 U.S. 23, 83 S.Ct. 1623 (warrantless and unannounced entry of dwelling by police to prevent imminent destruction of evidence). Similarly, in the regulatory field, our cases have recognized the importance of "prompt inspections, even without a warrant * * * in emergency situations." *Camara*, supra, at 539, citing North American Cold Storage Co. v. City of Chicago, 211 U.S. 306, 29 S.Ct. 101 (seizure of unwholesome food); Jacobson v. Mas-

sachusetts, 197 U.S. 11, 25 S.Ct. 358 (compulsory smallpox vaccination); Compagnie Francaise v. Board of Health, 186 U.S. 380, 22 S.Ct. 812 (health quarantine).

A burning building clearly presents an exigency of sufficient proportions to render a warrantless entry "reasonable." Indeed, it would defy reason to suppose that firemen must secure a warrant or consent before entering a burning structure to put out the blaze. And once in a building for this purpose, firefighters may seize evidence of arson that is in plain view. * * * Thus, the Fourth and Fourteenth Amendments were not violated by the entry of the firemen to extinguish the fire at Tyler's Auction, nor by Chief See's removal of the two plastic containers of flammable liquid found on the floor of one of the showrooms.

* * *

The entries occurring after January 22, however, were clearly detached from the initial exigency and warrantless entry. Since all of these searches were conducted without valid warrants and without consent, they were invalid under the Fourth and Fourteenth Amendments, and any evidence obtained as a result of those entries must, therefore, be excluded at the respondents' retrial.

In summation, we hold that an entry to fight a fire requires no warrant, and that once in the building, officials may remain there for a reasonable time to investigate the cause of the blaze. Thereafter, additional entries to investigate the cause of the fire must be made pursuant to the warrant procedures governing administrative searches. * * * Evidence of arson discovered in the course of such investigations is admissible at trial, but if the investigating officials find probable cause to believe that arson has occurred and require further access to gather evidence for a possible prosecution, they may obtain a warrant only upon a traditional showing of probable cause applicable to searches for evidence of crime. * * *

These principles require that we affirm the judgment of the Michigan Supreme Court ordering a new trial.

Affirmed.

Mr. Justice BRENNAN took no part in the consideration or decision of this case.

Mr. Justice STEVENS, concurring in part and concurring in the judgment.

Because [p]art * * * of the Court's opinion in this case, like the opinion in Camara v. Municipal Court, 387 U.S. 523, 87 S.Ct. 1727, seems to assume that an official search must either be conducted pursuant to a warrant or not take place at all, I cannot join its reasoning.

In particular, I cannot agree with the Court's suggestion that, if no showing of probable cause could be made, "the warrant procedures governing administrative searches," * * * would have complied with the Fourth Amendment. In my opinion, an "administrative search warrant" does not satisfy the requirements of the Warrant Clause. * * * Nor does such a warrant make an otherwise unreasonable search reasonable.

A warrant provides authority for an unannounced, immediate entry and search. No notice is given when an application for a warrant is made and no notice precedes its execution; when issued, it authorizes entry by force. In my view, when there is no

probable cause to believe a crime has been committed and when there is no special enforcement need to justify an unannounced entry, the Fourth Amendment neither requires nor sanctions an abrupt and peremptory confrontation between sovereign and citizen. In such a case, to comply with the constitutional requirement of reasonableness, I believe the sovereign must provide fair notice of an inspection.

The Fourth Amendment interests involved in this case could have been protected in either of two ways—by a warrant, if probable cause existed; or by fair notice, if neither probable cause nor a special law enforcement need existed. Since the entry on February 16 was not authorized by a warrant and not preceded by advance notice, I concur in the Court's judgment and in [p]arts * * * of its opinion.

Mr. Justice WHITE, with whom Mr. Justice MARSHALL joins, concurring in part and dissenting in part.

* * *

The Michigan Supreme Court found that the warrantless searches, at 8 and 9 a.m. were not, in fact, continuations of the earlier entry under exigent circumstances and therefore ruled inadmissible all evidence derived from those searches. The Court offers no sound basis for overturning this conclusion of the state court that the subsequent re-entries were distinct from the original entry. Even if, under the Court's "reasonable time" criterion, the firemen might have stayed in the building for an additional four hours—a proposition which is by no means clear—the fact remains that the firemen did not choose to remain and continue their search, but instead locked the door and departed from the premises entirely. The fact that the firemen were willing to leave demonstrates that the exigent circumstances justifying their original warrantless entry were no longer present. * * *

To hold that some subsequent re-entries are "continuations" of earlier ones will not aid firemen, but confuse them, for it will be difficult to predict in advance how a court might view a re-entry. In the end, valuable evidence may be excluded for failure to seek a warrant that might have easily been obtained.

Those investigating fires and their causes deserve a clear demarcation of the constitutional limits of their authority. Today's opinion recognizes the need for speed and focuses attention on fighting an ongoing blaze. The fire truck need not stop at the courthouse in rushing to the flames. But once the fire has been extinguished and the firemen have left the premises, the emergency is over. Further intrusion on private property can and should be accompanied by a warrant indicating the authority under which the firemen presume to enter and search.

* * *

Mr. Justice REHNQUIST, dissenting.

I agree with my Brother STEVENS, for the reasons expressed in his dissenting opinion in Marshall v. Barlow's, Inc., 436 U.S. 307, 98 S.Ct. 1816 (1978) (STEVENS, J., dissenting), that the "Warrant Clause has no application to routine, regulatory inspections of commercial premises." Since in my opinion the searches involved in this case fall within that category, I think the only appropriate inquiry is whether they were reasonable. The Court does not dispute

that the entries which occurred at the time of the fire and the next morning were entirely justified, and I see nothing to indicate that the subsequent searches were not also eminently reasonable in light of all the circumstances.

In evaluating the reasonableness of the later searches, their most obvious feature is that they occurred after a fire which had done substantial damage to the premises, including the destruction of most of the interior. Thereafter the premises were not being used and very likely could not have been used for business purposes, at least until substantial repairs had taken place. Indeed, there is no indication in the record that after the fire Tyler ever made any attempt to secure the premises. As a result, the fire department was forced to lock up the building to prevent curious bystanders from entering and suffering injury. And as far as the record reveals, Tyler never objected to this procedure or attempted to reclaim the premises for himself.

Thus, regardless of whether the premises were technically "abandoned" within the meaning of the Fourth Amendment, * * * it is clear to me that no purpose would have been served by giving Tyler notice of the intended search or by requiring that the search take place during the hours which in other situations might be considered the only "reasonable" hours to conduct a regulatory search. In fact, as I read the record, it appears that Tyler not only had notice that the investigators were occasionally entering the premises for the purpose of determining the cause of the fire, but he never voiced the slightest objection to these searches and actually accompanied the investigators on at least one occasion. * * * In fact, while accompanying the investigators during one of these searches, Tyler himself suggested that the fire very well may have been caused by arson. * * * This observation, coupled with all the other circumstances, including Tyler's knowledge of, and apparent acquiescence in, the searches, would have been taken by any sensible person as an indication that Tyler thought the searches ought to continue until the culprit was discovered; at the very least they indicated that he had no objection to these searches. Thus, regardless of what sources may serve to inform one's sense of what is reasonable, in the circumstances of this case I see nothing to indicate that these searches were in any way unreasonable for purposes of the Fourth Amendment.

Since the later searches were just as reasonable as the search the morning immediately after the fire in light of all these circumstances, the admission of evidence derived therefrom did not, in my opinion, violate respondents' Fourth and Fourteenth Amendment rights. I would accordingly reverse the judgment of the Supreme Court of Michigan which held to the contrary.

TERRY v. OHIO

Supreme Court of the United States, 1968
392 U.S. 1, 88 S.Ct. 1868, 20 L.Ed.2d 889

At approximately 2:30 one afternoon, Detective Martin McFadden was patrolling in downtown Cleveland. His attention was attracted by two men, petitioner Terry and his cohort. McFadden testified that he had never seen the men before but that routine habits of observation which he had developed in over forty years with the police force led him to conclude that they "didn't look right." He took up an observation post in a doorway several hundred yards away and continued to watch them. His suspicions were aroused further when he saw one of the men walk past some stores, pause, look in a store window, walk on a short distance, turn around, pause, look in the same window and then rejoin his companion at the corner. In all, this ritual was repeated about a dozen times. At one point the two men were joined by a third, and they conferred together at the corner. These observations led McFadden to surmise that the men were "casing" the store for a prospective robbery. He decided to investigate. McFadden approached the three men he had seen at the corner, identified himself as a police officer, and asked for their names, an inquiry to which he received a mumbled response. Because he thought they might have a gun, McFadden "grabbed * * * Terry, spun him around * * * and patted down the outside of his clothing." He felt a pistol in Terry's left breast pocket but could not remove the gun by reaching inside to the coat pocket, so he told the men to step into a store where he took off Terry's coat and confiscated the revolver. After "patting down" the other two men, McFadden found another gun. He then asked the proprietor of the store to call the police, and the men were taken to the police station where Terry and his companions were booked for carrying concealed weapons. Both were convicted on the charge and sentenced to from one to three years' imprisonment. Defendants moved before the trial to suppress the evidence on grounds McFadden's actions constituted an unreasonable search and seizure under the Fourth and Fourteenth Amendments. A state appellate court later affirmed the convictions, and the Ohio Supreme Court dismissed the appeal.

Mr. Chief Justice WARREN delivered the opinion of the Court.

* * *

* * * We granted certiorari to determine whether the admission of the revolvers in evidence violated petitioner's rights under the Fourth Amendment, made applicable to the States by the Fourteenth. * * *

* * * The question is whether in all the circumstances of this on-the-street encounter, [Terry's] right to personal security was violated by an unreasonable search and seizure.

We would be less than candid if we did not acknowledge that this question thrusts to the fore difficult and troublesome issues regarding a sensitive area of police activity—issues which have never before been squarely presented to this Court. Reflective of the tensions involved are the practical and constitutional arguments pressed with great vigor on both sides of the public debate over the power of the police to "stop and frisk"—as it is sometimes euphemistically termed—suspicious persons.

* * *

Our first task is to establish at what point in this encounter the Fourth Amendment becomes relevant. That is, we must decide whether and when Officer McFadden "seized" Terry and whether and when he conducted a "search." * * * It is quite plain that the Fourth Amendment governs "seizures" of the person which do not eventuate in a trip to the station house and prosecution for crime— "arrest" in traditional terminology. It must be recognized that whenever a police officer accosts an individual and restrains his freedom to walk away, he has "seized" that person. And it is nothing less than sheer torture of the English language to suggest that a careful exploration of the outer surfaces of a person's clothing all over his or her body in an attempt to find weapons is not a "search." Moreover, it is simply fantastic to urge that such a procedure performed in public by a policeman while the citizen stands helpless, perhaps facing a wall with his hands raised, is a "petty indignity." It is a serious intrusion upon the sanctity of the person, which may inflict great indignity and arouse strong resentment, and it is not to be undertaken lightly.

The danger in the logic which proceeds upon distinctions between a "stop" and an "arrest," or "seizure" of the person, and between a "frisk" and a "search" is twofold. It seeks to isolate from constitutional scrutiny the initial stages of the contact between the policeman and the citizen. And by suggesting a rigid all-or-nothing model of justification and regulation under the Amendment, it obscures the utility of limitations upon the scope, as well as the initiation, of police action as a means of constitutional regulation. * * *

The distinctions of classical "stop-and-frisk" theory thus serve to divert attention from the central inquiry under the Fourth Amendment—the reasonableness in all the circumstances of the particular governmental invasion of a citizen's personal security. "Search" and "seizure" are not talismans. We therefore reject the notions that the Fourth Amendment does not come into play at all as a limitation upon police conduct if the officers stop short of something called a "technical arrest" or a "full-blown search."

* * *

[W]e cannot blind ourselves to the need for law enforcement officers to protect themselves and other prospective victims of violence in situations where they may lack probable cause for an arrest. When an officer is justified in believing that the individual whose suspicious behavior he is investigating at close range is armed and presently dangerous to the officer or to others, it would appear to be clearly unreasonable to deny the officer the power to take necessary measures to determine whether the person is in fact carrying a weapon and to neutralize the threat of physical harm.

We must still consider, however, the nature and quality of the intrusion on individual rights which must be accepted if police officers are to be conceded the right to search for weapons in situations where probable cause to arrest for crime is lacking. Even a limited search of the outer clothing for weapons constitutes a severe, though brief, intrusion upon cherished personal security, and it must surely be an annoying, frightening, and perhaps humiliating experience. * * *

* * *

We conclude that the revolver seized from Terry was properly admitted in evidence against him. At the time he seized petitioner and searched him for weapons, Officer McFadden had reasonable grounds to believe that petitioner was armed and dangerous, and it was necessary for the protection of himself and others to take swift measures to discover the true facts and neutralize the threat of harm if it materialized. The policeman carefully restricted his search to what was appropriate to the discovery of the particular items which he sought. Each case of this sort will, of course, have to be decided on its own facts. We merely hold today that where a police officer observes unusual conduct which leads him reasonably to conclude in light of his experience that criminal activity may be afoot and that the persons with whom he is dealing may be armed and presently dangerous, where in the course of investigating this behavior he identifies himself as a policeman and makes reasonable inquiries, and where nothing in the initial stages of the encounter serves to dispel his reasonable fear for his own or others' safety, he is entitled for the protection of himself and others in the area to conduct a carefully limited search of the outer clothing of such persons in an attempt to discover weapons which might be used to assault him.

Such a search is a reasonable search under the Fourth Amendment, and any weapons seized may properly be introduced in evidence against the person from whom they were taken.

Affirmed.

Mr. Justice HARLAN, concurring.

While I unreservedly agree with the Court's ultimate holding in this case, I am constrained to fill in a few gaps, as I see them, in its opinion. I do this because what is said by this Court today will serve as initial guidelines for law enforcement authorities and courts throughout the land as this important new field of law develops.

A police officer's right to make an on-the-street "stop" and an accompanying "frisk" for weapons is of course bounded by the protections afforded by the Fourth and Fourteenth Amendments. The Court holds, and I agree, that while the right does not depend upon possession by the officer of a valid warrant, nor upon the existence of probable cause, such activities must be reasonable under the circumstances as the officer credibly relates them in court. Since the question in this and most cases is whether evidence produced by a frisk is admissible, the problem is to determine what makes a frisk reasonable.

* * *

The state courts held * * * that when an officer is lawfully confronting a possibly hostile person in the line of duty he has a right, springing only from the necessity of the situation and not from any broader right to disarm, to frisk for his own protection. This holding, with which I agree and with which I think the Court agrees, offers the only satisfactory basis I can think of for affirming this conviction. The holding has, however, two logical corollaries that I do not think the Court has fully expressed.

In the first place, if the frisk is justified in order to protect the officer during an encounter with a citizen, the officer must first have constitutional grounds to insist on an encounter, to make a *forcible* stop. Any person, including a policeman, is at liberty to avoid a person he considers dangerous. If and when a policeman has a right instead to disarm such a person for his own protection, he must first have a right not to avoid him but to be in his presence. That right must be more than the liberty (again, possessed by every citizen) to address questions to other persons, for ordinarily the person addressed has an equal right to ignore his interrogator and walk away; he

certainly need not submit to a frisk for the questioner's protection. I would make it perfectly clear that the right to frisk in this case depends upon the reasonableness of a forcible stop to investigate a suspected crime.

Where such a stop is reasonable, however, the right to frisk must be immediate and automatic if the reason for the stop is, as here, an articulable suspicion of a crime of violence. Just as a full search incident to a lawful arrest requires no additional justification, a limited frisk incident to a lawful stop must often be rapid and routine. There is no reason why an officer, rightfully but forcibly confronting a person suspected of a serious crime, should have to ask one question and take the risk that the answer might be a bullet.

* * * Officer McFadden's right to interrupt Terry's freedom of movement and invade his privacy arose only because circumstances warranted forcing an encounter with Terry in an effort to prevent or investigate a crime. Once that forced encounter was justified, however, the officer's right to take suitable measures for his own safety followed automatically.

* * *

Mr. Justice WHITE, concurring.

* * *

* * * I think an additional word is in order concerning the matter of interrogation during an investigative stop. There is nothing in the Constitution which prevents a policeman from addressing questions to anyone on the streets. Absent special circumstances, the person approached may not be detained or frisked but may refuse to cooperate and go on his way. However, given the proper circumstances, such as those in this case, it seems to me the person may be briefly detained against his will while pertinent questions are directed to him. Of course, the person stopped is not obliged to answer, answers may not be compelled, and refusal to answer furnishes no basis for an arrest, although it may alert the officer to the need for continued observation. In my view, it is temporary detention, warranted by the circumstances, which chiefly justifies the protective frisk for weapons. Perhaps the frisk itself, where proper, will have beneficial results whether questions are asked or not. If weapons are found, an arrest will follow. If none are found, the frisk may nevertheless serve preventive ends because of its unmistakable message that suspicion has been aroused. But if the investigative stop is sustainable at all, constitutional rights are not necessarily violated if pertinent questions are asked and the person is restrained briefly in the process.

Mr. Justice DOUGLAS, dissenting.

I agree that petitioner was "seized" within the meaning of the Fourth Amendment. I also agree that frisking petitioner and his companions for guns was a "search." But it is a mystery how that "search" and that "seizure" can be constitutional by Fourth Amendment standards, unless there was "probable cause" to believe that (1) a crime had been committed or (2) a crime was in the process of being committed or (3) a crime was about to be committed.

The opinion of the Court disclaims the existence of "probable cause." If loitering were in issue and that was the offense charged, there would be "probable cause" shown. But the crime here is carrying concealed weapons; and there is no basis for concluding that the officer had "probable cause" for believing that that crime was being committed. Had a warrant been sought, a magistrate would, therefore, have been unauthorized to issue one, for he can act only if there is a showing of "probable cause." We hold today that the police have greater authority to make a "seizure" and conduct a "search" than a judge has to authorize such action. We have said precisely the opposite over and over again.

* * *

SIBRON v. NEW YORK
PETERS v. NEW YORK

Supreme Court of the United States, 1968
392 U.S. 40, 88 S.Ct. 1889, 20 L.Ed.2d 917

These controversies were companion cases to *Terry* v. *Ohio* (p. 1138). They involved the application of a New York statute, the provisions of which were substantially identical to the guidelines enunciated by the Supreme Court in *Terry*. Both Sibron and Peters were convicted in state courts on the basis of evidence taken from them by police under "stop-and-frisk" conditions. Both challenged the statute as unconstitutional on its face.

Mr. Chief Justice WARREN delivered the opinion of the Court.

The facts in these cases may be stated briefly. Sibron, the appellant in No. 63, was convicted of the unlawful possession of heroin. He moved before trial to suppress the heroin seized from his person by the arresting officer, Brooklyn Patrolman Anthony Martin. [T]he trial court denied his motion. * * *
At the hearing on the motion to suppress, Officer Martin testified that while he was patrolling his beat in uniform on March 9, 1965, he observed Sibron "continually from the hours of 4:00 P.M. to 12:00, midnight * * * in the vicinity of 742 Broadway." He stated that during this period of time he saw Sibron in conversation with six or eight persons whom he (Patrolman Martin) knew from past experience to be narcotics addicts. The officer testified that he did not overhear any of these conversations, and that he did not see anything pass between Sibron and any of the others. Late in the evening Sibron entered a restaurant. Patrolman Martin saw Sibron speak with three more known addicts inside the restaurant. Once again, nothing was overheard and nothing was seen to pass between Sibron and the addicts. Sibron sat down and ordered pie and coffee, and, as he was eating Patrolman Martin approached him and told him to come outside. Once outside, the officer said to Sibron, "You know what I am after." According to the officer, Sibron "mumbled something and reached into his pocket." Simultaneously, Patrolman Martin thrust his hand into the same pocket, discovering several glassine envelopes, which, it turned out, contained heroin.

* * *

Peters, the appellant in No. 74, was convicted of possessing burglary tools under circumstances evincing an intent to employ them in the commission of a crime. The tools were seized from his person at the time of his arrest, and like Sibron he made a pretrial motion to suppress them. [T]he trial court denied the motion. * * * Officer Samuel Lasky of the New York City Police Department testified at the hearing on the motion that he was at home in his apartment in Mount Vernon, New York, at about 1 p.m. on July 10, 1964. He had just finished taking a shower and was drying himself when he heard a noise at his door. His attempt to investigate was interrupted by a telephone call, but when he returned and looked through the peephole into the hall, Officer Lasky saw "two men tiptoeing out of the alcove toward the stairway." He immediately called the police, put on some civilian clothes and armed himself with his service revolver. Returning to the peephole, he saw "a tall man tiptoeing away from the alcove and followed by this shorter man, Mr. Peters, toward the stairway." Officer Lasky testified that he had lived in the 120-unit building for 12 years and that he did not recognize either of the men as tenants. Believing that he had happened upon the two men in the course of an attempted burglary, Officer Lasky opened his door, entered the hallway and slammed the door loudly behind him. This precipitated a flight down the stairs on the part of the two men, and Officer Lasky gave chase. His apartment was located on the sixth floor, and he apprehended Peters between the fourth and fifth floors. Grabbing Peters by the collar, he continued down another flight in unsuccessful pursuit of the other man.

Peters explained his presence in the building to Officer Lasky by saying that he was visiting a girl friend. However, he declined to reveal the girl friend's name, on the ground that she was a married woman. Officer Lasky patted Peters down for weapons, and discovered a hard object in his pocket. He stated at the hearing that the object did not feel like a gun, but that it might have been a knife. He removed the object from Peters' pocket. It was an opaque plastic envelope, containing burglar's tools.

* * *

The parties on both sides of these two cases have urged that the principal issue before us is the constitutionality of [the New York "stop-and-frisk" statute] "on its face." We decline, however, to be drawn into what we view as the abstract and unproductive exercise of laying the extraordinarily elastic categories of [the statute] [a] next to the categories of the Fourth Amendment in an effort to determine whether the two are in some sense compatible. The constitutional validity of a warrantless search is pre-eminently the sort of question which can only be decided in the concrete factual context of the individual case. In this respect it is quite different from the question of the adequacy of the procedural safeguards written into a statute which purports to authorize the issuance of search warrants in certain circumstances. * * *

* * *

Turning to the facts of Sibron's case, it is clear that the heroin was inadmissible in evidence against him. The prosecution has quite properly abandoned the notion that there was probable cause to arrest Sibron for any crime at the time Patrolman Martin accosted him in the restaurant, took him outside and searched him. The officer was not acquainted with Sibron and had no information concerning him. He merely saw Sibron talking to a number of known narcotics addicts over a period of eight hours. It must be emphasized that Patrolman Martin was completely ignorant regarding the content of these conversations, and that he saw nothing pass between Sibron and the addicts. So far as he knew, they might * * * "have been talking about the World Series." The inference that persons who talk to narcotics addicts are engaged in the criminal traffic in narcotics is simply not the sort of reasonable inference required to support an intrusion by the police upon an individual's personal security. Nothing resembling probable cause existed until after the search had turned up the envelopes of heroin. It is axiomatic that an incident search may not precede an arrest and serve as part of its justification. * * *

If Patrolman Martin lacked probable cause for an arrest, however, his seizure and search of Sibron might still have been justified at the outset if he had reasonable grounds to believe that Sibron was armed and dangerous. * * * In the case of the self-protective search for weap-

---

a. As described by the Court, the New York statute "deals with the substantive validity of certain types of seizures and searches without warrants. It purports to authorize police officers to 'stop' people, 'demand' ex-

planations of them and 'search [them] for dangerous weapon[s]' in certain circumstances upon 'reasonable suspicion' that they are engaged in criminal activity and that they represent a danger to the policeman."

ons, he must be able to point to particular facts from which he reasonably inferred that the individual was armed and dangerous. * * * Patrolman Martin's testimony reveals no such facts. The suspect's mere act of talking with a number of known narcotics addicts over an eight-hour period no more gives rise to reasonable fear of life or limb on the part of the police officer than it justifies an arrest for committing a crime. Nor did Patrolman Martin urge that when Sibron put his hand in his pocket, he feared that he was going for a weapon and acted in self-defense. His opening statement to Sibron—"You know what I am after"—made it abundantly clear that he sought narcotics, and his testimony at the hearing left no doubt that he thought there were narcotics in Sibron's pocket.

Even assuming *arguendo* that there were adequate grounds to search Sibron for weapons, the nature and scope of the search conducted by Patrolman Martin were so clearly unrelated to that justification as to render the heroin inadmissible. The search for weapons approved in *Terry* consisted solely of a limited patting of the outer clothing of the suspect for concealed objects which might be used as instruments of assault. Only when he discovered such objects did the officer in *Terry* place his hands in the pockets of the men he searched. In this case, with no attempt at an initial limited exploration for arms, Patrolman Martin thrust his hand into Sibron's pocket and took from him envelopes of heroin. His testimony shows that he was looking for narcotics, and he found them. The search was not reasonably limited in scope to the accomplishment of the only goal which might conceivably have justified its

inception—the protection of the officer by disarming a potentially dangerous man. Such a search violates the guarantee of the Fourth Amendment. * * *

We think it is equally clear that the search in Peters' case was wholly reasonable under the Constitution. * * * By the time Officer Lasky caught up with Peters on the stairway between the fourth and fifth floors of the apartment building, he had probable cause to arrest him for attempted burglary. The officer heard strange noises at his door which apparently led him to believe that someone sought to force entry. When he investigated these noises he saw two men, whom he had never seen before in his 12 years in the building, tiptoeing furtively about the hallway. They were still engaged in these maneuvers after he called the police and dressed hurriedly. And when Officer Lasky entered the hallway, the men fled down the stairs. It is difficult to conceive of stronger grounds for an arrest, short of actual eyewitness observation of criminal activity. As the trial court explicitly recognized, deliberately furtive actions and flight at the approach of strangers or law officers are strong indicia of mens rea [criminal intent], and when coupled with specific knowledge on the part of the officer relating the suspect to the evidence of crime, they are proper factors to be considered in the decision to make an arrest. * * *

As we noted in Sibron's case, a search incident to a lawful arrest may not precede the arrest and serve as part of its justification. It is a question of fact precisely when, in each case, the arrest took place. * * * And while there was some inconclusive discussion in the trial court concerning when Officer Lasky "arrested" Peters, it is clear that the arrest had, for purposes of constitutional justification, already taken place before the search commenced. When the policeman grabbed Peters by the collar, he abruptly "seized" him and curtailed his freedom of movement on the basis of probable cause to believe that he was engaged in criminal activity. * * * At that point he had the authority to search Peters, and the incident search was obviously justified "by the need to seize weapons and other things which might be used to assault an officer or effect an escape, as well as by the need to prevent the destruction of evidence of the crime." * * * Moreover, it was reasonably limited in scope by these purposes. Officer Lasky did not engage in an unrestrained and thorough-going examination of Peters and his personal effects. He seized him to cut short his flight, and he searched him primarily for weapons. While patting down his outer clothing, Officer Lasky discovered an object in his pocket which might have been used as a weapon. He seized it and discovered it to be a potential instrument of the crime of burglary.

* * *

Conviction in No. 74 affirmed, and conviction in No. 63 reversed.

Mr. Justice WHITE, concurring.

* * * With respect to appellant Peters, I join the affirmance of his conviction, not because there was probable cause to arrest, a question I do not reach, but because there was probable cause to stop Peters for questioning and thus to frisk him for dangerous weapons. * * *

Mr. Justice FORTAS, concurring.

* * * I would explicitly reserve the possibility that a statute purporting to authorize a warrantless search might be so extreme as to justify our concluding that it is unconstitutional "on its face," regardless of the facts of the particular case. * * *

Mr. Justice HARLAN, concurring in the result.

I fully agree with the results the Court has reached in these cases. * * * For reasons I do not understand, however, the Court has declined to rest the judgments here upon the principles of *Terry*. In doing so it has, in at least one particular, made serious inroads upon the protection afforded by the Fourth and Fourteenth Amendments.

* * *

Mr. Justice BLACK, concurring and dissenting.

I concur in the affirmance of the judgment against Peters but dissent from the reversal of No. 63, *Sibron* v. *New York*, and would affirm that conviction. * * *

* * *

I think there was probable cause for the policeman to believe that when Sibron reached his hand to his coat pocket, Sibron had a dangerous weapon which he might use if it were not taken away from him. * * *

* * *

DUNAWAY v. NEW YORK

Supreme Court of the United States, 1979
442 U.S. 200, 99 S.Ct. 2248, 60 L.Ed.2d 824

Following the death of a pizza parlor proprietor during an armed robbery, a police detective learned from another officer that an informant had supplied a possible lead implicating Dunaway in the crime. After questioning the informant, who was then in jail awaiting trial on a burglary charge, the detective still lacked "enough information to get a warrant" for Dunaway's arrest. Nonetheless, he instructed other detectives to "pick up" Dunaway and "bring him in." Dunaway was taken into custody, and although he was not told he was under arrest, he would have been restrained had he attempted to leave. He was given the *Miranda* warnings and taken to an interrogation room at police headquarters where he was questioned by several officers. Dunaway waived his right to counsel and subsequently made statements and drew sketches which incriminated him. At trial, he moved to suppress the statements and sketches. The motion was denied, and he was eventually convicted. Two state appellate courts affirmed the conviction, but the U.S. Supreme Court vacated the judgment and remanded the case for further consideration in light of its ruling in Brown v. Illinois, 422 U.S. 590, 95 S.Ct. 2254 (1975).

Like Dunaway, Brown had made incriminating statements during custodial interrogation after having first received *Miranda* warnings. But in that case, Brown was formally arrested, though on less than probable cause. Overturning Brown's conviction, the Supreme Court held that the Illinois courts erred in adopting an absolute rule that the giving of *Miranda* warnings sufficed to correct the Fourth Amendment violation. Declining to adopt a reverse absolute rule, however, the Court said in *Brown*: "The *Miranda* warnings are an important factor, to be sure, in determining whether the confession is obtained by exploitation of an illegal arrest. But they are not the only factor to be considered. The temporal proximity of the arrest and the confession, the presence of intervening circumstances, * * * and, particularly, the purpose and flagrancy of the official misconduct are all relevant. * * * The voluntariness of the statement is a threshold requirement. * * * And the burden of showing admissibility rests, of course, on the prosecution." In other words, the Court held that in order to use the incriminating statements the prosecution was constitutionally obliged to show not only that the statements had been made voluntarily, but also that the taint of illegal arrest had been purged by an act of free will.

On remand, a county court found that Dunaway's suppression motion should have been granted: (1) since this was not a case where an individual had voluntarily appeared at the police station in response to a police request; (2) since no probable cause existed for the detention; (3) since the Court in *Brown* had indicated "disdain for custodial questioning without probable cause to arrest"; and (4) since there was nothing which showed attenuation in Dunaway's illegal detention. A state appellate court reversed, citing a New York Court of Appeals ruling that "[l]aw enforcement officials may detain an individual upon reasonable suspicion for questioning for a reasonable and brief period of time under carefully controlled conditions which are ample to protect the individual's Fifth and Sixth Amendment Rights." The appellate court held that the taint of illegal detention was sufficiently attenuated and took pains to note that Dunaway was never threatened or abused by the interrogating police officers. The U.S. Supreme Court granted certiorari "to clarify the Fourth Amendment's requirements as to the permissible grounds for custodial interrogation and to review the New York court's application of Brown v. Illinois."

Mr. Justice BRENNAN delivered the opinion of the Court.

We decide in this case the question reserved 10 years ago in Morales v. New York, 396 U.S. 102, 90 S.Ct. 291 (1969), namely, "the question of the legality of custodial questioning on less than probable cause for a full-fledged arrest."
*   *   *

*   *   *

We first consider whether the Rochester police violated the Fourth and Fourteenth Amendments when, without probable cause to arrest, they took petitioner into custody, transported him to the police station, and detained him there for interrogation.

*   *   *

Terry [v. Ohio, 392 U.S. 1, 88 S.Ct. 1868 (1968)] for the first time recognized an exception to the requirement that Fourth Amendment seizures of persons must be based on probable cause. * * * *Terry* departed from traditional Fourth Amendment analysis in two respects. First, it defined a special category of Fourth Amendment "seizures" so substantially less intrusive than arrests that the general rule requiring probable cause to make Fourth Amendment "seizures" reasonable could be replaced by a balancing test. Second, the application of this balancing test led the Court to approve this narrowly defined less intrusive seizure on grounds less rigorous than probable cause, but only for the purpose of a pat-down for weapons.

Because *Terry* involved an exception to the general rule requiring probable cause, this Court has been careful to maintain its narrow scope.

Terry itself involved a limited, on-the-street frisk for weapons. Two subsequent cases which applied *Terry* also involved limited weapons frisks. See Adams v. Williams, 407 U.S. 143, 92 S.Ct. 1921 (1972) (frisk for weapons on basis of reasonable suspicion); Pennsylvania v. Mimms, 434 U.S. 106, 98 S.Ct. 330 (1977) (order to get out of car is permissible "de minimis" intrusion after car is lawfully detained for traffic violations; frisk for weapons justified after "bulge" observed in jacket). United States v. Brignoni-Ponce, 422 U.S. 873, 95 S.Ct. 2574 (1975), applied *Terry* in the special context of roving border patrols stopping automobiles to check for illegal immigrants. The investigative stops usually consumed less than a minute and involved "a brief question or two." *   *   * The Court stated that "[b]ecause of the limited nature of the intrusion, stops of this sort may be justified on facts that do not amount to the probable cause required for an arrest." * * * See also United States v. Martinez-Fuerte, 428 U.S. 543, 96 S.Ct. 3074 (1976) (fixed checkpoint to stop and check vehicles for aliens); Delaware v. Prouse, 440 U.S. 648, 99 S.Ct. 1391 (1979) (random checks for drivers' licenses and proper vehicle registration not permitted on less than articulable reasonable suspicion).

Respondent State now urges the Court to apply a balancing test, rather than the general rule, to custodial interrogations, and to hold that "seizures" such as that in this case may be justified by mere "reasonable suspicion." *Terry* and its progeny clearly do not support such a result. The narrow intrusions involved in those cases were judged by a balancing test rather than by the general principle that Fourth Amendment seizures must be supported by the "long prevailing standards" of probable cause * * * only because these intrusions fell far short of the kind of intrusion associated with an arrest. Indeed, *Brignoni-Ponce* expressly refused to extend *Terry* in the manner respondent now urges. The Court there stated: "The officer may question the driver and passengers about their citizenship and immigration status, and he may ask them to explain suspicious circumstances, *but any further detention or search must be based on consent or probable cause.*" * * *

In contrast to the brief and narrowly circumscribed intrusions involved in those cases, the detention of petitioner was in important respects indistinguishable from a traditional arrest. Petitioner was not questioned briefly where he was found. Instead, he was taken from a neighbor's home to a police car, transported to a police station, and placed in an interrogation room. He was never informed that he was "free to go"; indeed, he would have been physically restrained if he had refused to accompany the officers or had tried to escape their custody. The application of the Fourth Amendment's requirement of probable cause does not depend on whether an intrusion of this magnitude is termed an "arrest" under state law. The mere facts that petitioner was not told he was under arrest, was not "booked," and would not have had an arrest record if the interrogation had proved fruitless, while not insignificant for all purposes * * * obviously do not make petitioner's seizure even roughly analogous to the narrowly defined intrusions involved in *Terry* and its progeny. In-

deed, any "exception" that could cover a seizure as intrusive as that in this case would threaten to swallow the general rule that Fourth Amendment seizures are "reasonable" only if based on probable cause.

The central importance of the probable cause requirement to the protection of a citizen's privacy afforded by the Fourth Amendment's guarantees cannot be compromised in this fashion. * * * Hostility to seizures based on mere suspicion was a prime motivation for the adoption of the Fourth Amendment, and decisions immediately after its adoption affirmed that "common rumor or report, suspicion, or even 'strong reason to suspect' was not adequate to support a warrant for arrest." * * * The familiar threshold standard of probable cause for Fourth Amendment seizures reflects the benefit of extensive experience accommodating the factors relevant to the "reasonableness" requirement of the Fourth Amendment, and provides the relative simplicity and clarity necessary to the implementation of a workable rule. * * *

In effect, respondents urge us to adopt a multifactor balancing test of "reasonable police conduct under the circumstances" to cover all seizures that do not amount to technical arrests. But the protections intended by the Framers could all too easily disappear in the consideration and balancing of the multifarious circumstances presented by different cases, especially when that balancing may be done in the first instance by police officers engaged in the "often competitive enterprise of ferreting out crime." * * * A single, familiar standard is essential to guide police officers, who have only limited time and expertise to reflect on and balance the social and individual interests involved in the specific circumstances they confront. Indeed, our recognition of these dangers, and our consequent reluctance to depart from the proven protections afforded by the general rule, is reflected in the narrow limitations emphasized in the cases employing the balancing test. For all but those narrowly defined intrusions, the requisite "balancing" has been performed in centuries of precedent and is embodied in the principle that seizures are "reasonable" only if supported by probable cause.

Moreover, two important decisions since *Terry* confirm the conclusion that the treatment of petitioner, whether or not it is technically characterized as an asset, must be supported by probable cause. Davis v. Mississippi, 394 U.S. 721, 89 S.Ct. 1394 (1969), decided the term after *Terry*, considered whether fingerprints taken from a suspect detained without probable cause must be excluded from evidence. The State argued that the detention "was of a type which does not require probable cause," * * * because it occurred during an investigative, rather than accusatory stage, and because it was for the sole purpose of taking fingerprints. Rejecting the State's first argument, the Court warned:

"[T]o argue that the Fourth Amendment does not apply to the investigatory stage is fundamentally to misconceive the purposes of the Fourth Amendment. Investigatory seizures would subject unlimited numbers of innocent persons to the harassment and ignominy incident to involuntary detention. Nothing is more clear than that the Fourth Amendment was meant to prevent wholesale in-

trusions upon the personal security of our citizenry, whether these intrusions be termed 'arrests' or 'investigatory detentions.'" * * *

The State's second argument in *Davis* was more substantial, largely because of the *distinctions* between taking fingerprints and interrogation:

"Fingerprinting involves none of the probing into an individual's private life and thoughts that marks an interrogation or search. Nor can fingerprint detention be employed repeatedly to harass any individual, since the police need only one set of each person's prints. Furthermore, fingerprinting is an inherently more reliable and effective crime-solving tool than eyewitness identifications or confessions and is not subject to such abuses as the improper line-up and the 'third degree.' Finally, because there is no danger of destruction of fingerprints, the limited detention need not come unexpectedly or at an inconvenient time." * * *

In *Davis*, however, the Court found it unnecessary to decide the validity of a "narrowly circumscribed procedure for obtaining" the fingerprints of suspects without probable cause— in part because, as the Court emphasized, "petitioner was not merely fingerprinted during the * * * detention but *also subjected to interrogation*." * * * (Emphasis added.) The detention therefore violated the Fourth Amendment.

Brown v. Illinois, 422 U.S. 590, 95 S.Ct. 2254 (1975) * * * similarly disapproved arrests made for "investigatory" purposes on less than probable cause. Although Brown's arrest had more of the trappings of a technical formal arrest than petitioner's, such differences in form must not be exalted over substance. Once in the police station, Brown was taken to an interrogation room, and his experience was indistinguishable from petitioner's. Our condemnation of the police conduct in *Brown* fits equally the police conduct in this case:

"The impropriety of the arrest was obvious; awareness of the fact was virtually conceded by the two detectives when they repeatedly acknowledged, in their testimony, that the purpose of their action was 'for investigation' or for 'questioning.' * * * The arrest, both in design and in execution, was investigatory. The detectives embarked upon this expedition for evidence in the hope that something might turn up." * * *

These passages from *Davis* and *Brown* reflect the conclusion that detention for custodial interrogation— regardless of its label—intrudes so severely on interests protected by the Fourth Amendment as necessarily to trigger the traditional safeguards against illegal arrest. We accordingly hold that the Rochester police violated the Fourth and Fourteenth Amendments when, without probable cause, they seized petitioner and transported him to the police station for interrogation.

There remains the question whether the connection between this unconstitutional police conduct and the incriminating statements and sketches obtained during petitioner's illegal detention was nevertheless sufficiently attenuated to permit the use at trial of the statements and sketches. See Wong Sun v. United States, 371 U.S. 471, 83 S.Ct. 407 (1963); Nardone v. United States, 308 U.S. 338, 60 S.Ct. 266 (1939);

Silverthorne Lumber Co. v. United States, 251 U.S. 385, 40 S.Ct. 182 (1920).

The New York courts have consistently held, and petitioner does not contest, that proper *Miranda* warnings were given and that his statements were "voluntary" for purposes of the Fifth Amendment. But *Brown* v. *Illinois*, supra, settled that "[t]he exclusionary rule, * * * when utilized to effectuate the Fourth Amendment, serves interests and policies that are distinct from those it serves under the Fifth," 422 U.S., at 601, 95 S.Ct., at 2260, and held therefore that "*Miranda* warnings, and the exclusion of a confession made without them, do not alone sufficiently deter a Fourth Amendment violation." * * *

* * *

The situation in this case is virtually a replica of the situation in *Brown*. Petitioner was also admittedly seized without probable cause in the hope that something might turn up, and confessed without any intervening event of significance. Nevertheless, three members of the Appellate Division purported to distinguish *Brown* on the ground that the police did threaten or abuse petitioner (presumably putting aside his illegal seizure and detention) and that the police conduct was "highly protective of defendant's Fifth and Sixth Amendment rights." 61 App. Div.2d, at 303, 402 N.Y.S.2d, at 493. This betrays a lingering confusion between "voluntariness" for purposes of the Fifth Amendment and the "causal connection" test established in *Brown*. Satisfying the Fifth Amendment is only the "threshold" condition of the Fourth Amendment analysis required by

Brown. No intervening events broke the connection between petitioner's illegal detention and his confession. To admit petitioner's confession in such a case would allow "law enforcement officers to violate the Fourth Amendment with impunity, safe in the knowledge that they could wash their hands in the 'procedural safeguards' of the Fifth."

Reversed.

Mr. Justice POWELL took no part in the consideration or decision of this case.

Mr. Justice REHNQUIST, with whom THE CHIEF JUSTICE [BURGER] joins, dissenting.

If the Court did no more in this case than it announced in the opening sentence of its opinion—"decide * * * the question reserved 10 years ago in Morales v. New York, 396 U.S. 102, 90 S.Ct. 291 (1969), namely 'the question of the legality of custodial questioning on less than probable cause for a full fledged arrest' "—I would have little difficulty joining its opinion. The decision of this question, however, does not, contrary to the implication in the Court's opening sentence, decide this case. For the Court goes on to conclude that petitioner Dunaway was in fact "seized" within the meaning of the Fourth Amendment, and that the connection between Dunaway's purported detention and the evidence obtained therefrom was not sufficiently attenuated as to dissipate the taint of the alleged unlawful police conduct. * * * I cannot agree with either conclusion, and accordingly, I dissent.

There is obviously nothing in the Fourth Amendment that prohibits police from calling from their vehicle to a particular individual on the street and asking him to come over and talk with them; nor is there anything in the Fourth Amendment that prevents the police from knocking on the door of a person's house and when the person answers the door, inquiring whether he is willing to answer questions that they wish to put to him. "Obviously, not all personal intercourse between policemen and citizens involves 'seizures' of persons." Terry v. Ohio, 392 U.S., at 19 n. 16, 88 S.Ct., at 1879. Voluntary questioning not involving any "seizure" for Fourth Amendment purposes may take place under any number of varying circumstances. And the occasions will not be few when a particular individual agrees voluntarily to answer questions that the police wish to put to him either on the street, at the station, or in his house, and later regrets his willingness to answer those questions. However, such morning-after regrets do not render involuntary responses that were voluntary at the time they were made. In my view, this is a case where the defendant voluntarily accompanied the police to the station to answer their questions.

In *Terry* v. *Ohio*, supra, the Court set out the test for determining whether a person has been "seized" for Fourth Amendment purposes. "Only when the officer, by means of physical force or show of authority, has in some way restrained the liberty of a citizen may we conclude that a 'seizure' has occurred." * * * In this case, three police officers were dispatched to petitioner's house to question him about his participation in a robbery. According to the testimony of the police officers, one officer approached a house where petitioner was thought to be located and knocked on the door. When a person answered the door, the officer identified himself and asked the individual his name. * * * After learning that the person who answered the door was petitioner, the officer asked him if he would accompany the officers to police headquarters for questioning, and petitioner responded that he would. * * * Petitioner was not told that he was under arrest or in custody and was not warned not to resist or flee. No weapons were displayed and petitioner was not handcuffed. Each officer testified that petitioner was not touched or held during the trip downtown; his freedom of action was not in any way restrained by the police. * * * In short, the police behavior in this case was entirely free of "physical force or show of authority."

* * *

Therefore, although I agree that the police officers in this case did not have that degree of suspicion or probable cause that would have justified them in physically compelling petitioner to accompany them to the police station for questioning, I do not believe that the record demonstrates as a fact that this is what happened. No involuntary detention for questioning was shown to have taken place. The Fourth Amendment, accordingly, does not require suppression of petitioner's statements.

Assuming *arguendo* that there was a "seizure" in this case, I still cannot agree with the Court that the Fourth Amendment requires suppression of petitioner's statements and sketches. Relying on Brown v. Illinois, 422 U.S. 590, 95 S.Ct. 2254

(1975), the Court concludes that this evidence must be suppressed primarily, it seems, because no intervening events broke the connection between petitioner's detention and his confession. * * * In my view, the connection between petitioner's allegedly unlawful detention and the incriminating statements and sketches is sufficiently attenuated to permit their use at trial. * * *

* * *

The Court concedes that petitioner received proper *Miranda* warnings and that his statements were "voluntary" for purposes of the Fifth Amendment. * * * And the police acted in good faith. * * * At the time of petitioner's detention, the New York Court of Appeals had held that custodial questioning on less than probable cause for an arrest was permissible under the Fourth Amendment. People v. Morales, 22 N.Y.2d 55, 238 N.E.2d 307 (1968). Petitioner testified that the police never threatened or abused him. * * * Petitioner voluntarily gave his first statement to police about an hour after he reached the police station and then gave another statement to police the following day. Contrary to the Court's suggestion, the police conduct in this case was in no manner as flagrant as that of the police in *Brown* v. *Illinois*, supra. * * * Thus, in my view, the record convincingly demonstrates that the statements and sketches given police by petitioner were of sufficient free will as to purge the primary taint of his alleged illegal detention. I would, therefore, affirm the judgment of the Appellate Division of the Supreme Court of New York.

MORE RECENT RULINGS DRAWING UPON *TERRY* v. *OHIO*

Case	Ruling	Vote
Brown v. Texas, 443 U.S. 47, 99 S.Ct. 2637 (1979)	Defendant was unconstitutionally convicted under a Texas statute for refusing to comply with a policeman's demand that he identify himself when he was stopped on a hunch by the police officer. Police were without any articulable suspicion in stopping the defendant where, on patrol, they observed defendant and another man walking away from each other in an alley in an area known to have a high volume of drug traffic and had no basis for suspecting defendant of any criminal activity or of being armed other than that the circumstances "looked suspicious" and because the officers "had never seen that subject in that area before." The Court expressly reserved the question "whether an individual may be punished for refusing to identify himself in the context of a lawful investigative stop which satisfies Fourth Amendment requirements."	9–0
Ybarra v. Illinois, 444 U.S. 85, 100 S.Ct. 338 (1979)	Where police, armed with a warrant to search a tavern and the bartender for drugs, simply frisked all of the patrons in a cursory search for weapons, they violated the Fourth Amendment since none of the customers were implicated or even mentioned in the events leading to the issuance of the warrant. Nor did the conduct of the defendant (who was a customer in the bar at the time the search warrant was executed) give the police cause to frisk him since: (1) he was not known as a person with a criminal history who might try to attack the police, his hands were empty, and he "gave no indication of possessing a weapon, made no gestures or other actions indicative of an intent to commit an assault, and acted generally in a manner that was not threatening"; and (2) the police did not have reason to believe he was engaged in criminal conduct, and "he made no gestures indicative of criminal conduct, made no movements that might suggest an attempt to conceal contraband, and said nothing of a suspicious nature to the police officers."	6–3; Chief Justice Burger and Justices Blackmun and Rehnquist dissented

Following her arrival at the Detroit airport on an early morning flight, Sylvia Mendenhall was approached by two agents of the federal Drug Enforcement Administration (DEA). What triggered the agents' interest was the similarity of her behavior to that suggested by the "drug courier profile." [b] The agents

---

b. As Justice Stewart explained in a footnote, the "drug courier profile" is "an informally compiled abstract of characteristics thought typical of persons carrying illicit

stopped Ms. Mendenhall as she was walking through the concourse of the airport, identified themselves as federal narcotics agents, and asked to see her airline ticket and some personal identification. When it turned out that the name on the ticket did not jibe with that on her driver's license, after she indicated that she had stayed in California for only two days, and in light of the fact that she appeared quite shaken, extremely nervous, and was so upset she could hardly speak, the agents asked her to come with them to the airport DEA office, which she did. At the office, an agent asked if she would allow a search of her person and handbag and told her that she had the right to refuse. She replied by saying, "Go ahead." A policewoman arrived shortly after that and asked the agents if the respondent had consented to the search. After the agents indicated that she had, the two women went into a separate room. There the policewoman again asked Ms. Mendenhall if she consented to the search, and she responded affirmatively. When she was asked to disrobe, the respondent expressed apprehension about missing her flight, and the policewoman told her that there would be no problem if she had no narcotics. In the course of disrobing, the respondent removed two small packages from her undergarments and handed them to the policewoman. Ms. Mendenhall was subsequently arrested and convicted for possession of heroin. A federal district court denied a defense motion to suppress the evidence: (1) because the agents' conduct constituted a permissible investigative stop based upon "specific and articulable facts that justified a suspicion of criminal activity"; (2) because no arrest had been effected until after the heroin was found; and (3) because Ms. Mendenhall had voluntarily accompanied the agents to the DEA office and voluntarily consented to the search. A federal appellate court reversed on the grounds that: (1) the correspondence between the defendant's behavior and that described in the drug courier profile constituted inadequate suspicion of criminal activity; (2) the request to accompany the agents to the DEA office amounted to an arrest requiring probable cause; and (3) the consent to search was invalid because it was the fruit of an unconstitutional detention. On rehearing en banc, the appellate court reaffirmed the judgment of the panel based on the conclusion that the respondent had not consented to the search.

The Supreme Court reversed the ruling of the appeals court in United States v. Mendenhall, 446 U.S. 554, 100 S.Ct. 1870 (1980). The judgment of the Court was announced by Justice Stewart in an opinion in which he was joined by Justice Rehnquist and also in part by Chief Justice Burger and Justices Blackmun and Powell. Since only "seizures" are subject to constitutional safeguards and reasoning that it would be "wholly unrealistic" to "characteriz[e] every street encounter between a citizen and the police as a 'seizure,'" Justice Stewart began by "adher[ing] to the view that a person is 'seized' only when by means of physical force or a show of authority, his freedom of movement is restrained." He continued:

> We conclude that a person has been "seized" within the meaning of the Fourth Amendment only if, in view of all of the circumstances surrounding the incident, a reasonable person would have believed that he was not free

---

drugs. In this case the agents thought it relevant that (1) the respondent was arriving on a flight from Los Angeles, a city believed by the agents to be the place of origin for much of the heroin brought to Detroit; (2) the respondent was the last person to leave the plane, 'appeared to be very nervous' and 'completely scanned the whole area where [the agents] were standing'; (3) after leaving the plane the respondent proceeded past the baggage area without claiming any luggage; and (4) the respondent changed airlines for her flight out of Detroit."

to leave. Examples of circumstances that might indicate a seizure, even where the person did not attempt to leave, would be the threatening presence of several officers, the display of a weapon by an officer, some physical touching of the person of the citizen, or the use of language or tone of voice indicating that compliance with the officer's request might be compelled. * * * In the absence of some such evidence, otherwise inoffensive contact between a member of the public and the police cannot, as a matter of law, amount to a seizure of that person.

On the facts of this case, no "seizure" of the respondent occurred. The events took place in the public concourse. The agents wore no uniforms and displayed no weapons. They did not summon the respondent to their presence, but instead approached her and identified themselves as federal agents. They requested, but did not demand to see the respondent's identification and ticket. Such conduct, without more, did not amount to an intrusion upon any constitutionally protected interest. The respondent was not seized simply by reason of the fact that the agents approached her, asked her if she would show them her ticket and identification, and posed to her a few questions. Nor was it enough to establish a seizure that the person asking the questions was a law enforcement official. * * * In short, nothing in the record suggests that the respondent had any objective reason to believe that she was not free to end the conversation in the concourse and proceed on her way, and for that reason we conclude that the agents' initial approach to her was not a seizure.

Having disposed of the question whether the initial encounter between the agents and Ms. Mendenhall amounted to an unlawful seizure, Justice Stewart proceeded to consider if "respondent's Fourth Amendment protections were violated when she went from the concourse to the DEA office." Addressing this question, he explained:

The question whether the respondent's consent to accompany the agents was in fact voluntary or was the product of duress or coercion, express or implied, is to be determined by the totality of all the circumstances. Schneckloth v. Bustamonte, 412 U.S. 218, 227, 93 S.Ct. 2041 and is a matter which the government has the burden of proving. * * * The respondent herself did not testify at the hearing. The Government's evidence showed that the respondent was not told that she had to go to the office, but was simply asked if she would accompany the officers. There were neither threats nor any show of force. The respondent had been questioned only briefly, and her ticket and identification were returned to her before she was asked to accompany the officers.

On the other hand, it is argued that the incident would reasonably have appeared coercive to the respondent, who was 22 years old and had not been graduated from high school. It is additionally suggested that the respondent, a female and a Negro, may have felt unusually threatened by the officers, who were white males. While these factors were not irrelevant, * * * neither were they decisive, and the totality of the evidence in this case was plainly adequate to support the District Court's finding that the respondent voluntarily consented to accompany the officers to the DEA office.

Given that "the search of the respondent's person was not preceded by an impermissible seizure of her person," and therefore, since "it cannot be contended that her apparent consent to the subsequent search was infected by an unlawful detention," there only remained to be considered whether Ms. Mendenhall's consent to the strip search was otherwise invalid. Relying upon the Supreme Court's previous ruling in *Schneckloth* v. *Bustamonte*, the district court found that " 'consent was freely and voluntarily given.' " Commenting on this finding, Justice Stewart wrote:

> There was more than enough evidence in this case to sustain that view. First, we note that the respondent, who was 22 years old and had an 11th grade education, was plainly capable of a knowing consent. Second, it is especially significant that the respondent was twice expressly told that she was free to decline to consent to the search, and only thereafter explicitly consented to it. Although the Constitution does not require "proof of knowledge of a right to refuse as the *sine qua non* of an effective consent to a search, * * * such knowledge was highly relevant to the determination that there had been consent. And, perhaps more important for present purposes, the fact that the officers themselves informed the respondent that she was free to withhold her consent substantially lessened the probability that their conduct could reasonably have appeared to her to be coercive.
>
> Counsel for the respondent has argued that she did in fact resist the search, relying principally on the testimony that when she was told that the search would require the removal of her clothing, she stated to the female police officer that "she had a plane to catch." But the trial court was entitled to view the statement as simply an expression of concern that the search be conducted quickly. The respondent had twice unequivocally indicated her consent to the search, and when assured by the police officer that there would be no problem if nothing were turned up by the search, she began to undress without further comment.
>
> Counsel for the respondent has also argued that because she was within the DEA office when she consented to the search, her consent may have resulted from the inherently coercive nature of those surroundings. But in view of the District Court's finding that the respondent's presence in the office was voluntary, the fact that she was there is little or no evidence that she was in any way coerced. And in response to the argument that the respondent would not voluntarily have consented to a search that was likely to disclose the narcotics that she carried, we repeat that the question is not whether the respondent acted in her ultimate self-interest, but whether she acted voluntarily.
>
> We conclude that the District Court's determination that the respondent consented to the search of her person "freely and voluntarily" was sustained by the evidence and that the Court of Appeals was, therefore, in error in setting it aside. Accordingly, the judgment of the Court of Appeals is reversed, and the case is remanded to that court for further proceedings.

In a concurring opinion, Justice Powell, joined by Chief Justice Burger and Justice Blackmun, did "not reach the Government's contention that the agents did not 'seize' the respondent within the meaning of the Fourth Amendment[,] * * * assume[d] for present purposes that the stop did constitute a seizure[,]" and concluded "that the federal agents had reasonable suspicion that the respondent was engaging in criminal activity * * *." Consequently, "they did not violate the Fourth Amendment by stopping the respondent for routine questioning."

Justice White dissented in an opinion in which Justices Brennan, Marshall, and Stevens joined. Since the government sought reversal of the judgment below by arguing for the first time before the Supreme Court that no seizure of Ms. Mendenhall had in fact occurred (as opposed to its repeated contention in the courts below that the initial encounter between the agents and Ms. Mendenhall was justified by reasonable suspicion), the dissenters would have remanded the case to the district court for an evidentiary hearing on the question of whether the encounter on the concourse constituted a "seizure" within the meaning of the Fourth Amendment. Alternatively, the dissenters concluded that, consistent with the holdings of *Terry* v. *Ohio* and its progeny, "seizure" extends to include "stops" of which the encounter on the concourse was one. If so, the dissenters reasoned, there were no " 'specific and articulable facts, which taken together with rational inferences from those facts, reasonably warrant[ed] that intrusion.' " Justice White explained:

At the time they stopped Ms. Mendenhall, the DEA agents' suspicion that she was engaged in criminal activity was based solely on their brief observations of her conduct at the airport. The officers had no advance information that Ms. Mendenhall, or anyone on her flight, would be carrying drugs. What the agents observed Ms. Mendenhall do in the airport was not "unusual conduct" which would lead an experienced officer reasonably to conclude that criminal activity was afoot, * * * but rather the kind of behavior that could reasonably be expected of anyone changing planes in an airport terminal.

None of the aspects of Ms. Mendenhall's conduct, either alone or in combination, were sufficient to provide reasonable suspicion that she was engaged in criminal activity. The fact that Ms. Mendenhall was the last person to alight from a flight originating in Los Angeles was plainly insufficient to provide a basis for stopping her. Nor was the fact that her flight originated from a "major source city," for the mere proximity of a person to areas with a high incidence of drug activity or to persons known to be drug addicts, does not provide the necessary reasonable suspicion for an investigatory stop. Ybarra v. Illinois, 444 U.S. 85, 100 S.Ct. 338 (1979); Brown v. Texas, 443 U.S. 47, 99 S.Ct. 2637 (1979); Sibron v. New York, 392 U.S. 40, 62, 88 S.Ct. 1889 (1968). Under the circumstances of this case, the DEA agents' observations that Ms. Mendenhall claimed no luggage and changed airlines were also insufficient to provide reasonable suspicion. Unlike the situation in *Terry* v. *Ohio*, * * * where "nothing in [the suspects'] conduct from the time [the officer] first noticed them until the time he confronted them and identified himself as a police officer gave him sufficient reason to negate [his] hypothesis" of criminal behavior, Ms. Mendenhall's subsequent conduct negated any reasonable inference that she was travelling a long distance without luggage or changing her ticket to a different airline to avoid detection. Agent Anderson testified that he heard the ticket agent tell Ms. Mendenhall that her ticket to Pittsburgh already was in order and that all she needed was a boarding pass for the flight. Thus it should have been plain to an experienced observer that Ms. Mendenhall's failure to claim luggage was attributable to the fact that she was already ticketed through to Pittsburgh on a different airline. Because Agent Anderson's suspicion that Ms. Mendenhall was transporting narcotics could be based only on "his inchoate and unparticularized suspicion or 'hunch,' " rather than "specific reasonable inferences which he is entitled to draw from the facts in light of his experience," * * * he was not justified in "seizing" Ms. Mendenhall.

Even putting aside the question of whether the initial encounter was tantamount to a "seizure," the dissenters concluded that Ms. Mendenhall "undoubtedly was 'seized' within the meaning of the Fourth Amendment, when the agents escorted her from the public area of the terminal to the DEA office for questioning and a strip search of her person." Relying on its decision in *Dunaway* v. *New York*, where the Court found that the defendant (1) "was not told that he was under arrest"; (2) "was never informed that he was 'free to go'"; and (3) "would have been physically restrained if he had refused to accompany the officers or had tried to escape their custody," Justice White reasoned that

the nature of the intrusion to which Ms. Mendenhall was subjected when she was escorted by DEA agents to their office and detained there for questioning and a strip search was so great that it "was in important respects indistinguishable from a traditional arrest." * * * Although Ms. Mendenhall was not told that she was under arrest, she in fact was not free to refuse to go to the DEA office and was not told that she was. Furthermore, once inside the office, Ms. Mendenhall would not have been permitted to leave without submitting to a strip search. * * *

As for the majority's finding that Ms. Mendenhall had consented to go to the DEA office, the dissenters concluded that such a statement was "inconsistent with *Dunaway* and unsupported in the record." Observing that "[t]he evidence of consent here is even flimsier than that we rejected in *Dunaway* where it was claimed that the suspect made an affirmative response when asked if he would accompany the officers to the police station," Justice White asserted, "On the record before us, the Court's conclusion can only be based on the notion that consent can be assumed from the absence of proof that a suspect resisted police authority. This is a notion that we have squarely rejected." He concluded, "Because Ms. Mendenhall was being illegally detained at the time of the search of her person, her suppression motion should have been granted in the absence of evidence to dissipate the taint."

DELAWARE v. PROUSE

Supreme Court of the United States, 1979
440 U.S. 648, 99 S.Ct. 1391, 59 L.Ed.2d 660

A patrolman in a police cruiser stopped the automobile driven by the respondent. As the officer walked toward the stopped vehicle, he smelled marijuana smoke and subsequently seized marijuana that was in plain sight on the floor of respondent's car. At a hearing on a motion to suppress the evidence, the officer testified that he did not observe any traffic or equipment violations or any suspicious activity prior to stopping the vehicle. He said he made the stop only to spot check the driver's license and vehicle registration. He was not acting pursuant to any department procedures or guidelines regarding such spot checks. The patrolman characterized the stop as "routine" and something he did because he was not busy at the time responding to a complaint. The trial court granted respondent's motion to suppress the evidence, and the Delaware Supreme Court affirmed. The state then sought certiorari from the U. S. Supreme Court.

Mr. Justice WHITE delivered the opinion of the Court.

The question is whether it is an unreasonable seizure under the Fourth and Fourteenth Amendments to stop an automobile, being driven on a public highway, for the purpose of checking the driving license of the operator and the registration of the car, where there is neither probable cause to believe nor reasonable suspicion that the car is being driven contrary to the laws governing the operation of motor vehicles or that either the car or any of its occupants is subject to seizure or detention in connection with the violation of any other applicable law. ·

*   *   *

The Fourth and Fourteenth Amendments are implicated in this case because stopping an automobile and detaining its occupants constitute a "seizure" within the meaning of those Amendments, even though the purpose of the stop is limited and the resulting detention quite brief. United States. v. Martinez-Fuerte, 428 U.S. 543, 556–558, 96 S.Ct. 3074, 3082–3083 (1976); United States v. Brignoni-Ponce, 422 U.S. 873, 878, 95 S.Ct. 2574, 2578 (1975); cf. Terry v. Ohio, 392 U.S. 1, 16, 88 S.Ct. 1868, 1877 (1968). The essential purpose of the proscriptions in the Fourth Amendment is to impose a standard of "reasonableness" upon the exercise of discretion by government officials, including law-enforcement agents, in order " 'to safeguard the privacy and security of individuals against arbitrary invasions.' " * * * Marshall v. Barlow's, Inc., 436 U.S. 307, 312, 98 S.Ct. 1816, 1820 (1978), quoting Camara v. Municipal Court, 387 U.S. 523, 528, 87 S.Ct. 1727, 1730 (1967). Thus, the permissibility of a particular law-enforce-

ment practice is judged by balancing its intrusion on the individual's Fourth Amendment interests against its promotion of legitimate governmental interests. Implemented in this manner, the reasonableness standard usually requires, at a minimum, that the facts upon which an intrusion is based be capable of measurement against "an objective standard," whether this be probable cause or a less stringent test. In those situations in which the balance of interests precludes insistence upon "some quantum of individualized suspicion," other safeguards are generally relied upon to assure that the individual's reasonable expectation of privacy is not "subject to the discretion of the official in the field," Camara v. Municipal Court, supra, 387 U.S. at 532, 87 S.Ct. at 1733.
*   *   *

In this case, however, the State of Delaware urges that patrol officers be subject to no constraints in deciding which automobiles shall be stopped for a license and registration check because the State's interest in discretionary spot checks as a means of ensuring the safety of its roadways outweighs the resulting intrusion on the privacy and security of the persons detained.

*   *   *

Although not dispositive, * * * [earlier] decisions undoubtedly provide guidance in balancing the public interest against the individual's Fourth Amendment interests implicated by the practice of spot checks such as occurred in this case. We cannot agree that stopping or detaining a vehicle on an ordinary city street is less intrusive than a roving patrol stop on a major highway and that it bears greater resemblance to a permissible stop and secondary detention at a checkpoint near the border. In this regard, we note that *Brignoni-Ponce* was not limited to roving patrol stops on limited access roads, but applied to any roving patrol stop by border patrol agents on any type of roadway on less than reasonable suspicion. * * * We cannot assume that the physical and psychological intrusion visited upon the occupants of a vehicle by a random stop to check documents is of any less moment than that occasioned by a stop by border agents on roving patrol. Both of these stops generally entail law-enforcement officers signaling a moving automobile to pull over to the side of the roadway, by means of a possibly unsettling show of authority. Both interfere with freedom of movement, are inconvenient, and consume time. Both may create substantial anxiety. For Fourth Amendment purposes, we also see insufficient resemblance between sporadic and random stops of individual vehicles making their way through city traffic and those stops occasioned by roadblocks where all vehicles are brought to a halt or to a near halt, and all are subjected to a show of the police power of the community. "At traffic checkpoints, the motorist can see that other vehicles are being stopped, he can see visible signs of the officer's authority, and he is much less likely to be frightened or annoyed by the intrusion." * * *

* * *

The question remains * * * whether in the service of * * * important ends [e.g., "that only those qualified to do so are permitted to operate motor vehicles, that these vehicles are fit for safe operation, and hence that licensing, registration, and vehicle inspection requirements

are being observed"] the discretionary spot check is a sufficiently productive mechanism to justify the intrusion upon Fourth Amendment interests which such stops entail. On the record before us, that question must be answered in the negative. Given the alternative mechanisms available, both those in use and those that might be adopted, we are unconvinced that the incremental contribution to highway safety of the random spot check justifies the practice under the Fourth Amendment.

The foremost method of enforcing traffic and vehicle safety regulations, it must be recalled, is acting upon observed violations. Vehicle stops for traffic violations occur countless times each day; and on these occasions, licenses and registration papers are subject to inspection and drivers without them will be ascertained. Furthermore, drivers without licenses are presumably the less safe drivers whose propensities may well exhibit themselves. Absent some empirical data to the contrary, it must be assumed that finding an unlicensed driver among those who commit traffic violations is a much more likely event than finding an unlicensed driver by choosing randomly from the entire universe of drivers. If this were not so, licensing of drivers would hardly be an effective means of promoting roadway safety. It seems common sense that the percentage of all drivers on the road who are driving without a license is very small and that the number of licensed drivers who will be stopped in order to find one unlicensed operator will be large indeed. The contribution to highway safety made by discretionary stops selected from among drivers generally will therefore be marginal at best. Furthermore, and again absent something more than mere assertion to the contrary, we find it difficult to believe that the unlicensed driver would not be deterred by the possibility of being involved in a traffic violation or having some other experience calling for proof of his entitlement to drive but that he would be deterred by the possibility that he would be one of those chosen for a spot check. In terms of actually discovering unlicensed drivers or deterring them from driving, the spot check does not appear sufficiently productive to qualify as a reasonable law-enforcement practice under the Fourth Amendment.

Much the same can be said about the safety aspects of automobiles as distinguished from drivers. Many violations of minimum vehicle safety requirements are observable, and something can be done about them by the observing officer, directly and immediately. Furthermore, in Delaware, as elsewhere, vehicles must carry and display current license plates, which themselves evidence that the vehicle is properly registered; and, under Delaware law, to qualify for annual registration a vehicle must pass the annual safety inspection and be properly insured. It does not appear, therefore, that a stop of a Delaware-registered vehicle is necessary in order to ascertain compliance with the State's registration requirements; and because there is nothing to show that a significant percentage of automobiles from other States do not also require license plates indicating current registration, there is no basis for concluding that stopping even out-of-state cars for document checks substantially promotes the State's interest.

The marginal contribution to roadway safety possibly resulting from a system of spot checks cannot justify subjecting every occupant of every vehicle on the roads to a seizure—limited in magnitude compared to other intrusions but nonetheless constitutionally cognizable— at the unbridled discretion of law-enforcement officials. To insist upon neither an appropriate factual basis for suspicion directed at a particular automobile nor upon some other substantial and objective standard or rule to govern the exercise of discretion "would invite intrusions upon constitutionally guaranteed rights based on nothing more substantial than inarticulate hunches." * * * Terry v. Ohio, supra, 392 U.S. at 22, 88 S.Ct. at 1880. By hypothesis, stopping apparently safe drivers is necessary only because the danger presented by some drivers is not observable at the time of the stop. When there is not probable cause to believe that a driver is violating any one of the multitude of applicable traffic and equipment regulations— nor other articulable basis amounting to reasonable suspicion that the driver is unlicensed or his vehicle unregistered—we cannot conceive of any legitimate basis upon which a patrolman could decide that stopping a particular driver for a spot check would be more productive than stopping any other driver. This kind of standardless and unconstrained discretion is the evil the Court has discerned when in previous cases it has insisted that the discretion of the official in the field be circumscribed, at least to some extent. Almeida-Sanchez v. United States, 413 U.S. 266, 270, 93 S.Ct. 2535, 2538 (1973); Camara v. Municipal Court, supra, 387 U.S. at 532–533, 87 S.Ct. at 1733.

* * *

An individual operating or travelling in an automobile does not lose all reasonable expectation of privacy simply because the automobile and its use are subject to government regulation. Automobile travel is a basic, pervasive, and often necessary mode of transportation to and from one's home, workplace, and leisure activities. Many people spend more hours each day travelling in cars than walking on the streets. Undoubtedly, many find a greater sense of security and privacy in travelling in an automobile than they do in exposing themselves by pedestrian or other modes of travel. Were the individual subject to unfettered governmental intrusion every time he entered an automobile, the security guaranteed by the Fourth Amendment would be seriously circumscribed. As *Terry* v. *Ohio*, supra, recognized, people are not shorn of all Fourth Amendment protection when they step from their homes onto the public sidewalks. Nor are they shorn of those interests when they step from the sidewalks into their automobiles. * * *

Accordingly, we hold that except in those situations in which there is at least articulable and reasonable suspicion that a motorist is unlicensed or that an automobile is not registered, or that either the vehicle or an occupant is otherwise subject to seizure for violation of law, stopping an automobile and detaining the driver in order to check his driver's license and the registration of the automobile are unreasonable under the Fourth Amendment. This holding does not preclude the State of Delaware or other States from developing methods for spot checks that involve less intrusion or that do not involve the unconstrained exercise of discretion. Questioning of all oncoming

traffic at roadblock-type stops is one possible alternative. We hold only that persons in automobiles on public roadways may not for that reason alone have their travel and privacy interfered with at the unbridled discretion of police officers. The judgment below is affirmed.

So ordered.

* * *

Mr. Justice REHNQUIST, dissenting.

The Court holds, in successive sentences, that absent an articulable, reasonable suspicion of unlawful conduct, a motorist may not be subjected to a random license check, but that the States are free to develop "methods for spot checks that * * * do not involve the unconstrained exercise of discretion," such as "[q]uestioning * * * all oncoming traffic at roadblock-type stops." * * * Because motorists, apparently like sheep, are much less likely to be "frightened" or "annoyed" when stopped en masse, a highway patrolman needs neither probable cause nor articulable suspicion to stop *all* motorists on a particular thoroughfare, but he cannot without articulable suspicion stop *less* than all motorists. The Court thus elevates the adage "misery loves company" to a novel role in Fourth Amendment jurisprudence. The rule becomes "curiouser and curiouser" as one attempts to follow the Court's explanation for it.

As the Court correctly points out, people are not shorn of their Fourth Amendment protection when they step from their homes onto the public sidewalks or into their automobiles. But a random license check of a motorist operating a vehicle on highways owned and maintained by the State is quite different from a random stop designed to uncover violations of laws that have nothing to do with motor vehicles. No one questions that the State may require the licensing of those who drive on its highways and the registration of vehicles which are driven on those highways. If it may insist on these requirements, it obviously may take steps necessary to enforce compliance. The reasonableness of the enforcement measure chosen by the State is tested by weighing its intrusion on the motorists' Fourth Amendment interests against its promotion of the State's legitimate interests. * * *

In executing this balancing process, the Court concludes that given the alternative mechanisms available, discretionary spot checks are not a "sufficiently productive mechanism" to safeguard the State's admittedly "vital interest in ensuring that only those qualified to do so are permitted to operate motor vehicles, that these vehicles are fit for safe operation, and hence that licensing, registration, and vehicle inspection requirements are being observed." * * * Foremost among the alternative methods of enforcing traffic and vehicle safety regulations, according to the Court, is acting upon observed violations, for "drivers without licenses are presumably the less safe drivers whose propensities may well exhibit themselves." * * * Noting that "finding an unlicensed driver among those who commit traffic violations is a much more likely event than finding an unlicensed driver by choosing randomly from the entire universe of drivers," * * * the Court concludes that the contribution to highway safety made by random stops would be marginal at best. The State's primary

interest, however, is in traffic safety, not in apprehending unlicensed motorists for the sake of apprehending unlicensed motorists. The whole point of enforcing motor vehicle safety regulations is to remove from the road the unlicensed driver before he demonstrates why he is unlicensed. The Court would apparently prefer that the State check licenses and vehicle registrations as the wreckage is being towed away.

Nor is the Court impressed with the deterrence rationale, finding it inconceivable that an unlicensed driver who is not deterred by the prospect of being involved in a traffic violation or other incident requiring him to produce a license would be deterred by the possibility of being subjected to a spot check. The Court arrives at its conclusion without the benefit of a shred of empirical data in this record suggesting that a system of random spot checks would fail to deter violators. In the absence of such evidence, the State's determination that random stops would serve a deterrence function should stand.

On the other side of the balance, the Court advances only the most diaphanous of citizen interests. Indeed, the Court does not say that these interests can never be infringed by the State, just that the State must infringe them en masse rather than citizen by citizen. To comply with the Fourth Amendment, the State need only subject *all* citizens to the same "anxiety" and "inconvenien[ce]" to which it now subjects only a few.

* * * Although a system of discretionary stops could conceivably be abused, the record before us contains no showing that such abuse is probable or even likely. Nor is there

evidence in the record that a system of random license checks would fail adequately to further the State's interest in deterring and apprehending violators. Nevertheless, the Court concludes "on the record before us" that the random spot check is not "a sufficiently productive mechanism to justify the intrusion upon Fourth Amendment interests which such stops entail." * * * I think that the Court's approach reverses the presumption of constitutionality accorded acts of the States. The burden is not upon the State to demonstrate that its procedures are consistent with the Fourth Amendment, but upon respondent to demonstrate that they are not. "On this record" respondent has failed to make such a demonstration.

Neither the Court's opinion, nor the opinion of the Supreme Court of Delaware, suggests that the random stop made in this case was either authorized or carried out in a manner inconsistent with the Equal Protection Clause of the Fourteenth Amendment. Absent an equal protection violation, the fact that random stops may entail "a possibly unsettling show of authority," * * * and "may create substantial anxiety," * * * seems an insufficient basis to distinguish for Fourth Amendment purposes between a roadblock stopping all cars and the random stop at issue here. Accordingly, I would reverse the judgment of the Supreme Court of Delaware.

OTHER AUTO "STOP-AND-FRISK" CASES

Case	Ruling	Vote
United States v. Robinson, 414 U.S. 218, 94 S.Ct. 467 (1973); Gustafson v. Florida, 414 U.S. 260, 94 S.Ct. 488 (1973)	Where a police officer has probable cause to stop a vehicle and arrest the driver for driving without a license, a full search of the driver's person may be made incident to taking him into custody.	6–3; Douglas, Brennan, and Marshall dissented
Pennsylvania v. Mimms, 434 U.S. 106, 98 S.Ct. 330 (1977)	Where a police officer stopped an automobile to issue a citation for an expired license plate, he was entitled to ask the driver to step out of the car and produce his driver's license and vehicle registration. Where, as a consequence, he noticed a large bulge under the driver's sports jacket, the officer was entitled to protect himself by frisking the driver.	6–3; Brennan, Marshall, and Stevens dissented

In recent years, considerable attention and concern has focused on the large flow of illegal aliens entering the country. As the U.S. Border Patrol has stepped up its measures to prevent illegal aliens, principally from Mexico, from slipping past border areas, a flurry of cases raising important Fourth Amendment issues have reached the Court. A sketch of the Supreme Court decisions in those cases is set out below:

Case	Ruling	Vote
Almeida-Sanchez v. United States, 413 U.S. 266, 93 S.Ct. 2535 (1973)	Warrantless auto *search* conducted by *roving* Border Patrol agents without probable cause and at best twenty miles from Mexican border unconstitutional	5–4; Burger, White, Blackmun, and Rehnquist dissenting
United States v. Brignoni-Ponce, 422 U.S. 873, 95 S.Ct. 2574 (1975)	Except at the border or its functional equivalent, roving Border Patrol agents may *stop* vehicles only if they are aware of "specific and articulable facts," together with rational inferences from those facts, that reasonably warrant suspicion that vehicles contain illegal aliens; mere Mexican ancestry of occupants of a car does not constitute a "founded suspicion"	Unanimous
United States v. Ortiz, 422 U.S. 891, 95 S.Ct. 2585 (1975)	Vehicle *searches* at traffic checkpoints removed from the border or its functional equivalents, like searches conducted by roving patrols, must be based on probable cause	Unanimous
United States v. Martinez-Fuerte, 428 U.S. 543, 96 S.Ct. 3074 (1976)	A vehicle may be *stopped* at a fixed checkpoint for *brief questioning* of its occupants even though there is no reason to believe the particular car contains illegal aliens; further, motorists can be referred selectively to secondary inspection area "even if it be assumed that such referrals are made largely on the basis of apparent Mexican ancestry"; operation of a fixed checkpoint need not be authorized in advance by a judicial warrant	7–2; Brennan and Marshall dissenting

c. WIRETAPPING AND EAVESDROPPING

OLMSTEAD v. UNITED STATES

Supreme Court of the United States, 1928
277 U.S. 438, 48 S.Ct. 564, 72 L.Ed. 944

Roy Olmstead and several accomplices were convicted in federal district court of importing and selling liquor in violation of the National Prohibition Act. Incriminating evidence, obtained by federal officers who wiretapped telephone lines at points between defendants' homes and their offices, was presented by the government at the trial. A U. S. Court of Appeals affirmed the convictions over objections that this evidence was inadmissible under the Fourth Amendment guarantee against unreasonable searches and seizures and the Fifth Amendment protection

from being compelled to testify against one's self. The Supreme Court granted certiorari.

Mr. Chief Justice TAFT delivered the opinion of the Court.

* * *

There is no room in the present case for applying the Fifth Amendment, unless the Fourth Amendment was first violated. There was no evidence of compulsion to induce the defendants to talk over their many telephones. They were continually and voluntarily transacting business without knowledge of the interception. Our consideration must be confined to the Fourth Amendment.

* * *

The well-known historical purpose of the Fourth Amendment, directed against general warrants and writs of assistance, was to prevent the use of governmental force to search a man's house, his person, his papers, and his effects, and to prevent their seizure against his will. * * *

* * *

The amendment itself shows that the search is to be of material things—the person, the house, his papers, or his effects. The description of the warrant necessary to make the proceeding lawful is that it must specify the place to be searched and the person or *things* to be seized.

* * *

* * * The amendment does not forbid what was done here. There was no searching. There was no seizure. The evidence was secured by the use of the sense of hearing and that only. There was no

entry of the houses or offices of the defendants.

* * *

The language of the amendment cannot be extended and expanded to include telephone wires, reaching to the whole world from the defendant's house or office. The intervening wires are not part of his house or office, any more than are the highways along which they are stretched.

* * *

Congress may, of course, protect the secrecy of telephone messages by making them, when intercepted, inadmissible in evidence in federal criminal trials, by direct legislation, and thus depart from the common law of evidence. But the courts may not adopt such a policy by attributing an enlarged and unusual meaning to the Fourth Amendment. The reasonable view is that one who installs in his house a telephone instrument with connecting wires intends to project his voice to those quite outside, and that the wires beyond his house, and messages while passing over them, are not within the protection of the Fourth Amendment. Here those who intercepted the projected voices were not in the house of either party to the conversation.

* * *

We think, therefore, that the wire tapping here disclosed did not amount to a search or seizure within the meaning of the Fourth Amendment.

What has been said disposes of the only question that comes within the terms of our order granting certi-orari in these cases. But some of our number, departing from that order, have concluded that there is merit in the twofold objection, overruled in both courts below, that evidence obtained through intercepting of telephone messages by government agents was inadmissible, because the mode of obtaining it was unethical and a misdemeanor under the law of Washington.   *   *   *

*   *   *

The common-law rule is that the admissibility of evidence is not affected by the illegality of the means by which it was obtained.   *   *   *

*   *   *

[W]ithout the sanction of congressional enactment [we cannot] subscribe to the suggestion that the courts have a discretion to exclude evidence, the admission of which is not unconstitutional, because unethically secured. This would be at variance with the common-law doctrine generally supported by authority. There is no case that sustains, nor any recognized text-book that gives color to, such a view. Our general experience shows that much evidence has always been receivable, although not obtained by conformity to the highest ethics. The history of criminal trials shows numerous cases of prosecutions of oathbound conspiracies for murder, robbery, and other crimes, where officers of the law have disguised themselves and joined the organizations, taken the oaths, and given themselves every appearance of active members engaged in the promotion of crime for the purpose of securing evidence. Evidence secured by such means has always been received.

*   *   *

The judgments of the Circuit Court of Appeals are affirmed.
*   *   *

Mr. Justice BRANDEIS (dissenting).

*   *   *

The government makes no attempt to defend the methods employed by its officers. Indeed, it concedes that, if wire tapping can be deemed a search and seizure within the Fourth Amendment, such wire tapping as was practiced in the case at bar was an unreasonable search and seizure, and that the evidence thus obtained was inadmissible. But it relies on the language of the amendment, and it claims that the protection given thereby cannot properly be held to include a telephone conversation.

*   *   *

When the Fourth and Fifth Amendments were adopted, "the form that evil had theretofore taken" had been necessarily simple. Force and violence were then the only means known to man by which a government could directly effect self-incrimination. It could compel the individual to testify—a compulsion effected, if need be, by torture. It could secure possession of his papers and other articles incident to his private life—a seizure effected, if need be, by breaking and entry. Protection against such invasion of "the sanctities of a man's home and the privacies of life" was provided in the Fourth and Fifth Amendments by specific language. Boyd v. United States, 116 U.S. 616, 630, 6 S.Ct. 521. But "time works changes, brings into existence new conditions and purposes." Subtler and more far-reaching means of invading privacy have become available to the government. Discovery and invention have made it possible for the government, by means far more effective than stretching upon the rack, to obtain disclosure in court of what is whispered in the closet.

Moreover, "in the application of a Constitution, our contemplation cannot be only of what has been, but of what may be." The progress of science in furnishing the government with means of espionage is not likely to stop with wire tapping. Ways may some day be developed by which the government, without removing papers from secret drawers, can reproduce them in court, and by which it will be enabled to expose to a jury the most intimate occurrences of the home. Advances in the psychic and related sciences may bring means of exploring unexpressed beliefs, thoughts and emotions. * * * Can it be that the Constitution affords no protection against such invasions of individual security?

* * *

Time and again this court, in giving effect to the principle underlying the Fourth Amendment, has refused to place an unduly literal construction upon it. * * *

* * *

The protection guaranteed by the amendments is much broader in scope. The makers of our Constitution undertook to secure conditions favorable to the pursuit of happiness. They recognized the significance of man's spiritual nature, of his feelings and of his intellect. They knew that only a part of the pain, pleasure and satisfactions of life are to be found in material

things. They sought to protect Americans in their beliefs, their thoughts, their emotions and their sensations. They conferred, as against the government, the right to be let alone—the most comprehensive of rights and the right most valued by civilized men. To protect that right, every unjustifiable intrusion by the government upon the privacy of the individual, whatever the means employed, must be deemed a violation of the Fourth Amendment. And the use, as evidence in a criminal proceeding, of facts ascertained by such intrusion must be deemed a violation of the Fifth.

Applying to the Fourth and Fifth Amendments the established rule of construction, the defendants' objections to the evidence obtained by wire tapping must, in my opinion, be sustained. It is, of course, immaterial where the physical connection with the telephone wires leading into the defendants' premises was made. And it is also immaterial that the intrusion was in aid of law enforcement. Experience should teach us to be most on our guard to protect liberty when the government's purposes are beneficent. Men born to freedom are naturally alert to repel invasion of their liberty by evil-minded rulers. The greatest dangers to liberty lurk in insidious encroachment by men of zeal, well-meaning but without understanding.

* * *

* * * Here the evidence obtained by crime was obtained at the government's expense, by its officers, while acting on its behalf; the officers who committed these crimes are the same officers who were charged with the enforcement of the Prohibition Act; the crimes of these officers were committed for the pur-

pose of securing evidence with which to obtain an indictment and to secure a conviction. The evidence so obtained constitutes the warp and woof of the government's case. * * * There is literally no other evidence of guilt on the part of some of the defendants except that illegally obtained by these officers. As to nearly all the defendants * * * the evidence relied upon to secure a conviction consisted mainly of that which these officers had so obtained. by violating the state law.

* * *

When these unlawful acts were committed they were crimes only of the officers individually. The government was innocent, in legal contemplation; for no federal official is authorized to commit a crime on its behalf. When the government, having full knowledge, sought, through the Department of Justice, to avail itself of the fruits of these acts in order to accomplish its own ends, it assumed moral responsibility for the officers' crimes. * * * [A]nd if this court should permit the government, by means of its officers' crimes, to effect its purpose of punishing the defendants, there would seem to be present all the elements of a ratification. If so, the government itself would become a lawbreaker.

Will this court, by sustaining the judgment below, sanction such conduct on the part of the executive? The governing principle has long been settled. It is that a court will not redress a wrong when he who invokes its aid has unclean hands. * * * Its common application is in civil actions between private parties. Where the government is the actor, the reasons for applying it are even more persuasive. 'Where the reme-

dies invoked are those of the criminal law, the reasons are compelling.

The door of a court is not barred because the plaintiff has committed a crime. The confirmed criminal is as much entitled to redress as his most virtuous fellow citizen; no record of crime, however long, makes one an outlaw. The court's aid is denied only when he who seeks it has violated the law in connection with the very transaction as to which he seeks legal redress. Then aid is denied despite the defendant's wrong. It is denied in order to maintain respect for law; in order to promote confidence in the administration of justice; in order to preserve the judicial process from contamination. * * *

Decency, security, and liberty alike demand that government officials shall be subjected to the same rules of conduct that are commands to the citizen. In a government of laws, existence of the government will be imperiled if it fails to observe the law scrupulously. Our government is the potent, the omnipresent teacher. For good or for ill, it teaches the whole people by its example. Crime is contagious. If the government becomes a lawbreaker, it breeds contempt for law; it invites every man to become a law unto himself; it invites anarchy. To declare that in the administration of the criminal law the end justifies the means—to declare that the government may commit crimes in order to secure the conviction of a private criminal—would bring terrible retribution. Against that pernicious doctrine this court should resolutely set its face.

[Justices HOLMES and STONE also dissented agreeing with Justice BRANDEIS.]

Mr. Justice BUTLER (dissenting). I sincerely regret that I cannot support the opinion and judgments of the court in these cases.

* * *

Telephones are used generally for transmission of messages concerning official, social, business and personal affairs including communications that are private and privileged—those between physician and patient, lawyer and client, parent and child, husband and wife. The contracts between telephone companies and users contemplate the private use of the facilities employed in the service. The communications belong to the parties between whom they pass. During their transmission the exclusive use of the wire belongs to the persons served by it. Wire tapping involves interference with the wire while being used. Tapping the wires and listening in by the officers literally constituted a search for evidence. As the communications passed, they were heard and taken down.

* * *

When the facts in these cases are truly estimated, a fair application of that principle decides the constitutional question in favor of the petitioners. * * *

BERGER v. NEW YORK

Supreme Court of the United States, 1967
388 U.S. 41, 87 S.Ct. 1873, 18 L.Ed.2d 1040

New York judges were authorized by provision of a state statute to permit wiretaps and buggings "upon oath or affirmation * * * that there is reasonable ground to believe that evidence of crime" may be obtained by such means. Officers applying for warrants were also required to "particularly [describe] the person or persons whose communications, conversations, or discussions are to be overheard or recorded and the purpose" of the eavesdrop. Ralph Berger was convicted of conspiring to bribe the chairman of the state's liquor authority on evidence obtained by a recording device installed for sixty days under a court order. Berger contended that the statute was unconstitutional because, among other things, it failed to require a particular description of the conversations to be seized and a showing of probable cause. Two state courts affirmed the conviction before the U. S. Supreme Court granted certiorari.

Mr. Justice CLARK delivered the opinion of the Court.

[The Court began by observing that the holding in *Olmstead* had been largely washed out by legislation and judicial rulings since then and that interception of conversations by use of electronic devices also had been brought within the scope of Fourth and Fourteenth Amendment protections.]

* * *

While New York's statute satisfies the Fourth Amendment's requirement that a neutral and detached authority be interposed between the police and the public, * * * the broad sweep of the statute is immediately observable. * * *

* * *

The Fourth Amendment commands that a warrant issue not only upon probable cause supported by oath or affirmation, but also "particularly describing the place to be searched, and the persons or things to be seized." New York's statute lacks this particularization. It merely says that a warrant may issue on reasonable ground to believe that evidence of crime may be obtained by the eavesdrop. It lays down no requirement for particularity in the warrant as to what specific crime has been or is being committed, nor "the place to be searched," or "the persons or things to be seized" as specifically required by the Fourth Amendment. The need for particularity and evidence of reliability in the showing required when judicial authorization of a search is sought is especially great in the case of eavesdropping. By its very nature eavesdropping involves an intrusion on privacy that is broad in scope. * * * Moreover, the statute permits, and there were authorized here, extensions of the original two-month period—presumably for two months each—on a mere showing that such extension is "in the public interest." Apparently the original grounds on which the eavesdrop order was initially issued also form the basis of the renewal. This we believe insufficient without a showing of present probable cause for the continuance of the eavesdrop. [Also] the statute places no termination date on the eavesdrop once the conversation sought is seized. This is left entirely in the discretion of the officer. Finally, the statute's procedure, necessarily because its success depends on secrecy, has no requirement for notice as do conventional warrants, nor does it overcome this defect by requiring some showing of special facts. On the contrary, it permits uncontested entry without any showing of exigent circumstances. Such

a showing of exigency, in order to avoid notice would appear more important in eavesdropping, with its inherent dangers, than that required when conventional procedures of search and seizure are utilized. Nor does the statute provide for a return on the warrant thereby leaving full discretion in the officer as to the use of seized conversations of innocent as well as guilty parties. In short, the statute's blanket grant of permission to eavesdrop is without adequate judicial supervision or protective procedures.

* * *

* * * Some may claim that without the use of such devices crime detection in certain areas may suffer some delays since eavesdropping is quicker, easier, and more certain. However, techniques and practices may well be developed that will operate just as speedily and certainly and—what is more important—without attending illegality.

It is said that neither a warrant nor a statute authorizing eavesdropping can be drawn so as to meet the Fourth Amendment's requirements. If that be true then the "fruits" of eavesdropping devices are barred under the Amendment. On the other hand this Court has in the past, under specific conditions and circumstances, sustained the use of eavesdropping devices * * * where the "commission of a specific offense" was charged, its use was "under the most precise and discriminate circumstances" and the effective administration of justice in a federal court was at stake. The States are under no greater restrictions. The Fourth Amendment does not make the "precincts of the home or the office * * * sanctuaries where the law can never reach," * * * but it does prescribe a constitutional standard that must be met before official invasion is permissible. Our concern with the statute here is whether its language permits a trespassory invasion of the home or office, by general warrant, contrary to the command of the Fourth Amendment. As it is written, we believe that it does.

Reversed.

Mr. Justice DOUGLAS, concurring.

I join the opinion of the Court because at long last it overrules *sub silentio Olmstead* v. *United States* * * * and its offspring and brings wiretapping and other electronic eavesdropping fully within the purview of the Fourth Amendment. I also join the opinion because it condemns electronic surveillance, for its similarity to the general warrants out of which our Revolution sprang and allows a discreet surveillance only on a showing of "probable cause." These safeguards are minimal if we are to live under a regime of wiretapping and other electronic surveillance.

Yet there persists my overriding objection to electronic surveillance, viz., that it is a search for "mere evidence" which, as I have maintained on other occasions * * * is a violation of the Fourth and Fifth Amendments no matter with what nicety and precision a warrant may be drawn. * * *

A discreet selective wiretap or electronic "bugging" is of course not rummaging around, collecting everything in the particular time and space zone. But even though it is limited in time, it is the greatest of all invasions of privacy. It places a government agent in the bedroom, in the business conference, in the social

hour, in the lawyer's office—everywhere and anywhere a "bug" can be placed.

If a statute were to authorize placing a policeman in every home or office where it was shown that there was probable cause to believe that evidence of crime would be obtained, there is little doubt that it would be struck down as a bald invasion of privacy, far worse than the general warrants prohibited by the Fourth Amendment. I can see no difference between such a statute and one authorizing electronic surveillance, which, in effect, places an invisible policeman in the home. If anything, the latter is more offensive because the homeowner is completely unaware of the invasion of privacy.

*   *   *

[Justice STEWART concurred in the result but rejected the majority's conclusion that the statute was *per se* unconstitutional. While he agreed with the dissenters that it was compatible with the Fourth Amendment on its face, he found that there were no "reasonable grounds" for authorizing the bugging in this particular instance.]

Mr. Justice BLACK, dissenting.

*   *   *

While the electronic eavesdropping here bears some analogy to the problems with which the Fourth Amendment is concerned, I am by no means satisfied that the Amendment controls the constitutionality of such eavesdropping. As pointed out, the Amendment only bans searches and seizures of "persons, houses, papers, and effects." This literal language imports tangible things, and it would require an expansion of the language used by the framers, in the interest of "privacy" or some equally vague judge-made goal, to hold that it applies to the spoken word. It simply requires an imaginative transformation of the English language to say that conversations can be searched and words seized. * * *

[Justice BLACK then went on to discuss what he saw as the correctness and the continuing viability of the Court's ruling in *Olmstead*.]

* * *

As I see it, the differences between the Court and me in this case rest on different basic beliefs as to our duty in interpreting the Constitution. This basic charter of our Government was written in few words to define governmental powers generally on the one hand and to define governmental limitations on the other. I believe it is the Court's duty to interpret these grants and limitations so as to carry out as nearly as possible the original intent of the Framers. But I do not believe that it is our duty to go further than the Framers did on the theory that the judges are charged with responsibility for keeping the Constitution "up to date." Of course, where the Constitution has stated a broad purpose to be accomplished under any circumstances, we must consider that modern science has made it necessary to use new means in accomplishing the Framers' goal. * * * There are * * * some constitutional commands that leave no room for doubt—certain procedures must be followed by courts regardless of how much more difficult they make it to convict and punish for crime. These commands we should enforce firmly and to the letter. But my objection to what the Court does today is the

picking out of a broad general provision against unreasonable searches and seizures and the erecting out of it a constitutional obstacle against electronic eavesdropping that makes it impossible for lawmakers to overcome. Honest men may rightly differ on the potential dangers or benefits inherent in electronic eavesdropping and wiretapping. * * * But that is the very reason that legislatures, like New York's should be left free to pass laws about the subject. * * *

Mr. Justice HARLAN, dissenting.

The Court in recent years has more and more taken to itself sole responsibility for setting the pattern of criminal law enforcement throughout the country. Time-honored distinctions between the constitutional protections afforded against federal authority by the Bill of Rights and those provided against state action by the Fourteenth Amendment have been obliterated, thus increasingly subjecting state criminal law enforcement policies to oversight by this Court. * * * Newly contrived constitutional rights have been established without any apparent concern for the empirical process that goes with legislative reform. * * *

Today's decision is in this mold. Despite the fact that the use of electronic eavesdropping devices as instruments of criminal law enforcement is currently being comprehensively addressed by the Congress and various other bodies in the country, the Court has chosen, quite unnecessarily, to decide this case in a manner which will seriously restrict, if not entirely thwart, such efforts, and will freeze further progress in this field, except as the Court may it-

self act or a constitutional amendment may set things right.

*   *   *

[Justice WHITE also dissented.]

KATZ v. UNITED STATES

Supreme Court of the United States, 1967
389 U.S. 347, 88 S.Ct. 507, 19 L.Ed.2d 576

Charles Katz was convicted in United States District Court for telephoning information on bets and wagers from a telephone booth in Los Angeles to Boston and
Miami in violation of a federal statute. A recording of his phone conversations
made by FBI agents using an electronic listening device attached to the outside of
the booth was presented as evidence by the government at the trial. A U. S. Court
of Appeals affirmed the conviction over Katz's contention that the evidence was
obtained at the expense of his Fourth Amendment right to be secure against
unreasonable searches and seizures, and he appealed to the Supreme Court.

Mr. Justice STEWART delivered
the opinion of the Court.

*   *   * We granted certiorari in
order to consider the constitutional
questions thus presented.

The petitioner has phrased those
questions as follows:

"A. Whether a public telephone
booth is a constitutionally protected
area so that evidence obtained by attaching an electronic listening recording device to the top of such a
booth is obtained in violation of the
right to privacy of the user of the
booth.

"B. Whether physical penetra-
tion of a constitutionally protected
area is necessary before a search and
seizure can be said to be violative of
the Fourth Amendment to the United
States Constitution."

We decline to adopt this formulation of the issues. In the first place
the correct solution of Fourth
Amendment problems is not necessarily promoted by incantation of the
phrase "constitutionally protected
area." Secondly, the Fourth Amendment cannot be translated into a general constitutional "right to privacy."
That Amendment protects individual

privacy against certain kinds of governmental intrusion, but its protections go further, and often have
nothing to do with privacy at all.
Other provisions of the Constitution
protect personal privacy from other
forms of governmental invasion.
But the protection of a person's *general* right to privacy—his right to be
let alone by other people—is, like the
protection of his property and of his
very life, left largely to the law of
the individual States.

Because of the misleading way
the issues have been formulated
*   *   * attention [has been deflect-
ed] from the problem presented by
this case. For the Fourth Amendment protects people, not places.
What a person knowingly exposes to
the public, even in his own home or
office, is not a subject of Fourth
Amendment protection. *   *   *
But what he seeks to preserve as private, even in an area accessible to
the public, may be constitutionally
protected. *   *   *

The Government stresses the fact
that the telephone booth from which
the petitioner made his calls was constructed partly of glass, so that he
was as visible after he entered it as

he would have been if he had remained outside. But what he sought
to exclude when he entered the booth
was not the intruding eye—it was
the uninvited ear. He did not shed
his right to do so simply because he
made his calls from a place where he
might be seen. No less than an individual in a business office, in a
friend's apartment, or in a taxicab, a
person in a telephone booth may rely
upon the protection of the Fourth
Amendment. * * *

* * *

We conclude that the underpinnings of *Olmstead* and *Goldman* [v.
United States, 316 U.S. 129, 62 S.Ct.
993] have been so eroded by our subsequent decisions that the "trespass"
doctrine there enunciated can no
longer be regarded as controlling.
The Government's activities in elec-
tronically listening to and recording
the petitioner's words violated the
privacy upon which he justifiably relied while using the telephone booth
and thus constituted a "search and
seizure" within the meaning of the
Fourth Amendment. The fact that
the electronic device employed to
achieve that end did not happen to
penetrate the wall of the booth can
have no constitutional significance.

The question remaining for decision, then, is whether the search and
seizure conducted in this case complied with constitutional standards.
In that regard, the Government's position is that its agents acted in an
entirely defensible manner: They did
not begin their electronic surveillance until investigation of the petitioner's activities had established a
strong probability that he was using
the telephone in question to transmit
gambling information to persons in
other States, in violation of federal

law. Moreover, the surveillance was
limited, both in scope and in duration, to the specific purpose of
establishing the contents of the petitioner's unlawful telephonic communications. The agents confined their
surveillance to the brief periods during which he used the telephone
booth, and they took great care to
overhear only the conversations of
the petitioner himself.

* * *

The Government urges that, because its agents relied upon the decisions in *Olmstead* and *Goldman*,
and because they did no more here
than they might properly have done
with prior judicial sanction, we
should retroactively validate their
conduct. That we cannot do. It is
apparent that the agents in this case
acted with restraint. Yet the inescapable fact is that this restraint was
imposed by the agents themselves,
not by a judicial officer. They were
not required, before commencing the
search, to present their estimate of
probable cause for detached scrutiny
by a neutral magistrate. They were
not compelled, during the conduct of
the search itself, to observe precise
limits established in advance by a
specific court order. Nor were they
directed, after the search had been
completed, to notify the authorizing
magistrate in detail of all that had
been seized. In the absence of such
safeguards, this Court has never sustained a search upon the sole ground
that officers reasonably expected to
find evidence of a particular crime
and voluntarily confined their activities to the least intrusive means consistent with that end. * * *

* * *

Judgment reversed.

Mr. Justice MARSHALL took no part in the consideration or decision of this case.

Mr. Justice HARLAN, concurring.

I join the opinion of the Court, which I read to hold only (a) that an enclosed telephone booth is an area where, like a home, Weeks v. United States, 232 U.S. 383, 34 S.Ct. 341, and unlike a field, Hester v. United States, 265 U.S. 57, 44 S.Ct. 445, a person has a constitutionally protected reasonable expectation of privacy; (b) that electronic as well as physical intrusion into a place that is in this sense private may constitute a violation of the Fourth Amendment; and (c) that the invasion of a constitutionally protected area by federal authorities is, as the Court has long held, presumptively unreasonable in the absence of a search warrant.

As the Court's opinion states, "the Fourth Amendment protects people, not places." The question, however, is what protection it affords to those people. Generally, as here, the answer to that question requires reference to a "place." My understanding of the rule that has emerged from prior decisions is that there is a twofold requirement, first that a person have exhibited an actual (subjective) expectation of privacy and, second, that the expectation be one that society is prepared to recognize as "reasonable." Thus a man's home is, for most purposes, a place

where he expects privacy, but objects, activities, or statements that he exposes to the "plain view" of outsiders are not "protected" because no intention to keep them to himself has been exhibited. On the other hand, conversations in the open would not be protected against being overheard, for the expectation of privacy under the circumstances would be unreasonable. * * *

* * *

Mr. Justice BLACK, dissenting.

* * *

Since I see no way in which the words of the Fourth Amendment can be construed to apply to eavesdropping, that closes the matter for me. In interpreting the Bill of Rights, I willingly go as far as a liberal construction of the language takes me, but I simply cannot in good conscience give a meaning to words which they have never before been thought to have and which they certainly do not have in common ordinary usage. I will not distort the words of the Amendment in order to "keep the Constitution up to date" or "to bring it into harmony with the times." It was never meant that this Court have such power, which in effect would make us a continuously functioning constitutional convention.

* * *

RECENT DECISIONS ON ELECTRONIC SURVEILLANCE

Case	Ruling	Dissents
Dalia v. United States, 441 U.S. 238, 99 S.Ct. 1682 (1979)	"The Fourth Amendment does not prohibit *per se* a covert entry performed for the purpose of installing otherwise legal electronic bugging equipment" because " 'of-	Justices Brennan, Stewart, Marshall, and Stevens

ELECTRONIC SURVEILLANCE (*Cont.*)

Case	Ruling	Dissents
Dalia (*Cont.*)	ficers need not announce their purpose before conducting an otherwise [duly] authorized search if such an announcement would provoke the escape of the suspect or the destruction of critical evidence' " and because "Title III [of the Omnibus Crime Control and Safe Streets Act of 1968] provide[s] a constitutionally adequate substitute for advance notice by requiring that once the surveillance operation is completed the authorizing judge must cause notice to be served on those subjected to surveillance." Moreover, "the Fourth Amendment does not require that a Title III electronic surveillance order include a specific authorization to enter covertly the premises described in the order" because the mode of executing the warrant traditionally lies within the officers' discretion subject to the reasonableness requirement of the Fourth Amendment; because the particular means of execution cannot always be anticipated; and because precision in describing the mode of executing the order would render the protection afforded by the Warrant Clause unacceptably rigid and extreme.	
Smith v. Maryland, 442 U.S. 735, 99 S.Ct. 2577 (1979)	Installation and use of a pen register (a device which, when hooked up to the appropriate phone lines, records the phone numbers but not the content of outgoing calls) does not constitute a "search" within the meaning of the Fourth and Fourteenth Amendments. Telephone users entertain no subjective expectation of privacy because pen registers and similar devices are routinely employed by the phone company for billing, investigative, and repair purposes, and phone subscribers are given notice of this in their phone book and could otherwise conclude that the phone company regularly obtains information about outgoing calls simply by looking at their phone bills. Nor does the phone subscriber have an objective expectation of privacy in the numbers he calls (as distinguished from the content of those calls) because he has voluntarily exposed this information to a third party, the phone company, and necessarily assumes the risk that the phone company may turn such information over to the police. The phone subscriber waives his privacy interest in the numbers	Justices Brennan, Stewart, and Marshall

ELECTRONIC SURVEILLANCE (*Cont.*)

Case	Ruling	Dissents
Smith (*Cont.*)	he calls which are recorded by a pen register just as surely as he would if he placed the calls through an operator.	

UNITED STATES v. UNITED STATES DISTRICT COURT FOR EASTERN DISTRICT OF MICHIGAN

Supreme Court of the United States, 1972
407 U.S. 297, 92 S.Ct. 2125, 32 L.Ed.2d 752

The United States filed charges against three defendants in federal district court for the destruction of government property. One of the defendants was indicted for the bombing of a Central Intelligence Agency office in Ann Arbor, Michigan. At pretrial proceedings the defense moved to compel disclosure of certain wiretap information which the government had accumulated. The purpose of requesting disclosure was to allow a determination as to whether the electronic surveillance had tainted the evidence upon which the indictment was based or which the government would offer at the trial. The government produced a sealed exhibit containing the wiretap logs and offered them for inspection by the judge *in camera* but refused to permit disclosure to the defense on grounds secrecy was essential to national security. The government also submitted an affidavit by the Attorney General certifying that the wiretapping had been carried out lawfully under his authorization, though without prior judicial approval and pursuant to Title III of the Omnibus Crime Control and Safe Streets Act of 1968. The district court ruled that the surveillance violated the Fourth Amendment and ordered full disclosure, whereupon the government sought a writ of mandamus from the U. S. Sixth Circuit Court of Appeals directing the district court to vacate its order. The appellate court denied the government's petition, and the government appealed.

Mr. Justice POWELL delivered the opinion of the Court.

The issue before us is an important one for the people of our country and their Government. It involves the delicate question of the President's power, acting through the Attorney General, to authorize electronic surveillance in internal security matters without prior judicial approval. Successive Presidents for more than one-quarter of a century have authorized such surveillance in varying degrees, without guidance from the Congress or a definitive decision of this Court. This case brings the issue here for the first time. * * *

Title III of the Omnibus Crime Control and Safe Streets Act, 18 U.S. C.A. §§ 2510–2520, authorizes the use of electronic surveillance for classes of crimes carefully specified in 18 U.S.C.A. § 2516. Such surveillance is subject to prior court order. Section 2518 sets forth the detailed and particularized application necessary to obtain such an order as well as carefully circumscribed conditions for its use. The Act represents a comprehensive attempt by Congress to promote more effective control of crime while protecting the privacy of individual thought and expression. Much of Title III was drawn to meet the constitutional requirements for electronic surveillance enunciated by this Court in Berger v. New York, 388 U.S. 41, 87 S.Ct. 1873 (1967), and Katz v. United States, 389 U.S. 347, 88 S.Ct. 507 (1967).

Together with the elaborate surveillance requirements in Title III, there is the following proviso, 18 U.S.C.A. § 2511(3):

"Nothing contained in this chapter or in section 605 of the Communications Act of 1934 (48 Stat. 1143; 47 U.S.C.A. 605) shall limit the constitutional power of the President to take such measures as he deems necessary to protect the Nation against actual or potential attack or other hostile acts of a foreign power, to obtain foreign intelligence information deemed essential to the security of the United States, or to protect national security information against foreign intelligence activities. *Nor shall anything contained in this chapter be deemed to limit the constitutional power of the President to take such measures as he deems necessary to protect the United States against the overthrow of the Government by force or other unlawful means, or against any other clear and present danger to the structure or existence of the Government.* The contents of any wire or oral communication intercepted by authority of the President in the exercise of the foregoing powers may be received in evidence in any trial hearing, or other proceeding only where such interception was reasonable, and shall not be otherwise used or disclosed except as is necessary to implement that power." (Emphasis supplied.)

The Government relies on § 2511(3). It argues that "in excepting national security surveillances from the Act's warrant requirement Congress recognized the President's authority to conduct such surveillances without prior judicial approval." * * * The section thus is viewed as a recognition or affirmance of a constitutional authority in the President to conduct warrantless domestic security surveillance such as that involved in this case.

We think the language of § 2511 (3), as well as the legislative history of the statute, refutes this interpretation. * * *

* * *

Though the Government and respondents debate their seriousness and magnitude, threats and acts of sabotage against the Government exist in sufficient number to justify investigative powers with respect to them. The covertness and complexity of potential unlawful conduct against the Government and the necessary dependency of many conspirators upon the telephone make electronic surveillance an effective investigatory instrument in certain circumstances. The marked acceleration in technological developments and sophistication in their use have resulted in new techniques for the planning, commission and concealment of criminal activities. It would be contrary to the public interest for Government to deny to itself the prudent and lawful employment of those very techniques which are employed against the Government and its law abiding citizens.

But a recognition of these elementary truths does not make the employment by Government of electronic surveillance a welcome development—even when employed with restraint and under judicial supervision. There is, understandably, a deep-seated uneasiness and apprehension that this capability will be used to intrude upon cherished privacy of law-abiding citizens. * * *

National security cases, moreover, often reflect a convergence of First and Fourth Amendment values not present in cases of "ordinary" crime. Though the investigative duty of the executive may be stronger in such cases, so also is there greater jeopardy to constitutionally protected speech. * * * History abundantly documents the tendency of Government—however benevolent and benign its motives—to view with suspicion those who most fervently dispute its policies. Fourth Amendment protections become the more necessary when the targets of official surveillance may be those suspected of unorthodoxy in their political beliefs. The danger to political dissent is acute where the Government attempts to act under so vague a concept as the power to protect "domestic security." Given the difficulty of defining the domestic security interest, the danger of abuse in acting to protect that interest becomes apparent. * * * The price of lawful public dissent must not be a dread of subjection to an unchecked surveillance power. Nor must the fear of unauthorized official eavesdropping deter vigorous citizen dissent and discussion of Government action in private conversation. For private dissent, no less than open public discourse, is essential to our free society.

As the Fourth Amendment is not absolute in its terms, our task is to examine and balance the basic values at stake in this case: the duty of Government to protect the domestic security, and the potential danger posed by unreasonable surveillance to individual privacy and free expression. If the legitimate need of Government to safeguard domestic se-

curity requires the use of electronic surveillance, the question is whether the needs of citizens for privacy and free expression may not be better protected by requiring a warrant before such surveillance is undertaken. We must also ask whether a warrant requirement would unduly frustrate the efforts of Government to protect itself from acts of subversion and overthrow directed against it.

These Fourth Amendment freedoms cannot properly be guaranteed if domestic security surveillances may be conducted solely within the discretion of the executive branch. The Fourth Amendment does not contemplate the executive officers of Government as neutral and disinterested magistrates. Their duty and responsibility is to enforce the laws, to investigate and to prosecute. * * *

* * *

* * * We recognize * * * the constitutional basis of the President's domestic security role, but we think it must be exercised in a manner compatible with the Fourth Amendment. In this case we hold that this requires an appropriate prior warrant procedure.

We cannot accept the Government's argument that internal security matters are too subtle and complex for judicial evaluation. Courts regularly deal with the most difficult issues of our society. There is no reason to believe that federal judges will be insensitive to or uncomprehending of the issues involved in domestic security cases. Certainly courts can recognize that domestic security surveillance involves different considerations from the surveillance of ordinary crime. If the threat is too subtle or complex for our senior law enforcement officers to convey its significance to a court, one may question whether there is probable cause for surveillance.

Nor do we believe prior judicial approval will fracture the secrecy essential to official intelligence gathering. The investigation of criminal activity has long involved imparting sensitive information to judicial officers who have respected the confidentialities involved. Judges may be counted upon to be especially conscious of security requirements in national security cases. * * *

* * *

We emphasize [that] our decision * * * involves only the domestic aspects of national security. We have not addressed, and express no opinion as to, the issues which may be involved with respect to activities of foreign powers or their agents. * * *

* * *

Given those potential distinctions between Title III criminal surveillances and those involving the domestic security, Congress may wish to consider protective standards for the latter which differ from those already prescribed for specified crimes in Title III. Different standards may be compatible with the Fourth Amendment if they are reasonable both in relation to the legitimate need of Government for intelligence information and the protected rights of our citizens. For the warrant application may vary according to the governmental interest to be enforced and the nature of citizen rights deserving protection. * * *

[In footnotes to its opinion, the Court added:

Section 2511(3) refers to "the constitutional power of the President" in two types of situations: (i) where necessary to protect against attack, other hostile acts or intelligence activities of a "foreign power"; or (ii) where necessary to protect against the overthrow of the Government or other clear and present danger to the structure or existence of the Government. Although both of the specified situations are sometimes referred to as "national security" threats, the term "national security" is used only in the first sentence of § 2511(3) with respect to the activities of foreign powers. This case involves only the second sentence of § 2511(3), with the threat emanating—according to the Attorney General's affidavit—from "domestic organizations." Although we attempt no precise definition, we use the term "domestic organization" in this opinion to mean a group or organization (whether formally or informally constituted) composed of citizens of the United States and which has no significant connection with a foreign power, its agents or agencies. No doubt there are cases where it will be difficult to distinguish between "domestic" and "foreign" unlawful activities directed against the Government of the United States where there is collaboration in varying degrees between domestic groups or organizations and agents or agencies of foreign powers. But this is not such a case.

For the view that warrantless surveillance, though impermissible in domestic security cases, may be constitutional where foreign powers are involved, see Smith v. United States, 330 F.Supp. 867 (D.C.1971); and American Bar Association Criminal Justice Project, Standards Relating to Electronic Surveillance, Feb. 1971, pp. 11, 120, 121. See also United

States v. Clay, 5 Cir., 430 F.2d 165 (1970).]

Affirmed.

The CHIEF JUSTICE [BURGER] concurs in the result.

Mr. Justice REHNQUIST took no part in the consideration or decision of this case.

Mr. Justice DOUGLAS, concurring.

While I join in the opinion of the Court, I add these words in support of it.

This is an important phase in the campaign of the police and intelligence agencies to obtain exemptions from the Warrant Clause of the Fourth Amendment. For, due to the clandestine nature of electronic eavesdropping, the need is acute for placing on the Government the heavy burden to show that "exigencies of the situation [make its] course imperative." * * *

Here federal agents wish to rummage for months on end through every conversation, no matter how intimate or personal, carried over selected telephone lines simply to seize those few utterances which may add to their sense of the pulse of a domestic underground.

We are told that one national security wiretap lasted for 14 months and monitored over 900 conversations. Senator Edward Kennedy found recently that "warrantless devices accounted for an average of 78 to 209 days of listening per device, as compared with a 13-day per device average for those devices installed under court order." He concluded that the Government's revelations posed "the frightening possibility that the conversations of untold thousands of citizens of this country are being monitored on secret devices which no judge has authorized and which may remain in operation for months and perhaps years at a time." Even the most innocent and random caller who uses or telephones into a tapped line can become a flagged number in the Government's data bank. See Laird v. Tatum, 408 U.S. 1, 92 S.Ct. 2318 (1972).

* * *

Six years later, Congress passed the Foreign Intelligence Surveillance Act, 92 Stat. 1783, in an effort to control electronic surveillance conducted in the United States for purposes of national security. The statute reaffirmed the principle that no bugging or wiretapping without prior judicial approval was to be initiated by federal intelligence or law enforcement agents against an American citizen, a lawfully resident alien, or any of various incorporated and unincorporated domestic orgainizations. The law required that agents seeking a warrant for any electronic surveillance of the above parties first produce evidence of criminal activity. The law also imposed stiff criminal penalties for violations and provided for the recovery of compensatory and punitive damages and legal and investigative fees by an aggrieved party. As distinguished from its stringent regulation of surveillance of "U.S. persons" believed to be engaged in intelligence operations on behalf of a foreign power, the legislation provided more relaxed oversight of bugging and wiretapping activities by federal agents directed at a "foreign power" or an "agent of a foreign power." In such instances, although a warrant was required—except in a specially recognized but secret category of NSA (National Security Agency) probes—court authorization did not hinge upon the government's showing of criminal activity but only upon a demonstration that there was "probable cause" to believe that the target of surveillance was a "foreign power" or the "agent of a foreign power." The statute also did not allow foreign powers or their agents to recover damages or fees for any violation of the act. Other provisions of the law: (1) provided for special courts to authorize warrants and hear government appeals from their denial in matters of such national-security-related electronic surveillance; (2) specified procedures governing the issuance, execution, and extension of such warrants; (3) minimized, closely regulated the disclosure of, and potentially mandated the suppression of intercepted communications involving innocent American individuals; and (4) required regular reports to Congress from the Attorney General concerning all electronic surveillance conducted pursuant to the statute. Although the act purposely eschewed any mention or recognition of any inherent constitutional power of the President to conduct warrantless electronic surveillance in the name of national security, it did—in addition to the NSA exception noted earlier—empower the President to authorize electronic surveillance without a court order for up to fifteen days following a declaration of war by Congress.

HOFFA v. UNITED STATES

Supreme Court of the United States, 1966
385 U.S. 293, 87 S.Ct. 408, 17 L.Ed.2d 374

James Hoffa was tried for violations of the Taft-Hartley Act in federal district court in Nashville late in 1962. That proceeding, known as the *Test Fleet* case, ended in a hung jury. Hoffa and others were indicted and convicted two years later of attempting to bribe jurors in that trial. Their convictions were upheld by a U. S. Circuit Court of Appeals. A significant factor in the conviction of the four defendants was the testimony of one Edward Partin who told of several incriminating statements which defendants had made in his presence during the *Test Fleet* trial. Hoffa and the other defendants challenged the admissibility of Partin's testimony because, when they freely admitted him to their conversations, they did not know he was working closely with the government as an informer and was being compensated for his services as such.

Mr. Justice STEWART delivered the opinion of the Court.

* * *

It is contended that only by violating the petitioner's rights under the Fourth Amendment was Partin able to hear the petitioner's incriminating statements in the hotel suite, and that Partin's testimony was therefore inadmissible under the exclusionary rule of Weeks v. United States, 232 U.S. 383, 34 S.Ct. 341. The argument is that Partin's failure to disclose his role as a government informer vitiated the consent that the petitioner gave to Partin's re-

peated entries into the suite, and that by listening to the petitioner's statements Partin conducted an illegal "search" for verbal evidence.

The preliminary steps of this argument are on solid ground. A hotel room can clearly be the object of Fourth Amendment protection as much as a home or an office. * * * The Fourth Amendment can certainly be violated by guileful as well as by forcible intrusions into a constitutionally protected area. * * * And the protections of the Fourth Amendment are surely not limited to tangibles, but can extend as well to oral statements.

Silverman v. United States, 365 U.S. 505, 81 S.Ct. 679.

Where the arguments falls is in its misapprehension of the fundamental nature and scope of Fourth Amendment protection. What the Fourth Amendment protects is the security a man relies upon when he places himself or his property within a constitutionally protected area, be it his home or his office, his hotel room or his automobile. There he is protected from unwarranted governmental intrusion. And when he puts something in his filing cabinet, in his desk drawer, or in his pocket, he has the right to know it will be secure from an unreasonable search or an unreasonable seizure. * * *

In the present case, however, it is evident that no interest legitimately protected by the Fourth Amendment is involved. It is obvious that the petitioner was not relying on the security of his hotel suite when he made the incriminating statements to Partin or in Partin's presence. Partin did not enter the suite by force or by stealth. He was not a surreptitious eavesdropper. Partin was in the suite by invitation, and every conversation which he heard was either directed to him or knowingly carried on in his presence. The petitioner, in a word, was not relying on the security of the hotel room; he was relying upon his misplaced confidence that Partin would not reveal his wrongdoing. As counsel for the petitioner himself points out, some of the communications with Partin did not take place in the suite at all, but in the "hall of the hotel," in the "Andrew Jackson Hotel lobby," and "at the courthouse."

Neither this Court nor any member of it has ever expressed the view that the Fourth Amendment protects a wrongdoer's misplaced belief that a person to whom he voluntarily confides his wrongdoing will not reveal it. Indeed, the Court unanimously rejected that very contention less than four years ago in Lopez v. United States, 373 U.S. 427, 83 S.Ct. 1381. In that case the petitioner had been convicted of attempted bribery of an internal revenue agent named Davis. The Court was divided with regard to the admissibility in evidence of a surreptitious electronic recording [made by instruments concealed in Davis' pocket] of an incriminating conversation Lopez had had in his private office with Davis. But there was no dissent from the view that testimony about the conversation by Davis himself was clearly admissible.

As the Court put it, "Davis was not guilty of an unlawful invasion of petitioner's office simply because his apparent willingness to accept a bribe was not real. * * * He was in the office with petitioner's consent, and while there he did not violate the privacy of the office by seizing something surreptitiously without petitioner's knowledge. * * * The only evidence obtained consisted of statements made by Lopez to Davis, statements which Lopez knew full well could be used against him by Davis if he wished." * * * 373 U.S. at 438, 83 S.Ct. at 1387. In the words of the dissenting opinion in *Lopez*, "The risk of being overheard by an eavesdropper or betrayed by an informer or deceived as to the identity of one with whom one deals is probably inherent in the conditions of human society. It is the kind of risk we necessarily assume whenever we speak." * * *

Adhering to these views, we hold that no right protected by the Fourth

Amendment was violated in the present case.

The petitioner argues that his right under the Fifth Amendment not to "be compelled in any criminal case to be a witness against himself" was violated by the admission of Partin's testimony. The claim is without merit.

There have been sharply differing views within the Court as to the ultimate reach of the Fifth Amendment right against compulsory self-incrimination. * * * [A]ll have agreed that a necessary element of compulsory self-incrimination is some kind of compulsion. * * *

In the present case no claim has been or could be made that the petitioner's incriminating statements were the product of any sort of coercion, legal or factual. The petitioner's conversations with Partin and in Partin's presence were wholly voluntary. For that reason, if for no other, it is clear that no right protected by the Fifth Amendment privilege against compulsory self-incrimination was violated in this case.

The petitioner makes two separate claims under the Sixth Amendment, and we give them separate consideration.

During the course of the *Test Fleet* trial the petitioner's lawyers used his suite as a place to confer with him and with each other, to interview witnesses, and to plan the following day's trial strategy. Therefore, argues the petitioner, Partin's presence in and around the suite violated the petitioner's Sixth Amendment right to counsel, because an essential ingredient thereof is the right of a defendant and his counsel to prepare for trial without intrusion upon their confidential relationship by an agent of the govern-

ment, the defendant's trial adversary. Since Partin's presence in the suite thus violated the Sixth Amendment, the argument continues, any evidence acquired by reason of his presence there was constitutionally tainted and therefore inadmissible against the petitioner in this case. We reject this argument.

* * *

The petitioner's second argument under the Sixth Amendment needs no extended discussion. That argument goes as follows: Not later than October 25, 1962, the Government had sufficient ground for taking the petitioner into custody and charging him with endeavors to tamper with the *Test Fleet* jury. Had the Government done so, it could not have continued to question the petitioner without observance of his Sixth Amendment right to counsel. Massiah v. United States, 377 U.S. 201, 84 S.Ct. 1199; Escobedo v. State of Illinois, 378 U.S. 478, 84 S.Ct. 1758. Therefore, the argument concludes, evidence of statements made by the petitioner subsequent to October 25 was inadmissible, because the Government acquired that evidence only by flouting the petitioner's Sixth Amendment right to counsel.

Nothing in *Massiah*, in *Escobedo*, or in any other case that has come to our attention, even remotely suggests this novel and paradoxical constitutional doctrine, and we decline to adopt it now. There is no constitutional right to be arrested. The police are not required to guess at their peril the precise moment at which they have probable cause to arrest a suspect, risking a violation of the Fourth Amendment if they act too soon, and a violation of the Sixth Amendment if they wait too long. Law enforcement officers are under no constitutional duty to call a halt to a criminal investigation the moment they have the minimum evidence to establish probable cause, a quantum of evidence which may fall far short of the amount necessary to support a criminal conviction.

Finally, the petitioner claims that * * * [t]he "totality" of the Government's conduct during the *Test Fleet* trial operated * * * to " 'offend those canons of decency and fairness which express the notions of justice of English-speaking peoples even toward those charged with the most heinous offenses' (Rochin v. [People of] California, 342 U.S. 165, 169 [72 S.Ct. 205, 208])."

The argument boils down to a general attack upon the use of a government informer as "a shabby thing in any case," and to the claim that in the circumstances of this particular case the risk that Partin's testimony might be perjurious was very high. Insofar as the general attack upon the use of informers is based upon historic "notions" of "English-speaking peoples," it is without historical foundation. * * *

This is not to say that a secret government informer is to the slightest degree more free from all relevant constitutional restrictions than is any other government agent. * * * It *is* to say that the use of secret informers is not *per se* unconstitutional.

* * *

Affirmed.

Mr. Justice WHITE and Mr. Justice FORTAS took no part in the consideration or decision of these cases.

Mr. Chief Justice WARREN, dissenting.

I cannot agree either with the opinion of the Court affirming these convictions or with the separate opinions of Mr. Justice CLARK and Mr. Justice DOUGLAS to the effect that the writs of certiorari were improvidently granted.

* * *

* * * Here, Edward Partin, a jailbird languishing in a Louisiana jail under indictments for such state and federal crimes as embezzlement, kidnapping, and manslaughter (and soon to be charged with perjury and assault), contacted federal authorities and told them he was willing to become, and would be useful as, an informer against Hoffa who was then about to be tried in the *Test Fleet* case. A motive for his doing this is immediately apparent—namely, his strong desire to work his way out of jail and out of his various legal entanglements with the State and Federal Governments. And it is interesting to note that, if this was his motive, he has been uniquely successful in satisfying it. In the four years since he first volunteered to be an informer against Hoffa he has not been prosecuted on any of the serious federal charges for which he was at that time jailed, and the state charges have apparently vanished into thin air.

* * *

This type of informer and the uses to which he was put in this case evidence a serious potential for undermining the integrity of the truth-finding process in the federal courts. Given the incentives and background of Partin, no conviction should be allowed to stand when based heavily on his testimony. And that is exactly the quicksand upon which these convictions rest, because without Partin, who was the principle government witness, there would probably have been no convictions here. Thus, although petitioners make their main arguments on constitutional grounds and raise serious Fourth and Sixth Amendment questions, it should not even be necessary for the Court to reach those questions. For the affront to the quality and fairness of federal law enforcement which this case presents is sufficient to require an exercise of our supervisory powers.   *   *   *

I do not say that the Government may never use as a witness a person of dubious or even bad character. In performing its duty to prosecute crime the Government must take the witnesses as it finds them. They may be persons of good, bad, or doubtful credibility, but their testimony may be the only way to establish the facts, leaving it to the jury to determine their credibility. In this case, however, we have a totally different situation. Here the Government reaches into the jailhouse to employ a man who was himself facing indictments far more serious, (and later including one for perjury) than the one confronting the man

against whom he offered to inform. It employed him not for the purpose of testifying to something that had already happened, but rather for the purpose of infiltration to see if crimes would in the future be committed. The Government in its zeal even assisted him in gaining a position from which he could be a witness to the confidential relationship of attorney and client engaged in the preparation of a criminal defense. And, for the dubious evidence thus obtained, the Government paid an enormous price. Certainly if a criminal defendant insinuated his informer into the prosecution's camp in this manner he would be guilty of obstructing justice. I cannot agree that what happened in this case is in keeping with the standards of justice in our federal system and I must, therefore, dissent.

Mr. Justice CLARK, joined by Mr. Justice DOUGLAS.

I would dismiss the writs of certiorari as improvidently granted.

*   *   *

Chapter 12

The Right of Privacy

As Justice Stewart's opinion for the Court in *Katz* v. *United States* (p. 1175) indicates, the contours of the constitutional debate about the protection of privacy heretofore were largely defined by litigating the question of whether or not a given place constituted a "constitutionally protected area." As contrasted with such a place-oriented conception of privacy, in which the constitutional right became heavily suffused with property interests, the more modern notion of the right to privacy has come increasingly to focus on privacy as a *personal* right. Writing nearly eight decades before the *Katz* majority, Louis Brandeis, as a legal scholar, suggested in a now famous article entitled, "The Right to Privacy," 4 Harvard Law Review 193 (1890), which he coauthored with Samuel Warren, that the assertion of traditional property interests was only of limited utility in the protection of privacy. What was important was "not the principle of private property but that of an inviolate personality." In sum, the right to privacy meant "the right to be let alone." As the forerunner of the argument Brandeis was to make nearly forty years later in his dissent in the *Olmstead* case (p. 1166), he and Warren showed that if the protection of privacy was to become a reality, legal protections must reach beyond the reified concepts of property rights to develop as human rights against the ever growing threat of technological and psychological intrusions. Brandeis, then, as scholar and judge, was one of the earliest architects of a person-oriented constitutional right of privacy.

But where do the implications of such a conception lead? As Christian Bay has shown in his book, *The Structure of Freedom* (1958), the notion would certainly take us beyond the circumscription of wiretapping and eavesdropping to include protection against psychological hurt and political manipulation. The materials which follow suggest another slant on the person-oriented conception of privacy: Do the rights embodied in a personal right to privacy compel limits on the legislative power of govern-

1189

ment, particularly on the enactment of laws aimed solely at the enforcement of a certain code of morality?

The "right to be let alone" certainly implies freedom from governmental intrusion. The fact that a person is alone when exercising this right further suggests that government—particularly if, as in a constitutional democracy, it is a *limited* government—has no valid interests to protect by intruding. To what degree, do you think, our concept of limited government means that government may use its police power only when human behavior has spill-over effects, i.e., when your actions effect others?

Also, consider what we mean by saying privacy is a personal right. Isn't privacy the negative side of a coin the positive side of which we call volition or consent? Privacy establishes a barrier against intrusion from the outside world; our own volition determines what we will do in that realm of protected behavior. This, then, brings us to a consideration of the question we posed above but in other words: Given the right of privacy as a *personal* right, is it constitutional for government to punish "crimes without victims," i.e., behaviors which, because of a certain notion of morality that the state is enforcing, are called "crimes" but which in objective terms would seem not be because the individuals involved freely consented (e.g., prostitution, homosexual behavior, drug addiction, etc.)? The cases which follow deal with the problem of governmental regulation in the area of sexual behavior. At stake in virtually all of these cases is the constitutionality of some kind of "morals legislation." As you read them, consider to what extent the Court's decisions recognizing a right of privacy in such matters implicitly adopt the following view articulated by John Stuart Mill as the thesis of his classic essay, *On Liberty*:

The object of this Essay is to assert one simple principle, as entitled to govern absolutely the dealings of society with the individual by way of compulsion and control, whether the means used be physical force in the form of legal penalties, or the moral coercion of public opinion. That principle is, that * * * the only purpose for which power can be rightfully exercised over any member of a civilized community, against his will, is to prevent harm to others. His own good, either physical or moral, is not a sufficient warrant.

The first decision outside of the context of search and seizure or libel cases in which the Court spoke to the question of a protected right of privacy was *Griswold* v. *Connecticut* (p. 1192) in 1965. In that case the Court confronted the constitutionality of Connecticut's birth control statute. What contribution, if any, do you think Justice Douglas's opinion makes toward the development of a right of privacy? Does either the majority opinion or the concurring opinion of Justice Goldberg lead you to believe privacy is a personal right? Or do they suggest that the Constitution protects only the marital relationship as opposed to individual privacy in general? In other words, what precisely is the "fundamental right" the Court is bent on protecting in *Griswold*?

As in other instances (see the *Youngstown* case, p. 272) where the opinion of the Court seemed weak and unduly vague because it was a kind of lowest common denominator among the majority, the principal concurring opinion—here, the opinion written by Justice Goldberg—took on added importance. How good an argument do you think Goldberg makes for the right of privacy inhering in the Ninth Amendment? How accurate is Justice Black's argument that all this talk of "fundamental rights" and the use of the Ninth Amendment smacks of substantive due process all over again? Does the Court's position in *Griswold*, particularly insofar as it relies on some categorical right to procreate in privacy, raise other kinds of problems in light of, say, the population crisis? Also, how can advocates of the Goldberg position boldly claim that the Ninth Amendment is a source of power to assert against governmental regulation and, at the same time, agree with Chief Justice Stone's statement in the *Darby* case (p. 488) that the Tenth Amendment "states but a truism"? If the Ninth Amendment means something, why doesn't the Tenth also?

Justice Stewart, dissenting in *Griswold*, faults the majority for its failure to identify which of the six amendments cited is infringed by Connecticut's statute. The gist of his criticism—that the Court has failed to identify a specific and consistent source of the right—is a theme which also marks subsequent rulings on the privacy issue. Thus, in *Eisenstadt* v. *Baird* (p. 1200), the Court veers off into a discussion that advances the protection of privacy by way of validating an equal protection claim. And in its controversial abortion decision, *Roe* v. *Wade* (p. 1204), the Court finds the relevant protection of privacy emanating from the Fourteenth Amendment's Due Process Clause.

Beyond this concern over the orderly exposition of the right, the abortion ruling in *Roe* raises other questions. To begin with, does the Court persuasively demonstrate why abortion involves a claim of privacy—why a controversy involving even part of the pregnancy term ought to be considered in the category of "crimes without victims"? In other words, *can* the Court successfully avoid discussing the question of whether or not the fetus is a person?

Subsequent Court decisions have disposed of several issues related to the right to privacy recognized in *Roe*. In *Planned Parenthood of Central Missouri* v. *Danforth* (p. 1212), which involved the constitutionality of a state attempt comprehensively to regulate the abortion process in the aftermath of *Roe*, the Court most notably struck down the requirement that the abortion prerogative be conditioned upon spousal consent if the woman was married or upon parental consent if she was underage. Succeeding cases have addressed in more detail the constitutionality of state statutes regulating the performance of abortions on unmarried, dependent, female minors (p. 1213). With respect to minors, too, the Court has ruled that the Constitution protects their access to contraceptives and birth control information (p. 1214). The Court also declared, in a series of 1977 rulings (p. 1215), that while a state may not infringe the abortion prerogative during the first trimester, the ruling in *Roe* v. *Wade* does not oblige the states to facilitate elective abortions. Three years later the

Court upheld congressional legislation which severely restricted federal funding of abortions (p. 1217).

In the wake of the apparent modifications grafted on to the holding in *Griswold* by the Court's decisions in *Eisenstadt* and *Roe*, culminating in the legacy of the abortion decisions that the right to privacy is a *personal* right, the New York Court of Appeals in *People* v. *Onofre* (p. 1221) struck down that state's sodomy statute as violative of both the right to privacy and equal protection of the laws. But, as the dissent in that case points up, sharp dispute persists over whether and to what extent *Griswold* was modified. Regardless of any judicial interest in promulgating criminal law reform by employing the right to privacy to abolish "crimes without victims," it is clear from a canvass of state codes that the legislatures themselves are instituting change in that direction (p. 1232).

In his classic discussion of adjudication, *The Nature of the Judicial Process*, published some sixty years ago, Justice Cardozo remarked on the tendency of a principle in law "to expand itself to the limit of its logic." The state court decision in *Onofre* would appear to illustrate this tendency rather well. In *Matter of Quinlan* (p. 1233), however, the personal right of privacy was recognized by the New Jersey Supreme Court so as to allow the suspension of life support apparatus for a comatose and incurably ill individual by action of her guardian. Does the New Jersey court demonstrate to you with sufficient persuasiveness why the right to privacy extends to determine the matter at issue—and the granting of relief through a guardian—in that case?

Finally, in light of the tendency observed by Justice Cardozo, does it seem to you desirable or possible for the Court to aim at a coherent and integrated doctrine surrounding a constitutionally protected personal right to privacy? Or will it remain in its present state, a funny little excursus in the law? As Justice Douglas acknowledged in *Griswold*, privacy interests are implicated in the provisions of half a dozen amendments. Would it materially advance the cause of securing privacy if the Court built a coherent theory of the right, knitting together in one principled approach the various guarantees contained in the penumbras? Or, is the protection of privacy better served, as some have suggested, by dealing with such issues as they arise under the respective amendments, where, they argue, difficult questions posed by conflicting interests are better resolved by recourse to less structured statements of doctrine, that is by principles remote from a general theory of a right to privacy but, more helpfully, closer to the facts of a given case?

GRISWOLD v. CONNECTICUT

Supreme Court of the United States, 1965
381 U.S. 479, 85 S.Ct. 1678, 14 L.Ed.2d 510

A Connecticut statute outlawed the use of birth control devices and also made it a criminal offense for anyone to give information or instruction on their use. Estelle Griswold, executive director of a planned parenthood league, and Dr. Buxton, its medical director, were convicted for dispensing such information to married persons in violation of the law and fined $100. A state appellate court

and the Connecticut Supreme Court of Errors affirmed the convictions, whereupon defendants appealed to the U. S. Supreme Court.

Mr. Justice DOUGLAS delivered the opinion of the Court.

* * *

[W]e are met with a wide range of questions that implicate the Due Process Clause of the Fourteenth Amendment. Overtones of some arguments suggest that Lochner v. State of New York, 198 U.S. 45, 25 S.Ct. 539, should be our guide. But we decline that invitation as we did in West Coast Hotel Co. v. Parrish, 300 U.S. 379, 57 S.Ct. 578. * * * We do not sit as a super-legislature to determine the wisdom, need, and propriety of laws that touch economic problems, business affairs, or social conditions. This law, however, operates directly on an intimate relation of husband and wife and their physician's role in one aspect of that relation.

The association of people is not mentioned in the Constitution nor in the Bill of Rights. The right to educate a child in a school of the parents' choice—whether public or private or parochial—is also not mentioned. Nor is the right to study any particular subject or any foreign language. Yet the First Amendment has been construed to include certain of those rights.

* * *

[Previous] cases suggest that specific guarantees in the Bill of Rights have penumbras, formed by emanations from those guarantees that help give them life and substance. * * * Various guarantees create zones of privacy. The right of association contained in the penumbra of the First Amendment is one, as we

have seen. The Third Amendment in its prohibition against the quartering of soldiers "in any house" in time of peace without the consent of the owner is another facet of that privacy. The Fourth Amendment explicitly affirms the "right of the people to be secure in their persons, houses, papers, and effects, against unreasonable searches and seizures." The Fifth Amendment in its Self-Incrimination Clause enables the citizen to create a zone of privacy which government may not force him to surrender to his detriment. The Ninth Amendment provides: "The enumeration in the Constitution, of certain rights, shall not be construed to deny or disparage others retained by the people."

The Fourth and Fifth Amendments were described in Boyd v. United States, 116 U.S. 616, 630, 6 S.Ct. 524, 532, as protection against all governmental invasions "of the sanctity of a man's home and the privacies of life." We recently referred in Mapp v. Ohio, 367 U.S. 643, 656, 81 S.Ct. 1684, 1692, to the Fourth Amendment as creating a "right to privacy, no less important than any other right carefully and particularly reserved to the people."
* * *

We have had many controversies over these penumbral rights of "privacy and repose." See, e.g., Breard v. City of Alexandria, 341 U.S. 622, 626, 644, 71 S.Ct. 920, 923, 933; Public Utilities Comm. v. Pollak, 343 U.S. 451, 72 S.Ct. 813; * * * Skinner v. State of Oklahoma, 316 U.S. 535, 541, 62 S.Ct. 1110, 1113. These cases bear witness that the right of privacy which presses for recognition here is a legitimate one.

The present case, then, concerns a relationship lying within the zone of privacy created by several fundamental constitutional guarantees. And it concerns a law which, in forbidding the *use* of contraceptives rather than regulating their manufacture or sale, seeks to achieve its goals by means having a maximum destructive impact upon that relationship. Such a law cannot stand in light of the familiar principle, so often applied by this Court, that a "governmental purpose to control or prevent activities constitutionally subject to state regulation may not be achieved by means which sweep unnecessarily broadly and thereby invade the area of protected freedoms." NAACP v. Alabama, 377 U.S. 288, 307, 84 S.Ct. 1302, 1314. Would we allow the police to search the sacred precincts of marital bedrooms for telltale signs of the use of contraceptives? The very idea is repulsive to the notions of privacy surrounding the marriage relationship.

We deal with a right of privacy older than the Bill of Rights—older than our political parties, older than our school system. Marriage is a coming together for better or for worse, hopefully enduring, and intimate to the degree of being sacred. It is an association that promotes a way of life, not causes; a harmony in living, not political faiths; a bilateral loyalty, not commercial or social projects. Yet it is an association for as noble a purpose as any involved in our prior decisions.

Reversed.

Mr. Justice GOLDBERG, whom The CHIEF JUSTICE [WARREN] and Mr. Justice BRENNAN join, concurring.

I agree with the Court that Connecticut's birth-control law unconstitutionally intrudes upon the right of marital privacy, and I join in its opinion and judgment. Although I have not accepted the view that "due process" as used in the Fourteenth Amendment includes all of the first eight Amendments * * * I do agree that the concept of liberty protects those personal rights that are fundamental, and is not confined to the specific terms of the Bill of Rights. My conclusion that the concept of liberty is not so restricted and that it embraces the right of marital privacy though that right is not mentioned explicitly in the Constitution is supported both by numerous decisions of this Court, referred to in the Court's opinion, and by the language and history of the Ninth Amendment. In reaching the conclusion that the right of marital privacy is protected, as being within the protected penumbra of specific guarantees of the Bill of Rights, the Court refers to the Ninth Amendment. * * * I add these words to emphasize the relevance of that Amendment to the Court's holding.

The Court stated many years ago that the Due Process Clause protects those liberties that are "so rooted in the traditions and conscience of our people as to be ranked as fundamental." Snyder v. Com. of Massachusetts, 291 U.S. 97, 105, 54 S.Ct. 330, 332. * * *

This Court, in a series of decisions, has held that the Fourteenth Amendment absorbs and applies to the States those specifics of the first eight amendments which express fundamental personal rights. The language and history of the Ninth Amendment reveal that the Framers of the Constitution believed that there are additional fundamental rights, protected from governmental infringement, which exist alongside those fundamental rights specifically mentioned in the first eight constitutional amendments.

* * * It was proffered to quiet expressed fears that a bill of specifically enumerated rights could not be sufficiently broad to cover all essential rights and that the specific mention of certain rights would be interpreted as a denial that others were protected.

* * *

* * * The Ninth Amendment to the Constitution may be regarded by some as a recent discovery but since 1791 it has been a basic part of the Constitution which we are sworn to uphold. To hold that a right so basic and fundamental and so deeprooted in our society as the right of privacy in marriage may be infringed because that right is not guaranteed in so many words by the first eight amendments to the Constitution is to ignore the Ninth Amendment and to give it no effect whatsoever. Moreover, a judicial construction that this fundamental right is not protected by the Constitution because it is not mentioned in explicit terms by one of the first eight amendments or elsewhere in the Constitution would violate the Ninth Amendment, which specifically states that "[t]he enumeration in the Constitution, of certain rights shall not be *construed* to deny or disparage others retained by the people." (Emphasis added.)

A dissenting opinion suggests that my interpretation of the Ninth Amendment somehow "broaden[s] the powers of this Court." * * * With all due respect, I believe that it misses the import of what I am saying. I do not take the position of my Brother Black in his dissent in Adam-

son v. People of State of California, 332 U.S. 46, 68, 67 S.Ct. 1672, 1683, that the entire Bill of Rights is incorporated in the Fourteenth Amendment, and I do not mean to imply that the Ninth Amendment is applied against the States by the Fourteenth. Nor do I mean to state that the Ninth Amendment constitutes an independent source of rights protected from infringement by either the States or the Federal Government. Rather, the Ninth Amendment shows a belief of the Constitution's authors that fundamental rights exist that are not expressly enumerated in the first eight amendments and an intent that the list of rights included there not be deemed exhaustive. As any student of this Court's opinions knows, this Court has held, often unanimously, that the Fifth and Fourteenth Amendments protect certain fundamental personal liberties from abridgment by the Federal Government or the States. * * * The Ninth Amendment simply shows the intent of the Constitution's authors that other fundamental personal rights should not be denied such protection or disparaged in any other way simply because they are not specifically listed in the first eight constitutional amendments. I do not see how this broadens the authority of the Court; rather it serves to support what this Court has been doing in protecting fundamental rights.

Nor am I turning somersaults with history in arguing that the Ninth Amendment is relevant in a case dealing with a *State's* infringement of a fundamental right. While the Ninth Amendment—and indeed the entire Bill of Rights—originally concerned restrictions upon *federal* power, the subsequently enacted Fourteenth Amendment prohibits the States as well from abridging funda-

mental personal liberties. And, the Ninth Amendment, in indicating that not all such liberties are specifically mentioned in the first eight amendments, is surely relevant in showing the existence of other fundamental personal rights, now protected from state, as well as federal, infringement. In sum, the Ninth Amendment simply lends strong support to the view that the "liberty" protected by the Fifth and Fourteenth Amendments from infringement by the Federal Government or the States is not restricted to rights specifically mentioned in the first eight amendments.
* * *

In determining which rights are fundamental, judges are not left at large to decide cases in light of their personal and private notions. Rather, they must look to the "traditions and [collective] conscience of our people" to determine whether a principle is "so rooted [there]   *   *   * as to be ranked as fundamental." *Snyder* v. *Com. of Massachusetts* [supra]. The inquiry is whether a right involved "is of such a character that it cannot be denied without violating those 'fundamental principles of liberty and justice which lie at the base of all our civil and political institutions.'"   *   *   * Powell v. State of Alabama, 287 U.S. 45, 67, 53 S.Ct. 55, 63.   *   *   *

* * *

The entire fabric of the Constitution and the purposes that clearly underlie its specific guarantees demonstrate that the rights to marital privacy and to marry and raise a family are of similar order and magnitude as the fundamental rights specifically protected.

Although the Constitution does not speak in so many words of the right of privacy in marriage, I cannot

believe that it offers these fundamental rights no protection. The fact that no particular provision of the Constitution explicitly forbids the State from disrupting the traditional relation of the family—a relation as old and as fundamental as our entire civilization—surely does not show that the Government was meant to have the power to do so. Rather, as the Ninth Amendment expressly recognizes, there are fundamental personal rights such as this one, which are protected from abridgment by the Government though not specifically mentioned in the Constitution.

* * *

The logic of the dissents would sanction federal or state legislation that seems to me even more plainly unconstitutional than the statute before us. Surely the Government, absent a showing of a compelling subordinating state interest, could not decree that all husbands and wives must be sterilized after two children have been born to them. Yet by their reasoning such an invasion of marital privacy would not be subject to constitutional challenge because, while it might be "silly," no provision of the Constitution specifically prevents the Government from curtailing the marital right to bear children and raise a family. While it may shock some of my Brethren that the Court today holds that the Constitution protects the right of marital privacy, in my view it is far more shocking to believe that the personal liberty guaranteed by the Constitution does not include protection against such totalitarian limitation of family size, which is at complete variance with our constitutional concepts. Yet, if upon a showing of a slender basis of rationality, a law outlawing voluntary birth control by married persons is valid, then, by the same reasoning, a law requiring compulsory birth control also would seem to be valid. In my view, however, both types of law would unjustifiably intrude upon rights of marital privacy which are constitutionally protected.

In a long series of cases this Court has held that where fundamental personal liberties are involved, they may not be abridged by the States simply on a showing that a regulatory statute has some rational relationship to the effectuation of a proper state purpose. * * *

* * *

[I]t is clear that the state interest in safeguarding marital fidelity can be served by a more discriminately tailored statute, which does not, like the present one, sweep unnecessarily broadly, reaching far beyond the evil sought to be dealt with and intruding upon the privacy of all married couples. * * *

Finally, it should be said of the Court's holding today that it in no way interferes with a State's proper regulation of sexual promiscuity or misconduct. As my Brother Harlan so well stated in his dissenting opinion in Poe v. Ullman, 367 U.S. at 553, 81 S.Ct. at 1782.

"Adultery, homosexuality and the like are sexual intimacies which the State forbids * * * but the intimacy of husband and wife is necessarily an essential and accepted feature of the institution of marriage, an institution which the State not only must allow, but which always and in every age it has fostered and protected. It is one thing when the State exerts its power either to forbid extra-marital sexuality * * * or to say who may marry, but it is quite

another when, having acknowledged a marriage and the intimacies inherent in it, it undertakes to regulate by means of the criminal law the details of that intimacy."

In sum, I believe that the right of privacy in the marital relation is fundamental and basic—a personal right "retained by the people" within the meaning of the Ninth Amendment. Connecticut cannot constitutionally abridge this fundamental right, which is protected by the Fourteenth Amendment from infringement by the States. I agree with the Court that petitioners' convictions must therefore be reversed.

Mr. Justice HARLAN, concurring in the judgment.

I fully agree with the judgment of reversal, but find myself unable to join the Court's opinion. * * *

* * *

In my view, the proper constitutional inquiry in this case is whether this Connecticut statute infringes the Due Process Clause of the Fourteenth Amendment because the enactment violates basic values "implicit in the concept of ordered liberty," Palko v. State of Connecticut, 302 U.S. 319, 325, 58 S.Ct. 149, 152. * * * I believe that it does. While the relevant inquiry may be aided by resort to one or more of the provisions of the Bill of Rights, it is not dependent on them or any of their radiations. The Due Process Clause of the Fourteenth Amendment stands, in my opinion, on its own bottom.

* * *

While I could not more heartily agree that judicial "self restraint" is an indispensable ingredient of sound constitutional adjudication, I do submit that the formula suggested for achieving it is more hollow than real. "Specific" provisions of the Constitution, no less than "due process," lend themselves as readily to "personal" interpretations by judges whose constitutional outlook is simply to keep the Constitution in supposed "tune with the times." * * *

Judicial self-restraint will not, I suggest, be brought about in the "due process" area by the historically unfounded incorporation formula long advanced by my Brother Black, and now in part espoused by my Brother Stewart. It will be achieved in this area, as in other constitutional areas, only by continual insistence upon respect for the teachings of history, solid recognition of the basic values that underlie our society, and wise appreciation of the great roles that the doctrines of federalism and separation of powers have played in establishing and preserving American freedoms. * * * Adherence to these principles will not, of course, obviate all constitutional differences of opinion among judges, nor should it. Their continued recognition will, however, go farther toward keeping most judges from roaming at large in the constitutional field than will the interpolation into the Constitution of an artificial and largely illusory restriction on the content of the Due Process Clause.

Mr. Justice WHITE concurring in the judgment.

In my view this Connecticut law as applied to married couples deprives them of "liberty" without due process of law, as that concept is used in the Fourteenth Amendment. I therefore concur in the judgment of the Court. * * *

* * *

Mr. Justice BLACK, with whom Mr. Justice STEWART joins, dissenting.

I agree with my Brother Stewart's dissenting opinion. And like him I do not to any extent whatever base my view that this Connecticut law is constitutional on a belief that the law is wise or that its policy is a good one. In order that there may be no room at all to doubt why I vote as I do, I feel constrained to add that the law is every bit as [personally] offensive to me as it is my Brethren. * * *

* * *

* * * I get nowhere in this case by talk about a constitutional "right of privacy" as an emanation from one or more constitutional provisions. I like my privacy as well as the next one, but I am nevertheless compelled to admit that government has a right to invade it unless prohibited by some specific constitutional provision. For these reasons I cannot agree with the Court's judgment and the reasons it gives for holding this Connecticut law unconstitutional.

* * *

I realize that many good and able men have eloquently spoken and written, sometimes in rhapsodical strains, about the duty of this Court to keep the Constitution in tune with the times. The idea is that the Constitution must be changed from time to time and that this Court is charged with a duty to make those changes. For myself, I must with all deference reject that philosophy. The Constitution makers knew the need for change and provided for it. Amendments suggested by the people's elected representatives can be submitted to the people or their selected agents for ratification. That method of change was good for our Fathers, and being somewhat old-fashioned I must add it is good enough for me. And so, I cannot rely on the Due Process Clause or the Ninth Amendment or any mysterious and uncertain natural law concept as a reason for striking down this state law. The Due Process Clause with an "arbitrary and capricious" or "shocking to the conscience" formula was liberally used by this Court to strike down economic legislation in the early decades of this century, threatening, many people thought, the tranquility and stability of the Nation. See, e.g., Lochner v. State of New York, 198 U.S. 45, 25 S.Ct. 539. That formula, based on subjective considerations of "natural justice," is no less dangerous when used to enforce this Court's views about personal rights than those about economic rights. I had thought that we had laid that formula, as a means for striking down state legislation, to rest once and for all in cases like West Coast Hotel Co. v. Parrish, 300 U.S. 379, 57 S.Ct. 578. * * *

* * *

Mr. Justice STEWART, whom Mr. Justice BLACK joins, dissenting.

Since 1879 Connecticut has had on its books a law which forbids the use of contraceptives by anyone. I think this is an uncommonly silly law. As a practical matter, the law is obviously unenforceable, except in the oblique context of the present case. * * * But we are not asked in this case to say whether we think this law is unwise, or even asinine. We are asked to hold that it violates the United States Constitution. And that I cannot do.

In the course of its opinion the Court refers to no less than six

Amendments to the Constitution: the First, the Third, the Fourth, the Fifth, the Ninth, and the Fourteenth. But the Court does not say which of these Amendments, if any, it thinks is infringed by this Connecticut law.

* * *

The Court also quotes the Ninth Amendment, and my Brother GOLDBERG's concurring opinion relies heavily upon it. But to say that the Ninth Amendment has anything to do with this case is to turn somersaults with history. The Ninth Amendment, like its companion the Tenth, which this Court held "states but a truism that all is retained which has not been surrendered," United States v. Darby, 312 U.S. 100, 124, 61 S.Ct. 451, 462, was framed by James Madison and adopted by the States simply to make clear that the adoption of the Bill of Rights did not alter the plan that the *Federal* Government was to be a government of express and limited powers, and that all rights and powers not delegated to it were retained by the people and the individual States. Until today no member of this Court has ever suggested that the Ninth Amendment meant anything else, and the idea that a federal court could ever use the Ninth Amendment to annul a law passed by the elected representatives of the people of the State of Connecticut would have caused James Madison no little wonder.

What provision of the Constitution, then, does make this state law invalid? The Court says it is the right of privacy "created by several fundamental constitutional guarantees." With all deference, I can find no such general right of privacy in the Bill of Rights, in any other part of the Constitution, or in any case ever before decided by this Court.

* * *

EISENSTADT v. BAIRD

Supreme Court of the United States, 1972
405 U.S. 438, 92 S.Ct. 1029, 31 L.Ed.2d 349

Massachusetts law made it a felony to give anyone other than a married person contraceptive medicines or devices, and even then such distribution was to be only through a registered pharmacist or on prescription of or administration by a licensed physician. William Baird was convicted for exhibiting contraceptive articles during his lecture to a group of students at Boston University and for giving away a package of Emko vaginal foam to a woman at the close of his remarks. The Massachusetts Supreme Judicial Court struck down his conviction for exhibiting the contraceptives as a violation of freedom of speech under the First and Fourteenth Amendments but upheld his conviction for distributing the foam. Baird subsequently filed a petition for habeas corpus in federal district court which was dismissed but later granted on appeal by the U. S. First Circuit Court of Appeals. Eisenstadt, the sheriff of Suffolk County appealed, and the Supreme Court granted certiorari.

[After concluding at the outset of its opinion that Baird, who was neither unmarried nor an authorized distributor of contraceptive materials named in the statute, still had standing to challenge its constitutionality, (because he was acting in the role of "an advocate of the rights of persons to obtain contraceptives and those desirous of doing so," and the fact that enforcement of the law would "naturally impair the ability of single persons to obtain contraceptives"), the Court proceeded to decide the case on the merits.]

Mr. Justice BRENNAN delivered the opinion of the Court.

*   *   *

The legislative purposes that the statute is meant to serve are not altogether clear. In Commonwealth v. Baird [355 Mass. 746, 753, 247 N.E.2d 574, 578], the Supreme Judicial Court noted only the State's interest in protecting the health of its citizens. * * * In a subsequent decision, Sturgis v. Attorney General, Mass., 260 N.E.2d 687, 690 (1970), the court, however, found "a second and more compelling ground for upholding the statute"—namely, to protect morals through "regulating the private sexual lives of single persons." The Court of Appeals, for reasons that will appear, did not consider the promotion of health or the protection of morals through the de-

terrence of fornication to be the legislative aim. Instead, the court concluded that the statutory goal was to limit contraception in and of itself—a purpose that the court held conflicted "with fundamental human rights" under *Griswold* v. *Connecticut*.
*   *   *

We agree that the goals of deterring premarital sex and regulating the distribution of potentially harmful articles cannot reasonably be regarded as legislative aims of [the state law]. And we hold that the statute, viewed as a prohibition on contraception *per se*, violates the rights of single persons under the Equal Protection Clause of the Fourteenth Amendment.

*   *   *

The basic principles governing application of the Equal Protection

Clause of the Fourteenth Amendment are familiar. * * *

The question for our determination in this case is whether there is some ground of difference that rationally explains the different treatment accorded married and unmarried persons under Massachusetts General Laws c. 272, §§ 21 and 21A [the statutes governing the distribution of contraceptives]. For the reasons that follow, we conclude that no such ground exists.

First. Section 21 stems from [a law enacted in] 1879 which prohibited, without exception, distribution of articles intended to be used as contraceptives. In [1917] the Massachusetts Supreme Judicial Court explained that the law's "plain purpose is to protect purity, to preserve chastity, to encourage continence and self restraint, to defend the sanctity of the home, and thus to engender in the State and nation a virile and virtuous race of men and women." Although the State clearly abandoned that purpose with the enactment of § 21A at least insofar as the illicit sexual activities of married persons are concerned, * * * the court reiterated in *Sturgis* v. *Attorney General*, supra, that the object of the legislation is to discourage premarital sexual intercourse. Conceding that the State could, consistently with the Equal Protection Clause, regard the problems of extramarital and premarital sexual relations as "[e]vils * * * of different dimensions and proportions, requiring different remedies," * * * we cannot agree that the deterrence of premarital sex may reasonably be regarded as the purpose of the Massachusetts law.

It would be plainly unreasonable to assume that Massachusetts has prescribed pregnancy and the birth of an unwanted child as punishment for fornication, which is a misdemeanor under Massachusetts [law]. * * *

* * * The very terms of the State's criminal statutes, coupled with the *de minimis* effect of §§ 21 and 21A in deterring fornication, * * * compel the conclusion that such deterrence cannot reasonably be taken as the purpose of the ban on distribution of contraceptives to unmarried persons.

Second. Section 21A [the provision confining distribution to pharmacists and doctors] was added to the Massachusetts General Laws by Stat.1966, c. 265, § 1. The Supreme Judicial Court in *Commonwealth* v. *Baird*, supra, held that the purpose of the amendment was to serve the health needs of the community by regulating the distribution of potentially harmful articles. It is plain that Massachusetts had no such purpose in mind before the enactment of § 21A. As the Court of Appeals remarked, "Consistent with the fact that the statute was contained in a chapter dealing with 'Crimes Against Chastity, Morality, Decency and Good Order,' it was cast only in terms of morals. A physician was forbidden to prescribe contraceptives even when needed for the protection of health." * * *

* * *

Third. If the Massachusetts statute cannot be upheld as a deterrent to fornication or as a health measure, may it, nevertheless, be sustained simply as a prohibition on contraception? * * * We need not and do not, however, decide that important question in this case because, whatever the rights of the individual to access to contraceptives may be, the rights must be the same for the unmarried and the married alike.

If under *Griswold* the distribution of contraceptives to married persons cannot be prohibited, a ban on distribution to unmarried persons would be equally impermissible. It is true that in *Griswold* the right of privacy in question inhered in the marital relationship. Yet the marital couple is not an independent entity with a mind and heart of its own, but an association of two individuals each with a separate intellectual and emotional make-up. If the right of privacy means anything, it is the right of the *individual*, married or single, to be free from unwarranted governmental intrusion into matters so fundamentally affecting a person as the decision whether to bear or beget a child. * * *

On the other hand, if *Griswold* is no bar to a prohibition on the distribution of contraceptives, the State could not, consistently with the Equal Protection Clause, outlaw distribution to unmarried but not to married persons. In each case the evil, as perceived by the State, would be identical, and the under-inclusion would be invidious. * * *

* * *

Affirmed.

Mr. Justice POWELL and Mr. Justice REHNQUIST took no part in the consideration or decision of this case.

Mr. Justice DOUGLAS, concurring.

While I join the opinion of the Court, there is for me a narrower ground for affirming the Court of Appeals. This to me is a simple First Amendment case, that amendment being applicable to the States by reason of the Fourteenth. * * *

* * *

Baird gave an hour's lecture on birth control and as an aid to understanding the ideas which he was propagating he handed out one sample of one of the devices whose use he was endorsing. A person giving a lecture on coyote-getters would certainly improve his teaching technique if he passed one out to the audience; and he would be protected in doing so unless of course the device was loaded and ready to explode, killing or injuring people. The same holds true in my mind for mousetraps, spray guns, or any other article not dangerous *per se* on which speakers give educational lectures.

It is irrelevant to the application of these principles that Baird went beyond the giving of information about birth control and advocated the use of contraceptive articles. The First Amendment protects the opportunity to persuade to action whether that action be unwise or immoral, or whether the speech excites to action. See, e.g., Brandenburg v. Ohio, 395 U.S. 444, 89 S.Ct. 1827. * * *

In this case there was not even incitement to action. There is no evidence or finding that Baird intended for the young lady to take the foam home with her when he handed it to her or that she would not have examined the article and then returned it to Baird, had he not been placed under arrest immediately upon handing the article over.

* * *

Mr. Justice WHITE, with whom Mr. Justice BLACKMUN joins, concurring in the result.

* * *

I assume that a State's interest in the health of its citizens empowers it to restrict to medical channels the distribution of products whose use should be accompanied by medical advice. I also do not doubt that various contraceptive medicines and articles are properly available only on prescription. * * * Had Baird distributed a supply of the so-called "pill," I would sustain his conviction under this statute. Requiring a prescription to obtain potentially dangerous contraceptive material may place a substantial burden upon the right recognized in *Griswold*, but that burden is justified by a strong State interest and does not, as did the statute at issue in *Griswold*, sweep unnecessarily broadly or seek "to achieve its goals by means having the maximum destructive impact upon" a protected relationship. * * *

Baird, however, was found guilty of giving away vaginal foam. Inquiry into the validity of this conviction does not come to an end merely because some contraceptives are harmful and their distribution may be restricted. Our general reluctance to question a State's judgment on matters of public health must give way where, as here, the restriction at issue burdens the constitutional rights of married persons to use contraceptives. In these circumstances we may not accept on faith the State's classification of a particular contraceptive as dangerous to health. Due regard for protecting constitutional rights requires that the record contain evidence that a restriction on distribution of vaginal foam is essential to achieve the statutory purpose, or the relevant facts concerning the product must be such as to fall within the range of judicial notice.

* * *

That Baird could not be convicted for distributing Emko to a married person disposes of this case. Assuming *arguendo* that the result would be otherwise had the recipient been unmarried, nothing has been placed in the record to indicate her marital status. The State has maintained that marital status is irrelevant because an unlicensed person cannot legally dispense vaginal foam either to married or unmarried persons. This approach is plainly erroneous and requires the reversal of Baird's conviction; for on the facts of this case, it deprives us of knowing whether Baird was in fact convicted for making a constitutionally protected distribution of Emko to a married person.

* * *

Because this case can be disposed of on the basis of settled constitutional doctrine, I perceive no reason for reaching the novel constitutional question whether a State may restrict or forbid the distribution of contraceptives to the unmarried. * * *

Mr. Chief Justice BURGER, dissenting.

* * * It is undisputed that appellee is not a physician or pharmacist and was prohibited under Massachusetts law from dispensing contraceptives to anyone, regardless of marital status. To my mind the validity of this restriction on dispensing medicinal substances is the only issue before the Court, and appellee has no standing to challenge that part of the statute restricting the persons to whom contraceptives are available. There is no need to labor this point, however, for everyone seems to agree that if Massachusetts

has validly required, as a health measure, that all contraceptives be dispensed by a physician or pursuant to a physician's prescription, then the statutory distinction based on marital status has no bearing on this case. * * *

* * *

* * * I see nothing in the Fourteenth Amendment or any other part of the Constitution which even vaguely suggests that these medicinal forms of contraceptives must be available in the open market. I do not challenge *Griswold* v. *Connecticut*, supra, despite its tenuous moorings to the text of the Constitution,

but I cannot view it as controlling authority for this case. * * *

* * * I am constrained to suggest that if the Constitution can be strained to invalidate the Massachusetts statute underlying appellee's conviction, we could quite as well employ it for the protection of a "curbstone quack," reminiscent of the "medicine man" of times past, who attracted a crowd of the curious with a soapbox lecture and then plied them with "free samples" of some unproven remedy. Massachusetts presumably outlawed such activities long ago, but today's holding seems to invite their return.

ROE v. WADE

Supreme Court of the United States, 1973
410 U.S. 113, 93 S.Ct. 705, 35 L.Ed.2d 147

Texas abortion law, typical of that in effect in most states for over a century, made it a felony for anyone to destroy a fetus except on "medical advice for the purpose of saving the life of the mother." Three plaintiffs brought suit against Wade, the District Attorney of Dallas County, for declaratory and injunctive relief: an unmarried pregnant woman, a licensed physician, and a childless married couple fearing future pregnancy because of the wife's deteriorated health. [At the outset of its opinion, the U. S. Supreme Court subsequently determined that only Jane Roe (a pseudonym for the unmarried pregnant woman) had the requisite standing to sue.] The statute was challenged on grounds it denied equal protection (by forcing women who did not have the money to have a baby when those who had money could go elsewhere and procure a safe, legal abortion), due process (because the statute was vague as to what preserving the life of the mother actually meant), and the mother's right of privacy guaranteed under the First, Fourth, Fifth, Ninth and Fourteenth Amendments. A three-judge federal district court found the statute unconstitutional, and the Supreme Court granted review as a matter of right.

Mr. Justice BLACKMUN delivered the opinion of the Court.

We forthwith acknowledge our awareness of the sensitive and emotional nature of the abortion controversy, of the vigorous opposing views, even among physicians, and of the deep and seemingly absolute convictions that the subject inspires. One's philosophy, one's experiences,

one's exposure to the raw edges of human existence, one's religious training, one's attitudes toward life and family and their values, and the moral standards one establishes and seeks to observe, are all likely to influence and to color one's thinking and conclusions about abortion.

In addition, population growth, pollution, poverty, and racial overtones tend to complicate and not to simplify the problem.

Our task, of course, is to resolve the issue by constitutional measurement free of emotion and of predilection. We seek earnestly to do this, and, because we do, we have inquired into, and in this opinion place some emphasis upon, medical and medical-legal history and what that history reveals about man's attitudes toward the abortive procedure over the centuries. We bear in mind, too, Mr. Justice Holmes' admonition in his now vindicated dissent in Lochner v. New York, 198 U.S. 45, 76, 25 S.Ct. 539, 547 (1905):

"It [the Constitution] is made for people of fundamentally differing views, and the accident of our finding certain opinions natural and familiar, or novel, and even shocking, ought not to conclude our judgment upon the question whether statutes embodying them conflict with the Constitution of the United States."

* * *

The principal thrust of appellant's attack on the Texas statutes is that they improperly invade a right, said to be possessed by the pregnant woman, to choose to terminate her pregnancy. Appellant would discover this right in the concept of personal "liberty" embodied in the Fourteenth Amendment's Due Process Clause; or in personal, marital, familial, and sexual privacy said to be protected by the Bill of Rights or its penumbras * * *; or among those rights reserved to the people by the Ninth Amendment. * * * Before addressing this claim, we feel it desirable briefly to survey, in several aspects, the history of abortion, for such insight as that history may afford us, and then to examine the

state purposes and interests behind the criminal abortion laws.

[The Court then turned to an extensive scholarly examination of abortion in Western thought and ethics, focusing substantially on a distinction developed at common law as to the status given to "quickening" in the fetus (i.e., "the first recognizable movement of the fetus *in utero*"). The Court noted that before this point—"usually from the 16th to 18th week of pregnancy"— abortion was not considered an indictable offense and after this point it was prevalently treated as a misdemeanor. The Court also examined the positions of several professional organizations (the American Medical Association, the American Bar Association and others) on the abortion issue.]

* * *

Three reasons have been advanced to explain historically the enactment of criminal abortion laws in the 19th century and to justify their continued existence.

It has been argued occasionally that these laws were the product of a victorian social concern to discourage illicit sexual conduct. Texas, however, does not advance this justification in the present case, and it appears that no court or commentator has taken the argument seriously.
* * *

A second reason is concerned with abortion as a medical procedure. When most criminal abortion laws were first enacted, the procedure was a hazardous one for the woman.
* * * Thus it has been argued that a State's real concern in enacting a criminal abortion law was to protect the pregnant woman, that is, to restrain her from submitting to a

procedure that placed her life in serious jeopardy.

* * *

The third reason is the State's interest—some phrase it in terms of duty—in protecting prenatal life. Some of the argument for this justification rests on the theory that a new human life is present from the moment of conception. The State's interest and general obligation to protect life then extends, it is argued, to prenatal life. Only when the life of the pregnant mother herself is at stake, balanced against the life she carries within her, should the interest of the embryo or fetus not prevail. Logically, of course, a legitimate state interest in this area need not stand or fall on acceptance of the belief that life begins at conception or at some other point prior to live birth. In assessing the State's interest, recognition may be given to the less rigid claim that as long as at least *potential* life is involved, the State may assert interests beyond the protection of the pregnant woman alone.

* * *

It is with these interests, and the weight to be attached to them, that this case is concerned.

The Constitution does not explicitly mention any right of privacy. In a line of decisions, however, going back perhaps as far as [1891], the Court has recognized that a right of personal privacy, or a guarantee of certain areas or zones of privacy, does exist under the Constitution. In varying contexts the Court or individual Justices have indeed found at least the roots of that right in the First Amendment, Stanley v. Georgia, 394 U.S. 557, 564, 89 S.Ct. 1243, 1247 (1969); in the Fourth and Fifth Amendments, Terry v. Ohio, 392 U.S. 1, 8–9, 88 S.Ct. 1868, 1872–1873 (1968); Katz v. United States, 389 U.S. 347, 350, 88 S.Ct. 507, 510 (1967); Boyd v. United States, 116 U.S. 616, 6 S.Ct. 524 (1886), see Olmstead v. United States, 277 U.S. 438, 478, 48 S.Ct. 564, 572 (1928) (Brandeis, J., dissenting); in the penumbras of the Bill of Rights, Griswold v. Connecticut, 381 U.S. 479, 484–485, 85 S.Ct. 1678, 1681–1682 (1965); in the Ninth Amendment, *id.*, at 486, 85 S.Ct. at 1682 (Goldberg, J., concurring); or in the concept of liberty guaranteed by the first section of the Fourteenth Amendment, see Meyer v. Nebraska, 262 U.S. 390, 399, 43 S.Ct. 625, 626 (1923). These decisions make it clear that only personal rights that can be deemed "fundamental" or "implicit in the concept of ordered liberty," Palko v. Connecticut, 302 U.S. 319, 325, 58 S.Ct. 149, 152 (1937), are included in this guarantee of personal privacy. They also make it clear that the right has some extension to activities relating to marriage, Loving v. Virginia, 388 U.S. 1, 12, 87 S.Ct. 1817, 1823 (1967), procreation, Skinner v. Oklahoma, 316 U.S. 535, 541–542, 62 S.Ct. 1110, 1113–1114 (1942), contraception, Eisenstadt v. Baird, 405 U.S. 438, 453–454, 92 S.Ct. 1029, 1038–1039 (1972); *id.*, at 460, 463–465, 92 S.Ct. at 1042, 1043–1044 (White, J., concurring), family relationships, Prince v. Massachusetts, 321 U.S. 158, 166, 64 S.Ct. 438, 442 (1944), and child rearing and education, Pierce v. Society of Sisters, 268 U.S. 510, 535, 45 S.Ct. 571, 573 (1925), *Meyer* v. *Nebraska*, supra.

This right of privacy, whether it be founded in the Fourteenth Amendment's concept of personal liberty and restrictions upon state action, as we feel it is, or, as the District Court determined, in the Ninth Amendment's reservation of rights to the people, is broad enough to encompass a woman's decision whether or not to terminate her pregnancy. The detriment that the State would impose upon the pregnant woman by denying this choice altogether is apparent. Specific and direct harm medically diagnosable even in early pregnancy may be involved. Maternity, or additional offspring, may force upon the woman a distressful life and future. Psychological harm may be imminent. Mental and physical health may be taxed by child care. There is also the distress, for all concerned, associated with the unwanted child, and there is the problem of bringing a child into a family already unable, psychologically and otherwise, to care for it. In other cases, as in this one, the additional difficulties and continuing stigma of unwed motherhood may be involved. All these are factors the woman and her responsible physician necessarily will consider in consultation.

On the basis of elements such as these, appellants and some *amici* argue that the woman's right is absolute and that she is entitled to terminate her pregnancy at whatever time, in whatever way, and for whatever reason she alone chooses. With this we do not agree. Appellants' arguments that Texas either has no valid interest at all in regulating the abortion decision, or no interest strong enough to support any limitation upon the woman's sole determination, is unpersuasive. The Court's decisions recognizing a right of privacy also acknowledge that some state regulation in areas protected by that right is appropriate. As noted above, a state may properly assert important interests in safeguarding health, in maintaining medical standards, and in protecting potential life. At some point in pregnancy, these respective interests become sufficiently compelling to sustain regulation of the factors that govern the abortion decision. The privacy right involved, therefore, cannot be said to be absolute. In fact, it is not clear to us that the claim asserted by some *amici* that one has an unlimited right to do with one's body as one pleases bears a close relationship to the right of privacy previously articulated in the Court's decisions. The Court has refused to recognize an unlimited right of this kind in the past. Jacobson v. Massachusetts, 197 U.S. 11, 25 S.Ct. 358 (1905) (vaccination); Buck v. Bell, 274 U.S. 200, 47 S.Ct. 584 (1927) (sterilization).

We therefore conclude that the right of personal privacy includes the abortion decision, but that this right is not unqualified and must be considered against important state interests in regulation.

* * *

Where certain "fundamental rights" are involved, the Court has held that regulation limiting these rights may be justified only by a "compelling state interest," Kramer v. Union Free School District, 395 U.S. 621, 627, 89 S.Ct. 1886, 1890 (1969); Shapiro v. Thompson, 394 U.S. 618, 634, 89 S.Ct. 1322, 1331 (1969); Sherbert v. Verner, 374 U.S. 398, 406, 83 S.Ct. 1790, 1795 (1963), and that legislative enactments must be narrowly drawn to express only the legitimate state interests at stake. Griswold v. Connecticut, 381 U.S. 479, 485, 85 S.Ct. 1678, 1682 (1965); Aptheker v. Secretary of State, 378 U.S. 500, 508, 84 S.Ct. 1659, 1664 (1964). * * *

* * *

The District Court held that the appellee failed to meet his burden of demonstrating that the Texas statute's infringement upon Roe's rights was necessary to support a compelling state interest, and that, although the defendant presented "several compelling justifications for state presence in the area of abortions," the statutes outstripped these justifications and swept "far beyond any areas of compelling state interest." * * * Appellant and appellee both contest that holding. Appellant, as has been indicated, claims an absolute right that bars any state imposition of criminal penalties in the area. Appellee argues that the State's determination to recognize and protect prenatal life from and after conception constitutes a compelling state interest. [W]e do not agree fully with either formulation.

A. The appellee and certain *amici* argue that the fetus is a "person" within the language and meaning of the Fourteenth Amendment. In support of this they outline at length and in detail the well-known facts of fetal development. If this suggestion of personhood is established, the appellant's case, of course, collapses, for the fetus' right to life is then guaranteed specifically by the Amendment. The appellant conceded as much on reargument. On the other hand, the appellee conceded on reargument that no case could be cited that holds that a fetus is a person within the meaning of the Fourteenth Amendment.

[The use of the word "person" in the provisions of the Constitution only in a postnatal sense] together with our observation * * * that throughout the major portion of the 19th century prevailing legal abortion practices were far freer than they are today, persuades us that the word "person," as used in the Fourteenth Amendment, does not include the unborn. * * *

This conclusion, however, does not of itself fully answer the contentions raised by Texas, and we pass on to other considerations.

B. The pregnant woman cannot be isolated in her privacy. She carries an embryo and, later, a fetus, if one accepts the medical definitions of the developing young in the human uterus. * * * The situation therefore is inherently different from marital intimacy, or bedroom possession of obscene material, or marriage, or procreation, or education, with which *Eisenstadt, Griswold, Stanley, Loving, Skinner, Pierce,* and *Meyer* were respectively concerned. As we have intimated above, it is reasonable and appropriate for a State to decide that at some point in time another interest, that of health of the mother or that of potential human life, becomes significantly involved. The woman's privacy is no longer sole and any right of privacy she possesses must be measured accordingly.

Texas urges that, apart from the Fourteenth Amendment, life begins at conception and is present throughout pregnancy, and that, therefore, the State has a compelling interest in protecting that life from and after conception. We need not resolve the difficult question of when life begins. When those trained in the respective disciplines of medicine, philosophy, and theology are unable to arrive at any consensus, the judiciary, at this point in the development of man's knowledge, is not in a position to speculate as to the answer.

* * *

In view of * * * this, we do not agree that, by adopting one theory of life, Texas may override the rights of the pregnant woman that are at stake. We repeat, however, that the State does have an important and legitimate interest in preserving and protecting the health of the pregnant woman, whether she be a resident of the State or a nonresident who seeks medical consultation and treatment there, and that it has still *another* important and legitimate interest in protecting the potentiality of human life. These interests are separate and distinct. Each grows in substantiality as the woman approaches term and, at a point during pregnancy, each becomes "compelling."

With respect to the State's important and legitimate interest in the health of the mother, the "compelling" point, in the light of present medical knowledge, is at approximately the end of the first trimester. This is so because of the now established medical fact * * * that until the end of the first trimester mortality in abortion is less than mortality in normal childbirth. It follows that, from and after this point, a State may regulate the abortion procedure to the extent that the regulation reasonably relates to the preservation and protection of maternal health. Examples of permissible state regulation in this area are requirements as to the qualifications of the person who is to perform the abortion; as to the licensure of that person; as to the facility in which the procedure is to be performed, that is, whether it must be a hospital or may be a clinic or some other place of less-than-hospital status; as to the licensing of the facility; and the like.

This means, on the other hand, that, for the period of pregnancy prior to this "compelling" point, the attending physician, in consultation with his patient, is free to determine, without regulation by the State, that in his medical judgment the patient's pregnancy should be terminated. If that decision is reached, the judgment may be effectuated by an abortion free of interference by the State.

With respect to the State's important and legitimate interest in potential life, the "compelling" point is at viability. This is so because the fetus then presumably has the capability of meaningful life outside the mother's womb. State regulation protective of fetal life after viability thus has both logical and biological justifications. If the State is interested in protecting fetal life after viability, it may go so far as to proscribe abortion during that period except when it is necessary to preserve the life or health of the mother.

Measured against these standards, Art. 1196 of the Texas Penal Code, in restricting legal abortions to those "procured or attempted by medical advice for the purpose of saving the life of the mother," sweeps too broadly. The statute makes no distinction between abortions performed early in pregnancy and those performed later, and it limits to a single reason, "saving" the mother's life, the legal justification for the procedure. The statute, therefore, cannot survive the constitutional attack made upon it here.

* * *

To summarize and to repeat:

1. A state criminal abortion statute of the current Texas type, that excepts from criminality only a *life*

saving procedure on behalf of the mother, without regard to pregnancy stage and without recognition of the other interests involved, is violative of the Due Process Clause of the Fourteenth Amendment.

(a) For the stage prior to approximately the end of the first trimester, the abortion decision and its effectuation must be left to the medical judgment of the pregnant woman's attending physician.

(b) For the stage subsequent to approximately the end of the first trimester, the State, in promoting its interest in the health of the mother, may, if it chooses, regulate the abortion procedure in ways that are reasonably related to maternal health.

(c) For the stage subsequent to viability the State, in promoting its interest in the potentiality of human life, may, if it chooses, regulate, and even proscribe, abortion except where it is necessary, in appropriate medical judgment, for the preservation of the life or health of the mother.

* * *

This holding, we feel, is consistent with the relative weights of the respective interests involved, with the lessons and example of medical and legal history, with the lenity of the common law, and with the demands of the profound problems of the present day. The decision leaves the State free to place increasing restrictions on abortion as the period of pregnancy lengthens, so long as those restrictions are tailored to the recognized state interests. The decision vindicates the right of the physician to administer medical treatment according to his professional judgment up to the points where important state interests provide compel-

ling justifications for intervention. Up to those points the abortion decision in all its aspects is inherently, and primarily, a medical decision, and basic responsibility for it must rest with the physician. If an individual practitioner abuses the privilege of exercising proper medical judgment, the usual remedies, judicial and intra-professional, are available.

* * *

We find it unnecessary to decide whether the District Court erred in withholding injunctive relief, for we assume the Texas prosecutorial authorities will give full credence to this decision that the present criminal abortion statutes of that State are unconstitutional.

* * *

Mr. Justice DOUGLAS, concurring.

While I join the opinion of the Court, I add a few words.

* * *

The Ninth Amendment obviously does not create federally enforceable rights. It merely says, "The enumeration in the Constitution of certain rights, shall not be construed to deny or disparage others retained by the people." But a catalogue of these rights includes customary, traditional, and time-honored rights, amenities, privileges, and immunities that come within the sweep of "the Blessings of Liberty" mentioned in the preamble to the Constitution. Many of them in my view come within the meaning of the term "liberty" as used in the Fourteenth Amendment.

First is the autonomous control over the development and expres-

sion on one's intellect, interests, tastes, and personality.

These are rights protected by the First Amendment and in my view they are absolute, permitting of no exceptions. * * *

Second is freedom of choice in the basic decisions of one's life respecting marriage, divorce, procreation, contraception, and the education and upbringing of children.

These rights, unlike those protected by the First Amendment, are subject to some control by the police power. Thus the Fourth Amendment speaks only of "unreasonable searches and seizures" and of "probable cause." These rights are "fundamental" and we have held that in order to support legislative action the statute must be narrowly and precisely drawn and that a "compelling state interest" must be shown in support of the limitation. * * *

* * *

Third is the freedom to care for one's health and person, freedom from bodily restraint or compulsion, freedom to walk, stroll, or loaf.

These rights, though fundamental, are likewise subject to regulation on a showing of "compelling state interest." * * *

* * *

In summary, the enactment [here] is overbroad. It is not closely correlated to the aim of preserving pre-natal life. In fact, it permits its destruction in several cases, including pregnancies resulting from sex acts in which unmarried females are below the statutory age of consent. At the same time, however, the measure broadly proscribes aborting other pregnancies which may cause severe

mental disorders. Additionally, the statute is overbroad because it equates the value of embryonic life immediately after conception with the worth of life immediately before birth.

* * *

Mr. Justice WHITE, with whom Mr. Justice REHNQUIST joins, dissenting.

* * *

With all due respect, I dissent. I find nothing in the language or history of the Constitution to support the Court's judgment. The Court simply fashions and announces a new constitutional right for pregnant mothers and, with scarcely any reason or authority for its action, invests that right with sufficient substance to override most existing state abortion statutes. * * *

* * *

Mr. Justice REHNQUIST, dissenting.

* * *

[L]iberty is not guaranteed absolutely against deprivation, but only against deprivation without due process of law. The test traditionally applied in the area of social and economic legislation is whether or not a law such as that challenged has a rational relation to a valid state objective. * * * The Due Process Clause of the Fourteenth Amendment undoubtedly does place a limit on legislative power to enact laws such as this, albeit a broad one. If the Texas statute were to prohibit an abortion even where the mother's life is in jeopardy, I have little doubt that such a statute would lack a rational relation to a valid state objective under the test stated. * * * But the Court's sweeping invalidation of any restrictions on abortion during the first trimester is impossible to justify under that standard, and the conscious weighing of competing factors which the Court's opinion apparently substitutes for the established test is far more appropriate to a legislative judgment than to a judicial one.

In Doe v. Bolton, 410 U.S. 179, 93 S.Ct. 756 (1973), a companion case to *Roe*, the Court considered the constitutionality of a very recently enacted Georgia statute which, while allowing abortion when the woman's life was endangered or when the child would be born with a severe and permanent defect or when pregnancy resulted from rape, nevertheless provided that the operation be performed in a specially state-accredited hospital, be approved by a hospital staff abortion committee, and that the attending physician's judgment be confirmed by two additional practitioners. The Court, speaking again through Justice Blackmun, invalidated the statute as unjustifiably infringing on the patient's rights and unduly intruding on the right of her doctor to practice medicine. The state may not confine the performance of abortions, the Court announced, to only certain specially accredited hospitals without showing that such accreditation meets its interest in fully protecting the patient, or interpose examination of the abortion request by a hospital abortion committee, or require approval of the abortion decision by two other doctors. Justices White and Rehnquist again dissented.

Three years later the Court turned its attention to issues which presented "logical and anticipated corollar[ies]" to *Roe* v. *Wade* and *Doe* v. *Bolton*. In Planned Parenthood of Central Missouri v. Danforth, 428 U.S. 52, 96 S.Ct. 2831 (1976), the Court addressed a number of conditions imposed by Missouri on the conduct of abortions particularly during the first trimester of pregnancy. While the Court upheld the statute's flexible definition of viability, affirmed the state's right to require the informed, voluntary, and written consent of the woman, and sustained the reporting and record-keeping provisions of the law, the Court declared the following elements of the statute unconstitutional: (1) the requirement that written consent also be obtained from the spouse if the woman were married and the abortion were not necessary to save her life; (2) the requirement that written consent be obtained from the woman's parents if she were under eighteen and unmarried except in a lifesaving situation; (3) the blanket prohibition on the use of saline amniocentesis as the technique for inducing abortion; and (4) the imposition of a criminal penalty on the attending physician for any failure on his part to exercise due care and skill to preserve the life and health of the fetus insofar as that is possible. Speaking for the Court, Justice Blackmun wrote with respect to the spousal consent requirement: "We are not unaware of the deep and proper concern and interest that a devoted and protective husband has in his wife's pregnancy and in the growth and development of the fetus she is carrying. Neither has this Court failed to appreciate the importance of the marital relationship in our society. See, e.g., Griswold v. Connecticut, 381 U.S. 479, 486, 85 S.Ct. 1678, 1682 (1965). * * * Moreover, we recognize that the decision whether to undergo or to forego an abortion may have profound effects on the future of any marriage, effects that are both physical and mental, and possibly deleterious. Notwithstanding these factors, we cannot hold that the State has the constitutional authority to give the spouse unilaterally the ability to prohibit the wife from terminating her pregnancy, when the State itself lacks that right." And, as to the parental consent requirement, Justice Blackmun observed: "One suggested interest is the safeguarding of the family unit and of parental authority. * * * It is difficult, however, to conclude that providing a parent with absolute power to overrule a determination, made by the physician and his minor patient, to terminate the patient's pregnancy will serve to strengthen the family unit. Neither is it likely that such veto power will enhance parental authority or control where the minor and the nonconsenting parent are so fundamentally in conflict and the very existence of the pregnancy already has fractured the family structure. Any independent interest the parent may have in the termination of the minor daughter's pregnancy is no more weighty than the right of privacy of the competent minor mature enough to have become pregnant." Warning that the Court verged on becoming "not only the country's continuous constitutional convention but also its *ex officio* medical board," Justice White dissented in an opinion in which Chief Justice Burger and Justice Rehnquist joined. Concluding that the majority's findings of unconstitutionality were unjustified, the dissenters emphasized the deference which they felt should be shown to rational legislative choices of policy, pausing to observe at one point: "These are matters which a State should be able to decide free from the suffocating power of the federal judge, purporting to act in the name of the Constitution." Justice Stevens, dissenting in part, voted to uphold the constitutionality of the parental consent provisions.

CASES ON THE CONSTITUTIONALITY OF STATE STATUTES REGULATING THE PERFORMANCE OF ABORTIONS ON UNMARRIED FEMALE MINORS

Bellotti v. Baird, 443 U.S. 622, 99 S.Ct. 3035 (1979)	Facts and Decision	The Supreme Court declared unconstitutional a Massachusetts law which required, as a prerequisite to the performance of an abortion on an unmarried female minor, the consent of her parents or guardian or, if they refused, an order from a superior court judge obtainable on a showing of good cause.
	Plurality Opinion	Justice Powell announced the judgment of the Court, joined by Chief Justice Burger and Justices Stewart and Rehnquist, and concluded that where the state requires parental consent, it must provide for an alternative authorizing procedure so that the pregnant minor can show she is sufficiently mature and knowledgeable to make her own decision or that, if she is not, the desired abortion would be in her best interests. Parental consent cannot be a requirement tantamount to an absolute veto. The Massachusetts law fails in two respects: "First, it permits judicial authorization for an abortion to be withheld from a minor who is found by the superior court to be mature and fully competent to make this decision independently. Second, it requires parental consultation or notification in every instance, without affording the pregnant minor an opportunity to receive an independent judicial determination that she is mature enough to consent or that an abortion would be in her best interests."

Bellotti (*Cont.*)	Opinion Concurring in the Judgment	Justice Stevens, speaking also for Justices Brennan, Marshall, and Blackmun, was of the view that "this case is governed by *Danforth*" and that the statute in this instance was unconstitutional because "[i]n every instance, the minor's decision to secure an abortion is subject to an absolute, third-party veto," whether of parent, guardian, or judge, regardless of "how mature and capable of informed decision-making she may be."
	Dissent	Justice White dissented.
H. L. v. Matheson, 450 U.S. 398, 101 S.Ct. 1164 (1981)	Facts and Decision	As applied only to an unemancipated, female minor who made no claim or showing as to either her maturity or her relations with her parents, a Utah statute which required a physician to "notify, if possible," the parents or guardian of a minor upon whom an abortion is to be performed was held to be constitutional.
	Opinion of the Court	Chief Justice Burger, speaking for the Court, concluded that the law advanced important state interests (such as enhancing the integrity of the family, protecting immature adolescents, and providing an opportunity for the parents to supply useful medical and other information to the physician), was narrowly drawn so as to further only those interests, and did not give parents a veto power over the minor's abortion decision. The Court also held that the statute was not unconstitutional because it failed to indicate what kind of information the parents might give the physician, or required a period of delay following notification of the parents, or allowed a minor to consent to other medical procedures in the absence of formal notice to the parents if she carried the child to term, or inhibited some minors from procuring abortions.
	Dissents	Justices Brennan, Marshall, and Blackmun dissented.

In Carey v. Population Services International, 431 U.S. 678, 97 S.Ct. 2010 (1977), the Supreme Court struck down a New York statute which made it a crime "(1) for any person to sell or distribute any contraceptive of any kind to a minor under the age of 16 years; (2) for anyone other than a licensed pharmacist to distribute contraceptives to persons over 16; and (3) for anyone, including licensed pharmacists, to advertise or display contraceptives." Speaking in part for the Court and in part for a plurality including Justices Stewart, Marshall, and Blackmun, Justice Brennan reasoned, with respect to the total ban on the sale of contraceptives to minors under sixteen years of age: "Since the State may not impose a blanket prohibition, or even a blanket requirement of parental consent, on the choice of a minor to terminate her pregnancy, the constitutionality of a blanket prohibition of the distribution of contraceptives to minors is *a fortiori* foreclosed. The State's interests in protection of the mental and physical health of the pregnant minor, and in protection of potential life are clearly more implicated by the abortion decision than by the decision to use a nonhazardous contraceptive." This conclusion was reached from two premises which the Court reaffirmed: (1) "Read in light of its progeny, the teaching of *Griswold* is that the Constitution protects individual decisions in matters of childbearing from unjustified intrusion by the State"; and (2) "the right to privacy in connection with decisions affecting procreation extends to minors as well as to adults." Responding to the argument advanced by the State that "minors' sexual activity may be deterred by increasing the hazards attendant on it," the Court quoted its earlier rejection of this proposition in *Eisenstadt* v. *Baird*: "It would be plainly unreasonable to assume that [the State] has prescribed pregnancy and birth of an unwanted child [or the physical and psychological dangers of an abortion] as punishment for fornication."

With respect to the second provision of the statute, Justice Brennan observed: "Limiting the distribution of nonprescription contraceptives to licensed pharmacists clearly imposes a significant burden on the right of individuals to use contraceptives if they choose to do so." This burden, the Court held, was not justified in any compelling way by the arguments advanced by the State (that it inhibits young people from selling contraceptives, that it permits customers to inquire about the relative merits of different brands of contraceptives, that it prevents tampering with products, etc.). And as for the ban on advertising and display of contraceptives, the Court found that provision of the statute unconstitutional for the reasons elaborated at length in both Bigelow v. Virginia, 421 U.S. 809, 95 S.Ct. 2222 (1975), and Virginia State Board of Pharmacy v. Virginia Citizens Consumer Council, 425 U.S. 748, 96 S.Ct. 1817 (1976). Chief Justice Burger and Justice Rehnquist dissented.

Near the conclusion of its October 1976 Term, the Court handed down several rulings directed toward answering the question of how far states and their political subdivisions had to go in facilitating elective abortions. In Beal v. Doe, 432 U.S. 438, 97 S.Ct. 2366 (1977), the Court, speaking through Justice Powell, concluded that, as a matter of statutory interpretation, Title XIX of the Social Security Act, did not require that states participating in the federal grant-in-aid Medicaid program fund the cost of nontherapeutic abortions. In Maher v. Roe, 432 U.S. 464, 97 S.Ct. 2376 (1977), the Court, again speaking through Justice Powell, ruled that there was no violation of the Equal Protection Clause where states subsidize therapeutic abortions but do not elect to pay for elective abortions. Addressing the argument that funding only therapeutic abortions results in making it much more difficult for an indigent woman to procure an elective abortion, the Court observed in terms of constitutional interpretation: "This case involves no discrimination against a suspect class. An indigent woman desiring an abortion does not come within the limited category of disadvantaged classes so recognized by our cases. Nor does the fact that the impact of the regulation falls upon those who cannot pay lead to a different conclusion. In a sense, every denial of welfare to an indigent creates a wealth classification as compared to non-indigents who are able to pay for the desired goods or services. But this Court has never held that financial need alone identifies a suspect class for purposes of equal protection analysis." The allegation that the limitation on funding impaired the fundamental right of a woman to elect abortion, recognized in *Roe* v. *Wade*, was rebutted by Chief Justice Burger in terse fashion in his concurring opinion: "Like the Court, I do not read any decision of this Court as requiring a State to finance a nontherapeutic abortion. The Court's holdings in *Roe* and *Doe*, supra, simply require that a State not create an absolute barrier to a woman's decision to have an abortion. These precedents do not suggest that the State is constitutionally required to assist her in procuring it." Finally, in a third case, Poelker v. Doe, 432 U.S. 519, 97 S.Ct. 2391 (1977), the Court held in a *per curiam* opinion that a city may constitutionally refuse to permit the performance of elective abortions in city-owned hospitals while at the same time providing hospital services to women carrying their pregnancies to childbirth.

Justices Brennan, Marshall, and Blackmun dissented in all three cases. In his dissenting opinion in *Maher*, Justice Brennan argued that sanctioning the state's policy of not funding elective abortions while funding childbirth not only "makes access to competent licensed physicians not merely 'difficult' but 'impossible' " for "too many, not just 'some' indigent pregnant woman" but also "[t]his disparity in funding by the State clearly operates to coerce indigent pregnant women to bear children they would not otherwise choose to have." "[J]ust as clearly," continued Justice Brennan, "this coercion can only operate upon the poor, who are uniquely the victims of this form of financial pressure." It was Justice Blackmun who voiced the sharpest dissent. Often trenchant and sometimes poignant, Justice Blackmun's dissent, appended to the *Beal* case, read in part as follows:

> The Court today, by its decisions in these cases, allows the States, and such municipalities as choose to do so, to accomplish indirectly what the Court in Roe v. Wade, 410 U.S. 113 (1973), and Doe v. Bolton, 410 U.S. 179 (1973)—by a substantial majority and with some emphasis, I had thought—said they could not do directly. The Court concedes the existence of a constitutional right but denies the realization and enjoyment of that right on the ground that existence and realization are separate and distinct. For the individual woman concerned, indigent and financially helpless, as the Court's opinions in the three cases concede her to be, the result is punitive and tragic. Implicit in the Court's holdings is the condescension that she may go elsewhere for her abortion. I find that disingenuous and alarming, almost reminiscent of "let them eat cake."

> The result the Court reaches is particularly distressing in *Poelker* v. *Doe*, where a presumed majority, in electing as mayor one whom the record shows campaigned on the issue of closing public hospitals to nontherapeutic abortions, punitively impresses upon a needy minority its own concepts of the socially desirable, the publicly acceptable, and the morally sound, with a touch of the devil-take-the-hindmost. This is not the kind of thing for which our Constitution stands.

> The Court's financial argument, of course, is specious. To be sure, welfare funds are limited and welfare must be spread perhaps as best meets the community's concept of its needs. But the cost of a nontherapeutic abortion is far less than the cost of maternity care and delivery, and holds no comparison whatsoever with the welfare costs that will burden the State for the new indigents and their support in the long, long years ahead.

> Neither is it an acceptable answer, as the Court well knows, to say that the Congress and the States are free to authorize the use of funds for nontherapeutic abortions. Why should any politician incur the demonstrated wrath and noise of the abortion opponents when mere silence and nonactivity accomplish the results the opponents want?

> There is another world "out there," the existence of which the Court, I suspect, either chooses to ignore or fears to recognize. And so the cancer of poverty will continue to grow. This is a sad day for those who regard the Constitution as a force that would serve justice to all evenhandedly and, in so doing, would better the lot of the poorest among us.

In 1965, Congress created the Medicaid program as Title XIX of the Social Security Act to provide federal financial assistance to states that chose to reimburse certain costs of medical treatment for needy persons. Since 1976, Congress has passed various versions of the so-called Hyde Amendment (named for its sponsor in the House) which severely restrict the use of any federal funds to reimburse the cost of abortions under the program. Specifically, the amendment bars the use of federal funds "to perform abortions except where the life of the mother would be endangered if the fetus were carried to term." A more recent version also "except[s] * * * medical procedures necessary for the victims of rape or incest when such rape or incest has been reported promptly to a law enforcement agency or public health service." Plaintiffs, including several indigent pregnant women, brought suit attacking the Hyde Amendment as a violation of the Due Process Clause of the Fifth Amendment and the Religion Clauses of the First Amendment and on grounds that a participating state remains obligated, despite the restriction, to fund all medically necessary abortions. A federal district court rejected any such statutory obligation on the part of the states but held the Hyde Amendment unconstitutional as an infringement of the plaintiffs' First and Fifth Amendment rights, whereupon the Secretary of the Department of Health and Human Services (formerly HEW) appealed.

In Harris v. McRae, 448 U.S. 297, 100 S.Ct. 2671 (1980), the Supreme Court upheld the Hyde Amendment and reversed the district court's award of injunctive relief. Justice Stewart, who spoke for the Court, began by considering the statutory issue. Because the "system of 'cooperative federalism'" reflected in the structure of the Medicaid program made it clear that "the Congress that enacted Title XIX did not intend a participating State to assume a unilateral funding obligation for any health service * * *," he concluded, "* * * Title XIX does not require a participating State to pay for those medically necessary abortions for which federal reimbursement is unavailable under the Hyde Amendment." Turning to the constitutional questions, he "address[ed] first the appellees' argument that the Hyde Amendment, by restricting the availability of certain medically necessary abortions under Medicaid, impinges on the 'liberty' protected by the Due Process Clause as recognized in Roe v. Wade, 410 U.S. 113, 93 S.Ct. 705 (1973), and its progeny." After a review of the Court's holdings both in that landmark case and in Maher v. Roe, 432 U.S. 464, 97 S.Ct. 2376 (1977), he explained:

The Hyde Amendment, like the Connecticut welfare regulation at issue in *Maher*, places no governmental obstacle in the path of a woman who chooses to terminate her pregnancy, but rather, by means of unequal subsidization of abortion and other medical services, encourages alternative activity deemed in the public interest. The present case does differ factually from *Maher* insofar as that case involved a failure to fund nontherapeutic abortions, whereas the Hyde Amendment withholds funding of certain medically necessary abortions. Accordingly, the appellees argue that because the Hyde Amendment affects a significant interest not present or asserted in *Maher*—the interest of a woman in protecting her health during pregnancy—and because that interest lies at the core of the personal constitutional freedom recognized in *Wade*, the present case is constitutionally different from *Maher*. It is the appellees' view that to the extent that the Hyde Amendment withholds funding for certain medically necessary abortions, it clearly impinges on the constitutional principle recognized in *Wade*.

While it is clear that *Roe* barred state interference with a woman's decision to abort a fetus in the first trimester of her pregnancy, Justice Stewart concluded:

> [I]t simply does not follow that a woman's freedom of choice carries with it a constitutional entitlement to the financial resources to avail herself of the full range of protected choices. The reason why was explained in *Maher*: although government may not place obstacles in the path of a woman's exercise of her freedom of choice, it need not remove those not of its own creation. Indigency falls in the latter category. The financial constraints that restrict an indigent woman's ability to enjoy the full range of constitutionally protected freedom of choice are the product not of governmental restrictions on access to abortions, but rather of her indigency. Although Congress has opted to subsidize medically necessary services generally, but not certain medically necessary abortions, the fact remains that the Hyde Amendment leaves an indigent woman with at least the same range of choice in deciding whether to obtain a medically necessary abortion as she would have had if Congress had chosen to subsidize no health care costs at all. We are thus not persuaded that the Hyde Amendment impinges on the constitutionally protected freedom of choice recognized in *Wade*.

Justice Stewart dispatched the challenges predicated on the Religion Clauses of the First Amendment by pointing out, on the one hand, "that the fact that the funding restrictions in the Hyde Amendment may coincide with the religious tenets of the Roman Catholic Church does not, without more, contravene the Establishment Clause" and, on the other hand, that "appellees lack standing to raise a free exercise challenge to the Hyde Amendment." Confronting the contention, finally, that the Hyde Amendment "violates the equal protection component of the Fifth Amendment," Justice Stewart concluded that it did not because "it is not predicated on a constitutionally suspect classification." He elaborated:

> It is our view that the present case is indistinguishable from *Maher* in this respect. Here, as in *Maher*, the principal impact of the Hyde Amendment falls on the indigent. But that fact does not itself render the funding restriction constitutionally invalid, for this Court has held repeatedly that poverty, standing alone, is not a suspect classification. See, e.g., James v. Valtierra, 402 U.S. 137, 91 S.Ct. 1331. That *Maher* involved the refusal to fund nontherapeutic abortions, whereas the present case involves the refusal to fund medically necessary abortions, has no bearing on the factors that render a classification "suspect" within the meaning of the constitutional guarantee of equal protection.

Absent the necessity for strict scrutiny, then, the Hyde Amendment has only to be "rationally related to a legitimate governmental objective." "By subsidizing the medical expenses of indigent women who carry their pregnancies to term while not subsidizing the comparable expenses of women who undergo abortions (except those whose lives are threatened)," the legislation "establishe[s] incentives that make childbirth a more attractive alternative than abortion" and so furthers the legitimate goal of "protecting potential life." It was not irrational for Congress to have chosen this means "because no other procedure [than abortion] involves the purposeful termination of potential life." It is not for the Court, declared Justice Stewart, to sit in judgment about the *wisdom* of such public policy.

In a dissenting opinion in which he also spoke for Justices Marshall and Blackmun, Justice Brennan faulted the majority for its "mischaracterization of the nature of the fundamental right recognized in *Roe* v. *Wade* * * * and its misconception of the manner in which that right is infringed by federal and state legislation withdrawing all funding for medically necessary abortions." He wrote:

> *Roe* v. *Wade* held that the constitutional right to personal privacy encompasses a woman's decision whether or not to terminate her pregnancy. *Roe* and its progeny established that the pregnant woman has a right to be free from state interference with her choice to have an abortion—a right which, at least prior to the end of the first trimester, absolutely prohibits any governmental regulation of that highly personal decision. The proposition for which these cases stand thus is not that the State is under an affirmative obligation to ensure access to abortions for all who may desire them; it is that the State must refrain from wielding its enormous power and influence in a manner that might burden the pregnant woman's freedom to choose whether to have an abortion. The Hyde Amendment's denial of public funds for medically necessary abortions plainly intrudes upon this constitutionally protected decision, for both by design and in affect it serves to coerce indigent pregnant woman to bear children that they would otherwise elect not to have.

> * * * [T]he Hyde Amendment is a transparent attempt by the Legislative Branch to impose the political majority's judgment of the morally acceptable and socially desirable preference on a sensitive and intimate decision that the Constitution entrusts to the individual. Worse yet, the Hyde Amendment does not foist that majoritarian viewpoint with equal measure upon everyone in our Nation, rich and poor alike; rather, it imposes that viewpoint only upon that segment of our society which, because of its position of political powerlessness, is least able to defend its privacy rights from the encroachments of state-mandated morality. The instant legislation thus calls for more exacting judicial review than in most other cases.

> A poor woman in the early stages of pregnancy confronts two alternatives: she may elect either to carry the fetus to term or to have an abortion. In the abstract, of course, this choice is hers alone, and the Court rightly observes that the Hyde Amendment "places no governmental obstacle in the path of a woman who chooses to terminate her pregnancy." * * * But the reality of the situation is that the Hyde Amendment has effectively removed this choice from the indigent woman's hands. By funding all of the expenses associated with childbirth and none of the expenses incurred in terminating pregnancy, the government literally makes an offer that the indigent woman cannot afford to refuse. It matters not that in this instance the government has used the carrot rather than the stick. What is critical is the realization that as a practical matter, many poverty-stricken women will choose to carry their pregnancy to term simply because the government provides funds for the associated medical services, even though these same women would have chosen to have an abortion if the government had also paid for that option, or indeed if the government had stayed out of the picture altogether and had defrayed the costs of neither procedure.

> The fundamental flaw in the Court's due process analysis, then, is its failure to acknowledge that the discriminatory distribution of the benefits of governmental largesse can discourage the exercise of fundamental liberties just as effectively as can an outright denial of those rights through criminal and regulatory sanctions. Implicit in the Court's reasoning is the notion that as long as the government is not obligated to provide its citizens

with certain benefits or privileges, it may condition the grant of such benefits on the recipient's relinquishment of his constitutional rights.

* * *

* * * Here * * * the government withholds financial benefits in
a manner that discourages the exercise of a due process liberty: The indigent woman who chooses to assert her constitutional right to have an abortion can do so only on pain of sacrificing health care benefits to which she
would otherwise be entitled. * * *

Justice Marshall in a separate dissent added a protest to what he regarded as
"perhaps the most dramatic illustration to date of the deficiencies of the Court's
obsolete 'two-tiered' approach to the Equal Protection Clause." He went on forcefully to point out that "[t]he class burdened by the Hyde Amendment consists of
indigent women, a substantial proportion of whom are members of minority
races" such that "nonwhite women obtain abortions at nearly double the rate of
whites." Justice Marshall emphasized that he "continue[s] to believe that 'a showing that state action has a devastating impact on the lives of minority racial
groups must be relevant' for purposes of equal protection analysis."

Beginning from the premise that "[w]hen the sovereign provides a special benefit or a special protection for a class of persons, it must define the membership in
the class by neutral criteria; it may not make special exceptions for reasons that
are constitutionally insufficient," Justice Stevens, dissenting separately, reasoned:

The question is whether certain persons who satisfy those criteria may be
denied access to benefits solely because they must exercise the constitutional right to have an abortion in order to obtain the medical care they
need. Our prior cases plainly dictate the answer to that question.

A fundamentally different question was decided in Maher v. Roe, 432
U.S. 464, 97 S.Ct. 2376. Unlike these plaintiffs, the plaintiffs in *Maher* did
not satisfy the neutral criterion of medical need; they sought a subsidy for
nontherapeutic abortions—medical procedures which by definition they did
not need. In rejecting that claim, the Court held that their constitutional
right to choose that procedure did not impose a duty on the State to subsidize the exercise of that right. Nor did the fact that the State had undertaken to pay for the necessary medical care associated with childbirth
require the State also to pay for abortions that were not necessary; for
only necessary medical procedures satisfied the neutral statutory criteria.
Nontherapeutic abortions were simply outside the ambit of the medical benefits program. Thus, in *Maher*, the plaintiffs' desire to exercise a constitutional right gave rise to neither special access nor special exclusion from the
pool of benefits created by Title XIX.

This case involves a special exclusion of women who, by definition, are
confronted with a choice between two serious harms: serious health damage to themselves on the one hand and abortion on the other. The competing interests are the interest in maternal health and the interest in
protecting potential human life. It is now part of our law that the pregnant
woman's decision as to which of these conflicting interests shall prevail is
entitled to constitutional protection.

He noted that in *Roe* v. *Wade*, "the Court held that a woman's freedom to elect to
have an abortion prior to viability has absolute constitutional protection, subject
only to valid health regulations." "Indeed," he pointed out, "the Court held that

even after viability, a State may 'regulate, and even proscribe, abortion *except where it is necessary, in appropriate medical judgment, for the preservation of the life or health of the mother.'* " Declaring that "we have a duty to respect that holding" and that "[t]he Court shirks that duty in this case," he continued:

If a woman has a constitutional right to place a higher value on avoiding either serious harm to her own health or perhaps an abnormal childbirth than on protecting potential life, the exercise of that right cannot provide the basis for the denial of a benefit to which she would otherwise be entitled. The Court's sterile equal protection analysis evades this critical though simple point. The Court focuses exclusively on the "legitimate interest in protecting the potential life of the fetus." * * * It concludes that since the Hyde amendments further that interest, the exclusion they create is rational and therefore constitutional. But it is misleading to speak of the Government's legitimate interest in the fetus without reference to the context in which that interest was held to be legitimate. For *Roe* v. *Wade* squarely held that the States may not protect that interest when a conflict with the interest in a pregnant woman's health exists. It is thus perfectly clear that neither the Federal Government nor the States may exclude a woman from medical benefits to which she would otherwise be entitled solely to further an interest in potential life when a physician, "in appropriate medical judgment," certifies that an abortion is necessary "for the preservation of the life or health of the mother." * * * The Court totally fails to explain why this reasoning is not dispositive here.

* * *

Having decided to alleviate some of the hardships of poverty by providing necessary medical care, the Government must use neutral criteria in distributing benefits. It may not deny benefits to a financially and medically needy person simply because he is a Republican, a Catholic, or an Oriental—or because he has spoken against a program the Government has a legitimate interest in furthering. In sum, it may not create exceptions for the sole purpose of furthering a governmental interest that is constitutionally subordinate to the individual interest that the entire program was designed to protect. The Hyde amendments not only exclude financially and medically needy persons from the pool of benefits for a constitutionally insufficient reason; they also require the expenditure of millions and millions of dollars in order to thwart the exercise of a constitutional right, thereby effectively inflicting serious and long lasting harm on impoverished women who want and need abortions for valid medical reasons. In my judgment, these amendments constitute an unjustifiable, and indeed blatant, violation of the sovereign's duty to govern impartially.

PEOPLE v. ONOFRE

Court of Appeals of New York, 1980
51 N.Y.2d 476, 434 N.Y.S.2d 947, 415 N.E.2d 936

Ronald Onofre was convicted of violating § 130.38 of the New York State Penal Code which punished consensual sodomy after he admitted engaging in acts of what the statute defined as "deviate sexual intercourse" in his home with another male. He attacked the constitutionality of the statute on grounds that it infringed his right to privacy by criminalizing sexual acts between consenting adults and denied him equal protection of the laws by exempting from any criminal sanction acts of "deviate sexual conduct" between persons married to each other. An intermediate state appellate court reversed the trial court and declared the statute

unconstitutional, and, in the opinion which follows, the New York Court of Appeals affirmed that judgment. Five months later, the U. S. Supreme Court denied certiorari, 451 U.S. 987, 101 S.Ct. 2323 (1981).

The conclusions drawn by the New York Court of Appeals were quite different from those reached by a divided three-judge federal district court in Doe v. Commonwealth's Attorney for City of Richmond, 403 F.Supp. 1199 (E.D.Va.1975). Responding to a suit brought by two adult males who challenged the constitutionality of Virginia's sodomy statute as it applied to punish consensual homosexual relations in private, the federal court denied the declaratory and injunctive relief sought. The majority reasoned that *Griswold* protected only privacy inhering in the marital relationship and concluded that the statute reflected a "rationally supportable" decision about public policy properly for the legislature and not the courts to determine. The U. S. Supreme Court affirmed the judgment of the district court without argument or opinion, 425 U.S. 901, 96 S.Ct. 1489 (1976). Justices Brennan, Marshall, and Stevens, however, voted to note probable jurisdiction and set the case for oral argument.

By also denying certiorari in *Onofre* without offering any explanation, the Court appears to have let stand two squarely contradictory decisions. Speaking for the New York Court of Appeals in the opinion below, Judge Jones addresses this conflict and attempts to harmonize the two decisions. But explanations of this sort notwithstanding, many observers have criticized the Court for what they see as its persistent pattern of ducking cases involving the rights of gays. In fact, some of that criticism has come from within the Court.[a] Dissenting from a decision to deny certiorari in a case involving the right of a homosexual organization to recognition on campus, Justice Rehnquist wrote: "Unlike * * * [lower federal courts], Congress has accorded to us through the Judiciary Act of 1925, 28 U.S.C.A. § 1254, the discretion to decline to hear a case such as this on the merits without explaining our reasons for doing so. But the existence of such discretion does not imply that it should be used as a sort of judicial storm cellar to which we may flee to escape from controversial or sensitive cases." Ratchford v. Gay Lib, 434 U.S. 1080, 1081, 98 S.Ct. 1276, 1277 (1978).

One explanation for the seeming inability of the Court to muster the four votes necessary to grant certiorari in such cases is that neither the two Justices who are most likely to favor expansion of constitutional rights nor the two Justices most likely to uphold restrictions on them are willing to risk a possibly adverse decision. Justices Brennan and Marshall may prefer to accept the existing contradiction in decisions below rather than risk a final resolution that might curtail civil liberties. Chief Justice Burger and Justice Rehnquist, on the other hand, may not be sure they have the votes necessary to once and for all overturn expansive constitutional rulings handed down by lower courts. The other five members of the Court may simply have decided not to become involved because rulings on gay rights are likely to put the Court in a no-win position.[b]

OPINION OF THE COURT

JONES, Judge.

These appeals, argued together, present a common question—viz., whether the provision of our State's Penal Law that makes consensual sodomy a crime is violative of rights protected by the United States Constitution. We hold that it is.

* * *

---

a. Morton Mintz, "The Supreme Court: Remaining Silent on Homosexual Rights," *Washington Post*, Dec. 11, 1979, p. A3.

b. Ibid.

* * * Because the statutes are broad enough to reach noncommercial, cloistered personal sexual conduct of consenting adults and because it permits the same conduct between persons married to each other without sanction, we agree with defendants' contentions that it violates both their right of privacy and the right to equal protection of the laws guaranteed them by the United States Constitution.

As to the right of privacy. At the outset it should be noted that the right addressed in the present context is not, as a literal reading of the phrase might suggest, the right to maintain secrecy with respect to one's affairs or personal behavior; rather, it is a right of independence in making certain kinds of important decisions, with a concomitant right to conduct oneself in accordance with those decisions, undeterred by governmental restraint—what we referred to in People v. Rice, 41 N.Y.2d 1018, 1019, 395 N.Y.S.2d 626, 363 N.E.2d 1371 as "freedom of conduct." * * *

* * *

The People are in no disagreement that a fundamental right of personal decision exists; the divergence of the parties focuses on what subjects fall within its protection, the People contending that it extends to only two aspects of sexual behavior—marital intimacy (by virtue of the Supreme Court's decision in Griswold v. Connecticut, 381 U.S. 479, 85 S.Ct. 1678) and procreative choice (by reason of Eisenstadt v. Baird, 405 U.S. 438, 92 S.Ct. 1029 and Roe v. Wade, 410 U.S. 113, 93 S.Ct. 705). Such a stance fails however adequately to take into account the decision in Stanley v. Georgia, 394 U.S. 557, 89 S.Ct. 1243 and the explication

of the right of privacy contained in the court's opinion in *Eisenstadt.* In *Stanley* the court found violative of the individual's right to be free from governmental interference in making important, protected decisions a statute which made criminal the possession of obscene matter within the privacy of the defendant's home. Although the material itself was entitled to no protection against government proscription * * * the defendant's choice to seek sexual gratification by viewing it and the effectuation of that choice within the bastion of his home, removed from the public eye, was held to be blanketed by the constitutional right of privacy. That the right enunciated in Griswold v. Connecticut, 381 U.S. 479, 85 S.Ct. 1678, to make decisions with respect to the consequence of sexual encounters and, necessarily, to have such encounters, was not limited to married couples was made clear by the language of the court in Eisenstadt v. Baird, 405 U.S. 438, 453, 92 S.Ct. 1029, 1038: "It is true that in *Griswold* the right of privacy in question inhered in the marital relationship. Yet the marital couple is not an independent entity with a mind and heart of its own, but an association of two individuals each with a separate intellectual and emotional makeup. If the right of privacy means anything, it is the right of the *individual,* married or single, to be free from unwarranted governmental intrusion into matters so fundamentally affecting a person as the decision whether to bear or beget a child. See Stanley v. Georgia, 394 U.S. 557, 89 S.Ct. 1243 (1969)." * * *

In light of these decisions, protecting under the cloak of the right of privacy individual decisions as to indulgence in acts of sexual intimacy by unmarried persons and as to satisfaction of sexual desires by resort to material condemned as obscene by community standards when done in a cloistered setting, no rational basis appears for excluding from the same protection decisions—such as those made by defendants before us—to seek sexual gratification from what at least once was commonly regarded as "deviant" conduct,[3] so long as the decisions are voluntarily made by adults in a noncommercial, private setting. Nor is any such basis supplied by the claims advanced by the prosecution—that a prohibition against consensual sodomy will prevent physical harm which might otherwise befall the participants, will uphold public morality and will protect the institution of marriage. Commendable though these objectives clearly are, there is nothing on which to base a conclusion that they are achieved by section 130.38 of the Penal Law. No showing has been made, even in references tendered in the briefs that physical injury is a common or even occasional consequence of the prohibited conduct, and there has been no demonstration ei-

ther that this is a danger presently addressed by the statute or was one apprehended at the time the statutory section was enacted contemporaneously with the adoption of the new Penal Law in 1965. Indeed, the proposed comprehensive penal statute submitted to the Legislature by the Temporary Commission on Revision of the Penal Law and Criminal Code dropped all proscription against private acts of consensual sodomy. That the enactment of section 130.38 of the Penal Law was prompted by something other than fear for the physical safety of participants in consensual sodomy is suggested by the statement contained in the memorandum prepared by the chairman of the Temporary Commission: "It would appear that the Legislature's decision to restore the consensual sodomy offense was, as with adultery, based largely upon the premises that deletion thereof might ostensibly be construed as legislative approval of deviate conduct" (N.Y.Legis.Ann., 1965, pp. 51–52).

Any purported justification for the consensual sodomy statute in terms of upholding public morality is

---

3. We express no view as to any theological, moral or psychological evaluation of consensual sodomy. These are aspects of the issue on which informed, competent authorities and individuals may and do differ. Contrary to the view expressed by the dissent, although on occasion it does serve such ends, it is not the function of the Penal Law in our governmental policy to provide either a medium for the articulation or the apparatus for the intended enforcement of moral or theological values. Thus, it has been deemed irrelevant by the United States Supreme Court that the purchase and use of contraceptives by unmarried persons would arouse moral indignation among broad segments of our community or that the viewing of pornographic materials even within the privacy of one's home would not evoke general approbation (Eisenstadt v. Baird, 405 U.S. 438, 92 S.Ct. 1029; Stanley v.

Georgia, 394 U.S. 557, 89 S.Ct. 1243). We are not unmindful of the sensibilities of many persons who are deeply persuaded that consensual sodomy is evil and should be prohibited. That is not the issue before us. The issue before us is whether, assuming that at least at present it is the will of the community (as expressed in legislative enactment) to prohibit consensual sodomy, the Federal Constitution permits recourse to the sanctions of the criminal law for the achievement of that objective. The community and its members are entirely free to employ theological teaching, moral suasion, parental advice, psychological and psychiatric counseling and other noncoercive means to condemn the practice of consensual sodomy. The narrow question before us is whether the Federal Constitution permits the use of the criminal law for that purpose.

belied by the position reflected in the *Eisenstadt* decision in which the court carefully distinguished between public dissemination of what might have been considered inimical to public morality and individual recourse to the same material out of the public arena and in the sanctum of the private home. There is a distinction between public and private morality and the private morality of an individual is not synonymous with nor necessarily will have effect on what is known as public morality (see State v. Saunders, 75 N.J. 200, 218–220, 381 A.2d 333). So here, the People have failed to demonstrate how government interference with the practice of personal choice in matters of intimate sexual behavior out of view of the public and with no commercial component will serve to advance the cause of public morality or do anything other than restrict individual conduct and impose a concept of private morality chosen by the State.

Finally, the records and the written and oral arguments of the District Attorneys as well are devoid of any support for the statement that a prohibition against consensual sodomy will promote or protect the institution of marriage, venerable and worthy as is that estate. Certainly there is no suggestion that the one is a substitute or alternative for the other nor is any empirical data submitted which demonstrates that marriage is nothing more than a refuge for persons deprived by legislative fiat of the option of consensual sodomy outside the marital bond.

In sum, there has been no showing of any threat, either to participants or the public in general, in consequence of the voluntary engagement by adults in private, discreet, sodomous conduct. Absent is the factor of commercialization with the attendant evils commonly attached to the retailing of sexual pleasures; absent the elements of force or of involvement of minors which might constitute compulsion of unwilling participants or of those too young to make an informed choice, and absent too intrusion on the sensibilities of members of the public, many of whom would be offended by being exposed to the intimacies of others. Personal feelings of distaste for the conduct sought to be proscribed by section 130.38 of the Penal Law and even disapproval by a majority of the populace, if that disapproval were to be assumed, may not substitute for the required demonstration of a valid basis for intrusion by the State in an area of important personal decision protected under the right of privacy drawn from the United States Constitution—areas, the number and definition of which have steadily grown but, as the Supreme Court has observed, the outer limits of which it has not yet marked.

The assertion in the dissent that validation of the consensual sodomy statute is mandated by our recent decision in People v. Shepard, 50 N.Y.2d 640, 431 N.Y.S.2d 363, 409 N.E.2d 840 proceeds from a misconception of our holding in *Shepard*. In that case we upheld the constitutionality of the statutory proscription against the possession of marihuana as applied to possession by an individual in the privacy of his home, noting the existence of a legitimate controversy with respect to whether marihuana is a dangerous substance. The concurring opinion assembled the impressive evidence of the harmfulness which attends the use of marihuana. On such a record we sustained the right of the Legislature to reach the substantive conclusion that the use of marihuana was indeed harmful and accordingly to impose a criminal proscription based on that predicate. There is in the present case no basis for a counterpart to the statement in *Shepard* that "the Legislature, following extensive studies and hearings, has specifically found the drug to be sufficiently harmful to warrant punishing its possession in an effort to deter its use." * * * By critical contrast neither the People nor the dissent has cited any authority or evidence for the proposition that the practice of consensual sodomy in private is harmful either to the participants or to society in general; indeed, the dissent's appeal is only to the historical, conventional characterization which attached to the practice of sodomy. It surely does not follow that, because it is constitutionally permissible to enter the privacy of an individual's home to regulate conduct justifiably found to be harmful to him, the Legislature may also intrude on such privacy to regulate individual conduct where no basis has been shown for concluding that the conduct is harmful.

As to the denial of defendants' right to equal protection. Section 130.38 of the Penal Law on its face discriminates between married and unmarried persons, making criminal when done by the latter what is innocent when done by the former. With that distinction drawn, we look to see whether there is, as a minimum, "some ground of difference that rationally explains the different treatment accorded married and unmarried persons" under the statute (Eisenstadt v. Baird, 405 U.S. 438, 447, 92 S.Ct. 1029, 1035). In our view, none has been demonstrated or identified by the People in any of the cases before us. In fact, the only justifications suggested are a societal interest in protecting and nurturing the institution of marriage and what are termed "rights accorded married persons." As has been indicated, however, no showing has been made as to how, or even that, the statute banning consensual sodomy between persons not married to each other preserves or fosters marriage. Nor is there any suggestion how consensual sodomy relates to rights accorded married persons; certainly it is not evident how it adversely affects any such rights. Thus, even if it be assumed that the objectives tendered by the prosecution are legitimate matters of public concern, no relationship—much less rational relationship—between those objectives and the proscription of section 130.38 of the Penal Law is manifested. The statute therefore must fall as violative of the right to equal protection enjoyed by persons not married to each other.

Little more need be said to dispose of the contention made by the District Attorneys that the statute is a valid exercise of the police power vested in the State, which power, it is asserted, is authorized for the prevention of harm or for the preservation of public morality. No substantial prospect of harm from consensual sodomy nor any threat to public—as opposed to private—morality has been shown.

Finally, we do not plow new ground in the result we reach today. Most recently, the Supreme Court of Pennsylvania, for some of the same reasons that underlie our decision, has reached a similar conclusion even in a case in which the defendants were charged with commission of deviant acts of sexual conduct with members of the audience at performances in a public theatre for which an admission fee had been charged Commonwealth v. Bonadio, 490 Pa. 91, 415 A.2d 47. Also consistent with the result we reach are the decisions by the Iowa Supreme Court in State v. Pilcher, 242 N.W.2d 348 [Iowa] and by the New Jersey Superior Court in State v. Ciuffini, 164 N.J. Super. 145, 395 A.2d 904, relying on the earlier case of State v. Saunders, 75 N.J. 200, 381 A.2d 333, supra in which its Supreme Court had invalidated as contrary to the constitutionally protected right of privacy a statute making fornication a criminal offense. Nor is any contrary result compelled by Doe v. Commonwealth's Attorney for City of Richmond, D.C., 403 F.Supp. 1199, affd. 425 U.S. 901, 96 S.Ct. 1489, a civil action in which prayers for a declaratory judgment invalidating an injunction precluding prosecution under a Virginia sodomy statute which expressly included consensual sodomy, were denied. Although the District Court in its opinion addressed the constitutionality of the statute and concluded that it was not invalid, its disposition included no declaration of constitutionality, but merely denied the relief requested and dismissed the complaint. A summary affirmance of the dismissal without declaration followed in the United States Supreme Court. In that circumstance the disposition by the Supreme Court does not necessarily signify approval of the reasoning by which the lower court resolved the case. * * * Apart from the limited precedential value of a summary affirmance * * * in Doe there was lacking any evidence of threatened prosecution of the plaintiffs under the Virginia statute—a factor arguably relevant to their standing to maintain the action. * * * Thus,

the affirmance by the Supreme Court of the District Court's dismissal of the action may have been predicated on a lack of standing on the part of plaintiffs. Subsequent to the decision of the Doe case a member of that court stated that the court had not yet "definitively answered the difficult question whether and to what extent the Constitution prohibits state statutes regulating such behavior (private consensual sexual behavior) among adults" (Carey v. Population Servs. Int., 431 U.S. 678, 694, n. 17, 97 S.Ct. 2010, 2021 n. 17 [opn. by Brennan, J., concurred in by a plurality]).

That difficult question, to the extent that it is posed by these appeals, is before us now. For the reasons given above, we conclude that the imposition of criminal sanctions such as those contained in section 130.38 of the Penal Law is proscribed by the Constitution of the United States.

* * *

GABRIELLI, Judge (dissenting).

* * *

I begin with the premise that none of the cases relied upon by the majority stand for the proposition that there is a generalized right of privacy or personal autonomy implicit in the Federal Bill of Rights. Nor do the cases cited in the majority opinion provide support for the idea that the courts may invoke the due process clause of the Fourteenth Amendment as a predicate for striking down penal provisions which some members of the judiciary may find distasteful or inconsistent with their own notions of fundamental fairness. Indeed, were that not the case, we could not have held as we recently did in People v. Shepard, 50 N.Y.2d 640, 431 N.Y.S.2d 363, 409

N.E.2d 840 that the statutory ban on the private possession of marihuana (see Penal Law § 220.03) is not an unconstitutional infringement of the right of an individual to do as he pleases in his own home. To the contrary, had we concluded in *Shepard* as the majority seems to have concluded in this case that the freedom to choose one's own form of sensory gratification within the confines of one's own home is a constitutionally protected "fundamental" right, we could not have sustained the statute at issue in that case on the basis of mere "rationality," but would instead have been duty bound to conduct a more searching inquiry to determine whether the State's interest in the legislative ban was truly "compelling" (see, e.g., Roe v. Wade, 410 U.S. 113, 93 S.Ct. 705, Shapiro v. Thompson, 394 U.S. 618, 89 S.Ct. 1322, Griswold v. Connecticut, 381 U.S. 479, 85 S.Ct. 1678).

Arguing that the People have failed to demonstrate that individuals who engage in consensual acts of sodomy are likely to suffer any serious physical side effects, the majority has attempted to distinguish the statutory prohibition at issue in *Shepard* from that at issue in this case by stressing that the ban which we upheld in *Shepard* was justified by a rational legislative finding that marihuana use can be physically harmful. * * * This assertion, however, represents a seriously flawed understanding of the inquiry that must be pursued in identifying such rights.

* * *

Under the analysis utilized by the majority, *all* private, consensual conduct would necessarily involve the exercise of a constitutionally protected "fundamental right" unless the conduct in question jeopardizes the physical health of the participant. In effect, the majority has held that a State statute regulating private conduct will not pass constitutional muster if it is not designed to prevent physical harm to the individual. Such an analysis, however, can only be based upon an unnecessarily restrictive view of the scope of the State's power to regulate the conduct of its citizens. In my view, the so-called "police powers" of the State must include the right of the State to regulate the moral conduct of its citizens and "to maintain a decent society" (Jacobellis v. Ohio, 378 U.S. 184, 199, 84 S.Ct. 1676, 1684, quoted in Paris Adult Theatre I v. Slaton, 413 U.S. 49, 59–60, 93 S.Ct. 2628, 2635–36). Indeed, without mentioning specific provisions, it is apparent that our State's penal code represents, in part, an expression of our society's collective view as to what is or is not morally acceptable conduct. And, although the Legislature may not exercise this power in a manner that would impair a constitutionally protected "fundamental right," it begs the question to suggest, as the majority has, that such a right is necessarily involved whenever the State seeks to regulate conduct pursuant only to its interest in the moral well-being of its citizenry.

We may avoid the circularity in the majority's reasoning in cases such as this only if we utilize a two-tiered approach, taking care to ascertain at the outset whether a "fundamental right" is actually implicated without regard to the nature of the governmental interest involved in the challenged statute. If no such right is found to exist, we must refrain from interfering with the choice made by the Legislature and rest content upon the assurance that when the challenged statute is no longer palatable to the moral sensibilities of a majority of our State's citizens, it will simply be repealed.

Although our decision to sustain the statute challenged in *Shepard* under settled principles of judicial restraint would seem dispositive of the issue in this case, the majority has nonetheless adopted a contrary view and has placed the claim of personal autonomy asserted by defendants in the category of those ill-defined fundamental rights which are protected by the "penumbras" emanating from the Bill of Rights (Griswold v. Connecticut, supra, 381 U.S. at pp. 484–485, 85 S.Ct. at pp. 1681–1682) and by the concept of ordered liberty implicit in the due process clause of the Fourteenth Amendment (Roe v. Wade, supra, 410 U.S. at pp. 152–153, 93 S.Ct. at p. 726). I cannot agree, however, that the right of an individual to select his own form of sexual gratification should stand on any better footing than does the right of an individual to choose his own brand of intoxicant without governmental interference. Admittedly, the issue in this case is superficially distinguishable from the issue in *Shepard*, in that here we are concerned with a claim involving freedom of sexual expression, and it is therefore tempting to equate the "right" asserted by defendants with other well-established sexually related rights such as the right of an individual to obtain contraceptives (Griswold v. Connecticut, supra), the right of a woman to terminate an unwanted pregnancy (Roe v. Wade, supra; see Doe v. Bolton, 410 U.S. 179, 93 S.Ct. 739) and the right of a citizen to consume printed pornographic material in the privacy of his own home (Stanley v. Georgia, 394 U.S. 557, 89 S.Ct. 1243). But the decisions in

Griswold, Roe and *Stanley* cannot fairly be interpreted as collectively establishing an undifferentiated right to unfettered sexual expression. * * * Consequently, the majority's effort to justify its holding today as a mere extension of these decisions is, in the final analysis, entirely unconvincing.

The "fundamental" rights recognized in *Griswold, Roe* and their progeny are clearly not a product of a belief on the part of the Supreme Court that modern values and changing standards of morality should be incorporated wholesale into the due process clause of the Fourteenth Amendment. To the contrary, the language of the Supreme Court decisions makes clear that the rights which have so far been recognized as part of our due process guarantee are those rights to make certain familial decisions which have been considered sacrosanct and immune from governmental intrusion throughout the history of western civilization. * * *

This is not to suggest that the Federal Constitution protects only those sexually related decisions that are made within the context of the marital relationship. As the majority notes, such a conclusion was effectively foreclosed when the Supreme Court stated in Eisenstadt v. Baird, 405 U.S. 438, 453, 92 S.Ct. 1029, 1038, supra: "It is true that in *Griswold* the right of privacy in question inhered in the marital relationship. Yet the marital couple is not an independent entity with a mind and heart of its own, but an association of two individuals each with a separate intellectual and emotional makeup. If the right of privacy means anything, it is the right of the *individual*, married or single, to be free from unwarranted governmen-

tal intrusion into matters so fundamentally affecting a person as the
decision whether to bear or beget a
child" (emphasis in original).

Nevertheless, contrary to the position taken by the majority, I cannot
agree that this language foreshadows a recognition by the Supreme
Court of a generalized right to complete sexual freedom for all adults,
whether married or single. Instead,
as is suggested by the careful wording of the quoted paragraph, I would
conclude that *Eisenstadt* stands only
for the narrower proposition that the
ancient and "fundamental" right of
an individual to decide "whether to
bear or beget a child" cannot be limited to married adults. * * * Under this view, *Eisenstadt* may be regarded as a simple extension of a
long line of cases protecting "freedom of personal choice in matters of
marriage *and family life*" (Roe v.
Wade, 410 U.S. 113, 169, 93 S.Ct.
705, 734, supra [Stewart, J., concurring; emphasis supplied]; see Loving
v. Virginia, 388 U.S. 1, 87 S.Ct. 1817
[personal decisions relating to mar-
riage]; Prince v. Massachusetts, 321
U.S. 158, 64 S.Ct. 438 [decisions relating to family relationships]; Skinner v. Oklahoma, 316 U.S. 535, 62
S.Ct. 1110 [decisions relating to pro-
creation]; Pierce v. Society of Sisters, 268 U.S. 510, 45 S.Ct. 571; Meyer v. Nebraska, 262 U.S. 390, 43 S.Ct.
625 [decisions relating to childbearing and education]). Indeed, even
the highly controversial decision in
Roe v. Wade (supra) holding the freedom of women to obtain abortions to
be a constitutionally protected right
may be regarded as part of the continuum of cases that bring within the
ambit of the due process clause those
familial decisions that historically
have enjoyed immunity from governmental regulation. As the *Roe* court

was careful to point out: "It perhaps
is not generally appreciated that the
restrictive criminal abortion laws in
effect in a majority of States today
are of relatively recent vintage.
Those laws, generally proscribing
abortion or its attempt at any time
during pregnancy except when necessary to preserve the pregnant woman's life, are not of ancient or even
of common-law origin. Instead, they
derive from statutory changes effected, for the most part, in the latter
half of the 19th century." * * *

The majority impliedly recognizes
that the Supreme Court has to date
limited the protection of the Constitution to decisions relating to the traditionally protected areas of family
life, marital intimacy and procreation. Yet the majority has also concluded that there exists "no rational
basis * * * for excluding from
the same protection decisions
* * * to seek sexual gratification
from what at least once was commonly regarded as 'deviant' conduct." * * * I must disagree,
however, because my reading of the
recent Supreme Court cases leads me
to the conclusion that the distinction
repeatedly drawn in those cases between freedom of choice in the historically insulated areas of procreation, family life and marital
relationships on the one hand and the
general freedom of unfettered sexual
choice on the other is more than just
a temporary or artificial one.

The assertion that the theories espoused in *Griswold*, *Roe* and their
progeny may be likened to the discredited doctrine of "substantive due
process" (see, e.g., Coppage v. Kansas, 236 U.S. 1, 35 S.Ct. 240; Lochner v. New York, 198 U.S. 45, 25
S.Ct. 539; Allgeyer v. Louisiana, 165
U.S. 578, 17 S.Ct. 427 * * *)
would not come as a surprise to any

serious constitutional scholar. Many have made the observation that the modern notion of "fundamental rights" bears a striking resemblance to the *Lochner* doctrine under which State economic and social regulations were routinely struck down as violative of certain basic, substantive freedoms that were thought to inhere in the due process clauses of the Fifth and Fourteenth Amendments. * * * The *Lochner* doctrine was ultimately rejected by the Supreme Court, in part because it had placed the court in the position of a "superlegislature" enabling it to use the "vague contours" of the due process clause as a vehicle for striking down State legislation which it found to be inconsistent with its own contemporary views of natural law (Ferguson v. Skrupa, 372 U.S. 726, 83 S.Ct. 1028; accord Williamson v. Lee Opt. Co., 348 U.S. 483, 488, 75 S.Ct. 461, 464; Day-Brite Light. v. Missouri, 342 U.S. 421, 423, 72 S.Ct. 405, 407). Indeed, inherent in the *Lochner* doctrine was the very real danger that a countermajoritarian institution such as the court would impose upon the elected officials of State government its *ad hoc* notions regarding the substantive content of the term "liberty" and would place restrictions upon the States' power to govern over and above those mandated by the specific provisions contained in the body of the Constitution and the Bill of Rights. It was out of a recognition of this danger that the rule of judicial restraint and minimal judicial scrutiny of State legislation was born. * * *

In the wake of *Griswold* and *Roe*, it is no longer an intellectually defensible position to suggest that the once discredited doctrine of "substantive due process" is entirely dead and buried. On the other hand, it is far from clear that those two cases heralded an unqualified return to the days when a Judge acted as "a knight-errant roaming at will in pursuit of his own ideal of beauty or of goodness" (Cardozo, Selected Writings, Nature of the Judicial Process, at p. 164, quoted in People v. Shepard, 50 N.Y.2d 640, 646, 43 N.Y.S.2d 363, 409 N.E.2d 840, supra). As the language of those decisions and their forerunners indicates, the "fundamental" rights so far recognized by the Supreme Court under the modern version of "substantive due process" have been strictly limited to those that may be traced to matters that were traditionally insulated from governmental intrusion. In my view, it is precisely this limitation that differentiates the relatively recent "fundamental right" concept from the long discarded and truly pernicious doctrine enunciated in Lochner v. New York (supra).

To suggest, as the majority does, that the concept of "fundamental rights" should be expanded to include a generalized right to sexual gratification in whatever form would be, in effect, to bring the law of "substantive due process" full circle by eliminating all of its present salutary limitations and restoring it to its former status as a vehicle for lawmaking by judicial fiat. The majority acknowledges in passing that the sexual choice the defendants now assert as a matter of constitutional right was once regarded as "'deviant' conduct" * * * but it erroneously ascribes no legal significance to the fact, relegating it instead to an irrelevant phenomenon of theology and privately held moral beliefs. This rather glib refusal to take account of the historical treatment of consensual sodomy as criminally punishable conduct has left a gaping hole in the majority's analysis.

In contrast to decisions relating to family life, matrimony and procreation, decisions involving pure sexual gratification have been subject to State intervention throughout the history of western civilization. * * * [A]lthough some may take offense at the persistence of the proscriptions against consensual sodomy in our modern law, the fact remains that western man has never been free to pursue his own choice of sexual gratification without fear of State interference. Consequently, it simply cannot be said that such freedom is an integral part of our concept of ordered liberty as embodied in the due process clauses of the Fifth and Fourteenth Amendments.

In view of the continuous and unbroken history of antisodomy laws in the United States, the majority's decision to strike down New York's statute prohibiting consensual sod-

omy can only be regarded as an act of judicial legislation creating a "fundamental right" where none has heretofore existed. As such, today's decision represents a radical departure from cases such as *Griswold* and *Roe*, in which the Supreme Court merely swept aside State laws which impaired or prohibited entirely the free exercise of rights that traditionally had been recognized in western thought as being beyond the reach of government. I cannot concur in the majority's conclusion. * * *

* * *

WACHTLER, FUCHSBERG and MEYER, JJ., concur with JONES, J.

JASEN, J., concurs in result in a separate opinion.

GABRIELLI, J., dissents and votes to reverse in another opinion in which COOKE, C.J., concurs.

In People v. Onofre: Order affirmed.

A canvass of state criminal codes as of January 1, 1983 reveals that, whatever may be the interest of the judiciary in invoking a right of privacy to circumscribe the scope of legitimate state regulation of sexual activities, the state legislatures themselves are enacting widespread reforms. Although the chart below focuses on private, consensual relations between adults of the same sex, state legislative change usually extends in parallel manner to the punishment of fornication and adultery as well. Moreover, many of the same states that have repealed or substantially reduced penalties for what are popularly called "crimes without victims" in the area of sex have also scaled down drug offenses, particularly with respect to the private possession of small amounts of marijuana.

States which have repealed statutes penalizing sexual activities between consenting adults of the same sex and the year in which the state legislature voted repeal	Alaska, 1978 California, 1975 Colorado, 1971 Connecticut, 1969 Delaware, 1972 Hawaii, 1972 Illinois, 1961 Indiana, 1976 Iowa, 1976 Maine, 1975

Repealed statutes (*Cont.*)	Nebraska, 1977 New Hampshire, 1975 New Jersey, 1978 New Mexico, 1975 Ohio, 1972 Oregon, 1971 South Dakota, 1976 Vermont, 1977 Washington, 1975 West Virginia, 1976 Wyoming, 1977
States whose laws punishing sexual relations between consenting adults of the same sex have been declared unconstitutional	New York (People v. Onofre, 51 N.Y.2d 476, 434 N.Y.S.2d 947, 415 N.E.2d 936 [1980]) Pennsylvania (Commonwealth v. Bonadio, 490 Pa. 91, 415 A.2d 47 [1980]) Texas (Baker v. Wade, — F.Supp. — [N.D.Tex.1982])
States which punish sexual activities between consenting adults of the same sex as a misdemeanor (i.e., with a fine and/or confinement in county jail for up to one year) together with the year in which such change was adopted	Arizona, 1977 Arkansas, 1977 Florida, 1971 Kansas, 1969 Kentucky, 1971 Minnesota, 1977 Missouri, 1977 North Dakota, 1973 Utah, 1973 Wisconsin, 1977
States which still punish sexual activities between consenting adults of the same sex as a felony (i.e., by incarceration in state prison for a maximum of beyond one year)	Alabama Georgia Idaho Louisiana Maryland Massachusetts Michigan Mississippi Montana Nevada North Carolina Oklahoma Rhode Island South Carolina Tennessee Virginia

MATTER OF QUINLAN

Supreme Court of New Jersey, 1976
70 N.J. 10, 355 A.2d 647

Joseph Quinlan sought adjudication of his daughter's incompetency following extensive physical damage which left her comatose and, as later described by the court, "in a chronic and persistent 'vegetative' state." He also asked to be appointed guardian of her person and property and proposed that such letters of guardianship, if granted, expressly empower him to discontinue procedures prolonging her life, among other things by disconnecting the respirator. A New Jersey superior court found Karen Ann incompetent and appointed her father as guardian of her property but, finding no authority in law for suspending the life-support measures, refused to appoint him guardian of her person. Instead, the court appointed a third party. Joseph Quinlan appealed to the state supreme court.

The excerpts of the opinion reproduced below focus on the right to privacy as a basis for reversing the superior court's decision as to the appointment of Mr. Quinlan as guardian of Karen Ann's person. For coverage of other constitutional questions raised in this litigation, such as freedom of religion and cruel and unusual punishment, for the opinion of Judge Muir, the trial judge, and for additional commentary, see Dionisopoulos and Ducat, The Right to Privacy: Essays and Cases (1976).

HUGHES, C. J.

THE LITIGATION

The central figure in this tragic case is Karen Ann Quinlan, a New Jersey resident. At the age of 22, she lies in a debilitated and allegedly moribund state at Saint Clare's Hospital in Denville, New Jersey. The litigation has to do, in final analysis, with her life,—its continuance or cessation,—and the responsibilities, rights and duties, with regard to any fateful decision concerning it, of her family, her guardian, her doctors, the hospital, the State through its law enforcement authorities, and finally the courts of justice.

*   *   *

The matter is of transcendent importance, involving questions related to the definition and existence of death, the prolongation of life through artificial means developed by medical technology undreamed of in past generations of the practice of the healing arts; the impact of such durationally indeterminate and artificial life prolongation on the rights of the incompetent, her family and society in general; the bearing of constitutional right and the scope of judicial responsibility, as to the appropriate response of an equity court of justice to the extraordinary prayer for relief of the plaintiff. Involved as well is the right of the plaintiff, Joseph Quinlan, to guardianship of the person of his daughter.

*   *   *

Essentially * * * appealing to the power of equity, and relying on claimed constitutional rights of free exercise of religion, of privacy and of protection against cruel and unusual punishment, Karen Quinlan's father sought judicial authority to withdraw the life-sustaining mechanisms temporarily preserving his daughter's life, and his appointment as guardian of her person to that end. His request was opposed by her doctors, the hospital, the Morris County Prosecutor, the State of New Jersey, and her guardian *ad litem*.

*   *   *

CONSTITUTIONAL AND LEGAL ISSUES

At the outset we note the dual role in which plaintiff comes before the Court. He not only raises, derivatively, what he perceives to be the constitutional and legal rights of his daughter Karen, but he also claims certain rights independently as parent.

Although generally litigant may assert only his own constitutional rights, we have no doubt that plaintiff has sufficient standing to advance both positions.

* * *

The father of Karen Quinlan is certainly no stranger to the present controversy. His interests are real and adverse and he raises questions of surpassing importance. Manifestly, he has standing to assert his daughter's constitutional rights, she being incompetent to do so.

* * *

It is the issue of the constitutional right of privacy that has given us most concern, in the exceptional circumstances of this case. Here a loving parent, *qua* parent and raising the rights of his incompetent and profoundly damaged daughter, probably irreversibly doomed to no more than a biologically vegetative remnant of life, is before the court. He seeks authorization to abandon specialized technological procedures which can only maintain for a time a body having no potential for resumption or continuance of other than a "vegetative" existence.

* * *

We have no hesitancy in deciding * * * that no external compelling interest of the State could compel Karen to endure the unendurable, only to vegetate a few measurable months with no realistic possibility of returning to any semblance of cognitive or sapient life. We perceive no thread of logic distinguishing between such a choice on Karen's part and a similar choice which, under the evidence in this case, could be made by a competent patient terminally ill, riddled by cancer and suffering great pain; such a patient would not be resuscitated or put on a respirator * * * and *a fortiori* would not be kept *against his will* on a respirator.

Although the Constitution does not explicitly mention a right of privacy, Supreme Court decisions have recognized that a right of personal privacy exists and that certain areas of privacy are guaranteed under the Constitution. Eisenstadt v. Baird, 405 U.S. 438, 92 S.Ct. 1029 (1972); Stanley v. Georgia, 394 U.S. 557, 89 S.Ct. 1243 (1969). The Court has interdicted judicial intrusion into many aspects of personal decision, sometimes basing this restraint upon the conception of a limitation of judicial interest and responsibility, such as with regard to contraception and its relationship to family life and decision. Griswold v. Connecticut, 381 U.S. 479, 85 S.Ct. 1678 (1965).

The Court in *Griswold* found the unwritten constitutional right of privacy to exist in the penumbra of specific guarantees of the Bill of Rights "formed by emanations from those guarantees that help give them life and substance." 381 U.S. at 484, 85 S.Ct. at 1681. Presumably this right is broad enough to encompass a patient's decision to decline medical treatment under certain circumstances, in much the same way as it is broad enough to encompass a woman's decision to terminate pregnancy under certain conditions. Roe v. Wade, 410 U.S. 113, 153, 93 S.Ct. 705, 727 (1973).

Nor is such right of privacy forgotten in the New Jersey Constitution. N.J.Const. (1947), Art. I, par. 1.

The claimed interests of the State in this case are essentially the preservation and sanctity of human life and defense of the right of the physician to administer medical treatment according to his best judgment. In this case the doctors say that removing Karen from the respirator will conflict with their professional judgment. The plaintiff answers that Karen's present treatment serves only a maintenance function; that the respirator cannot cure or improve her condition but at best can only prolong her inevitable slow deterioration and death; and that the interests of the patient, as seen by her surrogate, the guardian, must be evaluated by the court as predominant, even in the face of an opinion *contra* by the present attending physicians. Plaintiff's distinction is significant. The nature of Karen's care and the realistic chances of her recovery are quite unlike those of the patients discussed in many of the cases where treatments were ordered. In many of those cases the medical procedure required (usually a transfusion) constituted a minimal bodily invasion and the chances of recovery and return to functioning life were very good. We think that the State's interest *contra* weakens and the individual's right to privacy grows as the degree of bodily invasion increases and the prognosis dims. Ultimately there comes a point at which the individual's rights overcome the State interest. It is for that reason that we believe Karen's choice, if she were competent to make it, would be vindicated by the law. Her prognosis is extremely poor,—she will never resume cognitive life. And the bodily invasion is very great,—she requires 24 hour intensive nursing care, antibiotics, the assistance of a respirator, a catheter and feeding tube.

Our affirmation of Karen's independent right of choice, however, would ordinarily be based upon her competency to assert it. The sad truth, however, is that she is grossly incompetent and we cannot discern her supposed choice based on the testimony of her previous conversations with friends, where such testimony is without sufficient probative weight. 137 N.J.Super. at 260, 348 A.2d 801. Nevertheless we have concluded that Karen's right of privacy may be asserted on her behalf by her guardian under the peculiar circumstances here present.

If a putative decision by Karen to permit this non-cognitive, vegetative existence to terminate by natural forces is regarded as a valuable incident of her right of privacy, as we believe it to be, then it should not be discarded solely on the basis that her condition prevents her conscious exercise of the choice. The only practical way to prevent destruction of the right is to permit the guardian and family of Karen to render their best judgment, subject to the qualifications hereinafter stated as to whether she would exercise it in these circumstances. If their conclusion is in the affirmative this decision should be accepted by a society the overwhelming majority of whose members would, we think, in similar circumstances, exercise such a choice in the same way for themselves or for those closest to them. It is for this reason that we determine that Karen's right of privacy may be asserted in her behalf, in this respect, by her guardian and family under the particular circumstances presented by this record.

Regarding Mr. Quinlan's right of privacy, we agree with Judge Muir's conclusion that there is no parental constitutional right that would entitle him to a grant of relief *in propria persona.* * * * Insofar as a parental right of privacy has been recognized, it has been in the context of determining the rearing of infants and, as Judge Muir put it, involved "continuing life styles." See

Wisconsin v. Yoder, 406 U.S. 205, 92 S.Ct. 1526 (1972); Pierce v. Society of Sisters, 268 U.S. 510, 45 S.Ct. 571 (1925); Meyer v. Nebraska, 262 U.S. 390, 43 S.Ct. 625 (1923). Karen Quinlan is a 22 year old adult. Her right of privacy in respect of the matter before the Court is to be vindicated by Mr. Quinlan as guardian, as hereinabove determined.

*   *   *

Perhaps * * * [some] confusion * * * stems from mention by some courts of statutory or common law condemnation of suicide as demonstrating the state's interest in the preservation of life. We would see, however, a real distinction between the self-infliction of deadly harm and a self-determination against artificial life support or radical surgery, for instance, in the face of irreversible, painful and certain imminent death. * * *

*   *   *

DECLARATORY RELIEF

We thus arrive at the formulation of the declaratory relief which we have concluded is appropriate to this case. Some time has passed since Karen's physical and mental condition was described to the Court. At that time her continuing deterioration was plainly projected. Since the record has not been expanded we assume that she is now even more fragile and nearer to death than she was then. Since her present treating physicians may give reconsideration to her present posture in the light of this opinion, and since we are transferring to the plaintiff as guardian the choice of the attending physician and therefore other physicians may be in charge of the case who may take a different view from that of

the present attending physicians, we herewith declare the following affirmative relief on behalf of the plaintiff. Upon the concurrence of the guardian and family of Karen, should the responsible attending physicians conclude that there is no reasonable possibility of Karen's ever emerging from her present comatose condition to a cognitive, sapient state and that the life-support apparatus now being administered to Karen should be discontinued, they shall consult with the hospital "Ethics Committee" or like body of the institution in which Karen is then hospitalized. If that consultative body agrees that there is no reasonable possibility of Karen's ever emerging from her present comatose condition to a cognitive, sapient state, the present life-support system may be withdrawn and said action shall be without any civil or criminal liability therefor on the part of any participant, whether guardian, physician, hospital or others. We herewith specifically so hold.

CONCLUSION

We therefore remand this record to the trial court to implement (without further testimonial hearing) the following decisions:

1. To discharge, with the thanks of the Court for his service, the present guardian of the person of Karen Quinlan, Thomas R. Curtin, Esquire, a member of the Bar and an officer of the court.

2. To appoint Joseph Quinlan as guardian of the person of Karen Quinlan with full power to make decisions with regard to the identity of her treating physicians.

We repeat for the sake of emphasis and clarity that upon the concurrence of the guardian and family of

Karen, should the responsible attending physicians conclude that there is no reasonable possibility of Karen's ever emerging from her present comatose condition to a cognitive, sapient state and that the life-support apparatus now being administered to Karen should be discontinued, they shall consult with the hospital "Ethics Committee" or like body of the institution in which Karen is then hospitalized. If that consultative body agrees that there is no reasonable possibility of Karen's ever emerging from her present comatose condition to a cognitive, sapient state, the present life-support system may be withdrawn and said action shall be without any civil or criminal liability therefor on the part of any participant, whether guardian, physician, hospital or others.

By the above ruling we do not intend to be understood as implying that a proceeding for judicial declaratory relief is necessarily required for the implementation of comparable decisions in the field of medical practice.

Modified and remanded.

Chapter 13

Freedom of Speech

In the abstract, few of us would deny that freedom of speech is one of the fundamentals of democracy. Almost all of us would agree with Justice Black that "Freedom to speak and write about public questions is as important to the life of our government as is the heart to the human body. In fact, this privilege is the heart of our government. If the heart is weakened, the result is debilitation; if it be stilled, the result is death." Milk Wagon Drivers Union v. Meadowmoor Dairies, 312 U.S. 287, 301, 61 S.Ct. 552, 559 (1941) (dissenting opinion). The First Amendment reflects this sentiment by the use of an absolute: "Congress shall make no law * * * abridging the freedom of speech * * *." But, in reality, we have often taken a different view.

Throughout our history we have ignored or tolerated violations of the principle in the name of order, national security, or some other social goal. We have been vigilant in curbing dangerous, subversive, or libelous expressions which, at a certain time and place, seemed to call for repression. This paradox is undoubtedly a function of man's tendency to, as Robert Dahl notes, "qualify universals in application while leaving them intact in rhetoric." The cause of the paradox lies in the fact that freedom of expression is not the only desirable goal of democratic society.

Individuals in a society prize other values such as order, justice, and equality. Any of these values, may at some time conflict with the principle of free expression. Accommodating all of the varied social interests with freedom of expression necessarily involves drawing boundary lines for free expression. The task is never easy, and the results can never satisfy all concerned.

The alternatives to the process of line drawing are, however, more unpalatable. It is possible to curtail all speech to promote some higher goals. Totalitarianism would be the obvious result. On the other hand, we could grant expression unbridled freedom and thereby open the door to anarchy. Clearly, the middle option, involving compromise as it must, provides the best chance for accommodating all of the competing values sought by those in society.

As you read the cases in this section pay particular attention to the conflicting interests involved in each case. Determine for yourself the value of the competing interests. Should the exercise of expression always prevail? More important, are free speech and governmental regulation always antithetical interests?

a. The Rise and Fall of the "Clear and Present Danger" Test

Despite the numerous possibilities over the course of American history, questions involving the regulation of speech did not find their way to the Court until World War I. The Sedition Act of 1798 provided the most conspicuous instance in our experience of interference with freedom of expression, and yet the Act was never challenged in the Supreme Court. Ten persons were convicted under the Act which made it unlawful to, among other things, publish "false, scandalous, and malicious" writings against the government, Congress, or the President if the publication intended to defame any of them or to promote hatred against them among the people. Upon assuming office, President Jefferson pardoned all persons imprisoned under provisions of the Act, and years later Congress refunded with interest all fines which had been imposed.

By the time a question of curtailing freedom of expression finally reached the Court, it was met by a judiciary which showed little interest in civil liberties. Complicating matters even more was the fact that the original challenges to the curtailment of speech occurred during a time of national emergency. Neither the country nor the Court possessed any burning desire to be watchful of violations to personal rights.

The first and perhaps most significant attempt at establishing a standard for evaluating statutes limiting free speech appeared in 1919 with the creation of the "clear and present danger" doctrine. See *Schenck* v. *United States* (p. 1249). Significantly, in authoring the Court's opinion Justice Holmes paid no regard to the possibility that the right to speak was absolute. The Court disavowed the idea that speech was immune from all restriction. At the outset, then, the absolutist position, later to be held by Justice Black, was rejected in favor of a philosophy of balancing the interests.

Deceptively simple, the "clear and present danger" test rested on the plain assertion that before an utterance could be restricted by government, it must have occurred "in such circumstances or have been of such a nature as to create a clear and present danger" that it would bring about "substantive evils" within the power of government to control. Actually, in formulating the test Holmes adopted long-accepted tenets of criminal attempt and applied them to constitutional law. The similarity between the two doctrines is easily seen if we examine the two-part test contained in the concept. One of the requirements of criminal attempt is that there must be a sizeable risk that a prohibited act would be the result of a specific action. The counterpart to this in the Holmes doctrine is that the circumstances must be such "as to create a clear and present danger that they will bring about the substantive evils that Congress has a right to prevent." Criminal attempt also requires that there must be a specific intent to carry forward the forbidden act. While Holmes did not stress this aspect in his original formulation of the doctrine, it is quite apparent in his dissent in *Abrams* v. *United States* (p. 1251).

In devising the "clear and present danger" test, Holmes was endeavoring to make a distinction which would protect the state from harmful speech and yet give free speech the widest latitude possible. Do you feel he was successful in striking a balance? In considering the question you should examine whether conviction in the *Abrams* case seems clearly wrong as opposed to the outcome in *Schenck*.

Regardless of Holmes's intentions in framing the doctrine, it is obvious that for approximately the next twenty years the Court majority rejected any formula which placed primary emphasis on free speech. This is not to say that "clear and present danger" faded into oblivion. On the contrary, the phrase appeared often in the Court's opinions, but the Court of this period used it as a conclusion rather than a test. "Clear and present danger" became the peg onto which the Court's decisions were finally placed after a decision had been reached by other avenues.

This trend is reflected clearly in *Gitlow* v. *New York* (p. 1254). In that case the Court dramatically substituted the "bad tendency" concept in place of the "clear and present danger" test. This same standard was applied again by the Court two years later in *Whitney* v. *California* (p. 1258). The Court announced that it was no longer concerned with the proximity of the speech to the prohibited evil. All that need be shown was that the speech had a tendency, even if it be remote, to advance the prohibited action.

The critical change in direction so apparent here is not solely the result of the majority's disdain for civil liberties issues. Rather it is the natural consequence of the majority's acceptance of judicial self-restraint in regard to civil liberties (to be contrasted, of course, with its activism in vindicating economic liberties). Acting on the basis of self-restraint in this area, the Court was limited to assessing only the reasonableness of the statute at issue. Thus, once certain speech was made illegal by statute, as was the case in *Gitlow*, the Court's only choice was to determine if the statute could have been enacted by reasonable men.

Justice Sanford, speaking for the Court in *Gitlow*, argued that the "clear and present danger" test is applicable in situations where a statute makes certain actions unlawful since the purpose of the test was to determine at what point words become the equivalent of unlawful deeds, but it is not applicable in situations in which the state has previously determined that certain words of incitement are dangerous. In the latter case the Court must defer to the legislature so long as the statute could have been the product of reasonable men's judgment.

Is the majority right in claiming that the question in *Gitlow* was entirely different than that posed by *Schenck*? Does the Holmes dissent in *Gitlow* face this problem squarely? You should notice here that Holmes does not challenge the validity of the New York statute. He merely doubts that Gitlow's action constitutes a violation of the statute. Compare the Holmes dissent in *Gitlow* with Brandeis's concurring opinion in *Whitney*.

The Brandeis concurrence represents an attempt to save the "clear and present danger" test and to inject into it the maximum protection possible by once again emphasizing the proximity of the speech to the prohibited act. Do you feel that by requiring restrictions on free speech to be justified by some emergency Brandeis has provided in the "clear and imminent danger" test an adequate method for evaluating statutes curtailing speech? Has he faced the problem posed by the *Gitlow* majority more successfully than Holmes did in *Gitlow*?

After the Court of the 1920s and 1930s had routinely discounted the "clear and present danger" test, the Court of the 1940s revived and tried to shore up the doctrine. "Clear and present danger" became one element of the preferred freedoms concept as you can see from reading *Thomas* v. *Collins* (p. 53). The appearance of a "bad tendency" was no longer sufficient to justify an infringement on the exercise of speech. The preferred position commanded by speech demanded that the danger be more immediate than that required by the "bad tendency" test. Again, the Court's changing philosophy was the product of an alteration in the Court's composition.

Do you find the preferred freedoms test an adequate safeguard to protect free speech? Why does free speech merit a preferred position? Because of its value to society or because of its value to the individual? Does it make a difference which of these interests is relied upon as the foundation for the preferred freedoms concept?

Before you reach any definite conclusions on the value of the preferred freedoms approach, especially in free speech cases, we suggest that you examine *Terminiello* v. *Chicago* (p. 1260). Are you satisfied with the decision rendered by the Court? Do you have the feeling that the majority may have ignored the very real danger of the situation? Notice Jackson's account of the facts. Consider his insights on how political extremists use constitutional guarantees. Are the values of free speech and governmental regulation necessarily in conflict?

Dissenting in Bridges v. California, 314 U.S. 252, 62 S.Ct. 190 (1941), Justice Frankfurter charged that application of the "clear and present danger" test as embodied in the preferred freedoms concept was an unthinking "recitation of phrases that are the short-hand of a complicated historic process." Is the Court guilty of this in *Terminiello*? Can preferred freedoms become a mechanical approach?

Compare the *Terminiello* case with *Feiner* v. *New York* (p. 1265). Did Feiner present a greater danger than Terminiello, or can the difference in the majority opinions be understood in a different light? Note the composition of the Court in 1951. What are the consequences of the Court's automatic acceptance of the facts of the case in *Feiner* as determined by the trial court?

Clearly *Feiner* marked another turning point in the Court's zeal to protect free speech. Self-restraint again became the majority's guiding light, and greater latitude was given to those who desired to curtail speech. Significantly, the "clear and present danger" test underwent redefinition. The Court's new standard was proclaimed in the lower court by Judge Learned Hand. It is echoed by the majority in the Court's opinion disposing of *Dennis* v. *United States* (p. 1267). Is there any difference between the "clear and probable danger" test devised by Hand and adopted by the Court and the earlier "bad tendency" test?

Consider Chief Justice Vinson's criticism of "clear and present danger" as being limited in application only to isolated events. Would you consider this merely a rationalization for substituting a test more akin to the majority's philosophy, or is it a valid criticism?

Following the *Dennis* case, a majority on the Court persistently declined to formulate a doctrine which would fit all free speech circumstances. Instead the judges appeared to take each case and judge it on its own merits. Justice Harlan succinctly described this process some years later in Noto v. United States, 367 U.S. 290, 81 S.Ct. 1517 (1961), "It need hardly be said that it is upon the particular evidence in a particular record that a particular defendant must be judged, and not upon evidence in some other record or upon what may be supposed to be the tenets of the Communist Party."

Supposedly, this process was at work in *Yates* v. *United States* (p. 1275). Justice Harlan, speaking for the Court, did not use any of the familiar phrases in holding that the Smith Act could only forbid advocacy of the overthrow of the government as it amounted to actual incitement to action. But does *Yates* really seem to be in line with *Dennis*? Despite the lack of reference to "clear and present danger," do you perceive a shift back toward Holmes's formulation?

Consider the further refinement of the Smith Act in *Scales* v. *United States* (p. 1280). It is true that, like most security cases, the Court validated both the conviction and the statute, but the Court read into the Act a stipulation which was not there. Is the requirement of active and purposeful membership akin to showing evidence of "a clear and present danger"? What of *Dennis*? Is *Dennis* still good law?

The Warren Court came to endorse the preferred freedoms approach on speech questions (incorporating as that concept does the element of "clear and present danger") as the binding constitutional standard. Do you find it ironic that, at long last when a majority on the Court was prepared to go this far, the Court's two senior libertarians, Black and Douglas, came to the opposite conclusion about the acceptability of "clear and present danger" as a standard? See *Brandenburg* v. *Ohio* (p. 1283). What would they have replaced the "clear and present danger" test with? Why? Relying on *Brandenburg's* reading of the First Amendment, both in spirit and in word, the Burger Court in *NAACP* v. *Claiborne Hardware Co.* (p.1284) significantly narrowed the possible scope of damages liability for blacks boycotting white-owned commercial establishments in one Mississippi county in a concerted effort to secure equality and racial justice.

It is important for you in reviewing these cases to follow the ups and downs of the "clear and present danger" test and what such a pattern tells you about the relation of the Court's composition to its policy. It is also important for you to consider how much of the Court's difficulty with the "clear and present danger" test was political and how much was the product of the faulty notion that one free speech standard could be used to evaluate regulation in all speech situations. Would it have been more successful, do you think, had the Court formulated alternative tests for dealing with different kinds of speech problems? In order to consider the latter question thoroughly, see Thomas Emerson's excellent article (later published as a book), "Toward a General Theory of the First Amendment," 72 *Yale Law Journal* 877 (1963), as well as the cases which follow in the succeeding portions of this chapter.

b. Free Speech—Where and When

All of the speech cases which have been reviewed so far have dealt with what the Court has labelled "pure speech." But what about other forms of expression such as mass demonstrations and picketing? That such activities mix elements of speech and action complicates our efforts to weigh competing interests when expression by those means collides, for example, with the interest of the public in the free and unobstructed movement of traffic or with the interest of those who own property. How far does the state's obligation to protect citizens from interference with their daily lives empower restriction on this variety of expression? At the least, it is suggested, such kinds of speech are conditioned in their exercise by some considerations of time and place.

During the 1940s the Court settled many questions concerning restrictions on the exercise of free speech in public places. The cases of this period largely involved the activism of Jehovah's Witnesses as they attempted to spread their gospel. The issues in their cases typically revolved around an individual selling pamphlets, soliciting house to house, or speaking on street corners. The Court of the 1960s faced questions of greater magnitude. The Court in these later years was confronted with masses attempting to hold parades and vigils in public places. It became much tougher to argue that the state had an insubstantial interest in restricting the exercise of speech under these circumstances.

Since its decision in Cox v. Louisiana, 379 U.S. 559, 85 S.Ct. 476 (1965), the Court has taken the position that the "clear and present danger" test is not applicable in assessing regulation of this type of speech. The majority in that case rejected the contention that it should be used in judging the applicability of a statute which prohibited obstructing the administration of justice where participants engaged in a mass demonstration held on courthouse grounds. The Court rejected the test because the expression involved was not pure speech. Rather, it was "conduct of a totally different character." Would you agree? Would you regard the use of a balancing test in such cases as acceptable? If so, are there any guidelines you would want to specify in the use of such an approach?

A situation similar to that in the *Cox* case appeared in *Adderley* v. *Florida* (p. 1287). Would you agree with the argument that the state has a very special interest in restricting this type of demonstration in the vicinity of jails? What other kinds of public places do you think are also affected with such a special interest that they should be considered off limits for demonstrations? Is Justice Douglas correct in assuming that the case is the same as if the demonstration had taken place outside of a public building housing both a jail and a legislative body? What do you feel would have been the result had the Court applied the "clear and present danger" test? Would it have necessarily reversed Adderley's conviction? Also, do you perceive a basic difference in the way the majority and the dissenters view the facts? Did the majority ignore the connection between the demonstrators and their selection of the jailhouse as the place for their activities? Or, would you say that the dissenters, by placing an emphasis upon the purposes of the demonstration, attempted to justify the means by the ends to be achieved? Do the circumstances in more recent "public forum" cases (p. 1291) present a clearer case for the need of time, place, and manner restrictions on speech?

It may seem ironic that at about the same time the Court ruled that the right to demonstrate on public property was limited, it recognized a right to protest on private property in Amalgamated Food Employees Union v. Logan Valley Plaza, 391 U.S. 308, 88 S.Ct. 1601 (1968). The focus of the Warren Court's concern there was simply that if the property rights associated with a privately owned shopping mall could be asserted to ban picketers from the plaza area, individuals who sought to convey a message to the public about the nonunion practices of a supermarket in the mall would be relegated to ineffectually demonstrating along a public highway at a substantial distance from the store and thus well-removed from the object of their grievance. Eight years later in *Hudgens* v. *National Labor Relations Board* (p. 1292), the Burger Court overruled *Logan Valley Plaza*, agreeing with Justice Black who, dissenting from the earlier decision, had written: "To hold that store owners are compelled by law to supply picketing areas for pickets to drive store customers away is to create court-made law wholly disregarding the constitutional basis on which ownership of private property rests in this country. * * * These pickets do have a constitutional right to speak about Weis' [the supermarket] refusal to hire union labor, but they do not have a constitutional right to compel Weis to furnish them a place to do so on its property." *Hudgens*, however, has been the last word only as a matter of *federal* constitutional protection for any free speech rights on private property. As the Court's decision in *PruneYard Shopping Center* v. *Robins* (p. 1299) recognizes, the states retain considerable latitude as a matter of *state* constitutional law to secure such rights.

A third kind of "where and when" problem in freedom of speech is presented in *Cohen* v. *California* (p. 1302). How satisfied are you with the Court's accommodation of the conflicting interests here? Does the state have no right to protect the sensibilities of those who found Cohen's jacket upsetting—especially in a public place? Consider the bearing which the content of the defendant's speech had on the result. Is it significant that his jacket blared a political message? Would the result have been different had the reference to the draft been omitted? The Court, in *Erznoznik* v. *City of Jacksonville* (p. 1305), relies on the holding in *Cohen*. How would you appraise the Court's resolution of the competing interests here? Does the decision in *Erznoznik* reflect the wisdom or foolishness of the constitutional doctrine adopted in *Cohen*?

Door-to-door solicitations are also protected by the First Amendment as the Court makes clear in *Village of Schaumburg* v. *Citizens for a Better Environment* (p. 1306). Since money is being sought by the canvassers, why isn't this a case of commercial speech? Would it have made a difference if it were? Why does the Court conclude that the ordinance is overbroad? In dissent, Justice Rehnquist faults the Court for what he sees as its failure to confront the definition of a "charitable" organization and for its lapse in regard for the fact that the definition and regulation of such organizations is a prerogative of the states in our system. In your judgment, does he make some telling points against the majority position?

c. Symbolic Speech

Another mode of expression which received a significant push from the protest activities of the 1960s was symbolic speech. As with the varieties of speech discussed in the preceding section, symbolic speech cases also intertwine elements of expression and action and, for that reason, present similarly complex questions. The perception that speech need not be oral was recognized at least as far back as the decision in Stromberg v. California, 283 U.S. 359, 51 S.Ct. 532 (1931), which held unconstitutional a state statute prohibiting the display of a red flag as a symbol of opposition to organized government. The Court in that case reversed the defendant's conviction for having raised a red flag as part of the daily activities at a Communist youth camp. Writing for the Court, Chief Justice Hughes found the statute objectionable because its vagueness permitted punishment for the fair use of "the opportunity for free political discussion."

A decade later the Court again reiterated its conclusion that speech could be nonverbal in its invalidation of West Virginia's flag salute ritual in the public schools. In *West Virginia State Board of Education* v. *Barnette* (p. 1313) the Court, however, did more than merely affirm the possibility of nonverbal speech. For the first time the Court recognized that government could not enforce participation in a symbolic act. Be careful to note that the holding in *Barnette* rests clearly on speech grounds and *not* on the free exercise of the plaintiffs' religious beliefs (see p. 1314, col. 2). The same principle, that government may not force unwilling individuals to become couriers of an ideology, was recently reaffirmed by the Court in *Wooley* v. *Maynard* (p. 1317).

Without a doubt the Court has accepted symbolic speech as a form of expression protected by the First Amendment, but that is not to say that symbolic expression any more than pure speech is protected absolutely. The opinion in *Street* v. *New York* (p. 1322) makes it abundantly clear that government cannot constitutionally punish the mere expression of contempt for the flag. But clearly Street did more than that. Why did the Court fail to reach the issue Chief Justice Warren would have it decide? Is there a similarity of approach between the Court's decision in *Street* and its ruling in *Terminiello*? The Court has also held that expression which makes nondestructive use of the flag as an instrument of protest is also protected. Do you think the result in *United States* v. *O'Brien* (p. 1318) can be squared with the decision in *Street*? If *Street* stands for the proposition that statutes which directly infringe a preferred freedom must be subjected to "strict scrutiny," why does the Court sustain O'Brien's conviction for draft card burning in an antiwar protest on the grounds that the law furthered administrative convenience?

When we considered the practices of juvenile courts, we had occasion to confront the question of to what extent rights which adults possess should also be similarly extended to minors. Are you content with the accommodation of interests reached by the Court in the *Tinker* case (p. 1327)? Do the values of academic freedom and free speech necessarily support protest in the classroom even if it is of the quiet, symbolic variety? Consider the Illinois Supreme Court's decision in *Village of Skokie* v. *National Socialist Party* (p. 1330). Would display of the swastika still have been viewed as protected symbolic expression if children had gone to school wearing that insignia rather than the black arm bands in *Tinker*?

Finally, the disposition of the speech cases in this and the preceding section prompts one final comment. A legacy of their dissents together from Court decisions which were inhospitable to civil liberties during the Cold War era was the commonly held belief that Justices Black and Douglas were of one mind on free speech matters. Compare the voting records of Black and Douglas in section "a" of this chapter and in the *Barnette* case, on the one hand, with the decisions in sections "b" and "c" in which they participated, on the other. The comparison is instructive because it points up the essential importance of the difference between "pure speech" and "speech plus" to Black's conception of his role as a judge in interpreting the First Amendment. To call Justice Black an "absolutist," as many people do, is somewhat misleading, at least without qualifying the label by saying exactly *what kind* of speech was absolutely protected.

d. Campaign Financing, Party Patronage, and the First Amendment

The clash between government regulation and freedoms of speech and association during the Cold War era focused mainly on the alleged threat of subversive activities, as the decisions in *Dennis, Yates, Scales,* and *Barenblatt* (p. 210), among others, attest. With the retirement of Justices Whittaker and Frankfurter in 1962 and the appointment of Justice White and Justice Goldberg, who was subsequently replaced by Justice Fortas, the face of the Court changed significantly. Driven still further leftward by the nomination of Justice Marshall in 1967 to fill the spot vacated by Justice Clark, the Court maintained a staunch libertarian majority for most of the decade with the net effect of firmly establishing the dominance of the preferred freedoms approach in the constitutional evaluation of government action touching the face of First Amendment liberties. In the 1970s, however, the focus of the cases on political expression and association changed dramatically. Given the extent to which the influence of "big money" was thought to corrupt the political process, thus generating major attempts on both the national and state level at campaign finance reform, the Court was impelled to assess the constitutionality of such legislation by invoking "strict scrutiny." The Court's disposition of *Buckley* v. *Valeo* (p. 1331), a complex case which consumed nearly 300 pages of the *U.S. Reports* and involved over half a dozen different provisions of the Federal Election Campaign Act, stands as the prime example. The excerpt which appears highlights the Court's discussion of the statute's limitations on political contributions and campaign spending as they impact on free speech. On what basis does the Court sustain the law's limitations on contributions but declare unconstitutional various provisions regulating campaign spending?

In *First National Bank of Boston* v. *Bellotti* (p. 1342), the Court struck down a Massachusetts statute that severely limited political contributions by corporations. The majority clearly felt that such a result was required by certain neutral principles protecting freedom of speech. Would you agree? Or does Justice White develop some relevant distinctions between political spending by individuals and corporations? To what extent does the difference between Justice Powell's position and that of Justice White turn upon the acceptance of one theory over another of the function to be served by freedom of speech? Are you surprised to find Justice Rehnquist in dissent? To what extent have the Court's decisions in *Buckley, Bellotti, Consolidated Edison* (p. 1350), and *Citizens Against Rent Control* (p. 1354) left the electoral process to the tender mercies of "big money"?

In *Elrod* v. *Burns* (p. 1358), the Court found significant constitutional flaws in the patronage system. Why do political firings of opposition party members simply on the basis of their party affiliation violate the First Amendment? To what kind of government offices does the Court's ruling apply, at least in the eyes of the plurality opinion? Unlike *Elrod*, the Court in *Branti* v. *Finkel* (p. 1365) mustered a majority behind one opinion. Does Justice Stevens, speaking for the Court, give us more solid clues as to when political party affiliation can be a constitutionally relevant consideration in public employment?

e. Commercial Speech

Most recently, the Court has become involved in rolling back the proposition that advertising is not protected speech. Blanket bans on the dissemination of commercial information, as the Court points out in *Virginia State Board of Pharmacy* v. *Virginia Citizens Consumer Council* (p. 1367), bear a very substantial burden of justification. And commercial speech does not necessarily have to include some additional information of public interest above and beyond the advertisement of a commodity or service to qualify for First Amendment protection. Still, while a total ban on commercial speech may be quite difficult to justify—even for worthy motives, as in *Linmark Associates, Inc.* v. *Township of Willingboro* (p. 1379)—the Court has made it quite clear that government can legitimately regulate the manner and style of such speech and require that it not be false or deceptive. Four years after *Virginia Pharmacy*, the Court codified its approach in *Central Hudson Gas & Electric* v. *Public Service Com'n* (p. 1374). Without much doubt, however, Justice Rehnquist has been the Court's most persistent critic of the "commercial speech" concept. What problems does he see in the creation of such a doctrine? To what extent do the decisions in *Virginia Pharmacy, Central Hudson Gas & Electric,* and *Metromedia* (p. 1380) provide support for his contention that the concept invites a return to the sort of *laissez-faire* economic orientation that got the Court into so much hot water in the 1930s?

Principal targets of challenge to government-sanctioned prohibitions on certain varieties of commercial speech have been the strictures against solicitation of business by professionals, notably lawyers. Close on the heels of its decision in *Goldfarb* v. *Virginia State Bar* (p. 439), which brought the minimum fee schedules imposed by bar associations within the purview of the antitrust statutes, the Court in *Bates* v. *State Bar of Arizona* (p. 1384) sustained the constitutionality of in-print advertising of the prices charged for routine legal services. Two subsequent rulings of the Court explore the problems presented by in-person solicitation of clients by attorneys. On what basis does the Court distinguish punishment of the "ambulance chaser" in the *Ohralik* case (p. 1385) from the legitimate exercise of freedom of speech by the "civil liberties lawyer" in *In re Primus* (p. 1387)?

a. THE RISE AND FALL OF THE "CLEAR AND PRESENT DANGER" TEST

SCHENCK v. UNITED STATES

Supreme Court of the United States, 1919
249 U.S. 47, 39 S.Ct. 247, 63 L.Ed. 470

The facts are set out in the opinion.

Mr. Justice HOLMES delivered the opinion of the Court.

This is an indictment in three counts. The first charges a conspiracy to violate the Espionage Act of June 15, 1917, c. 30, tit. 1, § 3, 40 Stat. 217, 219 * * * by causing and attempting to cause insubordination, &c., in the military and naval forces of the United States, and to obstruct the recruiting and enlist-

ment service of the United States, when the United States was at war with the German Empire, to-wit, that the defendant wilfully conspired to have printed and circulated to men who had been called and accepted for military service * * * a document set forth and alleged to be calculated to cause such insubordination and obstruction. The count alleges overt acts in pursuance of the conspiracy, ending in the distribution of the document set forth. The second count alleges a conspiracy to commit an offense against the United States, to-wit, to use the mails for the transmission of matter declared to be non-mailable * * * to-wit, the above mentioned document, with an averment of the same overt acts. The third count charges an unlawful use of the mails for the transmission of the same matter and otherwise as above. The defendants were found guilty on all the counts. They set up the First Amendment to the Constitution forbidding Congress to make any law abridging the freedom of speech, or of the press, and bringing the case here on that ground have argued some other points. * * *

* * * According to the testimony Schenck said he was general secretary of the Socialist party and had charge of the Socialist headquarters from which the documents were sent. He identified a book found there as the minutes of the Executive Committee of the party. The book showed a resolution of August 13, 1917, that 15,000 leaflets should be printed * * * to be mailed to men who had passed exemption boards, and for distribution. Schenck personally attended to the printing. On August 20 the general secretary's report said "Obtained new leaflets from printer and started work addressing envelopes" &c.; and there was a resolve that Comrade Schenck be allowed $125 for sending leaflets through the mail. * * * There were files of the circular in question in the inner office. * * * [C]opies were proved to have been sent through the mails to drafted men. * * *

* * *

The document in question upon its first printed side recited the first section of the Thirteenth Amendment, said that the idea embodied in it was violated by the conscription act and that a conscript is little better than a convict. In impassioned language it intimated that conscription was despotism in its worst form and a monstrous wrong against humanity in the interest of Wall Street's chosen few. It said, "Do not submit to intimidation," but in form at least confined itself to peaceful measures such as a petition for the repeal of the act. The other and later printed side of the sheet was headed "Assert Your Rights." It stated reasons for alleging that any one violated the Constitution when he refused to recognize "your right to assert your opposition to the draft," and went on, "If you do not assert and support your rights, you are helping to deny or disparage rights which it is the solemn duty of all citizens and residents of the United States to retain." It described the arguments on the other side as coming from cunning politicians and a mercenary capitalist press, and even silent consent to the conscription law as helping to support an infamous conspiracy. It denied the power to send our citizens away to foreign shores to shoot up the people of other lands, and added that words could not express the condemnation such cold-blooded ruthlessness deserves, &c., &c., winding up, "You must do your share to maintain, support and uphold the rights of the people of this country." Of course the document would not have been sent unless it had been intended to have some effect, and we do not see what effect it could be expected to have upon persons subject to the draft except to influence them to obstruct the carrying of it out. The defendants do not deny that the jury might find against them on this point.

But it is said, suppose that that was the tendency of this circular, it is protected by the First Amendment to the Constitution. Two of the strongest expressions are said to be quoted respectively from well-known public men. It well may be that the prohibition of laws abridging the freedom of speech is not confined to previous restraints, although to prevent them may have been the main purpose. * * * We admit that in many places and in ordinary times the defendants in saying all that was said in the circular would have been within their constitutional rights. But the character of every act depends upon the circumstances in which it is done. * * * The most stringent protection of free speech would not protect a man in falsely shouting fire in a theatre and causing a panic. It does not even protect a man from an injunction against uttering words that may have all the effect of force. * * * The question in every case is whether the words used are used in such circum-

stances and are of such a nature as to create a clear and present danger that they will bring about the substantive evils that Congress has a right to prevent. It is a question of proximity and degree. When a nation is at war many things that might be said in time of peace are such a hindrance to its effort that their utterance will not be endured so long as men fight and that no Court could regard them as protected by any constitutional right. It seems to be admitted that if an actual obstruction of the recruiting service were proved, liability for words that produced that effect might be enforced. The statute of 1917 in section 4 * * * punishes conspiracies to obstruct as well as actual obstruction. If the act, (speaking, or circulating a paper,) its tendency and the intent with which it is done are the same, we perceive no ground for saying that success alone warrants making the act a crime. * * *

* * *

Judgments affirmed.

Abrams and several other Russian immigrants, who were avowed anarchists and revolutionaries, were charged under the Espionage Act as amended in 1918 with writing, publishing, and disseminating some 5,000 circulars which (1) used "scurrilous and abusive language" to characterize the American form of government, (2) brought the government into disrespect, (3) intended to incite and encourage resistance to the war, and (4) advocated curtailment in the production of materials necessary to fight the war. The defendants condemned as hyprocrisy American participation in the World War and efforts of the Wilson Administration to aid in crushing the Russian Revolution, referring in their leaflets to the President as a "coward" and to his administration as "the plutocratic gang in Washington." The leaflets also appealed to soldiers and to workers in the munitions factories to stop killing their Russian comrades. The defendants were convicted in federal district court on all four counts and sentenced to twenty years in prison; they appealed to the Supreme Court. In Abrams v. United States, 250 U.S. 616, 40 S.Ct. 17 (1919), the Court, per Justice Clarke, upheld the convictions focusing principally on the third and fourth counts and noting particularly that defendants' circulars, in which they sounded a call for a general strike, were distributed "in the greatest port of our land, from which great numbers of soldiers were at the time taking ships daily, and in which great quantities of war supplies were at the time being manufactured for transportation overseas."

Justice Holmes dissented and was joined in his opinion by Justice Brandeis. He first gave a careful and detailed portrayal of the defendants' behavior and then proceeded to explain the nature of the "clear and present danger" test and its application:

> [T]o make the[ir] conduct criminal th[e] statute requires that it should be "with intent by such curtailment to cripple or hinder the United States in the prosecution of the war." It seems to me that no such intent is proved.
>
> I am aware of course that the word "intent" as vaguely used in ordinary legal discussion means no more than knowledge at the time of the act that the consequences said to be intended will ensue. Even less than that will satisfy the general principle of civil and criminal liability. A man may have to pay damages, may be sent to prison, at common law might be hanged, if at the time of his act he knew facts from which common experience showed that the consequences would follow, whether he individually could foresee them or not. But, when words are used exactly, a deed is not done with intent to produce a consequence unless that consequence is the aim of the deed. It may be obvious, and obvious to the actor, that the consequence will follow, and he may be liable for it even if he regrets it, but he does not do the act with intent to produce it unless the aim to produce it is the proximate motive of the specific act, although there may be some deeper motive behind.
>
> It seems to me that this statute must be taken to use its words in a strict and accurate sense. They would be absurd in any other. A patriot might think that we were wasting money on aeroplanes, or making more cannon of a certain kind than we needed, and might advocate curtailment with success, yet even if it turned out that the curtailment hindered and was thought by other minds to have been obviously likely to hinder the United States in the prosecution of the war, no one would hold such conduct a crime. * * *
>
> * * * I do not doubt for a moment that by the same reasoning that would justify punishing persuasion to murder, the United States constitutionally may punish speech that produces or is intended to produce a clear and imminent danger that it will bring about forthwith certain substantive evils that the United States constitutionally may seek to prevent. The power undoubtedly is greater in time of war than in time of peace because war opens dangers that do not exist at other times.
>
> But as against dangers peculiar to war, as against others, the principle of the right to free speech is always the same. It is only the present danger of immediate evil or an intent to bring it about that warrants Congress in setting a limit to the expression of opinion where private rights are not concerned. Congress certainly cannot forbid all effort to change the mind of the country. Now nobody can suppose that the surreptitious publishing of a silly leaflet by an unknown man, without more, would present any immediate danger that its opinions would hinder the success of the government arms or have any appreciable tendency to do so. Publishing those opinions for the very purpose of obstructing, however, might indicate a greater danger and at any rate would have the quality of an attempt. So I assume that the second leaflet if published for the purposes alleged in the fourth count might be punishable. But it seems pretty clear to me that

nothing less than that would bring these papers within the scope of this law. An actual intent in the sense that I have explained is necessary to constitute an attempt, where a further act of the same individual is required to complete the substantive crime.   *   *   *   It is necessary where the success of the attempt depends upon others because if that intent is not present, the actor's aim may be accomplished without bringing about the evils sought to be checked. An intent to prevent interference with the revolution in Russia might have been satisfied without any hindrance to carrying on the war in which we were engaged.

I do not see how anyone can find the intent required by the statute in any of the defendant's words. The second leaflet is the only one that affords even a foundation for the charge, and there, without invoking the hatred of German militarism expressed in the former one, it is evident from the beginning to the end that the only object of the paper is to help Russia and stop American intervention there against the popular government—not to impede the United States in the war that it was carrying on. To say that two phrases taken literally might import a suggestion of conduct that would have interference with the war as an indirect and probably undesired effect seems to me by no means enough to show an attempt to produce that effect.

I return for a moment to the third count. That charges an intent to provoke resistance to the United States in its war with Germany. Taking the clause in the statute that deals with that in connection with the other elaborate provisions of the Act, I think that resistance to the United States means some forcible act of opposition to some proceeding of the United States in pursuance of the war. I think the intent must be the specific intent that I have described and for the reasons that I have given I think that no such intent was proved or existed in fact. I also think that there is no hint at resistance to the United States as I construe the phrase.

*   *   *   Even if I am technically wrong and enough can be squeezed from these poor and puny anonymities to turn the color of legal litmus paper;   *   *   *   the most nominal punishment seems to me all that possibly could be inflicted, unless the defendants are to be made to suffer not for what the indictment alleges but for the creed that they avow—a creed that I believe to be the creed of ignorance and immaturity when honestly held, as I see no reason to doubt that it was held here but which, although made the subject of examination at the trial, no one has a right even to consider in dealing with the charges before the Court.

Persecution for the expression of opinions seems to me perfectly logical. If you have no doubt of your premises or your power and want a certain result with all your heart you naturally express your wishes in law and sweep away all opposition. To allow opposition by speech seems to indicate that you think the speech impotent, as when a man says that he has squared the circle, or that you do not care whole heartedly for the result, or that you doubt either your power or your premises. But when men have realized that time has upset many fighting faiths, they may come to believe even more than they believe the very foundations of their own conduct that the ultimate good desired is better reached by free trade in ideas—that the best test of truth is the power of the thought to get itself accepted in the competition of the market, and that truth is the only ground upon which their wishes safely can be carried out. That at any rate is the theory of our Constitution. It is an experiment, as all life is an experiment. Every year if not every day we have to wager our salvation upon some prophecy based upon imperfect knowledge. While that experiment is part of our system I think that we should be eternally vigilant against attempts to check the expression of opinions that we loathe and believe to be fraught with death, unless they so imminently threaten immediate interference with the lawful and pressing purposes of the law that an immediate check is required to save the country. * * *

GITLOW v. NEW YORK

Supreme Court of the United States, 1925
268 U.S. 652, 45 S.Ct. 625, 69 L.Ed. 1138

Benjamin Gitlow, a leader of the Left Wing Section of the Socialist party which had been formed to oppose "moderate socialism," was tried and convicted by a New York court of violating the state's criminal anarchy statute. The indictment, which specifically charged that by publishing and disseminating "The Left Wing Manifesto," a compendium of the section's beliefs, in *The Revolutionary Age*, the movement's paper, Gitlow had distributed materials which advocated, advised, and taught "the doctrine that organized government should be overthrown by force, violence and unlawful means." The publication sounded a general call to emulate the Russian Revolution and to throw off capitalism which it described as being "in the process of disintegration and collapse." As a start, it called for using "mass industrial revolts to broaden the strike [the then recent labor disputes in Seattle and Winnipeg], make it general and militant, and develop it into mass political strikes and revolutionary mass action for the annihilation of the parliamentary state." There was no evidence that publication of the manifesto had any effect. Gitlow did not challenge the accuracy of the state's factual assertions but defended by attacking the constitutionality of the statute. His conviction was affirmed by the New York Court of Appeals, and he appealed to the United States Supreme Court.

Mr. Justice SANFORD delivered the opinion of the Court.

* * *

The contention here is that the statute, by its terms and as applied in this case, is repugnant to the due process clause of the Fourteenth Amendment. * * *

* * *

* * * The sole contention here is, essentially, that as there was no evidence of any concrete result flowing from the publication of the Manifesto or of circumstances showing the likelihood of such result, the statute as construed and applied by the trial court penalizes the mere utterance, as such, of "doctrine" having no quality of incitement, without regard either to the circumstances of its utterance or to the likelihood of unlawful sequences. * * *

* * *

The statute does not penalize the utterance or publication of abstract "doctrine" or academic discussion having no quality of incitement to any concrete action. It is not aimed against mere historical or philosophical essays. It does not restrain the advocacy of changes in the form of government by constitutional and lawful means. What it prohibits is language advocating, advising or teaching the overthrow of organized government by unlawful means. These words imply urging to action.
* * *

The Manifesto, plainly, is neither the statement of abstract doctrine nor, as suggested by counsel, mere prediction that industrial disturbances and revolutionary mass strikes will result spontaneously in an inevitable process of evolution in the economic system. It advocates and urges in fervent language mass action which shall progressively foment industrial disturbances and through political mass strikes and revolutionary mass action overthrow and destroy organized parliamentary government. It concludes with a call to action in these words:

"The proletariat revolution and the Communist reconstruction of society—*the struggle for these*—is now indispensable. * * * The Communist International calls the proletariat of the world to the final struggle!"

This is not the expression of philosophical abstraction, the mere prediction of future events; it is the language of direct incitement.

The means advocated for bringing about the destruction of organized parliamentary government, namely, mass industrial revolts usurping the functions of municipal government, political mass strikes directed against the parliamentary state, and revolutionary mass action for its final destruction, necessarily imply the use of force and violence, and in their essential nature are inherently unlawful in a constitutional government of law and order. That the jury were warranted in finding that the Manifesto advocated not merely the abstract doctrine of overthrowing organized government by force, violence and unlawful means, but action to that end, is clear.

For present purposes we may and do assume that freedom of speech and of the press—which are protected by the First Amendment from abridgment by Congress—are among the fundamental personal rights and "liberties" protected by the due process clause of the Fourteenth Amendment from impairment by the States. * * *

It is a fundamental principle, long established, that the freedom of speech and of the press which is secured by the Constitution, does not confer an absolute right to speak or publish, without responsibility, whatever one may choose, or an unrestricted and unbridled license that gives immunity for every possible use of language and prevents the punishment of those who abuse this freedom. * * *

That a State in the exercise of its police power may punish those who abuse this freedom by utterances inimical to the public welfare, tending to corrupt public morals, incite to crime, or disturb the public peace, is not open to question. * * *

And, for yet more imperative reasons, a State may punish utterances endangering the foundations of organized government and threatening its overthrow by unlawful means. These imperil its own existence as a constitutional State. Freedom of speech and press * * * does not protect disturbances to the public peace or the attempt to subvert the government. It does not protect publications or teachings which tend to subvert or imperil the government or to impede or hinder it in the performance of its governmental duties. * * * In short this freedom does not deprive a State of the primary and essential right of self preservation; which, so long as human governments endure, they cannot be denied. * * *

By enacting the present statute the State has determined, through its legislative body, that utterances advocating the overthrow of organized government by force, violence and unlawful means, are so inimical to the general welfare and involve such danger of substantive evil that they may be penalized in the exercise of its police power. That determination must be given great weight. Every presumption is to be indulged in favor of the validity of the statute. * * * That utterances inciting to the overthrow of organized government by unlawful means, present a sufficient danger of substantive evil to bring their punishment within the range of legislative discretion, is clear. Such utterances, by their very nature, involve danger to the public peace and to the security of the State. They threaten breaches of the peace and ultimate revolution. And the immediate danger is none the less real and substantial, because the effect of a given utterance cannot be accurately foreseen. The State cannot reasonably be required to measure the danger from every such utterance in the nice balance of a jeweler's scale. A single revolutionary spark may kindle a fire that, smouldering for a time, may burst into a sweeping and destructive conflagration. It cannot be said that the State is acting arbitrarily or unreasonably when in the exercise of its judgment as to the measures necessary to protect the public peace and safety, it seeks to extinguish the spark without waiting until it has enkindled the flame or blazed into the conflagration. It cannot reasonably be required to defer the adoption of measures for its own peace and safety until the revolutionary utterances lead to actual disturbances of the public peace or imminent and imme-

diate danger of its own destruction; but it may, in the exercise of its judgment, suppress the threatened danger in its incipiency. * * *

We cannot hold that the present statute is an arbitrary or unreasonable exercise of the police power of the State unwarrantably infringing the freedom of speech or press; and we must and do sustain its constitutionality.

This being so it may be applied to every utterance—not too trivial to be beneath the notice of the law—which is of such a character and used with such intent and purpose as to bring it within the prohibition of the statute. * * * In other words, when the legislative body has determined generally, in the constitutional exercise of its discretion, that utterances of a certain kind involve such danger of substantive evil that they may be punished, the question whether any specific utterance coming within the prohibited class is likely, in and of itself, to bring about the substantive evil, is not open to consideration. It is sufficient that the statute itself be constitutional and that the use of the language comes within its prohibition.

It is clear that the question in such cases is entirely different from that involved in those cases where the statute merely prohibits certain acts involving the danger of substantive evil, without any reference to language itself, and it is sought to apply its provisions to language used by the defendant for the purpose of bringing about the prohibited results. There, if it be contended that the statute cannot be applied to the language used by the defendant because of its protection by the freedom of speech or press, it must necessarily be found, as an original question, without any previous determination by the legislative body, whether the specific language used involved such likelihood of bringing about the substantive evil as to deprive it of the constitutional protection. In such case it has been held that the general provisions of the statute may be constitutionally applied to the specific utterance of the defendant if its natural tendency and probable effect was to bring about the substantive evil which the legislative body might prevent. * * * And the general statement in the *Schenck* Case * * * that the "question in every case is whether the words used are used in such circumstances and are of such a nature as to create a clear and present danger that they will bring about the substantive evils,"—upon which great reliance is placed in the defendant's argument—was manifestly intended, as shown by the context, to apply only in cases of this class, and has no application to those like the present, where the legislative body itself has previously determined the danger of substantive evil arising from utterances of a specified character.

* * * It was not necessary, within the meaning of the statute, that the defendant should have advocated "some definite or immediate act or acts" of force, violence or unlawfulness. It was sufficient if such acts were advocated in general terms; and it was not essential that their immediate execution should have been advocated. Nor was it necessary that the language should have been "reasonably and ordinarily calculated to incite certain persons" to acts of force, violence or unlawfulness. The advocacy need not be addressed to specific persons. Thus, the publication and circulation of a

newspaper article may be an encouragement or endeavor to persuade to murder, although not addressed to any person in particular. * * *

* * *

Affirmed.

Mr. Justice HOLMES (dissenting).

Mr. Justice BRANDEIS and I are of opinion that this judgment should be reversed. The general principle of free speech, it seems to me, must be taken to be included in the Fourteenth Amendment, in view of the scope that has been given to the word "liberty" as there used, although perhaps it may be accepted with a somewhat larger latitude of interpretation than is allowed to Congress by the sweeping language that governs or ought to govern the laws of the United States. If I am right then I think that the criterion sanctioned by the full Court in *Schenck* v. *United States* * * * applies. * * *

* * * If what I think the correct test is applied it is manifest that there was no present danger of an attempt to overthrow the government by force on the part of the admittedly small minority who shared the defendant's views. It is said that this manifesto was more than a theory, that it was an incitement. Every idea is an incitement. It offers itself for belief and if believed it is acted on unless some other belief outweighs it or some failure of energy stifles the movement at its birth. The only difference between the expression of an opinion and an incitement in the narrower sense is the speaker's enthusiasm for the result. Eloquence may set fire to reason. But whatever may be thought of the

redundant discourse before us it had no chance of starting a present conflagration. If in the long run the beliefs expressed in proletarian dictatorship are destined to be accepted by the dominant forces of the community, the only meaning of free speech is that they should be given their chance and have their way.

If the publication of this document had been laid as an attempt to induce an uprising against government at once and not at some indefinite time in the future it would have presented a different question. The object would have been one with which the law might deal, subject to the doubt whether there was any danger that the publication could produce any result, or in other words, whether it was not futile and too remote from possible consequences. But the indictment alleges the publication and nothing more.

Along with other radicals who split off from the Socialist party, Charlotte Whitney formed the Communist Labor party. The party espoused revolutionary goals and methods, on the order of those at issue in *Gitlow*, and in contrast to the democratic propensities of the old-line socialists. Miss Whitney was convicted on several counts under California's criminal syndicalism statute for helping to form and becoming a member of an organization which was "advocating, teaching or aiding and abetting the commission of crime, sabotage, or unlawful acts of force and violence * * * as a means of accomplishing a change in industrial ownership or control, or effecting any political change." The California Supreme Court affirmed the conviction.

In Whitney v. California, 274 U.S. 357, 47 S.Ct. 641 (1927), the United States Supreme Court upheld the constitutionality of the statute against a challenge predicated on the due process clause of the Fourteenth Amendment. Justice Sanford, on behalf of the majority, sustained the regulation as a valid protection of state interests:

> The essence of the offense denounced by the Act is the combining with others in an association for the accomplishment of the desired ends through the advocacy and use of criminal and unlawful methods. It partakes of the nature of a criminal conspiracy. * * * That such united and joint action involves even greater danger to the public peace and security than the isolated utterances and acts of individuals is clear. We cannot hold that, as here applied, the Act is an unreasonable or arbitrary exercise of the police power of the State, unwarrantably infringing any right of free speech, assembly or association, or that those persons are protected from punishment by the due process clause who abuse such rights by joining and furthering an organization thus menacing the peace and welfare of the State.

Justice Brandeis, in an opinion also representing the views of Justice Holmes, concurred in the judgment of the Court. He cautioned:

> The felony which the statute created is a crime very unlike the old felony of conspiracy or the old misdemeanor of unlawful assembly. The mere act of assisting in forming a society for teaching syndicalism, of becoming a member of it, or assembling with others for that purpose is given the dynamic quality of crime. There is guilt although the society may not con-

template immediate promulgation of the doctrine. Thus the accused is to be punished, not for attempt, incitement or conspiracy, but for a step in preparation, which, if it threatens the public order at all, does so only remotely. The novelty in the prohibition introduced is that the statute aims, not at the practice of criminal syndicalism, nor even directly at the preaching of it, but at association with those who propose to preach it.

[A]lthough the rights of free speech and assembly are fundamental, they are not in their nature absolute. Their exercise is subject to restriction, if the particular restriction proposed is required in order to protect the state from destruction or from serious injury, political, economic or moral. That the necessity which is essential to a valid restriction does not exist unless speech would produce, or is intended to produce, a clear and imminent danger of some substantive evil which the state constitutionally may seek to prevent has been settled.   *   *   *

*   *   *

This court has not yet fixed the standard by which to determine when a danger shall be deemed clear; how remote the danger may be and yet be deemed present; and what degree of evil shall be deemed sufficiently substantial to justify resort to abridgment of free speech and assembly as the means of protection. To reach sound conclusions on these matters, we must bear in mind why a state is, ordinarily, denied the power to prohibit dissemination of social, economic and political doctrine which a vast majority of its citizens believes to be false and fraught with evil consequence.

Those who won our independence believed that the final end of the state was to make men free to develop their faculties, and that in its government the deliberative forces should prevail over the arbitrary. They valued liberty both as an end and as a means. They believed liberty to be the secret of happiness and courage to be the secret of liberty. They believed that freedom to think as you will and to speak as you think are means indispensable to the discovery and spread of political truth; that without free speech and assembly discussion would be futile; that with them, discussion affords ordinarily adequate protection against the dissemination of noxious doctrine; that the greatest menace to freedom is an inert people; that public discussion is a political duty; and that this should be a fundamental principle of the American government. They recognized the risks to which all human institutions are subject. But they knew that order cannot be secured merely through fear of punishment for its infraction; that it is hazardous to discourage thought, hope and imagination; that fear breeds repression; that repression breeds hate; that hate menaces stable government; that the path of safety lies in the opportunity to discuss freely supposed grievances and proposed remedies; and that the fitting remedy for evil counsels is good ones. Believing in the power of reason as applied through public discussion, they eschewed silence coerced by law—the argument of force in its worst form. Recognizing the occasional tyrannies of governing majorities, they amended the Constitution so that free speech and assembly should be guaranteed.

Fear of serious injury cannot alone justify suppression of free speech and assembly. Men feared witches and burnt women. It is the function of speech to free men from the bondage of irrational fears. To justify suppression of free speech there must be reasonable ground to fear that serious evil will result if free speech is practiced. There must be reasonable ground to believe that the danger apprehended is imminent. There must be reasonable ground to believe that the evil to be prevented is a serious one. Every denunciation of existing law tends in some measure to increase the probability that there will be violation of it. Condonation of a breach enhances the probability. Expressions of approval add to the probability. Propagation of the criminal state of mind by teaching syndicalism increases it. Advocacy of law-breaking heightens it still further. But even advocacy of violation, however reprehensible morally, is not a justification for denying free speech where the advocacy falls short of incitement and there is nothing to indicate that the advocacy would be immediately acted on. The wide difference between advocacy and incitement, between preparation and attempt, between assembling and conspiracy, must be borne in mind. In order to support a finding of clear and present danger it must be shown either that immediate serious violence was to be expected or was advocated, or that the past conduct furnished reason to believe that such advocacy was then contemplated.

* * * Only an emergency can justify repression. * * * The fact that speech is likely to result in some violence or in destruction of property is not enough to justify its suppression. There must be the probability of serious injury to the State. Among free men, the deterrents ordinarily to be applied to prevent crime are education and punishment for violations of the law, not abridgment of the rights of free speech and assembly.

* * *

Justice Brandeis, however, found that the evidence in this case established that the group had transgressed the bounds of a political party and had, in fact, become a conspiracy to commit serious crimes.

THOMAS v. COLLINS

Supreme Court of the United States, 1945
323 U.S. 516, 65 S.Ct. 315, 89 L.Ed. 430

See p. 53.

TERMINIELLO v. CHICAGO

Supreme Court of the United States, 1949
337 U.S. 1, 69 S.Ct. 894, 93 L.Ed. 1131

Arthur Terminiello was charged with disorderly conduct when he was arrested for violating Chicago's "breach of the peace" ordinance.' His arrest grew out of a speech that he gave which attracted considerable public attention. The auditorium in which he spoke was filled with about 800 people, almost all of them admirers, while outside the hall a hostile crowd approximately double the size angrily milled about, protesting the meeting. Terminiello in vigorous and sometimes vicious terms castigated certain political and racial groups. Specifically, he assailed several prominent figures in the Roosevelt Administration as Communists and tauntingly portrayed those of a leftist persuasion as "scum" and by other names. He also lashed out at and villified people of the Jewish faith. Despite efforts of the police to cordon off the area, there were several disturbances in the crowd. There was much pushing and shoving, rocks were thrown, twenty-eight windows were broken, stink bombs were set off, and there were efforts to break in through the back door of the meeting hall. Though the defendant continually asserted that the application of the ordinance to his behavior violated the Constitution's guarantee of free speech, the jury returned a verdict of guilty, and he was fined $100. The Illinois Supreme Court upheld the conviction, and Terminiello appealed.

Mr. Justice DOUGLAS delivered the opinion of the Court.

* * *

The argument here has been focused on the issue of whether the content of petitioner's speech was composed of derisive, fighting words, which carried it outside the scope of the constitutional guarantees. See Chaplinsky v. New Hampshire, 315 U.S. 568, 62 S.Ct. 766. * * * We do not reach that question, for there is a preliminary question that is dispositive of the case.

As we have noted, the statutory words "breach of the peace" were defined in instructions to the jury to include speech which "stirs the public to anger, invites dispute, brings about a condition of unrest, or creates a disturbance." * * * That construction of the ordinance is a ruling on a question of state law that is as binding on us as though the precise words had been written into the ordinance. * * *

The vitality of civil and political institutions in our society depends on free discussion. * * * [I]t is only through free debate and free exchange of ideas that government remains responsive to the will of the people and peaceful change is effected. The right to speak freely and to promote diversity of ideas and programs is therefore one of the chief distinctions that sets us apart from totalitarian regimes.

Accordingly a function of free speech under our system of government is to invite dispute. It may indeed best serve its high purpose when it induces a condition of unrest, creates dissatisfaction with conditions as they are, or even stirs people to anger. Speech is often provocative and challenging. It may strike at prejudices and preconceptions and have profound unsettling effects as it presses for acceptance of an idea. That is why freedom of speech, though not absolute * * * is nevertheless protected against censorship or punishment, unless shown likely to produce a clear and present danger of a serious sustantive evil that rises far above public inconvenience, annoyance, or unrest. * * * There is no room under our Constitution for a more restrictive view. For the alternative would lead to standardization of ideas either by legislatures, courts, or dominant political or community groups.

The ordinance as construed by the trial court seriously invaded this province. It permitted conviction of petitioner if his speech stirred people to anger, invited public dispute, or brought about a condition of unrest. A conviction resting on any of those grounds may not stand.

* * *

* * * For all anyone knows [Terminiello] was convicted under the parts of the ordinance (as construed) which, for example, make it an offense merely to invite dispute or to bring about a condition of unrest. * * *

Reversed.

[Chief Justice VINSON dissented.]

Mr. Justice FRANKFURTER, dissenting.

For the first time in the course of the 130 years in which State prosecutions have come here for review, this Court is today reversing a sentence imposed by a State court on a ground that was urged neither here nor below and that was explicitly disclaimed on behalf of the petitioner at the bar of this Court.

*　*　*

*　*　*　The relation of the United States and the courts of the United States to the States and the courts of the States is a very delicate matter. It is too delicate to permit silence when a judgment of a State court is reversed in disregard of the duty of this Court to leave untouched an adjudication of a State unless that adjudication is based upon a claim of a federal right which the State has had an opportunity to meet and to recognize. If such a federal claim was neither before the State court nor presented to this Court, this Court unwarrantably strays from its province in looking through the record to find some federal claim that might have been brought to the attention of the State court and, if so, brought, fronted, and that might have been, but was not, urged here. This is a court of review, not a tribunal unbounded by rules. We do not sit like a kadi under a tree dispensing justice according to considerations of individual expediency.

Freedom of speech undoubtedly means freedom to express views that challenge deep-seated, sacred beliefs and to utter sentiments that may provoke resentment. But those indulging in such stuff as that to which this proceeding gave rise are hardly so deserving as to lead this Court to single them out as beneficiaries of the first departure from the restrictions that bind this Court

in reviewing judgments of State courts. *　*　*

*　*　*

On the merits of the issue reached by the Court I share Mr. Justice JACKSON'S views. *　*　*

Mr. Justice JACKSON and Mr. Justice BURTON join this dissent.

Mr. Justice JACKSON, dissenting.

The Court reverses this conviction by reiterating generalized approbations of freedom of speech with which, in the abstract, no one will disagree. Doubts as to their applicability are lulled by avoidance of more than passing reference to the circumstances of Terminiello's speech and judging it as if he had spoken to persons as dispassionate as empty benches, or like a modern Demosthenes practicing his Philippics on a lonely seashore.

But the local court that tried Terminiello was not indulging in theory. It was dealing with a riot and with a speech that provoked a hostile mob and incited a friendly one, and threatened violence between the two. When the trial judge instructed the jury *　*　* [h]e was saying *　*　* in effect, that if this particular speech added fuel to the situation already so inflamed as to threaten to get beyond police control, it could be punished as inducing a breach of peace. When the light of the evidence not recited by the Court is thrown upon the Court's opinion, it discloses that underneath a little issue of Terminiello and his hundred-dollar fine lurk some of the most far-reaching constitutional questions that can confront a people who value both liberty and order. This Court seems to regard these as enemies of each other and to be of the view that we must forego order to achieve liberty. So it fixes its eyes on a conception of freedom of speech so rigid as to tolerate no concession to society's need for public order.

An old proverb warns us to take heed lest we "walk into a well from looking at the stars." To show why I think the Court is in some danger of doing just that, I must bring these deliberations down to earth by a long recital of facts.

[Several pages follow containing excerpts from Terminiello's caustic speech and details of the incidents which occurred in and about the meeting hall.]

*   *   *

Hitler summed up the strategy of the mass demonstration as used by both fascism and communism: "We should not work in secret conventicles but in mighty mass demonstrations, and it is not by dagger and poison or pistol that the road can be cleared for the movement but *by the conquest of the streets.* We must teach the Marxists that the future *master of the streets* is National Socialism, just as it will some day be the master of the state." [Emphasis supplied.]   *   *   *   from *Mein Kampf.* First laughed at as an extravagant figure of speech, the battle for the streets became a tragic reality when an organized *Sturmabteilung* began to give practical effect to its slogan that "possession of the streets is the key to power in the state."   *   *   *

The present obstacle to mastery of the streets by either radical or reactionary mob movements is not the opposing minority. It is the authority of local governments which represent the free choice of democratic and law-abiding elements, of all shades of opinion but who, whatever their differences, submit them to free elections which register the results of their free discussion. The fascist and communist groups, on the contrary, resort to these terror tactics to confuse, bully and discredit those freely chosen governments. Violent and noisy shows of strength discourage participation of moderates in discussions so fraught with violence and real discussion dries up and disappears. And people lose faith in the democratic process when they see public authority flouted and impotent and begin to think the time has come when they must choose sides in a false and terrible dilemma such as was posed as being at hand by the call for the Terminiello meeting: "Christian Nationalism or World Communism—Which?"

This drive by totalitarian groups to undermine the prestige and effectiveness of local democratic governments is advanced whenever either of them can win from this Court a ruling which paralyzes the power of these officials. This is such a case. The group of which Terminiello is a part claims that his behavior, because it involved a speech, is above the reach of local authorities.

If the mild action those authorities have taken is forbidden, it is plain that hereafter there is nothing effective left that they can do. If they can do nothing as to him, they are equally powerless as to rival totalitarian groups. Terminiello's victory today certainly fulfills the most extravagant hopes of both right and left totalitarian groups, who want nothing so much as to paralyze and discredit the only democratic authority that can curb them in their battle for the streets.

I am unable to see that the local authorities have transgressed the Federal Constitution. Illinois imposed no prior censorship or suppression upon Terminiello. On the contrary, its sufferance and protection was all that enabled him to speak. It does not appear that the motive in punishing him is to silence the ideology he expressed as offensive to the State's policy or as untrue, or has any purpose of controlling his thought or its peaceful communication to others. There is no claim that the proceedings against Terminiello are designed to discriminate against him or the faction he represents or the ideas that he bespeaks. There is no indication that the charge against him is a mere pretext to give the semblance of legality to a covert effort to silence him or to prevent his followers or the public from hearing any truth that is in him.

* * *

Rioting is a substantive evil, which I take it no one will deny that the State and the City have the right and the duty to prevent and punish. Where an offense is induced by speech, the Court has laid down and often reiterated a test of the power of the authorities to deal with the speaking as also an offense. "The question in every case is whether the words *used are used in such circumstances* and are of *such a nature* as to create a *clear and present danger* that they will bring about the substantive evils that Congress [or the State or City] has a right to prevent." [Emphasis supplied.] Mr. Justice Holmes in Schenck v. United States, 249 U.S. 47, 52, 39 S.Ct. 247, 249. No one ventures to contend that the State on the basis of this test, for whatever it may be worth,

was not justified in punishing Terminiello. In this case the evidence proves beyond dispute that danger of rioting and violence in response to the speech was clear, present and immediate. If this Court has not silently abandoned this long standing test and substituted for the purposes of this case an unexpressed but more stringent test, the action of the State would have to be sustained.

Only recently this Court [unanimously] held that a state could punish as a breach of the peace use of epithets such as "damned racketeer" and "damned fascists," addressed to only one person, an official, because likely to provoke the average person to retaliation. But these are mild in comparison to the epithets "slimy scum," "snakes," "bedbugs," and the like, which Terminiello hurled at an already inflamed mob of his adversaries. * * *

* * *

However, these wholesome principles are abandoned today and in their place is substituted a dogma of absolute freedom for irresponsible and provocative utterance which almost completely sterilizes the power of local authorities to keep the peace as against this kind of tactics.

* * *

This Court has gone far toward accepting the doctrine that civil liberty means the removal of all restraints from these crowds and that all local attempts to maintain order are impairments of the liberty of the citizen. The choice is not between order and liberty. It is between liberty with order and anarchy without either. There is danger that, if the Court does not temper its doctrinaire logic with a little practical wisdom, it will convert the constitutional Bill of Rights into a suicide pact.

I would affirm the conviction.

Mr. Justice BURTON joins in this opinion.

Another case of provocative oratory, Feiner v. New York, 340 U.S. 315, 71 S.Ct. 303 (1951), grew out of the following circumstances: In an effort to give some publicity to a meeting of the Young Progressives of America to be held later in the evening at a downtown hotel, the theme of which meeting was to be racial discrimination and civil liberties, Irving Feiner, a college student, gave a street-corner speech in a largely Negro neighborhood of Syracuse, New York. In the words of Chief Justice Vinson, who spoke for the Court as it reviewed Feiner's conviction for disorderly conduct:

At approximately 6:30 p.m., the police received a telephone complaint concerning the meeting, and two officers were detailed to investigate. * * * They found a crowd of about seventy-five or eighty people, both Negro and white, filling the sidewalk and spreading out into the street. Petitioner, standing on a large wooden box on the sidewalk, was addressing the crowd through a loud-speaker system attached to an automobile. Although the purpose of his speech was to urge his listeners to attend [the] meeting * * * in its course he was making derogatory remarks concerning President Truman, the American Legion, the Mayor of Syracuse, and other local political officials. [Feiner referred to the mayor as "a champagne-sipping bum" and called President Truman and New York Mayor O'Dwyer "bums." He also made reference to the American Legion as a "Nazi Gestapo."]

The police officers made no effort to interfere with petitioner's speech, but were first concerned with the effect of the crowd on both pedestrian and vehicular traffic. They observed the situation from the opposite side of the street, noting that some pedestrians were forced to walk in the street to avoid the crowd. Since traffic was passing at the time, the officers attempted to get the people listening to petitioner back on the sidewalk. The crowd was restless and there was some pushing, shoving and milling around. * * *

At this time, petitioner was speaking in a "loud, high-pitched voice." He gave the impression that he was endeavoring to arouse the Negro people against the whites, urging that they rise up in arms and fight for equal rights. The statements before such a mixed audience "stirred up a little excitement." Some of the onlookers made remarks to the police about their inability to handle the crowd and at least one threatened violence if the police did not act. There were others who appeared to be favoring petitioner's arguments. Because of the feeling that existed in the crowd both for and against the speaker, the officers finally "stepped in to prevent it from resulting in a fight." One of the officers approached the petitioner, not for the purpose of arresting him, but to get him to break up the crowd. He asked petitioner to get down off the box, but the latter refused to accede to his request and continued talking. The officer waited for a minute and then demanded that he cease talking. Although the officer had thus twice requested petitioner to stop over the course of several minutes, petitioner not only ignored him but continued talking. During all this time, the crowd was pressing closer around petitioner and the officer. Finally, the officer told petitioner he was under arrest and ordered him to get down from the box, reaching up to grab him. Petitioner stepped down, announcing over the microphone that "the law has arrived, and I suppose they will take over now." In all, the officer had asked petitioner to get down off the box three times over a space of four or five minutes. Petitioner had been speaking for over a half hour.

The Supreme Court affirmed Feiner's conviction explaining, again per Chief Justice Vinson:

The courts below recognize petitioner's right to hold a street meeting at this locality, to make use of loud-speaking equipment in giving his speech, and to make derogatory remarks concerning public officials and the American Legion. They found that the officers in making the arrest were motivated solely by a proper concern for the preservation of order and protection of the general welfare, and that there was no evidence which could lend color to a claim that the acts of the police were a cover for suppression of petitioner's views and opinions. Petitioner was thus neither arrested nor convicted for the making or the content of his speech. Rather, it was the reaction which it actually engendered.

The language of Cantwell v. State of Connecticut, 1940, 310 U.S. 296, 60 S.Ct. 900, is appropriate here. "The offense known as breach of the peace embraces a great variety of conduct destroying or menacing public order and tranquility. It includes not only violent acts but acts and words likely to produce violence in others. No one would have the hardihood to suggest that the principle of freedom of speech sanctions incitement to riot or that religious liberty connotes the privilege to exhort others to physical attack upon those belonging to another sect. When clear and present danger of riot, disorder, interference with traffic upon the public streets, or other immediate threat to public safety, peace, or order, appears, the power of the State to prevent or punish is obvious." * * *

We are well aware that the ordinary murmurings and objections of a hostile audience cannot be allowed to silence a speaker, and are also mindful of the possible danger of giving overzealous police officials complete discretion to break up otherwise lawful public meetings. * * * But we are not faced here with such a situation. It is one thing to say that the police cannot be used as an instrument for the suppression of unpopular views, and another to say that, when as here the speaker passes the bounds of argument or pursuasion and undertakes incitement to riot, they are powerless to prevent a breach of the peace. Nor in this case can we condemn the considered judgment of three New York courts approving the means which the police, faced with a crisis, used in the exercise of their power and duty to preserve peace and order. * * *

After firing an opening salvo at what he saw as the majority's blind deference to the assessment of the facts by the state courts, Justice Black, in dissent, scorned the Court's conclusion as "far-fetched to suggest that the 'facts' show any imminent threat of riot or uncontrollable disorder." He continued:

It is neither unusual nor unexpected that some people at public street meetings mutter, mill about, push, shove, or disagree, even violently, with the speaker. Indeel, it is rare where controversial topics are discussed that an outdoor crowd does not do some or all of these things. Nor does one isolated threat to assault the speaker forebode disorder. Especially should the danger be discounted where, as here, the person threatening was a man whose wife and two small children accompanied him and who, so far as the record shows, was never close enough to petitioner to carry out the threat.

Moreover, assuming that the "facts" did indicate a critical situation, I reject the implication of the Court's opinion that the police had no obligation to protect petitioner's constitutional right to talk. The police of course have power to prevent breaches of the peace. But if, in the name of preserving order, they ever can interfere with a lawful public speaker, they first must make all reasonable efforts to protect him. Here the policemen did not even pretend to try to protect petitioner. According to the officers' testimony, the crowd was restless but there is no showing of any attempt to quiet it; pedestrians were forced to walk into the street, but there was no effort to clear a path on the sidewalk; one person threatened to assault petitioner but the officers did nothing to discourage this when even a word might have sufficed. Their duty was to protect petitioner's right to talk, even to the extent of arresting the man who threatened to interfere. Instead, they shirked that duty and acted only to suppress the right to speak.

In another dissenting opinion, Justice Douglas, joined by Justice Minton, added:

A speaker may not, of course, incite a riot any more than he may incite a breach of the peace by the use of "fighting words." See Chaplinsky v. State of New Hampshire, 315 U.S. 568, 62 S.Ct. 766. But this record shows no such extremes. It shows an unsympathetic audience and the threat of one man to haul the speaker from the stage. It is against that kind of threat that speakers need police protection. If they do not receive it and instead the police throw their weight on the side of those who would break up the meetings, the police become the new censors of speech.

DENNIS v. UNITED STATES

Supreme Court of the United States, 1951
341 U.S. 494, 71 S.Ct. 857, 95 L.Ed. 1137

Eugene Dennis and ten other top-ranking members of the U. S. Communist Party were indicted under provisions of the Smith Act of 1940. Specifically the indictment charged the defendants with

wilfully and knowingly conspiring (1) to organize as the Communist Party of the United States of America a society, group and assembly of persons who teach and advocate the overthrow and destruction of the Government of the United States by force and violence, and (2) knowingly and wilfully to advocate and teach the duty and necessity of overthrowing and destroying the Government of the United States by force and violence

The trial lasted some nine months and was occasionally marked by tumult in the courtroom. At its conclusion, the jury found the defendants guilty. These convictions were upheld by the U. S. Court of Appeals for the Second Circuit in an opinion by Judge Learned Hand. As Chief Justice Vinson later paraphrased their findings of fact concerning the Communist Party, the Court of Appeals concluded that

By virtue of their control over the political apparatus of the Communist Political Association, petitioners were able to transform that organization into the Communist Party; that the policies of the Association were changed from peaceful cooperation with the United States and its economic and political structure to a policy which had existed before the United States and the Soviet Union were fighting a common enemy, namely, a policy which worked for the overthrow of the Government by force and violence; that the Communist Party is a highly disciplined organization, adept at infiltration into strategic positions, use of aliases, and double-meaning language; that the Party is rigidly controlled; that Communists, unlike other political parties, tolerate no dissension from the policy laid down by the guiding forces, but that the approved program is slavishly followed by the members of the Party; that the literature of the Party and the statements and activities of its leaders, petitioners here, advocate, and the general goal of the Party was, during the period in question, to achieve a successful overthrow of the existing order by force and violence.

On argument to the Supreme Court consideration was limited to the constitutional issue of whether (1) the relevant positions of the Smith Act infringed freedom of speech as protected by the First Amendment, and (2) the applicable statutes were void for vagueness in contravention of First and Fifth Amendment protections.

Mr. Chief Justice VINSON announced the judgment of the Court and an opinion in which Mr. Justice REED, Mr. Justice BURTON and Mr. Justice MINTON join.

* * *

I.

It will be helpful in clarifying the issues to treat next the contention that the trial judge improperly interpreted the statute by charging that the statute required an unlawful intent before the jury could convict.
* * *

* * * The structure and purpose of the statute demand the inclusion of intent as an element of the crime. Congress was concerned with those who advocate and organize for the overthrow of the Government. Certainly those who recruit and combine for the purpose of advocating overthrow intend to bring about that overthrow. We hold that the statute requires as an essential element of the crime proof of the intent of those who are charged with its violation to overthrow the Government by force and violence. * * *

* * *

II.

The obvious purpose of the statute is to protect existing Government, not from change by peaceable, lawful and constitutional means, but from change by violence, revolution and terrorism. That it is within the *power* of the Congress to protect the Government of the United States from armed rebellion is a proposition which requires little discussion. Whatever theoretical merit there may be to the argument that there is a "right" to rebellion against dictatorial governments is without force where the existing structure of the government provides for peaceful and orderly change. We reject any principle of governmental helplessness in the face of preparation for revolution, which principle, carried to its logical conclusion, must lead to anarchy. No one could conceive that it is not within the power of Congress to prohibit acts intended to overthrow the Government by force and violence. The question with which we are concerned here is not whether Congress has such *power*, but whether the *means* which it has employed conflict with the First and Fifth Amendments to the Constitution.

One of the bases for the contention that the means which Congress has employed are invalid takes the form of an attack on the face of the statute on the grounds that by its terms it prohibits academic discussion of the merits of Marxism-Leninism, that it stifles ideas and is contrary to all concepts of a free speech and a free press.   *   *   *

The very language of the Smith Act negates the interpretation which petitioners would have us impose on that Act. It is directed at advocacy, not discussion. Thus, the trial judge properly charged the jury that they could not convict if they found that petitioners did "no more than pursue peaceful studies and discussions or teaching and advocacy in the realm of ideas."   *   *   *   Congress did not intend to eradicate the free discussion of political theories, to destroy the traditional rights of Americans to discuss and evaluate ideas without fear of governmental sanction. Rather Congress was concerned with the very kind of activity in which the evidence showed these petitioners engaged.

III.

*   *   *

[T]he basis of the First Amendment is the hypothesis that speech can rebut speech, propaganda will answer propoganda, free debate of ideas will result in the wisest governmental policies. It is for this reason that this Court has recognized the inherent value of free discourse. An analysis of the leading cases in this Court which have involved direct limitations on speech, however, will demonstrate that both the majority of the Court and the dissenters in particular cases have recognized that this is not an unlimited, unqualified right, but that the societal value of speech must, on occasion, be subordinated to other values and considerations.

*   *   *

The rule we deduce from [*Schenck* v. *United States* and the other Espionage Act] cases is that where an offense is specified by a statute in nonspeech or nonpress terms, a conviction relying upon speech or press as evidence of violation may be sustained only when the speech or publication created a "clear and present danger" of attempting or accomplishing the prohibited crime, e.g., interference with enlistment. The dissents,   *   *   * in emphasizing the value of speech, were addressed to the argument of the sufficiency of the evidence.

*   *   *

Although no case subsequent to *Whitney* and *Gitlow* has expressly overruled the majority opinions in those cases, there is little doubt that subsequent opinions have inclined toward the Holmes-Brandeis rationale. *   *   *   [N]either Justice Holmes nor Justice Brandeis ever envisioned that a shorthand phrase should be crystallized into a rigid rule to be applied inflexibly without regard to the circumstances of each case. Speech is not an absolute, above and beyond control by the legislature when its judgment, subject to review here, is that certain kinds of speech are so undesirable as to warrant criminal sanction. Nothing is more certain in modern society than the principle that there are no absolutes, that a name, a phrase, a standard has meaning only when associated with the considerations which gave birth to the nomenclature. * * * To those who would paralyze our Government in the face of impending threat by encasing it in a semantic straitjacket we must reply that all concepts are relative.

In this case we are squarely presented with the application of the "clear and present danger" test, and must decide what that phrase imports. We first note that many of the cases in which this Court has reversed convictions by use of this or similar tests have been based on the fact that the interest which the State was attempting to protect was itself too insubstantial to warrant restriction of speech. In this category we may put such cases as Schneider v. State, 1939, 308 U.S. 147, 60 S.Ct. 146; Cantwell v. State of Connecticut, 1940, 310 U.S. 296, 60 S.Ct. 900; * * * West Virginia State Board of Education v. Barnette, 1943, 319 U.S. 624, 63 S.Ct. 1178; Thomas v. Collins, 1945, 323 U.S. 516, 65 S.Ct. 315. * * * Overthrow of the Government by force and violence is certainly a substantial enough interest for the Government to limit speech. Indeed, this is the ultimate value of any society, for if a society cannot protect its very structure from armed internal attack, it must follow that no subordinate value can be protected. If, then, this interest may be protected, the literal problem which is presented is what has been meant by the use of the phrase "clear and present danger" of the utterances bringing about the evil within the power of Congress to punish.

Obviously, the words cannot mean that before the Government may act, it must wait until the putsch is about to be executed, the plans have been laid and the signal is awaited. If Government is aware that a group aiming at its overthrow is attempting to indoctrinate its members and to commit them to a course whereby they will strike when the leaders feel the circumstances permit, action by the Government is required. The argument that there is no need for Government to concern itself, for Government is strong, it possesses ample powers to put down a rebellion, it may defeat the revolution with ease needs no answer. For that is not the question. Certainly an attempt to overthrow the Government by force, even though doomed from the outset because of inadequate numbers or power of the revolutionists, is a sufficient evil for Congress to prevent. The damage which such attempts create both physically and politically to a nation makes it impossible to measure the validity in terms of the probability of success, or the immediacy of a successful attempt. In the instant case the trial judge charged the jury that they could not convict unless they found that petitioners intended to overthrow the Government "as speedily as circumstances would permit." This does not mean, and could not properly mean, that they would not strike until there was certainty of success. What was meant was that the revolutionists would strike when they thought the time was ripe. We must therefore reject the contention that success or probability of success is the criterion.

The situation with which Justices Holmes and Brandeis were concerned in *Gitlow* was a comparatively isolated event, bearing little relation in their minds to any substantial threat to the safety of the community. * * * They were not confronted with any situation comparable to the instant one—the development of an apparatus designed and dedicated to the overthrow of the Government, in the context of world crisis after crisis.

Chief Judge Learned Hand, writing for the majority below, interpreted the phrase as follows: "In each case [courts] must ask whether the gravity of the 'evil,' discounted by its improbability, justifies such invasion of free speech as is necessary to avoid the danger." 183 F.2d at 212. We adopt this statement of the rule. As articulated by Chief Judge Hand, it is as succinct and inclusive as any other we might devise at this time. It takes into consideration those factors which we deem relevant, and relates their significances. More we cannot expect from words.

Likewise, we are in accord with the court below, which affirmed the trial court's finding that the requisite danger existed. The mere fact that from the period 1945 to 1948 petitioners' activities did not result in an attempt to overthrow the Government by force and violence is of course no answer to the fact that there was a group that was ready to make the attempt. The formation by petitioners of such a highly organized conspiracy, with rigidly disciplined members subject to call when the leaders, these petitioners, felt that the time had come for action, coupled with the inflammable nature of world conditions, similar uprisings in other countries, and the touch-and-go nature of our relations with countries with whom petitioners were in the very least ideologically attuned, convince us that their convictions were justified on this score. And this analysis disposes of the contention that a conspiracy to advocate, as distinguished from the advocacy itself, cannot be constitutionally restrained, because it comprises only the preparation. It is the existence of the conspiracy which creates the danger. * * * If the ingredients of the reaction are present, we cannot bind the Government to wait until the catalyst is added.

IV.

Although we have concluded that the finding that there was a sufficient danger to warrant the application of the statute was justified on the merits, there remains the problem of whether the trial judge's treatment of the issue was correct. * * * [At trial, Judge Medina informed the jury that the sole question before them was whether they were "satisfied beyond a reasonable doubt that (the defendants) conspired to organize a society, group, and assembly of persons" who taught and advocated the overthrow of the government. This was a question of fact and thus within the purview of the jury. Defendants asserted that the question of whether or not such an association of the defendants produced a "clear and present danger" was the issue which should have been submitted. The Supreme Court rejected this claim, finding that this question was a matter of law and thus one to be left to the judge for his determination, i.e., whether, as a matter of law, the Constitution forbade the punishment of all such conspiracies once they had been shown to exist. And so the Court concluded:]

* * *

The question in this case is whether the statute which the legislature has enacted may be constitutionally applied. In other words, the Court must examine judicially the application of the statute to the particular situation, to ascertain if the Constitution prohibits the conviction. We hold that the statute may be applied where there is a "clear and present danger" of the substantive evil which the legislature had the right to prevent. Bearing, as it does, the marks of a "question of law," the issue is properly one for the judge to decide.

V.

There remains to be discussed the question of vagueness—whether the statute as we have interpreted it is too vague, not sufficiently advising those who would speak of the limitations upon their activity. It is urged that such vagueness contravenes the First and Fifth Amendments. * * *

We agree that the standard as defined is not a neat, mathematical formulary. Like all verbalizations it is subject to criticism on the score of indefiniteness. But petitioners themselves contend that the verbalization, "clear and present danger" is the proper standard. We see no difference, from the standpoint of vagueness, whether the standard of "clear and present danger" is one contained in *haec verba* within the statute, or whether it is the judicial measure of constitutional applicability. We have shown the indeterminate standard the phrase necessarily connotes. We do not think we have rendered that standard any more indefinite by our attempt to sum up the factors which are included within its scope. We think it well serves to indicate to those who would advocate constitutionally prohibited conduct that there is a line beyond which they may not go—a line which they, in full knowledge of what they intend and the circumstances in which their activity

takes place, will well appreciate and understand. * * *

* * *

We hold that [the relevant sections] of the Smith Act, do not inherently, or as construed or applied in the instant case, violate the First Amendment and other provisions of the Bill of Rights, or the First and Fifth Amendments because of indefiniteness. Petitioners intended to overthrow the Government of the United States as speedily as the circumstances would permit. Their conspiracy to organize the Communist Party and to teach and advocate the overthrow of the Government of the United States by force and violence created a "clear and present danger" of an attempt to overthrow the Government by force and violence. They were properly and constitutionally convicted for violation of the Smith Act. The judgments of conviction are affirmed.

Mr. Justice CLARK took no part in the consideration or decision of this case.

Mr. Justice FRANKFURTER, concurring in affirmance of the judgment.

* * *

[After a detailed discussion of the Court's First Amendment decisions according to the interests involved, Justice FRANKFURTER continued:] I must leave to others, the ungrateful task of trying to reconcile all these decisions.

* * * Viewed as a whole, however, the decisions express an attitude toward the judicial function and a standard of values which for me are decisive of the case before us.

* * * Free-speech cases are not an exception to the principle that

we are not legislators, that direct policy-making is not our province. How best to reconcile competing interests is the business of legislatures, and the balance they strike is a judgment not to be displaced by ours, but to be respected unless outside the pale of fair judgment.

* * *

Mr. Justice JACKSON, concurring.

* * *

I would save [the "clear and present danger" test] unmodified, for application as a "rule of reason" in the kind of case for which it was devised. When the issue is criminality of a hot-headed speech on a street corner, or circulation of a few incendiary pamphlets, or parading by some zealots behind a red flag, or refusal of a handful of school children to salute our flag, it is not beyond the capacity of the judicial process to gather, comprehend, and weigh the necessary materials for decision whether it is a clear and present danger of substantive evil or a harmless letting off of steam. * * *

I think reason is lacking for applying that test to this case.

If we must decide that this Act and its application are constitutional only if we are convinced that petitioner's conduct creates a "clear and present danger" of violent overthrow, we must appraise imponderables, including international and national phenomena which baffle the best informed foreign offices and our most experienced politicians. We would have to foresee and predict the effectiveness of Communist propaganda, opportunities for infiltration, whether, and when, a time will come that they consider propitious for ac-

tion, and whether and how fast our existing government will deteriorate. And we would have to speculate as to whether an approaching Communist *coup* would not be anticipated by a nationalistic fascist movement. No doctrine can be sound whose application requires us to make a prophecy of that sort in the guise of a legal decision. The judicial process simply is not adequate to a trial of such far-flung issues. The answers given would reflect our own political predilections and nothing more.

The authors of the clear and present danger test never applied it to a case like this, nor would I. * * *

* * *

What really is under review here is a conviction of conspiracy. * * *

The Constitution does not make conspiracy a civil right. The Court has never before done so and I think it should not do so now. Conspiracies of labor unions, trade associations, and news agencies have been condemned, although accomplished, evidenced and carried out, like the conspiracy here, chiefly by letter-writing, meetings, speeches and organization. Indeed, this Court seems, particularly in cases where the conspiracy has economic ends, to be applying its doctrines with increasing severity. While I consider criminal conspiracy a dragnet device capable of perversion into an instrument of injustice in the hands of a partisan or complacent judiciary, it has an established place in our system of law, and no reason appears for applying it only to concerted action claimed to disturb interstate commerce and withholding it from those claimed to undermine our whole Government.

* * *

* * * The Communist Party realistically is a state within a state, an authoritarian dictatorship within a republic. It demands [constitutional] freedoms, not for its members, but for the organized party. It denies to its own members at the same time the freedom to dissent, to debate, to deviate from the party line, and enforces its authoritarian rule by crude purges, if nothing more violent.

The law of conspiracy has been the chief means at the Government's disposal to deal with the growing problems created by such organizations. I happen to think it is an awkward and inept remedy, but I find no constitutional authority for taking this weapon from the Government. There is no constitutional right to "gang up" on the Government.

While I think there was power in Congress to enact this statute and that, as applied in this case, it cannot be held unconstitutional, I add that I have little faith in the long-range effectiveness of this conviction to stop the rise of the Communist movement. Communism will not go to jail with these Communists. No decision by this Court can forestall revolution whenever the existing government fails to command the respect and loyalty of the people and sufficient distress and discontent is allowed to grow up among the masses. Many failures by fallen governments attest that no government can long prevent revolution by outlawry. Corruption, ineptitude, inflation, oppressive taxation, militarization, injustice, and loss of leadership capable of intellectual initiative in domestic or foreign affairs are allies on which the Communists count to bring opportunity knocking to their door. Sometimes I think they may be mistaken. But

the Communists are not building just for today—the rest of us might profit by their example.

Mr. Justice BLACK, dissenting.

* * *

At the outset I want to emphasize what the crime involved in this case is, and what it is not. These petitioners were not charged with an attempt to overthrow the Government. They were not charged with overt acts of any kind designed to overthrow the Government. They were not even charged with saying anything or writing anything designed to overthrow the Government. The charge was that they agreed to assemble and to talk and publish certain ideas at a later date: The indictment is that they conspired to organize the Communist Party and to use speech or newspapers and other publications in the future to teach and advocate the forcible overthrow of the Government. No matter how it is worded, this is a virulent form of prior censorship of speech and press, which I believe the First Amendment forbids. * * *

* * * The opinions for affirmance indicate that the chief reason for jettisoning the ["clear and present danger"] rule is the expressed fear that advocacy of Communist doctrine endangers the safety of the Republic. Undoubtedly, a governmental policy of unfettered communication of ideas does entail dangers. To the Founders of this Nation, however, the benefits derived from free expression were worth the risk. They embodied this philosophy in the First Amendment's command that "Congress shall make no law * * * abridging the freedom of speech, or of the press." * * * I have always believed that the First Amendment is the keystone of our

Government, that the freedoms it guarantees provide the best insurance against destruction of all freedom. At least as to speech in the realm of public matters, I believe that the "clear and present danger" test does not "mark the furthermost constitutional boundaries of protected expression" but does "no more than recognize a minimum compulsion of the Bill of Rights." * * *

So long as this Court exercises the power of judicial review of legislation, I cannot agree that the First Amendment permits us to sustain laws suppressing freedom of speech and press on the basis of Congress' or our own notions of mere "reasonableness." Such a doctrine waters down the First Amendment so that it amounts to little more than an admonition to Congress. The Amendment as so construed is not likely to protect any but those "safe" or orthodox views which rarely need its protection. * * *

Public opinion being what it now is, few will protest the conviction of these Communist petitioners. There is hope, however, that in calmer times, when present pressures, passions and fears subside, this or some later Court will restore the First Amendment liberties to the high preferred place where they belong in a free society.

Mr. Justice DOUGLAS, dissenting.

If this were a case where those who claimed protection under the First Amendment were teaching the techniques of sabotage, the assassination of the President, the filching of documents from public files, the planting of bombs, the art of street warfare, and the like, I would have no doubts. The freedom to speak is not absolute; the teaching of methods of terror and other seditious conduct should be beyond the pale along with obscenity and immorality. This case was argued as if those were the facts. The argument imported much seditious conduct into the record. That is easy and it has popular appeal, for the activities of Communists in plotting and scheming against the free world are common knowledge. But the fact is that no such evidence was introduced at the trial. There is a statute which makes a seditious conspiracy unlawful. Petitioners, however, were not charged with a "conspiracy to overthrow" the Government. They were charged with a conspiracy to form a party and groups and assemblies of people who teach and advocate the overthrow of our Government by force or violence and with a conspiracy to advocate and teach its overthrow by force and violence. It may well be that indoctrination in the techniques of terror to destroy the Government would be indictable under either statute. But the teaching which is condemned here is of a different character.

* * *

The same year that the Court handed down its decision in *Dennis*, the government brought Smith Act prosecutions against fourteen second-string functionaries of the Communist party. Oleta Yates and the other defendants were indicted on the same counts as had been those in the *Dennis* case. Yates and the others were found guilty in federal district court, and each was sentenced to serve five years and pay a $10,000 fine. Their convictions were affirmed by the U.S. Court of Appeals, Ninth Circuit.

Speaking for the Supreme Court in Yates v. United States, 354 U.S. 298, 77 S.Ct. 1064 (1957), Justice Harlan began by examining the competing interpretations given the word "organize" by the defendants and the government:

> Petitioners claim that "organize" means to "establish," "found," or "bring into existence," and that in this sense the Communist Party was organized by 1945 at the latest. On this basis petitioners contend that this part of the indictment, returned in 1951, was barred by the three-year statute of limitations. The Government, on the other hand, says that "organize" connotes a continuing process which goes on throughout the life of an organization, and that, in the words of the trial court's instructions to the jury, the term includes such things as "the recruiting of new members and the forming of new units, and the regrouping or expansion of existing clubs, classes and other units of any society, party, group or other organization." * * * Stated most simply, the problem is to choose between two possible answers to the question: when was the Communist Party "organized"? Petitioners contend that the only natural answer to the question is the formation date—in this case, 1945. The Government would have us answer the question by saying that the Party today is still not completely "organized"; that "organizing" is a continuing process that does not end until the entity is dissolved.

Finding "dictionary definitions," "the legislative history of the Smith Act," and lower court decisions unhelpful in answering the question, the Court settled the matter, Justice Harlan saying:

We think, however, that petitioners' position must prevail, upon principles stated by Chief Justice Marshall more than a century ago in United States v. Wiltberger, 5 Wheat. 76, 95, 5 L.Ed. 37, as follows:

> "The rule that penal laws are to be construed strictly, is perhaps not much less old than construction itself. It is founded on the tenderness of the law for the rights of individuals; and on the plain principle that the power of punishment is vested in the legislative, not in the judicial department. It is the legislature, not the Court, which is to define a crime, and ordain its punishment." * * *

                              * * *

We conclude, therefore, that since the Communist Party came into being in 1945, and the indictment was not returned until 1951, the three-year statute of limitations had run on the "organizing" charge, and required the withdrawal of that part of the indictment from the jury's consideration.

The bulk of the Court's opinion, however, was given to consideration of the second count—conspiring to advocate the overthrow of the government. As to it, Justice Harlan sketched out the rival contentions and summed up the problem:

> Petitioners contend that the instructions to the jury were fatally defective in that the trial court refused to charge that, in order to convict, the jury must find that the advocacy which the defendants conspired to promote was of a kind calculated to "incite" persons to action for the forcible overthrow of the Government. It is argued that advocacy of forcible overthrow

as mere *abstract doctrine* is within the free speech protection of the First Amendment; that the Smith Act, consistently with that constitutional provision, must be taken as proscribing only the sort of advocacy which incites to illegal *action*; and that the trial court's charge, by permitting conviction for mere advocacy, unrelated to its tendency to produce forcible action, resulted in an unconstitutional application of the Smith Act. The Government, which at the trial also requested the court to charge in terms of "incitement," now takes the position, however, that the true constitutional dividing line is not between inciting and abstract advocacy of forcible overthrow, but rather between advocacy as such, irrespective of its inciting qualities, and the mere discussion or exposition of violent overthrow as an abstract theory.

* * *

There can be no doubt from the record that in so instructing the jury the court regarded as immaterial, and intended to withdraw from the jury's consideration, any issue as to the character of the advocacy in terms of its capacity to stir listeners to forcible action. Both the petitioners and the Government submitted proposed instructions which would have required the jury to find that the proscribed advocacy was not of a mere abstract doctrine of forcible overthrow, but of action to that end, by the use of language reasonably and ordinarily calculated to incite persons to such action. The trial court rejected these proposed instructions on the ground that any necessity for giving them which may have existed at the time the *Dennis* case was tried was removed by this Court's subsequent decision in that case. The court made it clear in colloquy with counsel that in its view the illegal advocacy was made out simply by showing that what was said dealt with forcible overthrow and that it was uttered with a specific intent to accomplish that purpose, insisting that all such advocacy was punishable "whether it is language of incitement or not." * * *

We are thus faced with the question whether the Smith Act prohibits advocacy and teaching of forcible overthrow as an abstract principle, divorced from any effort to instigate action to that end, so long as such advocacy or teaching is engaged in with evil intent. We hold that it does not.

The Court then went on to resolve the issue by at once affirming *Dennis* but more carefully circumscribing its holding. Justice Harlan continued:

The distinction between advocacy of abstract doctrine and advocacy directed at promoting unlawful action is one that has been consistently recognized in the opinions of this Court, beginning with * * * Schenck v. United States, 249 U.S. 47, 39 S.Ct. 247. This distinction was heavily underscored in Gitlow v. People of State of New York, 268 U.S. 652, 45 S.Ct. 625, in which the statute involved was nearly identical with the one now before us. * * *

We need not, however, decide the issue before us in terms of constitutional compulsion, for our first duty is to construe this statute. In doing so we should not assume that Congress chose to disregard a constitutional danger zone so clearly marked, or that it used the words "advocate" and "teach" in their ordinary dictionary meanings when they had already been construed as terms of art carrying a special and limited connotation. * * * The *Gitlow* case and the New York Criminal Anarchy Act there involved, which furnished the prototype for the Smith Act, were both known and adverted to by Congress in the course of the legislative proceedings. * * * The legislative history of the Smith Act and related bills shows beyond all question that Congress was aware of the distinction between the advocacy or teaching of abstract doctrine and the advocacy or teaching of action, and that it did not intend to disregard it. The statute was aimed at the advocacy and teaching of concrete action for the forcible overthrow of the Government, and not of principles divorced from action.

The Government's reliance on this Court's decision in *Dennis* is misplaced. The jury instructions which were refused here were given there, and were referred to by this Court as requiring "the jury to find the facts *essential* to establish the substantive crime." * * * (emphasis added). It is true that at one point in the late Chief Justice's opinion it is stated that the Smith Act "is directed at advocacy, not discussion," * * * but it is clear that the reference was to advocacy of action, not ideas, for in the very next sentence the opinion emphasizes that the jury was properly instructed that there could be no conviction for "advocacy in the realm of ideas." The two concurring opinions in that case likewise emphasize the distinction with which we are concerned. * * *

In failing to distinguish between advocacy of forcible overthrow as an abstract doctrine and advocacy of action to that end, the District Court appears to have been led astray by the holding in *Dennis* that advocacy of violent action to be taken at some future time was enough. It seems to have considered that, since "inciting" speech is usually thought of as something calculated to induce immediate action, and since *Dennis* held advocacy of action for future overthrow sufficient, this meant that advocacy, irrespective of its tendency to generate action, is punishable, provided only that it is uttered with a specific intent to accomplish overthrow. In other words, the District Court apparently thought that *Dennis* obliterated the traditional dividing line between advocacy of abstract doctrine and advocacy of action.

This misconceives the situation confronting the Court in *Dennis* and what was held there. Although the jury's verdict, interpreted in light of the trial court's instructions, did not justify the conclusion that the defendants' advocacy was directed at, or created any danger of, immediate overthrow, it did establish that the advocacy was aimed at building up a seditious group and maintaining it in readiness for action at a propitious time. * * * The essence of the *Dennis* holding was that indoctrination of a group in preparation for future violent action, as well as exhortation to immediate action, by advocacy found to be directed to "action for the accomplishment" of forcible overthrow, to violence as "a rule or principle of action," and employing "language of incitement," * * * is not constitutionally protected when the group is of sufficient size and cohesiveness, is sufficiently oriented towards action, and other circumstances are such as reasonably to justify apprehension that action will occur. This is quite a different thing from the view of the District Court here that mere doctrinal justification of forcible overthrow, if engaged in with the intent to accomplish overthrow, is punishable *per se* under the Smith Act. That sort of advocacy, even though uttered with the hope that it may ultimately lead to violent revolution, is too remote from concrete action to be regarded as the kind of indoctrination preparatory to action which was condemned in *Dennis*. As one of the concurring opinions in *Dennis* put it: "Throughout our decisions there has recurred a distinction between the statement of an idea which may prompt its hearers to take unlawful action, and advocacy that such action be taken." * * * There is nothing in *Dennis* which makes that historic distinction obsolete.

* * *

In light of the foregoing we are unable to regard the District Court's charge upon this aspect of the case is adequate. The jury was never told that the Smith Act does not denounce advocacy in the sense of preaching abstractly the forcible overthrow of the Government. We think that the trial court's statement that the proscribed advocacy must include the "urging," "necessity," and "duty" of forcible overthrow, and not merely its "desirability" and "propriety," may not be regarded as a sufficient substitute for charging that the Smith Act reaches only advocacy of action for the overthrow of government by force and violence. The essential distinction is that those to whom the advocacy is addressed must be urged to *do* something, now or in the future, rather than merely to *believe* in something. At best the expressions used by the trial court were equivocal, since in the absence of any instructions differentiating advocacy of abstract doctrine from advocacy of action, they were as consistent with the former as they were with the latter. Nor do we regard their ambiguity as lessened by what the trial court had to say as to the right of the defendants to announce their beliefs as to the inevitability of violent revolution, or to advocate other unpopular opinions. Especially when it is unmistakable that the court did not consider the urging of action for forcible overthrow as being a necessary element of the proscribed advocacy, but rather considered the crucial question to be whether the advocacy was uttered with a specific intent to accomplish such overthrow, we would not be warranted in assuming that the jury drew from these instructions more than the court itself intended them to convey.

* * *

We recognize that distinctions between advocacy or teaching of abstract doctrines, with evil intent, and that which is directed to stirring people to action, are often subtle and difficult to grasp, for in a broad sense, as Mr. Justice Holmes said in his dissenting opinion in *Gitlow* * * * "Every idea is an incitement." But the very subtlety of these distinctions required the most clear and explicit instructions with reference to them, for they concerned an issue which went to the very heart of the charges against these petitioners. The need for precise and understandable instructions on this issue is further emphasized by the equivocal character of the evidence in this record. * * * Instances of speech that could be considered to amount to "advocacy of action" are so few and far between as to be almost completely overshadowed by the hundreds of instances in the record in which overthrow, if mentioned at all, occurs in the course of doctrinal disputation so remote from action as to be almost wholly lacking in probative value. Vague references to "revolutionary" or "militant" action of an unspecified character, which are found in the evidence, might in addition be given too great weight by the jury in the absence of more precise instructions. Particularly in light of this record, we must regard the trial court's charge in this respect as furnishing wholly inadequate guidance to the jury on this central point in the case. We cannot allow a conviction to stand on such "an equivocal direction to the jury on a basic issue." * * *

* * *

Based upon these determinations, the Court directed new trials for nine of the defendants, including Yates, and acquittal for the remaining five (since the evidence in their cases "would be palpably insufficient" to convict). Justices Black and Douglas concurred in part and dissented in part. (They voted to direct all the defendants be acquitted on First Amendment grounds as per their opinions in *Dennis*.) Justice Clark dissented. (He voted to convict all fourteen defendants.) Justices Brennan and Whittaker did not participate.

In Scales v. United States, 367 U.S. 203, 81 S.Ct. 1469 (1961), the Court took the opportunity to review a conviction under the membership clause of the Smith Act, which clause makes it a felony to acquire or hold knowing membership in any organization that advocates the overthrow of the government by force and violence. Scales was indicted for having been a member of the Communist party since 1946 "with knowledge of the Party's illegal purpose and a specific intent to accomplish overthrow 'as speedily as circumstances would permit.'" The Supreme Court affirmed the conviction.

Justice Harlan spoke for the five-man majority. He began with the observation that the following charge by the trial judge to the jury properly construed the criminal requisites of the membership clause:

> The jury was instructed that in order to convict it must find that within the three-year limitations period (1) the Communist Party advocated the violent overthrow of the Government, in the sense of present "advocacy of action" to accomplish that end as soon as circumstances were propitious; and (2) petitioner was an "active" member of the Party, and not merely "a nominal, passive, inactive or purely technical" member, with knowledge of the Party's illegal advocacy and a specific intent to bring about violent overthrow "as speedily as circumstances would permit."

Scales's constitutional objections that the clause infringed the Fifth Amendment protection against imputing guilt by association and First Amendment rights of expression and association were without merit. As to the first claim, Justice Harlan found nothing incompatible between the criterion of "active," "knowing" membership which lends support to an enterprise of the kind government can justifiably prohibit and "our jurisprudence" where "guilt is personal." Indeed,

> we can perceive no reason why one who actively and knowingly works in the ranks of that organization, intending to contribute to the success of those specifically illegal activities, should be any more immune from prosecution than he to whom the organization has assigned the task of carrying out the substantive criminal act.

This being the case, the remaining critical problem of delineating degrees of participation was well satisfied by the distinction between "active" membership, on the one hand, which has a sufficiently close nexus to the illegitimate activity, and "nominal," passive membership on the other hand—"what otherwise might be regarded as merely an expression of sympathy with the alleged criminal enterprise, unaccompanied by any significant action in its support or any commitment to undertake such action." As to the second contention—the alleged abridgement of First Amendment rights—Justice Harlan wrote:

> Little remains to be said concerning the claim that the statute infringes First Amendment freedoms. It was settled in *Dennis* that the advocacy with which we are here concerned is not constitutionally protected speech, and it was further established that a combination to promote such advocacy, albeit under the aegis of what purports to be a political party, is not such association as is protected by the First Amendment. We can discern no reason why membership, when it constitutes a purposeful form of complicity in a group engaging in this same forbidden advocacy, should receive any greater degree of protection from the guarantees of that Amendment.
>
> If it is said that the mere existence of such an enactment tends to inhibit the exercise of constitutionally protected rights, in that it engenders an unhealthy fear that one may find himself unwittingly embroiled in criminal liability, the answer surely is that the statute provides that a defendant must be proven to have knowledge of the proscribed advocacy before he may be convicted. It is, of course, true that quasi-political parties or other groups that may embrace both legal and illegal aims differ from a technical conspiracy, which is defined by its criminal purpose, so that *all* knowing association with the conspiracy is a proper subject for criminal proscription as far as First Amendment liberties are concerned. If there were a similar blanket prohibition of association with a group having both legal and illegal aims, there would indeed be a real danger that legitimate political expression or association would be impaired, but the membership clause, as here construed, does not cut deeper into the freedom of association than is necessary to deal with "the substantive evils that Congress has a right to prevent." * * * The clause does not make criminal all association with an organization which has been shown to engage in illegal advocacy. There must be clear proof that a defendant "specifically intend[s] to accomplish [the aims of the organization] by resort to violence." * * * Thus the member for whom the organization is a vehicle for the advancement of legitimate aims and policies does not fall within the ban of the statute: he lacks the requisite specific intent "to bring about the overthrow of the government as speedily as circumstances would permit." Such a person may be foolish, deluded, or perhaps merely optimistic, but he is not by this statute made a criminal.

Justice Harlan found *Yates* a helpful guide in evaluating the evidence as to when one, through group association, forms the necessary specific intent thereby transgressing the line between protected expression and association and "advocacy to action." He pointed out:

> The decision in *Yates* rested on the view (not articulated in the opinion, though perhaps it should have been) that the Smith Act offenses, involving as they do subtler elements than are present in most other crimes, call for strict standards in assessing the adequacy of the proof needed to make out a case of illegal advocacy. This premise is as applicable to prosecutions under the membership clause of the Smith Act as it is to conspiracy prosecutions under that statute as we had in *Yates*.
>
> * * * Yates also articulates general criteria for the evaluation of evidence in determining whether this requirement is met. The *Yates* opinion

* * * indicates what type of evidence is needed to permit a jury to find that (a) there was "advocacy of action" and (b) the Party was responsible for such advocacy.

First, *Yates* makes clear what type of evidence is not *in itself* sufficient to show illegal advocacy. This category includes evidence of the following: the teaching of Marxism-Leninism and the connected use of Marxist "classics" as textbooks; the official general resolutions and pronouncements of the Party at past conventions; dissemination of the Party's general literature, including the standard outlines on Marxism; the Party's history and organizational structure; the secrecy of meetings and the clandestine nature of the Party generally; statements by officials evidencing sympathy for an alliance with U.S.S.R. It was the predominance of evidence of this type which led the Court to order the acquittal of several *Yates* defendants, with the comment that they had not themselves "made a single remark or been present when someone else made a remark which would tend to prove the charges against them." However, this kind of evidence, while insufficient in itself to sustain a conviction, is not irrelevant. Such evidence, in the context of other evidence, may be of value in showing illegal advocacy.

Second, the *Yates* opinion also indicates what kind of evidence is sufficient. There the Court pointed to two series of events which justified the denial of directed acquittals as to nine of the *Yates* defendants. The Court noted that with respect to seven of the defendants, meetings in San Francisco which were described by the witness Foard might be considered to be "the systematic teaching and advocacy of illegal action which is condemned by the statute." * * * In those meetings, a small group of members were not only taught that violent revolution was inevitable, but they were also taught techniques for achieving that end. For example, the *Yates* record reveals that members were directed to be prepared to convert a general strike into a revolution and to deal with Negroes so as to prepare them specifically for revolution. In addition to the San Francisco meetings, the Court referred to certain activities in the Los Angeles area "which might be considered to amount to 'advocacy of action'" and with which two *Yates* defendants were linked. * * * Here again, the participants did not stop with teaching of the inevitability of eventual revolution, but went on to explain techniques, both legal and illegal, to be employed in preparation for or in connection with the revolution. * * * Viewed together, these events described in *Yates* indicate at least two patterns of evidence sufficient to show illegal advocacy: (a) the teaching of forceful overthrow, accompanied by directions as to the type of illegal action which must be taken when the time for the revolution is reached; and (b) the teaching of forceful overthrow, accompanied by a contemporary, though legal, course of conduct clearly undertaken for the specific purpose of rendering effective the later illegal activity which is advocated. * * *

Finally, *Yates* is also relevant here in indicating, at least by implication, the type and quantum of evidence necessary to attach liability for illegal advocacy to the Party. In discussing the Government's "conspiratorial-nexus theory" the Court found that the evidence there was insufficient because the incidents of illegal advocacy were infrequent, sporadic, and not fairly related to the period covered by the indictment. In addition, the Court indicated that the illegal advocacy was not sufficiently tied to officials who spoke for the Party as such.

Chief Justice Warren and Justices Black, Douglas, and Brennan dissented. The Chief Justice and Justice Brennan differed with the majority principally on statutory grounds; Justices Black and Douglas dissented on First Amendment grounds.

BRANDENBURG v. OHIO

Supreme Court of the United States, 1969
395 U.S. 444, 89 S.Ct. 1827, 23 L.Ed.2d 430

Charles Brandenburg, the leader of a local Ku Klux Klan group, was convicted under the Ohio Criminal Syndicalism statute for "advocat[ing] * * * the duty, necessity, or propriety of crime, sabotage, violence, or unlawful methods of terrorism as a means of accomplishing industrial or political reform" and for "voluntarily assembl[ing] with any society, group, or assemblage of persons formed to teach or advocate the doctrines of criminal syndicalism." The prosecution's case rested most heavily on two films which had been taken at a rally by a Cincinnati television reporter attending the gathering at Brandenburg's request. The first film aired by the prosecution showed twelve hooded men, some of whom carried firearms, standing around a burning cross. Most of what the men said was inaudible, but a few scattered phrases could be understood as being derogatory toward Negroes and, in one instance, Jews. The same film showed Brandenburg making a speech before those assembled at the rally. During the course of his remarks, Brandenburg suggested that if the President, Congress, and the Court continued "to suppress the white, Caucasian race, it's possible that there might have to be some revengeance taken." The speech ended with Brandenburg's announcement that they were planning a march on Washington for July 4 and separate marches in St. Augustine, Florida and in Mississippi. A second film presented by the prosecution showed Brandenburg delivering essentially the same speech to five hooded men. Again, some of the men carried firearms, but Brandenburg did not. During this second speech Brandenburg omitted the reference to the possibility of "revengeance" but added, "Personally, I believe the nigger should be returned to Africa, the Jew returned to Israel." Appealing his conviction, Brandenburg challenged the constitutionality of the statute under the First and Fourteenth Amendments. An intermediate Ohio appellate court affirmed his conviction, and the state supreme court dismissed his appeal as failing to raise a substantial constitutional question. Brandenburg then sought review by the U. S. Supreme Court.

PER CURIAM.

* * *

The Ohio Criminal Syndicalism Statute was enacted in 1919. From 1917 to 1920, identical or quite similar laws were adopted by 20 States and two territories. * * * In 1927, this Court sustained the constitutionality of California's Criminal Syndicalism Act, Cal.Penal Code §§ 11400–11402, the text of which is quite similar to that of the laws of Ohio. Whitney v. California, 274 U.S. 357, 47 S.Ct. 641 (1927). The Court upheld the statute on the ground that, without more, "advocating" violent means to effect political and economic change involves such danger to the security of the State that the State may outlaw it. * * * But *Whitney* has been thoroughly discredited by later decisions. * * * These later decisions have fashioned the principle that the constitutional guarantees of free speech and free press do not permit a State to forbid or proscribe advocacy of the use of force or of law violation except where such advocacy is directed to inciting or producing imminent lawless action and is likely to incite or produce such action. * * *

* * *

[W]e are here confronted with a statute which, by its own words and as applied, purports to punish mere advocacy and to forbid, on pain of criminal punishment, assembly with others merely to advocate the described type of action. Such a statute falls within the condemnation of the First and Fourteenth Amendments. The contrary teaching of *Whitney* v. *California*, supra, cannot be supported, and that decision is therefore overruled.

Reversed.

Mr. Justice BLACK, concurring.

I agree with the views expressed by Mr. Justice DOUGLAS in his concurring opinion in this case that the "clear and present danger" doctrine should have no place in the interpretation of the First Amendment. I join the Court's opinion, which, as I understand it, simply cites Dennis v. United States, 341 U.S. 494, 71 S.Ct. 857 (1951), but does not indicate any agreement on the Court's part with the "clear and present danger" doctrine on which *Dennis* purported to rely.

Mr. Justice DOUGLAS, concurring.

* * *

My own view is quite different. I see no place in the regime of the First Amendment for any "clear and present danger" test, whether strict and tight as some would make it, or

free-wheeling as the Court in *Dennis* rephrased it.

When one reads the opinions closely and sees when and how the "clear and present danger" test has been applied, great misgivings are aroused. First, the threats were often loud but always puny and made serious only by judges so wedded to the *status quo* that critical analysis made them nervous. Second, the test was so twisted and perverted in *Dennis* as to make the trial of those teachers of Marxism on all-out political trial which was part and parcel of the cold war that has eroded substantial parts of the First Amendment.

* * *

The example usually given by those who would punish speech is the case of one who falsely shouts fire in a crowded theatre.

This is, however, a classic case where speech is brigaded with action. See Speiser v. Randall, 357 U.S. 513, 536–537, 78 S.Ct. 1332, 1346 (Douglas, J., concurring). They are indeed inseparable and a prosecution can be launched for the overt acts actually caused. Apart from rare instances of that kind, speech is, I think, immune from prosecution. Certainly there is no constitutional line between advocacy of abstract ideas as in *Yates* and advocacy of political action as in *Scales*. The quality of advocacy turns on the depth of the conviction; and government has no power to invade that sanctuary of belief and conscience.

In NAACP v. Claiborne Hardware Co., — U.S. —, 102 S.Ct. 3409 (1982), the Supreme Court addressed the question whether and to what extent a state court could award damages to merchants for economic losses sustained in the course of a seven-year political boycott of white-owned businesses by blacks engaged in an effort in one Mississippi county to put pressure on business and civic leaders so as to secure compliance with a lengthy list of demands for equality and racial justice, including among other things: desegregation of public schools and public facilities, public improvements in black residential areas, selection of blacks to serve on juries, integration of bus stations, and an end to verbal abuse by the police. In the original complaint, seventeen white merchants named two organizations and 146 individuals as defendants. The trial court awarded the plaintiff merchants some $1¼ million in damages, plus interest and costs, and injunctive relief against certain of defendants' actions it concluded were coercive and intimidating. Although the state supreme court narrowed the number of individuals who could properly be named as defendants and remanded the case for recomputation of damages, it affirmed the imposition of liability on the basis of common-law tort theory (i.e., traditional personal injury law predicated on an intent to inflict injury) when it concluded that the defendants had, through violence and the threat of violence, caused some blacks to withhold their patronage from white businesses and, therefore, that the entire boycott was illegal.

Speaking for the Court, Justice Stevens acknowledged at the start that the boycott "included elements of criminality and elements of majesty." Among the latter, he identified behavior—such as meetings, speeches, publication of demands, and nonviolent picketing—"ordinarily entitled to protection under the First and Fourteenth Amendments." Justice Stevens wrote, "The right to associate does not lose all constitutional protection merely because some members of the group may have participated in conduct or advocated doctrine that itself is not protected." But peaceful assembly and picketing, he noted, are clearly protected. He continued:

> Speech itself also was used to further the aims of the boycott. Nonparticipants repeatedly were urged to join the common cause, both through public address and through personal solicitation. These elements of the boycott involve speech in its most direct form. In addition, names of boycott violators were read aloud at meetings at the First Baptist Church and published in a local black newspaper. Petitioners admittedly sought to persuade others to join the boycott through social pressure and the "threat" of social ostracism. Speech does not lose its protected character, however, simply because it may embarrass others or coerce them into action.
> * * *

"In sum," he wrote, "the boycott clearly involved constitutionally protected activity. * * * Through speech, assembly, and petition—rather than through riot or revolution—petitioners sought to change a social order that had consistently treated them as second-class citizens."

Turning to the less "majestic" acts, Justice Stevens declared: "The First Amendment does not protect violence. * * * Although the extent and significance of the violence in this case is vigorously disputed by the parties, there is no question that acts of violence occurred. No federal rule of law restricts a State from imposing tort liability for business losses that are caused by violence and by threats of violence." However, citing NAACP v. Button, 371 U.S. 415, 83 S.Ct. 328 (1963), Justice Stevens continued, "When such conduct occurs in the context of constitutionally protected activity, * * * 'precision of regulation' is demanded. * * * Specifically, the presence of activity protected by the First Amendment imposes restraints on the grounds that may give rise to damage liability and on the persons who may be held accountable for those damages." As to the behavior that might give rise to an award of damages, Justice Stevens pointed out: "While the State legitimately may impose damages for the consequences of violent conduct, it may not award compensation for the consequences of nonviolent, protected activity. Only those losses proximately caused by unlawful conduct may be recovered." And, with respect to who among the defendants may be required to pay damages, he said:

> Civil liability may not be imposed merely because an individual belonged to a group, some members of which committed acts of violence. For liability to be imposed by reason of association alone, it is necessary to establish that the group itself possessed unlawful goals and that the individual held a specific intent to further those illegal aims. "In this sensitive field, the State may not employ 'means that broadly stifle fundamental personal liberties when the end can be more narrowly achieved.' Shelton v. Tucker, 364 U.S. 479, 488, 81 S.Ct. 247, 252 (1960)." * * *

With this framework in place, the Court went on to overturn judgments of liability predicated on various unconstitutional grounds. For example, the Court, reversing the state courts' finding that the merchants were entitled to recover all losses for the seven-year period, rejected the proposition that the success of the boycott was due to "coercion, intimidation, and threats." Said Justice Stevens, "It is * * * inconceivable that a boycott launched by the unanimous vote of several hundred people succeeded solely through fear and intimidation." Furthermore, the state courts "completely failed to demonstrate" that business losses occurring years after 1966, the latest year during which there was any finding of acts of violence, "were proximately caused by any acts of violence found in 1966." "It is impossible to conclude," wrote Justice Stevens, "that state power has not been exerted to compensate respondents for the direct consequences of nonviolent, constitutionally protected activity." Nor could damages be levied on the boycotters for their "[r]egular attendance and participation at the Tuesday meetings of the Claiborne County Branch of the NAACP" in the absence of proof of "any discussion of unlawful activity" or "evidence that the association possessed unlawful aims." Nor could damages be awarded against the "store watchers," individuals who stood outside the boycotted stores and took down the names of blacks trading at those stores. Said the Court, "There is nothing unlawful in standing outside a store and recording names." Where, however, such individuals engaged in acts of violence and intimidation, "a judgment tailored to the consequences of their unlawful conduct may be sustained." And as to the liability imposed on Charles Evers, one of the leaders of the boycott, for his rousing speeches, Justice Stevens pointed out: "This Court has made clear * * * that mere *advocacy* of the use of force or violence does not remove speech from the protection of the First Amendment. * * * The emotionally charged rhetoric of Charles Evers' speeches did not transcend the bounds of protected speech set forth in *Brandenburg* [v. Ohio, 395 U.S. 444, 89 S.Ct. 1827 (1969)]. * * * If * * * [the impassioned] language had been followed by acts of violence, a substantial question would be presented whether Evers could be held liable for the consequences of that unlawful conduct. * * * An advocate must be free to stimulate his audience with spontaneous and emotional appeals for unity and action in a common cause. When such appeals do not incite lawless action, they must be regarded as protected speech." Finally, with respect to damages awarded against the NAACP, there was "no finding that Charles Evers or any other NAACP member had either actual or apparent authority to commit acts of violence or to threaten violent conduct. * * * Similarly, there is no evidence that the NAACP ratified—or even had specific knowledge of—any of the acts of violence or threats of discipline associated with the boycott. * * * The NAACP supplied no financial aid to the boycott. * * * [There was] no finding that the national organization was involved in any way with the boycott." Summing up, Justice Stevens wrote:

> In litigation of this kind the stakes are high. Concerted action is a powerful weapon. History teaches that special dangers are associated with conspiratorial activity. And yet one of the foundations of our society is the right of individuals to combine with other persons in pursuit of a common goal by lawful means.
>
> At times the difference between lawful and unlawful collective action may be identified easily by reference to its purpose. In this case, however, petitioners' ultimate objectives were unquestionably legitimate. The charge of illegality—like the claim of constitutional protection—derives from the means employed by the participants to achieve those goals. The use of speeches, marches, and threats of social ostracism cannot provide the basis for a damage award. But violent conduct is beyond the pale of constitutional protection.
>
> The taint of violence colored the conduct of some of the petitioners. They, of course, may be held liable for the consequences of their violent deeds. The burden of demonstrating that it colored the entire collective effort, however, is not satisfied by evidence that violence occurred or even that violence contributed to the success of the boycott. A massive and prolonged effort to change the social, political, and economic structure of a local environment cannot be characterized as a violent conspiracy simply by reference to the ephemeral consequences of relatively few violent acts. Such a characterization must be supported by findings that adequately disclose the evidentiary basis for concluding that specific parties agreed to use unlawful means, that carefully identify the impact of such unlawful conduct, and that recognize the importance of avoiding the imposition of punishment for constitutionally protected activity. The burden of demonstrating that fear rather than protected conduct was the dominant force in the movement is heavy. A court must be wary of a claim that the true color of a forest is better revealed by reptiles hidden in the weeds than by the foliage of countless free-standing trees. * * *

Justice Rehnquist concurred in the result. Justice Marshall did not participate in the consideration or decision of the case.

b. FREE SPEECH—WHERE AND WHEN

ADDERLEY v. FLORIDA

Supreme Court of the United States, 1967
385 U.S. 39, 87 S.Ct. 242, 17 L.Ed.2d 149

Harriett Adderley and other university students gathered at a jail in Tallahassee to protest continuing state and local policies of racial segregation, including segregation in the jail itself, and to protest against earlier arrests of demonstrators. The county sheriff warned the students that he would arrest them if they did not leave the premises. Those that remained were arrested and later convicted for violating a state statute prohibiting trespass "committed with a malicious and mischievous intent." Two state courts affirmed the convictions, and the U. S. Supreme Court granted certiorari.

Mr. Justice BLACK delivered the opinion of the Court.

Petitioners have insisted from the beginning of this case that it is controlled by and must be reversed because of our prior cases of Edwards v. South Carolina, 372 U.S. 229, 83 S.Ct. 680, and Cox v. State of Louisiana, 379 U.S. 536, 559, 85 S.Ct. 453, 476. We cannot agree.

The *Edwards* case, like this one, did come up when a number of persons demonstrated on public property against their State's segregation policies. They also sang hymns and danced, as did the demonstrators in this case. But here the analogies to this case end. In *Edwards*, the demonstrators went to the South Carolina State Capitol grounds to protest. In this case they went to the jail. Traditionally, state capitol grounds are open to the public. Jails, built for security purposes, are not. The demonstrators at the South Carolina Capitol went in through a public driveway and as they entered they were told by state officials there that they had a right as citizens to go through the State House grounds as long as they were peaceful. Here the demonstrators entered the jail grounds through a driveway used only for jail purposes and without warning to or permission from the sheriff. More importantly, South Carolina sought to prosecute its State Capitol demonstrators by charging them with the common-law crime of breach of the peace. This Court in *Edwards* took pains to point out at length the indefinite, loose, and broad nature of this charge; indeed, this Court pointed out * * *

that the South Carolina Supreme Court had itself declared that the "breach of the peace" charge is "not susceptible of exact definition." South Carolina's power to prosecute, it was emphasized * * * would have been different had the State proceeded under a "precise and narrowly drawn regulatory statute evincing a legislative judgment that certain specific conduct be limited or proscribed" such as, for example, "limiting the periods during which the State House grounds were open to the public." * * * The South Carolina breach-of-the-peace statute was thus struck down as being so broad and all-embracing as to jeopardize speech, press, assembly and petition. * * * And it was on this same ground of vagueness that in Cox v. State of Louisiana * * * the Louisiana breach-of-the-peace law used to prosecute Cox was invalidated.

The Florida trespass statute under which these petitioners were charged cannot be challenged on this ground. It is aimed at conduct of one limited kind, that is, for one person or persons to trespass upon the property of another with a malicious and mischievous intent. There is no lack of notice in this law, nothing to entrap or fool the unwary.

Petitioners seem to argue that the Florida trespass law is void for vagueness because it requires a trespass to be "with a malicious and mischievous intent." * * * But these words do not broaden the scope of trespass so as to make it cover a multitude of types of conduct as does the common-law breach-of-the-peace charge. On the contrary, these words narrow the scope of the offense. The trial court charged the jury as to their meaning and petitioners have not argued that this definition * * * is not a reasonable and clear definition of the terms. The use of these terms in the statute, instead of contributing to uncertainty and misunderstanding, actually makes its meaning more understandable and clear.

* * *

[P]etitioners' summary of facts, as well as that of the Circuit Court, shows an abundance of facts to support the jury's verdict of guilty.
* * *

* * *

[The only question remaining is] whether conviction of the state offense * * * unconstitutionally deprives petitioners of their rights to freedom of speech, press, assembly or petition. We hold it does not. The sheriff, as jail custodian, had power, as the state courts have here held, to direct that this large crowd of people get off the grounds. There is not a shred of evidence in this record that this power was exercised, or that its exercise was sanctioned by the lower courts, because the sheriff objected to what was being sung or said by the demonstrators or because he disagreed with the objectives of their protest. The record reveals that he objected only to their presence on that part of the jail grounds reserved for jail uses. There is no evidence at all that on any other occasion had similarly large groups of the public been permitted to gather on this portion of the jail grounds for any purpose. Nothing in the Constitution of the United States prevents Florida from even-handed enforce-

ment of its general trespass statute against those refusing to obey the sheriff's order to remove themselves from what amounted to the curtilage of the jailhouse. The State, no less than a private owner of property, has power to preserve the property under its control for the use to which it is lawfully dedicated. For this reason there is no merit to the petitioners' argument that they had a constitutional right to stay on the property, over the jail custodian's objections, because this "area chosen for the peaceful civil rights demonstration was not only 'reasonable' but also particularly appropriate." * * * Such an argument has as its major unarticulated premise the assumption that people who want to propagandize protests or views have a constitutional right to do so whenever and however and wherever they please. That concept of constitutional law was vigorously and forthrightly rejected in [the very] cases petitioners rely on. * * * We reject it again. The United States Constitution does not forbid a State to control the use of its own property for its own lawful nondiscriminatory purpose.

These judgments are affirmed.

Mr. Justice DOUGLAS, with whom The CHIEF JUSTICE [WARREN], Mr. Justice BRENNAN, and Mr. Justice FORTAS concur, dissenting.

* * *

The jailhouse, like an executive mansion, a legislative chamber, a courthouse, or the statehouse itself (*Edwards* v. *South Carolina*, supra) is one of the seats of governments whether it be the Tower of London, the Bastille, or a small county jail. And when it houses political prisoners or those who many think are unjustly held, it is an obvious center for protest. The right to petition for the redress of grievances has an ancient history and is not limited to writing a letter or sending a telegram to a congressman; it is not confined to appearing before the local city council, or writing letters to the President or Governor or Mayor. * * * Conventional methods of petitioning may be, and often have been, shut off to large groups of our citizens. Legislators may turn deaf ears; formal complaints may be routed endlessly through a bureaucratic maze; courts may let the wheels of justice grind very slowly. Those who do not control television and radio, those who cannot afford to advertise in newspapers or circulate elaborate pamphlets may have only a more limited type of access to public officials. Their methods should not be condemned as tactics of obstruction and harassment as long as the assembly and petition are peaceable, as these were.

There is no question that petitioners had as their purpose a protest against the arrest of Florida A. & M. students for trying to integrate public theatres. * * * There was no violence; no threat of violence; no attempted jail break; no storming of a prison; no plan or plot to do anything but protest. The evidence is uncontradicted that the petitioners' conduct did not upset the jailhouse routine; things went on as they normally would. * * *

* * *

* * * When we allow Florida to construe her "malicious trespass" statute to bar a person from going on property knowing it is not his own and to apply that prohibition to public property, we discard *Cox* and *Edwards*. Would the case be any dif-

ferent if, as is common, the demonstration took place outside a building which housed both the jail and the legislative body? I think not.

There may be some public places which are so clearly committed to other purposes that their use for the airing of grievances is anomalous. There may be some instances in which assemblies and petitions for redress of grievances are not consistent with other necessary purposes of public property. A noisy meeting may be out of keeping with the serenity of the statehouse or the quiet of the courthouse. No one, for example, would suggest that the Senate gallery is the proper place for a vociferous protest rally. And in other cases it may be necessary to adjust the right to petition for redress of grievances to the other interests inhering in the uses to which the public property is normally put. * * * But this is quite different from saying that all public places are off limits to people with grievances. * * *

* * *

Today a trespass law is used to penalize people for exercising a constitutional right. Tomorrow a disorderly conduct statute, a breach-of-the-peace statute, a vagrancy statute will be put to the same end. It is said that the sheriff did not make the arrests because of the views which petitioners espoused. That excuse is usually given, as we know from the many cases involving arrests of minority groups for breaches of the peace, unlawful assemblies, and parading without a permit. The charge against William Penn, who preached a nonconformist doctrine in a street in London, was that he caused "a great concourse and tumult of people" in contempt of the King and "to the great disturbance of his peace." * * * That was in 1670. In modern times, also, such arrests are usually sought to be justified by some legitimate function of government.

Yet by allowing these orderly and civilized protests against injustice to be suppressed, we only increase the forces of frustration which the conditions of second-class citizenship are generating amongst us.

RECENT "PUBLIC FORUM" CASES

Case	Holding	Dissents
Greer v. Spock, 424 U.S. 828, 96 S.Ct. 1211 (1976)	Army post regulations banning "[d]emonstrations, picketing, sit-ins, protest marches, political speeches and similar activities" and permitting the posting of publications and the distribution of literature only with the prior written approval of the commanding officer do not violate the First Amendment. Since it is the primary function of the armed forces to be ready to fight wars, such regulations are consistent with the fact that it is the business of military installations to train soldiers, not to provide a public forum. There was no evidence that authorities discriminated among candidates for public office in enforcing the regulations. Although authorities may not ban the distribution of conventional literature and may not prevent the circulation of materials simply because they do not like their contents, authorities may ban publications which constitute "a clear danger to [military] loyalty, discipline, or morale."	Brennan and Marshall
Brown v. Glines, 444 U.S. 348, 100 S.Ct. 594 (1980)	Air Force regulations which prohibit the circulation of petitions on military bases without first obtaining the approval of the base's commanding officer do not violate the First Amendment. Although "members of the military services are entitled to the protections of the First Amendment, 'the different character of the military community and the military mission requires a different application of those protections.'" "Speech likely to interfere with * * * overriding demands of discipline and duty * * * can be excluded from a military base." The regulations "prevent commanders from interfering with the circulation of any materials other than those posing a clear danger to military loyalty, discipline, or morale."	Brennan and Stewart; Marshall did not participate
United States Postal Service v. Council of Greenburgh Civic Ass'ns, 453 U.S. 114, 101 S.Ct. 2676 (1981)	Postal regulations making it an offense to deposit unstamped mailable matter in home mailboxes do not violate the First Amendment because mailboxes are not a public forum. "[W]hen a letter box is designated [an 'authorized depository'], it becomes an es-	Marshall and Stevens

"PUBLIC FORUM" CASES (*Cont.*)

Case	Holding	Dissents
United States Postal Service (*Cont.*)	sential part of the Postal Service's nation-wide system for the delivery and receipt of mail" with the effect that "the postal customer, although he pays for the physical components of the 'authorized depository,' agrees to abide by the Postal Service's regulations in exchange for the Postal Service agreeing to deliver and pick up his mail." Congress was entitled to conclude that postal service efficiency and security would be enhanced by such a measure and could authorize the Postal Service's promulgation of such regulations as incident to its Art. I, § 8 power "to establish post offices and post roads."	

HUDGENS v. NATIONAL LABOR RELATIONS BOARD

Supreme Court of the United States, 1976
424 U.S. 507, 96 S.Ct. 1029, 47 L.Ed.2d 196

Striking employees of the Butler Shoe Company decided to picket not only the company's warehouse but also all nine of its retail stores. When several employees showed up to picket Butler's store in the North DeKalb Shopping Plaza located outside Atlanta, Georgia, the shopping center manager informed them that they could not picket within the mall or parking lot and threatened them with arrest for trespassing should they choose to do so. After a second warning, the picketers left, but the union filed an unfair labor practice complaint with the National Labor Relations Board against Hudgens, the owner of the shopping center. Relying upon a previous Supreme Court decision in Amalgamated Food Employees Union Local 590 v. Logan Valley Plaza, Inc., 391 U.S. 308, 88 S.Ct. 1601 (1968), the board entered a cease-and-desist order against Hudgens, who appealed to the U. S. Court of Appeals, Fifth Circuit. Though the appeals court ultimately affirmed the board's order, its decision to do so was the result of a lengthy process during which the case was passed back and forth between the appeals court and the board, with the movement of the board being steadily away from reliance upon a constitutional basis for its decision to one of its interpretation of statutes governing labor-management relations. Hudgens sought further review, and the Supreme Court granted certiorari. In its opinion, the Court recounts the origin and substance of its *Logan Valley Plaza* decision, traverses the modification that holding subsequently underwent, and spells out reasons why it finally decided to overrule *Logan Valley Plaza*.

Mr. Justice STEWART delivered the opinion of the Court.

* * *

It is, of course, a commonplace that the constitutional guarantee of free speech is a guarantee only against abridgment by government, federal or state. * * * Thus, while statutory or common law may in some situations extend protection or provide redress against a private corporation or person who seeks to abridge the free expression of others, no such protection or redress is provided by the Constitution itself.

This elementary proposition is little more than a truism. But even truisms are not always unexceptionably true, and an exception to this one was recognized almost 30 years ago in the case Marsh v. Alabama, 326 U.S. 501, 66 S.Ct. 276. In *Marsh*, a Jehovah's Witness who had distributed literature without a license on a sidewalk in Chickasaw, Ala., was convicted of criminal trespass. Chickasaw was a so-called company town, wholly owned by the Gulf Shipbuilding Corporation. * * *

The Court pointed out that if the "title" to Chickasaw had "belonged not to a private but to a municipal corporation and had appellant been arrested for violating a municipal ordinance rather than a ruling by those appointed by the corporation to manage a company town it would have been clear that appellant's conviction must be reversed." * * * Concluding that Gulf's "property interests" should not be allowed to lead to a different result in Chickasaw, which did "not function differently from any other town," * * * the Court invoked the First and Fourteenth Amendments to reverse the appellant's conviction.

It was the *Marsh* case that in 1968 provided the foundation for the Court's decision in Amalgamated Food Employees Union Local 590 v. Logan Valley Plaza, Inc., 391 U.S. 308, 88 S.Ct. 1601. That case involved peaceful picketing within a large shopping center near Altoona, Pa. One of the tenants of the shopping center was a retail store that employed a wholly nonunion staff. Members of a local union picketed the store, carrying signs proclaiming that it was nonunion and that its employees were not receiving union wages or other union benefits. The picketing took place on the shopping center's property in the immediate vicinity of the store. A Pennsylvania court issued an injunction that required all picketing to be confined to public areas outside the shopping center, and the Supreme Court of Pennsylvania affirmed the issuance of this injunction. This Court held that the doctrine of the *Marsh* case required reversal of that judgment.

The Court's opinion pointed out that the First and Fourteenth Amendments would clearly have protected the picketing if it had taken place on a public sidewalk:

"It is clear that if the shopping center premises were not privately owned but instead constituted the business area of a municipality, which they to a large extent resemble, petitioners could not be barred from exercising their First Amendment rights there on the sole ground that title to the property was in the municipality. * * * The essence of those opinions is that streets, sidewalks, parks, and other similar public places are so historically associated with the exercise of First Amendment rights that access to them for the purpose of exercising such rights cannot constitutionally be denied broadly and absolutely." * * *

The Court's opinion then reviewed the *Marsh* case in detail, emphasized the similarities between the business block in Chickasaw, Ala., and the Logan Valley shopping center and unambiguously concluded:

"The shopping center here is clearly the functional equivalent of the business district of Chickasaw involved in *Marsh*." * * *

Upon the basis of that conclusion, the Court held that the First and Fourteenth Amendments required reversal of the judgment of the Pennsylvania Supreme Court.

* * *

Four years later the Court had occasion to reconsider the *Logan Valley* doctrine in Lloyd Corp. v. Tanner, 407 U.S. 551, 92 S.Ct. 2219. That case involved a shopping center covering some 50 acres in downtown Portland, Ore. On a November day in 1968 five young people entered the mall of the shopping center and distributed handbills protesting the then ongoing American military operations in Vietnam. Security guards told them to leave, and they did so, "to avoid arrest." * * * They subsequently brought suit in a federal district court, seeking declaratory and injunctive relief. The trial court ruled in their favor, holding that the distribution of handbills on the shopping center's property was protected by the First and Fourteenth Amendments. The Court of Appeals for the Ninth Circuit affirmed the judgment * * * expressly relying on this Court's *Marsh* and *Logan Valley* decisions. This Court reversed the judgment of the Court of Appeals.

The Court in its *Lloyd* opinion did not say that it was overruling the *Logan Valley* decision. Indeed a substantial portion of the Court's opinion in *Lloyd* was devoted to pointing out the differences between the two cases, noting particularly that, in contrast to the handbilling in *Lloyd*, the picketing in *Logan Valley* had been specifically directed to a store in the shopping center and the picketers had had no other reasonable opportunity to reach their intended audience. * * * But the fact is that the reasoning of the Court's opinion in *Lloyd* cannot be squared with the reasoning of the Court's opinion in *Logan Valley*.

It matters not that some members of the Court may continue to believe that the *Logan Valley* case was rightly decided. Our institutional duty is to follow until changed the law as it now is, not as some members of the Court might wish it to be. And in the performance of that duty we make clear now, if it was not clear before, that the rationale of *Logan Valley* did not survive the Court's decision in the *Lloyd* case. Not only did the *Lloyd* opinion incorporate lengthy excerpts from two of the dissenting opinions in *Logan Valley*, * * * the ultimate holding in *Lloyd* amounted to a total rejection of the holding in *Logan Valley:*

"The basic issue in this case is whether respondents, in the exercise of asserted First Amendment rights, may distribute handbills on Lloyd's private property contrary to its wishes and contrary to a policy enforced against *all* handbilling. In addressing this issue, it must be remembered that the First and Fourteenth Amendments safeguard the rights of free speech and assembly by limitations on *state* action, not on action by the owner of private property used nondiscriminatorily for private purposes only." * * *

* * *

"Respondents contend * * * that the property of a large shopping center is 'open to the public,' serves the same purposes as a 'business district' of a municipality, and therefore has been dedicated to certain types of public use. The argument is that such a center has sidewalks, streets, and parking areas which are functionally similar to facilities customarily provided by municipalities. It is then asserted that all members of the public, whether invited as customers or not, have the same right of free speech as they would have on the similar public facilities in the streets of a city or town.

"The argument reaches too far. The Constitution by no means requires such an attenuated doctrine of dedication of private property to public use. The closest decision in theory, *Marsh* v. *Alabama, supra,* involved the assumption by a private enterprise of all of the attributes of a state-created municipality and the exercise by that enterprise of semi-official municipal functions as a delegate of the State. In effect, the owner of the company town was performing the full spectrum of municipal powers and stood in the shoes of the State. In the instant case there is no comparable assumption or exercise of municipal functions or power."

*   *   *

*   *   *

"We hold that there has been no such dedication of Lloyd's privately owned and operated shopping center to public use as to entitle respondents to exercise therein the asserted First Amendment rights." *   *   *

If a large self-contained shopping center *is* the functional equivalent of a municipality, as *Logan Valley* held, then the First and Fourteenth Amendments would not permit control of speech within such a center to depend upon the speech's content. For while a municipality may constitutionally impose reasonable time, place, and manner regulations on the use of its streets and sidewalks for First Amendment purposes, see Cox v. New Hampshire, 312 U.S. 569, 61 S.Ct. 762; Poulos v. New Hampshire, 345 U.S. 395, 73 S.Ct. 760, and may even forbid altogether such use of some of its facilities, see Adderley v. Florida, 385 U.S. 39, 87 S.Ct. 242,

what a municipality may *not* do under the First and Fourteenth Amendments is to discriminate in the regulation of expression on the basis of the content of that expression. Erznoznik v. City of Jacksonville, 422 U.S. 205, 95 S.Ct. 2268. "[A]bove all else, the First Amendment means that government has no power to restrict expression because of its message, its ideas, its subject matter, or its content." Police Department of Chicago v. Mosley, 408 U.S. 92, 95, 92 S.Ct. 2286, 2290. It conversely follows, therefore, that if the respondents in the *Lloyd* case did not have a First Amendment right to enter that shopping center to distribute handbills concerning Vietnam, then the respondents in the present case did not have a First Amendment right to enter this shopping center for the purpose of advertising their strike against the Butler Shoe Company.

We conclude, in short, that under the present state of the law the constitutional guarantee of free expression has no part to play in a case such as this.

From what has been said it follows that the rights and liabilities of the parties in this case are dependent exclusively upon the National Labor Relations Act. Under the Act the task of the Board, subject to review by the courts, is to resolve conflicts between § 7 rights [the rights of employees acting through labor unions] and private property rights, "and to seek a proper accommodation between the two." Central Hardware Co. v. NLRB, 407 U.S. 539, 543, 92 S.Ct. 2238, 2241. What is "a proper accommodation" in any situation may largely depend upon the content and the context of the § 7 rights being asserted. The task of the Board and the reviewing courts under the

Act, therefore, stands in conspicuous contrast to the duty of a court in applying the standards of the First Amendment, which requires "above all else" that expression must not be restricted by government "because of its message, its ideas, its subject matter, or its content."

* * *

For * * * reasons stated in this opinion, the judgment is vacated and the case is remanded to the Court of Appeals with directions to remand to the National Labor Relations Board, so that the case may be there considered under the statutory criteria of the National Labor Relations Act alone.

It is so ordered.

Vacated and remanded.

Mr. Justice STEVENS took no part in the consideration or decision of this case.

Mr. Justice WHITE, concurring in the judgment.

While I concur in the result reached by the Court, I find it unnecessary to inter Amalgamated Food Employees Union Local 590 v. Logan Valley Plaza, Inc., 391 U.S. 308, 88 S.Ct. 1601, * * * and therefore do not join the Court's opinion. I agree that "the constitutional guarantee of free expression has no part to play in a case such as this," * * * but Lloyd Corp. v. Tanner * * * did not overrule Logan Valley, either expressly or implicitly, and I would not, somewhat after the fact, say that it did.

One need go no further than Logan Valley itself, for the First Amendment protection established by Logan Valley was expressly limited to the picketing of a specific store for the purpose of conveying information with respect to the oper-

ation in the shopping center of *that* store:

"The picketing carried on by petitioners was directed specifically at patrons of the Weis Market located within the shopping center and the message sought to be conveyed to the public concerned the manner in which that particular market was being operated. We are, therefore, not called upon to consider whether respondents' property rights could, consistently with the First Amendment, justify a bar on picketing which was not thus directly related in its purpose to the use to which the shopping center property was being put." * * *

On its face, Logan Valley does not cover the facts of this case. The pickets of the Butler Shoe Company store in the North DeKalb Shopping Center were not purporting to convey information about the "manner in which that particular [store] was being operated" but rather about the operation of a warehouse not located on the Center's premises. The picketing was thus not "directly related in its purpose to the use to which the shopping center property was being put."

The First Amendment question in this case was left open in Logan Valley. I dissented in Logan Valley * * * and I see no reason to extend it further. Without such extension, the First Amendment provides no protection for the picketing here in issue and the Court need say no more. Lloyd v. Tanner is wholly consistent with this view. There is no need belatedly to overrule Logan Valley, only to follow it as is.

Mr. Justice MARSHALL, with whom Mr. Justice BRENNAN joins, dissenting.

* * *

It is inescapable that after *Lloyd*, *Logan Valley* remained "good law," binding on the state and federal courts. Our institutional duty in this case, if we consider the constitutional question at all, is to examine whether *Lloyd* and *Logan Valley* can continue to stand side-by-side, and if they cannot, to decide which one must fall. I continue to believe that the First Amendment principles underlying *Logan Valley* are sound, and were unduly limited in *Lloyd*. But accepting *Lloyd*, I am not convinced that *Logan Valley* must be overruled.

The foundation of *Logan Valley* consisted of this Court's decisions recognizing a right of access to streets, sidewalks, parks, and other public places historically associated with the exercise of First Amendment rights. * * * Thus, the Court in *Logan Valley* observed that access to such forums "cannot constitutionally be denied broadly and absolutely." * * * The importance of access to such places for speech-related purposes is clear, for they are often the only places for effective speech and assembly.

Marsh v. State of Alabama, 326 U.S. 501, 66 S.Ct. 276 (1946), which the Court purports to leave untouched, made clear that in applying those cases granting a right of access to streets, sidewalks and other public places, courts ought not let the formalities of title put an end to analysis. The Court in *Marsh* observed that "the town and its shopping district are accessible to and freely used by the public in general and there is nothing to distinguish them from any other town and shopping center except the fact that the title to the property belongs to a pri-

vate corporation." * * * That distinction was not determinative:

"Ownership does not always mean absolute dominion. The more an owner, for his advantage, opens up his property for use by the public in general, the more do his rights become circumscribed by the statutory and constitutional rights of those who use it." * * *

Regardless of who owned or possessed the town in *Marsh*, the Court noted, "the public * * * has an identical interest in the functioning of the community in such manner that the channels of communication remain free," * * * and that interest was held to prevail.

The Court adopts the view that *Marsh* has no bearing on this case because the privately owned property in *Marsh* involved all the characteristics of a typical town. But there is nothing in *Marsh* to suggest that its general approach was limited to the particular facts of that case. The underlying concern in *Marsh* was that traditional public channels of communication remain free, regardless of the incidence of ownership. Given that concern, the crucial fact in *Marsh* was that the company owned the traditional forums essential for effective communication; it was immaterial that the company also owned a sewer system and that its property in other respects resembled a town.

In *Logan Valley* we recognized what the Court today refuses to recognize—that the owner of the modern shopping center complex, by dedicating his property to public use as a business district, to some extent displaces the "state" from control of historical First Amendment forums, and may acquire a virtual monopoly of places suitable for effective communication. The roadways, parking lots and walkways of the modern shopping center may be as essential for effective speech as the streets and sidewalks in the municipal or company-owned town. I simply cannot reconcile the Court's denial of any role for the First Amendment in the shopping center with *Marsh's* recognition of a full rule for the First Amendment on the streets and sidewalks of the company-owned town.

My reading of *Marsh* admittedly carried me farther than the Court in *Lloyd*, but the *Lloyd* Court remained responsive in its own way to the concerns underlying *Marsh*. *Lloyd* retained the availability of First Amendment protection when the picketing is related to the function of the shopping center, and when there is no other reasonable opportunity to convey the message to the intended audience. Preserving *Logan Valley* subject to *Lloyd's* two related criteria guaranteed that the First Amendment would have application in those situations in which the shopping center owner had most clearly monopolized the forums essential for effective communication. This result, although not the optimal one in my view, * * * is nonetheless defensible.

* * *

In the final analysis, the Court's rejection of any role for the First Amendment in the privately owned shopping center complex stems, I believe, from an overly formalistic view of the relationship between the institution of private ownership of property and the First Amendment's guarantee of freedom of speech. No one would seriously question the legitimacy of the values of privacy and individual autonomy traditionally associated with privately owned property. But property that is privately owned is not always held for private use, and when a property owner opens his property to public use the force of those values diminishes. A degree of privacy is necessarily surrendered; thus, the privacy interest that petitioner retains when he leases space to 60 retail businesses and invites the public onto his land for the transaction of business with other members of the public is small indeed. * * * And while the owner of property open to public use may not automatically surrender any of his autonomy interest in managing the property as he sees fit, there is nothing new about the notion that that autonomy interest must be accommodated with the interests of the public. As this Court noted some time ago, albeit in another context:

"Property does become clothed with a public interest when used in a manner to make it of public consequence, and affect the community at large. When, therefore, one devotes his property to a use in which the public has an interest, he, in effect, grants to the public an interest in that use, and must submit to be controlled by the public for the common good, to the extent of the interest he has thus created." Munn v. Illinois, 94 U.S. 113, 126, 24 L.Ed. 77, 84.

The interest of members of the public in communicating with one another on subjects relating to the businesses that occupy a modern shopping center is substantial. Not only employees with a labor dispute, but also consumers with complaints against business establishments, may look to the location of a retail store as the only reasonable avenue for effective communication with the public. As far as these groups are concerned, the shopping center owner has assumed the traditional role of the state in its control of historical First Amendment forums. *Lloyd* and *Logan Valley* recognized the vi-

tal role the First Amendment has to play in such cases, and I believe that this Court errs when it holds otherwise.

PruneYard is a privately owned, twenty-one-acre shopping center, open to the public for the purpose of patronizing its more than sixty-five specialty shops, ten restaurants, and movie theater. The shopping center maintained a nondiscriminatory policy of not permitting any visitor or tenant to engage in expressive activity, including the circulation of petitions, not directly related to the conduct of business. Robins and other high school students, attempting to gain support for their opposition to a United Nations resolution condemning "Zionism," set up a card table in a corner of the central courtyard of the shopping center and began to distribute pamphlets and solicit signatures for petitions addressed to the President and Congress. The students were promptly informed by a security guard that these activities violated shopping center regulations and were asked to leave. It was suggested that the students move to a public sidewalk on the perimeter of the shopping center. The students left and subsequently filed suit to enjoin the shopping center from denying them access in order to circulate their petitions. A state superior court rendered judgment for the shopping center, but this ruling was later reversed by the California Supreme Court on state constitutional grounds. The owner of the shopping center then appealed to the U.S. Supreme Court.

In its disposition of this case, PruneYard Shopping Center v. Robins, 447 U.S. 74, 100 S.Ct. 2035 (1980), the Supreme Court considered "whether state constitutional provisions [as construed by the state supreme court], which permit individuals to exercise free speech and petition rights on the property of a privately owned shopping center to which the public is invited, violate the shopping center owner's property rights under the Fifth and Fourteenth Amendments or his free speech rights under the First and Fourteenth Amendments." Speaking for the Court, Justice Rehnquist noted that neither *Lloyd* nor *Hudgens* controlled this case because the holdings in those cases were predicated on *federal* constitutional law, whereas here the decision below was specifically grounded in construction of the *state* constitution. Said Justice Rehnquist, "It is, of course, well-established that a State in the exercise of its police power may adopt reasonable restrictions on private property so long as the restrictions do not amount to a taking without just compensation or contravene any other federal constitutional provision." Addressing the first of the two constitutional contentions, Justice Rehnquist noted that, while "[i]t is true that one of the essential sticks in the bundle of property rights is the right to exclude others," nevertheless "it is well-established that 'not every destruction or injury to property by governmental action has been held to be a "taking" in the constitutional sense.' Armstrong v. United States, 364 U.S. 40, 48, 80 S.Ct. 1563, 1568 (1960)." Although Robins and the other students "may have 'physically invaded' appellants' property," the intrusion here was simply not comparable to that in *Kaiser Aetna* v. *United States* (see p. 506) where "reasonable investment backed expectations" were so extensively damaged when the "right to exclude others" was destroyed that the government-mandated intrusion amounted to a "taking." In this case, "[t]here is nothing to suggest that preventing appellants from prohibiting this sort of activity will unreasonably impair the value or use of their property as a shopping center. The PruneYard is a large commercial complex that covers several city blocks, contains numerous separate business establishments, and is open to the public at large." The Court also pointed out that Robins and the others conducted themselves in an orderly fashion and that the California court made clear that PruneYard was entitled to impose reasonable time, place, and manner restrictions to minimize disruption of its commercial function.

Turning to the First and Fourteenth Amendment challenge, the Court rejected the contention that, like the message challenged as unconstitutionally imposed in *Wooley* v. *Maynard* (see p. 1317), PruneYard was made "to participate in the dissemination of an ideological message by displaying it on [its] private property in a manner and for the express purpose that it be observed and read by the public." The Court went on to point out several factors that distinguished this case from that case where the State of New Hampshire had the statutory authority to impose criminal sanctions on persons who covered the state motto "Live Free or Die" on their passenger car license plates. In the first place, noted the Court, the message in *Wooley* was displayed on appellant's "personal property that was used 'as part of his daily life,' " while here "the shopping center by choice of its owner is not limited to * * * personal use * * * [but] is instead a business establishment that is open to the public to come and go as they please." Consequently, "[t]he view expressed by members of the public in passing out pamphlets or seeking signatures for a petition * * * will not likely be identified with those of the owner." Secondly, unlike *Wooley*, "no specific message is dictated by the State to be displayed on appellants' property" so there is "no danger of governmental discrimination for or against a particular message." Finally, the owners of the PruneYard "can expressly disavow any connection with the message by simply posting signs in the area where the speakers or handbillers stand * * * disclaim[ing] any sponsorship of the message" and indicating that these individuals are espousing their own messages as is their prerogative under state law.

In a concurring opinion, Justice Marshall reaffirmed his "belie[f] that *Logan Valley* was rightly decided, and that both *Lloyd* and *Hudgens* were incorrect interpretations of the First and Fourteenth Amendments." "State action," he reasoned, "was present in all three cases." Justice Marshall explained: "In all of them the shopping center owners had opened their centers to the public at large, effectively replacing the State with respect to such traditional First Amendment forums as streets, sidewalks, and parks. The State had in turn made its law of trespass available to shopping center owners, enabling them to exclude those who wished to engage in expressive activity on their premises. Rights of free expression become illusory when a State has operated in such a way as to shut off effective channels of communication." Alternatively, he "applaud[ed] the [California] court's decision, which is part of a very healthy trend of affording state constitutional provisions a more expansive interpretation than this Court has given to the Federal Constitution."

In another concurring opinion, in which he was joined by Justice White, Justice Powell emphasized that he joined parts of the Court's opinion "on the understanding that our decision is limited to the type of shopping center involved in this case." He thought that "[s]ignificantly different questions would be presented if a State authorized strangers to picket or distribute leaflets in privately owned, freestanding stores and commercial premises." He added, "Nor does the decision today apply to all shopping centers." Justice Powell thought "some of the language in the Court's opinion [was] unnecessarily and confusingly broad." In his view, "state action that transforms privately owned property into a forum for the expression of the public's views could raise serious First Amendment questions."

Said Justice Powell with respect to the perplexing potential of one such controversy:

> If a state law mandated public access to the bulletin board of a freestanding store, hotel, office, or small shopping center, customers might well conclude that the messages reflect the view of the proprietor. The same would be true if the public were allowed to solicit or distribute pamphlets in the entrance area of a store or in the lobby of a private building. The property owner or proprietor would be faced with a choice: he either could permit his customers to receive a mistaken impression or he could disavow the messages. Should he take the first course, he effectively has been compelled to affirm someone else's belief. Should he choose the second, he had been forced to speak when he would prefer to remain silent. In short, he has lost control over his freedom to speak or not to speak on certain issues. The mere fact that he is free to dissociate himself from the views expressed on his property, * * * cannot restore his "right to refrain from speaking at all." Wooley v. Maynard, supra, 430 U.S., at 714, 97 S.Ct., at 1435.
>
> A property owner also may be faced with speakers who wish to use his premises as a platform for views tht he finds morally repugnant. Numerous examples come to mind. A minority-owned business confronted with distributors from the American Nazi Party or the Ku Klux Klan, a church-operated enterprise asked to host demonstrations in favor of abortion, or a union compelled to supply a forum to right-to-work advocates could be placed in an intolerable position if state law requires it to make its private property available to anyone who wishes to speak. The strong emotions evoked by speech in such situations may virtually compel the proprietor to respond.
>
> The pressure to respond is particularly apparent when the owner has taken a position opposed to the view being expressed on his property. But an owner who strongly objects to some of the causes to which the state-imposed right of access would extend may oppose ideological activities "of *any* sort" that are not related to the purposes for which he has invited the public onto his property. * * * To require the owner to specify the particular ideas he finds objectionable enough to compel a response would force him to relinquish his "freedom to maintain his own beliefs without public disclosure." * * * Thus, the right to control one's own speech may be burdened impermissibly even when listeners will not assume that the messages expressed on private property are those of the owner.

RECENT CASES ON TIME, PLACE, AND MANNER LIMITATIONS

Case	Facts	Outcome	Vote	Reasoning	Dissents
Carey v. Brown, 447 U.S. 455, 100 S.Ct. 2286 (1980)	An Illinois statute prohibited all picketing of residences or dwellings but exempted from its prohibition "the peaceful picketing of a place of employment involved in a labor dispute."	Struck down	6–3	The statute denied equal protection by placing an unjustified premium on one kind of speech, namely that related to labor disputes. The law was insufficiently tailored in its subject matter discrimination to support any such valid interest as, for example, the protection of privacy.	Burger, Blackmun, and Rehnquist

TIME, PLACE, AND MANNER LIMITATIONS (*Cont.*)

Case	Facts	Outcome	Vote	Reasoning	Dissents
Schad v. Borough of Mt. Ephraim, 452 U.S. 61, 101 S.Ct. 2176 (1980)	A local ordinance banned "live entertainment," including nude dancing.	Struck down	7–2	By excluding "live entertainment," the ordinance proscribes a wide range of expression protected by the First Amendment. Nude (as distinguished from "obscene") dancing is not without First Amendment protection. The zoning ordinance is neither narrowly drawn nor in furtherance of a "sufficiently substantial govermental interest." The asserted justification that permitting live entertainment would conflict with the borough's plan to create a commercial area catering only to the most immediate needs of its residents is patently insufficient. There was also no evidence to show that live entertainment, as distinguished from some of the presently permitted uses, would increase problems associated with parking, trash, police protection, and medical facilities. Finally, the borough did not demonstrate what interests supporting the ordinance as a time, place, or manner limitation made it reasonable to exclude "live entertainment" but permitted a wide variety of commercial uses.	Burger and Rehnquist

COHEN v. CALIFORNIA

Supreme Court of the United States, 1971
403 U.S. 15, 91 S.Ct. 1780, 29 L.Ed.2d 284

Cohen was convicted in Los Angeles Municipal Court for violating a provision of the California Penal Code which made it a misdemeanor to "maliciously and willfully disturb the peace or quiet of any neighborhood or person * * * by * * * offensive conduct * * * " and he was sentenced to thirty days' imprisonment. He had been arrested and charged with this offense for wearing a jacket with the words "Fuck the Draft" emblazoned on it in a corridor of the Los Angeles County Courthouse. Women and children were present in the corridor. A California appellate court noted, however, that Cohen "did not engage in nor threaten to engage in, or did anyone as the result of his conduct in fact commit or threaten to commit any act of violence." Nor did Cohen make any "loud or unusual noise." He testified that the words on his jacket were a straightforward expression of his strongly felt sentiments about the Vietnam war. The U. S. Supreme Court granted certiorari to review the conviction.

Mr. Justice HARLAN delivered the opinion of the Court.

This case may seem at first blush too inconsequential to find its way into our books, but the issue it presents is of no small constitutional significance.

*   *   *

The conviction quite clearly rests upon the asserted offensiveness of the *words* Cohen used to convey his message to the public. The only "conduct" which the State sought to punish is the fact of communication. Thus, we deal here with a conviction resting solely upon "speech" * * * not upon any separately identifiable conduct which allegedly was intended by Cohen to be perceived by others as expressive of particular views but which, on its face, does not necessarily convey any message and hence arguably could be regulated without effectively repressing Cohen's ability to express himself. Cf. United States v. O'Brien, 391 U.S. 367, 88 S.Ct. 1673 (1968). Further, the State certainly lacks power to punish Cohen for the underlying content of the message the inscription conveyed. At least so long as there is no showing of an intent to incite disobedience to or disruption of the draft, Cohen could not, consistently with the First and Fourteenth Amendments, be punished for asserting the evident position on the inutility or immorality of the draft his jacket reflected. * * *

Appellant's conviction, then, rests squarely upon his exercise of the "freedom of speech" protected from arbitrary governmental interference by the Constitution and can be justified, if at all, only as a valid regulation of the manner in which he exercised that freedom, not as a permissible prohibition on the substantive message it conveys. This does not end the inquiry, of course, for the First and Fourteenth Amendments have never been thought to give absolute protection to every individual to speak whenever or wherever he pleases or to use any form of address in any circumstances that he chooses. In this vein, too, however, we think it important to note that several issues typically associated with such problems are not presented here.

In the first place, Cohen was tried under a statute applicable throughout the entire State. Any attempt to support this conviction on the ground that the statute seeks to preserve an appropriately decorous atmosphere in the courthouse where Cohen was arrested must fail in the absence of any language in the statute that would have put appellant on notice that certain kinds of otherwise permissible speech or conduct would nevertheless, under California law, not be tolerated in certain places. See Edwards v. South Carolina, 372 U.S. 229, 236–237, 83 S.Ct. 680, 683–684 (1963). Cf. Adderley v. Florida, 385 U.S. 39, 87 S.Ct. 242 (1966). No fair reading of the phrase "offensive conduct" can be said sufficiently to inform the ordinary person that distinctions between certain locations are thereby created.

In the second place, as it comes to us, this case cannot be said to fall within those relatively few categories of instances where prior decisions have established the power of government to deal more comprehensively with certain forms of individual expression simply upon a showing that such a form was employed. This is not, for example, an obscenity case. Whatever else may be necessary to give rise to the States' broader power to prohibit obscene expression, such expression must be, in some significant way, erotic. Roth v. United States, 354 U.S. 476, 77 S.Ct. 1304 (1957). It cannot plausibly be maintained that this vulgar allusion to the Selective Service System would conjure up such psychic stimulation in anyone likely to be confronted with Cohen's crudely defaced jacket.

This Court has also held that the States are free to ban the simple use, without a demonstration of additional justifying circumstances, of so-called "fighting words," those personally abusive epithets which, when addressed to the ordinary citizen, are, as a matter of common knowledge, inherently likely to provoke violent reaction. Chaplinsky v. New Hampshire, 315 U.S. 568, 62 S.Ct. 766 (1942). While the four-letter word displayed by Cohen in relation to the draft is not uncommonly employed in a personally provocative fashion, in this instance it was clearly not "directed to the person of the hearer." * * * No individual actually or likely to be present could reasonably have regarded the words on appellant's jacket as a direct personal insult. Nor do we have here an instance of the exercise of the State's police power to prevent a speaker from intentionally provoking a given group to hostile reaction. Cf. Feiner v. New York, 340 U.S. 315, 71 S.Ct. 303 (1951); Terminiello v. Chicago, 337 U.S. 1, 69 S.Ct. 894 (1949). There is, as noted above, no showing that anyone who saw Cohen was in fact violently aroused or that appellant intended such a result.

Finally, in arguments before this Court much has been made of the claim that Cohen's distasteful mode of expression was thrust upon unwilling or unsuspecting viewers, and that the State might therefore legitimately act as it did in order to protect the sensitive from otherwise unavoidable exposure to appellant's crude form of protest. Of course,

the mere presumed presence of unwitting listeners or viewers does not serve automatically to justify curtailing all speech capable of giving offense. * * * While this Court has recognized that government may properly act in many situations to prohibit intrusion into the privacy of the home of unwelcome views and ideas which cannot be totally banned from the public dialogue, * * * we have at the same time consistently stressed that "we are often 'captives' outside the sanctuary of the home and subject to objectionable speech." * * * The ability of government, consonant with the Constitution, to shut off discourse solely to protect others from hearing it is, in other words, dependent upon a showing that substantial privacy interests are being invaded in an essentially intolerable manner. Any broader view of this authority would effectively empower a majority to silence dissidents simply as a matter of personal predilections.

In this regard, persons confronted with Cohen's jacket were in a quite different posture than, say, those subjected to the raucous emissions of sound trucks blaring outside their residences. Those in the Los Angeles courthouse could effectively avoid further bombardment of their sensibilities simply by averting their eyes. And, while it may be that one has a more substantial claim to a recognizable privacy interest when walking through a courthouse corridor than, for example, strolling through Central Park, surely it is nothing like the interest in being free from unwanted expression in the confines of one's own home. * * *

[W]e cannot overemphasize that, in our judgment, most situations where the State has a justifiable interest in regulating speech will fall within one or more of the various established exceptions, discussed above but not applicable here, to the usual rule that governmental bodies may not prescribe the form or content of individual expression. * * *

* * *

[W]e discern certain more particularized considerations that peculiarly call for reversal of this conviction. First, the principle contended for by the State seems inherently boundless. How is one to distinguish this from any other offensive word? Surely the State has no right to cleanse public debate to the point where it is grammatically palatable to the most squeamish among us. Yet no readily ascertainable general principle exists for stopping short of that result were we to affirm the judgment below. For, while the particular four-letter word being litigated here is perhaps more distasteful than most others of its genre, it is nevertheless often true that one man's vulgarity is another's lyric. Indeed, we think it is largely because governmental officials cannot make principled distinctions in this area that the Constitution leaves matters of taste and style so largely to the individual.

* * *

It is, in sum, our judgment that, absent a more particularized and compelling reason for its actions, the State may not, consistently with the First and Fourteenth Amendments, make the simple public display here involved of this single four-letter expletive a criminal offense. * * *

Reversed.

Mr. Justice BLACKMUN, with whom The CHIEF JUSTICE [BURGER] and Mr. Justice BLACK join.

I dissent, and I do so for two reasons:

1. Cohen's absurd and immature antic, in my view, was mainly conduct and little speech. * * * The California Court of Appeal appears so to have described it * * * and I cannot characterize it otherwise. Further, the case appears to me to be well within the sphere of Chaplinsky v. New Hampshire, 315 U.S. 568, 62 S.Ct. 766 (1942). * * * As a consequence, this Court's agonizing over First Amendment values seems misplaced and unnecessary.

2. I am not at all certain that the California Court of Appeal's construction of [the statute] is now the authoritative California construction. * * * Inasmuch as this Court does not dismiss this case, it ought to be remanded to the California Court of Appeal for reconsideration in the light of [a] subsequently rendered decision by the State's highest tribunal. * * *

Mr. Justice WHITE concurs in Paragraph 2 of Mr. Justice BLACKMUN'S dissenting opinion.

Pending prosecution, Richard Erznoznik, manager of a Jacksonville, Florida drive-in, brought suit for a declaration as to the constitutionality of a city ordinance making it a public nuisance and a punishable offense to exhibit any motion picture containing nudity where the screen is visible from a public street. Erznoznik was alleged to have permitted the showing of "Class of '74", a movie in which "female buttocks and bare breasts were shown." Two state courts upheld the ordinance as a valid exercise of the police power, and the Florida Supreme

Court, with three Justices dissenting, refused to hear the case, whereupon Erznoznik appealed to the U.S. Supreme Court.

In Erznoznik v. City of Jacksonville, 422 U.S. 205, 95 S.Ct. 2268 (1975), the Supreme Court found the ordinance unconstitutional. Speaking for the Court, Justice Powell concluded that the ordinance, which "discriminates among movies solely on the basis of content" and sweeps broadly so as to ban the showing of "movies containing any nudity, however innocent or even educational," was justified neither "as a means of preventing significant intrusions on privacy" nor "as an exercise of the city's undoubted police power to protect children." As to the first of these aims, the Court reasoned that the putative poor taste of otherwise protected expression was no justification for its suppression and that, at any rate, "the screen of a drive-in theater is not 'so obtrusive as to make it impossible for an unwilling individual to avoid exposure to it.'" In terms of the second justification offered for the ordinance, the Court held that the ban on all nudity was overbroad. The Court observed that the ordinance "would bar a film containing a picture of a baby's buttocks, the nude body of a war victim, or scenes from a culture in which nudity is indigenous." And it concluded, "Clearly all nudity cannot be deemed obscene even as to minors. * * * Speech that is neither obscene as to youths nor subject to some other legitimate proscription cannot be suppressed solely to protect the young from ideas or images that a legislative body thinks unsuitable for them." "Moreover," added Justice Powell, "the deterrent effect of this ordinance is both real and substantial," for the owners and operators of drive-in theaters "are faced with an unwelcome choice: to avoid prosecution of themselves and their employees they must either restrict their movie offerings or construct adequate protective fencing which may be extremely expensive or even physically impracticable." Although Justice Douglas in a concurring opinion pointed out that "under proper circumstances, a narrowly drawn ordinance could be utilized within constitutional boundaries to protect the interests of captive audiences or to promote highway safety," Justice Powell noted that "Nothing in the record or in the text of the ordinance suggests it is aimed at traffic regulation."

Chief Justice Burger dissented in an opinion in which Justice Rehnquist joined, explaining that whatever may be said of the leather jacket in *Cohen* v. *California,* "it distorts reality to apply that notion to the outsize screen of a drive-in movie theater" that produces "giant displays which through technology are capable of revealing and emphasizing the most intimate details of human anatomy." Justice White, dissenting separately, observed that, applying the same logic as that found in the majority opinion, "the State may not forbid 'expressive' nudity on the public streets, in the public parks or any other public place since other persons in those places at that time have a 'limited privacy interest' and may merely look the other way." Said Justice White, "I am not ready to take this step with the Court."

VILLAGE OF SCHAUMBURG v. CITIZENS FOR A BETTER ENVIRONMENT

Supreme Court of the United States, 1980
444 U.S. 620, 100 S.Ct. 826, 62 L.Ed.2d 73

A municipal ordinance prohibited door-to-door and on-the-street solicitation of contributions by charitable organizations which do not use 75-percent of their receipts for "charitable purposes," that is for purposes other than solicitation expenses, salaries, overhead, and other administrative costs. After the village government denied the Citizens for a Better Environment (CBE) a permit to solicit because it could not meet the ordinance's 75-percent requirement, the nonprofit environmental protection organization brought suit for declaratory and injunctive relief in federal district court alleging a violation of the First and Fourteenth

Amendments. The district court granted summary judgment for the organization, and a federal appellate court affirmed the decision, whereupon the village sought certiorari from the Supreme Court.

Mr. Justice WHITE delivered the opinion of the Court.

*   *   *

It is urged that the ordinance should be sustained because it deals only with solicitation and because any charity is free to propagate its views from door to door in the Village without a permit as long as it refrains from soliciting money. But this represents a far too limited view of our prior cases relevant to canvassing and soliciting by religious and charitable organizations.

*   *   *

Prior *   *   * [cases] clearly establish that charitable appeals for funds, on the street or door to door, involve a variety of speech interests—communication of information, the dissemination and propagation of views and ideas, and the advocacy of causes—that are within the protection of the First Amendment. Soliciting financial support is undoubtedly subject to reasonable regulation but the latter must be undertaken with due regard for the reality that solicitation is characteristically intertwined with informative and perhaps persuasive speech seeking support for particular causes or for particular views on economic, political or social issues, and for the reality that without solicitation the flow of such information and advocacy would likely cease. Canvassers in such contexts are necessarily more than solicitors for money. Furthermore, because charitable solicitation does more than inform private economic decisions and is not primarily con-

cerned with providing information about the characteristics and costs of goods and services, it has not been dealt with in our cases as a variety of purely commercial speech.

The issue before us, then, is not whether charitable solicitations in residential neighborhoods are within the protections of the First Amendment. It is clear that they are. "[O]ur cases long have protected speech even though it is in the form of *   *   * a solicitation to pay or contribute money, New York Times Co. v. Sullivan, [376 U.S. 254, 84 S.Ct. 710 (1964)]." Bates v. State Bar of Arizona, 433 U.S. 350, 363, 97 S.Ct. 2691, 2699 (1977).

The issue is whether the Village has exercised its power to regulate solicitation in such a manner as not unduly to intrude upon the rights of free speech. *   *   * In pursuing this question we must first deal with the claim of the Village that summary judgment was improper because there was an unresolved factual dispute concerning the true character of CBE's organization. Although CBE's affidavits in support of its motion for summary judgment and describing its interests, the activities of its canvassers and the percentage of its receipts devoted to salaries and administrative expenses were not controverted, the District Court made no findings with respect to the nature of CBE's activities; and the Court of Appeals expressly stated that the facts with respect to the internal affairs and operations of the organization were immaterial to a proper resolution of the case. The Village claims, however, that it should have had a chance to prove that the 75-percent requirement is valid as applied to CBE because CBE spends so much of its resources for the benefit of its employees that it may appropriately be deemed an organization existing for private profit rather than for charitable purposes.

We agree with the Court of Appeals that CBE was entitled to its judgment of facial invalidity if the ordinance purported to prohibit canvassing by a substantial category of charities to which the 75-percent limitation could not be applied consistently with the First and Fourteenth Amendments, even if there was no demonstration that CBE itself was one of these organizations. Given a case or controversy, a litigant whose own activities are unprotected, may nevertheless challenge a statute by showing that it substantially abridges the First Amendment rights of other parties not before the court. * * * In these First Amendment contexts, the courts are inclined to disregard the normal rule against permitting one whose conduct may validly be prohibited to challenge the proscription as it applies to others because of the possibility that protected speech or associative activities may be inhibited by the overly broad reach of the statute.

We have declared the overbreadth doctrine to be inapplicable in certain commercial speech cases, Bates v. State Bar of Arizona, 433 U.S., at 381, 97 S.Ct., at 2707, but as we have indicated, that limitation does not concern us here. The Court of Appeals was thus free to inquire whether [the ordinance] was overbroad, a question of law that involved no dispute about the characteristics of CBE. On this basis, proceeding to rule on the merits of the summary judgment was proper. As we have

indicated, we also agree with the Court of Appeals' ruling on the motion.

Although indicating that the 75-percent limitation might be enforceable against "the more traditional charitable organizations" or "where solicitors represent themselves as mere conduits for contributions," * * * the Court of Appeals identified a class of charitable organizations as to which the 75-percent rule could not constitutionally be applied. These were the organizations whose primary purpose is not to provide money or services for the poor, the needy or other worthy objects of charity, but to gather and disseminate information about and advocate positions on matters of public concern. These organizations characteristically use paid solicitors who "necessarily combine" the solicitation of financial support with the "functions of information dissemination, discussion, and advocacy of public issues." * * * These organizations also pay other employees to obtain and process the necessary information and to arrive at and announce in suitable form the organizations' preferred positions on the issues of interest to them. Organizations of this kind, although they might pay only reasonable salaries, would necessarily spend more than 25% of their budgets on salaries and administrative expenses and would be completely barred from solicitation in the Village. The Court of Appeals concluded that such a prohibition was an unjustified infringement of the First and Fourteenth Amendments.

We agree with the Court of Appeals that the 75-percent limitation is a direct and substantial limitation on protected activity that cannot be sustained unless it serves a sufficiently strong, subordinating interest that the Village is entitled to protect. We also agree that the Village's proffered justifications are inadequate and that the ordinance cannot survive scrutiny under the First Amendment.

The Village urges that the 75-percent requirement is intimately related to substantial governmental interests "in protecting the public from fraud, crime and undue annoyance." These interests are indeed substantial, but they are only peripherally promoted by the 75-percent requirement and could be sufficiently served by measures less destructive of First Amendment interests.

Prevention of fraud is the Village's principal justification for prohibiting solicitation by charities that spend more than one-quarter of their receipts on salaries and administrative expenses. The submission is that any organization using more than 25% of its receipts on fund-raising, salaries and overhead is not a charitable, but a commercial, for profit enterprise and that to permit it to represent itself as a charity is fraudulent. But, as the Court of Appeals recognized, this cannot be true of those organizations that are primarily engaged in research, advocacy or public education and that use their own paid staff to carry out these functions as well as to solicit financial support. The Village, consistently with the First Amendment, may not label such groups "fraudulent" and bar them from canvassing on the streets and house to house. Nor may the Village lump such organizations with those that in fact are using the charitable label as a cloak for profitmaking and refuse to employ more precise measures to separate one kind from the other. The Village may serve its legitimate interests, but it must do so by narrow-

ly drawn regulations designed to serve those interests without unnecessarily interfering with First Amendment freedoms. * * * "Broad prophylactic rules in the area of free expression are suspect. Precision of regulation must be the touchstone." * * * NAACP v. Button, 371 U.S. 415, 438, 83 S.Ct. 328, 340 (1963) (citations omitted).

The Village's legitimate interest in preventing fraud can be better served by measures less intrusive than a direct prohibition on solicitation. Fraudulent misrepresentations can be prohibited and the penal laws used to punish such conduct directly. * * * Efforts to promote disclosure of the finances of charitable organizations also may assist in preventing fraud by informing the public of the ways in which their contributions will be employed. Such measures may help make contribution decisions more informed, while leaving to individual choice the decision whether to contribute to organizations that spend large amounts on salaries and administrative expenses.

We also fail to perceive any substantial relationship between the 75-percent requirement and the protection of public safety or of residential privacy. There is no indication that organizations devoting more than one-quarter of their funds to salaries and administrative expenses are any more likely to employ solicitors who would be a threat to public safety than are other charitable organizations. Other provisions in the ordinance that are not challenged here, such as the provision making it unlawful for charitable organizations to use convicted felons as solicitors, * * * may bear some relation to public safety; the 75-percent requirement does not.

The 75-percent requirement is related to the protection of privacy only in the most indirect of ways. As the Village concedes, householders are equally disturbed by solicitation on behalf of organizations satisfying the 75-percent requirement as they are by solicitation on behalf of other organizations. The 75-percent requirement protects privacy only by reducing the total number of solicitors, as would any prohibition on solicitation. The ordinance is not directed to the unique privacy interests of persons residing in their homes because it applies not only to door-to-door solicitation, but also to solicitation on "public streets and public ways." * * * Other provisions of the ordinance, which are not challenged here, such as the provision permitting homeowners to bar solicitors from their property by posting signs reading "No Solicitors or Peddlers Invited," * * * suggest the availability of less intrusive and more effective measures to protect privacy. * * *

The 75-percent requirement in the Village ordinance plainly is insufficiently related to the governmental interests asserted in its support to justify its interference with protected speech. "Frauds may be denounced as offenses and punished by law. Trespasses may similarly be forbidden. If it is said that these means are less efficient and convenient than * * * [deciding in advance] what information may be disseminated from house to house, and who may impart the information, the answer is that considerations of this sort do not empower a municipality to abridge freedom of speech and press." Schneider v. State (Town of Irvington), 308 U.S., at 164, 60 S.Ct., at 152.

We find no reason to disagree with the Court of Appeals' conclusion that [the ordinance] * * * is unconstitutionally overbroad. Its judgment is therefore affirmed.

It is so ordered.

Mr. Justice REHNQUIST, dissenting.

The Court holds that Art. III of the Schaumburg Village Code is unconstitutional as applied to prohibit respondent Citizens for a Better Environment (CBE) from soliciting contributions door to door. If read in isolation, today's decision might be defensible. When combined with this Court's earlier pronouncements on the subject, however, today's decision relegates any local government interested in regulating door-to-door activities to the role of Sisyphus.

The Court's opinion [in portions which have been deleted] first recites the litany of language from 40 years of decisions in which this Court has considered various restrictions on the right to distribute information or solicit door to door, concluding from these decisions that "charitable appeals for funds, on the street or door to door, involve a variety of speech interests * * * that are within the protection of the First Amendment." * * * I would have thought this proposition self-evident now that this Court has swept even the most banal commercial speech within the ambit of the First Amendment. See Virginia Board of Pharmacy v. Virginia Consumer Council, 425 U.S. 748, 96 S.Ct. 1817 (1976). But, having arrived at this conclusion on the basis of earlier cases, the Court effectively departs from the reasoning of those cases in discussing the limits on Schaumburg's authority to place limitations on so-called "charitable" solicitors who go from house to house in the village.

The Court's neglect of its prior precedents in this regard is entirely understandable, since the earlier decisions striking down various regulations covering door-to-door activities turned upon factors not present in the instant case. A plurality of these decisions turned primarily, if not exclusively, upon the amount of discretion vested in municipal authorities to grant or deny permits on the basis of vague or even non-existent criteria. See Schneider v. State (Town of Irvington), 308 U.S. 147, 163–164, 60 S.Ct. 146, 151–152 (1939); Cantwell v. Connecticut, 310 U.S. 296, 305–306, 60 S.Ct. 900, 904 (1940); Largent v. Texas, 318 U.S. 418, 422, 63 S.Ct. 667, 669 (1943); Hynes v. Mayor of Oradell, 425 U.S. 610, 620–621, 96 S.Ct. 1755, 1760–1761 (1976). In *Schneider*, for example, the Court invalidated such an ordinance as applied to Jehovah's Witnesses because "[i]n the end, [the applicant's] liberty to communicate with the residents of the town at their homes depends upon the exercise of the officer's discretion." Schneider v. State (Town of Irvington), supra, at 164, 60 S.Ct., at 152. These cases clearly do not control the validity of Schaumburg's ordinance, which leaves virtually no discretion in the hands of the licensing authority.

Another line of earlier cases involved the distribution of information, as opposed to requests for contributions. Martin v. Struthers, 319 U.S. 141, 63 S.Ct. 862 (1943), for example, dealt with Jehovah's Witnesses who had gone door to door with invitations to a religious meeting despite a local ordinance prohibiting distribution of any "handbills, circulars, or other advertisements" door

to door. The Court noted that such an ordinance "limits the dissemination of knowledge," and that it could "serve no purpose but that forbidden by the Constitution, the naked restriction of the dissemination of ideas." * * *

Here, however, the challenged ordinance deals not with the dissemination of ideas, but rather with the solicitation of money. That the *Martin* Court would have found this distinction important is apparent not only from *Martin's* emphasis on the dissemination of knowledge, but also from various other decisions of the same period. * * *

Shunning the guidance of these cases, the Court sets out to define a new category of solicitors who may not be subjected to regulation. According to the Court, Schaumburg cannot prohibit door-to-door solicitation for contributions by "organizations whose primary purpose is * * * to gather and disseminate information about and advocate positions on matters of public concern." * * * In another portion of its opinion, the majority redefines this immunity as extending to all organizations "primarily engaged in research, advocacy, or public education and that use their own paid staff to carry out these functions as well as to solicit financial support." * * * This result—or perhaps, more accurately, these results—seem unwarranted by the First and Fourteenth Amendments for three reasons.

First, from a legal standpoint, the Court invites municipalities to draw a line it has already erased. Today's opinion strongly, and I believe correctly, implies that the result here would be otherwise if CBE's primary objective were to provide "information about the characteristics and

costs of goods and services,"
* * * rather than to "advocate
positions on matters of public concern." * * * Four years ago,
however, the Court relied upon the
supposed bankruptcy of this very distinction in overturning a prohibition
on advertising by pharmacists. See
Virginia Pharmacy Board v. Virginia
Consumer Council, 425 U.S. 748, 96
S.Ct. 1817 (1976). According to *Virginia Pharmacy*, while "not all commercial messages contain the same
or even a very great public interest
element[,] [t]here are few to which
such an element * * * could not
be added." * * * This and other
considerations led the Court in that
case to conclude that "no line between publicly 'interesting' or 'important' commercial advertising and the
[other] kind could ever be drawn."
* * * To the extent that the
Court found such a line elusive in
Virginia Pharmacy, I venture to
suggest that the Court, as well as local legislators, will find the line
equally elusive in the context of
door-to-door solicitation.

Second, from a practical standpoint, the Court gives absolutely no
guidance as to how a municipality
might identify those organizations
"whose primary purpose is * * *
to gather and disseminate information about and advocate positions on
matters of public concern," and
which are therefore exempt from
[the ordinance]. Earlier cases do
provide one guideline: the municipality must rely on objective criteria,
since reliance upon official discretion
in any significant degree would
clearly run afoul of *Schneider,
Cantwell, Largent,* and *Hynes.* In
requiring municipal authorities to
use "more precise measures to separate" constitutionally preferred organizations from their less preferred

counterparts, * * * the Court
would do well to remember that
these local bodies are poorly
equipped to investigate and audit the
various persons and organizations
that will apply to them for preferred
status. Stripped of discretion, they
must be able to resort to a line-drawing test capable of easy and reliable
application without the necessity for
an exhaustive case-by-case investigation of each applicant.

Finally, I believe that the Court
overestimates the value, in a constitutional sense, of door-to-door solicitation for financial contributions and
simultaneously underestimates the
reasons why a village board might
conclude that regulation of such activity was necessary. * * *
While such activity may be worthy of
heightened protection when limited
to the dissemination of information,
* * * or when designed to propagate religious beliefs, * * * I believe that a simple request for money
lies far from the core protections of
the First Amendment as heretofore
interpreted. In the case of such solicitation, the community's interest in
ensuring that the collecting organization meet some objective financial
criteria is indisputably valid. Regardless whether one labels nonchar-
itable solicitation "fraudulent," nothing in the United States Constitution
should prevent residents of a community from making the collective judgment that certain worthy charities
may solicit door to door while at the
same time insulating themselves
against panhandlers, profiteers, and
peddlers.

The central weakness of the
Court's decision, I believe, is its failure to recognize, let alone confront,
the two most important issues in this
case: how does one define a "charita-

ble" organization, and to which authority in our federal system is application of that definition confided? I would uphold Schaumburg's ordinance as applied to CBE because that ordinance, while perhaps too strict to suit some tastes, affects only door-to-door solicitation for financial contributions, leaves little or no discretion in the hands of municipal authorities to "censor" unpopular speech, and is rationally related to the community's collective desire to bestow its largess upon organizations that are truly "charitable." I therefore dissent.

c. SYMBOLIC SPEECH

WEST VIRGINIA STATE BOARD OF EDUCATION v. BARNETTE

Supreme Court of the United States, 1943
319 U.S. 624, 63 S.Ct. 1178, 87 L.Ed. 1628

In Minersville School Dist. v. Gobitis, 310 U.S. 586, 60 S.Ct. 1010 (1940), the Supreme Court per Justice Frankfurter sustained the constitutionality of the directive by a local board of education in a small Pennsylvania town to compel students and teachers in the public schools to salute the flag. Following that decision, the West Virginia legislature passed an act requiring all schools in the state to conduct classes in civics, history, and the federal and state constitutions "for the purpose of teaching, fostering and perpetuating the ideals, principles and spirit of Americanism" and increasing knowledge of the structure and operations of government. Pursuant to this legislation the State Board of Education directed that all students and teachers in West Virginia's public schools salute the flag as part of regular school activities. The prescribed ritual entailed the recitation of the pledge of allegiance while maintaining the "stiff arm" salute. Failure to comply constituted insubordination for which a student was to be expelled and thereafter treated as a delinquent. Parents were liable to prosecution and a penalty of thirty days in jail and a fifty-dollar fine.

Walter Barnette, a Jehovah's Witness, brought suit to enjoin this compulsory flag salute on grounds that to have his children comply would violate a religious commandment not to worship any graven image. The State Board of Education moved to dismiss the complaint, but a federal district judge granted the injunction whereupon the Board appealed.

You will want to note especially the explanations offered in the concurring opinions setting forth the views of Justices Black, Douglas, and Murphy, who were the only members of the Court in *Barnette* to change from the votes they cast upholding the flag salute in *Gobitis*. With the exceptions of Justices Jackson and Rutledge, who were not appointed until after 1940, the remaining members of the Court in *Barnette* were consistent with the positions they had taken in *Gobitis*: Chief Justice Stone, who had dissented in *Gobitis*, was in the majority in *Barnette*, and Justices Roberts, Reed, and Frankfurter, who were in the majority in *Gobitis*, dissented in *Barnette*.

Mr. Justice JACKSON delivered the opinion of the Court.

* * *

The freedom asserted by these appellees does not bring them into collision with rights asserted by any other individual. It is such conflicts which most frequently require intervention of the State to determine where the rights of one end and those of another begin. But the refusal of these persons to participate in the ceremony does not interfere with or deny rights of others to do so. Nor is there any question in this case that their behavior is peaceable and orderly. The sole conflict is between authority and rights of the individual. The State asserts power to condition access to public education on making a prescribed sign and profession and at the same time to coerce attendance by punishing both parent and child. The latter stand on the right of self-determination in matters that touch individual opinion and personal attitude.

As the present Chief Justice said in dissent in the *Gobitis* case, the State may "require teaching by instruction and study of all in our history and in the structure and organization of our government, including the guaranties of civil liberty which tend to inspire patriotism and love of country." * * * Here, however, we are dealing with a compulsion of students to declare a belief. They are not merely made acquainted with the flag salute so that they may be informed as to what it is or even what it means. The issue here is whether this slow and easily neglected route to aroused loyalties constitutionally may be short-cut by substituting a compulsory salute and slogan. * * *

There is no doubt that, in connection with the pledges, the flag salute is a form of utterance. Symbolism is a primitive but effective way of communicating ideas. The use of an emblem or flag to symbolize some system, idea, institution, or personality, is a short-cut from mind to mind. Causes and nations, political parties, lodges and ecclesiastical groups seek to knit the loyalty of their followings to a flag or banner, a color or design. The State announces rank, function,

and authority through crowns and maces, uniforms and black robes; the church speaks through the Cross, the Crucifix, the altar and shrine, and clerical raiment. Symbols of State often convey political ideas just as religious symbols come to convey theological ones. Associated with many of these symbols are appropriate gestures of acceptance or respect: a salute, a bowed or bared head, a bended knee. A person gets from a symbol the meaning he puts into it, and what is one man's comfort and inspiration is another's jest and scorn.

Over a decade ago Chief Justice Hughes led this Court in holding that the display of a red flag as a symbol of opposition by peaceful and legal means to organized government was protected by the free speech guaranties of the Constitution. Stromberg v. California, 283 U.S. 359, 51 S.Ct. 532. * * *

[H]ere the power of compulsion is invoked without any allegation that remaining passive during a flag salute ritual creates a clear and present danger that would justify an effort even to muffle expression. To sustain the compulsory flag salute we are required to say that a Bill of Rights which guards the individual's right to speak his own mind, left it open to public authorities to compel him to utter what is not in his mind.

Whether the First Amendment to the Constitution will permit officials to order observance of ritual of this nature does not depend upon whether as a voluntary exercise we would think it to be good, bad or merely innocuous. * * *

Nor does the issue as we see it turn on one's possession of particular religious views or the sincerity with which they are held. While religion supplies appellees' motive for enduring the discomforts of making the issue in this case, many citizens who do not share these religious views hold such a compulsory rite to infringe constitutional liberty of the individual. It is not necessary to inquire whether non-conformist beliefs will exempt from the duty to salute unless we first find power to make the salute a legal duty.

* * * We * * * re-examine specific grounds assigned for the *Gobitis* decision.

1. It was said that the flag-salute controversy confronted the Court with "the problem which Lincoln cast in memorable dilemma: 'Must a government of necessity be too *strong* for the liberties of its people, or too *weak* to maintain its own existence?'" and that the answer must be in favor of strength. * * *

* * *

It may be doubted whether Mr. Lincoln would have thought that the strength of government to maintain itself would be impressively vindicated by our confirming power of the state to expel a handful of children from school. Such oversimplification, so handy in political debate, often lacks the precision necessary to postulates of judicial reasoning. If validly applied to this problem, the utterance cited would resolve every issue of power in favor of those in authority and would require us to override every liberty thought to weaken or delay execution of their policies.

* * *

2. It was also considered in the *Gobitis* case that functions of educational officers in states, counties, and school districts were such that to interfere with their authority "would in effect make us the school board for the country." * * *

The Fourteenth Amendment, as now applied to the States, protects the citizen against the State itself and all of its creatures—Boards of Education not excepted. These have, of course, important, delicate, and highly discretionary functions, but none that they may not perform within the limits of the Bill of Rights. That they are educating the young for citizenship is reason for scrupulous protection of Constitutional freedoms of the individual, if we are not to strangle the free mind at its source and teach youth to discount important principles of our government as mere platitudes.

* * *

3. The *Gobitis* opinion reasoned that this is a field "where courts possess no marked and certainly no controlling competence," that it is committed to the legislatures as well as the courts to guard cherished liberties and that it is constitutionally appropriate to "fight out the wise use of legislative authority in the forum of public opinion and before legislative assemblies rather than to transfer such a contest to the judicial arena," since all the "effective means of inducing political changes are left free." * * *

The very purpose of a Bill of Rights was to withdraw certain subjects from the vicissitudes of political controversy, to place them beyond the reach of majorities and officials and to establish them as legal principles to be applied by the courts. One's right to life, liberty, and property, to free speech, a free press, freedom of worship and assembly, and other fundamental rights may not be submitted to vote; they depend on the outcome of no elections.

*   *   *

4. Lastly, and this is the very heart of the *Gobitis* opinion, it reasons that "National unity is the basis of national security," that the authorities have "the right to select appropriate means for its attainment," and hence reaches the conclusion that such compulsory measures toward "national unity" are constitutional. * * * Upon the verity of this assumption depends our answer in this case.

National unity as an end which officials may foster by persuasion and example is not in question. The problem is whether under our Constitution compulsion as here employed is a permissible means for its achievement.

Struggles to coerce uniformity of sentiment in support of some end thought essential to their time and country have been waged by many good as well as by evil men. Nationalism is a relatively recent phenomenon but at other times and places the ends have been racial or territorial security, support of a dynasty or regime, and particular plans for saving souls. As first and moderate methods to attain unity have failed, those bent on its accomplishment must resort to an ever-increasing severity. As governmental pressure toward unity becomes greater, so strife becomes more bitter as to whose unity it shall be. Probably no deeper division of our people could proceed from any provocation than from finding it necessary to choose what doctrine and whose program public educational officials shall compel youth to unite in embracing. Ultimate futility of such attempts to compel coherence is the lesson of every such

effort from the Roman drive to stamp out Christianity as a disturber of its pagan unity, the Inquisition, as a means to religious and dynastic unity, the Siberian exiles as a means to Russian unity, down to the fast failing efforts of our present totalitarian enemies. Those who begin coercive elimination of dissent soon find themselves exterminating dissenters. Compulsory unification of opinion achieves only the unanimity of the graveyard.

It seems trite but necessary to say that the First Amendment to our Constitution was designed to avoid these ends by avoiding these beginnings. There is no mysticism in the American concept of the State or of the nature or origin of its authority. We set up government by consent of the governed, and the Bill of Rights denies those in power any legal opportunity to coerce that consent. Authority here is to be controlled by public opinion, not public opinion by authority.

The case is made difficult not because the principles of its decision are obscure but because the flag involved is our own. * * * To believe that patriotism will not flourish if patriotic ceremonies are voluntary and spontaneous instead of a compulsory routine is to make an unflattering estimate of the appeal of our institutions to free minds. * * * [F]reedom to differ is not limited to things that do not matter much. That would be a mere shadow of freedom. The test of its substance is the right to differ as to things that touch the heart of the existing order.

If there is any fixed star in our constitutional constellation, it is that no official, high or petty, can prescribe what shall be orthodox in politics, nationalism, religion, or other matters of opinion or force citizens to confess by word or act their faith therein. If there are any circumstances which permit an exception, they do not now occur to us.

* * *

Affirmed.

Mr. Justice BLACK and Mr. Justice DOUGLAS, concurring.

We are substantially in agreement with the opinion just read, but since we originally joined with the Court in the *Gobitis* case, it is appropriate that we make a brief statement of reasons for our change of view.

Reluctance to make the Federal Constitution a rigid bar against state regulation of conduct thought inimical to the public welfare was the controlling influence which moved us to consent to the *Gobitis* decision. Long reflection convinced us that although the principle is sound, its application in the particular case was wrong. * * *

* * *

No well-ordered society can leave to the individuals an absolute right to make final decisions, unassailable by the State, as to everything they will or will not do. The First Amendment does not go so far. Religious faiths, honestly held, do not free individuals from responsibility to conduct themselves obediently to laws which are either imperatively necessary to protect society as a whole from grave and pressingly imminent dangers or which, without any general prohibition, merely regulate time, place or manner of religious activity. Decision as to the constitutionality of particular laws which strike at the substance of religious tenets and practices must be made by this Court. The duty is a solemn one, and in meeting it we cannot say that a failure, because of religious scruples, to assume a particular physical position and to repeat the words of a patriotic formula creates a grave danger to the nation. Such a statutory exaction is a form of test oath, and the test oath has always been abhorrent in the United States.

Mr. Justice MURPHY, concurring.

I agree with the opinion of the Court and join in it.

* * *

* * * I am impelled to conclude that such a requirement is not essential to the maintenance of effective government and orderly society. To many it is deeply distasteful to join in a public chorus of affirmation of private belief. By some, including the members of this sect, it is apparently regarded as incompatible with a primary religious obligation and therefore a restriction on religious freedom. Official compulsion to affirm what is contrary to one's religious beliefs is the antithesis of freedom of worship. * * *

[Justices ROBERTS and REED dissented and would have reversed the district court's decision on the basis of *Gobitis*. Justice FRANKFURTER's dissenting opinion appears on p. 46.]

Relying substantially on the holding in the flag salute case, supra, the Court in Wooley v. Maynard, 430 U.S. 705, 97 S.Ct. 1428 (1977), answered in the negative the question "whether the State of New Hampshire may constitutionally enforce criminal sanctions against persons who cover the [state] motto 'Live Free or Die' on passenger vehicle license plates because that motto is repugnant to their moral and religious beliefs." (The Maynards were Jehovah's Witnesses.) The Court found insufficient the two interests advanced by New Hampshire—"that display of the motto (1) facilitates the identification of passenger vehicles, and (2) promotes appreciation of history, individualism and state pride." As to the first of these assertions by the state, the Court found the configurations of letters and numbers normally comprising passenger license plates sufficient to serve the purpose of distinguishing those vehicles and as such constituted a "less drastic means for achieving the same basic purpose." And, with respect to the second aim, the Court per Chief Justice Burger concluded that "where the State's interest is to disseminate an ideology, no matter how acceptable to some, such interest cannot outweigh an individual's First Amendment right to avoid becoming the courier for such message." Arguing that "[t]he logic of the Court's opinion leads to startling, and I believe totally unacceptable, results," namely that the provision of the U.S. Code proscribing defacement of U.S. currency could not be enforced to prevent an atheist from obscuring the display of the mottos "In God We Trust" and "E pluribus unum" on American coins and paper money, Justice Rehnquist, joined by Justice Blackmun, dissented. In none of these contexts, he explained, was any affirmation of belief implicated. Justice White also dissented.

UNITED STATES v. O'BRIEN

Supreme Court of the United States, 1968
391 U.S. 367, 88 S.Ct. 1673, 20 L.Ed.2d 672

The facts are set out in the opinion.

Mr. Chief Justice WARREN delivered the opinion of the Court.

On the morning of March 31, 1966, David Paul O'Brien and three companions burned their Selective Service registration certificates on the steps of the South Boston Courthouse. A sizable crowd, including several agents of the Federal Bureau of Investigation, witnessed the event. Immediately after the burning, members of the crowd began attacking O'Brien and his companions. An FBI agent ushered O'Brien to safety inside the courthouse. After he was advised of his right to counsel and to silence, O'Brien stated to FBI agents that he had burned his registration certificate because of his beliefs, knowing that he was violating federal law. He produced the charred remains of the certificate,

which, with his consent, were photographed.

For this act, O'Brien was indicted, tried, convicted, and sentenced in the United States District Court for the District of Massachusetts. He did not contest the fact that he had burned the certificate. He stated in argument to the jury that he burned the certificate publicly to influence others to adopt his antiwar beliefs, as he put it, "so that other people would reevaluate their positions with Selective Service, with the armed forces, and reevaluate their place in the culture of today, to hopefully consider my position."

The indictment upon which he was tried charged that he "willfully and knowingly did mutilate, destroy, and change by burning * * * [his] Registration Certificate (Selective Service System Form No. 2); in violation of Title 50, App., United States Code, Section 462(b)." Section 462(b) is part of the Universal Military Training and Service Act of 1948. Section 462(b)(3), one of six numbered subdivisions of § 462(b), was amended by Congress in 1965, 79 Stat. 586 (adding the words italicized below), so that at the time O'Brien burned his certificate an offense was committed by any person,

"who forges, alters, *knowingly destroys, knowingly mutilates*, or in any manner changes any such certificate." * * * (Italics supplied.)

In the District Court, O'Brien argued that the 1965 Amendment prohibiting the knowing destruction or mutilation of certificates was unconstitutional because it was enacted to abridge free speech, and because it served no legitimate legislative purpose. The District Court rejected these arguments, holding that the statute on its face did not abridge First Amendment rights, that the court was not competent to inquire into the motives of Congress in enacting the 1965 Amendment, and that the Amendment was a reasonable exercise of the power of Congress to raise armies.

On appeal, the Court of Appeals for the First Circuit held the 1965 Amendment unconstitutional as a law abridging freedom of speech. At the time the Amendment was enacted, a regulation of the Selective Service System required registrants to keep their registration certificates in their "personal possession at all times." * * * Wilful violations of regulations promulgated pursuant to the Universal Military Training and Service Act were made criminal by statute. * * * The Court of Appeals, therefore, was of the opinion

that conduct punishable under the 1965 Amendment was already punishable under the nonpossession regulation, and consequently that the Amendment served no valid purpose; further, that in light of the prior regulation, the Amendment must have been "directed at public as distinguished from private destruction." On this basis, the court concluded that the 1965 Amendment ran afoul of the First Amendment by singling out persons engaged in protests for special treatment. The court ruled, however, that O'Brien's conviction should be affirmed under the statutory provision, 50 U.S.C.A. App. § 462(b)(6), which in its view made violation of the nonpossession regulation a crime, because it regarded such violation to be a lesser included offense of the crime defined by the 1965 Amendment.

* * *

O'Brien first argues that the 1965 Amendment is unconstitutional as applied to him because his act of burning his registration certificate was protected "symbolic speech" within the First Amendment. His argument is that the freedom of expression which the First Amendment guarantees includes all modes of "communication of ideas by conduct," and that his conduct is within this definition because he did it in "demonstration against the war and against the draft."

We cannot accept the view that an apparently limitless variety of conduct can be labeled "speech" whenever the person engaging in the conduct intends thereby to express an idea. However, even on the assumption that the alleged communicative element in O'Brien's conduct is sufficient to bring into play the First Amendment, it does not necessarily follow that the destruction of a registration certificate is constitutionally protected activity. This Court has held that when "speech" and "nonspeech" elements are combined in the same course of conduct, a sufficiently important governmental interest in regulating the nonspeech element can justify incidental limitations on First Amendment freedoms. To characterize the quality of the governmental interest which must appear, the Court has employed a variety of descriptive terms: compelling; substantial; subordinating; paramount; cogent; strong. Whatever imprecision inheres in these terms, we think it clear that a government regulation is sufficiently justified if it is within the constitutional power of the Government; if it furthers an important or substantial governmental interest; if the governmental interest is unrelated to the suppression of free expression; and if the incidental restriction on alleged First Amendment freedoms is no greater than is essential to the furtherance of that interest. We find that the 1965 Amendment to § 12(b) (3) of the Universal Military Training and Service Act meets all of these requirements, and consequently that O'Brien can be constitutionally convicted for violating it.

The constitutional power of Congress to raise and support armies and to make all laws necessary and proper to that end is broad and sweeping. * * * The power of Congress to classify and conscript manpower for military service is "beyond question." * * * Pursuant to this power, Congress may establish a system of registration for individuals liable for training and service, and may require such individuals within reason to cooper-

ate in the registration system. * * *

[Chief Justice WARREN then reviewed extensively how particular items of information contained on the card, such as classification, address of the local board, and continual reminders about the necessity of notifying the local board of changes in circumstances that might alter the registrant's classification, contributed to the effective functioning of the draft system.]

* * *

We think it apparent that the continuing availability to each registrant of his Selective Service certificates substantially furthers the smooth and proper functioning of the system that Congress has established to raise armies. We think it also apparent that the Nation has a vital interest in having a system for raising armies that functions with maximum efficiency and is capable of easily and quickly responding to continually changing circumstances. For these reasons, the Government has a substantial interest in assuring the continuing availability of issued Selective Service certificates.

It is equally clear that the 1965 Amendment specifically protects this substantial governmental interest. We perceive no alternative means that would more precisely and narrowly assure the continuing availability of issued Selective Service certificates than a law which prohibits their wilful mutilation or destruction. * * * The 1965 Amendment prohibits such conduct and does nothing more. * * *

* * *

O'Brien finally argues that the 1965 Amendment is unconstitutional as enacted because what he calls the "purpose" of Congress was "to suppress freedom of speech." We reject this argument because under settled principles the purpose of Congress, as O'Brien uses that term, is not a basis for declaring this legislation unconstitutional.

It is a familiar principle of constitutional law that this Court will not strike down an otherwise constitutional statute on the basis of an alleged illicit legislative motive. * * *

Inquiries into congressional motives or purposes are a hazardous matter. When the issue is simply the interpretation of legislation, the Court will look to statements by legislators for guidance as to the purpose of the legislature, because the benefit to sound decision-making in this circumstance is thought sufficient to risk the possibility of misreading Congress' purpose. It is entirely a different matter when we are asked to avoid a statute that is, under well-settled criteria, constitutional on its face, on the basis of what fewer than a handful of Congressmen said about it. What motivates one legislator to make a speech about a statute is not necessarily what motivates scores of others to enact it, and the stakes are sufficiently high for us to eschew guesswork. We decline to void essentially on the ground that it is unwise legislation which Congress had the undoubted power to enact and which could be reenacted in its exact form if the same or another legislator made a "wiser" speech about it.

O'Brien's position, and to some extent that of the court below, rest upon a misunderstanding of Grosjean v. American Press Co., 297 U.S. 233, 56 S.Ct. 444 (1936), and Gomil-

lion v. Lightfoot, 364 U.S. 339, 81 S.Ct. 125 (1960). These cases stand, not for the proposition that legislative motive is a proper basis for declaring a statute unconstitutional, but that the inevitable effect of a statute on its face may render it unconstitutional. * * * In these cases, the purpose of the legislation was irrelevant, because the inevitable effect—the "necessary scope and operation" * * * —abridged constitutional rights. The statute attacked in the instant case has no such inevitable unconstitutional effect, since the destruction of Selective Service certificates is in no respect inevitably or necessarily expressive. Accordingly, the statute itself is constitutional.

We think it not amiss, in passing, to comment upon O'Brien's legislative-purpose argument. * * * It is principally on the basis of the statements by these three Congressmen that O'Brien makes his congressional-"purpose" argument. We note that if we were to examine legislative purpose in the instant case, we would be obliged to consider not only these statements but also the more authoritative reports of the Senate and House Armed Services Committees. * * * While both reports make clear a concern with the "defiant" destruction of so-called "draft cards" and with "open" encouragement to others to destroy their cards, both reports also indicate that this concern stemmed from an apprehension that unrestrained destruction of cards would disrupt the smooth functioning of the Selective Service System.

Since the 1965 Amendment to § 12(b)(3) of the Universal Military Training and Service Act is constitutional as enacted and as applied, the Court of Appeals should have affirmed the judgment of conviction entered by the District Court. Accordingly, we vacate the judgment of the Court of Appeals, and reinstate the judgment and sentence of the District Court. This disposition makes unnecessary consideration of O'Brien's claim that the Court of Appeals erred in affirming his conviction on the basis of the nonpossession regulation.

* * *

Mr. Justice MARSHALL took no part in the consideration or decision of these cases.

Mr. Justice DOUGLAS, dissenting.

The Court states that the constitutional power of Congress to raise and support armies is "broad and sweeping" and that Congress' power "to classify and conscript manpower for military service is 'beyond question.'" This is undoubtedly true in times when, by declaration of Congress, the Nation is in a state of war. The underlying and basic problem in this case, however, is whether conscription is permissible in the absence of a declaration of war. That question has not been briefed nor was it presented in oral argument; but it is, I submit, a question upon which the litigants and the country are entitled to a ruling. * * * [T]his Court has never ruled on the question. It is time that we made a ruling. This case should be put down for reargument and heard with Holmes v. United States and with Hart v. United States, 390 U.S. 956, 88 S.Ct. 1851, in which the Court today denies certiorari.

* * *

STREET v. NEW YORK

Supreme Court of the United States, 1969
394 U.S. 576, 89 S.Ct. 1354, 22 L.Ed.2d 572

A New York statute made it a misdemeanor to "publicly mutilate, deface, defile, or defy, trample upon, or cast contempt upon either by words or act" an American flag. When Sidney Street, a black, heard over an afternoon radio broadcast that James Meredith, a figure in the civil rights movement, had been shot by a sniper in Mississippi, he took an American flag, which he had heretofore displayed on national holidays, from his apartment and proceeded to a nearby street corner. Motivated by feelings of resentment that the government had not lived up to its promise to protect Meredith, Street struck a match to the flag and, dropping it to the pavement, let it burn. A policeman subsequently saw the burning flag and soon approached a small crowd which had gathered near the corner. The behavior of the group was not menacing or threatening, nor did the people block the street or sidewalk. As the officer neared he heard Street say, "We don't need no damn flag." And, after inquiring as to whether Street had burned the flag and receiving a forthright admission, the officer arrested him. Street was found guilty at a bench trial, and his conviction was affirmed on appeal to the New York Court of Appeals. The Supreme Court granted certiorari.

Mr. Justice HARLAN delivered the opinion of the Court.

* * *

Street argues that his conviction was unconstitutional for three different reasons. *First*, he claims that § 1425, subd. 16, par. d [that portion of the state penal code under which Street was convicted] is overbroad, both on its face and as applied, because the section makes it a crime "publicly [to] defy * * * or cast contempt upon [an American flag] *by words.*" * * * (Emphasis added.) *Second,* he contends that § 1425, subd. 16, par. d, is vague and imprecise because it does not clearly define the conduct which it forbids. *Third,* he asserts that New York may not constitutionally punish one who publicly destroys or damages an American flag as a means of protest, because such an act constitutes expression protected by the Fourteenth Amendment. We deem it unnecessary to consider the latter two arguments, for we hold that § 1425, subd. 16, par. d, was unconstitutionally applied in appellant's case because it permitted him to be punished merely for speaking defiant or contemptuous words about the American flag. In taking this course, we resist the pulls to decide the constitutional issues involved in this case on a broader basis than the record before us imperatively requires.

* * *

[I]n the present case the general verdict was rendered by a judge, not a jury. However, if the ground of the judge's decision cannot be ascertained from the record, then the danger of unconstitutional conviction is [significant]. * * * Nor would it be appropriate to remand the case to the trial judge for a *post hoc* explanation of the grounds of his decision. * * * Hence, we conclude that * * * appellant's conviction must be set aside if we find that it could have been based solely upon his words and that a conviction resting on such a basis would be unconstitu-

tional—a matter to which we shall turn in a moment.

Moreover, even assuming that the record precludes the inference that appellant's conviction might have been based *solely* on his words, we are still bound to reverse if the conviction could have been based upon *both* his words and his act. * * *

* * *

In the face of an information explicitly setting forth appellant's words as an element of his alleged crime, and of appellant's subsequent conviction under a statute making it an offense to speak words of that sort, we find this record insufficient to eliminate the possibility either that appellant's words were the sole basis of his conviction or that appellant was convicted for both his words and his deed.

We come finally to the question whether, in the circumstances of this case, New York may constitutionally inflict criminal punishment upon one who ventures "publicly [to] defy * * * or cast contempt upon [any American flag] by words." * * *

* * *

In [the context of the] circumstances [which led to defendant's arrest] we can think of four governmental interests which might conceivably have been furthered by punishing appellant for his words: (1) an interest in deterring appellant from vocally inciting others to commit unlawful acts; (2) an interest in preventing appellant from uttering words so inflammatory that they would provoke others to retaliate physically against him, thereby causing a breach of the peace; (3) an interest in protecting the sensibilities of passers-by who might be shocked by appellant's words about the American flag; and (4) an interest in assuring that appellant, regardless of the impact of his words upon others, showed proper respect for our national emblem.

In the circumstances of this case, we do not believe that any of these interests may constitutionally justify appellant's conviction under § 1425, subd. 16, par. d, for speaking as he did. We begin with the interest in preventing incitement. Appellant's words, taken alone, did not urge anyone to do anything unlawful. They amounted only to somewhat excited public advocacy of the idea that the United States should abandon, at least temporarily, one of its national symbols. It is clear that the Fourteenth Amendment prohibits the States from imposing criminal punishment for public advocacy of peaceful change in our institutions. * * * Even assuming that appellant's words might be found incitive when considered together with his simultaneous burning of the flag, § 1425, subd. 16, par. d, does not purport to punish only those defiant or contemptuous words which amount to incitement, and there is no evidence that the state courts regarded the statute as so limited. Hence, a conviction for words could not be upheld on this basis. * * *

Nor could such a conviction be justified on the second ground mentioned above: the possible tendency of appellant's words to provoke violent retaliation. Though it is conceivable that some listeners might have been moved to retaliate upon hearing appellant's disrespectful words, we cannot say that appellant's remarks were so inherently inflammatory as to come within that small class of "fighting words" which are "likely to provoke the av-

erage person to retaliation, and thereby cause a breach of the peace." * * * And even if appellant's words might be found within that category, § 1425, subd. 16, par. d, is not narrowly drawn to punish only words of that character, and there is no indication that it was so interpreted by the state courts. * * *

Again, such a conviction could not be sustained on the ground that appellant's words were likely to shock passers-by. Except perhaps for appellant's incidental use of the word "damn," upon which no emphasis was placed at trial, any shock effect of appellant's speech must be attributed to the content of the ideas expressed. * * *

Finally, such a conviction could not be supported on the theory that by making the above-quoted remarks about the flag appellant failed to show the respect for our national symbol which may properly be demanded of every citizen. [See] West Virginia State Board of Educ. v. Barnette. * * *

We have no doubt that the constitutionally guaranteed "freedom to be intellectually * * * diverse or even contrary," and the "right to differ as to things that touch the heart of the existing order," encompass the freedom to express publicly one's opinions about our flag, including those opinions which are defiant or contemptuous.

Since appellant could not constitutionally be punished under § 1425, subd. 16, par. d, for his speech, and since we have found that he may have been so punished, his conviction cannot be permitted to stand. In so holding, we reiterate that we have no occasion to pass upon the validity of this conviction insofar as it was sus-

tained by the state courts on the basis that Street could be punished for his burning of the flag, even though the burning was an act of protest.
* * *

* * *

Reversed and remanded.

Mr. Chief Justice WARREN, dissenting.

I dissent from the reversal of this judgment * * * because the Court in my opinion * * * has declined to meet and resolve the basic question presented in the case. * * * The court below employed the following statement of the question:

"We are called upon to decide whether the deliberate act of burning an American flag in public as a 'protest' may be punished as a crime."
* * *

* * * But the Court specifically refuses to decide this issue. Instead, it searches microscopically for the opportunity to decide the case on [a] peripheral * * * ground, holding that it is impossible to determine the basis for appellant's conviction. In my opinion a reading of the short trial record leaves no doubt that appellant was convicted solely for burning the American flag.

* * *

I am in complete agreement with the general rule that this Court should not treat broad constitutional questions when narrow ones will suffice to dispose of the litigation. However, where only the broad question is presented, it is our task and our responsibility to confront that question squarely and resolve it.
* * *

* * * Since I am satisfied that

the constitutionality of appellant's conduct should be resolved in this case and am convinced that this conduct can be criminally punished, I dissent.

[Justice BLACK dissented.]

Mr. Justice WHITE, dissenting.

* * *

The Court's schema is this: the statute forbids insults to the flag either by act or words; the charge alleged both flag burning and speech; the court rendered a general judgment; since the conviction might logically have been for speech alone or for both words and deeds and since in either event the conviction is invalid, the judgment of the New York courts must be set aside without passing upon the validity of a conviction for burning the flag. I reach precisely the opposite conclusion; before Street's conviction can be either reversed or affirmed, the Court *must* reach and decide the validity of a conviction for flag burning.

* * *

Mr. Justice FORTAS, dissenting.

* * *

If a state statute provided that it is a misdemeanor to burn one's shirt or trousers or shoes on the public thoroughfare, it could hardly be asserted that the citizen's constitutional right is violated. If the arsonist asserted that he was burning his shirt or trousers or shoes as a protest against the Government's fiscal policies, for example, it is hardly possible that his claim to First Amendment shelter would prevail against the State's claim of a right to avert danger to the public and to avoid obstruction to traffic as a result of the fire. This is because action, even if clearly for serious protest purposes, is not entitled to the pervasive pro-

tection that is given to speech alone. * * *

* * *

Subsequent Court decisions have also turned decisively on due process or free speech considerations although it seems apparent from a reading of the opinions in those cases that malicious destruction of the flag is a legitimately punishable offense.

Smith v. Goguen, 415 U.S. 566, 94 S.Ct. 1242 (1974)	Facts	Defendant was convicted under a Massachusetts flag desecration statute for "publicly treat[ing] contemptuously the flag of the United States" when he wore a 4" x 4" flag sewn to the seat of his blue jeans
	Ruling	The statute is void for vagueness because it "fails to draw reasonably clear lines between the kinds of nonceremonial treatment that are criminal and those that are not." While a policeman must often have leeway to permit on-the-spot assessment of the need to keep public order, "there is no comparable reason for committing broad discretion to law enforcement officials in the area of flag contempt. Indeed, because display of the flag is so common and takes so many forms, changing from one generation to another and often difficult to distinguish in principle, a legislature should define with some care the flag behavior it intends to outlaw."
	Other opinions	Justice White concurred on the grounds that punishment for casting contempt on the flag, as distinguished from destroying it, infringed legitimate exercise of free speech by its overbreadth.
		Justice Rehnquist, joined by Chief Justice Burger, dissented, voting to uphold the statute on grounds that "The flag of the United States is not just another 'thing,' and it is not just another 'idea'; * * * [but] a unique national symbol which has been given content by generations of his and our forebearers * * *."
		Justice Blackmun also dissented
Spence v. Washington, 418 U.S. 405, 94 S.Ct. 2727 (1974)	Facts	Defendant displayed from his apartment window an upside down American flag to which, on front and back, he had taped peace symbols. For this protest of the invasion of Cambodia and the eruption of violence at Kent State, he was convicted under a Washington flag defacement statute
	Ruling	Conviction reversed. The flag was privately owned and displayed on private property. The record shows no risk of breach of the peace from display of the flag in this case. Furthermore, the defendant

Spence (*Cont.*)	Ruling (*Cont.*)	did not "permanently disfigure the flag or destroy it. He displayed it as a flag of his country in a way closely analogous to the manner in which flags have always been used to convey ideas."
	Other opinions	Justice Rehnquist, joined by Chief Justice Burger and Justice White, dissented. He observed that "Virtually any law enacted by a State, when viewed with sufficient ingenuity, could be thought to interfere with some citizen's preferred means of expression" and concluded that, while the state "presumably cannot punish criticism of the flag, or the principles for which it stands, anymore than it could punish criticism of this country's policies or ideas," it does act legitimately when it "withdraws a unique national symbol from the roster of materials that may be used as a background for communications."

TINKER v. DES MOINES INDEPENDENT COMMUNITY SCHOOL DISTRICT

Supreme Court of the United States, 1969
393 U.S. 503, 89 S.Ct. 733, 21 L.Ed.2d 731

This suit was brought to recover nominal damages and for injunctive relief against school officials from enforcing a regulation which barred the wearing of armbands in school by students. John Tinker, a high school student, and his sister Mary Beth, who was in junior high school, wore black armbands to school to protest the continuing hostilities in Vietnam. When they refused to remove the armbands, they were sent home under suspension until they decided to comply. A federal district court dismissed the Tinkers' complaint finding that the interest in preventing disturbances in school and distraction from academic work countervailed any asserted abridgement of First and Fourteenth Amendment rights. On appeal, the U.S. Court of Appeals, Eighth Circuit, sitting en banc, divided evenly. The Supreme Court subsequently granted certiorari.

Mr. Justice FORTAS delivered the opinion of the Court.

* * *

[T]he wearing of armbands in the circumstances of this case was entirely divorced from actually or potentially disruptive conduct by those participating in it. It was closely akin to "pure speech" which, we have repeatedly held, is entitled to comprehensive protection under the First Amendment. * * *

First Amendment rights, applied in light of the special characteristics of the school environment, are available to teachers and students. It can hardly be argued that either students or teachers shed their constitutional rights to freedom of speech or expression at the schoolhouse gate. This has been the unmistakable holding of this Court for almost 50 years. In Meyer v. Nebraska, 262 U.S. 390, 43 S.Ct. 625 (1923), and Bartels v. Iowa, 262 U.S. 404, 43 S.Ct. 628 (1923), this Court, in opinions by Mr. Justice McReynolds, held that the Due Process Clause of the Fourteenth Amendment prevents States from forbidding the teaching of a foreign language to young students. Statutes to this effect, the Court held, unconstitutionally interfere with the liberty of teacher, student, and parent. * * *

The problem posed by the present case does not relate to regulation of the length of skirts or the type of clothing, to hair style, or deportment. * * * It does not concern aggressive, disruptive action or even group demonstrations. * * *
Our problem involves direct, primary First Amendment rights akin to "pure speech."

* * *

[I]n our system, undifferentiated fear or apprehension of disturbance is not enough to overcome the right to freedom of expression. Any departure from absolute regimentation may cause trouble. Any variation from the majority's opinion may inspire fear. Any word spoken, in class, in the lunchroom, or on the campus, that deviates from the views of another person may start an argument or cause a disturbance. But our Constitution says we must take this risk * * *; and our history says that it is this sort of hazardous freedom—this kind of openness— that is the basis of our national strength and of the independence and vigor of Americans who grow up and live in this relatively permissive, often disputatious, society.

In order for the State in the person of school officials to justify prohibition of a particular expression of opinion, it must be able to show that its action was caused by something more than a mere desire to avoid the discomfort and unpleasantness that always accompany an unpopular viewpoint. Certainly where there is no finding and no showing that engaging in the forbidden conduct would "materially and substantially

interfere with the requirements of appropriate discipline in the operation of the school," the prohibition cannot be sustained. * * *

In the present case, the District Court made no such finding, and our independent examination of the record fails to yield evidence that the school authorities had reason to anticipate that the wearing of the armbands would substantially interfere with the work of the school or impinge upon the rights of other students. Even an official memorandum prepared after the suspension that listed the reasons for the ban on wearing the armbands made no reference to the anticipation of such disruption.

On the contrary, the action of the school authorities appears to have been based upon an urgent wish to avoid the controversy which might result from the expression, even by the silent symbol of armbands, of opposition to this Nation's part in the conflagration in Vietnam. * * *

It is also relevant that the school authorities did not purport to prohibit the wearing of all symbols of political or controversial significance. The record shows that students in some of the schools wore buttons relating to national political campaigns, and some even wore the Iron Cross, traditionally a symbol of Nazism. The order prohibiting the wearing of armbands did not extend to these. Instead, a particular symbol—black armbands worn to exhibit opposition to this Nation's involvement in Vietnam—was singled out for prohibition. Clearly, the prohibition of expression of one particular opinion, at least without evidence that it is necessary to avoid material and substantial interference with schoolwork or discipline, is not constitutionally permissible.

In our system, state-operated schools may not be enclaves of totalitarianism. School officials do not possess absolute authority over their students. Students in school as well as out of school are "persons" under our Constitution. They are possessed of fundamental rights which the State must respect, just as they themselves must respect their obligations to the State. In our system, students may not be regarded as closed-circuit recipients of only that which the State chooses to communicate. They may not be confined to the expression of those sentiments that are officially approved. In the absence of a specific showing of constitutionally valid reasons to regulate their speech, students are entitled to freedom of expression of their views.
* * *

* * *

* * *   The principal use to which the schools are dedicated is to accommodate students during prescribed hours for the purpose of certain types of activities. Among those activities is personal intercommunication among the students. This is not only an inevitable part of the process of attending school; it is also an important part of the educational process. A student's rights, therefore, do not embrace merely the classroom hours. When he is in the cafeteria, or on the playing field, or on the campus during the authorized hours, he may express his opinions, even on controversial subjects like the conflict in Vietnam, if he does so without "materially and substantially interfer[ing] with the requirements of appropriate discipline in the operation of the school" and without collid-

ing with the rights of others.
* * *

* * *

Reversed and remanded.

Mr. Justice BLACK dissenting.

* * *

As I read the Court's opinion it relies upon the following grounds for holding unconstitutional the judgment of the Des Moines school officials and the two courts below. First, the Court concludes that the wearing of armbands is "symbolic speech" which is "akin to 'pure speech'" and therefore protected by the First and Fourteenth Amendments. Secondly, the Court decides that the public schools are an appropriate place to exercise "symbolic speech" as long as normal school functions are not "unreasonably" disrupted. Finally, the Court arrogates to itself, rather than to the State's elected officials charged with running the schools, the decision as to which school disciplinary regulations are "reasonable."

Assuming that the Court is correct in holding that the conduct of wearing armbands for the purpose of conveying political ideas is protected by the First Amendment, * * * the crucial remaining questions are whether students and teachers may use the schools at their whim as a platform for the exercise of free speech—"symbolic" or "pure"—and whether the courts will allocate to themselves the function of deciding how the pupils' school day will be spent. While I have always believed that under the First and Fourteenth Amendments neither the State nor the Federal Government has any authority to regulate or censor the content of speech, I have never believed that any person has a right to give speeches or engage in demonstrations where he pleases and when he pleases. * * *

* * *

Mr. Justice HARLAN, dissenting.

I certainly agree that state public school authorities in the discharge of their responsibilities are not wholly exempt from the requirements of the Fourteenth Amendment respecting the freedoms of expression and association. At the same time I am reluctant to believe that there is any disagreement between the majority and myself on the proposition that school officials should be accorded the widest authority in maintaining discipline and good order in their institutions. To translate that proposition into a workable constitutional rule, I would, in cases like this, cast upon those complaining the burden of showing that a particular school measure was motivated by other than legitimate school concerns—for example, a desire to prohibit the expression of an unpopular point of view, while permitting expression of the dominant opinion.

Finding nothing in this record which impugns the good faith of respondents in promulgating the armband regulation, I would affirm the judgment below.

Skokie, a suburb of Chicago, has a population of approximately 70,000 of whom about 40,500 residents are Jewish and of those between 5,000 and 7,000 are survivors of the Nazi holocaust. The village sought an injunction to prevent a demonstration in Skokie by uniformed members of the American Nazi party. Various Jewish organizations, including the militant Jewish Defense League, and other groups announced plans for a counterdemonstration. The prospect of demonstration and counterdemonstration precipitated forecasts of violence and bloodshed. After a Cook County circuit court enjoined the Nazi march, both an appellate court and the Illinois Supreme Court refused to stay the judgment pending an appeal. The U.S. Supreme Court reversed the state supreme court's ruling and, in view of the important First Amendment issues at stake, ordered the higher state courts to proceed promptly to a consideration of the merits. On remand, the state appeals court reversed those portions of the circuit court order barring the Nazis from "marching, walking, or parading, from distributing pamphlets or displaying materials, and from wearing the uniform of the National Socialist Party of America." The appellate court held, however, that the village had met "the heavy burden" of showing that, particularly in Skokie, wearing or displaying the swastika constituted the use of a symbol tantamount to "fighting words" and was therefore not protected by the First Amendment. Calling the display of that symbol "a personal affront to every member of the Jewish faith," the court concluded that "Skokie's Jewish residents must feel gross revulsion for the swastika and would immediately respond to the personally abusive epithets slung their way in the form of the defendants' chosen symbol, the swastika." The appeals court thus affirmed the remaining portion of the circuit court's injunction prohibiting the Nazis from displaying that symbol during the demonstration.

In a per curiam opinion announcing its judgment in this controversy, Village of Skokie v. National Socialist Party, 69 Ill.2d 605, 14 Ill.Dec. 890, 373 N.E.2d 21 (1978), the Illinois Supreme Court, with one Justice dissenting, concluded that "[t]he decisions of * * * [the United States Supreme Court], particularly Cohen v. California, 403 U.S. 15, 91 S.Ct. 1780 (1971), in our opinion compel us to permit the demonstration as proposed, including display of the swastika." After quoting at length from the decision in *Cohen*, the Illinois court explained its reversal of the appellate court judgment enjoining display of the swastika as follows:

> The display of the swastika, as offensive to the principles of a free nation as the memories it recalls may be, is symbolic political speech intended to convey to the public the beliefs of those who display it. It does not, in our opinion, fall within the definition of "fighting words," and that doctrine cannot be used here to overcome the heavy presumption against the constitutional validity of a prior restraint.

> Nor can we find that the swastika, while not representing fighting words, is nevertheless so offensive and peace threatening to the public that its display can be enjoined. We do not doubt that the sight of this symbol is abhorrent to the Jewish citizens of Skokie, and that the survivors of the Nazi persecutions, tormented by their recollections, may have strong feelings regarding its display. Yet it is entirely clear that this factor does not justify enjoining defendants' speech.   *   *   *

*   *   *

> In summary, as we read the controlling Supreme Court opinions, use of the swastika is a symbolic form of free speech entitled to first amendment protections. Its display on uniforms or banners by those engaged in peaceful demonstrations cannot be totally precluded solely because that display may provoke a violent reaction by those who view it. Particularly is this true where, as here, there has been advance notice by the demonstrators of their plans so that they have become, as the complaint alleges, "common knowledge" and those to whom sight of the swastika banner or uniforms would be offense are forewarned and need not view them. A speaker who gives prior notice of his message has not compelled a confrontation with those who voluntarily listen.

Subsequently, in connection with a parallel suit lodged in federal district court attacking the constitutionality of several Skokie ordinances precluding the Nazi march, the U.S. Supreme Court denied certiorari with respect to a federal appellate court judgment affirming the unconstitutionality of the ordinances. Smith v. Collin, 439 U.S. 916, 99 S.Ct. 291 (1978).

d. CAMPAIGN FINANCING, PARTY PATRONAGE, AND THE FIRST AMENDMENT

BUCKLEY v. VALEO

Supreme Court of the United States, 1976
424 U.S. 1, 96 S.Ct. 612, 46 L.Ed.2d 659

Senator James Buckley, former Senator Eugene McCarthy, and others brought suit against Francis Valeo, the Secretary of the United States Senate, the Clerk of the House of Representatives, and others challenging the constitutionality of the Federal Election Campaign Act of 1971, as amended. The Act, characterized by a federal appeals court as "by far the most comprehensive reform legislation [ever]

passed by Congress concerning the election of the President, Vice-President, and members of Congress," contained the following provisions:

(1) the Act limits political contributions by individuals and groups to $1,000 each and by political committees to $5,000 each for any single candidate in any one election, with an annual limit of $25,000 on any individual contributor;

(2) the Act limits independent spending by an individual or group "relative to a clearly identified candidate" to $1,000 each per election;

(3) the Act sets limits, which vary with the office, on personal contributions by both the candidate himself and his family toward his campaign;

(4) the Act establishes a ceiling on overall primary and general election expenditures by a candidate in any one election according to the office sought;

(5) the Act requires political committees to keep detailed contribution and expenditure records, publicly disclosing the identity of the contributors and the nature of expenditures above a certain level;

(6) the Act creates an eight-member commission to oversee enforcement of the regulations: two to be appointed by the President, two by the President *pro tempore* of the Senate, and two by the Speaker of the House, all to be confirmed by both Houses of Congress, and the Secretary of the Senate and Clerk of the House to be *ex officio* members; and

(7) the Act amends the Internal Revenue Code to provide for some financing of primary and general election campaigns from public funds, major party candidates to receive "full" funding and "minor" and "new" party candidates to receive a reduced proportion of funding (the funding to be on a dollar-matching basis).

Buckley and the other plaintiffs sought declaratory and injunctive relief, alleging mostly that the act violated the First Amendment, the Fifth Amendment, and Art. II, § 2, cl. 2, the constitutional provision governing appointment to federal office. The U.S. Court of Appeals for the District of Columbia Circuit upheld nearly all of the Act's provisions, and the plaintiffs appealed.

PER CURIAM.

*   *   *

I. CONTRIBUTION AND EXPENDITURE LIMITATIONS

*   *   *

B. Contribution Limitations

*   *   *

[T]he primary First Amendment problem raised by the Act's contribution limitations is their restriction of one aspect of the contributor's freedom of political association. The Court's decisions involving associational freedoms establish that the right of association is a "basic constitutional freedom" that is "closely allied to freedom of free speech and a right which, like free speech, lies at the foundation of a free society." * * * In view of the fundamental nature of the right to associate, governmental "action which may have the effect of curtailing the freedom to associate is subject to the closest scrutiny." * * * Yet, it is clear that "[n]either the right to associate nor the right to participate in political activities is absolute." United States Civil Service Comm'n v. National Association of Letter Carriers, 413 U.S. 548, 567, 93 S.Ct. 2880, 2891 (1973). Even a " 'significant interference' with protected rights of political association" may be sustained if the State demonstrates a sufficiently important interest and employs means closely drawn to avoid unnecessary abridgment of associational freedoms. * * *

Appellees argue that the Act's restrictions on large campaign contributions are justified by three governmental interests. According to the parties and *amici*, the primary interest served by the limitations and, indeed, by the Act as a whole, is the prevention of corruption and the appearance of corruption spawned by the real or imagined coercive influence of large financial contributions on candidates' positions and on their actions if elected to office. Two "ancillary" interests underlying the Act are also allegedly furthered by the $1,000 limits on contributions. First, the limits serve to mute the voices of affluent persons and groups in the election process and thereby to equalize the relative ability of all citizens to affect the outcome of elections. Second, it is argued, the ceilings may to some extent act as a brake on the skyrocketing cost of political campaigns and thereby serve to open the political system more widely to candidates without access to sources of large amounts of money.

It is unnecessary to look beyond the Act's primary purpose—to limit the actuality and appearance of corruption resulting from large individual financial contributions—in order to find a constitutionally sufficient justification for the $1,000 contribution limitation. Under a system of private financing of elections, a candidate lacking immense personal or family wealth must depend on financial contributions from others to provide the resources necessary to conduct a successful campaign. The

increasing importance of the communications media and sophisticated mass mailing and polling operations to effective campaigning make the raising of large sums of money an ever more essential ingredient of an effective candidacy. To the extent that large contributions are given to secure political *quid pro quos* from current and potential office holders, the integrity of our system of representative democracy is undermined. Although the scope of such pernicious practices can never be reliably ascertained, the deeply disturbing examples surfacing after the 1972 election demonstrate that the problem is not an illusory one.

Of almost equal concern as the danger of actual *quid pro quo* arrangements is the impact of the appearance of corruption stemming from public awareness of the opportunities for abuse inherent in a regime of large individual financial contributions. In *Civil Service Comm'n* v. *Letter Carriers*, supra, the Court found that the danger to "fair and effective government" posed by partisan political conduct on the part of federal employees charged with administering the law was a sufficiently important concern to justify broad restrictions on the employees' right of partisan political association. Here, as there, Congress could legitimately conclude that the avoidance of the appearance of improper influence "is also critical * * * if confidence in the system of representative Government is not to be eroded to a disastrous extent." * * *

Appellants contend that the contribution limitations must be invalidated because bribery laws and narrowly-drawn disclosure requirements constitute a less restrictive means of dealing with "proven and suspected *quid pro quo* arrangements." But laws making criminal the giving and taking of bribes deal with only the most blatant and specific attempts of those with money to influence governmental action. And while disclosure requirements serve the many salutary purposes discussed elsewhere in this opinion, Congress was surely entitled to conclude that disclosure was only a partial measure, and that contribution ceilings were a necessary legislative concomitant to deal with the reality or appearance of corruption inherent in a system permitting unlimited financial contributions, even when the identities of the contributors and the amounts of their contributions are fully disclosed.

The Act's $1,000 contribution limitation focuses precisely on the problem of large campaign contributions—the narrow aspect of political association where the actuality and potential for corruption have been identified—while leaving persons free to engage in independent political expression, to associate actively through volunteering their services, and to assist to a limited but nonetheless substantial extent in supporting candidates and committees with financial resources. Significantly, the Act's contribution limitations in themselves do not undermine to any material degree the potential for robust and effective discussion of candidates and campaign issues by individual citizens, associations, the institutional press, candidates, and political parties.

We find that, under the rigorous standard of review established by our prior decisions, the weighty interests served by restricting the size of financial contributions to political candidates are sufficient to justify the limited effect upon First Amend-

ment freedoms caused by the $1,000 contribution ceiling.

* * *

C. Expenditure Limitations

* * *

1. The $1,000 Limitation on Expenditures "Relative to a Clearly Identified Candidate."

Section 608(e)(1) provides that "[n]o person may make any expenditure * * * relative to a clearly identified candidate during a calendar year which, when added to all other expenditures made by such person during the year advocating the election or defeat of such candidate, exceeds $1,000." The plain effect of § 608(e)(1) is to prohibit all individuals, who are neither candidates nor owners of institutional press facilities, and all groups, except political parties and campaign organizations, from voicing their views "relative to a clearly identified candidate" through means that entail aggregate expenditures of more than $1,000 during a calendar year. The provision, for example, would make it a federal criminal offense for a person or association to place a single one-quarter page advertisement "relative to a clearly identified candidate" in a major metropolitan newspaper.

Before examining the interests advanced in support of § 608(e)(1)'s expenditure ceiling, consideration must be given to appellants' contention that the provision is unconstitutionally vague. Close examination of the specificity of the statutory limitation is required where, as here, the legislation imposes criminal penalties in an area permeated by First Amendment interests. * * * The test is whether the language of § 608(e)(1) affords the "[p]recision of regulation [that] must be the touchstone in an area so closely touching our most precious freedoms." NAACP v. Button, 371 U.S., at 438, 83 S.Ct., at 340.

The key operative language of the provision limits "any expenditure * * * relative to a clearly identified candidate." Although "expenditure," "clearly identified," and "candidate" are defined in the Act, there is no definition clarifying what expenditures are "relative to" a candidate. The use of so indefinite a phrase as "relative to" a candidate fails to clearly mark the boundary between permissible and impermissible speech, unless other portions of § 608(e)(1) make sufficiently explicit the range of expenditures covered by the limitation. The section prohibits "any expenditure * * * relative to a clearly identified candidate during a calendar year which, *when added to all other expenditures * * * advocating the election or defeat of such candidate*, exceeds, $1,000." (Emphasis added.) This context clearly permits, if indeed it does not require, the phrase "relative to" a candidate to be read to mean "advocating the election or defeat of" a candidate.

But while such a construction of § 608(e)(1) refocuses the vagueness question, the Court of Appeals was mistaken in thinking that this construction eliminates the problem of unconstitutional vagueness altogether. * * * For the distinction between discussion of issues and candidates and advocacy of election or defeat of candidates may often dissolve in practical application. Candidates, especially incumbents, are intimately tied to public issues involving legislative proposals and governmental actions. Not only do candidates campaign on the basis of their positions on various public issues, but campaigns themselves generate issues of public interest. In an analogous context, this Court in *Thomas* v. *Collins* observed:

"[W]hether words intended and designed to fall short of invitation would miss the mark is a question both of intent and of effect. No speaker, in such circumstances, safely could assume that anything he might say upon the general subject would not be understood by some as an invitation. In short, the supposedly clear-cut distinction between discussion, laudation, general advocacy, and solicitation puts the speaker in these circumstances wholly at the mercy of the varied understanding of his hearers and consequently of whatever inference may be drawn as to his intent and meaning.

"Such a distinction offers no security for free discussion. In these conditions it blankets with uncertainty whatever may be said. It compels the speaker to hedge and trim." 323 U.S. 516, 535, 65 S.Ct. 315, 325 (1945).

The constitutional deficiencies described in *Thomas* v. *Collins* can be avoided only by reading § 608(e)(1) as limited to communications that include explicit words of advocacy of election or defeat of a candidate, much as the definition of "clearly identified" in § 608(e)(2) requires that an explicit and unambiguous reference to the candidate appear as part of the communication. This is the reading of the provision suggested by the the non-governmental appellees in arguing that "[f]unds spent to propagate one's views on issues without expressly calling for a candidate's election or defeat are thus not covered." We agree that in order to preserve the provision against invalidation on vagueness grounds, § 608(e)(1) must be construed to apply only to expenditures for communications that in express terms advocate the election or defeat of a clearly identified candidate for federal office.

* * *

* * * The markedly greater burden on basic freedoms caused by § 608(e)(1) * * * cannot be sustained simply by invoking the interest in maximizing the effectiveness of the less intrusive contribution limitations. Rather, the constitutionality of § 608(e)(1) turns on whether the governmental interests advanced in its support satisfy the exacting scrutiny applicable to limitations on core First Amendment rights of political expression.

We find that the governmental interest in preventing corruption and the appearance of corruption is inadequate to justify § 608(e)(1)'s ceiling on independent expenditures. First, assuming *arguendo* that large independent expenditures pose the same dangers of actual or apparent *quid pro quo* arrangements as do large contributions, § 608(e)(1) does not provide an answer that sufficiently relates to the elimination of those dangers. Unlike the contribution limitations' total ban on the giving of large amounts of money to candidates, § 608(e)(1) prevents only some large expenditures. So long as persons and groups eschew expenditures that in express terms advocate the election or defeat of a clearly identified candidate, they are free to spend as much as they want to promote the candidate and his views. The exacting interpretation of the statutory language necessary to avoid unconstitutional vagueness thus undermines the limitation's effectiveness as a loophole-closing provision by facilitating circumvention by those seeking to exert improper influence upon a candidate or officeholder. It would naively underestimate the ingenuity and resourcefulness of persons and groups desiring to buy influence to believe that they would have much difficulty devising expenditures that skirted the restriction on express advocacy of election or defeat but nevertheless benefited the candidate's campaign. Yet no substantial societal interest would be served by a loophole-closing provision designed to check corruption that permitted unscrupulous persons and organizations to expend unlimited sums of money in order to obtain improper influence over candidates for elective office. * * *

* * *

While the independent expenditure ceiling thus fails to serve any substantial governmental interest in stemming the reality or appearance of corruption in the electoral process, it heavily burdens core First Amendment expression. For the First Amendment right to " 'speak one's mind * * * on all public institutions' " includes the right to engage in " 'vigorous advocacy' no less than 'abstract discussion.' " New York Times Co. v. Sullivan, 376 U.S., at 269, 84 S.Ct., at 721, quoting Bridges v. California, 314 U.S. 252, 270, 62 S.Ct. 190, 197 (1941), and NAACP v. Button, 371 U.S., at 429, 83 S.Ct., at 335. Advocacy of the election or defeat of candidates for federal office is no less entitled to protection under the First Amendment than the discussion of political policy generally or advocacy of the passage or defeat of legislation.

It is argued, however, that the ancillary governmental interest in equalizing the relative ability of individuals and groups to influence the outcome of elections serves to justify the limitation on express advocacy of the election or defeat of candidates imposed by § 608(e)(1)'s expenditure ceiling. But the concept that government may restrict the speech of some elements of our society in order to enhance the relative voice of others is wholly foreign to the First Amendment, which was designed "to secure 'the widest possible dissemination of information from diverse and antagonistic sources,' " and " 'to assure unfettered interchange of ideas for the bringing about of political and social changes desired by the people.' " New York Times Co. v. Sullivan, supra, 376 U.S., at 266, 269, 84 S.Ct., at 718, quoting Associated Press v. United States, 326 U.S. 1, 20, 65 S.Ct. 1416, 1424 (1945), and Roth v. United States, 354 U.S., at 484, 77 S.Ct., at 1308. The First Amendment's protection against governmental abridgement of free expression cannot properly be made to depend on a person's financial ability to engage in public discussion.
* * *

The ceiling on personal expenditures by candidates on their own behalf, like the limitations on independent expenditures contained in § 608(e)(1), imposes a substantial restraint on the ability of persons to engage in protected First Amendment expression. The candidate, no less than any other person has a First Amendment right to engage in the discussion of public issues and vigorously and tirelessly to advocate his own election and the election of other candidates. Indeed, it is of particular importance that candidates have the unfettered opportunity to make their views known so that the electorate may intelligently evaluate the candidates' personal qualities and their positions on vital public issues before choosing among them on election day. Mr. Justice Brandeis' observation that in our country "public discussion is a political duty," Whitney v. California, 274 U.S. 357, 375, 47 S.Ct. 641, 648 (1927) (concurring opinion), applies with special force to candidates for public office. Section 608(a)'s ceiling on personal expenditures by a candidate in furtherance of his own candidacy thus clearly and directly interferes with constitutionally protected freedoms.

The primary governmental interest served by the Act—the prevention of actual and apparent corruption of the political process—does not support the limitation on the candidate's expenditure of his own personal funds. As the Court of Appeals concluded, "[m]anifestly, the core problem of avoiding undisclosed and undue influence on candidates from outside interests has lesser application when the monies involved come from the candidate himself or from his immediate family." 519 F.2d, at 855. Indeed, the use of personal funds reduces the candidate's dependence on outside contributions and thereby counteracts the coercive pressures and attendant risks of abuse to which the Act's contribution limitations are directed.

The ancillary interest in equalizing the relative financial resources of candidates competing for elective office, therefore, provides the sole relevant rationale for [an] * * * expenditure ceiling. That interest is clearly not sufficient to justify the provision's infringement of fundamental First Amendment rights. First, the limitation may fail to promote financial equality among candidates. A candidate who spends less of his personal resources on his campaign may nonetheless outspend his rival as a result of more successful fundraising efforts. Indeed, a candidate's personal wealth may impede his efforts to persuade others that he needs their financial contributions or volunteer efforts to conduct an effective campaign. Second, and more fundamentally, the First Amendment simply cannot tolerate * * * [a] restriction upon the freedom of a candidate to speak without legislative limit on behalf of his own candidacy. We therefore hold that * * * restrictions on a candidate's personal expenditures is unconstitutional.

* * *

In sum, the provisions of the Act that impose a $1,000 limitation on contributions to a single candidate, § 608(b)(1), a $5,000 limitation on contributions by a political committee to a single candidate, § 608(b)(2), and a $25,000 limitation on total contributions by an individual during any calendar year, § 608(b)(3), are constitutionally valid. These limitations along with the disclosure provisions, constitute the Act's primary weapons against the reality or appearance of improper influence stemming from the dependence of candidates on large campaign contributions. The contribution ceilings thus serve the basic governmental interest in safeguarding the integrity of the electoral process without directly impinging upon the rights of individual citizens and candidates to engage in political debate and discussion. By contrast, the First Amendment requires the invalidation of the Act's independent expenditure ceiling, § 608(e)(1), its limitation on a candidate's expenditures from his own

personal funds, § 608(a), and its ceilings on overall campaign expenditures, § 608(c). These provisions place substantial and direct restrictions on the ability of candidates, citizens, and associations to engage in protected political expression, restrictions that the First Amendment cannot tolerate.

* * *

CONCLUSION

In summary, we sustain the individual contribution limits, the disclosure and reporting provisions, and the public financing scheme. We conclude, however, that the limitations on campaign expenditures, on independent expenditures by individuals and groups, and on expenditures by a candidate from his personal funds are constitutionally infirm. Finally, we hold that most of the powers conferred by the Act upon the Federal Election Commission can be exercised only by "Officers of the United States," appointed in conformity with Art. II, § 2, cl. 2, of the Constitution, and therefore cannot be exercised by the Commission as presently constituted.

* * * The mandate shall issue forthwith, except that our judgment is stayed, for a period not to exceed 30 days, insofar as it affects the authority of the Commission to exercise the duties and powers granted it under the Act.

So ordered.

Mr. Justice STEVENS took no part in the consideration or decision of these cases.

Mr. Chief Justice BURGER, concurring in part and dissenting in part.

* * * I dissent from those parts of the Court's holding sus-

taining the Act's provisions (a) for disclosure of small contributions, (b) for limitations on contributions, and (c) for public financing of Presidential campaigns. In my view, the Act's disclosure scheme is impermissibly broad and violative of the First Amendment as it relates to reporting $10 and $100 contributions. The contribution limitations infringe on First Amendment liberties and suffer from the same infirmities that the Court correctly sees in the expenditure ceilings. The Act's system for public financing of Presidential campaigns is, in my judgment, an impermissible intrusion by the Government into the traditionally private political process.

More broadly, the Court's result does violence to the intent of Congress in this comprehensive scheme of campaign finance. By dissecting the Act bit by bit, and casting off vital parts, the Court fails to recognize that the whole of this Act is greater than the sum of its parts. Congress intended to regulate all aspects of federal campaign finances, but what remains after today's holding leaves no more than a shadow of what Congress contemplated. I question whether the residue leaves a workable program.

* * *

* * * I doubt that the Court would tolerate for an instant a limitation on contributions to a church or other religious cause; however grave an "evil" Congress thought the limits would cure, limits on religious expenditures would most certainly fall as well. To limit either contributions or expenditures as to churches would plainly restrict "the free exercise" of religion. In my view Congess can no more ration political expression than it can ration religious expression; and limits on political or religious

contributions and expenditures effectively curb expression in both areas. There are many prices we pay for the freedoms secured by the First Amendment; the risk of undue influence is one of them, confirming what we have long known: freedom is hazardous, but some restraints are worse.

Mr. Justice WHITE, concurring in part and dissenting in part.

* * *

Since the contribution and expenditure limitations are neutral as to the content of speech and are not motivated by fear of the consequences of the political speech of particular candidates or of political speech in general, this case depends on whether the nonspeech interests of the Federal Government in regulating the use of money in political campaigns are sufficiently urgent to justify the incidental effects that the limitations visit upon the First Amendment interests of candidates and their supporters.

Despite its seeming struggle with the standard by which to judge this case, this is essentially the question the Court asks and answers in the affirmative with respect to the limitations on contributions which individuals and political committees are permitted to make to federal candidates. In the interest of preventing undue influence that large contributors would have or that the public might think they would have, the Court upholds the provision that an individual may not give to a candidate, or spend on his behalf if requested or authorized by the candidate to do so, more than $1,000 in any one election. This limitation is valid although it imposes a low ceiling on what individuals may deem to be their most effective means of supporting or speaking on behalf of the candidate—i. e., financial support given directly to the candidate. The Court thus accepts the congressional judgment that the evils of unlimited contributions are sufficiently threatening to warrant restriction regardless of the impact of the limits on the contributor's opportunity for effective speech and in turn on the total volume of the candidate's political communications by reason of his inability to accept large sums from those willing to give.

The congressional judgment, which I would also accept, was that other steps must be taken to counter the corrosive effects of money in federal election campaigns. One of these steps is § 608(e), which, aside from those funds that are given to the candidate or spent at his request or with his approval or cooperation limits what a contributor may independently spend in support or denigration of one running for federal office. Congress was plainly of the view that these expenditures also have corruptive potential; but the Court strikes down the provision, strangely enough claiming more insight as to what may improperly influence candidates than is possessed by the majority of Congress that passed this Bill and the President who signed it. Those supporting the Bill undeniably included many seasoned professionals who have been deeply involved in elective processes and who have viewed them at close range over many years.

It would make little sense to me, and apparently made none to Congress, to limit the amounts an individual may give to a candidate or spend with his approval but fail to limit the amounts that could be spent on his behalf. Yet the Court permits the former while striking down the

latter limitation. No more than $1,000 may be given to a candidate or spent at his request or with his approval or cooperation; but otherwise, apparently, a contributor is to be constitutionally protected in spending unlimited amounts of money in support of his chosen candidate or candidates.

Let us suppose that each of two brothers spends one million dollars on TV spot annoucements that he has individually prepared and in which he appears, urging the election of the same named candidate in identical words. One brother has sought and obtained the approval of the candidate; the other has not. The former may validly be prosecuted under § 608(e); under the Court's view, the latter may not, even though the candidate could scarcely help knowing about and appreciating the expensive favor. For constitutional purposes it is difficult to see the difference between the two situations. I would take the word of those who know— that limiting independent expenditures is essential to prevent transparent and widespread evasion of the contribution limits.

* * *

Mr. Justice REHNQUIST, concurring in part and dissenting in part.

* * *

The limits imposed by the First and Fourteenth Amendments on governmental action may vary in their stringency depending on the capacity in which the Government is acting. The Government as proprietor, Adderley v. Florida, 385 U.S. 39, 87 S.Ct. 242 (1966), is, I believe, permitted to affect putatively protected interests in a manner in which it might not do if simply proscribing conduct across the board. Similarly, the Government as employer, Pickering v. Board of Education, 391 U.S. 563, 88 S.Ct. 1731 (1968), and United States Civil Service Comm'n v. Letter Carriers, 413 U.S. 548, 93 S.Ct. 2880 (1973), may prescribe conditions of employment which might be constitutionally unacceptable if enacted into standards of conduct made applicable to the entire citizenry.

For the reasons stated in the dissenting opinion of Mr. Justice Jackson in Beauharnais v. Illinois, 343 U.S. 250, 288–295, 72 S.Ct. 725, 746–750 (1952), and by Mr. Justice Harlan in his dissenting opinion in Roth v. United States, 354 U.S. 476, 500–503, 77 S.Ct. 1304, 1317–1318 (1957), I am of the opinion that not all of the strictures which the First Amendment imposes upon Congress are carried over against the States by the Fourteenth Amendment, but rather that it is only the "general principle" of free speech, Gitlow v. New York, 268 U.S. 652, 672, 45 S.Ct. 625, 632 (1925) (Holmes, J., dissenting), that the latter incorporates. See Palko v. Connecticut, 302 U.S. 319, 324–325, 58 S.Ct. 149, 151–152 (1937).

Given this view, cases which deal with state restrictions on First Amendment freedoms are not fungible with those which deal with restrictions imposed by the Federal Government, and cases which deal with the Government as employer or proprietor are not fungible with

those which deal with the Government as a lawmaker enacting criminal statutes applying to the population generally. The statute before us was enacted by Congress, not with the aim of managing the Government's property nor of regulating the conditions of Government employment, but rather with a view to the regulation of the citizenry as a whole. The case for me, then, presents the First Amendment interests of the appellants at their strongest, and the legislative authority of Congress in the position where it is most vulnerable to First Amendment attacks.

While this approach undoubtedly differs from some of the underlying assumptions in the opinion of the Court, opinions are written not to explore abstract propositions of law but to decide concrete cases. I therefore join in all of the Court's opinion except [that part] which sustains, against appellants' First and Fifth Amendment challenges, the disparities found in the congressional plan for financing general Presidential elections between the two major parties, on the one hand and minor parties and candidacies on the other.

* * *

[The opinions of Justices MARSHALL and BLACKMUN, concurring in part and dissenting in part, are omitted.]

It is noteworthy that in the discussion in *Buckley* v. *Valeo*, supra, with respect to "substantial restraints on the quantity of political speech" no mention is made of limitations on free speech for the purposes of achieving fairness and to expedite certain activities which have long been practiced in some of our institutions. For example, debate is commonly limited in the House of Representatives, as is the time for presentation of oral arguments before the Supreme Court. Justice

White, however, in his opinion, did endeavor to distinguish between the control of *content* of speech and other limitations:

> Concededly, neither the limitations on contributions nor those on expenditures directly or indirectly purport to control the content of political speech by candidates or by their supporters or detractors. What the Act regulates is giving and spending money, acts that have First Amendment significance not because they are themselves communicative with respect to the qualifications of the candidate, but because money may be used to defray the expenses of speaking or otherwise communicating about the merits or demerits of federal candidates for election. * * *

Would it or would it not be a worthy consideration that limitations on the quantity of free speech to achieve fairness are constitutionally different from limitations on content?

FIRST NATIONAL BANK OF BOSTON v. BELLOTTI

Supreme Court of the United States, 1978
435 U.S. 765, 98 S.Ct. 1407, 55 L.Ed.2d 707

A Massachusetts statute imposes stiff criminal penalties on business corporations and management which spend corporate funds "for the purpose of * * * influencing or affecting the vote on any question submitted to the voters, other than one materially affecting any of the property, business or assets of the corporation." Additionally, the law specifies that "[n]o question submitted to the voters solely concerning the taxation of income, property or transactions of individuals shall be deemed materially to affect the property, business or assets of the corporation."

The First National Bank of Boston and other financial institutions and corporations wished to disseminate their views in opposition to a proposed amendment to the Commonwealth's constitution to be voted on at the November 1976 general election, authorizing the levy of a graduated personal income tax. The plaintiff corporations brought suit against the Attorney General of Massachusetts alleging that the law violated the First Amendment and seeking a judgment declaring the statute unconstitutional. The Massachusetts Supreme Judicial Court upheld the statute, and the plaintiffs appealed.

Mr. Justice POWELL delivered the opinion of the Court.

* * *

The court below framed the principal question in this case as whether and to what extent corporations have First Amendment rights. We believe that the court posed the wrong question. The Constitution often protects interests broader than those of the party seeking their vindication. The First Amendment, in particular, serves significant societal interests.

The proper question therefore is not whether corporations "have" First Amendment rights and, if so, whether they are coextensive with those of natural persons. Instead, the question must be whether § 8 [the statute] abridges expression that the First Amendment was meant to protect. We hold that it does.

The speech proposed by appellants is at the heart of the First Amendment's protection.

* * *

We * * * find no support in the First or Fourteenth Amendments, or in the decisions of this Court, for the proposition that speech that otherwise would be within the protection of the First Amendment loses that protection simply because its source is a corporation that cannot prove, to the satisfaction of a court, a material effect on its business or property. The "materially affecting" requirement is not an identification of the boundaries of corporate speech etched by the Constitution itself. Rather, it amounts to an impermissible legislative prohibition of speech based on the identity of the interests that spokesmen may represent in public debate over controversial issues and a requirement that the speaker have a sufficiently great interest in the subject to justify communication.

Section 8 permits a corporation to communicate to the public its views on certain referendum subjects— those materially affecting its business—but not others. It also singles out one kind of ballot question—individual taxation—as a subject about which corporations may never make their ideas public. The legislature has drawn the line between permissible and impermissible speech according to whether there is a sufficient nexus, as defined by the legislature, between the issue presented to the voters and the business interests of the speaker.

In the realm of protected speech, the legislature is constitutionally disqualified from dictating the subjects about which persons may speak and the speakers who may address a public issue. * * * If a legislature may direct business corporations to "stick to business," it also may limit other corporations—religious, charitable, or civic—to their respective "business" when addressing the public. Such power in government to channel the expression of views is unacceptable under the First Amendment. Especially where, as here, the legislature's suppression of speech suggests an attempt to give one side of a debatable public question an advantage in expressing its views to the people, the First Amendment is plainly offended. Yet the State contends that its action is necessitated by governmental interests of the highest order. We next consider these asserted interests.

The constitutionality of § 8's prohibition of the "exposition of ideas" by corporations turns on whether it can survive the exacting scrutiny necessitated by a state-imposed restriction of freedom of speech. Especially where, as here, a prohibition is directed at speech itself, and the speech is intimately related to the process of governing, "the State may prevail only upon showing a subordinating interest which is compelling," Bates v. City of Little Rock, 361 U.S. 516, 524, 80 S.Ct. 412, 417 (1960); see NAACP v. Button, 371 U.S. 415, 438–439, 83 S.Ct. 328, 340–341 (1963); NAACP v. Alabama ex rel. Patterson, 357 U.S., at 463, 78 S.Ct., at 1172; Thomas v. Collins, 323 U.S. 516, 530, 65 S.Ct. 315, 322 (1945), "and the burden is on the Government to show the existence of such an interest." Elrod v. Burns, 427 U.S. 347, 362, 96 S.Ct. 2673 (1976). Even then, the State must employ means "closely drawn to avoid unnecessary abridgment." * * * Buckley v. Valeo, 424 U.S. 1, 25, 96 S.Ct. 612, 638 (1976); see NAACP v. Button, supra, 371 U.S. at 438, 83 S.Ct. at 340; Shelton v. Tucker, 364 U.S. 479, 488, 81 S.Ct. 247, 252 (1960).

* * * Appellee * * * advances two principal justifications for the prohibition of corporate speech. The first is the State's interest in sustaining the active role of the individual citizen in the electoral process and thereby preventing diminution of the citizen's confidence in government. The second is the interest in protecting the rights of shareholders whose views differ from those expressed by management on behalf of the corporation. However weighty these interests may be in the context of partisan candidate elections, they either are not implicated in this case or are not served at all, or in other than a random manner, by the prohibition in § 8.

Preserving the integrity of the electoral process, preventing corruption, and "sustain[ing] the active, alert responsibility of the individual citizen in a democracy for the wise conduct of government" are interests of the highest importance. * * Preservation of the individual citizen's confidence in government is equally important. * * *

Appellee advances a number of arguments in support of his view that these interests are endangered by corporate participation in discussion of a referendum issue. They hinge upon the assumption that such participation would exert an undue influence on the outcome of a referendum vote, and—in the end—destroy the confidence of the people in the democratic process and the integrity of government. According to appellee, corporations are wealthy and powerful and their views may drown out other points of view. If appellee's arguments were supported by record or legislative findings that corporate advocacy threatened imminently to undermine democratic processes, thereby denigrating rather than serving First Amendment interests, these arguments would merit our consideration. * * * But there has been no showing that the relative voice of corporations has been overwhelming or even significant in influencing referenda in Massachusetts, or that there has been any threat to the confidence of the citizenry in government. * * *

Nor are appellee's arguments inherently persuasive or supported by the precedents of this Court. Referenda are held on issues, not candidates for public office. The risk of corruption perceived in cases involving candidate elections, e.g., * * * simply is not present in a popular vote on a public issue. To be sure, corporate advertising may influence the outcome of the vote; this would be its purpose. But the fact that advocacy may persuade the electorate is hardly a reason to suppress it: The Constitution "protects expression which is eloquent no less than that which is unconvincing." Kingsley Int'l Pictures Corp. v. Regents, 360 U.S., at 689, 79 S.Ct., at 1365. We noted only recently that "the concept that government may restrict the speech of some elements of our society in order to enhance the relative voice of others is wholly foreign to the First Amendment." * * * Buckley, supra, 424 U.S., at 48–49, 96 S.Ct., at 649. Moreover, the people in our democracy are entrusted with the responsibility for judging and evaluating the relative merits of conflicting arguments. They may consider, in making their judgment, the source and credibility of the advocate. But if there be any danger that the people cannot evaluate the information and arguments advanced by appellants, it is a danger contemplated by the Framers of the First

Amendment. * * * In sum, "[a] restriction so destructive of the right of public discussion [as § 8], without greater or more imminent danger to the public interest than existed in this case, is incompatible with the freedoms secured by the First Amendment."

Finally, the State argues that § 8 protects corporate shareholders, an interest that is both legitimate and traditionally within the province of state law. * * The statute is said to serve this interest by preventing the use of corporate resources in furtherance of views with which some shareholders may disagree. This purpose is belied, however, by the provisions of the statute, which are both under- and over-inclusive.

The under-inclusiveness of the statute is self-evident. Corporate expenditures with respect to a referendum are prohibited, while corporate activity with respect to the passage or defeat of legislation is permitted, * * * even though corporations may engage in lobbying more often than they take positions on ballot questions submitted to the voters. Nor does § 8 prohibit a corporation from expressing its views, by the expenditure of corporate funds, on any public issue until it becomes the subject of a referendum, though the displeasure of disapproving shareholders is unlikely to be any less.

The fact that a particular kind of ballot question has been singled out for special treatment undermines the likelihood of a genuine state interest in protecting shareholders. It suggests instead that the legislature may have been concerned with silencing corporations on a particular subject. Indeed, appellee has conceded that "the legislative and judicial history of the statute indicates * * *

that the second crime was 'tailor-made' to prohibit corporate campaign contributions to oppose a graduated income tax amendment." Brief for Appellee 6.

Nor is the fact that § 8 is limited to banks and business corporations without relevance. Excluded from its provisions and criminal sanctions are entities or organized groups in which numbers of persons may hold an interest or membership, and which often have resources comparable to those of large corporations. Minorities in such groups or entities may have interests with respect to institutional speech quite comparable to those of minority shareholders in a corporation. Thus the exclusion of Massachusetts business trusts, real estate investment trusts, labor unions, and other associations undermines the plausibility of the State's purported concern for the persons who happen to be shareholders in the banks and corporations covered by § 8.

The over-inclusiveness of the statute is demonstrated by the fact that § 8 would prohibit a corporation from supporting or opposing a referendum proposal even if its shareholders unanimously authorized the contribution or expenditure. Ultimately shareholders may decide, through the procedures of corporate democracy, whether their corporation should engage in debate on public issues. Acting through their power to elect the board of directors or to insist upon protective provisions in the corporation's charter, shareholders normally are presumed competent to protect their own interests. In addition to intra-corporate remedies, minority shareholders generally have access to the judicial remedy of a derivative suit to challenge corporate disbursements alleged to have been made for improper corporate purposes or merely to further the personal interests of management.

Assuming, *arguendo*, that protection of shareholders is a "compelling" interest under the circumstances of this case, we find "no substantially relevant correlation between the governmental interest asserted and the State's effort" to prohibit appellants from speaking. Shelton v. Tucker, 364 U.S., at 485, 81 S.Ct., at 250.

Because § 8 prohibits protected speech in a manner unjustified by a compelling state interest, it must be invalidated. The judgment of the Supreme Judicial Court is Reversed.

[The concurring opinion of Chief Justice BURGER appears at p. 1425.]

Mr. Justice WHITE, with whom Mr. Justice BRENNAN and Mr. Justice MARSHALL join, dissenting.

* * *

There is now little doubt that corporate communications come within the scope of the First Amendment. This, however, is merely the starting point of analysis, because an examination of the First Amendment values corporate expression furthers and the threat to the functioning of a free society it is capable of posing reveals that it is not fungible with communications emanating from individuals and is subject to restrictions which individual expression is not. Indeed, what some have considered to be the principal function of the First Amendment, the use of communication as a means of self-expression, self-realization and self-fulfillment, is not at all furthered by corporate speech. It is clear that the communications of profitmaking corporations are not "an integral part of the development of ideas, of mental exploration and of the affirmation of self." They do not represent a manifestation of individual freedom or choice. Undoubtedly, as this Court has recognized, see NAACP v. Button, 371 U.S. 415, 83 S.Ct. 328 (1963), there are some corporations formed for the express purpose of advancing certain ideological causes shared by all their members, or, as in the case of the press, of disseminating information and ideas. Under such circumstances, association in a corporate form may be viewed as merely a means of achieving effective self-expression. But this is hardly the case generally with corporations operated for the purpose of making profits. Shareholders in such entities do not share a common set of political or social views, and they certainly have not invested their money for the purpose of advancing political or social causes or in an enterprise engaged in the business of disseminating news and opinion. In fact, * * * the government has a strong interest in assuring that investment decisions are not predicated upon agreement or disagreement with the activities of corporations in the political arena.

Of course, it may be assumed that corporate investors are united by a desire to make money, for the value of their investment to increase. Since even communications which have no purpose other than that of enriching the communicator have some First Amendment protection, activities such as advertising and other communications integrally related to the operation of the corporation's business may be viewed as a means of furthering the desires of individual shareholders. This unanimity of purpose breaks down, however, when corporations make expenditures or undertake activities designed to influence the opinion or votes of the general public on political and social issues that have no material connection with or effect upon their business, property, or assets. Although it is arguable that corporations make such expenditures because their managers believe that it is in the corporations' economic interest to do so, there is no basis whatsoever for concluding that these views are expressive of the heterogeneous beliefs of their shareholders whose convictions on many political issues are undoubtedly shaped by considerations other than a desire to endorse any electoral or ideological cause which would tend to increase the value of a particular corporate investment. This is particularly true where, as in this case, whatever the belief of the corporate managers may be, they have not been able to demonstrate that the issue involved has any material connection with the corporate business. Thus when a profitmaking corporation contributes to a political candidate this does not further the self-expression or self-fulfillment of its shareholders in the way that expenditures from them as individuals would.

The self-expression of the communicator is not the only value encompassed by the First Amendment. One of its functions, often referred to as the right to hear or receive information, is to protect the interchange of ideas. Any communication of ideas, and consequently any expenditure of funds which makes the communication of ideas possible, it can be argued, furthers the purposes of the First Amendment. This proposition does not establish, however, that the right of the general public to receive communications financed by means of corporate expenditures is of the same dimension as that to hear other forms of expression. In the first place, * * *, corporate expenditures designed to further political causes lack the connection with individual self-expression which is one of the principal justifications for the constitutional protection of speech provided by the First Amendment. Ideas which are not a product of individual choice are entitled to less First Amendment protection. Secondly, the restriction of corporate speech concerned with political matters impinges much less severely upon the availability of ideas to the general public than do restrictions upon individual speech. Even the complete curtailment of corporate communications concerning political or ideological questions not integral to day-to-day business functions would leave individuals, including corporate shareholders, employees, and customers, free to communicate their thoughts. Moreover, it is unlikely that any significant communication would be lost by such a prohibition. These individuals would remain perfectly free to communicate any ideas which could be conveyed by means of the corporate form. Indeed, such individuals could even form associations for the very purpose of promoting political or ideological causes.

* * *

The governmental interest in regulating corporate political communications, especially those relating to electoral matters, also raises considerations which differ significantly from those governing the regulation of individual speech. Corporations are artificial entities created by law for the purpose of furthering certain economic goals. In order to facilitate the achievement of such ends, special rules relating to such matters as limited liability, perpetual life, and the accumulation, distribution, and taxation of assets are normally applied to them. States have provided corporations with such attributes in order to increase their economic viability and thus strengthen the economy generally. It has long been recognized however, that the special status of corporations has placed them in a position to control vast amounts of economic power which may, if not regulated, dominate not only the economy but also the very heart of our democracy, the electoral process. Although Buckley v. Valeo, 424 U.S. 1, 96 S.Ct. 612 (1976), provides support for the position that the desire to equalize the financial resources available to candidates does not justify the limitation upon the expression of support which a restriction upon individual contributions entails, the interest of Massachusetts and the many other States which have restricted corporate political activity is quite different. It is not one of equalizing the resources of opposing candidates or opposing positions but rather of preventing institutions which have been permitted to amass wealth as a result of special advantages extended by the State for certain economic purposes from using that wealth to acquire an unfair advantage in the political process, especially where, as here, the issue involved has no material connection with the business of the corporation. The State need not permit its own creation to consume it. Massachusetts could permissibly conclude that not to impose limits upon the political activities of corporations would have placed it in a position of departing from neutrality and indirectly assisting the propagation of corporate views because of the advantages its laws give to the corporate acquisition of funds to finance

such activities. Such expenditures may be viewed as seriously threatening the role of the First Amendment as a guarantor of a free marketplace of ideas. Ordinarily, the expenditure of funds to promote political causes may be assumed to bear some relation to the fervency with which they are held. Corporate political expression, however, is not only divorced from the convictions of individual corporate shareholders, but also, because of the ease with which corporations are permitted to accumulate capital, bears no relation to the conviction with which the ideas expressed are held by the communicator.

The Court's opinion appears to recognize at least the possibility that fear of corporate domination of the electoral process would justify restrictions upon corporate expenditures and contributions in connection with referenda but brushes this interest aside by asserting that "there has been no showing that the relative voice of corporations has been overwhelming or even significant in influencing referenda in Massachusetts," * * and by suggesting that the statute in issue represents an attempt to give an unfair advantage to those who hold views in opposition to positions which would otherwise be financed by corporations. * * * It fails even to allude to the fact, however, that Massachusetts' most recent experience with unrestrained corporate expenditures in connection with ballot questions establishes precisely the contrary. In 1972, a proposed amendment to the Massachusetts Constitution which would have authorized the imposition of a graduated income tax on both individuals and corporations was put to the voters. The Committee for Jobs and Government Economy, an organized political committee, raised and expended approximately $120,000 to oppose the proposed amendment, the bulk of it raised through large corporate contributions. Three of the present appellant corporations each contributed $3,000 to this committee. In contrast, the Coalition for Tax Reform, Inc., the only political committee organized to support the 1972 amendment, was able to raise and expend only approximately $7,000. * * * Perhaps these figures reflect the Court's view of the appropriate role which corporations should play in the Massachusetts electoral process, but it nowhere explains why it is entitled to substitute its judgment for that of Massachusetts and other States, as well as the United States, which have acted to correct or prevent similar domination of the electoral process by corporate wealth.

This Nation has for many years recognized the need for measures designed to prevent corporate domination of the political process. The Corrupt Practices Act, first enacted in 1907, has consistently barred corporate contributions in connection with federal elections. This Court has repeatedly recognized that one of the principal purposes of this prohibition is "to avoid the deleterious influences on federal elections resulting from the use of money by those who exercise control over large aggregations of capital." United States v. International Union United Auto. Workers, 352 U.S. 567, 585, 77 S.Ct. 529, 538 (1937). * * * Although this Court has never adjudicated the constitutionality of the Act, there is no suggestion in its cases construing it, * * * that this purpose is in any sense illegitimate or deserving of other than the utmost respect; indeed, the thrust of its opinions, until today, has been to the contrary. * * *

There is an additional overriding interest related to the prevention of corporate domination which is substantially advanced by Massachusetts' restrictions upon corporate contributions: assuring that shareholders are not compelled to support and financially further beliefs with which they disagree where, as is the case here, the issue involved does not materially affect the business, property, or other affairs of the corporation. The State has not interfered with the prerogatives of corporate management to communicate about matters that have material impact on the business affairs entrusted to them, however much individual stockholders may disagree on economic or ideological grounds. Nor has the State forbidden management from formulating and circulating its views at its own expense or at the expense of others, even where the subject at issue is irrelevant to corporate business affairs. But Massachusetts has chosen to forbid corporate management from spending corporate funds in referenda elections absent some demonstrable effect of the issue on the economic life of the company. In short, corporate management may not use corporate monies to promote what does not further corporate affairs but in the last analysis are the purely personal views of the management, individually or as a group.

* * *

I would affirm the judgment of the Supreme Judicial Court for the Commonwealth of Massachusetts.

Mr. Justice REHNQUIST, dissenting.

* * *

The question presented today, whether business corporations have a constitutionally protected liberty to engage in political activities, has never been squarely addressed by any previous decision of this Court. However, the General Court of the Commonwealth of Massachusetts, the Congress of the United States, and the legislatures of 30 other States of this Republic have considered the matter, and have concluded that restrictions upon the political activity of business corporations are both politically desirable and constitutionally permissible. The judgment of such a broad consensus of governmental bodies expressed over a period of many decades is entitled to considerable deference from this Court. I think it quite probable that their judgment may properly be reconciled with our controlling precedents, but I am certain that under my views of the limited application of the First Amendment to the States, which I share with the two immediately preceding occupants of my seat on the Court, but not with my present colleagues, the judgment of the Supreme Judicial Court of Massachusetts should be affirmed.

*   *   *

*   *   * A State grants to a business corporation the blessings of potentially perpetual life and limited liability to enhance its efficiency as an economic entity. It might reasonably be concluded that those properties, so beneficial in the economic sphere, pose special dangers in the political sphere: Furthermore, it might be argued that liberties of political expression are not at all necessary to effectuate the purposes for which States permit commercial corporations to exist. So long as the Judicial Branches of the State and Federal Governments remain open to protect the corporation's interest in its property, it has no need, though it may have the desire, to petition the political branches for similar protection. Indeed, the States might reasonably fear that the corporation would use its economic power to obtain further benefits beyond those already bestowed. I would think that any particular form of organization upon which the State confers special privileges or immunities different from those of natural persons would be subject to like regulation, whether the organization is a labor union, a partnership, a trade association, or a corporation.

*   *   *

I can see no basis for concluding that the liberty of a corporation to engage in political activity with regard to matters having no material effect on its business is necessarily incidental to the purposes for which the Commonwealth permitted these corporations to be organized or admitted within its boundaries. Nor can I disagree with the Supreme Judicial Court's factual finding that no such effect has been shown by these appellants. Because the statute as construed provides at least as much protection as the Fourteenth Amendment requires, I believe it is constitutionally valid.

*   *   *

Along with the January 1976 utility bills it mailed to its customers, Consolidated Edison Company inserted into the envelopes a statement of its views on nuclear power, the gist of which was that nuclear power is essential to the goal of energy independence; that nuclear power plants are safe, clean, and economical; and that the benefits of nuclear power far outweigh the potential risks. The National Resources Defense Council (NRDC), an environmental group, subsequently requested the utility to enclose a rebuttal statement prepared by NRDC in its next monthly billing. When Consolidated Edison refused, the environmental group asked the state Public Service Commission to compel the utility to open its billing envelopes to contrasting views on controversial public issues. The Commission denied NRDC's request, but instead ordered public utilities to stop using billing inserts that discuss "controversial matters of public policy." Consolidated Edison then took the matter to the New York courts. An initial judgment finding the Commission's order unconstitutional was overturned by an intermediate state appellate court, and this ruling favorable to the Commission was affirmed by the New York Court of Appeals on grounds the order was "a valid time, place, and manner regulation designed to protect the privacy of Consolidated Edison's customers."

In Consolidated Edison Co. of New York v. Public Serv. Comm'n of the State of New York, 447 U.S. 530, 100 S.Ct. 2326 (1980), the Supreme Court reversed the judgment of the New York Court of Appeals and declared the order unconstitutional. Observing at the beginning that "[i]n First National Bank of Boston v. Bellotti, 435 U.S. 765, 98 S.Ct. 1407 (1978), we rejected the contention that a State may confine corporate speech to specific issues" and that "state action [which] limited protected speech * * * could not stand absent a showing of a compelling state interest," Justice Powell, speaking for the Court, wrote, "We must determine whether the prohibition [here] is (i) a reasonable time, place, or manner restriction, (ii) a permissible subject-matter regulation, or (iii) a narrowly-tailored means of serving a compelling state interest." Addressing the first of these issues, Justice Powell emphasized that

> A restriction that regulates only the time, place or manner of speech may be imposed so long as it's reasonable. But when regulation is based on the content of speech, governmental action must be scrutinized more carefully to ensure that communication has not been prohibited "merely because public officials disapprove the speaker's views." Niemotko v. Maryland, 340 U.S. 268, 282, 71 S.Ct. 325 (1951) (Frankfurter, J., concurring in the result). As a consequence, we have emphasized that time, place, and manner regulations must be "applicable to all speech regardless of content." Erznoznick v. City of Jacksonville, 422 U.S. 205, 209, 95 S.Ct. 2268 (1975). * * * Governmental action that regulates speech on the basis of its subject matter " 'slip[s] from the neutrality of time, place, and circumstances into a concern about content.' " Police Department v. Mosley, 408 U.S. 92, 99, 92 S.Ct. 2286 (1972), quoting Kalven, The Concept of the Public Forum: Cox v. Louisiana, 1965 Sup.Ct.Rev. 29. Therefore, a constitutionally permissible time, place, or manner restriction may not be based upon either the content or subject matter of speech.

Applying these precepts to the case at hand, he explained:

> The Commission does not pretend that its action is unrelated to the content or subject matter of bill inserts. Indeed, it has undertaken to suppress certain bill inserts precisely because they address controversial issues of public policy. The Commission allows inserts that present information to consumers on certain subjects, such as energy conservation measures, but it forbids the use of inserts that discuss public controversies. The Commis-

sion, with commendable candor, justifies its ban on the ground that consumers will benefit from receiving "useful" information, but not from the prohibited information. * * * The Commission's own rationale demonstrates that its action cannot be upheld as a content-neutral time, place, or manner regulation.

As to the second issue, the Court rejected the Commission's contention "that its order is acceptable because it applies to all discussion of nuclear power, whether pro or con," * * * because the prohibition "is related to subject matter rather than to the views of a particular speaker" and, therefore, because "the regulation does not favor either side of a political controversy * * *." Said Justice Powell, "The First Amendment's hostility to content regulation extends not only to restrictions on particular viewpoints but also to prohibition of public discussion on an entire topic." He continued, "To allow a government the choice of permissible subjects for public debate would be to allow that government control over the search for political truth." Finally, the Court considered the compelling state interests advanced by the Commission as well served by its order: (a) "to avoid forcing Consolidated Edison's view on a captive audience"; (b) "to allocate limited resources in the public interest"; and (c) "to ensure that ratepayers do not subsidize the cost of the bill inserts." Focusing on the first of these interests, Justice Powell wrote:

> Even if a short exposure to Consolidated Edison's views may offend the sensibilities of some consumers, the ability of government "to shut off discourse solely to protect others from hearing it [is] dependent upon a showing that substantial privacy interests are being invaded in an essentially intolerable manner." Cohen v. California, 403 U.S., at 21, 91 S.Ct., at 1786. A less stringent analysis would permit a government to slight the First Amendment's role "in affording the public access to discussion, debate and the dissemination of information and ideas." First National Bank of Boston v. Bellotti, 435 U.S., at 783, 98 S.Ct. at 1419. * * * Where a single speaker communicates to many listeners, the First Amendment does not permit the government to prohibit speech as intrusive unless the "captive" audience cannot avoid objectionable speech.

> Passengers on public transportation * * * or residents of a neighborhood disturbed by the raucous broadcasts from a passing soundtruck * * * may well be unable to escape an unwanted message. But customers who encounter an objectionable billing insert may "effectively avoid further bombardment of their sensibilities simply by averting their eyes." Cohen v. California, 403 U.S., at 21, 91 S.Ct., at 1786. * * * The customer of Consolidated Edison may escape exposure to objectionable material simply by transferring the bill insert from envelope to wastebasket.

He also rejected the contention that the actions of the Public Service Commission were rather like that of the Federal Communications Commission in its regulation of radio and television broadcast frequencies. As Justice Powell pointed out, the federal government's "unusual authority over speech" in the broadcast industry did not by analogy support the Commission's order because

> billing envelopes differ from broadcast frequencies in two ways. First, a broadcaster communicates through use of a scarce, publicly owned resource. No person can broadcast without a license, whereas all persons are free to send correspondence to private homes through the mails. Thus,

it cannot be said that billing envelopes are a limited resource comparable to the broadcast spectrum. Second, the Commission has not shown on the record before us that the presence of the bill inserts at issue would preclude the inclusion of other inserts that Consolidated Edison might be ordered lawfully to include in the billing envelope. Unlike radio or television stations broadcasting on a single frequency, multiple bill inserts will not result in a "cacophony of competing voices." * * *

And, finally, as to contention (c), the Court pointed out that "there is no basis on this record to assume that the Commission could not exclude the cost of these bill inserts from the utility's rate base." Said Justice Powell, "Mere speculation of harm does not constitute a compelling state interest."

Concurring in the judgment of the Court, Justice Stevens wrote to take issue with the majority for resting their conclusion as to the unconstitutionality of the Commission's order on the fact that the order was based on the content or subject matter of speech. He wrote:

> Any student of history who has been reprimanded for talking about the World Series during a class discussion of the First Amendment knows that it is incorrect to state that a "time, place, or manner restriction may not be based upon either the content or subject matter of speech." * * * And every lawyer who has read our Rules, or our cases upholding various restrictions on speech with specific reference to subject matter must recognize the hyperbole in the dictum, "But, above all else, the First Amendment means that Government has no power to restrict expression because of its message, its ideas, its subject matter or its content." Police Department v. Mosley, 408 U.S. 92, 95, 92 S.Ct. 2286, quoted in part. * * * Indeed, if that were the law, there would be no need for the Court's detailed rejection of the justifications put forward by the State for the restriction involved in this case. * * *

> There are, in fact, many situations in which the subject matter, or, indeed, even the point of view of the speaker, may provide a justification for a time, place and manner regulation. Perhaps the most obvious example is the regulation of oral argument in this Court; the appellant's lawyer precedes his adversary solely because he seeks reversal of a judgment. As is true of many other aspects of liberty, some forms of orderly regulation actually promote freedom more than would a state of total anarchy.

> Instead of trying to justify our conclusion by reasoning from honeycombed premises, I prefer to identify the basis of decision in more simple terms. * * * A regulation of speech that is motivated by nothing more than a desire to curtail expression of a particular point of view on controversial issues of general interest is the purest example of a "law abridging the freedom of speech, or of the press." A regulation that denies one group of persons the right to address a selected audience on "controversial issues of public policy" is plainly such a regulation.

In an opinion in which, at one point, he termed Consolidated Edison's practice an "abuse of monopoly power," Justice Blackmun dissented and was joined in part by Justice Rehnquist. Justice Blackmun said in generally summing up his views:

> I cannot agree with the Court that the New York Public Service Commission's ban on the utility bill insert somehow deprives the utility of its First

and Fourteenth Amendment rights.   Because of Consolidated Edison's monopoly status and its rate structure, the use of the insert amounts to an exaction from the utility's customers by way of forced aid for the utility's speech.   And, contrary to the Court's suggestion, an allocation of the insert's cost between the utility's shareholders and the ratepayers would not eliminate this coerced subsidy.

MORE RECENT CASES ON THE FIRST AMENDMENT AND LEGISLATION DEALING WITH "CORRUPTION" OF THE ELECTORAL PROCESS

Citizens Against Rent Control/ Coalition For Fair Housing v. City of Berkeley, 454 U.S. 290, 102 S.Ct. 434 (1981)	Facts	A city ordinance imposes a $250 ceiling per contributor on contributions to committees organized to support or oppose issues on the ballot to be submitted to a popular vote. When the plaintiff organization, which received several contributions in excess of the $250 limit, was ordered to pay the excess in each instance to the city treasury by the Berkeley Fair Campaign Practices Commission, the organization sued challenging the ordinance as a facial infringement of the First Amendment.
	Decision	Ordinance declared unconstitutional
	Vote	8–1
	Opinion of the Court	Speaking for the Court, Chief Justice Burger concluded that the ordinance violated First Amendment rights both of association and expression. Since the ordinance imposes a limitation on contributions to committees but none on individuals acting alone, it clearly places a restraint on the right of association. Although Buckley v. Valeo, 424 U.S. 1, 96 S.Ct. 612 (1976), held that contributions to candidates or their committees could be restricted so as to prevent corruption or the appearance of corruption, here, as in First National Bank of Boston v. Bellotti, 435 U.S. 765, 98 S.Ct. 1407 (1978), the prospect of corruption is significantly lessened because the ordinance deals with contributions to committees formed to support or oppose propositions on the ballot rather than candidates. The city's argument that the portion of the ordinance in question "is necessary as a prophylactic measure to make known the identity of supporters and opponents of ballot measures" is unconvincing because "there is no risk that the Berkeley voters will be in doubt as to the identity of those whose money supports or opposes a given ballot measure since contributors must make their identities known under * * * [another section] of the ordinance which requires publication of lists of contributors in advance of the voting." The asserted means for "preserv[ing] voters' confidence in the ballot measure process * * * does not advance a legitimate governmental interest significant enough to

Citizens Against Rent Control/ Coalition For Fair Housing (*Cont.*)	Opinion of the Court (*Cont.*)	justify its infringement of First Amendment rights." In the context of this case, the rights of association and expression "overlap and blend" because "[t]he contribution limit * * * automatically affects expenditures and limits on expenditures operate as a direct restraint on freedom of expression of a group or committee desiring to engage in political dialogue concerning a ballot measure."
	Concurring Opinion	Reconciling his vote to strike down the ordinance in this case with his vote to uphold the statute in *Bellotti*, Justice Rehnquist explained: "Unlike the factual situation * * * [there], the Berkeley ordinance was not aimed only at corporations, but sought to impose an across-the-board limitation on the size of contributions to committees formed to support or oppose ballot measure referenda. * * * Therefore, my dissenting opinion in * * * *Bellotti* * * * which relied on the corporate shield which the state had granted to corporations as a form of *quid pro quo* for the limitation does not come into play."
	Opinion Concurring in the Judgment	Observing that "this Court has *always* drawn a distinction between restrictions on contributions, and direct limitations on the amount an individual can expend for his own speech" and in light of the fact that "the Court's opinion is silent on the standard of review it is applying to this contributions limitation," which led him to the "assum[ption] that the Court is following our consistent position that this type of governmental action is subjected to less rigorous scrutiny than a direct restriction on expenditures," Justice Marshall concluded there was insufficient evidence in the record to support the city's asserted governmental interest. He emphasized that it was a lower level standard of review which the evidence failed to meet: "As we noted last term in California Medical Assn. v. Federal Election Commission, 453 U.S. 182, 101 S.Ct. 2712 (1980), * * * 'speech by proxy' that is achieved through contributions to a political campaign committee 'is not the sort of political advocacy that this Court in *Buckley* found entitled to full First Amendment protection.'"
	Opinion Concurring in the Judgment	Applying "exacting scrutiny" because "[t]he contribution limitations at issue here encroach directly on political expression and association," Justice Blackmun, joined by Justice O'Connor, thought "that Berkeley has neither demonstrated a genuine threat to its important governmental interests nor employed means closely drawn to avoid unnecessary abridgment of protected activity."
	Dissenting Opinion	In the lone dissent, Justice White explained: "The Berkeley ordinance does not control the quantity or content of speech. Unlike the statute in *Bellotti*, it does not completely prohibit contributions or expend-

Citizens Against Rent Control/ Coalition For Fair Housing (*Cont.*)	Dissenting Opinion (*Cont.*)	itures. Any person or company may contribute up to $250. If greater spending is desired, it must be made as an expenditure, and expenditures are not limited or otherwise controlled. Individuals also remain completely unfettered in their ability to join interested groups or otherwise directly participate in the campaign." Believing that "the Court overstates the extent to which First Amendment interests are implicated," Justice White thought that the lesser level of scrutiny for evaluating "'speech by proxy'" in the form of contributions to political committees was met here. Taking note of the "[s]taggering disparities [which] have developed between spending for and against various ballot measures" such that "[l]arge contributions, mainly from corporate sources, have skyrocketed as the role of individuals has declined," he observed that "[b]y restricting the size of contributions, the Berkeley ordinance requires major contributors to communicate directly with the voters. If the ordinance has an ultimate impact on speech, it will be to assure that a diversity of views will be presented to the voters. * * * [T]he inadequacy of disclosure laws was a major reason for the adoption of the Berkeley ordinance" and although "neither the City of Berkeley or the State of California can 'prove' that elections have been or can be unfairly won by special interest groups spending large sums of money, there is a widespread conviction in legislative halls, as well as among citizens, that the danger is real."
		Quoting a statement he made when the Court decided *Buckley*, he added: "I continue to believe that because the limitations are content-neutral, and because many regulatory actions will indirectly affect speech in the same manner as regulations in the sphere of campaign finance, 'the argument that money is speech and that limiting the flow of money to the speaker violates the First Amendment proves entirely too much.' * * * Every form of regulation—from taxes to compulsory bargaining—has some effect on the ability of individuals and corporations to engage in expressive activity. We must therefore focus on the extent to which expressive and associational activity is restricted by the Berkeley ordinance. That first amendment interests are implicated should begin, not end our inquiry. When the infringement is as slight and ephemeral as it is here, the requisite state interest to justify the regulation need not be so high."
Brown v. Hartlage, — U.S. —, 102 S.Ct. 1523 (1982)	Facts	A candidate for county commissioner pledged at a televised news conference to lower commissioners' salaries if elected. When he learned that his statement of such a commitment might conceivably violate the Kentucky Corrupt Practices Act which, on its face, bars a candidate from offering material benefits to voters in consideration for their votes, the candidate retracted his statement. After he won the election,

Brown (*Cont.*)

Facts (*Cont.*)	his opponent (the incumbent) sued to have the election nullified on grounds the statement made by the victorious candidate to have his salary reduced to less than that "fixed by law" violated the state statute.
Decision	That provision of the state Corrupt Practices Act, as applied in this case, infringed the First Amendment.
Vote	9–0
Opinion of the Court	Justice Brennan, speaking for the Court, began "by acknowledging that the States have a legitimate interest in preserving the integrity of the electoral processes" yet "[w]hen a State seeks to restrict directly the offer of ideas by a candidate to the voters, the First Amendment surely requires that the restriction be demonstrably supported not only by a legitimate state interest, but a compelling one, and that the restriction operate without unnecessarily circumscribing protected expression." The Court "discern[ed] three bases upon which the application of the statute to [the candidate's] promise might conceivably be justified: first, as a prohibition on buying votes; second, as facilitating the candidacy of persons lacking independent wealth; and third, as an application of the State's interests and prerogatives with respect to factual misstatements."

As to the first of these bases for applying the statute, "there is no *constitutional* basis upon which [the candidate's] pledge to reduce his salary might be equated with a candidate's promise to pay voters for their support from his own pocketbook." "Like a promise to lower taxes, to increase efficiency in government, or indeed to increase taxes in order to provide some group with a desired public benefit or service, [the candidate's] promise to reduce his salary cannot be deemed beyond the reach of the First Amendment, or considered as inviting the kind of corrupt arrangement the appearance of which a State may have a compelling interest in avoiding."

In response to the second conceivable basis for invoking the statute, "[t]he State might legitimately fear that such emphasis on free public service might result in persons of independent wealth but less ability being chosen over those who, though better qualified, could not afford to serve at a reduced salary. But if [the statute] was designed to further this interest, it chooses a means unacceptable under the First Amendment. In barring certain public statements with respect to this issue, the State ban runs directly counter to the fundamental premises underlying the First Amendment as the guardian of our democracy. That Amendment embodies our trust in the free exchange of ideas as the means by which the people are to choose between good ideas and bad, and between candidates for political office. The

Brown (*Cont.*)	Opinion of the Court (*Cont.*)	State's fear that voters might make an ill-advised choice does not provide the State with a compelling justification for limiting speech. It is simply not the function of government to 'select which issues are worth discussing or debating' * * * in the course of a political campaign."
		And, with respect to the third and last justification offered, that of preventing factual misstatements (such as that contained in the candidate's pledge but where his salary is "fixed by law" and he cannot therefore deliver on it), erroneous statement is inevitable in robust political debate and the exchange of ideas must be given "breathing space." There was no evidence that the disputed statement was made "other than in good faith and without knowledge of its falsity or that he made the statement with reckless disregard whether it was false or not. Moreover, [the candidate] retracted the statement promptly after discovering it might have been false."
	Other Statements	Chief Justice Burger concurred in the judgment. Justice Rehnquist concurred in the result.

ELROD v. BURNS

Supreme Court of the United States, 1976
427 U.S. 347, 96 S.Ct. 2673, 49 L.Ed.2d 547

Burns and other Republican noncivil service employees of the Cook County, Illinois sheriff's office were discharged from their jobs solely on the basis of their political party affiliation. They brought suit against Elrod, a Democrat and the newly elected sheriff, alleging infringement of their First and Fourteenth Amendment rights and violation of, among other statutes, the Civil Rights Act of 1871. After the district court dismissed the complaint, plaintiff sought review from the federal appeals court which reversed the lower court decision and instructed the district court to grant preliminary injunctive relief. The sheriff appealed.

In reading the case, you should consider the tremendous impact on the American political system that the Court's sweeping opinion promises to make. Fortunately, for the purpose of making value judgments on the question raised in the case, the issues are exceptionally well drawn in both the majority opinion and the dissent.

———

Mr. Justice BRENNAN announced the judgment of the Court and delivered an opinion in which Mr. Justice WHITE and Mr. Justice MARSHALL joined.

This case presents the question whether public employees who allege they were discharged or threatened with discharge solely because of their partisan political affiliation or nonaffiliation state a claim for deprivation of constitutional rights secured by the First and Fourteenth Amendments.

* * *

The cost of the practice of patronage is the restraint it places on freedoms of belief and association. In order to maintain their jobs, respondents were required to pledge their political allegiance to the Democratic Party, work for the election of other candidates of the Democratic Party, contribute a portion of their wages to the Party, or obtain the sponsorship of a member of the Party, usually at the price of one of the first three alternatives. Regardless of the incumbent party's identity, Democratic or otherwise, the consequences for association and belief are the same. An individual who is a member of the out-party maintains affiliation with his own party at the risk of losing his job. He works for the election of his party's candidates and espouses its policies at the same risk. The financial and campaign assistance that he is induced to provide to another party furthers the advancement of that party's policies to the detriment of his party's views and ultimately his own beliefs, and any assessment of his salary is tantamount to coerced belief. See Buckley v. Valeo, 424 U.S. 1, 13–14, 96 S.Ct. 612, 631–632. Even a pledge of allegiance to another party, however ostensible, only serves to compromise the individual's true beliefs. Since the average public employee is hardly in the financial position to support his party and another, or to lend his time to two parties, the individual's ability to act according to his beliefs and to associate with others of his political persuasion is constrained, and support for his party is diminished.

It is not only belief and association which are restricted where political patronage is the practice. The free functioning of the electoral process also suffers. Conditioning public employment on partisan support prevents support of competing political interests. Existing employees are deterred from such support, as well as the multitude seeking jobs. As government employment, state or federal, becomes more pervasive, the greater the dependence on it becomes, and therefore the greater becomes the power to starve political opposition by commanding partisan support, financial and otherwise. Patronage thus tips the electoral process in favor of the incumbent party, and where the practice's scope is substantial relative to the size of the electorate, the impact on the process can be significant.

Our concern with the impact of patronage on political belief and association does not occur in the abstract, for political belief and association constitute the core of those activities protected by the First Amendment. Regardless of the nature of the inducement, whether it be by the denial of public employment or, as in West Virginia State Board of Education v. Barnette, 319 U.S. 624, 63 S.Ct. 1178, by the influence of a teacher over students, "[i]f there is any fixed star in our constitutional constellation, it is that no official, high or petty, can prescribe what shall be orthodox in politics, nationalism, religion, or other matters of opinion or force citizens to confess by word or act their faith therein." Id., at 642. And, though freedom of belief is central, "[t]he First Amendment protects political association as well as political expression." *Buckley* v. *Valeo*, supra, at 11. "There can no longer be any doubt that freedom to associate with others for the common advancement of political beliefs and ideas is a form of 'orderly activity' protected by the First and Fourteenth Amendments. NAACP v. Button, 371 U.S. 415, 430, 83 S.Ct. 328, 336; Bates v. Little Rock, 361 U.S. 516, 522–523, 80 S.Ct. 412, 416–417; NAACP v. Alabama, 357

U.S. 449, 460–461, 78 S.Ct. 1163, 1171. The right to associate with the political party of one's choice is an integral part of this basic constitutional freedom." Kusper v. Pontikes, 414 U.S. 51, 56–57, 94 S.Ct. 303, 307.

These protections reflect our "profound national commitment to the principle that debate on public issues should be uninhibited, robust, and wide-open." New York Times Co. v. Sullivan, 376 U.S. 254, 270, 84 S.Ct. 710, 721, a principle itself reflective of the fundamental understanding that "[c]ompetition in ideas and governmental policies is at the core of our electoral process." * * * Williams v. Rhodes [393 U.S. 23 (1968)] at 32, 89 S.Ct., at 11. Patronage, therefore, to the extent it compels or restrains belief and association, is inimical to the process which undergirds our system of government and is "at war with the deeper traditions of democracy embodied in the First Amendment." Illinois State Employees Union v. Lewis [473 F.2d 561 (CA 7 1972)] at 576. As such, the practice unavoidably confronts decisions by this Court either invalidating or recognizing as invalid government action that inhibits belief and association through the conditioning of public employment on political faith.

* * *

* * * It is firmly established that a significant impairment of First Amendment rights must survive exacting scrutiny. Buckley v. Valeo, supra, at 59; NAACP v. Alabama, supra, at 460–461. "This type of scrutiny is necessary even if any deterrent effect on the exercise of First Amendment rights arises, not through direct government action, but indirectly as an unintended but inevitable result of the government's

conduct." * * * Buckley v. Valeo, supra, at 59. Thus encroachment "cannot be justified by a mere showing of some legitimate governmental interest." Kusper v. Pontikes, 414 U.S. 51, 58, 94 S.Ct. 303, 308. The interest advanced must be paramount, one of vital importance, and the burden is on the Government to show the existence of such an interest. * * * In the instant case, care must be taken not to confuse the interest of partisan organizations with governmental interests. Only the latter will suffice. Moreover, it is not enough that the means chosen in furtherance of the interest be rationally related to that end. * * * The gain to the subordinating interest provided by the means must outweigh the incurred loss of protected rights, * * * and the Government must "employ[ ] means closely drawn to avoid unnecessary abridgement." * * * Buckley v. Valeo, supra, at 20. "[A] State may not choose means that unnecessarily restrict constitutionally protected liberty. 'Precision of regulation must be the touchstone in an area so closely touching most precious freedoms.' If the State has open to it a less drastic way of satisfying its legitimate interests, it may not choose a legislative scheme that broadly stifles the exercise of fundamental personal liberties." * * * In short, if conditioning the retention of public employment on the employee's support of the in-party is to survive constitutional challenge, it must further some vital government end by a means that is least restrictive of freedom of belief and association in achieving that end, and the benefit gained must outweigh the loss of constitutionally protected rights.

One interest which has been offered in justification of patronage is the need to insure effective government and the efficiency of public employees. It is argued that employees of political persuasions not the same as that of the party in control of public office will not have the incentive to work effectively and may even be motivated to subvert the incumbent administration's efforts to govern effectively. We are not persuaded. The inefficiency resulting from the wholesale replacement of large numbers of public employees every time political office changes hands belies this justification. And the prospect of dismissal after an election in which the incumbent party has lost is only a disincentive to good work. Further, it is not clear that dismissal in order to make room for a patronage appointment will result in replacement by a person more qualified to do the job since appointment often occurs in exchange for the delivery of votes, or other party service, not job capability. More fundamentally, however, the argument does not succeed because it is doubtful that the mere difference of political persuasion motivates poor performance; nor do we think it legitimately may be used as a basis for imputing such behavior. The Court has consistently recognized that mere political association is an inadequate basis for imputing disposition to ill-willed conduct. * * * At all events, less drastic means for insuring government effectiveness and employee efficiency are available to the State. Specifically, employees may always be discharged for good cause, such as insubordination or poor job performance, when those bases in fact exist.

Even if the first argument that patronage serves effectiveness and efficiency be rejected, it still may be argued that patronage serves those

interests by giving the employees of an incumbent party the incentive to perform well in order to insure their party's incumbency and thereby their jobs. Patronage, according to the argument, thus makes employees highly accountable to the public. But the ability of officials more directly accountable to the electorate to discharge employees for cause and the availability of merit systems, growth in the use of which has been quite significant, convince us that means less intrusive than patronage still exist for achieving accountability in the public work force and, thereby, effective and efficient Government. The greater effectiveness of patronage over these less drastic means, if any, is at best marginal, a gain outweighed by the absence of intrusion on protected interests under the alternatives.

* * *

A second interest advanced in support of patronage is the need for political loyalty of employees, not to the end that effectiveness and efficiency be insured, but to the end that representative government not be undercut by tactics obstructing the implementation of policies of the new administration, policies presumably sanctioned by the electorate. The justification is not without force, but is nevertheless inadequate to validate patronage wholesale. Limiting patronage dismissals to policymaking positions is sufficient to achieve this governmental end. Nonpolicymaking individuals usually have only limited responsibility and are therefore not in a position to thwart the goals of the in-party.

No clear line can be drawn between policymaking and nonpolicymaking positions. While nonpolicymaking individuals usually have limited responsibility, that is not to say that one with a number of responsibilities is necessarily in a policymaking position. The nature of the responsibilities is critical. Employee supervisors, for example, may have many responsibilities, but those responsibilities may have only limited and well-defined objectives. An employee with responsibilities that are not well defined or are of broad scope more likely functions in a policymaking position. In determining whether an employee occupies a policymaking position, consideration should also be given to whether the employee acts as an adviser or formulates plans for the implementation of broad goals. Thus the political loyalty "justification is a matter of proof, or at least argument, directed at particular kinds of jobs." *Illinois State Employees Union* v. *Lewis,* supra, at 574. Since, as we have noted, it is the Government's burden to demonstrate an overriding interest in order to validate an encroachment on protected interests, the burden of establishing this justification as to any particular respondent will rest on the petitioners on remand, cases of doubt being resolved in favor of the particular respondent.

It is argued that a third interest supporting patronage dismissals is the preservation of the democratic process. According to petitioners, " 'we have contrived no system for the support of party that does not place considerable reliance on patronage. The party organization makes a democratic government work and charges a price for its service.' " The argument is thus premised on the centrality of partisan politics to the democratic process.

Preservation of the democratic process is certainly an interest protection of which may in some instances justify limitations on First Amendment freedoms.   *   *   *
But however important preservation of the two-party system or any system involving a fixed number of parties may or may not be,   *   *   *
we are not persuaded that the elimination of patronage practice or, as is specifically involved here, the interdiction of patronage dismissals, will bring about the demise of party politics. Political parties existed in the absence of active patronage practice prior to the administration of Andrew Jackson, and they have survived substantial reduction in their patronage power through the establishment of merit systems.

Patronage dismissals thus are not the least restrictive alternative to achieving the contribution they may make to the democratic process. The process functions as well without the practice, perhaps even better, for patronage dismissals clearly also retard that process. Patronage can result in the entrenchment of one or a few parties to the exclusion of others. And most indisputably, as we recognized at the outset, patronage is a very effective impediment to the associational and speech freedoms which are essential to a meaningful system of democratic government. Thus, if patronage contributes at all to the elective process, that contribution is diminished by the practice's impairment of the same. Indeed, unlike the gain to representative government provided by the Hatch Act   *   *   * the gain to representative government provided by the practice of patronage, if any, would be insufficient to justify its sacrifice of First Amendment rights.

*   *   *

In summary, patronage dismissals severely restrict political belief and association. Though there is a vital need for government efficiency and effectiveness, such dismissals are on balance not the least restrictive means for fostering that end. There is also a need to insure that policies which the electorate has sanctioned are effectively implemented. That interest can be fully satisfied by limiting patronage dismissals to policymaking positions. Finally, patronage dismissals cannot be justified by their contribution to the proper functioning of our democratic process through their assistance to partisan politics since political parties are nurtured by other, less intrusive and equally effective methods. More fundamentally, however, any contribution of patronage dismissals to the democratic process does not suffice to override their severe encroachment on First Amendment freedoms. We hold, therefore, that the practice of patronage dismissals is unconstitutional under the First and Fourteenth Amendments, and that respondents thus stated a valid claim for relief.

*   *   *

The judgment of the Court of Appeals is

Affirmed.

Mr. Justice STEVENS did not participate in the consideration or decision of this case.

Mr. Justice STEWART, with whom Mr. Justice BLACKMUN joins, concurring in the result.

Although I cannot join the Court's wide-ranging opinion, I can and do concur in its judgment.

This case does not require us to consider the broad contours of the so-called patronage system, with all its variations and permutations. In particular, it does not require us to consider the constitutional validity of a system that confines the hiring of some governmental employees to those of a particular political party, and I would intimate no views whatever on that question.

The single substantive question involved in this case is whether a nonpolicy making, nonconfidential government employee can be discharged from a job that he is satisfactorily performing upon the sole ground of his political beliefs. I agree with the Court that he cannot.

*   *   *

Mr. Chief Justice BURGER, dissenting.

The Court's decision today represents a significant intrusion into the area of legislative and policy concerns—the sort of intrusion Mr. Justice BRENNAN has recently protested in other contexts. I therefore join Mr. Justice POWELL'S dissenting opinion, and add a few words simply to emphasize an aspect that seems particularly important to me.

The Illinois Legislature has pointedly decided that roughly half of the Sheriff's staff shall be made up of tenured career personnel and the balance left exclusively to the choice of the elected head of the department. The Court strains the rational bounds of First Amendment doctrine and runs counter to longstanding practices that are part of the fabric of our democratic system to hold that the Constitution *commands* something it has not been thought to require for 185 years. For all that time our system has wisely left these matters to the States and, on the federal level, to the Congress. The Court's action is a classic example of trivializing constitutional adjudication—a function of the highest importance in our system.

Only last week, in National League of Cities v. Usery, 426 U.S. 833, 96 S.Ct. 2465 (1976), we took steps to arrest the denigration of States to a role comparable to the departments of France, governed entirely out of the national capital. Constant inroads on the powers of the States to manage their own affairs cannot fail to complicate our system and centralize more power in Washington. For the reasons Mr. Justice POWELL persuasively adduces, the First Amendment neither requires nor justifies such inroads in this case. In my view, the issue is not so much whether the patronage system is "good" or "bad," as the plurality characterizes the problem, but whether the choice of its use in the management of the very government of each State was not, in the words of the Tenth Amendment, "reserved to the States * * * or to the people."

Congress long ago, as a matter of policy, opted for a federal career service with a small number of purely political appointments in the Executive Branch, and many governmental departments have a limited number of positions in which the persons appointed have no tenure but serve at the pleasure of the cabinet officer or agency chief, who in turn serves at the pleasure of the President.
* * *

The considerations leading to these legislative conclusions are—for me— not open to judicial scrutiny under the guise of a First Amendment claim, any more than is the right of a newly elected Representative or Senator, for example, to have a staff made up of persons who share his political philosophy and affiliation and are loyal to him. It seems to me that the Illinois Legislature's choice is entitled to no less deference.

Mr. Justice POWELL, with whom THE CHIEF JUSTICE [BURGER] and Mr. Justice REHNQUIST join, dissenting.

The Court holds unconstitutional a practice as old as the Republic, a practice which has contributed significantly to the democratization of American politics. This decision is urged on us in the name of First Amendment rights, but in my view the judgment neither is constitutionally required nor serves the interest of a representative democracy. It also may well disserve—rather than promote—core values of the First Amendment. I therefore dissent.

* * *

It might well be possible to dispose of this case on the ground that it implicates no First Amendment right of the respondents, and therefore that they have failed to state a cause of action. They are employees seeking to avoid discharge—not citizens desiring an opportunity to be hired by the county without regard to their political affiliation or loyalty.
* * *

We thus have complaining employees who apparently accepted patronage jobs knowingly and willingly, while fully familiar with the "tenure" practices long prevailing in the Sheriff's Office. Such employees have *benefited* from their political beliefs and activities; they have not been penalized for them. In these circumstances, I am inclined to agree with the holding of the Supreme Court of Pennsylvania in American Federation of State Employees v. Shapp, 443 Pa. 527, 280 A.2d 375 (1971), that beneficiaries of a patronage system may not be heard to challenge it when it comes their turn to be replaced.
* * *

* * *   * * *

The question is whether it is consistent with the First and Fourteenth Amendments for a State to offer some employment conditioned, explicitly or implicity, on partisan political affiliation and on the political fortunes of the incumbent officeholder. This is to be determined, as the plurality opinion agrees, by whether patronage hiring practices sufficiently advance important state interests to justify the consequent burdening of First Amendment interests. * * * It is difficult to disagree with the view, as an abstract proposition, that government employment ordinarily should not be conditioned upon one's political beliefs or activities. But we deal here with a highly practical and rather fundamental element of our political system, not the theoretical abstractions of a political science seminar. In concluding that patronage hiring practices are unconstitutional, the plurality seriously underestimates the strength of the government interest—especially at the local level—in allowing some patronage hiring practices, and it exaggerates the perceived burden on First Amendment rights.

On the assumption that we must reach the constitutional issue at the behest of respondents, I would hold that a state or local government may elect to condition employment on the political affiliation of a prospective employee and on the political fortunes of the hiring incumbent. History and long prevailing practice across the country support the view that patronage hiring practices make a sufficiently substantial contribution to the practical functioning of our democratic system to support their relatively modest intrusion on First Amendment interests. The judgment today unnecessarily constitutionalizes another element of American life—an element certainly not without its faults but one which generations have accepted on balance as having merit. We should have heeded, instead, the admonition of Mr. Justice Holmes that "[i]f a thing has been practiced for two hundred years by common consent, it will need a strong case for the Fourteenth Amendment to affect it." * * * Jackman v. Rosenbaum Co., 260 U.S. 22, 31, 43 S.Ct. 9, 9, * * *

Finkel and Tabakman, two assistant public defenders, brought suit against Branti, the newly appointed public defender and their superior, for firing them because of their political party affiliation. Branti, a Democrat, was appointed to office by the county legislature which had recently passed from Republican to Democratic control. Finkel and Tabakman were appointees of Branti's predecessor, a Republican. A federal district court found that the plaintiffs were competent lawyers whose employment had been terminated solely because of their political affiliation. The court reasoned that the discharges would be permissible, in light of *Elrod* v. *Burns*, only if Finkel and Tabakman could be shown to be "policymaking, confidential employees." It concluded the plaintiffs were not policy makers because, although they enjoyed broad responsibilities with respect to particular cases, they had negligible, if any, responsibility for the overall operation of the public defender's office, and the confidential character of their work related to observance of the attorney-client privilege, not to any confidential relationship to policy-making deliberations. Accordingly, the district court rendered judgment for the plaintiffs, and this ruling was affirmed on appeal.

In Branti v. Finkel, 445 U.S. 507, 100 S.Ct. 1287 (1980), the Supreme Court affirmed the decision below. Addressing the first of two arguments proffered by Branti, Justice Stevens, speaking for the Court, said:

> Petitioner argues that *Elrod* v. *Burns* should be read to prohibit only dismissals resulting from an employee's failure to capitulate to political coercion. This, he argues that, so long as an employee is not asked to change his political affiliation or to contribute to or work for the party's candidates, he may be dismissed with impunity—even though he would not have been dismissed if he had had the proper political sponsorship and even though the sole reason for dismissing him was to replace him with a person who did have such sponsorship. Such an interpretation would surely emasculate the principles set forth in *Elrod*. While it would perhaps eliminate the more blatant forms of coercion described in *Elrod*, it would not eliminate the coercion of belief that necessarily flows from the knowledge that one must have a sponsor in the dominant party in order to retain one's job. More importantly, petitioner's interpretation would require the Court to repudiate entirely the conclusion of both Mr. Justice Brennan and Mr. Justice Stewart that the First Amendment prohibits the dismissal of a public employee solely because of his private political beliefs.
>
> In sum, there is no requirement that dismissed employees prove that they, or other employees, have been coerced into changing, either actually or ostensibly, their political allegiance. To prevail in this type of an action, it was sufficient, as *Elrod* holds, for respondents to prove that they were discharged "solely for the reason that they were not affiliated with or sponsored by the Democratic Party." * * *

Branti also contended that "even if party sponsorship is an unconstitutional condition of continued public employment for clerks, deputies, and janitors, it is an acceptable requirement for an assistant public defender." Disposing of appellant's argument on this score, Justice Stevens wrote:

> Both opinions in *Elrod* recognize that party affiliation may be an acceptable requirement for some types of government employment. Thus, if an employee's private political beliefs would interfere with the discharge of his public duties, his First Amendment rights may be required to yield to the State's vital interest in maintaining governmental effectiveness and efficiency. * * * In *Elrod*, it was clear that the duties of the employees— the chief deputy of the process division of the sheriff's office, a process server and another employee in that office, and a bailiff and security guard at the Juvenile Court of Cook County—were not of that character, for they were, as Mr. Justice Stewart stated, "nonpolicymaking, nonconfidential" employees. * * *
>
> As Mr. Justice Brennan noted in *Elrod*, it is not always easy to determine whether a position is one in which political affiliation is a legitimate factor to be considered. * * * Under some circumstances, a position may be appropriately considered political even though it is neither confidential nor policymaking in character. As one obvious example, if a State's election laws require that precincts be supervised by two election judges of different parties, a Republican judge could be legitimately discharged solely for changing his party registration. That conclusion would not depend on

any finding that the job involved participation in policy decisions or access to confidential information. Rather, it would simply rest on the fact that party membership was essential to the discharge of the employee's governmental responsibilities.

It is equally clear that party affiliation is not necessarily relevant to every policymaking or confidential position. The coach of a state university's football team formulates policy, but no one could seriously claim that Republicans make better coaches than Democrats, or vice versa, no matter which party is in control of the state government. On the other hand, it is equally clear that the governor of a state may appropriately believe that the official duties of various assistants who help him write speeches, explain his views to the press, or communicate with the legislature cannot be performed effectively unless those persons share his political beliefs and party commitments. In sum, the ultimate inquiry is not whether the label "policymaker" or "confidential" fits a particular position; rather, the question is whether the hiring authority can demonstrate that party affiliation is an appropriate requirement for the effective performance of the public office involved.

Having thus framed the issue, it is manifest that the continued employment of an assistant public defender cannot properly be conditioned upon his allegiance to the political party in control of the county government. The primary, if not the only, responsibility of an assistant public defender is to represent individual citizens in controversy with the State. * * *

Thus, whatever policymaking occurs in the public defender's office must relate to the needs of individual clients and not to any partisan political interests. Similarly, although an assistant is bound to obtain access to confidential information arising out of various attorney-client relationships, that information has no bearing whatsoever on partisan political concerns. Under these circumstances, it would undermine, rather than promote, the effective performance of an assistant public defender's office to make his tenure dependent on his allegiance to the dominant political party.

Justice Powell dissented in an opinion joined by Justice Rehnquist and, in part, by Justice Stewart. Justice Powell objected to the "constitutionalized civil service standard" promulgated by the majority because: (1) it was "framed in vague and sweeping language certain to create vast uncertainty" (for example: Would United States Attorneys, traditionally appointed by the President very much with an eye to their political party affiliation, fall within the Court's standard?); (2) it was justified by recourse to freedom of speech precedents "in which patronage was neither involved nor discussed"; and (3) it was arrived at without adequate reflection on the relationship between patronage and the need for a stable party system and, in turn, on the contribution of party responsibility to the operation of the American political system.

e. COMMERCIAL SPEECH

VIRGINIA STATE BOARD OF PHARMACY v. VIRGINIA CITIZENS CONSUMER COUNCIL

Supreme Court of the United States, 1976
425 U.S. 748, 96 S.Ct. 1817, 48 L.Ed.2d 346

Virginia law punishes as unprofessional conduct advertising by pharmacists of the prices on prescription drugs. Seeking to promote competition and thus, hopefully, lower prices, the Virginia Citizens Consumer Council and others, consumers of prescription drugs, brought suit to have the statute declared unconstitutional and to enjoin the Virginia State Board of Pharmacy from enforcing it. The consumer group alleged a violation of the First and Fourteenth Amendments. A three-judge federal district court struck down the statute and enjoined the board from enforcing it, whereupon the state pharmacy board appealed to the Supreme Court.

Mr. Justice BLACKMUN delivered the opinion of the Court.

* * *

The * * * attack on the statute is one made not by one directly subject to its prohibition, that is, a pharmacist, but by prescription drug consumers who claim that they would greatly benefit if the prohibition were lifted and advertising freely allowed. The plaintiffs are an individual Virginia resident who suffers from diseases that require her to take prescription drugs on a daily basis, and two nonprofit organizations. Their claim is that the First Amendment entitles the user of prescription drugs to receive information, that pharmacists wish to communicate to them through advertising and other promotional means, concerning the prices of such drugs.

* * *

Last Term, in Bigelow v. Virginia, 421 U.S. 809, 95 S.Ct. 2222, the notion of unprotected "commercial speech" all but passed from the scene. We reversed a conviction for violation of a Virginia statute that made the circulation of any publication to encourage or promote the processing of an abortion in Virginia a misdemeanor. The defendant had published in his newspaper the availability of abortions in New York. The advertisement in question, in addition to announcing that abortions were legal in New York, offered the services of a referral agency in that State. We rejected the contention that the publication was unprotected because it was commercial. * * * We concluded that "the Virginia courts erred in their assumptions that advertising, as such, was entitled to no First Amendment protection," and we observed that the "relationship of speech to the marketplace of products or of services does not make it valueless in the marketplace of ideas." Id., at 825–826.

Some fragment of hope for the continuing validity of a "commercial speech" exception arguably might have persisted because of the subject matter of the advertisement in *Bigelow*. We noted that in announcing the availability of legal abortions in New York, the advertisement "did more than simply propose a commercial transaction. It contained factual material of clear 'public interest.'" Id., at 822. And, of course, the advertisement related to activity with which, at least in some respects, the State could not interfere. See Roe v. Wade, 410 U.S. 113, 93 S.Ct. 705; Doe v. Bolton, 410 U.S. 179, 93 S.Ct. 739. Indeed, we observed: "We need not decide in this case the precise extent to which the First Amendment permits regulation of advertising that is related to activities the State may legitimately regulate or even prohibit." Id., at 825.

Here, in contrast, the question whether there is a First Amendment exception for "commercial speech" is squarely before us. Our pharmacist does not wish to editorialize on any subject, cultural, philosophical, or political. He does not wish to report any particularly newsworthy fact, or to make generalized observations even about commercial matters. The "idea" he wishes to communicate is simply this: "I will sell you the X prescription drug at the Y price." Our question, then, is whether this communication is wholly outside the protection of the First Amendment.

We begin with several propositions that already are settled or beyond serious dispute. It is clear, for example, that speech does not lose its First Amendment protection because money is spent to project it, as in a paid advertisement of one form or another. * * * Speech likewise is protected even though it is carried in a form that is "sold" for profit, Smith v. California, 361 U.S. 147, 150, 80 S.Ct. 215, 217 (books); Joseph Burstyn, Inc. v. Wilson, 343 U.S. 495, 501, 72 S.Ct. 777, 780 (motion pictures); Murdock v. Pennsylvania, 319 U.S., at 111, 63 S.Ct., at 874 (religious literature), and even though it may involve a solicitation to purchase or otherwise pay or contribute money. * * *

If there is a kind of commercial speech that lacks all First Amendment protection, therefore, it must be distinguished by its content. Yet the speech whose content deprives it of protection cannot simply be speech on a commercial subject. No one would contend that our pharmacist may be prevented from being heard on the subject of whether, in general, pharmaceutical prices should be regulated, or their advertisement forbidden. Nor can it be dispositive that a commercial advertisement is uneditorial, and merely reports a fact. Purely factual matter of public interest may claim protection. * * *

Our question is whether speech which does "no more than propose a commercial transaction," * * * is so removed from any "exposition of ideas," * * * and from " 'truth, science, morality, and arts in general, in its diffusion of liberal sentiments on the administration of Government' " * * * that it lacks all protection. Our answer is that it is not.

Focusing first on the individual parties to the transaction that is proposed in the commercial advertisement, we may assume that the advertiser's interest is a purely economic one. That hardly disqualifies him for protection under the First Amendment. The interests of the contestants in a labor dispute are primarily economic, but it has long been settled that both the employee and the employer are protected by the First Amendment when they express themselves on the merits of the dispute in order to influence its outcome. * * * We know of no requirement that, in order to avail themselves of First Amendment protection, the parties to a labor dispute need address themselves to the merits of unionism in general or to any subject beyond their immediate dispute. * * *

As to the particular consumer's interest in the free flow of commercial information, that interest may be as keen, if not keener by far, than his interest in the day's most urgent political debate. Appellees' case in this respect is a convincing one. Those whom the suppression of prescription drug price information hits the hardest are the poor, the sick, and particularly the aged. A disproportionate amount of their income tends to be spent on prescription drugs; yet they are the least able to learn, by shopping from pharmacist to pharmacist, where their scarce dollars are best spent. When drug prices vary as strikingly as they do, information as to who is charging what becomes more than a convenience. It could mean the alleviation of physical pain or the enjoyment of basic necessities.

Generalizing, society also may have a strong interest in the free flow of commercial information. Even an individual advertisement, though entirely "commercial," may be of general public interest. The facts of decided cases furnish illustrations: advertisements stating that referral services for legal abortions are available, * * * that a manufacturer of artificial furs promotes his product as an alternative to the extinction by his competitors of fur-bearing mammals, * * * that a domestic producer advertises his product as an alternative to imports that tend to deprive American residents of their jobs. * * * Obviously, not all commercial messages contain the same or even a very great public interest element. There are few to which such an element, however, could not be added. Our pharmacist, for example, could cast himself as a commentator on store-to-store disparities in drug prices, giving his own and those of a competitor as proof. We see little point in requiring him to do so, and little difference if he does not.

Moreover, there is another consideration that suggests that no line between publicly "interesting" or "important" commercial advertising and the opposite kind could ever be drawn. Advertising, however tasteless and excessive it sometimes may

seem, is nonetheless dissemination of information as to who is producing and selling what product, for what reason, and at what price. So long as we preserve a predominantly free enterprise economy, the allocation of our resources in large measure will be made through numerous private economic decisions. It is a matter of public interest that those decisions, in the aggregate, be intelligent and well informed. To this end, the free flow of commercial information is indispensable. * * * And if it is indispensable to the proper allocation of resources in a free enterprise system, it is also indispensable to the formation of intelligent opinions as to how that system ought to be regulated or altered. Therefore, even if the First Amendment were thought to be primarily an instrument to enlighten public decisionmaking in a democracy, we could not say that the free flow of information does not serve that goal.

Arrayed against these substantial individual and societal interests are a number of justifications for the advertising ban. These have to do principally with maintaining a high degree of professionalism on the part of licensed pharmacists. Indisputably, the State has a strong interest in maintaining that professionalism. It is exercised in a number of ways for the consumer's benefit. There is the clinical skill involved in the compounding of drugs, although, as has been noted, these now make up only a small percentage of the prescriptions filled. Yet, even with respect to manufacturer-prepared compounds, there is room for the pharmacist to serve his customer well or badly. Drugs kept too long on the shelf may lose their efficacy or become adulterated. They can be packaged for the user in such a way that the same results occur. The expertise of the pharmacist may supplement that of the prescribing physician, if the latter has not specified the amount to be dispensed or the directions that are to appear on the label. The pharmacist, a specialist in the potencies and dangers of drugs, may even be consulted by the physician as to what to prescribe. He may know of a particular antagonism between the prescribed drug and another that the customer is or might be taking, or with an allergy the customer may suffer. The pharmacist himself may have supplied the other drug or treated the allergy. Some pharmacists, concededly not a large number, "monitor" the health problems and drug consumptions of customers who come to them repeatedly. A pharmacist who has a continuous relationship with his customer is in the best position, of course, to exert professional skill for the customer's protection.

Price advertising, it is argued, will place in jeopardy the pharmacist's expertise and, with it, the customer's health. It is claimed that the aggressive price competition that will result from unlimited advertising will make it impossible for the pharmacist to supply professional services in the compounding, handling, and dispensing of prescription drugs. Such services are time-consuming and expensive; if competitors who economize by eliminating them are permitted to advertise their resulting lower prices, the more painstaking and conscientious pharmacist will be forced either to follow suit or to go out of business. It is also claimed that prices might not necessarily fall as a result of advertising. If one pharmacist advertises, others must, and the resulting expense will inflate the cost of drugs. It is further claimed

that advertising will lead people to shop for their prescription drugs among the various pharmacists who offer the lowest prices, and the loss of stable pharmacist-customer relationships will make individual attention—and certainly the practice of monitoring—impossible. Finally, it is argued that damage will be done to the professional image of the pharmacist. This image, that of a skilled and specialized craftsman, attracts talent to the profession and reinforces the better habits of those who are in it. Price advertising, it is said, will reduce the pharmacist's status to that of a mere retailer.

The strength of these proffered justifications is greatly undermined by the fact that high professional standards, to a substantial extent, are guaranteed by the close regulation to which pharmacists in Virginia are subject. And this case concerns the retail sale by the pharmacist more than it does his professional standards. Surely, any pharmacist guilty of professional dereliction that actually endangers his customer will promptly lose his license. At the same time, we cannot discount the Board's justifications entirely.
* * *

The challenge now made, however, is based on the First Amendment. This casts the Board's justifications in a different light, for on close inspection it is seen that the State's protectiveness of its citizens rests in large measure on the advantages of their being kept in ignorance. The advertising ban does not directly affect professional standards one way or the other. It affects them only through the reactions it is assumed people will have to the free flow of drug price information. There is no claim that the advertising ban in any way prevents the cutting of corners by the pharmacist who is so inclined. That pharmacist is likely to cut corners in any event. The only effect the advertising ban has on him is to insulate him from price competition and to open the way for him to make a substantial, and perhaps even excessive, profit in addition to providing an inferior service. The more painstaking pharmacist is also protected but, again, it is a protection based in large part on public ignorance.

It appears to be feared that if the pharmacist who wishes to provide low cost, and assertedly low quality, services is permitted to advertise, he will be taken up on his offer by too many unwitting customers. They will choose the low-cost, low-quality service and drive the "professional" pharmacist out of business. They will respond only to costly and excessive advertising, and end up paying the price. They will go from one pharmacist to another, following the discount, and destroy the pharmacist-customer relationship. They will lose respect for the profession because it advertises. All this is not in their best interests, and all this can be avoided if they are not permitted to know who is charging what.

There is, of course, an alternative to this highly paternalistic approach. That alternative is to assume that this information is not in itself harmful, that people will perceive their own best interests if only they are well enough informed, and that the best means to that end is to open the channels of communication rather than to close them. If they are truly open, nothing prevents the "professional" pharmacist from marketing his own assertedly superior product, and contrasting it with that of the low-cost, high-volume prescription drug retailer. But the choice among

these alternative approaches is not ours to make or the Virginia General Assembly's. It is precisely this kind of choice, between the dangers of suppressing information, and the dangers of its misuse if it is freely available, that the First Amendment makes for us. Virginia is free to require whatever professional standards it wishes of its pharmacists; it may subsidize them or protect them from competition in other ways. * * * But it may not do so by keeping the public in ignorance of the entirely lawful terms that competing pharmacists are offering. In this sense, the justifications Virginia has offered for suppressing the flow of prescription drug price information, far from persuading us that the flow is not protected by the First Amendment, have re-enforced our view that it is. We so hold.

In concluding that commercial speech, like other varieties, is protected, we of course do not hold that it can never be regulated in any way. Some forms of commercial speech regulation are surely permissible. We mention a few only to make clear that they are not before us and therefore are not foreclosed by this case.

* * *

[The Court went on to recognize a legitimate state interest in regulating commercial speech with respect to: (1) time, place, and manner of advertising; (2) misleading, deceptive, and false messages; (3) illegal transactions and commodities; and (4) special problems posed by the use of the broadcast media.]

What is at issue is whether a State may completely suppress the dissemination of concededly truthful information about entirely lawful activity, fearful of that information's effect upon its disseminators and its recipients. Reserving other questions,[25] we conclude that the answer to this one is in the negative.

The judgment of the District Court is affirmed.

It is so ordered.

Mr. Justice STEVENS took no part in the consideration or decision of this case.

Mr. Justice REHNQUIST, dissenting.

The logical consequences of the Court's decision in this case, a decision which elevates commercial intercourse between a seller hawking his wares and a buyer seeking to strike a bargain to the same plane as has been previously reserved for the free marketplace of ideas, are far reaching indeed.   *   *   *

*   *   *

[T]he issue on the merits is not, as the Court phrases it, whether "our pharmacist" may communicate the fact that he "will sell you the X prescription drug at Y price." No pharmacist is asserting any such claim to so communicate. The issue is rather whether appellee consumers may override the legislative determination that pharmacists should not advertise even though the pharmacists themselves do not object. In deciding that they may do so, the Court necessarily adopts a rule which cannot be limited merely to dissemination of price alone, and

which cannot possibly be confined to pharmacists without likewise extending to lawyers, doctors and all other professions.

*   *   *

Both Congress and state legislatures have by law sharply limited the permissible dissemination of information about some commodities because of the potential harm resulting from those commodities, even though they were not thought to be sufficiently demonstrably harmful to warrant outright prohibition at their sale. Current prohibitions on television advertising of liquor and cigarettes are prominent in this category, but apparently under the Court's holding so long as the advertisements are not deceptive they may no longer be prohibited.

This case presents a fairly typical First Amendment problem—that of balancing interests in individual free speech against public welfare determinations embodied in a legislative enactment. As the Court noted in American Comm. Assn. v. Douds, 339 U.S. 382, 399, 70 S.Ct. 674, 684,

"[L]egitimate attempts to protect the public, not from the remote possible effects of noxious ideologies, but from the present excesses of direct, active conduct are not presumptively bad because they interfere with and, in some of its manifestations, restrain the exercise of First Amendment rights."

Here the rights of the appellees seem to me to be marginal at best.

---

25. We stress that we have considered in this case the regulation of commercial advertising by pharmacists. Although we express no opinion as to other professions, the distinctions, historical and functional, between professions, may require consideration of quite different factors. Physicians and lawyers,

for example, do not dispense standardized products; they render professional *services* of almost infinite variety and nature, with the consequent enhanced possibility for confusion and deception if they were to undertake certain kinds of advertising.

There is no ideological content to the information which they seek and it is freely available to them—they may even publish it if they so desire. The only persons directly affected by this statute are not parties to this lawsuit. On the other hand, the societal interest against the promotion of drug use for every ill, real or imaginary, seems to me extremely strong. I do not believe that the First Amendment mandates the Court's "open door policy" toward such commercial advertising.

In Central Hudson Gas & Electric Corp. v. Public Service Commission of New York, 447 U.S. 557, 100 S.Ct. 2343 (1980), the Supreme Court addressed the question whether a Commission regulation completely banning advertising by an electrical utility promoting the use of electricity violated the First and Fourteenth Amendments. Justice Powell, speaking for the Court, traversed the Court's rulings in its "commercial speech" cases and distilled from that survey the following standard:

> In commercial speech cases, then, a four-part analysis has developed. At the outset, we must determine whether the expression is protected by the First Amendment. For commercial speech to come within that provision, it at least must concern lawful activity and not be misleading. Next, we ask whether the asserted governmental interest is substantial. If both inquiries yield positive answers, we must determine whether the regulation directly advances the governmental interest asserted, and whether it is not more extensive than is necessary to serve that interest.

He then turned to the application of this four-step analysis. Initially focusing on whether Central Hudson's advertising was protected commercial speech, Justice Powell noted the court below concluded that "the Commission's order restricts no commercial speech of any worth" because "appellant holds a monopoly over the sale of electricity in its service area" and because "advertising in a 'noncompetitive market' could not improve the decisionmaking of consumers." He responded:

> This reasoning falls short of establishing that appellant's advertising is not commercial speech protected by the First Amendment. Monopoly over the supply of a product provides no protection from competition with substitutes for that product. Electric utilities compete with suppliers of fuel oil and natural gas in several markets, such as those for home heating and industrial power. * * * Each energy source continues to offer peculiar advantages and disadvantages that may influence consumer choice. For consumers in those competitive markets, advertising by utilities is just as valuable as advertising by unregulated firms.
>
> Even in monopoly markets, the suppression of advertising reduces the information available for consumer decisions and thereby defeats the purpose of the First Amendment. The New York court's argument appears to assume that the providers of a monopoly service or product are willing to pay for wholly ineffective advertising. Most businesses—even regulated monopolies—are unlikely to underwrite promotional advertising that is of no interest or use to consumers. Indeed, a monopoly enterprise legitimately may wish to inform the public that it has developed new services or terms of doing business. A consumer may need information to aid his deci-

sion whether or not to use the monopoly service at all, or how much of the service he should purchase. In the absence of factors that would distort the decision to advertise, we may assume that the willingness of a business to promote its products reflects a belief that consumers are interested in the advertising. Since no such extraordinary conditions have been identified in this case, appellant's monopoly position does not alter the First Amendment's protection for its commercial speech.

The Court found, secondly, that the two state interests advanced by the Commission in support of its order were "clear and substantial." The first and foremost of these was the state's interest in promoting energy conservation to reduce dependence on foreign supplies. Also important, in the Court's view, was "the State's concern that rates be fair and efficient." The Commission had argued "that promotional advertising will aggravate inequities caused by the failure to base the utility's rates on marginal cost." This would mean that "extra costs would be borne by all consumers through higher overall rates." Next, the Court focused "on the relationship between the State's interest and the advertising ban." Justice Powell termed "[t]he impact of promotional advertising on the equity of appellant's rates * * * speculative" but, in contrast, found "an immediate connection between advertising and demand for electricity." Consequently, the Court affirmed "a direct link between the state interest in conservation and the Commission's order." Finally, the Court came "to the critical inquiry in this case: whether the Commission's complete suppression of speech ordinarily protected by the First Amendment is no more extensive than necessary to further the State's interest in energy conservation." Faulting the Commission's order in this respect, Justice Powell wrote:

> The Commission's order reaches all promotional advertising, regardless of the impact of the touted service on overall energy use. But the energy conservation rationale, as important as it is, cannot justify suppressing information about electric devices or services that would cause no net increase in total energy use. In addition, no showing has been made that a more limited restriction on the content of promotional advertising would not serve adequately the State's interests.
>
> Appellant insists that but for the ban, it would advertise products and services that use energy efficiently. These include the "heat pump," which both parties acknowledge to be a major improvement in electric heating, and the use of electric heat as a "back-up" to solar and other heat sources. Although the Commission has questioned the efficiency of electric heating before this Court, neither the Commission's Policy Statement nor its order denying rehearing made findings on this issue. In the absence of authoritative findings to the contrary, we must credit as within the realm of possibility the claim that electric heat can be an efficient alternative in some circumstances.
>
> The Commission's order prevents appellant from promoting electric services that would reduce energy use by diverting demand from less efficient sources, or that would consume roughly the same amount of energy as do alternative sources. In neither situation would the utility's advertising endanger conservation or mislead the public. To the extent that the Commission's order suppresses speech that in no way impairs the State's interest in energy conservation, the Commission's order violates the First and Fourteenth Amendments and must be invalidated. * * *

The Commission also has not demonstrated that its interest in conservation cannot be protected adequately by more limited regulation of appellant's commercial expression. To further its policy of conservation, the Commission could attempt to restrict the format and content of Central Hudson's advertising. It might, for example, require that the advertisements include information about the relative efficiency and expense of the offered service, both under current conditions and for the foreseeable future. * * * In the absence of a showing that more limited speech regulation would be ineffective, we cannot approve the complete suppression of Central Hudson's advertising.

Justice Blackmun, joined by Justice Brennan, concurred in the judgment because, although he "agree[d] with the Court that th[e] level of intermediate scrutiny is appropriate for a restraint on commercial speech designed to protect consumers from misleading or coercive speech, or a regulation related to the time, place, or manner of commercial speech," he "d[id] not agree * * * that the Court's four-part test is the proper one to be applied when a State seeks to suppress information about a product in order to manipulate a private economic decision that the State cannot or has not regulated or outlawed directly." Noting that the Court failed to cite any empirical data or other authority linking advertising and energy consumption, Justice Blackmun disagreed that "the State may suppress advertising of electricity in order to lessen the demand for electricity." He maintained, "If the First Amendment guarantee means anything it means that, absent a clear and present danger, government has no power to restrict expression because of the effect its message is likely to have on the public." He added:

It appears that the Court would permit the State to ban all direct advertising of air conditioning, assuming that a more limited restriction on such advertising would not effectively deter the public from cooling its homes. In my view, our cases do not support this type of suppression. If a governmental unit believes that use or over-use of air conditioning is a serious problem, it must attack that problem directly, by prohibiting air conditioning or regulating thermostat levels. * * *

Justice Stevens, also joined by Justice Brennan, concurred in the result too. What prompted him to write was a concern that "[b]ecause 'commercial speech' is afforded less constitutional protection than other forms of speech, it is important that the commercial speech concept not be defined too broadly lest speech deserving of greater constitutional protection be inadvertently suppressed." He continued:

The issue in this case is whether New York's prohibition on the promotion of the use of electricity through advertising is a ban on nothing but commercial speech.

In my judgment one of the two definitions the Court uses in addressing that issue is too broad and the other may be somewhat too narrow. The Court first describes commercial speech as "expression related solely to the economic interests of the speaker and its audience." * * * Although it is not entirely clear whether this definition uses the subject matter of the speech or the motivation of the speaker as the limiting factor, it seems clear to me that it encompasses speech that is entitled to the maximum protection afforded by the First Amendment. Neither a labor leader's exhortation to strike, nor an economist's dissertation on the money supply, should receive any lesser protection because the subject matter concerns only the economic interests of the audience. Nor should the economic motivation of a speaker qualify his constitutional protection; even Shakespeare may have been motivated by the prospect of pecuniary reward. Thus, the Court's first definition of commercial speech is unquestionably too broad.

The Court's second definition refers to "speech proposing a commercial transaction." * * * A salesman's solicitation, a broker's offer, and a manufacturer's publication of a price list or the terms of his standard warranty would unquestionably fit within this concept. Presumably, the definition is intended to encompass advertising that advises possible buyers of the availability of specific products at specific prices and describes the advantages of purchasing such items. Perhaps it also extends to other communications that do little more than make the name of a product or a service more familiar to the general public. Whatever the precise contours of the concept, and perhaps it is too early to enunciate an exact formulation, I am persuaded that it should not include the entire range of communication that is embraced within the term "promotional advertising."

This case involves a governmental regulation that completely bans promotional advertising by an electric utility. This ban encompasses a great deal more than mere proposals to engage in certain kinds of commercial transactions. It prohibits all advocacy of the immediate or future use of electricity. It curtails expression by an informed and interested group of persons of their point of view on questions relating to the production and consumption of electrical energy—questions frequently discussed and debated by our political leaders. For example, an electric company's advocacy of the use of electric heat for environmental reasons, as opposed to wood-burning stoves, would seem to fall squarely within New York's promotional advertising ban and also within the bounds of maximum First Amendment protection. The breadth of the ban thus exceeds the boundaries of the commercial speech concept, however that concept may be defined.

The justification for the regulation is nothing more than the expressed fear that the audience may find the utility's message persuasive. Without the aid of any coercion, deception, or misinformation, truthful communication may persuade some citizens to consume more electricity than they otherwise would. I assume that such a consequence would be undesirable and that government may therefore prohibit and punish the unnecessary or excessive use of electricity. But if the perceived harm associated with greater electrical usage is not sufficiently serious to justify direct regulation, surely it does not constitute the kind of clear and present danger that can justify the suppression of speech.

"In sum," wrote Justice Stevens, "I concur in the result because I do not consider this to be a 'commercial speech' case."

In a lengthy and lone dissenting opinion, Justice Rehnquist presented a number of objections both to the disposition of the case at hand and to the generation of "commercial speech" doctrine. He wrote in part:

The Court's analysis in my view is wrong in several respects. Initially, I disagree with the Court's conclusion that the speech of a state-created monopoly, which is the subject of a comprehensive regulatory scheme, is entitled to protection under the First Amendment. I also think that the

Court errs here in failing to recognize that the state law is most accurately viewed as an economic regulation and that the speech involved (if it falls within the scope of the First Amendment at all) occupies a significantly more subordinate position in the hierarchy of First Amendment values than the Court gives it today. Finally, the Court in reaching its decision improperly substitutes its own judgment for that of the State in deciding how a proper ban on promotional advertising should be drafted. With regard to this latter point, the Court adopts as its final part of a four-part test a "no more extensive than necessary" analysis that will unduly impair a state legislature's ability to adopt legislation reasonably designed to promote interests that have always been rightly thought to be of great importance to the State.

* * *

The Court today holds not only that commercial speech is entitled to First Amendment protection, but also that when it is protected a State may not regulate it unless its reason for doing so amounts to a "substantial" governmental interest, its regulation "directly advances" that interest, and its manner of regulation is "not more extensive than necessary" to serve the interest. * * * The test adopted by the Court thus elevates the protection accorded commercial speech that falls within the scope of the First Amendment to a level that is virtually indistinguishable from that of non-commercial speech. I think the Court in so doing has effectively accomplished the "devitalization" of the First Amendment that it counseled against in *Ohralik* [v. Ohio State Bar Ass'n, 436 U.S. 447, 98 S.Ct. 1912 (1978)]. I think it has also by labeling economic regulation of business conduct as a restraint on "free speech" gone far to resurrect the discredited doctrine of cases such as *Lochner* [v. New York, 198 U.S. 45, 25 S.Ct. 539 (1905)] and Tyson & Brother v. Banton, 273 U.S. 418, 47 S.Ct. 426 (1927). New York's order here is in my view more akin to an economic regulation to which virtually complete deference should be accorded by this Court.

* * *

I remain of the view that the Court unleashed a Pandora's box when it "elevated" commercial speech to the level of traditional political speech by according it First Amendment protection in *Virginia State Board of Pharmacy* v. *Virginia Citizens Consumer Council, Inc.*, [425 U.S. 748, 96 S.Ct. 1817 (1976)]. The line between "commercial speech," and the kind of speech that those who drafted the First Amendment had in mind, may not be a technically or intellectually easy one to draw, but it surely produced far fewer problems than has the development of judicial doctrine in this area since *Virginia Board.* For in the world of political advocacy and *its* marketplace of ideas, there is no such thing as a "fraudulent" idea: there may be useless proposals, totally unworkable schemes, as well as very sound proposals that will receive the imprimatur of the "marketplace of ideas" through our majoritarian system of election and representative government. The free flow of information is important in this context not because it will lead to the discovery of any objective "truth," but because it is essential to our system of self-government.

The notion that more speech is the remedy to expose falsehood and fallacies is wholly out of place in the commercial bazaar, where if applied logically the remedy of one who was defrauded would be merely a statement, available upon request, reciting the Latin maxim *"caveat emptor."* But since "fraudulent speech" in this area is to be remediable under *Virginia Board,* supra, the remedy of one defrauded is a lawsuit or an agency proceeding based on common law notions of fraud that are separated by a world of difference from the realm of politics and government. What time, legal decisions, and common sense have so widely severed, I declined to join in *Virginia Board,* and regret now to see the Court reaping the seeds that it there sowed. For in a democracy, the economic is subordinate to the political, a lesson that our ancestors learned long ago, and that our descendants will undoubtedly have to relearn many years hence.

OTHER RECENT CASES RELATING TO COMMERCIAL SPEECH

Linmark Associates, Inc. v. Township of Willingboro, 431 U.S. 85, 97 S.Ct. 1614 (1977)	Facts	Fearful that the integrated community was becoming all black and that property values would decline, the township, in an effort to stem what it thought was "panic selling" by whites, banned the placing of "For Sale" signs on all but model homes.
	Decision	Ordinance declared unconstitutional
	Vote	8–0; Justice Rehnquist did not participate
	Opinion of the Court	Justice Marshall reasoned that this ordinance was not distinguishable from the legislation struck down in *Bigelow* and *Virginia Pharmacy.* The ordinance could not be upheld on the grounds that it restricts only one mode of communication while leaving other channels of communication open since the other options—newspaper advertising and realtor listings—were not only more costly but less likely to reach people who did not deliberately seek sales information. The ordinance was also not genuinely connected with the place or manner of speech but was directed at the content of the signs. In the Court's view, the township was not concerned "that the place or manner of speech produces a detrimental 'secondary effect' on society" but rather feared the signs' primary effect—that people would act on the information communicated. Finally, there was no convincing evidence that the placement of "For Sale" signs in front of 2 percent of the homes in Willingboro contributed meaningfully to "panic selling." Apart from the fact that the ordinance seemed unrelated to maintaining the integrated nature of the community, the First Amendment denies government the power to prevent the free flow of information to the township's citizens. The township's concern "was not with any commercial aspect of 'For Sale' signs—with offerors communicating offers to offerees—but with the substance of the information communicated to Willingboro citizens."

Metromedia, Inc. v.
City of San Diego,
453 U.S. 490, 101
S.Ct. 2882 (1981)

Facts	A San Diego city ordinance substantially prohibited the erection of outdoor advertising display signs in order "to eliminate hazards to pedestrians and motorists brought about by distracting sign displays" and "to preserve and improve the appearance of the City." The ordinance permitted on-site commercial advertising (i.e., a sign advertising goods or services available on the property where the sign was located) but otherwise banned commercial and noncommercial fixed-structure signs unless they fell within twelve recognized exceptions, such as government signs; commemorative historical plaques; religious symbols; time, temperature, and news signs; for sale and for rent signs; and temporary political campaign signs. A company engaged in the outdoor advertising business challenged the billboard ordinance on grounds the legislation amounted to an unconstitutional use of the city's police power and an abridgment of the company's First Amendment rights.
Decision	Ordinance declared unconstitutional
Vote	6–3
Plurality Opinion	Justice White announced the judgment of the Court in an opinion in which Justices Stewart, Marshall, and Powell joined. The plurality concluded that although the ordinance met the constitutional requirements recognized in Central Hudson Gas & Electric Corp. v. Public Service Comm'n, 447 U.S. 557, 100 S.Ct. 2343 (1980), in advancing substantial governmental interests and was no broader than necessary to serve those ends, "[i]t does not follow, however, that San Diego's general ban on signs carrying noncommercial advertising is also valid under the First and Fourteenth Amendments." Justice White pointed out that "recent commercial speech cases have consistently accorded noncommercial speech a greater degree of protection than commercial speech." Observing that "San Diego effectively inverts this judgment by affording a greater degree of protection to commercial than to noncommercial speech," the plurality continued: "There is a broad exception for on-site commercial advertisements, but there is no similar exception for noncommercial speech. The use of on-site billboards to carry commercial messages related to the commercial use of the premises is fully permitted, but the use of otherwise identical billboards to carry noncommercial messages is generally prohibited. The city does not explain how or why noncommercial billboards located in places where commercial billboards are permitted would be more threatening to safe driving or would detract more from the beauty of the city. Insofar as the city tolerates billboards at all, it cannot choose to limit their content to commercial messages; the city may not conclude that the com-

Metromedia, Inc.
(*Cont.*)

Plurality
Opinion
(*Cont.*)

munication of commercial information concerning goods and services connected with a particular site is of greater value than the communication of noncommercial messages."

"Furthermore, the ordinance contains exceptions that permit various kinds of noncommercial signs, whether on property where goods and services are offered or not, that would otherwise be within the general ban." Justice White noted that "[a]lthough the city may distinguish between the relative value of different categories of commercial speech, the city does not have the same range of choice in the area of noncommercial speech to evaluate the strength of, or distinguish between, various communicative interests. With respect to noncommercial speech, the city may not choose the appropriate subjects for public discourse. * * * Because some noncommercial messages may be conveyed on billboards throughout the commercial and industrial zones, San Diego must similarly allow billboards conveying other noncommercial messages throughout those zones."

The plurality also pointed out that the ordinance did not constitute a reasonable "time, place and manner" restriction because "the ordinance distinguishes in several ways between permissible and impermissible signs at a particular location by reference to their content. Whether or not these distinctions are themselves constitutional, they take the regulation out of the domain of time, place, and manner restrictions."

Opinion
Concurring
in the
Judgment

Justice Brennan, joined by Justice Blackmun, agreed with the plurality that "billboards are a medium of communications warranting First Amendment protection." As contrasted with the plurality's view that the question of a total ban was not presented because the ordinance provided for exceptions, Justice Brennan thought that "the *practical* effect of the San Diego ordinance is to eliminate the billboard as an effective medium of communication for * * * [all] sorts of messages * * * and that the exceptions do not alter the overall character of the ban." Unless a commercial or noncommercial billboard advertiser "chooses to buy or lease premises in the city, or unless his message falls within one of the narrowly exempted categories, he is foreclosed from announcing either commercial or noncommercial ideas through a billboard." Justice Brennan would have held "that a city may totally ban [billboards] if it can show that a sufficiently substantial governmental interest is directly furthered by the total ban and that any more narrowly drawn restriction, i.e., anything less than a total ban, would promote less well the achievement of that goal." In his judgment, San Diego's ordinance failed this test because: (1) the city failed to pro-

Metromedia, Inc. (*Cont.*)	Opinion Concurring in the Judgment (*Cont.*)	duce evidence showing the relationship between billboards and traffic safety; (2) the ordinance was not narrowly drawn in its advancement of the traffic safety interest; and (3) the city failed to demonstrate that its asserted interest in aesthetics was sufficiently substantial in its commercial and industrial areas. Furthermore, an ordinance totally banning commercial billboards but allowing noncommercial billboards would also not be constitutional since it would give city officials wide latitude in the first instance in determining whether a given message was "commercial" or "noncommercial."
	Dissenting Opinions	Chief Justice Burger objected that the majority's rigid and doctrinaire application of broad First Amendment statements announced initially in very different contexts allowed the billboard industry here to "escape the real and growing problems every municipality faces in protecting safety and preserving the environment in an urban area." "[T]he long arm and voracious appetite of federal [judicial] power" as reflected in this decision forced American cities "as a matter of *federal constitutional law*" to choose "between two unsatisfactory options: (a) allowing all 'noncommercial' signs, no matter how many, how dangerous, or how damaging to the environment; or (b) forbidding signs altogether."
		Justice Rehnquist concluded that "the aesthetic justification alone is sufficient to sustain a total prohibition of billboards within a community."
		Since Justice Stevens was "persuaded * * * that a wholly impartial total ban on billboards would be permissible," he found "it * * * difficult to understand why the exceptions in San Diego's ordinance present any additional threat to the interests protected by the First Amendment." He continued: "The essential concern embodied in the First Amendment is that government not impose its viewpoint on the public or select the topics on which public debate is permissible." He concluded that the "neutral exceptions" in the San Diego ordinance "simply [do] not implicate this concern" unlike government's attempt "to limit discussion of controversial topics" reflected in the facts of Consolidated Edison Co. v. Public Service Comm'n, 447 U.S. 530, 100 S.Ct. 2326 (1980).
Village of Hoffman Estates v. Flipside, Hoffman Estates, Inc., 455 U.S. 489, 102 S.Ct. 1186 (1982)	Facts	A village ordinance required a business to obtain a license if it sold any items "designed or marketed for use with illegal cannabis or drugs." The ordinance set out guidelines defining items such as "roach clips," "pipes," and "paraphernalia," whose sale was required to be licensed. The license fee was $150. The ordinance also forbade sales of any regulated items to minors, required affidavits from the licensee and its employees that they had not been convicted of any drug-related offense, and mandat-

Village of Hoffman Estates (*Cont.*)	Facts (*Cont.*)	ed that the business keep a record of each sale of a regulated item (including the name and address of the purchaser) to be open to police inspection. A local "headshop," which sold a variety of merchandise including "roach clips" and pipes especially designed for the smoking of marijuana, brought suit for declaratory and injunctive relief, contending that the ordinance was unconstitutionally vague and overbroad.
	Decision	Ordinance upheld
	Vote	8–0; Justice Stevens did not participate
	Opinion of the Court	Justice Marshall observed at the outset that in a facial challenge to a statute involving contentions of overbreadth and vagueness a court must first determine whether the law touches a substantial amount of protected conduct. If it does not, the overbreadth challenge fails. A court should then take up the vagueness contention, and it should uphold the law unless the enactment is impermissibly vague in all its applications. This ordinance does not infringe the retailer's First Amendment rights, nor is it overbroad because it inhibits the rights of other people. The law does not restrict speech but instead regulates the sale of items whose labels disclose possible use for an unlawful purpose. This ordinance does not implicate noncommercial speech, and, with respect to commercial speech, its restriction on the marketing of regulated items does not substantially limit communication of information by the retailer except to the extent that it is aimed at marketing and sales encouraging the illegal use of drugs which, if it can be said to be speech, is speech proposing an illegal transaction and hence is subject to governmental regulation or prohibition. Whether the ordinance is overbroad with respect to the commercial speech of other people is irrelevant since the concept of overbreadth does not apply to commercial speech. As to the vagueness challenge, the statute was not shown to be impermissibly vague in all of its applications. The phrase "designed * * * for use" in the ordinance is not vague on its face because it covers several items designed by the manufacturer principally for use with illegal drugs and is sufficiently clear to apply to "roach clips" and specially designed pipes sold by the retailer. With respect to the "marketed for use" phrase, such language "describes a retailer's intentional display and marketing of merchandise. The guidelines refer to the display of paraphernalia and to the proximity of covered items to otherwise uncovered items. A retail store therefore must obtain a license if it deliberately displays its wares in a manner that appeals to or encourages illegal drug use." This standard

Village of Hoffman Estates (*Cont.*)	Opinion of the Court (*Cont.*)	requires scienter (proof of knowledge) on the retailer's part "since a retailer could scarcely 'market' items 'for' a particular use without intending that use." Here, "Flipside" had ample warning that its marketing activities brought it within the ambit of the ordinance. Magazines and books encouraging the illegal use of drugs were located "physically close to pipes and colored rolling papers, in clear violation of the guidelines." Also, the retailer "sold 'roach clips' which are principally used for illegal purposes." "The language of the ordinance is sufficiently clear that the speculative danger of arbitrary enforcement does not render the ordinance void for vagueness."
	Concurring Opinion	Justice White would have confined discussion of the ordinance to the vagueness contention. In his view, "[t]here [was] * * * no need to go any further: If it is 'transparently clear' that some particular conduct is restricted by the ordinance, the ordinance survives a facial challenge on vagueness grounds."

Bates and O'Steen, two lawyers in Phoenix, opened a legal aid clinic aimed at providing at high volume routine legal services at modest fees to middle-income individuals who did not qualify for legal aid furnished by the government. After a couple of less-than-brisk years of business, they concluded that the legal aid clinic could survive only if they advertised the availability of low-cost legal services including the fees charged. Such an advertisement was run in the *Arizona Republic*, whereupon the president of the state bar association filed a complaint with a bar association committee that the two had violated a rule of practice adopted by the state supreme court inveighing against the advertisement of legal services. The bar committee recommended a short suspension from practice. On appeal to the Arizona Supreme Court, the Justices rejected both the claims of Bates and O'Steen: That the regulation constituted a violation of the Sherman Act and that the ban on advertising violated the First and Fourteenth Amendments.

In Bates v. State Bar of Arizona, 433 U.S. 350, 97 S.Ct. 2691 (1977), the U.S. Supreme Court affirmed in part and reversed in part the decision of the state supreme court. Looking to Parker v. Brown, 317 U.S. 341, 63 S.Ct. 307 (1943), which held that the Sherman Act was not intended to apply to certain state action, and subsequent decisions interpreting the state action exemption, including Goldfarb v. Virginia State Bar, 421 U.S. 773, 95 S.Ct. 2004 (1975), the Court ruled that the ban on the advertisement of legal services could not be attacked under the Sherman Act since "the challenged restraint is the affirmative command of the Arizona Supreme Court" and "[t]hat Court is the ultimate body wielding the State's power over the practice of law, * * * thus, the restraint is 'compelled by direction of the State acting as a sovereign.'" Where the U. S. Supreme Court did agree with the appellants Bates and O'Steen was with respect to their second assertion. As the Court narrowed the First Amendment issue for consideration in its opinion, "The heart of the dispute before us today is whether lawyers also may constitutionally advertise the *prices* at which certain routine services will be performed." The Court then considered at length "[n]umerous justifications * * * proffered for the restriction of such price advertising" (the adverse effect on professionalism, the inherently misleading nature of attorney advertising, the adverse effect on the administration of justice, the undesirable economic effects of advertising, the adverse effect of advertising on the quality of service, and the difficulties of enforcement) and concluded, speaking through Justice Blackmun, "[W]e are not persuaded that any of the proffered justifications rises to the level of an acceptable reason for the suppression of all advertising by attorneys." The Court reached this conclusion not by applying the traditional and rigidly set test of "overbreadth" common to "pure speech" cases but in light of many of the precepts set out in Virginia State Board of Pharmacy v. Virginia Citizens Consumer Council, 425 U.S. 748, 96 S.Ct. 1817 (1976), in which the Court clearly acknowledged that commercial speech, while protected by the First Amendment, must necessarily be balanced against a greater need for regulation than noncommercial varieties. "[M]ention[ing] some of the clearly permissible limitations on advertising not foreclosed by our holding" (for example, restrictions on advertising that is "false, deceptive, or misleading," restrictions as to "time, place, and manner," and restrictions on advertising "transactions that are themselves illegal"), the Court concluded, "[W]e, of course, do not hold that advertising by attorneys may not be regulated in any way."

In his opinion concurring in part (with the state action exception under the Sherman Act) and dissenting in part (to the First Amendment ruling)—an opinion in which Justice Stewart joined—Justice Powell, a past President of the American Bar Association himself, took exception at length to the Court's dismissal of the justifications offered to support the wholesale ban on advertising by attorneys. Calling the First Amendment interest in this case "marginal," Justice Powell predicted "today's decision will effect profound changes in the practice of law." Chief Justice Burger and Justice Rehnquist similarly concurred in part and dissented in part, though in separate opinions.

————

In a pair of cases from its October 1977 Term, the Court confronted the potential for conflict between state efforts to regulate in-person solicitation of business by lawyers and the free speech and association guarantees of the First Amendment. At the beginning of his opinion for the Court in Ohralik v. Ohio State Bar Ass'n, 436 U.S. 447, 98 S.Ct. 1912 (1978), Justice Powell observed, "The solicitation of business by a lawyer through direct, in-person communication with the prospective client has long been viewed as inconsistent with the profession's ideal of the attorney-client relationship and as posing a significant potential for harm to the prospective client. It has been proscribed by the organized Bar for many years." In the *Ohralik* case, which presented two instances of what Justice Marshall in a concurring opinion called "classic examples of 'ambulance chasing,'" an attorney was indefinitely suspended from practice after following two auto accident victims to the hospital and offering his services on a contingent basis, i.e., for one-third of the award or settlement for damages. The lawyer was soon discharged by his two clients after they had second thoughts about his eagerness to have them sue. After he subsequently demanded one-third of their recovery from the insurance company, alleging that they had breached their oral contracts with him, the two accident victims filed a complaint with the bar association. The Court rejected the attorney's contention that such disciplinary action infringed his First Amendment rights. Upholding the power of the bar association to impose sanctions for in-person solicitation of business, Justice Powell explained that this form of commercial speech posed special problems beyond those of the straightforward newspaper advertisement allowed in Bates v. State Bar of Arizona, 433 U.S. 350, 97 S.Ct. 2691 (1977): (1) "Unlike a public advertisement, which simply provides information and leaves the recipient free to act upon it or not, in-person solicitation may exert pressure and often demands an immediate response, without providing an opportunity for comparison or reflection"; and (2) "In-person solicitation is as likely as not to discourage persons needing counsel from engaging in a critical comparison of the 'availability, nature, and prices' of legal services * * * [and] it actually may disserve the individual and societal interest * * * in facilitating 'informed and reliable decisionmaking.'" Observing that "state interests implicated in this case are particularly strong," the Court went on to point out:

> The substantive evils of solicitation have been stated over the years in sweeping terms: stirring up litigation, assertion of fraudulent claims, debasing the legal profession, and potential harm to the solicited client in the form of overreaching, overcharging, underrepresentation, and misrepresentation. The American Bar Association, as *amicus curiae*, defends the rule against solicitation primarily on three broad grounds: It is said that the prohibitions embodied in Disciplinary Rules 2–103(A) and 2–104(A) serve to reduce the likelihood of overreaching and the exertion of undue influence on lay persons; to protect the privacy of individuals; and to avoid situations where the lawyer's exercise of judgment on behalf of the client will be clouded by his own pecuniary self-interest.

> We need not discuss or evaluate each of these interests in detail as appellant has conceded that the State has a legitimate and indeed "compelling" interest in preventing those aspects of solicitation that involve fraud, undue influence, intimidation, overreaching, and other forms of "vexatious conduct." * * * We agree that protection of the public from these aspects of solicitation is a legitimate and important state interest.

Conceding that the dangers of in-person solicitation "are amply present in the *Ohralik* case," Justice Marshall, who concurred in part in the Court's opinion and in its judgment, found "somewhat disturbing the Court's suggestion * * * that in-person solicitation of business, though entitled to some degree of constitutional protection as 'commercial speech,' is entitled to less protection under the First Amendment than is 'the kind of advertising approved in *Bates.*'" He continued, "The First Amendment informational interests served by solicitation, whether or not it occurs in a purely commercial context, are substantial, and they are entitled to as much protection as the interests we found to be protected in *Bates.*" Justice Marshall explained:

> Not only do prohibitions on solicitation interfere with the free flow of information protected by the First Amendment, but by origin and in practice they operate in a discriminatory manner. * * * [T]hese constraints developed as rules of "etiquette" and came to rest on the notion that a lawyer's reputation in his community would spread by word-of-mouth and bring business to the worthy lawyer. * * * The social model on which this conception depends is that of the small cohesive and homogeneous community; the anachronistic nature of this model has long been recognized. * * * If ever this conception were more generally true, it is now valid only with respect to those persons who move in the relatively elite social and educational circles in which knowledge about legal problems, legal remedies and lawyers is widely shared. * * *

> The impact of the nonsolicitation rules, moreover, is discriminatory with respect to the suppliers as well as the consumers of legal services. Just as the persons who suffer most from lack of knowledge about lawyers' availa-

bility belong to the less privileged classes of society, * * * so the disciplinary rules against solicitation fall most heavily on those attorneys engaged in a single practitioner or small partnership form of practice—attorneys who typically earn less than their fellow practitioners in larger, corporate-oriented firms. * * * Indeed, some scholars have suggested that the rules against solicitation were developed by the professional bar to keep recently immigrated lawyers, who gravitated toward the smaller, personal injury practice, from effective entry into the profession. * * * In light of this history, I am less inclined than the majority appears to be * * * to weigh favorably in the balance of the State's interests here the longevity of the ban on attorney solicitation.

Concluded Marshall, "While the State's interest in regulating in-person solicitation may * * * be somewhat greater than its interest in regulating print advertisements, these concededly legitimate interests might well be served by more specific and less restrictive rules than a total ban on pecuniary solicitation" (for example, permitting " 'all solicitation and advertising except the kinds that are false, misleading, undignified, or champertous' ").

In the second case, In re Primus, 436 U.S. 412, 98 S.Ct. 1893 (1978), the Court found the South Carolina Bar's sanction of a public reprimand for an alleged violation of the ban on solicitation of business to be an infringement of the attorney's First Amendment rights. In this case an attorney, cooperating with the ACLU and working free of charge in that capacity but who was otherwise paid by a nonprofit civil rights group, contacted by mail a woman who had been induced to undergo sterilization as the price of receiving continued medicaid benefits for pregnant women on public assistance. The attorney's letter inquired whether the woman would like the ACLU to file a suit for damages on her behalf against the doctor and thus join the organization's effort in the interest of others similarly situated to recover for the injury done to them and to bring the state's policy to a halt. At the outset, the Court noted three features which distinguished the attorney's conduct in *Primus* from that of the attorney in *Ohralik*: (1) the solicitation took the form of a letter; (2) the lawyer did not make the inquiry for financial gain; and (3) the lawyer's efforts "were undertaken to express personal political beliefs and to advance the civil-liberties objectives of the ACLU * * *." Relying on its decision in NAACP v. Button, 371 U.S. 415, 83 S.Ct. 328 (1963) (where the Court sustained, as an exercise of freedom of speech and association, efforts of that group to aid blacks by facilitating suits challenging segregation) and its progeny, which "establish[ed] the principle that 'collective activity undertaken to obtain meaningful access to the courts is a fundamental right within the protection of the First Amendment,' " the Court concluded that South Carolina's disciplinary rules, as employed in this case, swept too broadly and thus infringed constitutional rights. Quoting *Button*, Justice Powell, speaking for the Court, pointed out that " '[b]road prophylactic rules in the area of free speech are suspect,' and that '[p]recision of regulation must be the touchstone in an area so closely touching our most precious freedoms.' " The disciplinary rules also failed to survive "exacting scrutiny" in this case because of the absence of any "compelling" state interest. Justice Powell wrote, "The record does not support * * * [the Bar's] contention that undue influence, overreaching, misrepresentation, or invasion of privacy actually occurred in this case." Likewise, "The State's interests in preventing the 'stirring up' of frivolous or vexatious litigation and minimizing commercialization of the legal profession offer no further justification for the discipline administered in this case." In short, concluded the Court:

> Where political expression or association is at issue, this Court has not
> tolerated the degree of imprecision that often characterizes government

regulation of the conduct of commercial affairs. The approach we adopt today in *Ohralik*, * * * that the State may proscribe in-person solicitation for pecuniary gain under circumstances likely to result in adverse consequences, cannot be applied to appellant's activity on behalf of the ACLU. Although a showing of potential danger may suffice in the former context, appellant may not be disciplined unless her activity in fact involved the type of misconduct at which South Carolina's broad prohibition is said to be directed.

Although concurring in *Ohralik*, Justice Rehnquist dissented from the Court's decision in *Primus*. He observed that the Court's decisions in these two cases seemed more concerned with identifying good guys and bad guys and he lamented the "develop[ment of] a jurisprudence of epithets and slogans in this area, in which 'ambulance chasers' suffer one fate and 'civil liberties lawyers' another." The Court's "tale of two lawyers" was visibly marred, in Rehnquist's view, by the "absence of any principled distinction between the two cases * * *." The effects of the decisions were especially disturbing, he believed, because of "the radical difference in scrutiny brought to bear upon state regulation in each area." He expressed reservation.

> that any State will be able to determine with confidence the area in which it may regulate prophylactically and the area in which it may regulate only upon a specific showing of harm. Despite the Court's assertion to the contrary, * * * the difficulty of drawing distinctions on the basis of the content of the speech or the motive of the speaker *is* a valid reason for avoiding the undertaking where a more objective standard is readily available. I believe that constitutional inquiry must focus on the character of the conduct which the State seeks to regulate, and not on the motives of the individual lawyers or the nature of the particular litigation involved. The State is empowered to discipline for conduct which it deems detrimental to the public interest unless foreclosed from doing so by our cases construing the First and Fourteenth Amendments.

And he concluded:

> As the Court understands the disciplinary rule enforced by South Carolina, "a lawyer employed by the ACLU or a similar organization may never give unsolicited advice to a lay person that he or she retain the organization's free services." * * * That prohibition seems to me entirely reasonable. A State may rightly fear that members of its Bar have powers of persuasion not possessed by laymen * * * and it may also fear that such persuasion may be as potent in writing as it is in person. Such persuasion may draw an unsophisticated layman into litigation contrary to his own best interests * * * and it may force other citizens of South Carolina to defend against baseless litigation which would not otherwise have been brought. I cannot agree that a State must prove such harmful consequences in each case simply because an organization such as the ACLU or the NAACP is involved.

> I cannot share the Court's confidence that the danger of such consequences is minimized simply because a lawyer proceeds from political conviction rather than for pecuniary gain. A State may reasonably fear that a lawyer's desire to resolve "substantial civil liberties questions," * * * may occasionally take precedence over his duty to advance the interests of

his client. It is even more reasonable to fear that a lawyer in such circumstances will be inclined to pursue both culpable and blameless defendants to the last ditch in order to achieve his ideological goals. Although individual litigants, including the ACLU, may be free to use the courts for such purposes, South Carolina is likewise free to restrict the activities of the members of its Bar who attempt to persuade them to do so.

* * *

Chapter 14

Freedom of the Press

The famous epigram on the masthead of *The New York Times* proudly proclaims that the pages of that newspaper contain "All the news that's fit to print." But what is "news"? What kind of "news" is "fit to print"? And, most important, *who* shall decide what kind of "news" is "fit to print"? These are questions which any constitutional democracy must answer when it attempts to reconcile the exercise of freedom of the press with a multitude of competing social values. The freedom to print, like the freedom to speak, inescapably involves the Court in the business of line drawing that allocates the rights and responsibilities of those who publish. As with freedom of speech, such accommodations must also acknowledge the fundamental quality of the right.

But a factor of considerable significance surfaces in many if not most free press problems and distinguishes them from virtually all of the controversies involving free speech. The simple fact of the matter is that today the dissemination of news is big business, and the difficulty of reconciling the competing interests presented in free press cases is, therefore, compounded by the concentration of power in the media. A First Amendment guarantee written with the aim of protecting the lone pamphleteer now operates to shield large commercial enterprises. Increasingly, libertarians, once sympathetic to the argument that the absolute protection of a free press was indispensable to securing the integrity of the small town newspaper publisher and the independent journalist, now see that such a comprehensive guarantee today more often amounts to sanctioning *laissez-faire* capitalism for the media conglomerate. The dilemma posed for the First Amendment by the development of a media establishment is especially perplexing, for the hazards of regulation are well-known; yet, on its face, the First Amendment applies with equal force to both the political essayist and the newspaper syndicate. Ironically, one of the chief obstacles to the exercise of a wide freedom of the press has turned out to be the exercise of freedom by the giants of the media. Such was the concern three decades ago of a most prestigious Commission on Freedom of the Press. Despite the passage of years, their report, *A Free and Responsible Press*, is still relevant and worthy of review.

a. Censorship and Prior Restraint

The First Amendment's prohibition on the enactment of statutes abridging freedom of the press has lent itself, of course, to many of the same interpretations that have been placed on freedom of speech. And, as in free speech cases, the overwhelming majority of Justices on the Court have never acceded to the idea that freedom of the press is absolute, despite the fact that one of the most oft-quoted notions of freedom of the press is that supplied by Blackstone. In the words of the revered eighteenth-century English legal scholar as they appear in his *Commentaries*, "The liberty of the press * * * consists in laying no *previous* restraints upon publications, and not in freedom from censure for criminal matter when published * * * ." Speaking for a majority in Near v. Minnesota, 283 U.S. 697, 51 S.Ct. 625 (1931), the earliest decision in which the Court focused on freedom of the press as a fundamental right applicable against state as well as federal infringement, Chief Justice Hughes rejected Blackstone's formulation not only because "the protection * * * as to previous restraint is not absolutely unlimited" but also, and indeed, "chiefly because that immunity cannot be deemed to exhaust the conception of the liberty guaranteed by State and Federal Constitutions." He continued, "The point of criticism has been 'that the mere exemption from previous restraints cannot be all that is secured by the constitutional provisions,' and that 'the liberty of the press might be rendered a mockery and a delusion, and the phrase itself a by-word, if, while every man was at liberty to publish what he pleased, the public authorities might nevertheless punish him for harmless publications.' " Instructive in this respect are the facts of the controversy at hand which occasioned Chief Justice Hughes's remarks. Near, the owner of a rather shrill and sensationalistic, municipal reform-minded, but anti-Semitic newspaper, had been enjoined from any further publication of articles after the Minnesota courts had determined that the paper fell within the ambit of a state law which provided for the abatement as a public nuisance of any "malicious, scandalous and defamatory newspaper, magazine or other periodical." Although the Court recognized that, under certain circumstances it clearly labeled "exceptional" (for example, the publication of obscenity, libel, or incitements to violence or subversion), certain post publication penalties might legitimately be imposed by government on the publisher, it struck down the Minnesota statute (albeit by a slim majority) on the grounds that—to use the words here that later Courts would employ—it had a "chilling effect" on the rightful exercise of constitutional liberties.

As is clear from the decision in *Times Film Corp.* v. *Chicago* (p. 1400), some members of the Warren Court were willing to accept the proposition of absolutely no prior restraint, but the majority of Justices were not. Compare the tenor of the *Times Film Corp.* decision with that in *Freed-*

man v. *Maryland* (p. 1402) four years later. If the Court could not subscribe to the proposition that those who distributed motion pictures were absolutely entitled to one showing before the state intervened, it did come to impose exacting requirements on the activities of censorship agencies. What were these stringent standards that the Court imposed? Why are these procedural requirements especially important to check censorship activities? Do you find the restrictions placed on such practices to be similar to those imposed on the regulation of other constitutional rights? What mode of constitutional interpretation is exemplified in the *Freedman* decision?

The problems posed by censorship and post-publication penalties are equally apparent in government efforts to keep certain information from the media, either as a matter of national security, as in *New York Times Co.* v. *United States* (p. 1404), or in order not to sully the reputation of innocent individuals, as in *Cox Broadcasting Corp.* v. *Cohn* (p. 1411), *Landmark Communications, Inc.* v. *Commonwealth of Virginia* (p. 1413), and *Smith* v. *Daily Mail Publishing Co.* (p. 1413). Although these decisions run against the imposition of censorship and post-publication sanctions, they are distinguishable one from another on the basis of the availability of the information as a matter of public record—at least this factor distinguishes *Cox Broadcasting*. In the absence of this factor, to what extent do you think the Court has implicitly adopted a "hide and go seek" view on the question of newspaper publication of sensitive information? In other words, without impinging on government's right to withhold information not a matter of public record, what limits, if any, has the Court placed on the media's right to publish such information when and by whatever manner (including theft) such information falls into its hands?

If what is at stake in the aforementioned cases is the access of the media to government decisions, an interesting twist on this issue of access is supplied by the controversy in *Miami Herald Publishing Co.* v. *Tornillo* (p. 1421) and by Chief Justice Burger's concurring opinion in *First National Bank of Boston* v. *Bellotti* (p. 1425). In *Tornillo*, the question is simply one of access by the private citizen to newspaper decision making: Can the First Amendment be interpreted as guaranteeing a right of access to the media so as to insure a right of reply by the citizen to a public attack? Although the Court rejected such mandatory access, the opinions of Chief Justice Burger—for the Court in *Tornillo* and, more explicitly, concurring in *Bellotti*—manifest deep concern about the concentration of power and influence in media conglomerates. In his view, such business enterprises, with vast wealth and power, shielded by the First Amendment, pose significant threats to society that, in some instances, rival the benefits they contribute. In the Chief Justice's view, these dangers may well overshadow the potential for mischief in the hands of ordinary, commercial enterprises which we have traditionally regulated.

It is one thing to say that the First Amendment guarantees a broad, if not unlimited right to publish; it is something else, the Court has said, to adopt the view of many journalists and argue that freedom of the press encompasses "the public's right to know." Although Congress has recognized a *statutory* "right to know" with its passage of the Freedom of Information Act (p. 1411) as amended, the Court has never recognized the existence of a broad-based *constitutional* "right to know." As the Court has pointed out repeatedly—especially and most explicitly in *Houchins* v. *KQED* (p. 1428) and less pointedly in both *Branzburg* v. *Hayes* (p. 1414) and *Tornillo*—the First Amendment does not guarantee to the press any right of special access to information not available to the public generally. Nor do the cases on commercial speech, notably *Virginia State Board of Pharmacy* v. *Virginia Citizens Consumer Council* (p. 1367), support the recognition of any "right to know" since there the government's restraint on publication of price information was imposed *despite* the fact that the parties concerned wanted public disclosure not because they sought to maintain secrecy. Neither can it be argued that the framers of the Amendment—by and large the same individuals responsible for drafting the Constitution proper—favored such a right in view both of the fact that Article I, section 4 provides with respect to Congress that "Each House shall keep a Journal of its Proceedings, and from time to time publish the same, excepting such Parts as may in their Judgment require Secrecy" and the fact that the Constitutional Convention itself was held behind closed doors. More important, could the press as agent of "the public's right to know" act as trustee of that right and still hope to exercise the very kind of independent editorial judgment the Court felt compelled to recognize in *Tornillo?* Ultimately, the Court recognized some right of access emanating from the First Amendment—to criminal trials, at least—in *Richmond Newspapers, Inc.* v. *Virginia* (p. 1509). Justice Stevens is quick to call this "a watershed case." Is it? How broad is the right recognized in *Richmond Newspapers?* A spirited debate on a kindred theme is reflected in the Court's disposition of the *Pico* case (p. 1438). What is the extent of the right of access developed by the Court here?

A final aspect of press immunity, which constitutes the focus of discussion in *Branzburg* v. *Hayes* (p. 1414) and *Matter of Farber and the New York Times Co.* (p. 1417) and which is touched upon by some of the dissenters in *Zurcher* v. *Stanford Daily* (p. 1125), presents an inverted version of the "right to know" issue to which we have just alluded. Briefly put, does government have the right to demand and acquire information held by a journalist when such disclosures may reveal his confidential news sources? In *Branzburg,* this boils down to the issue of whether a reporter can be compelled to divulge information he possesses to a grand jury. Would you agree that not to vindicate government's right to know here would place the reporter in a specially privileged position? And consider the issue as it is presented in the *Farber* case where the reporter is believed to possess information thought useful to the defense in a criminal trial. Would it be possible to conduct fair trials had the Court not held as it did in *Branzburg?* Note the relevance of the Supreme Court's decision in *United States* v. *Nixon* (p. 288). Is the claim of press immunity here consistent with the simultaneous claim of the press as agent of "the public's right to know," mentioned above?

b. Obscenity

Though the Burger Court's recent decisions regarding obscenity substantially overturned earlier rulings of the Warren Court, we have reproduced or otherwise drawn your attention to most of the Supreme Court's principal decisions, both past and present. A panorama of cases is essential to an understanding of the wide range of issues which the Court's struggle with the obscenity problem illumines. The Court's decisions concerning obscenity, in sum, are a microcosm of the problems of law itself and its development.

Until 1957, when the Supreme Court entered the field, American courts based their decisions as to what was obscene on the standard articulated in a nineteenth-century English case, Regina v. Hicklin, L.R. 3 Q.B. 360 (1868). In that case, the facts of which are unimportant here, the standard laid out was "whether the tendency of the matter charged as obscenity is to deprave and corrupt those whose minds are open to such immoral influences, and into whose hands a publication of this sort may fall." The application of this test had a particularly unfortunate antilibertarian thrust to it because, in addition to judging the obscenity of the material in terms of the most peripheral social group who might have contact with it (i.e., children), the judges looked only at the objectionable parts of the material and did so without any regard to any artistic or literary merit the work might have. Although some American judges struggled with the Hicklin test trying to liberalize it, notably by demanding that the work be considered as a whole and that expert testimony be taken into account concerning its artistic or literary value, the standard for the determination of obscenity remained the same until the Supreme Court held that it swept so broadly and indiscriminately as to violate the First Amendment. As Justice Frankfurter noted, writing for the Court in Butler v. Michigan, 352 U.S. 380, 77 S.Ct. 524 (1957), a case involving the validity of a statute embodying the Hicklin test, "The incidence of this enactment is to reduce the adult population of Michigan to reading only what is fit for children."

Beginning with its decision in Roth v. United States (p. 1443) and a companion case, Alberts v. California, the Supreme Court formulated a new constitutional standard. What was this standard, and how would you say it differed from the old Hicklin test? In its construction of this new test does the Court lay the proper foundation? That is, does the Court ever offer any justification as to why obscenity should be regulated beyond merely assuming that it is not protected by the First Amendment? Consider thoroughly the implications of the Court's failure to do so. If the Court did not understand exactly why and under what circumstances obscenity might bear regulation, how could it formulate a constitutional test? Contrast Douglas's dissent with Brennan's insistence that material have "redeeming social value." Which position is most consistent with the concept of limited government? Why?

Read with care Justice Harlan's concurring and dissenting opinion. When you examine later the recent decisions of the Burger Court, consider to what extent Harlan's two-tier approach to obscenity has been accepted.

Note that the difference in the substance of his constitutionally permissible standards leads Harlan to vote differently in *Roth* and *Alberts*. What is Harlan's view of a national obscenity standard?

Note how substantially Chief Justice Warren diverges from the majority on what exactly the issue is in these cases. On what basis would Warren vote to affirm Roth's and Albert's convictions? Compare Warren's formulation of the obscenity problem with the majority in *Ginzburg* v. *United States* (p. 1451). He anticipated what would become the dominant view on the Court by nearly a decade.

From the decision in *Roth* until the trilogy of cases decided in 1966 (*Memoirs*, *Ginzburg*, and *Mishkin*), the drift of the Court was to accepting what two leading constitutional authorities, Professors William Lockhart and Robert McClure (in their article, "Censorship of Obscenity: The Developing Constitutional Standards," 45 Minnesota Law Review 5 [1960], characterized as the concept of "constant obscenity." The fundamental premise underlying this notion was that what was obscene was so at all times, in all places, and for all people. The efforts of several of the Justices turned, therefore, to more exactly describing this quality and to applying it as a standard of judgment against the books, magazines, and movies which came before the Court. By the time the Court took up *Memoirs* v. *Attorney General of Massachusetts* (p. 1449), the Fanny Hill case, the *Roth* test had been expanded to comprise a tripartite standard, the independent parts of which had emerged incrementally from rulings subsequent to 1957. With the sole exception of a 1959 case, Kingsley International Pictures Corp. v. Regents of the University of the State of New York, 360 U.S. 684, 79 S.Ct. 1362, in which the Court unanimously ruled that no work (in this case the film "Lady Chatterly's Lover") could be banned on the basis of "ideological obscenity," i.e., the inherent immorality of an idea, the Court was so fractured on the probelm of developing obscenity standards in the decade following *Roth* that it disposed of cases involving the substantive issue of obscenity either by a plurality opinion or without any written opinion at all. The futility of trying to define obscenity once and for all led Justice Stewart to confess in a 1964 case involving a motion picture entitled "The Lovers": "I shall not attempt further to define the kinds of material I understand to be embraced within that short-hand description [i.e., hard-core pornography]; and perhaps I could never succeed in intelligibly doing so. But I do know it when I see it, and the motion picture involved in this case is not that." (Jacobellis v. Ohio, 378 U.S. 184, 197, 84 S.Ct. 1676, 1683).

By 1966, however, the Court had come to appreciate the limitations and false assumptions of the constant obscenity concept. Without changing a word of the threefold *Roth* test, the Court sufficiently reworked interpretation and application of the standards to recast its policy in favor of what Professors Lockhart and McClure have labeled the "variable obscenity" approach. As contrasted with constant obscenity, the variable approach begins with the premise that obscenity has a chameleonlike quality and differs according to time and place in appeal. As Chief Justice Warren remarked in *Roth*, something which is obscene in one context may not be in another. Professors Lockhart and McClure suggested that a variable concept could be applied by first isolating the primary audience to whom the material in question was directed and, secondly, by examining the nature of the appeal made to an average member of that group. Consider both *Ginzburg* v. *United States* (p. 1451) and *Mishkin* v. *New York* (p. 1455). How has the Court reinterpreted the threefold *Roth* test to fit its new conception of obscenity? Note also the Court's decision two years later in *Ginsberg* v. *New York* (p. 1456). Does the Court's decision here convince you of the superior understanding of obscenity which the variable concept demonstrates over the constant approach?

The Court's adoption of the variable approach, however, did not quell objections even though a majority of Justices now found it possible to agree on a position. As Justices Black and Harlan make quite clear in *Ginzburg,* when the Court formulates new policy without adequate notice and at the expense of the defendant, certain elementary questions of justice have to be considered. Would you agree that Ginzburg's conviction was essentially *ex post facto?* Is this kind of inequity a necessary concomitant of judicial policy making? Nor was everyone on the Court agreed that the variable approach was any more justified than constant obscenity. Consider Justice Marshall's opinion for the Court in *Stanley* v. *Georgia* (p. 1457). To what extent does the opinion here discredit the *Roth* standards? To what extent does it alter the burden of proof in an obscenity case? Wouldn't the Court have been better off—not to mention Ralph Ginzburg—had it twelve years earlier dealt with the arguments Justice Marshall raises? Given the drift of the opinion in *Stanley,* could the Court have been moving to a place-oriented conception of obscenity—that the right to see or read material was to be conditioned on where it was done and so long as it was done with consent? The *Stanley* case might also be considered a case on the right of privacy, too.

The most recent phase of the Court's obscenity policy was inaugurated with the Burger Court's decisions of June 1973. The impact of the Nixon appointees has been significant in this area, if not others, in reformulating constitutional doctrine. After reading *Miller* v. *California* (p. 1459) and *Paris Adult Theatre I* v. *Slaton* (p. 1463), would you say the Court has gone all the way back to the original *Roth* position? And, if so, to whose opinion? Can the Court's process of decision stop with such a policy or, as the dissenters suggest, will the present Court be dragged inevitably into a repetition of past distinctions and, therefore, past mistakes? What does Justice Brennan, the architect of so many of those past decisions, appear to have learned from the Court's attempt to make policy regarding obscenity? An interesting sidelight to this controversy is provided by the Court's recent decision in *Federal Communications Comm'n* v. *Pacifica Foundation* (p. 1468), in which the Justices addressed the legitimacy of an effort by the FCC to enforce a ban on the use of "indecent" language over the airways during daytime and prime time radio broadcasts.

c. **Libel**

The free press questions which we have been considering have dealt with the traditional clash of individual and governmental interests. Questions of libel present a different problem, for they pit individual rights against individual rights, specifically the value of freedom of the press against the right of privacy. If you will recall Blackstone's conception of a free press quoted earlier, you will remember that he assumed publications were not to be free from punishment after the publication of unprotected matter, and, until recently, the Supreme Court accepted this position by allowing wide latitude in state libel laws. Like obscenity, libel was not considered within the parameters of the First Amendment. The Warren Court, however, began to scrutinize the effect of libel laws on the right of free press.

The Court's effort to narrow the reach of state libel laws began in *New York Times* v. *Sullivan* (p. 1470) by focusing on the right of public officials to recover damages. How did the new standard announced by the Court differ from the existing basis for recovery under Alabama law? The cases which followed expanded the application of the *New York Times* rule. What began as a doctrine marking the bounds of fair comment public officials would have to tolerate evolved to apply also for other categories of newsworthy individuals. The Court next extended the constitutional limitation on the recovery of damages for libel to public figures who were not public officials, as exemplified by the rulings in *Curtis Publishing Co.* v. *Butts* (p. 1476) and a companion case, *Associated Press* v. *Walker*. Four years later in Rosenbloom v. Metromedia, Inc., 403 U.S. 29, 91 S.Ct. 1811 (1971), the Court went the full distance, applying the *New York Times* rule to govern recovery of damages "by a private individual for a defamatory falsehood uttered in a news broadcast by a radio station about the individual's involvement in an event of public or general interest." But, sensing that it had gone too far in making recovery difficult for private individuals who had been victimized by irresponsible attacks by the media, the Court quickly retreated from its *Rosenbloom* holding in *Gertz* v. *Robert Welch, Inc.* (p. 1482, footnote d).

In *Gertz* and *Time, Inc.* v. *Firestone* (p. 1481), the Court summed up its current views on the constitutional requirements of any law allowing recovery for libel. Where does the court stand today on the essential basis for imposing any liability for libelous statements; on the different basis for recovery allowed public officials and public figures, on the one hand, and private individuals, on the other; and on the correlation of less demanding standards of fault with the ability to collect only compensatory damages? Since the Court has held that damages for defamation may not be awarded without some showing of fault and since proof of some kind of intent is necessary to any such demonstration, the Court inevitably came to address the question whether the plaintiff in a libel suit could direct inquiries at news media defendants about editorial decisions they reached prior to publishing or broadcasting the allegedly defamatory material. In *Herbert* v. *Lando* (p. 1494), the Court upheld the constitutionality of such inquiries.

The Court's bifurcated libel standards leave public figures with substantially less protection than the average citizen, a result justified as a necessary price which the celebrity pays for the notoriety he or she has achieved. But as the facts in *Galella* v. *Onassis* (p. 1497) show, this can be a high price indeed. This is not a libel case, of course, but a suit revolving around the question of an invasion of privacy. Apart from illustrating the potentially devastating intrusiveness of the media, the *Galella* case is interesting because of the remedy imposed by the district court—the issuance of an injunction rather than the award of damages. In your view, was the relief granted by the district court consistent with First Amendment values? The appeals court found the remedy excessive and substantially reduced the distances between the photographer and Mrs. Onassis required by the district judge. Would you agree? In your view, do these decisions on libel and privacy reflect a genuine if tough-minded appreciation for what Justice Brennan called "a profound national commitment to the principle that debate on public issues should be uninhibited, robust, and wide-open * * * " or do they demonstrate an insensitive regard for the value of the individual's reputation and his privacy in the face of irresponsible attacks by the media?

d. Fair Trial—Free Press

We have repeatedly pointed out that, while in a democracy freedom of the press must be accorded high regard, other values sometimes conflict. The choice between values becomes tougher, as we noted with regard to libel, when the competing interest is another civil liberty. The Court, as we have shown there, has largely vindicated the free press interest at some expense—perhaps, some would argue, at too great expense—to personal privacy. The Court's accommodation of the conflict between free press and the individual's right to a fair trial, however, came to be resolved very much the other way.

While a number of cases have shown the Court to be most reluctant to uphold use of the contempt power to regulate press criticism of the conduct of trials, it had throughout the 1960s been much more willing to undertake a searching examination of convictions resulting from trials in which press coverage was alleged to have endangered the integrity of the verdict. The Court came to regard the right to a fair trial as a paramount right.

The first case in which the Court reversed a conviction because of pretrial publicity was Irvin v. Dowd, 366 U.S. 717, 81 S.Ct. 1639 (1961). The defendant in that case was a man accused of six murders whose confession had been issued to the press by the police. Publicity had been so intense that he was granted a change of venue, but the situation proved to be little better at the new location. It took four weeks to select a jury from a panel of 430, of whom 268 members were excused because of fixed opinions of guilt. Of the twelve jurors finally selected, eight admitted to believing that the defendant was guilty. Taking notice of the extensive publicity previous to the trial, the Court unanimously reversed the state conviction concluding that, "With his life at stake, it is not requiring too much that petitioner be tried in an atmosphere undisturbed by so huge a wave of public passion and by a jury other than one in which two-thirds of the members admit, before hearing any testimony, to possessing a belief in his guilt."

Two years later the Court faced the same question with the exception that the press coverage involved was by television. In Rideau v. Louisiana, 373 U.S. 723, 83 S.Ct. 1417 (1963), a man accused of murder made a confession which was filmed in a television interview with the sheriff. Once again the Court reversed the conviction on the ground that a change of venue should have been granted so that the jury could have been selected from persons who had not witnessed his televised confession.

A third case, Estes v. Texas, 381 U.S. 532, 85 S.Ct. 1628 (1965), presented the question as to whether the defendant, an alleged swindler, was constitutionally compelled to undergo a trial the proceedings of which were being televised. During the pretrial hearing at least twelve cameramen operated within the courtroom leading to considerable disruption of the hearings. At the trial itself the situation improved because the cameramen were assigned to operate at the rear of the courtroom. The Supreme Court, nevertheless, reversed Estes's conviction on grounds that the presence of television equipment and personnel, even discreetly positioned, raised an issue of possibly distracting influence. Writing for the majority, Justice Clark concluded, "A defendant on trial for a specific crime is entitled to his day in court, not in a stadium or a city or nation-wide arena." The dissenters agreed in principle with regard to the disruptive potential of the media but found no specific effect in that case to warrant reversal. The Court has since shaken off the undue nervousness about televising criminal trials apparent in *Estes*. Without directly overruling *Estes*, the court in Chandler v. Florida, 449 U.S. 560, 101 S.Ct. 802 (1981), upheld a rule adopted by the Florida Supreme Court allowing for experimental, controlled television coverage of trials in that state. In *Chandler*, the Court ruled that television coverage does not *per se* impair the fairness of a criminal trial and defendants challenging such coverage must be able to show "that their trial was affected adversely by the impact on any of the participants of the presence of cameras and the prospect of broadcast." The Court distinguished *Estes* on the grounds that there was specific evidence of adverse impact in that case.

The Sam Sheppard murder trial, which furnished the basic plot line for a popular movie of some years ago entitled "The Lawyer," probably constituted the most infamous example of media impact on the conduct of criminal proceedings. In support of its finding that "massive, pervasive and prejudicial publicity   *   *   *   attended his prosecution," the Court's opinion in Sheppard v. Maxwell, 384 U.S. 333, 86 S.Ct. 1507 (1966), recounted numerous examples of the local news media's continuous editorializing about Sheppard's guilt, sensationalistic coverage of developments in the case, and extraordinary intrusion into all facets of the trial itself. In the face of the carnival-like atmosphere that permeated the proceedings—especially the inquest convened to explore the mysterious circumstances surrounding the death of Sheppard's wife—and in view of the options available to minimize the impact of such shrill and polemical media coverage, the Court, speaking through Justice Clark, concluded that "the state trial judge did not fulfill his duty to protect Sheppard from the inherently prejudicial publicity which saturated the community and to control disruptive influences in the courtroom * * *." Justice Black dissented alone *and without opinion.*

The line of thought culminating in the *Sheppard* opinion appeared to suggest that the right to a fair trial was paramount. The Court's opinion in *Nebraska Press Ass'n* v. *Stuart* (p. 1502) assumes a different tenor. At the least, it suggests that the occasion for choice between the vindication of First or Sixth Amendment rights should prove to be rare because of the options open to a trial judge to mitigate the effect of extensive media coverage. Justice Brennan argues that *no* such choice is necessary. Would you agree? The Burger Court's more recent decisions in *Richmond Newspapers* (p. 1509) and *Globe Newspaper Co.* (p. 1521) have accentuated the trend away from the seemingly automatic preference for the "fair trial" interest which marked the decisions of the Warren Court during the 1960s. *Richmond Newspapers* makes it clear that there is a First Amendment expectation that criminal trials are to be open to the press. If, as Justice Frankfurter once forcefully argued, "A trial is not a free trade in ideas," what justifications does the Court offer for a constitutional right of access by the press? How persuasively does the Court recognize a legitimate public interest in press access to trials as opposed to, say, the private interest of the press in capitalizing on the sensationalism of the moment?

a.   CENSORSHIP AND PRIOR RESTRAINT

TIMES FILM CORP. v. CHICAGO

Supreme Court of the United States, 1961
365 U.S. 43, 81 S.Ct. 391, 5 L.Ed.2d 403

A Chicago ordinance required submission of all motion pictures to be shown in the city for examination prior to their exhibition. Times Film Corporation, a New York outfit which owned the rights to distribute the movie "Don Juan," paid the required license fee but refused to submit the film for review. As a consequence, the appropriate city official denied a permit to show the film, and his decision was upheld under the ordinance's authorized appeal to the mayor. Times Film then brought this suit for injunctive relief contending that the ordinance was unconstitutional on its face because it imposed prior restraint on the exhibition of films in contravention of the protections contained in the First and Fourteenth Amendments. A federal district court dismissed the complaint, and this decision was affirmed by a U.S. Court of Appeals. The Supreme Court granted certiorari.

Mr. Justice CLARK delivered the opinion of the Court.

* * *

* * * Admittedly, the challenged section of the ordinance imposes a previous restraint, and the broad justiciable issue is therefore present as to whether the ambit of constitutional protection includes complete and absolute freedom to exhibit, at least once, any and every kind of motion picture. It is that question alone which we decide. We have concluded that * * * Chicago's ordinance requiring the submission of films prior to their public exhibition is not, on the grounds set forth, void on its face.

Petitioner's narrow attack upon the ordinance does not require that any consideration be given to the validity of the standards set out therein. They are not challenged and are not before us. Prior motion picture censorship cases which reached this Court involved questions of standards. The films had all been submitted to the authorities and permits for their exhibition were refused because of their content. Obviously, whether a particular statute is "clearly drawn," or "vague," or "indefinite," or whether a clear standard is in fact met by a film are different questions involving other constitutional challenges to be tested by considerations not here involved.

Moreover, there is not a word in the record as to the nature and content of "Don Juan." We are left entirely in the dark in this regard, as were the city officials and the other reviewing courts. Petitioner claims that the nature of the film is irrelevant, and that even if this film contains the basest type of pornography, or incitement to riot, or forceful overthrow of orderly government, it may nonetheless be shown without prior submission for examination. The challenge here is to the censor's basic authority; it does not go to any statutory standards employed by the censor or procedural requirements as to the submission of the film.

* * *

Petitioner would have us hold that the public exhibition of motion pictures must be allowed under any circumstances. The State's sole remedy, it says, is the invocation of criminal process under the Illinois pornography statute * * * and then only after a transgression. But this position * * * is founded upon the claim of absolute privilege against prior restraint under the First Amendment—a claim without sanction in our cases. * * * Chicago emphasizes here its duty to protect its people against the dangers of obscenity in the public exhibition of motion pictures. To this argument petitioner's only answer is that regardless of the cpacity for, or extent of, such an evil, previous restraint cannot be justified. With this we cannot agree. We recognized in Burstyn [v. Wilson, 343 U.S. 495, 72 S.Ct. 777 (1952)] that "capacity for evil * * * may be relevant in determining the permissible scope of community control," * * * and that motion pictures were not "necessarily subject to the precise rules governing any other particular method of expression. Each method," we said, "tends to present its own peculiar problems." * * * Certainly petitioner's broadside attack does not warrant, nor could it justify on the record here, our saying that—aside from any consideration of the other "exceptional cases" mentioned in our decisions—the State is stripped of all constitutional power to prevent, in the most effective fashion, the utterance of this class of speech. It is not for this Court to limit the State in its selection of the remedy it deems most effective to cope with such a problem, absent, of course, a showing of unreasonable strictures on individual liberty resulting from its application in particular circumstances. * * *

As to what may be decided when a concrete case involving a specific standard provided by this ordinance is presented, we intimate no opinion. The petitioner has not challenged all—or for that matter any—of the ordinance's standards. Naturally we could not say that every one of the standards, including those which Illinois' highest court has found sufficient, is so vague on its face that the entire ordinance is void. At this time we say no more than this—that we are dealing only with motion pictures and, even as to them, only in the context of the broadside attack presented on this record.

Affirmed.

Mr. Chief Justice WARREN, with whom Mr. Justice BLACK, Mr. Justice DOUGLAS and Mr. Justice BRENNAN join, dissenting.

I cannot agree either with the conclusion reached by the Court or with the reasons advanced for its support. To me, this case clearly presents the question of our approval of unlimited censorship of motion pictures before exhibition through a system of administrative licensing. Moreover, the decision presents a real danger of eventual censorship for every form of communication, be it newspapers, journals, books, magazines, television, radio or public speeches. The Court purports to leave these questions for another day, but I am aware of no constitutional principle which permits us to hold that the communication of ideas through one medium may be censored while other media are immune. Of course each medium presents its own peculiar problems, but they are not of the kind which would authorize the censorship of one form of communication and not others. * * *

The censor performs free from all of the procedural safeguards afforded litigants in a court of law. * * * The likelihood of a fair and impartial trial disappears when the censor is both prosecutor and judge. There is a complete absence of rules of evidence; the fact is that there is usually no evidence at all as the system at bar vividly illustrates. How different from a judicial proceeding where a full case is presented by the litigants. The inexistence of a jury to determine contemporary community standards is a vital flaw. * * *

Mr. Justice DOUGLAS, with whom THE CHIEF JUSTICE and Mr. Justice BLACK concur, dissenting.

* * *

The First Amendment was designed to enlarge, not to limit, freedom in literature and in the arts as well as in politics, economics, law, and other fields. * * * Its aim was to unlock all ideas for argument, debate, and dissemination. No more potent force in defeat of that freedom could be designed than censorship. It is a weapon that no minority or majority group, acting through government, should be allowed to wield over any of us.

Freedman v. Maryland, 380 U.S. 51, 85 S.Ct. 734 (1965), took the Court beyond the petitioner's claim in *Times Film* of an absolute right to a first showing to an attack on the review procedures which were part of a state censorship program. In that case, Freedman, the owner of a Baltimore movie theater, exhibited the film

"Revenge at Daybreak" without first submitting it to the Maryland Board of Censors for review and approval as required by state law. (The state subsequently conceded that the film would have received a license had it been submitted.) As a defense to prosecution for noncompliance with the statute, Freedman asserted that the Maryland scheme presented the danger of prior censorship because of the extensive, time-consuming (the only reported case running the gauntlet on appeal took six months), and burdensome features of appellate review from any possible adverse ruling by the board. The U. S. Supreme Court reversed the decision of the Maryland Court of Appeals affirming Freedman's conviction and found the review procedures unconstitutional.

Speaking for the Court's unanimous decision, Justice Brennan wrote:

> Applying the settled rule of our cases, we hold that a noncriminal process which requires the prior submission of a film to a censor avoids constitutional infirmity only if it takes place under procedural safeguards designed to obviate the dangers of a censorship system. First, the burden of proving that the film is unprotected expression must rest on the censor. As we said in Speiser v. Randall, 357 U.S. 513, 526, 78 S.Ct. 1332, 1342, "Where the transcendent value of speech is involved, due process certainly requires * * * that the State bear the burden of persuasion to show that the appellants engaged in criminal speech." Second, while the State may require advance submission of all films, in order to proceed effectively to bar all showings of unprotected films, the requirement cannot be administered in a manner which would lend an effect of finality to the censor's determination whether a film constitutes protected expression. The teaching of our cases is that, because only a judicial determination in an adversary proceeding ensures the necessary sensitivity to freedom of expression, only a procedure requiring a judicial determination suffices to impose a valid final restraint. * * * To this end, the exhibitor must be assured, by statute or authoritative judicial construction, that the censor will, within a specified brief period, either issue a license or go to court to restrain showing the film. Any restraint imposed in advance of a final judicial determination on the merits must similarly be limited to preservation of the status quo for the shortest fixed period compatible with sound judicial resolution. Moreover, we are well aware that, even after expiration of a temporary restraint, an administrative refusal to license, signifying the censor's view that the film is unprotected, may have a discouraging effect on the exhibitor. * * * Therefore, the procedure must also assure a prompt final judicial decision, to minimize the deterrent effect of an interim and possibly erroneous denial of a license.

> Without these safeguards, it may prove too burdensome to seek review of the censor's determination. Particularly in the case of motion pictures, it may take very little to deter exhibition in a given locality. The exhibitor's stake in any one picture may be insufficient to warrant a protracted and onerous course of litigation. The distributor, on the other hand, may be equally unwilling to accept the burdens and delays of litigation in a particular area when, without such difficulties, he can freely exhibit his film in most of the rest of the country; for we are told that only four States and a handful of municipalities have active censorship laws.

Justices Black and Douglas concurred favoring an absolutist reading of the First Amendment that would not countenance "any form of censorship—no matter how speedy or prolonged it may be." * * *

NEW YORK TIMES CO. v. UNITED STATES
[THE PENTAGON PAPERS CASE]

Supreme Court of the United States, 1971
403 U.S. 713, 91 S.Ct. 2140, 29 L.Ed.2d 822

The United States government brought suit to restrain the New York Times from publishing excerpts of a classified study, "History of U.S. Decision-Making Process on Viet Nam Policy." The Times came to have possession of a copy of this multivolume analysis, more popularly known as "The Pentagon Papers," as a consequence of the efforts of one of the study's contributors, Daniel Ellsberg. In a companion proceeding the government sought similar injunctive relief against publication in another newspaper, *The Washington Post.* The federal district courts in which the suits were brought refused to issue orders halting publication, and the government appealed. The U.S. Court of Appeals for the District of Columbia affirmed the ruling of one district court, but the Court of Appeals for the Second Circuit remanded the New York Times case to the lower court for further hearings. Both the New York Times and the government sought review by the Supreme Court.

PER CURIAM.

We granted certiorari * * * in these cases in which the United States seeks to enjoin the New York Times and the Washington Post from publishing the contents of a classified study entitled "History of U. S. Decision-Making Process on Viet Nam Policy."

"Any system of prior restraints of expression comes to this Court bearing a heavy presumption against its constitutional validity." Bantam Books, Inc. v. Sullivan, 372 U.S. 58, 70, 83 S.Ct. 631, 639 (1963); see also Near v. Minnesota ex rel. Olson, 283 U.S. 697, 51 S.Ct. 625 (1931). The Government "thus carries a heavy burden of showing justification for the imposition of such a restraint." Organization for a Better Austin v. Keefe, 402 U.S. 415, 419, 91 S.Ct. 1575, 1578 (1971). The District Court for the Southern District of New York in the *New York Times* case, 328 F.Supp. 324, and the District Court for the District of Columbia and the Court of Appeals for the District of Columbia Circuit, 446 F.2d 1327, in the *Washington Post* case

held that the Government had not met that burden. We agree.

The judgment of the Court of Appeals for the District of Columbia Circuit is therefore affirmed. The order of the Court of Appeals for the Second Circuit is reversed, 444 F.2d 544, and the case is remanded with directions to enter a judgment affirming the judgment of the District Court for the Southern District of New York. The stays entered June 25, 1971, by the Court are vacated. * * *

* * *

Mr. Justice BLACK, with whom Mr. Justice DOUGLAS joins, concurring.

* * * I believe that every moment's continuance of the injunctions against these newspapers amounts to a flagrant, indefensible, and continuing violation of the First Amendment. * * * In my view it is unfortunate that some of my Brethren are apparently willing to hold that the publication of news may sometimes be enjoined. Such a holding

would make a shambles of the First Amendment.

* * *

In seeking injunctions against these newspapers and in its presentation to the Court, the Executive Branch seems to have forgotten the essential purpose and history of the First Amendment. * * *

In the First Amendment the Founding Fathers gave the free press the protection it must have to fulfill its essential role in our democracy. The press was to serve the governed, not the governors. The Government's power to censor the press was abolished so that the press would remain forever free to censure the Government. The press was protected so that it could bare the secrets of government and inform the people. Only a free and unrestrained press can effectively expose deception in government. And paramount among the responsibilities of a free press is the duty to prevent any part of the government from deceiving the people and sending them off to distant lands to die of foreign fevers and foreign shot and shell. In my view, far from deserving condemnation for their courageous reporting, the New York Times, the Washington Post, and other newspapers should be commended for serving the purpose that the Founding Fathers saw so clearly. In revealing the workings of government that led to the Vietnam war, the newspapers nobly did precisely that which the Founders hoped and trusted they would do.

* * *

[W]e are asked to hold that despite the First Amendment's emphatic command, the Executive Branch, the Congress, and the Judiciary can make laws enjoining publication of current news and abridging freedom of the press in the name of "national security." The Government does not even attempt to rely on any act of Congress. Instead it makes the bold and dangerously far-reaching contention that the courts should take it upon themselves to "make" a law abridging freedom of the press in the name of equity, presidential power and national security, even when the representatives of the people in Congress have adhered to the command of the First Amendment and refused to make such a law. * * * No one can read the history of the adoption of the First Amendment without being convinced beyond any doubt that it was injunctions like those sought here that Madison and his collaborators intended to outlaw in this Nation for all time.

The word "security" is a broad, vague generality whose contours should not be invoked to abrogate the fundamental law embodied in the First Amendment. The guarding of military and diplomatic secrets at the expense of informed representative government provides no real security for our Republic. The Framers of the First Amendment, fully aware of both the need to defend a new nation and the abuses of the English and Colonial Governments, sought to give this new society strength and security by providing that freedom of speech, press, religion, and assembly should not be abridged. * * *

Mr. Justice DOUGLAS, with whom Mr. Justice BLACK joins, concurring.

* * *

The Government says that it has inherent powers to go into court and obtain an injunction to protect the national interest, which in this case is alleged to be national security.

Near v. Minnesota ex rel. Olson, 283 U.S. 697, 51 S.Ct. 625, repudiated that expansive doctrine in no uncertain terms.

* * *

Secrecy in government is fundamentally anti-democratic, perpetuating bureaucratic errors. Open debate and discussion of public issues are vital to our national health. On public questions there should be "uninhibited, robust, and wide-open" debate. * * *

* * *

The stays in these cases that have been in effect for more than a week constitute a flouting of the principles of the First Amendment. * * *

Mr. Justice BRENNAN, concurring.

I write separately in these cases only to emphasize what should be apparent: that our judgments in the present cases may not be taken to indicate the propriety, in the future, of issuing temporary stays and restraining orders to block the publication of material sought to be suppressed by the Government. So far as I can determine, never before has the United States sought to enjoin a newspaper from publishing information in its possession. The relative novelty of the questions presented, the necessary haste with which decisions were reached, the magnitude of the interests asserted, and the fact that all the parties have concentrated their arguments upon the question whether permanent restraints were proper may have justified at least some of the restraints heretofore imposed in these cases. * * * But even if it be assumed that some of

the interim restraints were proper in the two cases before us, that assumption has no bearing upon the propriety of similar judicial action in the future. * * * [W]hatever values there may be in the preservation of novel questions for appellate review may not support any restraints in the future. * * * [T]he First Amendment stands as an absolute bar to the imposition of judicial restraints in circumstances of the kind presented by these cases.

* * *

Mr. Justice STEWART, with whom Mr. Justice WHITE joins, concurring.

In the governmental structure created by our Constitution, the Executive is endowed with enormous power in the two related areas of national defense and international relations. This power, largely unchecked by the Legislative and Judicial branches, has been pressed to the very hilt since the advent of the nuclear missile age. For better or for worse, the simple fact is that a President of the United States possesses vastly greater constitutional independence in these two vital areas of power than does, say, a prime minister of a country with a parliamentary form of government.

In the absence of the governmental checks and balances present in other areas of our national life, the only effective restraint upon executive policy and power in the areas of national defense and international affairs may lie in an enlightened citizenry—in an informed and critical public opinion which alone can here protect the values of democratic government. For this reason, it is perhaps here that a press that is alert, aware, and free most vitally serves the basic purpose of the First

Amendment. For without an informed and free press there cannot be an enlightened people.

Yet it is elementary that the successful conduct of international diplomacy and the maintenance of an effective national defense require both confidentiality and secrecy. Other nations can hardly deal with this Nation in an atmosphere of mutual trust unless they can be assured that their confidences will be kept. And within our own executive departments, the development of considered and intelligent international policies would be impossible if those charged with their formulation could not communicate with each other freely, frankly, and in confidence. In the area of basic national defense the frequent need for absolute secrecy is, of course, self-evident.

I think there can be but one answer to this dilemma, if dilemma it be. The responsibility must be where the power is. If the Constitution gives the Executive a large degree of unshared power in the conduct of foreign affairs and the maintenance of our national defense, then under the Constitution the Executive must have the largely unshared duty to determine and preserve the degree of internal security necessary to exercise that power successfully. It is an awesome responsibility, requiring judgment and wisdom of a high order. I should suppose that moral, political, and practical considerations would dictate that a very first principle of that wisdom would be an insistence upon avoiding secrecy for its own sake. For when everything is classified, then nothing is classified, and the system becomes one to be disregarded by the cynical or the careless, and to be manipulated by those intent on self-protection or self-promotion I

should suppose, in short, that the hallmark of a truly effective internal security system would be the maximum possible disclosure, recognizing that secrecy can best be preserved only when credibility is truly maintained. But be that as it may, it is clear to me that it is the constitutional duty of the Executive—as a matter of sovereign prerogative and not as a matter of law as the courts know law—through the promulgation and enforcement of executive regulations, to protect the confidentiality necessary to carry out its responsibilities in the fields of international relations and national defense.

*   *   *

[I]n the cases before us we are asked neither to construe specific regulations nor to apply specific laws. We are asked, instead, to perform a function that the Constitution gave to the Executive, not the Judiciary. We are asked, quite simply, to prevent the publication by two newspapers of material that the Executive Branch insists should not, in the national interest, be published. I am convinced that the Executive is correct with respect to some of the documents involved. But I cannot say that disclosure of any of them will surely result in direct, immediate, and irreparable damage to our Nation or its people. That being so, there can under the First Amendment be but one judicial resolution of the issues before us. I join the judgments of the Court.

Mr. Justice WHITE, with whom Mr. Justice STEWART joins, concurring.

I concur in today's judgments, but only because of the concededly extraordinary protection against prior restraints enjoyed by the press under our constitutional system. I do not say that in no circumstances would the First Amendment permit an injunction against publishing information about government plans or operations. Nor, after examining the materials the Government characterizes as the most sensitive and destructive, can I deny that revelation of these documents will do substantial damage to public interests. Indeed, I am confident that their disclosure will have that result. But I nevertheless agree that the United States has not satisfied the very heavy burden that it must meet to warrant an injunction against publication in these cases, at least in the absence of express and appropriately limited congressional authorization for prior restraints in circumstances such as these.

Mr. Justice MARSHALL, concurring.

The Government contends that the only issue in these cases is whether in a suit by the United States, "the First Amendment bars a court from prohibiting a newspaper from publishing material whose disclosure would pose a 'grave and immediate danger to the security of the United States.'" * * * With all due respect, I believe the ultimate issue in this case is even more basic than the one posed by the Solicitor General. The issue is whether this Court or the Congress has the power to make law.

* * *

It would * * * be utterly inconsistent with the concept of separation of powers for this Court to use its power of contempt to prevent behavior that Congress has specifically declined to prohibit. There would be a similar damage to the basic concept of these co-equal branches of Government if when the Execu-

tive Branch has adequate authority granted by Congress to protect "national security" it can choose instead to invoke the contempt power of a court to enjoin the threatened conduct. The Constitution provides that Congress shall make laws, the President execute laws, and courts interpret laws. * * * It did not provide for government by injunction in which the courts and the Executive Branch can "make law" without regard to the action of Congress. It may be more convenient for the Executive Branch if it need only convince a judge to prohibit conduct rather than ask the Congress to pass a law, and it may be more convenient to enforce a contempt order than to seek a criminal conviction in a jury trial. Moreover, it may be considered politically wise to get a court to share the responsibility for arresting those who the Executive Branch has probable cause to believe are violating the law. But convenience and political considerations of the moment do not justify a basic departure from the principles of our system of government.

* * *

[Justice MARSHALL then discussed at some length Congress's explicit rejection on two occasions, once in 1917 and again in 1957, of proposals to give the President the power to prohibit the publication during any national emergency emanating from war of any information which might endanger the national security.]

Mr. Chief Justice BURGER, dissenting.

* * *

I suggest * * * these cases have been conducted in unseemly haste. * * * The prompt settling of these cases reflects our universal abhorrence of prior restraint. But prompt judicial action does not mean unjudicial haste.

Here, moreover, the frenetic haste is due in large part to the manner in which the Times proceeded from the date it obtained the purloined documents. It seems reasonably clear now that the haste precluded reasonable and deliberate judicial treatment of these cases and was not warranted. * * *

The newspapers make a derivative claim under the First Amendment; they denominate this right as the public "right to know"; by implication, the Times asserts a sole trusteeship of that right by virtue of its journalistic "scoop." The right is asserted as an absolute. Of course, the First Amendment right itself is not an absolute, as Justice Holmes so long ago pointed out in his aphorism concerning the right to shout "fire" in a crowded theater if there was no fire. There are other exceptions, some of which Chief Justice Hughes mentioned by way of example in Near v. Minnesota ex rel. Olson. * * * An issue of this importance should be tried and heard in a judicial atmosphere conducive to thoughtful, reflective deliberation, especially when haste, in terms of hours, is unwarranted in light of the long period the Times, by its own choice, deferred publication.

It is not disputed that the Times has had unauthorized possession of the documents for three to four months, during which it has had its expert analysts studying them, presumably digesting them and preparing the material for publication. During all of this time, the Times, presumably in its capacity as trustee of the public's "right to know," has held up publication for purposes it considered proper and thus public knowledge was delayed. No doubt this was for a good reason; the analysis of 7,000 pages of complex material drawn from a vastly greater volume of material would inevitably take time and the writing of good news stories takes time. But why should the United States Government, from whom this information was illegally acquired by someone, along with all the counsel, trial judges, and appellate judges be placed under needless pressure? After these months of deferral, the alleged "right to know" has somehow and suddenly become a right that must be vindicated instanter.

Would it have been unreasonable, since the newspaper could anticipate the Government's objections to release of secret material, to give the Government an opportunity to review the entire collection and determine whether agreement could be reached on publication? Stolen or not, if security was not in fact jeopardized, much of the material could no doubt have been declassified, since it spans a period ending in 1968. With such an approach—one that great newspapers have in the past practiced and stated editorially to be the duty of an honorable press—the newspapers and Government might well have narrowed the area of disagreement as to what was and was not punishable, leaving the remainder to be resolved in orderly litigation, if necessary. To me it is hardly believable that a newspaper long regarded as a great institution in American life would fail to perform one of the basic and simple duties of every citizen with respect to the discovery or possession of stolen property or secret government documents. That duty, I had thought—perhaps naively—was to report forthwith, to responsible public officers. This duty rests on taxi drivers, Justices, and the New York Times. The course followed by the Times, whether so calculated or not, removed any possibility of orderly litigation of the issues. If the action of the judges up to now has been correct, that result is sheer happenstance.

* * *

Mr. Justice HARLAN, with whom THE CHIEF JUSTICE and Mr. Justice BLACKMUN join, dissenting.

* * * With all respect, I consider that the Court has been almost irresponsibly feverish in dealing with these cases.

* * *

This frenzied train of events took place in the name of the presumption against prior restraints created by the First Amendment. Due regard for the extraordinarily important and difficult questions involved in these litigations should have led the Court to shun such a precipitate timetable. In order to decide the merits of these cases properly, some or all of the following questions should have been faced:

1. Whether the Attorney General is authorized to bring these suits in the name of the United States. * * *

2. Whether the First Amendment permits the federal courts to enjoin publication of stories which would present a serious threat to national security. * * *

3. Whether the threat to publish highly secret documents is of itself a sufficient implication of national security to justify an injunction on the theory that regardless of the contents of the documents harm enough

results simply from the demonstration of such a breach of secrecy.

4. Whether the unauthorized disclosure of any of these particular documents would seriously impair the national security.

5. What weight should be given to the opinion of high officers in the Executive Branch of the Government with respect to questions 3 and 4.

6. Whether the newspapers are entitled to retain and use the documents notwithstanding the seemingly uncontested facts that the documents, or the originals of which they are duplicates, were purloined from the Government's possession and that the newspapers received them with knowledge that they had been feloniously acquired. * * *

7. Whether the threatened harm to the national security or the Government's possessory interest in the documents justifies the issuance of an injunction against publication in light of—

a. The strong First Amendment policy against prior restraints on publication;

b. The doctrine against enjoining conduct in violation of criminal statutes; and

c. The extent to which the materials at issue have apparently already been otherwise disseminated.

These are difficult questions of fact, of law, and of judgment; the potential consequences of erroneous decision are enormous. The time which has been available to us, to the lower courts, and to the parties has been wholly inadequate for giving these cases the kind of consideration they deserve. It is a reflection on the stability of the judicial process that these great issues—as important as any that have arisen during my time on the Court—should have been decided under the pressures engendered by the torrent of publicity that has attended these litigations from their inception.

Forced as I am to reach the merits of these cases, I dissent from the opinion and judgments of the Court.

*   *   *

[Justice BLACKMUN also dissented.]

Congress, in 1966, created a *statutory* "right to know" when it passed the Freedom of Information Act, which now constitutes § 552 of Title 5 of the United States Code Annotated. The aim of the law was to enhance public access to and understanding of the operation of federal agencies both in respect to the information held by them and in the formulation of public policy. With this in mind, Congress required federal agencies to publish in the Federal Register: descriptions of an agency's central and field organization, together with an explanation of how individuals might obtain information, make requests, or obtain judgments; statements with respect to the general functioning and operation of the agency; procedures and forms by which to do business with the agency; and statements of substantive policy, regulations, and rules of interpretation. The law also mandated federal agencies to make available for inspection and copying by the public: final opinions of all kinds and orders in the adjudication of cases; policy statements, regulations, and interpretive rules not published in the Federal Register; and staff manuals and staff instructions that affect any member of the public. The act further authorized any party who alleged that he was prohibited access to these materials to file suit in federal district court for an order directing their disclosure. The law also assigned such suits priority hearing in the federal courts. A final section of the act excluded from public disclosure among other things such items as: defense and foreign policy secrets, internal agency personnel rules and practices, employees' personnel and medical files, trade secrets, investigatory files, and geological maps.

As uneasiness over governmental secrecy grew with the transgressions of the Watergate era, Congress amended the act significantly in 1974. Highlighting this effort to penetrate bureaucratic secrecy were provisions which: (1) required agencies to maintain indices available to the public of all materials open to public inspection; (2) provided for *de novo* determination by the federal courts as to whether agency materials in question were justifiably classified and thus legitimately to be kept from public view; (3) specified contempt of court or disciplinary measures to be taken against recalcitrant federal employees judged to have withheld public materials; (4) mandated a timely response and devised appropriate procedures for agency response to a request for information by a member of the public; (5) directed the Attorney General annually to report to Congress on the disposition of all FOIA cases; and (6) extended the meaning of the term "agency" in the act to include all establishments in the executive branch, including the Executive Office of the President.

In August 1971, Martin Cohn's seventeen-year-old daughter, Cynthia, was raped. She suffocated in the course of the attack. While covering the criminal proceedings against the six youths who were subsequently indicted for her rape and murder, Wassell, a reporter, learned the victim's name. The same day he broadcasted her name as part of a news report over a television station operated by his employer, Cox Broadcasting Corporation. Georgia law made it a misdemeanor to publicize the name of a rape victim, and Cohn, relying upon that statute and alleging that his privacy had been invaded by its violation, brought an action for money damages. The trial court agreed and awarded a summary judgment to Cohn with damages to be determined later by jury trial. On appeal and subsequent rehearing the Georgia Supreme Court held: (1) that the misdemeanor statute failed to support a cause for civil action but that a civil suit was supported by a common-law tort for invasion of privacy; (2) that the case was not appropriate for summary judgment but should have been sent to a jury for a determination of the facts; (3) that Cohn should be required to establish that the reporter and broadcasting company "invaded his privacy with willful or negligent disregard for the fact that reasonable men would find the invasion highly offensive"; and (4) that the name of a rape victim was not a matter of public concern and hence not necessarily within the range of journalistic activity protected by the First Amendment. On appeal the U.S. Supreme Court in the initial segment of its opinion concluded that it had jurisdiction since the state supreme court had rendered a final judgment as to the constitutional issue raised in the case. The Supreme Court in Cox Broadcasting Corp. v. Cohn, 420 U.S. 469, 95 S.Ct. 1029 (1975), reversed the judgment below. Addressing the question "whether the State may impose sanctions on the accurate publication of the name of a rape victim obtained from public records—more specifically, from judicial records which are maintained in connection with a public prosecution and which themselves are open to public inspection," the Court, per Justice White, held that "the State may not do so." Observing at the outset that, "[w]ith respect to judicial proceedings in particular, the function of the press serves to guarantee the fairness of trials and to bring to bear the beneficial effects of public scrutiny upon the administration of justice" and that "even the prevailing law of invasion of privacy generally recognizes that the interests in privacy fade when the information involved already appears on the public record," Justice White reasoned:

> By placing the information in the public domain on official court records, the State must be presumed to have concluded that the public interest was thereby being served. Public records by their very nature are of interest to those concerned with the administration of government, and a public benefit is performed by the reporting of the true contents of the records by the media. The freedom of the press to publish that information appears to us to be of critical importance to our type of government in which the citizenry is the final judge of the proper conduct of public business. In preserving that form of government the First and Fourteenth Amendments command nothing less than that the States may not impose sanctions for the publication of truthful information contained in official court records open to public inspection.

> We are reluctant to embark on a course that would make public records generally available to the media but forbid their publication if offensive to the sensibilities of the supposed reasonable man. Such a rule would make it very difficult for the press to inform their readers about the public business and yet stay within the law. The rule would invite timidity and self-censorship and very likely lead to the suppression of many items that would otherwise be put into print and that should be made available to the public. At the very least, the First and Fourteenth Amendments will not allow exposing the press to liability for truthfully publishing information released to the public in official court records. If there are privacy interests to be protected in judicial proceedings, the States must respond by means which

avoid public documentation or other exposure of private information. Their political institutions must weigh the interests in privacy with the interests of the public to know and of the press to publish. Once true information is disclosed in public court documents open to public inspection, the press cannot be sanctioned for publishing it. In this instance as in others reliance must rest upon the judgment of those who decide what to publish or broadcast. * * *

CASES ON THE CONSTITUTIONALITY OF CRIMINAL SANCTIONS IMPOSED FOR NEWSPAPER PUBLICATION OF LAWFULLY OBTAINED CONFIDENTIAL INFORMATION

Case	Ruling
Landmark Communications, Inc. v. Commonwealth of Virginia, 435 U.S. 829, 98 S.Ct. 1535 (1978)	Where a Virginia law that made it a criminal offense to divulge information relating to an inquiry underway by the state's commission on judicial conduct was applied to punish third persons, including news media, for divulging or publishing truthful information regarding such confidential proceedings, the Court held that "neither the Commonwealth's interest in protecting the reputation of its judges nor in maintaining the institutional integrity of its courts is sufficient to justify the subsequent punishment of speech at issue here, even on the assumption that criminal sanctions do in fact enhance the guarantee of confidentiality." This was not a case involving "the possible applicability of the statute to one who secures information by illegal means and thereafter divulges it." Articulating the principle implicit in previous cases, Chief Justice Burger, for the Court, wrote: "What emerges from these cases is the 'working principle that the substantive evil must be extremely serious and the degree of imminence extremely high before utterances can be punished.' * * *."
Smith v. Daily Mail Publishing Co., 443 U.S. 97, 99 S.Ct. 2667 (1979)	Newspapers were indicted for violating a West Virginia statute that made it a misdemeanor to publish the name of any youth charged as a juvenile without first obtaining permission from the juvenile court when, after obtaining the name of a juvenile arrested in the shooting death of another junior high school student by monitoring police radio band frequencies and by asking several eyewitnesses, they published the arrested juvenile's name in articles on the shooting. After observing that there was no issue in this case of unlawful press access to confidential proceedings or of privacy or prejudicial pretrial publicity but only "the power of a state to punish the truthful publication of an alleged juvenile delinquent's name lawfully obtained by the newspaper," the Court, per Chief Justice Burger, noted that "if a newspaper lawfully obtains truthful information about a matter of public significance then state officials may not constitutionally punish publication of the information, absent a need to further a state interest of the highest order."

SANCTIONS FOR PUBLICATION (*Cont.*)

Case	Ruling
Smith (*Cont.*)	The Court found the asserted state interests here insufficient and the statute flawed because it applied only to newspapers but not to dissemination of the information by the electronic media or other sorts of publications. "In addition," the Court added, "there is no evidence to demonstrate that the imposition of criminal penalties is necessary to protect the confidentiality of juvenile proceedings."

BRANZBURG v. HAYES

Supreme Court of the United States, 1972
408 U.S. 665, 92 S.Ct. 2646, 33 L.Ed.2d 626

The Supreme Court granted certiorari to review several cases involving the refusal of newsmen to reveal the identity of confidential sources of information before grand jury investigations of criminal activity. In one case, Paul Branzburg, a reporter for the *Louisville Courier-Journal*, who had written an article on processing hashish from marijuana, was ordered by a judge to answer questions of a grand jury concerning the identity of the individuals he had observed making the hashish. Branzburg refused to comply and brought proceedings to restrain Judge John Hayes from imposing a contempt ruling. The Kentucky Court of Appeals denied Branzburg's petition for relief rejecting his claim that immunity against such compelled testimony flowed from the guarantees of a free press contained in the First and Fourteenth Amendments.

In the companion cases two newsmen, Pappas and Caldwell, refused to testify before grand juries whose inquiries touched on the Black Panthers. Pappas declined to answer questions about what he saw and heard during the time he remained in Panther headquarters while covering "civil disorders" in New Bedford, Massachusetts even though no articles or publications were produced by him following the events. And, in response to queries put to him by a federal panel investigating threats against the President and interstate travel to incite riots, Caldwell refused to discuss interviews he had had with militants.

Opinion of the Court by Mr. Justice WHITE, announced by The CHIEF JUSTICE [BURGER].

The issue in these cases is whether requiring newsmen to appear and testify before State or federal grand juries abridges the freedom of speech and press guaranteed by the First Amendment. We hold that it does not.

* * *

Petitioners * * * press First Amendment claims that may be simply put: that to gather news it is oft-

en necessary to agree either not to identify the source of information published or to publish only part of the facts revealed, or both; that if the reporter is nevertheless forced to reveal these confidences to a grand jury, the source so identified and other confidential sources of other reporters will be measurably deterred from furnishing publishable information, all to the detriment of the free flow of information protected by the First Amendment. Although petitioners do not claim an absolute privilege against official interrogation in all circumstances, they assert that the reporter should not be forced either to appear or to testify before a grand jury or at trial until and unless sufficient grounds are shown for believing that the reporter possesses information relevant to a crime the grand jury is investigating, that the information the reporter has is unavailable from other sources, and that the need for the information is sufficiently compelling to override the claimed invasion of First Amendment interests occasioned by the disclosure. Principally relied upon are prior cases emphasizing the importance of the First Amendment guarantees to individual development and to our system of representative government, decisions requiring that official action with adverse impact on First Amendment rights be justified by a public interest that is "compelling" or "paramount," and those precedents establishing the principle that justifiable governmental goals may not be achieved by unduly broad means having an unnecessary impact on protected rights of speech, press, or association. The heart of the claim is that the burden on news gathering resulting from compelling reporters to disclose confidential information outweighs any public interest in obtaining the information.

* * *

It is clear that the First Amendment does not invalidate every incidental burdening of the press that may result from the enforcement of civil or criminal statutes of general applicability. Under prior cases, otherwise valid laws serving substantial public interests may be enforced against the press as against others, despite the possible burden that may be imposed. The Court has emphasized that "[t]he publisher of a newspaper has no special immunity from

the application of general laws. He has no special privilege to invade the rights and liberties of others." Associated Press v. NLRB, 301 U.S. 103, 132–133, 57 S.Ct. 650, 656 (1937). It was there held that the Associated Press * * * was not exempt from the requirements of the National Labor Relations Act. * * * Associated Press v. United States, 326 U.S. 1, 65 S.Ct. 1416 (1945), similarly overruled assertions that the First Amendment precluded application of the Sherman Act to a news gathering and disseminating organization. * * * Likewise, a newspaper may be subjected to nondiscriminatory forms of general taxation. Grosjean v. American Press Co., 297 U.S. 233, 250, 56 S.Ct. 444, 449. * * *

The prevailing view is that the press is not free with impunity to publish everything and anything it desires to publish. Although it may deter or regulate what is said or published, the press may not circulate knowing or reckless falsehoods damaging to private reputation without subjecting itself to liability for damages, including punitive damages, or even criminal prosecution. * * * A newspaper or a journalist may also be punished for contempt of court, in appropriate circumstances. Craig v. Harney, 331 U.S. 367, 377–378, 67 S.Ct. 1249, 1255–1256 (1947).

It has generally been held that the First Amendment does not guarantee the press a constitutional right of special access to information not available to the public generally. * * *

Despite the fact that news gathering may be hampered, the press is regularly excluded from grand jury proceedings, our own conferences, the meetings of other official bodies gathered in executive session, and the meetings of private organizations. Newsmen have no constitutional right of access to the scenes of crime or disaster when the general public is excluded, and they may be prohibited from attending or publishing information about trials if such restrictions are necessary to assure a defendant a fair trial before an impartial tribunal. * * *

It is thus not surprising that the great weight of authority is that newsmen are not exempt from the normal duty of appearing before a grand jury and answering questions relevant to a criminal investigation. At common law, courts consistently refused to recognize the existence of any privilege authorizing a newsman to refuse to reveal confidential information to a grand jury. * * *

* * *

A number of States have provided newsmen a statutory privilege of varying breadth, but the majority have not done so, and none has been provided by federal statute. Until now the only testimonial privilege for unofficial witnesses that is rooted in the Federal Constitution is the Fifth Amendment privilege against compelled self-incrimination. We are asked to create another by interpreting the First Amendment to grant newsmen a testimonial privilege that other citizens do not enjoy. This we decline to do. * * *

* * *

Finally, as we have earlier indicated, news gathering is not without its First Amendment protections, and grand jury investigations if instituted or conducted other than in good faith, would pose wholly different issues for resolution under the First Amendment. Official harassment of the press undertaken not for purposes of law enforcement but to disrupt a reporter's relationship with his news sources would have no justification. * * * We do not expect courts will forget that grand juries must operate within the limits of the First Amendment as well as the Fifth.

[Affirmed.]

Mr. Justice STEWART, with whom Mr. Justice BRENNAN and Mr. Justice MARSHALL, join, dissenting.

The Court's crabbed view of the First Amendment reflects a disturbing insensitivity to the critical role of an independent press in our society. * * * [T]he Court in these cases holds that a newsman has no First Amendment right to protect his sources when called before a grand jury. The Court thus invites state and federal authorities to undermine the historic independence of the press by attempting to annex the journalistic profession as an investigative arm of government. Not only will this decision impair performance of the press' constitutionally protected functions, but it will, I am convinced, in the long run, harm rather than help the administration of justice.

* * *

The impairment of the flow of news cannot, of course, be proven with scientific precision, as the Court seems to demand. Obviously, not every news-gathering relationship requires confidentiality. And it is difficult to pinpoint precisely how many relationships do require a promise or understanding of nondisclosure. But we have never before demanded that First Amendment rights rest on elaborate empirical studies demonstrating beyond any conceivable doubt that deterrent effects exist; we have never before required proof of the exact number of people potentially affected by governmental action, who would actually be dissuaded from engaging in First Amendment activity.

* * *

Accordingly, when a reporter is asked to appear before a grand jury and reveal confidences, I would hold that the government must (1) show that there is probable cause to believe that the newsman has information which is clearly relevant to a specific probable violation of law; (2) demonstrate that the information sought cannot be obtained by alternative means less destructive of First Amendment rights; and (3) demonstrate a compelling and overriding interest in the information.

* * *

Mr Justice DOUGLAS, dissenting.

* * *

The intrusion of government into this domain is symptomatic of the disease of this society. As the years pass the power of government becomes more and more pervasive. It is a power to suffocate both people and causes. Those in power, whatever their politics, want only to perpetuate it. Now that the fences of the law and the tradition that has protected the press are broken down, the people are the victims. The First Amendment, as I read it, was designed precisely to prevent that tragedy.

Myron Farber, a reporter, and the New York Times Company, his employer, were each charged with civil and criminal contempt for refusal to produce certain subpoenaed materials for *in camera* inspection by the judge in the murder trial of Dr. Mario E. Jascalevich. Jascalevich was alleged to have brought about the deaths of several of his patients by administering doses of the drug curare. Farber's investigative reporting was said to have contributed significantly to the decision to prosecute Dr. Jascalevich. Indeed, Farber was alleged to have worked closely with the prosecutor's office for some time and, in the defense's view, was the driving force in getting the case to court. The defense contended that Farber had in his possession notes, statements, and other materials relevant to information supplied by half a dozen of the state's witnesses (one of whom had died and others of whom had made themselves inaccessible to the defense) presumed to bear directly on the guilt or innocence of the defendant. For willful violation of the trial judge's order, the New York Times Company was fined $100,000, and Farber was ordered ultimately to serve a six-month jail sentence and to pay a $1,000 fine. Furthermore, in order to compel production of the materials, the Times was ordered to pay $5,000 a day for each day that elapsed until compliance with the court order, and Farber was jailed until he decided to comply with the subpoena. A New Jersey appellate court denied applications to stay the order, as did two separate Justices of the U. S. Supreme Court. Farber and the Times subsequently appealed to the New Jersey Supreme Court. They argued that the contempt citations could not stand because the trial judge's order to produce the materials for *in camera* inspection violated both the First Amendment and a New Jersey "shield law" which guaranteed the confidentiality of a reporter's source materials.

In Matter of Farber and the New York Times Co., 78 N.J. 259, 394 A.2d 330 (1978), the New Jersey Supreme Court upheld both the subpoena *duces tecum* and the contempt citations. The court found the First Amendment contention already settled by decision of the U. S. Supreme Court. Said the New Jersey court:

> In our view the Supreme Court of the United States has clearly rejected this claim and has squarely held that no such First Amendment right exists. * * *

* * *

> [W]e do no weighing or balancing of societal interests in reaching our determination that the First Amendment does not afford appellants the privilege they claim. The weighing and balancing has been done by a higher court. Our conclusion that appellants cannot derive the protection they seek from the First Amendment rests upon the fact that the ruling in *Branzburg* is binding upon us and we interpret it as applicable to, and clearly including, the particular issues framed here. It follows that the obligation to appear at a criminal trial on behalf of a defendant who is enforcing his Sixth Amendment rights is at least as compelling as the duty to appear before a grand jury.

The court then turned its attention to the statutory provision, observing, "In *Branzburg* no shield law was involved. Here we have a shield law, said to be as strongly worded as any in the country." In pertinent part, the statute reads as follows:

> [A] person * * * connected with, or employed by news media for the purpose of gathering * * * or disseminating news for the general public or on whose behalf news is so gathered * * * or disseminated has a privilege to refuse to disclose, in any legal or quasi-legal proceeding or before any investigative body, including, but not limited to, any court, grand jury, petit jury, administrative agency, the Legislature or legislative committee, or elsewhere
>
>   a. The source * * * from or through whom any information was procured [;] * * * and
>
>   b. Any news or information obtained in the course of pursuing his professional activities whether or not it is disseminated.

Although it observed that the legislation was facially constitutional, the New Jersey court believed that it conflicted with the Sixth Amendment guarantee for the defendant at trial "to have compulsory process for obtaining witnesses in his favor" and an identical provision contained in Article 1, ¶ 10 of the state constitution. As the New Jersey court took pains to note, the Sixth Amendment guarantee was incorporated into the Due Process Clause of the Fourteenth and thus made applicable to the states in Washington v. Texas, 388 U.S. 14, 87 S.Ct. 1920 (1967). The court found further support for subordinating the statutory privilege to Sixth Amendment considerations citing the Supreme Court's decision in United States v. Nixon, 418 U.S. 683, 94 S.Ct. 3090 (1974), about which it said, "Despite th[e] conclusion that at least to some extent a president's executive privilege derives from the Constitution, the Court nonetheless concluded that the demands of our criminal justice system required that the privilege must yield." Resting its decision ultimately on the parallel confrontation and compulsory process provision of the state constitution, the New Jersey court explained:

> We interpret it as affording a defendant in a criminal prosecution the right to compel the attendance of witnesses and the production of documents and other material for which he may have, or may believe he has, a legitimate need in preparing or undertaking his defense. It also means that witnesses properly summoned will be required to testify and that material demanded by a properly phrased *subpoena duces tecum* will be forthcoming and available for appropriate examination and use.

Although the court held that "Article 1, ¶ 10 of our Constitution prevails over this statute," it prescribed several safeguards "in recognition of the strongly expressed legislative viewpoint favoring confidentiality * * *." Chief among these was the guarantee of a full hearing *in camera* "on the issues of relevance, materiality, and overbreadth of the subpoena." The court continued:

> The trial court recognized its obligation to conduct such a hearing, but the appellants have aborted that hearing by refusing to submit the material subpoenaed for an *in camera* inspection by the court to assist it in determining the motion to quash. That inspection is no more than a procedural tool, a device to be used to ascertain the relevancy and materiality of that material. Such an *in camera* inspection is not in itself an invasion of the statutory privilege. Rather it is a preliminary step to determine whether, and if so to what extent, the statutory privilege must yield to the defendant's constitutional rights.

> Appellants' position is that there must be a full showing and definitive judicial determination of relevance, materiality, absence of less intrusive access, and need, prior to any *in camera* inspection. The obvious objection to such a rule, however, is that it would, in many cases, effectively stultify the judicial criminal process. It might well do so here. The defendant properly recognizes Myron Farber as a unique repository of pertinent information. But he does not know the extent of this information nor is it possible for him to specify all of it with particularity, nor to tailor his subpoena to precise materials of which he is ignorant. Well aware of this, Judge Arnold refused to give ultimate rulings with respect to relevance and other preliminary matters until he had examined the material. We think he had no other course. It is not rational to ask a judge to ponder the relevance of the unknown.

> The same objection applies with equal force to the contention that the subpoena is overbroad. Appellants do not assert that the subpoena is vague and uncertain, but that the data requested may not be relevant and material. To deal effectively with this assertion it is not only appropriate but absolutely necessary for the trial court to inspect *in camera* the subpoenaed items so that it can make its determinations on the basis of concrete materials rather than in a vacuum. * * *

The court also held that in deference "to the very positively expressed legislative intent to protect the confidentiality and secrecy of sources from which the media derive information," newsmen in such situations are entitled to a preliminary hearing "before being compelled to submit the subpoenaed material to a trial judge for such inspection." The court explained:

> The threshold determination would normally follow the service of a subpoena by a defendant upon a newspaper, a reporter or other representative of the media. The latter foreseeably would respond with a motion to quash. If the status of the movant—newspaper or media representative—were not conceded, then there would follow the taking of proofs leading to a determination that the movant did or did not qualify for the statutory privilege. Assuming qualification, it would then become the obligation of the defense to satisfy the trial judge, by a fair preponderance of the evidence including all reasonable inferences, that there was a reasonable probability or likelihood that the information sought by the subpoena was material and relevant to his defense, that it could not be secured from any less intrusive source, and that the defendant had a legitimate need to see and otherwise use it.

And the court added a caveat:

> The manner in which the obligation of the defendant is to be discharged in the proceedings leading to this threshold determination will depend largely upon the facts of the particular case. We wish to make it clear, however, that this opinion is not to be taken as a license for a fishing expedition in every criminal case where there has been investigative reporting, nor as permission for an indiscriminate rummaging through newspaper files.

Two Justices on the seven-man New Jersey court dissented, largely on the grounds that Farber and the New York Times "were denied 'an opportunity to be heard' prior to the imposition of sanctions against them   *   *   *" as to the possible invalidity of the subpoenas *duces tecum* and the applicability of the newsman's privilege and that, in view of the lack of adequate fact finding prior to ordering *in camera* inspection of the materials, the present record was insufficient "to justify the judgments of contempt." When Farber and the New York Times sought review by the Supreme Court, the Court denied certiorari, 439 U.S. 997, 99 S.Ct. 598 (1978).

Following the decision in *Farber*, the New Jersey legislature passed amendments to the shield statute requiring the party seeking enforcement of such a subpoena to show that the materials sought were necessary to the defense and were not available from any less intrusive source or that clear and convincing evidence demonstrated that the privilege had been waived. Such a determination was to precede any *in camera* inspection of material by the trial judge. The New Jersey Supreme Court subsequently applied and upheld the amended statute in the context of another criminal case in State v. Boiardo, 82 N.J. 446, 414 A.2d 14 (1980). In Maressa v. New Jersey Monthly, 89 N.J. 176, 445 A.2d 376 (1982), a libel case, the New Jersey Supreme Court held "that the New Jersey Shield Law affords newspersons an absolute privilege not to disclose confidential sources and editorial processes, absent any conflicting constitutional right." Since plaintiffs in defamation suits have no overriding constitutional interests at stake, inquiry into the editorial processes was absolutely precluded by the shield law in such a suit.

See *Zurcher* v. *Stanford Daily* at p. 1125 and the note following it on the Privacy Protection Act of 1980 at p. 1128.

MIAMI HERALD PUBLISHING CO. v. TORNILLO

Supreme Court of the United States, 1974
418 U.S. 241, 94 S.Ct. 2831, 41 L.Ed.2d 730

A Florida "right to reply" statute required any newspaper attacking a candidate for public office to make available to him equal space to rebut the criticism. Noncompliance constituted a misdemeanor. Pat Tornillo, the Executive Director of the Classroom Teachers Association and a candidate for election to the Florida House of Representatives, was the butt of a Miami Herald editorial questioning his fitness for office and castigating his leadership as a bargaining agent for the teachers union as inimical to the public welfare. After the paper refused to print his reply, Tornillo brought suit in a state court. That court held the statute an infringement of the First Amendment guarantee of a free press, but the ruling was overturned on appeal by the Florida Supreme Court. The newspaper obtained certiorari from the United States Supreme Court.

Mr. Chief Justice BURGER delivered the opinion of the Court.

The issue in this case is whether a state statute granting a political candidate a right to equal space to reply to criticism and attacks on his record by a newspaper, violates the guarantees of a free press.

* * *

The challenged statute creates a right to reply to press criticism of a candidate for nomination or election. The statute was enacted in 1913 and this is only the second recorded case decided under its provisions.

Appellant contends the statute is void on its face because it purports to regulate the content of a newspaper in violation of the First Amendment. Alternatively it is urged that the statute is void for vagueness since no editor could know exactly what words would call the statute into operation. It is also contended that the statute fails to distinguish between critical comment which is and is not defamatory.

The appellee and supporting advocates of an enforceable right of access to the press vigorously argue that Government has an obligation to ensure that a wide variety of views reach the public. The contentions of access proponents will be set out in some detail. It is urged that at the time the First Amendment to the Constitution was enacted in 1791 as part of our Bill of Rights the press was broadly representative of the people it was serving. While many of the newspapers were intensely partisan and narrow in their views, the press collectively presented a broad range of opinions to readers. Entry into publishing was inexpensive; pamphlets and books provided meaningful alternatives to the organized press for the expression of unpopular ideas and often treated events and expressed views not covered by conventional newspapers. A true marketplace of ideas existed in which there was relatively easy access to the channels of communication.

Access advocates submit that although newspapers of the present are superficially similar to those of 1791 the press of today is in reality very different from that known in the early years of our national existence. In the past half century a communications revolution has seen the introduction of radio and television into our lives, the promise of a global community through the use of communications satellites, and the spectre of a "wired" nation by means of an expanding cable television network with two-way capabilities. The printed press, it is said, has not escaped the effects of this revolution. Newspapers have become big business and there are far fewer of them to serve a larger literate population. Chains of newspapers, national newspapers, national wire and news services, and one-newspaper towns, are the dominant features of a press that has become noncompetitive and enormously powerful and influential in its capacity to manipulate popular opinion and change the course of events. Major metropolitan newspapers have collaborated to establish news services national in scope. Such national news organizations provide syndicated "interpretative reporting" as well as syndicated features and commentary, all of which can serve as part of the new school of "advocacy journalism."

The elimination of competing newspapers in most of our large cities, and the concentration of control of media that results from the only newspaper being owned by the same interests which own a television station and a radio station, are important components of this trend toward concentration of control of outlets to inform the public.

The result of these vast changes has been to place in a few hands the power to inform the American people and shape public opinion. Much of the editorial opinion and commentary that is printed is that of syndicated columnists distributed nationwide and, as a result, we are told, on national and world issues there tends to be a homogeneity of editorial opinion, commentary, and interpretative

analysis. The abuses of bias and manipulative reportage are, likewise, said to be the result of the vast accumulations of unreviewable power in the modern media empires. In effect, it is claimed, the public has lost any ability to respond or to contribute in a meaningful way to the debate on issues. The monopoly of the means of communication allows for little or no critical analysis of the media except in professional journals of very limited readership.

"This concentration of nationwide news organizations—like other large institutions—has grown increasingly remote from and unresponsive to the popular constituencies on which they depend and which depend on them." Report of the Task Force, The Twentieth Century Fund Task Force Report for a National News Council, A Free and Responsive Press 4 (1973).

Appellees cite the report of the Commission on Freedom of the Press, chaired by Robert M. Hutchins, in which it was stated, as long ago as 1947, that "The right of free public expression has * * * lost its earlier reality." Commission on Freedom of the Press, A Free and Responsible Press 15.

The obvious solution, which was available to dissidents at an earlier time when entry into publishing was relatively inexpensive, today would be to have additional newspapers. But the same economic factors which have caused the disappearance of vast numbers of metropolitan newspapers, have made entry into the marketplace of ideas served by the print media almost impossible. It is urged that the claim of newspapers to be "surrogates for the public" carries with it a concomitant fiduciary obligation to account for that stewardship. From this premise it is reasoned that the only effective way to insure fairness and accuracy and to provide for some accountability is for government to take affirmative action. The First Amendment interest of the public in being informed is said to be in peril because the "marketplace of ideas" is today a monopoly controlled by the owners of the market.

Proponents of enforced access to the press take comfort from language in several of this Court's decisions which suggests that the First Amendment acts as a sword as well as a shield, that it imposes obligations on the owners of the press in addition to protecting the press from government regulation. * * *

* * *

Access advocates note that Mr. Justice Douglas a decade ago expressed his deep concern regarding the effects of newspaper monopolies:

"Where one paper has a monopoly in an area, it seldom presents two sides of an issue. It too often hammers away on one ideological or political line using its monopoly position not to educate people, not to promote debate, but to inculcate its readers with one philosophy, one attitude—and to make money. * * * The newspapers that give a variety of views and news that is not slanted or contrived are few indeed. And the problem promises to get worse." * * * The Great Right (Ed. by E. Cahn) 124–125, 127 (1963).

They also claim the qualified support of Professor Thomas I. Emerson, who has written that "[a] limited right of access to the press can be safely enforced," although he believes that "[g]overnment measures to encourage a multiplicity of outlets, rather than compelling a few

outlets to represent everybody, seems a preferable course of action." T. Emerson, The System of Freedom of Expression 671 (1970).

However much validity may be found in these arguments, at each point the implementation of a remedy such as an enforceable right of access necessarily calls for some mechanism, either governmental or consensual. If it is governmental coercion, this at once brings about a confrontation with the express provisions of the First Amendment and the judicial gloss on that amendment developed over the years.

* * *

Even if a newspaper would face no additional costs to comply with a compulsory access law and would not be forced to forego publication of news or opinion by the inclusion of a reply, the Florida statute fails to clear the barriers of the First Amendment because of its intrusion into the function of editors. A newspaper is more than a passive receptacle or conduit for news, comment, and advertising. The choice of material to go into a newspaper, and the decisions made as to limitations on the size of the paper, and content, and treatment of public issues and public officials—whether fair or unfair—constitutes the exercise of editorial control and judgment. It has yet to be demonstrated how governmental regulation of this crucial process can be exercised consistent with First Amendment guarantees of a free press as they have evolved to this time. Accordingly, the judgment of the Supreme Court of Florida is reversed.

* * *

Reversed.

Mr. Justice BRENNAN, with whom Mr. Justice REHNQUIST joins, concurring.

I join the Court's opinion which, as I understand it, addresses only "right of reply" statutes and implies no view upon the constitutionality of "retraction" statutes affording plaintiffs able to prove defamatory falsehoods a statutory action to require publication of a retraction. See generally Note, Vindication of the Reputation of a Public Official, 80 Harv.L. Rev. 1730, 1739–1747 (1967).

Mr. Justice WHITE, concurring.

The Court today holds that the First Amendment bars a State from requiring a newspaper to print the reply of a candidate for public office whose personal character has been criticized by that newspaper's editorials. According to our accepted jurisprudence, the First Amendment erects a virtually insurmountable barrier between government and the print media so far as government tampering, in advance of publication, with news and editorial content is concerned. * * * A newspaper or magazine is not a public utility subject to "reasonable" governmental regulation in matters affecting the exercise of journalistic judgment as to what shall be printed. * * * We have learned, and continue to learn, from what we view as the unhappy experiences of other nations where government has been allowed to meddle in the internal editorial affairs of newspapers. Regardless of how beneficent-sounding the purposes of controlling the press might be, we prefer "the power of reason as applied through public discussion" and remain intensely skeptical about those measures that would allow government to insinuate itself into the editorial rooms of this Nation's press.

* * *

Of course, the press is not always accurate, or even responsible, and may not present full and fair debate on important public issues. But the balance struck by the First Amendment with respect to the press is that society must take the risk that occasionally debate on vital matters will not be comprehensive and that all viewpoints may not be expressed. The press would be unlicensed because, in Jefferson's words, "[w]here the press is free, and every man able to read, all is safe." Any other accommodation—any other system that would supplant private control of the press with the heavy hand of government intrusion—would make the government the censor of what the people may read and know.

* * *

But though a newspaper may publish without government censorship, it has never been entirely free from liability for what it chooses to print. * * * Among other things, the press has not been wholly at liberty to publish falsehoods damaging to individual reputation. At least until today, we have cherished the average citizen's reputation interest enough to afford him a fair chance to vindicate himself in an action for libel characteristically provided by state law. He has been unable to force the press to tell his side of the story or to print a retraction, but he has had at least the opportunity to win a judgment if he can prove the falsity of the damaging publication, as well as a fair chance to recover reasonable damages for his injury.

* * *

One need not think less of the First Amendment to sustain reasonable methods for allowing the average citizen to redeem a falsely tarnished reputation. Nor does one have to doubt the genuine decency, integrity and good sense of the vast majority of professional journalists to support the right of any individual to have his day in court when he has been falsely maligned in the public press. The press is the servant, not the master, of the citizenry, and its freedom does not carry with it an unrestricted hunting license to prey on the ordinary citizen.

"In plain English, freedom carries with it responsibility even for the press; freedom of the press is not a freedom from responsibility for its exercise. * * *

" * * * Without * * * a lively sense of responsibility a free press may readily become a powerful instrument of injustice." Pennekamp v. Florida, 328 U.S. 331, 356, 365, 66 S.Ct. 1029, 1042 (1946) (Frankfurter, J., concurring) (footnote omitted).

To me it is a near absurdity to so deprecate individual dignity * * * and to leave the people at the complete mercy of the press, at least in this stage of our history when the press, as the majority in this case so well documents, is steadily becoming more powerful and much less likely to be deterred by threats of libel suits.

FIRST NATIONAL BANK OF BOSTON v. BELLOTTI

Supreme Court of the United States, 1978
435 U.S. 765, 98 S.Ct. 1407, 55 L.Ed.2d 707

For a description of the facts in this case, see p. 1342.

Mr. Chief Justice BURGER, concurring.

I join the opinion and judgment of the Court but write separately to raise some questions likely to arise in this area in the future.

A disquieting aspect of Massachusetts' position is that it may carry the risk of impinging on the First Amendment rights of those who employ the corporate form—as most do—to carry on the business of mass communications, particularly the large media conglomerates. This is so because of the difficulty, and perhaps impossibility, of distinguishing, either as a matter of fact or constitutional law, media corporations from corporations such as the appellants in this case.

Making traditional use of the corporate form, some media enterprises have amassed vast wealth and power and conduct many activities, some directly related—and some not—to their publishing and broadcasting activities. See Miami Herald Publishing Co. v. Tornillo, 418 U.S. 241, 248–254, 94 S.Ct. 2831, 2835–2838 (1974). Today, a corporation might own the dominant newspaper in one or more large metropolitan centers, television and radio stations in those same centers and others, a newspaper chain, news magazines with nationwide circulation, national or worldwide wire news services, and substantial interests in book publishing and distribution enterprises. Corporate ownership may extend, vertically, to pulp mills and pulp timber lands to insure an adequate, continuing supply of newsprint and to trucking and steamship lines for the purpose of transporting the newsprint to the presses. Such activities would be logical economic auxiliaries to a publishing conglomerate. Ownership also may extend beyond to business activities unrelated to the task of publishing newspapers and magazines or broadcasting radio and television programs. Obviously, such far-reaching ownership would not be possible without the state-provided corporate form and its "special rules relating to such matters as limited liability, perpetual life, and the accumulation, distribution, and taxation of assets." * * * (WHITE, J., dissenting).

In terms of "unfair advantage in the political process" and "corporate domination of the electoral process," * * * it could be argued that such media conglomerates as I describe pose a much more realistic threat to valid interests than do appellants and similar entities not regularly concerned with shaping popular opinion on public issues. * * *

In terms of Massachusetts' other concern, the interests of minority shareholders, I perceive no basis for saying that the managers and directors of the media conglomerates are more or less sensitive to the views and desires of minority shareholders than are corporate officers generally. Nor can it be said, even if relevant to First Amendment analysis—which it is not—that the former are more virtuous, wise or restrained in the exercise of corporate power than are the latter. * * * Thus, no factual distinction has been identified as yet

that would justify government restraints on the right of appellants to express their views without, at the same time, opening the door to similar restraints on media conglomerates with their vastly greater influence.

Despite these factual similarities between media and nonmedia corporations, those who view the Press Clause as somehow conferring special and extraordinary privileges or status on the "institutional press"—which are not extended to those who wish to express ideas other than by publishing a newspaper—might perceive no danger to institutional media corporations flowing from the position asserted by Masachusetts. Under this narrow reading of the Press Clause, government could perhaps impose on nonmedia corporations restrictions not permissible with respect to "media" enterprises. * * * The Court has not yet squarely resolved whether the Press Clause confers upon the "institutional press" any freedom from government restraint not enjoyed by all others.

I perceive two fundamental difficulties with a narrow reading of the Press Clause. First, although certainty on this point is not possible, the history of the Clause does not suggest that the authors contemplated a "special" or "institutional" privilege. * * *

Indeed most pre-First Amendment commentators "who employed the term 'freedom of speech' with great frequency, used it synonymously with freedom of the press." L. Levy, Legacy of Suppression: Freedom of Speech and Press in Early American History 174 (1963).

Those interpreting the Press Clause as extending protection only to, or creating a special role for, the "institutional press" must either (a) assert such an intention on the part of the Framers for which no supporting evidence is available, * * * (b) argue that events after 1791 somehow operated to "constitutionalize" this intepretation, * * * or (c) candidly acknowledging the absence of historical support, suggest that the intent of the Framers is not important today. * * *

To conclude that the Framers did not intend to limit the freedom of the press to one select group is not necessarily to suggest that the Press Clause is redundant. The Speech Clause standing alone may be viewed as a protection of the liberty to express ideas and beliefs, while the Press Clause focuses specifically on the liberty to disseminate expression broadly and "comprehends every sort of publication which affords a vehicle of information and opinion." Lovell v. Griffin, 303 U.S. 444, 452, 58 S.Ct. 666, 669 (1938). Yet there is no fundamental distinction between expression and dissemination. The liberty encompassed by the Press Clause, although complementary to and a natural extension of Speech Clause liberty, merited special mention simply because it had been more often the object of official restraints. Soon after the invention of the printing press, English and continental monarchs, fearful of the power implicit in its use and the threat to Establishment thought and order— political and religious—devised restraints, such as licensing, censors, indices of prohibited books, and prosecutions for seditious libel, which generally were unknown in the pre-printing press era. Official restrictions were the official response to the new, disquieting idea that this in-

vention would provide a means for mass communication.

The second fundamental difficulty with intepreting the Press Clause as conferring special status on a limited group is one of definition. * * * The very task of including some entities within the "institutional press" while excluding others, whether undertaken by legislature, court or administrative agency, is reminiscent of the abhorred licensing system of Tudor and Stuart England—a system the First Amendment was intended to ban from this country. * * * Further, the officials undertaking that task would be required to distinguish the protected from the unprotected on the basis of such variables as content of expression, frequency or fervor of expression, or ownership of the technological means of dissemination. Yet nothing in this Court's opinions supports such a confining approach to the scope of Press Clause protection. Indeed, the Court has plainly intimated the contrary view:

"Freedom of the press is a 'fundamental personal right' which 'is not confined to newspapers and periodicals. It necessarily embraces pamphlets and leaflets. * * * The press in its historic connotation comprehends every sort of publication which affords a vehicle of information and opinion.' * * * The information function asserted by representatives of the organized press * * * is also performed by lecturers, political pollsters, novelists, academic researchers, and dramatists. Almost any author may quite accurately assert that he is contributing to the flow of information to the public." * * * Branzburg v. Hayes, 408 U.S. 665, 704–705, 92 S.Ct. 2646,

2668 (1972), quoting Lovell v. Griffin, supra, 303 U.S., at 450, 452, 58 S.Ct., at 668, 669.

The meaning of the Press Clause, as a provision separate and apart from the Speech Clause, is implicated only indirectly by this case. Yet Massachusetts' position poses serious questions. The evolution of traditional newspapers into modern corporate conglomerates in which the daily dissemination of news by print is no longer the major part of the whole enterprise suggests the need for caution in limiting the First Amendment rights of corporations as such. Thus, the tentative probings of this brief inquiry are wholly consistent, I think, with the Court's refusal to sustain § 8's serious and potentially dangerous restriction on the freedom of political speech.

Because the First Amendment was meant to guarantee freedom to express and communicate ideas, I can see no difference between the right of those who seek to disseminate ideas by way of a newspaper and those who give lectures or speeches and seek to enlarge the audience by publication and wide dissemination. "[T]he purpose of the Constitution was not to erect the press into a privileged institution but to protect all persons in their right to print what they will as well as to utter it. ' * * * the liberty of the press is no greater and no less * * *' than the liberty of every citizen of the Republic." Pennekamp v. Florida, 328 U.S. 331, 364, 66 S.Ct. 1029, 1046 (1946) (Frankfurter, J., concurring).

In short, the First Amendment does not "belong" to any definable category of persons or entities: it belongs to all who exercise its freedoms.

HOUCHINS v. KQED

Supreme Court of the United States, 1978
438 U.S. 1, 98 S.Ct. 2588, 57 L.Ed.2d 553

In the wake of a prisoner's suicide allegedly prompted by conditions at a portion (Little Greystone) of the Alameda county jail, station KQED asked for and was refused permission to inspect and photograph that area of the detention facility. The broadcasting company, joined by local branches of the NAACP, brought suit under the federal civil rights statutes against Houchins, the county sheriff, alleging abridgment of First Amendment rights. The plaintiffs argued that such a restriction thwarted efforts to report on the condition of the facility and to bring the prisoners' grievances to the public's attention. The sheriff subsequently inaugurated a regular program of monthly tours—open to the public and representatives of the media—of part of the jail (not including Little Greystone). Cameras and sound recording equipment were not allowed on these tours, nor were interviews permitted with the inmates. However, members of the public and representatives of the media who knew a prisoner were allowed to visit him. A federal district court enjoined the sheriff from denying the media reasonable access to the jail (including Little Greystone), from preventing the use of photographic and audio recording equipment, and from barring the conduct of interviews with inmates. The court of appeals affirmed this judgment.

Mr. Chief Justice BURGER announced the judgment of the Court and delivered an opinion, in which

Mr. Justice WHITE and Mr. Justice REHNQUIST joined.

The question presented is whether the news media have a constitutional right of access to a county jail, over and above that of other persons, to interview inmates and make sound recordings, films, and photographs for publication and broadcasting by newspapers, radio and television.

* * *

Notwithstanding our holding in *Pell* v. *Procunier*,[a] respondents assert that the right recognized by the Court of Appeals flows logically from our decisions construing the First Amendment. They argue that there is a constitutionally guaranteed right to gather news under Pell v. Procunier, supra, 417 U.S., at 835, 94 S.Ct., at 2810, and Branzburg v. Hayes, 408 U.S. 665, 681, 707, 92 S.Ct. 2646, 2656–2669. From the right to gather news and the right to receive information, they argue for an implied special right of access to government controlled sources of information. This right, they contend, compels access as a *constitutional* matter. Respondents suggest further support for this implicit First Amendment right in the language of Grosjean v. American Press Co., 297 U.S. 233, 250, 56 S.Ct. 444, 449, and Mills v. Alabama, 384 U.S. 214, 219, 86 S.Ct. 1434, 1437, which notes the importance of an informed public as a safeguard against "misgovernment" and the crucial role of the media in providing information. Re-

spondents contend that public access to penal institutions is necessary to prevent officials from concealing prison conditions from the voters and impairing the public's right to discuss and criticize the prison system and its administration.

We can agree with many of the respondents' generalized assertions; conditions in jails and prisons are clearly matters "of great public importance." Pell v. Procunier, supra, 417 U.S., at 830 n. 7, 94 S.Ct., at 2808 n. 7. Penal facilities are public institutions which require large amounts of public funds, and their mission is crucial in our criminal justice system. Each person placed in prison becomes, in effect, a ward of the state for whom society assumes broad responsibility. It is equally true that with greater information, the public can more intelligently form opinions about prison conditions. Beyond question, the role of the media is important; acting as the "eyes and ears" of the public, they can be a powerful and constructive force, contributing to remedial action in the conduct of public business. They have served that function since the beginning of the Republic, but like all other components of our society media representatives are subject to limits.

The media are not a substitute for or an adjunct of government, and like the courts, they are "ill-

<hr>

a. 417 U.S. 817, 94 S.Ct. 2800 (1974). Proceeding from the premises that "prison restrictions that are asserted to inhibit First Amendment interests must be analyzed in terms of the legitimate policies and goals of the corrections system, to whose custody and care the prisoner has been committed in accordance with due process of law" and that "[t]he Constitution does not * * * require government to accord the press special access to information not shared by members of the

public generally," the Court upheld the constitutionality of an order issued by the Director of the California Department of Corrections barring "[p]ress and other media interviews with specific individual inmates * * *." In a companion case, Saxbe v. Washington Post Co., 417 U.S. 843, 94 S.Ct. 2811 (1974), the Court also sustained the validity of a comparable ban on interviews with specifically named prisoners at federal medium and maximum-security institutions.

equipped" to deal with problems of prison administration. * * * We must not confuse the role of the media with that of government; each has special, crucial functions each complementing—and sometimes conflicting with—the other.

The public importance of conditions in penal facilities and the media's role of providing information afford no basis for reading into the Constitution a right of the public or the media to enter these institutions, with camera equipment, and take moving and still pictures of inmates for broadcast purposes. This court has never intimated a First Amendment guarantee of a right of access to all sources of information within government control. Nor does the rationale of the decisions upon which respondents rely lead to the implication of such a right.

Grosjean v. *American Press*, supra, and *Mills* v. *Alabama*, supra, emphasized the importance of informed public opinion and the traditional role of a free press as a source of public information. But an analysis of those cases reveals that the Court was concerned with the freedom of the media to *communicate* information once it is obtained; neither case intimated that the Constitution *compels* the government to provide the media with information or access to it on demand. * * *

* * *

The right to *receive* ideas and information is not the issue in this case. See, e.g., Virginia State Board of Pharmacy v. Virginia Citizens Consumer Council, 425 U.S. 748, 96 S.Ct. 1817; Procunier v. Martinez, supra, at 408–409, 94 S.Ct., at 1808, 1809; Kleindienst v. Mandel, 408 U.S. 753, 762–763, 92 S.Ct. 2576, 2581. The issue is a claimed special privilege of access which the Court rejected in *Pell* and *Saxbe*, a right which is not essential to guarantee the freedom to communicate or publish.

The respondents' argument is flawed, not only because it lacks precedential support and is contrary to statements in this Court's opinions, but also because it invites the Court to involve itself in what is clearly a legislative task which the Constitution has left to the political processes. Whether the government should open penal institutions in the manner sought by respondents is a question of policy which a legislative body might appropriately resolve one way or the other.

A number of alternatives are available to prevent problems in penal facilities from escaping public attention. The early penal reform movements in this country and England gained impetus as a result of reports from citizens and visiting committees who volunteered or received commissions to visit penal institutions and make reports. * * * Citizen task forces and prison visitation committees continue to play an important role in keeping the public informed on deficiencies of prison systems and need for reforms. Grand juries, with the potent subpoena power—not available to the media—traditionally concern themselves with conditions in public institutions; a prosecutor or judge may initiate similar inquiries and the legislative power embraces an arsenal of weapons for inquiry relating to tax supported institutions. In each case, these public bodies are generally compelled to publish their findings, and if they default, the power of the media is always available to generate public pressure for disclosure. But the choice as to the most effective

CHAPTER 14   FREEDOM OF THE PRESS   1431

and appropriate method is a policy decision to be resolved by legislative decision. We must not confuse what is "good," "desirable" or "expedient" with what is constitutionally commanded by the First Amendment. To do so is to trivialize constitutional adjudication.

Unarticulated but implicit in the assertion that media access to the jail is essential for informed public debate on jail conditions is the assumption that media personnel are the best qualified persons for the task of discovering malfeasance in public institutions. But that assumption finds no support in the decisions of this Court or the First Amendment. Editors and newsmen who inspect a jail may decide to publish or not to publish what information they acquire. * * * Public bodies and public officers, on the other hand, may be coerced by public opinion to disclose what they might prefer to conceal. No comparable pressures are available to anyone to compel publication by the media of what they might prefer not to make known.

There is no discernable basis for a constitutional duty to disclose, or for standards governing disclosure of or access to information. Because the Constitution affords no guidelines, absent statutory standards, hundreds of judges would, under the Court of Appeals' approach, be at large to fashion ad hoc standards, in individual cases, according to their own ideas of what seems "desirable" or "expedient." We, therefore, reject the Court of Appeals' conclusory assertion that the public and the media have a First Amendment right to government information regarding the conditions of jails and their inmates and presumably all other pub-

lic facilities such as hospitals and mental institutions.

The First Amendment is "neither a Freedom of Information Act nor an Official Secrets Act." Stewart, Or of the Press, 26 Hast.L.J. 631, 636 (1975). The guarantee of "freedom of speech" and "of the press" only "establishes the contest [for information] not its resolution. * * * For the rest, we must rely, as so often in our system we must, on the tug and pull of the political forces in American society." Ibid.

Petitioner cannot prevent respondents from learning about jail conditions in a variety of ways, albeit not as conveniently as they might prefer. Respondents have a First Amendment right to receive letters from inmates criticizing jail officials and reporting on conditions. * * * Respondents are free to interview those who render the legal assistance to which inmates are entitled. * * * They are also free to seek out former inmates, visitors to the prison, public officials, and institutional personnel, as they sought out the complaining psychiatrist here.

Moreover, California statutes currently provide for a prison Board of Corrections that has the authority to inspect jails and prisons and *must* provide a public report at regular intervals. * * * Health inspectors are required to inspect prisons and provide reports to a number of officials, including the State Attorney General and the Board of Corrections. * * * Fire officials are also required to inspect prisons. * * * Following the reports of the suicide at the jail involved here, the County Board of Supervisors called for a report from the County Supervisor, held a public hearing on the report, which was open to the media, and called for further reports when the initial report failed to describe the conditions in the cells in the Greystone portion of the jail.

Neither the First Amendment nor Fourteenth Amendment mandates a right of access to government information or sources of information within the government's control. Under our holdings in *Pell* v. *Procunier* supra, and *Saxbe* v. *Washington Post*, supra, until the political branches decree otherwise, as they are free to do, the media has no right special of access to the Alameda County Jail different from or greater than that accorded the public generally.

The judgment of the Court of Appeals is reversed and the case is remanded for further proceedings.

Reversed.

Mr. Justice MARSHALL and Mr. Justice BLACKMUN took no part in the consideration or decision of this case.

Mr. Justice STEWART, concurring in the judgment.

I agree that the preliminary injunction issued against the petitioner was unwarranted, and therefore concur in the judgment. In my view, however, KQED was entitled to injunctive relief of more limited scope.

The First and Fourteenth Amendments do not guarantee the public a right of access to information generated or controlled by government, nor do they guarantee the press any basic right of access superior to that of the public generally. The Constitution does no more than assure the public and the press equal access once government has opened its doors. Accordingly, I agree substantially with what the opinion of THE

CHIEF JUSTICE has to say on that score.

We part company, however, in applying these abstractions to the facts of this case. Whereas he appears to view "equal access" as meaning access that is identical in all respects, I believe that the concept of equal access must be accorded more flexibility in order to accommodate the practical distinctions between the press and the general public.

When on assignment, a journalist does not tour a jail simply for his own edification. He is there to gather information to be passed on to others, and his mission is protected by the Constitution for very specific reasons. "Enlightened choice by an informed citizenry is the basic ideal upon which an open society is premised." * * * Branzburg v. Hayes, 408 U.S. 665, 726, 92 S.Ct. 2646 (concurring opinion). Our society depends heavily on the press for that enlightenment. Though not without its lapses, the press "has been a mighty catalyst in awakening public interest in governmental affairs, exposing corruption among public officers and employees, and generally informing the citizenry of public events and occurrences." * * * Estes v. Texas, 381 U.S. 532, 539, 85 S.Ct. 1628, 1631. See Mills v. Alabama, 384 U.S. 214, 219, 86 S.Ct. 1434, 1437; Grosjean v. American Press Co., 297 U.S. 233, 250, 56 S.Ct. 444, 449.

That the First Amendment speaks separately of freedom of speech and freedom of the press is no constitutional accident, but an acknowledgement of the critical role played by the press in American society. The Constitution requires sensitivity to that role, and to the special needs of the press in performing it effectively. A person touring Santa Rita jail can grasp its reality with his own eyes and ears. But if a television reporter is to convey the jail's sights and sounds to those who cannot personally visit the place, he must use cameras and sound equipment. In short, terms of access that are reasonably imposed on individual members of the public may, if they impede effective reporting without sufficient justification, be unreasonable as applied to journalists who are there to convey to the general public what the visitors see.

Under these principles, KQED was clearly entitled to some form of preliminary injunctive relief. At the time of the District Court's decision, members of the public were permitted to visit most parts of the Santa Rita jail, and the First and Fourteenth Amendments required the Sheriff to give members of the press *effective* access to the same areas. The Sheriff evidently assumed that he could fulfill this obligation simply by allowing reporters to sign up for tours on the same terms as the public. I think he was mistaken in this assumption, as a matter of constitutional law.

The District Court found that the press required access to the jail on a more flexible and frequent basis than scheduled monthly tours if it was to keep the public informed. By leaving the "specific methods of implementing such a policy * * * [to] Sheriff Houchins," the Court concluded that the press could be allowed access to the jail "at reasonable times and hours" without causing undue disruption. The District Court also found that the media required cameras and recording equipment for effective presentation to the viewing public of the conditions

at the jail seen by individual visitors, and that their use could be kept consistent with institutional needs. These elements of the Court's order were both sanctioned by the Constitution and amply supported by the record.

In two respects, however, the District Court's preliminary injunction was overbroad. It ordered the Sheriff to permit reporters into the Little Greystone facility and it required him to let them interview randomly encountered inmates. In both these respects, the injunction gave the press access to areas and sources of information from which persons on the public tours had been excluded, and thus enlarged the scope of what the Sheriff and Supervisors had opened to public view. The District Court erred in concluding that the First and Fourteenth Amendments compelled this broader access for the press.

Because the preliminary injunction exceeded the requirements of the Constitution in these respects, I agree that the judgment of the Court of Appeals affirming the District Court's order must be reversed. But I would not foreclose the possibility of further relief for KQED on remand. In my view, the availability and scope of future permanent injunctive relief must depend upon the extent of access then permitted the public, and the decree must be framed to accommodate equitably the constitutional role of the press and the institutional requirements of the jail.

Mr. Justice STEVENS, with whom Mr. Justice BRENNAN and Mr. Justice POWELL join, dissenting.

* * *

For two reasons, which shall be discussed separately, the decisions in *Pell* and *Saxbe* do not control the propriety of the District Court's preliminary injunction. First, the unconstitutionality of petitioner's policies which gave rise to this litigation does not rest on the premise that the press has a greater right of access to information regarding prison conditions than do other members of the public. Second, relief tailored to the needs of the press may properly be awarded to a representative of the press which is successful in proving that it has been harmed by a constitutional violation and need not await the grant of relief to members of the general public who may also have been injured by petitioner's unconstitutional access policy but have not yet sought to vindicate their rights.

* * *

It is well settled that a defendant's corrective action in anticipation of litigation or following commencement of suit does not deprive the court of power to decide whether the previous course of conduct was unlawful. See United States v. W. T. Grant Co., 345 U.S. 629, 73 S.Ct. 894, and cases cited, at 632–633, 73 S.Ct. at 897. The propriety of the court's exercise of that power in this case is apparent. When this suit was filed, there were no public tours. Petitioner enforced a policy of virtually total exclusion of both the public and the press from those areas within the Santa Rita jail where the inmates were confined. At that time petitioner also enforced a policy of reading all inmate correspondence addressed to persons other than lawyers and judges and censoring those portions that related to the conduct of the guards who controlled their daily existence. Prison policy as well as

prison walls significantly abridged the opportunities for communication of information about the conditions of confinement in the Santa Rita facility to the public. Therefore, even if there would not have been any constitutional violation had the access policies adopted by petitioner following commencement of this litigation been in effect all along, it was appropriate for the District Court to decide whether the restrictive rules in effect when KQED first requested access were constitutional.

In Pell v. Procunier, 417 U.S. 817, 834, 94 S.Ct. 2800, 2810, the Court stated that "newsmen have no constitutional right of access to prisons or their inmates beyond that afforded the general public." But the Court has never intimated that a nondiscriminatory policy of excluding entirely both the public and the press from access to information about prison conditions would avoid constitutional scrutiny. Indeed, *Pell* itself strongly suggests the contrary.

In that case, representatives of the press claimed the right to interview specifically designated inmates. In evaluating this claim, the Court did not simply inquire whether prison officials allowed members of the general public to conduct such interviews. Rather, it canvassed the opportunities already available for both the public and the press to acquire information regarding the prison and its inmates. And the Court found that the policy of prohibiting interviews with inmates specifically designated by the press was "not part of an attempt by the state to conceal the conditions in its prisons." The challenged restriction on access, which was imposed only after experience revealed that such interviews posed disciplinary problems, was an isolated limitation on the efforts of the press to gather information about those conditions. It was against the background of a record which demonstrated that both the press and the general public were "accorded full opportunities to observe prison conditions," that the Court considered the constitutionality of the single restraint on access challenged in *Pell*.

The decision in *Pell*, therefore, does not imply that a state policy of concealing prison conditions from the press, or a policy denying the press any opportunity to observe those conditions, could have been justified simply by pointing to like concealment from, and denial to, the general public. If that were not true, there would have been no need to emphasize the substantial press and public access reflected in the record of that case. What *Pell* does indicate is that the question whether respondents established a probability of prevailing on their constitutional claim is inseparable from the question whether petitioner's policies unduly restricted the opportunities of the general public to learn about the conditions of confinement in Santa Rita jail. As in *Pell*, in assessing its adequacy, the total access of the public and the press must be considered.

Here, the broad restraints on access to information regarding operation of the jail that prevailed on the date this suit was instituted are plainly disclosed by the record. The public and the press had consistently been denied any access to those portions of the Santa Rita facility where inmates were confined and there had been excessive censorship of inmate correspondence. Petitioner's no-access policy, modified only in the wake of respondents' resort to the courts, could survive constitutional scrutiny only if the Constitution af-

fords no protection to the public's right to be informed about conditions within those public institutions where some of its members are confined because they have been charged with or found guilty of criminal offenses.

The preservation of a full and free flow of information to the general public has long been recognized as a core objective of the First Amendment to the Constitution. It is for this reason that the First Amendment protects not only the dissemination but also the receipt of information and ideas. See, e.g., Virginia Pharmacy Board v. Virginia Consumer Council, 425 U.S. 748, 756, 96 S.Ct. 1817, 1822; Procunier v. Martinez, 416 U.S. 396, 408–409, 94 S.Ct. 1800, 1808–1809; Kleindienst v. Mandel, 408 U.S. 753, 762–763, 92 S.Ct. 2576, 2581. Thus, in Procunier v. Martinez, supra, the Court invalidated prison regulations authorizing excessive censorship of outgoing inmate correspondence because such censorship abridged the rights of the intended recipients. * * * So here, petitioner's prelitigation prohibition on mentioning the conduct of jail officers in outgoing correspondence must be considered an impingement on the noninmate correspondent's interest in receiving the intended communication.

In addition to safeguarding the right of one individual to receive what another elects to communicate, the First Amendment serves an essential societal function. Our system of self-government assumes the existence of an informed citizenry. * * *

It is not sufficient, therefore, that the channels of communication be free of governmental restraints. Without some protection for the ac-

quisition of information about the operation of public institutions such as
prisons by the public at large, the
process of self-governance contemplated by the Framers would be
stripped of its substance.

For that reason information-gathering is entitled to some measure of
constitutional protection. See, e.g.,
Branzburg v. Hayes, 408 U.S. 665,
681, 92 S.Ct. 2646, 2656; Pell v.
Procunier, 417 U.S., at 833, 94 S.Ct.,
at 2809. As this Court's decisions
clearly indicate, however, this protection is not for the private benefit of
those who might qualify as representatives of the "press" but to insure that the citizens are fully informed regarding matters of public
interest and importance.

* * *

A recognition that the "underlying right is the right of the public
generally" is also implicit in the doctrine that "newsmen have no constitutional right of access to prisons or
their inmates beyond that afforded
the general public." Pell v.
Procunier, supra, 417 U.S., at 834, 94
S.Ct., at 2810. In Pell it was unnecessary to consider the extent of the
public's right of access to information regarding the prison and its inmates in order to adjudicate the
press claim to a particular form of
access, since the record demonstrated that the flow of information to the
public, both directly and through the
press, was adequate to survive constitutional challenge; institutional
considerations justified denying the
single, additional mode of access
sought by the press in that case.

Here, in contrast, the restrictions
on access to the inner portions of the
Santa Rita jail that existed on the
date this litigation commenced concealed from the general public the
conditions of confinement within the
facility. The question is whether petitioner's policies, which cut off the
flow of information at its source,
abridged the public's right to be informed about those conditions.

The answer to that question does
not depend upon the degree of public
disclosure which should attend the
operation of most governmental activity. Such matters involve questions of policy which generally must
be resolved by the political branches
of government. Moreover, there are
unquestionably occasions when governmental activity may properly be
carried on in complete secrecy. For
example, the public and the press are
commonly excluded from "grand jury proceedings, our own conferences,
[and] the meetings of other official
bodies gathering in executive session." * * * Branzburg v.
Hayes, 408 U.S., at 684, 92 S.Ct., at
2658; Pell v. Procunier, 417 U.S., at
834, 94 S.Ct., at 2810. In addition,
some functions of government—essential to the protection of the public
and indeed our country's vital interests—necessarily require a large
measure of secrecy, subject to appropriate legislative oversight. In such
situations the reasons for withholding information from the public are
both apparent and legitimate.

In this case, however, "[r]espon-
dents do not assert a right to force
disclosure of confidential information
or to invade in any way the decision-
making processes of governmental
officials." They simply seek an end
to petitioner's policy of concealing
prison conditions from the public.
Those conditions are wholly without
claim to confidentiality. While prison officials have an interest in the
time and manner of public acquisition of information about the institutions they administer, there is no le-

gitimate, penological justification for concealing from citizens the conditions in which their fellow citizens are being confined.

The reasons which militate in favor of providing special protection to the flow of information to the public about prisons relate to the unique function they perform in a democratic society. Not only are they public institutions, financed with public funds and administered by public servants; they are an integral component of the criminal justice system. The citizens confined therein are temporarily, and sometimes permanently, deprived of their liberty as a result of a trial which must conform to the dictates of the Constitution. By express command of the Sixth Amendment the proceeding must be a "public trial." It is important not only that the trial itself be fair, but also that the community at large have confidence in the integrity of the proceeding. That public interest survives the judgment of conviction and appropriately carries over to an interest in how the convicted person is treated during his period of punishment and hoped-for rehabilitation. While a ward of the State and subject to its stern discipline, he retains constitutional protections against cruel and unusual punishment, * * * a protection which may derive more practical support from access to information about prisons by the public than by occasional litigation in a busy court.

Some inmates—in Santa Rita, a substantial number—are pretrial detainees. Though confined pending trial, they have not been convicted of an offense against society and are entitled to the presumption of innocence. Certain penological objectives, i.e., punishment, deterrence and rehabilitation, which are legiti-

mate in regard to convicted prisoners, are inapplicable to pretrial detainees. Society has a special interest in ensuring that unconvicted citizens are treated in accord with their status.

In this case, the record demonstrates that both the public and the press had been consistently denied any access to the inner portions of the Santa Rita jail, that there had been excessive censorship of inmate correspondence, and that there was no valid justification for these broad restraints on the flow of information. An affirmative answer to the question whether respondent established a likelihood of prevailing on the merits did not depend, in final analysis, on any right of the press to special treatment beyond that accorded the public at large. Rather, the probable existence of a constitutional violation rested upon the special importance of allowing a democratic community access to knowledge about how its servants were treating some of its members who have been committed to their custody. An official prison policy of concealing such knowledge from the public by arbitrarily cutting off the flow of information at its source abridges the freedom of speech and of the press protected by the First and Fourteenth Amendments to the Constitution.

The preliminary injunction entered by the District Court granted relief to KQED without providing any specific remedy for other members of the public. Moreover, it imposed duties on petitioner that may not be required by the Constitution itself. The injunction was not an abuse of discretion for either of these reasons.

If a litigant can prove that he has suffered specific harm from the application of an unconstitutional policy, it is entirely proper for a court to grant relief tailored to his needs without attempting to redress all the mischief that the policy may have worked on others. Though the public and the press have an equal right to receive information and ideas, different methods of remedying a violation of that right may sometimes be needed to accommodate the special concerns of the one or the other. Preliminary relief could therefore appropriately be awarded to KQED on the basis of its proof of how it was affected by the challenged policy without also granting specific relief to the general public. Indeed, since our adversary system contemplates the adjudication of specific controversies between specific litigants, it would have been improper for the District Court to attempt to provide a remedy to persons who have not requested separate relief. According-

ly, even though the Constitution provides the press with no greater right of access to information than that possessed by the public at large, a preliminary injunction is not invalid simply because it awards special relief to a successful litigant which is a representative of the press.

* * * It follows that if prison regulations and policies have unconstitutionally suppressed information and interfered with communication in violation of the First Amendment, the District Court has the power to require, at least temporarily, that the channels of communication be opened more widely than the law would otherwise require in order to let relevant facts, which may have been concealed, come to light. * * *

I would affirm the judgment of the Court of Appeals.

RICHMOND NEWSPAPERS, INC. v. VIRGINIA

Supreme Court of the United States, 1980
448 U.S. 555, 100 S.Ct. 2814, 65 L.Ed.2d 973

See p. 1509.

Steven Pico and other high school and junior high school students brought suit against the members of the local board of education for their action removing nine books—including Kurt Vonnegut's Slaughter House Five, Eldridge Cleaver's Soul on Ice, Richard Wright's Black Boy, Desmond Morris's The Naked Ape, and Bernard Malamud's The Fixer—from school libraries and use in the curriculum. The board's action, which came after it rejected a report by a committee of citizens and staff it appointed, was taken because the board concluded the books were "anti-American, anti-Christian, anti-Semitic, and just plain filthy." The plaintiff students alleged that the motivation behind the board's action was that "particular passages in the books offended their social, political, and moral tastes and not because the books, taken as a whole, were lacking in educational value." A federal district court granted summary judgment for the board members, finding that "the board acted not on religious principles but on its conservative educational philosophy, and on its belief that the nine books removed from the school library and curriculum were irrelevant, vulgar, immoral, and in bad taste, making them educationally unsuitable for the district's junior and senior high school students." A fragmented federal appeals court reversed and remanded the case for trial, apparently on the grounds that the board had not offered sufficient proof that its decision to remove the books was motivated by a concern about vulgarity and sexual explicitness and to give the plaintiff students an opportunity to demonstrate that this justification offered by the board was instead a pretext for the suppression of ideas. The board members petitioned the Supreme Court for certiorari.

In Board of Education, Island Trees Union Free School District Number 26 v. Pico, —— U.S. ——, 102 S.Ct. 2799 (1982), the Supreme Court affirmed the judgment of the federal appellate court. Announcing the judgment of the Court in an opinion in which Justices Marshall and Stevens joined and in which Justice Blackmun joined in part, Justice Brennan emphasized at the outset that the present case did not involve textbooks or other required reading but *library* books and that it did not involve the acquisition of such books but their *removal*. Characterizing the issue in this case as "a narrow one, both substantively and procedurally," Justice Brennan phrased it in terms of "two distinct questions": "First, Does the First Amendment impose *any* limitations upon the discretion of petitioners to remove library books from the Island Trees High School and Junior High School? Second, If so, do the affidavits and other evidentiary materials before the District Court, construed most favorably to respondents, raise a genuine issue of fact whether petitioners might have exceeded those limitations?" (Because the petitioner school board members moved for and obtained summary judgment in their favor from the district court, any disputed questions of fact must be considered in a light most favorable to the respondent students.)

Addressing the first question, the plurality, although "recogniz[ing] that local school boards have broad discretion in the management of school affairs," reaffirmed the proposition adopted by the Court in Tinker v. Des Moines Independent Community School District, 393 U.S. 503, 89 S.Ct. 733 (1969), that "students do not 'shed their rights to freedom of speech or expression at the schoolhouse gate'" and that school authorities must operate within the confines of the First Amendment. Justice Brennan continued, "[W]e think that the First Amendment rights of students may be directly and sharply implicated by the removal of books from the shelves of a school library" because—quoting controlling principles of prior First Amendment cases— "'the State may not * * * contract the spectrum of available knowledge'" and because "'the Constitution protects the right to receive information and ideas.'" He went on to say, "In sum, just as access to ideas makes it possible for citizens generally to exercise their rights to free speech and press in a meaningful manner, such access prepares students for active and effective participation in the pluralistic, often contentious society in which they will soon be adult members. Of course all First Amendment rights accorded to students must be construed 'in light of the special characteristics of the school environment.' * * * But the special characteristics of the school *library* make that environment especially appropriate for the recognition of the First Amendment rights of students." In response to the board's contention that it "be allowed *unfettered* discretion to 'transmit community values' through the Island Trees schools," the plurality pointed out that such a "sweeping claim overlooks the unique role of the school library" where the selection of books is "wholly optional" and "entirely a matter of free choice." Said the plurality: "Petitioners might well defend their claim of absolute discretion in matters of *curriculum* by reliance upon their duty to inculcate community values. But we think that petitioners' reliance upon that duty is misplaced where, as here, they attempt to extend their claim of absolute discretion beyond the compulsory environment of the classroom, into the school library and the regime of voluntary inquiry that there holds sway." With respect to the extent to which the First Amendment places limitations upon the discretion of board members to remove books from their libraries, Justice Brennan wrote:

> Petitioners rightly possess significant discretion to determine the content of their school libraries. But that discretion may not be exercised in a narrowly partisan or political manner. If a Democratic school board, motivated by party affiliation, ordered the removal of all books written by or in favor of Republicans, few would doubt that the order violated the constitutional rights of the students denied access to those books. The same conclusion would surely apply if an all-white school board, motivated by racial animus, decided to remove all books authored by blacks or advocating racial equality and integration. Our Constitution does not permit the official suppression of *ideas*. Thus whether petitioners' removal of books from their school libraries denied respondents their First Amendment rights depends upon the motivation behind petitioners' actions. If petitioners *intended* by their removal decision to deny respondents access to ideas with which petitioners disagreed, and if this intent was the decisive factor in petitioners' decision, then petitioners have exercised their discretion in violation of the Constitution. To permit such intentions to control official actions would be to encourage the precise sort of officially prescribed orthodoxy unequivocally condemned in *Barnette*. On the other hand, respondents implicitly concede that an unconstitutional motivation would *not* be demonstrated if it were shown that petitioners had decided to remove the books at issue because those books were pervasively vulgar. * * * And again, respondents concede that if it were demonstrated that the removal decision was based solely upon the "educational suitability" of the books in question, then their removal would be "perfectly permissible." * * * In other words, in respondents' view such motivations, if decisive of petitioners' actions, would not carry the danger of an official suppression of ideas, and thus would not violate respondents' First Amendment rights.
>
> As noted earlier, nothing in our decision today affects in any way the discretion of a local school board to choose books to *add* to the libraries of their schools. Because we are concerned in this case with the suppression of ideas, our holding today affects only the discretion to *remove* books. In brief, we hold that local school boards may not remove books from school library shelves simply because they dislike the ideas contained in those books and seek by their removal to "prescribe what shall be orthodox in politics, nationalism, religion, or other matters of opinion." West Virginia [State Board of Education] v. Barnette, 319 U.S., at 642, 63 S.Ct., at 1187. Such purposes stand inescapably condemned by our precedents.

As to the second question, the plurality concluded that a real question of fact existed about the board's motivation, and the plurality cited the following facts in the record as tending to contradict the "vulgarity" and "educational suitability" reasons offered by the board: (1) when a public explanation was first offered by the board, it characterized excerpts from some of the books as "anti-American"; (2) the recommendation of the Book Review Committee empaneled initially by the board, which applied standards such as "educational suitability," "good taste," "relevance," and "appropriateness to age and grade level" and which subsequently recommended that five of the books be retained and only two removed, was rejected without any statement of reasons by the board"; (3) the board's book removal decision ignored the advice and views of literary experts, librarians, and teachers; (4) the board's decision followed soon after some members attended a conference of "a politically conservative organization of parents concerned about education legislation in the State of New York"; and (5) the board's action empaneling the Book Review Committee, whose recommendation was subsequently rejected, was contrary to established procedures. Said the plurality: "[S]ome of the evidence before the District Court might lead a finder of fact to accept petitioners' claim that their removal decision was based upon constitutionally valid concerns. But that evidence at most creates a genuine issue of material fact on the critical question of the credibility of petitioners' justification for their decision: On that issue, it simply cannot be said that there is no genuine issue as to any material fact."

Justice White concurred in the judgment, saying: "I am not inclined to disagree with the Court of Appeals on such a fact-bound issue and hence concur in the judgment of affirmance. Presumably this will result in a trial and the making of a full record and findings on the critical issues." He continued, "We should not decide constitutional questions until it is necessary to do so, or at least until there is better reason[s] to address them than are evident here." In another concurring opinion, Justice Blackmun took exception to Justice Rehnquist's attack in dissent on the usefulness of "the suppression of ideas" as an analytical tool in First Amendment cases. Said Justice Blackmun, "In my view, we strike a proper balance here by holding that school officials may not remove books for the *purpose* of restricting access to the political ideas or social perspectives discussed in them, when that action is motivated simply by the officials' disapproval of the ideas involved."

Chief Justice Burger and Justices Powell, Rehnquist, and O'Connor dissented, each writing separate opinions, although Burger's and Rehnquist's dissents each carried the approval of all or most of the other dissenters. Chief Justice Burger decried the Court's "lavish expansion" of the First Amendment and feared it "would come perilously close" to making the Court "a 'super censor' of school board library decisions." He also objected to the "plurality['s] suggest[ion] * * * that if a writer has something to say, the government through its schools must be the courier." Finally, the Chief Justice protested the Court's activism in a field where he thought democratic accountability should be the norm:

We can all agree that as a matter of *educational policy* students should have wide access to information and ideas. But the people elect school boards, who in turn select administrators, who select the teachers, and these are the individuals best able to determine the substance of that policy. The plurality fails to recognize the fact that local control of education involves democracy in a microcosm. In most public schools in the United States the *parents* have a large voice in running the school. Through participation in the election of school board members, the parents influence, if not control, the direction of their childrens' education. A school board is not a giant bureaucracy far removed from accountability for its actions; it is truly "of the people and by the people." A school board reflects its constituency in a very real sense and thus could not long exercise unchecked discretion in its choice to acquire or remove books. If the parents disagree with the educational decisions of the school board, they can take steps to remove the board members from office. Finally, even if parents and students cannot convince the school board that book removal is inappropriate, they have alternative sources to the same end. Books may be acquired from book stores, public libraries, or other alternative sources unconnected with the unique environment of the local public schools.

Justice Powell, himself the former President of a school board, viewed the Court's decision "with genuine dismay." Said Powell:

> School boards are uniquely local and democratic institutions. Unlike the governing bodies of cities and counties, school boards have only one responsibility: the education of the youth of our country during their most formative and impressionable years. Apart from health, no subject is closer to the hearts of parents than their children's education during those years. For these reasons, the governance of elementary and secondary education traditionally has been placed in the hands of a local board, responsible locally to the parents and citizens of school districts. Through parent-teacher associations (PTAs), and even less formal arrangements that vary with schools, parents are informed and often may influence decisions of the board. Frequently, parents know the teachers and visit classes. It is fair to say that no single agency of government at any level is closer to the people whom it serves than the typical school board.
>
> * * * Whatever the final outcome of this suit and suits like it, the resolution of educational policy decisions through litigation, and the exposure of school board members to liability for such decisions, can be expected to corrode the school board's authority and effectiveness. As is evident from the generality of the plurality's "standard" for judicial review, the decision as to the educational worth of a book is a highly subjective one. Judges rarely are as competent as school authorities to make this decision; nor are judges responsive to the parents and people of the school district.

The most vigorous attack on the plurality's opinion, however, came from Justice Rehnquist who offered at least half a dozen criticisms of it. He objected, first, to the plurality's "combing through the record of affidavits, school bulletins, and the like for bits and snatches of dispute" that presented a version of the facts far more favorable to the students than that to which they had stipulated. Second, although the plurality might cite *Tinker* in support of the First Amendment rights of students, Justice Rehnquist pointed out that the right discussed there was a freedom of expression, not a right of access to information. He also observed, as a third matter, that such a right to receive ideas was basically incompatible with the educational process, at least at the junior high and high school level. He wrote:

> Education consists of the selective presentation and explanation of ideas. The effective acquisition of knowledge depends upon an orderly exposure to relevant information. Nowhere is this more true than in elementary and secondary schools, where, unlike the broad-ranging inquiry available to university students, the courses taught are those thought most relevant to the young students' individual development. Of necessity, elementary and secondary educators must separate the relevant from the irrelevant, the appropriate from the inappropriate. Determining what information *not* to present to the students is often as important as identifying relevant material. This winnowing process necessarily leaves much information to be discovered by students at another time or in another place, and is fundamentally inconsistent with any constitutionally required eclecticism in public education.

Fourth, Justice Rehnquist took the plurality to task for what he saw as the highly artificial and illogical restraints it fastened on the newly created right of access.

For example, he thought the limitation of the decision to include only the removal of *library* books was both unsupported by precedent and deficient in failing to recognize that, since elementary and secondary schools are significantly involved with the socializing of children, i.e., with the inculcation of values, it must be seen that "[t]he libraries of such schools serve as supplements to this inculcative role." And he failed to see why the plurality limited its access right to the *removal* of books and did not accept the logic implicit in the principle which would extend it as well to their *acquisition*, at which point he argued the unacceptability and unworkability of the principle was manifest. A fifth target of his criticism was the plurality's reliance upon the "suppression of ideas" as a principle. Expressing "doubt that it is really a useful tool in solving First Amendment problems," he characterized it as both novel and rudderless. Finally, Justice Rehnquist faulted the plurality for not recognizing the implications which flowed from the fact that government wears two different hats—"educator" and "sovereign":

> After all else is said, however, the most obvious reason that petitioners' removal of the books did not violate respondents' right to receive information is the ready availability of the books elsewhere. Students are not denied books by their removal from a school library. The books may be borrowed from a public library, read at a university library, purchased at a bookstore, or loaned by a friend. The government as educator does not seek to reach beyond the confines of the school. Indeed, following the removal from the school library of the books at issue in this case, the local public library put all nine books on display for public inspection. Their contents were fully accessible to any inquisitive student.

And he continued:

> I think the Court will far better serve the cause of First Amendment jurisprudence by candidly recognizing that the role of government as sovereign is subject to more stringent limitations than is the role of government as employer, property owner, or educator. It must also be recognized that the government as educator is subject to fewer strictures when operating an elementary and secondary school system than when operating an institution of higher learning. * * * With respect to the education of children in elementary and secondary schools, the school board may properly determine in many cases that a particular book, a particular course, or even a particular area of knowledge is not educationally suitable for inclusion within the body of knowledge which the school seeks to impart. Without more, this is not a condemnation of the book or the course; it is only a determination akin to that referred to by the Court in Village of Euclid v. Ambler Realty Co., 272 U.S. 365, 388, 47 S.Ct. 114, 118 (1926): "A nuisance may be merely a right thing in the wrong place—like a pig in the parlor instead of the barnyard."

b. OBSCENITY

ROTH v. UNITED STATES
ALBERTS v. CALIFORNIA

Supreme Court of the United States, 1957
354 U.S. 476, 77 S.Ct. 1304, 1 L.Ed.2d 1498

Samuel Roth was indicted under the federal statute which makes it a criminal offense to send "obscene, lewd, lascivious, or filthy" matter or advertisements for

such matter through the mail. Among the materials he sold and advertised for sale were "American Aphrodite," a quarterly publication dealing in literary erotica which appeared in bound volumes retailing for a price of ten dollars each, and sets of nude photographs. Roth was convicted on counts concerning the sale and advertisement of "American Aphrodite" but acquitted on charges involving the obscenity of the photographs. The conviction was affirmed by a U.S. Court of Appeals.

A companion case heard by the Supreme Court involved the indictment and subsequent conviction of David Alberts under California's obscenity law. Unlike Roth, Alberts disseminated pictures of "nude and scantily-clad women," sometimes depicted in bizarre poses and without any literary pretentions. His conviction in municipal court was affirmed by a state superior court.

Mr. Justice BRENNAN delivered the opinion of the Court.

The constitutionality of a criminal obscenity statute is the question in each of these cases. In *Roth*, the primary constitutional question is whether the federal obscenity statute violates the provision of the First Amendment that "Congress shall make no law * * * abridging the freedom of speech, or of the press." * * * In *Alberts*, the primary constitutional question is whether the obscenity provisions of the California Penal Code invade the freedoms of speech and press as they may be incorporated in the liberty protected from state action by the Due Process Clause of the Fourteenth Amendment.

Other constitutional questions are: whether these statutes violate due process, because too vague to support conviction for crime; whether power to punish speech and press offensive to decency and morality is in the States alone, so that the federal obscenity statute violates the Ninth and Tenth Amendments (raised in *Roth*); and whether Congress, by enacting the federal obscenity statute, under the power delegated by Art. I, § 8, cl. 7, to establish post offices and post roads, pre-empted the regulation of the subject matter (raised in *Alberts*).

* * *

The dispositive question is whether obscenity is utterance within the area of protected speech and press. Although this is the first time the question has been squarely presented to this Court, either under the First Amendment or under the Fourteenth Amendment, expressions found in numerous opinions indicate that this Court has always assumed that obscenity is not protected by the freedoms of speech and press. * * *

The guaranties of freedom of expression in effect in 10 of the 14 States which by 1792 had ratified the Constitution, gave no absolute protection for every utterance. Thirteen of the 14 States provided for the prosecution of libel, and all of those States made either blasphemy or profanity, or both, statutory crimes. As early as 1712, Massachusetts made it criminal to publish "any filthy, obscene, or profane song, pamphlet, libel or mock sermon" in imitation or mimicking of religious services. * * * Thus, profanity and obscenity were related offenses.

In light of this history, it is apparent that the unconditional phrasing of the First Amendment was not intended to protect every utterance. This phrasing did not prevent this

Court from concluding that libelous utterances are not within the area of constitutionally protected speech. Beauharnais v. People of State of Illinois, 343 U.S. 250, 266, 72 S.Ct. 725, 735. At the time of the adoption of the First Amendment, obscenity law was not as fully developed as libel law, but there is sufficiently contemporaneous evidence to show that obscenity, too, was outside the protection intended for speech and press.

The protection given speech and press was fashioned to assure unfettered interchange of ideas for the bringing about of political and social changes desired by the people. * * *

All ideas having even the slightest redeeming social importance—unorthodox ideas, controversial ideas, even ideas hateful to the prevailing climate of opinion—have the full protection of the guaranties, unless excludable because they encroach upon the limited area of more important interests. But implicit in the history of the First Amendment is the rejection of obscenity as utterly without redeeming social importance. This rejection for that reason is mirrored in the universal judgment that obscenity should be restrained, reflected in the international agreement of over 50 nations, in the obscenity laws of all of the 48 States, and in the 20 obscenity laws enacted by the Congress from 1842 to 1956. This is the same judgment expressed by this Court in Chaplinsky v. New Hampshire, 315 U.S. 568, 571–572, 62 S.Ct. 766, 769:

" * * * There are certain well-defined and narrowly limited classes of speech, the prevention and punishment of which have never been thought to raise any Constitutional problem. *These include the*

lewd and obscene. * * * *It has been well observed that such utterances are no essential part of any exposition of ideas, and are of such slight social value as a step to truth that any benefit that may be derived from them is clearly outweighed by the social interest in order and morality."* * * * (Emphasis added.)

We hold that obscenity is not within the area of constitutionally protected speech or press.

It is strenuously urged that these obscenity statutes offend the constitutional guaranties because they punish incitation to impure sexual *thoughts*, not shown to be related to any overt antisocial conduct which is or may be incited in the persons stimulated to such *thoughts.* * * * It is insisted that the constitutional guaranties are violated because convictions may be had without proof either that obscene material will perceptibly create a clear and present danger of antisocial conduct, or will probably induce its recipients to such conduct. But, in light of our holding that obscenity is not protected speech, the complete answer to this argument is in the holding of this Court in *Beauharnais* v. *People of State of Illinois,* supra:

"Libelous utterances not being within the area of constitutionally protected speech, it is unnecessary, either for us or for the State courts, to consider the issues behind the phrase 'clear and present danger.' Certainly no one would contend that obscene speech, for example, may be punished only upon a showing of such circumstances. Libel, as we have seen, is in the same class."

However, sex and obscenity are not synonymous. Obscene material is material which deals with sex in a manner appealing to prurient interest.[20] The portrayal of sex, e.g., in art, literature and scientific works, is not itself sufficient reason to deny material the constitutional protection of freedom of speech and press. Sex, a great and mysterious motive force in human life, has indisputably been a subject of absorbing interest to mankind through the ages; it is one of the vital problems of human interest and public concern. * * *

* * *

The early leading standard of obscenity allowed material to be judged merely by the effect of an isolated excerpt upon particularly susceptible persons. Regina v. Hicklin, [1868] L.R. 3 Q.B. 360.[b] Some American courts adopted this standard but later decisions have rejected it and substituted this test: whether to the average person, applying contemporary community standards, the dominant theme of the material taken as a whole appeals to prurient interest. The *Hicklin* test, judging obscenity by the effect of isolated passages up-

on the most susceptible persons, might well encompass material legitimately treating with sex, and so it must be rejected as unconstitutionally restrictive of the freedoms of speech and press. On the other hand, the substituted standard provides safeguards adequate to withstand the charge of constitutional infirmity.

Both trial courts below sufficiently followed the proper standard. Both courts used the proper definition of obscenity. * * *

It is argued that the statutes do not provide reasonably ascertainable standards of guilt and therefore violate the constitutional requirements of due process. * * * The thrust of the argument is that these words are not sufficiently precise because they do not mean the same thing to all people, all the time, everywhere.

Many decisions have recognized that these terms of obscenity statutes are not precise. This Court, however, has consistently held that lack of precision is not itself offen-

---

20. I.e., material having a tendency to excite lustful thoughts. Webster's New International Dictionary (Unabridged, 2d ed., 1949) defines *prurient*, in pertinent part, as follows:

" * * * Itching; longing; uneasy with desire or longing; or persons, having itching, morbid, or lascivious longings; of desire, curiosity, or propensity, lewd * * *."

Pruriency is defined, in pertinent part, as follows:

" * * * Quality of being prurient; lascivious desire or thought. * * * "

See also Mutual Film Corp. v. Industrial Comm., 236 U.S. 230, 242, 35 S.Ct. 387, 390, where this Court said as to motion pictures: " * * * They take their attraction from the general interest, eager and wholesome it may be, in their subjects, but a *prurient interest may be excited and appealed to * * *.*" (Emphasis added.)

We perceive no significant difference between the meaning of obscenity developed in the case law and the definition of the A.L.I., Model Penal Code, § 207.10(2) (Tent.Draft No. 6, 1957), viz.:

" * * * A thing is obscene if, considered as a whole, its predominant appeal is to prurient interest, i.e., a shameful or morbid interest in nudity, sex, or excretion, and if it goes substantially beyond customary limits of candor in description or representation of such matters. * * * " See comment, id., at 10, and the discussion at page 29 et seq.

b. The English court hearing that case held that in such controversies each of the questionable passages in a book which is challenged must be judged as to "whether the tendency of the matter charged as obscenity is to deprave and corrupt those whose minds are open to such immoral influences, and into whose hands a publication of this sort may fall." L.R. 3 Q.B. 360, 371.

sive to the requirements of due process. * * * These words, applied according to the proper standard for judging obscenity, already discussed, give adequate warning of the conduct proscribed and mark " * * * boundaries sufficiently distinct for judges and juries fairly to administer the law. * * * That there may be marginal cases in which it is difficult to determine the side of the line on which a particular fact situation falls is no sufficient reason to hold the language too ambiguous to define a criminal offense." * * *

[The Court found no merit to the other contentions raised.]

* * *

The judgments are affirmed.

* * *

Mr. Chief Justice WARREN, concurring in the result.

I agree with the result reached by the Court in these cases, but, because we are operating in a field of expression and because broad language used here may eventually be applied to the arts and sciences and freedom of communication generally, I would limit our decision to the facts before us and to the validity of the statutes in question as applied.

The line dividing the salacious or pornographic from literature or science is not straight and unwavering. Present laws depend largely upon the effect that the materials may have upon those who receive them. It is manifest that the same object may have a different impact, varying according to the part of the community it reached. But there is more to these cases. It is not the book that is on trial; it is a person. The conduct of the defendant is the central issue, not the obscenity of a book or

picture. The nature of the materials is, of course, relevant as an attribute of the defendant's conduct, but the materials are thus placed in context from which they draw color and character. A wholly different result might be reached in a different setting.

* * * The defendants in both these cases were engaged in the business of purveying textual or graphic matter openly advertised to appeal to the erotic interest of their customers. They were plainly engaged in the commercial exploitation of the morbid and shameful craving for materials with prurient effect. I believe that the State and Federal Governments can constitutionally punish such conduct. That is all that these cases present to us, and that is all we need to decide.

* * *

Mr. Justice HARLAN, concurring in the result in [*Alberts*] and dissenting in [*Roth*].

I regret not to be able to join the Court's opinion. I cannot do so because I find lurking beneath its disarming generalizations a number of problems which not only leave me with serious misgivings as to the future effect of today's decisions, but which also, in my view, call for different results in these two cases.

* * * The Court seems to assume that "obscenity" is a peculiar *genus* of "speech and press," which is as distinct, recognizable, and classifiable as poison ivy is among other plants. * * * But surely the problem cannot be solved in such a generalized fashion. Every communication has an individuality and "value" of its own. The suppression of a particular writing or other tangible form of expression is, therefore,

an *individual* matter, and in the nature of things every such suppression raises an individual constitutional problem, in which a reviewing court must determine for *itself* whether the attacked expression is suppressable within constitutional standards. Since those standards do not readily lend themselves to generalized definitions, the constitutional problem in the last analysis becomes one of particularized judgments which appellate courts must make for themselves.

* * *

* * * I do not think it follows that state and federal powers in this area are the same, and that just because the State may suppress a particular utterance, it is automatically permissible for the Federal Government to do the same. I agree with Mr. Justice Jackson that the historical evidence does not bear out the claim that the Fourteenth Amendment "incorporates" the First in any literal sense. See Beauharnais v. People of State of Illinois, supra.
* * *

The Constitution differentiates between those areas of human conduct subject to the regulation of the States and those subject to the powers of the Federal Government. The substantive powers of the two governments, in many instances, are distinct. And in every case where we are called upon to balance the interest in free expression against other interests, it seems to me important that we should keep in the forefront the question of whether those other interests are state or federal. Since under our constitutional scheme the two are not necessarily equivalent, the balancing process must needs often produce different results. Whether a particular limitation on

speech or press is to be upheld because it subserves a paramount governmental interest must, to a large extent, I think, depend on whether that government has, under the Constitution, a direct substantive interest, that is, the power to act, in the particular area involved.

The Federal Government has, for example, power to restrict seditious speech directed against it, because that Government certainly has the substantive authority to protect itself against revolution. Cf. Commonwealth of Pennsylvania v. Nelson, 350 U.S. 497, 76 S.Ct. 477. But in dealing with obscenity we are faced with the converse situation, for the interests which obscenity statutes purportedly protect are primarily entrusted to the care, not of the Federal Government, but of the States. Congress has no substantive power over sexual morality. Such powers as the Federal Government has in this field are but incidental to its other powers, here the postal power, and are not of the same nature as those possessed by the States, which bear direct responsibility for the protection of the local moral fabric. * * *

* * * Different States will have different attitudes toward the same work of literature. The same book which is freely read in one State might be classed as obscene in another. And it seems to me that no overwhelming danger to our freedom to experiment and to gratify our tastes in literature is likely to result from the suppression of a borderline book in one of the States, so long as there is no uniform nation-wide suppression of the book, and so long as other States are free to experiment with the same or bolder books.

[Justice HARLAN went on to conclude that while the states might be allowed fairly substantial latitude in the obscenity standards they promulgated, the national government was limited to proscribing only "hard-core pornography."]

Mr. Justice DOUGLAS, with whom Mr. Justice BLACK concurs, dissenting.

When we sustain these convictions, we make the legality of a publication turn on the purity of thought which a book or tract instills in the mind of the reader. I do not think we can approve that standard and be faithful to the command of the First Amendment. * * *

* * *

By these standards punishment is inflicted for thoughts provoked, not for overt acts nor antisocial conduct. This test cannot be squared with our decisions under the First Amendment. Even the ill-starred *Dennis* case conceded that speech to be punishable must have some relation to action which could be penalized by government. * * *

The absence of dependable information on the effect of obscene literature on human conduct should make us wary. It should put us on the side of protecting society's interest in literature, except and unless it can be said that the particular publication has an impact on action that the government can control.

* * *

The legality of a publication in this country should never be allowed to turn either on the purity of thought which it instills in the mind of the reader or on the degree to which it offends the community conscience. By either test the role of the censor is exalted, and society's values in literary freedom are sacrificed.

* * *

I would give the broad sweep of the First Amendment full support. I have the same confidence in the ability of our people to reject noxious literature as I have in their capacity to sort out the true from the false in theology, economics, politics, or any other field.

The Supreme Court found occasion to restate and apply its evolving, cumulative obscenity standards nearly a decade later in A Book Named "John Cleland's Memoirs of a Woman of Pleasure" v. Attorney General of Massachusetts, 383 U.S. 413, 86 S.Ct. 975 (1966). The book, a classic eighteenth-century novel detailing the adventures of a young prostitute as she wends her way through life, was itself the object of proceedings brought by the state. A Massachusetts superior court found the book obscene, and the Commonwealth's Supreme Judicial Court affirmed the judgment.

The U.S. Supreme Court reversed. In a plurality opinion which announced the judgment of the Court and spoke also for Chief Justice Warren and Justice Fortas, Justice Brennan reiterated the burgeoning *Roth* criteria and explained their misapplication by the Massachusetts High Court:

We defined obscenity in *Roth* in the following terms: "[W]hether to the average person, applying contemporary community standards, the dominant theme of the material taken as a whole appeals to prurient interest."

* * * Under this definition, as elaborated in subsequent cases, three elements must coalesce: it must be established that (a) the dominant theme of the material taken as a whole appeals to a prurient interest in sex; (b) the material is patently offensive because it affronts contemporary community standards relating to the description or representation of sexual matters; and (c) the material is utterly without redeeming social value.

The Supreme Judicial Court purported to apply the *Roth* definition of obscenity and held all three criteria satisfied. We need not consider the claim that the court erred in concluding that *Memoirs* satisfied the prurient appeal and patent offensiveness criteria; for reversal is required because the court misinterpreted the social value criterion. The court applied the criterion in this passage:

> "It remains to consider whether the book can be said to be 'utterly without social importance.' We are mindful that there was expert testimony, much of which was strained, to the effect that Memoirs is a structural novel with literary merit; that the book displays a skill in characterization and a gift for comedy; that it plays a part in the history of the development of the English novel; and that it contains a moral, namely, that sex with love is superior to sex in a brothel. But the fact that the testimony may indicate this book has some minimal literary value does not mean it is of any social importance. We do not interpret the 'social importance' test as requiring that a book which appeals to prurient interest and is patently offensive must be unqualifiedly worthless before it can be deemed obscene." 349 Mass., at 73, 206 N.E.2d, at 406.

The Supreme Judicial Court erred in holding that a book need not be "unqualifiedly worthless before it can be deemed obscene." A book cannot be proscribed unless it is found to be *utterly* without redeeming social value. This is so even though the book is found to possess the requisite prurient appeal and to be patently offensive. Each of the three federal constitutional criteria is to be applied independently; the social value of the book can neither be weighed against nor canceled by its prurient appeal or patent offensiveness. Hence even on the view of the court below that *Memoirs* possessed only a modicum of social value, its judgment must be reversed as being founded on an erroneous interpretation of a federal constitutional standard.

It does not necessarily follow from this reversal that a determination that *Memoirs* is obscene in the constitutional sense would be improper under all circumstances. On the premise, which we have no occasion to assess, that *Memoirs* has the requisite prurient appeal and is patently offensive, but has only a minimum of social value, the circumstances of production, sale, and publicity are relevant in determining whether or not the publication or distribution of the book is constitutionally protected. Evidence that the book was commercially exploited for the sake of prurient appeal, to the exclusion of all other values, might justify the conclusion that the book was utterly without redeeming social importance. It is not that in such a setting the social value test is relaxed so as to dispense with the requirement that a book be *utterly* devoid of social value, but rather that, as we elaborate in Ginzburg v. United States, * * * where the purveyor's sole emphasis is on the sexually provocative aspects of his publications, a court could accept his evaluation at its face value. In this proceeding, however, the courts were asked to judge the obscenity of

Memoirs in the abstract, and the declaration of obscenity was neither aided nor limited by a specific set of circumstances of production, sale, and publicity. All possible uses of the book must therefore be considered, and the mere risk that the book might be exploited by panderers because it so pervasively treats sexual matters cannot alter the fact—given the view of the Massachusetts court attributing to *Memoirs* a modicum of literary and historical value—that the book will have redeeming social importance in the hands of those who publish or distribute it on the basis of that value.

Justices Black, Douglas, and Stewart concurred separately. Justice Clark dissented in an opinion in which he protested having to "stomach" "the continuous flow of pornographic material reaching this Court and the increasing problem States have in controlling it." He objected particularly to the use of the redeeming social value condition to evade the original *Roth* holding, thus lowering the standard and thereby giving "the smut artist free rein to carry on his dirty business." Justices Harlan and White also dissented.

GINZBURG v. UNITED STATES

Supreme Court of the United States, 1966
383 U.S. 463, 86 S.Ct. 942, 16 L.Ed.2d 31

A federal district judge convicted Ralph Ginzburg on all twenty-eight counts of an indictment charging violations of the federal obscenity law by mailing certain publications or advertisements for them. A federal appellate court affirmed the convictions, and Ginzburg sought review by the Supreme Court.

Mr. Justice BRENNAN delivered the opinion of the Court.

* * *

In the cases in which this Court has decided obscenity questions since *Roth*, it has regarded the materials as sufficient in themselves for the determination of the question. In the present case, however, the prosecution charged the offense in the context of the circumstances of production, sale, and publicity and assumed that, standing alone, the publications themselves might not be obscene. We agree that the question of obscenity may include consideration of the setting in which the publications were presented as an aid to determining the question of obscenity, and assume without deciding that the prosecution could not have succeeded otherwise. * * * [W]e view the publications against a background of commercial exploitation of erotica solely for the sake of their prurient appeal. The record in that regard amply supports the decision of the trial judge that the mailing of all three publications offended the statute.

The three publications were EROS, a hard-cover magazine of expensive format; Liaison, a bi-weekly newsletter; and *The Housewife's Handbook on Selective Promiscuity* (hereinafter the *Handbook*), a short book. The issue of EROS specified in the indictment, Vol. 1, No. 4, contains 15 articles and photo-essays on the subject of love, sex, and sexual relations. The specified issue of Liaison, Vol. 1, No. 1, contains a prefatory "Letter from the Editors" announcing its dedication to "keeping sex an art and preventing it from becoming a science." The remainder of the issue consists of digests of two articles concerning sex and sexual relations which had earlier appeared in professional journals and a report of an interview with a psychotherapist who favors the broadest license in sexual relationships. As the trial judge noted, "[w]hile the treatment is largely superficial, it is presented entirely without restraint of any kind. According to defendants' own expert, it is entirely without literary merit." The *Handbook* purports to be a sexual autobiography detailing with complete candor the author's sexual experiences from age 3 to age 36. The text includes, and prefatory and concluding sections of the book elaborate, her views on such subjects as sex education of children, laws regulating private consensual adult sexual practices, and the equality of women in sexual relationships. It was claimed at trial that women would find the book valuable, for example as a marriage manual or as an aid to the sex education of their children.

Besides testimony as to the merit of the material, there was abundant evidence to show that each of the accused publications was originated or sold as stock in trade of the sordid business of pandering—"the business of purveying textual or graphic matter openly advertised to appeal to the erotic interest of their customers." EROS early sought mailing privileges from the postmasters of Intercourse and Blue Ball, Pennsylvania. The trial court found the obvious, that these hamlets were chosen only for the value their names would have in furthering petitioners' efforts to sell their publications on the basis of salacious appeal; the facilities of the post offices were inadequate to handle the anticipated volume of mail, and the privileges were denied. Mailing privileges

were then obtained from the postmaster of Middlesex, New Jersey. EROS and Liaison thereafter mailed several million circulars soliciting subscriptions from that post office; over 5,500 copies of the Handbook were mailed.

The "leer of the sensualist" also permeates the advertising for the three publications. The circulars sent for EROS and Liaison stressed the sexual candor of the respective publications, and openly boasted that the publishers would take full advantage of what they regarded as an unrestricted license allowed by law in the expression of sex and sexual matters. The advertising for the *Handbook*, apparently mailed from New York, consisted almost entirely of a reproduction of the introduction of the book, written by one Dr. Albert Ellis. Although he alludes to the book's informational value and its putative therapeutic usefulness, his remarks are preoccupied with the book's sexual imagery. The solicitation was indiscriminate, not limited to those, such as physicians or psychiatrists, who might independently discern the book's therapeutic worth. Inserted in each advertisement was a slip labeled "GUARANTEE" and reading, "Documentary Books, Inc. unconditionally guarantees full refund on the price of THE HOUSEWIFE'S HANDBOOK ON SELECTIVE PROMISCUITY if the book fails to reach you because of U. S. Post Office censorship interference." Similar slips appeared in the advertising for EROS and Liaison; they highlighted the gloss petitioners put on the publications, eliminating any doubt what the purchaser was being asked to buy.

This evidence, in our view, was relevant in determining the ultimate question of obscenity and, in the context of this record, serves to resolve all ambiguity and doubt. The deliberate representation of petitioners' publications as erotically arousing, for example, stimulated the reader to accept them as prurient; he looks for titillation, not for saving intellectual content. Similarly, such representation would tend to force public confrontation with the potentially offensive aspects of the work; the brazenness of such an appeal heightens the offensiveness of the publications to those who are offended by such material. And the circumstances of presentation and dissemination of material are equally relevant to determining whether social importance claimed for material in the courtroom was, in the circumstances, pretense or reality—whether it was the basis upon which it was traded in the marketplace or a spurious claim for litigation purposes. Where the purveyor's sole emphasis is on the sexually provocative aspects of his publications, that fact may be decisive in the determination of obscenity. Certainly in a prosecution which, as here, does not necessarily imply suppression of the materials involved, the fact that they originate or are used as a subject of pandering is relevant to the application of the *Roth* test.

A proposition argued as to EROS, for example, is that the trial judge improperly found the magazine to be obscene as a whole, since he concluded that only four of the 15 articles predominantly appealed to prurient interest and substantially exceeded community standards of candor, while the other articles were admittedly non-offensive. But the trial judge found that "[t]he deliberate and studied arrangement of EROS is editorialized for the purpose of appealing predominantly to prurient in-

terest and to insulate through the inclusion of non-offensive material." 224 F.Supp., at 131. However erroneous such a conclusion might be if unsupported by the evidence of pandering, the record here supports it. EROS was created, represented and sold solely as a claimed instrument of the sexual stimulation it would bring. Like the other publications, its pervasive treatment of sex and sexual matters rendered it available to exploitation by those who would make a business of pandering to "the widespread weakness for titillation by pornography." * * *

A similar analysis applies to the judgment regarding the *Handbook*. The bulk of the proofs directed to social importance concerned this publication. Before selling publication rights to petitioners, its author had printed it privately; she sent circulars to persons whose names appeared on membership lists of medical and psychiatric associations, asserting its value as an adjunct to therapy. * * * Petitioners, however, did not sell the book to such a limited audience, or focus their claims for it on its supposed therapeutic or educational value; rather, they deliberately emphasized the sexually provocative aspects of the work, in order to catch the salaciously disposed. They proclaimed its obscenity; and we cannot conclude that the court below erred in taking their own evaluation at its face value and declaring the book as a whole obscene despite the other evidence.

* * *

We perceive no threat to First Amendment guarantees in thus holding that in close cases evidence of pandering may be probative with respect to the nature of the material in question and thus satisfy the *Roth* test. No weight is ascribed to the fact that petitioners have profited from the sale of publications which we have assumed but do not hold cannot themselves be adjudged obscene in the abstract; to sanction consideration of this fact might indeed induce self-censorship, and offend the frequently stated principle that commercial activity, in itself, is no justification for narrowing the protection of expression secured by the First Amendment. Rather, the fact that each of these publications was created or exploited entirely on the basis of its appeal to prurient interests strengthens the conclusion that the transactions here were sales of illicit merchandise, not sales of constitutionally protected matter. * * *

It is important to stress that this analysis simply elaborates the test by which the obscenity vel non of the material must be judged. Where an exploitation of interests in titillation by pornography is shown with respect to material lending itself to such exploitation through pervasive treatment or description of sexual matters, such evidence may support the determination that the material is obscene even though in other contexts the material would escape such condemnation.

* * *

Affirmed.

Mr. Justice BLACK, dissenting.

Only one stark fact emerges with clarity out of the confusing welter of opinions and thousands of words written in this and two other cases today. That fact is that Ginzburg, petitioner here, is now finally and authoritatively condemned to serve five years in prison for distributing printed matter about sex which

neither Ginzburg nor anyone else could possibly have known to be criminal. [Moreover] as I have said many times, I believe the Federal Government is without any power whatever under the Constitution to put any type of burden on speech and expression of ideas of any kind (as distinguished from conduct) * * * and I would reverse Ginzburg's conviction on this ground alone. * * *

* * *

* * * I think that the criteria declared by a majority of the Court today as guidelines for a court or jury to determine whether Ginzburg or anyone else can be punished as a common criminal for publishing or circulating obscene material are so vague and meaningless that they practically leave the fate of a person charged with violating censorship statutes to the unbridled discretion, whim and caprice of the judge or jury which tries him. * * *

* * *

Mr. Justice HARLAN, dissenting.

* * * I believe that under this statute the Federal Government is constitutionally restricted to banning from the mails only "hardcore pornography." * * * Because I do not think it can be maintained that the material in question here falls within that narrow class, I do not believe it can be excluded from the mails.

The Court recognizes the difficulty of justifying these convictions. * * * In fact, the Court in the last analysis sustains the convictions on the express assumption that the items held to be obscene are not, viewing them strictly, obscene at all. * * *

This curious result is reached through the elaboration of a theory of obscenity entirely unrelated to the language, purposes, or history of the federal statute now being applied, and certainly different from the test used by the trial court to convict the defendants. * * *

* * *

Mr. Justice STEWART, dissenting.

* * * There was testimony at his trial that these publications pos-sess artistic and social merit. Personally, I have a hard time discerning any. Most of the material strikes me as both vulgar and unedifying. But if the First Amendment means anything, it means that a man cannot be sent to prison merely for distributing publications which offend a judge's esthetic sensibilities, mine or any other's.

* * *

[Justice DOUGLAS also dissented.]

Edward Mishkin was indicted and convicted on 141 counts of violating New York's statute prohibiting possession, publication, or hiring others to prepare obscene or pornographic material. While some of his books were directed toward conventional heterosexual tastes, many of these cheap paperbacks had strong themes of homosexuality, fetishism, bondage, and sado-masochism. Typical of the titles were: *Dance with the Dominant Whip, Bound in Rubber, I'll Try Anything Twice, Swish Bottom,* and *The Strap Returns.* Miskin was convicted by a New York City court, and that judgment was affirmed by the Appellate Division of the New York Supreme Court. He sought review by the U.S. Supreme Court contending that the law was invalid on its face due to a lack of reasonable certainty in defining the terms "obscenity" and "hard-core pornography."

Speaking for the Court in Mishkin v. New York, 383 U.S. 502, 86 S.Ct. 958 (1966), Justice Brennan affirmed the conviction. In accord with the "variable obscenity" approach manifest in *Memoirs* and *Ginzburg,* he noted that several factors evident in the record disclosed the requisite knowledge that the materials were obscene and intent to purvey them so as to appeal to "a prurient interest in sex": defendant's efforts to hide his relationship with the enterprise, the explicit content and repetitive character of the books, the quantity of books produced, and the fantastic mark-ups in price which resulted in enormous profits. Embellishing the *Roth* test, Justice Brennan found this ample evidence to convict.

[A]ppellant's * * * contention regarding the nature of the material is that some of the books involved in this prosecution, those depicting various deviant sexual practices, such as flagellation, fetishism, and lesbianism, do not satisfy the prurient-appeal requirement because they do not appeal to a prurient interest of the "average person" in sex, that "instead of stimulating the erotic, they disgust and sicken." We reject this argument as being founded on an unrealistic interpretation of the prurient-appeal requirement.

Where the material is designed for and primarily disseminated to a clearly defined deviant sexual group, rather than the public at large, the prurient-appeal requirement of the *Roth* test is satisfied if the dominant theme of the material taken as a whole appeals to the prurient interest in sex of the members of that group. The reference to the "average" or "normal" person in *Roth* * * * does not foreclose this holding. * * *

We adjust the prurient-appeal requirement to social realities by permitting the appeal of this type of material to be assessed in terms of the sexual interests of its intended and probable recipient group; and since our holding requires that the recipient group be defined with more specificity than in terms of sexually immature persons, it also avoids the inadequacy of the most-susceptible-person facet of the *Hicklin* test.

No substantial claim is made that the books depicting sexually deviant practices are devoid of prurient appeal to sexually deviant groups. The evidence fully establishes that these books were specifically conceived and marketed for such groups. Appellant instructed his authors and artists to prepare the books expressly to induce their purchase by persons who would probably be sexually stimulated by them. It was for this reason that appellant "wanted an emphasis on beatings and fetishism and clothing—irregular clothing, and that sort of thing, and again sex scenes between women; always sex scenes had to be very strong." * * *

Justices Black, Douglas, and Stewart dissented separately. As to the Court's holding in *Mishkin*, Justice Douglas wrote:

Some of the tracts for which these publishers go to prison concern normal sex, some homosexuality, some the masochistic yearning that is probably present in everyone and dominant in some. Masochism is a desire to be punished or subdued. In the broad frame of reference the desire may be expressed in the longing to be whipped and lashed, bound and gagged, and cruelly treated. Why is it unlawful to cater to the needs of this group? They are, to be sure, somewhat offbeat, nonconformist, and odd. But we are not in the realm of criminal conduct, only ideas and tastes. Some like Chopin, others like "rock and roll." Some are "normal," some are masochistic, some deviant in other respects, such as the homosexual. Another group also represented here translates mundane articles into sexual symbols. This group, like those embracing masochism, are anathema to the so-called stable majority. But why is freedom of the press and expression denied them? Are they to be barred from communicating in symbolisms important to them? When the Court today speaks of "social value," does it mean a "value" to the majority? Why is not a minority "value" cognizable? The masochistic group is one; the deviant group is another. Is it not important that members of those groups communicate with each other? Why is communication by the "written word" forbidden? If we were wise enough, we might know that communication may have greater therapeutical value than any sermon that those of the "normal" community can ever offer. But if the communication is of value to the masochistic community or to others of the deviant community, how can it be said to be "utterly without redeeming social importance"? "Redeeming" to whom? "Importance" to whom?

———

In Ginsberg v. New York, 390 U.S. 629, 88 S.Ct. 1274 (1968), the Court upheld the constitutionality of a New York statute prohibiting the dissemination of certain kinds of material to minors under seventeen years of age. Ginsberg, the owner and operator of "Sam's Stationery and Luncheonette," was convicted for selling two "girlie" magazines to a sixteen-year-old boy. The Court, per Justice Brennan, affirmed the conviction acknowledging that while the sale of such material to an adult could not be deemed obscene, the New York legislature could justifiably have regarded such magazines as obscene when directed to youths. The Court predicated this ruling on the well-established difference in the degree of protection afforded children as distinguished from adults applied in the framework of "variable obscenity."

STANLEY v. GEORGIA

Supreme Court of the United States, 1969
394 U.S. 557, 89 S.Ct. 1243, 22 L.Ed.2d 542

Stanley was charged under a Georgia statute with possession of obscene matter. His arrest on that charge stemmed from a search of his home by police officers executing a warrant to seize evidence of bookmaking activity. While they found little trace of that for which they were looking, they did stumble upon three rolls of motion picture film and several other items of an allegedly obscene nature. Stanley was convicted in a state superior court, and the conviction was upheld by the Georgia Supreme Court. The U. S. Supreme Court granted certiorari.

Mr. Justice MARSHALL delivered the opinion of the Court.

* * *

* * * Appellant argues here, and argued below, that the Georgia obscenity statute, insofar as it punishes mere private possession of obscene matter, violates the First Amendment, as made applicable to the States by the Fourteenth Amendment. For reasons set forth below, we agree that the mere private possession of obscene matter cannot constitutionally be made a crime.

[W]e do not believe that this case can be decided simply by citing *Roth*. *Roth* and its progeny certainly do mean that the First and Fourteenth Amendments recognize a valid governmental interest in dealing with the problem of obscenity. But the assertion of that interest cannot, in every context, be insulated from all constitutional protections. * * * That holding cannot foreclose an examination of the constitutional implications of a statute forbidding mere private possession of such material.

It is now well established that the Constitution protects the right to receive information and ideas. * * *

This right to receive information and ideas, regardless of their social worth * * * is fundamental to our free society. Moreover, in the context of this case—a prosecution for mere possession of printed or filmed matter in the privacy of a person's own home—that right takes on an added dimension. For also fundamental is the right to be free, except in very limited circumstances, from unwanted governmental intrusions into one's privacy. * * * See *Griswold v. Connecticut.* * * *

These are the rights that appellant is asserting in the case before us. He is asserting the right to read or observe what he pleases—the right to satisfy his intellectual and emotional needs in the privacy of his own home. He is asserting the right to be free from state inquiry into the contents of his library. Georgia contends that appellant does not have these rights, that there are certain types of materials that the individual may not read or even possess. Georgia justifies this assertion by arguing that the films in the present case are obscene. But we think that mere categorization of these films as "obscene" is insufficient justification for such a drastic invasion of personal liberties guaranteed by the First and Fourteenth Amendments. Whatever may be the justifications for other statutes regulating obscenity, we do not think they reach into the privacy of one's own home. If the First Amendment means anything, it means that a State has no business telling a man, sitting alone in his own house, what books he may read or what films he may watch. Our whole constitutional heritage rebels at the thought of giving government the power to control men's minds.

And yet, in the face of these traditional notions of individual liberty, Georgia asserts the right to protect the individual's mind from the effects of obscenity. We are not certain that this argument amounts to anything more than the assertion that the State has the right to control the moral content of a person's thoughts. To some, this may be a noble purpose, but it is wholly inconsistent with the philosophy of the First Amendment. * * * Nor is it relevant that obscene materials in general, or the particular films before the Court, are arguably devoid of any ideological content. The line between the transmission of ideas and mere entertainment is much too elusive for this Court to draw, if indeed such a line can be drawn at all. * * * Whatever the power of the state to control public dissemination of ideas inimical to the public morality, it cannot constitutionally premise legislation on the desirability of controlling a person's private thoughts.

Perhaps recognizing this, Georgia asserts that exposure to obscene materials may lead to deviant sexual behavior or crimes of sexual violence. There appears to be little empirical basis for that assertion. * * * Given the present state of

knowledge, the State may no more prohibit mere possession of obscene matter on the ground that it may lead to antisocial conduct than it may prohibit possession of chemistry books on the ground that they may lead to the manufacture of home-made spirits.

It is true that in *Roth* this Court rejected the necessity of proving that exposure to obscene material would create a clear and present danger of antisocial conduct or would probably induce its recipients to such conduct. * * * But that case dealt with public distribution of obscene materials and such distribution is subject to different objections. For example, there is always the danger that obscene material might fall into the hands of children * * * or that it might intrude upon the sensibilities or privacy of the general public. * * * No such dangers are present in this case.

*   *   *

We hold that the First and Fourteenth Amendments prohibit making mere private possession of obscene material a crime. *Roth* and the cases following that decision are not impaired by today's holding. As we have said, the States retain broad power to regulate obscenity; that power simply does not extend to mere possession by the individual in the privacy of his own home. * * *

*   *   *

Judgment reversed and case remanded.

[Justice STEWART concurred in the result and, in an opinion in which Justices BRENNAN and WHITE joined, voted to reverse on Fourth Amendment grounds.]

MILLER v. CALIFORNIA

Supreme Court of the United States, 1973
413 U.S. 15, 93 S.Ct. 2607, 37 L.Ed.2d 419

A jury found Miller guilty of mailing unsolicited brochures advertising four "adult"-type books and a film in violation of California's obscenity law. Besides some printed matter which described the items offered for sale, the pamphlets contained pictures and drawings explicitly portraying men and women in groups of two or more engaged in sexual acts frequently with genitals clearly shown. Miller's conviction was summarily affirmed by a state appellate court, and he petitioned the U. S. Supreme Court for certiorari.

Mr. Chief Justice BURGER delivered the opinion of the Court.

This is one of a group of "obscenity-pornography" cases being reviewed by the Court in a re-examination of standards enunciated in earlier cases involving what Mr. Justice Harlan called "the intractable obscenity problem." * * *

* * *

Apart from the initial formulation in the *Roth* case, no majority of the Court has at any given time been able to agree on a standard to determine what constitutes obscene, pornographic material subject to regulation under the States' police power. * * * We have seen "a variety of views among the members of the Court unmatched in any other course of constitutional adjudication. * * * This is not remarkable, for in the area of freedom of speech and press the courts must always remain sensitive to any infringement on genuinely serious literary, artistic, political, or scientific expression. This is an area in which there are few eternal verities.

The case we now review was tried on the theory that the California Penal Code § 311 [the statute applied here] approximately incorporates the three-stage *Memoirs* test. But now the *Memoirs* test has been aban-

doned as unworkable by its author and no member of the Court today supports the *Memoirs* formulation.

This much has been categorically settled by the Court, that obscene material is unprotected by the First Amendment. * * * "The First and Fourteenth Amendments have never been treated as absolutes." * * * We acknowledge, however, the inherent dangers of undertaking to regulate any form of expression. State statutes designed to regulate obscene materials must be carefully limited. * * * As a result, we now confine the permissible scope of such regulation to works which depict or describe sexual conduct. That conduct must be specifically defined by the applicable state law as written or authoritatively construed. A state offense must also be limited to works which, taken as a whole, appeal to the prurient interest in sex, which portray sexual conduct in a patently offensive way, and which, taken as a whole, do not have serious literary, artistic, political, or scientific value.

The basic guidelines for the trier of fact must be: (a) whether "the average person, applying contemporary community standards" would find that the work, taken as a whole, appeals to the prurient interest. * * * (b) whether the work depicts or describes, in a patently offensive way, sexual conduct specifically defined by the applicable state law, and (c) whether the work, taken as a whole, lacks serious literary, artistic, political, or scientific value. We do not adopt as a constitutional standard the *"utterly* without redeeming social value" test of *Memoirs* v. *Massachusetts* * * *; that concept has never commanded the adherence of more than three Justices at one time. * * * If a state law that regulates obscene material is thus limited, as written or construed, the First Amendment values applicable to the States through the Fourteenth Amendment are adequately protected by the ultimate power of appellate courts to conduct an independent review of constitutional claims when necessary. * * *

We emphasize that it is not our function to propose regulatory schemes for the States. That must await their concrete legislative efforts. It is possible, however, to give a few plain examples of what a state statute could define for regulation under the second part (b) of the standard announced in this opinion, supra:

(a) Patently offensive representations or descriptions of ultimate sexual acts, normal or perverted, actual or simulated.

(b) Patently offensive representations or descriptions of masturbation, excretory functions, and lewd exhibition of the genitals.

Sex and nudity may not be exploited without limit by films or pictures exhibited or sold in places of public accommodation any more than live sex and nudity can be exhibited or sold without limit in such public places. At a minimum, prurient, pa-

tently offensive depiction or description of sexual conduct must have serious literary, artistic, political, or scientific value to merit First Amendment protection. * * *

* * *

Under the holdings announced today, no one will be subject to prosecution for the sale or exposure of obscene materials unless these materials depict or describe patently offensive "hard core" sexual conduct specifically defined by the regulating state law, as written or construed. We are satisfied that these specific prerequisites will provide fair notice to a dealer in such materials that his public and commercial activities may bring prosecution. * * *

* * *

Under a national Constitution, fundamental First Amendment limitations on the powers of the States do not vary from community to community, but this does not mean that there are, or should or can be, fixed, uniform national standards of precisely what appeals to the "prurient interest" or is "patently offensive." These are essentially questions of fact, and our nation is simply too big and too diverse for this Court to reasonably expect that such standards could be articulated for all 50 States in a single formulation, even assuming the prerequisite consensus exists. When triers of fact are asked to decide whether "the average person, applying contemporary community standards" would consider certain materials "prurient," it would be unrealistic to require that the answer be based on some abstract formulation. The adversary system, with lay jurors as the usual ultimate factfinders in criminal prosecutions, has historically permitted triers-of-fact to draw on the standards of their community, guided always by limiting instructions on the law. To require a State to structure obscenity proceedings around evidence of a *national* "community standard" would be an exercise in futility.

As noted before, this case was tried on the theory that the California obscenity statute sought to incorporate the tripartite test of *Memoirs*. This, a "national" standard of First Amendment protection enumerated by a plurality of this Court, was correctly regarded at the time of trial as limiting state prosecution under the controlling case law. The jury, however, was explicitly instructed that, in determining whether the "dominant theme of the material as a whole * * * appeals to the prurient interest" and in determining whether the material "goes substantially beyond customary limits of candor and affronts contemporary community standards of decency" it was to apply "contemporary community standards of the State of California."

During the trial, both the prosecution and the defense assumed that the relevant "community standards" in making the factual determination of obscenity were those of the State of California, not some hypothetical standard of the entire United States of America. Defense counsel at trial never objected to the testimony of the State's expert on community standards or to the instructions of the trial judge on "state-wide" standards. * * *

We conclude that neither the State's alleged failure to offer evidence of "national standards," nor the trial court's charge that the jury consider state community standards, were constitutional errors. Nothing

in the First Amendment requires that a jury must consider hypothetical and unascertainable "national standards" when attempting to determine whether certain materials are obscene as a matter of fact. * * *

* * * People in different States vary in their tastes and attitudes, and this diversity is not to be strangled by the absolutism of imposed uniformity. * * *

The dissenting Justices sound the alarm of repression. But, in our view, to equate the free and robust exchange of ideas and political debate with commercial exploitation of obscene material demeans the grand conception of the First Amendment and its high purposes in the historic struggle for freedom. It is a "misuse of the great guarantees of free speech and free press." * * * The First Amendment protects works which, taken as a whole, have serious literary, artistic, political or scientific value, regardless of whether the government or a majority of the people approve of the ideas these works represent. "The protection given speech and press was fashioned to assure unfettered interchange of *ideas* for the bringing about of political and social changes desired by the people," *Roth* v. *United States*. * * * But the public portrayal of hard core sexual conduct for its own sake, and for the ensuing commercial gain, is a different matter.

* * *

* * * One can concede that the "sexual revolution" of recent years may have had useful byproducts in striking layers of prudery from a subject long irrationally kept from needed ventilation. But it does not follow that no regulation of pa-

tently offensive "hard core" materials is needed or permissible; civilized people do not allow unregulated access to heroin because it is a derivative of medicinal morphine.

*   *   *

Vacated and remanded for further proceedings.

Mr. Justice DOUGLAS, dissenting.

*   *   *

Today the Court retreats from the earlier formulations of the constitutional test and undertakes to make new definitions. This effort, like the earlier ones, is earnest and well-intentioned. The difficulty is that we do not deal with constitutional terms, since "obscenity" is not mentioned in the Constitution or Bill of Rights. And the First Amendment makes no such exception from "the press" which it undertakes to protect nor, as I have said on other occasions, is an

exception necessarily implied, for there was no recognized exception to the free press at the time the Bill of Rights was adopted which treated "obscene" publications differently from other types of papers, magazines, and books. So there are no constitutional guidelines for deciding what is and what is not "obscene." The Court is at large because we deal with tastes and standards of literature. What shocks me may be sustenance for my neighbor. What causes one person to boil up in rage over one pamphlet or movie may reflect only his neurosis, not shared by others. We deal here with problems of censorship which, if adopted, should be done by constitutional amendment after full debate by the people.

*   *   *

[Justices BRENNAN, STEWART, and MARSHALL also dissented.]

In New York v. Ferber, —— U.S. ——, 102 S.Ct. 3348 (1982), the Supreme Court upheld a state criminal law aimed at preventing the exploitation of children which prohibits the knowing production, direction, or promotion of visual material depicting sexual conduct by children below the age of sixteen, regardless of whether the material is obscene in the legal sense, i.e., within the meaning of *Miller* v. *California*. Speaking for the Court, Justice White acknowledged that "[i]n recent years, the exploitive use of children in the production of pornography has become a serious national problem" and noted that the federal government and forty-seven states have sought to combat child pornography by adopting statutes specifically directed at it. The Court concluded that "the States are entitled to greater leeway in the regulation of pornographic depictions of children" than that furnished by the decision in *Miller* for the following reasons: (1) A "state's interest in 'safeguarding the physical and psychological well being of a minor' is 'compelling'"; (2) "The distribution of photographs and films depicting sexual activity by juveniles is intrinsically related to the sexual abuse of children" because "the materials produced are a permanent record of the children's participation and the harm to the child is exacerbated by their circulation" and because "the distribution network for child pornography must be closed if the production of material which requires the sexual exploitation of children is to be effectively controlled"; (3) "The advertising and selling of child pornography provides an economic motive for and is thus an integral part of the production of such materials, an activity illegal throughout the nation"; (4) "The value of permitting live performances and photographic reproductions of children engaged in lewd sexual conduct is exceedingly modest, if not *de minimis*"; and (5) "Recognizing and classifying child pornography as a category of material outside the protection of the First Amendment is not incompatible with our earlier decisions." Justice White then declared:

> The test for child pornography is separate from the obscenity standard enunciated in *Miller*, but may be compared to it for purpose of clarity. The *Miller* formulation is adjusted in the following respects: A trier of fact need not find that the material appeals to the prurient interest of the average person; it is not required that sexual conduct portrayed be done so in a patently offensive manner; and the material at issue need not be considered as a whole. We note that the distribution of descriptions or other depictions of sexual conduct, not otherwise obscene, which do not involve live performance or photographic or other visual reproduction of live performances, retains First Amendment protection. As with obscenity laws, criminal responsibility may not be imposed without some element of scienter [i.e., of acting knowingly] on the part of the defendant. * * *

The Court went on to uphold the constitutionality of the statute's definition of "sexual conduct" as "actual or simulated sexual intercourse, deviate sexual intercourse, sexual bestiality, masturbation, sadomasochistic abuse, or lewd exhibition of the genitals" against attack on grounds of overbreadth.

PARIS ADULT THEATRE I v. SLATON

Supreme Court of the United States, 1973
413 U.S. 49, 93 S.Ct. 2628, 37 L.Ed.2d 446

Lewis Slaton, the district attorney for an area including the City of Atlanta, and others brought suit under a Georgia civil statute to enjoin operators of a movie house from showing two allegedly obscene films, "Magic Mirror" and "It All Comes Out in the End." At a bench trial the judge dismissed the complaint ruling that exhibition of the pictures to consenting adults in the confines of a commercial theater was "constitutionally permissible." Moreover, he did not require any "expert testimony" as to the obscenity of the films in order to reach his conclusion. On appeal, the Georgia Supreme Court reversed, holding that the sex activity portrayed in the motion pictures was "hard-core pornography," whereupon operators of the theater sought review by the U. S. Supreme Court.

Mr. Chief Justice BURGER delivered the opinion of the Court.

* * *

We categorically disapprove the theory, apparently adopted by the trial judge, that obscene, pornographic films acquire constitutional immunity from state regulation simply because they are exhibited for consenting adults only. This holding was properly rejected by the Georgia Supreme Court. Although we have often pointedly recognized the high importance of the state interest in regulating the exposure of obscene materials to juveniles and unconsenting adults, * * * this Court has never delared these to be the only legitimate state interests permitting regulation of obscene material. The States have a long-recognized legitimate interest in regulating the use of obscene material in local commerce and in all places of public accommodation, as long as these regulations do not run afoul of specific constitutional prohibitions. * * *

In particular, we hold that there are legitimate state interests at stake in stemming the tide of commercialized obscenity, even assuming it is feasible to enforce effective safeguards against exposure to juveniles and to the passerby. * * * These include the interest of the public in the quality of life and the total community environment, the tone of commerce in the great city centers, and, possibly, the public safety itself. The Hill-Link Minority Report of the Commission on Obscenity and Pornography indicates that there is at least an arguable correlation between obscene material and crime. * * *

But, it is argued, there is no scientific data which conclusively demonstrates that exposure to obscene materials adversely affects men and women or their society. It is urged on behalf of the petitioner that, absent such a demonstration, any kind of state regulation is "impermissible." We reject this argument. It is not for us to resolve empirical uncertainties underlying state legislation, save in the exceptional case where that legislation plainly impinges upon rights protected by the Constitution itself. * * * Although there is no conclusive proof of a connection between antisocial behavior and obscene material, the legislature of Georgia could quite reasonably determine that such a connection does or might exist. In deciding *Roth*, this Court implicitly accepted that a legislature could legitimately act on such a conclusion to protect "*the social interest in order and morality.*" Roth v. United States, supra, 354 U.S., at 485 (1957), quoting Chaplinsky v. New Hampshire, 315

U.S. 568, 572 (1942) (emphasis added in *Roth*).

From the beginning of civilized societies, legislators and judges have acted on various unprovable assumptions. Such assumptions underlie much lawful state regulation of commercial and business affairs. * * * On the basis of these assumptions both Congress and state legislatures have, for example, drastically restricted associational rights by adopting antitrust laws, and have strictly regulated public expression by issuers of and dealers in securities, profit sharing "coupons," and "trading stamps," commanding what they must and may not publish and announce. * * *

* * * The fact that a congressional directive reflects unprovable assumptions about what is good for the people, including imponderable aesthetic assumptions, is not a sufficient reason to find that statute unconstitutional.

* * * The sum of experience, including that of the past two decades, affords an ample basis for legislatures to conclude that a sensitive, key relationship of human existence, central to family life, community welfare, and the development of human personality, can be debased and distorted by crass commercial exploitation of sex. Nothing in the Constitution prohibits a State from reaching such a conclusion and acting on it legislatively simply because there is no conclusive evidence or empirical data.

It is argued that individual "free will" must govern, even in activities beyond the protection of the First Amendment and other constitutional guarantees of privacy, and that Government cannot legitimately impede an individual's desire to see or acquire obscene plays, movies, and books. * * * States are told by some that they must await a "laissez faire" market solution to the obscenity-pornography problem, paradoxically "by people who have never otherwise had a kind word to say for laissez-faire," particularly in solving urban, commercial, and environmental pollution problems. * * *

The States, of course, may follow such a "laissez faire" policy and drop all controls on commercialized obscenity, if that is what they prefer, just as they can ignore consumer protection in the market place, but nothing in the Constitution *compels* the States to do so with regard to matters falling within state jurisdiction. * * *

It is asserted, however, that standards for evaluating state commercial regulations are inapposite in the present context, as state regulation of access by consenting adults to obscene material violates the constitutionally protected right to privacy enjoyed by petitioners' customers. Even assuming that petitioners have vicarious standing to assert potential customers' rights, it is unavailing to compare a theatre, open to the public for a fee, with the private home of Stanley v. Georgia, 394 U.S. 557, 568 (1969), and the marital bedroom of Griswold v. Connecticut, 381 U.S. 479, 485–486 (1965). This Court, has, on numerous occasions, refused to hold that commercial ventures such as a motion-picture house are "private" for the purpose of civil rights litigation and civil rights statutes. * * *

Our prior decisions recognizing a right to privacy guaranteed by the Fourteenth Amendment included "only those personal rights that can be deemed 'fundamental' or 'implicit

in the concept of ordered liberty.' Palko v. Connecticut, 302 U.S. 319, 325." Roe v. Wade, 410 U.S. 113, 152 (1973). This privacy right encompasses and protects the personal intimacies of the home, the family, marriage, motherhood, procreation, and child rearing. * * * Nothing, however, in this Court's decisions intimates that there is any "fundamental" privacy right "implicit in the concept of ordered liberty" to watch obscene movies in places of public accommodation.

[W]e have declined to equate the privacy of the home relied on in *Stanley* with a "zone" of "privacy" that follows a distributor or a consumer of obscene materials wherever he goes. See United States v. Orito, 413 U.S. 139 (pp. 2–4) (1973); United States v. Twelve 200-Ft. Reels, 413 U.S. 123 (pp. 3–6) (1973); United States v. Thirty-Seven Photographs, 402 U.S. 363, 376–377 (1971) (opinion of WHITE, J.); United States v. Reidel, 402 U.S. 351, 355 (1971). The idea of a "privacy" right and a place of public accommodation are, in this context, mutually exclusive. Conduct or depictions of conduct that the state police power can prohibit on a public street does not become automatically protected by the Constitution merely because the conduct is moved to a bar or a "live" theatre stage, any more than a "live" performance of a man and woman locked in a sexual embrace at high noon in Times Square is protected by the Constitution because they simultaneously engage in a valid political dialogue.

It is also argued that the State has no legitimate interest in "control [of] the moral content of a person's thoughts," * * * and we need not quarrel with this. But we reject the claim that the State of Georgia is here attempting to control the minds or thoughts of those who patronize theatres. Preventing unlimited display or distribution of obscene material, which by definition lacks any serious literary, artistic, political, or scientific value as communication, * * * is distinct from a control of reason and the intellect. * * * Where communication of ideas, protected by the First Amendment, is not involved, nor the particular privacy of the home protected by *Stanley*, nor any of the other "areas or zones" of constitutionally protected privacy, the mere fact that, as a consequence, some human "utterances" or "thoughts" may be incidentally affected does not bar the State from acting to protect legitimate state interests. * * * The fantasies of a drug addict are his own and beyond the reach of government, but government regulation of drug sales is not prohibited by the Constitution. * * *

Finally, petitioners argue that conduct which directly involves "consenting adults" only has, for that sole reason, a special claim to constitutional protection. * * * Commercial exploitation of depictions, descriptions, or exhibitions of obscene conduct on commercial premises open to the adult public falls within a State's broad power to regulate commerce and protect the public environment. The issue in this context goes beyond whether someone, or even the majority, considers the conduct depicted as "wrong" or "sinful." The States have the power to make a morally neutral judgment that public exhibition of obscene material, or commerce in such material, has a tendency to injure the community as a whole, to endanger the public safety, or to jeopardize, in Chief Justice Warren's words, the States' "right

* * * to maintain a decent society." * * *

* * * In this case we hold that the States have a legitimate interest in regulating commerce in obscene material and in regulating exhibition of obscene material in places of public accommodation, including so-called "adult" theatres from which minors are excluded. In light of these holdings, nothing precludes the State of Georgia from the regulation of the allegedly obscene materials exhibited in Paris Adult Theatre I or II, provided that the applicable Georgia law, as written or authoritatively interpreted by the Georgia courts, meets the First Amendment standards set forth in *Miller* v. *California*, supra. * * *

Vacated and remanded for further proceedings.

Mr. Justice DOUGLAS, dissenting.

* * *

I applaud the effort of my Brother BRENNAN to forsake the low road which the Court has followed in this field. The new regime he would inaugurate is much closer than the old to the policy of abstention which the First Amendment proclaims. But since we do not have here the unique series of problems raised by government imposed or government approved captive audiences * * * I see no constitutional basis for fashioning a rule that makes a publisher, producer, bookseller, librarian, or movie house criminally responsible, when he or she fails to take affirmative steps to protect the consumer against literature or books offensive to those who temporarily occupy the seats of the mighty.

* * *

Mr. Justice BRENNAN, with whom Mr. Justice STEWART and Mr. Justice MARSHALL join, dissenting.

* * * I am convinced that the approach initiated 15 years ago in Roth v. United States * * * and culminating in the Court's decision today, cannot bring stability to this area of the law without jeopardizing fundamental First Amendment values, and I have concluded that the time has come to make a significant departure from that approach.

* * *

[A]fter 15 years of experimentation and debate I am reluctantly forced to the conclusion that none of the available formulas, including the one announced today, can reduce the vagueness to a tolerable level while at the same time striking an acceptable balance between the protections of the First and Fourteenth Amendments, on the one hand, and on the other the asserted state interest in regulating the dissemination of certain sexually oriented materials. Any effort to draw a constitutionally acceptable boundary on state power must resort to such indefinite concepts as "prurient interest," "patent offensiveness," "serious literary value," and the like. The meaning of these concepts necessarily varies with the experience, outlook, and even idiosyncracies of the person defining them. Although we have assumed that obscenity does exist and that we "know it when [we] see it," Jacobellis v. Ohio, 378 U.S. 184, 197 (1964) (STEWART, J., concurring) we are manifestly unable to describe it in advance except by reference to concepts so elusive that they fail to distinguish clearly between protected and unprotected speech.

* * *

The problems of fair notice and chilling protected speech are very grave standing alone. But it does not detract from their importance to recognize that a vague statute in this area creates a * * * more subtle set of problems. These problems concern the institutional stress that inevitably results where the line separating protected from unprotected speech is excessively vague. In Roth we conceded that "there may be marginal cases in which it is difficult to determine the side of the line on which a particular fact situation falls." * * * Our subsequent experience demonstrates that almost every case is "marginal." And since the "margin" marks the point of separation between protected and unprotected speech, we are left with a system in which almost every obscenity case presents a constitutional question of exceptional difficulty. * * *

* * * The number of obscenity cases on our docket gives ample testimony to the burden that has been placed upon this Court.

* * *

The severe problems arising from the lack of fair notice, from the chill on protected expression, and from the stress imposed on the state and federal judicial machinery persuade me that a significant change in direction is urgently required. * * *

* * *

Our experience since Roth requires us not only to abandon the effort to pick out obscene materials on a case-by-case basis, but also to reconsider a fundamental postulate of Roth: that there exists a definable class of sexually oriented expression that may be totally suppressed by the Federal and State Governments. Assuming that such a class of expression does in fact exist, I am forced to conclude that the concept of "obscenity" cannot be defined with sufficient specificity and clarity to provide fair notice to persons who create and distribute sexually oriented materials, to prevent substantial erosion of protected speech as a by-product of the attempt to suppress unprotected speech, and to avoid very costly institutional harms. Given these inevitable side-effects of state efforts to suppress what is assumed to be *unprotected* speech, we must scrutinize with care the state interest that is asserted to justify the suppression. * * *

* * *

[V]irtually all of the interests that might be asserted in defense of suppression, laying aside the special interests associated with distribution to juveniles and unconsenting adults, were also posited in *Stanley* v. *Georgia* * * * where we held that the State could not make the "mere private possession of obscene material a crime." * * * That decision presages the conclusions I reach here today.

* * *

* * * Like the proscription of abortions, the effort to suppress obscenity is predicated on unprovable, although strongly held, assumptions about human behavior, morality, sex, and religion. The existence of these assumptions cannot validate a statute that substantially undermines the guarantees of the First Amendment, any more than the existence of similar assumptions on the issue of abortion can validate a statute that infringes the constitutionally-protected privacy interests of a pregnant woman.

* * *

* * * Even a legitimate, sharply focused state concern for the morality of the community cannot, in other words, justify an assault on the protections of the First Amendment. * * * Where the state interest in regulation of morality is vague and ill-defined, interference with the guarantees of the First Amendment is even more difficult to justify.

In short, while I cannot say that the interests of the State—apart from the question of juveniles and unconsenting adults—are trivial or nonexistent, I am compelled to conclude that these interests cannot justify the substantial damage to constitutional rights and to this Nation's judicial machinery that inevitably results from state efforts to bar the distribution even of unprotected material to consenting adults. * * * I would hold, therefore, that at least in the absence of distribution to juveniles or obtrusive exposure to unconsenting adults, the First and Fourteenth Amendments prohibit the state and federal governments from attempting wholly to suppress sexually oriented materials on the basis of their allegedly "obscene" contents. * * *

* * *

About midafternoon one weekday, a New York radio station broadcast a twelve-minute monologue entitled "Filthy Words" from an album of comedy routines by George Carlin. A listener, who was driving in his car with his young son, tuned in in the midst of the broadcast, became upset about the language used in the monologue, and filed a complaint with the FCC. The agency subsequently informed the station that it considered the words used to be "patently offensive" and, while not "obscene," certainly "indecent" within the meaning of the federal statutes. Although it did not take immediate action against the station, the commission indicated that it would include the complaint in the station's license file and, in the event further complaints were received, would consider whether to employ "any of the available sanctions * * * granted by Congress." Clarifying its ruling on the matter, the FCC later indicated that it did not seek to place an "absolute prohibition on the broadcast of this type of language but rather sought to channel it to times of the day when children most likely would not be exposed to it." A divided federal appellate court reversed the FCC's ruling. In Federal Communications Commission v. Pacifica Foundation, 438 U.S. 726, 98 S.Ct. 3026 (1978), the Supreme Court overturned the lower court's judgment.

Speaking in part for the Court and in part for a plurality composed of Chief Justice Burger, Justice Rehnquist, and himself, Justice Stevens concluded that the FCC had the power to proscribe a radio broadcast that was indecent but not obscene. After finding: (1) that federal statutes do "not limit the Commission's authority to impose sanctions on licensees who engage in obscene, indecent, or profane broadcasting," and (2) that the terms "indecent" and "obscene" are not identical within the meaning of the statutes because there was no indication either from prior decisions or the legislative history "that prurient appeal [which is an identifying characteristic of obscenity] is an essential component of indecent language, * * * " the Court turned to constitutional considerations. Directing its attention to several words—"the seven dirty words"—"that referred to excretory or sexual activities or organs," the plurality observed that if the offensiveness ruling could be traced to a monologue's political content or to a satirization of four-letter words, "First Amendment protection might be required. But that is simply not this case." As deliberately and repetitively used in Carlin's comedy sketch, "[t]hese words offend for the same reasons that obscenity offends." Asserting that the words had very " 'slight social value' " and ranked near the bottom of priorities in First Amendment expression, the plurality looked to the context of their use in assessing their marginally protected use over the airwaves. The plurality then reasoned that two factors supported the FCC's ruling in this case: first, "[p]atently offensive, indecent material presented over the airwaves confronts the citizen, not only in public, but also in the privacy of the home, where the individual's right to be alone plainly outweighs the First Amendment right of an intruder." Even a prior warning, such as that given by the station in this instance, was insufficient to countervail this interest "[b]ecause the broadcast audience is constantly tuning in and out" and, therefore, "cannot completely protect the listener or viewer from unexpected program content." And "[s]econd, broadcasting is uniquely accessible to children * * * "

Justice Powell, joined by Justice Blackmun, referring to the repetitious use of the proscribed words "as a sort of verbal shock treatment," concurred but took exception to the plurality's notion that the result in this case turned "on whether Carlin's monologue, viewed as a whole, or the words that comprise it, have more or less 'value' than a candidate's campaign speech." Instead, he concluded that the decisive issues were the privacy and child-protection interests already cited.

In a tart dissenting opinion in which Justice Marshall joined, Justice Brennan began by confessing that he "found the Court's misapplication of First Amendment principles so patent, and its attempt to impose *its* notions of propriety on the whole of the American people so misguided, that I am unable to remain silent."

In rejoinder to the weight to be accorded factors a majority of the Court thought to be decisive, Justice Brennan turned first to the asserted interest in privacy. Said Brennan:

* * * I believe that an individual's actions in switching on and listening to communications transmitted over the public airways and directed to the public at-large do not implicate fundamental privacy interests, even when engaged in within the home. Instead, because the radio is undeniably a public medium, these actions are more properly viewed as a decision to take part, if only as a listener, in an ongoing public discourse. * * *

Even if an individual who voluntarily opens his home to radio communications retains privacy interests of sufficient moment to justify a ban on protected speech if those interests are "invaded in an essentially intolerable manner," * * * the very fact that those interests are threatened only by a radio broadcast precludes an intolerable invasion of privacy; for unlike other intrusive modes of communications, such as sound trucks, "[t]he radio can be turned off," * * *—and with a minimum of effort. * * * Whatever the minimal discomfort suffered by a listener who inadvertently tunes into a program he finds offensive during the brief interval before he can simply extend his arm and switch stations or flick the "off" button, it is surely worth the candle to preserve the broadcaster's right to send, and the right of those interested to receive, a message entitled to First Amendment protection. * * *

The Court's balance, of necessity, fails to accord proper weight to the interests of listeners who wish to hear broadcasts the FCC deems offensive. It permits majoritarian tastes completely to preclude a protected message from entering the homes of a receptive, unoffended minority. No decision of this Court supports such a result. * * * And, as to the child-protection argument, he responded that, in view of the Court's own past rulings which prevent children only from gaining access to obscene materials, "[t]he Court's refusal to follow its own pronouncements * * * has the * * * anomalous * * * effect, at least in the radio context at issue here, of making completely unavailable to adults material which may not be kept even from children." Drawing his attack on the First Amendment faults of the plurality and concurring opinions to a close, he observed "another vein I find equally disturbing: a depressing inability to appreciate that in our land of cultural pluralism, there are many who think, act, and talk differently from the Members of this Court, and who do not share their fragile sensibilities. It is only an acute ethnocentric myopia that enables the Court to approve the censorship of communications solely because of the words they contain."

In a second dissenting opinion, which addressed purely statutory issues, Justice Stewart, joined by Justices Brennan, White, and Marshall, concluded "that Congress intended, by using the word 'indecent' * * * to prohibit nothing more than obscene speech" and "[u]nder that reading of the statute" would have held that the commission's order was not authorized.

c. LIBEL

NEW YORK TIMES CO. v. SULLIVAN

Supreme Court of the United States, 1964
376 U.S. 254, 84 S.Ct. 710, 11 L.Ed.2d 686

The facts are contained in the Court's opinion given on the following page.

Mr. Justice BRENNAN delivered the opinion of the Court.

We are required in this case to determine for the first time the extent to which the constitutional protections for speech and press limit a State's power to award damages in a libel action brought by a public official against critics of his official conduct.

Respondent L. B. Sullivan is one of the three elected Commissioners of the City of Montgomery, Alabama. He testified that he was "Commissioner of Public Affairs and the duties are supervision of the Police Department, Fire Department, Department of Cemetery and Department of Scales." He brought this civil libel action against the four individual petitioners, who are Negroes and Alabama clergymen, and against petitioner the New York Times Company, a New York corporation which publishes the New York Times, a daily newspaper. A jury in the Circuit Court of Montgomery County awarded him damages of $500,000, the full amount claimed, against all the petitioners, and the Supreme Court of Alabama affirmed.

Respondent's complaint alleged that he had been libeled by statements in a full-page advertisement that was carried in the New York Times on March 29, 1960. Entitled "Heed Their Rising Voices," the advertisement began by stating that "As the whole world knows by now, thousands of Southern Negro students are engaged in widespread non-violent demonstrations in positive affirmation of the right to live in human dignity as guaranteed by the U. S. Constitution and the Bill of Rights." It went on to charge that "in their efforts to uphold these guarantees, they are being met by an unprecedented wave of terror by those who would deny and negate that document which the whole world looks upon as setting the pattern for modern freedom." * * * Succeeding paragraphs purported to illustrate the "wave of terror" by describing certain alleged events. The text concluded with an appeal for funds for three purposes: support of the student movement, "the struggle for the right-to-vote," and the legal defense of Dr. Martin Luther King, Jr., leader of the movement, against a perjury indictment then pending in Montgomery.

* * *

Of the 10 paragraphs of text in the advertisement, the third and a portion of the sixth were the basis of respondent's claim of libel. They read as follows:

Third paragraph:

"In Montgomery, Alabama, after students sang 'My Country, 'Tis of Thee' on the State Capitol steps, their leaders were expelled from school, and truckloads of police armed with shotguns and tear-gas ringed the Alabama State College Campus. When the entire student body protested to state authorities by refusing to re-register, their dining hall was padlocked in an attempt to starve them into submission."

Sixth paragraph:

"Again and again the Southern violators have answered Dr. King's peaceful protests with intimidation and violence. They have bombed his home almost killing his wife and child. They have assaulted his person. They have arrested him seven times—for 'speeding,' 'loitering' and similar 'offenses.' And now they have charged him with 'perjury'—a *felony* under which they could imprison him for *ten years.*" * * *

Although neither of these statements mentions respondent by name, he contended that the word "police" in the third paragraph referred to him as the Montgomery Commissioner who supervised the Police Department, so that he was being accused of "ringing" the campus with police. He further claimed that the paragraph would be read as imputing to the police, and hence to him, the padlocking of the dining hall in order to starve the students into submission. As to the sixth paragraph, he contended that since arrests are ordinarily made by the police, the statement "They have arrested [Dr. King] seven times" would be read as referring to him; he further contended that the "They" who did the arresting would be equated with the "They" who committed the other described acts and with the "Southern violators." Thus, he argued, the paragraph would be read as accusing the Montgomery police, and hence him, of answering Dr. King's protests with "intimidation and violence," bombing his home, assaulting his person, and charging him with perjury. Respondent and six other Montgomery residents testified that they read some or all of the statements as referring to him in his capacity as Commissioner.

It is uncontroverted that some of the statements contained in the two paragraphs were not accurate descriptions of events which occurred in Montgomery. Although Negro students staged a demonstration on the State Capitol steps, they sang the National Anthem and not "My Country, 'Tis of Thee." Although nine students were expelled by the State Board of Education, this was not for leading the demonstration at the

Capitol, but for demanding service at a lunch counter in the Montgomery County Courthouse on another day. Not the entire student body, but most of it, had protested the expulsion, not by refusing to register, but by boycotting classes on a single day; virtually all the students did register for the ensuing semester. The campus dining hall was not padlocked on any occasion, and the only students who may have been barred from eating there were the few who had neither signed a preregistration application nor requested temporary meal tickets. Although the police were deployed near the campus in large numbers on three occasions, they did not at any time "ring" the campus, and they were not called to the campus in connection with the demonstration on the State Capitol steps, as the third paragraph implied. * * *

* * *

Because of the importance of the constitutional issues involved, we granted * * * certiorari. * * * We reverse the judgment. We hold that the rule of law applied by the Alabama courts is constitutionally deficient for failure to provide the safeguards for freedom of speech and of the press that are required by the First and Fourteenth Amendments in a libel action brought by a public official against critics of his official conduct. We further hold that under the proper safeguards the evidence presented in this case is constitutionally insufficient to support the judgment for respondent.

We may dispose at the outset of two grounds asserted to insulate the judgment of the Alabama courts from constitutional scrutiny. The first is the proposition relied on by the State Supreme Court—that "The Fourteenth Amendment is directed against State action and not private action." That proposition has no application to this case. Although this is a civil lawsuit between private parties, the Alabama courts have applied a state rule of law which petitioners claim to impose invalid restrictions on their constitutional freedoms of speech and press. * * *

The second contention is that the constitutional guarantees of freedom of speech and of the press are inapplicable here, at least so far as the Times is concerned, because the allegedly libelous statements were published as part of a paid, "commercial" advertisement. * * *

* * * That the Times was paid for publishing the advertisement is as immaterial in this connection as is the fact that newspapers and books are sold. * * * Any other conclusion would discourage newspapers from carrying "editorial advertisements" of this type, and so might shut off an important outlet for the promulgation of information and ideas by persons who do not themselves have access to publishing facilities—who wish to exercise their freedom of speech even though they are not members of the press. * * * The effect would be to shackle the First Amendment in its attempt to secure "the widest possible dissemination of information from diverse and antagonistic sources." * * * To avoid placing such a handicap upon the freedoms of expression, we hold that if the allegedly libelous statements would otherwise be constitutionally protected from the present judgment, they do not forfeit that protection because they were published in the form of a paid advertisement.

Under Alabama law as applied in this case, a publication is "libelous per se" if the words "tend to injure a person * * * in his reputation" or to "bring [him] into public contempt"; the trial court stated that the standard was met if the words are such as to "injure him in his public office, or impute misconduct to him in his office, or want of official integrity, or want of fidelity to a public trust." * * * The jury must find that the words were published "of and concerning" the plaintiff, but where the plaintiff is a public official his place in the governmental hierarchy is sufficient evidence to support a finding that his reputation has been affected by statements that reflect upon the agency of which he is in charge. Once "libel per se" has been established, the defendant has no defense as to stated facts unless he can persuade the jury that they were true in all their particulars. * * * His privilege of "fair comment" for expressions of opinion depends on the truth of the facts upon which the comment is based. * * * Unless he can discharge the burden of proving truth, general damages are presumed, and may be awarded without proof of pecuniary injury. A showing of actual malice is apparently a prerequisite to recovery of punitive damages, and the defendant may in any event forestall a punitive award by a retraction meeting the statutory requirements. Good motives and belief in truth do not negate an inference of malice, but are relevant only in mitigation of punitive damages if the jury chooses to accord them weight. * * *

The question before us is whether this rule of liability, as applied to an action brought by a public official against critics of his official conduct,

1474 CIVIL RIGHTS AND LIBERTIES PART III

abridges the freedom of speech and of the press that is guaranteed by the First and Fourteenth Amendments.

Respondent relies heavily, as did the Alabama courts on statements of this Court to the effect that the Constitution does not protect libelous publications. Those statements do not foreclose our inquiry here. None of the cases sustained the use of libel laws to impose sanctions upon expression critial of the official conduct of public officials. * * * Like insurrection, contempt, advocacy of unlawful acts, breach of the peace, obscenity, solicitation of legal business, and the various other formulae for the repression of expression that have been challenged in this Court, libel can claim no talismanic immunity from constitutional limitations. It must be measured by standards that satisfy the First Amendment.

* * *

[W]e consider this case against the background of a profound national commitment to the principle that debate on public issues should be uninhibited, robust, and wide-open, and that it may well include vehement, caustic, and sometimes unpleasantly sharp attacks on government and public officials. * * *

* * *

* * * A rule compelling the critic of official conduct to guarantee the truth of all his factual assertions—and to do so on pain of libel judgments virtually unlimited in amount—leads to * * * "self-censorship." Allowance of the defense of truth, with the burden of proving it on the defendant, does not mean that only false speech will be deterred. Even courts accepting this defense as an adequate safeguard

have recognized the difficulties of adducing legal proofs that the alleged libel was true in all its factual particulars. * * * Under such a rule, would-be critics of official conduct may be deterred from voicing their criticism, even though it is believed to be true and even though it is in fact true, because of doubt whether it an be proved in court or fear of the expense of having to do so. * * * The rule thus dampens the vigor and limits the variety of public debate. It is inconsistent with the First and Fourteenth Amendments.

The constitutional guarantees require, we think, a federal rule that prohibits a public official from recovering damages for a defamatory falsehood relating to his official conduct unless he proves that the statement was made with "actual malice"—that is, with knowledge that it was false or with reckless disregard of whether it was false or not. * * *

Such a privilege for criticism of official conduct is appropriately analogous to the protection accorded a public official when *he* is sued for libel by a private citizen. In Barr v. Matteo, 360 U.S. 564, 575, 79 S.Ct. 1335, 1341, this Court held the utterance of a federal official to be absolutely privileged if made "within the outer perimeter" of his duties. The States accord the same immunity to statements of their highest officers, although some differentiate their lesser officials and qualify the privilege they enjoy. But all hold that all officials are protected unless actual malice can be proved. The reason for the official privilege is said to be that the threat of damage suits would otherwise "inhibit the fearless, vigorous, and effective administration of policies of government" and "dampen the ardor of all but the most resolute, or the most irresponsible, in the unflinching discharge of their duties." * * * Analogous considerations support the privilege for the citizen-critic of government. It is as much his duty to criticize as it is the official's duty to administer. * * * It would give public servants an unjustified preference over the public they serve, if critics of official conduct did not have a fair equivalent of the immunity granted to the officials themselves.

We conclude that such a privilege is required by the First and Fourteenth Amendments.

We hold today that the Constitution delimits a State's power to award damages for libel in actions brought by public officials against critics of their official conduct. Since this is such an action, the rule requiring proof of actual malice is applicable. While Alabama law apparently requires proof of actual malice for an award of punitive damages, where general damages are concerned malice is "presumed." Such a presumption is inconsistent with the federal rule. * * * Since the trial judge did not instruct the jury to differentiate between general and punitive damages, it may be that the verdict was wholly an award of one or the other. But it is impossible to know, in view of the general verdict returned. Because of this uncertainty, the judgment must be reversed and the case remanded. * * *

Since respondent may seek a new trial, we deem that considerations of effective judicial administration require us to review the evidence in the present record to determine whether it could constitutionally support a judgment for respondent. This

Court's duty is not limited to the elaboration of constitutional principles; we must also in proper cases review the evidence to make certain that those principles have been constitutionally applied. This is such a case, particularly since the question is one of alleged trespass across "the line between speech unconditionally guaranteed and speech which may legitimately be regulated." * * *

Applying these standards, we consider that the proof presented to show actual malice lacks the convincing clarity which the constitutional standard demands, and hence that it would not constitutionally sustain the judgment for respondent under the proper rule of law. * * *

[Since Sullivan was not identified in the advertisement either personally or by position, the Court also found the evidence to be "constitutionally defective" because of only a remote relationship between the criticism contained in the advertisement and any interest asserted by the plaintiff.]

Mr. Justice BLACK, with whom Mr. Justice DOUGLAS joins (concurring).

* * * I base my vote to reverse on the belief that the First and Fourteenth Amendments not merely "delimit" a State's power to award damages to "public officials against critics of their official conduct" but completely prohibit a State from exercising such a power. The Court goes on to hold that a State can subject such critics to damages if "actual malice" can be proved against them. "Malice," even as defined by the Court, is an elusive, abstract concept, hard to prove and hard to disprove. The requirement that malice be proved provides at best an evanescent protection for the right critically

to discuss public affairs and certainly does not measure up to the sturdy safeguard embodied in the First Amendment. Unlike the Court, therefore, I vote to reverse exclusively on the ground that the Times and the individual defendants had an ab-solute, unconditional constitutional right to publish in the Times advertisement their criticisms of the Montgomery agencies and officials. * * *

* * *

CURTIS PUBLISHING CO. v. BUTTS
ASSOCIATED PRESS v. WALKER

Supreme Court of the United States, 1967
388 U.S. 130, 87 S.Ct. 1975, 18 L.Ed.2d 1094

In an article entitled, "The Story of a College Football Fix," *The Saturday Evening Post* published accusations that Wally Butts, football coach at the University of Georgia, conspired to rig a game in 1962 between his team and another representing the University of Alabama. Stemming from information supplied by one George Burnett, an Atlanta insurance salesman who accidently overheard a telephone conversation between Butts and Alabama coach Paul Bryant, the article charged that a week before the teams were to play Butts had revealed to Bryant Georgia's offensive and defensive game plans. After his resignation from the coaching position, ostensibly for health and business reasons, Butts brought suit for $10 million in compensation and punitive damages against Curtis Publishing Company, owner of *The Saturday Evening Post.*

At trial, Curtis Publishing offered only the defense of truth, but the content of the telephone conversation at issue was hotly disputed by Butts, who contended that he and Bryant had engaged in nothing more than general talk about football, and by expert witnesses, who analyzed Burnett's notes of the conversation in the context of films of the game. Aside from relating the usual standards concerning truth as a defense to libel, the federal district judge who presided in this diversity proceeding additionally instructed the jury that it could award punitive damages at any figure in its discretion if it found that malice (defined by the judge as "ill will, spite, hatred and an intent to injure" or "wanton or reckless indifference * * * with regard to the rights of others") had been proved. The jury voted $60,000 in general damages and $3 million in punitive damages, reduced subsequently by the trial judge to a total award of $460,000. A U. S. Court of Appeals affirmed, explicitly rejecting defendant's motion for a new trial. Even though the *New York Times* decision was handed down very soon after the damages had been awarded in this case, the appellate court ruled that the judgment should be allowed to stand: (1) because Butts was not a public official, and (2) because Curtis Publishing had knowingly waived defense as to malice in spite of the fact that many of the very same lawyers defending it here were also engaged in litigating the *Times* case and Curtis Publishing was, therefore, well aware of it as a factor to be considered in the developing constitutional standard of libel.

On hearing before the Supreme Court, *Butts* was scheduled for argument with a suit brought by Edwin Walker, who as a former Army general gained considerable fame heretofore in attacks on what he termed as the efforts of civilian leadership in the Pentagon to "muzzle the military" (i.e., control the expressions of opinion by military personnel on controversial issues of the day). His suit against the Associated Press grew out of the dissemination of an AP news dispatch which contained an eyewitness account of efforts by federal authorities to enforce a court order enrolling James Meredith, a Negro, at the University of Mississippi. The news report stated that Walker was present on the campus the night Meredith arrived and that he personally "took command" of a violent crowd which had gathered "encouraging rioters to use violence and giving them technical advice on combatting the effects of tear gas." Walker, who was a private citizen, had an established record as an enthusiast of right-wing causes including vigorous opposition to federal efforts at forcing desegregation. At the conclusion of trial, instructions relatively similar to those in *Butts* were given, and the jury returned awards of $500,000 in compensatory and $300,000 in punitive damages. The trial judge, however, ruled that as a matter of law no evidence could be found to support a finding of malice and, as a consequence, struck the award of punitive damages. A Texas appellate court affirmed, and the Supreme Court of Texas denied certiorari.

Mr. Justice HARLAN announced the judgments of the Court and delivered an opinion in which Mr. Justice CLARK, Mr. Justice STEWART, and Mr. Justice FORTAS join.

* * * We brought these two cases here * * * to consider the impact of [the] decision [in *New York Times* v. *Sullivan*] on libel actions instituted by persons who are not public officials, but who are "public figures" and involved in issues in which the public has a justified and important interest. * * *

* * *

* * * Powerful arguments are brought to bear for the extension of the *New York Times* rule in both cases. In *Butts* it is contended that the facts are on all fours with those of Rosenblatt v. Baer[c] * * * since Butts was charged with the important responsibility of managing the athletic affairs of a state university. It is argued that while the Athletic Association is financially independent from the State and Butts

was not technically a state employee, as was Baer, his role in state administration was so significant that this technical distinction from *Rosenblatt* should be ignored. Even if this factor is to be given some weight, we are told that the public interest in education in general, and in the conduct of the athletic affairs of educational institutions in particular, justifies constitutional protection of discussion of persons involved in it equivalent to the protection afforded discussion of public officials.

A similar argument is raised in the *Walker* case where the important public interest in being informed about the events and personalities involved in the Mississippi riot is pressed. In that case we are also urged to recognize that Walker's claims to the protection of libel laws are limited since he thrust himself into the "vortex" of the controversy.

We are urged by the respondents, Butts and Walker, to recognize society's "pervasive and strong interest in preventing and redressing attacks

---

c. Rosenblatt v. Baer, 383 U.S. 75, 86 S.Ct. 669 (1966), involved a suit brought by a former county recreation supervisor who alleged libel by a local newspaper columnist. Though the article in question made no personal reference to Baer, the author professed amazement at the success of managing the recreation area under his successor and the new county commissioners. The column observed that in a season which was notably poorer for skiing weatherwise, the cash in-

come was "Simply fantastic"—"literally hundreds of per cent better than last year." By way of concluding, the article wondered aloud, "What happened to all the money last year? and every other year? What magic has [the new management] wrought to make such a tremendous difference in net cash results?" The U. S. Supreme Court reversed an award for damages which had been upheld by the New Hampshire Supreme Court. It found *New York Times* controlling.

upon reputation," and the "important social values which underline the law of defamation." * * * It is pointed out that the publicity in these instances was not directed at employees of government and that these cases cannot be analogized to seditious libel prosecutions. * * *

We fully recognize the force of these competing considerations and the fact that an accommodation between them is necessary not only in these cases, but in all libel actions arising from a publication concerning public issues. * * *

* * *

In the cases we decide today none of the particular considerations involved in *New York Times* is present. These actions cannot be analogized to prosecutions for seditious libel. Neither plaintiff has any position in government which would permit a recovery by him to be viewed as a vindication of governmental policy. Neither was entitled to a special privilege protecting his utterances against accountability in libel. We are prompted, therefore, to seek guidance from the rules of liability which prevail in our society with respect to compensation of persons injured by the improper performance of a legitimate activity by another. Under these rules, a departure from the kind of care society may expect from a reasonable man performing such activity leaves the actor open to a judicial shifting of loss. In defining these rules, and especially in formulating the standards for determining the degree of care to be expected in the circumstances, courts have consistently given much attention to the importance of defendants' activities. * * * The courts have also, especially in libel cases, investigated the plaintiff's position to determine

whether he has a legitimate call upon the court for protection in light of his prior activities and means of self-defense. * * * We note that the public interest in the circulation of the materials here involved, and the publisher's interest in circulating them, is not less than that involved in *New York Times*. And both Butts and Walker commanded a substantial amount of independent public interest at the time of the publications; both, in our opinion, would have been labeled "public figures" under ordinary tort rules. * * *

These similarities and differences between libel actions involving persons who are public officials and libel actions involving those circumstanced as were Butts and Walker, viewed in light of the principles of liability which are of general applicability in our society, lead us to the conclusion that libel actions of the present kind cannot be left entirely to state libel laws, unlimited by any overriding constitutional safeguard, but that the rigorous federal requirements of *New York Times* are not the only appropriate accommodation of the conflicting interests at stake. We consider and would hold that a "public figure" who is not a public official may also recover damages for a defamatory falsehood whose substance makes substantial danger to reputation apparent, on a showing of highly unreasonable conduct constituting an extreme departure from the standards of investigation and reporting ordinarily adhered to by responsible publishers. * * *

* * *

Having set forth the standard by which we believe the constitutionality of the damage awards in these cases must be judged, we turn now, as the Court did in *New York Times*, to the question whether the evidence and findings below meet that standard. We find the standard satisfied in * * * *Butts*, and not satisfied by either the evidence or the findings in * * * *Walker*.

* * *

The evidence showed that the *Butts* story was in no sense "hot news" and the editors of the magazine recognized the need for a thorough investigation of the serious charges. Elementary precautions were, nevertheless, ignored. The Saturday Evening Post knew that Burnett had been placed on probation in connection with bad check charges, but proceeded to publish the story on the basis of his affidavit without substantial independent support. * * *

* * * In short, the evidence is ample to support a finding of highly unreasonable conduct constituting an extreme departure from the standards of investigation and reporting ordinarily adhered to by responsible publishers.

* * *

In contrast to the *Butts* article, the dispatch which concerns us in *Walker* was news which required immediate dissemination. The Associated Press received the information from a correspondent who was present at the scene of the events and gave every indication of being trustworthy and competent. His dispatches in this instance with one minor exception, were internally consistent and would not have seemed unreasonable to one familiar with General Walker's prior publicized statements on the underlying controversy. Considering the necessity for rapid dissemination, nothing in this series of events gives the slightest hint of a severe departure from accepted publishing standards. We therefore conclude that General Walker should not be entitled to damages from the Associated Press.

We come finally to Curtis' contention that whether or not it can be required to compensate Butts for any injury it may have caused him, it cannot be subjected to an assessment for punitive damages limited only by the "enlightened conscience" of the community. Curtis recognizes that the Constitution presents no general bar to the assessment of punitive damages in a civil case * * * but contends that an unlimited punitive award against a magazine publisher constitutes an effective prior restraint by giving the jury the power to destroy the publisher's business. We cannot accept this reasoning. * * *

* * *

Where a publisher's departure from standards of press responsibility is severe enough to strip from him the constitutional protection our decision acknowledges, we think it entirely proper for the State to act not only for the protection of the individual injured but to safeguard all those similarly situated against like abuse. Moreover, punitive damages require a finding of "ill will" under general libel law and it is not unjust that a publisher be forced to pay for the "venting of his spleen" in a manner which does not meet even the minimum standards required for constitutional protection. Especially in those cases where circumstances outside the publication itself reduce its impact sufficiently to make a compensatory imposition an inordinately light burden, punitive damages serve a wholly legitimate purpose in the

protection of individual reputation.
* * *

* * *

Judgment of Court of Appeals for
the Fifth Circuit in [*Butts*] affirmed;
judgment of Texas Court of Civil Appeals in [*Walker*] reversed and case
remanded with directions.

Mr. Chief Justice WARREN, concurring in the result.

* * *

* * * Mr. Justice HARLAN'S
opinion departs from the standard of
New York Times and substitutes in
cases involving "public figures" a
standard that is based on "highly unreasonable conduct" and is phrased
in terms of "extreme departure from
the standards of investigation and reporting ordinarily adhered to by responsible publishers." * * * I
cannot believe that a standard which
is based on such an unusual and uncertain formulation could either
guide a jury of laymen or afford the
protection for speech and debate that
is fundamental to our society and
guaranteed by the First Amendment.

* * *

I therefore adhere to the *New
York Times* standard in the case of
"public figures" as well as "public
officials." * * *

I have no difficulty in concluding
that * * * *Associated Press* v.
Walker must be reversed since it is
in clear conflict with *New York
Times.* * * * The trial judge expressly ruled that no showing of malice in any sense had been made, and
he reversed an award of punitive
damages for that reason. * * *
Under any reasoning, General Walk-

er was a public man in whose public
conduct society and the press had a
legitimate and substantial interest.

* * *

I am satisfied that the evidence
[in *Butts*] discloses that degree of
reckless disregard for the truth of
which we spoke in *New York Times.*
* * * Freedom of the press under
the First Amendment does not include absolute license to destroy
lives or careers.

Mr. Justice BLACK, with whom
Mr. Justice DOUGLAS joins, concurring in the result in [*Walker*] and dissenting in [*Butts*].

* * * I do not recede from any
of the views I have previously expressed about the much wider press
and speech freedoms I think the
First and Fourteenth Amendments
were designed to grant to the people
of the Nation. * * *

These cases illustrate, I think, the
accuracy of my prior predictions that
the *New York Times* constitutional
rule concerning libel is wholly inadequate to save the press from being
destroyed by libel judgments.
* * *

* * *

[Justice BRENNAN, in an opinion
in which he was joined by Justice
WHITE, concurred in the result in
Walker and dissented in *Butts*. He
agreed with THE CHIEF JUSTICE
that the *New York Times* standard
should be applied in both cases but
would have remanded the *Butts* case
for a new trial rather than have the
Court usurp the jury's function by directly affirming the award as consistent with the *Times* rule.]

TIME, INC. v. FIRESTONE

Supreme Court of the United States, 1976
424 U.S. 448, 96 S.Ct. 958, 47 L.Ed.2d 154

Mary Alice Firestone brought suit against Time, Inc. because of the following squib which it ran in the "Milestones" section of its magazine, alleging that it was "false, malicious, and defamatory":

"DIVORCED. By Russell A. Firestone Jr., 41, heir to the tire fortune: Mary Alice Sullivan Firestone, 32, his third wife; a one-time Palm Beach schoolteacher; on grounds of extreme cruelty and adultery; after six years of marriage, one son; in West Palm Beach, Fla. The 17-month intermittent trial produced enough testimony of extramarital adventures on both sides, said the judge, 'to make Dr. Freud's hair curl.'"

The Supreme Court of Florida affirmed a $100,000 award of damages against the publisher, and Time, Inc. appealed, arguing that the libel judgment infringed the First and Fourteenth Amendments.

She had married Russell Firestone, scion of a famous industrial family, in 1961. In 1964, they separated and she subsequently filed a complaint against him in a Florida circuit court for separate maintenance; he counterclaimed for divorce on grounds of cruelty and adultery. Charges of infidelity abounded on both sides. The circuit court judge finally granted the husband a divorce, finding "[t]hat the equities in this cause" were with him and concluding that:

"In the present case, it is abundantly clear from the evidence of marital discord that neither of the parties has shown the least susceptibility to domestication, and that the marriage should be dissolved."

Mr. Justice REHNQUIST delivered the opinion of the Court.

* * *

Petitioner initially contends that it cannot be liable for publishing any falsehood defaming respondent unless it is established that the publication was made "with actual malice," as that term is defined in New York Times Co. v. Sullivan, 376 U.S. 254, 84 S.Ct. 710 (1964). Petitioner advances two arguments in support of this contention: that respondent is a "public figure" within this Court's decisions extending *New York Times* to defamation suits brought by such individuals * * * and that the Time item constituted a report of a judicial proceeding, a class of subject matter which petitioner claims deserves the protection of the "actual malice" standard even if the story is proven to be defamatorily false or in-

accurate. We reject both arguments.

* * *

Petitioner contends that because the Firestone divorce was characterized by the Florida Supreme Court as a "cause célèbre," it must have been a public controversy and respondent must be considered a public figure. But in so doing petitioner seeks to equate "public controversy" with all controversies of interest to the public. Were we to accept this reasoning, we would reinstate the doctrine advanced in the plurality opinion in Rosenbloom v. Metromedia, Inc., 403 U.S. 29, 91 S.Ct. 1811 (1971), which concluded that the *New York Times* privilege should be extended to falsehoods defamatory of private persons whenever the statements concern matters of general or public interest. In Gertz [v. Robert Welch, Inc., 418

U.S. 323, 94 S.Ct. 2997 (1974)],[d] however, the Court repudiated this position, stating that "extension of the *New York Times* test proposed by the *Rosenbloom* plurality would abridge [a] legitimate state interest to a degree that we find unacceptable." * * *

Dissolution of a marriage through judicial proceedings is not the sort of "public controversy" referred to in *Gertz*, even though the

---

d. In that case, Richard Nuccio, a Chicago police officer, was tried and found guilty of second-degree murder in the shooting of a youth by the name of Nelson. Subsequently, the Nelson family retained Elmer Gertz, an attorney, to represent them in a suit for damages against Nuccio. As part of a continuing attempt during the 1960s to warn of what it saw as a concerted effort by Communists to discredit local law enforcement, *American Opinion* magazine, an arm of the John Birch Society published by Robert Welch, carried a story in its March 1969 issue on the Nuccio murder trial. The article purported to show that the evidence against Nuccio was false and contrived and that the officer had been framed. Gertz, who had only a very remote connection with the criminal proceedings, was nonetheless assailed as an architect of the frame-up. The article said that Gertz had been at one time a leader in the Marxist League for Industrial Democracy, described as a group which once advocated a violent takeover of the government, and called him a "Leninist" and a "Communist-fronter." The story went on to say that he had also been an officer of the National Lawyers Guild, which it portrayed as an organization that "probably did more than any other outfit to plan the Communist attack on the Chicago police during the 1968 Democratic convention." The assertion that Gertz had been a member and official of the League was false as were additional allegations to the effect that he had a criminal record. No evidence could be found that Gertz was a Communist, and while he had indeed been a member and officer of the Lawyers Guild for some fifteen years, there was no proof that the organization had any connection with planning demonstrations in Chicago in 1968. Though the article passed itself off as the product of "extensive research," the managing editor made no attempt to check out any of the story. Because of a diversity in state citizenship, Gertz filed a libel action in federal district court, and the case was tried to a jury which later returned an award of $50,000. After the verdict was rendered, the trial judge, on further reflection, held as a matter of law that the *New*

York Times standard should apply—a decision which anticipated the Supreme Court's decision in *Rosenbloom*—and he set aside the award. The U. S. Court of Appeals for the Seventh Circuit affirmed, though it expressed doubt about the district court decision.

In *Gertz*, the Court held that the *New York Times* rule regarding fair comment did not extend to individuals who were neither public officials nor public figures. Though the Court's decision allowed such private individuals to collect damages under a standard something less than "actual malice," it did make clear that: (1) states may not allow damages to be recovered without a showing of some kind of fault; and (2) "the private defamation plaintiff who establishes liability under a less demanding standard than that stated by *New York Times* may recover only such damages as are sufficient to compensate him for actual injury" (though the Court left the door open to the collection of punitive damages also but under a much stiffer standard).

The Court also went on to point out that a private individual could become a public figure (and thus bring the *New York Times* rule into play) if: (1) he "achieve[s] such pervasive fame or notoriety that he becomes a public figure for all purposes in all contexts"; or (2) he "voluntarily injects himself or is drawn into a particular public controversy and thereby becomes a public figure for a limited range of issues." Considering Gertz's involvement against this background, the Court per Justice Powell, speaking for a bare majority, concluded: "In this context it is plain that petitioner was not a public figure. He played a minimal role at the coroner's inquest, and his participation related solely to his representation of a private client. He took no part in the criminal prosecution of officer Nuccio. Moreover, he never discussed either the criminal or civil litigation with the press and was never quoted as having done so. He plainly did not thrust himself into the vortex of this public issue, nor did he engage the public's attention in an attempt to influence its outcome."

marital difficulties of extremely wealthy individuals may be of interest to some portion of the reading public. Nor did respondent freely choose to publicize issues as to the propriety of her married life. She was compelled to go to court by the State in order to obtain legal release from the bonds of matrimony. We have said that in such an instance "[r]esort to the judicial process * * * is no more voluntary in a realistic sense than that of the defendant called upon to defend his interests in court." Boddie v. Connecticut, 401 U.S. 371, 376, 91 S.Ct. 780, 785 (1971). Her actions, both in instituting the litigation and in its conduct, were quite different from those of General Walker in Curtis Publishing Co. [v. Butts, 388 U.S. 130, 87 S.Ct. 1975 (1967)]. * * * She assumed no "special prominence in the resolution of public questions." Gertz, 418 U.S., at 351, 94 S.Ct., at 3013. We hold respondent was not a "public figure" for the purpose of determining the constitutional protection afforded petitioner's report of the factual and legal basis for her divorce.

For similar reasons we likewise reject petitioner's claim for automatic extension of the New York Times privilege to all reports of judicial proceedings. It is argued that information concerning proceedings in our Nation's courts may have such importance to all citizens as to justify extending special First Amendment protection to the press when reporting on such events. We have recently accepted a significantly more confined version of this argument by holding that the Constitution precludes States from imposing civil liability based upon the publication of truthful information contained in official court records open to public in-

spection. Cox Broadcasting Corp. v. Cohn, 420 U.S. 469, 95 S.Ct. 1029 (1975).

Petitioner would have us extend the reasoning of Cox Broadcasting to safeguard even inaccurate and false statements, at least where "actual malice" has not been established. But its argument proves too much. It may be that all reports of judicial proceedings contain some informational value implicating the First Amendment, but recognizing this is little different from labeling all judicial proceedings matters of "public or general interest," as that phrase was used by the plurality in Rosenbloom. Whatever their general validity, use of such subject matter classifications to determine the extent of constitutional protection afforded defamatory falsehoods may too often result in an improper balance between the competing interests in this area. It was our recognition and rejection of this weakness in the Rosenbloom test which led us in Gertz to eschew a subject matter test for one focusing upon the character of the defamation plaintiff. * * *

* * *

* * * Imposing upon the law of private defamation the rather drastic limitations worked by New York Times cannot be justified by generalized references to the public interest in reports of judicial proceedings. The details of many, if not most, courtroom battles would add almost nothing towards advancing the uninhibited debate on public issues thought to provide principal support for the decision in New York Times. * * * And while participants in some litigation may be legitimate "public figures," either generally or for the limited purpose of that

litigation, the majority will more likely resemble respondent, drawn into a public forum largely against their will in order to attempt to obtain the only redress available to them or to defend themselves against actions brought by the State or by others. There appears little reason why these individuals should substantially forfeit that degree of protection which the law of defamation would otherwise afford them simply by virtue of their being drawn into a courtroom. * * *

Petitioner has urged throughout this litigation that it could not be held liable for publication of the "Milestones" item because its report of respondent's divorce was factually correct. In its view the Time article faithfully reproduced the precise meaning of the divorce judgment. But this issue was submitted to the jury under an instruction intended to implement Florida's limited privilege for accurate reports of judicial proceedings. * * * By returning a verdict for respondent the jury necessarily found that the identity of meaning which petitioner claims does not exist even for laymen. The Supreme Court of Florida upheld this finding on appeal, rejecting petitioner's contention that its report was accurate as a matter of law. Because demonstration that an article was true would seem to preclude finding the publisher at fault, * * * we have examined the predicate for petitioner's contention. We believe the Florida courts properly could have found the "Milestones" item to be false.

For petitioner's report to have been accurate, the divorce granted Russell Firestone must have been based on a finding by the divorce court that his wife had committed extreme cruelty towards him *and* that

she had been guilty of adultery. This is indisputably what petitioner reported in its "Milestones" item, but it is equally indisputable that these were not the facts. Russell Firestone alleged in his counterclaim that respondent had been guilty of adultery, but the divorce court never made any such finding. Its judgment provided that Russell Firestone's "counterclaim for divorce be and the same is hereby granted," but did not specify that the basis for the judgment was either of the two grounds alleged in the counterclaim. The Supreme Court of Florida on appeal concluded that the ground actually relied upon by the divorce court was "lack of domestication of the parties," a ground not theretofore recognized by Florida law. The Supreme Court nonetheless affirmed the judgment dissolving the bonds of matrimony because the record contained sufficient evidence to establish the ground of extreme cruelty. 263 So.2d 223, 225 (1972).

Petitioner may well argue that the meaning of the trial court's decree was unclear, but this does not license it to choose from among several conceivable interpretations the one most damaging to respondent. Having chosen to follow this tack, petitioner must be able to establish not merely that the item reported was a conceivable or plausible interpretation of the decree, but that the item was factually correct. We believe there is ample support for the jury's conclusion, affirmed by the Supreme Court of Florida, that this was not the case. There was, therefore, sufficient basis for imposing liability upon petitioner if the constitutional limitations we announced in *Gertz* have been satisfied. These are a prohibition against imposing liability without fault, * * * and the requirement that compensatory awards "be supported by competent evidence concerning the injury." * * *

As to the latter requirement little difficulty appears. Petitioner has argued that because respondent withdrew her claim for damages to reputation on the eve of trial, there could be no recovery consistent with *Gertz*. Petitioner's theory seems to be that the only compensable injury in a defamation action is that which may be done to one's reputation, and that claims not predicated upon such injury are by definition not actions for defamation. But Florida has obviously decided to permit recovery for other injuries without regard to measuring the effect the falsehood may have had upon a plaintiff's reputation. This does not transform the action into something other than an action for defamation as that term is meant in *Gertz*. In that opinion we made it clear that States could base awards on elements other than injury to reputation, specifically listing "personal humiliation, and mental anguish and suffering" as examples of injuries which might be compensated consistently with the Constitution upon a showing of fault. Because respondent has decided to forgo recovery for injury to her reputation, she is not prevented from obtaining compensation for such other damages that a defamatory falsehood may have caused her.

The trial court charged, consistently with *Gertz*, that the jury should award respondent compensatory damages in "an amount of money that will fairly and adequately compensate her for such damages," and further cautioned that "It is only damages which are a direct and natural result of the alleged libel which may be recovered." There was competent evidence introduced to permit the jury to assess the amount of injury. Several witnesses testified to the extent of respondent's anxiety and concern over Time inaccurately reporting that she had been found guilty of adultery, and she herself took the stand to elaborate on her fears that her young son would be adversely affected by this falsehood when he grew older. The jury decided these injuries should be compensated by an award of $100,000. We have no warrant for re-examining this determination. * * *

Gertz established, however, that not only must there be evidence to support an award of compensatory damages, there must also be evidence of some fault on the part of a defendant charged with publishing defamatory material. No question of fault was submitted to the jury in this case, because under Florida law the only findings required for determination of liability were whether the article was defamatory, whether it was true, and whether the defamation, if any, caused respondent harm.

The failure to submit the question of fault to the jury does not, of itself establish noncompliance with the constitutional requirements established in *Gertz*, however. Nothing in the Constitution requires that assessment of fault in a civil case tried in a state court be made by a jury, nor is there any prohibition against such a finding being made in the first instance by an appellate, rather than a trial, court. The First and Fourteenth Amendments do not impose upon the States any limitations as to how, within their own judicial systems, factfinding tasks shall be allocated. If we were satisfied that one of the Florida courts which considered this case had supportably ascertained petitioner was at fault, we would be required to affirm the judgment below.

But the only alternative source of such a finding, given that the issue was not submitted to the jury, is the opinion of the Supreme Court of Florida. That opinion appears to proceed generally on the assumption that a showing of fault was not required, but then in the penultimate paragraph it recites:

"Furthermore, this erroneous reporting is clear and convincing evidence of the negligence in certain segments of the news media in gathering the news. *Gertz* v. *Welch, Inc.,* supra. Pursuant to Florida law in effect at the time of the divorce judgment (Section 61.08, Florida Statutes), a wife found guilty of adultery could not be awarded alimony. Since petitioner had been awarded alimony, she had not been found guilty of adultery nor had the divorce been granted on the ground of adultery. A careful examination of the final decree prior to publication would have clearly demonstrated that the divorce had been granted on the grounds of extreme cruelty, and thus the wife would have been saved the humiliation of being accused of adultery in a nationwide magazine. This is a flagrant example of 'journalistic negligence.'" 305 So.2d, at 178.

It may be argued this is sufficient indication the court found petitioner at fault within the meaning of *Gertz*. Nothing in that decision or in the First or Fourteenth Amendments requires that in a libel action an appellate court treat in detail by written opinion all contentions of the parties, and if the jury or trial judge had found fault in fact, we would be quite willing to read the quoted passage as affirming that conclusion. But without some finding of fault by the judge or jury in the Circuit Court, we would have to attribute to the Supreme Court of Florida from the quoted language not merely an intention to affirm the finding of the lower court, but an intention to find such a fact in the first instance.

* * *

It may well be that petitioner's account in its "Milestones" section was the product of some fault on its part, and that the libel judgment against it was, therefore, entirely consistent with *Gertz*. But in the absence of a finding in some element of the state court system that there was fault, we are not inclined to canvass the record to make such a determination in the first instance. * * * Accordingly, the judgment of the Supreme Court of Florida is vacated and the case remanded for further proceedings not inconsistent with this opinion.

So ordered.

Mr. Justice STEVENS took no part in the consideration or decision of this case.

Mr. Justice POWELL, with whom Mr. Justice STEWART joins, concurring.

* * *

In *Gertz* we held that "so long as they do not impose liability without fault, the States may define for themselves the appropriate standard of liability for a publisher or broadcaster of defamatory falsehood injurious to a private individual." * * * Thus, while a State may elect to hold a publisher to a lesser duty of care, there is no First Amendment constraint against allowing recovery upon proof of negligence. The applicability of such a fault standard was expressly limited to circumstances where, as here, "the substance of the defamatory [falsehood] 'makes substantial danger to reputation apparent.' " * * * By requiring a showing of fault the Court in *Gertz* sought to shield the press and broadcast media from a rule of strict liability that could lead to intolerable self-censorship and at the same time recognize the legitimate state interest in compensating private individuals for wrongful injury from defamatory falsehoods.

In one paragraph near the end of its opinion, the Supreme Court of Florida cited *Gertz* in concluding that Time was guilty of "journalistic negligence." But, as the opinion of the Court recognizes, * * * it is not evident from this single paragraph that any type of fault standard was in fact applied. Assuming that Florida now will apply a negligence standard in cases of this kind, the ultimate question here is whether Time exercised due care under the circumstances: did Time exercise the reasonably prudent care that a State may constitutionally demand of a publisher or broadcaster prior to a publication whose content reveals its defamatory potential?

* * *

There was substantial evidence, much of it uncontradicted, that the editors of Time exercised considerable care in checking the accuracy of the story prior to its publication. The Milestones item appeared in the December 22, 1967, issue of Time. This issue went to press on Saturday, December 16, the day after the Circuit Court rendered its decision at about 4:30 in the afternoon. The evening of the 15th the Time editorial staff in New York received an Associated Press dispatch stating that

Russell A. Firestone, Jr., had been granted a divorce from his third wife, whom "he had accused of adultery and extreme cruelty." Later that same evening, Time received the New York Daily News edition for December 16, which carried a special bulletin substantially to the same effect as the AP dispatch.

On the morning of December 16, in response to an inquiry sent to its Miami Bureau, Time's New York office received a dispatch from the head of that Bureau quoting excerpts from the Circuit Court's opinion that strongly suggested adultery on the part of both parties. Later that day the editorial staff received a message from Time's Palm Beach stringer that read, in part: "The technical grounds for divorce according to Joseph Farrish, Jr., attorney for Mary Alice Firestone, were given as extreme cruelty and adultry [*sic*]." * * * The stringer's dispatch also included several quotations from the Circuit Court opinion. At trial the senior editor testified that although no member of the New York editorial staff had read the Circuit Court's opinion, he had believed that both the stringer and the chief of Time's Miami Bureau had read it.

The opaqueness of the Circuit Court's decree is also a factor to be considered in assessing whether Time was guilty of actionable fault under the *Gertz* standard. Although it appears that neither the head of the Miami Bureau nor the stringer personally read the opinion or order, the stringer testified at trial that respondent's attorney Farrish and others read him portions of the decree over the telephone before he filed his dispatch with Time. The record does not reveal whether the limited portions of the decree that shed light on the grounds for the granting of the divorce were read to the stringer. But the ambiguity of the divorce decree may well have contributed to the stringer's view, and hence the Time editorial staff's conclusion, that a ground for the divorce was adultery by respondent.

However one may characterize it, the Circuit Court decision was hardly a model of clarity. * * * There is no reference whatever in the "order" portion of the decision either to "extreme cruelty" or "adultery," the only grounds relied upon by the husband. But the divorce was granted to him following an express finding "that the equities * * * are with the defendant [the husband]."

Thus, on the face of the opinion itself, the husband had counterclaimed for divorce on the grounds of extreme cruelty and adultery, the court had found the equities to be with him, and had granted his counterclaim for divorce. Apart from the awarding of alimony to the wife there is no indication, either in the opinion or accompanying order, that the husband's counterclaim was not granted on both of the grounds asserted. This may be a redundant reading, as either ground would have sufficed. But the opinion that preceded the order was full of talk of adultery and made no explicit reference to any other type of cruelty. In these circumstances, the decision of the Circuit Court may have been sufficiently ambiguous to have caused reasonably prudent newsmen to read it as granting divorce on the ground of adultery.

As I join the opinion of the Court remanding this case, it is unnecessary to decide whether the foregoing establishes as a matter of law that Time exercised the requisite care under the circumstances. Nor have I

undertaken to identify all of the evidence that may be relevant or to point out conflicts that arguably have been resolved against Time by the jury. My point in writing is to emphasize that, against the background of a notorious divorce case, * * * and a decree that invited misunderstanding, there *was* substantial evidence supportive of Time's defense that it was not guilty of actionable negligence. At the very least the jury or court assessing liability in this case should have weighed these factors and this evidence before reaching a judgment. There is no indication in the record before us that this was done in accordance with *Gertz.*

Mr. Justice BRENNAN, dissenting.

*   *   *

At stake in the present case is the ability of the press to report to the citizenry the events transpiring in the Nation's judicial systems. There is simply no meaningful or constitutionally adequate way to report such events without reference to those persons and transactions that form the subject matter in controversy. This Court has long held that

"[a] trial is a public event. What transpires in the court room is public property. * * * Those who see and hear what transpired can report it with impunity. There is no special perquisite of the judiciary which enables it, as distinguished from other institutions of democratic government, to suppress, edit, or censor events which transpire in proceedings before it." Craig v. Harney, 331 U.S. 367, 374, 67 S.Ct. 1249, 1254 (1947).

The Court has recognized that with regard to the judiciary, no less than other areas of government, the press performs an indispensable role by "subjecting the * * * judicial processes to extensive public scrutiny and criticism." Sheppard v. Maxwell, 384 U.S. 333, 350, 86 S.Ct. 1507, 1515 (1966). And it is critical that the judicial processes be open to such scrutiny and criticism, for, as the Court has noted in the specific context of labor disputes, the more acute public controversies are, "the more likely it is that in some aspect they will get into court." Bridges v. California, 314 U.S. 252, 268–269, 62 S.Ct. 190, 196 (1941). Indeed, slight reflection is needed to observe the insistent and complex interaction between controversial judicial proceedings and popular impressions thereof and fundamental legal and political changes in the Nation throughout the 200 years of evolution of our political system. With the judiciary as with all other aspects of government, the First Amendment guarantees to the people of this Nation that they shall retain the necessary means of control over their institutions that might in the alternative grow remote, insensitive, and finally acquisitive of those attributes of sovereignty not delegated by the Constitution.

Also no less true than in other areas of government, error in reporting and debate concerning the judicial process is inevitable. Indeed, in view of the complexities of that process and its unfamiliarity to the laymen who report it, the probability of inadvertent error may be substantially greater. * * *

For precisely such reasons, we have held that the contempt power may not be used to punish the reporting of judicial proceedings merely because a reporter "missed the essential point in a trial or failed to summarize the issues to accord with

the views of the judge who sat on the case." Craig v. Harney, *supra,* at 375, 67 S.Ct., at 1254. * * * The First Amendment insulates from defamation liability a margin for error sufficient to ensure the avoidance of crippling press self-censorship in the field of reporting public judicial affairs. To be adequate, that margin must be both of sufficient breadth and predictable in its application. In my view, therefore, the actual malice standard of *New York Times* must be met in order to justify the imposition of liability in these circumstances.

Mr. Justice WHITE, dissenting.

I would affirm the judgment of the Florida Supreme Court because First Amendment values will not be furthered in any way by application to this case of the fault standards newly drafted and imposed by Gertz v. Robert Welch, Inc., 418 U.S. 323, 94 S.Ct. 2997, upon which my Brother REHNQUIST relies, or the fault standards required by Rosenbloom v. Metromedia, Inc., 403 U.S. 29, 91 S.Ct. 1811, upon which my Brother BRENNAN relies; and because, in any event, any requisite fault was properly found below.

* * *

Mr. Justice MARSHALL, dissenting.

* * * Because I consider the respondent, Mary Alice Firestone, to be a "public figure" within the meaning of our prior decisions, Gertz v. Robert Welch, Inc., 418 U.S. 323, 94 S.Ct. 2997 (1974); Curtis Publishing Co. v. Butts, 388 U.S. 130, 87 S.Ct. 1975 (1967), I respectfully dissent.

Mary Alice Firestone was not a person "first brought to public attention by the defamation that is the subject of the lawsuit." Rosenbloom

v. Metromedia, Inc., 403 U.S. 29, 78, 86, 91 S.Ct. 1811, 1841 (1971) (Marshall, J., dissenting). On the contrary, she was "prominent among the '400' of Palm Beach Society," and an "active [member] of the sporting set," Firestone v. Time, Inc., 271 So. 2d 745, 751 (Fla.1972), whose activities predictably attracted the attention of a sizeable portion of the public. Indeed, Mrs. Firestone's appearances in the printed press were evidently frequent enough to warrant her subscribing to a press clipping service.

Mrs. Firestone brought suit for separate maintenance, with reason to know of the likely public interest in the proceedings. As the Supreme Court of Florida noted, Mr. and Mrs. Firestone's "marital difficulties were * * * well-known," and the lawsuit became "a veritable *cause celebre* in social circles across the country." *Ibid.* The 17-month trial and related events attracted national news coverage, and elicited no fewer than 43 articles in the Miami Herald and 45 articles in the Palm Beach Post and Palm Beach Times. Far from shunning the publicity, Mrs. Firestone held several press conferences in the course of the proceedings.

These facts are sufficient to warrant the conclusion that Mary Alice Firestone was a "public figure" for purposes of reports on the judicial proceedings she initiated. In *Gertz v. Robert Welch, Inc., supra,* * * * we noted that an individual can be a public figure for some purposes and a private figure for others. And we found two distinguishing features between public figures and private figures. First, we recognized that public figures have less need for judicial protection because of their greater ability to resort to

self-help: "public figures usually enjoy significantly greater access to the channels of effective communication and hence have a more realistic opportunity to counteract false statements than private individuals normally enjoy." * * *

As the above recital of the facts makes clear, Mrs. Firestone is hardly in a position to suggest that she lacked access to the media for purposes relating to her lawsuit. It may well be that she would have had greater difficulty countering alleged falsehoods in the national press than in the Miami and Palm Beach papers that covered the proceedings so thoroughly. But presumably the audience Mrs. Firestone would have been most interested in reaching could have been reached through the local media. In any event, difficulty in reaching all those who may have read the alleged falsehood surely ought not preclude a finding that Mrs. Firestone was a public figure under *Gertz*. *Gertz* set no absolute requirement that an individual be able fully to counter falsehoods through self-help in order to be a public figure. We viewed the availability of the self-help remedy as a relative matter in *Gertz*, and set it forth as a minor consideration in determining whether an individual is a public figure.

The second, "more important," consideration in *Gertz* was a normative notion that public figures are less deserving of protection than private figures: that although "it may be possible for someone to become a public figure through no purposeful action of his own," generally those classed as public figures have "thrust themselves to the forefront of particular public controversies" and thereby "invite[d] attention and comment." * * * And even if they have not, "the communications media are entitled to act on the assumption that * * * public figures have voluntarily exposed themselves to increased risk of injury from defamatory falsehood concerning them." * * *

We must assume that it was by choice that Mrs. Firestone became an active member of the "sporting set"—a social group with "especial prominence in the affairs of society," * * * whose lives receive constant media attention. Certainly there is nothing in the record to indicate otherwise, and Mrs. Firestone's subscription to a press clipping service suggests that she was not altogether uninterested in the publicity she received. Having placed herself in a position in which her activities were of interest to a significant segment of the public, Mrs. Firestone chose to initiate a lawsuit for separate maintenance, and most significantly, held several press conferences in the course of that lawsuit. If these actions for some reason fail to establish as a certainty that Mrs. Firestone "voluntarily exposed [herself] to increased risk of injury from defamatory falsehood," surely they are sufficient to entitle the press to act on the assumption that she did. Accordingly, Mrs. Firestone would appear to be a public figure under *Gertz*.

The Court resists this result by concluding that the subject matter of the alleged defamation was not a "public controversy" as that term was used in *Gertz*. In part, the Court's conclusion rests on what I view as an understatement of the degree to which Mrs. Firestone can be said to have voluntarily acted in a manner that invited public attention.

But more fundamentally its conclusion rests on a reading of *Gertz* that differs from mine. The meaning that the Court attributes to the term "public controversy" used in *Gertz* resurrects the precise difficulties that I thought *Gertz* was designed to avoid.

* * *

If there is one thing that is clear from *Gertz*, it is that we explicitly rejected the position of the plurality in Rosenbloom v. Metromedia, Inc., 403 U.S. 29, 91 S.Ct. 1811 (1971), that the applicability of the *New York Times* standard depends upon whether the subject matter of a report is a matter of "public or general concern." * * *

If *Gertz* is to have any meaning at all, the focus of analysis must be on the actions of the individual, and the degree of public attention that had already developed, or that could have been anticipated, before the report in question. Under this approach, the class of public figures must include an individual like Mrs. Firestone, who acquired a social prominence that could be expected to attract public attention, initiated a lawsuit that predictably attracted more public attention, and held press conferences in the course of and in regard to the lawsuit. I would hold that, for purposes of this case, Mrs. Firestone is a public figure, who must demonstrate that the report in question was published with "actual malice"—that is, with knowledge that it was false or with reckless disregard of whether it was false or not.

* * *

RECENT SUPREME COURT DECISIONS ON WHO IS A "PUBLIC FIGURE"

Case	Nature of the Controversy	Decision and Reasons	Vote
Hutchinson v. Proxmire, 443 U.S. 111, 99 S.Ct. 2675 (1979)	A U.S. Senator gave his "Golden Fleece of the Month" Award to the National Science Foundation for funding Hutchinson's research. The award is given to point up what the Senator thinks are egregious examples of wasteful government spending. Hutchinson was given an NSF grant to study emotional behavior, particularly aggression. On the Senate floor and in a news release, a newsletter, and a TV interview, Proxmire characterized the research as transparently worthless and ridiculed it as studying why monkeys "grind their teeth." Hutchinson sued, alleging that he was humiliated by the Senator's attack, held up to public ridicule and scorn, and that his professional and scholarly reputation had been damaged	Hutchinson was not a "public figure" simply because he received federal funds. "Neither his applications for federal grants nor his publications in professional journals can be said to have invited that degree of public attention and comment on his receipt of federal funds essential to meet the public figure level." Nor did his response to Proxmire's criticism make him a "public figure." " * * * Hutchinson's activities and public profile are much like those of countless members of his profession. [He was a research scientist.] His published writings reach a relatively small category of professionals concerned with research in human behavior. To the extent the subject of his published writings became a matter of controversy, it was a consequence of the Golden Fleece Award. Clearly those charged with defamation cannot, by their own conduct, create their own defense by making the claimant a public figure"	8–1; Brennan dissented
Wolston v. Reader's Digest Assn., Inc., 443 U.S. 157, 99 S.Ct. 2701 (1979)	Wolston was mentioned in a book as having been indicted for espionage and was named as one of several postwar Soviet agents in the U.S. He sued, charg-	"[T]he mere fact that petitioner voluntarily chose not to appear before the grand jury, knowing that his action might be attended by publicity, is not decisive	8–1; Brennan dissented

"PUBLIC FIGURE" (*Cont.*)

Case	Nature of the Controversy	Decision and Reasons	Vote
Wolston (*Cont.*)	ing that these statements were defamatory and false. As a result of a grand jury investigation in 1957–58, his aunt and uncle were arrested on and pleaded guilty to espionage charges. He was called several times to appear before the grand jury and, on one occasion, refused. He was subsequently found guilty of contempt and given a suspended sentence. While there were several news stories in the New York and Washington papers at the time, the publicity subsided after his sentencing, and he returned to lead a private life	on the question of public figure status." "[P]etitioner never discussed this matter with the press and limited his involvement to that necessary to defend himself on the contempt charge. It is clear that petitioner played only a minor role in whatever public controversy there may have been concerning the investigation of Soviet espionage. We decline to hold that his mere citation for contempt rendered him a public figure for purposes of comment on the investigation of Soviet espionage." "A private individual is not automatically transformed into a public figure just by becoming involved in or associated with a matter that attracts public attention." "His failure to respond to the grand jury's subpoena was in no way calculated to draw attention to himself in order to invite public comment or influence the public with respect to any issue. He did not in any way seek to arouse public sentiment in his favor and against the investigation. * * * [T]his is not a case where a defendant invites a citation for contempt in order to use the contempt citation as a fulcrum to create public discussion about the methods being used in connection with an investigation or prosecution. To the	

"PUBLIC FIGURE" (*Cont.*)

Case	Nature of the Controversy	Decision and Reasons	Vote
Wolston (*Cont.*)		contrary, petitioner's failure to appear before the grand jury appears simply to have been the result of his poor health"	

Anthony Herbert, a retired Army officer who saw extended wartime duty in Vietnam, received national attention in the media in 1969 and 1970 when he charged that his superior officers covered up reports of atrocities and other war crimes. CBS broadcast a report on Herbert and his allegations three years later on its television program, "60 Minutes." The segment was produced and edited by Barry Lando and narrated by Mike Wallace. Lando later published an article with much the same focus in *Atlantic Monthly* magazine. Herbert subsequently sued Lando, Wallace, CBS, and *Atlantic Monthly* for defamation in federal court, predicating jurisdiction on diversity of citizenship. He contended that both the program and the article falsely and with malice portrayed him as a liar and as an individual who had made war crimes charges to explain his relief from command. Conceding that he was a "public figure" and therefore that the *New York Times* rule precluded recovery in the absence of a showing that the defendants had disseminated a damaging falsehood with "actual malice," Herbert set about proving his case in light of that requirement. In preparation for the trial, Herbert sought a deposition from Lando including statements with respect to inquiries about his conclusions about people or leads to be pursued or not pursued, his opinions as to the veracity and accuracy of various persons interviewed, and discussions about material to be included and excluded from the broadcast publication. In view of Rule 26(b) of the Federal Rules of Civil Procedure which allows discovery of any matter "relevant to the subject matter involved in the pending action" if it either would be admissible as evidence or "appears reasonably calculated to lead to the discovery of admissible evidence," the district court judge ruled that since the defendant's state of mind was of "central importance" to establishing malice, Herbert's questions were relevant and proper. A divided federal appellate court reversed, finding the First Amendment privilege not to answer absolute and concluding that the Constitution protected Lando from any inquiry about his thoughts, opinions, and conclusions during the editorial process. Herbert then petitioned the Supreme Court for certiorari.

In Herbert v. Lando, 441 U.S. 153, 99 S.Ct. 1635 (1979), the Supreme Court rejected the proposition "that when a member of the press is alleged to have circulated damaging falsehoods and is sued for injury to the plaintiff's reputation, the plaintiff is barred from inquiry into the editorial processes of those responsible for the publication, even though the inquiry would produce evidence material to the proof of a critical element of this cause of action." Given that "*New York Times* and its progeny make it essential to proving liability that plaintiffs focus on the conduct and state of mind of the defendant," the Court reasoned that the suggested immunity from inquiry into the editorial processes "would constitute a substantial interference with the ability of a defamation plaintiff to establish the ingredients of malice as required by *New York Times*." The Court concluded that direct inquiry into the editorial processes was justified in the interests of both equity and accuracy. Acknowledging that "[t]he evidentiary burden Herbert must carry to prove at least reckless disregard for the truth is substantial indeed," Justice White, speaking for the Court, explained that "[p]ermitting plaintiffs such as Herbert to prove their cases by direct as well as indirect evidence is consistent with the balance struck by our prior decisions." Justice White observed that the Court was urged by the defendants "to override [the] important interests of [the plaintiffs] because requiring disclosure of editorial conversations and of a reporter's conclusions about the veracity of the material he had gathered will have an intolerable chilling effect on the editorial process and editorial decisionmaking." To this he responded: "But if the claimed inhibition flows from the fear of damages liability for publishing knowing or reckless falsehoods, those effects are precisely what *New York Times* and other cases have held to be consistent with the First Amendment. Spreading false information in and of itself carries no First Amendment credentials." Justice White continued:

> Realistically, however, some error is inevitable; and the difficulties of separating fact from fiction convinced the Court in *New York Times*, *Butts*, *Gertz*, and similar cases to limit liability to instances where some degree of culpability is present in order to eliminate the risk of undue self-censorship and the suppression of truthful material. Those who publish defamatory falsehoods with the requisite culpability, however, are subject to liability, the aim being not only to compensate for injury but also to deter publication of unprotected material threatening injury to individual reputation. * * * If * * * proof results in liability for damages which in turn discourages the publication of erroneous information known to be false or probably false, this is no more than what our cases contemplate and does not abridge either freedom of speech or of the press.

> Of course, if inquiry into editorial conclusions threatens the suppression not only of information known or strongly suspected to be unreliable but also of truthful information, the issue would be quite different. But as we have said, our cases necessarily contemplate examination of the editorial process to prove the necessary awareness of probable falsehood, and if indirect proof of this element does not stifle truthful publication and is consistent with the First Amendment, as respondents seem to concede, we do not understand how direct inquiry with respect to the ultimate issue would be substantially more suspect. Perhaps such examination will lead to liability that would not have been found without it, but this does not suggest that the determinations in these instances will be inaccurate and will lead to the suppression of protected information. On the contrary, direct inquiry from the actors, which affords the opportunity to refute inferences that might otherwise be drawn from circumstantial evidence, suggests that more accurate results will be obtained by placing all, rather than part, of the evidence before the decisionmaker. Suppose, for example, that a reporter has two contradictory reports about the plaintiff, one of which is false and damaging, and only the false one is published. In resolving the issue whether the publication was known or suspected to be false, it is only common sense to believe that inquiry from the author, with an opportunity to explain, will contribute to accuracy. If the publication is false but there is an exonerating explanation, the defendant will surely testify to this effect. Why should not the plaintiff be permitted to inquire before trial? On the other hand, if the publisher in fact had serious doubts about accuracy, but published nevertheless, no undue self-censorship will result from permitting the

relevant inquiry. Only knowing or reckless error will be discouraged; and unless there is to be an absolute First Amendment privilege to inflict injury by knowing or reckless conduct, which respondents do not suggest, constitutional values will not be threatened.

Disallowing direct inquiry about the editorial process would, the Court believed, be tantamount to according the press an absolute privilege, a position clearly inconsistent with past rulings. Justice White added:

> Evidentiary privileges in litigation are not favored, and even those rooted in the Constitution must give way in proper circumstances. The President, for example, does not have an absolute privilege against disclosure of materials subpoenaed for a judicial proceeding. United States v. Nixon, 418 U.S. 683, 94 S.Ct. 3090 (1974). In so holding, we found that although the President has a powerful interest in confidentiality of communications between himself and his advisers, that interest must yield to a demonstrated specific need for evidence. As we stated, in referring to existing limited privileges against disclosure, "[w]hatever their origins, these exceptions to the demand for every man's evidence are not lightly created nor expansively construed, for they are in derogation of the search for truth." Id., at 710, 94 S.Ct., at 3108.

Justice Brennan dissented in part. Beginning from the premise that it was "a great mistake to understand * * * the First Amendment solely through the filter of individual rights" and that greater regard should be given to the function filled by the press in "serv[ing] democratic values" and "attain[ing] social ends," Justice Brennan contended that *United States* v. *Nixon* articulated a more exact principle—that "[a] general claim of executive privilege, for example, will not stand against a 'demonstrated, specific need for evidence * * * .' " He continued:

> [In my judgment the existence of a privilege protecting the editorial process must, in an analogous manner, be determined with reference to the circumstances of a particular case. In the area of libel, the balance struck by *New York Times* between the values of the First Amendment and society's interest in preventing and redressing attacks upon reputation must be preserved. This can best be accomplished if the privilege functions to shield the editorial process from general claims of damaged reputation. If, however, a public figure plaintiff is able to establish, to the prima facie satisfaction of a trial judge, that the publication at issue constitutes defamatory falsehood, the claim of damaged reputation becomes specific and demonstrable, and the editorial privilege must yield. Contrary to the suggestion of the Court, an editorial privilege so understood would not create "a substantial interference with the ability of a defamation plaintiff to establish the ingredients of malice as required by *New York Times*." * * * Requiring a public figure plaintiff to make a prima facie showing of defamatory falsehood will not constitute an undue burden, since he must eventually demonstrate these elements as part of his case-in-chief. And since editorial privilege protects only deliberative and policymaking processes and not factual material, discovery should be adequate to acquire the relevant evidence of falsehood. A public figure plaintiff will thus be able to redress attacks on his reputation, and at the same time the editorial process will be protected in all but the most necessary cases.

Justice Stewart dissented on the grounds that since "inquiry into the broad 'editorial process' is simply not relevant in a libel suit brought by a public figure against a publisher * * * it is not permissible." He explained:

> Although I joined the Court's opinion in *New York Times*, I have come greatly to regret the use in that opinion of the phrase "actual malice." For the fact of the matter is that "malice" as used in the *New York Times* opinion simply does not mean malice as that word is commonly understood. In common understanding, malice means ill will or hostility, and the most relevant question in determining whether a person's action was motivated by actual malice is to ask "why." As part of the constitutional standard enunciated in the *New York Times* case, however, "actual malice" has nothing to do with hostility or ill will, and the question "why" is totally irrelevant.
>
> Under the constitutional restrictions imposed by *New York Times* and its progeny, a plaintiff who is a public official or public figure can recover from a publisher for a defamatory statement upon convincingly clear proof of the following elements:
>
> (1) the statement was published by the defendant,
>
> (2) the statement defamed the plaintiff,
>
> (3) the defamation was untrue,
>
> (4) and the defendant knew the defamatory statement was untrue, or published it in reckless disregard of its truth or falsity. * * *
>
> The gravamen of such a lawsuit thus concerns that which was in fact published. What was *not* published has nothing to do with the case. And liability ultimately depends upon the publisher's state of knowledge of the falsity of what he published, not at all upon his motivation in publishing it—not at all, in other words, upon actual malice as those words are ordinarily understood.

Justice Marshall also dissented.

GALELLA v. ONASSIS

United States District Court
Southern Dist. of New York, 1972
353 F.Supp. 196

Ronald Galella, a photographer, brought suit in federal district court for $1.3 million in damages against Jacqueline Onassis and three Secret Service agents assigned to protect her and her two children, Caroline and John F. Kennedy, Jr., alleging false arrest and malicious prosecution and seeking an injunction to prohibit Mrs. Onassis and the agents from interfering with the practice of his trade. In a countersuit, Mrs. Onassis sought injunctive relief and damages in the amount of $1.5 million for invasion of privacy, assault, harassment, and intentional infliction of emotional distress. The United States intervened as a third party to represent the interests of the agents assigned to protect the former First Lady and the children, pursuant to federal law.

In the words of the opinion subsequently rendered by the appeals court, "Galella fancies himself as a 'paparazzo' (literally a kind of annoying insect, perhaps roughly equivalent to the English 'gadfly'). Paparazzi make themselves as visible to the public and obnoxious to their photographic subjects as possible to aid in the advertisement and wide sale of their works." The technique apparently entails pursuing the individual to be photographed everywhere, manufacturing bizarre situations which startle the subject, and then capturing the subject's surprise on film—a technique once practiced by Galella on Marlon Brando who was so incensed that he punched the photographer and broke his jaw.

On countless occasions Galella followed Mrs. Onassis to restaurants and on her other outings, lunging at her as she was getting into or alighting from her car, leaping and jumping about wildly, grunting and making loud noises, and clicking his camera constantly, frequently with the blinding aftereffects of flash bulbs. Several times he surprised her inside restaurants and theaters, popping out at her from behind coatracks or running up and down the aisles. He followed her closely at high speeds and, in one episode, came uncomfortably close to her in a power boat while she was swimming. In another instance, he jumped out from behind a bush and into the path of John, Jr., who was riding his bicycle in Central Park, making him swerve suddenly and nearly fall off. With alleged frequency he seduced or bribed employees so as to be apprised of Mrs. Onassis's every move. On numerous occasions Galella came so close in snapping pictures that he brushed against people, pushing them and knocking them around, and touched Mrs. Onassis. Finally, still another incident illustrative of what the district court described as the "ersatz happenings" into which "Galella forces his subjects" is revealed in the following excerpt from the lower court opinion:

> * * * Accompanied by Mr. Andre Meyer on December 17, 1970 defendant went first to the "21" Club and then to the theatre. As soon as they left her apartment building, they saw plaintiff and some one in a Santa Claus costume whom plaintiff had paid to pose with Mrs. Onassis. She testified:
>
>> Santa Claus lunges up at me, pushing, trying to get next to me, pushing Mr. Meyer, scuffling, the doorman is there, too. This strange Santa Claus is running up at us.
>
> At the same time, she testified, while Galella leaped around her photographing her, he said: " * * * come on, Jackie, be nice to Santa, won't you? Come on, Jackie, snuggle up to Santa."
>
> Plaintiff and his Santa followed them to "21". Dinner over, they exited the restaurant accompanied by the witness Snyder (a "21" executive) who tried to keep Santa away from defendant, but Santa kept pushing and shoving in his efforts to get next to her and finally succeeded in getting within a few inches.
>
> When she reached her car, plaintiff pressed against it with his flash. From "21" they drove to the theatre. Plaintiff followed. He leaped around them in the lobby while they tried to take their seats; he rushed down the aisle twice (she believes) to take photographs of her. His behavior compelled her to remain in her seat during intermission. * * *
>
> After theatre, she returned home. For her the evening was "a wreck."

Several of these episodes occurred after and despite temporary restraining orders which had been issued prohibiting Galella from such close, unsolicited contact with Mrs. Onassis and the children.

COOPER, District Judge.

* * *

Any injunction which would absolutely or effectively prevent plaintiff from photographing Mrs. Onassis or her children would raise a problem of prior restraint. This is true whether the Government is the sole beneficiary (the classic prior restraint), New York Times Co. v. United States, 403 U.S. 713, 91 S.Ct. 2140 (1971), or whether the relief runs in favor of Mrs. Onassis and her children, either apart from or joined with the Government. Organization for a Better Austin v. Keefe, 402 U.S. 415, 419, 91 S.Ct. 1575 (1971); see Shelley v. Kraemer, 334 U.S. 1, 68 S.Ct. 836 (1948).

Accordingly, we must determine whether the paramount protections of the First Amendment to photograph and gather news are infringed by the relief which we have considered granting. Galella asserts that the First Amendment is a complete defense to the counterclaim and intervenor complaint. We reject this contention; it is unsupported by legal authority.

The proposition that the First Amendment gives the press wide liberty to engage in any sort of conduct, no matter how offensive, in gathering news has been flatly rejected.

Restricted areas. Several decisions have established that news gathering in certain places, especially by photography, may be absolutely barred, no matter how circumspect the deportment of the reporter or photographer may be. * * *

* * *

The Ninth Circuit [in Dietemann v. Time, Inc., 449 F.2d 245 (1971)] * * * expressly rejected the proposition that freedom of the press is a license to commit torts with impunity. * * *

* * *

We conclude that the First Amendment does not license Galella to trespass inside private buildings, such as the children's schools, lobbies of friends' apartment buildings and restaurants. Nor does that Amendment command that Galella be permitted to romance maids, bribe employees and maintain surveillance in order to monitor defendant's leaving, entering and living inside her own home.

* * *

[W]e said at trial * * * and now repeat, that [Mrs. Onassis] is a public figure. Nevertheless, the First Amendment does not immunize all conduct designed to gather information about or photographs of a public figure. There is no general constitutional right to assault, harass, or unceasingly shadow or distress public figures.

Balancing the right of privacy against the impingement on "speech." [F]oregoing authorities have dealt with "speech" of substantial or even great public interest and concern. The trial record before us, however, warrants the inquiry: Should the unremitting tortious and criminal behavior of plaintiff towards defendant over the past few years, with a very strong likelihood of its continuance, be a mandatory sacrifice she is compelled to make in order that some portion of the public may learn what she wore while walking on the public streets, or her appearance at the theater and public functions, or her department store purchases, or what she ate in restaurants? Does the Constitution insist on that too? Surely, such a contention belittles the great wisdom that is the hallmark of the Constitution.

In this case, photographs of defendant walking in Central Park, riding in automobiles, eating in restaurants, picnicking with her children, and the like, and his photograph captions indicating what magazines she has bought and what she has put in her coffee are of miniscule importance to the public. The torment inflicted upon her in the course of Galella's obtaining these photographs and bits of information clearly outweighs any interest in his obtaining such information.

Most of the courts which have considered this problem have concluded that just such a balancing test must be applied. * * *

* * *

The balancing test is responsive both to the protection of the individual's right to privacy and to the purposes of the First Amendment. * * *

* * *

It might be argued that the Court should not place itself in the position of drawing lines and of weighing the value of various communications so as to deny to some of them, under certain circumstances, the protection of the First Amendment. But that is what courts are for. * * *

[In its subsequent decision the appellate court summed up the ruling of Judge Cooper as follows: "[T]he [district] court dismissed Galella's claim and granted relief to both the defendant and the intervenor. Galella was enjoined from (1) keeping the defendant and her children under surveillance or following any of them; (2) approaching within 100 yards of the home of defendant or her children, or within 100 yards of either child's school or within 75 yards of either child or 50 yards of defendant; (3) using the name, portrait or picture of defendant or her children for advertising; (4) attempting to communicate with defendant or her children except through her attorney."]

On appeal, the U. S. Court of Appeals for the Second Circuit, in Galella v. Onassis, 487 F.2d 986 (1973), affirmed in part and reversed in part the judgment of the district court. The appeals court agreed with the reasoning of the lower court both as to the lack of any absolute press immunity from regulation under the First Amendment and as to an accommodation of the competing claims through an interest-balancing methodology. Speaking for the court, Judge J. Joseph Smith said:

Of course legitimate countervailing social needs may warrant some intrusion despite an individual's reasonable expectation of privacy and freedom from harassment. However the interference allowed may be no greater than that necessary to protect the overriding public interest. Mrs. Onassis was properly found to be a public figure and thus subject to news coverage. * * * Nonetheless, Galella's action went far beyond the reasonable bounds of news gathering. When weighed against the *de minimis* public importance of the daily activities of the defendant, Galella's constant surveillance, his obtrusive and intruding presence, was unwarranted and unreasonable. If there were any doubt in our minds, Galella's inexcusable conduct toward defendant's minor children would resolve it.

Galella does not seriously dispute the court's finding of tortious conduct. Rather, he sets up the First Amendment as a wall of immunity protecting newsmen from any liability for their conduct while gathering news. There is no such scope to the First Amendment right. Crimes and torts committed in news gathering are not protected. * * * There is no threat to a free press in requiring its agents to act within the law.

While the court also accepted the proposition that "[i]njunctive relief is appropriate," it nonetheless adjusted the parameters of relief afforded by the district court opinion:

> The injunction   *   *   *   is broader than is required to protect the defendant. Relief must be tailored to protect Mrs. Onassis from the "paparazzo" attack which distinguishes Galella's behavior from that of other photographers; it should not unnecessarily infringe on reasonable efforts to "cover" defendant. Therefore, we modify the court's order to prohibit only (1) any approach within twenty-five (25) feet of defendant or any touching of the person of the defendant Jacqueline Onassis; (2) any blocking of her movement in public places and thoroughfares; (3) any act foreseeably or reasonably calculated to place the life and safety of defendant in jeopardy; and (4) any conduct which would reasonably be foreseen to harass, alarm, or frighten the defendant.
>
> Any further restriction on Galella's taking and selling pictures of defendant for news coverage is, however, improper and unwarranted by the evidence.   *   *   *
>
> Likewise, we affirm the grant of injunctive relief to the government modified to prohibit any action interfering with Secret Service agents' protective duties. Galella thus may be enjoined from (a) entering the children's schools or play areas; (b) engaging in action calculated or reasonably foreseen to place the children's safety or well being in jeopardy, or which would threaten or create physical injury; (c) taking any action which could reasonably be foreseen to harass, alarm, or frighten the children; and (d) from approaching within thirty (30) feet of the children.

Judge Timbers of the U. S. Circuit Court concurred in part and dissented in part. He accepted the court's characterization and over all treatment of the constitutional issue but vigorously dissented from any modification of the district court order, arguing that the court ought to defer to the judgment of Judge Cooper in the court below absent any abuse of discretion on his part. Judge Timbers found "unexplained and anomalous" the "84% reduction of the distance Galella is required to keep away from Mrs. Onassis   *   *   *   and an equally implausible 87% reduction of the distance he is required to keep away from the children   *   *   *." Judge Timbers was also disturbed that the order "further results in no restriction whatsoever against Galella's hovering at the entrance to the home of Mrs. Onassis and her children   *   *   *, or at the schools attended by the children—just so he does not physically enter their schools or play areas." Given Galella's past conduct *"in the teeth of previous restraining orders of the district court,"* Judge Timbers found these modifications "an invitation for trouble." On a final modification contained in the majority opinion which he thought particularly vexing, Judge Timbers added:

> *   *   *   As I read the majority's modification of the injunction, to the extent that it distinguishes between protection for Mrs. Onassis and that for the children, limiting the latter to the grant of injunctive relief to the government, the net effect is to strip the children of any protection under the injunction after they reach age 16 when their protection by the Secret Service ceases. 18 U.S.C.A. 3056 (1970). For Caroline, who was born November 27, 1957, this means that one of her birthday presents—less than two months away—will be exposure to the resumed predatory conduct of the paparazzo Galella who will be totally unrestrained with respect to her by the injunction as modified by the majority. For John, who was born Nov-

ember 25, 1960, he has only three years to wait for similar exposure. To strip these children, before they reach their majority, of the protection of the injunction of the United States District Court below, is to deny to them and to their mother the very least to which they are entitled under the law.

d. FAIR TRIAL—FREE PRESS

NEBRASKA PRESS ASS'N v. STUART

Supreme Court of the United States, 1976
427 U.S. 539, 96 S.Ct. 2791, 49 L.Ed.2d 683

Following the arrest and arraignment of Simants, the suspected murderer of six members of a family in a small Nebraska farm community, and after hearing arguments on the issue of potentially prejudicial pretrial publicity, Judge Stuart, the trial judge, imposed restrictions on press and media coverage of the case until a jury had been impaneled. Specifically, the judge banned reporting on five topics. As summarized later by the Supreme Court, they included: "(1) the existence or contents of a confession Simants had made to law enforcement officers, which had been introduced in open court at arraignment; (2) the fact or nature of statements Simants had made to other persons; (3) the contents of a note he had written the night of the crime; (4) certain aspects of the medical testimony at the preliminary hearing; (5) the identity of the victims of the alleged sexual assault and the nature of the assault."

On appeal of the judge's orders, the Nebraska Supreme Court upheld but narrowed the constraints on reporting to three matters: "(a) the existence and nature of any confessions or admissions made by the defendant to law enforcement officers, (b) any confessions or admissions made to any third parties, except members of the press, and (c) other facts 'strongly implicative' of the accused." The U. S. Supreme Court granted certiorari to determine whether Judge Stuart's orders, as modified, constituted a violation of the First Amendment.

Mr. Chief Justice BURGER delivered the opinion of the Court.

* * *

The problems presented by this case are almost as old as the Republic. Neither in the Constitution nor in contemporaneous writings do we find that the conflict between these two important rights was anticipated, yet it is inconceivable that the authors of the Constitution were unaware of the potential conflicts between the right to an unbiased jury and the guarantee of freedom of the press. The unusually able lawyers who helped write the Constitution and later drafted the Bill of

Rights were familiar with the historic episode in which John Adams defended British soldiers charged with homicide for firing into a crowd of Boston demonstrators; they were intimately familiar with the clash of the adversary system and the part that passions of the populace sometimes play in influencing potential jurors. They did not address themselves directly to the situation presented by this case; their chief concern was the need for freedom of expression in the political arena and the dialogue in ideas. But they recognized that there were risks to private rights from an unfettered press. Jefferson, for example, writing from

Paris in 1786 concerning press attacks on John Jay, stated:

"In truth it is afflicting that a man who has past his life in serving the public * * * should yet be liable to have his peace of mind so much disturbed by any individual who shall think proper to arraign him in a newspaper. It is however an evil for which there is no remedy. Our liberty depends on the freedom of the press, and that cannot be limited without being lost." * * * 9 Papers of Thomas Jefferson (Boyd, ed.) 239. * * *

* * *

The authors of the Bill of Rights did not undertake to assign priorities as between First Amendment and Sixth Amendment rights, ranking one as superior to the other. In this case, the petitioners would have us declare the right of an accused subordinate to their right to publish in all circumstances. But if the authors of these guarantees, fully aware of the potential conflicts between them, were unwilling or unable to resolve the issue by assigning to one priority over the other, it is not for us to rewrite the Constitution by undertaking what they declined. It is unnecessary, after nearly two centuries, to establish a priority applicable in all circumstances. Yet it is nonetheless clear that the barriers to prior restraint remain high unless we are to abandon what the Court has said for nearly a quarter of our national existence and implied throughout all of it. The history of even wartime suspension of categorical guarantees, such as habeas corpus or the right to trial by civilian courts, see Ex parte Milligan, 4 Wall. 2, 18 L.Ed. 281 (1867), cautions against suspending explicit guarantees.

* * *

We turn now to the record in this case to determine whether, as Learned Hand put it, "the gravity of the 'evil,' discounted by its improbability, justifies such invasion of free speech as is necessary to avoid the danger." Dennis v. United States, 183 F.2d 201, 212 (1950), aff'd, 341 U.S. 494, 71 S.Ct. 857 (1951); see also L. Hand, The Bill of Rights 58–61 (1958). To do so, we must examine the evidence before the trial judge when the order was entered to determine (a) the nature and extent of pretrial news coverage; (b) whether other measures would be likely to mitigate the effects of unrestrained pretrial publicity; (c) how effectively a restraining order would operate to prevent the threatened danger. The precise terms of the restraining order are also important. We must then consider whether the record supports the entry of a prior restraint on publication, one of the most extraordinary remedies known to our jurisprudence.

In assessing the probable extent of publicity, the trial judge had before him newspapers demonstrating that the crime had already drawn intensive news coverage, and the testimony of the County Judge, who had entered the initial restraining order based on the local and national attention the case had attracted. The District Judge was required to assess the probable publicity that would be given these shocking crimes prior to the time a jury was selected and sequestered. He then had to examine the probable nature of the publicity and determine how it would affect prospective jurors.

Our review of the pretrial record persuades us that the trial judge was justified in concluding that there would be intense and pervasive pretrial publicity concerning this case. He could also reasonably conclude, based on common human experience, that publicity might impair the defendant's right to a fair trial. He did not purport to say more, for he found only "a clear and present danger that pretrial publicity *could* impinge upon the defendant's right to a fair trial." (Emphasis added.) His conclusion as to the impact of such publicity on prospective jurors was of necessity speculative, dealing as he was with factors unknown and unknowable.

We find little in the record that goes to another aspect of our task, determining whether measures short of an order restraining all publication would have insured the defendant a fair trial. Although the entry of the order might be read as a judicial determination that other measures would not suffice, the trial court made no express findings to that effect; the Nebraska Supreme Court referred to the issue only by implication. See 194 Neb., at 797–798, 236 N.W.2d, at 803.

Most of the alternatives to prior restraint of publication in these circumstances were discussed with obvious approval in Sheppard v. Maxwell, 384 U.S., at 357–362, 86 S.Ct., at 1519–1522: (a) change of trial venue to a place less exposed to the intense publicity that seemed imminent in Lincoln County; (b) postponement of the trial to allow public attention to subside; (c) use of searching questioning of prospective jurors, as Chief Justice Marshall did in the *Burr* case, to screen out those with fixed opinions as to guilt or innocence; (d) the use of emphatic and clear instructions on the sworn duty of each juror to decide the issues on-

ly on evidence presented in open court. Sequestration of jurors is, of course, always available. Although that measure insulates jurors only after they are sworn, it also enhances the likelihood of dissipating the impact of pretrial publicity and emphasizes the elements of the jurors' oaths.

This Court has outlined other measures short of prior restraints on publication tending to blunt the impact of pretrial publicity. See Sheppard v. Maxwell, 384 U.S., at 361–362, 86 S.Ct., at 1521–1522. Professional studies have filled out these suggestions, recommending that trial courts in appropriate cases limit what the contending lawyers, the police, and witnesses may say to anyone. See American Bar Association, Standards for Criminal Justice, Fair Trial and Free Press 2–15 (Approved Draft, 1968).

We have noted earlier that pretrial publicity, even if pervasive and concentrated, cannot be regarded as leading automatically and in every kind of criminal case to an unfair trial. The decided cases "cannot be made to stand for the proposition that juror exposure to information about a state defendant's prior convictions or to news accounts of the crime with which he is charged alone presumptively deprives the defendant of due process." Murphy v. Florida, 421 U.S. 794, 799, 95 S.Ct. 2031, 2036. Appellate evaluations as to the impact of publicity take into account what other measures were used to mitigate the adverse effects of publicity. The more difficult prospective or predictive assessment that a trial judge must make also calls for a judgment as to whether other precautionary steps will suffice.

We have therefore examined this record to determine the probable efficacy of the measures short of prior restraint on the press and speech. There is no finding that alternative measures would not have protected Simants' rights, and the Nebraska Supreme Court did no more than imply that such measures might not be adequate. Moreover, the record is lacking in evidence to support such a finding.

We must also assess the probable efficacy of prior restraint on publication as a workable method of protecting Simants' right to a fair trial, and we cannot ignore the reality of the problems of managing and enforcing pretrial restraining orders. The territorial jurisdiction of the issuing court is limited by concepts of sovereignty, see, e.g., Hanson v. Denckla, 357 U.S. 235, 78 S.Ct. 1228; Pennoyer v. Neff, 95 U.S. 714, 24 L.Ed. 565 (1878). The need for *in personam* jurisdiction also presents an obstacle to a restraining order that applies to publication at-large as distinguished from restraining publication within a given jurisdiction. See generally American Bar Association, Legal Advisory Committee on Fair Trial and Free Press, Recommended Court Procedures to Accommodate Rights of Fair Trial and Free Press (Revised Draft, November 1975); Rendleman, Free Press-Fair Trial: Review of Silence Orders, 52 N.C.L. Rev. 127, 149–155 (1973).

The Nebraska Supreme Court narrowed the scope of the restrictive order, and its opinion reflects awareness of the tensions between the need to protect the accused as fully as possible and the need to restrict publication as little as possible. The dilemma posed underscores how difficult it is for trial judges to predict what information will in fact undermine the impartiality of jurors, and the difficulty of drafting an order that will effectively keep prejudicial information from prospective jurors. When a restrictive order is sought, a court can anticipate only part of what will develop that may injure the accused. But information not so obviously prejudicial may emerge, and what may properly be published in these "gray zone" circumstances may not violate the restrictive order and yet be prejudicial.

Finally, we note that the events disclosed by the record took place in a community of 850 people. It is reasonable to assume that, without any news accounts being printed or broadcast, rumors would travel swiftly by word of mouth. One can only speculate on the accuracy of such reports, given the generative propensities of rumors; they could well be more damaging than reasonably accurate news accounts. But plainly a whole community cannot be restrained from discussing a subject intimately affecting life within it.

Given these practical problems, it is far from clear that prior restraint on publication would have protected Simants' rights.

Finally, another feature of this case leads us to conclude that the restrictive order entered here is not supportable. At the outset the County Court entered a very broad restrictive order, the terms of which are not before us; it then held a preliminary hearing open to the public and the press. There was testimony concerning at least two incriminating statements made by Simants to private persons; the statement—evidently a confession—that he gave to law enforcement officials was also introduced. The State District Court's later order was entered after this public hearing and, as modified by the Nebraska Supreme Court, enjoined reporting of (1) "[c]onfessions or admissions against interests made by the accused to law enforcement officials"; (2) "[c]onfessions or admissions against interest, oral or written, if any, made by the accused to third parties, excepting any statements, if any, made by the accused to representatives of the news media"; and (3) all "[o]ther information strongly implicative of the accused as the perpetrator of the slayings."

To the extent that this order prohibited the reporting of evidence adduced at the open preliminary hearing, it plainly violated settled principles: "there is nothing that proscribes the press from reporting events that transpire in the courtroom." Sheppard v. Maxwell, 384 U.S., at 362–363, 86 S.Ct., at 1522. See also *Cox Broadcasting Corp.* v. *Cohn*, supra; *Craig* v. *Harney*, supra. The County Court could not know that closure of the preliminary hearing was an alternative open to it until the Nebraska Supreme Court so construed state law; but once a public hearing had been held, what transpired there could not be subject to prior restraint.

The third prohibition of the order was defective in another respect as well. As part of a final order, entered after plenary review, this prohibition regarding "implicative" information is too vague and too broad to survive the scrutiny we have given to restraints on First Amendment rights. See, e.g., Hynes v. Oradell Mayor & Council, 425 U.S. 610, 96 S.Ct. 1755; Buckley v. Valeo, 424 U.S. 1, 76–82, 96 S.Ct. 612, 662–665; NAACP v. Button, 371 U.S. 415, 83 S.Ct. 328. The third phase of the order entered falls outside permissible limits.

The record demonstrates, as the Nebraska courts held, that there was indeed a risk that pretrial news accounts, true or false, would have some adverse impact on the attitudes of those who might be called as jurors. But on the record now before us it is not clear that further publicity, unchecked, would so distort the views of potential jurors that 12 could not be found who would, under proper instructions, fulfill their sworn duty to render a just verdict exclusively on the evidence presented in open court. We cannot say on this record that alternatives to a prior restraint on petitioners would not have sufficiently mitigated the adverse effects of pretrial publicity so as to make prior restraint unnecessary. Nor can we conclude that the restraining order actually entered would serve its intended purpose. Reasonable minds can have few doubts about the gravity of the evil pretrial publicity can work, but the probability that it would do so here was not demonstrated with the degree of certainty our cases on prior restraint require. Of necessity our holding is confined to the record before us. But our conclusion is not simply a result of assessing the adequacy of the showing made in this case; it results in part from the problems inherent in meeting the heavy burden of demonstrating, in advance of trial, that without prior restraint a fair trial will be denied. The practical problems of managing and enforcing restrictive orders will always be present. In this sense, the record now before us is illustrative rather than exceptional. It is significant that when this Court has reversed a state conviction because of prejudicial publicity, it has carefully noted that some course of action short of prior restraint would have made a critical difference. See Sheppard v. Maxwell, 384 U.S., at 363, 86 S.Ct., at 1522; Estes v. Texas, 381 U.S., at 550–551, 85 S.Ct., at 1636–1637; Rideau v. Louisiana, 373 U.S., at 726, 83 S.Ct., at 1419; Irvin v. Dowd, 366 U.S., at 728, 81 S.Ct., at 1645. However difficult it may be, we need not rule out the possibility of showing the kind of threat to fair trial rights that would possess the requisite degree of certainty to justify restraint. This Court has frequently denied that First Amendment rights are absolute and has consistently rejected the proposition that a prior restraint can never be employed. * * *

Our analysis ends as it began, with a confrontation between prior restraint imposed to protect one vital constitutional guarantee and the explicit command of another that the freedom to speak and publish shall not be abridged. We reaffirm that the guarantees of freedom of expression are not an absolute prohibition under all circumstances, but the barriers to prior restraint remain high and the presumption against its use continues intact. We hold that, with respect to the order entered in this case prohibiting reporting or commentary on judicial proceedings held in public, the barriers have not been overcome; to the extent that this order restrained publication of such material, it is clearly invalid. To the extent that it prohibited publication based on information gained from other sources, we conclude that the heavy burden imposed as a condition to securing a prior restraint was not met and the judgment of the Nebraska Supreme Court is therefore

Reversed.

Mr. Justice BRENNAN, with whom Mr. Justice STEWART and Mr. Justice MARSHALL concur, concurring in the judgment.

* * *

* * * The right to a fair trial by a jury of one's peers is unquestionably one of the most precious and sacred safeguards enshrined in the Bill of Rights. I would hold, however, that resort to prior restraints on the freedom of the press is a constitutionally impermissible method for enforcing that right; judges have at their disposal a broad spectrum of devices for ensuring that fundamental fairness is accorded the accused without necessitating so drastic an incursion on the equally fundamental and salutary constitutional mandate that discussion of public affairs in a free society cannot depend on the preliminary grace of judicial censors.

* * *

No one can seriously doubt, however, that unmediated prejudicial pretrial publicity may destroy the fairness of a criminal trial, see, e.g., *Sheppard* v. *Maxwell*, supra, and the past decade has witnessed substantial debate, colloquially known as the Free Press/Fair Trial controversy, concerning this interface of First and Sixth Amendment rights. In effect, we are now told by respondents that the two rights can no longer coexist when the press possesses and seeks to publish "confessions and admissions against interest" and other information "strongly implicative" of a criminal defendant as the perpetrator of a crime, and that one or the other right must therefore be subordinated. I disagree. Settled case law concerning the impropriety and constitutional invalidity of prior restraints on the press compels the conclusion that there can be no prohibition on the publication by the press of any information pertaining to pending judicial proceedings or the operation of the criminal justice system, no matter how shabby the means by which the information is obtained. This does not imply, however, any subordination of Sixth Amendment rights, for an accused's right to a fair trial may be adequately assured through methods that do not infringe First Amendment values.

* * *

I unreservedly agree with Mr. Justice Black that "free speech and fair trials are two of the most cherished policies of our civilization, and it would be a trying task to choose between them." Bridges v. California, 314 U.S. 252, 260, 62 S.Ct. 190, 192. But I would reject the notion that a choice is necessary, that there is an inherent conflict that cannot be resolved without essentially abrogating one right or the other. To hold that courts cannot impose any prior restraints on the reporting of or commentary upon information revealed in open court proceedings, disclosed in public documents, or divulged by other sources with respect to the criminal justice system is not, I must emphasize, to countenance the sacrifice of precious Sixth Amendment rights on the altar of the First Amendment. For although there may in some instances be tension between uninhibited and robust reporting by the press and fair trials for criminal defendants, judges possess adequate tools short of injunctions against reporting for relieving that tension. To be sure, these alternatives may require greater sensitivity and effort on the part of judges conducting criminal trials than would the stifling of publicity through the simple expedient of issuing a restric-

tive order on the press; but that sensitivity and effort is required in order to ensure the full enjoyment and proper accommodation of both First and Sixth Amendment rights.

There is, beyond peradventure, a clear and substantial damage to freedom of the press whenever even a temporary restraint is imposed on reporting of material concerning the operations of the criminal justice system, an institution of such pervasive influence in our constitutional scheme. And the necessary impact of reporting even confessions can never be so direct, immediate and irreparable that I would give credence to any notion that prior restraints may be imposed on that rationale. It may be that such incriminating material would be of such slight news value or so inflammatory in particular cases that responsible organs of the media, in an exercise of self-restraint, would choose not to publicize that material, and not make the judicial task of safeguarding precious rights of criminal defendants more difficult. Voluntary codes * * * are a commendable acknowledgement by the media that constitutional prerogatives bring enormous responsibilities, and I would encourage continuation of such voluntary cooperative efforts between the bar and the media. However, the press may be arrogant, tyrannical, abusive, and sensationalist, just as it may be incisive, probing, and informative. But at least in the context of prior restraints on publication, the decision of what, when, and how to publish is for editors, not judges. * * * Every restrictive order imposed on the press in this case was accordingly an unconstitutional prior restraint on the freedom of the press, and I would therefore reverse the judgment of the Nebraska Supreme

Court and remand for further proceedings not inconsistent with this opinion.

Mr. Justice WHITE, concurring.

Technically there is no need to go farther than the Court does to dispose of this case, and I join the Court's opinion. I should add, however, that for the reasons which the Court itself canvasses there is grave doubt in my mind whether orders with respect to the press such as were entered in this case would ever be justifiable. It may be the better part of discretion, however, not to announce such a rule in the first case in which the issue has been squarely presented here. Perhaps we should go no farther than absolutely necessary until the federal courts, and ourselves, have been exposed to a broader spectrum of cases presenting similar issues. If the recurring result, however, in case after case is to be similar to our judgment today, we should at some point announce a more general rule and avoid the interminable litigation that our failure to do so would necessarily entail.

Mr. Justice STEVENS, concurring in the judgment.

For the reasons eloquently stated by Mr. Justice BRENNAN, I agree that the judiciary is capable of protecting the defendant's right to a fair trial without enjoining the press from publishing information in the public domain, and that it may not do so. Whether the same absolute protection would apply no matter how shabby or illegal the means by which the information is obtained, no matter how serious an intrusion on privacy might be involved, no matter how demonstrably false the information might be, no matter how prejudicial it might be to the interests of innocent persons, and no matter how perverse the motivation for publishing it, is a question I would not answer without further argument. See Ashwander v. Valley Authority, 297 U.S. 288, 346–347, 56 S.Ct. 466, 482–483 (Brandeis, J., concurring). I do, however, subscribe to most of what Mr. Justice BRENNAN says and, if ever required to face the issue squarely, may well accept his ultimate conclusion.

RICHMOND NEWSPAPERS, INC. v. VIRGINIA

Supreme Court of the United States, 1980
448 U.S. 555, 100 S.Ct. 2814, 65 L.Ed.2d 973

At the beginning of the defendant Stevenson's fourth trial on a murder charge (his conviction at the first trial having been reversed on appeal and two subsequent retrials having ended in mistrials), the Virginia trial judge granted a defense motion to close the trial to the public. Apparently referring to § 19.2–266 of the Virginia Code, he announced, "[T]he statute gives me that power specifically and the defendant has made the motion." No objection was made either by the prosecutor or by two newspaper reporters who were present. Later that day the newspaper sought and received a hearing on a motion to vacate the closure order. Counsel for the newspaper argued that federal constitutional guarantees required that the judge examine alternative methods of protecting the defendant's rights and conclude that no other effective alternative existed before closing the trial to the public. Asserting that if he felt the defendant's rights were infringed in any way, he would be "inclined to go along with the defendant's motion," the judge ordered the trial to continue "with the press and public excluded." The following day the judge granted a defense motion to strike the prosecution's evidence, excused the jury, and found the defendant not guilty. The trial judge then granted the newspaper's motion to intervene in the case. On appeal, the Virginia Supreme Court denied the newspaper's appeal from the closure order.

Mr. Chief Justice BURGER announced the judgment of the Court and delivered an opinion in which Mr. Justice WHITE and Mr. Justice STEVENS joined.

The narrow question presented in this case is whether the right of the public and press to attend criminal trials is guaranteed under the United States Constitution.

* * *

We begin consideration of this case by noting that the precise issue presented here has not previously been before this Court for decision. In Gannett Co., Inc. v. DePasquale, 443 U.S. 368, 99 S.Ct. 2898 (1979), the Court was not required to decide whether a right of access to *trials*, as distinguished from hearings on *pre*trial motions, was constitutionally guaranteed. The Court held that the Sixth Amendment's guarantee to the accused of a public trial gave neither the public nor the press an enforceable right of access to a *pre*trial suppression hearing. One concurring opinion specifically emphasized that "a hearing on a motion before trial to suppress evidence is not a *trial*. * * *" 443 U.S., at 394, 99 S.Ct., at 2913 (Burger, C. J., concurring).[e]

Moreover, the Court did not decide whether the First and Fourteenth Amendments guarantee a right of the public to attend trials, * * * nor did the dissenting opinion reach this issue. * * *

In prior cases the Court has treated questions involving conflicts between publicity and a defendant's right to a fair trial; as we observed in Nebraska Press Assn. v. Stuart, 427 U.S. 539, 547, 96 S.Ct. 2791 (1976), "[t]he problems presented by this [conflict] are almost as old as the Republic." See also, e.g., *Gannett*, supra; Murphy v. Florida, 421 U.S. 794, 95 S.Ct. 2031 (1975); Sheppard v. Maxwell, 384 U.S. 333, 86 S.Ct. 1507 (1966); Estes v. Texas, 381 U.S. 532, 85 S.Ct. 1628 (1965). But here for the first time the Court is asked to decide whether a criminal trial itself may be closed to the public upon the unopposed request of a defendant, without any demonstration that closure is required to protect the defendant's superior right to a fair trial, or that some other overriding consideration requires closure.

* * *

[After a survey of developments from the time of the Norman con-

---

e. In his concurring opinion in *Gannett*, Chief Justice Burger, going to the heart of the matter, also observed:

When the Sixth Amendment was written, and for more than a century after that, no one could have conceived that the Exclusionary Rule and pretrial motions to suppress evidence would be part of our criminal jurisprudence. The authors of the Constitution, imaginative, far-sighted, and perceptive as they were, could not conceivably have anticipated the paradox inherent in a judge-made

rule of evidence that excludes undoubted truth from the truth-finding processes of the adversary system. Nevertheless, as of now, we are confronted not with a legal theory but with the reality of the unique strictures of the Exclusionary Rule and they must be taken into account in this setting. To make public the evidence developed in a motion to suppress evidence * * * would, so long as the Exclusionary Rule is not modified, introduce a new dimension to the problem of conducting fair trials.

quest of England through the American colonial era, the Chief Justice continued:]

As we have shown, and as was shown in both the Court's opinion and the dissent in *Gannett*, * * * the historical evidence demonstrates conclusively that at the time when our organic laws were adopted, criminal trials both here and in England had long been presumptively open. This is no quirk of history; rather, it has long been recognized as an indispensible attribute of an Anglo-American trial. Both Hale in the 17th century and Blackstone in the 18th saw the importance of openness to the proper functioning of a trial; it gave assurance that the proceedings were conducted fairly to all concerned, and it discouraged perjury, the misconduct of participants, and decisions based on secret bias or partiality. See, e.g., M. Hale, The History of the Common Law of England, 343–345 (6th ed. 1820); 3 W. Blackstone, Commentaries 372–373. Jeremy Bentham not only recognized the therapeutic value of open justice but regarded it as the keystone:

"Without publicity, all other checks are insufficient: in comparison of publicity, all other checks are of small account. Recordation, appeal, whatever other institutions might present themselves in the character of checks, would be found to operate rather as cloaks than checks; as cloaks in reality, as checks only in appearance." 1 J. Bentham, Rationale of Judicial Evidence 524 (1827).

Panegyrics on the values of openness were by no means confined to self-praise by the English. Foreign observers of English criminal procedure in the 18th and early 19th centuries came away impressed by the very fact that they had been freely admitted to the courts, as many were not in their own homelands. * * * The nexus between openness, fairness, and the perception of fairness was not lost on them:

"[T]he judge, the counsel, and the jury, are constantly exposed to public animadversion; and this greatly tends to augment the extraordinary confidence, which the English repose in the administration of justice." [C. Goede, A Foreigner's Opinion of England 215 (Horne trans. 1822).]

This observation raises the important point that "[t]he publicity of a judicial proceeding is a requirement of much broader bearing than its mere effect on the quality of testimony." 6 J. Wigmore, Evidence § 1834, at p. 435 (Chadbourn rev. 1976). The early history of open trials in part reflects the widespread acknowledgement, long before there were behavioral scientists, that public trials had significant community therapeutic value. Even without such experts to frame the concept in words, people sensed from experience and observation that, especially in the administration of criminal justice, the means used to achieve justice must have the support derived from public acceptance of both the process and its results.

When a shocking crime occurs, a community reaction of outrage and public protest often follows. See H. Weihofen, The Urge to Punish 130–131 (1956). Thereafter the open processes of justice serve an important prophylactic purpose, providing an outlet for community concern, hostility, and emotion. Without an awareness that society's responses to criminal conduct are underway, natural human reactions of outrage and protest are frustrated and may manifest themselves in some form of vengeful "self-help," as indeed they did regularly in the activities of vigilante "committees" on our frontiers. "The accusation and conviction or acquittal, as much perhaps as the execution of punishment, operate[ ] to restore the imbalance which was created by the offense or public charge, to reaffirm the temporarily lost feeling of security, and, perhaps, to satisfy that latent 'urge to punish.'" Mueller, Problems Posed by Publicity to Crime and Criminal Proceedings, 110 U.Pa.L.Rev. 1, 6 (1961).

Civilized societies withdraw both from the victim and the vigilante the enforcement of criminal laws, but they cannot erase from people's consciousness the fundamental, natural yearning to see justice done—or even the urge for retribution. The crucial prophylactic aspects of the administration of justice cannot function in the dark; no community catharsis can occur if justice is "done in a corner [or] in any covert manner." * * * It is not enough to say that results alone will satiate the natural community desire for "satisfaction." A result considered untoward may undermine public confidence, and where the trial has been concealed from public view an unexpected outcome can cause a reaction that the system at best has failed and at worst has been corrupted. To work effectively, it is important that society's criminal process "satisfy the appearance of justice," Offutt v. United States, 348 U.S. 11, 14, 75 S.Ct. 11, 13 (1954), and the appearance of justice can best be provided by allowing people to observe it.

* * *

People in an open society do not demand infallibility from their institutions, but it is difficult for them to accept what they are prohibited from observing. When a criminal trial is conducted in the open, there is at least an opportunity both for understanding the system in general and its workings in a particular case. * * *

In earlier times, both in England and America, attendance at court was a common mode of "passing the time." * * * With the press, cinema, and electronic media now supplying the representations or reality of the real life drama once available only in the courtroom, attendance at court is no longer a widespread pastime. * * * Instead of acquiring information about trials by firsthand observation or by word of mouth from those who attended, people now acquire it chiefly through the print and electronic media. In a sense, this validates the media claim of functioning as surrogates for the public. While media representatives enjoy the same right of access as the public, they often are provided special seating and priority of entry so that they may report what people in attendance have seen and heard. This "contribute[s] to public understanding of the rule of law and to comprehension of the functioning of the entire criminal justice system." * * * Nebraska Press Assn. v. Stuart, 427 U.S. 539, 587, 96 S.Ct. 2791, 2816 (Brennan, J., concurring).

From this unbroken, uncontradicted history, supported by reasons as valid today as in centuries past, we are bound to conclude that a presumption of openness inheres in the very nature of a criminal trial under our system of justice. This conclusion is hardly novel; without a direct holding on the issue, the Court has voiced its recognition of it in a variety of contexts over the years. * * *

Despite the history of criminal trials being presumptively open since long before the Constitution, the State presses its contention that neither the Constitution nor the Bill of Rights contains any provision which by its terms guarantees to the public the right to attend criminal trials. Standing alone, this is correct, but there remains the question whether, absent an explicit provision, the Constitution affords protection against exclusion of the public from criminal trials.

The First Amendment, in conjunction with the Fourteenth, prohibits governments from "abridging the freedom of speech, or of the press; or the right of the people peaceably to assemble, and to petition the Government for a redress of grievances." These expressly guaranteed freedoms share a common core purpose of assuring freedom of communication on matters relating to the functioning of government. Plainly it would be difficult to single out any aspect of government of higher concern and importance to the people than the manner in which criminal trials are conducted; as we have shown, recognition of this pervades the centuries-old history of open trials and the opinions of this Court. * * *

The Bill of Rights was enacted against the backdrop of the long history of trials being presumptively open. Public access to trials was then regarded as an important aspect of the process itself; the conduct of trials "before as many of the people as chuse to attend" was regarded as one of "the inestimable advantages of a free English constitution of government." 1 Journals of the Continental Congress, * * * at 106, 107. In guaranteeing freedoms such as those of speech and press, the First Amendment can be read as protecting the right of everyone to attend trials so as to give meaning to those explicit guarantees. "[T]he First Amendment goes beyond protection of the press and the self-expression of individuals to prohibit government from limiting the stock of information from which members of the public may draw." First National Bank of Boston v. Bellotti, 435 U.S. 765, 783, 98 S.Ct. 1407, 1419 (1978). Free speech carries with it some freedom to listen. "In a variety of contexts this Court has referred to a First Amendment right to 'receive information and ideas.'" Kleindienst v. Mandel, 408 U.S. 753, 762, 92 S.Ct. 2576, 2581 (1972). What this means in the context of trials is that the First Amendment guarantees of speech and press, standing alone, prohibit government from summarily closing courtroom doors which had long been open to the public at the time that amendment was adopted. "For the First Amendment does not speak equivocally. * * * It must be taken as a command of the broadest scope that explicit language, read in the context of a liberty-loving society, will allow." Bridges v. California, 314 U.S. 252, 263, 62 S.Ct. 190, 194 (1941).

It is not crucial whether we describe this right to attend criminal trials to hear, see, and communicate observations concerning them as a "right of access," cf. *Gannett*, supra, 443 U.S., at 397, 99 S.Ct., at 2914 (Powell, J., concurring); Saxbe v. Washington Post Co., 417 U.S. 843, 94 S.Ct. 2811 (1974); Pell v. Procunier, 417 U.S. 817, 94 S.Ct. 2800 (1974), or a "right to gather information," for we have recognized that "without some protection for seeking out the news, freedom of the press could be eviscerated." Branzburg v. Hayes, 408 U.S. 665, 681, 92 S.Ct. 2646, 2656 (1972). The explicit, guaranteed rights to speak and to publish concerning what takes place at a trial would lose much meaning if access to observe the trial could, as it was here, be foreclosed arbitrarily.

The right of access to places traditionally open to the public, as criminal trials have long been, may be seen as assured by the amalgam of the First Amendment guarantees of speech and press; and their affinity to the right of assembly is not without relevance. From the outset, the right of assembly was regarded not only as an independent right but also as a catalyst to augment the free exercise of the other First Amendment rights with which it was deliberately linked by the draftsmen. "The right of peaceable assembly is a right cognate to those of free speech and free press and is equally fundamental." DeJonge v. Oregon, 299 U.S. 353, 364, 57 S.Ct. 255, 260 (1937). People assemble in public places not only to speak or to take action, but also to listen, observe, and learn; indeed, they may "assembl[e] for any lawful purpose," Hague v. C. I. O., 307 U.S. 496, 519, 59 S.Ct. 954, 965 (1939) (opinion of Stone, J.). Subject to the traditional time, place, and manner restrictions, see, e.g., Cox v. New Hampshire, 312 U.S. 569, 61 S.Ct. 762 (1941); see also Cox v. Louisiana, 379 U.S. 559, 560–564, 85 S.Ct. 476, 478–480 (1965), streets, sidewalks, and parks are places traditionally open, where First Amendment rights may be exercised, see Hague v. C. I. O., 307 U.S. 496, 515, 59 S.Ct. 954, 963 (1939) (opinion of Roberts, J.); a trial courtroom also is a public place where the people generally—and representatives of the media—have a right to be present, and where their presence historically has been thought to enhance the integrity and quality of what takes place.

The State argues that the Constitution nowhere spells out a guarantee for the right of the public to attend trials, and that accordingly no such right is protected. The possibility that such a contention could be made did not escape the notice of the Constitution's draftsmen; they were concerned that some important rights might be thought disparaged because not specifically guaranteed. It was even argued that because of this danger no Bill of Rights should be adopted. * * *

But arguments such as the State makes have not precluded recognition of important rights not enumerated. Notwithstanding the appropriate caution against reading into the Constitution rights not explicitly defined, the Court has acknowledged that certain unarticulated rights are implicit in enumerated guarantees. For example, the rights of association and of privacy, the right to be presumed innocent and the right to be judged by a standard of proof beyond a reasonable doubt in a criminal trial, as well as the right to travel, appear nowhere in the Constitution or Bill of Rights. Yet these important but unarticulated rights have nonetheless been found to share constitutional protection in common with explicit guarantees. * * * [F]undamental rights, even though not expressly guaranteed, have been recognized by the Court as indispensable to the enjoyment of rights explicitly defined.

We hold that the right to attend criminal trials is implicit in the guarantees of the First Amendment; without the freedom to attend such trials, which people have exercised for centuries, important aspects of freedom of speech and "of the press could be eviscerated." *Branzburg*, supra, 408 U.S. at 681, 92 S.Ct., at 2656.

Having concluded there was a guaranteed right of the public under the First and Fourteenth Amendments to attend the trial of Stevenson's case, we return to the closure order challenged by appellants. The Court in *Gannett*, supra, made clear that although the Sixth Amendment guarantees the accused a right to a public trial, it does not give a right to a private trial. * * * Despite the fact that this was the fourth trial of the accused, the trial judge made no findings to support closure; no inquiry was made as to whether alternative solutions would have met the need to ensure fairness; there was no recognition of any right under the Constitution for the public or press to attend the trial. In contrast to the pretrial proceeding dealt with in *Gannett*, supra, there exist in the context of the trial itself various tested alternatives to satisfy the constitutional demands of fairness. See, e.g., Nebraska Press Association v. Stuart, 427 U.S., at 563–565, 96 S.Ct., at 2804–2805; Sheppard v. Maxwell, 384 U.S., at 357–362, 86 S.Ct., at 1519–1522. There was no suggestion that any problems with witnesses could not have been dealt with by their exclusion from the courtroom or their sequestration during the trial. * * * Nor is there anything to indicate that sequestration of the jurors would not have guarded against their being subjected to any improper information. All of the alternatives admittedly present difficulties for trial courts, but none of the factors relied on here was beyond the realm of the manageable.

Absent an overriding interest articulated in findings, the trial of a criminal case must be open to the public. Accordingly, the judgment under review is reversed.

Reversed.

Mr. Justice POWELL took no part in the consideration or decision of this case.

Mr. Justice WHITE, concurring.

This case would have been unnecessary had Gannett Co. v. DePasquale, 443 U.S. 368, 99 S.Ct. 2898 (1979), construed the Sixth Amendment to forbid excluding the public from criminal proceedings except in narrowly defined circumstances. But the Court there rejected the submission of four of us to this effect, thus requiring that the First Amendment issue involved here be addressed. On this issue, I concur in the opinion of The Chief Justice.

Mr. Justice STEVENS, concurring.

This is a watershed case. Until today the Court has accorded virtually absolute protection to the dissemination of information or ideas, but never before has it squarely held that the acquisition of newsworthy matter is entitled to any constitutional protection whatsoever. An additional word of emphasis is therefore appropriate.

Twice before, the Court has implied that any governmental restriction on access to information, no matter how severe and no matter how unjustified, would be constitutionally acceptable so long as it did not single out the press for special disabilities not applicable to the public at large. In a dissent joined by Mr. Justice Brennan and Mr. Justice Marshall in Saxbe v. Washington Post Co., 417 U.S. 843, 850, 94 S.Ct.

2811, 2815, Mr. Justice Powell unequivocally rejected the conclusion "that *any* governmental restriction on press access to information, so long as it is not discriminatory, falls outside the purview of First Amendment concern." * * * And in Houchins v. KQED, Inc., 438 U.S. 1, 19–40, 98 S.Ct. 2588, 2599–2610, I explained at length why Mr. Justice Brennan, Mr. Justice Powell, and I were convinced that "[a]n official prison policy of concealing * * * knowledge from the public by arbitrarily cutting off the flow of information at its source abridges the freedom of speech and of the press protected by the First and Fourteenth Amendments to the Constitution." * * * Since Mr. Justice Marshall and Mr. Justice Blackmun were unable to participate in that case, a majority of the Court neither accepted nor rejected that conclusion or the contrary conclusion expressed in the prevailing opinions. Today, however, for the first time, the Court unequivocally holds that an arbitrary interference with access to important information is an abridgment of the freedoms of speech and of the press protected by the First Amendment.

It is somewhat ironic that the Court should find more reason to recognize a right of access today than it did in *Houchins.* For *Houchins* involved the plight of a segment of society least able to protect itself, an attack on a long-standing policy of concealment, and an absence of any legitimate justification for abridging public access to information about how government operates. In this case we are protecting the interests of the most powerful voices in the community, we are concerned with an almost unique exception to an established tradition of openness in the conduct of criminal trials, and it is

likely that the closure order was motivated by the judge's desire to protect the individual defendant from the burden of a fourth criminal trial.

In any event, for the reasons stated in [p]art * * * of my *Houchins* opinion * * * as well as those stated by The Chief Justice today, I agree that the First Amendment protects the public and the press from abridgment of their rights of access to information about the operation of their government, including the Judicial Branch; given the total absence of any record justification for the closure order entered in this case, that order violated the First Amendment.

Mr. Justice BRENNAN, with whom Mr. Justice MARSHALL joins, concurring in the judgment.

Gannett Co. v. DePasquale, 443 U.S. 368, 99 S.Ct. 2898 (1979), held that the Sixth Amendment right to a public trial was personal to the accused, conferring no right of access to pretrial proceedings that is separately enforceable by the public or the press. The instant case raises the question whether the First Amendment, of its own force and as applied to the States through the Fourteenth Amendment, secures the public an independent right of access to trial proceedings. Because I believe that the First Amendment—of itself and as applied to the States through the Fourteenth Amendment—secures such a public right of access, I agree with those of my Brethren who hold that, without more agreement of the trial judge and the parties cannot constitutionally close a trial to the public.

While freedom of expression is made inviolate by the First Amendment, and, with only rare and stringent exceptions, may not be suppressed, * * * the First Amendment has not been viewed by the Court in all settings as providing an equally categorical assurance of the correlative freedom of access to information. * * * Yet the Court has not ruled out a public access component to the First Amendment in every circumstance. Read with care and in context, our decisions must therefore be understood as holding only that any privilege of access to governmental information is subject to a degree of restraint dictated by the nature of the information and countervailing interests in security or confidentiality. * * * These cases neither comprehensively nor absolutely deny that public access to information may at times be implied by the First Amendment and the principles which animate it.

The Court's approach in right of access cases simply reflects the special nature of a claim of First Amendment right to gather information. Customarily, First Amendment guarantees are interposed to protect communication between speaker and listener. When so employed against prior restraints, free speech protections are almost insurmountable. * * * But the First Amendment embodies more than a commitment to free expression and communicative interchange for their own sakes; it has a *structural* role to play in securing and fostering our republican system of self-government. See United States v. Carolene Prods. Co., 304 U.S. 144, 152–153, n. 4, 58 S.Ct. 778, 783–784, n. 4 (1938); Grosjean v. American Press Co., 297 U.S. 233, 249–250, 56 S.Ct. 444, 448–449 (1936); * * * Ely, Democracy and Distrust 93–94 (1980); Emerson, The System of Freedom of Expression 7 (1970); Meiklejohn, Free Speech and Its Relation to Self-Government

(1948); Bork, Neutral Principles and Some First Amendment Problems, 47 Ind.L.J. 1, 23 (1971). Implicit in this structural role is not only "the principle that debate on public issues should be uninhibited, robust, and wide-open," New York Times Co. v. Sullivan, 376 U.S. 254, 270, 84 S.Ct. 710, 721 (1964), but the antecedent assumption that valuable public debate—as well as other civic behavior—must be informed. The structural model links the First Amendment to that process of communication necessary for a democracy to survive, and thus entails solicitude not only for communication itself, but for the indispensable conditions of meaningful communication.

However, because "the stretch of this protection is theoretically endless," * * * it must be invoked with discrimination and temperance. For so far as the participating citizen's need for information is concerned, "[t]here are few restrictions on action which could not be clothed by ingenious argument in the garb of decreased data flow." * * * An assertion of the prerogative to gather information must accordingly be assayed by considering the information sought and the opposing interests invaded.

This judicial task is as much a matter of sensitivity to practical necessities as it is of abstract reasoning. But at least two helpful principles may be sketched. First, the case for a right of access has special force when drawn from an enduring and vital tradition of public entree to particular proceedings or information. * * * Such a tradition commands respect in part because the Constitution carries the gloss of history. More importantly, a tradition of accessibility implies the favorable judgment of experience. Second, the value of access must be measured in specifics. Analysis is not advanced by rhetorical statements that all information bears upon public issues; what is crucial in individual cases is whether access to a particular government process is important in terms of that very process.

To resolve the case before us, therefore, we must consult historical and current practice with respect to open trials, and weigh the importance of public access to the trial process itself.

* * *

This Court * * * has persistently defended the public character of the trial process. *In re Oliver* established that the Due Process Clause of the Fourteenth Amendment forbids closed criminal trials. Noting the "universal rule against secret trials," 333 U.S., at 266, 68 S.Ct., at 504, the Court held that

"[i]n view of this nation's historic distrust of secret proceedings, their inherent dangers to freedom, and the universal requirement of our federal and state governments that criminal trials be public, the Fourteenth Amendment's guarantee that no one shall be deprived of his liberty without due process of law means at least that an accused cannot be thus sentenced to prison." * * *

Even more significantly for our present purpose, *Oliver* recognized that open trials are bulwarks of our free and democratic government: public access to court proceedings is one of the numerous "checks and balances" of our system, because "contemporaneous review in the forum of public opinion is an effective restraint on possible abuse of judicial power." * * * Indeed, the Court focused

with particularity upon the public trial guarantee "as a safeguard against any attempt to employ our courts as instruments of persecution," or "for the suppression of political and religious heresies." * * * Thus, *Oliver* acknowledged that open trials are indispensable to First Amendment political and religious freedoms.

By the same token, a special solicitude for the public character of judicial proceedings is evident in the Court's rulings upholding the right to report about the administration of justice. While these decisions are impelled by the classic protections afforded by the First Amendment to pure communication, they are also bottomed upon a keen appreciation of the structural interest served in opening the judicial system to public inspection. So, in upholding a privilege for reporting truthful information about judicial misconduct proceedings, Landmark Communications, Inc. v. Virginia, 435 U.S. 829, 98 S.Ct. 1535 (1978), emphasized that public scrutiny of the operation of a judicial disciplinary body implicates a major purpose of the First Amendment—"discussion of governmental affairs." * * * Again, *Nebraska Press Assn.* v. *Stuart*, supra, * * * noted that the traditional guarantee against prior restraint "should have particular force as applied to reporting of criminal proceedings." * * * And Cox Broadcasting Corp. v. Cohn, 420 U.S. 469, 492, 95 S.Ct. 1029, 1044 (1975), instructed that

"[w]ith respect to judicial proceedings in particular, the function of the press serves to guarantee the fairness of trials and to bring to bear the beneficial effects of public scrutiny upon the administration of justice." * * *

Tradition, contemporaneous state practice, and this Court's own decisions manifest a common understanding that "[a] trial is a public event. What transpires in the court room is public property." Craig v. Harney, 331 U.S. 367, 374, 67 S.Ct. 1249, 1254 (1947). As a matter of law and virtually immemorial custom, public trials have been the essentially unwavering rule in ancestral England and in our own Nation. * * * Such abiding adherence to the principle of open trials "reflect[s] a profound judgment about the way in which law should be enforced and justice administered." Duncan v. Louisiana, 391 U.S. 145, 155, 88 S.Ct. 1444, 1451 (1968).

* * *

Mr. Justice STEWART, concurring in the judgment.

In Gannett Co. v. DePasquale, 443 U.S. 368, 99 S.Ct. 2898, the Court held that the Sixth Amendment, which guarantees "the accused" the right to a public trial, does not confer upon representatives of the press or members of the general public any right of access to a trial. But the Court explicitly left open the question whether such a right of access may be guaranteed by other provisions of the Constitution. * * *

* * * [T]he First and Fourteenth Amendments clearly give the press and the public a right of access to trials themselves, civil as well as criminal. * * * With us, a trial is by very definition a proceeding open to the press and to the public.

In conspicuous contrast to a military base, Greer v. Spock, 424 U.S. 828, 96 S.Ct. 1211; a jail, Adderley v. Florida, 385 U.S. 39, 87 S.Ct. 242; or a prison, Pell v. Procunier, 417 U.S. 817, 94 S.Ct. 2800, a trial courtroom is a public place. Even more than city streets, sidewalks, and parks as areas of traditional First Amendment activity, e.g., Shuttleworth v. Birmingham, 394 U.S. 147, 89 S.Ct. 935, a trial courtroom is a place where representatives of the press and of the public are not only free to be, but where their presence serves to assure the integrity of what goes on.

But this does not mean that the First Amendment right of members of the public and representatives of the press to attend civil and criminal trials is absolute. Just as a legislature may impose reasonable time, place and manner restrictions upon the exercise of First Amendment freedoms, so may a trial judge impose reasonable limitations upon the unrestricted occupation of a courtroom by representatives of the press and members of the public. * * * Much more than a city street, a trial courtroom must be a quiet and orderly place. * * * Moreover, every courtroom has a finite physical capacity, and there may be occasions when not all who wish to attend a trial may do so. And while there exist many alternative ways to satisfy the constitutional demands of a fair trial, those demands may also sometimes justify limitations upon the unrestricted presence of spectators in the courtroom.

Since in the present case the trial judge appears to have given no recognition to the right of representatives of the press and members of the public to be present at the Virginia murder trial over which he was presiding, the judgment under review must be reversed.

It is upon the basis of these principles that I concur in the judgment.

* * *

Mr. Justice BLACKMUN, concurring in the judgment.

My opinion and vote in partial dissent last Term in Gannett Co. v. DePasquale, 443 U.S. 368, 406, 99 S.Ct. 2898, 2919 (1979), compels my vote to reverse the judgment of the Supreme Court of Virginia.

* * *

The Court's ultimate ruling in *Gannett*, with such clarification as is provided by the opinions in this case today, apparently is now to the effect that there is no *Sixth* Amendment right on the part of the public—or the press—to an open hearing on a motion to suppress. I, of course, continue to believe that *Gannett* was in error, both in its interpretation of the Sixth Amendment generally, and in its application to the suppression hearing, for I remain convinced that the right to a public trial is to be found where the Constitution explicitly placed it—in the Sixth Amendment.[3]

The Court, however, has eschewed the Sixth Amendment route. The plurality turns to other possible constitutional sources and invokes a veritable potpourri of them—the speech clause of the First Amendment, the press clause, the assembly clause, the Ninth Amendment, and a cluster of penumbral guarantees recognized in past decisions. This course is troublesome, but it is the route that has been selected and, at least for now, we must live with it. No purpose would be served by my spelling out at length here the reasons for my saying that the course is

troublesome. I need do no more than observe that uncertainty marks the nature—and strictness—of the standard of closure the Court adopts.

* * *

Having said all this, and with the Sixth Amendment set to one side in this case, I am driven to conclude, as a secondary position, that the First Amendment must provide some measure of protection for public access to the trial. The opinion in partial dissent in *Gannett* explained that the public has an intense need and a deserved right to know about the administration of justice in general; about the prosecution of local crimes in particular; about the conduct of the judge, the prosecutor, defense counsel, police officers, other public servants, and all the actors in the judicial arena; and about the trial itself. * * * It is clear and obvious to me, on the approach the Court has chosen to take, that, by closing this criminal trial, the trial judge abridged these First Amendment interests of the public.

I also would reverse, and I join the judgment of the Court.

Mr. Justice REHNQUIST, dissenting.

In the Gilbert & Sullivan operetta *Iolanthe*, the Lord Chancellor recites:

"The Law is the true embodiment of everything that's excellent,

It has no kind of fault or flaw,

And I, my lords, embody the law."

---

3. I shall not again seek to demonstrate the errors of analysis in the Court's opinion in *Gannett*. I note, however, that the very existence of the present case illustrates the utter fallacy of thinking, in this context, that "the

public interest is fully protected by the participants in the litigation." Gannett Co. v. DePasquale, 443 U.S. 368, 384, 99 S.Ct. 2898, 2908 (1979). * * *

It is difficult not to derive more than a little of this flavor from the various opinions supporting the judgment in this case. * * *

* * *

We have at present 50 state judicial systems and one federal judicial system in the United States, and our authority to reverse a decision by the highest court of the State is limited to only those occasions when the state decision violates some provision of the United States Constitution. And that authority should be exercised with a full sense that the judges whose decisions we review are making the same effort as we to uphold the Constitution. As said by Mr. Justice Jackson, concurring in the result in Brown v. Allen, 344 U.S. 443, 540, 73 S.Ct. 397, 427 "we are not final because we are infallible, but we are infallible only because we are final."

The proper administration of justice in any nation is bound to be a matter of the highest concern to all thinking citizens. But to gradually rein in, as this Court has done over the past generation, all of the ultimate decisionmaking power over how justice shall be administered, not merely in the federal system but in each of the 50 States, is a task that no Court consisting of nine persons, however gifted, is equal to. Nor is it desirable that such authority be exercised by such a tiny numerical fragment of the 220 million people who compose the population of this country. In the same concurrence just quoted, Mr. Justice Jack-

son accurately observed that "[t]he generalities of the Fourteenth Amendment are so indeterminate as to what state actions are forbidden that this Court has found it a ready instrument, in one field or another, to magnify federal, and incidentally its own, authority over the states."
* * *

However high minded the impulses which originally spawned this trend may have been, and which impulses have been accentuated since the time Justice Jackson wrote, it is basically unhealthy to have so much authority concentrated in a small group of lawyers who have been appointed to the Supreme Court and enjoy virtual life tenure. Nothing in the reasoning of Chief Justice Marshall in Marbury v. Madison, 5 U.S. (1 Cranch) 137 (1803) requires that this Court through ever broadening use of the Supremacy Clause smother a healthy pluralism which would ordinarily exist in a national government embracing 50 States.

The issue here is not whether the "right" to freedom of the press conferred by the First Amendment to the Constitution overrides the defendant's "right" to a fair trial conferred by other amendments to the Constitution; it is instead whether any provision in the Constitution may fairly be read to prohibit what the trial judge in the Virginia state court system did in this case. Being unable to find any such prohibition in the First, Sixth, Ninth, or any other Amendments to the United States Constitution, or in the Constitution itself, I dissent.

In Globe Newspaper Co. v. Superior Court for Suffolk County, —— U.S. ——, 102 S.Ct. 2613 (1982), the Supreme Court addressed the question whether a Massachusetts statute, construed so that it "requires trial judges, at trials for specified sexual offenses involving a victim under the age of 18, to exclude the press and general public from the courtroom during the testimony of that victim," violates the First Amendment as made applicable to the states through the Fourteenth. Relying principally on *Richmond Newspapers*, Justice Brennan, writing for the Court, held the statute unconstitutional as so construed. He found both interests asserted by the Commonwealth to support such a construction—safeguarding the physical and emotional well-being of a minor victim and encouraging minor victims of sex crimes to come forward and file a complaint—important but insufficient to support *automatic* exclusion of the press and public. As to the first of these interests, the Court concluded that the statute "cannot be viewed as a narrowly tailored means of accommodating the State's asserted interest: That interest could be served just as well by requiring the trial court to determine on a case-by-case basis whether the State's legitimate concern for the well-being of the minor necessitated closure." And with respect to the second interest proffered by the Commonwealth, Justice Brennan pointed out that it "has offered no empirical support for the claim" but such a proposition "is also open to serious question as a matter of logic and common sense." He observed that "the press is not denied access to the transcript, court personnel, or any other possible source that could provide an account of the minor victim's testimony. Thus [the statute] cannot prevent the press from publishing the substance of a minor victim's testimony, as well as his or her identity." As a result, the statute "hardly advances that interest in an effective manner," and even if it did, such an interest would probably not be sufficient to support *automatic* closure.

Chief Justice Burger, joined by Justice Rehnquist, dissented. He regarded the Court's ruling as an unwarranted extension of *Richmond Newspapers* and observed: "[T]oday the Court holds unconstitutional a state statute designed to protect not the *accused*, but the minor *victims* of sex crimes. In doing so, it advances a disturbing paradox. Although states are permitted, for example, to mandate the closure of all proceedings in order to protect a 17-year-old charged with rape, they are not permitted to require the closing of part of criminal proceedings in order to protect an innocent child who has been raped or otherwise sexually abused." Justice Stevens also dissented but did so on the grounds that, at least in terms of the facts of this case, "the Court's comment on the First Amendment issues implicated by the Massachusetts statute is advisory, hypothetical, and, at best, premature."

Chapter 15

Freedom of Religion

Freedom to worship as one saw fit was one of the dominant motives behind the founding of the American colonies. As a consequence, it might be expected that some provision guaranteeing that right would have been included in the Constitution. However, the original Constitution made mention of religion on only one occasion. Article VI requires in part that "no religious test shall ever be required as a qualification to any office or public trust under the United States." Yet again, the protection of a vital freedom was left to be included in the amendments to the Constitution.

Protection of religious freedom was embodied in the First Amendment's prohibition that "Congress shall make no law respecting an establishment of religion, or prohibiting the free exercise thereof * * *." As we have pointed out on previous occasions, however, the rights contained in the First Amendment have seldom, if ever, been enforced as absolutes. This is so, we said, because these rights often conflict with important social interests or other individual rights. Thus we saw, for example, that the exercise of free speech came into conflict at some point with a popular demand for public order and security and, in a second instance, the right to publish collided with the individual's right of privacy.

As regards religion, the tension surrounding the realization of First Amendment guarantees is particularly acute, for the Amendment contains two distinct prohibitions which often appear directly to contradict one another. Both the Establishment and the Free Exercise Clauses were intended to provide the greatest latitude in religious freedom. Yet a governmental policy which is helpful to one man in the exercise of his religious belief is the establishment of a religion to another; and the removal of some vestige of support for a religious institution which is the actualization of the establishment prohibition to one person is for another individual the impairment of a right to worship.

1523

Where do we draw the line as these two conflicting constitutional requirements affect governmental policy? Chief Justice Burger on at least one occasion has said that such a boundary "cannot be an absolutely straight line." Would you agree? Is the absolutist approach here even less useful than it was elsewhere? If so, then what kind of balance between these diametrically opposed interests would you have the Court strike?

a. The Establishment of Religion

The First Amendment forbids "the establishment of religion." But what constitutes the establishment of a religion? Historically, the Establishment Clause has provoked two different views as to its interpretation. One view of this prohibition holds that the word "establishment" should be interpreted narrowly. Persons holding this view contend that the phrase prohibits only the kind of establishment which existed in Europe prior to the American Revolution. Thus Congress was barred by the First Amendment from establishing an official, publicly supported church. Nothing comparable to the Church of England, for example, could be instituted by the Congress. However, nothing in the Establishment Clause forbids state support of religious activities so long as all religions are treated equally.

A second view results in a much broader interpretation of the Establishment Clause. Individuals of this persuasion contend that the Clause prohibits *any* governmental support of religion. Government is barred from supporting or becoming involved with religion in any manner. The fact that its support may be distributed equally to all religions is irrelevant.

Over the years the Supreme Court has seemed consistently to espouse the latter position, demanding what Justice Black termed "a wall of separation between Church and State." Yet decisions in some cases appear contradictory and may indicate that the Court has not been so totally dedicated to the latter theory as to exclude all of the former. As you read the cases which follow, see if you can determine which position the Justices seem to be acting upon. Can both positions be held logically and consistently?

One of the Court's early bouts with the problems of the Establishment Clause was brought by a New Jersey taxpayer in Everson v. Board of Education, 330 U.S. 1, 67 S.Ct. 504 (1947). The statute at issue contained a very controversial provision which allowed school boards to reimburse parents of both public and parochial school students for transportation costs incurred to and from school on the public transportation system. Everson contended that the reimbursement to parochial school students amounted to an establishment of religion. However, the Court in a 5–4 decision, Justice Black writing the opinion, rejected that contention. Said Justice Black delineating the requirements of the Establishment Clause:

Neither a state nor the Federal Government can set up a church. Neither can pass laws which aid one religion, aid all religions, or prefer one religion over another. Neither can force nor influence a person to go to or to remain away from church against his will or force him to profess a belief or disbelief in any religion. No person can be punished for entertaining or professing religious beliefs or disbeliefs, for church attendance or non-attendance. No tax in any amount, large or small, can be levied to support any religious activities or institutions, whatever they may be called, or whatever form they may adopt to teach or practice religion. Neither a state nor the Federal Government can, openly or secretly, participate in the affairs of any religious organizations or groups and vice versa. In the words of Jefferson, the clause against establishment of religion by law was intended to erect "a wall of separation between Church and State."

Black's interpretation of the Establishment Clause might well lead one to expect that the majority would have declared the New Jersey statute unconstitutional, but such was not the case. Admitting that the statute approached the verge of constitutional power, Black explained that it was saved because it provided benefits to the pupil, not the school. In this manner Black likened the statute to general public welfare legislation. Thus, to deny parents of parochial school students a reimbursement allowed other parents would have been tantamount to denying welfare benefits on the basis of religious faith—an act which would have clearly resulted in an impairment of the Free Exercise Clause.

Justice Black contended that the wall between church and state had been kept high and impregnable, but the four dissenting Justices saw the result differently. Justice Jackson forcefully argued that the Black opinion was inconsistent with the Black decision. Concluding with one of his typical literary allusions, Jackson remarked that the Court's decision reminded him of "Julia who, according to Byron's reports, 'whispering "I will ne'er consent,"—consented.' "

Following its initial posture in the *Everson* case, the Court was approached with more efforts to litigate the meaning of the establishment prohibition. In an early line of cases the Court dealt with claims that government was using its power to bolster religious practices. More recently, it has been pressed by contentions that public tax monies were going to support religious education. Whatever the issue, the Court has been dogged at every turn by those who seek a stringent reading of the First Amendment on the one hand and those who favor a permissive reading of *Everson* on the other. We turn presently to the first series of cases.

Within a year after its ruling in the *Everson* case, the Court was hearing arguments on the constitutionality of a "released time" program of religious instruction undertaken by the Champaign, Illinois Board of Education. The gist of the arrangement was that students, on the consent of their parents, would be allowed time off from class in order to receive instruction in their respective religions. Instructors in these religion classes were not paid by the school, but classes were held in the school building and the instructors were required to take attendance.

In this case, People of State of Illinois ex rel. McCollum v. Board of Education, 333 U.S. 203, 68 S.Ct. 461 (1948), Justice Black, speaking once again for the Court, found that the board's practice had indeed violated the Establishment Clause. The eight-man majority was not only distressed by the fact that a tax-supported building had been used for the propagation of religious doctrine but also that the state's compulsory school attendance machinery had been used so effectively to provide students for religion classes. As you might guess, considerable uproar followed the *McCollum* ruling, and the concept of "released time" was forced through some rethinking.

Four years later in Zorach v. Clauson, 343 U.S. 306, 72 S.Ct. 679 (1952), the Court had occasion to review a modified "released time" program which did not entail what were thought to be the objectionable features of the Champaign plan. Under a plan implemented for the New York City public schools, students, again with the consent of their parents, were released during the school day. However, they went to centers off school grounds to receive religious instruction. Those students not participating were required to remain at school to study as directed by their teacher. Significantly, those students who remained were not given any work which would have advanced them beyond their classmates. In other words, students who were released from school under the New York plan missed a study hall rather than a regular class. Religion instructors were also required by the board of education to take attendance and forward their reports to the student's homeroom teacher or the principal.

Speaking for the Court, Justice Douglas distinguished *Zorach* from *McCollum* by emphasizing the differences between the two plans noted above. More important than these distinctions was Justice Douglas's contention that the establishment prohibition did not preclude government from accommodating the interests of religion. Conceding that government could not finance religious groups or undertake religious instruction, he added, "But we find no constitutional requirement which makes it necessary for government to be hostile to religion and to throw its weight against efforts to widen the effective scope of religious influence" for "[t]hat would be preferring those who believe in no religion over those who do believe." Rather, concluded Douglas, "We are a religious people whose institutions presuppose a Supreme Being." Justices Black, Frankfurter, and Jackson found the New York plan unconstitutional.

If religious groups were heartened by the Vinson Court's stand in *Zorach*, their ire was rekindled nearly a decade later by two rulings of the Warren Court. One of these involved the invalidation of a prayer written by the New York State Board of Regents for recitation in the state's schools. Is there much doubt in your mind that the Court in *Engel* v. *Vitale* (p. 1531) accurately found this to be an abridgement of the First Amendment? The majority felt hard pressed to conjure up a clearer case of establishment.

Less clear-cut and more embittering was the Court's decision in two cases concerning the legitimacy of Bible reading and the recitation of the Lord's Prayer in public schools. See *Abington School District* v. *Schempp* and *Murray* v. *Curlett* (p. 1534). Were these rulings a logical extension of *Engel*? Or would you agree with the position of Justice Stewart, articulated in dissent, that so long as no student is compelled to participate, such practices as Bible reading should be sustained?

A strong negative reaction followed the Court's decisions in *Schempp* and *Murray*. Typical of the congressional criticisms which the Justices received were Senator Goldwater's statement that the Court had "ruled against God" and the remarks of other legislators to the effect that the Court had no business taking God out of the public schools. A surprisingly strong letter-writing campaign flooded Congress with messages of support for passage of a constitutional amendment to allow voluntary prayer in the schools. Despite the introduction of well over a hundred such proposals and the boost given such a move by its inclusion in the 1964 Republican platform, both of the major attempts to overturn the Court's rulings and modify the First Amendment failed. In 1964, the House Judiciary Committee, chaired by one of the Court's staunchest supporters, Representative Emanuel Celler, failed to report out any of the resolutions despite a strong effort by conservatives to discharge one of the proposals so that it could be brought to the floor for a vote. Two years later Senator Everett Dirksen's attempt to secure approval of such legislation by the Senate failed by nine votes to get the necessary two-thirds majority. The hostility of the Court's critics, of course, lingered on—the school prayer decisions essentially reinforcing the already negative reaction of most conservatives to an institution which they perceived had sacrificed the interests of the majority of the people time and again to the preferred interests of racial minorities, criminal suspects, smut peddlers, subversives, and now, atheists.

Not all of the Court's rulings concerning the Establishment Clause involved public education, however. In *McGowan* v. *Maryland* (p. 1537), the Court was asked to consider the constitutionality of Sunday Closing laws which were prevalent throughout the country. In addressing that question the Court once again applied the "purpose and primary effect" test of its Bible-reading decision. Would you accept the majority's view that the purpose and primary effect of the Maryland statute was secular? Or would you agree with the position articulated by Justice Douglas in dissent that any religious practice, whatever the utilitarian rationalization that might be conjured up, should be held unconstitutional when it has the sanction of law behind it? Is the Douglas position practical?

A second series of rulings handed down by the Court, as we pointed out earlier, bears on the constitutionality of using public revenues to aid the education of students attending church-related schools. The legislation at issue in these cases stemmed principally from efforts to do something about the increasing financial plight of parochial schools and the frightening prospect that large numbers of students housed in such private educational institutions would suddenly be dumped on the already overburdened public school system. Consider the textbook program designed by the New York State legislature and challenged in *Board of Education* v. *Allen* (p. 1540). Given the fact that in *Everson* the Court rejected an absolute application of the establishment prohibition in favor of some distinction in the degree of support given religious schools, who draws this line more helpfully—the majority in its blend of the purpose and primary effect test and the child benefit theory, or Justice Douglas in the difference he sees between aid in the form of bus transportation and aid in the form of textbooks? What kind of protection do you think the majority's approach affords against the enlargement of such aid programs eventually to include teachers' salaries or to avoid the kind of politicization which Douglas forecasts?

The criteria of applying the establishment prohibition came to be more clearly and fully defined following the appearance of a new Chief Justice at the Court's October 1969 Term. The first occasion of the Burger Court's formulation of the establishment problem came in a 1970 decision, *Walz* v. *Tax Commission* (p. 1545), which concerned the constitutionality of property tax exemptions given religious institutions. The modulated tone of the majority's opinion was unmistakable. As contrasted with what critics saw as the hostile tenor of some of the Warren Court's decisions, the new Chief Justice portrayed the constitutional relationship between church and state as one of "benevolent neutrality." At the outset of the Court's opinion, Chief Justice Burger summarized what he saw as the legacy of past decisions:

> The Establishment and Free Exercise Clause of the First Amendment are not the most precisely drawn portions of the Constitution. The sweep of the absolute prohibitions in the Religion Clauses may have been calculated; but the purpose was to state an objective not to write a statute. In attempting to articulate the scope of the two Religion Clauses, the Court's opinions reflect the limitations inherent in formulating general principles on a case-by-case basis. The considerable internal inconsistency in the opinions of the Court derives from what, in retrospect, may have been too sweeping utterances on aspects of these clauses that seemed clear in relation to the particular cases but have limited meaning as general principles.

> The Court has struggled to find a neutral course between the two Religion Clauses, both of which are cast in absolute terms, and either of which, if expanded to a logical extreme would tend to clash with the other.

Concluding, therefore, that "[t]he course of constitutional neutrality in this area cannot be an absolutely straight line," the Chief Justice exhorted the Court to adopt a more flexible balancing approach. That approach is developed in *Walz* and succeeding decisions of the Burger Court. Do you think this position reflects a genuinely more insightful understanding of the judicial process, or is this just a sophisticated attempt by an appointee of a new and more conservative administration to secure an interpretation of these Clauses more favorable to the support of religious interests?

Apart from assailing the ridigity of past religion rulings, the Burger Court generated a new test by which further to measure establishment—whether the practice in question invites "excessive governmental entanglement with religion." Why does the Court reason that granting the tax exemption results in less of an entanglement with religion than not granting an exemption?

By the conclusion of its October 1970 Term, the Court, relying on *Allen* and *Walz*, had formulated a three-part Establishment Clause test which it announced in *Lemon* v. *Kurtzman* (p. 1548): (1) whether the program at issue has a secular purpose, (2) if the primary effect is neither to advance nor inhibit religion, and (3) whether the legislation fosters "an excessive government entanglement with religion." This tripartite standard was applied not only in *Lemon* and its companion case, *Tilton* v. *Richardson* (p. 1555), but has since dominated the Court's Establishment Clause jurisprudence. Does the Court draw a convincing distinction between the facts of *Lemon* and *Tilton* to account for the different outcomes of these cases? As applied in succeeding cases, does the three-part test provide a clear sense of what does and what does not constitute an establishment of religion? Should the Court's application of the test—at least through 1977—have allayed the fears expressed by Justices Black and Douglas, dissenting in *Allen*, that the textbook decision was "the entering edge of the wedge" in terms of a dangerous church-state relationship? Would the apprehensions of Black and Douglas have been greater after the Court's decision in *Committee for Public Education and Religious Liberty* v. *Regan* (p. 1562)? Finally, are the decisions of the Burger Court themselves free of the "considerable internal inconsistency" charge it flung at previous decisions?

b. The Free Exercise of Religious Belief

In what appear to be equally absolute terms, the First Amendment also prohibits government from abridging the free exercise of religious belief. As has already been suggested by some of the establishment cases, there appears to be an inevitable clash between the interests protected under that Clause and those safeguarded by this. In *Thomas* v. *Indiana Employment Security Review Board* (p. 1574), the Court reviews and applies the approach developed in Sherbert v. Verner, 374 U.S. 398, 83 S.Ct. 1790 (1963), to deal with free exercise questions. What is this approach? In dissent, Justice Rehnquist argues that the Court's approach in this area, together with its reading of the Establishment Clause, has caused unnecessary problems. Why? When he suggests that the Court emulate its past performance in Braunfeld v. Brown, 366 U.S. 599, 81 S.Ct. 1144 (1961), what does he mean? Justice Rehnquist, of course, urges that a more restrained reading of both Religion Clauses would avert the collision spotlighted by Chief Justice Burger in *Walz*; but is his approach itself free of costs, or does it simply impose different costs? As an illustration, consider the Court's decisions in *McGowan* and *Braunfeld*. Presumably, the result reached by the Court in *McGowan* pleases Justice Rehnquist as much as that in *Braunfeld*, but does the interface between the Religion Clauses demonstrated by these two decisions seem preferable to that adopted by the Court later which Justice Rehnquist criticizes?

Protection of the public health, safety, and welfare has long been viewed as a legitimate function of state government implicitly recognized by the Tenth Amendment. The exercise of religious belief, however, occasionally collides with the states' use of the police power to advance these interests. The conflict is highlighted in three cases, *Wisconsin* v. *Yoder* (p. 1584), *United States* v. *Lee* (p. 1589), and *State ex rel. Swann* v. *Pack* (p. 1591). What kinds of considerations does the Court in *Yoder* recognize as sufficient to overcome the state's significant interest in fostering education? Does the Court's treatment of the issues involved in the case, in light of Justice Douglas's dissent, lead you to conclude that the decision is a libertarian one or not? How persuasively does the Court distinguish the result announced in *Lee* from that reached in *Yoder*? Upholding the public interest proffered by the state in *Pack*, the Tennessee Supreme Court addressed the competing interests in terms of a distinction between belief and action analogous to the dichotomy between speech and action frequently employed by the Court in resolving free speech controversies. This, as the Tennessee court indicates, has been the traditional mode of analysis invoked by judges when asked to assess the limits of the Free Exercise Clause *vis-à-vis* the state police power.

United States v. *Ballard* (p. 1594) raises a somewhat different, though equally intriguing issue: may juries be allowed to examine the credibility of one's religious beliefs in a criminal prosecution for fraud? Note the difference between what the trial judge considered fit issues for the judgment of the jury and what the appeals court would have allowed. The trial judge in this case would have confined the jury to examining the same question of sincerity of belief which draft boards came to consider in an analogous circumstance in applications for conscientious objector status. Is it possible to draw a durable line between the credibility of one's beliefs and the sincerity with which they are held? Suppose X kills Y and says that God came to him in a vision and told him to do it. Assuming X did, in fact, kill Y, could the jury avoid the credibility question—especially if asked to choose between returning a verdict of "murder in the first degree" or one of "not guilty by reason of insanity"? In other words, can we afford ourselves the luxury of—as Justice Jackson put it—"hav[ing] done with this business of judicially examining other people's faiths"? A contemporary and equally controversial variation on the theme in *Ballard* is the issue before a California appellate court in *Katz* v. *Superior Court* (p. 1598), one of several cases involving attempts to "deprogram" several "Moonies." Although the California court recognized that "the state may have a compelling * * * interest in preventing fraud under the guise of religious belief," it also observed that "the question of proof was not settled by *United States* v. *Ballard* * * *." Ruling in favor of the petitioners and against enforcement of a lower court's orders to place the "Moonies" in the custody of their parents, the appeals court, siding with Justice Jackson in *Ballard*, concluded by quoting with approval the following excerpt from his dissent: "The wrong of these things, as I see it, is not in the money the victims part with half so much as in the mental and spiritual poison they get. But that is precisely the thing the Constitution put beyond the reach of the prosecutor, for the price of freedom of religion or of speech or of the press is that we must put up with, and even pay for, a good deal of rubbish."

a. THE ESTABLISHMENT OF RELIGION

ENGEL v. VITALE

Supreme Court of the United States, 1962
370 U.S. 421, 82 S.Ct. 1261, 86 L.Ed.2d 601

Steven Engel and other parents brought action against members of the board of education of a New York school district to compel them to retract their requirement that a prayer be recited in classrooms before each school day. (Student participation in that exercise was voluntary.) The practice was adopted by the board pursuant to a recommendation of the state Board of Regents that the following prayer, composed by the Regents, be read in public schools: "Almighty God, we acknowledge our dependence upon Thee, and we beg Thy blessings upon us, our parents, our teachers and our country." The school board's order was upheld in the state courts, and the U. S. Supreme Court granted certiorari.

Mr. Justice BLACK delivered the opinion of the Court.

*   *   *

We think that by using its public school system to encourage recitation of the Regents' prayer, the State of New York has adopted a practice wholly inconsistent with the Establishment Clause. There can, of course, be no doubt that New York's program of daily classroom invocation of God's blessings as prescribed in the Regents' prayer is a religious activity.   *   *   *

The petitioners contend among other things that the state laws requiring or permitting use of the Regents' prayer must be struck down as a violation of the Establishment Clause because that prayer was composed by governmental officials as a part of a governmental program to further religious beliefs. For this reason, petitioners argue, the State's use of the Regents' prayer in its public school system breaches the constitutional wall of separation between Church and State. We agree with that contention since we think that the constitutional prohibition against laws respecting an establishment of religion must at least mean that in this country it is no part of the business of government to compose official prayers for any group of the American people to recite as a part of a religious program carried on by government.

*   *   *

There can be no doubt that New York's state prayer program officially establishes the religious beliefs embodied in the Regents' prayer. The respondents' argument to the contrary, which is largely based upon the contention that the Regents' prayer is "non-denominational" and the fact that the program, as modified and approved by state courts, does not require all pupils to recite the prayer but permits those who wish to do so to remain silent or be excused from the room, ignores the essential nature of the program's constitutional defects. Neither the fact that the prayer may be denominationally neutral nor the fact that its observance on the part of the students is voluntary can serve to free it from the limitations of the Establishment Clause, as it might from the Free Exercise Clause of the First Amendment, both of which are operative against the States by virtue of the Fourteenth Amendment. Although these two clauses may in certain instances overlap, they forbid two quite different kinds of governmental encroachment upon religious freedom. The Establishment Clause, unlike the Free Exercise Clause, does not depend upon any showing of direct governmental compulsion and is violated by the enactment of laws which establish an official religion whether those laws operate directly to coerce nonobserving individuals or not. This is not to say, of course, that laws officially prescribing a particular form of religious worship do not involve coercion of such individuals. When the power, prestige and financial support of government is placed behind a particular religious belief, the indirect coercive pressure upon religious minorities to conform to the prevailing officially approved religion is plain. But the purposes underlying the Establishment Clause go much further than that. Its first and most immediate purpose rested on the belief that a union of government and religion tends to destroy government and to degrade religion. The history of governmentally established religion, both in England and in this country, showed that whenever government had allied itself with one particular form of religion, the inevitable result had been that it had incurred the hatred, disrespect and even contempt of those who held contrary beliefs. That same history showed that many people had lost their respect for any religion that had relied upon the support of government to spread its faith. The Establishment Clause thus stands as an expression of principle on the part of the Founders of our Constitution that religion is too personal, too sacred, too holy, to permit its "unhal-

lowed perversion" by a civil magistrate. Another purpose of the Establishment Clause rested upon an awareness of the historical fact that governmentally established religions and religious persecutions go hand in hand. * * * The New York laws officially prescribing the Regents' prayer are inconsistent both with the purposes of the Establishment Clause and with the Establishment Clause itself.

It has been argued that to apply the Constitution in such a way as to prohibit state laws respecting an establishment of religious services in public schools is to indicate a hostility toward religion or toward prayer. Nothing, of course, could be more wrong. * * * It is neither sacrilegious nor antireligious to say that each separate government in this country should stay out of the business of writing or sanctioning official prayers and leave that purely religious function to the people themselves and to those the people choose to look to for religious guidance.

* * * To those who may subscribe to the view that because the Regents' official prayer is so brief and general there can be no danger to religious freedom in its governmental establishment, however, it may be appropriate to say in the words of James Madison, the author of the First Amendment:

"[I]t is proper to take alarm at the first experiment on our liberties. * * * Who does not see that the same authority which can establish Christianity, in exclusion of all other Religions, may establish with the same ease any particular sect of Christians, in exclusion of all other Sects? That the same authority which can force a citizen to contribute three pence only of his property for the support of any one establishment, may force him to conform to any other establishment in all cases whatsoever?"

The judgment of the Court of Appeals of New York is reversed and the cause remanded. * * *

* * *

Mr. Justice FRANKFURTER took no part in the decision of this case.

Mr. Justice WHITE took no part in the consideration or decision of this case.

Mr. Justice DOUGLAS, concurring.

It is customary in deciding a constitutional question to treat it in its narrowest form. Yet at times the setting of the question gives it a form and content which no abstract treatment could give. The point for decision is whether the Government can constitutionally finance a religious exercise. Our system at the federal and state levels is presently honeycombed with such financing. Nevertheless, I think it is an unconstitutional undertaking whatever form it takes.

* * *

* * * The First Amendment leaves the Government in a position not of hostility to religion but of neutrality. The philosopy is that the atheist or agnostic—the nonbeliever—is entitled to go his own way. The philosophy is that if government interferes in matters spiritual, it will be a divisive force. The First Amendment teaches that a government neutral in the field of religion better serves all religious interests.

* * *

Mr. Justice STEWART, dissenting.

* * * The Court today decides that in permitting this brief non-denominational prayer the school board has violated the Constitution of the United States. I think this decision is wrong.

* * *

With all respect, I think the Court has misapplied a great constitutional principle. I cannot see how an "official religion" is established by letting those who want to say a prayer say it. On the contrary, I think that to deny the wish of these school children to join in reciting this prayer is to deny them the opportunity of sharing in the spiritual heritage of our Nation.

* * *

At the opening of each day's Session of this Court we stand, while one of our officials invokes the protection of God. Since the days of John Marshall our Crier has said, "God save the United States and this Honorable Court." Both the Senate and the House of Representatives open their daily Sessions with prayer. Each of our Presidents, from George Washington to John F. Kennedy, has upon assuming his Office asked the protection and help of God.

* * *

Countless similar examples could be listed, but there is no need to belabor the obvious. It was all summed up by this Court just ten years ago in a single sentence: "We are a religious people whose institutions presuppose a Supreme Being." Zorach

v. Clauson, 343 U.S. 306, 313, 72 S.Ct. 679, 684.

I do not believe that this Court, or the Congress, or the President has by the actions and practices I have mentioned established an "official re-ligion" in violation of the Constitution. And I do not believe the State of New York has done so in this case. * * *

* * *

ABINGTON SCHOOL DISTRICT v. SCHEMPP
MURRAY v. CURLETT

Supreme Court of the United States, 1963
374 U.S. 203, 83 S.Ct. 1560, 10 L.Ed.2d 844

Both of these cases, reviewed together by the Supreme Court, raised challenges to Bible reading in the public schools. In *School District of Abington Township* **v.** *Schempp,* **the Schempp family, members of the Unitarian church, brought suit against their school district challenging a Pennsylvania law that required readings at the beginning of each school day. Student participation was voluntary, how-ever. A three-judge federal district court found the law an abridgment of the Establishment Clause of the First Amendment, applicable to the states through the Fourteenth, and granted the requested injunctive relief. In the second case,** *Murray* **v.** *Curlett,* **Mrs. Madalyn Murray and her son William, two professed athe-ists, challenged a similar enactment adopted by the Baltimore school board. The trial court found the practice constitutional, and this judgment was affirmed on appeal to the Maryland Court of Appeals, but by a narrow vote.**

Mr. Justice CLARK delivered the opinion of the Court.

* * *

The wholesome "neutrality" of which this Court's cases speak * * * stems from a recognition of the teachings of history that power-ful sects or groups might bring about a fusion of governmental and religious functions or a concert or de-pendency of one upon the other to the end that official support of the State or Federal Government would be placed behind the tenets of one or of all orthodoxies. This the Estab-lishment Clause prohibits. And a further reason for neutrality is found in the Free Exercise Clause, which recognizes the value of reli-gious training, teaching and obser-vance and, more particularly, the right of every person to freely choose his own course with reference thereto, free of any compulsion from the state. This the Free Exercise Clause guarantees. Thus, * * * the two clauses may overlap. * * * [T]he Establishment Clause has been directly considered by this Court eight times in the past score of years and, with only one Justice dis-senting on the point, it has consis-tently held that the clause withdrew all legislative power respecting reli-gious belief or the expression there-of. The test may be stated as fol-lows: what are the purpose and the primary effect of the enactment? If either is the advancement or inhibi-tion of religion then the enactment exceeds the scope of legislative pow-er as circumscribed by the Constitu-tion. That is to say that to with-stand the strictures of the Establishment Clause there must be a secular legislative purpose and a primary effect that neither advances nor inhibits religion. * * * The Free Exercise Clause, likewise considered many times here, withdraws from legislative power, state and federal, the exertion of any restraint on the free exercise of religion. Its purpose is to secure religious liberty in the individual by prohibiting any invasions thereof by civil authority. Hence it is necessary in a free exercise case for one to show the coercive effect of the enactment as its operates against him in the practice of his religion. The distinction between the two clauses is apparent—a violation of the Free Exercise Clause is predicated on coercion while the Establishment Clause violation need not be so attended.

Applying the Establishment Clause principles to the cases at bar we find that the States are requiring the selection and reading at the opening of the school day of verses from the Holy Bible and the recitation of the Lord's Prayer by the students in unison. These exercises are prescribed as part of the curricular activities of students who are required by law to attend school. They are held in the school buildings under the supervision and with the participation of teachers employed in those schools. * * * The trial court in [*Schempp*] has found that such an opening exercise is a religious ceremony and was intended by the State to be so. We agree with the trial court's finding as to the religious character of the exercises. Given that finding, the exercises and the law requiring them are in violation of the Establishment Clause.

There is no such specific finding as to the religious character of the exercises in [*Murray*] and the State contends (as does the State in

[*Schempp*]) that the program is an effort to extend its benefits to all public school children without regard to their religious belief. Included within its secular purposes, it says, are the promotion of moral values, the contradiction to the materialistic trends of our times, the perpetuation of our institutions and the teaching of literature. The case came up on demurrer, of course, to a petition which alleged that the uniform practice under the rule had been to read from the King James version of the Bible and that the exercise was sectarian. The short answer, therefore, is that the religious character of the exercise was admitted by the State. But even if its purpose is not strictly religious, it is sought to be accomplished through readings, without comment, from the Bible. Surely the place of the Bible as an instrument of religion cannot be gainsaid, and the State's recognition of the pervading religious character of the ceremony is evident from the rule's specific permission of the alternative use of the Catholic Douay version as well as the recent amendment permitting nonattendance at the exercises. None of these factors is consistent with the contention that the Bible is here used either as an instrument for nonreligious moral inspiration or as a reference for the teaching of secular subjects.

The conclusion follows that in both cases the laws require religious exercises and such exercises are being conducted in direct violation of the rights of the appellees and petitioners. Nor are these required exercises mitigated by the fact that individual students may absent themselves upon parental request, for that fact furnishes no defense to a claim of unconstitutionality under the Establishment Clause. * * *

Further, it is no defense to urge that the religious practices here may be relatively minor encroachments on the First Amendment. The breach of neutrality that is today a trickling stream may all too soon become a raging torrent and, in the words of Madison, "it is proper to take alarm at the first experiment on our liberties." * * *

It is insisted that unless these religious exercises are permitted a "religion of secularism" is established in the schools. We agree of course that the State may not establish a "religion of secularism" in the sense of affirmatively opposing or showing hostility to religion, thus "preferring those who believe in no religion over those who do believe." * * * We do not agree, however, that this decision in any sense has that effect. In addition, it might well be said that one's education is not complete without a study of comparative religion or the history of religion and its relationship to the advancement of civilization. It certainly may be said that the Bible is worthy of study for its literary and historic qualities. Nothing we have said here indicates that such study of the Bible or of religion, when presented objectively as part of a secular program of education, may not be effected consistently with the First Amendment. But the exercises here do not fall into those categories. They are religious exercises, required by the States in violation of the command of the First Amendment that the Government maintain strict neutrality, neither aiding nor opposing religion.

Finally, we cannot accept that the concept of neutrality, which does not permit a State to require a religious exercise even with the consent of the majority of those affected, collides with the majority's right to free exercise of religion. While the Free Exercise Clause clearly prohibits the use of state action to deny the rights of free exercise to *anyone*, it has never meant that a majority could use the machinery of the State to practice its beliefs. Such a contention was effectively answered by Mr. Justice JACKSON for the Court in *West Virginia Board of Education v. Barnette.* * * *

The place of religion in our society is an exalted one, achieved through a long tradition of reliance on the home, the church and the inviolable citadel of the individual heart and mind. We have come to recognize through bitter experience that it is not within the power of government to invade that citadel, whether its purpose or effect be to aid or oppose, to advance or retard. In the relationship between man and religion, the State is firmly committed to a position of neutrality. Though the application of that rule requires interpretation of a delicate sort, the rule itself is clearly and concisely stated in the words of the First Amendment. Applying that rule to the facts of these cases, we affirm the judgment in [*Schempp*]. In [*Murray*] the judgment is reversed and the cause remanded to the Maryland Court of Appeals for further proceedings consistent with this opinion.

[Justice STEWART dissented.]

McGOWAN v. MARYLAND

Supreme Court of the United States, 1961
366 U.S. 420, 81 S.Ct. 1101, 6 L.Ed.2d 393

Margaret McGowan and six other employees of a large discount department store were indicted and convicted for selling "a three-ring, loose-leaf binder, a can of floor wax, a stapler and staples, and a toy submarine" in violation of Maryland's Sunday Closing laws. These statutes, with some exceptions, proscribed labor, business, and commercial activity on Sunday. The convictions were affirmed by the state Court of Appeals, and the U. S. Supreme Court granted certiorari. Before reaching the appellants' claim that such laws violated the First Amendment's prohibition on the establishment of a religion, the Court discussed and rejected as without merit assertions that classifications contained in the statutes permitting certain exceptions were a violation of equal protection of the laws or were vague.

Mr. Chief Justice WARREN delivered the opinion of the Court.

* * *

The essence of appellants' "establishment" argument is that Sunday is the Sabbath day of the predominant Christian sects; that the purpose of the enforced stoppage of labor on that day is to facilitate and encourage church attendance; that the purpose of setting Sunday as a day of universal rest is to induce people with no religion or people with marginal religious beliefs to join the predominant Christian sects; that the purpose of the atmosphere of tranquility created by Sunday closing is to aid the conduct of church services and religious observance of the sacred day. In substantiating their "establishment" argument, appellants rely on the wording of the present Maryland statutes, on earlier versions of the current Sunday laws and on prior judicial characterizations of these laws by the Maryland Court of Appeals. * * * There is no dispute that the original laws which dealt with Sunday labor were motivated by religious forces. But what we must decide is whether present Sunday legislation, having undergone extensive changes from the earliest forms, still retains its religious character.

* * *

But, despite the strongly religious origin of these laws, beginning before the eighteenth century, nonreligious arguments for Sunday closing began to be heard more distinctly and the statutes began to lose some of their totally religious flavor.
* * *

More recently, further secular justifications have been advanced for making Sunday a day of rest, a day when people may recover from the labors of the week just passed and may physically and mentally prepare for the week's work to come. In England, during the First World War, a committee investigating the health conditions of munitions workers reported that "if the maximum output is to be secured and maintained for any length of time, a weekly period of rest must be allowed. * * * On economic and social grounds alike this weekly period of rest is best provided on Sunday."

The proponents of Sunday closing legislation are no longer exclusively representatives of religious interests. Recent New Jersey Sunday legislation was supported by labor groups and trade associations * * *; modern English Sunday legislation was promoted by the National Federation of Grocers and supported by the National Chamber of Trade, the Drapers' Chamber of Trade, and the National Union of Shop Assistants. * * *

* * *

This Court has considered the happenings surrounding the Virginia General Assembly's enactment of "An act for establishing religious freedom," * * * written by Thomas Jefferson and sponsored by James Madison, as best reflecting the long and intensive struggle for religious freedom in America, as particularly relevant in the search for the First Amendment's meaning. * * * In 1776, nine years before the bill's passage, Madison co-authored Virginia's Declaration of Rights which provided, *inter alia*, that " all men are equally entitled to the free exercise of religion, according to the dictates of conscience." * * * Virginia had had Sunday legislation since early in the seventeenth century; in 1776, the laws penalizing "maintaining any opinions in matters of religion, *forbearing to repair to church*, or the exercising any mode of worship whatsoever" (emphasis added), were repealed, and all dissenters were freed from the taxes levied for the support of the established church. * * * The Sunday labor prohibitions remained; apparently, they were not believed to be inconsistent with the newly enacted Declaration of Rights. * * *

* * *

[T]he "Establishment" Clause does not ban federal or state regulation of conduct whose reason or effect merely happens to coincide or harmonize with the tenets of some or all religions. In many instances, the Congress or state legislatures conclude that the general welfare of society, wholly apart from any religious considerations, demands such regulation. Thus, for temporal purposes, murder is illegal. And the fact that this agrees with the dictates of the Judaeo-Christian religions while it may disagree with others does not invalidate the regulation. So too with the questions of adultery and polygamy. * * * The same could be said of theft, fraud, etc., because those offenses were also proscribed in the Decalogue.

* * *

In light of the evolution of our Sunday Closing Laws through the centuries, and of their more or less recent emphasis upon secular considerations, it is not difficult to discern that as presently written and administered, most of them, at least, are of a secular rather than of a religious character, and that presently they bear no relationship to establishment of religion as those words are used in the Constitution of the United States.

* * *

Considering the language and operative effect of the current statutes, we no longer find the blanket prohibition against Sunday work or bodily labor. To the contrary, we find that § 521 of Art. 27, the section which appellants violated, permits the Sunday sale of tobaccos and sweets and a long list of sundry articles which we have enumerated above; we find that § 509 of Art. 27 permits the

Sunday operation of bathing beaches, amusement parks and similar facilities; we find that Art. 2B, § 28, permits the Sunday sale of alcoholic beverages, products strictly forbidden by predecessor statutes; we are told that Anne Arundel County allows Sunday bingo and the Sunday playing of pinball machines and slot machines, activities generally condemned by prior Maryland Sunday legislation. Certainly, these are not works of charity or necessity. Section 521's current stipulation that shops with only one employee may remain open on Sunday does not coincide with a religious purpose. These provisions, along with those which permit various sports and entertainments on Sunday, seem clearly to be fashioned for the purpose of providing a Sunday atmosphere of recreation, cheerfulness, repose and enjoyment. Coupled with the general proscription against other types of work, we believe that the air of the day is one of relaxation rather than one of religion.

The existing Maryland Sunday laws are not simply verbatim re-enactments of their religiously oriented antecedents. Only § 492 retains the appellation of "Lord's day" and even that section no longer makes recitation of religious purpose. It does talk in terms of "profan[ing] the Lord's day," but other sections permit the activities previously thought to be profane. Prior denunciation of Sunday drunkenness is now gone. Contemporary concern with these statutes is evidenced by the dozen changes made in 1959 and by the recent enactment of a majority of the exceptions.

* * *

But this does not answer all of appellants' contentions. We are told that the State has other means at its disposal to accomplish its secular purpose, other courses that would not even remotely or incidentally give state aid to religion. On this basis, we are asked to hold these statutes invalid on the ground that the State's power to regulate conduct in the public interest may only be executed in a way that does not unduly or unnecessarily infringe upon the religious provisions of the First Amendment. * * * It is true that if the State's interest were simply to provide for its citizens a periodic respite from work, a regulation demanding that everyone rest one day in seven, leaving the choice of the day to the individual, would suffice.

However, the State's purpose is not merely to provide a one-day-in-seven work stoppage. In addition to this, the State seeks to set one day apart from all others as a day of rest, repose, recreation and tranquility—a day which all members of the family and community have the opportunity to spend and enjoy together, a day on which there exists relative quiet and disassociation from the everyday intensity of commercial activities, a day on which people may visit friends and relatives who are not available during working days.

Obviously, a State is empowered to determine that a rest-one-day-in-seven statute would not accomplish this purpose; that it would not provide for a general cessation of activity, a special atmosphere of tranquility, a day which all members of the family or friends and relatives might spend together. Furthermore, it seems plain that the problems involved in enforcing such a provision would be exceedingly more difficult than those in enforcing a common-day-of-rest provision.

* * *

Finally, we should make clear that this case deals only with the constitutionality of § 521 of the Maryland statute before us. We do not hold that Sunday legislation may not be a violation of the "Establishment" Clause if it can be demonstrated that its purpose—evidenced either on the face of the legislation, in conjunction with its legislative history, or in its operative effect—is to use the State's coercive power to aid religion.

* * *

Affirmed.

Mr. Justice DOUGLAS, dissenting.

The question is not whether one day out of seven can be imposed by a State as a day of rest. The question is not whether Sunday can by force of custom and habit be retained as a day of rest. The question is whether a State can impose criminal sanctions on those who, unlike the Christian majority that makes up our society, worship on a different day or do not share the religious scruples of the majority.

* * *

The institutions of our society are founded on the belief that there is an authority higher than the authority of the State; that there is a moral law which the State is powerless to alter; that the individual possesses rights, conferred by the Creator, which government must respect.
* * *

* * *

But those who fashioned the First Amendment decided that if and when God is to be served, His service will not be motivated by coercive measures of government. * * *

The First Amendment commands government to have no interest in theology or ritual; it admonishes government to be interested in allowing religious freedom to flourish—whether the result is to produce Catholics, Jews, or Protestants, or to turn the people toward the path of Buddha, or to end in a predominantly Moslem nation, or to produce in the long run atheists or agnostics. On matters of this kind government must be neutral. * * *

* * *

BOARD OF EDUCATION v. ALLEN

Supreme Court of the United States, 1968
392 U.S. 236, 88 S.Ct. 1923, 20 L.Ed.2d 1060

A local school board brought action against Dr. James E. Allen, the New York State Commissioner of Education, challenging the constitutionality of § 701 of the state Education Law. The statute in question required school districts to purchase and loan textbooks upon request for use by all students attending parochial, other private, and public schools. In addition to a declaratory judgment that the statute contravened the First and Fourteenth Amendments, the suit sought to enjoin Commissioner Allen from expending state funds pursuant to that portion of the Education Law and to restrain him from removing the local board members because of their noncompliance. The trial court held the statute unconstitutional, but this decision was reversed by an intermediate state appellate tribunal. On a hearing before the state's highest court, the reversal was affirmed, whereupon the school board appealed to the Supreme Court.

Mr. Justice WHITE delivered the opinion of the Court.

A law of the State of New York requires local public school authorities to lend textbooks free of charge to all students in grades seven through 12; students attending private schools are included. This case presents the question whether this statute is a "law respecting an establishment of religion, or prohibiting the free exercise thereof," and so in conflict with the First and Fourteenth Amendments to the Constitution, because it authorizes the loan of textbooks to students attending parochial schools. We hold that the law is not in violation of the Constitution.

*   *   *

Everson v. Board of Education, 330 U.S. 1, 67 S.Ct. 504 (1947), is the case decided by this Court that is most nearly in point for today's problem. New Jersey reimbursed parents for expenses incurred in busing their children to parochial schools. The Court stated that the Establishment Clause bars a State from passing "laws which aid one religion, aid all religions, or prefer one religion over another," and bars too any "tax in any amount, large or small * * * levied to support any religious activities or institutions, whatever they may be called, or whatever form they may adopt to teach or practice religion." * * * Nevertheless, said the Court, the Establishment Clause does not prevent a State from extending the benefits of state laws to all citizens without regard for their religious affiliation and does not prohibit "New Jersey from spending tax-raised funds to pay the bus fares of parochial school pupils as a part of a general program under which it pays the fares of pupils attending public and other schools."

The statute was held to be valid even though one of its results was that "children are helped to get to church schools" and "some of the children might not be sent to the church schools if the parents were compelled to pay their children's bus fares out of their own pockets." * * * As with public provision of police and fire protection, sewage facilities, and streets and sidewalks, payment of bus fares was of some value to the religious school, but was nevertheless not such support of a religious institution as to be a prohibited establishment of religion within the meaning of the First Amendment.

Everson and later cases have shown that the line between state neutrality to religion and state support of religion is not easy to locate. "The constitutional standard is the separation of Church and State. The problem, like many problems in constitutional law, is one of degree." Zorach v. Clauson, 343 U.S. 306, 314, 72 S.Ct. 679, 684 (1952). * * * Based on *Everson, Zorach, McGowan*, and other cases, *Abington Tp. School District* v. *Schempp* * * * fashioned a test subscribed to by eight Justices for distinguishing between forbidden involvements of the State with religion and those contacts which the Establishment Clause permits:

"The test may be stated as follows: what are the purpose and the primary effect of the enactment? If either is the advancement or inhibition of religion then the enactment exceeds the scope of legislative power as circumscribed by the Constitution. That is to say that to withstand the strictures of the Establishment Clause there must be a secular legislative purpose and a primary effect that neither advances nor inhibits religion. Everson v. Board of Education." * * *

This test is not easy to apply, but the citation of *Everson* by the *Schempp* Court to support its general standard made clear how the *Schempp* rule would be applied to the facts of *Everson*. The statute upheld in *Everson* would be considered a law having "a secular legislative purpose and a primary effect that neither advances nor inhibits religion." We reach the same result with respect to the New York law requiring school books to be loaned free of charge to all students in specified grades. The express purpose of § 701 was stated by the New York Legislature to be furtherance of the educational opportunities available to the young. Appellants have shown us nothing about the necessary effects of the statute that is contrary to its stated purpose. The law merely makes available to all children the benefits of a general program to lend school books free of charge. Books are furnished at the request of the pupil and ownership remains, at least technically, in the State. Thus no funds or books are furnished to parochial schools, and the financial benefit is to parents and children, not to schools. Perhaps free books make it more likely that some children choose to attend a sectarian school, but that was true of the state-paid bus fares in *Everson* and not alone demonstrate an unconstitutional degree of support for a religious institution.

Of course books are different from buses. Most bus rides have no inherent religious significance, while religious books are common. However, the language of § 701 does not authorize the loan of religious books, and the State claims no right to distribute religious literature. Although the books loaned are those required by the parochial school for use in specific courses, each book loaned must be approved by the public school authorities; only secular books may receive approval. * * *

The major reason offered by appellants for distinguishing free textbooks from free bus fares is that books, but not buses, are critical to the teaching process, and in a sectarian school that process is employed to teach religion. However this Court has long recognized that religious schools pursue two goals, religious instruction and secular education. * * *

* * *

[W]e cannot agree with appellants * * * that all teaching in a sectarian school is religious or that the processes of secular and religious training are so intertwined that secular textbooks furnished to students by the public are in fact instrumental in the teaching of religion. * * * Nothing in this record supports the proposition that all textbooks, whether they deal with mathematics, physics, foreign languages, history, or literature, are used by the parochial schools to teach religion. No evidence has been offered about particular schools, particular courses, particular teachers, or particular books. We are unable to hold, based solely on judicial notice that this statute results in unconstitutional involvement of the State with religious instruction or that § 701, for this or the other reasons urged, is a law respecting the establishment of religion within the meaning of the First Amendment.

* * *

Mr. Justice HARLAN, concurring.

Although I join the opinion and judgment of the Court * * * I would hold that where the contested governmental activity is calculated to achieve nonreligious purposes otherwise within the competence of the State, and where the activity does not involve the State "so significantly and directly in the realm of the sectarian as to give rise to * * * divisive influences and inhibitions of freedom," * * * it is not forbidden by the religious clauses of the First Amendment.

* * *

Mr. Justice BLACK, dissenting.

* * * I believe the New York law * * * is a flat, flagrant, open violation of the First and Fourteenth Amendments which together forbid Congress or state legislatures to enact any law "respecting an establishment of religion." For that reason I would reverse the New York Court of Appeals' judgment. This, I am confident, would be in keeping with the deliberate statement we made in Everson v. Board of Education, 330 U.S. 1, 15–16, 67 S.Ct. 504, 511 (1947), and repeated in People of State of Illinois ex rel. McCollum v. Board of Education, 333 U.S. 203, 210–211, 68 S.Ct. 461, 464–465 (1948), that:

"Neither a state nor the Federal Government can set up a church. Neither can pass laws which aid one religion, aid all religions, or prefer one religion over another. Neither can force nor influence a person to go to or to remain away from church against his will or force him to profess a belief or disbelief in any religion. No person can be punished for entertaining or professing religious beliefs or disbeliefs, for church attendance or non-attendance. No tax in any amount, large or small, can be levied to support any religious activities or institutions, whatever they may be called, or whatever form they may adopt to teach or practice religion. Neither a state nor the Federal Government can, openly or secretly, participate in the affairs of any religious organizations or groups and *vice versa*. In the words of Jefferson, the clause against establishment of religion by law was intended to erect 'a wall of separation between Church and State.' "

* * *

It is true, of course, that the New York law does not as yet formally adopt or establish a state religion. But it takes a great stride in that direction and coming events cast their shadows before them. * * *

I still subscribe to the belief that tax-raised funds cannot constitutionally be used to support religious schools, buy their school books, erect their buildings, pay their teachers, or pay any other of their maintenance expenses, even to the extent of one penny. The First Amendment's prohibition against governmental establishment of religion was written on the assumption that state aid to religion and religious schools generates discord, disharmony, hatred, and strife among our people, and that any government that supplies such aids is to that extent a tyranny. And I still believe that the only way to protect minority religious groups from majority groups in this country is to keep the wall of separation between church and state high and impregnable as the First and Fourteenth Amendments provide. The Court's affirmance here bodes nothing but evil to religious peace in this country.

Mr. Justice DOUGLAS, dissenting.

* * *

Whatever may be said of *Everson*, there is nothing ideological about a bus. There is nothing ideological about a school lunch, or a public nurse, or a scholarship. The constitutionality of such public aid to students in parochial schools turns on considerations not present in this textbook case. The textbook goes to the very heart of education in a parochial school. It is the chief, although not solitary, instrumentality for propagating a particular religious creed or faith. How can we possibly approve such state aid to a religion? A parochial school textbook may contain many, many more seeds of creed and dogma than a prayer. Yet we struck down in Engel v. Vitale * * * an official New York prayer for its public schools, even though it was not plainly denominational. * * *

* * *

Even where the treatment given to a particular topic in a school textbook is not blatantly sectarian, it will necessarily have certain shadings that will lead a parochial school to prefer one text over another.

* * *

The initiative to select and requisition "the books desired" is with the parochial school. Powerful religious-political pressures will therefore be on the state agencies to provide the books that are desired.

These then are the battlegrounds where control of textbook distribution will be won or lost. Now that "secular" textbooks will pour into religious schools, we can rest assured that a contest will be on to provide those books for religious schools which the dominant religious group concludes best reflect the theocentric or other philosophy of the particular church.

The stakes are now extremely high—just as they were in the school prayer cases * * *—to obtain approval of what is "proper." For the "proper" books will radiate the "correct" religious view not only in the parochial school but in the public school as well.

Even if I am wrong in that basic premise, we still should not affirm the judgment below. Judge Van Voorhis, dissenting in the New York Court of Appeals, thought that the result of tying parochial school textbooks to public funds would be to put nonsectarian books into religious schools, which in the long view would tend towards state domination of the church. * * * [H]owever the case be viewed—whether sectarian groups win control of school boards or do not gain such control—the principle of separation of church and state, inherent in the Establishment Clause of the First Amendment, is violated by what we today approve.

* * *

Mr. Justice FORTAS, dissenting.

* * *

This case is not within the principle of Everson v. Board of Education, 330 U.S. 1, 67 S.Ct. 504 (1947). Apart from the differences between textbooks and bus rides, the present statute does not call for extending to children attending sectarian schools the same service or facility extended to children in public schools. This statute calls for furnishing special, separate, and particular books, specially, separately, and particularly chosen by religious sects or their representatives for use in their sectarian schools. This is the infirmity, in my opinion. This is the feature that makes it impossible, in my view, to reach any conclusion other than that this statute is an unconstitutional use of public funds to support an establishment of religion.

This is the feature of the present statute that makes it totally inaccurate to suggest, as the majority does here, that furnishing these specially selected books for use in sectarian schools is like "public provision of police and fire protection, sewage facilities, and streets and sidewalks." * * * These are furnished to all alike. They are not selected on the basis of specification by a religious sect. And patrons of any one sect do not receive services or facilities different from those accorded members of other religions or agnostics or even atheists.

* * *

WALZ v. TAX COMMISSION OF CITY OF NEW YORK

Supreme Court of the United States, 1970
397 U.S. 664, 90 S.Ct. 1409, 25 L.Ed.2d 697

Walz owned real estate on Staten Island in New York City. He brought suit against city officials to enjoin the granting of tax exemption on property utilized solely for purposes of religious worship. Walz asserted that the exemption given to religious property constituted a clear violation of the First Amendment's Establishment Clause. The New York courts granted summary judgment for the commission, and Walz appealed.

Mr. Chief Justice BURGER delivered the opinion of the Court.

* * *

I

Prior opinions of this Court have discussed the development and historical background of the First Amendment in detail. * * * It would therefore serve no useful purpose to review in detail the background of the Establishment and Free Exercise Clauses of the First Amendment or to restate what the Court's opinions have reflected over the years.

* * *

The course of constitutional neutrality in this area cannot be an absolutely straight line; rigidity could well defeat the basic purpose of these provisions, which is to insure that no religion be sponsored or favored, none commanded, and none inhibited. The general principle deducible from the First Amendment and all that has been said by the Court is this: that we will not tolerate either governmentally established religion or governmental interference with religion. Short of those expressly proscribed governmental acts there is room for play in the joints productive of a benevolent neutrality which will permit religious exercise to exist without sponsorship and without interference.

Each value judgment under the Religion Clauses must therefore turn on whether particular acts in question are intended to establish or interfere with religious beliefs and practices or have the effect of doing so. Adherence to the policy of neutrality that derives from an accommodation of the Establishment and Free Exercise Clauses has prevented the kind of involvement that would tip the balance toward government control of churches or governmental restraint on religious practice.

Adherents of particular faiths and individual churches frequently take strong positions on public issues including, as this case reveals in the several briefs *amici*, vigorous advocacy of legal or constitutional positions. Of course, churches as much as secular bodies and private citizens have that right. No perfect or absolute separation is really possible; the very existence of the Religion Clauses is an involvement of sorts—one that seeks to mark boundaries to avoid excessive entanglement.

* * *

II

The legislative purpose of a property tax exemption is neither the advancement nor the inhibition of religion; it is neither sponsorship nor hostility. New York, in common with the other States, has determined that certain entities that exist in a harmonious relationship to the community at large, and that foster its "moral or mental improvement," should not be inhibited in their activities by property taxation or the hazard of loss of those properties for nonpayment of taxes. It has not singled out one particular church or religious group or even churches as such; rather, it has granted exemp-

tion to all houses of religious worship within a broad class of property owned by nonprofit, quasi-public corporations which include hospitals, libraries, playgrounds, scientific, professional, historical, and patriotic groups. The State has an affirmative policy that considers these groups as beneficial and stabilizing influences in community life and finds this classification useful, desirable, and in the public interest. Qualification for tax exemption is not perpetual or immutable; some tax-exempt groups lose that status when their activities take them outside the classification and new entities can come into being and qualify for exemption.

Governments have not always been tolerant of religious activity, and hostility toward religion has taken many shapes and forms—economic, political, and sometimes harshly oppressive. Grants of exemption historically reflect the concern of authors of constitutions and statutes as to the latent dangers inherent in the imposition of property taxes; exemption constitutes a reasonable and balanced attempt to guard against those dangers. The limits of permissible state accommodation to religion are by no means co-extensive with the noninterference mandated by the Free Exercise Clause. To equate the two would be to deny a national heritage with roots in the Revolution itself. * * * We cannot read New York's statute as attempting to establish religion; it is simply sparing the exercise of religion from the burden of property taxation levied on private profit institutions.

* * *

Granting tax exemptions to churches necessarily operates to afford an indirect economic benefit and also gives rise to some, but yet a lesser, involvement than taxing them. In analyzing either alternative the questions are whether the involvement is excessive, and whether it is a continuing one calling for official and continuing surveillance leading to an impermissible degree of entanglement. * * *

* * * The exemption creates only a minimal and remote involvement between church and state and far less than taxation of churches. It restricts the fiscal relationship between church and state, and tends to complement and reinforce the desired separation insulating each from the other.

Separation in this context cannot mean absence of all contact; the complexities of modern life inevitably produce some contact and the fire and police protection received by houses of religious worship are no more than incidental benefits accorded all persons or institutions within a State's boundaries, along with many other exempt organizations. * * *

* * *

Nothing in this national attitude toward religious tolerance and two centuries of uninterrupted freedom from taxation has given the remotest sign of leading to an established church or religion and on the contrary it has operated affirmatively to help guarantee the free exercise of all forms of religious belief. Thus, it is hardly useful to suggest that tax exemption is but the "foot in the door" or the "nose of the camel in the tent" leading to an established church. If tax exemption can be seen as this first step toward "establishment" of religion, as Mr. Justice DOUGLAS fears, the second step has been long in coming. * * *

* * *

The argument that making "fine distinctions" between what is and what is not absolute under the Constitution is to render us a government of men, not laws, gives too little weight to the fact that it is an essential part of adjudication to draw distinctions, including fine ones, in the process of interpreting the Constitution. We must frequently decide, for example, what are "reasonable" searches and seizures under the Fourth Amendment. Determining what acts of government tend to establish or interfere with religion falls well within what courts have long been called upon to do in sensitive areas.

* * *

Affirmed.

Mr. Justice BRENNAN, concurring.

* * *

As I said [concurring] in *Schempp* the First Amendment does not invalidate "the propriety of certain tax * * * exemptions which incidentally benefit churches and religious institutions, along with many secular charities and nonprofit organizations. * * * [R]eligious institutions simply share benefits which government makes generally available to educational, charitable, and eleemosynary groups. There is no indication that taxing authorities have used such benefits in any way to subsidize worship or foster belief in God." * * *

Mr. Justice DOUGLAS, dissenting.

* * * The question in the case therefore is whether believers—organized in church groups—can be

made exempt from real estate taxes, merely because they are believers, while non-believers, whether organized or not, must pay the real estate taxes.

* * *

In Torcaso v. Watkins, 367 U.S. 488, 81 S.Ct. 1680, we held that a State could not bar an atheist from public office in light of the freedom of belief and religion guaranteed by the First and Fourteenth Amendments. Neither the State nor the Federal Government, we said, "can constitutionally pass laws or impose requirements which aid all religions as against non-believers, and neither can aid those religions based on a belief in the existence of God as against those religions founded on

different beliefs." * * *

That principle should govern this case.

* * *

This case * * * is quite different [from *Everson*]. Education is not involved. The financial support rendered here is to the church, the place of worship. A tax exemption is a subsidy. Is my Brother BRENNAN correct in saying that we would hold that state or federal grants to churches, say, to construct the edifice itself would be unconstitutional? What is the difference between that kind of subsidy and the present subsidy?

* * *

LEMON v. KURTZMAN [a]

Supreme Court of the United States, 1971
403 U.S. 602, 91 S.Ct. 2105, 29 L.Ed.2d 745

Pennsylvania and Rhode Island each embarked upon programs of aid to church-affiliated elementary and secondary schools. The statutes of both states were attacked in the federal courts as abridging the Religion Clauses of the First Amendment, applicable to the states through the Due Process Clause of the Fourteenth Amendment. In the Pennsylvania case, Alton Lemon and other taxpayers brought suit against David Kurtzman, the state Superintendent of Public Instruction, and others to enjoin the expenditure of state funds. In the Rhode Island case, considered together by the U. S. Supreme Court with *Lemon*, Joan DiCenso and other taxpayers brought similar actions likewise to restrain the state Commissioner of Education, the Treasurer, and the Controller. A three-judge federal district court dismissed the complaint regarding the Pennsylvania statute while a similarly constituted federal panel sitting in Rhode Island struck down that state's aid plan. These cases were consolidated for argument also with *Tilton* v. *Richardson* (p. 1555). The opinions of Justices Brennan and White appear with the opinions in *Tilton* (see p. 1558) and are applicable both here and there.

Mr. Chief Justice BURGER delivered the opinion of the Court.

* * *

Pennsylvania has adopted a statutory program that provides financial support to nonpublic elementary and secondary schools by way of reim-

***

a. Together with *Early* v. *DiCenso* and *Robinson* v. *DiCenso*.

bursement for the cost of teachers' salaries, textbooks, and instructional materials in specified secular subjects. Rhode Island has adopted a statute under which the State pays directly to teachers in nonpublic elementary schools a supplement of 15% of their annual salary. Under each statute state aid has been given to church-related educational institutions. We hold that both statutes are unconstitutional.

I

The Rhode Island Statute

The Rhode Island Salary Supplement Act was enacted in 1969. It rests on the legislative finding that the quality of education available in nonpublic elementary schools has been jeopardized by the rapidly rising salaries needed to attract competent and dedicated teachers. The Act authorizes state officials to supplement the salaries of teachers of secular subjects in nonpublic elementary schools by paying directly to a teacher an amount not in excess of 15% of his current annual salary. As supplemented, however, a nonpublic school teacher's salary cannot exceed the maximum paid to teachers in the State's public schools, and the recipient must be certified by the state board of education in substantially the same manner as public school teachers.

In order to be eligible for the Rhode Island salary supplement, the recipient must teach in a nonpublic school at which the average per-pupil expenditure on secular education is less than the average in the State's public schools during a specified period. Appellant State Commissioner of Education also requires eligible schools to submit financial data. If this information indicates a per-pupil expenditure in excess of the statutory limitation, the records of the school in question must be examined in order to assess how much of the expenditure is attributable to secular education and how much to religious activity.

The Act also requires that teachers eligible for salary supplements must teach only those subjects that are offered in the State's public schools. They must use "only teaching materials which are used in the public schools." Finally, any teacher applying for a salary supplement must first agree in writing "not to teach a course in religion for so long as or during such time as he or she receives any salary supplements" under the Act.

* * *

A three-judge federal court * * * found that Rhode Island's nonpublic elementary schools accommodated approximately 25% of the State's pupils. About 95% of these pupils attended schools affiliated with the Roman Catholic church. To date some 250 teachers have applied for benefits under the Act. All of them are employed by Roman Catholic schools.

* * *

The Pennsylvania Statute

Pennsylvania has adopted a program that has some but not all of the features of the Rhode Island program. The [1968] Pennsylvania [act was also] passed * * * in response to a crisis that the Pennsylvania Legislature found existed in the State's nonpublic schools due to rapidly rising costs. * * *

The statute authorizes [the] state Superintendent of Public Instruction to "purchase" specified "secular educational services" from nonpublic schools. Under the "contracts" authorized by the statute, the State directly reimburses nonpublic schools solely for their actual expenditures for teachers' salaries, textbooks, and instructional materials. A school seeking reimbursement must maintain prescribed accounting procedures that identify the "separate" cost of the "secular educational service." These accounts are subject to state audit. * * *

There are several significant statutory restrictions on state aid. Reimbursement is limited to courses "presented in the curricula of the public schools." It is further limited "solely" to courses in the following "secular" subjects: mathematics, modern foreign languages, physical science, and physical education. Textbooks and instructional materials included in the program must be approved by the state Superintendent of Public Instruction. Finally, the statute prohibits reimbursement for any course that contains "any subject matter expressing religious teaching, or the morals or forms of worship of any sect."

* * * It appears that some $5 million has been expended annually under the Act. The State has now entered into contracts with some 1,181 nonpublic elementary and secondary schools with a student population of some 535,215 pupils—more than 20% of the total number of students in the State. More than 96% of these pupils attend church-related schools, and most of these schools are affiliated with the Roman Catholic church.

* * *

II

* * * Candor compels acknowledgment, moreover, that we can only dimly perceive the lines of demarcation in this extraordinarily sensitive area of constitutional law.

The language of the Religion Clauses of the First Amendment is at best opaque, particularly when compared with other portions of the Amendment. Its authors did not simply prohibit the establishment of a state church or a state religion, an area history shows they regarded as very important and fraught with great dangers. Instead they commanded that there should be "no law *respecting* an establishment of religion." A law may be one "respecting" the forbidden objective while falling short of its total realization. A law "respecting" the proscribed result, that is, the establishment of religion, is not always easily identifiable as one violative of the Clause. A given law might not *establish* a state religion but nevertheless be one "respecting" that end in the sense of being a step that could lead to such establishment and hence offend the First Amendment.

* * *

Every analysis in this area must begin with consideration of the cumulative criteria developed by the Court over many years. Three such tests may be gleaned from our cases. First, the statute must have a secular legislative purpose; second, its principal or primary effect must be one that neither advances nor inhibits religion * * *; finally, the statute must not foster "an excessive government entanglement with religion." * * *

Inquiry into the legislative purposes of the Pennsylvania and Rhode Island statutes affords no basis for a conclusion that the legislative intent was to advance religion. On the contrary, the statutes themselves clearly state that they are intended to enhance the quality of the secular education in all schools covered by the compulsory attendance laws. There is no reason to believe the legislatures meant anything else. * * *

* * * The legislatures of Rhode Island and Pennsylvania have concluded that secular and religious education are identifiable and separable. In the abstract we have no quarrel with this conclusion.

The two legislatures, however, have also recognized that church-related elementary and secondary schools have a significant religious mission and that a substantial portion of their activities is religiously oriented. They have therefore sought to create statutory restrictions designed to guarantee the separation between secular and religious educational functions and to ensure that State financial aid supports only the former. * * * We need not decide whether these legislative precautions restrict the principal or primary effect of the programs to the point where they do not offend the Religion Clauses, for we conclude that the cumulative impact of the entire relationship arising under the statutes in each State involves excessive entanglement between government and religion.

III

[The holding in *Walz*] tended to confine rather than enlarge the area of permissible state involvement with religious institutions by calling for close scrutiny of the degree of entan- glement involved in the relationship. The objective is to prevent, as far as possible, the intrusion of either into the precincts of the other.

Our prior holdings do not call for total separation between church and state; total separation is not possible in an absolute sense. Some relationship between government and religious organizations is inevitable. * * * Fire inspections, building and zoning regulations, and state requirements under compulsory school-attendance laws are examples of necessary and permissible contacts. * * * Judicial caveats against entanglement must recognize that the line of separation, far from being a "wall," is a blurred, indistinct, and variable barrier depending on all the circumstances of a particular relationship.

This is not to suggest, however, that we are to engage in a legalistic minuet in which precise rules and forms must govern. A true minuet is a matter of pure form and style, the observance of which is itself the substantive end. Here we examine the form of the relationship for the light that it casts on the substance.

In order to determine whether the government entanglement with religion is excessive, we must examine the character and purposes of the institutions that are benefited, the nature of the aid that the State provides, and the resulting relationship between the government and the religious authority. * * * Here we find that both statutes foster an impermissible degree of entanglement.

(a) *Rhode Island program*

* * *

The church schools involved in the program are located close to parish churches. * * * The school buildings contain identifying religious symbols such as crosses on the exterior and crucifixes, and religious paintings and statues either in the classrooms or hallways. Although only approximately 30 minutes a day are devoted to direct religious instruction, there are religiously oriented extracurricular activities. Approximately two-thirds of the teachers in these schools are nuns of various religious orders. Their dedicated efforts provide an atmosphere in which religious instruction and religious vocations are natural and proper parts of life in such schools. * * *

* * * This process of inculcating religious doctrine is, of course, enhanced by the impressionable age of the pupils, in primary schools particularly. In short, parochial schools involve substantial religious activity and purpose.

The substantial religious character of these church-related schools gives rise to entangling church-state relationships of the kind the Religion Clauses sought to avoid. * * *

The dangers and corresponding entanglements are enhanced by the particular form of aid that the Rhode Island Act provides. Our decisions from *Everson* to *Allen* have permitted the States to provide church-related schools with secular, neutral, or nonideological services, facilities, or materials. Bus transportation, school lunches, public health services, and secular textbooks supplied in common to all students were not thought to offend the Establishment Clause. * * *

In *Allen* the Court refused to make assumptions, on a meager record, about the religious content of the textbooks that the State would

be asked to provide. We cannot, however, refuse here to recognize that teachers have a substantially different ideological character from books. In terms of potential for involving some aspect of faith or morals in secular subjects, a textbook's content is ascertainable, but a teacher's handling of a subject is not. We cannot ignore the danger that a teacher under religious control and discipline poses to the separation of the religious from the purely secular aspects of precollege education. The conflict of functions inheres in the situation.

In our view the record shows these dangers are present to a substantial degree. * * *

* * *

Several teachers testified, however, that they did not inject religion into their secular classes. * * * But what has been recounted suggests the potential if not actual hazards of this form of state aid. The teacher is employed by a religious organization, subject to the direction and discipline of religious authorities, and works in a system dedicated to rearing children in a particular faith. These controls are not lessened by the fact that most of the lay teachers are of the Catholic faith. Inevitably some of a teacher's responsibilities hover on the border between secular and religious orientation.

We need not and do not assume that teachers in parochial schools will be guilty of bad faith or any conscious design to evade the limitations imposed by the statute and the First Amendment. We simply recognize that a dedicated religious person, teaching in a school affiliated with his or her faith and operated to inculcate its tenets, will inevitably experience great difficulty in remaining religiously neutral. Doctrines and faith are not inculcated or advanced by neutrals. With the best of intentions such a teacher would find it hard to make a total separation between secular teaching and religious doctrine. * * * Further difficulties are inherent in the combination of religious discipline and the possibility of disagreement between teacher and religious authorities over the meaning of the statutory restrictions.

* * * The Rhode Island Legislature has not, and could not, provide state aid on the basis of a mere assumption that secular teachers under religious discipline can avoid conflicts. The State must be certain, given the Religion Clauses, that subsidized teachers do not inculcate religion—indeed the State here has undertaken to do so. To ensure that no trespass occurs, the State has therefore carefully conditioned its aid with pervasive restrictions. * * *

A comprehensive, discriminating, and continuing state surveillance will inevitably be required to ensure that these restrictions are obeyed and the First Amendment otherwise respected. Unlike a book, a teacher cannot be inspected once so as to determine the extent and intent of his or her personal beliefs and subjective acceptance of the limitations imposed by the First Amendment. These prophylactic contacts will involve excessive and enduring entanglement between state and church.

There is another area of entanglement in the Rhode Island program that gives concern. The statute excludes teachers employed by nonpublic schools whose average per-pupil expenditures on secular education equal or exceed the comparable figures for public schools. In the event that the total expenditures of an otherwise eligible school exceed this norm, the program requires the government to examine the school's records in order to determine how much of the total expenditures is attributable to secular education and how much to religious activity. This kind of state inspection and evaluation of the religious content of a religious organization is fraught with the sort of entanglement that the Constitution forbids. It is a relationship pregnant with dangers of excessive government direction of church schools and hence of churches. * * *

(b) *Pennsylvania program*

* * *

[T]he very restrictions and surveillance necessary to ensure that teachers play a strictly nonideological role give rise to entanglements between church and state. The Pennsylvania statute, like that of Rhode Island, fosters this kind of relationship. * * *

The Pennsylvania statute, moreover, has the further defect of providing state financial aid directly to the church-related schools. This factor distinguishes both *Everson* and *Allen*, for in both those cases the Court was careful to point out that state aid was provided to the student and his parents—not to the church-related school. * * * The history of government grants of a continuing cash subsidy indicates that such programs have almost always been accompanied by varying measures of control and surveillance. The government cash grants before us now provide no basis for predicting that comprehensive measures of surveil-

lance and controls will not follow.
* * *

IV

A broader base of entanglement of yet a different character is presented by the divisive political potential of these state programs. In a community where such a large number of pupils are served by church-related schools, it can be assumed that state assistance will entail considerable political activity. Partisans of parochial schools, understandably concerned with rising costs and sincerely dedicated to both the religious and secular educational missions of their schools, will inevitably champion this cause and promote political action to achieve their goals. Those who oppose state aid, whether for constitutional, religious, or fiscal reasons, will inevitably respond and employ all of the usual political campaign techniques to prevail. Candidates will be forced to declare and voters to choose. It would be unrealistic to ignore the fact that many people confronted with issues of this kind will find their votes aligned with their faith.

Ordinarily political debate and division, however vigorous or even partisan, are normal and healthy manifestations of our democratic system of government, but political division along religious lines was one of the principal evils against which the First Amendment was intended to protect. * * * The potential divisiveness of such conflict is a threat to the normal political process. * * * It conflicts with our whole history and tradition to permit questions of the Religion Clauses to assume such importance in our legislatures and in our elections that they could divert attention from the myri-

ad issues and problems that confront every level of government. * * * The history of many countries attests to the hazards of religion's intruding into the political arena or of political power intruding into the legitimate and free exercise of religious belief.

* * *

The potential for political divisiveness related to religious belief and practice is aggravated in these two statutory programs by the need for continuing annual appropriations and the likelihood of larger and larger demands as costs and populations grow. * * *

V

* * *

* * * We have already noted that modern governmental programs have self-perpetuating and self-expanding propensities. These internal pressures are only enhanced when the schemes involve institutions whose legitimate needs are growing and whose interests have substantial political support. Nor can we fail to see that in constitutional adjudication some steps, which when taken were thought to approach "the verge," have become the platform for yet further steps. A certain momentum develops in constitutional theory and it can be a "downhill thrust" easily set in motion but difficult to retard or stop. * * * The dangers are increased by the difficulty of perceiving in advance exactly where the "verge" of the precipice lies. As well as constituting an independent evil against which the Religion Clauses were intended to protect, involvement or entanglement between government and religion serves as a warning signal.

* * *

* * * Under our system the choice has been made that government is to be entirely excluded from the area of religious instruction and churches excluded from the affairs of government. The Constitution decrees that religion must be a private matter for the individual, the family, and the institutions of private choice, and that while some involvement and entanglement are inevitable, lines must be drawn.

The judgment of the Rhode Island District Court * * * is affirmed. The judgment of the Pennsylvania District Court * * * is reversed, and the case is remanded. * * *

Mr. Justice MARSHALL took no part in the consideration or decision of [*Lemon*].

TILTON v. RICHARDSON

Supreme Court of the United States, 1971
403 U.S. 672, 91 S.Ct. 2091, 29 L.Ed.2d 790

Title I of the Higher Education Facilities Act of 1963 provided aid for the construction of college and university buildings and facilities solely for secular educational purposes. In order to receive the loans and grants available, applicant schools were required to give assurances that no facility constructed with such funds would be used "for sectarian instruction or as a place of religious worship, or * * * primarily in connection with any part of the program of a school or department of divinity." The federal government retained an interest in the buildings and facilities for twenty years and, if a college or university violated the statutory conditions during that period, the government would be entitled to recover funds. Four church-affiliated schools in Connecticut receiving funds under the act were the focus of attention in this suit brought by Tilton and other U. S. citizens and taxpayers, residents of Connecticut, to enjoin Secretary of Health, Education, and Welfare Elliott Richardson from administering the act. The taxpayers attacked the constitutionality of the Act via the Establishment Clause. A three-judge U. S. District Court sustained the constitutionality of the act, finding that neither its purpose nor effect promoted religion. Tilton and the other taxpayers sought review by the Supreme Court.

Mr. Chief Justice BURGER announced the judgment of the Court and an opinion in which Mr. Justice HARLAN, Mr. Justice STEWART and Mr. Justice BLACKMUN join.

* * *

We are satisfied that Congress intended the Act to include all colleges and universities regardless of any affiliation with or sponsorship by a religious body. Congress defined "institutions of higher education," which are eligible to receive aid under the Act, in broad and inclusive terms.

* * * [T]he Act makes no reference to religious affiliation or nonaffiliation. Under these circumstances "institutions of higher education" must be taken to include church-related colleges and universities.

Against this background we consider four questions: First, does the Act reflect a secular legislative purpose? Second, is the primary effect of the Act to advance or inhibit religion? Third, does the administration of the Act foster an excessive government entanglement with religion? Fourth, does the implementation of the Act inhibit the free exercise of religion?

The stated legislative purpose * * * expresses a legitimate secular objective entirely appropriate for governmental action.

* * *

The Act itself was carefully drafted to ensure that the federally subsidized facilities would be devoted to the secular and not the religious function of the recipient institutions. It authorizes grants and loans only for academic facilities that will be used for defined secular purposes and expressly prohibits their use for religious instruction, training, or worship. These restrictions have been enforced in the Act's actual administration, and the record shows that some church-related institutions have been required to disgorge benefits for failure to obey them.

Finally, this record fully supports the findings of the District Court that none of the four church-related institutions in this case has violated the statutory restrictions. The institutions presented evidence that there had been no religious services or worship in the federally financed facilities, that there are no religious symbols or plaques in or on them, and that they had been used solely for nonreligious purposes. * * *

* * *

Rather than focus on the four defendant colleges and universities involved in this case, however, appellants seek to shift our attention to a "composite profile" that they have constructed of the "typical sectarian" institution of higher education. We are told that such a "composite" institution imposes religious restrictions on admissions, requires attend-

ance at religious activities, compels obedience to the doctrines and dogmas of the faith, requires instruction in theology and doctrine, and does everything it can to propagate a particular religion. Perhaps some church-related schools fit the pattern that appellants describe. * * * But appellants do not contend that these four institutions fall within this category. * * * We cannot, however, strike down an Act of Congress on the basis of a hypothetical "profile."

Although we reject appellants' broad constitutional arguments we do perceive an aspect in which the statute's enforcement provisions are inadequate to ensure that the impact of the federal aid will not advance religion. If a recipient institution violates any of the statutory restrictions on the use of a federally financed facility, § 754(b)(2) permits the Government to recover an amount equal to the proportion of the facility's present value that the federal grant bore to its original cost.

* * *

Limiting the prohibition for religious use of the structure to 20 years obviously opens the facility to use for any purpose at the end of that period. It cannot be assumed that a substantial structure has no value after that period and hence the unrestricted use of a valuable property is in effect a contribution of some value to a religious body. Congress did not base the 20-year provision on any contrary conclusion. If, at the end of 20 years, the building is, for example, converted into a chapel or otherwise used to promote religious interests, the original federal grant will in part have the effect of advancing religion.

To this extent the Act therefore trespasses on the Religion Clauses. The restrictive obligations of a recipient institution under § 751(a)(2) cannot, compatibly with the Religion Clauses, expire while the building has substantial value. This circumstance does not require us to invalidate the entire Act [but only this single provision]. * * *

* * *

We next turn to the question of whether excessive entanglements characterize the relationship between government and church under the Act. * * * Our decision today in *Lemon* v. *Kurtzman* and *Robinson* v. *DiCenso* has discussed and applied this independent measure of constitutionality under the Religion Clauses. * * *

* * *

There are generally significant differences [however] between the religious aspects of church-related institutions of higher learning and parochial elementary and secondary schools. * * * There is substance to the contention that college students are less impressionable and less susceptible to religious indoctrination. Common observation would seem to support that view, and Congress may well have entertained it. The skepticism of the college student is not an inconsiderable barrier to any attempt or tendency to subvert the congressional objectives and limitations. Furthermore, by their very nature, college and postgraduate courses tend to limit the opportunities for sectarian influence by virtue of their own internal disciplines. Many church-related colleges and universities are characterized by a high degree of academic freedom and

seek to evoke free and critical responses from their students.

* * *

Since religious indoctrination is not a substantial purpose or activity of these church-related colleges and universities, there is less likelihood than in primary and secondary schools that religion will permeate the area of secular education. This reduces the risk that government aid will in fact serve to support religious activities. Correspondingly, the necessity for intensive government surveillance is diminished and the resulting entanglements between government and religion lessened. Such inspection as may be necessary to ascertain that the facilities are devoted to secular education is minimal and indeed hardly more than the inspections that States impose over all private schools within the reach of compulsory education laws.

The entanglement between church and state is also lessened here by the nonideological character of the aid that the Government provides. * * *

[G]overnment entanglements with religion are reduced by the circumstance that, unlike the direct and continuing payments under the Pennsylvania program, and all the incidents of regulation and surveillance, the Government aid here is a one-time, single-purpose construction grant. There are no continuing financial relationships or dependencies, no annual audits, and no government analysis of an institution's expenditures on secular as distinguished from religious activities. Inspection as to use is a minimal contact.

No one of these three factors standing alone is necessarily controlling; cumulatively all of them shape a narrow and limited relationship with government which involves fewer and less significant contacts than the two state schemes before us in *Lemon* and *DiCenso*. The relationship therefore has less potential for realizing the substantive evils against which the Religion Clauses were intended to protect.

We think that cumulatively these three factors also substantially lessen the potential for divisive religious fragmentation in the political arena. * * * The potential for divisiveness inherent in the essentially local problems of primary and secondary schools is significantly less with respect to a college or university whose student constituency is not local but diverse and widely dispersed.

* * * Appellants claim that the Free Exercise Clause is violated because they are compelled to pay taxes, the proceeds of which in part finance grants under the Act. Appellants, however, are unable to identify any coercion directed at the practice or exercise of their religious beliefs. * * * Their share of the cost of the grants under the Act is not fundamentally distinguishable from the impact of the tax exemption sustained in *Walz* or the provision of textbooks upheld in *Allen*.

We conclude that the Act does not violate the Religion Clauses of the First Amendment except that part * * * providing a 20-year limitation on the religious use restrictions. * * * We remand to the District Court with directions to enter a judgment consistent with this opinion.

* * *

Mr. Justice DOUGLAS, with whom Mr. Justice BLACK and Mr.

Justice MARSHALL concur, dissenting in part.

* * *

* * * The Federal Government is giving religious schools a block grant to build certain facilities. The fact that money is given once at the beginning of a program rather than apportioned annually as in *Lemon* and *DiCenso* is without constitutional significance. The First Amendment bars establishment of a religion. * * *

Mr. Justice BRENNAN.

I agree that the judgments in [*DiCenso*] must be affirmed. In my view the judgment in [*Lemon*] must be reversed outright. I dissent in [*Tilton*] insofar as the plurality opinion and the opinion of my Brother WHITE sustain the constitutionality, as applied to sectarian institutions, of the Federal Higher Education Facilities Act of 1963. * * * In my view that Act is unconstitutional insofar as it authorizes grants of federal tax monies to sectarian institutions, but is unconstitutional only to that extent. I therefore think that our remand of the case should be limited to the direction of a hearing to determine whether the four institutional appellees here are sectarian institutions.

* * *

Mr. Justice WHITE, concurring in the judgments in [*Lemon* and *Tilton*] and dissenting in [*DiCenso*].

* * *

[T]he decision of the Court is * * * surely quite wrong in overturning the Pennsylvania and Rhode Island statutes on the ground that they amount to an establishment of religion forbidden by the First Amendment.

* * *

It is enough for me that the States and the Federal Government are financing a separable secular function of overriding importance in order to sustain the legislation here challenged. That religion and private interests other than education may substantially benefit does not convert these laws into impermissible establishments of religion.

* * *

The Court * * * creates an insoluble paradox for the State and the parochial schools. The State cannot finance secular instruction if it permits religion to be taught in the same classroom; but if it exacts a promise that religion not be so taught—a promise the school and its teachers are quite willing and on this record able to give—and enforces it,

it is then entangled in the "no entanglement" aspect of the Court's Establishment Clause jurisprudence.

* * *

I find it very difficult to follow the distinction between the federal and state programs in terms of their First Amendment acceptability. My difficulty is not surprising, since there is frank acknowledgment that "we can only dimly perceive the boundaries of permissible government activity in this sensitive area of constitutional adjudication." * * * I find it even more difficult, with these acknowledgments in mind, to understand how the Court can accept the considered judgment of Congress that its program is constitutional and yet reject the equally considered decisions of the Rhode Island and Pennsylvania legislatures that their programs represent a constitutionally acceptable accommodation between church and state.

STATE AID TO RELIGIOUS SCHOOLS AFTER *LEMON* AND *TILTON*

Committee for Public Education and Religious Liberty v. Nyquist, 413 U.S. 756, 93 S.Ct. 2955 (1973)	Type of Aid in Question	(1) Direct money grants to qualifying nonpublic schools primarily in low-income, urban areas for "maintenance and repair of * * * school facilities and equipment to ensure the health, welfare and safety of enrolled pupils," graduated on per pupil per year basis depending on the age of the building; (2) tuition reimbursements to parents earning less than $5,000 a year whose children attend nonpublic schools (the maximum grants to be $50 or $100 per child depending on whether the school attended was elementary or secondary); (3) tax credits on tuition payments to nonpublic schools for parents not qualifying for reimbursements at a rate of $50 per child, the total deduction declining as the parents' income increased.
	Ruling	All three programs failed the "effects" test. Regardless of the adequacy of the legitimate nonsectarian state interests which were advanced to support these programs (e.g., fostering and maintaining a diverse populace, making viable the selection of alternative

Committee for Public Education and Religious Liberty (*Cont.*)	Ruling (*Cont.*)	education programs for lower-income families, preventing a massive increase in public school enrollments and the likely consequent financial crisis), the primary effect was to advance religion. While the facilities maintenance program had a legitimate public welfare purpose, no provision was made in the present instance of a *direct* grant to isolate the expenditure of public monies so that they would bolster only secular educational activities. By the same token, the tuition reimbursements were unconstitutional because, even if given to the parents, such indirect aid still had the primary effect of promoting religiously affiliated education. Finally, the Court rejected the tax credit, distinguishing it from the exemption approved in *Walz* on the following grounds: (1) unlike the exemption in *Walz* where the "aid" minimized the entanglement between church and state, here it would tend to increase the involvement between church and state; and (2) unlike the exemption in *Walz* which was not restricted to a class composed exclusively or predominantly of religious institutions, this exemption flows primarily to parents of children attending religious schools.
	Vote	6–3; Burger, White, and Rehnquist dissented.
Meek v. Pittenger, 421 U.S. 349, 95 S.Ct. 1753 (1975)	Type of Aid in Question	(1) Providing various "auxiliary services" including counseling, testing and psychological services, speech and hearing therapy, teaching and related services for exceptional children, for remedial students, and for the educationally disadvantaged as well as other unspecified "nonideological services" of benefit to the children; (2) lending of secular textbooks without charge to children attending nonpublic elementary and secondary schools; (3) lending of certain "instructional materials and equipment" including "periodicals, photographs, maps, charts, sound recordings, films" as well as projectors, tape recorders, laboratory equipment, and other instructional aids.
	Ruling	All of the aid provisions except that regarding the loan of secular textbooks violated the First Amendment. Although acknowledging that a state may include church-related schools in programs of bus transportation, school lunches, and health facilities, the Court held that the "massive aid" provided here is "neither indirect nor incidental." The Court observed that for the 1972–73 school year just under $12 million had been appropriated for direct aid predominantly to church-related nonpublic schools in loans of instructional materials and equipment. Given the *pervasive* religious influence in the recipient schools, it "would simply ignore reality to separate secular educational functions from the predominantly religious role" performed by such elementary and secondary schools in the face of the *large volume* of *direct* aid. "Sub-

Meek (*Cont.*)	Ruling (*Cont.*)	stantial aid to the educational function of such schools * * * necessarily results in aid to the sectarian enterprise as a whole." The supervision required to ensure that personnel furnishing the auxiliary services play a strictly nonideological role would also give rise to a constitutionally intolerable degree of entanglement between church and state. Furthermore, "the recurrent nature of the appropriation process provides successive opportunities for political fragmentation and division along religious lines, one of the principal evils against which the Establishment Clause was intended to protect."
	Vote	6–3; Douglas, Brennan, and Marshall dissented with respect to upholding the textbook loan provisions; Burger, White, and Rehnquist dissented with respect to holding the other provisions of the aid program unconstitutional.
Wolman v. Walter, 433 U.S. 229, 97 S.Ct. 2593 (1977)	Type of Aid in Question	"[B]ooks, instructional materials and equipment, standardized testing and scoring, diagnostic services, therapeutic services, and field trip transportation."
	Ruling	The Court held constitutional those parts of the statute providing nonpublic school pupils "with books, standardized testing and scoring, diagnostic services, and therapeutic and remedial services" but held unconstitutional those portions "relating to instructional materials and equipment and field trip services." The Court distinguished diagnostic services from teaching or counseling on the grounds that: (1) "diagnostic services * * * have little or no educational content," and (2) "the diagnostician has only limited contact with the child, and that contact involves chiefly the use of objective and professional testing methods to detect students in need of treatment." While "unlike the diagnostician, the therapist may establish a relationship with the pupil in which there might be opportunity to transmit ideological views," this danger is unlikely to arise as long as "therapeutic and remedial services [are provided] at a neutral site off the premises of the nonpublic schools * * *." In addition to not having the impermissible effect of advancing religion, "neither will there be any excessive entanglement arising from the supervision of public employees to insure that they maintain a neutral stance" since "[i]t can hardly be said that the supervision of public employees performing public functions on public property creates an excessive entanglement between church and state."
	Vote	6–3; Brennan, Marshall, and Stevens dissented.

COMMITTEE FOR PUBLIC EDUCATION AND RELIGIOUS LIBERTY v. REGAN

Supreme Court of the United States, 1980
444 U.S. 646, 100 S.Ct. 840, 63 L.Ed.2d 94

In 1970, the New York legislature appropriated public funds to reimburse church-affiliated and secular nonpublic schools for performing various state-mandated services. The most expensive of these was the "administration, grading and the compiling and reporting of the results of tests and examinations." The tests included were both state-prepared examinations and more common, teacher-prepared tests. Although the legislation stipulated that no payments were to be made for religious worship or instruction, the statute did not provide for any audit of school financial records to guarantee that public funds were being used only for secular purposes. In Levitt v. Committee for Public Education and Religious Liberty, 413 U.S. 472, 93 S.Ct. 2814 (1973), the Supreme Court ruled that the legislation constituted an impermissible aid to religion because "despite the obviously integral role of such testing in the total teaching process, no attempt is made under the statute, and no means are available, to assure that internally prepared tests are free of religious instruction."

The legislature responded promptly by enacting a new law in 1974 designed to eliminate these defects. The legislation directed the state Commissioner of Education to reimburse nonpublic schools for the actual costs incurred in meeting certain state-mandated requirements, including "the requirements of the state's pupil evaluation program, the basic educational data system, regents examinations, the statewide evaluation plan, the uniform procedure for pupil attendance reporting, and other similar state prepared examinations and reporting procedures." By comparison, "the new scheme did not reimburse nonpublic schools for the preparation, administration, or grading of teacher-prepared tests," and it "provide[d] a means by which payments of state funds [were] audited, thus ensuring that only the actual costs incurred in providing the covered secular services [were] reimbursed out of state funds." Despite these modifications, a federal district court held the legislation unconstitutional on the basis of its reading of the Supreme Court's decision in Meek v. Pittenger, 421 U.S. 349, 95 S.Ct. 1753 (1975). On appeal to the Supreme Court, the Court vacated the district court's judgment and remanded the case for further consideration in light of the more recent decision in Wolman v. Walter, 433 U.S. 229, 97 S.Ct. 2593 (1977). On remand, the district court, reasoning that *Wolman* embodied a "more flexible concept," upheld New York's reimbursement program against allegations that the enactment violated the Establishment Clause.

Mr. Justice WHITE delivered the opinion of the Court.

* * *

Under the precedents of this Court a legislative enactment does not contravene the Establishment Clause if it has a secular legislative purpose, if its principal or primary effect neither advances nor inhibits religion, and if it does not foster an excessive government entanglement with religion. * * *

* * *

We agree with the District Court that *Wolman* v. *Walter* controls this case. Although the Ohio statute under review in *Wolman* and the New York statute before us here are not identical, the differences are not of constitutional dimension. Addressing first the testing provisions, we note that here, as in *Wolman*, there is clearly a secular purpose behind the legislative enactment: "To provide educational opportunity of a quality which will prepare [New York] citizens for the challenges of American life in the last decades of the twentieth century." New York Laws 1974, ch. 507, § 1. Also like the Ohio statute, the New York plan calls for tests that are prepared by the State and administered on the premises by nonpublic school personnel. The nonpublic school thus has no control whatsoever over the content of the tests. The Ohio tests, however, were graded by the State; here there are three types of tests involved, one graded by the State and the other two by nonpublic school personnel, with the costs of the grading service, as well as the cost of administering all three tests, being reimbursed by the State. In view of the nature of the tests, the District Court found that the grading of the examinations by nonpublic school employees afforded no control to the school over the outcome of any of the tests.

* * *

We see no reason to differ with the factual or legal characterization of the testing procedure arrived at by the District Court. As in *Wolman* v. *Walter*, * * * "[t]he non-public school does not control the content of the test or its result"; and here, as in *Wolman*, this factor "serves to prevent the use of the test as a part of religious teaching," * * * thus avoiding the kind of direct aid forbidden by the Court's prior cases. The District Court was correct in concluding that there was no substantial risk that the examinations could be used for religious educational purposes.

The District Court was also correct in its characterization of the recordkeeping and reporting services

for which the State reimburses the nonpublic school. Under the New York law, "[e]ach year, private schools must submit to the State a Basic Educational Data System (BEDS) report. This report contains information regarding the student body, faculty, support staff, physical facilities, and curriculum of each school. Schools are also required to submit annually a report showing the attendance record of each minor who is a student at the school." * * * Although recordkeeping is related to the educational program, the District Court characterized it and the reporting function as "ministerial [and] lacking in ideological content or use." * * * These tasks are not part of the teaching process and cannot "be used to foster an ideological outlook." * * * Reimbursement for the costs of so complying with state law, therefore, has primarily a secular, rather than a religious, purpose and effect.

The New York statute, unlike the Ohio statute at issue in *Wolman*, provides for direct cash reimbursement to the nonpublic school for administering the state-prescribed examinations and for grading two of them. We agree with the District Court that such reimbursement does not invalidate the New York statute. If the State furnished state-prepared tests, thereby relieving the nonpublic schools of the expense of preparing their own examinations, but left the grading of the tests to the schools, and if the grading procedures could be used to further the religious mission of the school, serious Establishment Clause problems would be posed under the Court's cases, for by furnishing the tests it might be concluded that the State was directly aiding religious education. But as we have already concluded, grading the secular tests furnished by the State in this case is a function that has a secular purpose and primarily a secular effect. This conclusion is not changed simply because the State pays the school for performing the grading function. As the District Court observed, "[p]utting aside the question of whether direct financial aid can be administered without excessive entanglement by the State in the affairs of a sectarian institution, there does not appear to be any reason why payments to sectarian schools to cover the cost of specified activities would have the impermissible effect of advancing religion if the same activities performed by sectarian school personnel without reimbursement but with State-furnished materials have no such effect." * * *

A contrary view would insist on drawing a constitutional distinction between paying the nonpublic school to do the grading and paying state employees or some independent service to perform that task, even though the grading function is the same regardless of who performs it and would not have the primary effect of aiding religion whether or not performed by nonpublic school personnel. In either event, the nonpublic school is being relieved of the cost of grading state-required, state-furnished examinations. We decline to embrace a formalistic dichotomy that bears so little relationship either to common sense or to the realities of school finance. None of our cases requires us to invalidate these reimbursements simply because they involve payments in cash. * * * Because the recordkeeping and reporting functions also have neither a religious purpose nor a primarily religious effect, we reach the same re-

sults with respect to the reimbursements for these services.

Of course, under the relevant cases the outcome would likely be different were there no effective means for insuring that the cash reimbursements would cover only secular services. * * * But here, as we shall see, the New York law provides ample safeguards against excessive or misdirected reimbursement.

The District Court recognized that "[w]here a state is required in determining what aid, if any, may be extended to a sectarian school, to monitor the day-to-day activities of the teaching staff, to engage in onerous, direct oversight, or to make on-site judgments from time to time as to whether different school activities are religious in character, the risk of entanglement is too great to permit governmental involvement." * * * After examining the New York statute and its operation, however, the District Court concluded that "[t]he activities subsidized under the Statute here at issue * * * do not pose any substantial risk of such entanglement." * * *

The District Court described the process of reimbursement:

"Schools which seek reimbursement must 'maintain a separate account or system of accounts for the expenses incurred in rendering' the reimbursable services, and they must submit to the N. Y. State Commissioner of Education an application for reimbursement with additional reports and documents prescribed by the Commissioner. * * * Reimbursable costs include proportionate share of the teachers' salaries and fringe benefits attributable to administration of the examinations and reporting of State-required data on pupil attendance and performance, plus the cost of supplies and other contractual expenditures such as data processing services. Applications for reimbursement cannot be approved until the Commissioner audits vouchers or other documents submitted by the schools to substantiate their claims. * * * The Statute further provides that the State Department of Audit and Control shall from time to time inspect the accounts of recipient schools in order to verify the cost to the schools of rendering the reimbursable services. If the audit reveals that a school has received an amount in excess of its actual costs, the excess must be returned to the State immediately." * * *

We agree with the District Court that "[t]he services for which the private schools would be reimbursed are discrete and clearly identifiable." * * * The reimbursement process, furthermore, is straightforward and susceptible to the routinization that characterizes most reimbursement schemes. On its face, therefore, the New York plan suggests no excessive entanglement, and we are not prepared to read into the plan as an inevitability the bad faith upon which any future excessive entanglement would be predicated.

It is urged that the District Court judgment is unsupportable under *Meek* v. *Pittenger*, supra, which is said to have held that any aid to even secular educational functions of a sectarian school is forbidden, or more broadly still, that any aid to a sectarian school is suspect since its religious teaching is so pervasively intermixed with each and every one of its activities. * * * The difficulty with this position is that a majority of the Court, including the author of *Meek* v. *Pittenger*, upheld in *Wol-*

man a state statute under which the State, by preparing and grading tests in secular subjects, relieved sectarian schools of the cost of these functions, functions that they otherwise would have had to perform themselves and that were intimately connected with the educational processes. Yet the *Wolman* opinion at no point suggested that this holding was inconsistent with the decision in *Meek*. * * *

That *Meek* was understood more narrowly was suggested by Mr. Justice Powell in his separate opinion in *Wolman*: "I am not persuaded," he said, "nor did *Meek* hold, that all loans of secular instructional material and equipment" inescapably have the effect of direct advancement of religion. * * * And obviously the testing services furnished by the State in *Wolman* were approved on the premise that those services did not and could not have the primary effect of advancing the sectarian aims of the nonpublic schools. With these indicators before it, the District Court properly put the two cases together and sustained the reimbursements involved here because it had been shown with sufficient clarity that they would serve the State's legitimate secular ends without any appreciable risk of being used to transmit or teach religious views.

This is not to say that this case, any more than past cases, will furnish a litmus-paper test to distinguish permissible from impermissible aid to religiously oriented schools. But Establishment Clause cases are not easy; they stir deep feelings; and we are divided among ourselves, perhaps reflecting the different views on this subject of the people of this country. What is certain is that our decisions have tended to avoid categorical imperatives and absolutist approaches at either end of the range of possible outcomes. This course sacrifices clarity and predictability for flexibility, but this promises to be the case until the continuing interaction between the courts and the States—the former charged with interpreting and upholding the Constitution and the latter seeking to provide education for their youth—produces a single, more encompassing construction of the Establishment Clause.

The judgment of the District Court is

Affirmed.

Mr. Justice BLACKMUN, with whom Mr. Justice BRENNAN and Mr. Justice MARSHALL join, dissenting.

The Court in this case, I fear, takes a long step backwards in the inevitable controversy that emerges when a state legislature continues to insist on providing public aid to parochial schools.

I thought that the Court's judgments in Meek v. Pittenger, 421 U.S. 349, 95 S.Ct. 1753 (1975), and in Wolman v. Walter, 433 U.S. 229, 97 S.Ct. 2593 (1977), * * * at last had fixed the line between that which is constitutionally appropriate public aid and that which is not. The line necessarily was not a straight one.
* * *

* * *

I have no trouble in agreeing with the Court that Chapter 507 [the New York statute] manifests a clear secular purpose. * * * I therefore would evaluate Chapter 507 under the two remaining inquiries of the three-part test.

In deciding whether Chapter 507 has an impermissible primary effect

of advancing religion, or whether it fosters excessive government entanglement with sectarian affairs, one must keep in focus the nature of the assistance prescribed by the New York statute. The District Court found that $8–10 million annually would be expended under Chapter 507, with the great majority of these funds going to sectarian schools to pay for personnel costs associated with attendance reporting. The court found that such payments would amount to from 1% to 5.4% of the personnel budget of an individual religious school receiving assistance under Chapter 507. Moreover, Chapter 507 provides direct cash payments by the State of New York to religious schools, as opposed to providing services or providing cash payments to third parties who have rendered services. And the money paid sectarian schools under Chapter 507 is designated to reimburse costs that are incurred by religious schools in order to meet basic state testing and reporting requirements, costs that would have been incurred regardless of the availability of reimbursement from the State.

This direct financial assistance provided by Chapter 507 differs significantly from the types of state aid to religious schools approved by the Court in *Wolman* v. *Walter*. For example, in *Wolman* the Court approved that portion of the Ohio statute that provided to religious schools the standardized tests and scoring services furnished to public schools. But, unlike New York's Chapter 507, Ohio's statute provided only the tests themselves and scoring by employees of neutral testing organizations. It did not authorize direct financial aid of any type to religious schools.
* * *

Similarly, the other forms of assistance upheld in *Wolman* did not involve direct cash assistance. * * *

It is clear * * * that none of the programs upheld in *Wolman* provided direct financial support to sectarian schools. At the very least, then, the Court's holding today goes further in approving state assistance to sectarian schools than the Court had gone in past decisions. But beyond merely failing to approve the type of direct financial aid at issue in this case, *Wolman* reaffirmed the finding of the Court in *Meek* v. *Pittenger* that *direct* aid to the educational function of religious schools necessarily advances the sectarian enterprise as a whole. * * *

* * *

Under the principles announced in these decided cases, I am compelled to conclude that Chapter 507, by providing substantial financial assistance directly to sectarian schools, has a primary effect of advancing religion. The vast majority of the schools aided under Chapter 507 typify the religious-pervasive institution the very purpose of which is to provide an integrated secular and sectarian education. The aid provided by Chapter 507 goes primarily to reimburse such schools for personnel costs incurred in complying with state reporting and testing requirements, costs that must be incurred if the school is to be accredited to provide a combined sectarian-secular education to school-age pupils. To continue to function as religious schools, sectarian schools thus are required to incur the costs outlined in § 3 of Chapter 507, or else lose accreditation by the State of New York. * * * These reporting and testing requirements would be met by the

schools whether reimbursement were available or not. As such, the attendance, informational, and testing expenses compensated by Chapter 507 are essential to the overall educational functioning of sectarian schools in New York in the same way instruction in secular subjects is essential. Therefore, just as direct aid for ostensibly secular purposes by provision of instructional materials or direct financial subsidy is forbidden by the Establishment Clause, so direct aid for the performance of recordkeeping and testing activities that are an essential part of the sectarian school's functioning also is interdicted. * * *

It is also true that the keeping of pupil attendance records is essential to the religious mission of sectarian schools. To ensure that the school is fulfilling its religious mission properly, it is necessary to provide a way to determine whether pupils are attending the sectarian classes required of them. Accordingly, Chapter 507 not only advances religion by aiding the educational mission of the sectarian school as a whole; it also subsidizes directly the religious mission of such schools. Chapter 507 makes no attempt, and none is possible, to separate the portion of the overall expense of attendance-taking attributable to the desire to ensure that students are attending religious instruction from that portion attributable to the desire to ensure that state attendance laws are complied with. This type of direct aid the Establishment Clause does not permit. * * *

I thus would hold that the aid provided by Chapter 507 constitutes a direct subsidy of the operating costs of the sectarian school that aids the school as a whole, and that the statute therefore directly advances religion in violation of the Establishment Clause of the First Amendment.

Beyond this, Chapter 507 also fosters government entanglement with religion to an impermissible extent. Unlike *Wolman*, under Chapter 507 sectarian employees are compensated by the State for grading examinations. In some cases, such grading requires the teacher to exercise subjective judgment. For the State properly to ensure that judgment is not exercised to inculcate religion, a "comprehensive, discriminating, and continuing state surveillance will inevitably be required." Lemon v. Kurtzman, 403 U.S. 602, 619, 91 S.Ct. 2105, 2114 (1971).

Moreover, Chapter 507 provides for continuing reimbursement with regard to examinations in which the questions may vary from year to year, and for examinations that may be offered in the future. This will require the State continually to evaluate the examinations to ensure that reimbursement for expenses incurred in connection with their administration and grading will not offend the First Amendment. This, too, fosters impermissible government involvement in sectarian affairs, since it is likely to lead to continuing adjudication of disputes between the State and others as to whether certain questions or new examinations present such opportunities for the advancement of religion that reimbursement for administering and grading them should not be permitted. * * *

Finally, entanglement also is fostered by the system of reimbursement for personnel expenses. The State must make sure that it reimburses sectarian schools only for those personnel costs attributable to the sectarian employees' secular ac-

tivities described in § 3 of Chapter 507. It is difficult to see how the State adequately may discover whether the time for which reimbursement is made available was devoted only to secular activities without some type of ongoing surveillance of the sectarian employees and religious schools at issue. It is this type of extensive entanglement that the Establishment Clause forbids. * * *

Mr. Justice STEVENS, dissenting.

Although I agree with Mr. Justice Blackmun's demonstration of why today's holding is not compelled by precedent, my vote also rests on a more fundamental disagreement with the Court. The Court's approval of a direct subsidy to sectarian schools to reimburse them for staff time spent in taking attendance and grading standardized tests is but another in a long line of cases making largely ad hoc decisions about what payments may or may not be constitutionally made to nonpublic schools. In groping for a rationale to support today's decision, the Court has taken a position that could equally be used to support a subsidy to pay for staff time attributable to conducting fire drills or even for constructing and maintaining fireproof premises in which to conduct classes. Though such subsidies might represent expedient fiscal policy, I firmly believe they would violate the Establishment Clause of the First Amendment.

The Court's adoption of such a position confirms my view, expressed in Wolman v. Walter, 433 U.S. 229, 264, 97 S.Ct. 2593, 2614 (Stevens, J., dissenting), and Roemer v. Board of Public Works, 426 U.S. 736, 775, 96 S.Ct. 2337, 2358 (Stevens, J., dissenting), that the entire enterprise of trying to justify various types of subsidies to nonpublic schools should be abandoned. Rather than continuing with the sisyphean task of trying to patch together the "blurred, indistinct, and variable barrier" described in Lemon v. Kurtzman, 403 U.S. 602, 614, 91 S.Ct. 2105, 2112, I would resurrect the "high and impregnable" wall between church and state constructed by the Framers of the First Amendment. See Everson v. Board of Education, 330 U.S. 1, 18, 67 S.Ct. 504, 512.

RECENT ESTABLISHMENT CLAUSE RULINGS

Case	Facts	Holding/Reasoning	Vote
National Labor Relations Board v. Catholic Bishop of Chicago, 440 U.S. 490, 99 S.Ct. 1313 (1979)	The National Labor Relations Board certified unions as bargaining agents for lay teachers in several church-operated schools. When school and church officials refused to recognize the unions, the board held hearings and ultimately directed school and church officials to cease and desist from their "unfair labor practices" and to recognize and bargain with the unions. A federal appeals court subsequently ruled that the First Amendment barred any exercise of NLRB jurisdiction over church-operated schools. The board argued that while its jurisdiction concededly did not extend to "completely religious" schools, it did include "religiously associated" schools, i.e., schools in which both religious and secular subjects were taught.	Church-operated schools which teach both religious and secular subjects are beyond the jurisdiction of the NLRB, and the board was therefore without authority to issue the orders. If the National Labor Relations Act conferred jurisdiction over church-operated schools, there would be significant risk of infringing the Religion Clauses of the First Amendment. Neither the language of the statute nor a canvass of its legislative history reveals any clear intention of Congress so to extend the board's jurisdiction, and, in the absence of any clearly expressed congressional intent to do so, the Court will not construe the act in such a way as to give rise to conflict implicating sensitive First Amendment questions.	5–4; Brennan, White, Marshall, and Blackmun dissented.
Stone v. Graham, 449 U.S. 39, 101 S.Ct. 192 (1980)	A Kentucky statute required the posting of a copy of the Ten Commandments, purchased with private funds, on the wall of	The statute violates the Establishment Clause because it has "no secular legislative purpose" and "is plainly religious in	5–4; Burger, Stewart, Blackmun, and Rehnquist dissented.

ESTABLISHMENT CLAUSE RULINGS (*Cont.*)

Case	Facts	Holding/Reasoning	Vote
Stone (*Cont.*)	every public school classroom throughout the state.	nature." Collision with the First Amendment could not be averted either by including in small print at the bottom of each display the statement that "The secular application of the Ten Commandments is clearly seen in its adoption as the fundamental legal code of Western Civilization and the Common Law of the United States" or by the fact that copies were provided by private funding. While some of the Commandments "confine themselves to arguably secular matters," others concern "the religious duties of believers." Here exhibition of the Commandments was not for educational purposes—in the sense of enhancing the study of history, comparative religion, or literature—but if it has any effect at all, "it will be to induce the schoolchildren to read, meditate upon, and perhaps to venerate and obey, the Commandments."	
Widmar v. Vincent, 454 U.S. 263, 102 S.Ct. 269 (1981)	Although a state university made its facilities generally available to registered student groups for their activities, a registered religious student group was denied access to university facilities because a university regulation prohibited	The university's exclusionary policy violates the fundamental First Amendment principle that governmental regulation of speech be content-neutral. Having created a forum open to registered student groups, the university cannot deny access based up-	8–1; White dissented.

ESTABLISHMENT CLAUSE RULINGS (*Cont.*)

Case	Facts	Holding/Reasoning	Vote
Widmar (*Cont.*)	the use of university buildings or grounds "for purposes of religious worship or religious teaching."	on the religious content of speech without demonstrating a compelling state interest. Although the university asserts that its regulation fulfills the compelling interest of preserving the separation of church and state, such is not the case because a policy of equal access to university facilities for all registered student groups—religious and secular alike—does not offend the three-pronged Establishment Clause test. The university concedes that an equal access policy has both a secular legislative purpose and would not foster "an excessive government entanglement with religion." Neither would a policy of *equal access* have the *primary* effect of either advancing or inhibiting religion.	
Larson v. Valente, — U.S. —, 102 S.Ct. 1673 (1982)	A provision of Minnesota's charitable contributions act specifies that only those religious organizations which receive more than half of their total contributions from members or affiliated organizations are exempt from the statute's registration and reporting requirements. The Unification Church argued that the statute was overbroad and therefore violative of the	This statute permits the very sort of denominational preference prohibited by the First Amendment and therefore must be evaluated according to strict scrutiny. Assuming for the sake of argument that the prevention of fraudulent solicitations constitutes a "compelling governmental interest," no substantial support has been demonstrated here for the three	5–4; Burger, White, Rehnquist, and O'Connor dissented.

ESTABLISHMENT CLAUSE RULINGS (*Cont.*)

Case	Facts	Holding/Reasoning	Vote
Larson (*Cont.*)	Establishment Clause of the First Amendment.	necessary premises upon which this legislation would appear to be based, i.e., "that members of a religious organization can and will exercise supervision and control over the organization's solicitation activities when membership contributions exceed fifty per cent; that membership control, assuming its existence, is an adequate safeguard against abusive solicitations of the public by the organization; and that the need for public disclosure rises in proportion with the *percentage* of non-member contributions." The excessive governmental entanglement component of the Establishment Clause test is particularly implicated in this statute. Where the act's registration and reporting requirements are imposed on some religious denominations and not on others, the "risk of politicizing religion" is obvious.	

In McLean v. Arkansas Board of Education, 529 F.Supp. 1255 (E.D.Ark.1982), a federal district court held unconstitutional a state statute aimed at affording equal time in the classroom for "creation science" when evolution is presented or discussed. The legislation was attacked in a suit by nonfundamentalist religious leaders and organizations, schoolchildren, and teachers as a violation of the Establishment Clause. "Creation science," as defined by the statute, "means the scientific evidences for creation and inferences from those scientific evidences." Included within this rubric are: "(1) Sudden creation of the universe, energy, and life from nothing; (2) The insufficiency of mutation and natural selection in bringing about development of all living kinds from a single organism; (3) Changes only within fixed limits of originally created kinds of plants and animals; (4) Separate ancestry for man and apes; (5) Explanation of the earth's geology by catastrophism, including the occurrence of a worldwide flood; and (6) A relatively recent inception of the earth and living kinds."

After surveying the history, tenets, and methods of "creation science" and noting parenthetically that Arkansas fundamentalists had tried previously to outlaw the teaching of evolution in public schools (a statutory undertaking held unconstitutional by the Supreme Court in Epperson v. Arkansas, 393 U.S. 97, 89 S.Ct. 266 [1968]), the district court concluded that "creation science * * * is simply not a science." The district court examined the half dozen tenets of "creation science" identified in the statute and found that they failed to accord with "the[se] essential characteristics of science": "(1) It is guided by natural law; (2) It has to be explanatory by reference to natural law; (3) It is testable against the empirical world; (4) Its conclusions are tentative, i.e., are not necessarily the final word; and (5) It is falsifiable. * * *" The court pointed out: "The methodology employed by creationists is another factor which is indicative that their work is not a science. A scientific theory must be tentative and always subject to revision or abandonment in light of facts that are inconsistent with, or falsify, the theory. A theory that is by its own terms dogmatic, absolutist and never subject to revision is not a scientific theory." The court added, "The creationists' methods do not take data, weigh it against the opposing scientific data, and thereafter reach * * * conclusions. * * * Instead, they take the literal wording of the Book of Genesis and attempt to find scientific support for it." Against this background and applying the three-part Establishment Clause test formulated in *Lemon* v. *Kurtzman*, the court reasoned as follows:

The conclusion that creation science has no scientific merit or educational value as science has legal significance in light of the Court's previous conclusion that creation science has, as one major effect, the advancement of religion. The second part of the three-pronged test for establishment reaches only those statutes having as their *primary* effect the advancement of religion. Secondary effects which advance religion are not constitutionally fatal. Since creation science is not science, the conclusion is inescapable that the *only* real effect of Act 590 is the advancement of religion. The Act therefore fails both the first and second portions of the test in *Lemon* v. *Kurtzman*, 403 U.S. 602, 91 S.Ct. 2105 (1971).

Act 590 mandates "balanced treatment" for creation science and evolution science. The Act prohibits instruction in any religious doctrine or references to religious writings. The Act is self-contradictory and compliance is impossible unless the public schools elect to forego significant portions of subjects such as biology, world history, geology, zoology, botany, psychology, anthropology, sociology, philosophy, physics and chemistry. Presently, the concepts of evolutionary theory * * * permeate the public school textbooks. There is no way teachers can teach the Genesis account of creation in a secular manner.

The State Department of Education, through its textbook selection committee, school boards and school administrators will be required to constantly monitor materials to avoid using religious references. The school boards, administrators and teachers face an impossible task. How is the teacher to respond to questions about a creation suddenly and out of nothing? How will a teacher explain the occurrence of a world-wide flood? How will a teacher explain the concept of a relatively recent age of the earth? The answer is obvious because the only source of this information is ultimately contained in the Book of Genesis.

References to the pervasive nature of religious concepts in creation science texts amply demonstrate why State entanglement with religion is inevitable under Act 590. Involvement of the State in screening texts for impermissible religious references will require State officials to make delicate religious judgments. The need to monitor classroom discussion in order to uphold the Act's prohibition against religious instruction will necessarily involve administrators in questions concerning religion. These continuing involvements of State officials in questions and issues of religion create an excessive and prohibited entanglement with religion. * * *

b. THE FREE EXERCISE OF RELIGIOUS BELIEF

THOMAS v. INDIANA EMPLOYMENT SECURITY REVIEW BOARD

Supreme Court of the United States, 1981
450 U.S. 707, 101 S.Ct. 1425, 67 L.Ed.2d 624

Thomas, a Jehovah's Witness, who was employed by the Blaw-Knox Foundry and Machinery Company, was transferred about a year after he was hired from the roll foundry, whose function was to fabricate sheet steel for industrial purposes, to a department that was engaged in the manufacture of turrets for military tanks. After checking to see whether it might be possible to transfer to another department that was not engaged in armaments production and finding that all of the other company departments were directly involved in the manufacture of weapons, Thomas asked for a layoff. When the request was denied, he quit, saying that he could not work on the production of weapons without violating his religious beliefs.

After leaving Blaw-Knox, he applied for unemployment compensation from the State of Indiana. At an administrative hearing on his application for benefits, the hearing referee determined: (1) that Thomas's religious beliefs specifically precluded work in weapons production; (2) that Thomas had indeed left work for religious reasons; and (3) that the reason Thomas had ended his employment was not a "good cause [arising] in connection with [his] work," as required by Indiana's unemployment compensation law. A state appellate court ordered the state review board to grant Thomas the benefits since to deny them would improperly burden his free exercise of religious belief. The Indiana Supreme Court, however, reversed this judgment and denied him the benefits on grounds: (1) that his decision to quit was "a personal-philosophical choice rather than a religious choice"; (2) that denying him unemployment compensation created only an indirect burden on his First Amendment right which was outweighed by the state's interest in preserving the financial integrity of the insurance fund and in not encouraging workers to leave their jobs for personal reasons; and (3) that awarding unemployment compensation to an individual who terminated his employment for reasons such as Thomas gave would violate the Establishment Clause. Thomas subsequently sought review of this decision by the U. S. Supreme Court.

Chief Justice BURGER delivered the opinion of the Court.

We granted certiorari to consider whether the State's denial of unemployment compensation benefits to the petitioner, a Jehovah's Witness who terminated his job because his religious beliefs forbade participation in the production of armaments, constituted a violation of his First Amendment right to free exercise of religion. * * *

* * *

The judgment under review must be examined in light of our prior decisions, particularly Sherbert v. Verner, 374 U.S. 398, 83 S.Ct. 1790 (1963).[b]

Only beliefs rooted in religion are protected by the Free Exercise Clause, which, by its terms, gives special protection to the exercise of religion. *Sherbert* v. *Verner,* supra; Wisconsin v. Yoder, 406 U.S. 205, 215–216, 92 S.Ct. 1526, 1533 (1971). The determination of what is a "religious" belief or practice is more often than not a difficult and delicate task, as the division in the Indiana Supreme Court attests. However, the resolution of that question is not to turn upon a judicial perception of the particular belief or practice in question; religious beliefs need not be acceptable, logical, consistent, or comprehensible to others in order to merit First Amendment protection.

In support of his claim for benefits, Thomas testified:

"Q. And then when it comes to actually producing the tank itself, hammering it out; that you will not do. * * *

"A. That's right, that's right when * * * I'm daily faced with the knowledge that these are tanks. * * *

* * *

"A. I really could not, you know, conscientiously continue to work with armaments. It would be against all of the * * * religious principles that * * * I have come to learn." * * *

Based upon this and other testimony, the referee held that Thomas "quit due to his religious convictions." The Review Board adopted that finding, and the finding is not challenged in this Court.

The Indiana Supreme Court apparently took a different view of the record. It concluded that "although the claimant's reasons for quitting were described as religious, it was unclear what his belief was, and what the religious basis of his belief was." In that court's view, Thomas had made a merely "personal philosophical choice rather than a religious choice."

In reaching its conclusion, the Indiana court seems to have placed considerable reliance on the facts that Thomas was "struggling" with his beliefs and that he was not able to "articulate" his belief precisely. It noted, for example, that Thomas

---

b. In that case, a Seventh Day Adventist was dismissed by her employer for refusing to work on Saturday, the Sabbath Day in her faith. When she was subsequently refused work at other textile plants because she would not work Saturdays, she made application for unemployment compensation benefits. The South Carolina Employment Security Commission denied her request for benefits because it found she was ineligible under a provision of the state unemployment compensation act which provided that one who is "able to work and * * * is available for work" cannot receive benefits "[i]f * * *

he has failed, without good cause * * * to accept available suitable work when offered him by the employment office or the employer." The Supreme Court, reversing a state court ruling upholding the commission's denial of benefits, found the asserted state interest ("a possibility that the filing of fraudulent claims by unscrupulous claimants feigning religious objections to Saturday work" might "dilute the unemployment compensation fund" and "also hinder the scheduling by employers of necessary Saturday work") insufficiently compelling to override Sherbert's First Amendment right.

admitted before the referee that he would not object to

"working for United States Steel or Inland Steel * * * produc[ing] the raw product necessary for the production of any kind of tank * * * [because I] would not be a direct party to whoever they shipped it to [and] would not be * * * chargeable in * * * conscience." * * *

The court found this position inconsistent with Thomas' stated opposition to participation in the production of armaments. But, Thomas' statements reveal no more than that he found work in the roll foundry sufficiently insulated from producing weapons of war. We see, therefore, that Thomas drew a line, and it is not for us to say that the line he drew was an unreasonable one. Courts should not undertake to dissect religious beliefs because the believer admits that he is "struggling" with his position or because his beliefs are not articulated with the clarity and precision that a more sophisticated person might employ.

The Indiana court also appears to have given significant weight to the fact that another Jehovah's Witness had no scruples about working on tank turrets; for that other Witness, at least, such work was "scripturally" acceptable. Intrafaith differences of that kind are not uncommon among followers of a particular creed, and the judicial process is singularly ill equipped to resolve such differences in relation to the Religion Clauses. One can, of course, imagine an asserted claim so bizarre, so clearly nonreligious in motivation, as not to be entitled to protection under the Free Exercise Clause; but that is not the case here, and the guarantee of free exercise is not limited to beliefs which are shared by all of the members of a religious sect. Particularly in this sensitive area, it is not within the judicial function and judicial competence to inquire whether the petitioner or his fellow worker more correctly perceived the commands of their common faith. Courts are not arbiters of scriptural interpretation.

The narrow function of a reviewing court in this context is to determine whether there was an appropriate finding that petitioner terminated his work because of an honest conviction that such work was forbidden by his religion. Not surprisingly, the record before the referee and the Review Board was not made with an eye to the microscopic examination often exercised in appellate judicial review. However, judicial review is confined to the facts as found and conclusions drawn. On this record, it is clear that Thomas terminated his employment for religious reasons.

More than 30 years ago, the Court held that a person may not be compelled to choose between the exercise of a First Amendment right and participation in an otherwise available public program. A state may not

"exclude individual Catholics, Lutherans, Mohammedans, Baptists, Jews, Methodists, Non-believers, Presbyterians, or the members of any other faith, because of their faith, or lack of it, from receiving the benefits of public welfare legislation." Everson v. Board of Education, 330 U.S. 1, 16, 67 S.Ct. 504, 511 (1947).

Later, in *Sherbert*, supra, the Court examined South Carolina's attempt to deny unemployment compensation benefits to a Sabbatarian who declined to work on Saturday.

In sustaining her right to receive benefits, the Court held:

"The ruling [disqualifying Mrs. Sherbert from benefits because of her refusal to work on Saturday in violation of her faith] forces her to choose between following the precepts of her religion and forfeiting benefits, on the one hand, and abandoning one of the precepts of her religion in order to accept work, on the other hand. Governmental imposition of such a burden puts the same kind of burden upon the free exercise of religion as would a fine imposed against [her] for her Saturday worship." * * *

The respondent Review Board argues, and the Indiana Supreme Court held, that the burden upon religion here is only the indirect consequence of public welfare legislation that the state clearly has authority to enact. "Neutral objective standards must be met to qualify for compensation." * * * Indiana requires applicants for unemployment compensation to show that they left work for "good cause in connection with the work." * * *

A similar argument was made and rejected in *Sherbert*, however. It is true that, as in *Sherbert*, the Indiana law does not *compel* a violation of conscience. But, "this is only the beginning, not the end, of our inquiry." * * * In a variety of ways we have said that "a regulation neutral on its face may, in its application, nonetheless offend the constitutional requirement for governmental neutrality if it unduly burdens the free exercise of religion." Wisconsin v. Yoder, 406 U.S. 205, 220, 92 S.Ct. 1526, 1535 (1972). * * *

Here, as in *Sherbert*, the employee was put to a choice between fidelity to religious belief or cessation of work; the coercive impact on Thomas is indistinguishable from *Sherbert*, where the Court held:

"[N]ot only is it apparent that appellant's declared ineligibility for benefits derives solely from the practices of her religion, but the pressure upon her to forego that practice is unmistakable." * * *

Where the state conditions receipt of an important benefit upon conduct proscribed by a religious faith, or where it denies such a benefit because of conduct mandated by religious belief, thereby putting substantial pressure on an adherent to modify his behavior and to violate his beliefs, a burden upon religion exists. While the compulsion may be indirect, the infringement upon free exercise is nonetheless substantial.

The State also contends that *Sherbert* is inapposite because, in that case, the employee was dismissed by the employer's action. But we see that Mrs. Sherbert was dismissed because she refused to work on Saturdays after the plant went to a six-day workweek. Had Thomas simply presented himself at the Blaw-Knox plant turret line but refused to perform any assigned work, it must be assumed that he, like Sherbert, would have been terminated by the employer's action, if no other work was available. In both cases, the termination flowed from the fact that the employment, once acceptable, became religiously objectionable because of changed conditions.

The mere fact that the petitioner's religious practice is burdened by a governmental program does not mean that an exemption accommodating his practice must be granted. The state may justify an inroad on religious liberty by showing that it is the least restrictive means of achieving some compelling state interest. However, it is still true that "[t]he essence of all that has been said and written on the subject is that only those interests of the highest order can overbalance legitimate claims to the free exercise of religion." Wisconsin v. Yoder, supra, 406 U.S., at 215, 92 S.Ct., at 1533.

The purposes urged to sustain the disqualifying provision of the Indiana unemployment compensation scheme are two-fold: (1) to avoid the widespread unemployment and the consequent burden on the fund resulting if people were permitted to leave jobs for "personal" reasons; and (2) to avoid a detailed probing by employers into job applicants' religious beliefs. These are by no means unimportant considerations. When the focus of the inquiry is properly narrowed, however, we must conclude that the interests advanced by the state do not justify the burden placed on free exercise of religion.

There is no evidence in the record to indicate that the number of people who find themselves in the predicament of choosing between benefits and religious beliefs is large enough to create "widespread unemployment," or even to seriously affect unemployment—and no such claim was advanced by the Review Board. Similarly, although detailed inquiry by employers into applicants' religious beliefs is undesirable, there is no evidence in the record to indicate that such inquiries will occur in Indiana, or that they have occurred in any of the states that extend benefits to people in the petitioner's position. Nor is there any reason to believe that the number of people terminating employment for religious reasons will be so great as to

motivate employers to make such inquiries.

Neither of the interests advanced is sufficiently compelling to justify the burden upon Thomas' religious liberty. Accordingly, Thomas is entitled to receive benefits unless, as the state contends and the Indiana court held, such payment would violate the Establishment Clause.

The respondent contends that to compel benefit payments to Thomas involves the state in fostering a religious faith. There is, in a sense, a "benefit" to Thomas deriving from his religious beliefs, but this manifests no more than the tension between the two Religious Clauses which the Court resolved in *Sherbert*:

"In holding as we do, plainly we are not fostering the 'establishment' of the Seventh Day Adventist religion in South Carolina, for the extension of unemployment benefits to Sabbatarians in common with Sunday worshippers reflects nothing more than the governmental obligation of neutrality in the face of religious differences, and does not represent that involvement of religious with secular institutions which it is the object of the Establishment Clause to forestall." Sherbert v. Verner, supra, 374 U.S., at 409, 83 S.Ct., at 1796.
* * *

Unless we are prepared to overrule *Sherbert*, supra, Thomas cannot be denied the benefits due him on the basis of the findings of the referee, the Review Board and the Indiana Court of Appeals that he terminated his employment because of his religious convictions.

Reversed.

Justice BLACKMUN joins [p]arts * * * of the Court's opinion. As to [other parts] * * * he concurs in the result.

Justice REHNQUIST, dissenting.

The Court today holds that the State of Indiana is constitutionally required to provide direct financial assistance to a person solely on the basis of his religious beliefs. Because I believe that the decision today adds mud to the already muddied waters of First Amendment jurisprudence, I dissent.

The Court correctly acknowledges that there is a "tension" between the Free Exercise and Establishment Clauses of the First Amendment of the United States Constitution. Although the relationship of the two clauses has been the subject of much commentary, the "tension" is a fairly recent vintage, unknown at the time of the framing and adoption of the First Amendment. The causes of the tension, it seems to me, are three-fold. First, the growth of social welfare legislation during the latter part of the 20th century has greatly magnified the potential for conflict between the two clauses, since such legislation touches the individual at so many points in his life. Second, the decision by this Court that the First Amendment was "incorporated" into the Fourteenth Amendment and thereby made applicable against the States, Stromberg v. California, 283 U.S. 359, 51 S.Ct. 532 (1931); Cantwell v. Connecticut, 310 U.S. 296, 60 S.Ct. 900 (1940), similarly multiplied the number of instances in which the "tension" might arise. The third, and perhaps most important, cause of the tension is our overly expansive interpretation of *both* clauses. By broadly construing both clauses, the Court has constantly narrowed the channel between the Scylla and Charybdis through which

any state or federal action must pass in order to survive constitutional scrutiny.

None of these developments could have been foreseen by those who framed and adopted the First Amendment. The First Amendment was adopted well before the growth of much social welfare legislation and at a time when the Federal Government was in a real sense considered a government of limited delegated powers. Indeed, the principal argument against adopting the Constitution *without* a "Bill of Rights" was not that such an enactment would be *undesirable* but that it was *unnecessary* because of the limited nature of the Federal Government. So long as the government enacts little social welfare legislation, as was the case in 1791, there are few occasions in which the two clauses may conflict. Moreover, as originally enacted, the First Amendment applied only to the Federal Government, not the government of the States. Barron v. Baltimore, 32 U.S. (7 Pet.) 243, 8 L.Ed. 672 (1933). The Framers could hardly anticipate *Barron* being superseded by the "selective incorporation" doctrine adopted by the Court, a decision which greatly expanded the number of statutes which would be subject to challenge under the First Amendment. Because those who drafted and adopted the First Amendment could not have foreseen either the growth of social welfare legislation or the incorporation of the First Amendment into the Fourteenth Amendment, we simply do not know how they would view the scope of the two clauses.

The decision today illustrates how far astray the Court has gone in interpreting the Free Exercise and Establishment Clauses of the First Amendment. Although the Court holds that a State is constitutionally required to provide direct financial assistance to persons solely on the basis of their religious beliefs and recognizes the "tension" between the two clauses, it does little to help resolve that tension or to offer meaningful guidance to other courts which must decide cases like this on a day-by-day basis. Instead, it simply asserts that there is no Establishment Clause violation here and leaves tension between the two Religion Clauses to be resolved on a case-by-case basis. As suggested above, however, I believe that the "tension" is largely of this Court's own making, and would diminish almost to the vanishing point if the clauses were properly interpreted.

Just as it did in Sherbert v. Verner, 374 U.S. 398, 83 S.Ct. 1790 (1963), the Court today reads the Free Exercise Clause more broadly

than is warranted. As to the proper interpretation of the Free Exercise Clause, I would accept the decision of Braunfeld v. Brown, 366 U.S. 599, 81 S.Ct. 1144 (1961),[c] and the dissent in *Sherbert*. In *Braunfeld*, we held that Sunday Closing laws do not violate the First Amendment rights of Sabbatarians. Chief Justice Warren explained that the statute did not make unlawful any religious practices of appellants; it simply made the practice of their religious beliefs more expensive. We concluded that "to strike down, without the most critical scrutiny, legislation which imposes only an indirect burden on the exercise of religion, *i.e.* legislation which does not make unlawful the religious practice itself, would radically restrict the operating latitude of the legislature." * * * Likewise in this case, it cannot be said that the State discriminated against

---

c. Braunfeld and other merchants brought suit against Philadelphia's police commissioner to enjoin enforcement of Pennsylvania's Sunday Closing Law. As Orthodox Jews whose religious tenets forbade conduct of any commercial activity each week from nightfall Friday until nightfall Saturday, they asserted that the additional prohibition of doing business on Sunday impaired their ability to earn a living and thus resulted in a penalty to them solely because of their religious beliefs. The Court affirmed a federal district court judgment dismissing the complaint. As a later opinion of the Court summarized the holding in *Braunfeld*: despite the fact that it made the plaintiffs' " 'religious beliefs more expensive' * * * the statute was nevertheless saved by a countervailing factor * * *—a strong state interest in providing one uniform day of rest for all workers. That secular objective could be achieved, the Court found, only by declaring Sunday to be that day of rest. Requiring exemptions for Sabbatarians, while theoretically possible, appeared to present an administrative problem of such magnitude, or to afford the exempted class so great a competitive advantage, that such a requirement would have rendered the

entire statutory scheme unworkable." Sherbert v. Verner, 374 U.S. 398, 408–409, 83 S.Ct. 1790, 1796 (1963). Speaking for a four-Justice plurality in *Braunfeld*, Chief Justice Warren wrote:
[T]he statute at bar does not make unlawful any religious practices of appellants; the Sunday law simply regulates a secular activity and, as applied to appellants, operates so as to make the practice of their religious beliefs more expensive. Furthermore, the law's effect does not inconvenience all members of the Orthodox Jewish faith but only those who believe it necessary to work on Sunday. And even these are not faced with as serious a choice as forsaking their religious practices or subjecting themselves to criminal prosecution. Fully recognizing that the alternatives open to appellants and others similarly situated—retaining their present occupations and incurring economic disadvantage or engaging in some other commercial activity which does not call for either Saturday or Sunday labor—may well result in some financial sacrifice in order to observe their religious beliefs, still the option is wholly different than when the legislation attempts to make a religious practice itself unlawful.

Thomas on the basis of his religious beliefs or that he was denied benefits *because* he was a Jehovah's Witness. Where, as here, a State has enacted a general statute, the purpose and effect of which is to advance the State's secular goals, the Free Exercise Clause does not in my view require the State to conform that statute to the dictates of religious conscience of any group. As Justice Harlan recognized in his dissent in Sherbert v. Verner, 374 U.S. 398, 83 S.Ct. 1790 (1963) "Those situations in which the Constitution may require special treatment on account of religion are * * * few and far between." Like him I believe that although a State could choose to grant exemptions to religious persons from state unemployment regulations, a State is not constitutionally compelled to do so. * * *

The Court's treatment of the Establishment Clause issue is equally unsatisfying. Although today's decision requires a State to provide direct financial assistance to persons solely on the basis of their religious beliefs, the Court nonetheless blandly assures us, just as it did in *Sherbert*, that its decision "plainly" does not foster the "establishment" of religion. * * * I would agree that the Establishment Clause, properly interpreted, would not be violated if Indiana voluntarily chose to grant unemployment benefits to those persons who left their jobs for religious reasons. But I also believe that the decision below is inconsistent with many of our prior Establishment Clause cases. Those cases, if faithfully applied, would require us to hold that such voluntary action by a State *did* violate the Establishment Clause.

Justice STEWART noted this point in his concurring opinion in *Sherbert*. * * * He observed that decisions like *Sherbert*, and the one rendered today, squarely conflict with the more extreme language of many of our prior Establishment Clause cases. In Everson v. Board of Education, 330 U.S. 1, 67 S.Ct. 504 (1961), the Court stated that the Establishment Clause bespeaks a "government * * * stripped of all power * * * to support, or otherwise to assist any or all religions * * *," and no State "can pass laws which aid one religion [or] all religions." * * * In Torcaso v. Watkins, 367 U.S. 488, 495, 81 S.Ct. 1680, 1683 (1961), the Court asserted that the government cannot "constitutionally pass laws or impose requirements which aid all religions as against non-believers." And in School District of Abington Township v. Schempp, 374 U.S. 203, 217, 83 S.Ct. 1560, 1568 (1963), the Court adopted Justice Rutledge's words in *Everson* that the Establishment Clause forbids "every form of public aid or support for religion." See also Engel v. Vitale, 370 U.S. 421, 431, 82 S.Ct. 1261, 1267 (1962).

In recent years the Court has moved away from the mechanistic "no-aid-to-religion" approach to the Establishment Clause and has stated a three-part test to determine the constitutionality of governmental aid to religion. See Lemon v. Kurtzman, 403 U.S. 602, 91 S.Ct. 2105 (1971); Committee for Public Education & Religious Liberty v. Nyquist, 413 U.S. 756, 772–773, 93 S.Ct. 2955, 2965 (1973). First, the statute must serve a secular legislative purpose. Second, it must have a "primary effect" that neither advances nor inhibits religion. And third, the State and its administration must avoid excessive entanglement with religion. Walz v.

Tax Commission, 397 U.S. 664, 90 S.Ct. 1409 (1970).

It is not surprising that the Court today makes no attempt to apply those principles to the facts of this case. If Indiana were to legislate what the Court today requires—an unemployment compensation law which permitted benefits to be granted to those persons who quit their jobs for religious reasons—the statute would "plainly" violate the Establishment Clause as interpreted in such cases as *Lemon* and *Nyquist*. First, although the unemployment statute as a whole would be enacted to serve a secular legislative purpose, the proviso would clearly serve only a religious purpose. It would grant financial benefits for the sole purpose of accommodating religious beliefs. Second, there can be little doubt that the primary effect on the proviso would be to "advance" religion by facilitating the exercise of religious belief. Third, any statute including such a proviso would surely "entangle" the State in religion far more than the mere grant of tax exemptions, as in *Walz*, or the award of tuition grants and tax credits, as in *Nyquist*. By granting financial benefits to persons solely on the basis of their religious beliefs, the State must necessarily inquire whether the claimant's belief is "religious" and whether it is sincerely held. Otherwise any dissatisfied employee may leave his job without cause and claim that he did so because his own particular beliefs required it.

It is unclear from the Court's opinion whether it has temporarily retreated from its expansive view of the Establishment Clause, or wholly abandoned it. I would welcome the latter. Just as I think that Justice Harlan in *Sherbert* correctly stated

the proper approach to free exercise questions, I believe that Justice Stewart, dissenting in School District v. Schempp, 374 U.S. 203, 204, 83 S.Ct. 1560, 1562 (1963), accurately stated the reach of the Establishment Clause. He explained that the Establishment Clause is limited to "government support of proselytizing activities of religious sects by throwing the weight of secular authorities behind the dissemination of religious tenets." See McCollum v. Board of Education, 333 U.S. 203, 248 68 S.Ct. 461, 483 (1948) (Reed, J., dissenting) (impermissible aid is only "purposeful assistance directly to the church itself or to some religious group * * * performing ecclesiastical functions.") Conversely, governmental assistance which does not have the effect of "inducing" religious belief, but instead merely "accommodates" or implements an independent religious choice does not impermissibly involve the government in religious choices and therefore does not violate the Establishment Clause of the First Amendment. I would think that in this case, as in *Sherbert*, had the state voluntarily chosen to pay unemployment compensation benefits to persons who left their jobs for religious reasons, such aid would be constitutionally permissible because it redounds directly to the benefit of the individual. Accord, Wolman v. Walter, 433 U.S. 229, 97 S.Ct. 2593 (1977) (upholding various disbursements made to pupils in parochial schools).

In sum, my difficulty with today's decision is that it reads the Free Exercise Clause too broadly and it fails to squarely acknowledge that such a reading conflicts with many of our Establishment Clause cases. As such, the decision simply exacerbates the "tension" between the two clauses. If the Court were to construe the Free Exercise Clause as it did in *Braunfeld* and the Establishment Clause as Justice Stewart did in *Schempp*, the circumstances in which there would be a conflict between the two clauses would be few and far between. Although I heartily agree with the Court's tacit abandonment of much of our rhetoric about the Establishment Clause, I regret that the Court cannot see its way clear to restore what was surely intended to have been a greater degree of flexibility to the federal and state governments in legislating consistently with the Free Exercise Clause. Accordingly, I would affirm the judgment of the Indiana Supreme Court.

In McDaniel v. Paty, 435 U.S. 618, 98 S.Ct. 1322 (1978), the Supreme Court struck down a Tennessee statute barring clergymen from serving as delegates to the state's constitutional convention. A provision of the state constitution, dating from the time Tennessee joined the Union, similarly banned clergymen from occupying seats in the state legislature. These prohibitions were intended to preserve the wall of separation between church and state. In a plurality opinion announcing the judgment of the Court, Chief Justice Burger concluded that the statute ran afoul of the First Amendment because it conditioned the right to hold public office upon the surrender of the right to freely exercise one's religion. Without passing on the question of whether the exclusion of the clergy from public office ever constituted permissible public policy, the plurality found that whatever may have been the anxieties of those eighteenth-century statesmen who fostered the idea behind the prohibition, "the American experience provides no persuasive support for the fear that clergymen in public office will be less careful of antiestablishment interests or less faithful to their oaths of civil office than their unordained counterparts." The plurality disclaimed any reliance on Torcaso v. Watkins, 367 U.S. 488, 81 S.Ct. 1680 (1961), which declared unconstitutional a provision of the Maryland constitution that required state officials, as a test of office, to declare a belief in the existence of God. The Chief Justice reasoned that while the holding in that case absolutely precluded the use of religious belief as a criterion for eligibility to hold public office, what was at issue in this case was not religious belief *per se* but conduct or status in the form of occupying a position as a clergyman.

Concurring in the judgment, Justice Brennan, joined by Justice Marshall, concluded that the Tennessee statute violated both the Free Exercise and the Establishment Clauses. As to the first ground, Justice Brennan found *Torcaso* dispositive "[b]ecause the challenged provision establishes as a condition of office the willingness to eschew certain protected religious practices * * *." Said Justice Brennan:

The plurality recognizes that *Torcaso* held "categorically forbid[den]," a provision disqualifying from political office on the basis of religious belief, but draws what I respectfully suggest is a sophistic distinction between that holding and Tennessee's disqualification provision. The purpose of the Tennessee provision is not to regulate activities associated with a ministry, such as dangerous snake-handling or human sacrifice, which the State validly could prohibit, but to bar from political office persons regarded as deeply committed to religious participation because of that participation—

participation itself not regarded as harmful by the State and which there-fore must be conceded to be protected. As the plurality recognizes, peti-tioner was disqualified because he "fill[ed] a 'leadership role in religion' and * * * 'dedicated [himself] to the full time *promotion* of the religious objectives of a particular religious sect.' 547 S.W.2d at 903 (emphasis added)." * * * According to the plurality, McDaniel could not be and was not in fact barred for *his* belief in religion, but was barred because of his commitment to persuade or lead others to accept that belief. I simply cannot fathom why the Free Exercise Clause "categorically forbids" hing-ing qualification for office on the *act* of declaring a belief in religion, but not on the act of discussing that belief with others. * * *

And with respect to the violation of the Establishment Clause, Justice Brennan wrote that "the exclusion manifests patent hostility toward, not neutrality in respect of, religion, forces or influences a minister or priest to abandon his minis-try as the price of public office, and in sum, has a primary effect which inhibits religion." In a separate opinion concurring in the judgment, Justice Stewart endorsed Justice Brennan's position on the Free Exercise question, saying he believed "that *Torcaso* * * * controls this case."

In another opinion concurring in the judgment, Justice White rested his deci-sion against the Tennessee statute on the grounds that it violated the Equal Pro-tection Clause. Justice White observed that the statute was fatally flawed because it erected an irrebuttable presumption against fitness for public office which could not survive strict scrutiny. He justified reliance upon the strict scru-tiny standard by analogizing the deprivation here to cases in which state legisla-tion *absolutely* excluded individuals from a position on the ballot. Justice Blackmun did not participate in the decision.

WISCONSIN v. YODER

Supreme Court of the United States, 1972
406 U.S. 205, 92 S.Ct. 1526, 32 L.Ed.2d 15

Wisconsin law compels children to attend either public or private school until they are sixteen years old. Yoder and other members of the Amish Church, how-ever, refused to send their children, ages fourteen and fifteen, to school beyond the eighth grade. Subsequent to a complaint filed by an administrator of the local school district, a county court found Yoder and the other parents to be in viola-tion of the law and fined them five dollars each. In response to the charges the parents asserted that the compulsory school attendance law violated their First and Fourteenth Amendment rights, and the state stipulated to the sincerity of the defendants' beliefs that they risked not only censure by their community but the prospect of salvation for themselves and their children by continuing to send them to school. The Wisconsin Supreme Court reversed the convictions, and the state sought review by the U. S. Supreme Court.

Mr. Chief Justice BURGER deliv-ered the opinion of the Court.

* * *

Amish objection to formal educa-tion beyond the eighth grade is firm-ly grounded in these central religious concepts. They object to the high school and higher education general-ly because the values it teaches are in marked variance with Amish val-ues and the Amish way of life; they view secondary school education as an impermissible exposure of their children to a "worldly" influence in conflict with their beliefs. The high school tends to emphasize intellectual and scientific accomplishments, self-distinction, competitiveness, worldly success, and social life with other students. Amish society emphasizes informal learning-through-doing, a life of "goodness," rather than a life of intellect, wisdom, rather than technical knowledge, community welfare rather than competition, and separation, rather than integration with contemporary worldly society.

Formal high school education beyond the eighth grade is contrary to Amish beliefs not only because it places Amish children in an environment hostile to Amish beliefs with increasing emphasis on competition in class work and sports and with pressure to conform to the styles, manners and ways of the peer group, but because it takes them away from their community, physically and emotionally, during the crucial and formative adolescent period of life. During this period, the children must acquire Amish attitudes favoring manual work and self-reliance and the specific skills needed to perform the adult role of an Amish farmer or housewife. They must learn to enjoy physical labor. Once a child has learned basic reading, writing, and elementary mathematics, these traits, skills, and attitudes admittedly fall within the category of those best learned through example and "doing" rather than in a classroom. And, at this time in life, the Amish child must also grow in his faith and his relationship to the Amish community if he is to be prepared to accept the heavy obligations imposed by adult baptism. * * *

The Amish do not object to elementary education through the first eight grades as a general proposition because they agree that their children must have basic skills in the "three R's" in order to read the Bible, to be good farmers and citizens and to be able to deal with non-Amish people when necessary in the course of daily affairs. They view such a basic education as acceptable because it does not significantly expose their children to worldly values or interfere with their development in the Amish community during the crucial adolescent period. * * * In the Amish belief higher learning tends to develop values they reject as influences that alienate man from God.

On the basis of such considerations, [an expert witness] testified that compulsory high school attendance could not only result in great psychological harm to Amish children, because of the conflicts it would produce, but would, in his opinion, ultimately result in the destruction of the Old Order Amish church community as it exists in the United States today. * * * [Another expert witness] described their system of learning-through-doing the skills directly relevant to their adult roles in the Amish community as "ideal" and perhaps superior to ordinary high school education. The evidence also showed that the Amish have an excellent record as law-abiding and generally self-sufficient members of society.

* * *

[A] State's interest in universal education, however highly we rank it, is not totally free from a balancing process when it impinges on other fundamental rights and interests, such as those specifically protected by the Free Exercise Clause of the First Amendment. * * *

It follows that in order for Wisconsin to compel school attendance beyond the eighth grade against a claim that such attendance interferes with the practice of a legitimate religious belief, it must appear either that the State does not deny the free exercise of religious belief by its requirement, or that there is a state interest of sufficient magnitude to override the interest claiming protection under the Free Exercise Clause. * * *

The essence of all that has been said and written on the subject is that only those interests of the highest order and those not otherwise served can overbalance legitimate claims to the free exercise of religion. We can accept it as settled, therefore, that however strong the State's interest in universal compulsory education, it is by no means absolute to the exclusion or subordination of all other interests. * * *

* * * In evaluating * * * claims [at issue here] we must be careful to determine whether the Amish religious faith and their mode of life are, as they claim, inseparable and interdependent. A way of life, however virtuous and admirable, may not be interposed as a barrier to reasonable state regulation of education if it is based on purely secular considerations; to have the protection of the Religion Clauses, the claims must be rooted in religious belief. Although a determination of what is a "religious" belief or practice entitled to constitutional protection may present a most delicate question, the very concept of ordered liberty precludes allowing every person to make his own standards on matters of conduct in which society as a whole has important interests. Thus, if the Amish asserted their claims because of their subjective

evaluation and rejection of the contemporary secular values accepted by the majority, much as Thoreau rejected the social values of his time and isolated himself at Walden Pond, their claim would not rest on a religious basis. Thoreau's choice was philosophical and personal rather than religious, and such belief does not rise to the demands of the Religion Clause.

Giving no weight to such secular considerations, however, we see that the record in this case abundantly supports the claim that the traditional way of life of the Amish is not merely a matter of personal preference, but one of deep religious conviction, shared by an organized group, and intimately related to daily living. * * *

[T]he unchallenged testimony of acknowledged experts in education and religious history, almost 300 years of consistent practice, and strong evidence of a sustained faith pervading and regulating respondents' entire mode of life support the claim that enforcement of the State's requirement of compulsory formal education after the eighth grade would gravely endanger if not destroy the free exercise of respondents' religious beliefs.

* * *

We turn, then to the State's broader contention that its interest in its system of compulsory education is so compelling that even the established religious practices of the Amish must give way. Where fundamental claims of religious freedom are at stake, however, we cannot accept such a sweeping claim; despite its admitted validity in the generality of cases, we must searchingly examine the interests which the State seeks to promote by its requirement

for compulsory education to age 16, and the impediment to those objectives that would flow from recognizing the claimed Amish exemption.
* * *

The State advances two primary arguments in support of its system of compulsory education. It notes, as Thomas Jefferson pointed out early in our history, that some degree of education is necessary to prepare citizens to participate effectively and intelligently in our open political system if we are to preserve freedom and independence. Further, education prepares individuals to be self-reliant and self-sufficient participants in society. We accept these propositions.

However, the evidence adduced by the Amish in this case is persuasively to the effect that an additional one or two years of formal high school for Amish children in place of their long established program of informal vocational education would do little to serve those interests.
* * * It is one thing to say that compulsory education for a year or two beyond the eighth grade may be necessary when its goal is the preparation of the child for life in modern society as the majority live, but it is quite another if the goal of education be viewed as the preparation of the child for life in the separated agrarian community that is the keystone of the Amish faith. * * *

* * *

Contrary to the suggestion of the dissenting opinion of Mr. Justice DOUGLAS, our holding today in no degree depends on the assertion of the religious interest of the child as contrasted with that of the parents. It is the parents who are subject to prosecution here for failing to cause their children to attend school, and it

is their right of free exercise, not that of their children, that must determine Wisconsin's power to impose criminal penalties on the parent. The dissent argues that a child who expresses a desire to attend public high school in conflict with the wishes of his parents should not be prevented from doing so. There is no reason for the Court to consider that point since it is not an issue in the case. The children are not parties to this litigation. The State has at no point tried this case on the theory that respondents were preventing their children from attending school against their expressed desires, and indeed the record is to the contrary.
* * *

Our holding in no way determines the proper resolution of possible competing interests of parents, children, and the State in an appropriate state court proceeding in which the power of the State is asserted on the theory that Amish parents are preventing their minor children from attending high school despite their expressed desires to the contrary. Recognition of the claim of the State in such a proceeding would, of course, call into question traditional concepts of parental control over the religious upbringing and education of their minor children recognized in this Court's past decisions. It is clear that such an intrusion by a State into family decisions in the area of religious training would give rise to grave questions of religious freedom. * * * On this record we neither reach nor decide those issues.

* * *

For the reasons stated we hold, with the Supreme Court of Wisconsin, that the First and Fourteenth Amendments prevent the State from compelling respondents to cause their children to attend formal high school to age 16. * * *

* * *

Affirmed.

Mr. Justice POWELL and Mr. Justice REHNQUIST took no part in the consideration or decision of this case.

Mr. Justice DOUGLAS, dissenting in part.

* * * The Court's analysis assumes that the only interests at stake in the case are those of the Amish parents on the one hand, and those of the State on the other. The difficulty with this approach is that, despite the Court's claim, the parents are seeking to vindicate not only their own free exercise claims, but also those of their high-school-age children.

* * *

* * * If the parents in this case are allowed a religious exemption, the inevitable effect is to impose the parents' notions of religious duty upon their children. Where the child is mature enough to express potentially conflicting desires, it would be an invasion of the child's rights to permit such an imposition without canvassing his views. * * * As the child has no other effective forum, it is in this litigation that his rights should be considered. And, if an Amish child desires to attend high school, and is mature enough to have that desire respected, the State may well be able to override the parents' religiously motivated objections.

Religion is an individual experience. It is not necessary, nor even appropriate, for every Amish child to express his views on the subject in a prosecution of a single adult. Cru-

cial, however, are the views of the child whose parent is the subject of the suit. Frieda Yoder has in fact testified that her own religious views are opposed to high-school education. I therefore join the judgment of the Court as to respondent Jonas Yoder. But Frieda Yoder's views may not be those of [the other children whose parents are involved here].

* * *

On this important and vital matter of education, I think the children should be entitled to be heard. While the parents, absent dissent, normally speak for the entire family, the education of the child is a matter on which the child will often have decided views. He may want to be a pianist or an astronaut or an ocean geographer. To do so he will have to break from the Amish tradition.

It is the future of the student, not the future of the parents, that is imperilled in today's decision. If a parent keeps his child out of school beyond the grade school, then the child will be forever barred from entry into the new and amazing world of diversity that we have today. The child may decide that that is the preferred course, or he may rebel. It is the student's judgment, not his parent's, that is essential if we are to give full meaning to what we have said about the Bill of Rights and of the right of students to be masters of their own destiny. If he is harnessed to the Amish way of life by those in authority over him and if his education in truncated, his entire life may be stunted and deformed. The child, therefore, should be given an opportunity to be heard before the State gives the exemption which we honor today.

* * *

Lee, a self-employed farmer and carpenter and a member of the Old Order Amish, employed several other Amish to work on his farm and in his carpentry shop but failed to withhold social security tax from their wages or to contribute the employer's share or to file quarterly social security tax returns. When the government assessed him $27,000 in unpaid employment taxes, he sued, defending his failure to comply on grounds that the Amish believe it is sinful not to provide for their own elderly and needy and, therefore, are religiously opposed to the Social Security System. A federal district court upheld Lee's claim, relying in part on the First Amendment, and the government directly appealed to the Supreme Court.

Speaking for the Court in United States v. Lee, 252 U.S. 455, 102 S.Ct. 1051 (1982), Chief Justice Burger wrote:

> The conclusion that there is a conflict between the Amish faith and the obligations imposed by the social security system is only the beginning, however, and not the end of the inquiry. Not all burdens on religion are unconstitutional. * * * The state may justify a limitation on religious liberty by showing that it is essential to accomplish an overriding governmental interest. *Thomas* [v. Review Bd. of Indiana Employment Sec., 450 U.S. 707, 101 S.Ct. 1425 (1981)] * * *; Wisconsin v. Yoder, 406 U.S. 205, 92 S.Ct. 1526 (1972). * * *
>
> Because the social security system is nationwide, the governmental interest is apparent. The social security system in the United States serves the public interest by providing a comprehensive insurance system with a variety of benefits available to all participants, with costs shared by employers and employees. The social security system is by far the largest domestic governmental program in the United States today, distributing approximately $11 billion monthly to 36 million Americans. The design of the system requires support by mandatory contributions from covered employers and employees. This mandatory participation is indispensable to the fiscal vitality of the social security system. "[W]idespread individual voluntary coverage under social security * * * would undermine the soundness of the social security program." S.Rep.No. 404, 89th Cong., 1st Sess., Pt. III, U.S.Code Cong. & Admin.News (1965), pp. 1943, 2056. Moreover, a comprehensive national social security system providing for voluntary participation would be almost a contradiction in terms and difficult, if not impossible, to administer. Thus, the government's interest in assuring mandatory and continuous participation in and contribution to the social security system is very high.
>
> The remaining inquiry is whether accommodating the Amish belief will unduly interfere with fulfillment of the governmental interest. In Braunfeld v. Brown, 366 U.S. 599, 605, 81 S.Ct. 1144, 1146 (1961), this Court noted that "to make accommodation between the religious action and an exercise of state authority is a particularly delicate task * * * because resolution in favor of the State results in the choice to the individual of either abandoning his religious principle or facing * * * prosecution." The difficulty in attempting to accommodate religious beliefs in the area of taxation is that "we are a cosmopolitan nation made up of people of almost every conceivable religious preference." * * * The Court has long recognized that balance must be struck between the values of the comprehensive social system, which rests on a complex of actuarial factors, and the consequences of allowing religiously based exemptions. To maintain an

organized society that guarantees religious freedom to a great variety of faiths requires that some religious practices yield to the common good. Religious beliefs can be accommodated, * * * but there is a point at which accommodation would "radically restrict the operating latitude of the legislature." * * *

Unlike the situation presented in *Wisconsin* v. *Yoder*, supra, it would be difficult to accommodate the comprehensive social security system with myriad exceptions flowing from a wide variety of religious beliefs. The obligation to pay the social security tax initially is not fundamentally different from the obligation to pay income taxes; the difference—in theory at least—is that the social security tax revenues are segregated for use only in furtherance of the statutory program. There is no principled way, however, for purposes of this case, to distinguish between general taxes and those imposed under the Social Security Act. If, for example, a religious adherent believes war is a sin, and if a certain percentage of the federal budget can be identified as devoted to war-related activities, such individuals would have a similarly valid claim to be exempt from paying that percentage of the income tax. The tax system could not function if denominations were allowed to challenge the tax system because tax payments were spent in a manner that violates their religious belief. * * * Because the broad public interest in maintaining a sound tax system is of such a high order, religious belief in conflict with the payment of taxes affords no basis for resisting the tax.

Congress has accommodated, to the extent compatible with a comprehensive national program, the practices of those who believe it a violation of their faith to participate in the social security system. In [26 U.S.C.A.] § 1402(g) Congress granted an exemption, on religious grounds, to self-employed Amish and others. Confining the § 1402(g) exemption to the self-employed provided for a narrow category which was readily identifiable. Self-employed persons in a religious community having its own "welfare" system are distinguishable from the generality of wage earners employed by others.

Congress and the courts have been sensitive to the needs flowing from the Free Exercise Clause, but every person cannot be shielded from all the burdens incident to exercising every aspect of the right to practice religious beliefs. When followers of a particular sect enter into commercial activity as a matter of choice, the limits they accept on their own conduct as a matter of conscience and faith are not to be superimposed on the statutory schemes which are binding on others in that activity. Granting an exemption from social security taxes to an employer operates to impose the employer's religious faith on the employees. Congress drew a line in § 1402(g), exempting the self-employed Amish but not all persons working for an Amish employer. The tax imposed on employers to support the social security system must be uniformly applicable to all, except as Congress provides explicitly otherwise.

* * *

Justice Stevens rejected the application of the "compelling interest" test in such cases and was of the view that, since "the Amish have demonstrated their capacity to care for their own, the social cost of eliminating this relatively small group of dedicated believers would be minimal," the government had not met its burden of proof under that standard. Instead, he believed that "it is the objector who must shoulder the burden of demonstrating that there is a unique reason for allowing him special exemption from a valid law of general applicability." In light of "the difficulties associated with processing other claims to tax exemption on religious grounds * * *" Justice Stevens concluded that "there is virtually no room for a 'constitutionally-required exemption' on religious grounds from a valid tax law that is entirely neutral in its general application."

STATE EX REL. SWANN v. PACK

Supreme Court of Tennessee, 1975
527 S.W.2d 99

Swann, a district attorney general, brought suit against Pack, pastor of The Holiness Church of God in Jesus Name, to enjoin the sect from engaging in its religious practice of handling poisonous snakes on grounds such activity constituted a public nuisance in violation of a state statute prohibiting the handling or exhibition of poisonous snakes "in such a manner as to endanger the life and health of any person." The state also sought to bar the church from the use of strychnine or other poisonous medicines. The suit was prompted by a church ritual at which a boy had been bitten by a snake and two church members died after consuming strychnine. The trial court enjoined the church from engaging in these practices, but a state appellate court later held this ruling to be overbroad and narrowed the order to forbid the handling or exhibition of poisonous snakes only to individuals who did not consent. The state then sought review by the Tennessee Supreme Court.

HENRY, Justice.

We granted certiorari in this case to determine whether the State of Tennessee may enjoin a religious group from handling snakes as a part of its religious service and in accordance with its Articles of Faith, on the basis of such action constituting a public nuisance.

*   *   *

[T]his is not a conventional religious group and its members are few. There is, however, no requirement under our State or Federal Constitution that any religious group be conventional or that it be numerically strong in order that its activities be protected. Nor is there any requirement that its practices be in accord with prevailing views.

*   *   *

A "mode of worship", even of a religious group wherein the handling of serpents is central to its Articles of Faith, is constitutionally protected under the Constitutions of Tennessee and of the United States.

*   *   *

Under our constitutions, a citizen may be a devout Christian, a dedicated Jew or a consummate infidel—or he may be a member of the Holiness Church of God in Jesus Name. The government must view all citizens and all religious beliefs with absolute and uncompromising neutrality. The day this Country ceases to countenance irreligion or unusual or bizarre religions, it will cease to be free for all religions. We must prefer none and disparage none.

We, therefore, hold that the Holiness Church of God in Jesus Name, is a constitutionally protected religious group.

This is not to say, however, that this or any other religious group has an absolute and unbridled right to pursue any practice of its own choosing. The right to believe is absolute; the right to act is subject to reasonable regulation designed to protect a compelling state interest. This belief-action dichotomy has been the subject of numerous decisions of the Supreme Court of the United States.

An early case dealing with the belief-action dichotomy is Reynolds v. United States, 98 U.S. 145, 25 L.Ed. 244 (1878), wherein the defendant, a member of the Church of Jesus Christ of Latter-Day Saints, commonly called the Mormon Church, was indicted for polygamy and defended upon the ground that, under his religious faith, it was his duty to practice polygamy. In disposing of this contention and in holding that a religious belief cannot be a justification for a criminal violation, the Court said:

Laws are made for the government of actions, and while they cannot interfere with mere religious belief and opinions, they may with practices. Suppose one believed that human sacrifices were a necessary part of religious worship, would it be seriously contended that the civil government under which he lived could not interfere to prevent a sacrifice? Or if a wife religiously believed it was her duty to burn herself upon the funeral pile [*sic*, pyre] of her dead husband, would it be beyond the power of the civil government to prevent her carrying her belief into practice?

So here, as a law of the organization of society under the exclusive dominion of the United States, it is provided that plural marriages shall not be allowed. Can a man excuse his practices to the contrary because of his religious belief? To permit this would be to make the professed doctrines of religious belief superior to the law of the land, and in effect to permit every citizen to become a law unto himself. Government could exist only in name under such circumstances. 98 U.S. 166, 167.

* * *

In Cantwell v. State of Connecticut, 310 U.S. 296, 60 S.Ct. 900 (1940), the Court succinctly stated the belief-action doctrine and simultaneously recognized the delicate balance which must be preserved, in these words:

Thus the Amendment embraces two concepts,—freedom to believe and freedom to act. The first is absolute but, in the nature of things, the second cannot be. Conduct remains subject to regulation for the protection of society. The freedom to act must have appropriate definition to preserve the enforcement of that protection. In every case the power to regulate must be so exercised as not, in attaining a permissible end, unduly to infringe the protected freedom. 310 U.S. 303, 304, 60 S.Ct. 903.

This was the first case to apply the "clear and present danger doctrine" in the context of First Amendment freedoms of religion, vis-à-vis a "substantial interest of the state." In this respect the Court said:

When *clear and present danger* of riot, disorder, interference with traffic upon the public steets, or other immediate threat to public safety, peace, or order, appears, the power of the state to prevent or punish is obvious. (Emphasis supplied) 310 U.S. 308, 60 S.Ct. 905.

* * *

We hold that under the First Amendment to the Constitution of the United States and under the substantially stronger provisions of Article 1, Section 3 of the Constitution of Tennessee, a religious practice may be limited, curtailed or restrained to the point of outright prohibition, where it involves a clear and present danger to the interests of society; but the action of the state must be reasonable and reasonably dictated by the needs and demands of society as determined by the nature of the activity as balanced against societal interests. Essentially, therefore, the problem becomes one of a balancing of the interests between religious freedom and the preservation of the health, safety and morals of society. The scales must be weighed in favor of religious freedom, and yet the balance is delicate.

The right to the free exercise of religion is not absolute and unconditional. Nor is its sweep susceptible of discrete and concrete compartmentalization. It is perforce, of necessity, a vague and nebulous notion, defying the certainties of definition and the niceties of description. At some point the freedom of the individual must wane and the power, duty and interest of the state becomes compelling and dominant.

Certain guidelines do, however, emerge under both constitutions.

Free exercise of religion does not include the right to violate statutory law.

It does not include the right to commit or maintain a nuisance.

The fact that one acts from the promptings of religious beliefs does not immunize against lawless conduct.

But, again, the scales are always weighted in favor of free exercise and the state's interest must be compelling; it must be substantial; the danger must be clear and present and so grave as to endanger paramount public interests.

* * *

This is a suit to abate a nuisance.

The right of the District Attorney General to institute and maintain such an action inheres in his office. It is his duty to investigate, prosecute and insure against all infractions of the public peace and all acts which are against the peace and dignity of the state.

We hold that the handling of snakes as a part of a religious ritual is a common law nuisance, wholly independent of any state statute.

* * *

In Yarbrough v. Louisville and Nashville Ry. Co., 11 Tenn.App. 456 (1930) a common law nuisance is defined as follows:

(a) nuisance in legal parlance, extends to everything that endangers life or health, gives offense to the senses, violates the laws of decency, or obstructs the reasonable or comportable use of property.

Under this record, showing as it does, the handling of snakes in a crowded church sanctuary, with virtually no safeguards, with children roaming about unattended, with the handlers so enraptured and entranced that they are in a virtual state of hysteria and acting under the compulsion of "anointment," we would be derelict in our duty if we did not hold that respondents and their confederates have combined and conspired to commit a public nuisance and plan to continue to do so. The human misery and loss of life at their "Homecoming" of April 7, 1970 is proof positive.

Our research confirms the general pattern.

Tennessee has the right to guard against the unnecessary creation of widows and orphans. Our state and nation have an interest in having a strong, healthy, robust, taxpaying citizenry capable of self-support and of bearing arms and adding to the resources and reserves of manpower. We, therefore, have a substantial and compelling state interest in the face of a clear and present danger so grave as to endanger paramount public interests.

It has been held that a state may compel polio shots, McCartney v. Austin, 57 Misc.2d 525, 293 N.Y.S.2d 188 (Sup.Ct.1968); may regulate child labor, Prince v. Massachusetts, 321 U.S. 158, 64 S.Ct. 438 (1944); may require compulsory chest x-rays, State ex rel. Holcomb v. Armstrong, 39 Wash.2d 860, 239 P.2d 545 (1955); may decree compulsory water fluoridation, Kraus v. City of Cleveland, 163 Ohio St. 559, 127 N.E.2d 609 (1955); may mandate vaccinations as a condition of school attendance, Wright v. Dewitt School District, 238 Ark. 906, 385 S.W.2d 644 (1965); and may compel medical care to a dying patient, Application of President and Directors of Georgetown College, Inc., 118 U.S. App.D.C. 80, 331 F.2d 1000 (1964).

This holding is in no sense dependent upon the way or manner in which snakes are handled since it is not based upon the snake handling statute. Irrespective of its import, we hold that those who publicly handle snakes in the presence of other persons and those who are present aiding and abetting are guilty of creating and maintaining a public nuisance. * * *

* * *

On remand the trial judge will enter an injunction perpetually enjoining and restraining all parties respondent from handling, displaying or exhibiting dangerous and poisonous snakes or from consuming strychnine or any other poisonous substances, within the confines of the State of Tennessee.

* * *

Reversed.

FONES, C. J., and COOPER, BROCK and HARBISON, JJ., concurring.

UNITED STATES v. BALLARD

Supreme Court of the United States, 1944
322 U.S. 78, 64 S.Ct. 882, 88 L.Ed. 1148

The facts are set out in the Court's opinion below, and additional background appears in Justice Jackson's dissent.

———————

Mr. Justice DOUGLAS delivered the opinion of the Court.

Respondents were indicted and convicted for using, and conspiring to use, the mails to defraud. * * * The indictment was in twelve counts.

It charged a scheme to defraud by organizing and promoting the I Am movement through the use of the mails. The charge was that certain designated corporations were formed, literature distributed and

sold, funds solicited, and memberships in the I Am movement sought "by means of false and fraudulent representations, pretenses and promises." The false representations charged were eighteen in number. It is sufficient at this point to say that they covered respondents' alleged religious doctrines or beliefs.
* * *

Each of the representations enumerated in the indictment was followed by the charge that respondents "well knew" it was false.
* * *

* * *

[In statements to the jury, the trial judge said in part:]

"First, the defendants in this case made certain representations of belief in a divinity and in a supernatural power. Some of the teachings of the defendants' representations, might seem extremely improbable to a great many people. For instance, the appearance of Jesus to dictate some of the works that we have had introduced in evidence, as testified to here at the opening transcription, or shaking hands with Jesus, to some people that might seem highly improbable. I point that out as one of the many statements.

"Whether that is true or not is not the concern of this Court and is not the concern of the jury—and they are going to be told so in their instructions. As far as this Court sees the issue, it is immaterial what these defendants preached or wrote or taught in their classes. They are not going to be permitted to speculate on the actuality of the happening of those incidents. Now, I think I have made that as clear as I can. Therefore, the religious beliefs of

these defendants cannot be an issue in this court.

"The issue is: Did these defendants honestly and in good faith believe those things? If they did, they should be acquitted. I cannot make it any clearer than that."

* * *

The Circuit Court of Appeals reversed the judgment of conviction and granted a new trial, one judge dissenting. 138 F.2d 540. * * *

[T]he Circuit Court of Appeals held that the question of the truth of the representations concerning respondent's religious doctrines or beliefs should have been submitted to the jury. And it remanded the case for a new trial. It may be that the Circuit Court of Appeals took that action because it did not think that the indictment could be properly construed as charging a scheme to defraud by means other than misrepresentations of respondents' religious doctrines or beliefs. Or that court may have concluded that the withdrawal of the issue of the truth of those religious doctrines or beliefs was unwarranted because it resulted in a substantial change in the character of the crime charged. But on whichever basis that court rested its action, we do not agree that the truth or verity of respondents' religious doctrines or beliefs should have been submitted to the jury. Whatever this particular indictment might require, the First Amendment precludes such a course, as the United States seems to concede. "The law knows no heresy, and is committed to the support of no dogma, the establishment of no sect." * * * The First Amendment has a dual aspect. It not only "forestalls compulsion by law of the acceptance of any creed or the practice of any form of worship" but also "safeguards the free exercise of the chosen form of religion." Cantwell v. State of Connecticut, 310 U.S. 296, 303, 60 S.Ct. 900, 903. "Thus the Amendment embraces two concepts,—freedom to believe and freedom to act. The first is absolute but, in the nature of things, the second cannot be." * * * Freedom of thought, which includes freedom of religious belief, is basic in a society of free men. * * * It embraces the right to maintain theories of life and of death and of the hereafter which are rank heresy to followers of the orthodox faiths. Heresy trials are foreign to our Constitution. Men may believe what they cannot prove. They may not be put to the proof of their religious doctrines or beliefs. Religious experiences which are as real as life to some may be incomprehensible to others. Yet the fact that they may be beyond the ken of mortals does not mean that they can be made suspect before the law. Many take their gospel from the New Testament. But it would hardly be supposed that they could be tried before a jury charged with the duty of determining whether those teachings contained false representations. The miracles of the New Testament, the Divinity of Christ, life after death, the power of prayer are deep in the religious convictions of many. If one could be sent to jail because a jury in a hostile environment found those teachings false, little indeed would be left of religious freedom. The Fathers of the Constitution were not unaware of the varied and extreme views of religious sects, of the violence of disagreement among them, and of the lack of any one religious creed on which all men would agree. They fashioned a charter of government which envisaged the widest possible toleration of conflicting views. Man's relation to his God was made no concern of the state. He was granted the right to worship as he pleased and to answer to no man for the verity of his religious views. The religious views espoused by respondents might seem incredible, if not preposterous, to most people, But if those doctrines are subject to trial before a jury charged with finding their truth or falsity, then the same can be done with the religious beliefs of any sect. When the triers of fact undertake that task, they enter a forbidden domain. The First Amendment does not select any one group or any one type of religion for preferred treatment. It puts them all in that position. * * * "With man's relations to his Maker and the obligations he may think they impose, and the manner in which an expression shall be made by him of his belief on those subjects, no interference can be permitted, provided always the laws of society, designed to secure its peace and prosperity, and the morals of its people, are not interfered with." * * * So we conclude that the District Court ruled properly when it withheld from the jury all questions concerning the truth or falsity of the religious beliefs or doctrines of respondents.

Respondents maintain that the reversal of the judgment of conviction was justified on other distinct grounds. The Circuit Court of Appeals did not reach those questions. * * * But since attention was centered on the issues which we have discussed, the remaining questions were not fully presented to this Court either in the briefs or oral argument. In view of these circumstances we deem it more appropriate to remand the cause to the Circuit

Court of Appeals so that it may pass on the questions reserved. * * *

* * *

Reversed.

Mr. Chief Justice STONE, dissenting.

I am not prepared to say that the constitutional guaranty of freedom of religion affords immunity from criminal prosecution for the fraudulent procurement of money by false statements as to one's religious experiences, more than it renders polygamy or libel immune from criminal prosecution. * * * I cannot say that freedom of thought and worship includes freedom to procure money by making knowingly false statements about one's religious experiences. To go no further, if it were shown that a defendant in this case had asserted as a part of the alleged fraudulent scheme, that he had physically shaken hands with St. Germain in San Francisco on a day named, or that, as the indictment here alleges, by the exertion of his spiritual power he "had in fact cured * * * hundreds of persons afflicted with diseases and ailments," I should not doubt that it would be open to the Government to submit to the jury proof that he had never been in San Francisco and that no such cures had ever been effected. In any event I see no occasion for making any pronouncement on this subject in the present case.

* * *

On the issue submitted to the jury in this case it properly rendered a verdict of guilty. As no legally sufficient reason for disturbing it appears, I think the judgment below should be reversed and that of the District Court reinstated.

Mr. Justice ROBERTS and Mr. Justice FRANKFURTER join in this opinion.

Mr. Justice JACKSON, dissenting.

I should say the defendants have done just that for which they are indicted. If I might agree to their conviction without creating a precedent, I cheerfully would do so. I can see in their teachings nothing but humbug, untainted by any trace of truth. But that does not dispose of the constitutional question whether misrepresentation of religious experience or belief is prosecutable; it rather emphasizes the danger of such prosecutions.

The Ballard family claimed miraculous communication with the spirit world and supernatural power to heal the sick. They were brought to trial for mail fraud on an indictment which charged that their representations were false and that they "well knew" they were false. The trial judge, obviously troubled, ruled that the court could not try whether the statements were untrue, but could inquire whether the defendants knew them to be untrue; and, if so, they could be convicted.

I find it difficult to reconcile this conclusion with our traditional religious freedoms.

* * *

Prosecutions of this character easily could degenerate into religious persecution. I do not doubt that religious leaders may be convicted of fraud for making false representations on matters other than faith or experience, as for example if one represents that funds are being used to construct a church when in fact they are being used for personal purposes. But that is not this case, which reaches into wholly dangerous ground. When does less than full belief in a professed credo become actionable fraud if one is soliciting gifts or legacies? Such inquiries may discomfort orthodox as well as unconventional religious teachers, for even the most regular of them are sometimes accused of taking their orthodoxy with a grain of salt.

I would dismiss the indictment and have done with this business of judicially examining other people's faiths.

In Heffron v. International Soc'y for Krishna Consciousness, Inc., 452 U.S. 640, 101 S.Ct. 2259 (1981), the Supreme Court addressed the question "whether a State, consistent with the First and Fourteenth Amendments, may require a religious organization desiring to distribute and sell religious literature and to solicit donations at a state fair to conduct those activities only at an assigned location within the fairgrounds even though application of the rule limits the religious practices of the organization." Specifically, the religious organization in this case argued that the rule, applicable to nonprofit, charitable, and commercial organizations alike, which required any exhibitor to conduct sales, literature distributions, and fund solicitations from rented booths at the Minnesota state fair, suppressed its "practice of Sankirtan, one of its religious rituals, which enjoins its members to go into public places to distribute or sell religious literature and so solicit donations for the support of the Krishna religion." Reversing the judgment of the Minnesota Supreme Court, the U. S. Supreme Court rejected the state supreme court's conclusions that the regulation unconstitutionally trenched upon the religious ritual of the Krishnas, that it was inadequately justified, and that the state's interests could be protected by means less restrictive of First Amendment rights.

Writing for the Court, Justice White found the rule to be an evenhanded, nondiscriminatory time, place, and manner regulation which advanced a substantial governmental interest in crowd control. Observing that this interest is even more important at a fair than it is in ensuring the movement of traffic on a public street, Justice White noted, "The Minnesota Fair * * * is a temporary event attracting great numbers of visitors who come to the event for a short period to see and experience the host of exhibits and attractions at the Fair. The flow of the crowd and demands of safety are more pressing in the context of the Fair." The Court also took notice of the fact that booths at the fair were allocated in a nondiscriminatory first-come, first-served fashion. Characterizing the fair as "a limited public forum," the Court rejected the argument that the state should have chosen a less restrictive approach, pointing out that the regulation did not bar the Krishnas from practicing Sankirtan outside the fairgrounds or from mingling with patrons inside the fair orally to propagate their beliefs.

Justices Brennan, Marshall, Blackmun, and Stevens concurred in part and dissented in part. They concluded that the three justifications offered by the state for the booth rule (maintaining the orderly movement of crowds at the fair, protecting fairgoers from deceptive or fraudulent solicitations, and protecting patrons as members of a "captive audience" from annoyance and harrassment) supported restrictions on sales and fund solicitations but could not constitutionally justify limitation on the distribution of literature.

Katz and four others, all twenty-one years old and followers of Rev. Sun Myung Moon's Unification church, popularly known as "Moonies," brought suit to

bar the enforcement of court orders appointing their respective parents as temporary conservators (guardians) of their persons and estates. Arguing that their
children had been "brainwashed" by the religious cult, the parents sought the
court orders to force their allegedly mesmerized offspring to submit to
"deprogramming." The parents asserted in their applications for conservatorship
(a legal procedure normally employed in those instances where an individual is
thought to be mentally incompetent and thus unable to manage his own affairs or
care for himself) that each of the proposed wards was "unable to properly care for
* * * [his] person or * * * property * * * and is likely to be deceived
by artful and designing persons." Katz and the other young adults argued that
such a basis for invoking the state's conservatorship laws was both unconstitutionally vague and a violation of the First Amendment's guarantee against the
infringement of religious belief.

Disposing of this controversy in Katz v. Superior Court, 73 Cal.App.3d 952, 141
Cal.Rptr. 234 (1977), a California appellate court ruled in favor of the "Moonies."
Addressing the vagueness contention first, the court observed that applications
for conservatorships were usually directed at individuals who were so incapaci-
tated as to lack the ability to manage their property. In this regard the court
pointed out that the relative clarity of the law in that context paled where the
behavior of the affected individual was motivated by religious belief:

> Although the words "likely to be decieved or imposed upon by artful or
> designing persons" may have some meaning when applied to the loss of
> property which can be measured, they are too vague to be applied in the
> world of ideas. In an age of subliminal advertising, television exposure,
> and psychological salesmanships, everyone is exposed to artful and design-
> ing persons at every turn. It is impossible to measure the degree of likeli-
> hood that some will succumb. In the field of beliefs, and particularly
> religious tenets, it is difficult, if not impossible, to establish a universal
> truth against which deceit and imposition can be measured.

The court concluded that "the evidence was insufficient to sustain a finding that
there was any emergency authorizing good cause for appointment of a temporary
conservator * * *." Said the court, "Here it is not the conservatee's estate
that is to be protected, but his mind." As to the law's provision for a guardian of
the persons (as distinguished from a concern principally with the protection of an
individual's property), the court noted that "[t]here is no real showing here that
the conservatees are physically unhealthy, or actually deprived of, or unable to
secure food, clothing and shelter." "Justification for the appointment," continued
the court, "can only be attributed to a necessity to secure treatment medical or
otherwise, which it cannot be gainsaid, is to affect the conservatee's mental
health." Speaking to this contention, the court said:

> If an adult person is less than gravely disabled we find no warrant for
> depriving him or her of liberty and freedom of action under either the for-
> mer provisions of the Probate Code, or the Welfare and Institutions Code.
> If there is coercive persuasion or brainwashing which requires treatment,
> the existence of such a mental disability and the necessity of legal control
> over the mentally disabled person for the purpose of treatment should be
> ascertained after compliance with the protection of civil liberties provided
> by the Welfare and Institutions Code. To do less is to license kidnaping for
> the purpose of thought control. We conclude that the provisions of the Pro-

bate Code could not be applied to justify the appointment of a conservator of the person on the evidence presented in this case.

Turning its attention to the second challenge pressed by the petitioners, the court delineated the conflicting claims as follows:

> As an alternative ground of decision we are asked to find that the temporary orders violated the conservatees' rights to freedom of religion and association under the federal and state Constitutions. * * * The parents claim that there is no freedom of action, freedom of religion, or freedom of assembly involved, that the sole issue is whether or not the conservatees have been deprived of their reasoning powers by artful and designing persons. On behalf of the conservatees it is urged that since an alleged religious group is involved, there can be no inquiry into the validity of the beliefs held by the members of that group, and the proceedings below trespassed into that field. We find that the law applicable to this case is not as myopic, but is more perceptive than the conservatees assert, and that the facts cannot be as simply interpreted as the parents contend.

The court went on to underscore certain precepts governing application of the Free Exercise Clause, notably that it absolutely bars government regulation of religious *beliefs* but that it permits regulation of certain overt acts even though they stem from religious beliefs. The court continued:

> [W]here does belief end and action begin? * * * Evidence was introduced of the actions of the proposed conservatees in changing their life style. When the court is asked to determine whether that change was induced by faith or by coercive persuasion is it not in turn investigating and questioning the validity of that faith? At the same time the trier of fact is asked to adjudge the good faith and bona fideness of the beliefs of the conservatees' preceptors. If it be assumed that certain leaders were using psychological methods to proselytize and hold the allegiance of recruits to the church or cult, call it what we will, can it be said their actions were not dictated by faith merely because others who engaged in such practices have recanted? The total picture disclosed must be tested by principles applicable to the regulation of acts of religious organizations and their members.

Such principles, the court observed, were not unlike those governing interference with political beliefs and associations. It continued, "The test of interference with action in the above fields, which are protected by the First Amendment, is a compelling state interest." In this light—and fully cognizant "that the state has an interest in the health of its citizens"—the court "conclude[d] that in the absence of such actions as render the adult believer himself gravely disabled as defined in the law of this state, the processes of this state cannot be used to deprive the believer of his freedom of action and to subject him to involuntary treatment."

Appendix A

A Time Chart of the United States Supreme Court

The following table is designed to aid the user in identifying the composition of the Court at any given time in American history. Each listing is headed by the Chief Justice, whose name is italicized. Associate Justices are listed following the Chief Justice in order of seniority. In addition to dates of appointment, the table provides information on political party affiliation. Following each Justice is a symbol representing his party affiliation at the time of appointment:

F = Federalist	W = Whig
DR = Democratic Republican (Jeffersonian)	R = Republican
	I = Independent
D = Democrat	

This chart will aid you in accounting for all of the votes cast in any of the major decisions included in this casebook. In order to identify how each Justice voted in a given case, find the listing of the Court's membership for the year in which the case was decided. The process of identifying the votes then proceeds by elimination: since all dissenting votes have been noted as well as any nonparticipations, all of the remaining members of the court can be counted as voting to join the judgment of the Court, although since all concurring opinions have not been included or noted throughout the casebook, all of the remaining Justices may not necessarily have also joined in the Opinion of the Court.

1789	1790–91	1792	1793–94
Jay (F)	*Jay* (F)	*Jay* (F)	*Jay* (F)
J. Rutledge (F)	J. Rutledge (F)	Cushing (F)	Cushing (F)
Cushing (F)	Cushing (F)	Wilson (F)	Wilson (F)
Wilson (F)	Wilson (F)	Blair (F)	Blair (F)
Blair (F)	Blair (F)	Iredell (F)	Iredell (F)
	Iredell (F)	T. Johnson (F)	Paterson (F)

1795	1807–10	1835	1845
J. Rutledge (F) [a]	*J. Marshall* (F)	*J. Marshall* (F)	*Taney* (D)
Cushing (F)	Cushing (F)	Duvall (DR)	McLean (D)
Wilson (F)	S. Chase (F)	Story (DR)	Wayne (D)
Blair (F)	Washington (F)	Thompson (DR)	Catron (D)
Iredell (F)	W. Johnson (DR)	McLean (D)	McKinley (D)
Paterson (F)	Livingston (DR)	Baldwin (D)	Daniel (D)
	Todd (DR)	Wayne (D)	Nelson (D)
1796–97			Woodbury (D)
Ellsworth (F)	**1811–22**		
Cushing (F)	*J. Marshall* (F)	**1836**	**1846–50**
Wilson (F)	Washington (F)	*Taney* (D)	*Taney* (D)
Iredell (F)	W. Johnson (DR)	Story (DR)	McLean (D)
Paterson (F)	Livingston (DR)	Thompson (DR)	Wayne (D)
S. Chase (F)	Todd (DR)	McLean (D)	Catron (D)
	Duvall (DR)	Baldwin (D)	McKinley (D)
1798–99	Story (DR)	Wayne (D)	Daniel (D)
Ellsworth (F)		Barbour (D)	Nelson (D)
Cushing (F)	**1823–25**		Woodbury (D)
Iredell (F)	*J. Marshall* (F)		Grier (D)
Paterson (F)	Washington (F)	**1837–40**	
S. Chase (F)	W. Johnson (DR)	*Taney* (D)	**1851–52**
Washington (F)	Todd (DR)	Story (DR)	*Taney* (D)
	Duvall (DR)	Thompson (DR)	McLean (D)
1800	Story (DR)	McLean (D)	Wayne (D)
Ellsworth (F)	Thompson (DR)	Baldwin (D)	Catron (D)
Cushing (F)		Wayne (D)	McKinley (D)
Paterson (F)	**1826–28**	Barbour (D)	Daniel (D)
S. Chase (F)	*J. Marshall* (F)	Catron (D)	Nelson (D)
Washington (F)	Washington (F)	McKinley (D)	Grier (D)
Moore (F)	W. Johnson (DR)		Curtis (W)
	Duvall (DR)		
1801–03	Story (DR)	**1841–43**	**1853–57**
J. Marshall (F)	Thompson (DR)	*Taney* (D)	*Taney* (D)
Cushing (F)	Trimble (DR)	Story (DR)	McLean (R) [b]
Paterson (F)		Thompson (DR)	Wayne (D)
S. Chase (F)	**1829**	McLean (D)	Catron (D)
Washington (F)	*J. Marshall* (F)	Baldwin (D)	Daniel (D)
Moore (F)	Washington (F)	Wayne (D)	Nelson (D)
	W. Johnson (DR)	Catron (D)	Grier (D)
1804–05	Duvall (DR)	McKinley (D)	Curtis (W)
J. Marshall (F)	Story (DR)	Daniel (D)	Campbell (D)
Cushing (F)	Thompson (DR)		
Paterson (F)	McLean (D)		**1858–60**
S. Chase (F)		**1844**	*Taney* (D)
Washington (F)	**1830–34**	*Taney* (D)	McLean (R)
W. Johnson (DR)	*J. Marshall* (F)	Story (DR)	Wayne (D)
	W. Johnson (DR)	McLean (D)	Catron (D)
1806	Duvall (DR)	Baldwin (D)	Daniel (D)
J. Marshall (F)	Story (DR)	Wayne (D)	Nelson (D)
Cushing (F)	Thompson (DR)	Catron (D)	Grier (D)
S. Chase (F)	McLean (D)	McKinley (D)	Campbell (D)
Washington (F)	Baldwin (D)	Daniel (D)	Clifford (D)
W. Johnson (DR)			
Livingston (DR)			

a Rutledge was a recess appointment whose confirmation was rejected by the Senate after the 1795 Term.

b After 1853–54 Justice McLean identified with the Republican Party. Although doubtless it was the case that he came to find far greater ideological compatibility with the Republican Party, especially given his pronounced anti-slavery views, it was equally true that he possessed an overwhelming ambition to be President. Although appointed to the Court when he was a Democrat, his four presidential candidacies demonstrated a remarkable freedom from the encumbrance of party loyalty. In his announced tries for a presidential nomination, McLean was respectively an anti-Mason (1832), an independent (1836), a Whig and Free Soiler (1852), and a Republican (1856).

1861 *Taney* (D) McLean (R) Wayne (D) Catron (D) Nelson (D) Grier (D) Campbell (D) Clifford (D)	**1867–69** *S. P. Chase* (R) Nelson (D) Grier (D) Clifford (D) Swayne (R) Miller (R) Davis (R) Field (D)	**1880** *Waite* (R) Clifford (D) Swayne (R) Miller (R) Field (D) Bradley (R) Hunt (R) Harlan (Ky.) (R) Woods (R)	**1890–91** *Fuller* (D) Field (D) Bradley (R) Harlan (Ky.) (R) Gray (R) Blatchford (R) L. Lamar (D) Brewer (R) Brown (R)
1862 *Taney* (D) Wayne (D) Catron (D) Nelson (D) Grier (D) Clifford (D) Swayne (R) Miller (R) Davis (R)	**1870–71** *S. P. Chase* (R) Nelson (D) Clifford (D) Swayne (R) Miller (R) Davis (R) Field (D) Strong (R) Bradley (R)	**1881** *Waite* (R) Miller (R) Field (D) Bradley (R) Hunt (R) Harlan (Ky.) (R) Woods (R) Matthews (R) Gray (R)	**1892** *Fuller* (D) Field (D) Harlan (Ky.) (R) Gray (R) Blatchford (R) L. Lamar (D) Brewer (R) Brown (R) Shiras (R)
1863 *Taney* (D) Wayne (D) Catron (D) Nelson (D) Grier (D) Clifford (D) Swayne (R) Miller (R) Davis (R) Field (D)	**1872–73** *S. P. Chase* (R) Clifford (D) Swayne (R) Miller (R) Davis (R) Field (D) Strong (R) Bradley (R) Hunt (R)	**1882–87** *Waite* (R) Miller (R) Field (D) Bradley (R) Harlan (Ky.) (R) Woods (R) Matthews (R) Gray (R) Blatchford (R)	**1893** *Fuller* (D) Field (D) Harlan (Ky.) (R) Gray (R) Blatchford (R) Brewer (R) Brown (R) Shiras (R) H. Jackson (D)
1864–65 *S. P. Chase* (R) Wayne (D) Catron (D) [c] Nelson (D) Grier (D) Clifford (D) Swayne (R) Miller (R) Davis (R) Field (D)	**1874–76** *Waite* (R) Clifford (D) Swayne (R) Miller (R) Davis (R) Field (D) Strong (R) Bradley (R) Hunt (R)	**1888** *Fuller* (D) Miller (R) Field (D) Bradley (R) Harlan (Ky.) (R) Matthews (R) Gray (R) Blatchford (R) L. Lamar (D)	**1894** *Fuller* (D) Field (D) Harlan (Ky.) (R) Gray (R) Brewer (R) Brown (R) Shiras (R) H. Jackson (D) E. White (D)
1866 *S. P. Chase* (R) Wayne (D) [c] Nelson (D) Grier (D) Clifford (D) Swayne (R) Miller (R) Davis (R) Field (D)	**1877–79** *Waite* (R) Clifford (D) Swayne (R) Miller (R) Field (D) Strong (R) Bradley (R) Hunt (R) Harlan (Ky.) (R)	**1889** *Fuller* (D) Miller (R) Field (D) Bradley (R) Harlan (Ky.) (R) Gray (R) Blatchford (R) L. Lamar (D) Brewer (R)	**1895–97** *Fuller* (D) Field (D) Harlan (Ky.) (R) Gray (R) Brewer (R) Brown (R) Shiras (R) E. White (D) Peckham (D)

c Upon the deaths of Catron in 1865 and Wayne in 1867 their positions were abolished according to a congressional act of 1866. The Court's membership was reduced to eight until a new position was created by Congress in 1869. The new seat has generally been regarded as a re-creation of Wayne's seat.

1898–1901	1910–11	1922	1937
Fuller (D)	*E. White* (D)	*Taft* (R)	*Hughes* (R)
Harlan (Ky.) (R)	Harlan (Ky.) (R)	McKenna (R)	McReynolds (D)
Gray (R)	McKenna (R)	Holmes (R)	Brandeis (R)
Brewer (R)	Holmes (R)	Van Devanter (R)	Sutherland (R)
Brown (R)	Day (R)	Pitney (R)	Butler (D)
Shiras (R)	Lurton (D)	McReynolds (D)	Stone (R)
E. White (D)	Hughes (R)	Brandeis (R)	Roberts (R)
Peckham (D)	Van Devanter (R)	Sutherland (R)	Cardozo (D)
McKenna (R)	J. Lamar (D)	Butler (D)	Black (D)
1902	**1912–13**	**1923–24**	**1938**
Fuller (D)	*E. White* (D)	*Taft* (R)	*Hughes* (R)
Harlan (Ky.) (R)	McKenna (R)	McKenna (R)	McReynolds (D)
Brewer (R)	Holmes (R)	Holmes (R)	Brandeis (R)
Brown (R)	Day (R)	Van Devanter (R)	Butler (D)
Shiras (R)	Lurton (D)	McReynolds (D)	Stone (R)
E. White (D)	Hughes (R)	Brandeis (R)	Roberts (R)
Peckham (D)	Van Devanter (R)	Sutherland (R)	Cardozo (D)
McKenna (R)	J. Lamar (D)	Butler (D)	Black (D)
Holmes (R)	Pitney (R)	Sanford (R)	Reed (D)
1903–05	**1914–15**	**1925–29**	**1939**
Fuller (D)	*E. White* (D)	*Taft* (R)	*Hughes* (R)
Harlan (Ky.) (R)	McKenna (R)	Holmes (R)	McReynolds (D)
Brewer (R)	Holmes (R)	Van Devanter (R)	Butler (D)
Brown (R)	Day (R)	McReynolds (D)	Stone (R)
E. White (D)	Hughes (R)	Brandeis (R)	Roberts (R)
Peckham (D)	Van Devanter (R)	Sutherland (R)	Black (D)
McKenna (R)	J. Lamar (D)	Butler (D)	Reed (D)
Holmes (R)	Pitney (R)	Sanford (R)	Frankfurter (I)
Day (R)	McReynolds (D)	Stone (R)	Douglas (D)
1906–08	**1916–20**	**1930–31**	**1940**
Fuller (D)	*E. White* (D)	*Hughes* (R)	*Hughes* (R)
Harlan (Ky.) (R)	McKenna (R)	Holmes (R)	McReynolds (D)
Brewer (R)	Holmes (R)	Van Devanter (R)	Stone (R)
E. White (D)	Day (R)	McReynolds (D)	Roberts (R)
Peckham (D)	Van Devanter (R)	Brandeis (R)	Black (D)
McKenna (R)	Pitney (R)	Sutherland (R)	Reed (D)
Holmes (R)	McReynolds (D)	Butler (D)	Frankfurter (I)
Day (R)	Brandeis (R) [d]	Stone (R)	Douglas (D)
Moody (R)	Clarke (D)	Roberts (R)	Murphy (D)
1909	**1921**	**1932–36**	**1941–42**
Fuller (D)	*Taft* (R)	*Hughes* (R)	*Stone* (R)
Harlan (Ky.) (R)	McKenna (R)	Van Devanter (R)	Roberts (R)
Brewer (R)	Holmes (R)	McReynolds (D)	Black (D)
E. White (D)	Day (R)	Brandeis (R)	Reed (D)
McKenna (R)	Van Devanter (R)	Sutherland (R)	Frankfurter (I)
Holmes (R)	Pitney (R)	Butler (D)	Douglas (D)
Day (R)	McReynolds (D)	Stone (R)	Murphy (D)
Moody (R)	Brandeis (R)	Roberts (R)	Byrnes (D)
Lurton (D)	Clarke (D)	Cardozo (D)	R. Jackson (D)

d According to Professor Henry Abraham, "Many—and with some justice—consider Brandeis a Democrat; however, he was in fact a registered Republican when nominated." Freedom and the Court 455 (3d ed., 1977).

TIME CHART OF THE SUPREME COURT

1943–44	1955	1965–67	19.
Stone (R)	*Warren* (R)	*Warren* (R)	*Bur.*
Roberts (R)	Black (D)	Black (D)	Doug.
Black (D)	Reed (D)	Douglas (D)	Brenna
Reed (D)	Frankfurter (I)	Clark (D)	Stewart
Frankfurter (I)	Douglas (D)	Harlan (N.Y.) (R)	B. White
Douglas (D)	Burton (R)	Brennan (D)	T. Marshal.
Murphy (D)	Clark (D)	Stewart (R)	Blackmun (l.
R. Jackson (D)	Minton (D)	B. White (D)	
W. Rutledge (D)	Harlan (N.Y.) (R)	Fortas (D)	**1972–75**
			Burger (R)
1945	**1956**	**1967–69**	Douglas (D)
Stone (R)	*Warren* (R)	*Warren* (R)	Brennan (D)
Black (D)	Black (D)	Black (D)	Stewart (R)
Reed (D)	Reed (D)	Douglas (D)	B. White (D)
Frankfurter (I)	Frankfurter (I)	Harlan (N.Y.) (R)	T. Marshall (D)
Douglas (D)	Douglas (D)	Brennan (D)	Blackmun (R)
Murphy (D)	Burton (R)	Stewart (R)	Powell (D)
R. Jackson (D)	Clark (D)	B. White (D)	Rehnquist (R)
W. Rutledge (D)	Harlan (N.Y.) (R)	Fortas (D)	
Burton (R)	Brennan (D)	T. Marshall (D)	**1975–1981**
			Burger (R)
1946–48	**1957**	**1969**	Brennan (D)
Vinson (D)	*Warren* (R)	*Burger* (R)	Stewart (R)
Black (D)	Black (D)	Black (D)	B. White (D)
Reed (D)	Frankfurter (I)	Douglas (D)	T. Marshall (D)
Frankfurter (I)	Douglas (D)	Harlan (N.Y.) (R)	Blackmun (R)
Douglas (D)	Burton (R)	Brennan (D)	Powell (D)
Murphy (D)	Clark (D)	Stewart (R)	Rehnquist (R)
R. Jackson (D)	Harlan (N.Y.) (R)	B. White (D)	Stevens (R)
W. Rutledge (D)	Brennan (D)	Fortas (D)	
Burton (R)	Whittaker (R)	T. Marshall (D)	**1981– ——**
			Burger (R)
1949–52	**1958–61**	**1969–70**	Brennan (D)
Vinson (D)	*Warren* (R)	*Burger* (R)	B. White (D)
Black (D)	Black (D)	Black (D)	T. Marshall (D)
Reed (D)	Frankfurter (I)	Douglas (D)	Blackmun (R)
Frankfurter (I)	Douglas (D)	Harlan (N.Y.) (R)	Powell (D)
Douglas (D)	Clark (D)	Brennan (D)	Rehnquist (R)
R. Jackson (D)	Harlan (N.Y.) (R)	Stewart (R)	Stevens (R)
Burton (R)	Brennan (D)	B. White (D)	O'Connor (R)
Clark (D)	Whittaker (R)	T. Marshall (D)	
Minton (D)	Stewart (R)		
		1970	
1953–54	**1962–65**	*Burger* (R)	
Warren (R)	*Warren* (R)	Black (D)	
Black (D)	Black (D)	Douglas (D)	
Reed (D)	Douglas (D)	Harlan (N.Y.) (R)	
Frankfurter (I)	Clark (D)	Brennan (D)	
Douglas (D)	Harlan (N.Y.) (R)	Stewart (R)	
R. Jackson (D)	Brennan (D)	B. White (D)	
Burton (R)	Stewart (R)	T. Marshall (D)	
Clark (D)	B. White (D)	Blackmun (R)	
Minton (D)	Goldberg (D)		

Appendix B

Biographical Chart of the Justices

The following chart summarizes in easy-to-read form certain basic biographical information about the past and present members of the Supreme Court. Chief Justices are identified by an asterisk. Attendance at law school is noted only for those Justices who graduated from a program of formal study. The numbers in parentheses following each entry regarding prior experience show the approximate number of years spent. Membership in the U. S. House of Representatives or Senate is indicated by "House" and "Senate"; membership in the upper and/or lower house of a state legislature is denoted simply by "state legislature." Although several Justices, including Jay, Byrnes, and Goldberg to name only a few, continued their careers of public service after resigning, information on this chart is restricted to that occurring before appointment to the Court. Four Presidents made no appointments to the Court and are, therefore, not included on this chart: William Henry Harrison (March–April 1841); Zachary Taylor (1849–1850); Andrew Johnson (1865–1869); and Jimmy Carter (1977–1981).

While the entries for each Justice are self-explanatory, in the aggregate the data yield several general observations. First, a significant majority of Justices have had some experience in public life before coming to the Court which suggests that they have had more than a nodding acquaintance with the political process and belies the icy remoteness we frequently attribute to judges. Second, Presidents overwhelmingly appoint Justices of their own political party since they want to leave their mark on the political complexion of the Court, and—some notable exceptions to the contrary notwithstanding—they usually succeed. The impact, in fact, is sometimes still felt decades after a President has left office. Third, the formal study of law (i.e., following a prescribed program of study at a law school eventuating in conferral of a law degree) is a comparatively modern route of entry into the legal profession. Before well into the twentieth century, those lawyers who became Justices, like the vast majority of their colleagues, got into the profession by what was called "reading the law," that is by studying law books and clerking for a practicing attorney who supervised their on-the-job training to a point where the young aspiring lawyer could pass the bar exam and be entitled to practice on his own. Justice Jackson was the last member of the Court who did not have a law degree, and he left the Court as recently as 1954. By the way, the lack of a law degree did not prevent Jackson from becoming one of the most skilled and effective advocates to argue before the Court or from becoming one of its most gifted and literate members once he ascended to the Bench. All of the Justices, of course, have been lawyers, but the Constitution does not require it. Fourth and finally, there is absolutely no correlation between prior experience as a judge and judicial "greatness" among the Justices. Holmes and Cardozo together spanned nearly four decades of prior judicial experience; the cumulative total for Marshall, Story, Brandeis, Black, and Frankfurter was a year and a half. All of these men, however, are widely acclaimed as among the very best to have graced the Court.

PRESIDENT Party Dates of his Administration	JUSTICE Political Party Years of Service	Born/Died · Law School · Residence Prior Experience
GEORGE WASHINGTON Fed. 1789–1797	* JOHN JAY Fed. 1789–1795	1745–1829 · · · N.Y. Cont.Cong. (5); N.Y. prov. cong. (1); State judge (2); Minister to Spain (1); U.S. Sec'y of Foreign Affairs (5)
	JOHN RUTLEDGE Fed. 1789–1791	1739–1800 · · · S.C. Confirmed but never sat with the Court. Col. legis. (15); Col.Atty.Gen. (1); Cont.Cong. (3); State legis. (9); Gov. (3); Const.Conn., 1787; State judge (1)
	WILLIAM CUSHING Fed. 1789–1810	1732–1810 · · · Mass. Local judge (1); State judge (17)
	JAMES WILSON Fed. 1789–1798	1724–1798 · · · Pa. Cont.Cong. (4); Const.Conv., 1787
	JOHN BLAIR Fed. 1789–1796	1732–1800 · · · Va. House of Burgesses (4); Clerk, Va. council (5); State privy council (1); Const.Conv., 1787; State judge (11)
	JAMES IREDELL Fed. 1790–1799	1750–1799 · · · N.C. Customs collector (3); State judge (1); State Atty. Gen. (1); State council (1)

PRESIDENT Party Dates of his Administration	JUSTICE Political Party Years of Service	Born/Died Law School Residence Prior Experience
WASHINGTON (*Cont.*)	THOMAS JOHNSON Fed. 1791–1793	1732–1819 Md. Cont.Cong. (2)
	WILLIAM PATERSON Fed. 1793–1806	1745–1806 N.J. State legis. (2); State Atty. Gen. (7); Const.Conv., 1787; Senate (1); Gov. (3)
	* JOHN RUTLEDGE Fed. 1795	1739–1800 S.C. (See entry above) Unconfirmed recess appointment Since 1791: State judge (4)
	SAMUEL CHASE Fed. 1796–1811	1741–1811 Md. Col. & state legis. (20); Cont.Cong. (6); Local judge (1); State judge (5)
	* OLIVER ELLSWORTH Fed. 1796–1800	1745–1807 Conn. State legis. (1); State's atty. (1); Cont.Cong. (6); Gov's. council (4); State judge (5); Const.Conv., 1787; Senate (7)
JOHN ADAMS Fed. 1797–1801	BUSHROD WASHINGTON Fed. 1798–1829	1762–1829 Pa. State legis. (1)
	ALFRED MOORE Fed. 1799–1804	1755–1810 N.C. State legis. (2); State Atty. Gen. (9); State judge (1)
	* JOHN MARSHALL Fed. 1801–1835	1755–1835 Va. House of Burgesses (7); Gov's. council (13); City recorder (2); House (1); Mem., special comm'n to France, XYZ Affair (1); Sec'y of State (1)
THOMAS JEFFERSON Dem.-Rep. 1801–1809	WILLIAM JOHNSON Dem.-Rep. 1804–1834	1771–1834 S.C. State legis. (4); State judge (6)
	[HENRY] BROCKHOLST LIVINGSTON Dem.-Rep. 1806–1823	1757–1823 N.Y. State judge (5)

PRESIDENT Party Dates of his Administration	JUSTICE Political Party Years of Service	Born/Died Law School Residence Prior Experience
JEFFERSON (*Cont.*)	THOMAS TODD Dem.-Rep. 1807–1826	1765–1826 Ky. Court clerk (14); State judge (6)
JAMES MADISON Dem.-Rep. 1809–1817	GABRIEL DUVALL Dem.-Rep. 1811–1835	1752–1844 Md. Gov's. council (2); State legis. (7); House (1-1/2); State judge (6); Comptr., U.S. Treasury (9)
	JOSEPH STORY Dem.-Rep. 1811–1845	1779–1845 Mass. State legis. (4); House (1)
JAMES MONROE Dem.-Rep. 1817–1825	SMITH THOMPSON Dem.-Rep. 1823–1843	1768–1843 N.Y. State legis. (1); State judge (16); Sec'y of the Navy (4)
JOHN QUINCY ADAMS Dem.-Rep. 1825–1829	ROBERT TRIMBLE Dem.-Rep. 1826–1828	1777–1828 Ky. State legis. (1); State judge (2); U.S. atty. (4); Fed. judge (9)
ANDREW JACKSON Dem. 1829–1837	JOHN McLEAN Dem., later Rep. 1829–1861	1785–1861 Ohio House (3-1/2); State judge (6); Fed. agency (1); Post. Gen. (4)
	HENRY BALDWIN Dem. 1830–1844	1780–1844 Pa. House (5)
	JAMES M. WAYNE Dem. 1835–1867	1790–1867 Ga. State legis. (1); Mayor (1); State judge (5); House (6)
	* ROGER B. TANEY Dem. 1836–1864	1777–1864 Md. State legis. (5); State Atty. Gen. (4); U.S. Atty. Gen. (4); Acting Sec'y of War (1); Sec'y of the Treasury (1)
	PHILIP P. BARBOUR Dem. 1836–1841	1783–1841 Va. State legis. (2); House (14); Fed. judge (6)
MARTIN VAN BUREN Dem. 1837–1841	JOHN CATRON Dem. 1837–1865	1778–1865 Tenn. State judge (10)

PRESIDENT Party Dates of his Administration	JUSTICE Political Party Years of Service	Born/Died Law School Residence Prior Experience
VAN BUREN (*Cont.*)	JOHN McKINLEY Dem. 1837–1852	1780–1852 Ky. State legis. (1); Senate (5); House (2)
	PETER V. DANIEL Dem. 1841–1860	1784–1860 Va. State legis. (1); State privy council (23); Lt. Gov. (1); Fed. judge (4)
JOHN TYLER Whig 1841–1845	SAMUEL NELSON Dem. 1845–1872	1792–1873 N.Y. State judge (22)
JAMES KNOX POLK Dem. 1845–1849	LEVI WOODBURY Dem. 1845–1851	1789–1851 N.H. State judge (6); Gov. (1); State legis. (1); Senate (10); Sec'y of the Navy (3); Sec'y of the Treasury (7)
	ROBERT C. GRIER Dem. 1846–1870	1794–1870 Pa. Local judge (13)
MILLARD FILLMORE Whig 1850–1853	BENJAMIN R. CURTIS Whig 1851–1857	1809–1874 Mass. State legis. (1)
FRANKLIN PIERCE Dem. 1853–1857	JOHN A. CAMPBELL Dem. 1853–1861	1811–1889 Ala. State legis. (2)
JAMES BUCHANAN Dem. 1857–1861	NATHAN CLIFFORD Dem. 1858–1881	1803–1881 Maine State legis. (4); State Atty. Gen. (4); House (4); U.S. Atty. Gen. (2)
ABRAHAM LINCOLN Rep. 1861–1865	NOAH H. SWAYNE Rep. 1862–1881	1804–1884 Ohio Pros. atty. (1); State legis. (1); U.S. atty. (9)
	SAMUEL F. MILLER Rep. 1862–1890	1816–1890 Iowa Private practice
	DAVID DAVIS Rep., later Dem. 1862–1877	1815–1886 Ill. State legis. (1); State judge (14)

PRESIDENT Party Dates of his Administration	JUSTICE Political Party Years of Service	Born/Died Law School Residence Prior Experience
LINCOLN (*Cont.*)	STEPHEN J. FIELD Dem. 1863–1897	1816–1899 Calif. State legis. (1); State judge (6)
	* SALMON P. CHASE Rep. 1864–1873	1808–1873 Ohio Senate (7); Gov. (4); Sec'y of the Treasury (3)
ULYSSES S. GRANT Rep. 1869–1877	WILLIAM STRONG Rep. 1870–1880	1808–1895 Pa. House (4); State judge (11)
	JOSEPH P. BRADLEY Rep. 1870–1892	1803–1892 N.J. Private practice
	WARD HUNT Rep. 1872–1882	1810–1886 N.Y. State legis. (1); Mayor (1); State judge (8)
	* MORRISON WAITE Rep. 1874–1888	1816–1888 Ohio State legis. (1)
RUTHERFORD B. HAYES Rep. 1877–1881	JOHN MARSHALL HARLAN Rep. 1877–1911	1833–1911 Ky. Local judge (1); State Atty. Gen. (4); Repub. cand. for Gov., 1871, 1875
	WILLIAM B. WOODS Rep. 1880–1887	1824–1887 Ga. Private practice
JAMES A. GARFIELD Rep. 1881	STANLEY MATTHEWS Rep. 1881–1889	1824–1889 Ohio Asst. pros. atty. (1); Local judge (4); State legis. (3); U.S. atty. (3); Senate (2)
CHESTER ALAN ARTHUR Rep. 1881–1885	HORACE GRAY Rep. 1881–1902	1828–1902 Mass. Court reporter (7); State judge (18)

PRESIDENT Party Dates of his Administration	JUSTICE Political Party Years of Service	Born/Died Law School Residence Prior Experience
ARTHUR (*Cont.*)	SAMUEL BLATCHFORD Rep. 1882–1893	1820–1893 N.Y. Resident minister to the Vatican (1); Fed. judge (15)
GROVER CLEVELAND Dem. 1885–1889	LUCIUS Q. C. LAMAR Dem. 1888–1893	1825–1893 Miss. Coll. prof. (2); State legis. (1); House (8); Law prof. (1); Senate (8); Sec'y of the Interior (3)
	* MELVILLE W. FULLER Dem. 1888–1910	1833–1910 Ill. City atty. & councilman (1); State legis. (2)
BENJAMIN HARRISON Rep. 1889–1893	DAVID J. BREWER Rep. 1889–1910	1837–1910 Kan. U.S. commissioner (1); Local judge (1); County atty. (1); State judge (18); Fed. judge (5)
	HENRY B. BROWN Rep. 1890–1906	1836–1913 Mich. Dep. U.S. marshal (2); Asst. U.S. atty. (5); Local judge (½); Fed. judge (15)
	GEORGE SHIRAS Rep. 1892–1903	1832–1924 Yale Pa. Private practice
	HOWELL E. JACKSON Dem. 1893–1895	1832–1895 Tenn. State judge (4); State legis. (1); Senate (5); Fed. judge (7)
GROVER CLEVELAND Dem. 1893–1897	EDWARD D. WHITE Dem. 1894–1910	1845–1921 La. State legis. (1); State judge (1); Senate (3) Promoted to Chief Justice, 1910
	RUFUS W. PECKHAM Dem. 1895–1909	1838–1909 N.Y. Dist. atty. (1); City atty. (1); State judge (12)
WILLIAM McKINLEY Rep. 1897–1901	JOSEPH McKENNA Rep. 1898–1925	1843–1926 Calif. Dist. atty. (2); State legis. (1); House (7); Fed. judge (5); U.S. Atty. Gen. (1)

PRESIDENT Party Dates of his Administration	JUSTICE Political Party Years of Service	Born/Died Law School Residence Prior Experience
THEODORE ROOSEVELT Rep. 1901–1908	OLIVER WENDELL HOLMES, Jr. Rep. 1902–1932	1841–1935 Harvard Mass. Law prof. (2); State judge (20)
	WILLIAM R. DAY Rep. 1903–1922	1849–1923 Ohio Local judge (4); Asst. Sec'y of State (1); Sec'y of State (½); Fed. judge (4)
	WILLIAM H. MOODY Rep. 1906–1910	1853–1917 Mass. City atty. (2); Dist. atty. (5); House (7); Sec'y of the Navy (2); U.S. Atty. Gen. (1-½)
WILLIAM HOWARD TAFT Rep. 1909–1913	HORACE H. LURTON Dem. 1909–1914	1844–1914 Cumberland Tenn. State judge (10); Law prof. & dean (12); Fed. judge (17)
	CHARLES EVANS HUGHES Rep. 1910–1916	1862–1948 Columbia N.Y. Spec. counsel to legis. invest. comms. (2); Law prof. (4); Gov. (2) Later appointed Chief Justice
	* EDWARD D. WHITE Dem. 1910–1921	1845–1921 La. Promoted from Associate Justice
	WILLIS VAN DEVANTER Rep. 1910–1937	1859–1941 Cincinnati Wyo. City atty. (1); Terr. legis. (1); State judge (1); Chmn., Rep. state comm. (1); Chmn., Rep. nat. comm. (1); Asst. U.S. Atty. Gen. (6); Fed. judge (7)
	JOSEPH R. LAMAR Dem. 1910–1916	1857–1916 Ga. State legis. (3); State judge (4)
	MAHLON PITNEY Rep. 1912–1922	1858–1924 N.J. House (4); State legis. (2); State judge (14)
WOODROW WILSON Dem. 1913–1921	JAMES C. McREYNOLDS Dem. 1914–1940	1862–1946 Virginia Tenn. Asst. U.S. Atty. Gen. (4); U.S. Atty. Gen. (1)

PRESIDENT Party Dates of his Administration	JUSTICE Political Party Years of Service	Born/Died Law School Residence Prior Experience
WILSON (*Cont.*)	LOUIS D. BRANDEIS Rep. 1916–1939	1856–1941 Harvard Mass. Private practice and public interest law in antitrust, labor, and consumer matters. Counsel for fed. and state govts. in rate regulation, minimum wage, and maximum hours cases.
	JOHN H. CLARKE Dem. 1916–1922	1857–1945 Ohio Railroad counsel (13); Fed. judge (2)
WARREN G. HARDING Rep. 1921–1923	* WILLIAM HOWARD TAFT Rep. 1921–1930	1857–1930 Cincinnati Ohio Asst. pros. atty. (3); County atty. (2); Local judge (3); U.S. Sol. Gen. (2); Fed. judge (8); Law prof. & dean (4); Gov. of Philippines (4); Sec'y of War (3-1/2); President (4); Law prof. (8)
	GEORGE SUTHERLAND Rep. 1922–1938	1862–1942 Utah State legis. (1); House (2); Senate (12)
	PIERCE BUTLER Dem. 1922–1939	1866–1939 Minn. Private practice
	EDWARD T. SANFORD Rep. 1923–1930	1865–1930 Harvard Tenn. Asst. U.S. Atty. Gen. (1); Fed. judge (15)
CALVIN COOLIDGE Rep. 1923–1929	HARLAN F. STONE Rep. 1925–1941	1872–1946 Columbia N.Y. Law prof. & dean (24); U.S. Atty. Gen. (1) Promoted to Chief Justice, 1941
HERBERT HOOVER Rep. 1929–1933	* CHARLES EVANS HUGHES Rep. 1930–1941	1862–1948 Columbia N.Y. (See entry above) Since 1916: Repub. pres. candid., 1916; Sec'y of State (4); Perm. Court of Arbitration (4); World Court (2)
	OWEN J. ROBERTS Rep. 1930–1945	1875–1955 Pennsylvania Pa. Dist. atty. (3); Law prof. (20)

PRESIDENT Party Dates of his Administration	JUSTICE Political Party Years of Service	Born/Died Law School Residence Prior Experience
HOOVER (*Cont.*)	BENJAMIN N. CARDOZO Dem. 1932–1938	1870–1938 N.Y. State judge (18)
FRANKLIN D. ROOSEVELT Dem. 1933–1945	HUGO L. BLACK Dem. 1937–1971	1886–1971 Alabama Ala. Local judge (1-1/2); Pros. atty. (2); Senate (10)
	STANLEY F. REED Dem. 1938–1957	1884–1980 Ky. State legis. (4); Counsel, fed. agencies (6); Sol. Gen. (3)
	FELIX FRANKFURTER Ind. 1939–1962	1882–1965 Harvard Mass. Asst. U.S. atty. (4); Fed. agencies (3); Law prof. (25)
	WILLIAM O. DOUGLAS Dem. 1939–1975	1898–1980 Columbia Wash. Law prof. (9); SEC, chmn. and commn'r (3)
	FRANK MURPHY Dem. 1940–1949	1893–1949 Michigan Mich. Asst. U.S. atty. (1); Local judge (7); Mayor (3); Gov. (3); U.S. Atty. Gen. (1)
	JAMES F. BYRNES Dem. 1941–1942	1879–1972 S.C. Senate (12)
	* HARLAN F. STONE Rep. 1941–1946	1872–1946 Columbia N.Y. Promoted from Associate Justice
	ROBERT H. JACKSON Dem. 1941–1954	1892–1954 N.Y. Counsel, IRS (2); Asst. U.S. Atty. Gen. (2); Sol. Gen. (1); U.S. Atty. Gen. (1-1/2)
	WILEY B. RUTLEDGE Dem. 1943–1949	1894–1949 Colorado Iowa Law prof. & dean (15); Fed. judge (4)

PRESIDENT Party Dates of his Administration	JUSTICE Political Party Years of Service	Born/Died Law School Residence Prior Experience
HARRY S. TRUMAN Dem. 1945–1953	HAROLD H. BURTON Rep. 1945–1958	1888–1964 Harvard Ohio State legis. (1); City atty. (3); Mayor (5); Senate (4)
	* FRED M. VINSON Dem. 1946–1953	1890–1953 Centre College, Ky. Ky. City atty. (1); Pros. atty. (3); House (14); Fed. judge (5); Fed. agencies (2); Sec'y of the Treasury (1)
	TOM C. CLARK Dem. 1949–1967	1899–1977 Texas Tex. Dist. atty. (6); U.S. Justice Dept. (8); U.S. Atty. Gen. (4)
	SHERMAN MINTON Dem. 1949–1956	1890–1965 Indiana Ind. Senate (6); Fed. judge (8)
DWIGHT D. EISENHOWER Rep. 1953–1961	* EARL WARREN Rep. 1953–1969	1891–1974 California Calif. Dep. city atty. (1); Dep. dist. atty. (5); Dist. atty. (14); State Atty. Gen. (4); Gov. (10); Repub. vice-pres. cand., 1948
	JOHN MARSHALL HARLAN Rep. 1955–1971	1899–1971 New York Law School N.Y. Asst. U.S. atty. (2); Spec. asst. state At- ty. Gen. (4); Chief counsel, state crime comm'n (2); Fed. judge (1)
	WILLIAM J. BRENNAN, Jr. Dem. 1956–	1906– Harvard N.J. State judge (7)
	CHARLES E. WHITTAKER Rep. 1957–1962	1901–1973 Univ. of Kansas City Mo. Fed. judge (3)
	POTTER STEWART Rep. 1958–1981	1915– Yale Ohio City council (3); Fed. judge (4)
JOHN F. KENNEDY Dem. 1961–1963	BYRON R. WHITE Dem. 1962–	1917– Yale Colo. Dep. U.S. Atty. Gen. (1)

PRESIDENT Party Dates of his Administration	JUSTICE Political Party Years of Service	Born/Died Law School Residence Prior Experience
KENNEDY (*Cont.*)	ARTHUR J. GOLDBERG Dem. 1962–1965	1908– Northwestern Ill. Counsel to AFL–CIO (13); Sec'y of Labor (1)
LYNDON B. JOHNSON Dem. 1963–1969	ABE FORTAS Dem. 1965–1969	1910–1982 Yale Tenn. Law prof. (4); Fed. agencies (4); Under sec'y of the Interior (4)
	THURGOOD MARSHALL Dem. 1967–	1908– Howard N.Y. Counsel, NAACP (25); Sol. Gen. (2); Fed. judge (4)
RICHARD M. NIXON Rep. 1969–1974	* WARREN E. BURGER Rep. 1969–	1907– St. Paul College of Law Minn. Asst. U.S. Atty. Gen. (3); Fed. judge (13)
	HARRY A. BLACKMUN Rep. 1970–	1908– Harvard Minn. Counsel, Mayo Clinic (9); Fed. judge (11)
	LEWIS F. POWELL, Jr. Dem. 1972–	1907– Washington & Lee Va. Private practice
	WILLIAM H. REHNQUIST Rep. 1972–	1924– Stanford Ariz. Asst. U.S. Atty. Gen. (2)
GERALD R. FORD Rep. 1974–1977	JOHN PAUL STEVENS Rep. 1975–	1920– Northwestern Ill. Fed. judge (5)
RONALD REAGAN Rep. 1981–	SANDRA DAY O'CONNOR Rep. 1981–	1930– Stanford Ariz. Asst. state Atty. Gen. (4); State legis. (5); State judge (7)

Appendix C

The Constitution of the United States

Preamble

We the People of the United States, in Order to form a more perfect Union, establish Justice, insure domestic Tranquility, provide for the common defence, promote the general Welfare, and secure the Blessings of Liberty to ourselves and our Posterity, do ordain and establish this Constitution for the United States of America.

Article I

Section 1. All legislative Powers herein granted shall be vested in a Congress of the United States, which shall consist of a Senate and House of Representatives.

Section 2. [1] The House of Representatives shall be composed of Members chosen every second Year by the People of the several States, and the Electors in each State shall have the Qualifications requisite for Electors of the most numerous Branch of the State Legislature.

[2] No Person shall be a Representative who shall not have attained to the Age of twenty five Years, and been seven Years a Citizen of the United States, and who shall not, when elected, be an Inhabitant of that State in which he shall be chosen.

[3] Representatives and direct Taxes shall be apportioned among the several States which may be included within this Union, according to their respective Numbers, which shall be determined by adding to the whole Number of free Persons, including those bound to Service for a Term of Years, and excluding Indians not taxed, three fifths of all other Persons. The actual Enumeration shall be made within three Years after the first Meeting of the Congress of the United States, and within every subsequent Term of ten Years, in such Manner as they shall by Law direct.

The Number of Representatives shall not exceed one for every thirty Thousand, but each State shall have at Least one Representative; and until such enumeration shall be made, the State of New Hampshire shall be entitled to chuse three, Massachusetts eight, Rhode Island and Providence Plantations one, Connecticut five, New York six, New Jersey four, Pennsylvania eight, Delaware one, Maryland six, Virginia ten, North Carolina five, South Carolina five, and Georgia three.

[4] When vacancies happen in the Representation from any State, the Executive Authority thereof shall issue Writs of Election to fill such Vacancies.

[5] The House of Representatives shall chuse their Speaker and other Officers; and shall have the sole Power of Impeachment.

Section 3.   [1] The Senate of the United States shall be composed of two Senators from each State, chosen by the Legislature thereof, for six Years; and each Senator shall have one Vote.

[2] Immediately after they shall be assembled in Consequence of the first Election, they shall be divided as equally as may be into three Classes. The Seats of the Senators of the first Class shall be vacated at the Expiration of the Second Year, of the second Class at the Expiration of the fourth Year, and of the third Class at the Expiration of the sixth Year, so that one third may be chosen every second Year; and if Vacancies happen by Resignation, or otherwise, during the Recess of the Legislature of any State, the Executive thereof may make temporary Appointments until the next Meeting of the Legislature, which shall then fill such Vacancies.

[3] No Person shall be a Senator who shall not have attained to the Age of thirty Years, and been nine Years a Citizen of the United States, and who shall not, when elected, be an Inhabitant of that State for which he shall be chosen.

[4] The Vice President of the United States shall be President of the Senate, but shall have no Vote, unless they be equally divided.

[5] The Senate shall chuse their other Officers, and also a President pro tempore, in the Absence of the Vice President, or when he shall exercise the Office of President of the United States.

[6] The Senate shall have the sole Power to try all Impeachments. When sitting for that Purpose, they shall be on Oath or Affirmation. When the President of the United States is tried, the Chief Justice shall preside: And no Person shall be convicted without the Concurrence of two thirds of the Members present.

[7] Judgment in Cases of Impeachment shall not extend further than to removal from Office, and disqualification to hold and enjoy any Office of honor, Trust, or Profit under the United States: but the Party convicted shall nevertheless be liable and subject to Indictment, Trial, Judgment, and Punishment, according to Law.

Section 4.   [1] The Times, Places and Manner of holding Elections for Senators and Representatives, shall be prescribed in each State by the Legislature thereof; but the Congress may at any time by Law make or alter such Regulations, except as to the Places of chusing Senators.

[2] The Congress shall assemble at least once in every Year, and such Meeting shall be on the first Monday in December, unless they shall by Law appoint a different Day.

Section 5. [1] Each House shall be the Judge of the Elections, Returns, and Qualifications of its own Members, and a Majority of each shall constitute a Quorum to do Business; but a smaller Number may adjourn from day to day, and may be authorized to compel the Attendance of absent Members, in such Manner, and under such Penalties as each House may provide.

[2] Each House may determine the Rules of its Proceedings, punish its Members for disorderly Behavior, and, with the Concurrence of two thirds, expel a Member.

[3] Each House shall keep a Journal of its Proceedings, and from time to time publish the same, excepting such Parts as may in their Judgment require Secrecy; and the Yeas and Nays of the Members of either House on any question shall, at the Desire of one fifth of those Present, be entered on the Journal.

[4] Neither House, during the Session of Congress, shall, without the Consent of the other, adjourn for more than three days, nor to any other Place than that in which the two Houses shall be sitting.

Section 6. [1] The Senators and Representatives shall receive a Compensation for their Services, to be ascertained by Law, and paid out of the Treasury of the United States. They shall in all Cases, except Treason, Felony and Breach of the Peace, be privileged from Arrest during their Attendance at the Session of their respective Houses, and in going to and returning from the same; and for any Speech or Debate in either House, they shall not be questioned in any other Place.

[2] No Senator or Representative shall, during the Time for which he was elected, be appointed to any civil Office under the Authority of the United States, which shall have been created, or the Emoluments whereof shall have been increased during such time; and no Person holding any Office under the United States, shall be a Member of either House during his Continuance in Office.

Section 7. [1] All Bills for raising Revenue shall originate in the House of Representatives; but the Senate may propose or concur with Amendments as on other Bills.

[2] Every Bill which shall have passed the House of Representatives and the Senate, shall, before it becomes a Law, be presented to the President of the United States; If he approve he shall sign it, but if not he shall return it, with his Objections to the House in which it shall have originated, who shall enter the Objections at large on their Journal, and proceed to reconsider it. If after such Reconsideration two thirds of that House shall agree to pass the Bill, it shall be sent together with the Objections, to the other House, by which it shall likewise be reconsidered, and if approved by two thirds of that House, it shall become a Law. But in all such Cases the Votes of both Houses shall be determined by yeas and Nays, and the Names of the Persons voting for and against the Bill shall

be entered on the Journal of each House respectively. If any Bill shall not be returned by the President within ten Days (Sundays excepted) after it shall have been presented to him, the Same shall be a Law, in like Manner as if he had signed it, unless the Congress by their Adjournment prevent its Return in which Case it shall not be a Law.

[3] Every Order, Resolution, or Vote, to Which the Concurrence of the Senate and House of Representatives may be necessary (except on a question of Adjournment) shall be presented to the President of the United States; and before the Same shall take Effect, shall be approved by him, or being disapproved by him, shall be repassed by two thirds of the Senate and House of Representatives, according to the Rules and Limitations prescribed in the Case of a Bill.

Section 8. [1] The Congress shall have Power To lay and collect Taxes, Duties, Imposts and Excises, to pay the Debts and provide for the common Defence and general Welfare of the United States; but all Duties, Imposts and Excises shall be uniform throughout the United States;

[2] To borrow money on the credit of the United States;

[3] To regulate Commerce with foreign Nations, and among the several States, and with the Indian Tribes;

[4] To establish an uniform Rule of Naturalization, and uniform Laws on the subject of Bankruptcies throughout the United States;

[5] To coin Money, regulate the Value thereof, and of foreign Coin, and fix the Standard of Weights and Measures;

[6] To provide for the Punishment of counterfeiting the Securities and current Coin of the United States;

[7] To Establish Post Offices and Post Roads;

[8] To promote the Progress of Science and useful Arts, by securing for limited Times to Authors and Inventors the exclusive Right to their respective Writings and Discoveries;

[9] To constitute Tribunals inferior to the supreme Court;

[10] To define and punish Piracies and Felonies committed on the high Seas, and Offenses against the Law of Nations:

[11] To declare War, grant Letters of Marque and Reprisal, and make Rules concerning Captures on Land and Water;

[12] To raise and support Armies, but no Appropriation of Money to that Use shall be for a longer Term than two Years;

[13] To provide and maintain a Navy;

[14] To make Rules for the Government and Regulation of the land and naval Forces;

[15] To provide for calling forth the Militia to execute the Laws of the Union, suppress Insurrections and repel Invasions;

[16] To provide for organizing, arming, and disciplining, the Militia, and for governing such Part of them as may be employed in the Service of the United States, reserving to the States respectively, the Appointment of

the Officers, and the Authority of training the Militia according to the discipline prescribed by Congress;

[17] To exercise exclusive Legislation in all Cases whatsoever, over such District (not exceeding ten Miles square) as may, by Cession of particular States, and the Acceptance of Congress, become the Seat of the Government of the United States, and to exercise like Authority over all Places purchased by the Consent of the Legislature of the State in which the Same shall be, for the Erection of Forts, Magazines, Arsenals, dock-Yards, and other needful Buildings;—And

[18] To make all Laws which shall be necessary and proper for carrying into Execution the foregoing Powers, and all other Powers vested by this Constitution in the Government of the United States, or in any Department or Officer thereof.

Section 9. [1] The Migration or Importation of Such Persons as any of the States now existing shall think proper to admit, shall not be prohibited by the Congress prior to the Year one thousand eight hundred and eight, but a Tax or duty may be imposed on such Importation, not exceeding ten dollars for each Person.

[2] The privilege of the Writ of Habeas Corpus shall not be suspended, unless when in Cases of Rebellion or Invasion the public Safety may require it.

[3] No Bill of Attainder or ex post facto Law shall be passed.

[4] No Capitation, or other direct, Tax shall be laid, unless in Proportion to the Census or Enumeration herein before directed to be taken.

[5] No Tax or Duty shall be laid on Articles exported from any State.

[6] No Preference shall be given by any Regulation of Commerce or Revenue to the Ports of one State over those of another: nor shall Vessels bound to, or from, one State be obliged to enter, clear, or pay Duties in another.

[7] No money shall be drawn from the Treasury, but in Consequence of Appropriations made by Law; and a regular Statement and Account of the Receipts and Expenditures of all public Money shall be published from time to time.

[8] No Title of Nobility shall be granted by the United States: And no Person holding any Office of Profit or Trust under them, shall, without the Consent of the Congress, accept of any present, Emolument, Office, or Title, of any kind whatever, from any King, Prince, or foreign State.

Section 10. [1] No State shall enter into any Treaty, Alliance, or Confederation; grant Letters of Marque and Reprisal; coin Money; emit Bills of Credit; make any Thing but gold and silver Coin a Tender in Payment of Debts; pass any Bill of Attainder, ex post facto Law, or Law impairing the Obligation of Contracts, or grant any Title of Nobility.

[2] No State shall, without the Consent of the Congress, lay any Imposts or Duties on Imports or Exports, except what may be absolutely necessary for executing it's inspection Laws: and the net Produce of all Duties and Imposts, laid by any State on Imports or Exports, shall be for

the Use of the Treasury of the United States; and all such Laws shall be subject to the Revision and Controul of the Congress.

[3] No State shall, without the Consent of Congress, lay any Duty of Tonnage, keep Troops, or Ships of War in time of Peace, enter into any Agreement or Compact with another State, or with a foreign Power, or engage in War, unless actually invaded, or in such imminent Danger as will not admit of delay.

Article II

Section 1.   [1] The executive Power shall be vested in a President of the United States of America. He shall hold his Office during the Term of four Years, and, together with the Vice President, chosen for the same Term, be elected, as follows:

[2] Each State shall appoint, in such Manner as the Legislature thereof may direct, a Number of Electors, equal to the whole Number of Senators and Representatives to which the State may be entitled in the Congress; but no Senator or Representative, or Person holding an Office of Trust or Profit under the United States, shall be appointed an Elector.

[3] The Electors shall meet in their respective States, and vote by Ballot for two Persons, of whom one at least shall not be an Inhabitant of the same State with themselves. And they shall make a List of all the Persons voted for, and of the Number of Votes for each; which List they shall sign and certify, and transmit sealed to the Seat of the Government of the United States, directed to the President of the Senate. The President of the Senate shall, in the Presence of the Senate and House of Representatives, open all the Certificates, and the Votes shall then be counted. The Person having the greatest Number of Votes shall be the President, if such Number be a Majority of the whole Number of Electors appointed; and if there be more than one who have such Majority, and have an equal Number of Votes, then the House of Representatives shall immediately chuse by Ballot one of them for President; and if no Person have a Majority, then from the five highest on the List the said House shall in like Manner chuse the President. But in chusing the President, the Votes shall be taken by States the Representation from each State having one Vote; A quorum for this Purpose shall consist of a Member or Members from two thirds of the States, and a Majority of all the States shall be necessary to a Choice. In every Case, after the Choice of the President, the Person having the greater Number of Votes of the Electors shall be the Vice President. But if there should remain two or more who have equal Votes, the Senate shall chuse from them by Ballot the Vice President.

[4] The Congress may determine the Time of chusing the Electors, and the Day on which they shall give their Votes; which Day shall be the same throughout the United States.

[5] No person except a natural born Citizen, or a Citizen of the United States, at the time of the Adoption of this Constitution, shall be eligible to the Office of President; neither shall any Person be eligible to that Office

who shall not have attained to the Age of thirty-five Years, and been fourteen Years a Resident within the United States.

[6] In case of the removal of the President from Office, or of his Death, Resignation or Inability to discharge the Powers and Duties of the said Office, the Same shall devolve on the Vice President, and the Congress may by Law provide for the Case of Removal, Death, Resignation or Inability, both of the President and Vice President, declaring what Officer shall then act as President, and such Officer shall act accordingly, until the Disability be removed, or a President shall be elected.

[7] The President shall, at stated Times, receive for his Services, a Compensation, which shall neither be increased nor diminished during the Period for which he shall have been elected, and he shall not receive within that Period any other Emolument from the United States, or any of them.

[8] Before he enter on the Execution of his Office, he shall take the following Oath or Affirmation: "I do solemnly swear (or affirm) that I will faithfully execute the Office of President of the United States, and will to the best of my Ability, preserve, protect and defend the Constitution of the United States."

Section 2.   [1] The President shall be Commander in Chief of the Army and Navy of the United States, and of the militia of the several States, when called into the actual Service of the United States; he may require the Opinion, in writing, of the principal Officer in each of the Executive Departments, upon any Subject relating to the Duties of their respective Offices, and he shall have Power to grant Reprieves and Pardons for Offenses against the United States, except in Cases of Impeachment.

[2] He shall have Power, by and with the Advice and Consent of the Senate to make Treaties, provided two thirds of the Senators present concur; and he shall nominate, and by and with the Advice and Consent of the Senate, shall appoint Ambassadors, other public Ministers and Consuls, Judges of the supreme Court, and all other Officers of the United States, whose Appointments are not herein otherwise provided for, and which shall be established by Law; but the Congress may by Law vest the Appointment of such inferior Officers, as they think proper, in the President alone, in the Courts of Law, or in the Heads of Departments.

[3] The President shall have Power to fill up all Vacancies that may happen during the Recess of the Senate, by granting Commissions which shall expire at the End of their next Session.

Section 3.   He shall from time to time give to the Congress Information of the State of the Union, and recommend to their Consideration such Measures as he shall judge necessary and expedient; he may, on extraordinary Occasions, convene both Houses, or either of them, and in Case of Disagreement between them, with Respect to the Time of Adjournment, he may adjourn them to such Time as he shall think proper; he shall receive Ambassadors and other public Ministers; he shall take Care that the Laws be faithfully executed, and shall Commission all the Officers of the United States.

Section 4. The President, Vice President and all civil Officers of the United States, shall be removed from Office on Impeachment for, and Conviction of, Treason, Bribery, or other high Crimes and Misdemeanors.

Article III

Section 1. The judicial Power of the United States, shall be vested in one supreme Court, and in such inferior Courts as the Congress may from time to time ordain and establish. The Judges, both of the supreme and inferior Courts, shall hold their Offices during good Behaviour, and shall, at stated Times, receive for their Services a Compensation, which shall not be diminished during their Continuance in Office.

Section 2. [1] The judicial Power shall extend to all Cases, in Law and Equity, arising under this Constitution, the Laws of the United States, and Treaties made, or which shall be made, under their Authority;—to all Cases affecting Ambassadors, other public Ministers and Consuls;—to all Cases of admiralty and maritime Jurisdiction;—to Controversies to which the United States shall be a Party;—to Controversies between two or more States;—between a State and Citizens of another State;—between Citizens of different States;—between Citizens of the same State claiming Lands under the Grants of different States, and between a State, or the Citizens thereof, and foreign States, Citizens or Subjects.

[2] In all Cases affecting Ambassadors, other public Ministers and Consuls, and those in which a State shall be a Party, the supreme Court shall have original Jurisdiction. In all the other Cases before mentioned, the supreme Court shall have appellate Jurisdiction, both as to Law and Fact, with such Exceptions, and under such Regulations as the Congress shall make.

[3] The trial of all Crimes, except in Cases of Impeachment, shall be by Jury; and such Trial shall be held in the State where the said Crimes shall have been committed; but when not committed within any State, the Trial shall be at such Place or Places as the Congress may by Law have directed.

Section 3. [1] Treason against the United States, shall consist only in levying War against them, or, in adhering to their Enemies, giving them Aid and Comfort. No Person shall be convicted of Treason unless on the Testimony of two Witnesses to the same overt Act, or on Confession in open Court.

[2] The Congress shall have Power to declare the Punishment of Treason, but no Attainder of Treason shall work Corruption of Blood, or Forfeiture except during the Life of the Person attainted.

Article IV

Section 1. Full Faith and Credit shall be given in each State to the public Acts, Records, and judicial Proceedings of every other State. And the Congress may by general Laws prescribe the Manner in which such Acts, Records and Proceedings shall be proved, and the Effect thereof.

Section 2. [1] The Citizens of each State shall be entitled to all Privileges and Immunities of Citizens in the several States.

[2] A Person charged in any State with Treason, Felony, or other Crime, who shall flee from Justice, and be found in another State, shall on demand of the executive Authority of the State from which he fled, be delivered up, to be removed to the State having Jurisdiction of the Crime.

[3] No Person held to Service or Labour in one State, under the Laws thereof, escaping into another, shall, in Consequence of any Law or Regulation therein, be discharged from such Service or Labour, but shall be delivered up on Claim of the Party to whom such Service or Labour may be due.

Section 3. [1] New States may be admitted by the Congress into this Union; but no new State shall be formed or erected within the Jurisdiction of any other State; nor any State be formed by the Junction of two or more States, or Parts of States, without the Consent of the Legislatures of the States concerned as well as of the Congress.

[2] The Congress shall have Power to dispose of and make all needful Rules and Regulations respecting the Territory or other Property belonging to the United States; and nothing in this Constitution shall be so construed as to Prejudice any Claims of the United States, or of any particular State.

Section 4. The United States shall guarantee to every State in this Union a Republican Form of Government, and shall protect each of them against Invasion; and on Application of the Legislature, or of the Executive (when the Legislature cannot be convened) against domestic Violence.

Article V

The Congress, whenever two thirds of both Houses shall deem it necessary, shall propose Amendments to this Constitution, or, on the Application of the Legislatures of two thirds of the several States, shall call a Convention for proposing Amendments, which, in either Case, shall be valid to all Intents and Purposes, as part of this Constitution, when ratified by the Legislatures of three fourths of the several States, or by Conventions in three fourths thereof, as the one or the other Mode of Ratification may be proposed by the Congress; Provided that no Amendment which may be made prior to the Year One thousand eight hundred and eight shall in any Manner affect the first and fourth Clauses in the Ninth Section of the first Article; and that no State, without its Consent, shall be deprived of its equal Suffrage in the Senate.

Article VI

[1] All Debts contracted and Engagements entered into, before the Adoption of this Constitution shall be as valid against the United States under this Constitution, as under the Confederation.

[2] This Constitution, and the Laws of the United States which shall be made in Pursuance thereof; and all Treaties made, or which shall be made, under the Authority of the United States, shall be the supreme Law

of the Land; and the Judges in every State shall be bound thereby, any Thing in the Constitution or Laws of any State to the Contrary notwithstanding.

[3] The Senators and Representatives before mentioned, and the Members of the several State Legislatures, and all executive and judicial Officers, both of the United States and of the several States, shall be bound by Oath or Affirmation, to support this Constitution; but no religious Test shall ever be required as a Qualification to any Office or public Trust under the United States.

Article VII

The Ratification of the Conventions of nine States shall be sufficient for the Establishment of this Constitution between the States so ratifying the Same.

ARTICLES IN ADDITION TO, AND AMENDMENT OF, THE
CONSTITUTION OF THE UNITED STATES OF AMERICA,
PROPOSED BY CONGRESS, AND RATIFIED BY THE
LEGISLATURES OF THE SEVERAL STATES PURSUANT
TO THE FIFTH ARTICLE OF THE ORIGINAL CONSTITUTION.

Amendment I [1791]

Congress shall make no law respecting an establishment of religion, or prohibiting the free exercise thereof; or abridging the freedom of speech, or of the press; or the right of the people peaceably to assemble, and to petition the Government for a redress of grievances.

Amendment II [1791]

A well regulated Militia, being necessary to the security of a free State, the right of the people to keep and bear Arms, shall not be infringed.

Amendment III [1791]

No Soldier shall, in time of peace be quartered in any house, without the consent of the Owner, nor in time of war, but in a manner to be prescribed by law.

Amendment IV [1791]

The right of the people to be secure in their persons, houses, papers, and effects, against unreasonable searches and seizures, shall not be violated, and no Warrants shall issue, but upon probable cause, supported by Oath or affirmation, and particularly describing the place to be searched, and the persons or things to be seized.

Amendment V [1791]

No person shall be held to answer for a capital, or otherwise infamous crime, unless on a presentment or indictment of a Grand Jury, except in cases arising in the land or naval forces, or in the Militia, when in actual service in time of War or public danger; nor shall any person be subject for the same offence to be twice put in jeopardy of life or limb; nor shall be compelled in any criminal case to be a witness against himself, nor be deprived of life, liberty, or property, without due process of law; nor shall private property be taken for public use, without just compensation.

Amendment VI [1791]

In all criminal prosecutions, the accused shall enjoy the right to a speedy and public trial, by an impartial jury of the State and district wherein the crime shall have been committed, which district shall have been previously ascertained by law, and to be informed of the nature and cause of the accusation; to be confronted with the witnesses against him; to have compulsory process for obtaining witnesses in his favor, and to have the Assistance of Counsel for his defence.

Amendment VII [1791]

In Suits at common law, where the value in controversy shall exceed twenty dollars, the right of trial by jury shall be preserved, and no fact tried by jury, shall be otherwise re-examined in any Court of the United States, than according to the rules of the common law.

Amendment VIII [1791]

Excessive bail shall not be required, nor excessive fines imposed, nor cruel and unusual punishments inflicted.

Amendment IX [1791]

The enumeration in the Constitution, of certain rights, shall not be construed to deny or disparage others retained by the people.

Amendment X [1791]

The powers not delegated to the United States by the Constitution, nor prohibited by it to the States, are reserved to the States respectively, or to the people.

Amendment XI [1798]

The Judicial power of the United States shall not be construed to extend to any suit in law or equity, commenced or prosecuted against one of the United States by Citizens of another State, or by Citizens or Subjects of any Foreign State.

Amendment XII [1804]

The Electors shall meet in their respective states and vote by ballot for President and Vice-President, one of whom, at least, shall not be an inhabitant of the same state with themselves; they shall name in their ballots the person voted for as President, and in distinct ballots the person voted for as Vice-President, and they shall make distinct lists of all persons voted for as President, and of all persons voted for as Vice-President, and of the number of votes for each, which lists they shall sign and certify, and transmit sealed to the seat of the government of the United States, directed to the President of the Senate;—The President of the Senate shall, in the presence of the Senate and House of Representatives, open all the certificates and the votes shall then be counted;—The person having the greatest number of votes for President, shall be the President, if such number be a majority of the whole number of Electors appointed; and if no person have such majority, then from the persons having the highest numbers not exceeding three on the list of those voted for as President, the House of Representatives shall choose immediately, by ballot, the President. But in choosing the President, the votes shall be taken by states, the representation from each state having one vote; a quorum for this purpose shall consist of a member or members from two-thirds of the states, and a majority of all the states shall be necessary to a choice. And if the House of Representatives shall not choose a President whenever the right of choice shall devolve upon them before the fourth day of March next following, then the Vice-President shall act as President, as in the case of the death or other constitutional disability of the President.—The person having the greatest number of votes as Vice-President, shall be the Vice-President, if such number be a majority of the whole number of Electors appointed, and if no person have a majority, then from the two highest numbers on the list, the Senate shall choose the Vice-President; a quorum for the purpose shall consist of two-thirds of the whole number of Senators, and a majority of the whole number shall be necessary to a choice. But no person constitutionally ineligible to the office of President shall be eligible to that of Vice-President of the United States.

Amendment XIII [1865]

Section 1. Neither slavery nor involuntary servitude, except as a punishment for crime whereof the party shall have been duly convicted, shall exist within the United States, or any place subject to their jurisdiction.

Section 2. Congress shall have power to enforce this article by appropriate legislation.

Amendment XIV [1868]

Section 1. All persons born or naturalized in the United States, and subject to the jurisdiction thereof, are citizens of the United States and of the State wherein they reside. No State shall make or enforce any law which shall abridge the privileges or immunities of citizens of the United States; nor shall any State deprive any person of life, liberty, or property, without due process of law; nor deny to any person within its jurisdiction the equal protection of the laws.

Section 2. Representatives shall be apportioned among the several States according to their respective numbers, counting the whole number of persons in each State, excluding Indians not taxed. But when the right to vote at any election for the choice of electors for President and Vice President of the United States, Representatives in Congress, the Executive and Judicial officers of a State, or the members of the Legislature thereof, is denied to any of the male inhabitants of such State, being twenty-one years of age, and citizens of the United States, or in any way abridged, except for participation in rebellion, or other crime, the basis of representation therein shall be reduced in the proportion which the number of such male citizens shall bear to the whole number of male citizens twenty-one years of age in such State.

Section 3. No person shall be a Senator or Representative in Congress, or elector of President and Vice President, or hold any office, civil or military, under the United States, or under any State, who having previously taken an oath, as a member of Congress, or as an officer of the United States, or as a member of any State legislature, or as an executive or judicial officer of any State, to support the Constitution of the United States, shall have engaged in insurrection or rebellion against the same, or given aid or comfort to the enemies thereof. But Congress may by a vote of two-thirds of each House, remove such disability.

Section 4. The validity of the public debt of the United States, authorized by law, including debts incurred for payment of pensions and bounties for services in suppressing insurrection or rebellion, shall not be questioned. But neither the United States nor any State shall assume or pay any debt or obligation incurred in aid of insurrection or rebellion against the United States, or any claim for the loss or emancipation of any slave; but all such debts, obligations and claims shall be held illegal and void.

Section 5. The Congress shall have power to enforce, by appropriate legislation, the provisions of this article.

Amendment XV [1870]

Section 1. The right of citizens of the United States to vote shall not be denied or abridged by the United States or by any State on account of race, color, or previous condition of servitude.

Section 2. The Congress shall have power to enforce this article by appropriate legislation.

Amendment XVI [1913]

The Congress shall have power to lay and collect taxes on incomes, from whatever source derived, without apportionment among the several States, and without regard to any census or enumeration.

Amendment XVII [1913]

[1] The Senate of the United States shall be composed of two Senators from each State, elected by the people thereof, for six years; and each Senator shall have one vote. The electors in each State shall have the qualifications requisite for electors of the most numerous branch of the State legislatures.

[2] When vacancies happen in the representation of any State in the Senate, the executive authority of such State shall issue writs of election to fill such vacancies: *Provided*, That the legislature of any State may empower the executive thereof to make temporary appointments until the people fill the vacancies by election as the legislature may direct.

[3] This amendment shall not be so construed as to affect the election or term of any Senator chosen before it becomes valid as part of the Constitution.

Amendment XVIII [1919]

Section 1. After one year from the ratification of this article the manufacture, sale, or transportation of intoxicating liquors within, the importation thereof into, or the exportation thereof from the United States and all territory subject to the jurisdiction thereof for beverage purposes is hereby prohibited.

Section 2. The Congress and the several States shall have concurrent power to enforce this article by appropriate legislation.

Section 3. This article shall be inoperative unless it shall have been ratified as an amendment to the Constitution by the legislatures of the several States, as provided in the Constitution, within seven years from the date of the submission hereof to the States by the Congress.

Amendment XIX [1920]

[1] The right of citizens of the United States to vote shall not be denied or abridged by the United States or by any State on account of sex.

[2] Congress shall have power to enforce this article by appropriate legislation.

Amendment XX [1933]

Section 1. The terms of the President and Vice President shall end at noon on the 20th day of January, and the terms of Senators and Representatives at noon on the 3d day of January, of the years in which such terms would have ended if this article had not been ratified; and the terms of their successors shall then begin.

Section 2. The Congress shall assemble at least once in every year, and such meeting shall begin at noon on the 3d day of January, unless they shall by law appoint a different day.

Section 3. If, at the time fixed for the beginning of the term of the President, the President elect shall have died, the Vice President elect shall become President. If the President shall not have been chosen before the time fixed for the beginning of his term, or if the President elect shall have failed to qualify, then the Vice President elect shall act as President until a President shall have qualified; and the Congress may by law provide for the case wherein neither a President elect nor a Vice President elect shall have qualified, declaring who shall then act as President, or the manner in which one who is to act shall be selected, and such person shall act accordingly until a President or Vice President shall have qualified.

Section 4. The Congress may by law provide for the case of the death of any of the persons from whom the House of Representatives may choose a President whenever the right of choice shall have devolved upon them, and for the case of the death of any of the persons from whom the

Senate may choose a Vice President whenever the right of choice shall have devolved upon them.

Section 5. Sections 1 and 2 shall take effect on the 15th day of October following the ratification of this article.

Section 6. This article shall be inoperative unless it shall have been ratified as an amendment to the Constitution by the legislatures of three-fourths of the several States within seven years from the date of its submission.

Amendment XXI [1933]

Section 1. The eighteenth article of amendment to the Constitution of the United States is hereby repealed.

Section 2. The transportation or importation into any State, Territory, or possession of the United States for delivery or use therein of intoxicating liquors, in violation of the laws thereof, is hereby prohibited.

Section 3. This article shall be inoperative unless it shall have been ratified as an amendment to the Constitution by conventions in the several States, as provided in the Constitution, within seven years from the date of the submission hereof to the States by the Congress.

Amendment XXII [1951]

Section 1. No person shall be elected to the office of the President more than twice, and no person who has held the office of President, or acted as President, for more than two years of a term to which some other person was elected President shall be elected to the office of President more than once. But this Article shall not apply to any person holding the office of President when this Article was proposed by the Congress, and shall not prevent any person who may be holding the office of President, or acting as President, during the term within which this Article becomes operative from holding the office of President or acting as President during the remainder of such term.

Section 2. This article shall be inoperative unless it shall have been ratified as an amendment to the Constitution by the legislatures of three-fourths of the several States within seven years from the date of its submission to the States by the Congress.

Amendment XXIII [1961]

Section 1. The District constituting the seat of Government of the United States shall appoint in such manner as the Congress may direct:

A number of electors of President and Vice President equal to the whole number of Senators and Representatives in Congress to which the District would be entitled if it were a State, but in no event more than the least populous state; they shall be in addition to those appointed by the states, but they shall be considered, for the purposes of the election of President and Vice President, to be electors appointed by a state; and they shall meet in the District and perform such duties as provided by the twelfth article of amendment.

Section 2. The Congress shall have power to enforce this article by appropriate legislation.

Amendment XXIV [1964]

Section 1. The right of citizens of the United States to vote in any primary or other election for President or Vice President, for electors for President or Vice President, or for Senator or Representative in Congress, shall not be denied or abridged by the United States, or any State by reason of failure to pay any poll tax or other tax.

Section 2. The Congress shall have power to enforce this article by appropriate legislation.

Amendment XXV [1967]

Section 1. In case of the removal of the President from office or of his death or resignation, the Vice President shall become President.

Section 2. Whenever there is a vacancy in the office of the Vice President, the President shall nominate a Vice President who shall take office upon confirmation by a majority vote of both Houses of Congress.

Section 3. Whenever the President transmits to the President pro tempore of the Senate and the Speaker of the House of Representatives his written declaration that he is unable to discharge the powers and duties of his office, and until he transmits to them a written declaration to the contrary, such powers and duties shall be discharged by the Vice President as Acting President.

Section 4. Whenever the Vice President and a majority of either the principal officers of the executive departments or of such other body as Congress may by law provide, transmit to the President pro tempore of the Senate and the Speaker of the House of Representatives their written declaration that the President is unable to discharge the powers and duties of his office, the Vice President shall immediately assume the powers and duties of the office as Acting President.

Thereafter, when the President transmits to the President pro tempore of the Senate and the Speaker of the House of Representatives his written declaration that no inability exists, he shall resume the powers and duties of his office unless the Vice President and a majority of either the principal officers of the executive department or of such other body as Congress may by law provide, transmit within four days to the President pro tempore of the Senate and the Speaker of the House of Representatives their written declaration and the President is unable to discharge the powers and duties of his office. Thereupon Congress shall decide the issue, assembling within forty-eight hours for that purpose if not in session. If the Congress, within twenty-one days after receipt of the latter written declaration, or, if Congress is not in session, within twenty-one days after Congress is required to assemble, determines by two-thirds vote of both Houses that the President is unable to discharge the powers and duties of his office, the Vice President shall continue to discharge the same as Acting President; otherwise, the President shall resume the powers and duties of his office.

Amendment XXVI [1971]

Section 1. The right of citizens of the United States, who are eighteen years of age or older, to vote shall not be denied or abridged by the United States or by any State on account of age.

Section 2. The Congress shall have power to enforce this article by appropriate legislation.

Proposed Constitutional Amendment *

Section 1. For purposes of representation in Congress, election of the President and Vice President, and Article V of this Constitution, the District constituting the seat of government of the United States shall be treated as though it were a State.

Section 2. The exercise of the rights and powers conferred under this article shall be by the people of the District constituting the seat of government and shall be as provided by Congress.

Section 3. The twenty-third Amendment to the Constitution is hereby repealed.

Section 4. This article shall be inoperative, unless it shall have been ratified as an amendment to the Constitution by the legislatures of three-fourths of the several States within seven years from the date of its submission.

---

* Congress submitted this proposed amendment to the states for ratification in August 1978.

Index

References are to pages

[*Subjects listed in the Table of Contents are not duplicated in the entries below*]